BLOOMSBURY
REFERENCE
DICTIONARY

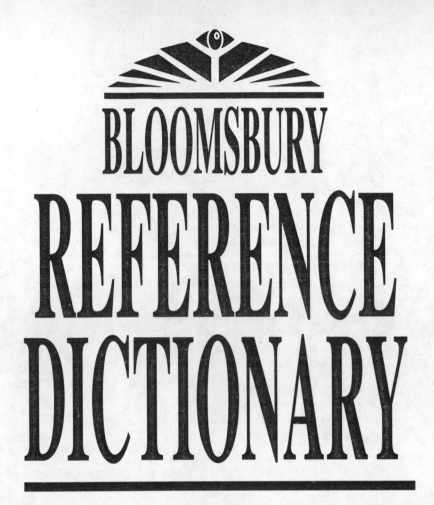

BLOOMSBURY
REFERENCE
DICTIONARY

BLOOMSBURY BOOKS

This edition published 1994 by
Bloomsbury Books, an imprint of
The Godfrey Cave Group, 42 Bloomsbury
Street, London, WC1B 3QJ.

ISBN 1 85471 283 7

Printed and bound in Finland

Using the Dictionary

The order of entries is by strict alphabetical order of the headword, ignoring hyphens and spaces. Words of identical spelling but with different origins are listed separately with superscript numerals. Guide words are printed at the top of each page to show the first and last entries on it.

Irregular plurals of nouns, and regular plurals which might cause confusion, are given in bold type in parentheses following the part of speech label. The standard *-y* ending with the plural *-ies* is not, however, included. Irregular spellings of the present and past participles and tenses of verbs are also included.

Abbreviations of part of speech labels are listed in the abbreviations overleaf. Where a part of speech changes within an entry, this is marked by a dash —.

At the back of the book (starting on page 995) is a list of current abbreviations, contractions and acronyms.

Abbreviations in the Dictionary

adj	adjective	*med*	medicine
adv	adverb	*milit*	military
anat	anatomy	*mineral*	mineralogy
arch	archaic	*mus*	music
archit	architecture	*myth*	mythology
art	article	*n*	noun
astrol	astrology	*naut*	nautical term
astron	astronomy	*npl*	plural noun
auto	automobile	*p*	participle
aux	auxiliary	*pers*	person, personal
biol	biology	*philos*	philosophy
bot	botany	*photog*	photography
chem	chemistry	*physics*	physics
colloq	colloquial term	*pl*	plural
com	commerce	*poet*	poetical
compar	comparative	*poss*	possessive
comput	computer term	*pp*	past participle
conj	conjunction	*ppr*	present participle
demons	demonstrative	*prep*	preposition
derog	derogatory, derogatorily	*pret*	preterit (past tense)
e.g.	*exempli gratia*, for example	*print*	printing
econ	economics	*pron*	pronoun
elect	electricity	*psychol*	psychology
exclam	exclamation	*RC*	Roman Catholic
f	feminine	*refl*	reflexive
fig	figurative use	*Scots*	a Scottish term
geog	geography	*sing*	singular
geol	geology	*sl*	slang
geom	geometry	*superl*	superlative
gram	grammar	*UK*	United Kingdom
heral	heraldry	*US*	United States
hist	history	*USA*	United States of America
i.e.	*id est*, that is	*vb*	verb
imper	imperative	*verb aux*	auxiliary verb
interj	interjection	*vi*	intransitive verb
law	law term	*vt*	transitive verb
m	masculine	*vti*	transitive or intransitive verb
math	mathematics	*vulg*	vulgar
mech	mechanics	*zool*	zoology

A

A the first letter in the English and other alphabets derived from the Latin and Greek alphabets; (*mus*) the sixth note of the modal or diatonic scale of C, the note sounded by the open second string of the violin.

a the indefinite article, a contraction of **an**, used before nouns singular beginning with a consonant.

A1 a character attached to a ship of the first-class in Lloyd's register of shipping.

aardvark *n* the groundhog of South Africa, a burrowing, insectivorous, edentate animal.

aardwolf *n* the earth wolf of South Africa, an animal allied to the hyaenas and civets.

aback *adv* backwards, (*naut*) catching the wind so as to urge a vessel backwards (of sails); (*fig*) by surprise; unexpectedly, as, *to take a person aback.*

abacus *n* a device on a frame with beads on rods for reckoning on; the Pythagorean multiplication table; (*archit*) a slab or table forming the crowning of a column and its capital.

abaft *adv*, *prep* on or towards the aft or hinder part of a ship.

abandon *vt* to detach or withdraw oneself from; desert; forsake; give up; resign; yield up; (*refl*) to yield oneself up without attempt at restraint, as *to abandon oneself to grief.*—*n* abandonment; heartiness; frank, unrestrained demeanour.

abandoned *adj* given up to vice; shamelessly and recklessly wicked; profligate; depraved; vicious.

abandonment *n* the act of abandoning or state of being abandoned; relinquishment; desertion; giving up.

abase *vt* (**abased, abasing**) to lower or depress (of material objects); to reduce lower, as in rank; humble; degrade.

abasement *n* the act of abasing; a state of depression, degradation or humiliation.

abash *vt* to confuse or confound, as by consciousness of guilt, inferiority, etc; to make ashamed; to put to confusion; a stronger word than *confuse*, but not so strong as *confound.*

abatable *adj* capable of being abated.

abate *vt* (**abated, abating**) to beat down; to lessen; to diminish; to remit; to moderate (zeal, a demand, a tax); (*law*) to annul; to put an end to.—*vi* to decrease or become less in strength or violence.

abatement *n* the act of abating or state of being abated; decrease; decline; mitigation; amount or sum deducted; deduction; decrease.

abattoir *n* a public slaughterhouse.

abbacy *n* the dignity, rights and privileges of an abbot.

abbé *n* in France, especially before the Revolution, one who devoted himself to divinity or who had pursued a course of study in a theological seminary.

abbess *n* a woman superior of an abbey, possessing, in general, the same dignity and authority as an abbot, except that she cannot exercise the spiritual functions appertaining to the priesthood.

abbey *n* a monastery or monastic establishment of the highest rank; a society of persons of either sex, secluded from the world and devoted to religion and celibacy, governed by an abbot or abbess.

abbot *n* the male head or superior of an abbey or monastery.

abbreviate *vt* (**abbreviated, abbreviating**) to make briefer; to shorten; to abridge; to reduce to smaller compass.

abbreviation *n* act of abbreviating, shortening or contracting; that which is abbreviated; a syllable, letter or series of letters, standing for a word or words, as, *esq.* for *esquire*; *FRS.* for *Fellow of the Royal Society.*

abdicate *vt* (**abdicated, abdicating**) to give up, renounce, lay down or withdraw from in a voluntary, public or formal manner, as a throne, duties, etc; to vacate; to resign.—*vi* to renounce or give up power voluntarily.

abdication *n* the act of abdicating an office, especially the throne.

abdomen *n* that part of the human body which lies between the thorax and the pelvis, containing the stomach, liver, spleen,

aardvark

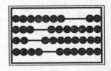

abacus

pancreas, kidneys, bladder and intestines; the posterior of the three parts of a perfect insect.

abdominal *adj* pertaining to the abdomen or belly.

abduce *vt* (**abduced, abducing**) to draw or conduct away.

abduct *vt* to draw or lead away; to take away surreptitiously and by force.

abduction *n* the act of abducting; (*law*) the unlawful leading away of a person by fraud, persuasion or open violence.

abeam *adv* (*naut*) in the direction of the beams, that is, at right angles to the keel of a ship.

abed *adv* in bed; gone to bed.

Aberdeen terrier *n* the Scotch terrier.

aberdevine *n* the siskin, a common song-bird.

aberrant *adj* characterized by aberration; wandering; straying from the right way; differing from a common type.

aberration *n* the act of wandering from the right way; deviation from truth or rectitude or from a type or standard; partial alienation of mind; mental wandering; the difference between the true and the observed position of a heavenly body.

Aberdeen terrier

abet *vt* (**abetted, abetting**) to encourage by aid or approval (used chiefly in a bad sense); to incite; to support; to encourage; to back up.

abetter, abettor *n* one who abets or incites; a supporter or encourager, generally of something bad.

abeyance *n* a state of expectation or waiting for an occupant or holder (said of lands, honours or dignities); a state of temporary suspension.

abhor *vt* (**abhorred, abhorring**) to hate extremely or with loathing; to loathe, detest or abominate; to shrink from with horror; to fill with horror and loathing.

abhorrence *n* extreme hatred; detestation; great aversion.

abhorrent *adj* struck with abhorrence; hating; detesting; utterly repugnant (in the last sense used formerly with *from*, now with *to*).

abhorrer *n* one who abhors.

abide *vi* (*pret, pp* **abode** *or* **abided**, *ppr* **abiding**) not to depart.—**to abide by**, to remain beside; to adhere to; to maintain; to remain satisfied with.—*vt* to be prepared for; to await; to be able to endure or sustain; to remain firm under; to put up with; to tolerate.

abider *n* one who abides.

abiding *adj* continuing; permanent; steadfast, as *an abiding faith*.

abies *n* the genus of trees to which the fir belongs; a tree of this genus.

abies

abigail *n* a waiting-woman.

ability *n* the state or condition of being able;

power, whether bodily or mental; (*pl*) talents; powers of the mind; mental gifts or endowments.

abiogenesis *n* the doctrine that living matter may be produced by non-living matter.

abject *adj* sunk to a low condition; worthless, mean, despicable; low, grovelling.— *n* a person in a low or abject condition.

abjection *n* a low state; meanness of spirit; abjectness.

abjectly *adv* in an abject or contemptible manner; meanly; servilely.

abjectness *n* the state of being abject; meanness; servility.

abjuration *n* the act of abjuring; a renunciation on oath; a rejection or denial with solemnity; a total abandonment.

abjure *vt* (**abjured, abjuring**) to renounce on oath; to reject or withdraw from with solemnity; to abandon (as allegiance, errors); to recant or retract.

abjurement *n* the act of abjuring; renunciation.

abjurer *n* one who abjures.

ablative *adj* taking or tending to take away, applied to a case of nouns in Sanskrit, Latin and some other languages, originally given to the case in Latin because separation from was considered to be one of the chief ideas expressed by it.

ablaut *n* (*philol*) a substitution of one vowel for another in the body of a word, to indicate a corresponding modification of use or meaning, as, *bind, band, bound, bond*; especially the change of a vowel to indicate tense change in verbs, instead of the addition of a syllable (*-ed*), as, *sink, sank, sunk*.

ablaze *adv, adj* in a blaze; in a state of eager excitement or desire.

able *adj* having the power, means or qualification sufficient; competent; qualified; having strong or unusual powers of mind or intellectual qualifications; gifted; vigorous; active.

able-bodied *adj* healthy, fit; without a physical disability.

able-bodied seaman, able seaman *n* a seaman who is well skilled in seamanship and classed in the ship's books as AB.

ableness *n* ability of body or mind; force; vigour.

ably *adv* in an able manner; with ability.

ablution *n* the act of washing; cleansing or purification by water or other liquid; specifically, a washing of the body preparatory to religious rites.

abnegate *vt* (**abnegated, abnegating**) to deny; to renounce.

abnegation *n* the act of abnegating; denial; renunciation.

abnormal *adj* not conforming to rule; deviating from a type or standard; irregular; contrary to system or law.

abnormality *n* the state or quality of being abnormal; deviation from a standard, rule or type; irregularity; that which is abnormal.

aboard *adv* on board; within a ship or boat.—*prep* on board; into (*to go aboard a ship*).

abode *n* a residence or place of residence; a place where a person abides; a dwelling; habitation.

abolish *vt* to do away with; to put an end to; to destroy; to efface or obliterate; to make void; to annul; to put out of existence.

abolition *n* the act of abolishing or the state of being abolished.

abolitionist *n* a person who favours the abolition of anything, applied especially to those who favoured the abolition of slavery in the United States.

abominate *vt* (**abominated, abominating**) to hate extremely; to abhor; to detest.

abominable *adj* deserving or liable to be abominated; detestable; loathsome; odious in the utmost degree; execrable.

abominable snowman *n* the yeti.

abomination *n* that which is abominated or abominable.

aboriginal *adj* inhabiting a country from the earliest known times, as, *aboriginal tribes*.—*n* an original inhabitant; one of an aboriginal race.

Aboriginal *n* a member of the race which originally inhabited Australia before the arrival of European settlers.

aborigines *npl* the people found in a country at the time of the earliest known settlement.

abort *vi* to miscarry in giving birth; to appear in a rudimentary or undeveloped state.—*vt* to cause or bring about a miscarriage; to terminate (a project) prematurely, usually because of failure.

abortion *n* the act of miscarrying or producing young before the natural time or before the foetus is perfectly formed; the product of untimely birth; a misshapen being; a monster; anything which fails before it is matured or perfect, as a design.

abortive *adj* brought forth in an immature state; rudimentary; imperfectly formed or developed; producing or intended to produce abortion; not brought to completion or to a successful issue; coming to nought.

abound *vi* to be in great plenty; to be very prevalent; to have or possess in great quantity; to be copiously supplied (in the latter sense followed by *with* or *in*).

about *prep* around; on the outside or surface of; in a circle surrounding; round (*two yards about the stem*); near to in place, time, size, number, quantity, etc; near to in action; on the point of (*to be about to speak*), in this sense followed by the infinitive; concerned in; engaged in (*what is he about?*) concerning; relating to; respecting.—*adv* around the outside; in circuit; in a circle; near to in number, time, place, quality or degree (*about as high*); here and there; around; in one place and another; in different directions.

above *prep* in or to a higher place than; superior to in any respect; too high for (*above mean actions*); more in number, quantity or degree than; in excess of (*above a ton*).—**above all** above or before everything else; before every other consideration.—*adv* in or to a higher place; overhead; before, in rank or order, especially in a book or writing (*what has been said above*); besides, in the expression *over and above*; *above* is often used elliptically as a noun, meaning (1) heaven; (2) the aforesaid (*from the above you will learn*).—it is equal to an adjective in such phrases as, *the above particulars*, in which cited or mentioned is understood.

aboveboard *adj*, *adv* honest; in open sight; without tricks or disguise.

abracadabra *n* a word of eastern origin used in incantations and, when written down, worn as an amulet.

abrade *vt* (**abraded, abrading**) to rub or wear down; to rub or grate off.

abrasion *n* the act of abrading, wearing or rubbing off; an injury of the skin by removal of cuticle.

abrasive *adj* causing scraping or grazing; annoying in speech or behaviour; arousing friction or irritation.—*n* a material for grinding, such as sand, powdered glass, etc.

abranchiate *adj* devoid of branchiae or gills.—*n* a vertebrate animal (mammal, bird, reptile) that at no period of its existence possesses gills.

abreast *adv* side by side, hence, up to a level or standard (*to keep abreast of science*).

abridge *vt* (**abridged, abridging**) to make shorter; to curtail; to epitomize; to shorten by using fewer words; to condense; to lessen; to diminish.

abridgement *n* the act of abridging or state of being abridged; that which is abridged; an epitome; a summary, as of a book; an abstract.

abroad *adv* at large; without being confined to narrow limits; with expansion (*to spread its branches abroad*); beyond the walls of a house or other enclosure; beyond the bounds of a country; in foreign countries.

abrogate *vt* (**abrogated, abrogating**) to repeal; to make void; to do away with; to annul by an authoritative act.

abrogation *n* the act of abrogating; repeal by authority.

abrupt *adj* steep; craggy (of rocks, preci-

Aboriginal

pices, etc); sudden; without notice to prepare the mind for the event (*an abrupt entrance*); disconnected; making sudden transitions (*an abrupt style*).

abruptness *n* the state or quality of being abrupt; precipitousness; suddenness; unceremonious haste or vehemence.

abscess *n* a collection of purulent matter in the tissue of an organ or part, with pain and heat.

abscind *vt* to cut off.

abscissa *n* (*pl* **abscissae**) in coordinate geometry, the x of a point, or distance of the point from the y-axis, measured parallel to the x-axis.

abscond *vi* to withdraw or absent oneself in a private manner; to run away in order to avoid a legal process or a punishment; to decamp.

abseil *vi* to descend a rock face or steep surface by means of a double rope attached to a higher point.

absence *n* the state of being absent; opposite of presence; the state of being at a distance in place; the state of being lacking; non-existence within a certain sphere (*absence of evidence*); inattention.—**absence of mind** attention not to things or objects present, but to others distant or foreign.

absent *adj* not present; away; somewhere else; lacking; having the mind withdrawn from what is passing; characterized by absence of mind (*an absent man*).

absent *vt* to keep away intentionally, used (*refl*), as, *to absent oneself from a meeting*.

absentee *n* one who is absent; one who absents himself (often applied to landlords who, deriving their income from one country, reside and spend it in another).

absinthe *n* a popular French liqueur or cordial consisting of brandy flavoured with wormwood.

absolute *adj* freed from limitation or condition; unconditional (*an absolute promise*); unlimited by extraneous power or control (*an absolute government or prince*); complete in itself; finished; perfect (*absolute beauty*); free from mixture (*absolute alcohol*); positive; decided; (*metaph*) not relative; considered without reference to other things (*absolute knowledge*); existing independent of any other cause; self-existing; unconditioned; (*gram*) applied to the case which is not determined by any other word in the sentence.

absolutely *adv* in an absolute manner; completely; without restriction, limitation or qualification; unconditionally; positively.

absolute zero *n* the lowest temperature theoretically possible, equal to 0° Kelvin, -273.15° C, -459.67° F.

absolution *n* the act of absolving or state of being absolved; specifically, in the Roman Catholic and some other churches, a remission of sins pronounced by a priest in favour of a penitent.

absolutism *n* state of being absolute or principles of absolute government.

absolve *vt* (**absolved, absolving**) to set free or release from some duty, obligation or responsibility (*to absolve a person from a promise*); to acquit; to forgive or grant remission of sins to; to pronounce forgiveness of sins to (with *from*).

absorb *vt* to drink in; suck up; imbibe, as a sponge; take in by capillarity; swallow up; engross or engage wholly.

absorbable *adj* capable of being absorbed or imbibed.

absorbent *adj* capable of absorbing fluids; performing the function of absorption.—*n* anything which absorbs; a vessel in an animal body which takes in nutritive matters into the system; a substance applied to a wound to staunch or arrest the flow of blood.

absorption *n* the act or process of absorbing; state of being absorbed or engrossed.

abstain *vi* to forbear or refrain voluntarily; to withhold

abstainer *n* one who abstains; specifically, one who abstains from the use of intoxicating liquors.

abstention *n* the act of holding off or abstaining; abstinence.

abstinence *n* the act or practice of voluntarily refraining from the use of anything within our reach, especially from some bodily indulgence; partaking sparingly of food or drink.

abstemious *adj* temperate; very moderate and plain; very sparing (*abstemious diet*).

abstergent *adj* having cleansing or purgative properties.—*n* something that aids in scouring or cleansing; a detergent.

abstract *vt* to draw or take away; to withdraw; to purloin; to take away mentally; consider separately; to epitomize or reduce to a summary.—*adj* considered or thought of in itself; not concrete; considered and treated apart from any particular object (*abstract mathematics*; *abstract logic*).—*n* a summary or epitome containing the substance; a bare or brief statement of facts detailed elsewhere.

abstracted *adj* absent in mind; inattentive.

abstraction *n* the act of abstracting or separating; the act of withdrawing; the act of considering separately what is united in a complex object; something abstract; an idea or notion of an abstract character; absence of mind; the state of being entirely engrossed in thought.

abstract noun *n* a name of a quality, in opposition to a *concrete noun*.

abstruse *adj* remote from ordinary minds or notions; difficult to be comprehended or understood; profound; recondite.

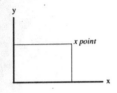

abscissa

abseil

abstrusely *adv* in an abstruse manner; profoundly; with terms or notions remote from such as are obvious.

abstruseness *n* the quality of being abstruse.

absurd *adj* inconsistent with reason or common sense; ridiculous; nonsensical; logically contradictory.

absurdity *n* the state or quality of being absurd; that which is absurd; an absurd action, statement, etc.

absurdly *adv* in an absurd manner.

absurdness *n* the quality of being absurd.

abundance *n* a fullness or plenteousness great to overflowing; ampleness; plenteousness; copiousness.

abundant *adj* plentiful; ample; fully sufficient; abounding; overflowing.

abundantly *adv* in a plentiful or sufficient degree; amply; plentifully.

abusable *adj* capable of being abused.

abuse *n* improper treatment or employment; improper use or application; misuse; a corrupt practice or custom (*the abuses of government*); injury; scurrilous or insulting language; ill-treatment or maltreatment, especially physical or sexual.—*vt* (**abused, abusing**) to ill-treat or maltreat, especially physically, mentally or sexually; to misuse; to put to a wrong or bad use; to do wrong to; to injure; to dishonour; to violate; to deceive; to impose on; to take undue advantage of.

abuser *n* one who abuses in speech or behaviour.

abusive *adj* practising abuse; offering harsh words or ill-treatment; scurrilous; opprobrious; insulting.

abusiveness *n* the quality of being abusive; rudeness of language.

abut *vi* (**abutted, abutting**) to be contiguous; to join at a border or boundary; to form a point or line of contact (with *on, upon, against*).

abutment *n* the solid part of a pier or wall against which an arch abuts or from which it springs.

abysmal *adj* pertaining to an abyss; profound; immeasurable.

abyss *n* a bottomless gulf; anything profound and unfathomable, literally or figuratively.

Abyssinian *adj* belonging to Abyssinia or its inhabitants.—*n* a native or inhabitant of Abyssinia.

acacia *n* any of a genus of ornamental plants, some species of which produce catechu and some exude gum arabic.

acacia tree *n* a name sometimes given to the locust tree.

academe, academia *n* the world of higher education; the academic environment.

academic *adj* belonging to the school or philosophy of Plato; belonging to an academy or to a college or university (*academic studies*).—*n* a member of an college or university; a scholarly person.

academical *adj* academic.—*n* (*pl*) the costume proper to the officers and students of a school or college.

academician *n* a member of an academy or society for promoting arts and sciences.

academy *n* the members of the philosophical school founded by the Greek philosopher Plato; in Scotland, a school holding a rank between a college and an elementary school; a specialized college; an association for the promotion of literature, science or art, established by government or by the voluntary union of private individuals.

acajou *n* a kind of heavy red mahogany; gum and resin from the stem of the mahogany tree.

acantha *n* a prickle of a plant; a spine of an animal.

acanthaceous *adj* armed with prickles, as a plant.

acanthine *adj* pertaining to or resembling the plant acanthus; prickly.

acanthopterygian *adj* of or belonging to a large group of bony fishes characterized by having one or more of the first rays of the fins in the form of spines.

acanthus *n* the plant bear's-breech or brankursine; an architectural ornament used in capitals of the Corinthian and Composite orders and resembling the foliage of this plant.

acarid, acaridan *n* any of that branch of arachnids that includes mites, ticks and water-mites, the mouth in all of which is formed for suction.

acarus *n* the genus to which the true mites belong; a mite or tick generally.

accede *vi* (**acceded, acceding**) to agree or assent, as to a proposition or to terms proposed by another; to become a party by agreeing to terms; to join or be added; to succeed, as an heir; to come to by inheritance (said especially of a sovereign).

accelerate *vt* (**accelerated, accelerating**) to make quicker; to cause to move or advance faster; to hasten; to add to the velocity of; to bring about or help to bring about more speedily.

acceleration *n* the act of accelerating or state of being accelerated; increase of velocity; rate of change of velocity in magnitude, direction, or both.

accelerator *n* one who or that which accelerates; a hastener; a device for producing greater speed in a machine, e.g. a motor car; (*physics*) an apparatus that imparts high velocities to elementary particles.

accent *n* a superior stress or force of voice on certain syllables of words, which distinguishes them from the other syllables

acacia

11

and forms an element in correct pronunciation; a mark or character used in writing to direct the stress of the voice in pronunciation or to mark a particular tone, length of vowel sound, etc; a peculiar or characteristic modulation or modification of the voice, such as that found in a given district; (*pl*) words or expressions; (*mus*) stress or emphasis on particular notes.—*vt* to give an accent or accents to in speaking; to mark with an accent or accents.

accentor *n* any of several songbirds resembling the sparrow found in mountainous regions.

accentual *adj* pertaining to accent.

accentuate *vt* (**accentuated, accentuating**) to mark or pronounce with an accent or with accents; to emphasize or give prominence to.

accentuation *n* the act of accentuating or state of being accentuated.

accept *vt* to take or receive, as something offered; to receive with approbation or favour; to take as it comes; to accede or assent to (a treaty, a proposal); to acknowledge, especially by signature, and thus to promise to pay (a bill of exchange).

acceptable *adj* capable, worthy or sure of being accepted or received; pleasing to a receiver; gratifying; agreeable; welcome.

acceptance *n* the act of accepting; a taking or receiving; favourable reception; an agreeing to terms; a written engagement to pay money, made by a person signing his or her name across or at the end of a bill of exchange; an accepted bill or the amount contained in it.

access *n* a coming to; near approach; admittance; admission; the means or way of approach; passage allowing communication; increase or accession; attack or return fit of a disease.

accessibility *n* the condition or quality of being accessible or of admitting approach.

accessible *adj* capable of being approached or reached; easy of access; approachable; attainable.

accession *n* the act of acceding; the act of agreeing or assenting; increase by something added; that which is added; the act of succeeding to a throne, office or dignity; the attack or commencement of a disease.

accessory, accessary *adj* contributing; aiding in producing some effect or acting in subordination to the principal agent; contributing to a general effect; belonging to something else as principal; accompanying.—*n* one who aids or gives countenance to a crime; that which belongs to something else as its principal; that which contributes to the effect of something more important; an accompaniment.

accidence *n* that part of grammar which deals with the inflection of words or the declension of nouns, adjectives, etc and the conjugation of verbs.

accident *n* chance or what happens by chance; an event that happens when quite unlooked for; an unforeseen and undesigned injury to a person; casualty; mishap; a property or quality of a thing which is not essential to it nor is one of its invariable signs.

accidental *adj* happening by chance or accident or unexpectedly; casual; fortuitous; nonessential; not necessarily belonging; adventitious.—*n* a casualty; a property not essential; (*mus*) a sharp, flat or natural which does not occur in the clef and which implies some change of key or modulation different from that in which the piece began.

accidentally *adv* in an accidental manner; by chance; fortuitously; not essentially.

accipiter *n* any of a genus of hawks characterized by short wings and a long tail.

acclaim *vt* to applaud; to declare or salute by acclamation.

acclamation *n* a shout or other demonstration of applause made by a multitude, indicating joy, hearty assent, approbation or good wishes.

acclimatization *n* the act or process of acclimatizing or state of being acclimatized.

acclimatize *vt* (**acclimatized, acclimatizing**) to habituate to a foreign climate; to render proof against the prejudicial influences of a foreign climate; to adapt for permanent existence in any new environment.

accolade *n* a ceremony used in conferring knighthood, anciently consisting in putting the hand on the knight's neck, now usually a tap on the shoulder with the flat of a sword.

accommodate *vt* (**accommodated, accommodating**) to make suitable, correspondent or consistent; to fit; to adapt; to conform; to adjust; to reconcile (with *to* after the object); to supply or furnish with required conveniences (with *with* after the object, as *to accommodate a friend with money*).

accommodating *adj* obliging; yielding to the desires of others; disposed to comply and to oblige another.

accommodation *n* the act of accommodating; adjustment; adaptation; adjustment of differences; anything which supplies a lack, as in respect of ease, refreshment, etc; a convenience; lodgings; a loan of money.

accompanier *n* one who accompanies.

accompaniment *n* something that attends as a circumstance or which is added by way of ornament to the principal thing, or for the sake of symmetry; the subordinate part or parts performed by instruments ac-

accolade

companying a voice, several voices or a principal instrument.

accompanist *n* the performer in music who plays the accompaniment.

accompany *vt* (**accompanied, accompanying**) to go with or attend as a companion or associate; to go together; to be associated or connected with; to play a subordinate musical part to, as to a singer or other performer of a musical composition.

accomplice *n* an associate or confederate, especially in a crime; a partner in guilt.

accomplish *vt* to complete; to finish entirely; to execute; to carry out; to fulfil or bring to pass.

accomplished *adj* perfected; finished; consummate; having the attainments and graces regarded as necessary for cultivated or fashionable society.

accomplishment *n* the act of accomplishing or carrying into effect; fulfilment; acquirement; attainment, especially such as belongs to cultivated or fashionable society.

accord *n* agreement; harmony of minds, as, *to do a thing with one accord*; just correspondence of things; concord; harmony of sound; voluntary or spontaneous impulse or act (*of my, of his, of its, of their own accord*).—*vt* to make to agree or correspond; to grant; to give; to concede (*to accord to one due praise*).—*vi* to be in correspondence or harmony.

accordance *n* the state of being in accord; agreement with a person; conformity with a thing.

according *adj* agreeing; agreeable; in accordance.—**according as** agreeably, conformably or proportionately as.—**according to** agreeably to or in accordance with (*zeal according to knowledge*); followed by a personal object it refers to a statement of the person (*according to him you are wrong*).

accordingly *adv* agreeably; suitably; in a manner conformable; consequently.

accordion *n* a small keyed wind instrument, the tones of which are generated by the play of wind on metallic reeds.

accost *vt* to speak first to; to address before oneself is addressed.

account *n* a reckoning, enumeration or computation; a list of debts and credits or charges; a statement of things bought or sold, of payments, services, etc; an explanatory statement of particulars, facts or events; narrative; relation; description; reason or consideration; ground (*on all accounts*); profit; advantage (*to turn to account*); regard; behalf; sake (*trouble incurred on one's account*).

account *vt* to deem, judge, think or hold in opinion.—*vi* to render an account or relation of particulars; to answer in a responsible character; to give reasons; to explain

(followed by *to* before a person, *for* before a thing).

accountability *n* the state of being accountable or answerable.

accountable *adj* liable to pay or make good in case of loss; responsible for a trust; liable to be called to account; answerable to a superior.

accountant *n* one who makes the keeping or examination of accounts his or her profession; a person in a public office who has charge of the accounts.

account book *n* a book in which accounts are kept.

accoutre *vt* (**accoutred, accoutring**) to equip or furnish with personal trappings; especially to array in military dress and arms; to equip for military service.

accoutrements *npl* military dress and arms; fighting array.

accredit *vt* to send with credentials, as an envoy.

accrete *vi* (**accreted, accreting**) to adhere, to grow together; to be added.—*vt* to cause to grow or unite.—*adj* (*bot*) grown into one.

accretion *n* the act of accreting; a growing to; an increase by natural growth; an increase by an accession of parts externally; (*med*) the growing together of parts naturally separate, as the fingers or toes; the thing added by growth; an accession.

accrue *vi* (**accrued, accruing**) to be gained or obtained; to proceed, arise or spring (*a profit* or *a loss accrues from a commercial transaction*).

accumulate *vt* (**accumulated, accumulating**) to heap or pile up; to amass; to collect or bring together.—*vi* to grow to be extensive in number or quantity; to increase greatly.

accumulation *n* the act of accumulating; a collecting or being heaped up; that which has accumulated; a mass that has been collected.

accumulative *adj* causing accumulation; heaping up.

accumulator *n* one who or that which accumulates; a contrivance, such as a spring, that by being coiled up serves as a store of force; a kind of electric battery by which electric energy may be kept in store.

accuracy *n* the condition or quality of being accurate; extreme precision or exactness; exact conformity to truth or to a rule or model; correctness.

accurate *adj* in exact conformity to truth or to a standard or rule, or to a model; free from error or defect; exact; precise; strictly correct; adhering to exactness or correctness.

accurse *vt* (**accursed, accursing**) to call down curses on; to curse.

accursed, accurst *adj* lying under a curse; blasted; ruined; cursed.

accordion

account book

13

accuse *vt* (**accused, accusing**) to charge with a crime, offence or fault; to blame (with *of* before the crime or offence).

accusant *n* one who accuses.

accusation *n* the act of accusing; the offence of which one is accused; a charge brought against one.

accusative *n* the third case of nouns and other declinable words in Latin, Greek, etc, corresponding to the objective in English.

accused *pp used as a noun* a person or persons charged with a crime.

accuser *n* one who accuses; one who formally brings a charge.

accustom *vt* to familiarize by use or habit; to habituate or inure.

accustomed *adj* often practised; customary; habitual; wonted; familiar, as *in their accustomed manner.*

ace *n* a unit; a single pip on a card or die, or the card or face of a die so marked; a trifle or insignificant quantity or distance (*within an ace of it*); in military aviation, the name given to a pilot who has brought down ten enemy machines; the ace in certain card games counting as ten; (*colloq*) an expert.—*adj* (*colloq*) excellent, expert.

acephala *npl* molluscous animals, like the oyster and scallop, that have not a distinct head.

acephalous *adj* without a head; headless.

acerbic *adj* bitter and harsh to the taste; astringent; cutting in speech.

acerbity *n* sourness, with roughness or astringency of taste; poignancy or severity; painfulness; sharpness; harshness or severity of temper; sourness.

acetate *n* a salt formed by the union of acetic acid with a base.

acetic *adj* having the properties of vinegar; sour.

acetic acid *n* an acid often prepared by the oxidation of alcohol (acetous fermentation) and along with water forming the chief ingredient of vinegar.

acetification *n* the act of acetifying or making acetous or sour; the process of becoming acetous; the operation of making vinegar.

acetify *vt* (**acetified, acetifying**) to convert into acid or vinegar.—*vi* to become acid; to be converted into vinegar.

acetone *n* a liquid of pungent odour, the lowest of the ketones and related to acetic acid.

acetous, acetose *adj* having a sour taste; having the character of vinegar; acid; causing or connected with acetification.

acetylene *n* an inflammable gas made with calcium carbide and water and used for cutting or welding metals.

ache *n* pain or continued pain, in opposition to sudden twinges or spasmodic pain; a

ace

acetylene

continued gnawing pain as in *toothache* or *earache*; feeling of distress (*heartache*).— *vi* (**ached, aching**) to suffer from an ache or pain; to be distressed.

achieve *vt* (**achieved, achieving**) to perform or execute; to finish or carry on to a final and prosperous close; to obtain or bring about, as by effort.

achievement *n* the act of achieving or performing; accomplishment; an exploit; a great or heroic deed; an escutcheon or ensign armorial; a hatchment.

achiever *n* one who achieves or accomplishes.

achromatic *adj* lacking colour; transmitting light without decomposing it into its primary colours, as, *an achromatic lens or telescope.*

achromatism *n* the state of being achromatic; lack of colour.

achromatize *vt* (**achromatized, achromatizing**) to deprive of colour; to render achromatic.

acid *adj* sour, sharp or biting to the taste; not sweet; not alkaline.—*n* a sour substance; (*chem*) a compound of which hydrogen is an essential constituent; acids possess a sour taste, change blue vegetable colours to red and combine with bases to form salts; (*colloq*) LSD.

acidic *adj* (*chem*) pertaining to acid; containing a large amount of an acid constituent.

acidiferous *adj* bearing, producing or containing acids or an acid.

acidify *vt* (**acidified, acidifying**) to make acid; to convert into an acid.

acidity, acidness *n* the quality of being acid or sour; sourness; tartness.

acid rain *n* rain containing high levels of acids discharged into the atmosphere by the effluent from industrial processes and harmful to crops etc.

acidulate *vt* (**acidulated, acidulating**) to make acid in a moderate degree.

acidulent *adj* somewhat acid or sour; tart; peevish.

acidulous *adj* slightly sour; subacid (as cream of tartar, oranges, etc).

acknowledge *vt* (**acknowledged, acknowledging**) to own or recognize by avowal or by some act; to assent to the truth or claims of; to admit to be; to own or confess; to avow receiving.

acknowledgment, acknowledgement *n* the act of acknowledging; owning; recognition; avowal; confession; expression of thanks; a printed recognition by an author of others' works used or referred to; something given or done in return for a favour; a receipt for money received.

acme *n* the top or highest point; the furthest point attained; maturity or perfection; the height or crisis of a disease.

acne *n* an eruption of hard, inflamed tubercles or pimples on the face.

acolyte *n* an attendant; (*RC Church*) one of a lower order of clergy who attends during service; a lay attendant so employed.

acondylous, acondylose *adj* jointless.

aconite *n* a plant of a genus with hooded flowers, including wolfsbane and monkshood; a drug prepared from some of these plant.

acorn *n* the fruit of the oak; a one-celled, one-seeded oval nut which grows in a permanent cup.

acotyledon *n* (*bot*) a plant with seeds, called spores, which do not have cotyledons or seed lobes.

acotyledonous *adj* having no seed lobes.

acoustic *adj* pertaining to the sense or organs of hearing or to the science of acoustics.

acoustics *n* the science of sound, teaching the cause, nature and phenomena of the vibrations of elastic bodies which affect hearing; the properties of a room, oncert hall, etc, determining clarity of sounds.

acquaint *vt* to make to know; to make aware of; to apprise; to make familiar; to inform (*with* is used before the subject of information, if a noun, as *acquaint a person with facts*).

acquaintance *n* a state of being acquainted or of having more or less intimate knowledge; knowledge; familiarity (followed by *with*); a person known to one; the whole body of those with whom one is acquainted.

acquaintanceship *n* state of being acquainted.

acquainted *adj* having personal knowledge of; knowing, but not closely or intimately; known, familiar (with *of* or *with*).

acquiesce *vi* (**acquiesced, acquiescing**) to rest satisfied or apparently satisfied, or to rest without opposition and discontent; to assent quietly; to agree.

acquiescence *n* the act of acquiescing or giving a quiet assent.

acquiescent *adj* disposed to acquiesce; disposed to submit; quietly assenting.

acquirable *adj* capable of being acquired.

acquire *vt* (**acquired, acquiring**) to get or gain, the object being something which is more or less permanent (as fortune, title, habits, etc): a mere temporary possession is not expressed by *acquire*, but by *obtain*, *procure*, etc, as, *to obtain* (not *acquire*) *a book on loan*.—**acquired character** a character acquired by an individual plant or animal in relation to its surroundings, e.g. thickenings of epidermis on hands from use of a spade.

acquired immune deficiency syndrome *see* **AIDS**.

acquirement *n* the act of acquiring or of making acquisition; that which is acquired; attainment, especially personal attainment (as contrasted with a natural gift or endowment).

acquisition *n* the act of acquiring; the thing acquired or gained, generally applied to material gains.

acquisitive *adj* disposed to make acquisitions; having a propensity to acquire property.

acquisitiveness *n* quality of being acquisitive; a propensity to acquire property.

acquit *vt* (**acquitted, acquitting**) to release or discharge from an obligation, accusation, etc; to pronounce not guilty (with *of* before the thing); (*refl*) to behave; to bear or conduct oneself.

acquittal *n* the act of acquitting; a judicial setting free from the charge of an offence.

acquittance *n* an acquitting or discharging from a debt or any other liability; the writing which is evidence of such a discharge.

acre *n* a definite quantity of land: the British imperial acre contains 4840 square yards or 40468659 metres.

acreage *n* the number of acres in a piece of land; acres taken collectively.

acred *adj* possessing acres or landed property.

acrid *adj* sharp or biting to the taste; pungent; bitter; virulent (as in temper or disposition).

acrid *n* an acrid or irritant poison.

acridity, acridness *n* the quality of being acrid or pungent.

acrimonious *adj* abounding in acrimony; severe; bitter; virulent; caustic; stinging.

acrimony *n* acridity; pungency; sharpness or severity of temper; bitterness of expression; acerbity; asperity.

acrobat *n* an entertainer who performs vaulting, tumbling, somersaults and other spectacular feats.

acrobatic *adj* of or pertaining to an acrobat or his or her performance.

acrocephalic *adj* high-skulled; having the top of the skull high or pyramidal.

acrolith *n* (*arch, sculp*) a statue, of which only the extremities are stone.

acromegaly *n* a disease associated with overgrowth of bone, especially in the jaws, hands and feet.

acrophobia *n* abnormal fear of being at a great height.

acropolis *n* the citadel or highest part of a Grecian city, usually situated on an eminence commanding the town.

across *prep, adv* from side to side, opposed to *along*; athwart; quite over; intersecting; passing over at any angle; from one side to another; crosswise.

across-the-board *adj* applying equally in all cases.

acrostic *n* a composition in verse, in which

acne

acrobat

the first, or the first and last, or certain other letters of the lines, taken in order, form a name, title, motto, etc, which is the subject of the poem.

act *vi* to exert power; to produce effects; to be in action or motion; to carry into effect a purpose or determination of the mind; to behave, demean or conduct oneself; to perform, as an actor.—*vt* to transact; to do or perform; to represent as real; to perform on or as on the stage; to play, hence, to feign or counterfeit.—*n* that which is being done or which has been done; a deed; an exploit; the exertion of power; the effect of which power exerted is the cause; a state of reality or real existence as opposed to a possibility; actuality; a part or division of a play, generally subdivided into smaller portions called *scenes*; a decree, edict or law, especially one proceeding from a legislative body; action.—**in the act** in the actual performance or commission of some misdeed.

actable *adj* capable of being acted or performed; practically possible.

acting *adj* performing duty, service or functions; doing the real work of an office for a nominal or honorary holder of the post.—*n* a playing on the stage.

actinia

actinia *n* (*pl* **actiniae**) a sea anemone; a polyp having the mouth surrounded by tentacles in concentric circles, which when spread resemble the petals of a flower (often of brilliant colours).

actinic *adj* pertaining to rays; pertaining to the chemical rays of the sun.

actinism *n* the radiation of heat or light; the property of the chemical part of the sun's rays, which, as seen in photography, produces chemical combinations and decompositions.

actinium *n* a radioactive element occurring as a decayed product of uranium.

actinozoan *n* same as **anthozoan**.

action *n* the state or manner of acting or being active, as opposed to *rest*; activity; an act or thing done; the performance of a function; a deed; an exploit; a battle or engagement; the mechanism or movement of a compound instrument, etc; agency; operation; impulse; the connected series of events on which the interest of a drama or work of fiction depends; gesture or gesticulation; a suit or process at law; (*physics*) twice the time-integral of the kinetic energy of a system.

actionable *adj* furnishing ground for an action at law.

acupuncture

active *adj* having the power or property of acting; exerting or having the power to exert an influence (as opposed to *passive*); performing actions quickly; quick; nimble; brisk; agile; constantly engaged in action; busy; assiduous; accompanied or characterized by action, work or by the performance of business (*an active demand for goods*); actually proceeding (*active hostilities*); (*gram*) expressing action, especially action affecting an object; transitive.

activity *n* the state or quality of being active; the active faculty; active force; nimbleness; agility; briskness.

actor *n* one who acts or performs; one who represents a character or acts a part in a play.

actress *n* a female actor.

actual *adj* acting or existing really and objectively; real; effectively operative; effectual; opposed to potential or nominal; now existing; present.—*n* something actual or real.

actuality *n* the state of being actual; that which is real or actual.

actually *adv* in fact; really; with active manifestation.

actuarial *adj* of or pertaining to an actuary or to his or her business.

actuary *n* a person who calculates insurance risks, premiums, etc.

actuate *vt* (**actuated, actuating**) to put into action; to move or incite to action.

actuation *n* the state of being put in action.

aculeate, aculeated *adj* (*bot*) having prickles or sharp points; (*zool*) having a sting.

aculeiform *adj* formed like a prickle.

acumen *n* quickness of perception; mental acuteness or penetration; keenness of insight; sagacity.

acupressure *n* the Japanese technique known as shaitsu in which pressure is applied to specific pressure points on the body to relieve symptoms of an illness or disorder.

acupuncture *n* the Chinese technique of puncturing the skin with needles to reach the nerve areas, used as an anaesthetic or as a treatment for some illnesses and disorders.

acute *adj* sharp at the end; ending in a sharp point, opposed to *blunt* or *obtuse*; intellectually sharp; perceiving minute distinctions, or characterized by the use of such; characterized by keenness of insight; opposed to *dull* or *stupid*; having quick sensibility; susceptible of slight impressions (*acute hearing*); keen; sharp, said of pain; high in pitch; shrill, said of sound; (*med*) a term applied to a disease which is attended with more or less violent symptoms and comes speedily to a crisis; (*geom*) less than a right angle.

acutely *adv* in an acute manner; sharply; keenly; with quick discrimination.

acuteness *n* the quality of being acute; sharpness; keenness; sagacity; acumen.

adage *n* a proverb; an old saying which has obtained credit by long use.

adagio *adj, adv* (*mus*) slow; slowly, leisurely and with grace.—*n* (*pl* **adagios**) (*mus*) a slow movement.

adamant *n* any substance of impenetrable hardness, chiefly a rhetorical or poetical word; (*formerly*) diamond.

adamantine *adj* made of adamant; having the qualities of adamant; impenetrable.

Adam's apple the prominence on the fore part of the throat.

Adam's needle the popular name of the plants otherwise called *yucca*.

adapt *vt* to make suitable; to make to correspond; to fit or suit; to proportion; to remodel, work up and render fit for representation on the stage, as a play from a novel.

adaptability *n* the quality of being capable of adaptation.

adaptable *adj* capable of being adapted.

adaptation *n* the act of adapting or making suitable; the state of being suitable or fit; that which is adapted; of organisms, adjustment to surroundings by structural modifications.

adapter, adaptor *n* one who or that which adapts; a device that allows an item of equipment to be put to a new use; a device for connecting parts of different size and shape; an electrical plug using one socket for different appliances.

add *vt* to set or put together; to join or unite; to put into one sum; to annex; to subjoin; to say further.—*vi* to be or serve as an addition (with *to*); also, to perform the arithmetical operation of addition.

addax *n* a species of large antelope inhabiting Africa, with long and beautifully twisted horns.

addendum *n* (*pl* **addenda**) a thing to be added; an addition; an appendix to a work.

adder *n* a venomous snake, the common viper, found in Britain and over Europe.

addict *vt* to apply habitually; to habituate; to devote or give oneself up to (usually in a bad sense and followed by *to*, as, *to addict oneself to intemperance*).—*n* a person who is unable to free himself or herself from a particular habit, such as smoking, drug-taking etc.

addicted *adj* habitually practising; given up; devoted; habituated (followed by *to*).

addiction *n* the state of being addicted to something; a dependence on something, such as smoking or drugs.

Addison's disease *n* a disease caused by loss of function in the suprarenal glands.

addition *n* the act or process of adding; the uniting of two or more numbers in one sum; the rule or branch of arithmetic which treats of adding numbers; an increase; something added; a title coming after a personal name

additional *adj* added; supplementary.

additive *n* a substance added to food as a preservative or to improve colour or texture.

addle *vt* (**addled, addling**) to make rotten, as eggs; to cause perplexity or confusion

addled *adj* having lost the power of development and become rotten; putrid (applied to eggs); barren; producing nothing.

addle-headed, addle-pated *adj* stupid; muddled.

address *vt* to direct or aim words to; to pronounce; to apply to by words or writings; to accost; to speak to; to direct in writing; to write an address on; to court or make suit to.—**to address oneself to** to speak to; to address (task).—*n* the act of addressing oneself to a person; a speaking to; any speech or writing in which one person or set of persons makes a communication to another person or set of persons; manner of speaking to another; a person's bearing in conversation; courtship (in this sense generally in the plural); skill; dexterity; adroitness; direction of a letter.

addressee *n* a person or company to whom a letter, etc, is addressed.

adduce *vt* (**adduced, adducing**) to cite; to name or instance as authority or evidence; to bring to notice as bearing on a subject.

adenoids *npl* gland-like enlarged growths in the throat behind the soft palate.

adept *n* one fully skilled or well versed in any art; a proficient.—*adj* well skilled.

adequacy *n* the state of being adequate; a sufficiency for a particular purpose.

adequate *adj* equal; proportionate; exactly correspondent; fully sufficient.

adequately *adv* in an adequate manner; sufficiently.

adhere *vi* (**adhered, adhering**) to stick together; to cleave; to become closely joined or united; to be fixed in attachment or devotion.

adherence *n* the quality or state of adhering; fidelity; steady attachment.

adherent *n* one who adheres; one who follows a leader, party or profession; a follower or partisan.—*adj* sticking fast to something; clinging; attached.

adhesion *n* the act or state of adhering or being united and attached; a sticking together of the surface of bodies; close connection or association; steady attachment of the mind or feelings; assent; concurrence (*adhesion to a treaty*); of flowers, the union of unlike parts, as stamens with petals; (*physics*) the attractive force between two bodies of different kinds in close contact; (*med*) the abnormal union of two surfaces as the result of inflammation.

adhesive *adj* sticky; tenacious.—*n* an adhesive substance.

adhesiveness *n* the state or quality of being adhesive.

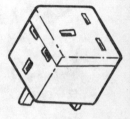

adaptor

addax

adiabatic *n* of physical changes without gain or loss of heat.

adiabatic curve a curve showing relation between the volume and the pressure of a fluid which changes its volume without gain or loss of heat.

adieu *n* (*pl* **adieux, adieus**) farewell; good-bye; an expression of kind wishes at the parting of friends.

adipocere *n* a soft, unctuous or waxy substance into which the flesh of dead animals is converted when protected from atmospheric air and under certain circumstances of temperature and humidity.

adipose *adj* fatty; consisting of or resembling fat.—*n* fat; the fat on the kidneys.

adit *n* approach; access; passage; a more or less horizontal passage into a mine.

adjacent *adj* lying near or close; bordering on; neighbouring; adjoining.

adjectival *adj* belonging to or like an adjective; having the import of an adjective.

adjective *n* (*gram*) a word used with a noun to express a quality of the thing named or something attributed to it, or to specify or describe a thing as distinct from something else and so to limit and define it.

adjoin *vt* to join or add; to unite; to annex or append.—*vi* to lie or be next or in contact; to be contiguous.

adjoining *adj* adjacent; contiguous; neighbouring.

adjutant bird

adjourn *vt* to put off or defer to another day or till a later period; to suspend the meeting of, as of a public or private body, to a future day; to postpone to a future meeting of the same body.—*vi* to cease sitting and carrying on business for a time.

adjournment *n* the act of adjourning; the period during which a public body adjourns its sittings.

adjudge *vt* (**adjudged, adjudging**) to award judicially; to adjudicate on; to settle.

adjudicate *vt* (**adjudicated, adjudicating**) to adjudge; to award judicially.—*vi* to sit in judgment; to give a judicial decision.

adjudication *n* the act of adjudicating; the act or process of trying and determining judicially; judgment or decision of a court.

adjudicator *n* one who adjudicates.

adjunct *n* something added to another, but not essentially a part of it.—*adj* united with in office or in action of any kind; conjoined with.

adjuration *n* the act of adjuring; a solemn charging on oath; a solemn oath.

adjure *vt* (**adjured, adjuring**) to charge, bind or command, earnestly and solemnly.

admiral

adjust *vt* to fit; to make correspondent; to adapt; to accommodate; to put in order; to regulate or reduce to system; to settle or bring to a satisfactory state, so that parties are agreed on the result.

adjustable *adj* capable of being adjusted.

adjustment *n* the act of adjusting.

adjutancy *n* the office of an adjutant.

adjutant *n* (*milit*) an officer whose business is to assist a commanding officer by receiving and communicating orders.

adjutant bird, adjutant crane, adjutant stork *n* a very large long-legged, wading bird allied to the storks, a native of the warmer parts of India.

administer *vt* to manage or conduct as chief agent or directing and controlling official; to direct or superintend the execution of, as of laws; to afford, give, furnish or supply; to give, as a dose of medicine; to dispense or distribute; to tender, as an oath; (*law*) to manage, as the estate of a deceased person, collecting debts, paying legacies, etc.—*vi* to contribute assistance; to bring aid or supplies (with *to*, as, *to administer to one's necessities*); (*law*) to perform the office of administrator.

administration *n* the act of administering; direction; management; government of public affairs; the executive functions of government; the persons, collectively, who are entrusted with such functions; the executive; (*law*) the management of the estate of a deceased person, consisting in collecting debts, paying debts and legacies, and distributing the property among the heirs.

administrative *adj* pertaining to administration.

administrator *n* one who administers or who directs, manages, distributes or dispenses; one who has the charge of the goods and estate of a person dying without a will.

admirable *adj* worthy of admiration; most excellent.

admirably *adv* in an admirable manner; excellently; exceedingly well.

admiral *n* a naval officer of the highest rank; a commander-in-chief of a fleet or navy, there being four grades of this rank, namely, admiral of the fleet, admiral, vice-admiral and rear-admiral; the ship which carries the admiral; also, the most considerable ship of any fleet; either of two species of butterflies, red admiral and white admiral.

admiralty *n* the office and jurisdiction of the officials appointed to take the general management of the naval affairs of a state; the officials collectively; the building in which they transact business.

admiration *n* wonder; wonder mingled with pleasing emotions, as approbation, esteem, love or veneration; an emotion excited by something beautiful or excellent.

admire *vt* (**admired, admiring**) to wonder at; to regard with wonder mingled with approbation, esteem, reverence or affection;

to take pleasure in the beauty of; to look on or contemplate with pleasure.—*vi* to feel or express admiration.

admirer *n* one who admires; one who esteems greatly; one who openly shows his or her admiration of another; a lover.

admissible *adj* capable of being admitted, allowed or conceded.

admission *n* the act of admitting; power or permission to enter; entrance; access; power to approach; the granting of an argument or position not fully proved; a point or statement admitted; acknowledgement; confession of a charge, error or crime.

admit *vt* (**admitted, admitting**) to allow to enter; to grant entrance to; to give right of entrance to; to grant in argument; to receive as true; to permit, grant or allow, or to be capable of; to acknowledge; to own; to confess.—*vi* to give warrant or allowance; to grant opportunity; to permit, with *of* (*the words do not admit of this interpretation*).

admittance *n* the act of admitting; permission to enter; entrance.

admixture *n* the act of mingling or mixing; that which is formed by mingling.

admonish *vt* to warn or notify of a fault; to reprove with mildness; to counsel against wrong practices; to caution or advise; to instruct or direct; to remind; to recall or incite to duty.

admonition *n* the act of admonishing; counsel or advice; gentle reproof; instruction in duties; caution; direction.

admonitory *adj* containing admonition; tending or serving to admonish.

ado *n* bustle; trouble; labour; difficulty.

adobe *n* a sun-dried brick.

adolescence *n* the state of growing, applied to young human beings; youth or the period of life between childhood and full development.

adolescent *adj* growing up; advancing from childhood to adulthood.—*n* an adolescent person.

Adonis *n* a young handsome man.

adopt *vt* to take into one's family and treat as one's own child; to take to oneself by choice or approval, as principles, opinions, a course of conduct, etc.

adoptable *adj* capable of, fit for or worthy of being adopted.

adopter *n* one who adopts.

adoption *n* the act of adopting or the state of being adopted.

adoptive *adj* resulting from adoption; adopting or adopted; assumed.

adore *vt* (**adored, adoring**) to worship with profound reverence; to pay divine honours to; to regard with the utmost esteem, love and respect; to love in the highest degree, as a man a woman.

adorable *adj* demanding adoration; worthy of being adored.

adoration *n* the act of adoring; the act of paying honours, as to a divine being; worship addressed to a deity; the highest degree of love, as of a man for a woman.

adorer *n* one who adores; one who worships or honours as divine; a lover; an admirer.

adorn *vt* to deck or decorate; to add to the attractiveness of by dress or ornaments; to set off to advantage; to beautify; to embellish.

adorning *n* orname.   decoration.

adornment *n* an ornament or decoration.

adrenal *adj* of or near the kidney.—*n* an adrenal gland.

adrenal gland *n* one of two glands situated above the kidneys which secrete adrenaline.

adrenaline, adrenalin *n* a hormone that stimulates the heart rate, blood pressure, etc, in response to stress and that is secreted by the adrenal glands or manufactured synthetically.

adrift *adj*, *adv* floating at random; impelled or moving without direction; at the mercy of winds and currents; swayed by any chance impulse; at sea; at a loss.

adroit *adj* dexterous; skilful; expert; inventive.

adroitness *n* the quality of being adroit; dexterity; readiness.

adsorption *n* condensation of gases or dissolved substances on the surfaces of solids.

adulate *vt* to show feigned devotion to; to flatter servilely.

adulation *n* servile flattery; praise in excess or beyond what is merited; high compliment.

adulator *n* a flatterer.

adulatory *adj* flattering.

adult *adj* having arrived at mature years or to full size and strength; pertaining or relating to full strength; suitable for an adult.—*n* a person grown to full size and strength.

adulterant *n* the person or thing that adulterates.

adulterate *vt* (**adulterated, adulterating**) to debase or deteriorate by an admixture of foreign or baser materials.

adulteration *n* the act of adulterating or the state of being adulterated or debased by foreign mixture.

adulterer *n* a man guilty of adultery.

adulteress *n* a woman guilty of adultery.

adulterous *adj* guilty of adultery; pertaining to adultery; illicit.

adultery *n* sexual intercourse between someone who is married and someone who is not his or her legal partner.

adumbrate *vt* (**adumbrated, adumbrat-**

adobe

Adonis

ing) to give a faint shadow of; to exhibit a faint resemblance of, like a shadow; to shadow forth.

adumbration *n* the act of adumbrating or shadowing forth; a faint or imperfect representation of a thing.

advance *vt* (**advanced, advancing**) to bring forward; to move further in front; to promote; to raise to a higher rank; to forward or further; to encourage the progress of; to raise (price); to accelerate the growth of; to offer or propose; to bring to view or notice, as something one is prepared to abide by; to allege; to supply beforehand; to furnish on credit or before goods are delivered or work done.—*vi* to move or go forward; to proceed; to make progress; to grow better, greater, wiser or older; to rise in rank, office or consequence.—*n* a moving forward or towards the front; a march forward; gradual progression; improvement; advancement; promotion; a proposal; a first step towards; addition to price; rise in price; a giving beforehand; that which is given beforehand, especially money.—**in advance** in front, before; beforehand; before an equivalent is received.

advancement *n* the act of advancing; the state of being advanced; the act of promoting; preferment; promotion; improvement; furtherance.

advantage *n* any state, condition, circumstance, opportunity or means specially favourable to success, prosperity or any desired end (*the advantage of a good constitution, of an excellent education*); superiority; benefit; gain; profit.—*vt* (**advantaged, advantaging**) to bring advantage to; to be of service to; to benefit; to yield profit or gain to.

advantageous *adj* being of advantage; profitable; useful; beneficial.

advent *n* a coming; approach; visitation.

Advent *n* the coming of Christ; an ecclesiastical division of the year covering the four weeks before Christmas.

adventitious *adj* added extrinsically; not essentially inherent; accidentally or casually acquired.

adventure *n* hazard; risk; chance; a hazardous enterprise; a bold and dangerous undertaking of uncertain issue; a commercial speculation; a speculation in goods sent abroad; a remarkable occurrence in one's personal history; a noteworthy event or experience in one's life.—*vt* (**adventured, adventuring**) to risk or hazard; to venture on; to attempt.

adventurer *n* one who engages in an adventure or speculation; one who attempts or takes part in bold, novel or extraordinary enterprises; one who lives by underhand means or by imposing on others.

adventuress *n* a female adventurer.

adventurer

adventurous *adj* daring; courageous; enterprising; full of hazard; attended with risk.

adverb *n* (*gram*) a part of speech joined to verbs, adjectives, other adverbs, clauses, etc, for the purpose of limiting, extending or modifying meaning.

adverbial *adj* pertaining to or having the character or structure of an adverb.

adversary *n* an enemy; a foe; an antagonist; an opponent.

adverse *adj* acting in a contrary direction; counteracting; opposing (*adverse winds*); hostile; inimical (a party, criticism); unfortunate; calamitous; unprosperous (fate or circumstances).

adversity *n* an event or series of events which oppose success or desire; misfortune; calamity; affliction; distress; state of unhappiness.

advert[1] *vi* to turn the mind or attention; to regard, observe or notice; to refer or allude (followed by *to*).

advert[2] *n* a colloquial shortened form of **advertisement**.

advertence *n* attention; notice; regard; heedfulness.

advertent *adj* attentive; heedful.

advertise *vt* (**advertised, advertising**) to inform or give notice; to make public intimation of, especially by printed notice.—*vi* to announce one's wishes or intentions by a public and usually a printed notice.

advertisement *n* a written or printed notice intended to make something known to the public, especially a printed and paid notice in a newspaper, magazine, etc; a short accouncement on radio or film on television promoting a product, etc.

advertiser *n* one who advertises.

advice *n* an opinion recommended or offered as worthy to be followed; counsel; suggestion; information; notice; intelligence; a notification in respect of a business transaction.—**to take advice** to consult with others; specifically, to take the opinion of a professional person, as a physician or lawyer.

advisability *n* advisableness; expediency.

advisable *adj* to be done or practised; deserving; sensible; open to advice.

advise *vt* (**advised, advising**) to give counsel to; to counsel; to give information to; to inform; to acquaint.—*vi* to consider; to reflect; to take counsel.

advised *adj* cautious; prudent; done, formed or taken with advice or deliberation (*an advised act*).

adviser *n* one who gives advice; a counsellor.

advisory *adj* having power to advise; containing advice.

advocacy *n* the act of pleading for; intercession; defence.

advocate *n* one who pleads the cause of another in a court of law; one who defends, vindicates or espouses a cause by argument; a pleader in favour of something; an upholder; a defender.—*vt* (**advocated, advocating**) to plead in favour of (a thing, not a person); to defend by argument before a tribunal; to support or vindicate.

adytum *n* (*pl* **adyta**) an innermost sanctuary or shrine; the chancel or altar-end of a church.

adze *n* an instrument of the axe kind used for chipping the surface of timber, the cutting edge being at right angles to the handle.—*vt* (**adzing, adzed**) to chip or shape with an adze.

aedile same as **edile**.

aegis *n* among the ancient Greeks, the shield of Zeus; in later times part of the armour of Pallas Athena, a kind of breastplate; hence, anything that protects or shields; protecting power or influence.

Aeolian, Eolian *adj* pertaining to Aeolus, the god of the winds.

Aeolian lyre, Aeolian harp *n* a simple instrument that sounds by the air sweeping across its strings.

Aeolian mode *n* (*mus*) the fifth of the authentic Gregorian modes; it consists of the natural notes A B C D E F G.

aeon, eon *n* a long indefinite space of time; a great cycle of years; an age; an era.

aepyornis *n* one of a genus of gigantic birds found fossil in Madagascar.

aerate *vt* (**aerated, aerating**) to combine with carbonic acid or other gas, or with air.—**aerated waters** acidulous and alkaline beverages more or less impregnated with carbonic acid, including lemonade, soda water, etc.

aeration *n* the act or operation of aerating.

aerial *adj* belonging or pertaining to the air or atmosphere; inhabiting or frequenting the air; produced by or in the air; reaching far into the air; high; lofty; possessed of a light and graceful beauty.—*n* a device which receives or sends out radio waves.

aerify *vt* (**aerified, aerifying**) to infuse air into; to fill with air or to combine air with.

aerie, eyrie *n* the nest of a bird of prey, as of an eagle or hawk; a brood of eagles or hawks.

aerobic *adj* requiring air or free oxygen in order to live and thrive, as certain bacteria; (of exercise) conditioning the heart and lungs by increasing the efficient intake of oxygen by the body.

aerobics *npl* a system of physical exercises, sometimes combined with dance routines and often performed to music, that increases bodily fitness and improves the condition of the heart and lungs through increasing oxygen intake.

aerodrome *n* an area for aeroplanes to land.

aerodynamics *n* the science treating of the motion of the air and gases and of their effects when in motion.

aerolite, aerolith *n* a meteoric stone; a meteorite.

aerometer *n* an instrument for weighing air or for ascertaining the density of air and gases.

aerometric *adj* pertaining to aerometry.

aerometry *n* the science of measuring the weight or density of air and gases.

aeronaut *n* an aerial navigator; a balloonist.

aeronautic, aeronautical *adj* pertaining to aeronautics or aerial sailing.

aeronautics *n* the science, study or art of flight.

aerophyte *n* same as **epiphyte**.

aeroplane *n* any flying machine in which the carrying or supporting surfaces are of the nature of planes, depending on the kite principle and driven by power.

aerose *adj* containing copper or brass; coppery.

aerosiderite *n* an iron meteorite.

aerosiderolite *n* a meteor containing both stone and iron.

aerosol *n* a suspension of fine solid or liquid particles in gas, especially when stored under pressure in a container with a device for releasing it in a fine spray; the container storing this.

aerospace *n* the earth's atmosphere and the space beyond; technology for flight in aerospace.

aerostat *n* a machine or vessel sustaining weight in the air; an air balloon, a dirigible.

aerostatics *n* the science which treats of the weight, pressure and equilibrium of air and other elastic fluids, and of the equilibrium of bodies sustained in them.

aeruginous, aerugineous *adj* pertaining to or resembling verdigris, the rust of copper.

aery *adj* airy; breezy; aerial.

Aesculapian *adj* of or pertaining to Aesculapius, or Asclepius, the Greek god of medicine.

aesthesia *n* perception; feeling; sensibility.

aesthete *n* one devoted to the principles or doctrines of aesthetics; a lover of the beautiful.

aesthetic, aesthetical *adj* pertaining to the science of taste or beauty; pertaining to the sense of the beautiful.

aesthetically *adv* according to the principles of aesthetics; with reference to the sense of the beautiful.

aestheticism *n* the principles or doctrines of aesthetics; attachment to aesthetics.

aesthetics *n* the theory of the fine arts; the science or that branch of philosophy which deals with the beautiful; the doctrines of taste.

aetiology, etiology *n* the study of the causes of anything, especially of diseases.

adze

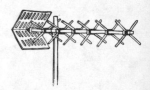

aerial

afar *adv* at a distance; to or from a distance (often with *from* preceding or *off* following, or both).

affability *n* the quality of being affable.

affable *adj* easy of conversation; admitting others to friendly conversation; courteous; of easy manners.

affably *adv* in an affable manner; courteously.

affair *n* business of any kind; that which is done or is to be done; matter; concern; sometimes used by itself in the plural with the specific sense of public affairs or financial affairs; special business; personal concern; a skirmish; a love affair; a relationship involving adultery.—**affair of honour** a duel.

affect *vt* to act on; to produce an effect or change on; to influence; to move or touch by exciting the feelings; to aspire to; to endeavour after; to choose commonly; habitually to follow after; to make a show of; to assume the appearance of; to pretend.

affectation, affectedness *n* an attempt to assume or exhibit what is not natural or real; false pretence, especially of what is praiseworthy or uncommon; artificial appearance or show.

affection

affected *adj* given to affectation; assuming or pretending to possess what is not natural or real; assumed artificially; not natural.

affecting *adj* having power to excite emotion; pathetic; moving.

affection *n* the state of having one's feelings affected in some way; a feeling of tenderness, love or attachment; an abnormal state of the body (*a gouty affection*).

affectionate *adj* having great love or affection; warmly attached; fond; kind; loving; proceeding from affection; tender.

affectionately *adv* in an affectionate manner; fondly; tenderly; kindly.

affectionateness *n* the quality of being affectionate; fondness; affection.

affiance *vt* (**affianced, affiancing**) to betroth; to bind by promise of marriage.

affianced *n* one bound by a promise of marriage.

affidavit *n* a written declaration on oath; a statement of facts in writing signed by the party and sworn to or confirmed by declaration before an authorized magistrate.

affiliate *vt* (**affiliated, affiliating**) to adopt; to receive into a family as a son; to establish the paternity of, as of a bastard child; to connect in the way of descent; to receive into a society as a member.—*n* an affiliated person, club, etc.

affiliation *n* the act of one who affiliates; the settlement of the paternity of a child on its true father.

affinity *n* a feeling of liking inclining one towards a person or thing; the relation contracted by marriage, as opposed to *consan-*

guinity; relation, connection or alliance in general (as of languages, sounds, etc); similarity in kind or nature; (*chem*) that force by which bodies of dissimilar nature unite in certain definite proportions to form a compound different in its nature from any of its constituents.

affirm *vt* to assert positively; to tell with confidence; to aver; to declare; to allege, opposed to *deny*; to confirm or ratify.—*vi* to make a solemn assertion or declaration; to make a legal affirmation.

affirmation *n* the act of affirming or asserting as true; that which is asserted; averment; confirmation; ratification; a solemn declaration made in lieu of an oath by one who has scruples about taking the oath.

affirmative *adj* affirming or asserting, opposed to *negative*.—*n* a word or phrase expressing assent or affirmation or answering a question affirmatively; the opposite of a *negative*.—**the affirmative** that side of a debated question which maintains the truth of the affirmative proposition.

affirmative action *n* positive action taken to improve opportunities for members of minority groups and women in an attempt to avoid racism, sexism etc.

affix *vt* to subjoin, annex, unite or add at the close or end; to append; to attach.—*n* a syllable or letter added to the end of a word; a suffix.

afflatus *n* inspiration; the inspiration of the poet.

afflict *vt* to give (to the body or mind) pain which is continued or of some permanence; to trouble, grieve, harass or distress.

affliction *n* the state of being afflicted; a state of acute pain or distress of body or mind; the cause of continued pain of body or mind.

affluence *n* an abundant supply; great plenty of worldly goods; wealth.

affluent *adj* flowing to; wealthy; abundant.—*n* a tributary stream.

afford *vt* to give forth; to yield, supply or produce (fruit, profit); to grant or confer (as consolation, gratification); to buy, sell, expend, etc, from having a sufficiency of means; to bear the expense of (with *can, could, may, might*, etc).

afforest *vt* to convert into a forest; to turn into forest land.

afforestation *n* the act of afforesting.

affray *n* fear; a noisy quarrel; a brawl; a tumult; disturbance.

affront *vt* to offend openly; to insult; to put out of countenance.—*n* disrespect deliberately shown to someone; an outrage to the feelings; an insult; anything producing a feeling of shame or disgrace.

afield *adv* to the field; in the field; away from home; astray.

afire *adj, adv* on fire.

aflame *adj, adv* flaming; glowing.

afloat *adj, adv* borne on the water; floating; passing from one person to another; in circulation (as a rumour).

afoot *adj, adv* on foot; borne by the feet; walking; in a state of being planned.

afore *adv* before in time or place, now mainly a nautical term; in the fore part of a vessel—*prep* before in time, position, rank, etc; in presence of, now a nautical term; more towards the head of a ship than; nearer the bow than.

aforegoing *adj* going before.

aforementioned, aforenamed, aforesaid *adj* mentioned before in the same document or discourse.

aforethought *adj* thought of beforehand; premeditated.

afraid *adj* full of fear or apprehension; frightened.

afresh *adv* anew; again; after intermission.

African *adj* pertaining to Africa.—*n* a native of Africa.

Afrikaner *n* a native of South Africa born of white parents.

aft *adj, adv* (*naut*) a word used to denote position at, near, or towards the stern of a ship.

after *adj* later in time; subsequent; succeeding, as, *an after period of life* (in this sense often combined with the following noun).—*prep* behind in place; later in time; in pursuit of; in search of; with or in desire for; in imitation of, or in imitation of the style of (*after a model*); according to; in proportion to (*after our deserts*); below in rank or excellence; next to; concerning (*inquire after*).—**after all** at last; in the end; at the most; notwithstanding.—*adv* later in time; afterwards; behind; in pursuit.

afterbirth *n* that which is expelled from the uterus after the birth of a child.

aftercare *n* care following hospital treatment, etc.

afterglow *n* the glow in the west after sunset.

aftergrowth *n* a second growth or crop springing up after a previous one has been removed.

after-hours *npl* hours that follow business; time following.

afterimage *n* the image of a bright object left for a time on the retina.

afterlife *n* future life; remainder of life; the life after death.

aftermath *n* the later consequences of an event; a second mowing of grass from the same land in the same season.

afternoon *n* the part of the day which follows noon, between noon and evening.

afterpains *npl* the pains which succeed childbirth.

afterpiece *n* a short dramatic entertainment performed after the principal performance.

afterthought *n* reflection after an act; a thought that occurs to one's mind too late to be useful.

aftermost *adj superl* hindmost, opposed to *foremost*.

afterward, afterwards *adv* at a later or subsequent time.

aga, agha *n* a Turkish commander or chief officer.

again *adv* a second time; once more; on another occasion; on the other hand; moreover; besides; further; in return; back; in answer.

against *prep* in opposition to; adverse or hostile to (*against law* or *public opinion*); towards or on; so as to meet (*to strike against a rock*); bearing or resting on (*to lean against*); in preparation for (an event).

agami *n* a bird of the crane family, native to South America.

agape *adv, adj* gaping as with wonder; having the mouth wide open.

Agape *n* among the primitive Christians a love-feast or feast of charity, held before or after the communion, when contributions were made for the poor.

agaric *n* a name of various fungi, many of which species are edible like the common mushroom, while others are deleterious and even poisonous.

agate *n* a semi-pellucid mineral, consisting of bands or layers of various colours blended together, the base generally being chalcedony, and this mixed with jasper, amethyst, quartz, opal, etc.

agave *n* one of a genus of plants including the American aloe.

age *n* a period of time representing the whole or a part of the duration of any individual thing or being; the time during which an individual has lived; the latter part of life; the state of being old; oldness; old people collectively; the state of having arrived at legal maturity (the completion of the first eighteen years of one's life); a great length of time; a long or protracted period; a historical epoch; an epoch having a particular character; the people who live at a particular period.—**the age** the times we live in.—*vi* (**aged, aging**) to grow old; to assume the appearance of old age.—*vt* to give the character of age or ripeness to (*to age wine*).

aged *adj* old; having lived long; having a certain age (*aged forty years*).

ageism, agism *n* discrimination on the grounds of age.—**ageist, agist** *adj*.

agency *n* the state of being in action or of exerting power; operation; instrumentality; the office or business of an agent or factor.

agami

agaric

agenda *npl* memoranda; business to be transacted at a meeting.

agent *n* one who or that which acts; an actor; one that exerts power or has the power to act; an active power or cause; a body or substance that causes a certain action to begin; a person entrusted with the business of another.

agglomerate *vt* (**agglomerated, agglomerating**) to collect or gather into a mass.—*vi* to become collected into a ball or mass.—*n* (*geol*) a collective name for masses consisting of angular fragments ejected from volcanoes.

agglutinate *vt* (**agglutinated, agglutinating**) to unite or cause to adhere, as with glue or other viscous substance; to glue together.—*adj* united as by glue; joined.

agglutinate language *n* (*philol*) a language in which the suffixes for inflection retain a kind of independence and are felt to be distinct from the root or main significant element of the word.

agglutination *n* the act of agglutinating or the state of being agglutinated; adhesion of parts; the marked feature of an agglutinate language.

aggrandize *vt* (**aggrandized, aggrandizing**) to make great or greater; especially to make greater in power, wealth, rank or honour; to exalt; to elevate; extend; enlarge.

aggrandizement *n* the act of aggrandizing; the act of increasing one's own power, rank or honour; advancement.

aggravate *vt* (**aggravated, aggravating**) to make worse, more severe or less tolerable; to make more enormous or less excusable; to intensify; to exaggerate; to provoke; to irritate; to tease.

aggravation *n* the act of aggravating or making worse; addition to that which is evil or improper; provocation; irritation.

aggregate *vt* (**aggregated, aggregating**) to bring together; to collect into a sum, mass or body.—*adj* formed by the conjunction or collection of particulars into a whole mass or sum; total.—*n* a sum, mass or assemblage of particulars; a whole or total.—**in the aggregate** taken altogether; considered as a whole; collectively.

aggregation *n* the act of aggregating; the state of; an aggregate.

aggress *vi* to make a first attack; to commit the first act of hostility or offence.—*vt* to attack.

aggression *n* the first attack or act of hostility; the first act leading to a war or controversy.

aggressive *adj* characterized by aggression; acting in a hostile manner.

aggressor *n* the person who attacks first; an assaulter; an invader.

aggrieve *vt* (**aggrieved, aggrieving**) to give

aggressive

pain or sorrow; to afflict; to grieve; to bear hard on; to oppress or injure the rights of.

aghast *adj* struck with amazement; stupefied with sudden fright or horror.

agile *adj* nimble; quick in movement; brisk; active.

agility *n* the state or quality of being agile; nimbleness; briskness; activity.

agio *n* the difference in value between one sort of money and another, especially between paper money and metallic coin.

agism *n* same as **ageism**.

agitate *vt* (**agitated, agitating**) to move or force into violent irregular action; to shake or move briskly; to disturb; to perturb; to discuss; to debate; to arouse public attention to, as by speeches, pamphlets, etc.—*vi* to engage in agitation.

agitated *adj* disturbed; perturbed; excited; expressing or displaying agitation.

agitation *n* the act of agitating or state of being agitated; perturbation of mind or feelings; commotion; disturbance.

agitator *n* one who or that which agitates, rouses or stirs up, especially one who wants to stir up political strife.

aglow *adj* in a glow; glowing.

agnate *n* any male relation by the father's side.—*adj* related or akin by the father's side.

agnomen *n* an additional name or epithet conferred on a person.

agnostic *n* one who disclaims any knowledge of God or of the origin of the universe or of anything but material phenomena, holding that with regard to such matters nothing can be known.—*adj* pertaining to the agnostics or their doctrines.

agnosticism *n* the doctrines or belief of agnostics.

agnus castus *n* a shrub of the verbena family, a native of the Mediterranean countries, with white flowers and acrid, aromatic fruits.

Agnus Dei a medal, or more frequently a cake of wax, consecrated by the pope, stamped with the figure of a lamb supporting the banner of the cross; the first words of a Roman Catholic chant or Anglican anthem.

ago *adv* past; gone, as, *a year ago.*

agog *adv* in eager excitement; highly excited by eagerness or anticipation.

agonic *adj* not forming an angle.

agonic line *n* one of two lines on the earth's surface, on which the magnetic needle points to the true north, or where the magnetic meridian coincides with the geographical.

agonize *vi* (**agonized, agonizing**) to writhe with agony or extreme pain.—*vt* to distress with extreme pain; to torture.

agonizing *adj* giving extreme pain.

agony *n* a violent contest or striving; the

struggle, frequently unconscious, that precedes natural death; the death throe or pang (often in plural); extreme bodily or mental pain; intense suffering; anguish; torment.

agony aunt *n* a person who gives advice to readers in an agony column.

agony column *n* a feature in a newspaper, magazine, etc, giving advice to readers on personal problems in response to letters.

agoraphobia *n* an abnormal fear of open spaces.

agouti *n* the native American name of several species of rodent mammals allied to the guinea pig.

agrarian *adj* relating to lands, especially public lands; growing wild in fields.—*n* one in favour of an equal division of landed property.

agrarianism *n* the upholding of an equal division of lands and property; the principles of one who does so.

agrarian law *n* any of various laws in ancient Rome for regulating the distribution of the public lands among the citizens.

agree *vi* (**agreed, agreeing**) to be of one mind; to harmonize in opinion; to live in concord or without contention; to come to an arrangement or understanding; to arrive at a settlement (*agree to a proposal*; *agree with a person*); to be consistent; to harmonize; not to contradict or be repugnant (*stories agree with each other*); to tally; to match; to correspond; to suit; to be accommodated or adapted (*food agrees with a person*); (*gram*) to correspond in number, case, gender or person.

agreeable *adj* suitable; conformable; correspondent; pleasing, either to the mind or senses (*agreeable manners*; *agreeable to the taste*); willing or ready to agree or consent; giving consent (with *to*).

agreeably *adv* in an agreeable manner; suitably; consistently; conformably; in a manner to give pleasure; pleasingly.

agreement *n* the state of agreeing or being agreed; harmony; conformity; union of opinions or sentiments; bargain; compact; contract.

agriculture *n* the cultivation and planting of the ground in large areas or fields, also including the raising and feeding of cattle or other livestock; husbandry; tillage; farming.

agricultural *adj* pertaining to, connected with or engaged in agriculture.

agriculturalist *n* one engaged or skilled in agriculture.

agrimony *n* a British plant, formerly used as a medicine, whose leaves and root stock are astringent, the latter yielding a yellow dye.

aground *adv, adj* on the ground; run ashore; stranded.

ague *n* the cold fit or rigor which precedes a fever or a paroxysm of fever; a fever coming in periodical fits accompanied by shivering; a chill or state of shaking.

ah *exclam* expressing pain, surprise, pity, compassion, complaint, contempt, dislike, joy, exultation, etc, according to the tone of voice.

aha *exclam* expressing triumph, contempt, surprise, etc.

ahead *adv* headlong; head foremost; in or to the front; in advance; before; further on (*to walk ahead of a person*); (*naut*) opposite to *astern*.

-aholic *suffix* modelled on *alcoholic*, indicating an addiction to something (*a workaholic*).

ahoy *exclam* a word used chiefly at sea in hailing.

ai *n* the three-toed sloth, so called from its cry.

aid *vt* to help; to assist; to come to the support or relief of; to succour.—*n* help; succour; support; assistance; the person or thing that aids or yields assistance; a helper; an auxiliary; an assistant; a subsidy or tax formerly granted by parliament to the crown; a tax paid by a feudal tenant to his lord.

aide-de-camp *n* (*pl* **aides-de-camp**) (*milit*) an officer whose duty is to receive and communicate the orders of a general officer, to act as his secretary, etc.

AIDS *n* a serious disease caused by a virus which hinders the production of the body's antibodies and so lessens and destroys immunity to infection.

aigret, aigrette *n* a plume or ornament for the head composed of feathers or precious stones.

ail *vt* to affect with pain or uneasiness, either of body or mind; to trouble; to be the matter with (*what ails you?*).—*vi* to be in pain or trouble.

ailment *n* disease; indisposition; a minor illness.

aim *vi* to direct a missile towards an object; to direct the mind or intention; to make an attempt; to endeavour (followed by *at* before the object).—*vt* to direct or point to a particular object with the intention of hitting it; to level at.—*n* the pointing or directing of a missile; the point intended to be hit or object intended to be achieved; the mark; a purpose; intention; design; scheme.

aimless *adj* without aim; purposeless.

air *n* the mixture of gases that we breathe; an odourless, invisible, tasteless, colourless, elastic compound of oxygen, nitrogen, etc, essential to life; air in motion; a light breeze; a tune; a short song or piece of music adapted to words; a melody; the soprano part in a harmonized piece of mu-

agouti

sic; the look, appearance and bearing of a person; the general character or complexion of anything; appearance; semblance; an affected manner; manifestation of pride or vanity (chiefly in the phrase *to give oneself airs*).—**to take the air** to go out of doors; to walk or ride a little distance.—*vt* to expose to the air; to ventilate; to display; to bring before public notice; to make dry and comfortable by heating (*to air sheets*).

air bag *n* a safety device built in to the steering column of a motor vehicle which in the event of collision inflates with air and comes between the steering column and the torso of the driver.

air bed *n* an inflatable mattress, used as a spare bed or for sunbathing.

air bladder *n* a vesicle filled with air; a bag situated under the backbone of certain fish, which, being full of air, assists in regulating buoyancy.

air chief marshal *n* an officer in the Royal Air Force, ranking equivalent to an admiral in the Navy or general in the Army.

air commodore *n* an officer in the Royal Air Force, ranking equivalent to a commodore in the Navy or a brigadier in the Army.

aircraft

air-condition *vt* to install an air-conditioning system.

air-conditioning *n* a system regulating air temperature and humidity in buildings and vehicles.

aircraft *n* a general name for craft designed for flight, such as aeroplanes or helicopters.

Airedale *n* a large breed of terrier, long in the legs and with a hard, close coat.

air filter *n* a contrivance for filtering or purifying air.

air force *n* the aviation branch of the military forces of a country.

air gun *n* a gun in which highly compressed air is used to fire the missile.

airily *adv* in an airy manner; in a light, bright manner.

airiness *n* the state or quality of being airy.

airing *n* a short walk or drive out of doors.

airline *n* an organization which provides scheduled transport by air between specified points.

airman *n* (*pl* **airmen**) one who flies, especially in an air force.

air marshal *n* an officer in the Royal Air Force, ranking equivalent to a vice-admiral in the Navy or a lieutenant-general in the Army.

air plant *n* a plant that derives its nourishment from the air, an epiphyte.

air pocket *n* a place in the air where pressure is abnormally low, so that an aeroplane entering it drops suddenly.

air sac *n* one of the sacs or bags for air in the

alarm clock

hollow bones and cavities of the body of birds, communicating with the lungs.

air shaft *n* a passage for air into a mine.

airship *n* a lighter-than-air vessel driven by mechanical power and depending on gas for buoyancy.

airside *n* the part of an airport complex nearest the aircraft, reached after going through security checks and passport control.

airspace *n* the space above a country over which it exercises jurisdiction.

airtight *adj* so tight or close as to be impermeable to air.

air vice-marshal *n* an officer in the Royal Air Force, ranking equivalent to a rear-admiral in the Navy or a major-general in the Army.

airy *adj* consisting of or having the character of air; ethereal; unsubstantial; relating to the air; high in air; open to a free current of air; exposed to all winds (*an airy situation*); bright and sprightly; full of vivacity; lively; casual; unconcerned.

aisle *n* a lateral division of a cathedral or other church, separated from the central part, called the nave, by pillars or piers.

ajar *adv* neither quite open nor shut; partly opened (said of a door).

akimbo *adj*, *adv* with the elbow pointing outwards and the hand resting on the hip (said of the arm).

akin *adj*, *adv* related by blood; allied by nature; having like properties.

alabaster *n* a soft, semitransparent, marble-like chalky stone.

alack *interj* an exclamation expressive of sorrow; alas.

alacrity *n* a cheerful readiness or promptness to do some act; cheerful willingness; briskness.

alar *adj* pertaining to wings; having the character of a wing.

alarm *n* an outcry or other notice of approaching danger; a tumult; a disturbance; a sudden fear excited by an apprehension of danger; apprehension; terror; a mechanical contrivance for awakening persons from sleep or rousing their attention.—*vt* to give notice of danger; to rouse to vigilance; to disturb with terror; to fill with anxiety.

alarm clock a clock with an apparatus that can be set to awaken sleepers at a given time by ringing or buzzing.

alarmed *adj* indicating or expressive of alarm (look, countenance).

alarming *adj* calculated to rouse alarm; causing apprehension.

alarmist *n* one who excites alarm; one prone to take alarm and to circulate and exaggerate bad news.

alas *exclam* expressing sorrow, grief, pity, concern or apprehension of evil.

alate *adj* winged; having membranous expansions like wings.

alb *n* a clerical vestment worn by priests, a long robe of white linen bound with a girdle.

albacore, albicore *n* a name given to several fishes of the tunny kind, especially to the Pacific tunny.

albatross *n* a bird of the ocean, the largest sea bird known; a heavy and inescapable burden.

albeit *conj* even although; notwithstanding.

albert *n* a short chain attaching the watch to a waistcoat buttonhole.

Albigenses *npl* a party of religious reformers in the twelfth century in southern France, who were ruthlessly persecuted.

Albigensian *adj* of or pertaining to the Albigenses.

albino *n* (*pl* **albinos**) a person of abnormally pale, milky complexion, with light hair and pink eyes; an animal lacking pigment in skin, hair and eyes.

albinism *n* the state or condition of an albino.

album *n* a book, originally blank, for inserting autographs of celebrated persons and friends or favourite pieces of poetry or prose; a book for preserving photographs, stamps, etc; a long-playing record.

albumin, albumen *n* the white of an egg; the substance surrounding the yolk.

albuminous *adj* pertaining to or having the properties of albumin (applied to plants whose seeds have a store of albumin, as all kinds of grain, palms, etc).

albuminuria *n* (*pathol*) a condition in which the urine contains albumin, indicating a diseased state of the kidneys.

alburnum *n* the white and softer part of the wood of exogenous plants between the inner bark and the heartwood; the sapwood.

Alcaic *adj* pertaining to Alcaeus, a lyric poet of Mitylene.

Alcaic verse *n* a variety of verse used in Greek and Latin poetry.

alcalde, alcaide *n* in Spain, Portugal, etc, a commander of a fortress; the chief civil magistrate of a town, also, a jailer.

alchemy *n* the art which had for its main objects the transmuting of the baser metals into gold or silver, the discovery of an elixir of life, a universal solvent, etc.

alchemist *n* one who practises alchemy.

alcohol *n* a liquid forming the intoxicating principle of all vinous and spirituous liquors and obtained by distillation, first procured from wine.

alcohol abuse *n* excessive consumption of alcohol, often leading to illness.

alcoholic *adj* pertaining to alcohol or partaking of its qualities.—*n* a person addicted to alcohol.

alcoholism *n* an addiction to alcohol; a disease caused by excessive consumption of alcoholic drinks.

alcoholize *vt* (**alcoholized, alcoholizing**) to convert into alcohol; to rectify (spirit) till it is wholly purified.

Alcoran *n* the Koran.

alcove *n* a wide and deep recess in a room, intended for a bed or seats, etc; any natural recess.

aldehyde *n* a transparent colourless liquid produced by the oxidation of pure alcohol; one of a class of organic compounds, derived from alcohol by the abstraction of two atoms of hydrogen and converted into acids by the addition of one atom of oxygen.

alder *n* the popular name of a tree or shrub with toothed leaves and usually growing in moist land.

alder buckthorn *n* a British shrub with small flowers.

alderman *n* (*pl* **aldermen**) (*hist*) an Anglo-Saxon nobleman, often a governor of a shire; until 1974, a magistrate or officer of a town, next in rank below the mayor.

Aldine *adj* of or from the printing press of Aldus Manutius, of Venice, and his family, from 1490 to 1597.

ale *n* a liquor made from an infusion of malt by fermentation; beer or a kind of beer.

alecost *n* costmary, a plant put into ale to give it an aromatic flavour.

alee *adv* (*naut*) on the lee side; on the side opposite to that on which the wind strikes, opposite of *aweather*.

alert *adj* watchful; vigilant; brisk; nimble.—**on the alert** on the watch; on the lookout; guarding against surprise or danger.

alewife *n* a fish of the shad genus, caught in the Severn; also a similar North American fish much used as food.

Alexandrian *adj* pertaining to Alexandria in Egypt, especially ancient Alexandria.

Alexandrine *n* a line of verse consisting of twelve syllables in English poetry, or in French of twelve and thirteen in alternate couplets.

alfa, alfa-grass *adj* a North African name for one of the varieties of esparto and its fibre.

alfalfa *n* a common name in the United States for the fodder plant lucerne.

alga *n* (*pl* **algae**) a seaweed; one of an order of cryptogamic plants found for the most part in the sea and fresh water, comprising seaweeds.

algebra *n* that branch of mathematical analysis in which signs are employed to denote arithmetical operations and letters are used to represent numbers and quantities; a kind of universal arithmetic.

algebraic, algebraical *adj* pertaining to algebra; containing an operation of algebra.

alb

albatross

algebraist *n* one versed in the science of algebra.

algid *adj* cold.

algorism *n* Arabic decimal notation; arithmetic.

algorithm *n* the art of computing or reckoning in reference to some particular subject or in some particular way (*the algorithm of the differential calculus*).

alias *adv* otherwise (used especially of persons who assume various names, as *John Smith alias Thomas Jones*).—*n* (*pl* **aliases**) an assumed name; another name.

alibi *n* (*law*) a plea stating that the accused was in another place at the time of the offence and therefore cannot be guilty.

alien *adj* not belonging to the same country, land or government; foreign; different in nature; estranged; adverse (with *to* or *from*).—*n* a foreigner; one born in or belonging to another country; one who is not, as a foreigner, entitled to the privileges of a citizen; in science fiction, a being from another planet or world.

alienability *n* the state of being alienable.

alienable *adj* capable of being alienated, sold or transferred to another.

alienate *vt* (**alienated, alienating**) to transfer or convey, as title, property or other right, to another; to withdraw, as the affections; to make indifferent or averse; to estrange.

alienation *n* estrangement; transference; diversion to another purpose; mental derangement.

alienism *n* the study and treatment of mental alienation.

alienist *n* in USA, a specialist in mental illness for legal purposes.

alight[1] *vi* to get down, descend or step from a vehicle; to settle, as a bird on a tree; to land.

alight[2] *adj, adv* lighted; made to burn by having a light applied.

align *vt* to lay out or regulate by a line; to form in line, as troops; to join, unite or agree with a cause, group, etc (with *with*).

alignment *n* the act of aligning; an adjusting to a line; the line of adjustment; the ground plan of a railway or road, distinct from the gradients or profile; a row of things; an alliance or agreement for a cause.

alike *adj* having resemblance; similar; without difference.—*adv* in the same manner, form or degree; in common (*all have erred alike*).

aliment *n* that which nourishes; food; nutriment.

alimental *adj* of or pertaining to aliment; supplying food; having the quality of nourishing.

alimentary *adj* pertaining to aliment or food; nourishing.

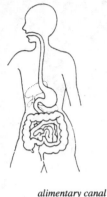
alimentary canal

aliped

alimentary canal *n* the tube extending within the body from the mouth to the anus, through which food passes and is absorbed.

alimony *n* an allowance out of her husband's estate made for the support of a woman legally separated from him.

aliped *adj* wing-footed; having the toes connected by a membrane, which serves as a wing, as bats.—*n* an animal whose toes are so connected.

alive *adj* having life; living; not dead; in a state of action; in force or operation (*keep an agitation alive*); sprightly (*alive with excitement*); sensitive to; susceptible (*alive to the beauties of nature*); full of or teeming with life.

alkali *n* one of an important class of bases which combine with acids to form salts, turn vegetable yellows to red and vegetable blues to green, and unite with oil or fat to form soap.

alkaline *adj* having the properties of an alkali.

alkaline earth *n* lime, magnesiium, barium, strontium, radium.

alkane *n* (*chem*) see **paraffin**.

alkaloid *n* any of a class of nitrogenized compounds found in living plants and containing their active principles, such as morphine, quinine, aconitine, caffeine, etc.—*adj* relating to or containing alkali.

Alkoran *n* the Koran.

all *adj* every one of; the whole number or quantity of: it goes before an article or adjective belonging to the same noun—*all the men, all good men, all my labour*, etc; with nouns of time it is equivalent to during the whole (*all day, all night*).—*adv* wholly; completely; entirely; altogether; quite (*all alone, all unarmed*).—**all but** nearly; almost; not quite.—**all one** the same thing in effect; quite the same.—*n* the whole number; the entire thing; the aggregate; the total.—**at all** in the least degree; to the least extent; under any circumstances.—**in all** everything reckoned or taken into account; all included.—**all in** composition, has often the force of an adverb, as in *almighty, all-powerful, all-perfect, all-important*; sometimes of a noun in the objective case, as, *all-seeing*.—**all along** *adv* throughout; from the beginning onwards.—**all-in-all** *n* everything to a person; everything in all respects.—*adv* altogether; as a whole.

Allah *n* the Arabic name for God.

allay *vt* to make quiet; to pacify or appease (a tumult); to abate, mitigate or subdue; to relieve or alleviate (grief, thirst).—*vi* to subside; to grow calm.

allayment *n* the act of allaying; the state of being allayed.

allegation *n* the act of alleging; affirmation;

declaration; that which is affirmed or asserted.

allege *vt* (**alleged, alleging**) to assert without proof; to produce as an argument, plea or excuse in court.

allegiance *n* the tie or obligation of a subject to his or her sovereign or government; the duty of fidelity to a sovereign, government or state.

allegoric, allegorical *adj* pertaining to allegory; in the manner of allegory.

allegorize *vt* (**allegorized, allegorizing**) to turn into allegory; to narrate in allegory; to explain in an allegorical sense.—*vi* to use allegory.

allegory *n* a figurative discourse, in which the principal subject is described by another subject resembling it in its properties and circumstances; a narrative in which abstract ideas are personified; a continued metaphor.

allegretto *adj, adv* (*mus*) of a time quicker than andante, but not so quick as allegro.—*n* (*pl* **allegrettos**) a piece of music played in this way.

allegro *adj, adv* (*mus*) a word denoting a brisk movement; a sprightly part or strain. —*n* (*pl* **allegros**) a composition performed in a sprightly manner.

allergenic *adj* causing an allergic reation.

allergic *adj* pertaining to or charactgerizing allergy; having an allergy; antipathetic.

allergy *n* an abnormal reaction of the body to substances (certain foods, pollen, etc) normally harmless; antipathy.

alleviate *vt* (**alleviated, alleviating**) to make light, in a figurative sense; to lessen, mitigate or make easier to be endured (sorrow, pain, distress).

alleviation *n* the act of alleviating; that which lessens, mitigates or makes more tolerable.

alley *n* a passage; especially, a narrow passage or way in a town.

All Fools' Day *n* the first day of April.

all fours *n* all four legs of an animal; the two legs and two arms or hands of a person.

Allhallows *n* All Saints' Day.

alliaceous *adj* pertaining to garlic and allied plants; having the properties of garlic.

alliance *n* the state of being allied or connected; the relation or union between families, contracted by marriage; a union between nations, contracted by compact, treaty or league; any union or connection of interests; a compact or treaty; the persons or parties allied; (*bot*) a group of allied families or orders.

Allies *npl* in the First World War, all the nations allied against the alliance of Germany, Austria-Hungary, Bulgaria and Turkey; in the Second World War, the nations allied against the alliance of Germany

and Italy and later Japan and other nations.

alligator *n* a large reptile of the crocodile family found in tropical America, differing from the true crocodiles in having a shorter and flatter head, cavities or pits in the upper jaw, into which the long canine teeth of the underjaw fit, and having the feet much less webbed.

alligator pear *n* same as **avocado pear**.

alliteration *n* the repetition of the same letter at the beginning of two or more words immediately succeeding each other, or at short intervals (as in *apt alliteration's artful aid*).

allocate *vt* (**allocated, allocating**) to assign or allot to a person or persons; to set apart for a particular purpose; to apportion or distribute (shares in a public company or the like).

allocation *n* the act of allocating, allotting or assigning; allotment; assignment; apportionment.

allodial *adj* pertaining to allodium or freehold; held independent of an overlord; opposed to *feudal*.

allodium *n* freehold estate; real estate held in absolute independence, without being subject to any rent, service or acknowledgment to a superior.

allomorphic *adj* pertaining to or possessing the qualities of allomorphism.

allomorphism *n* that property of certain substances of assuming a different form, the substance remaining otherwise unchanged.

allopathy *n* the method of treating disease by producing a condition of the system either different from, opposite to or incompatible with the condition essential to the disease: it is opposed to *homoeopathy* and is the common method of treatment.

allot *vt* (**allotted, allotting**) to distribute or parcel out in parts or portions; to assign; to set apart; to destine.

allotment *n* the act of allotting; that which is allotted; a share, part or portion granted or distributed; a piece of ground rented by a person for cultivating.

allotropic *adj* of or pertaining to allotropy.

allotropy, allotropism *n* the capability exhibited by some substances of existing in more than one form and with different characteristics (thus carbon forms both the diamond and charcoal).

allow *vt* to grant, give or make over; to assign (*to allow him £300 a year*); to admit; to own or acknowledge (*allow a claim*); to abate or deduct; to set apart (*allow so much for loss*); to grant permission to; to permit.—*vi* to concede; to make abatement or concession.

allowable *adj* capable of being allowed or permitted; not forbidden; permissible.

allowance *n* permission; licence; sanction;

alley

alligator

a quantity allowed or granted; relaxation of severity in censure; a deduction before tax assessment.

alloy *n* a baser metal mixed with a finer; a mixture of different metals; any metallic compound; (*fig*) evil mixed with good.—*vt* to reduce the purity of (a metal) by mixing with it a portion of less valuable metal; to reduce, abate or impair by mixture.

All Saints' Day *n* a church festival held on 1st November for all saints.

All Souls' Day a church festival held on 2nd November, when prayers are offered up for the dead.

allspice *n* a spice of a mildly pungent taste, the fruit of a West Indian tree, so called from being regarded as combining many different flavours; pimento.

allude *vi* (**alluded, alluding**) to refer to something not directly mentioned; to hint at by remote suggestions (followed by *to*).

allure *vt* (**allured, alluring**) to tempt by the offer of something good, real or apparent; to draw or try to draw by some proposed pleasure or advantage; to entice, decoy, tempt, attract.

alluring *adj* inviting; having the quality of attracting or tempting.

allusion *n* the act of alluding; a reference to something not explicitly mentioned; an indirect or incidental suggestion; a hint.

alluvium *n* (*pl* **alluviums, alluvia**) soil deposited by means of the action of water, often washed down from mountains or high grounds.

alluvial *adj* pertaining to or having the character of alluvium; deposited by the action of waves or currents of water.

ally *vt* (**allied, allying**) to unite by marriage, treaty, league or confederacy; to connect by formal agreement; to bind together or connect (as by friendship, marriage, treaty, etc).—*vi* to be closely united.—*n* a state united by treaty or league; a confederate.

alma mater *n* the name applied by students to their own university.

almanac, almanack *n* a table, book or publication, generally annual, comprising a calendar of days, weeks and months, with the times of the rising of the sun and moon, changes of the moon, eclipses, stated festivals of churches, etc, for a certain year or years.

almighty *adj* possessing all power; omnipotent; being of unlimited might.

Almighty *n* God, the all-powerful.

almond *n* the seed or kernel of a tree allied to the peach; the tree itself, of which there are two varieties, sweet and bitter.—*adj* (of eyes, etc) oval and pointed at one or both ends.

almond oil *n* a bland, fixed oil obtained from almonds.

almoner *n* originally, a dispenser of alms or

charity; formerly, a medically trained social worker attached to a hospital to help patients with social problems.

almonry *n* the place where an almoner resided or where alms were distributed.

almost *adv* nearly; well nigh; for the greatest part.

alms *npl* anything given gratuitously to relieve the poor; a charitable dole; charity.

alms-deed *n* an act of charity; a charitable gift.

alms-gate *n* the gate of religious or great houses, at which alms were distributed to the poor.

almshouse *n* a house appropriated for the use of the poor who are supported by the public or by a revenue derived from public endowment; a poorhouse.

aloe *n* the common name of plants of the lily family, natives of warm climates and especially abundant in Africa, several species yielding aloes, a bitter purgative medicine.

aloft *adv* on high; in the air; high above the ground; (*naut*) on or in the rigging.

alone *adj, adv* apart from another or others; single; solitary (*to remain alone, to walk alone*); only; to the exclusion of other persons or things; solely (*he alone remained, two men alone returned*).—**to let alone** to leave untouched or not meddled with.

along *adv* by the length; lengthwise; in a line with the length (*stretched along*); in a line or with a progressive motion; onward (*to walk along*); in company; together (followed by *with*).—*prep* by the length of, as distinguished from *across*; in a longitudinal direction over or near.

alongshore *adv* by or near the shore.

alongside *adv* along or by the side; beside each other (*to lie alongside* or *alongside of*).—*prep* beside; by the side of.

aloof *adv* at a distance, but within view; apart; separated.—*prep* away or apart from.

aloud *adv* in a normal tone of voice.

alow *adv* in a low place or a lower part, opposed to *aloft*.

alp *n* a high mountain.

alpaca *n* a ruminant mammal of the camel family, a native of the Andes, valued for its long, soft and silky wool, which is woven into fabrics of great beauty; a fabric manufactured from the wool of the alpaca.

alpenhorn, alphorn *n* a very long, powerful, nearly straight horn, but curving slightly and widening towards its extremity, used on the Alps to convey signals.

alpenstock *n* a strong tall stick with a pointed iron-tipped end, used in climbing mountains.

alpha *n* the first letter in the Greek alphabet or A, sometimes used to denote first or top grade, e.g. in examinations.

alpha and omega the first and last letters of

alpaca

alpenhorn

the Greek alphabet; the beginning and the end; that which comprises all.

alphabet *n* the letters of a language arranged in a particular order; any series of elementary signs or symbols used for a similar purpose; hence, first elements; simplest rudiments.

alphabetic, alphabetical *adj* pertaining to an alphabet; furnished with an alphabet; expressed by an alphabet; in the order of an alphabet.

alphabetically *adv* in an alphabetical order of the letters.

alpha ray *n* a ray emitted by radium and other radioactive substances, consisting of positively charged atoms of helium.

alphorn *n* same as **alpenhorn**.

alpine *adj* of or pertaining to the Alps or any high mountain; (of plants) growing above the treeline.—*n* an alpine plant.

already *adv* before the present time; before some specified time.

Alsatian *adj* of or pertaining to Alsace in France.—*n* a native of Alsace; a large breed of dog, the German shepherd.

also *adv, conj* in like manner; likewise; in addition; too; further.

also-ran *n* a defeated contestant in a race, an election, etc.

Altaic *n* a family of languages which includes Hungarian, Finnish, Turkish, etc.—*adj* pertaining to Altaic or to the Altai, a vast range of mountains in Eastern Asia.

altar *n* an elevated place on which sacrifices were offered or incense burned to a deity; a table in a church for the celebration of the eucharist.

altar cloth *n* the cloth that covers the altar and hangs down in front.

altarpiece *n* a painting or piece of sculpture placed behind or above an altar in a church.

altazimuth *n* an astronomical instrument for determining the altitude and azimuth of heavenly bodies, consisting of a vertical circle and attached telescope, the two having both a vertical and a horizontal motion.

alter *vt* to make other or different; to make some change in; to vary in some degree, without an entire change.—*vi* to become, in some respects, different; to vary; to change.

alteration *n* the act of altering; the state of being altered; also, the change made.

alterative *adj* causing alteration; having the power to alter; (*med*) having the power to restore the healthy functions of the body.—*n* a medicine or drug having this character.

altercate *vi* to argue; to wrangle.

altercation *n* the act of altercating; heated argument; a wrangle.

alternate *adj* being by turns; following one

another in time or place by turns; first one, then another successively; reciprocal; having one intervening between each pair; occupying every second place; consisting of parts or members proceeding in this way (*an alternate series*).—*vt* (**alternated, alternating**) to perform by turns or in succession; to cause to succeed or follow by turns.—*vi* to follow one another in time or place by turns.

alternate generation *n* that species of generation among animals by which the young do not resemble their parent, but their grandparent or some remote ancestor; heterogenesis.

alternating current *n* (*elect*) a current which changes periodically in magnitude and direction.

alternation *n* the act of alternating or state of being alternate; the act of following and being followed in turn.

alternation of generation *n* in organisms, alternation of sexual and asexual stages in the life history.

alternative *adj* offering a choice or possibility of one of two things; offering or following a different approach from the conventional or established one.—*n* a choice between two things, so that if one is taken the other must be left; a possibility of one of two things, so that if one is false the other must be true.

alternative medicine *n* a form of treatment not based on traditional medical or surgical techniques or on the use of chemical drugs but using such techniques as osteopathy, acupuncture, aromatherapy, herbal remedies, etc.

alternator *n* an electric generator for producing alternating currents.

although *conj* grant all this; be it so; suppose that; admit all that; *although* differs very little from *though*, but is perhaps rather stronger.

altimeter *n* an instrument for taking altitudes by geometrical principles, as a sextant or a quadrant; an instrument for indicating the height of an aeroplane above the ground.

altimetry *n* the art of ascertaining altitudes.

altitude *n* height; amount of space to a point above from one below; measure of elevation.

alto *n* (*mus*) contralto; the deepest voice among women and boys, and the highest among men, a special voice above the tenor; a singer in this voice.—*adj* pertaining to this voice.

altogether *adv* wholly; entirely; completely; quite.

alto-rilievo, alto-relievo *n* (*pl* **alto-rilievi, alto-relievos**) high relief; sculpture in which the figures stand out prominently from the background.

Alsatian

altar

altruism *n* devotion to others or to humanity; the opposite of *selfishness*.

altruist *n* one who practises altruism.

altruistic *adj* pertaining to altruism; regardful of others.

alum *n* a general name for a class of double sulphates containing aluminium and such metals as potassium, ammonium, iron, etc, common or potash alum being used medicinally as an astringent and a styptic, in dyeing as a mordant, and in tanning for restoring the cohesion of skins.—*vt* to steep in or impregnate with a solution of alum.

alumina *n* the oxide of aluminium, the most abundant of the earths, widely diffused in the shape of clay, loam, etc.

aluminium *n* the metallic base of alumina; a white metal with a bluish tinge and a lustre somewhat resembling, but far inferior to, that of silver.

aluminium bronze *n* an alloy of aluminium and copper, possessed of great tenacity, for industrial purposes.

aluminium gold *n* an alloy of 10 parts of aluminium to 90 of copper.

alumnus *n* (*pl* **alumni**) a pupil; a graduate or undergraduate of a university, regarded as his or her alma mater.

always *adv* perpetually; uninterruptedly; continually (*always the same*); as often as occasion recurs (*he is always late*).

alveolus *n* (*pl* **alveoli**) a small pit, cell, cavity or socket; the socket in which a tooth is fixed; an air sac from a bronchiole end in the lungs; the cell of a honeycomb.

Alzheimer's disease *n* a degenerative disorder of the brain resulting in premature progressive senility.

am the first person of the verb to be, in the indicative mood, present tense.

amadavat, avadavat *n* a small grain-eating bird of India, with a red conical beak and red and black plumage, kept as a cage bird.

amalgam *n* a compound of mercury with another metal; any metallic alloy of which mercury forms an essential constituent part; a mixture or compound of different things.

amalgamate *vt* (**amalgamated, amalgamating**) to compound or mix (a metal) with mercury; to blend, unite or combine generally into one mass or whole.—*vi* to combine to form an amalgam; to unite or coalesce generally; to become mixed or blended together.

amalgamation *n* the act or operation of amalgamating; the state of being amalgamated; union or junction into one body or whole; the process of separating gold and silver from their ores by combining them with mercury, which dissolves and separates the other metal and is afterwards driven off by heat.

amanuensis *n* (*pl* **amanuenses**) a person who writes down what another dictates or copies what has been written by another.

amaranth *n* (*poet*) a flower supposed never to fade; a red colouring added to food.

amaranthine *adj* belonging to, consisting of or resembling amaranth; never-fading; of a purplish colour.

amass *vt* to collect into a heap; to gather a great quantity or number of; to accumulate.

amateur *n* one who cultivates a study, art or pursuit, e.g. sport, without pursuing it professionally or with a view to gain; any non-professional or non-expert.

amateurish *adj* pertaining to or characteristic of an amateur; lacking the skill, finish or other faculties of a professional.

amative *adj* full of love; amorous; amatory.

amatory *adj* pertaining to or producing love; expressive of love (verses, sighs, etc).

amaurosis *n* a partial or complete loss of sight from loss of power in the optic nerve or retina without any visible defect in the eye except an immovable pupil.

amaze *vt* (**amazed, amazing**) to confound with fear, sudden surprise or wonder; to confuse utterly; to perplex; to astound; to astonish; to surprise.—*n* astonishment; confusion; amazement (used chiefly in poetry).

amazement *n* the state of being amazed or astounded; astonishment; great surprise.

amazing *adj* very wonderful; exciting astonishment.

Amazon *n* one of a fabled race of female warriors mentioned by the ancient Greek writers; a warlike or masculine woman; a virago.

ambassador *n* a minister of the highest rank sent to represent a sovereign or state in another country and to transact state affairs.

amber *n* a mineralized pale-yellow, and sometimes reddish or brownish, resin of extinct pine trees, found most abundantly on the shores of the Baltic.

ambergris *n* a solid, opaque, ash-coloured inflammable substance used in perfumery, a secretion obtained from the sperm whale.

ambidextrous *adj* having the faculty of using both hands with equal ease; double-dealing.

ambient *adj* surrounding; encompassing on all sides (applied to fluids or diffusible substances, as *the ambient air*).

ambiguity, ambiguousness *n* the state or quality of being ambiguous; doubtfulness or uncertainty, particularly of meaning.

ambiguous *adj* doubtful or uncertain, especially in respect to meaning; liable to be interpreted two ways; equivocal; indefinite.

ambit *n* compass or circuit; circumference; scope; sphere; extent.

ambition *n* an eager and sometimes inordinate desire after honour, power, fame or whatever confers distinction; desire to distinguish oneself among others.

ambitious *adj* possessing ambition; eagerly or inordinately desirous of power, honour, fame, office, superiority or distinction; strongly desirous (with *of* or *after*); springing from, indicating or characterized by ambition; showy; pretentious (*ambitious ornament*).

amble *vi* (**ambled, ambling**) to move by lifting both legs on each side alternately (said of horses, etc); hence, to move easily and gently.—*n* the pace of a horse or like animal when ambling; easy motion; gentle pace.

ambo *n* in early Christian churches a raised desk or pulpit.

amboyna wood *n* a beautifully mottled and curled wood employed in cabinet work.

ambrosia *n* the fabled food of the ancient Greek gods, which conferred immortality on those who partook of it; hence, anything pleasing to the taste or smell.

ambrosial *adj* of or pertaining to ambrosia; anointed or fragrant with ambrosia; delicious; fragrant.

ambry *n* an almonry; a niche or recess in the wall of ancient churches near the altar in which the sacred utensils were deposited.

ambsace *n* double ace; complete bad luck, the two aces being the lowest throw at dice.

ambulance *n* a a vehicle for for conveying the sick and injured to hospital;.

ambulant *adj* (of a patient) able to walk, not bed-ridden; moving from place to place.

ambulatory *adj* of or pertaining to walking; movable; temporary; capable of walking.—*n* a place for walking in; a covered way.

ambuscade *n* a lying in wait concealed for the purpose of attacking an enemy by surprise; a place where one party lies concealed with a view to attack another by surprise; those lying so concealed; ambush.—*vti* (**ambuscaded, ambuscading**) to lie in wait in order to attack from a concealed position.

ambush *n* same as ambuscade.—*vt* to post or place in ambush.—*vi* to lie or be posted in ambush.

ameer, amir *n* a nobleman; a chief; a ruler; an emir.

ameliorate *vt* (**ameliorated, ameliorating**) to make better; to improve; to meliorate.—*vi* to grow better; to meliorate.

amelioration *n* the act of ameliorating; improvement; melioration.

ameliorative *adj* producing or having a tendency to produce, amelioration.

amen *interj* so be it.—*n* a saying of this; any expression of assent.

amenability *n* the state of being amenable.

amenable *adj* ready to yield or submit, as to advice; submissive; liable to answer or be called to account; responsible.

amend *vt* to make better or change for the better, by removing what is faulty; to correct; to improve; to reform.—*vi* to grow or become better by reformation or rectifying something wrong in manners or morals.

amendable *adj* capable of being amended or corrected.

amender *n* one who amends.

amendment *n* the act of amending or changing for the better, in any way; the act of becoming better or state of having become better; an alteration proposed to be made in the draft of a parliamentary bill or in the terms of any motion under discussion before a meeting.

amends *npl* compensation for a loss or injury; recompense; satisfaction; equivalent.

amenity *n* the quality of being pleasant or agreeable, in respect of situation, prospect, climate, etc, as also of temper, disposition or manners.

amenorrhoea *n* (*med*) abnormal absence of menstruation.

amentia *n* serious or congenital illness.

American *adj* pertaining to America or the United States.—*n* a native of America or the United States.

American Indian *n* any member of the original native peoples of North America, Central America or South America, excluding the Inuit.

Americanism *n* the feelings of nationality which distinguish American citizens; a word, phrase or idiom peculiar to Americans.

Americanize *vt* (**Americanized, Americanizing**) to render American or like what prevails in or is characteristic of America.

Amerindian *n* an American Indian.

amethyst *n* a violet-blue or purple variety of quartz used in articles of jewellery.

amiable *adj* worthy of love; delightful or pleasing (said of things); having a friendly and attractive disposition; lovable.

amiability, amiableness *n* the quality of being amiable or lovable; sweetness of temper.

amicable *adj* characterized by or exhibiting friendship, peaceableness or harmony; friendly; peaceable; harmonious in social or mutual transactions.

amicability *n* quality of being amicable.

amicably *adv* in an amicable or friendly manner; with harmony.

amice *n* a flowing cloak formerly worn by priests and pilgrims; an oblong embroidered piece or strip of fine linen, falling down the shoulders like a cope, worn un-

ambulance

American Indian

der the alb by priests in the service of the Mass.

amid, amidst *prep* in the midst or middle of; surrounded or encompassed by; mingled with; among.

amidships *adv* in or towards the middle or the middle line of a ship.

amide, amine *n* (*chem*) any of a series of salts produced by the substitution of elements or radicals for the hydrogen atoms of ammonia, often used as terminations of the names of such salts.

amidogen *n* the radical NH_2, the characteristic part of amides and amines.

amino acid (*chem*) an acid derived from a fatty or dibasic acid by exchanging one or more hydrogen atoms of the hydrocarbon radical or radicals for the amino group (NH_2).

amiss *adj* wrong; faulty; out of time or order; improper.—*adv* in a faulty manner.

amity *n* friendship; harmony; good understanding, especially between nations.

ammeter *n* an instrument for measuring an electric current (in amperes).

ammonal *n* a blasting explosive, a mixture of ammonium nitrate, powdered aluminium and charcoal.

ammonia *n* a pungent coulouless gas composed of nitrogen and hydrogen, used in medicine and chemistry.

ammonite *n* a fossil shell of an extinct cuttlefish, coiled in a plane spiral and chambered within like that of the nautilus, to which the ammonites were allied.

ammonium *n* the chemical ion of ammonia.

ammonium carbonate *n* a carbonate of ammonia; a solution of carbonate of ammonia flavoured with aromatics, used as a remedy for faintness; sal volatile.

ammonium hydroxide *n* an alkaline solution of ammonia mixed with water used as a cleansing agent and in the manufacture of rayong, plastic, etc.

ammunition *n* articles used in the discharge of weapons of all kinds, as bullets, shells, bombs, (nuclear) missiles, rockets, etc.

amnesia *n* loss of memory.

amnesty *n* a general pardon of the offences of subjects against the government or the proclamation of such pardon.

amniocentesis *n* a medical technique involving the extraction by a hollow needle of some of the amniotic fluid surrounding a foetus in the uterus to test for foetal abnormality.

amnion *n* the thin sac surrounding the foetus in the uterus and containing the amniotic fluid.

amniotic fluid *n* the watery fluid surrounding the foetus in the uterus contained in the amnion and expelled before birth.

amoeba *n* any of a genus of a microscopic protozoan one of which is common in

ammonite

amoeba

freshwater ponds and ditches, consisting of a gelatinous mass which continually alters its shape.

amok *n* same as **amuck**.

among, amongst *prep* mixed or mingled with (implying a number); in or into the midst of; in or into the number of (*one among a thousand*); jointly or with a reference to someone or other (*they killed him among them*).

amontillado *n* a dry kind of sherry of a light colour.

amorous *adj* inclined to love persons of the opposite sex; having a propensity to love or to sexual enjoyment; loving; fond; pertaining or relating to love; produced by love; indicating love; enamoured (in this sense with *of*).

amorphous *adj* having no determinate form; of irregular shape; not having the regular forms exhibited by the crystals of minerals; being without crystallization; formless; characterless.

amount *vi* to reach a certain total by an accumulation of particulars; to come in the aggregate or whole; to result in; to be equivalent (followed by *to*).—*n* the sum total of two or more particular sums or quantities; the aggregate; the effect, substance or result.

amour *n* a love intrigue; an affair.

amp *n* a short form of **ampere**.

ampere *n* (*elect*) the SI unit employed in measuring the strength of an electric current.

ampersand *n* the sign &, meaning 'and'.

amphetamine *n* a drug used especially as a stimulant and to suppress appetite.

amphibian *n* an animal which possesses both gills and lungs, whether at different stages of its existence or simultaneously, and lives on land and breeds in water, e.g. frogs and toads.

amphibious *adj* having the power of living in two elements, air and water; having the characteristics of amphibians; adapted for living on land or at sea; (*milit*) involving both land and sea forces.

amphibology *n* a phrase open to two interpretations; a phrase of uncertain meaning.

amphibolous *adj* susceptible of two meanings; ambiguous; equivocal.

amphibrach *n* (*pros*) a foot of three syllables, the middle one long, the first and last short.

amphigory *n* a meaningless rigmarole; a nonsensical parody.

amphioxus *n* a kind of fish of a very rudimentary type, the lancelet.

amphipod *n* one of an order of small crustaceous animals common in fresh and salt water, including the sand-hopper.

amphisbaena *n* one of a genus of small snake-like lizards.

amphitheatre *n* an ancient edifice of an oval form, having a central area surrounded by rows of seats, rising higher as they receded from the centre, for viewing spectacles; a similar modern edifice; anything, as a natural hollow among hills, resembling an amphitheatre in form.

amphora *n* (*pl* **amphorae**) among the Greeks and Romans, a vessel, usually tall and narrow, with two handles or ears and a narrow neck, used for holding wine, oil, honey, etc.

amphoteric *adj* (*chem*) both basic and acid.

ample *adj* large in dimensions; of great size, extent, capacity or bulk; wide; spacious; extended (*ample room*); fully sufficient for some purpose intended; abundant; copious; plentiful (*an ample supply*; *ample justice*).

ampleness *n* the state of being ample; largeness; sufficiency; abundance.

amplification *n* the act of amplifying; an enlargement; extension; additional description for the sake of clarity.

amplifier *n* one who amplifies or enlarges; a device that increases electric voltage, current or power, or the loudness of sound.

amplify *vt* (**amplified, amplifying**) to make more ample, larger, more extended, more copious, full, etc.—*vi* to grow or become ample or more ample; to be diffuse in argument or description.

amplitude *n* state of being ample; largeness of dimensions; extent of surface or space; greatness; (*astron*) an arc of the horizon intercepted between the east or west point and the centre of the sun or star at its rising or setting.

amply *adv* in an ample manner; largely; sufficiently; copiously.

ampulla *n* (*pl* **ampullae**) a bottle used by the Romans for holding oil; a vessel for holding the consecrated oil used in various church rites and at a coronation; (*anat*) a small swelling in a duct or canal, especially of the ear.

amputate *vt* (**amputated, amputating**) to cut off, especially a human limb.

amputation *n* the act of amputating; the operation of cutting off a limb or other projecting part of the body.

amuck, amok *n* a furious, reckless onset.—**to run amuck** to rush about frantically, attacking all that come in the way; to attack all and sundry.

amulet *n* something worn or carried to act as a charm or preservative against evils or mischief, such as diseases and witchcraft.

amuse *vt* (**amused, amusing**) to entertain agreeably; to hold the attention of in a pleasant manner or with agreeable objects; to divert; entertain (often reflexively).

amusement *n* the act of amusing or state of being amused; a slight amount of mirth or tendency towards merriment; that which amuses; entertainment; sport; pastime.

amusement arcade *n* an indoor or roofed area containing mechanical games, usually operated by the insertion of coins.

amusing *adj* giving amusement; pleasing; diverting.

amyl *n* formerly, the alcohol radical of many chemical compounds, as amylic alcohol, etc.

amylene *n* a hydrocarbon obtained from amylic alcohol and possessing anaesthetic properties.

amyl nitrite *n* a drug inhaled to relieve spasms.

amylopsin *n* an enzyme in the pancreatic juice by which starch is converted into sugar.

an, a *indef art* a word used before nouns in the singular number to denote an individual as one among more belonging to the same class and not marking singleness like *one*, nor pointing to something known and definite like *the*; in such phrases as *once an hour*, *a pound an ounce*, *an* has a distributive force, being equivalent to *each*, *every*; the form *a* is used before consonants (including the name sound of *u*, as in *unit*, *European* = yu); *an* is used before words beginning with a vowel sound or the sound of *h* when the accent falls on any syllable except the first, as, *an inn*, *an umpire*, *an heir*.

ana *npl* the sayings of notable men; personal gossip or anecdotes.

Anabaptist *n* one who holds the invalidity of infant baptism and the necessity of rebaptism, generally by immersion, as an adult.

anabolic steroid *n* any of a group of synthetic steroid hormones used to stimulate a rapid increase in muscle size and strength.

anabolism *n* upbuilding chemical changes in living bodies.

anachronism *n* an error which implies the misplacing of persons or events in time; anything foreign to or out of keeping with a specified epoch (as where Shakespeare makes Hector quote Aristotle).

anacoluthon *n* (*gram*) lack of sequence in a sentence, owing to the latter member of it belonging to a different grammatical construction from the preceding.

anaconda *n* a large, non-poisonous South American snake that kills by constricting.

anacrusis *n* the unstressed syllable at the beginning of a verse.

anadem *n* a band, fillet, garland or wreath.

anaemia *n* (*med*) a deficiency of blood; a state of the system marked by a deficiency in certain constituents of the blood.

anaemic *adj* pertaining to or affected with anaemia.

amphitheatre

amphora

anaerobic *adj* (of bacteria) only active in the absence of oxygen.

anaesthesia, anaesthesis *n* diminished or lost sense of feeling; an artificially produced state of insensibility, especially to the sense of pain.

anaesthetic *adj* of or belonging to anaesthesia; having the power of depriving of feeling or sensation.—*n* a substance which has the power of depriving of feeling or sensation.

anaesthetize *vt* (**anaesthetized, anaesthetizing**) to bring under the influence of an anaesthetic agent; to render insensible to the feeling of pain.

anaglyph *n* an ornament in relief chased or embossed.

anagram *n* a transposition of the letters of a word or sentence, to form a new word or sentence.

anal *adj* pertaining to or situated near the anus.

analect *n* a selected piece; an extract.

analecta, analects *npl* extracts or small pieces selected from different authors.

analectic *adj* relating to analecta; made up of selections.

analgesia *n* (*pathol*) incapacity for feeling pain in some part of the body.

analgesic *adj* pertaining to analgesia; insensible to pain.

analogous *adj* having analogy; bearing some resemblance in the midst of differences (followed by *to* or *with*).

analogue clock *n* one which indicates the time by means of a pointer moving round a numbered dial.

analogy *n* an agreement or likeness between things in some circumstances or effects, when the things are otherwise entirely different; relationship; conformity; parallelism; likeness.

analyse *vt* (**analysed, analysing**) to resolve into its elements; to separate, as a compound subject, into its parts or propositions.

analysis *n* (*pl* **analyses**) the resolution of a compound object whether of the senses or the intellect into its constituent elements or component parts; a consideration of anything in its separate parts and their relation to each other, opposed to *synthesis*; the process of subjecting to chemical tests to determine ingredients; that one of the two great branches of mathematics—the other being geometry—which is based on arithmetic and algebra; a syllabus or table of the principal heads of a discourse or treatise; psychoanalysis.

analyst *n* one who analyses or is versed in analysis; one who subjects articles to chemical tests to find out their ingredients; a psychoanalyst.

analytic, analytical *n* pertaining to analysis; resolving into first principles or elements.

analytics *n* the science of analysis.

ananas *n* the pineapple.

anapest, anapaest *n* a poetical foot consisting of three syllables, the first two short or unaccented, the last long or accented.

anapestic *adj* pertaining to an anapest; consisting of anapests.

anaphrodisiac *n* a substance capable of dulling sexual appetite.

anaplasty *n* plastic surgery.

anarchic, anarchical *adj* of or pertaining to anarchy or anarchism; in a state of anarchy or confusion; lawless.

anarchism *n* the doctrine of the abolition of formal government, free action for the individual, land and other resources being common property.

anarchist *n* one who excites disorder in a state; an advocate of anarchy or anarchism.

anarchy *n* lack of government; a state of society when there is no law or supreme power; political confusion.

anastomose *vi* (**anastomosed, anastomosing**) (*anat, bot*) to unite or run into each other, to communicate with each other by minute branches or ramifications, as the arteries and veins.

anastomosis *n* the uniting of vessels in vegetable or animal bodies.

anastomotic *adj* pertaining to anastomosis.

anastrophe, anastrophy *n* an inversion of the natural order of words.

anathema *n* one who or that which is hated; a curse or denunciation pronounced with religious solemnity by ecclesiastical authority and accompanied by excommunication; execration generally; curse.

anathematize *vt* (**anathematized, anathematizing**) to pronounce an anathema against.—*vi* to pronounce anathemas; to curse.

anatomic, anatomical *adj* belonging to anatomy or dissection.

anatomist *n* one who is skilled in dissection or in the doctrine and principles of anatomy.

anatomize *vt* (**anatomized, anatomizing**) to cut up or dissect for the purpose of displaying or examining the structure; (*fig*) to lay open or expose minutely; to analyse (*to anatomize an argument*).

anatomy *n* the art of dissecting or artificially separating the different parts of the human body, to discover their situation and structure; the science which deals with the internal structure of human, animal or vegetable bodies, as shown by dissection; the act of taking to pieces something for the purpose of examining in detail (*the anatomy of a discourse*); a skeleton; a human body.

analogue clock

ancestor *n* one from whom a person descends, either by the father or mother, at any distance of time; a progenitor; a forefather; one from whom an inheritance is derived.

ancestral *adj* pertaining to ancestors; claimed or descending from ancestors.

ancestress *n* a female ancestor.

ancestry *n* a series of ancestors; lineage; honourable descent; high birth.

anchor *n* an iron implement, consisting usually of a straight bar called the shank, at the upper end of which is a transverse piece called the stock, and of two curved arms at the lower end of the shank, each of which arms terminates in a triangular plate called a fluke, and used for holding a ship or other vessel at rest in comparatively shallow water; something serving a purpose analogous to that of a ship's anchor; (*fig*) that which gives stability or security; that on which we place dependence for safety.—**at anchor** floating attached to an anchor; anchored.—*vt* to hold at rest by lowering the anchor; to place at anchor; (*fig*) to fix or fasten on; to fix in a stable condition.—*vi* to cast anchor; to come to anchor.

anchorage *n* anchoring ground; a place where a ship can anchor; a duty imposed on ships for anchoring in a harbour.

anchorite *n* a hermit; a recluse; one who retires from society to devote himself or herself to religious duties.

anchoress *n* a female anchorite.

anchovy *n* a small fish of the herring family, caught in vast numbers in the Mediterranean and pickled for export and from which a well-known paste is also made.

ancient *adj* that happened or existed in former times, usually at a great distance of time; associated with or bearing marks of the times of long ago (*ancient authors*); of long standing; having lasted from a remote period; of great age; old (*an ancient city*); having lived long (*an ancient man*—poetical).—*n* a person living at an early period of history (generally in plural and opposed to *moderns*); a very old man; an elder or person of influence.

ancillary *adj* subservient; aiding; auxiliary; subordinate.

and *conj* a particle joining words and sentences and expressing the relations of connection or addition; sometimes used to introduce interrogative and other clauses.

andalusite *n* a pellucid mineral of the garnet family, of a grey, green, bluish, flesh or rose-red colour (so called from Andalusia in Spain, where it was first discovered).

andante *adj* (*mus*) moving with a moderate, even, graceful progression.—*n* a movement or piece composed in andante time.

andiron *n* a horizontal iron bar raised on short legs, with an upright standard at one end, used to support pieces of wood when burning on an open hearth, one being placed on each side; a firedog.

androecium *n* (*pl* **androecia**) (*bot*) the male system of a flower; the assemblage of the stamens.

androgynous *adj* having two sexes; being male and female; hermaphrode; having or partaking of the mental characteristics of both sexes.

anecdotage *n* a collection of anecdotes; the garrulity of old age.

anecdotal *adj* pertaining to anecdotes; consisting of or of the nature of anecdotes; (of evidence, etc) obtained from experience, not scientific.

anecdote *n* a short story, narrating a detached incident or fact of an interesting or amusing nature; a biographical incident.

anele *vt* (**aneling, aneled**) to anoint; to give extreme unction.

anemograph *n* an instrument for measuring and recording the force and direction of the wind.

anemology *n* the study of or a treatise on winds.

anemometer *n* an instrument for measuring the force and velocity of the wind.

anemometry *n* the process of determining the pressure or force of the wind.

anemone *n* windflower, a genus of plants of which three species occur in Britain, but only one, the wood anemone, is truly a native.

anemophilous *adj* (*bot*) having the pollen conveyed and fertilization effected by the wind.

anemoscope *n* a contrivance which shows the direction of the wind; a weathercock; a wind vane.

anent *prep* about; respecting; regarding.

aneroid *adj* having no fluid.

aneroid barometer *n* a barometer the action of which depends on the pressure of the atmosphere on a circular metallic box exhausted of air, hermetically sealed and having a slightly elastic top, the vacuum serving the purpose of the column of mercury in the ordinary barometer.

aneurism *n* (*med*) the swelling of an artery or the dilatation and expansion of some part of an artery, often a very dangerous ailment.

anew *adv* over again; in a new form; afresh.

anfractuous *adj* winding; full of windings and turnings; sinuous.

angel *n* a divine messenger; a spiritual being employed in the service of God; a gold coin, formerly current in England, bearing the figure of the archangel Michael.

angelfish *n* a fish nearly allied to the sharks, so called from its pectoral fins, which are so large as to spread like wings.

anchor

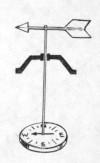

anemoscope

angelic, angelical *adj* resembling or belonging to or partaking of the nature and dignity of angels.

angelica *n* the name of two umbelliferous plants, one of which is common in Britain and used in preparing gin and bitters, etc; the other, garden angelica, possesses calming and tonic properties.

angelus *n* (*RC Church*) a solemn devotion in memory of the incarnation; the bell tolled to indicate the time when the angelus is to be recited.

anger *n* a violent passion or emotion of the mind, excited by a real or supposed injury to oneself or others; passion; ire; choler; rage; wrath: *anger* is more general and expresses a less strong feeling than *wrath* and *rage*, both of which imply a certain outward manifestation, and the latter violence and lack of self-command.—*vt* to excite to anger; to rouse resentment in; to make angry; to exasperate.

angina *n* (*med*) an inflammatory affection of the throat or fauces.

angina pectoris *n* a fatal disease characterized by paroxysms of intense pain and a feeling of constriction in the chest.

angiogram *n* an X-ray photograph of the blood vessels which have been injected with a substance opaque to X-rays.

angiology *n* (*med*) a description of the vessels of the body.

angioplasty *n* a non-surgical procedure to widen or clean out blood vessels using balloon dilatation or laser.

angiosperm *n* (*bot*) a plant which has its seeds enclosed in a seed vessel.

angle¹ *n* the point where two lines or planes meet that do not run in the same straight line; a corner; the degree of opening or divergence of two straight lines which meet one another.

angle² *vi* (**angled, angling**) to fish with line and hook.

Angle *n* a member of a Low German tribe which in the fifth century and subsequently crossed over to Britain along with bands of Saxons, Jutes and others, and colonized a great part of what from them has received the name of England.

angle bar *n* a bar fitting into an angle or corner to connect the side pieces.

angled *adj* having angles (used chiefly in compounds).

angle iron *n* a piece of rolled iron in the shape of the letter L, used for forming the joints of iron plates in girders, boilers, etc, to which it is riveted.

angle of repose *n* the angle of inclination to the horizontal of an inclined plane when the force of gravity is just sufficient to overcome friction.

angler *n* one who fishes with hook and line; a fish having long filaments in its head,

angle

angler

which attract the smaller fishes and thus provide it with prey.

Anglican *adj* English; pertaining to the English Church.—*n* a member of the Anglican Church.

Anglican Church *n* the Church of England and the Protestant Episcopal churches in communion with it.

Anglicanism *n* the principles of or adherence to the Anglican Church.

Anglice *adv* in English; in the English manner.

Anglicism *n* the quality of being English; an English idiom.

anglicize, anglify *vt* (**anglicized, anglicizing; anglified, anglifying**) to make English; to render conformable to the English idiom or to English analogies.

anglification *n* the art of converting into English.

angling *n* the act or art of fishing with a rod and line; rod-fishing.

Anglo- *prefix* signifying English or connected with England.

Anglophile *n* a person who loves England or anything English.

Anglophobe *n* one who hates or fears England and the English.

Anglophone *adj* of, pertaining to, or being an English-speaking person or population.

Anglo-Saxon *n* one of the Saxons of Britain as distinct from the continental Saxons; one belonging to the English race; the language of the Anglo-Saxons, or the English language in its first stage.—*adj* pertaining to the Anglo-Saxons or to the oldest form of English.

angora *n* a light cloth, made from the wool or long silky hair of the Angora goat, a native of Asia Minor.

angriness *n* the state of being angry.

angry *adj* feeling resentment; provoked; showing anger; caused by anger; raging; tumultuous.

angstrom, ångström *n* one hundred millionth of a centimetre, a unit used in measuring the length of light waves.

anguish *n* extreme pain, either of body or mind; any keen affection of the emotions or feelings.

angular *adj* having an angle or angles; having corners; pointed; consisting of or forming an angle.

angularity *n* the quality of being angular.

anhydride *n* a compound derived from another by the abstraction of water.

anhydrite *n* anhydrous sulphate of calcium, a mineral resembling a coarse-grained granite.

anhydrous *adj* lacking water; specifically, (*chem*) lacking the water of crystallization.

anil *n* a shrub from whose leaves and stalks the West Indian indigo is made.

anile *adj* old-womanish; aged; imbecile.

aniline *n* a substance obtained from indigo and other organic substances, though the aniline of commerce is obtained from benzole, a product of coal tar: it furnishes a number of brilliant dyes.

anility *n* the state of being anile.

animadversion *n* the act of one who animadverts; a remark by way of criticism or censure; stricture; censure.

animadvert *vi* to perceive or take cognizance; usually, to make remark by way of criticism; to pass strictures or criticisms (followed by *on, upon*).

animal *n* a living being characterized by sensation and voluntary motion; any mammal except humankind; an inferior or irrational being, in contradistinction to human beings.—*adj* belonging or relating to animals (*animal functions*); pertaining to the merely sentient part of a living being, as distinguished from the intellectual or spiritual part (*animal passions*); of or pertaining to, or consisting of, the flesh of animals.

animal magnetism *n* attractiveness to the opposite sex; sensuality; (*arch*) hypnotism.

animalcule *n* a minute animal, especially one that is microscopic or invisible to the naked eye.

animate *vt* (**animated, animating**) to give natural life to; to quicken; to make alive; to give life, spirit or liveliness to; to heighten the powers or effect of; to stimulate or incite; to inspirit; rouse.

animate *adj* alive; possessing animal life.

animated *adj* endowed with animal life; lively; vigorous; full of spirit (*an animated discourse*).

animation *n* the act of animating or state of being animated; state of having life; liveliness; briskness; vivacity.

animism *n* the old hypothesis of a force (*anima mundi*, soul of the world) immaterial but inseparable from matter and giving to matter its form and movements; the attribution of spirit or soul to inanimate things.

animist *n* one who holds to or believes in animism.

animosity *n* rancorous feeling; bitter and active enmity.

animus *n* intention; purpose; spirit; temper; hatred; hostility.

anion *n* (*elect*) the element of an electrolyte which is evolved at the positive pole or anode.

anise *n* an annual plant, the seeds of which have an aromatic smell and a liquorice taste and are employed in the manufacture of liqueurs.

aniseed *n* the seed of the anise.

ankle *n* the joint which connects the foot with the leg.

anklet *n* an ornament, support or protection for the ankle.

annals *npl* a history or relation of events in chronological order, each event being recorded under the year in which it happened.

annalist *n* a writer of annals.

annats, annates *npl* the first year's income of a spiritual living, formerly vested in the sovereign, but in the reign of Queen Anne appropriated to the augmentation of poor livings.

anneal *vt* to heat, as glass or iron vessels, in an oven or furnace, and then cool slowly, for the purpose of rendering less brittle; to temper by a gradually diminishing heat; to heat in order to fix colours; to bake.

annelid, annelidan *n* one of an extensive division or class of annulose animals, so called because their bodies are formed of a great number of small rings, as in the earthworm.

annex *vt* to unite at the end; to subjoin; to unite, as a smaller thing to a greater; to connect, especially as a consequence (*to annex a penalty*).—*n* something annexed.

annexation *n* the act of annexing; what is annexed; addition; union.

annexe *n* a wing or subsidiary building communicating with the main edifice.

annihilate *vt* (**annihilated, annihilating**) to reduce to nothing; to destroy the existence of; to cause to cease to be; to destroy the form or peculiar distinctive properties of.

annihilation *n* the act of annihilating or the state of being annihilated.

anniversary *adj* returning with the year at a stated time; annual; yearly.—*n* a stated day on which some event is annually celebrated; the annual celebration in honour of an event.

annotate *vt* (**annotated, annotating**) to comment on; to make remarks on by notes.—*vi* to act as an annotator; to make annotations or notes (with *on*).

annotation *n* the act of annotating or making notes on; an illustrative note on some passage of a book.

annotator *n* a writer of annotations or notes; a commentator.

announce *vt* (**announced, announcing**) to publish; to proclaim; to give notice or first notice of.

announcement *n* the act of announcing or giving notice; proclamation; publication.

announcer *n* one who announces, especially a newsreader or introducer of programmes on radio or television; a proclaimer.

annoy *vt* to torment or disturb, especially by continued or repeated acts; to tease, vex, pester or molest.

annoyance *n* the act of annoying; the state

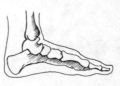

ankle

of being annoyed; that which annoys; trouble.

annoying *adj* vexatious; troublesome.

annual *adj* returning every year; coming yearly; lasting or continuing only one year or one yearly season; performed in a year; reckoned by the year.—*n* a plant that grows from seed, flowers and perishes in the course of the same season; a literary production published annually.

annually *adv* yearly; returning every year; year by year.

annuitant *n* one receiving an annuity.

annuity *n* a yearly payment of money which a person receives for life or for a term of years, the person being usually entitled to such payment in consideration of money advanced to those who pay.

annul *vt* (**annulled, annulling**) to reduce to nothing or annihilate; to make void; to nullify; to abrogate; to cancel (laws, decrees, compacts, etc).

annular *adj* having the form of a ring; pertaining to a ring.

annular eclipse *n* an eclipse of the sun in which a ring of light formed by the sun's disc is visible around the dark shadow of the moon.

annulose *adj* composed of a succession of rings; segmented.

annunciate *vt* (**annunciated, annunciating**) to bring tidings of; to announce.

annunciation *n* the act of announcing; announcement.

Annunciation *n* the tidings brought by the angel to the Virgin Mary of the incarnation of Christ; the church festival in memory of this announcement falling on 25th March.

anode *n* the part of the surface of an electrolyte which the electric current enters, opposed to *cathode*.

anode ray *n* any of a stream of charged atoms and molecules given off at the anode of an electric discharge tube.

anodyne *n* any medicine which allays pain. —*adj* assuaging pain.

anoint *vt* to pour oil on; to smear or rub with oil or unctuous substances; to consecrate by unction or the use of oil.

anointment *n* the act of anointing.

anomalous *adj* forming an anomaly; deviating from a general rule, method or analogy; irregular; abnormal.

anomaly *n* deviation from the common rule; something abnormal; irregularity; (*astron*) the angular distance of a planet from its perihelion, as seen from the sun; also the angle measuring apparent irregularities in the motion of a planet.

anon *adv* soon, shortly.

anonymity *n* the state of being anonymous.

anonymous *adj* lacking a name; without any name acknowledged as that of author, contributor, etc.

annular eclipse

ant

anonymously *adv* in an anonymous manner; without a name.

anopheles *n* the genus containing the species of mosquito by which malarial germs are distributed.

anorexia, anorexia nervosa *n* an eating disorder involving the avoidance of food, sometimes to the point of starvation and even death, because of an abnormal and often irrational fear of being overweight.

another *adj* not the same; different; one more, in addition to a former number; any other; any one else (often used without a noun, as a substitute for the name of a person or thing and much used in opposition to *one*: as, *one went one way, another another*; also frequently used with *one* in a reciprocal sense: as, *love one another*).

anserine *adj* relating to or resembling a goose, or the skin of a goose (applied to the skin when roughened by cold or disease).

answer *vt* to speak or write in return to; to reply to; to refute; to say or do in reply; to act in compliance with, or in fulfilment or satisfaction of; to render account to or for; to be equivalent or adequate to; to serve; to suit.—*vi* to reply; to speak or write by way of return; to respond to some call; to be fit or suitable.—**to answer for** to be accountable for; to guarantee.—**to answer to** to be known by; to correspond to, in the way of resemblance, fitness or correlation.

answer *n* a reply; that which is said, written or done, in return to a call, question, argument, challenge, allegation, petition, prayer or address; the result of an arithmetical or mathematical operation; a solution; something done in return for, or in consequence of, something else; (*law*) a counterstatement of facts in a course of pleadings.

answerable *adj* capable of being answered; obliged to give an account; amenable; responsible; correspondent.

ant *n* an emmet; a pismire; a hymenopterous insect living in communities which consist of males, females and neuters: the name is also given to the neuropterous insects more correctly called *termites*.

antacid *n* an alkali or a remedy for acidity in the stomach.—*adj* counteracting acidity.

antagonism *n* character of being an antagonist or antagonistic; counteraction or contrariety of things or principles.

antagonist *n* one who contends with another; an opponent; a competitor; an adversary.—*adj* counteracting; opposing (said of muscles).

antagonistic *adj* contending against; acting in opposition; opposing.

antagonize *vi* (**antagonized, antagonizing**) to contend against; to act in opposition.

antalkali *n* a substance which neutralizes an alkali.

antalkaline *adj* having the property of neutralizing alkalies.

Antarctic *adj* opposite to the northern or Arctic pole; relating to the southern pole or to the region near it and applied to a circle parallel to the equator and distant from the pole 23° 28´.—*n* the Antartic region; the Antartic Ocean.

ant bear *n* a kind of large anteater.

anteater *n* a quadruped that eats ants, especially an edentate animal which feeds on ants and other insects, catching them by thrusting among them its long tongue covered with a viscid saliva.

antecede *vt* (**anteceded, anteceding**) to go before in time; to precede.

antecedent *adj* going before; prior; anterior; preceding.—*n* one who or that which goes before in time or place; (*gram*) the noun to which a relative or other pronoun refers; (*pl*) the earlier events of a person's life; (*pl*) previous course, conduct or avowed principles; (*pl*) ancestry.

antechamber, anteroom *n* a chamber or room leading to another apartment.

antedate *n* prior date; a date before another.—*vt* (**antedated, antedating**) to date before the true time or beforehand; to give an earlier date than the real one to; to anticipate or give effect to before the due time.

antediluvian *adj* existing, happening or relating to what happened before the Flood; belonging to very ancient times; antiquated; primitive.—*n* one who lived before the Flood; an old-fashioned person.

ant egg *n* a small white body found in the hillocks of ants, popularly supposed to be its egg but really its larva.

antelope *n* a name applied to many species of ruminant mammals resembling the deer in general appearance, but essentially different in nature from them, having hollow, unbranched horns that are not deciduous.

antemeridian *adj* being before noon; pertaining to the forenoon.

antemundane *adj* being before the creation of the world.

antenatal *adj* existing or happening previous to birth.

antenna *n* (*pl* **antennae**) one of the hornlike filaments that project from the head in insects, crustaceans and myriapods, and are considered as organs of touch and hearing; a feeler; (*radio*) an aerial.

antenuptial *adj* occurring or done before marriage; preceding marriage.

antepenultimate *adj* pertaining to the last but two.

anteprandial *adj* relating to the time before dinner; occurring before dinner.

anterior *adj* before in time; prior; antecedent; before in place; in front.

anteroom *n* same as **antechamber**.

anthelion *n* (*pl* **anthelia**) a luminous ring, or rings, caused by the diffraction of light, seen in alpine and polar regions opposite the sun when rising or setting.

anthelminthic, anthelmintic *adj* (*med*) destroying or expelling worms in the intestines.—*n* a vermifuge; a remedy for worms in the intestines.

anthem *n* a hymn sung in alternate parts; in modern usage, a sacred tune or piece of music set to words taken from the Psalms or other parts of the Scriptures.

anther *n* the essential part of the stamen of a plant containing the pollen or fertilizing dust.

antheridium *n* in lower plants, a male sexual organ, usually producing motile male cells.

ant hill *n* a little tumulus or hillock formed by ants for their habitation and composed of earth, leaves, twigs, etc.

anthoid *adj* having the form of a flower; resembling a flower.

antholite *n* (*geol*) the impress of the inflorescence of plants on rocks.

anthology *n* a collection of passages from authors; a collection of selected poems.

anthophyllite *n* a clove-brown variety of hornblende occurring in radiating columnar aggregates.

anthozoan, actinozoan *n* any of a class of radiated soft marine zoophytes which includes the sea anemones, corals, etc.

anthracene *n* a hydrocarbon obtained from coal tar.

anthracite *n* glance or blind coal, a nonbituminous coal of a shining lustre, approaching to metallic, which burns without smoke, with a weak or no flame and with intense heat.

anthrax *n* (*med*) a carbuncle; a malignant disease in cattle sometimes communicated to man with fatal results.

anthropoid *adj* resembling man, specifically applied to such apes as most closely approach the human race.

anthropological *adj* pertaining to anthropology.

anthropologist *n* one who writes on or studies anthropology.

anthropology *n* the scientific study of human beings, their origins, distribution, physical attributes and culture.

anthropometry *n* the measurement of the human body.

anthropomorphism *n* the representation or conception of God or an animal under a human form or with human attributes.

anthropomorphic *adj* relating to or characterized by anthropomorphism; resembling a human being.

anthropophagi *npl* (*sing* **anthropophagus**) cannibals; people who eat human flesh.

anteater

ant hill

anthropophagous *adj* feeding on human flesh.

anthropophagy *n* cannibalism.

antiar *n* a milky juice which exudes from wounds made in the upas tree, an acrid and virulent vegetable poison.

anti-aircraft *adj* used in defence against attacks from the air, as guns, searchlights, etc.

antibody *n* (*med*) a substance formed in the blood which combats disease germs.

antibiotic *n* a substance, such as penicillin, used to kill or prevent the growth of bacterial or fungal organisms and used to cure diseases involving these.

antic *n* an absurd or ridiculous gesture; an odd gesticulation; a caper.

Antichrist *n* an opponent of Christ; a person or power antagonistic to Christ.

anticipant *adj* anticipating, anticipative.

anticipate *vt* (**anticipated, anticipating**) to be before in doing something; to prevent or preclude by prior action; to forestall; to realize beforehand; to foretaste or foresee; to look forward to; to expect.—*vi* to treat of something, as in a narrative, before the proper time.

anticipation *n* the act of anticipating; expectation; foretaste; realization beforehand; previous notion; preconceived opinion.

anticipative *adj* anticipating or tending to anticipate; containing anticipation.

anticipatively *adv* by anticipation.

anticipator *n* one who anticipates.

anticipatory *adj* anticipative.

anticlastic *adj* of a surface curved in opposite directions, like a saddle, contrasted with *synclastic*.

anticlimax *n* a sentence in which the ideas first increase in force and then terminate in something less important and striking, opposed to *climax*.

anticlinal *adj* inclining in opposite directions, opposed to *synclinal*.—*n* an anticlinal line or axis.

anticlinal axis n (*geol*) a line from which strata dip on either side as from the ridge of a house.

anticlockwise *adj, adv* moving in a direction contrary to the hands of a clock as viewed from the front.

anticyclone *n* a meteorological phenomenon consisting of a region of high barometric pressure, the pressure being greatest in the centre, with light winds flowing outwards from the centre and not inwards as in the cyclone.

antidepressant *n* any of various drugs used in the treatment of clinical depression.

antidote *n* a medicine to counteract the effects of poison or of anything noxious taken into the stomach; (*fig*) anything that prevents or counteracts evil.

anticlockwise

antifebrile *adj* having the quality of abating fever; opposing or tending to cure fever.

antifreeze *n* a substance used in a vehicle's radiator to prevent it freezing up.

antigen *n* a substance introduced into the blood to stimulate the production of antibodies.

antigraph *n* (*law*) a copy or counterpart of a deed.

antihistamine *n* any of a group of drugs which inhibit the production of histamines and used in the treatment of allergies, such as hay fever.

antilogous *adj* contradictory; (*elect*) applied to that pole of a crystal which is negative when being electrified by heat and afterwards, when cooling, positive.

antilogy *n* a contradiction between any words or passages in an author, or between members of the same body.

antimacassar *n* a covering for chairs, sofas, couches, etc, made of open cotton or worsted work, to preserve them from being soiled.

antimonial *adj* pertaining to antimony; composed of or containing antimony.—*n* a preparation of antimony; a medicine in which antimony is a principal ingredient.

antimony *n* a brittle metal of a bluish-white or silvery-white colour and laminated or scaly texture, much used in the arts in the construction of alloys and also in medicine.

antinomian *adj* opposed to law; pertaining to the antinomians.—*n* one of a sect who maintain that, under the gospel dispensation, the moral law is of no use or obligation.

antinomianism *n* the tenets of the antinomians.

antinomy *n* the opposition of one law or rule to another law or rule; anything, as a law, statement, etc, opposite or contrary.

antipasto *n* (*pl* **antipastos**) an appetizer, an hors d'oeuvre.

antipathetic, antipathetical *adj* having or causing antipathy.

antipathy *n* natural aversion; instinctive contrariety or opposition in feeling; an aversion felt at the presence of an object; repugnance; contrariety in nature (commonly with *to* before the object).

antiphlogistic *adj* counteracting inflammation or an excited state of the system.—*n* a medicine which checks inflammation.

antiphon *n* the answer of one choir or one portion of a congregation to another when an anthem or psalm is sung alternately; a short versicle sung before and after the psalms.

antiphonal *adj* pertaining to an antiphon or antiphony.—*n* a book of antiphons or anthems.

antiphony *n* the alternate or responsive rendering of psalms or chants by a dual choir; a musical setting of sacred verses arranged for alternate singing.

antiphrasis *n* (*rhet*) the use of a word or phrase in a sense opposite to the proper meaning, often for an ironic or humours affect (*his mother is ninety years young today*).

antipodal, antipodean *adj* pertaining to antipodes.

antipode *n* one who or that which is in opposition or opposite; (*pl*) those who live on the opposite side of the globe; the region directly on the opposite side of the globe; (*fig*) anything diametrically opposite or opposed to another; a contrary.

Antipodes *npl* Australia and New Zealand.

antipope *n* one who usurps the papal power in opposition to the pope; a pretender to the papacy.

antipyretic *n* (*med*) a remedy effective against fever.

antiquarian *adj* pertaining to antiquaries or to antiquity.—*n* an antiquary.

antiquarianism *n* character of an antiquarian; love or study of antiquities.

antiquary *n* one devoted to the study of ancient times through their relics; one versed in antiquity; an archaeologist.

antiquated *adj* grown old-fashioned; obsolete; out of use; behind the times.

antique *adj* having existed in ancient times; belonging to or having come down from antiquity; ancient (*an antique statue*); having the characteristics of an earlier day; smacking of bygone days; of old fashion (*an antique robe*).—*n* anything very old; specifically, a term applied to the remains of ancient art, more especially to the works of Grecian and Roman antiquity.

antiquity *n* the quality of being ancient; ancientness; great age; ancient times; former ages; the people of ancient times; (*pl*) the remains of ancient times; institutions, customs, etc, belonging to ancient nations.

antirrhinum *n* snapdragon, the generic name of various plants with showy flowers, much cultivated in gardens.

antiscorbutic *adj* (*med*) counteracting scurvy or a scorbutic tendency.—*n* a remedy for or preventive of scurvy.

anti-Semite *n* one opposed to the Semitic or Jewish race.

anti-Semitic *adj* displaying hatred of or discrimination against Jews.

antiseptic *adj* opposing or counteracting putrefaction or a putrescent tendency.—*n* a substance which resists or corrects putrefaction.

antiserum *n* (*med*) a blood preparation containing an antibody and used in the treatment of bacterial diseases, e.g. diphtheria.

antistrophe *n* a part of an ancient Greek choral ode alternating with the strophe.

antistrophic *adj* relating to the antistrophe.

antithesis *n* (*pl* **antitheses**) opposition; contrast; (*rhet*) a figure by which contraries are opposed to contraries; a contrast or opposition of words or sentiments, as, *the prodigal robs his heir, the miser robs himself.*

antithetic, antithetical *adj* pertaining to or characterized by antithesis.

antitoxin *n* (*med*) a fluid introduced into the blood to counteract the poison of a disease.

antitype *n* that which is correlative to a type; that which is prefigured or represented by the type.

antitypical *adj* pertaining to an antitype; explaining the type.

antivivisectionist *n* one who is opposed to scientific experiments being conducted on live animals.

antler *n* a branch of the horn of a deer, particularly of a stag; one of the horns of the cervine animals.

antlia *n* (*pl* **antliae**) the spiral tongue or proboscis of butterflies and moths, by which they suck the juices of plants.

antonomasia, antonomasy *n* (*rhet*) the use of the name of some office, dignity, profession, etc, instead of the name of the person; or, conversely, the use of a proper noun instead of a common noun (as *a Solomon* for *a wise man*).

antonym *n* a word of directly contrary meaning to another ('black' is an antonym for 'white', 'fast' is an antonym for 'slow'), the opposite of a *synonym*.

anuran *n* any of an order of amphibians which lose the tail when they reach maturity, as the toad and frog.

anurous *adj* of or pertaining to a anuran.

anus *n* (*anat*) (*pl* **anuses**) the opening at the bottom of the alimentary canal for excretion.

anvil *n* an iron block with a smooth, usually steel, face and often a projecting horn, on which metals are hammered and shaped.

anxiety *n* pain or uneasiness of mind respecting some event, future or uncertain; concern; solicitude; care; disquiet.

anxious *adj* full of anxiety or solicitude respecting something future or unknown; being in painful suspense (of persons); attended with or proceeding from solicitude or uneasiness (of things), followed often by *for*, *about*, *on account of*.

anxiously *adv* in an anxious manner; solicitously.

any *adj* one out of many indefinitely (*any man*); some; an indefinite number or quantity (*any men, any money*), often used as a pronoun, the noun being understood.—*adv* in any degree; to any extent; at all (*any better*).

anybody *n* any one person.

anvil

43

anyhow *adv* in any manner; at any rate; in any event; on any account.

anywhere *adv* in any place.

aorist *n* (*gram*) a tense in the Greek verb which expresses past time indefinitely.

aorta *n* (*anat*) the great artery or trunk of the arterial system, proceeding from the left ventricle of the heart and giving origin to all the arteries except the pulmonary.

apace *adv* with a quick pace; fast; speedily; with haste.

Apache *n* one of a tribe of American Indians.

apache *n* a French street ruffian or desperado.

apart *adv* separately; in a state of separation; taken to pieces; distinct or away from others; at some distance.

apartment *n* a room in a building; a division in a house separated from others by partitions; a flat; (*pl*) a suite, or set, of rooms; lodgings.

apathetic *adj* affected with or proceeding from apathy; devoid of feeling; insensible.

apathy *n* lack of feeling; privation of passion, emotion or excitement; insensibility; indifference.

apatite *n* a mineral consisting chiefly of phosphate of lime, used as manure.

aphid

ape *n* a primate mammal with teeth of the same number and form as in human beings and possessing neither tails nor cheek pouches; (*fig*) one who imitates servilely.—*vt* (**aped, aping**) to imitate servilely; to mimic.

apish *adj* having the qualities of an ape; inclined to imitate; affected.

apeak *adv* (*naut*) perpendicular or inclining to the perpendicular (said of the anchor or yards).

aperient *adj* (*med*) gently purgative; having the quality of opening; laxative.—*n* a medicine which gently opens the bowels; a laxative.

aperitif *n* a drink, usually alcoholic, taken before a meal.

aperture *n* an opening; a mouth, entrance, gap, cleft, etc; a passage; a perforation; the diameter of the exposed part of the object glass of a telescope or other optical instrument.

apex *n* (*pl* **apices, apexes**) the tip, point or summit of anything.

apiary

aphaeresis, apheresis *n* (*gram*) the taking of a letter or syllable from the beginning of a word.

aphanite *n* a name of fine-grained minerals whose structure cannot be detected by the naked eye.

aphasia *n* loss of the faculty of speech, or of connecting words and ideas, owing to an abnormal condition of the brain, while the speech organs and general intelligence remain unaffected.

aphelion *n* (*pl* **aphelia**) that point of a planet's or comet's orbit which is most distant from the sun, opposed to *perihelion*.

aphesis *n* loss of a short unaccented syllable at the beginning of a word, as *squire* for *esquire*.

aphetic *adj* pertaining to aphesis.

aphetize *vt* to shorten by aphesis.

aphid *n* any of various small insects, some of them wingless, which suck the juice of plants and are highly destructive, almost every species of plant supporting a different variety.

aphis *n* (*pl* **aphides**) an aphid.

aphorism *n* a precept or principle expressed in a few words; a brief sentence containing some important truth; a maxim.

aphorist *n* a writer of aphorisms.

aphorize *vi* to make aphorisms.

aphrodisiac *adj* exciting sexual desire.—*n* food or a medicine exciting sexual desire.

aphtha *n* (*pl* **aphthae**) (*med*) a small white ulcer on the tongue or inside of the mouth.

apiarian *adj* relating to bees.—*n* a beekeeper; an apiarist.

apiarist *n* one who keeps bees.

apiary *n* the place where bees are kept; a stand or shed for bees.

apical *adj* relating to the apex or top; belonging to the pointed end of a cone-shaped body.

apiculture *n* the art of managing bees in hives; beekeeping.

apiece *adv* to each; as the share of each; each by itself; by the individual.

aplomb *n* self-possession springing from perfect self-confidence; assurance.

apocalypse *n* revelation; discovery; disclosure.

Apocalypse *n* the name applied to the Book of Revelation, the last book of the New Testament.

apocalyptic, apocalyptical *adj* containing or pertaining to revelation; anticipating the end of the world.

apocope *n* the cutting off or omission of the last letter or syllable of a word, as *th'* for *the*.

Apocrypha *n* the collective name of certain books admitted by the Roman Catholics into the Old Testament canon, but whose authenticity as inspired writings is not generally admitted.

apocryphal *adj* pertaining to the Apocrypha; not canonical; of uncertain authority or credit; fictitious.

apodeictic *adj* demonstrative; evident beyond contradiction.

apodosis *n* (*gram*) the latter part of a conditional sentence (or one beginning with *if, though*, etc), dependent on the protasis or condition.

apogee *n* that point in the orbit of a planet or other heavenly body which is at the greatest distance from the earth; properly this particular point of the moon's orbit.

apologetic *adj* of or pertaining to or containing apology; regretful; defending by words or arguments.

apologetics *n* that branch of theology by which Christians are enabled scientifically to justify and defend the peculiarities of their faith and to answer its opponents.

apologist *n* one who makes an apology.

apologize *vi* (**apologized, apologizing**) to express regret; to make an apology.

apologue *n* a moral fable; a relation of fictitious events intended to convey useful truths, such as the fables of Aesop.

apology *n* something said or written in defence; justification; vindication; an acknowledgment, usually accompanied by an expression of regret, for some improper remark or act; a temporary substitute or makeshift.

apophthegm *n* a short, pithy and instructive saying; a sententious precept or maxim.

apoplectic *adj* pertaining to or consisting in apoplexy; predisposed to apoplexy.

apoplexy *n* abolition or sudden diminution of sensation and voluntary motion, resulting from congestion or rupture of the blood vessels of the brain.

aposiopesis *n* (*rhet*) sudden stopping short and leaving a statement unfinished for the sake of effect.

apostasy *n* an abandonment of what one has professed; a total desertion or departure from one's faith, principles or party.

apostate *n* one who has forsaken his or her faith, principles or party.—*adj* false, traitorous.

apostatize *vi* (**apostatized, apostatizing**) to turn apostate; to abandon principles, faith or party.

aposteme *n* an abscess; a swelling filled with purulent matter.

a posteriori a phrase applied to a mode of reasoning founded on observation of effects, consequences or facts, whereby we reach the causes; inductive, opposed to *a priori*.

apostle *n* a person regarded as having a mission similar to that of the Apostles.

Apostle *n* one of the twelve disciples of Christ who were commissioned to preach the gospel.

apostolate *n* the dignity or office of an apostle; a mission; the dignity or office of the pope, the holder of the Apostolic See.

apostolic, apostolical *adj* pertaining or relating to or characteristic of an apostle, more especially of the twelve Apostles; according to the doctrines of the apostles; proceeding from an apostle.

Apostolic See *n* the see of the bishop of Rome, as directly founded by the apostle Peter.

Apostolic succession *n* the uninterrupted succession of bishops and, through them, of priests and deacons in the church by regular ordination from the Apostles down to the present day.

apostrophe *n* a sudden change in discourse; a sudden and direct address to a person or thing in the course of a speech; (*gram*) the omission of a letter or letters from a word marked by a sign ('); the sign used to mark the omission, or merely as the sign of the possessive case in nouns.

apostrophize *vt* (**apostrophized, apostrophizing**) to address by apostrophe; to make a direct address to in course of a speech; to mark with an apostrophe.—*vi* to make an apostrophe in speaking.

apothecary *n* formerly, one who practises pharmacy; a skilled person who prepared and sold drugs for medicinal use; a chemist.

apotheosis *n* deification; the placing or ranking of a person among deities.

appal *vt* (**appalled, appalling**) to impress with overpowering fear; to confound with terror; to dismay.

appalling *adj* calculated to cause dismay or horror.

apparatus *n sing and pl* (*pl* rarely **apparatuses**) things provided as means to some end; a collection or combination of articles or materials for the accomplishment of some purpose, operation or experiment; (*physiol*) a collection of organs all ministering to the same function.

apparel *n* clothing; garments; dress; external array; the furniture of a ship.—*vt* (**apparalled, apparelling**) to dress or clothe; to cover as with garments.

apparent *adj* visible to the eye; within sight or view; appearing to the eye or to the judgment; seeming (often in distinction to *real*); obvious; plain; evident.

apparently *adv* openly; evidently; seemingly; in appearance.

apparition *n* the act of appearing; the thing appearing; especially a ghost; a spectre; a visible spirit.

apparitor *n* a messenger or officer who serves the process of a spiritual court; the beadle in a university.

appeal *vi* to call, as for aid, mercy, sympathy, etc; to refer to another person or authority for the decision of a question controverted; to refer to a superior judge or court for a final settlement; to give pleasure to; to allure or interest.—*vt* to summon or to challenge; to remove (a cause) from an inferior to a superior judge or court; to charge with a crime; to accuse.—*n* a call for sympathy, mercy, aid, etc; a supplication; an entreaty; the removal of a cause or suit from an inferior to a superior tribunal, that the latter may, if needful, amend the decision of the former; a challenge; a reference to another for proof or decision; resort; recourse (*appeal to arms*); attraction and the ability to attract or arouse interest.

appear *vi* to come into or be in sight; to be or become visible to the eye; to stand in the presence of someone; to be obvious; to be clear or made clear by evidence; to seem; to look like.

appearance *n* the act of appearing or coming into sight; a coming into the presence of a person or persons; the thing seen; a phenomenon; an apparition; external show; semblance, in opposition to *reality* or *substance*; mien; build and carriage; figure; demeanour.

appease *vt* (**appeased, appeasing**) to make quiet; to still; to assuage (hunger); to tranquillize; to calm or pacify (a person, anger).

appeasement *n* act of appeasing; appeased state.

appellant *n* one who appeals; one who removes a cause from a lower to a higher tribunal.

appellation *n* the word by which a thing or person is known; name; title.

appellative *adj* serving as an appellation; naming or marking out; denominative.—*n* an appellation; a general name.

apple

append *vt* to hang on or attach; to add, as accessory or adjunct to a thing; to subjoin; to annex.

appendage *n* something appended or attached; what is attached to a greater thing.

appendicitis *n* inflammation of the vermiform appendix, a small hollow blind process attached to the caecum in human beings and some animals.

appendix *n* (*pl* **appendices, appendixes**) something appended or added; an addition appended to a book relating, but not essential, to the main work; (*anat*) an appendage, process or projecting part.

apperception *n* perception that reflects on itself; consciousness; spontaneous thought.

appertain *vi* to belong or pertain (with *to*).

appetite *n* the natural desire of pleasure or good; taste; inclination; a desire to supply a bodily need or craving; a desire for food or drink; eagerness or longing.

appetizer *n* a food or drink that stimulates the appetite served before a meal.

apple pie

appetizing *adj* whetting the appetite.

applaud *vt* to show approbation of by clapping the hands, acclamation or other significant sign; to praise highly; to extol.—*vi* to give praise; to express approbation.

applause *n* loud praise by clapping the hands or by shouting; commendation; approval.

apple *n* a fruit of a well-known fruit tree or the tree itself; also a name popularly given

to various exotic fruits or trees having little or nothing in common with the apple, as the pineapple, etc.—**apple of one's eye** someone or something beloved above all.

apple pie *n* a pie made of apples, covered with pastry.

apple-pie order *n* perfect order.

appliance *n* the act of applying; the thing applied; means to an end; a device or machine with a special pupose.

applicable *adj* capable of being applied; fit to be applied; having relevance.

applicant *n* one who applies; a petitioner; a candidate.

application *n* the act of applying or putting to; the thing applied; the act of making request or soliciting; the employment of means; close study; attention; the testing of something theoretical by applying it in practice.

apply *vt* (**applied, applying**) to lay on; to put or place on another thing; to use or employ for a particular purpose or in a particular case (a remedy, a sum of money); to put, refer or use as suitable or relative to some person or thing; to engage and employ with attention; to occupy (the mind, or *refl*).—*vi* to suit; to agree; to have some connection, agreement, analogy or reference; to make request; to solicit; to have recourse with a view to gain something (followed by *to*).

appoggiatura *n* (*pl* **appoggiaturas, appoggiature**) (*mus*) a grace note immediately preceding a principal note with which it is connected, and taking its time from the latter.

appoint *vt* to make firm, establish or secure; to constitute, ordain or decree; to allot, set apart or designate; to nominate, as to an office; to settle; to fix, name or determine by authority or on agreement; to equip.—*vi* to ordain; to determine.

appointer *n* one who appoints.

appointment *n* the act of appointing; designation to office; an office held; the act of fixing by mutual agreement; arrangement to meet; decree; direction; command; (usually *pl*) equipment, furniture, fittings, etc.

apportion *vt* to divide and assign in just proportion; to distribute in proper shares; to allot.

apposite *adj* suitable; fit; appropriate; very applicable; well adapted (followed by *to* and said of answers, arguments, etc).

apposition *n* the act of adding to; addition; a setting to; (*gram*) the relation in which a noun or a substantive phrase or clause stands to a noun or pronoun when it explains without being a predicate of it, at the same time agreeing in case, as, *Cicero, the orator, was there.*

appraise *vt* (**appraised, appraising**) to set

a price on; to estimate the value of under the direction of a competent authority; to estimate generally.

appraisement *n* the act of appraising; the value fixed; the valuation.

appraiser *n* one who appraises; a person licensed and sworn to estimate and fix the value of goods and estate.

appreciable *adj* capable of being appreciated or estimated; sufficiently great to be capable of estimation.

appreciably *adv* to a degree that may be appreciated or estimated; perceptibly.

appreciate *vt* (**appreciated, appreciating**) to set a just price, value or estimate on; to estimate or value properly.—*vi* to rise in value; to become of more value.

appreciation *n* the act of appreciating; the act of valuing or estimating; the act of setting a due price or value on.

appreciative *adj* capable of appreciating; manifesting due appreciation; grateful.

apprehend *vt* to take or seize (a person); to arrest; to take or lay hold of by the mind; to become cognizant of; to understand; to entertain suspicion or fear of; to dread or be apprehensive of.—*vt* to form a conception; to conceive; to believe or be of opinion without positive certainty; to be apprehensive; to be in fear of a future evil.

apprehension *n* the act of apprehending; a seizing or arresting by legal process; the operation of the mind in contemplating ideas, or merely taking them into the mind; opinion; belief; the power of perceiving and understanding; distrust or fear at the prospect of future evil, accompanied with uneasiness of mind.

apprehensive *adj* inclined to fear or dread; anticipating or in expectation of evil (*apprehensive of evil*; *apprehensive for our lives*).

apprentice *n* one bound, often by legal document, to learn some art, trade or profession; a learner in any subject; one not well versed in a subject.—*vt* (**apprenticed, apprenticing**) to make an apprentice of; to put under the care of a master, for the purpose of learning a trade or profession.

apprenticeship *n* the state or condition of an apprentice; the term during which one is an apprentice.

apprise *vt* (**apprised, apprising**) to give notice, verbal or written; to inform (followed by *of* before that of which notice is given).

approach *vi* to come or go near in place or time; to draw near; to advance nearer; to approximate.—*vt* to bring near; to advance or put near; to come or draw near to, either literally or figuratively; to come near to, so as to be compared with.—*n* the act of approaching or drawing near; a coming or

advancing near; access; a passage or avenue by which buildings are approached.

approachable *adj* capable of being approached; accessible; of a friendly disposition.

approbation *n* the act of approving; approval; praise.

appropriate *vt* (**appropriated, appropriating**) to claim or take to oneself in exclusion of others; to claim or use as by an exclusive right; to set apart for or assign to a particular purpose.—*adj* set apart for a particular use or person; hence, belonging peculiarly; peculiar; suitable; fit; proper.

appropriation *n* the act of appropriating; application to a special use or purpose; the act of making one's own; anything appropriated or set apart.

approval *n* the act of approving; approbation; commendation; sanction; ratification.—**on approval** for testing by a customer without the obligation to buy.

approve *vt* (**approved, approving**) to admit the propriety or excellence of; to think or judge well or favourably of; to find to be satisfactory.—*vi* to be pleased; to feel or express approbation; to think or judge well or favourably (followed by *of*).

approximate *vt* (**approximated, approximating**) to carry or advance near; to cause to approach (especially said of amount, state or degree).—*vi* to come near; to approach (especially as regards amount, state or character).—*adj* being near in state, place or quantity; approaching; nearly equal, like or accurate.

approximately *adv* in an approximate manner; almost exactly.

approximation *n* the act of approximating; an approximate estimate or amount; approach.

appurtenance *n* that which appertains or belongs to something else; something belonging to another thing as principal; an adjunct; an appendage.

appurtenant *adj* appertaining or belonging; pertaining; being an appurtenance.

apricot *n* a roundish fruit of a delicious flavour, the produce of a tree of the plum kind.

April *n* the fourth month of the year, having 30 days.

April fool *n* the victim of a practical joke, conventionally allowed to be played on the 1st of April.

a priori a phrase applied to a mode of reasoning proceeding from the cause to the effect, as opposed to *a posteriori* reasoning, proceeding from the effect to the cause; also a term applied to knowledge independent of all experience.

apron *n* a piece of cloth or leather worn on the fore part of the body to keep the clothes clean or defend them from injury;

apricot

apron

a covering for the front part of a body; anything resembling the shape of an apron used for protection; the paved surface on an airfield where aircraft are parked, etc. —*vt* to put an apron on; to furnish with an apron.

apropos *adj* opportune; seasonable; to the purpose (*an apropos remark*).—**apropos of** *prep* regarding, in reference to.

apse *n* a portion of any building forming a termination or projection semicircular or polygonal in plan and having a dome or vaulted roof; especially such a structure at the east end of a church.

apsis *n* (*pl* **apsides**) (*archit*) an apse; (*astron*) one of the two points in the orbit of a heavenly body which marks its greatest and its least distance from the primary round which it revolves.

apt *adj* fit; suitable; apposite; pertinent; appropriate; having a tendency; liable; inclined; disposed; ready; prompt.

apteral, apterous *adj* lacking wings.

apteran *n* any of an order of insects that have no wings.

apteryx *n* the kiwi.

aptitude *n* the state or quality of being apt; disposition; tendency; fitness; suitableness; readiness in learning.

aptly *adv* in an apt or suitable manner; justly; pertinently; readily; quickly; cleverly.

aptness *n* the state or quality of being apt; fitness; tendency; quickness of apprehension; readiness in learning.

apyretic *adj* without fever; marked by the absence of fever.

apyrexia, apyrexy *n* the absence of intermission of fever.

aqua *n* water, a word forming an element in various terms.

aqua fortis *n* (= 'strong water') a name given to weak and impure nitric acid.

aquamarine *n* the finest beryl, so called from its bluish or sea-green tint; its colour.

aqua regia *n* (= 'royal water') a mixture of nitric and hydrochloric acids, so called from its power of dissolving gold and other metals.

aquarelle *n* watercolour painting; a painting in watercolour.

aquarium *n* (*pl* **aquariums, aquaria**) a case, vessel, tank, etc, in which aquatic plants and animals are kept; a place containing a collection of such vessels or tanks.

Aquarius *n* the Water Bearer; a sign in the Zodiac which the sun enters about the 21st of January.

aquatic *adj* pertaining to water; living in or frequenting water.—*n* a plant which grows in water; (*pl*) sports or exercises practised on or in water, as rowing or swimming.

aquatint *n* a method of etching on copper by which a beautiful effect is produced, resembling a fine drawing in watercolours or Indian ink.

aqua vitae *n* (= 'water of life'), spirits, as whisky, brandy, etc.

aqueduct *n* a conduit or channel for conveying water from one place to another; a structure for conveying water for the supply of a town.

aqueous *adj* of the nature of water, or abounding with or formed by it; watery.

aquiline *adj* of or belonging to the eagle; resembling an eagle's beak; curving; hooked.

arab *n* a neglected outcast boy or girl of the streets

Arab *n* a native of Arabia; a small breed of Arabian horse.—*adj* of or pertaining to the Arabs or Arabia.

arabesque *n* a species of architectural ornamentation for enriching flat surfaces, either painted, inlaid or wrought in low relief, often consisting of fanciful figures, human or animal, combined with floral forms; in ballet, a posture in which the dancer balances on one leg with one arm extending forwards and the other arm and leg extending backwards.

Arabian *adj* pertaining to Arabia.—*n* a native of Arabia; an Arab.

Arabic *adj* belonging to Arabia or the language of its inhabitants.—*n* the language of the Arabians.

arable *adj* fit for ploughing or tillage.

arachnid *n* any of a class of wingless animals, intermediate between insects and crustaceans, including spiders, mites and scorpions.

arachnoid *adj* pertaining to spiders; resembling a spider's web.—*n* the enveloping membrane of the brain and spinal cord, between the dura mater and the pia mater.

Aramaic *n* a language or group of languages anciently spoken in Syria, the earliest specimens being the Chaldee passages in the Old Testament and Apocrypha; Chaldaic; Chaldee.

araneid *n* an animal of the spider family.

araucaria *n* the generic name of some fine coniferous trees found chiefly in South America, but now also commonly grown in Britain, e.g. the monkey puzzle.

arbalist, arbalest *n* a kind of powerful crossbow of medieval times.

arbiter *n* a person appointed or chosen by parties in controversy to decide their differences; one who judges and determines without control; one whose power of deciding and governing is not limited; an arbitrator.

arbitrage *n* the calculation of the best mode by which advantage may be taken of differences in the value of money, stocks, etc, at different places in the same time; the

arachnid

aquarium

dealing in bills of exchange, stocks, etc, for the purpose of making profit by such calculations.

arbitrament *n* determination; decision; settlement; award (*the arbitrament of the sword*).

arbitrary *adj* given, adjudged or done according to one's will or discretion; exercised according to one's will or discretion; capricious; despotic; imperious; tyrannical; uncontrolled.

arbitrate *vi* (**arbitrated, arbitrating**) to act as an arbiter or umpire; to hear and decide in a dispute.—*vt* to hear and decide on.

arbitration *n* the act of arbitrating; the hearing and determination of a cause between parties in controversy, by a person or persons chosen by the parties.

arbitrator *n* one who arbitrates; an arbiter.

arbor *n* the principal spindle or axis of a machine communicating motion to the other moving parts.

arboreous, arboreal *adj* pertaining to trees; living on or among trees; having the character of a tree.

arboretum *n* (*pl* **arboretums, arboreta**) a place in which a collection of different trees and shrubs is cultivated for scientific or educational purposes.

arboriculture *n* the cultivation of trees; the art of planting, dressing and managing trees and shrubs.

arbour *n* a seat in the open air sheltered by intertwining branches or climbing plants; a bower.

arbutus *n* (*pl* **arbutuses**) the generic name of an evergreen tree or shrub with bright red or yellow berries somewhat like the strawberry, having an unpleasant taste and narcotic properties.

arc *n* (*geom*) a curved line forming or that might form part of the circumference of a circle; formerly also an arch; (*elect*) a discharge, continuous or alternating, of electricity through a gas, accompanied by a brilliant light and partial volatilization of the electrodes.

arcade *n* a series of arches supported on pillars, often used as a roof support or as an ornamental dressing to a wall; a covered-in passage containing shops or stalls.

Arcadian *adj* pertaining to Arcadia, a mountainous district in southern Greece; rustic; rural; pastoral.

arch¹ *n* a structure composed of separate wedge-shaped pieces arranged on a curved line so as to retain their position by mutual pressure; a covering or structure of a bow shape; a vault.—*vt* to cover or span with an arch; to curve or form into the shape of an arch.

arch² *adj* cunning, sly, shrewd; waggish; mischievous; roguish.

arch³ *adj* chief; of the first class or rank,

principally used in composition as the first part of many words; as, *archbishop*, *archpriest*, etc.

archaean *adj* (*geol*) applied to the oldest rocks of the earth's crust, crystalline in character and embracing granite, syenite, gneiss.

archaeological *adj* pertaining to archaeology.

archaeologist *n* one skilled in archaeology.

archaeology *n* the science of antiquities, especially prehistoric antiquities, which investigates the history of peoples by the remains belonging to the earlier periods of their existence.

archaeopteryx *n* a fossil bird of the size of a rook, having two claws representing the thumb and forefinger projecting from the wing and about twenty tail vertebrae prolonged as in mammals.

archaic *adj* old-fashioned; obsolete; antiquated.

archaism *n* an ancient or obsolete word or idiom; antiquity of style or use; obsoleteness.

archangel *n* an angel of the highest order in the celestial hierarchy.

archbishop *n* a bishop who has the supervision of other bishops (the sees of whom form his province) and also exercises episcopal authority in his own diocese.

archbishopric *n* the jurisdiction, office or see of an archbishop.

archdeacon *n* in England, an ecclesiastical dignitary who has jurisdiction, under the bishop, either over a part of or over the whole diocese.

archdeaconate, archdeaconry *n* the office, jurisdiction or residence of an archdeacon.

archducal *adj* pertaining to an archduke.

archduchess *n* the wife of an archduke.

archduke *n* formerly, a prince belonging to the reigning family of the Austrian empire.

archer *n* one who uses or is skilled in the use of the bow and arrow; a bowman.

archerfish *n* a small fish of Asia which shoots drops of water at insects, causing them to fall into the water and become its prey.

archery *n* the practice, art or skill of shooting with a bow and arrow.

archetype *n* a model or first form; the original pattern after which a thing is made, or to which it corresponds.

archidiaconal *adj* pertaining to an archdeacon.

archiepiscopacy, archiepiscopate *n* the dignity, office or province of an archbishop.

archiepiscopal *adj* belonging to an archbishop.

archil *n* same as **orchil**.

Archimedean *adj* pertaining to Archimedes, the Greek philosopher.

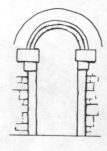

arch

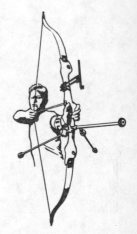

archer

Archimedean screw *n* an ancient instrument for raising water, formed by winding a flexible tube round a cylinder in the form of a screw.

archipelago *n* (*pl* **archipelagoes, archipelagos**) an expanse of water interspersed with many islands; a group of many islands.

architect *n* a person skilled in the art and science of building; one who draws plans and designs of buildings and superintends their erection; any former, maker or planner.

architectonic *adj* pertaining to or skilled in architecture.

architectonics *n* the science of architecture.

architectural *adj* pertaining to architecture or the art of building.

architecture *n* the art or science of building; that branch of the fine arts which has for its object the designing of beautiful buildings; construction.

architrave *n* (*archit*) the lower division of an entablature or that part which rests immediately on the column.

archive *n* a record or document preserved in evidence of something (almost always in plural and signifying documents or records relating to the affairs of a family, corporation, community, city or state).

archivist *n* the keeper of archives or records.

archly *adv* in an arch or roguish manner.

archway *n* a passage under an arch.

arc lamp, arc light *n* a lamp, the intense light from which is produced by an electric arc.

arctic *adj* northern; surrounding or lying near the North Pole.

Arctic circle *n* a circle parallel to the equator, 23° 28′ from the North Pole.

Arcturus *n* a fixed star of the first magnitude near the tail of the Great Bear.

arcuate *adj* bent or curved in the form of a bow.

ardent *adj* burning; causing a sensation of burning; warm, applied to the passions and affections; vehement; passionate; eager; fervent; fervid; zealous.

ardent spirits *npl* alcoholic drinks, as brandy, whisky, rum, etc.

ardour *n* heat in a literal sense; warmth or heat, as of the passions and affections; eagerness.

arduous *adj* steep and therefore difficult of ascent; hard to climb; attended with great labour; difficult; hard (task or employment).

are[1] the present tense plural of the verb to be.

are[2] *n* a metric unit of square measure, containing 100 square metres.

area *n* any plain surface within boundaries, as the floor of a hall, etc; a space sunk below the general surface of the ground before windows in the basement storey of a building; a yard; the superficial contents of any space; a surface as given in square inches, feet, yards, etc.

areca *n* a genus of palms, including the betel nut and cabbage trees.

arena *n* the enclosed space (usually covered with sand) in the central part of Roman amphitheatres; the scene or theatre of exertion or contest of any kind.

areola *n* (*pl* **areolae**) a small area or space; a small interstice; the coloured circle or halo surrounding the nipple or surrounding a pustule.

areometer *n* an instrument for measuring the specific gravity of liquids; a hydrometer.

Areopagite *n* a member of the Areopagus.

Areopagus *n* a tribunal at ancient Athens, so called because held on a hill of this name.

argal, argol *n* unrefined or crude tartar; a hard crust formed on the sides of vessels in which wine has been kept.

argali *n* a species of wild Asiatic sheep with very large horns, nearly as bulky as a moderately sized ox.

argent *n* silver; whiteness, like that of silver; (*heral*) the white colour in coats of arms, intended to represent silver, etc— *adj* resembling silver; bright like silver; silvery.

argil *n* clay or potter's earth; sometimes, pure clay or alumina.

argillaceous *adj* of the nature of or composed of argil or clay; clayey.

argon *n* a gas existing in the atmosphere in very small quantities; an inert chemical element.

Argonaut *n* one of the persons of Greek legend who sailed with Jason in the ship *Argo* in quest of the Golden Fleece; a kind of cuttlefish, the paper nautilus or paper sailor of the Mediterranean, the female having a boat-like shell in which its eggs are received (said to float with its arms extended to catch the breeze and with other arms as oars).

argosy *n* formerly, a large merchantman or other ship especially if richly laden.

argot *n* slang.

arguable *adj* capable of being argued.

argue *vi* (**argued, arguing**) to offer reasons to support or overthrow a proposition, opinion or measure; to reason; to discuss; to debate; to dispute.—*vt* to debate or discuss (*argue a cause in court*); to prove, show or evince; to cause to be inferred (*his conduct argued suspicion*).

argument *n* the subject of a discourse or writing; an abstract or summary of a book or section of a book; a reason offered for or against something; a debate, contro-

Archimedean screw

Artic circle

versy or discussion; a process of reasoning.

argumentative *adj* consisting of argument; addicted to argument, disputing or debating.

argumentum ad hominem *n* an argument which presses a man with consequences drawn from his own principles and concessions or his own conduct.

argus *n* a species of pheasant having its plumage marked with eye-like spots.

Argus *n* a being in Greek mythology having a hundred watchful eyes; any watchful person.

Argus-eyed *adj* vigilant; watchful; extremely observant.

aria *n* in opera, cantata, etc, a song for solo voice.

Arian *n* one maintaining the doctrines of Arius (fourth century), who held Christ to be a created being inferior to God.— *adj* pertaining to Arius or to his doctrines.

Arianism *n* the doctrines of the Arians.

arid *adj* dry; without moisture; parched with heat; uninteresting.

aridity *n* the state of being arid; dryness; lack of interest.

Aries *n* the Ram, a northern constellation, the first of the twelve signs in the Zodiac, which the sun enters at the vernal equinox.

arietta *n* a short song or aria.

aright *adv* in a right way or form; properly; correctly; rightly.

aril *n* an extra covering of the seed of some plants (as the nutmeg) outside the true seed coats, falling off spontaneously.

arise *vi* (*pret* **arose**, *pp* **arisen**, *ppr* **arising**) to move to a higher place; to mount up; to ascend; to come into view; to get out of bed or quit a sitting or lying posture; to spring; to originate; to start into action; to rise.

aristocracy *n* government by the nobility or persons of rank in the state; the nobility or chief persons in a state.

aristocrat *n* a member of the aristocracy; one who favours an aristocracy.

aristocratic, aristocratical *adj* pertaining or belonging to the aristocracy or to the rule of aristocrats; resembling the aristocracy in manner, behaviour and elegance.

Aristotelian *adj* pertaining to Aristotle (born 384 BC), the celebrated Greek philosopher and founder of the Peripatetic school.—*n* a follower of Aristotle; a peripatetic.

Aristotelianism *n* the philosophy or doctrines of Aristotle.

arithmetic *n* the science of numbers or the art of computation by figures or numerals.

arithmetical *adj* pertaining to arithmetic; according to the rules or methods used in arithmetic.

arithmetical progression *n* a series of numbers showing increase or decrease by a constant quantity, as 1, 2, 3, 4, etc—9, 7, 5, 3, opposed to *geometrical progression*.

arithmetically *adv* by the rules or methods of arithmetic.

arithmetician *n* one skilled in arithmetic.

ark *n* a small chest or coffer; a place of safety or shelter.

Ark *n* (*Scrip*) the repository of the covenant or tables of the law, over which was placed the golden covering or mercy seat; the large floating vessel in which Noah and his family were preserved during the deluge.

arm[1] *n* the limb of the human body which extends from the shoulder to the hand; an anterior limb; anything projecting from a main body, as a branch of a tree, a narrow inlet of the sea; (*fig*) power, might, strength.

arm[2] *n* a weapon; a branch of the military service; (*pl*) war; the military profession; armour; armorial bearings.—**small arms** arms that can be carried by those who use them.—**side-arms** arms worn at the side, as a sword or bayonet.—*vt* to furnish or equip with arms or weapons; to cover or provide with whatever will add strength, force or security; to fortify.—*vi* to provide oneself with arms; to take arms.

armada *n* a fleet of armed ships; a squadron, usually applied (*with cap*) to the Spanish fleet intended to act against England in the reign of Queen Elizabeth, 1588.

armadillo *n* (*pl* **armadillos**) a mammal of South America covered with a hard bony shell divided into belts and composed of small separate plates like a coat of mail.

armament *n* weapons carried by military vehicles, ships, etc; a fighting force; equipment for war.

armature *n* armour; hence, anything serving as a defence, as the prickles and spines of plants; a piece of iron connecting the two poles of a magnet; (*elect*) that part of a dynamo or motor which carries the conductors in which the generation of electricity takes place or in which the main currents act.

armchair *n* a chair with arms to support the elbows.

Armenian *adj* pertaining to Armenia, a country in Asia.—*n* a native of Armenia; the language of the country; an adherent of the Christian Church of Armenia.

armful *n* as much as the arms can hold; that which is embraced by the arms.

armhole *n* a hole for the arm in a garment.

Arminian *n* a member of the Protestant sect who follows the teaching of Arminius, a Dutch theologian (died 1609), specially opposed to the Calvinistic doctrine of predestination.—*adj* pertaining to Arminius or his principles.

armidillo

armchair

51

Arminianism *n* the doctrines or tenets of the Arminians.

armistice *n* a temporary suspension of hostilities by agreement of the parties; a truce.

armless *adj* without arms.

armlet *n* a little arm; a piece of armour for defending the arm; an ornament worn on the arm; a bracelet.

armorial *adj* belonging to armour or to the arms or escutcheon of a family.

Armoric, Armorican *adj* pertaining to the northwestern part of France, formerly called Armorica, now Brittany.—*n* the language of the Celtic inhabitants of Brittany, allied to the Welsh.

armour *n* defensive arms; any covering worn to protect the body in battle; the steel or iron covering intended as a protection for a ship of war or a tank.

armour-bearer *n* one who carried the armour of another.

armourer *n* a maker of armour or arms, or one who keeps them in repair; one who has the care of arms and armour.

armour plate *n* an iron or steel plate of great thickness covering the side of a ship or tank.

armour-plated, armoured *adj* covered or protected by armour plates; iron-clad.

armoury *n* a place where arms and instruments of war are made or deposited for safe-keeping; a collection of arms.

armpit *n* the cavity under the shoulder or upper arm.

army *n* a collection or body of men armed for war and organized in regiments, brigades or similar divisions under officers; a host; a vast multitude; a great number.

army corps *n* section of the army, complete in itself, embracing infantry, cavalry, artillery.

Army List *n* an official publication with names of all commissioned officers.

arnica *n* a composite plant, otherwise called mountain tobacco, the roots of which yield tannin, and a tincture of the plants is used as an application to wounds and bruises.

aroma *n* an agreeable odour; fragrance; perfume; (*fig*) delicate intellectual quality; flavour.

aromatherapy *n* the massage of fragrant oils into the skin to relieve tension and promote wellbeing.

aromatic *adj* giving out an aroma; fragrant; sweet-scented; odoriferous.

around *prep* about; on all sides; encircling; encompassing.—*adv* in a circle; on every side.

arouse *vt* (**aroused, arousing**) to excite into action that which is at rest; to stir or put in motion or exertion; to rouse; to animate; to awaken.

arousal *n* the act of arousing.

arpeggio *n* (*pl* **arpeggios**) the distinct sound of the notes of a chord heard when the notes are struck in rapid succession.

arquebus *n* an old-fashioned handgun fired from a rest.

arrack *n* a spirituous liquor distilled in the East Indies from rice, the juice of the coconut and other palms, etc.

arraign *vt* to call or set at the bar of a court of justice; to accuse or charge; to censure publicly; to impeach.

arrange *vt* (**arranged, arranging**) to put in proper order; to dispose or set out; to adjust; to settle; to come to an agreement or understanding regarding; (*mus*) to prepare a composition for different instruments from those intended.—*vi* to make or come to terms; to come to a settlement or agreement.

arrangement *n* the act of arranging; disposition in suitable form; that which is arranged; preparatory measure; preparation; settlement; adjustment; (*pl*) plans.

arrant *adj* notorious; thorough; out-and-out; downright.

arras *n* tapestry; hangings consisting of woven stuffs ornamented with figures.

array *n* a collection or assemblage of men or things disposed in regular order, as an army in order of battle; raiment; dress; apparel.—*vt* to place or dispose in order, as troops for battle; to marshal; to deck or dress; to attire.

arrear *n* the state of being behindhand; that which remains unpaid or undone when the due time is past (usually in the plural).

arrest *vt* to check or hinder the motion or action of; to stop; to seize or apprehend by a warrant from authority; to seize and fix (attention); to engage; to secure; to catch.—*n* the act of arresting; apprehension; stoppage; stay; restraint.

arresting *adj* striking or attracting to the mind or eye; impressive.

arrival *n* the act of arriving; a coming to or reaching; attainment; the person or thing which arrives.

arrive *vi* (**arrived, arriving**) to come to a certain place or point; to get to a destination; to reach a point or stage; to attain to a certain result or state (followed by *at*).

arrogance *n* the disposition to make exorbitant claims of rank, dignity or estimation; the pride which exalts one's own importance; pride with contempt of others; presumption; haughtiness; disdain.

arrogant *adj* making exorbitant claims on account of one's rank, power, worth; presumptuous; haughty; overbearing; proud and assuming.

arrogate *vt* (**arrogated, arrogating**) to claim or demand unduly or presumptuously; to lay claim to in an overbearing manner.

arrondissement *n* in France, an administra-

armour

tive district forming a subdivision of a department.

arrow *n* a missile weapon, straight, slender, pointed and barbed, to be shot from a bow; anything resembling this.

arrowroot *n* a flour or starch obtained from the root stocks of several West Indian reed-like plants and used as food.

arsenal *n* a repository or magazine of arms and military stores for land or naval service; a public establishment where arms or warlike equipment are manufactured or stored.

arsenic *n* a chemical element of a steel-blue colour, quite brittle: combined with oxygen it forms arsenious oxide, which is the white arsenic, a virulent poison.

arsenical *adj* of or pertaining to arsenic; containing arsenic.

arsis *n* elevation of the voice at a word or syllable, in distinction from *thesis*, or its depression; (*pros*) a greater stress or force on a syllable.

arson *n* the malicious burning of property which by common law is felony.

art *n* the use or employment of things to answer some special purpose; the employment of means to accomplish some end, opposed to *nature*; a system of rules to facilitate the performance of certain actions; skill in applying such rules (*the art of building* or *of engraving*; *the fine arts*), opposed to *science*; one of the fine arts or the fine arts collectively, that is, those that appeal to the taste or sense of beauty, as painting, sculpture, music; the profession of a painter or sculptor; the special skill required by those who practise these arts; artistic faculty; skill; dexterity; knack; artfulness; cunning; duplicity.

Art Deco *n* a style of design and architecture popular in the 1920s and 1930s and characterized by bold geometrical lines.

artefact *n* same as **artifact**.

arterial *adj* pertaining to or contained in an artery or the arteries; (of blood) oxygenated, of a lighter red colour than blood in the veins; major, with many branches (*arterial road*).

arterialization *n* the conversion of the venous into the arterial blood.

artery *n* one of a system of cylindrical vessels or tubes, which convey the blood from the heart to all parts of the body, to be brought back again by the veins.

artesian *adj* (of a well) formed by a perpendicular boring into the ground, often of great depth, through which water rises to the surface of the soil by natural gravitation, producing a constant flow or stream.

artful *adj* cunning; sly; deceitful; crafty.

artfully *adv* in an artful manner; cunningly; craftily.

artfulness *n* the quality of being artful.

arthritic *adj* pertaining to or affecting the joints; pertaining to arthritis and gout.

arthritis *n* any inflammation of the joints caused by gout.

artichoke *n* a composite plant somewhat resembling a thistle, cultivated in gardens for the thick and fleshy receptacle (or part supporting the flower), which is eaten: the *Jerusalem artichoke* is quite different, being a species of sunflower whose roots are used like potatoes.

article *n* a single clause, item, point or particular; a point of faith, doctrine or duty; a prose contribution to a newspaper, magazine or other periodical; a particular commodity or substance; a part of speech used before nouns to limit or define their application—in English *a* or *an* and *the*.—*vt* (**articled, articling**) to draw up under distinct heads or particulars; to bind, as an apprentice; to indenture.

articular *adj* belonging to the joints or to a joint.

articulate *adj* jointed; formed with joints (*an articulate animal*); formed by the distinct and intelligent movement of the organs of speech; pronounced distinctly; expressed clearly; distinct (*articulate speech* or *utterance*); (of an invertebrate animal) with an external skeleton forming a series of rings articulated together and enveloping the body, such as crustaceans, insects, worms, etc.—*vt* (**articulated, articulating**) to joint; to unite by means of a joint; to utter by intelligent and appropriate movement of the vocal organs; to enunciate, pronounce or speak.—*vi* to utter articulate sounds; to utter distinct syllables or words.

articulation *n* the act or manner of articulating or being articulated; a joining or juncture, as of the bones; a joint; a part between two joints.

artifact, artefact *n* a product of human workmanship, especially those of interest to archaeologists.

artifice *n* artful, skilful or ingenious contrivance; a crafty device; trick; shift; stratagem; deception; cunning; guile; fraud.

artificer *n* a skilful or artistic worker; a constructor; a maker; a contriver; an inventor; a mechanic or handicraftsman.

artificial *adj* made or contrived by art or by human skill and labour; feigned; fictitious; assumed; affected; not genuine or natural.

artificiality *n* the quality of being artificial.

artificial silk *n* a fabric manufactured from wood pulp or cotton cellulose by forcing it through capillaries and allowing it to dry.

artillery *n* heavy guns; ordnance; ordnance and its equipment both in men and material; the soldiers and officers who manage

artery

Art Deco

heavy guns; the science which deals with their use and management.

artiodactyle *n* a hoofed mammal in which the number of toes is even (two or four), as the ox and other ruminants, the pig, etc.

artisan *n* one skilled in any trade; a handicraftsman; a mechanic.

artist *n* one skilled in an art or profession, especially one who professes and practises one of the fine arts, as painting, sculpture, engraving and architecture; specifically and most frequently a painter.

artiste *n* a professional, usually musical or theatrical, entertainer.

artistic, artistical *adj* pertaining to art or artists; trained in art; conformable to or characterized by art.

artless *adj* devoid of art, skill or cunning; natural; simple.

artlessly *adv* in an artless manner; naturally; simply.

artlessness *n* naturalness; simplicity; ingenuousness.

Art Nouveau *n* a style of art and decoration that developed in the late 19th century, characterized by flowing curves and designs in imitation of nature.

artwork *n* work in the graphic or plastic artsl (print) the decorative and graphic portions of a publication, as opposed to the text.

arum *n* the generic name of certain plants, one of which, the common arum, wake-robin or lords-and-ladies, is abundant in woods and hedges in England and Ireland.

arundinaceous *adj* pertaining to reeds; resembling a reed.

arundineous, arundinose *adj* abounding with reeds.

Aryan *n* formerly, an Indo-European; in Nazi belief, a Caucasian, especially of the Nordic type with no Jewish blood.—*adj* pertaining or belonging to the Aryans; Indo-European.

aryl *n* a certain type of univalent aromatic hydrocarbon radical.

as[1] *adv, conj* a word expressing equality, similarity of manner or character, likeness, proportion, accordance; in the same manner in which (*ye shall be as gods*; *I live as I did*); while; when (*he whistled as he went*); for example; for instance; thus; because; since (*as the wind was fair we set sail*); often equivalent to the relative *that* after *such* (*give us such things as you please*).

as[2] *n* (*pl* **asses**) a Roman weight of 12 ounces; a Roman copper or bronze coin.

asafetida, asafoetida *n* a fetid sap from a large plant found in Central Asia, used in medicine as an antispasmodic, in flatulence, hysteric paroxysms, etc.

asbestos *n* a fibrous variety of several hornblendes with fine, elastic, flexible, flax-like incombustible filaments, for-

merly made into fireproof cloth, paper, etc.

ascend *vi* to move upwards; to mount; to go up from a lower to a higher place; to rise; to proceed from an inferior to a superior degree, from mean to noble objects, from particulars to generals, etc; to pass from a grave tone to one more acute.—*vt* to go or move upwards on; to climb; to move upwards along; to go towards the source of (a river).

ascendancy *n* governing or controlling influence; power; sway; control.

ascendant *n* superiority or commanding influence; predominance.

ascension *n* the act of ascending; a rising.

Ascension *n* the visible elevatio of Christ to heaven.

Ascension Day *n* the day on which the Ascension of Christ is commemorated, falling on the Thursday but one before Whitsuntide.

ascent *n* the act of rising; motion upwards; rise; the way by which one ascends; acclivity; an upward slope; the act of proceeding from an inferior to a superior degree, from particulars to generals, etc.

ascertain *vt* to make certain; to make sure or find out by trial or examination; to establish; to determine with certainty.

ascertainable *adj* capable of being ascertained or certainly known.

ascetic *adj* excessively strict or rigid in devotions or mortifications; severe; austere.—*n* one who retires from the world and devotes himself to a strictly devout life; one who practises excessive rigour and self-denial; a hermit; a recluse.

asceticism *n* the condition or practice of ascetics.

ascian *n* one who has no shadow; an inhabitant of the torrid zone when the sun is in the zenith.

ascidian *n* one of certain marine molluscous animals of a low type, having frequently the shape of a double-necked bottle, often found on the beach at low water or attached to rocks, shells, etc; a sea-squirt, a tunicate animal.

ascites *n* (*med*) dropsy of the abdomen or of the peritoneal cavity.

ascitic, ascitical *adj* relating to ascites; dropsical.

ascorbic acid *n* vitamin C, found especially in citrus fruit and fresh green vegetables.

ascribable *adj* capable of being ascribed or attributed.

ascribe *vt* (**ascribed, ascribing**) to attribute, impute or refer, as to a cause; to assign; to set down; to attribute, as a quality or appurtenance.

ascription *n* the act of ascribing.

aseptic *adj* free from disease germs, especially in aseptic surgery.

artist

Art Nouvea

asexual *adj* not sexual; having no distinctive organs of sex, or imperfect organs; performed without the union of males and females.

ash[1] *n* a common tree cultivated extensively for its hard and tough timber; the timber of this tree.—*adj* pertaining to or like the ash; made of ash.

ash[2] *n* what remains of something that is burnt; the dust or powdery substance to which a thing is reduced by the action of fire (generally used in the plural); incombustible residue; the remains of a human body when burnt or otherwise decayed; (*fig*) a corpse.

ashamed *adj* affected or touched by shame; feeling shame; exhibiting shame (*an ashamed look*): with *of* before the object.

ashen[1] *adj* pertaining to or like the ash; made of ash.

ashen[2] *adj* pale, colourless, especially of complexion; pallid

ashlar *n* common freestones rough from the quarry; a facing made of squared stones on the front of buildings; hewn stone for such facing.

ashore *adv* on the shore, bank or beach; on the land adjacent to water; to the shore.

Ash Wednesday *n* the first day of Lent, so called from the ancient custom of sprinkling ashes on the heads of penitents on that day.

ashy *adj* composed of or resembling ashes; lifeless and pale.

Asian *adj* pertaining to Asia, one of the continents of the globe.—*n* a native of Asia.

Asiatic *adj* belonging to Asia or its inhabitants.—*n* a native of Asia.

aside *adv* on or to one side; to or at a short distance off; apart; away from some normal direction; out of one's thoughts, consideration or regard; away; off (*to lay cares aside*); so as not to be heard, or supposed not to be heard, by someone present.—*n* something spoken and not heard, or supposed not to be heard, by someone present, as something uttered by an actor on the stage.

asinine *adj* belonging to or having the qualities of an ass; absurdly stupid or obstinate.

ask *vt* to request; to seek to obtain by words; to petition (with *if* before the person); to require, expect or claim; to demand; to interrogate or inquire of; to question; to inquire concerning; to seek to be informed about (*to ask the way*); to invite.—*vi* to make a request or petition (with *for* before an object); to inquire or seek by request (often followed by *after*).

askance *adv* sideways; obliquely; out of one corner of the eye.

askew *adv* in an oblique position; obliquely; awry.

aslant *adj, adv* slantwise; on one side; obliquely; not perpendicular or at right angles.

asleep *adj, adv* in or into a state of sleep; at rest.

asp *n* a deadly species of viper found in Egypt; also, a species of viper found on the continent of Europe.

asparagus *n* a perennial plant of the lily family cultivated for its young edible shoots.

aspect *n* look; view; appearance to the eye or the mind (*to present a subject in its true aspect*); countenance; look or particular appearance of the face; mien; air (*a severe aspect*); view commanded; prospect; outlook (*a house with a southern aspect*); (*astrol*) the situation of one planet with respect to another.

aspen *n* a species of poplar the leaves of which tremble with the slightest breath of air.

asperity *n* the quality or state of being rough; roughness or harshness to the touch, taste, hearing or feelings; tartness; crabbedness; severity; acrimony.

aspersion *n* the spread of false and injurious reports or charges; calumny; censure.

asphalt *n* the most common variety of bitumen; mineral pitch; a black or brown substance which melts readily and has a strong pitchy odour; a mixture of asphalt or bitumen and sand or other substances, used for pavements, roads and roofs.

asphodel *n* the name given to various species of plants of the lily family: the asphodel of the older English poets is the daffodil.

asphyxia *n* suspended animation or loss of consciousness, with temporary stoppage of the heart's action, caused by interrupted respiration, particularly from suffocation or drowning or the inhalation of irrespirable gases.

asphyxiate *vt* (**asphyxiating, asphyxiated**) to bring to a state of asphyxia; to cause asphyxia in.

asphyxiation *n* the act of causing asphyxia; a state of asphyxia.

aspic *n* a dish consisting of a clear, savoury, meat jelly and containing fowl, game, fish, etc.

aspidistra *n* a flowering plant with variegated leaves, originally from China and Japan.

aspirant *n* one who aspires or seeks with eagerness; a candidate.

aspirate *vt* (**aspirated, aspirating**) to pronounce with a breathing or audible emission of breath; to pronounce with such a sound as letter *h* has; to add an *h*-sound to ('horse' is aspirated but not 'hour').—*n* an aspirated sound like that of *h*; the letter *h* itself; or any mark of aspiration.

aspidistra

aspiration *n* the act of aspirating; an aspirated sound; the act of aspiring or ardently desiring; an ardent wish or desire chiefly after what is great and good.

aspire *vi* (**aspired, aspiring**) to desire with eagerness; to pant after a great or noble object; to aim at something elevated or above one; to be ambitious (followed by *to* or *after*); to ascend; to tower; to point upward; to soar.

aspirin *n* acetylsalicylic acid, a pain-relieving drug.

ass *n* a quadruped of the horse family, supposed to be a native of Asia, in parts of which vast troops roam in a wild state; from the supposed slowness and lack of spirit of the domestic ass, obstinacy and stupidity; a dull, stupid fellow; a dolt; a blockhead.

assail *vt* to fall on with violence; to set upon; assault; to attack with actual weapons or with arguments, censure, abuse, criticism, entreaties, etc.

assailant *n* one who assails, attacks or assaults.

assassin *n* one of a sect in Palestine in the time of the Crusades distinguished for their secret murders; one who kills or attempts to kill by surprise or secret assault; a murderer, especially of a public figure.

assassinate *vt* (**assassinated, assassinating**) to kill by surprise or secret assault; to murder by sudden violence; to defame; to slander; to libel.

assassination *n* the act of assassinating; a killing or murdering by surprise or secret assault.

assault *n* an attack or violent onset; an onslaught; a violent attack with the intention of injuring a person; a sudden and vigorous attack on a fortified post; a storm.—*vt* to fall on by violence or with a hostile intention; to fall on with force; to assail.

assay *n* examination; trial; the trial of the goodness, purity, weight, value, etc, of metals or metallic substances, especially gold and silver, their ores and alloys.—*vt* to make any assay of; to examine by trial; to test the purity or metallic constituents of; to attempt, endeavour, essay.

assayer *n* one who assays.

assegai *n* a South African spear.

assemblage *n* the act of assembling or state of being assembled; a collection of individuals or of particular things; a gathering or company.

assemble *vt* (**assembled, assembling**) to collect into one place or body; to bring or call together; to convene; to congregate; to fit together (pieces of a mechanism, a product, etc).—*vi* to meet or come together; to gather; to convene.

assembly *n* a company or collection of human beings in the same place, usually for the same purpose; the name given to the legislative body or one of the divisions of it in various states; a ball, especially a subscription ball.

assembly line *n* a series of machines, equipment and workers through which a product passes in successive stages to be assembled.

assent *n* the admitting or agreeing to the truth of a proposition; consent; concurrence; acquiescence; agreement to a proposal; accord; agreement; approval.—*vi* to express agreement to what is alleged or proposed; to concur; to acquiesce.

assert *vt* to support the cause or claims of (rights, liberties); to vindicate a claim or title to; to affirm positively; to asseverate; to aver; (*refl*) to come forward and assume one's rights, claims, etc.

assertion *n* the act of affirming; the maintaining of a claim; a positive declaration or averment; an affirmation.

assess *vt* to set, fix or charge a certain sum on (a person) by way of tax; to value, as property or the amount of yearly income, for the purpose of being taxed; to settle or determine the amount of (damages).

assessable *adj* capable of being assessed; liable to be assessed.

assessment *n* the act of assessing; a valuation of property, profits or income for the purpose of taxation; a tax or specific sum charged on a person or property.

assessor *n* one appointed to make assessments; an officer of justice who sits to assist a judge.

asset *n* an article of goods or property available for the payment of a person's obligations or debts (generally used in the plural); any portion of the entire effects belonging to a person.

asset-stripping *n* the practice of buying a company simply to sell off its assets at a profit.

asseverate *vt* (**asseverated, asseverating**) to affirm or aver positively or with solemnity.

asseveration *n* the act of asseverating; positive affirmation or assertion.

assiduity, assiduousness *n* the quality of being assiduous; constant or diligent application to any business or enterprise; diligence.

assiduous *adj* constant in application; attentive; devoted; unremitting; performed with constant diligence or attention.

assign *vt* to mark out as a portion allotted; to apportion; to allot; to fix or specify; (*law*) to transfer or make over to another.—*n* a person to whom property or an interest is transferred; an assignee.

assignable *adj* capable of being assigned.

assignation *n* the act of assigning or allotting; the act of fixing or specifying; a mak-

aspirin

ing over by transfer of title; an appointment of time and place for meeting (used chiefly of love meetings).

assignee *n* a person to whom an assignment is made; a person appointed or deputed to perform some act or business or enjoy some right.

assignment *n* the act of assigning, fixing or specifying; the writing by which an interest is transferred.

assimilable *adj* capable of being assimilated.

assimilate *vt* (**assimilated, assimilating**) to make alike; to cause to resemble; to absorb and incorporate (food) into the system; to incorporate with organic tissues; to liken or compare.—*vi* to become similar; to harmonize; to become incorporated with the body; to perform the act of converting food to the substance of the body.

assimilation *n* the act or process of assimilating or being assimilated; the process by which animals and plants convert and absorb nutriment so that it becomes part of the substances composing them.

assist *vt* to help; to aid; to succour.—*vi* to lend aid; to be present; to take part in a ceremony or discussion.

assistance *n* help; aid; succour; a contribution in aid.

assistant *adj* helping; lending aid or support; auxiliary.—*n* one who aids or assists another; one engaged to work along with another; an auxiliary.

assize *n* formerly, the periodical sessions held at stated intervals in the counties of England and Wales for the purpose of trying criminal and certain other cases before a jury (generally in the plural), now dealt with by crown courts.

associate *vt* (**associated, associating**) to join in company (another with ourselves); to adopt as a partner, companion, etc; to join or connect intimately (things together); to unite; to combine.—*vi* to unite in company; to join in a confederacy or association.—*adj* joined in interest, object, office, etc; combined together; joined with another or others.—*n* a companion; a mate; a fellow; a partner; a confederate; an accomplice; an ally.

association *n* the act of associating or state of being associated; connection; union; a society, the members of which are united by mutual interests or for a common purpose; (*pscychol*) the tendency which one idea, feeling, etc, has for one reason or another to recall another.

association football *n* one of the two principal varieties of football, played by eleven men a side, with a round ball, handling (except by the goalkeeper) being forbidden.

assonance *n* resemblance of sounds; (*pros*) a species of imperfect rhyme which consists in using the same vowel with different consonants.

assonant *adj* having a resemblance of sounds; (*pros*) rhyming only so far as the vowels are concerned.

assort *vt* to separate and distribute into sorts, classes or kinds; to furnish with a suitable variety of goods (*to assort a cargo*); to adapt or suit.—*vi* to agree; to suit together.

assortment *n* the act of assorting; a collection of assorted things.

assuage *vt* (**assuaged, assuaging**) to allay, mitigate, ease or lessen (pain or grief); to moderate; to appease or pacify (passion or tumult).

assume *vt* (**assumed, assuming**) to take on oneself; to take on; to appear in (*assume a figure* or *shape*); to appropriate; to take for granted; to suppose as a fact; to pretend to possess; to put on (*assume a wise air*).—*vi* to be arrogant; to claim more than is due; (*law*) to undertake or promise.

assuming *adj* putting on airs of superiority; haughty; arrogant; overbearing.

assumption *n* the act of assuming; a taking on oneself; the act of taking for granted; supposition; the thing supposed; a postulate or proposition assumed.

assurable *adj* capable of being assured; suitable for insurance.

assurance *n* the act of assuring; a pledge furnishing ground of full confidence; firm persuasion; certain expectation; undoubting steadiness; intrepidity; excess of boldness; impudence; laudable confidence; self-reliance; insurance against what is certain rather than probable (e.g. death).

assure *vt* (**assured, assuring**) to make (a person) sure or certain; to convince (*to assure a person of a thing*); to declare or affirm solemnly to; to confirm; to ensure; to secure (*to assure success to a person*); to insure (one's life); to embolden or make confident.

assured *adj* certain; convinced; not doubting or doubtful; bold to excess; confident; having life or goods insured (in this sense often a noun, *sing* or *pl*).

assuredly *adv* certainly; indubitably.

assurer *n* one who assures; an insurer or underwriter.

Assyrian *adj* pertaining or relating to Assyria or to its inhabitants.—*n* a native or inhabitant of Assyria; the language of the Assyrians.

Assyriologist *n* one skilled in the antiquities, language (as exhibited in the cuneiform inscriptions), etc, of ancient Assyria.

aster *n* a large genus of composite plants, the flowers of which somewhat resemble stars.

association football

asterisk *n* the figure of a star (*) used in printing and writing as a reference to a note or to fill the space where something is omitted.

astern *adv* in or at or towards the stern of a ship; behind a ship; backward; with the stern foremost.

asteroid *n* one of the small planets between the orbits of Mars and Jupiter.

asthma *n* a chronic disorder of respiration, characterized by difficulty of breathing, a cough and expectoration.

asthmatic *adj* pertaining to asthma; affected by asthma.—*n* a person troubled with asthma.

astigmatism *n* a malformation of the lens of the eye, such that rays of light are not brought to converge in the same point.

astir *adv*, *adj* on the move; stirring; active.

astonish *vt* to strike or impress with wonder, surprise or admiration; to surprise; to amaze; to stun; to confound.

astonishing *adj* calculated to astonish; amazing; wonderful.

astonishment *n* the state or feeling of being astonished; amazement; great surprise; a cause or matter of astonishment.

astound *vt* to astonish; to strike dumb with amazement.

astronaut

astounding *adj* fitted or calculated to astound; causing terror; astonishing.

astraddle *adv* straddling; with one leg on either side; astride.

astragal *n* a small semicircular moulding separating the shaft of a column from the capital; one of the bars which hold the panes of a window; the huckle or anklebone; the upper bone of the foot.

astrakhan *n* the pelt of lambs from Astrakhan in Russia, which is black with small tight curls; a rough kind of cloth with a curled pile.

astral *adj* belonging to the stars; starry.

astral body *n* an ethereal body supposed by theosophists to exist along with, but more or less independently of, an ordinary material body.

astray *adv* having strayed; out of the right way or proper place.

astride *adv* with one leg on each side; with the legs wide apart.

astringent *adj* contracting; especially contracting the organic tissues and canals of the body, thereby checking or diminishing excessive discharges; severe, stern.—*n* an astringent substance.

astrological chart

astrolabe *n* an instrument formerly used for taking the altitude of the sun or stars at sea, now superseded by the quadrant and sextant.

astrologer *n* one who practises astrology.

astrological *adj* pertaining to astrology.

astrologize *vt* (**astrologized, astrologizing**) to practise astrology.

astrology *n* the study of the supposed effects and influences of planetary positions and motions on human beings and human affairs.

astronaut *n* one trained to make flights in outer space.

astronautics *n* sing the scientific study of space flight and technology.

astronomer *n* one who studies astronomy.

astronomic, astronomical *adj* pertaining to astronomy; (*colloq*) huge.

astronomical unit *n* a unit of length used in astronomy, equal to the mean distance of the earth from the sun.

astronomy *n* the scientific investigation of the celestial bodies, their nature, magnitudes, motions, distances, periods of revolution, etc.

astrophysics *n* the branch of astronomy that deals with the physical and chemical structure of the heavenly bodies.

astute *adj* shrewd; penetrating; sagacious; keen.

astutely *adv* in an astute manner; shrewdly; sharply.

astuteness *n* the quality of being astute; shrewdness.

asunder *adv* apart; into parts.

asylum *n* a sanctuary or place of refuge; any place of retreat and security; formerly, an institution for the mentally ill.

asymmetrical *adj* not having symmetry.

asymmetry *n* the lack of symmetry or proportion between the parts of a thing.

asymptote *n* (*math*) a line which approaches nearer and nearer to a curve, but though infinitely extended would never meet it.

asymptotic *adj* belonging to or having the character of an asymptote.

asyndeton *n* a figure of speech by which conjunctions are omitted.

at *prep* denoting coincidence or contiguity, in time (*at first*); in space (*at home*, *at church*); in occupation or condition (*at work*, *at prayer*); in degree or condition (*at best*, *at the worst*); in effect, as coincident with the cause (*at the sight*); in relation, as existing between two objects (*at your command*); in value (*at a pound a head*); also, direction towards (*fire at the target*).—**at large** at liberty, unconfined; also, generally; as a whole (*the country at large*).

atavism *n* the resemblance of offspring to a remote ancestor; the return or reversion among animals to the original type.

atelier *n* a workshop; specifically, the workroom of sculptors and painters.

Athanasian *adj* pertaining to Athanasius, bishop of Alexandria, in the fourth century.

Athanasian Creed *n* a creed of the Christian church erroneously attributed to

Athanasius and also ascribed to Hilary, bishop of Arles (about AD 430), defining the doctrines of the trinity and the incarnation in very precise and emphatic language, declaring damnation to be the lot of those who do not hold the right faith.

atheism *n* disbelief in the existence of a God or a god.

atheist *n* one who professes atheism or disbelief in God.

atheistic, atheistical *adj* pertaining to, implying or containing atheism; disbelieving the existence of God or a god.

atheling, aetheling *n* in Anglo-Saxon times, a prince; one of the royal family.

athenaeum *n* an institution for the encouragement of literature and art, where a library, periodicals, etc, are kept for the use of the members.

Athenian *adj* pertaining to Athens.—*n* a native or inhabitant of Athens.

athirst *adj, adv* thirsty; lacking drink; having a keen appetite or desire (with *for*).

athlete *n* one trained to to compete in sports and exercises of speed and strength.

athletic *adj* pertaining to athletes or exercises practised by athletes; strong; robust; vigorous.

athletics *npl* athletic exercises and competitive sporting events.

athleticism *n* the practice of athletics; the strength and vigour of an athlete.

at home *n* an informal reception or party held at the host's or hostess's own home.

athwart *prep* across; from side to side of; (*naut*) across the line of a ship's course.— *adv* in a manner to cross and perplex; crossly; wrong.

atilt *adv* tilted up.

atlas *n* a collection of maps in a volume; a volume of plates or tables illustrative or explanatory of some subject; the first vertebra of the neck (so named because it supports the head).

atlantes *npl* (*sing* **atlas**) sculptured figures or half figures of men used in the place of columns or pilasters in buildings, supporting or seeming to support an entablature.

Atlantic *adj* pertaining to that division of the ocean which lies between Europe and Africa on the east and America on the west.—*n* the Atlantic Ocean.

atmosphere *n* the gaseous mass surrounding the earth extending to 40 or 50 miles above its surface; any similar gaseous envelope or medium; the amount of pressure of a column of the atmosphere on a square inch (= 15 pounds); (*fig*) pervading influence, feeling or mood (*to live in an atmosphere of doubt*).

atmospheric, atmospherical *adj* pertaining to, existing in or consisting of the atmosphere; caused, produced or operated on by the atmosphere.

atmospherics *npl* (*radio*) disturbances, resembling actual signals, produced in the receiving circuits by electrical action in the atmosphere or in the earth's crust.

atoll *n* a coral island consisting of a strip or ring of coral surrounding a central lagoon or lake: such islands are very common in the Pacific Ocean.

atom *n* the smallest particle that makes up all matter and still retains the chemical properties of the element; anything extremely small; a minute quantity (*not an atom of sense*).

atomic *adj* pertaining to atoms; consisting of atoms; extremely minute.

atomic bomb *n* a bom whose explosive power derives from the atomic energy released during nuclear fission or fusion.

atomic energy *n* energy derived from nuclear fission.

atomic heat *n* the product of the specific heat and atomic weight of an element, equal to about 6.4 for practically all elements.

atomic mass unit *n* one twelfth of the mass of an atom of the carbon isotope.

atomic number *n* the number of protons in the nucleus of an atom, marking the place of an element in the periodic table.

atomic theory *n* the theory that all chemical combinations take place in a definite manner between the atoms of bodies.

atomic volume *n* the number obtained by dividing the atomic weight of an element by its density.

atomic weight *n* the former name of **relative atomic mass**, the mass of atoms of an element given in atomic mass units.

atomizer *n* one who or that which atomizes or reduces to atoms; an apparatus for reducing a liquid into spray for disinfecting, cooling, perfuming, etc.

atonable *adj* capable of being atoned for.

atone *vi* (**atoned, atoning**) to make reparation, amends or satisfaction, as for an offence or a crime.—*vt* to expiate.

atonement *n* the act of atoning; reparation; specifically, the reconciliation of God with man through Christ; satisfaction; expiation.

atop *adv* on or at the top.

atrium *n* (*pl* **atria**) the entrance hall and usually the most splendid apartment of an ancient Roman house; (*anat*) an auricle of the heart; (*zool*) the chamber into which the intestine opens in ascidians.

atrocious *adj* extremely heinous, criminal or cruel; enormously or outrageously wicked; horrifying.

atrociousness *n* the quality of being atrocious.

atrocity *n* the state or quality of being atrocious; enormous wickedness or cruelty; an act of extreme heinousness or cruelty.

athlete

atoll

atrophy *n* a wasting of the flesh with loss of strength; emaciation.

atropin, atropine *n* a very poisonous substance obtained from the deadly nightshade.

attach *vt* to make to adhere; to tie, bind or fasten; to connect or associate; to gain over, win, charm or attract.—*vi* to be attached or connected; to be joined or bound up with; to belong (with *to*, as *interest attaches to a subject*).

attachable *adj* capable of being attached.

attaché *n* one attached to an embassy or legation to a foreign court.

attaché case *n* a travelling case, similar to a suitcase but smaller, and suitable for carrying papers or documents.

attachment *n* the act of attaching; the state of being attached; close adherence or affection; any passion or liking which binds one person to another or to a place, etc; love; regard; that which attaches one object to another; the object attached; an adjunct; (*law*) a taking of a person or goods by legal means to secure a debt.

attaché case

attack *vt* to assault; to fall on with force or violence; to make a hostile onset on; to assail; to endeavour to injure by an act, speech or writing; to come or fall upon; to seize, as a disease.—*vi* to make an attack or onset; to begin an assault.—*n* a falling on, with force or violence, or with calumny, satire, etc; an onset; an assault; a seizure by a disease.

attain *vt* to reach by effort; to achieve or accomplish; to acquire; to gain (said of an end or object); to come to; to arrive at; to reach (said of a place).—*vi* to reach; to come or arrive (followed by *to*).

attainable *adj* capable of being attained, reached, achieved or accomplished.

attainment *n* the act of attaining; that which is attained; an acquisition; an accomplishment.

attainder *n* formerly, the act or legal process of subjecting a person to the consequences of judgment of death or outlawry pronounced in respect of treason or felony; forfeiture of civil privileges.

attar *n* a perfumed oil from flowers.

attar or roses, otto of roses *n* an essential oil made from various species of roses, which forms a valuable perfume.

attic

attempt *vt* to make an effort to effect; to endeavour to perform; to undertake; to try; to make an effort upon (a person's life); to try to win or seduce.—*n* an essay, trial or endeavour; an effort to gain a point; an attack, onset or assault.

attend *vt* to accompany or be present with, as a companion or servant; to be present at or in for some purpose (church, a concert, etc); to accompany or follow in immediate sequence, especially from a causal connection (*a cold attended with fever*); to wait for.—*vi* to pay regard or heed; to be present, in pursuance of duty; to act as an attendant; to be concomitant (by itself or followed by *on* or *upon*).

attendance *n* the act of attending or attending on; the act of waiting on or serving; service; ministry; the persons attending for any purpose.

attendant *adj* accompanying; being present or in attendance on; connected with, or immediately following.—*n* one who attends or accompanies another; one who is present or regularly present; that which accompanies or is consequent on.

attention *n* the act of attending or heeding; the application of the ear to sounds or of the mind to objects presented to its study; heedfulness; observation; an act of civility or courtesy

attentive *adj* paying or giving attention; heedful; intent; observant; regarding with care; mindful; habitually heedful or mindful; sedulous.

attenuate *vt* (**attenuated, attenuating**) to make thin, fine or slender; to reduce the thickness of either liquids or solid bodies; to reduce the strength of.—*vi* to become thin, slender or fine; to diminish; to lessen.

attest *vt* to bear witness to; to certify; to affirm to be true or genuine; to declare the truth of; to manifest (one's joy, etc).

attestation *n* the act of attesting; a solemn declaration, verbal or written, in support of a fact; evidence; testimony.

attic *n* (*archit*) a low storey erected over a principal; an apartment in the uppermost part of a house, with windows in the cornice or the roof; a garret.

Attic *adj* pertaining to Attica in Greece or to its principal city, Athens; marked by the qualities characteristic of the Athenians. —*n* the dialect spoken in Attica or Athens; the chief literary and the purest dialect of ancient Greece.

Attic wit, Attic salt *n* a dry delicate wit as that for which the Athenians were famous.

attire *vt* (**attired, attiring**) to dress; to deck; to array; to adorn with elegant or splendid garments.—*n* (no *pl*) dress; clothes; garb; apparel.

attitude *n* posture or position of a person or the manner in which the parts of his or her body are disposed; viewpoint, state, condition or conjuncture, as likely to have a certain result; aspect (*the attitude of affairs*).

attitudinize *vi* (**attitudinized, attitudinizing**) to assume affected attitudes, airs or postures.

attorney *n* (*pl* **attorneys**) (*law*) one who is appointed or admitted in the place or admitted in the place of another to transact any business for him or her; one who acts for another, as in a court of law; a solicitor.

Attorney General *n* in England, the chief ministerial law officer of the crown; the public prosecutor on behalf of the crown.

attract *vt* to draw to or towards, either in a physical or mental sense; to cause to draw near or close to by some influence; to invite or allure; to entice; to win.—*vi* to possess or exert the power of attraction; to be attractive or winning.

attraction *n* the act, power or property of attracting; (*physics*) the tendency, force or forces through which all particles of matter, as well as all individual masses of matter, are attracted or drawn towards each other; the inherent tendency in bodies to approach each other to unite and to remain united; the power or act of alluring, drawing to, inviting or engaging; allurement; enticement; that which attracts; a charm; an allurement.

attractive *adj* having the quality of attracting; having the power of charming or alluring; inviting; engaging; enticing.

attractiveness *n* the quality of being attractive or engaging.

attributable *adj* capable of being or liable to be attributed; ascribable; imputable.

attribute *vt* (**attributed, attributing**) to ascribe; to impute; to consider as belonging or as due; to assign.—*n* any property, quality or characteristic that can be ascribed to a person or thing.

attribution *n* the act of attributing; that which is ascribed; attribute.

attrition *n* the act of wearing or rubbing down; the state of being worn down or smoothed by friction; weakening by continual wearing down (*war of attrition*).

attune *vt* (**attuned, attuning**) to tune or put in tune; to adjust one sound to another; to make accordant; (*fig*) to arrange fitly; to bring into harmony, concord or agreement.

aubergine *n* a pear-shaped or globe-shaped vegetable with a dark purple skin and a pale firm flesh; a dark purple colour.

auburn *adj* reddish brown or rich chestnut, generally applied to hair.

auction *n* a public sale of property to the highest bidder.—*vt* to sell by auction.

auctioneer *n* one whose business it is to sell things by auction.

audacious *adj* overbold or daring; bold in wickedness; insolent; impudent; shameless; unabashed.

audacity *n* the quality of being audacious; impudence; effrontery; insolence.

audible *adj* capable of being heard; perceivable by the ear; loud enough to be heard.

audibility *n* the quality of being audible.

audience *n* the act of listening; a hearing; liberty or opportunity of being heard before a person or assembly; an assembly of listeners (*concert audience, radio audience*); a devoted following..

audiofrequency *n* any frequency which is audible by the human ear.

audiotape *n* a sound tape recording, a cassette tape.

audit *n* an examination of accounts or dealings with money or property by persons, especially accountants, appointed for that purpose; a calling to account; an examination into one's actions.—*vt* to make an audit of; to examine, as an account or accounts.

audition *n* the act of hearing; a hearing or listening; a testing of an actor for a role or a performer for an engagement.

auditor *n* a hearer; a listener; a person appointed and authorized to audit or examine an account or accounts.

auditorium *n* in an opera house, public hall, etc, the space allotted to the audience.

auditory *adj* relating to hearing or to the sense or organs of hearing.

Augean stables *n* the stables of mythical King Augeas of Elis in Greece, in which he kept 3000 oxen, and the cleaning out of which, after it had remained uncleaned for thirty years, was assigned as a task to Hercules, who accomplished it in a single day, hence *cleaning the Augean stables* became a synonym for the removal of accumulated nuisances, abuses, etc.

auger *n* an instrument for boring holes larger than those bored by a gimlet, chiefly used by carpenters, joiners, etc; any instrument on the same plan used for boring into the soil.

aught *n* anything, indefinitely; any part or quantity.

augment *vt* to increase; to enlarge in size or extent; to swell; to make bigger.—*vi* to increase; to grow larger.—*n* (*gram*) an increase at the beginning of certain inflectional forms of a verb, as the *e* prefixed in certain tenses of the Greek verb.

augmentation *n* the act of augmenting; the act of adding to or enlarging; the state or condition of being made larger; increase; enlargement; accession; the thing added by way of enlargement; addition.

augur *n* among the ancient Romans one whose duty was to derive signs concerning future events from the flight or other actions of birds, etc, and hence, one who foretells future events by omens; a soothsayer; a prophet.—*vi* to guess; to conjecture, as from signs or omens; to be a sign; to bode (*to augur well* or *ill for a project*).—*vt* to guess or conjecture; to predict; to anticipate (said of persons); to betoken; to forebode (said of things).

augury *n* the art or practice of an augur; that which forebodes; that from which a prediction is drawn; a prognostication.

august *adj* grand; magnificent; majestic; inspiring reverence.

audiotape

August *n* the eighth month of the year, containing thirty-one days.

Augustan *adj* pertaining to the Emperor Augustus.

Augustan age *n* the most brilliant period in Roman literature; any brilliant period in the literary history of a country, as the reign of Queen Anne in England.

Augustin, Augustine, Augustinian *n* a member of one of the fraternities who follow rules framed by St Augustine or deduced from his writings.

auk *n* one of various swimming birds found in British seas, having their legs placed so far back as to cause them to stand nearly upright, and with very short wings more useful for swimming and diving than for flight.

aunt *n* the sister of one's father or mother.

Aunt Sally *n* a dummy figure at which balls, etc, are thrown, the object being to knock a pipe out of its mouth; any person or institution which becomes a target for popular abuse.

au pair *n* a person, especially a young woman, from abroad who performs domestic chores, child-minding, etc, in return for board and lodging.

aura *n* an air; an effluvium or odour; an exhalation; the symptoms immediately preceding attacks of certain diseases, especially epilepsy; a particular quality or atmosphere surrounding someone or something.

aural *adj* relating to the ear (*aural surgery*).

aurist *n* one skilled in disorders of the ear, or who professes to cure them.

aureate *adj* golden; gilded.

aureole *n* in painting, an illumination surrounding a holy person, as Christ, a saint, etc; a halo.

auricle *n* the external ear or that part which is prominent from the head; either of the two cavities in the mammalian heart placed above the two ventricles and resembling in shape the external ear.

auricula *n* a garden flower of the primrose family, found native in the Swiss Alps, and sometimes called bear's-ear from the shape of its leaves.

auricular *adj* pertaining to the ear or the sense of hearing, or to an auricle; confided to one's ear, especially privately.

aurochs *n* a species of wild bull or buffalo now extinct, once abundant on the continent of Europe.

aurora *n* (*pl* **auroras, aurorae**) either of the two luminous bands seen in the night sky in the polar regions.

Aurora *n* the goddess of the morning or dawn deified.

aurora australis *n* the aurora of the southern hemisphere, a similar phenomenon to that of the aurora borealis.

aurora borealis *n* the northern lights or streamers, a luminous meteoric phenomenon of varying brilliance seen in the northern heavens and in greatest magnificence in Arctic regions.

auroral *adj* belonging to or resembling the dawn; belonging to or resembling the polar lights; roseate; rosy.

auspices *npl* protection, patronage; favourable influence or omens.

auspicious *adj* having omens of success or favourable appearances; propitious; favourable; prosperous; happy.

austere *adj* severe; harsh; rigid; rigorous; stern; self-disciplined; simple, unelaborate, e.g. in style.

austerely *adv* in an austere manner; severely; rigidly.

austerity *n* the state or quality of being austere; severity; rigour; strictness; harshness.

austral *adj* southern; lying or being in the south.

Australasian *adj* relating to Australia, New Zealand and the adjacent islands.—*n* a native of Australasia.

Australian *adj* pertaining to Australia.—*n* a native or inhabitant of Australia.

Australian sloth *n* the koala.

autarky *n* self-sufficiency; ability to stand on one's own feet.

authentic *adj* being what it purports to be; not false or fictitious; genuine; valid; authoritative; reliable.

authenticate *vt* (**authenticated, authenticating**) to render authentic; to give authority to by proof, attestation, etc; to prove authentic; to determine as genuine.

authentication *n* the act of authenticating; the giving of proof or authority.

authenticity *n* the quality of being authentic; the quality of being genuine; genuineness.

author *n* an originator or creator; the original composer of a literary work; the writer of a book or other literary production.

authoress *n* a female author

authoritative *adj* having authority; recognised as true or as being expert; positive; peremptory; dictatorial.

authority *n* power or right to command or act; dominion; control; the power derived from opinion, respect or esteem; influence conferred by character, station, mental superiority, etc; a person or persons exercising power or command (generally in the plural, as *the civil and military authorities*); that to which or one to whom reference may be made in support of any fact, opinion, action, etc (*a person's authority for a statement*); credit or credibility (*a work of no authority*).

authorization *n* the act of authorizing

authorize *vt* (**authorized, authorizing**) to give authority, warrant or legal power to;

auk

to give a right to act; to empower; to make legal; to establish by authority or by usage or public opinion (*an authorized idiom*); to warrant; to sanction; to justify.

authorship *n* the character or state of being an author; the source from which a work proceeds.

autobiography *n* biography or memoirs of a person written by himself of herself.

autobiographer *n* one who writes an autobiography

autobiographic, autobiographical *adj* pertaining to, consisting of, or containing autobiography.

autochthon *n* (*pl* **autochthones**) one of the primitive inhabitants of a country; an aboriginal inhabitant; that which is original to a particular country.

autoclave *n* a strong metallic vessel, used for heating liquids under high pressure.

autocracy *n* supreme power invested in a single person; the government or power of an absolute monarch.

autocrat *n* an absolute sovereign; a monarch who governs without being subject to restriction; one who assumes unlimited authority in any sphere.

autocratic *adj* pertaining to autocracy; absolute; domineering.

auto-da-fé *n* (*pl* **autos-da-fé**) formerly, a public ceremony held by the courts of the Inquisition in Spain at the execution of heretics condemned to the stake.

autograph *n* a person's own handwriting; an original manuscript or signature.—*vt* to sign; to write one's signature.

automatic *adj* belonging to or proceeding by spontaneous movement; having the power of self-motion; self-acting (said especially of mechanism); not depending on the will; instinctive; applied to actions; of firearms, after the first shot firing others in rapid succession.—*n* a pistol (Colt, Browning, etc) with magazine in the butt and reloaded by means of the recoil.

automatism *n* automatic action; theory regarding automatic actions.

automaton *n* (*pl* **automata, automatons**) that which is self-moving; a self-acting machine or mechanical device which imitates the movements of living beings; a robot; a person who acts mechanically.

automobile *n* a motorcar.

autonomous *adj* independent; self-governing.

autonomy *n* the power or right of self-government.

autopsy *n* (*med*) a post-mortem examination.

autosuggestion *n* (*psychol*) suggestion, akin to hypnotic suggestion, made to oneself consciously or unconsciously with a view to producing a desired frame of mind or bodily condition.

autumn *n* the third season of the year or the season between summer and winter, popularly regarded in the Northern hemisphere as comprising August, September and October, but astronomically beginning at the autumnal equinox, 23rd September, and ending at the winter solstice, 21st December.

autumnal *adj* belonging to autumn; produced or gathered in autumn; (*fig*) belonging to the period past the middle stage of life.

auxiliary *adj* conferring aid or support; helping; aiding; assisting; subsidiary.—*n* a helper; an assistant; an associate in some undertaking; (*pl*) foreign troops in the service of a nation at war; (*gram*) a verb which helps to form the moods and tenses of other verbs, as, *have, may, shall* and *will.*

avadavat *n* same as **amadavat**.

avail *vt* to be for the advantage of; to assist or profit; to benefit.—**to avail oneself of** to turn to one's profit or advantage; to take advantage of.—*vi* to be of use, benefit or advantage; to answer a purpose; to have strength, force or efficacy sufficient.—*n* advantage tending to promote success; benefit; service; utility; efficacy (used in such phrases as, *of little avail*; *of no avail*).

available *adj* having efficacy; capable of being used; attainable; accessible.

avalanche *n* a vast body of snow or ice sliding down a mountain or over a precipice; a sudden overwhelming accumulation or influx.

avarice *n* an inordinate desire of gaining and possessing wealth; covetousness; cupidity; greediness.

avaricious *adj* characterized by avarice; greedy of gain; miserly; covetous.

avast *exclam* (*naut*) stop! hold! cease!.

avatar *n* a descent from heaven, the incarnation of the Hindu deities or their appearance in some manifest shape on earth.

avaunt *interj* begone; depart, an exclamation of contempt or abhorrence.

ave *interj* hail! farewell! God bless you!

Ave *n* a short form of **Ave Maria**.

Ave Maria *n* (*RC Church*) devotional words often repeated, chaplets and rosaries being divided into a certain number of Ave Marias and Paternosters.

avenge *vt* (**avenged, avenging**) to vindicate by inflicting pain or evil on the wrongdoer; to deal punishment for injury done to (with a person as object); to take satisfaction for, by pain or punishment inflicted on the injuring party; to deal punishment on account of.

avenger *n* one who avenges; one who takes vengeance.

avens *n* the popular name of several species of rosaceous plants growing wild.

avenue *n* a passage; a way or opening for

automobile

entrance; a wide straight roadway or street; an alley or walk planted on each side with trees; (*fig*) means of access or attainment.

aver *vt* (**averred, averring**) to affirm with confidence; to declare in a positive or peremptory manner; to assert.

average *n* a sum or quantity intermediate to a number of different sums or quantities; a mean or medial amount; a general estimate based on comparison of a number of diverse cases; a medium; (*com*) a contribution falling on the owners of a ship's freight and cargo, in proportion to their several interests, to make good a loss that has been sustained.—*adj* exhibiting a mean proportion or mean quality; forming an average; medium; not extreme; ordinary; (*com*) estimated in accordance with the rules of average.—*vt* (**averaged, averaging**) to find the average of; to reduce to a mean sum or quantity; to show or have as an average or mean (*trees average 50 feet in height*).

averse *adj* unwilling; opposed, having repugnance (followed by *to*).

averseness *n* the state of being averse.

aversion *n* opposition or repugnance of mind; dislike; disinclination; reluctance; hatred; the cause of dislike; the object of repugnance.

avert *vt* to turn or direct away from; to turn or to cause to turn off or away (the eyes, calamity, etc).

Avesta *n* the sacred writings attributed to Zoroaster; the Zendavesta.

Avestan, Avestic *n* the language of the Avesta; Zend.

avian *adj* pertaining to birds.

aviary *n* a building or enclosure for the breeding, rearing and keeping of birds.

aviation *n* the art or science of aerial navigation.

aviator *n* one who engages in aviation.

aviculture *n* the breeding and rearing of birds.

avid *adj* eager; greedy (with *for*).

avidity *n* greediness; strong appetite; eagerness; intenseness of desire.

avizandum *n* (*Scots law*) the private consideration by a judge of a case that has been heard in court.

avocado pear, alligator pear *n* the fruit of a small tree of the laurel family common in tropical America and the West Indies.

avocation *n* formerly, a distraction from work; a hindrance; a person's business, pursuit or occupation; vocation or calling.

avocet *n* a wading bird of the size of a lapwing with very long legs, feathers variegated with black and white, and a long slender bill bent upwards towards the tip.

avoid *vt* to make void (in legal phraseology); to shun; to keep away from; to es-

avocado pear

aviator

chew; to evade; to elude (expense, danger, bad company).—*vi* to become void or vacant.

avoidable *adj* that may be annulled; capable of being avoided, shunned or escaped.

avoidance *n* the act of annulling or making void; the act of avoiding or shunning.

avoirdupois *n* a system of weight of which 1 pound contains 16 ounces, in distinction to troy weight which has only 12—the system by which commodities in general are weighed.

avouch *vt* to affirm openly; to avow; to maintain, vindicate or justify (a statement); to establish; guarantee; substantiate.

avow *vt* to declare openly; to acknowledge; to own.

avowal *n* an open declaration; frank acknowledgment.

avowed *adj* declared; open (*an avowed enemy*).

avuncular *adj* of or pertaining to an uncle.

await *vt* to wait for; to look for or expect; to be in store for; to be ready for (*a reward awaits him*).

awake *vt* (*pret* **awoke** *pp* **awaked, awoken,** *ppr* **awaking**) to rouse from sleep or from a state resembling sleep; to put into action or new life.—*vi* to cease to sleep; to bestir or rouse oneself from sleep.—*adj* not sleeping; in a state of vigilance or action.

awaken *vi* to become awake; to awake.—*vt* to rouse from sleep; to awake.

awakening *n* act of awaking from sleep; a revival of religion.—*adj* rousing; alarming.

award *vt* to give as a reward or prize; to adjudge; to assign judicially or by sentence (as an arbitrator pronouncing on the rights of parties).—*vi* to make an award.—*n* a prize; a judgment; decision; the decision of arbitrators on points submitted to them.

aware *adj* apprised; cognizant; informed; conscious (followed by *of*).

away *adv* absent; at a distance; apart; to a distance (*to go away*); often used elliptically (*whither away so fast?*): with many verbs it conveys a notion of using up or consuming (*to squander away, to idle away*); it has also merely an intensive force (*eat away, laugh away*).—*interj* begone! depart! go away!

awe *n* admiration or reverence; feeling inspired by something sublime.—*vt* (**awed, awing**) to strike with awe; to influence by fear, reverence or respect.

aweather *adj, adv* (*naut*) on or to the weather side of a ship, opposed to *alee*.

awesome *adj* inspiring awe; (*colloq*) marvellous, terrific.

awestruck *adj* struck with awe.

awful *adj* striking or inspiring with awe; horrible, terrible, ugly.

awhile *adv* for a space of time; for some time.

awkward *adj* lacking dexterity in the use of the hands or of instruments; bungling; clumsy; ungraceful in manners; uncouth; not cooperative, dangerous.

awl *n* a pointed instrument for piercing small holes in leather, wood, etc.

awn *n* the bristle or beard of corn or grass, or any similar bristle-like appendage.

awning *n* a covering of canvas or other cloth on a frame spread or projecting over any place as a protection from the sun's rays.

awry *adj*, *adv* turned or twisted towards one side; crooked; perverse; wrong.

axe *n* an instrument, consisting of a head, with an arching edge of steel in the plane of the sweep of the tool, attached to a handle and used for hewing timber and chopping wood.

axehead *n* the head or iron of an axe.

axestone *n* the mineral nephrite or jade.

axiom *n* a self-evident truth or proposition; a proposition whose truth is so evident at first sight that no process of reasoning or demonstration can make it plainer; an established principle in some art or science; a principle universally received.

axiomatic *adj* pertaining to, consisting of, or having the character of an axiom.

axis *n* (*pl* **axes**) the straight line, real or imaginary, passing through a body or magnitude, on which it revolves, or may be supposed to revolve; (*bot*) the central line or column about which other parts are arranged; (*anat*) the second vertebra of the neck.

axle, axletree *n* a piece of timber or bar of iron on which the wheels of a vehicle, etc, turn.

axle nut *n* a screw nut on the end of an axle to keep the wheel in place.

axle pin *n* same as linchpin.

axolotl *n* a remarkable member of the tailed amphibians found in Mexican lakes, possessing four limbs resembling those of a frog and usually having throughout life both lungs and gills, but sometimes losing the latter.

ay, aye *adv* yes; yea; a word expressing assent or affirmation; truly; certainly; indeed.—*n* the word by which assent is expressed in Parliament; hence, an affirmative vote.—**the ayes have it** the affirmative votes are in a majority.

ayah *n* in India, etc, a waiting-woman, governess, nursemaid or lady's maid.

aye *adv* always; for ever; continually; for an indefinite time (used mostly in poetry).

aye-aye *n* a nocturnal quadruped about the size of a hare found in Madagascar, allied to the lemurs and in its habits resembling the sloth.

azalea *n* any of certain plants belonging to the heath family, remarkable for the beauty and fragrance of their flowers and distinguished from the rhododendrons chiefly by the flowers having five stamens instead of ten.

azimuth *n* (*astron*) an arc of the horizon intercepted between the meridian of a place and the vertical circle passing through the centre of a celestial object and the zenith.

azo dye *n* any of a class of synthetic organic colouring compounds, containing nitrogen combined in a special way.

azoic *adj* lacking any vestige of organic life (applied to rocks, especially some very old rocks, in which no fossils have as yet been found).

Aztec *n*, *adj* one of or pertaining to the Aztecs, the people of Mexico or their empire at the time of the Spanish invasion.

azure *adj* resembling the clear blue colour of the sky; sky-blue.—*n* the fine blue colour of the sky; a name common to several sky-coloured or blue pigments; the sky or vault of heaven.—*vt* to colour blue.

azurite, azure stone *n* a blue mineral, an ore of copper, composed chiefly of hydrous carbonate.

an Aztec mask

B

B the second letter and the first consonant in the English and most other alphabets; (*mus*) the seventh note of the model diatonic scale or scale of C.

baa *n* the bleating of a sheep.

Baal *n* a deity worshipped among the Canaanites, Phoenicians, etc, and supposed to represent the sun.

Babbitt metal *n* an alloy of copper, zinc, tin and lead, used for obviating friction in the bearings of cranks, axles, etc.

babble *vi* to utter words imperfectly or indistinctly; to talk idly or irrationally; to make a continuous murmuring sound; to prate; to tell secrets.—*vt* to utter idly or irrationally.—*n* idle talk; senseless prattle; murmur as of a stream.

babbler *n* one who babbles; a teller of secrets.

babe *n* a baby; a naive person; (*sl*) a girl or young woman..

Babel *n* the city mentioned in Scripture where the confusion of tongues took place; any great city where confusion may be supposed to prevail; a confused mixture of sounds; confusion; disorder.

baboon *n* a monkey of the Old World with an elongated muzzle, strong canine teeth, a short tail, cheek pouches, small deep eyes with huge eyebrows and naked callosities on the hips.

baby *n* a newborn child or infant; a very young animal; (*sl*) a girl or young woman; a personal project.—*vt* (**babied, babying**) to pamper..

babyhood *n* the state of being a baby; infancy.

babyish *adj* like a babe; childish.

baby

Babylonian *adj* of or pertaining to the ancient kingdom of Babylonia; magnificent luxurious.—*n* an inhabitant of Babylonia; its language.

babysit *vt* (**babysitted, babysitting**) to look after (a child) temporarily while the parents are absent.—*vi* to act as a babysitter.

babysitter *n* one who looks after a child temporarily while the parents are absent.

baccarat *n* a game of cards played by any number of players.

bacchanal, bacchanalian *adj* revelling in or characterized by intemperate drinking; riotous; noisy.

bacchanalia *npl* feasts or festive rites in honour of Bacchus, the god of wine.

bacchant, bacchante *n* a priest or priestess of Bacchus, the god of wine; one who joined in the feasts of Bacchus; one in a state of Bacchic frenzy.

Bacchic, Bacchical *adj* relating to Bacchus, the god of wine; jovial; drunken; mad with intoxication.

bachelor *n* formerly, a young man in the first or probationary stage of knighthood; a man who has not been married; a person who has taken the degree below that of master or doctor in arts, science, or other subjects at a university.

bacillus *n* (*pl* **bacilli**) a microscopic organism that often swarms in the blood of animals in abnormal states; a bacterium.

back *n* the posterior part of the trunk; the region of the spine; the hinder part of the body in humans and the upper in other animals; that which is behind or farthest from the face or front; the rear (*the back of a house*); that which is behind or in the farthest distance; the part which comes behind in the ordinary movements of a thing, or when it is used (*the back of the hand, a knife, saw*, etc); a reserve or secondary resource; a support or second; in football, hockey, etc, a player stationed in a defensive position, usually near his or her own goal.—**behind one's back** in secret, or when one is absent.—*adv* to or towards a former place, state or condition; not advancing; in a state of restraint or hindrance (*to keep back*); toward times or things past (*to look back*); again; in return (*to give back*); away from contact; by reverse movement; in withdrawal from an undertaking or engagement (*to draw back*).—**to go back** to retreat, to recede; to give way; to succumb.—*adj* belonging to the back; lying in the rear; remote; in a backward direction (chiefly in compounds).—*vt* to furnish with a back or backing; to support; to second or strengthen by aid (often with *up*); to bet or wager in favour of; to get on the back of; to mount; to write something on the back of; to endorse; to put backward; to cause to move backwards or recede.—*vi* to move or go back; to move with the back foremost; (*meteor*) to shift in a anticlockwise direction (said of wind), the opposite of *veer*.

backbencher *n* a British member of parliament who is not a minister or shadow minister and therefore is not entitled to sit on the front benches in the House of Commons.

backbite *vt* (*pret* **backbit**, *pp* **backbit** *or* **backbitten** *ppr* **backbiting**) to censure, slander, or speak evil of, in the absence of the person.

backbiter *n* one who backbites.

backbiting *n* malicious gossip or slander behind someone's back.

backbone *n* the bone of the back; the spine; the vertebral column; firmness; decision of character; resolution.

backchat *n* interchange of facetious or insolent remarks between two persons; impudence.

backcomb *vt* to fluff up (hair) by combing it towards the roots.

back door *n* a door in the back part of a building.

backdoor *adj* secret, clandestine.

backer *n* one who backs or gets on the back; one who supports another; one who bets in favour of a particular party in a contest; one who provides financial support.

backfire *vi* (**backfired**, **backfiring**) of motor vehicles, to ignite prematurely, causing a loud bang from the exhaust; to have the opposite effect from that intended, usually with unfortunate or disastrous consequences.

backgammon *n* a game played by two persons on a table or board made for the purpose, with pieces or men, dice boxes and dice.

background *n* the part of a picture represented as farthest from the spectator; (*fig*) a situation little seen or noticed; a state of being out of view (*to keep a fact in the background*); social class; education and training; the circumstances leading up to an event.

backhand *n* (in tennis, etc) a stroke played with the hand turned outwards; writing sloping backwards or to the left.

backhanded *adj* with the hand turned backward (*a backhanded blow*); unfair; oblique; indirect; (of writing) sloping back or to the left; dubious or ambiguous (*a backhanded compliment*).

backhander *n* a blow with the back of the hand; a bribe.

backing *n* something put at or attached to the back of something else by way of support or finish; support; financial support.

backlash *n* a reaction or consequence, often violent.

backlog *n* an accumulation of things which have to be done but which have been left unattended to.

backpack *n* a kind of bag of various sizes designed for carrying on the back.—*vi* to carry a backpack; to go hiking or travelling with one's possessions in a backpack.

back-seat driver *n* a passenger in a car who irritates the driver with persistent unwanted advice.

backside *n* the back part of anything; the side opposite to the front or behind that which is presented to the spectator.

backslide *vi* (**backslid**, **backsliding**) to slide back; to fall off or turn away from religion or morality; to apostatize.

backslider *n* one who backslides; one who falls away from religion or morality.

backsliding *adj* apostatizing from faith or practice.

backstage *adv* behind the stage of a theatre in areas hidden from the audience; (*colloq*) away from public view.

backstair, backstairs *n* a stair or stairs in the back part of a house; private stairs.—*adj* of or pertaining to backstairs; hence, indirect; underhand; secret and unfair (*backstairs influence*).

backstroke *n* (in swimming) a stroke using backward circular sweeps of the arms while lying face upward.

backtrack *vi* to go back along the way one has come; to reverse one's opinions, actions, etc.

backward *adj* being in the back or at the back; turned or directed back (*a backward look*); unwilling; reluctant; slow; dull; not quick to learn; late; behind in time.—*adv* backwards.

backwardation *n* a consideration paid to purchasers for an extension of time by speculators on the Stock Exchange unable to supply the stock or shares they have contracted to deliver.

backwards *adv* with the back in advance; towards the back; in a direction opposite to forward; towards past times or events; from a better to a worse state; in a contrary or reverse manner, way or direction.

backwater *n* currentless water beside a stream; metaphorically, a stagnant place.

backwoods *npl* woody or forest districts of a country situated away from the more thickly settled parts (especially used in the USA and Canada); a remote or isolated district, particularly one that is unsophisticated.

backwoodsman *n* (*pl* **backwoodsmen**) an inhabitant of the backwoods; a voter in the House of Lords appearing only on special occasions.

backbone

backhand

bacon *n* swine's flesh salted or pickled and dried, usually in smoke.

bacteriologist *n* one who investigates bacteria, especially in relation to disease.

bacteriology *n* the doctrine or study of bacteria.

bacterium *n* (*pl* **bacteria**) a name applied to certain very minute organisms which appear in infusions of organic matter, in fluids exposed to the air, in diseased animal tissues, etc.

bad *adj*, *compar* (from quite a different root) **worse**, *superl* **worst**) the opposite of *good*; lacking good qualities, physical or moral; not coming up to a certain type or standard or the average of individuals of the particular class; wicked, unprincipled, depraved, immoral, vicious; pernicious, debasing, corrupting (influence, habits); ill, infirm (health); unwholesome, noxious (air, climate, food); defective, insufficient (work, crop); infertile, sterile (soil); unfortunate or unhappy (result, marriage); incompetent (workman), etc.—*n* that which is bad.—**to go to the bad** to fall into bad company, bad ways or bad circumstances; to fall into vicious ways and ruin one's life.

baddish *adj* somewhat bad.

badge *n* a mark, sign, token, etc, worn to show membership or the relation of the wearer to any person, occupation or order.

badger *n* a carnivorous mammal belonging to a family intermediate between the bears and the weasels, living in a burrow, nocturnal in habits and feeding on vegetables, small quadrupeds, etc.—*vt* to attack (a person), as the badger is attacked when being drawn or baited; to assail (as with importunities, commands, etc); to worry; to pester.

badinage *n* light or playful discourse.

badly *adv* in a bad manner; not well; unskilfully.

badminton *n* a game similar to lawn tennis but played with shuttlecocks; a kind of claret cup or summer beverage.

badness *n* the state of being bad; lack of good qualities, physical or moral.

baffle *vt* (**baffled, baffling**) to elude; to foil; to frustrate; to defeat; to thwart; to puzzle or perplex.

baffle *n* (*engin*) a plate or wall for deflecting or checking the flow of gases or liquids.

bag *n* a sack; a wallet; a pouch; what is contained in a bag (as the animals shot by a sportsman); a definite quantity of certain commodities.—*vt* (**bagged, bagging**) to put into a bag; to distend; to swell; to shoot or otherwise lay hold of (game).—*vi* to swell or hang like a bag.

bagatelle *n* a trifle; a thing of no importance; a game played on a board having at

badger

bagpipe

the end nine holes, into which balls are to be struck with a cue.

baggage *n* the necessaries of an army, or other body of people on the move; luggage; things required for a journey; a low worthless woman; a strumpet (an old, playful term applied familiarly to any young woman).

bagginess *n* character of being baggy.

bagging *n* the cloth or other materials for bags.

baggy *adj* having the appearance of a bag; puffy; loose; wide.

bag lady *n* a homeless woman who carries her possessions in shopping bags or carrier bags.

bagman *n* (*pl* bagmen) formerly, a travelling salesman; a person who collects or distributes illegally obtained money for another.

bagnio *n* (*pl* bagnios) a brothel.

bagpipe *n* a wind instrument consisting of a leather bag which receives the air from the mouth or from a bellows, and of pipes into which the air is pressed from the bag by the performer's elbow.

bagpiper *n* one who plays on a bagpipe.

baguette *n* a type of bread loaf that is long and thin.

bah *interj* an exclamation expressing contempt, disgust, or incredulity.

bail[1] *vt* (*law*) to liberate from arrest and imprisonment on security that the person liberated shall appear and answer in court.—*n* the person or persons who procure the release of a prisoner from custody by becoming surety for his or her appearance in court; the security given for the release (not used with a plural termination, as *we were his bail*).

bail[2] *vt* to empty (a boat) of water with a bucket or other utensil.

bail[3] *n* a little stick laid on the tops of the stumps in playing cricket: the two bails and the three stumps together form a wicket.

bailable *adj* capable of being admitted to bail; admitting of bail (*a bailable offence*).

bail bond *n* a bond given for the appearance in court of a person who is bailed.

bailee *n* a person to whom goods are committed for the purposes of a trust.

bailer *n* one who or that which bails.

bailie, baillie *n* a magistrate in Scotland corresponding to an alderman in England.

bailiff *n* a civil officer or functionary, subordinate to someone else; an overseer or understeward on an estate.

Bairam, Beiram *n* the name of two Muslim festivals, one held at the close of the fast Ramadan, the other seventy days after.

bairn *n* (*Scot*) a child.

bait *vt* to furnish with a piece of flesh or other substance which acts as a lure to fish or other animals (*to bait a hook*); to provoke and harass by dogs (as a bull, badger, or bear); to annoy.—*n* any substance used as a lure to catch fish or other animals; an allurement; enticement.

baize *n* a coarse woollen stuff with a long nap, usually green, used for billiard tables, etc.

bake *vt* (**baked, baking** (*old pp* **baken**) to dry and harden by heat in an oven, kiln or furnace or by solar rays (as bread, bricks, pottery); to prepare in an oven.—*vi* to do the work of baking; to dry and harden in heat.

baked meat, bake meat *n* meat cooked in an oven; a meat pie.

bakehouse *n* a house or building for baking.

Bakelite *n* (*trademark*) a hard, insoluble, infusible substance derived by heat treatment from phenol and formaldehyde.

baker *n* one whose occupation is to bake bread, biscuit, etc.

baker's dozen thirteen.

bakery *n* a place used for the business of baking bread, etc; a bakehouse.

baking *n* a quantity baked at once.

bakshish, baksheesh *n* a present or gratuity of money, used in Eastern countries.

balalaika *n* an instrument of the guitar family often used by gypsies and for Russian folk music.

balance *n* an instrument for ascertaining the weight of bodies, consisting in its common form of a beam or lever suspended exactly at the middle and having a scale or basin hung to each extremity of exactly the same weight, so that the beam rests horizontally when nothing is in either scale or when they are loaded with equal weights; the excess by which one thing is greater than another; surplus; the difference of two sums; the sum due on an account; an equality of weight, power, advantage, etc; the part of a clock or watch which regulates the beats; the balance wheel.—*vt* (**balanced, balancing**) to bring to an equipoise; to keep in equilibrium on a small support; to poise; to compare by estimating the relative importance or value of; to weigh; to serve as a counterpoise to; to settle (an account) by paying what remains due; to examine (the books of a business) by summations and show how debits and credits stand.—*vi* to be in equipoise; to have equal weight or importance; to be employed in finding balances on accounts.

balancer *n* one who or that which balances; an organ of an insect useful in balancing the body.

balance sheet *n* a statement of the assets and liabilities of a trading concern.

balance wheel *n* that part of a watch or chronometer which, like a pendulum, regulates the beat or strike.

balas *n* a variety of spinel ruby, of a pale rose-red colour, sometimes inclining to orange.

balata *n* a gum obtained from a South American tree used for purposes similar to those of indiarubber.

balcony *n* a platform projecting from the front of a building, supported by columns, pillars or consoles, and encompassed with a balustrade, railing, or parapet; a projecting gallery in the interior of a building, as of a theatre.

bald *adj* having white on the face, (said of animals); lacking hair, especially on the top and back of the head; lacking natural growth, as of a hill; unadorned (said of style or language); (*bot*) lacking beard or awn.

baldachin, baldachino, baldaquin *n* a canopy or covering; a canopy on four poles held over the pope; a canopy on four columns over an altar; a canopy over a throne.

bald eagle *n* the white-headed erne or sea eagle of America.

balderdash *n* senseless talk; nonsense.

baldly *adv* nakedly; meanly; bluntly.

baldness *n* the state or quality of being bald.

baldric *n* a broad belt, stretching from the right or left shoulder diagonally across the body, either as an ornament or to suspend a sword, dagger or horn.

bale[1] *n* a bundle or package of goods.—*vt* (**baled, baling**) to make up into a bale or bundle.

bale[2] *vt* (**baled, baling**) to empty of water; to bail.

bale[3] *n* misery; calamity; that which causes ruin, destruction, or sorrow.

baleen *n* whalebone.

baleful *adj* destructive; pernicious; deadly.

balk *n* a ridge of land left unploughed; an uncultivated strip of land serving as a boundary; a beam or piece of timber of considerable length and thickness; a barrier or check; a disappointment.—*vt* to bar the way of; to disappoint; to frustrate.—*vi* to turn aside or stop in one's course (as a horse).

ball[1] *n* a round body; a small spherical body often covered with leather and used in many games; any part of a thing that is rounded or protuberant; in veterinary science, a form of medicine, corresponding to the term bolus in pharmacy; (*metal*) a mass of half-melted iron; a loop; the projectile of a firearm; a bullet (in this sense also used collectively).—*vt* to make into a ball.—*vi* to form or gather into a ball.

ball[2] *n* a social assembly of persons of both sexes for the purpose of dancing.

ballad *n* a short narrative poem, formerly sun; a sentimental song.

ballade *n* a poem normally of three stanzas

bald eagle

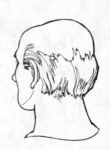

bald

of eight lines each, with a closing stanza or envoy of four lines, the rhymes throughout being not more than three.

balladmonger *n* formerly, a dealer in ballads; an inferior poet.

ball-and-socket joint *n* a joint (as in the human hip) formed by a ball or rounded end playing within a socket so as to allow motion in all directions.

ballast *n* heavy matter, as stone, sand or iron, carried in the bottom of a ship or other vessel for stability (the vessel being said to be *in ballast* when she sails without a cargo); material forming the foundation of a road or railway to make it firm and solid.—*vt* to place ballast in or on; (*fig*) to steady; to counterbalance.

ball bearing *n* a bearing in which the revolving part turns on loose hardened steel balls rolling in a race.

ball cock *n* a kind of self-acting stopcock opened and shut by means of a hollow sphere or ball of metal floating on the surface of a liquid and attached to the end of a lever connected with the cock.

ballet *n* an elaborate style of dancing with conventional steps and graceful, flowing gestures; a theatrical representation in which a story is told by gesture accompanied with dancing, scenery, etc.

ballet

ball game *n* any of various games played with a ball; a situation, a state of affairs (*colloq*).

ballista, balista *n* (*pl* **ballistae, balistae**) a military engine used by the ancients for discharging heavy stones or other missiles especially against a besieged place.

ballistic *adj* pertaining to the ballista or its use.

ballistic missile *n* a missile which is guided in the initial stages of its course.

ballistics *n* the science which deals with projectiles in motion.

ballonet *n* the name of the separate bags, or small balloons, that contain the gas within the envelope of a dirigible.

balloon *n* a large hollow spherical body; a very large bag, usually made of silk or other light fabric, and filled with hydrogen gas or any lighter-than-air gas causing it to rise and float in the atmosphere; a toy or decoration consisting of a small coloured inflatable rubber bag.—*vi* to travel in a balloon; to swell, to expand.

balloon sail *n* a light triangular sail used by yachts in a light breeze.

ballot *n* a paper, etc, by which one votes and which gives no indication of who the voter is; the system of voting by this means.—*vi* to vote or decide by ballot (frequently with *for*).

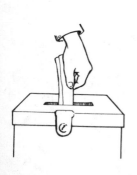

ballot box

ballot box *n* a box for receiving ballot papers.

ballpoint pen *n* a pen with a tiny ball, which rotates against an inking cartridge as its writing tip.

ballroom dancing *n* formal, social dancing with traditional steps.

ballyhoo *n* noisy demonstration to attract attention; sensational propaganda.

balm *n* a name common to several species of fragrant or aromatic trees or shrubs, and to the medicinal fragrances they exude; any fragrant or valuable ointment; anything which heals, soothes, or mitigates pain.—*vt* to anoint as with balm or with anything fragrant or medicinal; to soothe; to mitigate; to assuage; to heal.

balmy *adj* having the qualities of balm; aromatic; fragrant; healing; soothing; (of weather) mildly warm.

balsam *n* an oily, aromatic, resinous substance obtained from certain plants and used in medicine and perfumery; balm.

baluster *n* a small column or pilaster of various forms and dimensions used for balustrades.

balustrade *n* a row of small columns or pilasters joined by a rail, serving as an enclosure for altars, balconies, staircases, terraces, etc, or as an ornament.

bambino *n* (*pl* **bambinos, bambini**) in Roman Catholic countries the figure of Christ represented as an infant in swaddling clothes, often surrounded by a halo and watched over by angels; a young Italian child.

bamboo *n* a tropical plant of the family of grasses with large jointed stems, used for building purposes, furniture, fences, walking sticks, etc.

bamboozle *vt* (**bamboozled, bamboozling**) to hoax; to puzzle, to mystify; to deceive.

ban *n* an edict or proclamation in general; an edict of interdiction or proscription; interdiction; prohibition; (*pl*) proclamation of marriage (bans).—*vt* (**banned, banning**) to prohibit; to interdict.

banal *adj* hackneyed; commonplace.

banana *n* a herbaceous plant closely allied to the plantain, and extensively cultivated in tropical countries for its soft yellow fruit.

band¹ *n* that which binds together; a bond or means of attachment in general; a fetter or similar fastening; a narrow strip or ribbon-shaped ligature, tie, or connection; a fillet; a border or strip on an article of dress; that which resembles a band, tie, or ligature; a limited part of a series; a range of wavelengths; a track on a gramophone record; (*pl*) the linen ornament about the neck of a clergyman, with the ends hanging down in front.

band² *n* a company of persons united together by some common bond, especially a body of armed soldiers; a company of soldiers; an organized body of instrumental musicians; an orchestra.—*vt* to bind with a band; to mark with a band; to unite in a troop, company, or confederacy.—*vi* to associate or unite for some common purpose.

bandage *n* a strip of cloth used in dressing and binding up wounds, restraining haemorrhages, etc; a band or ligature in general; that which is bound over something else.—*vt* (**bandaged, bandaging**) to put a bandage on.

B and B, B & B an abbreviation for **bed and breakfast.**

bandanna, bandana *n* a large colourful handkerchief.

bandbox *n* a box made of pasteboard or thin flexible pieces of wood and paper, for holding collars, hats or other light articles.

bandeau *n* (*pl* **bandeaux**) a headband.

banderole *n* a little flag or streamer fixed to a mast, a military weapon or a trumpet; a pennon.

bandicoot *n* a large species of rat, a native of India and Sri Lanka.

bandit *n* (*pl* **bandits, banditti**) an outlaw; more commonly a robber; a highwayman.

bandmaster *n* the conductor and trainer of a band of musicians.

bandoleer, bandolier *n* a shoulder belt for carrying cartridges.

bandore, pandore *n* a bass musical instrument resembling the lute, with metal strings.

band saw *n* a saw formed of a long flexible belt of steel revolving on pulleys.

bandsman *n* (*pl* **bandsmen**) a player in a band of musicians.

bandy *adj* bent or curved outwards; bandy-legged.—*vt* (**bandied, bandying**) to toss from one to another; to exchange contentiously; to give and receive reciprocally (words, etc).—*vi* to contend; to strive.

bandy-legged *adj* having bandy legs.

bane *n* any cause of unhappiness, injury, or destruction; ruin; destruction; a deadly poison.

baneful *adj* destructive; pernicious; poisonous.

bang *vt* to beat, as with a club or cudgel; to thump; to cudgel; to beat or handle roughly or with violence; to make a loud noise, as in slamming a door, etc.—*vi* to resound with a loud noise; to produce a loud noise; to thump violently.—*n* a loud, sudden, resonant sound; a blow as with a club; a heavy blow.

bangle *n* an ornamental ring worn on the arms or ankles.

banish *vt* to condemn to exile; to send (a person) from a country as a punishment; to drive away; to exile; to cast from the mind (thoughts, care, business).

banishment *n* the act of banishing; the state of being banished; enforced absence; exile.

banister, bannister *n* a baluster; an upright in a stair rail.

banjo *n* (*pl* **banjos**) a musical instrument with six strings, a body like a tambourine and a neck like a guitar.

bank *n* a mound or heap of earth; any steep acclivity, as one rising from a river, the sea or forming the side of a ravine, etc; a rising ground in the sea, partly above water or covered everywhere with shoal water; a shoal; the face of coal at which miners work; a bench or seat for the rowers in a galley; one of the rows of oars; an establishment which trades in money; an establishment for the deposit, custody, remittance and issue of money; the office in which the transactions of a banking company are conducted; the funds of a gaming establishment; a fund in certain games at cards; a supply or store for future use (*blood bank*).—*vt* to enclose, defend, or fortify with a bank; to embank; to lay up or deposit in a bank.—*vi* to deposit money in a bank.—**to bank on** *or* **upon** to stake or rest hopes on an event.

bankbook *n* the book given to a customer, in which his debits and credits are entered.

banker *n* one who keeps a bank; one who traffics in money, receives and remits money, negotiates bills of exchange, etc; the person who looks after the bank in (gambling) games.

bank holiday a statutory annual holiday, on which the banks are closed.

banking *n* the business or profession of a banker; the system followed by banks in carrying on their business; the tilting up of an aeroplane at a sharp angle sideways when flying swiftly round a curve, on the same principle as that on which a cycle track is 'banked' steeply at corners rounded at high speed.

bank manager *n* a person employed by a bank to conduct its banking operations in a branch office.

banknote *n* a promissory note issued by a banking company payable at the bank on demand.

bankrupt *n* a person declared by legal authority unable to pay his or her debts; popularly, one who has wholly or partially failed to pay his or her debts; one who has compounded with his or her creditors; an insolvent.—*adj* insolvent; unable to meet one's obligations.

bankruptcy *n* the state of being a bankrupt; inability to pay all debts; failure in trade.

banner *n* a piece of cloth usually bearing some heraldic device or national emblem, attached to the upper part of a pole or staff; an ensign; a standard; a square flag.

bannock *n* an unleavened cake of oatmeal or other meal baked on an iron plate or griddle.

banjo

banner

banns *npl* the proclamation in church previous to a marriage, made by calling over the names of the parties intending matrimony.

banquet *n* a feast; a rich entertainment of meat and drink for a large company; something specially delicious or enjoyable.—*vt* to treat with a feast or rich entertainment.—*vi* to feast; to regale oneself.

banshee *n* a female fairy believed in Ireland and some parts of Scotland to attach herself to a particular house and to wail before the death of one of the family.

bantam *n* a small, spirited breed of domestic fowl with feathered shanks; a small belligerent person.

bantamweight *n* a class for boxers weighing about 54 kilograms.

banter *vt* to address humorous raillery to; to attack with jokes or jests; to make fun of; to rally.—*n* a joking or jesting; humorous teasing; pleasantry with which a person is attacked.

banyan, banyan tree *n* an Indian tree of the fig genus, remarkable for its horizontal branches sending down shoots which take root when they reach the ground and enlarge into trunks, which in their turn send out branches, the tree in this manner covering a prodigious extent of ground.

banyan tree

baobab *n* a large African tree having an oblong pulpy fruit called monkey bread.

bap *n* a small bread roll.

baptise, baptize *vt* (**baptised, baptising**) to administer the sacrament of baptism to; to christen.

baptism *n* the application of water by sprinkling or immersion to a person, as a sacrament or religious ceremony.

baptism of fire martyrdom by fire, regarded as an equivalent of baptism; a soldier's first experience of battle; a testing or challenging ordeal, especially a first experience of this.

Baptist *n* one who administers baptism, specifically applied to John, the forerunner of Christ.

baptistery *n* a building or a portion of a building in which is administered the rite of baptism.

baptize *vt* (**baptised, baptising**) same as **baptise**.

bar[1] *n* a piece of wood, metal, or other solid matter, long in proportion to its thickness; a pole; a connecting piece in various positions and structures, often for a hindrance or obstruction; anything which obstructs, hinders or impedes; an obstruction; an obstacle; a barrier; a bank of sand, gravel, or earth forming an obstruction at the mouth of a river or harbour; the railing enclosing the place which counsel occupy in courts of justice; the place in court where prisoners are stationed for arraignment, trial or sentence; all those who can plead in a

barb

court; (*with cap*) barristers in general; the profession of barrister; the railing or partition which separates a space near the door from the body of either house of parliament; a tribunal in general; a public house; a place where alcoholic drinks are served; the counter over which such drinks are served out; a military mark of distinction, added to a medal; (*mus*) a line drawn perpendicularly across the staff dividing it into equal measures of time; the space and notes included between two such lines.— *vt* (**barred, barring**) to fasten with a bar or as with a bar; to hinder; to obstruct; to prevent; to prohibit; to restrain; to except; to exclude by exception; to provide with a bar or bars; to mark with bars; to cross with one or more stripes or lines.

bar[2] *n* a standard unit of barometric pressure equal to a million dynes per square centimetre.

barb *n* the sharp point projecting backwards from the penetrating extremity of an arrow, fish-hook, or other instrument for piercing, intended to prevent its being extracted; a barbel; one of the flattened branches of a feather; a sharp, hurtful remark.—*vt* to shave or dress the beard; to furnish with barbs, as an arrow.

barbarian *n* a person in a rude savage state; an uncivilized person; a cruel, savage, brutal person; one lacking pity or humanity.— *adj* of or pertaining to savages; rude; uncivilized; cruel; inhuman.

barbaric *adj* of or pertaining to or characteristic of a barbarian; uncivilized; savage; wild.

barbarism *n* an uncivilized state; lack of civilization; rudeness of manners; an act of barbarity, cruelty or brutality; an outrage; an offence against purity of style or language; any form of speech contrary to correct idiom.

barbarity *n* the state of being barbarous; barbarousness; savageness; ferociousness; inhumanity; a barbarous act.

barbarization *n* the act or process of rendering barbarous or of becoming barbarous.

barbarize *vi* (**barbarized, barbarizing**) to become barbarous.—*vt* to make barbarous.

barbarous *adj* unacquainted with arts and civilization; uncivilized; rude and ignorant; pertaining to or characteristic of barbarians; adapted to the taste of barbarians; barbaric; cruel; ferocious; inhuman.

barbarously *adv* in a barbarous manner; without knowledge or arts; savagely; cruelly; ferociously; inhumanely.

barbarousness *n* the state or quality of being barbarous; barbarity.

barbecue *n* a metal frame for grilling food over an open fire; an open-air meal or party where food is cooked on a barbecue.— vt (**barbecued, barbecuing**) to cook on a barbecue.

barbel n a freshwater fish with four beard-like appendages on its upper jaw; a vermiform process appended to the mouth of certain fishes, serving as an organ of touch.

barbell n a metal rod with weights at each end, used in weightlifting.

barber n one whose occupation is to shave the beard or to cut and dress hair.—vt to shave and dress the hair of.

barberry n a shrubby plant bearing small acid and astringent red berries, common in hedges.

barbican n. a kind of watchtower, an advanced work defending the entrance to a castle or fortified town, as before the gate or drawbridge.

barcarole, barcarolle n a simple song or melody sung by Venetian gondoliers; a piece of instrumental music composed in imitation of such a song.

bar code n an arrangement of parallel lines printed on the packaging of goods giving information as to price, etc, that is readable by computer.

bard n a poet and singer among the ancient Celts; a poet generally.

bardic adj pertaining to bards or to their poetry.

bare adj naked; without covering; laid open to view; detected; no longer concealed; poor; destitute; indigent; ill-supplied; empty; unfurnished; unprovided (often followed by of, as bare of furniture); threadbare; much worn.—vt (**bared, baring**) to strip off the covering from; to make naked.

barebacked adj having the back uncovered; unsaddled.

barefaced adj having the face uncovered; hence undisguised; unreserved; shameless; impudent; audacious (barefaced robbery).

barefacedness n effrontery; assurance.

barefoot, barefooted adj, adv with the feet bare; without shoes or stockings.

barely adv in a bare manner; nakedly; poorly; without decoration; scarcely; hardly.

bareness n the state of being bare; lack of clothing or covering; nakedness; deficiency of appropriate covering, ornament, etc; poverty; indigence.

bargain n a contract or agreement between two or more parties; a compact settling that something shall be done, sold, transferred, etc; the thing purchased or stipulated for; what is obtained by an agreement; something bought or sold at a low price.—vi to make a bargain or agreement; to make an agreement about the transfer

of property.—vt to sell; to transfer for a consideration (generally followed by away).

barge n a vessel or boat fitted up and decorated and used on occasions of state and pomp; a flat-bottomed vessel for loading and unloading ships or conveying goods from one place to another.—vi to lurch clumsily; to interrupt (a conversation) rudely (with in); to enter abruptly (with into).—vt to convey by barge.

bargee n one of charge of or one of the crew of a barge or canal boat.

barite n a white crystalline mineral of great weight.

baritone n a male voice ranging between tenor and bass; a man with a voice of this compass.

barium n a white metallic element, the basis of baryta (which is an oxide of barium).

barium meal n a mixture of barium sulphate which is opaque to X-rays and which a patient swallows in order to show up any obstruction there may be in the alimentary canal.

bark[1] n the outer rind of a tree, shrub, etc; the exterior covering of exogenous plants, composed of cellular and vascular tissue. —vi to strip bark off; to peel; to scrape (the knees, etc); to apply bark to; to treat with bark in tanning.

bark[2] vi to emit the cry of a dog or a similar sound.—n the cry of the dog, fox, etc; a cry resembling that of the dog.

barley n a kind of grain commonly grown and used especially for making malt; the plant yielding the grain.

barleycorn n a grain of barley; formerly, a measure equal to the third part of an inch.—**John Barleycorn** n a personification of malted drink.

barley sugar n sugar boiled till it is brittle (formerly with a decoction of barley), and candied.

barley water n a decoction of pearl barley used in medicine as an emollient.

barm n yeast.

barmaid n a woman who serves at the bar of an inn, pub, etc.

barman n (pl **barmen**) a man who serves at the bar of a pub.

Barmecide, Barmecidal adj disappointing; fallacious.

Barmecide feast n a rich apparent feast given in the Arabian Nights by a prince to guests, with nothing but names for the dishes.

bar mitzvah, bar mizvah n (often with caps) the Jewish ceremony marking the thirteenth birthday of a boy who then assumes full religious responsibility and obligations.

barmy adj silly; mad.

barn n a covered building for securing

ISBN 1-85534-490-4

9 781855 344907

bar code

barley

grain, hay or other farm produce.—*vt* to store up in a barn.

barnacle *n* a marine crustacean that attaches itself to the bottoms of ships, on timber fixed below the surface of the sea, etc; a species of goose found in the northern seas but visiting more southern climates in winter.

barn owl *n* the common white owl often found in barns.

barometer *n* an instrument for measuring the weight or pressure of the atmosphere, consisting ordinarily of a glass tube containing a column of mercury, its lower end dipping into a cup containing the same metal; the mercury in the tube, having a vacuum above it, rises and falls according to the varying pressure of the air on the mercury in the cup: in the aneroid barometer no fluid is used; something that indicates a change.

baron *n* in Great Britain, a title or degree of nobility; one who holds the lowest rank in the peerage; a title of certain judges or officers (as, *barons of the exchequer*, the judges of the court of exchequer); a rich, often despotic businessman.—**baron of beef** *n* two sirloins not cut asunder.

baronage *n* the whole body of barons or peers; the dignity or condition of a baron.

baroness *n* a baron's wife or lady; a holder of the title in her own right.

baronet *n* one who possesses a hereditary rank or degree of honour next below a baron, and therefore not a member of the peerage; one belonging to an order founded by James I in 1611.

baronetcy *n* the title and dignity of a baronet.

baronial *adj* pertaining to a baron or a barony.

barony *n* the title or honour of a baron; also the territory or lordship of a baron; in Ireland, a territorial division corresponding nearly to the English hundred.

baroque *adj* extravagantly ornamented, especially in architecture and decorative art.

barouche *n* a four-wheeled carriage with a falling top.

barque *n* (*naut*) a three-masted vessel with only fore-and-aft sails on the mizzenmast, the other two masts being square-rigged.

barrack *n* a hut or house for soldiers; permanent buildings in which both officers and soldiers are lodged; a large building or a collection of huts for a body of work people (generally in *pl*).—*vi* (*cricket sl*) to cheer derisively or jeer at a team in order to put them off their game; to shout or protest at.

barrage *n* an artificial dam across a river; heavy artillery fire; continuous and heavy delivery, for example of questions or critical remarks.

barn owl

barrier

barrage balloon a large balloon anchored to the ground and trailing cables or nets, used as a defence against low-flying enemy aircraft.

barrel *n* a cylindrical wooden vessel made of staves and bound with hoops; a cask; anything resembling a barrel in shape; a hollow cylinder or tube (*the barrel of a gun*).—*vt* (**barrelled, barrelling**) to put in a barrel.

barrel organ *n* an organ in which a barrel or cylinder furnished with pegs or staples, when turned round, opens a series of valves to admit a current of air to a set of pipes or acts on wires like those of the piano so as to produce a tune.

barren *adj* incapable of producing children of offspring; not prolific (applied to animals and vegetables); unproductive; unfruitful; sterile (applied to land); not producing or leading to anything (*barren speculation*, *barren of ideas*); unsuggestive; uninstructive.

barrenness *n* the state or quality of being barren; sterility; lack of fertility, instructiveness, interest, etc (*barrenness of invention*).

barrette *n* a small clasp used to hold hair in place.

barricade *n* a temporary fortification made of trees, earth, stones or anything that will obstruct the progress of an enemy or serve for defence or security against shot; a fence around or along the side of a space to be kept clear; any barrier or obstruction.—*vt* (**barricaded, barricading**) to stop up by a barricade; to erect a barricade across; to obstruct.

barrier *n* a fence; a railing; any obstruction; what hinders approach, attack, or progress; what stands in the way; an obstacle; a limit or boundary of any kind; a line of separation.

barrister *n* a counsellor or advocate admitted to plead at the bar of a court of law in protection and defence of clients, a term more especially used in England and Ireland, the corresponding term in Scotland being advocate, in the USA counsellor.

barroom *n* the room in a public house, hotel, etc, containing the bar or counter where refreshments are served out.

barrow[1] *n* a light small, usually two-wheeled cart; when having one wheel it is a *wheelbarrow*.

barrow[2] *n* a prehistoric or at least ancient sepulchral mound formed of earth or stones, found in Britain and elsewhere, and met with in various forms, often containing remains of the dead, implements, etc.

barter *vi* to traffic or trade by exchanging one commodity for another (and not for money).—*vt* to give in exchange; to exchange, as one commodity for another.—*n* the act of exchanging commodities; the thing given in exchange.

baryta *n* oxide of barium, a grey powder with a sharp caustic alkaline taste, called sometimes *heavy earth*, generally found in combination with sulphuric and carbonic acids, forming sulphate and carbonate of baryta, the former of which is called *heavy spar*.

barytes *n* a name of baryta or its sulphate (heavy spar).

basalt *n* a common igneous dark grey or black rock remarkable as often assuming the form of regularly prismatic columns, such as at Fingal's Cave in Staffa, or the Giant's Causeway in the north of Ireland.

basaltic *adj* pertaining to basalt; formed of or containing basalt.

base[1] *n* the bottom of anything, considered as its support or the part of a thing on which it stands or rests; the opposite extremity to the apex; (*archit*) the part between the bottom of a column and the pedestal or the floor; (*chem*) one of those compound substances which unite with acids to form salts; dyeing, a mordant; (*geom*) the line or surface forming that part of a figure on which it is supposed to stand; (*mus*) the bass; (*milit*) a location from which the operations of an army proceed; the place from which racers start; a starting post; (in baseball) one of the four corners of the diamond.—*vt* (**based, basing**) to lay the base or foundation of; to place on a basis; to found.

base[2] *adj* of little or no value; coarse in comparison (*the base metals*); worthless; fraudulently debased in value; spurious (*base coin*); of or pertaining to humble or illegitimate birth; of low station; lowly; of mean spirit; morally low; showing or proceeding from a mean spirit; deep; grave (applied to sounds).

baseball *n* a game somewhat similar to rounders, played with a short bat and a ball by two sides of nine or ten players each.

baseball cap *n* a close-fitting cap with a deep peak at the front.

baseless *adj* without a base; without grounds or foundation (*a baseless rumour*).

baseline *n* a line adopted as a base or foundation from which future operations are carried on or on which they depend or rest, as in surveying, military affairs, etc; the line at each end of a tennis court; the line between any two consecutive bases on a baseball field.

basely *adv* in a base manner or condition; meanly; humbly; vilely.

basement *n* (*archit*) the lowest storey of a building, whether above or below the ground.

baseness *n* the state or quality of being base; meanness; lowness; vileness; worthlessness.

bash *vt* to beat violently; to knock out of shape.

bashful *adj* easily put to confusion; modest to excess; diffident; shy.

basic *adj* relating to a base; fundamental; (*chem*) performing the place of a base in a salt, or having the base in excess.

basic slag *n* the slags or refuse matter got in making steel, a valuable fertilizer from the phosphate of lime it contains.

basil *n* a plant cultivated as an aromatic pot herb and used for flavouring dishes.

basilica *n* originally, the name applied by the Romans to their public halls, usually of rectangular form, with a middle and two side aisles and an apse at the end: the ground plan of these was followed in the early Christian churches, and the name is now applied to some of the churches in Rome by way of distinction or to other churches built in imitation of the Roman basilicas.

basilisk *n* a legendary creature variously regarded as a kind of serpent, lizard or dragon, and sometimes identified with the cockatrice; a name of several reptiles of the lizard family with a crest or hood.

basin *n* a vessel or dish, usually circular, rather broad and not very deep, used to hold water for washing and for various other purposes; any reservoir for water, natural or artificial; the whole tract of country drained by a river and its tributaries; (*geol*) an aggregate of strata dipping towards a common axis or centre; strata or deposits lying in a depression in older rocks.

basis *n* (*pl* **bases**) a base; a foundation or part on which something rests; grounds or foundation; base.

bask *vi* to lie in warmth; to be exposed to genial heat; to be at ease and thriving under benign influences.

basket *n* a vessel made of twigs, rushes, thin strips of wood or other flexible materials interwoven; as much as a basket will hold.—*vt* to put in a basket.

basketball *n* a game played with an inflated ball which is tossed into goals resembling baskets.

basking shark *n* a species of shark so called from its habit of lying on the surface of the water basking in the sun.

Basque *n* a language of unknown affinities spoken in parts of France and Spain on both sides of the Pyrenees at the angle of the Bay of Biscay, supposed to represent the tongue of the ancient Iberians, the primitive inhabitants of Spain; Biscayan or Euskarian.—*adj* pertaining to the people or language of Biscay.

baseball cap

bas-relief *n* same as **basso-rilievo**.

bass[1] *n* (*mus*) the lowest part in the harmony of a musical composition, whether vocal or instrumental; the lowest male voice.—*adj* (*mus*) low; deep; grave.

bass[2] *n* any of various British and American sea fishes allied to the perch, some of them of considerable size and used as food.

bass[3] *n* the American linden or lime tree; a mat made of bast; a hassock.

bass clef *n* the character shaped like an inverted C put at the beginning of the bass staff.

basset *n* a small, short-legged hound of French origin.

basset horn *n* a musical instrument, a sort of clarinet of enlarged dimensions and extended compass.

bassinet *n* a wickerwork or wooden cradle with a covering or hood over one end; a perambulator of similar shape.

bassoon *n* a musical wind instrument of the reed order, blown with a bent metal mouthpiece, holed and keyed like the clarinet and serving for the bass among woodwind instruments, as hautboys, flutes, etc.

basso-rilievo, bas-relief *n* a sculpture in low relief; a mode of sculpting figures on a flat surface, the figures being raised above the surface but not so much as in high-relief or *alto-rilievo*.

bass staff *n* the staff on which are written the notes belonging to the bass of a harmonized composition.

bass viol *n* a violoncello.

bast *n* the inner bark of various trees, especially of the lime, consisting of several layers of fibres; rope or matting made of this.

bastard *n* a natural child; a child born out of wedlock; an illegitimate child; what is spurious or inferior in quality.—*adj* born out of lawful matrimony; illegitimate; spurious; not genuine; false; adulterate; impure; not of the first or usual order or character.

baste[1] *vt* (**basted, basting**) to beat with a stick; to cudgel; to give a beating to; to drip butter or fat on meat in roasting it.

baste[2] *vt* to sew with long stitches, usually to keep parts together temporarily; to tack.

bastinado *n* (*pl* **bastinadoes**) a sound beating with a stick or cudgel; a mode of punishment in Oriental countries by beating the soles of the feet with a rod.—*vt* (**bastinadoed, bastinadoing**) to beat with a stick or cudgel; to beat on the soles of the feet as a judicial punishment.

basting *n* the long stitches by which pieces of garments are loosely attached to each other.

bastion *n* a huge mass of earth faced with sods, brick or stones, standing outside an angular form from the rampart at the angles of a fortification.

bat[1] *n* a heavy stick or club; a piece of wood shaped somewhat like the broad end of an oar and with a round handle, used in driving the ball in cricket and similar games; a batsman or batter; a piece of a brick; a brickbat.—*vi* (**batted, batting**) to be the batsman at cricket.

bat[2] *n* one of a group of mammals possessing a pair of leathery wings which extend between the fore and the posterior limbs, the former being specially modified for flying, the bones of the forefeet being extremely elongated.

batch *n* the quantity of bread baked at one time; any quantity of a thing made at once; a number of individuals or articles similar to each other.

bate *vt* (**bated, bating**) to abate, lessen or reduce.

bath *n* the immersion of the body or a part of it in water or other fluid or medium; a vessel for holding water in which to wash the body; an apparatus or contrivance for exposing the surface of the body to water or other diffusible body (as oil, medicated fluids, steam, etc); a building in which people may bathe; an apparatus for regulating the heat in chemical processes by interposing a quantity of sand, water, etc, between the fire and the vessel to be heated.

Bath brick *n* a preparation of siliceous earth in the form of a brick, used for cleaning knives, etc.

bath bun *n* a light sweet bun, generally mixed with currants, etc.

Bath chair *n* a small wheeled carriage used by invalids.

bathe *vt* (**bathed, bathing**) to immerse in water for pleasure, health or cleanliness; to wash, moisten, or suffuse with any liquid; to immerse in or surround with anything analogous to water.—*vi* to take a bath; to be or lie in a bath; to be in water or in other liquid; to be immersed or surrounded as if with water.

bathing costume, bathing suit *n* a garment that is worn for swimming, a swimsuit.

bathing machine *n* a covered vehicle, driven into the water, in which bathers formerly dressed and undressed.

bathometer *n* an apparatus for taking soundings, especially one in which a sounding line is dispensed with.

bathos *n* a ludicrous descent from the elevated to the mean in writing or speech; a sinking; anticlimax.

bathroom *n* a room for bathing in.

Bath stone *n* a variety of limestone extensively worked near Bath, and belonging to the oolite formation.

batik *n* a method of printing on fabric using

bassoon

bath

wax and dyes to make a pattern; a fabric printed in this way.

batiste *n* a fine linen cloth made in Flanders and Picardy, a kind of cambric.

batman *n* (*pl* **batmen**) an officer's servant.

baton *n* a staff or club; a truncheon, the official badge of various officials of widely different rank; the stick with which a conductor of music beats time.

batrachian *n* a frog-like animal; a member of a group of amphibious animals, as frogs, toads, etc.

batsman *n* (*pl* **batsmen**) cricket, the player who wields the bat.

battalion *n* a body of infantry, varying from about 300 to 1000 soldiers.

batten[1] *n* a long piece of wood; a plank; (*naut*) one of the slips of wood used to keep a tarpaulin close over a hatchway; (*weav*) a lathe.—*vt* to fasten with battens (*to batten down the hatches*).

batten[2] *vt* to make fat by rich living; to fertilize or enrich.—*vi* to grow or become fat; to live on and prosper at someone else's expense.

batter[1] *vt* to beat with successive blows; to beat with violence so as to bruise or seriously injure; to assail by a battering ram; to wear or impair, as by beating, long service, etc.—*vi* to make attacks, as by a battering ram.

batter[2] *n* a mixture of several ingredients, as flour, eggs, etc, beaten together with some liquid into a paste and cooked.

battering ram *n* an engine formerly used to beat down the walls of besieged places, consisting of a large beam with a head of iron somewhat resembling the head of a ram.

battery *n* the act of battering; a number of guns, etc, placed near each other and intended to act in concert; (*elect*) an electric cell that supplies current; an arrangement of hens' cages designed to increase egg laying; (*law*) the unlawful beating of a person.

battery hen *n* a hen kept with many others in a battery and mechanically fed throughout its life to increase egg production.

battle *n* a fight or encounter between enemies or opposing armies; an engagement; more especially a general engagement between large bodies of troops; a combat, conflict, or struggle.—**to give battle** to attack; to join battle, to meet in hostile encounter.—*vi* (**battled, battling**) to join in battle; to contend; to struggle; to strive or exert oneself.

battle cruiser *n* a heavy-gunned ship with a higher speed and lighter armour than a battleship.

battle cry *n* a war cry; a slogan used to rally supporters of a political campaign, etc.

battledore *n* an instrument with a handle and a flat board or palm, used to strike a ball or shuttlecock; a racquet.

battlefield *n* the land on which a battle is fought.

battlement *n* a notched or indented parapet, originally constructed for defence, afterwards for ornament.

battleship *n* a large, heavily armoured warship.

bauble *n* a short stick with a fool's head, formerly carried by jesters; a trifling piece of finery; something showy without real value; a gewgaw; a trifle.

bawd *n* a person who keeps a house of prostitution or acts as a go-between in illicit amours.

bawdy *adj* obscene; lewd; indecent; smutty; unchaste.

bawl *vi* to cry out with a loud full sound; to make vehement or clamorous outcries; to shout.—*vt* to proclaim by outcry; to shout out.—*n* a vehement cry or clamour.

bay[1] *n* a wide recess in the shore of a sea or lake; the expanse of water between two capes or headlands; a gulf; any recess resembling a bay.

bay[2] *n* the laurel tree or sweet bay; a garland or crown bestowed as a prize for victory or excellence, consisting of branches of the laurel; hence, fame or renown; laurels (in this sense chiefly in plural).

bay[3] *n* the bark of a dog; especially, a deep-toned bark.—**at bay** so hard pressed by enemies as to be compelled to turn round and face them from impossibility of escape.—*vi* to bark; to bark with a deep sound.—*vt* to bark at; to follow with barking; to express by barking.

bay[4] *n* red or reddish, inclining to a chestnut colour; a horse of this colour.

bay leaf *n* the leaf of the laurel dried and used as a herb in cooking.

bayonet *n* a short sword or dagger, made so that it may be fixed on the muzzle of a rifle.—*vt* to stab with a bayonet; to compel or drive by the bayonet.

bay rum *n* a spirituous liquor containing the oil of a species of pimento, used in medicines and cosmetics.

bay window *n* a window forming a recess or bay in a room and projecting outwards on a generally polygonal plan.

bazaar *n* in the East, a place where goods are exposed for sale, usually consisting of small shops or stalls in a narrow street or series of streets; a series of connected shops or stalls in a European town; a sale of miscellaneous articles for some charitable or other purpose; a fair.

bazooka *n* a portable anti-tank weapon that fires rockets from a long tube.

bdellium *n* an aromatic gum resin.

be *vi* (substantive verb, *pres* **am, is, are**; *pret* **was, were**; *pp* **been**; *ppr* **being**) to

battleship

bayonet

have a real state or existence; to exist in the world of fact, whether physical or mental; to exist in or have a certain state or quality; to become; to remain: therefore the most common use of the verb *to be* is to assert connection between a subject and a predicate, as, *he is good*; *John was at home*; or to form the compound tenses of other verbs.

beach *n* that part of the shore of a sea or lake which is washed by the tide and waves; the strand.—*vt* to run (a vessel) onto a beach.

beachcomber *n* a long rolling wave breaking on the beach; one who lives on or wanders along the shore on the lookout for anything of value washed ashore.

beacon *n* an object visible at some distance and serving to notify the presence of danger, as a light or signal shown to notify the approach of an enemy or to warn seamen of the presence of rocks, shoals, etc; anything used as a guide or a helpful or warning purpose.

bead *n* a little perforated ball of gold, amber, glass, etc, strung with others on a thread and often worn round the neck as an ornament or used to form a rosary; any small globular body, as a drop of liquid, etc; the sight of a rifle; (*archit*) a small round moulding sometimes cut so as to resemble a series of beads or pearls.—*vt* to mark or ornament with beads.

beaded *adj* furnished with beads; beady.

beading *n* moulding or edging in the form of a series of beads; a wooden strip, rounded on one side, used for trimming.

beadle *n* formerly, a messenger or crier of a court; a parish officer whose business is to punish petty offenders; a church officer with various subordinate duties.

beadsman *n* (*pl* **beadsmen**) formerly, a man employed in praying, generally in praying for another; one privileged to claim certain alms or charities.

beady *adj* consisting of or containing beads; bead-like; (of eyes) small, round, sharp and bright.

beagle *n* a small smooth-haired hound kept to hunt hares.

beak *n* the bill or neb of a bird; anything resembling a bird's bill; the bill-like mouth of some fishes, reptiles, etc; a pointed piece of wood fortified with brass, fastened to the prow of ancient galleys, and intended to pierce the vessels of an enemy; a similar, but infinitely more powerful appendage of iron or steel in modern warships; a magistrate.

beaked *adj* having a beak or something resembling a beak; beak-shaped; rostrate.

beaker *n* a large drinking cup or glass; a cylindrical glass container with a lip used by scientists.

beam *n* a long straight and strong piece of wood or iron, especially when holding an important place in some structure, and serving for support or consolidation; a horizontal piece of timber in a structure; the part of a balance from the ends of which the scales are suspended; the pole of a carriage which runs between the horses; a cylindrical piece of wood, making part of a loom, on which the warp is wound before weaving; one of the strong timbers stretching across a ship from one side to the other to support the decks and retain the sides at their proper distance; the oscillating lever of a steam engine forming the communication between the piston rod and the crankshaft; a ray of light, or more strictly a collection of parallel rays emitted from the sun or other body.—*vi* to emit rays of light or beams; to give out radiance; to shine.

bean *n* a name given to several kinds of leguminous seeds contained in a bivalve pod and to the plants producing them, as the common bean, cultivated both in fields and gardens, the French bean, the kidney bean, etc.

bean bag *n* a small cloth bag filled with dried beans and used in games; a larger bag filled with plastic granules and used for sitting on.

beanfeast *n* an employer's annual feast to work people; any festive meal.

bean sprout *n* the young shoot of any of several beans used in Chinese cooking.

bear[1] *vt* (*pret* **bore**, *pp* **borne**, *ppr* **bearing**) to support, hold up, or sustain, as a weight; to suffer, endure, undergo or tolerate, as pain, loss, blame, etc; to carry or convey; to have, possess, have on or contain; to bring forth or produce, as the fruit of plants or the young of animals.—**to bear down** to overcome by force.—**to bear out** to give support or countenance to (a person or thing); to uphold, corroborate, establish, justify.—**to bear up** to support; to keep from sinking.—**to bear a hand** to lend aid; to give assistance.—to bear in mind, to remember.—*vi* to suffer, as with pain; to be patient; to endure; to produce (fruit); to be fruitful; to lean, weigh or rest heavily; to tend; to be directed or move in a certain way (*to bear back, to bear out to sea, to bear down on the enemy*); to relate; to refer (with *on* or *upon*); to be situated as to some point of the compass, with respect to something else.—**to bear up** to have fortitude; to be firm; not to sink.—**to bear with** to tolerate; to be indulgent; to forbear to resent, oppose or punish.

bear[2] *n* a name common to various quadrupeds of the carnivorous order and of the plantigrade group, having shaggy hair and a very short tail, the most notable being

beam

beak

the brown or black bear of Europe, the grisly bear of the Rocky Mountains, the white or Polar bear, etc; the name of two constellations in the northern hemisphere, called the Greater and Lesser Bear; (*fig*) a rude or uncouth man; in stock-exchange slang, a person who does all he or she can to bring down the price of stock in order that he or she may buy cheap, opposed to a *bull*, who tries to raise the price that he or she may sell dear.

bearable *adj* capable of being borne, endured or tolerated.

bear-baiting *n* formerly, the sport of baiting bears with dogs.

beard *n* the hair that grows on the chin and round the lips of male adults; anything resembling this; a hairy, bristly or threadlike appendage of various kinds, such as the filaments by which some shellfish attach themselves to foreign bodies, etc; the awn on the ears of grain; a barb, as of an arrow.—*vt* to take by the beard; to oppose to the face; to set at defiance.

bearer *n* one who or that which bears, sustains, supports, carries, conveys, etc.

bear garden *n* formerly a place in which bears were kept for sport, as bear-baiting, etc; (*fig*) a place of disorder or tumult.

bearing *n* the act of one who bears; the manner in which a person comports himself or herself; carriage, mien or behaviour; import, effect, or force (of words); that part of a shaft or axle which is in connection with its support; the direction or point of the compass in which an object is seen; relative position or direction; a figure on a heraldic shield.

bearing rein *n* the rein by which the head of a horse is held up in driving.

bearish *adj* resembling a bear; rude; violent in conduct; surly.

beast *n* any four-footed animal as distinguished from birds, insects, fishes and humans; as opposed to humans, any irrational animal; a brutal person; a disgusting person.

beastliness *n* the state or quality of being beastly; brutality; filthiness.

beastly *adj* like a beast; brutish; brutal; filthy; contrary to the nature and dignity of humans.

beat *vt* to strike repeatedly; to lay repeated blows on; to knock, rap or dash against often; to pound; to strike for the purpose of producing sound (a drum); to shape by hammer; to scour with outcry in order to raise game; to overcome, vanquish or conquer in a battle, contest, competition, etc; to surpass or excel; to be too difficult for; to be beyond the power or skill of; to baffle; to fatigue utterly; to prostrate; to flutter (the wings).—**to beat back** to compel to retire or return.—**to beat down** to dash

down by beating or battering, as a wall; to lay flat; to cause to lower a price by persuasion or argument; to lessen the price or value of; to depress or crush.—**to beat off** to repel or drive back.—**to beat out** to extend by hammering.—**to beat up** to attack suddenly and consistently so as to cause severe injury.—**to beat time** to regulate time in music by the motion of the hand or foot.—**to beat a retreat** to give a signal to retreat by a drum; hence, generally, to retreat or retire.—*vi* to strike or knock repeatedly; to move with pulsation; to throb (as the pulse, heart, etc); to dash or fall with force or violence (as a storm, flood, etc); to summon or signal by beating a drum; (*naut*) to make progress against the direction of the wind by sailing in a zigzag.—**to beat about** to make search by various means or ways.—*n* a stroke; a blow; a pulsation; a throb; a footfall; a round or course which is frequently gone over, as by a policeman, etc; (*mus*) the beating or pulsation resulting from the joint vibrations of two sounds of the same strength and all but in unison.

beaten *adj* made smooth by beating or treading; worn by use; conquered; vanquished; exhausted; baffled.

beater *n* one who or that which beats; an instrument or device for pounding substances; the striking part in various machines; a person who raises game birds from cover.

beatific, beatifical *adj* blessing or making happy; imparting bliss.

beatification *n* the act of beatifying; the state of being blessed; blessedness; (*RC Church*) an act of the pope by which he declares a person beatified; an inferior kind of canonization.

beatify *vt* (**beatified, beatifying**) to make happy; to bless with the completion of celestial enjoyment; (*RC Church*) to declare that a person is to be reverenced as blessed though not canonized.

beatitude *n* blessedness; felicity of the highest kind; consummate bliss; felicity.

Beatitude *n* one of the declarations of blessedness to particular virtues, made by Christ in the Sermon on the Mount.

beatnik *n* a member of the beat generation in the 1950s which originated in North America and consisted of young liberal, unconventional people who dissociated themselves from the aims of contemporary society; one who rejects conventional standards of dress, behaviour, etc, and leads rather a bohemian way of life.

beau *n* (*pl* **beaux**) a man whose great care is to dress according to the first fashion of the times; a fop; a dandy; a man who attends or is suitor to a lady; a male sweetheart or lover.

beard

Beaufort scale *n* an international system of indicating wind strength, ranging from 0 (calm) to 12 (hurricane force).

beauteous *adj* possessing beauty; beautiful.

beautician *n* a person whose work involves giving cosmetic treatment to improve people's appearance, such as skin treatment, facial make-up, manicures etc.

beautification *n* the act of beautifying or rendering beautiful; decoration; adornment; embellishment.

beautifier *n* one who or that which makes beautiful.

beautiful *adj* having the qualities that constitute beauty; highly pleasing to the eye, the ear or the mind (*a beautiful scene, melody, poem, character*, but not a *beautiful* taste or smell); beauteous; lovely; handsome; fair; charming; comely.—**the beautiful** all that possesses beauty; beauty in the abstract.

beautify *vt* (**beautified, beautifying**) to make or render beautiful; to adorn; to deck; to decorate; to embellish.

beauty *n* an assemblage of perfections through which an object is rendered pleasing to the eye; those qualities that together give pleasure to the aesthetic sense; qualities that delight the eye, the ear or the mind; loveliness; elegance; grace; a particular grace or ornament; that which is beautiful; a beautiful person, especially a beautiful woman.

beaver

beaver[1] *n* a large semiaquatic rodent with large webbed hind feet and a flat tail covered with scales on its upper surface, living in streams and lakes and now found in considerable numbers only in North America, and generally living in colonies; beaver fur.—*vi* to work hard at (usually with *away*).

beaver[2] *n* the face guard of a helmet, so constructed with joints or otherwise that the wearer could raise or lower it to eat and drink; a visor.

becalm *vt* to keep from motion for lack of wind (as a ship); to delay (a person) by a calm.

because *conj* by cause or by the cause that; on this account that; for the cause or reason next explained, as, *he fled because (as the reason given) he was afraid.*

beccafico *n* (*pl* **beccaficos**) a bird resembling the nightingale; the garden warbler, a summer visitor to England.

bêche-de-mer *n* (*pl* **bêches-de-mer, bêche-de-mer**) the trepang, a species of sea slug or sea cucumber obtained in Eastern seas and eaten by the Chinese; the jargon or trade speech of Melanesia.

beck *n* a small stream; a brook.

beckon *vi* to make a sign to another by a motion of the hand or finger, etc, intended as a hint or intimation.—*vt* to make a sig-

Bedlington terrier

nificant sign to; to direct by making signs (*beckon him to us*).

become *vi* (*pret* **became**, *pp* **become**, *ppr* **becoming**) to pass from one state to another; to change, grow or develop into (*the boy becomes a man*).—**to become of** (usually with *what* preceding) to be the fate of; to be the end of; to be the final or subsequent condition.—*vt* to suit or to be suitable to (*blue becomes her*); to befit; to accord with, in character or circumstances; to be worthy of or proper to; to grace or suit as regards outward appearance.

becoming *adj* suitable; meet; proper; appropriate; befitting; seemly.

bed *n* that on or in which one sleeps or which is specially intended to give ease to the body at night; a bedstead; a piece of tilled ground in a garden; the bottom of a river or stream, or of any body of water; a layer; a stratum; an extended mass of anything, whether on the earth or within it; that on which anything lies, rests or is supported.—*vt* (**bedded, bedding**) to place in, or as in, a bed; to plant, as flowers in beds.

bed and breakfast *n* overnight accommodation and breakfast the following morning, as offered by hotels and guest houses.

bedaub *vt* to daub over; to soil with anything thick, slimy and dirty.

bedazzle *vt* (**bedazzled, bedazzling**) to dazzle; to blind by excess of light.

bedchamber *n* a bedroom.

bedclothes *n* blankets, sheets, etc, for beds.

bedding *n* a bed and its furniture; materials of a bed.

bedeck *vt* to deck; to adorn; to grace.

bedew *vt* to moisten with or as with dew.

bedim *vt* (**bedimmed, bedimming**) to make dim; to obscure or darken.

bedizen *vt* to adorn or dress gaudily.

bedlam *n* formerly, a madhouse; any scene of wild uproar.

bed linen *n* sheets, pillow covers, etc, for beds.

Bedlington terrier *n* a medium-sized terrier with a grey, crisp coat.

Bedouin, Beduin *n* a nomadic Arab living in tents in Arabia, Syria, Egypt and elsewhere.

bedplate *n* (*engin*) a foundation plate of an engine or other machine.

bedpost *n* one of the posts forming part of the framework of a bed.

bedraggle *vt* (**bedraggled, bedraggling**) to soil by drawing along in mud.

bedridden *adj* long confined to bed by age or infirmity.

bedroom *n* a room intended for sleeping in; a bedchamber.

bedsitter, bedsit *n* a combined bedroom and sitting room, often having cooking facilities.

bedsore *n* a sore liable to occur on bedridden persons on the parts of the body sub-jected to most pressure.

bedstead *n* the framework of a bed.

bee *n* an insect, of which there are numerous species, the honey or hive bee being the most familiar and typical species, having been kept in hives from the earliest periods for its wax and honey.

beech *n* a large tree with a smooth bark yielding a hard timber made into tools, etc, and nuts from which an oil is expressed.

beechmast *n* the mast or nuts of the beech-tree.

beechnut *n* one of the nuts or fruits of the beech.

beef *n* originally an animal of the ox kind in the full-grown state (in this sense with the plural *beeves*, but the singular is no longer used); the flesh of a cow when killed for food.

beefburger *n* a round flat cake of minced beef and seasoning cooked by grilling or frying.

beefeater *n* a yeoman of the royal guard (of England), a body of soldiers who attend the sovereign at state banquets and on other occasions; an African bird that picks the larvae of insects from the hides of oxen.

beefsteak *n* a steak or slice of beef for grilling, frying, etc.

beef tea *n* a nutritious soup made from beef which, being easy to digest, is recommended for invalids and convalescents.

beefwood *n* the timber of some Australian trees of a reddish colour, hard, and with dark and whitish streaks, chiefly used in ornamental work.

beehive *n* a case or box intended as a habitation for bees, in which they may store honey.

beeline *n* the direct line or nearest distance between two places.

beer *n* a fermented alcoholic liquor made from any starchy grain, but generally from malted barley flavoured with hops, and yielding a spirit on being distilled; a fermented drink prepared with various substances (*ginger beer*).

beestings *npl* the first milk given by a cow after calving.

beeswax *n* the wax secreted by bees and of which their cells are constructed; this wax used in polishes, ointments, etc.

beeswing *n* a gauzy film in port wines indicative of age.

beet *n* a plant of various species cultivated for its thick fleshy roots, the red varieties of which are much used as a kitchen vegetable, while the white varieties yield a widely used variety of sugar.

beetle[1] *n* a general name of many insects having four wings, the anterior pair of which are of a horny nature and form a

sheath or protection to the posterior pair.—*vi* (*colloq*) to hurry away (with *off*).

beetle[2] *n* a heavy wooden mallet used to drive wedges and to pound or crush, etc.—*vt* to use a beetle on; to beat with a heavy wooden mallet as a substitute for mangling.

beetle[3] *vi* to be prominent (as a cliff, a battlement); to hang or extend out; to overhang; to jut.

beetling *adj* standing out from the main body; jutting; overhanging (said of cliffs, etc).

beetroot *n* the root of the beet plant; the plant itself.

befall *vt* (*pret* **befell**, *pp* **befallen**, *ppr* **befalling**) to happen to; to occur to.—*vi* to happen; to come to pass.

befit *vt* (**befitted, befitting**) to be fitting for; to suit; to be suitable or proper to.

befog *vt* (**befogged, befogging**) to involve in fog; hence, to confuse.

before *prep* in front of; preceding in space; in presence of; in sight of; under the cognizance or consideration of (a court, a meeting); preceding in time; earlier than; ere; in preference to; prior to; having precedence of in rank, dignity, etc.—*adv* further onward in place; in front; in the forepart; in time preceding; previously; formerly; already.

beforehand *adj, adv* in anticipation; in advance; early.

befriend *vt* to act as a friend to; to aid, benefit, or assist.

beg[1] *vt* (**begged, begging**) to ask or supplicate; to ask for earnestly; to ask earnestly (a person); to beseech; to implore; to entreat or supplicate; to take for granted; to assume without proof.—*vi* to ask for charity; to live by begging, especially in the street.

beg[2] *n* same as **bey**.

beget *vt* (*pret* **begot** or **begat**, *pp* **begot** or **begotten**, *ppr* **begetting**) to procreate as a father or sire; to produce, as an effect; to cause to exist; to generate.

beggar *n* one who begs; a person who lives by begging; one who supplicates with humility; a petitioner; (*colloq*) a person (*poor beggar, lucky beggar*).—*vt* to reduce to beggary; to impoverish; to exhaust the resources of (*to beggar description*); to exhaust.

beggarly *adj* like or belonging to a beggar; poor; mean; contemptible.

beggar-my-neighbour *n* a child's game at cards.

beggary *n* the state of a beggar; a state of extreme indigence.

begin *vi* (*pret* **began**, *pp* **begun**, *ppr* **beginning**) to take rise; to originate; to commence; to do the first act; to enter upon something new; to take the first step.—*vt*

bee

beetle

to do the first act of; to enter on; to commence.

beginner *n* a person who begins or originates; the agent who is the cause; one who first enters upon any art, science, or business; a young practitioner; a novice; a tyro.

beginning *n* the first cause; origin; the first state; commencement; entrance into being; that from which a greater thing proceeds or grows.

begone *interj* go away; hence!—the imperative *be* and pp *gone* combined.

begonia *n* the generic name of tropical plants much cultivated in hothouses for the beauty of their leaves and flowers.

begrudge *vt* (**begrudged, begrudging**) to grudge; to envy the possession of, with two objects (*to begrudge a person something*).

beguile *vt* (**beguiled, beguiling**) to fascinate; to practise guile on; to delude; to deceive; to cheat; to trick; to dupe; to impose on by artifice or craft; to dispel or render unfelt by diverting the mind (cares); to while away (time).

begum *n* a Muslim princess or woman of high rank.

belemnite

behalf *n* interest; profit; support; defence, always in such phrases as *in* or *on behalf of, in my, his, some person's behalf*).

behave *vt* (**behaved, behaving**) to conduct oneself.—*vi* to act; to conduct oneself.

behaviour *n* manner of behaving; conduct; deportment; mode of acting (of a person, a machine etc).

behaviourism *n* the doctrine that human action is governed by external stimuli.

behead *vt* to cut off the head of; to sever the head from the body of.

behest *n* a command; precept; mandate.

behind *prep* on the side opposite the front or nearest part of or opposite to that which fronts a person; at the back of; towards the back or back part of; remaining after; later in point of time than; farther back than; in an inferior position to.—*adv* at the back; in the rear; out of sight; not exhibited; remaining; towards the back part; backward; remaining after one's departure.—*n* (*colloq*) the buttocks.

behindhand *adv, adj* in a state in which means are not adequate to the supply of needs in arrears; in a backward state; not sufficiently advanced; not equally advanced with another; tardy.

behold *vt* (*pret, pp* **beheld**, *ppr* **beholding**) to look at with attention; to observe with care.—*vi* to fix the attention on an object; to attend or fix the mind (in this sense chiefly in the imperative, and used interjectionally).

beholden *adj* under obligation; bound in gratitude; obliged; indebted.

belfry

beholder *n* one who beholds; a spectator.

behoof *n* that which is advantageous to a person; behalf; interest; advantage; profit; benefit (always in such phrases as *in* or *for behoof of, for a person's behoof*).

behove *vt* (**behoved, behoving**) to be fit or meet for, with respect to necessity, duty, or convenience; to be necessary for (used impersonally, as *it behoves us*, etc).

beige *n* a fabric made of unbleached or undyed wool; a light brown colour.

being *n* existence, whether real or only in the mind; that which has life; a living existence; a creature.

belabour *vt* to beat soundly; to deal blows to; to thump.

belay *vt* (*naut*) to make fast by winding round something.

belaying pin *n* (*naut*) a pin for belaying ropes to.

belch *vt* to eject with violence, as from the stomach or from a deep hollow place; to cast forth (*a volcano belches flames or ashes*).—*vi* to eject wind from the stomach; to issue out, as with eructation.—*n* the act of one who or that which belches; eructation.

beldam, beldame *n* formerly, an old woman in general, especially an ugly old woman; a hag.

beleaguer *vt* to besiege; to surround with an army so as to preclude escape; to blockade; to harass.

belemnite *n* a straight, tapering, dart-shaped fossil, the internal bone or shell of animals allied to the cuttlefishes, common in the chalk formation; the animal to which such a bone belonged.

belfry *n* a bell tower generally attached to a church or other building; that part of a building in which a bell is hung.

belie *vt* (**belied, belying**) to show to be false; to be in contradiction to (*his terror belies his words*); to fail to equal or come up to; to disappoint (*belie one's hopes*).

belief *n* the acceptance of the mind to the truth of a declaration, proposition or alleged fact, on the ground of evidence distinct from personal knowledge; (*theol*) faith or a firm persuasion of the truths of religion; the thing believed; the object of belief; the body of tenets held by the professors of any faith; a creed.

believe *vt* (**believed, believing**) to credit on the ground of authority, testimony, argument or any other circumstances than personal knowledge; to expect or hope with confidence.—*vi* to be more or less firmly persuaded of the truth of anything.—**to believe in** to hold as an object of faith; to have belief of.

believer *n* one who believes; an adherent of a religious faith; a professor of Christianity.

belittle *vt* (**belittled, belittling**) to make smaller; to lower; speak disparagingly of.

bell[1] *n* a metallic vessel which gives forth a clear, musical, ringing sound on being struck, generally cup-shaped; anything in the form of a bell; (*pl*) the phrase employed on a ship to denote the divisions of daily time from their being marked by strokes on a bell each half-hour.—*vt* to put a bell on.

bell[2] *vi* to roar; to bellow, as a bull or a deer in rutting time.

belladonna *n* deadly nightshade, a perennial plant of the potato family, a native of Britain and throughout Europe: the whole plant is poisonous but it yields a useful and powerful drug.

bellbird *n* a South American bird whose song resembles a bell; an Australian bird with a similar call.

bellboy, bellhop *n* one who carries luggage, runs, errands, etc, in a hotel or club.

bell buoy *n* a buoy on which is fixed a bell, which is rung by the heaving of the sea.

belle *n* a woman of superior beauty and much admired; the most beautiful woman present in a gathering.

belles-lettres *n sing* polite or elegant literature, a term including rhetoric, poetry, history, criticism with the languages in which the literature is written.

bellfounder *n* a person who casts bells.

bellhop *n* same as **bellboy**.

bellicose *adj* inclined to war; warlike; pugnacious; indicating warlike feelings.

belligerent *adj* waging war; carrying on war; pertaining to war or warfare.—*n* a nation, power or state carrying on war; one engaged in fighting.

bell jar *n* a protective glass cover in the shape of a bell.

bellman *n* (*pl* **bellmen**) formerly, a public crier who used a bell.

bell metal *n* an alloy of copper and tin, used for making bells.

bellow *vi* to utter a deep, loud sound, as a bull; to make a loud noise or outcry; to roar.—*n* a loud outcry; roar.

bellows *n, sing, pl* an instrument for producing a strong current of air and principally used for blowing fire, either in private dwellings or in forges, furnaces, mines, etc, or for supplying the pipes of an organ with wind.

bell pull *n* that by which a bell is made to ring; a bell rope.

bellwether *n* a sheep which leads the flock, often with a bell on its neck.

belly *n* that part of the human body which extends from the breast to the thighs containing the bowels and the abdomen; the corresponding part of a beast; the part of anything which resembles the human belly in protuberance or cavity.—*vt* (**bellied,** **bellying**) to fill; to swell out.—*vi* to swell and become protuberant like the belly.

belong *vi* to be the property of; to appertain; to be the concern or affair; to be dependent or connected; to be suitable; to be due; to have a settled residence; to be a native of a place; to have original residence (in all senses followed by *to*).

belonging *n* that which belongs to one (used generally in plural); a person's property and possessions.

beloved *adj* loved; greatly loved; dear to the heart.

below *prep* under, in place; beneath; not so high as; inferior to in rank, excellence, or dignity.—*adv* in a lower place with respect to any object; beneath; on the earth, as opposed to the heavens; in hell or the regions of the dead; in a court of inferior jurisdiction.

belt *n* a girdle; a band of cloth, leather, etc, worn round the waist to hold up clothing, as decoration or to carry things or hang things from; anything resembling a belt; a strip; a stripe; a band; a band passing round two wheels and communicating motion from one to the other; (*sl*) a hard blow.—*vt* to surround or attach with a belt; to thrash with a belt; (*sl*) to deliver a hard blow; (*sl*) to hurry (with *along*); (*sl*) to sing or play loudly (with *out*); to fasten with a belt (with *up*).—*vi* (*colloq*) to wear a seat-belt; (*sl*) to be quiet (often imperative).

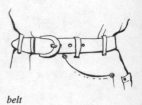

belt

Beltane *n* the name of a festival formerly observed among all the Celtic tribes of Europe, and celebrated in Scotland on 1st May (Old Style), and in Ireland on 21st June, by kindling fires on the hills.

beluga *n* a kind of whale found in northern seas, the white whale or white fish, killed for its oil and skin.

bemire *vt* (**bemired, bemiring**) to drag in the mire; to soil by mud or mire.

bemoan *vt* to moan or mourn for; to lament; to bewail; to express sorrow for.

bemused *adj* sunk in reverie; muddled; stupefied.

bench *n* a long seat; a strong table on which carpenters or other mechanics prepare their work; the seat on which judges sit in court; the seat of justice; the persons who sit as judges; the court.

bencher *n* one who sits on a bench; in England, one of the senior barristers in an Inn of Court, one of four societies that train barristers, who have the government of the society.

benchmark *n* a surveyor's mark for making measurements; something that serves as a standard.

bend *vt* (*pret, pp* **bent,** *ppr* **bending**) to curve or make crooked; to deflect from a normal condition of straightness; to direct

bellows

to a certain point (one's mind, course, steps); to subdue; to cause to yield.—*vi* to be or become curved or crooked; to incline; to lean or turn; to be directed; to bow or be submissive.—*n* a curve; a crook; a turn.

beneath *prep* under; lower in place than something which rests above; burdened or overburdened with; lower than in rank, dignity or excellence; below the level of.—*adv* in a lower place; below.

Benedictine *adj* pertaining to the monks of St Benedict.—*n* a member of the order of monks founded at Monte Casino about 530 by St Benedict, and wearing a loose black gown with large wide sleeves and a cowl on the head; a greenish-yellow liqueur made by the Benedictine monks at Fécamp, in Normandy.

benediction *n* the act of invoking a blessing; blessing, prayer or kind wishes uttered in favour of any person or thing; a solemn or affectionate invocation of happiness.

benefaction *n* the act of conferring a benefit; a benefit conferred, especially a charitable donation.

benefactor *n* one who confers a benefit.

benefice *n* an ecclesiastical living; a church endowed with a revenue for the maintenance of divine service or the revenue itself.

beneficence *n* the practice of doing good; active goodness, kindness, or charity.

beneficent *adj* doing good; performing acts of kindness and charity.

beneficial *adj* contributing to a valuable end; conferring benefit; advantageous; useful; profitable; helpful.

beneficially *adv* in a beneficial manner; advantageously; profitably; helpfully.

beneficiary *adj* connected with the receipt of benefits, profits, or advantages.—*n* one who holds a benefice; one who is in the receipt of benefits, profits, or advantages; one who receives something as a free gift.

benefit *n* an act of kindness; a favour conferred; whatever is for the good or advantage of a person or thing; advantage; profit; a performance at a theatre or other place of public entertainment, the proceeds of which go to one of the actors, or towards some charitable object.—*vt* to do good to; to be of service to; to advantage.—*vi* to gain advantage; to make improvement.

beret

benevolence *n* the disposition to do good; the love of mankind accompanied with a desire to promote their happiness; goodwill; kindness; charitableness; an act of kindness; historically, a contribution or tax illegally exacted by arbitrary kings of England.

benevolent *adj* possessing love to human-kind and a desire to promote their prosperity and happiness; inclined to charitable actions.

Bengalese *adj* of or pertaining to Bengal.—*n sing pl* a native or natives of Bengal.

Bengali *n* the language or dialect spoken in West Bengal and Bangladesh.

Bengal light *n* a kind of firework formerly used as signals, producing a steady and vivid blue-coloured light.

benighted *adj* unenlightened; ignorant.

benign *adj* of a kind disposition; gracious; kind (*benign despot*); proceeding from or expressive of gentleness, kindness or benignity; salutary (*benign influences*); (*med*) mild; not severe or violent; (of a tumour) not malignant.

benignant *adj* kind; gracious; favourable.

benignity *n* the state or quality of being benign or benignant; kindness of nature; graciousness.

bent *n* originally, a condition of being bent (as a bow); hence, turn; inclination; disposition; natural tendency; leaning or bias of the mind; bent grass.—*adj* curved or crooked; strongly determined (with *on*); (*sl*) dishonest; (*sl*) sexually deviant.

bent grass *n* a wiry grass such as grows on commons or neglected ground.

bentwood *adj* (of furniture) made of wood that is bent and shaped by heat.

benumb *vt* to make numb or torpid; to deprive of sensation; to stupefy; to render inactive.

benzene *n* a colourless liquid obtained in the destructive distillation of coal, a hydrocarbon important in organic chemistry as the basis of numerous compounds.

benzine *n* petrol or motor spirit derived by distillation from crude petroleum, and quite distinct from coal-tar benzene.

benzoin, benzoine *n* gum benjamin; a concrete resinous juice or balsam flowing from incisions made in the stem of a tree of Sumatra, etc, chiefly used in cosmetics and perfumes and in incense, having a fragrant and agreeable smell.

bequeath *vt* to give or leave by will; to devise by testament; to hand down; to transmit.

bequest *n* the act of bequeathing or leaving by will; something left by will; a legacy.

berate *vt* (**berated, berating**) to chide vehemently; to scold.

Berber *n* a person belonging to, or the language spoken by, certain tribes of North Africa (Barbary).

bereave *vt* (*pret, pp* **bereaved** *or* **bereft**, *ppr* **bereaving**) to deprive of something or someone that is prized, usually by death.

bereavement *n* deprivation, particularly by the loss of a friend or relative by death.

beret *n* a flat woollen cap, originally worn by Basque peasants.

bereft *adj* deprived (with *of*).

bergamot *n* a variety of pear; a kind of lemon, the rind of which yields an oil used in perfumery.

beriberi *n* a dangerous disease endemic eastern and southern Asia, characterized by paralysis, difficult breathing and swelling.

berlin *n* a four-wheeled vehicle of the chariot kind first made at Berlin.

berm *n* (*fort*) a space of ground between the rampart and the moat or fosse; the bank or side of a canal which is opposite to the towpath.

berry *n* a succulent or pulpy fruit containing many seeds and usually of no great size, such as the gooseberry, the strawberry, etc; what resembles a berry, as one of the eggs of the lobster or crayfish.

bersagliere *n* (*pl* **bersaglieri**) a rifleman or sharpshooter in the Italian army.

berserk *adj, adv* frenzied; destructively violent.

berth *n* a place where a ship can moor; a box or place for sleeping in a ship or railway carriage; a post or appointment; a situation.—*vt* to assign a berth or anchoring ground to; to allot a berth or berths to.

beryl *n* a colourless, yellowish, bluish or less brilliant green variety of emerald, the prevailing hue being green.

beseech *vt* (*pret, pp* **besought**, *ppr* **beseeching**) to entreat; to supplicate; to implore; to beg eagerly for; to solicit.

beset *vt* (*pret, pp* **beset, besetting**) to surround; to enclose; to hem in (*beset with enemies, a city beset with troops*); to press on all sides so as to perplex (*temptations that beset us*); to press hard on.

besetting *adj* habitually attending or assailing (*a besetting sin*).

beside *prep* at the side of a person or thing; near to; apart from; not connected with (*beside the point*).—**to be beside oneself** to be out of one's wits or senses; to be extremely agitated.

besides *adv* moreover; over and above; not included in the number, or in what has been mentioned.—*prep* over and above; separate or distinct from; in addition to.

besiege *vt* (**besieged, besieging**) to lay siege to; to beset or surround with armed forces for the purpose of compelling to surrender; to beset; to harass (*besieged with applications*).

besmear *vt* to smear all over; to bedaub; to overspread with some viscous, glutinous, or soft substance that adheres; to foul; to soil.

besom *n* a broom; a brush of twigs or other materials for sweeping.

besot *vt* (**besotted, besotting**) to make stupid, as with drink; to infatuate; to stupefy; to make dull, stupid, or senseless.

besotted *adj* made stupid by drink; indicating or proceeding from gross stupidity; stupid; infatuated.

bespangle *vt* (**bespangled, bespangling**) to adorn with spangles; to dot or sprinkle with something brilliant.

bespatter *vt* to soil by spattering; to slander or reproach.

bespeak *vt* (*pret* **bespoke**, *pp* **bespoke** *or* **bespoken**, *ppr* **bespeaking**) to speak for (something wanted) beforehand; to order or engage against a future time; to betoken; to indicate by outward appearance (*an action that bespoke a kind heart*).

bespread *vt* to spread over; to cover or form a coating over.

besprinkle *vt* to sprinkle over.

best *adj superl* most good; having good qualities or attainments in the highest degree; possessing the highest advantages.—*adv* in the highest degree.—*n* highest possible state of excellence; all that one can do or show in oneself (often used in this sense with the possessive pronouns *my, thy, his, their*, etc).—**at best** considered or looked at in the most favourable light.—**to make the best of** to use to the best advantage; to get all that one can out of; to put up with as well as one can.—*vt* to defeat, outdo.

bestial *adj* belonging to a beast or to the class of beasts; animals; having the qualities of a beast; brutal; brutish.

bestir *vt* to stir; to put into brisk or vigorous action (usually reflexive).

best man *n* the right-hand man or supporter of the bridegroom at a wedding.

bestow *vt* to give; to confer; to impart (followed by *on* or *upon* before the recipient).

bestowal *n* the act of bestowing.

bestrew *vt* to scatter over; to besprinkle; to strew.

bestride *vt* (*pret* **bestrode**, *pp* **bestridden**, *ppr* **bestriding**) to stride over; to stand or sit on with the legs on either side.

bet *vti* (**bet** *or* **betted, betting**) to lay or stake in wagering; to stake or pledge something on the outcome of a contest; to wager.—*n* a wager; that which is staked, or pledged on any uncertain question or event; the terms on which a bet is laid.

beta ray *n* a stream of penetrating rays emitted by radioactive substances.

betake *vt* (*pret* **betook**, *pp* **betaken**, *ppr* **betaking**) to repair; to resort; to have recourse (with the reflexive pronouns).

betel *n* a species of pepper, a creeping or climbing plant, cultivated throughout India, the Malayan Peninsula and Islands, for its leaf which is chewed with the betel nut and lime.

betel nut *n* the kernel of the fruit of a palm tree found in east and southeast Asia, which is eaten both in its unripe and mature state.

berth

betide *vt* (**betided, betiding**) to happen to; to befall; to come to.—*vi* to come to pass; to happen.

betimes *adv* in good time; early; at an early hour.

betoken *vt* to be or serve as a token of; to foreshow; to indicate as future by that which is seen.

betony *n* a British plant formerly used in medicine, and to dye wool dark yellow.

betray *vt* to deliver into the hands of an enemy by treachery in violation of trust; to violate by fraud or unfaithfulness (*to betray a cause* or *trust*); to play false to; to reveal or disclose (secrets, designs); to let appear or be seen inadvertently (*to betray ignorance*).

betroth *vt* to contract to anyone to a future marriage.

betrothal *n* the act of betrothing.

better[1] *adj* (*compar* of **good**) having good qualities in a greater degree than another; preferable (in regard to use, fitness, etc); improved in health.—**to be better off** to be in improved or in superior circumstances.—*adv* in a more excellent or superior manner; more correctly or fully; in a higher or greater degree; with greater advantage; more in extent or amount (*better than a mile*).—*vt* to make better; to improve; to ameliorate; to increase the good qualities of (soil, etc); to advance the interest or worldly position of; to surpass; to exceed; to improve on (as a previous effort).—*vi* to grow better; to become better; to improve.—*n* a superior; one who has a claim to precedence (generally in the plural, and with possessive pronouns).—**the better** a state of improvement (generally in adverbial phrase *for the better*, as *to alter a thing for the better*); advantage; superiority; victory (*to have* or *get the better of*).

better[2], **bettor** *n* one who lays bets or wagers.

better half *n* (*colloq*) one's spouse.

between *prep* in the space, place, or interval of any kind separating; in intermediate relation to; from one to another of (*letters passing between them*); in partnership among (*shared between them*); so as to affect both of; pertaining to one or other of two (*the blame lies between you*).

betwixt *prep* between; passing between; from one to another.

bevel *n* the inclination of one surface of a solid body to another surface of the same body; an instrument for drawing or measuring angles.—*adj* having the form of a bevel; slanting; not upright.—*vt* (**bevelled, bevelling**) to cut to a bevel.—*vi* to slant or incline off to a bevel angle.

beverage *n* drink; liquor for drinking; a liquid for drinking such as coffee or tea.

bevy *n* a flock of birds; a company of women.

bewail *vt* to wail or weep aloud for; to lament.

beware *vi* to be wary or cautious; to be suspicious of danger; to take care (now used only in imperative and infinitive with *of* before the noun denoting what is to be avoided).

bewilder *vt* to lead into perplexity or confusion; to perplex; to puzzle; to confuse.

bewilderment *n* state of being bewildered.

bewitch *vt* to subject to the influence of witchcraft; to throw a charm or spell over; to fascinate.

bey, beg *n* a Turkish title of respect; a title similar to Mr; formerly, a governor of a town or district in the Turkish dominions; also, a prince.

beyond *prep* on the further side of; out of reach of; further than the scope or extent of; above; in a degree exceeding or surpassing.

bezel *n* the part of a finger ring which surrounds and holds fast the stone; the grooved flange or rim in which the glass of a watch is set.

bezique *n* a game at cards played by two, three, or four persons.

bezoar *n* a name for certain concretions found in the intestines of some animals (especially ruminants).

bhang *n* an Indian variety of the common hemp, having highly narcotic and intoxicant properties; a drug prepared from the plant used as a narcotic, an anodyne, etc.

bhangra *n* a type of pop music which combines elements of Punjabi folk music with elements of Western pop and disco music.

biannual *adj* occurring twice a year.

bias *n* a weight on the side of a bowl which turns it from a straight line; that which causes the mind to incline towards a particular object or course; inclination; bent; prejudice.—*vt* (**biased** or **biassed, biasing** or **biassing**) to give a bias or particular direction to; to prejudice.—*adv* in a slanting manner; obliquely.

bib[1] *n* a small piece of cloth, plastic, etc, tied round a child to prevent food spilling on clothes; the upper part of dungarees or an apron.

bib[2] *n* a fish of the cod family found in the British seas.

bibelot *n* a knick-knack; a trinket.

Bible *n* the sacred book of the Christian church; the sacred Scriptures, consisting of two parts, the Old Testament, originally written in Hebrew, the New Testament in Greek; (*often without cap*) an authoritative text.

biblical *adj* pertaining to the Bible or to the sacred writings.

bibliographer *n* one versed in bibliogra-

bib

phy; one who composes or compiles the history of books.

bibliographic, bibliographical *adj* pertaining to bibliography.

bibliography *n* a history or description of books or manuscripts with lists of the different editions, the times when they were printed, etc.

bibliolatry *n* worship or homage paid to books; excessive reverence for any book, especially the Scriptures.

bibliomancy *n* divination performed by means of a book; divination by means of the Bible.

bibliomania *n* a passion for possessing rare and curious books.

bibliophile *n* a lover of books.

bibliopole *n* a bookseller, especially one dealing in rare books.

bibulous *adj* addicted to drinking intoxicants; pertaining to the drinking of intoxicants (*bibulous propensities*).

bicameral *adj* pertaining to or consisting of two legislative or other chambers.

bicarbonate *n* sodium bicarbonate used in baking powder or as an antacid digestive remedy.

bice *n* a name given to two colours used in painting, one blue, the other green, and both native carbonates of copper.

bicentenary *n* the period of two hundred years; the commemoration of an event that happened two hundred years before.—*adj* relating to a bicentenary; occurring once in two hundred years.

biceps *n* a muscle having two heads or origins; the name of two muscles, one of the arm the other of the thigh.

bicker *vi* to quarrel; to contend in words; to scold.—*n* a trivial quarrel.

bicycle *n* a vehicle consisting of two wheels, one behind the other, connected by a light metal frame carrying a seat, the vehicle being propelled by pedals.

bicyclist *n* one who rides on a bicycle.

bid *vt* (*pret* **bid bade**, *pp* **bid** *or* **bidden**, *ppr* **bidding**) to ask, request or invite (a person); to say to by way of greeting or benediction (*to bid good day, farewell*); to command; to order or direct; to enjoin (followed by an objective and infinitive without to, as *bid him come*); to offer; to propose as a price at an auction.—*n* an offer of a price, especially at an auction.

bidder *n* one who bids or offers a price.

bide *vi* (**bided, biding**) to be or remain in a place or state; to dwell; to inhabit.— *vt* to endure; to suffer; to bear; to wait for (chiefly in phrase *to bide one's time*).

bidet *n* a low bowl-shaped fixture on which one sits to wash one's genitals and bottom.

biennial *n* happening or taking place once in two years; (*bot*) continuing for two years and then perishing; taking two years

to produce its flowers and fruit.—*n* a biennial plant.

biennially *adv* once in two years; at the return of two years.

bier *n* a carriage or frame of wood for conveying a corpse to the grave.

bifurcate *adj* forked; divided into two branches.

big *adj* having great size; great; large; bulky; great with young; pregnant; important; teeming; distended; grown-up; haughty in air or mien; pompous; boastful.

bigamist *n* one who has committed bigamy.

bigamous *adj* of or pertaining to bigamy; guilty of bigamy.

bigamy *n* the crime, fact or state of having two (or more) wives or husbands at once.

big bang theory *n* (*astron*) the theory that the universe originated in a cataclysmic explosion and is still expanding.

Big Ben *n* a clock tower in the Houses of Parliament in London, England; the bell in this tower that tolls the hour.

big end *n* in an internal combustion engine, a bearing that connects the crankshaft and the connecting rod.

big dipper *n* a roller coaster.

Big Dipper *n* (*astron*) the seven main stars in the constellation Ursa Major.

big game *n* large animals or fish hunted for sport; an important, usually risky, objective.

bighorn *n* a large wild species of sheep with long horns, found in the western mountains of North America.

bight *n* a bend in a coastline; a bay; the double of a rope when folded; a bend anywhere except at the ends; a loop.

bigness *n* the state or quality of being big; size; bulk.

bignonia *n* one of a number of plants, inhabitants of hot climates, usually climbing shrubs with beautiful trumpet-shaped flowers, hence their name of *trumpet flower*.

bigot *n* a person obstinately and unreasonably wedded to a particular religious creed, opinion or practice; a person blindly attached to any opinion, system or party.

bigoted *adj* intolerant.

bigotry *n* the practice or tenets of a bigot; obstinate or blind attachment to a particular creed or to certain tenets; unreasoning zeal; intolerance.

big screen *n* (*colloq*) the cinema; the cinema industry.

big top *n* a large circus tent.

bigwig *n* a person of great importance, consequence or dignity.

bikini *n* a two-piece bathing costume for girls or women.

bilander *n* a small merchant vessel with two masts, used chiefly in the Dutch canals.

biceps

bicycle

bilateral *adj* two-sided.

bilberry *n* a dark blue or almost black berry, the fruit of a small shrub belonging to the cranberry family (akin to the heaths) growing on moors and woods in Britain; the shrub itself.

bile *n* a yellow bitter liquid separated from the blood by the action of the liver and discharged into the gall bladder, its most obvious use being to assist in the process of digestion; ill-nature; bitterness of feeling; spleen.

bilge *n* the protuberant part of a cask; the breadth of a ship's bottom, or that part of her floor which approaches to a horizontal direction; nonsense.—*vi* (*naut*) to spring a leak in the bilge.

bilge water *n* the water which enters a ship and lies in her bilge or bottom.

biliary *n* pertaining to or containing bile.

bilingual *adj* containing, or expressed in, two languages (*a bilingual dictionary*); able to speak two languages.

bilious *adj* consisting of or affected by bile; having an excess of bile; having the health affected by excess of bile in the system.

biliousness *n* the state or quality of being bilious, or of suffering from an excessive secretion of bile.

billboard

bilk *vt* to deceive or defraud by non-fulfilment of engagement; to leave in the lurch; to decamp without paying (a person).

bill[1] *n* a piece of paper containing a statement of certain particulars; a sheet containing a public notice or advertisement; a note of charges for goods supplied, work done, etc, with the amount due on each item; a declaration of certain facts in legal proceedings; a written promise to pay or document binding one to pay a specified sum at a certain date; a bill of exchange; a draft of a law presented to a legislature to be passed into an act (also applied to various measures that are really acts).—*vt* to make out a bill of (items); to present a statement of charges to; to advertise by bills; to book.

bill[2] *n* the beak of a fowl.—*vt* to join bills or beaks, as doves; to caress fondly.

bill[3] *n* a cutting instrument, hook-shaped towards the point or with a concave cutting edge, used in pruning, etc; a billhook; an ancient military weapon consisting of a broad hook-shaped blade with a short pike at the back and another at the summit attached to a long handle.

billhook

billboard *n* a large panel designed to carry outdoor advertising; a hoarding.

bill broker *n* one who buys, negotiates, or discounts bills of exchange, promissory notes, etc.

billet[1] *n* a small paper or note in writing; a short letter; a ticket directing soldiers at what house to lodge; lodgings especially for soldiers in private houses.—*vt* to quarter or place in lodgings, as soldiers in private houses.—*vi* to be quartered; to lodge (specifically applied to soldiers).—*vt* to assign to lodging by billet.

billet[2] *n* a small stick or round piece of wood used for various purposes.

billet-doux *n* (*pl* **billets-doux**) a love note or short love letter.

billhook *n* a small variety of hatchet with a hook at the end of the cutting edge.

billiards *n* a game played on a long, rectangular, cloth-covered table with cues and ivory balls which the players strike against each other and drive into pockets at the sides and corners of the table.

billingsgate *n* profane or foul language; ribaldry.

billion *n* in Britain, a million millions; in America and often now in Britain, a thousand millions.

bill of exchange *n* an order drawn by one person (the drawer) on another (the drawee) who is either in the same or in some distant country, requesting or directing him or her to pay money at a specified time to some person assigned (the payee), who may either be the drawer himself or herself or some other person: the person on whom the bill is drawn becomes the 'acceptor' by writing his or her name on it as such.

bill of fare *n* in a hotel, restaurant, etc, a list of refreshments ready to be supplied.

bill of health *n* a certificate affirming the health of a ship's company at the time of her clearing any port.—**a clean bill of health** a favourable report on a person's state of health.

bill of lading *n* a memorandum of goods shipped on board a vessel, signed by the master of the vessel.

bill of sale *n* a formal instrument for the transfer of personal property (as furniture, the stock in a shop), often given in security for a debt, empowering the receiver to sell the goods if the money is not repaid at the appointed time.

billow *n* a great wave or surge of the sea.—*vi* to swell; to rise and roll in large waves or surges.

billowy *adj* swelling into large waves.

billposter, billsticker *n* one who sticks up bills or advertising placards in public places.

billy *n* a tin can used as a camp kettle, etc.

billy goat *n* a male goat.

biltong *n* an African name for lean meat cut in strips and dried.

bimanous *adj* having two hands.

bimetallism *n* that system of currency which recognizes coins of two metals, as silver and gold, as legal tender to any amount.

bimetallist *n* one who favours bimetalism.

bin *n* a box or enclosed place used as a repository of any commodity; one of the subdivisions of a cellar for wine bottles; a dustbin; a container for waste paper or rubbish.—*vt* (**binned, binning**) to put or store in a bin; (*colloq*) to throw away.

binary *adj* consisting or composed of two or of two parts; double; two-fold; dual; denoting or of a number system in which the base is two, each number being expressed by using only two digits, specifically 0 and 1.

bind *vt* (*pret, pp* **bound**, *ppr* **binding**) to tie or confine with a cord, or anything that is flexible; to fasten or encircle as with a band or ligature; to put a ligature or bandage on; to put in bonds or fetters; to hold in, confine or restrain; to engage by a promise, agreement, vow, law, duty or any other moral or legal tie; to form a border on or strengthen by a border; to sew together and cover (a book).—*vi* to exercise an obligatory influence; to be obligatory; to tie up; to tie sheaves up; to grow hard or stiff (of soil).

binder *n* a person who binds; one whose occupation is to bind books; one who binds sheaves; anything that binds, as a fillet, cord, rope, band; a bandage; a folder for keeping loose papers together.

bindery *n* a place where books are bound.

binding *adj* serving to bind; having power to bind or oblige; obligatory; making fast; astringent.—*n* the act of one who binds; anything which binds; the cover of a book with the sewing and accompanying work; something that secures the edges of cloth.

bindweed *n* the common name for twining or trailing plants of the convolvulus family, common in cornfields and waste places and overrunning hedges.

bing *n* a large heap, as of corn, coal, ore, etc.

binnacle *n* the fixed case and stand in which the steering compass in any vessel is set.

binoculars *npl* a device for viewing with both eyes, consisting of two small telescope lenses joined together.

binomial *n* (*alg*) an expression or quantity consisting of two terms connected by the sign plus (+) or minus (-).—*adj* pertaining to binomials.

binomial theorem *n* a celebrated theorem by Sir Isaac Newton, for raising a binomial to any power or for extracting any root of it.

biochemistry *n* the study of chemical processes taking place in organisms.

biodegradable *adj* readily decomposed by bacterial action and so considered to be environmentally friendly.

biodynamics *n* the doctrine of vital forces or energy.

biogenesis *n* the origin of what has life

(vegetable or animal) from living matter; the doctrine which holds that living organisms can spring only from living parents.

biographer *n* one who writes a biography; a writer of lives.

biographic, biographical *adj* pertaining to biography; containing biography.

biography *n* the history of the life and character of a particular person; a life; a memoir; biographical writings in general, or as a department of literature.

biologic, biological *adj* pertaining to biology.

biological warfare *n* warfare using biological weapons, such as disease-producing micro-organisms or toxic chemical substances capable of killing living organisms.

biologist *n* one skilled in or who studies biology.

biology *n* the science of life, or which studies generally the life of animals and plants, including their morphology, physiology, origin, development and distribution.

bioplasm *n* the substance constituting the living matter of the elementary part or cell in plants and animals; germinal matter.

biopsy *n* the removal of parts of living tissue from the body for the purpose of medical diagnosis.

biparous *adj* bringing forth two at a birth.

bipartite *adj* in two parts; having two correspondent parts; double.

biped *n* an animal having two feet, as humans.

bipennate *adj* having two wings or organs resembling wings.

biplane *n* an aeroplane with an upper and an under plane or carrying surface.

biquadratic *n* (*math*) the fourth power, arising from the multiplication of a square by itself; the square of the square.—*adj* pertaining to this power.

birch *n* a graceful tree having small leaves, slender, often drooping branches and a smooth whitish bark; the tough, slender twig of the birch formerly used for punishment.

birchen *adj* made of birch; consisting of birch.

bird *n* a feathered, warm-blooded animal, with two legs and two wings, producing young from eggs.

bird call *n* the song or call of a bird; an instrument for imitating the cry of birds in order to attract or decoy them.

birdlime *n* a viscous substance prepared from holly bark, etc, used for entangling birds.

bird of paradise *n* one of a family of birds found in the islands of the Indian Archipelago, the male bird having colourful plumage.

bird of prey *n* a meat-eating bird (as a

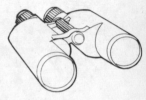

binoculars

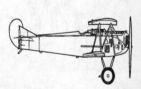

biplane

hawk, owl, falcon, etc) that hunts other animals for food.

bird's-eye view *n* a view or landscape shown as it might appear to a flying bird; hence, a rapid and comprehensive view of a subject.

bird's-foot *n* a common name for several plants, having pods somewhat resembling the claws of a bird.

birdsong *n* a bird's cry or song.

bird watcher *n* one who makes a study of birds in the wild.

bireme *n* an ancient Greek or Roman vessel with two banks or tiers of oars.

biretta *n* a square cap worn by ecclesiastics; priests have it black, bishops purple, cardinals red.

birr *n* a whirring noise.—*vt* to make a whirring noise.

birth *n* the act or process of being born; the occasion of an individual's coming into life; the act of bearing or bringing forth; parturition; the condition in which a person is born; lineage; extraction; descent; that which is born or produced; origin; beginning.

birth control *n* the use of contraceptive drugs or devices to limit reproduction.

birthday *n* the day on which any person is born, or the anniversary of the day; day or time of origin.

birthday suit *n* (colloq) a state of nakedness.

birthmark *n* some congenital mark or blemish on a person's body.

birthplace *n* the place of one's birth; place of origin.

birth rate *n* the number of births per thousand of population per year.

birthright *n* any right or privilege to which a person is entitled by birth; right of primogeniture.

birthstone *n* a gem symbolizing the month of one's birth.

biscuit *n* a kind of small, flat, baked cake; porcelain or earthenware after being first fired and before the application of glazing and embellishments; unglazed porcelain.

bisect *vt* to cut or divide into two equal parts.

bisection *n* the act of bisecting; the division of a line, angle, etc, into two equal parts.

bishop *n* a member of the highest order of the Christian ministry; a prelate having the spiritual direction and government of a diocese, the oversight of the clergy within it and with whom rests the power of ordination, confirmation and consecration; a piece in the game of chess having its upper section in the form of a bishop's mitre.

bishopric *n* the office or dignity of a bishop; the district over which the jurisdiction of a bishop extends; a diocese.

bismuth *n* a metal of a yellowish or reddish

biscuit

bishop

white colour and a lamellar texture, somewhat harder than lead and not malleable, used in the composition of pewter and in various other metallic mixtures.

bison *n* the name of two bovine quadrupeds, the European bison or aurochs and the American bison, usually but improperly called the buffalo, having short, black, rounded horns and on the shoulders a large hump.

bisque[1] *n* unglazed white porcelain; biscuit.

bisque[2] *n* a point given to another player in golf, tennis, croquet; the other player may take it when he or she chooses.

bisque[3] *n* a rich fish soup.

bissextile *n* leap year.—*adj* pertaining to leap year.

bistoury *n* a surgical instrument for making incisions.

bistre, bister *n* a brown pigment prepared from the soot of wood, especially of the beech.

bistro *n* (*pl* **bistros**) a small restaurant.

bisulcate *adj* cloven-footed.

bisulphate *n* (*chem*) a salt of sulphuric acid in which one half of the hydrogen of the acid is replaced by a metal.

bit *n* a small piece of anything; a piece, morsel, fragment, or part; any small coin; the metal part of a bridle which is inserted in the mouth of a horse and its appendages to which the reins are fastened; a boring tool for wood or metal, fixed in a stock, brace, lathe, etc; the part of a key which enters the lock and acts on the bolts and tumblers; the cutting blade of a plane; (*comput*) a unit of information equivalent to either of two digits, 0 or 1.

bitch *n* the female of canine animals, as of the dog, wolf and fox; a derogatory term for a woman.

bite *vt* (*pret* **bit**, *pp* **bitten** *or* **bit**, *ppr* **biting**) to cut, break or crush with the teeth; to penetrate or seize with the teeth; to cause a sharp or smarting pain to (*pepper bites the mouth*); to pinch or nip as with frost; to blast or blight; to grip or catch into or on so as to act with effect (as an anchor, a file, etc); to corrode or eat into, by aqua fortis or other acid.—*vi* to have a habit of biting persons; to seize a bait with the mouth; to grip or catch into another object so as to act on it with effect (*the anchor bites*).—*n* the seizure of anything by the teeth or with the mouth; a wound made by the mouth; a mouthful; a bit; a cheat, trick, fraud; catch or hold of one object on another.

biter *n* one who or that which bites; an animal given to biting; one who cheats or deceives (in phrase now, 'the biter bit').

biting *adj* sharp; severe; cutting; pungent; sarcastic.

bitingly *adv* in a biting manner; sarcastically; sneeringly.

bitt *n* (*naut*) a piece of wood or frame secured to the deck, on which to make fast the cables.

bitter *adj* acrid, biting, pungent to taste; keen, cruel, poignant, severe, sharp, harsh, painful, distressing, piercing to the feelings or to the mind; reproachful, sarcastic or cutting, as words.

bitterish *adj* somewhat bitter, especially to the taste.

bitterly *adj* in a bitter manner; keenly, sharply, severely, intensely.

bittern *n* a name given to several wading birds of the heron family: the common British species is known for the singular booming or drumming noise it makes.

bitterness *n* the state or quality of being bitter in all its senses, whether to the taste, feelings or mind.

bitters *npl* an alcoholic drink made from a mixture of spirits; a liquor prepared with bitter herbs or roots and used as a tonic, etc.

bittersweet *n* the woody nightshade.—*adj* of a bitter and also sweet taste; pleasant but also sad.

bitterwort *n* yellow gentian.

bitumen *n* a mineral substance of a resinous nature and highly inflammable, appearing in a variety of forms which are known by different names, naphtha being the most fluid, petroleum and mineral tar less so, and asphalt being solid.

bituminous *adj* having the qualities of bitumen; containing or yielding bitumen.

bivalve *n* a mollusc with two valves or a shell consisting of two parts which open by a flexible hinge and are closed by muscles, as the oyster, cockle, mussel, etc.

bivouac *n* an encampment of soldiers, climbers, etc, in the open air without tents or under an improvised shelter.—*vi* (**bivouacked, bivouacking**) to camp in bivouac; to pass the night in the open air without tents or with only scant facilities.

bizarre *adj* odd in appearance; fanciful; fantastical and amusing.

blab *vt* (**blabbed, blabbing**) to utter or tell in a thoughtless or unnecessary manner what ought to be kept secret; to let out (secrets).—*vi* to talk indiscreetly; to tattle; to tell tales.

blabber *n* a tattler; a telltale.

black *n* of the darkest colour; the opposite of white; very dark in hue (though not absolutely incapable of reflecting light); lacking light or nearly so; dismal, gloomy, sullen, forbidding, etc; lacking moral light or goodness; mournful; calamitous; evil; wicked; atrocious.—*n* the opposite of white; a black dye or pigment or a hue produced by such; a black part of something, as of the eye; a black dress or mourning; a small flake of soot.—*vt* to make black; to

apply blacking to (shoes); to blacken; to soil; to boycott; to impose a ban on.

Black *n* a member of one of the dark-skinned races; a Negro; an Australian Aboriginal.

black-and-tan *n* a variety of terrier.

Black-and-Tan *n* a member of a British police force sent to Ireland in 1921.

black art *n* the art of performing wonderful feats by supernatural means or aided by evil spirits; necromancy; magic.

blackball *vt* to reject as a proposed member of a club; to exclude by vote.

black beetle *n* a cockroach.

blackberry *n* the berry of the bramble.

blackbird *n* a bird of the thrush family, the male bird being characterized by its black plumage and its rich mellow note; the merle.

blackboard *n* a board used in schools and lecture rooms for writing or drawing on for instruction.

black body *n* (*physics*) an ideal body with surface so constituted as to absorb all the radiation which falls on it without reflecting any.

black box *n* a specially protected electronic device installed in an aircraft to record any information about its flight and used to find out the cause of a crash.

blackcap *n* a British bird of the warbler family.

blackcock *n* a bird of the grouse family, so called from the glossy black plumage of the male; the heath cock or black grouse.

blackcurrant *n* a garden plant and its fruit, so called from its black berries.

Black Death *n* an oriental plague which first visited Europe in the fourteenth century, characterized by inflammatory boils and black spots all over the skin.

black economy *n* the part of a country's economy relating to earned income that is illegally not declared for tax purposes.

blacken *vt* to make black; to sully; to stain; to defame; to vilify; to slander.—*vi* to become black or dark.

black flag *n* the flag formerly assumed by pirates; the Jolly Roger.

Black Friar *n* a friar of the Dominican order, so called from the colour of the dress.

blackguard *n* a person of coarse and offensive manners; a fellow of low character; a scamp; a scoundrel.—*vt* to revile in low or scurrilous language.

blackguardism *n* the conduct or language of a blackguard.

blackhead *n* a small pimple clogging a pore in the skin.

black hole *n* a theoretically possible region of space with a field of such strong gravitational pull that matter and energy cannot escape from it, presumed to exist where a massive star has collapsed.

blackcap

blackcurrent

black ice *n* a thin transparent coating of ice on roads, etc.

blacking *n* a composition for polishing boots, shoes, metals, etc, consisting usually of a mixture of lampblack, oil, vinegar, etc.

blackjack[1] *n* a gambling game with cards in which players try to obtain points better than the banker's but not more than 21; pontoon.

blackjack[2] *n* a tankard now made of tin but formerly of waxed leather.

black lead *n* graphite; plumbago.

blackleg *n* one who systematically tries to win money by cheating in connection with races or with cards, billiards or other game; one who works for an employer against a trade union during a strike.—*vti* (**blacklegged, blacklegging**) to act or injure, as a blackleg.

black letter *n* the old English or Gothic type used in early printed books, being an imitation of the written character in use before the art of printing.

blacklist *n* a printed list circulated by a government or business containing the names of persons who are politically suspect, have become bankrupt, etc.—*vt* to put on such a list.

blackly *adv* in a black manner; darkly; gloomily; threateningly; angrily; atrociously.

black magic *n* sorcery, witchcraft.

blackmail *n* extortion by means of intimidation, as by threats of accusation or exposure.—*vt* to extort money by threatening to disclose certain facts.

blackness *n* the state or quality of being black; black colour; darkness; gloominess; sombreness; sullen or severe aspect; atrocity.

blackout *n* the darkness when all lights are switched off; temporary loss of consciousness or electricity; a breakdown of communications between a spacecraft and ground control; a closing down of radio or television broadcasting due to strike action or government ban.

black pudding *n* a kind of sausage made of blood, suet thickened with meal, etc.

Black Rod *n* in England, the usher belonging to the order of the Garter and one of the official messengers of the House of Lords.

black sheep *n* a member of a family or society distinguished from his or her fellows by disreputable conduct.

Blackshirt *n* (*hist*) a fascist, especially a member of Mussolini's Italian Fascist party.

blacksmith *n* a smith who works in iron and makes iron utensils; an ironsmith.

black spot *n* a disease affecting leaves, especially of roses.

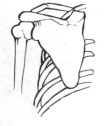

blade bone

blancmange

blackthorn *n* the sloe.

Black Watch *n* formerly, the 42nd Regiment of the British army, raised to protect the Highlands.

blackwater fever *n* an African fever in which the urine is dark-coloured.

bladder *n* a thin membranous bag in animals, which serves as the receptacle of some secreted fluid, as the urine, the gall, etc; any vesicle, blister, or pustule, especially if filled with air or a thin watery liquor; a hollow appendage in some plants.

blade *n* the leaf of a plant, especially of grass or corn plants; a thing resembling a blade in shape, as the cutting part of a knife, etc; the broad part of an oar; formerly, a rakish fellow.—*vt* to furnish with a blade.

blade bone *n* the scapula or upper bone in the shoulder; the shoulder blade.

blaeberry *n* (*Scots*) the whortleberry.

blain *n* a pustule; a blotch; a blister.

blame *vt* (**blamed, blaming**) to express disapprobation of (a person or thing); to find fault with; to censure; to reproach; to chide; to condemn; to upbraid.—*n* an expression of disapprobation for something deemed to be wrong; imputation of a fault; censure; reproach; reprehension; that which is deserving of censure (*the blame is yours*); fault; crime; sin.

blameable, blamable *adj* deserving of blame or censure; faulty; culpable; reprehensible; censurable.

blameful *adj* meriting blame; reprehensible; faulty; guilty; criminal.

blameless *adj* not meriting blame or censure; without fault; undeserving of reproof; innocent; guiltless.

blameworthy *adj* deserving blame; censurable; culpable; reprehensible.

blanch *vt* to whiten by depriving of colour; to render white, pale, or colourless (*fear blanches the cheek*); (*hortic*) to whiten or prevent from turning green by excluding the light, a process applied to kitchen vegetables, such as celery, lettuce, sea kale, etc; to whiten or make lustrous, as metals, by acids or other means; to scald.—*vi* to become white; to bleach.

blancmange *n* a preparation of the consistency of a jelly, composed of cornflour with milk and flavouring substances.

bland *adj* mild; soft; gentle (*bland zephyrs*); affable; suave (*his manner is very bland*); soothing; kindly.

blandish *vti* to render pleasing, alluring or enticing; to coax or flatter.

blandishment *n* words or actions expressive of affection or kindness with the intention of flattering or cajoling.

blank *adj* empty of written or printed characters, as paper; lacking something necessary to completeness; vacant; unoccupied;

void; empty; pale from fear or terror; hence, confused; confounded; dispirited; dejected; unrhymed (applied to verse).—*n* a piece of paper without writing or printed matter on it; a void space on paper or in any written or printed document; a document remaining incomplete till something essential is filled in; a void; a vacancy; a ticket in a lottery on which no prize is indicated; a lot by which nothing is gained; in archery, the white mark in the centre of a target; a piece of metal prepared to be formed into something useful by a further operation; a plate, or piece of gold or silver, cut and shaped, but not stamped into a coin.

blank cartridge *n* a cartridge filled with powder but having no bullet.

blank cheque *n* a signed cheque with the amount left blank to be filled by the payee; complete freedom of action.

blanket *n* a soft thick cloth made of wool loosely woven, and used as a covering in beds; any similar fabric used as covering, etc.—*vt* to cover as with a blanket; (*naut*) to take the wind out of the sails of (another yacht) by sailing to windward of her.

blank verse *n* unrhymed verse.

blare *vi* (**blared, blaring**) to give forth a loud sound like a trumpet; to give out a brazen sound; to bellow.—*vt* to sound loudly; to proclaim noisily.—*n* a sound like that of a trumpet; noise; roar.

blarney *n* excessively complimentary language; gross flattery; smooth, deceitful talk; gammon.

blasé *adj* bored, indifferent, usually from having had a surfeit of pleasure, etc.

blaspheme *vt* (**blasphemed, blaspheming**) to speak in terms of irreverence of; to revile (used of speaking against God or things sacred).—*vi* to utter blasphemy; to swear or curse against.

blasphemous *adj* containing or exhibiting blasphemy; impiously irreverent toward God.

blasphemy *n* the language of one who blasphemes; words uttered impiously against God; grossly irreverent or outrageous language.

blast *n* a sudden gust of wind; the sound made by blowing a wind instrument, as a horn or trumpet; the sound produced by one breath; a blight or sudden pernicious influence on animals or plants; a forcible stream of air from the mouth, bellows, etc; a violent explosion of gunpowder or other explosive in splitting rocks, etc.—*vt* to injure by a blast; to cause to fade, shrivel, or wither; to blight or cause to come to nothing; to ruin; to split by an explosion.—*vi* to wither or be blighted.

blast furnace *n* a smelting furnace operated by compressed air.

blastoderm *n* (*anat*) the germinal skin or membrane; the superficial layer of the embryo in its earliest condition.

blast-off *n* the launch of a space vehicle or rocket; the time when this takes place.

blastomere *n* one of the cells into which a fertilized ovum divides.

blatant *adj* glaringly conspicuous; noisy.

blaze[1] *n* the stream of light and heat from any body when burning; a flame; brilliant sunlight; effulgence; brilliance; a bursting out; an active or violent display (*a blaze of wrath*).—*vi* (**blazed, blazing**) to flame; to send forth or show a bright and expanded light.

blaze[2] *n* a white spot on the forehead or face of a horse or other quadruped; a white spot on a tree made by removing the bark with a hatchet.—*vt* to set a blaze on, by paring off part of the bark; to indicate or mark out, as a path, by paring off the bark of a number of trees in succession.

blaze[3] *vt* (**blazed, blazing**) to make known to all; to noise abroad; to proclaim.

blazer *n* that which blazes; a bright-coloured or striped jacket or short coat suited for sports, etc.

blazing *adj* emitting a blaze; flaming.

blazon *n* the drawing or representation on coats of arms; a heraldic figure; show; pompous display, by words or other means.—*vt* to explain, in proper terms, the figures on ensigns armorial; to deck; to embellish; to adorn; to display; to announce loudly and publicly (with *abroad*).

blazonry *n* the art of describing or explaining coats of arms in proper heraldic terms and method.

bleach *vt* to make white or whiter by taking out colour; to whiten; to blanch; to whiten by exposure to the action of the air and sunlight or of chemical preparations.—*vi* to grow white in any manner.—*n* a substance that bleaches.

bleacher *n* one who bleaches; one whose occupation is to whiten cloth.

bleaching *n* the act or art of making textiles and various other substances white.

bleaching powder *n* chloride of lime made by exposing slaked lime to the action of chlorine.

bleak[1] *adj* exposed to cold and winds (situation, tract of land); desolate; ungenial; cheerless; dreary; cold; chill (*bleak winds*).

bleak[2] *n* a small river fish belonging to the carp family, occurring in many European and English rivers.

bleary *adj* (of the eyes) sore, dim and watery.

bleat *vi* to utter the cry of a sheep; to whine or complain.

bleat, bleating *n* the cry of a sheep.

bleed *vi* (**bled, bleeding**) to lose blood; to

blazon

blazer

be drained of blood; to run with blood; to let sap or other moisture flow; to trickle or flow, as from an incision; to have money extorted or to part with it freely to some wheedling or unworthy party.—*vt* to take blood from by opening a vein; to emit or distil (*a tree bleeds juice, sap* or *gum*); to extort or extract money from.

bleeding *n* a running or issuing of blood; a haemorrhage; the operation of letting blood, as in surgery; the drawing of sap from a tree or plant.

bleep *vi* to emit a high-pitched sound or signal, as a car alarm.—*n* a small portable electronic radio receiver that emits a bleep to convey a message.

bleeper *n* a bleep.

blemish *vt* to deface; to sully; to tarnish, as reputation or character; to defame.—*n* a defect, flaw or imperfection; something that mars beauty, completeness, perfection or reputation.

blench *vi* to shrink; to start back; to flinch; to turn aside, as from pain, fear, repugnance, etc.

blend *vt* to mix or mingle together.—*vi* to be mixed; to become united; to merge the one into the other (as colours).—*n* a mixture, as of liquids, colours, spirits.

blende *n* a native sulphide of zinc.

blender *n* an electrical kitchen device for mixing or chopping foods.

blender

blenny *n* the name of several small fishes frequenting rocky coasts.

bless *vt* (**blessed** or **blest, blessing**) to invoke the divine favour on; to express a wish for the good fortune or happiness of; to bestow happiness, prosperity or good things of any kind on (*blessed with peace and plenty*); to make and pronounce holy; to consecrate; to glorify for benefits received; to extol for excellences (*to bless the Lord*); to esteem or account happy (with the reflexive pronoun).—**bless me! bless my soul!** expressions of surprise.

blessed *adj* enjoying happiness; favoured with blessings; highly favoured; happy; fortunate; enjoying spiritual blessings and the favour of God; sacred; hallowed; holy.

blessedness *n* the state of being blessed; happiness; felicity; heavenly joys; the favour of God.—**single blessedness** the unmarried state; celibacy.

blindworm

blessing *n* the act of one who blesses; a prayer or solemn wish imploring happiness for another; a benediction; the act of pronouncing a benediction or blessing; any good thing falling to one's lot; a mercy.

blight *n* something that nips, blasts or destroys plants; a diseased state of plants; smut, mildew or other plant diseases; (*fig*) something that frustrates, blasts, destroys, brings to nought, etc.—*vt* to affect with blight; to cause to wither or decay; to blast; to frustrate.—*vi* to injure or blast as blight does.

blind *adj* lacking sight; not having the faculty of discernment; lacking intellectual, moral, or spiritual light; not easily discernible; dark; obscure (*blind paths, blind mazes*); indiscriminate; heedless (*blind wrath*); without openings for admitting light (*blind window*) or otherwise lacking something ordinarily essential; closed at one end; having no outlet (*a blind alley*).—*vt* to make physically, morally, or intellectually blind; to render incapable of clear vision (*blinded by passion*); to darken; to obscure to the eye or to the mind.—*n* something to hinder sight, to intercept a view or keep out light; a screen to prevent too strong a light from shining in at a window or to keep people from seeing in; something ostensible to conceal a covert design; a cover; a pretext.

blind date *n* a social engagement with a person of the opposite sex whom one has not met before, usually arranged by a mutual friend or a by dating agency.

blindfold *adj* having the eyes covered, as with a bandage; having the mental eye darkened.—*vt* to cover the eyes of; to hinder from seeing by binding something round the eyes.—*n* a cloth or bandage used to blindfold.

blinding *adj* making blind; preventing from seeing clearly; depriving of sight or of understanding; dazzlingly bright.

blindly *adv* in a blind manner; without sight or understanding; without examination; regardlessly; recklessly.

blind man's buff *n* a game in which one person is blindfolded and tries to catch another player and tell who it is.

blindness *n* state of being blind; lack of sight; mental darkness; ignorance.

blind spot *n* a point on the retina of the eye that is insensitive to light; a place where vision is obscured; a subject on which someone is ignorant.

blindworm *n* a small harmless worm-like reptile, called also **slowworm**.

blink *vi* to wink; to twinkle; to see with the eyes half shut or with frequent winking; to get a glimpse; to peep; to intermit light; to glimmer.—*vt* to shut one's eyes to; to avoid or purposely evade (*to blink a question* or *topic*).—*n* a glance of the eye; a glimpse; a gleam; a glimmer; the gleam or glimmer reflected from ice in the Arctic regions.

blinker *n* one who blinks; a leather flap placed on either side of a horse's head, to prevent it from seeing sideways.

blip *n* a spot of light on a radar screen representing a particular object; a quick recurring sound; a sudden, unexpected, short-lived rise or fall in some form of statistics; an unexpected temporary problem or hitch.—*vi* (**blipped, blipping**) to make a blip.

bliss *n* the highest degree of happiness; blessedness; felicity, often specifically heavenly felicity.

blissful *adj* full of, abounding in, enjoying, or conferring bliss.

blister *n* a thin vesicle on the skin containing watery matter or serum; a pustule; an elevation made by the separation of an external film or skin, as on plants; something applied to the skin to raise a blister.—*vt* to raise a blister or blisters on.—*vi* to rise in blisters or become blistered.

blister pack *n* a transparent plastic dome on a firm backing for packaging small articles for sale.

blithe *adj* happy; merry; joyous; sprightly; heedless; casual.

blitheness *n* the quality of being blithe; gaiety; sprightliness.

blithesome *adj* full of blitheness or gaiety; happy; merry; cheerful.

blizzard *n* a biting-cold snowstorm.

bloat *vt* to make turgid or swollen, as with air, water, etc.

bloated *adj* swelled out; puffed up; unwieldy, especially from overindulgence in eating and drinking; unduly large; overgrown (*bloated armaments*).

bloater *n* a smoke-dried herring first soaked in brine.

blob *n* a small globe of liquid; a dewdrop; a blister; a bubble; (*cricket sl*) a score of nothing; a duck.

block *n* any solid mass of matter, usually with one or more plane or approximately plane faces; a lump; a stupid person; the mass of wood on which criminals laid their necks when they were beheaded; any obstruction or cause of obstruction; a stop; the state of being blocked or stopped up; a casing or shell containing one or more pulleys over which a rope or chain works; a connected mass of buildings; a portion of a city enclosed by streets; a mould or piece on which something is shaped or placed to make it keep in shape; a piece of wood on which an engraving is cut.—*vt* to hinder egress or passage from or to; to stop up or barricade; to obstruct; (in cricket) to stop a ball with the bat without striking it to a distance; to mould, shape or stretch on a block; (in bookbinding) to ornament by means of brass stamps.—**to block out** to begin to reduce to the required shape; to shape out.

blockade *n* the shutting up of a place by surrounding it with hostile troops or ships with a view to compel a surrender by hunger and want; any strategic barrier.—**to raise a blockade** to remove or break up a blockade.—*vt* (**blockaded, blockading**) to subject to a blockade; to prevent ingress to or egress from by warlike means; to shut up or in by obstacles of any kind; to obstruct.

blockbuster *n* a very heavy Second World War bomb able to penetrate concrete blockhouses; an exceptionally successful book, film or show.

blockhead *n* a stupid person; a dolt.

blockhouse *n* (*milit*) formerly, a strong building of one or more storeys constructed chiefly of logs or beams of timber, having loopholes for musketry; a concrete building with openings for guns and observation; one near a rocket-launching site for controlling and observing.

block letter *n* a handwritten capital letter similar to a printed letter.

block printing *n* the process or art of printing from engraved blocks of wood.

block system *n* the system of working the traffic on a railway, according to which the line is divided into short sections, and no train is allowed to enter any one section until it is signalled wholly clear.

blond, blonde *adj* of a fair colour or complexion.—*n* a person of very fair complexion, with light hair and usually light-blue or grey eyes.

blood *n* the fluid which circulates through the arteries and veins of the human body and that of other animals, and which is essential to life and nutrition—in humans and the higher animals of a more or less red colour; relationship by descent from a common ancestor (*allied by blood*); consanguinity; lineage; kindred; family; birth; extraction; often high birth; good extraction; natural disposition; temper; spirit (*to do a thing in hot blood* or *cold blood*, that is in anger or deliberately); mettle; passion; anger (*his blood was up*).—*vt* to let blood; to bleed; to stain with blood; to inure to blood; to give a taste of blood.

blood bank *n* a place where blood is taken from blood donors and stored.

blood count *n* a count of the number of red and white blood cells in a specific volume of blood.

blood donor *n* a person who donates his or her blood for transfusion.

blood group *n* any of the classes of human blood.

blood horse *n* a horse of a breed derived originally from a cross with the Arabian horse, combining lightness, strength, swiftness and endurance.

bloodhound *n* a large variety of dog with long smooth and pendulous ears, remarkable for the acuteness of its smell.

bloodiness *n* the state of being bloody.

bloodless *adj* without blood; drained of blood; dead; without shedding of blood or

bloodhound

slaughter (*a bloodless victory*); without spirit or liveliness.

blood-letting *n* the act of letting blood by opening a vein.

blood money *n* money earned by a hired killer or by laying, or supporting, a charge implying peril to the life of an accused person; money paid to a victim's relatives.

blood pressure *n* the pressure of the blood in the arterial system.

blood relation *n* one related by blood or descent.

bloodshed *n* the shedding or spilling of blood; slaughter; waste of life.

bloodshot *adj* red and inflamed by a turgid state of the blood vessels (said of the eye).

blood sport *n* any sport where blood is shed, such as fox hunting.

bloodstone *n* red hematite; a species of heliotrope dotted with spots of jasper as a gemstone.

bloodstream *n* the flow of blood through the blood vessels in the body.

bloodsucker *n* any animal that sucks blood, as a leech, a fly, etc; a hard niggardly person; an extortioner.

blood test *n* an examination of a specimen of blood to determine blood group, presence of bacteria, level of alcohol or drug intake, etc.

bloodthirsty *adj* desirous to shed blood; murderous.

blood vessel *n* any vessel in which blood circulates in an animal body; an artery or a vein.

bloody *adj* of or pertaining to blood; consisting of, containing or exhibiting blood; bloodstained; cruel; murderous; given to the shedding of blood; attended with much bloodshed.

bloom *n* a blossom; the flower of a plant; the act or state of blossoming; fullness of life and vigour; a period of high success; a flourishing condition; the delicate rose hue on the cheek indicative of youth and health; a glow; a flush; a superficial coating, as the delicate powdery coating on certain fruits when newly gathered.—*vi* to produce or yield blossoms; to blossom; to flower; to glow.

bloomer *n* (*colloq*) a blunder.

bloomers *npl* formerly, a costume for women consisting of a short skirt over loose trousers; (*colloq*) knickers.

blooming *adj* showing blooms; glowing as with youthful vigour.

blossom *n* the flower or flowers of a plant; the bloom; blooming state or period (*the plant is in blossom*).—*vi* to put forth blossoms or flowers; to bloom; to flourish.

blot *n* a spot or stain, as of ink on paper; a blur; an obliteration of something written or printed; a spot in reputation; a blemish.—*vt* (**blotted, blotting**) to spot, to

blowhole

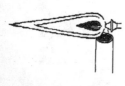

blowpipe

stain, as with ink; to stain with infamy; to tarnish; to obliterate or efface (with *out*); to dry by means of blotting paper, etc.

blotting paper *n* a kind of unsized paper serving to absorb superfluous ink.

blotch *n* a pustule or eruption on the skin; a stain.

blouse *n* a light shirt-like upper garment made of linen, cotton, etc, worn by women.

blow[1] *vi* (*pret* **blew**, *pp* **blown**, *ppr* **blowing**) to make a current of air, as with the mouth, a bellows, etc; to constitute or form a current of air; to be a wind (often used with an indefinite *it* for the subject, as *it blew strongly yesterday*); to pant; to puff; to breathe hard or quickly; to give out sound by being blown, as a horn or trumpet; (*colloq*) to boast; to brag.—**to blow over** to pass away after having spent its force (*the storm blew over*).—*vt* to throw or drive a current of air on; to drive by a current of air; to sound by the breath (a wind instrument); to form by inflating (*to blow a glass bottle*); to swell by injecting air into; to put out of breath by fatigue; to scatter or shatter by explosives (*to blow up, to blow to pieces*).—**to blow out** to extinguish by a current of air; to scatter (one's brains) by firearms.—**to blow up** to fill with air; to swell; to inflate; to puff up; to blow into a blaze; to burst in pieces and scatter by explosion; to exaggerate the importance of; to enlarge a photograph; (*colloq*) to scold.—*n* a gale of wind; a blast; the breathing or spouting of a whale.

blow[2] *n* a stroke with the hand or fist or a weapon; a knock; an act of hostility; a sudden calamity; a sudden or severe evil; mischief or damage received.

blow[3] *vi* (**blew, blown**) to flower; to blossom; to bloom, as plants.

blowfly *n* a name of various species of flies (dipterous insects) which deposit their eggs on flesh, and thus taint it.

blowhole *n* the nostril of a whale situated on the highest part of the head; a hole in the ice to which whales and seals come to breathe.

blowpipe *n* an instrument by which a current of air or gas is driven through a flame so as to direct it on a substance, an intense heat being created by the rapid supply of oxygen and the concentration of the flame; a pipe or tube through which poisoned arrows or darts are blown.

blowy *adj* windy; gusty.

blowzy, blowsy *adj* fat and ruddy; dishevelled, slatternly.

blubber *n* the fat of whales and other large sea animals.—*vi* to weep, especially in such a manner as to swell the cheeks or disfigure the face.

bludgeon *n* a short stick with one end

loaded or thicker and heavier than the other, used as a weapon.

blue *n* one of the primary colours; the colour of the clear sky or deep sea; azure; what is blue; a dye or pigment of this hue; one who represents his or her university (especially Oxford and Cambridge) at rowing, cricket, football, etc; (*pl*) depression, melancholy; a type of melancholy folk music.—*adj* of the colour of blue; sky-coloured; azure.—*vt* (**blued, blueing**) to make blue; to dye a blue colour.

Bluebeard *n* a person in mediaeval tale, synonymous with wife-murderer.

bluebell *n* the popular name given in England to the wild hyacinth and in Scotland to the harebell.

bluebird *n* a small bluish bird with a red breast very common in the United States; the blue robin.

bluebook *n* a name applied to British government official reports and other papers, because their covers are made of blue paper.

bluebottle *n* a fly with a large blue belly.

blue devils *npl* (*colloq*) dejection, hypochondria, or lowness of spirits; delirium tremens.

bluejacket *n* a sailor.

blue mould *n* a thread-like fungus growing on cheese and other food, leather, etc.

blue peter *n* (*naut*) a blue signal flag having a white square in the centre, flown by a boat leaving port.

blueprint *n* a print obtained by the action of light on prepared paper over which a transparent drawing is laid, the exposed part of the paper becoming covered with Prussian blue and the drawing showing in white; a detailed outline or plan; a basis or prototype for future development.

blue ribbon *n* the broad, dark-blue ribbon worn by members of the order of the Garter over the left shoulder and hanging down to the hip; a member of this order; (*fig*) what marks the attainment of an object of great ambition; the object itself.

bluestocking *n* a literary woman (applied usually with the imputation of pedantry).

bluff *adj* broad and full, specially applied to a full countenance, indicative of frankness and good humour; rough and hearty; somewhat boisterous and unconventional; having a steep front (*a bluff bank*).—*vt* to deceive or impose on by a false bold front.—*n* a high bank with a steep front; a bold headland; bold words or acts intended to daunt, deceive or test an opponent.

blunder *vi* to make a gross mistake, especially through mental confusion; to err stupidly; to move without direction or steady guidance; to flounder; to stumble, literally or figuratively.—*n* a mistake through precipitance or mental confusion; a tactless and stupid mistake.

blunderbuss *n* a short gun or firearm, with a large bore and usually a bell muzzle, now obsolete; a stupid, tactless person.

blunt *adj* having a thick edge or point, as an instrument; dull; not sharp; dull in understanding; slow of discernment; abrupt in address; plain; unceremonious.—*vt* to dull the edge or point of by making it thicker; to impair the force, keenness or susceptibility of.

bluntly *adv* in a blunt manner; plainly; abruptly; without delicacy or the usual forms of civility.

blur *n* something that obscures or soils; a blot; a stain; confused appearance as produced by indistinct vision.—*vt* (**blurred, blurring**) to obscure without quite effacing; to render indistinct; to confuse and dim; to cause imperfection of vision in; to dim.

blurb *n* a brief promotional description of a book, often printed on its jacket.

blurt *vt* to utter suddenly or inadvertently; to divulge unadvisedly (commonly with *out*).

blush *vi* to redden in the cheeks or over the face, as from guilt, shame, confusion or shyness; to exhibit a red or rosy colour; to bloom.—*n* the act of blushing; the suffusion of the cheeks or the face generally with a red colour through confusion, shame, diffidence, etc; a red or reddish colour; a rosy tint.

blusher *n* a cosmetic applied to the upper cheeks to add colour.

bluster *vi* to roar and be tumultuous, as wind; to be boisterous; to be loud, noisy or swaggering; to bully; to swagger.—*vt* to utter, protest in a blustering manner or with noise and violence (with *out*, or other *prep*).—*n* a violent blast of wind; a gust; noisy talk; swaggering; boisterousness.

boa *n* the generic and common name of certain snakes which have neither fangs nor poison but with a prehensile tail and including some of the largest species, the name being popularly given to any of the large snakes of similar habits and so including the python and the anaconda; a long scarf made of fur or feathers.

boar *n* the male pig: when applied to the wild species the term is used without reference to sex.

board *n* a piece of timber sawed thin and of greater length and breadth than thickness; a table; hence, what is served on a board or table; food; diet; specifically, daily food obtained for a stipulated sum at the table of another; a council table; a number of persons having the management, direction or superintendence of some public or private office or trust; the deck or side of a

blue peter

blunderbuss

ship or boat or its interior part (*on board*, *to fall overboard*); a flat rectangular piece of wood or other material designed for playing a game (chess, draughts, etc) on; a kind of thick stiff paper; a sheet of substance formed by layers of paper pasted together (usually in compounds, as *cardboard*, *millboard*); one of the two stiff covers on the sides of a book.—**the boards** the stage of a theatre.—*vt* to lay or spread with boards; to cover with boards; to provide with food or food and lodging for payment; to go on board a vessel; to enter a vessel by force in combat.—*vi* to live as a boarder.

boarder *n* one provided with food or food and lodging at another's house at a stated charge; one who boards a ship.

boarding house *n* a house where board or board and lodging are provided.

boarding school *n* a school which supplies board as well as tuition.

boast *vi* to speak in high praise of oneself or one's possessions; to use exulting, pompous or pretentious language; to brag; to exult; to glory; to vaunt; to bluster.—*vt* to display in ostentatious language; to speak of with pride, vanity or exultation; to magnify or exalt (strength, genius); to vaunt (often reflexive).—*n* a statement expressive of ostentation, pride or vanity; a vaunting or bragging; a brag; the cause of boasting; occasion of pride, vanity or laudable exultation.

boaster *n* one who boasts, glories or brags with exaggeration or ostentatiously.

boat

boat *n* a small open vessel or water craft, usually moved by oars or rowing; any sailing vessel, but usually described by another word denoting its use or mode of propulsion, as, a sailing boat, steamboat, etc.—*vt* to transport in a boat.—*vi* to go or sail in a boat.

boater *n* a stiff flat straw hat.

boathook *n* an iron hook with a point on the back fixed to a long pole to pull or push a boat.

boathouse *n* a house or shed for protecting boats from the weather.

boatman *n* (*pl* **boatmen**) a man who manages a boat; a rower of a boat.

boatswain *n* a ship's officer who is in charge of equipping and maintaining a boat.

boater

bob *n* a general name for any small round object playing loosely at the end of a cord, line, chain, etc, the ball or weight at the end of a pendulum, plumbline, etc; a short jerking action or motion; a shake or jog; a blow; a woman's short, even haircut; the refrain or burden of a song; formerly, a shilling; in bell-ringing, a peal of courses or sets of changes.—*vt* (**bobbed, bobbing**) to move in a short, jerking manner;

to perform with a jerky movement; to cut short, as hair or a horse's tail.—*vi* to play backward and forward; to play loosely against anything; to make a quick, jerky motion, as a rapid bow or obeisance; to angle or fish with a knot of worms on a string, or by giving the hook a jerking motion in the water.

bobbin *n* a small cylindrical piece of wood with a head or flange at one or both ends, on which thread or yarn is wound for use in sewing, weaving, etc.

bobolink, boblink *n* the ricebird or reedbird of the USA (so called from its cry).

bode *vt* (**boded, boding**) to portend; to foreshow; to presage; to indicate something future by signs; to be the omen of.—*vi* to be ominous.

bodice *n* the top part of a woman's dress.

bodiless *adj* having no body or material form; incorporeal.

bodily *adj* pertaining to or concerning the body; of or belonging to the body or to the physical constitution; not mental; corporeal.

bodkin *n* originally a dagger; now a pointed pin of steel, ivory, etc, for piercing holes in cloth; a blunted needle for drawing a ribbon, cord, or string through a loop.

body *n* the frame or substance of human being or animal, as distinct from the soul or spirit; the main central or principal part of anything, as distinguished from subordinate parts, such as the extremities, branches, wings, etc; a person; a human being (now generally forming a compound with *some* or *no* preceding); a number of individuals collectively, united by some common tie or occupation; a corporation; any extended solid substance; matter; any substance or mass distinct from others; a united mass; a general collection; a code; a system; a certain consistency or density; substance; strength (as of liquors, paper, etc); a garment that covers the torso; (*print*) the area occupied by a line of type over and above the area of the impression.—*vt* (**bodied, bodying**) to produce in some form; to embody; to invest with a body.

body building *n* the performing of regular physical exercises designed to increase the power of muscles and make them more conspicuous.

bodyguard *n* the guard that protects or defends one's person; lifeguard.

body language *n* gestures, unconscious bodily movements, etc, that function as a means of communication.

body shop *n* a garage that specializes in car body repair work.

body snatcher *n* formerly, one who robbed graves of dead bodies; a resurrectionist.

body stocking *n* a woman's tight-fitting

garment that covers the torso and sometimes the legs.

bodywork *n* the outer structure of a car, usually metal; the act or process of repairing the bodywork of a car.

Boeotian *adj* of or relating to Boeotia, thick-witted, dull, as distinct from Attic, the inhabitants of Attica.

Boer *n* the name applied to the Dutch colonists of South Africa.

boffin *n* (*colloq*) a scientist.

bog *n* a piece of wet, soft and spongy ground where the soil is composed mainly of decaying and decayed vegetable matter; a piece of mossy ground or where peat is found; a quagmire or morass.—*vt* (**bogged, bogging**) to plunge in mud or mire.—**to be bogged down** to be slowed or hindered.

bogey[1] *n* in golf, a fixed number of strokes for each hole against which players compete.

bogey[2], **bogy** *n* a hobgoblin; a wicked spirit.

bogey[3] n same as **bogie**.

boggle *vi* (**boggled, boggling**) to doubt; to hesitate; to stop, as if afraid to proceed or as if impeded by unforeseen difficulties; to waver; to shrink.

boggy *adj* pertaining to or resembling a bog; full of bogs; marshy; swampy; miry.

bogie, bogey *n* a four-wheeled truck supporting the front part of a locomotive and turning beneath it by means of a central pivot.

bog oak *n* the wood of trunks or large branches of oak trees found in peat bogs, of a deep black colour and is used for carved ornaments, etc.

bogus *adj* counterfeit; spurious; sham; pretended.

bohea *n* an inferior kind of black tea, sometimes applied to black teas in general.

Bohemian *n* a person, especially an artist or literary person, who leads a free life, despising conventionalities generally.

boil[1] *vi* to bubble by the action of heat, as water or other fluids; to exhibit a swirling or swelling motion; to seethe, as waves; to be violently agitated or excited, as the blood; to be subjected to the action of boiling water in cooking, etc, as meat.—*vt* to cause to be agitated or bubble by the application of heat; to collect, form, or separate by the application of heat, as sugar, salt; to subject to the action of heat in a boiling liquid, as meat in cooking; to prepare in a boiling liquid; to seethe.

boil[2] *n* an inflamed and painful pus-filled swelling on the skin.

boiler *n* a large vessel of iron, copper, etc, in which anything is boiled in great quantities; a strong metallic vessel, usually of iron or steel plates riveted together, in which steam is generated for driving en-

gines, etc ; a domestic vessel for providing hot water or central heating; an old and tough chicken for boiling.

boiling point *n* the point at which a liquid, especially water, boils; a point of crisis in a situation.

boisterous *adj* violent; stormy; turbulent; furious; tumultuous; noisy.

bold *adj* daring; courageous; brave; intrepid; fearless; requiring or exhibiting courage; executed with courage and spirit, as a deed; rude; forward; impudent; overstepping usual bounds; striking to the eye; markedly conspicuous; steep; abrupt; prominent; (of type) characterized by thick heavy strokes.

boldface type *n* type characters with thickened, heavy strokes.

boldly *adv* in a bold manner; courageously; intrepidly; forwardly; insolently; abruptly, etc.

boldness *n* the quality of being bold in all the senses of the word; courage; bravery; confidence; assurance; forwardness; steepness; abruptness.

bole *n* the body or stem of a tree.

bolero *n* a favourite dance in Spain; short coat worn by women.

boll *n* the pod or capsule of a plant, as of flax.

bollard *n* a strong post on a wharf around which mooring lines are secured; a post in a street to prevent driving or parking; a marker on a traffic island.

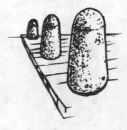

bollard

bologna sausage *n* polony.

Bolshevik *n* the Russian name for the majority party as opposed to the minority (*Mensheviki*) in the 1903 split of the social democrats; revolutionist, extreme socialist.

bolster *n* a long pillow or cushion used to support the head; a pad or quilt used to prevent pressure; a compress; a cushioned or padded part of a saddle; the part of a cutting tool which joins the end of the handle; a hollow tool for punching holes, etc.—*vt* to furnish or support with a bolster, pillow or any soft pad; to pad; to stuff; (*fig*) to support; to maintain (generally with *up*, as *to bolster up his courage*).

bolt[1] *n* an arrow; a thunderbolt; a stream of lightning; a stout metallic pin used for holding objects together, frequently screw-threaded at one extremity to receive a nut; a movable bar for fastening a door, gate, window sash, etc; especially that portion of a lock which is protruded from or retracted within the case by the action of the key.—*vt* to fasten or secure with a bolt or iron pin, as a door, etc; to swallow hurriedly or without chewing, as food; to start or spring game.—*vi* to shoot forth suddenly; to spring out with speed and suddenness; to start forth; to run out of the

bolt

regular path; to start and run off; to take flight; to make one's escape.

bolt² *vt* to sift or pass through a sieve so as to separate the coarser from the finer particles, as bran from flour; (*fig*) to separate good from bad, etc.

bolt-upright *adj, adv* as straight, upright and rigid; erect or erectly.

bolus *n* (*pl* **boluses**) a soft round mass of anything, as chewed food; a large pill.

bomb *n* a missile thrown by hand, propelled by other means or dropped from aircraft, filled with powerful explosive, incendiary material or chemicals, and constructed to detonate on impact or fitted with a time fuse; (*colloq*) a great deal of money.—**the bomb** the hydrogen or atomic bomb.—**to go like a bomb** to be very fast; to be very successful.—*vt* to attack with bombs.—*vi* to fail, to flop.

bomb

bombard *vt* to attack with bombs; to fire shells at or into; to assault with artillery of any kind; to subject to a succession of (blows, questions).

bombardier *n* in the British army, a non-commissioned artillery officer below sergeant in rank; in air crew, the one who releases bombs on a target.

bombardment *n* the act of bombarding; the consistent attack on a target.

bombardon *n* a large-sized and grave-toned musical instrument of the trumpet kind.

bombast *n* high-sounding words; inflated or turgid language.

bombastic *adj* characterized by bombast; high-sounding; turgid; inflated.

bombazine, bombasine *n* a twilled fabric of which the warp is silk (or cotton) and the weft worsted.

bomber *n* a person who bombs; an aeroplane equipped to carry bombs.

bomber jacket *n* a waist-length bloused jacket, often of leather, with a zip.

bombproof *adj* secure against the force of bombs; capable of resisting the shock or explosion of bombs.

bombshell *n* a spherical shell; a bomb; a shocking surprise.

bomb site *n* an area devastated by bombing; a vacant area cleared after a bombing raid.

bona fide with good faith; without fraud or deception.

bonbon *n* a sweet.

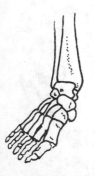

bone

bond *n* anything that binds, fastens, confines, or holds things together, as a cord, a chain, a rope; hence, (*pl*) fetters, chains, and so imprisonment, captivity; a binding power or influence; a uniting tie (*the bond of affection*); an obligation imposing a moral duty, as by a vow or promise; an obligation or deed by which a person binds himself or herself, his or her heirs, etc, to do or not to do a certain act, usually to pay a certain sum on or before a certain day; in masonry, the connection of one stone or brick with another by lapping them over each other in building so that an inseparable mass may be formed, which could not be the case if every vertical joint were over that below it; the state of being bonded, as goods in bond, i.e. stored in a bonded warehouse until customs or excise duties have been paid; (*chem*) a unit of combining power, such as is possessed by the hydrogen or other univalent atom; represented in formulae by a short line or dash.—*adj* in a state of servitude or slavery; captive.—*vt* to put in bond or into a bonded warehouse (goods liable for customs or excise duties, the duties remaining unpaid till the goods are taken out).

bondage *n* slavery, servitude; thraldom; captivity; imprisonment; restraint of a person's liberty by compulsion.

bonded warehouse *n* a licensed warehouse or store in which goods liable to government duties may be lodged after bond has been given on behalf of the owners of the goods for the payment of such duty on their removal.

bondholder *n* one who holds a government or corporation bond.

bonding *n* the process by which people form a relationship with one another, especially parent and child.

bondmaid *n* a female slave, or one bound to service without wages.

bondsman *n* (*pl* **bondsmen**) a male slave, or one bound to service without wages; one bound to act as surety for another.

bondservant *n* a slave.

bond service *n* the condition of a bondservant; slavery.

bone *n* one of the pieces of which the skeleton of vertebrates is composed; the substance of which the skeleton of vertebrates is composed; a firm hard substance of a dull white colour, more or less hollow or cellular internally and consisting of earthy matters (chiefly phosphate of lime and some carbonate of lime) about 65 per cent, and animal matter 33 per cent; (*pl*) the human body or skeleton; (*pl*) pieces of bone held between the fingers like castanets and struck together in time to music.—**to make no bones** to make no scruple.—*vt* (**boned, boning**) to take out the bones from, as in cookery; to put whalebone into (corsets).—**to bone up** (*colloq*) to study hard.

bone of contention *n* a subject of dispute and rivalry.

bonesetter *n* one whose occupation is to treat broken and dislocated bones.

bone shaker *n* an early type of bicycle before the invention of pneumatic tyres.

bonfire *n* a fire made as an expression of public joy and exultation.

bonito *n* one of several species of warm-sea game fishes allied to the tuna.

bon mot *n* (*pl* **bons mots**) a witty saying; a fitting remark.

bonnet *n* a cap; a covering for the head formerly worn by women, and distinguished from a hat by details which vary according to the fashion; anything that covers the head or top of an object, as the cowl or wind cap of a chimney, etc; (*engin*) a metal covering for a valve or other part; the metal shield over the engine of a motorcar.

bonny *adj* handsome; beautiful; fair or pleasant to look on; pretty; fine.

bonspiel *n* in Scotland, a match in the game of curling between parties belonging to different districts.

bonus *n* a sum given or paid over and above what is required to be paid, as a premium given for a loan, or for a charter or other privilege granted to a company; an extra dividend or allowance to the shareholders of a joint-stock company, holders of insurance policies, etc, out of accumulated profits; a sum paid to an employee over and above his or her stated pay as a reward for good service; an added, often unexpected, benefit.

bony *adj* pertaining to, consisting of or resembling bone; having prominent bones.

bonze *n* the European name for a priest or monk of the religion of Fo or Buddha in China, Japan, etc.

booby *n* a dunce; a stupid person; a bird allied to the gannet and included in the pelican family.

booby prize *n* a low-value or humorous prize for the lowest score or least success in a contest.

booby trap *n* a concealed device designed to be set off by some unsuspecting action of the intended victim; a trap for playing a practical joke on someone.

book *n* a number of sheets of paper or other material folded, stitched and bound together on one edge, blank, written or printed; a volume; a particular part (generally including several chapters or sections) of a literary composition; a division of a subject in the same volume; a register or record; a register containing commercial transactions or facts in proper form; a record of bets placed.—*vt* to enter, write, or register in a book; to engage or reserve in advance (as a hotel room, theatre tickets, etc); to take the name of for an alleged offence.

bookbinder *n* one whose occupation is to bind books.

bookbinding *n* the act or practice of binding books by sewing the sheets and covering them with leather or other material.

bookcase *n* an upright case with shelves for holding books.

book club *n* an organization that sells books to its members at cheaper prices, usually by mail order.

book collector *n* one who collects books, especially rare and fine editions; a bibliophile.

bookend *n* a prop at the end of a row of books to keep them upright.

bookie *n* same as **bookmaker**.

booking office *n* an office where passengers receive tickets for conveyance by rail, sea or air or where seats are engaged for a concert or play.

bookish *adj* given to reading or study; more acquainted with books than with the world; pertaining to, contained in, or learned from books; theoretical.

bookkeeper *n* one who keeps accounts; a person who has the charge of entering or recording business transactions or items of debit and credit in the regular set of books belonging to business houses.

bookkeeping *n* the art of recording business transactions in a regular and systematic manner; the art of keeping accounts in a book or set of books in such a manner as to give a permanent record of business transactions so that at any time the true state of one's financial affairs and commercial dealings may be shown.

booklet *n* a small book, usually with a paper cover.

bookmaker *n* one who writes and publishes books; especially, a compiler; (*often* **bookie**) in betting, a person, generally a professional, who wagers on the defeat of a specified horse or other competitor in a race; a layer as opposed to a backer.

bookmark *n* a thing to mark a place in a book.

bookseller *n* one whose occupation is to sell books.

bookstall *n* a stall on which books are offered for sale.

book token *n* a voucher which can be exchanged for books.

bookworm *n* a worm or mite that eats holes in books; a person much addicted to books or study.

boom[1] *vi* to make a sonorous, hollow, humming or droning sound.—*n* a deep hollow noise, as the roar of waves or the sound of distant guns.

boom[2] *n* a long pole or spar run out from various parts of a vessel for extending the bottom of particular sails, as the jib boom, main boom, etc; a strong beam or an iron chain or cable extended across a river or harbour to prevent ships from passing.

boom[3] *vi* to flourish or prosper, especially suddenly.—*n* a period, often sudden, of increased activity or prosperity in business, etc; a sudden rise in price or value.

boomerang *n* a missile formed generally of a piece of hard wood, parabolic in shape,

bookend

boomerang

used by the Australian aborigines: when thrown to a distance it rises into the air then returns to the thrower or to hit an object behind the thrower if skilfully handled.—*vi* to recoil, to backfire.

boon *n* a petition; a favour; a grant; a benefaction; a benefit; a blessing; a great privilege.

boor *n* a person who is rude and insensitive in manners.

boorish *adj* awkward in manners; rude.

boost *vt* to increase (sales, etc); to promote or advance the interests of (someone or something); to encourage; to improve; to push.—*n* a push.

booster *n* a thing or person that increases the effectiveness of another; the first stage of a rocket, which usually breaks away after launching; a substance that increases the efficacy of medication.

boot

boot[1] *n* an article of dress, generally of leather, covering the foot and extending to a greater or less distance up the leg; an instrument of torture fastened on to the leg to crush both muscles and bones; the rear compartment of a car used for carrying luggage, etc; (*pl* used as *sing*) a hotel servant who formerly cleaned the boots of guests.—*vt* to put boots on; to kick; (*colloq*) to get rid of, to sack (usually with *out*); to start up the initial programs on (a computer).

boot[2] *n* formerly, profit; gain; advantage.—**to boot** in addition to; over and above; into the bargain.—*vi* (*arch*) to avail.

booth *n* a temporary stall for the sale of goods in a fair or market; an enclosure for voting; a public telephone enclosure; a seating area in a restaurant.

bootjack *n* an instrument for drawing off boots.

bootlace *n* the string or cord for fastening a boot.

bootlegging *n* illicit trafficking in liquor in a prohibition country.

bootless *adj* unprofitable; unavailing; useless.

boot tree *n* an instrument consisting of two wooden blocks, which together form the shape of the leg and foot, and which are inserted into a boot and then driven apart by a wedge to stretch the boot.

booty *n* spoil taken from an enemy in war; that which is seized by violence and robbery; plunder; pillage.

booze *vi* (**boozed, boozing**) to drink alcohol, usually to excess.—*n* alcoholic liquor.

booze-up *n* a drinking session or party.

boracic *adj* of, pertaining to, or produced from borax.

boracic acid *n* a compound of boron with oxygen and hydrogen.

boracite *n* a mineral consisting of borate and chloride of magnesium.

borage *n* a plant allied to the forget-me-not used as a herb in salads.

borate *n* a salt formed by a combination of boracic acid with any base.

borax *n* a salt formed by the combination of boracic acid with soda occurring in a crude state (tincal) in India, Persia, China, Peru, Chile, etc, or prepared from a solution of boracic acid and of carbonate of soda combined and crystallized, used as a flux in soldering metals and in making glass and artificial gems.

border *n* the outer part or edge of anything, as of a garment, piece of cloth, a country, etc; margin; verge; brink; boundary; confine; frontier.—*vi* to have the edge or boundary adjoining; to be contiguous or adjacent; to approach; to come near (with *on* or *upon*).—*vt* to make a border to; to adorn with a border of ornaments; to form a border to; to touch at the edge or end; to be contiguous to; to limit.

borderland *n* land forming a border or frontier; an uncertain intermediate district.

bore[1] *vt* (**bored, boring**) to pierce or perforate and make a round hole in; to drill a hole in; to form by piercing or drilling (*to bore a hole*); to force a narrow and difficult passage through; to weary by tedious iteration or repetition; to tire by insufferable dullness; to tease; to annoy; to pester.—*vi* to pierce or enter by drilling, etc; to push forward towards a certain point.—*n* the hole made by boring; hence, the cavity or hollow of a gun or other firearm; the calibre; a person who tires or wearies, especially by trying the patience; a dull person who forces his or her company and conversation on others; anything troublesome or annoying.

bore[2] *n* a sudden influx of the tide into the estuary of a river from the sea, the inflowing water rising and advancing like a wall, rushing with tremendous noise against the current for a considerable distance.

boreal *adj* northern; pertaining to the north or the north wind.

boredom *n* the state of being bored.

boron *n* the characteristic element contained in borax, forming dark-coloured brilliant crystals or sometimes a darkbrown powder.

borough *n* a corporate town or township; a town with a properly organized municipal government.

borough-English *n* (*law*) formerly, a customary descent of estates to the youngest son instead of the eldest.

borrow *vt* to ask and obtain on loan, trust, or on credit with the intention of returning or giving an equivalent for; to take or adopt from another or from a foreign source and use as one's own; to adopt; to appropriate; to imitate; to copy.

borrower *n* one who borrows; one who takes what belongs to another and uses it as his or her own; a copier; an imitator; a plagiarist.

borstal *n* formerly, a system of imprisonment for young criminals based on indeterminate sentences.

bort *n* diamonds too coarse for ornamental setting, or small fragments of pure diamonds used, when reduced to a powder, for polishing and grinding.

borzoi *n* a Russian wolfhound.

bosh *n* nonsense; absurdity; trash.

bosom *n* the breast of a human being; the folds of the dress about the breast; the seat of the tender affections, passions, inmost thoughts, wishes, secrets, etc; embrace or compass (*the bosom of the church*); something likened to the human bosom (*the bosom of the earth, of a lake*, etc).—*adj* very dear or close (*a bosom friend*).

boss[1] *n* an employer; a master; a superintendent; a chief person.—*vt* to be in control; to domineer.

boss[2] *n* a protuberant part; a round, swelling body; a projecting mass; a stud or knob; a protuberant ornament of silver, ivory or other material, used on bridles, harness, etc; (*archit*) an ornament placed at the intersection of the ribs or groins in vaulted or flat roofs.

bossy *adj* domineering; fond of giving orders.

botanical, botanic *adj* pertaining to botany; relating to plants in general.

botanist *n* one skilled in botany; one versed in the knowledge of plants or vegetables, their structure and generic and specific differences.

botanize *vi* (**botanized, botanizing**) to study plants; to investigate the vegetable kingdom; to seek for plants with a view to study them.

botany *n* the science which treats of the vegetable kingdom, dealing with the forms, structure and tissues of plants, the laws or conditions which regulate their growth or development, the functions of their various organs, the classification of the various specific forms of plants, their distribution and their condition at various geological epochs.

botch *n* a clumsy repair; a part in any work bungled or ill-finished; bungled work generally.—*vt* to mend or patch in a clumsy manner; to perform in a bungling manner.

botcher *n* a clumsy worker at mending; a bungler.

both *adj, pron* the one and the other; the two; the pair or the couple.

bother *vt* to perplex; to perturb; to tease; to annoy.—*vi* to trouble or worry oneself; to make many much ado; to care and concern oneself about; to give time to.—*n* a trouble, vexation or plague; someone who causes problems, etc.

botheration *n* the act of bothering, or state of being bothered; annoyance; trouble; vexation; perplexity.

bothie, bothy *n* in Scotland, a building for a farm worker to lodge.

bottle *n* a hollow vessel of glass, plastic, etc, with a narrow mouth for holding and carrying liquors; the contents of a bottle; as much as a bottle contains; (*colloq*) courage.—**the bottle** strong drink in general; the practice of drinking (*to be fond of the bottle*); milk in a bottle for feeding a baby.—*vt* (**bottled, bottling**) to put into bottles.—**to bottle up** to keep things to oneself; to restrain oneself.

bottle glass *n* a coarse green glass used in the manufacture of bottles.

bottle-green *adj* of a dark green colour like common bottle glass.

bottleneck *n* a narrow stretch of a road where traffic is held up; a congestion in any stage of a process.

bottlenose *n* a whale having a beaked snout, occurring in high north latitudes; a dolphin with a sharp protruding beak.

bottler *n* one whose occupation is to bottle wines, spirits, beer, etc.

bottom *n* the lowest or deepest part of anything, as distinguished from the top; that on which anything rests or is founded; utmost depth either literally or figuratively; base; foundation; the ground under any body of water; the lower or hinder extremity of the trunk of an animal or human being; the buttocks; the portion of a chair for sitting on; the seat; low land formed by alluvial deposits along a river; a dale; a valley; the part of a ship below the waves; power of endurance; stamina; native strength.—*adj* at the bottom; lowest; undermost; having a low situation; alluvial.—*vt* to found or build on; to base; to furnish with a bottom.—*vi* to flatten off, level out after dropping sharply (with *out*).

bottomless *adj* without a bottom; fathomless; very deep.

bottom line *n* the last line of a firm's financial statement which indicates the net profit or loss; the final outcome or conclusion of something; the most important point of something; the last straw.

bottomry *n* the act of borrowing money, and pledging the bottom of the ship, that is, the ship itself as security for the repayment of the money.

botulism *n* severe food poisoning, producing the effects of paralysis without facial distortion and often fatal.

boudoir *n* a small private room to which a woman may retire.

bough *n* an arm or large branch of a tree.

bougie *n* a slender flexible cylinder in-

boss

bough

tended for introduction into the urethra, oesophagus or rectum.

boulder *n* a water-worn, roundish stone of considerable size; (*geol*) an ice-worn and smoothed block lying on the surface of the soil or embedded in the clays and gravels of the drift formation.

boulder clay *n* the stiff, unlaminated, tenacious clay of the glacial or drift epoch or ice age.

boulevard *n* a public walk or street, usually tree-lined, in a city.

bounce *vi* (**bounced, bouncing**) to rebound, to spring back; to make a sudden leap or spring; to jump or rush suddenly; to walk in a lively manner; (of a cheque) to be returned unpaid from a bank; to spring back after hitting something; to recover easily, e.g. from ill health or misfortune (with *back*); (*sl*) to put (a person) out by force; (*sl*) to fire from a job.—*vt* to cause a ball to bounce.—*n* a leap or springiness; capacity for bouncing; sprightliness; boastfulness, arrogance.

bouncer *n* one who or that which bounces; (*sl*) a person employed to keep people out of nightclubs, etc.

bouncing *adj* vigorous; strong; stout; exaggerated; excessive; big.

bound[1] *vi* to leap; to jump; to spring; to move forward by leaps; to rebound.—*n* a leap; a spring; a jump; a rebound.

bound[2] (*pp* and *pret* of **bind**) *adj* made fast by a band or by chains, fetters, etc; hemmed in; kept back; tied; having a binding; obliged by moral ties; confined; restrained: colloquially the word is often used as equivalent to certain, sure (as, *he is bound to succeed*; *the population is bound to increase*).

bound[3] *n* that which limits or circumscribes; the external or limiting line of any object or of space (*to pass beyond the bounds*); hence, that which keeps in or restrains; limit (*to set bounds to ambition*).—*vt* to set bounds or limits to; to act as a limit to; to limit; to terminate; to restrain or confine; to circumscribe.

bound[4] *adj* going or intending to go (*outward bound*); destined (often with *to* or *for*, as *a ship bound for London*).

boundary *n* that which marks a bound or limit; a limit; a bound.

bounden *adj* obliged or beholden; appointed; indispensable; obligatory (*our bounden duty*).

bounder *n* a loud-mannered and vulgar person.

boundless *adj* without bounds or limits.

bounteous *adj* disposed to give freely; free in bestowing gifts; bountiful; liberal; generous; munificent.

bountiful *adj* liberal in bestowing gifts, favours or bounties; munificent; generous.

bounty *n* liberality in bestowing gifts and favours; generosity; munificence; that which is given bounteously; a free gift; a premium offered to induce people to do something, for example to enlist into the public service or to encourage some branch of industry.

bouquet *n* a bunch of flowers; something resembling a bunch of flowers; an agreeable aromatic odour, such as that of the finer wines.

bouquet garni *n* (*pl* **bouquets garnis**) a bunch of herbs wrapped together and used as flavouring in cooking.

bourgeois *n* a member of the middle class.—*adj* conventional; without imagination.

bourgeoisie *n* the middle classes of a country, especially those dependent on trade.

Bourse *n* a stock exchange, especially in Paris.

bout *n* a period spent in some activity; a trial; a set-to; a contest.

boutique *n* a small fashionable shop, usually selling women's clothes or gifts.

bovine *adj* pertaining to cattle; stolid; dull.—*n* an ox, cow, etc.

bovine spongiform encephalopathy *n* a fatal infectious degenerative brain disease of cattle, originally caused by cattle feed made from the remains of sheep infected with scrapie—also known as **BSE** and **mad cow disease**.

bow[1] *vt* to make crooked or curved, to bend; to bend or incline, as the head or the body, in token of respect or civility; to bend or cause to yield; to subdue; to make a bow to (*to bow a person out*, etc).—*vi* to bend in token of reverence, respect or civility; to be bent or inflected; to curve.—*n* an inclination of the head or a bending of the body in token of reverence, respect or submission.

bow[2] *n* (*naut*) the forward, rounded part of a ship.

bow[3] *n* a weapon made of a strip of wood or other flexible material, which, being bent by means of a string fastened to its two ends, can discharge an arrow placed endwise on the string by the latter being drawn back and suddenly let go; anything bent or in the form of a curve, as the rainbow; an implement strung with horsehair, by means of which the tone is produced from instruments of the violin kind; an ornamental knot of ribbon or other material.

bowdlerize *vt* (**bowdlerized, bowdlerizing**) to abbreviate or expunge texts of objectionable matter on moral grounds.

bowel *n* the intestines; the interior part of anything (*the bowels of the earth*).

bower *n* a shelter made with boughs or twining plants; an arbour; a shady recess.

bouquet

bow

bowknot *n* a decorative slipknot made with ribbon or other material.

bowl[1] *n* a round concave vessel; a large cup with roundish outlines; a goblet; the hollow part of anything, as of a spoon, a pipe, a sports stadium, etc.

bowl[2] *n* a ball of wood or other material used in a game for rolling on a level surface; a ball of wood loaded on one side used in the game of bowls.—*vi* to roll a bowl, as in the games of bowls or bowling; to deliver the ball to be played by the batsman at cricket; to move rapidly and like a ball (*bowl along*).—*vt* to roll in the manner of a bowl.

bow-legged *adj* having crooked or bandy legs.

bowler[1] *n* one who plays at bowls; in cricket, the player who delivers the ball to be played by the batsman.

bowler[2] *n* a stiff round felt hat.

bowline *n* (*naut*) a knot used in making a fixed end loop; a rope fastened near the middle of the perpendicular edge of square sails, and used to keep the weather edge of the sails tight forward towards the bow.

bowling *n* a game played by rolling a ball down a wooden alley to knock down a group of pins.

bowling alley *n* a covered place for the game of bowls or bowling.

bowling green *n* a level piece of green turf kept smooth for bowls.

bowls *n sing* a game for two people or two teams played on a bowling green, the winner being the player whose bowl ends up closest to the jack.

bowman *n* (*pl* **bowmen**) one skilled in the use of the bow; an archer.

bowsprit *n* the large spar or boom projecting over the bow or stem of a vessel.

bow window *n* a window built so as to project in a curve from a wall.

box[1] *n* a case or receptacle of any size and made of any material; a present, now only a Christmas present; a compartment for a small number of people in a theatre; a narrow confined enclosed place; a place of shelter for one or two people on duty, as sentries, signalmen, etc; a small house for sportsmen during the shooting season.—*vt* to enclose, as in a box; to confine.—**to box the compass** to repeat the points of the compass in order; to perform a swift change in politics.

box[2] *n* a blow with the fist.—*vt* to strike with the fist or hand.—*vi* to fight with the fists.

box[3] *n* one of several species of trees or shrubs, the most important being a small evergreen tree with small shining leaves and yielding a hard close-grained wood, and the dwarf variety used as edgings of garden walks.

boxer *n* one who fights with his fists; a pugilist.

Boxing Day *n* the day after Christmas Day when Christmas boxes and presents used to be given.

boxing glove *n* a large padded glove used for sparring.

box office *n* a theatre ticket office; the popularity of a play, film, actor, etc.

boxroom *n* a room in which suitcases, boxes, etc, are stored.

boxwood *n* the fine hard-grained timber of the box.

boy *n* a male child from birth to the age of puberty; a lad; a man lacking in experience, judgment.

boycott *vt* to combine in refusing to work for, to buy from or sell to or to have any dealings with, on account of difference of opinion on social and political questions, etc.

boyfriend *n* a male friend with whom a person is romantically or sexually involved.

boyhood *n* the state of being a boy or of immature age.

boyish *adj* belonging to a boy; pertaining to boyhood ; having the attractive characteristics of a boy.

Boy Scout *n* a member of an organization founded in England in 1908 by Lord Baden-Powell with the object of promoting good citizenship, now called **Scout**.

bra *n* a short form of **brassiere**.

brace *n* a tool or device that holds anything tight, tense, firm or secure, or which supports, binds or strengthens, as a piece of timber placed near and across the angles in the frame of a building, a thick strap which supports a carriage on wheels, a strap passing over a person's shoulders for supporting his trousers; the crank-shaped stock in which boring tools, etc, are held, serving as a lever for turning them, etc; a mark ({ }) used in written or printed matter connecting two or more words or lines; a couple or pair, especially of game.—*vt* (**braced, bracing**) to bind or tie closely; to make tense; to strain up; to increase the tension, tone or vigour of (the nerves, the system); to strengthen; to invigorate; to steady.

brachiopod *n* an animal like a mollusc with two spirally coiled armlike appendages, one on each side of the mouth.

bracelet *n* an ornament encircling the wrist.

bracer *n* one who or that which braces; alcohol taken as a tonic.

brachycephalic *adj* (of a head) having a diameter from side to side not much less than that from front to back.

bracing *adj* giving vigour or tone to the bodily system; invigorating.

bracken *n* a large, tough fern.

bracket *n* a kind of short supporting piece

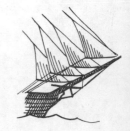

bowsprit

boxers

projecting from a perpendicular surface, either plain or ornamentally carved, as an ornamental projection from the face of a wall to support a statue; a triangular wooden support for a shelf, etc; an ornamental piece supporting a hammer beam; one of two projecting pieces attached to a wall, beam, etc, for carrying or supporting a line of shafting; printing, one of two marks [] or (), used to enclose a reference, note or explanation, to indicate an interpolation, rectify a mistake, etc; a gas pipe projecting from a wall, usually ornamental.—*vt* to furnish with a bracket or with brackets; (*print*) to place within brackets; to connect by brackets.

brackish *adj* possessing a salt or somewhat salt taste; salt in a moderate degree (applied to water).

bract *n* (*bot*) a modified leaf differing from other leaves in shape or colour, and generally situated on the peduncle near the flower.

brad *n* a kind of nail with little or no head .

bradawl *n* an awl to make holes for brads or other nails.

brae *n* (*Scots*) a hill; a sloping bank.

brag *vi* (**bragged, bragging**) to use boastful language; to boast; to vaunt; to swagger; to bluster.—*n* a boast or boasting; the thing boasted of; a game at cards (so called because one player brags he or she has a better hand than the others, staking a sum of money on the issue).

braggart *n* a boaster; a vain fellow.

Brahman *n* among the Hindus a member of the sacred or sacerdotal caste; a member of the highest Hindu caste.

Brahmanism *n* the religion or system of doctrines of the Brahmans.

braid *vt* to weave or intertwine, as hair, by forming three or more strands into one; to plait.—*n* a narrow textile band formed by plaiting or weaving several strands of silk, cotton, woollen, etc, together; a plait or plaited tress of hair.

braiding *n* braid, or trimming made of braid collectively.

brail *n* (*naut*) a rope attached to a fore-and-aft sail, or a jib to assist in taking in the sail.—*vt* to haul in by means of the brails (followed by *up*).

Braille *n* a system of reading with raised letters for the blind.

brain *n* the soft whitish mass enclosed in the skull in humans and other vertebrate animals, forming the centre of the nervous system and the seat of consciousness and volition, and in which the nerves and spinal marrow terminate; the cerebrum (sometimes used to include also the cerebellum); the understanding.—*vt* to dash out the brains of; to kill by beating out the brains.

braid

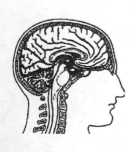
brain

brain death *n* the irreversible cessation of brain activity but not of the heartbeat, widely accepted as a criterion of death.

brain drain *n* the loss of highly skilled scientists, academics, etc, through emigration.

brainless *adj* without understanding or judgment; silly; stupid.

brainwashing *n* the changing of a person's ideas or beliefs by physical of mental conditioning, usually over a long period.

brainwave *n* an electrical impulse in the brain; (*colloq*) a bright idea.

brainy *adj* provided with brains; intellectual.

braise *vt* to fry (meat) lightly and stew slowly with herbs, spices and vegetables in a closely covered pan.

brake[1] *n* an instrument or machine to break flax or hemp; a large heavy harrow for breaking clods; a kind of wagon; an appliance used to stop or retard the motion of a machine or vehicle (often plural).

brake[2] *n* a fern; bracken; a place overgrown with brushwood, shrubs and brambles; a thicket.

bramble *n* a prickly trailing shrub of the rose family growing in hedges and waste places and bearing a black berry; the berry itself; the blackberry.

brambling *n* a finch inhabiting Britain, very like the chaffinch but larger.

bran *n* the outer coat of wheat, rye or other starchy grain, separated from the flour by grinding.

branch *n* a portion of a tree, shrub or other plant springing from the stem or from a part ultimately supported by the stem; a bough; a shoot; something resembling a branch; an offshoot or part extending from the main body of a thing; any member or part of a body or system; a department, section or subdivision; a line of family descent, as distinct from some other line or lines from the same stock.—*vi* to spread in branches; to send out branches, as a plant; to divide into separate parts or subdivisions; to diverge (*a road branches off*); to ramify.

branchia *n* (*pl* **branchiae**) one of the respiratory organs of fishes, etc; a gill.

branchial *adj* relating to the branchiae or gills; performed by means of branchiae.

branchiopod *n* any of an order of crustaceans, so called because their branchiae are situated on the feet, as in the waterfleas.

brand *n* a piece of wood burning or partly burned; a mark made by burning with a hot iron or by other means, as on sheep to indicate the owner, or formerly on criminals to indicate their crime or for identification; a trademark; hence, kind or quality; a mark of infamy; a stigma.—*vt* to burn or impress a mark on with a hot iron, or to distinguish by a similar mark; to fix a mark or character of infamy on; to stigmatize as infamous.

branding iron *n* an iron to brand with.

brandish *vt* to wave, as a weapon; to shake or flourish in triumph or threateningly.

brandling *n* a small red worm used for bait in freshwater fishing.

brand-new *adj* completely new.

brandy *n* a spirituous liquor obtained by the distillation of wine, or of the refuse of the wine press; a name also given to spirit distilled from other liquors or fruit juices.

brant goose *n* same as **brent goose**.

brasier *n* same as **brazier**.

brass *n* a malleable and fusible alloy of copper and zinc of a yellow colour, usually containing about one-third of its weight of zinc; a utensil, ornament or other article made of brass; officers of high rank or leading officials of an organization (often with *top*); (*pl*) musical instruments of the trumpet kind; brazenness or impudence; money.—*vt* to cover or coat with brass.

brass band *n* a company of musicians who perform on brass instruments.

brasserie *n* a bar and restaurant.

brass hat *n* a general or staff officer; (*colloq*) an important official.

brassiere *n* a woman's undergarment for protecting and supporting the breasts.

brassy *adj* resembling or composed of brass; brazen.—*n* a golf club shod with brass (also **brassie**).

brat *n* a child (so called in contempt).

bravado *n* arrogance intended to intimidate or to boost one's courage; a boast; a brag.

brave *adj* courageous; bold; daring; intrepid; high-spirited; valiant; fearless; making a fine display in bearing, dress, or appearance generally; excellent; capital.— *n* a North American Indian.—*vt* (**braved, braving**) to encounter with courage or without being moved; to defy; to dare.

bravely *adv* in a brave manner; courageously; gallantly; prosperously.

bravery *n* the quality of being brave; courage; undaunted spirit; intrepidity; gallantry; splendour; show; bravado.

bravo[1] *interj* well done!

bravo[2] *n* (*pl* **bravoes**) a daring villain; an assassin or murderer for hire.

brawl *vi* to be clamorous or noisy; to quarrel noisily.—*n* a noisy quarrel; loud angry contention; an uproar, row, or squabble.

brawler *n* one who brawls; a noisy person; a wrangler.

brawling *adj* given to indulge in brawls; contentious; quarrelsome.

brawn *n* the flesh of a pig's head and calf's feet cut in pieces and boiled, pickled and pressed into a shape; muscular strength; muscle; the arm.

brawny *adj* having large strong muscles; muscular; fleshy; bulky; strong.

bray[1] *vt* to pound, beat, or grind small.

bray[2] *vi* to utter a harsh cry (said especially of the ass).

braze *vt* (**brazed, brazing**) to solder with hard solder, such as an alloy of brass and zinc; to cover or ornament with brass; to harden; to harden to impudence.

brazen *adj* made of brass; proceeding from brass (*a brazen sound*); impudent; without shame.—*vt* to behave with insolence or effrontery (with an indefinite *it*).—**to brazen out** to persevere in treating with effrontery (with an indefinite *it*).

brazier, brasier *n* an open, metal, portable vessel for burning wood or coal.

brazil nut *n* the seeds of a very lofty tree growing throughout tropical America.

breach *n* the act of breaking in a figurative sense; the act of violating or neglecting some law, contract, promise, obligation or custom; a rupture; a break; a gap (*a breach in a wall*); separation between persons through ill-feeling.

breach of promise *n* the breaking of a promise to marry.

breach of the peace *n* a public disturbance.

bread *n* a food made by moistening and kneading the flour or meal of some species of grain, or that prepared from other plants, and baking it, the dough being often caused to ferment; food or sustenance in general.—*vt* to coat meat, fish, etc, with breadcrumbs before cooking.

breadfruit *n* the fruit of a tree which grows in the islands of the Pacific Ocean, producing a large round fruit used as a substitute for bread.

breadline *n* a queue for free food from a charity or government.—**on the breadline** poverty-stricken, only just able to subsist.

breadth *n* the measure or extent of any plane surface from side to side; width; largeness of mind; liberality; wide intellectual grasp.

breadwinner *n* one who works to support himself or herself and a family.

break *vt* (*pret* **broke**, *pp* **broken** or **broke**, *ppr* **breaking**) to part or divide by force and violence (as a stick, a rope); to sever or interrupt (connection, friendship); to cause to give way (*to break an enemy's lines*); to destroy, weaken, or impair (health, constitution); to subdue; to quell (*to break one's spirit*); to train to obedience; to make tractable (*to break a horse*); to reduce in rank or condition (an officer); to give a superficial wound to so as to lacerate (the skin); to violate, as a contract, law or promise; to stop; to interrupt (sleep); to cause to discontinue (*to break a person of a habit*); to check; to lessen the force of (a fall or a blow); to make a first

brawny

brazier

107

and partial disclosure of; to impart or tell cautiously so as not to startle or shock (*to break unwelcome news*); to destroy the completeness of; to remove a part from (a sum of money, a set of things).—**to break in** to intervene; to train.—**to break in** *or* **into** to enter illegally.—**to break off** to sever by breaking; to put a sudden stop to (a relationship); to discontinue; to leave off (intimacy, a conversation).—**to break up** to dissolve or put an end to (a meeting); to separate; to disband.—**to break the ice** to overcome obstacles and make a beginning; to get over the feeling of restraint caused by a new acquaintanceship.—*vi* to become broken; to burst forth violently (a storm, a deluge); to open spontaneously or by force from within; to burst (a bubble, a tumour); to show the first light of morning; to dawn (*the day, the morning breaks*); to become bankrupt; to decline or fail in health and strength; to fail, change in tone or falter, as the voice; to become known publicly in a sensational way (*the news broke*).—**to break down** to come down by breaking; to fail and be unable to proceed in an undertaking; to collapse in tears; to analyse.—**to break even** to suffer neither profit nor loss (after taking certain action).—**to break loose** to get free by force; to shake off restraint.—**to break off** to part; to become separated; to desist suddenly.—**to break out** to issue forth; to arise or spring up (fire, fever, sedition); to appear in eruptions.—**to break through** to break through an obstruction; to make an important advance or discovery.—**to break up** to dissolve and separate (as a company, a marriage); to disband; to disintegrate; to close for holidays (as a school).—*n* an opening made by force; a rupture; a breach; an interruption of continuity (*five years without a break*); a line in writing or printing, noting a suspension of the sense or a stop in the sentence; a contrivance to check the velocity of a wheeled carriage; a brake; a contrivance for interrupting or changing the direction of electric currents; a large high-set four-wheeled vehicle; a brake; in cricket, a sudden swerve of the ball after pitching, in the direction of the batsman; in billiards, a continuous score of points.

breakwater

breakable *adj* capable of being broken.—*n* a fragile object.

breakage *n* the act of breaking; allowance for what is accidentally broken.

breakaway *n* secession; disassociation.

breakdown *n* a failure; mechanical failure; a collapse, especially a nervous breakdown; an analysis.

breaker *n* the person who or that which breaks anything; a violator or transgressor; a wave broken into foam against the shore,

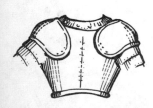

breastplate

a sandbank or a rock near the surface; a small flat water cask.

breakeven *n* the point at which costs are covered but no profit is made.

breakfast *n* the first meal of the day; the meal which enables one to break the fast lasting from the previous day; the food eaten at the first meal.—*vt* to furnish with breakfast.—*vi* to eat breakfast.

break-in *n* the unlawful entering of premises, especially by thieves.

breaking point *n* the point at which stress on a structure or material will cause it to break; the point at which emotional or psychological stress will cause a person to break down.

breakneck *adj* endangering the neck or life; extremely hazardous (especially of speed).

break of day *n* the dawn.

breakthrough *n* the action of breaking through an obstruction; an important advance or discovery.

break-up *n* separation of a mass into parts; a disintegration; a disbandment; separation; divorce.

breakwater *n* any structure or contrivance serving to break the force of waves and protect a harbour or anything exposed to the force of the waves.

bream *n* the name of several freshwater soft-finned fishes belonging to the carp family; the name is also given to some spiny-finned sea fishes resembling the perches.

breast *n* the soft protuberant body adhering to the thorax in females, in which the milk is secreted for the nourishment of infants; the chest; (*fig*) the seat of the affections and emotions; the seat of consciousness, designs and secrets; anything resembling or likened to the breast (*the breast of a hill*).—**to make a clean breast** to make full confession.—*vt* to meet in front boldly or openly; to oppose; to confront.

breastplate *n* a plate worn on the breast as a part of defensive armour.

breastwork *n* (*fort*) a work thrown up breast-high for defence.

breath *n* the air inhaled and expelled in respiration; the power of breathing; life; the state or power of breathing freely (*to be out of breath from violent exercise*); a pause; time to breathe; a single respiration; the time of a single respiration; a very slight breeze; air in gentle motion; an exhalation; an odour; a perfume.—**out of breath** breathless.

Breathalyser *n* a trademark for a device for measuring the amount of alcohol in a person's breath.

breathe *vi* (**breathed, breathing**) to respire; to inspire and expire air; to live; to make a single respiration; to take breath; to rest from action; to pass or blow gently, as air; to exhale, as odour; to emanate; (*fig*) to have life; to be alive.—*vt* to inhale and exhale in respiration; to inspire or infuse (*breathe life into*); to exhale; to send out; to utter; to speak; to whisper (vows, etc).

breathed *adj* (*philol*) uttered with breath as distinguished from voice; surd or mute.

breather *n* a pause during exercise to recover one's breath.

breathing *n* respiration; the act of inhaling and exhaling air; a gentle breeze; (*fig*) a gentle influence or operation; inspiration; soft or secret utterance; time taken to recover breath; a stop; a delay; (*gram*) an aspiration; an aspirate.

breathing space *n* a pause in which to recover, get organized or get going.

breathless *adj* being out of breath; spent with labour or violent action; without breath; dead; incapable of breathing, as with wonder or admiration.

breathtaking *adj* very exciting; very impressive.

breath test *n* examination of the breath of a driver by Breathalyser.

breccia *n* (*geol*) an aggregate composed of angular fragments of the same rock or of different rocks united by a matrix or cement.

breech *n* the lower part of the body behind; the hinder part of anything; the large thick end of a firearm.—*vt* to fit or furnish with a breech.

breech delivery, breech birth *n* the birth of a baby buttocks or feet first.

breeches *npl* trousers covering the hips and thighs.

breechloader *n* a firearm loaded at the breech instead of the muzzle.

breed *vt* (*pret, pp* **bred**, *ppr* **breeding**) to procreate; to engender; to hatch; to cause; to occasion; to produce; to originate (*to breed dissension*); to produce; to yield or give birth to; to bring up; to nurse and foster; to train; to rear, as livestock.—*vi* to bear a child or children; to be fruitful; to be produced; to take rise (*dissensions breed among them*); to engage in rearing livestock.—*n* a race or progeny from the same parents or stock; kind or sort in a general sense.

breeder *n* one who breeds, procreates, or produces young; one who or that which rears or brings up; one who or that which produces, causes, brings about; one who takes care to raise a particular breed or breeds, as of horses or cattle.

breeder reactor *n* a nuclear reactor that produces more fissile material than it consumes.

breeding *n* the act of generating or producing; the rearing of cattle or livestock of different kinds; upbringing; nurture; edu-

cation; deportment or behaviour in social life; manners, especially good manners.

breeze *n* a wind, generally a light or not very strong wind.

breeze block *n* a lightweight building brick made mainly of the ashes of coal and coke, bonded with cement.

breezy *adj* fanned with gentle winds or breezes; subject to frequent breezes; vivacious; nonchalant; light-hearted.

Bren gun *n* a light machine gun, air-cooled and capable of firing 120 rounds (or four magazines) a minute with accuracy.

brent goose, brant goose *n* a species of goose much smaller than the common goose which breeds in the far north but migrates for the winter as low down as the middle of France.

Breton *adj* relating to Brittany or the language of its people.—*n* the native language of Brittany.

breve *n* (*mus*) a note or character of time equivalent to two semibreves or four minims; (*print*) a mark (ˇ) used to indicate that the syllable over which it is placed is short.

brevet *n* a commission to an officer which entitles him temporarily to a rank in the army above that which he holds without conferring corresponding advance in pay.—*adj* conferred by brevet; honorary, nominal.—*vt* (**brevetted, brevetting**) to confer brevet rank on.

breviary *n* (*RC Church*) a book containing the daily offices which all clerics are bound to read.

brevity *n* the state or character of being brief; shortness; conciseness; fewness of words.

brew *vt* to prepare, as beer, ale or other similar liquor, from malt or other materials, by steeping, boiling and fermentation; to mingle; to mix; to infuse tea; to contrive; to plot.—*vi* to perform the business of brewing or making beer; to be mixing, forming, or collecting (*a storm brews*).—*n* the mixture formed by brewing.

brewer *n* one who brews; usually beer.

brewery *n* the establishment where brewing is carried on.

briar *n* same as **brier**.

bribable *adj* capable of being bribed; liable to be bribed.

bribe *n* a price, reward, gift, or favour bestowed or promised with a view to pervert the judgment or corrupt the conduct.—*vt* (**bribed, bribing**) to induce to a certain course of action, especially a wrong course, by the gift or offer of something valued; to gain over by a bribe.—*vi* to practise bribery; to give a bribe to a person.

bribery *n* the act or practice of giving or taking a bribe or bribes; the giving or re-

brent goose

ceiving of money by which one's conduct in some public capacity is influenced.

bric-à-brac *n* a collection of objects having a certain interest or value from their rarity, antiquity, etc.

brick *n* a block used in building made principally of clay moistened and made fine by kneading, formed usually into a rectangular shape in a mould and hardened by being burned in a kiln; bricks collectively or describing the material of which any structure is composed; a mass or object resembling a brick; (*colloq*) a good person.—*adj* made of brick; resembling brick.—*vt* to lay or pave with bricks, or to surround, close or wall in with bricks.

brickbat *n* a piece or fragment of a brick; a critical remark.

bricklayer *n* a person whose occupation is to build with bricks.

bridal *adj* relating to a bride or to a wedding.

bride *n* a woman newly married, or on the eve of being married.

bridegroom *n* a man newly married, or just about to be married.

bridesmaid *n* a woman or girl who attends on or accompanies a bride at her wedding.

bride and bridegroom

bridge[1] *n* any structure of wood, stone, brick, steel, etc, raised over a river, pond lake, road, valley, etc, for convenient passage; the part of a stringed instrument over which the strings are stretched and by which they are raised above the sounding board; a raised platform extending over and across part of a ship's deck, for the captain, etc; the upper and bony part of the nose.—*vt* (**bridged, bridging**) to build a bridge or bridges on or over; to make a bridge or bridges for (a road); (*fig*) to find a way of overcoming or getting over (generally with *over*, as *to bridge over a difficulty*).

bridge[2] *n* a game of cards resembling whist: in the variety called *auction bridge*, the declaration goes to the player engaging to score the highest number of points; in the variety of auction bridge called *contract*, only tricks contracted for are scored.

bridgehead *n* a defensive work covering the end of a bridge nearest the enemy; a foothold in enemy territory.

bridle *n* the gear or harness fitted to the head of a horse by which it is governed and restrained; a restraint; a curb; a check.—*vt* (**bridled, bridling**) to put a bridle on; to restrain, guide or govern; to check, curb or control.—*vi* to hold the head up and backwards; to assume a lofty manner so as to assert one's dignity or express indignation; to toss the head (generally with *up*).

bridle

bridle path *n* a path which can be travelled on horseback.

brief *adj* short in duration; lasting a short time; short in expression; using few words; concise; succinct.—**in brief** in few words; in short.—*n* an abridged relation of the facts of a litigated case drawn up for the instruction of an advocate or barrister in conducting proceedings in a court of justice; a formal letter from the pope on some matter of discipline.—*vt* to furnish (a barrister) with a brief.

briefly *adv* in a brief manner; concisely; in few words.

brier, briar *n* a prickly plant or shrub in general; the sweetbrier and the wild brier, species of the rose; the wild rose.

brig *n* a vessel with two masts, square-rigged nearly like a ship's mainmast and foremast.

brigade *n* a party or division of troops, consisting of several regiments, squadrons, or battalions; a body of individuals organized, generally wearing a uniform, and acting under authority (*a fire brigade*).—*vt* (**brigaded, brigading**) to form into brigade or into brigades.

brigade major *n* the staff officer (usually a captain in rank) who assists a brigadier in the management and ordering of his brigade.

brigadier *n* the officer who commands a brigade.

brigand *n* a robber; a freebooter; especially one of those robbers who live in gangs in secret retreats in mountains or forests.

brigandage *n* the life and practices of a brigand.

brigantine *n* a light sailing vessel formerly much used by corsairs; a two-masted vessel partly square-rigged and resembling a brig.

bright *adj* radiating or reflecting light; blazing with light; brilliant; shining; luminous; resplendent; sparkling; illustrious; glorious; quick in wit; witty; clever; not dull; lively; vivacious; animated; cheerful.

brighten *vt* to make bright or brighter; to shed light on; to make to shine; to cheer; make lively or cheerful; to heighten the splendour of; to add lustre to; to make acute or witty; to sharpen the faculties of.—*vi* to grow bright or more bright; to clear up; to become less dark or gloomy.

Bright's disease *n* granular kidney degeneration.

brill *n* a flat fish resembling the turbot but inferior to it both in size and quality.

brilliance, brilliancy *n* great brightness; splendour; lustre; outstanding intelligence.

brilliant *adj* sparkling or gleaming with lustre; glittering; bright; distinguished by such qualities as command admiration; splendid; shining (*a brilliant achievement, a brilliant writer*).—*n* a diamond of the finest cut, formed into faces and facets so as to reflect and refract the light in the most vivid manner possible; (*print*) a very small type, a size less than diamond.

brim *n* the brink, edge or margin of a river or sheet of water; the upper edge of anything hollow, as a cup; a projecting edge, border or rim round anything hollow, as a hat.—*vt* (**brimmed, brimming**) to fill to the brim, upper edge or top; to furnish with a brim, as a hat.—*vi* to be full to the brim; to be full to overflowing.—**to brim over** to run over the brim; to be so full as to overflow.

brimful *adj* full to the top; completely full.

brimstone *n* sulphur.

brimstone butterfly *n* a species of butterfly, so called from its yellow colour.

brindled *adj* of a grey or tawny colour with bars or streaks of a darker hue.

brine *n* water saturated or strongly impregnated with salt, like the ocean; salt water used in pickling food.

bring *vt* (*pret*, *pp* **brought**, *ppr* **bringing**) to bear or convey from a distant to a nearer place, or to a person; to fetch; to carry; to make to come (honour, wisdom, strength, sleep); to procure; to conduct or attend in going; to accompany; to change in state or condition (*bring to nought*, etc); to persuade (*bring to reason, to terms*).—**to bring about** to effect; to accomplish.—**to bring forth** to produce, as young or fruit; to cause.—**to bring forward** to produce to view or notice (*bring forward arguments*).—**to bring in** to introduce; to supply; to furnish (income, rent).—**to bring over** to convey over; to convert by persuasion or other means; to cause to change sides or an opinion.—**to bring (a ship) to** to check the course of (a ship) by making the sails counteract each other and keep her nearly stationary.—**to bring to light** to reveal.—**to bring to mind** to recall what has been forgotten.—**to bring to pass** to effect.—**to bring up** to nurse, feed and tend; to rear; to educate; to introduce to notice (*to bring up a subject*); to cause to advance near (troops); to cause to stop (a horse); to pull up.

brink *n* the edge, margin or border of a steep place, as of a precipice or the bank of a river; verge; close proximity to danger.

briny *adj* consisting of or resembling brine; of the nature of brine; salt.—*n* the sea.

brisk *adj* lively; active; nimble; sprightly; vivacious; effervescing vigorously; sparkling (liquor); burning freely; rapid; quick (movement, pace).

brisket *n* the breast of an animal, or that part of the breast that lies next to the ribs; the meat of this part.

briskly *adv* in a brisk manner; actively; vigorously; with life and spirit.

bristle *n* one of the stiff, coarse, glossy hairs as of the pig, especially one growing on the back; any similar stiff roundish hair as of a brush.—*vi* (**bristled, bristling**) to rise up or stand on end like bristles; to show anger, resentment or defiance (generally followed by *up*).

bristly *adj* thickset with bristles or with hairs like bristles; rough; resembling a bristle or bristles.

Brit *n* (*colloq*) a British person.

Britannia metal *n* a metallic compound or alloy of tin with a little copper and antimony.

Britannic *adj* pertaining to Britain.

British *adj* pertaining to Great Britain, its inhabitants and language.

Briton *n* a native of Britain.

brittle *adj* easily broken, or easily breaking; fragile; not tough or tenacious.

broach *n* a spit; a spire, especially a spire springing directly from a tower; a general name for all tapered boring bits or drills.—*vt* to open for the first time in order to use; to tap; to pierce, as a cask in order to draw the liquor; to begin conversation or discussion about; to open up (a topic or subject).—**to broach to** (*naut*) to incline suddenly to windward so as to lay the sails aback and expose the vessel to the danger of oversetting.

broad *adj* having extent from side to side, as distinguished from *long*, or extended from end to end; having breadth; having a great extent from side to side, as opposed to *narrow*; wide; extensive; vast; (*fig*) not limited or narrow; liberal; comprehensive; enlarged; widely diffused; open; full (*broad daylight*); plain or unmistakable; free; unrestrained (*broad humour*); somewhat coarse or unpolished; indelicate; indecent; bold; unreserved; characterized by vigour, boldness, or freedom of style, as in art, so that strong and striking effects or impressions are produced by simple unelaborate means.—*n* (*sl*) a woman; an area of land flooded by a river.

broad arrow *n* a stamp resembling the barbed head of an arrow formerly put on prison clothing, etc, belonging to the British government.

broadcast *vt* to scatter (seed); to make known widely; to transmit on radio or television.—*vi* to transmit on radio or television.—*n* a programme on radio or television.

Broad Church *n* a section of the Church of England contrasted with the High Church and the Low Church; a section of any church holding moderate or not very rigid views.

broadcloth *n* a kind of fine woollen cloth woven about twice the usual breadth and dyed in the piece.

broad arrow

broaden *vt* to make broad or broader; to increase the width of; to render more comprehensive, extensive, or open.—*vi* to become broad or broader.

broadly *adv* in a broad manner; widely; comprehensively; fully; openly; plainly.

broad-minded *adj* tolerant; liberal in outlook.

Broads *npl* wide spaces of water formed on the Norfolk coast by the expansion of a river.

broadside *n* the side of a ship above the water from the bow to the quarter; a simultaneous discharge of all the guns on one side of a ship; a strong verbal attack; a sheet of paper, one side of which is covered by printed matter often of a popular character.

broadsword *n* a sword with a broad blade and cutting edges, formerly the national weapon of the Highlanders.

Brobdingnagian *adj* gigantic, like an inhabitant of the fabled region of Brobdingnag in Swift's *Gulliver's Travels*.

brocade *n* silk material variegated with gold and silver or having raised flowers, foliage and other ornaments.

broccoli *n* one of the many varieties of the common cabbage closely resembling the cauliflower.

brooch

brochure *n* a pamphlet; a booklet.

brock *n* a badger.

brogue *n* a kind of shoe made of raw or half-tanned leather, of one entire piece; a stout, coarse shoe; a dialectical manner of pronunciation, especially the pronunciation peculiar to the Irish.

broil *vt* to grill; to subject to a strong heat.—*vi* to be subjected to the action of heat; to be greatly heated or to sweat with heat.

broiler *n* a grill, pan, etc, for broiling; a young chicken for roasting.

broke *adj* bankrupt, short of money.

broken *adj* parted by violence; separated into fragments, as by a blow; not entire; fractional, as numbers; humble; contrite; interrupted by sobs or imperfect utterance.

broker *n* an agent who buys and sells goods or shares or transacts other business for others, being generally paid at a rate per cent on the value of the transaction, such as shipbrokers, stockbrokers, etc; one who deals in second-hand household goods, clothes, etc.

broom

brokerage *n* the fee, reward or commission given or charged for transacting business as a broker; the business or employment of a broker.

brolly *n* (*colloq*) an umbrella.

bromate *n* a salt formed of bromic acid.

bromic acid *n* a compound of bromine and oxygen.

bromide *n* a compound formed by bromine with another element; a platitude.

bromine *n* a simple non-metallic element much resembling chlorine and iodine; at common temperatures it is a very dark reddish liquid of a powerful and suffocating odour and emitting red vapour.

bronchi *pl* of **bronchus**.

bronchia *npl* (*sing* **bronchium**) the two tubes with their ramifications arising from the bifurcation of the windpipe in the lungs and conveying air to the latter; the bronchi.

bronchial *adj* belonging to the bronchia.

bronchial tubes *npl* the ramifications of the bronchia, terminating in the bronchial cells, or air cells of the lungs.

bronchiole *n* a fine, thin-walled extension of a bronchus.

bronchitis *n* an inflammation of the lining membrane of the bronchi or bronchia.

bronchus *n* (*pl* **bronchi**) one of the two principal branches of the windpipe.

bronze *n* a compound or alloy of from 2 to 20 parts of copper to 1 of tin, to which other metallic substances are sometimes added, especially zinc, used for statues, bells, coins, etc; any statue, bust, urn, medal or other work of art cast in bronze; a brown colour resembling bronze.—*vt* (**bronzed, bronzing**) to give the appearance or colour of bronze to, by covering with bronze leaf, copper dust, etc; to make brown or tan, as the skin by exposure to the sun.

brooch *n* an ornamental pin or clasp.

brood *n* offspring; progeny; the young birds hatched at once; that which is bred or produced.—*vi* to sit on eggs or on young, as a hen for the purpose of hatching, warming or protecting them; hence, to remain steadfastly settled over something; to have the mind dwelling for a long time uninterruptedly on a subject (with *on* or *over*).—*vt* to sit over and cover.

brooding *adj* pondering; disposed to ponder or think deeply (*a brooding disposition*).

broody *adj* contemplative; moody; (*colloq*) wanting to have a baby.

brook[1] *n* a small natural stream of water.

brook[2] *vt* to bear; to endure; to support.

broom *n* a pod-bearing shrub growing abundantly on sandy pastures and heaths; a brush with a long handle for sweeping floors.

broomstick *n* the handle of a broom.

brose *n* a Scottish dish made by pouring boiling liquid on oatmeal or other meal and stirring.

broth *n* a soup in which meat is boiled, usually with vegetables.

brothel *n* a house of prostitution.

brother *n* (*pl* **brothers** *or* **brethren**) a human male born of the same father and mother; a male born of the same father or mother, a half-brother; a relation or kinsman; an associate; one of the same profession, occupation, etc; a fellow creature; a member of a religious order; one that resembles another in manners or disposition.

brotherhood *n* the state of being a brother or brotherly; an association of men for any purpose; a class of individuals of the same kind, profession or occupation; a fraternity.

brotherly *adj* pertaining to brothers; such as is natural for brothers; becoming brothers (*brotherly love*).

brother-in-law *n* (*pl* **brothers-in-law**) the brother of one's husband or wife; also, a sister's husband.

brougham *n* a one-horse close carriage, either two- or four-wheeled and adapted to carry either two or four persons.

brow *n* the prominent ridge over the eye; the arch of hair over the eye; the eyebrow; the forehead; the edge of a steep place; the upper portion of a slope.

browbeat *vt* (*pret* **browbeat**, *pp* **browbeaten**, *ppr* **browbeating**) to bully or domineer.

brown *adj* of a dark or dusky colour, inclining to redness.—*n* a dark colour inclining to red or yellow of various degrees of depth, and resulting from a mixture of red, black and yellow.—*vt* to make brown or dusky; to give a brown colour to; to make food brown by cooking.—*vi* to become brown.

brown bread *n* wheaten bread made from unbolted flour which includes the bran and hence is of a brown colour.

brownie *n* in folklore, a household servant of a fairy or goblin nature; a rich, flat chocolate cake.

Brownie Guide *n* a junior Girl Guide between the ages of 8 and 11.

browning *n* the act of making brown; a preparation for colouring and flavouring meat, gravy, etc.

Browning *n* a make of automatic pistol.

brown study *n* a fit of mental abstraction or meditation; a reverie.

browse *vt* (**browsed, browsing**) to feed on (said of cattle, deer, etc); to pasture; to graze.—*vi* to feed on pasture or on the leaves, shoots, etc, of shrubs and trees.

brucellosis *n* an infectious disease of livestock, especially cattle, that can be passed to human beings.

bruin *n* a name given to the bear.

bruise *vt* (**bruised, bruising**) to injure by a blow without laceration but usually with discoloration; to contuse; to crush by beating or pounding; to pound; to crush, as drugs or articles of food; to make a dent or dint in.—*vi* to fight with the fists; to box.—*n* a contusion; a hurt on the flesh of animals, on plants or other bodies, with a blunt or heavy object.

bruiser *n* a strong, hefty person; a pugilist, boxer, or prizefighter.

bruit *n* something noised abroad; report; rumour; fame.—*vt* to announce with noise; to report; to noise abroad.

brunette *n* a woman with a brown or dark hair.

brunt *n* the main and severest shock of a battle, struggle or blow; the hardest part (*he bears the brunt of the work*).

brush *n* an instrument made of bristles or wires, etc, bound together, used for various purposes, as for dressing the hair, removing dust from clothes, etc, laying on colours, paint, etc; the small trees and shrubs of a wood, or a thicket of small trees; the bushy tail of some animals, as the fox, squirrel, etc; the act of using a brush or of applying a brush to; a slight encounter; a skirmish; (*elect*) in a generator, a block of carbon or other suitable material, bearing on a commutator or slip ring and thus collecting the current from the revolving part.—*vt* to sweep or rub with a brush; to strike lightly by passing over the surface; to pass lightly over; to remove by brushing or by lightly passing over.—**to brush aside** to ignore; to regard as of little account.—**to brush off** to remove by brushing; to ignore; to dismiss curtly.—**to brush up** to furbish; to polish; to improve; especially to improve the appearance of; to refresh and revise one's knowledge.—*vi* to move nimbly in haste; to move so lightly as scarcely to be perceived; to move over lightly.

brush-off *n* a curt dismissal.

brushwood *n* small trees or shrubs forming a thicket or coppice; branches of trees cut off.

brusque *adj* abrupt in manner; blunt; rude.

brusqueness *n* a rude, abrupt or blunt manner.

brusquerie *n* brusqueness; a hasty or blunt expression.

Brussels sprout *n* a variety of cabbage, characterized by little clusters of leaves which form miniature heads of cabbage.

brutal *adj* pertaining to a brute; like a brute; savage; cruel; inhuman; brutish.

brutality *n* inhumanity; savageness; gross cruelty; insensibility to pity or shame; a savage, shameless or inhuman act.

brutalize *vt* (**brutalized, brutalizing**) to make brutal, coarse, gross or inhuman; to degrade to the level of a brute.

brutally *adv* in a brutal manner; cruelly; inhumanely; in a coarse, gross or unfeeling manner.

brute *n* a beast; any animal lacking reason; a brutal person; a savage in disposition or manners; a low-bred, unfeeling human being.—*adj* insensible, irrational or unintelligent; not proceeding from or inspired by

brush

Brussels sprout

113

reason and intelligence (*brute force, the brute earth*).

brutish *adj* pertaining to or resembling a brute; uncultured; ignorant; stupid; unfeeling; savage; brutal; gross; carnal; bestial.

bryology *n* the science of mosses, their structure, affinities, classification, etc.

bryony *n* a climbing plant of various species.

byrozoan *n* same as **polyzoan**.

BSE an abbreviation of **bovine spongiform encephalopathy**.

bubble *n* a small vesicle of water or other fluid inflated with air; a blob of air in a fluid; (*fig*) something that lacks firmness or solidity; a vain project; a false show; a delusive or fraudulent scheme of speculation; a fraud.—*vi* (**bubbled, bubbling**) to rise in bubbles, as liquid when boiling or agitated; to run with a gurgling noise; to gurgle.—*vt* to cause to bubble.

bubo *n* (*pl* **buboes**) a tumour or abscess with inflammation affecting certain glands, as in the groin or armpit.

bubonic plague *n* see **plague**.

buccaneer *n* a pirate; a sea robber; one who made depredations on the Spaniards in America in the 17th and 18th centuries.—*vi* to act like or be a buccaneer.

buck *n* the male of the fallow deer, rabbit and hare; a roebuck; formerly, a dashing fellow, a fop; (*sl*) a dollar.—*vti* to rear of quickly (of a horse); to resist.—**to buck up** to make or become more cheerful; to hurry up; to pull oneself together.

bucket *n* a vessel made of wood, leather, metal, or plastic, for drawing or holding water or other liquids; one of the cavities on the circumference of a waterwheel; a scoop; (*comput*) a direct-access storage area from which data can be retrieved; (*colloq*) a wastepaper basket; (*pl*) (*colloq*) large quantities.

bucket seat *n* a single, contoured seat with an adjustable back as in a car, etc.

bucket shop *n* a travel agency that sells air tickets at greatly reduced prices; (*sl*) a dishonest brokerage firm.

buckhound *n* a kind of hound, smaller than the staghound, for hunting bucks or fallow deer.

buckle *n* a fastening or clasp for a strap or band; a bend or bulge.—*vt* (**buckled, buckling**) to fasten with a buckle or buckles; to twist out of shape.—*vi* to bend or bow with pressure.—**to buckle down** to apply oneself diligently.

buckler *n* a kind of shield, a piece of defensive armour formerly worn on the left arm.

buckram *n* a coarse linen cloth stiffened with glue, used as lining and in bookbinding.

buckshot *n* a large kind of shot used for killing deer or other large game.

bucket

Buddhist

buckskin *n* a soft, yellowish or greyish leather originally made of the skin of deer but now of sheepskin; (*pl*) breeches made of this leather.

buckthorn *n* a spiny shrub of various species.

buckwheat *n* a plant bearing small triangular seeds which are ground into meal.

bucolic *adj* pastoral; relating to country affairs; rustic, rural.

bud *n* a small protuberance on the stem or branches of a plant from which leaves or flowers grow; a prominence or outgrowth, as polyps.—*vi* (**budded, budding**) to put forth or produce buds; to sprout; to begin to grow from a stock like a bud, as a horn; (*fig*) to be in an early stage of development.—*vt* to graft by inserting a bud under the bark of another tree.

budding *adj* being at an early stage of development; showing promise.—*n* (*hortic*) a mode of grafting, in which a leaf bud is inserted as a graft instead of a young shoot, the bud sending out a stem.

Buddhism *n* the religious system founded by Buddha.

Buddhist *n* a worshipper of Buddha; one who adheres to the system of Buddhism.

budge[1] *vi* (**budged, budging**) to move off; to stir; to alter one's opinion (usually used negatively).

budge[2] *n* lambskin with the wool dressed outwards.

budgerigar *n* the grass or zebra parakeet; the Australian lovebird.

budget *n* the annual financial statement which the Chancellor of the Exchequer makes in the House of Commons; the sum of money allowed for a particular purpose; any restricted spending allowance.

buff *n* leather prepared from the skin of the buffalo, ox, etc; the colour of buff; a light yellow; the bare skin; a buff stick; (*colloq*) an enthusiast, a fan.—*adj* made of buff; of the colour of buff.—*vt* to clean or shine, originally with leather.

buffalo *n* a ruminant mammal of the ox family somewhat larger than the common ox and with stouter limbs and with horns curving upwards; the name is also applied to the bison of North America.

buffer[1] *n* any apparatus for deadening the concussion between a moving body and the one on which it strikes; an apparatus with powerful springs attached to railway carriages to prevent injury from violent contact; a temporary storage area in a computer.

buffer[2] *n* an old fellow, usually stupid and muddled.

buffer state *n* a state between two rival nations.

buffet[1] *n* the space set apart for refreshments in public places; a meal set out on a table at which people serve themselves and often eat standing up.

buffet² *n* a blow with the fist; a box; a cuff; a slap; hence, hard usage of any kind suggestive of blows (*Fortune's buffets*).—*vt* to strike with the hand or fist; to box; to beat; to beat in contention; to contend against (*buffet the billows*).—*vi* to deal blows or buffets; to make one's way by buffeting.

buffoon *n* a person who amuses others by tricks, gestures, postures and jokes, etc; a clown; a jester.—*vt* to make ridiculous.—*vi* to play the buffoon.—*adj* characteristic of a buffoon.

buffoonery *n* the arts and practices of a buffoon; jests; ridiculous pranks.

buff stick *n* a stick covered with leather, velveteen, etc, and powdered with emery, used in polishing.

bug *n* a name applied to insects of various kinds, as the maybug, the ladybug; particularly applied to an insect which infests the furniture, beds and walls of houses and inflicts severe bites; (*colloq*) a germ or virus; (*sl*) a fault or defect in a machine; (*sl*) a hidden microphone.—*vt* (**bugged, bugging**) (*sl*) to annoy; to irritate; (*sl*) to plant a hidden microphone.

bugbear *n* something real or imaginary that causes terror.

buggy *n* a light one-horse carriage or gig; a lightweight collapsible pushchair for a baby; a small vehicle with a motor used only for one purpose (*golf buggy, beach buggy*).

bugle¹ *n* a hunting horn; a military wind instrument.

bugle² *n* a shining elongated glass bead, usually black, sewn on clothing.

bugler *n* one who plays a bugle; a soldier whose duty is to convey the commands of the officers by sounding a bugle.

bugloss *n* a bristly plant of several species.

buhl *n* unburnished gold, brass or mother-of-pearl worked into complicated and ornamental patterns, used for inlaying; articles ornamented in this style.

build *vi* (**built, building**) to construct and raise, as an edifice or fabric of almost any kind; to construct; to frame; to raise on a support or foundation; to rear; to erect; to settle or establish (fame, hopes, etc); to create; to develop by stages.—*vi* to exercise the art or to practise the business of building; to rest or depend (*to build on another's foundation*); to base; to rely.—*n* construction; make; form; physique.

builder *n* one who builds; one whose occupation is to build, as an architect, shipwright, mason, etc.

building *n* the act of one who builds; the thing built, as a house, a church, etc; fabric; edifice.

built *adj* formed; shaped (of the human body, etc), frequently in composition; constructed of different pieces instead of one, as a mast, beam, etc.

built-in *adj* incorporated as an integral part of a main structure; inherent.

built-up *adj* made higher, stronger, etc, with added parts; having many buildings on it (*a built-up area*).

bulb *n* the rounded part or head of an onion or similar plant; strictly, a modified leaf bud consisting of scales or concentric coats or layers formed on a plant usually beneath the surface of the ground, producing roots from its base and a stem from its centre, as in the onion, lily, hyacinth, etc; any protuberance or expansion resembling a bulb, especially an expansion at the end of a stalk or long and slender body, as in the tube of a thermometer; a glass bulb in an electric light.

bulbous *adj* having or pertaining to bulbs or a bulb; growing from bulbs; resembling a bulb in shape; swelling out.

bulbul *n* the Persian name of the nightingale.

Bulgarian *adj* pertaining to Bulgaria.—*n* a member of the Bulgarian race; the language of the Bulgarians, a Slavonic tongue.

bulge *vi* (**bulged, bulging**) to swell out; to be protuberant.—*n* a swelling or curving out; an increase in population.

bulimia nervosa *n* an eating disorder characterized by alternately overeating or bingeing and vomiting.

bulk *n* magnitude of material substance; whole dimensions; size; the gross; the majority; the main mass or body (*the bulk of a nation*); the whole contents of a ship's hold.—**in bulk** in large quantities; loose or open, that is not packed in bags, boxes, etc.—*vi* to grow large; to swell; to appear large or important.

bulkhead *n* one of several upright partitions dividing the various compartments of a ship, aircraft or vehicle.

bulky *adj* of great bulk or dimensions; of great size; large and unwieldy.

bull¹ *n* the male of any bovine quadruped or animal of the ox or cow kind; a male whale or elephant; in stock-exchange slang, one who operates in order to effect a rise in the price of stock, the opposite of a bear; army discipline; (*colloq*) nonsense.—*adj* male, or of large size; characteristic of a bull, as coarse, loud, obstinate, etc: used in composition (*bull trout, bullhead*, etc).

bull² *n* a gross inconsistency in language; a ludicrous blunder involving a contradiction in terms.

bull³ *n* originally the seal appended to the edicts and briefs of the pope; hence, a letter or edict of the pope, published or trans-

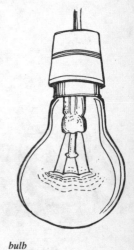

bulb

bull

mitted to the churches over which he is head, containing some decree, order, or decision.

bullace *n* the wild plum.

bull-baiting *n* the practice of baiting or attacking bulls with trained dogs.

bulldog *n* a very strong muscular breed of dog with a large head, broad muzzle, short hair and of great courage and ferocity.

bulldozer *n* a tractor with caterpillar tracks, having a large, broad, blunt metal blade for moving earth and rocks; (*colloq*) an overbearing or bullying person.

bullet *n* a small ball; a projectile of metal discharged from small arms, as rifles, pistols, etc.

bulletin *n* an official report concerning some public event; a news broadcast; a periodical published by a society, organization, etc.

bullfight *n* a combat between armed men and bulls in a closed arena, a popular amusement in Spain.

bullfinch *n* a finch distinguished by the large size of the head, the stoutness of the bill and by having the beak and crown of the head black; it is a British songbird.

bullfrog *n* a large frog living in marshy places in North America, having a loud bass voice which resembles the bellowing of a bull.

bullion *n* uncoined gold or silver in the mass; gold or silver not in the form of current coin; the precious metals in bars, ingots or in any uncoined form; foreign or uncurrent coins; a kind of heavy twisted fringe frequently made of silk and covered with fine gold or silver wire.

bullish *adj* of or resembling a bull; (of stocks and shares) rising or expected to rise; optimistic, hopeful.

bullock *n* a castrated bull; a full-grown steer.

bullring *n* an arena where a bullfight is held.

bullroarer *n* a flat piece of wood with a string passing through a hole in it; when swung round the head it gives out a roaring sound, and is used in religious ceremonies by Australian aborigines.

bull's-eye *n* (*archit*) any circular opening for the admission of light or air; a round piece of thick glass, convex on one side, let into the deck, port or skylight of a vessel to admit light; a small lantern with a lens on one side to concentrate the light in a given direction; the centre of a target of a different colour from the rest of it, and usually round; a shot that hits the bull's eye.

bull terrier *n* a variety of dog, a crossbreed between a bulldog and a terrier.

bull trout *n* a large fish of the salmon family, thicker and clumsier than the salmon.

bulldog

bungalow

bully *n* one who hurts or persecutes the weak or more timid; a blustering, quarrelsome, overbearing person; one who domineers or browbeats.—*vt* to act the bully towards.

bulrush *n* a name given to large rush-like plants of various genera growing in marshes.

bulwark *n* a rampart; a fortification; that which protects or secures against attack; means of protection and safety; the boarding round the sides of a ship above the level of the decks to prevent them being swept by the waves, etc.

bumblebee *n* any of various large bees of which many species are found in Britain.

bumbledom *n* a term applied to fussy official pomposity and incapacity.

bumboat *n* a boat for carrying provisions to a ship at a distance from shore.

bump *vt* to come in violent contact; to give a shock to; to strike; to thump.—*vi* to come in collision; to strike against something.—*n* a swelling or protuberance (especially on the body); (*phren*) one of the natural protuberances on the surface of the skull regarded as indicative of distinct qualities, affections, propensities, etc, of the mind; a shock from a collision.

bumper *n* a cup or glass filled to the brim; something well or completely filled; a shock-absorbing bar fixed to the front and rear of a motor vehicle.—*adj* large; abundant (*a bumper crop*).

bumpkin *n* an awkward, clumsy rustic; a clown or country lout.

bumptious *adj* offensively self-assertive; disposed to quarrel; domineering.

bun *n* a kind of cake; a kind of sweet bread; a bun-shaped coil of hair.

bunch *n* a collection, cluster or tuft of things of the same kind connected, grown or tied together; any cluster or aggregate.—*vi* to cluster, as into bunches.

bundle *n* a number of things bound or rolled into a convenient form for conveyance or handling; a package.—*vt* (**bundled, bundling**) to tie or bind in a bundle or roll (often followed by *up*); to place or dispose of in a hurried unceremonious manner.—**to bundle off** to send a person off in a hurry; to send off unceremoniously.—**to bundle out** to expel summarily.—*vi* to depart in a hurry or unceremoniously (often with *off*).

bung *n* a large cork or stopper for closing the hole in a cask through which it is filled.—*vt* to stop the orifice of with a bung; to close up.

bungalow *n* a single-storeyed house.

bungee jumping *n* the sport of jumping from a height with strong rubber ropes or cables attached to the ankles so that the person jumping springs back before reaching the ground.

bunghole *n* the hole or orifice in a cask through which it is filled and which is closed by a bung.

bungle *vi* (**bungled, bungling**) to perform in a clumsy, awkward or unsuccessful manner.—*vt* to make or mend clumsily; to botch; to manage awkwardly; to perform inefficiently.—*n* a clumsy performance; a piece of awkward or unsuccessful work; a botch.

bungler *n* one who bungles; one who performs without skill.

bungling *adj* prone to bungle; clumsy; characterized by bungling.

bunion *n* an excrescence or knob on some of the joints of the feet, generally at the side of the ball of the great toe.

bunk *n* a wooden box or case, serving as a seat during the day and a bed at night; one of a series of sleeping berths arranged above each other.

bunker *n* a sort of fixed chest or box; a large bin or receptacle (*a coal bunker*); a sandy hollow in golf links as an obstacle; an underground shelter.—*vt* to block, to check.

bunkum *n* talking for talking's sake; bombastic speechmaking; mere words.

bunny *n* a pet name for the rabbit.

bunsen *n* a kind of lamp or gas burner producing an intensely hot flame.

bunt[1] *n* (*naut*) the middle part, cavity, or belly of a sail.—*vi* to swell out.

bunt[2] *n* a disease of wheat; smut.

bunting[1] *n* a cotton material of which the colours or flags and signals of ships are made; a vessel's flags collectively; any string of flags or pennants.

bunting[2] *n* the popular name of a number of seed-eating birds closely allied to finches and sparrows.

buntline *n* (*naut*) one of the ropes fastened on the bottoms of square sails to draw them up to their yards.

buoy *n* a floating object fixed at a certain place to show the position of hazards, as shoals, rocks, etc, or to mark out the course a ship is to follow, etc; a floating object to throw to a person overboard to keep him or her afloat: more particularly called a *lifebuoy*.—*vt* to fix buoys as a direction to mariners.—**to buoy up** to keep afloat in a fluid, as in water or air; (*fig*) to keep from sinking into despondency.

buoyancy *n* the ability to float on the surface of water or in the atmosphere; (*fig*) light-heartedness; cheerfulness; hopefulness; elasticity of spirit.

buoyant *adj* floating; light; having the quality of rising or floating in a fluid; (*fig*) cheerful; hopeful; not easily depressed.

bur, burr *n* a rough prickly covering of the seeds of certain plants, as of the chestnut and burdock; the plant burdock; in engrav-

ing, a slight ridge of metal on the edges of a line which is removed by a scraper; the guttural pronunciation of the letter *r* common in some of the northern counties of England.

burble *vi* (**burbled, burbling**) to make a bubbling sound; to speak confusedly and unintelligently.

burbot *n* a fish of the cod family, found in several English rivers and lakes.

burden[1], **burthen** *n* that which is borne or carried; a load; that which is grievous, wearisome or oppressive; the quantity or number of tons a vessel will carry.—*vt* to load; to lay a heavy load on; to encumber with weight; to oppress.

burden[2] *n* the part in a song which is repeated at the end of each verse; the chorus or refrain; a subject on which one dwells.

burdensome *adj* weighing like a heavy burden; causing uneasiness or fatigue; oppressive; heavy; wearisome.

burdock *n* the popular name of a large rough-leaved perennial plant belonging to the composite family, common on roadsides and waste places and a troublesome weed in cultivated grounds.

bureau *n* (*pl* **bureaux, bureaus**) a desk or writing table with drawers or pigeonholes for papers; an office or place where business is transacted; a department for the transaction of public business; a chest of drawers for clothes, etc.

bureaucracy *n* the system of centralizing the administration of a country through regularly graded series of government officials; such officials collectively.

bureaucrat *n* an official in or a supporter of bureaucracy.

burette *n* a tube used in chemistry for accurately measuring out quantities of fluids.

burgee *n* a flag or pennant which ends in two points.

burgeon *vi* to sprout; to put forth buds; to flourish (often with *forth*).—*n* a bud.

burgess *n* an inhabitant of a borough; a citizen or freeman of a borough.

burgh *n* a corporate town or borough (the Scottish term corresponding to the English *borough*).

burglar *n* one guilty of housebreaking.

burglary *n* the act or crime of housebreaking, with an intent to commit a felony.

burgomaster *n* the chief magistrate of a municipal town in Holland, Flanders, and Germany.

Burgundy *n* a red or white wine from Burgundy, in France.

burial *n* the act of burying, especially the act of burying a deceased person; interment; the act of depositing a dead body in the earth, a tomb or in the water.

buried *adj* interred; hidden by the lapse of time; forgotten.

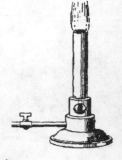

bunsen

buoy

117

burin *n* an instrument for engraving made of tempered steel.

burlesque *adj* tending to excite laughter by ludicrous images or by a contrast between the subject and the manner of treating it.—*n* a literary composition which exhibits a contrast between the subject and the manner of treating it so as to excite laughter or ridicule; travesty; caricature; a dramatic extravaganza; a ludicrous or debasing caricature of any kind; a gross perversion.—*vt* (**burlesqued, burlesquing**) to make ridiculous by burlesque representation; to turn into a burlesque.

burly *adj* great in bodily size; bulky; stout.

Burmese *adj* of or pertaining to Burma.—*n* an inhabitant or inhabitants of Burma; the language of the people of Burma.

burn[1] *vt* (**burned** *or* **burnt, burning**) to consume with fire; to reduce to ashes; to injure by fire; to scorch; to act on with fire; to expose to the action of fire; to affect with a burning sensation; to apply a cautery to; to cauterize.—*vi* to be on fire; to flame; to suffer from or be injured by an excess of heat; to shine; to sparkle; to glow; to gleam; to be inflamed with passion or desire; to be affected with strong emotion; to rage; to be affected with a sensation of heat (*the cheeks burn*).—**to burn off** to clear ground by burning all vegetation; to get rid of (surplus gas, energy) by burning or using up.—**to burn out** (of a fire) to go out; (of a person) to lose efficiency through exhaustion, excess or overwork.—*n* a hurt or injury of the flesh caused by the action of fire.

burn[2] *n* a rivulet; a brook.

burner *n* the part of a lamp, stove, etc, from which the flame issues; the jet piece from which a gas flame issues.

burning *adj* much heated; flaming; scorching; vehement; powerful; causing excitement, ardour, or enthusiasm; crucial (*a burning question*).

burning glass *n* a double-convex lens of glass which, when exposed to the direct rays of the sun, collects them into a focus, where an intense heat is produced so that combustible matter may be set on fire.

burnish *vt* to cause to glow or become resplendent; to polish and make shining by friction; to make smooth and lustrous.—*n* lustre; polish.

burnoose, burnous, burnouse *n* a white woollen mantle with a hood, woven in one piece, worn by the Arabs.

burnt sienna *n* earth of Siena burnt to convert it into a fine orange-red pigment.

burr *n* same as **bur**.

burrow *n* a hole in the ground excavated by rabbits and some other animals as a refuge and habitation.—*vi* to make a hole or burrow to lodge in; to work a way into or under something; to lodge in a burrow or in any deep or concealed place; to hide.

bursar *n* a treasurer or cash-keeper of a college or of a monastery; a purser; a student to whom a bursary is paid.

bursarship *n* the office of a bursar.

bursary *n* the treasurer of a college or monastery; an exhibition or scholarship in a Scottish academy or university.

burst *vi* (**burst, bursting**) to fly or break open from internal force and with sudden violence; to suffer a violent disruption; to explode; to become suddenly manifest; to rush (with prepositions, adverbs, and adverbial phrases, as *to burst out, to burst into life*).—*vt* to break or rend by force or violence; to open suddenly (*to burst one's bonds*).—*n* a sudden disruption; a violent rending; a sudden explosion or shooting forth; a volley of shots; a rush; an outburst.

bury *vt* (**buried, burying**) to cover with earth or other matter; to deposit in a grave when dead; to inter; to entomb; to hide; to conceal; to withdraw or conceal in retirement (used reflexively); to hide in oblivion (*to bury injuries*, etc).

bus *n* a motor coach for transporting a number of passengers, often operating on a regular route.

busby *n* a military headdress consisting of a fur hat with a bag, of the same colour as the facings of the regiment, hanging from the top over the right side.

bush[1] *n* a shrub with branches; a thick shrub; a stretch of shrubby vegetation; a district covered with brushwood or shrubs, trees, etc.—**to beat about the bush** to use circumlocution; to dilly-dally.—*vi* to grow thick or bushy.—*vt* to set bushes about; to support with bushes.

bush[2] *n* a lining of harder material let into an orifice (as for an axle) to guard against wearing by friction.—*vt* to furnish with a bush.

bush baby *n* a small tree-dwelling nocturnal lemur from Africa.

bushbuck *n* the name given to several species of South African antelopes.

bushel *n* a dry measure containing 8 gallons or 4 pecks.

bushman *n* (**bushmen**) a woodsman; a settler in the bush or forest districts of Australia, New Zealand.

Bushman *n* (**Bushman, Bushmen**) an Aboriginal of South Africa, near the Cape of Good Hope.

bushranger *n* in Australia, one who took to the 'bush', or woods, and lived by robbery.

bushy *adj* full of bushes; overgrown with shrubs; resembling a bush; thick and spreading, like a bush.

business *n* a matter or affair that engages a person's time, care and attention; occupation; employment; mercantile concerns, or

bus

burnoose

traffic in general; the proper duty; what belongs to one to do; task or object undertaken; a firm; a concern; right of action or interposing; affair; point; matter.

busk *vi* to prepare; to equip; to dress; to entertain in the street.

buskin *n* a kind of half-boot or high shoe covering the foot and leg to the middle of the calf; the high shoe worn by ancient tragic actors; the tragic drama as opposed to comedy.

buss *n* a kiss; a salute with the lips.—*vt* to kiss.

bust *n* a sculptured figure of a person showing only the head, shoulders and breast; the chest or thorax; a woman's bosom.

bustard *n* a bird belonging to the order of the runners, but approaching the waders (the great bustard is the largest European bird).

bustle[1] *vi* (**bustled, bustling**) to display activity with a certain amount of noise or agitation; to be active and stirring.—*n* activity with noise and agitation; stir; hurry-scurry; tumult.

bustle[2] *n* a pad, cushion, or wire framework worn at one time, about 1880, beneath the skirt of a woman's dress, expanding and supporting it behind.

bustling *adj* moving actively with noise or agitation; active; busy; stirring.

busy *adj* employed with constant attention; engaged about something that renders interruption inconvenient; occupied without cessation; constantly in motion; meddling with or prying into the affairs of others; officious; causing or spent in much employment (*a busy day*); (of a painting, design, etc) with much or too much detail.—*vt* (**busied, busying**) to employ with constant attention; to keep engaged; to make or keep busy (often reflexive).

busybody *n* one who officiously meddles in the affairs of others.

but (*originally a prep and still often to be so regarded, though also an adv and frequently a conj*) except; besides; unless (all, *none but one*); save or excepting that; were it not (commonly followed by *that*); only; merely; simply (*I do but jest*); something equivalent to, that . . . not (*who knows but* or *but that he may*); as an adversative conj equivalent to, on the contrary; on the other hand; yet; still; however; nevertheless.

butcher *n* one whose trade is to kill beasts for food; one who deals in meat; one who kills in a cruel or bloody manner.—*vt* to kill or slaughter for food or for market; to murder in a bloody or barbarous manner.

butcherbird *n* a name given to the shrikes.

butchery *n* the business of slaughtering cattle for the market; murder committed with unusual barbarity; great slaughter.

butler *n* a servant or officer in a household whose principal business is to take charge of the liquors, plate, etc; the head servant of a large household.

butt[1] *n* the end or extremity of a thing, particularly the larger end of a thing, as of a piece of timber or of a felled tree; the thick end of a gun, etc; the stub or end of something, as a cigarette; the end of a plank or piece of timber which unites with another endways in a ship's side or bottom; also, the joining of two such pieces; a mark to be shot at; the point where a mark is set or fixed to be shot at; the object of aim; the person at whom ridicule, jests, or contempt is directed; a bound; in rifle practice, the hut, embankment or other protection in which the marker sits.

butt[2] *vti* to strike by thrusting the head against, as a goat or ram; to interpose; to intrude or meddle (with *in*).

butt[3] *n* a large cask; a measure of 126 gallons of wine or 2 hogsheads or 108 gallons of beer.

butter *n* an oily or fatty substance obtained from cream or milk by churning.—*vt* to spread with butter; to flatter grossly (with *up*).

buttercup *n* a name given to several common field plants with bright yellow flowers.

butterfly *n* the common English name of a diurnal insect in its last and fully developed state, having four wings often brightly coloured; (*fig*) a person whose attention is given up to trifles; a showily dressed, vain and giddy person; a swimming stroke; (*pl*) (often *butterflies in the stomach*) nervous tremors.

butterknife *n* a blunt and generally ornamented knife used for cutting butter at table.

buttermilk *n* the milk that remains after the butter is separated from it.

butterscotch *n* a kind of brittle toffee containing brown sugar and butter.

buttery *n* a room for storing wines, liquors and provisions; in some colleges, a room where food is sold to students.

buttock *n* the rump or the protuberant part of a human behind.

button *n* a small round or roundish object of bone, ivory, metal, wood, mother-of-pearl, etc, used for fastening the parts of dress, by being passed into a hole, slit, or loop, or sometimes attached as ornament; something resembling a button; a round knob or protuberance; the small disc at the end of fencing foils, etc; (*pl used as sing*) (*colloq*) a page boy (from the buttons on his jacket).—*vt* to fasten with a button or buttons; to enclose or make secure with buttons.

buttonhole *n* the hole or loop in which a

butterfly

button

button or flower is fastened.—*vt* (**button-holed, buttonholing**) to seize a person by the button or buttonhole and detain him or her in conversation against his or her will.

buttress *n* a projecting support of masonry built on to the exterior of a wall, especially common in churches in the Gothic style; (*fig*) any prop or support (*a buttress of the constitution*).—*vt* to support by a buttress; to prop.

buxom *adj* well-built; plump and healthy (applied especially to women).

buy *vt* (*pret, pp* **bought**, *ppr* **buying**) to acquire by paying a price to the satisfaction of the seller; to purchase, opposed to *sell*; to get, acquire, or procure for any kind of equivalent (*to buy favour with flattery*); to bribe; to corrupt or pervert by paying a consideration.—**to buy off** to release from military service by a payment; to get rid of opposition by paying; to purchase the non-intervention of.

buzz *vi* to make a low humming sound, as that of bees; to whisper.—*vt* to whisper; to spread or report by whispers; to spread secretly.—*n* a continuous humming sound, as of bees; a low whispering hum; a report circulated secretly and cautiously; a general confused conversation.

buzzard *n* a name for several large raptorial birds of the falcon family, with short weak toes.

buzzer *n* (*elect*) an apparatus for producing high-frequency interruptions of current, e.g. the trembler of an induction coil; a device producing a buzzing sound, e.g. as an alternative to a doorbell, etc.

by *prep* near; close to; near along with motion past; through or with, denoting the author, producer, or agent, means, instrument, or cause; according to; by direction, authority, or example of (*by his own account, ten by the clock, a rule to live by*); at the rate of; in the ratio or proportion of (*by the yard, by the dozen*); to the amount or number of (*larger by half, older by ten years*); during the course of; within the compass or period of (*by day*); not later than (*by this time, by two o'clock*).—*adj* side; secondary (used only in composition, as *bypath, by-play, bystreet*, etc.—*adv*

near; in the same place with; at hand; aside (*to stand by, to lay a thing by*); so as to pass (*to run by*); so as to be past or over (*the time went by*).—**by and by** in the near future; soon; presently.—*n* a bye.

bye, by *n* a thing not directly aimed at; something not the immediate object of regard, as, *by the by*, or *by the bye*, that is, by the way, in passing; an odd or side run gained at cricket; the odd man in a game where the players pair off in couples; in golf, the holes remaining after a match is decided.

bygone *adj* past; gone by.

bygones *npl* what is gone by and past.

bylaw, bye-law *n* a local or private law; a law made by an incorporated body, as a railway company, for the regulation of its own affairs, or the affairs entrusted to its care.

bypass *n* a main road built to avoid a town or city; (*coronary bypass*) a surgical operation to redirect blood flow by bypassing a blocked coronary artery using a grafted blood vessel taken, for example, from the patient's leg; a secondary channel or outlet for a liquid or gas flowing through a pipe.—*vt* to go round or avoid; to get round, ignore.

bypath, byroad, bystreet, byway *n* a path, road, street, or way which is secondary to a main road, street, etc; a lesser, private, or obscure way.

by-play *n* action carried on aside, and commonly in dumb show, while the main action proceeds; action not intended to be observed by some of the persons present.

by-product *n* a secondary product; something obtained, as in a manufacturing process, in addition to the principal product or material.

byre *n* a cowhouse.

bystander *n* one who stands by or near; an onlooker or spectator; one present but taking no part in what is going on.

byword *n* a common saying; a proverb; an object of derision.

Byzantine *adj* pertaining to Byzantium, at one time the capital of the Eastern Roman Empire, afterwards Constantinople, its art, architecture and church.

buttress

C

C the third letter in the English alphabet and the second of the consonants, originally having the sound of *k*, now having also the sharp sound of *s* (before *e*, *i* and *y*); (*mus*) the name of the first or key note of the modern normal scale, answering to the *do* of the Italians and the *ut* of the French.

Caaba *n* same as **Kaaba**.

cab *n* a kind of hackney carriage with two or four wheels, drawn by one horse; a taxi; the compartment for the driver in a lorry, railway locomotive, etc.

cabal *n* a number of persons united in some common aim, especially by secret methods.

cabala, cabbala *n* a mystic learning among Jewish rabbis, transmitted by oral tradition, serving for the interpretation of difficult passages of Scripture.

cabalistic *adj* containing an occult meaning.

cabaret *n* a tavern; a restaurant or nightclub in which singing and dancing performances are given; the performances themselves.

cabbage *n* a common vegetable of several varieties, the kinds most cultivated being the common cabbage, the savoy, the broccoli and the cauliflower; the common cabbage forms its leaves into dense rounded heads, the inner leaves being blanched; (*colloq*) a dull, inactive person; one who is severely brain-damaged.

cabby *n* the driver of a cab.

caber *n* in Highland games, a long undressed stem of a tree used for tossing as a feat of strength.

cabin *n* a small room or enclosed place; a cottage; a hut or small house or habitation, especially one that is poorly constructed; an apartment in a ship for officers or passengers.

cabin boy *n* a boy whose duty is to wait on the officers and passengers on board ship.

cabinet *n* a small room or closet; a private room in which consultations are held; hence, the select or secret counsel of a prince or executive government; the collective body of ministers who direct the government of a nation or country, so called from the apartment in which the meetings were originally held; a piece of furniture consisting of a chest or box with drawers and doors.

cabinet-maker *n* a person who makes household furniture, such as cabinets, sideboards, tables, etc.

cable *n* a large strong rope, usually of 3 or 4 strands of hemp, or a chain, such as is used to retain a vessel at anchor; a cablegram; (*archit*) a moulding with its surface cut in imitation of the twisting of a rope; also, a cylindrical moulding in the flute of a column and partly filling it; an insulated cord that carries electric current; a bundle of insulated wires for carrying cablegrams, television signals, etc.—*vt* (**cabled, cabling**) to fasten with a cable; to send a message by electric cable; (*archit*) to fill (the flutes of columns) with cables or cylindrical pieces.

cablegram *n* a message by cable.

cable's length *n* a nautical measure, one-tenth of a sea mile or about 100 fathoms.

cable television *n* television transmission to subscribers by cable.

caboose *n* the cook room or kitchen of a ship; the galley.

cabriolet *n* a one-horse carriage; a cab.

cacao *n* the chocolate tree, a native of the West Indies, with seeds from which cocoa and chocolate are prepared.

cachalot *n* the blunt-headed sperm whale.

cache *n* a secret hiding place for treasure, etc; a store or hoard.

cachet *n* a seal; a distinguishing mark or characteristic; prestige.

cachinnation *n* loud or immoderate laughter.

cachou *n* a sweetmeat generally in the form of a pill, used to sweeten the breath.

cachucha *n* a Spanish dance similar to the bolero; a piece of music for it.

cackle *vi* (**cackled, cackling**) to utter a noisy cry as that made by a goose or a hen; to laugh raucously; to giggle; to prattle.—*n* the broken cry of a goose or hen; raucous laughter; silly prattle.

cab

cacophonous *adj* sounding harshly.

cacophony *n* a disagreeable vocal sound; discord.

cactus *n* (*pl* **cactuses, cacti**) a succulent, spiny and usually leafless shrub of numerous species, natives of tropical America.

cad *n* a dishonourable man, the opposite of a gentleman.

cadaverous *adj* pertaining to a dead body; especially having the appearance or colour of a dead human body; pale; wan; gaunt, haggard.

caddie *n* an attendant at golf links, especially one who carries a golfer's clubs.

caddis *n* the larva of the caddis fly.

caddis fly *n* an insect, the larva or grub of which forms a case of small roots, stalks, stones, shells, etc, and lives underwater until ready to emerge from the pupa state.

caddy *n* a small box for keeping tea.

cadence *n* a decline; a state of falling or sinking, as in the pitch of the voice at the end of a sentence; the general tone or modulation of the voice in reading or reciting; tone; sound; rhythm; measure; (*mus*) a short succession of notes or chords at the close of a musical passage or phrase; also a shake or trill, run or division introduced as an ending or as a means of return to the first subject.

cadenza *n* (*mus*) an embellishment made at the end of a melody, either actually extempore or of an impromptu character; a running passage at the conclusion of a vocal piece.

cadet *n* a younger or youngest son; a junior male member of a noble family; a young person in training for the rank of an officer in the army or navy.

cadge *vti* (**cadging, cadged**) to go about begging; to sponge; to borrow.

cadger *n* a sponger; a persistent borrower.

cadmium *n* a ductile, malleable and fusible metal of a fine white colour with a shade of bluish-grey, resembling that of tin.

caecum *n* (*pl* **caeca**) the blind gut or intestine.

Caesarean section *n* the operation by which the foetus is taken out of the uterus by an incision through the abdomen and uterus, when delivery of a living child is otherwise impossible or difficult (said to be so named because Julius Caesar was brought into the world in this way).

caesium *n* a rare metal originally discovered in mineral waters and so named because its spectrum exhibits two characteristic blue lines.

caesura *n* a pause or division in a verse; a separation, by the ending of a word or by a pause in the sense, of syllables rhythmically connected.

café *n* a coffee house; a small, informal restaurant.

cafetiere *n* a kind of coffee pot in which boiling water is poured over coffee grounds and a plunger with a metal filter is pressed down pushing the grounds to the bottom of the pot.

caffeine *n* a slightly bitter alkaloid found in coffee, tea, etc.

caftan, kaftan *n* a loose, usually full-length garment with long wide sleeves.

cage *n* a box or enclosure, a large part of which consists of lattice work of wood, wicker, wire or iron bars, for confining birds or beasts; a prison; a skeleton framework of various kinds; the framework of a hoisting apparatus, as the framework in which miners ascend and descend the shaft.—*vt* (**caged, caging**) to confine in a cage; to shut up or confine.

cagey *adj* secretive, not giving anything away; wary, cautious.

caginess *n* the quality of being cagey; secretiveness; wariness, caution.

cagoule, kagoule *n* a lightweight loose-fitting outer garment with hood attached, made of waterproof material, often nylon, and worn by walkers, mountaineers etc.

cahoots *npl*: **in cahoots** in league or partnership, usually for an illegal, underhand etc, purpose.

Cainozoic *adj* same as **Cenozoic**.

caique *n* a light skiff used in the Black Sea.

cairn *n* a heap of stones, especially of those conical in form and erected as a gravestone, a landmark or to commemorate some events.

cairngorm *n* a yellow or brown variety of rock crystal, found on Cairngorm and the neighbouring mountains in Scotland.

cairn terrier *n* a small shaggy-coated variety of Scotch terrier.

caisson *n* a kind of floating dock; a watertight box or cylindrical casing used in founding and building structures in water too deep for the cofferdam, such as piers of bridges, quays, etc.

cajole *vt* (**cajoled, cajoling**) to coax or persuade by flattery, specious promises, etc; to wheedle.

cajolery *n* the act of cajoling; coaxing language or tricks.

Cajun *n* a descendant of the French Canadians who settled in Louisiana in America in the eighteenth century.—*adj* relating to the language, music or food of the Cajuns.

cake *n* a mass of fine light dough baked and generally sweetened or flavoured with various ingredients; something made in the form of a cake, as soap or chocolate.— **to take the cake** to complete the victory, to surpass.—*vt* (**caked, caking**) to form into a cake or mass.—*vi* to become formed into a hard mass, as dough in an oven, etc.

calabash *n* a gourd shell dried and sometimes used as a vessel.

cactus

cairn

calamari *n* squid eaten as food.

calamine lotion *n* a soothing liquid made from zinc oxide used on the skin to relieve rashes, sunburn etc.

calamity *n* any great misfortune or cause of misery; a disaster.

calamitous *adj* producing or resulting from calamity; disastrous.

calash *n* a light carriage with very low wheels and a folding top.

calcareous *adj* of the nature of lime; containing lime.

calceolaria *n* any of a number of ornamental herbaceous or shrubby plants, natives of South America.

calcification *n* a changing into lime; the process of changing into a stony substance by the deposition of lime.

calcify *vi* (calcified, calcifying) to become gradually changed into a stony condition by the deposition or secretion of lime.

calcine *vt* (calcined, calcining) to reduce to a powder or to a friable state by the action of heat.—*vi* to be converted into a powder or friable substance by the action of heat.

calcite *n* a term applied to various minerals, including limestone, all the white and most of the coloured marbles, chalk, Iceland spar, etc.

calcium *n* the metallic basis of lime and the most widely diffused of the alkaline metals.

calcium carbide *n* a compound of calcium and carbon made by heating lime and carbon together and used for generating acetylene.

calculable *adj* capable of being calculated or ascertained by calculation.

calculate *vt* (calculated, calculating) to compute; to reckon up; to estimate (value, cost); to make the necessary or usual computations regarding; to make suitable or adapt (*a scheme calculated to do much mischief*).—*vi* to make a computation; to weigh all the circumstances; to deliberate; to suppose, to think.

calculated *adj* deliberate, premeditated.

calculating *adj* having the power or habit of making arithmetical calculations; quick at arithmetical calculations; given to forethought and calculation; deliberate and selfish; scheming (*a calculating disposition*).

calculation *n* the act of calculating; computation; a series of arithmetical processes set down in figures and bringing out a certain result; an estimate formed by comparing the circumstances bearing on the matter in hand.

calculus *n* (pl calculi) a general term for hard concretions of various kinds formed in various parts of the body, the more important being those formed in the gall bladder, called *biliary calculi* or *gall-*

stones, and those formed by a deposition from the urine in the kidney or bladder, called *urinary calculi*; the stone; gravel; a method of computation in the higher branches of mathematics.

Caledonian *adj* pertaining to Caledonia, an ancient name of Scotland; Scottish.—*n* a native of Caledonia, now Scotland; a Scotsman.

calendar *n* a register of the year, in which the months, weeks and days are set down in order, sometimes with the feasts observed by the church, etc; an orderly table or enumeration of persons or things, as a list of criminal cases which stand for trial; a list; a catalogue; a register; a list of scheduled events.

calendar month *n* a solar month reckoned according to the calendar, as distinct from a lunar month.

calender *n* a machine consisting of two or more cylinders revolving so nearly in contact with each other that cloth or paper passing through between them is smoothed or glazed by their pressure.

calends *n* among the Romans the first day of each month.

calenture *n* a kind of fever caused in the tropics, especially on board ship, by exposure to excessive heat.

calf[1] *n* (pl calves) the young of the cow or cattle; the young of the whale, elephant or buffalo; leather made from the skin of a calf.

calf[2] *n* (pl calves) the thick fleshy part of the leg behind and below the knee.

calf

calf love *n* a youthful romantic passion or affection.

calibre *n* the diameter of a body, as of a column or a bullet; usually the diameter of the bore of a firearm; (*fig*) compass or capacity of mind; the extent of one's intellectual endowments; the degree of excellence of a person.

calibre compasses, callipers *npl* compasses made either with arched legs to measure the diameters of cylinders or globular bodies, or with straight legs and points turned outwards to measure the interior diameter or bore of anything.

calico *n* a white or unprinted cotton cloth.

calif *n* same as caliph.

calipash *n* that part of a turtle which belongs to the upper shield, consisting of an edible fatty, gelatinous substance of a dull greenish colour.

calipee, callipee *n* that part of a turtle which belongs to the lower shield, of a light yellow colour and edible.

caliph, calif, kalif, khalif *n* formerly, a title given to a spiritual leader of Islam; a sultan of Turkey.

call *vt* to name; to pronounce the name of; to designate or characterize as; to affirm to

calibre compasses

123

be; to invite or command to come or assemble (a person, a cab, a meeting); to select or appoint, as for an office, duty or employment; to invoke or appeal to; to arouse, as from sleep; to awaken; to proclaim or utter loudly.—**to call names** to use abusive names to.—**to call off** to cancel; not to go ahead with.—**to call to mind** to recollect; to revive in memory.—**to call to the bar** to admit to the rank of barrister or advocate.—**to call up** to summons for military service; to telephone.—*vi* to utter a loud sound or to draw a person's attention by name (often with *to*); to make a short stop or pay a short visit (often followed by *at, for* or *on*).—**to call at** to visit a place in passing; **to call for** (a person or thing) to visit in order to obtain the company of the person to some other place or to get something; to demand, require, claim (*crime calls for punishment*).—**to call on** or **upon** to visit (a person); to demand from or appeal to; to invoke.—*n* a summons or invitation made vocally or by an instrument; a demand; requisition; claim (*the calls of justice* or *humanity*; *calls on one's time*); divine vocation or summons; invitation or request to a clergyman by a congregation to become their minister; a short or passing visit paid to a person; the cry of a bird to its mate or young.

callboy *n* a person who calls actors on to the stage at the proper moment.

callgirl *n* a prostitute, formerly especially one who made appointments by telephone.

calling *n* a vocation; profession; trade.

calligraphy *n* the art of beautiful writing; fair or elegant writing or penmanship.

calliper *n* a brace or support, such as worn to support or straighten a leg; (*pl*) calibre compasses.

callisthenics *n* the art or practice of taking exercise for health, strength or grace of movement.

callous *adj* hardened or thickened from continuous pressure or friction (said of the skin); hard, unfeeling, unsympathetic.

callousness *n* hardness; lack of feeling or sympathy.

callow *adj* immature; inexperienced.

calm *adj* still; not stormy (said of the weather, the sea, etc); not agitated or excited; tranquil and serene of mind or temper.—*n* freedom from motion, agitation or disturbance; stillness; a state or period at sea when there is neither wind nor waves.—*vt* to make calm; to appease, allay or pacify (grief, anger, anxiety, etc); to becalm.—*vi* to become calm or serene.

calmness *n* the state of being calm, quiet or unruffled; stillness.

calomel *n* a preparation of mercury.

Calorgas *n* the trademark of a type of bottled liquefied butane used for lighting, heating and cooking in caravans, tents, boats etc.

caloric *adj* pertaining to hear or calories.

calorie *n* a unit of energy which is the heat required to raise the temperature of one gram of water from 0° to 1° C.

Calorie, kilocalorie, large calorie *n* a unit of heat equivalent to 1000 calories, used to express the heat output of an organism or the energy value of food.

calorific *adj* capable of producing heat; causing heat; heating.

calorimeter *n* an apparatus for measuring absolute quantities of heat.

calumet *n* the North American Indians' pipe of peace.

calumniate *vt* (**calumniated, calumniating**) to speak falsely of; to speak maliciously of; to cast aspersions on; to slander.

calumny *n* false accusation of a crime or offence, knowingly or maliciously made or reported to the injury of another; a defamatory or slanderous report; slander.

Calvary *n* Golgotha, the place where Christ was crucified, west of Jerusalem; a representation of Christ's crucifixion.

calve *vi* (**calved, calving**) to bring forth a calf or calves (used specifically of cows, whales and seals).

Calvinism *n* the theological tenets or doctrines of John Calvin (1509–64), among the distinguishing doctrines of whose system are predestination, original sin, effectual calling and the final perseverance of the saints.

Calvinist *n* a follower of Calvin; one who embraces the theological doctrines of Calvin.

calx *n* (*pl* **calxes, calces**) a metal or mineral which remains after being subjected to violent heat.

calyx *n* (*pl* **calyces, calyxes**) (*bot*) the exterior covering of a flower within the bracts and external to the corolla, which it encloses and supports, and consisting of several whorls of leaves called sepals, either united or distinct, usually of a green colour and of a less delicate texture than the corolla.

calypso (*pl* **calypsos**) *n* a type of music from the West Indies having a strong rhythm and topical lyrics.

cam *n* (*mach*) a projecting part of a wheel or other revolving piece so placed as to give an alternating motion, especially in a rectilinear direction, to another piece (often a rod) that comes in contact with it and is free to move only in a certain direction.

camaraderie *n* mutual good fellowship as comrades.

camber *n* a convexity on an upper surface, as on a road, beam, ship's deck, etc.

124

cambium *n* (*bot*) a substance interspersed between the wood and bark of exogenous trees.

Cambrian *adj* relating or pertaining to Wales or Cambria; (*geol*) of the earliest Palaeozoic period before the Silurian.—*n* a Welshman.

cambric *n* a fine white linen.

camcorder *n* a piece of photographic equipment consisting of a video camera and a recorder in one portable unit.

camel *n* a large hoofed quadruped of the ruminant class, with one or two humps on its back, used in Asia and Africa for carrying burdens and for riding on.

camellia *n* a genus of flowering shrubs belonging to the tea family.

camelopard *n* the giraffe.

cameo *n* a stone or shell composed of several different coloured layers having a subject in relief cut on one or more of the upper layers, an under layer of a different colour forming the ground; a brooch, ring, etc, featuring a head in profile in relief; a short drama or piece of writing; a small part in a play, film, etc, taken by a celebrated actor.

camera *n* a device which records a photographic image by allowing a focused beam of light to fall on a sensitized material, such as film; an apparatus for converting a pattern of light into a pattern of electrical impulses for television transmission.—**in camera** (*law*) privately; in a judge's private room.

camera obscura *n* an apparatus in which the images of external objects received through a double-convex lens are exhibited in their natural colours on a white surface placed at the focus of the lens.

camisole *n* a loose bodice worn by women under their dress.

camomile, chamomile *n* a much-branched, perennial composite herb with daisy-like flowers.

camouflage *n* a method of disguise in which an object assumes the colour, texture, etc, of its surroundings and thus appears part of them; the art of disguising.—*vt* (**camouflaging, camouflaged**) to disguise by means of camouflage.

camp¹ *n* the place where an army or other group is or has been encamped; the collection of tents or other erections for the accommodation of a group, particularly troops in a temporary station; a group of tents or caravans.—*vi* to live in a camp, as an army; to encamp; to live temporarily, as on holiday, in a tent.

camp² *adj* exaggerated, theatrical; artificial; effeminate; homosexual.—**to camp up** to exaggerate; to make theatrical or artificial; to exhibit camp characteristics.

campaign *n* the active operations of an army during the time it keeps the field in one season; a series of organized operations for a particular purpose, as *political campaign, advertising campaign*.—*vi* to take part in or conduct a campaign.

campaigner *n* one who has served in several military campaigns; one who conducts a campaign.

campanile *n* (*archit*) a clock or bell tower.

campanologist *n* one skilled in the art of bell ringing or campanology.

campanology *n* the art or principles of bell ringing; a treatise on the art.

campanula *n* any of the bellflowers, a large genus of herbaceous plants with bell-shaped flowers usually of a blue or white colour.

camp bed *n* a bed made to fold up within a narrow space.

camper *n* one who lives in a tent; a person on a camping holiday; a vehicle equipped with all domestic facilities.

campfire *n* a fire out of doors at a camp; a social gathering around such a fire.

camp follower *n* one who follows or attaches himself or herself to a camp or army without serving; a personal associated with a group without being an active member; a hanger-on.

camphor *n* a whitish translucent essential oil with a bitterish aromatic taste and a strong characteristic smell, found in many plants and sometimes secreted naturally in masses, obtained also by distillation of the wood of the camphor tree and used to repel insects, as a stimulant in medicine, etc.

camphor tree *n* a species of laurel that yields camphor.

campion *n* any of various wild plants of the pink family, the commonest having red or pink flowers.

campsite *n* a place for camping, often with facilities for holiday-makers.

camp stool *n* a stool with crossed legs, so made as to fold up when not used.

campus *n* the grounds of a university or college.

can¹ *vi* (*pret* **could**) (a verb now used only as an auxiliary and in the indicative mood) to be able, physically, mentally, morally, legally, etc; to possess the qualities, qualifications or resources necessary for the attainment of any end or the accomplishment of any purpose, the specific end or purpose being indicated by the verb with which *can* is joined.

can² *n* a metal container such as one in which fruit, meat, etc, are hermetically sealed; the contents of such a container.—**to carry the can** to bear the responsibility or blame for.—*vt* (**canned, canning**) to put into a can (*to can preserved meat, fruit*, etc).

Canaanite *n* an inhabitant of the land of

camel

camera

Canaan; specifically, one of the inhabitants before the return of the Israelites from
Egypt.

Canadian *adj* pertaining to Canada.—*n* an
inhabitant or native of Canada.

canaille *n* the rabble.

canal *n* an artificial watercourse, particularly one constructed for the passage of
boats or ships; (*archit*) a channel; a groove
or a flute; (*anat*) any cylindrical or tubular
cavity in the body through which solids,
liquids or certain organs pass; a duct;
(*zool*) a groove observed in different parts
of certain univalve shells.

canalize *vt* (**canalizing, canalized**) to make
a canal through (*to canalize an isthmus*);
to make like a canal (*to canalize a river*).

canapé *n* a thin piece of bread spread with
one of a variety of foodstuffs such as
cheese, pâté, caviar etc, often served with
drinks at parties.

canard *n* an absurd story; a false rumour.

canary *n* wine made in the Canary Islands;
a singing bird, belonging to the finch family, a native of those islands.

cancan *n* an energetic French dance involving high kicks.

cancel *vt* (**cancelled, cancelling**) to draw
lines across (something written) so as to
deface; to blot out or obliterate; to annul or
destroy (an obligation, a debt); to call off
(an engagement, performance, etc); to balance or compensate for.

cancellation *n* the act of cancelling.

cancer *n* a malignant growth on the body or
on some internal part that grows and
spreads rapidly; a disease, sometimes fatal, involving a malignant growth; a destructive or evil influence.

Cancer *n* a genus of crustaceans, including
some edible species of crabs; one of the
twelve signs of the zodiac, represented by
the form of a crab.

cancerous *adj* like a cancer; having the
qualities of a cancer; virulent.

candela *n* the basic SI unit of luminous intensity.

candelabrum *n* (*pl* **candelabra**) a
branched, highly ornamental candlestick.

candid *adj* honest and frank; outspoken;
fair.

candidate *n* a person who seeks or is put
forward by others for a certain position,
office or honour.

candidature *n* the state of being, or act of
standing as, a candidate.

candle *n* a cylindrical body of tallow, wax,
spermaceti or other fatty material, formed
on a wick and used for a portable light.

Candlemas *n* an ecclesiastical festival held
on the second day of February in honour
of the purification of the Virgin Mary.

candlepower *n* the illuminating power of a
candle or source of light.

candle

cannon

candlestick *n* a holder for a candle.

candour *n* the quality of character of being
candid; frankness.

candy *n* a solid sweet of sugar or molasses,
either alone or in combination with other
substances, to flavour, colour or give it the
desired consistency; confectionery.—*vt*
(**candied, candying**) to conserve with
sugar so as to form a thick mass; to boil in
sugar; to boil down to crystalline form; to
preserve by coating with candy.—*vi* to become encrusted by candied sugar; to become crystallized or congealed.

candyfloss *n* a fluffy kind of sweet made
from coloured spun sugar and usually
eaten on a stick.

candytuft *n* the popular name of a tufted
flower brought from the island of Crete.

cane *n* a term applied to the stems of some
palms, grasses and other plants, such as
the bamboo, rattan and sugar cane; a cane
used as a walking stick.—*vt* (**caned, caning**) to beat with a cane or walking stick;
to furnish or complete with cane (as
chairs).

canine *adj* of or like a dog; of the family of
animals that includes dogs, foxes and
wolves.—*n* a dog or other member of the
same family of animals; in humans, a
pointed tooth next to the incisors.

canister *n* a small box or case, usually of
tin, for tea, coffee, etc; a case containing
shot which bursts on being discharged.

canker *n* a kind of erosive or ulcerous sore
or disease in animals or plants; anything
that insidiously or persistently destroys,
corrupts or irritates.

cannabis *n* a drug obtained from Indian
hemp and smoked or chewed to induce a
sense of euphoria or relaxation.

canned *adj* packed in cans; pre-recorded
(*canned music, canned laughter*)

cannel coal *n* a glistening greyish-black
hard bituminous coal.

cannelloni *npl* tubular rolls of pasta filled
with a savoury mixture of meat or vegetables.

cannibal *n* a human being that eats human
flesh; an animal that eats the flesh of its
own or kindred species.

cannibalism *n* the act or practice of eating
human flesh by mankind; anthropophagy.

cannon *n* (*pl* **cannons** *or* **cannon**) a large
military firearm for throwing shells and
other missiles; a big gun or piece of ordnance; in billiards, the act of hitting one of
the other two balls with one's own so that
the ball flies off and strikes the third ball.
—*vi* to make a cannon at billiards; to fly
off or asunder from the force of collision.

cannonade *n* the act of discharging cannon
or artillery generally.

cannonball *n* a ball or solid projectile to be
thrown from cannon.

cannula, canula *n* a small tube used by surgeons for various purposes.

canny *adj* cautious; prudent; shrewd; thrifty.

canoe *n* a light boat narrow in the beam and propelled by paddles.

canon *n* a law or rule in general; a decree of the Church; the books of the Holy Scriptures universally received as genuine by Christian churches; the catalogue of saints acknowledged in the Roman Catholic Church.

cañon *n* same as **canyon**.

canonical, canonic *adj* pertaining or according to a canon or rule, especially according to ecclesiastical canons or rules; belonging to the canon of Scripture.

canonicals *npl* the dress or habit prescribed by canon to be worn by the clergy when they officiate.

canonization *adj* the act of canonizing a person; the act of ranking a deceased person in the canon of saints.

canonize *vt* (**canonized, canonizing**) to declare a person a saint.

canon law *n* a collection of ecclesiastical constitutions for the regulation of a church; specifically those of the Roman Catholic Church.

canonry *n* the benefice filled by a canon.

canopy *n* a covering fixed at some distance above a throne or a bed; any similar covering; the transparent cover of an aeroplane's cockpit; the tops of trees in a forest; the sky regarded as a covering.—*vt* (**canopied, canopying**) to cover with or as with a canopy.

cant[1] *n* insincere or hypocritical speech; the language or jargon spoken by gypsies, thieves, professional beggars, etc; a kind of slang; the words and phrases peculiar to or characteristic of a sect, party or profession.—*adj* of the nature of cant or slang.

cant[2] *n* an inclination from a perpendicular or horizontal line.—*vt* to cause to assume an inclining position.

cantaloupe *n* a round, ribbed variety of musk melon.

cantankerous *adj* ill-natured; cross; contentious; disputatious.

cantata *n* (*mus*) a short composition in the form of an oratorio set to a religious text.

canteen *n* a cafeteria, originally in a military establishment but now also in a factory, office building, etc; a vessel used by soldiers on the march or in the field for carrying liquid drink; a box containing a set of cutlery.

canter *vi* to move in a moderate gallop.—*n* a moderate gallop.

canticle *n* a song taken from the Bible, e.g. the Magnificat.

cantilever *n* a wooden or iron bracket projecting from a wall, to carry mouldings, eaves, balconies, etc; a long projecting arm to support the roadway of a bridge.

canto *n* (*pl* **cantos**) a part or division of a poem of some length.

canton *n* a distinct or separate portion or district of territory; one of the states of the Swiss republic.

cantonment *n* a permanent military station of a slighter character than barracks; formerly, in India, military towns at some distance from any city.

cantrip *n* a spell; a witch's trick; any mischievous trick.

canula *n* same as **cannula**.

canvas *n* a coarse cloth made of hemp or flax, used for tents, sails of ships, painting on and other purposes; hence sails in general; a painting.—**under canvas** in a tent or tents; (*naut*) with sails spread.

canvasback *n* a sea duck of North America with a distinctively sloped beak.

canvass *vt* to visit or apply to in order to obtain orders for goods, votes or support for a candidate for an office or appointment, etc.—*vi* to seek or go about to solicit votes or interest or to obtain orders.—*n* the act of canvassing; solicitation of votes, orders for goods, etc.

canyon, cañon *n* a long and narrow steep-sided river valley.

caoutchouc *n* raw, untreated rubber.

cap *n* a part of dress made to cover the head, generally of softer material than a hat and without a brim; the summit, top or crown; anything resembling a cap in appearance, position or use; the removable part of a pen, jar, etc; a percussion cap.—*vt* (**capped, capping**) to put a cap on; to cover with a cap or as with a cap; to cover the top or end of; to place a cap on the head of when conferring official distinction, admitting to professional honours, etc; to complete; to consummate; to crown; to follow up with something more remarkable than what has previously been done; to impose an upper limit on.

capability *n* the state or quality of being capable.

capable *adj* susceptible; admitting (with *of*, as *capable of pain, of being broken*); having sufficient power, skill, ability (with *of*, as *capable of judging*); able; competent.

capacious *adj* capable of containing much; roomy.

capacity *n* the power of receiving or containing; specifically, the power of containing a certain quantity exactly; cubic contents; the extent or comprehensiveness of the mind; the power of receiving ideas or knowledge; the receptive faculty; active power; ability (*a person with the capacity of judging*); ability in a moral or legal sense; legal qualification (*to attend a meeting in the capacity of an elector*);

canoe

character (*to give advice in the capacity of a friend*).

caparison *n* a cloth or covering, more or less ornamented, laid over the saddle of a horse; hence, clothing, especially bright clothing.—*vt* to cover with a caparison; to adorn with rich dress.

cape[1] *n* a loose cloak or garment, hung from the shoulders.

cape[2] *n* a piece of land jutting into the sea or a lake beyond the rest of the coastline; a headland; a promontory.

caper[1] *n* a leap; a skip; a spring, as in dancing or mirth; a sportive or capricious action; a prank.—**to cut capers** to leap or dance in a frolicsome manner; to act sportively or capriciously.—*vi* to cut capers; to skip or jump; to prance; to spring.

caper[2] *n* a low Mediterranean shrub; its pickled bud used as a condiment (*caper sauce*).

capercailzie *n* the Scottish name for the wood grouse.

capillarity *n* the state or condition of being capillary; capillary action.

capillary *adj* resembling a hair; fine, minute, small in diameter; (*anat*) pertaining to capillary tubes or to the capillary vessels or capillaries in organic structures.—*n* a minute blood vessel constituting the termination of an artery or vein; one of the minute vessels which intervene between the terminal arteries and veins.

capillary tube *n* a tube with a very minute bore.

capital *adj* first in importance; chief; principal; incurring the forfeiture of life (*a capital offence*), punishable with death; excellent; a term applied to a type or letter of a certain form and a larger size than that generally used in the body of written or printed matter.—*n* (*archit*) the uppermost part of a column, pillar or pilaster, serving as the head or crowning and placed immediately over the shaft and under the entablature; the chief city or town in a kingdom or state; a metropolis; a type or letter of a certain form and of a larger size than that commonly used in the body of a piece of writing or printing; a capital letter; money or wealth in some shape employed in trade, manufacture or in any business; (*fig*) stock of any kind, whether physical or moral; means of influence or of increasing one's power.

capitalist *n* a person who has a large capital or stock in trade; a person of large property which is or may be employed in business.

capitalize *vt* (**capitalized, capitalizing**) to write or print in capital letters; to provide with capital; to convert into money or capital.-*vi* to profit by (with *on*); to take advantage of.

cape

capitation *n* numeration by the head; a numbering of persons.

capitation tax *n* a tax levied on each head or person; a poll tax.

Capitol *n* in ancient Rome, the name of a hill crowned by a temple dedicated to Jupiter; the temple itself, in which the senate assembled.

capitulate *vi* (**capitulated, capitulating**) to surrender, usually on certain stipulated conditions.

capitulation *n* the act of capitulating; the treaty or instrument containing the conditions of surrender.

capon *n* a chicken castrated for the purpose of improving the flesh for eating.

cappuccino *n* (*pl* **cappuccinos**) frothy milky coffee sometimes sprinkled with chocolate powder.

caprice *n* a sudden change of opinion or humour; a whim; capriciousness; fickleness.

capricious *adj* apt to change opinions suddenly; unsteady; changeable; fickle; subject to change or irregularity.

Capricorn *n* one of the twelve signs of the zodiac, the Goat; the tenth sign, marking the winter solstice.

capsicum *n* a kind of tropical plant with bell-shaped or pod-shaped fruits containing mild or hot seeds and used as a vegetable or flavouring agent.

capsize *vt* (**capsized, capsizing**) to upset or overturn.—*vi* to be upset or overturned.

capstan *n* an apparatus working on the principle of the wheel and axle and consisting of a cylinder or barrel adjusted on an upright axis, the barrel being made to turn round by means of horizontal bars or levers, the ends of which are inserted in holes near the top of the barrel so that a rope is thus wound round it and a weight, such as an anchor, raised or moved.

capsule *n* (*bot*) a dry fruit, containing seeds and opening of itself by valves or pores when mature; a metallic seal or cover for going over the cork or stopper of a bottle; a small soluble container for a dose of medicine; the part of a spacecraft containing the instruments and crew.

captain *n* one who is at the head of or has authority over others; a chief; a leader; a commander; more specifically, the military officer next in rank below a major; an officer in the navy commanding a ship of war; the commander or master of a merchant vessel.

captaincy *n* the rank, post or commission of a captain.

caption *n* a heading, short title or description, especially one accompanying an illustration or cartoon.

captious *adj* disposed to find or raise objections; difficult to please; carping.

captivate *vt* (**captivated, captivating**) to

overpower with excellence or beauty; to charm, to enchant; to engage the affections of.

captive *n* one who is taken prisoner, especially a prisoner taken in war; one who is charmed or subdued by beauty or excellence.—*adj* made prisoner in war; kept in confinement; unable to refuse what is offered (*a captive audience, a captive market*); bound by the ties of love or admiration; captivated.

captivity *n* the state of being a captive; subjection; a state of being under control.

captor *n* one who captures or takes by force, stratagem, etc.

capture *n* the act of one who captures; the act of making a prize of something; seizure; arrest; the thing taken; a prize.—*vt* (**captured, capturing**) to take or seize by force, surprise or stratagem, as an enemy or his or her property; to represent in fixed form (*capture her beauty on canvas*).

Capuchin *n* a monk of the order of St Francis.

capybara *n* a rodent quadruped, allied to the guinea pig, abounding in rivers of South America.

car *n* a motorcar, a light two-wheeled carriage for one horse; a chariot of war or state; a tramway carriage; a carriage with a particular purpose for passengers on a railway train (*dining car, observation car*).

caracal *n* a species of lynx, about the size of a fox and of a deep brown colour, a native of Northern Africa and Southwestern Asia.

caracole, caracol *n* in dressage, a half-turn which a horse and rider make, either to the right or left; (*archit*) a spiral staircase.—*vi* (**caracoled, caracoling**) to move in a caracole; to wheel.

carafe *n* a glass water bottle or wine decanter.

caramel *n* burnt sugar used to flavour desserts and to colour spirits and wines; a sweet made from burnt sugar; a pale golden-brown colour.

carapace *n* the shell which protects the body of chelonian reptiles; also the covering of the anterior upper surface of the crustaceans.

carat *n* a weight, about $3^1/_6$ grains, used in weighing precious stones and pearls; a term used to express the proportionate fineness of gold, gold of twenty-four carats being pure gold, gold of eighteen (for instance) have six parts of alloy.

caravan *n* a group of people travelling together across a desert, often with camels, for greater security; a large close carriage for conveying travelling exhibitions, etc, from place to place; a vehicle in which people may live, designed to be drawn either by a motor vehicle or horses, sometimes now called a *mobile home*.

caravanserai *n* in the East, a place appointed for receiving and lodging travellers.

caravel, carvel *n* a small galley-rigged ship formerly used by the Spanish and Portuguese; also a small fishing vessel.

caraway *n* a biennial plant with a taper root like a parsnip, the pungent seeds of which are used to flavour cakes, etc, and a volatile oil being obtained by distillation.

carbide *n* a compound of carbon with a metal.

carbine *n* a short-barrelled rifle used by cavalry, police, etc.

carbohydrate *n* a chemical compound of carbon, hydrogen and oxygen, the two latter being commonly in the same proportion as in water, found in starch, sugars and cellulose.

carbolic acid *n* an acid obtained from the distillation of coal tar, an oily, colourless liquid with a burning taste, used as an antiseptic and disinfectant.

carbon *n* a non-metallic chemical element, a black, brittle, light and odourless substance which is a constituent of all organic matter; a carbon copy.

carbonate *n* (*chem*) a compound formed by the union of carbonic acid with a base.

carbon copy *n* a copy made with carbon paper; any exact copy.

carbon dioxide *n* a colourless gas formed by combustion and respiration and absorbed by plants.

carbonic *adj* pertaining to carbon or obtained from it.

carbonic acid *n* a weakly acidic solution of carbon dioxide in water.

carbon monoxide *n* a colourless, odourless, poisonous gas which forms when carbon burns in an insufficient supply of oxygen.

car-boot sale *n* a sale at which people sell second-hand goods from their car boots.

Carborundum *n* a trademark for a compound of silicon and carbon, a very hard substance used for polishing and grinding.

carboy *n* a large, strong, glass bottle, protected by an outside covering and used chiefly for corrosive liquids, as vitriol.

carbuncle *n* a beautiful gem of a deep red colour; an inflammatory area of infection in the skin, producing pus.

carburettor *n* a device for vaporizing the light oil fuel used in the engines of motorcars, aeroplanes, etc.

carcass, carcase *n* the body, usually the dead body, of an animal; a corpse; the decaying remains of a bulky thing; the frame or main parts of a thing unfinished.

carcinogen *n* any substance that causes cancer in organisms.

carcinogenic *adj* causing cancer.

carcinoma *n* a cancerous or malignant tumour; cancer.

capybara

caravan

129

card¹ *n* a rectangular piece of thick paper or pasteboard; such a piece with certain devices, marks or figures, used for playing games; a piece having one's name, etc, written or printed on it; a larger piece written or printed and conveying an invitation or some intimation or statement, such as a greeting; the dial or face of the mariner's compass.

card² *n* an instrument for combing, opening and breaking wool or flax, freeing it from the coarser parts and from extraneous matter.—*vti* to comb or open wool, flax, hemp, etc, with a card.

cardamom *n* the aromatic capsule of various plants of the ginger family.

cardboard *n* a stiff kind of paper or pasteboard for making cards, etc.

card case *n* a small pocket case, generally ornamental, for holding visiting cards.

cardiac *adj* of the heart.

cardigan *n* a kind of knitted jacket fastened with buttons.

cardinal *adj* chief, principal, pre-eminent or fundamental.—*n* an ecclesiastical prince in the Roman Catholic Church, next in rank to the pope and having a distinguishing dress of a red colour.

cardinal bird *n* a North American bird with red plumage.

cardinal number *n* one of the numbers one, two, three, etc, in distinction from first, second, third, etc, called *ordinal numbers*.

cardinal points *npl* north and south, east and west.

cardsharp, cardsharper *n* one who cheats in card games.

care *n* a mental trouble; anxiety; solicitude; attention or heed; caution; watchfulness; charge or oversight, implying concern for safety and prosperity; supervision; the object of care or watchful regard and attention.—*vi* (**cared, caring**) to be anxious or solicitous; to be concerned; to be inclined or disposed; to look after (with *for*); to like, to love (with *for*).—**to take into care** to take (a child) into the charge of a local authority.

careen *vt* to heave or bring (a ship) to lie on one side.—*vi* to incline to one side.

career *n* a race or running; course of proceeding; a specific course of action or occupation forming the object of one's life.—*vi* to move or run rapidly (as a horse, a ship, etc).

careful *adj* full of care; anxious; solicitous; attentive to support and protect; giving good heed; watchful; cautious; showing or done with care or attention (with *of*).

careless *adj* free from care or anxiety; heedless; negligent; unthinking; inattentive; regardless; unmindful (with *of*); done or said without care; unconsidered.

carer *n* one who looks after someone, espe-

cardinal points

caribou

cially one who looks after an elderly, ill or disabled relative at home.

caress *n* any physical act or expression of affection.—*vt* to fondle; to touch or embrace with tender affection.

caret *n* in writing, a mark made thus (^), which shows where something omitted is to be inserted.

caretaker *n* a person employed to look after a building and to be responsible for maintenance and security.

careworn *adj* worn, oppressed or burdened with care; showing marks of care or anxiety.

cargo *n* the lading or freight of a ship.

caribou *n* an American variety of the reindeer.

caricature *n* a representation, pictorial or descriptive, in which beauties are concealed and peculiarities or defects exaggerated so as to make the person or thing ridiculous, while a general likeness is retained.—*vt* (**caricatured, caricaturing**) to make or draw a caricature of; to represent in a ridiculous and exaggerated fashion.

caricaturist *n* one who caricatures others.

caries *n* decay in a tooth or bone.

carillon *n* a simple air adapted to be performed on a set of bells.

Carlovingian *adj* pertaining to or descended from Charlemagne.

Carmelite *n* a mendicant friar of the order of White Friars founded at Mount Carmel.

carminative *n* a medicine which tends to expel wind from the stomach and remedy flatulence.

carmine *n* the pure colouring matter of cochineal; a red or crimson pigment made from cochineal; a deep purplish-red colour.

carnage *n* slaughter; great destruction of people.

carnal *adj* pertaining to the body, its passions and appetites; not spiritual; fleshly; sensual; lustful; impure.

carnation *n* flesh colour; a pink colour; a perennial plant found in many varieties, much prized for the colours of its sweet-scented double flowers.

carnelian, cornelian *n* a variety of chalcedony, of a deep red, flesh-red or reddish-white colour.

carnival *n* feasting or revelry; a fair or amusement show.

carnivorous *adj* eating or feeding on flesh, as the lion, tiger, wolf, dog, etc; also applied to some plants that can assimilate animal substances.

carnivore *n* a carnivorous animal.

carob *n* the edible pod of a Mediterranean tree, sometimes used as a substitute for chocolate.

carol *n* originally, a song, especially one expressive of joy; a religious song or ballad in celebration of Christmas.—*vi* (**carolled,**

carolling) to sing; to warble; to sing in joy or festivity.

carotid artery *n* one of the two great arteries, one on either side of the neck, which convey the blood from the aorta to the head and brain.

carouse *vi* (**caroused, carousing**) to drink freely and with jollity; to revel.

carousal *n* a feast or festival; a noisy drinking bout or revelling.

carousel *n* a merry-go-round; a revolving circular platform.

carp[1] *vi* to censure, cavil or find fault, particularly without reason or petulantly; to nag.

carp[2] *n* a freshwater fish found in lakes, rivers, ponds, etc.

car park *n* an area reserved for parking motor vehicles, for which a fee is often charged.

carpel *n* (*bot*) a single-celled ovary or seed vessel.

carpenter *n* a tradesman who works in timber; one who builds or repairs wooden structures.

carpentry *n* the art of cutting, framing and joining timber.

carper *n* one who carps; a fault-finder, a nag; a caviller.

carpet *n* a thick fabric used for covering floors, stairs, etc; a covering resembling a carpet (*a carpet of moss*).

carpetbag *n* a travelling bag made of the same material as carpets.

carpetbagger *n* a newcomer to a place, having all his or her property in a carpetbag; a political candidate who has had no previous connection with the constituency; one who moves into an area seeking political or financial advantage.

carping *adj* cavilling; captious; censorious.

carpus *n* (*pl* **carpi**) (*anat*) that part of the skeleton between the forearm and hand; the wrist in a human and the corresponding bones in other animals.

carrageen, carragheen *n* a seaweed which, when dried, becomes whitish and is used for making soups, jellies, etc.

carriage *n* the act of carrying, bearing, transporting or conveying; the price or expense of carrying; the manner of carrying oneself, deportment; behaviour; conduct; a wheeled vehicle, usually horse-drawn, for carrying passengers, especially a four-wheeled vehicle supported on springs and with a cover; a rail coach or compartment; in composition, a wheeled stand or support (*a gun carriage*); (*print*) the frame on rollers by which the bed carrying the type is run in and out from under the cylinder; the moving part of a typewriter.

carriageway *n* the part of a road for use by vehicles.

carrier *n* one who or that which carries or conveys; one who for hire undertakes the conveyance of goods or persons; the name of a particular part in various machines; a person or animal who may transmit an infectious disease without being affected by it; a plastic or paper bag with hands for holding things.

carrier pigeon *n* a variety of pigeon capable of finding its way home from great distances, often used to carry messages, etc.

carrion *n* the dead and putrefying body or flesh of animals.—*adj* feeding on carrion.

carrion crow *n* the common crow.

carrot *n* a plant having a long cone-shaped root of a reddish colour, used as a culinary vegetable; an inducement.

carroty *adj* like a carrot in colour.

carry *vt* (**carried, carrying**) to bear, convey, transport or take; to drive, drag or fetch (*carry a person off prisoner*); to transfer, as from one column, page, book, etc, to another; to convey or take with one generally (as a message, news, etc); to urge, impel, lead or draw, in a moral sense (*anger carried him too far*); to effect, accomplish, achieve, bring to a successful issue (a purpose, etc); to gain; to extend or continue in any direction, in time, in space or otherwise (commonly with such words as *up*, *back*, *forward*, etc, as *to carry a history on to the present, to carry improvements far*); to bear; to have in or on; to bear or bring as a result (*words carry conviction*); to import, contain or comprise (*the words carry a promise*); to manage; to conduct (matters or affairs); to accept, to adopt (*carry the motion*); to travel, to be transmitted (*a voice that carries*).

carse *n* in Scotland, a stretch of fertile, alluvial land along the side of a river.

cart *n* a carriage usually without springs for the conveyance of heavy goods.—*vt* to carry or convey on a cart; (*colloq*) to carry, often with difficulty.

carte blanche *n* a blank paper; a paper duly authenticated with signature, etc, and entrusted to a person to be filled up as he or she pleases; hence, unconditional terms, unlimited power to decide.

carter *n* one who drives a cart.

carthorse *n* a horse that draws a cart or is intended for such work.

Carthusian *n* one of an order of monks, founded in 1086 by St Bruno; a pupil of Charterhouse School.

cartilage *n* an elastic tissue occurring in vertebrate animals and forming the tissue from which bone is formed by a process of calcification; gristle.

cartilaginous *adj* pertaining to or resembling a cartilage; gristly; consisting of cartilage; having cartilage only and not true bones (as many fishes).

cartload *n* a load borne on a cart; as much as is usually carried at once on a cart; (*colloq*) a great deal or quantity.

carp

carrier pigeon

cartographer *n* one who prepares or publishes maps or charts.

cartography *n* the art or practice of drawing up maps or charts.

cartoon *n* a pictorial design drawn on strong paper as a study for a picture intended to be painted of the same size, and more especially for a picture to be painted in fresco; a humorous sketch relating to any current topic or event; a comic strip; a film made by photographing a series of drawings, giving the illusion of movement, known as *animated cartoon*.

cartouche, cartouch *n* formerly, a case of wood filled with shot to be fired from a cannon; on Egyptian monuments, papyri, etc, a group of hieroglyphics in a small oval area; (*archit*) a sculptured ornament in the form of a scroll unrolled.

cartridge *n* a cylindrical case containing the charge of powder, primer and bullet or shot for a gun or rifle; a similar object, such as a disposable ink container in a fountain pen; a sealed case of film for a camera; the device containing the stylus on the end of the pick-up arm of a record player.

cartridge paper *n* a thick sort of paper originally manufactured for soldiers' cartridges but extensively used in the arts.

caruncle *n* a small fleshy excrescence; a fleshy excrescence on the head of a fowl, as a wattle, etc.

carve *vt* (**carved, carving**) to cut (some solid material) in order to produce the representation of an object or some decorative design; to make or shape by cutting; to form by cutting or hewing; to cut into, hew or slash; to cut into small pieces or slices, as meat; to divide into shares.—*vi* to engrave or cut figures; to cut up meat.

carvel *n* same as **caravel**.

carvel-built *adj* (of ship or boat) built with the planks flush and not overlapping, as in clinker-built boats.

carver *n* one who carves, as one who cuts ivory, wood, etc, in a decorative way; one who cuts meat; a large table knife for carving; a dining chair with arms.

carving *n* a branch of sculpture usually limited to works in wood, ivory, etc; the device or figure carved.

caryatid *n* (*pl* **caryatids, caryatides**) (*archit*) a figure of a woman dressed in long robes, serving to support entablatures.

cascade *n* a fall or flowing of water over a precipice in a river or other stream; a waterfall; something resembling a waterfall.—*vi* (**cascaded, cascading**) to fall in a cascade.

cascara sagrada *n* a purgative medicine obtained from the bark of an American tree.

case[1] *n* particular state, condition or circumstances; an individual occurrence or specific instance, as of disease; a question or group of facts involving a question for discussion or decision; a cause or suit in court; a cause; a lawsuit; an argument for one side; (*med*) a patient under treatment; (*gram*) one of the forms in the declension of a noun, pronoun or adjective.—**in case** in order to prevent; lest.

case[2] *n* a covering, envelope, box, frame or sheath; that which encloses or contains; a suitcase or briefcase; a case with its contents; hence, a certain quantity; (*print*) the receptacle for the type.—*vt* (**cased, casing**) to cover with a case; to put in a container; to coat or cover over; (*sl*) to watch (a house, etc) when planning a crime.

case-hardened *adj* having the surface hardened by being converted into steel; (*fig*) shameless; brazen-faced.

case history *n* all the relevant information about a person relating to his or her background, especially medical or social background.

casein *n* that ingredient in milk which when coagulated forms curd and the main part of cheese.

casemate *n* (*fort*) a bomb-proof vault for the protection of a garrison.

cash *n* money, primarily ready money; money in the form of banknotes or coins, as opposed to cheques; immediate payment rather than hire purchase or credit.—*vt* to turn into money or to exchange for money (*to cash a banknote*).

cash-book *n* a book in which is kept a register or account of money received and paid.

cash dispenser *n* a device, usually set in a wall, provided by financial institutions such as banks for the withdrawal of money on insertion of a card and the keying in of a number (pin number), also called automated teller machine.

cashew *n* the tree which produces cashew nuts, a native of tropical America.

cashew nut *n* a small kidney-shaped edible nut.

cash flow *n* money which is paid into and out of a business during its operations.

cashier[1] *n* one who has charge of cash; one who keeps an account of the monetary transactions of a commercial or trading establishment; one who receives and pays out money, as in a bank or shop.

cashier[2] *vt* to dismiss from an office, place of trust or service for bad conduct.

cash register *n* a machine used to record cash sales equipped with a drawer to keep banknotes and coins from which change is given.

casino *n* a gaming saloon.

cask *n* a barrel for containing liquids, formed by staves, heading and hoops.

casket *n* a small chest or box for jewels, etc.

cartoon

cash

casque *n* a helmet; (*zool*) a helmet-like protuberance.

cassava *n* a slender erect shrub belonging to the spurge family, cultivated in tropical America and the West Indies.

casserole *n* a kind of covered fireproof dish in which food is both cooked and served; a dish cooked in this way.

cassette *n* a case containing magnetic tape or film for loading into a tape recorder, camera or video recorder.

cassia *n* a tropical leguminous plant of many species.

cassiterite *n* the most common ore of tin.

cassock *n* a long coat or tight-fitting garment worn by clergymen and choristers.

cassowary *n* a large flightless bird resembling the ostrich, inhabiting Australia and New Guinea.

cast *vt* (**cast, casting**) to throw, fling or send; to shed or throw off (leaves, the skin); to discard, dismiss or reject; to shed or impart (*cast light*); to turn or direct (a look, the eyes); to throw down (as in wrestling); to bring forth abortively (young); to form by pouring liquid metal, etc, into a mould; to compute, reckon or calculate; to distribute (the parts of a drama) among the actors; to assign a part to; to throw (a fishing line) into the water.—**to cast off** to discard or reject; (in knitting) to loop off stitches from a needle without letting them unravel; (*naut*) to loosen from or let go from a mooring; (print) to calculate the space (a manuscript) will take when set in type.—**to cast up** to compute; to calculate; to eject; to vomit; to bring up or mention (a past misdeed, mistake, etc) in reproach.—**to cast oneself on** *or* **upon** to resign or yield oneself to the disposal of.—**to cast (something) in the teeth** to upbraid (with something); to charge.—*vi* to throw or fling; to throw the line in angling; to work arithmetical calculations; to turn or revolve in the mind; to warp or twist.—*n* the act of casting; a throw; the distance passed by a thing thrown; motion or turn of the eye; direction, look or glance; a throw of dice; the form or shape into which something is cast; anything formed in a mould, as a figure in bronze, plaster, etc; (*fig*) shape; mould; impression generally; manner; style; the company of actors to whom the parts of a play are assigned.—**cast in the eye** squint.

castanet *n* one of a pair of small concave pieces of ivory or hard wood, shaped like spoons, fastened to the thumb and clapped together by the middle finger in certain Spanish dances.

castaway *n* one who or that which is cast away or shipwrecked; one ruined in fortune or character.—*adj* thrown away; rejected; useless.

caste *n* one of the classes into which the Hindus are divided according to the religious law of Brahmanism.

caster *n* one who or that which casts; specifically, one who makes castings; a founder; a small cruet or bottle for holding sauce, pepper, etc, for the table, spelled also **castor**; a small wheel attached by a vertical pivot to the legs of a chair, sofa, table, etc, to facilitate them being moved without lifting, spelled also **castor**.

castigate *vt* (**castigated, castigating**) to chastise; to punish; to correct.

castigation *n* the act of castigating; punishment; correction; chastisement; discipline; a stern rebuke.

casting *n* the act of one who casts; that which is cast; especially, something cast or formed in a mould; something formed of cast metal.

casting vote *n* a vote given by a president or chairman which decides when the votes are equally divided.

cast iron, cast metal, cast steel *n* iron, metal and steel melted and cast into pigs, ingots or moulds, which renders the metal hard and non-malleable.

castle *n* a building or series of connected buildings fortified for defence against an enemy; a house with towers, often surrounded by a wall and moat and having a donjon or keep in the centre; a fortified residence; a fortress; the large, imposing mansion of a person of rank or wealth; a large, imposing building; a piece made in the form of a castle, used in the game of chess; the rook.—*vti* (**castled, castling**) (in chess) to move the king two squares to the right or left and bring up the castle to the square the king has passed over.

castle in the air *n* a visionary project; a scheme that has no solid foundation.

cast-off *adj* laid aside as worn out or useless; rejected.

castor *n* see **caster**.

castor oil *n* oil from the seeds of a tropical tree used in medicine as a purgative.

castrate *vt* (**castrated, castrating**) to deprive of the testicles; to geld; to take the vigour or strength from; to emasculate.

castration *n* the act of castrating.

casual *adj* happening or coming to pass without design in the person or persons affected and without being foreseen or expected; accidental; fortuitous; coming by chance; occasional; incidental; careless; informal, especially of dress.—*n* a person who is in casual employment.

casualty *n* an unfortunate chance, especially one resulting in death or bodily injury; loss suffered by a group from death, wounds, etc; a person injured or killed.

casuistry *n* the science, doctrine or department of ethics dealing with cases of con-

cassowary

castanets

science (frequently used in a bad sense for quibbling in matters of morality or making too fine moral distinctions).

cat *n* a common domestic animal kept as a pet; any of a family of wild animals related to this, such as lions, tigers, etc; a cat-o'-nine-tails; a spiteful woman.—**to let the cat out of the bag** to disclose a trick; to let out a secret.

catabolism *n* a downward series of changes by which complex bodies are broken down into simpler forms; destructive metabolism.

cataclysm *n* a deluge, flood or inundation; any serious disturbance or overthrow, especially in politics.

catacomb *n* a cave or subterranean place for the burial of the dead, the most notable being those in Rome.

catafalque *n* a temporary structure representing a tomb placed over the coffin of a distinguished person in churches or over the grave.

catalepsy *n* a nervous condition characterized by a state of temporary rigidity and unconsciousness.

catamaran

catalogue *n* a list or enumeration of the names of people or things set out in a certain order, often in alphabetical order; a list; a register.—*vt* (**catalogued, cataloguing**) to make a catalogue of.

catalogue raisonné *n* a catalogue of books, paintings, etc, classed according to their subjects.

catalysis *n* (*pl* **catalyses**) (*chem*) a decomposition and new combination produced by the mere presence of substances which do not of themselves enter into combination.

catalyst *n* (*chem*) a substance which causes or increases the rate of a chemical reaction, itself remaining unchanged at the end of the reaction; any person or thing that causes or accelerates change.

catalytic *adj* relating to catalysis.

catamaran *n* a kind of float or raft consisting usually of three pieces of wood lashed together; a sailing boat with twin hulls.

catamount, catamountain *n* the cat of the mountain; the wild cat; the North American puma or cougar.

catapult *n* a military device of ancient times used for discharging missiles against a besieged place; originally a device of the nature of a powerful bow; a toy in the shape of a Y-shaped stick with elastic fixed to the two top ends for shooting small stones.

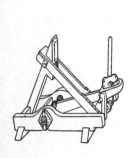

catapult

cataract *n* a waterfall; any strong rush or downpour of water; a disease of the eye consisting in an opacity of the crystalline lens or its capsule.

catarrh *n* a discharge or increased secretion of mucus from the membranes of the nose, throat and bronchia.

catastrophe *n* in Greek drama, the winding up of the plot of a dramatic piece; a calamity or great disaster.—**catastrophic** *adj*.

catatonia *n* a form of schizophrenia in which the sufferer remains in a rigid, trance-like state for long periods of time which are sometimes alternated by periods of excessive activity.

catatonic *adj* of, pertaining to or suffering from catatonia.

cat burglar *n* a burglar who enters a house by climbing.

catcall *n* a sound like the cry of a cat, such as that made by a dissatisfied audience in a theatre.

catch *vt* (*pret, pp* **caught**, *ppr* **catching**) to lay sudden hold on; to seize, especially with the hand; to snatch; to perceive or apprehend; to seize, as in a snare or trap; to entangle; to get entangled with or to come into contact or collision with (*the branch caught his hat*); to get; to receive (*to catch the sunlight*), especially, to take or receive as by contagion or infection; to take hold of; to communicate to; to fasten on (*the flames caught the woodwork*); to seize the affections of; to captivate; to be on time for; to begin to burn; to become popular.—**to catch it** to get a scolding, a beating or other unpleasant treatment.—**to catch hold of** to take or lay hold of.—*vi* to take or receive something; to be entangled or impeded; to spread by or as by infection; to be eager to get, use or adopt (with *at*)—**to catch on** to understand; to become popular.—**to catch up** to reach or overtake someone ahead; to attend to a backlog.—*n* the act of seizing; seizure; anything that seizes or takes hold, that checks motion, etc, as a hook, a ratchet, a springbolt for a door or lid, etc; a device for fastening; a snag or difficulty; a choking or stoppage of the breath; something caught or to be caught, especially anything valuable or desirable obtained or to be obtained; a gain or advantage; someone desirable, as a rich husband or wife; (*mus*) a kind of canon or round for three or four voices.

catching *adj* communicating, or liable to be communicated, by contagion; infectious; captivating; charming.

catchment *n* a surface of ground of which the drainage is capable of being directed into a common reservoir.

catchment area *n* the drainage area of a river and its tributaries; a geographic area served by a particular institution, e.g. a school.

catch-22 *n* a situation from which there is no escape; a regulation or procedure which offers the person subject to it no hope of meeting its conditions.

catchword *n* a well-known phrase or slogan.

catchy *adj* easily picked up or remembered (of tunes and songs).

catechism *n* a book containing a summary of principles in any science or art but especially in religion, reduced to the form of questions and answers.

catechize *vt* (**catechising, catechizing**) to instruct by asking questions, receiving answers and offering explanations and corrections; to interrogate; to examine or try by questions, especially such questions as would implicate the answerer.

catechumen *n* one who is under instruction in the first rudiments of Christianity; a neophyte.

categorical *adj* pertaining to a category; absolute; not relative or hypothetical (statement, answer).

categorize *vt* (**categorized, categorizing**) to place in a category; to classify.

category *n* a division or class within a particular field.

catenary *adj* relating to a chain; like a chain.

cater *vi* to buy or provide something for use, enjoyment or entertainment; to purvey food, provisions, amusement, etc (followed by *for*).

caterer *n* one who caters; a provider or purveyor of provisions; one who provides for any want or desire.

caterpillar *n* properly, the hairy, worm-like larva or grub of butterflies and moths but also sometimes applied to the larvae of other insects; (*engin*) a traction device consisting of an endless chain encircling the wheels of the tractor.

caterwaul *vi* to utter noisy and disagreeable cries (said of cats); to make a disagreeable howling or screeching.

catfish *n* a large, usually freshwater, fish with whisker-like feelers around the mouth.

catgut *n* the intestines of sheep (sometimes of the horse or the ass) dried and twisted into strings for the violin and for other purposes.

catharsis *n* (*pl* **catharses**) emotional relief brought about by art, especially dramatic tragedy; purgation; relief brought about by the uncovering of buried repressions.

cathartic *adj* bringing about catharsis; purgative.—*n* a purgative.

cathedra *n* the throne or seat of a bishop in the cathedral or episcopal church of his diocese.—**ex cathedra** by authority.

cathedral *n* the principal church in a diocese, that which is specially the church of the bishop.

Catherine wheel *n* a wheel-shaped firework; (*archit*) a circular window with radiating divisions or spokes.

catheter *n* (*surg*) a tubular instrument to be introduced through the urethra into the bladder to draw off the urine when the natural discharge is arrested.

cathode *n* the negative pole of an electric current or that by which the current leaves, opposed to *anode*.

cathode ray *n* one of the electrons in a stream of electrons emitted by a cathode in a vacuum tube.

cathode-ray tube a vacuum tube in which a beam of electrons produces a bright spot on a luminescent screen at the front of the tube, as used in television sets.

catholic *adj* universal or general; embracing all true Christians (*the catholic church* or *faith*); free from prejudice; liberal or wide-ranging (*catholic tastes* or *sympathies*);

Catholic *adj* pertaining to or affecting the Roman Catholic Church.—*n* a member of the Roman Catholic Church.

Catholicism *n* adherence to the Roman Catholic Church; the Roman Catholic faith.

cation *n* a positively charged ion.

catkin *n* the blossom of the willow, birch, hazel, etc, which resembles a kitten's or cat's tail.

cat litter *n* porous granular matter kep in a tray in which house pets excrete.

catnap *vi* (**catnapping, catnapped**) to take a short, light sleep, usually on a chair etc. —*n* a brief sleep.

catnip, catmint *n* a strongly scented plant attractive to cats.

cat-o'-nine-tails *n* an instrument consisting generally of nine pieces of knotted cord formerly used to flog offenders on the bare back.

cat's-eye *n* a hard and semitransparent variety of quartz.

Cat's-eye *n* a trademark for a reflector set in a road to mark lanes at night.

cat's-paw *n* a person used as a tool; a dupe; a light breeze, just strong enough to ruffle the water.

cat's whisker (*radio*) a thin wire, usually in the form of a spiral, which makes contact with the crystal in a crystal detector.

cattle *npl* a term applied collectively to domestic quadrupeds, such as serve for tillage or other labour or for food to humans, including camels, horses, asses, cows, sheep, goats, etc, but now chiefly restricted to domestic cows and bulls.

cattle show *n* an exhibition of farm animals for prizes; an agricultural show.

catty *adj* spiteful, mean.

Caucasian *n* a member of the light-skinned racial group of humankind.

caucus *n* (*pl* **caucuses**) a private meeting of citizens to agree on candidates to be proposed for election to offices or to concert measures for supporting a party or to form policy.

caterpillar

caudal *adj* pertaining to a tail.

caudate *adj* having a tail.

caudle *n* a kind of warm drink made of spiced and sugared wine or ale.

caul *n* a portion of the amnion or membrane enveloping the foetus, sometimes encompassing the head of a child when born and superstitiously supposed to be a protection against drowning.

cauldron *n* a large pot for cooking, associated traditionally with witches.

cauliflower *n* a garden variety of cabbage, with a white compact head of many sections or florets.

caulk *vt* to fill seams or a joint, such as gaps between planks in a boat, for example with pitch, to make them watertight.

causal *adj* relating to a cause or causes; implying, containing or expressing a cause or causes.—*n* a verb meaning to make to do something, as *fell*, to make to fall.

causality *n* the state of being causal; the fact of acting as a cause; the action or power of a cause in producing its effect; the doctrine or principle that every change implies the operation of a cause.

causation *n* the act of causing or producing; the doctrine as to the connection of causes and effects.

causative *adj* effective as a cause or agent (often followed by *of*); (*gram*) expressing a cause or reason; causal.—*n* a word expressing a cause.

cause *n* that which produces an effect; that which brings about a change; that from which anything proceeds and without which it would not exist; the reason or motive that urges, moves or impels the mind to act or decide; a suit or action in court; any legal process which a party institutes to obtain a demand or seek a right; any subject of question or debate; case; interest; matter; affair; that object or side of a question to which the efforts of a person or party are directed.—*vt* (**caused, causing**) to be the cause of; to effect by agency; to bring about; to be the occasion of; to produce.

causerie *n* talk; a chat; an informal lecture or essay.

causeway *n* a road or path raised above the natural level of the ground by stones, earth, timber, etc, serving as a passage over wet or marshy ground, etc; a raised and paved roadway.

caustic *adj* capable of burning, corroding or destroying organic matter; (*fig*) severe; cutting; sarcastic.

caustic soda *n* a white solid substance, largely used in soapmaking.

cauterize *vt* (**cauterized, cauterizing**) to burn or sear with fire or a hot iron or with a caustic substance so as to destroy dead tissue, stop bleeding, etc.

cave

cautery *n* a burning or searing; an instrument or drug used for such a purpose.

caution *n* care; prudence in regard to danger; wariness; watchfulness, forethought or vigilance; a measure taken for security; a security or guarantee; a warning or admonition.—*vt* to give notice of danger to; to warn; to exhort to take heed.

cautious *adj* possessing or exhibiting caution; attentive to examine probable effects and consequences of actions with a view to avoiding danger or misfortune; prudent; circumspect; wary; watchful; vigilant; careful.

cavalcade *n* a procession of persons on horseback or consisting mostly of persons on horseback.

cavalier *n* a horseman, especially an armed horseman; a knight; a gentleman attending on or escorting a lady.—*adj* sprightly; free and easy; offhand; haughty; supercilious (*a cavalier answer*).

Cavalier *n* at the time of the English Civil War, a partisan of Charles I, as opposed to a Roundhead or adherent to the Parliament.

cavalry *n* a body of troops, or soldiers, that serve on horseback; horse soldiers.

cave *n* a hollow place in the earth; a subterranean cavern; a den.—*vti* (**caved, caving**) to collapse or cause to collapse; to admit defeat (with *in*).

caveat *n* in law, a process in a court to stop proceedings; hence, an intimation of caution; hint; warning; admonition.

caveman *n* (*pl* **cavemen**) a name given to such of the earliest races of prehistoric man as dwelt in natural caves.

cavern *n* a deep hollow place in the earth; a cave.

caviar, caviare *n* the roe of the sturgeon, prepared and salted.

cavil *vi* (**cavilled, cavilling**) to raise trifling objections; to find fault without good reason (frequently followed by *at*).—*n* a trifling objection.

cavity *n* a hollow place; a hollow; a void or empty space in a body; an opening; a hollow part of the human body.

cavy *n* the name common to certain South American rodent animals, the most familiar species being the guinea pig.

caw *vi* to cry like a crow, rook or raven.—*n* the cry of the rook or crow.

cay, key *n* an islet; a range or reef of rocks lying near the surface of the water, used especially in the West Indies.

cayenne *n* a hot red pepper made from the ground pods and seeds of certain varieties of capsicum.

cayman, caiman *n* (*pl* **caymans, caimans**) a name applied popularly to the alligator of the West Indies and South America.

cease *vi* (**ceased, ceasing**) to stop moving,

acting or speaking; to leave off; to give over; to desist (followed by *from* before a noun); to come to an end; to terminate; to become extinct; to pass away (*the storm ceases*).—*vt* to put a stop to; to put an end to; to desist from.

cease-fire *n* the end of military hostilities; a truce

cedar *n* a coniferous evergreen tree which grows to a great size and is remarkable for its durability.—*adj* made of cedar; belonging to cedar.

cede *vt* (**ceded, ceding**) to yield; to surrender; to give up; to resign; to relinquish.

cedilla *n* a mark placed under the letter *c*, especially in French (ç), to show that it is to be sounded like *s*.

Ceefax *n* the trademark of a teletext system operated by the BBC.

ceilidh *n* in Scotland, an evening of storytelling, music, song and dance.

ceiling *n* the inner upper surface of a room, usually finished with plastered work; maximum height to which an aeroplane can climb; any upper limit.

celandine *n* either of to two British plants of the poppy family, which yield an acrid juice formerly used in medicine.

celebrate *vt* (**celebrated, celebrating**) to praise; to distinguish by any kind of observance or ceremony (*to celebrate a birthday*).

celebrated *adj* distinguished; well-known.

celebration *n* the act of celebrating; the act of praising or extolling; honour or distinction bestowed; the act of observing with appropriate rites or ceremonies.

celebrity *n* the condition of being celebrated; fame; renown; a person of distinction.

celerity *n* rapidity of motion; swiftness; speed.

celery *n* a plant cultivated as a salad and culinary vegetable.

celestial *adj* heavenly; belonging or relating to heaven; dwelling in heaven; supremely excellent or delightful; belonging to the sky.

celibacy *n* the state of being celibate, unmarried; a single life; sexual abstinence.

celibate *n* one who adheres to or practises celibacy.—*adj* unmarried; single; abstaining from sexual relations.

cell *n* a small apartment, as in a convent or a prison; a small or mean place of residence, such as a cave or hermitage; a small cavity or hollow place (*the cells of the brain*, *the cells of a honeycomb*, *a voltaic cell*); (*eccles*) a lesser religious house, especially one subordinate to a greater; a small group of people with common aims within an organization or political party; (*biol*) a microscopic unit of living matter.

cellar *n* a room in a house or other building, either wholly or partly underground, used for storage purposes.

cello *n* (*pl* **cellos**) the violoncello.

Cellophane *n* the trademark of a thin, waterproof paper obtained from wood cellulose, used for wrapping.

cellular *adj* consisting of or containing cells.

cellular radio *n* a communication system based on a network of transmitters, each serving a small area known as a cell, used in car phones.

cellule *n* a small cell or cavity.

celluloid *n* a plastic substance, made of cellulose camphor, used as a substitute for ivory, bone, coral, etc; a plastic coating on film; cinema film.

cellulose *n* the substance of which the permanent cell membranes of plants are always composed, in many respects allied to starch, used in the manufacture of paper, plastics and explosives.

Celsius *adj* of or pertaining to a scale of temperature with 0° as the freezing point and 100° as the boiling point.

celt *n* a cutting implement resembling an axe head, made of stone or metal, found in ancient tumuli and barrows.

Celt *n* one of a distinct race of people inhabiting the south and west of Europe; the Celts now speaking a distinctive language are the Bretons, Welsh, Scottish Highlanders and a portion of the Irish.

Celtic *adj* pertaining to the Celts or to their language.—*n* the language or group of dialects spoken by the Celts.

cement *n* any glutinous or other substance capable of joining bodies closely together; a kind of mortar consisting of those hydraulic limes which contain silica and therefore set quickly; (*fig*) bond of union; that which unites persons firmly together.—*vt* to unite by cement or other matter that produces joining of bodies; (*fig*) to unite firmly or closely.—*vi* to unite or become solid; to unite and cohere.

cemetery *n* a place set apart for interment; a graveyard; a necropolis.

cenobite *n* one of a religious order living in a convent or in community.

cenotaph *n* a monument erected to one who is buried elsewhere.

Cenozoic, Cainozoic *adj* (*geol*) of or belonging to the latest of the three divisions into which strata have been arranged, with reference to the age of the fossils they include, embracing the Tertiary and post-Tertiary systems.

censer *n* a vessel for burning and wafting incense; a thurible.

censor *n* a person empowered to examine all manuscripts, pamphlets, newspapers and books before they are published to see that they contain nothing obnoxious; a war official employed to open, destroy or re-

Celt

vise correspondence or sources of information calculated to instruct the enemy.—*vt* to revise in this sense; one who censures, blames or reproves.

censorious *adj* apt to blame or condemn; ready to pass severe remarks on a person's conduct; implying or expressing censure.

censorship *n* the office or dignity of a censor; the period of his office.

censure *n* the act of blaming or finding fault and condemning as wrong; expression of blame or disapprobation.—*vt* (**censured, censuring**) to find fault with and condemn as wrong; to blame; to express disapprobation of.

census *n* an official count of the population of a country.

cent *n* a hundred, commonly used with *per*, as, *ten per cent*, that is, in the proportion of ten to the hundred; in various countries a coin equal to the hundredth part of the monetary unit; in the United States the hundredth part of the dollar.

centaur *n* in Greek myth a member of a race of fabulous beings supposed to be half man and half horse.

centaury *n* the popular name of an annual herb of the gentian family.

centaur

centenarian *n* a person a hundred years old or upwards.

centenary *n* the space of a hundred years; the commemoration of any event which occurred a hundred years before.—*adj* relating to a hundred years.

centigrade *adj* Celsius.

centimetre *n* a measure of length, the hundredth part of a metre, rather more than 0.39 of an inch.

centipede *n* one of various crawling creatures with a long body divided into numerous segments each with a pair of legs.

cento *n* (*pl* **centos**) a composition (whether literary or musical) made up of selections from the works of various authors or composers.

central *adj* relating or pertaining to the centre; placed in the centre or middle; constituting or containing the centre; originating or proceeding from the centre.

central heating *n* a system of heating a building from one source by circulating hot water, steam or hot air.

centralization *n* the act of centralizing or bringing to one centre.

centipede

centralize *vt* (**centralized, centralizing**) to draw to a central point; to bring to a centre; to render central; to concentrate in some particular part, often applied to the process of transferring local administration to the capital or seat of government of a country.

central nervous system the brain and spinal cord which coordinates activity in humans and animals.

centre *n* that point of a line, plane figure or solid body which is equally distant from the extremities; the middle point, portion or place; the middle or central object; a point of concentration; the nucleus around which or into which things are collected (*a centre of attraction*); the part of a target next the bull's-eye; the members of the moderate party in parliament or of the moderate section in a political party.—*vt* (**centred, centring**) to place on a centre; to fix on a central point; to collect to a point.—*vi* to be placed in a centre or in the middle; to be collected to one point; to be concentrated or united in one.

centre bit *n* a carpenter's tool for boring large circular holes, which turns on an axis or central point when in operation.

centreboard *n* a kind of movable keel in yachts, capable of being raised and lowered in a well extending longitudinally amidships, to prevent leeway.

centre of gravity *n* the point of a body about which all the parts of the body exactly balance each other and which being supported the whole body will remain at rest though acted on by gravity.

centrifugal *adj* tending to move away from the centre; acting by or depending on centrifugal force or action; (*bot*) expanding first at the summit and later at the base, as an inflorescence.

centrifugal force *n* that force by which all bodies moving round another body in a curve tend to fly off at any point of their motion in the direction of a tangent to the curve.

centripetal *adj* tending towards the centre; progressing by changes from the exterior of an object to its centre; (*bot*) expanding first at the base of the inflorescence and later at the summit.

centripetal force *n* that force which draws a body towards a centre and thereby acts as a counterpoise to the centrifugal force in circular motion.

centrosome *n* in cells, a minute particle outside the nucleus which plays an active part in indirect division.

centuple *adj* multiplied or increased a hundred-fold.

centurion *n* in ancient Rome, a military officer who commanded a century or company of infantry consisting of a hundred men.

century *n* an aggregate of a hundred; anything consisting of a hundred in number; a period of a hundred years, often such a period reckoned from the birth of Christ; in cricket, a hundred runs.

cephalic *adj* pertaining to the head.

cephalic index *n* a number denoting the ratio of the transverse to the longitudinal (front to back) diameter of the skull and according to which skulls and races of people are called brachycephalic or dolichocephalic.

cephalopod n any of a group of marine molluscs including octopus, squid and cuttlefish, which have tentacles attached to their heads.

ceramic adj pertaining to the manufacture of porcelain and earthenware; earthenware or porcelain.

ceramics n the art of the potter; pottery.

Cerberus n in Classical myth, the three-headed watchdog of the infernal regions; hence, any watchful and dreaded guardian.

cereal adj pertaining to edible grain, as wheat, rye, barley, oats, maize, rice, millet.—n a grain plant, such as wheat, oats, barley, etc; a breakfast food made from such grains.

cerebellum n (pl **cerebellums, cerebella**) the little brain; that portion of the brain in vertebrate animals which is posterior to and underlies the great cerebral mass or cerebrum.

cerebral adj pertaining to the cerebrum or brain; acting or guided by intelligence as opposed to emotions.

cerebral palsy n a disability caused by brain damage before, during or immediately after birth resulting in poor muscle coordination.

cerebrum n (pl **cerebrums, cerebra**) the superior and chief portion of the brain, occupying the whole upper cavity of the skull.

cerecloth, cerement n cloth dipped in melted wax, in which dead bodies are wrapped when embalmed; (pl) grave clothes.

ceremonial adj relating to ceremonies or external forms or rites; ritual.—n a system of rites; ceremonies or formalities to be observed on any occasion.

ceremonious adj full of ceremony; accompanied with rites; according to prescribed or customary formalities or punctilios; formally respectful or polite; observant of conventional forms; fond of using ceremony.

ceremony n a religious or other rite or observance; a solemn or formal display or performance; a solemnity; a usage of politeness or such usages collectively; formality; punctiliousness.

Ceres n a Roman goddess watching over the growth of grain and other plants.

cerise n cherry colour.—adj of the colour of cerise; cherry-coloured.

cerium adj a rare metal discovered in 1803, of a colour between that of iron and that of lead; specific gravity 6.9.

certain adj sure; undoubtedly true; established as a fact; undoubtedly existing or impending (death, danger); capable of being counted or depended on; unfailing; infallible (of things, as a sign, a remedy); capable of being counted on or able to count on (of persons, as *he is certain to be there, you are certain to find him*); assured in mind; free from doubt; having no doubt or suspicion regarding (often with *of*); stated; fixed; determinate; definite (*a certain rate*); not specifically named; indefinite; one or some (*a certain person, a certain pleasure in something*).—**for certain** certainly.

certainly adv without doubt or question; in truth and fact; without fail; assuredly; of a certainty.

certainty n the fact of being certain; exemption from failure to happen or produce the natural result; a fact or truth certainly established; that which cannot be questioned; full assurance of mind; exemption from doubt.

certificate n a written testimony to the truth of a certain fact or facts; a testimonial; a legally authenticated voucher or testimony of certain facts; sometimes a kind of licence.—vt to give a certificate to, as to one who has passed an examination; to attest or certify by certificate.

certify vt (**certified, certifying**) to assure or make certain; to give certain information to (a person); to give certain information of; to make clear or definite; to testify to in writing; to make known or establish as a fact; to state a person is legally insane.

certitude n certainty; assurance; freedom from doubt.

cerulean adj sky-coloured; azure; blue.

cerumen n the wax or yellow matter secreted by certain glands lying in the external canal of the ear.

ceruse n white lead composed of hydroxide and carbonate of lead.

cervical adj belonging to the neck; belonging to the cervix.

cervine adj pertaining to the deer family.

cervix n the cylindrical opening of the uterus which opens into the vagina; the neck.

cessation n a ceasing; a stop; a rest; the act of discontinuing motion or action of any kind, whether temporary or final.

cession n the act of ceding, yielding or surrendering, as of territory, property or rights; a giving up, resignation or surrender.

cesspool n a cavity, well or cistern into which drains and sewage empty.

cetacean n a member of an order of aquatic, usually marine, mammals that includes whales, dolphins and porpoises.

CFC an abbreviation of **chlorofluorocarbon**.

Chablis n a dry white wine from Chablis in France.

chafe vt (**chafed, chafing**) to cause heat in

cephalopod

(some part of the body) by friction; to stimulate to warmth by rubbing; to irritate; to cause to rage (*the wind chafes the ocean*); to fret and wear by rubbing (*the rope was chafed*).—*vi* to feel irritation; to be fretted and worn by rubbing.—*n* a state of being irritated; fret.

chafer *n* any of various large beetles.

chaff[1] *n* the husks of corn and grasses, especially the husks when separated from the corn by thrashing, sifting or winnowing; worthless matter.

chaff[2] *vti* to banter; to tease good-humouredly; to make game of.—*n* banter.

chaffer *vi* to bargain; to haggle.

chaffinch *n* a common British bird of the finch family.

chafing dish *n* a dish for heating or cooking food at table; a portable grate for coals.

chagrin *n* ill humour, as from disappointment, wounded vanity, etc; vexation; peevishness; mortification.—*vt* to excite ill humour in; to vex; to mortify.

chain *n* a series of links or rings connected or fitted into one another, generally of metal and used for various purposes; (*fig*) that which binds, restrains, confines or fetters; a bond; a fetter; bondage; slavery (often in the plural, as *the chains of evil habit*); a series of things linked together; a series, line or range of things connected or following in succession (*chain of causes, events*, etc); a group of shops, hotels, etc, belonging to the same owner or company; in weaving, the warp threads of a web, so called because they form a long series of links or loops; (*pl*) (*naut*) strong links or plates of iron bolted to a ship's sides and forming part of the attachments of the shrouds; (*surv*) a measuring instrument, generally consisting of 100 links and having a total length of 66 feet.—*vt* to fasten, bind, restrain or fetter with a chain or chains; to put in chains; to restrain; to hold in control; to unite firmly; to link.

chain

chain letter *n* a letter requesting the recipient to send it to someone else or to send out a number of copies to other people.

chain reaction *n* a process in which a chemical, atomic or other reaction stimulates further reactions, e.g. combustion or nuclear fission; a series of events, each of which stimulates the next.

chain-smoke *vti* to smoke (cigarettes) one after the other.

chain store *n* one of a series of retail stores owned by own company or owner.

chair

chair *n* a movable seat, with a back, for one person; a seat of office or authority; hence, the office itself, especially the office of a professor; so the person occupying the chair at a meeting, etc; a chairman or president; the electric chair.—*vt* to place or carry in a chair; to carry publicly in a chair in triumph; to act as chairperson at a meeting, etc.

chair lift *n* a series of seats suspended from a cable for carrying skiers or sightseers uphill.

chairman, chairperson, chairwoman *n* (*pl* **chairmen, chairpersons, chairwomen**) the presiding officer of an assembly, association, or company, committee or public meeting.

chaise *n* a two-wheeled carriage drawn by one or more horses.

chalcedony *n* a kind of quartz, resembling milk diluted with water and more or less clouded or opaque, with veins, circles and spots.

chalcedony *n* a variety of agate, in which white and grey layers alternate.

chalet *n* a cottage, cabin or hut for sheltering herdsmen and their cattle in the Swiss mountains; a small dwelling house built in a similar style; a cabin used as a holiday house.

chalice *n* a drinking cup or bowl; a cup used to administer the wine in the celebration of Mass.

chalk *n* earthy limestone, an impure carbonate of lime of an opaque white colour, soft and admitting no polish.—*vt* to rub with chalk; to mark with chalk; to trace out; to describe (from the use of chalk in marking lines.—**to chalk up** to record a score; to achieve; to credit or charge money.

challenge *n* an invitation to a contest or trial of any kind; a calling or summons to fight in a single combat; the letter or message containing the summons to a contest; the calling in question or taking exception to something; the hailing and interrogating by a sentry; the claim of a party that certain jurors shall not sit at his or her trial; a test of one's abilities, stamina, etc.—*vt* (**challenged, challenging**) to address a challenge to; to call to a contest; to summon to fight or to a duel; to demand the password from; to hail and interrogate; to claim as due; to demand as a right; (*law*) to demand the removal of from among the jurymen; to object to (a person or thing); to take exception to; to call in question (a statement).

challenged *adj* a politically correct term for disabled or handicapped, as *visually challenged* for blind, the idea being that it is a more positive term.

challenger *n* one who challenges; one who summons another to a contest; an objector; one who calls in question.

chalybeate *adj* impregnated with iron (applied to medicines containing iron and especially to springs and waters impregnated with iron).

chamber *n* a room of a dwelling house, especially a bedroom; an apartment; a room where professional people, as lawyers, conduct their business; especially, the room in which judges sit for the disposing of matters not sufficiently important to be heard in court; a hall or place where an assembly, association or body of people meets; the assembly or body itself, as *a chamber of commerce*; a hollow or cavity in a thing, especially when of definite form and use; the part of a pump in which the bucket or plunger works; that part of a firearm where the cartridge lies.

chamberlain *n* a person charged with the direction and management of a chamber or chambers; specifically, an officer charged with the direction and management of the private apartments of a monarch or nobleman; the treasurer of a city, corporation, etc.

chambermaid *n* a woman who makes beds and cleans bedrooms in a hotel, etc.

chamber music *n* any music composed for a small group of instruments, originally for performance in a private house or small concert hall.

chamber pot *n* a bowl for urine used in a bedroom.

chameleon *n* a lizard capable of changing colour to match its surroundings; a person of variable moods or behaviour.

chamfer *n* a small gutter or furrow cut in wood or other hard material; a bevel or slope; the corner of anything originally right-angled cut aslant equally on the two sides which form it.

chamois *n* a species of goat-like antelope inhabiting high inaccessible mountains in Europe and Western Asia; a kind of soft leather made from various skins dressed with fish oil (in this sense often written **shammy**).

chamomile *n* same as **camomile**.

champ *vt* to bite with repeated action of the teeth and with a snapping noise; to bite into small pieces; to chew; to munch; to crunch.

champagne *n* a kind of light sparkling wine made in the department of Marne in the Champagne district of France.

champion *n* one who comes forward in defence of any cause; especially originally one who engages in single combat in the cause of another; one who has acknowledged superiority in certain matters decided by public contest or competition; one open to contend with all comers or otherwise requiring to resign the title.—*vt* to come forward and maintain or support (a cause or a person).

championship *n* state of being a champion; support or maintenance of a cause; a contest deciding who is the champion.

chance *n* the random or unexpected nature of events; accident; what fortune may bring; fortune; possibility of an occurrence; opportunity (*to lose a chance*).—*vi* (**chancing, chanced**) to happen; to come or arrive without design or expectation.—*vt* to put under the influence of chance; to risk; to hazard.—**to chance upon** to meet or find unexpectedly.—*adj* happening by chance; unexpected.

chancel *n* that part of the choir of a church between the altar or communion table and the balustrade or railing that encloses it or that part where the altar is placed.

chancellor *n* a high government official in some countries; in some universities, the honorary head.

Chancellor of the Exchequer *n* the principal finance minister of the government in Britain.

Chancery *n* in England, formerly the highest court of justice next to Parliament but since 1873 a division of the High Court of Justice.

chancre *n* a sore or ulcer caused by a venereal disease.

chandelier *n* a large hanging decorative holder with branches to hold a number of candles or light bulbs.

chandler *n* one who makes or sells candles; a dealer in general, the particular meaning of the term being determined by a prefix, as, tallow-chandler; ship-chandler, etc.

change *vt* (**changed, changing**) to cause to turn or pass from one state to another; to vary in form or essence; to alter or make different; to substitute another thing or things for (*to change the clothes*); to shift; to give or procure another kind of money for (*to change a banknote*); to give away for a money equivalent of a different kind; to exchange (*to change places with a person*).—*vi* to suffer change; to be altered; to undergo variation; to be partially or wholly transformed; to begin a new revolution or to pass from one phase to another, as the moon.—*n* any variation or alteration in form, state, quality or essence; a passing from one state or form to another; small money, which may be given for larger pieces; the balance of a sum of money returned when the price of goods is deducted.

changeable *adj* liable to change; subject to alteration; fickle; inconstant; mutable; variable.

changeling *n* a child supposed to be substituted by fairies for another.

channel *n* the bed of a stream of water; the hollow or course in which a stream flows; the deeper part of an estuary, bay, etc, where the current flows or which is most convenient for shipping; a strait or narrow sea between two islands, two continents or a continent and an island; that by which something passes or is transmitted (as

chameleon

news, information); means of passing, conveying or transmitting; a furrow or groove.—*vt* (**channelling, channelled**) to form a channel in; to groove; to direct.

chant *vt* to utter with a melodious voice; to sing; to celebrate in song; to repeat the words of in a kind of intoning voice or in a style between air and recitative.—*vi* to sing; to intone or perform a chant.—*n* a song or singing; melody; specifically, a short musical composition consisting generally of a long reciting note on which an indefinite number of words may be intoned and a melodic phrase or cadence.

chanter *n* in bagpipes, the tube with finger-holes for playing the melody.

chanterelle *n* a type of edible yellow mushroom.

chanticleer *n* a cock, so called from the clearness or loudness of its call.

chaos *n* that confusion or confused mass out of which the universe was created; a confused mixture of parts or elements; a scene of extreme confusion; disorder.

chaos theory *n* (*physics*) the theory that the behaviour of dynamic systems is haphazard rather than mathematical.

chaotic *adj* resembling chaos; confused.

chap[1] *n* a crack in the surface of the hands or feet.

chap[2], **chop** *n* the upper or lower part of the mouth; the jaw.

chap[3] *n* a man or a boy; (*colloq*) a youth.

chapbook *n* a kind of small book or tract; a small book of ballads, etc.

chapel *n* a subordinate place of worship usually attached to a large church or cathedral, connected with a palace or private residence, or subsidiary to a parish church; a place of worship used by dissenters from the Church of England; a meeting house; a union or society formed by the workers in a printing office.

chaperon *n* a woman, especially a married woman, who attends a young woman or a young couple to public places as a guide or protector.—*vt* to attend on as chaperon, guide, etc.

chapfallen, chopfallen *adj* dejected.

chaplain *n* an ecclesiastic who officiates at court, in the household of a nobleman or in an army, garrison, ship, institution, etc.

chaplet *n* a garland or wreath worn on the head; a rosary; a round moulding carved into beads, olives, etc.

chapman *n* (*pl* **chapmen**) formerly, a hawker, pedlar or travelling dealer.

chapter *n* a division of a book or treatise; the council of a bishop, consisting of the canons and other clergymen attached to a collegiate or cathedral church and presided over by a dean; the meeting of certain organized orders and societies; a branch of some society or brotherhood.

chapter house *n* the building in which a chapter meets for the transaction of business.

char[1] *vt* (**charred, charring**) to reduce to charcoal; to burn (wood) slightly or partially and on the surface.

char[2] *n* a charwoman.—*vi* (**charring, charred**) to act or be employed as a charwoman.

char[3] *n* a red-bellied fish related to the trout.

charabanc *n* a bus or motor coach used for outings.

character *n* a distinctive mark made by cutting, stamping or engraving, as on stone, metal or other hard material; a mark or figure, written or printed and used to form words and communicate ideas; a letter, figure or sign; the peculiar form of letters, written or printed, used by a particular person or people (*the Greek character*); the peculiar qualities impressed by nature or habit on a person, which distinguish him or her from others; a distinctive quality assigned to a person by repute; reputation, sometimes restricted to good qualities or reputation; strongly marked distinctive qualities of any kind; an account or statement of qualities or peculiarities; especially, an oral or written account of a person's character or qualifications; a person; a personage, especially applied to individuals represented in action or history, to persons of eminence and to persons marked by some prominent or idiosyncratic trait.

characteristic *adj* pertaining to or serving to constitute the character; exhibiting the peculiar qualities of a person or thing; peculiar; distinctive.—*n* that which serves to constitute a character; that which characterizes; that which distinguishes a person or thing from another.

characterize *vt* (**characterizing, characterized**) to give a special stamp or character to; to constitute a peculiar characteristic or the peculiar characteristics of; to stamp or distinguish (*characterized by benevolence*).

charade *n* a travesty; an absurd pretence; one part of charades.

charades *npl* a game in which a word of two or more syllables each is acted followed by the acting of the whole word.

charcoal *n* the black carbon matter produced by partially burning wood and used as fuel, as a filter and for drawing; a drawing made with charcoal; a dark grey colour.

charge *vt* (**charged, charging**) to lay a load or burden on; to burden; to load; to fill; to occupy (*to charge the memory*); to impute or register as a debt; to put down to the debt of; to register as indebted or as forming a debt (*to charge a person for a thing*;

chanterelle

to charge a thing to or *against a person*); to fix the price of (with *at* before the price or rate); to accuse; to impeach (*to charge a person with a crime*); to lay to one's charge; to impute; to ascribe the responsibility of (*to charge guilt on a person*); to entrust; to commission (a person with); to command; to enjoin; to instruct; to urge earnestly; to exhort; to adjure; to give directions to (a jury, etc); to instruct authoritatively; to attack by rushing against violently; to build up an electric charge in.—*vi* to rush to an attack; to place the price of a thing to one's debit.—*n* that which is laid on or in; any load or burden; the quantity of anything which an apparatus, as a gun, an electric battery, etc, is intended to receive and fitted to hold, or what is actually in as a load; an attack, onset or rush; an order, injunction, mandate or command; hence, a duty enjoined on or entrusted to one; care, custody; the person or thing committed to another's custody, care or management; a trust; instructions given by a judge to a jury or an exhortation given by a bishop to his clergy; what is alleged or brought forward by way of accusation; accusation; the sum payable as the price of anything bought; cost; expense; rent, tax or whatever constitutes a burden or duty.

chargeable *adj* capable of being charged; falling to be set, laid or imposed, as a tax or duty.

chargé d'affaires *n* (*pl* **chargés d'affaires**) one who transacts diplomatic business at a foreign court during the absence of his superior the ambassador or at a court where no functionary so high as an ambassador is appointed.

charger *n* a large dish; a warhorse; a device for charging a battery.

chariot *n* a four-wheeled pleasure or state carriage having one seat; a car or vehicle formerly used in war, in processions and for racing, drawn by two or more horses.

charioteer *n* formerly, the person who drove a chariot.

charisma *n* a special quality or power by which a person attracts or influences other people and inspires their devotion.

charismatic *adj* inspiring attraction, devotion etc.

charity *n* loving kindness towards one's fellow human beings; benevolence; liberality in thinking or judging; liberality in giving to the poor; whatever is bestowed gratuitously on the poor for their relief; any act of kindness or benevolence; a charitable institution; a hospital.

charitable *adj* pertaining to or characterized by charity; full of goodwill or loving kindness; benevolent and kind; liberal in gifts to the poor and in relieving them in distress; pertaining to relief to the poor;

springing from charity or intended for charity; lenient in judging of others; not harsh; favourable.

charlatan *n* a quack; a mountebank.

charlatanism *n* undue pretensions to skill; quackery.

Charleston *n* a lively dance in which the dancers make kicks to the side, popular in the 1920s.

charlock *n* a weedy annual of the mustard family with bright yellow flowers.

charm *n* anything believed to possess some occult or supernatural power, such as an amulet or spell or some mystic observance; something which exerts an irresistible power to please and attract; fascination; allurement; a trinket.—*vt* to subdue or control by incantation or magical or supernatural influence; to fortify or make invulnerable with charms; to subdue or soothe as if by magic; to give exquisite pleasure to; to fascinate; to enchant.—*vi* to act as a charm or spell; to produce the effect of a charm.

charmer *n* one who charms, fascinates or attracts.

charming *adj* delighting; fascinating; enchanting; alluring.

charnel house *n* formerly, a place under or near churches where the bones of the dead were deposited.

chart *n* a sheet of any kind on which information is exhibited in a methodical or tabulated form; specifically, a marine map with the coasts, islands, rocks, soundings, etc, to regulate the courses of ships; (*pl*) a list of the most popular pop music recordings.—*vt* to delineate, as on a chart; to map out.

charter *n* a writing given as evidence of a grant, contract, etc; any instrument executed with form and solemnity bestowing or granting powers, rights and privileges; privilege; immunity; exemption.—*vt* to hire or let (a ship, boat, etc) by charter or contract; to establish by charter; to grant.

Chartism *n* the political principles or opinions of the Chartists.

Chartist *n* one of a body of political reformers in England that sprang up about the year 1838 and advocated as their leading principles universal suffrage, no property qualification for a seat in parliament, annual parliaments, equal representation, payment of members and vote by ballot, all which privileges they demanded as constituting the people's charter.

chartulary *n* a record or register, as of a monastery.

charwoman *n* (*pl* **charwomen**) a woman employed by the day on odd jobs about a house.

chary *adj* careful; cautious; frugal; sparing (with *of* before an object).

chariot

chase¹ *vt* (**chased, chasing**) to pursue for the purpose of taking or capturing; to hunt; to follow after or search for with eagerness; to pursue for any purpose; to follow with hostility; to drive off.—*n* pursuit; hunting; search for or following after; that which is pursued or hunted; an open piece of ground or place well stocked with game and belonging to a private proprietor.

chase² *n* an iron frame used by printers to hold type when set in columns or pages; the part of a gun between the trunnions and the muzzle; a wide groove.

chase³ *vt* to cut a thread on, so as to make a screw.

chaser *n* a person or thing that chases; a drink taken after strong liquor, as beer after whisky.

chasm *n* a gaping or yawning opening, as in the earth; an abyss; a wide and deep cleft; a fissure; a void space; a fundamental difference in opinion, outlook, interest, etc.

chassis *n* the framework of a motorcar carrying the body and other parts.

chaste *adj* pure; virtuous; refraining from sexual intercourse outside marriage; restrained, simple and unadorned.

chasten *vt* to correct by disciplining; to chastise; to punish; to restrain.

chastise *vt* (**chastised, chastising**) to punish; to beat; to scold.

chastisement *n* the act of chastising; punishment; scolding.

chastity *n* the state or property of being chaste; sexual purity.

chastity belt *n* a device designed to prevent women having sexual intercourse, common in the Middle Ages when husbands were away on military campaigns.

chasuble *n* a rich vestment or garment worn by a priest at the celebration of the Eucharist.

chat¹ *vi* (**chatted, chatting**) to talk idly or in a familiar manner—**to chat up** to talk in a flirtatious way to someone of the other sex.—*n* free, familiar or informal talk; idle talk.

chat² *n* one of several small, lively birds of the warbler family, three species of which are found in Britain, namely, the stonechat, the whinchat and the wheatear.

château *n* (*pl* **châteaux**) a French castle or large country house.

chat show *n* a television or radio programme with informal interviews and conversation.

chattel *n* an item or article of goods, specifically applied in law to goods movable or immovable, except such as have the nature of freehold.

chatter *vi* to utter sounds rapidly and indistinctly, as a magpie or a monkey; to make a noise by repeated rapid striking together of the teeth, as from excessive cold; to talk idly, carelessly or rapidly; to jabber.—*n* sounds like those of a magpie or monkey; idle talk.

chatterbox *n* one who talks incessantly.

chatty *adj* inclined to chat; talkative.

chauffeur *n* a person regularly employed to drive a private motorcar.—*vt* to drive as a chauffeur.

chauvinism *n* absurdly exaggerated patriotism or military enthusiasm; jingoism; an excessive loyalty or devotion to a cause or belief, especially a man's belief in the supremacy of men over women.—**chauvinist** *n*.—**chauvinistic** *adj*.

cheap *adj* capable of being purchased at a low price, either as compared with the usual price of the commodity or with the real value, or more vaguely with the price of other commodities; being of small value; common; not respected.

cheapen *vt* to beat down the price of; to lessen the value of; to depreciate.

cheap-jack *adj* cheap and worthless; inferior.

cheat *vt* to deceive and defraud; to impose on; to trick (*to cheat a person of* or *out of something*); to mislead.—*vi* to act dishonestly; to practise fraud or trickery.—*n* a fraud committed by deception; a trick, imposition or imposture; a person who cheats; a swindler.

check *n* the act of suddenly stopping or restraining; a stop; hindrance; restraint; obstruction; a term or word of warning in chess when one player obliges the other either to move or guard his or her king; a reprimand; slight; cloth in which coloured lines or stripes cross each other rectangularly, making a pattern resembling the squares of a chessboard; the pattern of such cloth; a mark put against names or items on going over a list; a duplicate or counterpart used for security or verification; a counterfoil; a ticket or token given for identification.—*vt* to stop or moderate the motion of; to restrain in action; to hinder; to curb; to rebuke; in chess, to make a move which puts the adversary's king in check; to compare with a counterfoil or something similar with a view to ascertain authenticity or accuracy.—*vi* to make a stop; to stop; to pause.—**to check in** to register as having arrived at a hotel, airport desk etc.—**to check out** at a hotel to pay the bill and leave.—*adj* made of check; chequered.

checkmate *n* in chess, the position of a king when in check and unable to be moved, which brings the game to a close; hence, defeat; overthrow.—*vt* (**checkmated, checkmating**) to put in check, as an opponent's king in chess, so that it cannot be released; hence, to defeat; to thwart; to frustrate.

chasuble

checkout *n* the place in a shop, particularly a supermarket, where goods are paid for.

checkpoint *n* a place where people or vehicles may be stopped so that passports or other documents may be checked.

Cheddar *n* a rich fine-flavoured cheese made at Cheddar in Somerset, England; any cheese of similar character.

cheek *n* the side of the face below the eyes on each side; cool confidence; brazen-faced impudence; impudent or insulting talk.

cheeky *adj* disrespectful; impudent.

cheep *vti* to chirp, as a young bird; to squeak.—*n* a chirp; a squeak.

cheer *n* a state of gladness or joy; gaiety; animation; that which makes cheerful or promotes good spirits; provisions for a feast; fare; a shout of joy, encouragement, applause or acclamation.—*vt* to gladden; to make cheerful; to encourage; to salute with shouts of joy or cheers; to applaud.—*vi* to grow cheerful; to become more cheerful (often with *up*); to utter a cheer or shout of acclamation or joy.

cheerful *adj* being in good spirits; merry; lively; animated; promoting or causing cheerfulness; genial.

cheerio *interj* goodbye.

cheers *interj* an expression used when drinking a toast; goodbye; thank you.

cheery *adj* showing cheerfulness or good spirits; promoting cheerfulness.

cheese *n* an article of food consisting of the curd or casein of milk, coagulated by rennet or some acid, separated from the whey and usually pressed into a solid mass in a mould.

cheesecake *n* a cake on a base of biscuit made with cream cheese or cottage cheese topped often with fruit.

cheese-paring *adj* meanly economical; parsimonious.

cheetah *n* the hunting leopard, the swiftest of the mammals, light brown in colour with dark spots.

chef *n* professional cook; the head cook in a hotel, restaurant, etc.

chef-d'oeuvre *n* (*pl* **chefs-d'oeuvre**) a masterpiece; a fine work in art, literature, etc.

chela *n* (*pl* **chelae**) one of the prehensile claws possessed by certain crustaceans, as the crab, lobster, etc.

chelonian *adj* pertaining to or designating animals of the tortoise kind.—*n* a tortoise or turtle.

chemical *n* a substance used or arising from a chemical process.—*adj* of, used in or produced by chemistry.

chemical reaction *n* an interaction between substances that changes their chemical structure or energy content.

chemical warfare *n* warfare in which poisonous gases and other chemicals are used.

chemise *n* an undergarment or smock worn by women.

chemist *n* a person skilled in chemistry; one whose business is to make chemical examinations or investigations; one who deals in drugs and medicines, a pharmacist.

chemistry *n* the study of the composition of substances and their combinations and reactions; chemical structure.

chemotherapy *n* the treatment of disease, especially cancer, by chemicals such as drugs.

chenille *n* a tufted cord of silk or worsted.

cheque *n* an order for money drawn on a banker or bank, payable to the bearer.

chequebook *n* a book containing blank bank cheques.

chequer, checker *n* one of the pieces used in the game of Chinese chequers; a chess or draught board; (*pl*) the game of draughts (*Amer*); one of the divisions of a pattern that consists of squares; the pattern itself.—*vt* to mark with little squares, like a chessboard, by lines or stripes of different colours; to mark with different colours; (*fig*) to variegate with different qualities, scenes or events; to diversify; to impart variety to (*events that chequer one's career*).

cheetah

chequered, checkered *adj* marked with or exhibiting squares of different colours; varied with a play of different colours; (*fig*) variegated with different qualities, scenes or events; experiencing both good and bad fortune (*a chequered life*).

cherish *vt* to treat with tenderness and affection; to take care of; to foster; to hold as dear; to indulge and encourage in the mind; to harbour; to cling to.

cheroot *n* a kind of cigar of a cylindrical or often somewhat tapering shape, with both ends cut square off.

cherry *n* the fruit of a tree of the plum family, with a pulpy drupe enclosing a one-seeded smooth stone; the tree itself; also the name of other fruits.—*adj* like a red cherry in colour; red; ruddy.

cherry picker *n* a crane, usually on a truck, with a long elbow-jointed arm carrying a platform that can be raised and lowered.

chert *n* a variety of quartz.

cherub *n* (*pl* **cherubs, cherubim**) one of an order of angels; a beautiful child.

cherubic *adj* pertaining to or resembling cherubs; angelic.

chervil *n* an aromatic herb used in cooking and salads.

chess *n* a game of skill played by two players with different pieces on a chequered board divided into sixty-four squares.

chessboard *n* the board used in the game of chess.

chessman *n* (*pl* **chessmen**) a piece used in playing the game of chess.

chessboard

chest *n* a large, strong box; a case in which certain kinds of goods are packed for transit; the trunk of the body from the neck to the belly; the thorax.

chesterfield *n* a sofa with two upright ends.

chestnut *n* the seed or nut of a forest tree allied to the beech, enclosed in a prickly pericarp, containing two or more edible seeds; the tree itself or its timber; the colour of the husk of a chestnut; a reddish-brown colour; an old joke.—*adj* of the colour of a chestnut; reddish-brown.

chest of drawers *n* a piece of furniture with sliding drawers for holding various articles of dress, linen, etc.

cheval glass *n* a looking glass large enough to reflect the whole figure and mounted on a frame that can be swivelled.

chevalier *n* a horseman; a knight.

Cheviot *n* a variety of sheep noted for its large carcass and valuable wool.

chevron *n* (*heral*) a figure on a shield representing two rafters of a house meeting at the top; (*archit*) a variety of fret ornament; a zigzag; (*milit*) the V-shaped distinguishing marks on the sleeves of non-commissioned officers' jackets to indicate rank.

chicken

chew *vt* to bite and grind with the teeth; to masticate.—**to chew the cud** to ruminate; (*fig*) to ruminate or meditate on something.—*vi* to perform the act of chewing; to champ.—*n* that which is chewed; a quid of tobacco.

chewing gum *n* a preparation of various gums, sweetened and flavoured, used for chewing.

chiaroscuro *n* (*pl* **chiaroscuros**) the art of judiciously distributing the lights and shadows in a picture.

chic *n* elegance; style; smartness.—*adj* elegant, stylish; smart.

chicane *n* a hand at bridge without trumps; a barrier or obstacle on a motor-racing circuit; chicanery.

chicanery *n* underhand dealing; trickery; verbal subterfuge.

chick *n* a chicken.

chicken *n* a young domestic fowl.

chicken feed *n* a very small insignificant amount, especially of money.

chicken-hearted *adj* timid; cowardly.

chickenpox *n* a mild contagious viral disease causing an itchy rash and generally appearing in children.

child

chickpea *n* an edible pea-like seed of a bushy plant found in Mediterranean countries, Asia and the Middle East.

chickweed *n* a common weed with small white blossoms.

chicory *n* a plant with leaves used in salads and a fleshy tapering root used as a substitute for coffee or to mix with coffee.

chide *vt* (*pret* **chidded** *or* **chid**, *pp* **chidded**, **chid** *or* **chidden**, *ppr* **chiding**) to scold; to find fault with or take exception to (a thing); to strike as punishment or admonition.—*vi* to scold; to find fault.

chiding *n* a scolding.

chief *adj* highest in office, authority or rank; principal or most eminent in any quality or action; most important; at the head; leading; main.—*n* the person highest in authority, the head or head person; a military commander; the person who heads an army; the principal person of a clan, tribe, family, etc.

chiefly *adv* principally; mainly; for the most part; mostly.

chieftain *n* a leader or commander; a chief; the head of a clan or family.

chiffon *n* a thin gauzy material.—*adj* made of chiffon; (of a pie filling, etc) having a light, fluffy texture.

chignon *n* the term applied to a woman's back hair when raised and rolled up.

Chihuahua *n* a breed of very small short-haired dog with large eyes and pointed ears, originally from Mexico.

chilblain *n* an inflamed sore on the hands or feet produced by cold.

child *n* (*pl* **children**) a son or a daughter of any age; a male or female descendant in the first degree; a very young person of either sex; one of immature knowledge, experience or attainments; (*pl*) descendants; offspring.—**with child** pregnant.

child abuse *n* maltreatment of a child, especially through physical injury or sexual interference.

child-bearing *n* the act of producing or bringing forth children; parturition.

childbed *n* the state of a woman who is in labour.

childbirth *n* the act of bringing forth a child; labour.

childhood *n* the state of a child; the time in which persons are still classed as children.

childish *adj* of or belonging to a child or to childhood; like a child or what is proper to childhood (with the disparaging sense of trifling, puerile, ignorant, silly, weak).

childlike *adj* resembling a child or that which belongs to children; meek; submissive; innocent; trusting.

child's play *n* anything easily accomplished or surmounted.

chiliad *n* a thousand; a collection or sum containing a thousand individuals or particulars; the period of a thousand years.

chill *n* a shivering with cold; a cold fit; sensation of cold in an animal body; chilliness; coldness or absence of heat in a substance; (*fig*) the feeling of being damped or discouraged; a depressing influence.—*adj* cold; tending to cause shivering (*chill winds*); experiencing cold; shivering with cold; (*fig*) depressing; discouraging; distant; formal; not warm (*a chill recep-*

tion).—*vt* to affect with chill; to make chilly; to make cold, as by placing in ice; (*fig*) to check in enthusiasm or warmth; to discourage; to dispirit; to depress; (*metal*) to reduce suddenly the temperature of (a piece of cast iron) with the view of hardening (*a chilled shot*).

chilli *n* the hot-tasting pod of some of the capsicums, often dried and used as a flavouring for spicy foods.

chilling *adj* cooling; causing to shiver; (*fig*) tending to repress enthusiasm or warmth; cold; distant (*a chilling manner* or *address*); frightening.

chilly *adj* experiencing or causing the sensation of chilliness; disagreeably cold; chilling.—*adv* in a chill or chilly manner.

Chiltern Hundreds *n* a hilly district of Buckinghamshire belonging to the British crown, the stewardship of which is accepted by a member of parliament who wishes to resign his seat, this being regarded as an office of profit under the crown and so compelling resignation.

chimaera *n* same as **chimera**.

chime *n* the harmonious sound of bells or musical instruments; a set of bells (properly five or more) tuned to a musical scale and struck by hammers, not by the tongues.—*vi* (**chiming, chimed**) to sound in consonance, rhythm or harmony; to give out harmonious sounds; hence, to accord; to agree; to suit; to harmonize; to express agreement (often with *in with*, as *to chime in with one's sentiments* or *humour*).—*vt* to cause to sound harmoniously, as a set of bells.

chimera, chimaera *n* in Classical myth, a fire-breathing monster, the foreparts of whose body were those of a lion, the middle of a goat and the hinder of a dragon; a vain or idle fancy; a wild product of the imagination.

chimere *n* the upper robe, to which the lawn sleeves of a bishop are attached.

chimerical *adj* merely imaginary; fanciful; fantastic.

chimney *n* an erection, generally of stone or brick, containing a passage by which the smoke of a fire or furnace escapes to the open air; a chimney stack; a flue; the funnel of a steam engine; a tall glass to surround the flame of a lamp to protect it and promote combustion.

chimney corner *n* the corner of a fireplace; the fireside or a place near the fire.

chimneypiece *n* the assemblage of architectural dressings around the fireplace in a room; a mantelpiece.

chimney pot *n* a pipe of earthenware or sheet metal placed on the top of chimneys to prevent smoking.

chimney stack *n* a group of chimneys carried up together.

chimney stalk *n* a long chimney such as that connected with factories.

chimney sweep *n* one whose occupation is to clear chimneys of soot.

chimpanzee *n* a large West African ape belonging to the anthropoid or manlike monkeys and most nearly related to the gorilla.

chin *n* the lower part of the face below the mouth; the point of the under jaw in humans or a corresponding part in other animals.

china *n* fine porcelain; articles made from this.

china shop *n* a shop in which china, crockery, glassware, etc, are sold.

chinchilla *n* a genus of rodent animals peculiar to the South American continent, one species of which has fine pearly-grey fur; the fur of the chinchilla.

chine *n* the backbone or spine of an animal; a piece of the backbone of an animal, with the adjoining parts, cut for cooking.

Chinese *adj* pertaining to China.—*n sing, pl* a native of China; the language of China.

Chinese chequers *n* a board game played with marbles or pegs.

Chinese lantern *n* a lantern made of coloured paper used in illuminations.

chink *n* a narrow aperture; a cleft, rent or fissure of greater length than breadth; a cranny, gap or crack.

chink *vi* to make a small sharp metallic sound.—*vt* to cause to sound as by shaking coins or small pieces of metal.—*n* a short, sharp, clear, metallic sound; the reed bunting.

chintz *n* cotton cloth or calico printed with flowers or other devices in at least five different colours and now generally glazed.

chip *vt* (**chipped, chipping**) to cut into small pieces; to diminish by cutting away a little at a time or in small pieces; to knock a small piece off.—*vi* to break or fly off in small pieces.—*n* a piece of wood, stone or other substance separated from a body by a blow of an instrument; a mark or dent caused by breaking off a small piece; a small disc or counter used in some gambling games; a thin slice of deep-fried potato; a tiny piece of semiconducting material, such as silicon, printed with a microcircuit and used as part of an integrated circuit.

chipmunk *n* the popular name of the ground squirrel, a rodent animal very common in North America.

Chippendale *adj* of the light style of furniture introduced in the middle of the eighteenth century by the designer Thomas Chippendale.

chiromancy *n* divination by the hand; the art or practice of foretelling a person's fortune by inspecting the lines and lineaments of the hand; palmistry.

chimney

chinchilla

chiropodist *n* one who treats minor complains of the feet, such as corns.

chiropteran *n* a bat.

chiropterous *adj* belonging to the bat family.

chirp *vi* to make a short sharp shrill sound, as of small birds or certain insects; to cheep.—*n* a short, shrill note, as of certain birds or insects.

chirrup *vi* to chirp.—*n* a chirp.

chisel *n* an instrument of iron or steel used in carpentry, joinery, cabinet work, masonry, sculpture, etc, for paring, hewing or gouging.—*vt* (**chiselled, chiselling**) to cut, pare, gouge or engrave with a chisel (*a statue chiselled out of marble*); (*fig*) to cheat, as in a bargain.

chit¹ *n* a note; an order or pass.

chit² *n* a child or babe; a young and insignificant person; a cheeky child or girl.

chitchat *n* prattle; familiar or trifling talk.—*vi* (**chitchatting, chitchatted**) to gossip.

chitin *n* an organic substance which forms the outer covering of many invertebrate animals.

chiton *n* the name of certain molluscs, the shell of which is formed of successive portions, often in contact and overlapping each other but never truly articulated.

chitterling *n* in cookery, part of the small intestines, as of pig, fried for food (generally used in the plural).

chivalrous *adj* pertaining to chivalry; gallant; generous to the weak.

chivalry *n* the system to which medieval knighthood with all its laws and usages belonged; the qualities of a knight, as courtesy, valour and dexterity in arms; gallantry; kindness to the weak.

chive *n* a plant whose grass-like leaves are used in cooking and salads.

chivvy *vt* (**chivvied, chivvying**) to make to hurry; to nag; to harass.

chlamydia *n* a sexually transmitted disease.

chlorate *n* a salt of chloric acid.

chloric *adj* pertaining to or containing chlorine.

chloride *n* a compound of chlorine with another element.

chlorinate *vt* (**chlorinated, chlorinating**) to treat with chlorine; to disinfect with chlorine; to combine with chlorine.

chlorine *n* a non-metallic element of a greenish-yellow colour contained in common salt, from which it is chiefly obtained, being used as a bleaching agent and disinfectant.

chlorofluorocarbon *n* any of various compounds containing carbon, chlorine, fluorine and hydrogen, used in refrigeration agents, aerosol propellants, etc, and considered to be harmful to the earth's atmosphere, particularly the ozone layer.

chloroform *n* a volatile colourless liquid,

formerly used as an anaesthetic, now as a solvent and refrigerant.

chlorophyll *n* the green colouring matter of plants which is developed by the influence of sunlight.

chlorosis *n* a form of anaemia which affects young women and is characterized by a pale greenish hue of the skin; (*bot*) lack of green pigment.

chock-full *adj* as full as possible.

chocolate *n* a paste or cake composed of the kernels of the cacao nut ground and combined with sugar and vanilla, cinnamon, cloves or other flavouring substances; the beverage made by dissolving chocolate in boiling water or milk.—*adj* having the colour of chocolate; of a dark, glossy brown.

choice *n* the act or power of choosing; a selecting or separating from two or more things that which is preferred; selection; election; option; preference; the thing chosen; the best part of anything.—*adj* carefully selected; worthy of being preferred; select; precious.

choiceness *n* the quality of being choice or select; excellence; value.

choir *n* a collection of singers, especially in a church; that part of a church appropriated for the singers in cruciform churches; that part eastward from the nave and separated from it usually by a screen of open work; a chancel.—*vti* to sing in company.

choir screen *n* an ornamental open screen of wood or stone between the choir or chancel and the nave.

choke *vt* (**choked, choking**) to deprive of the power of breathing by stopping the passage of the breath through the windpipe; to compress the windpipe of; to strangle; to stop by filling (any passage); to obstruct; to block up; to hinder by obstruction or impediments (as plants from growing).—*vi* to have the windpipe stopped; to have something stick in the throat.

choler *n* anger, wrath, irascibility.

choleric *adj* easily irritated; irascible; inclined to anger; proceeding from anger.

cholera *n* a severe, infectious intestinal disease characterized by copious vomiting and purging of bilious matter.

cholesterol *n* a substance found in some animal tissue, an excess of which is thought to be associated with hardening of the arteries or heart disease.

choose *vt* (*pret* **chose**, *pp* **chosen**, *ppr* **choosing**) to take by preference; to make choice or selection of; to pick out; to select; to prefer; to wish; to be inclined or have an inclination for.—*vi* to make a choice.

chop¹ *vt* (**chopped, chopping**) to cut into pieces; to mince; to sever or separate by

chisel

chop

striking with a sharp instrument (usually with *off*).—*n* a piece chopped off; a slice, particularly of meat; (*colloq*) food.—**the chop** (*colloq*) dismissal.

chop² *vt* (**chopped, chopping**) to change, especially direction.—**to chop and change** to keep changing.—**to chop logic** to dispute or argue in a sophistic manner or with an affectation of logical terms or methods.

chopfallen *adj* same as **chapfallen**.

chopper *n* one who or that which chops; a tool for chopping or mincing meat; a cleaver; (*colloq*) a helicopter.

choppy *adj* showing short broken waves.

chops *npl* the chap; the jaw.

chopstick *n* one of two small sticks of wood, ivory, etc, used by the Chinese and Japanese for conveying food to the mouth.

choral *adj* belonging, relating or pertaining to a chorus, choir or concert.—*n* a chorale.

chorale *n* a psalm or hymn tune, often sung in unison by the congregation, the organ supplying the harmony.

chord *n* the string of a musical instrument; (*mus*) the simultaneous combination of different sounds, consonant or dissonant; (*geom*) a straight line drawn from one end of an arc of a circle to the other; a feeling of sympathy, recognition or remembering.

chore *n* a piece of housework; a regular or tedious task.

chorea *n* (*med*) a neurological disorder characterized by jerky involuntary movements, especially of the arms, legs and face.

choreograph *vt* to devise and arrange the steps for a ballet or dance routine.

choreographer *n* one who devises and arranges ballet and dance routines.

choreographic *adj* pertaining to the arrangement of ballet and dance routines.

choreography *n* the art and practice of devising and arranging ballet and dance routines.

chorister *n* a singer in a choir or chorus; a singer generally.

chorography *n* the art or practice of making maps of or of describing particular regions, countries or districts.

chortle *vi* (**chortling, chortled**) to chuckle triumphantly; to give an exultant snort.—*n* a chuckle or series of chuckles.

chorus *n* the performers in a Greek play who observed and sang of the action of the play; the song between the acts; now, usually, verses of a song in which the company join the singer or the singing of the company with the singer; a union or chiming of voices in general (*a chorus of laughter* or *ridicule*); (*mus*) a composition in parts sung by many voices; the whole body of vocalists other than soloists in an oratorio, opera, musical or concert.—*vt* to

sing, speak or agree in chorus.

chough *n* a British bird of the crow family.

chow *n* a breed of thick-coated dog, originally from china; (*sl*) food.

chrestomathy *n* a book of extracts from a foreign language, with notes, intended to be used in acquiring the language.

chrism *n* holy or consecrated oil or unguent used in the administration of baptism, confirmation, ordination and extreme unction, more especially in the Latin and Greek churches.

Christ *n* Jesus of Nazareth, regarded by Christians as the Messiah.

christen *vt* to name and baptize; to baptize; to name or denominate generally.

Christendom *n* the territories, countries or regions chiefly inhabited by Christians; the whole body of Christians.

Christian *n* one who believes in the religion of Christ; a believer in Christ who is characterized by piety.—*adj* pertaining to Christ or to Christianity; kind; gentle; humane.

Christianity *n* the religion of Christians or the system of doctrines and precepts taught by Christ; conformity to the laws and precepts of the Christian religion.

Christian name *n* the name given or announced at baptism, as distinguished from the family name, now often *first name*.

Christian Science *n* a religious system founded in America by Mary Baker Eddy and inculcating the science of mind healing.

Christmas *n* the festival of the Christian church observed annually on the 25th day of December, in memory of the birth of Christ; Christmas Day; Christmastide.

Christmas card *n* a greetings card, usually decorative, sent at Christmas.

Christmas Day *n* the 25th day of December when Christmas is celebrated.

Christmas Eve *n* the evening of the day before Christmas.

Christmas pudding *n* a rich pudding of eggs, flour, suet, spices and dried fruit, cooked by steaming and traditionally eaten at Christmas.

Christmas rose *n* a plant of the hellebore genus, so called from its open rose-like flower which blossoms during winter.

Christmas stocking *n* a stocking hung by a child on Christmas for Father Christmas to fill with presents.

Christmastide *n* Christmas Eve (24th December) to Epiphany (6th January).

Christmas tree *n* a small evergreen tree decorated with lights and trinkets, set up at Christmas, from which are hung presents.

Christology *n* a discourse or treatise concerning Christ; that branch of divinity that deals directly with Christ.

Christ's-thorn *n* a deciduous shrub with

Christmas tree

chough

149

large hooked spines, a native of Palestine and the south of Europe (so named from a belief that it supplied the crown of thorns for Christ).

chromate *n* a salt of chromic acid.

chromatic *adj* relating to colour or to coloured inks or pigments; (*mus*) including notes not belonging to the diatonic scale.

chromatics *n* the science of colours; that part of optics which treats of the properties of the colours of light and of natural bodies.

chromatic scale *n* a scale made up of thirteen successive semitones, that is, the eight diatonic tones and the five intermediate tones.

chrome *n* chromium; a chromium pigment; something plated with an alloy of chromium.

chromic *adj* pertaining to chrome or obtained from it.

chromite *n* a mineral containing chromium.

chromium *n* a hard metallic element which forms very hard steel-grey masses and which is used in the manufacture of steel alloys and electroplating to give a tough surface.

chromolithograph *n* a picture obtained by means of chromolithography.

chromolithography *n* a method of producing coloured lithographic pictures by using stones having different portions of the picture drawn on them with inks of different colours and so arranged as to blend into a complete picture.

chromosomal *adj* pertaining to a chromosome or chromosomes.

chromosome *n* any of the microscopic thread-like bodies responsible for the transmission of hereditary characteristics usually occurring in pairs in the nuclei of most cells.

chromosphere *n* a gaseous envelope that surrounds the body of the sun and through which the light of the photosphere passes.

chronic *adj* continuing a long time, as a disease; habitual.

chronicle *n* an account of facts or events arranged in the order of time; a history, more especially one of a simple unpretentious character.—*vt* (**chronicled, chronicling**) to record in history or chronicle; to record; to register.

chronicler *n* one who chronicles; a writer of a chronicle.

Chronicles *n* the title of two books of the Old Testament consisting mainly of the annals of the kingdom of Judah.

chronogram *n* a word or words in which a date is expressed by the numeral letters occurring therein.

chronograph *n* a device of various kinds for measuring and registering very minute portions of time with extreme precision.

chrysalis

chronological *adj* relating to chronology; containing an account of events in the order of time; according to the order of time.

chronologist, chronologer *n* one skilled in chronology; a person who investigates the dates of past events and transactions.

chronology *n* the science of ascertaining the true periods or years when past events or transactions took place and arranging them in their proper order according to their dates.

chronometer *n* any instrument that measures time, as a clock, watch or dial; specifically, a timekeeper of great perfection of workmanship, made much on the principle of a watch but rather larger, used (in conjunction with observations of the heavenly bodies) in determining the longitude at sea.

chrysalis *n* (*pl* **chrysalises, chrysalides**) the form which butterflies, moths and most other insects assume when they change from the state of larva or caterpillar and before they arrive at their winged state.

chrysanthemum *n* the generic and common name of numerous species of composite plants, two of which are common weeds in Britain, the ox-eye daisy and the corn marigold, while the Chinese chrysanthemum in its numerous varieties is equally well known.

chrysoberyl *n* a gem of a yellowish-green colour, next to the sapphire in hardness.

chrysolite *n* a greenish, sometimes transparent, gem, composed of silica, magnesium and iron, not of great value.

chrysoprase *n* a translucent mineral of an apple-green colour, a variety of chalcedony much esteemed as a gem.

chub *n* a river fish of the carp family, having the body oblong, nearly round; the head and back green, the sides silvery and the belly white.

chubby *adj* having a round plump face or plump body; round and fat; plump.

chuck[1] *n* the voice or call of a hen and some other birds or a sound resembling that.—*vi* to make the noise which a hen and some other birds make when they call their chickens.

chuck[2] *n* (*engin*) a contrivance to hold work or a tool in a machine, especially in a lathe.

chuck[3] *vt* to strike, tap or give a gentle blow; to throw with quick motion a short distance; to pitch.—*n* a slight blow or tap under the chin; a toss; a short throw.

chuckle *vi* (**chuckled, chuckling**) to cackle, as a hen or other fowl; to laugh in a suppressed or broken manner; to feel inward triumph or exultation.—*n* a short, suppressed laugh, expressive of satisfaction, exultation, amusement.

chuffed *adj* (*colloq*) very pleased; delighted; thrilled.

chukka, chukker *n* one of the six periods into which a game of polo is usually divided.

chum *n* a close companion; a bosom friend. —*vi* (**chumming, chummed**) to be the chum of someone; to accompany someone somewhere.

chump *n* a short, thick, heavy piece of wood; a fool; the thick end of a loin of veal or mutton next the tail.

chunk *n* a lump, as of bread, cheese, wood.

church *n* a house consecrated to the worship of God among Christians; the collective body of Christians; a particular body of Christians united under one form of ecclesiastical government in one creed and using the same ritual and ceremonies; ecclesiastical power or authority.—*vt* to perform with or for anyone the office of returning thanks in the church, as a mother after childbirth.

churchman *n* (*pl* **churchmen**) an ecclesiastic or clergyman.

Church of England *n* the established church in England, organized on episcopal lines; the Anglican Church.

Church of Rome *n* the Roman Catholic Church.

Church of Scotland *n* the established church in Scotland, organized on presbyterian lines.

churchwarden *n* a functionary appointed by the minister or elected by the parishioners to superintend a church and its concerns, to represent the interests of the parish, etc; a clay pipe with a long stem.

churchyard *n* the ground in which the dead are buried adjoining a church.

churl *n* a rude, surly, sullen, selfish or rough-tempered man.

churlish *adj* rude; surly; sullen.

churn *n* a vessel in which cream or milk is vigorously turned to make milk or cream into butter.—*vt* to stir or agitate (milk or cream) in order to make into butter; to make (butter) by the agitation of milk or cream; to shake or agitate with violence or continued motion.—**to churn out** (*colloq*) to produce quickly or one after the other or without much effort.

chute *n* a river fall or rapid over which timber is floated; an inclined trough or tube through which articles are passed from a higher to a lower level; an inclined slide for children; a slide sloping down to a swimming pool.

chutney *n* an Indian condiment made from fruit, spices and herbs, etc.

chutzpah *n* audacity; presumption; effrontery; brazenness.

chyle *n* a white or milky fluid separated from food while in the intestines, taken up by the lacteal vessels and finally entering the blood.

chyme *n* the pulpy mass of partially digested food before the chyle is extracted from it.

ciao *interj* an Italian expression used in greeting or bidding farewell to someone.

cicada *n* (*pl* **cicadae, cicadas**) the popular and generic name of certain insects, the males of which have on each side of the body an organ with which they can make a considerable noise.

cicatrix *n* (*pl* **cicatrices**) a scar; a little seam or elevation of flesh remaining after a wound or ulcer is healed.

cicatrize *vt* (**cicatrized, cicatrizing**) to heal a wound by inducing the skin to form a cicatrix; to mark with scars.

cicely *n* popular name applied to several umbelliferous plants, sweet cicely or sweet chervil, being an aromatic plant with fine, fern-like foliage.

cicerone *n* a person who explains the curiosities or special interest of a place; a guide.

Ciceronian *adj* resembling the style of Cicero; eloquent.

cider *n* a fermented, slightly alcoholic drink prepared from the juice of apples.

cigar *n* a small roll of tobacco leaf with a pointed end for putting into the mouth for smoking.

cigarette *n* a little cut tobacco rolled up in thin paper, used for smoking.

cilia *npl* (*sing* **cilium**) the hairs which grow from the margin of the eyelids; eyelashes; hairs or bristles situated on the margin of a vegetable body; small, generally microscopic, vibrating hair-like filaments which line or cover certain organs.

cinch *n* in USA, a saddle girth; a firm hold; (*colloq*) a sure thing.

cinchona *n* any of a number of South American trees and shrubs, some of which yield the bark from which quinine is obtained; the bark of such trees.

cincture *n* a belt, girdle or something similar; that which rings, encircles or encloses; enclosure; (*archit*) a ring round a column.

cinder *n* a solid piece of matter remaining after having been subjected to combustion; especially a piece of coal more or less completely burnt but not reduced to ashes.

cine- *prefix* film or cinema (*cinecamera, cinefilm*).

cinema *n* a building for showing films; the film industry.

cinema vérité *n* cinema photography of real-life scenes and situations, etc, to create realism.

cinematography *n* the art, craft or process of making films.

cineraceous, cinereous *adj* like ashes; having the colour of the ashes of wood.

church

151

cineraria *n* the common and generic name of several species of composite plants (chiefly South African) many varieties of which are cultivated for their flowers of various colours.

cinerary *adj* pertaining to ashes; a term applied to the urns in which the ashes of bodies which had been burned were deposited.

cinnabar *n* red sulphide of mercury; a red pigment; vermilion.

cinnamon *n* a tree of the laurel family, a native of Sri Lanka and other parts of tropical Asia; its dried, aromatic edible inner bark with some degree of sweetness and astringency used as a spice; a yellowish brown colour.—*adj* yellowish-brown.

cinnamon stone *n* a variety of garnet of a cinnamon colour.

cinquefoil *n* an ornament in the pointed style of architecture somewhat resembling five leaves about a common centre; the name of various plants having leaves arranged in groups of five, as the five-bladed clover, etc.

cinquefoil

Cinque Ports *npl* five ports on the southern shore of England, towards France, namely Hastings, Romney, Hythe, Dover and Sandwich, to which were added Winchelsea, Rye and Seaford, all having royal grants of particular privileges on condition of providing a certain number of ships in war at their own expense.

cipher *n* the numerical character or figure 0 or nothing; any numerical character, 0–9; a person or thing of no consequence, importance or value; a monogram or literal device formed of the intertwined initials of a name; a kind of secret writing.—*vi* to use figures; to practise arithmetic.—*vt* to write in occult or secret characters.

Circean *adj* pertaining to Circe, in Greek mythology a celebrated sorceress who transformed the companions of Ulysses into swine by a magical beverage; hence, fascinating but brutish or poisonous; magical.

circle *n* a plane figure delineated by a single curve line called its circumference, every part of which is equally distant from a point within it called the centre; the line bounding or forming such a figure or something in a similar form; a ring; a round body; compass; circuit; a series (as of actions) ending where it begins; an ending where one began; a number of particulars regarded as having a central point; a number of persons associated by some tie; a coterie; a set.—*vt* (**circled**, **circling**) to encircle; to encompass; to surround; to enclose; to move round; to revolve round.—*vi* to move circularly; to circulate; to revolve.

circuit *n* the act of moving or passing round; a circular journey; a revolution; the distance round any space whether circular or otherwise; a boundary line encompassing an object; circumference; the journey of judges or other persons through certain appointed places for the purpose of holding courts or performing other stated duties; the district or portion of country in which a particular judge or judges hold courts and administer justice; the path of an electric current; a series of sporting events taking place regularly at the same venues; a motor racing track.

circuitous *adj* having a roundabout or devious course; not direct; roundabout.

circular *adj* in the form of a circle; round; circumscribed by a circle; passing over or forming a circle, circuit or round; addressed to a number of persons having a common interest (*a circular letter*).—*n* a letter, notice or intimation, such as an advertisement, sent to many people.

circularity *n* the state or quality of being circular; a circular form.

circulate *vi* (**circulated**, **circulating**) to move in a circle; to move round and return to the same point; to flow in the veins or channels of an organism; to pass from one person or place to another; to be diffused.—*vt* to cause to pass from place to place or from person to person; to put about; to spread.

circulating library *n* a library the books of which circulate among the subscribers.

circulation *n* the act of circulating or moving in a course which brings or tends to bring the moving body to the point where its motion began; the act of flowing through the veins or channels of an organism; recurrence in a certain order or series; the act of passing from place to place or from person to person (as of money, news, etc); the extent to which anything is circulated (*a newspaper with a large circulation*); currency; circulating coin or notes, bills, etc, current and representing coin.

circumambient *adj* enclosing or being surrounded on all sides.

circumcise *vt* (**circumcised**, **circumcising**) to cut off the foreskin of, a ceremony or rite among the Jews, Muslims and others; to cut off the clitoris, as a religious rite.

circumcision *n* the act of circumcising.

circumference *n* the line that bounds a circle or any regular curvilinear figure; periphery; the length round a circular or spherical body.

circumflex *n* an accent (^) placed only on long vowels and indicating different things in different languages.—*vt* to mark or pronounce with the circumflex.

circumlocution *n* a roundabout way of speaking; the use of more words than necessary to express an idea; a periphrasis.

circumnavigate *vt* (**circumnavigated**, **cir-**

cumnavigating) to sail round; to pass round by water (the globe, an island, etc).

circumnavigator *n* one who circumnavigates, generally applied to one who has sailed round the globe.

circumscribe *vt* (**circumscribed, circumscribing**) to inscribe or draw a line round; to mark out certain bounds or limits for; to enclose within certain limits; to limit, bound, confine, restrain (authority, etc).

circumscription *n* the act of circumscribing or state of being circumscribed; limitation; restriction; also a periphery or circumference.

circumspect *adj* examining carefully all the circumstances that may affect a determination; watchful on all sides; wary; vigilant; prudent; cautious.

circumspection *n* the quality of being circumspect; observation of the true position of circumstances; watchfulness; vigilance; wariness; caution.

circumstance *n* something relevant to a fact or case; something incidental; some fact giving rise to a certain presumption or tending to afford some evidence; detail; occurrence; incident; event; (*pl*) situation; surroundings; state of things; especially, condition in regard to worldly estate.

circumstantial *adj* consisting in or pertaining to circumstances; incidental; relating to but not essential; exhibiting all the circumstances; minute; particular; obtained or inferred from the circumstances of the case, not direct or positive (*circumstantial evidence*).—*n* something incidental and of subordinate importance, opposed to *essential*.

circumstantially *adv* in a circumstantial manner; minutely; in full detail; indirectly; not positively.

circumstantiate *vt* (**circumstantiating, circumstantiated**) to confirm by circumstances; to describe circumstantially or in full detail.

circumvent *vt* to gain advantage over by artfulness, stratagem or deception; to defeat or get the better of by cunning; to outwit; to overreach.

circumvention *n* the act of circumventing; outwitting or overreaching; stratagem.

circus *n* (*pl* **circuses**) among the ancient Romans, a theatre or amphitheatre adapted for horse races, the exhibition of athletic exercises, contests with wild beasts, etc; a place of amusement where feats of horsemanship, acrobatic displays and the antics of clowns and trained animals form the principal entertainment.

cirrate, cirrose, cirrous *adj* (*bot*) having a cirrus or tendril.

cirrhosis *n* a disease consisting of diminution and deformity of the liver, often caused by alcoholism.

cirripede, cirriped *n* a member of an order of crustaceans, so called from the cirri or filaments with which their transformed feet are fringed.

cirrose, cirrous *adj* same as **cirrate**.

cirrus *n* (*pl* **cirri**) a tendril; a long thread-like organ by which a plant climbs; a soft curled filamentary appendage to parts serving as the feet of certain lower animals, as barnacles, and the jaws of certain fishes; one of the forms which clouds assume; a light fleecy cloud at a high elevation, cirrocumulus and cirrostratus being intermediate forms partaking partly of this character, partly of that of the cumulus and stratus.

cisalpine *adj* on this side of the Alps, with regard to Rome; that is, on the south of the Alps.

cismontane *adj* existing on this side of the mountains; specifically, on this side of the Alps, opposed to *ultramontane*.

cissoid *n* (*geom*) a particular variety of curve with two branches meeting in a cusp.

cist *n* a place of interment of an early or prehistoric period, consisting of a stone chest formed of two parallel rows of stones fixed on their ends and covered by similar flat stones.

Cistercian *n* a member of a religious order which takes its name from its original convent near Dijon, where it was founded in 1098.

cistern *n* an artificial reservoir or receptacle for holding water, especially in a lavatory, or other liquid.

cistus *n* the rockrose.

citadel *n* a fortress or castle in or near a city.

cite *vt* (**cited, citing**) to call on officially or authoritatively to appear; to summon before a person or tribunal; to quote, adduce or bring forward; to refer to in support, proof or confirmation (*to cite an authority*).

citation *n* a summons; an official call or notice given to a person to appear, as in a court; the act of citing a passage from a book or person; the passage or words quoted; quotation.

cithara *n* an ancient stringed musical instrument resembling the more modern cittern or guitar.

cithern *n* same as **cittern**.

citizen *n* the native of a city or an inhabitant who enjoys the freedom and privileges of the city in which he resides; a member of a state with full political privileges.

citizen's arrest *n* an arrest, legally allowable, made by a member of the public on his or her own authority.

citizens' band radio a band of short-wave radio frequencies on which members of the public are permitted to broadcast personal messages etc.

cirrus clouds

cithara

153

citizenship *n* the status or principles of a citizen.

citric *adj* belonging to or derived from lemons or citrons.

citric acid *n* the acid of lemons and other citrus fruits.

citrine *n* lemon colour; a yellow pellucid variety of quartz.

citron *n* the fruit of the citron tree, a large species of lemon; the tree itself.

citronella *n* a fragrant Asian grass which yields a strong-smelling aromatic oil used in some soap, perfume and insect repellents.

citrus fruit *n* any of a range of fruits including oranges, lemons, limes, grapefruit and their hybrids.

cittern, cithern *n* an old instrument of the guitar kind strung with wire instead of gut.

city *n* in a general sense, a large and important town; in a narrower sense and as regards Great Britain, a town corporate that is or has been the seat of a bishop and of a cathedral church; in the USA, an incorporated town governed by a mayor and aldermen; the inhabitants of a city collectively. —*adj* pertaining to a city.

civet *n* one of several carnivorous mammals, natives of North Africa and Asia, having a gland near the anus secreting a strong-smelling substance; this substance, which is used in perfumery.

civic *adj* pertaining to a city or citizen; relating to civil affairs or honours.

civics *n* the science of the rights and duties of citizens.

civil *adj* relating to the community or to the policy and government of the citizens and subjects of a state (*civil rights, government*, etc); political; municipal or private, as opposed to criminal; not ecclesiastical or military; exhibiting some refinement of manners; civilized; courteous; obliging.

civil disobedience *n* a non-violent way of protesting against the measures and actions of a government, involving refusal to pay taxes, obey laws and regulations, etc.

civil engineering *n* that branch of engineering which relates to the forming of roads, bridges, railroads, canals, aqueducts, harbours, etc.

civilian *n* one whose pursuits are those of civil life, not military.

civility *n* the state of being civilized; good breeding; politeness or an act of politeness; courtesy; kind attention.

civilization *n* the act of civilizing or state of being civilized; the state of being refined in manners from the rudeness of savage life and improved in arts and learning.

civilize *vt* (**civilized, civilizing**) to reclaim from a savage state; to introduce order and civic organization among; to refine and enlighten; to elevate in social life.

civil law *n* the law of a state, city or country.

civil list *n* a yearly sum of money allotted to the sovereign of Britain, mainly for the expenses of the royal household, pensions, etc.

civilly *adv* in a civil manner; as regards civil rights or privileges; politely; courteously; in a well-bred manner.

civil rights *npl* the personal rights of a citizen or individual in society, sometimes established in a country's institution.

civil service *n* that branch of the public service in which the non-military employees of a government are engaged or those persons collectively.

civil war *n* a war between the people of the same state.

clachan *n* in Scotland, a small village or hamlet.

clack *vi* to make a sudden sharp noise, as by striking or cracking; to rattle; to utter sounds or words rapidly and continually or with sharpness and abruptness.—*vt* to cause to make a sharp, short sound; to clap; to speak without thought; to rattle out.—*n* a sharp, abrupt sound, continually repeated; continual talk; prattle.

clad[1] *pp* of **clothe**.

clad[2] *vt* (*pret, pp* **clad**, *ppr* **cladding**) to bond one material to another for protection (*iron cladding*).

claim *vt* to ask or seek to obtain by virtue of authority, right or supposed right; to assert a right to; to demand as due.—*vi* to be entitled to a thing; to have a right; to derive a right; to assert claims; to put forward claims.—*n* a demand of a right or supposed right; a calling on another for something due or supposed to be due; a right to claim or demand; a title to anything; the thing claimed or demanded.

claimant *n* a person who makes a claim; a person receiving or seeking social security payments.

clairvoyance *n* the alleged power by which a person discerns objects concealed from sight, tells what is happening at a distance, at a future time, etc.

clairvoyant *n* a person with the gift of clairvoyance.—*adj* possessing clairvoyance; having remarkable insight.

clam *n* the popular name of certain bivalve shellfish, of several genera and many species.

clamant *adj* clamorous; beseeching; pressing; urgent; crying.

clamber *vi* to climb with difficulty or with hands and feet.

clammy *adj* damp and sticky.

clamour *n* an outcry made by a loud human voice continued or repeated or by a number of voices; loud complaint; urgent demand; loud and continued noise.—*vi* to make a clamour; to utter loud sounds or

citrus fruit

clam

outcries; to make importunate complaints or demands; to influence by continuous demand.

clamp *n* something rigid that fastens or binds; a piece of wood or metal fastening two pieces together or strengthening any framework; an instrument of wood or metal used by joiners, etc, for holding pieces of timber closely together until the glue hardens; a wheel clamp.—*vt* to fasten with clamps; to fix a clamp on; to enforce some measure.

clan *n* a race; a family; a tribe; the common descendants of the same progenitor under the patriarchal control of a chief; a clique, sect, society or body of people closely united by a common interest or pursuit.

clannish *adj* affected with the feelings, sentiments and prejudices peculiar to clans; closely united and excluding all others.

clandestine *adj* secret; private; hidden.

clang *n* a loud sound produced from solid bodies, especially that produced by the collision of metallic bodies; a clank; clangour.—*vi* to give out a clang; to clank; to resound.—*vt* to cause to sound with a clang.

clangour *n* a sharp, hard, ringing sound as of a trumpet.

clank *n* the loud sound made by collision of metallic or other similarly sounding bodies (as chains, armour, etc), generally expressing a less resounding sound than *clang* and a deeper and stronger sound than *clink*.—*vt* to cause to sound with a clank.—*vi* to sound with or give out a clank.

clap *vt* (*pret, pp* **clapped** *or* **clapt**, *ppr* **clapping**) to strike with a quick motion; to slap; to thrust; to drive together; to shut hastily (followed by to, as *to clap to the door*); to place or put by a hasty or sudden motion (*to clap the hand to the mouth, to clap spurs to a horse*).—**to clap hands** to strike the palms of the hands together, as a mark of applause or delight.—*vi* to come together suddenly with noise; to clack; to strike the hands together in applause.—*n* a collision of bodies with noise; a bang; a slap; a burst or peal of thunder; a striking of hands to express approbation.

clapper *n* that which claps or strikes, as the tongue of a bell.

claptrap *n* high-flown sentiments or other rhetorical device by which a person panders to an audience; bunkum; empty words.

claque *n* an organized group of people who are hired to applaud the piece or the actors.

claret *n* the name given in England to the red wines of the Bordeaux district.—*adj* having the colour of claret, purple-red.

clarify *vt* (**clarified, clarifying**) to make clear; to purify from polluted matter; to re-

fine (liquor).—*vi* to grow or become clear or free from polluted matter; to become pure, as liquors.

clarinet, clarionet *n* a wind instrument made of wood with fingerholes and keys and a fixed mouthpiece, containing a reed forming the upper joint of the instrument.

clarion *n* an obsolete trumpet more acute and shrill than the common trumpet.—*adj* loud, ringing and attracting attention (*a clarion call*).

clash *vi* to make a loud, harsh noise, as from violent or sudden collision; to dash against an object with a loud noise; to come into violent collision; (*fig*) to act with opposite power or in a contrary direction; to meet in opposition (*their opinions and their interests clash together*).—*n* the noise made by the meeting of bodies with violence; a striking together with noise; collision or noisy collision of bodies; (*fig*) opposition; contradiction, as between differing or contending interests.

clasp *n* a catch to hold something together; a hook for fastening or for holding together, as the different parts of a garment, of a belt, etc; a clinging, grasping or embracing; a close embrace; a bar on medal ribbon for additional service in a campaign.—*vt* to shut or fasten together with a clasp; to catch and hold by twining or embracing; to surround and cling to; to embrace closely; to catch with the arms or hands; to grasp.

clasp knife *n* a knife the blade of which folds into the handle.

class *n* an order or rank of persons; a number of persons in society supposed to have some resemblance or equality in rank, education; property, talents, etc; standing in society, rank; a number of pupils in a schoolroom or students in a college of the same standing or pursuing the same studies; (*nat hist*) a large group of plants or animals; (*colloq*) style, excellence.—*vt* to arrange in a class or classes; to rank together; to refer to a class or group; to classify.

classic *n* an author or artist of the first rank; a writer whose style is pure, correct and refined, primarily, a Greek or Roman author of this character; a literary, artistic, or musical production of the first class or rank; **the classics** specifically, the literature of ancient Greece and Rome.—*adj* of the highest class or rank; of the best Greek and Roman writers; of music conforming to certain standards of form, complexity, etc; traditional; authoritative.

classical *adj* pertaining to writers of the first rank; being of the first order; more specifically relating to Greek and Roman authors of the first rank or estimation; pertaining to ancient Greece or Rome; relating to lo-

clamp

clarinet

calities associated with great ancient or modern authors or to scenes of great historical events; pure, chaste, correct or refined (taste, style, etc).

classification *n* the act of classifying or forming into a class or classes, so as to bring together those beings or things which most resemble each other and to separate those that differ; distribution into sets, sorts or ranks.

classify *vt* (**classified, classifying**) to arrange in a class or classes; to arrange in sets or ranks according to some method founded on common characteristics in the objects so arranged.

classism *n* prejudice or discrimination against someone on the grounds of social class.

classist *adj* showing prejudice or discrimination against someone on the grounds of social class.

classroom *n* a room where pupils or students are taught.

clatter *vi* to make rattling sounds; to make repeated sharp sounds, as when metallic bodies strike or are struck rapidly together; to rattle.—*vt* to strike so as to produce a rattling noise from.—*n* a rapid succession of abrupt, sharp sounds; rattling sounds; tumultuous and confused noise.

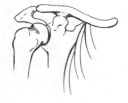
clavicle

clause *n* (*gram*) a member of a compound sentence containing both a subject and its predicate; (*law*) a distinct part of a contract, will, agreement, charter, treaty, law, commission, etc; a distinct stipulation, condition, proviso, etc.

claustral *adj* same as **cloistral**.

claustrophobia *n* an abnormal fear of confined spaces.

clavichord *n* an old stringed instrument, a precursor of the spinet and harpsichord.

clavicle *n* the collarbone.

clavier *n* the keyboard of a pianoforte or other instrument whose keys are arranged similarly; the instrument itself.

claw *n* the sharp hooked nail of a quadruped, bird or other animal; the whole foot of an animal with hooked nails; a hooked extremity belonging to any animal member or appendage; anything shaped like the claw of an animal, as the crooked forked end of a hammer used for drawing nails.—*vt* to tear, scratch, pull or seize with claws or nails; to scratch.

claw hammer

claw hammer *n* a hammer furnished with two claws, for drawing nails out of wood.

clay *n* the name common to various earths, compounds of silica and alumina; earth which is stiff, viscid and ductile when moistened and many kinds of which are used in the arts, as pipe clay, porcelain clay, etc; earth in general, especially as the material of the human body.—*adj* formed or consisting of clay.

clayey *adj* consisting of clay; abounding with clay; partaking of clay; like clay; bedaubed or besmeared with clay.

claymore *n* formerly the large two-handed sword of the Scottish Highlanders; now a basket-hilted, double-edged broadsword.

clay pigeon *n* a disc of baked clay propelled into the air as a target for shotguns.

clean *adj* clear of dirt or filth; having all impurities or foreign matter removed; pure; without fault, imperfection or defect (timber, a copy); well-proportioned; shapely (*clean limbs*); not bungling; dextrous; adroit (*a clean leap*); complete or thorough; free from moral impurity, guilt or blame; among the Jews, not defiled or polluted; not forbidden by the ceremonial law for use in sacrifice and for food.—*adv* quite; perfectly; wholly; entirely; fully.— *vt* to make clean; to remove all foreign matter from; to purify; to cleanse.—**to clean out** to exhaust the resources, goods, money of completely.

cleanliness *n* the state or quality of being clean.

cleanly *adv* in a clean manner; neatly; without filth; adroitly; dextrously.—*adj* free from dirt, filth or any foul matter; neat; carefully avoiding filth.

cleanness *n* the state or quality of being clean.

cleanse *vt* (**cleansed, cleansing**) to make clean; to free from filth or whatever is unseemly, noxious or offensive; to purify.

clear *adj* free from darkness or opacity; brilliant; light; luminous; unclouded; not obscured; free from what would dim transparency or bright colour (*clear water*); free from anything that confuses or obscures; acute, sagacious or discriminating (intellect, head); perspicuous; lucid (statement); evident; manifest; indisputable; undeniable; free from accusation, imputation, distress, imprisonment, etc (followed by *of* or *from*); free from impediment or obstruction; unobstructed (*a clear view*); sounding distinctly; distinctly audible; in full; net (*clear profit* or *gain*).—*vt* to make or render clear; to free from whatever diminishes brightness, transparency or purity of colour; to free from obscurity, perplexity or ambiguity (often followed by *up*); to free from any impediment or encumbrance or from anything noxious or injurious; to remove (with *off*, *away*, etc); to free from the imputation of guilt; to acquit; to make by way of gain or profit beyond all expenses and charges; to leap over or pass without touching or failure; (*naut*) to pay the customs on or connected with; to obtain permission to sail for (a cargo, a ship).—*vi* to become free from clouds or fog; to become fair or serene; to pass away or disappear from the sky (often followed by *up*, *off* or *away*); to exchange cheques and bills and settle balances, as is done in clearing houses; (*naut*) to leave a port (often followed by *out* or *outwards*).

clearance *n* the act of clearing; permission or authority to proceed; the space left between two moving objects.

clearing *n* the act of one who clears; among bankers, the act of exchanging drafts on each other's houses and settling the differences; a place or tract of land cleared of wood or cultivation.

clearing bank *n* a bank which uses a clearing house to exchange cheques and credits with another bank.

clearing house *n* a banking institution where cheques and bills are exchanged, only the balances paid in cash.

clearstory *n* same as **clerestory**.

clearway *n* a stretch of road where parking is prohibited; an area beyond an airport runway over which an aeroplane takes off.

cleat *n* a piece of wood or iron used in a ship to fasten ropes on; a piece of wood nailed on transversely to a piece of joinery for the purpose of securing it in its proper position or for strengthening; a piece of metal, leather, etc, fixed on the sole of a shoe to protect or aid grip.

cleavage *n* the act of cleaving or splitting; the manner in which rocks or mineral substances regularly cleave or split according to their natural joints or regular structure; in animals, early divisions of fertilized egg cell; the separation between a woman's breasts.

cleave *vi* (*pret* **clove** or **cleaved**; *pp* **cleaved**; *ppr* **cleaving**, **cleft** or **cloven**) to stick; to adhere; to be attached physically or by affection or other tie.—*vt* to part or divide by force; to split or rive; to sever forcibly; to hew; to cut.

cleaver *n* a butcher's instrument for cutting carcasses into joints or pieces.

cleek *n* a kind of golf club.

clef *n* a character in music placed at the beginning of a staff to determine the pitch of the notes.

cleft *n* a space or opening made by splitting; a crack; a crevice.

cleft palate *n* a malformation in which more or less of the palate is lacking so leaving a longitudinal gap in the upper jaw.

cleg *n* a bloodsucking fly; a horsefly.

clematis *n* the generic name of woody climbing plants, the only British species of which is the common traveller's joy.

clemency *n* mercy; leniency; softness or mildness of the weather.

clement *adj* mild in temper and disposition; gentle; lenient; merciful; kind; tender; compassionate; (of weather) mild.

clench *vt* to bring together and set firmly; to double up tightly (the teeth or the fists); to

grasp firmly.—*n* a grip; a persistent clutch.

clepsydra *n* (*pl* **clepsydras**, **clepsydrae**) a water clock.

clerestory, clearstory *n* the upper story of a cathedral or other church, perforated by a range of windows which form the principal means of lighting the central portions of the building.

clergy *n* the body of people set apart and consecrated by due ordination, to the service of God in the Christian church.

clergyman *n* (*pl* **clergymen**) a member of the clergy.

cleric *n* a clergyman.

clerical *adj* relating or pertaining to the clergy; relating to a clerk and the work of a clerk; relating to routine office work.

clerical error *n* an error in the text of a document made by carelessness on the part of the writer or transcriber.

clerk *n* a clergyman or ecclesiastic; a person in holy orders, especially in the Church of England; one who is employed in keeping records or accounts; an office worker who performs tasks such as filing; an officer attached to courts, municipal and other corporations, associations, etc, whose duty generally is to keep records of proceedings and transact business under direction of the court, body, etc, by whom he is employed; in USA, an assistant in a shop.

clergyman

clever *adj* performing or acting with skill or intelligence; possessing ability of any kind, especially such as involves quickness of intellect or mechanical dexterity; indicative of or exhibiting cleverness; dextrous; adroit; able.

cliché *n* a hackneyed jest or phrase; something that has become commonplace.

click *vi* to make a small sharp sound or a succession of small sharp sounds, as by a gentle striking; to tick; (*colloq*) to become plain or evident; (*colloq*) to get on well with another person.—*vt* to move with a clicking sound.—*n* a small sharp sound.

client *n* a person whose interests are represented by any professional person, such as a lawyer; a customer.

clientele *n* a body of clients or customers.

cliff *n* a precipice; the steep and rugged face of a rocky mass; a steep rock; a headland.

cliffhanger *n* something which is full of suspense or uncertainty, such as the situation at the end of an episode of an exciting serial or film; a situation which is full of suspense.

cliff

climacteric *n* a critical period in human life or a period in which some great change is supposed to take place in the human constitution, the grand or great climacteric being the 63rd year; the male menopause.

climactic *adj* of or relating to climax.

climate *n* the condition of a region in relation to the various phenomena of the atmosphere, as temperature, wind, moisture, etc, especially as they affect the life of animals or humans; the prevailing attitude, atmosphere or trend (*the economic climate*).

climatic *adj* of or pertaining to climate.

clime *n* (*poet*) a region of the earth.

climax *n* a figure of speech or rhetorical device in which the language rises step by step in dignity, importance and force; the highest point of anything; the culmination; acme; sexual orgasm.

climb *vi* to mount or ascend anything steep, often with labour and difficulty; to ascend by means of the hands and feet; of things, to rise with a slow motion; to ascend, as certain plants, by means of tendrils, etc.—*vt* to climb up.

climber *n* one who climbs; a mountaineer; a plant that rises by attaching itself to some support.

clinch *vt* to secure, confirm (a deal, argument, etc); to grip or hug (a boxing opponent) in order to prevent him delivering blows.—*n* the act of clinching; (*colloq*) a hug, embrace.

clincher *n* a decisive point in an argument.

cling *vi* (**clung, clinging**) to adhere closely; to stick; to hold fast, especially by winding round or embracing.

clinic *n* a centre to which patients go for medical care or advice; a private or specialized hospital; the teaching of medicine to students in the presence of patients.

clinical *adj* pertaining to a clinic; based on medical observation; objective, detached; unemotional; plain, stark.

clink *vi* to ring or jingle; to give out a small sharp sound or a succession of such sounds, as by striking small metallic bodies together.—*vt* to cause to produce a small sharp ringing sound.—*n* a sharp sound made by the collision of sonorous bodies; (*colloq*) prison.

clinker *adj* a partially vitrified brick; a kind of hard brick used for paving; a mass of incombustible slag which forms in grates and furnaces.

clinker-built *adj* (*naut*) built with the planks of the side so disposed that the lower edge of each overlies the upper edge of the next below it, like slates on a roof.

clinometer *n* an instrument for measuring the dip of rock strata.

clip *vt* (**clipped** *or* **clipt, clipping**) to cut off or sever with shears or scissors; to trim or make shorter (the hair) with scissors; to curtail; to cut short (words); to pronounce shortly and indistinctly; to punch a small hole in, as in a ticket; to strike sharply; to secure with a clip.—*n* the quantity of wool shorn at a single shearing of sheep; a season's shearing; a clasp or spring-holder for letters or papers; a magazine for a gun; a piece of jewellery attached with a clip; a

climber

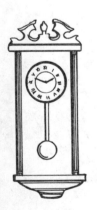

clock

short scene from a film; a passage cut from a newspaper.

clipboard *n* a portable writing board with a spring clip at the top for holding paper.

clipper *n* one who clips; a vessel with sharp bows raking forward and masts raking aft, built and rigged with a view to fast sailing.

clippers *npl* a hand tool, sometimes, electric, for cutting hair; a tool for cutting the nails.

clipping *n* that which is clipped off; a piece separated by clipping, e.g. a newspaper extract.

clique *n* a party; a set; a coterie (used generally in a bad sense).

clitoris *n* a small sensitive erectile organ situated above the vagina and urethra which plays a significant role in female orgasm.

cloaca *n* (*pl* **cloacae**) an underground conduit for drainage; a sewer; the cavity in birds, reptiles, many fishes and lower mammals which receives the alimentary canal and urinary duct.

cloak *n* a loose outer garment worn over other clothes; (*fig*) that which conceals; a disguise or pretext; an excuse.—*vt* to cover with a cloak; to hide; to conceal.

cloakroom *n* a room attached to any public place, as a railway station, theatre, etc, where cloaks, coats, etc, are deposited.

clobber[1] *vt* (*colloq*) to hit or strike heavily; to criticize severely; to defeat.

clobber[2] *n* (*colloq*) clothes; gear; personal belongings.

clock[1] *n* a device for measuring time, indicating the hours, minutes and often seconds by means of hands moving over a dial or by displayed numbers (*digital clock*).—*vt* to record time taken (of a race) with a stopwatch; (*sl*) to hit.

clock[2] *n* a figure or figured work embroidered on the ankle of a stocking.

clock[3] *n* a general name for a beetle.

clockwork *n* the machinery of a clock; a complex mechanism of wheels producing regularity of movement; perfect regularity.

clod *n* a lump or mass in general; a lump of earth or earth and turf; a lump of clay; a dull, gross, stupid fellow; a dolt.

clodhopper *n* a dolt; a clumsy person; a large heavy shoe or boot.

clog *n* an encumbrance that hinders motion or renders it difficult; hindrance; encumbrance; impediment; a sort of shoe with a wooden sole; a wooden shoe.—*vt* (**clogged, clogging**) to impede the movements of by a weight or by something that sticks or adheres; to encumber, restrain or hamper; to choke up (a tube, etc); to obstruct so as to hinder passage through; to throw obstacles in the way of; to hinder; to burden.—*vi* to become loaded or encumbered with extraneous matter.

cloister *n* an arched way or covered walk running round the walls of certain portions of monastic and collegiate buildings; a place of religious retirement; a monastery.

cloistered *adj* solitary, secluded.

cloistral, claustral *adj* relating to a cloister; cloister-like; secluded.

clone *n* a group of organisms or cells of the same genetic constitution that are derived from a common ancestor by asexual reproduction; an individual grown from a single cell of its parent and genetically identical to it; a group of plants grown from part of a single plant; a person or thing that bears a very close resemblance to another.—*vt* (**cloned, cloning**) to propagate a clone from; to make a copy of.

close[1] *vt* (**closed, closing**) to bring together the parts of; to shut (a door, window, book, eyes, hands); to make fast; to end, finish, conclude, complete; to fill or stop up; to consolidate (often followed by *up*); to encompass or enclose; to shut in.—*vi* to come together; to unite; to coalesce; to end, terminate or come to a period; to engage in close encounter; to grapple; to accede or consent to (*to close with terms*); to come to an agreement (*to close with a person*).—*n* conclusion; termination; end; pause; cessation; a grapple, as in wrestling.

close[2] *adj* shut fast; made fast so as to leave no opening; strictly confined; strictly watched (*a close prisoner*); retired; secluded; hidden; private; secret; having the habit or disposition to keep secrets; secretive; reticent; confined within narrow limits; narrow; without motion or ventilation; difficult to breathe; oppressive (of the air or weather); in direct contact or nearly so; adjoining; with little or no intervening distance in place or time; with little difference, as between antagonists or rival parties; almost evenly balanced (*close contest*); having the parts near each other; compact; dense; firmly attached; intimate; trusty; confidential (*close friends*); firmly fixed on a given object (*close attention*); keen and steady; not deviating from a model or original (*a close translation*); niggardly; stingy; penurious.—*n* an enclosed place; any place surrounded by a fence; specifically, the precinct of a cathedral or abbey; a narrow passage or entry leading off a street.—*adv* tightly, so as to leave no opening; in strict confinement; in contact or very near in space or time.

closed book *n* a matter which is completely finished and about which there will be no further discussion or investigation; something about which one knows very little or which one finds it difficult to understand.

closed-circuit television a television system in which signals are transmitted from the camera to the receivers by cables or telephone links forming a closed circuit, as used in shops for security purposes etc.

closed shop *n* a firm or industry which employs only workers who belong to a trade union.

close-fisted *adj* miserly; niggardly; penurious.

close-hauled *adj* (*naut*) sailing as nearly against the wind as possible.

closet *n* a small private room; (especially American) a cupboard for clothes, supplies, etc.—*vt* to enclose in a private place for confidential discussion.—*adj* secret, undeclared.

close-up *n* in cinematography, a picture taken at close range in order to show more detail.

closure *n* the act of closing; an end or conclusion; the act of bringing a parliamentary debate to an end, by special vote or otherwise, when a question or measure has been fairly discussed.

clot *n* a coagulated mass of soft or fluid matter, as of blood, cream, etc.

cloth *n* a fabric of wool or hair or of cotton, flax, hemp or other vegetable filaments formed by weaving; a tablecloth; a professional dress, specifically that of a clergyman.—**the cloth** the office of a clergyman; the members of the clerical profession.

clothe *vt* (**clothed** *or* **clad, clothing**) to put garments on; to dress; to furnish or supply with clothes; (*fig*) to cover or spread over with anything; to invest; to put on or over.

clothes *npl* garments for the human body; dress; vestments; bedclothes.

clotheshorse *n* a frame to hang clothes on; a person who is excessively interested in clothes.

clothesline *n* a rope on which washing is hung to dry.

clothes moth *n* a name for several moths whose larvae are destructive to woollen fabrics, furs, etc.

clothespeg, clothespin *n* a plastic, wooden or metal clip for attaching washing to a line.

clothier *n* a seller of cloth or of clothes.

clothing *n* garments in general; clothes.

cloud *n* a collection of visible vapour or watery particles suspended in the atmosphere at some altitude; that which obscures, darkens, sullies or threatens; a multitude; a collection; a mass.—*vt* to overspread with a cloud or clouds; hence, to obscure; to darken; to render gloomy or sullen; to darken in spots; to confuse.—*vi* to grow cloudy; to become obscured with clouds.

cloudberry *n* a plant of the bramble family with large white flowers and orange-red berries.

cloudburst *n* a tremendous downpour of rain over a limited area.

clothesline

cloud-cuckoo-land *n* a realm of fantasy; a world of dreams or unattainable hopes.

cloudy *adj* overcast with clouds; obscured with clouds, as the sky; consisting of a cloud or clouds; obscure; dark; not clear or transparent; not easily understood; gloomy; indicating gloom, anxiety, sullenness or ill-nature; marked with spots or areas of dark or various hues.

clout *n* any piece of cloth, especially a worthless piece; in archery, the mark fixed in the centre of a target; a clout nail; (*colloq*) a blow with the hand; (*colloq*) power, influence.—*vt* to hit.

clout nail *n* a short, large-headed nail worn in the soles of shoes.

clove *n* the dried flower bud of an evergreen tree of the myrtle family used as a pungent aromatic spice; the tree yielding cloves; a segment of a bulb such as garlic.

clove gillyflower, clove pink *n* popular names of the clove-scented, double-flowered whole-coloured varieties of the pink family of flowers.

cloven (*pp of* **cleave**) divided; parted.

cloven-hoofed *adj* having the hoof divided into two parts, as the pig, cow, deer, etc, the mark of the devil.

clover *n* a herbaceous leguminous plant of numerous species bearing three-lobed leaves and roundish heads or oblong spikes of small flowers, several species being widely cultivated for fodder.—**to be** or **to live in clover** to be in most enjoyable circumstances; to live luxuriously or in abundance.

clown *n* a jester or buffoon who entertains with humorous behaviour, as in a circus; a fool; a clumsy person.—*vi* to act as a clown; to behave comically or clumsily.

cloy *vt* to gratify to excess; to surfeit, satiate or glut.

club *n* a thick heavy stick used as a weapon; a cudgel; a staff with a crooked and heavy head for driving the ball in the game of golf, etc; a card of the suit that is marked with trefoils; (*pl*) the suit so marked; a select number of persons in the habit of meeting for the promotion of some common object, as social companionship, literature, science, politics; a meeting place for the members of such a group; a clubhouse.—*vi* (**clubbed, clubbing**) to form a club or combination for a common purpose; to combine to raise a sum of money (often with *for* before the object); to combine generally.—*vt* to beat with a club; to convert into a club; to add together, each contributing a certain sum.

clubbable *adj* having the qualities that make a person fit to be a member of a club; sociable.

club foot *n* a short, distorted foot, generally congenital.

clown

clubhouse *n* a building occupied by a club or in which a club assembles.

club law *n* government by clubs or violence; anarchy.

club sandwich *n* a sandwich which consists of three layers of bread rather than the usual two.

cluck *vi* to utter the call or cry of a brooding hen; to make a noise like this.—*n* a sound uttered by a hen; a noise sounding like this.

clue *n* anything that guides or directs to the solution of a mystery, puzzle or problem.

clueless *adj* without any knowledge or information about something; stupid; incompetent; useless.

clump *n* a shapeless mass; a lump; a cluster of trees or shrubs.

clumsy *adj* awkward; ungainly; ill-made; badly constructed; awkwardly done; unskilfully performed.

cluster *n* a number of things, as fruits, growing naturally together; a bunch; a number of individuals of any kind collected or gathered into a body; an assemblage; a group; a swarm; a crowd.—*vi* to grow or be assembled in clusters or groups.—*vt* to collect into a cluster or group; to produce in a cluster or clusters.

clustered column *n* (*archit*) a column or pier which appears to consist of several columns or shafts clustered together.

clutch[1] *vt* to seize, clasp or grip with the hand; to close tightly; to clench.—*n* a gripping or pinching with the fingers; seizure; grasp (*to fall into a person's clutches*); (*engin*) a coupling between two working parts of a machine or engine, allowing these parts to be thrown into or out of gear with each other.

clutch[2] *n* the eggs laid and hatched by a bird at one time.

clutter *n* a disordered mess, untidiness; confusion.—*vt* to put into disorder; to make untidy; to litter.

coach *n* a carriage (horse or motor) intended to carry passengers; more particularly a four-wheeled closed vehicle for carrying a number of passengers; a bus; a railway carriage; a private tutor; one who trains a person or team in certain sports.—*vt* to carry in a coach; to prepare for an examination by private instruction; to train.—*vi* to ride or travel in a coach.

coachman *n* (*pl* **coachmen**) the person who drives a coach.

coadjutor *n* the assistant of a bishop or other prelate.

coagulate *vt* (**coagulated, coagulating**) to change from a fluid into a curd-like or solid mass; to curdle, congeal or clot.—*vi* to curdle or congeal.

coagulant *n* that which produces coagulation.

coagulation *n* the act of coagulating or clotting; the state of being coagulated; the substance formed by coagulation.

coal *n* a solid black substance found in the earth, largely employed as fuel and formed from vast masses of vegetable matter deposited through the luxurious growth of plants in former epochs of the earth's history.—**to haul over the coals** to call to a strict or severe account; to reprimand.—**to carry coals to Newcastle** to take things where there are already plenty; to perform unnecessary labour.

coalesce *vt* (**coalesced, coalescing**) to unite by growth into one body; to grow together physically; to combine or be collected into one body or mass; to join or unite into one body, party, society, etc.

coalescence *n* the act of coalescing or uniting; the state of being united or combined.

coalfield *n* an extensive deposit or bed of coal; a district where coal abounds.

coal gas *n* gas obtained from coal and formerly used for lighting and heating.

coalition *n* union in a body or mass; voluntary union of individual persons, parties or states for a common object or cause.

coal mine *n* a mine or pit in which coal is dug.

coal tar *n* a thick, black, viscid, opaque liquid which condenses in pipes when gas is distilled from coal.

coal tit *n* one of the titmice, so called from its glossy black head and neck.

coaming *n* (*naut*) a raised border or edge round the hatches to keep out water.

coarse *adj* of ordinary or inferior quality; lacking in fineness of texture or structure or in elegance of form; rude; rough; unrefined; gross; indelicate (*coarse language*).

coarse fish *n* any freshwater fish that is neither salmon or trout.

coarse-grained *adj* having a coarse grain; ill-tempered.

coast *n* the exterior line, limit or border of a country; the edge or margin of the land next to the sea; the seashore.—**the coast is clear** danger is over; the enemies have gone.—*vi* to sail near a coast; to sail by or near the shore or in sight of land; to sail or trade from port to port in the same country; to travel downhill in a vehicle without using mechanical power; to proceed in a leisurely way.—*vt* to sail by or near to.

coaster *n* a vessel that is employed in sailing along a coast or in trading from port to port in the same country; a receptacle for a decanter or a wine bottle; a mat to put under a wine glass.

coastguard *n* an organization which monitors a coastline and provides help for ships in difficulties, prevents smuggling, etc.

coastline *n* the outline of a shore or coast.

coat *n* a sleeved outer garment for men or women; a man's jacket; an external covering; a layer of one substance covering another; a coating.—*vt* to cover with a coat; to spread over with a coating or layer of any substance such as paint.

coat armour *n* a coat of arms; armorial ensigns.

coat card *n* another name for **court card**.

coati *n* a raccoon-like, flesh-eating mammal belonging to the bear family.

coating *n* any substance spread over for cover or protection; a thin external layer, as of paint or varnish; cloth for coats.

coat of arms *n* a representation of the armorial insignia which used to be depicted on a coat worn by knights over their armour; an escutcheon or shield of arms.

coat of mail *n* armour worn on the upper part of the body and consisting of a network of iron or steel rings or of small plates, usually of tempered iron, laid over each other like the scales of a fish and fastened to a strong linen or leather jacket.

coax *vt* to persuade by flattery; to wheedle; to cajole.

coaxial *adj* having a common axis.

coaxial cable *n* a transmission cable having a double conductor separated by insulating material, as for a television.

cob *n* a roundish lump of anything; a short-legged stout horse or pony; a male swan; a corncob.

cobalt *n* a mineral of a reddish-grey or greyish-white colour, very brittle, never found in a pure state but usually as an oxide or combined with arsenic or its acid, with sulphur, iron, etc.

cobble[1] *n* a roundish stone used for paving.—*vt* (**cobbled, cobbling**) to pave with cobbles.

cobble[2] *vt* (**cobbled, cobbling**) to make or mend (shoes); to botch; to make or do clumsily.—*vi* to work as a cobbler; to do work badly.

cobbler *n* one who cobbles; a mender of boots and shoes; a clumsy workman; a cooling drink of wine, sugar, lemon and finely pounded ice.

coble *n* a flattish-bottomed boat, clinker-built, with a square stern.

cobra *n* the hooded snake, a venomous reptile found in hot countries, especially India.

cobweb *n* the network spun by a spider to catch its prey; something to entangle the weak or unwary; something flimsy; fustiness.

coca *n* the dried leaf of a South American plant which is chewed by the inhabitants of countries on the Pacific side of South America as a stimulant; the plant itself.

Coca-Cola *n* a trademark of a carbonated soft drink of a dark colour.

cobra

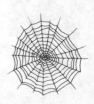

cobweb

cocaine *n* an addictive narcotic drug, the active principle of coca, used medicinally as a local anaesthetic.

coccus *n* (*pl* **cocci**) a spherical bacterium; one of the separable carpels of a dry fruit.

coccyx *n* (*pl* **coccyges**) an assemblage of small bones attached to the lower extremity of the backbone.

cochineal *n* a red dyestuff and food colouring obtained from the dried bodies of a species of insect, a native of the warmer climates of America.

cochlea *n* (*pl* **cochleae**) a bony structure in the internal ear resembling a snail shell.

cock[1] *n* the male of birds, particularly of domestic fowls (often used adjectivally and occasionally to signify the male of certain animals other than birds, as *cock lobster*); a kind of faucet or turn-valve for permitting or arresting the flow of fluids through a pipe; a prominent portion of the lock of a firearm, the hammer; the act of cocking or setting up or the effect or form produced by such an act (*a cock of the head, nose,* etc).—*vt* to set erect (the ears); to turn up with an air of pertness; to set or draw back the cock in order to fire (*to cock a gun*); (*colloq*) to make a mess of (with *up*).

cock

cock[2] *n* a small conical pile of hay, so shaped for shedding rain.

cockade *n* a ribbon or knot of ribbon worn in the hat.

cock-a-hoop *adj* triumphant.

cock-a-leekie *n* Scottish broth of fowl boiled with leeks.

cock-and-bull *adj* a term applied to idle or silly fictions, stories having no foundation, canards.

cockatoo *n* (*pl* **cockatoos**) any of numerous birds of the parrot kind chiefly inhabiting Australia and the Indian islands, having a crest composed of a tuft of feathers which it can raise or depress.

cockatrice *n* a fabulous monster said to be hatched by a serpent from a cock's egg and represented as possessing characters belonging to both animals; a basilisk.

cockchafer *n* a kind of beetle, the larvae or caterpillars of which feed on the roots of corn, etc, and the insects in their winged state do much injury to trees.

cockchafer

cockcrow, cockcrowing *n* the time at which cocks crow; early morning.

cocker *n* a dog of the spaniel kind used for raising game birds.

cockerel *n* a young cock.

cock-eyed *adj* crooked or twisted to one side; having a squint; absurd; foolish.

cockfight *n* an organized fight between gamecocks.

cockle *n* a heart-shaped mollusc with wrinkled shells, common on sandy shores and much used as food.—*vti* (**cockled, cockling**) to wrinkle or ridge; to give or assume a wrinkled or ridged surface (as a piece of paper).

cockney *n* a native or resident of the East End of London, especially one having a characteristic accent.

cockpit *n* a pit or area where gamecocks fight; an apartment under the lower gun deck of a ship of war; a small space in an aeroplane for accommodation of pilot or passenger; the driver's seat in a racing car.

cockroach *n* a nocturnal beetle-like insect.

cocksure *adj* confidently certain.

cocktail *n* a short drink or appetizer, usually consisting of spirits, bitters and some flavouring and often iced; a mixture, as of fruit for dessert.

coco *n* the coconut palm.

cocoa *n* the kernels of the cacao or chocolate tree ground into powder for making a beverage; the beverage itself.

coconut, cocoanut *n* the nut or fruit of the coconut palm, covered with a fibrous rind, having a white edible lining and containing a white milky liquid.

coconut oil *n* an orange-coloured oil obtained from the nuts of the coconut.

coconut palm *n* a palm found in most tropical regions growing on coasts and producing the coconut.

cocoon *n* the silky tissue or envelope which the larvae of many insects spin as a covering for themselves while they are in the chrysalis state; a cosy, secure covering.—*vt* to wrap in, or as if in, a cocoon; to protect oneself by cutting oneself off from one's surroundings, the outside world, etc.

cod *n* a species of fish of great commercial importance, inhabiting northern seas and used as food either fresh, salted or dried, and yielding cod-liver oil.

coddle *vt* (**coddled, coddling**) to treat tenderly like an invalid; to pamper.

code *n* a systematic collection or digest of laws; any system or body of rules or laws relating to one subject; a system of signals, etc, agreed on; a set of words representing others for purposes of secrecy; a set of rules or conventions; a set of computer program instructions.

codeine *n* a slightly bitter chemical made from opium and used as a painkiller.

codex *n* (*pl* **codices**) a manuscript volume, as of a Greek or Latin classic or of the Scriptures.

codger *n* a cross or eccentric old man; an old man.

codicil *n* a writing by way of supplement to a will, containing anything which the testator wishes to add or any revocation or explanation of what the will contains.

codification *n* the act or process of codifying.

codify *vt* (**codifying, codified**) to reduce to a code or digest, as laws.

codling *n* a term applied to several cultivated varieties of cooking apple.

cod-liver oil *n* a medical oil obtained from the liver of the cod.

codswallop *n* nonsense; rubbish.

coeducation *n* the teaching of pupils or students of both sexes in the same school or college.

coeducational *adj* (of a school) having pupils of both sexes.

coefficient *adj* cooperating; acting in union to the same end.—*n* that which unites in action with something else to produce the same effect; (*alg*) a number or known quantity put before letters or quantities, known or unknown, into which it is supposed to be multiplied.

coelacanth *n* a type of primitive fish that is extinct except for one species.

coelenterate *n* any of a large group of aquatic animals, such as the hydra, whose alimentary canal communicates freely with the general cavity of the body and which includes the corals, sea anemones, etc.

coeliac *adj* pertaining to the cavity of the abdomen.

coeliac disease *n* a chronic digestive disease of young children causing malnutrition and diarrhoea.

coemption *n* the buying up of the whole quantity of a commodity.

coenobite same as **cenobite**.

coenurus *n* (*pl* **coenuri**) the larval form of a tapeworm, producing staggers in sheep.

coequal *adj* equal with another person or thing; of the same rank, dignity or power. —*n* one who is equal to another.

coerce *vt* to restrain by force, particularly by moral force, as by law or authority; to repress; to compel to compliance; to constrain.

coercible *adj* capable of being coerced.

coercion *n* the act of coercing; restraint; compulsion; constraint.

coercive *adj* capable of coercing; restrictive; able to force into compliance. —*n* that which coerces; that which constrains or restrains.

coeval *adj* of the same age; having lived for an equal period; existing at the same time or of equal antiquity in general (*coeval with a person*).—*n* one who is coeval; one who lives at the same time.

coexist *vi* to exist at the same time with another (*to coexist with*).

coexistence *n* existence at the same time with another; contemporary existence.

coexistent *adj* existing at the same time with another.

coextensive *adj* equally extensive; having equal scope or extent.

coffee *n* the berries or the ground seeds of a tree, a native of Arabia and Abyssinia but now extensively cultivated throughout tropical countries, each berry containing two seeds (*coffee beans*); a drink made from the roasted and ground seeds of the coffee tree by infusion or decoction; a light brown colour.

coffee bean *n* a coffee seed.

coffee house *n* a place of refreshment where guests buy coffee and other refreshments, especially one that was a fashionable meeting place in eighteenth-century London.

coffee mill *n* a small machine or mill for grinding coffee.

coffee pot *n* a covered pot in which coffee is made or in which it is brought to the table for drinking.

coffee shop *n* a public room in an inn or hotel where guests are supplied with refreshments.

coffee table *n* a low table usually placed before a sofa.

coffer *n* a chest, trunk or casket for holding jewels, money or other valuables; a sunk panel or compartment in a ceiling of an ornamental character; a kind of caisson or floating dock.—*vt* to deposit or lay up in a coffer.

cofferdam *n* a wooden enclosure formed in a river, etc, by driving two or more rows of piles close together, with clay packed in between the rows to exclude the water and so obtain a firm and dry foundation for bridges, piers, etc.

coffin *n* the chest or box in which a dead human body is buried, cremated or deposited in a vault.—*vt* to put or enclose in a coffin.

cog *n* the tooth of a wheel by which it drives another wheel or body; any similar mechanical contrivance.

cogency *n* the quality of being cogent; power of moving the will or reason; power of compelling conviction; force; conclusiveness.

cogent *adj* convincing; powerful; not easily resisted; forcible; irresistible (of arguments, proofs, reasoning, etc).

cogitate *vi* (**cogitated, cogitating**) to think; to ponder.

cogitation *n* the act of cogitating or thinking; thought; meditation; contemplation.

cognac *n* a kind of French brandy, so called from the town of the same name in southwest France.

cognate *adj* allied by blood; kindred by birth; (*law*) connected by the mother's side; related in origin generally; coming from the same stock or root; of the same family (words, roots, languages); allied in nature; having affinity of any kind (*cognate sounds*). —*n* one connected with another by ties of kindred; anything related to another by origin or nature.

cognition *n* knowledge from personal view or experience; perception; a thing known.

coffee mill

cog

cognizable *adj* capable of being known, perceived or apprehended; capable of falling under judicial notice.

cognizance *n* knowledge or notice; perception; observation; (*law*) judicial or authoritative notice or knowledge, also right to try and determine causes; a heraldic crest; a badge.

cognizant *adj* acquainted with; having obtained knowledge of; competent to take legal or judicial notice.

cognomen *n* a surname or distinguishing name; a nickname.

cogwheel *n* a wheel with cogs or teeth.

cohabit *vi* to live together as husband and wife although not legally married.

cohabitation *n* the state of living together as husband and wife.

coheir *n* a joint heir; one who succeeds to a share of an inheritance divided among two or more.

cohere *vi* (**cohered, cohering**) to stick or cleave together; to be united; to keep in close contact as parts of the same mass or as two substances that attract each other; to hang well together; to agree or be consistent (as parts of a discourse or an argument).

coil

coherence *n* the state of cohering; a cleaving together of bodies by means of attraction; suitable connection or dependence; due agreement as of ideas; consistency.

coherent *adj* cohering or sticking together; united; having a due agreement of parts; hanging well together; consecutive; observing due agreement; logical; consistent (*a coherent argument* or *discourse, a coherent speaker*).

cohesion *n* the act or state of cohering, uniting or sticking together; logical connection; (*physics*) the state in which, or the force by which, the particles of bodies of the same nature are kept in contact so as to form a continuous mass.

cohesive *adj* causing cohesion.

cohort *n* in Roman armies, the tenth part of a legion, a body of about 500 or 600 men; a band or body of soldiers or people in general; a band of followers.

coif *n* a close-fitting cap or headdress.

coiffeur *n* a hairdresser.

coiffure *n* a manner of dressing the hair; a hairstyle.

coin

coil *vt* to gather (a rope, chain, etc) into a series of rings above one another; to twist or wind spirally.—*vi* to form rings or spirals; to wind.—*n* a ring or series of rings or spirals into which a rope or other pliant body is wound.

coin *n* a piece of metal, as gold, silver, copper or some alloy, converted into money by impressing some stamp on it; such pieces collectively; metallic currency; money.—*vt* to stamp and convert into money; to mint; to make, fabricate or invent (a word, phrase, etc).

coinage *n* the stamping of money; coin; money coined; the act of inventing, forming or producing; invention; fabrication; what is fabricated or produced.

coiner *n* one who coins; a maker of money; often a maker of base or counterfeit coin; an inventor or maker, as of words.

coincide *vi* (**coincided, coinciding**) to occupy the same place in space or the same position in a scale or series; to happen at the same point of time; to be exactly contemporaneous; to correspond exactly; to concur; to agree (*to coincide with a person in an opinion*).

coincidence *n* the fact of coinciding; exact correspondence in position; a happening or agreeing in time without apparent connection; contemporaneousness; agreement in circumstance, character, etc; exact correspondence generally or a case of exact correspondence.

coir *n* a yarn manufactured from the husk of coconuts and formed into cordage, sailcloth, matting, etc.

coition, coitus *n* a coming together; sexual intercourse.

coke[1] *n* coal deprived of its bitumen, sulphur or other extraneous or volatile matter by fire.—*vt* (**coked, coking**) to convert into coke; to deprive of volatile matter, as coal.

coke[2] *n* (*sl*) cocaine.

Coke *n* a trademark short form of **Coca-Cola**.

col *n* an elevated mountain pass between two higher summits; the most elevated part of a mountain pass.

colander *n* a vessel with a bottom perforated with little holes for straining liquids; a strainer.

cola nut, cola seed *n* a brownish bitter seed, about the size of a chestnut, produced by an African tree, containing much caffeine and used in some soft drinks.

cola tree *n* the tree which produces the cola nut.

colchicum *n* any of a genus of plants of the lily family, the most familiar species being the meadow saffron.

cold *adj* not warm or hot; frigid; chilling; cooling; having the sensation of coolness; lacking warmth or animal heat; chill; lacking passion, zeal or ardour; insensible; not animated or easily excited into action; not affectionate, cordial or friendly; unaffecting; not animated or animating; not able to excite feeling or interest; spiritless.—**in cold blood** without excitement, emotion or passion.—**to give, show** *or* **turn the cold shoulder** to treat a person with studied coldness, neglect or contempt.—*n* the relative absence or lack of heat; the cause of the sensation of coolness; the sensation produced in animal bodies by the escape of heat; an indisposition occasioned by cold; the common cold, characterized by coughing, sneezing, a running nose, etc.

cold-blooded *adj* having cold blood; without sensibility or feeling; (*zool*) a term applied to those animals the temperature of whose blood is a very little higher than that of their habitat.

cold chisel *n* a chisel for cutting metal in its cold state.

cold cream *n* a kind of cooling and cleansing unguent for the skin, variously prepared.

cold front *n* the forward edge of a cold air mass approaching a warmer mass.

cold-hearted *adj* unfeeling; stern.

coldness *n* the state or quality of being cold; frigidity; indifference.

cold shoulder *n* indifference; hostility.

cold-shoulder *vt* (*colloq*) to treat with indifference or hostility.

cold snap *n* a sudden short period of very cold weather.

cold sore *n* a viral skin infection causing sores on or near the lips .

cold turkey *n* the sudden withdrawal of addictive drugs from an addict, often as part of an attempted cure.

cold war *n* a state of hostility or enmity between nations which stops short of actual fighting.

cole *n* the general name of all sorts of cabbage.

coleopteran *n* any of the order of insects commonly known by the name of beetles and characterized by having four wings, of which the two anterior are not suited for flight but form a covering and protection to the two posterior and are of a hard and horny or parchment-like nature.

coleslaw *n* a salad made from raw, shredded cabbage and a creamy dressing.

colewort *n* a name applied to different varieties of cabbage.

colic *n* a painful spasmodic affection of the intestines, especially of the colon, sometimes attended with fever or inflammation.

colitis *n* inflammation of the large intestine, especially of its mucous membrane.

collaborate *vi* (**collaborating, collaborated**) to work jointly or together, especially in literature; to side with the invaders of one's country.

collaboration *n* the act of working together; united labour; cooperation with one's country's invaders or occupiers.

collaborator *n* an associate in work, especially in literary or scientific pursuits; one who sides with the invaders of his or her country.

collage *n* an art form in which various materials such as paper, cloth, string etc. are stuck onto a surface for artistic effect.

collagen *n* a protein present in protein, connective tissue and bones which forms gelatine when boiled.

collapse *vi* (**collapsed, collapsing**) to fall in or together, as the two sides of a vessel; to close by falling together; hence, to come to nothing; to break down physically or mentally; to fall down in a faint; to fold away storable articles, e.g. furniture.—*n* a falling in or together, as of the sides of a hollow vessel; a more or less sudden failure of the vital powers; a sudden and complete failure of any kind; a breakdown.

collapsible *adj* capable of collapsing or being made to collapse.

collar *n* something worn round the neck for use or ornament or both, or for restraint; a band or chain round an animal's neck to lead, restrain or identify; part of the harness of a draught animal; an article of dress or part of a garment going round the neck; something resembling a collar; something in the form of a ring, especially at or near the end of something else.—**to slip the collar** to escape or get free; to disentangle oneself.—*vt* to seize by the collar; to put a collar on; to catch and detain.

collar

collarbone *n* one of the two bones of the thorax in humans and many quadrupeds joined at one end to the shoulder bone and at the other to the breastbone; the clavicle.

collate *vt* (**collated, collating**) to bring together and compare; to examine critically, noting points of agreement and disagreement (manuscripts and books); to gather and place in order, as the sheets of a book for binding.

collateral *adj* at the side; belonging to the side or what is at the side; acting indirectly; acting through side channels; accompanying but subordinate; auxiliary; subsidiary; descending from the same ancestor but not in a direct line, as distinguished from lineal.—*n* a collateral relation or kinsman; security pledged by a borrower.

collation *n* the act of collating; a comparison, especially the comparison of manuscripts or editions of books; a light repast.

colleague *n* a partner or associate in the same office, employment or commission.

collect *vt* to gather into one body or place; to assemble or bring together; to gather (*to collect one's thoughts*).—**to collect oneself** to recover from surprise or a disconcerted state.—*vi* to run together; to accumulate.—*n* a short comprehensive prayer; a form of prayer adapted to a particular day or occasion.

cold sore

collectable, collectible *n* an object likely to be of interest to collectors; an object thought to be worth collecting.

collected *adj* gathered together; not disconcerted; self-possessed.

collection *n* the act or practice of collecting or of gathering; that which is collected or gathered together (as pictures or objects of interest); that which is collected for a charitable, religious or other purpose.

collective *adj* formed by collecting; gathered into a mass, sum or body; aggregate; (*gram*) expressing a number or multitude united, though in the singular number (*a collective noun*).—*n* (*gram*) a collective noun; a collective enterprise, such as a farm.

collectively *adv* in a collective manner; in a mass or body; in the aggregate; unitedly.

collective noun *n* (*gram*) a noun with a singular form including in its meaning several individuals, such as *family*, *flock*, *people*, *infantry*, *crowd*, etc.

collectivism *n* the political theory that the land and means of production should belong to the people collectively.

collector *n* one who collects; especially, one who collects objects of interest; one who collects things to inspect them, etc, as a ticket-collector.

college *n* a society of people engaged in some common pursuit or profession; a society or institution for purposes of instruction and study in the higher branches of knowledge; the building belonging to a college.

collegiate *adj* pertaining to a college (*collegiate studies*); constituted after the manner of a college.

collegiate church *n* a church that has no bishop's see but has nevertheless a college or chapter of dean, canons and prebendaries; in Scotland and the USA, a church under the joint pastorate of two or more clergymen.

collet *n* a band or collar; in jewellery, the horizontal face or plane at the bottom of brilliants and the part of a ring containing the bezel in which the stone is set.

collide *vi* (**collided, colliding**) to strike or dash against each other; to meet in shock; to meet in opposition or antagonism.

collie

collie *n* a variety of dog with a pointed muzzle and long hair used as a sheepdog.

collier *n* one who works in a coal mine; a vessel employed in the coal trade.

colliery *n* the place where coal is dug; a coal mine or pit.

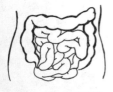

colon

colligate *vt* (**colligated, colligating**) to bind or fasten together.

collimation *n* the act of levelling or of directing the sight to a fixed object.

collimator *n* a small telescope used for adjusting the line of collimation; a tube with a convex lens at one end and a slit at the other end, exactly at the focus of the lens, used in spectroscopy to produce parallel light.

collinear *adj* pertaining to or situated in a corresponding line.

collision *n* the act of striking or dashing together; the meeting and mutual striking of two or more moving bodies or of a moving body with a stationary one; opposition; antagonism; interference.

collocate *vt* (**collocated, collocating**) to set or place; to set; to station.

collocation *n* the act of collocating, placing, disposing or arranging along with something else; the manner in which a thing is placed with regard to something else; disposition; arrangement.

collodion, collodium *n* a solution of pyroxylin used as an adhesive for surgical dressings, to coat the skin and as the basis of a photographic process.

colloid *adj* like glue or jelly; (*chem*) applied to uncrystallizable liquids; (*geol*) applied to partly amorphous minerals.—*n* the name given to a transparent, viscid, yellowish, structureless or slightly granular matter, resembling liquid gelatine.

colloidal *adj* of or pertaining to or of the nature of colloids.

collop *n* a slice or lump of meat.

colloquial *adj* pertaining to conversation; peculiar to the language of common conversation; (of language) informal.

colloquialism *n* a word or phrase peculiar to the language of common conversation.

colloquially *adv* in a colloquial or conversational manner; in colloquial language.

colloquy *n* the mutual discourse of two or more; a conference; a dialogue; a conversation.

collotype *n* thin gelatinous plate etched by actinic rays and then printed from.

collude *vi* (**colluded, colluding**) to conspire in a fraud; to act in concert; to connive.

collusion *n* secret agreement for a fraudulent purpose.

collusive *adj* fraudulently concerted between two or more.

cologne, Cologne water *n* eau de cologne

colon[1] *n* the largest portion of the human intestine, forming the middle section of the large intestine and terminating in the rectum.

colon[2] *n* a punctuation mark (:) used to mark a pause greater than that of a semicolon but less than that of a period.

colonel *n* an army or air force officer junior to a brigadier and senior to a lieutenant colonel.

colonial *adj* pertaining to a colony.—*n* one who helps to found or settles in a colony.

colonialism *n* a phrase, idiom or practice peculiar to a colony; the policy of a country of acquiring colonies.

colonist *n* an inhabitant of or settler in a colony; a member of a colonizing expedition.

colonization *n* the act of colonizing or state of being colonized.

colonize *vt* (**colonized, colonizing**) to plant or establish a colony in; to send a colony to; to migrate and settle in.—*vi* to remove and settle in a distant country.

colonizer *n* one who colonizes; one who establishes colonies.

colonnade *n* (*archit*) any series or range of columns placed at certain intervals from each other.

colony *n* a body of people transplanted from their mother country to a remote province or country; a body of settlers or their descendants; the country planted or colonized; a number of animals or plants living or growing together.

colophon *n* a publisher's device or emblem; formerly, a device or printer's name, place of publication and date put at the end of a book.

Colorado beetle *n* a yellowish beetle, a native of the southwestern states of North America, which works great havoc among potato crops.

coloration *n* colouring.

coloratura *adj* (*mus*) highly ornamented or florid.—*n* a vocal passage sung in this way; a singer, usually a soprano, specializing in ornamental trills or runs.

colossal *adj* like a colossus; very large; huge; gigantic.

colossus *n* a statue of a gigantic size or of size much greater than human size, such as the statue of Apollo which in ancient times stood at the entrance to the port of Rhodes.

colostomy *n* a surgical operation to produce an opening in the colon, forming an artificial anus.

colostrum *n* the first milk secreted in the breasts after childbirth.

colour *n* any tint or hue distinguished from white; that which is used for colouring; a pigment; paint; the blood-red hue of the face; redness; complexion; false show; pretence; guise; (*pl*) a flag, ensign or standard borne in an army or fleet; a colour used as a badge.—*vt* to impart colour to; to dye; to tinge; to paint; to stain; (*fig*) to clothe with an appearance different from the real; to give a specious appearance to; to make plausible.—*vi* to blush.

colour bar *n* discrimination based on colour, especially by the white races against other races.

colour-blind *adj* incapable of accurately distinguishing colours; having an imperfect perception of colours.

coloured *adj* having a colour; dyed, painted or stained; having some other colour than white or black; having a specious appearance; of a darker-skinned race of people.—*n* a person of a darker-skinned race.

colour-fast *adj* (of a material) coloured by dyes which will not run or come out on being washed.

colouring *n* the act or art of applying colours; colour applied; tints or hues collectively, as in a picture; a specious appearance; show.

colourize *vt* (**colourized, colourizing**) to add colour to (a black and white film) by a computerized process.

colour sergeant *n* (*milit*) prior to 1914, the senior sergeant in a company.

colporteur *n* a hawker of books and pamphlets, particularly religious ones.

colt *n* a young horse or a young animal of the horse genus, commonly and distinctively applied to the male, *filly* being the female.

coltsfoot *n* the popular name of a yellow-flowered plant whose leaves were once much used in medicine.

columbine *adj* like or pertaining to a pigeon or dove; of a dove colour; resembling the neck of a dove in colour.—*n* a plant of the buttercup family, so called from the curved petals being in shape somewhat like pigeons, the sepals forming the wings.

Columbine *n* the name of the sweetheart of Harlequin in pantomimes.

column *n* a solid body of considerably greater length than thickness, standing upright and generally serving as a support to something resting on its top; a pillar; anything resembling a column in shape (*a column of water, air* or *mercury*); (*bot*) the united stamens and styles of plants when they form a solid central body, as in orchids; a long line or file of people; (*milit*) a formation of troops, narrow in front and deep from front to rear; (*naut*) a body of ships, following each other; in printing and writing, a division of a page; a perpendicular set of lines separated from another set by a line or blank space; a regular feature article in a newspaper.

columnar *adj* formed in columns; like the shaft of a column.

columned *adj* furnished with columns; supported on or adorned by columns.

columnist *n* a journalist who writes a regular newspaper or magazine column.

colure *n* either of the two great circles supposed to intersect each other at right angles in the poles of the equator.

colza *n* the rape plant, its seed yielding an oil used for many purposes.

coma[1] *n* a state of more or less complete unconsciousness and loss of power of thought or motion.

coma[2] *n* (*bot*) the empty leaf or bract terminating the flowering stem of a plant, in a tuft or bush; also, the silky hairs at the end of some seeds; (*astron*) the nebulous hairlike envelope surrounding the nucleus of a comet.

Colorado beetle

comatose *adj* pertaining to coma; in a coma, unconscious; drowsy; lethargic.

comb *n* an instrument with teeth for separating, cleansing, adjusting or removing tangles from hair, wool or flax; also, an instrument used for keeping the hair in place; the crest or red fleshy tuft growing on a cock's head; the top or crest of a wave; honeycomb.—*vt* to dress or tidy with a comb; to remove tangles from; to examine or search thoroughly for.—*vi* to roll over, as the top of a wave, or to break with a white foam.

combat *vi* to fight; to struggle or contend.—*vt* to fight with; to oppose by force; to contend against; to resist, now chiefly *fig*, as *he combated their scruples*).—*n* a fight; a struggle to resist, overthrow or conquer; contest; engagement; battle.—**single combat** *n* a fight between two individuals; a duel.

combatant *adj* contending; disposed to combat or contend.—*n* a person who combats; any person engaged in active war; a person who contends with another in argument or controversy.

combat fatigue *n* a nervous disorder caused by the stress of battle.

comb

combative *adj* disposed to combat; showing such a disposition; pugnacious; aggressive.

combed *adj* having a comb or crest.

comber *n* one who combs; a machine that or one who combs wool, etc; a long wave.

combing *n* the act of using a comb; that which is removed by combing (in the latter sense, generally in the plural).

combination *n* the act of combining; the act of joining, coming together or uniting; concurrence; meeting; union or association of persons or things for effecting some object by joint operation; commixture; union of bodies or qualities in a mass or compound; chemical union; (*math*) the union of a number of individuals in different groups, each containing a certain number of the individuals; a sequence of numbers that opens a lock, especially of a safe.

combine *vt* (**combined, combining**) to unite or join; to link closely together.—*vi* to unite, agree or coalesce; to league together; to unite by affinity or chemical attraction.

combine harvester

combined *adj* united; associated; leagued; conjoined.

combine harvester *n* an agricultural machine which reaps, threshes and winnows grain in one process.

combustible *adj* capable of taking fire and burning; inflammable; (*fig*) fiery or irascible; hot-tempered.

combustion *n* the operation of fire on inflammable substances; burning.—**sponta-** neous **combustion** *n* the ignition of a body by the internal development of heat without the application of an external flame.

come *vi* (*pret* **came**, *pp* **come**, *ppr* **coming**) to move, advance nearer in any manner and from any distance; to approach the person speaking or writing, or the person addressed, opposed to *go*; to arrive; to take place; to reach a certain stage or point of progress; to arrive at (followed by an infinitive, as *I now come to consider the next subject*); to get into a certain state or condition (especially followed by *to be*); to happen or fall out (*come what will*); to advance or move into view; to appear (*colour comes into the face*); to accrue or result; to be formed (*knowledge comes*), frequently with *of* (*this comes of not taking heed*); to reach a sexual orgasm.—**come** (in the imperative) is used to excite attention or to invite to motion or joint action; or it expresses earnestness, haste, impatience, remonstrance, etc.—**to come and go** to alternate; to appear and disappear.—**to come about** to happen; to fall out (*how did these things come about?*).—**to come by** to pass near; to obtain, gain, acquire.—**to come down** to descend; to be humbled or abased.—**to come home** to come to one's dwelling; to touch nearly; to touch the feelings, interest or reason.—**to come in for** to get a share of; to get; to obtain.—**to come into** to acquire by inheritance or bequest.—**to come on** to advance; to progress; to thrive.—**to come out** to remove from within; to become public; to be introduced to general society; to declare or reveal that one is homosexual; to appear after being obscured by clouds (*the sun has come out*); to result from calculation.—**to come round** to recover; to revive; to regain one's former state of health.—**to come short** to fail; not to reach; to be inadequate.—**to come through** to survive.—**to come to** to fall or be allotted to; to amount to.—**to come to oneself** to get back one's consciousness; to recover.—**to come to pass** to happen.—**to come true** to be verified.—**to come** future; in future (*time to come*).—**to come up** to occur; to arise.

comedian *n* an actor or player in comedy; a writer of comedy; a person whose profession it is to tell jokes or funny stories, a comic; (*colloq*) a person who acts the fool.

comedienne *n* a female comedian or comic.

comedy *n* a dramatic composition of a light and amusing kind; drama consisting of amusing plays or films; an amusing occurrence; humour.

comeliness *n* the quality of being comely.

comely *adj* handsome; pretty and attractive.

comestible *n* an eatable; solid food (usually plural).

comet *n* the name given to certain celestial bodies consisting of a star-like nucleus, surrounded by a luminous envelope, called the *coma*, and usually accompanied by a tail or train of light, appearing at irregular intervals, moving through the heavens in paths which seem to correspond with parabolic curves or in a few instances in elliptical orbits of great eccentricity.

comeuppance *n* a deserved punishment; a deserved reprimand.

comfit *n* a bonbon; a sweet containing a nut.

comfort *vt* to raise from depression; to soothe when in grief or trouble; to bring solace or consolation to; to console; to cheer; to solace.—*n* relief from affliction, sorrow or trouble, etc; solace; consolation; a state of quiet or moderate enjoyment resulting from the possession of what satisfies bodily wants and freedom from all care or anxiety; a feeling or state of well-being, satisfaction or content; that which furnishes moderate enjoyment or content.

comfortable *adj* being in comfort or in a state of ease or moderate enjoyment; giving comfort; affording help, ease or consolation.

comforter *n* one who comforts; a knitted woollen scarf; in the USA, a baby's dummy; a quilted bedcover.

comfrey *n* a tall bell-flowered hairy plant, used in herbal medicine.

comic *adj* relating or belonging to comedy as distinct from tragedy; comical.—*n* a comic actor or singer; a person whose profession is to tell jokes or funny stories, a comedian; a funny person; a paper or book with stories told in comic strips.

comical *adj* exciting mirth; ludicrous; laughable; diverting; droll.

comic strip *n* a series of drawings which tell a story or joke by stages, often in the form of cartoons.

coming *adj* drawing nearer or nigh; approaching; moving towards; advancing; future; next in the future.

comity *n* courtesy; civility; good breeding.

comma *n* a punctuation mark (,) denoting the shortest pause in reading and separating a sentence into divisions according to the construction.

command *vt* to order with authority; to lay injunction on; to direct; to charge; to have or to exercise supreme authority, especially military authority, over; to have control over; to dominate through position, often specifically military position; to have within the range of the eye; to overlook; to exact or compel by moral influence; to challenge (*to command respect*); to have at one's disposal and service (*to command assistance*).—*vi* to act as or have the authority of a commander; to exercise influence or power.—*n* the power of governing with chief authority; supreme power; control; exercise of authority; a commandment; mandate; order; power or control, as from holding an advantageous military position; the power of overlooking from an elevated position; a force under the command of a particular officer.

commandant *n* a commander.

commandeer *vt* to seize for military purposes; to appropriate for one's own use.

commander *n* one who commands; a chief; one who has supreme authority; a leader; the chief officer of an army or of any division of it; a naval officer next in rank above lieutenant commander and under captain.

commander in chief *n* a supreme military commander; formerly, the highest staff appointment in the British army.

commanding *adj* governing; bearing rule; exercising supreme authority; controlling by influence, authority or dignity (*commanding eloquence*); dominating; overlooking a wide region without obstruction (*a commanding position* or *view*).

commandment *n* a command; a mandate; an order or injunction given by authority; charge; precept; one of the ten commandments of the Old Testament; authority; power of commanding.

command module *n* the operational part of a spacecraft.

commando *n* a member of an élite military force trained to raid enemy territory swiftly and destructively.

command performance *n* the performance of a variety show, play, film etc. at the request of a monarch or head of state.

commemorate *vt* (**commemorated, commemorating**) to preserve the memory of by a solemn act; to celebrate with honour and solemnity.

commemoration *n* the act of commemorating or calling to remembrance by some solemnity; the act of honouring the memory of some person or event by solemn celebration.

commence *vi* (**commenced, commencing**) to begin; to arise or originate; to have first existence; to begin to be, as in a new state or character.—*vt* to begin; to enter on; to perform the first act of.

commencement *n* the act or fact of commencing; beginning; rise; origin; first existence.

commend *vt* to entrust or give in charge; to represent as worthy of confidence, notice, regard or kindness; to recommend; with reflexive pronoun sometimes to call for notice or attention (*this subject commends itself to our attention*); to mention with approbation.

commendable *adj* capable or worthy of being commended or praised; praiseworthy; laudable.

commando

commendation *n* the act of commending; praise; favourable representation in words; declaration of esteem.

commendatory *adj* serving to commend; presenting to favourable notice or reception; containing praise.

commensal *n* one of two animals or plants that are always found together; an animal which lives on or in another without being parasitic.

commensurable *adj* having a common measure; reducible to a common measure; proportionate.

commensurate *adj* reducible to a common measure; of equal size; having the same boundaries; corresponding in amount, degree or magnitude; adequate; proportionate.

comment *vi* to make remarks or observations, either on a book or writing or on actions, events or opinions; to write notes on the works of an author with a view to illustrate his or her meaning or to explain particular passages; to make annotations.—*n* a remark or observation; a note intended to illustrate a difficult passage in an author; annotation; exposition; talk; discourse; opinion.

commentary *n* a series or collection of comments or annotations; a verbal description, as on radio or television, of an event as it happens.

commentate *vi* to act as commentator; to give a verbal description, as on radio or television, of an event as it is happening.

commentator *n* an annotator; one who comments on or analyses events, such as sporting events, on radio or television.

commerce *n* an interchange of goods, merchandise or property of any kind between countries or communities; trade; traffic; mutual dealings.

commercial *adj* pertaining to commerce or trade; dealing with or depending on commerce; carrying on commerce.

commercial art *n* the use of art and design in advertising, promotion or packaging of goods.

commercial artist *n* a person who is engaged in commercial art.

commercial traveller *n* a sales representative.

commination *n* a threat or threatening of punishment or vengeance.

commingle *vti* (commingled commingling) to mix together; to mingle in one mass or intimately; to blend.

comminute *vt* (comminuted, comminuting) to make small or fine; to reduce to minute particles or to a fine powder; to pulverize.

commiserate *vt* (commiserated, commiserating) to feel sorrow, pain or regret for through sympathy; to pity.

committee

commiseration *n* the act of commiserating; a feeling of sympathy for and empathy with, the pain, sorrow and afflictions of another; pity; compassion.

commissariat *n* the department of an army whose duties consisted in supplying transport, provisions and equipment to the troops; formerly, a department of government in the former USSR.

commissary *n* in a general sense, a commissioner; one to whom is committed some charge, duty or office by a superior power.

commission *n* the act of committing; the act of doing something; the act of perpetrating (*the commission of a crime*); the act of entrusting, as a charge or duty; the thing committed, entrusted or delivered; a duty, office, charge or piece of work entrusted to anyone; the warrant by which any trust is held or any authority exercised (as that of an officer in an army); mandate; authority given; a number of persons joined in an office or trust; commissioners; the state of acting in the purchase and sale of goods for another; position or business of an agent; agency; the allowance or percentage on sales paid to an agent.—*vt* to give a commission to; to empower or authorize by special commission; to send with a mandate or authority.

commissionaire *n* a uniformed doorman.

commissioner *n* one who commissions; a person who has a commission or warrant from proper authority to perform some office or execute some business; an officer having charge of some department of the public service, which is put into commission.

commit *vt* (**committed, committing**) to give in trust; to put into charge or keeping; to entrust; to surrender, give up, consign (with *to*); (*refl*) to bind to a certain line of conduct or to expose or endanger by a preliminary step or decision which cannot be recalled; to compromise; to order or send into confinement; to imprison (*the magistrate commits a guilty person*); to refer or entrust to a committee or select number of persons for their consideration and report; to do (generally something wrong); to perpetrate.—**to commit to memory** to learn by heart.

committee *n* a body of persons elected or appointed to attend to any matter or business referred to them, often a section of a larger body.

Committee of the Whole House *n* an arrangement by which matters are discussed in a particular manner in parliament, the chair being occupied by the chairman of committee and members being allowed to speak more than once on a question.

commix *vti* to mix or mingle; to blend.

commode *n* a chest of drawers; a low box-like stool or chair in which a chamber pot is fitted.

commodious *adj* roomy and convenient; spacious.

commodity *n* an article of merchandise; anything movable that is bought and sold, as goods, wares, produce of land and manufactures.

commodore *n* a courtesy title for the senior captain when three or more warships are cruising in company, for the senior captain of a line of merchant vessels and for the president of a yachting club.

common *adj* belonging or pertaining equally to more than one or to many indefinitely; belonging to all; general; universal; public; of frequent or usual occurrence; not extraordinary; frequent; usual; ordinary; habitual; not distinguished by rank or character; not of superior excellence; of low or mean rank or character; (*gram*) applied to such nouns as are both masculine and feminine and to those that are the names of all the objects possessing the attributes denoted by the noun (river, etc).—*n* a tract of ground, the use of which belongs to the public or to a number of people; (*pl*) the common people; the untitled; food provided at a common table, as at colleges; food or fare in general.

commonalty *n* the common people; all below the rank of nobility.

common cold *n* a viral respiratory infection characterized by sneezing, coughing and nasal congestion or a running nose.

commoner *n* a person under the degree of nobility or royalty.

common law *n* the unwritten law, the law that receives its binding force from immemorial usage and universal reception, in distinction from the written or statute law.

common-or-garden *adj* ordinary; not unusual or special in any way.

commonplace *adj* not new or extraordinary; common; trite.—*n* a passage, quotation, etc, to be included in a commonplace book; a well-known or customary remark; a trite saying; a platitude.

commonplace book *n* a book in which things to be remembered, passages, quotations, poems, etc, are recorded.

Commons *npl* the House of Commons.

common sense *n* sound practical judgment; a natural sagacity or understanding.

commonwealth *n* the body politic; a republican state; a political community; a federation of states.

Commonwealth *n* the form of government which existed in England from the death of Charles I in 1649 to the abdication of Richard Cromwell in 1659; the Commonwealth of Nations, an association of countries that are or have been ruled by the United Kingdom.

commotion *n* agitation; tumult of people; disturbance; perturbation; disorder of mind; excitement.

communal *adj* shared; for common use.

commune[1] *vi* (**communed, communing**) to talk together familiarly; to impart sentiments mutually; to interchange ideas or feelings; to communicate spiritually (*commune with nature*).—*n* familiar interchange of ideas or sentiments; communion; intercourse; friendly conversation (*to hold commune, to be in commune*).

commune[2] *n* a small territorial district in France and in some other countries under the government of a mayor; inhabitants of a commune; a group of people living together and sharing possessions and household chores.

communicable *adj* capable of being communicated or imparted from one to another; capable of being recounted; (of a disease) easily passed on.

communicant *n* one who partakes of the sacrament at Communion, the celebration of the Eucharist.

communicate *vt* (**communicated, communicating**) to impart to another or others; to bestow or confer for joint possession, generally or always something intangible, as intelligence, news, opinions or disease (with *to* before the receiver).—*vi* to share; to participate (followed by *in*); to have a connection or passage from one to another (*one room communicates with another*); to have or hold interchange of thoughts or ideas; to partake of the Eucharist or Communion; to succeed in conveying information.

communication *n* the act of communicating; means of communicating; connecting passage; means of passing from place to place; that which is communicated or imparted; information or intelligence imparted by word or writing; a document or message imparting information.

communicative *adj* inclined to communicate; ready to impart to others; free in communicating; not reserved; open; talkative.

communion *n* participation of something in common; fellowship; concord; bond or association; social communication between two or more persons; interchange of thoughts or acts; union in religious worship or in doctrine and discipline.

Communion *n* the act of partaking in the sacrament of the Eucharist; the celebration of the Lord's supper.

communiqué *n* an official communication, a statement given to the press.

communism *n* the system or theory which upholds the absorption of all proprietary rights in a common interest; the doctrine of common ownership of property.

Communion

communist *n* one who holds the doctrines of communism.

community *n* a society of people having common rights and privileges; a society of individuals of any kind; the body of people in a state; the public or people in general (used in this sense always with *the*); common character (*individuals distinguished by community of descent*); a group of plants and animals of a region dependent on each other for life and survival.

community nurse *n* a nurse employed by a local authority to visit patients in their own homes, staff various clinics etc.

community physician *n* a doctor appointed by a local authority with the administrative responsibility for the medical and social welfare of an area.

community policing *n* the provision of police officers in an area who are either from that area or are well-known to the residents of the area.

community service *n* unpaid work of a useful nature in the community, especially that undertaken by people found guilty of minor criminal offences as an alternative to prison sentences or fines.

community service order a court order directing someone to undertake community service.

commutable *adj* capable of being exchanged or mutually changed; interchangeable.

commutation *n* the act of commuting; the act of substituting one thing for another; the change of a penalty or punishment from a greater to a less; the act of substituting one sort of payment for another or of making a money payment in lieu of the performance of some sort of compulsory duty or labour.

commutative *adj* relating to exchange; interchangeable; mutual.

commutatively *adv* by way of exchange.

commutator *n* (*elect*) an instrument for converting an alternating current into a direct one.

commute *vt* (**commuted, commuting**) to exchange; to put one thing in the place of another; to give or receive one thing for another; to exchange, as one penalty or punishment for one of less severity; to pay in money instead of in kind or in duty; to pay a single sum as an equivalent for a number of successive payments.—*vi* to travel daily from home to work, often quite a distance.

compact[1] *adj* closely and firmly united, as the parts or particles of solid bodies; having the parts or particles close; solid; dense; concise.

compact[2] *n* an agreement; a contract, covenant, bargain or settlement between parties.

compact disc

compact disc *n* a small audio disc from which digitally recorded sound can be read by a laser beam.

compact disc player *n* a machine that plays compact discs by means of a laser beam.

compactly *adv* in a compact or condensed manner; closely; concisely; briefly; tersely; neat.

compact video *n* a disc, similar to a compact audio disc, that plays both sound and pictures.

companion[1] *n* one with whom a person frequently associates and converses; a friend; one who accompanies another; a person holding the third class of an order of knighthood (as of the Bath).—*adj* accompanying; united with.

companion[2] *n* (*naut*) a raised frame with windows on a quarterdeck, through which light passes to the cabins below; a raised cover to the cabin stair of a merchant vessel.

companionable *adj* fit for good fellowship; agreeable in company; sociable.

companion ladder *n* (*naut*) the steps or ladder between the main deck and the quarterdeck.

companionship *n* the state or fact of being a companion; fellowship; association; friendship.

companionway *n* (*naut*) the staircase at the entrance to the cabin of a vessel.

company *n* the state of being along with; companionship; fellowship; society; any gathering of persons; a collection of people or animals; guests at a person's house; a number of persons united for performing or carrying on anything jointly, as some commercial enterprise, the term being applicable to private partnerships or to incorporated bodies; a firm (but this word usually implies fewer partners than *company*); the members of a firm whose names do not appear in the style or title of the firm, usually contracted when written (*Messrs. Smith & Co.*); an army unit; the crew of a ship, including the officers.—**to bear** *or* **keep (a person) company** to accompany; to attend; to go with; to associate with.— **to be good company** to be an entertaining companion.

comparable *adj* capable of being compared; worthy of comparison; similar.

comparative *adj* estimated by comparison; not positive or absolute; proceeding by comparison; founded on comparison, especially founded on the comparison of different things belonging to the same science or study (*comparative anatomy*, etc); having the power of comparing different things (*the comparative faculty*); (*gram*) expressing a greater degree; expressing more than the positive but less than the superlative (applied to forms of adjectives and adverbs).—*n* (*gram*) the comparative degree.

comparatively *adv* by comparison; according to estimate made by comparison; not positively, absolutely or in itself; relatively.

compare *vt* (**compared, comparing**) to set or bring together to examine the relations they bear to each other, especially with a view to ascertain agreement or disagreement, resemblances or differences (*to compare one thing with another*); to liken; to represent as similar for the purpose of illustration (*to compare one thing to another*); (*gram*) to inflect by the degrees of comparison.—*vi* to hold or stand comparison; to contrast favourably.—*n* comparison; scope or room for comparison (*rich beyond compare*).

comparison *n* the act of comparing; the act of examining in order to discover how one thing stands with regard to another; the state of being compared; relation between things such as admits of their being compared; something with which another thing is compared; likeness or similarity; a parallel; (*gram*) the inflection of an adjective or adverb to express degrees of the original quality.

compartment *n* a division or separate part of a general structure, as of a building, railway carriage, etc; a separate section; a category.

compass *n* a limit or boundary; extent; range (applied to time, space, sound, etc); moderation; due limits (*to keep within compass*); an instrument consisting essentially of a magnet suspended so as to have as complete freedom of motion as possible and used to indicate the magnetic meridian or the position of objects with respect to that meridian; a mathematical instrument for describing circles, measuring figures, distances between two points, etc (often with the plural designation *compasses* or *a pair of compasses*).—*vt* to stretch round; to encompass; to enclose, encircle, environ, surround; to obtain; to attain to; to accomplish (*to compass one's purposes*).

compassion *n* a suffering with another; sympathy; pity; commiseration.

compassionate *adj* characterized by compassion; full of pity; tender-hearted; sympathetic.

compassion fatigue *n* an indifference towards the hardship of those in need and a consequent reluctance to give charitable donations to them, caused by having been exposed to many charitable appeals.

compatibility *n* the quality of being compatible; consistency; suitableness.

compatible *adj* capable of coexisting or being found together in the same subject; capable of existing together in harmony; suitable; agreeable; not incongruous (*things compatible with one another*).

compatriot *n* one of the same country.

compeer *n* an equal; a companion; an associate; a mate.

compel *vt* (**compelled, compelling**) to drive or urge with force; to constrain; to oblige; to necessitate.

compellable *adj* capable of being compelled or constrained.

compendious *adj* containing the substance or general principles of a subject or work in a narrow space; succinct; concise.

compendium *n* (*pl* **compendiums, compendia**) a brief compilation or composition containing the principal heads or general principles of a larger work or system; an abridgement; a summary; an epitome.

compensate *vt* (**compensated, compensating**) to recompense; to make up for; to counterbalance; to make amends for (losses, defects, etc).—*vi* to make amends; to supply or serve as an equivalent (followed by *for*).

compensation *n* the act of compensating; that which is given or serves as an equivalent for services, debt, lack, loss or suffering; amends; indemnity; recompense; that which supplies the place of something else or makes good a deficiency.

compere *n* a master of ceremonies.

compete *vi* (**competed, competing**) to seek or strive for the same thing as another; to carry on a contest or rivalry for a common object; to vie (*to compete with a person for a thing*); to take part in a competition or contest.

competition *n* the act of competing; mutual contest or striving for the same object; rivalry; a trial of skill held as a test of superiority or comparative fitness.

competitive *adj* relating to competition; carried out by competition; liking to compete; having the urge to compete against others; (of goods) able to be successful over those of rival firms because of low price or high quality; (of prices) low in comparison with those of rival firms.

competitor *n* one who competes; one who endeavours to obtain what another seeks; one who claims what another claims; a rival.

competence, competency *n* state of being competent; fitness; suitableness; adequateness; ability; sufficiency; such a quantity as is sufficient; especially, property or means of subsistence sufficient to furnish the necessaries and conveniences of life without superfluity.

competent *adj* answering all requirements; suitable; fit; sufficient or fit for the purpose; adequate; having legal capacity or power; rightfully or lawfully belonging.

compass

competently *adv* in a competent manner; sufficiently; adequately; suitably.

compilation *n* the act of compiling or collecting from written or printed documents or books; that which is compiled; a book or treatise drawn up by compiling.

compile *vt* (**compiled, compiling**) to draw up, write out or compose, especially by collecting materials from various sources; to collect or put together by utilizing the writings of others; to gather data, etc, for a book.

compiler *n* one who compiles.

complacence, complacency *n* a feeling of satisfaction; gratification; self-satisfaction, smugness.

complacent *adj* displaying complacency; gratified; satisfied; self-satisfied; smug.

complain *vi* to utter expressions of grief, pain, uneasiness, censure, resentment; to find fault; to grumble; to lament; to murmur; to bewail; to make a formal accusation against a person; to make a charge (now regularly followed by *of* before the cause of grief or censure).

complaint *n* an expression of grief, regret, pain, censure or resentment; lamentation; murmuring; a finding fault; grumbling; the cause or subject of complaint; a malady; an ailment; a disease (usually applied to disorders not violent); a charge; a representation of injuries suffered; accusation.

complaisance *n* a desire to please; disposition to oblige.

complaisant *adj* obliging; desirous to please; proceeding from an obliging disposition.

complement *n* full quantity or number; full amount; what is lacking to complete or fill up some quantity or thing; difference; (*math*) what is lacking in an arc or angle to make it up to 90°.

complementary *adj* completing; supplying a deficiency.

complementary medicine *n* a form of treatment, such as acupuncture, osteopathy, homeopathy, herbal medicine etc, which complements conventional forms of medicine.

complete *adj* having no deficiency; lacking no part or element; perfect; thorough; consummate; in every respect; finished; ended; concluded.—*vt* (**completed, completing**) to make complete; to finish; to end; to perfect; to fulfil; to accomplish; to realize.

completely *adv* in a complete manner; fully; perfectly; entirely; wholly; totally; utterly; thoroughly; quite.

completion *n* act of completing, finishing or perfecting; state of being complete or completed; perfect state; fulfilment; accomplishment.

complex *adj* composed of various parts or things; including sundry particulars connected; composite; not simple (*a complex being, a complex idea*); involved; intricate; complicated; perplexed (*a complex process*).—*n* assemblage of things related as parts of a system; a collection of interrelated units, buildings, etc, as a shopping complex; in psychoanalysis, a series of emotionally accentuated ideas in a repressed state; an abnormal preoccupation; a phobia.

complexion *n* physical character or nature; the colour or hue of the skin, particularly of the face; the general appearance of anything; character or aspect.

complexity *n* the state of being complex; anything complex or difficult; intricacy; involvement; entanglement.

compliance *n* the act of complying; a yielding as to a request, wish, desire, etc; a disposition to yield to others.

compliant *adj* given to comply; yielding to request or desire; ready to accommodate; obliging.

complicate *vt* (**complicated, complicating**) to intertwine; to interweave; to render complex or intricate; to involve; to make more difficult.

complicated *adj* involved; intricate.

complication *n* the act of complicating or state of being complicated; entanglement; complexity; something complicated; an aggregate of things involved, mixed up or mutually united; what complicates or causes complication; a difficulty; in medicine, a condition or illness following an original illness.

complicity *n* the state of being an accomplice; partnership in crime.

compliment *n* an act or expression of civility, respect or regard; delicate flattery; expression of commendation or admiration; praise.—*vt* to pay a compliment to; to flatter or gratify by expressions of approbation, esteem or respect.

complimentary *adj* full of or using compliments; intended to express or convey a compliment or compliments; expressive of civility, regard or praise; given free of charge (*a complimentary ticket*).

compline, complin *n* the last of the seven canonical hours in the Roman Catholic breviary.

comply *vi* (**complied, complying**) to adopt a certain course of action at the desire of another; to yield; to acquiesce; to consent; to agree (used alone or followed by *with*).

component *adj* composing; constituting; entering into as a part.—*n* a constituent part; the effective part of a force, velocity, etc, in a given direction; one of any number of constituent forces, velocities, etc, of which the given force, velocity, etc, is the resultant.

comport *vi* to be suitable; agree; accord; fit; suit.—*vt* to behave; to conduct (used reflexively).

comportment *n* behaviour; demeanour.

compose *vt* (**composed, composing**) to form by uniting two or more things; to form, frame or fashion; to form by being combined or united; to constitute; to make; to write, as an author; to become the author of (a book, a piece of music); to calm; to quiet; to appease; to settle; to adjust (differences, etc); to place in proper form; to dispose; in fine arts, to arrange the leading features of; (*print*) to set in proper order for printing, as type.—*vi* to write a musical composition.

composed *adj* free from disturbance or agitation; calm; sedate; quiet; tranquil.

composer *n* one who or that which composes; one who writes an original work; most commonly, one who composes musical pieces.

composite *adj* made up of distinct parts, elements or substances; compounded; (*bot*) having flowers forming dense heads composed of many florets, as in the daisy, dandelion, etc.—*n* anything made up of parts or of different elements; a compound; a composition; (*bot*) a composite flower.

Composite *adj* (*archit*) of the order in which the capital exhibits leaves, volutes, etc, blending Ionic and Corinthian forms.

composite number *n* an integer divisible by itself and at least one other number.

composition *n* the act of composing or compounding or the state of being composed or compounded; the act of producing some literary or musical piece; what is composed, as a literary, musical or artistic production; the act of writing for practice in English or a foreign language; the act of making a mutual agreement for the discharge of a debt or the agreement itself; the amount or rate paid in compounding with creditors; (*gram*) the act of forming compound words; the arrangement of parts in a whole; mode of arrangement; a material compounded of two or more ingredients; a compound; (*print*) the act of setting type or characters to form lines and of arranging the lines in a galley to make a column or page and from this to make a form.

compositor *n* (*print*) one who sets types and makes up the pages and forms.

composure *n* the state of being composed; a settled state of mind; sedateness; calmness; tranquillity.

compound[1] *adj* composed of two or more elements, parts or ingredients; not simple.—*n* something produced by compounding two or more ingredients, parts or elements, as a substance or a word.—*vt* to mix up or mingle together; to form by mingling two or more ingredients or elements into one; to combine; to settle amicably; to adjust by agreement (a difference or controversy); to discharge (a debt) by paying a part.—*vi* to agree on concession; to come to terms of agreement; to arrange or make a settlement by compromise; especially, to settle with creditors by agreement and discharge a debt by paying a part of its amount; to make an agreement to pay a debt by means or in a manner different from that stipulated or required by law (*to compound with a person* and *for a debt*).

compound[2] *n* an enclosure surrounding a building.

compound fracture *n* (*surg*) a fracture in which a bone is broken and there is also laceration of the tissues.

compound interest *n* that interest which arises from the principal with the interest added.

comprehend *vt* to take in or include within a certain scope; to include by implication or signification; to embrace; to comprise; to take into the mind; to grasp by the understanding; to understand.

comprehensible *adj* capable of being comprehended; capable of being understood; conceivable by the mind; intelligible.

comprehension *n* the act of comprehending, including or embracing; a comprising; inclusion; capacity of the mind to understand; power of the understanding to receive and contain ideas; capacity of knowing.

comprehensive *adj* having the quality of comprehending or embracing a great number or a wide extent; of extensive application; wide in scope; comprehending much in a comparatively small compass; having the power to comprehend or understand; (of a school) providing education for pupils of all levels of ability.

compress *vt* to press together; to force, urge or drive into a smaller compass; to condense.—*n* a pad used to apply pressure to a part of the body; a wet cloth applied to the skin to relieve inflammation, etc.

compressible *adj* capable of being compressed or forced into a narrow compass; yielding to pressure; condensable.

compression *n* the act of compressing; the act of forcing into closer union or density; the state of being compressed; condensation; one of the forms of stress, or more strictly of strain, consisting in a crushing action; the increase in pressure in an engine to compress the gases so that they explode.

comprise *vt* (**comprised, comprising**) to contain; to include; to consist of.

compromise *n* a settlement of differences by mutual concessions; a combination of two rival systems, principles, etc, in which a part of each is sacrificed to make the combination possible; what results from or is founded on such an agreement; a mutual concession.—*vt* (**compromised, compromising**) to adjust or combine by a compromise; to settle by mutual concessions; to put to risk or hazard or expose to serious consequences by some act or declaration which cannot be recalled; to put in jeopardy; to endanger the interests of (often reflexive, as *he compromised himself by his rash statements*).—*vi* to make a compromise; to settle by concession.

comptroller *n* a controller; an officer who examines the accounts of collectors of public money.

compulsion *n* the act of compelling or driving by force, physical or moral; constraint of the will.

compulsorily *adv* in a compulsory manner; by force or constraint.

compulsory *adj* exercising compulsion; compelling; constraining; enforced; due to compulsion; obligatory (*a compulsory contribution*).

compunction *n* the stinging or pricking of the conscience; regret, as for wrongdoing or for causing pain to someone; contrition; remorse.

computable *adj* capable of being computed, numbered or reckoned.

computation *n* the act or process of computing, reckoning or estimating; calculation; the result of a computation.

compute *vt* (**computed, computing**) to determine by calculation; to count; to reckon; to calculate; to estimate.—*vi* to reckon.

computer *n* a person or thing that computes; an electronic device that is capable of storing and processing data in accordance with programmed instructions.

computer

computer game *n* a game of skill recorded on a cassette or disc and played on a computer screen, the moves being made on a keyboard or by a joystick in response to the images appearing on the screen.

computer graphics *n* the production of pictorial images on a computer screen.

computerization *n* the carrying out of a process by means of computers; the storing or process of data by means of a computer system; the act of equipping with computers.

concave

computerize *vt* (**computerized, computerizing**) to carry out or control (a process) using computers; to store or process (data) by means of a computer system; to equip with computers.

computer virus *n* a computer program introduced into a computer system designed to sabotage it or destroy data.

comrade *n* a close companion; a mate; a friend; used as a term of address in some socialist or communist circles.

comradeship *n* the state or feeling of being a comrade; companionship; fellowship.

con[1] *adv, n* against, in the phrase *pro and con*, for and against, as a noun, a statement, argument, point or consideration supporting the negative side of a question (*to discuss the pros and cons*).

con[2] *vt* (**conned, conning**) to peruse carefully and attentively; to study over; to learn; to direct the steering of (a ship).

con[3] *vt* (**conned, conning**) to trick; to swindle; to deceive.—*n* a confidence trick.

conacre *n* in Ireland, the subletting of tilled land in small portions for a single crop.

con artist *n* a confidence trickster.

concatenate *vt* (**concatenated, concatenating**) to link together; to unite in a successive series or chain, as things depending on each other.

concatenation *n* the state of being concatenated or linked together; a series of links united.

concave *adj* curved or rounded inwards, as the inner surface of a spherical body.—*n* a concave line or surface.

conceal *vt* to hide; to withdraw from observation; to cover or keep from sight; to keep close or secret; to forbear to disclose.

concealment *n* the act of concealing, hiding or keeping secret; the state of being hidden or concealed; privacy; shelter from observation; cover from sight.

concede *vt* (**conceded, conceding**) to admit as true, just or proper; to grant; to let pass undisputed; to grant as a privilege; to yield up; to allow; to surrender.—*vi* to make concession; to grant a request or petition; to yield.

conceit *n* an ill-grounded opinion of one's own importance; self-conceit; vanity; a thought or expression intended to be striking or poetical but rather far-fetched, insipid or pedantic.

conceited *adj* entertaining a flattering opinion of oneself; self-conceited; vain; egotistical.

conceivable *adj* capable of being conceived, thought, imagined or understood; possible.

conceive *vt* (**conceived, conceiving**) to become pregnant with; to develop in the womb in an embryonic state; to form in the mind; to devise (an idea, a purpose); to realize in the mind; to form a conception of; to place distinctly before the thoughts; to comprehend (often used as a specific term in philosophy); to think; to imagine; to suppose possible.—*vi* to have a foetus formed in the womb; to become pregnant; to have or form a conception or idea; to think (*to conceive of a thing*); to formulate (an idea, etc).

concentrate *vt* (**concentrated, concentrating**) to bring to a common centre or point of union; to cause to come together to one spot or point; to bring to bear on one point; to direct towards one object; (*chem*) to intensify by removing non-essential matter; to reduce to a state of great strength and purity.—*vi* to approach or meet in a common point or centre; to direct one's thoughts, attention or actions towards something.—*n* a concentrated food reduced to its essential nutritiousness.

concentration *n* the act of concentrating; the act of collecting into a central point or of directing to one object; the state of being concentrated; the act of increasing the strength of fluids by volatilizing part of their water; the art of directing one's thoughts, attention, etc, towards something.

concentration camp *n* a prison camp for political prisoners and others, usually civilians, whom the authorities wish to segregate from the community.

concentric *adj* having a common centre (circles, etc).

concept *n* (*philos*) the subject of a conception; the object conceived by the mind; a general idea, especially an abstract one; a notion; an idea.

conception *n* the act of conceiving; the first formation of the embryo of an animal or human being; the act or power of conceiving in the mind; that which is conceived in the mind; product of the imaginative or inventive faculty; (*philos*) that mental act or combination of acts by which an absent object of perception is brought before the mind by the imagination; the mental operation by which such notions or conceptions are formed; a general notion; that which constitutes the meaning of a general term; thought, notion or idea in the loose sense (*you have no conception how clever he is*).

concern *vt* to relate, pertain or belong to; to affect the interest of; to be of importance to (*that does not concern me*); (*refl*) to take or have an interest in, occupy or busy oneself; to disturb, make uneasy or cause concern to.—*n* that which relates or belongs to one; business; affair; matter of importance; that which affects one's welfare or happiness; solicitude; anxiety; agitation or uneasiness of mind; disturbed state of feeling; an establishment, such as a manufacturing or commercial establishment.

concerned *adj* having concern; interested; engaged; anxious.

concerning *prep* in regard to; regarding; with relation to; about.

concert *vt* to contrive and settle by mutual communication of opinions or propositions; to plan; to devise.—*n* agreement of two or more in a design or plan; accordance in a scheme; cooperation; concord; the music of a company of players or singers or of both united; a public or private musical entertainment at which a number of vocalists or instrumentalists, or both, perform singly or combined; an entertainment at which a variety of acts are performed.

concerted *adj* mutually contrived or planned (*a concerted action*).

concerted piece *n* (*mus*) a composition in parts for several voices or instruments.

concertina *n* a musical instrument held between the hands in playing and composed of a bellows, with two faces or ends, in which are the keys or stops by pressing which with the fingers air is admitted to the free metallic reeds producing the sounds.

concerto *n* (*pl* **concertos, concerti**) a musical composition, usually in a symphonic form, written for one principal instrument, with accompaniments for a full orchestra.

concession *n* the act of conceding, admitting or granting; a yielding to demand or claim; the thing yielded; a grant; a right or privilege granted by a government institution, etc; a grant empowering some scheme or work to be done; a reduction in price for certain groups of people (*travel concessions for old-age pensioners*).

concessionary *adj* pertaining to a concession; of prices, reduced for particular groups of people, as old-age pensioners or students.

conch *n* a marine shell, especially a large spiral shell of a trumpet shape, which may be blown like a trumpet; the external portion of the ear, more especially the hollow part of it.

concha *n* (*pl* **conchae**) the external ear; (*archit*) the plain ribless surface of a vault; the semi-dome of an apse; the apse.

conchie *n* (*colloq*) a conscientious objector.

conchoid *n* the name of a special kind of curve used for finding two mean proportionals.

conchology *n* the study of the nature, formation and classification of shells.

concierge *n* a doorkeeper to a hotel, house, prison, etc; a janitor, male or female; a porter.

conciliate *vt* (**conciliated, conciliating**) to make friendly from being antagonistic; to pacify; to soothe; to win round.

conciliating *adj* winning; having the quality of gaining favour.

conciliation *n* the act of conciliating; the act of making friendly; the act of winning or gaining favour or esteem.

conciliatory *adj* tending to conciliate or bring to a friendly state or feeling; pacific.

concise *adj* brief and comprehensive; em-

concentric circles

conch

ploying as few words as possible; succinct.

concisely *adv* in a concise manner; briefly; in few words.

conclave *n* the assembly or meeting of the cardinals shut up for the election of a pope; hence, the body of cardinals; a private meeting; a close assembly.

conclude *vt* (**concluded, concluding**) to infer or arrive at by reasoning; to deduce, as from premises; to judge; to end, finish, bring to a conclusion; to settle or arrange finally (*to conclude an agreement* or *a peace*).—*vi* to infer; to form a final judgment; to come to a decision; to resolve; to determine (generally followed by an infinitive or a clause); to end; to make a finish.

conclusion *n* the end, close or termination; the last part; determination; final decision; inference; logic, the inference of a syllogism as drawn from the premises.—**in conclusion** finally, lastly.

conclusive *adj* putting an end to debate or argument; final; leading to a conclusion or determination; decisive; bringing out or leading to a logical conclusion; leaving no doubt.

concoct *vt* to form and prepare in the mind; to devise; to plan; to plot (a scheme, a conspiracy).

concoction *n* the act of concocting or devising; a made-up story.

concomitant *adj* accompanying; conjoined with; concurrent; attending (of things, circumstances, etc).—*n* a thing that accompanies another; an accompaniment; an accessory.

concord *n* agreement or union in opinions, sentiments, views or interests; harmony; agreement between things; suitableness; (*mus*) the pleasing combination of two or more sounds; the relation between two or more sounds which are agreeable to the ear; (*gram*) agreement of words in construction.

concordance *n* the state of being concordant; agreement; harmony; a book in which the principal words used in any work, as the Scriptures, Shakespeare, etc, are arranged alphabetically and the book, chapter, verse, act, scene, line or other subdivision in which each word occurs are noted.

concordant *adj* agreeing; agreeable; correspondent; harmonious.

concordat *n* an agreement; a compact; a convention; especially, a formal agreement between the pope and any secular government.

concourse *n* a moving, flowing or running together; confluence; a meeting or coming together of people; the people assembled; a throng; a crowd; an assemblage of things; agglomeration; a large open area or

a hall where people may gather, as at an airport.

concrete *adj* formed by union of separate particles in a mass; united in a solid form; in logic, a term applied to an object as it exists in nature, invested with all its attributes, or to the notion or name of such an object.—*n* a mass formed by concretion of separate particles of matter in one body; a compound; in logic, a concrete term; a compact mass of gravel, coarse pebbles or stone chippings, cemented together by hydraulic or other mortar, used extensively in building, especially under water.

concrete noun *n* a name of a thing as opposed to a quality.

concretion *n* the act of growing together so as to form one mass; the mass or solid matter formed by growing together; a clot; a lump; (*geol*) a lump or nodule formed by molecular aggregation as distinct from crystallization.

concubinage *n* the act or practice of having a concubine or concubines; the state of being a concubine; a living as husband and wife without being married.

concubine *n* a woman who cohabits with a man without being legally married to him; in polygamous societies, a wife of inferior status.

concupiscence *n* lustful feeling; lust; sinful desire.

concur *vi* (**concurred, concurring**) to run or meet together; to agree, join or unite, as in one action or opinion (*to concur with a person in an opinion*); to assent; to unite or be conjoined; to meet together; to be combined; to unite in contributing to a common object (*causes that concur to an effect*); to coincide or have points of agreement.

concurrence *n* the act of concurring; conjunction; combination of agents, circumstances or events; agreement in opinion; union or consent as to a design to be carried out; approbation; consent with joint aid or contribution of power or influence.

concurrent *adj* concurring or acting in conjunction; happening at the same time or in the same place; agreeing in the same act; contributing to the same event or effect; operating with; conjoined; associate; concomitant; joint and equal; existing together and operating on the same objects (*the concurrent jurisdiction of law courts*).

concussion *n* the shock occasioned by two bodies coming suddenly into collision; a shock; injury sustained by the brain usually with loss of consciousness caused by falls, blows, etc.

condemn *vt* to pronounce to be utterly wrong; to utter a sentence of disapprobation against; to pronounce to be guilty; to sentence to punishment; to utter sentence against judicially, opposed to *acquit* or *absolve*; to judge or pronounce to be unfit for use or service or to be forfeited.

condemnation *n* the act of condemning; the state of being condemned.

condensation *n* the act of condensing or making more dense or compact; the act of bringing into smaller compass; consolidation; the act of reducing a gas or vapour to a liquid or solid form.

condense *vt* (**condensed, condensing**) to make more dense or compact; to reduce the volume or extent of; to bring into closer union of parts; to consolidate; to compress (*to condense a substance*, *an argument*, etc); to reduce (a gas or vapour) to the condition of a liquid or solid; to abridge (a piece of writing).—*vi* to become close or more compact, as the particles of a body; to change from the vaporous to the liquid state.

condensed *adj* made dense or close in texture or composition; compressed; compact (a condensed style of composition).

condenser *n* one who or that which condenses; a pneumatic instrument or syringe in which air may be compressed; a vessel in which aqueous or spirituous vapours are reduced to a liquid form by coldness; a lens to gather and concentrate rays collected by a mirror and direct them on an object; (*elect*) an instrument for obtaining large electrical charges at comparatively small differences of potential.

condescend *vi* to descend voluntarily for a time to the level of an inferior; to stoop; to act in a patronizing manner; to lower oneself intentionally (often followed by the infinitive or a noun preceded by *to*).

condescending *adj* marked or characterized by condescension; stooping to the level of one's inferiors; patronizing.

condescension *n* the act of condescending; the act of voluntarily stooping to an equality with inferiors; affability on the part of a superior; patronizing manner or behaviour.

condign *adj* well-deserved; merited; suitable (applied to punishment).

condiment *n* something used to add flavour to food, such as salt, pepper or spices; seasoning.

condition *n* a particular mode of being; situation; predicament; case; state; state with respect to the orders or grades of society or to property; rank in society; that which is requisite to be done, happen, exist or be present prior to something else being done, taking effect or happening; a clause in a contract embodying some stipulation, provision or essential point.—*vt* to make accustomed; to bring about a desired effect by subjecting to various stimuli; to make fit, healthy or in good condition; to form

the condition or essential accompaniment of; to regulate or determine; to stipulate; to arrange.

conditional *adj* imposing conditions; containing or depending on a condition or conditions; made with limitations; not absolute; made or granted on certain terms; (*gram*, *logic*) expressing or involving a condition.

conditionally *adv* in a conditional manner; with certain limitations; on particular conditions, terms or stipulations.

conditioner *n* something that conditions; a substance for bringing something into good condition; something to improve the condition of, as *hair conditioner*.

conditioning *n* the act of conditioning; the bringing into a required state of fitness or health; a method of learning in which a response (called a *conditioned reflex*) comes to be associated with a stimulus which would not normally produce such a response.

condole *vi* (**condoled, condoling**) to express pain or grief at the distress or misfortunes of another; to express sympathy to one in grief or misfortune (followed by *with*).

condolence *n* the act of condoling; expression of sympathy with another's grief.

condom *n* a sheath made of thin rubber, used to cover the penis during sexual intercourse, as a barrier to contraception and the transmission of venereal disease.

condonation *n* the act of condoning or pardoning a wrong act; (*law*) an act or course of conduct by which a husband or a wife is held to have pardoned a matrimonial offence committed by the other, the party condoning being thus barred from a remedy for that offence.

condone *vt* (**condoned, condoning**) to pardon; to forgive; to overlook an offence (never with a personal object); (*law*) to forgive or to act so as to imply forgiveness of a violation of the marriage vow.

condor *n* a rare South American bird, one of the largest of the vultures.

condottiere *n* (*pl* **condottieri**) one of a class of mercenary Italian military adventurers of the thirteenth to sixteenth centuries.

conduce *vi* (**conduced, conducing**) to combine with other things in bringing about or tending to bring about a result; to lead or tend; to contribute (followed by the infinitive or a noun preceded by *to*).

conducive *adj* having the quality of conducing, promoting or furthering; tending to advance or bring about (followed by *to*).

conduct *n* mode of carrying on or conducting; handling; administration; management; personal behaviour.—*vt* to accompany and show the way; to guide; to lead;

condor

179

to escort; to lead, as a commander; to direct; to command; to manage (affairs, etc); (*refl*) to behave; (*physics*) to carry, transmit or propagate, as heat, electricity, etc; to lead or direct as musical conductor.—*vi* to carry, transmit or propagate heat, electricity, sound, etc; to act as musical conductor.

conduction *n* (*physics*) the mode of transference of heat through the substance of solids and of electricity through any suitable body called a conductor.

conductor *n* one who conducts; a leader; a guide; a commander; one who leads an army; a director or manager; the director of a chorus or orchestra; the person who attends to the passengers in a bus, coach, train, etc, and takes the fares or tickets; (*physics*) a body that receives and transmits or communicates heat, electricity or force in any of its forms; a lightning rod.

conduit *n* a pipe, tube or other channel for the conveyance of water or other fluid.

condyle *n* (*anat*) a protuberance on the end of a bone serving to form an articulation with another bone.

cone *n* a solid figure rising from a circular base and regularly tapering to a point; anything shaped like a cone; one of the fruits of fir trees, pines, etc; the hill surrounding the crater of a volcano, formed by the gradual accumulation of ejected material; a form of storm signal; a cone-shaped edible container for ice cream; a cone-shaped object used to mark off areas of roads, e.g. to designate no-parking areas.

coney *n* same as **cony**.

confab *n* a friendly conversation or chat; a discussion; confabulation.

confabulate *vi* to talk familiarly together.

confabulation *n* a talking together; familiar talk; easy, unrestrained conversation.

confection *n* anything prepared or preserved with sugar, as fruit; a sweetmeat; a sweet; a dessert.

confectioner *n* one whose occupation is to make or sell confections or sweets.

confectionery *n* sweetmeats; sweets; things prepared or sold by a confectioner; confections.

confederacy *n* a contract between two or more persons, bodies of men or states, combined in support of each other in some act or enterprise; a league; compact; alliance; the persons, states or nations united by a league.

confederate *adj* united in a league; allied by treaty; engaged in a confederacy; pertaining to a confederacy.—*n* one who is united with others in a league; a person or nation engaged in a confederacy; an ally; an accomplice.—*vi* (**confederated, confederating**) to unite in a league or confederacy.

confederation *n* a confederacy; a league;

alliance; the parties to a league; states united by a confederacy.

confer *vt* (**conferred, conferring**) to give or bestow (with *on* or *upon* before the recipient).—*vi* to consult together on some special subject; to compare opinions.

conference *n* the act of conferring or consulting together; a meeting for consultation, discussion or instruction; a meeting of the representatives of different foreign countries in regard to some matter of importance to all.

confess *vt* to own, acknowledge or avow, as a crime, a fault, a charge, a debt or something that is against one's interest or reputation; to own to; to disclose; (*eccles*) to disclose or recapitulate (sins) to a priest in private with a view to absolution; to hear or receive the confession of (said of a priest); to acknowledge as having a certain character or certain claims; to declare belief in; to grant, concede, admit.—*vi* to make confession or avowal; to disclose faults; to make known one's sins to a priest.

confession *n* the act of confessing; the act of making an avowal; a disclosing of sins or faults to a priest; the disburdening of the conscience privately to a confessor.—**confession of faith** the articles of faith that a person, a church, etc, accepts as true.

confessional *n* a compartment or cell in which a priest sits to hear confession, having a small opening or hole at each side through which a person makes confession.—*adj* of or pertaining to a confession.

confessor *n* a priest who hears confession and assumes power to grant absolution; one who made a profession of his faith in the Christian religion and adhered to it in the face of persecution.

confetti *npl* small pieces of coloured paper thrown at each other by revellers at carnivals or at the bride and groom by wedding guests.

confidant *n* (*masc*) **confidante** *n* (*fem*) a person entrusted with the confidence of another; one to whom secrets are confided; a confidential friend.

confide *vi* (**confided, confiding**) to rely with full assurance of mind; to rest the mind firmly without anxiety; to trust; to believe (followed by *in*).—*vt* to entrust; to commit with full reliance on the person to whom the thing is committed (*to confide a thing to a person*).

confidence *n* assurance of mind; firm belief; trust; reliance; reliance on one's own abilities, resources or circumstances; self-reliance; assurance; boldness; courage; that in which trust is placed; ground of trust; a secret; a private or confidential communication (*to exchange confidences together*).

conductor

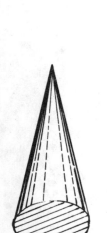

cone

confidence trick *n* a fraud carried out by first gaining the confidence of the person on whom the fraud is committed.

confidence trickster *n* one who carries out a confidence trick.

confident *adj* full of confidence; having full belief; fully assured; relying on oneself; full of assurance; bold.

confidential *adj* enjoying the confidence of another; entrusted with secrets or with private affairs; intended to be treated as private or kept in confidence; spoken or written in confidence; secret.

confidently *adv* in a confident manner; with firm trust; with strong assurance; positively; dogmatically.

confiding *adj* trusting; reposing confidence; trustful; credulous.

configuration *n* the external form, figure or shape of a thing as resulting from the disposition and shape of its parts; external aspect or appearance; shape or form.

confine *n* border; boundary; frontier; the part of any territory which is at or near the end or extremity (generally in the plural and in regard to contiguous regions).—*vt* (**confined, confining**) to restrain within limits; to circumscribe; hence, to imprison; to immure; to shut up; to limit or restrain voluntarily in some act or practice (*to confine oneself to a subject*).—**to be confined** to be in labour; to be in the process of childbirth.

confined *adj* restrained within limits; limited; circumscribed; narrow (*a confined scope* or *range*).

confinement *n* the state of being confined; restraint within limits; any restraint of liberty by force or other obstacle or necessity; imprisonment; childbirth; labour.

confirm *vt* to make firm or more firm; to add strength to; to strengthen; to settle or establish; to make certain; to put beyond doubt; to assure; to verify; to sanction; to ratify (an agreement, promise); to strengthen in resolution, purpose or opinion; to administer the rite of confirmation to.

confirmation *n* the act of confirming; the act of establishing; establishment; corroboration; the act of rendering valid or ratifying; the ceremony of laying on of hands by a bishop in the admission of baptised persons to the full enjoyment of Christian privileges, a rite of the Roman, Greek and English churches; that which confirms; additional evidence; proof; convincing testimony.

confirmed *adj* fixed; settled; settled in certain habits, state of health, etc (*a confirmed drunkard* or *invalid*); having received the rite of confirmation.

confiscate *vt* (**confiscated, confiscating**) to appropriate to public use by way of penalty; to appropriate under legal authority as forfeited.

confiscation *n* the act of confiscating or appropriating as forfeited.

conflagration *n* a great fire.

conflict *n* a fighting or struggle for mastery; a combat; a striving to oppose or overcome; active opposition; contention; strife; (*psychol*) antagonism between motives, e.g. between primitive instincts and acquired ideals.—*vi* to meet in opposition or hostility; to contend; to strive or struggle; to be in opposition; to be contrary.

conflicting *adj* being in opposition; contrary; contradictory; incompatible.

confluence *n* a flowing together; the meeting or junction of two or more streams of water; also, the place of meeting; the running together of people; a crowd; a concourse.

confluent *adj* flowing together; meeting in their course, as two streams; meeting; running together.

conflux *n* a flowing together; a crowd; a multitude collected.

conform *vt* to make like (*to conform anything to a model*); to bring into harmony or correspondence; to adapt; to submit (often reflexive).—*vi* to comply; (*eccles*) to comply with the usages of the established church.

conformable *adj* corresponding in form, character, manners, opinions, etc; in harmony or conformity; agreeable; suitable; consistent; adapted; compliant; submissive; disposed to obey.

conformation *n* the manner in which a body is formed; the particular disposition of the parts which compose it; configuration; form; structure.

conformist *n* one who conforms or complies; one who complies with the worship of the Church of England, as distinguished from a dissenter or nonconformist.

conformity *n* correspondence in form or manner; agreement; congruity; likeness; harmony; correspondence with decrees or dictates; submission; accordance; compliance with the usages or principles of an established church.

confound *vt* to mingle confusedly together; to mix in a mass or crowd so that individuals cannot be distinguished; to throw into disorder; to confuse; to mistake one for another; to make a mistake between; to throw into consternation; to perplex with terror, surprise or astonishment; to astound; to abash; to overthrow, ruin, baffle or bring to nought.

confounded *adj* excessive; odious; detestable.

confraternity *n* a fraternity or brotherhood.

confront *vt* to stand facing; to face; to stand in front of; to meet in hostility; to oppose;

to set face to face; to bring into the presence of (followed by *with*).

Confucian *n* a follower of Confucius, the famous Chinese philosopher.—*adj* relating to Confucius.

Confucianism *n* the doctrines or system of morality taught by Confucius.

confuse *vt* (**confused, confusing**) to mix up without order or clearness; to throw together indiscriminately; to disorder or jumble; to confound; to perplex or derange the mind or ideas of; to muddle; to embarrass; to disconcert.

confusion *n* a state in which things are confused; an indiscriminate or disorderly mingling; disorder; tumultuous condition; perturbation of mind; muddle; embarrassment; distraction; abashment; disconcertment; overthrow; defeat; ruin.

confutable *adj* capable of being confuted.

confutation *n* the act of confuting, disproving or proving to be false or invalid.

confute *vt* (**confuted, confuting**) to prove (an argument, statement, etc) to be false, defective or invalid; to disprove; to overthrow; to prove (a person) to be wrong; to convince of error by argument or proof.

conga *n* a dance, originating in Cuba, in which the dancers move along in a long line, holding onto the person in front; the music for such a dance.—*vi* to take part in such a dance.

congé *n* leave to depart; farewell; dismissal; a ceremonious leave-taking.

congeal *vt* to change from a fluid to a solid state by cold or a loss of heat; to freeze; to coagulate; to check the flow of; to make (the blood) run cold.—*vi* to pass from a fluid to a solid state by cold; to coagulate.

congener *n* a thing of the same kind or nearly allied; a plant or animal belonging to the same genus.

congenial *adj* pleasant; agreeable; to one's taste; sympathetic.

congenital *adj* belonging or pertaining to an individual from birth (*a congenital disease*).

conger, conger eel *n* the sea eel, a large voracious species of eel.

congeries *n sing, pl* a collection of several bodies in one mass or aggregate; an aggregate; a combination.

congest *vt* (*med*) to cause an unnatural accumulation of blood or mucus in an organ; to make overcrowded or too full (*holiday traffic congesting the roads*).

congested *adj* affected with congestion; affected with an accumulation of blood or mucus; clogged; packed closely together; overcrowded.

congestion *n* (*med*) an excessive accumulation of blood or mucus in an organ, the functions of which are thereby disordered; an excessive accumulation, as of traffic.

conger eel

congregation

conglomerate *adj* gathered into a ball or round body; crowded together; clustered.—*vt* (**conglomerated, conglomerating**) to gather or collect into a mass.—*n* a kind of rock made up of rounded fragments of various rocks cemented together by a matrix of siliceous, calcareous or other cement; gravel solidified by cement into a rock; pudding stone; something composed of different things; a large corporation consisting of a number of companies with varied interests.

conglomeration *n* the act of conglomerating; collection; accumulation; what is conglomerated; a mixed mass; a mixture.

congratulate *vt* (**congratulated, congratulating**) to address (a person) with expressions of pleasure on some piece of good fortune; to compliment on a happy event; to wish joy to; to felicitate; (*refl*) to have a lively sense of one's own good fortune; to consider oneself lucky.

congratulation *n* the act of congratulating; words used in congratulating; expression to a person of pleasure in his good fortune; felicitation.

congregate *vt* (**congregated, congregating**) to collect into a group; to assemble; to bring into one place or into a crowd or united body.—*vi* to come together; to assemble; to meet in a crowd.

congregation *n* the act of congregating; the act of bringing together or assembling; a collection or assemblage of persons or things; an assembly, especially an assembly of persons met for the worship of God; a number of people organized as a body for the purpose of holding religious services in common.

congregational *adj* pertaining to a congregation.

Congregational *adj* pertaining to Congregationalism.

Congregationalism *n* a system of administering church affairs by which each congregation has the right of regulating the details of its worship, discipline and government.

Congregationalist *n* one who belongs to a church practising Congregationalism.

congress *n* a meeting together of individuals; an assembly of envoys, commissioners, deputies, etc; a formal meeting of people with similar interests (*a medical congress*).

Congress *n* the legislative assembly of the United States of America, consisting of the Senate and House of Representatives.

Congressman, Congresswoman *n* a member of the United States Congress.

congruent *adj* suitable; agreeing; corresponding; identical in every aspect; (*math*) (of geometrical figures) identical in shape so as to correspond exactly.

congruity *n* the state or quality of being congruous; agreement between things; suitableness; pertinence; consistency; propriety.

congruous *adj* accordant; harmonious; well-adapted; appropriate; meet; fit.

conic *adj* having the form of a cone; conical; pertaining to a cone.—*n* a conic section.

conical *adj* having the form of a cone; cone-shaped.

conics *n* that part of geometry which treats of the cone and the several curve lines arising from the sections of it.

conic section *n* any of a group of figures formed by the outlines of the cut surfaces when a cone is cut by a plane, more especially the parabola, ellipse and hyperbola, the first of which is seen when the section is made parallel to the slope of the cone.

conifer *n* (*bot*) a plant producing cones or hard, dry, scaly seed vessels of a conical shape, as the pine, fir, etc.

conirostral *adj* (of birds) having a strong conical beak.

conjectural *adj* depending on conjecture; implying guess or conjecture.

conjecture *n* a guess or inference based on the supposed possibility or probability of a fact or on slight evidence; an opinion formed on insufficient or presumptive evidence; surmise.—*vt* (**conjectured, conjecturing**) to judge by guess or conjecture; to guess.—*vi* to form conjectures.

conjoin *vt* to join together or in one; to unite; to associate or connect.—*vi* to unite; to join; to league.

conjoint *adj* united; connected; associated.

conjointly *adv* in a conjoint manner; jointly; unitedly; in union; together.

conjugal *adj* belonging to marriage or married persons; matrimonial; connubial.

conjugate *vt* (**conjugated, conjugating**) (*gram*) to inflect (a verb) through its several voices, moods, tenses, numbers and persons.

conjugation *n* the inflection of a verb in its different forms; a class of verbs conjugated in the same way.

conjunct *adj* conjoined; united; concurrent.

conjunction *n* union; connection; association; (*astron*) that position of a planet in which it is in a line with the earth or another planet and the sun; (*gram*) an indeclinable particle, serving to unite words, sentences or clauses of a sentence and indicating their relation to one another.

conjunctiva *n* (*anat*) the mucous membrane which lines the inner surface of the eyelids and is continued over the forepart of the globe of the eye.

conjunctive *adj* uniting; serving to unite.

conjunctive mood *n* (*gram*) the mood which follows a conjunction or expresses some condition or contingency; the subjunctive.

conjunctivitis *n* inflammation of the conjunctiva.

conjuncture *n* combination of circumstances or affairs; especially a critical time proceeding from a union of circumstances; a crisis of affairs.

conjuration *n* the act of conjuring or imploring with solemnity; the act of binding by an oath; adjuration; an incantation; a spell.

conjure *vt* (**conjured, conjuring**) (with *pron*) to call on or summon by a sacred name or in a solemn manner; to implore with solemnity; to adjure (with *pron*) to affect or effect by magic or enchantment; to bring about as by the arts of a conjurer.— **to conjure up** to call up or bring into existence by conjuring or as if by conjuring.—*vi* to practise the arts of a conjurer; to use magic arts.

conjurer *n* one who practises magic; one who practises legerdemain; a juggler.

conjury *n* the act or art of a conjurer; magic; legerdemain.

conk *n* (*colloq*) the nose; a sharp blow.—*vt* to strike or hit.—**to conk out** to collapse in a faint; to become unconscious; (of a machine) to stop working.

conker *n* a horse chestnut; (*pl*) a children's game in which the children tie horse chestnuts to pieces of string and hit the horse chestnuts against each other to see which is the stronger.

con man, con woman *n* a confidence trickster.

connate *adj* belonging to from birth; implanted at birth.

connect *vt* to fasten together; to join or unite; to conjoin; to combine; to associate. —*vi* to join, unite or cohere.

connecting rod *n* a rod which connects a piston to a point outside the cylinder and either moved by the piston or moving it.

connection, connexion *n* the act of connecting or state of being connected; also that which connects; union by something physical or by relation of any kind; relationship by blood or marriage but more specifically by marriage; a person connected with another by this relationship; circle of persons with whom anyone is brought into contact.—**in this connection** in connection with what is now under consideration.

connective *adj* having the power of connecting; tending to connect; connecting.— *n* that which connects; (*gram*) a word that connects other words and sentences; a conjunction.

connivance *n* the act of conniving; voluntary blindness to an act.

connive *vi* (**connived, conniving**) to close

conifer

conker

the eyes to a fault or other act; to pretend ignorance or blindness; to forbear to see; to wink at or overlook a fault or other act and allow it to pass unnoticed (followed by *at*).

connoisseur *n* a critical judge; one competent to pass a critical judgment on anything; one who is experienced and discriminating in a particular field.

connote *vt* (**connoted, connoting**) to include in the meaning; to comprise among the attributes expressed; to imply.—*vi* to have a meaning or signification in connection with another word.

connotation *n* that which constitutes the meaning of a word; the attributes expressed by a word.

connubial *adj* pertaining to marriage; nuptial; belonging to the state of husband and wife.

conoid *n* (*geom*) a solid formed by the revolution of a conic section about its axis.

conquer *vt* to overcome in war; to vanquish; to gain by force; to overcome or surmount (obstacles, difficulties); to gain or obtain by effort.—*vi* to overcome; to gain the victory.

conqueror *n* one who conquers or gains a victory.

conquest *n* the act of conquering; the act of overcoming or vanquishing opposition by force, physical or moral; subjugation; that which is conquered; a possession gained by force.

consanguineous *adj* of the same blood; related by birth; descended from the same parent or ancestor.

consanguinity *n* the relation of persons by blood, the relation or connection of persons descended from the same stock or common ancestor, distinct from affinity or relation by marriage.

conscience *n* private or inward thoughts or real sentiments; the faculty, power or principle within one which decides on the rightness or wrongness of actions and affections; the sense of right and wrong; the moral sense; morality.

conscientious *adj* influenced by conscience; governed by a strict regard to the dictates of conscience; careful; scrupulous; industrious.

conscientiousness *n* the state or quality of being conscientious.

conscientious objector *n* one who refuses to take part in military service on the grounds of religious or moral beliefs.

conscionable *adj* governed by conscience; according to conscience; reasonable; just.

conscious *adj* knowing what affects or what goes on in one's own mind; having direct knowledge of a thing; having such a knowledge as is conveyed by immediate sensation or perception; aware; sensible (*conscious of something*); having become the subject of consciousness; known to oneself (*conscious guilt*).

consciously *adv* in a conscious manner; with knowledge of one's own mental operations or actions.

consciousness *n* the faculty of knowing what affects or what goes on in one's own mind; immediate knowledge, such as is given in sensation and perception; internal persuasion.

conscript *n* one who is compulsorily enrolled for military or naval service.

conscription *n* a compulsory enrolment of individuals of a certain age, held liable to be drafted for military or naval service.

consecrate *vt* (**consecrated, consecrating**) to make or declare to be sacred with certain ceremonies or rites; to appropriate to sacred uses; to enrol among deities or saints; to canonize; to give episcopal rank to; to dedicate with solemnity; to render venerable; to make respected; to hallow.

consecration *n* the act or ceremony of consecrating or separating from a common to a sacred use; dedication of a person or thing to the service and worship of God, by certain rites or solemnities; dedication; the ceremony of elevating a priest to the dignity of a bishop.

Consecration *n* the giving of the bread and wine of the Eucharist their sacred character in the Mass or Communion service.

consecutive *adj* uninterrupted in course or succession; succeeding one another in a regular order; successive; following; succeeding.

consensus *n* unanimity; agreement; concord.

consent *vi* to agree; to accord; to yield, as to persuasion or entreaty; to comply; to acquiesce or accede.—*n* voluntary accordance with what is done or proposed by another; a yielding of the mind or will to that which is proposed; acquiescence; concurrence; compliance; accord of minds; agreement in opinion or sentiment; (*law*) intelligent concurrence in the terms of a contract or agreement, of such a nature as to bind the party consenting.

consequence *n* that which follows from any act, cause, principles or series of actions; an event or effect produced by some preceding act or cause; inference; deduction; conclusion from premises; importance (*a matter of consequence, a person of great consequence*).—**in consequence of** as the effect of; by reason of; through.

consequent *adj* following as the natural effect (with *to* or *on*).—*n* that which follows; in logic, the part of a hypothesis that contains the conclusion.

consequential *adj* following as the effect; resultant; produced by the connection of

184

effects with causes; affecting airs of great self-importance or characterized by such affectation; pompous.

conservation *n* the act of conserving, preserving, guarding or protecting; preservation from loss, decay, injury or violation; preservation of the environment and natural resources.

conservationism *n* a movement designed to conserve the environment and natural resources.

conservationist *n* one who is actively interested in conservation, especially of the environment and natural resources.—*adj* pertaining to conservation.

conservatism *n* opposition to innovation or change, especially in politics.

Conservatism *n* the political principles and opinions maintained by the Conservative Party in Britain and elsewhere.

conservative *adj* tending to preserve; preservative; inclining to keep up old institutions, customs, etc; having a tendency to uphold and preserve entire the institutions of a country, both civil and ecclesiastical; opposed to radical changes or innovations.—*n* one who aims to preserve from innovation, injury or radical change; one who advocates conservatism.

Conservative *adj* pertaining to the Conservatives or their principles.—*n* a member of a Conservative Party; a Tory.

Conservative Party *n* the right-wing political party in Britain and elsewhere, formerly the Tories (in Britain).

conservator *n* one appointed to watch over anything.

conservatory *n* a large greenhouse attached to a house for preserving exotic plants and other plants requiring indoor care.

conserve *vt* (**conserved, conserving**) to keep in a safe or unimpaired state; to uphold and keep from decay, waste or injury; to guard or defend from destruction, harm, etc (institutions, customs, buildings, the environment, etc); to preserve with sugar, etc, as fruits.—*n* that which is conserved; a jam-like preserve made from fruit and sugar.

consider *vt* to fix the mind on with a view to a careful examination; to think on with care; to ponder; to study; to meditate on; to observe and examine; to regard with pity or sympathy and hence relieve; to have regard or respect to; to respect; to take into view or account or have regard to in examination or in forming an estimate; to judge to be; to reckon (*to consider a person wise*).—*vi* to think seriously, maturely or carefully; to reflect.

considerable *adj* worthy of consideration on account of its amount; more than a little; moderately large; somewhat important or valuable.

considerably *adv* to a degree deserving notice; to a significant degree.

considerate *adj* given to consideration or to sober reflection; characterized by consideration or regard for another's circumstances and feelings; thoughtful or mindful of others.

consideration *n* the act of considering; mental view; regard; notice; mature thought; serious deliberation; thoughtful, sympathetic, appreciative or due regard or respect; contemplation; meditation; some degree of importance or claim to notice or regard; motive of action; ground of conduct; ground of concluding; reason; recompense or remuneration.

considering *prep* having regard to; taking into account; making allowance for.

consign *vt* to give or hand over; to transfer or deliver over into the possession of another or into a different state (*to consign a body to the grave*); to deliver or transfer in charge or trust; to send or address (as goods for sale); to commit for permanent preservation (*to consign to writing*).

consignment *n* the act of consigning; the act of sending off goods to an agent for sale; goods sent or delivered for sale.

consist *vi* to hold together or remain fixed; to be, exist, subsist; to stand or be; to be comprised or contained (followed by *in*); to be composed; to be made up (followed by *of*); to be compatible, consistent or harmonious; to accord (followed by *with*).

consistence, consistency *n* an indefinite degree of density or viscosity; agreement or harmony of all parts of a complex thing among themselves or of the same thing with itself at different times; congruity, agreement or harmony.

consistent *adj* having a certain substance or firmness; standing in agreement; compatible; congruous; not contradictory or opposed; not out of harmony with other acts or professions of the same person.

consistory *n* a spiritual or ecclesiastical court.

consolation *n* the act of consoling; alleviation of misery or distress of mind.

consolation prize *n* a small prize given to the loser or runner-up in a competition or contest.

console[1] *vt* (**consoled, consoling**) to cheer the mind in distress or depression; to comfort; to soothe; to solace.

console[2] *n* the part of an organ containing the pedals, stops, etc; a radio or television cabinet designed to stand on the floor; an ornamental bracket supporting a shelf or table; a panel or cabinet with dials, switches, etc; the control unit of an electronic system.

consolidate *vt* (**consolidated, consolidating**) to make solid or compact; to harden or make dense and firm; to bring together

consolation

into one close mass or body; to make firm or establish (power).—*vi* to grow firm and hard; to unite and become solid.

consolidation *n* the act of consolidating; a making or process of becoming solid; the act of forming into a firm compact mass, body or system.

consommé *n* a clear, thin kind of soup.

consonance *n* accord or agreement of sounds; (*mus*) an accord of sounds which produces an agreeable sensation in the ear; agreement; accord; congruity; consistency; suitableness.

consonant *adj* like in sound; agreeing generally; according; congruous; consistent (followed by *to* or *with*).—*n* a letter that receives its proper sound only in connection with a vowel; one of the closings or junctions of the organs of speech which precede or follow the openings of the organs with which the vowels are uttered.

consort *n* a partner; a wife or husband; the wife or the husband of a reigning monarch; (*naut*) any vessel keeping company with another.—*vi* to associate; to unite in company; to keep company (followed by with.

consortium *n* (*pl* **consortia**) a temporary combination of banks or corporations to carry out some large-scale financial operation; a partnership.

conspectus *n* a comprehensive view of a subject; an abstract or sketch.

conspicuous *adj* obvious or prominent to the eye; easy to be seen; manifest; clearly or extensively known, perceived or understood; eminent; distinguished (*conspicuous abilities*).

conspiracy *n* a secret combination of people for an evil purpose; an agreement or combination to commit some crime in concert; a plot; concerted treason.

conspirator *n* one who conspires; one who engages in a plot to commit a crime, particularly treason.

conspire *vi* (**conspired, conspiring**) to agree with others to commit a crime; to plot; to form a secret plot; to hatch treason; to agree, concur or conduce to one end (*circumstances conspired to defeat the plan*).—*vt* to plot; to plan; to devise; to contrive; to concur to produce.

constable *n* an officer of high rank in several of the medieval monarchies; the keeper or governor of a castle belonging to the king or to a great baron; now usually a peace officer; a police officer.

constabulary *n* the body of constables of a district, city or country.

constancy *n* fixedness; a standing firm; immutability; steady, unshaken determination; fixedness or firmness of mind under sufferings; steadiness in attachments; perseverance in enterprise.

constable

constant *adj* not undergoing change; continuing the same; permanent; immutable; fixed or firm in mind, purpose or principle; not easily swayed; firm or unchanging in affection or duty; faithful; true; loyal.—*n* that which is not subject to change; (*math*) a quantity which remains the same throughout a problem.

constellation *n* a group of the fixed stars to which a definite name has been given.

consternation *n* astonishment; amazement or horror.

constipate *vt* (**constipated, constipating**) to cause constipation in; to make constipated.

constipation *n* a state of the bowels in which the evacuations do not take place as frequently as usual or are expelled with difficulty.

constituency *n* a body of constituents who appoint or elect persons to any office or employment, especially to municipal or parliamentary offices.

constituent *adj* forming or existing as an essential component or ingredient; composing or making up as an essential part; component, elementary (*the constituent parts of water*); having the power of constituting or appointing.—*n* one who or that which establishes or determines; that which constitutes or composes as a part or an essential part; an essential ingredient; one who has the power to vote.

constitute *vt* (**constituted, constituting**) to form or compose; to make up; to make a thing what it is.

constitution *n* the act of constituting, enacting, establishing or appointing; the peculiar structure and connection of parts which makes or characterizes a system or body; natural condition of the human body as regards general health or strength; the established form of government in a state; a system of fundamental rules, principles and ordinances for the government of a state or nation.

constitutional *adj* pertaining to a constitution; connected with the constitution or natural condition of body or mind; consistent with the constitution, of a state; authorized by the constitution or fundamental rules of a government; legal; based on a settled constitution proceeding ultimately from the people.—*n* a walk taken for health and exercise.

constitutive *adj* forming, composing, enacting or establishing; constituting; instituting.

constrain *vt* to compel or force; to urge with a power sufficient to produce the effect; to drive; to necessitate; to confine by force; to restrain, check, repress, confine, bind.

constrained *adj* with a certain constraint or lack of freedom; embarrassed; inhibited.

constraint *n* a constraining, compelling or restraining; force; compulsion; restraint; confinement; feeling of reserve or being embarrassed.

constrict *vt* to draw together; to cramp; to compress; to contract or cause to shrink (said of canals, etc, of the body).

constriction *n* the state of being constricted or drawn together as by some spasm; tightness.

constrictor *n* that which draws together or contracts; (*anat*) a muscle which draws together or closes an orifice of the body; one of the larger class of snakes which envelop and crush their prey.

construct *vt* to put together the parts of in their proper place and order; to build up; to erect; to form; to form by the mind.—*n* a structure; an interpretation; an arrangement, especially of words in a sentence.

construction *n* the act of building, devising or forming; fabrication; the form of building; the manner of putting together the parts; structure; conformation; the arrangement and connection of words in a sentence; syntactical arrangement; attributed sense or meaning to language; explanation; interpretation; the manner of describing a figure or problem in geometry for the purpose of any demonstration.

constructive *adj* pertaining to construction or building; having ability to construct; created or deduced by construction or mode of interpretation; helpful; intended to improve.

construe *vt* (**construed, construing**) to arrange words meaningfully; to analyse grammatically; as applied to a foreign language, to translate; to interpret or draw a certain meaning from; to explain (*to construe actions wrongly*).

consubstantiation *n* the doctrine that the body and blood of Christ are substantially present together with the substance of the Eucharistic bread and wine.

consuetude *n* custom; usage.

consul *n* the title of the two chief magistrates of the ancient Roman republic; a person commissioned by a government of a country to reside abroad as an agent or representative to protect the interests (especially commercial) and the citizens of the country.

consular *adj* pertaining to a consul.

consulate *n* the office or jurisdiction of a consul; the official dwelling or residence of a consul; consular government.

consult *vi* to seek the opinion or advice of another; to deliberate together.—*vt* to ask advice of; to seek the opinion of as a guide to one's own judgment; to have recourse to for information or instruction; to take professional advice from (a doctor, solicitor, etc).

consultation *n* the act of consulting; deliberation of two or more persons with a view to some decision; a meeting with a professional person such as a doctor, solicitor, etc, to obtain advice, a professional opinion, etc; a meeting of experts, as physicians or counsel, to consult about a specific case.

consultative *adj* having the privilege of consulting or deliberating; deliberative (often opposed to *executive*).

consume *vt* (**consumed, consuming**) to destroy by separating the component parts and destroying the form of the substance, as by fire or by eating; to destroy by use or by wasting; to expend; to waste; to spend; to pass (time); to eat or drink; to be a consumer of.—*vi* to waste away slowly; to be exhausted.

consumer *n* one who or that which consumes; one who uses goods and services as distinguished from the producer of them.

consumer goods *npl* goods bought for personal or domestic use as opposed to goods bought to produce other goods or services.

consummate *vt* (**consummated, consummating**) to finish by completing what was intended; (of marriage) to complete by sexual intercourse; to perfect; to bring or carry to the utmost point or degree; to make complete.—*adj* complete; perfect; carried to the utmost extent or degree; thorough.

consummation *n* completion; end; termination; perfection of a work, process or scheme.

consumption *n* the act of consuming or state of being consumed; a using up or wasting away; (*med*) tuberculosis; the use or expenditure of the products of industry or of all things having an exchangeable value.

consumptive *adj* consuming, wasting or exhausting; having the quality of consuming or wasting; affected with or having a tendency to the disease tuberculosis.

contact *n* a touching; touch; state of being so near as to touch; communication.—*vt* to establish contact with; to make communication with.

contact lens *n* a small, thin curved disc of glass or plastic with a central lens placed directly over the cornea of the eye to improve or correct the sight of the eye.

contagion *n* the communication of a disease by contact, direct or indirect; a disease spread in this way; a corrupting influence.

contagious *adj* communicated by contagion or contact; catching; containing contagion; spreading from one to another (*contagious fear*).

contain *vt* to hold within fixed limits; to comprehend; to comprise; to include; to

construction

hold or be capable of holding; to comprise, as a writing; to have for contents; to keep occupied, to hinder progress.—**to contain oneself** to restrain one's feelings or prevent them showing themselves.

container *n* an object, such as a tin, etc, designed to store or carry things; a receptacle; a standardized receptacle used for transporting goods.

containerize *vt* (**containerized, containerizing**) to put (freight) into large standardized containers.

containment *n* the act of containing; the policy or act of preventing the expansion of a hostile power by means other than war; the prevention of the release of dangerous quantities of radioactive material from a nuclear reactor.

contaminate *vt* (**contaminated, contaminating**) to defile; to pollute; to sully; to tarnish; to taint.

contamination *n* the act of contaminating; what contaminates; pollution; defilement; taint.

contemn *vt* to despise; to consider and treat as mean and despicable; to scorn; to reject with disdain.

containers

contemplate *vt* (**contemplated, contemplating**) to view or consider with continued attention; to study; to meditate on; to consider or have in view in reference to a future act or event; to intend.—*vi* to think studiously; to study; to muse; to meditate.

contemplation *n* the act of contemplating; meditation; continued attention of the mind to a particular subject; a looking forward to the doing or happening of something; expectation.

contemplative *adj* given to contemplation or continued application of the mind to a subject; thoughtful; meditative; having the power of thought or meditation (*the contemplative faculty*).

contemporaneous *adj* contemporary (most commonly of things).

contemporary *adj* living, existing or occurring at the same time (of persons and things); pertaining to or following present-day trends in fashion, art, etc.—*n* one who lives at the same time as another.

contempt *n* the feeling that causes people to consider and treat someone or something as mean, vile and worthless; disdain; scorn; the state of being despised; (*law*) disobedience to the rules or orders of a court or a disturbance of its proceedings.

contented

contemptible *adj* worthy of contempt; deserving scorn or disdain; despicable; mean; vile.

contemptuous *adj* showing or expressing contempt or disdain; scornful; apt to despise; haughty; insolent.

contend *vi* to strive; to struggle in opposition (absolutely or with *against* or *with* preceding an object); to use earnest efforts to obtain or to defend and preserve (with *for* before the object); to strive in debate; to wrangle.

content[1] *adj* having a mind at peace; satisfied, so as not to be unhappy, object or oppose; not disturbed; contented; easy.—*vt* to make content; to quiet so as to stop complaint or opposition; to appease; to make easy in any situation; to please or gratify.—*n* the state of being contented; contentment.

content[2] *n* that which is contained; the thing or things held, included or comprehended within a limit or line; (*geom*) the area or quantity of matter or space included in certain lines.

contented *adj* satisfied with what one has or with one's circumstances; easy in mind; not complaining, opposing or demanding more.

contention *n* the act of contending; contest, struggle or strife; strife in words; debate; angry contest; quarrel; controversy; competition; emulation; a point that a person maintains or the argument in support of it.

contentious *adj* apt to contend; given to angry debate; quarrelsome; perverse; relating to or characterized by contention or strife; involving contention.

contentment *n* the state or feeling of being contented; content; a resting or satisfaction of mind without disquiet or craving for something else; acquiescence in one's own circumstances.

conterminous, coterminous *adj* terminating at a common point; having common boundaries or limits; touching at the boundary.

contest *vt* to make a subject of contention or dispute; to enter into a struggle for; to struggle to defend; to controvert; to oppose; to call in question; to dispute (statements).—*vi* to strive; to contend (followed by *with*).—*n* a struggle for victory, superiority or in defence; struggle in arms; dispute; debate; controversy; strife in argument.

contestable *adj* capable of being disputed or debated; disputable; controvertible.

contested *adj* disputed; fought; litigated.

context *n* the parts of a book or other writing which immediately precede or follow a sentence quoted, contributing to its meaning.

contiguity *n* the state of being contiguous; closeness of situation or place; a linking together, as of a series of objects.

contiguous *adj* situated so as to touch; meeting or joining at the surface or border; close together; neighbouring; bordering or adjoining.

continence *n* the restraint which a person imposes on his or her desires and passions;

the restraint of the passion for sexual enjoyment; chastity; control over the bladder and bowels.

continent¹ *adj* refraining from sexual activity; chaste; also moderate or temperate in general; having control over one's bladder and bowels.

continent² *n* one of the great divisions of the earth's land.

Continent *n* the continent of Europe excluding the British Isles.

continental *adj* pertaining or relating to a continent; of or belonging to the continent of Europe, as distinguished from Britain.

contingency *n* the quality of being contingent; the possibility of happening or coming to pass; fortuitousness; something that may happen; a possible occurrence; a fortuitous event or one which may occur.

contingent *adj* possibly occurring; liable to occur; not determinable by any certain rule; accidental; casual; dependent on what is undetermined or unknown; dependent on the happening of something else.—*n* a contingency; a quota or suitable proportion, as of troops furnished for some joint enterprise.

continual *adj* proceeding without interruption or cessation; not intermittent; unceasing; of frequent recurrence; often repeated; incessant.

continually *adv* without pause or cessation; unceasingly; very often; in repeated succession; from time to time.

continuation *n* the act of continuing or prolonging; extension or carrying on to a further point; the portion continued or extended; a prolongation or extension.

continue *vi* (**continued, continuing**) to remain in a state or place; to abide for any time indefinitely; to last; to endure; to be permanent; to persevere; to be steadfast or constant in any course.—*vt* to protract or lengthen out; not to cease from or to terminate; to extend; to make longer; to persevere in; not to cease to do or use; to suffer or cause to remain as before.

continued *adj* protracted or extended; proceeding without cessation; unceasing.

continuing *adj* abiding; lasting; enduring; permanent.

continuity *n* uninterrupted connection; cohesion; close union of parts; unbroken texture; the complete script or scenario in a film or broadcast.

continuity girl, continuity man *n* a person who supervises continuity of dress, etc, in filming.

continuous *adj* joined without intervening space or time; proceeding from something else without interruption or without apparent interruption; uninterrupted; unbroken.

contort *vt* to twist together; to bend or curve in irregular forms; to writhe.

contortion *n* the act of contorting or state of being contorted; a twist or twisting; a writhing, especially spasmodic writhing; a twisted motion or position; (*med*) a twisting or wresting of a limb or member of the body out of its natural situation.

contortionist *n* an acrobat who practises contortions of the body.

contour *n* the outline of a figure or body; the line that defines or bounds a solid body; the periphery considered as distinct from the object.

contour line *n* a line on a map that passes through all points at the same altitude.

contra *n* a thing that may be argued against.

contra- *prefix* against.

contraband *adj* prohibited or excluded by proclamation, law or treaty.—*n* illegal or prohibited traffic; articles prohibited to be imported or exported.

contrabandist *n* one who deals in contraband goods.

contraception *n* the practice of preventing or avoiding conception; birth control.

contraceptive *adj* preventing conception.—*n* a device of any kind for preventing conception; a condom; a contraceptive pill.

contract *vt* to draw together or closer; to draw into less compass, either in length or breadth; to abridge, narrow, lessen; to wrinkle; to betroth; to incur, acquire (illness, debts); to shorten by omission of a letter or syllable.—*vi* to be drawn together; to become shorter or narrower; to shrink; to bargain; to make a mutual agreement as between two or more persons.—*n* an agreement or mutual promise on lawful consideration or cause which binds the parties; a bargain; a compact; the act by which a man and woman are betrothed to each other; the writing which contains the agreement of parties.

contract bridge *n* a form of bridge in which the players contract to take a certain number of tricks.

contracted *adj* narrow in scope or ideas; limited; mean (*contracted views*).

contractible *adj* capable of contraction

contractile *adj* tending to contract; having the power of shortening or of drawing into smaller dimensions.

contraction *n* the act of contracting, drawing together or shrinking; the act of shortening, narrowing or lessening dimensions by causing the parts to approach nearer to each other; the state of being contracted; (*pl*) the contracting of muscles in childbirth; an abbreviation; the shortening of a word by the omission of one or more letters or syllables.

contractor *n* one who contracts; one of the parties to a bargain; one who covenants to do anything for another; one who con-

continent

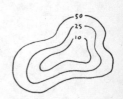

contour lines

tracts to perform any work or service or to furnish supplies at a certain price or rate.

contradict *vt* to assert not to be so or to assert to be the contrary to what has been asserted; to meet (a person, an assertion) with a statement quite different or opposite; to deny; to be directly contrary to.

contradiction *n* the act of contradicting; an assertion of the contrary to what has been said or affirmed; denial; contrary declaration; direct opposition or repugnance; inconsistency with itself; incongruity or contrariety of things, words, thoughts or propositions; the person who or thing that, contradicts or is inconsistent with him, her or itself.

contradictory *adj* contradicting; given to contradict; affirming the contrary; implying a denial of what has been asserted; inconsistent with one another; directly opposite.—*n* a proposition which denies or opposes another in all its terms.

contradistinction *n* distinction by opposite qualities or characteristics; a setting or bringing (terms, notions) into contrast or opposition.

contraflow *n* a stretch of motorway or dual carriageway in which two-way traffic travels on one carriageway to allow roadworks, etc, on the other.

contraflow

contraindicate *vt* (**contraindicated, contraindicating**) to point to (a drug, etc) as being unsuitable or inadvisable in the prevailing circumstances.

contraindication *n* a factor in a patient's condition which indicates that a certain drug or method of treatment is inadvisable, risky or dangerous.

contralto *n* (*pl* **contraltos**) (*mus*) the lowest voice of a woman, called also the *alto*; generally a female voice below the mezzo soprano and soprano; the person who sings with this voice.—*adj* pertaining to or possessed of the quality of contralto.

contraption *n* a contrivance.

contrariness *n* antagonism; opposition.

contrariwise *adv* on the contrary; in the opposite direction; on the other hand.

contrary *adj* opposite; adverse; moving against or in an opposite direction (*contrary winds*); contradictory; not merely different but inconsistent or repugnant; perverse.—*adv* in opposition to; in conflict with.—*n* a thing that is contrary or of opposite qualities; a proposition contrary to another or a fact contrary to what is alleged.

contrast *vt* to set in opposition so as to show the difference between and to exhibit the excellence of the one and the defects of the other; to compare so as to point out dissimilarity.—*vi* to stand in contrast or opposition to something else (followed by *with*).—*n* the viewing or comparing of

things together in order to render any difference between them more vividly marked; comparison by contrariety of qualities; opposition or dissimilitude of things or qualities.

contravene *vi* (**contravened, contravening**) to come or be in conflict with; to obstruct in operation; to act so as to violate; to transgress.

contravention *n* the act of contravening, violating or transgressing; violation; opposition.

contretemps *n* (*pl* **contretemps**) an unexpected and untoward accident; an embarrassing situation; a hitch.

contribute *vt* (**contributed, contributing**) to give or grant in common with others; to give to a common stock or cause or for a common purpose; to pay as a share; to give as a donation.—*vi* to give a part; to lend a portion of power, aid or influence; to have a share in any act or effect (with *to*); to write for a newspaper or magazine.

contribution *n* the act of contributing; something contributed; the payment of a share along with others; that which is given to a common stock or purpose, either by an individual or by many; the sum or thing contributed; a donation; an article written for a newspaper or magazine; a contributory cause.

contributor *n* one who contributes; one who gives or pays money to a common fund; one who gives aid to a common purpose; one who gives a donation; one who writes for a newspaper or magazine; a factor; a contributory cause.

contributory *adj* giving to a common fund or purpose; donating; partly responsible; being a factor in; of a pension scheme, in which the employer makes contributions as well as the employee.

contrite *adj* sincerely repentant; deeply affected with grief and sorrow; humble; penitent.—*n* a contrite person; a penitent.

contrition *n* sincere penitence and remorse.

contrivance *n* the act of contriving, inventing, devising or planning; the thing contrived; an artifice; scheme; invention.

contrive *vt* (**contrived, contriving**) to invent; to devise; to plan; to achieve, especially by some trick or scheme.—*vi* to form schemes or designs; to plan; to scheme; to succeed, especially by means of a trick or scheme.

contrived *adj* having been contrived; not spontaneous; laboured; artificially intricate.

control *n* restraining power or influence; check; restraint; power; authority; government; command.—*vt* (**controlled, controlling**) to exercise control over; to hold in restraint or check; to subject to authority; to regulate; to govern; to subjugate.

controller *n* one who controls; one that has the power or authority to govern or control; one who governs or regulates; an officer appointed to control finances; a comptroller.

control tower *n* a tower at an airport from which flight directions are given to pilots.

controversial *adj* relating to controversy; causing argument, debate or dispute.

controversialist *n* one who carries on a controversy; a disputant.

controversy *n* debate; agitation of contrary opinions; a dispute or discussion between parties, particularly in writing.

controvert *vt* to dispute; to oppose by reasoning; to contend against in words or writings; to deny and attempt to disprove or confute.

contumacious *adj* resisting legitimate authority; disobedient; (*law*) wilfully disobedient to the orders of a court.

contumacy *n* contumacious conduct; character or state of being contumacious; wilful and persistent resistance to legitimate authority; unyielding obstinacy; stubborn perverseness; (*law*) wilful disregard of the orders of a court.

contumelious *adj* indicating or expressive of contumely; contemptuous; insolent; rude and sarcastic; disposed to utter reproach or insult; insolent.

contumely *n* haughtiness and contempt in language or behaviour; contemptuous or insulting language; haughty insolence.

contuse *vt* (**contused, contusing**) to wound or injure by bruising; to injure without breaking the flesh.

contusion *n* a severe bruise on the body; a hurt or injury to the flesh or some part of the body without breaking the skin, as by a blunt instrument or by a fall.

conundrum *n* a riddle, the answer to which may involve a pun.

conurbation *n* a large urban area around a large town or city; a large urban area formed by a group of towns growing towards and meeting each other.

convalescence *n* the gradual recovery of health and strength after disease; the state of a person renewing his vigour after sickness or weakness.

convalescent *adj* recovering health and strength after sickness or debility.—*n* one who is recovering his or her health after sickness.

convection *n* the act of carrying or conveying; a process of transmission, as of heat or electricity by means of particles of matter affected by them.

convene *vi* (**convened, convening**) to come together; to meet; to meet in the same place; to assemble.—*vt* to cause to assemble; to call together; to convoke; to summon judicially to meet or appear.

convener, convenor *n* one who convenes or meets with others; one who convenes or calls a meeting.

convenience *n* the state or quality of being convenient; freedom from discomfort or trouble; ease; comfort; that which is suited to wants; suitability; something useful or labour-saving; a public lavatory.

convenience food *n* food requiring little preparation before it is eaten.

convenient *adj* suitable or proper; giving certain facilities or accommodation; commodious; opportune; at hand or readily available; useful or easy to use.

conveniently *adv* in a convenient manner or situation; suitably; with adaptation to the end or effect; with ease; without trouble or difficulty.

convent *n* a community of persons devoted to religion, a body of monks or nuns; a house for persons devoted to religion and celibacy; an abbey, monastery or nunnery.

conventicle *n* an assembly or gathering, especially a secret assembly; a meeting of dissenters from the Established Church for religious worship; a secret meeting for religious worship held by the Scottish Covenanters.

convention *n* the act of coming together; a meeting; an assembly; an assembly of delegates or representatives for consultation on important concerns, civil, political or ecclesiastical; a special agreement or contract between two countries or parties; an agreement previous to a definitive treaty; conventionality; established usage or custom.

conventional *adj* formed by agreement; tacitly understood; arising out of custom or tacit agreement; sanctioned by or depending on general concurrence and not on any principle; based on established usage or custom; not spontaneous or adventurous or original; (of weapons) not nuclear.

converge *vi* (**converged, converging**) to tend to one point; to incline and approach nearer together in position; to approach in character.

convergence *n* the quality of converging; tendency to one point.

convergent *adj* converging; tending to one point; approaching each other.

conversant *adj* acquainted by familiar use or study; having an intimate or thorough knowledge (of things), followed generally by *with*.

conversation *n* familiar discourse; general interchange of views or sentiments; chat; informal talk.

conversation piece *n* a painting of a number of people in their usual environment engaged in their usual pursuits; an unusual object that attracts interest and comment.

control tower

conversazione *n* (*pl* **conversazioni, conversaziones**) a meeting of a number of people for conversation or discussion, particularly on literary, scientific, antiquarian or artistic subjects.

converse[1] *vi* (**conversed, conversing**) to talk familiarly with; to exchange views, sentiments, etc; to chat; to discourse.—*n* interchange of thoughts or opinions; chat; discourse.

converse[2] *adj* turned so as to be transposed or inverted; put the opposite, reverse or contrary way (*converse statement, proposition, way*).—*n* something forming a counterpart; what is contrary or opposite; a statement or proposition produced by inversion or interchange of terms, thus the converse of 'religion is true wisdom', is 'true wisdom is religion'.

conversely *adv* in a converse manner; with inversion of order; put the converse way.

conversion *n* the act of turning or changing from one state to another; the state of being so turned or changed; transmutation; the act of changing or state of being changed in opinions or conduct; a change of heart or dispositions; a change from one religion to another; (*psychol*) a process by which a repressed idea is supposed to give rise to a hysterical symptom corresponding to it; an alteration in a building involving a change of function or use; (in rugby) a score following a try.

convert *vt* to change or turn into another substance or form; to change from one state to another; to change or turn from one religion to another or from one party or sect to another; to change from heathenism to Christianity; to turn from a bad life to a good, religious and holy one; to turn from one use or destination to another; to interchange conversely.—*vi* to turn or be changed; to undergo a change.—*n* a person who turns from one opinion or practice to another; a person who renounces one creed, religious system or party and embraces another; one who is turned from sin to holiness.

converter *n* one who converts; one who makes converts; that which converts, especially an iron retort used in the Bessemer process of steel-making; a kind of electrical induction coil.

convertible *adj* capable of being converted; susceptible of change; transmutable; transformable; capable of being used the one for the other, as terms of similar meaning; interchangeable.—*n* a motorcar with a roof which may be detached or folded back.

convex *adj* rising or swelling into a spherical or rounded form on the exterior surface, opposed to *concave*.—*n* a convex curve.

convex

convexity *n* state of being convex; the exterior surface of a convex body; roundness.

convey *vt* to carry, bear or transport; to transmit, hand over or transfer from one person to another (rights, landed estate); to transmit or carry by any medium (*air conveys sound, words convey meaning*).

conveyable *adj* capable of being conveyed or transferred.

conveyance *n* the act of conveying; the act of bearing, carrying or transporting; transmission; transference; the transmitting or transferring of property from one person to another; the document by which property is transferred; the means by which anything is conveyed, especially a vehicle or carriage of some kind.

conveyancer *n* one whose occupation is to draw conveyances of property, deeds, etc.

conveyancing *n* the act or practice of drawing deeds, leases or other writings for transferring the title to property from one person to another.

convict *vt* to prove or find guilty of a crime charged; to determine or decide to be guilty (with *of* before the crime).—*n* a person convicted or found guilty of a crime; a person undergoing a prison sentence.

conviction *n* the act of convicting or the state of being convicted; the act of a legal tribunal adjudging, finding or determining a person to be guilty of an offence charged against him or her; strong belief on the ground of satisfactory evidence; settled persuasion.

convince *vt* (**convinced, convincing**) to persuade or satisfy by evidence; to bring to full belief or acquiescence by satisfactory proofs or arguments; to compel to yield assent.

convivial *adj* relating to a feast or entertainment; social; sociable; jovial.

conviviality *n* the good humour or mirth indulged at an entertainment; a convivial spirit or disposition; sociability.

convoke *vt* (**convoked, convoking**) to call together; to summon to meet; to assemble by summons.

convocation *n* the act of convoking or assembling by summons; an assembly; a convention; a congress; a council; in England, an assembly of the clergy, by their representatives, to consult on ecclesiastical affairs—a sort of ecclesiastical parliament.

convoluted *adj* twisted, involved, hard to understand (of a style of writing or its meaning).

convolution *n* the act of rolling or winding together or one thing on another; a winding motion; the state of being rolled round on itself or rolled or wound together; a turn or winding; a twisted or tortuous part of something.

convolvulus *n* (*pl* **convolvuluses, convolvuli**) bindweed, a genus of plants consisting of slender twining herbs with milky juice and bell-shaped flowers.

convoy *vt* to accompany on the way for protection, either by sea or land; to escort, as a guard against enemies; to act as escort to.—*n* a protecting force accompanying ships or property on their way from place to place either by sea or land; that which is conducted by such a force; an escort.

convulse *vt* (**convulsed, convulsing**) to draw together or contract spasmodically, as the muscular parts of the body; to affect by irregular spasms; to affect by violent irregular action; to agitate violently.

convulsion *n* a violent and involuntary contraction of the muscular parts of the body, with alternate relaxations; violent and irregular motion; a violent and far-reaching disturbance in nature or among peoples; turmoil; a violent commotion.

cony, coney *n* a rabbit; a rabbit-like animal found in Syria and Palestine.

coo *vi* (**cooed, cooing**) to cry or make the characteristic sound uttered by pigeons or doves; to act in a loving manner.

cooee *n* a call used as a signal, originally used by Australian Aboriginals.

cook *vt* to prepare for the table by boiling, roasting, baking, stewing, etc; to dress up or give a colour to for some special purpose, especially, to tamper with accounts so as to give them a more favourable aspect; to falsify.—*n* one who cooks or prepares food for the table.

cookbook *n* a cookery book.

cook-chill *adj* (of food) prepared by cooking and chilling very rapidly, to be reheated in the future.

cooker *n* an electric or gas appliance for cooking.

cookery *n* the art or practice of dressing and preparing food for the table.

cookery book *n* a book containing recipes and other information for preparing food.

cookhouse *n* a kitchen, especially out of doors.

cookie *n* a biscuit; (*sl*) a person.

cool *adj* moderately cold; being of a temperature between hot and cold; not ardent or zealous; not excited by passion; not angry; indifferent; apathetic; chilling; frigid; deliberate; calm; quietly impudent and selfish (of persons and acts); (*colloq*) acceptable; (*colloq*) excellent.—*n* a moderate state of cold; moderate temperature of the air between hot and cold (*the cool of the day*); composure; self-possession.—*vt* to make cool; to reduce the temperature of; to moderate or allay, as passion of any kind; to calm; to abate, as desire, zeal or ardour; to render indifferent.—*vi* to become less hot; to lose heat; to lose the heat

of excitement, passion or emotion; to become less ardent, zealous or affectionate.

coolness *n* the state or quality of being cool; a moderate degree of cold; a moderate degree or a lack of passion; lack of ardour or zeal; indifference; lack of affection; composure; self-possession.

coomb *n* a valley between hills.

coop *n* a box of boards grated or barred on one side for keeping fowls in confinement; an enclosed place for small animals; a pen.—*vt* to put in a coop; to confine in a coop; to shut up or confine in a narrow compass (followed by *up*, *in* or *within*).

cooper *n* one whose occupation is to make barrels, tubs, etc.—*vti* to do the work of a cooper.

cooperate *vi* (**cooperated, cooperating**) to act or operate jointly with another or others to the same end; to work or labour to promote a common object; to unite in producing the same effect.

cooperation *n* the act of working or operating together to one end; joint operation; concurrent effort or labour.

cooperative *adj* operating jointly to the same end; established for the purpose of providing the members with goods at wholesale prices or at prime cost and cost of management (*cooperative societies* or *stores*).—*n* an organization or enterprise owned by and operated for the benefit of those using its services.

cooperator *n* one who cooperates.

coopt *vt* to elect into some body of which the electors are members.

coordinate *adj* being of equal order or of the same rank or degree; not subordinate. —*vt* (**coordinated, coordinating**) to make coordinate; to arrange in due and relative order; to integrate; to harmonize. —*vi* to function harmoniously; to be in harmony.—*n* that is coordinate; (*geom*) any straight line which, with another or others, serves to determine the position of certain points under consideration; (*pl*) separate items of clothing designed to harmonize with each other and to be worn together.

coordination *n* the act of making coordinate or state of being coordinated.

coot *n* a wading bird of the rail family with a bald forehead, black body and short tail.

cop *n* (*colloq*) a policeman; a police officer.—*vt* (**copped, copping**) to capture; to catch, to obtain; to get; to receive.—**to cop out** (*colloq*) to refuse to participate in; to renege.—**to cop it** (*colloq*) to receive punishment.

copaiba, copaiva *n* a liquid resinous juice or balsam flowing from incisions made in the stem of certain South American trees, used in ointment and varnishes and sometimes in medicine.

cook

cooker

copal *n* a hard, shining, transparent, citron-coloured and strong-smelling resinous substance, the product of several different tropical trees, when dissolved and diluted forming a transparent varnish.

coparcener *n* (*law*) a coheir.

cope[1] *vi* (**coped, coping**) to strive or contend on equal terms or with equal strength; to match; to oppose with success; to deal successfully with.

cope[2] *n* an ecclesiastical vestment resembling a cloak, worn in processions, at vespers, at consecration and other sacred functions; something spread or extended over the head; hence, the arch or concave of the sky, the roof or covering of a house, the arch over a door; a coping.—*vt* (**coped, coping**) to cover as with a cope.

copeck *n* same as **kopeck**.

copestone *n* a head or top stone as on a wall or roof.

copier, copyist *n* one who copies or transcribes; an imitator.

copilot *n* a second pilot in an aircraft.

coping *n* the act of coping; the covering course of a wall, parapet, buttresses, etc.

copious *adj* abundant; plentiful; in great quantities; furnishing abundant matter; rich in supplies.

copper *n* a ductile and malleable metal of a pale red colour, tinged with yellow, of great value both by itself and in alloys; a vessel made of copper, particularly a large boiler; a coin made of copper or partly of copper.—*adj* consisting of or resembling copper.—*vt* to cover or sheathe with sheets of copper (*to copper a ship*).

copperas *n* sulphate of iron or green vitriol, a salt of an astringent taste and of various colours but usually green.

copperhead *n* a poisonous American snake.

copperplate *n* a plate of polished copper on which some figure or design has been engraved and from which an impression can be printed; a print or impression from such a plate.—*adj* resembling an impression from a copperplate; beautifully formed, especially applied to handwriting.

coppersmith *n* one whose occupation is to manufacture copper utensils.

coppice, copse *n* a wood of small growth or consisting of underwood or brushwood; a wood cut at certain times for fuel or other purposes.

copra *n* the dried kernel of the coconut, from which the oil has yet to be extracted.

coprophilia *n* an abnormal interest in faeces.

copse *n* same as **coppice**.

Copt *n* a descendant of the ancient Egyptian race and usually professing Christianity.

Coptic *adj* pertaining to the Copts.—*n* the language of the Copts till superseded as a living language by Arabic.

copula *n* in logic, the word which unites the subject and predicate of a proposition (as in 'man is mortal', where *is* is the copula).

copulate *vi* (**copulated, copulating**) to have sexual intercourse.

copulation *n* the act of copulating; coition.

copulative *adj* uniting or coupling.

copy *n* a writing like another writing; a transcript from an original; a book printed according to the original; one of many books containing the same literary matter; what is produced by imitating; a thing made in close imitation of another; that which is to be imitated; a pattern; a model; an archetype; writing engraved or penned by a master to be imitated by a pupil; written or printed matter given to a printer to be put in type; a photocopy.—*vt* (**copied, copying**) to make a copy from; to write, print, engrave, construct, draw, paint, etc, according to an original; to transcribe; to imitate; to follow as in language, style, manners or course of life; take as one's model; to photocopy; to make a photocopy of.—*vi* to make or produce a copy.

copybook *n* a book in which copies are written or printed for learners to imitate.

copycat *n* (*colloq*) one who copies the actions of someone else; an imitator.

copycat crime *n* a crime thought to have been committed in imitation of another one, especially one that received a great deal of publicity in the press.

copyhold *n* (*law*) a tenure for which the tenant has nothing to show except the copy of the rolls made on the tenant being admitted to the possession of the subject; land held in copyhold.

copyist *n* same as **copier**.

copyright *n* the exclusive privilege which the law allows an author (or his or her assignee) of printing, reprinting, publishing and selling his or her own original work; an author's exclusive right of property in his or her work for a certain time.—*adj* relating to or protected by the law of copyright.—*vt* to secure by copyright, as a book.

copywriter *n* one who writes copy for advertisements or promotional material.

coq au vin *n* a dish made from chicken cooked in wine.

coquet *vt* (**coquetted, coquetting**) to flirt; to flirt with, to try to attract the attention of.—*vi* to endeavour to gain admirers.

coquetry *n* the arts of a coquette; flirting; attempts to attract admiration, notice or love.

coquette *n* a flirt.

coracle *n* an ancient form of boat made by covering a wicker frame with leather or oilcloth.

coral *n* a general term for the hard calcareous substance secreted by certain marine

coracle

polyps, exhibiting a great variety of forms and colours; the unimpregnated eggs in the lobster, so called from being of a reddish-pink colour after boiling.—*adj* made of coral; resembling coral; of the colour of coral; reddish-pink; deep pink.

coralline *adj* consisting of coral; like coral; containing coral.

coral reef, coral island *n* one of those reefs or islands of coral which are produced by the operation of species of polyps.

cor anglais *n* a long thin double-reed musical wind instrument with a lower pitch than an oboe.

corbeil *n* (*archit*) a carved basket with sculptured flowers and fruits.

corbel *n* (*archit*) a piece of stone, wood or iron projecting from the vertical face of a wall as a support.

cord *n* a string or thin rope composed of several strands twisted together; a quantity of wood; (*fig*) that which binds, restrains, draws, etc; corded cloth; corduroy; a thin electric cable; a ribbed cloth; (*pl*) corduroy trousers.—*vt* to bind with a cord or rope; to pile up for measurement and sale by the cord.

cordage *n* ropes or chords collectively; the rigging of a ship.

cordate, cordiform *adj* heart-shaped.

Cordelier *n* a Franciscan friar under the strictest rules and wearing a girdle of knotted cord.

cordial *adj* proceeding from the heart; hearty; sincere; not hypocritical; warm; affectionate; reviving the spirits; refreshing; invigorating (*a cordial liquor*).—*n* anything that strengthens, comforts, gladdens or exhilarates; an exhilarating liquor; an aromatic and sweetened spirit as a beverage.

cordiality *n* the state of being cordial; sincere affection and kindness; genial sincerity; hearty warmth of heart; heartiness.

cordially *adv* in a cordial manner; heartily; sincerely; without hypocrisy; with real affection.

cordillera *n* a ridge or chain of mountains.

cordite *n* a smokeless gunpowder, for use in small arms and ordnance.

cordon *n* a chain of police, soldiers, etc, enclosing or guarding any particular place; a ribbon worn across the breast by knights of the first class of an order; a ribbon as a fastening on a garment.—*vt* to prevent entry to an area (with *off*).

cordon bleu *adj* of a high degree of excellence, used especially of cooking or cooks.

cordon sanitaire *n* a barrier around an infected area; a buffer zone.

cordovan, cordwain *n* Spanish leather; goatskin tanned and dressed.

cordwainer *n* a worker in cordovan leather; a shoemaker.

corduroy *n* a thick cotton stuff corded or ribbed on the surface.

core *n* the heart or inner part of a thing; the central part of fruit containing the kernels or seeds; a centre or central part, as the iron bar of an electromagnet round which is wound a coil of insulated wire, the conducting wires of a submarine telegraph cable, the interior part of a column, the internal mould which forms a hollow in the casting of metals; the region of a nuclear reactor containing the fissile material; (*comput*) a form of magnetic memory used to store one bit of information; (*fig*) the heart or deepest and most essential part of anything (*the core of a question*).

co-respondent *n* (*law*) a person charged with adultery and made a party to a suit for dissolution of marriage.

corgi *n* a Welsh breed of dogs with short legs and a sturdy body.

coriaceous *adj* consisting of leather or resembling leather; tough and leathery.

coriander *n* an annual plant of the carrot family, with aromatic seeds and leaves which are used in cooking as a flavouring agent or garnish.

Corinthian *adj* pertaining to Corinth, a celebrated city of Greece.—*n* an inhabitant of Corinth.

Corinthian order *n* an architectural order distinguished by fluted columns and capitals adorned with acanthus leaves.

cork *n* the outer bark of the cork oak or cork tree growing in Spain and elsewhere, stripped off and made into such articles as stoppers for bottles and casks; a stopper for a bottle or cask cut out of cork.—*vt* to stop or fit with a cork; to confine or make fast with a cork.

corkage *n* a charge made by a restaurant for serving wine, especially when brought in by the customer from outside.

corked *adj* stopped or fitted with cork or a cork; having acquired the taste of cork (*corked wine*).

corkscrew *n* a spiral-shaped piece of metal with which to draw corks from bottles.—*vt* to direct or work along in a spiral; to wriggle forward.—*adj* spiral-shaped.

corm *n* (*bot*) a bulb-like part of a plant consisting of the dilated base of the stem, as in the crocus; a solid bulb.

cormorant *n* a web-footed sea bird of the pelican family, of several species, catching fish by swimming and diving and extremely voracious; (*fig*) a greedy person; a glutton.

corn[1] *n* a single seed of certain plants, especially of cereal plants; the seeds of cereal plants in general, in bulk or quantity; grain; especially in Britain, wheat, in America, maize (in this sense no plural); also, in collective sense, the plants which

coral reef

cormorant

produce corn and from which the grain is not yet separated (*a field* or *sheaf of corn*); (*colloq*) something overly sentimental, as a song, etc.—*vt* to preserve and season with salt.

corn² *n* a hard excrescence of the skin on the toes or some other part of the feet, caused by rubbing or the pressure of the shoes.

corn circle *n* same as **crop circle**.

corncob *n* the central woody stem on which kernels of maize or corn grow.

corncrake *n* the crake or land rail which frequents cornfields and is noted for its harsh cry.

cornea *n* the horny transparent membrane in the fore part of the eye through which the rays of light pass.

corned beef *n* beef preserved and seasoned with salt in grains; beef cured by salting.

cornel, cornel tree *n* a species of dogwood found in Europe and Northern Asia, which produces a small, red, acid, cherry-like fruit used in preserves and confectionery.

cornelian *n* same as **carnelian**.

corner *n* the point where two converging lines or surfaces meet or the space between; an angle; a secret place; a nook or out-of-the-way place; any part (*every corner of the forest*); a difficult situation; in sport, a free shot taken from the corner of the pitch in soccer or hockey; a combination to raise the price of goods in the market.—*vt* to buy up stock in the market at an advantage; to drive into a corner or into a position of great difficulty or necessary surrender.

cornerstone *n* the stone which forms the corner of the foundation of an edifice; hence, that which is of the greatest importance; that on which any system is founded.

cornet *n* a brass wind instrument; formerly, the title of the officer who carried the ensign or colours in a troop of horse in the British army; a cone to hold ice cream.

corn exchange *n* a place where grain is sold or bartered and samples shown and examined.

cornfield *n* a field in which corn is growing.

cornflakes *npl* a breakfast cereal made from split and toasted maize.

cornflour *n* the finely ground meal of Indian corn.

cornice *n* (*archit*) any moulded projection which crowns or finishes the part to which it is affixed; specifically, the highest part of an entablature resting on the frieze.

Cornish *adj* pertaining to Cornwall, in England.—*n* the ancient language of Cornwall, a dialect of the Celtic.

corn laws *npl* legislative enactments and restrictions relating to the exportation and importation of grain.

cornucopia *n* a wreathed horn filled to overflowing with fruit, flowers and grain, used in sculpture, etc, as a symbol of plenty, peace and concord; an unlimited supply.

corny *adj* of the nature of, or furnished with, grains of corn; producing corn; containing corn; produced from corn; tasting of corn or malt; hackneyed; banal; trite; overly sentimental; lacking subtlety.

corolla *n* (*bot*) the part of a flower inside the calyx, surrounding the fruiting parts and composed of one or more petals, generally distinguishable from the calyx by the fineness of its texture and its bright colours.

corollary *n* that which follows over and above what is directly demonstrated in a mathematical proposition; any consequence necessarily concurrent with or following from the main one; an inference; a conclusion; a surplus.

corona *n* a technical term for various things supposed to have some resemblance to a crown; (*astron*) a halo or luminous circle around one of the heavenly bodies; a luminous appearance observed during total eclipses of the sun, which lies outside the chromosphere; (*archit*) the lower member or drip of a classical cornice having a broad vertical face, usually of considerable projection; (*bot*) the circumference or margin of a radiated composite flower; also an appendage of the corolla or petals of a flower proceeding from the base of the limb.

coronach *n* a dirge; a lamentation for the dead among the Scottish Highlanders and Irish.

coronal *adj* pertaining to a corona; belonging to the crown or top of the head.—*n* a crown; wreath; garland.

coronary *adj* pertaining to the arteries which supply blood to the heart.—*n* a coronary artery; coronary thrombosis.

coronary artery *n* one of the arteries which supply blood to the heart from the aorta.

coronary artery bypass *n* a surgical procedure to redirect the flow of blood to the heart by which blocked coronary arteries are bypassed and lengths of vein taken from the leg, etc, are attached to the aorta.

coronary care unit *n* a hospital ward in which patients receive specialized care after suffering from a heart attack.

coronary thrombosis *n* a blockage in one of the arteries caused by a blood clot.

coronation *n* the act or solemnity of crowning a sovereign or investing him or her with the insignia of royalty; the pomp attending on a coronation.

coroner *n* an officer appointed to hold inquests on the bodies of people who die a sudden, accidental or violent death.

coroner's inquest *n* an inquest held by a coroner.

corncob

cornet

coronet *n* a small crown worn by princes and noblemen, bearing crosses, fleurs-de-lis, strawberry leaves, pearls; the lower part of the pastern of a horse.

corozo nut *n* the seed of a tropical American palm yielding oil.

corporal[1] *n* a non-commissioned officer next below a sergeant.

corporal[2] *n* a linen cloth on which the consecrated elements are placed during Mass.—*adj* belonging or relating to the body; bodily; material, not spiritual.

corporal punishment *n* punishment inflicted by striking someone on the body, as by smacking, beating, caning or flogging.

corporate *adj* united in a body, as a number of individuals who are empowered to transact business as an individual; formed into a body; united; collectively one; belonging to a corporation.

corporation *n* a body corporate, formed and authorized by law to act as a single person; a society having the capacity of transacting business as an individual; a town council.

corporeal *adj* of or pertaining to a body; having a body; consisting of a material body; material, as opposed to *spiritual*.

corposant *n* a name given to a ball of electric light often observed on dark tempestuous nights about a ship's rigging; St Elmo's fire.

corps *n* (*pl* **corps**) a body of troops; any division of an army.

corpse *n* the dead body of a human being.

corpulence *n* fleshiness or stoutness of body; excessive fatness.

corpulent *adj* stout; fat; obese.

corpus *n* (*pl* **corpora**) a collected whole; the collected writings of one author; a material substance.

Corpus Christi *n* (*RC Church*) the Eucharist; an annual festival in its honour.

corpuscle *n* a minute particle, molecule or atom; a minute animal cell generally enclosing granular matter and sometimes a spherical body called a nucleus; a red or white blood cell.

corpuscular *adj* relating to corpuscles or small particles, supposed to be the constituent materials of all large bodies.

corral *n* a pen or enclosure for horses or cattle; an enclosure formed of wagons; a strong stockade or enclosure.—*vt* (**corralled, corralling**) to form into a corral; to keep or enclose in a corral.

correct *adj* set right or made straight; in accordance with a certain standard; conformable to truth, rectitude or propriety; not faulty; free from error.—*vt* to make correct or right; to bring into accordance with a certain standard; to remove error or defect from; to amend or emend; to punish for faults; to chastise; to discipline; to

counteract, obviate, or neutralize by adding some new ingredient.

correction *n* the act of correcting; the removal of faults or errors; something written to point out an error or substituted in the place of what is wrong; punishment; discipline; chastisement; the counteraction of what is inconvenient or hurtful.

corrective *adj* having the power to correct; having the quality of removing or obviating what is wrong or injurious.—*n* that which has the power of correcting; that which has the quality of altering or obviating what is wrong or injurious.

correctly *adv* in a correct manner; according to a standard; in conformity with a copy or original; exactly; accurately; without fault or error.

correctness *n* the state of being correct; conformity to a standard or rule; exactness; accuracy.

corrector *n* one who corrects.

correlate *n* one who or that which stands in a reciprocal relation to something else.—*vi* (**correlated, correlating**) to have a reciprocal relation; to be reciprocally related, as father and son; to correspond to one another.—*vt* to place in reciprocal relation; to bring into mutual relation; to determine the relations between, as between several objects or phenomena which bear a resemblance to one another.

correlation *n* reciprocal relation; corresponding similarity or parallelism of relation or law; either of two things so related that one implies the other.

correlative *adj* having a reciprocal relation, so that the existence of one in a certain state depends on the existence of another; reciprocal.—*n* that which is correlative; that of which the existence implies the existence of something else; one of two terms either of which calls up the notion of the other, as husband and wife; (*gram*) the antecedent to a pronoun.

correspond *vi* to be adapted or suitable; to have a due relation; to be similar; to be adequate or proportionate; to accord; to agree; to answer; to fit (used absolutely or followed by *with* or *to*); to communicate with a person by letters sent and received.

correspondence *n* the state of corresponding or being correspondent; agreement; similarity; mutual adaptation of one thing or part to another; communication between persons by letter; the letters collectively which pass between correspondents.

correspondent *adj* corresponding; suitable; duly related; similar; congruous; agreeable; answerable; adapted.—*n* one who writes and receives letters; a person who sends regular communications to a newspaper or for broadcast on radio or television, usually from a foreign country.

coronet

corral

corridor *n* a passage in a building onto which rooms open; a passage into which compartments of a train open; a strip of land giving a country without a coastline access to the sea.

corrie *n* a steep hollow in a hill.

corrigendum *n* (*pl* **corrigenda**) something to be corrected or altered in a published book, etc.

corrigible *adj* capable of being corrected, amended or reformed.

corroborate *vt* (**corroborated, corroborating**) to strengthen or give additional strength to; to confirm; to make more certain; to add assurance to (*to corroborate testimony, news*).

corroboration *n* the act of corroborating; confirmation; that which corroborates.

corroborative *adj* having the power of corroborating or confirming.—*n* a medicine that strengthens.

corrode *vt* (**corroded, corroding**) to eat away by degrees; to wear away or diminish by gradually separating small particles (*nitric acid corrodes copper*); (*fig*) to gnaw or prey on; to consume by slow degrees; to embitter; to poison, blight, canker.

corrosion *n* the action of corroding, eating or wearing away by slow degrees, as by the action of acids on metals; (*fig*) the act of cankering, fretting, vexing or blighting.

corrosive *adj* having the power of corroding or eating into a substance; having the quality of fretting or blighting.—*n* that which has the quality of eating or wearing gradually; anything which irritates, preys on one or frets.

corrugate *vt* (**corrugated, corrugating**) to wrinkle; to draw or contract into folds.—*adj* wrinkled; showing wrinkles or furrows.

corrugated *adj* wrinkled; furrowed or ridged.

corrugated iron *n* common sheet iron or galvanized iron bent into a series of regular grooves and ridges by being passed between powerful rollers.

corrugated iron

corrugation *n* a wrinkling; contraction into wrinkles.

corrupt *vt* to change from a sound to a putrid or putrescent state; to cause to rot; (*fig*) to deprave; to pervert; to impair; to debase; to defile, taint, pollute or infect; to bribe; to debase or render impure by alterations or innovations (language); to falsify (a text).—*adj* changed from a sound to a putrid state; changed from the state of being correct, pure or true to a worse state; vitiated; perverted; debased; impure; ready to be influenced by a bribe; changed or made meaningless by errors or mistakes (*a corrupt text*).

corruptible *adj* capable of being made corrupt, putrid or rotten; subject to decay and destruction, debasement, depravation, etc.

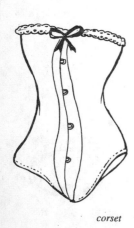

corset

corruption *n* the act of corrupting or state of being corrupt, putrid or rotten; putrid matter; pus; depravity; wickedness; loss of purity or integrity; debasement; impurity; depravation; pollution; defilement; vitiating influence; more specifically, bribery.

corsage *n* a small bunch or spray of flowers pinned to a woman's dress.

corsair *n* a pirate; a sea robber; a piratical vessel.

corselet *n* a small cuirass or armour to cover and protect the top part of the body; an undergarment combining a corset and brassiere.

corset *n* a stiffened bodice worn for support or to contain the figure.

cortège *n* a train of attendants; a funeral procession.

Cortes *n* the Spanish and the Portuguese legislative assembly.

cortex *n* (*pl* **cortices**) bark, as of a tree; hence, an outer covering; (*anat*) a membrane forming a covering or envelope for any part of the body.

corundum *n* a mineral, next in hardness to the diamond and consisting of nearly pure anhydrous alumina.

coruscate *vi* (**coruscated, coruscating**) to flash; to lighten; to gleam; to glitter.

coruscation *n* a sudden burst of light in the clouds or atmosphere; a flash; glitter; a blaze.

corvette *n* a warship that escorts a convoy.

corymb *n* (*bot*) an inflorescence in which the flowers or blossoms are so arranged as to form a mass of flowers with a convex or level top, as in the hawthorn, candytuft, etc.

coryphée *n* a leading ballet dancer.

coryza *n* (*med*) a cold in the head.

cosecant *n* (*geom*) the secant of an arc or angle which is the complement of another arc or angle, that is, when added to it makes up 90°.

cosh *n* a heavy, often flexible, weapon; a bludgeon; a truncheon.—*vt* to strike with a cosh; to bludgeon; to hit with a truncheon.

cosily *adv* in a cosy, snug or comfortable manner.

cosine *n* (*geom*) the sine of an arc or angle which is the complement of another, that is, when added to it makes 90°.

cos lettuce *n* a type of lettuce with long crisp leaves.

cosmetic *adj* beautifying; improving beauty, particularly the beauty of the complexion; improving the appearance; producing a superficial improvement.—*n* any preparation that renders, or is supposed to render, the skin soft, pure and white or helps to beautify and improve the complexion.

cosmetic surgery *n* a surgical operation carried out to improve a person's appearance rather than to cure disease.

cosmic *adj* relating to the universe and to the laws by which its order is maintained; hence, harmonious, as the universe; orderly.

cosmogony *n* the origin or creation of the world or universe; the doctrine of the origin or formation of the universe.

cosmography *n* a description of the world or universe; the science which treats of the construction of the universe.

cosmology *n* the science of the world or universe; or a theory relating to the structure of the universe and the laws which underlie it; cosmogony.

cosmopolitan *n* a person who is nowhere a stranger or who is at home in every place; a citizen of the world.—*adj* free from local, provincial or national prejudices or attachments; at home all over the world; common to all the world; well-travelled.

cosmos *n* the universe as an embodiment of order and harmony; the system of order and harmony combined in the universe.

Cossack *n* one of a warlike people, expert on horseback, inhabiting the steppes in the south of Russia.

cosset *n* a pet; a pet lamb; a lamb brought up by hand.—*vt* to pamper; to treat as a pet.

cost *n* the price, value or equivalent of a thing purchased; amount in value expended or to be expended; charge; expense; (*law*) the sum to be paid by the party losing in favour of the party prevailing, etc; outlay, expense or loss of any kind, as of time, labour, trouble, etc; detriment; pain; suffering (*he learned that to his cost*).—*vt* (*pret, pp* **cost**, *ppr* **costing**) to require to be given or expended in order to purchase; to be bought for; to require to be undergone, borne or suffered (often with two objects (*to cost a person money* or *labour*); (*pret* **costed**) to fix the price of something.

costal *adj* pertaining to the side of the body or the ribs.

cost-effective *adj* giving a satisfactory financial return for the amount of money laid out or invested.

coster, costermonger *n* a hawker who sells fruit or vegetables.

costing *n* preliminary estimate of the total cost of manufacture of an article.

costive *adj* suffering from an abnormal retention of faecal matter in the bowels; constipated.

costliness *n* the state or quality of being costly, high in price or expensive.

costly *adj* of a high price; costing much; expensive; dear.

costmary *n* a perennial composite plant, a native of the south of Europe, cultivated for the agreeable fragrance of the leaves.

cost price *n* the amount which a dealer or merchant pays for goods which will be sold by him/her.

costume *n* an established mode of dress; the style of dress peculiar to a people or nation, to a particular period or a particular class of people; clothes of a historical nature; fancy dress; a woman's suit; dress for a particular purpose, as a swimming costume.

costumed *adj* wearing a costume; dressed.

costumier *n* one who makes or deals in costumes, as for theatres, fancy-dress balls, etc.

cosy *adj* snug; comfortable.—*n* a padded covering put over a teapot to keep in the heat after the tea has been infused; a similar covering for an egg.

cot *n* a hut or cottage; a small bed or crib for a child to sleep in; a collapsible bed; (*naut*) a sort of bed frame suspended from the beams.

cotangent *n* the tangent of an arc or angle which is the complement of another, that is, when added to it makes 90°.

cot death *n* the sudden unexplained death of a sleeping baby.—also called **sudden infant death syndrome**.

cot

cote *n* a shelter or habitation for animals, as a dovecote; a sheepfold; a cottage or hut.

coterie *n* a set or circle of friends who are in the habit of meeting for social or literary intercourse or other purposes; a clique; a close, exclusive group of people.

coterminous *adj* same as **conterminous**.

cotillion *n* a kind of brisk dance; a tune which regulates the dance.

cottage *n* a small dwelling house, especially one in the country.

cottage cheese *n* a soft, white crumbly cheese made from milk curds.

cottage industry *n* manufacture of goods carried out in the home, such as pottery, weaving etc.

cottage piano *n* a small upright piano.

cottager *n* one who lives in a cottage.

cotter, cottier, cottar *n* a cottager; a farm labourer who has the use of a cottage as part of the terms of the job.

cotton *n* a soft downy substance resembling fine wool, growing in the pods or seed vessels of certain plants, being the material of a large proportion of cloth for apparel and furniture; cloth made of cotton.—*adj* pertaining to cotton; made of cotton.—**to cotton on** *vi* to understand; to become aware; to take a liking to.

cotton gin *n* a machine to separate the seeds from raw cotton.

cotton grass *n* a name of plants of the sedge family with white cottony spikes.

cottonwood *n* a tree of the poplar genus, a native of North America.

cottage

cotton wool *n* raw cotton with its wax removed and sterilized, used for surgical dressings, cleaning pads, etc; a state of overprotection.

cottony *adj* downy or soft like cotton; pertaining to or resembling cotton.

cotyledon *n* (*bot*) the seed leaf; the first leaf or leaves of an embryo.

cotyledonous *adj* pertaining to cotyledons; having cotyledons.

couch *vi* to lie down, as on a bed or place of repose; to recline; to lie or crouch with body close to the ground, as a beast.—*vt* to lay down; to spread on a bed or floor (*to couch malt*); to express in words; to put into words; (*surg*) to cure of cataract in the eye by depressing the crystalline lens.—*n* a bed; a piece of furniture with a back and armrests for seating several people; a sofa; a flat bed with a headrest used by doctors for patients; any place for repose, as the lair of a wild beast, etc; a heap of steeped barley spread out on a floor to allow germination to take place and so convert the grain into malt.

couchant *adj* (*heral*) lying down.

couch grass *n* a species of grass which infests arable land, spreading over a field with great rapidity, being propagated both by seed and by its creeping root stock.

couch

cougar *n* a quadruped of the cat kind, the puma.

cough *n* a deep inspiration of air followed by a spasmodic and noisy expiration, caused by some irritation in the air passages.—*vi* to give a cough; to expel the air from the lungs suddenly with noise.—*vt* to expel from the lungs by a violent effort with noise; to expectorate (with *up*, as *to cough up phlegm*).

could (*vb pret of* **can**) was able, capable or susceptible.

coulomb *n* the SI unit of electric charge.

coulter *n* an iron blade or knife inserted into the beam of a plough for cutting the ground and facilitating the separation of the furrow sliced by the ploughshare.

council *n* an assembly of people summoned or convened for consultation, deliberation and advice (*a common council, an ecumenical council, the privy council*); an elected or appointed legislative or advisory body; a central body uniting a group of organizations; a town council; act of deliberation; consultation, as of a council.

council of war *n* an assembly of officers of high rank called to consult on matters of supreme importance in wartime; an emergency meeting.

councillor *n* a member of a council.

council tax *n* a property-based tax charged to pay for local authority services.

counsel *n* opinion or advice given on request or otherwise for directing the judgment or conduct of another; consultation; interchange of opinions; deliberation; secret opinions or purposes (*to keep one's counsel*); intent or purpose; one who gives counsel in matters of law; any counsellor or advocate engaged in a case in court or the group of counsellors, barristers managing a case.—*vt* (**counselled, counselling**) to give advice or deliberate opinion to; to give counselling to; to advise, exhort, warn, admonish or instruct; to recommend or give an opinion in favour of.

counselling *n* professional guidance given by a trained person to someone who needs help in dealing with a personal problem, such as bereavement, marriage difficulties, war experiences, rape, etc.

counsellor *n* any person who gives counsel or advice; an adviser; one who gives counselling; one whose profession is to give advice in law and manage cases for clients; a barrister.

count¹ *vt* to reckon; to number; to compute; to esteem, account, think, judge or consider.—**to count out** to bring (a meeting) to a close by numbering the members and finding a quorum not present, as in the House of Commons, where this is done by the speaker.—*vi* to be added or reckoned in with others; to reckon; to rely (in this sense with *on* or *upon*, as *to count on assistance*).—*n* the act of numbering; reckoning; number; (*law*) a particular charge in an indictment or narration in pleading, setting forth the cause of complaint.

count² *n* a title of foreign nobility, equivalent to the English earl.

countdown *n* the final preparations for an event, especially the firing of a missile, launching a rocket, etc, the time of firing being taken as zero and the time being counted backwards from that; a descending count backwards to zero.

countenance *n* the whole form of the face; the features considered as a whole; the visage; the face; appearance or expression of the face; favour expressed towards a person; goodwill; support.—*vt* (**countenanced, countenancing**) to favour; to encourage; to aid; to abet; to support; to tolerate.

counter¹ *adv* in an opposite direction; in opposition; contrariwise; in the wrong way (*to run counter to wishes*).—*adj* adverse; opposite; opposing; antagonistic.

counter² *n* one who counts, numbers or reckons; that which is used to keep an account or reckoning, as in games, such as a small disc of metal, ivory, wood, plastic, etc; an imitation coin; a registering apparatus; a table or board on which money is counted; a table in a shop over which sales are made and on which goods are sometimes displayed for sale.

counteract *vt* to act in opposition to; to hinder, defeat or frustrate by contrary agency; to oppose, withstand, contravene or resist; to neutralize.

counterattack *n* an attack made in response to an attack.—*vt* to make a counterattack on.

counterattraction *n* an opposite or rival attraction.

counterbalance *vt* (**counterbalanced, counterbalancing**) to serve as a balance to; to weight against with an equal weight; to act against with equal power or effect.—*n* equal weight, power or agency acting in opposition to anything; counterpoise.

countercharge *n* a charge or claim made by an accused person in reply to the charge made against him or her; an opposing charge made by the accused against his or her accuser.

counterespionage *n* espionage directed against the enemy's spy system or action taken to counter the enemy's espionage activities in one's own country.

counterfeit *adj* made in imitation of something else with a view to passing the false copy as genuine or original; forged; not genuine; base; assuming the appearance of something; false; spurious; hypocritical.—*n* something made in imitation with a view to defraud by passing the false for the true.—*vt* to copy or imitate with a view to pass off as original or genuine; to make a likeness or resemblance of with a view to defraud; to forge; to imitate or copy generally; to sham or pretend.—*vi* to feign; to dissemble; to carry on a fiction or deception. .

counterfeiter *n* one who counterfeits; a forger; one who assumes a false appearance or who makes false pretences.

counterfoil *n* a portion of a document, such as a bank cheque, which is retained by the person giving the other part and on which is noted the main particulars contained in the principal document.

counterintelligence *n* a government organization whose work is to prevent the enemy from gathering information; activities intended to frustrate enemy espionage and intelligence gathering.

counterirritant *n* (*med*) an irritant substance employed to relieve another irritation or inflammation.

countermand *vt* to revoke, as a former command; to order or direct in opposition to an order before given, thereby annulling it.—*n* a contrary order; revocation of a former order or command by a subsequent order.

countermarch *vi* to march back.—*n* a marching back; a returning; a change of measures.

countermine *n* (*milit*) a mine sunk in search of the enemy's mine or till it meets it, to defeat its effect; (*fig*) a stratagem or project to frustrate any contrivance; an opposing scheme or plot.—*vt* (**countermined, countermining**) to mine so as to discover or destroy an enemy's mine; (*fig*) to frustrate by secret and opposite measures.—*vi* to make a countermine; to counterplot.

counterpane *n* a bedcover; a coverlet for a bed.

counterpart *n* a part that answers to or resembles another, as the several parts or copies of an indenture corresponding to the original; a thing or person exactly resembling another; a copy; a duplicate; the thing that supplements another thing or completes it; a complement.

counterplot *vi* (**counterplotted, counterplotting**) to oppose or frustrate by another plot or stratagem.—*n* a plot or artifice intended to oppose another.

counterpoint *n* the art of writing music in several distinct parts or themes proceeding simultaneously, as distinguished from harmony which depends more for its effects on the composition and progression of whole chords than on the melody of each separate part.

counterpoise *vt* (**counterpoised, counterpoising**) to weigh against with equal weight; to equal in weight; to counterbalance; to act against with equal power or effect; to balance.—*n* a weight equal to and acting in opposition to another weight; equal power or force acting in opposition; state of being in equilibrium by being balanced by another weight or force.

counterproductive *adj* producing a contrary effect on productivity or usefulness; hindering the desired end.

counter-revolution *n* a revolution opposed to a former one to restore a former state of things.

counterscarp *n* (*fort*) the slope of the ditch nearest the enemy and opposite the scarp; the face of the ditch sloping down from the covered way.

countersign *vt* to sign (a document) formally or officially in proof of its genuineness; to attest or witness by signature (another's signature).—*n* a password; a private sign or signal given in answer to a first sign.

countersink *vt* to form a cavity in timber or other materials so as to receive the head of a bolt, screw, etc, and make it flush with the surface; to sink below or even with a surface, as the head of a screw, bolt, etc, by making a depression for it in the material.—*n* a drill or brace-bit for countersinking; the cavity made by countersinking.

counterpane

countervail *vt* to act with equivalent force or effect against anything; to balance; to compensate; to equal.

countess *n* the wife of an earl or count or a lady possessed of the same dignity in her own right.

countless *adj* not capable of being counted; innumerable.

countrified *adj* having the airs, manner or style of the country; unsophisticated.

country *n* a tract of land; a region; the land occupied by a particular race of people; a state; a person's native or adopted land.—**the country** countryside; the people; the public; the parliamentary electors of a state or the constituencies of a state, collectively.—*adj* pertaining to the country or to a district at a distance from a city; rural; rustic.

country-and-western *n* a form of popular music based on the cowboy music of the southwest USA and influenced by rural ballads, folk music, gospel music, etc.

country cousin *n* an unsophisticated person from the country, unused to city life.

country dance *n* a dance in which the partners are arranged opposite to each other in lines.

countryman, countrywoman *n* (*pl* **countryman, countrywoman**) a person who lives in the country; one who comes from the same country as another.

countryside *n* the rural parts of a region, as opposed to cities or towns; the inhabitants of a region.

county *n* originally, the district or territory of a count or earl; now, a district or particular portion of a state or kingdom, separated from the rest of the territory for certain purposes, such as local government and the administration of justice; a shire.—*adj* pertaining to a county.

county town *n* the chief town of a county; that town where the various courts of a county are held.

coup *n* a French term for stroke or blow and used in various connections to convey the idea of promptness, force or violence; an unexpected or clever victory.

coup de grâce *n* (*pl* **coups de grâce**) the finishing stroke.

coup d'état *n* (*pl* **coups d'état**) a sudden decisive blow in politics; a stroke of policy; specifically, a daring or forcible alteration of the constitution of a country without the consent or concurrence of the people.

coupé *n* a closed two-seater motorcar.

couple *n* two of the same class or kind, connected or considered together; a brace; a pair; a male and female connected by marriage, engaged or otherwise allied; (*mech*) two equal and parallel forces acting in opposite directions; (*elect*) one of the pairs of plates of two metals which compose a battery, called a galvanic or voltaic couple; (*archit*) one of a pair of opposite rafters in a roof, united at the top where they meet.—*vt* (**coupled, coupling**) to link, chain or otherwise connect; to fasten together; to unite; to marry.—*vi* to copulate.

coupler *n* one who or that which couples; specifically, the mechanism by which any two of the ranks of keys or keys and pedals of an organ are connected together.

couplet *n* two verses or lines of poetry, especially two that rhyme together; a pair of rhymes.

coupling *n* the act of one who couples; that which couples or connects; a coupler; a contrivance for connecting one portion of a system of shafting with another; the chains or rods connecting the carriages, etc, of a train; linkage of two alternating electric circuits, causing the one to act inductively on the other.

coupon *n* one of a series of tickets which binds the issuer to make certain payments, perform some service or give value for certain amounts at different periods, in consideration of money received.

courage *n* that quality of mind which enables people to encounter danger and difficulties with firmness or without fear; bravery; intrepidity; valour; boldness; resolution.

courageous *adj* possessing or characterized by courage; brave; bold; daring; intrepid.

courgette, zucchini *n* a type of small edible marrow with a dark green skin and pale flesh.

courier *n* a messenger sent express with letters, despatches or packages; an attendant on a party travelling abroad whose especial duty is to make all arrangements at hotels and on the journey.

course *n* a running, race, flight, career, a moving or motion forward in any direction; a continuous progression or advance; the direction of motion; the line in which a body moves; the direction a ship is steered; the ground or path marked out for a race or sport (*golf course*); continuous or gradual advance; progress; order of succession; stated or orderly method of proceeding; customary or established sequence; series of successive and methodical proceedings; systematized order in arts or sciences for instruction (*course of studies*, etc); way of life or conduct; line of behaviour (*to follow evil courses*); the part of a meal served at one time; (*archit*) a continued range of stones or bricks of the same height throughout the face or faces of a building; (*naut*) one of the sails that hang from a ship's lowest yards; (*pl*) menstruation.—*vt* (**coursed, coursing**) to hunt; to pursue; to chase; to hunt (hares) with greyhounds; to drive with speed; to run through or over.—*vi* to move with speed; to run or move about.—**of course** by consequence; in regular or natural order; naturally; without special direction or provision.

courser *n* a swift horse.

court *n* an enclosed uncovered area, whether behind or in front of a house or surrounded by buildings; a courtyard; an alley, lane, close or narrow street; the place of residence of a king or sovereign prince; all the surroundings of a sovereign in his regal state; the collective body of persons who compose the retinue or council of a sovereign; a hall, chamber or place where justice is administered; the persons or judges assembled for hearing and deciding causes, as distinguished from the counsel or jury; any judicial body, civil, military or ecclesiastical; the sitting of a judicial assembly; attention directed to a person in power to gain favour; civility; flattery; address to gain favour (*to pay court to a person*).—*vt* to endeavour to gain the favour of or win over by attention and address; to flatter; to seek the affections or love of; to woo; to attempt to gain by address; to solicit; to seek (*to court applause*); to hold out inducements to; to invite.—*vi* to pay one's addresses; to woo.

court card *adj* in a pack of playing cards, the king, queen and jack.

court dress *n* a dress suitable for an appearance at court.

courteous *adj* characterized by courtesy; affable; polite.

courtesan, courtezan *n* a prostitute.

courtesy *n* politeness of manners, combined with kindness; an act of civility or respect; a favour or indulgence, as distinct from a right.

courtesy title *n* a title assumed or popularly accorded and to which the individual has no valid claim, as the title marquis to the eldest son of a duke, viscount to the eldest son of an earl, etc.

courthouse *n* a building in which established courts of law are held.

courtier *n* one who attends or frequents the court of a sovereign; one who courts or flatters another with a view to obtaining favour, etc.

courtly *adj* relating or pertaining to a prince's court; refined and dignified; elegant; polite; courteous.

court martial *n* (*pl* **courts martial**) a court consisting of military or naval officers, for the trial of military or naval offences.

court-martial *vt* (*pl* **court-martialled, court-martialling**) to try by court martial.

Court of Session *n* the supreme civil court of Scotland, having jurisdiction in all civil questions.

courtship *n* the act of courting or soliciting favour; wooing.

courtyard *n* a court or enclosure round a building or adjacent to it.

cousin *n* the son or daughter of an uncle or aunt.

couture *n* the business of designing and making fashionable clothes.

couturier *n* one who designs, makes or sells fashionable clothes.

couvade *n* a custom among some primitive races, by which, at the birth of a child, the father takes to bed and is attended by the mother.

cove *n* a small inlet, creek or bay.

coven *n* an assembly of witches.

covenant *n* a mutual consent or solemn agreement of two or more persons to some act; a contract; a compact; a bargain, arrangement or stipulation; a writing containing the terms of agreement or contract between parties.—*vi* to enter into a formal agreement; to contract; to bind oneself by contract.

covenanter *n* one who makes a covenant.

Covenanter *n* a person who joined in the Solemn League and Covenant in Scotland (1638).

cover *vt* to spread the surface of with another substance; to lay or set over; to conceal by covering; to envelop; to wrap up; to clothe; to shelter; to protect; to defend; to cloak; to screen; to invest with; to brood over; to be sufficient for; to include; to insure against; to comprehend; to be equal to; to be co-extensive with; to report for a newspaper; to understudy; (of a male animal) to copulate.—*vi* to spread over, as a liquid does; to provide an excuse or alibi (for); to work, e.g. as a salesman, in a certain area; to have within firing range.—*n* anything which is laid, set or spread over another thing; anything which veils or conceals; a screen; disguise; superficial appearance; shelter; defence; protection; something used or a character assumed to hide one's real actions, purpose or aims; concealment and protection; shrubbery, woods, underbrush, etc, which shelter and conceal game; the articles laid at table for the use of one person—plate, spoon, knife and fork, etc.

coverage *n* the extent or amount covered by something; the extent to which something is covered; the amount or scale of reporting of an event for newspapers, television, etc.

cover charge *n* a fixed charge made by a restaurant in addition to the cost of the meal.

covering *n* that which covers; anything spread or laid over another, whether for security, protection, shelter or concealment; clothing; dress; wrapper; envelope.

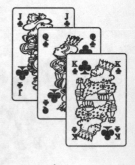

court cards

covering letter *n* a letter which accompanies something or is enclosed with it and explains something about it.

coverlet *n* the upper covering of a bed.

covert *adj* kept secret or concealed; not open (*covert fraud* or *enmity*); (*law*) under cover, authority or protection.—*n* a place which covers and shelters; a shelter; a defence; a thicket; a shady place or a hiding place; (*pl*) feathers covering the bases of the quills of the wing or tail of birds.

coverture *n* (*law*) the state of a married woman, who is considered as under the cover or power of her husband.

cover-up *n* the concealing of one's real activities; something used to conceal one's real activities; a concerted effort, as by a government, to prevent a situation, activity, etc, from being made public.

covet *vt* to desire or wish for with eagerness; to desire earnestly to obtain or possess; to desire with a greedy or envious longing; to long for; to hanker after.—*vi* to have or indulge inordinate desire.

covetous *adj* very desirous; eager to obtain; inordinately desirous; excessively eager to obtain and possess; avaricious.

covetousness *n* the state or quality of being covetous; avarice; cupidity; greediness; craving.

cowboy

covey *n* a small flock of partridges or grouse.

cow[1] *n* (*pl* **cows**, *old pl* **kine**) the female of domestic cattle; the female of the whale, elephant and seal.

cow[2] *vt* to sink the spirits or courage of; to daunt, dishearten, intimidate, overawe.

coward *n* a person who lacks courage to meet danger; a faint-hearted, timid or pusillanimous person.—*adj* lacking courage; timid; of, proceeding from or expressive of fear or timidity.

cowardice *n* lack of courage to face danger; timidity; pusillanimity; fear of exposing one's person to danger.

cowardly *adj* lacking courage to face danger; timid; timorous; pusillanimous; fainthearted; mean; base; proceeding from fear of danger; befitting a coward.

cowbane *n* a kind of hemlock, water hemlock, which is highly poisonous, being sometimes fatal to cattle.

crab

cowboy *n* boy who has charge of cows; a man who looks after cattle on a large stock farm and does this work on horseback; in stories and films about the old American West, a tough character who rides a horse, engages in gunfights and does battle with the Indians; (*colloq*) one who is engaged in dubious business activities; (*colloq*) one who drives an unsafe or overloaded lorry; (*colloq*) a workman who does shoddy, slapdash work and who is not properly qualified.

cowcatcher *n* a strong frame in front of locomotives for removing obstructions, such as strayed cattle, from the rails.

cower *vi* to stoop or sink downward, as from terror, discomfort, etc; to shrink back in fear; to cringe.

cowl *n* a hood, especially a monk's hood; a cowl-shaped covering for the top of a chimney, which turns with the wind; a wire cap or cage on the top of an engine funnel.

cow parsley *n* a popular name of several perennial herbs of the carrot family, said to be eaten by cattle.

cow parsnip *n* a plant of the carrot family, sometimes used in England for fattening pigs.

cowpox *n* a disease which appears on the teats of the cow in the form of blisters, the fluid or virus contained in which is capable of communicating the disease to humans and by injection providing for a time security against smallpox.

cowrie, cowry *n* a small univalve shell used for coin on the coast of Guinea and in many parts of Southern Asia.

cowslip *n* a perennial herb of the primrose family, growing in moist places in Britain.

coxswain *n* the person who steers a boat, especially in a race or on a lifeboat.

coy *adj* shy; modest; playfully or affectedly demure; bashful.

coyness *n* the quality of being coy; bashfulness; affected shyness.

coyote *n* the American prairie wolf.

coypu *n* the native name of a South American rodent, beaver-like, semi-aquatic mammal, valued for its fur.

cozen *vt* to cheat; to defraud; to deceive; to beguile.

crab[1] *n* any of numerous ten-footed, short-tailed crustaceans, having their tail folded under the body, the two forefeet not used for locomotion but furnished with strong claws or pincers and several species being highly esteemed as food; Cancer, a sign in the zodiac.

crab[2] *n* a small, wild, very sour apple; the tree producing the fruit.

crab apple *n* a wild apple.

crabbed, crabby *adj* irritable; cross; sour; peevish; morose; difficult; (of writing) cramped and hard to read.

crack *vt* to rend, break or burst; to break partially; to break without an entire severance of the parts; to throw out or utter with smartness (*to crack a joke*); to snap; to cause (a whip) to make a sharp sudden noise; to solve (a code, puzzle, etc); to open (a bottle).—*vi* to break with a sharp sound; to burst; to open in chinks; to be fractured without quite separating into different parts; to give out a loud or sharp sudden sound; to have a mental or nervous breakdown.—*n* a chink or fissure; a partial separation of the parts of a substance, with or without an opening; a burst of sound; a sharp or loud sound uttered suddenly; a violent report; injury or impairment to the intellect or to the character; flaw; blemish; an instant; a trice; (*colloq*) an attempt; (*colloq*) a wisecrack, a smart remark; (*colloq*) a highly addictive form of cocaine.—*adj* having qualities to be proud of; first-rate; excellent (*a crack regiment, a crack horse*); expert.

cracked *adj* burst or split; rent; broken; impaired; (*colloq*) crazy.

cracker *n* a small firework filled with powder, which explodes with a sharp crack or with a series of sharp cracks; a decorated paper tube that cracks open with a bang when pulled and releases a paper hat, a joke and a trinket; a thin, crisp biscuit.

crackers *adj* (*colloq*) crazy; mad.

crackle *vi* (**crackled, crackling**) to make slight cracks; to make a series of small abrupt noises.

crackling *n* a noise made up of small cracks or reports frequently repeated; the browned skin of roast pork.

crackpot *adj* (*colloq*) crazy; absurd; impractical, not workable.—*n* a crazy or eccentric person.

cradle *n* a small bed, crib or cot in which an infant is rocked; hence, the place where any person or thing is nurtured at an early stage; birthplace; something resembling a cradle in construction or use, as a case in which a broken limb is placed after being set; a rocking machine in which gold is washed from the earth, etc, containing it; a framework of timbers for supporting or transporting; a cage on a platform for hoisting workmen; the base on which a telephone rests.—*vt* (**cradled, cradling**) to lay in a cradle; to rock in a cradle; to compose or quiet by rocking; to nurse in infancy.

cradle-snatch *vt* to marry or have as a partner or lover, someone who is much younger than oneself.

craft *n* cunning art or skill; artifice; guile; dexterity in a particular manual occupation; hence, the occupation or employment itself; manual art; trade; the members of a trade collectively; (*naut*) a vessel (often used in a collective sense for vessels of any kind).

craftiness *n* the state or quality of being crafty.

craftsman *n* (*pl* **craftsmen**) an artificer; a mechanic; one skilled in a manual occupation.

craftsmanship *n* the skilled work of a craftsman.

crafty *adj* characterized by, having or using craft; cunning; wily; sly; deceitful.

crag *n* a steep, rugged rock; a rough broken rock or point of a rock; a cliff; (*geol*) shelly deposits in Norfolk and Suffolk, usually of gravel and sand, of the older Pliocene period.

cragsman *n* (*pl* **cragsmen**) one who is dextrous in climbing or descending rocks.

crake *n* a bird of various species belonging to the family of the rails, the best-known being the corncrake or land rail.

cram *vt* (**crammed, cramming**) to press or drive, particularly in filling or thrusting one thing into another; to stuff; to crowd; to fill to superfluity; to fill with food beyond satiety; to stuff; (*fig*) to endeavour to qualify for an examination in a short time by storing the memory with only such knowledge as is likely to be useful; to coach.—*vi* to eat greedily; to stuff; to prepare for an examination by rapidly storing the memory with facts.—*n* information acquired hurriedly for an examination or other special purpose.

crambo *n* a game in which one person or team gives a word, to which another finds a rhyme; a word rhyming with another.

crammer *n* one who crams or stuffs; one who crams in study.

cramp *n* the painful contraction of a limb or muscle of the body; spasm; a feeling of restraint; a piece of iron bent at the end, serving to hold together pieces of timber, stones, etc; a cramp-iron; a portable kind of iron screw press for closely compressing the joints of a timber framework.—*vt* to pain or affect with spasms or cramps; to confine, restrain or hinder from action or expansion.

crampon *n* a grappling iron; a spiked metal plate attached to boots to prevent slipping when mountaineering or walking or climbing on ice.

cran *n* in Scotland, a measure of capacity for fresh herrings.

cranberry *n* the dark red berry, about the size of a currant, produced by several species of small shrubs growing in peat bogs or swampy land in Europe and North America; the shrub producing this berry.

crane *n* a large migratory wading bird of several species, having long slender legs, a long neck and powerful wings; a machine for raising great weights and depositing them at some distance from their original place.—*vi* (**craned, craning**) to stretch out one's neck like a crane in order to see over; (of a horse) to pull up at a dangerous jump.

cranefly *n* a two-winged insect having very long legs and long spreading wings; the daddy-longlegs is a well-known species.

cranesbill *n* a popular name for a species of geranium, from the long slender beak of its fruit.

crampon

cranefly

craniology *n* the study of the size and shape of the cranium or skull.

cranium *n* (*pl* **crania**) the bones which enclose the brain; the skull.

crank¹ *n* an iron axis with the end bent like an elbow, serving as a handle for communicating circular motion, for changing circular motion into motion backwards and forwards or the reverse or for changing the direction of motion; any bend, turn, winding or involution; (*colloq*) a person with eccentric views.—*vt* to provide with a crank; to turn or wind.—**to crank up** to start (an engine) with a crank; (*colloq*) to speed up; (*sl*) to inject a narcotic drug.

crank² *adj* liable to be tipped over, as a sailing ship when she has insufficient ballast to carry full sail; in a shaky or crazy condition; loose; disjointed.

crankshaft *n* the main shaft in an internal combustion engine which is made to turn by the up-and-down motion of the pistons.

cranky *adj* (*colloq*) eccentric; cross.

cranny *n* a small narrow opening, fissure, crevice or chink, as in a wall.

crape *n* same as **crepe**.

crash¹ *vt* to break to pieces violently; to dash with noise and violence.—*vi* to make the loud sound of a thing or things falling and breaking; to make any similar noise.—*n* the loud sound of a thing or things falling and breaking; a sound made by dashing; the collapse of a commercial undertaking; bankruptcy; failure.

crash² *n* a coarse kind of linen cloth, mostly used for towels.

crash helmet *n* a form of protective headgear in the form of a fibreglass or metal cap worn by motor cyclists, cyclists, etc, to prevent or reduce injury to the head in case of accident.

crash-land *vi* to make a crash-landing.

crash-landing *n* an emergency landing of an aircraft, often without lowering the undercarriage.

crasis *n* (*pl* **crases**) (*gram*) a figure by which two different letters are contracted into one long letter or into a diphthong.

crass *adj* gross; thick; coarse; not thin, nor fine; applied to fluids and solids; (*fig*) gross; dense; stupid; obtuse.

crate *n* a container of wickerwork or slatted wood used for the transportation of china, glass, crockery and similar wares.

crater *n* the orifice or mouth of a volcano, often a circular cup-like hollow at the top of a volcanic cone; the cavity formed in the positive pole of an arc lamp by the passage of the current; the hole made by the explosion of a large shell or mine.

cravat *n* a neckcloth; a scarf of silk or wool worn by men about the neck.

crave *vt* (**craved, craving**) to ask for with earnestness or importunity; to ask (a thing) with submission or humility; to beg, entreat, implore, solicit; to call for, as a gratification; to long for; to require or demand, as a passion or appetite.—*vi* to beg, ask, beseech or implore; to long or hanker eagerly (with *for*).

craven *n* a coward; a weak-hearted, spiritless person.—*adj* cowardly; base.

craving *n* a very great desire; a longing.

craw *n* the crop or first stomach of fowls.

crawl *vi* to move slowly by drawing the body along the ground, as a worm; to move slowly on the hands and knees, as a human being; to creep; to move or walk weakly, slowly or timorously; to advance slowly and slyly; to insinuate oneself; to behave meanly, obsequiously or despicably.—*n* the act of crawling; slow creeping motion.

crayfish, crawfish *n* the river lobster, a ten-footed crustacean found in streams and resembling the lobster, but smaller, used as food; also the spiny lobster.

crayon *n* a pencil or cylinder of coloured chalk, wax, clay or charcoal, used in drawing on paper.—*vt* to sketch with a crayon.

craze *vt* (**crazed, crazing**) (of china) to produce or cover in many cracks; to make insane; to derange.—*n* an inordinate desire or longing; a passion; a wild fancy, notion or enthusiasm.

crazy *adj* disordered; deranged, mad; foolish, ridiculous.

crazy paving *n* paving for a garden path, etc, composed of irregularly shaped slabs, sometimes of various colours.

creak *vi* to make a sharp, harsh, grating sound, as by the friction of hard substances.—*vt* to cause to make a harsh protracted noise.—*n* a sharp, harsh, grating sound.

cream *n* any part of a liquid that separates from the rest, rises and collects on the surface; more particularly, the richer fatty part of milk; the best part of a thing; the choice part; a sweetmeat prepared from cream (*ice cream*); a creamy preparation as for the skin; a yellowish-white colour.—*vt* to skim; to take the cream off by skimming; to take off the best part of; to beat to a creamy consistency; to cover or spread with cream.—*vi* to gather cream; to gather a covering on the surface.

cream cheese *n* a cheese made with milk to which a certain quantity of cream is added.

creamery *n* an establishment to which farmers send their milk to be made into butter and cheese.

cream of tartar *n* purified tartar.

creamy *adj* full of cream; having the nature of or resembling cream; yellowish-white in colour.

crease¹ *n* a line or mark made by folding or doubling anything; hence, a similar mark,

crash helmet

crazy paving

however produced; specifically, the name given to certain lines marking boundaries near the wickets in the game of cricket.— *vt* (creased, creasing) to make a crease or mark in, as by folding or doubling; to wrinkle.

crease² *n* same as **kris**.

create *vt* (**created, creating**) to produce from nothing; to bring into being; to cause to exist; to make or form, by investing with a new character; to constitute; to appoint (*to create a peer*); to be the occasion of; to bring about; to cause; to produce (*create a disturbance*).

creation *n* the act of creating, producing or causing to exist; the act of investing with a new character; appointment; formation; the things created; that which is produced or caused to exist; the world; the universe.

Creation *n* the act of bringing this world into existence by God.

creative *adj* having the power to create or exerting the act of creating; having a talent for imaginative creation.

creative accounting *n* the use of loopholes and uncertainties in tax and financial legislation to make accounts seem misleadingly favourable.

creator *n* one who or that which creates, produces, causes or constitutes.

Creator *n* God.

creature *n* anything created; a thing; a created being; any living being; a human being, in contempt or endearment; a person who owes his or her rise and fortune to another; one who is entirely subject to the will or influence of another.—*adj* of or belonging to the body (*creature comforts*).

crèche *n* an institution or establishment where, usually for payment, children are taken care of during the day.

credence *n* reliance on evidence derived from other sources than personal knowledge, as from the testimony of others; belief or credit (*to give a story credence*); a credence table.

credence table *n* the small table by the side of the altar or communion table, on which the bread and wine are placed before they are consecrated.

credential *n* that which gives a title or claim to confidence; (*pl*) testimonials or documents given to a person as the warrant on which belief, credit or authority is claimed for him or her.

credibility *n* the quality or state of being credible or believable.

credibility gap *n* a situation arising when the claims of officials are obviously different from the known facts.

credible *adj* capable of being believed; such as one may believe; worthy of credit, reliance or confidence as to truth and correctness (applied to persons and things).

credibly *adv* in a credible manner; so as to command belief (*to be credibly informed*).

credit *n* reliance on testimony; belief; faith; trust; good opinion founded on a belief of a man's veracity, integrity, abilities and virtue; reputation derived from the confidence of others; esteem; honour; what brings some honour or estimation; reputation for commercial stability or solvency; the selling of goods or lending of money in confidence of future payment; in bookkeeping, the side of an account in which payment or other item lessening the claim against a debtor is entered, opposed to debit; the time given for payment for goods sold on trust.—*vt* to believe; to confide in the truth of; to sell or lend in confidence of future payment; to trust; to enter on the credit side of an account; to give credit for.

creditable *adj* accompanied with reputation or esteem; honourable; estimable; praiseworthy.

credit card *n* a card entitling the holder to purchase goods and services which are charged to his or her account.

creditor *n* one who gives goods or money on credit; one to whom money is due; one having a just claim for money (correlative to *debtor*).

credit rating *n* the assessment of a person's or a firm's creditworthiness.

creditworthy *adj* worthy of being given credit, as judged by one's earning capacity, record of paying debts promptly, etc.

credulity *n* the state or quality of being credulous; disposition or readiness to believe without sufficient evidence.

credulous *adj* apt to believe without sufficient evidence; unsuspecting; easily deceived.

creed *n* a brief and authoritative summary of the articles of Christian faith; hence, a statement or profession of fundamental points of belief.

creek *n* a small inlet, bay or cove; a recess in the shore of the sea or of a river; a small river; a brook.

creel *n* a wickerwork basket or pannier for fish.

creep *vi*, (*pret, pp* **crept**, *ppr* **creeping**) to move with the belly on the ground or any surface, as a reptile or as many insects with feet and very short legs; to crawl; to move along a surface in growth (as a vine); to move slowly, feebly or timorously; to move slowly and insensibly, as time; to move secretly or insidiously; to move or behave with extreme servility or humility; to cringe, to fawn; to have a sensation such as might be caused by worms or insects creeping on the skin.

creeper *n* one who or that which creeps; a creeping plant which moves along the sur-

credit card

face of the earth or attaches itself to some other body, as ivy; a popular name of birds which resemble the woodpeckers in their habits of creeping on the stems of trees in quest of insect prey.

creepy-crawly *n* (*colloq*) a small crawling insect.

cremate *vt* (**cremated, cremating**) to burn; to dispose of (a human body) by burning instead of interring.

cremation *n* the act or custom of cremating; the burning of a dead body instead of burial.

crenate, crenated *adj* (of leaves) scalloped.

crenelle *n* an embrasure in a battlement, parapet or breastwork to fire through; an indentation; a notch.

crenellate *vt* (**crenellated, crenellating**) to furnish with crenelles or similar openings; to embattle.

Creole *n* a person of pure European descent born in the West Indies or South America; a person of mixed European and Negro ancestry; the language of any of these groups.

creosote *n* an oily, heavy, colourless liquid obtained from wood tar used as a wood preservative.—*vt* (**creosoted, creosoting**) to treat with creosote.

crepe *n* a thin gauzy fabric made from cotton or silk and having a crinkly surface; crepe paper; a type of thin pancake.

crepe paper *n* a thin, soft, coloured, crinkly paper resembling the crepe.

crepuscular *adj* pertaining to twilight; glimmering; flying or appearing in the twilight or evening or before sunrise, as certain insects.

crescendo *adv* (*mus*) a term signifying that the notes of the passage are to be gradually swelled, usually written *cresc* and marked thus (<).—*n* (*pl* **crescendi, crescendos**) a piece of music so played.

crescent *adj* increasing; growing; waxing.—*n* the increasing or new moon, which, when receding from the sun, shows a curving rim of light terminating in points or horns; anything shaped like a new moon, as a range of buildings whose fronts form a concave curve; the figure or likeness of the new moon.

cress *n* the name of various plants in general use as a salad, such as watercress, common in streams and having a pungent taste; garden cress, a dwarf cultivated species; Indian cress, a showy garden annual whose fruits are made into pickles.

cresset *n* a light set on a beacon; an open frame of iron containing fire, used as a torch.

crest *n* a tuft, etc, on the top of an animal's head, as the comb of a cock, etc; anything resembling, suggestive of or occupying the same relative position as a crest, as the

cress

cresset

plume or tuft of feathers, etc, affixed to the top of the helmet; (*heral*) a figure placed on a wreath, coronet, etc, above both helmet and shield; the foamy, feather-like top of a wave; the highest part or summit of a hill, ridge, slope, etc; the rising part of a horse's neck.—*vt* to furnish with a crest; to serve as a crest for; to adorn as with a plume or crest.

crestfallen *adj* dejected; sunk; bowed; dispirited; spiritless.

cretaceous *adj* composed of or having the qualities of chalk; like chalk; abounding with chalk; chalky.

Cretaceous *adj* of or belonging to a geological group between the Jurassic and Tertiary formations.—n the Cretaceous formation.

cretin *n* a person suffering from mental and physical retardation caused by a lack of hormones produced by the thyroid gland; (*colloq*) an idiot, a fool.

cretonne *n* a cotton cloth with various textures of surface printed with pictorial and other patterns and used for curtains, covering furniture, etc.

crevasse *n* a fissure or rent, generally applied to a fissure across a glacier; a deep crack.

crevice *n* a crack; a cleft; a fissure; a cranny; a rent.

crew *n* a company of people; an assemblage; a crowd; a band; a gang; a herd; a horde; a company; the company of seamen who man a ship, vessel or boat; the company belonging to a vessel.

crew cut *n* a hairstyle in which the hair is cut extremely short.

crewel *n* a kind of fine worsted or thread of silk or wool, used in embroidery and fancy work.

crew neck *n* a round neck without a collar on a sweater, etc.

crib *n* a small cottage; the manger or rack of a stable or house for cattle; a feeding place for cattle; a small frame or bed for a child to sleep in; a theft or the thing stolen; a literal translation of a classic author for the use of students; in the game of cribbage, a set of cards made up of two thrown from the hand of each player.—*vt* (**cribbed, cribbing**) to shut or confine in a narrow habitation; to cage; to pilfer or purloin; to copy; to cheat by copying.

cribbage *n* a game at cards played with the whole pack by two, three or four persons, so called because the dealer receives a crib or additional hand partly drawn from the hands of his opponent or opponents.

cribbage board *n* a board used for marking in the game of cribbage.

crick *n* a spasmodic affection of some part of the body, as of the neck or back, making motion of the part difficult.

208

cricket¹ *n* a kind of insect nearly allied to the grasshoppers, noted for the chirping or creaking sound produced by the friction of the bases of its wing cases against each other.

cricket² *n* an outdoor game played by two sides of eleven each, with bats, ball and wickets.

cricketer *n* one who plays cricket.

crime *n* a violation of a law; specifically, a gross violation of law, as distinguished from a misdemeanour, trespass or other slight offence; any great wickedness or iniquity; a foul wrong; offence.

criminal *adj* guilty of a crime; culpable; wicked; iniquitous; atrocious; abandoned; villainous; felonious; nefarious; partaking of the nature of a crime; involving a crime; that violates public law, divine or human; relating to crime, opposed to civil.—*n* a person guilty of crime; a person indicted or charged with a public offence and found guilty; a culprit; a malefactor.

crimp *vt* to curl or crisp, as the hair; to flute or make regular ridges on, as on a frill; to pinch and hold; in cookery, to gash the flesh of fish or meat with a knife, to give it greater hardness and make it more crisp.—*n* a curl, as in the hair; a small fold.

crimson *n* a deep red colour; a rich red slightly tinged with blue; a red colour in general.—*adj* of a deep red colour.—*vt* to dye with crimson; to make red.—*vi* to become of a crimson colour; to be tinged with red; to blush.

cringe *vi* (**cringed, cringing**) to bend or crouch with servility; to fawn; to stoop or truckle.—*n* a mean or fawning obeisance.

cringle *n* (*naut*) an iron ring or a short rope worked into the bolt rope of a sail so as to form a ring or eye, etc.

crinkle *vi* (**crinkled, crinkling**) to bend; to wrinkle; to run in and out in little or short bends or turns; to curl.—*vt* to form with short turns or wrinkles.—*n* a wrinkle.

crinkly *adj* having been crinkled; wrinkled; creased; crimped; corrugated.

crinoid *n* an echinoderm having a star-shaped body supported by a long, slender, calcareous jointed stem.

crinoline *n* a stiff fabric of horsehair; etc; a skirt or petticoat stiffened by horsehair, hoops, etc.

cripple *n* one who limps; one who has lost or never enjoyed the use of his or her limbs; a lame person.—*adj* lame—*vt* (**crippled, crippling**) to disable by injuring the limbs, particularly the legs or feet; to lame; to deprive of the power of exertion; to disable (*a crippled fleet*).

crisis *n* (*pl* **crises**) the change of a disease which indicates recovery or death; the decisive state of things or the point of time when an affair has reached its height and must soon terminate or suffer a material change; turning point; conjuncture.

crisp *adj* curling in small stiff or firm curls; indented or winding; easily broken or crumbled; brittle; easily crumbled; possessing a certain degree of firmness and freshness; fresh; brisk.

crispbread *n* a brittle, unsweetened type of biscuit, made from rye or wheat and eaten instead of bread.

crispy *adj* crisp; easily crumbled; brittle; fresh.

criterion *n* (*pl* **criteria**) a standard of judging; any established law, rule, principle or fact by which a correct judgment may be formed.

critic *n* a person skilled in judging the merit of literary works; a judge of merit or excellence in the fine arts generally; a writer whose chief function it is to pass judgment on matters of literature, art, etc; a reviewer; one who judges with severity; one who censures or finds fault.

critical *adj* relating to criticism; belonging to the art of a critic; passing judgment on literary and artistic matters; inclined to make fine distinctions; exact; fastidious; inclined to find fault or to judge severely; (*med*) pertaining to the crisis or turning point of a disease; pertaining to any crisis; decisive; important as regards consequences (*a critical time*); momentous; attended with danger or risk; dangerous; hazardous (*a critical undertaking*).

criticism *n* the art of judging the merits and faults of a literary performance or of any production in the fine arts; the art of judging the merit of any performance; a critical judgment; a detailed critical examination; a critique.

criticize *vi* (**criticized, criticizing**) to judge critically, estimating good points and defects; to pick out faults; to utter censure.—*vt* to examine or judge critically; to point out merits and blemishes or faults in; to pass judgment on with respect to merit or blame.

critique *n* a written estimate of the merits of a performance, especially of a literary or artistic performance; a criticism.

croak *vi* to make a low, hoarse noise in the throat, as a frog, a raven or crow; to produce any low, harsh sound; to speak with a low, hollow voice; to die.—*vt* to utter in a low, hollow voice; to murmur out; to announce or herald by croaking.—*n* the low, harsh sound uttered by a frog or a raven or a like sound.

crochet *n* a style of knitting performed by means of a small hook, the material being cotton, wool, silk, etc.—*vt* to knit in this style.

crock *n* an earthen vessel; a pot or pitcher; a person broken down in health.

cricket

cricketer

cross

crockery *n* china dishes or earthenware vessels.

crocket *n* an architectural ornament, usually in imitation of curved and bent foliage, etc, placed on the angles of the inclined sides of pinnacles, canopies, gables, etc; one of the terminal snags on a stag's horn.

crocodile *n* a large aquatic reptile of the lizard kind, having a long and powerful tail flattened at the sides, the body covered with square bony plates, a tapering snout, the jaws long and the gape of enormous width; the best-known species haunt the Nile.—*adj* of or pertaining to or like a crocodile.

crocodile tears *npl* false or affected tears; in allusion to the old fiction that crocodiles shed tears over their victims.

crocus *n* (*pl* **crocuses**) a beautiful genus of European plants; saffron; the long orange-reddish stigmas of an autumnal species dried; the commercial name of a red or deep yellow polishing powder made with oxide of iron.

croft *n* a small piece of enclosed ground adjoining a dwelling house and used for pasture and tillage; a very small farm.

crofter *n* one who cultivates a croft.

croissant *n* a type of flaky bread roll baked in a crescent shape.

cromlech *n* an ancient structure (probably a sepulchral monument) consisting of two or more large unhewn stones fixed upright in the ground supporting a large flat stone in a horizontal position.

crone *n* a contemptuous term for an old woman.

crony *n* an intimate companion; an associate; a familiar friend.

crook *n* any bend, turn or curve; curvature; flexure; any bent or curved instrument; especially, a shepherd's staff, curving at the end, or the staff of a bishop or abbot, fashioned in the form of a shepherd's staff, as a symbol of his sway over and care for his flock; a pastoral staff; a small curved tube applied to a trumpet, horn, etc, to change its key; an artifice; a trick; a criminal.—*vt* to bend; to turn from a straight line; to make a curve or hook.—*vi* to bend or be bent; to be turned from a straight line; to curve; to wind.

crooked *adj* deviating from a straight line; bent, curved or winding; wry or deformed; deviating from the path of rectitude; perverse, deceitful or devious.

croon *vti* to sing in a low humming tone; to hum; to utter a low, continued, plaintive sound.

crop *n* the first stomach of a fowl; the craw; cultivated plants cut and gathered; the quantity of a particular kind of grain, fruit, etc, obtained in a single season; the corn or fruits of the earth collected; harvest; corn

croissant

and other cultivated plants while growing; the act of cutting or clipping off, as hair; a hunting crop.—**neck and crop** bodily; altogether; bag and baggage.—*vt* (**cropped, cropping**) to cut off the ends of; to eat off or browse; to pull off; to pluck; to mow; to reap; to cause to bear a crop; to raise crops on.—**to crop out** (*geol*) to appear on the surface; to appear incidentally and undesignedly; to come to light.

crop circle, corn circle *n* a circular patch in a field of crops, flattened by an unexplained circular motion, possibly as a hoax.

cropper *n* a breed of pigeons with a large crop; a fall as from horseback.—**to come a cropper** to fall heavily; to fail; to be unsuccessful.

croquet *n* an open-air game played by two or more persons with mallets, balls, pegs or posts and a series of iron hoops or arches, the object of each party being to drive their balls through the hoops and against the posts in a certain order before their opponents.

cross *n* an instrument on which wrongdoers of ancient times were put to death, consisting of two pieces of timber placed across each other, either in form of +, T or X, variously modified, such as that on which Christ suffered; hence, the symbol of the Christian religion; and hence, (*fig*) the religion itself; an ornament or medallion in the form of a cross; a monument with a cross on it to excite devotion, such as were formerly set in marketplaces; a focal point in a town where a monument in the form of a cross stands or once stood; any figure, mark or sign in the form of a cross or formed by two lines crossing each other, such as the mark made instead of a signature by those who cannot write; anything that thwarts, obstructs or perplexes; hindrance, vexation, misfortune or opposition; a mixing of breeds; a hybrid.—*adj* transverse; passing from side to side; falling athwart; adverse; thwarting; untoward; perverse; intractable; peevish; fretful; ill-humoured; contrary; contradictory; perplexing; made or produced by the opposite party, as a cross question or examination.—*vt* to draw or run a line or lay a body across another; to erase by marking crosses on or over, to cancel (usually with *out* or *through*); to make the sign of the cross on; to pass from side to side of; to pass or move over; to thwart, obstruct, hinder, embarrass; to contradict; to counteract; to clash with; to be inconsistent with; to cause to interbreed; to mix the breed of; to draw two lines across (a cheque) and write between the words 'and Co' as security that the sum shall be paid to the proper party.—*vi* to lie or be athwart; to move or pass across.—**to cross one's path** to thwart or oppose one's interest, purpose, designs, etc; to stand in one's way; to meet.

crossbill *n* a bird of several species belonging to the finch family, the mandibles curving opposite ways and crossing each other at the points.

crossbow *n* an ancient weapon formed by placing a bow crosswise on a stock.

cross-country *adj* across fields; denoting a sport (e.g. racing or skiing) across country.

cross-examination *n* the examination or interrogation of a witness called by one party by the opposite party or his or her counsel.

cross-examine *vt* to examine a witness of one party by the opposite party in the suit or his counsel.

cross-fertilize *vt* to fertilize (a plant) with pollen from another.

crossfire *n* converging gunfire from two or more positions; animated debate or argument.

crosshatch *vt* to shade with crossed lines.

crossing *n* the act of one who crosses; an intersection; a place specially set apart or adapted for passing across, as on a street or line of rails.

cross-purpose *n* a contrary purpose; a misunderstanding; an inconsistency; (*pl*) a sort of conversational game consisting in the mixing up of questions and answers.—**to be at cross-purposes** to misunderstand each other and so to act counter without intending it.

cross-question *vt* to cross-examine.

cross-reference *n* a reference from one part of a book to another where additional information on the subject is to be had.

crossroad *n* a road that crosses another or the place where one road intersects another.

cross section *n* strictly, the cutting of any body at right angles to its length but often used to denote the area of the surface thus exposed; a random selection of the population.

crosstalk *n* interference in lines of communication, especially telephone lines; a quick-witted flow of conversation; repartee.

crosstree *n* (*naut*) one of two horizontal pieces of timber at the upper ends of the lower and top masts, to sustain the frame of the tops and extend the shrouds.

crossword puzzle *n* a diagram of squares, each of which, except certain blanks, is to be filled with a letter so that the words formed, when read down and across, correspond to definitions given.

crotch *n* a fork or forking; the parting of two branches; the region of the body where the legs fork, the genital area.

crotchet *n* a perverse fancy; (*print*) a bracket; (*mus*) a black-faced note with a stem equal to a half minim.

crotchety *adj* full of crotchets; whimsical; fanciful; odd; cross; ill-tempered.

croton *n* a genus of East Indian shrubs from the seeds of which is extracted an oil formerly used as an extreme purgative.

crouch *vi* to bend down; to stoop low; to lie close to the ground, as an animal; to bend servilely; to cringe.—*vt* to bend or cause to bend down.

croup[1] *n* a disease mostly attacking children and consisting of inflammation of the windpipe, accompanied with a short barking cough and difficulty in breathing.

croup[2] *n* the rump or buttocks of certain animals, especially of a horse; hence, the place behind the saddle.

croupier *n* one who superintends and collects the money at a gaming table.

crow *n* the general name of such conical-beaked birds as the raven, rook, jackdaw, carrion crow, hooded crow, etc, usually black and having a harsh, croaking cry; the cry of the cock; a crowbar.—**as the crow flies** in a straight forward direction , resembling the flight of the crow.—*vi* (*pret* **crowed** or **crew**, *pp* **crowed**, *ppr* **crowing**) to cry or make a noise as a cock in joy, gaiety or defiance; to boast in triumph; to vaunt; to swagger; to utter a sound expressive of pleasure, as a young child.

crowbar *n* a bar of iron with a bent and sometimes forked end, used as a lever for forcing open doors or raising weights.

crowd *n* a number of persons or things collected or closely pressed together; a number of persons congregated without order; a throng; the populace; a mob.—*vt* to press into a crowd; to drive together; to fill by pressing numbers together without order; to fill to excess; to throng; to press upon; to encumber or annoy by multitudes or excess of numbers.—*vi* to press in numbers; to swarm; to press or urge forward.

crown *n* an ornament for the head, in the form of a wreath or garland, worn as a symbol of honour, victory, joy, etc; a rich head covering of gold, gems, etc, worn by monarchs on state occasions as a badge of sovereignty; hence, regal power; royalty; kingly government or executive authority; the wearer of a crown; the sovereign, as head of the state; honorary distinction; reward; honour; completion; accomplishment; highest or most perfect state; acme; the top part of anything, as of the head, or of a covering for the head, of a mountain or other elevated object; the portion of a tooth which appears above the gum; the end of the shank of an anchor or the point from which the arms proceed; a coin of ancient times stamped with a crown; paper

crossbill

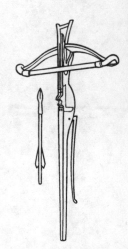

crossbow

of a particular size, so called from formerly having the watermark of a crown.—*vt* to cover, decorate or invest with, or as if with, a crown; hence, to invest with regal dignity and power; to honour; to reward; to dignify; to form the topmost or finishing part of; to terminate or finish; to complete; to consummate; to perfect.—*adj* relating to, pertaining to or connected with the crown or government.

crown court *n* in England and Wales, a judicial court held periodically to hear cases (formerly called *assize*).

crowning *adj* forming the crown or summit; completing; perfecting; final.

crown prince *n* the prince royal who is apparently successor to the crown.

crow's-feet *npl* wrinkles under and around the outer corners of the eyes.

crow's-nest *n* a platform fitted up on the main-topmast crosstrees of a sailing vessel for the shelter of the lookout.

crozier *n* a long staff surmounted by an ornamental cross or crucifix, borne by or before an archbishop on solemn occasions; also (and more properly) a bishop's pastoral staff terminating in a crook.

cruet

crucial *adj* relating to or like a cross; having the shape of a cross; transverse; intersecting; trying or searching, as if bringing to the cross; decisive (*a crucial experiment*); essential; very important; critical.

crucifer *n* a plant belonging to a very extensive order, all the members of which have flowers with six stamens, two of which are short, and four sepals and petals, the spreading limbs of which form a cross.

cruciform *adj* cross-shaped.

crucible *n* a heat-resistant container for melting ores, etc; a rigorous test.

crucifix *n* a cross with the figure of Christ crucified on it.

crucifixion *n* the act of nailing or fastening a person to a cross, for the purpose of putting him to death

Crucifixion *n* the death of Christ by crucifixion; a representation of this.

crucify *vt* (**crucified, crucifying**) to nail to a cross; to put to death by nailing the hands and feet to a cross or gibbet, sometimes by fastening a criminal to a cross with cords.

Crucifixion

crud *n* a deposit of encrusted dirt; excrement; anything dirty or filthy; anything disgusting; a contemptible person; radioactive waste.

crude *adj* raw; not cooked; in its natural state; not altered, refined or prepared by any artificial process (*crude oil*); not brought to perfection; unfinished; rough; lacking polish; not well formed, arranged or prepared (notions, plan, theory); vulgar; coarse.

crudités *npl* coarsely chopped salad vegetables usually dipped in a cold sauce before being eaten.

cruel *adj* disposed to give pain to others in body or mind; lacking pity, compassion or kindness; hard-hearted (applied to persons); exhibiting or proceeding from cruelty; causing pain, grief or distress; inhuman; tormenting, vexing or afflicting.

cruelty *n* the state or character of being cruel; savage or barbarous disposition; any act which inflicts unnecessary pain; a wrong; an act of great injustice or oppression.

cruet *n* a small bottle for holding vinegar, oil, etc.

cruise *vi* (**cruised, cruising**) to sail hither and thither or to rove on the ocean in search of an enemy's ships for capture, for protecting commerce, for pleasure or any other purpose; to go on a cruise; to move at the most efficient speed for sustained travel; (*colloq*) to wander the streets in search of a sexual partner.—*n* a voyage made in various courses; a sailing to and fro, as in search of an enemy's ships or for pleasure; a pleasure voyage on a ship which visits various ports.

cruise missile *n* a kind of subsonic, low-flying guided missile.

cruiser *n* a person or a ship that cruises; an armed ship that sails to and fro for capturing an enemy's ships, for protecting commerce or for plunder; a man-of-war less heavily armoured than a battleship.

crumb *n* a small fragment or piece; usually, a small piece of bread or other food, broken or cut off; the soft part of bread, opposed to crust; a very small piece.—*vt* to break into small pieces with the fingers; to cover (meat, etc) with breadcrumbs.

crumble *vt* (**crumbled, crumbling**) to break into crumbs or small pieces.—*vi* to fall into small pieces, as something friable; to moulder; to become frittered away; to disintegrate.

crummy *adj* (*colloq*) of very poor quality, dirty; squalid; rather ill.

crumpet *n* a sort of muffin; a kind of soft cake with holes in one side; a sexually attractive man or woman.

crumple *vt* (**crumpled, crumpling**) to draw or press into wrinkles or folds; to rumple; to crease.—*vi* to rumple; to crease; to contract; to shrink; to shrivel.

crunch *vt* to crush with the teeth; to chew with violence and noise.

crupper *n* the buttocks of a horse; a strap of leather buckled to a saddle and passing under a horse's tail to prevent the saddle from sliding forward on to the horse's neck.

crural *adj* belonging to the leg.

crusade *n* a enterprise undertaken through enthusiasm, especially for the defence of a

cause or for the advancement of an idea.—
vi (**crusaded, crusading**) to engage in a
crusade.

Crusade *n* a military expedition under the
banner of the cross, undertaken by Christians in the eleventh, twelfth and thirteenth
centuries, for the recovery of the Holy
Land from the power of infidels or Muslims.

crusader *n* a person engaged in a crusade.

cruse *n* a small cup; a bottle or cruet.

crush *vt* to press and bruise between two
hard bodies; to squeeze so as to force out
of the natural shape; to press with violence; to force together into a mass; to beat
or force down, by pressure, with breaking
or bruising; to bruise and break into fine
particles by beating or grinding; to comminute; to subdue or conquer beyond resistance.—*vi* to press, bruise or
squeeze.—*n* a violent pressing or squeezing; the act or effect of anything that
crushes; violent pressure caused by a
crowd; a crowding or being crowded together; a drink made from crushed fruit;
(*colloq*) a large party; (*colloq*) an infatuation.

crushing *adj* having the power to crush;
overwhelming.

crust *n* a hard or comparatively hard external coat or covering; a hard coating on a
surface; the hard outside portion of a loaf;
pastry; an encrustation; a deposit from
wine, as it ripens, collected on the interior
of bottles, etc; (*colloq*) means of livelihood.—*vt* to cover with a crust; to spread
over with hard matter; to encrust.—*vi* to
gather or form into a crust.

crustacean *n* a member of an important division of animals, comprising crabs, lobsters, crayfish, shrimp, etc.

crusty *adj* like crust; of the nature of a
crust; pertaining to a hard covering; hard;
peevish; snappish; surly.

crutch *n* a staff with a curving crosspiece at
the head, to be placed under the arm or
shoulder to support the lame in walking;
any fixture or adjustment of similar form
(used in various technical meanings);
something that supports; a prop; the
crotch.

crux *n* (*pl* **cruxes, cruces**) the essential
point; the deciding point; a difficult problem.

cry *vi* (**cried, crying**) to utter in a loud
voice; to speak, call or exclaim with vehemence; to utter in a loud voice in earnest
request or prayer; to lament; to weep or
shed tears; to give public notice in a loud
voice; to utter a loud inarticulate sound, as
a dog or other animal.—*vt* to utter loudly;
to sound abroad; to proclaim; to name
loudly and publicly, so as to give notice
regarding; to advertise by crying.—**to cry**

off to cancel; to renege on.—**to cry out
for** to be in dire need of.—*n* any loud
sound articulate or inarticulate uttered by
the mouth of an animal; a loud or vehement sound uttered in weeping or sorrow;
a fit of weeping; an exclamation as of
pain, triumph, etc; clamour.

crying *adj* claiming notice; calling for attention or action (*a crying need*); distressing, terrible (*a crying shame*).

cryogenics *n* a branch of physics which
studies phenomena at very low temperatures.

cryosurgery *n* surgery involving freezing to
destroy or remove diseased tissue.

crypt *n* a subterranean cell or cave, especially one constructed for the interment of
bodies; that part of a cathedral, church,
etc, below the floor, set apart for monumental purposes and sometimes used as a
chapel.

cryptic *adj* hidden; secret; occult; obscure.

cryptogam *n* any of those plant which do
not bear true flowers, consisting of stamens and pistils and which are divided
into *cellular* and *vascular cryptogams*, the
former including algae, fungi, lichens,
mosses, etc, the latter the ferns, horsetails,
etc.

cryptogram *n* something written in secret
characters or cipher.

crystal *n* a kind of glass more perfect in its
composition and manufacture than common glass; hence, collectively, all articles,
as decanters, cruets, etc, made of this material; (*chem, mineral*) an inorganic body,
which, by the operation of affinity, has assumed the form of a regular solid, terminated by a certain number of plane and
smooth surfaces.—*adj* consisting of crystal or like crystal; clear; transparent; pellucid.

crystal ball *n* a ball of crystal or glass into
which fortune tellers gaze, supposedly to
help them tell the future.

crystal detector *n* a detector of electromagnetic waves which depends on the property some crystals have of rectifying an
oscillating current by allowing it to pass
more readily in one direction than the
other.

crystalline *adj* consisting of crystal; relating or pertaining to crystals or
crystallography; resembling crystal; pure;
clear; transparent; pellucid.

crystalline lens *n* a lens-shaped pellucid
body situated in the anterior part of the eye
and serving to produce that refraction of
the rays of light which is necessary to
cause them to meet in the retina and form a
perfect image there.

crystallization *n* the act of crystallizing or
forming crystals; the act or process of becoming crystallized so that crystals are

crutch

produced with a determinate and regular form according to the nature of the substance; a body formed by the process of crystallizing.

crystallize *vt* (**crystallized, crystallizing**) to cause to form crystals; to make definite; to coat with sugar crystals.—*vi* to be converted into a crystal; to become solidified, as the separate particles of a substance into a determinate and regular shape; to take definite form or shape.

crystallography *n* the science of crystallization, teaching the principles of the process and the forms and structure of crystals.

crystal set *n* a simple early type of wireless receiving apparatus in which the rectifying agent was a crystal detector.

ctenoid *adj* comb-shaped; having the posterior edge with teeth (said of the scales of certain fishes).

cub *n* the young of certain quadrupeds, as of the lion, bear or fox; a young inexperienced person; a Cub Scout.

cube *n* a solid body that is exactly square; a regular solid body with six equal sides, all squares, and containing equal angles; the product of a number multiplied by itself and that product multiplied by the same number (4 x 4 = 16, and 16 x 4 = 64, the cube of 4).—*vt* (**cubed, cubing**) to raise to the cube or third power by multiplying by itself twice.

cubeb *n* the small spicy berry of a kind of pepper, a native of Java and other East India Isles.

cube root *n* the number or quantity which, multiplied by itself and then by the product, produces the cube (thus 4 is the cube root of 64).

cubic *adj* having the form or properties of a cube; pertaining to the measure of solids (*a cubic foot, cubic contents*).

cubicle *n* a small sleeping compartment, usually one of many which form a dormitory; a compartment in a room or hall for changing clothes, etc.

cubist *n* a follower of an early twentieth-century movement in art who seeks to express the underlying reality and rhythm of nature by the ordered arrangement of three dimensional forms.

cubit *n* formerly, a lineal measure, being the length of a man's arm from the elbow to the extremity of the middle finger.

Cub Scout *n* a member of the junior branch of the Scouting movement.

cucking stool *n* formerly, a chair in which an offender was placed to be hooted at or pelted by the mob, or used for ducking the occupant.

cuckold *n* a husband whose wife commits adultery.

cuckoo *n* a migratory bird remarkable for its striking call and its habit of depositing its eggs in the nests of other birds.

cucumber *n* an annual plant of the gourd family, extensively cultivated and used in salads and for pickling.

cud *n* the food taken into the first stomach of ruminating animals, afterwards brought up and chewed.—**to chew the cud** (*fig*), to ponder; to reflect; to ruminate.

cuddle *vi* (**cuddled, cuddling**) to lie close; to join in an embrace; to fondle.—*vt* to hug; to fondle; to press close.—*n* a hug; an embrace.

cuddy *n* (*naut*) a cabin abaft and under the poop deck.

cudgel *n* a short thick stick; a club.—**to take up the cudgels** to stand boldly forth in defence.—*vt* (**cudgelled, cudgelling**) to beat with a cudgel or thick stick; to beat in general.—**to cudgel one's brains** to reflect deeply and laboriously.

cue *n* a long roll of hair; a queue; the last words of a speech which the next actor takes as a signal to begin; a hint on which to act; the part which any person is to play in turn; turn or temper of mind; the straight tapering rod used in playing billiards.

cuff[1] *n* a blow with the fist; a stroke; a box.—*vt* to strike with the fist, as a person; to buffet.

cuff[2] *n* the fold at the end of a sleeve or trouser leg; a loose band worn round the wrist.

cuirass *n* a breastplate; a piece of defensive armour made of metal or leather covering the chest and back.

cuirassier *n* historically, a soldier who wore a cuirass or breastplate.

cuisine *n* manner or style of cooking; cookery; the food cooked.

Culdee *n* one of an ancient order of monks who formerly lived in Scotland, Ireland and Wales.

cul-de-sac *n* (*pl* **culs-de-sac, cul-de-sacs**) a place that has no thoroughfare; a blind alley; any natural cavity, bag or tubular vessel open only at one end.

culinary *adj* relating to the art of cooking; used in kitchens.

cull *vt* to pick out; to separate one or more things from others; to select from many; to pick up; to collect.

culm *n* (*bot*) the jointed stem of grasses, which is herbaceous in most but woody and tree-like in the bamboo.

culminate *vi* (**culminated, culminating**) to be in the highest point of altitude, as a planet; to reach the highest point, as of rank, power, size, numbers or quality; to come to the highest point.

culmination *n* the transit of a heavenly body over the meridian or highest point of altitude for the day; (*fig*) the highest or most brilliant or important point.

culpable *adj* deserving censure; blameable; blameworthy.

cub

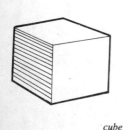

cube

culprit *n* a person arraigned in court for a crime; a criminal; a wrongdoer.

cult *n* a system of religious belief and worship; the rites and ceremonies employed in worship; a religion regarded as unorthodox; its body of adherents; a fashion.

cultivate *vt* (**cultivated, cultivating**) to till; to prepare for crops; to manure, plough, dress, sow and reap; to raise or produce by tillage; to improve by labour or study; to refine and improve; to labour to promote and increase; to cherish; to foster (*to cultivate a taste for poetry*); to devote study, labour or care to; to study (*to cultivate literature*); to study to conciliate or gain over; to labour to make better; to civilize; to try to get to know (someone); to seek the company of.

cultivation *n* the act or practice of cultivating; husbandry; study, care and practice directed to improvement or progress; the state of being cultivated or refined; culture; refinement.

cultivator *n* one who cultivates; especially, a farmer or agriculturist; a machine for breaking up the soil.

culture *n* training or discipline by which a person's moral and intellectual nature is raised; the result of such training; enlightenment; civilization; refinement; appreciation or understanding of the arts; the beliefs and customs, etc, of a group, especially racial or social; the cultivation of plants or breeding of animals by scientific means to improve or establish a new strain; a growth of bacteria in a prepared substance for study and as experiment.

cultured *adj* cultivated; having culture; refined; having an appreciation or understanding of the arts; artificially produced (*cultured pearls*).

culvert *n* an arched drain of brickwork or masonry carried under a road, railway, canal, etc, for the passage of water.

cumber *vt* to hamper; to burden; to check, stop or retard.

cumbersome *adj* troublesome; burdensome; embarrassing; vexatious; unwieldy; unmanageable.

cumin, cummin *n* a plant found wild in Egypt and Syria and cultivated for its aromatic seeds.

cummerbund *n* a sash worn as a waistband with a dinner jacket.

cumulate *vt* (**cumulated, cumulating**) to form a heap of; to heap together; to accumulate.

cumulative *adj* forming a mass; aggregated; increasing in force, weight or effect by successive additions (arguments, evidence).

cumulus *n* (*pl* **cumuli**) a cloud which assumes the form of dense convex or conical heaps resting on a flattish base.

cuneal *adj* having the form of a wedge.

cuneate *adj* wedge-shaped; cuneiform.

cuneiform *adj* having the shape or form of a wedge; wedge-shaped; describing the arrow-headed inscriptions found on old Babylonian and Persian monuments from the characters resembling a wedge.

cunning *adj* skilful; ingenious; shrewd; sly; crafty; astute; designing; subtle.—*n* skill; artifice; artfulness; craft; deceitfulness or deceit; fraudulent skill or dexterity.

cup *n* a small bowl-shaped container, usually with a handle, to drink from; a chalice; the contents of a cup; the liquid contained in a cup or that it may contain; the amount a cup holds; anything formed like a cup (*the cup of an acorn, of a flower*); an ornamental cup used as a trophy.—**in one's cups** intoxicated; tipsy.—*vt* (**cupped, cupping**) to curve the hands round like a cup; to perform the operation of cupping on.

cupboard *n* a cabinet with shelves to hold cups, plates, dishes, food, etc.

cupel *n* a small, shallow, porous, cup-like vessel, generally made of bone ash pressed into a mould and used in refining metals.

cupellation *n* the refining of gold or silver by a cupel.

Cupid *n* the god of love; (*fig*) love.

cupidity *n* an eager desire to possess something; unlawful desire, especially of wealth or power; avarice; covetousness.

cupola *n* (*archit*) a spherical vault on the top of an edifice; a dome or the round top of a dome; the round top of any structure, as of a furnace; the furnace itself.

cupping *n* (*surg*) formerly, blood-letting performed by scarifying into a glass (called a *cupping glass*) from which the air has been exhausted.

cupreous, cuprous *adj* coppery; consisting of copper; resembling copper.

cupric *adj* of or belonging to copper.

cupriferous *adj* producing or containing copper.

cuprite *n* the red oxide of copper; red copper ore.

cur *n* a dog, usually a mongrel and often savage; a worthless or contemptible man.

curable *adj* capable of being healed or cured; having a possible remedy.

curaçoa *n* a liqueur or cordial flavoured with orange peel.

curacy *n* the office or employment of a curate.

curare, curari *n* a brown-black resinous substance obtained from a small tropical tree, forming a deadly poison.

curassow *n* one of several species of birds found in the warmer parts of America, about the size of turkeys and easily domesticated and reared.

curate *n* a clergyman in episcopal churches who is employed to perform divine service

a cuneate leaf

a crested curassow

in the place of the incumbent, parson or vicar.

curative *adj* relating to the cure of diseases; tending to cure.

curator *n* one who has the care and superintendence of anything, as a public library, museum, fine art collection, etc; (*Scots law*) a guardian.

curb *vt* to check, restrain, hold back; to keep in subjection; to restrain (a horse) with a curb; to guide and manage by the reins; to strengthen by a kerbstone.—*n* what checks, restrains or holds back; restraint; check; hindrance; a chain or strap attached to a bridle and passing under the horse's lower jaw, against which it is made to press tightly when the rein is pulled; the edge stone of a pavement; a kerb.

curd *n* the coagulated or thickened part of milk; the coagulated part of any liquid.

curdle *vi* (**curdled, curdling**) to coagulate or concrete; to thicken or change into curd; to run slow with terror; to freeze; to congeal.—*vt* to change into curd; to coagulate; to congeal or make run slow.

curlew

cure *n* care; the spiritual charge and welfare of a parish; remedial treatment of disease; method of medical treatment; remedy for disease; restorative; that which heals; a healing; restoration to health from disease and to soundness from a wound.—*vt* (**cured, curing**) to restore to health or to a sound state; to heal; to remove or put an end to by remedial means; to heal, as a disease; to remedy; to prepare for preservation, as by drying, salting, etc.—*vi* to effect a cure.

curé *n* a curate; a parson.

curfew *n* a bell formerly rung in the evening as a signal to retire to rest; a regulation imposing restriction of movement at a certain time of night.

curia *n* (*pl* **curiae**) the Roman see in its temporal aspect, including the pope, cardinals, etc.

curie *n* a standard of radioactivity, being the quantity of radium emanation in equilibrium with 1 gram of radium.

curio *n* (*pl* **curios**) a curiosity; a small interesting article or object.

curiosity *n* the state or feeling of being curious; a strong desire to see something novel or to discover something unknown; inquisitiveness; a curious or singular object.

curious *adj* strongly desirous to discover what is novel or unknown; anxious to see or to know things; inquisitive; addicted to research or inquiry; singular; exciting surprise; awakening curiosity; odd or strange.

curl *vt* to bend or twist circularly; to bend or form into ringlets; to crimp (the hair); to writhe; to twist; to coil; to curve; to raise in breaking waves or undulations.—*vi* to bend or twist in curls or ringlets; to move

in or form curves or spirals; to rise in waves; to writhe; to twist; to play at the game of curling.—*n* a ringlet of hair or anything of a like form; something curled or bent round; a waving; sinuosity; flexure.

curler *n* one who or that which curls; one who engages in the sport of curling.

curlew *n* a bird allied to the snipe and woodcock with a long, slender, curved bill, longish legs and a short tail, frequenting moors and also the seaside.

curling *n* a winter sport on the ice (especially originally in Scotland), in which contending parties slide large smooth circular stones from one mark to another, called the tee.

curling tongs *n* an instrument for curling the hair.

curly *adj* having or forming curls; tending to curl.

curmudgeon *n* an avaricious churlish person; an ill-natured person.

currant *n* a small kind of dried grape, brought in large quantities from Greece; the name of several species of shrubs belonging to the gooseberry family.

currency *n* the state of being current; a passing from person to person; a passing from mouth to mouth among the public; a continual passing from hand to hand, as coin or bills of credit; circulation; that which is in circulation or is given and taken as having value or as representing property; circulating medium (*the currency of a country*).

current *adj* passing from person to person or from hand to hand (report, coin); circulating; common, general or fashionable; generally received, adopted or approved (opinions, beliefs, theories); popular; established by common estimation (*the current value of coin*); fitted for general acceptance or circulation; now passing or at present in its course (*the current month*).—*n* a flowing or passing; a stream; a body of water or air moving in a certain direction; course; progressive motion or movement; connected series; successive course (*the current of events*); general or main course (*the current of opinion*).—**electric current** *n* the passage of electricity from one pole of an apparatus to the other; often used for strength, amount or intensity of current, denoting the quantity of electricity which passes any particular section in unit time: the unit of current is the ampere.

current account *n* a type of bank account from which money is drawn by means of cash cards or writing cheques and which does not usually pay interest.

curricle *n* a chaise or carriage with two wheels, drawn by two horses abreast.

curriculum n (pl **curricula, curriculums**) a specified fixed course of study in a university, academy, school, etc.

curriculum vitae n (pl **curricula vitae**) (often abbreviated to **CV**) a summary of one's career up to the present time.

currier n a person who curries leather or a horse.

curry[1] n a dish of meat, chicken or vegetables originating in India and cooked with a variety of aromatic or hot spices, as cumin, coriander, turmeric, chilli, etc.—vt (**curried, currying**) to cook (meat, chicken, etc) with spices used in curry.

curry[2] vt (**curried, currying**) to dress leather after it is tanned by scraping, cleansing, beating and colouring; to rub and clean (a horse) with a comb.—**to curry favour** to seek favour by kindness, flattery, ingratiation, etc.

currycomb n an iron instrument or comb with very short teeth, for combing and cleaning horses.

curse vt (**cursed, cursing**) to utter a wish of evil against one; to imprecate evil on; to call for mischief or injury to fall on; to execrate; to bring evil to or on; to blast; to blight; to vex, harass or torment with great calamities.—vi to utter imprecations; to use blasphemous or profane language; to swear.—n a malediction; the expression of a wish of evil to another; an imprecation; evil solemnly or in passion invoked on one; that which brings evil or severe affliction; torment; great vexation; condemnation or sentence of divine vengeance on sinners.

cursed adj blasted by a curse; deserving a curse; execrable; hateful; detestable; abominable; wicked; vexatious; troublesome.

cursive adj running; flowing (said of handwriting).

cursor n a flashing indicator on a computer screen indicating position; the transparent slide on a slide-rule.

cursorial adj (of birds, etc) adapted to running.

cursory adj rapid or hurried; hasty; slight; superficial; careless; not exercising close attention (a cursory view, a cursory observer).

curt adj short; concise; brief and abrupt; short and sharp; rude.

curtly adv in a rudely brief manner.

curtail vt to cut off the end or a part of; to make shorter; to dock; to abridge; to diminish.

curtailment n the act of curtailing.

curtain n a hanging cloth or screen before a window that may be moved to admit or exclude the light, conceal or show anything; the movable screen in a theatre serving to conceal the stage from the audience; (pl) death; the end.—vt to enclose or furnish with curtains.

curtain call n in the theatre, a call from the audience for performers to appear to receive applause.

curtain wall n (fort) that part of a rampart which is between the flanks of two bastions or between two gates.

curtness n shortness; conciseness; abruptness, as of manner; rudeness.

curtsy, curtsey n a gesture of respect by women or girls, made by bending the knees and bowing the head.—vi (**curtsied, curtsying** or **curtseyed, curtseying**) to drop or make a curtsy.

curvature n a bending in a regular form; the manner or degree in which a thing is curved.

curve n a bending in a circular form; a bend or flexure such that no part forms a straight line; (geom) a line which may be cut by a straight line in more points than one; a line which changes its direction at every point.—vt (**curved, curving**) to bend into the form of a curve.—vi to have a curved or bent form; to bend round.

curvet n the leap of a horse when it raises both forelegs at once and as they are falling also its hind legs; a gambol; a leap.—vi (**curvetted, curvetting**) to make a curvet; to bound or leap; to prance; to frisk or gambol.—vt to cause to make a curvet.

curvilinear, curvilineal adj having the shape of a curved line; consisting of curved lines; bounded by curved lines.

cushat n the ring dove or wood pigeon.

cushion n a pillow for a seat; a soft pad to be placed on a chair or attached to some kind of seat; any stuffed or padded appliance; the padded side or edge of a billiard table.

cushy adj (colloq) comfortable; easy.

cusp n a sharp projecting point; the point or horn of the crescent moon or other similar point; a prominence on a molar tooth; a projecting point formed by the meeting of curves, as in heads of Gothic windows and panels, etc.

cusped adj furnished with a cusp or cusps; cusp-shaped.

custard n a mixture of milk and eggs, sweetened and baked or boiled, eaten as a pudding.

custard apple n the large, dark-brown, roundish fruit of a West Indian tree, now cultivated in all tropical countries.

custodian n one who has the care or custody of anything, as of a library, public building, etc; one who has charge of a prisoner.

custody n a keeping; a guarding; guardianship; care, watch, inspection, for keeping, preservation or security; restraint of liberty; confinement; imprisonment.

custom n frequent or common use or prac-

curtain

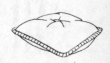

cushion

tice; established manner; habitual practice; a practice or usage; an established and general mode of action, which obtains in a community; practice of frequenting a shop, manufactory, etc, and purchasing or giving orders; tribute, toll or tax; (*pl*) the duties imposed by law on merchandise imported or exported.

customary *adj* according to custom or to established or common usage; wonted; usual; habitual; in common practice.

customer *n* a person who buys from a shop or business, especially regularly; purchaser; a buyer; a dealer; (*colloq*) a person.

custom house *n* a building where the customs on merchandise are paid or secured to be paid, especially at a port.

cutlass

cut *vt* (*pret, pp* **cut**, *ppr* **cutting**) to separate or divide the parts of by an edged instrument; to make an incision in; to sever; to sever and cause to fall for the purpose of removing; to fell, as wood; to mow or reap, as corn; to sever and remove, as the nails or hair; to fashion by, or as by, cutting or carving; to hew out; to carve; to wound the sensibilities of; to affect deeply; to intersect; to cross (*one line cuts another*); to have no longer anything to do with; to quit; to shun the acquaintance of; to edit film.—*vi* to do the work of an edged tool; to serve in dividing or gashing; to admit of incision or severance; to use a knife or edge tool; to divide a pack of cards, to determine the deal or for any other purpose; to move off rapidly; (in cinema) to switch abruptly to another scene; to stop photographing.—**to cut back** to prune (vegetation); to reduce expenditure; to economize.—**to cut the teeth** to have the teeth pierce the gums.—**to cut one's teeth on** to practise on or obtain early experience from.—*n* the opening made by an edged instrument; a gash; a notch; a wound; a stroke or blow as with an edged instrument; a sharp stroke or blow, as with a whip; anything that wounds one's feelings deeply, as sarcasm, criticism or act of discourtesy; a part cut off from the rest; a reduction in expenditure; a passage cut out or off; the block on which a picture is carved and by which it is impressed; the impression from such a block; the act of dividing a pack of cards; manner in which a thing is cut; form; shape; fashion; the act of passing a person without recognizing him or her or of avoiding him or her so as not to be recognized in turn; a share, e.g. of profits.

cutlery

cutaneous *adj* belonging to the skin; existing on or affecting the skin.

cutback *n* a reduction in expenditure.

cute *adj* acute; clever; sharp.

cuticle *n* (*anat*) the transparent skin at the base of the fingernail or toenail; the epi-

dermis; (*bot*) the thin external covering of the bark of a plant; the outer pellicle of the epidermis.

cutis *n* (*pl* **cutis, cutises**) (*anat*) the dense resisting skin which forms the general envelope of the body below the cuticle; the dermis or true skin.

cutlass *n* a broad curving sword formerly used by seamen, etc.

cutler *n* one whose occupation is to make or deal in knives and other cutting instruments; one who sharpens or repairs cutlery; a knife-grinder.

cutlery *n* the business of a cutler; edged or cutting instruments; implements, such as knives, forks and spoons, for eating food.

cutlet *n* a piece of meat, especially lamb, cut for cooking; generally a part of the rib with the meat belonging to it.

cut-off *n* that which cuts off or shortens; that which is cut off; the limit or point at which something ends or is completed; a device in some engines for switching them off by stopping the flow of air, fuel, steam, etc.

cut-out *n* (*elect*) a device to break the electrical continuity of a circuit when the current is excessive.

cutpurse *n* a pickpocket; a thief; a robber.

cutter *n* one who or that which cuts; one who cuts out cloth for garments according to measurements; (*naut*) a small boat used by ships of war; a vessel rigged nearly like a sloop, with one mast and a straight running bowsprit.

cutthroat *n* a murderer; an assassin; a folding razor with a long blade.—*adj* murderous; cruel; barbarous; merciless; (of prices) highly competitive.

cutting *adj* penetrating or dividing by the edge; serving to penetrate or divide; sharp; piercing the heart; wounding the feelings; sarcastic; satirical; severe.—*n* the act or operation of one who cuts; a piece cut off; a portion of a plant from which a new one is propagated; an excavation made through a hill or rising ground in constructing a road, railway, canal, etc; a piece cut from a newspaper article, etc.

cuttlebone *n* the internal calcareous plate of the cuttlefish, used for polishing wood and by caged birds to sharpen their beaks.

cuttlefish *n* a two-gilled mollusc having a body enclosed in a sac, eight arms or feet covered with suckers, used in locomotion and for seizing prey, a calcareous internal shell and a bag or sac from which the animal has the power of ejecting a black ink-like fluid (sepia) so as to darken the water and conceal it from pursuit.

cutty *n* short tobacco pipe.

cutty stool *n* formerly, a stool of repentance or of discipline in old Scottish ecclesiastical penance.

cutwater *n* the forepart of a ship's prow which cuts the water; the lower portion of the pier of a bridge formed with an angle or edge directed up stream.

CV an abbreviation of **curriculum vitae**.

cyan *n* a blue colour, one of the primary colours.

cyanic *adj* of or pertaining to the colour blue or azure; (*chem*) containing cyanogen (*cyanic acid*, *cyanic ether*).

cyanide *n* a combination of cyanogen with a metallic base and highly poisonous.

cyanide of potassium *n* a poisonous substance used in photography and electrotyping.

cyanide process *n* a method of extracting gold from its ores by treatment with dilute potassium cyanide.

cyanogen *n* a colourless poisonous gas burning with a purple flame and with the odour of peach blossom.

cyanosis *n* a disease in which the skin has a blue tint arising from the mingling of the venous and the arterial blood through defect in the heart.

cybernetics *n* the study of communication and control functions in living organisms and in mechanical and electronic systems.

cyclamen *n* one of a European genus of low-growing herbaceous plants with fleshy root stocks and very handsome flowers, several of them being favourite spring-flowering greenhouse plants; a reddish-purple colour.

cycle *n* a circle or orbit in the heavens; a circle or round of years or a period of time in which a certain succession of events or phenomena is completed; any complete period or course; a series of events which are repeated in a regular order; the aggregate of legendary or traditional lore accumulated round some mythical or heroic event or character (as the siege of Troy or King Arthur); a series of poems or songs; a bicycle or similar conveyance; (*elect, engin*) a set of changes after which initial conditions are restored. In any alternating phenomenon, the number of cycles (per second) is the number of periods per second, called the frequency.—*vi* (**cycled, cycling**) to use a bicycle or similar conveyance.

cyclic *adj* pertaining to or moving in a cycle or circle; connected with a cycle in the sense it has in literature.

cyclical *adj* pertaining to a cycle; cyclic.

cyclist *n* one who uses a cycle.

cycloid *n* a curve generated by a point in the circumference of a circle when the circle is rolled along a straight line and kept always in the same plane.

cyclone *n* a circular or rotary storm of immense force, revolving at an enormous rate round a calm centre and at the same time advancing at a rate varying from 2 to 30 miles an hour: in the northern hemisphere they rotate from right to left and in the southern from left to right.

cyclonic *adj* relating to a cyclone.

~~cyclopedia, cyclopaedia~~ *n* an encyclopedia.

cyclopedic, cyclopaedic *adj* belonging to an encyclopedia.

cyclopedist, cyclopaedist *n* a writer in an encyclopedia; a compiler of an encyclopedia.

Cyclops *n* (*pl* **Cyclopes, Cyclopses**) in classical mythology, one of a race of giants who had one circular eye in the middle of the forehead.

Cyclopean *adj* pertaining to the Cyclops; vast; gigantic.

cyclostyle *n* an apparatus for printing copies of writings from a stencil plate cut by a pen with a small toothed wheel.

cyclotron *n* a device which accelerates charged particles, used in nuclear research.

cygnet *n* a young swan.

cylinder *n* a body shaped like a roller; an elongated, round, solid body of uniform diameter throughout its length and terminating in two flat circular surfaces which are equal and parallel; the piston chamber of an engine; in certain printing machines, a roller by which the impression is made and on which plates are secured.

cylindrical, cylindric *adj* having the form of a cylinder or having its properties.

cyclorama *n* a series of moving pictures extended circularly so as to appear in natural perspective to the viewer standing in the centre; a painting or a series of paintings on the interior surface of a round or cylindrical wall, the point of view being in the axis of the cylinder.

cyma *n* (*pl* **cymae, cymas**) (*archit*) a moulding of a cornice, the profile of which is a double curve, concave joined to convex; an ogee moulding; (*bot*) a cyme.

cymbal *n* a musical instrument, circular and hollow like a dish, made of brass or bronze, two of which are struck together, producing a sharp ringing sound.

cyme *n* (*bot*) an inflorescence in which the flowers are in racemes, corymbs or umbels, the successive central flowers expanding first.

cymophane *n* a siliceous gem of a yellowish-green colour, the same as chrysoberyl.

Cymric *adj* of or pertaining to the Cymry, the name given to themselves by the Welsh; Welsh; pertaining to the ancient race to which the Welsh belong.—*n* the language of the Cymry or ancient Britons; Welsh.

cynic *n* one who is always sceptical about other people and their actions and motives; one who has no belief or trust in

cygnet

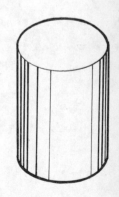

cylinder

goodness, honesty, sincerity; one of a sect of ancient Greek philosophers.

cynical *adj* sceptical about people and their motives; lacking belief in goodness, honesty, sincerity, etc; derisive.

cynicism *n* the practice of a cynic; the state of being cynical.

cynosure *n* an old name of the constellation Ursa Minor or the Little Bear, which contains the Pole Star and thus has long been noted by mariners and others; hence, anything that strongly attracts attention; a centre of attraction.

cypress *n* the popular name of any of a genus of coniferous trees, some species of which have attained much favour in shrubberies and gardens as ornamental evergreen trees, while the wood of others is highly valued for its durability; the emblem of mourning for the dead, cypress branches being used in ancient times at funerals.

cyprine *adj* pertaining to the carp or allied fishes.

Cyrillic *adj* the term applied to an alphabet adopted by all the Slavonic peoples belonging to the Eastern Church.

cyst *n* a closed sac or bag of vegetable or animal nature; a bladder-like body; a hollow organ with thin walls (as the urinary bladder); an abnormal closed bladder-like bag or vesicle containing fluid in animal bodies.

cystic *adj* pertaining to or contained in, a cyst; having cysts; formed in or shaped like a cyst.

cysticercus *n* (*pl* **cysticerci**) in tapeworms, a simple cyst with only one head.

cystic fibrosis *n* a congenital disorder involving chronic respiratory and digestive problems.

cystitis *n* inflammation of the bladder.

cytoblast *n* (*biol*) the nucleus, cellule or centre from which the organic cell is developed.

cytogenesis *n* (*biol*) the development of cells in animal and vegetable structures.,

cytology *n* the biological doctrine of cells; the study of cells.

cytoplasm *n* the substance of a cell, as opposed to its nucleus.

czar *n* same as **tsar**.

czarina *n* same as **tsarina**.

Czech *n* a native of the Czech Republic; the language of the Czech Republic.

D

D is the fourth letter in the English alphabet and the third consonant, representing a dental sound; as a numeral equivalent to 500; (*mus*) the second note of the natural scale, answering to the French and Italian *re*.

dab *vt* (**dabbed, dabbing**) to strike quickly but lightly with the hand or with some soft or moist substance.—*n* a gentle blow with the hand or some soft substance; a quick but light blow; an expert; a small lump or mass of anything soft or moist; a name common to many species of the flatfishes, but especially to a kind of flounder which is common in many parts of the British coast.

dabble *vt* (**dabbled, dabbling**) to wet; to moisten; to spatter; to sprinkle.—*vi* to play in water, as with the hands; to splash in mud or water; to do or engage in anything in a slight or superficial manner; to occupy oneself with slightly; to dip into; to meddle.

dabbler *n* one who dabbles in water or mud; one who engaged in something in a superficial way.

dabchick *n* the little grebe, a small swimming bird of the diver family.

dab hand *n* (*colloq*) an expert, a person who is very good at something.

da capo *adj, adv* (*mus*) a direction to repeat from the beginning of a passage or section.

dace *n* a small river fish resembling the roach, chiefly inhabiting the deep and clear waters of quiet streams.

dachshund *n* badger dog; a long-bodied, short-legged dog, with hanging ears and short hair.

dacoit, dakoit *n* an Indian name for robbers who plunder in bands, but seldom take life.

dactyl *n* a poetical foot consisting of three syllables, the first long and the others short, or the first accented, the others not.

dactylic *adj* pertaining to or consisting chiefly or wholly of dactyls.

dad, daddy *n* (*colloq*) father.

daddy-longlegs *n* a name given to species of the cranefly.

dado *n* (*pl* **dadoes, dados**) that part of a pedestal which is between the base and the cornice; the finishing of the lower part of the walls in rooms, made somewhat to represent a continuous pedestal and frequently formed by a lining of wood, by painting, or by a special wallpaper.

daffodil *n* the popular name of a British plant of the amaryllis family with large bright yellow bell-shaped flowers, growing in gardens, woods and meadows; its pale yellow colour.

daft *adj* silly; weak-minded; mad.

dagger *n* a weapon resembling a short sword, with usually a two-edged, sometimes a three-edged, sharp-pointed blade, used for stabbing at close quarters; (*print*) a mark of reference in the shape of a dagger (†).

daguerreotype *n* an early photographic process by which the picture was fixed on a chemically coated metallic plate solely by the action of the sun's actinic or chemical rays; a picture produced by the process.

dahlia *n* a tuberous plant with brightly coloured flowers related to the aster family.

daily *adj* happening, being or appearing every day; done day by day; bestowed or enjoyed every day.—*adv* every day; day by day.—*n* a newspaper published daily.

daintiness *n* the state or quality of being dainty.

dainty *adj* pleasing to the palate; of exquisite taste; delicious, as food; of acute sensibility; careful in selecting what is tender and good; delicate; squeamish; luxurious, as the palate or taste; scrupulous; affectedly fine; nice; ceremonious; elegant; pretty and slight; tender; effeminately beautiful.—*n* something delicate to the taste; that which is delicious; a delicacy.

dairy *n* the place where milk is kept and made into butter and cheese; a shop where milk, butter, etc, are sold.—also used as an *adj*.

dairy farm *n* a farm devoted to the keeping of cows and the sale of dairy produce.

dairymaid *n* a female servant whose busi-

dachshund

daffodil

dairyman

Dalmatian

ness is to milk cows and work in the dairy.

dairyman *n* (*pl* **dairymen**) one who keeps or works in a dairy farm or a dairy.

dais *n* a raised platform on which a speaker stands; the high table at the upper end of an ancient dining hall at which the chief persons sat; the raised floor on which the table stood; the chief seat at the high table, often with a canopy; a canopy.

daisy *n* a common wild plant with flowers of white petals and yellow centres; any similar cultivated plant.

daisy wheel *n* a component of some kinds of printer that carries the letter type to be printed and is shaped like a wheel with a different character at the end of each spike.

dakoit *n* same as **dacoit**.

dale *n* a low place between hills; a vale or valley.

dalesman *n* (*pl* **dalesman**) one living in a dale or valley.

dalliance *n* the act of dallying, caressing, fondling, trifling, deferring or delaying.

dally *vi* (**dallied, dallying**) to waste time in effeminate or voluptuous pleasures; to amuse oneself with idle play; to trifle; to linger; to delay; to toy and wanton; to interchange caresses; to fondle; to sport; to play; to frolic.

Dalmatian *adj* of or pertaining to Dalmatia.—*n* a large dog of a white colour, thickly marked with black rounded spots, usually kept as a coach dog.

dalmatic *n* the vestment used by the deacon at mass and worn also by bishops under the chasuble, long, loose and wide-sleeved.

dal segno (*mus*) a direction to go back to the sign § and repeat from thence to the close.

dam[1] *n* a bank, mound of earth, wall or other structure, built across a current of water, to raise its level for the purpose of driving millwheels or for other purposes.—*vt* (**dammed, damming**) to obstruct by a dam; to confine by constructing a dam.

dam[2] *n* a female parent (used now only of quadrupeds, unless in contempt).

damage *n* any hurt, injury or harm to person, property, character or reputation; the value in money of what is injured, harmed or lost; the estimated money equivalent for detriment or injury sustained (in this sense commonly in plural).—*vt* (**damaged, damaging**) to injure; to impair; to lessen the soundness, goodness or value of.—*vi* to become injured or impaired in soundness or value.

damascene *vt* (**damascened, damascening**) to ornament (particularly iron and steel) with designs produced by inlaying or encrusting with another metal, as gold, silver, etc, by etching, etc.—*n* an article or ornamentation produced in this way; a kind of plum; a damson.

damask *adj* of or belonging to Damascus; of the colour of the rose so called; pink or rosy.—*n* the name given to textile fabrics of various materials, more especially silk and linen ornamented with raised figures of flowers, etc; a pink colour, like that of the damask rose.—*vt* to form or imprint the figures of flowers on, as on cloth; to variegate; to diversify; to adorn with figures, as steelwork.

dame *n* a lady in rank; now more specifically, the wife of a knight or baronet or a member of the first or second class of the Victorian Order or the Order of the British Empire; a woman in general; formerly, the mistress of an elementary school; a comic female role in a pantomime, traditionally played by a male.

dammar *n* a gum or resin used as a colourless varnish and produced by various species of coniferous trees (*dammar* or *dammara pine*) belonging to the South Asiatic islands and New Zealand, kauri gum being a variety.

damn *vt* to consign or send to punishment in a future state; to send to hell; to condemn, censure, castigate severely; to condemn or destroy the success of by common consent, as by hissing in a theatre or by criticisms in the press.—*n* a profane oath; a curse or execration.

damnable *adj* liable to be damned or condemned; deserving damnation; odious, detestable or pernicious.

damnation *n* sentence to punishment in a future state or the state in which such punishment is undergone; eternal punishment; penalty inflicted for sin; condemnation.

damp *adj* being in a state between dry and wet; moderately wet; moist; humid; depressed or dejected.—*n* moist air; humidity; moisture; fog; dejection; depression of spirits; chill; a noxious exhalation issuing from the earth and deleterious or fatal to animal life, such as exists in old disused wells, in mines and coal pits.—*vt* to make damp; to moisten; to chill, deaden, depress or deject; to check or restrain; to discourage; to dispirit; to abate.

dampen *vt* to make damp or moist.—*vi* to grow or become damp.

damper *n* one who or that which damps; an iron plate sliding across a flue of a furnace, etc, to check or regulate the draught of air; a piece of mechanism in a pianoforte which, after the finger has left the key, checks a long-continued vibration of the strings; a cake made of flour and water without fermentation; a depressive influence.

dampness *n* the state or condition of being damp; moistness; humidity.

damsel *n* a young unmarried woman; a maiden; a virgin.

damson *n* a small black, dark-bluish, purple or yellow plum.

dance *vi* (**danced, dancing**) to leap or move with measured steps, regulated by music; to leap and frisk about; to move nimbly, as up and down, backwards and forwards.—*vt* to make to dance; to dandle.—*n* a leaping or stepping with motions of the body adjusted to the measure of a tune; the regular movements of one who dances; a tune by which dancing is regulated; an occasion at which there is dancing.

dandelion *n* a well-known composite plant, having a naked stalk, with one large bright yellow flower and a tapering milky perennial root of laxative and tonic properties.

dandle *vt* (**dandled, dandling**) to shake or jolt on the knee, as an infant; to fondle, amuse or treat as a child; to pet.

dandruff *n* a scurf which forms on the head and comes off in small scales or particles.

dandy *n* a man who pays excessive attention to dress; one who dresses with special finery; a fop; a coxcomb.—*adj* finely or foppishly dressed; foppish; trim.

Dane *n* a native or inhabitant of Denmark.

Danegelt, Danegeld *n* an annual tax laid on the English nation in early times for maintaining forces to oppose the Danes or to furnish tribute to procure peace.

Danish *adj* belonging to the Danes or Denmark.—*n* the language of the Danes.

danger *n* exposure to destruction, ruin, injury, loss, pain or other evil; peril; risk; hazard; jeopardy.

dangerous *adj* attended with danger; perilous; hazardous; unsafe; full of risk; creating danger; causing risk of evil.

dangle *vi* (**dangled, dangling**) to hang loose, flowing, shaking or waving; to hang and swing; to be a humble officious follower, or to hang about a person (with *about* or *after*).—*vt* to cause to dangle; to swing.

dank *adj* damp; moist; humid.

dap *vi* (**dapped, dapping**) to drop or let fall the bait gently into the water in angling.

dapper *adj* small and active; nimble; brisk; lively; neat.

dapple *adj* marked with spots; spotted; variegated with spots of different colours or shades of colour.—*vt* (**dappled, dappling**) to spot; to variegate with spots.

dare *vi* (*pret* **dared** *or* **durst**; *pp* **dared**; *ppr* **daring**) to have courage for any purpose; to make up the mind to undertake something hazardous or dangerous; to be bold enough; to venture.—*vt* (**dared, daring**) to challenge; to provoke; to defy.

daredevil *n* a desperado; one who fears nothing and will attempt anything.

daring *adj* bold; audacious; courageous; intrepid; adventurous.—*n* courage; boldness; fearlessness; audacity.

dark *adj* lacking light; not radiating or reflecting light; wholly or partially black; having the quality opposite to white; gloomy; disheartening; not cheerful; concealed; secret; mysterious; not easily understood; not enlightened with knowledge; rude; ignorant (*the dark ages*); morally black; atrocious; wicked; sinister; keeping designs concealed; not fair (said of the complexion).—*n* darkness; the absence of light; a dark hue; a dark part; secrecy; obscurity; a state of ignorance.

darken *vt* to make dark or black; to deprive of light; to obscure, cloud, make dim; to deprive of vision; to render gloomy; to render ignorant or stupid; to render less clear or intelligible; to make less white or clear; to tan; to sully; to taint.—*vi* to grow dark or darker.

darkness *n* the state or quality of being dark; the lack of physical light; gloom; obscurity; deepness of shade or colour; physical, intellectual or moral blindness; ignorance; sinfulness; secrecy; uncertainty; lack of clearness and intelligibility.

darling *adj* dearly beloved; dear; favourite.—*n* one much beloved; a favourite.

darn *vt* to mend a rent or hole in, by imitating the texture of the cloth or stuff with yarn or thread and a needle; to sew or repair by crossing and recrossing the stitches.—*n* a place mended by darning.

darnel *n* a kind of rye grass.

dart *n* a pointed missile weapon to be thrown by the hand; a short lance; anything which pierces and wounds; a sudden or rapid rush, leap, bound, spring or flight.—*vt* to throw (a dart, etc) with a sudden thrust; to throw swiftly; to shoot.—*vi* to fly, as a dart; to fly rapidly; to spring and run with velocity; to start suddenly and run.

Darwinian *adj* of or pertaining to Charles Darwin (1809–82), the celebrated naturalist.—*n* a believer in Darwinism.

Darwinism *n* the doctrine as to the origin and modifications of the species of animals and plants taught by Darwin.

dash *vt* to cause to strike or come against suddenly and with violence; to strike or throw violently or suddenly; to sprinkle or mix slightly; to disturb or frustrate (*to dash courage*); to confound, confuse, abash.—**to dash off** to form or sketch out in haste carelessly; to execute hastily or with careless rapidity.—*vi* to rush with violence; to strike or be cast violently; to rush.—*n* a violent striking together of two bodies; collision; something thrown into another substance; infusion; admixture; a sudden check; a rapid movement; a sudden onset; the capacity for unhesitating,

dance

dandelion

prompt action; vigour in attack; a flourish or ostentatious parade; a mark or line (—) in writing or printing noting a break or pause.

dashing *adj* impetuous; spirited; showy; brilliant.

dashboard *n* an instrument panel in a car; formerly, a board or leather apron on the forepart of a vehicle to prevent mud, etc, from being thrown on the occupants by the heels of the horses.

dastard *n* a coward; a poltroon; one who meanly shrinks from danger.—*adj* cowardly; meanly; shrinking from danger.

dastardly *adj* cowardly; meanly timid; base; sneaking.

data *npl* (*now frequently treated as sing*) (*sing* **datum**) the facts or information on a subject.

database *n* a large store of computerized information that can be retrieved when required.

data-capture *vt* to convert (information) to a machine-readable form on computer.—*n* the conversion of information to machine-readable form.

date[1] *n* that addition to a writing which specifies the year, month and day when it was given or executed; the time when any event happened, when anything was transacted or when anything is to be done; the period of time at or during which one has lived or anything has existed; era; age; (*colloq*) an appointment to meet someone; (*colloq*) a social engagement, often with a member of the other sex.—*vt* (**dated, dating**) to write down the date on; to append the date to; to note or fix the time of; to go out with (a member of the opposite sex) on a regular basis.—*vi* to reckon time; to begin at a certain date (*to date from the 10th century*); to have a certain date.

date[2] *n* the fruit of the date tree or date palm, consisting of a soft fleshy drupe enclosing a hard seed or stone and having a delicious perfume and taste, much used as food in North Africa and Western Asia.

date palm, date tree *n* a palm having a stem rising to the height of 50 or 60 feet, crowned with large feathery leaves, the female plant bearing a bunch of from 180 to 200 dates.

date rape *n* an instance of rape committed on a woman by her escort while on a date.

dative *adj* (*gram*) a term applied to the case of nouns which usually follows verbs that express giving or the doing of something to or for.—*n* the dative case.

datum *n* (*pl* **data**) a single unit of information; something given or admitted; some fact, proposition, quantity or condition granted or known, from which other facts, propositions, etc, are to be deduced.

daub *vt* to smear with soft adhesive matter, as with mud or slime; to plaster; to soil; to defile; to besmear; to paint coarsely; to lay or put on without taste; to load with affected finery.—*n* a smear or smearing; a rough painting.

daughter *n* a female child of any age; a female descendant; the female offspring of an animal or plant.

daughter-in-law *n* a son's wife.

daunt *vt* to repress or subdue the courage of; to intimidate; to dishearten; to check by fear.

dauntless *adj* bold; fearless; intrepid; not timid; not discouraged.

dauphin *n* the eldest son of the king of France prior to the revolution of 1830.

davit *n* (*naut*) either of the two projecting pieces of wood or iron on the side or stern of a vessel, used for suspending, lowering or hoisting boats by means of pulleys.

Davy lamp *n* a lamp whose flame is surrounded by wire, invented by Sir Humphry Davy to protect miners from explosions of firedamp.

daw *n* a jackdaw.

dawdle *vi* (**dawdled, dawdling**) to waste time; to trifle; to saunter.—*vt* to waste by trifling.

dawdler *n* one who dawdles; a trifler.

dawn *vi* to begin to grow light in the morning; to grow light; to begin to show intellectual light or knowledge; to begin to become visible or appear (*the truth dawns on me*).—*n* the break of day; the first appearance of light in the morning; first opening or expansion; beginning; rise; first appearance (*the dawn of civilization*, etc).

dawning *n* the growing light in the morning; dawn.

day *n* that space of time during which there continues to be light, in contradistinction to night; the time between the rising and setting of the sun; the period of one revolution of the earth on its axis or twenty-four hours; light; sunshine (*in the open day*); any period of time distinguished from other time (*the authors of that day*); age; era; epoch; in the plural often = lifetime, earthly existence; the contest of a day or day of combat (*to gain the day*); an appointed or fixed time; time of commemorating an event; anniversary.

daybook *n* a book in which are recorded the debts and credits or accounts of the day.

daybreak *n* the dawn or first appearance of light in the morning.

daydream *n* a reverie; a visionary fancy indulged in when awake.—*vi* to have one's mind on other things; to fantasize.

dayfly *n* a popular name for those insects which, though they may exist in the larva and pupa state for several years, in their perfect form exist only from a few hours to a few days.

date palm

davit

daylight *n* the light of the day; the light of the sun, as opposed to that of the moon or of a lamp or candle; enlightenment.

dayspring *n* the dawn; the beginning of the day.

daytime *n* the time of daylight.

daze *vt* (**dazed, dazing**) to stun or stupefy, as with a blow, liquor or excess of light; to blind by too strong a light.

dazzle *vt* (**dazzled, dazzling**) to overpower or blind with light; to dim by excess of light; (*fig*) to overpower or confound by splendour or brilliancy or with show or display of any kind.—*vi* to be overpoweringly bright or brilliant; to be overpowered or dimmed by light (as the eyes).—*n* a dazzling light; glitter.

dazzling *adj* so bright as to dazzle; excessively brilliant.

D-Day *n* 6th June 1944, the day the Allied troops landed in Europe in the Second World War, D being the military symbol for the day on which a planned operation is scheduled to begin; a date set aside for an important event.

DDT *n* dichlorodiphenyltrichloroethane, a chemical used as an insecticide, usually in the form of a white powder.

deacon *n* in the Roman and Anglican churches, a member of the lowest of the three orders of clergy (bishops, priests and deacons); in Presbyterian churches, a functionary who attends to the secular interests of the church; among Congregationalists, Baptists and others, one who looks after the spiritual as well as temporal concerns of the congregation under the minister.

dead *adj* deprived, devoid or lacking life; having lost the vital principle; lifeless; inanimate; hence, lacking animation, activity, spirit, vigour; numb; callous; void of perception; resembling death; deep and sound (*a dead sleep*); perfectly still or motionless (*a dead calm*); monotonous; unvarying or unbroken by apertures or projections (*a dead level* or *wall*); unemployed; useless (*dead capital* or *stock*); unreverberating, dull, heavy (*a dead sound*); tasteless, vapid, spiritless, flat, as liquors; producing death; sure or unerring as death (*a dead shot*); in a state of spiritual death; under the power of sin; no longer spoken or in common use by a people (*a dead language*); having no gloss, warmth or brightness (*a dead colour*).—*adv* to a degree approaching death; to the last degree; thoroughly; completely (*dead tired, dead drunk*).

dead beat *adj* (*colloq*) exhausted, very tired.

deaden *vt* to deprive of a portion of vigour, force or sensibility; to abate the vigour or action of; to destroy the acuteness, pun-gency, spirit or brilliancy of; to render dull, flat, heavy or vapid.

dead end *n* a street or passage with one end closed off, a cul-de-sac; a situation in which no progress can be achieved.

dead heat *n* the result, in a contest of speed, when two or more competitors finish at the same time, so that no one is the winner.

dead letter *n* a letter which cannot be delivered from lack of address and which is sent to the post office to be opened and returned to the writer; anything, as a condition, treaty, etc, which has lost its force or authority, by lapse of time or any other cause and has ceased to be acted on.

deadlight *n* (*naut*) a strong wooden shutter for protecting the windows of cabins, etc, in a storm.

deadline *n* the time by which something must be done.

deadlock *n* such a complicated state of affairs as renders action or progress impossible; complete obstruction or standstill.

deadly *adj* causing death; mortal; fatal; destructive; implacable.—*adv* in a manner resembling death (*deadly pale*); mortally; destructively.

deadly nightshade *n* belladonna.

deadpan *adj* without expression or reaction.

dead reckoning *n* the calculation of a ship's place at sea from the distance run by the log and the courses steered by the compass, rectified by allowances for drift, leeway, etc.

dead weight *n* a heavy or oppressive burden.

deaf *adj* lacking the sense of hearing, either wholly or in part; disinclined to hear; inattentive; unheeding; unconcerned.

deafen *vt* to make deaf; to deprive of the power of hearing; to stun; to prevent the passage of sound.

deafness *n* the state of being deaf or of being unable to hear sounds; lack of hearing; unwillingness to hear; inattention.

deaf-mute *n* a person who is both deaf and dumb.

deal *n* a portion or part; an indefinite quantity, degree or extent, generally implying that the amount is considerable (often qualified by *great*, which hardly adds to the sense); the division or distribution of playing cards; a board or plank of fir, of some length and at least 7 inches (17.75 cms) wide; fir or pine timber.—*vt* (**dealt, dealing**) to divide in portions; to give out; to part; to distribute; to scatter; to hurl (blows, destruction).—*vi* to distribute; to traffic; to trade; to negotiate; to transact; to have intercourse; to conduct oneself in relation to others; to act; to behave.

dealer *n* one who deals; one who has to do or has concern with others; a trader, mer-

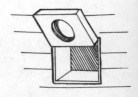

deadlight

daylight

chant or trafficker; one who distributes cards to the players.

dealing *n* conduct; behaviour; practice (*double-dealing*, *fair dealing*); traffic; business; intercourse or business of friendship; concern (commonly in plural).

dean *n* an ecclesiastical dignitary, ranking next to the bishop, who presides over the canons or prebendaries of a cathedral; in some universities, the chief or head of a faculty.

deanery *n* the office or jurisdiction of a dean; the official residence of a dean.

dear *adj* bearing a high price in comparison with the usual price or the real value; high-priced, opposite to cheap; characterized by high prices resulting from scarcity (*a dear year*); greatly valued; beloved; precious; heartfelt; passionate or intense.—*n* a darling; a term of affection or endearment.— *adv* dearly; tenderly; at a dear rate.

dearly *adv* with great affection; at a high price or rate.

dearth *n* scarcity, which makes food dear; lack, or time of lack; famine; lack or absence.

death *n* that state of a being, animal or vegetable, in which there is a total and permanent cessation of all the vital functions; the state of being dead; the state or manner of dying; cause, agent or instrument of death; total loss or extinction (*the death of one's faculties*); capital punishment.

deathblow *n* a blow causing death; a mortal blow; anything which extinguishes hope or blights one's prospects.

death duty *n* a tax paid on the inheritance of property.

deathless *adj* not subject to death, destruction or extinction; undying; immortal.

death rate *n* the proportion of deaths among the inhabitants of a town, country, etc.

death's-head *n* the skull of a human skeleton or a figure representing one.

death warrant *n* an order from the proper authority for the execution of a criminal.

deathwatch *n* a small beetle, the tapping noise made by which is superstitiously supposed to prognosticate death.

debacle *n* a sudden breaking up of ice in a river; (*geol*) a sudden outbreak of water, hurling before it stones and other debris; a confused rout; a sudden irretrievable disaster.

debar *vt* (**debarred, debarring**) to bar or cut off from entrance; to preclude; to hinder from approach, entry or enjoyment; to shut out or exclude.

debase *vt* (**debased, debasing**) to impart a certain baseness to; to reduce or lower in quality, dignity, character, etc; to degrade; to vitiate; to adulterate; to abase.

debatable *adj* capable of being debated; disputable; subject to controversy and contention.

debate *n* an argument or reasoning between persons of different opinions; dispute; controversy; quarrel; strife; contention.— *vt* (**debated, debating**) to discuss by arguments for and against; to dispute; to argue; to contest.—*vi* to discuss disputed points; to examine different arguments in the mind (*to debate with oneself whether*).

debauch *vt* to corrupt or vitiate (as principles, etc); to corrupt with lewdness; to bring to be guilty of unchastity; to seduce; to lead astray from duty or allegiance.—*n* excess or a fit of excess in eating or drinking; intemperance; drunkenness.

debauched *adj* corrupt in morals; given to debauchery; characterized by debauchery.

debauchery *n* excessive indulgence in sensual pleasures of any kind, as gluttony, intemperance, unlawful indulgence of lust.

debenture *n* a deed or document charging certain property with the repayment of money lent by a person therein named and with interest on the sum lent at a given rate; a certificate or drawback of customs duties on the exportation of certain goods.

debilitate *vt* (**debilitated, debilitating**) to weaken; to impair the strength of; to enfeeble; to make faint or languid.

debility *n* a state of general bodily weakness; feebleness; languor of body; faintness.

debit *n* that which is entered in an account as a debt; a recorded item of debt; that part of an account in which is entered any article of goods furnished or money paid to or on account of a person.—*vt* to charge with as a debt (*to debit a person for* or *with goods*); to enter on the debtor side of a book.

debonair *adj* characterized by courtesy, affability or gentleness; elegant; well-bred; winning; accomplished.

debouch *vi* to issue or march out of a narrow place, or from defiles, as troops.

debrief *vt* to gather information from (a soldier etc) at the end of a mission—**debriefing** *n*.

debris *n* fragments; rubbish; ruins.

debt *n* that which is due from one person to another; that which one person is bound to pay to or perform for another; what is incumbent on one to do or suffer; a due; an obligation; the state of owing something to another (*to be in debt*); a duty neglected or violated; a trespass; a sin.

debtor *n* a person who owes another either money, goods or services; the correlative of creditor; one who has received from another an advance of any kind; one indebted or in debt.

debug *vt* (**debugged, debugging**) to discover and remove faults in a computer

death's head

program, electronic device; to remove electronic listening devices from.

debunk *vt* to expose as false or exaggerated.

debut *n* entrance on anything; first appearance before the public, as that of an actor or actress on the stage.—*vi* to make one's debut.

debutant, debutante *n* one who makes a debut or first appearance before the public.

decade *n* the sum or number of ten; an aggregate or group consisting of ten; specifically, an aggregate of ten years.

decadence *n* decay; a falling into a lower state, especially in a moral or artistic sense.

decadent *adj* in decadence; decaying; deteriorating.—*n* an artist or writer of a morally weak fibre and style.

decaf *adj* (*colloq*) a shortened form of **decaffeinated**.

decaffeinated *adj* (of coffee) having had most of the caffeine removed.

Decalogue *n* the ten commandments or precepts given by God to Moses.

decamp *vi* to remove or depart from a camp or camping ground; to march off; to depart; to take oneself off, especially in a secret or clandestine manner.

decant *vt* to pour off gently, as liquor from its sediment or from one vessel into another.

decanter *n* one who decants; a vessel used to decant liquors or for receiving decanted liquors; a glass vessel or bottle used for holding wine or other liquors for filling drinking glasses.

decapitate *vt* (**decapitated, decapitating**) to behead; to cut off the head of.

decapitation *n* the act of beheading.

decapod *n* one of an order of crustaceans (crabs, lobsters) having ten feet; one of that division of the cuttlefishes which have ten prehensile arms.—*adj* having ten feet; belonging to the decapods.

decarbonate *vt* (**decarbonated, decarbonating**) to remove carbonic acid or carbon dioxide from.

decarbonization *n* the process of depriving of carbon.

decarbonize *vt* (**decarbonized, decarbonizing**) to take carbon or carbon deposit from.

decathlon *n* a contest in which athletes compete for the highest total score in ten separate events.

decay *vi* to pass gradually from a sound, prosperous or perfect state to a less perfect state or toward weakness or dissolution; to become decomposed or corrupted; to rot; to be gradually impaired; to waste or moulder away.—*n* the state or process of decaying; decline to a worse or less perfect state; decomposition; putrefaction; deterioration; wasting.

decease *n* departure from this life; death.—*vi* (**deceased, deceasing**) to depart from this life; to die.

deceased *adj* departed from life; dead (frequently used as a noun, the word *person* being understood).

deceit *n* the quality or act of deceiving; guilefulness; the act of misleading a person; any artifice, stratagem or practice which misleads another or causes him or her to believe what is false; act of fraud; cheat; fallacy.

deceitful *adj* given to deceive; full of deceit; tending to mislead, deceive or ensnare; trickish; fraudulent; cheating.

deceive *vt* (**deceived, deceiving**) to mislead the mind of, especially intentionally; to cause to believe what is false or disbelieve what is true; to cause to mistake; to impose on; to delude; to frustrate or disappoint (the hopes, etc).

decelerate *vi* (**decelerated, decelerating**) to reduce speed, to slow down—*vt* to reduce the speed of.

December *n* the twelfth and last month in the year.

decency *n* the state or quality of being decent; propriety in actions or discourse; decorum; modesty; freedom from ribaldry or obscenity; a decent or becoming ceremony or rite.

decent *adj* becoming; having a character or show that gains general approval; suitable, as to words, behaviour, dress and ceremony; seemly; decorous; free from immodesty; not obscene; modest; moderate, tolerable, passable, respectable.

decentralize *vt* (**decentralized, decentralizing**) to distribute what has been centralized; to remove from direct connection or dependence on a central authority.

decentralization *n* the act of decentralizing; in politics, the act of distributing among a number of places throughout a country the administration of its internal affairs.

deception *n* the act of deceiving or misleading; habit of deceiving; the state of being deceived or misled; that which deceives; artifice; cheat.

deceptive *adj* tending to deceive; having power to mislead or impress false opinions; misleading.

decide *vt* (**decided, deciding**) to determine, as a question, controversy or struggle, finally or authoritatively; to settle by giving the victory to one side or the other; to determine the issue or result of; to conclude; to end.—*vi* to determine; to form a definite opinion; to come to a conclusion; to pronounce a judgment.

decided *adj* well-marked; clear; unequivocal; that puts an end to doubt; free from ambiguity or uncertainty; unmistakable;

decanter

resolute; determined; free from hesitation or wavering.

deciduous *adj* not perennial or permanent; (*bot*) applied to trees whose leaves fall in autumn and to leaves or other parts of the plant that fall; (*zool*) applied to parts which fall off at a certain stage of an animal's existence as hair, horns, teeth.

decimal *adj* of or pertaining to tens; numbered or proceeding by tens; having a tenfold increase or decrease.—*n* a decimal fraction.

decimal fraction *n* a fraction whose denominator is 10, or some number produced by the continued multiplication of 10 as a factor, such as 100, 1000, etc, but written with the denominator omitted, its value being indicated by a point placed to the left of as many figures of the numerator as there are ciphers in the denominator; thus $^7/_{10}$, $^3/_{1000}$ are written .7, .003.

decimalization *n* the conversion (e.g. of a currency) to a decimal system; the expression of an amount in decimals.

decimalize *vt* (**decimalized, decimalizing**) to convert to a decimal system; to express in decimals.

decimal system *n* a system of weights, measures and moneys based on multiples of ten; the metric system.

decimate *vt* (**decimated, decimating**) to select by lot and punish with death every tenth man of, as was done by the Romans in punishing bodies of troops, etc; hence, to destroy a great but indefinite number of.

decimation *n* a selection of every tenth by lot, as for punishment, etc; the destruction of a great but indefinite proportion of people or things.

decipher *vt* to explain what is written in ciphers, by finding what each character or mark represents; to read what is written in obscure or badly formed characters; to discover or explain the meaning of, as of something difficult to be understood.

decision *n* the act of deciding; determination, as of a question or doubt; final judgment or opinion in a case which has been under deliberation or discussion; determination, as of a contest or event; arbitrament; the quality of being decided in character; unwavering firmness; prompt and fixed determination.

decisive *adj* having the power or quality of determining; final; conclusive; putting an end to controversy; marked by decision or prompt determination.

deck *vt* to clothe; to dress the person; but usually, to clothe with more than ordinary elegance; to array; to adorn; to embellish; to furnish with a deck, as a vessel.—*n* a horizontal platform or floor extending from side to side of a ship and formed of planking, supported by the beams; large

deciduous

deck

vessels having often upper, main and lower decks, with a quarterdeck over the upper deck towards the stern.—**to clear the decks** to prepare (a ship) for action.

deckle *n* a frame or rubber band on a paper-making machine to limit the size of sheet.—*adj* rough uncut edge (*deckle edge*).

declaim *vi* to speak a set oration in public; to make a formal speech or oration; to harangue; to inveigh; to speak or write for rhetorical display.—*vt* to utter with rhetorical force; to deliver with inflation of tone.

declamation *n* the act or art of declaiming or making a rhetorical harangue in public; the delivery of a speech or exercise in oratory, as by the students of a college, etc; a display of showy rhetorical oratory; pretentious rhetorical language, with more sound than sense.

declamatory *adj* relating to the practice of declaiming; pertaining to declamation; merely rhetorical, without solid sense or argument.

declaration *n* the act of declaring, making known or announcing; affirmation; explicit assertion; open expression; avowal; that which is declared; the document or instrument by which an announcement is authoritatively made; (*law*) that part of the process or pleadings in which the plaintiff sets forth at large his or her cause of complaint; a simple affirmation substituted in lieu of an oath, solemn affirmation or affidavit.

declare *vt* (**declared, declaring**) to make known by words; to tell explicitly; to manifest or communicate plainly in any way; to exhibit; to publish; to proclaim; to assert; to affirm; to make a full statement of, as of goods on which duty falls to be paid to the customhouse.—*vi* to make a declaration; to make known explicitly some determination; to proclaim oneself; to pronounce adhesion in favour of a party, etc (with *for* or *against*).

declared *adj* made known; told explicitly; avowed; manifested; proclaimed; openly professed (*a declared enemy*).

declension *n* the act of declining; declination; slope; a falling or declining towards a worse state; refusal; non-acceptance; (*gram*) the inflexion of nouns, adjectives and pronouns by change of termination to form the oblique cases; the act of declining a word; a class of nouns declined on the same type.

declination *n* (*astron*) the distance of a heavenly body from the celestial equator, measured on a great circle passing through the pole and also through the body; (*physics*) the variation of the magnetic needle from the true meridian of a place—declination of the compass or magnetic declination.

decline *vi* (**declined, declining**) to lean downward; to bend over; to hang down, as from weakness, despondency, submission, etc; to sink to a lower level; to stoop, as to an unworthy object; to approach or draw toward the close (*day declines*); to avoid or shun; to refuse; not to comply; to tend to a less perfect state; to sink in character or value; to become diminished or impaired (as health, reputation); to fail; to decay.—*vt* to bend downward; to cause to bend; to depress; to shun or avoid; to refuse; not to accept or comply with; (*gram*) to inflect, through cases and numbers; to change the termination of a word, for forming the oblique cases.—*n* a falling off; a tendency to a worse state; diminution or decay; deterioration; a popular name for almost all chronic diseases in which the strength and plumpness of the body gradually decrease, until the patient dies; consumption.

declivity *n* slope or inclination downwards; a slope or descent of the ground, opposed to *acclivity* or ascent.

decoct *vt* to prepare by boiling; to extract the strength or flavour of by boiling.

decoction *n* the act of boiling a substance in water, for extracting its virtues; the water in which a substance has been thus boiled.

decode *vt* to decipher (a telegram) in code; (*comput*) to convert data from one form to another.

décolleté *adj* having a low neckline; wearing a low-necked style of dress.

decompose *vt* (**decomposed, decomposing**) to separate the constituent parts or elementary particles of; to resolve into original elements.—*vi* to become resolved into constituent elements; to decay, rot or putrefy.

decomposition *n* the act of decomposing; analysis; resolution; the state of being decomposed; disintegration; decay; putrescence.

decontrol *vt* (**decontrolled, decontrolling**) to withdraw from governmental regulation.

decor *n* the general decorative style or colour scheme of a room etc.

decorate *vt* (**decorated, decorating**) to deck with something becoming or ornamental; to adorn; to beautify; to embellish; to honour with a badge or medal.

Decorated style *n* (*archit*) a style of Gothic architecture distinguished by the flowing or wavy lines of its tracery, especially of its windows, and generally by profuse and sometimes florid ornamentation.

decoration *n* the act of adorning; ornamentation; that which decorates or adorns; ornament; any badge, as a medal, cross of

honour, etc, bestowed for distinguished services.

decorative *adj* adorning; suited to embellish; ornamental; attractive.

decorator *n* one who decorates or embellishes, especially houses.

decorous *adj* suitable to a character or to the time, place and occasion; becoming; seemly; proper; befitting (speech, behaviour, dress, etc).

decorum *n* propriety of speech or behaviour; seemliness; decency; opposed to rudeness, licentiousness or levity.

decoy *n* a place into which wild fowls are enticed in order to be caught; a fowl, or the likeness of one, employed to entice other fowl into a net or within range of shot; a thing or person intended to lead into a snare; a stratagem employed to mislead or lead into danger; a lure.—*vt* to lead or lure by artifice into a snare with a view to catch; to entrap by any means which deceive; to allure, attract or entice.

decrease *vi* (**decreased, decreasing**) to be diminished gradually in extent, bulk, quantity or amount, or in strength, influence or excellence; to become less.—*vt* to lessen; to make smaller in dimensions, amount, quality or excellence, etc; to diminish gradually or by small deductions.—*n* a becoming less; gradual diminution; wane (as applied to the moon); decay.

decree *n* judicial decision or determination of a litigated cause; the judgment or award of an umpire in a case submitted to him or her; an edict, law or order by a superior authority as a rule to govern inferiors.—*vt* (**decreed, decreeing**) to determine judicially; to resolve by sentence; to determine or resolve legislatively; to fix or appoint; to determine or decide on.—*vi* to determine immutably; to make an edict; to appoint by edict.

decree absolute *n* (*law*) the final decree made by an English court of law which dissolves a marriage.

decree nisi *n* (*law*) the order made by an English court of divorce after satisfactory proof is given in support of a petition for dissolution of marriage.

decrepit *adj* broken down or weakened with age; wasted or worn by the infirmities of old age; being in the last stage of decay.

decrepitude *n* the state of being decrepit; the broken, crazy state of the body produced by decay and the infirmities of age.

decrial *n* the act of decrying or crying down.

decry *vt* (**decried, decrying**) to cry down; to censure as faulty, mean or worthless; to clamour against; to discredit by finding fault.

decussate *vt* (**decussated, decussating**) to

decoy

decoration

intersect so as to make right angles, thus x; to intersect; to cross, as lines, rays of light, leaves, or nerves in the body.—*adj* decussated.

decussated *adj* crossed; intersected; (*bot*) arranged in pairs alternately crossing each other at regular angles.

dedicate *vt* (**dedicated, dedicating**) to set apart and consecrate to God or to a sacred purpose; to appropriate to any person or purpose; to give wholly or earnestly up to (often reflexive); to inscribe or address to a patron, friend or public character (*to dedicate a book*).—*adj* dedicated.

dedicated *adj* consecrated; devoted; appropriated; wholly devoted to something.

dedication *n* the act of dedicating; consecration or devotion to a sacred use; solemn appropriation; an address prefixed to a book and inscribed to a friend of the author, some public character or other person, as a mark of esteem.

deduce *vt* (**deduced, deducing**) to draw; to draw, bring out or infer in reasoning; to attain or arrive at (a truth, opinion or proposition) from premises; to infer from what precedes.

deducible *adj* capable of being deduced; inferable.

deduct *vt* to take away, separate or remove, in numbering, estimating or calculating; to subtract.

deduction *n* the act of deducting or taking away; that which is deducted; sum or amount taken from another; abatement; the act or method of deducing from premises; that which is drawn from premises; inference; consequence drawn; conclusion.

deductive *adj* deducible; pertaining to deduction; that is or may be deduced from premises.

deductive reasoning *n* the process of deriving consequences from admitted or established premises, as distinguished from *inductive reasoning*, by which we arrive at general laws or axioms by an accumulation of facts.

deed *n* that which is done or performed; an act; a fact; anything that is done; an exploit; achievement; (*law*) a writing containing some contract or agreement and the evidence of its execution; particularly, an instrument conveying real estate to a purchaser, etc.

deed poll *n* a deed declaring formally and publicly a person's intentions or act, especially in the case of changing his or her name.

deem *vt* to think, judge, believe or consider to be so or so.—*vi* to think or suppose.

deemster, dempster *n* the name of two judges in the Isle of Man who act as the chief justices of the island.

deer

deep-fryer

deep *adj* extending or being far below the surface; descending far downwards; profound; (opposed to shallow, as *deep water*, *a deep pit*); low in situation; being or descending far below the adjacent land (*a deep valley*); entering far (*a deep wound*); absorbed; engrossed; wholly occupied; not superficial or obvious; hidden; abstruse; hard to penetrate or understand; profoundly learned; having the power to enter far into a subject; penetrating; artful; concealing artifice; insidious; designing; grave in sound; great in degree; intense; profound (silence, grief, poverty); measured back from the front.—*n* anything remarkable for depth; the sea; the abyss of waters; any abyss.—*adv* deeply; to a great depth; profoundly.

deepen *vt* to make deep or deeper; to sink lower; to increase; to intensify; to make more grave (sound).—*vi* to become more deep, in all its senses.

deep-freeze *n* an appliance in which foodstuffs or other perishable substances are stored at very low temperatures.— *vt* (*pret* **deep-froze** *or* **deep freezed**, *pp* **deep-frozen**, *ppr* **deep freezing**) to freeze (foodstuffs etc) for storage in a deep-freeze.

deep-fry *vt* (**deep-fried, deep-frying**) to cook (a foodstuff) by immersing it in hot fat.

deep-fryer, deep-frier *n* an appliance for deep-frying food.

deeply *adv* at or to a great depth; far below the surface; profoundly; thoroughly; to a great degree; intensely; gravely; with low or deep tone; with art or intricacy (*a deeply laid plot*).

deer *n sing and pl* a name of many ruminant quadrupeds, distinguished by having solid branching horns which they shed every year and eight cutting teeth in the lower jaw and none in the upper, such as the red deer, fallow deer, roebuck, reindeer, moose or elk, etc.

deerhound *n* a hound for hunting deer.

deerstalker *n* one who practises deerstalking; a kind of cap.

deerstalking *n* the hunting of deer (especially the red deer) on foot by hiding and stealing within shot of them unawares.

deface *vt* (**defaced, defacing**) to destroy or mar the face or surface of; to injure the beauty of; to disfigure; to erase or obliterate.

defaced *adj* injured on the surface; erased.

defacement *n* the act of defacing; injury to the surface or exterior; what mars or disfigures.

defamation *n* the uttering of slanderous words with a view to injure another's reputation; slander; calumny.

defamatory *n* containing defamation; slanderous.

defame *vt* (**defamed, defaming**) to slander; to speak evil of; to libel; to bring into disrepute.

default *n* a failing or failure; an omission of that which ought to be done; (*law*) a failure of appearance in court at a day assigned.—**in default of** in the absence or lack of; hence, in place of; in lieu of.—*vi* to fail in fulfilling or satisfying an engagement, claim, contract or agreement.—*vt* (*law*) to give judgment against on account of failing to appear and answer.

defaulter *n* one who makes default; a delinquent; one who fails to meet his or her claims or to fulfil engagements.

defeat *n* an overthrow; loss of battle; check, rout or destruction of an army by the victory of an enemy; a frustration by rendering null and void, or by prevention of success.—*vt* to overcome or vanquish; to overthrow; to frustrate; to prevent the success of; to disappoint; to render null and void; to resist with success (an attempt).

defeatist *n* one who takes for granted the defeat of his or her party or country in war or of his or her own plans and hopes.

defecate *vi* (**defecated, defecating**) to expel faeces from the bowels.

defect *n* lack or absence of something necessary or useful towards perfection; a fault; an imperfection; that which is lacking to make a perfect whole; blemish; deformity.—*vi* to revolt; to desert one's country or a case (for another).

defection *n* the act of abandoning a person or cause to which one is bound by allegiance or duty, or to which one has attached himself or herself; a falling away; apostasy; backsliding.

defective *adj* having some defect; lacking either in substance, quantity or quality, or in anything necessary; imperfect; faulty; (*gram*) lacking some of the usual forms of declension or conjugation (*a defective noun* or *verb*).

defence *n* the act of defending, upholding or maintaining; anything that opposes attack, violence, danger or injury; fortification; guard; protection; a speech or writing intended to repel or disprove a charge or accusation; vindication; apology; (*law*) the method adopted by a person against whom legal proceedings have been taken for defending himself or herself against them.

defend *vt* to protect or support against any assault or attack; to ward off an attack on; to protect by opposition or resistance; to vindicate, uphold or maintain uninjured by force or by argument (rights and privileges); (*law*) to come forward as defendant in (*to defend an action*).—*vi* to make opposition; to make defence.

defendant *n* one who defends; (*law*), the party that opposes a complaint, demand or charge; the party against whom the conclusions of a process or action are directed.

defender *n* one who defends; one who vindicates, either by arms or by arguments; a champion or an advocate; (*Scots law*) the defendant in a suit.

Defender of the Faith *n* a title peculiar to the sovereigns of England, first conferred by Pope Leo X on Henry VIII in 1521, as a reward for writing against Luther.

defensible *adj* capable of being defended, vindicated, maintained or justified.

defensive *adj* serving to defend; proper for or suited to defence; carried on in resisting attack or aggression, in distinction from *offensive*.—*n* that which defends.—**to be on the defensive** or **to stand on the defensive** to be or stand in a state or posture of defence or resistance, in opposition to aggression or attack.

defer¹ *vt* (**deferred, deferring**) to delay; to put off; to postpone to a future time.—*vi* to delay; to procrastinate.

defer² *vi* (**deferred, deferring**) to yield to another's opinion; to submit or give way courteously or from respect (*to defer to a friend's judgment*).

deference *n* a yielding in opinion; submission or judgment to the opinion or judgment of another; respect; courteous consideration; obedience.

deferential *adj* expressing deference; accustomed to defer.

defiance *n* the act of defying, daring or challenging; a challenge to fight; invitation to combat; a challenge to meet in any contest or to make good any assertion; contempt of opposition or danger; daring that implies the contempt of an adversary or of any opposing power.—**to bid defiance to** to defy; to brave.

defiant *adj* characterized by defiance, boldness or insolence.

deficiency *n* the state of being deficient; a failing or falling short; lack, either total or partial; defect; absence; something less than is necessary.

deficient *adj* lacking; defective; imperfect; not sufficient or adequate; not having a full or adequate supply (with *in*, as *deficient in strength*).

deficit *n* a falling short of a requisite sum or amount; a deficiency (*a deficit in revenue*).

defile¹ *vt* (**defiled, defiling**) to make unclean; to render foul or dirty; to soil or sully; to tarnish, as reputation, etc; to make ceremonially unclean; to pollute; to corrupt the chastity of; to debauch; to violate.

defile² *vi* (**defiled, defiling**) to march off in a line or file by file; to file off.—*n* a narrow passage or way, in which troops may march only in a file or with a narrow front; a long narrow pass, as between hills, etc.

defilement *n* the act of defiling or state of being defiled.

definable *adj* capable of being defined; capable of having the limits ascertained, fixed and determined; capable of having its meaning expressed with certainty or precision.

define *vt* (**defined, defining**) to determine or set down the limits of; to determine with precision; to mark the limit of; to circumscribe, mark or show the outlines of clearly; to determine the extent of the meaning of; to give or describe the meaning of; to enunciate or explain the distinctive properties of.—*vi* to give a definition.

defined *adj* having the limits marked; having a determinate limit; clearly marked out as to form.

definite *adj* having fixed or marked limits; bounded with precision; determinate; having well-marked limits in meaning; certain; precise; (*gram*) defining; limiting; applied to particular things; (*bot*) same as centrifugal.

definite article *n* (*gram*) the article *the*.

definition *n* the act of defining; a brief and precise description of a thing by its meaning; the quality or power in a telescope or other optical instrument of showing distinctly the outlines or features of any object; sharpness of outline, especially of a photograph, television image, etc.

definitive *adj* limiting; determinate; positive; express; conclusive; final.

deflate *vt* (**deflated, deflating**) to release the air or gas from a container such as a balloon or tyre; to reduce in importance; to reduce the money supply, restrict credit, etc, to reduce inflation in the economy.

deflation *n* the act of deflating; contraction of the amount of money in circulation, tending to lower prices and wages (the opposite of *inflation*).

deflect *vi* to turn away or aside; to deviate from a true course or right line; to swerve.—*vt* to cause to turn aside; to turn or bend from a straight line.

deflection *n* the strain produced by a transverse stress, such as the bending of a horizontal beam under a load; also used to denote amount of deflection.

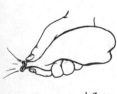

deflate

deflower *vt* to deprive of virginity; to violate, ravish, seduce.

defoliant *n* a substance, usually a chemical, that kills foliage.

defoliate *vt* (**defoliated, defoliating**) to strip (plants) of leaves, especially by using a chemical spray.—**defoliation** *n*.

deform *vt* to mar or injure the form of; to disfigure; to render ugly or unpleasing; to disfigure the moral beauty of (*vices deform the character*).

deformation *n* a disfiguring or defacing.

deformed *adj* disfigured; distorted; misshapen; ugly.

deformity *n* the state of being deformed; some deformed or misshapen part of the body; distortion; irregularity of shape or features; ugliness; anything that destroys beauty, grace or propriety.

defraud *vt* to deprive of right, either by obtaining something by deception or artifice, or by taking something wrongfully without the knowledge or consent of the owner; to cheat; to keep out of just rights (with *of* before the thing).

defray *vt* to pay for; to disburse the amount of; to discharge or bear (with cost, charge, expense as the object).

defrayal, defrayment *n* the act of defraying.

defrost *vt* to remove ice from (a refrigerator or freezer); to thaw out (frozen food).—*vi* (of frozen food) to thaw.

deft *adj* dextrous; clever; apt.

deftly *adv* in a deft manner; aptly; neatly; dextrously.

deftness *n* the quality of being deft; dexterity.

defunct *adj* having finished the course of life; dead; deceased.—*n* a dead person or dead persons; one deceased or persons deceased.

defuse *vt* to remove the fuse from (an explosive such as a bomb) and so render it harmless; to decrease tension in a difficult or crisis situation.

defy *vt* (**defied, defying**) to provoke to combat or strife, by appealing to the courage of another; to invite one to contest; to challenge; to dare; to brave; to set at nought; to despise or be regardless of; to challenge to say or do anything (*I defy you to say I did it*).

degeneracy *n* the state of degenerating or of being degenerate; a growing worse or inferior; a decline in good qualities; a state or condition of deterioration; lowness; meanness.

degenerate *vi* (**degenerated, degenerating**) to fall off from the qualities proper to the race or kind; to become of a lower type, physically or morally; to pass from a good to a worse state.—*adj* having fallen from a perfect or good state into a less excellent or worse state; having declined in natural or moral worth; characterized by or associated with degeneracy; base or mean (*degenerate arts* or *times*).

degeneration *n* the state or process of becoming degenerate; degeneracy; gradual deterioration from a state physiologically superior.

deglutition *n* the act or power of swallowing; the process by which animals swallow.

degradation *n* the act of degrading; a depriving of rank, dignity or office; the state of being reduced from an elevated or more honourable station to one that is meaner or humbler; a mean or abject state to which one has sunk; debasement; degeneracy; (*geol*) the lessening or wearing down of higher lands, rocks, strata, etc, by the action of water or other causes.

degrade *vt* (**degraded, degrading**) to reduce from a higher to a lower rank or degree; to strip of honours; to reduce in estimation; to lower or sink in morals or character; to debase.—*vi* to degenerate; to become lower in character.

degraded *adj* sunk to an abject or vile state; exhibiting degradation; debased; low.

degree *n* a step or single movement, upwards or downwards, towards any end; one of a series of progressive advances; measure, amount or proportion (*he is a degree worse*); measure of advancement; relative position attained; rank; station (*men of low degree*); a certain distance or remove in the line of family descent, determining the proximity of blood (*a relation in the third or fourth degree*); the 360th part of the circumference of any circle, a degree of latitude being the 360th part of any meridian on the earth's surface, a degree of longitude the same part of any given parallel of latitude; an interval of musical sound, marked by a line on the scale; a division, space or interval marked on a mathematical or other instrument, as a thermometer or barometer; in universities, a title of distinction (bachelor, master, doctor) conferred as a testimony of proficiency in arts and sciences or merely as an honour.—**by degrees** step by step; gradually; by moderate advances.

dehydrate *vt* (**dehydrated, dehydrating**) to remove water from.—*vi* to lose water, especially from body tissues.—**dehydration** *n*.

deification *n* the act of deifying.

deify *vt* (**deified, deifying**) to make a god of; to exalt to the rank of a deity; to enrol among deities; to treat as an object of supreme regard; to praise or revere as a deity; to make godlike; to elevate spiritually.

deign *vi* to vouchsafe; to condescend (generally followed by an infinitive).

deism *n* the doctrine or creed of a deist.

deist *n* one who believes in the existence of a God but denies revealed religion, basing his or her belief on the light of nature and reason.

deity *n* godhead; divinity; a fabulous god or goddess; a divinity.

Deity *n* the Supreme Being or infinite self-existing Spirit; God.

déjà vu *n* a feeling of familiarity when encountering a completely new scene or experience, as though one had encountered it before.

deject *vt* to cast down; to depress the spirits of; to dispirit, discourage, dishearten.

dejection *n* the state of being downcast; depression of mind; melancholy; lowness of spirits occasioned by grief or misfortune.

dekko *n* (*colloq*) a look.

delay *vt* to prolong the time of doing or proceeding with; to put off; to defer; to retard; to stop, detain or hinder for a time; to restrain the motion of.—*vi* to linger; to move slowly; to stop for a time.—*n* a lingering; a putting off or deferring; procrastination; protraction; hindrance.

delectable *adj* delightful; highly pleasing; affording great joy or pleasure.

delectation *n* a giving delight; delight.

delegate *vt* (**delegated, delegating**) to depute; to send on an embassy; to send with power to act as a representative; to entrust, commit or deliver to another's care and management (power, an affair).—*n* a person appointed and sent by another or by others, with powers to transact business as his, her or their representative; a deputy; a commissioner; a representative.

delegation *n* the act of delegating; appointment to act as deputy; a person or body of persons deputed to act for another or for others.

delete *vt* (**deleted, deleting**) to blot out; to erase; to strike or mark out, as with a pen, pencil, etc.

deleterious *adj* having the quality of destroying life; noxious; poisonous; injurious; pernicious.

deletion *n* the act of deleting; an erasure; a passage deleted.

delft, delftware *n* earthenware covered with enamel or white glazing in imitation of chinaware or porcelain, made at Delft, in Holland; glazed earthenware dishes.

deliberate *vi* (**deliberated, deliberating**) to weigh consequences or results in the mind previous to action; to pause and consider; to ponder, reflect, cogitate or debate with oneself.—*adj* weighing facts and arguments with a view to a choice or decision; carefully considering probable consequences; slow in determining; formed with deliberation; well advised or considered; not sudden or rash; not hasty.

deliberation *n* the act of deliberating; careful consideration; mature reflection; mutual discussion and examination of the reasons for and against a measure; the act or habit of doing anything coolly or without hurry or excitement.

deliberative *adj* pertaining to deliberation; proceeding or acting by deliberation or discussion; having or conveying a right or power to deliberate or discuss.

delicacy *n* the quality of being delicate or

highly pleasing to the taste or some other sense; fineness; smoothness; softness; tenderness; slenderness; that which is pleasing to the senses; a luxury; refined taste or judgment; nicety.

delicate *adj* pleasing to a cultivated taste; refinedly agreeable; dainty; of a fine texture; fine; soft; smooth; tender; sensitive; easily injured; not capable of standing rough handling; nice; accurate; light or softly tinted; slender; minute; peculiarly sensitive to beauty, harmony, or their opposites; refined in manner; polite.

delicatessen *n* a shop selling prepared cooked meats, prepared foods, cheese and other foods, often delicacies which have been imported.

delicious *adj* highly pleasing to the taste; most sweet or grateful to the senses; affording exquisite pleasure; charming; delightful; entrancing.

delight *vt* to affect with great pleasure; to please highly; to give or afford high satisfaction or joy.—*vi* to have or take great pleasure; to be greatly pleased or rejoiced (*to delight in a thing*).—*n* a high degree of pleasure or satisfaction of mind; joy; rapture; that which gives great pleasure; the cause of joy; charm.

delighted

delighted *adj* experiencing delight; overjoyed.

delightful *adj* giving delight; highly pleasing; charming; exquisite; delicious.

delimit *vt* to mark or settle distinctly the limits of.

delimitation *n* the act of delimiting; the fixing or settling of limits or boundaries.

delineate *vt* (**delineated, delineating**) to draw the lines which exhibit the form of; to make a draught of; to sketch or design; to represent in a picture; to draw a likeness of; to portray to the mind or understanding; to depict, sketch or describe.

delineation *n* the act or process of delineating; representation or portrayal, whether pictorially or in words; sketch; description.

delinquency *n* failure or omission of duty; a fault; a misdeed; an offence.

delinquent *adj* failing in duty; offending by neglect of duty; guilty of a misdeed or offence.—*n* one who fails to perform his or her duty; one guilty of a delinquency; an offender; a culprit; a malefactor.

delta

deliquesce *vi* (**deliquesced, deliquescing**) to melt gradually and become liquid by attracting and absorbing moisture from the air, as certain salts, acids and alkalis.

delirious *adj* affected with delirium; lightheaded; disordered in intellect; crazy; raving; frenzied; characterized by or proceeding from, delirium.

delirium *n* (*pl* **deliriums, deliria**) a temporary disordered state of the mental faculties occurring during illness, either of a febrile or of an exhausting nature; violent excitement; wild enthusiasm; mad rapture.

delirium tremens *n* an affection of the brain which arises from the inordinate and protracted use of alcoholic drinks.

deliver *vt* to release, as from restraint; to set at liberty; to free; to rescue or save; to transfer, hand over or commit (a letter, a person to enemies); to surrender, yield, give up, resign (often followed by *up*); to give birth to; to assist in the birth of; to utter, pronounce, speak (a sermon, address, etc); to direct, send forth or discharge (a blow, a broadside).

deliverance *n* the act of delivering or liberating; release or rescue, as from captivity, oppression, danger, etc.

deliverer *n* one who delivers; one who releases or rescues; a preserver; a saviour.

delivery *n* the act of delivering; release; rescue, as from slavery, restraint, oppression or danger; the act of handing over or transferring; surrender; a giving up; a giving or passing from one to another; specifically, the distribution of letters, etc, from a post office to a district or districts; utterance, pronunciation or manner of speaking; childbirth.

dell *n* a small narrow valley between hills or rising grounds; a ravine.

delta *n* the island formed by the alluvial deposits between the mouths of the Nile, from its resemblance in shape to this letter; any similar alluvial tract at the mouth of a river.

Delta *n* the name of the Greek letter Δ, answering to the English D; the island formed by the alluvial deposits between the mouths of the Nile, from its resemblance in shape to this letter; any similar alluvial tract at the mouth of a river.

delude *vt* (**deluded, deluding**) to cause to entertain foolish or erroneous notions; to impose on; to fool; to lead from truth or into error; to mislead; to beguile; to cheat (often reflexive, as *to delude oneself with vain hopes*).

deluder *n* one who deludes; a deceiver; an impostor; one who holds out false pretences.

delusion *n* the act of deluding; a misleading of the mind; false impression or belief; illusion; error or mistake proceeding from false views; the state of being deluded or misled.

deluge *n* an inundation; a flood; but specifically, the great flood or overflowing of the earth by water in the days of Noah; anything resembling an inundation; anything that overwhelms, as a great calamity.—*vt* (**deluged, deluging**) to overflow, as with water; to inundate; to drown; to overwhelm.

de luxe *adj* luxurious; of very high quality and so expensive.

delve *vt* (**delved, delving**) to search deeply; (*arch*) to turn up, as with a spade.—*vi* (*arch*) to dig (ground).

demagogue *n* a leader of the people; a person who sways the people by oratory; generally, an unprincipled factious orator; one who acquires influence with the populace by pandering to their prejudices or playing on their ignorance.

demand *vt* to claim or seek as due by right (*to demand a thing of a person*); to ask or claim generally (a price, a reward); to ask (a thing) by authority; to require as necessary or useful; to necessitate (*a task demands industry*).—*vi* to make a demand; to inquire; to ask.—*n* an asking for or claim made by virtue of a right or supposed right to the thing sought; an asking or request with authority; the asking or requiring of a price for goods offered for sale; question; interrogation; the calling for in order to purchase (*there is no demand for the goods*).

demarcate *vt* (**demarcated, demarcating**) to mark the limits or boundaries of.

demarcation *n* the act or process of marking off or of defining the limits or boundaries of anything; separation; distinction.

démarche *n* a fresh line of policy, especially a change from strained to better relations.

demean *vt* to behave; to carry; (*refl*) to conduct; to lower or degrade (oneself).

demeanour *n* behaviour, especially as regards air or carriage of the person, countenance, etc; carriage; deportment; conduct.

demented *adj* infatuated; mad; insane; crazy.

dementia *n* a decrease in or loss of mental powers.

demerit *n* the opposite or absence of merit; a fault; a defect.

demesne *n* an estate in land; the land adjacent to a manor house or mansion kept in the proprietor's own hands, as distinguished from lands held by tenants.

demi- *prefix* signifying half.

demigod *n* half a god; an inferior deity; one partaking partly of the divine partly of the human nature.

demijohn *n* a glass vessel or bottle with a large body and small neck, enclosed in wickerwork.

demise *n* the death of a person, especially of a person of distinction; decease (used with possessives); (*law*) a conveyance or transfer of an estate by lease or will.—*vt* (**demised, demising**) (*law*) to transfer or convey, as an estate; to bequeath; to grant by will.

demisemiquaver *n* (*mus*) the half of a semiquaver or one-fourth of a quaver.

demission *n* the act of demitting; a laying down office; resignation; transference.

demit *vt* (**demitted, demitting**) to lay down formally, as an office; to resign; to relinquish; to transfer.

demiurge *n* a maker or framer; the maker of the world; the Creator.

demobilization *n* the act of demobilizing.

demobilize *vt* (**demobilized, demobilizing**) to disarm and dismiss (troops) home; to disband.

democracy *n* that form of government in which the sovereignty of the state is vested in the people and exercised by them, either directly or indirectly, by means of representative institutions; in a collective sense, the people or populace, especially the populace regarded as rulers.

democrat *n* one who adheres to democracy.

Democrat *n* in UK, a member or adherent of the Liberal Democratic Party; in USA, a member of the Democratic Party.

democratic *adj* of, pertaining to or characteristic of democracy.

Democratic Party *n* one of the two American political parties (the other being the Republican) which lays greater strain on state rights of the individual states.

demography *n* the study of population statistics, such as births, deaths, illnesses etc.—**demographic** *adj*.

demoiselle *n* a young lady; a damsel; a small crane of North Africa, southeast Europe and central Asia.

demolish *vt* to throw or pull down; to raze; to destroy, as a structure or artificial construction; to ruin.

demolition *n* the act of demolishing; destruction; ruin.

demon *n* a spirit or immaterial being, holding a middle place between people and the celestial deities of the pagans; an evil or malignant spirit; a devil; a very wicked or cruel person.

demoniac *n* a human being possessed by a demon.

demonology *n* a treatise on evil spirits and their agency, or knowledge regarding them.

demonetize *vt* (**demonetize, demonetizing**) to deprive of standard value, as money; to withdraw from circulation.

demonstrate *vt* (**demonstrated, demonstrating**) to point out with perfect clearness; to show clearly; to make evident; to exhibit; to exhibit the parts of when dissected, as of a dead body; to show or prove to be certain; to prove beyond the possibility of doubt.

demonstration *n* the act of demonstrating; an exhibition; a manifestation; an outward show; the act of exhibiting proof beyond the possibility of doubt; a proof by logical or mathematical reasoning; the exhibition

demijohn

demoiselle

of parts dissected for the study of anatomy; (*milit*) an operation, such as the massing of soldiers at a certain point, performed for the purpose of deceiving the enemy.

demonstrative *adj* serving to demonstrate; showing or proving by certain evidence; invincibly conclusive; characterized by or given to the strong exhibition of any feeling; outwardly expressive of feelings or emotions.

demonstrative pronoun *n* a pronoun that clearly indicates the object to which it refers, as *this* man, *that* book.

demonstrator *n* one who demonstrates; a junior assistant to a professor in a laboratory.

demoralize *vt* (**demoralized, demoralizing**) to destroy or lessen the effect of moral principles on; to reduce the morale of, to deprive of courage and self-confidence.

demote *vt* (**demoted, demoting**) to lower in rank or position—**demotion** *n*.

demotic *adj* pertaining to the common people; popular; applied to the ordinary alphabet of ancient Egypt, as distinct from that used by the priestly caste, called the hieratic.

denarius

dempster *n* same as **deemster**.

demulcent *adj* softening; mollifying; lenient.—*n* any medicine which lessens the effects of irritation, as gums and other mucilaginous substances.

demur *vi* (**demurred, demurring**) to pause in uncertainty; to hesitate; to have or to state scruples or difficulties; to object hesitatingly; to take exceptions, *law*, to stop at any point in the pleadings.—*n* stop; pause; hesitation as to the propriety of proceeding; suspense of proceeding or decision; exception taken; objection stated.

demure *adj* affectedly modest or coy; making a show of gravity or decorousness; grave or reserved consciously and intentionally.

demurrage *n* the time during which a vessel is detained by the freighter beyond that originally stipulated, in loading or unloading; the compensation which the freighter has to pay for such delay or detention.

demurrer *n* one who demurs; (*law*) a stop at some point in the pleadings and a resting of the decision of the cause on that point; an issue on matter of law.

demy *n* a particular size of paper.

den *n* a cave or hollow place in the earth; a cave, pit or subterranean recess, used for concealment, shelter, protection or security; any squalid place of resort or residence; a dell, wooded hollow or ravine; a room in a house for study or relaxation.

denarius *n* (*pl* **denarii**) an ancient Roman silver coin.

denationalize *vt* (**denationalized, denationalizing**) to divest of national character or rights.

denaturalize *vt* (**denaturalized, denaturalizing**) to render unnatural; to alienate from nature; to deprive of naturalization or acquired citizenship in a foreign country.

dendriform *adj* having the form or appearance of a tree.

dendrite *n* a stone or mineral, on or in which are figures resembling shrubs, trees or, mosses.

dendrology *n* the natural history of trees.

dengue *n* a febrile epidemic disease of the East and West Indies.

denial *n* the act of denying; contradiction; a contradictory statement; refusal; rejection; disownment.

denizen *n* a citizen; a dweller; an inhabitant, especially a plant or an animal where it is not native.

denominate *vt* (**denominated, denominating**) to give a name or epithet to; to name, call, style or designate.

denomination *n* the act of naming; a name or appellation; a class, society or collection of individuals called by the same name; a religious sect.

denominator *n* one who or that which denominates; the number placed below the line in vulgar fractions, showing into how many parts the integer is divided.

denote *vt* (**denoted, denoting**) to signify by a visible sign; to indicate, mark or stand for; to be the name of or express; to be the sign or symptom of; to show; to indicate. denouement.—*n* the winding up of a plot, as of a novel, drama, etc; the solution of any mystery; the issue, as of any course of conduct; the event.

denounce *vt* (**denounced, denouncing**) to declare solemnly; to proclaim in a threatening manner; to announce or declare, as a threat; to threaten; to inform against; to accuse.

dense *adj* having its constituent parts closely united; close; compact; thick; crass; gross; crowded.

density *n* the quality of being dense, close or compact; closeness of constituent parts; compactness; either the mass of unit volume of a substance (*absolute density*) or the ratio of the mass of a given volume of the substance to that of an equal volume of some standard substance (*relative density*): the standard for solids and liquids is water; for gases, either air or (usually in *chem*) hydrogen.

dent *n* a mark made by a blow; especially, a hollow or depression made on the surface of a solid body.—*vt* to make a dent on or in.

dental *adj* of or pertaining to the teeth; having the characteristic sound given by the teeth and tip of the tongue (*d* and *t* are *dental* letters).—*n* a dental letter, as *d*, *t* and *th*.

dental floss *n* a kind of waxed thread used to clean between the teeth.

dental plaque *n* a sticky film which forms on teeth and which can cause gum disease.

dentifrice *n* a powder or other substance to be used in cleaning the teeth.

dentil *n* (*archit*) the name of the little cubes or square blocks often cut for ornament on Greek cornices.

dentine *n* the ivory tissue lying below the enamel and constituting the body of the tooth.

dentist *n* one whose business it is to clean and extract teeth, repair them when diseased and replace them when necessary by artificial ones.

dentistry *n* the art or profession of a dentist.

dentition *n* the breeding or cutting of teeth in infancy; the time of growing teeth; the system of teeth peculiar to an animal.

denture *n* a plate with one or more artificial teeth.

denudation *n* the act of stripping off covering; a making bare; (*geol*) the carrying away, by the action of running water, of a portion of the solid materials of the land, by which the underlying rocks are laid bare.

denude *vt* (**denuded, denuding**) to divest of all covering; to make bare or naked; to strip; to uncover or lay bare.

denunciation *n* the act of denouncing; proclamation of a threat; public menace.

deny *vt* (**denied, denying**) to declare not to be true; to affirm to be not so; to contradict; to gainsay; to refuse to grant; not to afford; to withhold (*Providence denies us many things*); to refuse or neglect to acknowledge; not to confess; to disavow; to disown; to reject.—**to deny oneself** to decline the gratification of appetites or desires.—**to deny oneself something** to abstain from something although desiring it.—*vi* to answer in the negative; to refuse; not to comply.

deodar *n* a kind of Indian cedar.

deodorant *n* a substance that removes or masks unpleasant smells, such as stale perspiration.

deodorize *vt* (**deodorized, deodorizing**) to deprive of odour or smell, especially of fetid odour resulting from impurities.

deontology *n* the science of duty.

deoxyribonucleic acid *n* see **DNA**.

depart *vi* to go or move away; to go elsewhere; to leave or desist, as from a practice; to forsake, abandon, deviate, not to adhere to or follow (commonly with *from* in these senses); to leave this world; to die; to decease.—*vt* to leave; to retire from (with ellipsis of *from*).

departed *adj* gone; vanished; dead; with the definite article used as a noun for a dead person.

department *n* a separate branch of business; a distinct province, in which a class of duties are allotted to a particular person; a distinct branch, as of science, etc; a division of territory, as in France; a district into which a country is formed for governmental or other purposes.

departmental *adj* pertaining to a department, branch, district, etc.

departure *n* the act of departing or going away; a moving from or leaving a place; death; decease; a forsaking; abandonment; deviation, as from a standard, rule or plan; (*navig*) the distance sailed east or west from a given meridian; the position in latitude and longitude of the starting point of a voyage.

depend *vi* to be sustained by being fastened or attached to something above; to hang down (followed by *from*); to be related to anything in regard to existence, operation or effects; to be contingent or conditioned (followed by *on* or *upon*, as *we depend on air for respiration*); to rest with confidence; to trust, rely or confide; to believe fully (with *on* or *upon*).

dependable *adj* capable of being depended on; trustworthy.

dependant *n* one who is sustained by another, or who relies on another for support or favour; a retainer; a follower; a servant.

dependence *n* a state of being dependent; connection and support; mutual connection; interrelation; a state of relying on another for support or existence; a state of being subject to the operation of any other cause; reliance; confidence; trust; a resting on.

dependent *adj* hanging down; subject to the power of or at the disposal of another; not able to exist or sustain itself alone; relying for support or favour (*dependent on another's bounty*).

depict *vt* to form a likeness of in colours; to paint; to portray; to represent in words; to describe.—**depiction** *n*.

depilate *vt* (**depilated, depilating**) to strip of hair.

depilatory *n* an application which is used to remove hair.

deplete *vt* (**depleted, depleting**) to empty, reduce or exhaust by draining away.—**depletion** *n*.

deplorable *adj* lamentable; sad; calamitous; grievous; miserable; wretched; contemptible or pitiable.

deplore *vt* (**deplored, deploring**) to feel or express deep and poignant grief for; to lament; to mourn; to grieve for; to bewail; to bemoan.

deploy *vt* (*milit*) to extend in a line of small depth, as a battalion which has been previ-

dentil

ously formed in one or more columns; to display; to open out.—*vi* to form a more extended front or line; to open out.

deployment *n* the act or state of deploying.

depopulate *vt* (**depopulated, depopulating**) to deprive of inhabitants, whether by death or by expulsion; to remove people from.

deport *vt* to carry, demean or behave (used reflexively); also, to transport; to carry away or from one country to another.

deportation *n* a removal from one country to another or to a distant place; exile; banishment.

deportment *n* manner of acting in relation to the duties of life; behaviour; demeanour; carriage; conduct.

deposal *n* the act of deposing or divesting of office.

depose *vt* (**deposed, deposing**) to remove from a throne or other high station; to dethrone; to divest of office; to give testimony on oath, especially in a court of law.

deposition *n* the act of deposing or giving testimony under oath; the attested written testimony of a witness; declaration; the act of dethroning a king or removing a person from an office or station.

deposit *vt* to lay down; to place; to put; to lay in a place for preservation; to lodge in the hands of a person for safekeeping or other purpose; to entrust; to commit as a pledge.—*n* that which is laid down; any matter laid or thrown down or lodged; matter that settles down and so is separated from a fluid, as (*geol*) an accumulation of mud, gravel, stones, etc, lodged by the agency of water; anything entrusted to the care of another; a pledge; a thing given as security or for preservation; a sum of money lodged in a bank; a sum of money given in part payment.

deposition *n* the act of depositing, laying or settling down; placing; that which is deposited, lodged or thrown down.

depositor *n* one who makes a deposit.

depository *n* a place where anything is lodged for safekeeping; a person to whom a thing is entrusted for safekeeping.

depot *n* a place of deposit; a building for receiving goods for storage or sale; a bus station.

deprave *vt* (**depraved, depraving**) to make bad or worse; to impair the good qualities of; to corrupt.

depravity *n* the state of being depraved; a corrupted state; especially, a state of corrupted morals; destitution of good principles; sinfulness; wickedness; vice; profligacy.

deprecate *vt* (**deprecated, deprecating**) to critize, especially mildly or politely; to belittle; to urge reasons against; to express disapproval of (as of anger, a scheme, etc).

depression

deprecatory *adj* apologetic; disapproving; belittling.

depreciate *vi* (**depreciated, depreciating**) to bring down the price or value of; to cause to be less valuable; to represent as of little value or merit or of less value than is commonly supposed; to lower in estimation, undervalue, decry, disparage or underrate.—*vi* to fall in value; to become of less worth.

depreciation *n* the act of depreciating; reduction in value or worth; a lowering or undervaluing in estimation; the state of being undervalued.

depredation *n* a robbing; a pillaging by people or animals; a laying waste.

depress *vt* to press down; to let fall to a lower state or position; to lower; to render dull or languid; to deject or make sad; to humble, abase, bring into adversity; to lower in value.

depression *n* the act of pressing down or depressing; a sinking or falling in of a surface; a hollow; the state or feeling of being depressed in spirits; a sinking of the spirits; dejection; a low state of strength; a state of debility; clinical depression, a condition characterized by a state of deep dejection, low self-esteem, apathy and loss of concentration; a state of dullness or inactivity (as in a trade); a period of commercial dullness; (*meteor*) a state of the atmosphere associated with low barometer and wet, stormy weather.

deprivation *n* the act of depriving; a taking away; a state of being deprived; loss; lack; bereavement; the act of divesting a clergyman of his spiritual promotion or dignity; the taking away of a preferment; deposition; hardship, lack of economic, social, etc, advantages.

deprive *vt* (**deprived, depriving**) to take from; to dispossess; to despoil; to bereave of something possessed or enjoyed (followed by *of*, as *to deprive a person of a thing*); to divest of an ecclesiastical preferment, dignity or office.

deprived *adj* having been deprived or dispossessed; suffering from hardship or economic or social, etc, disadvantage.

depth *n* the distance or measure of a thing from the highest part, top or surface to the lowest part or bottom, or to the extreme part downward or inward; the measure from the anterior to the posterior part; deepness; in a vertical direction opposed to *height*; a deep place; an abyss; a gulf; the inner, darker or more concealed part of a thing; the middle, darkest or stillest part (*the depth of winter* or *of a wood*); abstruseness; obscurity; immensity; infinity; intensity (*the depth of despair* or *of love*); extent of penetration or of the capacity of penetrating; profoundness.

deputation *n* the person or persons deputed to transact business for another.

depute *vt* (**deputed, deputing**) to appoint as a substitute or agent to act for another; to appoint and send with a special commission or authority to act for the sender.—*n* a deputy.

deputize *vi* (**deputized, deputizing**) to act as deputy or substitute (often with *for*).

deputy *n* a person appointed or elected to act for another; a representative, delegate, agent or substitute.

derange *vt* (**deranged, deranging**) to put out of order; to throw into confusion; to disorder; to confuse; to disturb; to unsettle; to embarrass; to discompose.

derangement *n* the act of deranging or state of being deranged; a putting out of order; embarrassment; confusion; disorder; delirium; insanity; mental disorder.

Derby *n* a famous British annual horse race; an important race; an important sporting contest, especially one between neighbouring teams.

derelict *adj* left; abandoned, especially abandoned at sea.—*n* an article abandoned by the owner, especially a vessel abandoned at sea.

dereliction *n* the act of leaving with an intention not to reclaim; desertion; relinquishment; abandonment (*a dereliction of duty*).

deride *vt* (**derided, deriding**) to laugh at in contempt; to turn to ridicule or make sport of; to treat with scorn by laughter; to mock; to ridicule.

de rigueur *adj* absolutely necessary; required by social convention or tradition

derision *n* the act of deriding or the state of being derided; contempt manifested by laughter; mockery; ridicule; scorn.

derisive *adj* expressing or characterized by derision; mocking; ridiculing.

derivation *n* the act of deriving, drawing or receiving from a source; the drawing or tracing of a word from its root or origin; etymology.

derivative *adj* taken or having proceeded from another or something preceding; derived; copied, not original; secondary.—*n* that which is derived; that which is deduced or comes by derivation from another; a word which takes its origin in another word or is formed from it.

derive *vt* (**derived, deriving**) to divert or turn aside from a natural course; to draw from, as in a regular course or channel; to receive from a source or as from a source or origin (*to derive power, knowledge, facts*); to deduce or draw from a root or primitive word; to trace the etymology of.

derma, dermis *n* the true skin, or underlayer of the skin, as distinguished from the cuticle, epidermis or scarf skin.

dermatitis inflammation of the skin.

dermatology *n* the branch of science which treats of the skin and its diseases.

derogate *vt* (**derogated, derogating**) to repeal, annul or revoke partially, as a law; distinguished from *abrogate*; to lessen the worth of; to disparage.—*vi* to detract; to have the effect of lowering or diminishing, as in reputation; to lessen by taking away a part (with *from*, as *something derogates from a person's dignity*).

derogation *n* the act of derogating; a taking away from or limiting in extent or operation; a lessening of value or estimation; detraction; disparagement.

derogatory *adj* having the effect of derogating or detracting from; lessening the extent, effect or value (with *to*).

derrick *n* an apparatus for hoisting heavy weights.

derrick crane *n* a kind of crane with a movable jib, combining the advantages of the derrick and of the crane.

derringer *n* a short-barrelled pistol of large calibre.

derv *n* a diesel oil for large road vehicles.

dervish *n* a Muslim ascetic, who professes extreme poverty and leads an austere life, partly in monasteries, partly itinerant.

descant *n* a discourse, discussion or disputation; (*mus*) an addition of a part or parts to a subject or melody; a song or tune with various modulations.—*vi* to discourse, comment or animadvert freely; to add a part or variation to a melody.

descend *vi* to move from a higher to a lower place; to move, come or go downward; to sink; to run or flow down; to invade or fall on hostilely; to proceed from a source or origin; to be derived; to pass from one heir to another; to pass, as from general to particular considerations; to lower or degrade oneself; to stoop.—*vt* to walk, move or pass downward on or along; to pass from the top to the bottom of.

descendant *n* an individual proceeding from an ancestor in any degree; offspring.

descent *n* the act of descending or passing from a higher to a lower place; inclination downward; slope; declivity; decline, as in station, virtue, quality, etc; an incursion, invasion or sudden attack on a country; transmission by succession or inheritance; a proceeding from a progenitor; extraction; lineage; pedigree.

describe *vt* (**described, describing**) to trace out; to form or trace by motion; to show or represent orally or by writing; to depict or portray in words.—*vi* to use the power of describing.

description *n* the act of describing; delineation; an account of the properties or appearance of a thing, so that another may form a just conception of it; the combina-

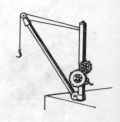

derrick crane

dervish

tion of qualities which constitute a class, species or individual; hence, class, species, variety, kind (*a person of this description*).

descriptive *adj* containing description; having the quality of representing.

descry *vt* (**descried, descrying**) to espy; to discover by the sight.

desecrate *vt* (**desecrated, desecrating**) to divert from a sacred purpose or sacred character; to render unhallowed; to profane.—**desecration** *n*.

deselect *vt* not to re-adopt as parliamentary candidate; not to choose as part of a team, group, etc, someone who was previously a member.

desert[1] *adj* lying waste; uncultivated and uninhabited; in the natural state and unimproved by man; pertaining to a wilderness (*the desert air*).—*n* an uninhabited tract of land; a wilderness; a solitude; often a vast sandy, stony or rocky expanse, almost lacking moisture and vegetation.

desert[2] *vt* to forsake; to leave utterly; to abandon; to quit, leave or depart from in defiance of duty.—*vi* to quit a service or post without permission; to run away.

desert[3] *n* the quality of deserving either reward or punishment; merit or demerit; what is deserved on account of good or evil done; reward or punishment merited; due return.

deserter *n* one who deserts; particularly, a soldier or seaman who quits the service without permission.

desertion *n* the act of deserting; the state of being deserted or forsaken.

deserve *vt* (**deserved, deserving**) to merit; to be worthy of, whether of good or evil; to merit by labour, services or qualities; to be worthy of or call for on account of evil acts or qualities (*actions that deserve censure*).—*vi* to merit; to be worthy of or deserving (*to deserve well of a person*).

deserving *adj* worthy of reward or praise; meritorious.

deshabille *n* same as **dishabille**.

desiccate *vt* (**desiccated, desiccating**) to exhaust of moisture; to exhale or remove moisture from; to dry.

desiderate *vt* (**desiderated, desiderating**) to feel the lack of; to miss; to want; to desire.

desideratum *n* (*pl* **desiderata**) that which is not possessed, but which is desirable; something much wanted.

design *vt* to plan and delineate by drawing the outline or figure of; to sketch, as for a pattern or model; to project or plan; to contrive for a purpose; to form in idea (*a scheme*); to set apart in intention; to intend; to purpose.—*vi* to intend; to purpose.—*n* a plan or representation of a thing by an outline; a first idea represented

desert

desk

by lines, as in painting or architecture; a sketch; a drawing; a tracing; a scheme or plan in the mind; purpose; intention; aim; the adaptation of means to a preconceived end; contrivance.

designate *vt* (**designated, designating**) to mark out or indicate by visible lines, marks, description, etc; to name and settle the identity of; to denominate; to select or distinguish for a particular purpose; to appoint, name or assign.

designation *n* the act of designating; a distinguishing from others; indication; appointment; assignment; distinctive appellation.

designer *n* one who designs, as clothes, furniture, etc.—*adj* designed by and bearing the name and label of a particular well-known designer; fashionable.

designing *adj* artful; insidious; intriguing; contriving schemes of mischief.—*n* the art or practice of making designs.

desire *vt* (**desired, desiring**) to wish for the possession or enjoyment of; to long for; to hanker after; to covet; to express a wish to obtain; to ask; to request; to petition.—*vi* to be in a state of desire or anxiety.—*n* an emotion or excitement of the mind, directed to the attainment or possession of an object from which pleasure is expected; a wish, craving or longing to obtain or enjoy; the object of desire; that which is desired.

desirous *adj* filled with a desire; wishing to obtain; wishful; covetous (often with *of*).

desist *vi* to cease to act or proceed; to forbear; to leave off; to discontinue; to cease.

desk *n* a kind of table or piece of furniture with a sloping upper surface for the use of writers and readers; a frame or case to be placed on a table for the same purpose.

desman *n* (*pl* **desmans**) the European muskrat.

desolate *vt* (**desolated, desolating**) to deprive of inhabitants; to make desert; to lay waste; to ruin; to ravage.—*adj* destitute or deprived of inhabitants; desert; uninhabited; laid waste; in a ruinous condition; without a companion; solitary; forsaken; forlorn; lonely.

desolation *n* the act of desolating; devastation; havoc; ravage; a place depopulated, ravaged or laid waste; the state of being desolate; gloominess; sadness; melancholy; destitution; ruin.

despair *vi* to give up all hope or expectation (followed by *of*); to be sunk in utter lack of hope.—*n* the state of being without hope, combined with a dread of coming evil; hopelessness; desperation; that which causes despair; (*theol*) loss of hope in the mercy of God.

despatch, dispatch *vt* to send or send away; particularly applied to the sending of messengers, agents and letters on special business and often implying haste; to hasten; to expedite; to speed; to send out of the world; to put to death; to slay; to kill; to perform or execute speedily; to finish.—*n* the act of despatching; the getting rid of or doing away with something; dismissal; riddance; speedy performance; speed; haste; expedition; a letter sent or to be sent with expedition by a special messenger; a letter on some affair of state or of public concern; a letter, message or document, sent by some public officer on public business.

desperado *n* (*pl* **desperadoes, desperados**) a desperate fellow; one fearless or regardless of safety; a reckless ruffian.

desperate *adj* without hope; regardless of safety; fearless of danger; reduced to extremity and reckless of consequences; frantic; proceeding from despair; reckless; beyond hope; irretrievable; past cure; hopeless (*desperate diseases, situation, undertaking*).

desperation *n* the state of being desperate; a giving up of hope.

despicable *adj* deserving of being despised; contemptible; base; mean; vile; worthless.

despise *vt* (**despised, despising**) to look down on; to have the lowest opinion of; to contemn; to disdain; to scorn.

despite *prep* in spite of; notwithstanding.—*n* extreme malice; malignity; contemptuous hate; aversion; spite.

despoil *vt* to take from by force; to rob; to strip; to divest; to deprive (*to despoil a person of a thing*).

despoliation *n* the act of despoiling; a stripping.

despond *vi* to be quite cast down; to feel depressed or dejected in mind; to lose hope, heart or resolution.

despondent *adj* losing courage at the loss of hope; sinking into dejection.

despot *n* a sovereign or monarch ruling absolutely or without control; a tyrant; one who enforces his or her will regardless of the interests or feelings of others.

despotic *adj* absolute in power; unrestrained by constitution, laws or people; arbitrary; tyrannical.

despotism *n* absolute power; unlimited or uncontrolled authority; an arbitrary government; the rule of a despot; absolutism; autocracy; tyranny.

des res *n* (*colloq*) a desirable residence.

dessert *n* a service of fruits or sweetmeats at the close of a dinner or entertainment.

dessertspoon *n* a spoon intermediate in size between a tablespoon and teaspoon, used for dessert.

destination *n* the act of destining; the purpose for which anything is intended or appointed; predetermined object or use; the place to which a thing is appointed; the predetermined end of a journey or voyage.

destine *vt* (**destined, destining**) to set, ordain or appoint to a use, purpose, state or place; to fix unalterably, as by a divine decree; to doom; to devote; to appoint inevitably.

Destinies *npl* the Fates.

destiny *n* a person's destined fate or lot; ultimate fate; doom; fortune; invincible necessity; fate; order of things fixed or established by divine decree or by connection of causes and effects.

destitute *adj* not having or possessing; lacking (with *of*); not possessing the necessaries of life; in abject poverty; entirely without the means of subsistence.

destitution *n* a state of utter want; poverty.

destroy *vt* to pull down; to knock to pieces; to demolish; to ruin; to annihilate; to put an end to; to cause to cease; to kill or slay; to ravage; to spoil.

destroyer *n* one who or that which destroys; a swift class of vessel intended for the destruction of torpedo craft and itself armed with guns and torpedoes.

destruction *n* the act of destroying; demolition; a pulling down; subversion; overthrow; ruin, by whatever means; extermination; death; murder; slaughter.

destructive *adj* causing destruction; having the quality of destroying; having a tendency to destroy; delighting in destruction; ruinous; mischievous; fatal; deadly (with *of* or *to*).

desuetude *n* a state of being no longer practised or customary; disuse; discontinuance of practice, custom or fashion.

desultory *adj* leaping or hopping about; passing from one thing or subject to another without order or natural connection; rambling; unconnected; unmethodical; inconstant; unsettled; hasty.

detach *vt* to separate or disunite; to disengage; to part from; to sever; to separate for a special purpose or service, especially some military purpose.

detached *adj* separated; disunited; standing apart or separately; drawn and sent on a separate service.

detachment *n* the act of detaching; a body of troops or number of vessels selected or taken from the main army or fleet and employed on some special service or expedition.

detail *vt* to relate, report or narrate in particulars; to recite the particulars of; to particularize; to relate minutely and distinctly; (*milit*) to appoint to a particular service.—*n* an individual fact, circumstance or portion going along with others; an item; a particular; a minute account; a narrative or report of particulars; (*milit*) an individual or small body; small detach-

dessert

ment on special service.—**in detail** circumstantially; item by item; individually; part by part.

detailed *adj* related in particulars; minutely recited; exact; minute; particular.

detain *vt* to keep back or from; to withhold; to retain or keep what belongs to another; to keep or restrain from proceeding; to hinder; to stay or stop; to hold in custody.

detainer *n* one who detains; (*law*) a holding or keeping possession of what belongs to another.

detent *n* a pin, stud or lever forming a check in a clock, watch, tumbler lock or other machine; a click or pawl.

detention *n* the act of detaining; a wrongful keeping of what belongs to another; state of being detained; confinement; restraint; delay from necessity or from accident.

detect *vt* to discover; to find out; to bring to light (an error, crime, criminal).

detection *n* the act of detecting; the finding out of what is concealed, hidden or formerly unknown; discovery.

detective *n* a police officer whose special duty it is to detect offences and to apprehend criminals; also a private person who engages to investigate cases, often of a delicate nature, for hire.

detector *n* one who or that which detects or brings to light; one who reveals; a discoverer; a device which records radio signals, currents, etc.

détente *n* a lessening in diplomatic tension between two countries.

deter *vt* (**deterred, deterring**) to discourage and prevent from acting or proceeding, the preventing agency being something anticipated as difficult, dangerous or unpleasant.

deterrent *adj* having the power or tendency to deter.—*n* that which deters or tends to deter.

detergent *adj* cleansing; purging.—*n* anything that has a strong cleansing power.

deteriorate *vi* (**deteriorated, deteriorating**) to grow worse or inferior in quality; to be impaired in quality; to degenerate.

deterioration *n* the process or state of growing worse.

determine *vt* (**determined, determining**) to fix the bounds of; to set bounds or limits to; to mark off, settle, fix, establish; to end or settle conclusively, as by the decision of a doubtful or controverted point; to settle ultimately; to come to a fixed resolution and intention in respect of; to give a bent or direction to; to influence the choice of; to cause to come to a conclusion or resolution.—*vi* to resolve; to conclude; to decide; to settle on some line of conduct; to decease; to terminate.

determination *n* the act of determining or deciding; decision in the mind; firm reso-

lution; settled purpose; the mental habit of settling on some line of action with a fixed purpose to adhere to it; adherence to aims or purposes; resoluteness.

determined *adj* having a firm or fixed purpose; manifesting firmness or resolution; resolute.

determinism *n* a system of philosophy which denies liberty of action to humans, holding that the will is not free but is invincibly determined by motives.

detest *vt* to abhor; to abominate; to hate extremely.

detestable *adj* extremely hateful; abominable; very odious; deserving abhorrence.

detestation *n* extreme hatred; abhorrence; loathing.

dethrone *vt* (**dethroned, dethroning**) to remove or drive from a throne, to depose; to divest of royal authority and dignity; to divest of rule or power, or of supreme power.

detonate *vti* (**detonated, detonating**) to explode or cause to explode; to burn with a sudden report.

detonation *n* an explosion or sudden report made by the inflammation of certain combustible bodies.

detonator *n* that which detonates; a device which sets off an explosion, torpedo, etc.

detour *n* a roundabout or circuitous way; a going round instead of by a direct road or route.

detract *vt* to take away from a whole; to withdraw; to disparage.—*vi* to take away a part; especially, to take away reputation; to derogate (followed by *from*, as *this detracts from his merit*).

detraction *n* the act of detracting; an attempt by injurious or carping statements to take something from the reputation of another; envious or malicious depreciation of a person or denial of his or her merits.

detractor *n* one who uses detraction; one who tries to take from the reputation of another injuriously.

detrain *vt* to remove from a train; to cause to leave a train.—*vi* to quit a train.

detriment *n* a certain degree of loss, damage or injury; injurious or prejudicial effect; harm; diminution.

detrimental *adj* injurious; hurtful; causing loss or damage.

detritus *n* (*geol*) a mass of substances worn off or detached from solid bodies by attrition; disintegrated materials of rocks.

deuce[1] *n* a playing card or a die with two spots; the two at dice; the score of 40 all at lawn tennis.

deuce[2] *exclam* the devil.

deuced *adj, adv,* (*sl*) devilish; excessive; confounded.

deuterium *n* a heavy hydrogen, used in nuclear reactors as a moderator to slow the rate of fission.

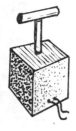

detonator

deuce

deuterogamy *n* a second marriage after the death of the first husband or wife.

Deuteronomy *n* the second law or second statement of the law in the fifth book of the Pentateuch.

Deutschmark *n* the basic monetary unit of German; the mark.

devastate *vt* (**devastated, devastating**) to lay waste; to ravage; to desolate.

devastation *n* the act of devastating; the state of being devastated; ravage; havoc; desolation.

devastator *n* one who or that which devastates.

develop *vt* to unfold gradually; to lay open part by part; to disclose or show all the ramifications of; (*biol*) to make to pass through the process of natural evolution.—*vi* to be unfolded; to become manifest in all its parts; to advance from one stage to another by a process of natural or inherent evolution; to grow or expand by a natural process; to be evolved; to proceed or come forth naturally from some vivifying source.

development *n* the act or process of developing; unfolding; the unravelling of a plot; a gradual growth or advancement through progressive changes; the organic changes which take place in animal and vegetable bodies, from their embryo state until they arrive at maturity; a new stage or event in the progress of something; (*photog*) the process following exposure, by which the image on the plate is rendered visible.

deviant *n* a person whose behaviour deviates from the accepted standards of society. —*adj* deviating from an accepted norm.

deviate *vi* (**deviated, deviating**) to turn aside or wander from the common or right way, course or line; to diverge; to err; to swerve; to vary from uniform state.—*vt* to cause to deviate.

deviation *n* a turning aside from the right way, course or line; variation from a common or established rule, standard, principle, etc.

deviation of the compass *n* the deviation of a ship's compass from the true magnetic meridian, caused by the near presence of iron.

device *n* that which is formed by design or invented; a scheme, contrivance, stratagem, project.

devil *n* an evil spirit or being; the evil one, represented in Scripture as the traducer, father of lies, tempter, etc; a very wicked person; a ferocious marsupial animal of Tasmania; a printer's errand boy.

devilish *adj* partaking of the qualities of the devil; pertaining to the devil; diabolical; very evil and mischievous.

devilment *n* trickery; roguishness; (*colloq*) a prank.

devil's advocate *n* (*RC Church*) a person appointed to raise doubts against the claims of a candidate for canonization; one who tests an argument or policy by putting forward the criticism likely to be made by its opponents.

devious *adj* out of the common way or track; following circuitous or winding paths; rambling; erring; going astray; cunning, crafty.

devise *vt* (**devised, devising**) to invent, contrive or form in the mind; to strike out by thought; to plan; to scheme; to excogitate; (*law*) to give or bequeath by will.—*vi* to consider; to contrive; to lay a plan; to form a scheme.—*n* the act of bequeathing by will; a will or testament; a share of estate bequeathed.

devoid *adj* destitute; not possessing (with *of* before the thing absent).

devoir *n* service or duty; an act of civility or respect; respectful notice due to another.

devolution *n* a transfer of authority, especially from a central government to regional governments.

devolve *vt* (**devolved, devolving**) to roll down; to move from one person to another; to deliver over or from one possessor to a successor.—*vi* to roll down; hence, to pass from one to another; to fall by succession from one possessor to a successor.

Devonian *adj* of or pertaining to Devonshire in England; (*geol*) a term applied to a great portion of the Palaeozoic strata of North and South Devon, lying between the Silurian and carboniferous rocks.

devote *vt* (**devoted, devoting**) to appropriate by vow; to set apart or dedicate by a solemn act; to consecrate; to give up wholly; to direct the attention wholly or chiefly (*to devote oneself* or *one's time to science*); to give up; to doom; to consign over (*to devote one to destruction*).

devoted *adj* strongly attached to a person or cause; ardent; zealous.

devotee *n* one who is wholly devoted; a votary; particularly, one who is superstitiously given to religious duties and ceremonies.

devotion *n* the state of being devoted or set apart for a particular purpose; a yielding of the heart and affections to God, with reverence, faith and piety, in religious duties, particularly in prayer and meditation; devoutness; performance of religious duties (now generally used in the plural); ardent attachment to a person or a cause; attachment, manifested by constant attention; earnestness; ardour; eagerness.

devour *vt* to eat up; to eat with greediness; to eat ravenously; to destroy or consume; to waste.

devout *adj* yielding a reverential devotion to God in religious exercises; pious; de-

devil

voted to religion; religious; expressing devotion or piety; solemn; earnest.

dew *n* the aqueous vapour or moisture which is deposited in small drops, especially during the night, from the atmosphere, on the surfaces of bodies when they have become colder than the surrounding atmosphere.—*vt* to wet with dew; to bedew.

dewberry *n* a species of bramble, the fruit of which is black, with a bluish bloom and an agreeable acid taste.

dew claw *n* the uppermost claw in a dog's foot, smaller than the rest and not touching the ground.

dewdrop *n* a drop or spangle of dew.

dewlap *n* the fold of skin that hangs from the throat of oxen or cows or a similar appendage in other animals.

dewy *adj* of or pertaining to dew; partaking of the nature or appearance of dew; like dew; moist with, or as with, dew.

dexterity *n* expertness; skill; that readiness in performing an action which proceeds from experience or practice, united with activity or quick motion; readiness of mind or mental faculties, as in contrivance or inventing means to accomplish a purpose; promptness in devising expedients.

dextrose *n* a form of sugar found in fruit, honey and animal tissues.

dextrous, dexterous *adj* characterized by dexterity; skilful and active with the hands; adroit; prompt in contrivance and management; expert; quick at inventing expedients; skilful; done with dexterity.

dey *n* the title of the old governors or sovereigns of Algiers, Tunis and Tripoli, under the Sultan of Turkey.

dhow *n* an Arab coastal vessel, generally with one mast and a large triangular sail.

dhurra *n* a kind of millet largely cultivated in Africa and elsewhere.

diabetes *n* (*med*) a metabolic disorder characterized by excessive and persistent discharge of urine.

diabetic *adj* pertaining to diabetes.—*n* a person with diabetes.

diabolic, diabolical *adj* devilish; pertaining to the devil; infernal; impious; atrocious.

diabolo *n* (*pl* **diabolos**) a kind of wooden reel which is spun on a string held by sticks at either end and tossed from one player to another.

diaconal *adj* pertaining to a deacon.

diaconate *n* the office or dignity of a deacon; a body of deacons.

diacritical, diacritic *adj* separating or distinguishing; distinctive.

diacritical mark *n* a mark used in some languages to distinguish letters which are similar in form.

diadem *n* a headband or fillet formerly worn as a badge of royalty; anything worn on the head as a mark or badge of royalty; a crown; a coronet.

diaeresis, dieresis *n* (*pl* **diaereses, diereses**) separation of one syllable into two; a mark which signifies such a division, as in naïf.

diagnosis *n* (*pl* **diagnosis**) the determination of diseases by their distinctive marks or symptoms.

diagnose *vt* (**diagnosed, diagnosing**) to ascertain from symptoms the true nature of a condition.

diagnostic *adj* distinguishing; characteristic; indicating the nature of a disease.—*n* a sign or symptom by which a disease is known.

diagonal *adj* extending from one angle to the opposite of a quadrilateral figure and dividing it into two triangles; lying in this direction.—*n* a straight line drawn between the opposite angles of a quadrilateral figure.

diagonally *adv* in a diagonal direction.

diagram *n* a figure or drawing for the purpose of demonstrating the properties of any geometrical figure, as a triangle, circle, etc; any illustrative figure wherein the outlines are exclusively or chiefly delineated.—*vt* (**diagrammed, diagramming**) to demonstrate in diagram form.

diagrammatic *adj* pertaining to or partaking of the nature of a diagram.

dial *n* an instrument for showing the hour of the day from the shadow thrown by means of a stile or gnomon on a surface; the face of a watch, clock or other timekeeper; any somewhat similar plate or face on which a pointer or index moves, as in a gas meter or telephone.—*vt* (**dialled, dialling**) to measure with, or as with, a dial; to make a telephone connection by using a dial or keypad.

dialect *n* the form or idiom of a language peculiar to a province or to a limited region or people, as distinguished from the literary language of the whole people; language; speech or manner of speaking.—**dialectal** *adj*.

dialectic *n* the pursuit of philosophical truth through logical debate; the interpretation of history, propounded by Marx and Engels, that sees it as a series of contradictions produced by the struggle between ruling and working classes.

dialectical *adj* pertaining to dialectics.

dialectician *n* one skilled in dialectics; a logician; a reasoner.

dialectics *n* the art of reasoning or disputing; that branch of logic which teaches the rules and modes of reasoning or of distinguishing truth from error; the art of using forms of reasoning so as to make fallacies pass for truth;.

dialogue *n* a conversation between two or

dhow

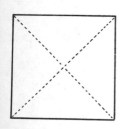

diagonal

more persons; a formal conversation in theatrical performances; a composition in which two or more persons are represented as conversing on some topic.

dialyse *vt* (**dialysed, dialysing**) to separate or purify by means of dialysis; to subject to dialysis.

dialysis *n* the separation of colloidal particles from dissolved substances in a solution by diffusion through a membrane; a treatment used in kidney disease in which blood is purified by filtering it through a membrane.

diamagnetic *adj* applied to a class of substances which, when under the influence of magnetism and freely suspended, take a position at right angles to the magnetic meridian, that is, point east and west.

diameter *n* a straight line passing through the centre of a circle or other curvilinear figure, terminated by the circumference and dividing the figure into two equal parts; a straight line through the centre of any body; the measure transversely through a cylindrical body; thickness.

diametric, diametrical *adj* of or pertaining to a diameter; directly opposed.—**diametrically** *adv*.

diamond *n* a most valuable gem of extreme hardness, usually clear and transparent, but sometimes yellow, blue, green, black, etc, consisting of pure carbon; a small diamond fixed to a handle and used for cutting glass; a four-sided figure with the sides equal or nearly so and having two obtuse and two acute angles, called also a lozenge or rhombus; one of a set of playing cards marked with one or more such figures in red.—*adj* resembling a diamond; consisting of diamonds; set with a diamond or diamonds.

diamond wedding *n* the sixtieth anniversary of a wedding.

dianoetic *adj* capable of thought; thinking; intellectual.

diapason *n* (*mus*) an old Greek term for the octave; proportion in the constituent parts of an octave; harmony; the entire compass of a voice or an instrument; a rule or scale by which the pipes of organs, the holes of flutes, etc, are correctly adjusted; a name of certain stops in the organ, given because they extend through the scales of the instrument.

diaper *n* (especially American), a baby's nappy.

diaphanous *adj* having power to transmit rays of light, as glass; pellucid; transparent; delicate.

diaphoresis *n* (*med*) a greater degree of perspiration than is natural.

diaphragm *n* the midriff, a muscular wall separating the chest or thorax from the abdomen; a partition or dividing substance,

as a circular ring used in telescopes, etc, to cut off marginal portions of a beam of light; a calcareous plate which divides the cavity of certain mollusc shells; a contraceptive cap covering the cervix; a thin vibrating disc used in a telephone, microphone etc.

diarrhoea *n* excessive looseness of bowel movements.

diary *n* a book in which daily events or transactions are noted; a journal; a blank book dated for the record of daily memoranda.

diarist *n* one who keeps a diary.

diastase *n* a substance existing in barley and oats after germination, so called because in solution it possesses the property of causing starch to break up.

diastole *n* (*physiol*) the dilatation of the heart with blood, opposed to *systole* or contraction; (*gram*) the lengthening of a syllable that is naturally short.

diathesis *n* (*pl* **diatheses**) (*med*) particular disposition or habit of body, good or bad.

diatom *n* one of a natural order of microscopic vegetable organisms with siliceous coverings, found in fresh and salt water and in moist places.

diatom

diatomic *adj* (*chem*) consisting of two atoms.

diatonic *adj* (*mus*) applied to the major or minor scales or to chords, intervals and melodic progressions belonging to one scale.

diatribe *n* a continued disputation; a lengthy invective; a harangue in which a person inveighs against something.

diazo compound *n* (*chem*) one of a group of organic substances containing the active azo group, important as intermediate products in many reactions.

dibasic *adj* (*chem*) of acids, containing two hydrogen atoms capable of being replaced by a base in forming salts.

dibble *n* a pointed instrument used in gardening and agriculture to make holes for planting seeds, bulbs, etc.

dicast *n* in Greek antiquity, an officer answering nearly to a modern member of a jury.

dice *npl* (*sing* **die**: *also now used in sing*) a small cube with numbered sides used in games of chance.—*vi* (**diced, dicing**) to play with dice; to gamble; to chop (food) into small cubes.

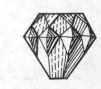

diamond

diced *adj* ornamented with square or diamond-shaped figures.

dicey *adj* (*colloq*) risky, dangerous.

dichroism *n* in optics, a property possessed by several crystallized bodies of appearing under two distinct colours according to the direction in which light is transmitted through them.

dickens *interj* devil; deuce.

dickey, dicky *n* an article of dress like the front of a dress shirt and worn instead; a space or seat at the back of a two-seater car.

dicky *adj* (*colloq*) shaky; unsound.

dicky-bird *n* a pet name for a little bird.

diclinic *adj* applied to crystals in which two of the axes are obliquely inclined.

dicotyledon *n* a plant whose seeds contain a pair of cotyledons or seed leaves, which are always opposite to each other.

dicotyledonous *adj* having two cotyledons.

Dictaphone *n* the trademark of a machine that records and replays dictation.

dictate *vt* (**dictated, dictating**) to deliver or announce with authority, as an order, command or direction; to instruct to be said or written; to utter, so that another may write out; to direct by impulse on the mind (*an action dictated by fear*); to instigate.—*n* an order delivered; a command; a rule, maxim or precept, delivered with authority; rule or direction suggested to the mind (*the dictates of reason*).

dictation *n* the act of dictating; the act or practice of speaking or reading that another may write down what is spoken.

dictator *n* one invested with absolute authority; a supreme leader or guide to direct the conduct or opinion of others.

dicotyledon

dictatorial *adj* pertaining to a dictator; imperious; overbearing.

dictatorship *n* the office of a dictator; authority; imperiousness.

diction *n* a person's choice or selection of words in speaking or writing; general mode of expressing oneself; style.

dictionary *n* a book containing the words of a language arranged in alphabetical order, with explanations or definitions of their meanings; a lexicon; a wordbook; any work which communicates information on an entire subject or branch of a subject, under entries or heads arranged alphabetically.—*adj* pertaining to, contained in or given by a dictionary or dictionaries.

dictum *n* (*pl* **dicta**) a positive assertion; an authoritative saying or decision.

didactic *adj* adapted to teach; containing doctrines, precepts, principles or rules; intended to instruct.

didactics *n* the art or science of teaching.

didapper *n* the dabchick or little grebe.

diet

diddle *vt* (**diddled, diddling**) to cheat or trick, especially in money matters.

die[1] *vi* (**died, dying**) to cease to live; to expire; to decease; to perish; to become dead; to lose life (said of both animals and plants); to come to an end; to cease to have influence or effect (*his fame will not die*); to sink; to faint (*his heart died within him*); to languish with pleasure, tenderness, affection, etc; to become gradually less distinct or perceptible to the sight or hearing, generally followed by *away* (*the sound died away*); (*theol*) to suffer divine wrath and punishment in the future world.—**to die out** to become extinct gradually.

die[2] *n* (*pl* **dice**) a small cube marked on its faces with numbers from one to six, used in gaming by being thrown from a box; a square body; (*pl* **dies**) (*archit*) the cubical part of a pedestal between its base and cornice; a stamp used in coining money, in foundries, etc.—**the die is cast** everything is now put to hazard; all will depend on fortune.

diecious *adj* same as **dioecious**.

dieresis *n* same as **diaeresis**.

die-sinker *n* an engraver of dies for stamping or embossing.

die-sinking *n* the process of engraving dies.

die-hard *n* an irreconcilable opponent of any measure in Parliament; usually applied only to uncompromising Tories.

dielectric *n* (*elect*) any medium through or across which electric induction takes place between two conductors.

diesel engine *n* an oil engine in which the vaporized oil is burned by being sprayed into air whose temperature has been raised by high compression.

diesel oil *n* a form of petroleum that ignites at a low temperature, used in diesel engines.

diet[1] *n* a person's regular food or victuals; manner of living as regards food and drink; course of food limited in kind and quantity; allowance of provision.—*vt* to furnish diet or meals for; to prescribe a particular diet for.—*vi* to eat according to rules prescribed; to limit one's intake of food in order to lose weight.

diet[2] *n* a meeting, as of dignitaries or delegates, held from day to day for legislative, ecclesiastical or other purposes; session; specifically, the legislative or administrative assemblies in pre-war Germany and Austria, etc.

dietary *adj* pertaining to diet or the rules of diet.—*n* a system or course of diet; allowance of food.

dietary fibre *n* a substance obtained from certain foods, such as cereals and vegetables, which cannot be digested and so adds roughage to the diet.

dietetic *adj* pertaining to diet or to the rules for regulating diet.

dietetics *n* that department of medicine which relates to the regulation of diet.

differ *vi* to be unlike, dissimilar, distinct or various, in nature, condition, form or qualities (*men and things differ greatly; they differ from each other*); to disagree; not to accord; to be of another opinion (*we differ with* or *from a person*); to contend; to be at variance; to dispute; to quarrel.

difference *n* the state or condition in virtue of which things differ from each other; a point or feature of disagreement; the being different; lack of sameness; variation; dissimilarity; distinction; a dispute, contention, quarrel, controversy; the point in dispute; the remainder of a sum or quantity after a lesser sum or quantity is subtracted; the quantity by which one quantity differs from another.—*vt* (**differenced, differencing**) to cause a difference or distinction in; to distinguish; to discriminate.

different *adj* distinct; separate; not the same; various; of various natures, forms or qualities; unlike; dissimilar.

differentia *n* (*pl* **differentiae**) in logic, the characteristic attribute of a species; specific difference.

differential *adj* making a difference; discriminating; distinguishing; (*math*) an epithet applied to an infinitely small quantity by which two variable quantities differ; pertaining to mathematical processes in which such quantities are employed.—*n* something that marks a difference between comparable things; a difference in wage rates; a differential gear; (*math*) an infinitesimal difference between two states of a variable quantity.

differential calculus *n* an important branch of higher mathematics which deals largely with the infinitely small differences of variable and mutually dependent quantities.

differential gear *n* (*mech*) an arrangement of gear wheels connecting two axles in one line, permitting one wheel to revolve faster than the other when necessary, as when a vehicle turns a corner.

differentiate *vt* (**differentiated, differentiating**) to produce or lead to, a difference in or between; to mark or distinguish by a difference; to set aside for a definite or specific purpose; (*math*) to obtain the differential of.—*vi* to acquire a distinct and separate character.

differentiation *n* the act of differentiating; the production or discrimination of differences or variations; the assignment of a specific agency to the discharge of a specific function; (*biol*) the formation of different parts, organs, species, etc, by the production or acquisition of a diversity of new structures, through a process of evolution or development; (*math*) the operation of finding the differential of any function.

difficult *adj* hard to make, do or perform; not easy; attended with labour and pains; arduous; hard to understand.

difficulty *n* hardness to be done or accomplished; the state of anything which renders its performance laborious or perplexing; opposed to *easiness* or *facility*; that which is hard to be performed or surmounted; perplexity; embarrassment of affairs; trouble; objection; cavil; obstacle to

belief; an embroilment; a falling out; a controversy; a quarrel.

diffidence *n* distrust; lack of confidence; especially distrust of oneself; a doubt respecting some personal qualification; modest reserve.

diffident *adj* characterized by diffidence; distrustful of oneself; not confident; backward; bashful.

diffract *vt* to break; to bend from a straight line; to deflect.

diffraction *n* in optics, the peculiar modifications which light undergoes when it passes by the edge of an opaque body, as e.g. through a slit or other small aperture.

diffuse *vt* (**diffused, diffusing**) to pour out and spread, as a fluid; to cause to flow and spread; to send out or extend in all directions (light, information, happiness).—*adj* widely spread; using too many words to express meaning; lacking conciseness and due condensation; verbose; prolix; (*bot*) spreading widely, horizontally and irregularly.

diffuseness *n* the quality of being diffuse; lack of conciseness or due concentration in expressing one's meaning.

diffusible *adj* capable of being diffused.

diffusion *n* the act of diffusing or process of being diffused; a spreading abroad or scattering; dispersion; dissemination; extension; propagation; the tendency of two different gases or miscible liquids to become uniformly intermingled.

dig *vt* (**digged** *or* **dug, digging**) to open and break, or turn up, with a spade or other sharp instrument; to excavate; to form in the ground by digging and removing loose soil; to raise from the earth by digging (*to dig coals, fossils*, etc).—*vi* to work with a spade or other similar instrument.

digamma *n* a letter which once belonged to the alphabet of the Greeks and appears to have had the force of *v* or *f*.

digest *vt* to arrange in suitable divisions or under proper heads or titles; to dispose in due method for being conveniently studied or consulted; to arrange methodically in the mind; to think out; to separate or dissolve in the stomach, preparing the nutritious elements for entering the system; (*chem*) to soften and prepare by a heated liquid; (*fig*) to bear with patience or with an effort; to brook; to put up with.—*vi* to undergo digestion, as food.—*n* a collection of Roman laws, digested or arranged under proper titles by order of the Emperor Justinian; any orderly or systematic summary, as of laws.

digester *n* one who digests or disposes in order; that which assists the digestion of food; a vessel in which bones or other substances may be subjected to heat in water or other liquid.

diffract

digestible *adj* capable of being digested.

digestion *n* the act of classifying or disposing in order; the process which food undergoes in the stomach, by which it is prepared for nourishing the body; (*chem*) the operation of exposing bodies to heat in a liquid to prepare them for some action on each other; or the slow action of a solvent on any substance.

digestive *adj* having the power to promote digestion in the stomach.—*n* any preparation or medicine which increases the tone of the stomach and aids digestion.

digger *n* one who or that which digs; a large machine with a shovel for digging.

digit *n* a finger, sometimes used scientifically to signify toe, when speaking of animals; the measure of a finger's breadth; (*astron*) the twelfth part of the diameter of the sun or moon; (*arith*) any integer under 10.

digital *adj* pertaining to the fingers or to digits; using numbers rather than a dial to display measurements.—*n* one of the keys of instruments of the organ or piano class.

digital clock, digital watch *n* a clock or watch on which the time is indicated directly by numbers rather than by means of a dial and pointers.

digital computer *n* a computer that processes information in the form of characters and digits in electronic binary code.

digitalin *n* a substance obtained from digitalis which acts as a heart stimulant.

digitalis *n* a genus of plants one species of which, the foxglove, is a common wild flower in Britain.

digital recording *n* the conversion of sound into discrete electronic pulses (representing binary digits) for recording.

digitigrade *n* an animal that walks on its toes, as the lion, wolf, etc.—*adj* walking on the toes.

dignify *vt* (**dignified, dignifying**) to invest with honour or dignity; to exalt in rank; to elevate to a high office; to honour; to make illustrious.

dignified *adj* invested with dignity; honoured; marked with dignity or loftiness; noble; stately in deportment.

dignitary *n* one who holds an exalted rank or office.

dignity *n* nobleness or elevation of mind; loftiness; honourable place or rank; degree of elevation; elevation of aspect; grandeur of mien; height or importance; an elevated office.

digraph *n* a union of two vowels or of two consonants, representing a single sound of the voice (as *ea* in head).

digress *vi* to depart or wander from the main subject or tenor of a discourse, argument or narration.

digression *n* the act of digressing; a depar-

digit

dill

ture from the main subject; the part or passage of a discourse, etc, which deviates from the main subject.

digs *npl* (*colloq*) lodgings.

dike, dyke *n* a ditch or channel for water; a barrier of earth, stones or other materials intended to prevent low lands from being inundated by the sea or a river; a low wall forming a fence.—*vt* (**diked, diking**) to surround with a dyke; to secure by a bank; to drain by one or more dykes or ditches.

dilapidate *vi* (**dilapidated, dilapidating**) to fall to ruin.—*vt* to suffer to go to ruin (buildings) by misuse or neglect.

dilapidated *adj* in a ruined condition; suffered to go to ruin; in a state of disrepair.

dilate *vt* (**dilated, dilating**) to expand or swell out, especially by filling; to distend; to enlarge in all directions, opposed to *contract*.—*vi* to expand, swell or extend in all directions; to speak largely and copiously; to dwell in narration; to descant (with *on* or *upon*).

dilatation, dilation *n* the act of expanding, dilating or state of being expanded or distended.

dilatory *adj* marked with or given to procrastination or delay; making delay or resulting in delay; slow; tardy; not proceeding with diligence (of persons or things).

dilemma *n* in logic, an argument in which the adversary is caught between two difficulties by being presented by two alternatives, each of which is equally conclusive; hence, a state of things in which evils or obstacles present themselves on every side and it is difficult to determine what course to pursue.

dilettante *n* (*pl* **dilettanti**) an admirer or lover of the fine arts; an amateur or trifler in art; one who pursues an art or other pursuit desultorily and for amusement.

dilettantism *n* the quality characteristic of a dilettante.

diligence[1] *n* steady application in business of any kind; constant effort to accomplish what is undertaken; due attention; industry; assiduity; care; heed; heedfulness; (*Scots law*) a kind of warrant and also a process by which persons or effects are attached.

diligence[2] *n* a kind of four-wheeled stagecoach.

diligent *adj* steady in application to business; constant in effort to accomplish what is undertaken; assiduous; attentive; industrious; not idle or negligent (of persons or things).

dill *n* an umbelliferous European plant, the fruits or seeds of which are moderately pungent and aromatic and are used to relieve flatulence.

dilly-dally *vi* (**dilly-dallied, dilly-dallying**) to loiter; to delay; to trifle.

dilute *vt* (**diluted, diluting**) to render liquid or more liquid, especially by mixing with water; to weaken (spirit, acid, etc) by an admixture of water.—*adj* diluted; reduced in strength by intermixture.

diluvial, diluvian *adj* pertaining to a flood or deluge, more especially to the deluge in Noah's days.

dim *adj* not seeing clearly; having the vision indistinct; not clearly seen; obscure; faint; vague; somewhat dark; not luminous; dull of apprehension; having the lustre obscured; tarnished; (*colloq*) stupid.—*vt* (**dimmed, dimming**) to render dim or less clear or distinct; to becloud; to obscure; to tarnish or sully.

dime *n* a silver coin of the United States, value ten cents; the tenth of a dollar.

dimension *n* extension in a single direction, as length, breadth and thickness or depth, a solid body having thus three dimensions; (*pl*) measure, size, extent, capacity; (*fig*) consequence; importance; (*alg*) same as degree.

dimeter *adj* having two poetical measures.—*n* a verse of two measures.

dimidiate *adj* divided into two equal parts; halved.

diminish *vt* to lessen; to make less or smaller by any means, opposed to *increase* and *augment*.—*vi* to lessen; to become or appear less or smaller; decrease.

diminuendo (*mus*) an instruction to the performer to lessen the volume of sound from loud to soft, opposite of *crescendo*.

diminution *n* the act of diminishing; a making smaller; the state of becoming or appearing less; discredit; loss of dignity; degradation.

diminutive *adj* considerably smaller than the normal size; small; little.—*n* (*gram*) a word formed from another word to express a little thing of the kind (as *manikin*, a little man).

dimissory *adj* sending away; dismissing to another jurisdiction; granting leave to depart.

dimity *n* a stout cotton fabric ornamented in the loom by raised stripes or fancy figures, rarely dyed, but usually employed white for beds, etc.

dimorphism *n* occurrence in two quite distinct forms.

dimple *n* a small natural depression in the cheek or other part of the face, as the chin; a slight depression or indentation on any surface.—*vi* (**dimpled, dimpling**) to form dimples; to sink into depressions or little inequalities.—*vt* to mark with dimples.

din *n* noise; a loud sound; particularly, a rattling, clattering or rumbling sound, long continued.—*vt* (**dinned, dinning**) to strike with continued or confused sound; to stun with noise; to harass with clamour.

dine *vi* (**dined, dining**) to eat the chief meal of the day; to take dinner.—*vt* to give a dinner to; to supply with dinner; to afford convenience for dining.

dining room *n* a room to dine in; a place for public dining.

dinner *n* the principal meal of the day, taken between morning and evening, or in the afternoon or evening.

dinner jacket *n* a black coat without tails worn by men in the evening.

ding *vi* to sound, as a bell, with a continuous monotonous tone.—*vt* to impress on by repetition.

ding-dong *n* the sound of bells or any similar sound of continuous strokes.

dinghy *n* a small open boat driven by oars or sails; an inflatable boat.

dingle *n* a narrow dale or valley between hills; a small secluded and embowered valley.

dingo *n* the wild Australian dog.

dingy *adj* of a dirty white or dusky colour; soiled; sullied; dusky.

dinornis *n* an extinct running bird of gigantic size which formerly inhabited New Zealand; the moa.

dinosaur *n* one of a group of huge terrestrial, fossil reptiles.

dinothere *n* a gigantic extinct mammal allied to the elephant.

dint *n* a blow or stroke; the mark made by a blow; a cavity or impression made by a blow or by pressure on a substance; a dent.—**by dint of** by the force or power of; by means of.—*vt* to make a dint in; to dent.

diocese *n* the circuit or extent of a bishop's jurisdiction; an ecclesiastical division of a state, subject to the authority of a bishop.

diocesan *adj* pertaining to a diocese.—*n* a bishop as related to his own diocese; one in possession of a diocese and having the ecclesiastical jurisdiction over it.

dioecious, diecious *adj* (*bot*) having stamens on one plant and pistils on another.

dioptric, dioptrical *adj* pertaining to dioptrics or to the passing of light through instruments or substances.

dioptrics *n* that part of optics which treats of the refractions of light passing through different mediums, as through air, water or glass and especially through lenses.

diorama *n* a scenic contrivance in which the scenes are viewed through a large aperture.

diorite *n* a tough crystalline trap rock of a whitish colour, speckled with black or greenish black.

dioxide *n* an oxide consisting of one atom of a metal and two atoms of oxygen.

dip *vt* (**dipped, dipping**) to plunge or immerse in water or other liquid; to put into a fluid and withdraw; to lift with a ladle or

dingo

dinosaur

other vessel (often with *out*); to baptize by immersion.—*vi* to plunge into a liquid and quickly emerge; to go into water and come out quickly; to suddenly drop down or sink out of sight; to sink, as below the horizon; to engage in a desultory way; to concern oneself to some little extent (*to dip into a subject*); to read passages here and there (*to dip into a volume*); (*geol*) to incline or slope.—*n* an immersion in any liquid; a plunge; a bath; an inclination or slope; a sudden drop; a mixture in which to dip something.

dipper *n* one who or that which dips; one of a sect of American Baptists; a name given to the water ouzel.

dipetalous *adj* having two flower leaves or petals.

diphtheria *n* an epidemic inflammatory disease of the air passages and especially of the throat, characterized by the formation of a false membrane.

diphthong *n* a union of two vowel sounds pronounced in one syllable (as in *bound*, *oil*); a ligature.

diploma *n* (*pl* **diplomas**) a letter or writing, usually under seal and signed by competent authority, conferring some power, privilege or honour, as that given to graduates of universities on their receiving the usual degrees, to physicians who are licensed to practise their profession, etc; (*pl* often **diplomata**) a charter.

diplomacy *n* the science or art of conducting negotiations, arranging treaties, etc, between nations; the forms of international negotiations; dexterity or skill in managing negotiations of any kind; artful management or manoeuvring with the view of securing advantages.

diplomat *n* a person skilled in diplomacy; a diplomatist.

diplomatic *adj* pertaining to diplomacy or to the management of any negotiations; skilful in gaining one's ends by tact and cleverness; conferred by diploma; relating to diplomatics.

diplomatics *n* the science of deciphering old writings, to ascertain their authenticity, date, etc; palaeography.

diplomatist *n* a diplomat.

dipsomania *n* a compulsive craving for alcohol.

dipsomaniac *n* a sufferer from dipsomania.

dipstick *n* a kind of rod with graduated markings to measure the level of a fluid, for example the level of oil in a car.

dipterous *adj* (*entom*) having two wings.

diptych *n* a painting or carved work, on two folding compartments or tablets.

dire *adj* dreadful; dismal; horrible; terrible; evil in a great degree.

direct *adj* straight; right, opposite to *crooked*, *circuitous*, *winding*, *oblique*;

dirty

(*astron*) appearing to move from west to east, opposed to retrograde; in the line of father and son, opposed to *collateral*; straightforward; open; ingenuous; plain; not ambiguous.—*vt* to point or aim in a straight line towards something; to make to act or work, towards a certain end or object; to show the right road or course to; to prescribe a course to; to regulate, guide, lead, govern; to order or instruct; to prescribe to; to inscribe (a letter) with the address.—*vi* to act as a guide; to point out a course.

direct current *n* (*elect*) an electric current flowing always in one direction, as distinguished from an alternating current.

direction *n* the act of directing; the course or line in which anything is directed; a being directed towards a particular end; the line in which a body moves or to which its position is referred; course; the act of governing; administration; management; guidance; superintendence; instruction in what manner to proceed; order; behest; the address on a letter, parcel, etc; a body or board of directors; directorate.

directly *adv* in a direct manner; in a straight line or course; straightway; immediately; instantly; soon; without delay; openly; expressly; without circumlocution or ambiguity.

director *n* one who or that which directs; one who superintends, governs or manages; specifically, one of a body appointed to direct, control or superintend the affairs of a company.

directorate *n* the office of a director; a body of directors.

directorship *n* the condition or office of a director.

directory *n* a book containing an alphabetical list, as of the inhabitants of a city, town, etc, with their telephone numbers.

dirge *n* a song or tune intended to express grief, sorrow and mourning.

dirigible *adj* that may be directed, turned or guided in any direction.—*n* a balloon or airship whose course can be directed by means of steering or directing apparatus.

dirk *n* a kind of dagger or poniard; a dagger worn as a sidearm by midshipmen; one worn as essential to complete the Highland costume.

dirt *n* any foul or filthy substance, as excrement, mud, mire, dust; whatever, adhering to anything, renders it foul or unclean; a gold miner's name for the material, as earth, gravel, etc, put into the cradle to be washed.—*vt* to soil; to dirty.

dirtiness *n* the condition of being dirty; filthiness; foulness; nastiness.

dirty *adj* foul; nasty; filthy; not clean; impure; turbid; mean; base; despicable; sleety, rainy or sloppy (weather).—*vt* (**dirtied, dirtying**) to defile; to make dirty or filthy; to soil.

disable *vt* (**disabled, disabling**) to render unable; to deprive of competent strength or power, physical or mental; to injure so as to be no longer fit for duty or service; to deprive of adequate means, instruments or resources; to impair; to deprive of legal qualifications; to incapacitate; to render incapable.

disability *n* the state or quality of being disabled or unable; a lack of physical, mental or social fitness; something that disables; a handicap; a learning difficulty.

disabuse *vt* (**disabused, disabusing**) to free from mistaken or erroneous notions or beliefs; to undeceive; to set right.

disadvantage *n* absence or deprivation of advantage; that which prevents success or renders it difficult; any unfavourable circumstance or state; prejudice to interest, fame, credit, profit or other good; loss; injury; harm; damage.

disadvantaged *adj* suffering unfavourable conditions or loss; deprived or discriminated against in economic or social terms.

disadvantageous *adj* attended with disadvantage; unfavourable to success or prosperity; prejudicial.

disaffect *vt* to alienate the affection of; to make less friendly or faithful, as to a person, party or cause; to make discontented or unfriendly.

disaffected *adj* having the affections alienated; indisposed to favour or support; unfriendly; hostile to the governing power.

disaffection *n* alienation of affection, attachment or goodwill; disloyalty.

disagree *vt* (**disagreed, disagreeing**) to be not accordant or coincident; to be not exactly similar; to differ; to be of an opposite or different opinion; to be unsuitable to the stomach; to be in opposition; not to accord or harmonize; to become unfriendly; to quarrel.

disagreeable *adj* the reverse of agreeable; unpleasing; offensive to the mind or to the senses; repugnant; obnoxious.

disagreement *n* lack of agreement; difference, as of form or character; difference of opinion or sentiments; a falling out; a quarrel; discord.

disallow *vt* to refuse permission or sanction for; not to grant; not to authorize; to disapprove of; to reject, as being illegal, unnecessary, unauthorized, etc.

disappear *vi* to cease to appear or to be perceived; to vanish from the sight; to go away or out of sight; to cease or seem to cease, to be or exist.

disappearance *n* act of disappearing; removal from sight.

disappoint *vt* to defeat of expectation, wish, hope, desire or intention; to frustrate; to balk; to hinder from the possession or enjoyment of that which was hoped or expected (*disappointed of the expected legacy*).

disappointment *n* the act of disappointing or feeling of being disappointed; defeat or failure of expectation, hope, wish, desire or intention.

disapprobation *n* the reverse of approbation; disapproval; censure, expressed or unexpressed.

disapprove *vt* (**disapproved, disapproving**) to censure; to regard as wrong or objectionable.—*vi* to express or feel disapproval (with *of* before the object).

disapproval *n* disapprobation; dislike.

disarm *vt* to take the arms or weapons from, usually by force or authority; to reduce to a peace footing, as an army or navy; to deprive of means of attack or defence or of annoyance or power to terrify; to render harmless; to conciliate; to charm; to win the affection of.—*vi* to lay down arms; to disband armed forces.

disarmament *n* act of disarming.

disarrange *vt* (**disarranged, disarranging**) to put out of order; to unsettle or disturb the order or due arrangement of.

disarray *vt* to undress; to divest of clothes; to throw into disorder.—*n* disorder; confusion; disordered dress.

disaster *n* any unfortunate event, especially a great and sudden misfortune; mishap; calamity; adversity; reverse.

disastrous *adj* occasioning or accompanied by disaster; calamitous.

disavow *vt* to deny to be true, as a fact or charge respecting oneself; to disown; to repudiate; to reject.

disavowal *n* denial; repudiation.

disband *vt* to dismiss from military service; to break up, as a band or body of people; to disperse.—*vi* to break up and retire from military service.

disbandment *n* the act of disbanding.

disbar *vt* (**disbarred, disbarring**) to expel from being a member of the bar; to remove from the list of barristers.

disbelief *n* refusal of credit or faith; denial of belief; unbelief; infidelity; scepticism.

disbelieve *vt* (**disbelieved, disbelieving**) to refuse belief to; to hold not to be true or not to exist; to refuse to credit.—*vi* to deny the truth of any position; to refuse to believe.

disburden *vt* to remove a burden from; to lay off or aside as oppressive; to get rid of.

disburse *vt* (**disbursed, disbursing**) to pay out, as money; to spend or lay out; to expend.

disbursement *n* the act of disbursing; a sum paid out.

disc, disk *n* a kind of ancient quoit; any flat circular plate or surface, as of a piece of metal, the face of the sun, moon or a planet as it appears to our sight, etc; (*bot*) the whole surface of a leaf; also, the central part of a radiate compound flower, the part surrounded by what is called the ray; one of the rings of cartilage in the vertebral column; a gramophone record; (*comput*) a disk.

discard *vti* to throw out of the hand such cards as are not played in the course of the game; to dismiss from service or employment or from society; to cast off.

discern *vt* to perceive or note as being different; to discriminate by the eye or the intellect; to distinguish or mark as being distinct; to discover by the eye; to see.—*vi* to see or understand differences; to make distinction; to have clearness of mental vision.

discerning *adj* having power to discern; capable of discriminating, knowing and judging; sharp-sighted; acute.

discernment *n* the act of discerning; the power or faculty of discerning by the mind; acuteness of judgment; power of perceiving differences of things or ideas and their relations; penetration.

disciple

discharge *vt* (**discharged, discharging**) to unload (a ship); to take out (a cargo); to free from any load or burden; to free of the missile with which anything is charged or loaded; to fire off; to let fly; to shoot; to emit or send out; (*lit, fig*) to give vent to; to deliver the amount or value of to the person to whom it is owing; to pay (a debt); to free from an obligation, duty or labour; to relieve (*to discharge a person from a task*); to clear from an accusation or crime; to acquit; to absolve; to set free; to perform or execute (a duty or office); to divest of an office or employment; to dismiss from service (a servant, a soldier, a jury); to release; to liberate from confinement.—*vi* to get rid of or let out a charge or contents.—*n* the act of discharging, unloading or freeing from a charge; a flowing or issuing out or a throwing out; emission; that which is thrown out; matter emitted; dismissal from office or service; release from obligation, debt or penalty; absolution from a crime or accusation; ransom; price paid for deliverance; performance; execution, as of an office, trust or duty; liberation; release from confinement; payment of a debt.

disciple *n* one who receives instruction from another; a learner; a scholar; a pupil; a follower; an adherent.

discipleship *n* the state of being a disciple.

disciplinarian *n* one who disciplines; one who instructs in military and naval tactics and manoeuvres; one who enforces rigid discipline; a martinet.

discipline *n* training; education; instruction

disc jockey

and the government of conduct or practice; the training to act in accordance with rules; drill; method of regulating principles and practice; punishment inflicted by way of correction and training; instruction by means of misfortune, suffering, etc; correction; chastisement.—*vt* (**disciplined, disciplining**) to subject to discipline; to apply discipline to; to train; to teach rules and practice and accustom to order and subordination; to drill; to correct, chastise, punish.

disc jockey *n* one who introduces and plays popular records on a radio programme or at a disco.

disclaim *vt* to deny or relinquish all claim to; to reject as not belonging to oneself; to renounce; to deny responsibility for or approval of; to disavow; to disown.

disclaimer *n* a person who disclaims; an act of disclaiming; abnegation of pretensions or claims; a denial of responsibility; (*law*) a renunciation, abandonment or giving up of a claim.

disclose *vt* (**disclosed, disclosing**) to uncover and lay open to the view; to cause to appear; to allow to be seen; to bring to light; to make known, reveal, tell, utter.

disclosure *n* the act of disclosing; exhibition; the act of making known or revealing; utterance of what was secret; a telling; that which is disclosed or made known.

disco *n* (*pl* **discos**) (originally **discotheque**) a dance at which a disc jockey plays recorded pop music and at which there is usually special lighting effects; a kind of nightclub at which such a dance takes place; the equipment and operator that provide the music for such a dance.

discolour *vt* to alter the hue or colour of; to change to a different colour or shade; to stain; to tinge.

discoloration *n* the act of discolouring; alteration of colour; a discoloured spot or marking.

discomfit *vt* to rout, defeat or scatter in flight; to cause to flee; to vanquish; to disconcert, foil or frustrate the plans of.

discomfiture *n* rout; defeat; overthrow; frustration; disappointment.

discomfort *n* absence or opposite of comfort or pleasure; uneasiness; disturbance of peace; pain, annoyance or anxiety.—*vt* to disturb the peace or happiness of; to make uneasy; to pain.

discompose *vt* (**discomposed, discomposing**) to disorder, disturb or disarrange; to disturb the peace and quietness of; to agitate, ruffle, fret or vex.

discomposure *n* the state of being discomposed; a certain agitation or perturbation of mind.

disconcert *vt* to throw into disorder or confusion; to undo, as a concerted scheme or plan; to defeat; to frustrate; to discompose or disturb the self-possession of; to confuse.

disconnect *vt* to separate or sever the connection between; to disunite; to detach.

disconnection *n* the act of disconnecting; separation; lack of union.

disconsolate *adj* lacking consolation; hopeless; sad; dejected; melancholy; cheerless; saddening; gloomy.

discontent *n* lack of content; uneasiness or anxiety of mind; dissatisfaction.

discontented *adj* not contented; dissatisfied; not pleased with one's circumstances; given to grumble.

discontinuance *n* lack of continuance; a breaking off; cessation; intermission; interruption.

discontinuation *n* discontinuance.

discontinue *vt* (**discontinued, discontinuing**) to continue no longer; to leave off or break off; to give up, cease from or abandon; to stop; to put an end to.—*vi* to cease; to stop.

discord *n* lack of concord or agreement; opposition of opinions; difference of qualities; disagreement; variance; contention; strife; (*mus*) a union of sounds disagreeable or grating to the ear; dissonance; each of the two sounds forming a dissonance.—*vi* to disagree; to be out of harmony or concord; to clash.

discordant *adj* disagreeing; incongruous; being at variance; dissonant; not in unison; not harmonious; not accordant; harsh; jarring.

discotheque *n* see **disco**.

discount *n* a certain sum deducted from the credit price of goods sold on account of prompt payment or any deduction from the customary price or from a sum due or to be due at a future time; a charge made to cover the interest of money advanced on a bill or other document not presently due; the act of discounting.—**at a discount** below par; hence, in low esteem; in disfavour.—*vt* to lend or advance the amount of (a bill or similar document), deducting the interest or other rate per cent from the principal; to leave out of account or disregard; to estimate or take into account beforehand; to enjoy or suffer by anticipation.

discountenance *vt* to put out of countenance; to put to shame; to abash; to set one's countenance against; to discourage, check or restrain by frowns, censure, arguments, cold treatment, etc.—*n* cold treatment; disapprobation.

discourage *vt* (**discouraged, discouraging**) to dishearten; to deprive of self-confidence; to attempt to repress or prevent by pointing out difficulties, etc; to dissuade.

discouragement *n* the act of discouraging;

the act of deterring or dissuading from an undertaking; that which discourages or damps ardour or hope; the state of being discouraged.

discouraging *adj* tending to discourage or dishearten; disheartening.

discourse *n* a running over a subject in speech; hence, a talking together or discussing; conversation; talk; speech; a treatise; a dissertation; a homily, sermon or other production.—*vi* (**discoursed, discoursing**) to communicate thoughts or ideas orally or in writing, especially in a formal manner; to hold forth; to expatiate; to converse.—*vt* to talk over or discuss; to utter or give forth.

discourteous *adj* lacking in courtesy; uncivil; rude.

discourtesy *n* lack of courtesy; incivility; rudeness of manner; act of disrespect.

discover *vt* to lay open to view; to disclose or reveal; to espy; to have the first sight of; to find out; to obtain the first knowledge of; to come to the knowledge of; to detect.

discoverer *n* one who discovers; one who first sees or espies; one who finds out or first comes to the knowledge of something.

discovery *n* the act of discovering; a disclosing or bringing to light; a revealing or making known; a finding out or bringing for the first time to sight or knowledge; what is discovered or found out.

discredit *n* lack of credit or good reputation; some degree of disgrace or reproach; disesteem; disrepute; lack of belief, trust or confidence; disbelief.—*vt* to give no credit to; not to credit or believe; to deprive of credit or good reputation; to bring into some degree of disgrace or disrepute; to deprive of credibility.

discreditable *n* injurious to reputation; disgraceful; disreputable.

discreet *adj* wise in avoiding errors or evil and in selecting the best course or means; prudent in conduct; circumspect; cautious; heedful; guarded.

discretion *n* the quality or attribute of being discreet; discernment to judge critically of what is correct and proper, united with caution; prudence; sound judgment; circumspection; wariness; caution; liberty or power of acting without other control than one's own judgment (*to leave an affair to one's discretion, to surrender at discretion*, that is without stipulating for terms).

discretionary *adj* left to a person's own discretion or judgment; to be directed according to one's own discretion (*discretionary powers*).

discrepancy *n* a difference or inconsistency between facts, stories, theories, etc; disagreement; divergence.

discrepant *adj* differing or diverging; not

discount

agreeing or according; disagreeing; dissimilar.

discrete *adj* separate; distinct; disjunctive.

discriminate *vt* (**discriminated, discriminating**) to distinguish from other things by observing differences; to perceive by a distinction; to discern; to separate; to select; to distinguish by some note or mark; to treat differently.—*vi* to make a difference or distinction; to observe or note a difference; to distinguish.

discriminating *adj* serving to discriminate; distinguishing; distinctive; able to make nice distinctions.

discrimination *n* the act of discriminating; the faculty of distinguishing or discriminating; penetration; discernment; the state of being discriminated or set apart.

discursive *adj* passing rapidly from one subject to another; desultory; rambling; digressional; argumentative; reasoning; rational.

discuss *vt* to debate; to argue; to make an end of, by eating or drinking; (*colloq*) to consume.

discussion *n* the act of discussing; debate; disquisition; the agitation of a point or subject with a view to elicit truth.

discussion

disdain *vt* to deem or regard as worthless; to consider to be unworthy of notice, care, regard, esteem or unworthy of one's character; to scorn; to contemn.—*n* a feeling of contempt, mingled with indignation; the looking upon anything as beneath one; haughtiness; contempt; scorn.

disease *n* an unhealthy state of part or all of the body, caused by a virus, bacterial infection, poisoning etc; an illness with distinctive symptoms.

diseased *adj* affected with disease.

disembark *vt* to remove from on board a ship to the land; to put on shore; to land.—*vi* to leave a ship and go on shore; to land.

disembody *vt* (**disembodied, disembodying**) to divest of the body (*a disembodied spirit* = a ghost); to set free from the flesh; to disband (military).

disembogue *vti* (**disembogued, disemboguing**) to pour out or discharge at the mouth, as a stream; to discharge water into the ocean or a lake.

disembowel *vt* (**disembowelled, disembowelling**) to deprive of the bowels or of parts analogous to the bowels; to eviscerate; to gut.

disenchant *vt* to free from enchantment; to deliver from the power of charms or spells; to free from fascination or pleasing delusion.

disencumber *vt* to free from encumbrance, clogs and impediments.

disenfranchise *vt* to disfranchise.

disengage *vt* (**disengaged, disengaging**) to separate or set free from union or attachment; to detach; to disunite; to free; to disentangle; to extricate; to clear, as from difficulties or perplexities; to free, as from anything that occupies the attention; to set free by dissolving an engagement.

disengaged *adj* being at leisure; not particularly occupied; not having the attention confined to a particular object.

disentail *vt* to free from being entailed; to break the entail of.

disentangle *vt* (**disentangled, disentangling**) to free from entanglement; to unravel; to extricate from perplexity or complications; to disengage.

disentomb *vt* to take out of a tomb; to disinter.

disestablish *vt* to cause to cease to be established; to withdraw (a church) from its connection with the state.

disestablishment *n* the act of disestablishing; the act of withdrawing a church from its connection with the state.

disesteem *n* lack of esteem; slight dislike; disregard.—*vt* to dislike in a moderate degree; to regard as unworthy of esteem.

disfavour *n* a feeling of some dislike or slight displeasure; unfavourable regard; disesteem; a state of being unacceptable or not favoured, patronized or befriended; a disobliging act.—*vt* to withdraw or withhold favour, friendship or support from.

disfiguration *n* the act of disfiguring; disfigurement.

disfigure *vt* (**disfigured, disfiguring**) to mar the external figure of; to impair the shape or form of; to injure the beauty, symmetry or excellence of; to deface; to deform.

disfigurement *n* the act of disfiguring or state of being disfigured; that which disfigures.

disfranchise *vt* (**disfranchised, disfranchising**) to deprive of the rights and privileges of a free citizen; to deprive of any franchise, more especially of the right of voting in elections, etc.

disgorge *vt* (**disgorged, disgorging**) to eject or discharge from, or as from, the stomach, throat or mouth; to vomit; to belch; to discharge violently (*a volcano disgorges lava*); to yield up, as what has been taken wrongfully; to give up; to surrender.—*vi* to give up plunder or ill-gotten gains.

disgrace *n* a state of being out of favour; disfavour; state of ignominy; dishonour; shame; infamy; cause of shame.—*vt* (**disgraced, disgracing**) to bring into disgrace; to put out of favour; to dismiss with dishonour; to treat ignominiously; to bring shame or reproach on; to humiliate or humble; to dishonour.

disgraceful *adj* entailing disgrace; shameful; infamous; dishonourable.

disgruntle *vt* (**disgruntled, disgruntling**) to put in a bad humour; to make dissatisfied.

disguise *vt* (**disguised, disguising**) to conceal the ordinary guise and appearance of by an unusual habit or mask; to hide by a counterfeit appearance; to cloak by a false show, false language or an artificial manner (anger, intentions, etc); to change in manners or behaviour by the use of spirituous liquor; to intoxicate.—*n* a counterfeit dress; a dress intended to conceal the identity of the person who wears it; a counterfeit show; artificial or assumed language or appearance intended to deceive.

disgust *n* aversion to the taste of food or drink; distaste; disrelish; nausea; aversion in the mind excited by something offensive in the manners, conduct, language or opinions of others; loathing; repugnance; strong dislike.—*vt* to cause to feel disgust; to excite aversion in the stomach of; to offend the taste of; to stir up loathing or repugnance in.

disgusting *adj* producing or causing disgust; nauseous; loathsome; nasty.

dish *n* a broad open vessel made of various materials, used for serving up meat and various kinds of food at the table; the meat or provisions served in a dish; hence, any particular kind of food; the concavity of certain wheels, as those of vehicles; a dish aerial.—*vt* to put in a dish after being cooked; (*sl*) to damage, ruin, completely overthrow.

dishabille, deshabille *n* the state of being in undress or of not being properly or fully dressed.

dish aerial *n* a microwave aerial in the form of a parabolic reflector used in radar, radio telescopes and satellite broadcasting reception.

dishearten *vt* to discourage; to deprive of courage; to depress the spirits of; to deject; to dispirit.

dishevel *vt* (**dishevelled, dishevelling**) to spread the locks or tresses of loosely and negligently; to suffer (the hair) to hang negligently and uncombed.

dishevelled *adj* unkempt; disarranged; untidy.

dishonest *adj* void of honesty, probity or integrity; not honest; fraudulent; inclined or apt to deceive, cheat, pilfer, embezzle or defraud; proceeding from or marked by fraud; knavish; unchaste.

dishonesty *n* the opposite of honesty; lack of probity or integrity; a disposition to cheat.

dishonour *n* the opposite of honour; lack of honour; disgrace; shame; anything that disgraces.—*vt* to disgrace; to bring shame on; to stain the character of; to lessen in reputation; to treat with indignity; to

refuse or decline to accept or pay (a bill of exchange).

dishonourable *adj* shameful; disgraceful; base; bringing shame; staining the character and lessening reputation.

disillusion *vt* to free from illusion; to disenchant.

disincentive *n* something which discourages action or effort.

disincline *vt* (**disinclined, disinclining**) to excite slight aversion in; to make unwilling; to cause to hang back; to alienate.

disinfect *vt* to cleanse from infection; to purify from contagious matter.

disinfectant *n* a substance that disinfects or is used for destroying the power or means of propagating diseases which spread by infection or contagion.

disingenuous *adj* not ingenuous; not open, frank and candid; meanly artful; insincere; sly; not candid.

disinherit *vt* to cut off from hereditary right; to deprive of the right to an inheritance.

disintegrate *vt* (**disintegrated, disintegrating**) to separate the component particles of; to reduce to powder or to fragments.

disinter *vt* (**disinterred, disinterring**) to take out of a grave or out of the earth; to take out, as from a grave; to bring from obscurity into view.

disinterment *n* the act of disinterring; exhumation.

disinterested *adj* free from self-interest; having no personal interest or private advantage in a question or affair; not influenced or dictated by private advantage; unselfish; uninterested.

disjoin *vt* to part asunder; to disunite; to separate; to detach; to sunder.—*vi* to be separated; to part.

disjointed *adj* unconnected; incoherent; out of joint; out of order; ill-joined together.

disjunctive *adj* disjoining; alternative; (*gram*) marking an adverse or oppositional sense; syntactically independent; (in logic) presenting alternative terms.—*n* (*gram*) a disjunctive sense.

disjunction, disjuncture *n* severance, disconnection.

disk *n* a thin, flat magnetic plate used as storage device in computers, sometimes rigid (hard), sometimes flexible (floppy). *See also* **disc.**

disk drive *n* a mechanism that allows a computer to write data on and extract data from a disk.

dislike *n* a feeling the opposite of liking; disinclination; aversion; distaste; antipathy; repugnance.—*vt* (**disliked, disliking**) to feel dislike towards; to regard with some aversion; to have a feeling against; to disrelish.

dislocate *vt* (**dislocated, dislocating**) to dis-

disguise

disk drive

255

place; to shift from the original site; particularly, to put out of joint; to move (a bone) from its socket, cavity or place of articulation.

dislocation *n* the act of dislocating; particularly, the act of removing or forcing a bone from its socket.

dislodge *vt* (**dislodged, dislodging**) to drive from the fixed position or place occupied; to drive (enemies) from any place of hiding or defence or from a position seized.—*vi* to go from a place of rest.

dislodgment, dislodgement *n* the act of dislodging.

disloyal *adj* not loyal or true to allegiance; false to a sovereign or country; faithless; false; perfidious; treacherous; not true to the marriage bed; false in love.

disloyalty *n* the character of being disloyal; lack of fidelity to a sovereign; violation of allegiance; lack of fidelity in love.

dismal *adj* dark, gloomy or cheerless to look at; depressing; sorrowful; dire; horrid; melancholy; calamitous; unfortunate; frightful; horrible.

dismantle *vt* (**dismantled, dismantling**) to deprive of dress; to strip; to divest; more generally, to deprive or strip (a thing) of furniture, equipment, fortifications, etc.

dismast *vt* to deprive of a mast or masts; to break and carry away the masts from.

dismay *vt* to discourage, with some feeling of dread or consternation; to confound; to daunt; to strike aghast.—*n* a complete giving way of boldness or spirit; loss of courage together with consternation; a yielding to fear.

dismember *vt* to divide limb from limb; to separate the members of; to mutilate; to sever and distribute the parts of; to divide into separate portions (a kingdom, etc).

dismiss *vt* to send away; to permit to depart, implying authority in a person to retain or keep; to discard; to remove from office, service or employment; (*law*) to reject as unworthy of notice or of being granted.

dismissal *n* the act of dismissing; discharge; liberation.

dismount *vi* to alight from a horse or other animal; to come or go down.—*vt* to throw or remove from a horse; to unhorse; to throw or remove (cannon or other artillery) from their carriages.

disobedience *n* neglect or refusal to obey; violation of a command or prohibition; the omission of that which is commanded to be done or the doing of that which is forbidden.

disobedient *adj* neglecting or refusing to obey; guilty of disobedience; not observant of duty or rules prescribed by authority.

disobey *vt* to neglect or refuse to obey; to omit or refuse obedience to; to transgress

or violate an order or injunction.—*vi* to refuse obedience; to disregard orders.

disobliging *adj* not obliging; not disposed to gratify the wishes of another; not accommodating.

disorder *n* lack of order or regular disposition; irregularity; unmethodical distribution; confusion; tumult; disturbance of the peace of society; disturbance or interruption of the functions of the animal economy or of the mind; distemper; sickness; derangement.—*vt* to break the order of; to derange; to throw into confusion; to disturb or interrupt the natural functions of; to produce sickness or indisposition in; to disturb as regards the reason or judgment; to craze.

disordered *adj* disorderly; irregular; deranged; crazed.

disorderly *adj* being without proper order; marked by disorder; confused; unmethodical; irregular; tumultuous; unruly; violating law and good order.

disorganize *vt* (**disorganized, disorganizing**) to disturb or destroy organic structure or connected system in; to throw out of regular system; to throw into confusion or disorder (a government, society, etc).

disown *vt* to refuse to acknowledge as belonging to oneself; to refuse to own; to deny; to repudiate (a child, a written work).

disparage *vt* (**disparaged, disparaging**) to dishonour by a comparison with something of less value or excellence; to treat with detraction or in a deprecatory manner; to undervalue; to decry; to vilify; to lower in estimation.

disparagement *n* the act of disparaging; the act of undervaluing or depreciating; detraction; what lowers in value or esteem; disgrace; dishonour.

disparate *adj* unequal; unlike; dissimilar.—*n* one of two or more things so unequal or unlike that they cannot be compared with each other.

disparity *n* inequality; difference in degree, in age, rank, condition or excellence; dissimilitude; unlikeness.

dispassionate *adj* free from passion; calm; composed; unmoved by feelings; not dictated by passion; not proceeding from temper or bias; impartial.

dispatch *vt*, *n* same as **despatch**.

dispel *vt* (**dispelled, dispelling**) to scatter by force; to disperse; to dissipate; to drive away (clouds, doubts, fears, etc).—*vi* to be dispersed; to disappear.

dispensable *adj* capable of being dispensed or administered; capable of being spared or dispensed with.

dispensary *n* a placer where medicines are dispensed.

dispensation *n* the act of dispensing or

dealing out; the distribution of good and evil in the divine government; system established by God settling the relations of man towards Him as regards religion and morality (*the Mosaic dispensation*); the granting of a licence or the licence itself, to do what is forbidden by laws or canons or to omit something which is commanded.

dispense *vt* (**dispensed, dispensing**) to deal or divide out in parts or portions; to distribute; to administer; to prepare and distribute (medicines); to apply, as laws to particular cases; to grant dispensation to; to relieve, excuse or set free from an obligation.—*vi* to bargain for, grant or receive a dispensation; to compound.—**to dispense with** to permit the neglect or omission of, as a ceremony, an oath, etc; to give up or do without, as services, attendance, articles of dress, etc.

dispersal *n* the act of dispersing or scattering; dispersion.

disperse *vt* (**dispersed, dispersing**) to scatter; to cause to separate and go far apart; to dissipate; to cause to vanish.—*vi* to scatter; to separate or move apart; to break up; to vanish, as fog or vapours.

dispersion *n* a state of being scattered or separated into remote parts; in optics, the separation of the different coloured rays of a beam of light by diffraction or refraction; in statistics, the scattering of data about a mean.

dispirit *vt* to depress the spirits of; to deprive of courage; to discourage; to dishearten; to deject; to cast down.

dispirited *adj* discouraged; depressed in spirits; spiritless; tame.

displace *vt* (**displaced, displacing**) to put out of the usual or proper place; to remove from its place; to remove from any state, condition, office or dignity.

displacement *n* the act of displacing; removal; the quantity of water displaced by a body floating at rest, as a ship.

display *vt* to spread before the view; to set in view ostentatiously; to show; to exhibit to the eyes or to the mind; to make manifest.—*vi* to make a show or display.—*n* an unfolding; an exhibition of anything to the view; ostentatious show; exhibition; parade.

displease *vt* (**displeased, displeasing**) to offend somewhat; to dissatisfy; to annoy; to make angry, usually in a slight degree; to excite aversion in; to be disagreeable to (the taste, the senses).

displeased *adj* not well pleased; offended; annoyed (*to be displeased with a person*).

displeasing *adj* offensive to the mind or any of the senses; disagreeable.

displeasure *n* the feeling of one who is displeased; dissatisfaction; anger; vexation; annoyance; that which displeases; offence.

dispone *vt* (**disponed, disponing**) (*Scots law*) to make over or convey (property) to another in a legal form.

disport *n* play; sport; pastime.—*vi* to play; to sport.

dispose *vt* (**disposed, disposing**) to arrange, place out or distribute; to set in a particular order; to apply to a particular end or purpose; to set the mind of in a particular frame; to incline.—*vi* to regulate, determine or settle.—**to dispose of** to part with; to alienate; to sell; to put into another's hand or power; to bestow; to do with, make use of, use or employ (oneself, one's time, etc); to put away or get rid of.

disposal *n* the act of disposing; a setting or arranging; power of ordering, arranging or distributing; government; management; power or right of bestowing; the act of selling or parting with; alienation.

disposition *n* the act of disposing or state of being disposed; manner in which things or the parts of a complex body are placed or arranged; order; method; distribution; arrangement; natural fitness or tendency; temper or natural constitution of the mind; inclination; propensity.

dispossess *vt* to put out of possession; to deprive of the occupancy or ownership; to dislodge; with *of* before the thing taken away.

disproportion *n* lack of proportion of one thing to another or between the parts of a thing; lack of symmetry; lack of proper quantity; according to rules prescribed; lack of suitableness or adequacy; disparity; inequality.—*vt* to violate due proportion or symmetry in.

disproportionate *adj* not having due proportion to something else; not having proportion or symmetry of parts; unequal; inadequate.

disprove *vt* (**disproved, disproving**) to prove to be false or erroneous; to confute; to refute.

disproof *n* confutation; refutation; a proving to be false or erroneous.

disputable *adj* capable of being disputed; liable to be called in question, controverted or contested; controvertible.

disputant *n* one who disputes; one who argues in opposition to another; a reasoner in opposition.

disputation *n* the act of disputing; controversy; verbal contest respecting the truth of some fact, opinion, proposition or argument.

dispute *vi* (**disputed, disputing**) to contend in argument; to reason or argue in opposition; to debate; to altercate; to wrangle; to contend in opposition to a competitor.—*vt* to attempt to disprove by arguments or statements; to attempt to overthrow by

displeased

reasoning; to controvert (an assertion, a claim, etc); to call in question; to strive to maintain; to contest (*to dispute every inch of ground*).—*n* strife or contest in words or by arguments; a difference of opinion vigorously maintained; controversy in words; a wordy war; contention; strife; contest.

disqualification *n* the act of disqualifying; the state of being disqualified; disability; legal disability or incapacity; that which disqualifies or incapacitates.

disqualify *vt* (**disqualified, disqualifying**) to make unfit; to deprive of natural power or the qualities or properties necessary for any purpose (*weakness disqualifies a person for labour*); to deprive of legal capacity, power or right; to deprive of the right to compete in a contest; to incapacitate.

disquiet *n* lack of quiet; uneasiness; anxiety.—*vt* to deprive of peace, rest or tranquillity; to make uneasy or restless; to disturb, harass, fret or vex.

disquieting *adj* tending to disquiet; disturbing the mind.

disquisition *n* a formal or systematic inquiry into any subject, by discussion of the facts and circumstances bearing on it; an argumentative inquiry; a formal discussion or treatise on any matter; dissertation; essay.

disregard *n* lack of regard, notice or attention; neglect; slight.—*vt* to omit to take notice of; to neglect to observe; to pay no heed to; to treat as unworthy of regard or notice.

disregardful *adj* neglectful; heedless.

disrelish *n* distaste; dislike of the palate; some degree of disgust; dislike of the mind; aversion; antipathy.

disrepair *n* a state of being not in repair or good condition; state of requiring to be repaired.

disreputable *adj* not reputable; disgracing reputation; dishonourable; discreditable; low; mean.

disrepute *n* loss or lack of reputation; disesteem; discredit; dishonour.

disrespect *n* lack of respect or reverence; incivility, irreverence or rudeness; a slight or neglect.—*vt* to have no respect or esteem for; to show disrespect to.

disrespectful *adj* lacking in respect; manifesting disrespect; irreverent; uncivil.

disrespectful

disrobe *vt* (**disrobed, disrobing**) to divest of a robe; to divest of garments; to undress; to strip of covering; to uncover.

disrupt *vt* to tear or rive away; to rend; to sever; to break asunder.

disruption *n* the act of rending asunder; the act of bursting and separating; breach; rent; break-up; the rupture which took place in the Established Church of Scotland in 1843, resulting in the foundation of the Free Church.

dissatisfaction *n* the feeling caused by lack of satisfaction; discontent; uneasiness proceeding from lack of gratification or from disappointed wishes and expectations.

dissatisfied *adj* not satisfied; not pleased; discontented.

dissatisfy *vt* (**dissatisfied, dissatisfying**) to fail to satisfy; to render discontented; to displease; to excite displeasure in by frustrating wishes or expectations.

dissect *vt* to cut up (an animal or vegetable) for the purpose of examining the structure and character of the several parts or to observe morbid affections; to anatomize; (*fig*) to analyse for the purpose of criticism; to describe with minute accuracy.

dissection *n* the act or art of dissecting or anatomizing.

dissector *n* one who dissects; an anatomist.

dissemble *vt* (**dissembled, dissembling**) to hide under an assumed manner; to conceal or disguise by a false outward show; to hide by false pretences (*to dissemble love, hate, opinions*, etc).—*vi* to try to appear other than reality; to put on an assumed manner or outward show; to conceal the real fact, motives, intention or sentiments under some pretence.

dissembler *n* one who dissembles; one who conceals his or her real thoughts or feelings.

disseminate *vt* (**disseminated, disseminating**) to spread by diffusion or dispersion; to diffuse; to spread abroad among people; to cause to reach as many persons as possible (religious doctrines, knowledge, etc).

dissension *n* disagreement in opinion, usually a disagreement producing warm debates or angry words; strife; discord; quarrel; breach of friendship and union.

dissent *vi* to disagree in opinion; to differ; to think in a different or contrary manner (with *from*); (*eccles*) to differ from an established church in regard to doctrines, rites or government.—*n* difference of opinion; disagreement; declaration of disagreement in opinion; (*eccles*) separation from an established church.

dissenter *n* one who dissents; one who differs in opinion or one who declares his or her disagreement; (*eccles*) one who separates from the service and worship of any established church.

dissentient *adj* disagreeing; declaring dissent; voting differently.—*n* one who disagrees and declares his or her dissent.

dissertation *n* a formal discourse, intended to illustrate or elucidate a subject; a written essay, treatise or disquisition.

disservice *n* an ill turn or injury; something done to one's injury.

dissidence *n* disagreement; dissent; nonconformity.

dissident *adj* dissenting; specifically, dissenting from an established church.—*n* one who dissents from others; a dissenter; one who separates from an established religion.

dissimilar *adj* not similar; unlike, either in nature, properties or external form.

dissimilarity *n* lack of similarity; unlikeness; lack of resemblance.

dissimulation *n* the act or practice of dissembling, usually from a mean or unworthy motive; a hiding under a false appearance; false pretension; hypocrisy.

dissipate *vt* (**dissipated, dissipating**) to scatter, to disperse, to drive away (mist, care, energy, etc); to scatter in wasteful extravagance; to waste.—*vi* to scatter, disperse, separate into parts and disappear; to vanish; to be wasteful or dissolute in the pursuit of pleasure.

dissipated *adj* given to extravagance in the expenditure of property; devoted to pleasure and vice; dissolute.

dissipation *n* the act of dissipating; the insensible loss of the minute particles of a body, which fly off, so that the body is diminished or may altogether disappear; indulgence in dissolute and irregular courses; a reckless and vicious pursuit of pleasure; dissolute conduct.

dissociate *vt* (**dissociated, dissociating**) to separate or take apart; to disunite; to part.

dissociation *n* the act of dissociating; a state of separation; disunion; (*chem*) the decomposition of a compound substance into its primary elements.

dissoluble *adj* capable of being dissolved or melted; having its parts separable, as by heat or moisture; susceptible of decomposition or decay.

dissolute *adj* loose in behaviour and morals; given to vice or profligacy; debauched; devoted to or occupied in dissipation.

dissoluteness *n* the state or character of being dissolute; looseness of manners and morals; vicious indulgence in pleasure, as in intemperance and debauchery; dissipation.

dissolution *n* the act of dissolving, liquefying or changing from a solid to a fluid state by heat; liquefaction; the reduction of a body into its smallest parts or into very minute parts; the separation of the parts of a body by natural decomposition; decomposition; death; the separation of the soul and body; the separation of the parts which compose a connected system or body; the breaking up of an assembly or the putting an end to its existence.

dissolve *vt* (**dissolved, dissolving**) to melt; to liquefy; to convert from a solid or fixed state to a fluid state, by means of heat or moisture; to disunite, break up, separate or loosen; to destroy any connected system or body (parliament, a government); to break or make no longer binding (an alliance, etc); to solve, explain or resolve (doubts).—*vi* to melt; to be converted from a solid to a fluid state; to fall asunder; to crumble; to waste away; to be decomposed; to be dismissed; to separate; to break up.

dissonance *n* discord; a mixture or union of harsh, inharmonious sounds; incongruity; inconsistency.

dissonant *adj* discordant; harsh; jarring; inharmonious; unpleasant to the ear; disagreeing; incongruous.

dissuade *vt* (**dissuaded, dissuading**) to advise or exhort against; to attempt to draw or divert from a measure by reasons or offering motives; to divert by persuasion; to turn from a purpose by argument; to render averse, the opposite of *persuade*.

dissuasion *n* advice or exhortation in opposition to something; the opposite of *persuasion*.

dissyllable *n* a word consisting of two syllables only.

distaff *n* the staff to which a bunch of flax or tow is tied and from which the thread is drawn to be spun by the spindle.

distaff side *n* the female side of a relationship, opposed to *spear* or male side.

distal *adj* applied to the end of a bone, limb or organ in plants and animals farthest removed from the point of attachment or insertion; situated away from or at the extremity most distant from the centre.

distance *n* an interval or space between two objects; the length of the shortest line which intervenes between things that are separate; remoteness of place; space of time, past or future; ideal space or separation, as between things that differ from each other; the remoteness or ceremonious avoidance of familiarity which respect requires; the remoteness or reserve which one assumes from being offended, from dislike, etc; (*mus*) the interval between two notes.—*vt* (**distanced, distancing**) to place at a distance or remote; to leave at a great distance; to outdo or excel greatly.

distant *adj* separate or apart, the intervening space being of any indefinite extent; remote in place; in time, past or future; in a line of succession or descent; in natural connection or consanguinity; in kind or nature, etc; as if remote or far off; hence, slight; faint (*a distant resemblance*); characterized by haughtiness, coldness, indifference or disrespect; reserved; shy.

distaste *n* aversion of the taste; dislike of food or drink; disrelish; disinclination; a lack of liking (*a distaste for rural sports*).

distasteful *adj* causing distaste; unpleasant to the taste or liking; disagreeable; slightly repulsive.

distemper[1] *n* an often fatal viral disease of

dissolve

distal

young dogs which causes catarrh and may lead to convulsions by affecting the central nervous system.

distemper² *n* in painting, a preparation of opaque colour, ground with size and water; tempera; a kind of painting in which the pigments are mixed with size and chiefly used for scene painting and interior decoration.

distend *vt* to stretch or swell out by force acting from within; to dilate; to expand; to swell; to puff out (a bladder, the lungs).—*vi* to become inflated or distended; to swell.

distension, distention *n* the act of distending; the state of being distended; extent or space occupied by the thing distended.

distich *n* a couplet.

distil *vi* (**distilled, distilling**) to drop; to fall in drops or in a small stream; to trickle; to use a still; to practise distillation.—*vt* to yield or give forth in drops or a small stream; to let fall in drops; to drop; to obtain or extract by distillation; to subject to the process of distillation.

distillate *n* a product of distillation.

distillation *n* the act of distilling or falling in drops; the volatilization and subsequent condensation of a liquid by means of an alembic or still, or of a retort and receiver; the operation of extracting spirit from a substance by evaporation and condensation.

distillery *n* the act or art of distilling; the building and works where distillation is carried on.

distinct *adj* separated or distinguished by some mark, note or character; marked out; not the same in number or kind; different; having well-marked characteristics; standing clearly or boldly out; well-defined; obvious; plain; unmistakable.

distinction *n* the act of separating or distinguishing; that which distinguishes or marks as different; a note or mark of difference; distinguishing quality; eminence or superiority; elevation or honourable estimation; that which confers or marks eminence or superiority; a title or honour of some kind.

distinctive *adj* marking or indicating distinction or difference.

distinguish *vt* to mark or set apart as different or separate from others; to perceive or recognize the individuality of; to note as differing from something else by some mark or quality; to know or ascertain difference by the senses or intellect; to classify or divide by any mark or quality which constitutes difference; to separate by definitions; to separate from others by a mark of honour or preference; to make eminent or known; to signalize.—*vi* to make a distinction; to find or show the difference.

distillation

DISTORTION

distortion

distinguishable *adj* capable of being distinguished or recognized; capable of being defined or classified; worthy of note or special regard.

distinguished *adj* separated from others by superior or extraordinary qualities; eminent; extraordinary; transcendent; noted; famous; celebrated.

Distinguished Conduct Medal *n* a medal that may be granted to non-commissioned officers and soldiers for individual acts of gallantry in the field.

Distinguished Service Cross *n* a naval decoration awarded for gallantry in action.

Distinguished Service Order *n* an honour bestowed on officers who have been mentioned in despatches for meritorious or distinguished services in war and often for conspicuous gallantry under fire.

distort *vt* to twist out of natural or regular shape; to force or put out of the true bent or direction; to bias (the judgment); to wrest from the true meaning, to misrepresent; to pervert.

distortion *n* the act of distorting; a twisting or writhing motion; an unnatural direction of parts from whatever cause, as a curved spine, a wry mouth; squinting, etc; a perversion of the true meaning of words.

distract *vt* to draw apart or pull separate; to turn or draw from any object or point; to divert toward various other objects (the attention); to perplex, confound or harass (the mind); to disorder the reason of; to render insane or frantic.

distraction *n* the act of distracting; the state of being distracted; confusion from a multiplicity of objects crowding the mind and calling the attention different ways; perplexity; embarrassment; madness; frenzy; insanity; extreme folly; extreme perturbation or agony of mind, as from pain or grief; anything giving the mind a new and less onerous occupation; a diversion.

distrain *vt* (*law*) to seize, as goods and chattels, for debt.

distraint *n* a distress or distraining.

distrait *adj* abstracted; absent-minded; inattentive.

distraught *adj* distracted; perplexed.

distress *n* extreme pain; anguish of body or mind; that which causes suffering; affliction; calamity; adversity; misery; a state of danger; (*law*) the act of distraining; the seizure of any personal chattel as a pledge for the payment of rent or debt or the satisfaction of a claim.—*vt* to afflict with pain or anguish; to harass; to grieve; to perplex; to make miserable.

distribute *vt* (**distributed, distributing**) to divide among two or more; to deal out; to give or bestow in parts or portions; to dispense; to administer; to divide, as into classes, orders, genera; (*print*) to separate types and place them in their proper boxes or compartments in the cases.

distribution *n* the act of distributing or dealing out; the act of dispensing or administering; the act of separating into distinct parts or classes; (*print*) the separating of the types and arranging of them in their proper places in the case; the manner of being distributed or spread over the earth (*the distribution of animals* or *plants*).

distributive *adj* serving to distribute; expressing separation or division; specifically, (*gram*) an epithet applied to certain words (as *each*, *every*) which denote the persons or things that make a number taken separately and singly.—*n* (*gram*) a distributive word, as *each* and *every*.

district *n* a part of a country, city, etc, distinctly defined or marked out; a portion of country without very definite limits; a tract; a region, locality, quarter.

distrust *vt* to doubt or suspect the truth, fidelity, firmness, sincerity, reality, sufficiency or goodness of; to have no faith, reliance or confidence in; to be suspicious of.—*n* doubt or suspicion; lack of confidence, faith or reliance.

disturb *vt* to excite from a state of rest or tranquillity; to stir; to move; to discompose; to agitate; to throw into confusion or disorder; to excite uneasiness in the mind of; to disquiet; to render uneasy; to ruffle; to move from any regular course; operation or purpose; to make irregular; to interfere with; to interrupt.

disturbance *n* the act of disturbing; interruption of peace or quiet; interruption of a settled state of things; violent change; derangement; perturbation; agitation; disorder of thoughts; confusion; agitation in the body politic; a disorder; a tumult.

disulphate *n* a sulphate with one atom of hydrogen, replaceable by a basic element.

disulphide *n* a sulphide in which two atoms of sulphur are contained.

disunion *n* a state of not being united; separation; disjunction; a breach of concord and its effect; contention; dissension.

disunite *vt* to separate; to disjoin; to part; to set at variance; to raise dissension between.—*vi* to fall asunder; to become separate.

disuse *n* cessation of use, practice or exercise.—*vt* to cease to use; to neglect or omit to practise.

ditch *n* a trench in the earth made by digging, particularly a trench for draining wet land or for making a fence to guard enclosures or for preventing an enemy from approaching a town or fortress; any long artificial channel dug to contain water.—*vi* to dig or make a ditch or ditches.—*vt* to dig a ditch or ditches in; to drain by a ditch; to surround with a ditch.

dithyramb *n* in ancient Greece, a hymn in honour of Bacchus, god of wine; a poem of an impetuous and irregular character.

dittany *n* a perennial plant of the Mediterranean region with numerous glands containing a fragrant and very volatile oil.

ditto a word used in lists, accounts, etc, to save writing, equivalent to same as above or aforesaid (often contracted into *Do, do*).

ditty *n* a song; a sonnet; a little poem to be sung.

diuretic *adj* having the power to simulate the secretion of urine; tending to produce discharges of urine.—*n* a medicine that stimulates secretion of urine or increases its discharges.

diurnal *adj* relating to a day; pertaining to the daytime; performed every day; daily.

divan *n* a long couch without back or sides; a bed of similar design.

divaricate *vi* (**divaricated, divaricating**) to fork; to part into two branches.

dive *vi* (**dived, diving**) to descend or plunge into water head first; to go under water for the purpose of executing some work; (of an aicraft) to descend or fall steeply; to go deep into any subject; to plunge into any business or condition; to sink; to penetrate.—*n* the act of diving; a headlong plunge; a sharp descent; (*sl*) a disreputable place.

diver *n* one who dives; one of a family of marine swimming birds, with short wings and tail, legs far back and toes completely webbed, preying on fish, which they pursue under water.

diverge *vt* (**diverged, diverging**) to tend or proceed from a common point in different directions; to deviate from a given course or line, opposed to *converge*; to differ or vary.

divergence *n* the act of diverging; a receding from each other; a going farther apart.

divergent *adj* diverging; separating or receding from each other, as lines which proceed from the same point.

divers *adj* different; various; several; sundry; more than one but not a great many.

diverse *adj* different; differing; unlike; not the same.

diversified *adj* distinguished by various forms or by a variety of objects.

diversify *vt* (**diversified, diversifying**) to make diverse or various in form or qualities; to give variety or diversity to; to variegate.

diversion *n* the act of diverting or turning aside from any course; that which diverts or turns the mind or thoughts away; what turns or draws the mind from care, business or study and thus relaxes and amuses; sport; play; pastime; a feint or other movement made to mislead an enemy as to the real point of attack.

diver

diversity *n* the state of being diverse; difference; dissimilitude; unlikeness; multiplicity with difference; variety; distinctness or separateness of being, as opposed to identity.

divert *vt* to turn off from any course, direction or intended application; to turn aside (*to divert a stream*, *traffic*, etc); to turn from business or study; to turn from care or serious thoughts; hence, to please; to amuse; to entertain.

divertimento *n* (*pl* **divertimenti, divertimentos**) a light, pleasant vocal or instrumental composition.

diverting *adj* causing diversion; amusing; entertaining.

divertissement *n* an amusement; a recreation; a short entertainment between the acts of longer theatrical pieces; (*mus*) a divertimento.

divest *vi* to strip; to strip of dress or of anything that surrounds or attends; to deprive (with *of* before the thing removed).

divide *vt* (**divided, dividing**) to part of separate into pieces; to cut or otherwise separate into two or more parts; to cause to be separate; to keep apart, as by a partition or by an imaginary line or limit; to make partition of among a number; to disunite in opinion or interest; to set at variance; to separate (an assembly) into two bodies for the purpose of voting.—*vi* to become separated; to part; to open; to cleave; to vote by the division of a legislative house into two parts.—*n* the watershed of a district or region.

dividend *n* a sum or a number to be divided; the profit or gain made by a joint-stock company and which falls to be divided among the shareholders according to the stock of each; the interest due to any holder of a share in the public debt.

divider *n* one who or that which divides; (*pl*) a pair of small compasses.

divination *n* the act of divining; a foretelling future events, or discovering things secret or obscure, by the aid of superior beings or by certain rites, experiments, observations, etc.

divine *adj* pertaining to God or to a heathen deity or false god; partaking of the nature of God; godlike; heavenly; sacred; holy; excellent in the highest degree; apparently above what is human; relating to divinity or theology.—*n* a minister of the gospel; a priest; a clergyman; a theologian.—*vt* (**divined, divining**) to foretell; to predict; to prognosticate; to conjecture; to guess.—*vi* to use or practise divination; to utter prognostications; to bode; to guess.

diviner *n* one who professes divination; a soothsayer; one who guesses or conjectures.

diving *n* the act or practice of descending into water; especially, the art of descending below the surface of the water and remaining there for some time in order to remove objects from the bottom, etc.

diving bell *n* an apparatus, originally bell-shaped, in which persons descend into the water and remain for a length of time, fresh air being pumped into the bell by assistants above.

diving suit *n* a waterproof garment used by professional divers, variously constructed.

divining rod *n* a rod, usually of hazel, which, if carried slowly along in suspension by an adept, dips and points downwards, it is affirmed, when brought over the spot where water or treasure is to be found.

divinity *n* the state of being divine; divineness; deity; godhead; divine element; divine nature; God; the Deity; a celestial being; one of the deities belonging to a polytheistic religion; supernatural power or virtue; awe-inspiring character or influence; sacredness; the science of divine things; theology.

divisible *adj* capable of division; that may be separated or disunited; separable.

division *n* the act of dividing or separating into parts; the state of being divided; separation; a dividing line; a partition; the part separated from the rest, as by a partition, line, etc, real or imaginary; a distinct segment or section; a part or distinct portion; a certain section or portion of an organized whole, as an army, a fleet; disunion; discord; dissension; variance; difference; the separation of members in a legislative house in order to ascertain the vote; (*arith*) one of the four fundamental rules, the object of which is to find how often one number is contained in another.

division lobby *n* a lobby in Parliament were Members record their votes on a division.

divisor *n* (*arith*) the number by which the dividend is divided.

divorce *n* a legal dissolution of the bond of marriage; a legal separation between husband and wife, after which either is free to marry again; the sentence or writing by which marriage is dissolved; disunion of things closely united; separation.—*vt* (**divorced, divorcing**) to dissolve the marriage contract between; to separate from the condition of husband and wife; to separate or disunite from close connection; to force asunder; to put away.

divot *n* a piece of turf cut out by a golfer when striking the ball.

divulge *vt* (**divulged, divulging**) to tell or make known what was before private or secret; to reveal; to disclose; to let be known.

dixie *n* a camp cauldron or two-handled cooking pot.

divining rod

dividers

dizziness *n* the state or feeling of being dizzy; giddiness; vertigo.

dizzy *adj* having a sensation of whirling in the head with instability or proneness to fall; giddy; vertiginous; causing giddiness (*a dizzy height*); arising from or caused by, giddiness; thoughtless; heedless; inconstant—*vt* (**dizzied, dizzying**) to make dizzy or giddy; to confuse.

DNA *n* deoxyribonucleic acid, the main component of chromosomes that stores genetic information.

DNA fingerprinting same as **genetic fingerprinting**.

do[1] *vt or auxiliary* (*pret* **did**; *pp* **done**; *ppr* **doing**—*the present tense singular is*: **I do, he does**) to perform; to execute; to carry into effect; to bring about, produce, effect; to give, confer or pay (*to do honour, reverence*, etc); to transact; to finish or complete; (*colloq*) to hoax, cheat, swindle; (*colloq*) to inspect the sights or objects of interest in; to prepare; to cook.—*vi* to act or behave in any manner, well or ill; to conduct oneself; to fare; to be in a state with regard to sickness or health (*how do you do?*); to succeed; to accomplish a purpose; to serve an end; to suffice (*will this plan do?*); to find means; to contrive; to shift (*how shall we do for money?*).—**do** is often used for a verb to save the repetition of it: as, *I shall probably come, but if I do not, you must not wait*, that is, *if I come not*.—as an auxiliary it is used most commonly in forming negative and interrogative sentences: as, *do you intend to go? does he wish me to come?* —**do** is also used to express emphasis: as, *I do love her*.—in the imperative, it expresses an urgent request or command: as, *do come; help me, do; make haste, do.*—in the past tense it is sometimes used to convey the idea that what was once true is not true now: 'My lord, you once did love me' (*Shak*).—the past participle **done**, besides being used for all the ordinary meanings of the verb, has some colloquial or familiar uses: as **done!** an exclamation expressing agreement to a proposal, that is, it is agreed or I accept; **done up** ruined in any manner, completely exhausted, very tired or fatigued.

do[2] *n* (*mus*) the name given to the first of the syllables used in solmization; the first or key note of the scale.

docile *adj* teachable; easily instructed; ready to learn; tractable; easily managed.—**docility** *n*.

dock[1] *n* the place where a prisoner stands in court; a place artificially formed on the side of a harbour or the bank of a river for the reception of ships, the entrance of which is generally closed by gates.—*vt* to bring, draw or place in a dock.

dock[2] *n* the common name of various species of perennial herbs, most of them troublesome weeds with stout root stalks, erect stems and broad leaves.

dock[3] *n* the tail of a beast cut short; the stump of a tail; the solid part of the tail.—*vt* to cut off, as the end of a thing; to curtail; to cut short; to clip; to shorten.

docker *n* a worker at a harbour docks.

docket *n* a summary of a larger writing; a small piece of paper or parchment containing the heads of a writing; an alphabetical list of cases in a court of law; a ticket attached to goods, containing the name of the owner, the place to which they are to be sent or specifying their measurement, etc.—*vt* to make an abstract of and enter, or write it down; to mark the contents of papers on the back; to add a docket to.

dockyard *n* a yard or repository near a harbour for containing all kinds of naval stores and timber.

Doc Martens *npl* the trademark for a brand of sturdy, high lace-up boots with thick lightweight soles.

doctor *n* a person who has received the degree of this name from a university, being thus a doctor of divinity, laws, medicine, etc, and supposed capable of teaching the particular subject; a person duly licensed to practise medicine; a physician; one who cures diseases.—*vt* to treat medically; hence, to repair or patch up; to drug or adulterate (wine); to falsify; to cook (in all senses *colloq*).

doctorate *n* the university degree of doctor.

doctrinaire *n* one who theorizes or advocates important changes in political or social matters without a sufficient regard to practical considerations; a political theorist.

doctrinal *adj* pertaining to doctrine; containing a doctrine; pertaining to the act or means of teaching.

doctrine *n* in a general sense, whatever is taught; hence, a principle, view or set of opinions maintained by any person or set of persons; whatever is laid down as true by an instructor or master; often instruction and confirmation in the truths of the gospel; one or more of the truths of the gospel.

document *n* any official or authoritative paper containing instructions or proof, for information, establishment of facts, etc; any written or printed paper.

documentary *adj* pertaining to documents or written evidence; consisting in documents.

dodder[1] *n* the name of certain slender, twining, leafless pink or white parasitic plants, the common English species of which are found on nettles, vetches, furze, flax, etc.

dodder[2] *vi* to walk or move shakily; to

DNA

tremble; to talk incoherently; to be enfeebled mentally.

dodecagon *n* a regular figure or polygon of twelve equal sides and angles.

dodecahedron *n* a regular solid contained under twelve equal and regular pentagons or having twelve equal bases.

dodge *vi* (**dodged, dodging**) to start suddenly aside; to follow the footsteps of a person, but so as to escape observation; to play tricks; to play fast and loose; to quibble.—*vt* to evade by a sudden shift of place; to escape by starting aside; to pursue by rapid movements in varying directions; to baffle by shifts and pretexts; to overreach by tricky knavery.—*n* a trick; an artifice; an evasion.

dodo *n* (*pl* **dodos, dodoes**) an extinct bird of Mauritius, having a massive, clumsy body covered with down, short and extremely strong legs and wings and tail so short as to be useless for flight.

doe *n* the female of the fallow deer, the hare and the rabbit.

doer *n* one who does, executes, performs or acts; one who performs what is required, as opposed to a mere talker or theorizer.

doff *vt* to put, take or lay off, as dress; to lay aside.—*vi* to lay off some article of dress; to take off the hat.

dog *n* a well-known domesticated carnivorous quadruped, closely allied to the wolf and the fox, noted for its sagacity, acute senses and great attachment to people; a term of reproach or contempt given to a man; a mean, worthless fellow; a lively young man; a buck; a name applied to several tools, articles, etc, generally iron, as, an andiron, a kind of trestle to lay wood on in a fireplace.—*vt* (**dogged, dogging**) to follow insidiously or indefatigably; to follow close; to hunt, to worry with importunity.

dogcart *n* a carriage with a box for holding sportsmen's dogs; a sort of double-seated gig, the occupants before and behind sitting back to back.

dog days *npl* the days when Sirius or the Dog Star (whence the term) rises and sets with the sun, extending from about 3rd July to about 11th August.

doge *n* the chief magistrate of the former republics of Venice (697–1797) and Genoa (1339–1797).

dogfish *n* a name given to several species of fishes closely allied to the sharks, but of no great size.

dogged *adj* having the qualities of a dog; surly; obstinate.

doggerel *adj* an epithet originally applied to a kind of loose irregular measure in burlesque poetry, but now more generally to mean verses defective in rhythm and sense.—*n* doggerel or mean verses.

dogma *n* a settled opinion or belief; a tenet; an opinion or doctrine received on authority, as opposed to one obtained from experience or demonstration.

dogmatic *adj* pertaining to a dogma or dogmas; having the character of a dogma; disposed to assert opinions with overbearing or arrogance; dictatorial; arrogant; authoritative; positive.

dogmatics *n* doctrinal theology; the essential doctrines of Christianity.

dogmatism *n* the quality of being dogmatic; arrogant assertion.

dogmatize *vi* (**dogmatized, dogmatizing**) to teach opinions with bold and undue confidence; to assert principles arrogantly or authoritatively.

dog rose *n* a common British wild rose; the wild briar, the fruit of which is known as the hip.

dog's-ear *n* the corner of a leaf in a book turned down, especially by careless handling.—*vt* to turn down in dog's ears.

dog's-tail grass *n* the popular name of several species of grasses common in Britain.

Dog Star *n* Sirius, a star of the first magnitude, whose rising and setting with the sun gives name to the dog days.

dogwatch *n* (*naut*) the name of the two watches of two hours each instead of four (between 4 and 8 p.m.) arranged so as to alter the watches kept from day to day by each portion of the crew, otherwise the same people would form the watch during the same hours for the whole voyage.

dogwood *n* a name of several trees or shrubs, one of them common in copses and hedges in England, with small cream-white flowers borne in dense roundish clusters.

doily, doyley *n* a small ornamental mat used at table under food dishes, such as cake plates; a table napkin.

doings *npl* things done; transactions; feats; actions, good or bad; behaviour; conduct.

doit *n* a small Dutch copper coin, being the eighth part of a stiver; the ancient Scottish penny piece, of which twelve were equal to a penny sterling; any small piece of money; a trifle.

doldrums *npl* (naut) the parts of the ocean near the equator that abound in calms, squalls and light baffling winds; (*colloq*) low spirits; the dumps.

dole¹ *n* that which is dealt out or distributed; a part, share or portion; lot; fortune; that which is given in charity; gratuity; a maintenance allowance made by the state under certain conditions to unemployed persons.—*vt* (**doled, doling**) to deal out; to distribute; especially, to deal out niggardly or in small quantities.

dole² *n* grief; sorrow.

doleful *adj* full of dole or grief; sorrowful;

dodecahedron

dodo

expressing grief; mournful; melancholy; sad; dismal; gloomy.

dolerite *n* a variety of dark-coloured igneous rock; basaltic greenstone.

~~dolichocephalic, dolichocephalous~~ *adj* a term used in ethnology to denote skulls in which the diameter from side to side bears a less proportion to the diameter from front to back than 8 to 10, as seen in West African tribes.

doll *n* a puppet or small image in the human form for the amusement of children; a girl or woman more remarkable for good looks than intelligence.

dollar *n* a banknote or silver coin of the USA, Canada, Australia.

dolman *n* (*pl* **dolmans**) a long outer robe, open in front and having narrow sleeves buttoned at the wrist, worn by Turks; a hussar's jacket.

dolmen *n* an ancient structure (probably of sepulchral origin) consisting of one large unhewn stone resting on two or more others placed erect; also applied to structures where several blocks are raised on pillars so as to form a sort of gallery; a cromlech.

dolomite *n* a granular, crystalline or schistose stone or rock, being a compound of carbonate of magnesia and carbonate of lime.

dolorous *adj* sorrowful; doleful; exciting sorrow or grief; painful; expressing pain or grief.

dolphin *n* a marine mammal with a beak-like snout, larger than a porpoise but smaller than a whale.

dolt *n* a heavy, stupid fellow; a blockhead.

dom *n* a Roman Catholic title of dignitaries of the Carthusian and Benedictine monks.

domain *n* the territory over which dominion is exercised; the territory ruled over; a dominion; an estate in land; the land about a mansion house and in the immediate occupancy of the owner; a demesne.

dome *n* a roof rising up in the form of an inverted cup; a large cupola; the hemispherical roof of a building.

domestic *adj* belonging to the house or home; pertaining to one's place of residence and to the family; devoted to home duties or pleasures; living in or about the habitations of humans; kept for the use of humans; tame; not wild; pertaining to one's own country; intestine; not foreign.—*n* one who lives in the family of another and is paid for some service; a household servant.

domesticate *vt* (**domesticated, domesticating**) to make domestic; to accustom to remain much at home; to accustom (animals) to live near the habitations of humans; to tame; to reduce from a wild to a cultivated condition (plants).

domicile *n* a place of residence; a dwelling house; the place where one lives in opposition to the place where one only remains for a time.—*vt* (**domiciled, domiciling**) to establish; to settle permanently.

dominant *adj* ruling; prevailing; governing; predominant; (of a genre) masking the expression of a recessive gene and establishing characteristics.—*n* (*mus*) the fifth tone of the diatonic scale; thus G is the dominant of the scale of C and D the dominant of the scale of G.

dominant chord *n* (*mus*) that which is formed by grouping three tones, rising gradually by intervals of a third from the dominant or fifth tone of the scale.

dominate *vt* (**dominated, dominating**) to have power or sway over; to govern; to prevail or predominate over.—*vi* to predominate.

domination *n* the exercise of power in ruling; dominion; government; arbitrary authority; tyranny.

domineer *vi* to rule with insolence or arbitrary sway; to bluster; to hector.—*vt* to govern harshly or overbearingly; to order or command insolently.

Dominican *n* a member of a religious order instituted in 1216 at Toulouse, called also Blackfriar, from the colour of the dress.

dominion *n* sovereign or supreme authority; the power of governing and controlling; government; sway; rule; ascendancy; predominance; territory under a government; country or district governed or within the limits of the authority of a prince or state.

domino *n* (*pl* **dominoes**) a masquerade dress, consisting of an ample cloak or mantle, with a cap and wide sleeves; frequently, though incorrectly, applied to a half-mask worn by ladies as a partial disguise for the features; a person wearing a domino; (*pl*) a game played with twenty-eight flat, oblong pieces of ivory or bone, dotted, after the manner of dice, with a certain number of points.

don[1] *vt* (**donned, donning**) to put on; to invest oneself with.

don[2] *n* a title in Spain, formerly given to noblemen and gentlemen only, but now used much more widely; a university lecturer.

donate *vt* (**donated, donating**) to give as a gift or donation, especially to a charity.

donation *n* the act of giving or bestowing; that which is gratuitously given; a grant; a gift.

donee *n* one who receives; (*med*) one who receives a transplant.

donor *n* one who gives, grants or bestows; a giver.

donjon *n* the principal tower of a castle

donkey *n* an ass; a stupid or obstinate and wrong-headed fellow.

doom *n* a judgment or judicial sentence; passing of sentence; the final judgment;

dolmen

dolphin

the state to which one is doomed or destined; fate; fortune, generally evil; adverse issue; ruin; destruction.—*vt* to condemn to any punishment; to consign by a decree or sentence; to pronounce sentence or judgment on; to ordain as a penalty; to decree; to destine.

doomsday *n* the day of doom or final judgment.

Doomsday Book *n* a book compiled by order of William the Conqueror containing a survey of all the lands in England, giving areas of estates, the amount of land under tillage, population, etc.

door *n* an opening or passage into a house or apartment by which persons enter; the frame of boards or other material that shuts such an opening and usually turns on hinges; means of approach or access.

doorkeeper *n* a porter; one who guards the entrance of a house or apartment.

doorstep *n* the stone at the threshold.

doorway *n* the passage of a door; the entrance way into a room or house.

dope n a thick pasty substance used for lubrication; (*colloq*) a drug, especially an illegal one; (*sl*) a stupid person; (*sl*) information.—*vt* (**doped, doping**) to drug; to dose; to inject petrol into an engine.

dor *n* an insect that makes a droning sound while flying.

Dorian mode *n* (*mus*) a composition in which the second note of the normal scale acquires something of the dignity or force of a tonic and on it the melody closes.

Doric *n* the language of the Dorians, a Greek dialect characterized by broadness and hardness; any dialect with similar characteristics, especially the Scottish.

Doric order *n* (*archit*) the oldest and simplest of the three orders of Grecian architecture, characterized by the columns having no base and the flutings few, large and not deep, the capital of simple character.

dorking *n* a species of domestic fowl, distinguished by having five claws on each foot, so named because bred largely at Dorking in Surrey.

dormant *adj* sleeping; sunk in the winter sleep or torpid state of certain animals; at rest; not in action (*dormant energies*); neglected; not claimed, asserted or insisted on (*a dormant title* or *privileges*); in heraldry, of beast with head on paws.

dormer *n* a window standing vertically on a sloping roof of a dwelling house.

dormitory *n* a place, building or room to sleep in.

dormouse *n* (*pl* **dormice**) a small rodent animal which passes the winter in a lethargic or torpid state.

dorsal *adj* of or pertaining to the back.

dory[1] *n* a European fish of a yellow colour with a protruding mouth, valued as food.

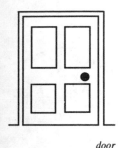

door

dory

dory[2] *n* a canoe or small boat.

dose *n* the quantity of medicine given or prescribed to be taken at one time; anything given to be swallowed; as much as a person can take; a quantity in general.—*vt* (**dosed, dosing**) to form into suitable doses; to give a dose or doses to.

dosh *n* (*sl*) money.

dossier *n* a collection of documents of information about a person or incident.

dot *n* a small point or spot made with a pen or other pointed instrument; a speck, used in marking a writing or other thing; a spot. —*vt* (**dotted, dotting**) to mark with dots; to mark or diversify with small detached objects (as clumps of trees).—*vi* to make dots or spots.

dotage *n* feebleness or imbecility of understanding or mind, particularly in old age; childishness of old age; senility; weak and foolish affection.

dotard *n* a person whose intellect is impaired by age.

dote *vi* (**doted, doting**) to have the intellect impaired by age, so that the mind wanders or wavers; to be in a state of senile silliness; to be excessively in love; to love to excess or extravagance (*to dote on a person*).

dotterel, dottrel *n* a species of plover, breeding in the highest latitudes of Asia and Europe and migrating to the shores of the Mediterranean; a booby; a dupe; a gull.

douane *n* foreign customhouse.

double *adj* forming a pair; consisting of two in a set together; coupled; composed of two corresponding parts; twofold; twice as much; multiplied by two (*a double portion*); acting two parts, one openly, the other in secret; deceitful; (*bot*) having two or more rows of petals produced by cultivation from stamens and carpels.—*vt* (**doubled, doubling**) to make double or twofold; to fold one part on another part of; to increase by adding an equal sum, value or quantity; to contain twice as much as; to pass round or by; to march or sail round, so as to proceed along both sides of (*to double a cape*).—*vi* to increase or grow to twice as much; to turn back or wind in running.—*n* twice as much; a turn in running to escape pursuers; a trick; a shift; an artifice to deceive; something precisely equal or like; a counterpart; a duplicate; a copy; a person's apparition or likeness; a wraith; a fold or plait; (*milit*) the quickest step in marching; a slow run.

double bass *n* the largest musical instrument of the viol kind.

double-breasted *adj* applied to a waistcoat or coat, either side of which may be made to lap over the other and button.

double-cross *vt* to betray an associate; to cheat.

double-dealer *n* one who deceitfully acts two different parts; a deceitful, trickish person; one who says one thing and thinks or intends another; one guilty of duplicity.

double entendre *n* a phrase with a double meaning, one of which is often more or less indecent.

double entry *n* a mode of bookkeeping in which two entries are made of every transaction, one on the debit side of one account and the other on the credit side of another account, in order that the one may check the other.

doublet *n* a close-fitting garment covering the body from the neck to a little below the waist, now superseded by the vest or waistcoat; one of a pair; one of two (or more) words really the same but different in form (as *ant* and *emmet*).

doubloon *n* an old gold coin of Spain.

doubt *vi* to waver or fluctuate in opinion; to be in uncertainty respecting the truth or fact; to be undetermined.—*vt* to question or hold questionable; to withhold assent from; to hesitate to believe; to suspect; to distrust; to be diffident of (*to doubt a person's ability*).—*n* a fluctuation of mind respecting the truth or correctness of a statement or opinion or the propriety of an action; uncertainty of mind; lack of belief; unsettled state of opinion; suspicion; apprehension.

doubtful *adj* entertaining doubt; not settled in opinion; undetermined; wavering; dubious; ambiguous; not clear in meaning; not obvious, clear or certain; questionable; not without suspicion; not confident; not without fear; not certain or defined.

doubtless *adv* without doubt or question; unquestionably.

douceur *n* a present, gift or gratuity; a bribe.

douche *n* a kind of bath consisting in a jet or current of water or vapour directed on some part of the body.

dough *n* paste of bread; a mass composed of flour or meal moistened and kneaded but not baked.

doughty *adj* brave; valiant; noble; illustrious; now seldom used except in irony or burlesque.

douse, dowse *vt* (**doused, dousing**) to thrust or plunge into water; to immerse; to dip; (*naut*) to strike or lower in haste; to slacken suddenly; to put out or extinguish.—*vi* to fall or be plunged suddenly into water.

dove *n* a pigeon, some varieties being distinguished by an additional term prefixed, as ring dove, turtledove, etc; a word of endearment.

dovecote, dovecot *n* a small building or box in which domestic pigeons breed; a house for doves.

dovetail *n* in carpentry, a method of fastening the ends of boards together at right angles by letting one piece, cut into projections somewhat like a dove's tail spread, into corresponding cavities in another.—*vt* to unite by the above method; (*fig*) to fit or adjust exactly and firmly.

dowager *n* a name given to the widow of a person of title, as a prince or nobleman, to distinguish her from the wife of her husband's heir bearing the same title; (*colloq*) a dignified elderly woman.

dowdy *adj* awkward; ill-dressed; lacking style; unfashionably dressed.

dowel *n* a wooden or iron pin or tenon used in joining together two pieces of any substance edgewise (as the pieces of a barrel end); a piece of wood driven into a wall to receive nails of skirtings, etc.—*vt* (**dowelled, dowelling**) to fasten by means of dowels, as two boards together by pins inserted in the edges.

dower *n* that with which one is endowed; the property which a woman brings to her husband in marriage; (*law*) the right which a wife has in the third part of the real estate of which her husband died possessed.—*vt* to furnish with dower or a portion; to endow.

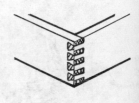

dovetail

down¹ *prep* along in descent; from a higher to a lower part of; towards the mouth of and in the direction of the current.—*adv* in a descending direction; from a higher to a lower position, degree or place in a series; from the metropolis of a country to the provinces or from the main terminus of a railway to the subordinate stations; on the ground or at the bottom; in a low condition; in humility, dejection, calamity, etc; below the horizon (*the sun is down*); into disrepute or disgrace (*to write down folly, vice, an author*); from a larger to a less bulk (*to boil down*); from former to more recent times; extended or prostrate on the ground or on any flat surface; paid or handed over in ready money (*a thousand pounds down*).—**up and down** here and there; everywhere.—**down in the mouth** (*colloq*) dispirited; dejected.—**to be down at heel** to have the back part of the upper, or heel, turned down, or to have on shoes with the heel turned down; to be slipshod or slovenly.

down² *n* the fine soft covering of birds under the feathers, particularly on the breasts of waterfowl, as the duck and swan; the soft hair of the human face when beginning to appear; the pubescence of plants, a fine hairy substance; any fine feathery or hairy substance of vegetable growth.—*vt* to cover, stuff or line with down.

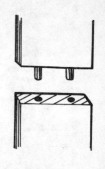

dowel

down³ *n* a hill or rising ground; a low, rounded, grassy hill; a tract of hilly land for pasturing sheep; a dune or sand hill.

downcast *adj* cast downward; directed to the ground (*downcast eyes*); in low spirits; dejected.

downfall *n* a falling down; a sudden descent or fall from a position of power, honour, wealth, fame, etc; loss of rank, reputation or fortune; loss of office; ruin; destruction.

downhearted *adj* dejected in spirits.

downhill *n* a declivity; slope.—*adj* sloping downwards; descending; sloping.—*adv* down a hill or slope.

downpour *n* a pouring down; especially a heavy or continuous shower.

downright *adv* right down; in plain terms; completely; thoroughly.—*adj* directed straight or right down; coming down perpendicularly; directly to the point; plain; open; mere; sheer (*downright nonsense*); straightforward; unceremonious; blunt (*a downright man*).

downside *n* the disadvantageous or less appealing aspect of something.

Down's syndrome *n* a condition caused by a chromosomal abnormality characterized by slanting eyes and mental retardation.

downtown *n* the main business or shopping centre of a city.

downtrodden *adj* trodden down; trampled on; tyrannized over.

downturn *n* a decline in economic prosperity or activity.

downward *adj* moving from a higher to a lower place, position or condition.—*adv* downwards.

downwards *adv* from a higher place to a lower; in a descending course; in a course or direction from a spring or source; in a course of descent from an ancestor.

downy *adj* covered with down or nap; covered with pubescence or soft hairs, as a plant; made of down; soft, calm, soothing (sleep); (*sl*) knowing, cunning or artful.

dowry *n* the money, goods or estate which a woman brings to her husband in marriage; dower.

dowsing rod *n* a name for the divining rod.

doxology *n* a short hymn or form of words ascribing glory to God and used in worship

doyen, doyenne *n* the senior member of a body or profession.

doyley *n* same as **doily**.

doze *vi* (**dozed, dozing**) to slumber; to sleep lightly; to live in a state of drowsiness; to be dull or half asleep.—*vt* to pass or spend in drowsiness; to make dull; to stupefy.—*n* a light sleep; a slumber.

dozen *n* a collection of twelve things of a like kind or regarded as forming an aggregate for the time being; an indefinite or round number comprising more or less than twelve units, as the case may be.

drab *adj* being of a dull-brown or pale-brown colour.

drachm *n* a unit of mass equal to about 3.89 g.

drachma *n* the basic unit of money in ancient and modern Greece.

draconian, draconic *adj* relating to Draco, the Athenian lawgiver; hence (applied to laws), extremely severe.

draff *n* refuse; dregs; hog's wash; the refuse of malt which has been brewed or distilled from, given to swine and cows.

draft *n* a selection of people or things for a special duty or purpose; a body of people drawn from a larger body; an order from one person to another directing the payment of money; an order authorizing a person to draw a certain sum of money; the first outlines of any writing, embodying an exposition of the purpose, as well as of the details, of the document; a drawing, delineation or sketch in outline.—*vt* to make a draft of; to compose and write the first outlines of; to delineate in outline; to draw from a larger body; to select.

drag *vt* (**dragged, dragging**) to pull; to haul; to draw along the ground by main force; to draw along slowly or heavily, as anything burdensome or troublesome; hence, to pass in pain or with difficulty; to search (a river, pond, etc) with a net, hooked instrument, etc, for drowned persons, etc.—*vi* to be drawn along or trail on the ground, as a dress or as an anchor that does not hold; to move or proceed slowly, heavily or laboriously; to move on lingeringly or with effort.—*n* a net or a kind of grapnel for recovering the bodies of drowned persons; an apparatus used to recover articles lost in the water or to dredge up oysters, etc; a kind of heavy harrow for breaking up ground; a long coach or carriage, generally drawn by four horses, uncovered and with seats round the sides; an apparatus for retarding or stopping the rotation of one wheel, or of several wheels of a vehicle, in descending hills, slopes, etc; a person or thing forming an obstacle to one's progress or prosperity; slow and difficult motion; (*colloq*) something very boring; (*colloq*) female clothing when worn by a man.

dragnet *n* a net to be drawn on the bottom of a river or pond for taking fish.

dragoman *n* (*pl* **dragomans, dragomen**) an interpreter and travellers' guide or agent in Eastern countries.

dragon *n* a fabulous animal, conceived as a sort of winged crocodile, with fiery eyes, crested head and enormous claws, spouting fire and often regarded as an embodiment of watchfulness; a kind of small lizard, having an expansion of the skin on each side, which forms a kind of wing, serving to sustain the animal when it leaps from branch to branch; a fierce, violent

dragon

person, male or female; more generally now, a spiteful, watchful woman.

dragonfly *n* the popular name of a family of insects, having large strongly reticulated wings, a large head with enormous eyes, a long body and strong horny mandibles.

dragoon *n* a cavalry soldier.—*vt* to harass with or abandon to the rage of soldiers; to harass; to persecute; to compel to submit by violent measures.

drain *vt* to cause to pass through some porous substance; to filter; to exhaust any body of a liquid; to exhaust (land) of excessive moisture by causing it to flow off in channels; to exhaust; to deprive by drawing off gradually (*to drain a country of men*).—*vi* to flow off gradually; to be emptied or deprived of liquor by flowing or dropping.—*n* the act of draining or drawing off or of emptying by drawing off; gradual or continuous outflow or withdrawal; a channel through which water or other liquid flows off; a trench or ditch to convey water from wet land; a watercourse; a sewer.

drainage *n* a draining; a gradual flowing off of any liquid; the system of drains and other works by which any town, surface, etc, is freed from water; the mode in which the waters of a country pass off by its streams and rivers; the water carried away from a district by natural or other channels.

drake *n* the male of the duck kind.

dram *n* apothecaries' weight, a weight of the eighth part of an ounce, or 60 grains; avoirdupois weight, the sixteenth part of an ounce; as much strong liquor as is drunk at once.

drama *n* a composition representing a picture of human life and accommodated to action, generally designed to be spoken in character and represented on the stage; a series of real events invested with dramatic unity and interest; dramatic composition or literature; dramatic representation and all that is connected with it.

dramatic, dramatical *adj* of or pertaining to the drama or plays represented on the stage; appropriate to or in the form of a drama; theatrical; characterized by the force and fidelity appropriate to the drama (*a dramatic description*).

dramatist *n* the author of a dramatic composition; a writer of plays.

dramatize *vt* (**dramatized, dramatizing**) to compose in the form of the drama; to adapt to the form of a play; to express in an exaggerated way.

dramaturge *n* a playwright; a literary adviser; an expert in dramaturgy.

dramaturgy *n* the science which treats of the rules of composing dramas and representing them on the stage.

drape *vt* (**draped, draping**) to cover or invest with clothing or cloth; to dispose drapery about for use or ornament.

draper *n* one who sells cloths; a dealer in cloths.

drapery *n* the occupation of a draper; cloth or textile fabrics; the clothes or hangings with which any object is draped or hung.

drastic *adj* acting with strength or violence; powerful; efficacious.—*n* a strong purgative.

draught *n* the act of drawing; the capacity of being drawn (*a cart* or *plough of easy draught*); the drawing of liquor into the mouth and throat; the act of drinking; the quantity of liquor drunk at once; the act of delineating or that which is delineated; a representation by lines; a drawing or first sketch; an outline; a sweeping of the water for fish with a net; that which is taken by sweeping with a net (*a draught of fishes*); the depth of water necessary to float a ship, or the depth a ship sinks in water, especially when laden; a current of air moving through an enclosed or confined space, as through a room or up a chimney; (*pl*) a game resembling chess played on a board divided into sixty-four chequered squares.—**on draught** drawn or to be had directly from the cask, as beer, etc.—*vt* to draw out; to sketch roughly; to draft.—*adj* used for drawing; drawn from the barrel or other receptacle in which it is kept (*draught ale*).

draughtsboard *n* a chequered board for playing draughts.

draughtsman *n* (*pl* **draughtsmen**) a man who draws plans or designs or one who is skilled in such drawings.

draughty *adj* of or pertaining to draughts of air; exposed to draughts.

draw *vt* (*pret* **drew**, *pp* **drawn**, *ppr* **drawing**) to pull along after one; to haul; to cause to advance by force applied in front of the thing moved or at the fore end; to pull out; to unsheathe; to bring out from some receptacle (*to draw water*); to let run out; to extract (blood, wine); to attract; to cause to move or tend towards; to allure; to lead by persuasion or moral influence; to lead, as a motive; to induce to move; to inhale; to take into the lungs; to pull more closely together or apart (*to draw a curtain*); to lengthen; to extend in length; to form by extension (*to draw wire*); to form (a line) between two points; to represent by lines drawn on a plain surface; to form a picture or image; to describe in words or to represent in fancy; to derive, deduce, have or receive from some source; to receive from customers or patrons; to receive or take (*to draw money from a bank*); to extort; to force out (groans, tears); to write in due form; to form in writing; to

dragonfly

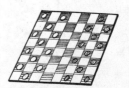

draughtsboard

take out of a box or wheel, as tickets in a lottery; to receive or gain by such drawing; to require (so many feet of water) for floating; to bend (*to draw the bow*); to eviscerate; to finish, as a game, battle, etc, so as neither party can claim the victory.—*vi* to pull; to exert strength in drawing; to act or have influence, as a weight; to shrink; to contract; to advance; to approach; to resort or betake oneself to; to unsheathe a sword; to use or practise the art of delineating figures; to form a picture; to make a draft or written demand for payment of a sum of money on a person.—*n* the act of drawing; the lot or chance drawn; a drawn game.

drawback *n* what detracts from profit or pleasure; a discouragement or hindrance; a disadvantage.

drawbridge *n* a bridge which may be drawn up or let down or opened or shut horizontally, to admit or hinder communication, as before the gate of a town or castle, or over a navigable river.

drawing board

drawer *n* one who draws or pulls; one who takes water from a well; one who draws liquor from a cask; (*Shak*) a waiter; one who draws a bill of exchange or an order for the payment of money; a sliding box in a table, desk, etc, which is drawn out at pleasure; one of a set of such boxes in a case or bureau; (*pl*) an undergarment worn on the legs and lower part of the body by both sexes.

drawing *n* the act of one who draws; the representation or delineation of an object on a plain surface, by means of lines and shades, as with a pencil, crayon, pen, etc; (*pl*) the amount of money taken for sales in a shop or other trading establishment.

drawing board *n* a board on which paper is stretched for drawing on or for painting in watercolours, etc.—**back to the drawing board** return to an early stage in a project because of a failure, hitch, etc.

drawing room *n* a room in a house appropriated for the reception of company.

drawn *adj* pulled, hauled, allured; unsheathed; extended; delineated, etc; not decided, from both parties having equal advantage and neither a victory (*a drawn battle*).

drawl *vt* to utter or pronounce in a slow lengthened tone.—*vi* to speak with slow utterance.—*n* a lengthened utterance of the voice.

dress

dray *n* a low cart or carriage on heavy wheels, such as those used by brewers.

drayhorse *n* a horse used in a dray.

dread *n* great fear or apprehension of evil or danger; terror; awe; fear united with respect; the cause of fear; the person or the thing dreaded (OT).—*adj* exciting great fear or apprehension; terrible; frightful; awful; venerable in the highest degree.—

vt to fear in a great degree.—*vi* to be in great fear.

dreadful *adj* impressing dread or great fear; terrible; formidable; awful; venerable.

dreadlocks *npl* a Rastafarian hairstyle in which the hair is twisted into long tight braids or strands.

dreadnought *n* a general term for a battleship.

dream *n* the thought or series of thoughts of a person in sleep; a matter which has only an imaginary reality; a visionary scheme or conceit; a vain fancy; an unfounded suspicion; anything very beautiful or delightful.—*vi* (**dreamed** *or* **dreamt, dreaming**) to have ideas or images in the mind in the state of sleep; with *of* before a noun; to think; to imagine; to think idly.—*vt* to see in a dream.—**to dream away** to pass in reverie or inaction; to spend idly.

dreamer *n* one who dreams; a visionary; one who forms or entertains vain schemes.

dreaminess *n* state of being dreamy.

dreamland *n* the land of dreams; the region of fancy or imagination; the region of reverie.

dreamy *adj* full of dreams; associated with dreams; giving rise to dreams; dream-like.

dreary *adj* dismal; gloomy; waste and desolate; distressing; oppressively monotonous.

dredge *n* a dragnet for taking oysters, etc; an apparatus for bringing up shells, plants and other objects from the bottom of the sea for scientific investigation; a machine for clearing the beds of canals, rivers, harbours, etc.—*vt* (**dredged, dredging**) to take, catch or gather with a dredge; to remove sand, silt, etc, from by the use of a dredge.

dregs *npl* the sediment of liquors; lees; grounds; any foreign matter of liquors that subsides to the bottom of a vessel; dross; sweepings; refuse; hence, the most vile and worthless among people.

drench *vt* to wet thoroughly; to soak; to saturate; to purge violently (an animal) with medicine.—*n* a draught; a dose of medicine for a beast, as a horse.

dress *vt* to make straight or in a straight line (troops); to put to rights; to put in good order; to till or cultivate; to treat (a wound or sore) with remedies or curative appliances; to prepare; to make suitable or fit for something (leather, a lamp, etc); to put clothes on; to invest with garments; to adorn; to deck.—*vi* to clothe oneself; to put on garments.—*n* clothes, garments or apparel; collectively, a suit of clothes; a costume; a lady's gown. **dress coat** *n* a coat with narrow pointed tails; a swallow-tailed coat.

dresser *n* one who dresses; one employed in preparing, trimming or adjusting anything;

a hospital assistant, whose office is to dress wounds, ulcers, etc; an attendant in a theatre who assists actors and actresses to dress and has charge of costumes, etc; a table or bench on which meat and other things are dressed or prepared for use; a kind of low cupboard for dishes and cooking utensils.

dressing *n* the act of one who dresses; what is used to dress; an application to a wound or sore; manure spread over land; gum, starch, paste, etc, used in stiffening or preparing silk, linen and other fabrics.

dressing gown *n* a light gown or wide and flowing coat worn by a person while dressing, etc.

dressing station *n* a place where wounded are collected and attended to by the personnel of a field ambulance.

dressing table *n* a piece of furniture with drawers and a mirror used when dressing, applying cosmetics, etc.

dressmaker *n* a maker of women's clothes.

dressy *adj* very attentive to dress; wearing rich or showy dresses.

drey *n* a squirrel's nest.

dribs and drabs *npl* very small irregular amounts.

dribble *vt* (**dribbled, dribbling**) to give out or let fall in drops; to take a football up the field by means of a series of short kicks, keeping the ball near to the foot and under control.—*vi* to fall in drops or small particles or in a quick succession of drops.

drift *n* a heap of matter driven together by the wind or water (*a snowdrift*); a driving or impulse; overbearing power or influence; course of anything; tendency; aim (*the drift of one's remarks*); intention; design; purpose; the deviation of an aircraft due to the wind; mining, a passage cut between shaft and shaft; (*naut*) the distance which a vessel drives through wind or current when lying to or hove to during a gale; (*geol*) earth and rocks which have been conveyed by icebergs and glaciers and deposited over a country while submerged.—*vi* to accumulate in heaps by the force of wind; to be driven into heaps; to float or be driven along by a current of water or air; to be carried at random by the force of the wind or tide; in mining, to make a drift; to search for metals or ores.—*vt* to drive into heaps.—*adj* drifted by wind or currents (*drift sand, drift ice*).

drill[1] *vt* to pierce or perforate by turning a sharp-pointed instrument of a particular form; to bore and make a hole by turning an instrument; (*agricul*) to sow in rows, drills or channels; to teach and train soldiers or others to their duty by frequent exercises; hence, to teach by repeated exercise or repetition of acts.—*vi* to go through the exercises prescribed to recruits, etc.—

n a pointed instrument used for boring holes, particularly in metals and other hard substances; the act of training soldiers, etc, to their duty or the exercises by which they are trained; (*agricul*) a row of seeds deposited in the earth or the trench or channel in which the seed is deposited; also a machine for sowing seeds in rows.

drill[2], **drilling** *n* a kind of coarse linen or cotton cloth.

drink *vi* (*pret* **drank** *or* **drunk**, *pp* **drunk** *or* **drunken**, *ppr* **drinking**) to swallow liquor, for quenching thirst or other purpose; especially, to take intoxicating liquor; to be intemperate in the use of intoxicating liquors; to be an habitual drunkard.—*vt* to swallow (liquids); to imbibe; to suck in; to absorb; to take in through the senses (*to drink delight*); to inhale.—*n* liquor to be swallowed; a draught of liquor; intoxicating liquors.

drip *vi* (**dripped, dripping**) to fall in drops; to have any liquid falling from it in drops.—*vt* to let fall in drops.—*n* a falling or letting fall in drops; a dripping; that which falls in drops; dripping or melted fat from meat while roasting; the edge of a roof; the eaves; (*colloq*) a weak or insipid person.

dripping *n* the fat which falls from meat in roasting.

dripstone *n* (*archit*) a projecting moulding or cornice over doorways, windows, etc, to throw off the rain.

drive *vt* (*pret* **drove**, *pp* **driven**, *ppr* **driving**) to impel or urge forward by force; to force or move by physical means; to propel; to compel or urge by other means than absolute physical force or by means that compel the will; to constrain; to press or carry to a great length (an argument); to chase or hunt; to keep horses or other animals moving onward while directing their course; to guide or regulate the course of the carriage drawn by them; to guide or regulate a machine; to convey in a carriage or other vehicle; to carry on, prosecute, engage in (a trade, a bargain); in mining, to dig horizontally; to cut a horizontal gallery or tunnel.—*vi* to be forced along or impelled (*a ship drives before the wind*); to rush and press with violence (*a storm drives against the house*); to go in a carriage; to travel in a vehicle drawn by horses or other animals; to aim or tend; to aim a blow; to make a stroke.—*n* a journey or airing in a vehicle; a course on which carriages are driven; a road prepared for driving; a strong or sweeping blow or impulsion; energy; ambition.

drivel *vi* (**drivelled, drivelling**) to slaver; to let spittle drop or flow from the mouth, like a child, idiot or dotard; to be weak or foolish; to dote.—*n* slaver; saliva flowing

drill

dressing gown

from the mouth; silly unmeaning talk; senseless twaddle.

driver *n* one who or that which drives; the person who drives a carriage; one who conducts a team; (*naut*) a large fore-and-aft quadrilateral sail, called also the spanker, on the mizzenmast; (*mach*) the main wheel by which motion is communicated to a train of wheels; a driving wheel; a wooden-headed golf club for long-distance driving from the tee.

driving wheel *n* (*mech*) a wheel that communicates motion to another or to others; the large wheel in a locomotive engine which is fixed on the crank axle or mainshaft.

drizzle *vi* (**drizzled, drizzling**) to rain in small drops; to fall from the clouds in very fine particles.—*vt* to shed in small drops or particles.—*n* a small or fine rain; mizzle.

droll *adj* odd; merry; facetious; comical; ludicrous; odd; laughable; ridiculous.—*n* one whose occupation or practice is to raise mirth by odd tricks; a jester; a buffoon; something exhibited to raise mirth or sport.—*vi* to jest; to play the buffoon.

drollery *n* the quality of being droll; something done to raise mirth; sportive tricks; buffoonery; fun; comicalness; humour.

dromedary *n* a species of camel, called also the Arabian camel, with one hump or protuberance on the back.

drone *n* the male of the honeybee; an idler; a lazy person; a good-for-nothing; a humming or low sound, or the instrument of humming; one of the largest tubes of the bagpipe, which emit a continued deep tone; a monotonous speech or tone of voice.—*vi* (**droned, droning**) to give forth a low, heavy, dull sound; to hum; to snore; to make use of a dull, monotonous tone; to live in idleness.—*vt* to read or speak in a dull, monotonous, droning manner.

droop *vi* to sink or hang down; to bend downward, as from weakness or exhaustion; to languish from grief or other cause; to fail or sink; to decline; to be dispirited.—*vt* to let sink or hang down.

drop *n* a small portion of any fluid in a spherical form, falling or pendent, as if about to fall; a small portion of water falling in rain; what resembles or hangs in the form of a drop, as a hanging diamond ornament, a glass pendant of a chandelier, etc; a very small quantity of liquor; a small quantity of anything; that part of a gallows which sustains the criminal before he is executed and which is suddenly dropped; also the distance which he has to fall; the curtain which conceals the stage of a theatre from the audience.—*vt* (**dropped, dropping**) to pour or let fall in drops; to let fall; lower or let down (*to drop the an-*

chor); to let go, dismiss, lay aside, break off from; to quit, leave, omit; to utter (words) slightly, briefly or casually; to send in an offhand informal manner (*drop me a few lines*).—*vi* to fall in small portions, globules or drops, as a liquid; to let drops fall; to drip; to discharge itself in drops; to fall; to descend suddenly or abruptly; to sink lower; to cease; to die suddenly; to fall, as in battle; to come to an end; to be allowed to cease; to be neglected and come to nothing; to come unexpectedly (with *in* or *into*).

drop kick *n* in rugby football, a kick in which the ball is kicked as it touches the ground, after being dropped from the player's hands.

dropping *n* the act of one who drops; a falling in drops; that which drops; (*pl*) the dung of animals.

dropsical *adj* diseased with dropsy.

dropsy *n* (*med*) an unnatural collection of water in any cavity of the body or in the cellular tissue.

droshky *n* a kind of light four-wheeled carriage used in Russia.

dross *n* the refuse or impurities of metals; rust; waste matter; refuse; any worthless matter separated from the better part.

drought *n* dry weather; lack of rain; such a continuance of dry weather as affects the crops; aridness; thirst; lack of drink; scarcity; lack.

drove *n* a number of animals, as oxen, sheep or swine, driven in a body; a collection of animals moving forward; a crowd of people in motion; a flock.

drover *n* one who drives cattle or sheep to market or from one locality to another.

drown *vt* to deprive of life by immersion in water or other fluid; to overflow, overwhelm or inundate; to put an end to, as if by drowning or overwhelming; to overpower (*to drown care*; *to drown one's voice*).—*vi* to be suffocated in water or other fluid; to perish in water.

drowse *vi* (**drowsed, drowsing**) to sleep imperfectly or unsoundly; to slumber; to be heavy with sleepiness; to be heavy or dull.—*vt* to make heavy with sleep; to make dull or stupid.—*n* a slight sleep; a doze; slumber.

drowsy *adj* inclined to sleep; sleepy; heavy with sleepiness; lethargic; sluggish; stupid; disposing to sleep; lulling.

drub *vt* (**drubbed, drubbing**) to beat with a stick; to thrash; to cudgel.

drubbing *n* a cudgelling; a sound beating.

drudge *vi* (**drudged, drudging**) to work hard; to labour in mean offices; to labour with toil and fatigue.—*n* one who labours hard in servile employment; a slave.

drudgery *n* ignoble toil; hard work in servile occupations.

dromedary

droshky

272

drug *n* any substance, vegetable, animal or mineral, used in the composition or preparation of medicines; an addictive substance, such as certain narcotics; any commodity that lies on hand or is not saleable; an article of slow sale or in no demand in the market.—*vi* (**drugged, drugging**) to prescribe or administer drugs or medicines.—*vt* to mix with drugs; to introduce some narcotic into with the design of rendering the person who drinks the mixture insensible; to dose to excess with drugs or medicines; to administer narcotics to; to render insensible with a narcotic drug.

drugget *n* a cloth or thin stuff of wool or of wool and thread, used for covering carpets.

druggist *n* one who deals in drugs.

druid *n* a priest who superintended the affairs of religion and morality and performed the office of judge among the ancient Celtic nations in Gaul, Britain and Germany.

druidism *n* the doctrines, rites and ceremonies of the druids.

drum *n* an instrument of music commonly in the form of a hollow cylinder, covered at the ends with vellum, the ends being beaten with sticks to produce the sound; a mechanical contrivance resembling a drum in shape and used in connection with machinery of various kinds, etc; the tympanum or barrel of the ear; a quantity packed in the form of a drum; a round box containing figs; a kettledrum; a name formerly given to a fashionable and crowded evening party.—*vi* (**drummed, drumming**) to beat a drum; to beat with rapid movements of the fingers; to beat with a rapid succession of strokes; to throb; to resound dully.—*vt* to perform on a drum; to expel with beat of drum (*he was drummed out of the regiment*); to summon by beat of drum; to din.

drummer *n* one who drums; one whose office is to beat the drum; (*colloq*) commercial traveller.

drumstick *n* the stick with which a drum is beaten; what resembles a drumstick, as the leg of a cooked chicken, etc.

drunk *adj* intoxicated; inebriated; overcome, stupefied or frenzied by alcoholic liquor.

drunkard *n* one given to an excessive use of strong liquor; a person who habitually or frequently is drunk.

drunken *adj* intoxicated; drunk; given to drunkenness; proceeding from intoxication; done in a state of drunkenness (*a drunken quarrel*).

drupe *n* (*bot*) a stone fruit, such as the cherry or plum; a fruit in which the outer part is fleshy while the inner hardens like a nut, forming a stone with a kernel.

dry *adj* lacking moisture; free from water or wetness; free from juice, sap or aqueous matter; not moist; arid; not giving milk; thirsty; craving drink; barren; jejune; plain; unembellished; lacking interest; quietly sarcastic; caustic; discouraging; expressive of a degree of displeasure; cold and not friendly (*a dry reception*); without alcohol; not allowing the sale of alcohol.—*vt* (**dried, drying**) to make dry; to free from water or from moisture of any kind; to desiccate; to expose in order to evaporate moisture; to deprive of natural juice, sap or greenness.—**dry out** to cause to be free of moisture; to become free of moisture; to undergo treatment to cure oneself of alcoholism; to subject to treatment for alcoholism.—**dry up** to become completely dry; to become fine after a spell of rain; (*colloq*) to forget what one was going to say; (*sl*) to be quiet, stop talking.—*vi* to grow dry; to lose moisture; to become free from moisture or juice; to evaporate wholly; sometimes with up.

dryad *n* (*myth*) a nymph of the woods.

dry-clean *vt* to clean (clothes, etc) using chemical solvents rather than by washing.

dry-cleaner's *n* a shop where dry-cleaning is carried out.

dry-cleaning *n* the process of cleaning using chemical solvents.

dry dock *n* a dock so constructed that the water may be excluded at pleasure, allowing the bottom of a vessel to be inspected and repaired.

dry measure *n* the measure for dry goods, by quarters, bushels, pecks, etc.

dry rot *n* a common disease affecting timber caused by various species of fungi, the mycelium of which penetrates the timber, destroying it.

drysalter *n* formerly a dealer in salted or dry meats, pickles, sauces, etc, but now a dealer in dry stuffs, chemical products, etc.

dual *adj* expressing the number two; existing as two; consisting of two; twofold; a term applied to a special form of a noun or verb used in some languages when two persons or things are spoken of.—*n* (*gram*) that number which is used when two persons or things are spoken of.

dualism *n* the belief in two antagonistic supernatural beings, the one good, the other evil; the doctrine of those who maintain the existence of spirit and matter as distinct substances, in opposition to idealism, which maintains we have no knowledge or assurance of the existence of anything but our own ideas or sensations.

duality *n* the state of being two or of being divided into two.

dub *vt* (**dubbed, dubbing**) to strike with a sword and make a knight; to confer any

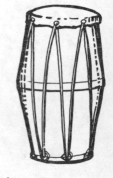

drum

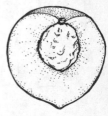

drupe

dignity or new character on; to entitle; to speak of as; to make smooth or of an equal surface, by some operation; to smooth with an adze; to rub with grease, as leather when being curried; to raise a nap on cloth by striking it with teasels.

dubiety *n* doubtfulness; a feeling of doubt.

dubious *adj* doubtful; wavering or fluctuating in opinion; uncertain; not ascertained or known exactly; not clear or plain; occasioning or involving doubt; of uncertain event or issue.

ducal *adj* pertaining to a duke

ducat *n* a gold or silver coin formerly common in several continental states.

duce *n* a leader, a chief.

Duce *n* the title of the leader of the Italian fascists, Benito Mussolini.

duchess *n* the consort or widow of a duke; a woman who has the sovereignty of a duchy

duchy *n* the territory or dominions of a duke; a dukedom.

duck[1] *vt* to dip or plunge in water and suddenly withdraw; to bow, stoop or nod in order to escape a blow or the like.—*vi* to plunge into water and immediately withdraw; to dip; to plunge the head in water or other liquid; to drop the head suddenly; to bow; to cringe.—*n* a name of various waterfowls akin to, but distinguished from, swans and geese by having broader bills, a more waddling gait from their legs being placed farther back, there being also a marked difference in the plumage of the sexes; the score of zero at cricket; (*colloq*) a term of endearment; an inclination of the head, resembling the motion of a duck in water.—**to make ducks and drakes** to throw a flat stone, piece of slate, etc, along the surface of water so as to cause it to strike and rebound repeatedly; hence, *to make ducks and drakes of one's money*, to squander it in a foolish manner.

duck[2] *n* a species of coarse cloth or canvas, used for sails, sacking of beds, etc.

duckbill, duck-billed platypus *n* an amphibious Australian mammal with dense fur, webbed feet and flat leathery jaws resembling a duck's bill, which lays eggs but nurses its young.

ducking stool *n* a stool or chair in which common scolds were formerly tied and plunged into water.

duckling *n* a young duck.

duck's egg *n* the score of zero at cricket, commonly termed 'a duck'.

duckweed *n* the popular name of several species of plants growing in ditches and shallow water.

duct *n* any tube or canal by which a fluid is conveyed, used especially of canals in the bodies of animals or in plants.

ductile *adj* easy to be led or influenced (per-

sons); tractable; yielding to persuasion or instruction; capable of being drawn out into wire or threads (used of metals).

ductility *n* the property of solid bodies, particularly metals, which renders them capable of being extended by drawing; a yielding disposition of mind; ready compliance.

ductless gland, endocrine gland *n* (*anat*) a gland of internal secretion, e.g. the adrenal, thyroid, parathyroid and pineal glands and the pituitary body or gland.

dud *n* a shell which fails to explode; an incompetent person or a defective thing.

dude *n* a dandy ; in USA, a city person who holidays at a ranch.

dudgeon *n* anger; resentment; malice; illwill; discord.

due *adj* falling to be paid or done to another; owed by one to another and by contract, justice or propriety required to be paid; liable or meriting to be given or devoted; owing to (*the attention due to one's studies*); proper; fit; appropriate; suitable; becoming; seasonable; required by the circumstances (*to behave with due gravity*); exact; correct; owing origin or existence; to be attributed or assigned as causing (*an effect due to the sun's attraction*); that ought to have arrived or to be present; bound or stipulated to arrive (*the mails are due*).—*adv* directly; exactly (*to sail due east*).—*n* what is owed or ought to be paid or done to another; that which justice, office, rank or station, social relations or established rules of decorum require to be given, paid or done; a toll, tribute, fee or other legal exaction.

duel *n* a premeditated combat between two persons with deadly weapons for the purpose of deciding some private difference or quarrel.—*vi* (**duelled, duelling**) to fight a duel.

duenna *n* an older female appointed to take charge of the younger female members of Spanish and Portuguese families; an older woman who is kept to guard a younger.

duet *n* a musical composition for two voices or two instruments.

duffel *n* a kind of coarse woollen cloth having a thick nap.

duffel coat *n* a kind of heavy woollen coat with a hood and fastened with toggles.

duffer *n* an incompetent or useless person; a pedlar; a hawker of cheap, flashy articles.

dug *n* the pap or nipple of a woman or (now generally) of an animal.

dugong *n* a herbivorous mammal of the Indian Seas, allied to the manatee or sea cow.

dugout *n* a rudely hollowed-out canoe from trunk of tree; an underground shelter from shells and bombs in time of war; an elderly officer who, during the First World War, emerged from retirement.

duffel coat

duke *n* in Great Britain, one of the highest order of nobility; a title of honour or nobility next below that of a prince; formerly, in other European countries, a sovereign prince, the ruler of a state.

dukedom *n* the seignory or possessions of a duke; the territory of a duke; the title or quality of a duke.

dulcet *adj* sweet to the taste; luscious; exquisite; sweet to the ear; melodious; harmonious; agreeable to the mind.

dulcify *vt* (**dulcified, dulcifying**) to sweeten

dulcimer *n* a musical instrument consisting in its modern form of a shallow quadrilateral box without a top, across which runs a series of wires, tuned by pegs at the sides and played on by being struck by two cork-headed hammers.

dulia *n* (*RC Church*) the worship offered to a saint.

dull *adj* stupid; doltish; slow of understanding; heavy; sluggish; without life or spirit; slow of motion; lacking sensibility or keenness in some of the senses (sight, hearing); not quick; sad; melancholy; depressing; dismal; gross; inanimate; insensible; not pleasing; not exhilarating; cheerless; not bright or clear; tarnished; dim; obscure; blunt; obtuse; having a thick edge; cloudy; overcast.—*vt* to make dull; to stupefy; to blunt; to render less acute; to make less eager; to make sad or melancholy; to make insensible or slow to perceive; to render dim; to sully; to tarnish or cloud.—*vi* to become dull.

dullard *n* a stupid person; a dolt; a blockhead; a dunce.

dulse *n* a kind of edible seaweed.

duma *n* the Russian parliament under the old regime.

dumb *adj* mute; silent; not speaking; lacking the power of speech; unable to utter articulate sounds; not accompanied with speech; effected by signs (*dumb show*).— **to strike dumb** to confound; to astonish; to render silent by astonishment.

dumbbell *n* a weight, usually consisting of two iron balls with a short piece for grasping between them, swung in the hands for developing the chest, the muscles of the arms, etc.

dumb show *n* a sort of dramatic representation performed in pantomime; gesture without words; pantomime.

dumb waiter *n* a small lift for carrying food, etc, between floors; a revolving stand for holding food; a side table or in a dining room, on which dessert, etc, is placed until required.

dumdum *n* a soft-nosed bullet which expands and lacerates on striking.

dumfound, dumbfound *vt* to strike dumb; to amaze; to confuse.

dummy *n* one who is dumb; the fourth or exposed hand when three persons play at whist; also, a game at whist when there are only three playing; one of the four hands at bridge, exposed on the table and played by the partner; a sham object doing service for a real one, as sham packages, etc, in shops; a figure of a person used to display clothes in a shop window, etc; a rubber teat given to a baby to suck in order to soothe him or her; (*colloq*) a stupid person.—*adj* silent; mute; sham; fictitious.

dump[1] *vt* to put or throw down with a bang; to deposit carelessly; to sell cheaply abroad through protection in the home market; (*colloq*) to dispose of, reject.

dump[2] *n* a large concentration of military stores, especially of ammunition, from which supplies are drawn as required; a place where things are discarded, a rubbish dump; a pile of discarded things; an unattractive, uninteresting place.

dump[3] *n* a dull, gloomy state of the mind; sadness; melancholy; low spirits; heaviness of heart (generally in the plural and now used only when a ludicrous effect is intended).

dumpling *n* a small ball of savoury or sweet dough.

dumpy *adj* short and thick.

dun[1] *adj* of a greyish-brown or dull-brown colour; of a smoky colour.

dun[2] *vt* (**dunned, dunning**) to clamour for payment of a debt from; to demand a debt in a pressing manner from; to call on for payment repeatedly; to urge importunately.—*n* one who duns.

dunce *n* an ignoramus; a pupil too stupid to learn; a dullard.

dunderhead *n* a dunce.

dune *n* a low hill of sand accumulated on the sea coast.

dung *n* the excrement of animals.—*vt* to manure with dung.—*vi* to void excrement.

dungarees *npl* overalls or trousers made from a coarse cotton fabric.

dung beetle *n* a beetle that rolls balls of dung in which to lay eggs.

dungeon *n* the innermost and strongest tower of a castle; the donjon; a close prison; a deep, dark place of confinement.

dunghill *n* a heap of dung; the place where dung is kept collected; a mean or vile abode or situation.

dunlin *n* a species of sandpiper.

dunnock *n* the common hedge-sparrow.

duodecimal *adj* proceeding in computation by twelves.—*n* a twelfth; a duodecimal number; a system of computing by twelves.

duodecimo *n* (*pl* **duodecimos**) a book in which a sheet is folded into twelve leaves; the size of a book consisting of sheets so folded, usually indicated thus, 12 *mo*.

dungarees

dunlin

duodenal *adj* connected with or relating to the duodenum.

duodenum *n* (*pl* **duodena, duodenums**) the first portion of the small intestines; the twelve-inch intestine.

duologue *n* a dialogue between two.

dupe *n* a person who is deceived or one easily led astray by credulity.—*vt* (**duped, duping**) to make a dupe of; to trick; to mislead by imposing on one's credulity.

duplex *adj* double; twofold.—*n* a flat on two floors.

duplicate *adj* double; twofold.—*n* another corresponding to the first; a second thing of the same kind; another example or specimen of the same kind of object; a copy; a transcript; a pawnbroker's ticket.—*vt* (**duplicated, duplicating**) to double; to make an exact copy of; to repeat; to fold.

duplication *n* the act of doubling; the multiplication of a number by 2; a folding; a doubling; a fold.

duplicity *n* the state of being doubled; doubleness; double-dealing; dissimulation; deceit.

durability *n* the quality of being durable.

durable *adj* having the quality of lasting or continuing long in being without perishing or wearing out; not perishable or changeable.

dura mater the outer membrane of the brain.

duramen *n* the central wood or heartwood in the trunk of an exogenous tree.

durance *n* imprisonment; restraint of the person; custody.

duration *n* continuance in time; length or extension of existence, indefinitely; power of continuance.

durbar *n* an audience room in the palace of an Indian prince; a state levee or audience held by the governor general of India or by an Indian prince; an official reception.

duress *n* imprisonment; restraint of liberty; (*law*) restraint or constraint by threats of personal injury.

durian *n* an Asian tree; also its oval fruit with a foul smell and pleasant taste.

during *prep* continuing; lasting; in the time of; throughout the course of.

durra *n* a species of grain widely cultivated in Africa, Asia and southern Europe.

dusk *adj* tending to darkness or moderately dark; tending to a dark or black colour; moderately black; swarthy.—*n* an approach to darkness; incipient or imperfect obscurity; a middle degree between light and darkness; twilight; darkness of colour.

dusky *adj* partially dark or obscure; not luminous; tending to blackness in colour; dark-coloured; not bright; gloomy.

dust *n* fine dry particles of earth or other matter, so attenuated that they may be raised and wafted by the wind; (*fig*) commotion and confusion accompanying a struggle; earth or earthy matter as symbolic of mortality; the body when it has mouldered in the grave; the grave; a low condition.—**to bite the dust** to die; to fall dead.—**to throw dust in one's eyes** to mislead; to blind as to the true character of something.—*vt* to free from dust; to brush, wipe or sweep away dust; to beat; to sprinkle with dust.

dustbin *n* a receptacle for ashes and other household rubbish.

dustcart *n* a cart for conveying dust and refuse from the streets.

duster *n* one who or that which clears from dust; a cloth used for removing dust.

dustman *n* (*pl* **dustmen**) a rubbish collector.

dustpan *n* a utensil to convey dust brushed from the floor, furniture, etc.

dusty *adj* filled, covered or sprinkled with dust; reduced to dust; like dust; of the colour of dust.

Dutch *npl* originally, the Germanic race; the German peoples generally, now only applied to the people of Holland; *n sing* the language spoken in Holland.—*adj* pertaining to Holland or its inhabitants.

Dutch auction *n* an auction at which the auctioneer starts with a high price and comes down till he or she meets with a bidder.

Dutch courage *n* false or artificial courage; boldness inspired by intoxicating spirits.

Dutchman *n* (*pl* **Dutchmen**) a native of Holland; a Hollander.

Dutch oven *n* a tin hanging screen for cooking before a kitchen range or ordinary fire grate.

Dutch treat *n* a meal or other social occasion at which everyone participating pays for himself or herself.

dutiable *adj* subject to the imposition of duty or customs.

dutiful *adj* performing the duties or obligations required by law, justice or propriety; obedient; submissive to superiors; expressive of respect or a sense of duty; respectful; reverential; required by duty.

duty *n* that which a person is bound by any natural, moral or legal obligation to do or perform; what has to be done as being due towards another; obligation to do something; obedience; submission; act of reverence or respect; any service, business or office; particularly military or similar service; a tax, toll or impost; any sum of money required by government to be paid on the importation, exportation or consumption of goods.

duty-free *adj* free from tax or duty.

duvet *n* a thick, soft quilt used instead of bedclothes; a continental quilt.

dustbin

dux *n* in Scotland, the head or chief pupil of a class or division in a school.

dwarf *n* a general name for an animal or plant which is much below the ordinary size of the species or kind; a very diminutive man or woman.—*vt* to hinder from growing to the natural size; to prevent the due development of; to stunt; to cause to look small or insignificant by comparison.—*vi* to become less; to become dwarfish or stunted.

dwarfish *adj* like a dwarf; below the common stature or size; very small; low; petty.

dwell *vi* (**dwelt** *or* **dwelled, dwelling**) to abide as a permanent resident; to live in a place; to have a habitation for some time or permanently; to be in any state or condition; to continue.—**to dwell on** *or* **upon** to keep the attention fixed on; to hang upon with fondness; to occupy a long time with; to be tedious over.

dweller *n* one who dwells; an inhabitant

dwelling *n* habitation; place of residence; abode; continuance; residence.

dwelling house *n* a house intended to be occupied as a residence, as opposed to a place of business, office or other building.

dwindle *vi* (**dwindled, dwindling**) to diminish gradually; to become small and insignificant; to shrink; to waste or consume away; to degenerate.—*vt* to cause to dwindle.

dye *vt* (**dyed, dyeing**) to give a new and permanent colour to; applied particularly to cloth or the materials of cloth, as wool, cotton, silk and linen; also to hair, skins, etc; to stain; to colour; to tinge.—*n* a colouring liquor; colour; stain; tinge.

dyer *n* one whose occupation is to dye cloth and the like.

dye-house *n* a building in which dyeing is carried on.

dying *adj* mortal; destined to death; given, uttered or manifested just before death (*dying words*); pertaining to or associated with death (*dying hours*); drawing to a close; fading away.—*n* the act of expiring; death.

dyke[1] *n, vt* (**dyked, dyking**) same as **dike**.

dyke[2] *n* (*sl*) a lesbian.

dynamic, dynamical *adj* pertaining to strength, power or force; relating to dynamics; relating to the effects of the forces or moving agencies in nature.

dynamics *n* the science which investigates the action of force, now usually divided into *statics* and *kinetics*, the former dealing with forces such as compel rest or prevent change of motion, the latter with forces that cause motion or change of motion, formerly the term was used as equivalent to the modern *kinetics*, *mechanics* being then equivalent to dynamics as now used.

dynamite *n* an explosive substance consisting of a siliceous earth and sometimes of charcoal, sawdust, etc, impregnated with nitroglycerine and having a disruptive force estimated at about eight times that of gunpowder.

dynamo *n* (*pl* **dynamos**) a machine for converting energy from a mechanical into an electric form by the use of electromagnets; an energetic person.

dynastic *adj* relating to a dynasty or line of rulers.

dynasty *n* a race or succession of rulers of the same line or family, who govern a particular region or country; the period during which they rule.

dyne *n* (*physics*) a unit of force, being that force which, acting on a gram for one second, generates a velocity of a centimetre per second.

dysentery *n* painful inflammation of the mucous membrane of the large intestine, accompanied generally with and diarrhoea.

dysfunction *n* a failure in the normal working of something, especially of any organ or part of the body.

dysfunctional *adj* having dysfunction; impaired.

dyslexia *n* a learning difficulty in which there is an impaired ability in reading or spelling.

dyslexic *adj* suffering from dyslexia.

dysmenorrhoea *n* painful menstruation

dyspepsia *n* indigestion or difficulty of digestion.

dyspeptic *adj* afflicted with dyspepsia; pertaining to or consisting in dyspepsia; morose, gloomy; bad-tempered.—*n* a person afflicted with dyspepsia.

dyspnoea *n* (*med*) difficulty of breathing.

dysuria *n* (*med*) difficulty in discharging the urine.

dziggetai *n* the wild ass of Central Asia.

dynamite

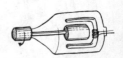

dynamo

E

E the second vowel and the fifth letter of the English alphabet, occurring more frequently than any other letter of the alphabet; (*mus*) the third note or degree of the natural or diatonic scale.

each *adj, pron* every one of any number separately considered or treated; every one of two or more considered individually (with *other* it is used reciprocally, as, *it is our duty to assist each other*, that is, *each to assist the other*).

eager[1] *adj* excited by ardent desire in pursuit of any object; keen to pursue, perform or obtain; ardently wishing or longing; vehement; fervid; earnest; impetuous; keen.

eager[2] *n* same as **eagre**.

eagerness *n* the state or character of being eager; keenness; ardour; zeal.

eagle *n* any of many large birds of prey, characterized by a hooked beak and curved, sharp and strong claws (talons) and by its great powers of flight and vision, often regarded as a symbol of royalty; a military standard having the figure of an eagle, such as that of ancient Rome and modern France.

eagle-eyed *adj* sharp-sighted as an eagle; having acute sight.

eagle owl *n* a horned owl almost as large as the golden eagle.

eagre, eager *n* a tidal wave moving up a river or estuary at spring tide, as in the Severn, Solway, etc; a bore.

ear[1] *n* the organ of hearing which in human beings and higher animals is composed of the external ear, a cartilaginous funnel for collecting the sound waves and directing them inwards; the middle ear, tympanum or drum and the internal ear or labyrinth; the sense of hearing; the power of distinguishing sounds; the power of perception of the differences of musical sounds; a favourable hearing; attention; heed; a part of any inanimate object resembling an ear; a projecting part from the side of anything, as a handle of a tub, pitcher, etc.—**to be all ears** to listen attentively.—**to be up to one's ears** to be very busy; to be deeply involved.

eagle

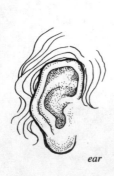

ear

ear[2] *n* a spike or head of corn or grain; that part of cereal plants which contains the flowers and seeds.

earache *n* pain in the ear.

eardrum *n* the tympanum.

earl *n* in Britain a nobleman, the third in rank, being next below a marquis and next above a viscount.

earldom *n* the jurisdiction or dignity of an earl.

earl marshal *n* an officer of state in Great Britain, who, as the head of the College of Arms, determines all rival claims to arms and grants armorial bearings through the medium of the King of Arms.

early *adj* in advance of something else as regards time; sooner than usual; produced or happening before the usual time (*early fruit, early maturity*); forward; being at the beginning; first (*in early manhood, early times*).—*adv* soon or sooner than usual or than others.

earmark *n* a mark on the ear for distinguishing sheep, pigs, cattle, etc; any mark for distinction or identification.—*vt* to distinguish by putting an earmark on; to set apart (money, etc) for a special purpose.

earn *vt* to merit or deserve by labour or by any performance; to gain by labour, service or performance; to deserve and receive as compensation.

earnest[1] *adj* sincere in the pursuit of an object; eager to obtain; having a longing desire; zealous; intent; serious; grave.—*n* seriousness; a reality; a real event, as opposed to jesting or feigned appearance.

earnest[2] *n* something given by way of token or pledge to bind a bargain and prove a sale; a part paid or delivered beforehand as a pledge and security for the whole or as a token of more to come; (*fig*) anything which gives assurance, promise or indication of what is to follow; token.

earnings *npl* that which is earned; what is gained or deserved by labour, services or performance; wages; reward; recompense.

earphone *n* a device held to or worn over the ear through which sound is transmitted.

earpiece *n* a telephone earphone; either of the two curved endpieces of the legs of the frame of glasses.

earring *n* an ornamental ring or other ornament worn hanging from the lobe of the ear.

earshot *n* the distance the ear can perceive sound; hearing distance.

earth *n* the particles which compose the mass of the globe but more particularly the particles which form the soil on the surface of the globe; the globe which we inhabit; the planet third in order from the sun; the world, as opposed to other scenes of existence; the inhabitants of the globe; dry land, as opposed to the sea; the ground; the hole in which a fox or other burrowing animal hides itself; (*chem*) one of the rare earths; (*elect*) the earth or ground considered as a conductor at zero potential.—*vt* (*elect*) to connect a conductor to the ground); to hide in the earth; to cover with earth or mould.—*vi* to retire underground; to burrow.

earthen *adj* made of earth; composed of clay or other like substance.

earthenware *n* every sort of household utensil made of clay hardened in the fire; crockery; pottery.

earthly *adj* pertaining to the earth or this world; worldly; temporal; gross; vile; carnal; mean; composed of earth; among the things of this earth; possible, conceivable (*earthly chance*).

earthquake *n* a shaking, trembling or concussion of the earth, sometimes a slight tremor, at other times a violent shaking or convulsion in which vast chasms open, swallowing up sometimes whole cities; at other times a rocking or heaving of the earth, due to internal igneous forces.

earth science *n* any of the sciences (e.g. geology) concerned with the nature and composition of the earth.

earthwork *n* a term applied to all operations where earth has to be removed or collected together, as in cuttings, embankments, etc; a fortification constructed of earth.

earthworm *n* the common worm found in the soil.

earthy *adj* of or pertaining to earth; composed of earth; of the nature of earth; like earth or having some of its properties; coarse; lacking refinement; crude.

ear trumpet *n* an instrument, usually in the shape of a cone-shaped tube, used to facilitate hearing.

earwig *n* one of a family of insects having a long narrow body and a pair of nippers at the extremity of the abdomen.

ease *n* freedom from labour or exertion or from physical pain, disturbance, excitement or annoyance; freedom from concern, anxiety, solicitude or anything that frets or ruffles the mind; tranquillity; repose; freedom from difficulty or great labour; facility; freedom from constraint, formality, stiffness, harshness, forced expressions or unnatural arrangement; unaffectedness.—*vt* (**eased, easing**) to free from pain, suffering, anxiety, care or any disquiet or annoyance; to relieve; to give rest to; to mitigate; to alleviate; to assuage; to allay; to abate or remove in part (*to ease pain, grief, a burden*, etc); to render less difficult; to facilitate; to release from pressure or restraint by moving gently; to shift a little.

easel *n* the wooden frame on which painters place pictures while at work on them.

easiness *n* the state or quality of being easy.

east *n* one of the four cardinal points, being the point in the heavens where the sun is seen to rise at the equinox or the corresponding point on the earth; that point of the horizon lying on the right hand when one's face is turned towards the north pole; the regions or countries which lie east of Europe; the oriental countries.—*adj* towards or in the direction of the rising sun; opposite from *west*.—*adv* in an easterly direction; eastwards.

Easter *n* a movable festival of the Christian Church observed in March or April in commemoration of Christ's resurrection.

easterly *adj* coming from the east; moving or directed eastward; situated or looking towards the east.—*adv* on the east; in the direction of east.

eastern *adj* being or dwelling in the east; oriental; situated towards the east; on the east part; going towards the east or in the direction of east.

Eastern Church *n* the Greek Church.

easting *n* the distance made good or gained by a ship to the eastward.

eastward *adj* facing, pointing or having its direction towards the east.

eastward, eastwards *adv* towards the east; in the direction of east from some point or place.

easy *adj* being at rest; having ease; free from pain, disturbance, suffering, annoyance, care, trouble, concern, anxiety, etc; quiet; tranquil; giving no pain or disturbance; requiring no great labour or exertion; not difficult; not steep, rough or uneven; gentle; not unwilling; ready; not constrained, stiff or formal; not rigid or strict; smooth; flowing; not straitened or restricted as regards money or means; affluent; comfortable.

easy chair *n* a comfortable chair.

easygoing *adj* placid, tolerant, relaxed.

eat *vt* (*pret* **ate**, *pp* **eaten**, *ppr* **eating**) to masticate and swallow; to partake of as food; said especially of solids; to corrode;

earring

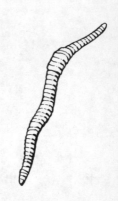

earthworm

to wear away; to gnaw into gradually.—*vi* to take food; to feed; to take a meal; to have a particular taste or character when eaten; to make way by corrosion; to gnaw; to enter by gradually wearing or separating the parts of a substance.

eatable *adj* capable of being eaten; esculent.—*n* anything that may be eaten; that which is used as food; an edible or comestible.

eating disorder *n* a medical condition in which people either undereat (anorexia) or overeat and deliberately vomit to get rid of the food consumed (bulimia) caused by an abnormal psychological fear of weight gain or an abnormal obsession with food.

eau de cologne a kind of perfume diluted with alcohol.

eaves *npl* that part of the roof of a building which projects beyond the wall and casts off the water that falls on the roof.

eavesdrop *vi* (**eavesdropped, eavesdropping**) to listen secretly to a private conversation; deliberately to overhear a private conversation.

eavesdropper *n* one who listens to a private conversation.

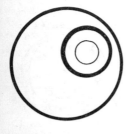

eccentric

ebb *n* the reflux of the tide; the return of tide water towards the sea, opposed to flood or flow; a flowing backward or away; decline; decay (*the ebb of prosperity* or *of life*).—*vi* to flow back; to return, as the water of a tide towards the ocean, opposed to *flow*; to recede; to decrease; to decay; to decline.

ebb tide *n* the reflux of tide water; the retiring tide.

ebony *n* a black-coloured wood of great hardness capable of taking on a fine polish.—*adj* made of ebony; black as ebony; black.

ebullience *n* the state of being ebullient; enthusiasm; exuberance.

ebullient *adj* boiling over; hence, over enthusiastic; over-demonstrative.

ebullition *n* the operation or phenomenon of boiling; an outward display of feeling, as of anger; a sudden outburst.

EC an abbreviation of **European Economic Community**.

écarté *n* a game of cards for two persons with thirty-two cards.

echelon

eccentric *adj* deviating or departing from the centre; not having the same centre; not concentric though situated one within the other; having the axis out of the centre; deviating from usual practice; given to act in a way peculiar to oneself and different from other people; unconventional; singular; odd; strange.—*n* an eccentric person.

eccentricity *n* the state of having a centre different from that of another related circle; the ratio, to the semi-major axis, of the distance of the centre of a planet's orbit

(an ellipse) from the centre of the sun (a focus); eccentric conduct; departure or deviation from what is regular or usual; singularity; strangeness; oddity; whimsicalness.

ecclesiastic, ecclesiastical *adj* pertaining or relating to the church; not civil or secular.

ecclesiastic *n* a person in orders or consecrated to the services of the church and the ministry of religion.

ecclesiasticism *n* strong adherence to the principles of the church or to ecclesiastical observances, privileges, etc.

ecclesiology *n* the science of antiquities as applied to churches and other ecclesiastical foundations.

echelon *n* (*milit*) the arrangement of troops, ships, guns, etc, in the form of steps or in parallel lines, each line being a little to the left or right of the preceding one; a level of authority in a hierarchy; a grade.

echidna *n* a nocturnal, burrowing, egg-laying, spine-covered mammal of Australia.

echinoderm *n* any of a class of marine invertebrate animals, characterized by having a tough integument in which lime is deposited as granules (as in the starfish and sea cucumber) or so as to form a kind of shell (like that of the sea urchin) and by the rayed arrangement of the parts of the adult; it includes the sea urchins, starfishes, sand stars, brittle stars, feather stars, sea cucumbers, etc.

echinoid *n* the generic name of the sea urchin.

echinus *n* (*pl* **echini**) (*archit*) an egg-shaped moulding or ornament, alternating with an anchor-shaped or dart-shaped body.

echo *n* (*pl* **echoes**) a sound reflected or reverberated from a distant surface; sound returned; repercussion of sound; repetition with assent; close imitation either in words or sentiments; a person who slavishly follows another in uttering sentiments.—*vi* (**echoed, echoing**) to give forth an echo; to resound; to reflect sound; to be sounded back; to produce a sound that reverberates; to give out a loud sound.—*vt* to reverberate or send back the sound of; to repeat with assent; to repeat; to adopt as one's own sentiments or opinion; to copy.

echo chamber *n* a room with walls that reflect sound, used for making acoustic measurements and for creating special sound effects.

echo sounder *n* an instrument for determining the depth beneath a ship using sound waves.

éclair *n* a small oblong shell of light pastry covered with chocolate and filled with cream.

eclampsia *n* a serious condition occurring in late pregnancy caused by toxins in the blood and giving rise to convulsions.

éclat *n* a burst, as of applause; acclamation; approbation; brilliancy of success; splendour of effect; lustre; renown; glory.

eclectic *adj* choosing from the doctrines, works, art, etc, of others; selecting from or using various styles, methods, etc; derived from a variety of sources.

eclipse *n* an interception of the light of the sun, moon or other luminous body by the intervention of some other body either between it and the eye or between the luminous body and that illuminated by it; an eclipse of the moon, for instance, being caused by the earth coming between it and the sun; (*fig*) a darkening or obscuring of splendour, brightness or glory.—*vt* (**eclipsed, eclipsing**) to cause the eclipse of; to cloud; to darken, obscure, throw into the shade; to surpass.—*vi* to suffer an eclipse.

ecliptic *n* a great circle of the celestial sphere supposed to be drawn through the middle of the zodiac, making an angle with the equinoctial of about 23° 27′; the path which the sun, owing to the annual revolution of the earth, appears to describe among the fixed stars; a great circle on the terrestrial globe, answering to and falling within the plane of the celestial ecliptic.

eclogue *n* a poetical composition with a pastoral theme.

ecological *adj* of or pertaining to ecology.

ecology *n* the study of the interaction of animals and plants with each other and with their environment.

economic *adj* of or relating to an economy; of or relating to economics; profitable; economical; inexpensive.

economical *adj* using the minimum amount required; not wasteful; thrifty; economic.

economics *n sing* the social science that studies the production, consumption and distribution of goods and services and the useful application of the wealth of material resources of a country; (*pl*) financial aspects.

economist *n* one who studies or is an expert in economics.

economize *vi* (**economized, economizing**) to manage financial concerns with thrift; to make prudent use of money or of the means of having or acquiring goods or property.—*vt* to use with prudence; to expend with frugality; to limit or reduce expenditure.

economy *n* a frugal and judicious use of money; that management which expends money to advantage and incurs no waste; saving; a judicious application of time, labour and the instruments of labour; the disposition or arrangement of any work or the system of rules and regulations which control it; the regulation and disposition of the financial affairs of a state or nation or of any business or department of government; the management of the financial affairs and resources of a country, organization, etc.

ecosphere *n* the parts of the universe where living organisms can exist.

ecosystem *n* a system comprising a community of living organisms and its surroundings.

ecstasy *n* a kind of trance; excessive joy; rapture; a degree of delight that fills the whole mind; extreme delight.

Ecstasy *n* the hallucinogenic drug methylenedioxymethamphetamine.

ecstatic *adj* pertaining to or resulting from ecstasy; entrancing; rapturous; transporting; experiencing delight beyond measure.

ECT an abbreviation of **electroconvulsive therapy**.

ectopic *adj* in an abnormal position; developing abnormally outside the uterus.

ectoplasm *n* (*biol*) the exterior portion of a cell; matter forming a cell wall; a bodily emanation supposedly issuing from a medium in a trance.

écu *n* an old French gold or silver coin.

ECU *n* a notional currency unit used in the European Community as a standard for the currencies of member countries, intended as the future common currency of EC countries, replacing that of individual countries.

ecumenical, ecumenic *adj* general; universal; specifically, an epithet applied to an ecclesiastical council regarded as representing the whole Christian Church or the whole Catholic Church.

eczema *n* an eruptive disease of the skin, characterized by minute vesicles which burst and discharge a thin acrid fluid.

Edda *n* the name of two Scandinavian books of mythology, dating from the eleventh to the thirteenth century.

eddy *n* a current of water or air moving circularly; a whirlpool.—*vi* (**eddied, eddying**) to move circularly or as an eddy.—*vt* to cause to move in an eddy; to collect as into an eddy.

edelweiss *n* an Alpine plant with white star-shaped flowers.

Eden *n* the garden in which Adam and Eve were placed by God; hence, a delightful region or residence.

edentate *n* one of an order of mammals, including the sloths, armadillos, pangolins and anteaters, some of the genera of which are toothless while the remainder have teeth of a rudimentary structure.

edge *n* the thin cutting side of an instrument; the abrupt border or margin of anything; the brink; the border or part adjacent to a line of division; the part nearest some limit; sharpness of mind or appetite; keenness; intensity of desire; sharpness;

eclipse

acrimony; the advantage.—*vt* (**edged, edging**) to sharpen; to furnish with an edge, fringe or border; to exasperate; to embitter; to incite; to provoke; to instigate; to move sideways; to move gradually.—*vi* to move sideways or gradually; to advance or retire gradually.

edgeways, edgewise *adv* with the edge turned forward or towards a particular point; in the direction of the edge; sideways; with the side foremost.

edible *adj* fit to be eaten as food; eatable; esculent.—*n* anything that may be eaten for food; an article of food; a comestible.

edict *n* an order, as a rule or law requiring obedience; a proclamation of command or prohibition; a decree.

edification *n* the act of edifying; improvement and progress of the mind in knowledge, in morals or in faith and holiness.

edify *vt* (**edified, edifying**) to build or construct; to instruct and improve in knowledge generally and particularly in moral and religious knowledge or in faith and holiness.—*vi* to cause or tend to cause moral or intellectual improvement.

edifying *adj* having the effect of instructing and improving.

edifice *n* a building; a structure; a fabric; chiefly applied to houses and other large structures.

edit *vt* to superintend the publication of; to prepare, as a book or paper, by writing, correcting or selecting the matter; to conduct or manage as regards literary contents or matter; to publish; to prepare the final version (of a film).

edition *n* a literary work bearing a special stamp or form when first published or subsequently; the whole number of copies of a work published at once.

editor *n* one who edits; a person who superintends, revises, corrects and prepares a book, newspaper or magazine for publication; a person in overall charge of a newspaper or radio or television programme; a person who prepares the final version of a film.

editorial *adj* pertaining to, proceeding from or written by an editor.—*n* an article, as in a newspaper, written by the editor; a leading article.

editorship *n* the business of an editor; the care and superintendence of a publication.

educate *vt* (**educated, educating**) to inform and enlighten the understanding of; to cultivate and train the mental powers of; to instruct; to train; to rear.

education *n* the act of educating, teaching or training; the act or art of developing and cultivating the various physical, intellectual, aesthetic and moral faculties; instruction and discipline; tuition; nurture; learning; erudition.

eel

educational *adj* pertaining to education; derived from education.

educationalist, educationist *n* one who is skilled in or who advocates or promotes education.

educative *adj* tending or having the power to educate.

educator *n* one who or that which educates.

EEC an abbreviation of **European Economic Community**.

EEG an abbreviation of **electroencephalogram**.

eel *n* a fish characterized by a snake-like elongated body, absence of ventral fins and continuity of the dorsal and anal fins round the extremity of the tail.

e'en *adv* (*poet*) a contraction for **even** or **evening**.

e'er *adv* (*poet*) a contraction for **ever**.

eerie *adj* calculated to inspire fear; weird.

eeriness *n* the state or quality of being eerie.

efface *vt* (**effaced, effacing**) to destroy or obliterate; to blot out; to erase, strike or scratch out; to remove from the mind; to make (oneself) unnoticeable.

effect *n* that which is produced by an operating agent or cause; consequence; result; power to produce consequences or results; force, validity or importance; purport, import, tenor or general intent; reality and not mere appearance; fact (preceded by *in*); the impression produced on the mind, as by natural scenery, a picture, musical composition or other work of art, by the object as a whole, before its details are examined; (*pl*) goods; movables; personal estate.—*vt* to produce, as a cause or agent; to bring about or cause to be; to bring to pass; to achieve; to accomplish.

effective *adj* having the power to cause or produce effect; efficacious; operative; active; efficient; having the power of active operation; fit for duty.

effectual *adj* producing an effect or the effect desired or intended; having adequate power or force to produce the effect.

effeminacy *n* the state or character of being effeminate.

effeminate *adj* having the qualities of a woman instead of those of a man; weak and unmanly; womanish.

effendi *n* a title of respect frequently attached to the official title of certain officers in the Middle East, especially learned men and ecclesiastics.

efferent *adj* (*anat*) conveying or discharging outwards.

effervesce *vi* (**effervesced, effervescing**) to bubble and hiss or froth and sparkle, as fermenting liquors or any fluid when some part escapes in a gaseous form; to work, as new wine; (*fig*) to exhibit signs of excitement; to exhibit feelings which cannot be suppressed.

effervescence *n* bubbling, frothing or sparkling of a liquid; strong excitement or manifestation of feeling; flow of lively spirits; exuberance.

effervescent *adj* effervescing.

effete *adj* having the energies or vigour worn out or exhausted; weak; ineffectual; decadent.

efficacious *adj* effectual; producing effects; producing the effect intended; having power adequate to the purpose intended.

efficacy *n* power to produce effects; production of the effect intended; effectiveness; efficiency; virtue; energy.

efficiency *n* the state or character of being efficient; effectual agency; power of producing the effect intended; competence for one's duties; in any mechanical device, the ratio of the useful work obtained to the energy expended.

efficient *adj* achieving results without waste of time or effort; efficacious; effectual; competent; able.

effigy *n* the image, likeness or representation of a person or thing; a likeness in sculpture, painting or otherwise; an image (frequently applied to the figures on sepulchral monuments); a crude likeness to display contempt.

effloresce *vi* (**effloresced, efflorescing**) to burst into bloom, as a flower; to break out into florid or excessive ornamentation; (*chem*) to change over the surface or throughout to a whitish or crystalline powder, from gradual decomposition or exposure to the air; to become covered with a whitish crust or light crystallization from a slow chemical change.

efflorescence *n* the act or process of efflorescing.

effluence, efflux *n* the act or state of flowing out or issuing in a stream; outflow; that which flows out; emanation.

effluent *adj* flowing out; emanating; emitted.—*n* (*geog*) a stream that flows out of another stream or out of a lake; liquid or nuclear waste.

effluvium *n* (*pl* **effluvia**) exhalation; emanation; especially applied to noxious or disagreeable exhalations.

effort *n* an exertion of strength or power, physical or mental; strenuous exertion to accomplish an object; a straining to do something; endeavour.

effortless *adj* making no effort; achieved with ease.

effrontery *n* audacious impudence or boldness; shamelessness; brazenness.

effulgence *n* a flood of light; a shining forth of light or glory; great lustre or brightness; splendour.

effulgent *adj* shining; bright; splendid; diffusing a flood of light.

effuse *vt* (**effused, effusing**) to pour out, as a fluid; to spill; to shed.—*vi* to emanate; to come forth.

effusion *n* the act of pouring out; that which is poured out; cordiality of manner; overflowing or demonstrative kindness.

effusive *adj* pouring out; pouring forth largely; showing overflowing kindness or cordiality of manner.

eft *n* a newt.

egad *exclam* (*arch*) expressing exultation or surprise.

egalitarian *adj* upholding the principle of equal rights for all.—*n* an egalitarian person.

egg[1] *n* a roundish body covered with a shell or membrane formed in a special organ of many female animals besides birds and in which the development of the young animal takes place; an ovum; the egg of domestic fowls used as food.

egg[2] *vt* to incite or urge on; to stimulate; to instigate; to provoke.

egg cup *n* a cup used to hold an egg at table.

egghead *n* (*colloq*) an intellectual.

eggplant *n* the aubergine.

eggshell *n* the shell or outside covering of an egg; (*fig*) anything very brittle, easily broken or destroyed.

egg spoon *n* a small spoon for eating eggs with.

eglantine *n* the sweetbrier or wild rose.

ego *n* (*philos*) the conscious thinking subject; the self; self-image; morale; conceit.

egoism *n* (*philos*) the doctrine which refers the elements of all knowledge to the phenomena of personal existence; subjective idealism; a passionate love of self; egotism; selfishness.

egoist *n* an egotist; a selfish person; one holding the doctrine of egoism.

egoistic, egoistical *adj* pertaining to egoism; addicted to or manifesting egoism; egotistic.

egotism *n* the practice of too frequently using the word *I*; hence, a speaking or writing much of oneself; a passionate and exaggerated love of self, leading one to refer all things to oneself and to judge everything by its relation to one's interests or importance.

egotist *n* one who repeats the word *I* very often in conversation or writing; one who speaks much of himself or herself or magnifies personal achievements.

egotistic, egotistical *adj* addicted to egotism; manifesting egotism.

egregious *adj* extraordinary; remarkable; enormous; now mostly used in a bad or ironical sense (*an egregious fool, blunder, impudence*).

egress *n* the act of going or issuing out; the way out.

egret *n* a small white heron; a plume of heron's feathers or of feathers, diamonds, etc.

effigy

283

Egyptian *n* pertaining to Egypt.—*n* a native of Egypt.

Egyptologist *n* one who studies the antiquities of Egypt, especially the hieroglyphic inscriptions and documents.

Egyptology *n* the science of Egyptian antiquities; that branch of knowledge which deals with the ancient language, history, etc, of Egypt.

eh *interj* expressive of doubt, inquiry, slight surprise.

eider, eiderduck *n* a species of large duck, with down that is much valued for its warmth, lightness and elasticity.

eiderdown *n* the down of the eider used for stuffing quilts, etc; a thick quilt for a bed with a soft filling.

eight *adj* one more than seven and one less than nine.—*n* the number composed of seven and one; the symbol representing this number, 8, VIII.

eighteen *adj* eight and ten.—*n* the sum of ten and eight; the symbol representing this sum, 18, XVIII.

eighteenth *adj* next in order after the seventeenth.—*n* one of eighteen equal parts.

eighth *adj* next in order after the seventh.—*n* one of eight equal parts of anything; an octave.

eightieth *adj* next in order to the seventyninth.—*n* one of eighty equal parts of anything.

eighty *adj* eight times ten; four score.—*n* a number composed of eight times ten; the symbol representing this, 80, LXXX.

eisteddfod *n* (*pl* **eisteddfods, eisteddfodau**) a meeting of bards and minstrels in Wales; a periodical Welsh festival of music, drama, poetry, etc.

either *adj, pron* one or the other; one of two things; each of two; the one and the other; both.—*conj* a disjunctive conjunction always used as correlative to and preceding *or* (*either the one or the other*).

ejaculate *vt* (**ejaculated, ejaculating**) to throw out, as an exclamation; to utter suddenly and briefly.—*vi* to utter ejaculations; to discharge semen from the penis.

ejaculation *n* the uttering of a short, sudden exclamation; the exclamation uttered; the discharge of semen from the penis.

eject *vt* to throw out; to cast forth; to thrust out; to drive away; to expel; to dismiss from office; to turn out.

ejection *n* the act of ejecting; dismissal; dispossession; expulsion; rejection.

eke *vt* (**eked, eking**) (usually with *out*) to add to (*he eked out his income by odd jobs*); to use (a supply) frugally.

elaborate *vt* (**elaborated, elaborating**) to work out or complete with great care; to work out fully or perfectly; to describe in detail.—*adj* planned with care; worked out with exactness; highly detailed; intricate.

elaboration *n* the act of elaborating; careful or laborious detail.

élan *n* unhesitating dash resulting from an impulsive imagination; style.

eland *n* an African species of antelope.

elapse *vi* (**elapsed, elapsing**) to pass by (said of time).

elastic *adj* returning to the form or size after stretching; rebounding; flying back; (*fig*) possessing the power or quality of recovering; adaptable.—*n* a piece of string, etc, made elastic by having a thin thread of rubber woven in it.

elasticity *n* the quality of being elastic.

Elastoplast *n* the trademark for a type of dressing for wounds consisting of a piece of dressing on an adhesive tape backing.

elate *vt* (**elated, elating**) to raise; to exalt; to elevate with success; to cause to exult; to make proud.

elated *adj* raised or lifted up; having the spirits lifted up; flushed, as with success; exultant.

elation *n* elevation of mind; high spirits; exultation, joy.

elbow *n* the outer angle made by the bend of the arm; the joint which unites the upper arm with the forearm; part of a structure somewhat resembling an elbow or which supports the arm or elbow, as the raised arm of a chair or sofa.—*vt* to push or jostle with the elbow; to make or gain (a path through a crowd) by pushing with the elbows.—*vi* to jut into an elbow or angle; to project; to bend; to push one's way.

elbow grease *n* hard work; effort.

elbow room *n* enough room to move and function freely.

elder *adj* having lived a longer time; of greater age; born, produced or formed before something else, opposed to younger; prior in origin; senior; pertaining to earlier times; earlier.—*n* one who is older than another or others; an ancestor; a person advanced in life and who, on account of his age, experience and wisdom, is selected for office; a lay official in Presbyterian churches.

elderly *adj* somewhat old; advanced beyond middle age; bordering on old age.

eldest *adj* oldest; most advanced in age; that was born first.

elder, elder tree *n* a well-known British tree or shrub of rapid growth with white flowers and purple berries and containing an unusual quantity of pith.

elderberry *n* the fruit of the elder.

El Dorado *n* a country formerly reputed to exist in South America and possessing immense stores of gold; hence, any region rich in gold or treasure of any kind.

elecampane *n* a British perennial plant formerly regarded as expectorant.

elect *vt* to pick out or select; especially, to

eland

elbow

select for an office or employment; to choose from among others; to appoint to an office by vote or designation; to choose by voting, as a politician; to choose; to determine in favour of (often with an infinitive, as *he elected to go*).—*adj* chosen or elected; especially, chosen but not inaugurated, consecrated or invested with office (*bishop elect*); (*theol*) chosen, selected or designated to eternal life; predestined in the divine counsels.—*n sing or pl* one of several chosen or set apart; (*theol*) those especially favoured by God.

election *n* the act of electing; the act of selecting one or more from others; the act of choosing a person to fill an office or employment, as by vote, uplifted hands, viva voce or ballot; the act of choosing (e.g. a politician) by voting; power of choosing or selecting; choice; voluntary preference; liberty to choose or act; (*theol*) predetermination of God, by which persons are distinguished as objects of mercy, become subjects of grace, are sanctified and prepared for heaven.

electioneer *vi* to work or exert oneself to obtain the election of a candidate.

elective *adj* chosen by election; dependent on choice; bestowed or passing by election; pertaining to or consisting in choice or right of choosing; exerting the power of choice.

elector *n* one who elects or has the right of electing; a person who has the right of voting for any functionary; specifically, one who has the right of voting for a representative in parliament; a voter.

electoral *adj* pertaining to election or electors; consisting of electors.

electoral college *n* in USA a group of representatives who vote to elect the President and Vice President.

Electra complex *n* an excessive attachment (in Freud's nomenclature) of a female child to her father.

electric, electrical *adj* containing electricity or capable of exhibiting it when excited by friction; pertaining to electricity; derived from or produced by electricity; worked or operated by electricity; conveying electricity; communicating a shock by electricity; (*fig*) full of fire, spirit or passion and capable of communicating it to others.

electrical engineering *n* that branch of engineering which deals with the uses and application of electricity.

electric blanket *n* a blanket which contains an electric heating element for warming a bed.

electric eye *n* a photoelectric cell.

electric guitar *n* a guitar which is electronically amplified, as opposed to an acoustic guitar.

electrician *n* one versed in the science of electricity; one who designs, sets up, repairs or attends to electrical appliances and machinery.

electricity *n* a form of energy comprising certain charged particles, such as electrons and protons; an electric current; emotional tension or excitement.

electrification *n* the act of electrifying or state of being electrified.

electrify *vt* (**electrified, electrifying**) to charge with electricity, to affect by electricity; to give an electric shock to; (*fig*) to give a sudden shock (as of surprise) to; to surprise with some sudden and brilliant effect; to thrill.—*vi* to become electric.

electrocardiogram *n* the tracing made by an electrocardiograph, a representation of the heartbeat made by recording the flow of electric currents in the heart muscle, used as a test for diagnosing heart disease.

electrocardiograph *n* a device for recording the electrical variations which occur during contractions of the muscle of the heart.

electroconvulsive therapy *n* the application of electric shocks to the brain, sometimes used in the treatment of clinical depression.

electrocute *vt* to execute by the agency of an electric current or shock.

electrocution *n* execution by an electric current.

electrode *n* one of the terminals or poles of the voltaic circuit.

electrodynamics *n* the science which treats of mechanical actions exerted on one another by electric currents.

electroencephalogram *n* the tracing produced by an electroencephalograph.

electroencephalograph *n* a device for recording small electrical impulses produced by the brain.

electrolysis *n* the passage of an electric current through an electrolyte to effect chemical change; the destruction of living tissue, especially hair roots, by electric current.

electrolyte *n* a solution that conducts electricity.

electromagnet *n* a bar of soft iron rendered temporarily magnetic by a current of electricity having been caused to pass through a wire coiled round it.

electromagnetic *adj* having to do with the relations between electricity and magnetism.

electromagnetic wave *n* a wave of alternating electric and magnetic force in the ether; the means, according to modern physical theory, whereby light and electrical influences are transmitted through space.

electromagnetism *n* that branch of electrical science which deals with the relation-

electric guitar

ships between electricity and magnetism, as shown, for example, in the action of dynamos and electric motors.

electrometallurgy *n* the use of electricity in depositing metals, as gold, silver, copper, etc, from solutions of their salts.

electrometer *n* an instrument for measuring potential or differences of electric potential between two conductors.

electromotive *adj* causing or tending to cause an electric current.

electromotive force *n* a force which determines the flow of electricity along a conductor; proportional to difference of potential and analogous to difference of level causing a flow of water and measured in volts.

electron *n* the stable, negatively charged elementary particle that orbits atomic nuclei.

electronic *adj* of or relating to electrons; of or relating to electronics; of or worked by streams of electrons flowing through semiconductor devices, vacuum or gas.

electronic mail *n* the transmission of information from one computer terminal to another, usually by means of a modem and telephone line.

electronic publishing *n* the publication of information on magnetic disks, on-line databases, CD ROM, etc, for access by computer.

electronics *n* the science and technology of the conduction of electricity in a vacuum, a gas or a semiconductor and of devices and systems to control and utilize it; the technique of manufacturing such devices, e.g. the semiconductors in transistors.

electroplate *vt* (**electroplated, electroplating**) to plate or give a coating of silver or other metal by means of electric currents. —*n* articles coated with silver or other metal by the process of electroplating.

electroscope *n* an instrument for observing or detecting the existence of free electricity and, in general, for determining its kind.

electrostatics *n* the science which treats of the phenomena occasioned by electricity at rest and of the production and discharge of stationary charges of electricity.

electrotype *n* the act of producing copies of types, woodcuts, medals, etc, by means of the electric deposition of copper on a mould taken from the original; a copy thus produced.—*vt* (**electrotyped, electrotyping**) to stereotype or take copies of by electrotype.

electuary *n* a medicine composed of powders or other ingredients, incorporated with some conserve, honey or syrup.

eleemosynary *adj* given in charity or alms; appropriated to charity; founded by charity.

elephant

elegance *n* the quality of being elegant; beauty resulting from grace, dignity, good taste; refinement; an elegant characteristic or feature; stylishness.

elegant *adj* having beauty or a pleasing effect resulting from grace, refinement or polish; pleasing to good taste; graceful; refined; having the words or style polished and appropriate (*an elegant speech*); giving expression to thought with propriety and grace; pleasing to the eye by grace of form or delicacy of colour; free from coarseness, blemish or other defect; showing fine harmony or symmetry; stylish.

elegiac *adj* belonging to elegy; plaintive; expressing sorrow or lamentation; used in elegies.

elegy *n* a mournful or plaintive poem or funeral song; a poem or a song expressive of sorrow and lamentation; a dirge; in classical poetry, any poem written in elegiac verse.

element *n* one of the simplest constituent principles or parts, of which anything consists or on which its constitution is based; a fundamental or ultimate part or principle, by the combination or aggregation of which any thing is composed; an ingredient; (*chem*) any of the 105 known substances composed of atoms with the same number of protons in their nuclei; a wire producing heat, e.g. in an electric kettle; (*pl*) the first or simplest rules or principles of an art or science; rudiments; one of the four constituents of the material world according to an old and still popular classification—fire, air, earth, water; atmospheric conditions, especially wind and rain; the state or sphere natural to anything or suited to its existence (hence, *out of one's element, out of one's natural sphere* or *position*); a datum or value necessary to be taken into consideration in making a calculation or coming to a conclusion; (*pl*) the bread and wine used in the Eucharist.

elemental *adj* pertaining to or produced by elements or primary ingredients; pertaining to the four so-called elements.

elementary *adj* primary; simple; not compounded; uncombined; initial; rudimentary; containing, teaching or discussing first principles, rules or rudiments.

elementary particle *n* any of the subatomic particles, such as electrons, protons and neutrons, not made up of other particles.

elephant *n* either of two species of huge quadrupeds, one Indian, one African, remarkable for having the nose prolonged into a long proboscis or trunk with the nostrils at its extremity and for their large tusks.

elephantiasis *n* (*med*) a skin disease in which the limbs, from their enlargement and the changed condition of the skin, have a slight resemblance to those of the elephant.

elephantine *adj* pertaining to the elephant; resembling an elephant; huge; immense.

elephant seal *n* a huge seal of the southern hemishere with a prolonged proboscis.

elevate *vt* (**elevated, elevating**) to raise; to raise from a low or deep place to a higher; to raise to a higher state or rank; to improve, refine or dignify; to improve by training or education; to exalt.

elevated *adj* raised; exalted; dignified.

elevation *n* the act of elevating; the act of raising or conveying from a lower place or degree to a higher; the state of being raised or elevated; exaltation; that which is raised or elevated; an elevated place; a rising ground; height; degree of height; height above the surface of the earth; altitude; (*astron*) altitude; the angle which the axis of the bore of a firearm makes with the plane of the horizon; (*archit*) a geometrical representation of a building in vertical section, as opposed to ground plan.

elevator *n* a mechanical device for raising passengers or goods from a lower place to a higher; a hoist; a lift; a tall building for the storage of grain.

eleven *adj* ten and one added.—*n* the sum of ten and one; a symbol representing eleven units, 11, XI; in cricket, the number of players selected from the members of a club to play in a match.

eleven plus *n* a former school exam taken at the age of 11 or 12 to decide the type of secondary school a pupil would attend.

elevenses *n* a snack, coffee, etc. taken mid-morning around 11 o'clock.

eleventh *adj, n* next in order after the tenth; one of eleven equal parts into which anything is divided.

eleventh hour *n* the very last possible moment for doing something.

elf *n* (*pl* **elves**) a mischievous fairy or goblin; a mischievous child.

elfin *adj* relating or pertaining to elves; small and winning.

elfish *adj* of or pertaining to elves; resembling an elf.

elflock *n* a knot of hair tangled as if by elves.

elicit *vt* to bring or draw out by reasoning, discussion, examination, etc; to deduce or educe (as truth, facts, etc).

elide *vt* (*gram*) to cut off or suppress, as a syllable.

eligibility *n* the state or condition of being eligible.

eligible *adj* fit to be chosen for some purpose or duty; worthy of choice; desirable; legally qualified to be chosen; acceptable or desirable as a marriage partner.

eliminate *vt* (**eliminated, eliminating**) to discharge or throw off (as a secretion of the human body); to take out or separate as not being an element of value or necessary; to set aside as unimportant or not to be considered; to leave out of account; to exclude (by defeating) from a competition.

elimination *n* the act of eliminating.

elision *n* (*gram*) the act of eliding; the cutting off or suppression of a vowel or syllable.

elite *npl* those who are choice or select or superior; the best; the flower.

elixir *n* a liquor sought for by the alchemists for transmuting metals into gold or prolonging life; quintessence; a cordial; (*med*) a tincture composed of various substances held in solution by alcohol in some form.

Elizabethan *adj* pertaining to Queen Elizabeth I of England or her period, especially its architecture and literature; pertaining to Queen Elizabeth II of Great Britain and her reign.—*n* a person alive in the reign of Elizabeth I.

elk *n* the largest existing species of the deer family, found in Europe and Asia but chiefly in North America, where it is called the *moose*.

ell *n* an old measure of different lengths in different countries, used chiefly for measuring cloth.

elk

ellipse *n* (*geom*) an oval figure produced when any cone is cut by a plane which passes through it, not parallel to nor cutting the base; a closed curve in which the distances of any point from two points called the foci have always the same sum.

ellipsis *n* (*gram*) the omission of one or more words which the hearer or reader may supply.

ellipsoid *n* (*geom*) a solid figure, all plane sections of which are ellipses or circles.

elliptic, elliptical *adj* pertaining to an ellipse; having the form of an ellipse; pertaining to ellipsis; having a word or words left out; (of writing or speech) so condensed as to be ambiguous or difficult to understand.

elm *n* a valuable European timber tree, species of which are also found in America.

Elmo's fire *n* a popular name for a meteoric appearance seen playing about the masts of a ship.

elocution *n* art or skill in delivering a discourse; mode of utterance or delivery of an address, accompanied by gestures.

ellipse

elocutionist *n* one who is versed in elocution; a teacher of elocution.

Elohim *n* one of the Hebrew names for God.

elongate *vt* (**elongated, elongating**) to lengthen; to extend.

elongation *n* the act of elongating or lengthening; the state of being stretched out or lengthened.

elope *vi* (**eloped, eloping**) to run away; to

run away with a lover secretly to be married.

elopement *n* the act of eloping; the running away of a couple to be married secretly.

eloquence *n* the art of expressing thoughts with conviction or persuasion; oratory; that which is expressed with eloquence.

eloquent *adj* having the power of expressing strong emotions vividly and appropriately; characterized by eloquence.

else *adj, adv* other; besides; in addition (as in *who else?, nothing* or *nobody else, nowhere else*).—*conj* otherwise; in the other case; if the fact were different (*he was ill, else he would have come*).

elsewhere *adv* in another place; somewhere else.

elucidate *vt* (**elucidated, elucidating**) to make clear or manifest; to explain; to remove obscurity from and render intelligible; to illustrate.

elucidation *n* the act of elucidating; explanation; exposition; illustration.

elude *vt* (**eluded, eluding**) to evade; to avoid by artifice, stratagem, wiles, deceit or dexterity; to remain unseen, undiscovered or unexplained by (*to elude scrutiny*).

embankment

elusive *adj* using arts to escape; baffling; difficult to find or contact.

elusory *adj* tending to elude; tending to deceive; evasive; fallacious.

Elysian *adj* pertaining to Elysium; exceedingly delightful.

Elysium *n* (*myth*) a place assigned to happy souls after death.

elytron *n* (*pl* **elytrons, elytra**) the wing sheath or horny membrane which forms the front wings in beetles, serving to cover and protect the hind wing.

em *n* (*print*) the unit of measurement, being a type whose breadth is equal to its depth.

emaciate *vi* (**emaciated, emaciating**) to lose flesh gradually; to become lean from loss of appetite or other cause.—*vt* to cause to lose flesh gradually; to reduce to leanness.—*adj* thin; wasted.

emaciation *n* the act of making or becoming lean or thin in flesh; the state of being reduced to leanness.

emanate *vi* (**emanated, emanating**) to flow forth or issue from a source (said of what is intangible, as light, heat, odour, power, etc); to proceed from something as the source, fountain or origin; to take origin; to arise; to spring.

emanation *n* the act of emanating; that which emanates, issues, flows or proceeds from any source, substance or body; effluence; effluvium; any person, power or thing emanating or proceeding from God.

emancipate *vt* (**emancipated, emancipat- ·ing**) to set free from servitude or slavery; to restore from bondage to freedom; to free from bondage, restriction or restraint

of any kind; to liberate from subjection, controlling power or influence.

emancipation *n* the act of emancipating; deliverance from bondage or controlling influence; liberation.

emasculate *vt* (**emasculated, emasculating**) to deprive of the properties of a male; to castrate; to geld; to deprive of masculine vigour; to render effeminate; to expurgate by removing coarse passages from (a book).

embalm *vt* to preserve (a dead body) from decay by removing the intestines and filling their place with chemicals, drugs, etc; to preserve from loss or decay; to cherish tenderly the memory of.

embankment *n* a mound or bank raised to protect land from being overflowed by a river or the sea or to enable a road or railway to be carried over a valley.

embargo *n* (*pl* **embargoes**) a restraint or prohibition imposed by the public authorities of a country on ships to prevent their leaving its ports; a ban or restriction on trade; a ban or restriction imposed on anything.—*vt* (**embargoed, embargoing**) to put an embargo on; to subject to an embargo.

embark *vt* to put or cause to enter on board a ship or boat; to engage, invest or enter on; to make a start on something.—*vi* to go on board a ship; to begin a journey; to engage or take a share in any affair.

embarkation *n* the act of embarking; that which is embarked or put on board.

embarrass *vt* to derange, confuse or entangle (affairs, business, etc), so as to make a course of action difficult; to involve in pecuniary difficulties; to perplex, disconcert or abash.

embarrassed *adj* entangled; involved; confused; disconcerted.

embarrassing *adj* perplexing; causing confusion or discomfort.

embarrassment *n* the state of being embarrassed; entanglement; perplexity arising from inability to pay one's debts; confusion of mind; abashment.

embassy *n* the mission of an ambassador; the charge or employment of an ambassador or envoy; the persons entrusted with ambassadorial functions; a legation; the official residence of an ambassador.

embed *vt* (**embedded, embedding**) to lay in or as in a bed; to lay in surrounding matter.

embellish *vt* to make beautiful; to adorn; to beautify; to decorate; to deck.

embellishment *n* the act of embellishing or adorning or state of being embellished; adornment; ornament; decoration.

ember *n* a small live coal, glowing piece of wood, etc; (*pl*) the smouldering remains of a fire.

Ember days *npl* days returning at certain

seasons, being the Wednesday, Friday and Saturday after the first Sunday in Lent, after Whitsunday, after Holyrood Day (14th September) and after St Lucia's day (13th December), appointed in the Church of England for fasting and abstinence.

embezzle *vt* (**embezzled**, **embezzling**) to appropriate fraudulently to one's own use what is entrusted to one's care; to apply to one's private use by a breach of trust, as an employee who misappropriates an employer's or firm's money or valuables.

embezzlement *n* the act by which a person fraudulently appropriates the money or goods entrusted to his or her care.

embitter *vt* to make bitter or more bitter; to make unhappy or resentful.

emblazon *vt* to adorn with figures of heraldry or ensigns armorial; to depict or represent, as an armorial ensign on a shield; to set off with ornaments; to celebrate in laudatory terms; to sing the praises of.

emblem *n* a picture, figure or other work of art representing something; a symbolic figure; a type; a symbol; a device as a balance used to symbolize justice.

emblematic, emblematical *adj* pertaining to or comprising an emblem; serving as an emblem or symbolic figure; symbolic.

embodiment *n* act of embodying or expressing in concrete form; bodily or material representation; the act of collecting or forming into a body or united whole.

embody *vt* (**embodied**, **embodying**) to invest with a material form; to render obvious to the senses or mental perception (*to embody thought in words*); to form or collect into a body or united mass; to collect into a whole; to personify.—*vi* to unite into a body, mass or collection; to coalesce.

embolden *vt* to give boldness or courage to; to encourage.

embolism *n* the insertion of days, months or years in an account of time, to produce regularity; intercalation; (*surg*) the obstruction of a blood vessel by a blood clot, air bubble, etc.

embolus *n* (*pl* **emboli**) material obstructing a blood vessel, e.g. a blood clot or air bubble.

embonpoint *n* plumpness; rotundity of figure; stoutness.

emboss *vt* to form bosses on; to fashion relief or raised work on; to cover with protuberances; to represent in relief or raised work; to represent in worked figures.

embouchure *n* a mouth of a river; the mouth hole of a musical wind instrument; the shaping of the lips to the mouthpiece.

embrace *vt* (**embraced**, **embracing**) to take, clasp or enclose in the arms; to press to the bosom in token of affection; to en-

close, encompass or contain; to encircle; to seize eagerly; to accept with cordiality (doctrines, religion); to comprehend, include or take in; to comprise.—*vi* to join in an embrace.—*n* enclosure or clasp with the arms; pressure to the bosom with the arms; sexual intercourse; conjugal endearment.

embracery *n* (*law*) an attempt to influence a jury corruptly to one side, by promises, persuasions, entreaties, money, threats, etc.

embrasure *n* (*fort*) an opening in a wall or parapet through which cannon or missiles were fired; a window or door opening with splayed sides.

embrocation *n* the liquid or lotion with which an affected part of the body is rubbed.

embroider *vt* to adorn with figures of needlework, often raised above the surface; to exaggerate or elaborate on a story, etc.

embroidery *n* work in gold, silver, silk or other thread, sewn on cloth into various figures; variegated needlework; exaggeration or elaboration for effect.

embroil *vt* to mix up or entangle in a quarrel or disturbance; to intermix confusedly; to involve in contention or trouble.

embryo *n* (*pl* **embryos**) the first rudiments of an animal in the womb; the rudimentary plant contained in the seed, produced by the action of the pollen on the ovule; the beginning or first state of anything; rudimentary state.

embryology *n* the study of the development of embryos, whether of plants or animals.

embryonic *adj* of or pertaining to an embryo or the embryo stage; existing at an early stage; immature.

emend *vt* to remove faults or blemishes from; to amend; especially to amend by editing a text.

emendation *n* the act of emending; removal of errors from the text of a book or writing; a textual alteration or correction.

emerald *n* a precious stone whose colour varies from green to a pale, yellowish, bluish or grass green, akin to the beryl, found especially in South America.—*adj* of a bright green, like emerald.

emerge *vi* (**emerged**, **emerging**) to rise from a liquid; to issue or proceed from something; to reappear or come into view; to rise out from obscurity; to come to notice; to be revealed or become apparent.

emergency *n* sudden occasion; unexpected casualty; unforeseen occurrence; any event or combination of circumstances calling for immediate action; pressing necessity.

emergent *adj* coming into existence; coming into view.

emeritus *adj* retired or discharged from the

embrasure

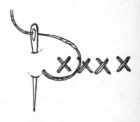

embroidery

performance of duty with honour (*a professor emeritus*).

emery *n* a hard granular mineral used for grinding and polishing metals, hard stones and glass; a hard abrasive powder.

emery paper *n* paper that has been first covered with a thin coating of glue and then dusted with emery powder, used for polishing.

emetic *adj* (*med*) inducing vomiting.—*n* a medicine that induces vomiting.

emigrate *vi* (**emigrated, emigrating**) to quit one country and settle in another.

emigrant *n* one who emigrates.

emigration *n* the act of emigrating; departure of inhabitants from one country or state to another for the purpose of residence.

émigré *n* an emigrant, usually one forced to emigrate.

eminence *n* a rising ground; a hill of moderate elevation; high rank; distinction; celebrity; conspicuousness.

Eminence *n* a title of honour given to cardinals and others.

eminent *adj* standing out above other things; prominent; lofty; exalted in rank; high in office or public estimation; distinguished.

emir *n* the title given to a Muslim ruler in parts of Asia and Africa.

emissary *n* a person sent on a mission; particularly, a secret agent or one who carries on private negotiations or business.

emit *vt* (**emitted, emitting**) to throw or give out (light, heat, steam, etc); to send forth; to vent; to cause or allow to issue or emanate.

emission *n* the act of emitting or of sending or throwing out; that which is emitted, issued, sent or thrown out.

emmenagogue *n* a medicine taken to induce menstrual discharge.

emmet *n* (*arch*) an ant.

emollient *adj* softening; making supple.—*n* a medicine which softens and relaxes living tissues that are inflamed or too tense; a cosmetic preparation used to soften the skin.

emolument *n* the profit arising from office or employment; compensation for services; remuneration; salary; income; profit; advantage or gain in general.

emotion *n* a state of excited feeling of any kind, as pleasure, pain, grief, joy, astonishment.

emotional *adj* pertaining to or characterized by emotion; attended by or producing emotion; tending to express excessive emotion.

emotive *adj* characterized by or arousing emotion.

empale *vt* same as **impale**.

empanel, impanel *vt* (**empanelled, empan-**elling) to form, complete or enrol the list of jurors in a court of justice.

emperor *n* the sovereign or supreme monarch of an empire.

emphasis *n* a particular stress given to something to underline its significance; force or vigour of expression or weight of thought; vividness.

emphasize *vt* (**emphasized, emphasizing**) to utter or pronounce with emphasis; to lay particular stress on; to render emphatic.

emphatic *adj* having emphasis; uttered with emphasis; forcible; expressive.

emphysema *n* a medical condition in which there is abnormal inflation of the air sacs in the lungs, causing breathlessness and increased susceptibility to infection.

empire *n* supreme power in governing; supreme dominion; sovereignty; imperial power; the territory or countries under the dominion of an emperor or other powerful sovereign; a large, far-flung business organization; supreme control; rule; sway.

empiric *n* one who relies only on experience and observation, as opposed to theory based on scientific conclusions; a medical quack; a charlatan.

empirical *adj* pertaining to experiments or experience; depending altogether on the observation of phenomena; depending on experience or observation alone.

empiricism *n* the quality or method of being empirical; the practice of an empiric; quackery.

emplacement *n* a position specially assigned to a gun or group of guns; a solid platform with accessories prepared for the support of a gun or guns.

employ *vt* to occupy the time, attention and labour of; to keep busy or at work; to make use of; to use as an instrument or means to, or as materials in forming anything; to engage in one's service; to use as an agent or substitute in transacting business; to apply or devote to an object; to occupy.—*n* a state of being employed; occupation; employment.

employee *n* one who works for an employer; a person working for a salary or wages.

employer *n* one who employs or uses; one who engages or keeps others in employment.

employment *n* the act of employing or using; the state of being employed; occupation; that which engages the head or hands; vocation; trade; profession; work.

emporium *n* a warehouse or large shop.

empower *vt* to give legal or moral power or authority to; to authorize, as by law, commission, letter of attorney, verbal licence, etc; to enable; to warrant; to license.

empress *n* the consort of an emperor; a woman who rules an empire.

emptiness *n* a state of being empty.

empty *adj* containing nothing; void of contents; lacking solid matter; not filled; void; devoid; lacking force or effect or sincerity; lacking substance or solidity; lacking reality; unsatisfactory; not able to fill the mind or the desires; lacking sense, knowledge or judgment; vain; ignorant.—*vt* (**emptied, emptying**) to remove the contents from; to discharge; to render void.—*vi* to pour out or discharge contents; to become empty.

empyrean *n* the highest and purest region of heaven.—*adj* pertaining to the highest heaven; celestial.

emu *n* a large Australian running bird closely related to the ostrich and the cassowary but having three toes.

emulate *vt* (**emulated, emulating**) to strive to equal or excel in qualities or actions; to vie with; to imitate; to copy.

emulation *n* the act of emulating; rivalry; desire of superiority, attended with effort to attain it; ambition to equal or excel.

emulator *n* one who emulates; a rival; a competitor.

emulous *adj* desirous or eager to imitate, equal or excel another; desirous of like excellence with another (*emulous of another's prowess*); rivalling; engaged in competition.

emulsion *n* a soft liquid remedy of a colour and consistency resembling milk; any milk-like mixture; a light-sensitive substance on photographic paper or film.

enable *vt* (**enabled, enabling**) to make able; to supply with power, physical, moral or legal; to furnish with sufficient power, ability or authority; to render fit or competent; to authorize.

enact *vt* to make into an act or established law; to give sanction to (a bill or legislative proposal); to decree; to perform or play a part in.

enactment *n* the passing of a bill or legislative proposal into a law; a law enacted; a decree; an act.

enamel *n* a coloured substance of the nature of glass, differing from it by a greater degree of fusibility or opacity, used as an ornamental coating for various articles; a smooth, glossy surface of various colours, resembling enamel, as paint; the smooth hard substance which covers the crown of a tooth.—*vt* (**enamelled, enamelling**) to lay enamel on; to paint in enamel; to form a glossy surface like enamel on; to variegate or adorn with different colours.—*vi* to practise the use of enamel or the art of enamelling.

enamour *vt* to inflame with love; to charm; to captivate (commonly in the past participle followed by *of*).

encamp *vi* to take up position in a camp; to make a camp.

encampment *n* the act of encamping; the place where a body of men is encamped; a camp.

encapsulate *vt* (**encapsulated, encapsulating**) to enclose in a capsule or similar small space; to describe succinctly; to summarize; to capture the essence of.

encase *vt* (**encased, encasing**) to enclose as in a case.

encaustic *adj* pertaining to the art of painting in colours that are fixed by burning.

enceinte[1] *n* (*fort*) the wall or rampart which surrounds a place; the area thus surrounded.

enceinte[2] *adj* pregnant; with child.

encephalic *adj* of or belonging to brain.

encephalitic *adj* relating to encephalitis; suffering from or affected by encephalitis.

encephalitis *n* inflammation of the brain.

encephalon *n* (*pl* **encephala**) the brain.

enchant *vt* to subdue by charms or spells; to hold as by a spell; to fascinate; to delight; to charm, captivate or enrapture.

enchanter *n* one who enchants; a sorcerer or magician; one who charms or delights.

enchanting *adj* charming; delighting; ravishing.

enchantment *n* the act of enchanting; the use of magic arts, spells or charms; incantation; that which enchants; an influence or power which fascinates or delights; overpowering influence of delight.

enchantress *n* a female enchanter.

encircle *vt* (**encircled, encircling**) to form a circle about; to enclose or surround; to encompass; to embrace.

enclave *n* a place or country which is entirely surrounded by the territories of another power; a district in a city, etc, inhabited by a minority group.

enclitic *adj* (*gram*) subjoined and as it were leaning (said of a word or particle which always follows another word and is so closely connected with the preceding word as to seem to be a part of it).

enclose *vt* to surround, shut in or confine on all sides; to shut up; to encompass; to separate an area of land by a fence; to put in a wrapper or envelope, usually with a letter.

enclosure *n* the act of enclosing; what is enclosed; a space enclosed or fenced; something enclosed in an envelope or parcel along with a letter.

encomium *n* a eulogy or commendation; a statement in praise of something or somebody; a panegyric.

encomiast *n* one who praises another; a panegyrist.

encompass *vt* to form a circle about; to encircle; to enclose or surround; to shut in; to go or sail round.

encore *adv* again; once more (used by an audience in calling for a repetition of a

emu

291

particular performance).—*vt* (**encored,
encoring**) to call for a repetition of; to call
on to repeat.—*n* applause demanding a repeat of or an extra performance; the performance given in response to this.

encounter *n* a meeting, particularly a sudden or accidental meeting of persons or
things; a meeting in contest; a fight; a conflict; a skirmish; a battle; an intellectual or
moral conflict or contest; controversy; debate.—*vt* to meet face to face; to meet suddenly or unexpectedly; to meet in opposition or in a hostile manner; to engage with
in battle; to come upon or light upon; to
meet with; to meet and oppose; to resist.—
vi to meet face to face; to meet unexpectedly; to meet in hostile fashion; to come
together in combat; to conflict.

encourage *vt* (**encouraged, encouraging**)
to give hope and confidence to; to help
forward; to give support or approval.

encouragement *n* the act of encouraging;
that which encourages; support; incentive.

encrinite *n* a fossil crinoid.

encroach *vi* to trespass or intrude on the
rights and possessions of another; to take
possession of what belongs to another by
gradual advances (*to encroach on one's
privileges*); to make inroads (*the sea
sometimes encroaches on the land*); to assail gradually and stealthily.

encroachment *n* the act of encroaching; undue or unlawful trespass on the privileges,
jurisdiction, etc, of another; that which is
taken by encroaching.

encrust, incrust *vt* to cover with a crust or
with a hard coat; to form a crust on the surface of.

encrustation, incrustation *n* the act of encrusting; a crust or hard coating on a surface; a covering or inlaying.

encumber *vt* to impede the motion of with a
load, burden or anything inconvenient; to
clog; to load; to embarrass; to load, as an
estate, with debts.

encumbrance *n* anything that impedes action or renders it difficult and laborious; a
load, burden, impediment; liability resting
on an estate; a legal claim on an estate for
the discharge of which the estate is liable,
as a mortgage, etc.

encyclical *adj* (of letters) intended for many
or for a whole order of people; circular.—
n a letter on some important issue or occasion sent by the pope to all bishops.

encyclopedia, encyclopaedia *n* a work in
which all branches of knowledge are discussed separately and usually in alphabetical order.

encyclopedic, encyclopaedic *adj* pertaining to an encyclopedia; universal as regards knowledge and information; comprehensive.

end *n* the extreme point of a line or of anything that has more length than breadth;
the termination, conclusion or last part of
anything, as of a portion of time, of an action, of a state of things, of a quantity of
materials; death; consequence; issue; result; the ultimate point or thing at which
one aims or directs one's views; purpose
intended; scope; aim; drift.—**on end** resting on one end; upright; also, continuously; uninterruptedly.—**to make both
ends meet** to keep one's expenditure
within one's income.—*vt* to put an end to
or be the end of; to finish; to close, conclude, terminate; to destroy; to put to
death.—*vi* to come to an end; to terminate;
to close; to conclude; to cease.

endanger *vt* to put in hazard; to bring into
danger or peril; to expose to loss or injury.

endangered species *n* a species of plant or
animal that is in danger of becoming extinct, e.g. from being hunted by people or
from the loss of its natural environment.

endear *vt* to make dear; to make more beloved; to bind by ties of affection and love.

endearing *adj* having a tendency to make
dear or beloved; tender; affectionate.

endearment *n* the act of endearing; the state
of being beloved; tender affection; a gesture of affection; words of affection.

endeavour *n* an exertion of physical
strength or the intellectual powers towards
the attainment of an object; an effort; an
essay; an attempt.—*vi* to labour or exert
oneself for the accomplishment of an object; to strive; to try; to attempt; to essay.—*vt* to try to effect; to strive after.

endemic *adj* peculiar to a people, locality or
region, especially applied to diseases to
which the inhabitants of a particular country are peculiarly subject; locally prevalent.—*n* a disease of an endemic nature.

ending *n* the act of putting or coming to an
end; conclusion; termination; the last part;
the final syllable or letter of a word.

endive *n* a plant with small crinkly leaves
used as a salad.

endless *adj* without end; having no end or
conclusion (applied to length and duration); perpetually recurring; interminable;
incessant; continuous; uninterrupted;
seeming as though without end; forming a
closed loop.

endocarditis *n* an inflammatory disease of
the internal parts of the heart, ending in the
deposit of fibrin on the valves.

endocardium *n* (**endocardia**) (*anat*) a colourless transparent membrane which lines
the interior of the heart.

endocarp *n* (*bot*) the inner layer of the
pericarp of fruits when its texture differs
from the outer layer, as the stone of a plum
or the flesh of an orange.

endocrine *adj* (*physiol*) of or relating to the
ductless glands.

endocrine gland *n* a ductless gland that secretes hormones directly into the bloodstream, e.g. the pituitary gland.

endocrinology *n* the study of endocrine glands and hormones.

endogamy *n* a custom among some peoples of marrying only within their own tribe; opposite of *exogamy*.

endogen *n* a monocotyledon.

endogenous *adj* growing from or on the inside.

endoplasm *n* (*biol*) internal matter of a cell; internal protoplasm.

endoscope *n* a medical instrument for examining the interior of the body.

endorse *vt* (**endorsed, endorsing**) to write something on the back of, as one's name on the back of a cheque; to sign by writing one's name on the back; to assign or transfer by endorsement; to sanction, ratify or approve; to record an offence on a driving licence.

endorsement *n* the act of endorsing; the signature of the holder of a cheque or bill of exchange written on the back; a record of an offence on a driving licence; ratification, sanction or approval.

endoscope *n* a medical instrument for examining the interior of the body.

endosmosis *n* the transmission of fluids or gases through porous septa or partitions, from the exterior to the interior.

endow *vt* to furnish with or bequeath a permanent fund or provision for support; to enrich or furnish with any gift, quality or faculty.

endowment *n* the act of endowing; property, fund or revenue permanently appropriated to any object; that which is given or bestowed on the person or mind; gift of nature; natural capacity.

endpaper *n* either of two folded sheets of paper pasted against the inside covers of a book and attached to the first and last pages.

endpiece *n* the piece at the end of something; an epilogue.

end product *n* the final product or result of something.

endue, indue *vt* (**endued, enduing**) to endow; to supply (as with virtue or other qualities).

endurance *n* a bearing or suffering; a continuing under pain or distress without sinking or yielding; sufferance; patience; fortitude.

endure *vi* (**endured, enduring**) to continue in the same state without perishing; to last; to remain; to abide; to suffer without resistance or without yielding; to hold out; to bear; to suffer.—*vt* to bear, sustain or support without breaking or yielding; to bear with patience; to undergo, suffer, experience.

enduring *adj* lasting long; permanent.

endways, endwise *adv* erectly; in an upright position; with the end forward.

enema *n* a liquid substance injected into the rectum; an appliance for giving injections.

enemy *n* one hostile to another; a foe; an adversary; an antagonist; a hostile force, army, etc.

energy *n* internal or inherent power; the power of operating, whether exerted or not; power exerted; vigorous operation; force; vigour; effectual operation; efficacy; strength or force; strength of expression; force of utterance; life; spirit; emphasis; (*physics*) power to do work (mechanical, electrical, thermal, chemical, nuclear, etc.).

energetic *adj* acting with or exhibiting energy; operating with force, vigour and effect; forcible; powerful; efficacious; working; active; operative; vigorous.

energize *vt* (**energized, energizing**) to act with energy or force; to act in producing an effect.—*vt* to give strength or force to; to give active vigour to.

enervate *vt* (**enervated, enervating**) to deprive of force or strength; to weaken; to render feeble; to debilitate.—*adj* without strength or force; weakened; debilitated.

enervation *n* the act of enervating; the state of being enervated.

enfant terrible *n* (*pl* **enfants terribles**) one who regularly behaves unconventionally and makes indiscreet remarks.

enfeeble *vt* (**enfeebled, enfeebling**) to make feeble; to deprive of strength; to weaken; to debilitate or enervate.

enfeoff *vt* (*law*) to give a fief or feu to; to invest with the fee of an estate; to give any corporeal hereditament to in fee.

enfeoffment *n* (*law*) the act of enfeoffing; the instrument or deed by which one is enfeoffed.

enfilade *vt* (**enfiladed, enfilading**) (*milit*) to rake or sweep with fire through the whole length of, as through a line of troops; to fire in the flank of a line.—*n* a firing in such a manner; the line of fire.

enfold, infold *vt* to fold in; to wrap up or enwrap; to clasp with the arms; to embrace.

enforce *vt* (**enforced, enforcing**) to make or gain by force or compulsion; to force; to compel, constrain or force; to put in execution; to cause to take effect (*to enforce the laws*).

enfranchise *vt* (**enfranchised, enfranchising**) to set free; to liberate from slavery; to free or release, as from custody or any restraining power; to confer the franchise on; to endow with the right of voting for a member of parliament.

engage *vt* (**engaged, engaging**) to bind or bring under an obligation, as by oath,

endoscope

pledge, contract or promise (generally with reflexive pronouns); to stake or pledge; to enlist; to bring into a party; to hire, as for service; to promise to marry; to win and attach (*to engage one's affections*); to attract and fix (attention); to occupy (*to engage a person in conversation*); to employ the attention or efforts of; to take concern in; to enter into contest with; to bring to conflict (*to engage an enemy*).—*vi* to promise or pledge one's word; to become bound; to embark in any business; to take a concern in; to undertake; to attack in conflict; to begin mutually a hostile encounter.

engaged *adj* pledged; pledged to be married; enlisted; attracted; occupied; employed.

engagement *n* the act of engaging; obligation by agreement or contract; a pledge to be married; the act of betrothing or state of being betrothed; occupation; employment of the attention; affair of business; an appointment; a combat between bodies of troops, etc; a fight; a conflict.

engaging *adj* winning; attractive; tending to draw the attention or the affections; pleasing.

engine

engender *vt* to produce; to cause to exist; to cause, excite, stir up.—*vi* to be caused or produced.

engine *n* a machine, tool, instrument or appliance by which any effect is produced; a person regarded as a tool or instrument; any mechanical instrument of complicated parts which produces an intended effect; a machine; especially, a machine to drive machinery, to propel vessels, trains, etc.—*vt* to furnish (a steam vessel) with an engine or engines.

engine driver *n* one who drives or manages an engine, especially a locomotive engine.

engineer *n* a person skilled in the principles and practice of engineering, either civil or military.—*vt* to direct or superintend the making of in the capacity of engineer; to perform the work of an engineer in respect of (*to engineer a canal*); to contrive; to succeed in bringing about.

engineering *n* the art of constructing and using engines or machines; the art of executing such works as are the objects of civil and military architecture, in which machinery is in general extensively employed.

English *adj* belonging to England or to its inhabitants.—*n* one of the Low German group of languages, spoken by the people of England, the USA, Canada, Australia, etc; as a collective noun, the people of England.

Englishman, Englishwoman *n* a native or naturalized inhabitant of England.

engraft, ingraft *vt* to graft; to attach by grafting; hence, to insert; to introduce; to set or fix deeply and firmly.

engrain *vt* same as **ingrain**.

engrave *vt* (*pp* engraved *or* engraven, engraving) to cut figures, letters or devices on, as on stone, metal, etc; to delineate, copy, picture or represent by incisions, as on stone, metal, wood, etc; to imprint; to impress deeply.

engraver *n* one who engraves; a cutter of letters, figures or devices on stone, metal or wood.

engraving *n* the art of cutting designs, writing, etc, on any hard substance; the art of forming designs on the surface of metal plates or blocks of wood for the purpose of taking off impressions or prints of these designs; that which is engraved; an engraved plate; an impression taken from an engraved plate; a print.

engross *vt* to seize, occupy or take up the whole of (one's attention, time, etc); to take or assume in undue quantity, proportion or degree; to write a fair correct copy of in large or distinct legible characters (*to engross a legal document*).—*vi* to be employed in engrossing or making fair copies of writings.

engulf, ingulf *vt* to swallow up in or as in a gulf or whirlpool; to overwhelm.

enhance *vt* (**enhanced, enhancing**) to heighten; to make greater; to increase (value, pleasure, beauty, etc); to heighten. —*vi* to increase or grow larger.

enigma *n* a saying in which something is concealed under obscure language; an obscure question; a riddle; something containing a hidden meaning; anything inexplicable to an observer, such as the means by which anything is effected, the motive for a course of conduct, the cause of any phenomenon, etc; a person whose conduct or disposition is inexplicable or puzzling.

enigmatic, enigmatical *adj* relating to or containing an enigma; obscure; ambiguous.

enjambment, enjambement *n* (*pros*) the prolongation of the words or sense beyond the second line of a couplet.

enjoin *vt* to prescribe or impose with some authority; to order or command; to put by way of injunction; to direct or urge (*to enjoin submission* or *obedience on a person*; *duties enjoined by law*); to instruct with authority.

enjoy *vt* to feel or perceive with pleasure; to take pleasure or satisfaction in the possession or experience of; to have, possess and use with satisfaction; to have, hold or occupy, as a good or profitable thing or as something desirable.

enjoyable *adj* capable of being enjoyed; giving enjoyment.

enjoyment *n* the condition of enjoying; the

possession of anything with satisfaction or pleasure; that which gives pleasure or satisfaction; cause of joy or gratification; delight.

enlarge *vt* (**enlarged, enlarging**) to make larger or greater in quantity or dimensions; to extend; to expand; to augment; to increase; to make more comprehensive (*to enlarge the mind*); to magnify to the eye; to reproduce a photograph in a larger size.—*vi* to grow large or larger; to extend; to dilate; to expand; to expatiate in speaking or writing; to speak or write at length or in full detail.

enlargement *n* an act, instance or state of enlarging; a photograph, etc, that has been enlarged.

enlighten *vt* to impart knowledge or practical wisdom to; to inform; to instruct; to enable to see or comprehend.

enlightenment *n* act of enlightening; state of being enlightened.

enlist *vt* to hire for public service, especially military service; to employ in advancing some interest; to engage the services of (*to enlist a person in the cause of truth*).—*vi* to engage in public service, especially military service, voluntarily.

enlistment *n* the act of enlisting; the raising of soldiers by enlisting.

enliven *vt* to give life, action or motion to; to make vigorous or active; to stimulate; to give spirit or vivacity to; to animate; to make sprightly or cheerful.

enmesh, immesh *vt* to entangle in the meshes of a net or anything similar.

enmity *n* the quality or state of being an enemy; hostile or unfriendly disposition; hostility; ill will.

ennoble *vt* (**ennobled, ennobling**) to make noble; to raise to nobility; to dignify; to exalt; to elevate in degree, qualities or excellence.

ennui *n* lack of interest in present scenes and surrounding objects; listlessness; weariness; tedium.

enormity *n* excessive degree; atrociousness; a very grave offence against order, right or decency; an atrocious crime; an atrocity.

enormous *adj* excessively large; huge.

enough *adj* satisfying need or desire; meeting reasonable expectations; answering the purpose; adequate to want or demand: (*enough* usually follows the noun with which it is connected).—*n* a sufficiency; a quantity of a thing which satisfies needs or wants; what is equal to the powers or abilities.—*exclam* denoting sufficiency.—*adv* sufficiently; in a quantity or degree that satisfies or is equal to the desires or wants; fully; quite; denoting a slight augmentation of the positive degree (*he was ready enough to embrace the offer*); in a toler-

able or passable degree (*the performance is good enough*).

enquire *vti* same as **inquire**.

enrage *vt* (**enraged, enraging**) to excite rage in; to exasperate; to provoke to fury or madness; to make furious.

enrapture *vt* (**enraptured, enrapturing**) to transport with rapture; to delight beyond measure.

enrich *vt* to make rich, wealthy or opulent; to supply with abundant property; to fertilize; to supply with an abundance of anything desirable; to fill or store; to supply with anything splendid or ornamental; to adorn.

enrichment *n* the act of enriching; something that enriches or adorns.

enrol, enroll *vt* (**enrolled, enrolling**) to write in a roll or register; to insert or enter the name of as a member; to record; to insert in records.

enrolment *n* the act of enrolling or registering; a register; the (total) number of people enrolled.

ens *n* (*pl* **entia**) entity; being; existence; an actually existing being.

ensconce *vt* (**ensconced, ensconcing**) to establish in a safe, secure or comfortable place (often with reflexive pronouns).

ensemble *n* all the parts of anything taken together so that each part is considered in relation to the whole; the general effect; an outfit; a group of musicians playing or singing together; the full number of musicians, dancers, etc.

enshrine *vt* (**enshrined, enshrining**) to enclose in or as in a shrine or chest; to preserve with care and affection; to cherish.

enshroud *vi* to cover with or as with a shroud; to envelop with anything which conceals from observation.

ensign *n* a flag or standard; the flag or banner distinguishing a company of soldiers, an army or vessel; the colours; formerly a commissioned officer of lowest rank in a British regiment of infantry, the equivalent rank now being that of second lieutenant.

ensilage *n* a mode of storing green fodder, vegetables, etc, by burying in pits or silos dug or built.

enslave *vt* (**enslaved, enslaving**) to make a slave of; to reduce to slavery or bondage; to subject to the dominant influence of; to master or overpower (*enslaved by his passions*).

ensnare, insnare *vt* (**ensnared, ensnaring**) to take in a snare; to entrap.

ensue *vi* (**ensued, ensuing**) to follow as a consequence; to follow in a train of events or course of time; to succeed; to come after.—*vt* to follow after.

en suite *adj, adv* in a single unit; in a series or succession.

ensure *vt* (**ensured, ensuring**) to make sure

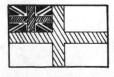

ensign

or secure; to make certain to turn out, arise or follow (*to ensure peace, to ensure a good crop*).

entablature *n* the superstructure which lies horizontally on the columns in classical architecture and consists of three principal divisions: the architrave, the frieze and the cornice.

entail *n* (*law*) an estate or fee entailed or limited in descent to a particular heir or heirs, male or female; rule of descent settled for an estate.—*vt* (*law*) to settle the descent of (lands and property) by gift so that neither the inheritor nor any subsequent possessor can bequeath it; to transmit in an unalterable course; to involve as a consequence or of necessity (*crimes entail punishment*).

entangle *vt* (**entangled, entangling**) to interweave in such a manner as not to be easily separated; to make confused or disordered; to involve in anything complicated and from which it is difficult to extricate oneself; to involve in difficulties or embarrassments; to puzzle; to perplex; to involve in contradictions; to hamper.

entanglement *n* the act of entangling or state of being entangled.

entelechy *n* the actuality of a thing as opposed to simple capability or potentiality.

entente *n* an understanding, a good feeling between two or more nations; relationship.

enter *vt* to come or go into in any manner whatever; to pierce; to penetrate; to begin or commence on, as a new period or stage in the progress of life, a new state of things, etc; to engage or become involved in; to join; to become a member of (an army, a profession, a college); to initiate into a business, service, society, method, etc; to set down in a book or other record; to enrol; to inscribe; to report (a ship) at the customhouse on arrival in port, by delivering a manifest; (*law*) to go in or on and take possession of (lands); to place in regular form before a court.—*vi* to come in; to go or pass in (sometimes with *in*); to embark or enlist in an affair; to become a member; (of an actor) to appear on stage.

enteric *adj* belonging to the intestines.

enteric fever *n* same as **typhoid fever.**

enteritis *n* (*med*) inflammation of the intestines.

enterprise *n* that which is undertaken or attempted to be performed; a project attempted; particularly, a bold, arduous or hazardous undertaking; a business project; an active and enterprising spirit; readiness to engage in undertakings of difficulty, risk or danger.

enterprising *adj* having a disposition for or tendency to engage in enterprises; ready to start and carry on untried schemes or new ventures.

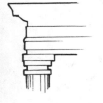

entablature

entertain *vt* to receive at home or elsewhere and treat with hospitality; to receive as a host; to engage the attention of agreeably; to amuse with anything that causes the time to pass pleasantly; to take into consideration; to hold or maintain in the mind with favour; to harbour; to cherish (*to entertain charitable sentiments*).—*vi* to give entertainment; to receive company.

entertaining *adj* affording entertainment; pleasing; amusing; diverting.

entertainment *n* the act of entertaining; the receiving and accommodating of guests; food, lodging or other things required by a guest; a hospitable repast; the pleasure which the mind receives from anything interesting and which holds or arrests the attention; that which entertains; that which serves for amusement, as a dramatic or other performance; reception; admission.

enthral *vt* (**enthralled, enthralling**) to captivate; to entrance; to capture one's interest totally.

enthralling *adj* captivating; spellbinding.

enthrone *vt* (**enthroned, enthroning**) to place on a throne; to invest with sovereign authority; to exalt to an elevated place or seat; to induct or install (a bishop) into the powers and privileges of a vacant see.

enthuse *vi* (**enthused, enthusing**) to be enthusiastic about; to show enthusiasm for (often with *over* or *about*).

enthusiasm *n* ardent zeal in pursuit of an object; passionate interest in or for; keenness; something that arouses keen or passionate interest.

enthusiast *n* one full of enthusiasm; one whose mind is completely possessed by any subject; one who is swayed to a great or undue extent by his or her feelings in any pursuit; a person of ardent zeal; one of elevated fancy; a highly imaginative person.

enthusiastic *adj* filled with or characterized by enthusiasm; prone to enthusiasm; ardent; devoted; very keen.

entice *vt* (**enticed, enticing**) to attract by exciting hope or desire; to allure, draw, invite; to lead astray; to induce to evil.

enticement *n* the act or means of enticing; allurement; attraction; seduction.

entire *adj* whole; unbroken; complete in its parts; perfect; not mutilated; mere; sheer.

entirely *adv* wholly; completely; fully; altogether.

entirety *n* the state of being entire or whole; wholeness; completeness; the whole.

entitle *vt* (**entitled, entitling**) to give a name or title to; to affix a name or appellation to; to designate; to denominate; to call; to name; to furnish with a title, right or claim (*a railway ticket entitles a person to travel*).

entity *n* being; character of existence; essence; a being or species of being; an existing thing.

entomb *vt* to deposit in a tomb; to bury; to inter.

entombment *n* the act of entombing; burial.

entomologist *n* one versed in entomology.

entomology *n* that branch of zoology which deals with the structure, habits and classification of insects.

entozoon, entozoan *n* (*pl* **entozoa**) an intestinal worm; an animal living in some part of another animal.

entr'acte *n* the interval between the acts of a drama; a short musical piece performed during such interval.

entrails *npl* the internal parts of animal bodies; the bowels; the viscera; the guts.

entrain *vt* to put on board a railway train, opposed to *detrain.*—*vi* to take places in a railway train.

entrammel *vt* (**entrammelled, entrammelling**) to trammel; to entangle.

entrance[1] *n* the act of entering into a place; the power or liberty of entering; admission; admission fee; the doorway or passage by which a place may be entered; initiation; beginning; the act of taking possession, as of property or an office.

entrance[2] *vti* (**entranced, entrancing**) to throw into a trance; to put into an ecstasy; to ravish with delight or wonder; to enrapture.

entrancement *n* the act of entrancing or the state of being entranced.

entrant *n* one who enters; one who begins a new course of life; one becoming a member for the first time of any association or body; a competitor.

entrap *vt* (**entrapped, entrapping**) to catch as in a trap; to ensnare; to catch by artifices; to entangle.

entreat *vt* to ask earnestly; to beseech; to supplicate; to beg.

entreaty *n* urgent prayer; earnest petition; pressing solicitation; supplication.

entrée *n* entry; freedom of access; a dish served before the main course.

entrench, intrench *vt* to dig or cut a trench or trenches round, as in fortification; to fortify with a ditch and parapet; to place (oneself) in a strong position.—*vi* to invade; to encroach (with *on* or *upon*).

entrenchment, intrenchment *n* the act of entrenching; (*fort*) a work consisting of a trench or ditch and a parapet (the latter formed of the earth dug out of the ditch), constructed for a defence against an enemy; an inroad or encroachment on the rights of others.

entrepôt *n* a warehouse for the depositing of goods; an emporium or centre for the distribution of merchandise.

entrepreneur *n* one who undertakes and controls an enterprise or business venture, especially one in which risk is involved.— **entrepreneurial** *adj.*

entresol *n* (*archit*) a low storey between two others of greater height.

entropy *n* a measure of the unavailable energy in a closed thermodynamic system; disorder, disorganization.

entrust, intrust *vt* to deliver in trust; to trust or confide to the care of; to commit with confidence (*to entrust a thing to a person* or *a person with a thing*).

entry *n* the act of entering; entrance; ingress; the act of recording in a book; any single item entered or set down; the passage into a house or other building or into a room; a beginning; a first attempt; the giving an account of a ship's cargo or exhibition of her papers and obtaining permission to land goods; anything which is entered or recorded in a register, diary, etc; (*law*) the act of taking possession of lands or tenements.

entwine *vt* (**entwined, entwining**) to twine; to twist round.—*vi* to become twisted or twined.

E number *n* a number preceded by the letter E used in lists of food ingredients to represent a food additive, E standing for European, E numbers being part of the EEC food regulations.

enumerate *vt* (**enumerated, enumerating**) to count number by number; to number; to count; to mention one by one; to recount.

enumeration *n* the act of enumerating; an account of a number of things one by one.

enunciate *vt* (**enunciated, enunciating**) to utter, as words or syllables; to pronounce clearly.—*vi* to utter words or syllables distinctly.

enunciation *n* the act of enunciating.

envelop *vt* to cover, as by wrapping or folding; to wrap up; to surround entirely; to cover on all sides; to form a covering about; to lie around and conceal; to outflank or turn the enemy's line, so that it is partially surrounded.

envelope *n* a flat paper container for a letter with a gummed flap for sealing; a wrapper; an enclosing cover; the outer covering of a balloon distended by means of enclosed gas.

envenom *vt* to taint or impregnate with venom; to poison; to imbue with bitterness or malice.

enviable *adj* exciting or capable of exciting envy.

envious *adj* feeling or harbouring envy; tinctured with envy.

environ *vt* to surround, encompass or encircle.

environment *n* act of surrounding; external conditions and surroundings, especially those that affect the lives of plants, animals and humans.

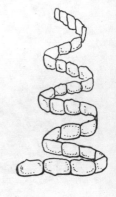

entozoon

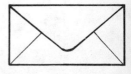

envelope

environs *npl* the parts or places which surround another place or lie in its neighbourhood; the outskirts; the suburbs.

envisage *vt* (**envisaged, envisaging**) to have a mental picture of; to imagine.

envoy *n* one despatched on an errand or mission; a messenger; a person deputed to negotiate a treaty or transact other business with a foreign ruler or government; a diplomatic agent sent on a special occasion; short poem or stanzas addressed by the author to the reader, sending him 'on his way' with the book, especially used of the concluding stanza of a ballade.

envy *n* pain, uneasiness, mortification or discontent excited by the sight of another's superiority or success; a feeling that makes a person begrudge another his good fortune; malice; object of envy.—*vt* (**envied, envying**) to feel envy towards or on account of; to repine at; to regard with malice and longing; to desire earnestly.—*vi* to be affected with envy; to have envious feelings.

enwrap *vt* (**enwrapped, enwrapping**) to envelop; to wrap up; to engross.

enzyme *n* an unorganized ferment, one of a group of complex nitrogenous substances similar to albumen which breaks up complex molecules and renders foodstuffs soluble and digestible.

Eocene *adj* (*geol*) of or pertaining to strata at the base of Tertiary formations, having a small proportion of living species among the fossils.—*n* the Eocene epoch.

Eolian *adj* same as **Aeolian**.

eolith *n* any of the oldest known type of prehistoric stone implements.

eon *n* same as **aeon**.

Eozoic *adj* of or pertaining to the oldest fossil-bearing rocks, postulated to contain the earliest traces of life.

epact *n* (*chron*) the excess of the solar month above the lunar month and of the solar year above the lunar year.

epaulet, epaulette *n* a shoulder piece; an ornamental badge worn on the shoulder by military and naval officers.

epergne *n* an ornamental stand with a large dish and branches for the centre of a table.

epexegesis *n* a full explanation or interpretation of something immediately preceding; exegesis.

ephemera *n* a small fly that lives for only a day or for a very short time; the mayfly.

ephemeral *adj* existing for a very short time; fleeting.

ephemeris *n* (*pl* **ephemerides**) an astronomical almanac showing the daily positions of the sun, moon and planets.

ephod *n* a kind of vestment worn by the Jewish high priest in ancient Israel.

epic *adj* composed in a lofty narrative style of poetry; pertaining to such a style; narrative; heroic; grand or impressive in scope; long in scope.—*n* a narrative poem of elevated character, describing often the exploits of heroes; a literary work, film, etc, dealing with heroic events or actions.

epicarp *n* (*bot*) the outer skin of fruits.

epicene *adj* having characteristics of both sexes; lacking characteristics of either sex; sexless; of indeterminate character, neither the one thing nor the other.

epicure *n* one devoted to sensual enjoyments; especially one who indulges in the luxuries of the table.

Epicurean *adj* pertaining to Epicurus or his teaching; luxurious; given to luxury.—*n* a follower of Epicurus; a man devoted to sensual pleasures or luxuries; an epicure.

epicycle *n* in old astronomy, a little circle, whose centre moves round in the circumference of a greater circle; a small circle, the centre of which is situated on the circumference of a larger circle.

epicycloid *n* (*geom*) a curve generated by the movement of a curve on the convex or concave side of another fixed curve.

epideictic *adj* serving to display or show off; having a rhetorical or declamatory character; demonstrative.

epidemic *adj* affecting a great number in a community (said of diseases); prevalent; general; generally prevailing.—*n* a disease which, arising from a widespread cause, attacks many people at the same period and in the same country.

epidermal *adj* of or pertaining to the **epidermis**.

epidermis *n* (*anat*) the cuticle or scarfskin of the body; a thin membrane covering the true skin of animals; (*bot*) the cellular integument or the exterior cellular coating of the leaf or stem of a plant.

epidural *n* a spinal anaesthetic used for the relief of pain in childbirth.

epigastric *adj* pertaining to the upper and anterior part of the abdomen.

epigastrium *n* (*pl* **epigastria**) the upper part of the abdomen.

epigenesis *n* (*biol*) the theory that organic bodies and parts are created by the division or segmentation of a fertilized egg cell and not merely developed from pre-existing bodies; (*geol*) a form of geological metamorphism of rock brought about by outside forces.

epiglottis *n* (*pl* **epiglottises, epiglottides**) (*anat*) a cartilaginous plate behind the tongue, which covers the glottis like a lid during swallowing.

epigram *n* a short poem usually satirical, the last line of which generally contains the sting or pointed allusion; an interesting thought represented happily in a few words, whether verse or prose; a pointed or antithetical saying.

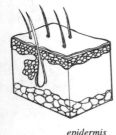

epidermis

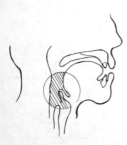

epiglottis

epigrammatic *adj* relating to, characterized by or producing epigrams; like an epigram; antithetical; pointed.

epigrammatist *n* one who composes epigrams.

epigraph *n* an inscription on a building, tomb, monument, statue, etc; a quotation or motto at the beginning of a work.

epilepsy *n* a disorder of the nervous system characterized by periodic bouts of unconsciousness with or without convulsions.

epileptic *adj* pertaining to or indicating epilepsy; affected with epilepsy.—*n* one who suffers from epilepsy.

epilogue *n* a speech or short poem addressed to the audience by one of the actors after the conclusion of a play; the concluding section of a book or other writing; a short religious broadcast at the end of the day.

Epiphany *n* an appearance or a becoming manifest; specifically, a Christian festival celebrated on the sixth day of January in commemoration of the manifestation of our Saviour's birth to the wise men of the East.

epiphyte, aerophyte *n* a plant growing on another plant but not deriving its nourishment from it; an air plant.

episcopacy *n* ecclesiastical government by bishops; bishops collectively; an episcopate.

episcopal *adj* belonging to or vested in bishops or prelates; characteristic of or pertaining to a bishop or bishops.

Episcopal Church *n* a church outside England in communion with the Anglican Church.

episcopalian *adj* pertaining to bishops or government by bishops; episcopal.—*n* one who favours episcopacy.

Episcopalian *adj* pertaining to an Episcopal Church.—*n* one who belongs to an Episcopal Church.

episcopate *n* a bishopric; the office and dignity of a bishop; bishops collectively.

episode *n* a separate incident, story or action in a book or programme; an incident or action more or less connected with a complete series of events; the section which follows on the entrance of the chorus into the orchestra; in Greek drama, the part of the play or dialogue between two choral odes, incident.

episodic, episodical *adj* pertaining to an episode; contained in an episode or digression; happening at irregular intervals.

epistaxis *n* bleeding from the nose.

epistemology *n* the theory of the method or ground of knowledge.

epistle *n* a writing, directed or sent, communicating information to a distant person; a letter (applied particularly in literary discourse; a letter in verse.

Epistle *n* a letter written by one of the Apostles to various churches and individuals.

epistolary *adj* pertaining to epistles or letters; suitable to letters; contained in or consisting of letters.

epitaph *n* an inscription on a tomb or monument in honour or memory of the dead.

epithalamium *n* (*pl* **epithalamia**) a wedding song or poem in praise of a bride and bridegroom; a poem in honour of a newly married pair.

epithelium *n* (*pl* **epitheliums, epithelia**) (*anat*) a thin and delicate kind of cuticle, like that which covers the nipple; the thin cellular layer which lines the internal cavities and canals of the body, as the mouth, nose, respiratory organs, blood vessels, etc.

epithet *n* an adjective expressing some real quality of the thing to which it is applied or some quality ascribed to it; any word or name implying a quality attached to a person or thing.

epitome *n* a brief summary or abstract of any book or writing; a compendium; an abridgement; a summary; anything which represents another or others in a condensed form; a typical example; personification.

epitomize *vt* (**epitomized, epitomizing**) to make an epitome of; to abstract in a summary the principal matters of; to be a typical example of.

epoch *n* a fixed point of time from which succeeding years are numbered; a point from which computation of years begins; any fixed time or period; a memorable term of years; era; age; date.

epode *n* the third or last part of an ode; a lyric poem in which a longer line is followed by a shorter one.

eponym *n* a person after whom something is named; a name derived in this way.

eponymous *adj* of or pertaining to a person after whom something is named (*in the film 'Hamlet', the eponymous hero was played by Laurence Olivier*).

Epsom salts *npl* sulphate of magnesia, used as a purgative and to reduce inflammation.

equable *adj* characterized by uniformity, invariability or evenness; uniform in action or intensity; not varying; steady; eventempered.

equal *adj* the same in size, value, qualities or degree; neither inferior nor superior, greater nor less, better nor worse; uniform; not variable; being in just relation or proportion; of the same interest or importance; not unduly favourable to any party; just; equitable; fair; having competent power, ability or means; adequate.—*n* one not inferior or superior to another; a person having the same or a similar age, rank, station, office, talents, strength etc; a compeer.—*vt* (**equalled, equalling**) to make equal; to make of the same quantity or quality; to (cause to) be commensurate with or unsurpassed by; to equalize; to be equal to; to be adequate to; to rise to the same state, rank, estimation or excellence with; to become equal to.

equality *n* the state of being equal; likeness in size, number, quantity, value, qualities or degree; the condition in which things or persons cannot be said to be inferior or superior, greater or less, one than another; parity; sameness in state or continued course.

equalize *vt* (**equalized, equalizing**) to make equal; to cause to be equal in amount or degree; to adjust so that there shall be equality between.

equally *adv* in an equal manner or degree; in the same degree with another; alike; in equal shares or proportions; impartially.

equanimity *n* evenness of temper or composure of mind.

equate *vt* (**equated, equating**) to make equal; to reduce to an average; to make such correction or allowance in as will reduce to a common standard of comparison or will bring to a true result; to treat or regard as comparable.

$$e = mc^2$$

equation

equation *n* the act of equating; (*alg*) a statement or expression asserting the equality of two quantities, equality being denoted by the sign = (equal to) between them; (*astron*) a quantity which from some imperfect method has to be taken into account in order to give a true result.

equator *n* the imaginary circle of the globe which divides it into two hemispheres (the northern and southern) and every point of which is 90° from the poles, which are also its poles, its axis being also the axis of the earth.

equatorial *adj* pertaining to the equator.—*n* an astronomical instrument contrived for the purpose of directing a telescope on any celestial object of which the right ascension and declination are known and of keeping the object in view for any length of time, notwithstanding the diurnal motion.

equator

equerry *n* formerly, an officer of nobles or princes who had the care and management of their horses: in Britain, an officer of the royal household who attends the sovereign.

equestrian *adj* pertaining to horses or horsemanship; consisting in or accompanied with performances on horseback; representing a person on horseback (*an equestrian statue*).—*n* a rider on horseback; one who earns his living by performing feats of agility and skill on horseback in a circus.

equestrianism *n* horsemanship

equidistance *n* equal distance.

equidistant *adj* being at an equal distance from some point or place.

equilateral *adj* having all the sides equal.

equilibrate *vt* (**equilibrated, equilibrating**) to balance equally; to keep in equipoise.

equilibrist *n* one who keeps his or her balance in unnatural positions and hazardous movements, as a tightrope walker.

equilibrium *n* (*pl* **equilibriums, equilibria**) equality of weight or force; a state of rest produced by two or more weights or forces counterbalancing each other, as the state of the two ends of a balance when both are charged with equal weights and they maintain an even or level position; a state of just poise; a position of due balance; psychological or emotional stability.

equine *adj* pertaining to or resembling a horse.

equinoctial *adj* pertaining to the equinoxes; occurring or manifested about that time (*equinoctial gales*); pertaining to the regions or climate under the equinoctial line or about the equator.—*n* the celestial equator, so called because, when the sun is on it, the days and nights are of equal length in all parts of the world.

equinox *n* the time when the sun reaches one of the two equinoctial points, or points in which the ecliptic and celestial equator intersect each other, the vernal equinox being about 21st March, the autumnal equinox about 23rd September, the day and the night being then of equal length all over the world.

equip *vt* (**equipped, equipping**) to dress; to prepare for some particular duty or service; to provide with everything necessary for an expedition, voyage, enterprise, etc; to provide with all the necessary tools or supplies.

equipage *n* formerly, equipment and supplies of an armed ship or military unit; a train of dependants accompanying or following a person; a carriage with the horse or horses, harness, etc; retinue.

equipment *n* the act of equipping or fitting out; anything that is used in equipping; things necessary for an expedition, voyage, enterprise, etc; the tools, supplies, etc, necessary to carry out a task, etc.

equipoise *n* equality of weight or force; due balance; equilibrium; a state in which the two ends or sides of a thing are balanced.

equipollent *adj* having equal power, force or meaning; equivalent.

equisetum *n* (*pl* **equisetums, equiseta**) any of a genus of many cryptogams, popularly known as horsetails.

equitable *adj* possessing or exhibiting equity; equal in regard to the rights of persons; giving each his due; just; fair; impartial.

equitation *n* the act or art of riding on horseback; horsemanship.

equity *n* the giving or disposition to give to each person his or her due; justice; impartiality; fairness; uprightness.

equities *npl* ordinary shares in a company.

equivalence *n* the condition of being equivalent; equality of value, signification or force.

equivalent *adj* equal in value, force, power, effect, excellence, import or meaning; interchangeable; virtually identical in function, effect, etc.—*n* something that is equivalent; that which is equal in value, weight, dignity, force, etc, with something else.

equivocal *adj* being of doubtful meaning; capable of being or liable to be understood in different senses; ambiguous; uncertain; dubious; unsatisfactory; deserving to be suspected; capable of being ascribed to different motives; doubtful; questionable.

equivocate *vi* (**equivocated, equivocating**) to use ambiguous expressions with a view to mislead; to prevaricate; to quibble.

equivocation *n* the act of equivocating; the use of words or expressions that are susceptible of a double meaning with a view to mislead; prevarication; quibbling.

era *n* a fixed point of time from which any number of years is begun to be counted; a succession of years proceeding from a fixed point or comprehended between two fixed points; an age or period.

eradicate *vt* (**eradicated, eradicating**) to pull up by the roots; to destroy at the roots; to root out; to destroy thoroughly; to extirpate.

erase *vt* (**erased, erasing**) to rub or scrape out, as letters or characters written, engraved or painted; to efface; to obliterate; to expunge; to remove or destroy, as by rubbing or blotting out; to remove (a recording) from magnetic tape; to remove (data) from a computer memory.

eraser *n* one who or that which erases; a piece of rubber, etc, for rubbing out writing or marks.

erasure *n* the act of erasing or scratching out; obliteration; the place where a word or letter has been erased.

erbium *n* a rare metal found, along with yttrium, terbium and other rare elements, in some minerals.

ere *adv, prep* before; sooner than.—*prep* before, in respect of time.

Erebus *n* according to the belief of the Greeks and Romans, a dark and gloomy region under the earth, through which the shades passed into Hades.

erect *adj* in a perpendicular posture; upright; directed upward; raised; uplifted; firm; bold; unshaken.—*vt* to raise and set in an upright or perpendicular position; to

set upright; to raise up; to construct; to set up; to build; to establish; to found; to form; to elevate; to exalt.

erectile *adj* able to raised upright; able to become enlarged and rigid.

erection *n* the act of erecting; a raising and setting perpendicular; a setting upright; the act of constructing or building; establishment; settlement; formation; anything erected; a building of any kind; a swelling of the penis due to sexual excitement.

eremite *n* one who lives in a wilderness or in retirement; a hermit.

erg *n* (*physics*) a unit of work.

ergo *adj* therefore.

ergonomics *n* the study of the physical relationship between people and their working environment.

erogenous *adj* arousing sexual feelings; sexually arousing; sensitive to sexual stimulation.

ergot *n* a diseased state of rye and other grasses, caused by the attack of a minute fungus on the seeds or grains; the diseased grain itself.

ergotism *n* a toxic condition in humans caused by ergot-infected food.

erica *n* a genus of flowering plants including the heaths.

ericaceous *adj* of or belonging to the natural order of heaths.

Erin *n* (*poet*) Ireland.

Erinyes *npl* (*sing* **Erinys**) in Greek myth, the Furies; goddesses of discord.

ermine *n* a quadruped of the weasel family found over temperate Europe but common only in the north; the fur of the ermine, white in winter; (*fig*) the office or dignity of a judge or other official, from his state robe being bordered with ermine.

erne *n* the white-tailed sea eagle, the bald eagle and other allied species.

erode *vt* (**eroded, eroding**) to eat into or away; to corrode; to wear away.

erosion *n* the act or operation of eating or wearing away; (*geol*) the wearing away of soil or rock by the influence of water and ice (especially in the form of glaciers).

erosive *adj* having the property of eating or wearing away.

erotic *adj* pertaining to or prompted by sexual love; treating of love.

err *vi* to wander from the right way; to go astray; to deviate from the path of duty; to fail morally; to transgress; to mistake in judgment or opinion; to blunder; to misapprehend.

errand *n* a special task entrusted to a messenger; something to be told or done by one sent for that purpose.

errant *adj* formerly, wandering, roving, rambling (applied particularly to medieval knights who wandered about to seek adventures); going astray; erring.

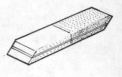

eraser

erratic *adj* wandering; devious; having no certain course; irregular or peculiar in movements or actions, eccentric; peculiar.

erratum *n* (*pl* errata) an error or mistake in writing or printing.

erroneous *adj* containing error or errors; wrong; mistaken; false; inaccurate.

error *n* a mistake; a misapprehension; a mistake made in writing, printing, calculation, etc; an inaccuracy; in statistics, the difference between an approximation of a value and the actual value, usually expressed as a percentage; an oversight; a transgression of law or duty; a fault; a sin.

Erse *n* the Gaelic language of Irish origin.

erstwhile *adv* till then or now; formerly.

erubescent *adj* red or reddish; blushing.

eruct *vt* to eject, as wind from the stomach; to belch.

eructation *n* the act of belching wind from the stomach; a belch; a violent bursting forth or ejection of matter from the earth.

erudite *adj* fully instructed; learned; deeply read; characterized by erudition.

erudition *n* knowledge gained by study or from books and instruction; scholarship.

erupt *vt* to throw out or emit by internal and especially by volcanic action; to cast out, as lava from a volcano; to burst forth violently; to break out in a rash.

eruption *n* the act of breaking or bursting forth from enclosure or confinement; a violent emission of lava, etc, from a volcano; a sudden or violent rushing forth of men or troops; the breaking out of a rash; a rash, pustules, vesicles, etc.

eruptive *adj* bursting forth; attended with eruption or rash or producing it; (*geol*) produced by eruption.

eryngo *n* (*pl* eryngoes) an umbelliferous plant of many species, found on the sandy shores of Britain and having thick and fleshy roots, called also *sea holly*.

erysipelas, *n* a disease characterized by diffused inflammation with fever and fiery eruptions chiefly on the face and head.

erythema *n* a superficial redness of some portion of the skin without blisters and not infectious.

escalade *n* an attack by troops on a fortified place in which ladders are used to pass a ditch or mount a rampart.—*vt* (escaladed, escalading) to mount and pass or enter by means of ladders; to scale.

escalate *vti* (escalated, escalating) to increase rapidly in scale or intensity.

escalation *n* the act of escalating; a rapid increase in scale or intensity.

escalator *n* a mechanism consisting of a series of steps which are carried up and down by means of a conveyor belt; a moving stairway.

escallonia *n* a South American genus of flowering plants.

escallop

escallop *n* a kind of bivalve, a scallop.

escalope *n* a thin cut of meat.

escapade *n* a mad prank; a wild or mischievous adventure.

escape *vt* (escaped, escaping) to flee from and avoid; to get out of the way of; to shun; to be unnoticed by; to obtain security from; to evade; to elude; (of liquid, gas) to seep or leak out.—*vt* to flee, shun and be secure from danger; to be free, or get free, from any injury; to hasten or get away; to free oneself from custody or restraint; to regain one's liberty.—*n* flight to shun danger or injury; the act of fleeing from danger or imprisonment; the condition of being passed by without receiving injury when danger threatens; a leaking of liquid or gas; a temporary break or respite from something, as work, reality, etc.

escapement *n* the general device in a timepiece by which the rotary motion of the wheels gives rise to or maintains the vibratory motion of the pendulum or balance wheel.

escapism *n* a withdrawing from reality or unpleasantness into entertainment or fantasy.

escapist *adj* providing entertainment as an alternative to reality (*escapist literature*).—*n* a person who seeks escapism.

escarpment *n* (*fort*) ground cut away nearly vertically about a position in order to make it inaccessible to an enemy; the precipitous side of any hill or rock; a steep ridge of land; a cliff.

eschar *n* the crust or scab caused on the skin by burns or caustic applications.

escharotic *adj* caustic; having the power of searing or destroying the flesh.—*n* an application which sears or destroys flesh.

eschatology *n* the doctrine of the last or final things, as death, judgment, etc

eschew *vt* to flee from; to shun; to seek to avoid; to avoid.

escort *n* a body of persons, soldiers, ships, planes to accompany, guard or protect something or something, or as a mark of respect, honour or attention; protection or safeguard on a journey or excursion; a person who accompanies another on a social occasion.—*vt* to attend and guard on a journey; to accompany as a guard or protector; to accompany (someone) on a social occasion.

escritoire *n* a desk or chest of drawers with compartments for writing materials; a writing desk.

esculent *adj* capable of or fit for being used by humans for food; edible.—*n* something that is eatable; an edible.

escutcheon *n* the shield on which a coat of arms is represented; a scutcheon; the shield of a family; a plate protecting the keyhole of a door or to which the handle is attached.

esker, eskar *n* in (*geol*) a term for a long linear ridge of sand and gravel, common in regions where ice sheets have prevailed and belonging to glacial phenomena.

Eskimo *n* (*pl* **Eskimos**) one of a race of people inhabiting the northern parts of North America and Greenland; the preferred term is now **Inuit**.

esoteric *adj* designed for and understood only by a select few; difficult; abstruse; obscure; private, opposed to *exoteric* or *public*.

ESP an abbreviation for **extrasensory perception**.

espadrille *n* a kind of sandal with a canvas or fabric upper and a rope sole.

espalier *n* a broad piece of trellis work on which the branches of fruit trees or bushes are trained.

esparto *n* a name of two or three species of grass used in the manufacture of paper, matting, baskets, etc.

especial *adj* of a distinct sort or kind; special; particular; marked; peculiar.

Esperanto *n* a language invented by Dr Zamenhof (about 1887) to enable the inhabitants of all countries to converse with each other.

espionage *n* the practice or employment of spies; the practice of watching the conduct of others as a spy to obtain information.

esplanade *n* a long open level space, especially a kind of terrace along the seaside, for walking.

espousal *n* the act of espousing or betrothing (frequently used in the plural); the adopting or taking up of a cause.

espouse *vt* (**espoused, espousing**) to give or take in marriage; to promise, engage or bestow in marriage by contract or pledge; to betroth; to marry; to wed; to become a partisan in; to embrace or to adopt (a cause, a quarrel).

espresso *n* (*pl* **espressos**) a strong coffee made by forcing steam under pressure through ground coffee beans.

espy *vt* (**espied, espying**) to see at a distance; to have the first sight of; to descry; to discover, as something concealed or as if unexpectedly or unintentionally; to inspect; to spy.

esquire *n* originally, a shield-bearer or armour-bearer; an attendant on a knight; hence, a title of dignity next in degree below a knight; a title now used as a complimentary adjunct to a name in addressing letters, etc.

essay *vt* to make an effort to perform; to try; to attempt; to endeavour to do; to make experiment of.—*n* a trial, attempt or endeavour; a test or experiment; a short literary composition intended to prove some particular point or illustrate a particular subject.

essence *n* that which constitutes the particular nature of a thing and which distinguishes it from all others; that which makes a thing what it is; existence; a being having existence; constituent substance; the predominant elements or principles of any plant or drug extracted, refined or rectified from grosser matter; an extract; perfume; odour; scent; the most important or fundamental doctrines, facts, ideas or conclusions (*the essence of a lecture, a statement*).

essential *adj* being of or pertaining to the essence; necessary to the constitution or existence of a thing; containing or constituting the essence of something; important in the highest degree; indispensable; volatile; diffusible (*essential oils*).—*n* what is essential; fundamental or constituent principle; distinguishing characteristic.

essential amino acid *n* any of eight amino acids that are required for normal health and growth and must be supplied by diet as they are manufactured in the body in insufficient quantities if at all.

essential oil *n* any of various plant oils used in perfumery.

establish *vt* to make steadfast, firm or stable; to settle on a firm or permanent basis; to set or fix unalterably; to institute and ratify; to enact or decree authoritatively and for permanence; to ordain; to strengthen; to prove; to confirm; to originate and secure the permanent existence of; to found permanently; to set up in connection with the state and endow (a church); to set up in business.

establishment *n* the act of establishing; the state of being established; settlement; fixed state; confirmation; a permanent civil or military force or organization, such as a fixed garrison or a local government; that form of doctrine and church government established by the legislature in any country; the place where a person is settled either for residence or for transacting business; a person's residence and everything connected with it; an institution, whether public or private.

Establishment *n* those people in institutions, such as the government, civil service and commerce, who use their power to preserve the social, economic and political status quo.

estate *n* condition or circumstances of any person or thing; state; rank; quality; possessions; property; a piece of landed property; a definite portion of land in the ownership of someone; an order or class of men constituting a state; one of the classes of the nation invested with political rights, the three estates of the realm, in Britain, being the lords spiritual, the lords temporal and the commons.

espadrille

estate agent *n* one who buys and sells houses on behalf of other people.

esteem *vt* to set a high value on; to regard with reverence, respect or friendship; to prize.—*n* high regard; favourable opinion.

estimable *adj* worthy of esteem or respect; deserving good opinion or regard.

estimate *vt* (estimated, estimating) to form a judgment or opinion regarding, especially applied to value, size, weight, degree, extent, quantity, etc; to rate by judgment, opinion or a rough calculation; to fix the worth of; to compute; to calculate; to reckon; to calculate approximately.—*n* an approximate judgment or opinion as to value, degree, extent, quantity, etc.

estimation *n* the act of estimating; calculation; computation; an estimate; esteem; regard; favourable opinion; honour.

estrange *vt* (estranged, estranging) to make to cease from being friendly; to alienate; to turn from kindness to indifference or malevolence.

estranged *adj* no longer friendly; no longer on friendly terms; (of marriage partners) separated.

estrangement *n* the act of estranging or state of being estranged; alienation.

estuary *n* the wide mouth of a river where the tide meets the currents or flows and ebbs; a firth.

etc, etc. an abbreviation of **et cetera**.

et cetera, etcetera *n* an expression used after the mention of certain individuals of a class, to indicate that others might also have been mentioned by name, commonly contracted **etc**.

etch *vti* to produce figures or designs on a plate of steel, copper, glass, etc, by means of lines drawn through a thin coating or ground covering the plate and bitten into by some strong acid, which can only affect the plate where the coating has been removed by the etching instrument.

etching *n* the art or operation of an etcher; a design or picture produced by an etcher.

eternal *adj* having no beginning or end of existence; everlasting; endless; continued without intermission; ceaseless; perpetual.—**the Eternal** an appellation of God.

eternal triangle *n* a situation which occurs when one person in a sexual relationship takes another lover whilst still retaining the first one, regarded as an ageless phenomenon.

eternity *n* the condition or quality of being eternal; duration or continuance without beginning or end; endless past time or endless future time; the state or condition which begins at death.

etesian *adj* recurring every year; blowing at stated times of the year (applied to the periodical winds in the Mediterranean).

estuary

ethane *n* a colourless gaseous hydrocarbon found in natural gas and used as a fuel.

ether *n* the upper regions of space; the supposed subtle atmosphere in space beyond the earth's atmosphere; an invisible medium of extreme tenuity and elasticity formerly believed to be diffused throughout all space; a very light, volatile and inflammable fluid obtained from alcohol, a solvent of fats and resins and used as a stimulant, antispasmodic and anaesthetic.

ethereal *adj* containing or filled with ether; belonging to the sky regions; heavenly; celestial; delicate; refined.

ethic *n* a moral principal or set of principles.—*adj* ethical.

ethical *adj* relating to morals; treating of morality; containing precepts of morality; moral; (*med*) legally available only on prescription (*an ethical drug*).

ethics *n* the science which deals with the nature and grounds of moral obligation; moral philosophy; moral principles.

Ethiopian *n* a native of Ethiopia.

ethnic, ethnical *adj* pertaining to race; ethnological; relating to or characteristic of any racial or cultural group; of or relating to a particular population, having a common language or common racial or cultural origins.

ethnography *n* that branch of science which has for its subject the description of the different races of men or the manners, customs, religion, etc, peculiar to different nations.

ethnology *n* that branch of science which investigates the mental and physical differences of mankind and the organic laws on which they depend.

ethology *n* the study of animal behaviour.

ethos *n* the distinguishing character, sentiment, moral nature or guiding believes of a person, group or institution.

ethyl *n* the radical of ordinary alcohol and ether.

ethylene *n* a gas to which is largely due the illuminating power of coal gas.

etiolate *vi* (etiolated, etiolating) to grow white from absence of the normal amount of green colouring matter in the leaves or stalks; to be whitened by excluding the light of the sun, as plants.—*vt* to blanch or whiten by excluding the light or by disease.

etiolation *n* the act of etiolating or state of being etiolated or pale.

etiology *n* same as **aetiology**.

etiquette *n* conventional forms of ceremony or decorum; social observances and conduct required by society, custom or authority.

etude *n* a musical composition for solo instrument designed to serve as a study and to display virtuosity.

étui *n* a pocket case for small articles, such as needles, pins, etc; a reticule.

etymologist *n* one who studies the origin of words.

etymology *n* the study of the origin and derivation of words; derivation.

etymon *n* (*pl* **etymons, etyma**) the root of a word.

eucalyptus *n* one of a genus of large mostly Australian trees of the myrtle order, cultivated for their resin, oil and wood; a medicinal oil obtained from its leaves.

Eucharist *n* the sacrament of the Lord's supper; the Communion; the consecrated elements especially the bread.

euchre *n* a game of cards, a modified form of écarté, played by two, three or four players with the thirty-two highest cards of the pack.

eudemonism *n* the system of philosophy which makes human happiness the highest object, declaring that the production of happiness is the foundation of virtue.

eugenics *n* the science of improving the human race by selective breeding.

eulogy *n* praise; encomium; panegyric; a speech or writing in commendation of a person on account of his valuable qualities or services.

eulogist *n* one who praises and commends another; one who pronounces a eulogy.

eulogistic *adj* containing or pertaining to eulogy or praise; laudatory.

eulogize *vt* (**eulogized, eulogizing**) to speak or write in commendation of another; to extol in speech or writing; to praise.

Eumenides *npl* (*lit*) the gracious goddesses, a Greek name of the Furies, because it was considered unlawful and dangerous to name them under their true designation Erinyes.

eunuch *n* a castrated human male, especially one formerly used as a harem attendant by some oriental rulers.

eupepsia *n* good digestion, the opposite of *dyspepsia*.

eupeptic *adj* having good digestion; easy of digestion.

euphemism *n* a figure of speech in which an inoffensive word or expression is substituted for one which is considered offensive; an expression used in this way.

euphonic, euphonious *adj* agreeable in sound.

euphonium *n* a brass bass instrument with three or four valves and a backward-facing tube, used in brass and military bands.

euphony *n* an agreeable sound; an easy, smooth enunciation of sounds; a pronunciation of letters, syllables and words which is pleasing to the ear.

euphorbia *n* any of a large genus of exogenous plants, some of which are found in Britain and are called spurges,

while the most remarkable are tropical shrubs or trees, often large, fleshy and leafless.

euphoria *n* a feeling of great happiness or elation.

euphoric *adj* of or pertaining to euphoria; very happy; elated; exhilarated.

euphrasy *n* (*arch*) a name for eyebright.

euphuism *n* excessive elegance and refinement of language; high-flown artificial diction.

euphuist *n* one addicted to euphuism.

Eurasian *adj* of Europe and Asia taken as one continent; of mixed European and Asian descent.—*n* one born in India of mixed Asian and European parentage.

eureka *n* an expression of triumph at a discovery or supposed discovery.

European *adj* pertaining to Europe; native to Europe.—*n* a native of Europe.

European Community, European Economic Community *n* an economic and political association of several European countries the aims of which are to eliminate all obstacles to the free movement of goods, services, capital and labour among the member countries and to set up common commercial, agricultural, etc, policies.

Eustachian tube *n* the tube which forms a communication between the internal ear and the back part of the mouth.

euthanasia *n* a putting to death by painless means; a means of putting to a painless death.

evacuate *vt* (**evacuated, evacuating**) to make empty; to make empty by removing oneself from (*an army evacuates a town* or *a country*); to void or discharge from the bowels.

evacuant *adj* producing evacuation; purgative.—*n* a medicine which promotes the natural secretions and excretions.

evacuation *n* the act of evacuating; that which is evacuated or discharged, especially from the bowels.

evade *vt* (**evaded, evading**) to avoid, escape from or elude in any way, as by dexterity, artifice, sophistry, address or ingenuity; to slip away from; to escape the grasp or comprehension of; to baffle or foil.—*vi* to escape; to slip away; to practise artifice or sophistry for the purpose of eluding.

evanescent *adj* vanishing; fleeting; passing; liable to disappear or come to an end.

Evangel *n* one of the four New Testament Gospels of Matthew, Mark, Luke or John.

evangelical, evangelic *adj* according to the four Gospels; adhering closely to the letter of the Gospels; fervent and devout.

evangelism *n* evangelical principles.

evangelist *n* a person engaged in preaching or missionary work.

Evangelist *n* one of the four writers of the Gospels.

The flag of the European Community

Eustachian tube

evaporate *vi* (**evaporated, evaporating**) to pass off in vapour; to escape and be dissipated, either in visible vapour or in particles too minute to be visible; (*fig*) to escape or pass off without effect; to be dissipated; to be wasted.—*vt* to convert into vapour; to cause to evaporate; to vaporize.

evaporated milk *n* tinned unsweetened milk thickened by means of evaporation.

evaporation *n* the act or process of evaporating; the conversion of a liquid by heat into vapour or steam, which becomes dissipated in the atmosphere in the manner of an elastic fluid; vaporization; the matter evaporated; vapour.

evasion *n* the act of evading, eluding, avoiding or escaping; shift; subterfuge; equivocation; prevarication.

evasive *adj* using evasion or artifice to avoid; equivocating; characterized by evasion.

eve *n* the close of the day; the evening; the day or the latter part of the day before a church festival; the period just preceding some event (*on the eve of a revolution*).

even[1] *adj* level; smooth; flat; devoid of irregularities; straight or direct; uniform; equal; not easily ruffled; on a level or on the same level; in the same or in an equally favourable position; on a level in advantage; having accounts balanced; square; adjusted; fair; equitable; capable of being divided by two without a remainder, opposed to *odd*.—*vt* to make even; to level; to smooth; to place in an equal state; to balance.—*adv* expressing a level or equality; just; exactly in consonance; according (*even as he wished*); expressing equality or sameness of time (*I knew it even then*); expressing emphatically the identity of a person (*even he did it*); expressing a strong assertion; not only this or so, but more or but also.

even[2] *n* (*arch*) evening.

evening *n* the close of the day and the beginning of darkness or night; the time from sunset till darkness; the latter part of the afternoon and the earlier part of the night; the decline or latter part of life, strength or glory.

evening primrose *n* a plant with yellow flowers that open in the evening.

evening primrose oil *n* an oil obtained from the evening primrose used medically and as a food supplement.

evening star *n* the planet Venus when visible in the evening.

evensong *n* a form of worship for the evening; vespers.

event *n* that which happens; any incident good or bad; an occurrence; a social or special occasion; the consequence of anything; one contest in a series of contests in a sports programme.

evergreen

eventful *adj* full of events or incidents; characterized by great changes either in public or private affairs; momentous.

eventide *n* (*poet*) evening.

eventing *n* taking part in riding events; the sport of horse riding in three-day events.

eventual *adj* coming or happening as a consequence or final result; consequential; final; ultimate.

eventuality *n* that which eventuates or happens; a possible occurrence; a contingent result.

eventually *adv*, *prep* in the event; in the final result or issue; ultimately.

eventuate *vi* (**eventuated, eventuating**) to issue as an event or consequence; to fall out; to happen; to come to pass.

ever *adv*, *prep* at any time past or future; at all times; always; eternally; constantly; incessantly; continually; in any degree.

evergreen *adj* always green; having green leaves throughout the year; (*fig*) always fresh, vigorous or in a good condition.—*n* a plant that retains its foliage through all the seasons.

everlasting *adj* lasting or enduring for ever; existing or continuing without beginning or end; eternal; perpetual; endless; continual.—*n* eternity; a plant whose flowers retain their form, colour and brightness for many months after being gathered.

evermore *adv* always; eternally; for ever; at all times; continually.

every *adj* each individual of the whole number; each of a number singly or one by one.

everybody, everyone *n* every person.

everyday *adj* used, occurring or that may be seen or met with every day; common; usual; ordinary.

everything *pron* all things, all; a thing of the utmost importance (*his children are everything to him*).

everywhere *adv*, *prep* in every place; in all places.

evict *vt* to dispossess by a judicial process or course of legal proceedings; to expel from lands or a building by legal proceedings.

eviction *n* the act of evicting; the expulsion of a tenant from lands or a building by legal proceedings.

evidence *n* that which demonstrates or makes clear that a fact is so; proof arising from one's own perceptions or from the testimony of others or from inductions of reason; testimony; (*law*) that which is legally submitted to a competent tribunal as a means of ascertaining the truth of any allegations under investigation.—*vt* (**evidenced, evidencing**) to render evident; to prove; to make clear.

evident *adj* open to be seen; clear; manifest; obvious; plain.

evil *adj* having qualities which tend to injury or to produce mischief; injurious; pernicious; mischievous; morally bad or wrong; wicked; corrupt; perverse; wrong; vile; vicious; unfortunate; not propitious; calamitous.—**the Evil One** the Devil.—*n* anything that causes injury, pain or suffering; misfortune; calamity; mischief; injury; depravity; corruption of heart or disposition to commit wickedness; malignity; the negation or contrary of good.—*adv* not well; ill.

evil eye *n* an influence superstitiously ascribed to certain persons, their glance being supposed to injure.

evince *vt* (**evinced, evincing**) to show; to prove; to manifest; to make evident; to display as something belonging to one's own nature or character (*to evince fear*).

eviscerate *vt* (**eviscerated, eviscerating**) to disembowel.

evocation *n* the act of evoking; a calling forth.

evoke *vt* (**evoked, evoking**) to call or summon forth.

evolution *n* a gradual development or working out; the extraction of arithmetical or algebraic roots; a regulated or systematic series of movements which a body of troops, a fleet or ship makes when changing a previous formation or position; that theory which sees in the history of all things, organic and inorganic, a development from simplicity to complexity, a gradual advance from a simple or rudimentary condition to one that is more complex and of a higher character.

evolutionist *n* a believer in the doctrine of evolution.

evolve *vt* (**evolved, evolving**) to develop; to cause to pass from a simple to a complex state.—*vi* to open or disclose itself.

ewe *n* a female sheep.

ewer *n* a large pitcher or jug with a wide spout.

exacerbate *vt* (**exacerbated, exacerbating**) to irritate, exasperate or inflame; to increase the malignant qualities of; to increase the violence of (a disease); to intensify; to make worse.

exact *adj* strictly correct or regular; accurate; precise; not different in the least; methodical; careful; observing strict method, rule or order; punctual; strict.—*vt* to force or compel to be paid or yielded; to extort by means of authority or compulsion; to order with pressing urgency.

exacting *adj* demanding or disposed to demand without pity or justice; extorting; making unreasonable claims.

exaction *n* the act of exacting; extortion; a wresting of contributions unjustly; that which is exacted; fees, rewards or contributions levied with severity or injustice.

exactitude *n* exactness; accuracy; nicety.

exactly *adv*, *prep* in an exact manner; precisely.

exactness *n* the state or quality of being exact; accuracy; correctness; preciseness; regularity.

exaggerate *vt* (**exaggerated, exaggerating**) to represent as greater than truth will warrant; to heighten unduly or beyond what is believable; to magnify.

exaggeration *n* the act of exaggerating; a representation of things beyond what is believable.

exalt *vt* to raise up; to elevate in power, wealth, rank or dignity; to elevate with joy, pride or confidence; to praise highly; to magnify; to extol; to elevate the tone of.

exaltation *n* the act of exalting or state of being exalted; elevated state; state of greatness or dignity; a state of great elation; mental elevation.

examination *n* the act of examining or state of being examined; a careful search or inquiry; careful and accurate inspection; a legal inquiry into facts by testimony; the formal questioning of witnesses under oath; an attempt to ascertain truth by inquiries and interrogation; a process for testing qualifications, knowledge, progress, of students, candidates, etc; a written or oral test of a person's knowledge or understanding of something; a physical inspection of a person's body, or part of it, by a doctor; investigation; scrutiny; trial.

examine *vt* (**examined, examining**) to inspect or observe carefully; to look into the state of; to view and consider in all its aspects; to question, as a witness or an accused person; to put judicial inquiries to; to inquire into the qualifications, capabilities, knowledge or progress of; to try or test; to set (someone) a written or oral test to find out the extent of a person's knowledge about something; to inspect a person's body, or part of it, to find out how healthy it is or to diagnose a disease.

examiner *n* one who examines; one who inspects; a person appointed to conduct an examination, as in a university.

example *n* a sample or specimen; a pattern worthy of imitation; a copy or model; a former instance.

exasperate *vt* (**exasperated, exasperating**) to irritate in a high degree; to provoke to rage; to enrage; to anger.

exasperation *n* the act of exasperating or state of being exasperated.

excavate *vt* (**excavated, excavating**) to cut, scoop, dig out the inner part of anything and make it hollow; to hollow; to form by scooping or hollowing out; to unearth.

excavation *n* the act of excavating; a hollow or a cavity formed by removing substance; the exposing of remains, etc, by digging.

ewe

excavation

excavator *n* one who or that which excavates; a machine for excavating.

exceed *vt* to pass or go beyond; to proceed beyond the given or supposed limit, measure or quantity of; to outdo; to surpass; to excel.—*vi* to go too far; to pass the proper bounds or limits.

exceeding *adj* great in extent, quantity, degree or duration; very large.

excel *vt* (**excelled, excelling**) to surpass in good qualities or laudable deeds; to outdo in comparison; to surpass; to transcend; to exceed.—*vi* to be eminent or distinguished; to surpass others.

excellence *n* the state of excelling in anything; the state of possessing good qualities to a very high degree; superiority; eminence; any valuable quality; anything highly laudable, meritorious or esteemed.

Excellency, Excellence *n* a title of honour given to governors, ambassadors, ministers, etc (with *Your, His, Her*, etc).

excellent *adj* being of great virtue or worth; eminent or distinguished for what is valuable or laudable; virtuous; good; worthy; excelling or surpassing in any quality, power or attainment; being of great value or use; remarkable for good properties.

except *vt* to take or leave out; to exclude.—*vi* to object; to take exception (usually followed by *to*).—*prep* being excepted or left out; with exception of; not including.—*conj* excepting; unless.

exception *n* the act of excepting or excluding; exclusion; that which is excepted or excluded; the person or thing specified as distinct or not included; an objection; that which is or may be offered in opposition to a rule, proposition, statement or allegation; offence; slight anger or resentment (*to take exception at a severe remark*; *to take exception to what was said*).

exceptional *adj* out of the ordinary; superior; relating to or forming an exception.

excerpt *n* an extract from an author or from a writing of any kind.

excess *n* that which exceeds any measure or limit; that which is beyond measure, proportion or due quantity; superfluity; superabundance; extravagance; wastefulness; riotous living; lack of restraint in gratifying the desires; intemperance; overindulgence; the amount by which one number or quantity exceeds another.

excessive *adj* beyond any given degree, measure or limit; beyond what is acceptable; immoderate; extravagant; extreme.

exchange *vt* (**exchanged, exchanging**) to give or take in return for another thing; to barter; to lay aside, quit or resign (a thing, state or condition) and take something else; to give and receive reciprocally; to give and take; to interchange.—*vi* to make an exchange; to pass or to be taken as an

equivalent.—*n* the act of giving one thing or commodity for another; barter; traffic by interchange of commodities; the act of giving up or resigning one thing or state for another; the act of giving and receiving reciprocally; the thing given or the thing received in return; the place where the merchants, brokers and bankers of a city meet to transact business; the difference of value in the respective currencies of different countries; a centre where telephone lines are interconnected.

exchange rate *n* the ratio used, or the price quoted, in exchanging one currency for another, as US dollars for pounds sterling.

exchequer *n* a state treasury; hence, financial property in general; a person's finances or financial resources.

Exchequer *n* the government department in Britain responsible for finances.

excisable *adj* liable or subject to excise tax.

excise[1] *n* a tax or duty imposed on certain commodities of home production and consumption, as beer, spirits, etc, or levied on persons for licences to pursue certain trades; that branch of the civil service which is connected with the collecting of such duties.—*vt* (**excised, excising**) to levy an excise on.

excise[2] *vt* (**excised, excising**) to cut out or off; to remove by cutting, as in surgery; to delete or expunge.

exciseman *n* (*pl* **excisemen**) formerly, an officer of the excise.

excision *n* the act of cutting out; removal by cutting; amputation; deletion.

excitable *adj* easily excited or stirred up; prone to or characterized by excitement.

excite *vt* (**excited, exciting**) to call into action; to animate; to rouse, provoke or to stir up; to cause to act, as that which is dormant, sluggish or inactive; to give new or increased action to; to stimulate; to call forth or increase the vital activity of; to raise, create or set afoot.

excitement *n* the act of exciting; stimulation; the state of being excited; agitation; sensation; commotion; a state of aroused or increased vital activity in the body or any of its tissues or organs; a vitiated and abnormal state of the actions and sensations, or both, produced by stimulants, irritants, etc; that which excites or rouses; that which moves, stirs or induces action.

exciting *adj* calling or rousing into action; producing excitement; deeply interesting; thrilling.

exclaim *vi* to utter with vehemence; to cry out; to shout; to declare loudly or excitedly.

exclamation *n* the act of exclaiming or making an outcry; noisy talk; a vehement cry; clamour; an emphatic or passionate utterance; the mark or sign in printing (!)

by which emphatic utterance or interjectional force is marked; (*gram*) a word expressing outcry; an interjection.

exclude *vt* (**excluded, excluding**) to hinder from entering or from admission; to shut out; to hinder from participation or enjoyment; to debar; to except; not to include in a privilege, grant, argument, description, etc; to thrust out; to eject.

exclusion *n* the act of excluding, shutting out, debarring, expelling, excepting or rejecting; the state of being excluded.

exclusive *adj* having the power or effect of excluding; possessed and enjoyed to the exclusion of others (*an exclusive privilege*); not taking into account something or certain individuals; not including certain things, as *an exclusive estimate* (often with *of*, as *500 men exclusive of officers*); reserved for certain persons; snobbish; unobtainable elsewhere; not shared or included elsewhere (*an exclusive story in a newspaper*); illiberal; narrow.—*n* an exclusive story.

excogitate *vt* (**excogitated, excogitating**) to strike out by thinking; to think out; to devise; to contrive.

excommunicate *vt* (**excommunicated, excommunicating**) to expel or eject from the communion of the church and deprive of spiritual advantages; hence, to expel from any association and deprive of the privileges of membership.—*n* one who is excommunicated; one cut off from any privilege.

excommunication *n* the act of excommunicating or state of being excommunicated; expulsion from the communion of a church and deprivation of its rights, privileges and advantages.

excrement *n* matter discharged from the bowels after digestion; faeces.

excrescence *n* anything which grows out of something else and is useless or disfiguring (as a wart or tumour); a useless or troublesome outgrowth.

excreta *npl* waste matter discharged from the body; faeces, urine.

excretion *n* a separation of some fluid from the blood by means of the glands; a discharge of fluids from the body; that which is discharged.

excruciate *vt* (**excruciated, excruciating**) to torment; to inflict severe pain on.

excruciating *adj* causing extreme pain or suffering; extremely painful; (*colloq*) very bad.

exculpate *vt* (**exculpated, exculpating**) to clear from a charge or imputation of fault or guilt; to vindicate from a charge of fault or crime; to relieve of or free from blame; to regard as innocent; to exonerate; to absolve; to excuse.

excursion *n* a wandering from a subject or main design; digression; a short journey for pleasure or health; a trip.

excursive *adj* given to making digressions; rambling; wandering.

excursus *n* a dissertation appended to a book, discussing some important point or topic more fully than could be done in the body of the work.

excusable *adj* capable of being excused; pardonable; admitting of excuse.

excuse *vt* (**excused, excusing**) to free from accusation or the imputation of fault or blame; to relieve from blame; to exculpate; to absolve; to justify; to pardon (a fault), to forgive; to agree to overlook; to free from an obligation or duty; to release by favour.—*n* a plea offered in extenuation of a fault or irregular behaviour; apology; that which lessens or justifies a fault.

execrable *adj* deserving to be execrated or cursed; very hateful; detestable; abominable.

execrate *vt* (**execrated, execrating**) to denounce evil against or to imprecate evil on; to curse; to detest utterly; to abhor; to abominate.

execration *n* the act of execrating; a curse pronounced; imprecation of evil; utter detestation; the object execrated.

executant *n* one who executes or performs; a performer.

execute *vt* (**executed, executing**) to follow out; to perform; to do; to carry into complete effect; to complete; to accomplish; to finish; to give effect to; to put in force (a law or measure); to inflict; to inflict capital punishment on; to put to death; to perform what is required to give validity to (a writing), as by signing and sealing; to perform (a piece of music) on an instrument or with the voice.

execution *n* the act of executing; performance; the mode of producing or performing an artistic work and the dexterity with which it is accomplished; the carrying out of the sentence of the law by putting a criminal to death; the infliction of capital punishment; the carrying out of the sentence of a court by arresting the goods or body of a debtor.

executioner *n* one who inflicts a capital punishment in pursuance of a legal warrant.

executive *adj* having the quality of executing or performing; designed or fitted for execution, administering or carrying into effect laws; governing.—*n* the person (or body of persons) who superintends the execution of the laws; the person or persons who administer the government.

executor *n* one who executes or performs; a performer or doer; (*law*) the person appointed by a testator to execute his or her will or to see it carried into effect.

executrix *n* a woman appointed by a testator to execute his or her will.

exegesis *n* the exposition or interpretation of any literary production, especially the exposition or interpretation of Scripture; also the principles of the art of sacred interpretation; exegetics; hermeneutics.

exegetics *n* the science which lays down the principles of the art of scriptural interpretation; exegesis; hermeneutics.

exemplar *n* a model, original or pattern to be copied or imitated; a person who serves as a pattern.

exemplary *adj* serving for a pattern or model for imitation; worthy of imitation; such as may serve for a warning to others; such as may deter.

exercise

exemplify *vt* (**exemplified, exemplifying**) to show or illustrate by example; to serve as an example or instance of; to make an attested copy or transcript of.

exempt *vt* to free or permit to be free from any charge, burden, restraint, duty, etc, to which others are subject; to privilege; to grant immunity (*no man is exempted from suffering*).—*adj* free from any service, charge, burden, tax, duty, requisition or evil of any kind to which others are subject; not subject; not liable; not included; freed; free.—*n* one who is exempted; one not subject.

exemption *n* the act of exempting; the state of being exempt; immunity; privilege.

exequies *npl* funeral rites; the ceremonies of burial; obsequies.

exercise *n* a putting in action the powers or faculties of (the eyes, the limbs, the mind); use; employment; practice or performance; a carrying out in action or performing the duties of anything (*the exercise of an art, trade, occupation*); exertion of the body to improve health or fitness; bodily exertion as a part of routine; systematic exertion of the body for amusement or in order to acquire some art, dexterity or grace; any such art or dexterity acquired by bodily training; training to acquire military skill; drill; moral training; discipline; a lesson or example for the practice of learners; a school task.—*vt* (**exercised, exercising**) to set in operation; to employ; to set or keep in a state of activity; to exert (the body, the mind) to put in practice; to carry out in action (*to exercise authority*); to train, discipline or improve by practice; to keep employed or busy; to cause to think earnestly and laboriously; to give anxiety to; to make uneasy; to pain or afflict.—*vi* to exercise oneself; to take exercise.

exhaust

exert *vt* to put forth (strength, force, ability); to put in action; to bring into active operation (the mind, the body); (*refl*) to use effort; to strive; to use one's powers.

exertion *n* the act of exerting; an effort; a striving or struggling; endeavour; trial.

exeunt they go out, a stage direction referring to more of the actors than one.

ex gratia *adj* (of a payment, etc) made without legal obligation or as a favour.

exhalation *n* the act or process of exhaling; that which is exhaled; that which is emitted or which rises in the form of vapour; emanation; effluvium.

exhale *vt* (**exhaled, exhaling**) to breathe or send out (something of a vaporous or gaseous character); to emit, as vapour; also, to cause to be emitted in vapour or minute particles.

exhaust *vt* to drain the energy of; to consume or use up; to empty by drawing out the contents; to use or expend the whole of by exertion; to wear out; to tire; to treat thoroughly; to leave nothing unsaid regarding.—*n* the escape of waste gas from an engine; the device through which this escapes; an exhaust pipe.

exhaustion *n* the act of exhausting; the state of being exhausted or emptied; the state of being deprived of strength or spirits; a state of complete fatigue and bodily weakness.

exhaustive *adj* causing exhaustion; tending to exhaust; treating a subject in such a way as to leave no part of it unexamined; thorough.

exhaust pipe *n* the pipe of an engine that conveys waste gases from the cylinder to the condenser or through which they escape to the atmosphere.

exhibit *vt* to present to view; to present for inspection; to show; to manifest publicly (*to exhibit a noble example*).—*vi* to show oneself in some particular capacity or character; to exhibit one's work or products at a public exhibition.—*n* anything exhibited, as at a public exhibition; anything shown in court as evidence.

exhibition *n* the act of exhibiting; a showing or presenting to view; that which is exhibited, especially a public display, as of works of art, natural products, manufactures, feats of skill, etc.

exhibitionism *n* attention seeking by bragging or outrageous behaviour; (*psychol*) a perverted condition in which pleasure is derived from immodest exposure of the body.

exhilarate *vt* (**exhilarated, exhilarating**) to make cheerful or merry; to make glad or joyous; to gladden; to cheer.

exhilaration *n* cheerfulness; joy; elation; gladness.

exhort *vt* to urge by words or advice; to urge, animate or urge by arguments; to advise, warn or caution; to admonish.—*vi* to use words or arguments to persuade.

exhortation *n* the act or practice of exhorting; language intended to persuade and encourage; a persuasive discourse; a homily; an admonition.

exhumation *n* the act of exhuming.

exhume *vt* (**exhumed, exhuming**) to dig up after having been buried; to disinter.

exigency, exigence *n* the state of being urgent or pressing; urgent demand; urgency; a pressing necessity; emergency.

exiguous *adj* small; slender; minute; meagre.

exiguity *n* smallness; slenderness.

exile *n* the state of being expelled from one's native country or place of residence by authority and forbidden to return, either for a limited time or for perpetuity; banishment; a removal to a foreign country for residence; a separation from one's country and friends by distress or necessity; the person banished or expelled from his country or who leaves his country and resides in another.—*vt* (**exiled, exiling**) to banish; to cause to be an exile.

exist *vi* to have actual existence or being; to be; to live; to continue to have life; to continue to be; to occur under specific circumstances or climate; to make a living with difficulty.

existence *n* the state of being or existing; continuance of being; that which exists; an entity; lifestyle.

exit *n* a way of departure; passage out of a place; the departure of a player from the stage when he or she has performed his or her part; a direction in a play to mark the time of an actor's quitting the stage; any departure; death; decease.—*vi* to leave or withdraw; to go offstage.

Exocet *n* a kind of rocket-propelled short-range guided missile; something unexpected and unwelcome; a critical or destructive remark.—*vt* to attack with an Exocet; to deliver a severe attack on.

exodus *n* departure from a place; especially, the emigration of large bodies of people from one country to another.

Exodus *n* the second book of the Old Testament.

ex officio *adj* because of or by virtue of one's office or position.

exogamy *n* a custom which prohibits a man from marrying a woman of his own tribe.

exogen *n* a plant in which the growth of the stem takes place by a succession of rings of new wood externally or from the central pith outwards to the bark or circumference.

exogenous *adj* (*biol*) produced by external growth; caused or influenced by external factors.

exonerate *vt* (**exonerated, exonerating**) to relieve of a charge or of blame; to clear of blame or imputation; to discharge of responsibility, obligation, duty or liability.

exoneration *n* the act of exonerating.

exorbitance *n* a going beyond rule or ordinary limits; excess; extravagance (*exorbitance of demands, of prices*).

exorbitant *adj* going beyond the established limits; excessive, especially of prices; enormous.

exorcise *vt* (**exorcised, exorcising**) to expel or cast out by prayers and ceremonies; to purify from unclean spirits by adjurations and ceremonies; to deliver from the influence or presence of malignant spirits or demons.

exorcism *n* the act of exorcising; a prayer or charm used to expel evil spirits.

exorcist *n* one who exorcises.

exordium *n* (*pl* **exordiums, exordia**) the beginning of anything; specifically, the introductory part of a speech, sermon, etc.

exoskeleton *n* all those structures which are produced by the hardening of the integument, as the shells of crustaceans, the scales and plates of fishes and reptiles.

exosmosis *n* the passage of gases or liquids through membranes or porous media from within outwards.

exoteric *adj* capable of being readily or fully comprehended, opposed to *esoteric*.

exotic *adj* introduced from a foreign country; not native; foreign; extraneous; attractive and exiting due to being unusual.—*n* anything of foreign origin, as a plant, tree, word, practice, introduced from a foreign country; an exotic person.

expand *vt* to spread out so as to give greater extent to; to open out; to cause the particles or parts of to spread or stand apart, thus increasing the bulk; to dilate; to enlarge in bulk; to distend; to widen or extend; to increase in size or scope; to describe more fully.—*vi* to become opened, spread apart, dilated, distended or enlarged; to increase in size or scope.

expanse *n* a widely expanded surface or space; a wide extent of land.

expansion *n* the act of expanding or spreading out; the state of being expanded; the increase of bulk which a body undergoes by the recession of its particles from one another so that it occupies a greater space, its weight remaining still the same; the act of increasing in size or scope; enlargement; dilatation; distension; an expanse or extended surface; extension; the further development of a business, etc.

expansive *adj* having the power of expanding or dilating; having the capacity of being expanded; embracing a large number of objects; wide-extending; comprehensive; communicative; friendly and frank.

ex parte *adj* proceeding only from one part or side of a matter in question; one-sided; partial; (*law*) made or done by or on behalf of one party in a suit.

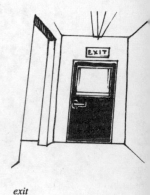

exit

exogen

311

expatiate *vi* (**expatiated, expatiating**) to speak or write at length on.

expatriate *adj* living in another country; self-exiled or banished.—*n* an expatriate person.—*vt* (**expatriated, expatriating**) to banish from one's native country; to exile (often reflexive).

expect *vt* to wait for; to await; to look forward to in the future; to look for to happen; to believe something to be likely to happen; to anticipate; to count on.

expectancy, expectance *n* the act or state of expecting; expectation; something on which expectations or hopes are founded; the object of expectation or hope.

expectant *adj* expecting; looking for.—*n* one who waits in expectation.

expectation *n* the act of expecting or looking forward to an event about to happen; the state of being expected or awaited; future prospect; wealth in prospect (usually plural).

expectorant *adj* producing or easing the expulsion of phlegm, etc, from the trachea or lungs.—*n* an expectorant medicine.

expectorate *vt* (**expectorated, expectorating**) to eject from the trachea or lungs; to discharge, as by coughing and spitting; to spit out.—*vi* to eject by coughing and spitting; to spit.

expediency, expedience *n* propriety under the particular circumstances of a case; advisability, all things being duly considered or taken into account; the seeking of immediate or selfish gain or advantage at the expense of genuine principle.

expedient *adj* proper or desirable under the circumstances; conducive or tending to selfish ends.—*n* that which serves to promote or advance; any means which may be employed to accomplish an end; means devised or employed in an exigency; shift; contrivance; resort; plan; device.

expedite *vt* (**expedited, expediting**) to free from impediments; to accelerate or facilitate the motion or progress of; to render quicker or easier in progress.—*adj* clear of impediments; easy; expeditious.

expedition *n* promptness in action; speed; quickness; despatch; the march of an army or the voyage of a fleet for hostile purposes; any organized journey or voyage for some end, especially exploration; a party making and equipped for such a journey.

expeditious *adj* performed with expedition or celerity; quick; hasty; speedy; nimble; active; swift.

expel *vt* (**expelled, expelling**) to drive or force out from any enclosed place; to eject; to cast or thrust out; to banish; to exclude; to drive out, as from a society or institution.

expend *vt* to lay out in paying, purchasing,

expiration

etc; to disburse; to spend; to deliver or distribute, either in payment or in donations; to use, employ, consume (time, labour, material).

expendable *adj* capable of being expended; that can be done without; not worth preserving; that can be sacrificed to achieve an aim.

expenditure *n* the act of expending; disbursement; that which is expended; expense.

expense *n* a laying out or expending; that which is expended, laid out or consumed; especially, money expended; cost; charge; cost, with the idea of loss, damage or discredit (*he did this at the expense of his character*); (*pl*) money spent by an employee, etc, on a business activity or trip; (*pl*) reimbursement of this money.

expense account *n* a list of expenses, such as travel or hotel expenses incurred by an employee in the course of his or her work and repayable by the employer.

expensive *adj* requiring much expense; costly; dear; extravagant; lavish.

experience *n* continued and varied observation; the knowledge gained by trial or observation; practical wisdom taught by life and the changes and trials of life; a particular event met with and undergone.—*vt* (**experienced, experiencing**) to make practical acquaintance with; to try or prove, by use, by suffering or by enjoyment; to have happen to or befall.

experienced *adj* taught by experience; skilful or wise by means of trials, use or observation.

experiment *n* an act or operation designed to discover some unknown truth, principle or effect, or to establish it when discovered; a trial.—*vi* to carry out a test or trial; to make an experiment.

experimental *adj* pertaining to, derived from, founded on or known by experiment; given to or skilled in experiment.

expert *adj* experienced; taught by use or practice; skilful; dextrous; adroit; having a facility of operation or performance from practice.—*n* a skilful or practised person; a scientific or professional witness who gives evidence on matters connected with his profession.

expiate *vt* (**expiated, expiating**) to atone for; to give satisfaction or make reparation for.

expiation *n* the act of atoning for a crime; the act of making reparation for an offence; atonement; satisfaction; the means by which atonement, satisfaction or reparation is made.

expiration *n* the act of breathing out or forcing the air from the lungs; emission of breath; exhalation; close, end, conclusion or termination; expiry.

expire *vt* (**expired, expiring**) to breathe out; to expel from the mouth or nostrils in the process of respiration, opposed to *inspire*; to emit in minute particles; to exhale.—*vi* to emit breath; to emit one's last breath; to die; to come to an end; to close or conclude, as a given period; to terminate; to end.

expiry *n* expiration; termination.

explain *vt* to make plain, manifest or intelligible; to clear of obscurity; to make clear or evident; to expound; to give or show the meaning or reason of.—*vi* to give explanations.

explanation *n* the act of explaining; a making clear or understood; exposition; interpretation; the clearing up of matters between parties who have been at variance.

expletive *n* an oath or a needless interjection; (*gram*) a word or syllable inserted to fill a vacancy.—*adj* (of words) added to fill a vacancy; superfluous.

expletory *adj* expletive.

explicate *vt* (**explicated, explicating**) to explain; to interpret.

explication *n* the act of explicating or explaining; explanation.

explicit *adj* not implied only but distinctly stated; plain in language; open to the understanding; clear; not obscure or ambiguous; open; unreserved; outspoken.

explode *vi* (**exploded, exploding**) to burst with a loud report; to burst and expand with force and noise; to detonate; to burst into activity or into a passion.—*vt* to cause to explode or burst with a loud report; to expose and bring into disrepute; to cause to be no longer practised, held or believed in (*to explode a theory*).

exploit *n* a deed or act of note; an heroic act; a notable feat; a great or noble achievement.—*vt* to make use of; to cultivate; to work up; to utilize; to take unfair advantage of.

exploitation *n* the act or process of exploiting or employing successfully; utilization; the successful application of industry on any object, as in the cultivation of land, the working of mines, etc; the act of taking unfair advantage of.

exploration *n* the act of exploring; close search; strict or careful examination.

explore *vt* (**explored, exploring**) to travel or range over with the view to making discovery, especially geographical discovery; to search by any means; to scrutinize; to inquire into with care; to examine closely with a view to discover truth.

explosion *n* the act of exploding; a bursting or sudden expansion of any elastic fluid with force and a loud report; a sudden and loud discharge caused by the application of fire, as of gunpowder or an inflammable gas; (*fig*) a violent outburst of feeling, as

of rage, generally accompanied by excited language or by violent actions.

explosive *adj* causing explosion; readily exploding.—*n*. anything liable or with a tendency to explode, as dynamite, etc.

exponent *n* one who expounds or explains anything; one who stands forth to explain the principles or doctrines of a party; one who champions or advocates something; one who exemplifies something; (*alg*) a small number placed above a quantity at the right hand to denote to what power the quantity must be understood to be raised, thus a^2 denotes a raised to the second power.

export *vt* to send (goods) for sale or consumption in foreign countries; to spread or transmit (ideas) abroad.—*n*. the act of exporting; exportation; the gross quantity of goods exported; that which is exported; a commodity that is exported.

exportation *n* the act of exporting; the act of conveying or sending abroad commodities in the course of commerce.

expose *vt* to set out or leave in a place unprotected and uncared for; to abandon; to make bare; to uncover; to disclose; to put forward or place in a position to be seen; to exhibit; to set out to view; to lay open to examination; to subject or place in the way of something to be avoided (*this exposed him to danger*); to put in danger; to hold up to censure by disclosing the faults of; to show the folly or ignorance of; (*refl*) to uncover or display one's sexual organs in public.

exposé *n* a revelation of crime, dishonesty, etc.

exposed *adj* put in danger; unprotected; liable; subject; open to the wind or the cold; unsheltered.

exposition *n* a laying open; a setting out to public view; explanation; interpretation; a laying open the sense or meaning; an exhibition or show.

expositor *n* one who expounds or explains; an interpreter.

exposure *n* the act of exposing; abandonment; the state of being exposed; openness to view; openness or liability to danger, inconvenience, etc; absence of shelter, especially from the cold; the position or aspect of a building; position in regard to the free access of light, air, etc; the uncovering or displaying of one's sexual organs in public; (*photog*) the time during which light reaches and acts on a photographic film, paper or plate; publicity, especially as given to a topical event or to a particular person in the news.

expostulate *vi* (**expostulated, expostulating**) to reason earnestly with a person; to remonstrate in order to dissuade.

expostulation *n* the act of expostulating; the

explosion

act of pressing on a person reasons or arguments against some action; an address containing expostulation.

expound *vt* to explain; to clear of obscurity; to interpret.

express *vt* to press or squeeze out; to force out by pressure; to give utterance to or declare by words; to represent in words; to intimate; to indicate; to make known; to tell; to represent; to exhibit; to denote; (*refl*) to make known one's ideas and thoughts.—*adj* given in direct terms; not implied or left to inference; clearly expressed; not ambiguous; plain; explicit; intended or sent for a particular purpose or on a particular errand; travelling with special speed with few or no stops (*an express train*); very fast.—*n* a messenger sent with haste on a particular errand or occasion; any regular provision made for the speedy transmission of messages; a railway train or coach which travels at a specially high rate of speed; a system or company for sending freight, etc, at quickly at rates higher than standard.

expression *n* the act of expressing or forcing out by pressure, as juices and oils; the act of uttering, declaring or representing; utterance; declaration; power of expressing one's thoughts, feelings, ideas, etc; something uttered; a phrase or mode of speech; the peculiar manner of utterance suited to the subject and sentiment; cast of countenance, as indicative of character; play of features, as expressive of feeling or emotion; the natural and lively representation of any state or condition, as in a picture by the pose of the figure, the conformation of the features, etc; the power or quality in a picture or other work of art of suggesting an idea; (*mus*) the tone, grace or modulation of voice or sound, suited to any particular subject; (*math*) a set of symbols serving to express something.

expressive *adj* serving to express, utter or represent (*words expressive of gratitude*); full of expression; vividly representing the meaning or feeling intended to be conveyed; emphatic.

expressly *adv* in an express manner; of set purpose; in direct terms; plainly.

expropriate *vt* to take away property from an owner; to dispossess.

expropriation *n* the act of dispossessing the owner of a property.

expulsion *n* the act of driving out or expelling; a driving away by violence; the state of being expelled, driven out or away.

expunge *vt* (**expunged, expunging**) to blot out; to rub out; to efface; to erase; to obliterate; to wipe out or destroy; to annihilate.

expurgate *vt* (**expurgated, expurgating**) to strike obscene, coarse or offensive passages out of (a book).

exquisite *adj* of great excellence or fineness; choice; select; consummate; perfect; of keen or delicate perception; keen; refined; delicate; pleasurable or painful in the highest degree; extreme.—*n* one who is fastidious in taste, dress, etc; a dandy.

extant *adj* still existing; in being; now subsisting; not destroyed or lost.

extemporaneous, extemporary *adj* performed, uttered or made at the time without previous thought or study; unpremeditated; offhand.

extempore *adv, prep* without previous thought, study or meditation; without preparation.—*adj* extemporaneous.

extemporize *vi* (**extemporized, extemporizing**) to speak without previous thought, study or preparation; to discourse without notes.—*vt* to make without forethought; to provide for the occasion; to prepare in great haste with the means within reach (*to extemporize a speech* or *a dinner*).

extend *vt* to stretch in any direction; to carry forward or continue in length, as a line; to spread in breadth; to expand or dilate in size; to hold out or reach forth; to expand; to enlarge; to widen; to diffuse; to continue; to prolong the time of; to communicate, bestow or impart.—*vi* to stretch; to reach; to be continued in length or breadth; to become larger or more comprehensive; to value land; to seize land for debt.

extended family *n* a family unit consisting not only of a couple and their children, or of a parent and children, but other relatives, such as grandparents.

extension *n* the act of extending; the state of being extended; enlargement; expansion; prolongation; that property of any body by which it occupies a portion of space, being one of the properties of matter; in logic, the extent of the application of a general term, that is, the objects collectively which are included under it; compass; a part added to a building; an additional telephone connected to the principal line; extra time to complete a project, etc.

extensive *adj* having great or considerable extent; wide; large; embracing a wide area or a great number of objects.

extent *n* the space or degree to which a thing is extended; extension; length; compass; bulk; size.

extenuate *vt* (**extenuated, extenuating**) to lessen or diminish; to weaken the import or force of; to make to seem less important, etc; to palliate; to mitigate; partially to justify.

extenuating *adj* serving to extenuate; mitigating.

extenuation *n* the act of extenuating; palliation; mitigation, as opposed to *aggravation*; partial justification.

exterior *adj* external; outer; outward;

bounding or limiting outwardly; situated beyond the limits of; on the outside; not arising or coming from within.—*n* the outer surface; the outside; the external features.

exterminate *vt* (**exterminated, exterminating**) to destroy utterly; to extirpate; to root out; to eradicate.

extermination *n* the act of exterminating; destruction; eradication; extirpation.

external *adj* on the outside, opposite to *internal*; on the exterior; superficial; visible; apparent; existing or situated outside; not being or arising within; pertaining to the outer part of the body; relating to or connected with foreign nations; foreign.—*n* an outward part; something pertaining to the exterior.

externally *adv* outwardly; on the outside; apparently.

extinct *adj* extinguished; quenched; having ceased; (of a volcano) inactive; being at an end; no longer in existence; having died out (*an extinct species*).

extinction *n* the act of putting out or quenching flame or fire; the state of being extinguished; a putting an end to or a coming to an end.

extinguish *vt* to put out; to quench; to stifle; to put an end to; to suppress; to destroy; to crush; to eclipse.

extinguisher *n* one who or that which extinguishes; a device for putting out a fire.

extirpate *vt* (**extirpated, extirpating**) to pull or pluck up by the roots; to root out; to eradicate; to destroy totally, exterminate.

extirpation *n* the act of rooting out; eradication; total destruction.

extol *vt* (**extolled, extolling**) to speak in laudatory terms of; to praise; to laud; to applaud; to eulogize; to magnify; to celebrate; to glorify.

extort *vt* to obtain from a person by force or compulsion; to wrest or wring from by physical force, by menace, torture or authority (*to extort contributions, a confession, a promise*, etc).

extortion *n* the act of extorting; the act or practice of extorting or wringing money from people by force; illegal compulsion to pay money.

extortionate *adj* characterized by extortion; oppressive in exacting money; exorbitant; excessively high in price.

extra *adj* extraordinary; more than what is usual; beyond what is due, appointed or expected; supplementary; additional.—*n* something in addition to what is due, expected or usual; something over and above; a special edition of a newspaper; a film actor with a non-speaking part or someone hired temporarily, e.g. for crowd scenes.

extract *vt* to draw out; to take out; to pull out or remove from a fixed position; to draw out by distillation or other chemical process; to select as a specimen or sample; to take (a passage or passages) from a book or writing; to ascertain the root of a number.—*n* that which is extracted or drawn from something; a passage taken from a book or writing; an excerpt; a quotation; anything drawn from a substance by heat, distillation or a chemical process, as an essence, a tincture, etc.

extraction *n* the act of extracting or drawing out; something extracted, e.g. a tooth; descent; lineage; the stock or family from which one has descended; (*arith, alg*) the operation of finding the root of a given number or quantity.

extracurricular *adj* outside the usual school timetable; not part of the regular school course; outside or beyond one's normal duties or activities.

extradite *vt* to deliver or give up (a criminal) to the authorities of the country from which he has come.

extradition *n* delivery of a criminal or fugitive from justice by one nation to another on sufficient grounds shown.

extradition treaty *n* a treaty by which either nation becomes bound to give up criminal refugees to the other.

extramural *adj* outside the usual courses run by a university or college.

extraneous *adj* foreign; not belonging to a thing; existing without; not intrinsic; not essential.

extraordinary *adj* beyond or out of the ordinary; not in the usual, customary or regular course; not ordinary; exceeding the common degree or measure; remarkable; uncommon; rare; wonderful; special; particular; sent for a special purpose or on a particular occasion (*an ambassador extraordinary*).

extrasensory perception *n* the claimed ability to obtain information or knowledge by means other than the ordinary physical senses.

extraterrestrial *adj* outside the earth; from outside the planet earth.

extravagance *n* lack of restraint; flamboyance; lavishness in spending; prodigality; excess; profusion; bombast.

extravagant *adj* exceeding due bounds; excessive; not within ordinary limits of truth or probability or other usual bounds; unrestrained; flamboyant; lavish in spending; wasteful; prodigal; profuse in expenses.

extravaganza *n* a lavish, extravagant, fanciful literary or musical composition; a burlesque.

extravasate *vt* (**extravasated, extravasating**) to force or let out of the proper vessels, as out of the blood vessels.

extreme *adj* outermost; furthest; at the utmost point, edge or border; worst or best that can exist or be supposed; greatest; most violent or urgent; utmost; last; beyond which there is none; carrying principles to the uttermost; holding the strongest possible views; ultra.—*n.* the utmost point of a thing; extremity; utmost limit or degree that can be supposed or tolerated; either of two states or feelings as different from each other as possible; height or extravagant pitch; (*math*) the first or the last term of a proportion.

extremely *adv* in the utmost degree; to the utmost point; very or exceedingly.

extreme unction *n* (*RC Church*) the ritual anointing of a person with oil when he or she is on the point of death.

extremist *n* a supporter of extreme doctrines or practice.

extremity *n* the utmost point or side; the verge; the point or border that terminates a thing; the highest degree; the most aggravated or intense form; extreme or utmost distress, straits or difficulties; a limb or organ of motion, as opposed to the trunk of the body and the head.

extricate *vt* (**extricated, extricating**) to free, as from difficulties or perplexities; to disengage; to disentangle; to clear.

extrication *n* the act of extricating, disentangling or setting free.

extrinsic *adj* external; outward; coming from without; not intrinsic; not contained in or belonging to a body.

extrude *vt* (**extruded, extruding**) to thrust out; to urge, force or press out; to expel; to drive away; to displace.

extrusion *n* the act of extruding; expulsion.

exuberance *n* the state of being exuberant; superfluous abundance; an overflowing quantity; high spirits; liveliness.

exuberant *adj* characterized by abundance, richness or luxuriance; high-spirited; in high spirits; lively.

exude *vt* (**exuded, exuding**) to discharge through the pores, as moisture or other liquid matter; to give out, like sweat or juice; to let ooze out.—*vi* to flow from a body through the pores; to ooze out like sweat.

exult *vi* to rejoice in triumph; to rejoice exceedingly; to be unusually glad; to triumph.

exultant *adj* rejoicing triumphantly.

exultation *n* the act of exulting; great gladness; rapturous delight; triumph.

exuviae *npl* cast skins, shells or coverings of animals; any parts of animals which are shed or cast off, as the skins of snakes, etc.

eye *n* the organ of vision, which in humans and the higher animals consists of a ball or globular body set in a socket and forming an optical apparatus by means of which the figures of external objects form sensible impressions; power of seeing; delicate or accurate perception; sight; ocular perception; notice; observation; regard; respect; anything resembling or suggesting an eye in shape or general appearance, as the bud or shoot of a plant or tuber, the hole or aperture in a needle, the circular catch of a hook and eye; (*archit*) the centre of something; thus, the eye of a dome is the circular aperture at its apex.—*vt* (**eyed, eyeing**) to fix the eye on; to look on; to observe or watch narrowly or with fixed attention; to look at flirtatiously.

eyeball *n* the ball, globe or apple of the eye.—**eyeball to eyeball** person to person; face to face.—*vt* (*colloq*) to stare at.

eyebright *n* a small annual herb common in meadows, heaths, etc, throughout Britain, which was formerly used for diseases of the eyes.

eyebrow *n* the brow or hairy arch above the eye.

eye-catching *adj* extremely attractive in appearance.

eyeglass *n* a glass to assist the sight; the lens of a telescope, microscope, etc, to which the eye is applied.

eyeglasses *npl* spectacles, glasses.

eyelash *n* the line of hair that edges the eyelid.

eyelet, eyelet-hole *n* a small hole or perforation to receive a lace or cord or for other purposes.

eyelid *n* that portion of movable skin that serves as a cover for the eyeball.

eyeliner *n* a cosmetic used to apply a line round the eye.

eye-opener *n* something that comes as a shock or surprise.

eyepiece *n* in an optical instrument the lens or combination of lenses to which the eye is applied.

eyeshadow *n* a coloured powder applied to accentuate the eyelids.

eyesight *n* the sight of the eye; view; observation; the sense of seeing.

eyesore *n* something offensive to the eye or sight.

eyetooth *n* (*pl* **eyeteeth**) one of the canine teeth in the upper jaw.

eyewash *n* (*colloq*) flattery; rubbish, nonsense.

eyewitness *n* one who sees an event or an action and can describe what happened.

eyot *n* a small island in a river.

eyrie *n* same as **aerie**.

eye

eyebrows

F

F the sixth letter of the English alphabet, a consonant, formed by the passage of breath between the lower lip and the upper front teeth; (*mus*) the fourth note of the diatonic scale.

fa *n* (*mus*) the name of the fourth note of the diatonic scale.

Fabian *n* a member of the Fabian Society (founded 1884) which advocates the gradual and non-revolutionary advance of socialism.

fable *n* a fictitious narration intended to enforce some useful truth or precept; a fabricated story; a fiction; the plot or connected series of events in an epic or dramatic poem.—*vi* (**fabled, fabling**) to tell fables or falsehoods.—*vt* to invent or fabricate; to speak of as true or real.

fabled *adj* celebrated in fables; fabulously imagined.

fabliau *n* (*pl* **fabliaux**) a kind of metrical tale common in French literature of the twelfth and thirteenth centuries.

fabulist *n* the inventor or writer of fables.

fabulous *adj* having the nature of a fable; fictitious; invented; not real; mythical; hardly to be received as truth; (*colloq*) very good, excellent.

fabric *n* a structure; a building, edifice or construction; the frame of a building; cloth manufactured; the structure of anything; the manner in which the parts are put together; texture.

fabricate *vt* (**fabricated, fabricating**) to frame, build, make or construct; to form into a whole by connecting the parts; to form by art and labour; to invent and form; to forge; to devise falsely.

fabrication *n* the act of fabricating; construction; making; the act of devising falsely; forgery; that which is fabricated; a falsehood.

façade, facade *n* the face or front view or elevation of an edifice; exterior front or face; a false or deceptive exterior.

face *n* the front part of a head, particularly of the human head, made up of the forehead, eyes, nose, mouth, cheeks, etc; the visage; aspect or air of the face; cast of features; look; countenance; expression of the face; the surface of a thing or the side which presents itself to the view of the spectator; the front; the forepart; a plane surface of a solid; one of the sides bounding a solid; appearance; aspect; effrontery; boldness; assurance; standing; reputation; the dial of a clock, watch, compass card or other indicator; the operating or working edge or surface of certain implements, e.g. a plane.—*vt* (**faced, facing**) to turn the face or front full toward; to meet in front; to stand up against in hostile encounter; to confront; to stand with the face or front toward; to finish or protect with a thin external covering over the front of; to smooth or dress the face of (a stone, etc).—*vi* to turn the face (*to face to the right* or left).

face cloth *n* a piece of towelling or other cloth for washing the face.

facet *n* a small flat portion of a surface; one of the small smooth surfaces on a gem or crystal.

facetious *adj* jocular, joking, especially in an inappropriate or irritating manner.

face value *n* the value indicated on the face of a coin or on a share document, etc; the apparent worth or significance of something.

facial *adj* of or pertaining to the face.

facile *adj* easy to be done or performed; dextrous (*an artist's facile pencil*); not difficult; easy to be dealt with; easily persuaded to good or bad; yielding.

facilitate *vt* (**facilitated, facilitating**) to make easy or less difficult; to lessen the labour of.

facility *n* easiness to be performed; freedom from difficulty; ease; ease in performance; readiness proceeding from skill or use; dexterity; pliancy in character; something that makes it easier to do things, services (in this sense usually in the plural, as *transport facilities, library facilities*).

facing *n* a covering in front for ornament, protection, defence or other purposes; the movement of soldiers in turning round to the left, right, etc; (*pl*) the distinctive trimmings on a regimental coat or jacket.

face

facsimile *n* an exact copy or likeness; an imitation of an original in all its proportions, traits and peculiarities; a method of transmitting printed matter through the telephone system.

fact *n* anything done or that comes to pass; an act; a deed; an effect produced or achieved; an event; reality; truth; a true statement.

faction *n* a party combined or acting in union, in opposition to another party or a government; a party unscrupulously promoting their private ends at the expense of the public good; a small discontented party within a larger group; discord; dissension.

factious *adj* given to faction; pertaining to faction; proceeding from faction.

factitious *adj* made by art, in distinction from what is produced by nature; artificial; conventional.

factor *n* an agent employed by businessmen residing in other places to buy and sell or transact other business on their account; in Scotland, a person appointed by a landholder or house proprietor to manage an estate, collect rents, etc; (*arith*) the multiplier or multiplicand, from the multiplication of which proceeds the product; (*alg*) any expression considered as part of a product; hence, generally, one of several elements or influences which tend to the production of a result.—*vt* to collect (money due) on behalf of another.—*vi* to act as a factor.

factory

factory *n* a building or collection of buildings for the manufacture or assembly of goods.

factotum *n* one who does a great variety of tasks for his or her employer.

factual *adj* based on or containing facts; actual.

faculty *n* any mental or bodily power; capacity for any action or function; skill derived from practice or practice aided by nature; special power or endowment; a right or power granted to a person by favour or indulgence, to do what by law he may not do; the body of individuals constituting one of the learned professions and more specifically the medical profession; the masters and professors of the several departments of a university or one of the departments themselves, as Faculty of Arts, Law, Medicine.

faggot

Faculty of Advocates *n* the Scottish bar.

fad *n* a whim; a temporary enthusiasm.

fade *vi* (**faded, fading**) to wither; to lose strength, health or vigour gradually; to decay; to lose freshness, colour or brightness; to tend from a stronger or brighter colour to a fainter shade of the same colour or to lose colour entirely; to grow dim or indistinct to view.—*vt* to cause to wither; to deprive of freshness or vigour.

fading *adj* liable to fade or lose freshness and vigour; not durable; transient.

faeces *npl* excrement; the solid waste material remaining after digestion of food, expelled from the anus.

faery *adj* pertaining to fairies; fairy.

fag *vi* (**fagged, fagging**) to become weary; to fail in strength; to be faint with weariness; to labour hard or assiduously; to work till wearied; to act as a fag.—*vt* to use or treat as a fag or drudge; to tire by labour; to exhaust.—*n.* a laborious drudge; a schoolboy who performs menial services for another boy who is in the highest or next highest form or class, a custom in some English public schools; (*colloq*) a cigarette; (*derog sl*) a male homosexual.

fag end *n* the end of a web of cloth; the useless remains of anything; (*sl*) a cigarette end.

faggot, fagot *n* a bundle of sticks or small branches used for fuel; a bundle of pieces of iron or steel in bars; (*colloq*) a male homosexual.

Fahrenheit *adj* of, using or being a temperature scale in which the space between the freezing and the boiling points of water is divided into 180 degrees, the freezing point being 32° and the boiling point 212°.

faience *n* a sort of fine pottery or earthenware glazed with a fine varnish and painted.

fail *vi* to become deficient; to be insufficient; to cease to be abundant for supply; to come short; not to have the due measure or degree; to decay, decline, sink or be diminished; to become weaker; to become extinct; to be entirely lacking; to be no longer produced, furnished or supplied; not to produce the effect; to miscarry; to be unsuccessful; to be unsuccessful in an exam, etc; not to pass an exam, etc; to be guilty of omission or neglect; to become insolvent or bankrupt.—*vt* to cease or to neglect or omit to afford aid or strength to; to be lacking to; to disappoint; to desert; not to be at hand when required; to be unsuccessful; to be unsuccessful in (an exam, etc); not to pass (an exam, etc).—*n* miscarriage; failure; deficiency; lack.

failing *n* imperfection; a weakness in character or disposition; foible; fault.

failure *n* a failing; deficiency; cessation of supply or total defect; omission; non-performance; decay or defect from decay; the act of failing or state of having failed to attain an object; lack of success; a becoming insolvent or bankrupt.

fain *adj* (*arch*) glad or pleased under some kind of necessity; inclined; content to accept of or do something for lack of better.—*adv* (*arch*) gladly; with joy or pleasure (with *would*).

faint *vi* to become temporarily unconscious; to swoon.—*adj* weak; languid; feeble; exhausted; inclined to swoon; hardly perceptible by or feebly striking the senses; indistinct; lacking in brightness or vividness, loudness, sharpness or force; not well defined; feeble; slight; imperfect; not carried on with vigour or energy; dejected; depressed; dispirited.—*n* a fainting fit; a swoon.

fair[1] *adj* pleasing to the eye; beautiful; handsome; white or light coloured in respect of skin or complexion; not dark or swarthy; not stormy or wet; not cloudy or overcast; clear (*fair weather*); free from obstruction, obstacle or anything to impede (*on the fair way to success*); open, frank or honest; not resorting to anything tricky or underhand; just; equitable; free from unfair or unfavourable circumstances or influences; civil, pleasing or courteous (*fair words*); free from deletions, blots, etc; perfectly or easily legible (*a fair copy*); free from stain or blemish; unspotted; untarnished (*one's fair name*); passably or moderately good; better than indifferent; average.

fair[2] *n* a market in a particular town or city; a meeting of buyers and sellers for trade; a gathering for the sale of a variety of goods, often for charity; a funfair.

Fair Isle *n* a complex, multicoloured pattern, knitted into a garment, originating on Fair Isle, Scotland.

fairness *n* the quality or character of being fair; lightness of complexion; beauty; honesty; justice.

fairway *n* the track or course that is clear of obstacles and is therefore taken by vessels in navigating a narrow bay, river or harbour; (*golf*) stretch of trimmed turf between tee and green.

fairy *n* an imaginary being or spirit having a human form, though of a stature much below human and with sundry superhuman attributes; an elf; any personage with superhuman power; fairyland; (*colloq*) an effeminate male; (*derog sl*) a male homosexual.—*adj* pertaining to or in some manner connected with fairies; coming from fairies; resembling a fairy.

fait accompli *n* (*pl* **faits accomplis**) something which has already occurred or been done and cannot be reversed.

faith *n* the assent of the mind to the truth of what is declared by another; firm and earnest belief on probable evidence of any kind; belief; belief in what is given forth as a revelation of man's relation to God and the infinite; a settled conviction in regard to religion; a system of religious belief; that which is believed on any subject, whether in science, politics or religion; a doctrine or system of doctrines believed;

faithfulness; fidelity; word or honour pledged; promise given.

faithful *adj* firm in faith; firmly adhering to religious or other duty; of true fidelity; loyal; true and constant to a person to whom one is bound; true to one's word; in conformity to the letter and spirit; conformable to truth; conformable to a prototype; true or exact; worthy of belief.

faithfulness *n* the quality or character of being faithful; fidelity; truth; loyalty; constancy.

fake *n* a sham, a fabrication, a forgery.—*vt* (**faked, faking**) to counterfeit; to reproduce or imitate something in order to deceive; to simulate.—*vi* to pretend; to put on an act.

fakir *n* an oriental ascetic or begging monk.

falcon *n* the common name of various raptorial birds inferior in size to the eagles and vultures; especially, one trained to hunt wild fowl or other game; a hawk.

falconer *n* a person who breeds and trains falcons or hawks for sport; one who follows the sport of fowling with hawks.

falconry *n* the art of training falcons to attack wild birds or game; the sport of pursuing wild fowl or game by means of falcons or hawks.

faldstool *n* a folding stool similar to a campstool; a small desk at which in churches litany is said.

fall *vi* (*pret* **fell**, *pp* **fallen**, *ppr* **falling**) to sink from a higher to a lower position; to descend by the power of gravity; to drop down; to sink; to ebb; to drop from an erect posture; to empty or discharge itself (said of a stream); to depart from the faith or from rectitude; to sink into sin; to die, particularly by violence; to come to an end suddenly; to perish, be overthrown or ruined; to sink into weakness; to become faint or feeble (*our hopes fall*); to sink into disrepute or disgrace; to decline in power, wealth or glory; to pass into a new state, especially with suddenness or through inadvertence or ignorance (*to fall asleep, to fall into error*); to decrease; to be diminished in weight, size, value or intensity (*the price falls, the wind falls*); to assume an expression of dejection, discontent, sorrow, shame, etc (applied to the countenance); to happen; to befall; to take place; to pass or be transferred by lot, inheritance or otherwise (*something falls to one's share*); to belong or appertain; to have to be reckoned to; to be dropped or uttered carelessly; to sink in tone or loudness.—*n* the act of one who or that which falls; a dropping or descending; descent; a tumble; death; destruction; overthrow; downfall; degradation; declension of greatness, power or dominion; ruin; diminution; decrease of price or value; a sinking of tone;

falcon

cadence; descent of water; a cascade or cataract; extent of descent; the distance through which anything falls or may fall; amount of slope; declivity; the season when leaves fall from trees (especially in USA); autumn; that which falls; a shower; lapse or declension from innocence or goodness, **the fall** being specifically the lapse into sin of Adam and Eve.

fallacious *adj* pertaining to or embodying something deceptive or misleading; based on fallacy; producing error or mistake; tending to mislead.

fallacy *n* a misleading or mistaken argument; an argument or proposition apparently sound but really containing some undetected error and therefore misleading; any unsound but specious mode of arguing.

fallen *adj* dropped; degraded; sunk in vice; lost to virtue; ruined; overthrown.

fall guy *n* a person who is left to take the blame or punishment for other people's wrongdoing or mistakes; a scapegoat; a person who is easily cheated or taken advantage of.

fallible *adj* liable to make mistakes; liable to be mistaken.

falling star

falling star *n* a meteor appearing as a luminous point darting through the sky and followed by a long train of light.

Fallopian tubes *n* (*anat*) one of the two tubes through which the egg cells or ova pass from the ovaries to the uterus.

fallow *adj* left to rest without a crop after tillage; untilled; uncultivated; pale red or pale yellow in colour, as some deer.—*vt* to leave fallow or ploughed but not sown in crop.

fallow deer *n* a European deer smaller than the red deer, of a brownish-bay colour, whitish beneath.

false *adj* not true; not conformable to fact; expressing what is contrary to that which exists, is done, said or thought; intended to mislead; counterfeit; forged; not real or genuine; hypocritical; feigned; not agreeable to rule or propriety (*false construction in language*); not honest or just; fraudulent; not faithful or loyal; treacherous; perfidious; deceitful; unfaithful; inconstant; not well founded or based (*false hopes*); constructed for show or a subsidiary purpose (*a false bottom, a false keel*).

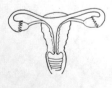

Fallopian tubes

falsehood *n* lack of conformity to fact or truth; falseness; lack of truth or veracity; untruthfulness; what is false or untrue; a lie; an untrue assertion; lack of honesty; deceitfulness; perfidy; imposture.

falseness *n* the state or quality of being false; untruthfulness; lack of veracity; duplicity; deceit; unfaithfulness; perfidy.

falsetto *n* the tones above the natural compass of the voice.

falsify *vt* (**falsified, falsifying**) to misrepresent; to alter fraudulently; to make not genuine; to disprove; to prove to be false.—*vi* to violate the truth.

falsity *n* the quality of being false; that which is false; a falsehood; a false assertion.

falter *vi* to hesitate in the utterance of words; to speak with a broken or trembling utterance; to stammer; not to be firm and steady; to stumble; to waver.—*n* the act of faltering; hesitation; trembling; quavering.

fame *n* public report or rumour; the condition of being widely known; the condition of being widely esteemed; renown; celebrity.

famed *adj* much talked of; renowned; celebrated.

familiar *adj* well acquainted; closely intimate; well versed (in a subject of study); exhibiting the manner of an intimate friend; affable; accessible; characterized by ease or absence of stiffness or pedantry; too informal; presumptuous; easy; well-known; well understood; of everyday occurrence or use.—*n* an intimate; a close companion; a familiar spirit.

familiarity *n* the state of being familiar; intimate acquaintance or knowledge; intimacy; over-informality; presumption; (*pl*) actions characterized by too much licence; liberties.

familiarize *vt* (**familiarized, familiarizing**) to make familiar or intimate with; to become familiar or intimate with; to habituate; to accustom; to make fully acquainted by practice or customary use.

familiar spirit *n* a spirit or demon supposed to be constantly at the command of some person.

family *n* the body of persons who live in one house; parents, or parent, and children, or child alone; the children as distinguished from the parents; those who descend from one common progenitor; a tribe or race; kindred; lineage; line of ancestors; honourable descent; noble or respectable stock (*a man of family*); in scientific classifications, a group of individuals more comprehensive than a genus and less so than an order.

family planning *n* the deliberate planning of the number of children born into a family, often by means of contraception; birth control.

family tree *n* a chart showing the descent and relationships of the members of a family.

famine *n* scarcity of food; dearth; a general lack of provisions; destitution.

famish *vt* to kill or destroy with hunger; to starve; to cause to suffer from hunger or thirst.—*vi* to die of hunger; to suffer extreme hunger or thirst.

famished *adj* (*colloq*) very hungry.

famous *adj* well-known; renowned; much talked of; distinguished in story.

fan[1] *n* the name of various instruments for exciting a current of air by the agitation of a broad surface, vanes or discs; a machine for winnowing grain; an instrument for agitating the air and cooling the face; anything resembling this; what fans or excites.—*vt* (**fanned, fanning**) to move or agitate as with a fan; to cool and refresh by moving the air with a fan; to winnow; to separate chaff from and drive it away by a current of air; (*fig*) to produce effects analogous to those of a fan in exciting flame; to excite or stir up to activity; to stimulate.

fan[2] *n* one who displays great enthusiasm for some sport, form of entertainment, etc (*a cricket fan, a film fan*).

fanatic, fanatical *adj* wild and extravagant in opinions, particularly in religious opinions; excessively enthusiastic about something.—*n* a person affected by excessive enthusiasm, particularly on religious subjects.

fanaticism *n* the state or character of a fanatic; excessive enthusiasm about or devotion to something, such as religion or a political ideology.

fanciful *adj* guided by fancy rather than by reason and experience; subject to the influence of fancy; whimsical (applied to persons); dictated or produced by fancy; appealing to or pleasing the fancy; full of wild images; curiously shaped (applied to things).

fancy *n* a phase of the intellectual faculty of a lighter and less impressive cast than the imagination or the active play of this lighter faculty; a new and pleasing thought or conception due to this faculty; the happy and poetical embodiment of such conception in words; a poetical illustration or ornament, as a simile, metaphor, etc; an opinion or notion; an impression or supposition; a whim or conceit; inclination; liking; fondness; preference.—**the fancy** a name for sporting characters, especially prizefighters.—*adj* fine; elegant; ornamental (*fancy goods*); beyond intrinsic value; extravagant (*a fancy price*).—*vi* (**fancied, fancying**) to imagine; to figure to oneself; to believe or suppose without proof.—*vt* to form a conception of; to portray in the mind; to imagine; to like; to be pleased with.

fancy-free *adj* free from the power of love.

fancywork *n* ornamental knitting, embroidery, etc.

fandango *n* a lively Spanish dance borrowed from the Moors, danced by two persons, male and female, the music being in triple time.

fane *n* (*arch*) a temple; a place consecrated to religion; a church.

fanfare *n* a flourish of trumpets; a short tune of a cheerful cast, played with hunting horns; an ostentatious parade or boast.

fang *n* the tusk of a boar or other animal by which the prey is seized and held; a long pointed tooth; the hollow poison tooth of a serpent; a claw or talon; the catch of a pump.

fanlight *n* a fan-shaped window situated over a door in a circular-headed opening; also any window over a door.

fantail *n* a variety of the domestic pigeon.

fantasia *n* a kind of musical composition having no particular theme but ranging amidst various airs and movements.

fantasize *vt* (**fantasized, fantasizing**) to imagine in an extravagant way.—*vi* to daydream.

fantastic *adj* fanciful; existing only in imagination; imaginary; chimerical; whimsical; capricious; indulging the vagaries of imagination; having oddness of figure or appearance; whimsically shaped; grotesque; unbelievable; (*colloq*) excellent, marvellous.

fantasy *n* imagination; fancy; a product of the imagination, such as a bizarre or extravagant notion; an imaginative poem, play or novel.

fanzine *n* a magazine produced for fans of a particular interest or hobby.

far *adj* distant; separated by a wide space; hence, remote as regards wishes, feelings, affections; more distant of the two (applied to the right side of a horse).—*adv* to a great extent or distance of space; to a remote period; in great part (*the day far spent*); in a great proportion; by many degrees; very much (*far better* or *higher*); to whatever point, degree or distance (*as far as*).

farad *n* the unit of electrical capacity in the practical system of units, being the capacity of a condenser which one coulomb of electricity raises to a potential of one volt.

farce *vt* (**farced, farcing**) to stuff with forcemeat; to fill with mingled ingredients.—*n* a dramatic composition of a broadly comic character; a comedy full of extravagant drollery; ridiculous parade; empty pageantry; mere show.

farcical *adj* belonging to a farce; of the character of a farce; droll; ludicrous; ridiculous.

farcy *n* a disease of horses closely related to glanders.

fardel *n* a bundle or pack; a burden; anything cumbersome or irksome.

fare *vi* (**fared, faring**) to be in any state, good or bad; to be in a certain condition as regards bodily or social comforts.—*n* the sum paid or due for conveying a person by

fan

fang

land, air or water; the person or persons conveyed in a vehicle; food; provisions of the table.

Far East *n* the countries of East and Southeast Asia including China, Japan, North and South Korea, Indochina, eastern Siberia and adjacent islands.

farewell *interj* may you fare or prosper well; a wish of happiness to those who leave or those who are left.—*n* goodbye; adieu; leave; departure.—*adj* leave-taking; valedictory.

far-fetched *adj* brought from a remote place; not easily or naturally introduced; elaborately strained (*a far-fetched explanation*).

farina *n* meal or flour; a soft, tasteless and commonly white powder obtained from the seeds of cereal and pod-bearing plants and of some roots, as the potato.

farinaceous *adj* consisting or made of meal or flour; containing or yielding farina or flour; mealy.

farm *n* a tract of land cultivated either by the owner of the land or a tenant and usually divided into fields.—*vt* to let to a tenant on condition of paying rent; to hold and cultivate either as tenant or as owner.—*vi* to be employed in agriculture; to cultivate the soil.

farmer *n* one who farms; one who cultivates a farm; an agriculturist.

farmhouse *n* a house attached to a farm for the residence of a farmer and family.

farming *adj* pertaining to agriculture.—*n* the business of a farmer; husbandry.

farmyard *n* the yard or enclosure surrounded by or connected with the farm buildings.

faro *n* a game of cards in which a person plays against the bank.

farrago *n* (*pl* **farragoes, farragos**) a mass composed of various materials confusedly mixed; a medley.

farrier *n* a shoer of horses; one who combines the art of horse-shoeing with the profession of veterinary surgery.—*vi* to practise as a farrier.

farrow *n* a litter of pigs.—*vti* to bring forth pigs.

far-sighted *adj* seeing to a great distance; calculating carefully the distant results of present conduct or action; not capable of perceiving objects near at hand distinctly.

farther *adj* more remote; more distant than something else; tending to a greater distance; additional.—*adv* at or to a greater distance; more remotely; beyond; by way of progression in a subject; moreover.

farthermost *adj* being at the farthest distance; most remote.

farthest *adj* at the greatest distance either in time or place.—*adv* at or to the greatest distance.

farthingale

farthing *n* a quarter of a penny; formerly, a small copper coin of Britain, the fourth or quarter of a penny in value.

farthingale *n* a hoop petticoat formerly worn by women or the circles of hoops used to extend the petticoat.

fasces *npl* (*sing* **fascis**) a bundle of rods, with an axe bound in along with them, in ancient times borne before the superior Roman magistrates as a badge of their power.

fascia *n* (*pl* **fasciae**) (*archit*) a long band of stone or brick forming a slight projection; the instrument panel of a motor vehicle; the dashboard; the flat surface above a shop front which displays the owner's name, etc.

fascicle *n* one of the separate divisions or numbers in which a book is published; a little bundle or collection; (*bot*) a cluster of leaves, roots, etc.

fasciculus *n* (*pl* **fasciculi**) (*anat*) a bundle of nerve fibres; a fascicle.

fascinate *vt* (**fascinated, fascinating**) to bewitch; to enchant; to operate on by some powerful or irresistible influence; to charm; to captivate; to allure irresistibly or powerfully; to interest greatly.—*vi* to exercise a bewitching or captivating power.

fascination *n* the act of fascinating, bewitching or enchanting; enchantment; a charm; that which fascinates.

fascine *n* (*fort*) a faggot or bundle of rods or small sticks, used in raising batteries, in filling ditches, in strengthening ramparts, etc

fascism *n* a form of extreme right-wing authoritarianism in which the government controls all the affairs of a country and restricts individual freedom, characterized by belligerent nationalism, racism and militarism; a set of extremely right-wing political beliefs which include excessive nationalism, racism, etc.

fascist *n* one who believes in and practises fascism; an exponent or supporter of fascism; a person with extreme right-wing, nationalist views.

fashion *n* the make or form of anything; external form; shape; pattern; make according to the custom of the time; the prevailing mode of dress or ornament; manner, sort, way or mode; custom; prevailing practice; genteel life or good breeding; genteel society.—*vt* to form; to give shape or figure to; to mould.

fashionable *adj* conforming to the fashion or established mode; taking the public taste and being in vogue; established by custom; current; prevailing; dressing or behaving according to the prevailing fashion; genteel; well-bred.—*n* a person of fashion.

fashionably *adv* in a manner according to fashion; according to the prevailing mode.

fast[1] *adj* swift; moving rapidly; quick in motion; rapid; dissipated; promiscuous.—*adv* in a fast or quick manner; swiftly; rapidly; with quick steps or progression; prodigally and wastefully; with dissipation.

fast[2] *adj* firmly fixed; close; tight; closely adhering; made close; strong against attack; firm in adherence; not easily alienated (*a fast friend*); steadfast; faithful; lasting; durable (*a fast colour*).—*adv* firmly; immovably.

fast[3] *vi* to abstain from food beyond the usual time; to go hungry; to abstain from food, or particular kinds of food, voluntarily, especially for religious reasons.—*n* abstinence from food; a withholding from the usual quantity of nourishment; voluntary abstinence from food as a religious mortification or humiliation; the time of fasting.

fast day *n* a day on which fasting is observed.

fasten *vt* to fix firmly; to make fast or close; to secure, as by lock, bolt, etc; to join in close union; to unite closely; to attach; to affix.—*vi* to fix oneself or itself; to become attached.

fastening *n* anything that fastens, binds, attaches, etc.

fast food *n* any type of food, that can be prepared and served quickly.

fastidious *adj* hard or difficult to please; squeamish; delicate to a fault; difficult to suit.

fastness *n* the state or quality of being fast, firm or secure; strength; security; a stronghold; a fortified place; a castle; a fortress.

fat *adj* fleshy; plump; obese; corpulent; the contrary to *lean*; oily; greasy; producing a large income; rich; fertile.—*n* a solid oily substance of whitish or yellow colour, a compound of carbon, hydrogen and oxygen, found in certain parts of animal bodies, lard and tallow being varieties of it; the best or richest part of a thing.—*vt* (**fatted, fatting**) to make fat; to fatten.—*vi* to grow fat.

fatal *adj* proceeding from fate or destiny; fraught with fate; fateful; causing death or destruction; deadly; mortal; destructive; calamitous; disastrous.

fatalist *n* one who maintains that all things happen by inevitable necessity.

fatality *n* the state of being fatal; a fixed unalterable course of things; a fatal occurrence; a calamitous accident.

fate *n* a fixed decree or sentence, by which the order of things is prescribed; inevitable necessity settling how events are to befall; unavoidable concatenation and succession of events; destiny; predetermined lot; human destiny; the final fortune of anything; final event; death; destruction.

Fates *npl* in classical myth, the Destinies or Parcae (Roman), Moirai (Greek), the three goddesses supposed to preside over the birth and life of humankind, called Clotho, Lachesis and Atropos.

father *n* a male parent; the founder of a race, family or line; a respectful mode of address to an old man; one who exercises paternal care over another; a guardian, protector or preserver; the first to practise any art; originator; cause; the title given to superiors of monasteries, confessors and priests; the eldest member of a profession or other body.—*vt* to beget as a father; to assume as one's own work; to profess or acknowledge oneself to be the author of; to ascribe or charge to one as his offspring or production (*to father a book on a person*).

Father *n* the appellation of the first person in the Trinity.

Father Christmas *n* a legendary fat, white-bearded old man who brings presents to children at Christmas; Santa Claus.

fatherhood *n* the state of being a father; the character or authority of a father.

father-in-law *n* (*pl* **fathers-in-law**) the father of one's husband or wife.

fatherland *n* one's native country; the country of one's parents or ancestors.

fatherly *adj* like a father in affection and care; paternal; protecting; pertaining to a father.—*adv* in the manner of a father.

fathom *n* a unit of length containing six feet, being originally the space to which the arms extend, used to measure depth of water.—*vi* to try the depth of; to find the bottom or extent of; to sound; (*fig*) to penetrate or comprehend.

fathomless *adj* that of which no bottom can be found; bottomless; not to be penetrated or comprehended.

fatigue *vt* (**fatigued, fatiguing**) to weary with labour or any bodily or mental exertion; to harass with toil; to exhaust the strength by severe or long-continued exertion; to tire or wear out.—*n* weariness from bodily labour or mental exertion; lassitude or exhaustion of strength; the cause of weariness; labour undergone; toil; a non-military task assigned to a soldier; the weakness caused in material by repeated stress, vibrations, etc (*metal fatigue*).

fatness *n* the state or quality of being fat; corpulence; plumpness; unctuousness; oiliness; richness; fertility.

fatten *vt* to make fat; to feed for slaughter; to enrich; to make fertile.—*vi* to grow fat; to become plump or fleshy.

fatty *adj* having the nature or qualities of fat; oily; greasy; composed of or containing much, fat.

fast food

fatuity *n* weakness or imbecility of mind; feebleness of intellect; foolishness.

fatuous *adj* feeble in mind; weak; idiotically silly; foolish.

fauces *npl* (*anat*) the gullet or windpipe; the posterior part of the mouth, terminated by the pharynx and larynx.

faucet *n* a pipe inserted into a cask for drawing liquid and stopped with a peg or spigot; the peg or spigot; in USA, a tap.

faugh *exclam* of contempt or abhorrence.

fault *n* a slight offence; a neglect of duty or propriety; something worthy of some blame or censure; a defect; a blemish; a flaw; (*geol, mining*) a break or dislocation of strata; an interruption in the continuity of strata such that the strata on either side appear elevated or depressed; in tennis, a misplaced serve.

faulty *adj* containing faults, blemishes or defects; defective; imperfect; guilty of a fault or of faults; blameable.

faun *n* in Roman myth, one of a kind of demigods or rural deities, differing little from satyrs.

fauna *n* (*pl* **faunas, faunae**) a collective term for the animals peculiar to a region or epoch, corresponding to the word flora in respect of plants.

faux pas *n* (*pl* **faux pas**) an indiscreet remark or action, especially a social indiscretion.

favonian *adj* pertaining to the west wind

favour *n* kind regard; friendly disposition; a state of being looked on with goodwill or kindness; a kind act or office; kindness done or granted; an act of grace or goodwill; leave; goodwill; pardon; a token of love; a knot of ribbons worn at a marriage or on other festive occasions; something worn as a token of affection; convenience afforded for success (*under favour of darkness*); partiality; bias; aspect, look or appearance.—*vt* to regard with favour or kindness; to support; to aid or have the disposition to aid; to be propitious to; to befriend; to show favour or partiality to; to afford advantages for success to; to render easier; to facilitate.

favourable *adj* kind; propitious; friendly; affectionate; manifesting partiality; conducive; contributing; tending to promote; advantageous; affording facilities.

favourite *n* a person or thing regarded with peculiar favour, preference and affection; one greatly beloved; often one unduly favoured; one treated with undue partiality.—**the favourite** the horse favoured by betting on a horse race.—*adj* regarded with particular affection or preference.

favouritism *n* the disposition to patronize favourites or to promote the interest of a person or persons to the neglect of others having equal claims.

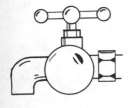

faucet

fax

fawn[1] *n* a young deer; a buck or doe of the first year.—*adj* resembling a fawn in colour; light brown.

fawn[2] *vi* to show a servile attachment; to court favour by low cringing, etc; to flatter meanly; to cringe and bow to gain favour.—*n* a servile cringe or bow; mean flattery.

fawning *adj* servilely courting or caressing; meanly flattering; cajoling in an abject manner.

fax *n* (short for **facsimile**) a machine which scans pieces of written information electronically and transfers the information to a receiving machine, sometimes at a considerable distance away, by telephone line; a copy of a document, picture, etc, sent in this way.—*vt* to send (a document, information, etc) by this means.

fealty *n* in the feudal system, faithful adherence of a tenant or vassal to the superior from whom he held his lands; faithfulness of any person to another; faith.

fear *n* a painful emotion excited by an expectation of evil or the apprehension of impending danger; anxiety; solicitude; holy awe and reverence for God and his laws; respect; due regard, as for persons of authority or worth.—*vt* to feel fear or a painful apprehension of; to be afraid of; to suspect; to doubt; to reverence; to have a reverential awe of; to venerate; to affright or to terrify—*vi* to be in fear; to be in apprehension of evil; to be afraid.

fearful *adj* affected by fear; apprehensive with anxiety; afraid; timorous; lacking courage; impressing fear; terrible; dreadful; awful; (*colloq*) very great, very bad.

fearsome *adj* alarming; terrible.

feasibility, feasibleness *n* the quality of being feasible.

feasible *adj* capable of being done, performed, executed or effected; practicable.

feast *n* a sumptuous repast or entertainment of which a number of guests partake; a banquet; a delicious meal; something particularly gratifying to the palate or the mind; a festival in commemoration of some great event or in honour of some distinguished personage; a periodical or stated celebration of some event.—*vi* to take a meal of rich or sumptuous viands; to dine or sup on rich provisions.—*vt* to entertain with sumptuous food.

feat *n* an act; a deed; an exploit; in particular, any extraordinary act of strength, skill or cunning.—*adj* neat; skilful; ingenious; deft.

feather *n* one of the growths which form the distinguishing covering of birds; a plume, consisting usually of a stem hollow at the lower part (called the quill) and having on each side of the upper part (called the shaft) the barbs, which with the shaft constitute the vane; something resembling a feather.—**a feather in the cap** an honour or mark of distinction.—**to show the white feather** to give indications of cowardice (a white feather in the tail of a fighting cock showed that it was not of the true game breed).—*vt* to dress in feathers; to fit with feathers; to cover with feathers.—**to feather one's nest** to collect wealth for oneself, especially at the expense of someone else, such as one's employer.—**to feather an oar** to turn the blade horizontally so as to lessen the resistance of the air on it.

featherweight *n* a weight as light as a feather; a boxer weighing less than nine stone (about 57 kg).

feathery *adj* clothed or covered with feathers; resembling feathers in appearance, softness or lightness.

feature *n* the make, form or cast of any part of the face; the make or form of any part of the surface of a thing, as of a country or landscape; a prominent part.—*vti* (**featured, featuring**) to make or be a feature of (something).

febrifuge *n* any medicine that mitigates or removes fever.—*adj* having the quality of mitigating or subduing fever.

febrile *adj* pertaining to fever; indicating fever or derived from it.

February *n* the second month in the year, consisting in common years of twenty-eight days, in leap years of twenty-nine.

feckless *adj* incompetent; untrustworthy; irresponsible.

feculent *adj* abounding with sediment, dregs or impure and extraneous matter; dreggy; muddy; turbid; foul.

fecundate *vt* (**fecundated, fecundating**) to make fruitful or prolific; to impregnate.

fecundity *n* the state or quality of being fecund or of bringing forth young abundantly; fertility; richness of invention.

federal *adj* pertaining to a league or contract, particularly between states or nations; united in a federation; founded on alliance between several states which unite for national or general purposes, each state retaining control of its home affairs, civil and criminal law, etc; of the joining of states or countries under one central government, as distinct from each other's separate government; of a union of states, etc, in which each state surrenders some of its power to a central authority.—*n* a member of the Northern party in the USA who during the civil war of 1861–65 maintained the integrity of the Union, in opposition to the Confederates, or the Southern party, who desired to secede.

federation *n* the act of uniting in a league; a federal government; a league; a federal union of states or countries; a union of states, countries, etc, in which each subordinates some of its power to a central authority.

fee *n* a reward or compensation for services; recompense (applied particularly to the reward of professional services); a fief or piece of land held of a superior on certain conditions; a feud; (*law*) a freehold estate liable to alienation at the pleasure of the proprietor, who is absolute owner of the soil; hence, absolute property, possession or ownership.—*vt* (*pret, pp* **feed** or **fee'd**, *ppr* **feeing**) to give a fee to; to pay for services; to reward; to hire; to bribe.

feeble *adj* lacking physical strength; infirm; debilitated; weak; lacking force, vigour, vividness or energy.

feeble-minded *adj* weak in mind; lacking firmness or constancy; irresolute.

feed *vt* (*pret, pp* **fed**, *ppr* **feeding**) to give food to; to supply with nourishment; (*fig*) to entertain, indulge, delight (*to feed oneself with hopes*); to furnish with anything of which there is constant consumption, waste, use or application for some purpose (*to feed a lake, a fire*); to supply.—*vi* to take food; to eat; to subsist by eating; to pasture; to graze; to satisfy a longing or craving.—*n* that which is eaten; food; fodder; an allowance of provender given to a horse, cow, etc; the material supplied at once to a machine or other contrivance to make it act.

feedback *n* information about the state or progress of something, such as a patient's response to treatment or the results of an advertising campaign, that helps to calculate the success of the action that is being taken.

feeder *n* one who feeds; one who gives food or nourishment; one who eats; that which supplies something (*the feeder of a lake*); a napkin tied round a child's neck at meal times, a bib.

feeding *n* food; that which furnishes food, especially for animals.

feel *vt* (*pret, pp* **felt**, *ppr* **feeling**) to perceive by the touch; to have sensation excited by contact of with the body or limbs; to have a sense of; to be affected by; to be sensitive of (pain, pleasure, disgrace); to experience; to suffer; to examine by touching.—*vi* to have perception by the touch or by the contact of any substance with the body; to have the sensibility or the passions moved or excited; to produce an impression on the nerves of sensation (*iron feels cold*); to perceive oneself to be (*to feel sick* or *well*); to know certainly or without misgiving.—*n* the act of feeling; sensation or impression on being touched.

feeler *n* one who feels; an organ of touch in insects and others of the lower animals, as antennae, palpi, etc; any device for the

feather

feeler

325

purpose of ascertaining the designs, opinions or sentiments of others.

feeling *adj* expressive of great sensibility; affecting; tending to excite the passions; possessing great sensibility; easily affected or moved.—*n* the sense of touch; the sense by which we perceive external objects which come in contact with the body and obtain ideas of their tangible qualities; the sensation conveyed by the sense of touch; physical sensation not due to sight, hearing, taste or smell (*a feeling of warmth, pain* or *drowsiness*); mental sensation or emotion; mental state or disposition; mental perception; consciousness; conviction; tenderness of heart; nice sensibility; the quality of exciting or expressing emotion; (*pl*) the emotional part of our nature; sensitiveness; susceptibility.

feign *vt* to invent or imagine; to make a show of; to pretend; to assume a false appearance of; to counterfeit.—*vi* to represent falsely; to pretend.

feint *n* a pretence; a mock attack; an appearance of aiming or thrusting at one part when another is intended to be struck.—*vi* to make a feint or mock attack.

feldspar, felspar *n* a mineral widely distributed and usually of a foliated structure, consisting of silicate and aluminium with potash, soda or lime, a principal constituent in granite, gneiss, porphyry, etc.

felicitate *vt* (**felicitated, felicitating**) to congratulate; to express joy or pleasure to another at his good fortune; (*refl*) to congratulate oneself.

felicitation *n* the act of felicitating; expression of joy at another's good fortune.

felicitous *adj* happy; extremely appropriate, suitable or well expressed; managed with extreme skill and success.

felicity *n* the state of being happy or in extreme enjoyment; happiness; bliss; blissfulness; blessing; source of happiness; skilfulness; a skilful or happy turn; appropriateness.

feline *adj* pertaining to cats or to their species; like a cat; belonging to the cat family.—*n* any of a family of carnivorous quadrupeds, including the lion, tiger, cat, leopard, panther, etc.

fell[1] *adj* cruel; barbarous; inhuman; fierce; savage.

fell[2] *n* a barren or stony hill; high land not fit for pasture.

fell[3] *vt* to cause to fall; to bring to the ground, either by cutting or by striking; to hew down; to knock down.

fell[4] *n* a skin or hide of an animal.

felloe *n* same as **felly**.

fellow *n* a companion; an associate; one of the same kind; an equal in rank, endowments, character, qualifications, etc; a peer; a compeer; one of a pair or of two things used together and suited to each other; an appellation of contempt for a man without good breeding or worth; (*colloq*) a man; a member of any incorporated society (as of the Royal Society of London); a postgraduate student receiving a stipend for a set period of time; a senior member of a college; a member of the governing body of a university or college.

fellow feeling *n* sympathy; a like feeling.

fellowship *n* the condition of being a fellow or associate; mutual association on equal and friendly terms; companionship; partnership; joint interest; an association of persons having the same tastes, occupations or interests; a brotherhood; an establishment in some colleges (as those in Cambridge and Oxford) which entitles the holder (called a fellow) to a share in their revenues.

felly, felloe *n* one of the curved pieces of wood which, joined together, form the circumference or circular rim of a wheel; the circular rim of a wheel.

felon *n* a person who has committed felony; a person guilty of heinous crimes; a criminal; a wrongdoer.

felony *n* a crime which occasions the forfeiture of lands or goods, or both; a serious crime.

felspar *n* same as **feldspar**.

felt *n* a cloth or stuff made of wool, or wool and hair or fur, matted or wrought into a compact substance by rolling, beating and pressure.

felucca *n* a long, narrow vessel, once common in the Mediterranean, with two large lateen sails and capable of being propelled by oars.

female *n* an animal of that sex which conceives and brings forth young; that plant which produces fruit; the flower that bears the pistil and receives the pollen of the male flowers.—*adj* belonging to the sex which produces young; feminine; delicate; weak; (*bot*) pistil-bearing.

feminine *adj* pertaining to a woman or to women or to the female sex; having the qualities belonging to a woman; womanly; effeminate; womanish; (*gram*) denoting the gender of words which signify females or the terminations of such words.

feminism *n* a movement designed to achieve political, economic and social equality for women; the principle or practice of political, economic and social equality for women.

feminist *adj* of or pertaining to feminism.—*n* one who advocates or practises feminism.

femme fatale *n* (*pl* **femmes fatales**) a dangerously attractive and seductive woman.

femoral *adj* belonging to the thigh.

fen *n* low land covered wholly or partially

with water but producing sedge, coarse grasses or other plants; boggy land; a marsh.

fence *n* a wall, hedge, bank, railing or paling forming a boundary to or enclosing some area; that which defends; defence; the art of fencing; skill in fencing or swordsmanship; hence, skill in argument and repartee; a purchaser or receiver of stolen goods.—*vt* (**fenced, fencing**) to enclose with a fence; to secure by an enclosure; to guard; to hedge in; to ward off or parry by argument or reasoning.—*vi* to use a sword or foil for the purpose of learning the art of attack and defence; to practise fencing; to fight and defend by giving and avoiding blows or thrusts; to parry arguments; to equivocate; to prevaricate.

fencer *n* one who fences; one who teaches or practises the art of fencing with sword or foil.

fencing *n* the art of using skilfully a sword or foil in attack or defence; material used in making fences; that which fences; a protection put round a dangerous piece of machinery.

fend *vt* to keep off; to ward off; to shut out (usually followed by *off*, as *to fend off blows*).

fender *n* one who or that which fends or wards off; a utensil employed to hinder coals of fire from rolling forward to the floor; also, a piece of timber, bundle of rope, etc, hung over the side of a vessel to prevent it from being injured by rubbing against any body.

fennec *n* a North African animal related to the fox.

fennel *n* a fragrant, perennial plant, having aromatic seeds and leaves that are used in sauces.

fenugreek *n* a pod-bearing annual plant resembling clover.

feoff *n* a fief or fee

feoffment *n* the legal gift or transference to a person of a fee or freehold estate; the instrument or deed by which such property is conveyed.

feral *adj* having become wild from a state of domestication, as animals or from a state of cultivation, as plants.

feretory *n* a shrine or repository for the relics of saints.

ferial *adj* pertaining to holidays or days in which business is not transacted.

ferine *adj* relating to or resembling a wild beast; wild; untamed; savage.

ferment *n* any substance, as a fungus, whose presence in another body produces the peculiar effervescence and decomposition called fermentation; commotion; heat; tumult; agitation (as of a crowd, of the feelings, etc).—*vt* to cause fermentation in; to set in brisk motion or agitation; to

warm; to excite.—*vi* to undergo fermentation; to work; to be in agitation or excited, as by violent emotions.

fermentation *n* the act or process of fermenting; the decomposition or conversion of an organic substance into new compounds in presence of a ferment, generally indicated by a sensible internal motion, the development of heat and the liberation of bubbles of gas; in common language, the process by which grape juice is converted into wine and the wort of malt into beer; (*fig*) the state of being in high activity or commotion; agitation; excitement.

fern *n* any of a large class of nonflowering plants with roots, stems and fronds and reproducing by spores.

ferocious *adj* fierce; savage; barbarous; ravenous; rapacious; indicating or expressive of ferocity.

ferocity *n* state of being ferocious; savage wildness or fierceness; fury; cruelty.

ferret *n* a domesticated variety of the polecat, usually of a pale yellow colour, with red eyes, used to drive rabbits out of their holes and to kill rats.—*vt* to hunt with ferrets; to drive out of a lurking place; to search out by perseverance and cunning (with *out*).

ferric *adj* of or containing iron.

ferriferous *adj* producing or yielding iron.

ferroconcrete *n* a building material consisting of concrete in which pieces of iron are embedded.

ferrous *adj* containing iron.

ferruginous *adj* partaking of iron; of the colour of rust or oxide of iron.

ferrule *n* a ring of metal put round the end of a walking stick or other thing to strengthen it or prevent its splitting.

ferry *n* the place or passage where boats pass over a narrow piece of water to convey passengers; the boat itself.—*vt* (**ferried, ferrying**) to carry or transport over a river, strait, etc, in a boat or other conveyance; to transport from one place to another, especially along a regular route.—*vi* to pass over a ferry.

ferry boat *n* a boat that plies at a ferry.

ferryman *n* (*pl* **ferrymen**) one who keeps a ferry.

fertile *adj* fruitful; producing fruit or crops in abundance; the opposite of *barren*; prolific or productive of anything, as of ideas, poetry, etc; inventive; able to produce abundantly; able to bear offspring; able to conceive offspring; capable of sexual reproduction; (*bot*) capable of producing fruit; fruit-bearing.

fertility *n* the state of being fertile or fruitful; fruitfulness; fecundity; productiveness; richness; fertile invention.

fertilization *n* the act or process of rendering fertile, fruitful or productive; (*bot*) the

fence

fern

application of the pollen to the stigma of a plant, by means of which a perfect seed containing an embryo is produced; fecundation.

fertilize *vt* (**fertilized, fertilizing**) to make fertile; to make fruitful or productive; to enrich; to fecundate.

fervency *n* the state of being fervent; heat of mind; ardour; animated zeal; warmth of devotion.

fervent *adj* hot; glowing; intensely warm; hot in temper; vehement; ardent; earnest; excited; animated; glowing with religious feeling; zealous.

fervid *adj* very hot; burning; glowing; fervent; very warm in zeal; vehement; ardent.

fervour *n* heat or warmth; intensity of feeling; ardour; burning zeal; extreme earnestness in religion, particularly in prayer.

fescue *n* a kind of grass, some species being excellent meadow and pasture grasses.

fesse *n* (*heral*) a band or girdle comprising the centre third part of the escutcheon, which it crosses horizontally.

festal *adj* pertaining to a feast; festive.

fester *vi* to suppurate; to discharge or become full of pus or purulent matter; to rankle (passions, a sense of wrong, etc).

festival *adj* pertaining to or befitting a feast; joyous; mirthful.—*n* a time of feasting; an anniversary day of joy, civil or religious; a festive celebration.

festive *adj* pertaining to or becoming a feast; joyous; mirthful.

festivity *n* the condition of being festive; social joy or exhilaration at an entertainment; something forming part of a festal celebration.

festoon *n* a string, chain or garland of flowers, foliage, etc, suspended so as to form one or more depending curves; (*archit*) a sculptured ornament in imitation of this.—*vt* to adorn with festoons; to connect by festoons.

feta cheese *n* a type of Greek, white, semisoft cheese made from either goat's milk or sheep's milk.

fetal *adj* some as **foetal**.

fetch *vt* to go and bring; to bring; to bear toward the person speaking; to recall or bring back; to make or perform, with certain objects (*to fetch a blow* or *stroke, to fetch a sigh*); to bring or obtain as its price.—*vi* to bring things; to move or turn.—*n* a stratagem by which a thing is indirectly brought to pass; a trick; an artifice; the apparition of a living person; a wraith.

fetch-candle *n* a light seen at night and believed by the superstitious to portend a person's death.

fête, fete *n* a feast; a holiday; a festival day; a small fair, often one held to raise money for an institution or a charity.—*vt* (**fêted,** **fêting**) to entertain with a feast; to honour with a festive entertainment.

fetid, foetid *adj* having an offensive smell; having a strong or rancid scent.

fetish *n* any object, animate or inanimate, natural or artificial, regarded by some uncivilized races with a feeling of awe, as having mysterious powers residing in it or as being the representative or habitation of a deity; hence, any object of exclusive or excessive devotion; an excessive devotion to something; a fixation.

fetlock *n* a tuft of hair growing behind the pastern joint of horses; the joint on which the hair grows.

fetter *n* a chain for the feet; a chain by which a person or animal is confined by the foot; anything that confines or restrains from motion; a restraint.—*vt* to put fetters on; to bind; to confine; to restrain.

fettle *n* condition; trim.

fetus *n* same as **foetus**.

feu *n* in Scotland a piece of ground (usually small) granted by a superior in perpetuity in consideration of an annual payment, called *feu duty*, and certain other contingent burdens.—*vt* to give or take in feu or by the payment of feu duty.

feud[1] *n* a contention or quarrel; hostility; often, hostility or declared warfare between families or parties in a state; a persistent state of hostility.—*vi* to carry on a state of hostility with another (party, state, etc).

feud[2] *n* a fief.

feudal *adj* pertaining to feuds or fiefs; founded on or pertaining to the system of holding lands by military services.

feudalism *n* the feudal system and its belongings; the system of holding lands by military services.

feudal system *n* a system according to which grants of land were made by the sovereign to the nobles and by them to an inferior class, on the condition that the possessor should take an oath of loyalty and do military service to him by whom the grant was made.

feudatory, feudatary *adj* holding from another by feudal tenure.—*n* a tenant or vassal holding his lands on condition of military service; the tenant of a feud or fief.

fever *n* an abnormally increased body temperature; a diseased state of the system, characterized by an accelerated pulse, with increase of heat, deranged functions, diminished strength and often with excessive thirst; agitation or excitement by anything that strongly affects the passions.—*vt* to put in a fever.—*vi* to be seized with fever.

feverfew *n* a European plant with much divided leaves and white flowers (once supposed to reduce fever).

feverish *adj* having fever; affected with fever, especially with a slight degree of fever; indicating or pertaining to fever; agitated; restless.

few *adj* not many; small in number (used frequently, by ellipsis of a noun, for not many persons or things)—**a few** is often used and generally means more than *few* alone.

fey *adj* on the verge of a sudden or violent death; fated soon to die and often showing this in some peculiar way; clairvoyant; strange.

fez *n* a brimless hat, originally Turkish, in the shape of a truncated cone with a tassel at the crown.

fiacre *n* a small four-wheeled carriage; a hackney coach or similar vehicle plying for hire.

fiancé, fiancée *n* an affianced or betrothed person.

fiasco *n* (*pl* **fiascos, fiascoes**) a failure in a musical performance; an ignominious and notorious failure generally.

fiat *n* a command to do something; a decisive or effective command; an order of a judge.

fib *n* a lie or falsehood (a word used as a softer expression than lie).—*vi* (**fibbed, fibbing**) to lie; to speak falsely.

fibre *n* a thread or filament; a natural or synthetic thread, e.g. from cotton or nylon, which is spun into yarn; a material made of such yarn; one of the fine slender thread-like or hair-like bodies of which the tissues of animals and plants are partly constituted; the small slender root of a plant; a substance obtained from certain foods, such as cereals and vegetables, which cannot be digested and so adds roughage to the diet; strength of character.

fibreglass *n* glass in fibrous form, often bonded with plastic, used in making various products.

fibre obtics *n* the transmission of information in the form of light signals along thin transparent fibres of glass.

fibrin *n* a white protein in the blood which causes coagulation.

fibrous *adj* containing or consisting of fibres.

fibula *n* (*pl* **fibulae**) an ancient clasp or buckle; (*anat*) the outer and lesser bone of the lower leg.

fichu *n* a light triangular scarf worn by women to cover the neck, throat and shoulders.

fickle *adj* wavering; inconstant; unstable; of a changeable mind; irresolute; capricious; liable to change.

fickleness *n* the state or quality of being fickle; inconstancy; unsteadiness in opinion or purpose; changeability.

fictile *adj* moulded into form by art; manufactured by pottery; suitable for pottery.

fiction *n* the act of inventing or imagining; that which is feigned, invented or imagined; a feigned or invented story; a tale or story composed for amusement or entertainment; fictitious literature; prose narrative in the form of romances, novels, tales, etc.

fictional *adj* pertaining to or characterized by fiction.

fictitious *adj* feigned; imaginary; not real; counterfeit; false; not genuine; invented to give literary pleasure; dealing with imaginary characters and events.

fid *n* (*naut*) a bar or short piece of wood or metal, helping to support a topmast; a wooden pin for various purposes on board ship.

fiddle *n* a stringed instrument of music; a violin; the wooden framework fixed on tables on board ship in rough weather, to keep the crockery from sliding off.—*vi* (**fiddled, fiddling**) to play on a fiddle or violin; to trifle; to falsify.

fiddle-faddle *adj* trifling; making a bustle about nothing.—*vi* (**fiddle-faddled, fiddle-faddling**) to trifle.

fiddler *n* one who plays on a fiddle.

fiddlestick *n* a fiddle bow.—**fiddlesticks** *interj* nonsense! pshaw! etc.

fiddling *adj* trifling; trivial; fussily busy with nothing.

fidelity *n* faithfulness; careful and exact observance of duty or performance of obligations; firm adherence to a person or to a party; loyalty; honesty; veracity; adherence to truth.

fidget *vi* to move uneasily one way and the other; to move irregularly or in fits and starts; to move restlessly, as with boredom, etc.—*n* irregular motion; restlessness.

fidgety *adj* given to fidget; restless; uneasy.

fiduciary *adj* confident in belief; trustful; undoubting; having the nature of a trust; held in trust; (of paper currency) deriving its value from the confidence of the public.—*n* one who holds a thing in trust; a trustee.

fie *interj* denoting contempt, dislike or impatience.

fief *n* an estate held of a superior on condition of military or other service; an estate held on feudal tenure.

field *n* a piece of land suitable for tillage or pasture; a distinct or separate division of a farm; cleared land; cultivated ground; the open country; the ground where a battle is fought or military operations carried on; hence, a battle or action (*the field is lost*); open space or unrestricted opportunity, for action or operation; scope; compass; extent; sphere (*a wide field for conjecture*); the ground or blank space on which figures are drawn; the general surface of a

fez

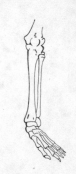

fibula

heraldic shield or escutcheon; in cricket, the fielders collectively; sporting, those taking part in a hunt; all the horses, dogs, etc, taking part in a race; all the competitors in a contest; (*physics*) a region of space, considered as the scene of certain physical phenomena; that part of an electrical generator which carries the magnetizing or field coils; area; area of interest or expertise; a division of activity.—*vi* in cricket, to be one of the field whose duty is to watch and catch or recover the ball as it is driven by the batsman.

field day *n* a day when troops are drawn out for instruction in field exercises; any day of unusual display; any day of unusual success.

field event *n* an athletic competition involving jumping or throwing, as opposed to running.

fielder *n* a player who fields at cricket.

fieldfare *n* a bird of the thrush family, a winter visitor to Britain.

field glasses *npl* a pair of binoculars for looking at objects at a considerable distance from the spectator.

field marshal *n* the highest rank conferred on military officers in the British and some foreign armies.

fieldmouse

fieldmouse *n* (*pl* **fieldmice**) one of several species of rodent animals that live in the field, burrowing in banks, etc.

field officer *n* a military officer above the rank of captain and below that of general, as a major or colonel.

fiend *n* an infernal being; a demon; the devil; a person with devilish qualities; a wicked, cruel or malicious person.

fiendish *adj* having the qualities of a fiend; infernal; excessively cruel; diabolic; devilish.

fierce *adj* vehement; violent; furious; savage; ferocious; easily enraged; indicating ferocity or a ferocious disposition; very eager; vehement in anger or cruelty.

fierceness *n* the quality of being fierce, furious or angry; violence; fury; ferocity; savageness.

fiery *adj* consisting of fire; burning; flaming; blazing; highly inflammable; hot; ardent; vehement; impetuous; passionate; irritable; fierce; like fire; bright; glaring.

fiery cross *n* a light wooden cross, the extremities of which were set fire to and then extinguished in blood (used in ancient times in Scotland as a signal to assemble under arms).

fife *n* a small musical instrument of the flute kind, having but one key and a compass of two octaves.—*vi* (**fifed, fifing**) to play on a fife.

fifteen *adj* five and ten.—*n* the number which consists of five and ten; a symbol representing this number, as 15 or XV.—**the fifteen, the '15** the Jacobite rebellion

of 1715.—**a fifteen** a rugby football team of fifteen players.

fifteenth *adj* the fifth in order after the tenth; being one of fifteen equal parts into which a whole is divided.—*n* a fifteenth part.

fifth *adj* the ordinal of five; next after the fourth; being one of five equal parts of a whole.—*n* one of five equal parts into which anything is divided; (*mus*) an interval consisting of three tones and a semitone.

fifth column *n* a group of people who are traitors to their own side; a subversive group within a country or organization whose members are willing to give help to the enemy or opposition.

fifth columnist *n* a member of a fifth column; a traitor.

fiftieth *adj* next in order after the forty-ninth; being one of fifty equal parts of a whole.—*n* one of fifty equal parts of a whole.

fifty *adj* five times ten.—*n* the number which consists of five times ten; a symbol representing this number, as 50 or L.

fifty-fifty *adj* in two equal portions; equally; with each person paying half the cost; having an equal possibility of winning or losing, as *fifty-fifty chance*.

fig *n* a fruit consisting of a hollow receptacle containing a great many minute flowers, the ripe carpels of which, erroneously called the seed, are embedded in the pulp; the tree that bears this fruit; a thing of no importance (*I do not care a fig for him*).

fight *vi* (*pret, pp* **fought**, *ppr* **fighting**) to contend for victory in battle or in single combat; to contend in arms or otherwise; to carry on active opposition; to strive or struggle to resist (with *with* or *against* before an object).—*vt* to carry on or wage (a battle); to win or gain by struggle (*to fight one's way*); to contend with; to war against; to do battle with; to quarrel with.—*n* a contest; a battle; an engagement; a struggle for victory; a quarrel.

figment *n* an invention; a fiction; something feigned or imagined.

figurative *adj* representing by means of a figure or type; typical; symbolical (used in a metaphorical sense); metaphorical, not literal; having the character of a figure or trope.

figure *n* the form of anything as expressed by the outline or contour; shape; fashion; form; any form made by drawing, painting, carving, embroidering, etc; especially the human body so represented; appearance or impression made by the conduct of a person (*to cut a poor figure*); a person; in logic, the form of a syllogism with respect to the relative position of the middle term; (*arith*) a character denoting or standing for a number; hence, value, as expressed in numbers; price; (*pl*) arithmetic calculation; in dancing or skating, a set of steps or movements; (*rhet*) a mode of speaking or writing in which words are deflected from their ordinary use or signification; a trope; a peculiar expression used for impressiveness as a metaphor, antithesis, etc—*vt* (**figured, figuring**) to make a figure or likeness of; to represent by drawing, sculpture, carving, embroidery, etc; to cover or adorn with figures or ornamental designs; to mark with figures; to represent by a typical or figurative resemblance; to typify; to imagine; to image in the mind; (*US colloq*) to believe.—*vi* to make a figure; to be a prominent figure or personage; to take a part in; to be conspicuous.—**to figure out** to solve.

figurehead *n* the ornamental figure on a ship immediately under the bowsprit; a nominal head or leader.

figure of speech *n* an expression not intended to be taken literally, as a metaphor or simile.

figure skating *n* skating in which prescribed figures are outlined.

figurine *n* a small ornamental figure or piece of statuary; a statuette.

filament *n* a thread; a fibre; a fine thread, of which flesh, nerves, skin, plants, roots, etc, and also some minerals, are composed; the fine wire in an electric bulb that is made incandescent by electric current.

filbert *n* the fruit of a cultivated variety of hazel.

filch *vt* to steal, especially something of little value; to pilfer.

file[1] *n* a container for keeping papers and documents in order for ready reference; a collection of papers arranged for ready reference; (*comput*) a collection of related data under a specified name; a line of people; (*milit*) a line of soldiers, one behind the other.—*vt* (**filed, filing**) to arrange or place in a file; to put on record; to bring before a court by presenting the proper papers (*to file a bill in chancery*).—*vi* to march in file as soldiers; to move in a line.

file[2] *n* a steel instrument, having minute teeth on the surface for cutting, abrading and smoothing metal, ivory, wood, etc—*vt* (**filed, filing**) to rub smooth or cut with a file, or as with a file; to polish.

filemot *adj* the colour of a plaid or pattern, of a yellowish-brown hue.

filial *adj* pertaining to a son or daughter; becoming a child in relation to parents; bearing the relation of a child.

filibuster *n* originally, a buccaneer of the West Indies, now applied to any lawless adventurers who invade, with the view of occupying, a foreign country.—*vi* to act as a filibuster; to obstruct business in parlia-

ment by making deliberately long speeches or other delaying tactics.

filical *adj* belonging to the family of ferns.

filigree *n* ornamental open work executed in fine gold or silver wire, formed into flowers and arabesques.

filing *n* a particle rubbed off by a file.

fill *vt* to make full; to cause to be occupied so that no space is left vacant; to put in so as to occupy a space; to occupy the whole space or capacity of; to occupy to a great extent; to pervade; to satisfy; to content; to glut; to press and dilate (a ship's sails); to supply with an occupant or holder; to possess and perform the duties of; to officiate in; to hold or occupy.—*vi* to grow or become full; to make something full.—*n* as much as fills or quite supplies; as much as gives complete satisfaction.

filler *n* a utensil for conveying a liquid into a bottle, cask, etc; something that fills; a substance used to fill holes or cracks; something that increases the bulk of something.

fillet *n* a little band to tie about the hair of the head; a band or narrow strip on various things and for various purposes; a thin boneless strip of meat or fish ready for cooking; (*archit*) a small moulding having the appearance of a narrow band, generally used to separate ornaments and mouldings; also the ridge between the flutes of a column.—*vt* to bind, furnish or adorn with a fillet or little band; to bone and slice (fish or meat).

filling *adj* calculated to fill, satisfy or satiate; (of food, a meat, etc) substantial.—*n* materials used for occupying some vacant space, stopping up a hole, etc; a substance used to fill a tooth cavity; the contents of a pie, tart, sandwich, etc.

fillip *vt* to strike with the fore or middle finger by jerking it away from the ball of the thumb; to strike with a smart stroke.—*n* a jerk of the finger forced suddenly from the thumb; a smart blow or stroke; something which sharply rouses or stimulates; a stimulus.

filly *n* a female or mare foal; a young mare; a young girl.

film *n* a thin skin or membrane; a haze, a mistiness; thin sheeting of plastic-based material used for wrapping; a flexible cellulose material covered with a light-sensitive substance used in photography; a series of images photographed (and recorded in sound) and projected in succession onto a screen to tell a story, present information on a subject, etc; a motion picture; this technique of storytelling, etc, as an art form or industry; the cinema.—*vt* to cover with a thin skin; to photograph or record on film; to make a motion picture of.—*vi* to be or become covered as by a film.

figurine

file

Filofax *n* the trademark of a kind of small, loose-leaf, portable filing system, containing an appointments diary, address book and other information which assists the owner to organize his or her time or business more effectively or efficiently; the trademark of a kind of personal organizer.

filo pastry *n* a kind of very thin, flaky pastry used in sheets and common in Greek and Middle Eastern cookery.

filter *n* a substance or apparatus for straining out solid particles, etc, from a liquid or gas; a device for removing or minimizing electrical oscillations, or sound or light waves, of certain frequencies; a traffic signal that allows vehicles to turn left or right while the main lights are red.—*vt* to purify by passing through a filter.—*vi* to percolate; to pass through a filter.

filtrate *vt* (**filtrated, filtrating**) to filter.—*n* the liquid which has been passed through a filter.

filtration *n* the act or process of filtering.

filth *n* anything that soils or defiles; dirt; foul matter; nastiness; corruption; pollution; obscenity; pornography.

filthiness *n* the state of being filthy; filth; foul matter; impurity.

filthy *adj* dirty; foul; unclean; nasty; morally impure; licentious; obscene; pornographic.

fimbriate, fimbriated *adj* (*bot*) having a fringe or border; having the edge surrounded by fibres, hairs or bristles.

fin *n* one of the projecting wing-like organs which enable fishes to balance themselves in an upright position and assist in regulating their movements; a fin-shaped object used as a stabilizer, as on an aircraft.

final *adj* pertaining to the end or conclusion; last; ultimate; conclusive; decisive; respecting a purpose or ultimate end in view (*a final cause*).

finale *n* (*mus*) the last part of a concerted piece, sonata, symphony or opera; hence, the last part, piece or scene in any public performance or exhibition.

finality *n* the state of being final; (*philos*) the doctrine that nothing exists or was made except for a determinate end.

finals *npl* the last deciding heat in a game; final or last, opposed to entrance, examinations.

finance *n* the system or science of public revenue and expenditure; the management of money; (*pl*) funds in the public treasury or accruing to it; public resources of money; the income or financial resources of individuals; money; capital.—*vi* (**financed, financing**) to conduct financial operations.—*vt* to provide the finance or capital for; to pay for; to raise money for.

financial *adj* pertaining to finance or public revenue; having to do with money matters.

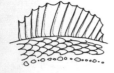

fin

finch

financier *n* one who is skilled in financial matters or in the principles or system of public revenue.

finch *n* the popular name given to any of a large family of small songbirds.

find *vt* (*pret, pp* **found**, *ppr* **finding**) to discover; to gain first sight or knowledge of (something lost); to recover; to get; to meet; to come or light upon; to gain, acquire or procure (leisure, happiness); to supply, provide or furnish (*to find money for a purpose*); to catch; to detect; (*law*) to determine and declare by verdict.—*vi* (*law*) to give judgment on the merits or facts of a case.—*n* a discovery of anything valuable; the thing found.

finder *n* one who or that which finds; (*astron*) a smaller telescope attached to a larger, for the purpose of finding an object more readily.

finding *n* discovery; that which is found; (*law*) the return of a jury to a bill; a verdict.

fine[1] *n* a payment of money imposed on a person as a punishment for an offence.—*vt* (**fined, fining**) to set a fine on by judgment of a court; to punish by fine.

fine[2] *adj* slender; minute; very small; of very small diameter; not coarse; in very small grains or particles; thin; keen; sharp; made of fine threads or material; delicate; pure; of excellent quality; refined; elegant; perceiving or discerning minute beauties or deformities (*fine taste*); handsome; beautiful; accomplished (*a fine gentleman*); elegant; showy; splendid; free from clouds or rain; sunshiny (*fine weather*); affectedly elegant; aiming too much at show or effect.—*vt* (**fined, fining**) to refine; to purify; to free from foreign matter.

fine art *n* one of the arts which depend chiefly on the mind or imagination, generally restricted to the imitative arts which appeal to us through the eye, such as painting and sculpture.

fine-drawn *adj* drawn out to too great a degree of fineness; drawn out with too much subtlety.

fineness *n* the state or quality of being fine; the quantity of pure metal in an alloy.

finery *n* fineness; ornament; showy or excessive decoration; elaborate clothes; the forge in ironworks at which the iron is hammered into what is called a bloom or square bar.

fine-spoken *adj* using fine phrases.

finespun *adj* drawn to a fine thread; minute; hence, over-refined; over-elaborate; subtle.

finesse *n* artifice; stratagem; subtlety of contrivance to gain a point.—*vi* (**finessed, finessing**) to use finesse.

finger *n* one of the five extreme members of the hand or any of them but the thumb; a digit; something resembling or serving the purpose of a finger.—*vt* to touch with the fingers; to handle; to toy or meddle with; to apply the fingers to in order to produce musical effects.—*vi* to use the fingers in playing on an instrument; (*sl*) to inform against.

fingerboard *n* the board at the neck of a violin, guitar, etc, where the fingers act on the strings; also the whole range of keys of a piano, organ, etc; a keyboard.

finger bowl *n* a bowl in which to rinse the fingers at dinner after eating food usually eaten with the fingers.

fingerhole *n* a hole in a wind instrument covered by a finger to modify the pitch.

fingering *n* the act of touching lightly or handling; (*mus*) the management of the fingers in playing a musical instrument; the marking of the notes of a piece of music to guide the fingers in playing; a thick loose worsted used for knitting stockings.

fingerplate *n* a plate fixed on the edge of a door where the handle is.

fingerpost *n* a post set up to guide travellers, generally where roads cross or divide.

fingerprint *n* an impression made by fingers, often serving to identify the person; the pattern formed by the tiny ridges on the tips of the fingers.—*vt* to take an impression of a person's fingerprints for purposes of identification.

finger stall *n* a cover of leather, etc, for protecting an injured finger.

finial *n* the ornamental termination of a pinnacle, canopy, gable, etc.

finical *adj* over-particular; fastidious; fussy; pernickety.

finis *n* an end; conclusion (often placed at the end of a book, film, etc).

finish *vt* to bring to an end; to make an end of; to arrive at the end of; to bestow the last required work on; to put a final coating or surface on; to perfect; to polish to a high degree; to elaborate carefully.—*vi* to come to an end; to terminate; to expire.—*n* the last touch to a work; polish; surface or coating; careful elaboration; sophistication.

finished *adj* polished to the highest degree of excellence; complete; perfect; provided with a particular surface treatment; destroyed; ruined.

finite *adj* having a limit; limited; bounded; opposed to *infinite*; (*gram*) a term applied to those moods of a verb which are limited by number and person, as the indicative, subjunctive and imperative.

Finn *n* a native of Finland or person of the same race.

Finnish *adj* relating to the Finns or Finland.—*n* the language spoken by the Finns.

finnan haddock *n* a split and cured haddock.

Finsen light *n* a powerful arc lamp used in treatment of skin diseases.

fiord *n* same as **fjord**.

fir *n* a kind of evergreen cone-bearing tree with short needle-like leaves.

fire *n* the flame, heat and light produced by burning; fuel in burning; the burning of a house, town, forest, etc; a conflagration; the discharge of a number of firearms; light; lustre; splendour; ardour of passion, whether of love, hate, anger, etc; consuming violence of temper; liveliness of imagination; vigour of fancy; animation; vivacity; force of sentiment or expression.—*vt* (**fired, firing**) to set on fire; to kindle; to inflame or irritate; to animate; to give life or spirit to; to cause to explode; to discharge (a gun, a shot); (*colloq*) to dismiss from a job.—*vi* to take fire; to be irritated or inflamed with passion; to discharge artillery or firearms.

firearm *n* any of various small arms, such as revolvers or light machine guns.

firebrand *n* a piece of wood kindled; an incendiary; one who inflames factions or causes contention and mischief.

firebrick *n* a brick of clay that will sustain intense heat without fusion.

fire brigade *n* a body of firefighters organized to work in extinguishing fires in particular towns or districts.

fireclay *n* a kind of clay capable of sustaining intense heat and used in making firebricks, gas retorts, crucibles, etc.

firedamp *n* a combustible gas, chiefly methane, found in mines and highly explosive when mixed with air.

fire-eater *n* a juggler who pretends to eat fire.

fire engine *n* an engine, acting on the force-pump principle, for throwing jets of water to extinguish fire and save buildings; a vehicle equipped for extinguishing fires.

fire escape *n* an exit, such as an outside staircase, for escaping from the upper storeys of a building when on fire.

firefighter *n* a person whose job is the putting out of fires and the rescuing of people involved in the fire.

firefighting *n* the job of a firefighter; the act of dealing with events as they arise rather than in practising long-term planning.

firefly *n* a name for any winged insect which possesses much luminosity.

fire hydrant *n* an outlet for drawing water from the pipes in the street to extinguish fire.

fire irons *npl* poker, tongs and shovel.

fireman *n* (*pl* **firemen**) a man whose business is to extinguish fires; a member of a fire brigade; a man employed in tending fires, as of a steam engine; the assistant driver of a railway locomotive.

fireplace *n* the lower part of a chimney

fingerboard

fingerprint

which opens into a room and in which fuel is burned; a hearth.

fireproof *adj* proof against fire; designed or constructed so as to resist fire.—*vt* to make fireproof.

fire raising *n* the name given in Scotland to the crime of arson.

fire ship *n* a vessel filled with combustibles to be set on fire for burning an enemy's ships.

fireside *n* the side of the fireplace; the hearth (often used adjectivally).

firewood *n* wood for fuel.

firework *n* (usually *pl*) any explosive device used to produce a bright light and sometimes a loud noise, often used to make a display; (*pl*) an outburst of anger, bad temper, etc.

fire worship *n* the worship of fire, the highest type being the adoration of the sun.

firing line *n* the point at which troops are close enough to the enemy to fire on them; the front line of a military position; the forefront of any area of activity; in a position of exposure to fierce criticism.

firkin *n* an old measure of capacity; a small wooden vessel or cask.

firm *adj* closely compressed; compact; hard; solid; fixed; steady; constant; stable; unshaken in purpose or will; resolute in mind; not easily moved; not giving way; definite; fixed.—*n* a partnership or association of two or more persons for carrying on a business; a commercial house; a business organization; the name or title under which a company transacts business.—*vt* to make firm or solid; to solidify.—*vi* to become firm.

firmament *n* the region of the air; the sky or heavens.

firmness *n* the state or quality of being firm; compactness; solidity; stability; steadfastness; resolution; definiteness.

first *adj* the ordinal of one; preceding all others in a series; advanced before or further than any other in progression; foremost in place; preceding all others in time, rank, dignity or excellence.—*adv* before all others in place, progression, rank, order of time, etc.

first-foot *n* in Scotland, the person who first enters a dwelling house after the coming in of the New Year.—*vt* to pay the first visit in the New Year.

first fruit, first fruits *n, npl* the fruit or produce first matured and collected in any season; the first profits of anything; the first or earliest effect of anything, in a good or bad sense.

first-hand *adj* obtained direct from the first source; obtained direct from the producer, maker, etc.

first-rate *adj* of the first class or rate; of the highest excellence.

firework

fist

fiscal *adj* pertaining to the public treasury or revenue.—*n* (*colloq*) in Scotland, an abbreviation of procurator fiscal.

fish *n* (*pl* **fishes, fish**) a vertebrate animal that lives in water, breathes by gills and has cold blood, with limbs in the form of fins; popularly applied also to whales and various other marine animals; a contemptuous or familiar term for a person (in such phrases as *a strange fish; a cold fish*); the flesh of fish used as food; (*naut*) a purchase used to raise the flukes of an anchor up to the gunwale.—*vi* to employ oneself in catching fish; to endeavour to take fish by a rod and line or other means; to seek to obtain by indirect methods (*to fish for compliments*).—*vt* to catch or attempt to catch fish; to draw out or up, especially when in water; to remove; to pull out; to search for.

fisher *n* one who fishes; one employed in catching fish.

fisherman *n* (pl **fishermen**) one whose occupation is to catch fish; an angler.

fishery *n* the business of catching fish; a place where fish are regularly caught, or other products of the sea or rivers are taken from the water; a place where fish are bred, hatched and reared.

fish-hook *n* a hook for catching fish.

fishing *n* the art or practice of catching fish.

fishing rod *n* a long slender rod to which a line is fastened for angling.

fishmonger *n* a seller of fish; a dealer in fish.

fishwife, fishwoman *n* (*pl* **fishwives, fishwomen**) a woman who hawks or retails fish; a coarse or abusive woman.

fishy *adj* pertaining to fishes; consisting of fish; having the qualities of fish; (*sl*) causing doubt or suspicion.

fissile *adj* capable of being split; capable of undergoing nuclear fission.

fission *n* the act of cleaving, splitting or breaking up into parts; (*biol*) a species of reproduction or multiplication by means of a process of self-division seen in animals of a low type, the body becoming divided into two parts, each of which then becomes a separate and independent individual; the splitting of the atomic nucleus, resulting in the release of energy; nuclear fission.

fissiparism, fissiparity *n* reproduction by fission.

fissiparous *adj* reproducing by fission or spontaneous division.

fissirostral *adj* (of birds) having a deeply cleft beak, as swallows, nightjars, etc.

fissure *n* a cleft; a crack; a narrow chasm made by the parting of any substance; a longitudinal opening.

fist *n* the hand clenched; the hand with the fingers doubled into the palm.

fisticuffs *npl* blows or a fight with the fists.

fistula *n* (*pl* **fistulas, fistulae**) a narrow passage or duct.

fit[1] *adj* conformable to a standard of right, duty, taste or propriety; of suitable kind; meet; becoming; appropriate; adapted to an end, object or design; suitable; qualified; competent; ready; healthy.—*vt* (**fitted, fitting**) to make fit or suitable; to bring into some required form; to adapt; to suit; to furnish or accommodate with anything; to prepare; to put in order for; to qualify; to be properly fitted for or adjusted to; to be the proper size, shape, etc, for; to suit; to become.—*vi* to be proper or becoming; to be adjusted to the shape intended; to have the proper size or shape; to suit or be suitable; to be adapted.—*n* nice adjustment; adaptation.

fit[2] *n* a sudden effort, activity or motion followed by an interval of relaxation; a temporary but violent mental affection or attack; a paroxysm; a temporary attack of a disease or pain; particularly a sudden and violent attack, accompanied with convulsions and loss of consciousness, as in hysteria, apoplexy, etc.

fitchet, fitchew *n* the polecat.

fitful *n* marked by intermittent activity; spasmodic; varied by events.

fitness *n* the state or quality of being fit; suitableness; adaptation; preparation; qualification.

fitter *n* one who fits; one who puts the parts of machinery together; one who specializes in fitting clothes.

fitting *adj* fit or appropriate; suitable; proper.—*n* a trying-on of altered clothes; something fitted on or attached as subsidiary to another thing; a small, often standardized, electrical part; a piece of equipment, as in a kitchen.

five *adj* four and one added; the half of ten.—*n* the number which consists of four and one; the number of the fingers and thumb of one hand; a symbol representing this number, as 5 or V.

fivefold *adj* consisting of five in one; five times repeated; in fives.

fives *n* a ball game so named probably because the ball is struck with the hand or five fingers.

fix *vt* to make stable, firm or fast; to set or place permanently; to establish firmly or immovably; to establish (a date, etc) definitely; to fasten; to attach firmly; to set in order; to repair, to mend; to direct steadily, as the eye, the mind, the attention, etc; to make solid; to congeal; to deprive of volatility; to stop or keep from moving; to prepare (e.g. food, a meal, etc); (*colloq*) to influence (e.g. a jury) by bribery; (*colloq*) to punish; to spay or castrate (an animal).—*vi* to settle or remain permanently;

to cease from wandering; to become firm, so as to resist volatilization; to cease to flow or be fluid; to congeal.—*n* the position of a ship, etc, determined from the bearings of two known positions; (*colloq*) a condition of difficulty, a dilemma; (*colloq*) a situation that has been fixed; (*colloq*) something whose supply becomes continually necessary or greatly desired, as a drug, entertainment, activity, etc.

fixed *adj* settled; established; firm; fast; stable; not volatile; definite; decided.

fixed star *n* an extremely distant star that appears to retain the same position and distance.

fixer *n* a chemical that fixes photographs, making the image permanent; (*sl*) a person who fixes something, especially illegally.

fixity *n* state of being fixed; fixed character; fixedness; stability.

fixture *n* anything placed in a firm or fixed position; that which is fixed to a building; any appendage or part of the furniture of a house which is fixed to it, as by nails, screws, etc; a fixed or appointed time or event, as a *football fixture*.

fizz *vi* to make a sputtering or hissing sound. —*n* this sound; an effervescent drink.

fizz

fizzle *vi* (**fizzled, fizzling**) to make a hissing sound; (*colloq*) to end feebly (with *out*); to fail, especially after a promising start (with *out*).

fjord, fiord *n* an inlet from the sea, usually long, narrow and very irregularly shaped, such as are common on the coast of Norway.

flabby *adj* soft and yielding to the touch; easily moved or shaken; hanging loose by its own weight; flaccid (said especially of flesh); fat and soft; weak and ineffectual.

flaccid *adj* soft and weak; lax; drooping; hanging down by its own weight; limp.

flag[1] *n* a cloth, usually bearing emblems or figures, borne on a staff and employed to distinguish one party or nationality from another; a standard on which are certain emblems expressive of nationality, party or opinion; a banner.—*vt* (**flagged, flagging**) to decorate with flags; to signal to (as if) with a flag.—**to flag down** to signal to stop.

flag

flag[2] *vi* (**flagged, flagging**) to grow limp; to become weak or listless; to lose strength.

flag[3] *n* a flat stone used for paving.

flag[4] *n* a popular name for many plants with sword-shaped leaves, mostly growing in moist situations; particularly appropriated to a species of iris.

flagellant *n* one who whips himself or herself in religious discipline or for sexual gratification.

flagellate *vt* (**flagellated, flagellating**) to whip; to scourge.

flagellation *n* a flogging; a whipping.

flageolet[1] *n* a small musical wind instrument which is holed and keyed like a flute.

flageolet[2] *n* a type of edible bean

flagitious *adj* deeply criminal; grossly wicked; vicious; abandoned; profligate; heinous; flagrant.

flag officer *n* a general distinguishing title for an admiral of any grade; the commanding officer of a squadron.

flagon *n* a vessel with a narrow mouth, used for holding and conveying water or other liquids.

flagrancy *n* heinousness; enormity.

flagrant *adj* glaring; conspicuous; deliberately obvious; notorious.

flagship *n* the ship that bears the flag officer and his flag; the most important vessel of a shipping line; the chief or leading item of a group or collection.

flagstaff *n* the staff or pole on which a flag is displayed.

flagstone *n* any sandstone that easily splits up into flags; a large flat paving stone.

flail *n* an instrument for thrashing or beating grain from the ear.—*vt* to beat with a flail; to wave (the arms, etc) wildly (usually with *about*).

flair *n* natural ability; talent; aptitude; stylishness.

flamingo

flake *n* a loose filmy or scale-like mass of anything; a scale; a small fleecy or feathery particle, as of snow; a small thin layer chipped from a larger mass of something.—*vi* (**flaked, flaking**) to break or separate in layers; to peel or scale off.

flambeau *n* (*pl* **flambeaux, flambeaus**) a flaming torch.

flamboyant *adj* florid; showy; loud; too highly coloured; courting publicity.

flame *n* a blaze; burning vapour or gas rising from matter in a state of visible combustion; fire in general; heat of passion; passionate excitement or strife; a state of ardour; the passion of love; (*colloq*) a sweetheart, a girlfriend or boyfriend.—*vi* (**flamed, flaming**) to blaze; to send out a flame or blaze; to shine like burning gas or any other luminous body; to break out in violence or passion; to become bright red with embarrassment, etc.

flaming *adj* of a bright red or yellow colour; burning; ardent; very hot; vehement.

flapper

flamingo *n* (*pl* **flamingos, flamingoes**) a web-footed tropical bird, with a long neck and long slender legs and having pink plumage.

flammable *adj* easily set on fire.

flan *n* an open savoury or sweet tart made usually with beaten eggs, cream or other ingredients baked in a pastry case.

flange *n* a projecting edge or rim on any object.

flank *n* the fleshy or muscular part of the side of an animal, between the ribs and the hip; the side of anything, particularly the extreme right or left of an army, brigade, regiment, etc, the outer ships of a fleet, or the place occupied by such forces; any part of a fortified work defending another work by a fire along its face.—*vt* to stand or be at the flank or side of; to place troops so as to command or attack the flank of; to pass round or turn the flank of.

flannel *n* a soft light woollen cloth of loose texture; (*pl*) trousers made of such material; a face cloth; nonsense; insincere talk; flattery.

flannelette *n* a cotton cloth with a soft nap.

flap *n* anything broad and flexible that hangs loose or is attached by one end or side and easily moved; a lappet, a lobe, a skirt or tail of a coat; the motion of anything broad and loose, or a stroke with it; (*colloq*) a panic, a state of agitation.—*vt* (**flapped, flapping**) to beat with or as with a flap; to move, as something broad or flap-like.—*vi* to move as wings, or as something broad or loose; to wave loosely or flutter; to panic.

flapper *n* one who or that which flaps; a young wild duck; a fashionable young woman of the 1920s.

flare *vi* (**flared, flaring**) to waver or flutter in burning; to burn with an unsteady light; to shine out with sudden and unsteady light or splendour; to give out a dazzling light; to burst into emotion, especially anger; to widen out gradually.—*n* a bright unsteady light; a gradually widening shape (as of a skirt, etc); (*pl*) (*colloq*) trousers widening to a very wide cuff.

flash *n* a sudden burst of light; a flood of light instantaneously appearing and disappearing; a gleam; a sudden burst of something regarded as resembling light, as wit, merriment, passion, etc; a short and brilliant burst; momentary brightness or show; the time occupied by a flash of light; an instant; a short item of urgent news or information.—*vi* to break or burst forth with a flash or flame; to give out a flash or gleam; to break forth into some new and dazzling condition; to burst out violently; to come, appear or pass suddenly; to dart (*a thought flashes through the mind*); (of a man) to expose the genitals in public.—*vt* to emit or send forth in a sudden flash or flashes; to convey or send instantaneously or startlingly.—*adj* showy or gaudy; forged; counterfeit (*flash notes*).

flashback *n* an interruption in the continuity of a story, etc, to tell about or show an episode or event that has taken place earlier in the story.

flashpoint *n* temperature at which vapour from oil or gaseous objects ignites; the point at which a situation erupts, or will erupt, into violence.

flashy *adj* showy or gaudy; tawdry; vulgarly ostentatious.

flask *n* a narrow-necked glass bottle; a small flat bottle of glass, metal, etc, for carrying liquids, as brandy, etc; a vacuum flask.

flat *adj* having an even and horizontal, or nearly horizontal, surface, without elevations or depressions, hills or valleys; level without inclination; level with the ground; prostrate; fallen; laid low; vapid; insipid; without interest, point or spirit; dull; absolute; downright (*a flat denial*); (*mus*) below the natural or the true pitch; not sharp or shrill; not acute; (of a tyre) deflated; (of a drink) not fizzy, having lost its fizz; (of a battery) drained of electric current.—*n* a flat surface; a surface without relief or prominences; a level; a plain; a low tract of land; a shoal; a shallow; a sandbank under water; the flat part or side of anything (*the flat of the hand, of a sword*); (*mus*) a mark placed on a line or in a space of the staff which indicates that all notes on the same degree (or their octaves) are lowered a semitone; a storey or floor of a building; a set of rooms on one floor of a building; one of the halves of such stage scenes or parts of scenes as are formed by two equal portions pushed from the sides of the stage and meeting in the centre; a shoe with a flat heel; a deflated tyre.—*vti* (**flatted, flatting**) to flatten.

flatfish *n* one of those fish which have their body of a flattened form, swim on the side and have both eyes on one side, as the flounder, turbot and sole.

flat race *n* a race over level or clear ground, as opposed to a hurdle race or steeplechase.

flatten *vt* to make flat or level; to lay flat; (*mus*) to lower in pitch; to render less acute or sharp.—*vi* to grow or become flat.

flatter *vt* to praise excessively or insincerely, especially to gain advantage or favour for oneself; to display to advantage; to represent as more attractive than is really the case; to encourage by favourable notice or by favourable representations or indications (*to flatter hopes*); to inspire with false hopes.

flattery *n* the act of one who flatters; false or insincere praise; adulation.

flatulence, flatulency *n* the state of being flatulent or affected with an accumulation of gases in the alimentary canal.

flatulent *adj* affected with gases generated in the alimentary canal; generating or apt to generate wind in the stomach; windy.

flaunt *vi* to make an ostentatious display; to move or act ostentatiously; to be glaring or gaudy.—*vt* to display ostentatiously; to display impudently or offensively.

flautist *n* a player on the flute.

flavour *n* the quality of any substance which affects the taste; that quality which gratifies the palate; relish; the quality of a substance which affects the smell; odour; fragrance; a characteristic quality.—*vt* to communicate flavour or some quality of taste or smell to.

flaw *n* a crack; a defect of continuity or cohesion; a gap or fissure; any blemish or imperfection; a defect; a fault; a sudden burst of wind.

flax *n* a wiry, erect-stemmed annual plant, the fibre of which is used for making linen thread and cloth, lace, etc; the fibrous part of the plant when broken and cleaned by scutching and hackling.

flaxen *adj* made of flax; resembling flax; of the colour of flax; fair; pale yellow in colour.

flay *vt* to skin; to strip off the skin of.

flea *n* an insect remarkable for its agility and its very troublesome bite.

fleabite *n* the bite of a flea; a trifling wound or pain; a slight inconvenience; a thing of no moment.

fleam *n* a sharp instrument for opening veins for letting blood; a lancet.

flea market *n* an open-air street market, usually selling second-hand goods.

fleck *n* a spot; a spot of colour; a dapple.—*vt* to spot with colour; to streak or stripe.

fledge *vt* (**fledged, fledging**) to furnish with feathers; to supply with the feathers necessary for flight (chiefly in *pp*).

fledgling *n* a young bird just fledged; a young inexperienced person.

flee *vi* (*pret, pp* **fled**, *ppr* **fleeing**) to hasten or run away, as from danger or evil; to resort to shelter (sometimes apparently transitive, *from* being omitted before the object).

fleece *n* the coat of wool that covers a sheep or that is shorn from a sheep at one time; any covering resembling wool; a fabric with a soft pile of the kind used for lining garments to make them warmer.—*vt* (**fleeced, fleecing**) to remove the fleece of; to strip of money or property; to rob or cheat heartlessly.

fleecy *adj* covered with wool; woolly; lined with a woolly fabric; resembling wool or a fleece.

fleer *vi* (*arch*) to sneer, mock or gibe.—*vt* (*arch*) to mock.

fleet[1] *n* a body or squadron of ships; a number of ships in company, more especially ships of war.

fleet[2] *adj* moving or able to move with rapidity; nimble; light and quick in motion.—*vi* to hasten; to flit, as a light substance.—*vt* to skim over the surface; to pass over rapidly.

fleet-footed *adj* swift of foot; running or able to run with rapidity.

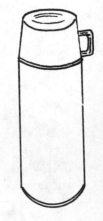

flask

flatfish

fleeting *adj* passing rapidly; transient; not durable (*the fleeting moments*).

fleetness *n* the quality of being fleet; swiftness; rapidity; velocity; celerity; speed.

Flemish *adj* pertaining to Flanders.—*n* the language of the Flemings, closely akin to Dutch; (*pl*) the people of Flanders.

flense *vt* (**flensed, flensing**) to cut up and obtain the blubber of (a whale).

flesh *n* the substance which forms a large part of an animal, consisting of the softer solids, as distinguished from the bones, the skin and the fluids; animal food, in distinction from vegetable; beasts and birds used as food, in distinction from fish; the body, as distinguished from the soul; the bodily frame; the human race; mankind; human nature; bodily appetite; kindred; family; the soft pulpy substance of fruit; also that part of a root, fruit, etc, which is fit to be eaten; the colour of flesh, a yellowish-pink colour.—*vt* to initiate to the taste of flesh (as dogs used in hunting).

fleshly *adj* pertaining to the flesh; corporeal; carnal; worldly; lascivious; human; not celestial; not spiritual or divine.

flesh wound *n* a superficial wound, a wound which does not reach beyond the flesh.

fleshy *adj* characterized by or consisting of flesh; full of flesh; plump; fat; corpulent; corporeal; human; pulpy, as fruit.

fleur-de-lis *n* (*pl* **fleurs-de-lis**) a heraldic figure representing either a lily or the head of a lance or some such weapon; the distinctive bearing of the kingdom of France; (*bot*) the iris.

fleur-de-lis

flexible *adj* capable of being flexed or bent; pliant; yielding to pressure; not stiff; capable of yielding to entreaties, arguments or other moral force; manageable; tractable; easy and compliant; capable of being moulded into different forms or styles; plastic; capable of being adapted or accommodated.

flexitime, flextime *n* a system of working by which employees can arrange their times of arrival and departure to suit themselves as long as they work a set number of hours per week or month.

flick *n* a sharp sudden stroke, as with a whip; a flip; (*colloq*) a film.—*vt* to strike with a flick; to flip.

flicker *vi* to fluctuate or waver, as a flame in a current of air or about to expire; to burn or shine unsteadily.—*n* a wavering or fluctuating gleam, as of a candle; a brief, unsteady movement, as of a flame.

flier, flyer *n* one that flies; something that moves very fast; one who flies; a fugitive; a part of a machine which by moving rapidly equalizes and regulates the motion of the whole; a pilot.

flight *n* the act of fleeing; hasty or precipi-

flipper

tate departure; the act or power of flying; the manner or mode of flying; a journey made by air; a flock of birds flying in company; the birds produced in the same season; a number of things flying together; a discharge; a volley; a shower, as of arrows; a mounting or soaring; an extravagant excursion or sally, as of the imagination; the series of steps from one platform or landing to another (*flight of stairs*).

flightless *adj* of birds, incapable of flight.

flight lieutenant *n* rank in the Royal Air Force, equivalent to captain in the army.

flighty *adj* indulging in flights or sallies of imagination, humour, caprice, etc; frivolous; fickle.

flimsy *adj* without strength or solid substance; of loose and insubstantial structure; without reason or plausibility.—*n* a thin sort of paper.

flinch *vi* to draw back from pain or danger; to show signs of yielding or of suffering; to shrink; to wince.

fling *vt* (**flung, flinging**) to cast, send or throw; to hurl; to send or shed forth; to emit; to scatter; to throw to the ground; to prostrate.—*vi* to flounce; to start away with a sudden motion, as in token of displeasure; to rush away angrily.—*n* a throw; a gibe; a severe or contemptuous remark; enjoyment of pleasure to the full extent of one's opportunities, a spree; (*colloq*) a love affair; a Scottish dance, the Highland fling.

flint *n* a species of quartz, of a yellowish or bluish-grey or greyish-black colour, very hard and used to form an ingredient in fine pottery; a piece of flint used to strike fire with steel or in a flintlock.

flint glass *n* a species of glass, of which flint was formerly an ingredient, now made with quartz and fine sand and used for tableware, etc.

flintlock *n* a musket lock in which fire is produced by a flint striking the steel pan.

flinty *adj* consisting or composed of flint; containing flints; like flints; very hard; cruel; unmerciful.

flip *n* a smart blow, as with a whip; a flick; an alcoholic drink containing beaten egg.—*vt* (**flipped, flipping**) to flick; to toss with a quick jerk; to turn over.—*vi* (*colloq*) to lose one's mind; (*colloq*) to burst into anger; to read quickly and superficially (with *through*).

flippant *adj* speaking fluently and confidently, without knowledge or consideration; heedlessly pert; showing undue levity; frivolous.

flipper *n* the paddle of a sea turtle; the broad fin of a fish; the arm of a seal; a flat rubber shoe expanded into a paddle and used in swimming underwater.

flip side *n* the reverse side of a gramophone

record; the side of a gramophone record that carries the less popular, successful, etc, song or tune; the less attractive, advantageous, well-known, etc, aspect of a person or thing.

flirt *vi* to toy or trifle with (with *with*); to make playful amorous approaches to.—*n* one who flirts; a coquette.

flirtation *n* the act of flirting; coquetry; a light-hearted, often brief, love affair.

flit *vi* (**flitted, flitting**) to fly away with a rapid motion; to move with speed through the air; to move rapidly about; to flutter; to migrate; to move from one dwelling place to another.—*n* the act of flitting; a removal.

flitch *n* the side of a hog salted and cured.

float *vi* to rest or glide on the surface of a fluid; to swim or be buoyed up; to move as if supported by a fluid; to move gently and easily through the air.—*vt* to cause to float; to cause to rest or be conveyed on the surface of a fluid; to flood; to inundate; to overflow.—*n* that which floats on the surface of a fluid; a collection of timber fastened together and floated down a stream; a raft; a buoy; the cork or quill on an angling line, to support it and indicate the bite of a fish; a large trailer; a low cart or platform drawn in processions; a small sum of money available for cash expenditures or from which to give change for first sales.

floating *adj* resting on and buoyed up by a fluid; circulating; available for use; not fixed or invested (*floating capital*; *floating debt*); disconnected; unattached (*floating ribs in fishes*); fluctuating; unsettled (*a floating population*).

flocculent *adj* coalescing and adhering in locks or flakes.

flock[1] *n* a company or collection of living creatures (especially applied to birds and sheep); a Christian congregation in relation to their minister or priest, who takes charge of them in spiritual things.—*vi* to gather in flocks or crowds.

flock[2] *n* a lock of wool or hair; the refuse of cotton and wool, or shreds of woollen goods, used for stuffing mattresses, etc.

floe *n* a large mass of ice floating in the ocean.

flog *vt* (**flogged, flogging**) to beat or whip; to chastise with repeated blows.

flood *n* a great flow of water; a body of water rising and overflowing the land; a river; the flowing in of the tide (opposed to *ebb*); a flow or stream of anything fluid; a great quantity; an overflowing; abundance; superabundance.—**the Flood** the deluge in the days of Noah.—*vt* to overflow; to inundate; to cause to be covered with water; to occur or arrive in great quantities.

floodgate *n* a gate to be opened for letting water flow or to be shut to prevent it; a sluice.

floor *n* that part of a building or room on which we walk; a platform; a storey in a building; a suite of rooms on a level.—*vt* to furnish with a floor; to strike or knock down level with the floor.

floor show *n* a form of entertainment, consisting of singing, dancing, comedy acts, etc, performed in a nightclub.

floozy, floosie *n* a disreputable woman; a tart; a loose woman; a vulgar woman; someone's mistress.

flop *vt* (**flopped, flopping**) to plump down suddenly.—*vi* to move in a heavy, clumsy or relaxed way; to fail.—*n* a sudden sinking to the ground; a flopping movement; a failure.

floppy disk see **disk**.

flora *n* a work describing the plants of a certain district or region; a collective term for the plants indigenous to any district, region or period.

floral *adj* containing or belonging to the flower; pertaining to flowers in general; made of flowers.

florescence *n* (*bot*) a bursting into flower; the season when plants expand their flowers; inflorescence.

floret *n* a single small flower in a compact inflorescence.

floribunda rose *n* any of several varieties of hybrid roses producing dense clusters of blooms.

florid *adj* flowery; bright in colour; flushed with red; of a lively red colour; embellished with profuse ornamentation, especially with high-flown or elaborately elegant language.

florin *n* a name given to different coins of gold or silver, of different values and to moneys of account, in different countries; a former British coin, value one-tenth of a pound sterling.

florist *n* a cultivator of flowers; one who deals in flowers.

floss *n* a downy or silky substance in the husks of certain plants; untwisted filaments of the finest silk, etc; any silky thread-like substance; dental floss.

flossy *adj* composed of or resembling floss.

flotilla *n* a little fleet; a fleet of small vessels.

flotsam *n* such a portion of the wreck of a ship and the cargo as continues floating on the surface of the water; rubbish floating on the sea.

flounce[1] *vi* (**flounced, flouncing**) to move or go about with jerks, as if in displeasure or agitation.—*n* a sudden jerking motion of the body.

flounce[2] *n* a strip of cloth sewed horizontally round a frock or gown, with the lower

floppy disk

border loose and spreading.—*vt* to deck with a flounce or flounces.

flounder[1] *vi* to make violent motions with the limbs and body when hampered in some manner; to roll or tumble about; to struggle helplessly or clumsily.

flounder[2] *n* one of the most common of the flatfishes, found in the sea and near the mouths of rivers.

flour *n* the finely ground meal of wheat or of any other grain; the finer part of meal separated by bolting; the fine and soft powder of any substance.—*vt* to convert into flour; to sprinkle with flour.

flourish *vi* to grow luxuriantly; to increase and enlarge; to thrive; to be prosperous; to increase in wealth, comfort, happiness or honour; to prosper; to live at a certain period (said of authors, painters, etc); to use florid language; to make ornamental strokes in writing; to move or be moved in fantastic irregular figures; to play a bold prelude or fanfare.—*vt* to adorn with flowers or beautiful figures; to ornament with anything showy; to give a fair appearance to; to make bold or irregular movements with; to hold in the hand and swing about; to brandish.—*n* an ostentatious embellishment; parade of words and figures; show; a fanciful stroke of the pen; a brandishing; the waving of a weapon or something held in the hand; the decorative notes which a singer or instrumental performer adds to a passage; a trumpet call, fanfare or prelude performed on the approach of a person of distinction (*a flourish of trumpets*); any ostentatious preliminary sayings or doings.

flour mill *n* a mill for grinding and sifting flour.

floury *adj* consisting of or resembling flour; covered with flour.

flout *vt* to mock or insult; to treat with contempt or disrespect; to jeer at; to disobey openly.—*vi* to behave with contempt (often with *at*)—*n* a mock; an insult.

flow *vi* to move along in the manner of liquids; to run like water; to proceed or issue as from a source; to abound; to have or be in abundance; to glide along smoothly, without harshness or roughness; to be smooth or pleasant to the ear; to be easily or smoothly uttered; to hang loose and waving; to rise, as the tide, opposed to *ebb*.—*vt* to cover with water; to overflow.—*n* a stream of water or other fluid; a current; an outflow; the rise of the tide; abundance; copiousness; undisturbed and even movement.

flow chart *n* a diagram representing the sequence of, and relationships between, the different steps or procedures in a complex process, e.g. a manufacturing process.

flower *n* the delicate and gaily coloured pet-

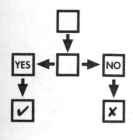

flow chart

als on a plant; a bloom or blossom; (*bot*) a bloom or blossom consisting of, when complete, stamens and pistils together with two sets of leaves which surround and protect them, the calyx and corolla; the early part of life or of manhood; the prime; youthful vigour; youth; the best or finest part; a figure of speech; an ornament of style; (*pl*) a powdery or mealy substance (as *flowers of sulphur*).—*vi* to blossom; to bloom; to flourish.—*vt* to embellish with figures of flowers; to adorn with imitated flowers.

floweret *n* a small flower; a floret.

floweriness *n* the state of being flowery; floridness of speech.

flower show *n* an exhibition of flowers, generally competitive.

flowery *adj* full of flowers; abounding with blossoms; richly embellished with figurative language; florid.

flu a contraction of **influenza**.

fluctuate *vi* (**fluctuated, fluctuating**) to move as a wave; to wave; to float backward and forward, as on waves; to be wavering or unsteady; to be irresolute; to rise and fall; to be in an unsettled state.—*vt* to put into a state of fluctuating or wave-like motion.

fluctuation *n* a motion like that of waves; a moving in this and that direction; a rising and falling; a wavering; unsteadiness.

flue *n* a passage for smoke in a chimney; a pipe or tube for conveying heat, as in certain kinds of steam boilers, etc.

fluency *n* the quality of being fluent; readiness of utterance; volubility.

fluent *adj* flowing; ready in the use of words; having words at command and uttering them with facility and smoothness; voluble; smooth.—*n* (*math*) the variable or flowing quantity in fluxions which is continually increasing or decreasing.

fluff *n* light down or nap such as rises from beds, cotton, etc.

fluffy *adj* containing or resembling fluff; giving off fluff; feathery; soft and downy; soft and light.

fluid *adj* capable of flowing or moving like water; liquid or gaseous.—*n* a fluid body or substance; a body whose particles on the slightest pressure move and change their relative position without separation; a liquid or a gas, opposed to a solid.

fluidity *n* the quality of being fluid; a liquid or gaseous state.

fluke[1] *n* the part of an anchor which catches in the ground; one of the two triangular divisions constituting the tail of a whale; in billiards, an accidental successful stroke; hence, any unexpected or accidental advantage.

fluke[2] *n* a flounder; a species of flattened parasitic worm which infests the ducts of the liver of various animals, especially sheep.

fluke³ *n* a stroke of luck.—*vti* (**fluked, fluking**) to make or score by a fluke.

flukey, fluky *adj* obtained by luck; uncertain.

flummery *n* a sort of jelly made of flour or meal; flour from oats steeped in water till sour and then boiled; flattery; empty compliment; nonsense.

flummox *vt* to bewilder; to confuse; to puzzle; to perplex.

flunky, flunkey *n* (*pl* **flunkies, flunkeys**) a servant in livery; a person who does menial work; a servile person, a toady.

fluorescence *n* the emission of bluish or greenish light by certain substances caused by the invisible rays of the solar spectrum at the violet end.

fluoride *n* any of various compounds of fluorine.

fluorinate *vt* (**fluorinated, fluorinating**) to treat or mix with fluorine.

fluorine *n* a chemical element, a pale greenish-yellow corrosive gas.

fluorspar *n* a mineral sometimes colourless and transparent but more frequently exhibiting tints of yellow, green, blue and red.

flurried *adj* put in agitation; agitated; discomposed; excited.

flurry *n* a sudden blast or gust of wind; a short sudden shower; agitation; commotion; bustle.—*vt* (**flurried, flurrying**) to put in agitation; to excite or alarm.

flush¹ *vi* to flow and spread suddenly, as the blood to the face; to become suffused; to become suddenly red; to blush.—*vt* to cause to blush or redden suddenly; to elate; to excite; to animate with joy; to wash out by drenching with copious supplies of water; sporting, to cause to start up or fly off; to spring.—*n* a sudden flow of blood to the face; the redness so produced; any warm colouring or glow; sudden thrill or shock of feeling; bloom; vigour; a rush or flow of water; a run of cards of the same suit.

flush² *adj* fresh; full of vigour; well supplied with money; having the surface even or level with the adjacent surface.

fluster *vt* to agitate; to confuse.—*n* heat; glow; agitation; confusion of mind.

flute *n* a musical wind instrument consisting of a tapering tube with six holes for the fingers and from one to fourteen keys which open other holes; a perpendicular furrow or channel cut along the shaft of a column or pilaster; any similar groove or channel in any material.—*vi* (**fluted, fluting**) to play on a flute.—*vt* to play or sing in notes resembling those of a flute; to form flutes or channels in.

flutter *vi* to move or flap the wings rapidly, without flying, or with short flights; to

move about with bustle; to move with quick vibrations or undulations; to be in agitation.—*vt* to agitate; to disorder; to throw into confusion.—*n* quick and irregular motion; vibration; agitation of the mind; confusion; disorder; (*colloq*) a betting transaction; fluttering of banknotes.

fluty *adj* soft and clear in tone, like a flute.

fluvial *adj* belonging to rivers; produced by river action; growing or living in freshwater rivers.

flux *n* the act of flowing; a flow; the flow of the tide, in opposition to the ebb; (*med*) an abnormal evacuation from the bowels or other part; that which flows or is discharged; in metallurgy, any substance or mixture used to promote the fusion of metals or minerals; a liquid state from the operation of heat.—*vt* to melt or to fuse; (*med*) to cause a flux or evacuation from; to purge.

fluxion *n* a flux or flowing; (*med*) a flow or determination of blood or other fluid towards any organ with greater force than natural; (*math*) a differential, *fluxions* being an old method of mathematical analysis superseded by differential calculus.

fly *vi* (*pret* **flew**, *pp* **flown**, *ppr* **flying**) to move through the air by the aid of wings; to move through the air by the force of wind or other impulse; to rise in the air, as light substances; to run or pass with swiftness; to depart swiftly; to run away; to flee; to escape; to become diffused or spread rapidly; to pass quickly from mouth to mouth; to burst in pieces; to flutter, vibrate or play, as a flag in the wind.—*vt* to flee from; to shun; to avoid; to cause to fly or float in the air.—*n* a winged insect of various species, whose distinguishing characteristics are that the wings are transparent and have no cases or covers; a hook dressed so as to resemble a fly or other insect used by anglers to catch fish; an arrangement of vanes on a revolving axis or other contrivance to regulate the motion of machinery; a flier; one of the arms that revolve round the bobbin in a spinning frame and twist the yarn as it is wound on the bobbin; a light carriage formed for rapid motion; a hackney coach; a cab; a gallery in a theatre running along the side of the stage at a high level, where the ropes for drawing up parts of the scenes, etc, are worked.

flyblow *n* the egg of a fly.

flyblown *adj* (of meat, etc) contaminated by having had eggs (especially of the blowfly) laid in it.

flycatcher *n* one who or that which catches flies; especially, a name of various perching birds which feed on flies and two species of which are British.

flyer *n* same as **flier**.

flute

fly

fly-fishing *n* the art or practice of angling for fish with flies, natural or artificial.

flying boat *n* a seaplane whose hull forms the support on water.

flying buttress *n* a buttress in the form of an arch springing from a solid mass of masonry and abutting against and serving to support another part of the structure.

flying fish *n* one of those fishes which have the power of sustaining themselves for a time in the air by means of their large pectoral fins.

flying fox *n* a bat found in tropical countries, so named from the resemblance of its head to that of a fox.

flying jib *n* (*naut*) a sail extended outside of the jib, on a boom called the flying-jib boom.

flying officer *n* a rank in the Royal Air Force, equivalent to lieutenant in the army.

flying saucer *n* a disc-shaped and unidentified object which some claim to have seen in the sky, assumed by some to have come from another planet; also called **unidentified flying object** or **UFO**.

flyleaf *n* a blank leaf at the beginning or end of a book, pamphlet, etc.

flypaper *n* a kind of porous paper impregnated with poison for destroying flies.

flysickness *n* a fatal tropical disease of horses, etc, caused by germs introduced by the bite of the tsetse fly.

flytrap *n* a trap to catch or kill flies; an American sensitive plant, the leaves of which close on and capture insects.

flywheel *n* a wheel with a heavy rim placed on the revolving shaft of any machinery put in motion by an irregular or intermitting force, for the purpose of rendering the motion equable and regular by means of its momentum.

f-number *n* (*photog*) a number used to calculate the ratio of light passing through a lens.

foal *n* the young of the horse, pony, donkey, etc, and of either sex; a colt; a filly.—*vt* to bring forth young (said of a mare or a she-ass).—*vi* to bring forth a foal.

foal

foam *n* froth; spume; the aggregation of bubbles which is formed on the surface of liquids by fermentation or violent agitation.—*vi* to gather foam; to froth; to be in a violent rage.—*vt* to cause to foam; to throw out with rage or violence (with *out*).

fob *n* the chain or ribbon for attaching a watch to a waistcoat; any object attached to a watch chain; a small pocket made in a waistcoat or trousers as a receptacle for a watch.

focal *adj* of or pertaining to a focus.

fo'c'sle *n* same as **forecastle**.

focus *n* (*pl* **focuses, foci**) a point of concentration; a central point; a centre of special activity; in optics, a point in which any

folder

number of rays of light meet after being reflected or refracted; (*geom*) a name of two important points on the principal axis of the ellipse.—*vt* to bring to a focus; to adjust to a focus.

fodder *n* food for cattle, horses and sheep, as hay, straw and other kinds of vegetables.—*vt* to feed with fodder.

foe *n* an enemy; one who entertains personal enmity; an enemy in war; a hostile or opposing army; an adversary; one who opposes anything (*a foe to virtue*).

foetal, fetal *adj* pertaining to the foetus.

foetid *adj* same as **fetid**.

foetus, fetus *n* the unborn young of an animal in the womb or in the egg, after it is perfectly formed.

fog *n* a dense watery vapour exhaled from the earth or from rivers and lakes, or generated in the atmosphere near the earth; a state of mental confusion or uncertainty.—*vti* (**fogged, fogging**) to make or become foggy.

fogbank *n* at sea a bank of fog sometimes resembling land at a distance.

fogey, fogy *n* an old-fashioned person.

foggy *adj* filled or abounding with fog; damp with humid vapours; misty; dull; stupid; beclouded.

foghorn *n* a horn to sound as a warning signal in foggy weather.

foible *n* the weak part of a sword, opposed to *forte*; a particular moral weakness; a weak point; a fault of a not very serious character.

foie gras *n* a kind of pâté made from the livers of specially fattened geese.

foil[1] *vt* to frustrate; to defeat; to render vain or unsuccessful, as an effort or attempt; to baffle; to balk.—*n* defeat; frustration; a blunt sword, or one that has a button at the end, used in fencing.

foil[2] *n* a leaf or thin plate of metal; a thin leaf of metal placed under precious stones to improve their appearance; anything of a different character which serves to set off something else to advantage.

foist *vt* to insert surreptitiously or without warrant; to pass off as genuine, true or worthy.

fold[1] *n* the doubling or double of any flexible substance, as cloth; a plait; one part turned or bent and laid on another.—*vt* to lap or lay double; to lay one part over another part of; to lay one over the other, as the hands or arms; to enfold; to embrace.—*vi* to become folded or doubled.

fold[2] *n* a pen or enclosure for sheep or like animals; a flock of sheep; hence, (*Scrip*) the church, the flock of Christ.—*vt* to confine in a fold.

folder *n* a folded piece of cardboard, plastic, etc, for holding loose papers or documents.

foliaceous *adj* leafy; of the nature or form of a leaf; consisting of leaves or thin laminae.

foliage *n* leaves collectively; the leaves of a plant; leaves or leafy growths, represented by sculpture, etc.

foliate *vt* (**foliated, foliating**) to beat into a leaf, thin plate or lamina; to cover with tinfoil, etc.—*adj* (*bot*) leafy; furnished with leaves.

foliation *n* the leafing of plants; the act of beating metal into a thin plate or foil; the operation of spreading foil over a surface; the property in certain rocks of dividing into laminae or plates; (*archit*) the foils, cusps, etc, in the tracery of Gothic windows.

folio *n* (*pl* **folios**) a book of the largest size, formed of sheets of paper once doubled, each sheet thus containing four pages; in bookkeeping, a page, or rather both the right- and left-hand pages, of an account book, expressed by the same figure; (*print*) the number appended to each page; (*law*) a written page of a certain number of words.

folk *n* people in general; a separate class of people; relatives; (*pl*) parents; folk music.

folklore *n* rural superstitions, tales, traditions or legends.

folk music, folk song *n, n* traditional music or song handed down through many generations of people in a particular country or region; music or song of a similar style.

follicle *n* a little bag or vesicle in animals and plants; a dry seed vessel or pod opening on one side only; a vessel distended with air; a gland; a minute secreting cavity.

follow *vt* to go or come after or behind; to move behind in the same direction; to pursue; to chase; to pursue as an object of desire; to go with (a leader); to be led or guided by; to accept as authority; to take as an example; to copy; to come after in order of time, rank or office; to result from, as an effect from a cause or an inference from premises; to keep the attention fixed on while in progress (a speech, piece of music, etc); to understand the meaning, connection or force of; to walk in (a road or course); to practise (a trade or calling).—**to follow suit** in card playing, to play a card of the same suit as that first played; hence, to follow the line of conduct adopted by a predecessor.—*vi* to go or come after another; to be posterior in time; to result, as an effect or an inference.

follower *n* one who follows; an adherent; a disciple; an imitator; a dependant; formerly, a servant girl's sweetheart.

following *n* a body of followers or retainers.— *adj* being next after; succeeding; related, described or explained next after.

follow-on *n* in cricket, a second innings immediately following the first by the side behind by a certain number of runs.

folly *n* weakness of intellect; a weak or foolish act; foolish, weak or light-minded conduct.

foment *vt* to abet (used especially in a bad sense, as *to foment quarrels*); to stir up (trouble); to apply warm lotions to; to bathe with warm medicated liquids or warm water.

fomentation *n* the act of fomenting; instigation; the application of a warm lotion to ease pain or swelling; what is used to foment; a warm lotion.

fond *adj* tender and loving; doting, indulgent; relishing highly; having a liking for (followed by *of*); (*arch*) foolish, indiscreet, imprudent.

fondle *vt* (**fondled, fondling**) to treat with tenderness; to caress.

fondness *n* the state of being fond; great affection or liking.

font[1] *n* the vessel used in churches as the receptacle of the baptismal water.

font[2] *n* a complete assortment of printing types of one size.

fontanel, fontanelle *n* (*anat*) an open space in the infant cranium between the frontal and parietal bones, and also between the parietal and occipital.

food *n* whatever supplies nourishment to organic bodies; nutriment; aliment; victuals; provisions; whatever feeds, sustains or nourishes.

food processor *n* an electric kitchen appliance with various attachments for mixing, blending, chopping, grating, etc.

fool *n* one who lacks reason or the common powers of understanding; an idiot; a person who acts absurdly, irrationally or unwisely; one who does not exercise his or her reason; a professional jester or buffoon.—**to make a fool of** to cause to appear ridiculous.—*vi* to act like a fool.—*vt* to make a fool of; to deceive; to impose on; to cheat.—**to fool around** to act jokingly; to idle one's time away; to meddle with; (*colloq*) to have a sexual affair; (*colloq*) to have an adulterous affair.

foolery *n* folly; the practice of folly; an act of folly; object of folly.

foolhardiness, foolhardihood *n* quality of being foolhardy; mad rashness.

foolhardy *adj* daring without judgment; madly rash and adventurous; foolishly bold.

foolish *adj* characterized by or exhibiting folly; weak in intellect; unwise; silly; vain; trifling; ridiculous.

foolscap *n* a large size of writing paper, 40.6 x 33 cm (16 x 13 inches).

fool's errand *n* an absurd or fruitless search or enterprise.

food processor

fool's paradise *n* illusory happiness.

fool's parsley *n* a poisonous plant resembling parsley.

foot *n* (*pl* **feet**) the lower extremity of an animal's leg; the part of the leg which treads the earth in standing or walking; that surface of the body by which progression is effected among the molluscs; step; tread; footfall; the part of a stocking, boot, etc, which receives the foot; the lower end of anything that supports a body; the part opposite to the head or top; the bottom; soldiers who march and fight on foot; infantry, as distinguished from cavalry; a measure consisting of 12 inches (30.48 cm), taken from the length of a man's foot; (*pros*) a certain number of syllables forming a distinct part of a verse.—**by foot** on foot, by walking.—**to put one's best foot foremost** to adopt all the means at command.—*vi* to dance; to walk, commonly followed by *it*.—*vt* to kick or spurn; to tread; to add or make a foot to (*to foot a stocking* or *boot*).

foot-and-mouth disease *n* a highly contagious disease which attacks the feet and mouths of animals, especially cattle.

football *n* a hollow globe of rubber, cased in leather, to be driven by the foot; a game played with a football by two teams of players, especially soccer.

football

footbridge *n* a bridge for pedestrians.

footcloth *n* a sumpter cloth, or housings of a horse, covering its body and reaching to its heels.

footfall *n* a footstep; tread of the foot.

foothill *n* a hill at the foot of a mountain or of a higher hill (usually in plural).

foothold *n* that on which one may tread or rest securely; firm standing; footing; stable position; settlement.

footing *n* a secure position of or for the feet; established place; foothold; basis; foundation; tread; walk; relative condition; state (*on a footing of equality*).

footlights *npl* a row of lights in a theatre on the front of the stage and serving to light it up.

footman *n* (*pl* **footmen**) a male servant whose duties are to attend the door, the carriage, the table, etc.

footmark *n* a track; mark of a foot.

footstool

footnote *n* a note of reference at the bottom of a page.

footpad *n* a highwayman that robs on foot.

footpath *n* a narrow path for walkers or pedestrians.

foot-pound *n* a British unit of work or energy; the work done in raising one pound weight through a height of one foot against the force of gravity.

footprint *n* the mark of a foot.

foot-race *n* a race performed by men on foot.

foot rot *n* a disease in the feet of sheep.

foot rule *n* a rule of 12 inches long; a rule for taking measurements in feet and inches.

foot soldier *n* a soldier that serves on foot.

footsore *adj* having the feet rendered sore or tender, as by much walking.

footstep *n* the mark or impression of the foot; footprint; tread; footfall; sound of the step.

footstool *n* a stool for the feet when sitting.

footwork *n* skilful use of the feet in boxing, football, dancing, etc; skilful manoeuvring.

fop *n* a vain man of weak understanding and much ostentation; a trifling man; a coxcomb; a dandy.

foppery *n* the characteristics of a fop; showy folly; idle affectation; dandyism.

foppish *adj* pertaining to a fop; vain of dress; dressing in the extreme of fashion; affected in manners.

for *prep* in the place of; instead of (indicating substitution or equivalence); corresponding to; accompanying (*groan for groan*); in the character of; as being (*he took it for truth*); toward; with the intention of going to; with a tendency to (*an inclination for drink*); conducive to; tending towards; in expectation of; with a view to obtain; in order to arrive at, get or procure (*to wait for money, he writes for money*); suitable or proper to; against; with a tendency to resist and destroy (*a remedy for headache*); because of; on account of; by reason of (*for lack of time*); on the part of; in relation to (*easy for you but difficult for me*); in proportion to (*tall for his age*); through a certain space; during a certain time; according to; as far as; so far as concerns; notwithstanding (*it may be so for anything I know*); in favour of; on the part or side of (*to vote for a person*); desirous to have; willing to receive; to take up the part or character of (*nature intended him for a usurer*); having so much laid to one's account; to the amount of (*he failed for ten thousand*).—*conj* for the cause or reason that; because (a word by which a reason is introduced of something before advanced, being really a preposition governing a clause).

forage *n* food of any kind for horses and cattle; the act of searching for provisions.—*vi* (**foraged, foraging**) to collect forage; to roam in search of food or provender; to hunt or search; to rummage about.—*vt* to collect forage from; to supply with forage.

foramen *n* (*pl* **foramina**) a small natural opening or perforation in parts of animals or plants; an opening by which nerves or blood vessels obtain a passage through bones.

foraminiferan, foraminifer *n* any of an order of minute animals belonging to the protozoa, furnished with a shell, simple or complex, usually perforated by pores.

forasmuch as *conj* in consideration that; seeing that; since.

foray *n* a sudden raid; an initial attempt at an endeavour.—*vti* to plunder.

forbear *vi* (*pret* **forbore**, *pp* **forborne**, *ppr* **forbearing**) to cease; to refrain from proceeding; to pause; to delay; to be patient; to restrain oneself from action or violence.—*vt* to avoid voluntarily; to abstain from; to omit; to avoid doing; to treat with indulgence.

forbearance *n* the act of forbearing; restraint of passions; indulgence towards those who injure one; lenity.

forbid *vt* (*pret* **forbade**, *pp* **forbid, forbidden**, *ppr* **forbidding**) to prohibit; to interdict; to command to forbear or not to do; to refuse access; to command not to enter or approach; to oppose; to hinder; to obstruct (*a river forbids approach*).

forbidden *adj* prohibited; interdicted.

forbidden fruit *n* the fruit of the tree of knowledge of good and evil prohibited to Adam and Eve in Paradise; a pleasure that is desirable but forbidden, especially illicit sexual pleasure; the fruit of the shaddock when of small size.

forbidding *adj* repelling approach; repulsive; raising fear, aversion or dislike.

force[1] *n* active power; vigour; might; strength; energy; that which is the source of all the active phenomena occurring in the material world; that which produces or tends to produce change; one of the modes or forms in which energy is exhibited in nature, as heat or electricity; momentum; the quantity of energy or power exerted by a moving body; violence; power exerted against will or consent; moral power to convince the mind; influence; validity; power to bind or hold (*the force of an agreement*); a military or naval armament; a body of troops; an army or navy; a body of men prepared for action in other ways (*a police force*).—*vt* (**forced, forcing**) to compel; to constrain to do or to forbear, by the exertion of a power not resistible; to impel; to press, drive, draw or push by main strength; to compel by strength of evidence (*to force conviction on the mind*); to ravish; to violate (a female); to twist, wrest or overstrain; to assume or compel oneself to give utterance or expression to (*to force a smile*); to ripen or bring to maturity by heat artificially applied.

force[2] *vt* to stuff; to farce.

forced *adj* compulsory; unnaturally assumed; constrained; affected; overstrained; unnatural; (*hortic*) raised outside the normal growing season.

forceful *adj* possessing force; powerful; driven with force; acting with power.

forcemeat *n* in cookery, meat chopped fine and seasoned, either served up alone or used as stuffing, farced meat, by corruption.

forceps *n* a two-bladed instrument on the principle of pincers or tongs for holding anything difficult to be held by the hand (used by surgeons, dentists, jewellers, etc).

forcible *adj* having force; exercising force; powerful; strong; marked by force or violence; violent.

forcing *n* (*hortic*) the art of raising plants, flowers and fruits at an earlier season than the natural one by artificial heat.

ford *n* a place in a river or other water where it may be passed by man or beast on foot or by wading.—*vt* to pass or cross (a stream) by wading; to wade through.

fore *adj* advanced, or, locally, in advance of something, opposed to *hind* or *hinder*; coming first in time, opposed to *after*; anterior; prior; antecedent; in front or towards the face; situated towards the stem of a ship.

forearm[1] *n* that part of the arm which is between the elbow and the wrist.

forearm[2] *vt* to arm or prepare for attack or resistance before the time of need.

forebode *vt* (**foreboded, foreboding**) to bode beforehand; foretell; to presage; to be a sign or warning of; to feel a secret sense of, as of a calamity about to happen.

foreboding *n* a feeling that something evil or disastrous is about to happen; a presentiment.

forecast *vt* (*pret, pp* **forecast**, *ppr* **forecasting**) to cast or scheme beforehand; to plan before execution; to calculate beforehand; to estimate in the future.—*vi* to form a scheme previously; to contrive beforehand.—*n* previous contrivance or determination; foresight; a guess or estimate of what will happen.

forecastle, fo'c'sle *n* a short raised deck in the forepart of a ship; the forepart of a vessel where the sailors live.

foreclose *vt* (**foreclosed, foreclosing**) to preclude; to stop; to prevent.—**to foreclose a mortgage** to compel the mortgagor to pay the money due on it or forfeit his or her right to the estate.

foreclosure *n* the act of foreclosing.

foredeck *n* the forepart of a deck of a ship.

foredoom *vt* to doom beforehand; to predestinate.

forefather *n* an ancestor.

forefend *vt* same as **forfend**.

forefinger *n* the finger next to the thumb; the index.

forefoot *n* (*pl* **forefeet**) one of the anterior feet of a quadruped or multiped.

forefront *n* the foremost part or place.

forceps

forearm

forego *vt* (*pret* **forewent**, *pp* **foregone**, *ppr* **foregoing**) to go before; to precede.

foregoing *adj* preceding; going before, in time or place; antecedent.

foregone *adj* past; preceding; predetermined; made up beforehand.

foregone conclusion *n* an inevitable result; a conclusion which is easily predictable.

foreground *n* the part of a picture which is represented so as to appear nearest the eye of the observer; a prominent position.

forehead *n* the part of the face which extends from the usual line of hair on the top of the head to the eyes; the brow.

foreign *adj* belonging or relating to another nation or country; not of the country in which one resides; alien; extraneous; not our own; remote; not belonging; not connected; irrelevant; not to the purpose (with *to* or *from*).

foreigner *n* a person born in or belonging to a foreign country; an alien.

forejudge *vt* (**forejudged, forejudging**) to judge beforehand or before hearing the facts and proof; to prejudge.

foreknow *vt* (*pret* **foreknew**, *pp* **foreknown**, *ppr* **foreknowing**) to have previous knowledge of; to know beforehand.

foreknowledge *n* knowledge of a thing before it happens; prescience.

foreland *n* a promontory or cape; a headland.

foreleg *n* one of the front or anterior legs, as of an animal, a chair, etc.

forelock *n* the lock or hair that grows from the forepart of the head.—**to take time by the forelock** to make prompt use of anything; to let no opportunity escape.

foreman, forewoman *n* (*pl* **foremen, forewomen**) the first or chief man or woman; the chief man or woman of a jury who acts as their speaker; a chief worker who superintends others.

foremast *n* the mast of a ship or other vessel which is placed before the other or the others.

foremost *adj* first in place, station, honour or dignity; most advanced; first in time.

forenoon *n* the part of the day that comes before noon; the part from morning to midday.

forensic *adj* belonging to courts of justice or to public discussion and debate; used in courts or legal proceedings or in public discussions.

forensic medicine *n* medical jurisprudence, the application of medical knowledge and information to legal proceedings, e.g. murder investigations and trials.

foreordain *vt* to ordain or appoint beforehand; to preordain; to predestinate.

forepart *n* the most advanced part or the first in time or place; the anterior part; the beginning.

forehead

forepeak *n* (*naut*) the part of a vessel in the angle of the bow.

forerunner *n* a messenger sent before to give notice of the approach of others; a harbinger; a sign foreshowing something to follow.

foresail *n* (*naut*) the principal sail set on the foremast.

foresee *vt* (*pret* **foresaw**, *pp* **foreseen**, *ppr* **foreseeing**) to see beforehand; to see or know before it happens; to have prescience of.—*vi* to exercise foresight.

foreshadow *vt* to shadow or typify beforehand.

foreshore *n* the sloping part of a shore between high and low water mark.

foreshorten *vt* in perspective, to represent or depict (as an arm, a branch, directed towards the spectator) with the due impression of length, prominence and relative position.

foreshow *vt* (*pret* **foreshowed**, *pp* **foreshown**, *ppr* **foreshowing**) to show, represent or exhibit beforehand; to prognosticate; to foretell.

foresight *n* the act or power of foreseeing; prescience; foreknowledge; provident care for the future; prudence in guarding against evil; wise forethought; the sight on the muzzle of a gun.

foreskin *n* the fold of skin that covers the anterior extremity of the penis; the prepuce.

forest *n* an extensive wood or a large tract of land covered with trees; a tract of mingled woodland and open uncultivated ground; a district wholly or chiefly devoted to the purposes of the chase; a royal domain kept separate for such purposes and subject to its own laws, courts and officers.—*adj* of or pertaining to a forest; sylvan; rustic.—*vt* to convert into a forest.

forestall *vt* to take too early action regarding; to realize beforehand; to anticipate; to take possession of in advance of something or somebody else; to hinder by preoccupation or prevention.

forester *n* an officer appointed to watch or attend to a forest; one who has the charge of a forest or forests; one whose occupation is to manage the timber on an estate.

forestry *n* the art of forming or of cultivating forests or of managing growing timber.

foretaste *n* a taste beforehand; anticipation; enjoyment in advance.—*vt* (**foretasted, foretasting**) to taste before possession; to have a foretaste of.

foretell *vt* (*pret*, *pp* **foretold**, *ppr* **foretelling**) to tell before happening; to predict; to prophesy; to foretoken or foreshow; to prognosticate.—*vi* to utter prediction or prophecy.

forethought *n* a thinking beforehand; provident care; foresight.

forewarn *vt* to warn beforehand; to give previous notice to.

foreword *n* a preface; an introduction to a book or reprint.

forfeit *vt* to lose the right to by some fault, crime or neglect; to become by misdeed liable to be deprived of (an estate, one's life).—*n* the act of forfeiting; that which is forfeited; a fine; a penalty; a sportive fine or penalty, whence the game of forfeits.—*adj* forfeited or subject to be forfeited; liable to deprivation or penal seizure.

forfeiture *n* the act of forfeiting; the losing of some right, privilege, estate, honour, etc, by an offence, crime, breach of condition or other act; that which is forfeited.

forfend, forefend *vt* to fend off; to avert; to prevent the approach of; to forbid or prohibit.

forgather *vi* to meet; to convene; to come or meet together accidentally.

forge[1] *n* a furnace in which iron or other metal is heated to be hammered into form; a workshop for this purpose; a smithy.—*vt* (**forged, forging**) to work into shape in a forge; to form or shape out in any way; to invent; to produce, as that which is counterfeit or not genuine; to counterfeit, as a signature or document.—*vi* to commit forgery.

forge[2] *vi* (**forged, forging**) (*naut*) to move on slowly and laboriously; to work one's way (usually with *ahead*, *off*, *past*, etc).

forger *n* one who forges; especially, a person guilty of forgery.

forgery *n* the act of forging, fabricating or producing falsely; the crime of counterfeiting a person's signature on a document; that which is forged, fabricated or counterfeited.

forget *vt* (*pret* **forgot**, *pp* **forgot, forgotten**, *ppr* **forgetting**) to lose the remembrance of; to let go from the memory; to cease to have in mind; not to remember or think of; to slight; to neglect; (*refl*) to be guilty of something unbecoming; to commit an oversight.

forgetful *adj* apt to forget; easily losing remembrance; careless; neglectful; inattentive.

forget-me-not *n* a well-known plant, having bright blue flowers with a yellow eye.

forgive *vt* (*pret* **forgave**, *pp* **forgiven**, *ppr* **forgiving**) to give up resentment or claim to requital on account of; to remit, as an offence, debt, fine or penalty; to pardon; to cease to feel resentment against; to free from a claim or the consequences of an injurious act or crime.

forgiveness *n* the act of forgiving; disposition or willingness to forgive.

forgiving *adj* disposed to forgive; inclined to overlook offences; mild; merciful; compassionate.

forgo *vt* (*pret* **forwent**, *pp* **forgone**, *ppr* **forgoing**) to forbear to enjoy or possess; voluntarily to avoid enjoying or possessing; to give up, renounce, resign.

fork *n* an instrument, consisting of a handle with a shank, terminating in two or more parallel prongs, used for holding or lifting something; anything similar in shape; one of the parts into which anything is bifurcated; a prong.—*vi* to divide into forks or branches.—*vt* to raise or pitch with a fork; to dig and break with a fork.

forked *adj* having prongs or divisions like a fork; opening into two or more prongs, points or shoots; furcated.

forlorn *adj* deserted; forsaken; abandoned; lost; helpless; wretched; solitary; bereft; destitute.

forlorn hope *n* a detachment appointed to lead in an assault or perform other dangerous and difficult task; a hope with very little chance of being realized.

form *n* the shape or external appearance of a body, as distinguished from its material; the figure, as defined by lines and angles; appearance to the eye; configuration; a shape; a phantom; manner of arranging particulars; disposition of particular things (*a form of words*); general system or arrangement (*a particular form of government*); something on or after which things are fashioned; a model, draft, pattern; proper shape or trim; high condition or fitness for any undertaking; external appearance without the essential qualities; stated method; established practice; ceremony; a long seat; a bench; a bench or class of pupils in a school; the bed of a hare; (*print*) the pages of type or stereotype plates arranged for printing a sheet and fastened in an iron frame or chase.—*vt* to give form or shape to; to shape; to mould; to arrange; to combine in any particular manner; to model by instruction and discipline; to mould; to train; to devise; to contrive; to frame; to create; to be an element or constituent of; to combine to make up; to answer as; to take the shape of.—*vi* to take a form.

formal *adj* given to outward forms, observances or ceremonies; strictly ceremonious; done or made in due form or according to regular method; acting according to rule or established mode; having the form or appearance without the substance or essence; conventional; ceremonial; punctilious; stiff; not spontaneous.

formalism *n* the quality of being formal or addicted to mere forms; strict observance of outward form or conventional usage, especially in religion.

formality *n* the condition or quality of being formal; form without substance; established order; rule of proceeding; mode;

fork

method; customary ceremony; ceremonial; conventionality; stiffness; lack of spontaneity.

format *n* size of a book as regards length and breadth; the style or presentation of something, e.g. a television programme; (*comput*) the arrangement of data on magnetic disk, etc, for access and storage.—*vt* (**formatted, formatting**) to arrange in a particular form, especially for a computer.

formation *n* the act of forming, making, creating, composing, shaping, etc; production; the manner in which a thing is formed; (*geol*) any series of rocks referred to a common origin or period; (*milit*) an arrangement of troops, as in a square, column, etc.

former *adj compar* before or preceding another in time, opposed to *latter*; ancient; long past (*former ages*); preceding; earlier, as between two things mentioned together; first mentioned.

formerly *adv* in time past, either in time immediately preceding or at an indefinite distance; of old; heretofore.

formic *adj* pertaining to or produced by ants.

formic acid *n* a pungent acid with a peculiar odour and acting as a corrosive on the skin, originally obtained from ants.

formidable *adj* exciting fear or apprehension; adapted to excite fear or deter from approach, encounter or undertaking.

formula *n* (*pl* **formulae, formulas**) a prescribed form; a prescribed form of words in which something is stated; an established procedure; a list of ingredients; a prescribed recipe for baby food; (*math*) a rule or principle expressed in algebraic symbols; (*chem*) an expression by means of symbols and letters of the constituents of a compound; in motor racing, any of the classes into which competing cars are divided.

formulate *vt* (**formulated, formulating**) to reduce to or express in a formula; to put into a precise and comprehensive statement; to state precisely; to devise.

formulize *vt* (**formulized, formulizing**) to reduce to a formula or formulas; to formulate.

fornicate *vi* (**fornicated, fornicating**) to have sexual intercourse with someone to whom one is not married.

fornication *n* sexual intercourse between people who are not married to each other.

forsake *vt* (*pret* **forsook**, *pp* **forsaken**, *ppr* **forsaking**) to quit or leave entirely, often to leave that to which we are bound by duty or natural affection; to desert; to abandon; to depart or withdraw from; to renounce; to reject.

forsooth *adv* in truth; in fact; certainly; very well (often ironic).

forswear *vt* (*pret* **forswore**, *pp* **forsworn**, *ppr* **forswearing**) to reject or renounce on oath; to renounce earnestly or with protestations; (*refl*) to swear falsely; to perjure oneself.—*vi* to swear falsely; to commit perjury.

fort *n* a fortified place; usually, a small fortified place, occupied only by troops.

fortalice *n* a small outwork of a fortification.

forte[1] *n* the strong portion of a sword blade or rapier; a peculiar talent or faculty a person has; a strong point; chief excellence.

forte[2] *adv* (*mus*) direction to sing or play with force of tone.

forth *adv* onward in time, place or order (*from that time forth*); in advance from a given point; forward; out; abroad; from a state of concealment; from an interior; out into view.

forthcoming *adj* ready to appear; making appearance.

forthright *adv* straightforward; straightaway.—*adj* straightforward; direct; immediate.

forthwith *adv* immediately; without delay; directly.

fortieth *adj* following the thirty-ninth; being one of forty equal parts into which anything is divided.—*n* one of forty equal parts into which a whole is divided.

fortification *n* the act of fortifying; the art or science of strengthening military positions in such a way that they may be readily defended; the works constructed for the purpose of strengthening a position; a fortified place; a fort.

fortify *vt* (**fortified, fortifying**) to add strength to; to strengthen (an argument, resolution); to furnish with strength or means of resisting (*to fortify one against cold*); to surround with a wall, ditch, palisades or other works, with a view to defend against the attacks of an enemy; to increase the alcoholic strength of (wine) by means of adventitious spirit.

fortissimo *adv* (*mus*) a direction to sing with the utmost strength or loudness.

fortitude *n* that strength or firmness of mind or soul which enables a person to encounter danger or to bear pain with coolness and courage; passive courage; resolute endurance.

fortnight *n* two weeks.

fortress *n* a fortified place, especially one of considerable extent and complication; a stronghold; a place of security.

fortuitous *adj* accidental; happening by chance; occurring without any known cause.

fortunate *adj* coming by good fortune or favourable chance; bringing some unexpected good; having good fortune; lucky; successful.

fortune *n* chance; accident; luck; fate; also, the personified or deified power regarded as determining the lots of life; the good or ill that befalls or may befall man; success, good or bad; what the future may bring; good success; prosperity; good luck; estate; possessions; especially, large estate; great wealth.

fortune teller *n* one who claims to foresee people's fortunes in life.

forty *adj* four times ten; thirty-nine and one added.—*n* the number which consists of four times ten; or a symbol expressing it, as 40 or XL.

forum *n* (*pl* **forums, fora**) a public place in Rome where causes were judicially tried and orations delivered to the people; a tribunal; a court; an assembly for discussion.

forward *adj* being at the front; anterior; fore; ready; prompt; ardent; eager; over bold; self-assertive; pert; saucy; advanced beyond the usual degree; advanced for the season.—*adv* towards a part or place before or in front; onward; progressively, opposed to *backward*.—*n* one in advance; a front player in football.—*vt* to advance or help onward; to further, promote, accelerate, hasten; to send toward the place of destination; to transmit.

forwards *adv* towards a part or place before or in front; onward; progressively.

fossil *adj* dug out of the earth; petrified and preserved in rocks.—*n* the petrified remains of plants and animals which occur in the strata that compose the surface of our globe; an old-fashioned person or thing.

fossilize *vt* (**fossilized, fossilizing**) to convert into a fossil; (*fig*) to render permanently antiquated; to cause to be out of harmony with present time and circumstances.—*vi* to become a fossil; to become antiquated, rigid and fixed.

foster *vt* to nourish or nurture; to bring up; to cherish; to promote the growth of; to encourage; to sustain and promote; to bring up (a child that is not one's one).

foster child *n* a child nurtured by one who is not its mother or father.

foster father, foster mother *n* one who takes the place of a father or mother in bringing up and educating a child.

foster parent *n* a foster father or foster mother.

foster son, foster daughter *n* one brought up like a son or daughter, though not the person's child by birth.

foul *adj* covered with or containing extraneous matter which is injurious, noxious or offensive; filthy; dirty; not clean; turbid; muddy; scurrilous; profane; abusive; stormy, rainy or tempestuous (*foul weather*); detestable; vile; shameful; odious; unfair; not lawful or according to es-

tablished rules or customs; obscene (*foul language*); (*naut*) entangled or in collision, opposed to clear.—**to fall foul of** to come into accidental contact; to clash with.—*vt* to make filthy; to defile; to dirty; to soil.—**to foul up** to cause to become entangled; to bungle: to ruin.—*vi* to become foul or dirty; (*naut*) to come into collision; to become entangled or clogged.—*n* the act of fouling; a colliding or otherwise impeding due motion or progress; a hit, blow, move, shot, etc, that is against the established rules.

foul-mouthed *n* using foul or vile language; uttering abuse or profane or obscene words.

foumart *n* the polecat.

found[1] *vt* to lay the basis of; to base; to establish on a basis literal or figurative; to take the first steps in erecting or building up; to originate.—*vi* to rest or rely (followed by *on* or *upon*, as *I found upon my own observation*).

found[2] *vt* to form by melting a metal and pouring it into a mould; to cast.

foundation *n* the act of founding, establishing or beginning to build; the masonry or the solid ground on which the walls of a building rest; the basis or groundwork of anything; that on which anything stands and is supported; a fund invested for a benevolent purpose; endowment; an endowed institution or charity.

foundation stone *n* a stone of a public building, laid in public with some ceremony.

founder[1] *n* one who founds; one who casts metals in various forms.

founder[2] *vi* to fill or be filled and sink; to go down (said of a ship); to fail; to miscarry; to go lame (said of a horse); to collapse; to fail.

foundling *n* a child found without a parent or anyone to take care of it.

foundry *n* the art of casting metals; the buildings and works occupied for casting metals.

fount[1] *n* a spring of water; a fountain; a source.

fount[2] *n* ʟame as **font**[2].

fountain *n* a spring or natural source of water; the head or source of a river; an artificial spout, jet or shower of water; a basin or other structure kept constantly supplied with water for use or for ornament; the origin or source of anything.

fountainhead *n* primary source; origin.

fountain pen *n* a writing pen with a reservoir for holding a continuous supply of ink.

four *adj* twice two; three and one.—*n* the number consisting of twice two; the symbol representing this number, as 4 or IV.

fourfold *adj* four times told; quadruple.

four-letter word *n* any of various words

fossil

fountain-pen

considered to be obscene or offensive, typically containing four letters.

fourposter *n* a large bed having four posts or pillars for curtains.

fourscore *adj* four times twenty; eighty (often elliptically for fourscore years).—*n* twenty taken four times; eighty units.

foursome *n* a game of golf between two pairs; a dance or reel of two pairs.

fourteen *n* the number consisting of ten and four, or the symbol representing it, 14 XIV.—*adj* four and ten; twice seven.

fourteenth *adj* the ordinal of fourteen; the fourth after the tenth.—*n* one of fourteen equal parts in which a whole is divided.

fourth *adj* the ordinal of four; the next after the third.—*n* one of four equal parts into which a whole is divided, a quarter; (*mus*) an interval composed of two tones and a semitone.

four-wheel drive *n* a drive mechanism in a motor vehicle connected to all four wheels instead of two.

fowl *n* a bird (often unchanged in the plural, as *the fowl of the air*); now very commonly a cock or hen; a barndoor or domestic fowl.—*vi* to catch or kill wild fowls.

fowler *n* a hunter who pursues wild fowls.

fowling piece *n* a light gun for shooting birds.

fox

fox *n* a carnivorous animal closely allied to the dog, with reddish-brown fur, a pointed muzzle and a bushy tail; a sly, cunning fellow.—*vti* to deceive by cunning; to puzzle; to turn sour (applied to beer when it sours in fermenting).—*vi* (of beer) to turn sour.

foxed *adj* marked with brownish stains or spots, as paper.

foxglove *n* a tall plant with spires of purple or white flowers, the leaves of which are used to produce a heart stimulant.

foxhound *n* a hound for chasing foxes, of great fleetness, strength and perseverance and with a keen scent.

foxhunt *n* the chase or hunting of a fox with hounds.

foxhunter *n* one who hunts or pursues foxes with hounds.

foxhunting *n* the pursuit of the fox.

foxtail grass *n* a name of various grasses having a close cylindrical panicle in which the spikelets of flowers are arranged.

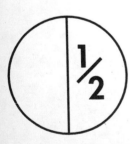
fraction

foxtrot *n* a dance for couples in quadruple time.—*vi* (**foxtrotted, foxtrotting**) to perform the foxtrot.

foxy *adj* pertaining to foxes; wily; suggestive of a fox or of cunning; sour (said of wine, beer, etc, which has soured in fermenting); physically attractive.

foyer *n* a part of the theatre for the use of the public, especially during the intervals; an entrance hallway, as in a theatre or hotel.

fracas *n* an uproar; a noisy quarrel; a disturbance.

fraction *n* the act of breaking; a fragment; a portion; a very small part; (*arith, alg*) one or more of the equal parts into which a unit or whole number is divided or supposed to be divided (as $^2/_5$, two-fifths, $^1/_4$, one-fourth, which are called *vulgar fractions*; .56, .004, *decimal fractions*).

fractional *adj* pertaining to fractions; constituting a fraction.

fractious *adj* apt to quarrel; cross; snappish; peevish; fretful.

fracture *n* a breakage; a breach in a body, especially caused by violence; a crack; a rupture; (*surg*) the breaking of a bone; (*mineral*) the characteristic manner in which a mineral breaks and by which its texture is displayed.—*vt* (**fractured, fracturing**) to cause fracture in; to break; to crack.

fragile *adj* brittle; easily broken; easily destroyed; frail.

fragility *n* the condition or quality of being fragile; brittleness; delicacy of substance.

fragment *n* a part broken off; a piece separated from anything by breaking; anything left uncompleted; a part separated from the rest.

fragmentary *adj* composed of fragments or broken pieces; broken up; not complete or entire; disconnected.

fragrance *n* the quality of being fragrant; sweetness of smell; pleasing scent; perfume.

fragrant *adj* sweet of smell; affecting the olfactory nerves agreeably; having an agreeable perfume; odoriferous.

frail[1] *adj* easily broken; fragile; liable to fail and decay; easily destroyed; perishable; not firm or durable; not strong against temptation; liable to fall from virtue.

frail[2] *n* a basket made of rushes.

frailty *n* the condition or quality of being frail; weakness of resolution; infirmity; liableness to be deceived or seduced; a fault proceeding from weakness; a foible.

framboesia *n* the yaws, an infectious tropical disease causing red skin eruptions and joint pain.

frame *vt* (**framed, framing**) to construct by fitting and uniting together the several parts; to make, compose, contrive, devise, invent, fabricate; (*sl*) to falsify evidence against (an innocent person); to fit, as for a specific end; to adjust, shape, conform; to surround or provide with a frame, as a picture.—*n* anything composed of parts fitted and united; fabric; structure; specifically, bodily structure; make or build of a person; the main timbers of a structure fitted and joined together for supporting and strengthening the whole; framework; some kind of case or structure for admitting, enclosing or supporting; particular state, as of the mind; temper or disposition.

350

frame house *n* a house constructed with a wooden skeleton.

frame-up *n* a plot; an underhand arranged scheme, especially one which is intended to make innocent persons appear guilty.

framework *n* a structure or fabric for supporting anything; a frame; fabric; structure.

franc *n* a French silver coin and money of account divided into 100 centimes.

franchise *n* a particular privilege or right granted by a sovereign or government; the right of voting for a parliamentary or other representative; authorization to sell the goods of a manufacturer in a particular area.—*vt* (**franchised, franchising**) to authorize a franchise.

Franciscan *n* a mendicant friar of the order founded by St Francis of Assisi about 1210.

francolin *n* a bird closely allied to the partridges.

frangible *adj* capable of being broken; brittle.

frangipani *n* a flowering tree that grows in tropical countries, the flowers of which are used to make a perfume.

frank *adj* free in uttering real sentiments; not reserved; open; candid; ingenuous; using no disguise; generous or liberal.—*n* a mark denoting that postage is free or has been paid; formerly, the signature of a Member of Parliament or other privileged person securing transmission of a letter free of postage.—*vt* to stamp or mark (a letter, etc) with a frank; to send by means of a frank; to transmit free of expense.

Frank *n* one of the ancient German race of the Franks; a native of Franconia.

frankincense *n* a gum resin obtained from a tree somewhat resembling the sumac, found in the mountains of India, which, when burned, emits a strong aromatic odour.

franklin *n* a freeholder; a yeoman; one whose estate was free of any feudal superior.

frantic *adj* mad; raving; furious; outrageous; distracted (*a frantic person*); characterized by violence, fury and disorder (*a frantic outburst*).

fraternal *adj* brotherly; pertaining to brothers; becoming or proceeding from brothers.

fraternity *n* the state or relationship of a brother; a body of men associated for their common interest, business or pleasure; a brotherhood; a society; a class or profession of men.

fraternize *vi* (**fraternized, fraternizing**) to associate with in a friendly way.

fratricide *n* the crime of murdering a brother; one who murders or kills a brother.

Frau *n* German married woman or widow; a title equivalent to Mrs and often applied also to unmarried women.

fraud *n* an act or course of deception deliberately practised with the view of gaining an unlawful or unfair advantage; deceit; deception; imposition.

fraudulence *n* the quality of being fraudulent.

fraudulent *adj* using fraud in making bargains, contracts, etc; given to using fraud; founded on fraud; proceeding from fraud; obtained by fraud.

fraught *adj* freighted; (*fig*) filled, stored, charged, abounding (*a scheme fraught with mischief*).

Fräulein *n* German unmarried woman; title equivalent to Miss.

fray[1] *vt* to rub; to rub away the surface of; to fret, as cloth by wearing or the skin by friction.

fray[2] *n* an affray; a broil, quarrel or violent riot.

freak *n* an unusual happening; any abnormal person, animal, etc; a deviation from the norm; an eccentric, unconventional person; (*colloq*) an enthusiast.

freakish *adj* very unusual; abnormal; changing suddenly; eccentric.

freckle *n* a spot of a brownish colour in the skin, particularly on the face, neck and hands; any small spot or discoloration.—*vti* (**freckled, freckling**) to mark or become marked with freckles.

free *adj* not being under necessity or restraint, physical or moral; exempt from subjection to the will of others; being at liberty; not in confinement; not under an arbitrary or despotic government; instituted by a free people; capable of being used, enjoyed or taken advantage of without charge; unrestricted; open; not obstructed; going beyond due limits in speaking or acting; candid; frank; without care; unconcerned; liberal; not parsimonious; profuse; gratuitous; given with readiness or goodwill; clear; exempt; having got rid; not encumbered, affected or oppressed (with *from* and sometimes *of*); invested with or enjoying certain immunities; having certain privileges (with *of*, as *a man free of the city of London*).—**to make free with** to intermeddle with; to take liberties with; to help oneself to.—*vt* (**freed, freeing**) to remove from a thing any encumbrance or obstruction; to disentangle; to disengage; to rid; to strip; to clear; to set at liberty; to rescue or release from slavery, captivity or confinement; to manumit; to loose; to exempt, as from some oppressive condition or duty; to clear from stain; to absolve from some charge.

freebie *n* (*colloq*) something that would normally be charged for given free, as a

framework

freckle

gift, holiday etc, given in the interests of advertising or promotion.

freeboard *n* (*naut*) the part of a ship's side between the gunwale and the line of flotation.

freebooter *n* one who wanders about for booty or plunder; a robber; a plunderer.

freeborn *adj* born free; not in vassalage; inheriting liberty.

freedman *n* (*pl* **freedmen**) a man who has been a slave and is manumitted.

freedom *n* the state of being free; exemption from slavery, servitude, confinement or constraint; liberty; independence; frankness; openness; outspokenness; unrestrictedness; permission; liberality; particular privileges (*the freedom of a city*); ease or facility of doing anything; licence; improper familiarity (in this sense with a plural).

free enterprise *n* private business or commerce in which competition is allowed to occur freely with no or little intervention or control from the government.

freehand *adj* applied to a drawing in which the hand is not assisted by any guiding or measuring instruments.

French horn

free-handed *adj* open-handed; liberal.

freehold *n* (*law*) an estate in real property, held either in fee simple or fee tail, or for life; an estate for which the owner owes no duty or service except to the crown; the tenure by which such an estate is held.

freelance *n* one of the mercenary soldiers of the middle ages; one unattached to any party; a journalist who is not attached to any particular paper; a person who pursues a profession without long-term commitment to any employer; a self-employed person.

free love *n* sexual intercourse without the restraints of marriage.

freeman *n* (*pl* **freemen**) a man who is free; one not a slave or vassal; one who enjoys or is entitled to a franchise or peculiar privilege.

freemartin *n* a cow calf twin born with a bull calf, generally barren.

Freemason *n* a person belonging to the society or organization of Freemasons which promotes mutual assistance and brotherly love among members.

free pass *n* a permission to pass free, as by railway, etc.

free-range *adj* of hens, allowed to roam freely, not confined to a battery; of eggs, produced by hens reared in this way.

freestone *n* any species of stone composed of sand or grit, so called because it is easily cut or wrought.

freethinker *n* a person who remains independent of or unaffected by tradition, authority, etc, in matters such as religion; a deist; an unbeliever; a sceptic.

free trade *n* trade or commerce free from restrictions and in particular from customs duties levied on foreign commodities.

free trader *n* an advocate of free trade.

free will *n* the power of directing our own actions without constraint by necessity or fate; voluntariness; spontaneousness.— *adj* voluntary; spontaneous.

freeze *vi* (*pret* **froze**, *pp* **frozen** *or* **froze**, *ppr* **freezing**) to be congealed by cold; to be changed from a liquid to a solid state by the abstraction of heat; to be hardened into ice; to be of that degree of cold at which water congeals (used impersonally, as *it freezes hard*); to become chilled in body with cold; to become blocked or ineffective due to frost, ice, etc.—*vt* to congeal or cause to freeze; to harden into ice; to chill; to give the sensation of cold and shivering.

freezing point *n* that degree of a thermometer at which a liquid begins to freeze; the temperature at which ordinarily water freezes (by the Celsius or centigrade thermometer the freezing point of water is 0° or zero; by Fahrenheit's thermometer 32° above zero).

freight *n* the cargo of a ship; lading; that which is carried by water; goods that are transported, as by train; the price paid for the use of a ship or part of a ship to transport goods; the sum charged or paid for the transportation of goods.—*vt* to load (a ship) with goods; to hire for the transportation of goods.

freightage *n* the act or process of freighting; money paid for freight.

French *adj* pertaining to France or its inhabitants.—*n* the language spoken by the people of France; collectively the French people.

French bean *n* a species of bean; the kidney bean.

French chalk *n* a variety of talc resembling chalk, of a pearly white or greyish colour.

French fries *npl* thin strips of potato deep-fried in fat or oil; chips; chipped potatoes.

French horn *n* a musical instrument of brass having several curves and gradually widening from the mouthpiece to the other end.

French letter *n* (*colloq*) a condom.

Frenchman, Frenchwoman *n* (*pl* **Frenchmen, Frenchwomen**) a person of the French nation; a native or naturalized inhabitant of France.

French polish *n* a shellac varnish used for coating wood with a fine glossy surface.

frenetic *adj* frantic; frenzied.

frenzy *n* distraction; delirium; madness; any violent agitation of the mind approaching to distraction or temporary derangement of the mental faculties.

frequency *n* the state of being frequent; a frequent return or occurrence; the condition of being often repeated at short intervals; (*physics*) in any form of periodic change, the number of complete periods which take place per second.

frequency modulation *n* the transmission of signals by radio waves the frequency of which varies according to the amplitude of the signal.

frequent *adj* often seen or done; often happening at short intervals; often repeated or occurring; doing a thing often; inclined to indulge in any practice.—*vt* to visit often; to resort to often or habitually.

frequently *adv* often; many times, at short intervals; repeatedly; commonly.

fresco *n* (*pl* **frescoes, frescos**) a method of painting on walls with mineral and earthy pigments on fresh plaster or on a wall laid with mortar not yet dry; a painting so made.—*vt* (**frescoed, frescoing**) to paint in fresco, as walls.

fresh *adj* full of health and strength; vigorous; strong; brisk; lively; bright; not faded; undecayed; unimpaired by time; in good condition; not stale; not exhausted with labour or exertion; renewed in strength; reinvigorated; refreshing; healthgiving (applied to pure cool water and also to a rather strong wind); vivid; clearly remembered; new; recently grown, made or obtained; not salt or salted; impertinent.— *n* a freshet; a spring of fresh water; a flood; an overflowing; an inundation.

freshen *vt* to make fresh; to give a fresh appearance or character to; to make to feel fresh; to refresh; to revive.—*vi* to grow fresh; to grow strong (*the wind freshens*).

freshet *n* a small stream of fresh water; a flood or overflowing of a river, by means of heavy rains or melted snow.

freshman *n* (*pl* **freshmen**) a novice; a student of the first year in a university.

freshwater *adj* pertaining to, produced by or living in water that is fresh or not salt.

fret[1] *vt* (**fretted, fretting**) to gnaw; to eat into; to rub or wear away; to fray; to chafe; to gall; to wear away so as to diminish; to impair; to agitate; to disturb (*to fret the surface of the sea*); (*fig*) to chafe the mind of; to irritate; to tease; to make angry.—*vi* to become frayed or chafed; to be chafed or irritated; to become vexed or angry; to utter peevish expressions; to boil or work as angry feelings; to rankle.—*n* a state of chafing or irritation; vexation; anger.

fret[2] *n* a kind of ornament formed of bands or fillets variously combined but most frequently arranged in rectangular forms; a piece of perforated ornamental work; one of the small cross bars or ridges on the fingerboards of some stringed instruments to regulate the pitch of the notes.—*vt* (**fretted, fretting**) to ornament or furnish with frets; to variegate; to diversify.

fretful *adj* disposed to fret; ill-humoured; peevish; in a state of vexation.

fret saw *n* a small saw for cutting fretwork.

fretwork *n* ornamental work consisting of a series or combination of frets; designs cut through a thin plate of wood.

Freudian *adj* of the theories of Sigmund Freud, Austrian neurologist, on hysteria, dreams and psychoanalysis.

Freudian slip *n* a slip of the tongue said to betray an unconscious feeling.

friable *adj* easily crumbled or pulverized; easily reduced to powder.

friar *n* a person belonging to one of the Roman Catholic mendicant religious orders or brotherhoods—Dominicans, Franciscans, Carmelites, Augustines, etc; a monk.

fricassee *n* a dish of food made by cutting meat or poultry into pieces and dressing them with a strong sauce in a frying pan or a like utensil.—*vt* (**fricasseed, fricasseeing**) to dress in fricassee.

friction *n* the act of rubbing the surface of one body against that of another; attrition; (*mech*) the effect of rubbing or the resistance which a moving body meets with from the surface on which it moves; conflict.

frictional *adj* relating to friction; moved by friction; produced by friction.

Friday *n* the sixth day of the week.

fridge *n* a refrigerator.

friend *n* one who is attached to another by affection; one who has esteem and regard for another and loves his or her society; one not hostile; one of the same nation, party or kin; one who looks with favour on a cause, institution, etc; also a term of salutation or familiar address; boyfriend, girlfriend, partner.

Friend *n* a Quaker, a member of the Society of Friends.

friendliness *n* the condition or quality of being friendly; a disposition to favour or befriend; goodwill; exercise of benevolence or kindness.

friendly *adj* having the temper and disposition of a friend; disposed to promote the good of another; kind; amicable; befitting friends; not hostile; favourable; propitious.

-friendly *adj suffix* meaning helpful, easy, advantageous, as in *user-friendly, child-friendly*.

friendly fire *n* an accidental attack or assault by someone from one's own side.

friendly society *n* an association, chiefly among tradesmen and mechanics, for the purpose of forming a fund for the assistance of members in sickness or of their relatives or others in case of death.

friendship *n* the feeling that exists between friends or binds them to one another; at-

friar

tachment to a person; mutual attachment; kind regard; intimacy; kindness.

Friesian *adj, n* same as **Frisian**.

frieze[1] *n* a decorative band along the top of the wall of a room; (*archit*) that part of the entablature of a column which is between the architrave and cornice, usually enriched with figures or other ornaments.

frieze[2] *n* a coarse woollen cloth having a shaggy nap on one side.

frigate *n* among ships of war of the older class, a vessel of a size larger than a sloop or brig and less than a ship of the line; a ship of war with a high speed and great fighting power.

frigate bird *n* a tropical sea bird related to the cormorant, remarkable for its powers of flight.

frigatoon *n* a ship-rigged sloop of war.

fright *n* sudden and violent fear; a sudden fit of fear or dread; terror; a person of a shocking, disagreeable or ridiculous appearance in person or dress.—*vt* to frighten; to affright; to scare.

frighten *vt* to strike with fright; to terrify; to scare; to alarm suddenly.

frightful *adj* causing fright; terrible; dreadful; awful; horrid; terrific.

frightfulness *n* the quality of being frightful; the German theory of war by terrorism.

frigid *adj* cold; lacking heat or warmth; of a very low temperature; cold in feeling or manner; lacking warmth of affection; unfriendly; sexually unresponsive; lacking zeal, fire, energy, spirit or animation; stiff; haughty; forbidding; lifeless.

frigidity *n* the state or quality of being frigid; coldness; lack of warmth; coldness of feeling or manner; lack of sexual responsiveness; lack of animation, ardour or vivacity.

Frigid Zone *n* (*geog*) one of the two zones comprehended between the poles and the polar circles, which are about 23° 28′ from the poles.

frill *n* a crimped or ornamental edging of fine linen on the bosom of a shirt; a somewhat similar trimming on something else; a ruffle.

fringe *n* an ornament to the borders of garments, furniture, etc, consisting of threads attached at one end, the other hanging loose; something resembling a fringe; hair falling over the forehead; an edging; margin; an outer edge; extremity; in optics, one of the coloured bands of light in the phenomena of diffraction.—*vt* (**fringed, fringing**) to adorn or border with or as with a fringe.

fringe benefit *n* anything received by an employee from his or her employer in addition to wages or salary, such as a company car, etc; any additional advantage.

frippery *n* useless things; trifles.

Frisbee *n* the trademark of a light plastic disc that is thrown with a spinning motion in a game.

Frisian, Friesian *adj* belonging to Friesland.—*n* a native of Friesland; the language of Friesland.

frisk *vi* to leap, skip, dance or gambol, as in gaiety or frolic; to frolic.—*vt* (*colloq*) to search by feeling for concealed weapons, etc.—*n* a frolic; a fit of wanton gaiety.

frisky *adj* fond of frisking or capering; lively; frolicsome.

frit *n* the matter of which glass is made after it has been calcined or baked in a furnace.

fritillary *n* the popular name of a genus of herbaceous bulbous plants, natives of north temperate regions; also of several British butterflies.

fritter *n* a small piece of anything, such as meat, fruit, etc, coated with batter and deep-fried.—*vt* to coat with batter and deep-fry.—**to fritter away** to waste or expend by little and little; to spend frivolously or in trifles.

frivolity *n* the condition or quality of being frivolous or trifling; insignificance; also, the act or habit of trifling; unbecoming levity of mind or disposition.

frivolous *adj* of little weight, worth or importance; not worth notice; trifling; trivial; given to trifling; characterized by unbecoming levity; silly; weak.

frizz, friz *vt* to curl; to crisp; to form into small curls or into little burs, as the nap of cloth.—*n* that which is frizzed or curled.

frizzle[1] *vt* (**frizzled, frizzling**) to curl or crisp, as hair; to frizz.

frizzle[2] *vti* (**frizzled, frizzling**) to sizzle, as in frying; to scorch by frying.

fro *adv* from; away; back or backward (as in the phrase *to and fro*).

frock *n* an ecclesiastical garment with large sleeves worn by monks; a woman's dress.

frockcoat *n* a coat with full skirts having the same length before and behind; a surtout.

frog[1] *n* the name of various amphibians, having four legs with four toes on the forefeet and five on the hind, more or less webbed, a naked body, no ribs and no tail, and with great powers of leaping; a sort of tender horn that grows in the middle of the sole of a horse's foot.

frog[2] *n* a fastening for a frock or coat in the form of a tassel or large button passed through a loop on the breast; the loop for the scabbard of a bayonet or sword.

frogmarch *vt* to carry (a resisting person) by the arms and legs face down; to move (a person) by force.

frolic *n* a wild or merry prank; a flight of levity or gaiety and mirth; a scene of gaiety and mirth; a merrymaking.—*vi* (**frol-**

frigate

frog

354

icked, **frolicking**) to play happily; to caper about; to play tricks of levity, mirth and gaiety.—*adj* merry; full of mirth; dancing, playing or frisking about.

frolicsome *adj* full of gaiety and mirth; given to frolics; sportive.

from *prep* out of the neighbourhood of; leaving behind; by reason of; out of; by aid of; denoting source, beginning, distance, absence, privation or departure, sometimes literally and sometimes figuratively, the antithesis and correlative of from is *to*.

fromage frais *n* a kind of smooth white cheese made from curd; a kind of low-fat dessert made from this with fruit, etc, added.

frond *n* (*bot*) a large leaf with many divisions, especially of a palm or fern.

frondescence *n* (*bot*) the precise time in which each species of plants unfolds its leaves; the act of bursting into leaf.

front *n* the part or side of anything which seems to look out or to be directed forward; the face or fore part; the foremost rank; position directly before the face of a person or the foremost part of anything; a set of false hair or curls; the van of war; the area of warfare in campaign; shirt front, real or false; the forehead, or part of the face above the eyes; the whole face; boldness of disposition; impudence.—*adj* relating to the front or face; having a position in the front; outward appearance; outward behaviour; cover, cloak (*a front for his drug-trading*).—*vt* to oppose face to face; to stand in front of or over against; to face; to appear in the presence of; to confront; to supply with a front; to adorn in front; to serve as a front for.—*vi* to have the face or front in some direction.

frontage *n* the front part of any structure or object; extent of front.

frontbencher *n* a Member of Parliament who is either a government minister or an opposition spokesman or spokeswoman and who sits on the front bench of the House of Commons.

frontier *n* that part of a country which fronts or faces another country; the confines or extreme part of a country bordering on another country; the marches; the border.

frontispiece *n* an ornamental figure or engraving fronting the first page of a book or at the beginning.

frost *n* that state or temperature of the air which occasions freezing or the solidification of water; freezing weather; frozen dew; rime; hoar frost; coldness or severity of manner or feeling.—*vt* to injure by frost; to cover or ornament with anything resembling hoar frost, as with white sugar; to give a frost-like opaque surface to (glass).

frostbite *n* a state of insensibility or deadness with arrested circulation in any part of the body, such as the nose and ears, occasioned by exposure to severe frost.

frostbitten *adj* affected by frostbite.

frosted glass *n* glass roughened on the surface, so as to destroy its transparency.

frostwork *n* the covering of hoar frost deposited on shrubs or other natural objects.

frosty *adj* accompanied with frost; of a freezing temperature; affected by frost; without warmth, affection or enthusiasm; resembling hoar frost; grey-haired.

froth *n* the bubbles caused in liquids by fermentation or agitation; spume; foam; empty talk; mere words without sense; light, insubstantial matter.—*vt* to cause to foam or produce froth; to vent or give expression to what is light, insubstantial or worthless.—*vi* to foam; to emit froth.

frothy *adj* full of or accompanied by froth; consisting of froth or light bubbles; foamy; light, empty or insubstantial; given to empty display.

froward *adj* (*arch*) not willing to comply with what is right or reasonable; perverse; ungovernable; refractory; disobedient; peevish.

frown *vi* to express displeasure, severity or sternness by contracting the brow; to put on a stern look; to scowl; to show displeasure or disapprobation; to be ominous of evil; to lower (*the clouds frown*).—*n* a contraction or wrinkling of the brow or a severe or stern look expressive of displeasure.

frowzy, frowsy *adj* dirty; dingy; slovenly; slatternly.

fructescence *n* (*bot*) the time when the fruit of a plant arrives at maturity and its seeds are dispersed; the fruiting season.

fructiferous *adj* bearing or producing fruit.

fructification *n* the act of forming or producing fruit; the act of fructifying or rendering productive of fruit; fecundation; the organs concerned in the production of the fruit of a plant.

fructify *vt* (**fructified, fructifying**) to make fruitful; to render productive; to fertilize.—*vi* to bear or produce fruit.

fructose *n* a type of sugar found in ripe fruit and honey.

frugal *adj* economical in regard to expenditure; thrifty; sparing; not profuse, prodigal or lavish; saving.

frugality *n* the quality of being frugal; a prudent and sparing use of anything.

fruit *n* (*pl* **fruit, fruits**) the reproductive product of a tree or other plant; especially, the edible succulent products of certain plants, generally covering and including their seeds; such products collectively; (*bot*) the seed of a plant, or the mature ovary, composed essentially of two parts, the pericarp and the seed; the produce of animals; offspring; young; something that results; effect, result or consequence.—*vi* to produce or yield fruit.

fruiterer *n* one who deals in fruit; a seller of fruits.

fruitful *adj* producing fruit in abundance; very productive; prolific; bearing children; not barren; producing or presenting in abundance; productive (*a fruitful meeting*).

fruitfulness *n* the state or quality of being fruitful; productiveness; fertility.

fruition *n* use or possession of anything, especially when accompanied by pleasure; the pleasure derived from use or possession; enjoyment; coming to fulfilment; realization.

fruitless *adj* not bearing fruit; lacking fruit or offspring; productive of no advantage or good effect; vain.

fruit machine *n* a coin-operated gambling machine in which a lever spins drums bearing symbols, such as fruit, dividends being paid for certain combinations of these when they come to rest.

fruit tree *n* a tree cultivated for its fruit or whose principal value consists in its fruit.

fruity *adj* resembling fruit; having the taste or flavour of fruit.

frumentaceous *adj* having the character of or resembling wheat or other cereal.

frumenty *n* a dish made of hulled wheat boiled in milk and seasoned; furmenty.

frump *n* a dowdy, old-fashioned woman.

frustrate *vt* (**frustrated, frustrating**) to make to be in vain or of no avail; to bring to nothing; to prevent from taking effect; to defeat; to balk.

frustration *n* the act of frustrating; something that frustrates.

frustum *n* (*pl* **frustums, frusta**) (*geom*) the part of a solid (as a cone or a pyramid) left by cutting off the top portion by a plane; a truncated solid.

fry¹ *vt* (**fried, frying**) to cook in hot fat or oil.—*vi* to be cooked as above.—*n* that which is fried; a dish of anything fried.

fry² *n* young of fishes at a very early stage; a swarm of little fishes; a swarm of small animals or of young people; small or insignificant objects collectively.

frying pan *n* a pan with a long handle, used for frying.

f-stop *n* any of the standard settings of the aperture in a camera lens.

fuchsia *n* a genus of beautiful flowering shrubs, natives of South America, Mexico and New Zealand, having a funnel-shaped, coloured, deciduous, four-parted calyx.

fuddle *vt* (**fuddled, fuddling**) to make foolish or stupid by drink; to make tipsy or intoxicated; to make confused.

fudge¹ *vt* (**fudged, fudging**) to make or do

anything in a bungling, careless manner; to fail; to obscure or cover up; to fake.

fudge² *n* a soft sweet made by boiling milk, sugar, butter and flavouring.

fuel *n* that which is used to feed fire, as wood, coal, peat, etc; that which serves to feed or increase heat, anger or excitement.—*vt* (**fuelled, fuelling**) to feed with fuel; to supply with fuel.

fuel-injection *adj* a method of spraying fuel directly into the manifold of an engine instead of using a carburettor.

fugacious *adj* flying or disposed to fly; volatile; fleeting.

fugitive *adj* apt to flee away or be dissipated; volatile; staying or lasting but a short time; fleeting; not fixed or durable (*fugitive dyes*); fleeing or running from danger or pursuit, duty or service.—*n* one who flees; a deserter; one who flees from danger or duty; one who flees for refuge.

fugue *n* (*mus*) a composition in parts that do not all begin at once but, as it were, follow or pursue each other successively.

fulcrum *n* (*pl* **fulcra, fulcrums**) (*mech*) a prop or support; (*mech*) that by which a lever is sustained; the point about which a lever turns in lifting a body.

fulfil *vt* (**fulfilled, fulfilling**) to accomplish or carry into effect, as a prophecy, promise, intention, design, desire, prayer, bargain, etc; to perform; to complete by performance; to complete (a term of years).

fulfilment *n* accomplishment; completion; execution; performance.

fulgent *adj* shining; dazzling; exquisitely bright.

fulguration *n* the flashing of lightning; assaying, the sudden brightening of the melted globules of gold and silver.

fuliginous *adj* pertaining to soot; sooty; smoky; resembling smoke; dusky.

full¹ *adj* having within its limits all that it can contain; replete; completely or largely supplied or furnished; abounding; supplied; occupied; not vacant; plump; filled out; inclined to be stout or corpulent; saturated; sated; abundant in quantity; plenteous; not defective or partial; entire; adequate; mature; perfect (*full supply, accomplishment, age; a full stop*); loud, clear and distinct (voice); giving ample details or arguments; copious (*a full account; the speech was full*).—**in full cry** a term in hunting signifying that all the hounds have caught the scent and give tongue in chorus; hence, hot pursuit; hard chase.—*n* the state of being full; complete measure; utmost extent; highest state or degree (*fed to the full; the full of the moon*).—**written in full** written without contractions; written in words, not in figures.—*adv* quite; fully; equally; completely; altogether; exactly (*full in the centre*); directly; straight (*he*

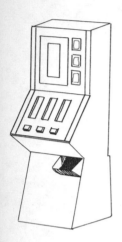

fruit machine

frying pan

looked him full in the face); to satiety (*to sup full of horrors*).

full² *vt* to thicken and condense the fibres of (woollen cloth) by wetting and beating; to scour, cleanse and thicken in a mill.—*vi* to become fulled or felted.

full-blooded *adj* having a full supply of blood; of pure blood or extraction; thoroughbred.

full-blown *adj* fully expanded, as a blossom; mature (*full-blown beauty*).

full-bound *adj* of a book, bound entirely in one material, especially leather.

fuller *n* one who fulls; one whose occupation is to full cloth; one who bleaches or whitens.

fuller's earth *n* a variety of clay or marl, useful in scouring and cleansing cloth.

full-grown *adj* grown to full size; accompanying fullness of growth.

full-length *adj* embracing the whole length or figure; extending the whole length (*a full-length portrait*).

full moon *n* the moon with its whole disc illuminated; also, the time when the moon is in this position.

fullness *n* the state or quality of being full or filled.—**in the fullness of time** at the proper or destined time.

full stop *n* the punctuation mark (.) at the end of a sentence; period.

fully *adv* in a full manner; to the full extent; so as to be full; without lack or defect; completely; entirely.

fulmar *n* a species of petrel which inhabits the northern seas in prodigious numbers and is valued for its feathers, down and the oil it yields.

fulminate *vi* (**fulminated, fulminating**) to thunder; to explode with a loud noise; to detonate; to issue threats, denunciations, censures, etc.—*vt* to cause to explode; to utter or hurl out (denunciation).—*n* a kind of explosive compound.

fulmination *n* the act of fulminating; that which is fulminated or thundered forth, as a menace or censure.

fulsome *adj* cloying; surfeiting; offensive from excess of praise; gross (flattery, compliments); nauseous; disgusting.

fulvous *adj* yellow; tawny; of a tawny yellow colour.

fumarole *n* a hole from which smoke or gases issue (in a volcanic locality).

fumble *vi* (**fumbled, fumbling**) to feel or grope about; to grope about in perplexity; to seek or search for something awkwardly; to employ the hands or fingers in an awkward fashion.

fume *n* smoky or vaporous exhalation, especially if possessing narcotic or other remarkable properties; volatile matter arising from anything; exhalation (generally in the plural); mental agitation clouding or

affecting the understanding.—*vi* (**fumed, fuming**) to yield fumes or exhalations; to pass off in vapours (with *away*); to be in a rage; to be hot with anger.

fumigate *vt* (**fumigated, fumigating**) to apply smoke to; to expose to fumes or vapours (as of sulphur) in cleansing infected apartments, clothing, etc

fumigation *n* the act of fumigating.

fumitory *n* a common garden and field plant with much divided leaves and purplish flowers, formerly much used in medicine.

fumy *adj* producing fumes; vaporous; apt to fume or fret.

fun *n* sport; mirthful drollery; amusement. —**to make fun of** to turn into ridicule.— **not to see the fun** to be unwilling to regard something in the light of a joke.

funambulist *n* a tightrope-walker or rope-dancer.

function *n* office, duty or business belonging to a person in virtue of a particular station or character; what a person or body of persons has specially to perform in some capacity (*the functions of a bishop, of a parent*); the specific office or action which any organ or system of organs performs in the animal or vegetable organism, as the body, the mind or a faculty of the mind (*the function of memory, of nutrition*); a formal ceremony; a formal social gathering; (*math*) a quantity so connected with another that no change can be made in the latter without producing a corresponding change in the former.—*vi* to perform a function; to carry out one's normal work or function; to work; to operate.

functional *adj* pertaining to a function or functions, thus a *functional disease* is one in which some one or other of the animal functions is deranged and is often opposed to an organic disease, in which an organ is directly affected; of, or designed for, a particular function; in working order; practical, not ornamental.

functionary *n* one who holds an office or trust; one who has a special office or duties.

fund *n* a stock or capital; a sum of money appropriated as the foundation of some commercial or other operation; money which an individual may possess or can employ for carrying on trade; money lent to government and constituting part of the national debt; a special branch or stock of a national debt; money set apart for any object more or less permanent; a store laid up from which one may draw at pleasure; stock; supply (*a fund of amusement, of anecdote*).—*vt* to provide and appropriate a fund or permanent revenue for the payment of the interest of; to put into the form of bonds or stocks bearing regular interest;

funambulist

to place in a fund; to provide money for; to pay for.

fundament *n* the part of the body on which one sits; the anus.

fundamental *adj* pertaining to a groundwork, root or basis; at the root or foundation of something; essential; elementary (*a fundamental truth* or *principle*).—*n* a leading or primary principle, rule, law or article; something essential; (*physics*) in any system capable of periodic changes, the natural vibration of lowest frequency.

fundamentalist *n* one who believes in the literal interpretation and the infallibility of the Bible, Koran or other holy book; an ultra-evangelical.

funeral *n* the ceremony of burying a dead human body; interment; burial; obsequies.—*adj* pertaining to burial; used at the interment of the dead.

funereal *adj* suiting a funeral; pertaining to or calling up thoughts of death or the grave; dismal; mournful; gloomy.

funfair *n* a collection of side-shows, rides and other amusements, usually one that travels from place to place around the country.

funfair

fungoid *adj* having the appearance or character of a fungus.

fungous *adj* like a fungus; having the character of one of the fungi; hence, growing or springing up suddenly but not substantial or durable.

fungus *n* (*pl* **fungi, funguses**) a member of a large natural order of plants that lack chlorophyll and reproduce by spores, typical forms of which being the numerous species of mushroom and the growths known as moulds, mildew, smut, rust, dry rot, etc; (*med*) a spongy abnormal excrescence; a diseased state dependent on the growth of vegetable parasites.

funicular *adj* consisting of a small rope or cord; dependent on the tension of a cord.

funicular railway *n* a short-distance railway system of cable-linked trains for ascending mountains or steep slopes.

funk *n* (*colloq*) fear, cowardice.—*vi* (*colloq*) to be in terror, to lose one's nerve.—*vt* (*colloq*) to fear.

funnel *n* a utensil for conveying fluids into vessels with small openings, being a kind of hollow cone with a pipe issuing from its apex; the shaft or hollow channel of a chimney; a cylindrical iron chimney in steam ships for the furnaces, rising above the deck.—*vt* (**funnelled, funnelling**) to pass through a funnel; to focus (attention) on.—*vi* to take the shape of a funnel.

funnel

funny *adj* making fun; droll; comical; odd.

funny bone *n* the shoulder bone at the elbow, (*os humeri*), with play on the sound of words.

fun run *n* a long-distance run in which participants run for entertainment or to raise funds rather than competitively.

fur *n* the short, fine, soft hair of certain animals growing thick on the skin and distinguished from the hair, which is longer and coarser; the skin of certain wild animals with the fur; a coating regarded as resembling fur, as abnormal matter collected on the tongue.—*adj* made of fur.—*vt* (**furred, furring**) to line, face or cover with fur.—*vi* to become covered in fur.

furbelow *n* a kind of flounce; the plaited border of a petticoat or gown.

furbish *vt* to rub or scour to brightness; to polish up; to burnish; (*fig*) to clear from taint or stain; to brighten.

furcate, furcated *adj* forked; branching like the prongs of a fork.

Furies *npl* in classical myth, the avenging deities, the daughters of Earth or of Night, three in number.

furious *adj* exhibiting fury; raging; violent; transported with passion; mad; frenzied; rushing with impetuosity; violent; boisterous.

furl *vt* (*naut*) to wrap or roll (a sail) close to the yard, stay or mast, and fasten; to draw into close compass.

furlong *n* a measure of length, being the eighth part of a mile (220 yards or 201 metres).

furlough *n* leave or licence given to a soldier to be absent from service for a certain time; leave of absence.

furmenty, furmity *n* same as **frumenty**.

furnace *n* an enclosed structure in which heat is produced for melting ores or metals, burning rubbish, etc.

furnish *vt* to supply with anything necessary or useful; to equip; to offer for use; to afford; to fit up; to supply with furniture.

furniture *n* that with which anything is furnished; movable equipment; specifically, the seats, tables, utensils, etc, necessary or convenient for housekeeping.

furore *n* rage; fury; great excitement; intense commotion; enthusiasm.

furrier *n* a dealer in or dresser of furs.

furrow *n* a trench in the earth made by a plough; a narrow trench or channel; a groove; a wrinkle in the face.—*vt* to make furrows in; to plough; to mark with or as with wrinkles.

further *adv* more in advance; still onwards; moreover; besides; farther (this word can hardly be said to differ in meaning from *farther*).—*adj* more distant; farther.—*vt* to help forward; to promote; to forward or assist.

furtherance *n* the act of furthering; promotion; advancement.

furthermore *adv* moreover; besides; in addition to what has been said.

furtive *adj* stealthy; thief-like; sly.

fury *n* rage; a storm of anger; madness; turbulence; a violent rushing; impetuous motion; inspired or supernatural excitement of the mind; a virago; an enraged woman; (*with cap*) one of the Furies.

furze *n* whin or gorse.

fuse[1] *vt* (**fused, fusing**) to melt or liquefy by heat; to render fluid; to dissolve; to blend or unite as if melted together.—*vi* to melt by heat; to become intermingled and blended; to cause to fail by blowing a fuse, as *fusing the lights.*—*n* (*elect*) a wire or strip of metal of low melting point, which melts and thus interrupts the circuit, if the current becomes too great for safety.

fuse[2], **fuze** *n* a tube filled with combustible matter, used in blasting or in discharging a shell, etc.

fusee, fuzee *n* a small musket or firelock; a fusil; a kind of large-headed match; a fuse; the conical piece in a watch or clock round which is wound the chain or cord.

fuselage *n* the long, narrow, somewhat spindle-shaped body of an aircraft.

fusel oil *n* a colourless oily spirit, of a strong and nauseous odour, separated in the rectification of ordinary distilled spirits.

fusible *adj* capable of being fused or melted.

fusil *n* a light musket or firelock formerly used.

fusilier *n* properly, a soldier armed with a fusil; an infantry soldier who bore firearms, as distinguished from a pikeman and archer.

fusillade *n* a simultaneous discharge of musketry.

fusion *n* the act or operation of fusing; the state of being melted or dissolved by heat; the act or process of uniting or blending as if melted together; complete union; nuclear fusion.

fuss *n* a tumult; a bustle; unnecessary bustle in doing anything; much ado about nothing.—*vi* to make much ado about trifles; to make a fuss or bustle.

fussy *adj* moving and acting with fuss; bustling; making more ado than is necessary; finicky; pernickety; over-elaborate.

fustian *adj* a coarse twilled cotton cloth with a pile like velvet but shorter, such as corduroy, moleskin, etc; an inflated style of writing; bombast.—*adj* made of fustian; ridiculously tumid; bombastic.

fustic *n* the wood of a tree growing in the West Indies, extensively used as an ingredient in making yellow dye.

fusty *adj* mouldy; musty; ill-smelling; rank; rancid.

futile *adj* serving no useful end; of no effect; answering no valuable purpose; worthless; trivial.

futility *n* the quality of being futile or producing no valuable effect; triflingness; unimportance.

futon *n* a padded quilt laid on the floor or on a mattress or light frame for sleeping on and rolled up during the day.

futtock *n* (*naut*) one of those timbers raised over the keel which form the breadth of the ship.

future *adj* that is to be or come hereafter; that will exist at any time after the present.—*n* time to come; time subsequent to the present; all that is to happen after the present time; the future tense.

future tense *n* that tense of a verb which expresses that something is yet to take place.

futurist *n* member of a school of recent art and literature.

futurity *n* the state of being future or yet to come; future time; time or event to come.

fuze *n* same as **fuse**[2].

fuzee *n* same as **fusee**.

fylfot *n* a rectangular cross with arms of equal lengths and each bent at right angles at the end; a swastika.

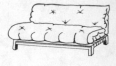

futon

G

G the seventh letter in the English alphabet, with two sounds, a hard (guttural), as in *good*; a soft (= *j*) as in *gem*, the former being the original sound; (*mus*) the fifth note and dominant of the normal scale of C.

gab *vi* (**gabbed, gabbing**) to talk much; to prate; to talk idly.—*n* the mouth; idle talk; chatter.

gabardine, gaberdine *n* formerly, a coarse frock or loose upper garment; a woollen or cotton twilled fabric.

gabble *vi* (**gabbled, gabbling**) to talk noisily and rapidly or without meaning; to utter rapid inarticulate sounds.—*n* loud or rapid talk without meaning; inarticulate sounds rapidly uttered, as of fowls.

gabbro *n* a dark crystalline igneous rock.

gaberdine *n* same as **gabardine**.

gabion *n* (*milit*) a large basket of wickerwork of a cylindrical form but without a bottom, filled with earth and serving to shelter soldiers from an enemy's fire.

gable

gable *n* (*archit*) the triangular end of a house from the level of the eaves to the top; also the end wall of a house.

gad[1] *vi* (**gadded, gadding**) to rove or ramble idly or without any fixed purpose; to act or move without restraint.

gad[2] *n* a spike, style or other sharp thing; a wedge or ingot of steel or iron; a pointed wedge-like tool used by miners.

gadabout *n* one who walks about idly.

gadfly *n* a two-winged insect which stings cattle and deposits its eggs in their skin; a provocative person.

gadget *n* a tool, appliance or contrivance.

gadwall *n* a duck belonging to Europe, Asia and North America.

Gael *n* a Scottish Highlander.

Gaelic *adj* of or pertaining to the Gaels, a Celtic race inhabiting Ireland, the Scottish Highlands and the Isle of Man.—*n* the language of the Celts inhabiting the Highlands of Scotland.

gaff *n* a harpoon; a gaff hook; (*naut*) a spar with a forked end used to extend the upper edge of some fore-and-aft sails.—*vt* to strike or secure (a salmon) by means of a gaff hook.

gaff hook

gaffer *n* an old man, often one living in the country; the foreman of a squad of workmen; an overseer.

gaff hook *n* an iron hook used to assist in landing large fish when they have been brought near the side by the angler.

gag *vt* (**gagged, gagging**) to stop the mouth of by thrusting something into it so as to hinder speaking but permit breathing; to silence by authority or violence.—*vi* to retch; to joke.—*n* something thrust into the mouth to hinder speaking; a restraint of free speech; a joke.

gaga *adj* (*colloq*) senile; not in possession of one's senses.

gage *n* something laid down or given as a security for the performance of some act by the person giving the gage; a pledge; something thrown down as a token of challenge to combat.—*vt* (**gaged, gaging**) to give or deposit as a pledge or security for some act; to pawn; to bind by pledge.

gaiety *n* the state of being gay (in the sense of merry); merriment; mirth; brightness; colourfulness.

gain *vt* to obtain by work or the employment of capital; to get as profit or advantage; to acquire, opposed to lose; to win or obtain by superiority or success (*to gain a battle, a prize*); to obtain in general; to procure (fame, favour); to win to one's side; to conciliate; to reach, attain to, arrive at (*to gain a mountain top*).—*vi* to reap advantage or profit; to acquire gain.—*n* something obtained as an advantage; anything opposed to loss; profit; benefit derived.

gainful *adj* producing profit or advantage; profitable; advantageous; lucrative.

gaining *n* that which one gains (usually in the plural); earnings.

gainsay *vt* (**gainsaid, gainsaying**) to contradict; to deny or declare not to be true; to controvert; to dispute.—*n* opposition in words; contradiction.

gainsayer *n* one who gainsays.

gait *n* walk; manner of walking or stepping; carriage.

gaiter *n* a covering of cloth for the leg, fitting over the shoe.

gala *n* an occasion of public festivity.

galactic *adj* of or pertaining to a galaxy; huge.

galago *n* (*pl* **galagos**) an African lemur, the bushbaby.

galangal *n* an Asian plant the aromatic dried root of which is used as a stimulant and seasoning.

galantine *n* a dish of veal, chicken or other white meat, boned and served cold.

galaxy *n* any of the systems of stars in the universe; an assemblage of splendid persons or things.

Galaxy *n* the Milky Way, the long, white, luminous tract which is seen at night stretching across the heavens and which is formed by a multitude of stars so distant and blended as to be distinguishable only by powerful telescopes.

galbanum *n* a fetid gum resin from Asian plants used in the manufacture of varnish and also as a medicine.

gale[1] *n* a strong wind; wind between a breeze and a storm or tempest; an outburst (*gales of laughter*).

gale[2] *n* a small shrub with an aromatic odour found in bogs and wet heaths.

galena *n* the principal ore of lead, of a lead-grey colour, with a metallic lustre.

galilee *n* a portico or chapel at the western end of some medieval churches.

Galilean[2] *n* a native or inhabitant of Galilee. —**the Galilean** Jesus Christ.—*adj* relating to Galilee.

Galilean[1] *adj* of or pertaining to Galileo, the Italian astronomer and mathematician.

galimatias *n* confused talk; nonsense; absurd mixture.

galingale *n* a rare marsh plant which occurs in the south of England.

galiot, galliot *n* a small galley; a two-masted Dutch cargo vessel.

gall[1] *n* a bitter fluid secreted in the liver of animals; bile; the gall bladder; (*fig*) bitterness of mind; rancour; nerve; impudence.

gall[2] *n* a growth produced by the deposit of the egg of an insect in the bark or leaves of a plant, especially the oak.

gall[3] *vt* to make a sore in the skin of by rubbing, fretting and wearing away; to vex; to chagrin; to cause to have a feeling of bitterness or annoyance; to irritate; to hurt the feelings of; to harass.—*n* a sore place caused by rubbing.

gallant *adj* splendid in attire or outward appearance; handsome; fine; brave; high-spirited; courageous; magnanimous; noble; chivalrous; courtly; polite and attentive to ladies; courteous.—*n* a sprightly man; a high-spirited brave young fellow; a daring spirit; a man who is polite and attentive to women; a wooer; a suitor.

gallantry *n* show; ostentatious finery; bravery; dash; intrepidity; polite attention to women; court paid to women for the purpose of winning illicit favours.

gall bladder *n* (*anat*) a small membranous sac shaped like a pear, which receives the gall or bile from the liver.

galleass, gallias *n* a large low-built three-masted vessel propelled by sails and oars, and carrying twenty or more guns.

galleon *n* a large sailing ship used as a warship and trading ship from the fifteenth to eighteenth centuries.

gallery *n* an apartment of much greater length than breadth, serving as a passage of communication between different rooms of a building; a room or building for the exhibition of paintings, statues and other works of art; a collection of paintings, statues, etc; a platform projecting from the walls of a building and overlooking a ground floor, as in a church, theatre, etc; (*fort*) any communication covered in both above and at the sides; (*mining*) a narrow passage; (*naut*) a frame like a balcony projecting from the stern and quarters of a ship; the spectators at a performance, match, etc.

galley *n* a low flat-built vessel with one deck and navigated with sails and oars, once commonly used in the Mediterranean; a ship of the ancient Greeks and Romans, propelled chiefly by oars; the boat of a warship appropriated for the captain's use; the cook room or kitchen on board ship; (*print*) a movable frame or tray which holds composed type.

galley slave *n* a slave or person condemned for a crime to work at the oar on board a galley.

gallfly, gall insect *n* an insect that punctures plants and causes galls.

galliard *n* a lively dance, originally Spanish; the dancer of a galliard; the music for such a dance.

Gallic, Gallican *adj* pertaining to Gaul or France (*the Gallican church* or *clergy*).

Gallicism *n* a mode of speech peculiar to the French nation; a custom or mode of thought peculiar to the French.

Gallicize *vt* (**Gallicized, Gallicizing**) to render conformable to the French idiom or language.

galligaskins *npl* large open breeches; wide hose; leather guards worn on the legs by sportsmen.

gallimaufry *n* a hash; a medley; a hotch-potch.

gallinaceous *adj* of or pertaining to an order of heavy-bodied largely land-loving birds including domestic fowl, pheasants, etc.

galling *adj* adapted to fret or chagrin; vexing; harassing; annoying.

gallinule *n* a wading bird closely allied to the coot; the water hen or moorhen.

gallipot *n* a small pot or vessel painted and

galleon

glazed, used by pharmacists for containing medicines.

gallium *n* a rare metallic element, of a greyish-white colour and brilliant lustre, exceedingly fusible.

gallivant *vi* to gad or run about; to go about in search of pleasure.

gallnut *n* a vegetable excrescence in plants.

galloglass *n* same as **gallowglass**.

gallon *n* a measure of capacity for dry or liquid goods but usually for liquids, containing 4 quarts or 4.54 litres (in USA 3.78 litres).

gallop *vi* to move or run with leaps, as a horse; to run with speed; to ride a horse that is galloping; to ride at a rapid pace; to scamper.—*n* the movement or pace of a horse, by springs or leaps.

Galloway *n* a small horse of great endurance, a breed of black cattle.

gallowglass, galloglass *n* an ancient heavy-armed foot soldier of Ireland and the Western Isles.

gallows *n* an instrument of punishment on which criminals are executed by hanging; a contrivance for suspending anything; one of a pair of braces for trousers.

gallstone *n* a concretion formed in the gall bladder.

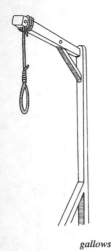

gallows

Gallup Poll *n* the trademark for a kind of public opinion poll, used, for example, to predict election results.

galop *n* a quick, lively dance, somewhat resembling a waltz; the music for the dance.

galore *n* abundance; plenty.

galosh, golosh *n* a shoe to be worn over another shoe to keep the foot dry; also a kind of gaiter.

galvanic *adj* pertaining to galvanism; containing or exhibiting galvanism; stimulating (people) into action.

galvanism *n* (*arch*) electricity produced by chemical action of certain bodies or an acid on a metal; the medical use of this.

galvanize *vt* (**galvanized, galvanizing**) to affect with galvanism; to electroplate by galvanism; to coat (sheets of iron) with tin or zinc in this way; to restore to consciousness by galvanic action, as from a state of suspended animation; to stimulate into action.

gambier, gambir *n* an earthy-looking substance obtained from the leaves of a tropical Asian shrub and used in tanning and dyeing.

gamekeeper

gambit *n* in chess, the sacrifice of a pawn early in the game for the purpose of taking up an attacking position; any action by which one hopes to gain an advantage.

gamble *vi* (**gambled, gambling**) to play for money or other stake, especially to be in the habit of doing so.—*vt* to lose or squander by gaming (with *away*).

gamboge *n* the hardened juice or sap yielded by several species of trees and used as a purgative in medicine and also in the arts, chiefly in watercolour painting.

gambol *vi* (**gambolled, gambolling**) to dance and skip about in sport; to frisk; to leap; to play in frolic.—*n* a skipping or leaping about in frolic; a skip, frisk, leap, prank.

gambrel *n* the hock of a horse; a stick crooked like a horse's leg, used by butchers for suspending carcasses.

game *n* sport of any kind; jest; play; some contrivance or arrangement for sport, recreation, testing skill, etc (*the game of cricket* or *of bowls*); a single contest in any such game; (*pl*) diversions or contests, as in wrestling, running and other athletic exercises; a scheme pursued or measures planned; such wild animals collectively as are usually pursued or hunted for sport (in this sense without a plural); the animals enumerated in the game laws.—*vi* (**gamed, gaming**) to gamble; to play at cards, dice, billiards, etc, for money; to be in the habit of so doing.—*adj* having the courageous spirit of a gamecock; courageous.

game bird *n* a bird hunted as game.

gamecock *n* a cock bred or used to fight; a cock of a good fighting breed.

gamekeeper *n* one who has the care of game; one who is employed to look after animals preserved for sport.

game laws *npl* laws enacted with regard to, or for the preservation of, the animals called game.

game leg *n* a crippled or bent leg.

gamesmanship *n* the art of winning games or competitions or of being generally successful against others, by questionable acts which are just short of cheating.

gamester *n* one who gambles; a person addicted to gambling; a gambler.

gamete *n* a reproductive cell that unites with another to form the cell that develops into a new individual.

gamin *n* a mischievous urchin.

gamine *n* a boyish girl or woman with impish appeal.

gaming house *n* a house where gambling is practised.

gamma ray *n* (*physics*) a penetrating ray emitted by radioactive substances of the same vibrational nature as an X-ray but with a higher frequency.

gammer *n* an old woman; the counterpart of *gaffer*.

gammon *n* the thigh of a pig, pickled and smoked or dried; a smoked ham.—*vt* to make into bacon; to pickle and dry in smoke.

gamut *n* (*mus*) a scale on which notes in music are written or printed, consisting of lines and spaces which are named after the first seven letters of the alphabet; the entire range of anything.

gander *n* the male of the goose.

gang *n* a number going in company; a company or number of people associated for a particular purpose, especially an illegal one; a group of people; a number of workers or labourers engaged on any piece of work under the supervision of one person; a squad.

ganger *n* one who superintends a gang of labourers.

ganglion *n* (*pl* **ganglia, ganglions**) (*anat*) an enlargement occurring somewhere in the course of a nerve; a mass of nervous matter containing nerve cells and giving origin to nerve fibres; (*surg*) a growth situated somewhere on a tendon.

gangrene *n* death of body tissue when the blood supply is obstructed; (*bot*) a disease ending in putrid decay.—*vt* (**gangrened, gangrening**) to produce a gangrene in.—*vi* to become affected by gangrene.

gangrenous *adj* attacked by gangrene; indicating gangrene.

gangster *n* a member of a gang of criminals.

gangue *n* the stony matrix of metallic ores.

gangway *n* a temporary means of access to some position, formed of planks or boards; a narrow framework or platform leading into or out of a ship or from one part of a ship to another; an opening in a ship's bulwarks and the steps leading to it; in House of Commons, the passage between rows of seats; the passage halfway down, giving access to back benches.

gannet *n* the solan goose, an aquatic bird of the pelican family, common on insular rocks in the northern seas; a very greedy person; a glutton.

ganoid *adj* belonging to an order of fishes, the majority of them extinct, characterized by scales composed of horny or bony plates, covered with glossy enamel.—*n* one of these fishes.

gaol *n* same as **jail**.

gap *n* a break or opening, as in a fence, wall, etc; a break in a mountain range; a breach; a chasm; a hiatus.

gape *vi* (**gaped, gaping**) to open the mouth wide, as indicative of drowsiness, dullness, surprise, expectation, etc; to stare with open mouth; to stare in amazement; to stand open; to show a fissure or chasm.—*n* the act of gaping; (*zool*) the width of the mouth when opened, as of birds, fishes, etc; (*pl*) a disease of young poultry characterized by much gaping.

garage *n* a place for housing or mending motorcars.

garage sale *n* a sale of used and unwanted household goods sold in a domestic garage.

garb *n* clothing; costume; habit; an official or other distinguishing dress; fashion or mode.

garbage *n* rubbish or offal; animal or vegetable refuse; any worthless, offensive matter; nonsense.

garble *vt* (**garbled, garbling**) to distort; to misrepresent or falsify by suppression or selection; to make (something) difficult to understand.

gardant *adj* (*heral*) same as **guardant**.

garden *n* a piece of ground appropriated to the cultivation of plants, fruits, flowers or vegetables; a rich well-cultivated spot or tract of country.—*vi* to lay out or cultivate a garden.

garden city *n* a town laid out with many gardens and open spaces.

gardener *n* one whose occupation or hobby is to keep a garden.

gardenia *n* a name of certain plants of Asia and Africa with large white or yellowish fragrant flowers.

gardening *n* the art or practice of cultivating gardens; horticulture.

Garden of Eden *n* see **Eden**.

garden party *n* a party held out of doors on the lawn or in the garden of a private residence.

garfish *n* a fish with an elongated body and a long, narrow, beak-like snout.

gargle *vt* (**gargled, gargling**) to wash or rinse (the mouth or throat) with a liquid preparation.—*n* any liquid preparation for washing the mouth and throat.

gargoyle *n* (*archit*) a projecting spout for draining water from the gutters of a building, generally carved into a grotesque figure from whose mouth the water gushes; a person with an ugly face.

garish *adj* gaudy; showy; staring; overbright; dazzling.

garland *n* a wreath or chaplet made of leaves, twigs, flowers, etc; a collection of little printed pieces; an anthology.—*vt* to deck with a garland or garlands.

garlic *n* a plant allied to the onion, leek, etc, with an acrid pungent taste and strong odour, used as a flavouring.

garment *n* any article of clothing or piece of dress, as a coat, a gown, etc.

garner *n* a granary; a building or place where grain is stored for preservation.—*vt* to store in, or as in, a granary.

garnet *n* the name common to a group or family of precious stones, varying considerably in composition, the prevailing colour being red of various shades.

garnish *vt* to adorn; to decorate with appendages; to set off; (in cookery) to ornament (a dish) with something, such as parsley.—*n* something added for embellishment; ornament; decoration; in cookery, something round a dish as an embellishment.

garnishee *n* a person warned not to pay money to another, because the other is

gannet

garland

363

himself a debtor to a third party, who gives the warning.

garret *n* that part of a house which is on the uppermost floor, immediately under the roof; a loft.

garrison *n* a body of troops stationed in a fort or fortified town; a fort, castle or fortified town furnished with troops.—*vt* to place a garrison in; to secure or defend by garrisons.

garrotte, garrote *n* a mode of capital punishment by strangling with an iron collar attached to a post; the instrument of this punishment.—*vt* (**garrotted, garrotting** *or* **garroted, garroting**) to strangle by means of the garrotte; to rob by suddenly seizing a person and compressing the windpipe till he or she becomes insensible or at least helpless, usually carried out by two or three accomplices.

garrulity *n* the quality of being garrulous; talkativeness; loquacity.

garrulous *adj* very talkative, often about unimportant matters.

garter *n* a string or band used to tie a stocking to the leg; the badge of the highest order of knighthood in Great Britain, called the Order of the Garter; hence, also, the order itself and the name given to the principal king of arms in England.—*vt* to bind with a garter.

gas *n* an elastic air-like fluid; a substance the particles of which tend to fly apart from each other, thus causing it to expand indefinitely; any gas, such as coal gas or natural gas or any mixture of gases, used for lighting and heating; any gas or mixture of gases used for anaesthetic purposes; poison disseminated in air by troops before an attack.—*vi* (**gassed, gassing**) to talk idly; to gossip.—*vt* to poison with gas in war.

gas chamber *n* an airtight room where animals or people are killed by poisonous gas.

gasconade *n* a boast or boasting; a vaunt; a bravado; a bragging.—*vi* (**gasconaded, gasconading**) to bluster, to boast.

gaselier *n* same as **gasolier**.

gaseous *adj* in the form of gas; of the nature of gas.

gasfitter *n* a worker who fixes pipes and fits burners and other appliances for gas.

gash *n* a deep and long cut; an incision of considerable length, particularly in flesh. —*vt* to make a gash or gashes in.

gasket *n* a piece or ring of rubber, metal, etc, sandwiched between metal surfaces to act as a seal; (*naut*) one of the plaited cords fastened to the yard of a ship to tie the sail to it.

gaslight *n* light produced by gas.

gas main *n* one of the principal pipes which convey gas from a gasworks to a place of consumption.

gas mask

gas mask *n* a face mask, usually provided with a filter containing charcoal and other chemicals, to purify the air inhaled and protect against dangerous gases; a respirator.

gas meter *n* an instrument through which the gas is made to pass in order to ascertain the quantity which is consumed at a particular place.

gasolier, gaselier *n* a hanging apparatus with brackets or branches adapted for burning gas.

gasoline, gasolene *n* an inflammable liquid obtained as one of the initial products in the distillation of petroleum, used as a solvent for oils, fats, etc, and also for lighting and heating; in the USA, petrol.

gasometer *n* an instrument or apparatus intended to measure, collect or mix gases; a reservoir or storehouse for the ordinary illuminating gas produced in gasworks.

gasp *vi* to open the mouth wide in laborious respiration; to labour for breath; to respire convulsively; to pant violently.—*vt* to emit or utter with gaspings or pantings (with *away, forth, out*, etc).—*n* a laboured respiration; a short painful catching of the breath.

gas stove *n* a stove heated by gas.

gassy *adj* relating to or containing gas; gaseous; (of a liquid for drinking) effervescent.

gasteropod *n* same as **gastropod**.

gastric *adj* of or pertaining to the belly or stomach.

gastritis *n* chronic inflammation of the stomach.

gastroenteritis *n* inflammation of the stomach and intestines.

gastronomer *n* one skilled in gastronomy; a judge of the art of cookery; a gourmet; an epicure.

gastronomy *n* the art or science of good living; the pleasures of eating; epicureanism.

gastropod, gasteropod *n* one of a class of molluscs, consisting of snails, periwinkles and other animals inhabiting a univalve shell (or lacking a shell), the distinguishing characteristic being the foot, a broad muscular organ attached to the abdomen.

gasworks *n sing* a place where gas is made.

gate *n* a large door such as gives entrance into a castle, palace or other large edifice; the entrance leading into such an edifice; any mans of access; a movable frame of timber or metal which opens or closes a passage into an enclosure of some kind, such as a garden; the frame which shuts or stops a passage for water, as at the entrance to a dock or in a canal; a device (as in a computer) that outputs a signal when specified input conditions are met; the total mount or number of paid admissions to a football match, etc.—*vt* (**gated, gating**) to supply with a gate; to keep within the gates (of a university) as a punishment.

-gate *suffix* indicating an alleged scandal, often a political scandal, derived from *Watergate*, a political scandal in America in 1972 which led to President Nixon's downfall.

gateau *n* (*pl* **gateaux**) a large cake, often decorated with cream, etc.

gate-crasher *n* an uninvited guest; one who obtains admission to a public entertainment without a ticket.

gatehouse *n* a house at a gate, as a porter's lodge at the entrance to the grounds of a mansion.

gateway *n* an opening which is or may be closed with a gate; a means of ingress or egress.

gather *vt* to bring together; to collect into one place or one aggregate; to assemble; to congregate; to pick; to pluck; to accumulate; to amass; to draw together; to bring together in folds or plaits, as a garment; hence, to plait; to pucker; to acquire or gain, with or without effort (*to gather strength*); to deduce by inference; to conclude.—*vi* to collect; to become assembled; to congregate; to take origin and grow; to come to a head (as a boil).—*n* a plait or fold in cloth held in position by a thread drawn through it; a pucker.

gathering *n* the act of collecting or assembling; that which is gathered; a crowd; an assembly; a collection of pus; an abscess.

Gatling gun *n* a machine gun with clustered barrels which are discharged in succession by turning a handle.

gauche *adj* socially inept; graceless, tactless.

gaucho *n* (*pl* **gauchos**) a cowboy of the pampas of South America.

gaudy *adj* showy; tastelessly or glaringly adorned; over-brightly coloured; flashy.—*n* a feast or festival.

gauffer *vt* same as **goffer**.

gauge *vt* (**gauged, gauging**) to measure or to ascertain the contents or capacity of; to measure in respect to capability, power, character, etc; to appraise; to estimate.—*n* a standard of measure; an instrument to determine dimensions or capacity; a measure; means of estimating; the distance between the rails of a railway; in joinery, a simple instrument made to strike a line parallel to the straight side of a board, etc.

gault *n* (*geol*) a series of stiff marls or calcareous clays, varying in colour from a light grey to a dark blue.

gaunt *adj* attenuated, as with fasting or suffering; haggard; lean; meagre; thin; slender.

gauntlet *n* a large iron glove with fingers covered with small plates, formerly worn as armour; a long glove for a lady, which

envelops the hand and wrist.—**to throw down the gauntlet** to issue a challenge.

gaur *n* one of the largest of the ox family, inhabiting the mountains and jungles of India.

gauze *n* a very thin, slight, transparent stuff, of silk, linen or cotton; any slight open material resembling this (*wire gauze*).

gauzy *adj* like gauze; thin as gauze.

gavial *n* a crocodile found in India.

gavotte *n* a sort of French dance; the music to which the dance was performed or a similar instrumental movement.

gawky *adj* awkward; clumsy; ungainly.

gay *adj* excited with merriment or delight; merry; frolicsome; bright and cheerful (*a gay dress*); homosexual.—*n* a homosexual.

gaze *vi* (**gazed, gazing**) to fix the eyes and look steadily and earnestly; to look with eagerness or curiosity.—*n* a fixed look; a look of eagerness, wonder or admiration.

gazebo *n* (*pl* **gazebos, gazeboes**) a summerhouse, tower, etc, commanding a wide prospect.

gazelle *n* an antelope about the size of a roebuck, of a graceful form and with long slender limbs.

gazette *n* a newspaper; especially an official or government newspaper containing public announcements; the title given to some newspapers.—*vt* (**gazetted, gazetting**) to insert or publish in a gazette; hence, *to be gazetted*, to have one's name announced in the gazette.

gazetteer *n* a book containing geographical and topographical information alphabetically arranged; a geographical dictionary.

gear *n* the harness or furniture of domestic animals; (*naut*) the ropes, blocks, etc, belonging to any particular sail or spar; any tools or apparatus for a particular purpose; clothing; dress; (*mach*) the appliances or furnishings connected with the acting portions of any piece of mechanism; a toothed wheel designed to mesh with another; (*pl*) a system of such gears meshed together to transmit motion.—**to throw machinery into** *or* **out of gear** to connect or disconnect wheels or couplings.—*vt* to put gear on; to harness.

gearing *n* harness; the parts by which motion is communicated from one portion of a machine to another; a train of connected toothed wheels.

gear lever *n* a lever used to engage or change gears in a motor vehicle.

gecko *n* a name of various nocturnal lizards of the warm parts of both hemispheres.

geezer *n* (*colloq*) an old man.

Geiger counter *n* a portable instrument used for detecting and measuring radiation.

geisha *n* a Japanese girl trained as an enter-

gateau

gauntler

tainer to serve as a hired companion to men.

gelatine, gelatin *n* a substance obtained from various animal tissues and employed in the arts and as human food, being known in its coarser forms as glue, size and isinglass, according to the sources whence it is obtained and the care exercised in its preparation.

gelatinous *adj* of or pertaining to or consisting of gelatine; resembling jelly; viscous.

geld *vt* to castrate; to emasculate.

gelding *n* a castrated animal; especially a castrated horse.

gelder-rose *n* same as **guelder-rose**.

gelid *adj* cold; very cold; icy or frosty.

gelignite *n* a nitroglycerine explosive.

gelsemium *n* (*pl* **gelsemiums, gelsemia**) a kind of twining shrub.

gem *n* a precious stone of any kind, as the ruby, topaz, emerald, etc, especially when cut or polished; a jewel; anything resembling a gem or remarkable for beauty, rarity or costliness.

gemination *n* a doubling; duplication; repetition.

Gemini *npl* the third sign of the zodiac, so named from its two brightest stars, Castor and Pollux.

gemmation *n* (*zool*) the process of reproduction by buds; the formation of a new individual by budding; (*bot*) the act of budding.

gemsbok *n* a fine large antelope inhabiting South Africa.

gen (*colloq*) *n* information.

gendarme *n* a private in the armed police of France.

gendarmerie *n* the body of gendarmes.

gender *n* kind or sort; a sex, male or female; (*gram*) one of those classes or categories into which words are divided according to the sex, natural or metaphorical, of the beings or things they denote; a grammatical category in which words of similar termination are classed together; such a distinction in words.

gene *n* any of the complex chemical units in the chromosomes by which hereditary characteristics are transmitted.

genealogist *n* one who traces descents of persons or families.

genealogy *n* an account or synopsis tracing the descent of a person or family from an ancestor; an enumeration or table of ancestors and their children in the order of succession; pedigree; lineage; the study of pedigrees or family history.

general *adj* relating to a whole genus, kind, class or order; relating to, affecting or comprehending the whole community; public; common to many or the greatest number; extensive though not universal; common, usual, ordinary (*a general opin-*

ion); not restrained or limited to a particular import; not specific (*a general term*); not directed to a single object; taken as a whole; regarded in the gross.—*n* a general or comprehensive notion; a military officer of the highest rank but one; the commander of an army, an army corps or division; the chief of an order of monks or of all the houses or congregations established under the same rule.—**in general** in the main; for the most part; not always or universally; in the aggregate or as a whole.

general anaesthetic *n* an anaesthetic affecting the whole body and producing unconsciousness.

General Assembly *n* the chief ecclesiastical court of the Church of Scotland.

generalissimo *n* (*pl* **generalissimos**) the chief commander of an army or military force which consists of two or more grand divisions under separate commanders.

generality *n* the state of being general; a statement which is general or not specific or which lacks application to any one case.—**the generality** the main body; the bulk; the greatest part.

generalization *n* the act or process of generalizing; a general inference.

generalize *vt* (**generalized, generalizing**) to reduce or bring under a general law, rule or statement; to bring into relation with a wider circle of facts; to deduce from the consideration of many particulars.—*vi* to form objects into classes; to bring or classify particulars under general heads or rules.

generally *adv* in general; commonly; ordinarily; extensively, though not universally; most frequently but not without exceptions; without detail; leaving particular facts out of account; in the whole taken together.

general practice *n* the work of a general practitioner; the branch of medicine carried out by a general practitioner.

general practitioner *n* a doctor who looks after the health needs of a community and deals with all types of illness, as opposed to one who specializes in a particular area of medicine or surgery.

generalship *n* the office of a general; the discharge of the functions of a general; military skill exhibited in the judicious handling of troops; management or judicious tactics generally.

generate *vt* (**generated, generating**) to procreate (young); to produce; to cause to be; to bring into existence; to cause (heat, vibrations).

generation *n* the act of generating; production; formation; a single succession of the human race in natural descent, calculated at thirty years; the average period of time between one succession of children and

the next following; people who are contemporary or living at the same time; a
race; progeny; offspring.

generative *adj* having the power of generating; belonging to generation or the act of
procreating.

generator *n* one who or that which begets,
causes or produces; a vessel or chamber in
which something is generated; (*elect*) a
machine for generating electric current
from mechanical energy.

generic *adj* pertaining to a genus; descriptive of, belonging to or comprehending the
genus, as distinct from the species or from
another genus; referring to a large class or
group; (of a drug, product, etc), not patented or sold as a proprietary name.

generosity *n* the quality of being generous;
nobleness of soul; liberality of sentiment;
a disposition to give liberally.

generous *adj* noble; honourable; magnanimous (of persons or things); liberal; bountiful; munificent; free in giving; strong;
full of spirit (*generous wine*).

genesis *n* the act of producing or giving origin; a taking origin; generation; origination.

Genesis *n* the first book of the Old Testament.

genet[1] *n* a carnivorous animal belonging to
the civet family, a native of western Asia;
the fur of the genet.

genet[2] *n* same as **jennet**.

genetic *adj* pertaining to genes; pertaining
to genetics; pertaining to the origin, causes
or development of something.

genetic counselling *n* advice based on investigation into chromosomes, etc, given
by specialists to prospective parents on
possible heritable defects in any children
born to them.

genetic engineering *n* the modification or
manipulation of the genetic constitution,
or DNA, of living things.

genetic fingerprinting *n* the identification
of a person's DNA pattern, obtained by
analysing samples of blood, saliva and semen and used, for example, in forensic
medicine to identify criminals.

genetics *n* the branch of biology which
deals with heredity; the inherited characteristics of an organism.

geneva *n* a spirit distilled from grain or
malt, with added juniper berries; gin.

genial *adj* characterized by kindly warmth
of disposition and manners such as promotes cheerfulness on the part of others;
cordial; kindly; sympathetically cheerful.

geniality *n* the state or quality of being genial; sympathetic cheerfulness or cordiality.

genie *n* a kind of spirit or demon, especially
one that is capable of changing into different shapes or one that can fulfil one's
wishes.

genital *adj* pertaining to the genitalia or
sexual organs; pertaining to reproduction.

genitalia, genitals *npl* the external sexual
organs.

genitive *adj* (*gram*) a term applied to a case
in the declension of nouns, adjectives, pronouns, etc, in English called the possessive case.—*n* (*gram*) the genitive case.

genius *n* an imaginary being ruling or protecting people, places or things; a good or
evil spirit supposed to be attached to a person and to influence his or her actions; intellectual endowment of the highest kind;
a man, woman or child thus intellectually
endowed; a natural ability for; peculiar
character or constitution; pervading spirit
or influence from associations or otherwise (*the special genius of a language*).

genocide *n* the systematic killing of a whole
race of people.

genome *n* the total genetic information
stored in the chromosomes of an organism, the number of chromosomes being
characteristic of that particular species.

genre *n* a category of literary or artistic
work; a style of painting in which scenes
of ordinary life are depicted realistically.

gent a vulgar abbreviation for gentleman.

genteel *adj* having the manners of well-bred
people; well-bred; refined; affectedly refined; of a station above the common people.

gentian *n* the name of certain bitter herbaceous plants with beautiful blue or yellow
flowers, the roots of some species being
highly valued as a tonic.

gentile *n* (*Scrip*) anyone belonging to the
non-Jewish nations; any person not a Jew.
—*adj* belonging to the non-Jewish nations; (*gram*) denoting one's race or country (*a gentile noun*).

gentility *n* the state or character of being
genteel; the manners or circumstances of
genteel people.

gentle *adj* well-born; of a good family; soft
and refined in manners; mild; meek; not
rough, harsh or severe; not wild, turbulent
or refractory; placid; bland; not rude or
violent.

gentlefolk, gentlefolks *npl* persons of good
breeding and family.

gentleman *n* (*pl* **gentlemen**) a man of good
family or good social position; a man of
good breeding and politeness; a courteous
and honourable man; often used almost as
a polite equivalent for 'man'; in the plural
the name by which men are addressed at
public gatherings, whatever may be their
condition or character.

gentleman's agreement *n* an agreement
guaranteed by trust and honour rather than
by legal contract.

gentlewoman *n* (*pl* **gentlewomen**) a woman of good family or good breeding.

genet

gently *adv* in a gentle manner; mildly; meekly; placidly.

gentry *n* (*colloq*) people of good position; wealthy or well-born people in general or a rank below the nobility.

gents', gents (*colloq*) *n* a public toilet for males.

genuflect *vi* to bend the knee, as in worship; to make a genuflection or genuflections.

genuflection, genuflexion *n* the act of bending the knee, particularly in worship.

genuine *adj* real; natural; true; pure; not spurious, false or adulterated.

genus *n* (*pl* **genera, genuses**) a kind, class or sort; a division of plants and animals below a family and above a species.

geocentric *adj* (*astron*) having reference to the earth for its centre; seen from the earth (applied to the place of a planet as seen from the centre of the earth).

geode *n* (*mineral*) a roundish hollow lump of agate or other mineral, having the cavity frequently lined with crystals.

geodesy *n* that branch of applied mathematics which determines the figures and areas of large portions of the earth's surface, the general figure of the earth and the variations of the intensity of gravity in different regions.

geodetic *adj* of, pertaining to, determined by or carried out by geodesy.

geographer *n* one who studies or specializes in geography.

geographic, geographical *adj* relating to geography; containing information regarding geography.

geography *n* the study of the physical nature of the earth, such as land and sea masses, climate, vegetation, etc, and their interaction with the human population; the physical features of a particular region.

geologist *n* one versed in geology.

geology *n* the science which deals with the structure, especially the internal structure, of the crust of the globe and of the substances which compose it; the science which treats of the minerals, rocks, earths or other substances composing the globe, the relations which the several constituent masses bear to each other, their formation, structure, position and history, together with the successive changes that have taken place in the organic and inorganic kingdoms of nature as illustrated by fossils or otherwise.

geometric, geometrical *adj* pertaining to geometry; according to the rules or principles of geometry; done or determined by geometry.

geometrical elevation *n* a design for the front or side of a building drawn according to the rules of geometry, as opposed to perspective or natural elevation.

geometrical progression *n* progression in which the terms increase or decrease by a common ratio, as 2, 4, 8, 16, etc.

geometrician, geometer *n* one skilled in geometry.

geometry *n* the science of magnitude; that science which treats of the properties of lines, angles, surfaces and solids; that branch of mathematics which treats of the properties and relations of magnitudes.

geomorphology *n* physical geography.

geoponic *adj* pertaining to tillage or agriculture.

geoponics *n* the art or science of cultivation.

Georgian *adj* belonging or relating to the reigns of the four Georges, kings of Great Britain from 1714 to 1830; a native of Georgia in the United States or of Georgia in the Caucasus.

georgic *n* a rural poem; a poetical composition on the subject of husbandry.

geotropism *n* disposition or tendency to turn or incline towards the earth, the characteristic exhibited in a young plant when deprived of light.

geranium *n* the cranesbill genus, a genus of herbaceous plants, natives of the temperate regions of the world, having flowers which are usually blue or red and often handsome; the geraniums of gardens belong, however, to a different genus (pelargonium).

gerfalcon *n* the gyrfalcon.

germ *n* (*physiol*) the earliest form under which any organism appears; the rudimentary or embryonic form of an organism; hence, that from which anything springs; origin; first principle; any micro-organism, especially any of the bacteria which produce diseases in human beings or the lower animals; a microbe.

german *adj* (*arch*) sprung from the same father and mother or from members of the same family.

German *n* a native or inhabitant of Germany; the language of the higher and more southern districts of Germany and the literary language of all Germany, called by the people themselves *Deutsch* (= Dutch). —*adj* belonging to Germany.

germander *n* an aromatic plant with two-lipped flowers, a few species of which are common in Britain.

germane *adj* closely akin; nearly related; allied; relevant; pertinent.

Germanic *adj* of Germany, Germans or of a German-speaking nation.—*n* the family of languages derived from Indo-European that comprises the English, Dutch, German, Scandinavian and Gothic languages.

German measles *n* a mild, infectious, viral disease, most common in children, characterized by a rash and likely to damage an unborn foetus if the mother contracts the disease (—also called **rubella**).

German shepherd *n* a breed of large, smooth-haired dog, often used by the police and to guard property; an Alsatian dog.

German silver *n* a white alloy of nickel, formed by fusing together 100 parts of copper, 60 of zinc and 40 of nickel.

germicide *n* a substance that destroys germs, especially disease germs.

germinate *vi* (**germinated, germinating**) to sprout; to bud; to shoot; to begin to vegetate, as a plant or its seed.

germination *n* the act of germinating; the first act of growth by an embryo plant.

germ warfare *n* a form of biological warfare using bacteria, viruses to destroy life.

gerrymander *vi* to rearrange the boundaries of a voting district or constituency in such a way as to favour a particular political party or candidate.

gerrymandering *n* the rearrangement of constituency boundaries to favour a particular political party or candidate.

gerund *n* a part of the Latin verb, or a kind of verbal noun, used to express the meaning of the present infinitive active; a term adopted into other languages to indicate various forms or modifications of the verb, in English being applied to verbal nouns such as 'teaching' in expressions like 'fit for teaching boys'.

gerundive *n* a name given originally by Latin grammarians to the future participle passive, a form similar to the gerund; sometimes used in regard to other languages.

Gestapo *n* the secret police in Germany from 1933-45, who worked to ensure obedience to the Nazi government.

gestation *n* the act of carrying young in the womb from conception to delivery; pregnancy.

gesticulate *vi* (**gesticulated, gesticulating**) to make gestures or motions by way of emphasis, explanation, etc.

gesticulation *n* the act of gesticulating or making gestures; a gesture.

gesture *n* a motion or action intended to express an idea or feeling or to enforce an argument or opinion; movement of the body or limbs; an action or statement for the sake of courtesy, diplomacy or the creating of an impression, etc.—*vt* (**gestured, gesturing**) to express by gesture.—*vi* to make gestures.

get *vt* (*pret* **got** (**gat**, *obs*), *pp* **got, gotten**, *ppr* **getting**) to procure; to obtain; to gain possession of by any means; to beget; to procreate; to commit to memory; to learn; to prevail on; to induce; to persuade; to procure or cause to be or occur (*to get a letter sent, to get things together*); (*refl*) to carry or betake oneself.—*vi* to make acquisition; to gain; to arrive at any place or state; to become (followed by some modifying word and sometimes implying difficulty or labour).

get-together *n* an informal social gathering; an informal meeting or discussion group.

get-up *n* equipment; dress and other accessories (*an actor's get-up*); (*colloq*) dress; outfit.

gewgaw *n* a showy trifle; a pretty thing of little worth; a toy; a bauble.

geyser *n* the name given to springs or fountains of hot water characterized by periodic eruptions, the water rising up in a column; a device for heating water by passing it over plates heated by gas.

ghastly *adj* terrible of countenance; death-like; dismal; horrible; shocking; dreadful.

ghee *n* the butter made from the milk of the buffalo converted into a kind of oil, much used in Indian cookery.

gherkin *n* a small-fruited variety of the cucumber used for pickling.

ghetto *n* formerly, the quarter in a city to which the Jews were confined; a section of a city inhabited by a particular racial, minority, etc, group, often because of economic or social considerations.

ghillie *n* same as **gillie**.

ghost *n* the soul or spiritual part of man; the visible spirit of a dead person; a disembodied spirit; an apparition; shadow (*not the ghost of a chance*).—**to give up the ghost** to yield up the spirit; to die.—*vt* to act as the ghost-writer of.

ghostly *adj* having to do with the soul or spirit; spiritual; not carnal or secular; pertaining to apparitions (*a ghostly visitant*); suggestive of ghosts (*ghostly gloom*).

ghostwrite *vt* (*pret* **ghostwrote**, *pp* **ghostwritten**, *ppr* **ghostwriting**) to act as the ghostwriter of.

ghostwriter *n* a person who writes a book which is published under the name of someone else who commissions the book.

ghoul *n* an imaginary evil being which is supposed to prey on human bodies; a person who enjoys horrific or macabre things.

ghyll *n* same as **gill**[3].

giant *n* a person of extraordinary bulk and stature; a person of extraordinary strength or powers, bodily or intellectual.—*adj* like a giant; extraordinary in size or strength.

giantess *n* a female giant.

giaour *n* a word used by the Turks to designate the adherents of all religions except Islam, more particularly Christians.

gibber *vi* to speak rapidly and inarticulately.

gibberish *n* rapid and inarticulate talk; unintelligible language; unmeaning words.

gibbet *n* a kind of gallows; a gallows with a crossbeam or an arm projecting from the top; the projecting beam or jib of a crane.—*vt* to hang on a gibbet or gallows; to hold up to ridicule, scorn, infamy, etc.

gherkin

gibbon *n* a name of various apes of the Indian archipelago, slender in form and with very long arms.

gibbous *adj* swelling out or protuberant; exhibiting a sort of hump or convex swelling; hunched (applied to the moon when more than half and less than full).

gibe, jibe *vi* (**gibed, gibing**) to utter taunting sarcastic words; to flout; to jeer.—*vt* to assail with contemptuous words; to mock; to flout; to treat with sarcastic reflections; to taunt.—*n* a taunt or sarcastic remark; a mocking jest; a scoff.

giblets *npl* the entrails of a goose or other fowl removed before cooking.

giddy *adj* having in the head a sensation of whirling or reeling about; affected by vertigo; dizzy; rendering giddy; inducing giddiness (*a giddy height*); suggesting giddiness from its motion; changeable; flighty.

gift *n* that which is given or bestowed; a present; a donation; the act, right or power of giving (*it is not in his gift*); a natural quality or endowment regarded as conferred; power; faculty; talent.—*vt* to confer as a gift; to make a gift or present to; to endow.

gifted *adj* endowed by nature with any power or faculty; largely endowed with intellect or genius; talented.

gig[1] *n* any little thing that is whirled round in play; a whirligig; a light one-horse carriage with two wheels; a long narrow rowing boat; a ship's boat suited for rowing speedily and generally having sails.

gig[2] *n* an engagement for a band or a pop group for one night; a single night's performance.

gigantic *adj* of the size or proportions of a giant; colossal; huge; enormous; immense.

giggle *n* a kind of laugh, with short catches of the voice or breath; a titter.—*vi* (**giggled, giggling**) to laugh with short catches of the breath or voice; to titter.

gigot *n* a leg of mutton or lamb.

gild *vt* (*pret, pp* **gilded** *or* **gilt**, *ppr* **gilding**) to overlay with gold, either in leaf or powder or in amalgam with quicksilver; to give a golden hue to; to illuminate; to brighten; to render bright; to give a fair and agreeable external appearance to.

gilding *n* the art of a gilder; what is laid on by the gilder; a thin coating of gold leaf; (*fig*) fair superficial show.

gill[1] *n* the respiratory organ of fishes and other animals which breathe the air that is mixed in water; (*pl*) the flap that hangs below the beak of a fowl; the flesh under or about a person's chin; the radiating plates on the underside of a fungus.

gill[2] *n* a measure of capacity containing the fourth part of a pint.

gill[3], **ghyll** *n* a ravine or chasm in a hill; a brook.

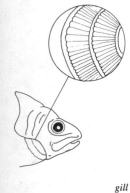

gill

giraffe

gillie, ghillie *n* in the Scottish Highlands, an outdoor male servant, especially one who attends a person while hunting or fishing.

gillyflower *n* the popular name given to certain plants, as the pink or clove pink.

gilt *adj* overlaid with gold.—*n* gold laid on the surface of a thing; gilding.

gilt-edged *adj* applied to securities favoured as safe by trustees, brokers and bankers.

gimbals *npl* a contrivance such as supports the mariner's compass and causes it to assume a constantly vertical position, notwithstanding the rolling of the ship.

gimcrack *adj* badly made or put together; shoddy; cheap and shoddy; worthless.

gimlet *n* a small instrument with a pointed screw at the end, for boring holes in wood by turning.

gimmick *n* a trick or device for attracting notice, advertising or promoting a person, product or service.

gimp *n* a kind of silk twist or edging.

gin[1] *n* a contraction of geneva, a distilled spirit.

gin[2] *n* a trap or snare; a machine for separating the seeds from cotton; a machine for driving piles.—*vt* (**ginned, ginning**) to catch in a gin; to clear of seeds by the cotton gin.

ginger *n* the underground stem of a perennial herb cultivated in most tropical countries, used in medicine and largely as a condiment.—*vt* to put life and vigour into a political party, quicken a policy.

ginger ale *n* a sparkling drink flavoured with ginger.

ginger beer *n* a beverage of sugar and water fermented and flavoured with ginger.

gingerbread *n* a kind of cake usually sweetened with treacle and variously flavoured.

gingerly *adv* cautiously; daintily (*to walk, to handle a thing gingerly*).

ginger wine *n* an alcoholic carbonated drink flavoured with ginger.

gingham *n* a kind of striped cotton or linen cloth.

ginseng *n* a name of two plants, the root of which is considered by the Chinese a panacea or remedy for all ailments or as a restorative.

gipsy *n* same as **gypsy**.

giraffe *n* a ruminant animal inhabiting Africa, the tallest of all animals (owing to the extraordinary length of the neck).

girandole *n* a branched chandelier; a revolving firework or water jet; a pendant or earring with small stones around a larger one; one of several mines connected in a group.

girasole *n* a variety of opal showing a reddish colour when turned towards the sun or any bright light.

gird *vt* (*pret, pp* **girded** *or* **girt**, *ppr* **gird-**

ing) to bind by surrounding with any flexible substance; to make fast by binding; to tie round; to surround; to encircle; to encompass; to prepare (oneself) for action.

girder *n* one who girds; a main beam, either of wood or metal, resting on a wall or pier at each end, used for supporting a superstructure or weight.

girdle *n* a band or belt for the waist; what girds or encloses; a kind of corset; a griddle.—*vt* (**girdled, girdling**) to bind with a girdle; to enclose or environ.

girl *n* a female child; a female not arrived at puberty; a young woman.

girlfriend *n* a female friend, especially one with whom one is romantically involved.

Girl Guide *n* formerly the name for a Guide.

girlhood *n* the state of being a girl; the time of being a girl.

girlish *adj* like or pertaining to a girl; befitting a girl.

Girondin, Girondist *n* a member of the moderate Republican party formed in the French Legislature Assembly of 1791.

girth *n* the band fastening the saddle on a horse's back; the measure round a person's body or anything cylindrical.

gist *n* the main point of a question or that on which it rests; the substance or pith of a matter.

gittern *n* an instrument of the guitar kind strung with wire; a cithern.

give *vt* (**gave** (*pret*), **given** (*pp*), **giving**) to convey to another; to bestow; to communicate (an opinion, advice); to utter; to pronounce (a cry, the word of command); to grant; to cause or enable (*he gave me to understand*); to surrender (with *up*); to excite (*to give offence*); to pledge (one's word); to propose as a toast; to ascribe; to pay; to yield, as a result or product.—*vi* to make gifts; to be liberal; to yield, as to pressure; to recede; to afford entrance or view; to face or be turned (as a house).

given *adj* bestowed; conferred; admitted or supposed; addicted; disposed (*much given to carping*); (*math*) supposed or held to be known.

given name *n* a first name; a Christian name.

gizzard *n* the third and principal stomach in birds, often very thick and muscular.

glabrous *adj* smooth; having a surface devoid of hair or pubescence.

glacé *adj* covered in icing, as fruit.—*vt* (**glacéed, glacéing**) to cover with icing.

glacial *n* pertaining to ice or to the action of ice; pertaining to glaciers; icy; frozen; having a cold glassy look; cold, unfriendly.

glacier *n* an immense accumulation of ice, or ice and snow, formed in high valleys above the snowline and slowly moving downwards into the lower valleys, reaching frequently to the borders of cultivation.

glacis *n* (*pl* **glacises, glacis**) (*fort*) a sloping bank.

glad *adj* affected with pleasure or satisfaction; pleased; joyful; gratified; well contented (often followed by *of* or *at*); cheerful; bright; wearing the appearance of joy (*a glad countenance*).—*vt* (**gladded, gladding**) to make glad; to gladden.

gladden *vt* to make glad; to cheer; to please; to exhilarate.

glade *n* an opening or passage through a wood; a kind of avenue in a wood or forest covered with grass.

gladiator *n* among the ancient Romans one who fought with deadly weapons in the amphitheatre and other places for the entertainment of the people; hence, a combatant in general.

gladiolus *n* (*pl* **gladioli**) an extensive and very beautiful genus of bulbous-rooted plants, found most abundantly in South Africa; sword lily.

gladly *adv* with pleasure; joyfully; cheerfully.

gladsome *adj* glad; cheerful; causing joy, pleasure or cheerfulness.

Glagolitic *adj* of or pertaining to Glagol, an ancient Slavonic alphabet.

glair *n* the white of an egg used as varnish to preserve paintings and as a size in gilding; any similar substance.—*vt* to varnish or smear with glair.

glaive, glave *n* a sword; a broadsword; a falchion; also a halberd or bill.

glamour *n* magical influence causing a person to see objects differently from how they really are; fascination; alluring charm; beauty, particularly of rather an artificial nature.

glance *n* a sudden dart or flash of light or splendour; a rapid or momentary casting of the eye; a name given to some minerals which possess a metallic lustre.—*vi* (**glanced, glancing**) to look briefly or quickly; to shoot or dart rays of light or splendour; to emit flashes or coruscations of light; to flash; to fly off in an oblique direction; to strike or graze; to dart aside.—*vt* to shoot or dart suddenly; to cast for a moment (*to glance the eye*).

gland *n* (*anat*) an organ that separates substances from the blood and synthesizes them for further use in or for elimination from, the body; (*bot*) a secreting organ occurring on the epidermis of plants; also, a kind of one-celled fruit, with a dry pericarp; (*engin*) the part of a stuffing box which is movable and compresses the packing.

glanders *n* a very dangerous and highly contagious disease, chiefly seen in horses

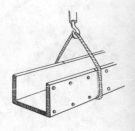

girder

but capable of being transmitted to humans, which especially affects the glands (whence the name), the mucous membranes of the nose, lungs, etc.

glandular *adj* consisting of a gland or glands; pertaining to glands.

glandular fever *n* a type of infectious, viral disease causing fever, swollen lymph glands and an increase in the white blood cells (also called **infectious mononucleosis**).

glare *n* a bright dazzling light; splendour that dazzles the eyes; a confusing and bewildering light; a fierce, piercing look.—*vi* (**glared, glaring**) to shine with a bright dazzling light; to look with fierce, piercing eyes; to look with great anger; to have a dazzling effect; to be ostentatiously splendid.

glaring *adj* shining with dazzling lustre; excessively bright; vulgarly splendid; forcing one's notice; notorious; open; barefaced (*a glaring crime*).

glass *n* a hard, brittle, transparent artificial substance formed by the fusion of siliceous matter (as powdered flint or fine sand) with some alkali; something made of glass; a mirror or looking glass; a glass vessel filled with running sand for measuring time; a drinking vessel made of glass; the quantity which such a vessel holds; an optical instrument, such as a lens or a telescope; a barometer or thermometer; (*pl*) spectacles.—*adj* made of glass.

glass-blower *n* one whose business it is to blow and fashion vessels of glass.

glass-cutter *n* one who cuts glass or grinds it into ornamental forms; an instrument for cutting glass.

glasses *npl* spectacles.

glasshouse *n* a large greenhouse; a house built largely of glass, as a conservatory or greenhouse; (*sl*) a prison.

glasspaper *n* a polishing paper made by strewing finely pounded glass on paper smeared with thin glue.

glasswort *n* a name of various plants common on the Mediterranean coasts yielding ashes containing much soda and hence used in making glass.

glassy *adj* made of glass; vitreous; resembling glass; having a lustre or surface like glass; expressionless.

glaucoma *n* a disease of the eye caused by increased pressure of the fluid in the eyeball.

glaucous *adj* of a sea-green colour; of a light green or bluish-green; (*bot*) covered with a fine bluish or greenish powder or bloom.

glave *n* same as **glaive**.

glaze *vt* (**glazed, glazing**) to furnish with glass or panes of glass; to encrust or overlay with glass or a vitreous coating; to give a glossy, or smooth, shining surface to.—

glengarry

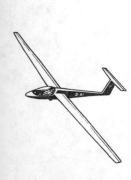

glider

vi to assume a dim, glassy lustre (said of the eye); to become expressionless.—*n* that which is used in glazing.

glazier *n* one whose business is to fix panes of glass in windows, etc.

glazing *n* the act or art of one who glazes; the substance with which anything is overlaid to give it a glassy appearance; enamel; glaze; (in painting) transparent or semi-transparent colours passed thinly over other colours to modify the effect.

gleam *n* a beam or flash of light; a ray; a small stream of light; brightness.—*vi* to dart or throw rays of light; to glimmer; to glitter; to shine.

gleaming *adj* beaming; shining clearly and brightly; radiant.

glean *vt* to gather after a reaper, or on a reaped cornfield, the ears of grain left ungathered; hence, to collect in scattered portions; to pick up here and there; to gather slowly and assiduously.—*vi* to gather ears of grain left by reapers.

glebe *n* soil; ground; earth; the land belonging to a parish church or ecclesiastical benefice.

glee *n* joy; merriment; mirth; gaiety; a musical composition consisting of two or more contrasted movements with the parts forming a series of interwoven melodies.

gleeful *adj* full of glee; merry; joyous.

glen *n* a secluded narrow valley; a dale; a depression or space between hills.

glengarry *n* a type of boat-shaped bonnet with a ribbon down the back, originating in the Scottish Highlands.

glib *adj* smooth; slippery, more commonly voluble; fluent; having words always ready.

glide *vi* (**glided, gliding**) to flow gently; to move along silently and smoothly; to pass along without apparent effort (*a river, a bird, a skater glides*); to fly on a descending path, when the aircraft machine is not under engine power.—*n* the movement of one who or that which glides; the joining or slurring together of two successive sounds; a kind of dance.

glider *n* one who glides; an aircraft which can travel through the air for a certain time without engine power.

glimmer *vi* to emit feeble or scattered rays of light; to shine faintly; to give a feeble light; to flicker.—*n* a faint and unsteady light; feeble scattered rays of light; glitter; twinkle; also, a name of mica.

glimmering *n* a glimmer; a gleam; a faint indication; an inkling; a glimpse.

glimpse *n* a gleam; a momentary flash; a short transitory view; a glance; a faint resemblance; a slight tinge.—*vt* (**glimpsed, glimpsing**) to see by a glimpse or glimpses.

glint *vi* to glance; to gleam; to give a flash of light.—*n* a glance; a flash; a gleam.

glissade *n* a sliding or gliding down a slope.

glissando *n* (*pl* **glissandi**, **glissandos**) (*mus*) a run by sliding the fingers over the keys of a piano; a quick slur on a violin.

glisten *vi* to shine; to sparkle with light; to shine with a scintillating light.

glister *vi* to shine; to glitter.—*n* lustre; glitter.

glitter *vi* to shine with a broken and scattered light; to emit rapid flashes of light; to gleam; to sparkle; to glisten; to be showy or brilliant.—*n* bright sparkling light; brilliancy; splendour; lustre.

glitz *n* showy glamour.

glitzy *adj* ostentatiously glamorous; flashy.

gloaming *n* the twilight; closing period.

gloat *vi* to gaze with admiration, eagerness or desire; to feast the eyes either actually or in thought; to contemplate with evil satisfaction.

global warming *n* a long-term increase in climatic temperatures, thought to be a result of the greenhouse effect.

globe *n* a round or spherical solid body; a ball; a sphere; the earth; an artificial sphere on whose convex surface is drawn a map or representation of the earth (*a terrestrial globe*) or of the heavens (*a celestial globe*).—*vt* (**globed**, **globing**) to gather into a round mass.

globetrotter *n* a person who travels widely.

globetrotting *adj* travelling widely.

globose, **globous** *adj* spherical; globular.

globular *adj* globe-shaped; having the form of a ball or sphere; round; spherical.

globule *n* a small particle of matter of a spherical form; a round body or corpuscle found in the blood.

globulin *n* any of a class of simple proteins that occur widely in plant and animal tissue.

glockenspiel *n* a percussion instrument of tuned metal bars played with small hammers.

glomerate *adj* congregated; gathered into a round mass or dense cluster.

glomeration *n* conglomeration; an aggregate.

gloom *n* obscurity; partial darkness; thick shade; dusk; cloudiness or heaviness of mind; heaviness, dejection, anger, sullenness; a depressing state of affairs; a dismal prospect.—*vi* to appear dimly; to be seen in an imperfect or waning light; to look gloomy, sad or dismal; to frown; to lower.—*vt* to make gloomy or dark; to fill with gloom or sadness.

gloomy *adj* involved in gloom; imperfectly illuminated; dusky or dark; characterized by gloom; wearing the aspect of sorrow; dejected; heavy of heart; dismal; doleful.

glorification *n* the act of glorifying or the state of being glorified.

glorify *vt* (**glorified**, **glorifying**) to give or ascribe glory to; to praise; to magnify and honour; to honour; to extol; to make glorious; to exalt to glory.

glorious *adj* characterized by attributes, qualities or acts that are worthy of glory; of exalted excellence and splendour; noble; illustrious; renowned; celebrated; magnificent; wonderful; splendid.

glory *n* praise, honour, admiration or distinction accorded by common consent to a person or thing; honourable fame; renown; celebrity; a state of greatness or renown; pomp; magnificence; brightness; lustre; splendour; brilliancy; the happiness of heaven; celestial bliss; distinguished honour or ornament; an object of which one is or may be proud; in painting, the radiation round the head or figure of a deity, saint, angel, etc.—*vi* (**gloried**, **glorying**) to exult with joy; to rejoice; to be boastful; to have pride.

gloss[1] *n* brightness or lustre of a body proceeding from a smooth and generally a soft surface; polish; sheen (*the gloss of silk*); a specious appearance or representation; external show that may mislead.—*vt* to give gloss to; to give a superficial lustre; to make smooth and shining.—**to gloss over** to hide (an error, etc) or make seem right or inconsequential.

gloss[2] *n* a marginal note or interlineation explaining the meaning of some word in a text; a remark intended to illustrate some point of difficulty in an author; comment; annotation; explanation.—*vt* to render clear by comments; to annotate; to illustrate.

glossary *n* a list of words, particularly technical or specialized words, with their definitions or explanations, either placed at the back of a book, etc, or published as a separate publication.

glossy *adj* having a gloss; having a soft, smooth and shining surface; lustrous with softness to the touch; specious or plausible.

glottal *adj* relating to the glottis.

glottis *n* (*pl* **glottises**, **glottides**) the opening at the upper part of the windpipe and between the vocal chords, which, by its dilatation and contraction, contributes to the modulation of the voice.

glove *n* a cover for the hand or for the hand and wrist, with a separate sheath for each finger.—*vt* (**gloved**, **gloving**) to cover with or as with a glove.

glover *n* one makes or sells gloves.

glow *vi* to burn with an intense or white heat and especially without flame; to give forth bright light and heat; to feel great heat of body; to be hot or flushed in person; to be bright or red, as with animation, blushes, etc; to exhibit brightness of colour; to feel pleased and happy; to feel the heat of passion; to be ardent; to burn or be vehement.

globe

gloves

—*n* shining heat or white heat; incandescence; brightness of colour; redness; vehemence of colour; ardour; animation.

glowing *adj* shining with intense heat; bright in colour; red; ardent; vehement; fervid; heated; fiery.

glow-worm *n* the wingless female of a kind of beetle, emitting a shining green light to attract the male.

gloxinia *n* a genus of almost stemless plants with fine bell-shaped flowers, natives of tropical America.

glucose *n* a naturally occurring sugar in animals and plants and an important primary energy source.

glue *n* common or impure gelatine, obtained by boiling animal substances, as the skins, hoofs, etc, of animals, with water (used for uniting pieces of wood or other materials); an adhesive.—*vt* (**glued, gluing**) to join with glue or other adhesive substance; to hold together, as if by glue; to fix; to rivet.

glum *adj* frowning; sullen; in low spirits.

glume *n* the husk of chaff or grain.

glumness *n* the condition or quality of being glum.

glut *vt* (**glutted, glutting**) to cloy, sate or disgust; to oversupply, as a market.—*n* a surfeit; superabundance; an oversupply of any commodity in the market.

gluten *n* a tough elastic substance of a greyish colour, which becomes brown and brittle by drying, found in the flour of wheat and other grain.

glutinous, glutinose *adj* gluey; viscous; viscid; tenacious; resembling glue; (*bot*) covered by a slippery moisture.

glutton *n* one who indulges to excess in eating, or eating and drinking; a gormandizer; one who has a tremendous capacity for something (e.g. work); the wolverine.

gluttonous *adj* characterized by gluttony; given to excessive eating; insatiable.

gluttony *n* the act or practice of a glutton; excess in eating, or eating and drinking.

glycerine, glycerin *n* the popular and commercial name for glycerol.

glycerol *n* a transparent colourless liquid with a very sweet taste, obtained from fats.

glycogen *n* a white insoluble starch-like substance stored in the liver to be converted into glucose when needed.

glycosuria *n* (*pathol*) the presence of glucose in the urine.

glyptic *adj* pertaining to the art of sculpture or engraving.

glyptodont *n* a gigantic fossil animal, closely allied to the armadillo, covered with an bony coat.

glyptography *n* the art or process of engraving on precious stones.

gnarl *n* a protuberance on the outside of a tree; a knot.

gnarled *adj* having many knots or knotty

gnu

protuberances; cross-grained; perverse.

gnash *vt* to strike together (the teeth) as in anger or pain.—*vi* to strike or dash the teeth together, as in rage or pain.

gnat *n* any of various small two-winged insects that bite or sting.

gnathic *adj* pertaining to the jaw or jaws.

gnaw *vt* to bite by little and little; to wear away by biting; to nibble at; to bite in agony or rage; to fret; to corrode;—*vi* to use the teeth in biting; to bite with repeated efforts; to cause or be affected with steady annoying pain.

gneiss *n* a kind of hard tough crystalline rock, composed in the main of quartz, feldspar and mica.

gnocchi *npl* small dumplings made from flour, semolina or potatoes.

gnome[1] *n* an imaginary being, said in legend to inhabit the inner parts of the earth and to be the guardian of mines, quarries, etc; a goblin; a small misshapen person; (*sl*) an international banker or financier.

gnome[2] *n* a brief reflection or maxim; a saw; an aphorism.

gnomic *adj* containing or dealing in maxims (*the ancient Greek gnomic poets*).

gnomon *n* the style or pin of a sundial, which by its shadow shows the hour of the day; a style consisting of a pillar, pyramid, etc, erected perpendicularly to the horizon, in order to find the altitudes, declinations, etc, of the sun and stars; the index of the hour circle of a globe.

Gnostic *n* one of a sect that arose in the first ages of Christianity, who pretended to be the only people who had a true knowledge of the Christian religion and professed a system of doctrines based partly on Christianity, partly on Greek and Oriental philosophy.—*adj* pertaining to the Gnostics or their doctrines.

Gnosticism *n* the doctrines or principles of the Gnostics.

gnu *n* a kind of large African antelope with a head like an ox (also called **wildebeest**).

go *vi* (*pret* **went**, *pp* **gone**, *ppr* **going**) to walk; to pass, proceed, move or be in motion; to work or function; to depart or move from a place, opposed to come; to have currency or use; to circulate (*the story goes*); to be reckoned or esteemed; to proceed or happen in a given manner; to have course; to turn out (*the case went against him*); to have recourse (*to go to law*); to be about to (in this usage a kind of auxiliary and usually in *ppr*, as—*going to say, going to begin*); to be guided or regulated (*to go by some rule*); to be with young, to be pregnant (*six months gone*); to be alienated, sold or disposed of (*it went for a trifle*); to extend, reach, lead (*this road goes to London*); to extend in effect, meaning or purport; to be of force or value; to proceed or tend towards a result or consequence; to contribute, conduce, concur (frequently with *to*, *towards*, etc); to perish; to sink or die; to become (*she has gone mad*).—**to go about** to handle (a task, etc) efficiently; to undertake (duties, etc); (*naut*) to change tack.—**to go off** to explode; to depart; (of food, etc) to become stale or rotten; to fall asleep; to proceed or occur in a certain manner; to take place as planned; to stop liking (someone or something).—**to go out** to depart; (of light, a fire, etc) to become extinguished; to cease to be fashionable; to socialize; (of a radio or television show) to be broadcast; to spend time with, especially a person of the opposite sex.—**to go slow** to work at a slow rate as part of an industrial dispute.— **to go without** to be deprived of or endure the lack of.—*n* (*pl* **goes**) stamina or power of endurance; energy or vitality; try or attempt; a turn in a game or series; a success.

goad *n* a pointed instrument used to stimulate a beast to move faster; hence, anything that urges or stimulates.—*vt* to drive with a goad; hence, to incite; to stimulate; to instigate; to urge forward.

go-ahead *adj* characterized by or disposed to progress; enterprising.—*n* permission to proceed.

goal *n* the point set to bound a race; the space between the two upright posts in the game of football, hockey, etc; also the act of driving the ball through between the posts; the end to which a design tends or which a person aims to reach or accomplish.

goalkeeper *n* a player whose special duty is to protect the goal, in soccer, hockey, etc.

goat *n* a horned ruminant quadruped, nearly of the size of a sheep but stronger and more agile.

goatee *n* a beard that hangs down from the chin without whiskers.

goatherd *n* one whose occupation is to tend goats.

goat moth *n* a large British moth, the larvae of which, about three inches long, damage trees by hollowing out galleries in them.

goatsucker *n* a name common to various species of birds which feed on nocturnal insects; the fern owl or nightjar.

gobbet *n* a mouthful; a morsel; a lump.

gobble *vt* (**gobbled, gobbling**) to swallow in large pieces; to swallow hastily.—*vi* to make a noise in the throat, as a turkey.—*n* a noise made in the throat, as that of a turkey cock.

gobbledygook *n* pompous and roundabout language that is difficult to understand.

Gobelin *n* a kind of rich tapestry.

go-between *n* an intermediary.

goblet *n* a kind of cup or drinking vessel without a handle.

goblin *n* an evil or mischievous sprite; a gnome; an elf; a malicious fairy.

gobsmacked *adj* (*colloq*) amazed; astonished.

goby *n* a name given to various rather small fishes.

go-by *n* a passing without notice; an intentional disregard or avoidance.

go-cart *n* a low flat vehicle with wheels for children to pull or ride in; a go-kart.

god *n* a being conceived of as possessing divine power; a divinity; a deity; any person or thing exalted too much in estimation or deified; (*pl*) the audience in the upper gallery of a theatre (so called from their elevated position).

God *n* the Supreme Being, Jehovah, the eternal and infinite Spirit, the Creator; Allah.

godchild *n* a godson or goddaughter.

goddaughter *n* a female for whom one becomes sponsor at baptism.

goddess *n* a female deity; a heathen deity of the female sex; a woman of superior charms or excellence.

godfather *n* a male godparent; (*sl*) the head of a Mafia crime family or other criminal organization.

god-fearing *adj* a term applied to one who fears or reverences God.

godhead *n* deity; divinity; divine nature or essence.

Godhead *n* God; the Supreme Being.

godless *adj* having or acknowledging no God; impious; ungodly; irreligious; wicked.

godlike *adj* resembling a god or God; divine; of superior excellence.

godly *adj* pious; reverencing God and his character and laws; devout; religious; righteous; conformed to or influenced by God's law.—*adv* piously; righteously.

godmother *n* a female godparent.

godparent *n* in several churches, a man or woman who at the baptism of a child makes a profession of the Christian faith in his or her name and guarantees his or her religious education.

God's acre *n* the churchyard.

godsend *n* an unlooked-for acquisition or piece of good fortune.

godson *n* a male for whom one has been sponsor at baptism.

Godspeed *n* success; prosperity; a prosperous journey, usually in phrase *to bid a person Godspeed*.

godwit *n* a name of several wading birds of no great size.

goffer, gauffer *vt* to plait; to crimp; to flute.

goffering *n* an ornamental plaiting, used for the frills and borders of women's caps, etc.

goffering iron *n* an iron used for plaiting or fluting frills, etc.

goggle *vi* (**goggled, goggling**) to stare with

goalkeeper

goblet

widely opened or bulging eyes.—*adj* full or prominent and rolling or staring (said of the eyes).—*n* a staring or bulging of the eyes; (*pl*) protective spectacles which fit snugly around the eyes; (*colloq*) spectacles.

go-go dancer *n* a scantily clad dancer employed in a nightclub or disco.

going *n* the act of moving in any manner; the state of the ground, as in horse-racing; departure; procedure.

goings-on *npl* actions; conduct (used mostly in a bad sense).

goitre *n* an abnormal enlargement of the thyroid gland.

go-kart *n* a low vehicle consisting of a frame with wheels, engine and steering wheel, used in racing.

gold *n* a precious metal of a bright yellow colour and the most ductile and malleable of all metals and one of the heaviest; money; riches; wealth; a symbol of what is valuable or much prized; a bright yellow colour, like that of the metal; archery, the exact centre of the target, marked with gold or of a gold colour.—*adj* made of gold; consisting of gold.

goldfish

goldcrest *n* one of the smallest British birds; the golden-crested wren.

gold-digger *n* a person who mines gold; a woman who is interested in a man because of his money and the gifts he gives her.

golden *adj* made of gold; of the colour or lustre of gold; yellow; shining; splendid; excellent; most valuable; precious; happy; marked by the happiness of mankind; preeminently favourable or auspicious (*a golden opportunity*).

golden eagle *n* a large eagle found in mountainous regions in the Northern hemisphere, so called because of a slight golden gleam about the head and neck.

goldeneye *n* one of two species of duck of northern regions with a rounded head, yellow eyes, a short bill and black and white plumage.

Golden Fleece *n* in Greek myth, a ram's fleece, the aim of the Argonauts under Jason.

golden handshake *n* a sum of money given to an employee on leaving a firm, sometimes in compensation for being declared redundant.

gondola

goldenrod *n* a name of certain composite plants with rod-like stems and terminal spikes or racemes of small yellow flowers.

golden rule *n* any basic or important rule; a guiding principle.

golden wedding *n* the fiftieth anniversary of a marriage.

gold fever *n* a mania for digging or otherwise searching for gold.

gold field *n* a district or region where gold is found.

goldfinch *n* a British songbird belonging to the finches, so named from the yellow markings on its wings.

goldfish, golden carp *n* a species of carp, so named from its colour, now largely bred in ponds, tanks or glass vessels.

gold leaf *n* gold beaten into an exceedingly thin sheet or leaf.

goldsmith *n* an artisan who manufactures vessels and ornaments of gold.

golf *n* a game played with clubs and balls, generally over large commons, downs or links; the object being to drive the ball, with as few strokes as possible, into holes placed at considerable distances apart.

golf ball *n* a hard dimpled ball used in golf; the spherical printing head in some printers.

golf club *n* a long-shafted club with a wooden or metal head used in golf; an association of people who play golf, usually having its own course and facilities; the premises of such an association.

golliwog *n* a soft black-faced doll.

golosh *n* same as **galosh**.

gonad *n* a reproductive gland such as the testes in the male and the ovary in the female.

gondola *n* a flat-bottomed boat, very long and narrow with high pointed ends, propelled from the stem with an oar and used chiefly at Venice; the passenger compartment hanging from an airship or balloon.

gondolier *n* a person who rows a gondola.

gone *pp* passed; vanished away; consumed; finished; dead; lost or destroyed; worn out, exhausted or overpowered.

gonfalon *n* an ensign or standard, the bearer of which in many of the medieval republican cities of Italy was often the chief personage in the state.

gonfalonier *n* one entrusted with a gonfalon; a chief magistrate in medieval Italian cities.

gong *n* a Chinese musical instrument of percussion, made of a mixed metal and shaped like a large round flat dish, used for making loud sonorous signals, for adding to the clangour of martial instruments, etc; a metal disc-shaped object struck with a hammer to summon people to meals.

goniometer *n* an instrument for measuring solid angles, particularly the angles formed by the faces of mineral crystals.

gonorrhoea *n* a sexually transmitted inflammatory ailment of the male urethra or the female vagina, attended with secretion of mucus intermingled with pus.

goo (*colloq*) *n* a thick, sticky substance; sentimentality.

good *adj* the opposite of *bad*; conducive, in general, to any useful end or purpose; serviceable; advantageous; beneficial; wholesome; suitable; useful; fit; proper;

right; possessing desirable or valuable physical or moral qualities; virtuous, righteous, dutiful, pious or religious; excellent, valuable, precious; kind, benevolent, humane, merciful or friendly; clever, skilful or dextrous; adequate, sufficient or competent; valid; of unimpaired credit; able to fulfil engagements; real, actual, serious (*good earnest*); considerable; more than a little; not deficient; full or complete; not blemished; unsullied; immaculate; honourable.—*n* what is good, especially a result that is so (*no good can come of it*); what is serviceable, fit, excellent, kind, benevolent, etc (*to do good*); benefit; advantage, opposed to evil, ill, harm, etc; welfare or prosperity (*the good of the state*); a valuable possession or piece of property (almost always in the plural in this sense and equivalent to wares, commodities, movables, household furniture, chattels, effects).

good afternoon *n*, *interj* a kind wish or salutation at meeting or parting.

goodbye a form of salutation at parting; farewell.

good day *n*, *interj* a kind wish or salutation at meeting or parting.

good evening *n*, *interj* a kind wish or salutation at meeting or parting.

good fellowship *n* merry society; friendliness.

good-for-nothing *adj* worthless; useless; lazy.—*n* a useless, lazy or idle person.

Good Friday *n* the Friday immediately preceding Easter, kept sacred as the day of Christ's crucifixion.

good humour *n* a cheerful temper or state of mind.

goodish *adj* pretty good; tolerable; fair.

goodly *adj* being of a handsome form; fair to look on; beautiful; graceful; well-favoured; pleasant; agreeable; large; considerable.

good morning *n*, *interj* a kind wish or salutation at meeting or parting.

good nature *n* natural mildness and kindness of disposition.

goodness *n* the state or quality of being good; a euphemism for God (*thank goodness*).

good night *n*, *interj* a kind wish between persons parting for the night.

goods *npl* commodities; articles of trade, especially those which are transportable; personal possessions or property; (*colloq*) the desired or required articles, information, etc.

goodwill *n* benevolence; kindly feelings; (*com*) the custom of any trade or business; the right to take up a trade or business connection, purchased of one who gives it up.

goody-goody *adj* excessively or annoyingly virtuous.

gooey (*colloq*) *adj* soft and sticky; sweet and sentimental.

goof *n* (*colloq*) a stupid person; a fool; a blunder.—*vi* to make a blunder; to bungle.

goofy *adj* stupid; foolish.

googly *n* at cricket, a ball which breaks in from the off while delivered with a leg-break action.

goon *n* a stupid person; a fool; a thug.

goosander *n* a swimming bird allied to the ducks and divers; the merganser.

goose *n* (*pl* **geese**) the name of several well-known swimming birds larger than ducks; a silly, stupid person; a tailor's smoothing iron.—**to cook one's goose** to do for one; to finish a person.

gooseberry *n* the edible fruit of a common prickly shrub either red, yellow or green in colour and hairy or smooth on the surface and when cooked used in jams, pies, etc; the shrub itself; an unwanted person in the company of a couple or group of couples.

goose bumps, goose flesh, goose pimples *npl* a peculiar roughness of the human skin produced by cold, fear, etc.

goose grass *n* a species of creeping plant on which geese feed.

goose step *n* the German or Russian military parade step made by alternately raising a stiffened leg to an exaggerated height.

gopher *n* the name given in America to several burrowing animals from their honey-combing the earth; also a species of burrowing tortoise of the Southern States.

Gordian knot *n* a knot tied by Gordius, king of Phrygia, which could be untied only by Alexander the Great; hence, any inextricable difficulty.—**to cut the Gordian knot** to remove a difficulty by bold or unusual measures.

gore[1] *n* blood that is shed; thick or clotted blood.

gore[2] *vt* (**gored, goring**) to stab; to pierce with a pointed instrument, as a spear, or with the horns (as an ox).

gore[3] *n* a triangular-shaped piece, as of cloth, let into or regarded as let into a larger piece; a gusset.—*vt* (**gored, goring**) to cut a gore in; to piece with a gore.

gorge *n* the throat or gullet; that which is swallowed; food caused to regurgitate through nausea or disgust; a narrow passage between hills or mountains; the entrance into a bastion or other outwork of a fort.—*vt* (**gorged, gorging**) to swallow, especially with greediness or in large quantities; to fill the stomach of; to satiate (often reflexive).—*vi* to feed greedily; to stuff oneself.

gorgeous *adj* exceedingly showy; splendid; magnificent; glittering with gay colours.

gorget *n* a piece of armour for defending the throat or neck; a small crescent-shaped

gooseberry

metallic ornament formerly worn on the breast by officers.

gorgon *n* someone like a Gorgon; an ugly or formidable woman.

Gorgon *n* in Greek myth, one of several monsters of terrific aspect, the sight of which turned the beholder to stone.

Gorgonzola *n* a kind of Italian ewe-milk cheese made at Gorgonzola, a village near Milan.

gorilla *n* the largest of the apes, very strong and fierce, found chiefly in the woody equatorial regions of Africa.

gormand *n* a gourmand.

gormandize *vi* (**gormandized, gormandizing**) to eat greedily; to swallow voraciously.

gorse *n* the common furze or whin.

gory *adj* covered with gore; bloody.

goshawk *n* a kind of large hawk used in falconry.

gosling *n* a young goose.

gospel *n* something which is accepted as being unquestionably true; any general doctrine (*a political gospel*).—*adj* accordant with a gospel; relating to a gospel; evangelical.

Gospel *n* the history of Jesus Christ; any of the four records of Christ's life left by His Apostles.—*adj* accordant with the Gospel; relating to the Gospel.

gossamer *n* a fine filmy substance, a kind of delicate cobwebs, floating in the air in calm clear weather, especially in autumn, formed by small species of spiders; any very light and flimsy material.—*adj* light as gossamer.

gossip *n* an idle carrier of tales; idle chat, especially about the affairs of others; mere tattle; groundless rumour.—*vi* to prate; to chat; to tell idle tales.

gossip column *n* a section of a newspaper or magazine devoted to gossip about celebrities.

Goth *n* one of an ancient Germanic race of people who overran and took an important part in subverting the Roman Empire; a barbaric person.

Gothic *adj* pertaining to the Goths; rude; barbarous; (*archit*) of a style characterized by pointed arches, steep roofs, elaborate stonework, etc; of a literary style that emphasizes the mysterious and the grotesque. —*n* the language of the Goths; (*print*) a bold type, used for titling; the Gothic style or order of architecture.

gouache *n* a method of painting with opaque watercolours.

Gouda

Gouda *adj* a kind of cheese from Gouda, in Holland.

gouge *n* a chisel with a hollow or grooved blade, used to cut holes, channels or grooves.—*vt* (**gouged, gouging**) to scoop out or turn with or as with a gouge.

gown

gourami *n* an oriental species of brightly coloured fish.

gourd *n* the popular name of the family of plants represented by the melon, cucumber, pumpkin, vegetable marrow, etc, or for their fruits.

gourmand *n* a glutton; a greedy feeder; a dainty feeder; an epicure; a gourmet.

gourmet *n* a person of keen palate; a connoisseur in wines and food; an epicure.

gout *n* a disease giving rise to paroxysms of acute pain with inflammation, affecting the small joints and generally the first joint of the great toe and often accompanied by concretions at the joints; a drop; a clot or coagulation.

gouty *adj* diseased with or subject to the gout; pertaining to the gout.

govern *vt* to direct and control; to regulate by authority; to keep within the limits prescribed by law or sovereign will; to influence; to direct; to restrain; to keep in due subjection; to steer or regulate the course of; (*gram*) to cause to be in a particular case or to require a particular case.—*vi* to exercise authority; to administer the laws; to maintain the superiority; to have the control.

governance *n* government; exercise of authority; control; management.

governess *n* a woman who has the care of educating or teaching children in their homes.

government *n* the act of governing; regulation; control; restraint; the exercise of authority; direction and restraint exercised over the actions of men in communities, societies or states; the administration of public affairs; the system of polity in a state; the mode or system according to which the sovereign powers of a nation, the legislative, executive and judicial powers, are vested and exercised; a body politic governed by one authority; a province or division of territory ruled by a governor; the persons or council who administer the laws of a kingdom or state; the administration; the executive power; (*gram*) the influence of a word in regard to construction.

governmental *adj* pertaining to government; made by government.

governor *n* a person appointed to govern a province, etc; the elected head of any state in the USA; the director or head of a governing body of an organization or institution; (*colloq*) an employer; a mechanical devise for automatically controlling the speed of an engine.

governor-general *n* a governor who has under him subordinate or deputy governors; a viceroy.

gown *n* a woman's outer garment; a dress; a frock; a dressing gown; the official dress worn by members of certain professions, as divinity, medicine, law, by magistrates, university professors and students, etc.—*vt* to put a gown on; to clothe or dress in a gown.—*vi* to put on a gown.

grab *vt* (**grabbed, grabbing**) to seize; to snatch; to grip suddenly; (*colloq*) to catch the interest of.—*n* a sudden grasp or seizure; a catch.

grace *n* favour, goodwill or kindness; disposition to oblige another; the love and favour of God; divine influence renewing the heart and restraining from sin; a state of reconciliation to God; virtuous or religious affection or disposition proceeding from divine influence; mercy; pardon; favour conferred; a licence, dispensation or peculiar privilege; a short prayer before or after meals acknowledging the grace or goodness of God; (with possessive pronouns) a title used in addressing or speaking of a duke or duchess; that external element in acting or speaking which renders it appropriate and agreeable; elegance with appropriate dignity; a beauty or element in what pleases the eye; an embellishment; an affectation of elegance, dignity or refinement (*a person's airs and graces*); dispensation by university authorities to take a degree; (*mus*) a turn, trill, shake, etc, introduced for embellishment.—*vt* (**graced, gracing**) to lend or add grace to; to adorn; to serve or embellish or dignify; to honour.

graceful *adj* displaying grace in form or action; possessing a peculiar elegance or attraction in mien or appearance .

graceless *adj* void of grace; somewhat careless in regard to religious matters; not at all devout; unregenerate; unsanctified.

grace note *n* (*mus*) a note added by way of ornament and printed or written in smaller characters; an appoggiatura.

Graces *npl* in Greek myth, three goddesses in whose gift were grace, loveliness and favour;

gracious *adj* favourable; benevolent; merciful; benign; kind; friendly; proceeding from, produced by or associated with divine grace; virtuous; good.

grackle *n* a name of various birds inhabiting Asia and Africa and belonging to the starling family.

gradation *n* the act of grading; the state of being graded; arrangement by grades or ranks; a regular advance from step to step; a degree or relative position in any order or series; the gradual blending of one tint into another.

grade *n* a degree in any series, rank or order; relative position or standing (officers, teachers, magnitudes, crimes of every grade); the degree of a slope; a mark or rating in an exam, etc.—*vt* (**graded, grad-**ing) to arrange in order according to size, quality, rank, degree of advancement, etc; to give a mark or rating to; to make level or evenly sloping.

gradient *n* the degree of slope or inclination of the ground over which a railway, road or canal passes; the rate of ascent or descent; the part of a road which slopes.

gradual *adj* proceeding by steps or degrees; advancing step by step; regular and slow; progressive.

graduate *vt* (**graduated, graduating**) to mark with degrees, regular intervals or divisions; to divide into small regular distances (*to graduate a thermometer*); to temper or modify by degrees; to characterize or mark with degrees or grades, as of intensity; to confer a university degree on; to reduce to a certain consistency by evaporation.—*vi* to receive a degree from a college or university; to pass by degrees; to change gradually; to shade off.—*n* one who has been admitted to a degree in a college or university or by some incorporated society.

graduation *n* the act of graduating or state of being graduated; the marks or lines made on an instrument to indicate degrees or other divisions.

graffiti *npl* any unofficial drawings or inscriptions, often obscene, on walls or other public places.

graft *n* a small shoot or scion of a tree, inserted in another tree and becoming part of it but retaining the characters of its own parent; the transplanting of tissue from another part of the body to replace diseased or damaged tissue; the tissue so transplanted; corrupt gains or practices in politics; hard work.—*vt* to insert a graft on; to propagate by a graft; to incorporate after the manner of a graft; to join on as if organically a part.

Grail *n* the holy vessel said to have been brought to England by Joseph of Arimathea, who had caught the last drops of Christ's blood in it and the object of many quests by medieval knights.

grain *n* a single seed of a plant, particularly of those plants whose seeds are used for food of man or beast; used collectively for corn in general or the fruits of cereal plants, as wheat, rye, barley, oats, etc, as also for the plants themselves; (*pl*) the husks or remains of grain used in brewing or distilling; any small hard particle, as of sand, sugar, salt, etc; a minute particle; an atom (*not a grain of sense*); a unit of weight equal to about 63.8 mg; the substance of a thing regarded with respect to the size, form or direction of the constituent particles; the fibres of wood or other fibrous substances, with regard to their arrangement or direction; texture (*stone or*

grain

wood of a fine grain).—vt to form into grains, as powder, sugar, etc; to paint so as to give the appearance of grains or fibres; (*tan*) to give a granular appearance to the surface; to prepare the hairy side as the outer side.

grainer *n* one who or that which grains; a peculiar brush or a toothed instrument used by painters.

grainy *n* full of grains or corn; full of kernels.

grallatorial *adj* (of birds) wading and having very long legs, long necks and long bills, including the cranes, storks, etc.

gralloch *vt* to remove the entrails from a deer.

gram[1], **gramme** *n* the basic unit of weight in the metric system.

gram[2] *n* the name of a chickpea extensively cultivated in India and used as food and fodder.

gramercy *interj* (*arch*) an expression of great thanks; expressing great surprise.

gramineous, gramineal, graminaceous *adj* like or pertaining to grass or to the family of grasses.

graminivorous *adj* feeding or subsisting on grass, as oxen, etc.

grammar *n* the exposition of the principles which underlie the use of language; a system of general principles and of particular rules for speaking or writing a language; a book containing such principles and rules; language as regulated by rules or usage; propriety of speech (*to violate grammar*); *good grammar, bad grammar*, correct or incorrect language); a treatise on the elements or principles of any science; an outline of the principles of any subject.—*adj* belonging to or contained in grammar.

grammarian *n* one versed in grammar.

grammar school *n* a kind of secondary school, usually with a selective entry system.

grammatical *adj* belonging to grammar; according to the rules of grammar.

gramme *n* same as **gram**[1].

gramophone *n* an instrument for recording and reproducing speech; a record player.

grampus *n* (*pl* **grampuses**) a marine mammal of the dolphin family; a person who snores.

gramophone

granary *n* a storehouse for grain after it is threshed.

grand *adj* great; illustrious; high in power or dignity; noble; splendid; magnificent; principal or chief (used largely in composition (grand juror, grand master); conceived or expressed with great dignity; implying an additional or second generation, as in grandfather, grandchild, etc.

grandam *n* an old woman; a grandmother.

grand-aunt *n* same as **great-aunt**.

grandchild *n* a son's or daughter's child.

granddaughter *n* the daughter of a son or daughter.

grand duke *n* formerly, the title of the sovereign of several of the states of Germany; also formerly applied to members of the imperial family of Russia.

grandee *n* formerly, a Spanish nobleman of the first rank; hence a nobleman or man of high rank in general.

grandeur *n* the state or quality of being grand.

grandfather *n* a father's or mother's father.

grandiloquent *adj* speaking in a lofty style; expressed in high-sounding words; bombastic; pompous.

grandiose *adj* impressive from inherent grandeur; imposing; commonly, aiming at or affecting grandeur; grandiloquent; bombastic; turgid.

grand juror *n* a member of a grand jury.

grand jury *n* a jury whose duty is to examine into the grounds of accusation against offenders, and if they see just cause, to find a true bill against them.

grandmother *n* a father's or mother's mother.

grandnephew *n* same as **great-nephew**.

grandness *n* grandeur; greatness with beauty; magnificence.

grandniece *n* same as **great-niece**.

grandparent *n* the parent of a parent.

grand piano *n* a large kind of piano, of great compass and strength, usually flat instead of upright.

Grand Prix *n* any of various major races for racing cars.

grandsire *n* a grandfather; any ancestor preceding a father.

grandson *n* the son of a son or daughter.

grandstand *n* an elevated erection on a racecourse or in a sports stadium, etc, whence a good view can be obtained.

granduncle *n* same as **great-uncle**.

grand vizier *n* formerly, the chief minister of the Turkish Empire and other Muslim states.

grange *n* a farm, with the dwelling house, stables, barns, etc; the dwelling of a yeoman or gentleman farmer.

granite *n* an unstratified rock, one of the most abundant in the earth's crust, composed generally of grains or crystals of quartz, feldspar and mica, united without regular arrangement.

granitic *adj* of or pertaining to granite; having the nature of granite; consisting of granite.

granivorous *adj* eating grain; feeding or subsisting on seeds.

granny *n* (*colloq*) grandmother.

granny flat *n* a self-contained flat within a family house for an elderly relative.

granny knot *n* a kind of knot similar to a reef knot but capable of slipping.

grant *vt* to transfer the title or possession of; to convey, give or make over; to bestow or confer, particularly in answer to prayer or request; to admit as true though not yet proved; to allow; to yield; to concede.—*vi* to make a grant; to consent.—*n* the act of granting, bestowing or conferring; the thing granted or bestowed.

grantee *n* the person to whom a grant or conveyance is made.

grantor *n* (*law*) the person who makes a grant or conveyance.

granular *adj* consisting of or resembling granules or grains.

granulate *vt* (**granulated, granulating**) to form into grains or small masses; to raise in granules; to make rough on the surface.—*vi* to collect or be formed into grains; to become granular.

granulation *n* the act of granulating; a reducing to the form of small grains; (*surg*) a process by which little granular fleshy bodies form on sores when healing; the fleshy grains themselves.

granule *n* a little grain; a small particle; a minute round body of vegetable, animal or mineral matter.

grape *n* a single berry of the vine; the fruit of the vine which yields wine; (*milit*) grapeshot.—**sour grapes** things professedly despised because they are beyond our reach (from Aesop's fable of 'The Fox and the Grapes').

grapefruit *n* a large citrus fruit, usually yellow in colour, with a thick skin and juicy acid flesh.

grapery *n* a place where grapes are grown; a vinery.

grapeshot *n* iron balls held in a frame and fired from a cannon, now superseded by shrapnel.

grapevine *n* a vine which bears grapes; any means by which secrets or rumours are passed on by informal word of mouth.

graph *n* a diagram representing the relation between two varying magnitudes by means of a curve or series of lines.

graphic, graphical *adj* pertaining to the art of writing, engraving or delineating; written; pictorial; describing with accuracy or vividly; vivid; portraying in vivid and expressive language.

graphics *npl* the use of drawings and lettering; the drawings, illustrations, etc, used in a newspaper, magazine, television programme, etc; information displayed in the form of diagrams, illustrations and animation on a computer monitor.

graphite *n* one of the forms under which carbon occurs, made into pencils and called also plumbago and black lead.

grapholite *n* a species of slate suitable for writing on.

graphology *n* the study of handwriting, es-pecially with a view to assessing the writer's character.

grapnel *n* a small anchor with four or five flukes or claws, used to hold boats or small vessels; a grappling iron.

grapple *vt* (**grappled, grappling**) to lay fast hold on, either with the hands or with hooks; to seize and hold.—*vi* to contend in close fight, as wrestlers; to struggle with.—**to grapple with**, to contend with; to struggle with; to confront boldly.—*n* a close seizure or hug; the wrestler's hold; close fight or encounter; a struggle; a hook by which one ship fastens on another.

grappling iron *n* an instrument consisting of four or more iron claws for grappling and holding fast.

grasp *vt* to seize and hold by the fingers or arms; to lay hold of; to take possession of; to begin to understand; to comprehend.—*vi* to make a clutch or catch; to grip.—*n* the grip or seizure of the hand; reach of the arms; hence, the power of seizing and holding; forcible possession; understanding; knowledge.

grasping *adj* covetous; rapacious; avaricious; greedy; miserly.

grass *n* in common usage (and without a plural), herbage; the green covering of the soil; also any plant of the family to which belong the grain-yielding and pasture plants; such plants grown as lawn or pasture; (*sl*) marijuana; (*sl*) a person who informs on another to the police.—*vt* to cover with grass; to furnish with grass; (*sl*) to inform (on someone) to the police.

grasshopper *n* a leaping insect allied to the locusts, commonly living among grass.

grasshopper

grass roots *npl* the common people; the ordinary members of an organization; the basic level; the essentials.

grass snake *n* a small non-poisonous European snake with a greenish body and yellow markings.

grass tree *n* an Australian plant of the lily family, having shrubby stems with tufts of long grass-like wiry foliage.

grass widow *n* a wife temporarily separated from her husband.

grate[1] *vt* (**grated, grating**) to rub hard or roughly together, as a body with a rough surface against another body; to wear away in small particles, as cheese, by rubbing with anything rough or indented; to offend or irritate.—*vi* to rub roughly with the surface in contact (*a body grates on another*); to have a galling or annoying effect (*to grate on the feelings*); to make a harsh sound by friction; to sound disagreeably.

grate

grate[2] *n* a series of parallel or crossed bars with interstices; a latticework; a grating; a metal receptacle for holding burning fuel and formed mainly of bars.

grateful *adj* having kind feelings and thankfulness towards one from whom a favour has been received; expressing gratitude; indicative of gratitude; affording pleasure; agreeable; pleasing to the taste or the intellect; gratifying.

gratification *n* the act of gratifying or pleasing; that which affords pleasure; enjoyment; satisfaction; delight.

gratify *vt* (**gratified, gratifying**) to please; to give pleasure to; to indulge, delight, humour, satisfy.

grating[1] *adj* irritating; harsh.—*n* the harsh sound or the feeling caused by strong attrition or rubbing.

grating[2] *n* a partition or frame of parallel or crossed bars.

gratis *adv* for nothing; freely; without recompense (*to give a thing gratis*).—*adj* given or done for nothing.

gratitude *n* the feeling of one who is grateful; a warm and friendly emotion awakened by a favour received; thankfulness.

gratuitous *adj* given without an equivalent or recompense; free; voluntary; not required, called for or warranted by the circumstances; adopted or asserted without any good ground (*a gratuitous assumption*).

gratuity *n* a free gift; a present; a donation.

gravamen *n* that part of an accusation which weighs most heavily against the accused; ground or burden of complaint in general.

grave[1] *n* an excavation in the earth in which a dead human body is deposited; hence, any place of interment; a tomb; a sepulchre.

grave[2] *adj* solemn; serious, opposed to *light* or *jovial*; important; momentous; having a serious and interesting import; (*mus*) low; depressed, opposed to sharp, acute or high.

grave[3] *vt* (*pret* **graved**, *pp* **graven** *or* **graved**, *ppr* **graving**) to carve or cut; to form or shape by cutting with a tool; to delineate by cutting; to engrave; hence, to impress deeply.

gravedigger *n* one whose occupation is to dig graves.

gravel *n* small stones or very small pebbles collectively; small stones, sand, etc, combined; (*pathol*) small concretions in the kidneys or bladder; the disease occasioned by such concretions.—*vt* (**gravelled, gravelling**) to cover with gravel; to cause to stick in the sand or gravel; to hurt the foot of (a horse) by gravel lodged under the shoe.

graveness *n* the state or quality of being grave; gravity.

graver *n* one who carves or engraves; an engraving tool; a burin.

gravestone *n* a stone placed at a grave as a monument to the dead.

gravestone

graveyard *n* a yard or enclosure for the interment of the dead.

gravid *adj* being with child, pregnant.

gravitate *vi* (**gravitated, gravitating**) to be affected by gravitation; to move under the influence of gravitation; (*fig*) to have a tendency towards some attracting influence; to move towards.

gravitation *n* the act of gravitating or tending to a centre of attraction; the force by which bodies are drawn or by which they tend towards the centre of the earth or other centre, or the effect of that force.

gravity *n* the state or character of being grave; solemnity of deportment, character or demeanour; seriousness; weight or weightiness; enormity (*the gravity of an offence*); the force which causes a mass of matter to tend towards a centre of attraction, especially towards the centre of the earth; the force by which the planets mutually attract each other and are attracted towards the sun; centripetal force.

gravy *n* a sauce, usually seasoned and thickened, made from the juices produced while cooking meat; (*colloq*) money easily obtained and in excess of what one needs or expects; (*colloq*) money or profit obtained by means of corrupt practices.

gravy train (*sl*) *n* a source of easy profit.

gray *adj* same as **grey**.

grayling *n* a fish of the salmon family found in streams in northern Europe.

graze[1] *vt* (**grazed, grazing**) to feed or supply with growing grass; to furnish pasture for; to feed on; to eat from the ground.—*vi* to eat grass; to feed on growing herbage; to eat snacks frequently rather than eating meals.—*n* the act of grazing or feeding on grass.

graze[2] *vt* (**grazed, grazing**) to rub or touch lightly in passing, as a missile does; to brush lightly the surface of; to scrape; to scratch.—*vi* to pass so as to touch or rub lightly—*n* the act of grazing; a slight rub or brush; an abrasion, especially on the skin, caused by scraping on a surface.

grazier *n* one who grazes or pastures cattle for the market; a farmer who raises and deals in cattle.

grazing *n* the act of feeding on grass; a pasture.

grease *n* animal fat in a soft state; particularly the fatty matter of land animals, as distinguished from the oily matter of marine animals; any soft, oily or fatty substance; a lubricant; a swelling and inflammation in a horse's legs attended with the secretion of oily matter and cracks in the skin.—*vt* (**greased, greasing**) to smear, anoint or daub with grease or fat.

greasepaint *n* make-up used by actors or performers.

greasy *adj* composed of or characterized by

grease; fatty; unctuous; having the appearance of fat or grease; seemingly unctuous to the touch, as some minerals; (of a horse) affected with the disease called grease.

great *adj* large in bulk, surface or linear dimensions; of wide extent; big; large in number; numerous; large, extensive or unusual in degree; long continued; of long duration; important; weighty; involving important interests; holding an eminent or prominent position in respect of mental endowments or acquirements, virtue or vice, rank, office, power, etc; eminent; distinguished; celebrated; notorious; of elevated sentiments; generous; noble; on an extensive scale; sumptuous; magnificent; wonderful; sublime; grand; (*colloq*) very good; pregnant; teeming; filled; denoting a degree of consanguinity in the ascending or descending line (*great-grandfather*).

great-aunt, grand-aunt *n* the aunt of one's father or mother.

greatcoat *n* an overcoat; a topcoat.

Great Dane *n* a breed of tall, strong, smooth-haired dogs.

greatness *n* the state or quality of being great; magnitude; dignity; eminence; distinguished rank or position; nobleness.

great-nephew, grandnephew *n* the grandson of a brother or sister.

great-niece, grandniece *n* the granddaughter of a brother or sister.

great-uncle, granduncle *n* the uncle of one's father or mother.

greave *n* armour worn on the front of the lower part of the leg, across the back of which it was buckled.

greaves *npl* the sediment of melted tallow.

grebe *n* an aquatic bird of various species, having almost no tail, toes separate but broadly fringed by a membrane and legs set so far back that on land it assumes the upright position of the penguin.

Grecian *adj* pertaining to Greece; Greek.

greed *n* an eager desire or longing; greediness.

greedy *adj* having a keen appetite for food or drink; ravenous; voracious; very fond of eating; gluttonous; having a keen desire for anything; covetous (*greedy of gain*).

Greek *adj* pertaining to Greece.—*n* a native of Greece; the language of Greece.

Greek calends *n* a supposed date, that never occurs, for payment, etc, there being calends only in the Roman calendar.

Greek Church *n* the eastern church which separated from the Roman or western church in the ninth century and comprises the great bulk of the Christians of Russia, Greece, Rumania, Turkey, etc.

green *adj* of the colour of grass or herbage and plants when growing; emerald; verdant; new; fresh; recent; fresh and vigorous; flourishing; undecayed (*a green old age*); containing its natural juices; not dry; not seasoned; unripe, immature (*green fruit*); immature in age; young; raw; inexperienced; easily imposed on; jealous; envious; supporting the conservation of the environment; not containing substances harmful to the environment.—*n* a green colour; a grassy plain, plot or common; a piece of ground covered with verdant herbage; a name of several pigments; a person concerned with conserving the environment; (*pl*) the leaves and stems of young plants used in cookery, especially certain plants of the cabbage kind.

Green *n* a member of a political party (the Green Party) concerned with conserving the environment.

green belt *n* an area round a city, including parks, playing fields and gardens, where building is not allowed.

greenery *n* a mass of green foliage; the green hue of such a mass.

greenfinch *n* a common British finch of a greenish colour; the green linnet or green grosbeak.

green fingers *npl* great skill in gardening and growing plants.

greenfly *n* the name given to various species of aphids which infest plants.

greengage *n* a species of plum having a juicy greenish pulp of an exquisite flavour.

greengrocer *n* a retailer of greens and other vegetables.

greenhorn *n* a person easily imposed on; a raw inexperienced person.

greenhouse *n* a building principally consisting of glazed frames or sashes for the purpose of cultivating exotic plants which are too tender to endure the open air (often artificially heated).

greenhouse effect *n* the warming-up of the earth's surface due to the trapping of long-wave radiation by carbon dioxide produced by various pollutants, such as chlorofluorocarbons, etc.

green light *n* the signal to go ahead or proceed.

greenroom *n* a room near the stage in a theatre, to which actors retire during the intervals of their parts in the play.

greensand *n* a name given (from the colour of some of the beds) to two groups of strata of Cretaceous origin, *lower greensand* and *upper greensand*.

greenshank *n* a common species of sandpiper with greenish legs.

greenstone *n* a form of jade commonly found in New Zealand; any green igneous rock.

greet *vt* to address with salutations or expressions of kind wishes; to pay respects or compliments to; to salute; to hail.—*vi* to meet and salute each other.

greeting *n* expression of kindness or joy;

greave

greenhouse

salutation at meeting; compliment sent by one absent.

gregarious *adj* having the habit of assembling or living in a flock or herd; not habitually solitary or living alone.

Gregorian *adj* pertaining to or established by Gregory, the name of various popes.

Gregorian calendar *n* the calendar as reformed by Pope Gregory XIII in 1582.

Gregorian chant *n* plainsong.

gremlin *n* an imaginary creature blamed for anything going wrong or breaking down, for example in an aircraft or machine.

grenade *n* a hollow ball or shell of iron or other metal, or of annealed glass, filled with powder, fired by means of a fuse and thrown among enemies.

grenadier *n* originally a soldier who threw hand grenades; afterwards a company of tall soldiers distinguished by a particular dress; now the title in the British army for a regiment of guards.

gressorial *adj* (of birds) having three toes forward (two of them connected) and one behind.

grenade

grey, gray *adj* of the colour of hair whitened by age; hoary; white with a mixture of black; of the colour of ashes; having grey hairs; old; mature (*grey experience*); (of a person) dreary, boring; (of an area of distinction) vague, indeterminate.—*n* a grey colour; a dull or neutral tint; an animal of a grey colour, as a horse.

greybeard *n* a man with a grey beard; an old man; a large earthen jar or bottle for holding liquor.

greyhen *n* the female of the black grouse, mate of the blackcock.

greyhound *n* a dog kept for the chase, remarkable for the symmetry and beauty of its form and its great fleetness.

grey matter *n* the parts of the central nervous system composed of nerve cells; (*colloq*) intelligence, brains.

greyness *n* the state or quality of being grey.

greystone *n* a greyish or greenish compact, volcanic rock.

greywacke *n* a hard conglomerate rock of pebbles and sand.

grid *n* a national network of transmission lines, pipes, etc, for electricity, water, gas, etc; a network of regular vertical and horizontal lines on a map, used for reference; a framework of parallel or crossed bars; a grill; a gridiron; a grating; an electrode for controlling the flow of electrons in an electron tube.

griffin

griddle *n* a broad disc of iron used for baking oatmeal cakes, etc.

gridiron *n* a framework of iron bars for cooking; anything resembling this, as a field used for American football; a frame of crossbeams on which a ship rests for inspection or repairs at low water.

gridlock *n* a traffic jam that halts all traffic at a street crossing; the breakdown of an organization or a system.

grief *n* pain of mind, arising from any cause; sorrow; sadness; cause of sorrow or pain; that which afflicts.

grievance *n* that which causes grief or uneasiness; wrong done and suffered; injury; circumstances thought to be unjust and cause for complaint.

grieve[1] *vt* (**grieved, grieving**) to cause to feel grief; to give pain of mind to; to make sorrowful; to afflict; to sorrow over; to deplore.—*vi* to feel grief; to sorrow; to mourn (followed by *at, for* and *over*).

grieve[2], **greeve** *n* in Scotland, a manager of a farm; a farm bailiff.

grievous *adj* causing grief or sorrow; afflictive; hard to bear; heavy; severe; harmful; great; atrocious; aggravated; full of grief; indicating great grief or affliction.

griffin, gryphon *n* a mythical animal, in the forepart represented as an eagle, in the hinder part as a lion.

grig *n* a cricket; a grasshopper; the sand eel; a small eel of lively and incessant motion.

grill *vt* to cook by means of a grill; (*colloq*) to question relentlessly.—*n* a utensil with parallel bars for cooking or heating food by direct heat; a device on a cooker that radiates heat downward to cook or heat food.

grille *n* a lattice or grating; a piece of grated work.

grilse *n* the young of the salmon on its first return from the sea to fresh water.

grim *adj* of a forbidding or fear-inspiring aspect; fierce; stern; sullen; sour; surly.

grimace *n* a distortion of the countenance expressive of affectation, scorn, distaste, disapprobation, self-satisfaction, etc; a smirk; a wry face.—*vi* (**grimaced, grimacing**) to make grimaces.

grime *n* foul matter; dirt; dirt deeply ingrained.—*vt* (**grimed, griming**) to sully or soil deeply; to dirt.

grimy *adj* full of grime; foul; dirty.

grin *vi* (**grinned, grinning**) to smile widely; to set the teeth together and open the lips; to show the teeth as in laughter, scorn or pain; to snarl and show the teeth, as a dog.—*vt* to show, set or snap (the teeth) in grinning; to express by grinning.—*n* the act of withdrawing the lips and showing the teeth; a wide smile.

grind *vt* (*pret, pp* **ground**, *ppr* **grinding**) to break and reduce to fine particles or powder by friction, as in a mill; to comminute by attrition; to triturate; to wear down, smooth or sharpen by friction; to whet; to oppress by severe exactions; to harass; (*sl*) to prepare for examination in some subject of study or to study.—*vi* to grind corn or other matter; to be rubbed together, as in the operation of grinding; to be ground or pulverized; to drudge or perform hard work; to study hard, especially for an examination.—*n* the act of one who grinds; a spell of work; (*colloq*) hard or monotonous work.

grinder *n* one who or that which grinds; a molar tooth.

grindstone *n* a revolving stone used for grinding or sharpening tools; (*colloq*) hard or monotonous work.—**to keep a person's nose to the grindstone** to oppress a person; to force a person to do hard or monotonous work.

grip *n* the act of grasping by the hand; handshake; a fast hold; a hilt or handle; control; understanding; a light travelling bag or sports bag.—*vt* (**gripped, gripping**) to grasp by the hand; to gripe; to seize forcibly; to hold fast.—*vi* to take hold; to hold fast.

gripe *vt* (**griped, griping**) to give pain in the bowels, as if by pressure or contraction; to distress; (*colloq*) to complain or grumble.—*vi* (*colloq*) to complain.—*n* grasp; seizure; grip; oppression; affliction; pinching distress; a kind of brake to act on a wheel; *pl* a pinching intermittent pain in the intestines, of the character of that which accompanies diarrhoea or colic.

grisly *adj* frightful; horrible; terrible; grim.

grist *n* corn ground in the mill or to be ground; the grain carried to the mill at one time or the meal it produces.—**to bring grist to the mill** to be a source of profit; to bring profitable business into one's hands.

gristle *n* cartilage.

gristly *adj* consisting of or like gristle; cartilaginous.

grit *n* sand or gravel; rough hard particles; any hard sandstone in which the component grains of quartz are less rounded or sharper than in ordinary sandstones; structure of a stone in regard to fineness and closeness of texture; strength; courage.

grits *npl* groats; grain hulled or coarsely ground.

gritty *adj* containing or consisting of grit; sandy; strong; courageous.

grizzle *n* a grey colour; a mixture of white and black; a mixture of white among dark hairs.—*vi* (**grizzled, grizzling**) to grow grey or grizzly; to become grey-haired; to fret; to complain.

grizzled *adj* of a greyish colour.

grizzly *adj* somewhat grey; greyish.

grizzly bear *n* a large and powerful bear of western North America.

groan *vi* to utter in a mournful voice, as in pain or sorrow; to utter a deep, low-toned, moaning sound.—*n* a deep, mournful sound uttered in pain, sorrow or anguish; a deep sound uttered in disapprobation or derision.

groat *n* an old English coin and money of account, equal to fourpence; hence, colloquially, fourpence.

groats *npl* oats or wheat with the husks taken off.

grocer *n* a trader who deals in tea, sugar, spices, coffee, liquors, fruits, etc.

grocery *n* a grocer's shop; (*pl*) the commodities sold by grocers.

grog *n* a mixture of spirit and water not sweetened; also used as a general term for strong drink.

groggy *adj* overcome with grog; tipsy; weak and unsteady; dazed; (of a horse) moving in an uneasy, hobbling manner owing to tenderness of the feet.

grogram *n* a kind of coarse stuff made of silk and mohair; also, a kind of strong, coarse silk.

groin *n* the hollow of the human body in front at the junction of the thigh with the trunk, where the genitals are situated; (*archit*) the angular projecting curve made by the intersection of simple vaults crossing each other at any angle.—*vt* (*archit*) to form into groins; to ornament with groins.

groining *n* (*archit*) the arrangement of groins; groins collectively.

grommet *n* a plastic or rubber ring used to protect wire, a cable, etc, passing through a hole; (*naut*) a ring of rope with or without a thimble; a loop formed at the end of a rope by splicing.

groom *n* a man or boy who has charge of horses; one who takes care of horses or the stable; a bridegroom.—*vt* to curry or care for (a horse); to make neat and tidy (as hair); to prepare and train (a person) for a particular purpose.

groomsman *n* (*pl* **groomsmen**) one who acts as attendant on a bridegroom at his marriage.

groove *n* a furrow or long hollow, such as is cut by a tool; a channel, usually an elongated narrow channel; a spiral track in a gramophone record for the stylus; the fixed routine of one's life.—*vt* (**grooved, grooving**) to cut a groove or channel in; to furrow.

grope *vi* (**groped, groping**) to search or attempt to find something in the dark or as a blind person, by feeling; to feel one's way; to search uncertainly; to attempt anything blindly.—*vt* to search out by feeling in or as in the dark (*to grope our way*); to fondle in a sexual way.

grosbeak *n* a name common to a group of finches distinguished by the thickness and strength of the bill.

gross *adj* coarse or rough; indelicate, obscene or impure; sensual; great, palpable or enormous; shameful; flagrant (*a gross mistake*; *gross injustice*); dense; not attenuated; whole; entire; total; bulky; of

grindstone

grizzly bear

some size.—*n* (no plural) main body; chief part; bulk; the number of twelve dozen (being the *gross* or *great hundred*).

grossbeak *n* same as **grosbeak**.

grotesque *adj* having a wild, extraordinary or extravagant form; of the utmost oddness; whimsical; extravagant.—*n* a capricious variety of arabesque ornamentation; a whimsical figure or scenery.

grotto *n* (*pl* **grottoes, grottos**) a cave or natural cavity in the earth, as in a mountain or rock; an artificial cavern decorated with rock work, shells, etc, constructed for coolness and pleasure.

grotty (*colloq*) *adj* dirty; nasty; unpleasant; ugly; unwell.

ground *n* the surface of the earth; the earth subject to tillage, etc; the soil; the soil of a particular country (*British ground*) or belonging to a particular person; land; estate; the place assigned to one in certain games, as cricket; an area used for a particular purpose; the position held by a person or group; that on which anything may rest, rise or originate; (often *pl*) basis, foundation; (often *pl*) reason; support; in painting, the first layer of colour on which the others are worked; the primary or predominating colour; a foil or background that sets off anything; (*pl*) sediment at the bottom of liquors; dregs; lees.—*vt* to lay or set on or in the ground; to cause to run (a ship) aground; to prevent (aircraft) from flying; to settle or establish, as on a foundation or basis; to fix or settle firmly; to found; to base; to instruct thoroughly in elements or first principles.—*vi* to run aground; to strike the ground and remain fixed (*the ship grounded in two fathoms*).

ground bait *n* bait scattered at the bottom of the water.

ground floor *n* the floor of a house on a level, or nearly so, with the exterior ground.

grounding *n* a basic general knowledge of a subject.

groundless *adj* lacking ground or foundation; lacking cause or reason; baseless; false.

groundnut *n* the peanut.

ground plan *n* a plan showing the divisions of a building on the same level as the surface of the ground.

ground rent *n* rent paid for the privilege of building on another man's land.

ground rule *n* a fundamental rule; a basic principle.

groundsel *n* a common annual weed, much used as food for caged birds.

ground sheet *n* waterproof sheet used by soldiers, campers, etc.

groundswell *n* a deep swell or rolling of the sea, caused by a distant storm or gale; a wave of popular feeling.

groundsheet

grouse

groundwork *n* the work which forms the foundation of anything; that to which the rest is additional; the basis.

group *n* an assemblage, either of persons or things; a number collected; a cluster; an artistic combination of figures; in scientific classifications, a number of individuals having some resemblance or common characteristic.—*vt* to form into a group; to arrange in a group or in groups.

group captain *n* rank in the Royal Air Force equivalent to a colonel in the army.

grouse[1] *n* the common name of a number of game birds, more particularly applied to the well-known moor fowl or red grouse of Britain.

grouse[2] *vi* (**groused, grousing**) to grumble; to murmur; to complain.—*n* a grumble; a complaint.

grout *n* coarse meal; a thin mortar used for pouring into the joints of masonry and brickwork and for filling in spaces between tiles; lees, grounds, dregs.—*vt* to fill with grout.

grove *n* a cluster of trees shading an avenue or walk; an assemblage of growing trees of no great extent; a small wood.

grovel *vi* (**grovelled, grovelling**) to lie prone or move with the body prostrate as a sign of respect or in fear or humility; to act in an excessively humble way.

grow *vi* (*pret* **grew**, *pp* **grown**, *ppr* **growing**) to become enlarged in bulk or stature, by a natural and organic process (said of animals and vegetables); to increase in any way; to become larger and stronger; to be augmented; to wax; to advance; to extend; to swell (*the wind grew to a hurricane*); to be changed from one state to another; to result, as from a cause or reason; to become (*to grow pale*).—*vt* to cause to grow; to cultivate; to produce; to raise.

grower *n* one who or that which grows or increases; one who grows, raises or produces; a cultivator.

growl *vi* to murmur or snarl, as a dog; to utter an angry, grumbling sound.—*vt* to express by growling; to utter in an angry or grumbling tone.—*n* the angry snarl of a dog; the inarticulate grumble of a discontented or angry person.

growler *n* one who growls; a small iceberg; a hansom cab with four wheels.

grown (*pp of* **grow**) increased in growth; having arrived at full size or stature.

growth *n* the process of growing; increase of bulk in animals and plants; gradual increase in any way, as in number, bulk, etc; that which has grown; something produced by growing; an abnormal formation of tissue, as a tumour.

groyne *n* a structure projecting into the sea or a river to check its encroachments.

grub *vi* (**grubbed, grubbing**) to dig in or

under the ground; to be occupied in digging.—*vt* to dig; to dig up by the roots; to root up by digging; generally followed by *up* or *out*.—*n* the larva of an insect, especially of beetles; a caterpillar; a maggot; (*sl*) food.

grubber *n* one who grubs; an instrument for grubbing out roots, weeds, etc.

grubby *adj* dirty; unwashed; grimy.

Grub Street *n* a street in London once inhabited by poor writers and literary adventurers.

grudge *vt* (**grudged, grudging**) to permit or grant with reluctance; to begrudge.—*vi* to be envious; to cherish ill-will.—*n* unwillingness to benefit; reluctance felt in giving; ill-will from envy or sense of injury.

grudgingly *adv* with reluctance or discontent.

gruel *n* a kind of broth made by boiling ingredients in water (usually made of the meal of oats).

gruesome *adj* causing one to shudder; frightful; horrible.

gruff *adj* of a rough or stern manner, voice or countenance; sour; surly.

grumble *vi* (**grumbled, grumbling**) to murmur with discontent; to utter in a low voice by way of complaint; to complain; to give vent to discontented expressions; to growl; to snarl; to rumble; to roar; to make a harsh and heavy sound.—*vt* to express or utter by grumbling.

grumpy *adj* surly; angry; gruff.

grunge *n* (*colloq*) dirt; grime; any unpleasant, nasty substance; second-hand clothes, often in bad repair.

grunt *vi* to snort or make a noise like a hog; to utter a short groan or a deep guttural sound, as of a hog.—*n* a deep guttural sound, as of a hog.

Gruyère *n* a kind of cheese made from a mixture of goats' and ewes' milk, from Gruyère in Switzerland.

gryphon *n* same as **griffin.**

G-string *n* a string on an instrument tuned to the note G; a strip of cloth between the legs and secured by a string round the waist.

G-suit *n* a suit designed to counteract the physiological effects of acceleration on astronauts and airmen.

guaiacum *n* a South American tree and the resin obtained from it, the latter, as well as the bark and wood, being of medicinal value.

guanaco *n* a quadruped closely allied to the llama and alpaca.

guano *n* (*pl* **guanos**) a substance found on many small islands, especially in the Pacific Ocean and on the west coast of South America, chiefly composed of the decomposed excrement of sea fowl and much used as a fertilizer.

guarantee *vt* (**guaranteed, guaranteeing**) to warrant; to pledge oneself for; to give a guarantee for; to promise; to become bound that an article shall be as good or useful 'as it is represented; to secure the performance of; to undertake to secure to another (claims, rights, possessions); to undertake to uphold or maintain.—*n* an undertaking that the engagement or promise of another shall be performed; a pledging of oneself as surety; one who binds himself to see the stipulations of another performed; a guarantor; a written promise to be responsible for someone else's debts or financial obligations if he or she does not pay them; a formal or official promise that something is made or will be done to specified standards; an assurance.

guarantor *n* a warrantor; one who gives a guarantee.

guard *vt* to secure against injury, loss or attack; to defend; to keep in safety; to accompany for protection; to provide or secure against objections or attacks.—*vi* to watch by way of caution or defence; to be cautious; to be in a state of caution or defence (*to guard against mistake*).—*n* a state of caution or vigilance or the act of observing what passes in order to prevent surprise or attack; defence; attention; watch; heed; in fencing or boxing, a posture of defence; the arms or weapon in such a posture; one who guards or keeps watch; one whose business is to defend or prevent attack or surprise; a person who has charge of a mail coach or a railway train; (*pl*) a body of select troops whose special duty is that of guarding the sovereign's person; that which guards or protects; caution of expression; any appliance or attachment designed to protect or secure against injury; part of a sword hilt which protects the hand; a chain or cord attached to a person's watch; an ornamental border, etc, on one's dress.

guardant, gardant *adj* (*heral*) (of a lion, etc) represented as looking with full face at the observer.

guarded *adj* protected; defended; cautious; circumspect (*guarded in language*); framed or uttered with caution.

guardian *n* one who guards; one to whom anything is committed for preservation from injury; one who has the charge or custody of any person or thing.—*adj* protecting; performing the office of a protector.

guardianship *n* the office of a guardian; protection; care; watch.

guardroom *n* a room for the accommodation of a guard of soldiers and where military defaulters are confined.

guardsman *n* (*pl* **guardsmen**) a watchman; an officer or private in a regiment of guards.

guardsman

guava *n* a small tropical tree of the myrtle family, the fruit of which is made into a delicious jelly.

gudgeon *n* a small freshwater fish which is very easily caught; hence, a person easily cheated or ensnared.

guelder-rose, gelder-rose *n* a shrub of the woodbine family with handsome flowers.

guerdon *n* a reward; requital; (*poet, rhet*) recompense, used both in a good and bad sense.—*vt* to give a guerdon to; to reward.

guernsey *n* a close-fitting woollen knitted jersey; a particular breed of dairy cattle.

guerrilla, guerilla *n* a member of an independent military force, often revolutionary, which makes surprise attacks on enemy positions, supplies, etc.

guess *vt* to form an opinion concerning, without good means of knowledge or sufficient evidence; to judge of at random; to conjecture; to solve by a correct conjecture; to think; to suppose; to imagine (often followed by a clause).—*vi* to form a conjecture; to judge at random or without any strong evidence (with *at*).—*n* a conjecture.

guesswork *n* mere conjecture; the act of working by hazard.

guided missile

guest *n* a visitor or friend entertained in the house or at the table of another; a lodger at a hotel or lodging house.

guesthouse *n* a private house or boarding house which gives temporary accommodation to paying visitors.

guffaw *n* a loud or sudden burst of laughter.—*vi* to burst into a loud or sudden laugh.

guidance *n* the act of guiding; direction; government; advice; counsel.

guide *vt* (guided, guiding) to lead or direct in a way; to conduct in a course or path; to direct; to regulate; to influence in conduct or actions; to give direction to; to instruct and direct; to superintend; to give advice to; to counsel.—*n* a person who guides; a leader or conductor; one who conducts travellers or tourists in particular localities; one who or that which directs another in his conduct or course of life; a director; a regulator; a guidebook; a book of basic instruction; a book with useful advice or information.

Guide *n* a member of the Guide Association, a youth organization for girls analogous to the Scout Association.

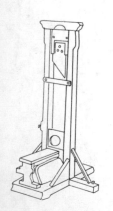

guillotine

guidebook *n* a book for giving travellers or tourists information about the places they visit.

guided missile *n* a type of missile whose direction is controlled throughout its flight by means of radar, internal instruments, etc.

guide dog *n* a dog, such as a Labrador, specially trained to lead a blind person.

guidepost *n* a post at the parting of roads for directing travellers; a fingerpost.

guidon *n* the flag of a troop of cavalry; a flag used to signal with at sea, etc.

guild *n* an association or incorporation of men belonging to the same class or engaged in similar pursuits, formed for mutual aid and protection.

guilder *n* a coin of the Netherlands.

guildhall *n* the hall where a guild or corporation usually assembles; a town or corporation hall.

guile *n* craft; cunning; artifice; duplicity; deceit.

guileful *adj* full of guile; intended to deceive; crafty; wily; deceitful; insidious; treacherous.

guillemot *n* a marine swimming bird allied to the auks and divers.

guillotine *n* an engine for beheading persons by means of a steel blade loaded with a mass of lead and sliding between two upright posts; a machine which consists of a knife descending between grooved posts, used for cutting paper, etc; a rule for limiting time for discussion in a legislature.—*vt* (guillotined, guillotining) to behead by the guillotine.

guilt *n* criminality; the feeling which results after the wilful or intentional commission of a crime or offence by one who knows it to be a crime or violation of law; a feeling of self-reproach from believing one has done a wrong.

guiltiness *n* the state of being guilty; wickedness; criminality; guilt.

guiltless *adj* free from guilt, crime or offence; innocent.

guilty *adj* having incurred guilt; not innocent; criminal; morally delinquent (with *of* before the crime); pertaining to guilt; indicating guilt (*a guilty look*).

guinea *n* a gold coin formerly current in the UK of the value of 21 shillings sterling; a sum of money of the same amount.

guinea fowl *n* a domestic African fowl closely allied to peacocks and pheasants.

guinea pig *n* a tailless rodent mammal originally from South America and often kept as a domestic pet or used in scientific experiments; a person used as the subject of an experiment.

guipure *n* a coarse lace in which the pattern is supported by bars connecting the motifs rather than founded on a net base.

guise *n* external appearance; an assumed appearance; dress; garb; manner; mien; cast or behaviour; custom; mode; practice.

guitar *n* a musical stringed instrument having six strings, which are played by plucking with the fingers of the right hand, while the notes are stopped by the fingers of the left.

gular *adj* pertaining to the gullet.

gulch *n* a deep, abrupt ravine caused by the action of water; the dry bed of a torrent; a gully.

gules *n* (*heral*) red.

gulf *n* a large indentation on the coastline of a country and the sea in it; a bay; a bight; an abyss, chasm or deep opening in the earth; what gulfs or swallows; a wide interval, as in station, education, etc.—*vt* to swallow up; to engulf.

Gulf Stream *n* a current of warm water flowing from the Gulf of Mexico through the channel between Cuba and America and northeastwards towards Europe.

gull[1] *n* any of numerous marine swimming birds with long wings and webbed feet and found in all latitudes.

gull[2] *n* a young unfledged bird; one easily cheated; a simpleton; a trick.—*vt* to make a fool of; to mislead by deception; to trick.

gullet *n* the passage in the neck of an animal by which food and liquor are taken into the stomach; the oesophagus; something resembling this.

gullibility *n* the quality of being gullible.

gullible *adj* easily gulled or cheated.

gully *n* a channel or hollow worn in the earth by a current of water; a ravine; a ditch; a gutter; a large knife.—*vt* (**gullied**, **gullying**) to wear into a gully or channel.

gulp *vt* to swallow eagerly or in large draughts; to gasp or choke.—*n* the act of taking a large swallow; the act of gasping or choking.

gum[1] *n* a juice which exudes from trees either spontaneously or after incisions are made and thickens on the surface or is obtained from their seeds or roots; an adhesive; chewing gum.—*vt* (**gummed**, **gumming**) to smear with gum; to unite or stiffen by gum or a gum-like substance; to stick with gum or an adhesive; (*colloq*) to make clogged; (*colloq*) to prevent from working properly; to ruin.—*vi* to exude or form gum.

gum[2] *n* the fleshy substance in the jaws which envelops the neck of the teeth.

gum arabic *n* the juice of various species of acacia, hardened in the air.

gumbo *n* (*pl* **gumbos**) a thick soup or stew; soil that becomes very sticky when wet.

gumboil *n* a boil or small abscess on the gum.

gumboot *n* a long waterproof boot made of rubber.

gummy *adj* consisting of gum; of the nature of gum; giving out gum; covered with gum or viscous matter; viscous; sticky; revealing the gums; toothless.

gumption *n* shrewdness; practical common sense; initiative.

gun *n* a name applied to every type of firearm for throwing projectiles by the explosion of gunpowder or other explosive.

gunboat *n* a boat or small vessel fitted to carry one or more guns of heavy calibre and from its light draught capable of running close inshore or up rivers.

gun carriage *n* the carriage on which a cannon is mounted or moved and from which it is fired.

guncotton *n* a highly explosive substance produced by soaking cotton or similar vegetable fibre in nitric and sulphuric acids and then leaving it to dry.

gung-ho *adj* excessively enthusiastic; over-zealous.

gunman *n* (*pl* **gunmen**) a man armed with a gun or revolver.

gunmetal *n* an alloy, generally of nine parts of copper and one part of tin, used for the manufacture of cannon, etc.

gunner *n* one who works a gun or cannon; formerly, a warrant officer in the navy responsible for training and overseeing gun crews and for ordnance; an officer or soldier in the Royal Artillery.

gunnery *n* the art of firing or managing guns; the science of artillery.

gunny *n* a strong coarse cloth of jute used for making into bags, sacks, etc.

gunport *n* an opening in the side of a ship through which cannon are discharged.

gunpowder *n* an explosive mixture of saltpetre, sulphur and charcoal, reduced to a fine powder, then granulated and dried.

gunrunner *n* one who runs or secretly conveys guns into a district.

gunshot *n* the firing of a gun; the distance to which shot can be thrown so as to be effective.—*adj* made by the shot of a gun (*gunshot wounds*).

gunsmith *n* one makes or repairs firearms.

gunwale, gunnel *n* (*naut*) the upper edge of a ship's or boat's side.

gurgle *vi* (**gurgled**, **gurgling**) to run or flow in an irregular, noisy current, as water from a bottle; to flow with a bubbling sound; to make a bubbling sound, as a baby.—*n* the sound made by a liquid flowing from the narrow mouth of a vessel or generally through any narrow opening; a bubbling sound like that made by a baby.

Gurkha *n* a native of Nepal in India; a soldier from Nepal in the Indian or British army.

gurnard *n* a spiny marine fish with an armoured head.

guru *n* (*pl* **gurus**) a Hindu spiritual guide; an influential leader or teacher, as of a religious cult, etc.

gush *vi* to rush forth, as a fluid from confinement; to flow suddenly or copiously; to issue plentifully; to be extravagantly and effusively sentimental.—*vt* to emit suddenly, copiously or with violence.—*n* a sudden and violent issue of a fluid; an emission of liquid in a large quantity and

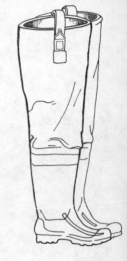

gumboot

guru

with force; an outpour; an effusive display of sentiment.

gusher *n* one who or that which gushes; an oil well from which oil spouts forth; a person who is demonstratively sentimental.

gushing *adj* rushing forth with violence, as a fluid; flowing copiously; exuberantly and demonstratively affectionate; extravagantly sentimental.

gusset *n* a triangular piece of cloth inserted in a garment for strengthening or enlarging some part; something resembling such a piece of cloth in shape or function.

gust *n* a violent blast of wind; a sudden rushing or driving of the wind, of short duration; a sudden violent burst of passion. —*vi* to blow in gusts.

gustatory *adj* pertaining to taste.

gusto *n* appreciation or enjoyment; keen relish; taste; fancy.

gusty *adj* subject to gusts or sudden blasts of wind; tempestuous; given to sudden bursts of passion.

gut *n* the intestinal canal of an animal from the stomach to the anus; an intestine; (*pl*) the stomach and digestive apparatus generally, the viscera or entrails; a preparation made from the intestines of an animal used for various purposes, as formerly for the strings of a fiddle; a channel or passage; (*pl*) (*colloq*) courage, daring.—*vt* (**gutted, gutting**) to take out the entrails of; to eviscerate; to plunder of contents; to destroy or take out the interior of.

gutta-percha *n* the hardened milky juice of a tree which grows in Southeast Asia, resembling rubber but stronger, more soluble and less elastic.

gutter *n* a channel at the side of a road, street, etc, also at the eaves of or on a roof of a building for conveying away water; a channel or groove to direct something, as in a bowling alley; the lowest condition of human life; social degradation or sordidness.—*vt* to cut or form gutters in.—*vi* to become channelled; to melt unevenly, as a candle.

guttural *adj* pertaining to the throat; uttered from the throat.—*n* a letter or combination of letters pronounced in the throat; any guttural sound.

guy[1] *n* a rope used to steady anything; a rope to steady an object which is being hoisted; a rope or rod to steady a suspension bridge.—*vt* to steady or direct by means of a guy.

guy[2] *n* a fright; a person of strange looks or dress (from the effigy of Guy Fawkes burned on 5th November); a chap; a fellow.—*vt* to make fun of; to ridicule.

guzzle *vi* (**guzzled, guzzling**) to swallow

liquid or food greedily.—*vt* to eat or drink greedily.

gybe *vt* (**gybed, gybing**) same as **jibe**[1].

gymkhana *n* a horse-riding competition consisting of various events.

gymnasium *n* (*pl* **gymnasiums, gymnasia**) a place where athletic exercises are performed.

gymnast *n* one who teaches or practises gymnastic exercises.

gymnastic *adj* pertaining to athletic exercises.

gymnastics *n* the art of performing athletic exercises; athletic exercises; any exercises which develop agility, suppleness and strength.

gymnocarpous *adj* (*bot*) having a naked fruit.

gynaecological *adj* pertaining to gynaecology.

gynaecologist *n* a doctor who specializes in gynaecology.

gynaecology *n* the branch of medicine that deals with diseases of women, especially diseases affecting the female productive system and adjacent organs.

gynandrous *n* (of a plant) having the stamens and pistil consolidated into a single body.

gypseous *adj* of the nature of gypsum; resembling gypsum.

gypsiferous *adj* producing gypsum.

gypsum *n* a mineral which is found in a compact and crystallized state, as alabaster, or in the form of a soft chalky stone which by heat becomes a fine white powder used to make plaster of Paris.

gypsy, gipsy *n* (*pl* **gypsies, gipsies**) one of a wandering race deriving their origin from India, now found mainly in Europe; a person who lives like a gypsy; a person who dresses looks like a gypsy.

gyrate *vi* (**gyrated, gyrating**) to turn round circularly; to revolve round a central point; to move spirally.—*adj* winding or going round, as in a circle.

gyration *n* a turning or whirling round; a circular motion.

gyratory *adj* moving in a circle or spirally.

gyre *n* a circular motion or a circle described by a moving body; a turn.

gyrfalcon, gerfalcon *n* a large, northern falcon, one of the boldest.

gyrocompass *n* a compass mounted of a gyroscope to keep it stable.

gyroidal *adj* spiral in arrangement or action.

gyroscope *n* a wheel mounted in a ring so that its axis is free to turn in any direction so that when spinning rapidly it keeps its original plane of rotation.

gymnast

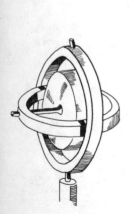

gyroscope

H

H the eighth letter of the English alphabet, a consonant often called the *aspirate*, as being a mere aspiration or breathing.

ha *exclam* denoting surprise, wonder, joy or other sudden emotion.

habeas corpus *n* (*law*) a writ ordering a person detained in custody to be brought before a judge or court so that the judge or court can decide whether the detention is lawful.

haberdasher *n* a dealer in drapery goods of various descriptions, as woollens, linens, silks, ribbons, etc.

haberdashery *n* the wares sold by a haberdasher.

habergeon *n* a short coat of mail or armour consisting of a jacket without sleeves.

habiliment *n* a garment; clothing (usually in the plural).

habit *n* the ordinary state or condition of the body, either natural or acquired; the bodily constitution or temperament; tendency or capacity resulting from frequent repetition of the same acts; practice; usage; a way of acting; a peculiar practice or custom; a characteristic item of behaviour; dress; garb; a distinctive costume, as of a nun or monk, etc; the outer dress worn by women on horseback.

habitable *adj* capable of being inhabited or dwelt in; capable of sustaining human beings.

habitant *n* an inhabitant; a dweller; a resident.

habitat *n* the natural abode or locality of a plant or animal.

habitation *n* act of inhabiting; occupancy; place of abode; a settled dwelling; a house or other place in which humans or animals dwell.

habitual *adj* formed or acquired by habit, frequent use or custom; constantly practised; customary; regular.

habituate *vt* (**habituated, habituating**) to accustom; to make familiar by frequent use or practice; to familiarize.—*adj* formed by habit.

habitude *n* customary manner or mode of living, feeling or acting; long custom; habit.

habitué *n* a habitual frequenter of any place, especially one of amusement, recreation, etc.

hacienda *n* in Spain, South America, etc, a farmhouse; a farm.

hack¹ *vt* to cut irregularly and into small pieces; to notch; to cough harshly; (*comput*) to gain illegal access to confidential data.—*n* a notch; a cut; a harsh cough.

hack² *n* a horse kept for hire; a worn-out horse; a person employed in dull and monotonous literary or writing work; a mediocre writer; (*colloq*) a journalist.—*adj* much used or worn, like a hired horse; hired.—*vt* to use as a hack; to let out for hire.

hack³ *n* a grated frame of various kinds; a frame for drying fish, etc; a rack for cattle fodder.

hackberry *n* a North American tree bearing sweet edible fruits.

hacker *n* (*comput*) a person who gains illegal access to confidential data.

hackee *n* the common ground squirrel of North America.

hackery *n* a two-wheeled cart of India drawn by oxen.

hacking *adj* short and interrupted (*a hacking cough*).

hackle *n* a comb for dressing flax; a long pointed feather on the neck of a fowl or any similar feather.—*vt* (**hackled, hackling**) to comb (flax or hemp).

hackney *n* a horse kept for riding or driving; a nag; a horse kept for hire; a hack; a carriage or vehicle for hire.—*adj* let out for hire; much used; common; trite—*vt* to use as a hackney; to devote to common or vulgar use.

hackneyed *adj* overused; banal; trite; commonplace.

hacksaw *n* a saw with a narrow blade set in a bow, used for cutting metal.

haddock *n* a fish of the cod family, smaller than the cod and having a dark spot on each side just behind the head.

Hades *n* in Greek mythology, the invisible abode of the dead; the place or state of departed souls; the world of spirits.

hacienda

hacksaw

hadj *n* same as **hajj**.

hadji *n* same as **hajji**.

haemal *adj* pertaining to the blood; connected with the blood vessels or the circulatory system.

haematite *n* same as **hematite**.

haematology *n* the study of the nature, function and diseases of the blood.

haematuria *n* a discharge of bloody urine.

haemoglobin *n* a combined protein which carries oxygen to the tissues and which is contained in the red corpuscles of the blood, to which it gives their colour.

haemophilia *n* (*med*) a hereditary tendency to excessive bleeding, to the point of being fatal, caused by slight injuries because the blood fails to clot normally, usually found only in males but transmitted by females.

haemorrhage *n* a discharge of blood from the blood vessels; heavy bleeding.

haemorrhoids *npl* piles.

hafnium *n* a silvery chemical element found in zirconium.

haft *n* a handle; that part of an instrument which is taken into the hand and by which it is held and used.—*vt* to set in a haft; to furnish with a handle.

hag *n* an ugly old woman; a witch; a sorceress; a she-monster; an eel-shaped fish which eats into and devours other fishes.

haggard *adj* having the expression of one wasted by want or suffering; having the face worn and pale; lean-faced; gaunt.

haggis *n* a Scottish dish, made from the heart, lungs and liver of a sheep minced with suet, onions, oatmeal, salt and pepper.

haggle *vi* (**haggled, haggling**) to argue over terms; to bargain; to barter. ·

Hagiographa *npl* the last of the three Jewish divisions of the Old Testament, comprising Psalms, Proverbs, Job, Daniel, Ezra, Nehemiah, Ruth, Esther, Chronicles, Canticles, Lamentations and Ecclesiastes.

hagiography *n* sacred writing; the lives of the saints or holy people.

hagiology *n* sacred literature; that branch of literature which has to do with the lives and legends of the saints.

hah *interj* expressing effort, surprise, etc.

ha-ha, haw-haw *n* a sunk fence or ditch.

haiku *n* a short Japanese poem of three unrhymed lines with an exact number of syllables per line in the pattern 5, 7, 5.

hail[1] *n* the small masses of ice or frozen vapour falling from the clouds in showers or storms; frozen rain.—*vi* to pour down hail.

hail[2] *interj* a term of greeting or salutation expressive of well-wishing.—*vt* to call to; to greet from a distance; to call to in order to arrest attention; to acclaim; to designate as; to salute or address as.—*vi* used only in the phrase *to hail from*, originally used of a ship, which is said to hail from the port whence she comes; hence to have as one's

halberd

residence or birthplace; to belong to.—*n* call.—**within hail** within call; within reach of the sound of the voice.

hailstone *n* a single ball or pellet of hail.

hailstorm *n* a storm of hail.

hair *n* a small filament issuing from the skin of an animal and from a bulbous root; the collection or mass of filaments growing from the skin of an animal and forming an integument or covering; such filaments in the mass; a filament resembling a hair; (*bot*) a species of down or pubescence.

hairdresser *n* one who dresses or cuts people's hair; a barber.

hairdressing *n* the art or practice of cutting, styling, colouring, perming, etc, the hair.

hairline *n* the natural border on the head formed by the growing hair; a line made of hair; a very slender line made in writing or drawing; a hair stroke.

hairpin *n* a pin used to keep the hair in a certain position; especially, a doubled pin or bent wire used by women.—*adj* resembling a U (*a hairpin bend*).

hair-raising *adj* frightening; terrifying; shocking.

hair's-breadth *n* the diameter or breadth of a hair; a minute distance.—*adj* of the breadth of a hair; very narrow (*a hair's-breadth escape*).

hair shirt *n* shirt or belt made of horsehair and worn by way of self-mortification.

hair space *n* the thinnest space used by printers.

hairspring *n* the fine hair-like spring giving motion to the balance wheel of a watch.

hair stroke *n* the fine up-stroke in penmanship.

hair trigger *n* a trigger to a gunlock, so delicately adjusted that the slightest touch will discharge the piece.

hairy *adj* overgrown with hair; covered with hair; abounding with hair; consisting of hair; resembling hair.

hajj, hadj *n* (*pl* **hajjes, hadjes**) the Muslim pilgrimage to Mecca and Medina.

hajji, hadji *n* (*pl* **hajjis, hadjis**) a Muslim who has made his pilgrimage to Mecca.

hake *n* a fish of the cod family, one species of which is known as king of herrings, on which it preys.

halal *n* meat from animals that have been slaughtered in accordance with Islamic law.—*adj* pertaining to such meat.

halberd, halbert *n* an ancient military weapon, a kind of combination of a spear and battle-axe, with a long shaft.

halberdier *n* one who is armed with a halberd.

halcyon *adj* calm; quiet; peaceful.

halcyon days *npl* days of peace and tranquillity.

hale *adj* sound; healthy; robust; not impaired in health.

half *n* (*pl* **halves**) one part of a thing which is divided into two equal parts.—*adv* in an equal part or degree; by half; to some extent (much used in composition and often indefinite, as *half-learned, half-hatched*).—*adj* consisting of a half.

half-and-half *adj* partly one thing and partly another.—*adv* in two equal parts.

halfback *n* player in football, immediately behind the forwards.

half-baked *adj* incomplete or immature; poorly planned or thought-out; stupid; foolish.

half-breed *n* one born of parents of different races or breeds.

half-brother *n* a brother by one parent, but not by both.

half-caste *n* one born of different races.

half-cock *n* the position of the hammer of a gun when it is elevated only halfway and retained by the first notch.

half-crown *n* formerly, a British silver coin.

half-hearted *adj* devoid of eagerness or enthusiasm; indifferent; lukewarm.

half holiday *n* a day on which work is carried on only during a portion of the usual working hours.

half-length *adj* of half the full or ordinary length; showing only the upper half of the body, as a portrait.

half-life *n* the period of time in which activity of a radioactive substance falls to half its value.

half-measure *n* an imperfect plan of operation; a feeble effort.

half-nelson *n* a wrestling hold in which one hand passes under an opponent's arm from behind and reaches forward to press the back of the opponent's neck.

half-pay *n* half wages or salary.

half-price *n* half the ordinary price; a reduced charge for admission.

half-seas-over *adj* pretty far gone in drunkenness; half-drunk; tipsy.

half-sister *n* a sister by the father's side only or by the mother's side only.

half-sovereign *n* formerly, a British gold coin.

half-timbered *adj* built with an exposed timber framework, as in Tudor architecture.

halftone *n* any tone or shade, intermediate between intense light and deep shade; a picture, such as a photograph in a newspaper, made up of tiny dots produced by reproducing the photograph through a fine mesh screen.

half-truth *n* a statement only partially true or that conveys only part of the truth.

halfway *adv* in the middle; at half the distance.—*adj* midway; equidistant from the extremes.

half-witted *adj* weak in intellect; silly; foolish.

halibut *n* one of the largest of the flatfish family, allied to the turbot, but less broad.

hall *n* a large room, especially a large public room; a room or building devoted to public business or in which meetings of the public or corporate bodies are held; a large room at the entrance of a house; a vestibule; an entrance lobby; a manor house.

hallelujah, halleluiah *n, interj* alleluia.

hallmark *n* an official stamp affixed to articles of gold and silver as a mark of their legal quality; a mark or symbol of high quality; a characteristic feature.

hallo *interj* same as **hello**.

halloo *interj, n* an exclamation, used as a call to invite attention; also, a hunting cry to set a dog on the chase.—*vi* to call halloo; to shout; to cry, as after dogs.—*vt* to shout to.

hallow *vt* to make holy; to consecrate; to set apart for holy or religious use; to reverence; to honour as sacred.

Hallowe'en, Halloween *n* the eve or vigil of All Saints' Day, 31st October.

hallucinate *vi* (**hallucinated, hallucinating**) to experience hallucinations.

hallucination *n* the experience of seeing or hearing things that seem to be real but do not actually exist.

hallucinatory *adj* pertaining to hallucination.

hallucinogenic *adj* producing hallucinations.

halm *n* same as **haulm**.

halo *n* (*pl* **haloes, halos**) a luminous ring, either white or coloured, appearing round the sun or moon; any circle of light, as that round the head of a saint; a coloured circle round the nipple; an ideal glory investing an object (*a halo of romance*).—*vt* to surround with a halo.

halo

halt *vi* to stop in marching or walking; to cease to advance; to stand in doubt whether to proceed or what to do; to hesitate; to limp; to be lame; to limp or be defective in regard to metre, versification or connection of ideas.—*vt* to stop; to cause to cease marching.—*adj* lame; not able to walk without limping.—*n* lameness; a limp; a stopping; a stop in walking or marching; a place on a railway line, bus route, etc, at which a halt is made.

halter *n* a cord or strap forming a head stall for leading or confining a horse or other animal; a style of women's dress or top tied behind the neck and waist, leaving the back and arms bare.—*vt* to put a halter on.

halve *vt* (**halved, halving**) to divide into two halves or equal parts; to join (timbers) by lapping or letting into each other.

halyard *n* (*naut*) a rope or tackle for hoisting and lowering sails, yards, gaffs, etc.

ham *n* the inner bend or hind part of the knee; the thigh of an animal, particularly

393

of a pig, salted and cured; (*colloq*) the back of the upper thigh; (*colloq*) an actor who uses too many stage clichés or gestures, or overacts; (*colloq*) a licensed amateur radio operator.—*vti* (**hammed, hamming**) to speak or move in an exaggerated manner, to overact.

hamadryad *n* (*pl* **hamadryads, hamadryades**) in classical mythology, a wood nymph believed to live and die with the tree to which she was attached; the king cobra of India.

hamadryas *n* a North African baboon, the male of which has a heavy mane of silvery hair, held sacred in ancient Egypt.

hamburger *n* a patty made from minced beef and flavouring, fried or grilled and often eaten in a bread roll with salad, pickles, etc.

ham-fisted, ham-handed *adj* clumsy; inept.

hamlet *n* a small village; a little cluster of houses in the country.

hammer *n* an instrument for driving nails, beating metals, etc, consisting usually of an iron head, fixed crosswise to a handle; a thing like this in shape or use; a striking piece in the mechanism of a clock and a piano; that part in the lock of a gun, rifle, etc, which when the trigger is pulled falls with a smart blow and causes detonation; a bone of the middle ear; a heavy metal ball attached to a wire thrown in athletic contests.—**hammer and tongs** with great force.—**to bring to the hammer** to sell by auction.—*vt* to beat, form or forge with a hammer; to contrive by intellectual labour; to excogitate (usually with *out*); to declare defaulting or bankrupt a member of the Stock Exchange; (*colloq*) to defeat utterly.—*vi* to strike anything repeatedly, as with a hammer; to work; to labour in contrivance.

hammer beam *n* a short projecting beam attached to the foot of a principal rafter in a roof, in the place of the tie beam.

hammerhead *n* the iron head of a hammer; a shark, the head of which resembles a hammer; a brown African and Asian wading bird; an African fruit bat with a nose shaped like a hammer.

hammerhead

hammock *n* a kind of hanging bed, consisting of a piece of cloth or network suspended by cords and hooks.

hamper *n* a kind of basket or wickerwork receptacle, chiefly used as a case for storing and transporting articles, such as food.—*vt* to put into a hamper.

hamper *vt* to impede in motion or progress; to render progress difficult to; to shackle; to embarrass; to encumber.—*n* something that hampers or encumbers; a clog.

hamster *n* a burrowing animal of the rat family.

handbell

hamstring *n* one of the tendons of the ham.—*vt* (*pret, pp* **hamstrung** *or* **hamstringed**, *ppr* **hamstringing**) to lame or disable by cutting the tendons of the ham; to render useless; to thwart.

hand *n* the extremity of the arm, consisting of the palm and fingers, connected to the arm at the wrist; the corresponding member in certain of the lower animals; a measure of 4 inches, a palm (applied chiefly to horses); side or direction, either right or left (*on the one hand or the other*); handiwork; style of penmanship; power of performance; skill; agency; part in performing (*to have a hand in mischief*); possession; power (*in the hands of the owner*); that which performs the office of the hand or of a finger in pointing (*the hands of a clock*); a male or female in relation to an employer; a person employed on board ship or in factories; a person with some special faculty or ability (*a good hand at a speech*); in card playing, the cards held by a single player; one of the players.—*vt* give or transmit with the hand (*hand me a book*); to lead, guide and lift with the hand; to conduct.—**to hand down** to transmit in succession, as from father to son or from predecessor to successor.—*adj* belonging to or used by the hand.

handbag *n* a woman's small bag for carrying personal items.

handball *n* a game in which players bat a ball against a single wall or walled court with the hand; the small hard rubber ball used in this.

handbell *n* a small bell rung when held by the hand.

handbill *n* a printed paper or sheet to be circulated for the purpose of making some public announcement.

handbook *n* a small book or treatise such as may be easily held in the hand; a manual; a guidebook.

handbrake *n* a brake in a motor vehicle operated by hand.

handbreadth, hand's-breadth *n* a space equal to the breadth of the hand; a palm.

handcart *n* a cart drawn or pushed by hand.

handcuff *n* either of a pair of connected steel rings for shackling the wrists of a prisoner.—*vt* to put a handcuff on; to manacle.

handfasting *n* (*arch*) an irregular marriage by agreement or mutual pledge.

handful *n* as much as the hand will grasp or contain; a small quantity or number.

hand grenade *n* a grenade to be thrown by the hand.

handicap *n* in racing, an allowance of a certain amount of time or distance to the inferior competitors in a race to bring all as nearly as possible to an equality or the extra weight imposed on the superior competitors with the same object; a race so arranged; a hindrance; a learning difficulty; a disadvantage.—*vt* (**handicapped, handicapping**) to put a handicap on; to equalize by a handicap; to hinder.

handicapped *adj* having a handicap.

handicraft *n* manual occupation; work performed by the hand.

handicraftsman *n* (*pl* **handicraftsmen**) a man employed in manual occupation; an artisan.

handiwork *n* work done by the hands; hence, the work or deed of any person.

handkerchief *n* a piece of cloth, usually silk, linen or cotton, carried about the person for blowing the nose, wiping the face, hands, etc; a similar piece worn round the neck.

handle *vt* (**handled, handling**) to bring the hand or hands in frequent contact with; to finger; to touch; to feel; to manage, ply or wield; to treat of or deal with, as a person or a topic.—*vi* to use the hands; to feel with the hands.—*n* that part of a thing which is intended to be grasped by the hand in using or moving it; the instrument or means of effecting a purpose.—**a handle to one's name** (*colloq*) a title.

handlebar *n* (often *pl*) the curved metal bar with a grip at each end used to steer a bicycle, etc.

handlebar moustache *n* a bushy moustache with curved ends.

handloom *n* a weaver's loom worked by the hand, as distinguished from a power loom.

handmade *adj* manufactured by the hand and not by a machine.

handmaid, handmaiden *n* a female servant or attendant.

handmill *n* a small mill for grinding grain, pepper, coffee, etc, moved by hand.

hand organ *n* a portable or barrel organ.

handout *n* anything which is given away; an item of food, clothing, etc given free to the needy; a prepared document given to the press to give information, promote a product, etc.

handrail *n* a rail or railing to hold by.

handsaw *n* a saw to be used with the hand.

handsel, hansel *n* an earnest, or earnest penny; a sale, gift or using, which is regarded as the first of a series; the first money received for the sale of goods.—*vt* to give a handsel to; to use or do for the first time.

handset *n* a telephone earpiece and mouthpiece as a single unit.

handsome *adj* good-looking; attractive; ample (*a handsome fortune*); generous.

hands-on *adj* having personal, especially practical, experience.

hand-to-mouth *adj* having barely enough food or money to survive.

handwork *n* work done by the hands.

handworked, hand-wrought *adj* made with the hands.

handwriting *n* writing done by hand; a style of such writing.

handy *adj* skilled to use the hand with ease; dextrous; ready; adroit; to hand; near; convenient.

hang *vt* (*pret, pp* **hung, hanged**—the latter being obsolete except in sense to put to death by the rope—*ppr* **hanging**) to suspend; to fasten to some elevated point without support from below (often with *up*); to put to death by suspending by the neck; to fit up so as to allow of free motion (a door, a gate, etc); to cover, furnish or decorate by anything suspended (*to hang an apartment with curtains*); to cause or suffer to assume a drooping attitude (*to hang the head*).—*vi* to be suspended; to be sustained wholly or partly by something above; to dangle; to depend; to bend forward or downward; to lean or incline; to be attached to or connected with in various ways; to hover; to impend (*dangers hang over us*); to linger, lounge, loiter; to incline; to have a steep declivity; to be put to death by suspension from the neck.—*n* the way a thing hangs; slope or declivity; inclination, bent or tendency.

hangar *n* a shed for housing aeroplanes.

hangdog *adj* abject or ashamed.

hanger *n* one who hangs; a metal, plastic or wooden shaped bar from which a garment, etc, is hung.

hanger-on *n* (*pl* **hangers-on**) a parasite; a dependant.

hanging *adj* such as to incur punishment by death (*a hanging matter*).—*n* death by suspension; what is hung up to drape a room, as tapestry, etc (usually plural).

hanging buttress *n* (*archit*) a merely decorative buttress supported on a corbel.

hanging garden *n* a garden formed in terraces rising one above the other.

hangman *n* (*pl* **hangmen**) one who hangs another; one employed to hang criminals.

hangnail *n* a fragment of torn skin attached to root of fingernail.

hang-up *n* an obsession; an emotional preoccupation with something; an inhibition.

hank *n* a coiled or looped bundle of wool, rope, etc.

hanker *vi* to long for; to think of with longing (followed by *after*).

hankering *n* the feeling of one who hankers; a longing.

hanky-panky *n* (*colloq*) mischievous behaviour; dishonest or illegal behaviour; illicit sexual intercourse.

Hansard *n* the published debates of the British Parliament.

hanse *n* a medieval guild of merchants; a confederacy; a fee paid by new members of such a guild.

handsaw

hank

Hanse *n* a town of the Hanseatic League; the Hanseatic League.

hanseatic *adj* of or pertaining to a hanse.

Hanseatic League *n* a confederacy of merchants or commercial cities in northern German and elsewhere, which lasted from the fourteenth to the nineteenth century.

hansom, hansom cab *n* a two-wheeled cab, so named after the inventor.

haphazard *adj* not planned; random; slipshod.

hapless *adj* luckless; unfortunate; unlucky; unhappy.

happen *vi* to come about by chance; to take place; to occur.—**to happen on** to meet with; to fall or light upon.

happy *adj* contented in mind; highly pleased with one's life, position, etc; satisfied; fortunate; bringing or attended with good fortune; prosperous; propitious; favourable; well suited for a purpose or occasion; well devised; felicitous; apt; living in concord or friendship (*a happy family*).

happy-go-lucky *adj* carefree; easy-going; taking things as they come.

happy hour *n* a period of time, usually in the early evening, when drinks are sold at a reduced price in bars.

happy medium *n* a middle course between two extremes; a compromise.

harangue *n* a tirade or declamation; a lengthy forceful speech.—*vi* (**harangued, haranguing**) to make a harangue; to address vehemently.—*vt* to address by a harangue.

hara-kiri, hari-kiri *n* formerly, a mode of suicide among Japanese military and civil officials who had been disgraced.

harass *vt* to perplex; to annoy by repeated attacks.

harassment *n* the act of harassing or state of being harassed.

harbinger *n* a forerunner; a precursor; that which precedes and gives notice of the expected arrival of something else.—*vt* to precede as harbinger; to presage or predetermine, as a harbinger.

harbour *n* a place of shelter, protection or refuge; a port or haven for ships.—*vt* to shelter or house; to protect; to entertain or cherish in the mind (*to harbour a grudge*).—*vi* to lodge or abide for a time for shelter or protection; to take shelter.

hard *adj* not easily penetrated or separated into parts; not yielding to pressure (applied to material bodies and opposed to *soft*); difficult to the understanding; not easy to the intellect; difficult of accomplishment; not easy to be done or executed; laborious; fatiguing; difficult to endure; oppressive; severe; cruel; distressing; painful; unfeeling; insensible; harsh; obdurate; exacting; avaricious; grasping; harsh or abusive (*hard words*); pinching

hardback

with cold; rigorous (*a hard winter*); austere; rough; acid or sour (*hard cider*); forced; constrained; unnatural; coarse, unpalatable or scanty (*hard fare*); (*gram*) applied to the consonants (also called surd) *f*, *k*, *p*, *s*, *t*, and the sound of *th* in *thin*, and also to the sound of *c* as in *corn* and *g* as in *get*, as distinguished from the sounds in *city* and *gin*; applied to water, not very suitable for washing from holding salts of lime or magnesia in solution; (of drugs) addictive and damaging to health; (of news, etc) definite, not speculative.—*adv* close; near (*hard by*); with urgency; vehemently; vigorously; energetically; violently; with great force; with difficulty or labour.

hardback *n* a book bound with a hard or stiff cover.—*adj* of a book, bound with a hard or stiff cover.

hard-bitten *adj* tough; seasoned.

hard-boiled *adj* of eggs, boiled until solid; of people, cynical; brazen.

hard-core *n* the inner group of an organization, etc that is stubborn and resistant to change.—*adj* deep-rooted or absolute; utterly entrenched; of pornography, explicit, obscene.

hard disk *n* (*comput*) a rigid magnetic disk in a sealed unit capable of much greater storage capacity than a floppy disk.

hard drug *n* any drug, such as heroin, considered to cause addiction.

harden *vt* to make hard or more hard; to confirm in effrontery, obstinacy, wickedness, opposition or enmity; to make insensible or unfeeling; to make firm; to inure.—*vi* to become hard or more hard; to acquire solidity or mere compactness; to become unfeeling; to become inured.

hard-hearted *adj* pitiless; unfeeling; inhuman; inexorable.

hardihood *n* boldness; bravery; intrepidity; venturesomeness; audacity.

hard-line *adj* (of a policy) aggressive or unyielding.

hardly *adv* scarcely; barely; not quite.

hardness *n* the condition or quality of being hard; resistance to scratching, especially of a mineral.

hard-nosed *adj* tough and stubborn; shrewd.

hardship *n* something hard, oppressive, toilsome, distressing, etc; lack or privation; grievance.

hard shoulder *n* a strip of land alongside a motorway where a vehicle can stop in an emergency.

hardware *n* articles of iron or other metal, as pots, kettles, saws, knives, etc; (*comput*) the mechanical and electronic components that make up a computer system.

hardwood *n* the close-grained wood of deciduous trees.

hardy *adj* bold; brave; stout; daring; resolute; intrepid; confident; full of assurance; inured to fatigue; proof against hardship; capable of bearing exposure to cold weather (*a hardy plant*).

hare *n* a rodent quadruped of various species, with long ears, a short tail, soft hair, a divided upper lip and long hind legs, often hunted for sport or for its flesh, which is excellent food.

harebell *n* a species of bellflower, also termed the common bellflower and Scottish bluebell; a name for the wild hyacinth.

harebrained *adj* foolish.

harelip *n* a malformation of the lip consisting of a fissure or vertical division of one or both lips, sometimes extending also to the palate.

hareld *n* a marine duck inhabiting the Arctic seas, the male having two very long feathers in the tail.

harem, hareem *n* the apartments appropriated to the female members of an Islamic family; the occupants.

haricot, haricot bean *n* a type of French bean with an edible light-coloured seed.

hari-kiri *n* same as **hara-kiri**.

hark *vi* to listen, to hearken (now used only in the imperative).—**to hark back** to retrace a course; to revert (to).

harl[1] *vt* to give a rough coating of lime to the stones of a house.

harl[2] *n* a filament, as of flax or hemp; a barb of one of the feathers from a peacock's tail, used in dressing fly-hooks.

harlequin *n* a clown; a fool.—*adj* fantastic or full of trickery; colourful.

Harlequin *n* a performer in a pantomime, masked, dressed in tight parti-coloured clothes, covered with spangles and armed with a magic wand or sword.

harlequin duck *n* a species of duck, the male of which has black and white marked plumage.

harlot *n* a prostitute.

harlotry *n* a trade or practice of prostitution.

harm *n* physical or material injury; hurt; damage; detriment; moral wrong; evil; mischief; wickedness.—*vt* to hurt; to injure; to damage.

harmattan *n* an extremely dry and hot wind which blows periodically from the interior parts of Africa towards the Atlantic Ocean.

harmful *adj* full of harm; hurtful; injurious; noxious.

harmless *adj* free from harm; uninjured; free from power or disposition to harm; not injurious; innocuous; inoffensive.

harmonic *adj* relating to harmony or music; concordant; musical; harmonious; in acoustics, denoting a secondary tone heard along with a fundamental tone, produced by secondary or partial vibrations.—*n*

(*mus*) a secondary and less distinct tone which accompanies any principal and apparently simple tone.

harmonica *n* a mouth organ.

harmonic progression *n* (*math*) a series of numbers the reciprocals of which are in arithmetical progression, e.g. 1, $\frac{1}{2}$, $\frac{1}{3}$, $\frac{1}{4}$, etc.

harmonics *n* the doctrine or science of musical sounds.

harmonious *adj* exhibiting or characterized by harmony; melodious; agreeing in ideas, interests, etc.

harmonist *n* one who harmonizes; one skilled in the principles of harmony; a writer of harmony.

harmonium *n* a musical instrument resembling a small organ and much used as a substitute for it, the tones being produced by the forcing of air through free reeds.

harmonization *n* the act of harmonizing.

harmonize *vi* (**harmonized, harmonizing**) to unite harmoniously or in harmony; to be in peace and friendship; to agree in action, effect, sense or purport; to be musically harmonious.—*vt* to bring to be harmonious; to cause to agree; to show the harmony or agreement of; to reconcile the contradictions between; (*mus*) to combine according to the laws of counterpoint; to set accompanying parts to, as to an air or melody.

harmony *n* the just adaptation of parts to each other, in any system or combination of things, or in things intended to form a connected whole; concord; consonance; concord or agreement in facts, views, sentiments, manners, interests, etc; peace and friendship; (*mus*) musical concord; the accordance of two or more sounds or that union of different sounds which pleases the ear or a succession of such sounds called chords; the science which treats of such sounds.

harness *n* the gear or tackle by which a horse or other animal is yoked and made to work; any arrangement of straps, etc, by which something is fastened or raised, as on a parachute; the apparatus in a loom by which the sets of warp thread are shifted alternately to form the shed.—*vt* to put harness on, as on a horse.

harp *n* a stringed musical instrument of great antiquity, now usually nearly triangular in form, with wire strings stretched from the upper part to one of the sides, played with both hands while standing upright or sitting, the strings being struck or plucked by fingers and thumb.—*vi* to play on the harp; to dwell on a subject tiresomely and vexatiously (usually with *on* or *upon*).

harpist, harper *n* a player on the harp.

harpoon *n* a spear or javelin used to strike

hare

harpoon

and kill whales and large fish.—*vt* to strike with a harpoon.

harpsichord *n* a horizontally strung musical instrument with a keyboard like that of the pianoforte, the strings being plucked by quills instead of struck by hammers.

harpy *n* a rapacious or ravenous animal; a grasping, vicious person.

Harpy *n* in classical myth, a name of three winged monsters having the face of a woman and the body of a bird, with feet and fingers armed with sharp claws.

harpy eagle *n* a large and very powerful bird of prey of Mexico and South America.

harridan *n* a hag; an odious old woman; a vixenish woman; a trollop.

harrier¹ *n* one who harries or pillages; a name for several species of birds of prey which strike their prey on the ground and generally fly very low.

harrier² *n* a breed of dog hound employed in hunting hares; a member of a cross-country running club.

harrow *n* an agricultural implement, usually formed of pieces of timber or metal crossing each other and set with iron teeth, called tines, used for covering seed when sown, etc.—*vt* to draw a harrow over; (*fig*) to lacerate (the feelings); to torment; to harass.

harrowing *adj* causing acute distress to the mind.

harry *vt* (**harried, harrying**) to pillage; to plunder; to rob; to harass.

harsh *adj* grating, either to the touch, to the taste or to the ear; austere; crabbed; morose; rough; rude; rigorous; severe.

hart *n* a stag or male deer, especially when he has passed his fifth year and the crown antler is formed.

hartal *n* in India, a stoppage of all work as a protest or as a sign of humiliation.

hartebeest, hartbeest *n* an antelope common in South Africa.

hartshorn *n* the horn of the hart or stag; an ammoniac preparation formerly obtained from the horn and used medicinally; solution of ammonia.

hart's-tongue *n* the popular name of a fern found in Britain.

harum-scarum *adj* harebrained; unsettled; giddy; rash.—*n* a giddy, harebrained or rash person.

harvest *n* the season of gathering a crop of any kind; the time of reaping and gathering corn and other grain; that which is reaped and gathered in; the product of any labour; gain; result; effect; consequence. —*vt* to reap or gather (corn and fruits).

harvester *n* one who or that which harvests; a mower; a reaper.

harvest home *n* the bringing home of the harvest; the harvest feast.

harrier

harvest mite, harvest tick *n* a species of tick which infests the skin in the autumn.

harvest moon *n* the full moon at the time of harvest or about the autumnal equinox, when it rises nearly at the same hour for several days.

has-been *n* a person or thing that is no longer successful, useful, popular, etc.

hash¹ *vt* to chop into small pieces; to mince and mix.—*n* that which is hashed or chopped up; meat which has been already cooked, chopped into small pieces and served up again; any second preparation of old matter; a repetition.

hash² *n* (*colloq*) hashish.

hashish *n* an intoxicating resin derived from the leaves and shoots of the hemp plant.

haslet *n* the cooked heart, liver, etc, of a hog.

hasp *n* a clasp that passes over a staple to be fastened by a padlock; a metal hook for fastening a door; the fourth part of a spindle (of yarn).—*vt* to shut or fasten with a hasp.

hassock *n* a thick mat or hard cushion on which persons kneel in church; a footstool stuffed with flock or other material.

haste *n* speed; swiftness; despatch; expedition; sudden excitement of passion; quickness; precipitance; the state of being pressed by business; hurry; urgency.—**to make haste** to hasten; to proceed rapidly.

hasten *vt* to drive or urge forward; to push on; to hurry; to expedite; with *me, him*, etc, to make haste; to be speedy or quick. —*vi* to move with celerity; to hurry.

hasty *adj* moving or acting with haste; quick; speedy; opposed to *slow*; precipitate, rash; inconsiderate; opposed to deliberate; irritable; easily excited to wrath; arising from or indicating passion (*hasty words*).

hasty pudding *n* a pudding made of milk and flour or semolina boiled quickly together and sweetened.

hat *n* a covering for the head; a headdress with a crown, sides and continuous brim, made of different materials and worn by men and women.

hatch¹ *vt* to produce young from eggs by incubation or by artificial heat; to contrive or plot; to originate and produce (a scheme, mischief, etc).—*vi* to perform or undergo the process of incubation.—*n* a brood; as many young birds as are produced at once; the act of hatching.

hatch² *n* the frame of crossbars laid over the opening in a ship's deck; the cover of a hatchway; the opening in a ship's deck; the hatchway; a similar opening in a floor; a trapdoor; a half-door or a door with an opening over it; a floodgate; a frame or weir in a river for catching fish.—*vt* to close with a hatch or hatches.

hatch³ *vt* to shade by lines crossing each other in drawing and engraving.

hatchback *n* a car with a sloping rear door which opens upwards.

hatcher *n* one who hatches; a contriver; a plotter.

hatchet *n* a small axe with a short handle, used with one hand.—**to bury the hatchet** to make peace.

hatchet-faced *adj* having a thin face with prominent features.

hatchet job *n* destructive verbal or written criticism, often malicious, and often on a person's reputation and standing; a severe critical attack; a severe reduction, as of jobs.

hatchet man *n* a person appointed to carry out an unpleasant task, such as declaring workers redundant; a person who mounts a severely critical and often malicious attack.

hatching *n* shading made by cross lines.

hatchment *n* the coat of arms of a dead person, placed on the front of a house, in a church, or elsewhere at funerals, notifying the death and the rank of the deceased.

hatchway *n* a square or oblong opening in a ship's deck for communication with the interior.

hate *vt* (**hated, hating**) to dislike greatly or intensely; to have a great aversion to; to detest.—*n* great dislike or aversion; hatred.

hateful *adj* causing hate; exciting great dislike; odious; detestable; feeling hatred; malevolent.

hatred *adj* great dislike or aversion; hate; detestation; active antipathy.

hatter *n* a maker or seller of hats.

hat trick *n* in cricket, the capture of three wickets by three successive balls bowled by the same bowler; the scoring of three successive goals or points in a match or contest; three wins or successes in a row.

hauberk *n* a coat of mail without sleeves, formed of steel rings interwoven.

haughty *adj* proud and disdainful; having a high opinion of oneself, with some contempt for others; lofty and arrogant; disdainful; supercilious.

haul *vt* to pull or draw with force; to transport by drawing; to drag; to tug.—*vi* (*naut*) to change the direction of sailing (with *off*, *up*, etc).—*n* a pulling with force; a violent pull; a draught of fish in a net; that which is caught by one haul; hence, that which is taken, gained or received at once.

haulage *n* the act of hauling or drawing; the force expended in hauling; dues or charges for hauling or towing.

haulm, halm *n* the stem or stalk of grain of all kinds or of peas, beans, hops, etc; dry stalks in general.

haunch *n* the hip; the bend of the thigh; part of the body of a human and of quadrupeds between the last ribs and the thigh; (*archit*) the middle part between the apex or crown and the springing of an arch; the flank.

haunt *vt* to frequent; to resort to much or often or to be much about; to visit customarily; to appear in or about, as a ghost; to be a frequent ghostly visitant of.—*vi* to be much about a place; to make frequent resort.—*n* a place to which one frequently resorts; a favourite resort; a common abiding place.

haunted *adj* frequently visited or resorted to, especially by ghosts.

hautboy, hautbois *n* an oboe; a wind instrument of wood, sounded through a double reed.

hauteur *n* pride; haughtiness; insolent manner or spirit.

Havana *n* a cigar made from Cuban tobacco.

have *vt* (*pret, pp* **had**, *ppr* **having**, *indicative pres* **I have, he has; we, they have**) to possess; to hold; to be in close relation to (*to have a son, a master, a servant*); to accept; to take as husband or wife; to hold or regard (*to have in honour*); to maintain or hold in opinion; to be under necessity or impelled by duty (*to have to do it*); to procure or make to be; to cause (*he had him murdered*); to gain, procure, receive, obtain; to bring forth (a child); to experience in any way, as to enjoy, to participate in, to suffer from; to understand.

haven *n* a harbour; a port; a bay, recess or inlet which affords anchorage and a station for ships; a shelter, asylum or place of safety.—*vi* to shelter, as in a haven.

haversack *n* a bag of strong cloth worn over the shoulder by soldiers in marching order for carrying their provisions; a light pack carried over the shoulder by hikers, etc.

having *n* the act or state of possessing; that which is had or possessed; goods; estate.

havoc *n* devastation; wide and general destruction.

haw¹ *n* a hedge; an enclosure; the hawthorn and its berry or seed.

haw² *n* an intermission or hesitation of speech (*hums and haws*).

hawfinch *n* a large finch with thick beak.

haw-haw *n* same has **ha-ha**.

hawk¹ *n* any of various diurnal birds of prey; a person who supports politics of aggression; a militant.—*vi* to hunt with a trained hawk; to practise falconry; to fly in the manner of the hawk; to strike like a hawk.

hawk² *vt* to sell, or try to sell, by offering goods at people's doors; to convey through town or country for sale; to spread gossip.—*vi* to peddle.

hawk³ *vi* to cough up phlegm noisily.—*vt* to raise by hawking.—*n* an effort to force up phlegm by coughing.

hatchet

hawk

hawker *n* one who travels selling wares.

hawkmoth *n* any of several moths with a large body and narrow front wings.

hawser *n* (*naut*) a small cable used in warping, etc.

hawthorn *n* a kind of small tree, one species of which is an excellent hedge plant, while some of its varieties are very beautiful when in full blossom; May.

hay *n* grass cut and dried for fodder.

haybox *n* a box packed with hay and so constructed that hot food placed in it continues to be cooked.

haycock *n* a conical pile or heap of hay.

hay fever *n* an allergic condition caused by a sensitivity to pollen and characterized by frequent sneezing and redness and watering of the eyes.

hayrack *n* a rack from which livestock on a farm can eat hay.

hayrick *n* a haystack.

haystack *n* a large pile of hay in the open air, laid up for preservation.

haywire *adj* out of control; out of order; disorganized.

hazard *n* danger; peril; risk; a game played with dice.—*vt* to put in danger of loss or injury; to risk.

hazardous *adj* exposing to peril or danger of loss or evil; dangerous; risky.

haze *n* fog; a greyish or dusky vapour in the air; hence, obscurity; dimness; mental fog. —*vi* (**hazed, hazing**) to make or become hazy.

hazel *n* a tree growing wild in Britain and yielding edible nuts, its wood being used for fishing rods, walking sticks, etc.—*adj* of a light-brown colour like the hazelnut.

hazelnut *n* the nut of the hazel.

hazy *adj* foggy; misty; thick with haze; mentally obscure or confused.

he *pron* (*possessive* **his**, *objective* **him**— *also dative*) the *masc sing* form of the pronoun of the 3rd person. It is sometimes used as a noun, being equivalent to *man* or *male person* and is often prefixed to the names of animals to designate the male kind (*a he-goat*).

head *n* the anterior part or extremity of animals; the part of the body above the neck, containing the eyes, mouth, etc; the part which forms the seat of the brain and mental faculties; hence, understanding, intellect, will or resolution, mind, an individual; a unit (*a thousand head of sheep*, used only in sing); a chief; a leader; a commander; the chief teacher in a school; what gives a striking appearance to the head, as the hair, antlers of a deer, etc; part of a thing resembling in position or otherwise the human head (*the head of a spear*, *of a nail*); the main point or part; the forepart (*the head of a ship*); the upper part (of a bed, etc); the top; the principal source of a stream; the part most remote from the mouth or opening; a headland; promontory; the foremost place; the place of honour or command; crisis; height; pitch; division of discourse; title of a subdivision; a small magnetic device across which the tape passes in a tape-recorder, video player, etc.—*vt* to be or put oneself at the head of; to lead; to direct; to behead; to decapitate; to form a head to; to fit or furnish with a head; to go in front of, so as to keep from advancing (*to head a drove of cattle*).—*adj* belonging to the head; chief; principal (often used in composition, as *head workman, a headmaster*, etc).

headache *n* pain in the head.

headdress *n* a covering for the head; an ornamented head covering; one denoting rank or occupation.

header *n* one who or that which puts a head on anything; a machine that trims heads from castings, etc; a tank or hopper; in soccer, the action of striking the ball with the head; a plunge or dive into water head-first; a beam placed between and at the top of two long beams; a brick laid across, not parallel to, a wall; a heading.

headfirst *adv* with the head first; rashly; precipitately.

headhunt *vt* to cut off and preserve as trophies the heads of enemies; to seek out and try to recruit (employees, especially executives) for a vacant post.

headhunter *n* a person who headhunts.

heading *n* that which stands at the head; a title of a section in a book, etc; the direction in which a vehicle is moving; a passage in the line of an intended tunnel.

headlamp *n* a light at the front of a vehicle.

headland *n* a cape; a promontory.

headline *n* printed lines at the top of a newspaper article giving the topic; a brief news summary.—*vi* (**headlined, headlining**) to give featured billing or publicity to.

headlock *n* in wrestling, a hold in which the arm encircles an opponent's head.

headlong *adv* with the head foremost; rashly; precipitately; without deliberation.—*adj* steep; precipitous; rash; precipitate.

headman *n* (*pl* **headmen**) the chieftain or leader of a tribe; a foreman or overseer.

headmaster, headmistress *n* the principal teacher of a school.

headmost *adj* most advanced; first.

head over heels *adv* as if somersaulting; completely, utterly, deeply.

headphone *n* one of two radio receivers held to the head by a band.

headquarters *npl* the quarters of the commander of an army; a centre of authority or order; the place where one chiefly resides.

head-sea *n* a sea that directly meets the head of a ship.

hazelnut

headship *n* the state or position of being a head or chief; authority; supreme power; government.

headsman *n* (*pl* **headsmen**) one that cuts off heads; an executioner.

headstone *n* the chief or corner stone; the keystone of an arch; the stone at the head of a grave.

headstrong *adj* obstinate; ungovernable; bent on pursuing one's own course.

headway *n* the progress made by a ship in motion; progress or success of any kind.

head wind *n* a wind directly opposed to a ship's course.

headwork *n* mental or intellectual labour.

heady *adj* hasty; precipitate; intoxicating; exciting.

heal *vt* to make hale, sound or whole; to cure of a disease or wound and restore to soundness; to reconcile, as a breach or difference.—*vi* to grow sound; to return to a sound state (sometimes with *up* or *over*).

health *n* that state of a being in which all the parts and organs are sound and in proper condition; physical and mental well-being; freedom from disease; the condition of body or mind; a wish for someone's health or happiness, as in a toast.

health farm *n* a residential place for improving health through a strict regime of diet and exercise.

health foods *npl* foods that are grown organically, not processed and free of additives.

healthy *adj* being in health; enjoying health; hale; sound; conducive to health; wholesome; salubrious.

heap *n* a pile or mass; a collection of things piled up; a large quantity; a great number.—*vt* to lay in a heap; to pile; to amass (often with *up* or with *on*); to round or form into a heap.

hear *vt* (*pret, pp* **heard**, *ppr* **hearing**) to perceive by the auditory sense; to take cognizance of by the ear; to give audience or allowance to speak; to listen to; to heed; to obey; to try judicially (a cause) in a court of justice; to listen to one repeating or going over, as a task, etc.—*vi* to enjoy the sense or faculty of perceiving sound; to listen; to hearken; to attend; to be told; to receive by report.

hearing *n* the act of perceiving sound; the faculty or sense by which sound is perceived; audience; an opportunity to be heard; a judicial investigation before a court; reach of the ear; extent within which sound may be heard.

hearing aid *n* a small electronic amplifier worn behind the ear to improve hearing.

hearken *vi* to listen; to lend the ear; to give heed to what is uttered; to hear with obedience or compliance.—*vt* to hear by listening; to hear with attention; to regard.

hearsay *n* report; rumour; common talk.

hearsay evidence *n* evidence repeated at second hand by one who heard the actual witness relate or admit what he or she knew of the transaction or fact in question, not generally admissible as evidence.

hearse *n* a vehicle for conveying a coffin to a funeral.

heart *n* a muscular organ, which is the propelling agent of the blood in the animal body, situated in the thorax of vertebrate animals; the mind, the soul, the consciousness; the seat of the affections and passions; the moral side of our nature in contradistinction to the intellectual; courage; spirit; the seat of the will or inclination; hence, disposition of mind; tendency; conscience or sense of good and ill; the inner part of anything; the part nearest the middle or centre; the vital or most essential part; the core; the very essence; that which has the shape or form of a heart or is regarded as representing the figure of a heart; one of a suit of playing cards marked with such a figure.—*vi* to form a close compact head, as a plant.

heartache *n* anguish.

heart attack *n* a sudden instance of abnormal heart function, especially coronary thrombosis.

heartbreak *n* overwhelming sorrow or grief.

heartbroken *adj* deeply grieved; in despair.

heartburn *n* an uneasy burning sensation in the stomach from indigestion and excess of acidity.

hearten *vt* to encourage; to cheer up.

heartfelt *adj* deeply felt; deeply affecting.

hearth *n* that portion of the floor of a room on which the fire stands, generally a pavement or floor of brick or stone below a chimney; the fireside; the domestic circle.

hearthrug *n* a small thick carpet laid before a fire.

hearthstone *n* the stone forming the hearth.

heartily *adv* in a vigorous or enthusiastic way; sincerely.

heartland *n* the central or most vital part of an area, region, etc.

heartless *adj* without a heart; lacking feeling or affection; cruel.

heart-rending *adj* breaking the heart; overpowering with anguish; very distressing.

heartsease, heart's-ease *n* ease of heart; a plant of the violet family; the pansy.

heartsick *adj* sick at heart; pained in mind; deeply depressed.

heartstrings *npl* hypothetical nerves or tendons supposed to brace and sustain the heart; strong emotions.

heart-throb *n* (*colloq*) the object of a person's infatuation.

heart-to-heart *n* an intimate conversation. —*adj* intimate; candid.

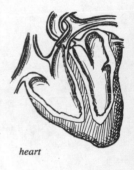

heart

hearth

heart-warming *adj* pleasing; inspiring sympathy; moving.

heart-whole *adj* not affected with love; having unbroken spirits or good courage.

heartwood *n* the central older part of the wood of trees; the duramen.

hearty *adj* enthusiastic; sound and healthy; large to satisfaction (*a hearty meal*); loud and unrestrained (*a hearty laugh*).

heat *n* a form of energy produced by agitation of the molecules of which a substance or body is composed; the sensation produced by substances or bodies that are hot; the sensation caused by exposure to fire, the sun's rays, etc; the reverse of cold; high temperature, as distinguished from low; hot weather; a hot period; a single effort, as in a race; utmost ardour or violence; rage; vehemence; agitation of mind; inflammation or excitement; exasperation; animation in thought or discourse; fervency; sexual excitement in animals; fermentation.—*vt* to make hot; to communicate heat to; to cause to grow warm; to make feverish; to excite; to warm with passion or desire; to animate.—*vi* to grow warm or hot.

heater *n* a device that provides heat.

heath *n* any of numerous shrubby plants that thrive on sandy soil, especially heather; a place overgrown with scrubby vegetation; a waste tract of land.

heath cock *n* the blackcock.

heathen *n* one who worships idols or does not acknowledge the true God; a pagan; an idolater; a rude, barbarous or irreligious person.—*adj* gentile; pagan.

heathendom *n* those parts of the world in which heathenism prevails.

heathenish *adj* belonging to heathens or their religions; barbarous; uncivilized; irreligious.

heathenism *n* the system of religion or the manners and morals of a heathen nation; paganism; barbarism.

heathenry *n* heathenism; heathens collectively.

heather *n* common heath, a low shrub with clusters of pink, purple or white flowers, covering tracts of waste land in Britain.

heatherbell *n* a blossom of a large-flowered British heath.

heathery *adj* abounding in heather.

heating *n* a system for providing warmth or heat (*central heating*); the warmth provided.

heat rash *n* miliaria.

heatwave *n* a prolonged period of unusually hot weather.

heave *vt* (*pret, pp* **heaved** *or* **hove**, *ppr* **heaving**) to lift; to raise; to elevate; to raise or utter (*to heave a sigh*); to throw; to cast; (*naut*) to apply power to, as by means of a windlass, in order to pull or force in

heatherbell

any direction.—**to heave to** to bring a ship's head to the wind and stop her motion.—*vi* to be thrown or raised up; to rise; to rise and fall with alternate motions; to swell up; to pant, as after severe labour or exertion; to make an effort to vomit; to retch.—**to heave in sight** to appear; to make its first appearance, as a ship at sea.—*n* an upward motion; swell, as of the waves of the sea; an effort of the lungs, etc; an effort to raise something.

heaven *n* the blue expanse which surrounds the earth and in which the sun, moon and stars seem to be set; the sky; the upper regions (often in the plural); the final abode of the blessed; the place where Christians believe that God manifests himself to the blessed (often used as equivalent to God or Providence); supreme felicity; bliss; a sublime or exalted condition.

heavenly *adj* pertaining to heaven; inhabiting heaven; celestial; supremely blessed; supremely excellent.—*adv* in a heavenly manner.

heaven-sent *adj* happening by a stroke of good fortune.

heaviness *n* the state or quality of being heavy; weight; severity; sadness; dullness or lifelessness.

heavy *adj* that can be lifted only with labour; ponderous; weighty, the opposite of light; large in amount or quantity (*a heavy rain*, *a heavy crop*); not easily borne; hard to endure; burdensome; oppressive; severe; hard to accomplish; weighted or bowed down; burdened with sorrow, sleep, weariness, etc; slow; sluggish; inactive; dull; lifeless; inanimate; impeding motion or action (*heavy roads*); acting or moving with violence (*a heavy sea*, *cannonade*); dark; gloomy; threatening; lowering (*a heavy sky*); not easily digested (food); deep and voluminous (sound).

heavy-duty *adj* made to withstand heavy or rough usage; durable.

heavy-laden *adj* laden with a heavy burden.

heavy metal *n* a style of loud, often much amplified, energetic rock music with a strong beat.

heavy spar *n* the sulphate of baryta, occurring in veins and in prismatic crystals.

heavy water *n* deuterium oxide, water in which the normal hydrogen content has been replaced by deuterium.

heavyweight *n* the heaviest weight division in boxing; a boxer of this weight.

hebdomadal *adj* weekly; consisting of seven days or occurring every seven days.

Hebe *n* in Greek myth, the goddess of youth.

hebetude *n* dullness; stupidity.

Hebraic *adj* pertaining to the Hebrews or their language.

Hebrew *n* one of the descendants of Jacob;

an Israelite; an ancient language of the Hebrews, now the official language of Israel, one of the Semitic tongues.—*adj* pertaining to the Hebrews.

hecatomb *n* a sacrifice of a hundred oxen or other beasts; hence, any great sacrifice of victims; a great number of persons or animals slaughtered.

heck[1] *interj* an expression of surprise or grief.

heck[2] *n* a device for catching fish; a rack; a hack.

heckle *n* a sort of comb for flax or hemp; a hackle.—*vt* (**heckled, heckling**) to dress with a heckle; (*fig*) to tease or vex; to disturb or harass with persistent questions, interruptions, etc.

heckler *n* one who heckles.

hectare *n* a metric measure equal to 10,000 square metres or 2.47 acres.

hectic *adj* full of energetic activity, haste, confusion, etc; feverish.—*n* a hectic fever.

hectogram *n* a metric weight containing 100 grams.

hectolitre *n* a metric measure for liquids, containing 100 litres .

hector *vt* to treat with insolence; to bully.—*vi* to play the bully; to bluster.—*n* a bully; a blustering, noisy person.

hederaceous *adj* pertaining to or resembling ivy.

hedge *n* a fence formed by bushes or small trees growing close together; any line of shrubbery closely planted.—*vt* (**hedged, hedging**) to enclose or fence with a hedge; to obstruct with a barrier; to stop by any means; to surround for defence; to hem in. —**to hedge a bet** to bet on both sides, thus guarding oneself against great loss, whatever may be the result.—*vi* to avoid direct commitment by evasive answers to questions, etc; to protect oneself from loss by cross-bets.

hedgehog *n* a small nocturnal insect-eating mammal, the upper part of whose body is covered with prickles or spines.

hedgerow *n* a row or series of shrubs or trees forming a hedge.

hedge-sparrow *n* a European bird with brownish plumage; the dunnock.

hedonism *n* the doctrine that the chief good of humans lies in the pursuit of pleasure.

hedonist *n* one who professes hedonism.

heed *vt* to regard with care; to take notice of; to attend to; to observe.—*n* care; attention; notice; observation; regard (usually with *give* or *take*).

heedful *adj* taking heed; attentive; watchful; cautious; wary.

heedless *adj* without heed; inattentive; careless.

heel[1] *n* the hinder part of the foot in humans or quadrupeds; the hinder part of a covering for the foot; something shaped like the human heel or that occupies a position corresponding to the heel; the latter or concluding part; (*colloq*) a despicable person.—*vt* to perform by the use of the heels, as a dance; to add a heel to.

heel[2] *vi* to incline or cant over from a vertical position, as a ship.—*n* the act of so inclining; a cant.

heel ball *n* a composition for blackening the heels of shoes; used also for taking impressions from engraved plates, monumental brasses, etc.

heeltap *n* the small portion of liquor left in a glass when the main portion has been drunk.

hegemony *n* leadership; predominance; preponderance of one state among others.

Hegira, Hejira *n* the flight of Mohammed from Mecca, adopted by the Muslims in reckoning their time, their era beginning 16th July 622; hence, any similar flight.

heifer *n* a young cow.

heigh-ho! *exclam* usually expressing some degree of languor, uneasiness or resignation.

height *n* the condition of being high; the distance which anything rises above its foot, basis or foundation or above the earth; altitude; an eminence; a summit; a hill or mountain; elevation or pre-eminence among other persons; elevation in excellence of any kind; elevation or dignity, as of sentiment, expression, etc; extent; degree; stage in progress or advancement.—**the height of** the utmost degree in extent, intensity or violence.

heighten *vt* to make high; to raise higher; to elevate; to increase; to augment; to intensify.

heinous *adj* hateful; odious; hence, notorious; enormous; aggravated (sin or crime, sinner).

heir *n* one who succeeds or is to succeed another in the possession of property; an inheritor; one who receives any endowment from an ancestor.

heir apparent *n* the heir who is certain to inherit if he survives the present holder.

heirdom *n* the state of an heir.

heiress *n* a female heir.

heirloom *n* a personal chattel that descends to an heir; any piece of personal property which has belonged to a family for a long time.

heir presumptive *n* one whose right of inheritance may be defeated by any contingency, as by the birth of a nearer relative.

heist *n* (*sl*) a robbery.—*vt* (*sl*) to steal.

Hejira *n* same as **Hegira**.

heliacal *adj* (*astron*) emerging from the light of the sun or passing into it; rising or setting at the same time, or nearly the same time, as the sun.

helianthus *n* any plant of the genus to

hedgehog

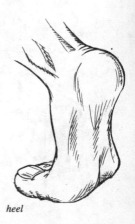

heel

403

which the sunflower and the Jerusalem artichoke belong.

helical *adj* of or resembling a helix; spiral.

helical gear *n* gearing in which the teeth of the gear wheels wind round the cylinder on which they are formed in the shape of a spiral or helix.

helicopter *n* a form of aircraft that can hover as well as fly horizontally and vertically, its support in the air derived from the vertical thrust of large air screws.

heliocentric *adj* (*astron*) relating to the sun as a centre; appearing as if seen from the sun's centre.

heliograph *n* an instrument used to send signals in Morse code by means of mirrors reflecting the sun's rays; a heliostat.—*vti* to convey or communicate by means of a heliograph or similar instrument.

heliolater *n* a worshipper of the sun.

heliolatry *n* the worship of the sun.

heliostat *n* a heliograph; any of various devices for reflecting the sun's light temporarily or continuously to an observer at a distance, used in astronomical observations, in experiments on light and for signalling in war. etc.

heliotrope *n* a variety of quartz, of a deep green colour, with bright red spots; bloodstone; a one of a genus of plants whose flowers follow the course of the sun; a bluish-purple colour.

heliotropism *n* the tendency of a plant to direct its growth towards the sun or towards light.

helium *n* a gas present in the air in small quantities, the lightest element next to hydrogen, one of the inert elements.

helix *n* (*pl* **helices, helixes**) a spiral line, as of wire in a coil; something that is spiral; a circumvolution; (*geom*) such a curve as is described by every point of a screw that is turned round in a fixed nut; (*archit*) a small volute or twist under the abacus of the Corinthian capital; (*anat*) the whole circuit of the external body of the ear; (*zool*) a genus of molluscs, comprising the land shell snails.

hell *n* the place of the dead or of souls after death; the place or state of punishment for the wicked after death; the infernal powers; (*colloq*) extreme pain or difficulty, intense suffering.

hellebore *n* any plant of two very different genera, the black hellebore or Christmas rose and the white hellebore or false helleborine.

Hellenes *npl* the inhabitants of Greece; the Greeks.

Hellenic *adj* pertaining to the Hellenes; Greek; Grecian.

Hellenism *n* the ideals, culture and spirit of the Greeks, ancient and modern; the love of Greek culture and art; the Greek idiom.

helicopter

helmet

Hellenist *n* a student of Greek history, civilization and language; one who affiliates with Greeks.

Hellenize *vi* (**Hellenized, Hellenizing**) to use the Greek language or adopt Greek culture or customs.

hellfire *n* the fire of hell; the torments of hell.

hellhole *n* a hellish place, especially one of great squalor or wickedness.

hellhound *n* a dog of hell; an agent of hell; a miscreant.

hellish *adj* pertaining to hell; infernal; malignant; very wicked; (*colloq*) very unpleasant.

hello, hallo, hullo *interj* a greeting; an exclamation of genial surprise or wonder (*hello, what's this?*); an exclamation to call attention.

helm[1] *n* the instrument by which a ship is steered, consisting of a rudder, a tiller, and in large vessels a wheel; in a narrower sense, the tiller; (*fig*) the place or post of direction or management.—*vt* to steer; to guide.

helm[2] *n* (*arch*) a helmet.—*vt* to cover or provide with a helmet.

helmet *n* a defensive covering for the head; head armour composed of metal, leather, etc.

helminthic *adj* relating to parasitic worms; expelling worms.—*n* a medicine for expelling worms; a vermifuge.

helminthology *n* the study of parasitic worms.

helmsman, helmswoman *n* (*pl* **helmsmen, helmswomen**) the person at the helm or wheel who steers a ship.

helot *n* a slave in ancient Sparta; hence, a slave in general.

helotism *n* the condition of a helot; slavery.

helotry *n* slavery; helots collectively; bondsmen.

help *vt* to give assistance or aid to; to aid; to assist; to succour; to relieve; to cure or mitigate (pain or disease); to avail against; to prevent; to remedy; to forbear; to avoid (*to help doing something*).—*vi* to lend aid; to be of use; to avail.—*n* aid furnished; deliverance from difficulty or distress; assistance; that which gives assistance; one who or that which contributes to advance a purpose; remedy; relief; a domestic servant or farm worker.

helper *n* one that helps, aids or assists; an assistant; an auxiliary.

helpful *adj* giving help; useful.

helpless *adj* lacking help or strength; needing help; feeble; weak; affording no help; beyond help.

helpmate *n* an assistant; a helper; a partner; a consort; a wife.

helpmeet *n* a helpmate.

helter-skelter *adv* with hurry and confusion.—*adj* disorderly.—*n* a kind of twisting slide found at funfairs.

Helvetic *adj* of or pertaining to Switzerland.

hem[1] *n* the border of a garment, doubled and sewn down to strengthen it; edge, border, margin.—*vt* (**hemmed, hemming**) to form a hem or border on; to border; to edge.—**to hem in** to enclose and confine; to surround closely; to environ.

hem[2] *interj* an exclamation consisting in a sort of half-cough, loud or subdued as the emotion may suggest (sometimes used as a noun).—*vi* (**hemmed, hemming**) to make the sound hem; hence, to hesitate or stammer in speaking.

hematite, haematite *n* either of two ores of iron, red hematite and brown hematite, so named from the blood-red colour of the former variety, which, as a source of iron, is one of the most important iron ores.

hemeralopia *n* difficulty in seeing in bright light, day blindness, the opposite of *nyctalopia*.

hemihedral *adj* (*mineral*) applied to a crystal having only half the number of faces required for complete symmetry.

hemihedron *n* a solid hemihedrally divided.

hemiplegia *n* paralysis of one side of the body.

hemiplegic *adj* relating to hemiplegia.

hemipteran, hemipteron *n* one of an order of four-winged insects, so named because many of them have the outer wings leathery at the base and transparent towards the tips, including the locusts, plant lice, etc.

hemipterous *adj* pertaining to the hemipterans.

hemisphere *n* a half sphere; one half of a sphere or globe; half the terrestrial sphere, divided into the northern and the southern hemispheres by the equator or into the eastern and western hemispheres by a meridian; half the celestial globe.

hemispheric, hemispherical *adj* pertaining to a hemisphere.

hemistich *n* half a line of verse or half a poetic verse; a verse or line of verse not completed.

hemlock *n* a poisonous umbelliferous Eurasian plant with small white flowers; any of several conifers originally mainly in North America and east Asia.

hemp *n* a widely cultivated Asian plant of the mulberry family; its fibre used to make rope, sailcloth, etc; a narcotic drug obtained from different varieties of this plan; cannabis; marijuana.

hempen *adj* made of hemp.

hemstitch *n* an ornamental stitch forming an open pattern.

hen *n* the female of any kind of bird; especially, the female of the domestic or barnyard fowl.

henbane *n* a poisonous plant found across Europe and west Asia, mostly in waste ground and sometimes fatal to domestic fowls, but yielding a juice, hyoscyamine, that is used as a sedative and narcotic.

hence *adv* from this place; from this time (*a week hence*); as a consequence, inference or deduction from something just before stated; from this source or origin.—**from hence** is sometimes used tautologically for *hence*.

henceforth, henceforward *adv* from this time forward.

henchman *n* (*pl* **henchmen**) a servant; a male attendant; a footman; a follower.

hendecagon *n* (*geom*) a plane figure of eleven sides and as many angles.

hendecasyllabic *adj* having eleven syllables.

hendecasyllable *n* a metrical line of eleven syllables.

hendiadys *n* a figure of speech by which two nouns and a conjunction are used instead of an adjective and a noun, as *through storm and weather* instead of *through stormy weather*.

henequen *n* an agave plant similar to sisal, the fibre of which is similarly used to make rope or coarse fabric.

hen harrier *n* a species of harrier, a bird of prey.

henhouse *n* a house or shelter for fowls.

henna *n* a plant cultivated in North Africa, the Middle East and India; a reddish-brown dye extracted from its leaves, used as hair tint.

hennery *n* an enclosed place for hens; a poultry farm.

henotheism *n* the worship of one deity as supreme among others.

henpeck *vt* to domineer and bully (said of a wife who has the upper hand of her husband).

henpecked *adj* domineered and bullied by one's wife.

hen roost *n* a place where poultry rest at night.

henry *n* the practical electric unit of self-inductance and mutual inductance.

hepatic *adj* pertaining to the liver.—*n* a medicine that acts on the liver.

hepatica *n* a species of anemone with trilobate leaves; any of an order of plants allied to the mosses and called liverworts.

hepatite *n* a variety of sulphate of baryta, which when rubbed or heated exhales a fetid odour.

heptachord *n* (*ancient mus*) a diatonic octave without the upper note; an instrument with seven strings.

heptad *n* a sum of seven; a series or group of seven.

heptaglot *adj* speaking, writing or written in seven languages.—*n* a book in seven languages.

hen

hen harrier

405

heptagon *n* (*geom*) a plane figure having seven sides and as many angles.

heptagonal *adj* having seven angles or sides.

heptahedron *n* a solid figure with seven sides.

heptahedral *adj* having seven sides.

heptamerous *adj* (*bot*) consisting of seven parts; having its parts in sevens.

heptangular *adj* having seven angles.

heptarchy *n* a government by seven persons or the country governed by seven persons (usually applied to the seven Anglo-Saxon kingdoms into which England was once divided).

Heptateuch *n* the first seven books of the Old Testament.

her *pron* a form answering to several cases of **she**; the possessive case of **she** (*her face*); the dative case of **she** (*give her that book*); the objective case of **she** (*I love her*).

herald *n* an officer whose business was to announce or proclaim war, to challenge to battle, to proclaim peace, to bear messages from the commander of an army, etc; an officer who marshals processions and superintends public ceremonies; one who records and blazons the arms of the nobility and gentry and regulates abuses therein; a proclaimer; one who makes public; a forerunner.—*vt* to introduce or to give tidings of, as by a herald; to proclaim; to usher in; to be the forerunner of.

heraldic *adj* pertaining to heralds or heraldry.

heraldry *n* the art or office of a herald; the art of blazoning arms or ensigns armorial or the knowledge pertaining thereto.

herb *n* any plant with a soft or succulent stem (or stems) which dies to the root every year, as distinguished from a tree and a shrub, which have woody stems; specifically, any of such plants that are aromatic and used in cookery and medicine.

herbaceous *adj* pertaining to herbs.

herbaceous plant *n* a plant which perishes annually down to the root; any plant used in medicine, cooking, etc.

herbage *n* herbaceous plants collectively; green food for beasts; grass; pasture.

herbal *adj* relating to herbs.—*n* a book containing the names and descriptions of plants; a collection of plants dried and preserved; a herbarium.

herbalist *n* a person who makes collections of plants; a dealer in medicinal plants; a person who practises healing by the use of herbs.

herbarium *n* (*pl* **herbariums, herbaria**) a collection of dried plants systematically arranged; a book or other contrivance for preserving dried specimens of plants.

heptagon

herbivore *n* an animal that feeds on grass and plants.

herbivorous *adj* eating grass and other plants; subsisting on plants (*a herbivorous animal*).

herculean *adj* pertaining to the Roman god Hercules; resembling Hercules in strength; very difficult or dangerous (*a herculean task*).

herd[1] *n* a number of beasts feeding or driven together; a company of people (in contempt or detestation); a crowd; a rabble.—*vi* to form or unite in a herd; to feed or run in herds; to associate; to unite in companies.—*vt* to gather together and move, as a herd; to tend, as a herdsman.

herd[2] *n* a keeper of cattle or sheep, now mostly in composition, as *shepherd, goatherd, swineherd*.

herdsman *n* (*pl* **herdsmen**) a man attending a herd.

here *adv* in this place; in the place where the speaker is present, opposed to *there*; in the present life or state; in this respect; to this place, hither (*come here*).

hereabout, hereabouts *adv* about this place; in this vicinity or neighbourhood.

hereafter *adv* in time to come; in some future time or state.—*n* a future state.

hereat *adv* (*arch*) at or by reason of this.

hereby *adv* by this; by means of this; close by; very near.

hereditable *adj* capable of being inherited; heritable.

hereditament *n* any species of property that may be inherited.

hereditary *adj* descended by inheritance; descending from an ancestor to an heir; that is or may be transmitted from a parent to a child.

heredity *n* hereditary transmission of qualities of like kind with those of the parent; the doctrine that the offspring inherits the characteristics of the parent or parents.

herein *adv* in this.

hereinafter *adv* in this afterwards (applied to something afterwards to be named or described in a writing).

hereinto *adv* into this.

hereof *adv* of this; concerning this; from this.

hereon *adv* on this.

heresiarch *n* a leader in heresy; a prominent or arch heretic.

heresy *n* a doctrine, principle or set of principles at variance with established or generally received principles; especially an opinion or opinions contrary to the established religious faith or what is regarded as the true faith; heterodoxy.

heretic *n* a person who holds heretical opinions; one who maintains heresy.

heretical *adj* containing or pertaining to heresy.

hereto *adv* to this.

heretofore *adv* before or up to this time; formerly.

hereunto *adv* unto this or this time; hereto.

hereupon *adv* upon this; hereon.

herewith *adv* with this.

heriot *n* (*law*) formerly, a chattel or payment given to the lord of a fee on the decease of the tenant or vassal.

heritable *adj* capable of being inherited; inheritable.

heritage *n* that which is inherited; inheritance; historical sites, traditions, practices, etc, regarded as the valuable inheritance of contemporary society.

heritor *n* in Scotland, a proprietor or landholder in a parish.

hermaphrodite *n* an animal in which the characteristics of both sexes are either really or apparently combined; (*bot*) a flower that contains both the stamen and the pistil, or the male and female organs. —*adj* including or being of both sexes.

hermeneutics *n* the art or science of interpretation, especially applied to the interpretation of the Scriptures; exegesis.

hermetic, hermetical *adj* sealed by fusing together the edges of an aperture, as of a bottle, can or tube, so that no air, gas or spirit can escape (*hermetically sealed*); of or pertaining to alchemy or the doctrines of the alchemists.

hermit *n* a person who retires from society and lives in solitude; a recluse; an anchorite.

hermitage *n* the habitation of a hermit.

hermit crab *n* a species of crustacean which takes possession of and occupies the cast-off shells of various molluscs, carrying it about with it and changing it for a larger one as it increases in size.

hern *n* (*arch*) a heron

hernia *n* (*surg*) a protrusion of some part from its natural cavity by an abnormal aperture; commonly the protrusion of viscera through an aperture in the wall of the abdomen; rupture.

hero *n* (*pl* **heroes**) in classical mythology, a kind of demigod; hence, a man of distinguished valour or intrepidity; a prominent or central personage in any remarkable action or event; the principal personage in a poem, play, novel, etc.

heroic *adj* pertaining to a hero; becoming a hero; characteristic of a hero; brave and magnanimous; intrepid and noble; reciting the achievements of heroes; epic.

heroic verse *n* in English poetry, the iambic verse of ten syllables, in French the iambic of twelve and in classical poetry the hexameter.

heroin *n* a sedative drug derived from morphine, now used illegally as a highly addictive hallucinatory drug.

heroine *n* a female hero.

heroism *n* the qualities of a hero; bravery; courage; intrepidity.

heron *n* any one of a family of large wading birds with long bills, long slender legs and long slim necks, usually grey or white plumage, found in many parts of the world.

heronry *n* a place where herons breed.

hero worship *n* the worship of heroes; excessive admiration of another person, often someone famous or successful or someone older.

herpes *n* any of several viral diseases characterized by small blisters on the skin or mucous membranes.

herpetology *n* the study of reptiles, snakes and amphibians.

herring *n* a food fish found in the North Sea, the northern parts of the Atlantic, etc, of great commercial importance.

herringbone *n* a pattern consisting of rows of slanted parallel lines, with the direction of the slant alternating from row to row, used in textiles, embroidery, etc.

hers *pron* a possessive pronoun used instead of **her** and a noun, as subject, object or predicate.

herself *pron* an emphasized or reflexive form of the 3rd person feminine pronoun, used in the same way as *himself*.

hertz *n* the SI unit of frequency equal to one cycle per second.

Hertzian wave *n* a long electromagnetic wave.

hesitancy *n* the act of hesitating or doubting.

hesitant *adj* hesitating; irresolute; lacking readiness.

hesitate *vi* (**hesitated, hesitating**) to stop or pause respecting decision or action; to be doubtful as to fact, principle or determination; to stammer; to stop in speaking.—*vt* to be undecided about.

hesitation *n* the act of hesitating; a stopping in speech; intermission between words; stammering.

hesitative *adj* showing hesitation.

Hesperian *adj* (*poet*) western; situated in the west.

Hesperides *npl* in Greek myth, the daughters of Hesperus, possessors of the garden of golden fruit, watched over by a dragon, at the western extremities of the earth.

Hesperus *n* the planet Venus, the evening star.

hessian *n* a coarse cloth made from jute.

Hessian fly *n* a small two-winged fly nearly black, the larva of which is very destructive to young wheat.

hest *n* (*arch*) command; precept; injunction; order.

hetero- *prefix* another; abnormal; different; other; unequal.

hermit crab

heron

407

heterocercal *adj* having the vertebral column running to a point in the upper lobe of the tail, as in the sharks and sturgeons, contrasted with *homocercal*.

heteroclite *n* a word which is irregular or anomalous either in declension or conjugation; something abnormal.

heterocyclic *adj* (*chem*) (of a ring) containing atoms of different kinds.

heterodont *adj* having teeth of different kinds, as molars, incisors and canines, opposed to *homodont*.

heterodox *adj* contrary to established or generally received opinions; contrary to some recognized standard of opinion, especially in theology; not orthodox.

heterodoxy *n* the holding of heterodox opinions; heresy.

heterodyne *adj* (*electronics*) of the production of beats by reaction between locally generated oscillations and those received.

heteroecism *n* in fungi, living on more than one kind of host in the course of the life history.

heterogamous *adj* (*bot*) irregular in regard to the arrangement of the sexes; having florets of different sexes in the same flower head.

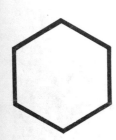

hexagon

heterogeneous *adj* differing in kind; composed of dissimilar or incongruous parts or elements, opposed to *homogeneous*.

heterogenesis, heterogeny *n* (*biol*) spontaneous generation; alternate generation.

heterologous *adj* different; not analogous or homologous.

heteromorphic, heteromorphous *adj* of an irregular or unusual form; having two or more diverse shapes.

heteromorphism, heteromorphy *n* the state or quality of being heteromorphic; existence under different forms at different stages of development.

heteronomous *adj* pertaining to or relating to heteronomy.

heteronomy *n* subordination to the law of another, opposed to *autonomy*.

heteronym *n* a word with the same spelling as another but a different pronunciation; a different name for the same thing.

heteroplasty *n* in surgery, transplantation of tissue from another person or from an animal.

hexastyle

heterosexism *n* discrimination in favour of heterosexual people.

heterosexual *adj* being sexually attracted to people of the opposite sex.—*n* a person who is sexually attracted to people of the opposite sex.

heterozygote *n* (*biol*) a Mendelian hybrid containing at least one recessive character and therefore with progeny not all true to type.

hetman *n* (*pl* **hetmans**) the title of the head (general) of the Cossacks.

heuristic *adj* aiding or leading on towards discovery or finding out.

hew *vt* (*pret* **hewed**, *pp* **hewed** *or* **hewn**, *ppr* **hewing**) to cut or fell with an axe or other like instrument; to shape with a sharp instrument (often with *out*).

hexachord *n* (*mus*) a series of six notes, each rising one degree over the other.

hexagon *n* (*geom*) a figure of six sides and six angles.

hexagonal *adj* having six sides and six angles; of a system of crystals (sometimes divided into two, hexagonal and trigonal) which may be referred to 4 equal axes, three equal and equally inclined in one plane, the fourth at right angles to that plane.

hexahedral *adj* of the figure of a hexahedron; cubic.

hexahedron *n* a regular solid body of six sides; a cube.

hexameter *n* a line of verse with six metrical feet.

hexapla *n* an edition of the Holy Scriptures in six languages or six versions in parallel columns.

hexapod *adj* having six feet.—*n* an animal having six feet.

hexastich *n* a poem consisting of six lines or verses.

hexastyle *n* a portico or temple which has six columns in front.

hexose *n* a sugar containing six carbon atoms in the molecule, as glucose and fructose.

hey *exclam* an exclamation of joy or surprise or to call attention.

heyday *n* the period of greatest prosperity, power, popularity, etc.

hiatus *n* (*pl* **hiatuses, hiatus**) an opening; a gap; a break in continuity; a lacuna; (*pros*) the coming together of two vowels in two successive syllables or words.

hibernal *adj* belonging or relating to winter; wintry.

hibernate *vi* (**hibernated, hibernating**) to winter; to pass the winter in sleep or seclusion, as some animals.

hibernation *n* the act of hibernating.

hibernaculum *n* (*pl* **hibernacula**) the winter retreat of an animal.

Hibernian *adj* pertaining to Hibernia, now Ireland; Irish.—*n* a native or inhabitant of Ireland.

Hibernianism, Hibernicism *n* a custom, an idiom or mode of speech peculiar to the Irish.

Hibernicize *vt* (**Hibernicized, Hibernicizing**) to make Irish; to render into the Irish language or idiom.

hiccup, hiccough *n* a spasmodic catching in the breath with a sudden sound; a convulsive catch of the respiratory muscles repeated at short intervals; a minor setback.—*vi* (**hiccuped, hiccuping**) to have hiccups.

hickory *n* a North American tree of the walnut family, the hard, strong wood of which is valued as timber and is used in smoking foods, to which it imports a good flavour.

hid, hidden *adj* concealed; placed in secrecy; secret; unseen; mysterious.

hidalgo *n* (*pl* **hidalgos**) formerly in Spain, a man belonging to the lower nobility; a gentleman by birth.

hide¹ *vt* (*pret* **hid**, *pp* **hid** *or* **hidden**, *ppr* **hiding**) to withhold or withdraw from sight or knowledge; to keep secret; to conceal.—*vi* to conceal oneself; to lie concealed.—*n* a place of concealment for birdwatchers, shooters of game birds, etc.

hide² *n* the skin of an animal; especially, the undressed skin of the larger domestic animals, as oxen, horses, etc; the human skin, in contempt.—*vt* (**hided, hiding**) to beat; to flog.

hide³ *n* an old measure of land .

hide-and-seek *n* a children's game in which one person looks for all the others who have gone into hiding.

hidebound *adj* rigidly conventional; obstinately conservative and narrow-minded.

hideous *adj* frightful to the sight; dreadful; shocking to the eye; shocking in any way; detestable; horrible.

hiding *n* a flogging or beating.

hiding place *n* a place of concealment.

hie *vi* (**hied, hieing**) to move or run with haste; to go in haste (often with *him, me*, etc, reflexively, as, *he hied him home*).

hiemal *adj* pertaining to winter; wintry.

hierarch *n* a person who has a high position of authority.

hierarchic, hierarchical *adj* pertaining to a hierarch or hierarchy.

hierarchy *n* a group of persons or things arranged in order of rank, grade, importance, etc.

hieratic, hieratical *adj* consecrated to sacred uses; pertaining to priests; sacred; sacerdotal; especially applied to the characters or mode of writing used by the ancient Egyptian priests, a development from the hieroglyphics.

hieroglyph, hieroglyphic *n* the figure of an animal, plant or other object intended to convey a meaning or stand for an alphabetical character; a figure implying a word, an idea or a sound, such as those in use among the ancient Egyptians; a figure having a hidden or enigmatic significance; a character difficult to decipher.

hieroglyphic, hieroglyphical *adj* forming a hieroglyphic; consisting of hieroglyphics; expressive of meaning by hieroglyphics.

hierogram *n* a species of sacred writing.

hierology *n* sacred lore; knowledge of hieroglyphics or sacred writing.

hierophant *n* a priest; one who teaches the mysteries and duties of religion.

hi-fi *n* (short for **high fidelity**) equipment for producing high-quality sound; a record or compact disc player and its equipment or similar sound-reproducing appliance.

higgledy-piggledy *adv* in confusion; topsy-turvy.

high *adj* having a great extent from base to summit; rising much above the ground or some other object; elevated, lofty, tall; exalted, excellent, superior (mind, attainments, art); elevated in rank, condition or office; difficult to comprehend; abstruse; arrogant, boastful, proud; loud, boisterous, threatening or angry (*high words*); extreme, intense, strong, forcible; exceeding the common measure or degree (*a high wind*; *high colour*); full or complete (*high time*); dear; of a great price or greater price than usual; remote from the equator north or south (*a high latitude*); (*mus*), acute or elevated in tone; capital; committed against the king, sovereign or state (*high treason*); (of meat, etc) beginning to go bad or become rotten; used substantively for people of rank or high station (*high and low*); (*colloq*) intoxicated; (*colloq*) under the influence of drugs; in a nervous state.—**on high** aloft; in a lofty position.—**high and dry** out of the water; out of reach of the current or waves.—**to be on the high horse** to mount one's high horse, to stand on one's dignity; to assume a lofty tone or manner; to take offence.—*adv* in a high manner; to a great altitude; highly; richly; luxuriously.

high altar *n* the chief altar in a church.

highborn *adj* being of noble birth or extraction.

highbred *adj* bred in high life; having very refined manners or breeding.

highbrow *n* an intellectual person; a person who has intellectual interests or is interested in subjects requiring learning.—*adj* intellectual; requiring learning.

High Church *n* the party in the Church of England that emphasizes links with Catholicism, exalts the authority of the Church and attaches great value to the episcopal office and the apostolic succession.

high day *n* a festival or gala day; high noon.

high explosive *n* an explosive of extremely powerful class, especially such as are based on nitroglycerine.

high-fidelity *n* the high-quality reproduction of sound.

high-flown *adj* elevated; proud; turgid; extravagant (*high-flown sentiment*).

high-flyer, high-flier *n* an ambitious person; a person of great ability in any profession.

high-flying *adj* ambitious; being promoted rapidly.

hierogylph

hi-fi

high frequency *n* any radio frequency between 3 and 30 megahertz.

high-handed *adj* overbearing; arbitrary.

highjack *vt*, **highjacker** *n* same as **hijack, hijacker**.

highland *n* an elevated or mountainous region (generally in plural).—*adj* pertaining to highlands.

Highland *adj* pertaining to the Highlands of Scotland.

highlander *n* an inhabitant of highlands.

Highlander *n* an of the Highlands of Scotland.

Highland fling *n* a sort of dance peculiar to the Scottish Highlanders, danced by one person.

Highlands *npl* the mountainous region occupying most of northern Scotland.

highlife *n* the style of living of the upper classes; a style of West African jazz-influenced music.

highlight *n* the lightest area of a painting, etc; the most interesting or important feature; (*pl*) a lightening of areas of the hair using a bleaching agent.—*vt* to bring to special attention; to give highlights to.

highlighter *n* a pen with fluorescent ink for marking text, etc, for attention; a cosmetic for creating highlights on the face.

high living *n* indulgence in rich or costly food and drink.

highly *adv* in a high manner or to a high degree; greatly; decidedly; markedly.

highly strung *adj* acutely tense, nervous or sensitive.

High Mass *n* principal mass, a solemn ceremony in which the priest is assisted by a deacon and subdeacon.

high-minded *adj* characterized by or pertaining to elevated principles and feelings; magnanimous; proud; arrogant.

highness *n* the state or quality of being high; a title of honour given to princes or other persons of rank (used with possessive pronouns *his*, *her*, etc).

high noon *n* the time when the sun is in the meridian; the most successful period of anything.

high place *n* in Scripture an eminence or mound on which sacrifices were offered, especially to heathen deities; (*pl*) offices or positions of authority or influence (*misconduct in high places*).

high-rise *adj* multi-storey; of a building, often a block of flats, having a large number of storeys.—*n* a multi-storey building, often a block of flats.

highroad *n* a highway; a much frequented road.

high seas *npl* the open sea or ocean; the area of sea outside the boundary claimed by any country as territorial waters.

high-sounding *adj* pompous; ostentatious; bombastic.

highwayman

high-spirited *adj* having a high spirit; bold; lively; vivacious; joyful.

high tea *n* a meal, usually eaten in the early evening, at which tea and a cooked dish are served.

high-tech *adj* (short for **high-technology**) pertaining to or using specialized complex modern technology; of a design of furniture, etc, imitative of industrial equipment.

high tide *n* the utmost flow or greatest elevation of the tide; the time when such flow or elevation occurs.

high water *n* high tide.

high-water mark *n* the highest point reached by a high tide; any maximum.

highway *n* a public road; a way open to all passengers.

highwayman *n* (*pl* **highwaymen**) formerly, one who often robbed on the public road or highway.

highway robbery *n* the practice of a highwayman; (*colloq*) blatant overpricing.

hijack, highjack *vt* to force (an aircraft, train or vehicle) to make an unscheduled journey to a destination of one's choice for political, etc, reasons; to stop and rob (a vehicle) etc, to steal (goods) in transit; (*colloq*) to take over a meeting, social event, etc.

hijacker, highjacker *n* a person who hijacks a vehicle or goods.

hike *vi* (**hiked, hiking**) to tramp; to go on a long or fairly long walking expedition.—*vt* (*colloq*) to pull up; to increase.—*n* a long walk, generally not on made-up roads.

hilarious *adj* merry; extremely funny; very amusing.

hilarity *n* mirth; merriment; laughter; amusement.

Hilary term *n* a law term beginning near the festival of St Hilary, which is 13th January.

hill *n* a natural elevation of less size than a mountain; an eminence rising above the level of the surrounding land; a heap (*a molehill*).

hillock *n* a small hill; a slight elevation.

hilly *adj* abounding with hills.

hilt *n* the handle of a sword, dagger, etc.

hilum *n* (*pl* **hila**) the mark or scar on a seed (as the black patch on a bean) produced by its separation from the placenta.

him *pron* the dative and objective case of **he**.

himself *pron* an emphatic and reflexive form of the 3rd personal *pron masc*, as *the man himself told me*; *it was himself*, or *he struck himself*, often implying that the person has command of himself or is possessed of his natural frame or temper, as *he is not himself at all* or *he soon came to himself*.

hind[1] *adj* backward; pertaining to the part

which follows or is behind, in opposition to *fore*.

hind² *n* the female of the red deer, the stag being the male.

hind³ *n* (*arch*) a labourer attached to a household; an agricultural labourer; a peasant; a rustic.

hinder¹ *vt* to prevent from proceeding or from starting; to stop; to interrupt; to obstruct; to impede; to check or retard in progression or motion; to debar; to shut out; to balk (often with *from* and a verbal noun, as *to hinder him from going*, the *from* is sometimes omitted).—*vi* to interpose obstacles or impediments.

hinder² *adj* belonging to that part which is in the rear; in the rear; following; after.

Hindi *n* one of the official languages of India; a group of languages spoken by northern Indians.

hindmost, hindermost *adj* farthest behind; behind all others; last.

hindrance *n* the act of hindering; that which hinders; impediment; obstruction; obstacle.

Hindu *n* (*pl* **Hindus**) a follower of Hinduism.

Hinduism *n* the dominant religion of India, characterized by an emphasis on religious law, a caste system and a belief in reincarnation.

Hindustani *n* a form of Hindi containing elements from other languages, used as a lingua franca in much of India and Pakistan.

hinge *n* the hook or movable joint on which a door, lid, gate or shutter, etc, turns; the joint of a bivalve shell; (*fig*) that on which anything depends or turns; a governing principle, rule or point.—*vt* (**hinged, hinging**) to furnish with hinges.—*vi* to stand, depend or turn, as on a hinge.

hinny¹ *n* the offspring of a male horse and a female donkey, as distinct from a mule, which is bred from a male donkey and a female horse.

hinny² *vi* (**hinnied, hinnying**) to neigh; to whinny.

hint *n* a distant allusion or slight mention; a word or two suggesting or insinuating something; a suggestion; a small amount of (*a hint of parsley*).—*vt* to bring to notice by a hint; to suggest indirectly.

hinterland *n* the land lying behind the coast.

hip¹ *n* the fleshy projecting part of the thigh; the haunch; (*archit*) the external angle at the junction of two sloping roofs or sides of a roof.—*vt* (**hipped, hipping**) to sprain or dislocate the hip.

hip² *n* the fruit of a rose, especially the dog rose or wild brier.

hip³ *adj* (*sl*) keeping up with the latest fashions in clothes, music, ideas, etc.

hip⁴ *interj* an exclamation expressive of a call to any one or to arouse attention (*hip, hip, hurrah!*).

hip bath *n* a portable bath in which the body can only be partially immersed.

hippie, hippy *n* in the 1960s and 1970s one of a group of people who rejected a conventional way of life and values, wore colourful clothes, believed in universal love and fellowship, favoured living in communes, experimented with psychedelic drugs and often turned to mysticism.

hippo *n* (*pl* **hippos**) (*colloq*) a hippopotamus.

hippocampus *n* (*pl* **hippocampi**) a small fish with a head and foreparts that resemble the head and neck of a horse and a prehensile tail; (*arch*) the sea horse, a mythological sea monster, part horse, part fish.

hippocras *n* an old English cordial of wine with an infusion of spices and other ingredients.

Hippocratic oath *n* an oath taken by a doctor to observe the code of medical ethics derived from Hippocrates, a Greek physician of the fifth century BC.

Hippocrene *n* in Greek myth, a fountain on Mount Helicon, the seat of the Muses in Boetia, produced by the stamp of the foot of the winged horse Pegasus; source of poetic inspiration.

hippodrome *n* in ancient times, a place in which horse races and chariot races were performed; a circus.

hippophagy *n* the act or practice of feeding on horseflesh.

hippopotamus *n* (*pl* **hippopotamuses, hippopotami**) a hoofed quadruped of great bulk inhabiting lakes and rivers in Africa, being an excellent swimmer and diver and feeding on herbage.

hippy *n* same as **hippie**.

hip rafter *n* the rafter which forms the hip of a roof.

hip roof, hipped roof *n* a roof the ends of which slope inwards with the same inclination to the horizon as its two other sides.

hircine *adj* pertaining to or resembling a goat; having a strong, rank smell like a goat; goatish.

hire *vt* (**hired, hiring**) to procure from another person and for temporary use at a certain price or equivalent; to engage in service for a stipulated reward; to grant the temporary use or service of for compensation; to let (in this sense usually with *out* and often reflexively).—*n* the compensation given for the temporary use of anything; the reward or recompense paid for personal service; wages.

hireling *n* one who is hired or who serves for wages; a venal or mercenary person.—*adj* venal; mercenary.

hire-purchase *n* purchase by instalments; a

hinge

hippopotamus

system of buying by which a person pays a proportion of the whole sum as a deposit and a specified number of instalments thereafter and has the use of the object after the deposit is paid.

hirsute *adj* rough with hair; hairy; shaggy.

hirundine *adj* swallow-like.—*n* a bird of the family of swallows and martins.

his *pron* the possessive case singular of the personal pronoun **he**; of or belonging to him; formerly also used for *its*.

hispid *adj* rough; shaggy; bristly; (*bot*) beset with stiff bristles.

hiss *vi* to make a sound like that of the letter *s*, in contempt or disapprobation; to emit a similar sound (said of snakes, of water thrown on hot metal, etc).—*vt* to condemn by hissing; to express disapproval of by hissing.—*n* the sound made by propelling the breath between the tongue and upper teeth, as in pronouncing the letter *s*, especially as expressive of disapprobation; any similar sound (*the hiss of steam*).

hist *exclam* a word commanding silence, equivalent to hush, be silent.

histology *n* the study of the tissues of living things.

historian *n* a writer or compiler of history; an historical writer; one who studies or conducts research into historical matters.

historic, historical *adj* pertaining to or connected with history; containing or contained in, deduced from, suitable to, representing, etc, history; memorable; important.

historiographer *n* a historian; particularly one who studies historical methods and writings.

historiography *n* the study of historical writing, method and research; the writing of history.

history *n* that branch of knowledge which deals with events that have taken place in the world's existence; the study or investigation of the past; a narrative or account of an event or series of events in the life of a nation, or that have marked the progress or existence of any community or institution; a verbal relation of facts or events; a narrative; an account of things that exist; a description; an account of an individual person.

hive

histrionic, histrionical *adj* pertaining to an actor or stage player; belonging to stage playing; theatrical; stagy; feigned for purposes of effect; overdone; melodramatic.

histrionics *n* the art of theatrical representation; exaggerated or overdramatic behaviour.

hit *vt* (**hit, hitting**) to strike or touch with some degree of force; to strike or touch (an object aimed at); not to miss; to give a blow to; to reach or attain to an object desired; to light upon; to get hold of or come

at (*to hit a likeness*); to suit with; to be conformable to; to fit; to agree with (*to hit the public taste*).—*vi* to strike; to meet or come in contact; to clash (followed by *against* or *on*); to succeed; to strike or reach the intended point; to agree; to suit; fit.—*n* the act of one who or that which hits; a striking of a mark; a stroke or blow; a lucky chance or fortunate event; a successful attempt; an expression or remark peculiarly applicable; a successful record, book, film, performance, etc; (*colloq*) an underworld killing; (*sl*) a dose of a drug.

hit-and-run *adj* (of a road accident) involving a driver who hits a pedestrian and drives on without stopping; (of a driver) having carried out such an action.

hitch *vi* to move by jerks or with stops; to become entangled; to be caught or hooked (*the cord hitched on a branch*); to be linked or yoked.—*vt* to fasten; to yoke; to make fast; to hook; to raise or pull up; to raise by jerks (*to hitch up one's trousers*); to hitchhike.—*n* a catch; an impediment; a breakdown, especially of a casual and temporary nature; a difficulty; a heave or pull up; temporary help or assistance (*to give one a hitch*); (*naut*) a kind of knot or noose in a rope for fastening it to an object.

hitchhike *vi* (**hitchhiked, hitchhiking**) to travel by soliciting free lifts from motorists along the way.

hitchhiker *n* one who travels by hitchhiking.

hither *adv* to this place; here (with verbs signifying motion).—*adj* on the side or in the direction towards the person speaking.

hitherto *adv* to this place; to this time; as yet; until now.

hitman *n* (*pl* **hitmen**) a hired assassin; a person hired to carry out any unpleasant task, such as to declare workers redundant, close a factory, etc.

hit parade *n* a weekly list of high-selling gramophone records of pop songs; a list of the most popular things of some kind.

hive *n* a structure in which social bees are kept for the purpose of collecting their honey and allowing them to breed and overwinter; the bees inhabiting a hive; a place swarming with busy occupants.—*vt* (**hived, hiving**) to collect into a hive; to cause to enter a hive; to lay up in store for future use.—*vi* to take shelter together; to reside in a collective body.—**to hive off** to separate from a group; to transfer (work, etc) elsewhere; to sell of (part of a business).

hives *n* a rash on the skin, often caused by an allergy; nettle rash.

ho, hoh *exclam* a cry or call to arrest attention.

hoar *adj* white (*hoarfrost*); grey or greyish-white; white with age; hoary.—*n* hoariness; antiquity.—*vi* to become mouldy or musty.

hoard *n* a store, stock or large quantity of anything accumulated or laid up; a hidden stock, especially of something valuable.—*vt* to collect and lay up in a hoard; to amass and deposit in secret (often followed by *up*).—*vi* to collect and form a hoard; to lay up a store of money.

hoarding *n* a timber enclosure round a building when the latter is in the course of erection or undergoing alteration or repair; a similar erection for the display of posters.

hoarfrost *n* the white particles of frozen dew; rime.

hoarse *adj* having a harsh, rough, grating voice, as when affected with a cold; giving out a harsh, rough cry or sound.

hoary *adj* white or grey with age; hence, (*fig*) remote in time past; (*bot*) covered with short, dense, greyish-white hairs.

hoax *n* something done for deception or mockery; a trick played in fun; a practical joke.—*vt* to play a trick on for fun or without malice.

hob *n* the part of a grate or fireplace on which things are placed in order to be kept warm; the flat surface on the top of a cooker, incorporating the cooking rings or hotplates.

hobble *vi* (**hobbled, hobbling**) to walk lamely, bearing chiefly on one leg; to limp; to walk awkwardly; to wobble.—*vt* to tie the legs of (a horse) to restrict movement.—*n* a halting gait; a difficulty; a scrape; a clog; a fetter; a rope used to hobble horses and other livestock.

hobbledehoy *n* a raw gawky youth approaching manhood.

hobby[1] *n* a spare-time activity carried out for personal pleasure.

hobby[2] *n* a small but strong-winged European falcon, a summer visitor to southern Britain.

hobbyhorse *n* a stick with a horse's head and sometimes with wheels on the other end, on which children ride; any favourite object, plan or pursuit; a favourite or obsessive interest.

hobgoblin *n* a goblin; an elf; an imp.

hobnail *n* a nail with a thick strong head used for shoeing horses or for the soles of heavy boots.

hobnailed *adj* set with hobnails; rough.

hobnob *vi* (**hobnobbed, hobnobbing**) to meet or associate with in a friendly way.

hock[1] *n* the joint bending backwards on the hind leg of a horse, etc, corresponding to the ankle in humans.—*vt* to hamstring.

hock[2] *n* a kind of German white wine.

hock[3] *vt* (*sl*) to give something in security for a loan.

hockey *n* a ball game involving two teams of 11 players played with a club curved at the lower end.

hocus-pocus *n* a meaningless phrase used by conjurers and magicians when performing sleight of hand; sleight of hand; deception; mumbo-jumbo.

hod *n* a kind of trough for carrying mortar and bricks to masons and bricklayers, fixed to the end of a pole and borne on the shoulder.

hodgepodge *n* same as **hotchpotch**.

hoe *n* an instrument for cutting up weeds and loosening the earth in fields and gardens.—*vt* (**hoed, hoeing**) to cut, dig, scrape or clean with a hoe.—*vi* to use a hoe.

hog *n* a swine; a pig; any animal of that species; a castrated boar; a sheep of a year old yet to be sheared; a selfish, greedy or filthy person.

hogbacked *adj* shaped like the back of a hog or sow.

hogget *n* a sheep two years old; a young boar of the second year.

hoggish *adj* having the qualities of a hog; brutish; filthy.

Hogmanay *n* the name given in Scotland to the last day of the year, New Year's Eve.

hog's-back *n* some thing shaped like the back of a hog; a ridge of a hill having this shape.

hogshead *n* a large cask or barrel; a measure of capacity.

hogskin *n* leather made of the skin of swine.

hogwash *n* the refuse of a kitchen or a brewery or like matter given to swine; swill; nonsense.

hogweed *n* a tall weedy plant with small white flowers; cow parsnip.

hoiden *n* same as **hoyden**.

hoist *vt* to heave or raise; especially to raise by means of block and tackle.—*n* the act of hoisting; that by which anything is hoisted; a machine for elevating goods, passengers, etc, in a warehouse, hotel, etc; an elevator.

hoity-toity *adj* haughty; arrogant.

hold *vt* (*pret*, *pp* **held**, *ppr* **holding**) to have or grasp in the hand; to grasp and retain (*to hold a sword, a pen, a candle*); to bear, put or keep in a certain position (*to hold the hands up*); to consider; to regard (*I hold him in honour*); to account (*I hold it true*); to contain or to have capacity to receive and contain; to retain within itself; to keep from running or flowing out; to keep possession of; to maintain, uphold, preserve; not to lose; to be in possession of; to possess, occupy, own, keep; to have or to entertain (*to hold enmity*); to derive or deduce title to (*he held lands of the king*); to stop, restrain, withhold; to keep fixed, as to a certain line of action; to bind or oblige

hobby horse

hoe

(*to hold one to his promise*); to keep in continuance or practice (*to hold discussions*); to prosecute or carry on, observe, pursue (a course, an argument); to celebrate, solemnize, carry out (a feast, a meeting); to occupy or keep employed; to engage the attention of.—*vi* to take or keep a thing in one's grasp; to maintain an attachment; to continue firm; not to give way or break; to adhere; to stand, be valid, apply (*the argument holds good*, *this holds true*); to stand one's ground (generally with *out*, as *the garrison held out*); to refrain; to be dependent on for possessions; to derive right or title (with *of*, sometimes *from*); to stop, stay or wait; to cease or give over (chiefly in the imperative).—*n* a grasp, grip, clutch (often in *to take hold, to lay hold*); (*fig*) mental grasp; grasp on, or influence working on, the mind; a strong influence or power; something which may be seized for support; power of keeping; authority to seize or keep; claim; a place of confinement; a position of strength, a keep, stronghold; the whole interior cavity of a ship between the bottom and deck or lowest deck.

holly

holder *n* one who or that which holds.

holdfast *n* something used to secure and hold in place something else.

holding *n* a tenure; a farm held of a superior; property owned, especially land, stocks and shares; that which holds, binds or influences.

hole *n* a hollow place or cavity in any solid body; a perforation, orifice, aperture, pit, rent, fissure, crevice, etc; the excavated habitation of certain wild beasts; a mean habitation; a wretched abode.—*vi* (**holed, holing**) to go into a hole.—*vt* to make a hole or holes in; to drive into a hole; in mining, to undercut a coal seam.

hole-and-corner, hole-in-the-corner *adj* clandestine; underhand.

holiday *n* a consecrated day; a religious anniversary; an occasion of joy and gaiety; a day, or a number of days, of freedom from work.—*adj* pertaining to or befitting a holiday; cheerful; joyous.

holiness *n* the state or quality of being holy or sinless; sanctity; godliness; sacredness. —**His Holiness** a title of the pope.

holster

holism *n* a philosophical theory according to which a fundamental feature of nature is the existence of 'wholes', which are more than assemblages of parts and which are always tending to become more highly developed and comprehensive.

holistic *adj* of or pertaining to holism.

holland *n* a kind of fine linen originally from Holland; also a coarser linen fabric used for covering furniture, carpets, etc.

hollow *adj* containing an empty space within; having a vacant space within; not solid; concave; sunken (eye, cheek); sounding as if reverberated from a cavity; deep or low; not sincere or faithful; false; deceitful.—*n* a depression or excavation below the general level or in the substance of anything; a cavity.—*vt* to make a hollow or cavity in; to excavate.—*adv* utterly; completely (*he beat him hollow*).

hollow-hearted *adj* insincere; deceitful; not true.

holly, holly tree *n* an evergreen tree or shrub with indented thorny leaves and which produces clusters of beautiful red berries; also a name sometimes given to the holm oak, an evergreen oak.

hollyhock *n* a tall single-stemmed biennial plant of the mallow family, a frequent ornament of gardens.

holm *n* a river island; a low flat tract of rich land by the side of a river.

holm oak *n* the evergreen oak.

holoblast *n* (*zool*) an ovum consisting entirely of germinal matter.

holocaust *n* a burnt sacrifice or offering the whole of which was consumed by fire; a great slaughter or sacrifice of life.

Holocaust *n* the attempt between 1933 and 1945 by the Nazis to exterminate European Jewry, to a great extent through the use of concentration camps.

Holocene *adj* of or denoting the second and most recent epoch of the Quaternary era. —*n* the Holocene epoch.

hologram *n* an image made without the use of a lens on photographic film by means of interference between two parts of a laser beam, the result appearing as a meaningless pattern until suitably illuminated, when it shows a three-dimensional image.

holograph *n* any document, as a letter, deed, etc, wholly written in its author's handwriting; an original manuscript; autograph.

holothurian *n* one of the sea cucumbers, an order of echinoderms, of which the bêche-de-mer or trepang is an example.

holster *n* a leather case for a pistol, usually on a belt.

holt *n* a wood or woodland; a grove; a plantation.

holus-bolus *adv* all at a gulp; altogether; all at once.

holy *adj* free from sin and sinful affections; pure in heart; pious; godly; hallowed; consecrated or set apart to a sacred use; having a sacred character.

Holy Ghost, Holy Spirit *n* the third person in the Trinity.

Holy Office *n* the Inquisition or the authorities at Rome who directed it.

holy of holies *n* the innermost apartment of the Jewish tabernacle or temple, where the Ark was kept; any place of special religious or other importance.

holy orders *npl* the clerical or ecclesiastical character conferred on a person by ordination or consecration to the ministry in the church.

Holy Spirit *n* same as **Holy Ghost**.

holystone *n* a soft sandstone used by sailors for cleaning the decks of ships.—*vt* to scrub with holystone.

Holy Thursday *n* Ascension Day; Maundy Thursday.

holy water *n* in the Roman Catholic and High Anglican Churches, water consecrated by the priest and used in various rites and ceremonies.

Holy Week *n* the week before Easter (the last week of Lent).

Holy Writ *n* the sacred Scriptures.

homage *n* acknowledgement of vassalage made by a feudal tenant to his lord on receiving investiture of a fee; hence, obeisance; respect paid by external action; reverence directed to God; reverential worship; deep respect; devout affection; an act or expression of respect or honour.

home *n* one's own abode or dwelling; the abode of the family or household of which one forms a member; abiding place; one's own country; the seat (*the home of war*); an institute or establishment for the homeless, sick or destitute (*a sailors' home, an orphans' home*, etc).—**at home** in or about one's own house or abode; available to visitors; in one's own country or environment.—**at home with a subject** conversant, familiar, thoroughly acquainted with it.—**to make oneself at home** to conduct oneself as unrestrainedly as if at home.—*adj* connected with one's home; domestic (often opposed to *foreign*).—*adv* to one's home or one's native country (often opposed to *abroad*); to oneself; to the point; to the mark aimed at; so as to produce an intended effect; effectively; thoroughly (*to strike home*).—*vi* (**homed, homing**) (of birds) to return home; (of a missile, etc) to be guided onto a target; to head for a destination; to send or go home. —*vt* to guide (a missile, etc) towards a target.

homebred *adj* bred at home; originating at home; not foreign.

home economics *n* the art and science of household management, nutrition, etc.

home help *n* a person employed to do household tasks in someone's home, especially a person employed by a local authority to help the elderly or infirm.

homely *adj* pertaining to home; domestic; of plain features; not handsome; like that which is made for common domestic use; plain, coarse; not fine or elegant.

home-made *adj* made at home; of domestic manufacture.

Home Office *n* the department of the Brit-

ish government which is broadly responsible for the domestic civil affairs of the country as a whole.

homeopath, homoeopath *n* one who practises or supports homeopathy.

homeopathic, homoeopathic *adj* relating to homeopathy.

homeopathy, homoeopathy *n* the system of treating disease by small quantities of drugs that cause symptoms similar to those of the disease itself.

Homeric *adj* pertaining to Homer, the great poet of Greece; resembling Homer's verse or style; grand, heroic, epic.

home rule *n* self-government for a part of a country seeking a separate parliament to manage its internal affairs.

Home Secretary *n* the Secretary of State for the British Home Office.

homesick *adj* sad from being absent from home; affected with homesickness.

homesickness *n* intense and uncontrolled sadness at a separation from one's home or native land; nostalgia; longing for home.

homespun *adj* spun or wrought at home; hence, plain; coarse; homely.—*n* cloth made at home.

homestead *n* a house with the grounds and buildings immediately contiguous; a home.

homeward, homewards *adv* toward home; toward one's abode or native country.—*adj* being in the direction of home.

homeward-bound *adj* bound or destined for home; returning from a foreign country.

homicidal *n* pertaining to homicide; murderous.

homicide *n* the killing of one human being by another; a person who kills another.

homiletics *n* the art of preaching; that branch of practical theology which treats of sermons and the best mode of composing and delivering them.

homilist *n* one that composes homilies; a preacher.

homily *n* a discourse or sermon read or pronounced to an audience; a sermon; a moralizing talk; a serious discourse.

hominy, hominy grits *n* maize hulled and coarsely ground and prepared for food by being boiled with water.

homo[1] *n* any member of the genus Homo that includes modern man.

homo[2] *n* (*pl* **homos**) (*derog*) a male homosexual.

homo- *prefix* same; like.

homocercal *adj* (of a fish) having the lobes of the tail diverging symmetrically from the backbone, as in the cod, herring, etc.

homodont *adj* having teeth all similar, opposed to *heterodont*.

homoeopath *n* same as **homeopath**.

homoeopathic *adj* same as **homeopathic**.

homoeopathy *n* same as **homeopathy**.

homogeneity *n* the state or character of being homogeneous.

homogeneous, homogenous *adj* of the same kind or nature; consisting of similar parts or of elements of the like nature, opposite of heterogeneous.

homogenize *vt* (**homogenized, homogenizing**) to break up the fat particles (in milk or cream) so they do not separate; to make or become homogeneous.

homogeny *n* (*biol*) sameness or correspondence in organs of animals as to structure and type but not function, thus the human arm corresponds to the foreleg of a quadruped and the wing of a bird; homology.

homograph *n* a word spelled the same as another word but with a different meaning and derived from a different root.

Homoiousian *n* a person holding the belief that the nature of Christ is not the same with, but only similar to, that of the Father.

homologate *vt* (**homologated, homologating**) to approve; to express approval of or assent to; to ratify; (in motor racing, etc) to recognize (a car) as a genuine production model, not a one-off or prototype.

honeycomb

homologous *adj* having the same relative position, proportion or structure; corresponding in use or general character; of similar type; (*biol*) having the same origin but different function.

homology *n* the quality of being homologous; correspondence in character or relation; homogeny.

homomorphic, homomorphous *adj* having the same external appearance or form.

homonym *n* a word which agrees with another in sound and perhaps in spelling, but differs from it in meaning; a homograph, as 'fair' *adj* and 'fair' *n*.

Homoousian *n* a person who maintains that the nature of the Father and the Son is the same, in opposition to the *Homoiousians*.

homophobia *n* technically, fear of the same or fear of mankind or men; specifically, dislike or fear of homosexual people; persecution of homosexual people.

homosexual *adj* being sexually attracted to people of one's own sex.—*n* a person who is sexually attracted to people of his or her own sex.

homunculus *n* (*pl* **homunculi**) a manikin; a midget; a miniature man.

hone *n* a stone of a fine grit, used for sharpening instruments that require a fine edge. —*vt* (**honed, honing**) to sharpen on, or as if on, a hone.

honest *adj* fair in dealing with others; free from dishonesty, deception, fraud or theft; upright; just; equitable; sincere, candid or unreserved; unpretentious; honourable; reputable; chaste or virtuous; pleasant-looking in features.

honesty *n* the state or quality of being honest; integrity; uprightness; fairness; candour; (*bot*) a common garden herb, with purple flowers and translucent seed pods.

honey *n* a sweet, viscid juice, collected from flowers by several kinds of insects, especially bees; (*fig*) sweetness or pleasantness; as a word of endearment, sweet one; darling.—*vt* to cover with or as with honey; to make agreeable; to sweeten.

honeycomb *n* the waxy structure containing rows of cells formed by bees for the reception of honey and for the eggs which produce their young; anything arranged like this.

honeycombed *adj* formed like a honeycomb; perforated with or containing many cavities.

honeydew *n* a sweet sugary substance exuded by trees and other plants in small drops like dew; a similar substance excreted by aphids and some other insects; a kind of tobacco which has been moistened with molasses.

honeydew melon *n* a variety of melon with yellowish skin and pale green flesh.

honeyed, honied *adj* covered with or as with honey; hence, sweet; soothing; full of compliments or tender words; flattering.

honeymoon *n* the interval spent by a newly married couple before settling down in a home of their own; a short period of harmony.—*adj* relating to a honeymoon (*honeymoon hotel*).—*vi* to have a honeymoon.

honeysuckle *n* any of a genus of upright or climbing shrubs of Europe, Southwest Asia, North Africa and Australia.

honied *adj* same as **honeyed**.

honorarium *n* (*pl* **honorariums, honoraria**) a fee to a professional person for professional services.

honorary *adj* done or made in honour; indicative of honour; intended merely to confer honour (*an honorary degree*); possessing a title or post without performing services or without receiving benefit or reward (*an honorary secretary* or *treasurer*).

honorific *adj* conferring honour.

honour *n* esteem paid to worth; high estimation; reverence; veneration; any mark of respect or estimation by words or actions; dignity; exalted rank or place; distinction; reputation; good name; a nice sense of what is right, just and true; scorn of meanness; a particular virtue, as bravery or integrity in men and chastity in women; one who or that which is a source of glory or esteem; he who or that which confers dignity (*an honour to his country*); title or privilege of rank or birth; a decoration or an appointment to an order; one of the highest trump cards, as the ace, king, queen or knave and, in bridge, ten; (*pl*) civilities paid, as at an entertainment; (*pl*) academic and university distinction or pre-eminence.—*vt* to regard or treat with honour; to revere; to respect; to reverence; to bestow honour on; to elevate in rank or station; to exalt; to render illustrious; (*com*) to accept and pay when due (*to honour a bill of exchange*).

Honour *n* a title of address or respect now restricted to the holders of certain offices (e.g. judges), with *his*, *her*, *your*, etc.

honourable *adj* worthy of being honoured; estimable; illustrious or noble; actuated by principles of honour; conferring honour; consistent with honour or reputation; regarded with esteem; accompanied with marks of honour or testimonies of esteem; upright and laudable; directed to a just and proper end; not base; a title of distinction applied to certain members of noble families, persons in high position, etc.

hooch *n* (*colloq*) any alcoholic liquor which is distilled or procured illicitly.

hood[1] *n* a soft covering for the head and back of the neck; a part of a monk's outer garment with which he covers his head; a cowl; a similar appendage to a cloak or overcoat; a garment worn as part of full academic dress; a covering for a bird of prey's head or eyes, used in falconry; anything that resembles a hood in form or use; the roof of a convertible; in USA, the bonnet of a car.—*vt* to dress in a hood or cowl; to put a hood on; to cover or hide.

hood[2] *n* (*colloq*) (short for **hoodlum**) a gangster or criminal, especially a violent one; a thug.

hoodlum *n* a gangster; a young hooligan.

hoodwink *vt* to deceive by external appearances or disguise; to trick.

hoof *n* (*pl* **hoofs**, **hooves**) the horny substance that covers the feet or the digits of the feet of ungulate animals, as horses, oxen, sheep, deer, etc.—**on the hoof** (of cattle, sheep, etc) alive, not slaughtered.—*vt* to kick with the hoofs.—**to hoof it** (*colloq*) to go on foot, to walk; to dance.

hook *n* a piece of iron or other metal bent into a curve for catching, holding or sustaining anything; any similar appliance; a curved instrument for cutting grass or grain; a sickle; an instrument for lopping; a small metallic fastening for dresses catching in an eye; a fish-hook.—**by hook or by crook** by some means or other.—*vt* to catch or fasten with a hook or hooks; to bend into the form of a hook; to furnish with hooks; to catch by artifice; to entrap.—*vt* to bend; to be curving; to catch into something.

hookah *n* an oriental pipe for tobacco, etc, with a long pliable tube and water vase so constructed that the smoke passes through the water before being inhaled; a hubble-bubble.

hooked *adj* shaped or curved like a hook.

hooker *n* in rugby, the central player in the front row of a scrum whose task it is to hook the ball; (*sl*) *n* a prostitute.

hook-nosed *adj* having a curved or aquiline nose.

hooligan *n* a street rough or rowdy; a young ruffian; a vandal.

hoop *n* a circular band or ring; a band of wood or metal used to confine the staves of casks, tubs, etc, or for other similar purposes; anything like this, as a child's toy or a ring, or one of a series of rings, used to expand the skirt of a dress.—*vt* to bind or fasten with hoops.

hoopoe *n* a pinkish-brown, medium-sized bird of the Middle East and parts of Africa, a summer visitor to Europe, remarkable for its long curved bill, black-and-white barred wings, and black-tipped crest which it can erect or fold at will.

hoorah, hooray *interj* same as **hurrah**.

hoot *vi* to cry out or shout in contempt; to laugh immoderately; to cry as an owl.—*vt* to utter cries or shouts in contempt of; to utter contemptuous cries or shouts at.—*n* a cry or shout in contempt; the cry of an owl; a similar sound, as made by a train whistle; (*colloq*) laughter; (*colloq*) an amusing person or thing.

Hoover *n* the trademark of a kind of vacuum cleaner.—*vi* to use such a vacuum cleaner on carpets, etc.—*vt* to clean (carpets, etc) by means of such a vacuum cleaner.

hop[1] *vi* (**hopped, hopping**) to move by successive leaps; to leap or spring on one foot; to skip, as birds; to limp; to dance; to climb or get into (usually with *in*); to jump or climb over (usually with *over*).—*n* a leap on one leg; a jump; a spring; a dance or dancing party.

hop[2] *n* a climbing plant of the hemp family; (*pl*) its dried flowers used to give the characteristic bitter taste to beers.—*vt* (**hopped, hopping**) to mix hops with.—*vi* to pick or gather hops.

hope *n* a desire of some good, accompanied with at least a slight expectation of obtaining it or a belief that it is obtainable; expectation of something desirable; confidence in a future event; trust; that which gives hope; one in whom trust or confidence is placed; a sportsman or sportsman tipped for success and fame; the object of hope; the thing hoped for.—*vi* (**hoped, hoping**) to entertain or indulge hope; to have confidence; to trust.—*vt* to entertain hope for; to desire with expectation.

hopeful *adj* full of or entertaining hope; having qualities which excite hope; promising.—*n* a boy or young man, the hope of his parents (often with the epithet *young* and used sarcastically).

hood

hoop

hopefully *adv* with hope (*travelling hopefully*); it is to be hoped that (*hopefully the goods will arrive safely*).

hopeless *adj* lacking hope; giving no grounds for hope; useless; incompetent.

hoplite *n* a heavily armed foot soldier of ancient Greece.

hopper *n* one who hops; a wooden trough through which grain passes into a mill, so named from its moving or shaking; any similar contrivance; a boat having a compartment with a movable bottom to convey matter dredged up and deposit it in deep water.

hop-picker *n* one who picks or gathers hops.

hopscotch *n* a children's game which consists in hopping over a sequence of squares drawn on the ground.

horde *n* a tribe, clan or race of Asiatic or other nomads; a rabble; a large crowd or throng; a swarm.—*vi* (**horded, hording**) to live in hordes; to huddle together.

horehound *adj* one of several European plants of the mint family, particularly the white horehound, which has an aromatic smell and bitter taste and was once much used for coughs and asthma.

horizon *n* the circle which bounds that part of the earth's surface visible from a given point; the apparent junction of the earth and sky (*the visible* or *apparent horizon*); an imaginary great circle, parallel to this, whose plane passes through the centre of the earth (*the celestial horizon*); the limits of a person's knowledge, ambition, achievement, etc.

horizontal *adj* pertaining to the horizon; on the same or a parallel plane with the horizon; parallel to the horizon; on a level; measured or contained in the plane of the horizon (*horizontal distance*).

hormone *n* a product of living cells formed in a ductless gland and affecting organs and tissues by way of the bloodstream; a synthetic product having the same purpose.

hormone replacement therapy *n* a treatment which boosts levels of oestrogen in women and thereby relieves some of the symptoms and results of the menopause.

horn *n* a hard projecting appendage growing on the heads of certain animals and particularly on cloven-hoofed quadrupeds; the material of which such horns are composed; a musical wind instrument, originally made of horn, now part of the brass section of an orchestra; a device to sound a warning, especially in a vehicle; a drinking cup of horn; a utensil for holding powder for immediate use, originally made of horn; a powder flask; something similar to a horn; the feeler of an insect, snail, etc; an extremity of the moon when waxing or

horn

hornet

waning.—**to draw in the horns** to repress one's ardour or to restrain pride (in allusion to the habit of the snail withdrawing its feelers when startled); to restrict one's spending.—*vt* to wound with a horn.—**to horn in** *vi* to intrude.

hornbeam *n* a small bushy tree with a hard white wood.

hornbill *n* a name of certain birds with very large bills surmounted by an extraordinary horny protuberance.

hornblende *n* a dark green or black lustrous mineral of several varieties, an important constituent of several rocks.

hornbook *n* in former times a child's alphabet book or primer, with a transparent sheet of horn placed over the single page of which it usually consisted, the whole being fixed to a wooden frame.

horned *adj* having horns or projections resembling them (*the horned moon*); wearing horns; made a cuckold.

horned owl *n* any of the large owls that have prominent ear tufts on the head, e.g. the European eagle owl.

hornet *n* any of several species of large wasps (in Britain, the largest), the sting of which is very painful; hence, anyone who gives particular annoyance.

hornpipe *n* an obsolete musical instrument formerly popular in Wales; a lively dance tune; a sprightly dance, usually performed solo, traditionally a sailor's dance.

hornwork *n* (*milit*) a fortified position with one front only, thrown out beyond the glacis, the front consisting of two demibastions connected by a curtain wall.

horny *adj* consisting or composed of horn; resembling horn in appearance or composition; exhibiting hardened skin or callosities (*a horny fist*); having horns; (*colloq*) sexually aroused.

horologe *n* (*arch*) a piece of mechanism for indicating the hours of the day; a timepiece of any kind.

horology *n* the science of measuring time; the art of constructing machines for measuring time, as clocks, watches, dials.

horoscope *n* a scheme or figure of the heavens at a given time, used by astrologers using zodiacal data for the time of birth plus data for the period under consideration to foretell future events and the fortunes of persons.

horrendous *adj* dreadful; horrible; terrible.

horrible *adj* exciting or tending to excite horror; dreadful; terrible; shocking; hideous; extremely unpleasant.

horribly *adv* in a horrible manner; excessively; very much.

horrid *adj* fitted to excite horror; dreadful; hideous; shocking; very offensive; extremely unpleasant.

horrify *vt* (**horrified, horrifying**) to strike

or impress with horror; to shock.

horror *n* a powerful feeling of fear, dread and abhorrence; a shuddering with terror and loathing; that which excites horror; something frightful or shocking; something or someone that causes horror, dislike, etc; (*colloq*) a wild or badly behaved person, especially a child; (*colloq*) a building, work of art, etc, of exceptional ugliness or lack of taste.—**the horrors** a state of extreme agitation felt by a drunkard on the withdrawal of the customary stimulus; frightening thoughts.—*adj* (of a film, story, etc) designed to frighten.

hors d'oeuvre *n* (*pl* **hors d'oeuvre, hors d'oeuvres**) a dish, usually cold, served at the beginning of a meal, consisting of a variety of things, such as tomatoes, olives, peppers, salami, sardines, hard-boiled egg, etc.

horse *n* a four-legged, solid-hoofed animal with a long mane and tail, used for riding and for drawing loads; the male animal, as distinct from the female mare; cavalry; troops serving on horseback (in this sense no plural termination); a wooden frame with legs for supporting something (*clotheshorse, sawhorse*); (*naut*) a rope attached to a yard to support the sailors while they loose, reef or furl the sails.—**to take horse** to mount or set out on horseback.—*vt* (**horsed, horsing**) to provide with a horse; to supply a horse or horses for; to sit astride; to bestride.

horse artillery *n* (*milit*) field artillery with lighter guns than ordinary field artillery and all the gunners mounted, usually attached to cavalry formations and sent into action well forward of heavier ordnance.

horseback *n* the back of a horse; that part on which the rider sits.—**on horseback** mounted or riding on a horse.

horsebox *n* a large motorized vehicle for transporting horses; a lighter closed trailer for the same purpose.

horse chestnut *n* any of several species of large or medium-sized flowering deciduous trees of North America, southern Europe and Asia, especially a European species with distinctive palmate leaves and shiny brown nuts enclosed in spiky green cases.

horse dealer *n* one who buys and sells horses.

horse doctor *n* one who treats the diseases of horses; a farrier; (*joc*) a vet.

horsefly *n* a large fly that sucks the blood of mammals, notably horses and cattle.

horsehair *n sing, pl* the hair of horses, more particularly of the mane and tail.

horseman, horsewoman *n* (*pl* **horsemen, horsewomen**) a person who rides on horseback; one who uses and manages a horse.

horsemanship *n* the art of riding and managing horses; equestrian skill.

horseplay *n* rough or rude practical jokes, etc; rude pranks.

horsepower *n* the power of a horse or its equivalent; the force with which a horse acts when drawing; the standard for estimating the power of a steam engine, each horsepower being estimated as equivalent to 746 watts or 33,000 pounds raised one foot high per minute.

horse racing *n* the practice or art of running horses in competition.

horseradish *n* a perennial plant of the cabbage family, the white cylindrical root of which has a pungent taste and is used as a condiment.

horseshoe *n* a shoe for horses, commonly a piece of iron, in shape resembling the letter U, nailed to the horse's foot; anything shaped like a horseshoe; something of this shape regarded as a symbol of good luck.

horseshoe magnet *n* an artificial steel magnet nearly in the form of a horseshoe.

horse soldier *n* a cavalry soldier.

horsewhip *n* a long whip for driving or striking horses.—*vt* (**horsewhipped, horsewhipping**) to lash or strike (especially a person) with a horsewhip.

horsewoman *see* **horseman**.

horst *n* (*geol*) a part of the earth's crust separated by faults from, and higher than, surrounding parts.

horsy, horsey *adj* connected with, fond of or much taken up with horses; horse-like in appearance

horticulture *n* the cultivation of a garden; the art of cultivating or managing gardens.

horticulturist *n* one who practises horticulture.

Hosanna *n* an exclamation of praise to God or an invocation of blessings.

hose *n* formerly, close-fitting trousers or breeches reaching to the knee; now any covering for the lower part of the legs, including the feet; socks, stockings and tights in general (used as a plural); a flexible tube or pipe for conveying water or other fluid to any required point.—*vt* (**hosed, hosing**) to spray with a hose (usually with *down*).

hosepipe *n* a hose for spraying water, etc.

hosier *n* one who deals in stockings or similar goods or in underclothing of every description.

hosiery *n* the goods sold by a hosier; knitted goods, etc.

hospice *n* a place of refuge and entertainment for travellers on some difficult road or pass, as among the Alps; a nursing home for patients in the later stages of a terminal illness, such as cancer.

hospitable *adj* receiving and entertaining strangers with kindness and without re-

horsehoe

hose

ward; kind to strangers and guests; pertaining to the liberal entertainment of guests.

hospital *n* a building or institution for treating the sick or injured.

hospitality *n* the kind and generous reception and entertainment of strangers or guests; fondness for entertaining guests; hospitable treatment or disposition.

hospitaller *n* a member of a usually religious community whose office it is to care for the poor, the stranger and the sick.

Hospitaller *n* a member of the medieval order of the Knights Hospitallers or Knights of St John of Jerusalem, later styled the Knights of Malta.

host[1] *n* one who receives and entertains a guest or guests either at his own house or at a restaurant, etc; a landlord, the counterpart of *guest*; an animal or organism in or on whose organs a parasite exists; a compere on a television or radio programme.—*vti* to act as a host (to a party, television programme, etc).

host[2] *n* an army; a number of people embodied for war; any great number or multitude.

Host *n* the altar bread or wafer in the Eucharist or in the Roman Catholic sacrament of the mass.

hostage *n* a person handed over to an enemy as a pledge for the performance of certain conditions; someone taken and held under threat of death for the purposes of advancing the ends (often political) of the hostage-taker.—**a hostage to fortune** something valued that one may lose.

hostel *n* a house for the board and lodging of students, workers, the homeless, etc, usually charging low rates.

hostelry *n* an inn; a lodging house.

hostess *n* a female host.

hostile *adj* belonging to an enemy; holding the position of an enemy or enemies; showing ill-will and malevolence.

hostility *n* state of being hostile; an act of an open enemy; an act of warfare (generally plural); antagonism; ill will.

hostler *n* same as **ostler**.

hot *adj* having great heat; exciting the feeling of warmth in a great or powerful degree; very warm; ardent in temper; easily excited or exasperated; vehement; violent; furious; animated; brisk; keen; lustful; lewd; acrid; biting; stimulating; pungent; spicy; (*colloq*) recent, new or popular; (*colloq*) angry; (*colloq*) radioactive; (*colloq*) stolen.

hotbed *n* (*hortic*) a bed of earth heated by fermenting substances and covered with glass, used for growing early or exotic plants; a place which favours rapid growth or development (generally in a bad sense, as *a hotbed of sedition*).

hot-blooded *adj* having hot blood; having warm passions; easily excited, volatile; irritable.

hotchpotch, hodgepodge *n* a mixed mass; a jumble of ingredients.

hotel *n* a house for entertaining strangers or travellers; an inn.

hotfoot *adv* in great haste.—**to hotfoot it** to go with all possible speed; to hurry; to hasten.

hot-headed *adj* violent; rash; impetuous.

hothouse *n* a greenhouse or house to shelter tender plants, artificially heated; a conservatory.

hotplate *n* a heated surface for cooking or keeping food warm; a small portable heating device.

hotpot *n* a dish of meat cooked with potatoes in a tight-lidded pan.

hot potato *n* (*colloq*) a problem that no one wants to handle.

hot-press *vt* to apply heat to in conjunction with mechanical pressure in order to produce a smooth and glossy surface (*to hot-press paper* or *cloth*).

hot water *n* heated water; (*fig*) strife; contention; difficulties or troubles; worry.

hough *n* the hock of a horse; the back part of the human knee joint; the ham.—*vt* to hamstring; to disable by cutting the sinews of the ham.

houmous, houmus *n* same as **hummous**.

hound *n* a term restricted to particular breeds or varieties of dogs used in the chase, as in hunting the deer, the fox, the hare; sometimes used as a term of contempt for a man.—*vt* to set on the chase; to incite to pursuit of animals; hence, to urge, incite or spur to action (usually with *on*); to pursue or harass relentlessly.

hour *n* the twenty-fourth part of a day; sixty minutes; the particular time of the day; a fixed or appointed time; a time, period or season; (*pl*) certain prayers in the Roman Catholic Church, to be repeated at stated times of the day.

hourglass *n* a glass in two compartments connected by a narrow neck, for measuring time by the running of a quantity of sand from one compartment to the other.—*adj* having the shape of an hourglass; narrow-waisted.

houri *n* a nymph of the Muslim paradise; (*colloq*) an attractive woman.

hourly *adj* happening or done every hour; frequent; often repeated; continual.—*adv* every hour; frequently; continually.

house *n* (*pl* **houses**) a building serving or intended to serve as an abode; a building for the habitation of people or for their use or accommodation; a dwelling; an abode; a household; a family; a family regarded as consisting of ancestors, descendants and kindred; especially a noble or illustri-

hourglass

ous family; a legislative body of people (*the House of Lords*); a quorum of a legislative body; the audience or attendance at a place of entertainment; a firm or commercial establishment; a twelfth part of the heavens as divided for astrological purposes.—*vt* (**housed, housing**) to put or receive into a house; to provide with a dwelling or residence; to shelter; to cause to take shelter.—*vi* to take shelter or lodgings; to take up abode.

house agent *n* a person whose job it is to buy, sell and rent out houses on behalf of clients; an estate agent.

houseboat *n* a moored boat serving as (and now usually designed to be) a home.

housebreaker *n* one who breaks into a house by day with intent to steal; a burglar.

household *n* those who dwell under the same roof and compose a family; those under the same domestic government; house; family.—*adj* pertaining to the house and family; domestic.

householder *n* the chief of a household; the occupier of a house.

housekeeper *n* a head female servant in a household; a person who looks after a household, especially one hired to do so.

housekeeping *n* the daily running of a household; (*colloq*) money used for domestic expenses; routine maintenance of equipment, records, etc, in an organization.

housel *n* (*arch*) the Eucharist.—*vt* (*arch*) to administer the Eucharist to.

housemaid *n* a female servant employed to keep a house clean, etc.

House of Commons *n* the lower house of the British Parliament, consisting of the representatives of constituencies (MPs).

House of Lords *n* that branch of the British legislature which consists of the lords spiritual and temporal assembled in one house; the upper chamber of Parliament.

Houses of Parliament *npl* in the UK, the House of Commons and the House of Lords; the building in which they meet.

housewife *n* (*pl* **housewives**) the mistress of a family; the wife of a householder; a female manager of domestic affairs; a little case for needles, thread, scissors, etc.

housing *n* houses collectively; the provision of accommodation; a casing enclosing a piece of machinery, etc.

hovel *n* a poor cottage; a small mean house.

hover *vi* to hang stationary in the air or on the wing; to be in doubt or hesitation; to be irresolute; to move to and fro threateningly or watchingly (*an army hovering on our borders*).

hovercraft *n* a land or water vehicle that travels supported on a cushion of air.

how *adv* in what manner; by what means or method; to what degree or extent; by what measure or quantity (*how long, how much better*); in what state, condition or plight.

howbeit *adv* (*arch*) however it be; be it as it may; nevertheless; however.

howdah *n* a seat erected on the back of an elephant for two or more persons to ride in, usually covered overhead.

however *adv* in whatever manner or degree; in whatever state.—*conj* nevertheless; notwithstanding; yet; still; though.

howitzer *n* a medium- to large-calibre artillery piece firing a heavy shell with a low velocity at a high angle to reach objects not to be reached with direct fire.

howl *vi* to utter a loud, protracted, mournful cry, as that of a dog or wolf; to produce any similar sound, as the wind; to wail or lament; to shout or laugh in pain, amusement, etc.—*vt* to utter in a loud or mournful tone.—*n* the cry of a dog or wolf or other similar sound; a cry of distress.

howler *n* one who howls; a name given to a monkey of South America from its cry; an error that cries aloud for correction.

howsoever *adj, conj* in what manner soever; however.

hoy *n* a small coasting vessel, usually rigged as a sloop.

hoyden, hoiden *n* a rude bold girl; a wild, tomboyish girl.

hub *n* the central cylindrical part of a wheel in which the spokes are set; the centre of activity (*the hub of the city*); the focal point; a block of wood for stopping a carriage wheel; a mark at which quoits, etc, are cast; the hilt of a weapon.

hubble-bubble *n* a kind of tobacco pipe so arranged that the smoke passes through water, making a bubbling noise, hence its name; a hookah.

hubbub *n* a noise of many confused voices; a tumult; uproar.

huckaback *n* a kind of linen cloth with raised figures on it, used principally for towels.

huckle *n* the hip; a part projecting like the hip.

huckster *n* a retailer of small articles; a hawker; one who haggles—*vi* to deal in small articles or in petty bargains; to haggle.—*vt* to hawk or peddle; to make a matter of bargain.

huddle *vi* (**huddled, huddling**) to crowd or press together without order or regularity; to curl up.—*vt* to crowd together without order.—*n* a crowd or crowded confused mass.

hue *n* colour or shade of colour; dye; tint.

hue and cry *n* formerly, the outcry raised by a person who knew that a felony had been committed legally requiring others to join the hunt for the criminal; a public clamour; a loud protest (*a hue and cry about the closure of the school*).

hub

huff *n* a fit of peevishness or petulance; anger at some offence, real or fancied; one filled with a false opinion of his or her own importance.—*vi* to swell up; to bluster; to take offence; to blow.

huffy *adj* disgruntled; moody.

hug *vt* (**hugged, hugging**) to press closely with the arms; to embrace closely; to clasp to the breast; to grasp or grip, as in wrestling; to cherish in the mind (*to hug fond memories*); to keep close to (*to hug the land* in sailing); (*refl*) to congratulate oneself.—*n* a close embrace; a clasp or grip.

huge *adj* having an immense bulk; very large or great; enormous; very great in any respect (*a huge difference*).

huggermugger *n* concealment; privacy; secrecy; confusion.—*adj* clandestine; secret; jumbled, confused.—*adv* in confusion.—*vt* to conceal.—*vi* to muddle.

Huguenot *n* a French Protestant, especially of the period of the religious wars in France in the sixteenth century.

hulk *n* a heavy ship; the body of a ship; the body of an old ship laid by as unfit for service; something bulky or unwieldy.—**the hulks** old or dismasted ships, formerly used as prisons.

hulking, hulky *adj* large and clumsy of body; unwieldy; loutish.

hull *n* the outer covering of something, particularly of fruits, grain, etc; the husk; the body of a ship exclusive of masts, yards and rigging.

hullabaloo *n* uproar; noisy confusion.

hullo *interj* same as **hello**.

hum *vi* (**hummed, humming**) to make a dull, prolonged sound, like that of a bee in flight; to utter a single note or a tune with the lips closed; to drone; to murmur; to buzz; to utter a similar sound with the mouth; to mumble; to make a drawling, inarticulate sound in speaking.—*vt* to sing wordlessly in a low voice; to murmur without articulation.—*n* the noise made by bees or any similar sound; a buzz; any inarticulate, low, murmuring or buzzing sound; a murmur of applause; a low inarticulate sound uttered by a speaker.—*interj* a sound with a pause, implying doubt and deliberation; ahem.

human *adj* belonging to a human being or mankind; having the qualities or attributes of a human being as opposed to an animal; kind; considerate.—*n* a human being.

human being *n* a member of the races of *Homo sapiens*; a man, woman or child.

humane *adj* having the feelings and dispositions proper to a human; kind; benevolent; tender; merciful; tending to humanize or refine.

humanism *n* belief in the promotion of human interests, intellect and welfare.

humanist *n* one who studies the humanities;

hummingbird

one versed in the knowledge of human nature; one who advocates humanism.

humanitarian *n* one who has a great regard or love for humanity; a philanthropist; (*theol*) one who denies the divinity of Christ and believes him to have been a man.

humanity *n* the quality of being human; humanness; mankind collectively; the human race; the quality of being humane; tenderness and kindness towards all created beings, opposed to *cruelty*; (*pl*) the study of literature and the arts, as opposed to the sciences (*the humanities*).

humanize *vt* (**humanized, humanizing**) to render human or humane.—*vi* to become more humane; to become more civilized.

humble *adj* of a low, mean or unpretending character; not grand, lofty, noble or splendid; having a low estimate of oneself; not proud, arrogant or assuming; lowly; modest; meek; submissive.—*vt* (**humbled, humbling**) to render humble; to reduce the power, independence or state of; to bring down; to abase; to lower; to bring down the pride of vanity of (often reflexive).

humblebee *n* the bumblebee.

humble pie *n* a pie made of humbles.—**to eat humble pie** to have to take a humble tone; to be made to apologize; to be humiliated.

humbles *npl* the heart, liver, kidneys, etc, of a deer.

humbug *n* a fraud; a sham; an insincere person.—*vt* (**humbugged, humbugging**) to impose on; to cajole or trick; to hoax.

humdrum *adj* commonplace; homely; dull; heavy.—*n* a droning tone of voice; dull monotony.

humerus *n* (*pl* **humeri**) (*anat*) the long cylindrical bone of the arm, situated between the shoulder blade and the forearm.

humid *adj* moist; damp; wet or watery.

humidity, humidness *n* the state of being humid; (*meteor*) the ratio of the amount of water vapour in the air to the amount that would saturate it at the same temperature, expressed as a percentage.

humiliate *vt* (**humiliated, humiliating**) to reduce to a lower position in one's own estimation or the estimation of others; to humble; to depress; to shame.

humiliation *n* the act of humiliating; the state of being humiliated, humbled or mortified.

humility *n* the state or quality of being humble; humbleness; lowliness of mind; a feeling of one's own insignificance.

humming *n* the sound of that which hums; a buzzing; a low murmuring sound.

hummingbird *n* a tiny, highly coloured tropical American bird, so called from the sound of its wings in flight.

humming top *n* a hollow spinning top

which, when spun, emits a loud humming noise.

hummock *n* a rounded knoll; a mound; a hillock; a protuberance on an ice field.

hummous, hummus, houmous, houmus *n* a spread or dip made from pureed chickpeas and tahini.

humorist *n* one who makes use of a humorous style in speaking or writing; one whose writings or conversation are full of humour; a performer or writer of comedy.

humorous *adj* full of humour; exciting laughter; jocular; governed by humour or caprice; capricious; whimsical.

humour *n* formerly, any of the four fluids of the body (blood, phlegm, yellow bile and black bile) that were thought to determine temperament; hence, turn or frame of mind; disposition or a peculiarity of disposition, often temporary (*not in the humour for reading*); a caprice, whim or fancy; temper (as regards anger or annoyance or the opposite); that mental quality which gives to ideas a ludicrous or fantastic turn and tends to excite laughter or mirth; writing or acting that is considered to be humorous.—*vt* to comply with the humour or inclination of; to soothe by compliance; to gratify; to indulge; to adapt oneself to.

humoresque *n* a light musical piece.

hump *n* a protuberance; especially, the protuberance formed by a crooked back; a rounded mass or bump; a hunch.

humpback *n* a back with a hump; a person who has such a back; a whale that has a hump on the back.

humph *interj* an exclamation expressive of disbelief, doubt, dissatisfaction, etc.

humus *n* vegetable mould; a dark-brown or blackish matter from decayed vegetable substances.

hunch *n* a hump; a lump; a feeling or suspicion about something.—*vt* to arch into a hump; to bend or draw up in a hump.

hunchback *n* a humpback; a humpbacked person.

hundred *adj* ten times ten; ninety and ten added.—*n* the product of ten multiplied by ten; a collection of ten times ten individuals or units; a division of a county in England, supposed to have originally contained a hundred families or freemen, still preserved in the *Chiltern Hundreds*.

hundredweight *n* a weight, usually denoted by *cwt*, containing 112 pounds or about 50.8 kilograms.

Hungarian *n* a native of Hungary; the language of the Hungarians.

hunger *n* an uneasy sensation occasioned by the lack of food; a craving for food; craving appetite; strong or eager desire.—*vi* to feel hunger; to crave food; to desire eagerly; to long.

hung jury *n* a jury that fails to reach a decision.

hungry *adj* feeling hunger; having a keen appetite; eagerly desirous; proceeding from hunger.

hunk *n* a large lump; a hunch; (*sl*) a sexually attractive man.

hunt *vt* to chase, search for or follow after (wild animals, particularly quadrupeds and especially with hounds) for the purpose of catching or killing; to search after, pursue, follow closely; to pursue game or wild animals over (*to hunt a district*); to send for; to look for.—*vi* to follow the chase; to go in pursuit of game or other wild animals; to seek by close pursuit; to search (with *after* or *for*).—*n* the chasing of wild animals; a pursuit; a chase; a pack of hounds; an association of huntsmen and huntswomen in a district.

hunter *n* one who hunts; a huntsman; a horse used in the chase; a watch whose glass is protected by a metal cover.

hunting box *n* a residence occupied for the purpose of hunting.

hunting crop *n* a riding whip with loop at end, with no lash.

huntress *n* a female that hunts or follows the chase.

huntsman, huntswoman *n* (*pl* **huntsmen, huntswomen**) one who hunts or who practises hunting; a person whose office it is to manage the chase.

hurdle *n* a movable frame made of interlaced twigs or sticks, or of bars or rods crossing each other, varying in form according to its use; a series of barriers across a racetrack to be jumped over by the competitors; a race involving such barriers; an obstacle; a hindrance.—*vt* (**hurdled, hurdling**) to jump over (a series of barriers); to overcome (obstacles).—*vi* to jump over barriers.

hurdy-gurdy *n* a barrel organ or similar musical instrument played by turning a handle.

hurl *vt* to send whirling or flying through the air; to throw or dash with violence; to emit or utter with vehemence.—*n* the act of throwing with violence.

hurling, hurley *n* an Irish ball game resembling hockey.

hurly-burly *n* tumult; bustle; confusion.

hurrah, hurray, hoorah, hooray *interj* an exclamation expressive of joy, applause or encouragement, also used as a noun.—*vi* to utter a hurrah.

hurricane *n* an extremely violent tempest or storm of wind (force 12 on the Beaufort scale); anything resembling a violent tempest.

hurry *vt* (**hurried, hurrying**) to impel to greater speed or haste; to urge to act or proceed with precipitance; to cause to be

hunter

hurdle

423

performed with great or undue rapidity; to impel to violent or thoughtless action.—*vi* to move or act with haste; to proceed with precipitation; to make great haste in going.—*n* the act of hurrying; urgency; bustle; confusion.

hurt *vt* (*pret, pp* **hurt**, *ppr* **hurting**) to cause physical pain to; to wound or bruise painfully; to cause mental pain; to wound the feelings of; to cause injury, loss or diminution to; to impair; to damage; to harm.—*n* a wound, a bruise, etc; injury; loss; damage; detriment.

hurtful *adj* causing hurt; harmful; injurious; mischievous; detrimental.

hurtle *vi* (**hurtled, hurtling**) to clash or meet in shock; to make a sound suggestive of hostile clash; to move with great speed and force; to throw with speed and great force.

husband *n* a man joined to a woman by marriage, the counterpart of *wife*.—*vt* to spend, apply or use with economy; to conserve (*to husband resources*).

husky

husbandman *n* (*pl* **husbandmen**) a farmer; a cultivator; one engaged in agriculture.

husbandry *n* domestic economy; good management; frugality; thrift; the business of a husbandman; agriculture.

hush *adj* silent; still; quiet.—*vt* to still; to silence; to make quiet; to repress the noise or clamour of.—**to hush up** to suppress; to procure silence concerning; to keep concealed.—*vi* to be still; to be silent (used chiefly in the imperative); to be still; to make no noise.—*n* stillness; quiet.

hush money *n* a bribe to secure silence.

husk *n* the external covering of certain fruits or seeds of plants; glume; hull; rind; chaff.—*vt* to deprive of the husk; to shell (peas, etc).

husky[1] *adj* rough in tone, as the voice; not clear; harsh; hoarse; strongly built.

husky[2] *n* an Arctic breed of dog used for drawing sledges.

hussar *n* originally one of the national cavalry of Hungary; now a light cavalry soldier of European armies.

Hussite *n* a follower of John Huss, the Bohemian religious reformer, burned in 1415.

hussy *n* a bad or worthless woman or girl; a forward girl.

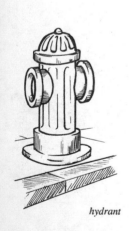

hydrant

hustings *npl* the temporary platform on which, previous to the Ballot Act of 1872, parliamentary candidates stood when addressing the electors; the campaigns, speeches, etc, which take place before a political election; the process of or place of political campaigning.

hustle *vt* (**hustled, hustling**) to push or elbow out or about rudely; to jostle; to bother; to cause to move or happen more quickly.—*vi* to push or crowd; to move or work speedily or energetically; to earn money by questionable or illegal means; (*sl*) to solicit, as a prostitute.

hustler *n* one who hustles, especially one who earns money by questionable means.

hut *n* a small simple house or cabin; a mean dwelling.—*vt* (**hutted, hutting**) to place in huts, as troops encamped in winter quarters.

hutch *n* a chest, box, coffer, bin or other receptacle in which things may be stored or animals confined (especially rabbits or guinea pigs); a low wagon in which coal is drawn up out of the pit.

huzza *interj* a form of **hurrah**.

hyacinth *n* a bulbous plant, of which there are many varieties cultivated, grown for their flowers and scent; a mineral, a variety of zircon, transparent or translucent, of a red colour tinged with yellow or brown; the name is also given to varieties of garnet, sapphire and topaz.

hyaena *n* same as **hyena**.

hybrid *n* a mongrel; an animal or plant, the produce of a female animal or plant which has been impregnated by a male of a different variety, species or genus; a word made up of elements from different languages; anything of mixed origin.—*adj* mongrel; produced from the mixture of two species; of mixed origin (*a hybrid word, a hybrid chassis*).

hydra *n* any of a genus of freshwater polyps of a very low type of structure and with a mouth surrounded by tentacles.

Hydra *n* in Greek myth, a monster destroyed by Hercules and represented as having many heads, one of which, being cut off, was immediately succeeded by another, unless the wound was cauterized; hence, evil or misfortune arising from many sources and not easily surmounted.

hydrangea *n* an Asiatic and American shrub cultivated in gardens for its large heads of white, pink or blue flowers.

hydrant *n* a pipe with suitable valves and a spout by which water is raised and discharged from a main pipe; a fire hydrant.

hydrate *n* a chemical compound in which water is a characteristic ingredient.—*vt* (**hydrate, hydrating**) to combine with or absorb, water.

hydraulic *adj* pertaining to fluids in motion or the action of water utilized for mechanical purposes.

hydraulics *n* that branch of science which treats of the motion of liquids and deals with the application of water in machinery.

hydride *n* a chemical compound of hydrogen and another element.

hydro *n* (*pl* **hydros**) formerly, an establishment in which persons were boarded to receive hydropathic treatment.

hydro- *prefix* water, fluids.

hydrocarbon *n* a chemical compound of hydrogen and carbon.

hydrocele *n* (*med*) an abnormal collection of serous fluid in the scrotum or testicle.

hydrocephalic *adj* pertaining to hydrocephalus.

hydrocephalus *n* (*med*) an accumulation of fluid within the cavity of the cranium, also called non-medically 'water on the brain'.

hydrochloric *adj* (*chem*) pertaining to or compounded of chlorine and hydrogen.

hydrochloric acid *n* a strong, highly corrosive acid that is a solution of the gas hydrogen chloride in water.

hydrocyanic *adj* derived from the combination of hydrogen and cyanogen

hydrocyanic acid, hydrogen cyanide *n* prussic acid, a colourless, volatile highly poisonous solution of hydrogen cyanide, found naturally and made synthetically and used in manufacturing plastics, etc.

hydrodynamic *adj* pertaining to the mechanical properties of fluids.

hydrodynamics *n* that branch of science which treats of the application of forces to fluids, especially when producing motion in fluids.

hydroelectric *adj* pertaining to the production of electric current by water power.

hydrofoil *n* one of a set of vanes or blades attached at an angle to the underside of a boat's hull which on impact with the water lifts the hull out of the water to allow fast cruising speeds; a vessel equipped with hydrofoils.

hydrofluoric *adj* consisting of fluorine and hydrogen (*hydrofluoric acid*, a most powerful corrosive).

hydrogen *n* one of the elements of water (the other being oxygen) and a component of all vegetable and animal products; the lightest and simplest chemical element known, its atom consisting of one proton and one electron.

hydrogen bomb *n* a powerful bomb that produces explosive energy through the fusion of hydrogen nuclei.

hydrogen cyanide *n* same as **hydrocyanic acid**.

hydrogenous *adj* pertaining to or containing hydrogen; formed or produced by the action of water (said of rocks).

hydrogen peroxide *n* a colourless oxiding compound used as an antiseptic, a bleach and an oxiding agent.

hydrography *n* that branch of science which deals with the measurement and description of the sea, lakes, rivers and other waters and includes marine surveying, the drawing of charts, etc.

hydrology *n* the science that treats of water.

hydrolysis *n* (*chem*) the resolution of an organic compound into other compounds by a reaction with water.

hydrometer *n* an instrument to measure the specific gravity or density of water and other fluids and hence the strength of spirituous liquors and of various solutions.

hydrometry *n* the art or operation of determining the specific gravity, density, force, etc, of fluids.

hydropathic *adj* relating to hydropathy.

hydropathy *n* the treatment of disease by the use of water externally or internally.

hydrophane *n* a variety of opal made transparent by immersion in water.

hydrophobia *n* an abnormal dread of water; a disease produced by the bite of a mad animal, especially of a mad or rabid dog, one of the characteristics of which is an aversion to or inability to swallow liquids.

hydrophyte *n* a plant which lives and grows in water.

hydrophytology *n* the botany of water plants.

hydropic, hydropical *adj* dropsical; pertaining to dropsy.

hydroplane *n* an external fin-like vane which governs the vertical course of a submarine; a motorboat that skims across water at high speed with its hull raised out of the water on hydrofoils; an attachment to an aircraft that enables it to glide along the surface of water.—*vi* (**hydroplaned, hydroplaning**) (of a boat) to rise above the surface in the manner of a hydroplane; (of a car) to be in an extremely dangerous condition where, on a wet road, speed is such that water pressure forces the front wheels off the road surface, akin to a hydroplaning boat.

hydropsy *n* dropsy.

hydrostatic *adj* relating to hydrostatics; pertaining to the principles of the equilibrium of fluids.

hydrostatics *n* the science that deals with the weight and equilibrium of fluids, particularly of water; that branch of science that deals with the properties of fluids at rest.

hydrosulphuric *adj* derived from or containing hydrogen and sulphur (*hydrosulphuric acid*).

hydrous *adj* containing water; watery.

hydroxide *n* a compound derived from water through the replacement of one of the hydrogen atoms by another atom or group.

hydrozoan *n* (*zool*) one of a class of animals consisting mostly of marine animals and including the jellyfishes, hydra, etc, many of them permanently attached to objects and somewhat resembling plants.

hyena, hyaena *n* a carnivorous animal of several species, belonging to Asia and Africa, strong and fierce, feeding chiefly on carrion and of nocturnal habits.

hygeian *adj* pertaining to health or its preservation.

hyena

hygiene *n* a system of principles or rules designed for the promotion of health, especially the health of households or communities; cleanliness.

hygienic *adj* relating to hygienic or sanitary matters; clean.

hygienics *n* the science of health; hygiene.

hygienist *n* one specializing in hygiene, especially dental hygiene.

hygrometer *n* an instrument for measuring the humidity of the atmosphere.

hygrometry *n* the determination of humidity or of the moisture of the atmosphere.

hygrophyte *n* a land plant adapted to moist surroundings.

hygroscope *n* an instrument for indicating the presence of moisture in the atmosphere.

hygroscopic *adj* readily absorbing and retaining moisture from the atmosphere.

hylozoism *n* (*philos*) the doctrine that matter possesses a species of life or that life and matter are inseparably connected.

hymen *n* (*anat*) the virginal membrane, situated at the entrance of the vagina; (*bot*) the fine pellicle which encloses a flower in the bud.

hymeneal *adj* (*arch poet*) pertaining to marriage.

hymenopteran, hymenopteron *n* a member of an order of insects, having four membranous wings and including the bees, wasps, ants, etc.

hymenopterous *adj* belonging or pertaining to the hymenopterans.

hymn *n* a song or ode in honour of God or in honour of some deity; a sacred lyric; a song of praise, adoration or thanksgiving. —*vt* to praise or celebrate in hymn or song; to sing.—*vi* to sing in praise or adoration.

hymnal, hymn book *n* a collection of hymns, generally for use in public worship.

hymnody *n* the composition or singing of hymns; a body of sacred lyrics composed by several authors of a particular period or country; hymns collectively.

hymnology *n* the study of hymns and hymn music.

hyoid bone *n* a movable bone, having somewhat the shape of the letter U, between the root of the tongue and the larynx.

hyoscine *n* same as **scopolamine**.

hyoscyamine *n* a poisonous alkaloid occurring in henbane and used in medicine.

hypaethral, hypethral *adj* (*archit*) (of a building) not covered by a roof, open to the sky.

hypallage *n* a figure of speech consisting of a transference of attributes from their proper subjects to others (*the water ruffled the air*).

hyper- *prefix* above; too; exceeding.

hyperactive *adj* overactive; abnormally active.

hyperaemia *n* an excessive accumulation of blood in a part of the body.

hyperaesthesia *n* an increased sensitivity of one of the sense organs.

hyperbaton *n* (*gram*) a figurative construction inverting the natural order of words and sentences (*him I dislike*).

hyperbola *n* (*pl* **hyperbolas, hyperbole**) (*geom*) a curve formed by a plane that cuts a cone in a direction parallel to its axis or so that the plane makes a greater angle with the base than the side of the cone makes.

hyperbole *n* a figure of speech which expresses much more or less than the truth; an exaggerated statement; deliberate exaggeration.

hyperbolic, hyperbolical *adj* belonging to or containing hyperbole; exaggerated in terms.

hyperbolize *vti* (**hyperbolized, hyperbolizing**) to speak or write with exaggeration; to exaggerate.

hypercritic *n* one who is critical beyond measure or reason; an over-rigid critic.

hypercritical *adj* overcritical; critical beyond use or reason.

hypercriticism *n* excessive rigour of criticism; excessive criticism.

hyperdulia *n* (*RC Church*) the worship offered to the Virgin Mary, so called because higher than that given to saints (*dulia*).

hyperplasia *n* (*pathol*) excessive growth of a part by multiplication of cells.

hypersensitive *adj* extremely vulnerable; abnormally sensitive to a drug, pollen, etc.

hypersthene *n* a mineral of the hornblende group, a constituent of some rocks.

hypertension *n* abnormally high blood pressure; (*colloq*) excessive tenseness.

hypertensive *adj* pertaining to abnormally high blood pressure; suffering from abnormally high blood pressure.

hyperthermia *n* an abnormally raised body temperature; a condition in which the body temperature is abnormally high.

hypertrophy *n* an abnormal enlargement of a part of the body from excessive nutrition.

hyphenate *vt* (**hyphenated, hyphenating**) to join or separate by a hyphen.

hyphenation *n* the act or practice of hyphenating.

hyphen *n* a mark or short line (-) made between two words to show that they form a compound word or used to connect the syllables of a divided word.—*vt* to hyphenate.

hypnosis *n* (*pl* **hypnoses**) the hypnotic state; a sort of sleep or relaxed state artificially induced, in which the person hypnotized responds to external suggestions.

hypnotic *adj* of or producing hypnosis; tending to produce sleep; soporific.—*n* a medicine that produces sleep; a soporific.

hypnotism *n* the art or practice of inducing hypnosis; the study and use of hypnosis.

hypnotize *vt* (**hypnotized, hypnotizing**) to affect with hypnotism; to fascinate.

hypo[1] *n* a compound of sodium used in photography as a fixing agent.

hypo[2] *n* (*pl* **hypos**) (*colloq*) a hypodermic syringe.

hypo- *prefix* below; slightly.

hypocaust *n* (*ancient archit*) an arched chamber in which a fire was kindled for the purpose of giving heat to the rooms above it.

hypochondria *n* (*med*) a disease characterized by chronic anxiety about health, etc, often involving imaginary illnesses.

hypochondriac *adj* pertaining to hypochondria or to the hypochondrium; affected with hypochondria.—*n* a person who suffers from hypochondria.

hypochondriac *n* a person affected with hypochondria.

hypochondrium *n* (*pl* **hypochondria**) (*anat*) the name of the two regions of the abdomen under the cartilages of the lowest ribs on the right and left sides.

hypocrisy *n* the act or practice of simulating or feigning to be what one is not; especially, the assuming of a false appearance of piety and virtue; dissimulation; insincerity.

hypocrite *n* a person who pretends to be what he or she is not.

hypocritical *adj* pertaining to or proceeding from, hypocrisy; characterized by hypocrisy; pretending goodness or religion; insincere.

hypocycloid *n* a curve generated by the movement of a circle on the concave side of a fixed circle.

hypodermal *adj* pertaining to or relating to parts under the skin or to the introduction of medicines under the skin.

hypodermic *adj* under the skin; subcutaneous; injected under the skin.—*n* a hypodermic syringe.

hypodermic needle *n* the hollow needle used with a hypodermic syringe.

hypodermic syringe *n* a syringe with a hollow needle for injecting a drug in solution under the skin or for drawing blood samples.

hypogastric *adj* relating to the hypogastrium.

hypogastrium *n* (*pl* **hypogastria**) (*anat*) the lower anterior region of the abdomen.

hypophysis *n* (*pl* **hypophyses**) the pituitary gland.

hypostasis *n* (*pl* **hypostases**) that which underlies something else; the reality underlying or assumed to underlie a phenomenon, whatever its apparent properties; (*theol*) the distinct substance or subsistence of the Father, Son and Holy Spirit in the Godhead.

hypostyle *n* (*archit*) a covered colonnade; a pillared hall.—*adj* having the roof supported by pillars.

hypotenuse *n* (*geom*) the longest side of a right-angled triangle; the line that subtends the right angle.

hypothermia *n* an abnormally low body temperature; a condition in which the body temperature is below normal.

hypothesis *n* (*pl* **hypotheses**) a supposition; something not proved, but assumed for the purpose of argument; a theory imagined or assumed to account for what is not understood.

hypothetical, hypothetic *adj* including or characterized by a supposition or hypothesis; conjectural; conditional.

hypsometry *n* the art of measuring the heights of places on the surface of the earth.

hyrax *n* a small rabbit-like herbivorous mammal of Southwest Asia, believed to be the 'coney' of Scripture; an allied species of southern Africa.

hyson *n* a species of green tea from China.

hyssop *n* an aromatic plant with blue flowers formerly used in medicine.

hysterectomy *n* the surgical removal of the uterus; an operation to remove the uterus.

hysteresis *n* (*pl* **hystereses**) (*physics*) the effect when a physical process lags behind its cause, resulting in a failure to return to a completely normal state or value.

hysteria *n* a condition characterized by excessive excitability, anxiety, imaginary organic disorders, etc; frenzied emotion or excitement, sometimes involving fits of laughter.

hysteric *n* a person suffering from hysteria; (*pl*) hysteria; (*pl*) (*colloq*) uncontrollable laughter.

hysterical *adj* pertaining to hysteria; affected by or subject to hysterics; (*colloq*) extremely funny.

hysteron-proteron *n* an inversion of the natural order in words (as *he worked for days and hours* instead of *hours and days*); a putting first what should be last; a false argument that seeks to use the proposition to be proved as the premise.

hypodermic

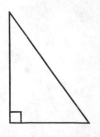

hypotenuse

I

ice cream

ice-hockey player

I¹ the ninth letter and the third vowel of the English alphabet, in which it represents not only several vowel sounds but also the consonantal sound of *y*.

I² (*possessive pron* **my** *or* **mine**, *dative and objective* **me**; *pl nominative* **we**, *possessive* **our** *or* **ours**, *dative and objective* **us**) the nominative case of the pronoun of the first person; the word by which a speaker or writer denotes himself or herself (sometimes used as a noun); the ego.

iaido *n* a Japanese form of fencing.

iambic *adj* pertaining to the iambus; composed of iambics.—*n* an iambic foot; a verse consisting of iambi.

iambus *n* (*pl* **iambuses**, **iambi**) (*pros*) a foot consisting of two syllables, the first short and the last long, or the first unaccented and the last accented, as in *delight*.

iatric, iatrical *adj* relating to medicine or physicians.

Iberian *adj* pertaining to Spain and Portugal; pertaining to Iberia, the ancient name of the southwest European peninsula now comprising Spain and Portugal.

ibex *n* a mountain goat of Europe, Asia and North Africa with large horns directed backwards and marked with prominent transverse ridges in front.

ibid *abbreviation of* **ibidem** in the same place; in the same book, page, etc.

ibis *n* a name of certain wading birds allied to the storks, the most remarkable species of which, the sacred ibis, was revered by the ancient Egyptians.

ice *n* water or other fluid congealed or in a solid state in consequence of the abstraction of the heat necessary to preserve its fluidity; cream or milk sweetened, variously flavoured and frozen; ice cream; (*sl*) diamonds.—**to break the ice** to make the first opening to any attempt; to open the way—**on ice** waiting in readiness; in reserve; postponed.—**on thin ice** in a risky situation.—*vt* (**iced**, **icing**) to cover with ice; to convert into ice; to cool with ice; to freeze; to cover with icing.

Ice Age *n* any of several periods of time when ice covered large areas of the earth.

iceberg *n* a great mass of ice floating on the ocean, having broken off from a glacier.

iceblink *n* a bright yellowish-white tint near the horizon, reflected from ice in Arctic regions.

icebreaker *n* a large and powerful steamer that smashes and forces a way through ice.

ice cream *n* a sweet frozen food, made from flavoured milk or cream.

iced *adj* covered with ice; cooled with ice; frosted; (of a cake, etc) covered with icing.

ice field *n* a large sheet of sea ice whose limits cannot be seen.

ice floe *n* a sheet of ice, smaller than an ice field but still of considerable size.

ice hockey *n* a kind of hockey played on ice by two teams of six players with curved sticks and a flat disc called a puck.

Icelander *n* a native of Iceland.

Icelandic *adj* pertaining to Iceland.—*n* the language of the Icelanders or of their literature.

ichneumon *n* a North African mongoose.

ichneumon fly *n* a kind of insect whose larvae are parasitic on other insects.

ichnite *n* (*geol*) a fossil footprint; the footprint of an extinct animal marked on rocks.

ichnography *n* the horizontal section of a building or other object, showing its true dimensions according to a geometric scale; a ground plan.

ichnolite *n* an ichnite or stone marked with an animal's footprint.

ichnology, ichnolithology *n* the study of the fossil footprints of animals.

ichor *n* an ethereal fluid that supplied the place of blood in the veins of the gods of the Greeks and Romans; (*med*) a thin watery humour, like serum or whey; a thin watery acrid discharge from an ulcer, wound, etc.

ichthyography *n* the description of fishes.

ichthyologist *n* one who specializes in ichthyology.

ichthyology *n* the science of fishes; that branch of zoology which treats of fishes.

ichthyophagous *adj* eating or subsisting on fish.

ichthyornis *n* an extinct bird with vertebrae like those of fishes and with teeth set in sockets.

ichthyosaur, ichthyosaurus *n* an immense, extinct, fish-like marine reptile, combining many of the characteristics of lizards and fishes.

ichthyosis *n* a disease of the skin, portions of which become hard and scaly, with a tendency to excrescences.

icicle *n* a hanging conical mass of ice formed by the freezing of water or other fluid as it drops from something.

iciness *n* the state of being icy or very cold.

icing *n* a semi-solid sugary mixture used to cover cakes, etc.

icon, ikon *n* an image or representation; a portrait; a picture of Christ, the Virgin or a saint, regarded as sacred in the Greek and Russian Churches; an emblem or epitome; (*comput*) a symbol to identify a program, file, etc.

iconoclasm *n* the act, principles or proceedings of an iconoclast.

iconoclast *n* a breaker of images; one who makes attacks on cherished or traditional beliefs.

iconoclastic *adj* pertaining to an iconoclast.

iconography *n* the art of representation by means of images, pictures or engravings; the study of symbols used in art.

iconolater *n* one who worships images.

iconolatry *n* the worship or adoration of images.

iconology *n* the study of icons.

icosahedral *adj* having twenty equal sides.

icosahedron *n* a solid of twenty equal sides.

icteric, icterical *adj* affected with jaundice; curing jaundice.

ictus *n* (*pl* **ictuses, ictus**) a stroke; the stress laid on an accented syllable.

icy *adj* pertaining to, composed of, produced by, resembling or abounding with ice; (*fig*) characterized by coldness or coolness, as of manner, etc; frigid; chilling; indifferent.

idea *n* the form, image or model in the mind of anything; that which is held or comprehended by the understanding or intellectual faculties; (*philos*) a subjective notion and representation, with or without objective validity; notion, conception, thought, opinion or belief.

ideal *adj* existing in idea; existing in fancy or imagination only; visionary; perfect; exactly suitable.—*n* an imaginary model of perfection; a standard of perfection or beauty.

idealism *n* that system of philosophy according to which nothing exists but the mind itself and ideas perceived by the mind, or which maintains that we have no rational grounds for believing in the reality of anything but percipient minds and ideas; the pursuit of high ideals; the pursuit of what one considers to be ideal.

idealist *n* one who holds the doctrines of idealism; one who idealizes; one who indulges in flights of fancy or imagination; a visionary.

ideality *n* the condition or quality of being ideal; the capacity to form ideals of beauty and perfection.

idealize *vt* (**idealized, idealizing**) to make ideal; to give form to in accordance with any preconceived ideal; to embody in an ideal form.—*vi* to form ideals.

ideation *n* the faculty of the mind for forming ideas; the establishment of a distinct mental representation or idea of an object.

idée fixe *n* (*pl* **idées fixes**) an obsession.

identical *adj* the same; not another or different.

identification *n* the act of identifying; the state of being identified; something which proves a person's identity.

identify *vt* (**identified, identifying**) to consider to be the same; to regard oneself as being similar to another; to unite or combine in such a manner as to make one; to determine or establish the identity of; to ascertain or prove to be the same with something described or claimed.—*vi* to become the same.

Identikit *n* a trademark for a device for building up a compound portrait from a large number of different features shown on transparent slips, by means of which a witness is assisted in producing a likeness of someone sought by the police.

identity *n* the state or fact of being identical; sameness, as distinguished from similitude and diversity; the state of being the same as a specified person or thing; the distinguishing characteristics of a person; who or what a person or thing is.

ideograph, ideogram *n* in some systems of writing, a character, symbol or figure which suggests the idea of an object without expressing its name; a hieroglyphic.

ideology *n* the science of ideas or of the understanding; that system of mental philosophy which exclusively derives our knowledge from sensation; the idea or ideas at the basis of some political system.—**ideological** *adj*.

Ides *npl* in the ancient Roman calendar the 13th of January, February, April, June, August, September, November and December, and the 15th of March, May, July and October.

idiocy *n* state of being an idiot; mental deficiency; foolishness; a stupid or foolish action.

idiom *n* a mode of expression peculiar to a language or to a person; a phrase or expression having a special meaning from usage or a special grammatical character;

icicle

the genius or peculiar cast of a language; a peculiar form of variety of language; a dialect.

idiomatic *adj* having the character of an idiom; pertaining to the particular modes of expression which belong to a language.

idiosyncrasy *n* a personal peculiarity of constitution or temperament; a mental or moral characteristic belonging to and distinguishing an individual; peculiar way of thinking or feeling; a quirk; eccentricity.

idiosyncratic *adj* pertaining to, having or showing idiosyncrasy; eccentric.

idiot *n* a person who is markedly mentally defective; a foolish or stupid person.—*adj* pertaining to an idiot; afflicted with idiocy.

idiotic *adj* like or relating to an idiot; foolish; utterly absurd.

idle *adj* not engaged in any occupation; unoccupied; doing nothing; slothful; averse to labour or employment; lazy; vacant or not spent in work (*idle hours*); remaining unused; producing no effect; useless, vain, ineffectual or fruitless (*idle rage*); trifling or irrelevant (*an idle story*).—*vi* (**idled, idling**) to lose or spend time in inaction or without being employed; (of an engine) to operate without transmitting power.—*vt* to spend in idleness (generally followed by *away*).

idleness *n* the condition or quality of being idle.

idler *n* one who idles.

idol *n* an image, representation or symbol of a deity which is not God made or consecrated as an object of worship; any person or thing on which we strongly set our affections; that to which we are excessively, often improperly, attached.

idolater *n* a worshipper of idols; one who worships as a deity that which is not God; a pagan; an adorer; a great admirer.

idolatrous *adj* pertaining to idolatry; partaking of the nature of idolatry; worshipping false gods; consisting in or partaking of an excessive attachment or reverence.

idolatry *n* the worship of idols, images or anything made by hands, or which is not God; excessive attachment to or admiration for any person or thing.

idolize *vt* (**idolized, idolizing**) to worship as an idol; to make an idol of; to love to excess; to love or reverence to adoration.

idyll *n* a short, highly wrought descriptive poem, consisting generally of scenes or events of pastoral life; a romantic or picturesque event or scene.

idyllic *adj* of or belonging to idylls or pastoral poetry; pastoral; romantic; picturesque.

if *conj* in case that; granting that; supposing that; even though; allowing that; whether; whenever.

igloo *n* an Inuit winter hut, made of blocks of frozen snow.

igloo

iguana

igneous *adj* pertaining to, consisting of or resembling fire; produced by or resulting from the action of fire.

ignis fatuus *n* (*pl* **ignes fatui**) a meteor or light that appears in the night and flits about in the air over marshy grounds; popularly known by such names as will-o'-the-wisp, jack-o'-lantern, etc.

ignite *vt* (**ignited, igniting**) to kindle or set on fire; to communicate fire to.—*vi* to take fire; to become red with heat.

ignition *n* the act of igniting; a means of igniting; the starting of an internal combustion engine; the mechanism that ignites an internal combustion engine.

ignoble *adj* of low birth or family; not noble; not illustrious; mean; worthless; not honourable; base.

ignominious *adj* marked with ignominy; shameful; dishonourable; infamous; despicable.

ignominy *n* public disgrace; shame; dishonour; infamy.

ignoramus *n* (*pl* **ignoramuses**) an ignorant person; a vain pretender to knowledge.

ignorance *n* the state of being ignorant; lack of knowledge; the condition of not being cognizant or aware.

ignorant *adj* lacking knowledge in general or with regard to some particular (with *of* before an object); uninstructed or uninformed; untaught; unenlightened; unacquainted; unconscious.

ignore *vt* (**ignored, ignoring**) to pass over or by without notice; to act as if one were unacquainted with; to shut the eyes to; to leave out of account; to disregard; to reject.

iguana *n* a reptile of the lizard family, a native of tropical America.

iguanodon *n* a colossal dinosaur.

ikon *n* same as **icon**.

iliac *adj* pertaining to the bowels, especially the lower bowels, or to the part of the abdomen containing them.

ilium *n* (*pl* **ilia**) (*anat*) a bone that forms the outer portion of the pelvis on either side; the hip bone.

ilk *n* a type or sort.—**of that ilk** in Scotland, a phrase sometimes used after the name of a landed person to denote that the surname and the title of the estate are the same.

ill *adj* bad or evil; the opposite of good; wicked; wrong (used of things rather than persons); producing evil or misfortune; calamitous or unfortunate (*an ill end*); cross, crabbed, surly or peevish (*ill nature, ill temper*); suffering from disease or sickness; sick or indisposed; unwell (*ill of a fever*); not proper; rude or unpolished (*ill manners, ill breeding*).—*n* wickedness; evil; misfortune; calamity; whatever annoys or impairs happiness or prevents success.—*adv* not well; not rightly or perfectly (*ill at ease*); not easily; with pain or difficulty (*he is ill able to sustain the burden*).

ill-advised *adj* badly advised; resulting from bad advice or the lack of good; injudicious.

illation *n* the act of inferring from premises or reasons; inference; an inference, deduction or conclusion.

ill-bred *adj* not well bred; badly educated or brought up; impolite.

illegal *adj* not legal; contrary to law; unlawful; illicit.

illegality *n* the condition or quality of being illegal.

illegibility, illegibleness *n* the state or quality of being illegible.

illegible *adj* incapable of being read.

illegitimacy *n* the state of being illegitimate; bastardy.

illegitimate *adj* not legitimate; born out of wedlock; not in conformity with law; not authorized; not legitimately inferred or deduced; not warranted (*an illegitimate inference*).

ill-favoured *adj* having ill features; ugly.

ill feeling *n* resentment; enmity.

ill-gotten *adj* gained by unfair or improper means.

illiberal *adj* not liberal; not free or generous; of narrow or contracted mind or opinions.

illicit *n* not permitted or allowed; prohibited; unlawful.

illimitable *adj* incapable of being limited or bounded; boundless; immeasurable.

illiteracy *n* the state of being illiterate.

illiterate *adj* unable to read or write; uneducated; unlearned; ignorant.—*n* an illiterate person.

ill nature *n* evil nature or disposition; bad temper; crossness; crabbedness.

illness *n* the state or condition of being ill; an ailment or sickness.

illogical *adj* ignorant or negligent of the rules of logic or correct reasoning; contrary to logic or sound reasoning.

ill-starred *adj* having an evil star presiding over one's destiny; fated to be unfortunate.

illude *vt* (**illuded, illuding**) to deceive; to mock; to make sport of.

illume *vt* (**illumed, illuming**) to illumine or illuminate.

illuminant *n* that which illuminates or affords light.

illuminate *vt* (**illuminated, illuminating**) to enlighten; to throw light on; to make clear; to supply with light; to light up with festal lamps, bonfires, etc; to adorn (a manuscript) with gilded and coloured decorations or illustrations.

illuminati *npl* (*sing* **illuminato**) a term formerly applied to certain sects and secret societies, now applied to persons who af-

fect to possess extraordinary knowledge whether justly or otherwise.

illumination *n* the act of illuminating or state of being illuminated; a festive display of lights, etc; an ornament or illustration in colours and gilding, such as those with which ancient manuscripts or books were embellished.

illuminative *adj* having the power of illuminating; tending to throw light; clarifying; illustrative.

illuminator *n* one who or that which illuminates.

illumine *vt* (**illumined, illumining**) to illuminate.

illusion *n* the act of deceiving or imposing upon; deception; mockery; a deceptive appearance; an unreal vision presented to the bodily or mental eye; hallucination; a false idea or conception; a conjuring trick.

illusive *adj* based on illusion; deceiving by false show; illusory; deceptive.

illusory *adj* causing illusion; deceiving or tending to deceive by false appearances; false and deceptive; fallacious.

illustrate *vt* (**illustrated, illustrating**) to make clear, intelligible or obvious; to throw light on by examples, by comparisons, etc; to ornament and elucidate by means of pictures, drawings, etc.

illustration *n* the act of illustrating; that which illustrates; a particular case or example intended to throw light on one's meaning; a picture accompanying and illustrating the text of a book.

illustrative *adj* tending to illustrate.

illustrator *n* one who illustrates.

illustrious *adj* distinguished by greatness, nobleness or eminence; conspicuous for praiseworthy qualities; renowned; eminent; glorious; brilliant (*an illustrious person, an illustrious action*).

ill will *n* a desire that evil will befall a person; enmity; malevolence.

image *n* a representation of any person or thing, sculpted, painted, photographed or otherwise made visible; a statue, picture, photograph or stamped representation; an effigy; an idol; what forms a counterpart or likeness of something else; likeness; embodiment; a picture drawn by fancy; semblance; show; appearance; the concept of a person, product, etc, held by the public at large; in optics, the figure or appearance of an object made by reflection or refraction.—*vt* (**imaged, imaging**) to represent by an image; to reflect the image or likeness of; to mirror; to represent to the mental vision; to form a likeness of in the mind.

imagery *n* images in general or collectively; forms of the fancy; imaginary phantasms; rhetorical figures collectively; comparisons, similes, etc, in discourse.

imaginable *adj* capable of being imagined or conceived.

imaginary *adj* existing only in imagination or fancy; conceived by the imagination; not real; fancied.

imagination *n* the power or faculty of the mind by which it conceives and forms ideas of things from knowledge communicated to it by the organs of sense; the faculty by which we can bring absent objects and perceptions forcibly before the mind; the power or faculty which enables a person to produce a new, impressive and artistic whole by selecting and working up ideas derived through observation and memory and which thus includes a certain share of invention; an image or conception in the mind; an idea; an unsolid or fanciful opinion; a scheme or plot.

imaginative *adj* forming imaginations; endowed with imagination; owing existence to, or characterized by, imagination.

imagine *vt* (**imagined, imagining**) to form a notion or idea of in the mind; to bring before the mind's eye; to produce by the imagination; to conceive in thought; to think, scheme or devise.—*vi* to conceive; to suppose; to fancy; to think.

imam

imago *n* (*pl* **imagos, imagines**) the last or perfect state of an insect, usually that in which it has wings.

imam, imaum *n* a minister or priest who performs the regular service of the mosque among Muslims; a title given to the successors of Mohammed.

imbecile *adj* mentally feeble; with mental faculties greatly impaired; foolish; stupid. —*n* a feeble-minded person; a fool; a dolt.

imbecility *n* the condition or quality of being imbecile.

imbibe *vt* (**imbibed, imbibing**) to drink in; to absorb; to receive or admit into the mind and retain.

imbricate *adj* formed like a bent or hollow tile; lapping over each other, like tiles on a roof or the scales of fishes and reptiles.

imbroglio *n* (*pl* **imbroglios**) an intricate and perplexing state of affairs; a misunderstanding between persons or nations of a complicated nature.

imbrue *vt* (**imbrued, imbruing**) to soak or drench in a fluid, as in blood.

imbue *vt* (**imbued, imbuing**) to soak, steep or tinge deeply; (*fig*) to inspire, impress or impregnate (the mind); to cause to become impressed or penetrated.

imitate *vt* (**imitated, imitating**) to follow as a model, pattern or example; to copy or endeavour to copy in acts, manners or otherwise; to produce a likeness of in form, colour, qualities, conduct, manners, etc; to counterfeit.

imitation *n* the act of imitating; that which is made or produced as a copy; a likeness; a copy; a counterfeit; (*mus*) the repetition of the same melodic idea by different parts or voices in a composition.

imitative *adj* inclined to imitate or copy; aiming at imitation; exhibiting an imitation of a pattern or model; formed after a model or original; intended to represent an actual sound by the sound of the letters (*an imitative word*).

imitator *n* one who imitates.

immaculate *adj* spotless; pure; unstained; undefiled; without blemish.

Immaculate Conception *n* the doctrine of the Roman Catholic Church (settled in 1854) that the Virgin Mary was conceived and born without original sin.

immanent *adj* remaining in or within; hence, not passing out of the subject; inherent and indwelling; internal or subjective, opposed to *transitive*.

immaterial *adj* not consisting of matter; incorporeal; spiritual; of no essential consequence; unimportant.

immaterialism *n* the doctrine that immaterial substances or spiritual beings exist or are possible; the doctrine that there is no material world but that all exists only in the mind.

immature *adj* not mature or ripe; unripe; not brought to a complete state; too early; premature.

immeasurable *adj* incapable of being measured.

immediacy *n* the state of being immediate; immediateness; proximity.

immediate *adj* not separated by anything intervening; placed in the closest relation; not separated by an interval of time; instant; done or occurring without delays; relating to the present time; acting without a medium or without the intervention of another object as a cause, means or condition; produced, acquired or obtained without the intervention of a medium; direct.

immediately *adv* in an immediate manner; without the intervention of anything; directly; without delay; instantly; forthwith.

immemorial *adj* beyond memory; extending beyond the reach of record or tradition.

immemorially *adv* beyond memory; from time out of mind.

immense *adj* vast in extent or bulk; very great; very large; boundless; huge; enormous.

immensity *n* the condition or quality of being immense; that which is immense; extent not to be measured; infinity.

immensurable *adj* not to be measured; immeasurable.

immerse *vt* (**immersed, immersing**) to plunge into anything that covers or surrounds, as into a fluid; to dip; (*fig*) to engage deeply; to involve (*to be immersed in business*).

immersion *n* the act of immersing or state of being immersed; a sinking or dipping into anything.

immersion heater *n* a hot-water system with an electric element inside the tank.

immesh *vt* same as **enmesh**.

immigrant *n* one who immigrates, the counterpart of *emigrant*.

immigrate *vi* (**immigrated, immigrating**) to remove into a country of which one is not a native for the purpose of permanent residence; to remove into and settle in another country.

immigration *n* the act of immigrating.

imminent *adj* hanging over; threatening to fall or occur (*imminent danger, war*); impending; near at hand; threatening evil.

immobile *adj* not mobile; immovable; fixed; stable.

immobility *n* the condition or quality of being immobile.

immoderate *adj* not moderate; exceeding just or usual bounds; excessive; extravagant; unreasonable.

immodest *adj* not modest; lacking in the reserve or restraint which decency requires; indelicate; unchaste.

immolate *vt* (**immolated, immolating**) to sacrifice; to kill, as a victim offered in sacrifice; to offer in sacrifice.

immolation *n* the act of immolating; a sacrifice offered.

immoral *adj* not moral; inconsistent with morality or rectitude; contrary to morals; wicked; unjust.

immorality *n* the quality of being immoral; an immoral act or practice.

immortal *adj* not mortal; having life that shall never end; undying; connected with immortality (*immortal hopes*); imperishable (*immortal fame*).—*n* one who is immortal, often applied to the gods of classical mythology.

immortality *n* the condition or quality of being immortal; exemption from death and annihilation; unending existence.

immortalize *vt* (**immortalized, immortalizing**) to render immortal; to make famous for ever.

immovable *adj* not movable; incapable of being moved in place; firmly fixed; fast; not to be moved from a purpose; steadfast; unalterable; unchangeable; not impressible; unfeeling.

immune *adj* proof against disease or poison; free from obligation.

immunity *n* exemption from obligation, duty, office, tax, etc; a particular privilege; freedom or exemption in general.

immunize *vt* (**immunized, immunizing**) to make immune (especially from a disease or infection by means of inoculation or vaccine).

immunology *n* the study of immunity from

disease and methods of producing this.

immure *vt* (**immured, immuring**) to enclose or imprison within walls; to shut up; to confine.

immutability, immutableness *n* the quality of being immutable.

immutable *adj* not mutable; not subject to mutation; unchangeable; invariable; unalterable.

imp *n* a young or little devil; a mischievous child.

impact *n* a collision; a violent contact; communicated force; (*mech*) the shock or collision occasioned by the meeting of two bodies; a shocking effect; an effect.

impacted *adj* pressed or forced closely together; (of a tooth) unable to emerge naturally through the gum because of an obstruction, especially the proximity of another tooth.

impair *vt* to make worse; to lessen in some good quality, as in quantity, value, excellence, strength; to deteriorate.

impale, empale *vt* (**impaled, impaling**) to fence or fortify with stakes or otherwise; to put to death by fixing on an upright sharp stake; to fix on or pierce through with something pointed; (*heral*) to join, as two coats of arms, by an upright line.

impalpable *adj* not to be felt; not easily or readily apprehended or grasped by the mind.

impanation *n* the supposed real presence in, and union of the body and blood of Christ with the bread and wine, after consecration, in the Eucharist.

impanel *vt* same as **empanel**.

imparity *n* inequality; disproportion; lack of equality; disparity.

impart *vt* to bestow a part, share or portion of; to give, grant, confer or communicate; to communicate the knowledge of; to make known; to show by words or tokens.—*vi* to give a part or share.

impartial *adj* not partial; not favouring one party more than another; unprejudiced; equitable; just.

impartiality *n* the quality of being impartial.

impartially *adv* in an impartial manner; without bias; fairly.

impassable *adj* not passable; incapable of being passed.

impasse *n* a position from which there is no escape; a deadlock.

impassioned *adj* actuated or animated by passion, ardour or warmth of feeling; animated; excited (*an impassioned orator* or *discourse*).

impassive *adj* not susceptible of pain or suffering; not exhibiting feeling or sensibility.

impatience *n* the condition or quality of being impatient.

impatient *adj* not patient; uneasy under given conditions and eager for change (followed by *of*, *at*, *for*, *under*); prompted by impatience; exhibiting or expressing impatience (*an impatient gesture*).

impeach *vt* to charge with a crime or misdemeanour; to accuse; specifically, to exhibit charges of maladministration against, as against a minister of state or other high official, before a competent tribunal; to call in question (motives, sincerity); to disparage or detract from.

impeachment *n* impediment or obstruction; the act of impeaching or state of being impeached.

impeccability *n* the condition or quality of being impeccable.

impeccable *adj* without defect or flaw; faultless.

impecuniosity *n* state of being impecunious.

impecunious *adj* not having money; hard-up; without funds.

impedance *n* the total resistance in an electric current to the flow of alternating current.

impede *vt* (**impeded, impeding**) to hinder; to stop or delay the progress of; to obstruct.

impediment *n* that which impedes; obstruction; a voice defect.

impedimenta *npl* baggage.

impel *vt* (**impelled, impelling**) to drive or urge forward; to press on; to excite to motion or action in any way.

impend *vi* to hang over; to threaten from near at hand; to be imminent.

impenetrable *adj* not penetrable; incapable of being penetrated or pierced; hence, incapable of intellectual or emotional impression; obtuse or unsympathetic.

impenitence *n* the condition of being impenitent.

impenitent *adj* not penitent; not repenting of sin; obdurate; of a hard heart.

imperative *adj* expressive of command; containing positive command; authoritative; not to be avoided or evaded; obligatory (*imperative duty*); essential; (*gram*) applied to the mood or form of a verb which expresses command, entreaty, advice or exhortation, as *go*, *write*, *attend* (in this sense often used substantively).

imperceptible *adj* not perceptible; not to be perceived; not discernible; not easily apprehended.

imperception *adj* lack of perception.

imperfect *adj* not perfect; not complete in all parts; lacking something necessary to completeness; defective; not reaching a certain standard or ideal; morally deficient or defective; not completely good; (*gram*) designating a verb tense that indicates a past action or state as incomplete or continuous.—*n* (*gram*) a tense expressing an uncompleted action or state, especially in time past.

imperfection *n* the condition or quality of being imperfect; defect; flaw; blemish.

imperfectly *adv* in an imperfect manner or degree; defectively; faultily.

imperforate *adj* not perforated or pierced; having no opening or pores.

imperial *adj* pertaining to an empire or to an emperor; pertaining to supreme authority or to one who wields it; sovereign; supreme; suitable for an emperor; of superior excellence.—*n* a tuft of hair on a man's lower lip as a style of beard.

imperialism *n* the policy of forming and maintaining an empire, as by subjugating territories, establishing colonies, etc.

imperialist *n* one favourable to empire or imperial government.

imperil *vt* (**imperilled, imperilling**) to bring into peril; to endanger.

imperious *adj* giving orders or commands in an arbitrary or absolute manner; dictatorial; haughty; arrogant; domineering; urgent, pressing or overmastering (*imperious necessity*).

imperishable *adj* not perishable; not subject to decay; indestructible; enduring permanently.

impermeable *adj* not permeable; impervious.

impersonal *adj* not having personal existence; not endued with personality; not influenced by personal feelings; not expressing personal feelings; cold; (*gram*) (of a verb) occurring only in the third person singular, usually with 'it' as the subject.—*n* that which lacks personality; (*gram*) a verb (such as *it rains*, *it becomes us to be modest*) which is used only with an impersonal nominative or subject.

impersonate *vt* (**impersonated, impersonating**) to assume the person or character of; to represent in character (as on the stage).

impersonation *n*. the act of impersonating; an instance of impersonating.

impertinence *n* the quality of being impertinent; that which is impertinent; impertinent conduct or language.

impertinent *adj* not pertinent or pertaining to the matter in hand; having no bearing on the subject; not to the point; irrelevant; presumptuous; rude; uncivil.

imperturbable *adj* incapable of being perturbed or agitated; unmoved; calm; cool.

impervious *adj* not pervious; not admitting entrance or passage; incapable of being passed through; unaffected (by); not receptive (to).

impetigo *n* (*pl* **impetigos**) (*med*) an eruption of itching pustules in clusters on the skin.

impetuosity *n* the quality of being impetuous; impetuousness; impulsiveness; rashness; hastiness.

impetuous *adj* rushing with force and violence; impulsive; hasty; rash.

impetus *n* (*pl* **impetuses**) force of motion; the force with which any body is driven or impelled; momentum.

impiety *n* the condition or quality of being impious; an act of wickedness or irreligion (in this latter sense with a plural).

impinge *vi* (**impinged, impinging**) to strike, knock or dash against; to have an effect or impact (on); to encroach (on); to strike.

impingement *n* act of impinging.

impious *adj* irreverent towards God; lacking in veneration for God and His authority; irreligious; irreverent; profane (*impious men*, *deeds*, *words*).

impiousness *n* impiety.

impish *adj* of or like an imp; mischievous.

implacable *adj* not to be appeased or pacified; inexorable; stubborn or constant in enmity.

implacability, implacableness *n* the quality of being implacable.

implant *vt* to plant; to set in soil; to insert; to fix firmly, as in the mind (*to implant truths*, *principles*, *virtue*, etc).—*n* something implanted in body tissue, as grafted tissue, a drug, etc.

implantation *n* the act of implanting.

implead *vt* to institute and prosecute a suit against in court; to sue at law.

implement *n* an instrument, tool or utensil.—*vt* to fulfil or perform; to put into effect (*to implement a bargain*); to carry out.

implicate *vt* (**implicated, implicating**) to entangle to a certain extent in some affair; to show or prove to be connected or concerned; to involve (*implicated in a conspiracy*).

implication *n* the act of implicating or state of being implicated; an implying or that which is implied but not expressed; an inference or something which may fairly be understood though not expressed in words.

implicit *adj* to be understood, though not expressed in words; implied, rather than stated explicitly (*an implicit promise*); free from doubt or questioning; unquestioning; absolute.

implode *vi* (**imploded, imploding**) to collapse inwards, usually suddenly and violently.

implore *vt* (**implored, imploring**) to call upon or for, in supplication; to beseech; to pray earnestly of someone; to entreat; to beg (*to implore forgiveness*, *to implore a person to forgive*).—*vi* to entreat; to beg.

implosion *n* the act of imploding; a collapsing inwards.

imply *vt* (**implied, implying**) to suggest in a subtle or indirect way; to hint; to include virtually (*words imply a promise*; *an effect implies a cause*); to involve logically or necessarily.

impolite *adj* not polite; uncivil; rude.

impolitic *adj* not politic; lacking policy or prudent management; unwise; imprudent; indiscreet; injudicious.

imponderable *adj* not ponderable; not able to be weighed or estimated.

import *vt* to bring into a place from abroad; to bring into one's own country, opposed to *export*; to bear or carry as a signification; to mean; to signify; to imply; to be of importance, moment or consequence to; to matter to.—*n* that which is imported or brought into a country from abroad; that which a word bears as its signification; purport; meaning; the application or interpretation of an action, of events, etc; bearing; importance, weight or consequence.

importance *n* the quality of being important; weight; consequence; moment.

important *adj* full of or bearing import, weight or consequence; momentous; weighty; material; influential; grave.

importation *n* the act or practice of importing; a quantity imported.

importunate *adj* troublesome by frequent demands; incessant in solicitation; urgent; unreasonable.

importune *vt* (**importuned, importuning**) to press with solicitation; to solicit or urge with frequent or unceasing application; to annoy with unremitting demands.—*vi* to solicit earnestly and repeatedly.

importunity *n* the quality of being importunate; application urged with troublesome pertinacity.

impose *vt* (**imposed, imposing**) to lay, set or place on (*to impose the hands*); to lay or enjoin as a burden, tax, penalty, command, law, etc; (*print*) to lay pages of type or film and secure them.—**to impose on** *or* **upon** *vi* to take advantage of; to make undue demands on.

imposing *adj* impressive in appearance; commanding; stately; majestic.

imposition *n* the act of imposing or laying on; that which is imposed, levied, inflicted, enjoined, etc; an unfair burden; a taking advantage of; (*print*) the arrangement of pages of type or film in the correct order for printing.

impossibility *n* the state or quality of being impossible; that which is impossible.

impossible *adj* not possible; not capable of being or being done; incapable of being accomplished, thought, endured, etc.

impost *n* that which is imposed or levied; a tax, tribute or duty; (*archit*) the point where an arch rests on a wall or column.

impostor *n* one who imposes on others; a person who assumes a character for the

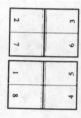

imposition

purpose of deception; a deceiver under a false character.

imposture *n* the act or conduct of an impostor; fraud or imposition.

impotence *n* the condition or quality of being impotent.

impotent *adj* entirely lacking power, strength or vigour of body or mind; deficient in capacity; weak; feeble; powerless; (of a man) unable to develop an erection in response to sexual stimuli.

impound *vt* to put in a pound (as a straying animal); to confine; to take possession of, as of a document, for use when necessary.

impoverish *vt* to make poor; to reduce to poverty or indigence; to exhaust the strength, richness or fertility of (*to impoverish land*).

impracticable *adj* not practicable; not to be performed or effected by human means or by the means at command; not to be dealt with or managed; unmanageable; incapable of being passed or travelled (*an impracticable road*).

impractical *adj* not practical; not taking a common-sense view of things; full of theories; unrealistic.

imprecation *n* the act of imprecating; a prayer that a curse or calamity may fall on any one; a curse.

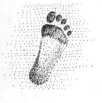

imprint

impregnable *adj* not to be taken; incapable of being reduced by force (*an impregnable fortress*); not to be moved, impressed or shaken.

impregnate *vt* (**impregnated, impregnating**) to make pregnant or with young; to cause to conceive; to transmit or infuse an active principle into; to saturate, soak (with); to imbue; to communicate qualities to by mixture.

impresario *n* (*pl* **impresarios**) a producer or manager of theatrical or musical entertainments.

impress[1] *vt* to press or stamp in or on; to mark by pressure; to make a mark or figure on; to stamp (*to impress a design on*; *to impress with a design*); to stamp on the mind; to inculcate (truth, facts, etc); to affect deeply the feelings or sentiments; to affect or influence the opinion of, especially favourably.—*n* a mark or figure made by pressure or as by pressure; stamp; impression.

impress[2] *vt* to compel to enter into public service, as a seaman; to seize and take into service by compulsion; to take for public use.—*n* the act of impressing; compulsion to serve.

impression *n* the act of impressing; that which is impressed, printed or stamped; (*print*) a copy taken by pressure from type, an engraved plate, etc; (*print*) the aggregate of copies taken at one time, edition; effect or influence on the senses, on the mind, feelings or sentiments; an indistinct notion, remembrance or belief; imitation.

impressionable *adj* susceptible of impression; having a mind or feelings easily affected.

impressionism *n* a style of painting, music or writing aimed at suggesting a mood or immediate feelings about a subject, rather than close detail or analysis.

impressionist *n* one who lays much stress on impressions; a person using the style of impressionism; a person who imitates someone or something.

impressive *adj* making or tending to make an impression; having the power of affecting or of exciting attention and feeling; arousing wonder or admiration.

imprimatur *n* a licence to print a book, etc; hence, a mark of approval in general.

imprimis *adv* in the first place; first in order.

imprint *vt* to mark by pressure; to stamp; to print; to fix indelibly or permanently, as on the mind or memory; to impress.—*n* whatever is impressed or printed; especially, the name of the printer or publisher on a book, with the place and often the time of publication; a mark made by imprinting; a lasting effect.

imprison *vt* to put into a prison; to incarcerate; to confine.

imprisonment *n* the act of imprisoning or state of being imprisoned.

improbability *n* the quality of being improbable.

improbable *adj* not probable; not likely to be true; unlikely.

improbity *n* lack of probity; lack of integrity or rectitude of principle; dishonesty.

impromptu *adv* spontaneous; unrehearsed; unprepared.—*n* a saying, poem, epigram, etc, made offhand or without previous rehearsal or preparation; an extemporaneous speech.—*adj* offhand; unrehearsed; unprepared; extempore.

improper *adj* not proper; not suitable, adapted or suited; unbecoming; indecent.

impropriety *n* the quality of being improper; that which is improper; an unsuitable act, expression, etc.

improve *vt* (**improved, improving**) to make better; to increase the value, worth or good qualities of; to use or employ to good purpose; to turn to profitable account (*to improve the time*).—*vi* to grow or become better; to advance in goodness, knowledge, wisdom or anything else desirable.

improvement *n* the act of improving or state of being improved; that which improves; that by which the value of anything is increased, its excellence enhanced, etc; a beneficial or valuable addition or alteration.

improvidence *n* the quality of being improvident.

improvident *adj* not provident; lacking foresight; lacking care to make provision for future exigencies; thriftless; thoughtless.

improvisation *n* the act or faculty of improvising; a song or other poem which is improvised.

improvise *vt* (**improvised, improvising**) to compose and recite or sing without preparation or practice; to speak extempore, especially in verse; to do or form on the spur of the moment for a special occasion; to do or create something with whatever is at hand.—*vi* to recite or sing compositions without previous preparation; to use whatever is at hand.

improviser *n* one who improvises.

imprudence *n* the quality of being imprudent; an imprudent act or course of conduct.

imprudent *adj* not prudent; lacking prudence or discretion; indiscreet; injudicious; rash; heedless.

impudence *n* the quality of being impudent; impudent language or behaviour; offensive forwardness.

impudent *adj* offensively forward in behaviour; intentionally treating others without due respect; lacking modesty; shameless; impertinent.

impugn *vt* to attack (a statement, truthfulness, etc) by words or arguments; to contradict; to call in question; to gainsay.

impulse *n* force communicated suddenly; motion produced by suddenly communicated force; thrust; push; influence acting on the mind suddenly or unexpectedly; sudden thought or determination; a sudden urge or desire; a force of infinitely large magnitude acting for an infinitely short time so as to produce a finite change of momentum.

impulsion *n* the act of impelling or state of being impelled; instigation; impulse.

impulsive *adj* having the power of impelling; actuated or liable to be actuated by impulses; tending to act on impulse; done on an impulse; rash; hasty; under the sway of one's emotions.

impunity *n* exemption from punishment or penalty; freedom or exemption from injury, suffering or loss.

impure *adj* not pure; mixed or impregnated with foul or extraneous substance; foul; obscene; unchaste; lewd; unclean; defiled by sin or guilt; unhallowed or unholy.

impurity *n* the condition or quality of being impure; foulness; that which is impure; foul matter.

imputation *n* the act of imputing; that which is imputed or charged; charge, as of evil; censure; reproach.

impute *vt* (**imputed, imputing**) to charge, attribute or ascribe; to set to the account of.

in *prep* within; inside of; surrounded by; indicating presence or situation within limits, whether of place, time or circumstances (*in the house, in the year, in sickness*), or existence as a part, constituent or quality of (*evil in a man's disposition*), or a certain state (*a vehicle in motion, to put in operation*).—*adv* in or within some place; in some state, affair or circumstances; not out (*he is in*, that is, in the house; *the Tories are in*, that is, in office; *the ship is in*, that is, in port); into some place or state, implying motion or change (*come in*, that is, into the house).—*adj* (*colloq*) fashionable; (*colloq*) popular.

inability *n* the state of being unable; lack of the necessary power or ability.

inaccessible *n* not accessible; not to be reached, obtained or approached.

inaccuracy *n* the state of being inaccurate; an inaccurate statement; a mistake in a statement; an error.

inaccurate *adj* not accurate, exact or correct; making or containing incorrect statements; not according to truth; erroneous.

inaction *n* lack of action; state of being inactive; idleness; rest.

inactive *adj* not active; inert; having no power to move; not engaged in action or effort; idle; indolent; sluggish; (*chem, med*) inoperative.

inactivity *n* the quality or condition of being inactive.

inadequacy, inadequateness *n* the state or quality of being inadequate.

inadequate *adj* not adequate; not equal to the purpose; insufficient; defective.

inadmissible *adj* not admissible; not proper to be admitted, allowed or received.

inadvertence *n* the quality of being inadvertent; an oversight, mistake or fault which proceeds from some degree of heedlessness.

inadvertent *adj* not paying strict attention; failing to notice or observe; heedless; unwary; due to oversight; unintentional.

inalienable *adj* incapable of being alienated or transferred to another; not able to be taken away.

inane *adj* empty; void; frivolous; worthless; void of sense or intelligence.

inanimate *adj* not animate; lacking life or animation; without vivacity or briskness; dull; inactive; sluggish.

inanity *n* the state of being inane; mental vacuity; silliness.

inapplicable *adj* not applicable; incapable of being applied; not suited or suitable to the purpose.

inapposite *adj* not apposite, fit or suitable; not pertinent.

inappreciable *adj* not appreciable; so small as hardly to be noticed or estimated.

inappropriate *adj* not appropriate; unsuited; unsuitable; not proper.

inapt *adj* not apt; unsuitable; unfit; not skilful.

inaptitude *n* inaptness; unfitness; unsuitableness, unsuitability.

inarch *vt* to graft by uniting to the stock without separating (for a time) the scion from its parent tree.

inarticulate *adj* not articulate; not uttered with distinctness of sounds or syllables; incapable of expressing oneself clearly or effectively; (*zool*) not jointed or articulated.

inasmuch *adv* to such a degree; in such wise; so (followed by *as*).

inattention *n* lack of attention; heedlessness.

inattentive *adj* not attentive; not fixing the mind on an object; heedless.

inaudibility *n* the quality of being inaudible.

inaudible *adj* not audible; incapable of being heard.

inaugural *adj* pertaining to an inauguration.

inaugurate *vt* (**inaugurated, inaugurating**) to introduce or induct into an office with solemnity or suitable ceremonies; to invest in a formal manner; to begin or set in progress with formality or some degree of solemnity, pomp or ceremony; to initiate; to perform in public initiatory ceremonies in connection with; to celebrate the completion of.

inauguration *n* the act of inaugurating or the ceremonies connected with such an act.

inauspicious *adj* not auspicious; ill-omened; unlucky; unfavourable.

in-between *adj* intermediate.

inboard *adj* within a ship or other vessel (*an inboard cargo*).—*adv* within the hold of a vessel; on board of a vessel.

inborn *adj* innate; implanted by nature; hereditary; present from birth.

inbred *adj* bred within; innate; natural; produced by inbreeding.

inbreed *vt* (*pret, pp* **inbred**, *ppr* **inbreeding**) to produce or generate within; to cross or mate closely related individuals.

Inca *n* a member of an American Indian people of Peru before the Spanish conquest; a prince of this people.

incalculable *adj* not calculable; beyond calculation; very great.

incandescence *n* the condition of being incandescent.

incandescent *adj* white or glowing with heat.

incantation *n* the act of using certain words and ceremonies for the purpose of raising spirits or performing magical actions; the form of words so used; a magical spell, charm or ceremony.

incapable *adj* not capable; possessing inadequate power; not admitting; not susceptible; not equal to anything; unable; unqualified or disqualified (generally followed by *of*).—*n* one physically or mentally unable to act with effect; an inefficient or silly person.

incapacitate *vt* (**incapacitated, incapacitating**) to deprive of capacity or natural power; to render or make unable or unfit; to disqualify or render incompetent.

incapacitation *n* the act of incapacitating.

incapacity *n* lack of capacity, power or ability; inability; incompetence.

incarcerate *vt* (**incarcerated, incarcerating**) to imprison; to confine in a jail; to shut up or enclose.

incarceration *n* the act of incarcerating; imprisonment.

incarnate *vt* (**incarnated, incarnating**) to clothe with flesh; to embody in flesh.—*adj* invested with flesh; embodied in flesh or a human body.

incarnation *n* the act of assuming flesh or taking a human body and the nature of humans; the state of being incarnated; a visible embodiment; a vivid exemplification in person or act (*he is the incarnation of wickedness*).

incendiarism *n* the act or practice of an incendiary.

incendiary *n* a person who wilfully and maliciously sets fire to a building, etc; one who sets fire to another's property; one who is guilty of arson; an arsonist; an incendiary substance or device; one who excites or inflames factions and promotes quarrels; an incendiary substance (as a bomb).—*adj* pertaining to wilful and malicious fireraising; relating to the starting of fires; tending to excite or inflame factions, sedition or quarrel.

incense[1] *n* the odours of spices and gums, burned in religious rites or as an offering to some deity; the materials burned for making perfumes.

incense[2] *vt* (**incensed, incensing**) to enkindle or inflame to violent anger; to excite to angry passions; to provoke, irritate, exasperate.

incentive *adj* inciting; encouraging or stirring up.—*n* that which incites or has a tendency to incite to determination or action; what prompts to good or ill; motive; spur.

inception *n* the act of beginning; a beginning; commencement; first stage.

inceptive *adj* pertaining to inception; beginning; (*gram*) applied to a verb which expresses the beginning of an action.—*n* (*gram*) an inceptive verb.

incertitude *n* uncertainty; doubtfulness; doubt.

incessant *adj* continuing without interruption; unceasing; unintermitted; uninterrupted; continual; ceaseless.

incest *n* the act of sexual intercourse between persons related within the degrees wherein marriage is prohibited by law.

incestuous *adj* guilty of incest; involving the crime of incest.

inch *n* a lineal measure, being the twelfth part of a foot, approximately 2.54 centimetres; proverbially, a small quantity or degree.—*vi* to move very slowly or by degrees.—*vt* to cause to move slowly.

inchoate *adj* recently or just begun; incipient; rudimentary; incomplete; immature.

incidence *n* the extent or frequency with which something occurs; occurrence; a falling or occurring; the manner of falling; (*physics*) the direction in which a body or a ray of light, heat, etc, falls on any surface, this direction, as regards the surface on which the body or ray falls, being called the *angle of incidence*.

incident *adj* liable to happen; apt to occur; hence, naturally happening (*ills incident to human life*); likely to happen as a result; falling or striking, as a ray of light on a surface.—*n* what happens or takes place; an event, especially a minor one; an unpleasant event, such as a fight.

incidental *adj* happening as an occasional event forming an incident; happening with or as a natural result of; accompanying, but not forming, a necessary or important part of; subsidiary; casual.

incinerate *vt* (**incinerated, incinerating**) to burn to ashes.

incineration *n* the act of incinerating.

incipient *adj* beginning; commencing; beginning to show itself.

incise *vt* (**incised, incising**) to cut into; to make a deep cut in; to carve.

incision *n* the act of cutting into a substance; that which is produced by incising; a cut; a gash; (*fig*) sharpness; trenchancy.

incisive *adj* cutting in; sharply and clearly expressive; trenchant (*incisive language* or *style*).

incisor *n* a foretooth; one of those teeth the special task of which is to cut or separate.

incite *vt* (**incited, inciting**) to move to action; to stir up; to stimulate, urge, provoke, spur on.

incitement *n* the act of inciting; that which incites or moves to action; incentive; impulse; spur; stimulus.

incivility *n* lack of courtesy; rudeness; impoliteness.

inclement *adj* not clement; unmerciful, severe or harsh; tempestuous, rough, stormy, boisterous or otherwise hard to bear (weather).

inclination *n* the act of inclining, leaning or bending; deviation from a direction regarded as the normal one; leaning; feeling in favour; propensity.

incline *vi* (**inclined, inclining**) to deviate from a direction which is regarded as normal; to bend, lean, tend; to tend, as towards an opinion, course of action, etc—*vt* to cause to deviate from a line, position or direction; to give a leaning to; to direct; to give a tendency or propensity to; to dispose; to bend, stoop or bow (the body, the head).—*n* an ascent or descent, as in a road or railway; a slope.

inclined *adj* having a disposition or tendency; disposed to; having a gradient; leaning; making an angle with a line or plane.

inclined plane *n* a plane inclined to the horizon or forming with a horizontal plane any angle except a right angle.

include *vt* (**included, including**) to confine, hold or contain; to comprise; to comprehend; to embrace or involve.

inclusion *n* the act of including.

inclusive *adj* enclosing; encircling; comprehended in the number or sum; comprehending the stated limit or extremes.

incognito *adj, adv* in disguise; in an assumed character and under an assumed name.—*n* (*fem* **incognita**) one unknown or in disguise or passing under an assumed name; assumption of a disguised or feigned character.

incoherence, incoherency *n* the quality of being incoherent.

incoherent *adj* not coherent; not cohering or attached together; unconnected (*incoherent particles*); lacking coherence or rational connection (ideas, language, etc); rambling and unintelligible.

incombustible *adj* not combustible; incapable of being burned or consumed by fire.

income *n* receipts or emoluments regularly accruing from work, investments, business operations, etc; the annual receipts derived from labour, trading or otherwise, by a person or body of persons; revenue.

incomer *n* one who comes in; a stranger, not a native.

income support *n* a kind of social security benefit paid to unemployed people who are not eligible for unemployment benefit or to certain people on low incomes.

income tax *n* a tax levied on incomes according to their amount.

incoming *adj* coming in, as an occupant (*an incoming tenant*).—*n* the act of coming in.

incommensurate *adj* not commensurate; not comparable; disproportionate; not adequate or of sufficient amount.

incommode *vt* (**incommoded, incommoding**) to give inconvenience to; to inconvenience; to put out; to trouble.

incommodious *adj* not commodious; inconvenient; tending to incommode.

incisor

incommunicable *adj* not communicable; incapable of being communicated, told or imparted to others.

incommunicado *adj, adv* without means of communication; not able or allowed to communicate with others.

incommunicative *adj* not communicative; not inclined to impart information to others; not disposed to hold communion or intercourse.

incommutable *adj* not commutable; incapable of being exchanged.

incomparable *adj* not comparable; admitting of no comparison with others; without a match, rival or peer; unequalled; transcendent.

incompatible *adj* not compatible; incapable of subsisting, of being possessed or of being made to accord with something else; incapable of existing in harmony (*feelings or tempers incompatible with each other*). —*n* a thing that is incompatible.

incompetence *n* the condition or quality of being incompetent.

incompetent *adj* not competent; lacking adequate strength, power, capacity, means, qualifications, etc; unable; incapable; inadequate; lacking necessary legal or constitutional qualifications (*an incompetent witness in a court*); not permissible or admissible (*an incompetent defence*).

incomplete *adj* not complete; not finished; imperfect; defective.

incomprehensible *adj* not comprehensible; incapable of being comprehended or understood; beyond the reach of human intellect; inconceivable.

incomprehension *n* lack of comprehension or understanding.

inconceivable *adj* not conceivable; incapable of being conceived or thought of; incomprehensible.

inconclusive *adj* not conclusive; not producing a conclusion; not settling a point in debate or a doubtful question.

incongruity *n* the quality of being incongruous; that which is incongruent; something exhibiting a lack of congruity.

incongruous *adj* not congruous; not of a kind or character to mingle well together; not such as to make a harmonious whole; not suiting each other; inharmonious; inconsistent (*incongruous parts, elements, mixtures*).

inconsequence *n* the condition or quality of being inconsequent; lack of logical sequence.

inconsequent *adj* not following from the premises; not in accordance with logical method; inconclusive.

inconsiderable *adj* not worthy of consideration or notice; unimportant; small; trivial; insignificant.

inconsiderate *adj* not considerate; not acting with due consideration; hasty; imprudent; thoughtless; heedless.

inconsistency, inconsistence *n* the condition or quality of being inconsistent; opposition or disagreement of particulars; self-contradiction; incongruity in action or conduct.

inconsistent *adj* not consistent; irreconcilable in conception or in fact; contrary; contradictory; incompatible; incongruous; not exhibiting uniformity of sentiment or conduct, steadiness to principle, etc; irregular; fickle.

inconsolable *adj* incapable of being consoled; grieved beyond consolation.

inconspicuous *adj* not conspicuous or readily noticed; not to be easily perceived.

inconstancy *n* the quality of being inconstant.

inconstant *adj* not constant; subject to change of opinion, inclination or purpose; not firm in resolution; unsteady; fickle; capricious (said of persons); mutable, changeable or variable (said of things).—*n* a thing which is not constant; a variable.

inconstantly *adv* in an inconstant manner.

incontestable *adj* not contestable; not to be disputed; too clear to be controverted; incontrovertible.

incontinence *n* the condition or quality of being incontinent.

incontinent *adj* not continent; not restraining the passions or appetites, particularly the sexual appetite; unchaste; lewd; immediate; (*med*) unable to control the excretion of bodily wastes.

incontrovertible *adj* not controvertible; too clear or certain to admit of dispute or controversy.

inconvenience *n* the quality of being inconvenient; something that incommodes or gives trouble or uneasiness.—*vt* (**inconvenienced, inconveniencing**) to put to inconvenience; to incommode.

inconvenient *adj* not convenient; giving some trouble; lacking due facilities; causing embarrassment; inopportune.

inconvertible *adj* not convertible; incapable of being converted into or exchanged for something else.

incorporate *vt* (**incorporated, incorporating**) to form into one body; to combine or mix into one mass; to unite with another body or substance; to combine or unite intimately (*to incorporate things together* or *one thing with another*); to embody or give material form to; to form into a corporation or body of individuals that can act as one.—*vi* to unite so as to form a part of another body; to be mixed or blended; to grow into (usually followed by *with*).— *adj* incorporated; united in one body.

incorporation *n* the act of incorporating or state of being incorporated; that which is incorporated; a society or body formed by the union of individuals and authorized by law to act as a single person.

incorporeal *adj* not corporeal; not consisting of matter; not having a material body; immaterial; intangible.

incorrect *adj* not correct; not exact; inexact; erroneous; faulty; not according to fact.

incorrigible *adj* incapable of being corrected or amended; bad beyond correction or reform.—*n* one who is bad beyond correction or reform.

incorrupt *adj* not corrupt or corrupted; not suffering from corruption or decay; not depraved; pure; untainted; above the influence of corruption or bribery.

incorruptible *adj* incapable of corruption, decay or dissolution; incapable of being corrupted or bribed; inflexibly upright.

increase *vi* (**increased, increasing**) to become greater; to grow; to augment; to advance; to multiply by the production of young; (*astron*) to show a gradually enlarging luminous surface; to wax (*the moon increases*).—*vt* to make greater or larger; to augment in bulk, quantity, amount or degree; to add to.—*n* augmentation; a growing greater or larger; enlargement; extension; the amount by which anything is augmented; increment; interest of money; produce; issue or offspring; (*astron*) the period of waxing, as of the moon.

incredibility *n* the quality of being incredible; that which is incredible.

incredible *adj* not credible; impossible to be believed; too extraordinary and improbable to admit of belief.

incredulous *adj* not credulous; not given to believing readily; refusing or withholding belief; sceptical.

increment *n* act or process of increasing; augmentation or growth; something added; increase; gain.

incriminate *vt* (**incriminated, incriminating**) to charge with a crime or fault; to involve or implicate in an accusation of wrongdoing.

incrust *vt* same as **encrust**.

incrustation *n* same as **encrustation**.

incubate *vi* (**incubated, incubating**) to sit on eggs for hatching; to keep at an even temperature and in a favourable environment for development, as premature babies, bacterial cultures, etc.

incubation *n* the act or process of incubating; the act of sitting on eggs for the purpose of hatching young; the length of time that it takes for an infection to develop to the stage of showing symptoms.

incubator *n* one who or that which incubates; an apparatus for hatching eggs by artificial heat; an apparatus which regulates temperature in an enclosed space; an apparatus for nurturing young babies until they can survive unaided.

incubus *n* (*pl* **incubuses, incubi**) nightmare; an imaginary being or demon, formerly supposed to be the cause of nightmare; hence, something that weighs heavily on the mind or feelings; an encumbrance of any kind; a dead weight.

inculcate *vt* (**inculcated, inculcating**) to impress by frequent admonitions; to teach and enforce by frequent repetitions; to urge on the mind.

inculpate *vt* (**inculpated, inculpating**) to show to be in fault; to accuse of crime; to impute guilt to; to incriminate, opposed to *exculpate*.

incumbency *n* the state of being incumbent; what is incumbent; (*eccles*) the state of holding or being in possession of a benefice.

incumbent *adj* lying or resting on; resting on a person as a duty or obligation to be performed; imposed and calling for performance.—*n* a person in possession of an ecclesiastical benefice or other office.

incunabulum *n* (*pl* **incunabula**) a book printed in the early times of printing; generally, a book printed before the year 1501; the earliest example of an art; (*pl*) the early stages of anything.

incur *vt* (**incurred, incurring**) to run in danger of or liability to; to expose oneself to; to become liable to; to become subject to (*to incur danger, inconvenience,* etc); to contract (*to incur a debt*).

incurable *adj* not curable; beyond the power of skill and medicine; not admitting remedy; unchangeable in attitude (*an incurable romantic*).—*n* a person diseased beyond the reach of cure.

incurious *adj* not curious or inquisitive; lacking curiosity.

incursion *n* an entering into a territory with hostile intention; an invasion not followed by continued occupation; an inroad.

incurvate *adj* curved inward or upward.—*vt* (**incurvated, incurvating**) to incurve.

incurve *vt* (**incurved, incurving**) to curve inwards; to make curved; to bend; to crook.

indebted *adj* being under a debt; having incurred a debt; held to payment or requital; obliged by something received, for which restitution or gratitude is due.

indecency *n* the quality of being indecent; what is indecent in language, actions or manners; grossness in speech or behaviour; immodesty.

indecent *adj* offending against decency; unfit to be seen or heard; offensive to modesty and delicacy; immodest; unseemly.

indecision *n* lack of decision or settled purpose; a wavering of mind; irresolution.

indecisive *adj* not decisive; not bringing to

incubate

a final close or ultimate issue; not having come to a decision; irresolute; vacillating; hesitating.

indecorous *adj* not decorous; violating decorum or propriety; unseemly; unbecoming.

indecorum *n* lack of decorum; impropriety of behaviour.

indeed *adv* in reality; in truth; in fact (sometimes used as intimating a concession or admission; sometimes interjectionally, as an expression of surprise or for the purpose of obtaining confirmation).

indefatigable *adj* incapable of being fatigued; not yielding to fatigue; unremitting in labour or effort; unwearied; untiring.

indefeasible *adj* not be defeated or made void (right, claim or title).

indefensible *adj* not defensible; incapable of being defended, vindicated or justified.

indefinable *adj* incapable of being defined; defying definition; not to be clearly explained by words.

indefinite *adj* not definite; not limited or defined; not precise or certain; having no determinate or certain limits.

indelible *adj* not to be blotted out; incapable of being effaced, cancelled or obliterated; permanent; enduring.

indelicacy *n* the condition or quality of being indelicate; a certain lack of modesty or purity of mind.

indelicate *adj* lacking delicacy; offensive to modesty or purity of mind; tending towards indecency or grossness; somewhat immodest; somewhat devoid of decency or tact.

indemnify *vt* (**indemnified, indemnifying**) to insure against loss, damage or penalty; to reimburse for expenditure made.

indemnity *n* security or exemption from damage, loss, injury or punishment; compensation or equivalent for loss, damage or injury sustained.

indent *vt* to notch, jag or cut into points or inequalities, like a row of teeth; to indenture; (*print*) to begin (a line) farther in from the margin than the rest of the paragraph.—*vi* to make an official demand for.—*n* a notch in a margin; an indentation; (*print*) the blank space at the beginning of a paragraph; (*com*) an order for goods.

index finger

indentation *n* the act of indenting; a cut or notch in a margin; an angular recess or depression like a notch in any border.

indented *adj* having notches or points like teeth on the margin; toothed; bound by indenture.

indenture *n* the act of indenting; an indentation; (*law*) a deed under seal, entered into between two or more parties, each party having a duplicate (so called from the duplicates having originally been writ-

ten on one skin, which was divided by a jagged cut, so that the correspondence of the two halves was at once manifest).

independence *n* the state of being independent; that which renders one independent; property or income sufficient to make one independent of others or of the need to work.

Independence Day *n* in the USA, the 4th day of July, 1776, and its yearly commemoration.

independent *adj* not dependent; not subject to the control of others; not relying on others (with *of* before an object); not subordinate; affording the means of independence (*an independent fortune*); moderately wealthy; acting and thinking for oneself; not swayed by bias or influence; self-directing; proceeding from or expressive of a spirit of independence (*an independent air* or *manner*).—*adv* irrespective; without taking note or regard; not to make mention (with *of*).—*n* a person who is independent in thinking, action, etc, especially in politics.

in-depth *adj* detailed; thorough.

indescribable *adj* not describable; incapable of being described.

indestructible *adj* not destructible; incapable of being destroyed.

indeterminable *adj* incapable of being determined, ascertained or fixed; not to be determined or ended; interminable.

indeterminate *adj* not determinate; not settled or fixed; not definite; uncertain; not precise; (*math*) applied to problems which have an indefinite number of solutions, not arbitrary but correlated; (*law*) (of a sentence) making the imprisonment or release of the prisoner dependent on his or her conduct and amendment.

index *n* (*pl* **indexes** *or* **indices**) something that points out, shows, indicates or manifests; a pointer or hand that points or directs to anything; a chart or table of relative levels of wages, prices, etc; a table of the contents of a book in alphabetical order; (*anat*) the forefinger; (*math*) the figure or letter which shows to what power any quantity is evolved; the exponent.—*vt* to provide with an index; to place in an index; to adjust wages, etc, to increases in the cost of living.

index finger *n* the forefinger.

Index Librorum Prohibitorum *n* Index of Prohibited Books, a catalogue of books which are forbidden by the Roman Catholic Church to be read by the faithful.

index-linked *adj* of wages, pensions, etc, directly linked to the cost-of-living index.

Indian *adj* pertaining to India or to either of the Indies, East or West; pertaining to American Indians; made of maize or Indian corn (*Indian meal*)—*n* a native of India or of the Indies, West or East; an American Indian, an Amerindian.

Indian corn *n* maize.

Indian file *n* single file; arrangement of persons in a line following one after another.

Indian ink *n* a black ink, originally from China and Japan.

Indian summer *n* a season of pleasant warm weather occurring late in autumn.

india-rubber *n* a former name for rubber; a piece of rubber or similar material used for erasing pencil marks.

indicate *vt* (**indicated, indicating**) to point out; to show; to direct the mind to a knowledge of; to intimate.

indication *n* the act of indicating or pointing out; what serves to indicate or point out; intimation; mark; token; sign; symptom.

indicative *adj* pointing out or indicating; serving as an indication; giving intimation or knowledge of (*movements indicative of uneasiness*); (*gram*) applied to that mood of the verb that declares directly or that asks questions.—*n* (*gram*) the indicative mood.

indicator *n* one who or that which indicates; a recording instrument of various kinds; a measuring device with a point, etc; an instrument showing the operating condition of a piece of machinery; a flashing light giving warning of a change of direction of a vehicle; a device giving updated information, such as a departure or arrival board at a railway station or airport; in ecology, a plant species that exists only in certain soil conditions and so indicates where those conditions are to be found; (*chem*) a substance used to indicate by changes of colour the condition of a solution as to acidity and alkalinity.

indict *vt* to accuse or charge with a crime or misdemeanour in due form of law.

indictable *adj* capable of being or liable to be indicted; that may bring an indictment on one (*an indictable offence*).

indictment *n* the act of indicting; a formal accusation or charge against a person; a written accusation.

indifference *n* the state or quality of being indifferent; absence of feeling or interest; unconcern; apathy; mediocrity.

indifferent *adj* not inclined to one side more than to another; impartial; unbiased; feeling no interest, anxiety or care; unconcerned; careless; having no difference that gives a preference; of no account or moment; neither very good nor very bad but rather bad than good; middling; tolerable.—formerly often used adverbially (*indifferent honest*).

indigence *n* the condition of being indigent; penury; poverty.

indigenous *adj* originating or produced naturally in a country or climate; native; not foreign or exotic.

indigent *adj* lacking the means of comfortable subsistence; needy; poor.

indigestible *adj* not digestible; digested with difficulty.

indigestion *n* incapability of or difficulty in digesting food; dyspepsia.

indignant *adj* displeased at what is unworthy or base; angry at something unjust, etc; affected with indignation.

indignation *n* a feeling of displeasure at what is unworthy or base; a feeling of anger at what is regarded as unjust, etc.

indignity *n* an action towards another which shows contempt for him or her or design to lower his or her dignity; an insult; an affront; an outrage; a blow to the pride, etc.

indigo *n* (*pl* **indigos, indigoes**) a blue dye, formerly extracted from plants; any of the plants yielding the dye; a dark-blue or purplish-blue colour now made artificially.

indirect *adj* not direct; deviating from a direct line or course; circuitous; not tending directly to an aim or end; roundabout; not open and straightforward; not resulting directly; having something interposed.

indiscernible *adj* incapable of being discerned; not discernible.

indiscreet *adj* not discreet; lacking in discretion or sound judgment; injudicious; inconsiderate.

indiscreetness *n* the quality of being indiscreet.

indiscretion *n* the condition or quality of being indiscreet; lack of discretion; an indiscreet act; an ill-judged act.

indiscriminate *adj* without discrimination or distinction; not making any distinction; not making a careful choice; random.

indiscrimination *n* lack of discrimination.

indispensability, indispensableness *n* the quality of being indispensable.

indispensable *adj* incapable of being dispensed with; absolutely necessary; essential.

indispose *vt* (**indisposed, indisposing**) to disincline; to render unfit or unsuited; to make unwell; to affect with indisposition.

indisposed *adj* not disposed; disinclined; averse; slightly unwell.

indisposition *n* the state of being indisposed; disinclination; a slight illness.

indisputable *adj* incapable of being disputed; incontrovertible; incontestable.

indissoluble *adj* not capable of being dissolved; not capable of being broken or rightfully violated; perpetually binding or obligatory (agreement, ties, etc); firm; stable.

indistinct *adj* not distinct; not readily distinguishable; faint to the sight; obscure to the mind; not clear; confused; imperfect or dim (*indistinct vision*).

Indian ink

indistinguishable *adj* incapable of being distinguished; not distinguishable; lacking identifying characteristics.

indite *vt* (**indited, inditing**) to compose or write; to direct, prompt or dictate.—*vi* to compose; to write; to pen.

individual *adj* subsisting as one indivisible entity or distinct being; single; one; pertaining to one only; peculiar to or characteristic of a single person or thing; distinctive.—*n* a being or thing forming one of its kind; a single person, animal or thing; especially, a human being; a person.

individualism *n* the quality of being individual; individuality; a system or condition in which each individual works for his or her own ends, in either social, political or religious matters; independence of thought and action.

individualistic *adj* pertaining to or characterized by individualism; showing independence of thought and action.

individuality *n* the condition of being individual; existence as an individual; oneness; distinctive character; the sum of the characteristics or traits peculiar to an individual.

individualize *vt* (**individualized, individualizing**) to mark as an individual; to distinguish by peculiar or distinctive characters.

individually *adv* in an individual manner; separately; each by itself; in a distinctive manner.

indivisible *adj* not divisible; not separable into parts.—*n* that which is indivisible.

indoctrinate *vt* (**indoctrinated, indoctrinating**) to instruct in any doctrine; to imbue or cause to imbibe certain principles; to instruct.

Indo-European *adj* a term applied to that family of languages which includes Sanskrit and the kindred tongues of India and Persia, Greek, Latin and the Romance tongues, the Germanic, Celtic and Slavonic tongues.—*n* an Aryan.

indolence *n* the condition or quality of being indolent; laziness; sloth.

indolent *adj* habitually idle or indisposed to labour; lazy; slothful; sluggish; idle (person, life); (*med*) causing little or no pain (*an indolent tumour*).

indomitable *adj* not to be tamed or subdued; unconquerable; untameable.

indoor *adj* being within doors; domestic (*an indoor servant*).

indoors *adv* within doors; inside a house.

indubitable *adj* too plain to admit of doubt; incontestable; unquestionable.

induce *vt* (**induced, inducing**) to lead by persuasion or argument; to prevail on; to impel; to bring on, produce, cause (*an ailment induced by cold*).

inducement *n* the act of inducing; that which induces or leads one to act; a mo-

tive; a consideration that leads to action.

induct *vt* to bring in or introduce; to introduce, as to a benefice or office; to put in possession of an ecclesiastical living or any other office.

inductance *n* the property of an electric circuit by which an electromotive force is produced by a variation in the current in the same or a neighbouring circuit.

induction *n* the act of inducting; introduction; the introduction of a clergyman into a benefice or of a person into an office, with the customary forms and ceremonies; in logic, the method of reasoning from particulars to generals; the deriving of a general principle or conclusion from particular facts, as that heat expands bodies, from observing its effect in particular cases; the conclusion or inference thus drawn or arrived at; (*mech*) that part of the cycle of an internal-combustion engine during which the fuel or air charge is drawn into the cylinder; (*physics*) the property by which one body, having electrical, galvanic or magnetic polarity, causes or induces it in another body without direct contact.

inductive *adj* proceeding by induction; employed in drawing conclusions by induction; (*elect*) able to produce electricity by induction; operating by induction; facilitating induction.

indue *vt* same as **endue**.

indulge *vt* (**indulged, indulging**) to give oneself up to; not to restrain or oppose; to give free course to (*to indulge the passions*); to gratify by compliance; to humour to excess (*to indulge children*).—*vi* to indulge oneself; to practise indulgence; to be self-indulgent (*to indulge in pleasure*); (*colloq*) to drink alcohol.

indulgence *n* the act or practice of indulging; an indulgent act; favour granted; intemperance in eating and drinking; readiness to forgive faults; tolerance; (*RC Church*) remission, by church authority, to a repentant sinner, of the penance attached to certain sins.

indulgent *adj* prone to indulge or humour; overcompliant; not strict.

indurate *vi* (**indurated, indurating**) to grow hard; to harden or become hard.—*vt* to make hard; to harden; to make unfeeling; to render obdurate.

indusium *n* (*pl* **indusia**) (*bot*) a collection of united hairs forming a sort of cup enclosing the stigma of a flower; the immediate covering of the capsules or spore cases in ferns.

industrial *adj* relating to or engaged in industry; used in industry.

industrious *adj* given to or characterized by industry or diligence; always working at something; assiduous.

industry *n* habitual diligence in any employment; steady attention to work or business; assiduity; any productive occupation, especially one in which considerable numbers of people are employed; organized production or manufacture of goods; manufacturing enterprises collectively; a branch of commercial enterprise producing a particular product.

inebriate *vt* (**inebriated, inebriating**) to make drunk; to intoxicate.—*n* an habitual drunkard.—*adj* inebriated.

inebriation *n* the act of inebriating or state of being inebriated.

inebriety *n* drunkenness; intoxication.

ineffable *adj* incapable of being expressed in words; beyond expression.

ineffective *adj* incapable of producing any effect or the effect intended; inefficient; useless; impotent; lacking energy.

ineffectual *adj* not effectual; futile; not producing the intended result.

inefficacious *adj* not efficacious; not producing the effect desired; of inadequate power.

inefficacy *n* lack of efficacy; ineffectualness; failure of effect.

inefficiency *n* the condition or quality of being inefficient.

inefficient *adj* not efficient; wasteful of resources; incapable of effective action; incompetent.

inelegance *n* the condition or quality of being inelegant; an inelegant point or feature.

inelegant *adj* not elegant; lacking in elegance; lacking in anything which correct taste requires.

ineligible *adj* not eligible; not capable of or fit for being elected or adopted; not worthy to be chosen or preferred, especially of a suitor.

inept *adj* unsuitable; awkward; clumsy; foolish; inefficient.

ineptitude, ineptness *n* the condition or quality of being inept; awkwardness; foolishness; unfitness.

inequality *n* the condition or quality of being unequal in status, size, etc; disparity; unevenness; lack of levelness; an elevation or a depression of a surface.

inequitable *adj* not equitable; not just or fair.

inequity *n* unfairness; injustice.

ineradicable *adj* incapable of being eradicated.

inert *adj* lacking the power of moving itself or of active resistance to motion impressed; not moving or acting; indisposed to move or act; sluggish; inactive.

inert gas, noble gas *n* any of the gaseous elements helium, neon, argon, krypton, xenon, which are chemically inert, not combining with any other elements.

inertia *n* passiveness; inactivity; inertness; sluggishness; (*physics*) the property of matter by which it retains its state of rest or of uniform rectilinear motion so long as no foreign cause occurs to change that state.

inessential *adj* not essential; unessential.

inestimable *adj* incapable of being estimated or computed; too valuable or excellent to be rated or fully appreciated; incalculable.

inestimably *adv* in a manner not to be estimated.

inevitability, inevitableness *n* unavoidableness; certainty.

inevitable *adj* incapable of being avoided; unavoidable; admitting of no escape or evasion; certain to befall.

inevitably *adv* unavoidably; certainly.

inexact *adj* not exact; not precisely correct or true.

inexcusable *adj* incapable of being excused or justified; unpardonable; indefensible.

inexhaustible *adj* not exhaustible; incapable of being exhausted or spent; unfailing.

inexorable *adj* incapable of being moved by entreaty or prayer; too firm and determined to yield to supplication; unyielding; unbending; implacable; unstoppable.

inexpedience, inexpediency *n* the condition or quality of being inexpedient.

inexpedient *adj* not expedient; inappropriate; unsuitable to time and place; not advisable.

inexpiable *adj* incapable of being expiated; not to be atoned for; unpardonable.

inexplicable *adj* incapable of being explained or interpreted; unaccountable; mysterious.

inexpressible *adj* not expressible; not to be uttered; unspeakable; unutterable.

inexpressive *adj* not expressive; lacking in expression; inexpressible; ineffable.

inextinguishable *adj* incapable of being extinguished; (of flame, thirst, desire) unquenchable.

inextricable *adj* incapable of being extricated or disentangled; not permitting extrication.

infallibility *n* the quality of being infallible.

infallible *adj* not fallible; not capable of erring or falling into error; not leading into error; perfectly reliable; certain (*infallible testimony*).

infamous *adj* having a reputation of the worst kind; scandalous; notoriously vile; shameful; branded with infamy.

infamy *n* total loss of reputation; public disgrace; bad or disgraceful repute; shamefulness; disgracefulness; scandalousness; extreme baseness or vileness.

infancy *n* the state of being an infant; the beginning or early existence of anything; earliest period of life.

infant *n* a child during the first two or three

infant

years of its life.—*adj* pertaining to infancy.

infanta *n* formerly, in Spain and Portugal, any princess of the royal blood.

infante *n* formerly in Spain and Portugal, any son of the king, except the eldest.

infanticide *n* the murder and also the murderer of an infant; child murder.

infantile *adj* pertaining to or characteristic of infancy or an infant; babyish; childish.

infantile paralysis *n* poliomyelitis.

infantry *n* the soldiers or troops that serve on foot, as distinguished from *cavalry*.

infarct, infarction *n* an area of dead tissue resulting from an interruption in blood flow to the affected region, as from a blood clot.

infatuate *vt* (**infatuated, infatuating**) to inspire with an intense, foolish and short-lived passion that cannot be controlled.

infatuation *n* the act of infatuating or state of being infatuated; intense, foolish and short-lived passion.

infect *vt* to taint with disease; to contaminate; to communicate bad qualities to; to corrupt.

infection *n* the act or process of infecting; that which infects (as distinguished from *contagion*, it does not imply actual contact, as the latter properly does).

infectious *adj* capable of infecting; likely to communicate disease; contagious; corrupting or contaminating; easily spread from person to person.

infectious hepatitis *n* an infectious disease which causes inflammation of the liver.

infectious mononucleosis *n* glandular fever.

infelicitous *adj* not felicitous; unhappy; unfortunate; ill-timed; (of writing) awkward, clumsy, tactless.

infelicity *n* the state of being unhappy; unhappiness; misery; unfavourableness.

infer *vt* (**inferred, inferring**) to gather or derive either by induction or deduction; to deduce, as a fact or consequence; to conclude or arrive at by reasoning.

inference *n* the act of inferring; conclusion drawn or inferred; deduction; consequence.

inferior *adj* lower in place, station, rank, value, importance, etc; subordinate; poor in quality.—*n* a person who is inferior to another or lower in station, rank, intellect, importance, etc.

inferiority *n* the condition of being inferior.

inferiority complex *n* an acute sense of inferiority expressed by an extreme lack of self-confidence and sometimes by extreme aggression or the adoption of a superior manner towards others.

infernal *adj* pertaining to the lower regions or regions of the dead; pertaining to hell; inhabiting hell; characteristic or worthy of

hell or the inhabitants of hell; hellish; diabolical; wicked and detestable.

inferno *n* (*pl* **infernos**) hell; intense heat; a terrible, destructive fire.

infest *vt* to make hostile attacks or depredations on; to overrun in large numbers (particularly of persistent, vermin, lice, cockroaches, etc); to harass, torment, disturb, annoy.

infidel *n* a disbeliever; a sceptic; one who does not believe in God or in Christianity or has no religious faith; an atheist; any one regarded as not holding the true faith, especially one opposed to the tenets of Islam.—*adj* unbelieving; sceptical.

infidelity *n* lack of faith or belief; atheism or disbelief in God; lack of religious faith; unbelief; scepticism; unfaithfulness in married persons; adultery; unfaithfulness to a charge or moral obligation; treachery; deceit.

infighting *n* in boxing, the exchange of punches at close quarters; intense competition or quarrelling within a group or organization.

infiltrate *vi* (**infiltrated, infiltrating**) to enter by penetrating the pores or interstices of a substance; to filter or pass gradually through or into; to penetrate gradually or stealthily (especially a clandestine or illegal organization).

infiltration *n* the process of infiltrating; that which infiltrates.

infinite *adj* not finite; without limits; not limited or circumscribed in time, space, etc; exceedingly great in excellence, degree, capacity, etc; boundless; limitless; immeasurable.—*n* that which is infinite; an infinite space or extent.

infinitesimal *adj* infinitely or indefinitely small; less than any assignable quantity.—*n* (*math*) a variable quantity which is imagined to become smaller and smaller without limit.

infinitive *adj* not limiting or restricting; (*gram*) applied to that mood of a verb which expresses the action of the verb without limitation of person or number.—*n* (*gram*) the infinitive mood.

infinity *n* unlimited extent of time, space, quantity, excellence, energy, etc; boundlessness; endless or indefinite number.

infirm *adj* not firm or sound; weak as regards the body; feeble; ill; not steadfast; irresolute; not solid or stable.

infirmary *n* a hospital; a place where the infirm or sick, or those suffering from accidents, are lodged and nursed or have their ailments attended to.

infirmity *n* the state of being infirm; an unsound or unhealthy state of the body; a disease; a malady; an ailment, weakness, failing, defect, foible.

in flagrante delicto *adv* in the very act of

committing a crime, offence or misdemeanour.

inflame *vt* (**inflamed, inflaming**) to set on
fire; to kindle; to redden or make fiery (the
eyes, the face); to excite or increase, as
passion or appetite; to rouse into violent
action; to enrage or exasperate; (*med*) to
make abnormally hot, red and swollen.—
vi to take fire; to grow angry; to grow hot
and painful.

inflammable *adj* capable of being set on
fire; easily kindled; combustible.

inflammation *n* the act of inflaming; (*med*)
a redness and swelling of any part of the
body, attended with heat, pain and febrile
symptoms.

inflammatory *adj* tending to inflame; tending to excite inflammation; tending to excite anger, animosity, etc; producing abnormal heat, redness and swelling in a part
of the body.

inflate *vt* (**inflated, inflating**) to swell or
distend by injecting air; to puff up; to
elate, as with pride; to raise above the real
value or value according to sound commercial principles (*inflated prices*).

inflated *adj* distended with air; puffed up;
turgid; tumid; bombastic (*an inflated style
of writing*); (of prices, the economy, etc)
having been inflated.

inflation *n* the act of inflating; the state of
being inflated; in economics, a general rise
in prices and fall in the value of money,
which may have various causes; such an
increase in the amount of currency in circulation, higher wages, unmatched by
higher productivity, etc.

inflationary *n* of, pertaining to or causing
inflation.

inflect *vt* to bend; to turn from a direct line
or course; to modulate (the voice); (*gram*)
to go over the inflections of; to decline or
conjugate.

inflection, inflexion *n* the act of inflecting
or the state of being inflected; modulation
or rise and fall of the voice; in optics, deflection or diffraction; (*gram*) the variation of nouns, etc, by declension and of
verbs by conjugation; (*math*) change of
the curvature of a curve from convex to
concave, or vice versa.

inflexible *adj* incapable of being bent; firm
in purpose; not to be prevailed on; incapable of being turned from a purpose; inexorable; unalterable; unyielding.

inflict *vt* to cause to bear or suffer from; to
cause to feel or experience; to impose
(pain, disgrace, punishment).

infliction *n* the act of inflicting or imposing;
that which is inflicted.

inflorescence *n* (*bot*) a mode of flowering
or the manner in which blossoms are arranged and supported on their foot stalks
or peduncles.

influence *n* a flowing in, into or upon;
agency or power serving to affect, modify
or sway in some way; ability or power sufficient to produce some effect; sway;
power or authority arising from elevated
station, wealth, etc; acknowledged ascendancy with people in power.—*vt* (**influenced, influencing**) to exercise influence
on; to modify or affect in some way; to act
on; to bias; to sway.

influential *adj* exerting influence, physical
or other; possessing power or influence.

influenza *n* an infectious viral disease causing symptoms such as fever, sneezing, catarrh, aching muscles, headache, etc, often
shortened to **flu**.

influx *n* the act of flowing in; infusion; a
coming in; introduction; importation in
abundance (*an influx of money*); the point
at which one stream runs into another or
into the sea.

infold *vt* same as **enfold**.

inform *vt* to animate; to communicate
knowledge to; to instruct; to tell, acquaint,
apprise (*to inform a person of something*).
—*vi* to give information, especially to the
police, often in accusing another.

informal *adj* not in the regular or usual
form; not in accordance with official, conventional or customary forms; without
ceremony; casual; (of speech) characteristic of ordinary conversation; colloquial.

informant *n* one who informs; a person
who gives information.

information *n* the act of informing; news or
intelligence communicated by word or
writing; intelligence; knowledge derived
from reading or instruction or gathered in
any way; data stored in or retrieved from a
computer; a statement of facts laid before
a court of justice.

information technology *n* technology relating to the gathering, recording, storing,
use and retrieval of information by electronic means, as by computer.

informer *n* one who informs; an accomplice who in order to escape punishment
gives evidence against another or others;
one who makes a business of informing
against others.

infraction *n* the act of infringing; breach;
violation; infringement.

infrangible *adj* not capable of being broken; not to be violated or infringed.

infrared *adj* the part of the spectrum lying
beyond the visible spectrum on the side of
the red.

infrastructure *n* the basic structure of any
system or organization; the basic installations, such as roads, railways, factories,
etc, that determine the economic power of
a country.

infrequence, infrequency *n* state of being
infrequent; rare occurrence.

447

infrequent *adj* not frequent; seldom happening or occurring; rare.

infrequently *adv* not frequently; seldom; rarely.

infringe *vt* (**infringed, infringing**) to break, as laws or contracts; to violate; to contravene; to impair or encroach on.—*vi* to encroach (followed by *on* or *upon*).

infringement *n* act of infringing or violating.

infuriate *vt* (**infuriated, infuriating**) to render furious or mad; to enrage.—*adj* enraged; mad; raging.

infuse *vt* (**infused, infusing**) to pour in as a liquid; to pour; to shed; to instil, as principles or qualities; to fill or inspire with; to introduce; to diffuse; to steep in liquor without boiling, in order to extract the essence.

infusion *n* the act or process of infusing; that which is infused or instilled; liquor obtained by infusing or steeping.

ingathering *n* the act of gathering in; the collecting and securing of the fruits of the earth; harvest.

ingeminate *vt* (**ingeminated, ingeminating**) to double or repeat.—*adj* redoubled; repeated.

ingemination *n* repetition; reduplication.

ingenious *adj* possessed of cleverness or ability; having the faculty of invention; skilful or prompt to invent; apt in contriving or forming new combinations of ideas; contrived with ingenuity; of curious design, structure or mechan ; witty or well-conceived (*an ing   s compliment*).

ingenue *n* an innocent youn   man, especially as represented by   ctress on a stage.

ingenuity *n* the quality or power of being ingenious; ready invention; skill in contrivance.

ingenuous *adj* honourable, noble or generous; open, frank or candid; free from reserve, disguise, equivocation or dissimulation; innocent; naive.

ingenuousness *n* the condition or quality of being ingenuous; openness of heart; frankness; innocence; naiveté.

inglorious *adj* not glorious; without renown; obscure; bringing disgrace rather than glory; disgraceful; ignominious.

ingoing *n* the act of entering; entrance.—*adj* going in; entering, as an office or position.

ingot *n* a mass or wedge of gold or silver cast in a mould; a mass of unworked metal.

ingraft *vt* same as **engraft**.

ingrain, engrain *vt* to fix firmly on; to make a deep impression on.

ingrate *n* an ungrateful person.

ingratiate *vt* (**ingratiated, ingratiating**) to introduce or commend to another's goodwill, confidence or kindness (always reflexive); to try to get into another's favour.

ingratitude *n* lack of gratitude; insensibility to favours and lack of a disposition to repay them; unthankfulness.

ingredient *n* that which enters into a compound or is a component part of any compound or mixture; one of the parts of a mixture, as of a mixture to be cooked; an element, component or constituent.

ingress *n* entrance; power or liberty of entrance; means of entering.—*vi* to go in or enter.

ingrowing *adj* (of a toe nail, etc) growing abnormally into the flesh.

inguinal *adj* pertaining to the groin.

ingulf *vt* same as **engulf**.

ingurgitate *vt* (**ingurgitated, ingurgitating**) to swallow eagerly or in great quantity.—*vi* to drink largely; to swill.

inhabit *vt* to live or dwell in; to occupy as a place of settled residence.—*vi* to dwell; to live; to abide.

inhabitable *adj* capable of being inhabited; habitable.

inhabitant *n* one who inhabits; one who dwells or resides permanently in a place, as distinguished from an occasional visitor.

inhalation *n* the act of inhaling.

inhale *vt* (**inhaled, inhaling**) to draw into the lungs; to breathe in; to suck in.

inharmonious *adj* not harmonious; discordant.

inhere *vi* (**inhered, inhering**) to exist or be fixed in; to be inherent; to belong, as attributes or qualities, to a subject.

inherence, inherency *n* the state of inhering; existence in something.

inherent *adj* inhering; inseparable; naturally pertaining; existing in something as a permanent and inseparable element, quality or attribute; inborn; innate.

inherently *adv* in an inherent manner.

inherit *vt* to receive or obtain by descent from an ancestor; to take by being the heir; to receive from a progenitor as part of one's nature; to come into possession of; to hold as belonging to one's lot.—*vi* to take an inheritance; to take the position of heir or heirs.

inheritable *adj* capable of being inherited; capable of being transmitted from parent to child.

inheritance *n* that which is or may be inherited; an estate derived or to be derived from an ancestor or relation to his or her heir; a possession received by gift or without purchase.

inheritor *n* one who inherits or may inherit; an heir.

inhibit *vt* to restrain by command or interdict; to hinder; to forbid, prohibit or inter-

ingot

dict; to repress; (*physiol*, *psychol*) to check or stop one mental or nervous process by another opposing process.

inhibition *n* the act of inhibiting; prohibition; a legal writ inhibiting a judge from further proceeding in a case; the act or process of inhibiting; the restraint of will over impulse; a mental process that restrains or represses an action, emotion or thought.

inhospitable *adj* not hospitable; lacking in hospitality; hence, affording no subsistence or shelter to strangers (*inhospitable shores*).

inhuman *adj* lacking the kindness and tenderness that belong to human beings; cruel; barbarous; savage; unfeeling.

inhumanity *n* the state of being inhuman.

inhumation *n* the act of burying; interment.

inimical *adj* unfriendly; hostile; adverse; hurtful (*inimical to commerce*).

inimitable *adj* incapable of being imitated or copied; surpassing imitation; unique.

iniquitous *adj* characterized by iniquity; unjust; wicked; unrighteous.

iniquity *n* lack of equity; a deviation from rectitude; unrighteousness; a sin or crime; wickedness; an act of injustice.

initial *adj* placed at the beginning (*an initial letter*); of or pertaining to the beginning; beginning; incipient.—*n* the first letter of a word (a person's initials are the first letters in proper order of the words composing his or her name).—*vt* (**initialled, initialling**) to put one's initials on or to; to sign or mark by initials.

initially *adv* in an initial manner; by way of beginning.

initiate *vt* (**initiated, initiating**) to begin or enter on; to set afoot; to be the first to practise or bring in; to guide or direct by instruction in rudiments or principles; to let into secrets; to introduce into a society or organization; to admit.—*adj* initiated; introduced to the knowledge of something.

initiation *n* the act or process of initiating.

initiative *adj* serving to initiate; initiatory.—*n* an introductory act or step; the first active procedure in any enterprise; power of taking the lead or of originating.

initiatory *adj* pertaining to initiation or introduction; introductory; initiating or serving to initiate.

inject *vt* to throw in; to cast in or into; to introduce fluid into the body, a cavity, etc; to introduce into.

injection *n* the act of injecting; the introduction of a liquid medicine into the body by a syringe or pipe; that which is injected.

injudicious *adj* not judicious; acting without judgment; not according to sound judgment or discretion; unwise; indiscreet; inconsiderate.

injunction *n* the act of enjoining or directing; that which is enjoined; a command, order, precept; (*law*) a writ requiring a person to do or refrain from doing certain acts.

injure *vt* (**injured, injuring**) to do harm or injury to; to impair the excellence, value, strength, etc, of; to hurt; to damage.

injurious *adj* tending to injure; hurtful; harmful; prejudicial.

injury *n* the doing of harm; harm or damage occasioned; a wrong or loss received; mischief; detriment.

injustice *n* lack of justice or equity; any violation of another's rights; iniquity; wrong.

ink *n* a coloured liquid used for writing, printing, etc; a pigment, as Indian ink.—*vt* to blacken, colour or daub with ink.

inkhorn *n* a small vessel used to hold ink on a writing table or desk.

inkling *n* a hint or whisper; an intimation.

inkstand *n* a vessel for holding ink and other writing utensils.

inkwell *n* an ink bottle fitted into a hole in the top of a writing desk.

inky *adj* consisting of ink; containing ink; smeared with ink; resembling ink; black.

inland *adj* interior; remote from the sea; carried on within a country; domestic, not foreign; confined to a country; drawn and payable in the same country (*an inland bill of exchange*).—*adv* in or towards the interior of a country.—*n* the interior part of a country.

Inland Revenue *n* in the UK, the revenue raised by taxes or duties on commodities or products made in the country or services provided, as opposed to customs duties on imported goods; the department in charge of raising this.

in-law *n* (*pl* **in-laws**) a relative by marriage.

inlay *vt* (*pret*, *pp* **inlaid**, *ppr* **inlaying**) to lay or insert in; to ornament or diversify by inserting precious stones, metals, fine woods, ivory, etc, in a groundwork of some other material.—*n* pieces inlaid and forming a pattern.

inlet *n* a passage or opening by which an enclosed place may be entered; place of ingress; entrance; a creek or narrow recess in a shore.

inmate *n* one of the occupants of a mental hospital, prison, etc

in memoriam in memory of.

inmesh *vt* same as **enmesh**.

inmost *adj* farthest within; remotest from the surface or external part.

inn *n* a public house or small hotel providing accommodation; a tavern.

innards *npl* (*colloq*) the internal parts of anything, especially the body.

innate *adj* inborn; belonging to the body or mind by nature; natural; derived from the constitution of the mind, as opposed to being derived from experience (*innate ideas*).

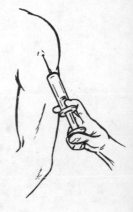

injection

injury

449

inner *adj* interior; farther inward than something else; internal; not outward (*the inner person*); not obvious; esoteric.—*n* the ring on a rifle target next the bull's-eye; a shot that strikes the target between the bull's-eye and this ring.

innermost *adj* farthest inward; deepest.

innings *npl* in cricket, the time or turn for using the bat, whether in the case of an individual player or of a side; a turn or period of some activity.

innkeeper *n* the keeper of an inn; a publican or hotel-keeper.

innocence *n* the quality of being innocent; harmlessness; freedom from crime, guilt or sin; freedom from the guilt of a particular crime.

innocent *adj* not noxious or hurtful; harmless; free from guilt; not having done wrong or violated any law; guiltless; sinless; pure; upright; free from the guilt of a particular crime or evil action.—*n* one free from guilt or harm; an innocent person; a simpleton.

innocuous *adj* harmless; producing no ill effect.

innovate *vt* (**innovated, innovating**) to change or alter by introducing something new.—*vi* to introduce novelties; to make changes in anything established.

innovation *n* the act of innovating; change made in established laws, customs, rites and practices by the introduction of something new; something new or different which is introduced.

innuendo *n* (*pl* **innuendoes**) an oblique hint; an intimation; an insinuation.

Innuit *n* same as **Inuit**.

innumerable *adj* incapable of being enumerated or numbered for multitude; hence, extremely numerous; countless.

innumerably *adv* without number.

inoculate *vt* (**inoculated, inoculating**) to graft by inserting a bud; to bud; (*med*) to introduce a mild form of a disease to so as to produce immunity, as by deliberately introducing a virus or bacteria into the body; to inject a vaccine or serum into, especially in order to create immunity.—*vi* to practise inoculation.

inoculation *n* the act or practice of inoculating; an injection of serum or vaccine.

inodorous *adj* lacking scent; having no smell.

inoffensive *adj* giving no offence or provocation; harmless; doing no injury or mischief.

inoperative *adj* not operative; not functioning; producing no effect.

inopportune *adj* not opportune; inconvenient; unseasonable.

inordinate *adj* excessive; immoderate; not limited by rules prescribed or usual boundaries.

inorganic *adj* having no organs; devoid of an organized structure or the structure of a living being; pertaining to or embracing the department of unorganized substances (*inorganic chemistry*).

input *n* what is put in, as data into a computer, power into a machine, etc.—*vt* (*pret, pp* **input** or **inputted**, *ppr* **inputting**) to put in; to enter (data) into a computer.

inquest *n* the act of inquiring; inquiry; search; quest; (*law*) a judicial inquiry, especially an inquiry held before a jury or by a coroner, especially into a case of violent or unexplained death; the jury itself; (*colloq*) any detailed inquiry or investigation.

inquire, enquire *vi* (**inquired, inquiring**) to ask a question or questions; to seek for information by asking questions; to seek for truth by argument or the discussion of questions or by investigation (*to inquire of a person*, but *after, concerning, into*, etc, *a thing*).—*vt* to ask about; to seek by asking (*to inquire the way of a person*).

inquiry, enquiry *n* the act of inquiring; a question or interrogation; search for information or knowledge; research; investigation.

inquisition *n* the act of inquiring; interrogation; inquiry; investigation; a judicial inquiry; an inquest.

Inquisition *n* (*RC Church*) formerly, a court or tribunal established for the examination and punishment of heretics which in some countries, especially in Spain from the fifteenth to the seventeenth centuries, was the means of great cruelties being perpetrated.

inquisitive *adj* addicted to inquiry; inclined to seek information; given to prying into anything; troublesomely curious; prying.

inquisitor *n* one whose official duty it is to inquire and examine.

Inquisitor *n* a member of the Inquisition.

inroad *n* the hostile entrance of an enemy into a country; a sudden incursion or invasion; an encroachment; loss or impairment (*to make inroads on one's health*).

insane *adj* not sane; unsound or deranged in mind or intellect; mad; crazy; delirious; distracted; intended for insane persons (*insane asylum*).

insanitary *n* not sanitary; unhealthy; unhygienic; injurious to health.

insanity *n* the state of being insane or of unsound mind; madness; lunacy.

insatiable *adj* incapable of being satiated, satisfied or appeased.

insatiate *adj* not satisfied; insatiable.

inscribe *vt* (**inscribed, inscribing**) to write down or engrave; to mark down (*to inscribe a motto*); to mark with characters or words (*to inscribe a monument*); to assign, address or dedicate (*to inscribe a poem to* *a person*); to imprint deeply; to impress; (*geom*) to draw or delineate within another figure so that the boundaries of the two are in contact at certain points.

inscription *n* the act of inscribing; any words or writing engraved on stone, metal or other hard substance for public inspection; an address of a book, poem, etc, to a person as a mark of respect, less formal than a dedication; (*numis*) the words placed in the middle of the reverse side of some coins and medals.

inscrutable *adj* incapable of being searched into and understood; incapable of being penetrated or understood by human reason; not to be satisfactorily accounted for or explained; enigmatic.

insect *n* one of a class of small animals that in their mature state have the three divisions of the body—the head, thorax and abdomen—always distinct from one another and usually have three pairs of legs and two pairs of wings, as flies, beetles, bees, etc; a puny contemptible person.

insectivore *n* any of an order of mammals that are small and nocturnal and feed on insects or other invertebrates; any insect-eating plant or animal.

insectivorous *adj* of or pertaining to insectivores; insect-eating.

insecure *adj* not secure; not confident of safety; apprehensive of danger or loss; not sufficiently strong or guarded; not furnishing security or safety; unsafe.

insecurity *n* the state of being insecure; lack of security.

inseminate *vt* (**inseminated, inseminating**) to introduce semen into the uterus of a female, sometimes artificially; to introduce (ideas, etc) to people's minds.

insemination *n* the act of inseminating.

insensate *adj* lacking sense or sensation; lacking sensibility; unfeeling; stupid.

insensible *adj* not apprehended by the senses; imperceptible; incapable of being felt or perceived; so slow or gradual that the stages are not noted; lacking the power of feeling or perceiving; numb or dead to pain; unconscious; not susceptible of emotion or passion; void of feeling; unfeeling; callous; apathetic; indifferent.

insensitive *adj* not sensitive; lacking sensitivity; unfeeling.

inseparable *adj* incapable of being separated or disjoined; not to be parted; always together.

insert *vt* to set in or among; to put or thrust in; to introduce.—*n* something inserted.

insertion *n* the act of inserting; something inserted.

in-service *adj* of training, given during employment.

insessorial *adj* (of birds) adapted to perching.

inset *vt* (*pret, pp* **inset**, *ppr* **insetting**) to set in; to infix or implant.—*n* that which is set in; insertion; an insert.

inshore *adj, adv* near the shore.

inside *adj* being within; interior; internal.—*n* that which is within; specifically, the entrails or bowels; an inside passenger in a vehicle.—*prep* in the interior of; within.

inside job *n* (*colloq*) a crime committed with the help of someone connected with the premises or victim involved.

insider dealing *n* the illegal use of confidential information on share-dealing on the stock market, usually for personal gain.

insidious *adj* characterized by treachery or stealthy and guileful acts; treacherous; guileful; working evil secretly (*an insidious person, plot, disease*).

insight *n* deep inspection or view; thorough knowledge; power of observation; discernment; penetration.

insignia *n* (*pl* **insignias, insignia**) a badge or distinguishing mark of office or honour; any characteristic mark or sign.

insignificance *n* the condition or quality of being insignificant.

insignificant *adj* lacking significance; having no weight or effect; unimportant; trivial or trifling; without weight or character; mean; contemptible.

insincere *adj* not sincere; dissembling; hypocritical; false; deceitful (of persons, statements, etc).

insincerity *n* the quality of being insincere.

insinuate *vt* (**insinuated, insinuating**) to introduce gently or as by a winding or narrow passage; hence, (*refl*) to push or work gradually into favour; to introduce oneself by slow or artful means; to infuse gently or artfully; to instil (*to insinuate a doubt*); to hint or suggest.—*vi* to creep or wind; to act by insinuation; to make an insinuation; to wheedle.

insinuating *adj* given to or characterized by insinuation; wheedling; gradually winning favour and confidence; hinting, suggestive.

insinuation *n* the act of insinuating; a wheedling manner; a suggestion, hint or innuendo.

insipid *adj* tasteless; lacking taste; vapid; lacking interest, spirit, life or animation; dull, heavy or uninteresting.

insist *vi* to rest or dwell on as a matter of special moment; to be persistent, urgent, peremptory or pressing (usually with *on* or *upon*).

insistence *n* act of insisting; persistency; urgency.

insnare *vt* same as **ensnare**.

insole *n* a loose, thin strip of leather, felt, etc, placed inside a shoe for warmth or comfort; the inner sole of a shoe, etc.

insignia (of an non-commissioned officer in the Royal Navy)

insolence *n* haughtiness manifested in contemptuous and overbearing treatment of others; insolent language.

insolent *adj* showing haughty disregard of others; using rude and haughty or defiant language; overbearing; saucy; proceeding from insolence.

insoluble *adj* incapable of being dissolved, particularly by a liquid; not to be solved or explained (*an insoluble problem*).

insolvency *n* the condition of being insolvent; inability of a person to pay all his or her debts.

insolvent *adj* not solvent; not having money, goods or estate sufficient to pay all debts.—*n* a debtor unable to pay his or her debts.

insomnia *n* lack of sleep; abnormal sleeplessness.

insomniac *n* a person who suffers from insomnia.

insouciant *adj* light-hearted and carefree; unconcerned about consequences, public opinion, etc.

inspect *vt* to view or examine for the purpose of ascertaining the quality or condition, discovering errors, etc; to examine officially.

inspection *n* the act of inspecting; official view or examination.

inspector *n* one who inspects or oversees; a police officer ranking below a superintendent.

inspiration *n* the act of inspiring; a stimulus to creative thought or work; the state of being inspired; an inspired idea.

inspire *vi* (**inspired, inspiring**) to draw in breath; to inhale air into the lungs.—*vt* to breathe in; to draw into the lungs; to infuse by or as if by breathing; to instil; to stimulate or motivate as to creative thought or work.

inspirit *vi* to infuse or excite spirit in; to enliven, animate, encourage, invigorate.

instability *n* lack of stability; inconstancy; changeability; lack of strength or firmness in construction.

install, instal *vt* (**installed, installing**) to place in a seat; to place in an office or post; to invest with any charge, office or rank with customary ceremonies; to fix in place (a piece of machinery, etc) and make operative; (*comput*) to load a program.

instalment *n* the act of installing; a part of a whole produced at stated periods; one of the parts of a sum paid at various times.

instance *n* the act or state of being instant or urgent; urgency; a case occurring; a case offered as an exemplification or precedent; an example; an occurrence.—*vt* (**instanced, instancing**) to mention as an instance, example or case in point.

instant *adj* pressing, urgent, importunate or earnest; immediate; without intervening

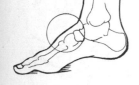
instep

time (*send him to instant execution*); quick; making no delay; present or current, usually abbreviated to *inst*, as *10th inst*, that is, 10th day of the present month.—*n* a point in duration; a moment; a part of duration that occupies the time of a single thought.

instantaneous *adj* done in an instant; occurring without any perceptible lapse of time.

instantly *adv* with urgency; instantaneously; immediately; forthwith; at once.

instate *vt* (**instated, instating**) to establish, as in a rank or condition; to install.

instead *adv* in the place or room.

instep *n* the upper part of the arch of the foot between the ankle and toes; that part of a shoe or stocking covering the instep.

instigate *vt* (**instigated, instigating**) to incite; to set on; to provoke; to urge (used chiefly or wholly in a bad sense).

instigation *n* the act of instigating; incitement, as to evil or wickedness.

instil *vt* (**instilled, instilling**) to pour in by drops; hence, to infuse slowly or by degrees into the mind; to cause to be imbibed; to insinuate imperceptibly.

instillation *n* the act of instilling.

instinct *n* the unlearned, natural responses or tendencies of people or animals; a natural aptitude or talent.

instinctive *adj* prompted by or proceeding from instinct; determined by natural impulse or propensity; spontaneous.

institute *vt* (**instituted, instituting**) to set up or establish; to ordain; to originate; to found; to set in operation; to begin (an investigation, etc).—*n* that which is instituted or formally established; an established law, precept or principle; a society established according to certain laws or regulations for the furtherance of some particular object.

institution *n* the act of instituting; something instituted or established; a permanent rule of conduct or of government; something forming a prominent or established feature in social or national life; a society or organization established for promoting any object, public or social; the building housing such a society or organization.

instruct *vt* to teach; to educate; to impart knowledge or information to; to coach; to train; to enlighten; to direct or command; to furnish with orders; to order or enjoin.

instruction *n* the act of instructing; that which is communicated for instructing; that with which one is instructed; information; order, mandate or direction.

instructive *adj* conveying knowledge; serving to instruct or inform.

instructor *n* one who instructs; a teacher; a coach or trainer.

instrument *n* that by which work is performed or anything is effected; a tool; a utensil; an implement; one who or that which is subservient to the execution of a plan or purpose; an agent; means used or contributing to an effect; any contrivance from which music is produced, as an organ, harp, violin, flute, etc; (*law*) a writing instructing one in regard to something that has been agreed on.

instrumental *adj* conducive as an instrument or means to some end; serving as a means; pertaining to instruments, especially musical instruments.

instrumentality *n* the condition of being instrumental; subordinate or auxiliary agency; agency as means to an end.

instrumentation *n* the art of arranging music for a combined number of instruments; the music for a number of instruments; execution of music on an instrument.

insubordinate *adj* not submitting to authority; disobedient; mutinous; riotous.

insubordination *n* the quality of being insubordinate.

insufferable *adj* not to be suffered, borne or endured; intolerable; unendurable.

insufficient *adj* not sufficient; inadequate to any need, use or purpose.

insular *adj* of or pertaining to an island; forming an island; pertaining to the opinions or views of people inhabiting an island; hence, narrow-minded (*insular prejudices*).

insulate *vt* (**insulated, insulating**) to make an island of; to place in a detached situation; to isolate; to separate, as an electrified or heated body, from other bodies by the interposition of nonconductors; to free from combination with other substances, as a chemical substance.

insulation *n* the act of insulating or state of being insulated; (*elect*) the substance or material used for the purpose of insulating.

insulator *n* one who or that which insulates; a body that interrupts the communication of electricity or heat to surrounding objects; a nonconductor.

insulin *n* a hormone secreted in the pancreas, controlling the amount of glucose in the blood and used to treat diabetes.

insult *n* any gross affront or indignity offered to another, either by words or actions; act or speech of insolence or contempt.—*vt* to treat with insult, gross abuse, insolence or contempt.—*vi* (*arch*) to behave with insolence.

insulting *adj* containing or conveying insult.

insuperable *adj* incapable of being overcome or surmounted; insurmountable (difficulties, objections, obstacles, etc).

insurance *n* the act of insuring; a contract by which a person or company, in consideration of a sum of money or percentage (technically called a premium) becomes

bound to indemnify the insured or his or her representatives against loss by certain risks; the premium paid for insuring property or life; a protective device or act (*an umbrella as insurance against rain*).

insure *vt* (**insured, insuring**) to make sure; to ensure; to contract for the payment of a certain sum in the event of loss or damage happening to (someone or something) or at the termination of (something) as *to insure a house against fire, a ship against damage, to insure one's life*; to make a subject of insurance; to assure (one's life).

insurgent *adj* rising in opposition to lawful civil or political authority; rebellious.—*n* a person who rises in opposition to civil or political authority.

insurmountable *adj* incapable of being surmounted, passed over or overcome.

insurrection *n* the open and active opposition of a number of persons to civil or political authorities ofin defiance of law and order; a revolt by a number of persons against constituted authorities.

insusceptible *adj* not susceptible; not capable of being affected or impressed (*a heart insusceptible of pity*).

intact *adj* untouched by anything that harms or defiles; uninjured; unimpaired; left complete, whole or unharmed.

intaglio *n* (**intaglios, intagli**) any figure engraved or cut into a substance so as to form a hollow; a gem with a figure or device sunk below the background; the reverse of *cameo*; a printing technique using engraved surfaces.

intake *n* the point at which water is taken from a main stream and directed into another channel; the act of taking in; anything which is taken in (*this year's intake of students*).

intangible *adj* not tangible; incapable of being touched; not perceptible to the touch; indefinable; evanescent.

integer *n* (*arith*) a whole number, as distinct from a fraction.

integral *adj* whole; entire; complete; belonging to or forming a necessary part of a whole; (*math*) pertaining to a whole number or undivided quantity; not fractional; pertaining to integration.—*n* a whole; an entire thing.

integral calculus *n* a branch of mathematical analysis which is the inverse of *differential calculus*, its object being the deriving of the primitive function from its differential or its differential coefficient.

integrate *vt* (**integrated, integrating**) to make whole or complete; to combine (parts) into a whole; to absorb into a culture or society; to abolish segregation in.—*vi* to become complete; to become part of a whole; to be absorbed into a culture or society.

integrated circuit *n* (*electron*) a complete circuit of many components etched on a minute silicon chip and much smaller than a printed circuit.

integration *n* the act of integrating; unification into a whole.

integrity *n* the state of being entire or complete; entireness; a genuine or unimpaired state; honesty; uprightness in mutual dealings; probity.

integument *n* (*anat*) the skin, membrane or shell which covers any part; (*bot*) the cellular skin of seed, leaf or stem.

intellect *n* that faculty of the human mind which receives or comprehends ideas, as distinguished from the power to feel and to will; the understanding faculty; also, the capacity for higher forms of knowledge; good mental power.

intellectual *adj* relating to the intellect or understanding; appealing to or engaging the intellect or higher capacities of humans; perceived by the intellect; existing in the understanding; ideal; having intellect; characterized by intellect.—*n* someone whose interest lies in, or whose living derives from, the exercise of the intellect.

intensive care

intellectuality *n* the state of being intellectual; intellectual power.

intelligence *n* the capacity to know, understand or comprehend; the capacity for the higher functions of the intellect; intellectual power; knowledge imparted or acquired; general information; information communicated by any means; news or notice; those engaged in gathering secret, especially military, information.

intelligence quotient *n* (short form **IQ**) an indicator of a person's intelligence as measured by an intelligence test and in relation to others of the same age.

intelligent *adj* endowed with the faculty of understanding or reason; endowed with a good intellect; having superior intellectual capacities; well-informed.

intelligentsia *n* the educated or intellectual classes.

intelligible *adj* capable of being understood or comprehended; comprehensible; perspicuous; clear.

intemperance *n* lack of moderation or due restraint; excess of any kind; specifically, habitual indulgence in the use of alcoholic liquors, especially with intoxication.

intemperate *adj* not exercising due moderation or restraint; addicted to an excessive or habitual use of alcoholic liquors; excessive, immoderate or inordinate (*intemperate language*).—*n* one who is not temperate.

intenable *adj* not tenable; untenable.

intend *vt* to fix the mind on, as the object to be effected or attained; to mean; to design; to purpose.

intended *adj* planned; betrothed; engaged.—*n* a person engaged to be married to another; an affianced lover.

intense *adj* extreme in degree; vehement; violent; severe (pain, cold, etc); characterized by strong feelings.

intensification *n* the act of intensifying or making more intense.

intensify *vt* (**intensified, intensifying**) to render intense or more intense.—*vi* to become intense or more intense.

intensity *n* the state of being intense; relative degree, vigour or activity; keenness or strength (of feeling, etc).

intensive *adj* concentrated; designed to produce maximum results (*an intensive course of study*); (*gram*) serving to give force or emphasis (*an intensive particle* or *prefix*).

intensive care *n* care of seriously ill hospital patients involving 24-hour monitoring and treatment; a unit in a hospital where such care is administered.

intent *adj* having the mind bent on an object; eager in pursuit of an object; firmly fixed or concentrated on.—*n* design, purpose or intention; meaning; drift; aim.

intention *n* determination to act in a particular manner; purpose; design; end; aim.

intentional *adj* done with intention, design or purpose; intended; designed.

intentionally *adv* with intention; by design; of purpose.

inter *vt* (**interred, interring**) to bury; to inhume.

interact *vi* to act reciprocally; to act on each other.

interaction *n* mutual or reciprocal action.

inter alia *adv* among other things.

intercalary *adj* inserted or introduced among others, as the odd day (29th February) inserted in a leap year.

intercalate *vt* (**intercalated, intercalating**) to insert between others; (*chron*) to insert between other days or other portions of time; (*geol*) to insert, as a layer or series of layers, between the regular series of the strata.

intercede *vi* (**interceded, interceding**) to act between parties with a view to reconciling those who differ or contend; to plead in favour of another; to interpose; to mediate or make intercession.

intercellular *adj* (*bot*, *zool*) lying between cells.

intercept *vt* to take or stop (someone or something) by the way; to interrupt the journey or passage of (a messenger, a letter, etc); to stop on its passage; to obstruct the progress of (rays of light, etc).

interception *n* the act of intercepting; obstruction of a course or proceeding.

intercession *n* the act of interceding; mediation.

intercessor *n* one who intercedes; a mediator.

interchange *vt* (**interchanged, interchanging**) to change reciprocally; to put each in the place of the other; to cause to succeed alternately.—*vi* to change reciprocally; to succeed alternately.—*n* the act or process of mutually giving and receiving; exchange between two or more; alternate succession; a road junction of interconnecting roads and bridges designed to prevent traffic crossing the routes of other traffic.

interchangeable *adj* capable of being interchanged.

intercolumniation *n* (*archit*) the space between two columns measured at the lowest part of their shafts.

intercommunicate *vti* (**intercommunicated, intercommunicating**) to communicate mutually; to hold mutual communication.

intercommunication *n* reciprocal communication.

intercourse *n* reciprocal dealings between persons or nations; interchange of thought and feeling; conversation, especially of mutual interest; communication; commerce; communion; sexual intercourse, copulation.

interdependence *n* reciprocal dependence; dependence each upon the others reciprocally.

interdependent *adj* reciprocally dependent.

interdict *vt* to debar, forbid, prohibit or prevent; to restrain by an interdict.—*n* a prohibition; a prohibiting order or decree; a papal prohibition of the performance of divine service and the administration of religious rites.

interdiction *n* the act of interdicting; prohibition.

interest *n* concern, sympathy or regard (*to excite one's interest*); advantage; good; profit (*it is in your interest to do so*); share, part or participation in value; the profit per cent derived from money lent or invested (which in reference to the interest is called the principal); hence, something in addition to a mere equivalent (*to repay injury with interest*); influence with a person, especially with persons in power (*to get a post by interest*); a collective name for those interested in any particular business (*the landed interest, the shipping interest*).—*vt* to engage the attention of; to awaken interest or concern in.

interested *adj* having an interest or share; affected; moved; having attention roused; concerned in a cause or in consequences; liable to be biased by personal considerations; chiefly concerned for one's own private advantage.

interesting *adj* engaging the attention or curiosity; exciting or adapted to excite attention and sympathy.

interface *n* a surface that forms a common boundary between two things; an electrical connection between one device and another, especially a computer.—*vt* (*elect*) to modify the input and output configurations of (devices) so that they may connect and communicate with each other; to connect using an interface; to be interactive (with).

interfere *vi* (**interfered, interfering**) to interpose; to meddle; to enter into or take a part in the concerns of others; to clash, come into collision or be in opposition; (*physics*) to act reciprocally on each other so as to modify the effect of each.

interference *n* the act of interfering or meddling; (*physics*) the mutual action of waves of any kind (water, sound, heat or light) on each other, by which the vibrations and their effects are increased, diminished or neutralized; the interruption of reception by a radio, television set, radar, etc, caused by atmospherics or unwanted signals.

interfuse *vt* (**interfused, interfusing**) to pour or spread between or among; to mix up together; to make interdependent.

interfusion *n* act of interfusing or that which is interfused.

interim *n* the meantime; time intervening.—*adj* belonging to an intervening time; belonging to the meantime; temporary.

interior *adj* internal; being within any limits, enclosure or substance, opposed to *exterior* or *superficial*; inland; remote from the frontiers or shore.—*n* the internal part of a thing; the inside; the inland part of a country; the department of a government having charge of home affairs.

interior decorator, interior designer *n* a person trained to design the inside decoration and furnishings of a building.

interject *vt* to throw between; to throw in between other words; to interrupt with.

interjection *n* the act of throwing between; a word or phrase thrown in between words connected in construction to express some emotion or passion, as exclamations of joy, grief, astonishment, etc; an interruption.

interknit *vt* (**interknitted, interknitting**) to knit, bind or weave together closely.

interlace *vt* (**interlaced, interlacing**) to weave or twine together; to entangle or interweave one thing with another.—*vi* to be intertwined or interwoven; to have parts crossing or intersecting.

interlard *vt* primarily, to mix fat with lean; hence, to mix by something frequently occurring; to diversify by mixture (*talk interlarded with oaths*).

interlace

interleave *vt* (**interleaved, interleaving**) to insert a blank leaf or blank leaves in; to insert between the other leaves of (a book).

interline *vt* (**interlined, interlining**) to write or print in alternate lines; to write or print between the lines of.

interlinear *adj* written or printed between lines already written or printed.

interlineation *n* the act of interlining; that which is interlined.

interlock *vi* to unite or be locked together by a series of connections.—*vt* to lock one in another firmly.

interlocution *n* dialogue; interchange of speech; (*law*) an intermediate act or decree before final decision.

interlocutor *n* one who speaks in a dialogue or conversation.

interlope *vi* (**interloped, interloping**) to intrude on a matter in which one has no concern.

interloper *n* one who unwarrantably intrudes or thrusts himself or herself into a business, position or matter.

interlude *n* a short lively entertainment performed between the acts of a play or between the play and the afterpiece; a piece of music played between the verses of a canticle or hymn, or between certain portions of a church service; an intervening episode or space.

intermarriage *n* marriage between two families, tribes, races, religions, nations, etc.

intermarry *vi* (**intermarried, intermarrying**) to marry together; to become connected by marriage, as two families, ranks, tribes, races, religions, etc.

intermediary *n* one who or that which interposes or is intermediate; an intervening agent.—*adj* acting as a mediator; intermediate.

intermediate *adj* lying or being between; in the middle place or degree between two extremes; intervening; interposed; intermediary.

intermediation *n* intervention; interposition; mediation between two or more parties.

intermediator *n* one who intervenes between parties; a peacemaker.

interment *n* the act of interring; burial.

intermezzo *n* (*pl* **intermezzos, intermezzi**) (*mus*) a short composition, generally of a light sparkling character, played between more important pieces; an interlude.

interminable *adj* boundless; endless; admitting no limit; wearisomely spun out or protracted.

intermingle *vt* (**intermingled, intermingling**) to mingle or mix together; to mix up; to intermix.—*vi* to be mixed or incorporated.

intermission *n* the act or state of

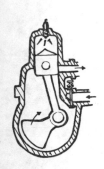
internal combustion

intermitting; cessation for a time; pause; an interval; the temporary subsidence of a fever or disease.

intermit *vt* (**intermitted, intermitting**) to cause to cease for a time; to interrupt; to suspend or delay.—*vi* to cease for a time; to cease or relax at intervals, as a fever.

intermittent *adj* ceasing at intervals.—*n* a fever which entirely subsides or ceases at certain intervals.

intermural *adj* lying between walls.

intern *vt* to send to or cause to remain in the interior of a country without permission to leave it; to disarm and quarter in some place, as a defeated body of troops; to imprison, often without trial.

internal *adj* inward; interior; being within any limit or surface; not external; pertaining to the mind or thoughts or to one's inner being; pertaining to itself, its own affairs or home interests (said of a country); domestic; not foreign.

internal combustion *n* the principle employed in the engines or motors of aircraft, motorcars, etc, by which a mixture of petrol or diesel gas and air is exploded in the cylinder, so that the explosive force acts directly on the piston.

internally *adv* inwardly; within the body; mentally; spiritually.

international *adj* pertaining to or reciprocally affecting nations; regulating the mutual intercourse between different nations.

internecine *adj* mutually destructive to both sides; marked by destructive hostilities or much slaughter; causing great slaughter, as between fellow citizens (*internecine war*); carried on within an organization (*internecine struggles*).

internment *n* the act of interning; the state of being interned.

interpellate *vt* (**interpellated, interpellating**) to question, especially to question (an official) about government policy or personal conduct; to interrupt by a question.

interpellation *n* the act of interrupting; an interruption by speaking; a question put by a member of a legislative assembly to a minister or member of the government.

interpenetrate *vti* (**interpenetrated, interpenetrating**) to penetrate between or within; to penetrate mutually.

interpenetration *n* the act of interpenetrating.

interplay *n* the effect of two or more things on each other; interaction.

Interpol *n* the International Crime Police Organization through which the police of member countries help each other in tracking down criminals and generally assist each other in dealing with crime.

interpolate *vt* (**interpolated, interpolating**) to insert, as a spurious word or passage in a manuscript or book; to insert or introduce (something) between parts already there; to estimate (an unknown quantity) within the limits of what is known; (*math, physics*) to fill up intermediate terms of, as of a series, according to the law of the series.

interpolation *n* the act of interpolating; that which is interpolated or inserted.

interpolator *n* one who interpolates.

interpose *vt* (**interposed, interposing**) to place between; (*fig, lit*) to present or bring forward by way of interruption or for some service (*to interpose one's hand, oneself, one's aid* or *services*).—*vi* to step in between parties at variance; to mediate; to interfere; to put in or make a remark by way of interruption.

interposer *n* one who interposes.

interposition *n* the act of interposing; a coming between; mediation; intervention.

interpret *vt* to explain the meaning of; to expound; to translate from an unknown to a known language or into intelligible or familiar words; to free from mystery or obscurity; to make clear; to unravel; to represent artistically (as by an actor on the stage).

interpretation *n* the act of interpreting; translation; explanation; the sense given by an interpreter; conception and representation of a character on the stage.

interpretative *adj* designed or fitted to explain; explanatory.

interpreter *n* one who or that which interprets.

interregnum *n* (*pl* **interregnums, interregna**) the time between the death or abdication of a monarch and the accession of his or her successor; the interval between the cessation of one government and the establishment of another.

interrelation *n* mutual, reciprocal or corresponding relation; correlation.

interrogate *vt* (**interrogated, interrogating**) to question, especially formally; to examine by asking questions.

interrogation *n* the act of questioning; a question put.

interrogation mark, interrogation point *n* the sign ?, indicating that the sentence immediately preceding it is a question or used to express doubt or to mark a query.

interrogative *adj* denoting a question; expressed in the form of a question.—*n* (*gram*) a word used in asking questions, as *who? what? which?*

interrogator *n* one who interrogates or asks questions.

interrogatory *n* a question; an interrogation.—*adj* containing a question; expressing a question.

interrupt *vt* to stop or hinder by breaking in on the course or progress of; to break the current or motion of; to cause to stop in

speaking; to cause to be delayed or given over; to break the uniformity of.

interrupter *n* one who interrupts.

interruption *n* the act of interrupting or breaking in on; a break or breach; intervention; interposition; obstruction or hindrance; cause of stoppage.

intersect *vt* to cut into or between; to cut or cross mutually; to divide into parts by crossing or cutting.—*vi* to cut into one another; to meet and cross each other.

intersection *n* the act or state of intersecting; the point or line in which two lines or two surfaces cut each other; the point at which two roads meet and cross each other.

interspace *n* a space between other things; intervening space.

intersperse *vt* (**interspersed, interspersing**) to scatter or set here and there among other things; to diversify by scattering objects here and there.

interspersion *n* the act of interspersing.

interstellar *adj* situated among the stars; beyond the solar system.

interstice *n* a narrow or small space between things close together or between the component parts of a body; a chink, crevice or cranny.

intertexture *n* the act of interweaving; state of things interwoven; what is interwoven.

intertwine *vt* (**intertwined, intertwining**) to unite by twining or twisting one with another; to interlace.—*vi* to be mutually interwoven.

intertwist *vt* to twist one with another; to interweave or interlace.

interval *n* a space or distance between things; an unoccupied space intervening; space of time between two definite points or events; intervening time or space; the lateral space between units having the same alignment or frontage; (*mus*) the difference in point of gravity or acuteness between two given sounds.

intervene *vi* (**intervened, intervening**) to come or be between persons or things; to be situated between; to occur, fall or come between points of time or events; to come in the way; to interpose.

intervention *n* the act of intervening; a coming between; interference that may affect the interest of others; interposition.

interview *n* a meeting between two or more persons face to face; a conference or mutual interchange of thoughts; a meeting in which a person is asked about his or her views, etc, as by a newspaper or television reporter; a published or transmitted account of this; a formal meeting at which a candidate for a job is questioned and assessed by a prospective employer.—*vt* to have an interview with; to wait or call on for the purpose of having an interview and getting information for publication or transmission.

interviewee *n* a person who is being interviewed.

interviewer *n* one who interviews; one who questions and writes an article about, or records an interview with, someone, often someone famous.

interweave *vt* (*pret* **interwove**, *pp* **interwoven**, *ppr* **interweaving**) to weave together; to intermingle as if by weaving; to unite intimately; to interlace.

intestacy *n* the state of being intestate.

intestate *adj* dying without having made a will; not disposed of by will; not devised or bequeathed.—*n* a person who dies without making a will or a valid will.

intestinal *adj* of or pertaining to the intestines.

intestine *adj* internal with regard to a state or country; domestic; not foreign.—*n* the canal or tube that extends with convolutions from the stomach to the anus; (*pl*) entrails or viscera in general.

intimacy *n* the state of being intimate.

intimate[1] *adj* inward or internal; close in friendship or acquaintance; on very friendly and familiar terms; very close as regards connection or relation (*an intimate union*).—*n* an intimate or familiar friend; a close associate.

intimate[2] *vt* (**intimated**, **intimating**) to hint, indicate or suggest; to announce; to make known.

intimation *n* the act of intimating; a hint; an explicit announcement or notification.

intimidate *vt* (**intimidated**, **intimidating**) to inspire with fear; to dishearten; to cow; to deter by threats.

intimidation *n* the act of intimidating; the deterring of a person by threats or otherwise.

into *prep* a compound preposition expressing motion or direction towards the inside of, whether literally or figuratively; or expressing a change of condition (*to go into a house, to fall into a fever*); (*colloq*) deeply involved or interested in (*he is into Bach*).

intolerable *adj* not to be borne or endured; unendurable; insufferable.

intolerance *n* the quality of being intolerant; lack of toleration; lack of capacity to endure.

intolerant *adj* not enduring; not able to endure (*an animal intolerant of cold*); refusing to tolerate others in the enjoyment of their opinions, rights or worship; unduly impatient of difference of opinion on the part of others; illiberal.

intonate *vi* (**intonated**, **intonating**) to modulate the voice; to sound the notes of the musical scale.—*vt* to pronounce with a certain tone or modulation.

intonation *n* the act or manner of intonating; modulation of the voice musically as in reading; the act of intoning; utterance with a special tone.

intone *vi* (**intoned**, **intoning**) to use a musical monotone in pronouncing or repeating; to chant.—*vt* to pronounce with a musical tone; to chant.

in toto *adv* wholly; as a whole; entirely; completely.

intoxicant *n* that which intoxicates; an intoxicating liquor or substance.

intoxicate *vt* (**intoxicated**, **intoxicating**) to inebriate; to make drunk, as with spirituous liquor; (*fig*) to excite the spirits of to a very high pitch; to elate to enthusiasm, frenzy or madness.—*vi* to have the power of intoxicating or making drunk.

intoxication *n* the act of intoxicating; the state of being intoxicated; inebriation; drunkenness.

intractable *adj* not tractable; not to be governed or managed; perverse; refractory; not docile.

intramural *adj* being within the walls or boundaries, as of a university, city or town.

intransigent *adj* refusing to agree or come to a settlement; irreconcilable (used especially of some extreme political party).—*n* an irreconcilable person.

intransitive *adj* (*gram*) expressing an action or state that is limited to the subject; not having an object (*an intransitive verb*).

intraparietal *adj* situated or happening within walls; shut out from public view; private.

intrauterine device *n* a contraceptive device consisting of a small loop or coil inserted into the uterus.

intravenous *adj* into a vein (*an intravenous injection*).

intrench *vt* same as **entrench**.

intrenchment *n* same as **entrenchment**.

intrepid *adj* fearless; bold; brave; undaunted.

intrepidity *n* fearlessness; fearless bravery in danger; undaunted courage.

intricacy *n* the state of being intricate or entangled; a winding or complicated arrangement; entanglement; complication.

intricate *adj* entangled; involved; difficult to unravel or follow out in all the windings; complicated.

intrigue *n* a plot or scheme of a complicated nature and especially political in character; an illicit affair between two persons of different sexes; a liaison.—*vi* (**intrigued**, **intriguing**) to form an intrigue; to engage in an intrigue; to carry on a liaison.

intrinsic, intrinsical *adj* inherent; essential; belonging to the thing in itself; not extrinsic or accidental (*the intrinsic value of gold* or *silver, intrinsic merit*).

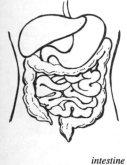

intestine

intrinsically *adv* by intrinsic character; in its nature; essentially; inherently.

introduce *vt* (**introduced, introducing**) to lead or bring in; to conduct or usher in; to pass in; to put in; to insert; to make known by stating one's name, often used of the action of a third party with regard to two others; to bring to be acquainted; to present (*to introduce one person, oneself, to another*); to bring into use or practice (a fashion, custom, etc); to bring before the public; to bring into a country; to bring forward (a topic) with preliminary or preparatory matter.

introduction *n* the act of introducing, bringing in, making persons acquainted, etc; the part of a book or discourse which precedes the main work and which gives some general account of its design and subject; a preface or preliminary discourse; a treatise introductory to more elaborate works on the same subject.

introductory *adj* serving to introduce something else; serving as or given by way of an introduction; prefatory; preliminary.

introit *n* (*RC Church*) a piece sung or chanted while the priest goes to the altar to celebrate Mass; in the Anglican Church, a piece sung at the beginning of a service.

intromission *n* the act of sending or letting in; admission.

intromit *vt* (**intromitted, intromitting**) to send in, put in or let in.

introspect *vt* to look into or within; to view the inside of.

introspection *n* the act of looking inwardly; examination of one's own thoughts or feelings; preoccupation with one's own thoughts.

introspective *adj* viewing inwardly; examining one's own thoughts; preoccupied with one's own thoughts.

intrude *vi* (**intruded, intruding**) to thrust oneself forwardly or unwarrantably into any place or position; to force oneself on others; to encroach; to enter unwelcome or uninvited into company; to enter someone else's property without authority; (*geol*) to penetrate, as into fissures or between the layers of rocks.—*vt* to thrust in or cause to enter without right or welcome (often with the reflexive pronoun).

intrusion *n* the act of intruding; unwarrantable entrance; unlawful entry into property without authority; (*geol*) the penetrating of one rock, while in a melted state, into fissures, etc, of other rocks.

intrusive *adj* characterized by intrusion; apt to intrude; of the nature of an intrusion.

intrust *vt* same as **entrust**.

intuition *n* an understanding or insight arrived at without conscious reasoning; the ability to perceive in this way; a hunch; an insight.

intuitive *adj* based on intuition; received or obtained by intuition.

Inuit, Innuit *n* the native people of the northern circumpolar regions, such as Greenland, Northern Canada and Alaska, formerly usually known as Eskimos.

inundate *vt* (**inundated, inundating**) to spread or flow over; to overflow; to deluge; to flood; to submerge; to fill with an overflowing abundance or superfluity.

inundation *n* the act of inundating or state of being inundated; a flood; a rising and spreading of waters over low grounds.

inure *vt* (**inured, inuring**) to apply or expose in use or practice till use gives little or no pain or inconvenience or makes little impression; to habituate; to accustom (to toil or hardships).

invade *vt* (**invaded, invading**) to enter with hostile intentions; to enter as an enemy, with a view to conquest or plunder; to enter by force; to make an inroad or incursion on; to intrude on; to infringe, encroach on or violate (rights or privileges).—*vi* to make an invasion.

invalid[1] *adj* not valid; of no force, weight or cogency; weak (*an invalid argument*); (*law*) having no force, effect or efficacy; void; null.

invalid[2] *n* a person who is weak and infirm; a sufferer from ill health.—*adj* in ill health; infirm; disabled for active service.—*vt* to render an invalid; to disable; to cause to retire from the armed forces because of ill health or injury.

invalidate *vt* (**invalidated, invalidating**) to render invalid or not valid; to deprive of legal force or effect.

invalidity *n* lack of validity; lack of cogency; lack of legal force or efficacy.

invaluable *adj* precious above estimation; so valuable that its worth cannot be estimated; inestimable.

Invar *n* a trademark for an alloy of nickel and steel which is practically unaffected by extremes of temperature.

invariable *adj* not variable; constant in the same state; always uniform; never varying.—*n* (*math*) an invariable quantity; a constant.

invariably *adv* constantly; uniformly; always.

invasion *n* the act of invading; a hostile entrance into the country or possessions of another; an attack on the rights of another.

invasive *adj* marked by military aggression; tending to spread; tending to infringe; (*surg*) affecting more than the area requiring attention; (*pathol*) affecting healthy tissue.

invective *n* a severe or violent utterance of censure or reproach; something uttered or written intended to cast opprobrium or censure on another; vituperation.

Inuit

inveigh *vi* to utter invectives; to exclaim or rail against a person or thing; to utter censorious or opprobrious words (with *against*).

inveigle *vt* (**inveigled, inveigling**) to persuade to something evil by deceptive arts or flattery; to cajole into wrongdoing; to entice; to seduce.

invent *vt* to contrive and produce; to devise, make or construct as the originator of something that did not before exist; to frame by the imagination; to excogitate; to concoct; to fabricate (a lie, etc).

invention *n* the act of inventing; the contrivance of that which did not before exist; origination; something invented or contrived; a contrivance; the power of inventing; that skill or ingenuity which is or may be employed in contriving anything new; a fabrication, a lie.

inventive *adj* able to invent; quick at invention or contrivance; ready at expedients.

inventor *n* one who invents or finds out something new.

inventory *n* a list containing a description, with the values, of goods and chattels, made on various occasions, as on the sale of goods or at the decease of a person; any catalogue of goods or wares; a catalogue or account of particular things.—*vt* (**inventoried, inventorying**) to make an inventory of; to enter in an inventory.

inverse *adj* opposite in order or relation; inverted; having what usually is or should be after placed before; proceeding the backward or reverse way; (*math*) opposite in nature and effect, thus, subtraction is *inverse* to addition, division to multiplication.—*n* a thing that is the direct opposite of another.

inverse proportion *n* proportion such that one thing is greater or less as another is less or greater.

inversion *n* the act of inverting or the state of being inverted; a change of order or position so that what was after is now before and vice versa; a making inverse in order; (*gram*, *rhet*) transposition of words so that they are out of their natural order ('wise was Solomon' for 'Solomon was wise'); (*mus*) change of position, as of an interval or a chord; (*math*) a change in the order of the terms of a proportion, so that the second takes the place of the first and the fourth of the third.

invert *vt* to turn upside down; to place in a contrary order or position; to put in inverse order or position.

invertebrate *adj* lacking a backbone or vertebral column; morally or mentally without stamina or backbone.—*n* an animal without a vertebral column or spine and in many cases no hard parts at all.

invest *vt* to put garments on; to clothe, to dress, to array (usually followed by *with*, sometimes by *in*, before the thing put on); to clothe, as with office or authority; to place in possession of an office, rank or dignity; (*milit*) to enclose or surround for the purpose of besieging; to lay siege to; to lay out (money or capital) on some species of property, usually of a permanent nature and with the purpose of getting a return (*to invest money in bank shares*).—*vi* to make an investment.

investigate *vt* (**investigated, investigating**) to search into; to inquire and examine into with care and accuracy; to make careful research or examination into.

investigation *n* the act of investigating; the process of inquiring into a subject; research; inquiry.

investigator *n* one who investigates.

investiture *n* the act of investing; the act or right of giving possession of an office, dignity, etc.

investment *n* the act of investing; the act of besieging by an armed force; the laying out of money in the purchase of some species of property; money laid out for profit; that in which money is invested.

investor *n* one who invests.

inveteracy *n* the state or quality of being inveterate; obstinacy confirmed by time.

inveterate *adj* firmly established by long continuance; deep-rooted or ingrained in a person's nature or constitution; firmly fixed by time or habit (*inveterate disease*, *custom*); confirmed in any habit by practice (*an inveterate liar*).

invidious *adj* envious; likely to bring on envy, ill-will or hatred; likely to provoke envy; entailing odium (*invidious distinctions*, *preference*, *position*).

invigilate *vi* (**invigilated, invigilating**) to watch diligently; to supervise an examination.

invigorate *vt* (**invigorated, invigorating**) to give vigour to; to cause to feel fresh and vigorous; to strengthen; to give life and energy to.

invincible *adj* incapable of being conquered or subdued; incapable of being overcome; unconquerable; insuperable.

inviolable *adj* not to be violated or profaned; not to be polluted or treated with irreverence; not to be broken or infringed (agreement, secrecy); not to be injured or tarnished (chastity, honour).

inviolate *adj* not violated; unprofaned; unpolluted; unbroken; inviolable.

invisible *adj* incapable of being seen; imperceptible by the sight.

invitation *n* the act of inviting; solicitation; the requesting of a person's company as to an entertainment, on a visit, etc; a card or letter containing such a request.

invite *vt* (**invited, inviting**) to ask, request,

⅃ꓤƎVNI

invert

invertebrate

bid or call on to do something; to summon; to ask to an entertainment or to pay a visit; to allure or attract; to tempt to come.—*vi* to give invitation; to allure or entice.—*n* (*colloq*) an invitation.

inviting *adj* attractive; enticing; tempting.

in vitro fertilization *n* (abbreviated form **IVF**) a treatment for infertility involving the fertilization outside the body of eggs from a woman's ovary and their re-implantation into her womb.

invocation *n* the act of invoking or addressing in prayer; the form or act of calling for the assistance or presence of any being, particularly of some divinity.

invoice *n* a written account of the particulars of merchandise sent to a purchaser, consignee, factor, etc, with the value or prices and charges annexed; a bill; a written statement of a fee or fees due.—*vt* (**invoiced, invoicing**) to submit an invoice for or to.

invoke *vt* (**invoked, invoking**) to address in prayer; to call on for assistance and protection; to call for solemnly or with earnestness.

involucre *n* (*bot*) any collection of bracts round a cluster of flowers; (*anat*) a membrane which surrounds or encloses a part, as the pericardium.

involuntary *n* not voluntary; not able to act or not acting according to will or choice (*an involuntary agent*); independent of will or choice (*an involuntary movement*); not proceeding from choice; not done willingly; unwilling.

involute, involuted *adj* involved; twisted; confusedly mingled; (*bot*) rolled inward from the edges (said of leaves and petals); (*zool*) turned inwards at the margin (said of the shells of molluscs).

involution *n* the action of involving or enfolding; the state of being entangled or involved or of being folded in; complication; (*arith, alg*) the raising of a quantity from its root to any power assigned; the multiplication of a quantity into itself a given number of times.

involve *vt* (**involved, involving**) to have or include as a part or element; to draw or get into a complicated or difficult situation; to make more complicated or difficult.

involved *adj* complicated; entangled; intricate.

invulnerable *adj* not vulnerable; incapable of being wounded or of receiving injury; unassailable, as an argument.

inward *adj* internal; interior; placed or being within; in or connected with the mind, thoughts, soul or feelings.—*adv* inwards. —*n* an inner part; inside; (*pl*) the viscera.

inwardly *adv* in an inward manner; internally; mentally; privately.

inwards *adv* towards the inside; towards the centre or interior; into the mind or thoughts.

inwrought *adj* wrought or worked in or among other things; adorned with figures worked in.

iodide *n* a compound of iodine and a metal.

iodine *n* a nonmetallic element, a solid substance of a bluish-black or greyish-black colour with a distinctive odour obtained from seaweed and in the form of compounds used in medicine and photography.

ion *n* an atom or group of atoms which has become electrically charged by losing (*positive ion*) or gaining (*negative ion*) one or more electrons.

Ionic order *n* one of the five orders of architecture, the distinguishing characteristic of which consists of ornamental volutes on its capital.

ionize *vi* (**ionized, ionizing**) to change or become changed into ions.

iota *n* the ninth letter of the Greek alphabet; a very small quantity; a jot.

IOU *n* (i.e. 'I owe you') a written note promising to pay a certain amount of money to the holder.

ipecacuanha *n* a substance extracted from the roots of various South American plants, used as an emetic.

ipso facto *adv* by that very fact; by the fact or act itself.

IQ abbreviation of **intelligence quotient.**

Iranian *adj* of or pertaining to Iran; applied to certain languages, including Persian and related tongues.—*n* a native or inhabitant of Iran; a branch of the Indo-European group of languages.

irascible *adj* readily made angry; easily provoked; apt to get into a passion; irritable.

irate *adj* angry; enraged; incensed.

ire *n* anger; wrath; keen resentment.

iridescent *adj* exhibiting or giving out colours like those of the rainbow; gleaming or shimmering with rainbow colours.

iridium *n* a rare metal of a whitish colour, not malleable and not readily affected by acids.

iridology *n* a method of alternative medicine in which diagnosis is made by examining the markings of the eye for indications of irregularities in the body.

iris *n* (*pl* **irises, irides**) the coloured circular part of the front of the eye, capable of contracting or expanding; the rainbow; an appearance resembling the rainbow; the hues of the rainbow as seen in sunlit spray, the spectrum of sunlight, etc; (*pl* **irises**) any of a group of plants with sword-shaped leaves and flowers of varied colours, such as dark blue.

Irish *adj* pertaining to Ireland or its inhabitants; Erse.—*n* the Irish language; the people of Ireland.

Iris

irk *vt* to weary; to give annoyance or uneasiness to; to be distressingly tiresome to; to annoy (used chiefly impersonally, as *it irks me*).

irksome *adj* wearisome; burdensome; vexatious; giving uneasiness (*irksome labour, delay*, etc).

iron *n* a common element of a livid whitish colour inclined to grey; an instrument or utensil made of iron; an instrument that when heated is used for smoothing cloth; a golf club with an iron head laid back; (*pl*) fetters; chains; manacles; handcuffs.—*adj* made of iron; consisting of iron; resembling iron, either really or metaphorically; hence, harsh, rude, severe; capable of great endurance; firm; robust; inflexible.—*vt* to smooth with an iron; to fetter or handcuff; to furnish or arm with iron.

iron

Iron Age *n* a period following the Bronze Age during which weapons and tools were first made of iron.

ironclad *adj* covered in iron; difficult to change or break (*an ironclad case*).—*n* a nineteenth-century naval vessel cased or covered, wholly or partially, with thick iron plates.

ironic, ironical *adj* relating to or containing irony; addicted to irony; using irony.

ironmonger *n* a dealer in iron wares or hardware.

iron pyrites *n* pyrites.

iron ration *n* a soldier's emergency ration.

ironstone *n* a type of iron ore; a type of hard-wearing earthenware.

irony *n* a mode of speech by which words are used that properly express a sense contrary to that which the speaker really intends to convey; a subtle kind of sarcasm, in which apparent praise really conveys disapprobation.

irradiance, irradiancy *n* emission of rays of light on an object; lustre; splendour.

irradiant *adj* emitting rays of light.

irradiate *vt* (**irradiated, irradiating**) to illuminate or shed a light on; to cast splendour or brilliancy on; to enlighten intellectually; to illuminate; to penetrate by radiation; to expose to X-rays or other radiation; to treat (food) with small doses of radiation to slow the rotting process.—*vi* to emit rays; to shine.

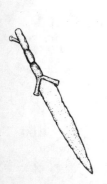

Iron Age tool

irradiation *n* the act of irradiating; illumination; brightness emitted; intellectual illumination.

irrational *adj* not rational; void of reason or understanding; contrary to reason; absurd; (*math*) not capable of being exactly expressed by an integral number or by a vulgar fraction; surd.

irreconcilable *adj* not reconcilable; not to be reconciled; implacable (an enemy, enmity); incapable of being made to agree or be consistent; inconsistent.

irrecoverable *adj* incapable of being recovered or regained; not capable of being restored, remedied or made good.

irredeemable *adj* not redeemable; not subject to be paid at its nominal value (specifically applied to a depreciated paper currency); (of a person) incapable of reform of salvation.

irreducible *adj* not reducible; incapable of being reduced.

irrefragable *adj* incapable of being refuted or overthrown; incontestable; undeniable; incontrovertible.

irrefutable *adj* not refutable; incapable of being refuted or disproved.

irregular *adj* not regular; not according to rules, established principles or customs; not conformable to the usual operation of natural laws; deviating from the rules of moral rectitude; vicious; not straight or uniform; (*gram*) deviating from the common form in respect to the inflectional terminations.—*n* one not conforming to settled rule; especially, a soldier not in regular service; a mercenary.

irregularity *n* state or character of being irregular; lack of regularity; that which is irregular; a part exhibiting or causing something to be irregular or impairing uniformity; an action or behaviour constituting a breach of morality; vicious conduct.

irrelevance, irrelevancy *n* the quality of being irrelevant.

irrelevant *adj* not relevant; not applicable or pertinent; not bearing on the case in point or matter in hand.

irreligion *n* lack of religion or contempt of it; impiety.

irreligious *adj* characterized by irreligion; disregarding or condemning religion; contrary to religion; profane; impious; ungodly.

irremediable *adj* incapable of being remedied or cured; not to be corrected or redressed; incurable; irreparable.

irremovable *adj* not removable; immovable; inflexible.

irreparable *adj* not reparable; incapable of being repaired; irremediable.

irrepressible *adj* not repressible; incapable of being repressed, restrained or kept under control; not easily depressed or cast down; buoyant.

irreproachable *adj* incapable of being reproached; upright; innocent; faultless; unblemished.

irresistance *n* forbearance to resist; nonresistance.

irresistible *adj* not resistible; incapable of being successfully resisted or opposed; resistless; invincible.

irresolute *adj* not resolute; not firm or constant in purpose; undecided; wavering; given to doubt or hesitation; vacillating.

462

irresolution *n* lack of resolution or decision; a fluctuation of mind; vacillation.

irresolvable *adj* incapable of being resolved.

irrespective *adj* having no relevance or regard to particular circumstances, generally used in the prepositional phrase *irrespective of*, that is, leaving out of account.

irresponsibility *n* lack of responsibility.

irresponsible *adj* not responsible; unable to bear responsibility; not liable to answer for consequences; heedless of consequences.

irresponsive *adj* not responsive.

irretrievable *adj* not retrievable; irrecoverable; irreparable.

irreverence *n* lack of reverence or veneration; lack of a due regard to the authority and character of a superior; irreverent conduct or an irreverent action.

irreverent *adj* exhibiting or marked by irreverence (person, conduct, words); lacking in respect to superiors.

irreversible *adj* not reversible; incapable of being reversed.

irrevocable *adj* not to be recalled or revoked; incapable of being reversed, repealed or annulled; irreversible (fate, decree, etc).

irrigate *vt* (**irrigated, irrigating**) to water (land) by causing a stream to flow on it and spread over it; to water by various artificial channels for water.

irrigation *n* the act or operation of irrigating.

irritable *adj* capable or susceptible of being irritated; readily provoked or exasperated; of a fiery temper.

irritant *adj* irritating; producing pain, heat or tension; producing inflammation (*an irritant poison*).—*n* that which excites or irritates; something that causes discomfort, such as itching.

irritate *vt* (**irritated, irritating**) to excite anger in; to provoke; to tease; to exasperate; to excite heat and redness or discomfort, such as itchiness, in, as in the skin or flesh; to inflame; to cause discomfort such as itching; to cause to exhibit irritation.

irritation *n* the act of irritating or state of being irritated; provocation; exasperation; angry feeling; feeling of heat and pain or discomfort, such as itchiness, in a part of the body; (*physiol*) the change or action which takes place in muscles or organs when a nerve or nerves are affected by the application of external bodies.

irruption *n* a bursting in; a breaking, or sudden, violent rushing into a place; a sudden invasion or incursion.

is the 3rd person sing of the verb to **be**.

ischuria *n* a stoppage, retention or suppression of urine.

isinglass *n* a gelatinous substance prepared from the air bladders of certain fishes; mica, especially in thin sheets.

Isis *n* one of the chief deities in the Egyptian mythology.

Islam *n* the Muslim religion, a monotheistic religion founded by Mohammed; the Muslim world.

Islamic *adj* of or pertaining to Islam; Muslim.

island *n* a tract of land surrounded by water, whether of the sea, a river or a lake; anything resembling an island.

islander *n* an inhabitant of an island.

isle *n* an island.

islet *n* a little isle or something similar.

isobar *n* a line drawn on a map connecting places at which the mean height of the barometer at sea level is the same.

isobarometric *adj* indicating equal barometric pressure.

isocheim *n* a line drawn on a map through places which have the same mean winter temperature.

isocheimal *adj* of the same mean winter temperature; marking places with the same mean winter temperature.

isochromatic *adj* having the same colour; marking correspondence in colour.

isochronal, isochronous *adj* uniform in time; of equal time; performed in equal times (as the oscillations of two pendulums).

isochronism *n* the state or quality of being isochronal.

isoclinal, isoclinic *adj* of equal inclination or dip.

isoclinal line, isoclinic line *n* a curve connecting places at which the dip of the magnetic needle is equal.

isodynamic *adj* having equal power or force.

isogon *n* (*math*) a polygonal figure whose angles are equal.

isogonic *adj* having equal angles.

isolate *vt* (**isolated, isolating**) to place or leave in a detached situation; to place apart; to quarantine; (*chem*) to obtain (a substance) free from all its combinations.

isolated *adj* standing detached from others of a like kind; placed by itself or alone; remote; lonely; lacking social contact.

isolation *n* state of being isolated or alone; the act of isolating.

isomer *n* any of two or more chemical compounds whose molecules contain the same atoms but in different arrangements.

isometric *adj* having equality of measure; (*physiol*) relating to muscular contraction involving little shortening of the muscle.

isometrics *npl* physical exercises in which muscles are contracted against each other or in opposition to fixed objects.

isomorphism *n* a similarity of crystalline form in minerals.

Isis

island

isomorphous *adj* exhibiting the property of isomorphism.

isonomy *n* equal law; equal distribution of rights and privileges.

isopod *n* one of an order of crustaceans, including those whose feet are of equal size and move in the same direction, such as woodlice.

isosceles *adj* having two legs or sides only that are equal (*an isosceles triangle*).

isoseismal, isoseismic *adj* marking equal earthquake disturbance on the earth's surface.

isotherm *n* an imaginary line on the earth's surface passing through places having a corresponding temperature either throughout the year or at any particular period.

isothermal *adj* pertaining to an isotherm or isotherms; marking correspondence in temperature.

isotonic *adj* (*mus*) having or indicating equal tones; (*physiol*) having the same tension; (*chem*) having the same osmotic pressure.

isotope *n* any of two or more forms of an element having the same atomic number but different atomic weights.

isotropic *adj* having properties alike in all directions.

Israelite *n* a descendant of Israel or Jacob; a Jew.

issue *n* the act of passing or flowing out; a moving out of any enclosed place; the act of sending out; delivery (of commands, money, etc); the whole quantity sent forth or issued at one time (*an issue of banknotes*; *yesterday's issue of a newspaper*); what happens or turns out; event; consequence; a point under dispute; progeny; a child or children; offspring; all persons descended from a common ancestor. —*vi* (**issued, issuing**) to pass, flow or run out, as from any enclosed place; to proceed, as from a source; to rush out; to proceed, as progeny; to be produced, as an effect or result; to close, end, terminate.—*vt* to send out; to deliver for use; to deliver authoritatively (orders etc); to put (notes, coin, newspapers) into circulation.

isthmus *n* (*pl* **isthmuses, isthmi**) a neck or narrow slip of land by which two continents are connected or by which a peninsula is united to the mainland.

it *pron* a pronoun of the neuter gender corresponding with the masculine *he* and the feminine *she*, having the same plural *they*. —*n* the player in a game who must catch another.

Italian *adj* pertaining to Italy.—*n* a native

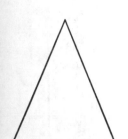

isosceles

ivy

of Italy; the language used in Italy or by the Italians.

italic *adj* (*print*) (of type) sloping towards the right, a style of type invented about 1500 by Aldus Manutius, a Venetian printer (*this is italic type*); a style of handwriting or calligraphy.—*n* italic type or handwriting (usually plural).

Italic *adj* pertaining to Italy.

italicize *vt* (**italicized, italicizing**) to write or print in italic characters; to distinguish by italics.

itch *n* a sensation in the skin causing a great desire to scratch or rub; a constant teasing desire (*an itch for praise*).—*vi* to feel an itch; to have an urge or desire to.

itching *n* the sensation of itch; an urge, desire or hankering.—*adj* having a sensation that leads to scratching; having an urge or desire.

item *n* a separate particular in a list or account; a paragraph; a scrap of news; an article; a piece of news or information.

itemize *vt* (**itemized, itemizing**) to specify the items of; to set down by items.

iterate *vt* (**iterated, iterating**) to utter or do a second time; to repeat.

iteration *n* repetition; recital or performance a second time.

itinerancy *n* a passing from place to place; the passing from place to place in the discharge of official duty.

itinerant *adj* passing or travelling about a country or district; wandering; not settled; strolling.—*n* one who travels from place to place.

itinerary *n* the route or plan of a journey.

itinerate *vi* (**itinerated, itinerating**) to travel from place to place; to wander without a settled habitation.

its *poss pron* of or belonging to **it**.

itself *pron* the neuter pronoun corresponding to himself, herself.

IVF an abbreviation of **in vitro fertilization.**

ivory *n* the substance composing the tusks of the elephant; a similar substance obtained from the tusks of the walrus, the hippopotamus, the narwhal, etc; a creamy white colour.—*adj* consisting or made of ivory; of a colour similar to that of ivory.

ivory tower *n* a place or situation which excludes the realities of everyday life.

ivy *n* an evergreen climbing plant growing on old buildings, rocks and trunks of trees.

ivied *adj* covered or overgrown with ivy.

izard, izzard *n* a wild goat, especially of the Pyrenees; the chamois.

J

J the tenth letter in the English alphabet and the seventh consonant, having a sound like that of *g* in *genius*.

jabber *vi* to talk rapidly, indistinctly or nonsensically; to utter gibberish; to chatter.— *n* rapid talk with indistinct utterance of words.

jabiru *n* a tall wading bird resembling the stork, a native of Africa and America; a similar bird of Australia.

jacamar *n* the name of certain climbing birds of tropical America, closely allied to the woodpeckers.

jacana *n* the name of sundry tropical wading birds, having very long toes, so that they can easily walk on the leaves of aquatic plants.

jacare *n* a species of Brazilian alligator.

jacinth *n* a gemstone, a variety of zircon, also called **hyacinth**.

jack *n* a popular name for a sailor; a name of various devices or implements; a device for raising great weights by the action of screws; a device for turning a spit; a device used to support a vehicle while changing a tyre or wheel; a coat quilted and covered with leather, formerly worn over a coat of mail; a pitcher of waxed leather; a blackjack; a small bowl thrown out for a mark to the players in the game of bowls; a flag displayed from a staff on the end of the bow of a ship; the Union Jack; the male of certain animals, as the ass; the fish more commonly called the pike; a young pike; any of the knaves in a pack of cards.

jackal *n* a flesh-eating animal closely allied to the dog and the wolf, native to parts of Africa and Asia.

jackanapes *n* an impertinent fellow; a conceited person.

jackass *n* the male of the ass; an ignorant or stupid person.

jackboot *n* a kind of large military boot reaching up to or over the knee.

jackdaw *n* a small species of crow.

jacket *n* a short outer garment extending downward to the hips; an outer casing of cloth, felt, wood, etc; a casing to prevent the radiation of heat from a water heater; an outer covering, as the removable paper cover of a book or the skin of a potato.—*vt* to cover or furnish with a jacket.

jacketed *adj* wearing or furnished with a jacket.

jack hare *n* a male hare.

jack-in-a-box *n* (*pl* **jacks-in-a-box, jack-in-a-boxes**) a kind of toy consisting of a box, out of which, when the lid is opened, a figure springs.

jack-in-office *n* one who is vain of his unimportant office.

jack ketch *n* a public hangman.

jackknife *n* (*pl* **jackknives**) a large strong clasp knife for the pocket.—*vi* (**jackknifed, jackknifing**) (of an articulated lorry) to go out of control so that the trailer and the cab swing together; to bend double like a jackknife.

jack of all trades *n* (*pl* **jacks of all trades**) a person who can do many different types of work.

jack-o'-lantern *n* will-o'-the-wisp, a phosphorescent light that appears in low moist lands.

jackpot *n* the accumulated stakes in certain games, as poker; the largest prize in a competition.—**to hit the jackpot** to win a prize; to receive a large sum of money as winnings; to achieve great success.

jacksnipe *n* a small species of snipe.

jackstraw *n* a figure of a man made of straw; a person without any substance or means; a dependant.

Jacobean *adj* (*archit*) the term sometimes applied to the later style of Elizabethan architecture prevailing in the age of James I of England.

Jacobite *n* a partisan or adherent of James II of England after he abdicated the throne and of his descendants.—*adj* pertaining to the Jacobites.

Jacobitical *adj* pertaining to the Jacobites.

Jacob's ladder *n* a cottage-garden plant with handsome blue (sometimes white) flowers; (*naut*) a rope ladder with wooden steps or spokes.

jacobus *n* (*pl* **jacobuses**) a gold coin struck

jacket

Jacob's ladder

in the reign of James I of England.

jaconet *n* a light soft muslin of an open texture, used for dresses, neckcloths, etc.

jacquard *n* a pattern woven on a jacquard loom.

jacquard loom *n* a loom for weaving patterns, fitted with a series of perforated cards which guide the warp threads.

jactitation *n* (*law*) a false claim of marriage, harmful to the interests of another; (*med*) extreme restlessness or tossing in bed, especially as a symptom of fever.

jaculatory *adj* throwing out suddenly, or suddenly thrown out; uttered in short sentences.

Jacuzzi *n* the trademark of a device that swirls water around in a bath or pool; the bath or pool containing such a device.

jade[1] *n* a semiprecious stone, light green in colour, used as an ornamental stone, as in jewellery; a light green colour.

jade[2] *n* a mean or poor horse; a hussy; a young woman (used in humour or slight contempt).—*vt* (**jaded, jading**) to weary or fatigue.—*vi* to become weary; to lose spirit or enthusiasm.

jaded *adj* worn out; fatigued; dispirited.

jag *vt* (**jagged, jagging**) to notch; to cut into notches or teeth like those of a saw; to prick.—*n* a notch or projection; a sharp protuberance or indentation; (*colloq*) an injection; (*colloq*) a binge, especially of drink or drugs.

jagged *adj* having notches or teeth; cleft; divided; sharp and ragged.

jaggery, jagghery *n* an unrefined brown sugar made from palm sap.

jaggy *adj* set with jags or teeth; notched; jagged; prickly.

jaguar *n* a large American black-spotted yellow wild cat similar to the leopard.

jail, gaol *n* a prison; imprisonment; a place where prisoners are kept.—*vt* to put in prison; to imprison.

Jain, Jaina *n* one of a Hindu religious sect believing doctrines similar to those of Buddhism.

jalap *n* the root of a Mexican plant formerly used as a purgative.

jalousie *n* a wooden frame or blind for shading from the sunshine, much used in hot countries; a Venetian blind.

jam[1] *n* a conserve of fruits boiled with sugar and water.

jam[2] *vt* (**jammed, jamming**) to wedge in; to squeeze tight; to press or thrust in; to block; to congest; to cause interference to (a radio signal).—*n* a crush; a squeeze; a crowded mass of people; a blockage; (*colloq*) congested road traffic (*a traffic jam*); (*colloq*) a difficult situation

jamb *n* the side or vertical piece of any opening in a wall, such as a door, window or chimney, supporting the lintel.

jaguar

jar

jamboree *n* a large rally or gathering, often of Scouts; a large party; a spree.

jammed *adj* wedged or blocked so as to be immovable.

jangle *vi* (**jangled, jangling**) to sound discordantly or harshly.—*vt* to cause to sound harshly or inharmoniously; to grate on (the nerves, etc).—*n* a discordant sound.

janissary, janizary *n* in history, a soldier of the Turkish footguards.

janitor *n* a doorkeeper; a porter; one who cleans and maintains property.

Jansenist *n* a follower of Jansen (d. 1638), Roman Catholic bishop of Ypres in Flanders, who leaned to the doctrine of irresistible grace as maintained by Calvin.

January *n* the first month of the year, having 31 days.

japan *n* work varnished and figured in the manner practised by the natives of Japan; the varnish employed in japanning articles; japan lacquer.—*vt* (**japanned, japanning**) to varnish or cover with japan lacquer.

Japanese *adj* pertaining to Japan or its inhabitants.—*n* a native or natives of Japan; the language of the inhabitants of Japan.

jape *n* a jest or joke.

japonica *n* a Japanese species of pear or quince.

jar[1] *n* a vessel of earthenware, glass or plastic, of various shapes and dimensions; the contents of a jar.

jar[2] *vi* (**jarred, jarring**) to strike together with a short rattle or tremulous sound; to give out a harsh sound; to sound discordantly; to vibrate from impact; to be irritating; to quarrel; to dispute.—*vt* to cause a short tremulous motion to; to cause to shake or tremble; to jolt; to have an irritating effect on.—*n* a rattling vibration of sound; a harsh sound; a vibration; a jolt.

jargon[1] *n* unintelligible talk or language; phraseology peculiar to a sect, profession, etc; professional slang.

jargon[2] *n* a variety of zircon.

jasmine *n* the name of several erect or climbing shrubs, with fragrant white or yellow flowers.

jasper *n* an impure opaque coloured quartz, which admits of a high polish and is used for vases, seals, etc.

jaundice *n* a disease characterized by yellowness of the eyes and skin, caused by an excess of bile in the bloodstream; bitterness; resentment; prejudice.—*vt* (**jaundiced, jaundicing**) to affect with jaundice; to affect with prejudice; to make bitter.

jaundiced *adj* affected with jaundice; jealous, envious; disillusioned.

jaunt *vi* to wander here and there; to make an excursion or trip.—*n* an excursion; a short journey, especially one taken for pleasure.

jaunting car *n* formerly, a light, two-wheeled, one-horse carriage used in Ireland in which the passengers ride back to back on folding-down seats placed at right angles to the axle.

jaunty *adj* light and easy in manner or actions; airy; sprightly; dapper.

javelin *n* a light spear thrown from the hand; the athletic field event in which such a spear is thrown.

jaw *n* the bones of the mouth in which the teeth are fixed; the upper or lower bony portion of the mouth; anything resembling a jaw in form or use (*the jaws of a vice*); (*colloq*) loquacity or talk; (*colloq*) a friendly chat.—*vi* (*colloq*) to talk or gossip; (*colloq*) to talk boringly and at length.

jawbone *n* the bone of the jaw in which the teeth are fixed.

jay *n* any of several birds of the crow family; a British bird with a crest of erect feathers; the blue jay, a native of North America.

jaywalk *vi* to cross a road carelessly, without regard to oncoming traffic.

jazz *n* a general term for various styles of American music characterized by improvisation and instrumental solos based on basic tunes and chord structures; (*sl*) pretentious talk, nonsense.—**to jazz up** *vt* (*colloq*) to play (music) in a jazz style; to enliven; to add colour to.

jazzy *adj* of or like jazz; (*colloq*) lively; (*colloq*) showy.

JCB *n* the trademark of an earth-moving vehicle with a large, hydraulically operated shovel mounted at the front.

jealous *adj* uneasy through fear of or on account of preference given to another; suspicious in love; apprehensive of rivalry; suspiciously vigilant; anxiously fearful or careful; possessive.

jealousy *n* the quality of being jealous; uneasiness from fear of being, or on account of being, supplanted by a rival; apprehension of another's superiority.

jean *n* a hard-wearing twilled cotton cloth.

jeans *npl* a pair of casual trousers made from jean or denim.

jeep *n* a small strong vehicle with heavy-duty tyres and four-wheel drive for use on rough terrain, originally and often still for military purposes.

jeer *vi* to utter severe sarcastic reflections; to scoff; to make a mock of some person or thing (*to jeer at a person*).—*vt* to treat with scoffs or derision; to make a mock of; to deride.—*n* a scoff; a taunt; a flout; a gibe; derision.

jehad *n* same as **jihad**.

Jehovah *n* a Scripture name of God.

jejune *adj* lacking interesting matter; dull; naive; lacking nourishment.

Jekyll and Hyde *n* a person who lives a double life; a person who has two completely different sides to his or her personality.

jelly *n* a soft but firm food made from fruit syrup and, usually, gelatine; a similar food made with meat juices; anything with the consistency of a jelly.—*vt* (**jellied, jellying**) to turn into jelly; to congeal.

jellyfish *n* any of various marine invertebrate animals which have a jelly-like appearance; a medusa.

jemmy *n* a short stout crowbar used by housebreakers for opening doors.

jennet, genet *n* a small-sized, well-proportioned Spanish horse; a female donkey.

jenny *n* a machine for spinning, moved by water or steam; a female of some animals, as a wren or donkey.

jeopardize *vt* (**jeopardized, jeopardizing**) to expose to loss or injury.

jeopardy *n* exposure to death, loss or injury; hazard; danger; peril.

jerboa *n* a name of certain small rodents of Asia and North Africa mainly characterized by the disproportionate length of the hind limbs.

jeremiad *n* a lamentation; a tale of grief, sorrow or complaint (used with a spice of ridicule or mockery).

jerk[1] *vt* to thrust with a sudden effort; to give a sudden pull, twitch, thrust or push to; to throw with a quick, smart motion.—*vi* to make a sudden motion; to give a start.—*n* a short sudden thrust, push or twitch; a jolt; a sudden spring; a start; a leap or bound; (*colloq*) a useless or stupid person.

jerk[2] *vt* to cut (beef) into long thin pieces and dry in the sun, as is done in South America.

jerkin *n* a jacket; a short coat; a close waistcoat.

jerky *adj* moving by or exhibiting jerks.

jerry-built *adj* badly or cheaply built; flimsily put together.

jersey *n* any plain machine-knitted fabric of natural or artificial fibres; a general term for knitted fabrics; a knitted woollen garment for the upper body; a sweater; a jumper.

Jerusalem artichoke *n* a plant, the tubers of which are of a sweetish farinaceous nature, somewhat akin to the potato.

jess *n* a short strap of leather fastened round each of the legs of a hawk or falcon to which the leash tied round the falconer's hand is attached.

jessamine *n* jasmine.

jest *n* a joke; something ludicrous uttered and meant only to excite laughter; the object of laughter; a laughing stock.—*vi* to make merriment by words or actions; to utter jests; to talk jokingly; to joke.

jester *n* one who jests; a person given to

javelin

jersey

jesting; a person formerly retained by royal households and persons of rank to entertain by humorous actions and talk.

Jesuit *n* one of the Society of Jesus, a religious order belonging to the Roman Catholic Church and founded by Ignatius Loyola in the sixteenth century.

Jesus, Jesus Christ *n* in the Christian religion, the Son of God; the founder of Christianity.

jet[1] *n* a shooting forth or spouting; that which issues or streams forth from an orifice, as water or other fluid, gas or flame; a spout or device which issues forth such a stream; an aeroplane operated by jet propulsion.—*vi* (**jetted, jetting**) to issue in a jet; to shoot out; to project; to jut.—*vt* to emit; to spout forth.

jet[2] *n* a highly compact type of coal capable of taking a good polish, deep black and glossy, used in jewellery and ornaments of various kinds.

jet-black *adj* of the deepest black, the colour of jet.

jet lag *n* fatigue caused by travelling through time zones at high speed and so disrupting the body rhythms.

jet-lagged *adj* affected by jet lag.

jet-propelled *adj* powered by jet propulsion.

jet propulsion *n* the propulsion of an aircraft or boat by the discharge of gases or fluid from a rear vent.

jigsaw puzzle

jettison, jetsam, jetson *n* the throwing of goods overboard in order to lighten a ship in danger; the goods thus thrown away.—*vt* to throw overboard; to throw away; to abandon.

jetty *n* a projecting portion of a building; a projecting structure (generally of piles), affording a convenient landing place for vessels or boats; a kind of small pier.

Jew *n* a person descended, or regarded as descended from the ancient Hebrews; a person whose religion is Judaism.

jewel *n* a personal ornament in which precious stones or metals form a principal part; a precious stone; anything of exceeding value or excellence.—*vt* (**jewelled, jewelling**) to adorn with jewels; to fit or provide with a jewel (as a watch).

jeweller *n* one who makes or deals in jewels and other ornaments.

jewellery, jewelry *n* the trade or occupation of a jeweller; jewels in general.

Jewish *adj* pertaining to the Jews or Hebrews.

jew's-harp *n* an instrument of music which is held between the teeth and, by means of a thin bent metal tongue struck by the finger, gives out a sound.

jib[1] *n* the foremost sail of a ship, triangular in shape and extended from the outer end of a jib boom towards the fore-topmast head; in sloops, a sail on the bowsprit and extending towards the lower masthead; the projecting beam or arm of a crane.

jib[2] *vi* (**jibbed, jibbing** *or* **jibed, jibing**) to pull against the bit, as a horse; to move restively sideways or backwards.

jib boom *n* a spar run out from the extremity of the bowsprit and which serves as a continuation of it.

jibe[1], **gybe** *vt* (**jibbed, jibbing**) (*naut*) to shift (a jib) from one side to the other; to alter course in this way.

jibe[2] *n, vi* (**jibed, jibing**) same as **gibe**.

jiffy *n* (*colloq*) a moment; an instant.

jig *n* a quick light Irish dance; a light quick tune or air, generally in triple time; a type of contrivance used in engineering shops for holding the work and guiding the cutting tools; any simple mechanical device.—*vi* (**jigged, jigging**) to dance a jig; to move with a light jolting motion.

jigger *n* (*mining*), a person who cleans ores by means of a wire-bottom sieve; the sieve itself; a kind of light tackle used in ships; a potter's wheel by which earthenware vessels are shaped.

jigsaw *n* a saw with a vertical motion, moved by a vibrating lever or crank rod.

jigsaw puzzle *n* a puzzle consisting of a picture mounted on board, etc, and cut into irregular pieces by a jigsaw, to be fitted together again by the person doing the puzzle.

jihad, jehad *n* a Muslim sacred or holy war against unbelievers.

jilt *n* a person who gives a lover hopes and then casts him or her aside.—*vt* to reject or cast aside (a lover whom one has given encouragement to).

jingle *vi* (**jingled, jingling**) to sound with a tinkling metallic sound; to clink, as money, chains or bells.—*vt* to cause to give a tinkling metallic sound.—*n* a rattling or clinking sound, as of metal; something that jingles; a little bell or rattle; correspondence of sound in rhymes; a short poem with a simple rhyme or rhythm, often set to music, e.g. for television advertisements.

jingo *n* an expletive used as a mild oath; (*pl* **jingoes**) a person eager for war.

jingoism *n* the advocacy of an aggressive foreign policy; aggressive nationalism.

jingoistic *adj* pertaining to jingoism; exhibiting jingoism.

jink *vi* to turn a corner deftly; to move deftly.—*vt* to dodge.

jinnee, djinni, djinny *n* (*pl* **jinn**) in Muslim myth, one of a race of angels or demons.

jinx *n* a person or thing believed to bring bad luck.—*vt* to bring bad luck to; to put an unlucky spell on.

jitters *n pl* nervousness; anxiety.

jittery *adj* nervous; anxious.

job *n* a piece of work undertaken; work turned out, especially when done for a fee or a wage; a particular kind of employment; work; employment; a thing or material being worked on; (*colloq*) a difficult task; (*sl*) a criminal undertaking.—*vt* (**jobbed, jobbing**) to let out to be done in several portions or jobs; to let out, as horses, carriages or other vehicles, for hire; to engage for one's own use for hire; to buy in large quantity and sell in smaller lots.—*vi* to work at chance jobs; to deal in the public stocks; to buy and sell as a broker; to let or hire horses, carriages, etc; to pervert some public undertaking to private advantage.—*adj* applied to goods bought and sold under special circumstances and generally under the ordinary trade price.

jockey *n* a person whose profession it is to ride horses in horse races.—*vi* to ride in a race; to manoeuvre for a more advantageous position.—*vt* to jostle by riding against; to trick.

jockstrap *n* a close-fitting protective support for the male genitalia, worn in athletics, sports, etc.

jocose *adj* given to jokes and jesting; merry; waggish; containing a joke; sportive; merry.

jocular *adj* given to jesting; jocose; merry; waggish; containing jokes; facetious.

jocund *adj* merry; cheerful; blithe; gleeful; gay; sprightly; sportive; light-hearted.

jodhpurs *npl* a pair of trousers that are loose to the thigh and then close-fitting to the ankle, worn when horse-riding.

jog *vt* (**jogged, jogging**) to push or shake with the elbow or hand; to give notice or excite attention by a slight push.—*vi* to move at a slow trot; to run at a relaxed trot as exercise; to walk or travel idly or slowly; to move along with but little progress (generally followed by *on*).—*n* a push; a slight shake; a shake or push intended to give notice or awaken attention; an exercise run; (*carp, masonry*), a square notch.

joggle *vt* (**joggled, joggling**) to shake slightly; to give a sudden but slight push.—*vi* to push; to shake; to totter.

jogtrot *n* a slow, easy trot; hence, a slow routine of daily duty to which one pertinaciously adheres.—*adj* monotonous; easygoing; humdrum.

John Bull *n* a humorous designation of the English people.

join *vt* to connect or bring together, physically or otherwise; to place in contiguity; to couple; to combine; to associate; to engage in (*to join the fray*); to make oneself a party in; to become connected with; to unite with; to enter or become a member of; to merge in (*to join the army*; *one river joins another*).—*vi* to be contiguous or in contact; to form a physical union; to coalesce; to unite or become associated, as in marriage, league, partnership, society; to confederate; to associate; to league.

joiner *n* one who joins; a worker who works with wood, especially in house interiors, as in fitting doors, window frames, building shelves, etc; a carpenter; a person who likes to join societies, etc.

joinery *n* the art of a joiner; carpentry.

joint *n* the place or part at which two separate things are joined or united; the mode of connection of two things; junction; articulation; one of the large pieces into which a carcass is cut up by the butcher; (*anat*) the joining of two or more bones, as in the elbow, the knee or the knuckle; (*bot*) a node or knot; also, the part between two nodes; (*geol*) a fissure or line of parting in rocks at any angle to the plane of stratification; (in building) the surface of contact between two bodies that are held firmly together by means of cement, mortar, etc; the place where or the manner in which one piece of timber is connected with another; (*sl*) a cigarette containing a drug such as hashish; (*sl*) a disreputable club, bar, etc.—*adj* shared by two or more (*joint property*); having an interest in the same thing (*joint owner*); united; combined; acting in concert (*a joint force*, *joint efforts*).—*vt* to form with a joint or joints; to articulate; to unite by a joint or joints; to fit together; to cut or divide into joints or pieces.—*vi* to coalesce by joints.

joint stock *n* stock held in company.

jointure *n* property settled on a woman in consideration of marriage and which she is to enjoy after her husband's decease.—*vt* (**jointured, jointuring**) to settle a jointure on.

joist

joist *n* one of the stout pieces of timber to which the boards of a floor or the laths of a ceiling are nailed and which are supported by the walls or on girders.—*vt* to fit or furnish with joists.

joke *n* something said for the sake of exciting a laugh; something witty or sportive; a jest; what is not in earnest or actually meant; (*colloq*) something ill-organized or useless.—*vi* (**joked, joking**) to jest; to utter jokes; to jest in words or actions.—*vt* to cast jokes at; to make merry with; to rally.

joker *n* a jester; a merry person; a clown; an extra playing card in a pack; a person who makes a show of cleverness; an unpredictable or contemptuous person.

jollification *n* a scene of merriment, mirth or festivity; a carouse; merrymaking.

jollity *n* the quality of being jolly; mirth; gaiety; festivity; joviality.

jolly *adj* merry; lively; full of life and mirth; jovial; expressing mirth; exciting mirth or gaiety.

joker

jollyboat *n* one of a ship's boats; a small boat carried on the stern of a larger ship.

jolt *vi* to shake with short abrupt risings and fallings, as a vehicle moving on rough ground; to move jerkily.—*vt* to shake with sudden jerks.—*n* a shock or shake by a sudden jerk, as in a carriage.

jonquil *adj* a species of narcissus or daffodil, with rush-like leaves and flowers that yield a fine perfume.

jorum *n* a bowl or drinking vessel with liquor in it.

jostle *vt* (**jostled, jostling**) to push or knock against; to crowd against; to elbow.—*vi* to shove about as in a crowd.

jot *n* an iota; the least quantity assignable.—*vt* (**jotted, jotting**) to write down briefly or quickly; to make a note of.

jotting *n* a brief note; a hurried or abbreviated writing.

joule *n* the SI unit of work and energy.

journal *n* a diary; an account of daily transactions and events or the book containing such account; a periodical or magazine, often one dealing with a learned or specialist subject; in bookkeeping, a book in which every particular article or charge is entered under each day's date or in groups at longer periods; (*naut*) a daily register of the ship's course and distance, etc; a log-book.

journalism *n* the work of writing, editing or publishing newspapers, magazines, etc.

joust

journalist *n* a person engaged in journalism; a person who writes or edits a newspaper or magazine; a reporter.

journey *n* travel from one place to another; a distance travelled at a time.—*vi* to travel from place to place; to pass from home to a distance.

journeyman *n* (*pl* **journeymen**) any workman who has served his apprenticeship.

joust *n* a combat between two knights at a tournament for sport or for exercise.—*vi* to engage in a mock fight on horseback; to tilt.

Jove *n* the chief god of the Romans; Jupiter.

jovial *adj* merry; joyous; jolly.

jowl *n* the cheek.

joy *n* excitement of pleasurable feeling caused by the acquisition or expectation of good; gladness; pleasure; delight; exultation; exhilaration of spirits; the cause of joy or happiness.—*vi* to rejoice; to be glad; to exult.

joyful *adj* full of joy; very glad; exulting; joyous; gleeful.

joyous *adj* glad; happy; merry; joyful; giving joy.

joyride *n* (*pret* **joyrode**, *pp* **joyridden**, *ppr* **joyriding**) a pleasure ride, often at great speed, in a vehicle without the owner's permission.—*vi* to take such a pleasure ride in a vehicle.

joystick[1] *n* a stick of incense.

joystick[2] *n* the control lever of an aircraft; in computing, a device for controlling cursor movement on a screen.

JP abbreviation of **justice of the peace**.

jubilant *adj* uttering songs of triumph; triumphant; rejoicing; shouting or singing with joy.

jubilation *n* rejoicing; triumph; exultation.

jubilee *n* any occasion of rejoicing or joy; a celebration of a marriage, etc, after it has lasted fifty years.

Judaic, Judaical *adj* pertaining to the Jews.

Judaism *n* the religious doctrines and rites of the Jews, as enjoined in the laws of Moses; conformity to the Jewish rites and ceremonies.

Judas *n* a treacherous person; one who betrays under the guise of friendship.

judge *n* a civil officer invested with power to hear and determine cases, civil and criminal, and to administer justice between parties in courts held for the purpose; one who has skill to decide on the merits of a question or on the value of anything; a person appointed to give a decision in the course of a competition or dispute; a person qualified to give an opinion; a critic; a connoisseur.—*vi* (**judged, judging**) to hear and determine, as in cases on trial; to pass judgment on any matter; to sit in judgment; to compare facts, ideas or propositions and perceive their agreement or disagreement; to form an opinion; to express censorious opinions; to determine; to estimate; to discern.—*vt* to hear and determine authoritatively, as a cause or controversy; to examine into and decide; to examine and pass sentence on; to try; to be censorious towards; to esteem, think, reckon.

Judges *npl* the name of the seventh book of the Old Testament.

judgeship *n* the office of a judge.

judgment, judgement *n* the act of judging; the act of deciding or passing decision on something; the act or faculty of judging truly, wisely or skilfully; good sense; discernment; understanding; opinion or notion formed by judging or considering; the act or mental faculty by which humans compare ideas and ascertain the relations of terms and propositions; (*law*) the sentence pronounced in a cause by the judge or court by which it is tried; hence, a calamity regarded as inflicted by God for the punishment of sinners; the final trial of the human race.

Judgment Day *n* the last day, when final judgment will be pronounced on men.

judicatory *n* a system of courts, a judiciary.—*adj* of or pertaining to the administration of justice.

judicature *n* the power of distributing justice; a court of justice; a judicatory; extent of jurisdiction of a judge or court.

judicial *adj* pertaining or appropriate to courts of justice or to a judge thereof; proceeding from, issued or ordered by, a court of justice; inflicted as a penalty or in judgment; enacted by law or statute.

judicial separation *n* the separation of a husband and wife by decree of a court.

judiciary *adj* pertaining to the courts of judicature or legal tribunals; judicial.—*n* the system of courts of justice in a government; the judges taken collectively.

judicious *adj* according to sound judgment; adapted to obtain a good end by the best means; well considered (said of things); acting according to sound judgment; possessing sound judgment; directed by reason and wisdom (said of persons).

judo *n* a Japanese system of unarmed combat adapted as a competitive sport from jujitsu.

jug *n* a vessel, usually of earthenware, metal, glass or plastic, of various sizes and shapes and generally with a handle or ear, used for holding and conveying liquids; a pitcher.—*vt* (**jugged, jugging**) to put in a jug; to cook by putting into a jug and this into boiling water (*jugged hare*).

juggernaut *n* a terrible irresistible, usually destructive, force; a large heavy lorry.

juggle *vi* (**juggled, juggling**) to play tricks by sleight of hand; to toss and catch several objects in the air in a sequence in order to keep them in continuous motion; to keep several activities in progress at the same time; to practise artifice or imposture.—*vt* to manipulate skilfully; to deceive by trick or artifice; to arrange and rearrange (appointments, etc) so as to accommodate alterations to them.—*n* a trick by legerdemain; an imposture.

juggler *n* one who juggles.

jugglery *n* the art or performances of a juggler; legerdemain; trickery; imposture.

jugular *adj* (*anat*) pertaining to the neck or throat.

jugular vein *n* one of the large veins (two on each side) by which the greater part of the blood that has circulated in the head, face and neck is returned to the heart.

juice *n* the sap or watery part of vegetables, especially of fruits; the fluid part of animal substances.

juicy *adj* abounding with juice; succulent; (*colloq*) (of gossip, etc) very interesting.

jujitsu, jujutsu *n* a style of Japanese unarmed defence in which techniques of balancing and leverage are used to overcome the opponent's strength.

jujube *n* the fruit of a spiny shrub or small tree of Southern Europe, Northern Africa and Western Asia; the tree itself; a confection made of gum arabic or gelatine.

juke box *n* a coin-operated record player or CD player equipped with a push-button system for selecting the records or discs.

julep *n* a sweet drink; a sweetened mixture in which medicine is taken; a kind of cocktail.

July *n* the seventh month of the year, having 31 days.

jumble *vt* (**jumbled, jumbling**) to mix in a confused mass; to put or throw together without order (often followed by *together* or *up*).—*vi* to meet, mix or unite in a confused manner.—*n* confused mixture, mass or collection without order; disorder; confusion.

jumble sale *n* a sale of assorted articles, such as second-hand clothes and bric-a-brac and home-made cakes and sweets, usually held in a hall in aid of charity.

jumbo *adj* (*colloq*) very large; outsize.—*n* (*pl* **jumbos**) (*colloq*) a very large thing; (*colloq*) elephant; a jumbo jet.

jumbo jet *n* (*colloq*) a very large jet aircraft capable of carrying several hundred passengers.

jump *vi* to throw oneself in any direction by lifting the feet wholly from the ground and again alighting on them; to leap; to spring; to bound; to give a start; to increase suddenly (as prices, etc); to accept or agree eagerly (with *at*); (*sl*) to be very lively.—*vt* to pass by a leap; to pass over eagerly or hastily; to skip over; to leap.—*n* the act of jumping; a leap; a spring; a bound; a start; a sudden increase.

jumped-up *adj* (*colloq*) conceited; upstart.

jumper *n* one who or that which jumps; a jersey.

jumpy *adj* nervous; easily startled.

junction *n* the act or operation of joining; the state of being joined; the place or point of union; joint; juncture; the place where two or more railway lines meet and unite.

juncture *n* the line or point at which two bodies are joined; a point of time; particularly, a point rendered critical or important by a concurrence of circumstances.

June *n* the sixth month of the year, having 30 days.

jungle *n* land covered with forest trees, thick, impenetrable brushwood or any coarse, rank vegetation; any wild or overgrown land; a scene of confusion or disorder; a situation in which there is ruthless competition.

junior *adj* younger; not as old as another (applied to distinguish the younger of two persons bearing the same name); opposed to senior; lower or younger in standing, as in a profession.—*n* a person younger than another; one of inferior standing in his or her profession to another; a young person employed in a minor capacity in an office, etc.

jug

jumbo jet

471

juniper *n* a coniferous shrub found throughout Europe, the berries of which are used in the preparation of gin and in cooking.

junk[1] *n* pieces of old cable or old cordage; salt beef supplied to vessels for long voyages (which is tough like junk); rubbish, useless stuff; (*colloq*) any narcotic drug.

junk[2] *n* a flat-bottomed ship used in China, Japan, Java, etc, often of large dimensions.

junket *n* curds mixed with cream, sweetened and flavoured; a feast; a lively entertainment of any kind.—*vi* to feast; to banquet; to take part in a lively entertainment.—*vt* to entertain; to feast.

Juno *n* in Roman myth, a goddess, the wife of Jupiter; a statuesque woman.

junta *n* a group of people, especially military, who assume responsibility for the government of a country following a revolution or coup d'état; a council; a junto.

junto *n* (*pl* **juntos**) a select council or assembly which deliberates in secret on any affair of government; a faction; a cabal.

Jupiter *n* in Roman myth, the supreme deity among the gods, the equivalent of the Greek Zeus; the largest planet in the solar system.

Jurassic system *n* the system of rocks of the Mesozoic era between the Triassic and the Cretaceous.

juridical *adj* acting in the distribution of justice; pertaining to a judge or the administration of justice; used in courts of law or tribunals of justice.

jurisdiction *n* the extent of the authority which a court has to decide matters tried before it; the right of exercising authority; the extent of the authority of a government, an officer, etc, to execute justice; the district or limit within which power may be exercised.

jurisprudence *n* the science of law; the knowledge of the laws, customs and rights of men, in a state or community, necessary for the due administration of justice.

jurist *n* a person who professes the science of law; one versed in the law, or more particularly in the civil law.

juror *n* one that serves on a jury; a member of a jury; a juryman.

jury[1] *n* a certain number of people selected according to law and sworn to inquire into or to determine facts and to declare the truth according to the evidence legally adduced; a body of people selected to adjudge prizes, etc, at a public exhibition.

jury[2] *adj* (*naut*) a term applied to a thing employed to serve temporarily in place of something broken or lost, as a jury mast, a jury rudder.

jurybox *n* the place in a court where the jury sit.

juryman, jurywoman *n* (*pl* **jurymen, jurywomen**) one who serves on a jury.

junk

just *adj* acting or disposed to act conformably to what is right; rendering or disposed to render to each one his or her due; equitable in the distribution of justice; upright; impartial; fair; blameless; righteous; conformed to rules or principles of justice; equitable; due; merited (*just reward* or *punishment*); rightful; proper; conformed to fact; exact.—*adv* exactly or nearly in time (*just at that moment*, *just now*); closely in place (*just by*, *just behind him*); exactly; nicely; accurately (*just as they were*); narrowly; barely; only; (*colloq*) really.

justice *n* the quality of being just; propriety; correctness; rightfulness; just treatment; vindication of right; requital of desert; merited reward or punishment; a judge holding a special office (used as an element in various titles, as *Lord Chief Justice*).

justice of the peace *n* a local judge or magistrate appointed to keep the peace, to inquire into felonies and misdemeanours and to discharge numerous other functions; an unpaid lay magistrate appointed by the Lord Chancellor (often abbreviated to **JP**).

justiciary *n* an administrator of justice.—*adj* of or pertaining to the administration of justice.

justifiable *adj* capable of being justified; defensible; warrantable; excusable.

justification *n* the act of justifying or state of being justified; (*theol*) acceptance of a sinner as righteous through the merits of Christ.

justify *vt* (**justified, justifying**) to prove or show to be just or conformable to law, right, justice, propriety or duty; to defend or maintain; to vindicate as right; to absolve or clear from guilt or blame; to prove by evidence; to verify; to adjust so as to fit exactly, as lines and words in printing.—*vi* to form an even surface or true line with something else.

jut *vi* (**jutted, jutting**) to shoot out or to project beyond the main body.—*n* that which juts; a projection.

jute *n* a fibrous substance resembling hemp, used in the manufacture of carpets, bagging, etc.

juvenile *adj* young; youthful; pertaining or suited to youth; immature; childish.—*n* a young person or youth.

juvenilia *npl* works produced in an author's or artist's youth.

juvenescent *adj* becoming young.

juxtapose *vt* (**juxtaposed, juxtaposing**) to place side by side, especially for comparison.

juxtaposition *n* the act of juxtaposing; the state of being placed close together; contiguity; proximity.

K

K the eleventh letter and the eighth consonant of the English alphabet; in Anglo-Saxon represented by *c*.

Kaaba, Caaba *n* an oblong stone building forming the great mosque at Mecca.

kaftan *n* same as **caftan**.

kagoule *n* same as **cagoule**.

Kaiser *n* formerly, the title of the emperors of Germany and Austria.

kaka *n* a New Zealand parrot.

kale, kail *n* cabbage having curled or wrinkled leaves but not a close head.

kaleidoscope *n* an optical instrument which exhibits, by reflection, a variety of beautiful colours and symmetrical forms, consisting in its simplest form of a tube containing two reflecting surfaces inclined to each other at a suitable angle, with loose pieces of coloured glass, etc, inside; something that constantly changes.

kaleidoscopic *adj* pertaining to a kaleidoscope; showing constant changes of form and colour.

kali *n* glasswort, a plant the ashes of which are used in making glass.

kalif *n* same as **caliph**.

kalmia *n* a genus of American evergreen shrubs of the heath family, with showy flowers in corymbs.

kalong *n* a large fruit bat of Southeast Asia; a flying fox.

kamikaze *n* in the Second World War, a Japanese airman who piloted an aircraft packed with explosives and deliberately crashed it on enemy ships and installations, so committing suicide.—*adj* pertaining to a kamikaze; pertaining to an attack made by a kamikaze; suicidal; self-destructive; foolhardy.

kamsin *n* same as **khamsin**.

kangaroo *n* a large marsupial of Australia, with long and powerful hind legs for leaping and small and short forelegs.

kangaroo court *n* an illegal court operated by an unauthorized body without regard for legal procedure and predisposed towards a verdict of guilty.

kangaroo grass *n* a valuable Australian fodder grass.

kangaroo rat *n* a small leaping rodent of North America.

kaolin *n* a fine variety of clay, resulting from the decomposition of the feldspar of a granitic rock under the influence of the weather; porcelain or China clay.

kapok *n* cotton-like fibre used for stuffing cushions, etc, and obtained from the silky fibres around the seeds of a tropical tree.

kaput *adj* (*colloq*) broken; ruined.

karaoke *n* a form of entertainment in bars or nightclubs in which people take it in turn to sing along with a vocal-less soundtrack of a popular song.

karate *n* a Japanese system of unarmed combat using sharp blows of the hands and feet.

karma *n* in Buddhism and Hinduism, the sum of a person's activities during one of his or her existences, held to determine his or her destiny in the next; a certain aura that a place or a person is felt to possess.

karoo, karroo *n* the name given to the immense arid tracts of clayey tablelands of South Africa, which are covered with verdure only in the wet season.

katydid *n* a species of grasshopper found in America; it gives out a loud sound which its name is intended to imitate.

kava *n* a Polynesian shrub of the pepper family and a beverage made from it.

kayak *n* a light fishing boat in Greenland, made of sealskins stretched round a wooden frame; a small, lightweight canoe with a small opening for the occupant.

KC an abbreviation of **King's Counsel**.

kebab *n* (*shish kebab*) a dish consisting of small cubes of meat and vegetables cooked and served on a skewer; (*doner kebab*) a dish consisting of thin slices cut from a block of seasoned lamb cooked on a spit and often eaten in a slice of pitta bread.

keblah *n* the direction of the Great Mosque at Mecca, being the point toward which Muslims turn their faces in prayer.

kedge *n* a small anchor used to keep a ship steady when riding in a harbour or river or to assist in warping her.—*vt* (**kedged**,

kangaroo

karate

473

kedging) to warp (a ship) by means of a rope attached to a kedge.

kedgeree *n* a dish made of boiled rice, fish and eggs.

keel *n* the principal timber in a ship, extending from stem to stern at the bottom and supporting the whole frame; any structure resembling this; the corresponding part in iron vessels; (*fig*) the whole ship; a projecting ridge on a surface; a low, flat-bottomed vessel used in the River Tyne for loading colliers; a coal barge.—*vi* to turn up the keel; to capsize.

keelhaul *vt* to punish by dropping into the sea on one side of a ship and hauling up on the other.

keelson, kelson *n* an internal keel laid on the middle of the floor timbers over the keel.

keen[1] *adj* acute of mind; penetrating; quickwitted; eager; vehement; full of relish or zest; devoted to; intense or strong; sharp (*a keen appetite*); having a very fine edge (*a keen razor*); piercing; penetrating; severe (cold or wind); bitter, acrimonious (*keen satire*); (of prices) competitive, low.

keen[2] *vi* to lament in a wailing tone.—*n* a dirge; a lament; wailing.

keenness *n* the state or quality of being keen; acuteness; eagerness.

keg

keep *vt* (*pret, pp* **kept,** *ppr* **keeping**) to hold; to retain in one's power or possession; not to lose or part with; to have in custody for security or preservation; to preserve; to protect; to guard; to restrain; to detain or delay; to tend or have the care of; to maintain, as an establishment, institution, etc; to manage; to hold in any state; to continue or maintain, as a state, course or action (*to keep silence*; *to keep the same pace*; *to keep step*); to remain confined to; not to quit (the house, one's bed); to observe in practice; not to neglect or violate; to fulfil; to observe or solemnize; to board, maintain, supply with necessaries of life; to have in the house; to entertain (*to keep lodgers, company*); to be in the habit of selling; to have a supply of for sale.—*vi* to remain in any position or state; to continue; to abide; to stay; not to be impaired; to continue fresh or wholesome; not to become spoiled.—*n* guard, care or heed; the state of being kept; the means by which one is kept; subsistence; provisions; the stronghold of an ancient castle; a donjon.

keeper *n* one who or that which keeps; one who has the care of a prison and the custody of prisoners; one who has the care, custody or superintendence of anything (*gamekeeper, goalkeeper, wicket keeper,* etc); something that keeps or holds safe; a ring which keeps another on the finger.

keeping *n* a holding; custody; guard; maintenance; support; food; just proportion; conformity; consistency; harmony.—**to be in keeping with** to accord or harmonize with; to be consistent with.

keepsake *n* anything kept or given to be kept for the sake of the giver; a token of friendship.

keg *n* a small cask or barrel.

kelp *n* the alkaline substance yielded by seaweed when burned, containing soda and iodine; any of a group of very large, brown seaweed.

kelpie, kelpy *n* in Scotland, a malignant spirit of the waters, generally seen in the form of a horse.

kelson *n* same as **keelson**.

kelvin *n* the basic SI unit of temperature equal to one degree Celsius.

Kelvin scale *n* a temperature scale in which absolute zero (-273.15° Celsius) is taken as zero degrees.

ken *n* cognizance; reach of sight or knowledge (as in *beyond our ken*).

kennel[1] *n* a shelter for a dog; (*pl*) a place where dogs are kept, boarded or bred.—*vt* (**kennelled, kennelling**) to keep or confine in a kennel.

kennel[2] *n* the watercourse of a street; a gutter.

kenosis *n* the renunciation for a time of the divine nature by Christ during the incarnation.

Kentish *adj* of or pertaining to the county of Kent.

keratin *n* the complex compound of which horny substances (e.g. hair and nails) are mainly composed.

kerb *n* the raised stone or concrete edge between a footpath or pavement and the roadway.

kerchief *n* a piece of cloth worn on the head; a similar piece of cloth worn round the neck.

kermes *n* a scarlet dyestuff consisting of the dried bodies of the females of certain insects found on various species of oak round the Mediterranean.

kern[1] *n* (*print*) the part of a type or character that overhangs the following piece of type or character.—*vt* (*print*) to adjust spacing between characters.

kern[2] *n* a lightly armed foot soldier of ancient Ireland and the Highlands of Scotland, opposed to *gallowglass*.

kernel *n* the edible substance contained in the shell of a nut or the stone of a fruit; anything enclosed in a shell, husk or integument; a grain of corn; the seed of pulpy fruit; a small mass around which other matter adheres; a nucleus; (*fig*) the main or essential point, as opposed to matters of less import; the core; the gist.

kerosene *n* a liquid hydrocarbon distilled from paraffin and used as a fuel in jet engines.

kerseymere *n* a thin twilled stuff woven from the finest wools, used for men's garments.

kestrel *n* a common small European falcon.

ketch *n* a kind of small two-masted sailing vessel.

ketchup *n* a kind of condiment in the form of a thick smooth sauce, usually made from tomatoes and flavouring.

ketone *n* (*chem*), one of a class of compounds, containing the carbonyl group (CO) united to two univalent hydrocarbon radicals.

kettle *n* a metal vessel with a handle and spout used for boiling water.

kettledrum *n* a drum consisting of a metal vessel, usually hemispherical, covered with parchment.

key *n* an instrument for shutting or opening a lock; that whereby any mystery is disclosed or anything difficult explained; a guide; a solution; an explanation; an instrument by which something is screwed or turned; something that fastens, keeps tight, prevents movement, etc; a binding or connecting piece; a movable piece in a musical instrument, struck or pressed by the fingers in playing to produce the notes; the keynote; a lever or button pressed to work something, such as a typewriter.—*adj* very important (*a key industry*); controlling.—*vt* to furnish or fasten with a key; to fasten or secure firmly.—**to key in** to capture (data) in a computer by using the keyboard.

keyboard *n* the series of levers in a keyed musical instrument, as a pianoforte, organ or harmonium, on which the fingers press; a similar series of levers on a typewriter or computer, etc.

keyhole *n* an opening (in a lock) into which a key is inserted.

keyhole surgery *n* a form of surgery performed through small incisions in the outer tissue using miniature instruments and fibre optic tubes.

keynote *n* (*mus*) the first note of any scale; the fundamental note or tone of the scale in which a piece is composed; the basic idea; the main element or principle.

keynote speech *n* an opening speech at a convention which sets out the issues to be discussed.

keystone *n* the stone at the apex of an arch which, when put in, keys or locks the whole.

khaki *n* a dull yellowish-brown colour; a material used for service dress uniforms in the army; any cloth of a dull yellowish-brown colour.—*adj* of a dull yellowish-brown colour, resembling dust or earth.

khalif *n* same as **caliph**.

khamsin, kamsin *n* a hot southerly wind, especially in Egypt; the simoom.

khan *n* in Asia, a governor; a king; a prince; a chief.

khedive *n* a title formerly applied to the viceroy of Egypt (1867-1914).

kibble *n* in mining, a large bucket, generally of iron, in which the ores, etc, are brought to the surface.

kibbutz *n* (*pl* **kibbutzim**) an agricultural commune in Israel.

kick *vt* to strike with the foot; to strike in recoiling, as a gun.—*vi* to strike with the foot or feet; to be in the habit of so striking; to manifest resistance to restraint; to be recalcitrant; to protest or rebel; to recoil, as a rifle or other firearm.—**to kick off** (in football) to give the ball the first kick to start play; (*colloq*) to start.—*n* a blow with the foot or feet; a striking or thrust of the foot; the recoil of a firearm; (*colloq*) a thrill; (*colloq*) an intoxicating effect.

kickoff *n* a kick putting the ball into play at football; the beginning of proceedings, e.g. a discussion.

kickshaw *n* a trinket; a bauble.

kid[1] *n* a young goat; leather made from the skin of a kid or in imitation of it; a child; a young person.

kid[2] *vi* (**kidded, kidding**) (*colloq*) to tease; to act the fool.—*vt* (*colloq*) to tease.

kidnap *vt* (**kidnapped, kidnapping**) to abduct forcibly or steal (a person) usually with a demand for a sum of money to secure the person's release; to seize and forcibly carry away.

kidney *n* either of the two oblong, flattened, bean-shaped glands which secrete the urine, situated in the belly on either side of the backbone; sometimes colloquially used for constitution, sort, kind, character or temper (*a man of that kidney*).

kidney bean *n* a culinary vegetable, of which there are two principal varieties; the French or haricot bean.

kilderkin *n* a small barrel; an old liquid measure.

kill *vt* to deprive of life, animal or vegetable, in any manner or by any means; to render inanimate; to put to death; to slay; to deprive of active qualities; to deaden (pain); to overpower; (*colloq*) to cause severe discomfort or pain to; (*colloq*) to cancel (a project etc); (*colloq*) to amuse greatly.

killing *adj* depriving of life; overpowering; irresistible; irresistibly fascinating; dangerous; too fast to last (*a killing pace*); tiring; (*colloq*) very amusing.

kiln *n* a fabric of brick or stone which may be heated for the purpose of hardening, burning or drying anything placed in it; a kind of large stove in which something is dried or baked.

kilocalorie *n* same as **Calorie**.

ketch

key

kilogram, kilogramme *n* a metric measure of weight, being 1000 grams or 2.2 pounds avoirdupois.

kilometre *n* a metric measure of length, 1000 metres, equivalent to about five-eighths of a mile.

kilowatt *n* an electric unit of power, equivalent to 1000 watts.

kilowatt hour *n* (*elect*) a unit of electrical energy, equal to the work done by an agent working at the rate of one kilowatt for one hour.

kilt *n* a kind of knee-length skirt made from tartan material and pleated at the back and sides, worn by men as part of the traditional dress of the Highlands of Scotland.—*vt* to tuck up like a kilt for greater freedom of movement.

kimono *n* a loose robe with short wide sleeves, worn by both sexes in Japan; a type of dressing gown.

kin *n* relationship; consanguinity or affinity; connection by blood; relatives collectively; kindred (used as a plural).—*adj* of the same nature or kind; kindred; congenial.

kind[1] *adj* disposed to do good to others and to make them happy; having tenderness or goodness of nature; sympathethic; gentle; benevolent; benignant; friendly; proceeding from or dictated by tenderness or goodness of heart.

kimono

kind[2] *n* race; genus; generic class; sort; variety; nature; style; manner; character.—**in kind** with produce or commodities, as opposed to in money (*to pay one in kind*).

kindergarten *n* a class or school for very young children.

kindle *vt* (**kindled, kindling**) to set on fire; to cause to burn with flame; to light; to inflame, as the passions; to rouse; to provoke; to excite to action.—*vi* to take fire; to grow warm or animated; to be roused or exasperated.

kindling *n* the act of one who kindles; materials for lighting a fire.

kindly *adv* in a kind manner.—*adj* of a kind disposition or character; sympathetic; congenial; benevolent; favourable; refreshing (*kindly showers*).

kindness *n* the state or quality of being kind; goodwill; benevolence; a kind act; an act of goodwill.

kindred *n* relationship by birth or marriage; consanguinity; kin; in plural sense, relatives by blood or marriage, more properly the former; relations or relatives.—*adj* related; congenial; allied.

kingfisher

kinematics *n* that branch of the science of mechanics which treats of motion, without reference to the forces producing it.

kinetic *adj* causing motion (applied to force actually exerted).

kinetics *n* that branch of the science of dynamics which treats of forces causing or changing motion in bodies.

king *n* the sovereign of a nation; a man invested with supreme authority over a nation, tribe or country; a monarch; a prince; a ruler; a man supreme in a certain sphere; something best in its class; a playing card having the picture of a king; the chief piece in the game of chess; a crowned piece in the game of draughts.

king crab *n* a kind of crustacean with a carapace of horseshoe shape and a long tail spine.

kingcraft *n* the art of governing; royal polity or policy.

kingdom *n* the power or authority of a king; the territory or country subject to a king; the dominion of a king or monarch; domain or realm in a general sense; (*natural hist*) one of the most extensive divisions into which natural objects are classified (*the animal, vegetable and mineral kingdoms*).

kingfisher *n* a brightly coloured, often crested, bird with a strong beak, which catches fish or insects.

kingly *adj* belonging or pertaining to a king or to kings; royal; monarchical; becoming a king; august; splendid.—*adv* with an air of royalty; as becoming a king.

King of Arms *n* (*pl* **Kings of Arms**) the chief heraldic officer in England whose business it is to direct the other heralds and who has jurisdiction in regard to coats of arms.

kingpin *n* the foremost pin in ten-pin bowling, skittles, etc; a pin on which an axle swivels; the chief person in an organization, etc.

king post, king piece *n* the middle post standing at the apex of a pair of rafters and having its lower end fastened to the middle of the tie beam.

Kings *npl* the title of two books in the Old Testament, relating particularly to the Hebrew kings.

King's Counsel *n* (abbreviated to **KC**) during the reign of a king, a barrister appointed counsel to the crown on the nomination of the Lord Chancellor and taking precedence over ordinary barristers.

king's evidence *n* during the reign of a king, evidence given by an accomplice, when the ordinary evidence is insufficient or defective, on the understanding that the accomplice shall not be prosecuted for sharing in the crime.

king's evil *n* a disease of the scrofulous kind, formerly believed curable by the touch of a king.

kingship *n* royalty; the state, office or dignity of a king.

kink *n* a twist in a rope or thread such as prevents it running freely; an unreasonable and obstinate notion; a personality quirk; a minor problem, a snag; (*colloq*) a sexual deviation.—*vi* to get into a kink; to twist or run into knots.

kinkajou *n* a nocturnal, long-tailed, flesh-eating mammal of South America, resembling the lemurs in structure and aspect but allied to the bear.

kinky *adj* having a kink or kinks; eccentric; (*colloq*) having bizarre tastes; (*colloq*) with unusual or deviant sexual tastes; (*colloq*) provocative.

kino *n* an astringent extract resembling gum, obtained from various tropical trees.

kinsfolk *npl* relations; kindred.

kinship *n* relationship; consanguinity.

kinsman, kinswoman *n* (*pl* **kinsmen, kinswomen**) a man or woman of the same race or family; one related by blood.

kiosk *n* a small open structure from which newspapers, cigarettes, sweets, snacks, etc, are sold; a booth; a public telephone booth.

kipper *n* a herring, split open, salted and smoked.—*vt* to cure (fish) by splitting open, salting and smoking.

kirk *n* a church (still in common use in Scotland).

kirk session *n* the lowest court of the Established Church of Scotland.

kirtle *n* a kind of short gown; a petticoat.—*vt* (**kirtled, kirtling**) to tuck up so as to give the appearance of a kirtle to.

kismet *n* an Islamic word for the will of Allah or for fate or destiny.

kiss *vt* to touch with the lips in salutation or as a mark of affection; to caress by joining lips; to touch gently; to touch lightly.—*vi* to join lips in love or respect; to meet or come in contact (as curved lines, etc).—*n* a salute given with the lips; a light, gentle touch.

kit *n* clothing and personal equipment; tools and equipment for a specific purpose; a set of parts ready to be assembled.

kitchen *n* the room of a house, hotel, etc, set aside for cookery.

kitchen garden *n* a garden set aside for the raising of vegetables for the table.

kite *n* a bird of prey with a long forked tail, long wings and comparatively weak bill and talons; a light frame of wood, cloth, paper, plastic, etc, constructed for flying in the air at the end of a long string.—**to fly a kite** to test opinion or response by starting a rumour about a project, etc.

kith *n* acquaintances or friends collectively.—**kith and kin** friends and relatives.

kitten *n* a young cat or the young of the cat.

kittiwake *n* a species of gull found in great abundance in the northern parts of the world.

kiwi *n* a flightless bird of New Zealand.

kiwi fruit *n* the edible green fruit of the Chinese gooseberry, having a greyish-brown, furry skin and pale green flesh.

kleptomania *n* an uncontrollable desire to steal.

kleptomaniac *n* a person who suffers from kleptomania.—*adj* pertaining to kleptomania.

knack *n* an ability to do something easily; a trick; a habit.

knacker *n* (*sl*) one who buys worn-out horses or old houses, ships, etc, for destruction.

knapsack *n* a bag of leather or strong cloth for carrying a soldier's necessaries, strapped to the back between the shoulders; any similar bag, such as those used by tourists and others for carrying light personal luggage.

knave *n* a boy; a male servant; a false deceitful fellow; a dishonest man or boy; a rascal; in a pack of playing cards, a card with a soldier or servant painted on it; a jack.

knavery *n* the conduct of a knave; dishonesty; deception; trickery; petty villainy; fraud.

knavish *adj* acting like or belonging to a knave; dishonest; fraudulent; mischievous.

knead *vt* to work and press into a mass; particularly, to work into a well-mixed mass, as the materials of bread, cake or paste; to beat or pommel.

knee *n* the joint connecting the two principal parts of the leg; the articulation of the thigh and bones of the lower leg; something resembling or suggestive of this; a piece of bent timber or iron used to connect the beams of a ship with her sides or timbers.

knee breeches *npl* breeches that do not reach farther down than the knee.

kneecap *n* the movable bone covering the knee joint in front; the knee pan; the patella; a leather cap or covering for the knee of a horse.

kneel *vi* (*pret, pp* **kneeled** *or* **knelt**, *ppr* **kneeling**) to bend the knee; to fall on the knees.

knell *n* the sound of a bell rung at a funeral; a passing bell; a death signal in general.—*vi* to sound as a funeral knell; to sound as an omen or warning of coming evil.—*vt* to summon by, or as by, a knell.

knickerbockers *npl* a kind of loose breeches, of American origin.

knickers *npl* an undergarment worn by women, covering the lower part of the trunk with openings for the legs; underpants for women.

knick-knack *n* a trifle or toy; any small article more for ornament than use.

knife *n* (*pl* **knives**) a cutting instrument con-

kite

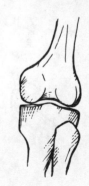

kneecap

sisting of a sharp-edged blade of small or moderate size attached to a handle.

knife edge *n* the sharp edge of a knife; anything resembling this, as the blade of an ice skate; a piece of steel with a fine edge, serving to support with the least friction an oscillating body, as the beam of a pair of scales; a critical or precarious situation.

knight *n* in feudal times, a man admitted to a certain military rank, with special ceremonies; in modern times, one who holds a certain dignity conferred by a sovereign and in the UK entitling the possessor to have the title of Sir prefixed to his Christian name but mainly not hereditary like the dignity of baronet; a member of an order of chivalry; a champion; one of the pieces in the game of chess, shaped like a horse's head.—*vt* to dub or create a knight; to confer the honour of knighthood on, the accolade or blow of a sword being commonly a part of the ceremony.

knight errant *n* a medieval knight who travelled in search of adventures and to exhibit his prowess.

knighthood *n* the character or dignity of a knight; the rank or honour accompanying the title of knight; knights collectively.

knightly *adj* pertaining to a knight; becoming a knight; chivalrous.—*adv* in a manner becoming a knight.

knitting

Knight of the Bath *n* one of a British order of knighthood instituted at the coronation of Henry IV in 1399 and revived by George I in 1725, receiving its name from the candidates for the honour being put into a bath the preceding evening to denote a purification or absolution from evil deeds.

knit *vt* (**knit** *or* **knitted, knitting**) to weave or form by looping or knotting a continuous thread by means of wires or needles; to cause to grow together; to join closely; to contract into folds or wrinkles (*to knit the brows*).—*vi* to make a fabric by interlooping yarn or thread by means of needles, etc; to unite closely; to grow together.

knitter *n* one who knits; a knitting machine.

knitting needle *n* a needle used for knitting, usually a straight piece of wire, plastic or other material with a pointed end.

knob *n* a hard protuberance; a hard swelling or rising; a round ball at the end of anything; the more or less ball-shaped handle for a door, drawer, etc; a boss; a knot; a bunch of foliage carved or cast for ornament.—*vi* (**knobbed, knobbing**) to grow into knobs; to bunch.

knobby *adj* full of knobs or hard protuberances.

knot

knock *vi* to strike or beat with something thick, hard or heavy; to drive or be driven so as to come in collision with something;

to strike against; to clash.—**to knock about** (*colloq*) to wander here and there; to move about in the world.—*vt* to dash; to drive; to cause to collide; to drive or force by a succession of blows.—**to knock down** to strike down; to fell; to prostrate by a blow; at auctions, to assign to a bidder, generally by a blow with a hammer.—**to knock out** to render unconscious by a blow or by blows; to defeat in a knockout competition.—**to knock on the head** to stun or kill by a blow or blows on the head; to frustrate, as a project or scheme; to render abortive.—*n* a blow; a stroke with something thick, hard or heavy; a stroke on a door, intended as a request for admittance; a rap.

knockdown *adj* a term applied to a blow which fells a person to the ground; (of furniture) easy to dismantle; (*colloq*) (of prices) cheap.

knocker *n* one that knocks; a contrivance fastened to a door to knock for admittance; (usually *pl*) (*sl*) a woman's breasts.

knock-kneed *adj* having the legs so much curved inwards that they touch or knock together in walking; hence, feeble (*a knock-kneed argument*).

knockout *n* a punch or blow that produces unconsciousness; a contest in which competitors are eliminated at each round; (*colloq*) an attractive or extremely impressive person or thing.

knoll[1] *n* the top or crown of a hill; a small or low round hill; a small elevation of earth.

knoll[2] *vti* to sound, as a bell.—*n* the ringing of a bell; a knell.

knot *n* a lump in a thread, cord or rope, made by tying, knitting or entangling; a fastening made by looping a cord or thread on itself; a tie; a figure with interlaced lines; a bond of association; a union (*the nuptial knot*); a cluster, collection, group; a difficulty or perplexity; something not easily solved; a hard part in timber caused by the shooting out of a branch; a protuberance; a nodule; a bunch; a knob; (*naut*) a division of the logline, forming the same fraction of a mile as half a minute is of an hour, that is, the hundred and twentieth part of a nautical mile, so that the number of knots run off the reel in half a minute shows the vessel's speed per hour in miles; hence, a nautical mile or 6080 feet; also, and more correctly, a speed of 1 nautical mile per hour.—*vt* (**knotted, knotting**) to tie in a knot or knots; to form a knot on; to entangle; to unite closely.—*vi* to become knotted; to form knots or joints, as in plants.

knotgrass *n* a common weed of low growth, with branched trailing stems and knotted joints.

knotted *adj* full of knots; having knots;

(*bot*) having knobs or enlargements as on a stem.

knotty *adj* full of knots; having many knots; difficult; intricate; involved; hard to unravel (*a knotty question* or *point*).

knout *n* a whip formerly used as an instrument of punishment in Russia; the punishment inflicted with the knout.—*vi* to punish with the knout.

know *vt* (*pret* **knew**, *pp* **known**, *ppr* **knowing**) to perceive with certainty; to understand clearly; to be convinced or satisfied regarding the truth or reality of; to be assured of; to be aware of; to distinguish (*to know a star from a planet*); to be familiar or acquainted with (a person, a topic, etc); to have experience of.—*vi* to have clear and certain perception; not to be doubtful; to be informed.

knowable *adj* capable of being known.

knowing *adj* well-informed; well-instructed; intelligent; sagacious; conscious; expressive of knowledge or cunning (*a knowing look*).

knowledge *n* the clear and certain perception of that which exists or of truth and fact; indubitable apprehension; cognizance; learning; erudition; information; skill in anything; familiarity gained by actual experience; acquaintance with any fact or person.

knuckle *n* the joint of a finger, particularly when protuberant by the closing of the fingers; the knee joint of a calf or pig (*a knuckle of veal*).—*vt* (**knuckled, knuckling**) to strike with the knuckles; to pommel.—**to knuckle down** (*colloq*) to apply oneself in earnest (to a duty, task, etc).—**to knuckle under** to yield; to submit; to acknowledge oneself beaten.

knuckle-duster *n* a metal instrument with knobs or points projecting, fitting over the knuckles and making a blow more powerful.

koala, koala bear *n* a tree-dwelling marsupial of Australia with thick grey fur.

kobold *n* a domestic spirit or elf in German mythology; a kind of goblin.

Kohinoor *n* a great Indian diamond owned by the Mogul kings which became, in 1849, the property of the British Crown.

kohl *n* a black pigment used as a cosmetic.

kohlrabi *n* a variety of cabbage distinguished by a globular swelling immediately above the ground, which is the part used.

koodoo *n* same as **kudu**.

kookaburra *n* an Australian kingfisher with a harsh cry that sounds like loud laughter.

kopeck, copeck *n* a Russian coin, the hundredth part of a rouble.

Koran *n* the sacred book of Islam which contains the religious and moral code of the Muslims and by which all their transactions, civil, legal, military, etc, are regulated; the Alkoran.

kosher *adj* prepared according to Jewish dietary laws; pure according to Jewish law; (*colloq*) genuine; (*colloq*) legitimate.—*n* kosher food.—*vt* to prepare food in the way prescribed by Jewish ceremonial rites.

kowtow *n* formerly the mode of saluting the Emperor of China by prostrating oneself and touching the ground with the forehead nine times.—*vi* to perform the kowtow; to show exaggerated respect; to behave in a servile way.

kraal *n* a native village or collection of huts in southern Africa.

kraft *n* a type of heavy brown wrapping paper made from wood pulp.

kraken *n* a huge legendary enormous sea monster, said to live in the sea off the coast of Norway.

krill *n* the tiny shrimp-like plankton eaten by many whales.

kris, crease *n* a Malayan dagger.

krone *n* the monetary unit of Denmark and Norway.

krypton *n* an inert gaseous element, occurring in minute quantities in the atmosphere.

kudos *n* glory; fame; renown.

kudu, koodoo *n* a striped antelope of southern Africa, the male of which has long and beautifully twisted horns.

kumiss *n* a liquor made from mare's milk fermented and distilled.

kümmel *n* a liqueur flavoured with caraway seeds.

kumquat *n* a small fruit like an orange with a sweet rind.

kung fu *n* a Chinese system of unarmed combat.

Kurd *n* an inhabitant of Kurdistan.

Kurdish *adj* of or relating to Kurdistan or the Kurds.

kyanize *vt* (**kyanized, kyanizing**) to preserve (timber) from dry rot by steeping in a solution of corrosive sublimate.

Kyrie eleison *n* a form of invocation ('Lord have mercy') in ancient Greek liturgies and still used in the Roman Catholic service; a musical setting of this; the response in an Anglican communion service.

koala

479

L

L the twelfth letter and ninth consonant of the English alphabet.

la (*mus*) the sixth of the seven syllables that represent the seven sounds in the diatonic scale.

laager *n* in South Africa, an encampment; a temporary defensive enclosure, formed of wagons.

lab *n* a laboratory.

labarum *n* (*pl* labara) a banner bearing the Greek letters XP (that is, *Chr*), joined so as to form a monogram of the name of Christ.

label *n* a slip of paper, parchment or other material, containing a name, title, address, statement of contents, nature, etc, affixed to anything; a tag; an epithet; a record or CD company trademark.—*vt* (labelled, labelling) to fix a label to; to designate or classify as.

labial *adj* pertaining to the lips; uttered by the lips; owing its special character to the lips (*a labial consonant*).—*n* a vowel or consonant formed chiefly by the lips, as *b*.

labiodental *adj* formed or pronounced by the lips and teeth.—*n* a sound thus formed (*f* and *v*).

laboratory *n* a building or room designed for investigation and experiment in chemistry, physics or other subject.

laborious *adj* requiring hard work; not easy; diligent in work or service; industrious; laboured.

labour *n* exertion, physical or mental, or both, undergone in the performance of some task or work; particularly, the exertion of the body in occupations by which one's living is earned; the performance of work; toil; work done or to be done; a particular task; workers collectively (*the claims* or *rights of labour*); travail; the pangs and efforts of childbirth.—*vi* to engage in labour; to work; to toil; to exert the body or mind, or both, in the carrying out of any purpose; to proceed or act with difficulty; to be burdened; to suffer (*to labour under a disease*); (*naut*) to pitch and roll heavily, as a ship in a rough sea.—*vt* to till; to cultivate; to carry out with effort.

Labour *n* the Labour Party.

Labrador

laburnum

laboured *adj* produced with labour; bearing the marks of constraint and effort, opposed to *easy* or *natural* (*a laboured speech*).

labourer *n* one who labours; a person who does work that requires little skill or special training.

Labour Exchange *n* formerly, an employment office run by the state.

Labour Party *n* a political party in Britain, formed in 1900 by trade unionists, etc; the socialist party of Britain.

labour-saving *adj* reducing or eliminating physical effort.

Labrador *n* a breed of large smooth-coated black or golden retrievers.

laburnum *n* a small deciduous tree with drooping yellow pea-shaped flowers and poisonous seeds.

labyrinth *n* a structure with numerous intricate winding passages through which it is hard to fine one's way; a place full of inextricable windings; an ornamental maze or wilderness in gardens; an intricate arrangement of bands or lines used for ornamentation; any intricate matter or business; any confusing entanglement; (*anat*) that part of the inner ear which lies behind the tympanum.

labyrinthine *adj* pertaining to or like a labyrinth; full of windings; intricate; mazy.

lac[1] *n* a resinous substance secreted by insects and used in preparing lacquers, varnishes, etc.

lac[2] *n* same as lakh.

lace *n* a string or cord used to fasten shoes or some other part of dress or plaited and otherwise ornamented and used for decoration; a delicate kind of openwork used for the decorating a dress, etc.—*vt* (laced, lacing) to fasten with a lace or string through eyelet holes; to adorn with lace or as with a lace; to strengthen beer, tea, etc, with whisky or other spirit.—*vi* to be fastened or tied by a lace; to have a lace.

lacerate *vt* (lacerated, lacerating) to tear; to rend; to make a ragged wound or gash in by violence or tearing; (*fig*) to torture; to harrow.

laceration *n* the act of lacerating; the breach made by rending.

lacertian, lacertilian *adj* belonging to the family of lizards.

lacertine *adj* like a lizard.

laches *n* (*law*) neglect; negligence; remissness; inexcusable delay.

lachrymal *adj* pertaining to tears; generating or secreting tears (*the lachrymal gland*); conveying tears (*lachrymal canal*).

lachrymose *adj* generating or shedding tears; appearing as if shedding or given to shed tears; tears; tearful.

lack *vt* to be without; not to have or possess; to want; to need; to require.—*vi* to be in want; to be wanting.—*n* want; destitution; need; failure.

lackadaisical *adj* showing lack of energy or interest; listless; careless or slapdash.

lackaday *exclam* of sorrow or regret; alas!—alas! the day.

lackey *n* an attending male servant; a footman; a servile follower.

lacklustre *n* lacking in brightness or vigour; dull.

laconic *adj* short; brief; concise; terse; sententious.

lacquer *n* a protective, usually transparent, coating made from a resin or artificial substance and capable of taking a high polish; a glossy varnish.—*vt* to varnish with lacquer.

lacrosse *n* a ball game in which the ball is carried or thrown through the enemy's goal by means of a long-handled racquet with a net.

lactate *n* (*chem*) a salt of lactic acid or acid of sour milk.

lactation *n* the act of giving suck or the time of suckling; the function of secreting and excreting milk.

lacteal *adj* pertaining to or resembling milk; milky; conveying chyle (*a lacteal vessel*).—*n* (*anat*) one of numerous minute tubes which absorb or take up the chyle from the alimentary canal and convey it to the thoracic duct.

lactescent *adj* becoming milky; having a milky appearance or consistence.

lactic *adj* pertaining to milk or procured from sour milk or whey (*lactic acid*).

lactose *n* the sugar present in milk.

lacuna *n* (*pl* **lacunae**) a small blank space; a gap; a missing portion in a text, etc; one of the spaces left among the tissues of the lower animals, serving in place of vessels for the circulation of the fluids.

lacustrine *adj* pertaining to a lake.

lacy *adj* made of lacy; resembling lace.

lad *n* a young man or boy.

ladder *n* an article of wood, metal or rope, consisting of two long side pieces connected by crosspieces at suitable dis-

tances, forming steps by which a person may ascend a building, etc; (*fig*) a means of rising to eminence; a hierarchy; in knitted fabrics, a defect due to the breaking of a thread, causing a loop to run down.

lade[1] *vt* (*pret* **laded**, *pp* **laden** *or* **laded, laden**, *ppr* **lading**) to load; to put a load or cargo on or in; to lift or throw in or out (a fluid) with some utensil.

lade[2] *n* a watercourse; a channel for water.

laden *adj* loaded; charged with a burden or freight; (*fig*) oppressed; burdened.

la-di-dah *adj* (*colloq*) pretentious in speech or actions; affected.

lading *n* that which constitutes a load or cargo; freight; burden.

ladle *n* a large spoon with a long handle, used for lifting or serving out liquids from a vessel.—*vt* (**ladled, ladling**) to lift or deal out with a ladle; to hand out in great quantities.

ladleful *n* the quantity contained in a ladle; a great deal.

lady *n* a woman of rank or distinction; the counterpart of *lord*; the proper title of any woman whose husband is a peer below the rank of duke, a baronet or a knight, or who is the daughter of a nobleman not lower than an earl; a term applied by courtesy to any woman; a woman of good breeding, education and refinement of mind, the counterpart of *gentleman*; the wife of a gentleman or man in good position; the mistress or possessor of an estate.

ladybird *n* a small beetle, the larva of which feeds on aphids.

ladybird

Lady Chapel *n* a chapel dedicated to the Virgin Mary, frequently attached to large churches.

Lady Day *n* the day of the Annunciation of the Virgin Mary, 25th March.

lady fern *n* a species of fern common in Great Britain.

lady-in-waiting *n* (*pl* **ladies-in-waiting**) a female attendant to a queen or princess.

lady-killer *n* a man who is, or thinks he is, very attractive to women.

ladylike *adj* like a lady in any respect.

ladylove *n* a female sweetheart.

ladyship *n* the condition or rank of a lady, employed as a title (with *her*, *your*, etc).

lady's fingers *n* same as **okra**.

lady's maid *n* a female attendant on a woman.

lady's-slipper *n* a rare British orchid with a conspicuous flower.

lady's-smock *n* a common European plant growing in meadows, with lilac or whitish flowers.

lag *vi* (**lagged, lagging**) to walk or move slowly; to loiter; to stay behind.—*n* a lagging behind in time or space in relation to something else; a delay.

lagan, ligan *n* goods sunk in the sea but

ladder

having something buoyant attached to mark their position.

lager *n* a light beer that has been aged for some months and stored at low temperatures.

laggard *adj* slow; sluggish; backward.—*n* one who lags; a loiterer; a lazy, slack person.

lagging *n* a covering of nonconducting material used to reduce loss of heat from a boiler or other hot body.

lagoon *n* a shallow lake or sheet of water connected with the sea or a river, found in low-lying regions; the sheet of water surrounded by an atoll or ring-shaped coral island.

laic, laical *adj* belonging to the laity or people, as distinct from the clergy.—*n* a layman.

laid back *adj* extremely relaxed or calm, easy-going.

lair *n* a place to lie or rest; especially the resting place of a wild beast, etc.

laissez faire, laisser faire *n* a letting alone; non-interference; a term especially used in regard to the interference of a government with social, commercial or other matters.

laity *n* collectively all people who do not belong to the clergy; people outside any profession as distinguished from those in it.

lake[1] *n* a sheet or body of water wholly surrounded by land; any large area of liquid or similar substance.

lake[2] *n* a pigment consisting of an earthy substance impregnated with red colouring matter of certain animal and vegetable substances (*lac lake, madder lake,* etc).

lake dwelling *n* the name given to an ancient habitation built on small islands in lakes or on platforms supported by piles near the shores of lakes.

lakh, lac *n* in India, a word used to denote 100,000, especially 100,000 rupees.

lama *n* a priest or ecclesiastic belonging to the form of Buddhism known as Lamaism.

Lamaism *n* a form of Buddhism chiefly prevailing in Tibet.

lamb *n* the young of the sheep; a person as gentle or innocent as a lamb.—*vi* to bring forth a lamb or lambs.

lambaste, lambast *vt* (**lambasted, lambasting**) to thrash severely; to scold severely; to criticize severely.

lambasting *n* the act of lambasting; a severe thrashing; a severe scolding; severe criticism.

lambent *adj* licking; playing about; touching lightly; gliding over (*a lambent flame*); gleaming; twinkling; flickering.

lambda *n* the Greek letter L.

lamb-like *adj* like a lamb; gentle; humble; meek.

lambskin *n* the skin of a lamb dressed with the fleece on or made into leather.

lamb

lamb's wool *n* a fine, soft wool obtained from lambs; spiced wine or beer with roasted apples.

lame *adj* crippled or disabled in one or more of the limbs; crippled; disabled (*a lame arm*); imperfect, defective, not sound or unassailable (*a lame excuse*).—*vt* (**lamed, laming**) to make lame; to cripple or disable; to render imperfect.

lamé *n* a fabric with silver or gold threads woven into it.

lame duck *n* an ineffectual person; a weak, unsuccessful person.

lamella *n* (*pl* **lamellae**) a thin plate or scale; one of an aggregate of thin plates; one of the thin plates which compose the gills of certain molluscs; one of the gills forming the spore-bearing layer of an agaric.

lamellar *adj* composed of thin plates or lamellae; disposed in thin plates or scales.

lamellate, lamellated *adj* formed in thin plates or lamellae or covered with them; furnished with lamellae.

lamellibranchiate *adj* having lamellar gills, especially having lamellar gills and bivalve shells as the molluscs of the class or order of which mussels, cockles and oysters are familiar examples.—*n* a lamellibranchiate animal.

lamellicorn *adj* having lamellar antennae; having antennae the three last joints of which are plate-like and disposed somewhat like the teeth of a comb (said of beetles, such as the cockchafers, etc).—*n* a lamellicorn animal.

lament *vi* to mourn; to weep or wail; to express sorrow; to regret deeply; to grieve.—*vt* to bewail; to mourn for; to bemoan; to deplore.—*n* lamentation; an elegy or mournful ballad or air.

lamentable *adj* to be lamented; causing or calling for sorrow; grievous; mournful; miserable; pitiful; wretched.

lamentation *n* the act of lamenting; a wailing; expression of sorrow; cries or words expressive of grief.

Lamentations *npl* a book of Scripture containing the lamentations of Jeremiah.

lamia *n* a mythological monster, half snake, half woman, said to suck the blood of infants.

lamina *n* (*pl* **laminae**) a thin plate or scale; a layer or coat lying over another (applied to the plates of minerals, bones, etc); (*bot*) the upper broad part of the petal in a corolla; the blade of a leaf.

laminar *adj* formed of laminae or plates; consisting of thin plates or layers.

laminaria *n* any of a genus of various seaweeds with no definite leaves but a plain ribless expansion which is either simple or cloven.

laminary *adj* composed of laminae or plates.

laminate *adj* consisting of laminae, scales or thin layers, one over another.—*vi* (**laminated, laminating**) to separate or split up into thin plates or layers; to cover or overlay with thin layers.

lamination *n* state of being laminated; arrangement in laminae or thin plates.

lammergeier, lammergeyer *n* the bearded vulture.

lamp *n* a vessel for containing oil or other liquid inflammable substance to be burned by means of a wick; any device adapted to contain an artificial light; something metaphorically communicating light.

lampblack *n* a fine soot formed by the condensation of the smoke of burning oil, pitch or resinous substances in a chimney terminating in a cone of cloth.

lamplighter *n* formerly, a person employed to light street or other public lamps.

lampoon *n* a personal satire in writing; a satiric or abusive attack in prose or verse.—*vt* to write a lampoon against; to assail in a lampoon.

lamppost *n* a post or pillar for supporting a street or other outdoor lamp.

lamprey *n* a jawless, eel-like, scaleless fish with a round sucking mouth, inhabiting both fresh and salt water.

lampshade *n* a shade placed over the flame or bulb of a lamp to mellow or intercept it.

lamp shell *n* one of the molluscs, a brachiopod.

lance *n* a weapon consisting of a long wooden shaft with a sharp-pointed head of steel or other metal; a spear; a lancet.—*vt* (**lanced, lancing**) to pierce with a lance or other pointed instrument; to open with a lancet or other sharp instrument.

lance corporal *n* a private soldier performing the duties of a corporal with a temporary rank as such.

lancelet *n* a small worm-like transparent fish, the lowest of the fish class.

lanceolate, lanceolated *adj* shaped like the head of a lance.

lancer *n* one who lances; one who carries a lance; a cavalry soldier armed with a lance.

lancers *n* a kind of dance.

lancet *n* a small surgical instrument, sharp-pointed and generally two-edged, used in opening boils, abscesses, etc.

lancet arch *n* an arch whose head is shaped like the point of a lancet, generally used in lancet windows.

lancet window *n* a high and narrow window pointed like a lancet.

lancewood *n* a kind of tough, elastic wood.

land *n* the solid or fixed part of the surface of the globe, as distinct from the sea or other waters which constitute the fluid part; a definite portion of the solid surface of the globe as set apart or belonging to any individual or a people, as a country, estate or farm (*to travel in all lands, his land adjoins mine*); ground or soil (*good land, poor land*).—*vt* to set on shore; to disembark; to set (an aircraft) down on the ground or water; to bring to or put in a certain place or condition (*to land a person at the theatre, in difficulties*); to catch (a fish); (*colloq*) to secure (a job, prize, etc); (*colloq*) to deliver (a blow).—*vi* to go on shore from a ship or boat; to disembark; to reach the ground (from a flight, jump, etc); to arrive; to reach.

landau *n* a kind of coach or carriage whose top may be opened and thrown back.

land breeze *n* a current of air setting from the land towards the sea.

land crab *n* a crustacean whose habits are terrestrial, as distinguished from one whose habits are aquatic.

landed *adj* having an estate in land; consisting in real estate or land (*landed property*).

landfall *n* the first land discovered after a voyage; a landslip.

landholder *n* a holder, owner or proprietor of land.

landing *adj* connected with the process of bringing to land or of unloading anything from a vessel, aircraft, etc.—*n* the act of going or setting on land; a place where persons land or where goods are set on shore; the first part of a floor at the end of a flight of steps; a resting place in a series or flight of steps.

landlady *n* a woman who lets rooms in her house to lodgers; a woman who lets out property to tenants; the mistress of an inn or of a lodging house, the counterpart of *landlord*.

landlocked *adj* enclosed or encompassed by land.

landlord *n* a man who lets rooms in his house to lodgers; a man who lets out property to tenants; the master of an inn, tavern, lodging house; a host.

landlubber *n* a contemptuous term among seamen for a landsman.

landmark *n* a mark to designate the boundary of land; any mark or fixed object by which the limits of a portion of territory may be known and preserved; any prominent and distinguishing feature of a locality; some elevated object on land that serves as a guide to sailors; what marks a stage in any course of development; any striking historical event to which others may be referred.

landowner *n* a proprietor of land.

land rail *n* the corncrake.

landscape *n* a picture representing a tract of country with the various objects it contains; such pictures in general or the painting of such pictures; a natural scene that might form the subject of such a picture.—

lamprey

lance

vt (**landscaped, landscaping**) to enhance the features of (a garden, park, etc) by shaping the contours, arranging plants and trees, etc.—*vi* to work in landscape gardening.

landscape gardening *n* the art of laying out grounds, arranging trees, shrubbery, etc, so as to produce the effect of natural landscape.

landslip, landslide *n* the slipping or sliding down of a considerable portion of land or earth from a higher to a lower level; the earth which so slides or slips.

landsman *n* (*pl* **landsmen**) one who lives on the land, opposed to *sailor*.

land surveying *n* the act of determining the boundaries and superficial extent of portions of land and of laying down an accurate map of the whole.

landward *adj* lying towards the land or towards the interior or away from the sea coast; situated in or forming part of the country, as opposed to the town; rural.

landwards *adv* towards the land.

lane *n* a narrow way or passage, as between hedges or buildings; a narrow street; an alley; a narrow pass; a path or strip specifically designated for ships, aircraft, cars, etc; one of the narrow strips dividing a running track, a swimming pool, etc, for competitors; one of the narrow passages along which balls are bowled in a bowling alley.

lane

language *n* human speech; the expression of thoughts by words or articulate sounds; the aggregate of the words employed by any community for intercommunication; the speech particular to a nation; words appropriate to or especially employed in any branch of knowledge (*the language of chemistry*); general style or manner of expression; the expression of thought in any way articulate or inarticulate (*the language of the eyes, of flowers*, etc).

languid *adj* flagging; drooping; weak; heavy; dull; indisposed to exertion; slow; tardy; without animation.

languish *vi* to lose strength or animation; to be or become dull, feeble or spiritless; to pine; to be or to grow heavy; to droop; to wither; to fade; to be no longer active and vigorous.—*n* the act of pining; a soft and tender look or appearance.

languishing *adj* losing strength; becoming feeble; pining; having a soft and tender expression (*a languishing eye*).

languor *n* the state of body induced by exhaustion of strength; feebleness; faintness; lassitude of body; dullness of intellect; listlessness; an agreeable listless or dreamy state.

lank *adj* of a thin or slender body; (of hair) straight and limp.

lanky *adj* tall and thin.

lantern

lanolin, lanoline *n* a grease obtained from unwashed wool, used in cosmetics, ointments, etc.

lantern *n* a case enclosing a light and protecting it from wind and rain, either portable or fixed; (*archit*) an erection on the top of a dome, the roof of an apartment, etc, to give light, for ventilation or for ornament; a tower which has the whole or a considerable portion of the interior open to view; a light, open erection on the top of a tower; the upper part of a lighthouse where the light is shown.

lantern fly *n* a four-winged insect of South America which emits a strong light in the dark.

lantern jaw *n* a protruding, square-shaped jaw.

lantern-jawed *n* having a lantern jaw; having a long thin face.

lanthanum *n* a metallic element, the second commonest of the rare earth group.

lanuginous, lanuginose *adj* downy; covered with down or fine soft hair.

lanyard *n* a cord worn round the neck to carry a whistle, etc; (*naut*) a short piece of rope or line used for fastening something in ships; (*milit*) a piece of strong twine with an iron hook at one end, formerly used in firing cannon.

laodicean *adj* lukewarm in religion; indifferent.

lap[1] *n* the lower part of a garment that hangs loosely; the part of clothes that lies on the knees when a person sits down; the upper part of the legs in this position.

lap[2] *n* the part of one body which lies on and covers a part of another (as a slate in roofing); a single circuit in a racetrack.—*vt* (**lapped, lapping**) to wrap or twist round; to enfold; to fold; to double over; to lay partly above; to get ahead of (a fellow competitor) by a lap or more of a racetrack.—*vi* to be spread or laid; to be turned over; to lie over something in part (as slates on a roof); to extend over something in space or time.

lap[3] *vi* (**lapped, lapping**) to take up liquid or food with the tongue; to feed or drink by licking up; to make a sound like that produced by taking up water by the tongue.—*vt* to take into the mouth with the tongue; to lick up.—*n* a lick, as with the tongue; a sound made in this way; a sound as of water rippling against the beach.

lap[4] *n* a wheel or revolving disc of soft metal which by means of a polishing powder is used in cutting glass, gems, etc.

lapdog *n* a small dog fondled in the lap; a pet dog.

lapel *n* that part of a garment which is made to lap or fold over; the part in the front of a coat or waistcoat that is folded back.

lapidary *n* a person who cuts, polishes and

engraves gems or precious stones; a dealer in precious stones.—*adj* of or pertaining to the art of polishing and engraving precious stones; inscribed on stone; concise, like an inscription.

lapis lazuli *n* an opaque semi-precious mineral of a rich blue colour used in mosaic work and other kinds of ornament and when powdered yielding ultramarine.

lap of honour a circuit of a sports field or stadium by a winning competitor or team.

Lapp *n* a native of Lapland.

lappet *n* a little lap or flap.

lapse *n* a gliding, slipping or gradually falling; an unobserved or very gradual advance; an unnoticed passing away (of time); a slip or error; a failing in duty; a deviation from truth or rectitude; (*eccles law*) the omission of a patron to present a clerk to a benefice within six months after it becomes void.—*vi* (**lapsed, lapsing**) to pass slowly, silently or by degrees; to glide away; to fall gradually; to slip in moral conduct; to fail in duty; to commit a fault; to fall or pass from one person to another, through some omission or negligence; (*law*) to become ineffectual or void.

lapsed *adj* exhibiting or having undergone a lapse; having fallen away from connection with any church (*a lapsed Catholic*).

lapwing *n* a bird belonging to the plover family, about the size of a pigeon, often called the peewit from its cry.

lar *n* (*pl* **lares**) a household deity among the ancient Romans, regarded as the spirit of a deceased ancestor.

larboard *n* (*naut*) the left-hand or port side of a ship, opposite of *starboard*, a term now given up in favour of *port*.

larceny *n* the unlawful taking and carrying away of any article or piece of goods with intent to deprive the rightful owner; theft.

larch *n* a deciduous coniferous tree with short needle-like leaves and hard durable wood.

lard *n* the fat from pigs after being melted and separated from the flesh.—*vt* to mix with lard or bacon; to stuff with pieces of bacon (as in cooking a fowl); to fatten; to enrich; to mix with something by way of improvement; to embellish.

larder *n* a room, house, box, etc, where food is kept.

large *adj* being of great size; having great dimensions; big; bulky; great; containing or consisting of a great quantity or number; abundant; plentiful; numerous; liberal, many-sided, comprehensive (*a large mind*); generous, noble, sympathetic (*a large heart*); bigger than others of its kind; operating on a big scale.—**at large** without restraint or confinement; diffusely; fully; with all details.

large calorie *n* same as **Calorie**.

large-hearted *adj* having a large heart; magnanimous; generous; sympathetic.

large intestine *n* the section of the digestive system which comprises the caecum, colon and rectum.

largely *adv* in a large manner; to a large or great degree or extent; widely; extensively; copiously; diffusely; amply; bountifully.

large-scale *adj* (of a map, etc) drawn on a big scale to reveal much detail; extensive.

largess, largesse *n* a present; a gift or donation; a bounty bestowed.

larghetto *adv* (*mus*) somewhat slowly but not so slowly as largo.—*n* (*pl* **larghettos**) a passage of music played in this way.

largo *adv* (*mus*) slowly; slowly, with breadth and dignity.—*n* (*pl* **largos**) a passage of music played in this way.

lariat *n* a lasso; a long cord or thong of leather with a noose used for catching horses, etc.

lark[1] *n* one of a genus of perching birds characterized by having a long straight hind claw and of which there are various species, as the skylark, woodlark, shore lark, etc, the skylark being celebrated for its song.

lark[2] *n* sport; frolic; a piece of merriment.—*vi* to sport; to make sport.

larkspur *n* the common name of a genus of plants, several species of which are common in gardens.

larrikin *n* (*Australian sl*) a hooligan.

larva *n* (*pl* **larvae**) the early form of any animal which during its development is unlike its parent; an insect in the caterpillar or grub state, i.e. the first stage after the egg, preceding the chrysalis and the perfect insect.

larval *adj* pertaining to a larva.

larynx *n* (*pl* **larynxes, larynges**) (*anat*) the upper part of the windpipe or trachea, a cartilaginous cavity which plays an important part in the utterance of articulate sounds.

laryngitis *n* an inflammation of the larynx of any sort.

lasagne *n* pasta in the form of flat broad sheets; a baked dish consisting of sheets of this pasta layered with a meat or vegetable sauce and cheese.

lascar *n* a sailor from the East Indies.

lascivious *adj* lecherous; lustful; exciting sexual desire.

laser *n* a device that produces an intense, narrow monochromatic beam of coherent light or other electromagnetic radiation, used extensively in electronic engineering, in certain surgical operations, etc.

laser printer *n* a computer printer that uses a laser beam and light-sensitive drum to produce high-quality text and graphic output.

lapwing

lapel

lash *n* the thong or cord at the point of a whip; any thong, cord, etc, for flogging; a whip; a scourge; a stroke with a whip or anything pliant and tough; a stroke of satire; a sarcastic or cutting remark; an eyelash.—*vt* to strike with a lash or anything pliant; to whip or scourge; to beat, as with something loose; to dash against (as waves); to satirize; to censure with severity; to tie, bind, secure or fasten with a rope or cord.—*vi* to ply the whip; to aim sarcasms; to hit.

lashing *n* a piece of rope binding or making fast one thing to another; a whipping or beating.

lashings *n* (*colloq*) an abundance; large quantities.

lass *n* a young woman; a girl; (*colloq*) a woman of any age.

lassie *n* a young girl; a term of endearment for a young woman.

lassitude *n* the state of having the energies weakened; weakness; weariness; languor of body or mind; enervation.

lasso *n* (*pl* **lassos, lassoes**) a rope or cord, with a noose, used for catching wild horses and other animals.—*vt* to catch with a lasso.

lasso

last[1] *adj* coming after all the others; latest; hindmost; closing; final; next before the present; most recent; utmost; extreme; lowest; meanest; farthest of all from possessing a given quality, character, use, etc; most unlikely (*you are the last man I should consult*).—*adv* on the last occasion; the time before the present; after all others; lastly; finally.—*n* the one coming last.

last[2] *vi* to continue in time; to endure; to remain in existence; not to decay or perish; to continue unimpaired.—*vt* to hold out and be sufficient in quantity (*provisions to last a week*); to continue during (*the journey lasts two hours*).

last[3] *n* a mould or form of the human foot on which boots and shoes are formed; an implement for repairing boots and shoes on.—*vt* to shape with a last.

last-ditch *adj* final and desperate (*a last-ditch attempt*).

lasting *adj* such as will or can continue or endure; durable; of long continuance (*lasting good, evil, impression*).

last name *n* a surname.

last straw *n* a final addition to existing burdens or problems which results in collapse, defeat, loss of temper, etc.

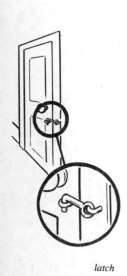

latch

latch *n* a simple device or catch for fastening a door.—*vt* to fasten with a latch.

latchet *n* the string or thong that fastens a shoe or sandal.

latchkey *n* the key of an outer door; the key to the front door.

late *adj* coming after the usual time; slow; tardy; long delayed; far advanced towards the end or close (*a late hour of the day*); existing not long ago but not now; deceased; departed; last or recently in any place, office or character.—*adv* after the usual time or the time appointed; after delay; not long ago; lately; far in the night, day, week or other particular period.—**of late** lately, in time not long past or near the present.

lateen *adj* a triangular sail with its foremost edge fastened to a yard which hoists obliquely to the mast, used in xebecs, feluccas, etc, in the Mediterranean.

lately *adv* not long ago; recently.

lateness *n* the state of being late; tardiness; far advanced period.

latent *n* a triangular sail.

latent heat *n* the heat required to change a solid into a liquid or a liquid into a gas, without change of temperature.

lateral *adj* pertaining to the side; directed to the side; proceeding from the side; situated on the side (as opposed to the front or back).

lateral thinking *n* a form of thinking which does not simply proceed by seemingly logical steps but seeks a new, often unorthodox, way of looking at a problem, issue, etc.

latex *n* (*bot*) the elaborated sap of plants, often a white milky fluid.

lath *n* a thin narrow board or slip of wood that is nailed to the rafters of a building to support the tiles or covering; a thin narrow slip of wood that is nailed to a wall to support the plastering; such slips collectively; any similar piece of wood.

lathe *n* an apparatus for turning and polishing wood, ivory, metals, etc, by supporting and causing the article to revolve while being operated on; the part of a loom to which the reed is fixed and by the movements of which the weft threads are driven home in weaving.

lather *n* foam or froth made by soap and water; foam or froth from profuse sweat, as of a horse.—*vi* to form a foam with soap and water; to foam or froth from profuse sweat, as of a horse.—*vi* to become frothy.—*vt* to spread over with lather.

Latin *adj* pertaining to or composed in the language spoken by the Romans.—*n* the language of the ancient Romans.

Latin races *npl* the Italian, French, Spanish, etc, whose language is based on Latin.

latitude *n* extent from side to side; breadth; width; room or scope; comprehensiveness or looseness of application; extent of deviation from a standard; freedom from rules or limits; laxity; extent; amplitude; distance north or south of the equator, measured on a meridian and expressed in degrees, minutes and seconds, the greatest possible latitude being 90° north or south; scope; freedom from restriction.

latitudinarian *adj* embracing a wide circle or range; having a wide scope; characterized by freedom, independence or lack of respect for the usual standards of belief or opinion; lax in religious principles or views; free-thinking; liberal.—*n* one who is liberal in his or her notions; one who has no respect for commonly accepted doctrines or opinions; one who indulges a latitude of thinking and is careless of orthodoxy.

latria *n* (*RC Church*) the worship offered to God alone.

latrine *n* a lavatory, especially one in a military camp.

latter *adj* more late or recent; the second of two, opposed to former; mentioned the last of two; modern; lately past (*in these latter ages*).

latter-day *adj* present-day; modern.

latterly *adv* of late; in time not long past; lately; ultimately; at last.

lattice *n* a structure of wood or iron made by crossing laths, rods or bars and forming open chequered or reticulated work; a window made of laths or strips of iron which cross one another like network so as to leave open interstices; in crystals, the regular linear geometrical form in which the particles are grouped in space.—*vt* (**latticed, latticing**) to give the form or appearance of a lattice to; to furnish with a lattice.

laud *vt* to praise in words alone or with words and singing; to extol; to celebrate.—*n* praise; a song or hymn of praise; (*pl*) a service of the church comprising psalms of praise and generally included in matins.

laudable *adj* praiseworthy; commendable.

laudanum *n* formally, any of various opium preparations; a solution of opium in alcohol.

laudatory *adj* containing or expressing praise; tending to praise.

laugh *vi* to make that convulsive or chuckling noise which sudden merriment, joy or derision causes.—*vt* to express by laughing; to ridicule or deride (with *out* or *down*).—**to laugh off** to dismiss as of little importance; to make a joke of.—**to laugh to scorn** to deride; to treat with mockery, contempt and scorn.—*n* the inarticulate expression of sudden mirth peculiar to humans; (*colloq*) an amusing person or thing.

laughable *adj* that may justly excite laughter; comical; ludicrous.

laughing gas *n* nitrous oxide (so called because, when inhaled, it usually produces exhilaration).

laughing stock *n* a person or thing that is an object of ridicule; a butt for laughter or jokes.

laughter *n* the act or sound of laughing; an expression of mirth, manifested chiefly in certain convulsive and partly involuntary actions of the muscles of breathing, which produce a succession of short abrupt sounds, with certain movements of the muscles of the face and often of other parts of the body; any expression of merriment perceivable in the countenance, as in the eyes.

launch *vt* to throw, as a lance; to dart; to let fly; to move or cause to slide from the land into the water; to set afloat for the first time after being built (*to launch a ship*); to propel (a rocket, spear, etc) into the air; to put into action; to get going; to put (a new product) onto the market.—*vi* to glide forward, as a ship into the water; to enter on a new field of activity; to begin enthusiastically on (*to launch into a discussion*).—*n* the setting afloat of a ship or boat; propulsion into the air (of a rocket, spear, etc); a kind of boat, longer, lower and more flat-bottomed than a longboat; the largest boat carried by a man-of-war; the advertisement and marketing of a new product.

launder *vt* to wash and iron (clothes); to handle and transfer (money obtained from criminal activity, etc) in such a way that the identity of the illegal source is not identified, for example by passing it gradually through foreign banks or investing it in legitimate businesses.—*vi* to wash and iron.

laundress *n* a woman who earns her living by doing laundry.

laundry *n* the place or room where clothes are washed and ironed; clothes, etc, to be washed and ironed.

laureate *adj* decked or invested with laurel.—*vt* (**laureated, laureating**) to honour with a wreath of laurel; to invest with the office of poet laureate.

laurel *n* an evergreen shrub with shiny leaves, used by the ancient Greeks and Romans to make victory wreaths; (*pl*) a crown of laurel, formerly bestowed as a distinction on poets, heroes, etc; (*pl*) honour, fame, distinction.

lava *n* the general term for all rock matter that flows in a molten state from volcanoes.

lavatory *n* a room with a toilet; a toilet.

lave *vt* (**laved, laving**) to wash; to bathe.—*vi* to wash oneself; to bathe; to wash, as the sea on the beach.

lavender *n* a shrub with spikes of fragrant, pale purple flowers, which yields an essential oil; a pale blue colour with a slight mixture of grey, like the flower of lavender.

lavender water *n* a perfume made from essential oil of lavender.

laver *n* an edible seaweed.

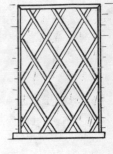

lattice

laurel

lavish *vt* to expend or bestow with profusion; to expend without necessity or use; to waste; to squander.—*adj* expending or bestowing with profusion; profuse; liberal to a fault; wasteful; being overflowing or in profusion; superabundant; superfluous.

law *n* a rule of action or conduct laid down or prescribed by authority; an edict or decree of a ruler or a government; a general command or order expressly laid down; such rules, edicts or decrees collectively; the whole body of rules regulating and controlling the individuals of a state or community (*to break the law, a violation of law, a father-in-law*); legal procedure; litigation; the science dealing with legal enactments and procedure; jurisprudence; rights established by law; justice; one of the rules or principles by which any matter or proceeding is regulated (*the laws of versification, of horse racing*); an allowance in distance or time granted to a weaker competitor in a race, etc; a theoretical principle deduced from practice or observation; a formal statement of facts invariably observed in natural phenomena (*the law of gravity*).

law-abiding *adj* observant of the law; obeying the law.

law-and-order *adj* advocating strong measures to keep order and reduce crime and violence.

lawful *adj* agreeable or conformable to law; allowed by law; legitimate; permissible (*lawful but not expedient*); competent; free from objection; rightful (*lawful owner*)

lawgiver *n* one who makes or enacts a law; a legislator.

lawless *adj* not obedient or conforming to law; contrary to or unauthorized by law; illegal; apparently uncontrolled by any law.

lawn[1] *n* a space of ground covered with grass and kept smoothly mown, generally in front of or around a house.

lawn[2] *n* a fine sheer cloth linen or cotton.—*adj* made of lawn.

lawn mower *n* a machine for mowing lawns.

lawn tennis *n* tennis played on grass court.

law of averages *n* the belief that an event will occur with a frequency approximating to its probability.

lawrencium *n* a radioactive metallic element.

lawsuit *n* a suit in law for the recovery of a supposed right; an action before a court instituted by a party to compel another to do him or her justice.

lawyer *n* one skilled in the laws or a practitioner of law; one whose profession is to institute suits in courts of law or to prosecute or defend the cause of clients.

lax *adj* loose; flabby; soft; not tense, firm or rigid; not tightly stretched or drawn; not rigidly exact or precise; not sufficiently strict or rigorous.

laxative *adj* having the power or quality of loosening or opening the bowels and relieving from constipation.—*n* a medicine that acts as a gentle purgative.

laxity *n* the state or quality of being lax; looseness; lack of strictness; remissness.

lay[1] *vt* (*pret, pp* **laid**, *ppr* **laying**) to place in a lying position; to cause to lie; to prostrate; to put, set or place in general; to impose (taxes, commands, blame, etc); to bring into a certain state (with various adjectives, as *to lay bare; to lay open*, etc); to settle (dust); to still (the wind); to allay (pain); to dispose with regularity in building or in other technical operations; to place at hazard; to wager; to stake; to contrive, scheme, plan (a plot); to place before a court of justice (an indictment, damages); (*sl*) to have sexual intercourse with.—*vi* to bring forth or produce eggs; (in betting) to wager; to bet; to stake money.—**to lay off** to suspend from work, sometimes temporarily, sometimes permanently; to stop (doing something).—**to lay out** to spread out, as for display; to arrange for display; to plan in detail; to prepare (a corpse) for burial; to spend (money) on.—**to lay up** to store for future use; to disable or confine to bed through illness.—*n* a stratum; a layer; a fold; the direction or lie in which the different strands of a rope are twisted; a way or position in which something is situated; (*sl*) an act of sexual intercourse; (*sl*) a partner in sexual intercourse.

lay[2] *adj* pertaining to the people, as distinct from the clergy; not clerical; not professional; not pertaining to one who has professional knowledge.

lay[3] *n* a song; a ballad; a narrative poem.

layabout *n* a loafer; a lazy person.

lay brother *n* a person received into a convent of monks under vows but not in holy orders.

layer *n* one who or that which lays; a single thickness, fold, etc; a stratum; a coat, as of paint; a row or course of masonry, brickwork, etc; a shoot or twig of a plant, not detached from the stock, partly laid under ground for growth or propagation.—*vt* to separate into layers; to form by superimposing layers; to propagate by bending the shoot of a living stem into the soil, the shoot striking root while being fed by the parent plant.

layette *n* a set of clothes, blankets, etc, for a newborn child.

lay figure *n* a jointed figure used by painters in imitation of the human body and which can be placed in any attitude so as to serve when clothed as a model for draperies, etc.

layman, laywoman *n* (**laymen, laywomen**)

lawn mower

lava

a person who is not in the clergy; one of the laity; a person not professionally or specially involved in a pursuit; anon-specialist.

layoff *n* a period of involuntary suspension from work.

layout *n* the manner in which something is laid out, as the arrangement of text and illustrations in a book, etc; the thing laid out; an arrangement; a plan.

lay sister *n* a woman received into a convent of nuns under vows but who does not perform any sacred office.

lazar *n* (*arch*) a leper.

lazy *adj* disinclined to action or exertion; sluggish; indolent; averse to labour; heavy in motion; moving slowly or apparently with labour.

lea *n* (*poet*) a meadow or grassy plain; land under grass or pasturage.

leach[1] *vt* to wash (soil, ore, etc) with a filtering liquid; to extract (a soluble substance) from some material.—*vi* to lose soluble matter through a filtering liquid.

leach[2] *n* same as **leech**[2].

lead[1] *vt* (*pret, pp* **led**, *ppr* **leading**) to guide by the hand; to guide or conduct by showing the way; to direct; to conduct, as a chief or commander; to be head of (an expedition, orchestra, etc); to direct and govern; to precede; to hold the first place in rank or dignity among; to show the method of attaining an object; to direct, as in an investigation; to draw, entice, allure; to induce; to prevail on; to influence; to pass or spend (*to lead a life of pleasure*); to cause to spend or endure (*he led his wife a sad life*); (in card playing) to commence a round or trick with.—*vi* to go before and show the way; to have precedence or pre-eminence; to take the first place; to have a position of authority; to be chief, commander or director; to conduct, bring, draw, induce (*gambling leads to other evils*); to guide a partner in a dance; (in card playing) to play the first card of a round or trick; (in boxing) to jab with a preferred hand.—*n* a going before; guidance; act of leading; the role of leader; precedence; the amount or distance ahead; a clue; the leading role in a play, film, etc; an animal's leash; the right of playing the first card in a round or trick.

lead[2] *n* a metallic element of a bluish-grey colour, characterized chiefly by its softness and fusibility; a plummet or mass of lead used in sounding at sea; (*print*) a thin plate of metal used to give space between lines; a small piece of graphite used in pencils; (*pl*) the leaden covering of a roof.—*adj* made or composed of lead; consisting more or less of lead; produced by lead.—*vt* (**leaded, leading**) to cover with lead; to fit with lead; (*print*) to widen the space between (lines) by inserting a lead or thin plate of type metal.

leaded *adj* covered with lead; fitted with lead; set in lead; (*print*) separated by thin plates of lead, as lines in printing.

leaden *adj* made of lead; resembling lead (*a leaden sky*); sluggish; slow; inert; heavy; dull; gloomy.

leader *n* one who leads or conducts; a guide; a conductor; a chief; a commander; the chief of a party, faction or any body of people; a musical performer who leads a band or choir; a leading article in a newspaper, i.e. an editor's own political or other statement; one of the front horses in a team.

leadership *n* the office of a leader; guidance; the leaders of an organization collectively.

lead-in *n* introductory material; the connection between a radio transmitter or receiver with an aerial or transmission cable.

leading *adj* guiding; conducting; chief; principal; most influential.

leading light *n* the most important member of a group or organization.

leading question *n* a question which suggests the answer.

lead pencil *n* an instrument for drawing or writing, usually made by enclosing a slip of plumbago or graphite (black lead) in a casing of wood.

leadsman *n* (*pl* **leadsmen**) (*naut*) the man who heaves the lead.

lead time *n* the period between the design of a product and its manufacture.

leaf *n* (*pl* **leaves**) one of the external parts of a plant, usually shooting from the sides of the stem and branches and ordinarily green in colour; something resembling a leaf; the part of a book or folded sheet containing two pages; a side, division or part of a flat body, the parts of which move on hinges, as folding doors, window shutters, etc; the part of a table which can be raised or lowered at will; a very thin plate of metal (*gold leaf*); the brim of a soft hat.—*vi* to shoot out leaves; to produce leaves.—**to leaf through** to turn the pages of.—**to turn over a new leaf** to adopt a different and better line of conduct.

leafage *n* leaves collectively; abundance of leaves; foliage.

leaf bud *n* a bud from which leaves only are produced.

leaf insect *n* the popular name of insects whose wings resemble or mimic leaves.

leaflet *n* a little leaf; a small pamphlet; (*bot*) one of the divisions of a compound leaf.

leaf mould *n* leaves decayed and reduced to the state of mould, used as manure for plants.

leafy *adj* full of leaves; abounding with leaves; resembling leaves.

leafage

lead pencil

league¹ *n* a combination or union of two or more parties for the purpose of promoting their mutual interest or for executing any design in concert; an alliance or confederacy between states for their mutual aid or defence; a national contract or compact; an association of sports clubs that organizes matches between members; a class or category.—*vi* (**leagued, leaguing**) to unite in a league or confederacy; to form a league; to confederate.

league² *n* a varying measure of length, averaging about 3 miles (5 km).

leak *n* a crack, fissure or hole in a vessel that admits water or permits a fluid to escape; the passing of liquid through such a crack or aperture; a disclosure of confidential information; confidential information disclosed either deliberately or accidentally.—*vi* to let water or other liquid in or out through a hole or crevice (*the vessel leaks*); to ooze or pass, as water or other fluid, through a crack, fissure or aperture in a vessel; to disclose (confidential information) either deliberately or accidentally.—**to leak out** to find vent; to find publicity in a clandestine or irregular way.

leakage *n* a leaking; something that leaks; the quantity of a liquid that enters or issues by leaking.

leaky *adj* letting water or other liquid pass in or out by leaks.

leal *adj* loyal; true; faithful; honest; upright.

lean¹ *vi* (*pret, pp* **leaned** *or* **leant** , *ppr* **leaning**) to slope or incline from a straight or perpendicular position or line; to slant; to incline in feeling or opinion; to tend towards; to rest as for support; to depend for consolation, comfort, etc (usually with *against, on* or *upon*).—*vt* to cause to lean; to incline; to support or rest.

lean² *adj* lacking flesh or fat on the body; meagre; not fat; not productive (*lean years*).—*n* that part of flesh which consists of muscle without fat.

lean-burn engine *n* an engine that uses a reduced proportion of fuel in the fuel-air mixture so lessening fuel consumption and pollution.

lean cuisine *n* a low-fat style of cooking which emphasizes the delicacy of flavour and the appearance of food.

lean-to *n* (*pl* **lean-tos**) a building whose rafters rest on another building; an open-sided shelter of branches.

leap *vi* (*pret, pp* **leaped**, rarely **leapt**, *ppr* **leaping**) to spring or rise from the ground with feet in the air; to move with springs or bounds; to jump, vault, bound, skip; to make a sudden transition.—*vt* to pass over by leaping; to spring or bound from one side to the other of; to cause (one's horse) to take a leap; to make to pass by leaping.—**to leap at** to accept something offered eagerly.—*n* the act of leaping; the space passed over or cleared in leaping; a jump; a spring; a bound; a sudden transition.

leapfrog *n* a game in which one player, by placing his or her hands on the back or shoulders of another in a stooping posture, leaps over his or her head.—*vi* (**leapfrogged, leapfrogging**) to play leapfrog. —*vt* to advance in alternate jumps.

leap year *n* a year in which February has an additional day and there are thus 366 days in all, so called because after February the days of the week leap an extra day as compared with other years.

learn *vt* (*pret, pp* **learned** *or* **learnt**, *ppr* **learning**) to gain or acquire knowledge of or skill in; to acquire by study; to teach.— *vi* to gain or receive knowledge, information or intelligence; to receive instruction; to be taught.

learned *adj* possessing knowledge; having a great store of information obtained by study; erudite; well acquainted; having much experience; skilful (often with *in*, as *learned in martial arts*); containing or indicative of learning (*a learned book*).

learner *n* a person who learns; one who is taught; a scholar; a pupil.

learning *n* acquired knowledge in any branch of science or literature; knowledge acquired by the study; erudition.

learning disability *n* any of various conditions, often involving the brain and nervous system, that interfere with the learning processes, such as mastering reading and writing.

lease *n* a letting or renting of property, vehicles, equipment, etc, to a person for a specified rent or compensation; the written contract for such letting or renting; any tenure by grant or permission; the time for which such a tenure holds good.—*vt* (**leased, leasing**) to grant by lease; to let for a specified rent; to let; to rent; to occupy in terms of a lease.

lease-back *n* the process of selling an asset, especially a building, and then renting it.

leasehold *n* the act of holding by lease; the land, buildings, etc, held by lease.

leash *n* a cord, strap or line by which a dog is held.—*vt* to hold or restrain on a leash.

least *adj* smallest; little beyond others, either in size, degree, value, worth, importance, etc.—*adv* in the smallest or lowest degree.

leather *n* the skin of animals dressed and prepared for use by tanning or other processes; tanned hide; an appliance made of this substance.—*adj* consisting of leather. —*vt* to furnish with leather; to beat as with a thong of leather.

leatherback *n* the largest existing sea turtle, having a flexible shell.

leapfrog

leash

Leatherette *n* a trademark of a kind of imitation leather.

leatherjacket *n* the larva of the cranefly or daddy-longlegs; a tropical fish with a leathery skin.

leathery *adj* pertaining to or resembling leather; tough and flexible.

leave[1] *n* liberty granted to act; permission; permission to be absent from duty, especially in the services; allowance; a formal parting of friends or acquaintances; farewell (*to take leave*).

leave[2] *vt* (*pret, pp* **left**, *ppr* **leaving**) to suffer to remain; not to take or remove; to have remaining at death; to commit or trust to, as a deposit; to bequeath; to give by will; to withdraw or depart from; to forsake, desert, abandon; to relinquish, resign, renounce; to refer; to commit for decision; to let remain without further discussion.—*vi* to set out; to take one's departure; to desist.

leave[3] *vi* (**leaved, leaving**) to put forth foliage, to leaf.

leaven *n* a substance that produces fermentation, as in dough, especially yeast; something that enlivens.—*vt* to mix with leaven; to impregnate or imbue; to enliven.

leave-taking *n* departure; farewell.

leavings *npl* something left disregarded; remnant; relic; refuse; offal.

lech, letch *vi* (*colloq*) to lust after, to practise lechery (usually with *after*).

lecher *n* a lecherous person.

lecherous *adj* characterized by lechery; lustful; lewd; encouraging lechery.

lechery *n* lustfulness; unrestrained sexuality; debauchery.

lecithin *n* any of a group of fatty compounds found in plant and animal tissues, used as an emulsifier and antioxidant.

lectern *n* a desk or stand on which the larger books used in church services are placed; any similar reading support.

lecture *n* a talk on some subject read or delivered before an audience; a formal or methodical talk intended for instruction; a lengthy rebuke.—*vt* (**lectured, lecturing**) to give a lecture to; to rebuke at length.—*vi* to read or deliver a formal discourse; to deliver lectures for instruction.

lecturer *n* one who lectures; a professor or instructor who delivers lectures to students.

ledge *n* a shelf on which articles may be placed; anything which resembles such a shelf; a part rising or projecting beyond the rest; a ridge or shelf of rocks; (*archit*) a small moulding; also, a string course; in joinery, a piece against which something rests.

ledger *n* a book in which a record of debts, credits, etc, is kept; a register; (*archit*) a

flat slab of stone, such as is laid horizontally over a grave; the covering slab of an altar tomb.

ledger line *n* (*mus*) a short line added above or below the staff for to extend its range for notes too high or too low for the staff.

lee *n* the side or part away from the wind, especially in a ship; shelter.—*adj* (*naut*) of or pertaining to the part or side towards which the wind blows, opposite to *weather*.

leech[1] *n* a small bloodsucking worm, formerly used in medicine; a person who clings to another person; a person who exploits another person.

leech[2], **leach** *n* (*naut*) the border or edge of a sail which is sloping or perpendicular.

leek *n* a culinary vegetable with a bulbous onion-like root; the national badge of the Welsh.

leer *n* a side glance expressive of amorousness, lust, slyness, etc.—*vi* to cast such a glance.

lees *npl* the parts of any liquid which have settled on the bottom of a vessel; dregs; sediment.

leeward *adj* in the direction towards which the wind blows.—*n* the quarter or direction towards the lee.

leeway *n* the drifting of a ship to the leeward of her course; the deviation from the true course which a vessel makes by drifting to leeward; scope; freedom of action.—**to make up leeway** to make up for lost time; to overtake work which has fallen behind.

left[1] *adj* denoting the part opposed to the right of the body; belonging to the side next which the heart is situated (*the left hand, arm* or *side*); of or relating to the left in politics; left-wing; socialist; radical; not conservative or reactionary.—*n* the side opposite to the right; that part which is on the left side; the left hand; a blow with the left hand; (sometimes with *cap*) a radical party, section, etc.

left[2] *pret* and *pp* of **leave**.

left-handed *adj* having the left hand more capable of being used than the right; using the left hand with more facility than the right; turned towards the left hand; (of a compliment) ambiguous.

left-hander *n* a left-handed person; a blow delivered with the left hand.

leftover *n* a remnant; a survival; (*usually pl*) unused portions of something, especially uneaten food.—*adj* remaining; unused; uneaten.

left wing *n* the most radical section of a political party or group.

left-wing *adj* tending towards the left wing of a political party or group; radical; socialist.

leg *n* the limb of an animal, used in supporting the body and in walking and running;

leek

leg

that part of the limb from the hip to the foot; a long slender support, as the leg of a chair or table; one of the sides of a triangle as opposed to the base; the part of a stocking or other article of dress that covers the leg; a section, as of a trip; any of a series of games or matches in a competition; in cricket, the part of the field that lies to the left and behind the batsman or as he faces the bowler.

legacy *n* a bequest; a particular thing or certain sum of money given by last will or testament; anything handed down by an ancestor or predecessor; something remaining from the past.

legal *adj* according to law; in conformity with law; permitted by law; pertaining to law; created by law.

legal aid *n* help given by the state towards the cost of legal proceedings given to certain people on low incomes.

legality *n* the state or quality of being legal.

legalize *vt* (**legalized, legalizing**) to make legal or lawful.

legally *adv* in a legal manner; by permission of or in conformity with law.

legal tender *n* a currency which a creditor is legally bound to accept in payment of a debt.

legate *n* an ambassador; especially, the pope's ambassador to a foreign state.

legume

legatee *n* one to whom a legacy is bequeathed.

legation *n* a person or persons sent as envoys or ambassadors to a foreign court; an embassy; a diplomatic minister and his or her suite; a district ruled by a papal legate.

legato *adj*, *adv* (*mus*) smoothly and evenly. —*n* (*pl* **legatos**) music played or sung in an even, smooth, gliding manner.

legend *n* a story handed down from the past; a notable person or the stories of his or her exploits; a tradition; an inscription on a coin; a caption.

legendary *adj* consisting of legends; like a legend; based on legend; presented in legend; famous.

legerdemain *n* sleight of hand; a deceptive performance which depends on dexterity of hand; trickery or deception generally.

leggings *npl* protective outer covering for the lower legs; footless tights.

leggy *adj* long-legged.

legibility *n* the quality of being legible.

legible *adj* capable of being read; consisting of letters or figures that may be easily seen by the eye.

lemon

legion *n* a body of ancient Roman infantry; a body of troops in general; a great number.

legionary *adj* belonging to a legion or legions.—*n* one of a legion; a Roman soldier belonging to a legion.

legionnaire *n* a member of certain military forces or associations.

legionnaire's disease *n* a kind of serious bacterial respiratory infection resembling pneumonia.

legislate *vi* (**legislated, legislating**) to make or enact a law or laws.

legislation *n* the act of legislating or enacting laws.

legislative *adj* enacting laws; having power or authority to enact laws; pertaining to the enacting of laws.

legislator *n* a lawgiver; one who frames or establishes the laws of a state; a member of a national or supreme legislative assembly.

legislature *n* the body of people in a state invested with power to make and repeal laws; the supreme legislating power of a state.

legitimacy *n* the state or quality of being legitimate.

legitimate *adj* born in wedlock; genuine; not false or spurious; following by logical or natural sequence; allowable (*a legitimate argument* or *influence*); reasonable; justifiable.

legitimize *vt* (**legitimized, legitimizing**) to make legitimate; to declare legitimate.

legume *n* (*bot*) a seed vessel of two valves, like the pod of a pea, in which the seeds are fixed to the ventral suture only; (*pl*) the fruit of leguminous plants of the pea kind; pulse.

leguminous *adj* pertaining to legumes or pulse; (*bot*) bearing legumes; pertaining to plants bearing legumes, as peas.

legwork *n* (*colloq*) work that involves a lot of walking; the gathering of small details.

lei *n* a garland of flowers for wearing around the neck, given as a token of affection in Hawaii.

leisure *n* freedom from occupation or business; time free from employment; relaxation.—*adj* not used or spent in labour or business; vacant (said of time).

leisurely *adv* not in haste or hurry; slowly; at leisure.—*adj* done at leisure; not hasty; deliberate.

leitmotif, leitmotiv *n* a recurring phrase in a musical composition, always associated with the same person or situation.

leman *n* an old term for a sweetheart of either sex.

lemma *n* (*pl* **lemmas, lemmata**) (*math*) a preliminary or preparatory proposition laid down and demonstrated for the purpose of facilitating something more important that follows.

lemming *n* a rodent mammal found in Norway, Lapland, Siberia, etc, vast hordes of which periodically migrate towards the sea, thus controlling the size of the population; anyone bent on wilful destruction.

lemon *n* a medium-size yellow citrus fruit having an acidic taste; the tree that produces lemons.—*adj* belonging to or made with lemon; pale yellow in colour.

lemonade *n* a drink consisting of lemon juice mixed with water and sweetened; an aerated drink flavoured with the juice or essence of lemons.

lemon peel *n* the rind of a lemon; the rind dried, preserved and candied, used in cooking.

lemon sole *n* a flat fish resembling a sole.

lemur *n* a small nocturnal, tree-dwelling monkey-like mammal with a long furry tail.

lend *vt* (*pret, pp* **lent**, *ppr* **lending**) to grant to another for temporary use; to provide (money) in return for payment with interest; to afford, grant or impart (assistance, an ear to a discourse, etc).

length *n* the longest measure of any object, as distinct from depth, thickness, breadth or width; extent from end to end; one of the three dimensions of space; distance to a place; a portion of space considered as measured longways; some definite long measure (*to cut a rope into lengths*); something of a certain length taken from a longer piece; long continuance; duration of any extent in time; detail or amplification in language; extent, degree, height, as in conduct or action (*to go to great lengths*); extent of progress.

lengthen *vt* to make long or longer; to extend in length (often followed by *out*).—*vi* to grow longer.

lengthways, lengthwise *adv* in the direction of the length; in a longitudinal direction.

lengthy *adj* long or moderately long; protracted; not short or brief (applied chiefly to discourses, arguments, proceedings, etc).

lenience, leniency *n* the quality of being lenient; clemency.

lenient *adj* acting without rigour or severity; gentle; merciful; clement.

lenitive *adj* having the quality of softening or mitigating, as pain; assuaging; emollient.—*n* a medicine or application of this kind.

lenity *n* gentleness; clemency; tenderness; mercy.

lens *n* (*pl* **lenses**) a transparent substance, usually glass or plastic, so formed that rays of light passing through it are made to change their direction and thus cause objects to appear magnified or diminished in size; one of the glasses of a telescope, microscope, etc; a device used to focus electromagnetic rays; the transparent part of the eye that focuses light rays on the retina.

lent *pret, pp* of **lend**.

Lent *n* a fast of forty days, beginning at Ash Wednesday and continuing till Easter, observed in the Christian Church in com-

memoration of the forty days' fast of Christ.

lenticular *adj* resembling a lentil in size or form; having the form of a double-convex lens.

lentiform, lentoid *adj* of the form of a lens; lenticular.

lentil *n* an annual pea-like leguminous plant having seeds used in food; these seeds used as food.

lento *adj, adv* (*mus*) to be performed slowly.—*n* (*pl* **lentos**) music played in this way.

Leo *n* the Lion, the fifth sign of the zodiac.

Leonid *n* (*pl* **Leonids, Leonides**) one of a group of meteors observed annually in November, which seem to radiate from the constellation Leo.

leonine *adj* belonging to a lion; resembling a lion or partaking of its qualities.

leopard *n* a carnivorous animal of the cat genus, inhabiting Africa, Persia, China and India, of a yellowish-fawn colour variegated with dark spots.

leper *n* a person affected with leprosy.

lepidopteran *n* any of an order of insects comprising the butterflies and moths in which the adult form has four scaly, membranous wings and which as larvae are caterpillars.

lepidosiren *n* a fish found of western Africa and South America with both gills and lungs and thus able to lie packed in the mud of their native rivers during the dry season.

leporine *adj* pertaining to a hare; having the qualities of the hare.

leprosy *n* a chronic infectious bacterial disease of the skin, often resulting in disfigurement.

leprous *adj* infected with leprosy.

lepton *n* (*physics*) any of various elementary particles, such as electrons, that participate in weak interactions with other elementary particles.

lesbian *n* a female homosexual.

lese-majesty *n* any crime committed against the sovereign power in a state; treason.

lesion *n* (*med*) injury; an abnormal change in the texture or substance of organs or tissue caused by injury or disease.

less *adj* serving as the comparative of *little*; smaller; not so large or great.—*adv* in a smaller or lower degree.—*prep* minus.—*n* not so much; a quantity not so great as another quantity; what is below a certain standard.—**no less** nothing of inferior consequence or moment; nothing else.

lessen *vt* to make less or smaller; to diminish; to reduce; to reduce in dignity; to depreciate; to disparage.—*vi* to become less or smaller; to decrease or diminish.

lesser *adj* less; smaller; especially common with the definite article and where there is

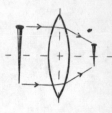

lens

leopard

opposition to *greater*, not used in comparisons with *than*.

lessee *n* the person to whom a lease is given.

lessor *n* one who leases or lets to a tenant for a term of years.

lesson *n* something to be learned or studied; a piece of instruction conveyed; a unit of learning or teaching; (*pl*) a course of instruction; what is learned or may be learned from experience; a portion of Scripture read in divine service; a doctrine or notion inculcated; a precept; a reproof, reprimand or rebuke.

lest *conj* for fear that; in case; that . . . not.

let[1] *vt* (*pret, pp* **let**, *ppr* **letting**) to permit; to allow; to suffer; to give leave; not to prevent; to lease; to grant possession and use of for a compensation.—in such phrases as *let us go*, *let* often expresses merely a suggestion for mutual action, in *let him go*, etc, it often has the force of a command; (when *let* governs an infinitive the later never takes *to*.).—*vi* to yield a certain rent by being hired out; to be taken on hire.—**to let down** to lower (*let down the flag*); to deflate (*let down a tyre*); to disappoint, to fail.—**to let up** to relax; to cease.

let[2] *vt* (**letted, letting**) to hinder; to impede; to interpose obstructions to.—*n* a hindrance; obstacle; impediment.

letch[1] *vt* to wash (wood ashes) by causing water to pass through them and thus to separate from them the alkali.

letch[2] *vi* same as **lech**.

let-down *n* a disappointment.

lethal *adj* deadly; mortal; fatal.

lethargic *adj* affected with lethargy; abnormally inclined to sleep; dull; heavy; pertaining to lethargy.

lethargy *n* unnatural sleepiness; abnormal drowsiness; profound sleep, from which a person can scarcely be awaked; dullness; inaction; inattention.

Lethe *n* in Greek myth, the river of oblivion; one of the streams of the infernal regions; hence, oblivion; a draught of oblivion.

letter *n* a mark or character used as the representative of a sound; a character standing for a vowel or a consonant; a written or printed message; an epistle; literal meaning; (*print*) a single type or character; types collectively; (*pl*) learning; erudition (*a man of letters*).—*vt* to impress or form letters on (*to letter a book*).

letter bomb *n* an explosive device concealed in an envelope and sent through the post.

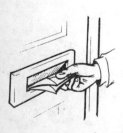
letterbox

letterbox *n* a slit in the door of a house or building through which letters and packages are delivered; a postbox.

lettered *adj* versed in literature or science; belonging to learning; marked or designated with letters.

letterhead *n* a name, address, etc, printed as a heading on stationery; stationery printed with a heading.

lettering *n* the act or process of inscribing with letters; the letter impressed; a title; an inscription.

letter of credit *n* an order given by bankers or others at one place to enable a specified person to receive money from their agents at another place.

letter-perfect *adj* accurate in the tiniest detail; word-perfect.

letterpress *n* words impressed by types; print; a copying press.—*adj* consisting of, relating to or employed in type printing.

letters patent *npl* official documentation conferring a right, patent or privilege.

lettuce *n* a plant whose succulent leaves are used in salads.

let-up *n* a relaxation of effort; cessation.

leucocyte *n* a white or colourless blood corpuscle.

leucorrhoea *n* (*med*) an abnormal discharge of a white or yellowish mucus from the female genital organs.

leukaemia *n* a cancerous disease involving the production of an excess of white blood cells in the body.

Levant *n* the eastern portion of the Mediterranean and its seaboard.

levanter *n* an easterly wind in the Mediterranean.

levator *n* (*pl* **levatores**) (*anat*) a muscle that serves to raise a part of the body.

levee[1] *n* a morning reception of visitors formerly held by a prince or great personage; any similar assemblage.

levee[2] *n* in USA, an embankment on the margin of a river to confine it within its natural channel.

level *n* an instrument by which to find or draw a straight line parallel to the plane of the horizon; a line or surface which coincides with the plane of the horizon; a surface without inequalities; usual elevation; customary height; equal elevation with something else; a state of equality; a position on a scale of values.—*adj* horizontal; coinciding with the plane of the horizon or parallel to it; not having one part higher than another; even; flat; on the same line or plane; equal in rank or degree; having no degree of superiority.—*vt* (**levelled, levelling**) to make level; to remove inequalities of surface in; to lay flat on the ground; to make equal in condition, state or degree; to point, in taking aim; to aim; to direct or point at.—*vi* to accord, agree or suit; to point a gun, etc, to the mark; to aim.

leveller *n* one who levels; one who would remove social distinctions and make all people equal.

levelling *n* the act of one who levels; the art

or operation of ascertaining the different elevations of objects on the surface of the earth, as in surveying.

lever *n* a bar of metal, wood or other substance turning on a support (called the fulcrum or prop) and used to overcome a certain resistance (called the weight) encountered at one part of the bar, by means of a force (called the power) applied at another part; a bar used for prying or moving something; a means to an end; a watch with a vibrating lever to connect the action of the escape wheel with that of the balance.—*vt* to raise or move, as with a lever.

leverage *n* the action of a lever; the mechanical advantage or power gained by using a lever; power; influence.

leveret *n* a hare in the first year of its life.

leviathan *n* an aquatic animal described in the book of Job; a fabulous sea monster of immense size.

levin *n* (*arch*) lightning.

levirate *n* marriage with a husband's brother.

Levis *npl* the trademark for a kind of jeans.

levitate *vt* (**levitated, levitating**) to cause to become buoyant in the atmosphere; to cause to float in the air without support.—*vi* to rise into the air and float without support.

levitation *n* the act of making light or buoyant; lightness; buoyancy.

Leviticus *n* a book of the Old Testament containing the ceremonial law or the laws and regulations relating to priests.

levity *n* lightness of temper or conduct; lack of seriousness; excessive frivolity.

levy *n* the act of raising, collecting or enlisting troops; the raising of taxes; that which is levied; a body of troops raised; an amount levied.—*vt* (**levied, levying**) to raise or enlist (troops); to collect (taxes).

lewd *adj* lustful; lecherous; lascivious; obscene; indecent.

lewdness *n* the state or quality of being lewd; lechery; lasciviousness; obscenity; indecency.

lexicographer *n* the author or compiler of a lexicon or dictionary.

lexicographic, lexicographical *adj* pertaining to lexicons or lexicography.

lexicography *n* the act or art of compiling a lexicon or dictionary; the occupation of composing dictionaries.

lexicology *n* the science of words, their derivation and meaning; that branch of learning which treats of the proper meaning and just application of words.

lexicon *n* a dictionary; a book containing an alphabetical arrangement of the words in a language, with the definition or an explanation of the meaning of each.

liability *n* the state of being liable; that for which one is liable; (*pl*) sums or amount which one is under obligation to pay; debts.

liable *adj* answerable for consequences; bound to make good a loss; responsible; apt or not unlikely to incur something undesirable; subject; exposed (with *to*).

liaise *vi* (**liaised, liaising**) to maintain contact with.

liaison *n* intercommunication as between units of a military force; a bond of union; an entanglement; an illicit affair between a man and a woman.

liaison officer *n* an officer employed in linking up troops under different commands; a member of a department of an organization forming a link with another department.

liana *n* a large climbing and twining plant of tropical forests.

liar *n* one who lies or tells lies; a person who knowingly utters falsehoods; one who declares to be a fact what he or she knows is not.

Lias *n* (*geol*) that series of strata lying at the basis of the oolite and above the Triassic or new red sandstone.

Liassic *adj* pertaining to or of the Lias.

libation *n* the act of pouring a liquid, usually wine, either on the ground or on a victim in sacrifice in honour of some deity; a portion of such wine; a drink.

libel *n* a defamatory writing; a malicious publication containing representations tending to bring a person into contempt or expose him or her to public hatred or derision; (*law*) the writ commencing a suit and containing the plaintiff's allegations.—*vt* (**libelled, libelling**) to publish a libel against; to defame by libel; to lampoon.

libellous *adj* containing matter of the nature of a libel; defamatory.

liberal *adj* bountiful; generous; ample, large, abundant, profuse (donation, supply, etc); not characterized by selfish, narrow or contracted ideas or feelings; favourable to civil, political and religious liberty; tolerant; favourable to reform or progress; not too literal or strict; free; contributing to a general broadening of the mind.—*n* an advocate of freedom from restraint, especially in politics and religion.

Liberal *n* a member of a political party that in a general way advocates democratic reform and individual liberty.

liberalism *n* liberal principles; the principles or practice of Liberals.

liberality *n* the quality of being liberal; largeness of mind or view; disposition to give largely; munificence; generosity.

liberalize *vt* (**liberalized, liberalizing**) to render liberal; to free from narrow views or prejudices.

liberally *adv* in a liberal manner; generously; bountifully; freely; largely.

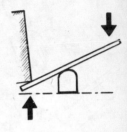

lever

liberate *vt* (**liberated, liberating**) to release from restraint or bondage; to set at liberty; to free.

liberation *n* the act of liberating.

libertarian *adj* pertaining to the doctrine of free will, as opposed to the doctrine of necessity.—*n* one who holds the doctrine of the freedom of the will.

libertine *n* one who indulges his or her lust without restraint; one who leads a dissolute, licentious life; a rake.—*adj* licentious; dissolute.

libertinism *n* the conduct of a libertine or rake.

liberty *n* the state or condition of one who is free; exemption from restraint; power of acting as one pleases; freedom; permission granted to do something; leave; immunity enjoyed; a special privilege or exemption; freedom of action or speech beyond the ordinary bounds of civility or decorum; freedom from occupation or engagements; state of being disengaged.

libidinous *adj* characterized by lust or lewdness; having an eager appetite for sexual indulgence; fitted to excite lustful desire; lustful; lewd.

libido *n* (*pl* **libidos**) a vital urge; sexual desire; sexual impulse.

Libra *n* the Balance, the seventh sign in the zodiac; a constellation represented as a pair of scales.

lid

librarian *n* the keeper of a library.

library *n* a collection of books, tapes, records, photographs, etc, for reference or borrowing; an apartment, suite of apartments or a whole building containing such a collection.

librate *vt* (**librated, librating**) to hold in equipoise; to poise; to balance.—*vi* to balance; to be poised.

libration *n* the act of balancing; a state of equipoise; (*astron*) a real or apparent motion like that of a balance before coming to rest; an apparent irregularity of the moon's motion, whereby those parts very near the border of the lunar disc alternately become visible and invisible.

libretto *n* (*pl* **librettos, libretti**) a book containing the words of an extended musical composition, as an opera; the words or text of an opera, oratorio, etc.

licence *n* authority given to act in a particular way; power conferred on a person by proper authority to do particular acts, practise in professions, conduct certain trades, etc; the document containing such authority; freedom to deviate from rule, practice, etc; excessive liberty; undue freedom; freedom abused or used in contempt of law or decorum; deviation from an artistic standard (*poetic licence*).

license *vt* (**licensed, licensing**) to permit or empower by licence; to grant a licence to.

licensed *adj* having a licence; permitted by authority.

licensee *n* one to whom a licence is granted.

licentiate *n* one who has a licence to practise some profession.

licentious *adj* characterized by licence; loose in behaviour; profligate; dissolute; libidinous.

lichen *n* (*bot*) one of an order of non-flowering plants without stem and leaves, growing on the bark of trees, on rocks, etc, and including rock moss, tree moss, etc.

lichee, lychee, litchi *n* a small fruit consisting of soft, sweet white pulp in a thin brown shell; the tree that bears this fruit.

lich gate, lych gate *n* a churchyard gate with a porch under which a coffin can be rested.

licit *adj* legal; lawful.

lick *vt* to pass or draw the tongue over the surface of; to lap; to take in by the tongue; to flicker around or touch lightly (*the flames licked the trees*); (*colloq*) to flog, beat or conquer.—*n* a rubbing or drawing of the tongue over anything; a slight smear or coat, as of paint; (*colloq*) a blow or stroke; (*colloq*) a short, rapid burst of activity.

lid *n* a removable cover for the opening of a vessel, box, etc; the cover of the eye; the eyelid.

lido *n* (*pl* **lidos**) a public open-air swimming pool or bathing beach, often with recreation facilities.

lie[1] *vi* (**lied, lying**) to utter a falsehood with an intention to deceive; knowingly to utter untruth.—*n* a falsehood uttered for the purpose of deception; an intentional violation of truth.

lie[2] *vt* (*pret* **lay**, *pp* **lain**,—*ppr* **lying**) to occupy a horizontal or nearly horizontal position; to rest lengthways or be flat on the surface of anything; to be placed and remain without motion; to lay or place oneself in a horizontal or nearly horizontal position (often with *down*); to be in bed; to sleep or pass the night; to lean or recline; to be situated; to have place or position (*Ireland lies west of England*); to remain or be in some condition (with words denoting the particular condition, as *to lie waste, to lie fallow, to lie open, to lie hid,* etc); to be present or contained; to be found; to exist; to depend (*it does not lie in my power; success lies in vigilance*); to weigh or press; to be sustainable in law; to be capable of being maintained (*an action will not lie*).—*n* the relative position of one object with regard to another or to a point of the compass; general bearing or direction; position or state of an affair; (*geol*) the manner in which strata are disposed.

lied *n* (*pl* **lieder**) a German song or ballad.

lie detector *n* a device that monitors sharp fluctuations in involuntary physiological responses as evidence of stress, guilt, etc, when deliberately lying.

lief *adv* (*arch*) gladly; willingly; readily (used in such phrases as *I had as lief go as not*).

liege *adj* (in feudalism) connected by loyalty or duty; bound by or resting on feudal ties (*a liege lord,*).—*n* (in feudalism) a vassal or person owing duties to his feudal lord; a lord or superior; a sovereign; a law-abiding citizen or citizen in general (usually plural).

lien *n* law, a legal claim; a right in one person to retain the property of another until some claim of the former is paid or satisfied.

lieu *n* place; room; stead (preceded by *in*, as *to give goods in lieu of wages*).

lieutenancy *n* the office or commission of a lieutenant.

lieutenant *n* an officer, civil or military, who takes the place of a superior in his or her absence; a commissioned officer in the army who is next in rank below a captain; a commissioned officer in the navy, next in rank below a lieutenant commander.

lieutenant colonel *n* an army officer next in rank below a colonel.

lieutenant commander *n* a naval officer immediately below the rank of commander and corresponding in rank to a major in the army.

lieutenantship *n* a lieutenancy.

life *n* (*pl* **lives**) that state of an animal or a plant in which its organs are capable of performing their functions or in which the performance of functions has not permanently ceased; animate existence; vitality; liveliness; the time during which such a state continues; the mundane existence of a human being; the period from birth to death; period during which anything continues to exist; outward manifestation of life; a person's condition or circumstances; mode, manner or course of living, as morally good or bad; social surroundings and characteristics (*high* or *low life*); that which makes alive; animating or inspiring principle; animation; vivacity; energy; the living form or nature itself, in opposition to a copy or imitation; a living person (*many lives were sacrificed*); collectively, human beings in any number (*a great loss of life*); animated beings in the aggregate (*the abundance of life on the globe*); narrative of a person's life; a biography or memoir; human affairs; course of things in the world; (*colloq*) a life sentence.

life assurance *n* insurance that pays a specified sum to a nominated beneficiary on the death of the insured party.

lifebelt *n* a small buoyant belt or ring worn to keep a person afloat in the water.

lifeblood *n* the blood necessary to life; vital blood; that which is essential to existence or strength.

lifeboat *n* a specially designed and equipped rescue vessel based on the coast and used to help those in distress at sea.

life expectancy *n* the average number of years, particularly when statistically calculated, that an individual can be expected to live.

lifeguard *n* an expert swimmer employed to rescue people in danger of drowning; a life-saver.

lifeless *adj* deprived of life; dead; inanimate; inorganic; lacking life or spirit; spiritless; dull; heavy; inactive.

lifelike *adj* like a living person; true to the life.

lifeline *n* a rope for raising or lowering a diver; a rope for rescuing a person, e.g. as attached to a lifebelt; a vitally important channel of communication or transport.

life peer *n* a British peer whose title lapses with death.

life preserver *n* one who or that which preserves life; a lifebelt; a short stick with a loaded head, used for defence against assailants.

life raft *n* a raft kept on board ship for use in emergencies.

life-saver *n* one who saves another's life; a lifeguard; (*colloq*) one who or that which helps at a time of trouble or need.

life science *n* one of the sciences, such as biology, which deal with living organisms and life processes.

life sentence *n* imprisonment for the rest of the prisoner's natural life or for a very long time (in Britain, usually now lasting approximately 15 years).

lifestyle *n* a person's typical way of life.

life-support system *n* a system designed to maintain human life in adverse situations, such as in people in comas, by providing oxygen, nourishment, etc.

lifetime *n* the time that life continues; duration of life.

lift *vt* to bring from a lower to a higher position or place; to raise or elevate; to elevate, exalt or improve, as in fortune, estimation, dignity or rank; to elate (often with *up*); to take and carry away; to remove by stealing (*to lift cattle*); to collect when due (*to lift rents, to lift accounts*).—*vi* to raise or try to raise; to rise or be raised or elevated (*the fog lifts*).—**to lift off** (of a rocket, etc) to take off.—*n* the act of manner of raising or lifting; elevation; a weight to be raised; assistance in lifting; assistance or aid in general; a device for raising persons or goods from a lower flat or storey of a house to a higher one; an elevator; an extra layer in a

lifebelt

shoe to give the wearer extra height; (*naut*) a rope from the cap and masthead to the extremity of a yard for supporting or raising it.

liftoff *n* the vertical thrust of a spacecraft, etc, at launching; the time of this.

ligament *n* what ties or unites one thing or part to another; a band; a bond; a strong flexible fastening; (*anat*) a strong, compact band of tissue binding one bone to another.

ligan *n* same as **lagan**.

ligature *n* something that binds; a cord, thong, band or bandage; a ligament; the act of binding; (*mus*) a line connecting notes; (*print*) a type consisting of two or more letters or characters cast on the same body, as *fi*, *fl*; (*surg*) a cord or string for tying blood vessels to prevent haemorrhage.

light[1] *n* that agent or force by the action of which on the organs of sight objects from which it proceeds are rendered visible; that from which this agent or force emanates or is supposed to emanate; a radiant body, as the sun, the moon, a candle, etc; a traffic signal; mental or spiritual illumination; enlightenment; knowledge; information; a person who is conspicuous or eminent in any study; a model or example; the phenomena constituting day; hence, open view, public observation, publicity; a compartment of a window; the illuminated part of an object or picture; the point of view or position in which or from which anything is looked at or considered; aspect.—*adj* bright; clear; not dark or obscure; white or whitish; not intense or deep, as a colour; not dark in hue.—*vt* (*pret, pp* **lighted** *or* **lit**, *ppr* **lighting**) to set fire to; to kindle; to ignite; to set burning; to give light to; to fill or spread over with light; to show the way to by means of a light; to illuminate.

light[2] *adj* not heavy; having little weight; not burdensome; easy to be lifted, borne or carried; not oppressive; easy to be suffered or endured; easy to be performed; not difficult; easy to be digested; not heavily armed, or armed with light weapons; swift; nimble; not dense or gross; not strong; not copious or vehement (*a light rain*); inconsiderable; easily influenced by trifling considerations; unsteady; volatile; trifling; happy; airy; not of legal weight (*light coin*); loose; sandy; easily pulverized (*a light soil*); having a sensation of giddiness; producing small products.

light[3] *vi* (*pret, pp* **lighted**, sometimes **lit**, *ppr* **lighting**) to descend, as from a horse or carriage (with *down, off, from*); to fly or fall and settle; to come to rest; to fall or come by chance; to happen to find (with *on* or *upon*).

lighten[1] *vi* to exhibit the phenomenon of lightning; to give out flashes; to flash; to

lighter

lighthouse

become lighter; to become less dark or gloomy; to clear.—*vt* to make light or clear; to dissipate darkness from; to illuminate; to enlighten.

lighten[2] *vt* to make lighter or less heavy; to relieve of a certain amount of weight; to make less burdensome or oppressive; to alleviate.

lighter[1] *n* one who or that which lights.

lighter[2] *n* a large open flat-bottomed barge, often used in lightening or unloading and loading ships.

light-fingered *adj* thievish; addicted to petty thefts.

light-footed *adj* nimble in running or dancing; active.

light-headed *adj* having dizziness or giddiness in the head; dizzy; delirious; thoughtless; heedless; weak; volatile; unsteady.

light-hearted *adj* free from grief or anxiety; happy; cheerful; merry.

lighthouse *n* a tower or other tall structure with a powerful light on top, erected as a guide or warning of danger to ships at night; a pharos.

lighting *n* the process of giving light; equipment for illuminating a stage, film set, etc; the distribution of light on an object, as in a work of art.

lightly *adv* in a light manner; with little weight; nimbly; airily; easily; slightly; cheerfully.

lightness[1] *n* lack of darkness or intensity; clearness.

lightness[2] *n* the condition or quality of being light; the opposite of *heaviness*; agility; briskness; levity.

lightning *n* a flash of light the result of a discharge of atmospheric electricity.

lightning conductor, lightning rod *n* a metallic rod attached to buildings or vessels to protect them from lightning by conducting it into the earth or water.

light pen *n* a pen-shaped photoelectric device used to communicate with a computer by pointing at the monitor; a similar device used for reading bar codes.

lights *npl* the lungs.

lightship *n* a ship anchored and hoisting a strong light to serve as a lighthouse.

light show *n* a spectacular display of lighting and laser effects.

lightweight *adj* of less than average weight; trivial, unimportant.—*n* a professional boxer weighing not less than 59 and not more than 61 kg; an amateur boxer weighing not less than 57 and not more than 60 kg.

light year *n* a unit of distance used in astronomy, being the distance which light can travel in a year, about 65,000 times the distance from the earth to the sun.

ligneous *adj* made of wood; consisting of wood; resembling wood; woody; wooden.

lignite *n* fossil wood, wood coal or brown coal, a combustible substance mineralized to a certain degree but retaining distinctly its woody texture.

lignum vitae *n* a small West Indian and South American tree yielding an extremely hard wood.

likable, likeable *adj* such as to attract liking; lovable.

like[1] *adj* equal; exactly corresponding; of the same kind; similar; resembling (*like passions*); probable; likely (*it is like he will*); feeling equal or disposed to.—**had like** was like; had nearly; came little short of.—*like* is frequently suffixed to nouns to form adjectives denoting resemblance, as *childlike*, etc.—*n* some person or thing resembling another; an exact counterpart.—*adv* in the same or a similar manner; similarly; likely; probably.

like[2] *vt* (**liked, liking**) to please or suit; to be pleased with in a moderate degree; to approve; to take satisfaction in; to enjoy.—*vi* to be pleased; to choose.—*n* a liking; a fancy.—**likes and dislikes** preferences.

likeable *adj* same as **likable**.

likelihood *n* likeliness; probability.

likeliness *n* the condition or quality of being likely.

likely *adj* like the truth; credible; probable (*a likely story*); giving a probability of something (*I am likely to be away from home tomorrow*); suitable, well-adapted or convenient for some purpose.—*adv* probably; as may be expected or reasonably thought.

liken *vt* to make like; to cause to resemble; to compare; to represent as resembling.

likeness *n* the condition or quality of being like; similarity; what exactly resembles something else, especially, a portrait.

likewise *adv* in like manner; also; moreover; too.

liking *n* inclination; desire; satisfaction (often with *for* or *to*, as *an amusement to your liking*).

lilac *n* a flowering shrub with flowers generally bluish or white; a pale purple colour.—*adj* of the colour of lilac.

Lilliputian *n* a member of the diminutive race of beings described in Swift's imaginary kingdom of Lilliput in *Gulliver's Travels*; a person of very small size.—*adj* very small; diminutive.

lilt *vti* to sing, especially in a cheerful manner; to give musical or harmonious utterance.—*n* a song; a tune.

lily *n* one of many bulbous plants with showy and fragrant flowers, as the white lily, orange lily, tiger lily, scarlet lily, etc.

limb *n* one of the jointed members of the human body or of any animal; an arm or leg, more especially the latter; a large or main branch of a tree; a participating member, an agent; an arm of a cross; (*geol*) the area between hinges in folded rocks; (*astron*) the rim of a heavenly body that has a visible disc.

limber[1] *adj* easily bent; flexible; pliant.—*vt* to make limber.—*vi* to become limber.—**to limber up** to stretch and warm the muscles in readiness for physical exercise.

limber[2] *n* the detachable wheeled section of a gun carriage.

limbo *n* (*pl* **limbos**) in Christianity, the abode after death for the souls of the unbaptized and those who have not offended by personal acts; a place for lost, unwanted or neglected persons or things; an intermediate stage or condition between extremes.

lime[1] *n* a viscous substance for catching birds; bird lime; a most useful caustic earth, obtained from chalk and other kinds of limestone, used in the manufacture of mortar and other cements and as a manure to fertilize land; mortar made with lime.—*vt* (**limed, liming**) to smear with bird lime; to entangle; to ensnare; to manure with lime; to cement or glue.

lime[2] *n* a species of tree cultivated in the south of Europe and producing a small green citrus fruit; the fruit itself.

lime[3] *n* the linden tree.

lime juice *n* the juice of the lime.

limekiln *n* a kiln in which limestone is exposed to a strong heat and reduced to lime.

limelight *n* formerly, a powerful light produced by heating a ball of lime and used to light a theatre stage; the state of being at the centre of attention; intense publicity.

limerick *n* a nonsense verse form of five lines, popularized by Edward Lear (1812–88) in his *Book of Nonsense*, 1840.

limestone *n* a kind of stone consisting of varieties of carbonate of lime.

limit *n* that which terminates, circumscribes or confines; bound, border, utmost extent; the greatest amount allowed; as much as one can tolerate.—*vt* to set limits or bounds to; to bound; to confine within certain bounds; to circumscribe; to restrain; to narrow or confine the meaning or significance of; to impose a limit on.

limitation *n* the act of limiting, bounding or circumscribing; the condition of being so limited; that which limits; limiting circumstances; restriction; qualification.

limited *adj* confined within limits; narrow; circumscribed; restricted; lacking intelligence, imagination, etc.

limited edition *n* an edition of a book, print, etc, that is issued in only a certain number of copies.

limited liability *n* such liability as that of a company whose partners or shareholders are liable only for the amount of the shares subscribed.

499

limn *vt* to draw or paint; to make a portrait or likeness of.

limner *n* one who limns; a painter of portraits or miniatures.

limp[1] *vi* to halt or walk lamely.—*n* the act of limping; a halt in one's gait.

limp[2] *adj* easily bent; flexible; pliant; lacking stiffness; flaccid.

limpet *n* a mollusc with a conical shell, found adhering to rocks.

limpid *adj* characterized by clearness or transparency; clear and bright; translucent; transparent (said of water).

limpidity *n* the state of being limpid.

linchpin *n* a pin used to prevent the wheel of a vehicle from sliding off the axle; an axle pin; a person regarded as vital to an organization.

linden *n* a tree with deciduous heart-shaped leaves and small fragrant yellow flowers.

line[1] *n* a small rope or cord; a thread-like marking, as with a pen, pencil, etc; a stroke or score; a marking or furrow on the hands or face; a mark traced or imagined to show latitude, longitude, temperature, etc, on a map or the globe (**the line** being specifically the equator); a row of things; a straight row of soldiers drawn up with an extended front; a similar disposition of ships in preparation for an engagement; a straight row of words or figures between two margins (*a page of thirty lines*); the words which form a certain number of poetical feet; a verse; an outline, contour, lineament (*a ship of fine lines*); a short note; course of thought, conduct, occupation, policy, etc, conceived as directed towards an end or object; a person's trade or occupation; a field of interest or experience; a continuous or connected series, as of descendants from a common progenitor; a series of public conveyances, as aircraft, buses, ships, etc, passing between places with regularity (*a line of ships to New Zealand*); an airline; (*pl*) (*fort*) works made to cover extended positions and presenting a front in only one direction to the enemy; (*pl*) all the speeches of a character in a play or film; (*colloq*) glib, persuasive talk; (*sl*) a measure of the drug cocaine laid in a strip ready for sniffing.—*vt* (**lined, lining**) to draw lines on; to mark with lines or thread-like strokes; to arrange in a line.—*vi* to align.

line[2] *vt* (**lined, lining**) to cover on the inside; to protect by a layer on the inside (*to line a garment*); to put in the inside of (*to line one's purse*).

lineage *n* descendants in a line from a common progenitor; line of descent from an ancestor; race; progeny.

lineal *adj* in a direct line from an ancestor; hereditary; linear.

lineament *n* the outline or contour of a body

limpet

linchpin

or figure, particularly of the face; a line of form or feature.

linear *adj* pertaining to a line; consisting of lines; lineal; narrow and long; in relation to length only (*linear measure*).

linear accelerator *n* a device for accelerating elementary particles in a straight line by successively activating electric fields at regular intervals along their path.

linear measure *n* a measure or a system of measures of length.

linen *n* cloth made of flax; a flaxen fabric or material; household articles (sheets, tablecloths, etc) made of linen or cotton.—*adj* made of flax or yarn from flax.

liner[1] *n* a large ocean-going passenger ship.

liner[2] *n* a material for lining a garment; a removable sleeveless padded garment for wearing under a jacket, etc; a protective sleeve for a part of an engine, etc.

linesman *n* (*pl* **linesmen**) in football and lawn tennis, an official who assists the referee or umpire, especially by noting when and where the ball goes out of play.

ling[1] *n* an edible fish of the cod family, rather long in proportion to its thickness, found in northern waters.

ling[2] *n* a type of heather.

lingam *n* a conventional symbol of the penis, held sacred among the Hindus.

linger *vi* to delay; to loiter; to lag or hang behind; to be slow to move or act; to hesitate; to remain long (*the disease lingers*); to dwell on in the mind; to remain alive though on the point of death.

lingerie *n* women's underclothing and nightclothes.

lingo *n* (*pl* **lingoes**) (*colloq*) a dialect, language, etc.

lingua franca *n* (*pl* **lingua francas, linguae francae**) a compound or mongrel language made up of words from different languages, serving as a common medium of communication.

lingual *adj* pertaining to the tongue; pronounced chiefly by means of the tongue.—*n* a letter pronounced chiefly by means of the tongue, as *l*, *r*.

linguiform *n* having the form or shape of a tongue.

linguist *n* a person skilled in languages; one who knows several languages.

linguistic *adj* relating to language or to the affinities of language; philological.

linguistics *n* the science and study of language.

liniment *n* an oily liquid of a stimulating or soothing character for rubbing into the skin.

lining *n* the covering of the inner surface of anything; a substance of some kind forming an inside and strengthening layer.

link[1] *n* a single ring or division of a chain; anything doubled and closed like a link;

something that serves to connect one thing or part with another; any constituent part of a connected series; in land measuring, a unit of length equal to 0.01 chain (20.1 cm); (*mach*) any straight rod connecting two rotating pieces by flexible joints.—*vt* to connect by, or as if by, a link or links; to unite or join.—*vi* to be joined or connected (with *together* or *in*).—**to link up** to meet; to (someone); to connect (things).

link² *n* a torch made of tow or other materials, with tar or pitch.

linkage *n* a linking; a series or system of links; in politics, a quid pro quo.

linkboy, linkman *n* formerly, a boy or man who carried a link to light passengers.

links *npl* a stretch of flat or slightly undulating ground on the seashore lying uncultivated; a golf course, especially by the sea.

linkup *n* a linking together; a connection of two machines or systems.

linn *n* a cataract or waterfall; the pool below a fall.

linnet *n* one of the commonest of British singing birds, frequenting open heaths and commons.

linoleum *n* a floor covering of coarse fabric backing with a smooth, hard decorative coating.

Linotype *n* (*print*) the trademark of a machine for setting and casting lines of type by the operation of a keyboard.

linseed *n* the seed of flax.

linseed oil *n* an oil obtained by pressing the seeds of flax and used in varnish and paint.

linsey-woolsey *n* a fabric made of linen and wool; an incongruous mixture.—*adj* made of linen and wool mixed; of different and unsuitable ingredients.

lint *n* flax; linen scraped into a soft substance and used for dressing wounds and sores; fluff.

lintel *n* the horizontal piece of timber or stone over a door, window or similar opening.

lion *n* a flesh-eating animal of a tawny colour with a full-flowing mane in the male and a tufted tail; a sign of the zodiac, Leo; an object of interest and curiosity.—**the lion's share** the whole or a very disproportionate share in advantages.

lioness *n* the female of the lion.

lion-hearted *adj* having a lion's courage; brave and magnanimous.

lionize *vt* (**lionized, lionizing**) to treat as a celebrity; to make a celebrity out of.

lip *n* the name of the two fleshy or muscular parts (upper and lower) covering the front teeth in humans and many other animals; something similar; the edge or border of something hollow (as a vessel, a wound); brink or margin; (*sl*) insolent talk.—*vt* (**lipped, lipping**) to touch, as with the lip; to kiss.

lip gloss *n* a soft cosmetic for colouring the lips.

lipid *n* an organic compound in fats which is soluble in solvents but insoluble in water.

liposuction *n* a kind of cosmetic surgery involving the removal of fat from under the skin by using a suction device inserted through an incision.

lip-reading *n* understanding what one says from the movement of the lips (used in regard to the deaf).

lip service *n* a merely verbal profession of service.

lipstick *n* a cosmetic used by women for heightening the colour of the lips.

liquate *vti* (**liquated, liquating**) to melt; to liquefy; to separate (a metal) from a less fusible metal by applying just sufficient heat to melt the more easily liquefiable.

liquefacient *n* that which causes to melt.

liquefaction *n* the act or operation of melting or dissolving; a becoming liquid; the state of being melted.

liquefiable *adj* capable of being liquefied.

liquefy *vt* (**liquefied, liquefying**) to convert from a solid form to that of a liquid; to melt by heat.—*vi* to be melted; to become liquid.

liquescent *adj* melting; becoming fluid.

liqueur *n* a sweet and variously flavoured alcoholic drink usually taken after dinner.

liquid *adj* composed of particles that move freely among each other on the slightest pressure; fluid; not solid; flowing smoothly or easily to the ear; devoid of harshness; pronounced with a slight contact of the organs of articulation; smooth in sound (*a liquid letter*); (of assets) readily converted into cash.—*n* a liquid; matter in the form of water, wine, milk, etc; a non-elastic fluid; a letter or sound pronounced with a smooth flowing sound, as *l* and *r*.

liquidambar *n* a kind of fragrant gum or resin from several trees.

liquidate *vt* (**liquidated, liquidating**) to make liquid; to dissolve or clear off (debts or liabilities); to pay; (*com*) to wind up, as the affairs of a firm or company, by settling with its debtors and creditors, apportioning the amount of profit and loss of each partner or shareholder, etc; to convert into cash; (*sl*) to kill or eliminate.

liquidation *n* the act of liquidating.

liquidator *n* one who liquidates; a person appointed to conduct the winding up of the affairs of a firm or company.

liquid-crystal display *n* an electronic display using a liquid with crystalline properties that changes its reflectivity when a signal is applied.

liquidize *vt* (**liquidized, liquidizing**) to make liquid; to pulverize (food) to a liquid.

lintel

lipstick

liquidizer *n* a domestic appliance for liquidizing and blending foods.

liquid measure *n* a unit or units for measuring volumes of liquid.

liquid paraffin *n* a colourless, slightly oily petroleum distillate used as a laxative.

liquor *n* a liquid or fluid substance; often specifically an intoxicating beverage; drink.

liquorice *n* a perennial plant of the bean family, the roots of which supply a sweet juice.

lira *n* (*pl* **lire**) the monetary unity of Italy and Turkey.

lisle *n* a fine, tightly twisted cotton thread.

lisp *vi* to pronounce the sibilant letters *s* and *z* imperfectly, as by giving the sound of *th* or *dh*; to speak imperfectly, as a child.—*vt* to pronounce with a lisp or imperfectly.—*n* the habit or act of lisping; the habitual utterance of *th* for *s*.

lissom, lissome *adj* supple; flexible; lithe; nimble; active.

list[1] *n* a series of things, such as names or numbers set down or stated one after the other.—*vt* to make a list of; to enter in a directory, catalogue, etc; to obtain a quotation in a stock exchange for (a security); to declare (a building) to be listed.

list[2] *n* a line enclosing a field of combat or tournament ground; (*pl*) ground or a field enclosed for a combat or competition.

list[3] *vi* to tilt to one side, as a ship.—*n* (of a ship) an inclination to one side.

list[4] *n vi* to hearken; to attend; to listen.—*vt* to listen to.

listed *adj* (of a company, etc) having its shares quoted on a stock exchange; (of a building) of architectural interested and protected from alteration or demolition without permission.

listed building *n* a building officially designated as of architectural or historic interest and protected from demolition or alteration.

listen *vi* to attend closely with a view to hear; to give ear; to hearken.

listener *n* one who listens; a person who listens to a radio broadcast.

listeriosis *n* a serious form of food poisoning with flu-like symptoms caused by the bacteria *Listeria*.

listing *n* a list or an individual entry in a list; the act of making a list; (*pl*) a guide giving details of events taking place in a particular area, published in a newspaper or magazine.

listless *adj* indifferent to or taking no pleasure in what is passing; languid and indifferent; uninterested; vacant.

litany *n* a solemn supplication used in public worship; a collection of short supplications in the Book of Common Prayer uttered by the priest and people alternately; any tedious or automatic recital.

litchi *n* same as **lichee**.

literal *adj* according to the letter or verbal expression; not figurative or metaphorical; following the letter or exact words; not free (*a literal translation*); in a strict or basic sense; prosaic; unimaginative.

literalism *n* the act of adhering to the letter; a mode of interpreting literally.

literally *adv* in a literal manner or sense; according to the primary and natural import of words; not figuratively.

literary *adj* pertaining to letters or literature; treating of or dealing with learning or learned people; engaged in literature; consisting in written or printed compositions (*literary property*).

literate *adj* able to read and write; educated.—*n* a literate person.

literatim *adv* letter for letter.

literature *n* learning; literary knowledge; literary productions collectively; the literary productions on a given subject or a particular branch of knowledge; the collective writings of a country or period; the class of writings in which beauty of style is a characteristic feature; belles lettres; the literary profession; the calling of authors of books, etc; (*colloq*) any printed matter.

litharge *n* an oxide of lead.

lithe *adj* easily bent; pliant; flexible; limber.

litheness *n* pliancy; flexibility; limberness.

lithesome *adj* pliant; lissom.

lithia *n* the oxide of the metal lithium,.

lithium *n* the metallic base of lithia, of a silver-white lustre, the lightest of the elements.

litho *n* (*pl* **lithos**) a lithograph; lithography.

lithoglyphics *n* the art of engraving on precious stones, etc.

lithograph *vt* to engrave or trace on stone and transfer to paper, etc, by printing.—*n* a print from a drawing on stone.

lithographer *n* one who practises lithography.

lithographic, lithographical *adj* pertaining to lithography; engraved on or printed from stone.

lithographic stone, lithographic slate *n* a slaty compact limestone, of a yellowish colour and fine grain, used for receiving the designs in lithography.

lithography *n* the art of writing or drawing with special pigments on a flat stone or metal plate, parts of which have been made receptive to ink, and of producing impressions from it on paper.

lithology *n* the science or natural history of stones; the study of the mineral structure of rocks.

lithotint *n* a tinted picture produced by lithography.

lithotripsy, lithotrity *n* the surgical operation of crushing a stone in the bladder.

litigant *adj* disposed to litigate; contending in law; engaged in a lawsuit.—*n* a person engaged in a lawsuit.

litigate *vt* (**litigated, litigating**) to make the subject of a lawsuit; to bring before a court of law for decision.—*vi* to carry on a suit by judicial process.

litigation *n* the act or process of litigating; the proceedings in a suit at law; a lawsuit.

litigious *adj* inclined to go to law; fond of litigation; given to bringing lawsuits; contentious.

litmus *n* a colouring matter obtained from certain lichens which turns red in acid solutions and blue in alkaline solutions.

litotes *n* (*rhet*) a figure of speech which expresses less than what is intended to be conveyed, thus, 'a citizen of no mean city' means 'of an illustrious or important city'.

litre *n* the metric standard measure of capacity, equal to 61.028 cubic inches.

litter[1] *n* a kind of frame for supporting a bed; a stretcher for carrying a sick or wounded person; straw, hay or other soft substance used as a bed for horses and other animals; porous granular matter kept in a tray in which house pets excrete (*cat litter*); articles scattered in a slovenly manner; scattered rubbish; a condition of disorder.—*vt* to provide (animals) with litter or bedding; to spread straw, etc, for; to scatter in a careless or slovenly manner; to make untidy.

litter[2] *n* the young produced at a birth by an animal which brings forth several at a birth; a birth or bringing forth, as of pigs, kittens, rabbits, puppies, etc.—*vt* to bring forth or give birth to (said of such animals as the sow, cat, rabbit).—*vi* to bring forth a litter.

litterateur *n* a literary man; one who adopts literature as a profession.

little *adj* (*compar* **less**, *superl* **least** *or* **littlest**) small in size or extent; not great or large; short in duration; small in quantity or amount; of small dignity, power or importance; of small force or weight; slight; inconsiderable; small in mind; petty; mean; narrow.—*n* that which is little; a small quantity, space, etc; small degree or scale; miniature.—**a little** somewhat; to or in a small degree; to a limited extent.—**by little and little** by slow degrees; gradually.—*adv* in a small quantity or degree.

littleness *n* the state or quality of being little.

littoral *adj* pertaining to a shore; inhabiting the seashore.—*n* a coastal strip or district.

liturgical *adj* pertaining to a liturgy or to public prayer and worship.

liturgics *n* the doctrine or theory of liturgics.

liturgist *n* one who favours or adheres to a liturgy.

liturgy *n* the ritual or established formulas for public worship in those churches which use prescribed forms.

livable, liveable *adj* worth living; suitable for living in.

live[1] *vi* (**lived, living**) to have life; to be capable of performing the vital functions; to continue; to remain still effective; not to perish; to pass or spend life in a particular manner; to conduct oneself in life; to regulate one's life; to abide, dwell, reside; to feed, subsist, be nourished and supported (*to live on grass* or *insects*); to acquire a livelihood; (*Scrip*) to be exempt from spiritual death.—*vt* to pass or spend (*to live a life of ease*).—**to live down** to survive or efface the effects of (a crime or mistake) by waiting until it is forgotten or forgiven.—**to live in** (of an employee, student, etc) to reside at one's place of work, study, etc.—**to live out** (of an employee, student, etc) to reside away from one's place of work, study, etc; to comply with, to do (*to live out one's fate*).—**to live together** (of an unmarried couple) to cohabit as man and wife.

live[2] *adj* having life; alive; not dead (*a live ox*; *a live plant*); ignited; not extinct (*a live coal*); vivid, as colour; carrying electric current; broadcast during the actual performance (*a live radio show*).

liveable *adj* same as **livable**.

lived *adj* having a life; existing, used in composition (*long-lived*, *short-lived*).

livelihood *n* means of maintaining life; support of life; maintenance.

livelong *adj* that endures long; lasting; durable.—**livelong day** day throughout its whole length; entire day.

lively *adj* brisk; vivacious; active; animated; spirited; living; lifelike; strong, energetic, keen (*a lively faith* or *hope*); fresh; bright; said of colours.—*adv* in a lively manner.

liven *vti* to make or become lively.

liver *n* the glandular organ which in animals secretes the bile and is important in metabolism (in humans placed in the right upper side and towards the front of the abdominal cavity); the liver of an animal used as food; a reddish-brown colour.

liverwort *n* one of an order of non-flowering plants closely related to the mosses.

livery *n* an allowance of food given out, as to a family, to servants, to horses, etc; hence, the state of a horse that is kept and fed at a certain rate (*to keep horses at livery*); a distinctive dress in which the male servants of some person of position are clad; a distinctive garb worn by any body or association of persons; the body or association of persons wearing such a garb; characteristic covering or outward appearance (*the livery of May, of grief*).

litter

lizard

lobster

livery stable *n* a stable where horses are kept for hire.

livid *adj* black and blue; of a lead colour; discoloured, as flesh by bruising; (*colloq*) extremely angry.

living *adj* having life; not dead; producing action, animation and vigour; quickening.—*n* means of subsistence; livelihood; power of continuing life; manner of life; the benefice of a clergyman.

living room *n* a room in a house used for general entertainment and relaxation.

living wage *n* a wage sufficient to maintain a reasonable standard of comfort.

lixivial, lixivious *adj* pertaining to lye.

lixiviate *vt* (**lixiviated, lixiviating**) to subject to the process of lixiviation.

lixiviation *n* the process of extracting alkaline salts from ashes by pouring water on them, the water passing through them taking up the salts and thus forming lye.

lixivium *n* lye.

lizard *n* any of various small or medium-sized reptiles with four legs, a slender body and a long tail.

llama *n* a hoofed ruminating animal of South America, related to the camel but smaller and without a hump.

llano *n* (*pl* **llanos**) a vast and almost entirely level grassy plain in the northern part of South America.

Lloyd's *n* a society of underwriters and others in London for the collection and diffusion of maritime intelligence, the insurance, classification and certification of vessels and the transaction of business of various kinds connected with shipping.

Lloyd's Register *n* a register of British and foreign shipping, published yearly.

lo *exclam* look! see! behold! observe!

loach *n* a small edible fish inhabiting clear streams in England.

load *n* what is laid on or put in anything for conveyance; a burden; as much as can be carried at one time by any conveyance; a grievous weight; an encumbrance; something that burdens or oppresses the mind or spirits; in building construction, the external forces acting on a structure and the weight of the structure itself.—*vt* to charge with a load; to lay a burden on; to weigh down, oppress, encumber; to bestow or confer in great abundance; to fill; to stuff; to make heavier for some purpose by adding special weight; to charge, as a gun with cartridges; to put film into (a camera); (*comput*) to install a program in memory.—*vi* to take on a load.

loaded *adj* (*sl*) having plenty of money; under the influence of drugs or drink.

load line *n* a line drawn on the side of a vessel to show the depth to which she may safely sink in the water.

loadstar *n* same as **lodestar**.

loadstone *n* same as **lodestone**.

loaf[1] *n* (*pl* **loaves**) a regularly shaped or moulded mass of bread of some size; a conical lump of sugar.

loaf[2] *vi* to lounge; to idle away one's time.—*vt* to pass or spend in idleness, as time; to spend lazily.

loafer *n* a lazy or disreputable person; a lazy person who picks up a living anyhow.

loam *n* a rich soil compounded of sand, clay, vegetable mould, etc; a mixture of sand, clay, etc, used for moulding in iron founding.—*vt* to cover with loam.

loan *n* the act of lending or condition of being lent; a lending; that which is lent; especially, a sum of money lent at interest.—*vti* to lend.

loath, loth *adj* filled with disgust or aversion; unwilling; not inclined; reluctant; averse.

loathe *vt* (**loathed, loathing**) to feel disgust at; to have an extreme aversion of the appetite towards; to dislike greatly; to abhor. —*vi* to feel nausea, disgust or abhorrence.

loathing *n* extreme disgust, nausea or aversion; abhorrence; detestation.

loathly *adj* loathsome.

loathness *n* the state of being loath.

loathsome *adj* causing to loathe; exciting disgust; disgusting; odious; detestable.

lob *n* a high-arching throw or kick.—*vti* (**lobbed, lobbing**) to toss or hit (a ball) in a high curve.

lobby *n* an enclosed space surrounding or communicating with one or more apartments; a small hall or waiting room; an entrance hall; that part of a hall of legislation not appropriated to the official use of the assembly; a person or group that tries to influence legislators on behalf of some cause.—*vt* (**lobbied, lobbying**) to interview or try to influence a member in the lobby of the Houses of Parliament or other legislature in support of a particular cause.

lobate, lobated *adj* consisting of or having lobes (applied to the foot of a bird).

lobe *n* a round projecting part of an organ, as of the liver, lungs, brain, etc; the lower soft part of the ear; (*bot*) a rounded projection or division of a leaf.

lobed *adj* lobate.

lobe-footed *adj* (of birds) having the toes lobate or bordered with membranes, as the grebes.

lobelia *n* one of a genus of plants belonging to the bellflower family, a blue species being common in gardens.

lobscouse *n* (*naut*) a hash of meat, biscuit, etc, baked.

lobster *n* a long-tailed, ten-footed crustacean with large claws, related to the crabs and used for food.

lobworm *n* same as **lugworm**.

local *adj* pertaining to a particular place;

limited or confined to a spot, place or definite district; (*med*) confined to a particular part or organ.—*n* an inhabitant of a particular place; a person who is local; a pub serving a particular district.

local anaesthetic *n* an anaesthetic that affects only a restricted part of the body.

local authority *n* a body responsible for the government of a region, etc.

local colour *n* a description in writing, etc, of the features and inhabitants of a specific locality.

locale *n* a place or area, especially in regard to the position or scene of some event.

local government *n* government of a region of a country by elected representatives.

locality *n* position; situation; place; district; geographical place or situation; neighbourhood; the state of being local.

localization *n* the act of localizing.

localize *vt* (**localized, localizing**) to fix in or assign to a particular place; to discover or detect the place of.

locally *adv* with respect to place; in place.

local option *n* the principle by which the inhabitants of an area vote directly on the sale there of alcohol.

locate *vt* (**located, locating**) to set in a particular spot or position; to place; to settle; to find or establish the position of.—*vi* to reside; to adopt a fixed residence.

location *n* the act of locating; situation with respect to place; place; a specific position or place; a place outside a studio where a film is shot; (*comput*) an area in memory where a single item of data is stored.

locative *adj* (*gram*) indicating place (*a locative adjective; a locative case*).—*n* the locative case; a case expressing position.

loch *n* (*Scot*) a lake; an arm of the sea running into the land, especially when narrow.

lock[1] *n* an appliance used for fastening doors, chests, drawers, etc, its main feature being a bolt moved with a key; the mechanism by which a firearm is discharged; a fastening together; a state of being closely entangled; a grapple in wrestling; an enclosure in a canal, with gates at each end, used in raising or lowering boats as they pass from one level to another.—*vt* to fasten with a lock and key; to fasten so as to impede motion (*to lock a wheel*); to shut up or confine with, or as with, a lock, or in an enclosed place; to close fast; to seal; to join or unite firmly, as by intertwining or enfolding; to embrace closely. —*vi* to become fast; to unite closely by mutual insertion of parts.—**to lock out** to close the doors of an industrial establishment against the operatives; to throw out of employment, so as to bring workers to the employer's terms.

lock[2] *n* a tuft of hair or wool; a tress; a ringlet; a tuft of hay or other like substance.

locker *n* a closed receptacle, as a drawer or small cupboard in a ship, that may be closed with a lock; a small cupboard, chest, etc, that can be locked, used especially for storing private possessions in a public place.

locket *n* a little case worn as an ornament, often pendent to a necklace.

lockjaw *n* tetanus.

lockkeeper *n* one who attends the locks of a canal.

lockout *n* the closing of a place of work against the workers on the part of the employers, in order to bring them to their terms as to hours, wages, etc.

locksmith *n* a person who makes locks.

lockup *n* a room or place in which persons under arrest are temporarily confined; a prison; a garage or storeroom which can be locked.

locomotion *n* the act or power of moving from place to place.

locomotive *adj* pertaining to locomotion; moving from place to place.—*n* an electric, diesel or steam engine used for drawing carriages on a railway; a steam engine that runs on a road.

locum *n* (*colloq*) a locum tenens.

locum tenens *n* (*pl* **locum tenentes**) one who temporarily acts for another; a deputy or substitute, especially of a doctor or clergyman.

locus *n* (*pl* **loci**) a place; (*geom*) the line traversed by a point which is constrained to move in accordance with certain determinate conditions.

locust *n* one of several large insects related to the grasshoppers and crickets, some of which appear in huge swarms and eat up every green thing.

locust tree *n* a type of hard-wooded, pod-bearing tree.

locution *n* a mode of speech; a phrase.

lode *n* an open ditch; a straight water channel; in mining, a metallic vein or any regular mineral vein.

lodestar, loadstar *n* a star that leads or serves to guide, especially the Pole Star.

lodestone, loadstone *n* an ore of iron; the magnetic oxide of iron, which possesses the property of attracting iron and the power of communicating this to iron and steel, thus forming artificial magnets; hence, a magnet.

lodge *n* a small house in a park, forest or domain; a small country residence; a temporary habitation; a hut; a small house connected with a larger (*a porter's lodge*); a place where a society or branch of a society, as freemasons, holds its meetings; the body of members who meet at such a place; a beaver's lair.—*vt* (**lodged, lodging**) to provide with temporary house accommodation; to provide with a tempo-

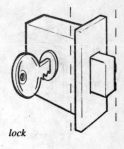

lock

locket

rary place of abode; to set, lay or deposit for keeping (*to lodge money in the bank*); to plant; fix or settle (*to lodge an arrow in one's breast*).—*vi* to have a temporary abode; to dwell at someone else's house; to be deposited or fixed; to settle; to reside; to dwell or have a fixed position.

lodgement *n* same as **lodgment**.

lodger *n* one who lodges; especially, one who lives in a hired room or rooms in the house of another.

lodging *n* a place of temporary rest or residence; a room or rooms hired for residence by a person in the house of another (usually plural).

lodging house *n* a house in which lodgers are accommodated.

lodgment, lodgement *n* the act of lodging; accumulation of something deposited; deposition; (*milit*) the occupation of a position, as in a siege, by the besieging party.

loess *n* a light brown deposit of fine silt and clay found in Asia, Europe and America.

loft *n* the room or space between a ceiling or flooring and the roof immediately above it; the space below and between the rafters; a gallery raised within a larger apartment, as in a church hall, etc.—*vt* to send into a high curve.

lofty *adj* greatly elevated in place; high; tall; elevated in condition or character; dignified; indicative of pride or haughtiness; proud; haughty; elevated in language or style; sublime; stately.

log *n* a bulky piece of timber unhewed; a large lump or piece of wood not shaped for any purpose; (*naut*) a device for measuring the rate of a ship's velocity through the water; the record of a ship's progress; a logbook.—**to log on** *or* **off** to begin or end a session at a computer terminal by performing the relevant set of operations.

logan, loggan *n* a rocking stone; a large stone or rock so balanced as to be easily moved.

loganberry *n* a cross between a blackberry and a raspberry.

logarithm *n* (*math*) the exponent of the power to which a given invariable number (or base) must be raised in order to reduce another given number, thus, in the common system of logarithms, in which the base is 10, the logarithm of 1000 is 3, because 10 raised to the third power is 1000.

logbook *n* (*naut*) an official record of a ship's or aircraft's voyage or flight.

log cabin, log house *n* a house the walls of which are composed of logs laid on each other.

loggerhead *n* (*arch*) a dunce; a dolt.—**at loggerheads with** in bitter dispute with; fighting with; quarrelling with.

loggia *n* (*pl* **loggias, loggie**) (*archit*) a term applied to a gallery or arcade in a building running along the front or part of the front and open on one side to the air, on which side are a series of pillars or slender piers.

logic *n* the science of reasoning; the science of the operations of the understanding subservient to the estimation of evidence; the science whose chief end is to ascertain the principles on which all valid reasoning depends and which may be applied to test the legitimacy of every conclusion that is drawn from premises; the art of practice of reasoning.

logical *adj* pertaining to logic; used in logic; according to the rules or principles of logic; skilled in logic; discriminating.

logician *n* a person skilled in logic.

logline *n* (*naut*) the line fastened to the log and wound on a reel by means of which the rate of sailing is ascertained from the knots into which it is divided.

logo *n* (*pl* **logos**) a symbol used to represent and identify a particular company, product, etc; a trademark; an emblem; a logotype.

logomachy *n* a contention about words; a war of words.

logotype *n* a logo.

logrolling *n* the act by a lumberjack of rolling a log down on another to cause it to move; the undemocratic trading of votes between politicians to pass legislation of mutual interest.

logwood *n* a dark-red wood, imported from Central America and the West Indies, used in dyeing and in calico printing to give a black or brown colour.

loin *n* the part of an animal on either side between the ribs and the haunch; the part on either side of the trunk from the ribs to the lower limbs.

loiter *vi* to be slow in moving; to delay; to spend time idly; to hang about.

loiterer *n* one who loiters.

loll *vi* to lie at ease; to lie in a careless attitude; to recline; to hang extended from the mouth as the tongue of the dog when hot from exertion.—*vt* to suffer to hang out, as the tongue.

lollipop a kind of sugar confectionery which dissolves easily in the mouth.

lolly *n* (*colloq*) a lollipop; (*sl*) money.

Londoner *n* a native or citizen of London.

London pride *n* a plant bearing pinkish-white flowers, common in cottage gardens.

lone *adj* solitary; retired; unfrequented; without any companion or fellow; not having others near; single; unmarried or in widowhood.

loneliness *n* the condition of being lonely.

lonely *adj* unfrequented by people; retired; sequestered; not having others near; apart from fellows or companions; sad from lack of companionship or sympathy.

log cabin

lollipop

loner *n* a person who avoids the company of others.

lonesome *adj* dreary from lack of company or animation; lonely.

long¹ *adj* drawn out in a line or in the direction of length, opposed to *short* and distinct from *broad* or *wide*; drawn out or extended in time; lasting during a considerable time; continued or protracted; extended to any specified measure; having certain linear extent (*a yard long*; *a mile long*); occurring after a protracted interval; late; containing much verbal matter (*a long speech* or *book*).—*adv* to a great extent in time; at a time far distant, either prior or posterior (*not long before* or *after*); throughout; without intermission (*all my life long*, *forty years long*).

long² *vi* to desire earnestly or eagerly (usually followed by the infinitive or *for* or *after*); to have an eager appetite; to have an abnormal craving (usually followed by *for*).

long ago *n* a time long or far past.

longboat *n* the largest and strongest boat belonging to a ship.

longbow *n* a large hand-drawn bow.—**to draw the longbow** to exaggerate; to tell improbable stories.

long-distance *adj* (of a driver, runner, etc) travelling long distances; (of a telephone call, system, etc) communicating or enabling communication over long distances.—*adv* by long-distance telephone.

long division *n* arithmetic division with the details of the calculations written down.

longevity *n* length or duration of life; more generally, great length of life.

longhand *n* ordinary written characters, as distinct from shorthand or stenography.

long-headed *adj* having a long head; dolichocephalic; shrewd.

long house *n* a long wooden structure used as a dwelling house by various peoples, often communally.

longicorn *adj* long-horned (applied to certain insects of the beetle family, from the length of their antennae).

longing *n* an eager desire; a craving or abnormal appetite.

longirostral *adj* having a long bill (applied to wading birds with long, slender, soft bills, such as the snipes, sandpipers, etc).

longitude *n* length; measure along the longest line; (*geog*) distance (in degrees, minutes and seconds) on the surface of the globe measured on an arc of the equator or a parallel of latitude, the meridian of Greenwich being selected as a starting point and called the first meridian, and longitude being called east or west accordingly; (*astron*) distance measured on the ecliptic from the first point of Aries.

longitudinal *adj* pertaining to longitude; running lengthways, as distinguished from transverse or across.

long johns *npl* (*colloq*) warm underpants with long legs.

long jump *n* an athletic event consisting of a horizontal running jump.

long-playing *adj* (of a record) playing at 33¹/₃ rpm.

longship *n* a long, narrow, open vessel propelled by oars and sails and used by the Vikings in the Middle Ages.

long shot *n* a wild guess; a competitor, etc, who is unlikely to win; a project that has little chance of success.

long-sighted *adj* able to see at a great distance; far-seeing; sagacious; of acute intellect.

long-suffering *adj* bearing injuries or provocation for a long time; patient; not easily provoked.

long suit *n* a hand in a card game with more than four of a suit; (*colloq*) a quality or talent.

long wave *n* a radio wave of a frequency less than 300 kilohertz.

longways, longwise *adv* in the direction of length; lengthways.

long-winded *adj* having the power of retaining the breath for a long time; tedious in speaking, argument or narration.

loo *n* (*pl* **loos**) an old game at cards; (*colloq*) a lavatory.

looby *n* an awkward, clumsy person.

loofah *n* the dried fibrous interior of a kind of gourd used as a sponge for scrubbing the skin when washing or bathing.

look *vi* to direct the eye towards an object; to gaze; to apply the mind or understanding; to consider; to have expectation or anticipation; to expect; to take heed or care; to mind; to have a particular direction or situation; to face; to front; to appear; to have a particular aspect; to give certain indications; to have or assume any air or manner.—*vt* to express or manifest by a look.—**to look after** to take care of.—**to look in** to pay a brief visit.—**to look on** to be a bystander or spectator.—**to look over** to examine.—**to look up** to improve in prospects; to research (for information, etc) in books; to visit.—*n* cast of countenance; air of the face; aspect; appearance; the act of looking or seeing.

looking glass *n* a mirror.

lookout *n* a careful looking or watching for any object or event; a place from which such observation is made; the person or party watching.

loom¹ *n* a frame or machine by means of which thread is worked into cloth, being either powered by hand or driven and worked by steam or other motive power; that part of an oar which is within the boat when used in rowing.

longbow

looking glass

507

loom² *vi* to appear larger than the real dimensions and indistinctly; to show large in darkness or fog (said of distant objects); to appear to the mind faintly or as at a distance; to come ominously close.

loon¹ *n* a bird, the great northern diver; also loosely applied to several other aquatic birds.

loon² *n* a clumsy or stupid person; a worthless fellow.

loony, looney *n* (*sl*) a lunatic.—*adj* (*sl*) crazy, demented.

loop *n* the doubled part of a string, rope, chain, etc; a noose; a bight; anything resembling a loop, as the bend of a river; (*comput*) a set of instructions in a program that are executed repeatedly; an intrauterine contraceptive device; a segment of film or magnetic tape.—*vt* to form into a loop or loops; to furnish or fasten with a loop or loops.—**to loop the loop** to make a complete circle vertically in the air, the pilot and his or her aircraft being temporarily upside-down.

loophole *n* a small aperture in the wall of a fortification through which small arms are fired at an enemy; a hole that gives a passage or the means of escape; (*fig*) a method of escape or evasion of obligations, etc, usually a cunning or clever one.

loop

loose *adj* not attached together or to something fixed; untied; not fastened or confined; (*fig*) free from ties; not tight or close (*a loose garment*); not dense, close or compact (*loose texture*); not precise or exact; vague; indeterminate; lax; careless; unconnected; rambling; having lax bowels; dissolute; debauched; immoral; (*colloq*) relaxed.—*vt* (**loosed, loosing**) to untie or unbind; to free from any fastening; to set free; to liberate; to relax; to loosen; to free from obligation, burden, etc; to discharge (a bullet, etc).—*vi* to become loose.

loosebox *n* a roomy stall in a stable for a horse that is not tied.

loose cannon *n* a person who acts independently and often obstreperously.

loose-leaf *adj* having pages or sheets that can easily be replaced or removed.

loosely *adv* in a loose manner; laxly; slackly; carelessly; negligently; dissolutely.

loosen *vt* to make loose; to untie; to unfix or unsettle; to free from restraint, tightness, tension, firmness or fixedness.—*vi* to become loose.

looseness *n* the state of being loose or relaxed; slackness; laxity; dissoluteness.

loot *n* booty; plunder such as is taken during warfare, civil unrest, burglary, etc; (*sl*) money.—*vt* to plunder, as a sacked city; to ransack in search of plunder.

lop¹ *vt* (**lopped, lopping**) to cut off, as the top or extreme part of anything or super-

fluous parts; to trim by cutting.—*n* the act of lopping; that which is lopped off.

lop² *vi* (**lopped, lopping**) to be pendulous, as the ears of some varieties of rabbits.

lope *vi* (**loped, loping**) to move or run with a long bounding stride.—*n* a long bounding stride.

lop-eared *adj* having hanging ears.

lopsided *adj* heavier at one side than the other; lying or inclining to one side.

loquacious *adj* talkative; given to continual talking; prating.

loquacity *n* the quality of being loquacious; talkativeness.

loquat *n* a Chinese and Japanese evergreen tree of the apple family, yielding a fruit the size of a large gooseberry, with the flavour of an apple.

lorcha *n* a light Chinese sailing vessel, carrying guns and built after the European model but rigged like a junk.

lord *n* a master; a person possessing supreme power and authority; a lady's husband; a ruler, governor, monarch; the proprietor of a manor; a nobleman; a title in Britain given to those who are noble by birth or creation, being thus applied to peers of the realm (dukes, marquises, earls, viscounts and barons) and by courtesy to the sons of dukes and marquises and to the eldest sons of earls; an honorary title of certain official personages, generally as part of a designation (*lord chancellor, lord mayor, lord provost*). —*vi* to domineer; to rule with arbitrary or despotic sway (often followed by *over* and an indefinite *it*, as *to lord it over us*).

Lord *n* a designation of God; Jehovah; or applied to Christ, especially in the expression *our Lord*.

Lord Advocate *n* the highest law officer of the Crown in Scotland.

Lord Chancellor *n* in England, the highest law officer of the Crown and speaker of the House of Lords.

Lord Chief Justice *n* in England, a senior judge next in precedence to the Lord Chancellor.

Lord Lieutenant *n* an official of high rank representing the sovereign, the principal official in a county.

lordly *adj* pertaining to, befitting or suitable for a lord; large; liberal; haughty; imperious.—*adv* proudly; imperiously; despotically.

Lords *n* the House of Lords.

Lord's Day *n* Sunday.

lordship *n* the state or quality of being a lord; dominion; sovereignty; the territory over which a lord holds jurisdiction.

Lordship *n* (with *his, your, their*), a title given to a lord; a title used in addressing judges and certain other persons in authority and office.

Lords Spiritual *npl* the archbishops and bishops who have seats in the House of Lords.

Lord's Supper *n* the sacrament of the Eucharist.

Lords Temporal *npl* those lay peers who have seats in the House of Lords.

lore *n* the store of knowledge which exists regarding anything; learning; erudition; knowledge.

lorgnette *n* an eyeglass, especially one with a long handle.

lorikeet *n* a small, brightly coloured Australian parrot.

loriot *n* the golden oriole of Europe.

loris *n* a small nocturnal, climbing mammal found in South and Southeast Asia.

lorn *adj* undone; forsaken; forlorn.

lorry *n* a large motor vehicle for transporting heavy loads; a truck.

lory *n* a small parrot with brilliant plumage.

lose *vt* (*pret, pp* **lost**, *ppr* **losing**) to cease to have in possession, as through accident; to become dispossessed or rid of unintentionally; to cease to possess; to forfeit, as by unsuccessful contest; not to gain or win; to wander from and not be able to find; to miss; to cease to perceive, as from distance or darkness; to cease or fail to see or hear.—*vi* to forfeit anything in contest; to fail in a competition; not to win; to suffer by comparison.

loser *n* one who loses or is deprived of anything by defeat, forfeiture, etc; one who takes loss (of a game) in a particular way; a person who is always unsuccessful; (*sl*) one who is found guilty of a crime a particular number of times.

losing *adj* causing or incurring loss; (of a business) unprofitable; (of a game) played with little success; (of a team) in the process of being defeated.—*n* the action of losing; (*pl*) losses, especially at gambling.

loss *n* the act of losing something; privation from something being lost; deprivation; forfeiture; failure to win or gain; that which is lost; quantity or amount lost; defeat; overthrow; ruin; misuse; failure to utilize (*loss of time*).—**to be at a loss** to be puzzled; to be unable to determine; to be in a state of uncertainty.

loss leader *n* a range of goods sold in a shop, etc, at a loss in order to attract customers who will then buy more profitable items also.

lost *adj* parted with; not to be found; no longer held or possessed; missing (*a lost book* or *sheep*); forfeited, as in an unsuccessful contest; not gained (*a lost prize, a lost battle*); not employed or enjoyed; misspent; squandered; wasted; having wandered from the way; bewildered; perplexed; ruined; quite undone; wrecked or drowned at sea; hardened beyond sensibility or recovery (*lost to shame*); no longer perceptible to the sense, not visible (*a person lost in a crowd*).

lot *n* something selected by or falling to a person by chance and adopted to determine his or her fate, portion or conduct; the part, fate or fortune which falls to one by chance; part in life allotted to a person; a distinct portion or parcel (*a lot of goods*); a large or considerable quantity or number (*a lot of people*) (often in plural in same sense, as *he has lots of money*).—*vt* (**lotted, lotting**) to allot; to assign; to distribute; to sort; to catalogue; to portion.

loth *adj* same as **loath**.

Lothario *n* (*pl* **Lotharios**) a libertine; a male seducer.

lotion *n* a liquid preparation for cosmetic or external medicinal use.

lottery *n* a system of raising money by selling numbered tickets that offer the chance of winning a prize; an enterprise which may or may not succeed.

lotus *n* in Greek myth and legend, one of a number of different plants, especially a tree the fruit of which was supposed to have the property of making people forget their country and friends and to remain idle in the lotus land; a type of water-lily.

lotus-eater *n* in Greek myth, one of a people who lived on lotus; a person dedicated to a life of idle pleasure.

lotus position *n* an erect sitting position in yoga with the legs crossed close to the body.

louche *adj* untrustworthy.

loud *adj* strong or powerful in sound; high-sounding; making use of high words; clamorous; vehement; obtrusive; flashy; showy.

louden *vi* to grow louder.—*vt* to make louder.

loudly *adv* in a loud manner; with great sound or noise; noisily; clamorously; vehemently.

loudmouth *n* (*colloq*) a person who talks offensively and excessively loudly.

loudness *n* the quality of being loud; noise; clamour.

loudspeaker *n* a device for converting electrical energy or electronic signals into audible sound, as in a public-address system, etc.

lough *n* the Irish form of **loch**.

louis d'or *n* (*pl* **louis d'or**) formerly, a gold coin of France, first struck in 1640.

lounge *vi* (**lounged, lounging**) to dawdle or loiter; to spend the time in idly moving about; to recline in a lazy manner; to loll.—*n* a sauntering or strolling; the act of reclining at ease or lolling; an apartment in a hotel, club or private house used for conversation, etc; a sitting room; a waiting room at an airport, etc.

lounger *n* a comfortable chair or couch for relaxing on; a person who lounges.

lorikeet

lorry

509

louse *n* (*pl* **lice**) any of various wingless insects that are parasitic on humans and other animals; any of sever similar but unrelated insects that are parasitic on plants; (*pl* **louses**) (*colloq*) a mean, contemptible person.—*vt* (**loused, lousing**) to clear of lice.

lousiness *n* the state of being lousy.

lousy *adj* swarming with lice; infested with lice; (*sl*) inferior, disgusting, very bad; (*sl*) well supplied (with).

lout *vi* to bend, bow or stoop down.—*n* a mean, awkward fellow; a bumpkin; a clown.

louvre *n* one of a set of parallel sloping slats placed across a door or window so as to admit air but exclude rain; a dome or turret rising out of the roof of a hall or other apartment, formerly open at the sides and intended to allow the smoke to escape.

lovable, loveable *adj* worthy of love; amiable.

lovage *n* a European herb used as a seasoning in food.

love *vt* (**loved, loving**) to regard with a strong feeling of affection; to have a devoted attachment to; to regard with the characteristic feelings of one sex towards the other; to like; to be pleased with; to delight in.—*vi* to be in love; to love each other; to be tenderly attached.—*n* a strong feeling or affection; devoted attachment to a person, especially one of the opposite sex; courtship; fondness; strong liking (*love of home*, *of art*, etc); the object beloved; a sweetheart; a representation or personification of love; a Cupid; (in lawn tennis) no score, nothing.

loveable *adj* same as **lovable**.

love affair *n* a romantic or sexual relationship between two people.

love apple *n* (*arch*) the tomato.

lovebird *n* any of various very small parrots, so called from the great attachment shown to each other by the male and female.

love child *n* an illegitimate child.

loveliness *n* the state of quality of being lovely; great beauty;

lovelock *n* a curl or lock of hair hanging by itself or so as to appear prominently.

lovely *adj* fitted to attract or excite love; exciting admiration through beauty; extremely beautiful.

lovemaking *n* amorous behaviour; sexual intercourse.

lover *n* one who loves or is attached to another; a person in love; a person having an extramarital sexual relationship with someone; one who likes or has a fondness for anything (*a lover of books*).

lovesick *adj* languishing because of love.

loving *adj* fond; affectionate; expressing love or kindness.

loving cup *n* a large cup containing liquor passed from guest to guest at a banquet; a loving cup used as a trophy.

low[1] *adj* not rising to any great elevation; of little height, the opposite of high; not of the usual height; much below the adjacent ground; not much above sea level; below the usual rate or amount (*low wages*; *a low estimate*); not loud; grave; depressed in the scale of sounds; indicative of a numerical smallness (*a low number*); near or not very distant from the equator (*a low latitude*, as opposed to *a high latitude*); dejected; depressed; humble in rank; in a mean condition; mean; vulgar; grovelling; base; dishonourable; feeble; having little vital energy (*a low pulse*; *a low state of health*); not excessive or intense; not violent (*a low temperature*); plain; not rich, high-seasoned or nourishing (*a low diet*).—*adv* not aloft or on high; near the ground; under the usual price; in a mean condition (in composition, as *a lowborn fellow*); with a depressed voice; not loudly.

low[2] *vi* to bellow, as an ox or cow.—*n* the sound uttered by a bovine animal, as a bull, ox, cow; a moo.

Low Church *n* the party in the Church of England which is opposed to the High Church.

lowdown *n* (*colloq*) the facts; all the relevant information.

low-down *adj* (*colloq*) mean, contemptible.

lower[1] *adj* below in place, rank, etc; less in amount, degree, etc.—*vt* to make lower in position; to let down; to take or bring down; to reduce or humble; to make less high or haughty; to reduce, as value or amount.—*vi* to become lower.

lower[2] *vi* to frown; to look sullen; to appear dark or gloomy; to be clouded; to threaten a storm.

lower case *n* (*print*) the case of boxes that contains the small letters of printing type; hence, small letters of printing type, as distinct from capitals.

lower-class *adj* pertaining to the class of people with the lowest status.

Lower House *n* the House of Commons.

lowering *adj* threatening a storm; cloudy; overcast.

lowest common denominator *n* (*math*) the smallest integer that is a multiple of each of the denominators of a set of fractions; (*colloq*) that which is acceptable to the greatest number of people.

low frequency *n* a radio frequency between 300 and 30 kilohertz.

lowing *n* the bellowing or cry of cattle.

lowland *n* land which is low with respect to the neighbouring country; a low or level country.

Lowlander *n* an inhabitant of the Lowlands.

louvre

lovebird

510

Lowlands *npl* the southern parts of Scotland.

lowly *adj* low or humble in position of life; not lofty or exalted; meek; free from pride.—*adv* in a low manner or condition.

Low Mass *n* the ordinary Mass performed by a priest assisted by one altar servant only.

lowness *n* the state of being low; lack of elevation; depression; dejection; meanness.

low profile *n* a position or way of life or activity intended to attract the least attention.

low-spirited *adj* cast down in spirit; dejected; depressed.

low tide *n* the lowest point of the ebb or receding tide; the time of this; a low point.

low water *n* low tide.

low-water mark *n* the level of low tide; the lowest or most degrading point.

loyal *adj* true or faithful in allegiance; faithful to a lawful government or to a superior; true to plighted faith, duty or love; not treacherous; constant.

loyalism *n* loyalty.

loyalist *n* a person who adheres to a constituted authority, especially during a revolt.

loyally *adv* in a loyal manner; faithfully.

loyalty *n* the state or quality of being loyal; fidelity; constancy.

lozenge *n* a rectilinear figure with four equal sides, having two acute and two obtuse angles (called also a *diamond*); a small cake of sugar, etc, originally in the form of a lozenge but now variously shaped, often used medicinally (*throat lozenge*, etc); a small diamond-shaped pane of glass in a window.

LSD an abbreviation of **lysergic acid diethylamide**.

lubber *n* a clumsy or awkward person, a term applied by sailors to one who does not know seamanship.

lubberly *adj* like a lubber; clumsy; clownish.

lubra *n* an Australian name for an Aboriginal woman.

lubricant *adj* lubricating.—*n* a substance that lubricates.

lubricate *vt* (**lubricated, lubricating**) to coat or treat (machinery, etc) with an oily or greasy substance to diminish friction; to make smooth, slippery or greasy.—*vi* to act as a lubricant.

lubrication *n* the act of lubricating.

lubricator *n* one who or that which lubricates; a device for oiling a machine.

lubricious *adj* slippery; oily; shifty; lascivious.

lubricity *n* smoothness or slipperiness; oiliness; shiftiness; lasciviousness.

lucerne *n* a pod-bearing plant valuable as fodder.

lucid *adj* shining; bright; resplendent; clear; transparent; bright with the radiance of intellect; not darkened or confused by delirium; easily understood; clearly expressed in words.

lucidity *n* the state or quality of being lucid; clearness; intelligibility.

lucifer *n* (*arch*) a match ignitable by friction.

Lucifer *n* the morning star; Satan (from an erroneous interpretation of the term as applied by Isaiah); a person of Satanic attributes.

luck *n* what is regarded as happening by chance; what chance or fortune sends; fortune; chance; accident; good fortune; success.

luckiness *n* the state or quality of being lucky.

luckless *adj* without luck; ill-fated; unfortunate.

lucky *adj* favoured by luck; fortunate; meeting with good success; sent by good luck; favourable; auspicious.

lucrative *adj* yielding lucre or gain; gainful; profitable.

lucre *n* gain in money; profit (often in sense of base or unworthy gain).

lucubrate *vi* (**lucubrated, lucubrating**) to study at night; to study laboriously.,

lucubration *n* nocturnal study; laborious study.

Luddite *n* one of a band, claiming to be under Captain Ludd, who in 1811–16 raised riots for the destruction of machinery as tending to diminish the demand for labour.

ludicrous *adj* adapted to raise good-humoured laughter; very ridiculous; comical; droll.

luff *n* (*naut*) the weather gauge; the weather part of a fore-and-aft sail or the side next the mast or stay to which it is attached.—*vi* to turn the head of a ship towards the wind; to sail near the wind.

Luftwaffe *n* the German air force before and during the Second World War.

lug *vt* (**lugged, lugging**) to haul; to drag; to pull along or carry, as something heavy and moved with difficulty.—*n* the ear; a projecting part of an object resembling the human ear, as the handle of a vessel.

luge *n* a small one-person toboggan.

luggage *n* a traveller's packages or baggage.

lugger *n* a vessel carrying either two or three masts with lugsails and a running bowsprit.

lugsail *n* a square sail bent on a yard that hangs obliquely to the mast at one-third of its length.

lugubrious *adj* mournful; indicating or expressive of sorrow; dismal; doleful.

lugworm, lobworm *n* an annelid or worm which burrows in the muddy sand of the shore and is much used for bait.

lukewarm *adj* moderately warm; tepid; not ardent; not zealous; cool; indifferent.

lucerne

511

lull *vt* to sing to in order to induce to sleep; to cause to rest by gentle, soothing means; to quiet; to compose; to calm the suspicions of, especially by deception.—*vi* to subside; to cease; to become calm (*the wind lulls*).—*n* a season of temporary quiet after storm, tumult or confusion.

lullaby *n* a song to lull or quiet babies; that which quiets.

lumbago *n* rheumatism or rheumatic pains affecting the region of the loins.

lumbar *adj* of or in the loins.

lumber *n* things bulky and thrown aside as of no use; old furniture, discarded utensils, etc; useless articles; timber sawed or split for use as beams, boards, planks, etc.—*vt* to heap together in disorder; to fill with lumber.—*vi* to move heavily, as a vehicle; in USA, to cut timber in the forest and prepare it for the market.

lumberjack *n* a person employed to fell trees and to transport and prepare timber.

lumen *n* the SI unit of light flux; (*anat*) a duct within a tubular organ.

luminary *n* any body that gives light but chiefly one of the heavenly bodies; a famous person; a celebrity.

luminescence *n* emission of light due to some other cause than incandescence, e.g. the glow of the firefly, the glow in electric discharge tubes, fluorescence and phosphorescence.

luminosity *n* the quality of being luminous; brightness; clearness; (*astron*) the degree of light emitted by a star when compared with the sun.

luminous *adj* shining; emitting light; bright; brilliant; giving mental light; clear (*a luminous essay* or *argument*).

lump *n* a small mass of matter of no definite shape; a mass of things blended or thrown together without order or distinction; an abnormal swelling; a stupid, clumsy or ungainly person.—*vt* to throw into a mass; to put together in one mass or group indiscriminately.—*vi* to form lumps; to become lumpy.

lumpectomy *n* the surgical removal of a lump or tumour, particularly from the breast.

lumpfish, lumpsucker *n* a fish of the northern seas, having the ventral fins modified into a sucker by means of which it adheres to bodies.

lumpish *adj* like a lump; heavy; dull; inactive.

lump sugar *n* loaf sugar in small lumps or pieces.

lumpy *adj* full of lumps or small compact masses; covered with lumps.

lunacy *n* the state or quality of being lunatic; insanity; madness; utter folly.

lunar *adj* pertaining to the moon; measured by the revolutions of the moon (*lunar days* or *years*).

lunar eclipse *n* an eclipse when the earth passes between the sun and the moon.

lunar month *n* a month measured by the complete revolution of the moon, 29.5 days.

lunatic *adj* affected by lunacy; mad; insane; utterly foolish.—*n* a person affected by lunacy; an insane person; an extremely foolish person.

lunation *n* the time from one new moon to the following.

lunch *n* the second meal of the day, eaten in the middle of the day.—*vi* to take a lunch.

luncheon *n* lunch, especially a formal lunch.

lune *n* anything in the shape of a crescent or half moon; a geometrical figure in shape of a crescent.

lunette *n* (*fort*) a work in the form of a redan with flanks, used as an advanced work; (*archit*) an aperture for the admission of light in a concave ceiling; (*archaeol*) a crescent-shaped ornament for the neck.

lung *n* one of the two organs of respiration in air-breathing animals, light and spongy and full of air cells.

lunge *n* a sudden thrust or pass, as with a sword; a sudden plunge forward.—*vi* (**lunged, lunging**) to make a thrust or pass, as with a sword or rapier; to plunge suddenly forward.

lungwort *n* a common garden flower with leaves speckled like lungs.

lupin *n* any of various pod-bearing plants, some of which are commonly cultivated in gardens for their brightly coloured flowers.

lupine *adj* like a wolf; wolfish; ravenous.

lupus *n* any of several diseases characterized by lesions in the skin; a disease of the connective tissues.

lurch[1] *vi* to roll suddenly to one side, as a ship in a heavy sea; to stagger to one side, as a tipsy person.—*n* a sudden roll of a ship; a roll or stagger of a person.

lurch[2] *n* in cribbage, the position of a player who has not made the thirty-one points when an opponent has made sixty-one.— **to leave in the lurch**, to leave in a difficult situation or in embarrassment; to leave in a forlorn state or without help.

lurcher *n* a mongrel dog, often half-collie and half-greyhound, frequently used by poachers.

lure *n* an object somewhat resembling a bird thrown into the air to recall a trained hawk; any enticement; that which invites by the prospect of advantage or pleasure.—*vt* (**lured, luring**) to attract by a lure or to a lure; to entice; to attract; to invite.

lurid *adj* pale yellow, as flame; glaring; sensationally vivid.

lurk *vi* to lie hid; to lie in wait; to lie concealed or unperceived.

lumberjack

lune

luscious *adj* very sweet; delicious; delightful.

lush[1] *adj* fresh, luxuriant and juicy; succulent.

lush[2] *n* (*sl*) an alcoholic.

lust *n* longing desire; eagerness to possess or enjoy; sexual appetite; unlawful desire of sexual pleasure; concupiscence.—*vi* to desire eagerly; to long; to have carnal desire (usually with *after* or *for*).

lustful *adj* inspired by lust or the sexual appetite; provoking to sensuality.

lustre *n* brightness; splendour; brilliance; sheen; a variation in the nature of the reflecting surface of minerals; the splendour of birth, of deeds or of fame; renown; distinction; a branched chandelier ornamented with drops or pendants of cut glass; a fabric with a lustrous surface; a metallic glaze on pottery.

lustreware *n* earthenware decorated with lustre.

lustring *n* a type of glossy silk cloth.

lustrous *adj* characterized by lustre; bright; shining; luminous.

lusty *adj* characterized by life, spirit, vigour, health, etc; stout; vigorous; robust; lustful; hot-blooded.

lute[1] *n* a stringed musical instrument of the guitar kind.

lute[2] *n* a composition of clay or other substance to make joints airtight, etc (also called **luting**).—*vt* (**luted, luting**) to close or coat with lute.

Lutheran *adj* pertaining to Martin Luther, the German religious reformer.—*n* a disciple or follower of Luther; one who adheres to the doctrines of Luther.

lux *n* a unit of illumination.

luxate *vt* (**luxated, luxating**) to put out of joint, as a limb; to dislocate.

luxation *n* the act of luxating; a dislocation.

luxuriance *n* the state of being luxuriant.

luxuriant *adj* exuberant in growth; rank; abundant; growing to excess; excessive or superfluous.

luxuriate *vi* (**luxuriated, luxuriating**) to grow rankly or exuberantly; to feed or live luxuriously; (*fig*) to indulge or revel without restraint.

luxurious *adj* characterized by indulgence in luxury; given to luxury; voluptuous; administering to luxury; furnished with luxuries; rich.

luxury *n* a free or extravagant indulgence in expensive food and drink, furnishings, clothes, etc; (often *pl*) something that is costly and pleasurable but not indispensable.—*adj* pertaining to luxury; expensive.

lycanthrope *n* formerly, a man believed to be transformed into a wolf; a werewolf; now, a person affected with lycanthropy.

lycanthropy *n* a kind of insanity in which the patient supposes himself or herself to be a wolf.

lyceum *n* a public lecture hall.

lychee *n* same as **lichee**.

lych gate *n* same as **lich gate**.

Lycra *n* a trademark for an elastic synthetic material used for tights and tight-fitting garments.

lyddite *n* an explosive prepared from picric acid.

lye *n* water impregnated with alkaline salt imbibed from the ashes of wood; a solution of an alkali used for cleaning purposes.

lying *ppr* of **lie**[1], **lie**[2].

lying-in *n* (*pl* **lyings-in**) childbirth.

lymph *n* water or a clear transparent fluid like water; a clear, yellowish body fluid drained from the tissues of the body and collected in the lymphatic vessels.

lymphatic *adj* pertaining to lymph; containing lymph; phlegmatic; sluggish.—*n* a vessel or duct containing or conducting lymph.

lymph node *n* any of numerous nodules of tissue distributed along the course of lymphatic vessels which produce lymphocytes.

lymphocyte *n* a white blood cell formed in the lymph nodes, which helps to protect against infection.

lynch *vt* to inflict punishment on or execute without the forms of law, as by a mob or by unauthorized persons.

lynch law *n* the practice of punishing people by unauthorized persons without a legal trial.

lynx *n* a name given to several carnivorous mammals of the cat family, remarkable for their sharp sight.

lynx-eyed *adj* having extremely acute sight.

Lyon King of Arms *n* the official in Scotland who has the chief supervision of coats of arms and other heraldic matters.

lyre *n* an ancient stringed instruments of the harp family.

lyrebird *n* an Australian bird somewhat smaller than a pheasant, with erect tail feathers in the form of a lyre.

lyric *adj* of or denoting poetry expressing the writer's emotion; of or having a high voice with a light, flexible quality.—*n* a lyric poem; (*pl*) the words of a song.

lyrical *adj* pertaining to a lyre or harp; pertaining to lyric poetry; lyric; expressing great enthusiasm; rapturous.

lyricism *n* lyric composition; a lyrical form of language; a lyrical quality.

lyricist *n* a person who writes lyrics, especially those of popular songs.

lyric poetry *n* songs and short poems having reference to the poet's own thoughts and feelings.

lyrist *n* a musician who plays the lyre.

lysergic acid diethylamide *n* (usually abbreviated to **LSD**) a kind of hallucinatory drug.

lynx

lyrebird

513

M

M the thirteenth letter and tenth consonant of the English alphabet, representing a labial and nasal articulation.

ma *n* a childish or shorter form of **mama**.

ma'am *n* (*colloq*) a contraction of **madam**.

macabre *adj* gruesome; terrible.

macadamize *vt* (**macadamized, macadamizing**) to cover, as a road, with small broken stones, which, when consolidated, form a firm surface.

macaroni *n* (*pl* **macaronis, macaronies**) a kind of pasta in tubular or pipe form, a name formerly given to fops or dandies.

macaroni

macaronic *adj* pertaining to the food macaroni; pertaining to or like a macaroni; applied to a species of burlesque verse, consisting of a mixture or jumble of ill-formed or ill-connected words.—*n* a confused mixture of several things; a macaronic verse or poem.

macaroon *n* a small sweet cake, with almonds in it.

macassar oil *n* an oil formerly used as a hair oil.

macaw *n* one of a genus of parrots with brightly coloured plumage and long tail feathers.

macaw tree *n* a name for several species of palm trees, natives of tropical America.

mace[1] *n* an ancient weapon of war consisting of a staff with a heavy metal head frequently in the form of a spiked ball; an ornamental staff of metal borne before magistrates and other persons in authority; a rod formerly used in place of a cue in billiards.

mace[2] *n* a spice, the dried aril or covering of the seed of the nutmeg, chiefly used in cooking or in pickles.

mace

macebearer *n* a person who carries a mace before public functionaries.

macerate *vt* (**macerated, macerating**) to steep almost to solution; to soften and separate the parts of by steeping in a fluid or by the digestive process.

maceration *n* the act of macerating; state of being macerated.

machete *n* a kind of large knife or cutlass used as a cutting tool and as a weapon.

Machiavellian *adj* crafty; ruled by expediency; unscrupulous in obtaining what one wants.—*n* one who adopts Machiavellian principles.

Machiavellianism *n* conduct based on expediency rather than on right and morality.

machicolation *n* (*milit archit*) a vertical opening in the floor of a projecting gallery, parapet, etc, for hurling missiles etc; a part thus projecting, as at the top of a tower, without any such opening.

machinate *vti* (**machinated, machinating**) to plan; to contrive; to form, as a plot or scheme.

machination *n* the act of machinating; a plot; an artful design or scheme formed with deliberation.

machine *n* any device or appliance which serves to increase or regulate the effect of a given force or to produce motion (simple machines or mechanical powers being such as the lever, pulley, etc); a structure of fixed and moving parts for doing useful work; an organization functioning like a machine; the controlling group in a political party.—*vt* to apply machinery to; to produce by machinery.

machine gun *n* a small-calibre firearm arranged to fire from a stand, carriage or tripod and provided with mechanical devices calculated to produce a very rapid rate of fire.

machine-readable *adj* directly usable by a computer.

machinery *n* a complicated apparatus or combination of mechanical powers, designed to increase, regulate or apply motion and force; machines in general; any complex system of means and appliances designed to carry on any particular work or effect a specific purpose; the framework for keeping something.

machine shop *n* a workshop in which machines are made.

machine tool *n* an adjustable machine for cutting metals into any required shape.

machinist *n* a constructor of machines; one who tends or works a machine.

machismo *n* exaggerated masculinity.

macho *adj* exaggeratedly masculine; displaying machismo.

mackerel *n* a common oily food fish.

mackintosh, macintosh *n* a kind of waterproof raincoat.

macle *n* a mineral, a variety of andalusite; (*pl*) a term applied to twin crystals united by simple contact, by penetration or by incorporation.

macrobiotic *adj* (of a diet or food) consisting largely of organically grown fruit, vegetables and whole grain.

macrocephalous *adj* having a long or large head.

macrocosm *n* the great world; the universe, regarded as analogous to the *microcosm* or little world constituted by human beings.

macrology *n* long and tedious talk; superfluity of words.

macron *n* a mark placed over a vowel (–) to show that it is long, as fate, me, note, tube.

macropod *n* an individual belonging to the kangaroo family.

macropterous *adj* (*zool*) having long wings or fins.

macrospore *n* (*bot*) a large (female) spore.

macruran *n* any of a family of stalk-eyed crustaceans with ten pincers, including the lobster, prawn and shrimp.

macula *n* (*pl* **maculae**) a spot, as on the skin.

maculate *vt* (**maculated, maculating**) to spot; to stain; to blur.

mad *adj* disordered in intellect; deprived of reason; distracted; crazy; insane; beside oneself; frantic; (of animals) furious; wildly frolicsome; infatuated; furious from disease or otherwise.—*vt* (**madded, madding**) to make mad; to madden.

madam *n* (*pl* **mesdames**) a term of compliment used in address to women; a woman in charge of a brothel.

madcap *n* a person of wild or eccentric behaviour; a flighty or hare-brained person; one who indulges in frolics.—*adj* pertaining to a madcap.

mad cow disease *n* an informal name for **bovine spongiform encephalopathy**.

madden *vt* to make mad; to craze; to excite with violent passion; to enrage.—*vi* to become mad; to act as if mad.

maddening *adj* making mad; exasperating.

madder *n* a climbing perennial plant, largely cultivated in Southern Europe, the root of which yields several dyes and pigments, such as madder red, madder lake, madder yellow; a synthetic pigment used in inks and paints.

madding *adj* (*arch*) raging; furious; wild; causing rage.

Madeira *n* a rich wine made in the island of Madeira.

mademoiselle *n* the title given to an unmarried woman in France; miss.

made-up *adj* wearing facial cosmetics; invented, fabricated; (of a road) surfaced with tarmac.

madhouse *n* (*colloq*) a lunatic asylum; a state of uproar.

madid *adj* wet; moist.

madly *adv* in a mad or frenzied manner; frantically; furiously.

madman *n* (*pl* **madmen**) a lunatic; a crazy person.

madness *n* the state or quality of being mad; lunacy; insanity; frenzy; extreme folly.

Madonna *n* the Virgin Mary; a picture; a representation of the Virgin Mary in painting, sculpture, etc.

madrepore *n* a common variety of reef coral, of a stony hardness and of a spreading or branching form; the coral-building polyp itself.

madrigal *n* an unaccompanied song in several parts in counterpoint; a lyrical poem suitable for such treatment.

maelstrom *n* a great whirlpool off the coast of Norway; (*fig*) a vortex or gulf; some dangerous movement or current in social life.

maenad, menad *n* (*pl* **maenads, maenades**) a female adherent of Bacchus; a raving, frenzied woman.

maestoso *adv* (*mus*) with grandeur and strength.—*n* (*pl* **maestosos**) a piece of music played in this way.

maestro *n* (*pl* **maestri, maestros**) a master of any art; specifically, a master in music; a musical composer, conductor or teacher.

Mafia *n* a secret society originating in Sicily and composed chiefly of criminal elements.

mafioso *n* (*pl* **mafiosi**) a member of the Mafia.

magazine *n* a military store; a place for storing quantities of gunpowder or other explosive substances; a supply chamber for ammunition in a rifle or film in a camera; a periodical publication containing a variety of articles and usually heavily illustrated.

magenta *n* a brilliant blue-red colour derived from coal tar.

maggot *n* the larva of a fly or other insect; a grub; a whim; an odd fancy; a crotchet.

magi *npl* (*sing* **magus**) holy men or sages of the East.

magic *n* the art of producing effects by superhuman means, as by spiritual beings or the occult powers of nature; sorcery; enchantment; necromancy; power or influence similar to that of enchantment; the art of producing illusions by sleight of hand.—*adj* pertaining to magic; used in magic; working or worked by or as if by magic; (*colloq*) wonderful.—*vt* (**magicking, magicked**) to influence, produce or take (away) by or as if by magic.

magical *adj* pertaining to magic; proceed-

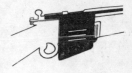

magazine

maggot

ing from magic; having supernatural qualities; acting or produced as if by magic; (*colloq*) wonderful.

magician *n* one skilled in magic; an enchanter; a necromancer; a conjurer.

magic lantern *n* an early form of slide projector using a lantern by means of which small pictures were projected onto the wall of a dark room or on a white sheet, magnified to any size.

megilp *n* same as **magilp**.

magisterial *adj* belonging to a master or ruler; pertaining to a magistrate or his or her office; authoritative; arrogant; imperious; domineering.

magistracy *n* the office or dignity of a magistrate; the body of magistrates.

magistrate *n* a public civil officer invested with the executive government or some branch of it; a justice of the peace; a person who dispenses justice in police courts, etc.

magma *n* (*pl* **magmas, magmata**) a mixture of mineral or other matters in a pasty state; a thick residuum separated from a fluid; a stratum of hot molten rock within the earth's crust which solidifies on the surface as lava.

magnanimity *n* the quality of being magnanimous; generosity; lack of pettiness.

magnanimous *adj* noble and generous; free from pettiness.

magnate *n* a person of rank; a noble or grandee; a person of note, distinction or wealth in any sphere.

magnesia *n* oxide of magnesium, a white tasteless earthy substance, possessing alkaline properties.

magnesium *n* the metallic base of magnesia, a white malleable metal, obtained by decomposing chloride of magnesium by means of potassium.

magnet *n* the lodestone; a bar or mass of iron or steel to which the particular properties of the lodestone have been imparted, either by contact or by other means.

magnetic *adj* pertaining to the magnet or magnetism; possessing the properties of the magnet or corresponding properties; pertaining to the earth's magnetism; attractive; having the ability to charm and fascinate people.

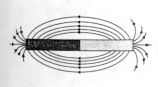

magnet

magnetic head *n* an electromagnet used in recording, retrieving or erasing information on magnetic tape, as in tape recorders and computer disks.

magnetic needle *n* any small magnetized iron or steel rod turning on a pivot, such as the needle of a compass.

magnetic north *n* that point of the horizon which is indicated by the direction of the magnetic needle.

magnetic pole *n* either of the ends of a thin bar magnet, at which the attractive or re-

pulsive force of the magnet may be regarded as concentrated; either of the nearly opposite points on the earth's surface where the dip of the needle is 90°, at some distance from the Earth's poles.

magnetics *n* the science or principles of magnetism.

magnetic storm *n* a violent disturbance in the earth's magnetism; a sudden alteration in the magnetic elements of a place.

magnetic tape *n* a thin plastic ribbon with a magnetized coating for recording sound, video signals, computer data, etc.

magnetism *n* a property possessed by certain bodies, whereby, under certain circumstances, they naturally attract or repel one another according to determinate laws; that branch of science which deals with the properties of the magnet and magnetic phenomena in general; power of attraction.

magnetite *n* a black oxide of iron, which sometimes possesses polarity and is highly magnetic; magnetic iron ore.

magnetization *n* the act of magnetizing or state of being magnetized.

magnetize *vt* (**magnetized, magnetizing**) to communicate magnetic properties to; to attract as if by a magnet; to attract strongly.

magneto *n* (*pl* **magnetos**) a type of combined dynamo and transformer used in internal-combustion engines to generate electrical pressures sufficient to cause a spark across the gap of a sparking plug.

magnetoelectricity *n* electricity evolved by the action of magnets.

magnetometer *n* an instrument for measuring any of the terrestrial magnetic elements, as the dip, inclination and intensity, especially the latter.

magnifiable *adj* capable or worthy of being magnified.

magnific, magnifical *adj* grand; splendid; illustrious.

Magnificat *n* canticle of the Virgin Mary in Luke, I, 46–55, 'My soul doth magnify (L. *magnificat*) the Lord'.

magnificence *n* the condition or quality of being magnificent.

magnificent *adj* grand in appearance; splendid; fond of splendour; showy; stately; of very high quality; excellent.

magnifico *n* (*pl* **magnificoes**) a grandee; a magnate; formerly, a title of a Venetian nobleman.

magnify *vt* (**magnified, magnifying**) to make great or greater; to increase the power or glory of; to sound the praises of; to extol; to exalt; to represent as greater than reality; to exaggerate.—*vi* to possess the quality of causing objects to appear larger than reality; to increase the apparent dimensions of objects.

magnifying glass *n* a lens that produces an enlarged image.

magniloquence *n* a lofty manner of speaking or writing; pompous words or style; grandiloquence; bombast.

magniloquent *adj* big in words; speaking loftily or pompously; grandiloquent.

magnitude *n* greatness; the comparative extent, bulk, size, quantity or amount of anything that can be measured; any quantity that can be expressed in terms of a quantity of the same kind taken as a unit; (*geom*) that which has one or more of the three dimensions, length, breadth and thickness; importance; (*astron*) the apparent brightness of a star; consequence (*an affair of magnitude*).

magnolia *n* one of a genus of trees and shrubs with deciduous or evergreen leaves and showy flowers.

magnum *n* a bottle holding two English quarts, about 2.27 litres.

magnum opus *n* (*pl* **magna opera**) a person's greatest achievement, especially a literary work.

magpie *n* a black and white bird of the crow family; an acquisitive person; a chatterer.

maharajah *n* the title of an Indian prince ruling over an extent of territory.

mahatma *n* a wise man; a sage; a man of great spirituality.

mah-jong *n* a Chinese game for four people played with pieces or tiles marked with suits or families.

mahlstick *n* same as **maulstick**.

mahogany *n* a valuable timber tree, the reddish wood of which is very hard and takes a fine polish; a dinner table or table in general (*over the mahogany*).

Mahomedan, Mahometan *n, adj* old words for **Muslim**.

mahout *n* in the East Indies, an elephant driver or keeper.

maid *n* a young unmarried woman; a virgin; a female servant.

maiden *n* a young unmarried woman; a virgin or maid; an instrument of capital punishment formerly used in Scotland resembling the guillotine.—*adj* pertaining to a maiden or virgin; consisting of virgins; like a maiden; fresh; unused; first (*maiden speech*).

maidenhair *n* a fern found growing on rocks and walls.

maidenhead *n* the hymen; virginity.

maidenhood *n* the state of being a maid or maiden; the state of an unmarried female; virginity.

maidenliness *n* behaviour that becomes a maid; modesty.

maidenly *adj, adv* like a maid; modest.

maiden over *n* in cricket, an over during whose delivery no runs are made.

maiden speech *n* the first public speech made by a person, especially in Parliament.

maid of all work *n* a female servant who does housework of every kind; a woman who can undertake many different tasks.

maidservant *n* a female servant; a female domestic.

maieutic *adj* aiding in bringing forth; of the Socratic method of teaching by means of questions.

mail[1] *n* letters, packages, etc, conveyed by the postal service; the person or conveyance by which the mail is conveyed.—*vt* to put in the mail; to post.

mail[2] *n* a body armour made of small metal rings or links; any defensive covering, as the shell of a lobster; in weaving, a glass or metal ring or eye through which the warp thread passes.—*vt* to put on mail or armour; to arm defensively.

mailbag *n* a bag in which the public mail is carried.

mailboat *n* a boat which carries the public mail.

mail order *n* an order for goods to be sent by post, often after having been selected from a catalogue or advertisement.

mail train *n* a railway train that conveys the mails.

maim *vt* to deprive of the use of a limb; to mutilate; to cripple; to disable.

main *adj* principal, chief or most important among other things; most to be regarded or considered; first in size, rank, importance, etc (*the main branch of a river, the main timbers of an edifice, the main consideration*); mighty; vast (*the main ocean*); directly applied; used with all one's might (*main strength*).—*n* all one's strength; violent effort (in the phrase *with might and main*); the chief or main portion; the gross, bulk, greater part; the ocean, the great sea, the high sea; a principal gas or water pipe in a street, as distinguished from the smaller ones supplied by it.—**in the main** for the most part; speaking generally.

mainframe *n* a large computer that can deal with several tasks concurrently.

mainland *n* the continent; territory of great extent as compared with an island near it.

mainline *vi* (**mainlined, mainlining**) to inject narcotic drugs directly into a vein.—*vt* to inject (drugs) directly into a vein.

mainly *adv* in the main; chiefly; principally.

mainmast *n* (*naut*) the principal mast in a ship or other vessel; the middle lower mast of a ship.

mainsail *n* (*naut*) the principal sail in a ship; the chief sail on the mainmast bent on the main yard.

mainsheet *n* (*naut*) a rope at one or both of the lower corners of a mainsail to keep it properly extended.

mainspring *n* the principal spring of any

magnifying glass

magnolia

piece of mechanism, as in a watch; (*fig*) the main cause of any action.

mainstay *n* (*naut*) the stay extending from the top of the mainmast to the deck; (*fig*) chief support.

maintain *vt* to preserve or keep in any particular state or condition; to keep up or in action or operation; to support; to keep possession of; not to lose or surrender; to continue (a conversation); to support with food, clothing, etc; to uphold; to vindicate or justify (one's right or cause); to assert, as a tenet or opinion; to allege.

maintenance *n* the act of maintaining, upholding or keeping up; support; vindication; that which maintains or supports; financial support, especially of a spouse after a divorce; alimony; (*law*) meddling in a suit in which the person has no interest by assisting either party with money or means to prosecute or defend it.

maize

maintop *n* (*naut*) a platform placed at the head of the mainmast.

main yard *n* (*naut*) the yard on which the mainsail is extended.

maisonette *n* a small house; self-contained living quarters, usually on two floors with a separate entrance and part of a larger building.

maître d' *n* (*colloq*) the head of a dining-room staff.

maître d'hôtel *n* (*pl* **maîtres d'hôtel**) a head waiter; a hotel manager or owner.

maize *n* a widely grown cereal plant producing a yellow cob which when cooked is eaten as a vegetable; corn.

majestic, majestical *adj* possessing majesty; having dignity of appearance; august; splendid; grand; sublime; stately.

majesty *n* grandeur or dignity of rank, character or manner; imposing loftiness of person or mien; stateliness; dignity or elevation of literary style; sublimity.

Majesty *n* a title of emperors, kings and queens (generally with a possessive pronoun, as *may it please your Majesty*).

majolica *n* a kind of earthenware resembling porcelain, used for making dishes, vases, etc.

major *adj* the greater in number, quantity, extent or dignity; the more important; very serious (*major surgery*); (*mus*) applied to the modes in which the third is four semitones above the tonic or keynote and to intervals consisting of four semitones.—*n* an officer in the army next in rank above a captain and below a lieutenant colonel; the lowest field officer; (*law*) a person of full age to manage his or her own concerns, which both in males and females is eighteen years complete; in logic, the first proposition of a regular syllogism, containing the major term.

major-domo *n* (*pl* **major-domos**) a person who takes charge of the management of a large household; a steward.

majority *n* the state of being major or greater; the greater number; more than half; the number by which one quantity which can be counted exceeds another; full age; the age at which the law permits a young person to manage his or her own affairs; the office, rank or commission of a major.—**to join the majority** to pass over to the dead.

majuscule *n* a capital letter, opposed to *minuscule*.

make *vt* (*pret, pp* **made**, *ppr* **making**) to cause to exist as a distinct thing; to create, frame, fashion, fabricate; to produce or effect, as agent or cause (*money makes friends*); to cause to be or to become (with words expressive of the result or condition of the object, as *to make a matter public*; *to make a man king*); to constrain, compel, cause, occasion (with infinitives after the object without *to*, as in *to make a person laugh*); to gain, acquire (money, profit, etc); to get or ascertain as the result of computation or calculation; to pass over in sailing or travelling; to put in a desired or desirable position or condition; to prepare for use (a bed, a fire); to compose, as parts united in a whole; to constitute; to serve or answer for (*she makes a good wife*); to complete, as by being added to a sum; to arrive at; to have within sight (*to make a port, land*); (*sl*) to have sexual intercourse with.—*vi* to act or do (often with adjectives to express the manner of acting, as *to make bold*, etc); to interfere; to proceed, move, direct one's course (*he made towards home*); to rise or flow towards land (said of the tide).—**to make away with** to take away; to steal.—**to make do** to manage with what one has; to get by.—**to make out** to discern; to identify; to decipher; to understand; to suggest, to hint; to write out; to complete (a form, etc) in writing.—**to make up** to create from parts or ingredients; to comprise; to invent; to fabricate; to prepare; to make complete; to put together; to make good (a deficit); to settle differences between; to apply cosmetics to the face.—*n* structure; construction; shape; form (*a man of slender make*).

make-believe *n* making believe or pretending; pretence; pretext; sham.—*adj* unreal; sham.

maker *n* one who makes; one who composes verses; a poet.

Maker *n* the Creator, God.

makeshift *n* something to serve a present purpose; a temporary substitute.

make-up *n* any product used on the face to improve its appearance; facial cosmetics; the cosmetics used by an actor.

makeweight *n* that which is thrown in to

make up weight; what contributes to something not sufficient of itself.

malachite *n* a mineral; a carbonate of copper found in solid masses of a green colour, the green carbonate of copper, used for many ornamental purposes.

malacology *n* the branch of zoology that studies molluscs or soft-bodied animals.

malacopterygian, malacopterygious *adj* (of bony fish) having all the rays of the fins soft.

maladjustment *n* a bad or wrong adjustment.

maladministration *n* faulty administration; bad management of public affairs.

maladroit *adj* not adroit or dextrous; awkward.

maladroitly *adv* clumsily; awkwardly.

malady *n* any disease of the human body; an ailment; an indisposition; moral or mental disorder.

malaise *n* state of being ill at ease; an abnormal and indefinite feeling of uneasiness.

malapropism *n* the ludicrous misuse of words as characterized by Mrs Malaprop in Sheridan's *Rivals*, e.g. 'an allegory on the banks of the Nile'.

malar *adj* pertaining to the cheek or cheekbone.—*n* (*anat*) the cheekbone.

malaria *n* an intermittent or remittent fever caused by a parasite which is communicated to the blood of human beings by the bite of the mosquito.

malarial, malarian, malarious *adj* pertaining to or infected by malaria.

malcontent *n* a discontented person; a discontented subject of a government.

male *adj* pertaining to or of the sex that fertilizes the ovum, as distinct from the female; masculine; (*bot*) having fertilizing organs but not fruit-bearing.—*n* a male person or animal; (*bot*) a plant which bears stamens.

male chauvinism *n* an entrenched belief in the superiority of men over women.

male chauvinist *n* one who practises male chauvinism; one who regards women as being inferior to men and treats them accordingly.

malediction *n* evil speaking; a curse or execration; an imprecation.

malefactor *n* one who commits a crime; a criminal.

malefic *adj* doing mischief.

maleficence *n* the quality of being maleficent.

maleficent *adj* doing evil; harmful.

malevolence *n* the quality of being malevolent; ill-will; personal hatred.

malevolent *adj* having an evil disposition towards another or others; malicious; spiteful.

malfeasance *n* (*law*) doing what a person ought not to do; illegal deed.

malformation *n* ill or wrong formation; a deviation from the normal structure of an organ.

malic *adj* pertaining to apples; obtained from the juice of apples.

malice *n* a disposition to injure others for mere personal gratification or from a spirit of revenge; spite; ill-will.

malice aforethought *n* (*law*) a formed design of doing mischief to another.

malicious *adj* indulging malice; harbouring ill-will without provocation; proceeding from ill-will; dictated by malice.

malign *adj* of an evil nature, disposition or character; malicious; pernicious; tending to injure or produce evil effects.—*vt* to speak evil of; to traduce, defame, vilify.

malignancy, malignance *n* the quality of being malignant; extreme malevolence; bitter enmity; (*med*) virulence.

malignant *adj* having extreme malevolence or enmity; malicious; exerting pernicious influence; (of a tumour, etc) cancerous; likely to cause death.

malignity *n* the state or quality of being malignant; evil disposition of heart towards another; malice without provocation; rancour; virulence.

malinger *vi* to feign illness in order to avoid work.

malingerer *n* a person who feigns illness in order to avoid work.

malison *n* a malediction; curse; execration.

mall *n* a heavy wooden beetle or hammer; a level shaded walk; a shopping street for pedestrians only; an enclosed shopping complex.

mallard *n* the common wild duck.

malleable *adj* (of metals) capable of being shaped or extended by beating with the hammer; pliable; (of a person) easily influenced or persuaded.

malleability *n* the quality of being malleable.

malleolus *n* (*pl* **malleoli**) one of the two projections of the leg bones at the ankle.

mallet *n* a wooden hammer, used chiefly by stonecutters, joiners, etc.

mallow *n* the common name of a number of plants, chiefly herbaceous or annual, some of them valuable for medicinal properties.

malm *n* a soil rich in lime, phosphoric acid and potash.

malmsey *n* a strong, sweet white wine made in Madeira.

malnutrition *n* lack of proper nutrition; poor nutrition due to a lack of the correct foods, especially vitamins or protein.

malodorous *adj* having a bad or offensive odour.

malpractice *n* misbehaviour; professional misconduct.

malt *n* grain, usually barley, steeped in water and made to germinate, the starch of

mallard

mallet

the grain being converted into saccharine matter, after which it is dried in a kiln and then used in brewing and distilling; liquor produced from malt; beer.—*vt* to make into malt.—*vi* to be converted into malt.

Malthusian *adj* of or pertaining to the economic theory of Thomas Malthus (1766–1834) which maintains that population tends to outgrow its means of subsistence and should be checked by means of birth control.—*n* an advocate of Malthusian theory.

maltose *n* malt sugar.

maltreat *vt* to treat badly or roughly.

maltreatment *n* the act of maltreating; ill-usage.

malt vinegar *n* vinegar made from an infusion of malt.

malvaceous *adj* pertaining to the plants of the mallow family.

malversation *n* evil conduct; fraudulent tricks; misbehaviour in an office or employment, as fraud, breach of trust, etc.

mama, mamma *n* mother (used chiefly by young persons).

mamelon *n* a small hill or mound with a rounded top.

mamillary *adj* pertaining to or resembling a nipple or pap; (*anat*) applied to two small protuberances like nipples in the brain; (of minerals) studded with protuberances.

mamma *n* same as **mama**.

mammal *n* an animal of the highest class in the animal kingdom, whose distinctive characteristic is that the female suckles the young.

mammalian *adj* pertaining to the mammals.

mammary *adj* pertaining to the female breasts.

mammary gland *n* the milk-producing gland in females, in humans called the breast, in other mammals called the udder.

mammee *n* an American tree yielding a large and nourishing fruit.

mammogram *n* an X-ray photograph of the breasts, taken to check for cancer.

Mammon *n* the Syrian god of riches, mentioned in the New Testament as a personification of worldliness; hence, riches; wealth.

mammoth *n* an extinct species of elephant of enormous size and covered with dense, shaggy hair.—*adj* resembling the mammoth in size; very large; gigantic.

man *n* (*pl* **men**) a human being; a person; particularly, a male adult of the human race; (*often with cap*) the human race; mankind; a male employee; a male servant; a member of certain sports teams; a husband or male partner; a piece with which a game, as chess or draughts, is played.—*vt* (**manned, manning**) to supply with people; to provide with a suffi-

mammoth

cient force or complement of people; to infuse courage into.

manacle *n* an instrument of iron for fastening the hands; handcuff; shackle (generally in plural).—*vt* (**manacled, manacling**) to put handcuffs or other fastening on; to shackle.

manage *vt* (**managed, managing**) to have under control and direction; to conduct, carry on, guide, administer; to make tractable or get under due control; to wield; to move or use in the manner desired (tools, etc); to treat (a person) with caution or judgment; to govern with address.—*vi* to direct or conduct affairs; to carry on concerns or business.

manageable *adj* capable of being managed; easily made subservient to one's views or designs.

management *n* the act of managing; the manner of treating, directing, carrying on or using for a purpose; conduct; administration; cautious handling or treatment; the body of directors or managers of any undertaking, concern or interest collectively.

manager *n* one who manages; one who has the guidance or direction of anything; one who is directly at the head of an undertaking, concern or interest collectively.

managerial *adj* of or belonging to a manager or management.

manakin *n* any of certain small tropical American birds with bright plumage and short beaks; a manikin.

man-at-arms *n* (*pl* **men-at-arms**) a fully equipped or heavily armed soldier of the Middle Ages.

manatee *n* the sea cow, an aquatic herbivorous mammal found off the coasts of South America, Africa and Australia.

manchineel *n* a tree of the West Indies and Central America exuding an acrid poisonous juice and yielding wood used for cabinet work.

manciple *n* a steward.

mandamus *n* (*pl* **mandamuses**) (*law*) a command or writ issuing from a superior court, directed to any person, corporation or inferior court, requiring them to do some specified act.

mandarin *n* a high-ranking bureaucrat of the Chinese empire; any high-ranking official or bureaucrat; a small kind of orange.

mandatary, mandatory *n* a person or state to whom a mandate or charge is given; one who receives special authority to act for another.

mandate *n* a command; an order, precept or injunction; written authority by one person to another to act for him or her; the instructions given by an electorate to its representatives, expressed by the results of a general election.—*vt* (**mandated, mandating**) to entrust by mandate.

mandatory *adj* containing a command; compulsory; obligatory.—*n* a mandatary.

mandible *n* an animal's jaw, particularly the under jaw of a mammal; the upper or lower jaw of a bird; one of the upper or anterior pair of jaws of an insect or other articulate animal.

mandolin, mandoline *n* a stringed musical instrument similar to a lute, with four or five pairs of strings.

mandragora *n* (*poet*) mandrake; a narcotic preparation obtained from the mandrake.

mandrake *n* a plant of the Mediterranean region with large thick roots and having strong purgative and narcotic properties.

mandrel, mandril *n* a bar of iron on which an article is fitted to be turned on a lathe; any straight bar on which a tube or ring is welded.

mandrill *n* the great blue-faced or rib-nosed baboon, the largest of the baboons.

mane *n* the long hair on the upper side of the neck of some animals, as the horse, lion, etc, usually hanging down on one side.

man-eater *n* an animal or fish that eats human flesh; a cannibal.

manège *n* a school for training horses and teaching horsemanship; the art of breaking, training and riding horses; the art of horsemanship.

manes *npl* in ancient Rome, the ghosts, shades or souls of deceased persons; the deified shades of the dead.

manful *adj* manly; bold; brave.

manganese *n* a metallic element of a dusky white or whitish-grey colour, with ores of great value in industry.

manganite *n* one of the ores of manganese, used in the manufacture of glass.

mange *n* a skin disease causing itching and loss of hair, to which horses, cattle, dogs and other beasts are subject.

mangelwurzel *n* a variety of beet, extensively cultivated as food for cattle.

manger *n* a trough or box in which fodder is laid for horses or cattle; the receptacle from which horses or cattle eat in a stable or cow house.

mangle[1] *vt* (**mangled, mangling**) to cut by repeated blows, making a ragged or torn wound or covering with wounds; to cut in a bungling manner; to hack; to lacerate; (*fig*) to destroy the symmetry or completeness of; to mutilate.

mangle[2] *n* a machine for smoothing tablecloths, sheets and other articles of linen or cotton.—*vt* (**mangled, mangling**) to smooth cloth with a mangle.

mango *n* (*pl* **mangoes, mangos**) a yellowish-red fleshy tropical fruit with a central stone.

mangosteen *n* a reddish-brown sweet, juicy fruit about the size of an orange.

mangrove *n* a tropical tree growing on the banks of rivers and on the sea coast, which has aerial roots growing from the stem and branches.

mangy *adj* infected with the mange; scabby; mean.

manhandle *vt* (**manhandled, manhandling**) to handle roughly; to move by physical force.

manhole *n* a hole through which a person may enter a drain, cesspool, steam boiler, etc, for cleaning or repairing.

manhood *n* the state of being a man; the qualities of or becoming a man.

mania *n* a mental disorder often characterized by very excited or violent behaviour; great excitement or enthusiasm; an eager desire for anything.

maniac *n* a mad person.

maniacal *adj* characteristic of mania; pertaining to mania; mad.

manic depression *n* a mental disorder marked by alternate moods of high excitement and deep depression.

manic-depressive *adj* a person who suffers from regular bouts of manic depression.—*adj* pertaining to manic depression.

manicure *n* the trimming, etc, of the nails. —*vt* (**manicured, manicuring**) to pare, clean and polish the nails.

manicurist *n* a person who practises manicure as a profession.

manifest *vt* to disclose to the eye or to the understanding; to show plainly; to display; to exhibit.—*adj* clearly visible to the eye or obvious to the understanding; not obscure or difficult to be seen or understood; evident; plain.—*n* a document listing the cargo or passengers of a ship or aircraft for the use of customs.—

manifestation *n* the act of manifesting; a making evident to the eye or to the understanding; the exhibition of anything by clear evidence; display; what is the means of displaying.

manifestly *adv* in a manifest manner; clearly; evidently; plainly.

manifesto *n* (*pl* **manifestos, manifestoes**) a public declaration of intent and policy, issued by a government or political party.

manifold *adj* numerous and various in kind or quality; many in number; exhibiting or embracing many points, features or characteristics (*the manifold wisdom of God*). —*adv* many times or by many times.—*n* a kind of pipe, e.g. in an engine, with many inlets and outlets.

manikin *n* a little man; a dwarf; a pygmy.

man in the street *n* one who is supposed to represent the views of the average person.

manioc *n* a plant cultivated in tropical America and the West Indies, from the large fleshy root of which tapioca and cassava are prepared.

mandolin

mangrove

maniple *n* formerly, a band worn on the left arm by a priest at Mass; a company of a Roman legion.

manipulate *vt* (**manipulated, manipulating**) to handle or operate with the hands, as in artistic or mechanical operations; to subject to certain processes; to manage and organize (people or things) to suit one's own ends; to operate on for the purpose of giving a false appearance to (*to manipulate accounts*).—*vi* to use the hands, as in artistic processes, mechanical operations, etc.

manipulation *n* the art or mode of manipulating or working by hand; cunning management and organization (of people or things) to suit one's own ends; the act of operating on skilfully, for the purpose of giving a false appearance to.

manipulative, manipulatory *adj* pertaining to or performed by manipulation.

mankind *n* the human race; human beings taken collectively.

manliness *n* the quality of being manly.

manly *adj* pertaining to or becoming a man; having the nobler attributes of a man; brave.

manna *n* in the Bible, a substance miraculously provided as food for the Israelites on their journey through the wilderness of Arabia; anything of value that comes unexpectedly.

mannequin *n* a model who wears dresses in order to display them before prospective purchasers; a life-size model of the human body used to display clothes for sale.

manner *n* the mode in which anything is done; the way of performing or effecting anything; a person's particular or habitual way of carriage; bearing or conduct; deportment; (*pl*) carriage or behaviour, considered as decorous or indecorous, polite or impolite, pleasing or displeasing; ceremonious behaviour; polite or becoming deportment (*he has no manners*); sort; kind (often with the sense of a plural = sorts, kinds, as in *all manner of things*).

mannered *adj* having manners of this or that kind; full of mannerisms; stylized; artificial.

mannerism *n* excessive adherence to a characteristic mode or manner of action or treatment; a personal and prominent peculiarity of style, as in a writer or an artist; an idiosyncrasy; an affected habit or style.

mannerly *adj* showing good manners; correct in deportment; polite; not rude or vulgar.

mannish *adj* characteristic of or resembling a man; (of a woman) masculine, unwomanly.

manoeuvre *n* a regulated dextrous movement, particularly in an army or navy; any movement of troops, ships, etc, for attack on or defence against an enemy; management with address or artful design; an adroit procedure; a skilful or shrewd move; intrigue; stratagem.—*vi* (**manoeuvred, manoeuvring**) to perform manoeuvres, especially military or naval manoeuvres; to employ intrigue or stratagem to effect a purpose.—*vt* to make to perform manoeuvres or evolutions; to manage or plan skilfully or shrewdly.

man-of-war *n* (*pl* **men-of-war**) a government vessel employed for the purposes of war.

manometer, manoscope *n* an instrument to measure the pressure of gases or vapours.

manor *n* the land belonging to a lord or nobleman or so much land as a lord formerly kept in his own hands for the use and subsistence of his family; a residence with a certain portion of land annexed to it; (*sl*) a police district.

manor house *n* the mansion belonging to a manor.

manorial *adj* pertaining to a manor.

mansard roof *n* a curb roof.

manse *n* in Scotland, properly the dwelling house of a minister of any Presbyterian church.

manservant *n* (*pl* **menservants**) a male servant.

mansion *n* a dwelling or residence, especially one of considerable size and pretension; a habitation; an abode.

mansion house *n* a mansion; a manor house.

Mansion House *n* the official residence of the Lord Mayor of London.

manslaughter *n* the slaughter or killing of a person or people; especially, the unlawful killing of a person without malice.

mantel, mantelpiece *n* the ornamental work above a fireplace; a narrow shelf or slab there.

mantelshelf *n* the shelf above the lintel of a fireplace.

mantilla *n* a hood; a Spanish head covering for women, which falls down onto the shoulders and may be used as a veil.

mantis *n* (*pl* **mantises, mantes**) a genus of carniverous tropical and subtropical insects, frequently resembling twigs and leaves (*praying mantis*).

mantissa *n* the decimal part of a logarithm following the integral part.

mantle *n* a kind of cloak or loose garment to be worn over other garments; a covering; something that covers and conceals; (*zool*) the external fold of the skin in most molluscs; a hood.—*vt* (**mantled, mantling**) to cloak or cover.—*vi* to be expanded or spread out like a mantle; to become covered with a coating, as a liquid; to send up froth or scum; to cream; to display superficial changes of hue.

mansard roof

mantlet *n* (*fort*) a kind of movable parapet or penthouse set on wheels for protecting sappers from musketry fire.

mantra *n* a devotional incantation used in prayer in Hinduism and Buddhism, meditation and in certain forms of yoga.

mantrap *n* a trap for catching trespassers.

mantua *n* a woman's loose gown worn open at the front to reveal an underskirt.

manual *adj* performed or done by the hand; such as to require bodily exertion (*manual labour*); used or made by the hand.—*n* a small book, such as may be carried in the hand or conveniently handled; a book or pamphlet containing instructions; the service book of the Roman Catholic Church; the keyboard of an organ, etc.

manually *adv* by hand.

manufacture *n* the operation of making goods of any kind; the operation of reducing raw materials into a form suitable for use, by more or less complicated operations; something made from raw materials.—*vt* (**manufactured, manufacturing**) to make or fabricate from raw materials, usually on a large scale, and work into forms convenient for use, especially by more or less complicated processes; to fabricate.—*vi* to be occupied in manufactures.

manufacturer *n* one who manufactures; one who employs a work force for manufacturing; the owner of a manufactory.

manumission *n* the act of manumitting; emancipation.

manumit *vt* (**manumitted, manumitting**) to release from slavery; to free, as a slave; to emancipate.

manure *vt* (**manured, manuring**) to cultivate by manual labour; to enrich (soils) with fertilizing substances; to treat with manure.—*n* any matter or substance added to the soil with the view of fertilizing it, such as guano, dung, bone dust, etc.

manuscript *n* a book or paper written with the pen or typewritten, as opposed to what is printed, often contracted to **MS**, (*pl*) **MSS**; an author's original copy to be submitted to a publisher for typesetting and publication.—*adj* written with the hand; not printed.

Manx *n* the native language of the inhabitants of the Isle of Man; (*pl*) the natives of the Isle of Man.—*adj* belonging to the Isle of Man or its language.

many *adj* numerous; forming or compromising a great number (*many men*), always followed by *an* or *a* before a noun in the singular number (*many a man*), and then with more of a distributive force.

Maori *n* one of the native inhabitants of New Zealand.—*adj* of or belonging to the native inhabitants of New Zealand.

map *n* a representation of the surface of the earth or of any part of it, or of the whole or any part of the celestial sphere, usually on paper or other material; a chart.—*vt* (**mapped, mapping**) to delineate in a map, as the figure of any portion of land; to sketch a plan of something.

maple *n* the name given to a genus of trees of the sycamore kind, the wood of which is valuable.

mar *vt* (**marred, marring**) to injure in any way; to spoil, impair, deface, deform.

marabou *n* either of two large African storks with handsome feathers and a short neck; their delicate white down from beneath the wing and tail used as a trimming, etc; a material produced from a fine raw silk.

marabout *n* in North Africa, a Muslim holy man or saint; the burial place or shrine of a marabout.

maraschino *n* a kind of liqueur made from cherries.

maraschino cherry *n* a cherry preserved in maraschino.

maraud *vi* to rove in quest of plunder; to make an excursion for booty.—*n* spoliation by marauders.

marauder *n* one who marauds; a rover in quest of booty or plunder; a plunderer.

marble *n* a hard limestone rock that takes a high polish; a block or work of art made of marble; a little ball of glass, etc, used by children in play; (*pl*) a children's game played with these balls; (*pl*) (*sl*) wits.—*adj* composed of marble; stained or veined like marble; hard or insensible like marble (*marble-hearted*, *marble-breasted*).—*vt* (**marbled, marbling**) to give an appearance of marble to; to stain or vein like marble.

marcasite *n* white iron pyrites; a white metal, especially steel, cut and polished for use in jewellery.

march[1] *vi* to move by steps and in order, as soldiers; to move in a military manner; to walk with a steady regular tread.—*vt* to cause to march.—*n* the measured and uniform walk of a body of people, as soldiers, moving simultaneously and in order; stately and deliberate walk; steady or laboured progression; an advance of soldiers from one halting place to another; the distance passed over; progressive advancement; progress (*the march of intellect*); a musical composition designed to accompany and regulate the movement of troops or other bodies of people.

march[2] *n* a frontier or boundary of a territory.—*vi* to be contiguous; to be situated next with a boundary line between.

March *n* the third month of the year having 31 days.

marching orders *npl* instructions to leave.

marchioness *n* the wife or widow of a mar-

map

quis; a woman having the rank of a marquis.

marchpane *n* same as **marzipan**.

march past *n* a march past the reviewing officer or some high dignitary on parade.

Mardi gras *n* the last day before Lent, Shrove Tuesday, in many places a day of carnival.

mare *n* the female of the horse.

mare's-nest *n* a discovery that is no discovery and that a person merely fancies he or she has made; a very complicated or disordered situation.

mare's-tail *n* a common marsh plant with tiny flowers and tapering leaves.

margarine *n* a fatty substance used as a butter substitute and made from vegetable or animal fats.

margay *n* a Brazilian carnivorous animal about the size of a cat.

margin *n* a border; edge; brink; verge (of a river, etc); the edge of the leaf or page of a book left blank or partly occupied by notes; a sum or quantity reserved to meet contingencies in addition to what is known to be necessary; the difference between the cost of an article and its selling price; (*fig*) a certain latitude to come and go.

marginal *adj* pertaining to a margin; written or printed in the margin of a page.

marginalia *npl* notes written on the margins of books.

margrave *n* originally, like marquis, a lord or keeper of the marches or borders; a title of nobility in Germany, etc.

marigold *n* a popular name for several composite plants bearing bright yellow flowers.

marijuana, marihuana *n* the dried flowers and leaves of the hemp plant, especially when taken as a non-medical drug.

marine *adj* pertaining to or in some way connected with the sea; found or formed in the sea; inhabiting the sea (*marine forms of life*); used at sea; suited for use at sea (*a marine engine*); naval; maritime (*a marine officer; marine forces*).—*n* the whole navy of a kingdom or state; the collective shipping of a country; a soldier trained for service on land or sea.

mariner *n* a seaman or sailor; one whose occupation is to assist in navigating ships.

Mariolatry *n* the adoration of the Virgin Mary.

marionette *n* a puppet moved by strings.

marital *adj* pertaining to a marriage, matrimonial.

maritime *adj* relating or pertaining to navigation or commerce by sea; connected or belonging to shipping; naval; having a navy and commerce by sea (*maritime powers*); bordering on the sea; situated near the sea (*a maritime town*).

marjoram *n* a kind of aromatic herb whose

leaves are used as a flavouring agent in cooking.

mark *n* a visible sign or impression on something, as a dot, line, streak, stamp, figure, etc; any sign by which a thing can be distinguished; a certain sign which a merchant puts on his or her goods in order to distinguish them from others; a trademark; an indication, visible token or evidence; pre-eminence, distinction, importance, eminent position (*a person of mark*); impression, influence, etc; respectful attention or regard; heed; anything to which a missile may be directed; the point to be reached; a target; the proper standard; the extreme estimate or allowance (*below* or *within the mark*); a grade given to academic work; a character, generally in the form of a cross, made by a person who cannot write his or her name and intended as a substitute for it; the basic monetary unit of Germany; the Deutschmark; the district of land held in possession by a Germanic village community.—*vt* to make a mark on; to single out, point out, stamp or characterize; to denote (often with *out*); to take particular observation of; to take note of; to regard, observe, heed.—*vi* to note; to observe critically; to take particular notice; to remark.—**to mark time** (*milit*) to lift and bring down the feet alternately at the same rate, as in marching.

marker *n* something that marks a place, as a bookmark, buoy, milestone, etc; one who marks, as the score at billiards or an examination paper; a counter used in card playing; a pen, usually with a broad felt nib, used for marking.

market *n* an occasion on which goods are publicly exposed for sale and buyers assemble to purchase; a fair; a public place in a city or town where goods are exposed for sale, whether a building or an open space; country or place of sale (*the British market, the foreign market*); purchase or sale, or rate of purchase and sale; demand for commodities.—*vi* to deal in a market; to make bargains for provisions or goods.—*vt* to offer for sale in a market; to vend; to sell.

marketable *adj* capable of being sold; saleable; fit for the market; current in the market.

market cross *n* a cross or small architectural structure set up where a market is held, sometimes of a very elaborate construction.

market economy *n* an economic system based on the free operation of the forces of demand and supply.

market garden *n* a garden in which vegetables and fruit are grown for sale.

market gardener *n* one who raises vegetables and fruit for sale.

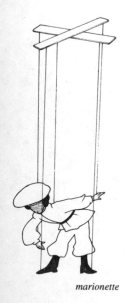
marionette

marketplace *n* a market in a public place; the world of economic trade and activity; a sphere in which ideas, opinions, etc, compete for acceptance.

market research *n* the gathering of factual information from consumers concerning their preferences for goods and services.

market town *n* a town in which markets are held, by privilege, at stated times.

market value *n* the amount obtained for goods and services on the open market.

marking *n* the act of impressing a mark; a mark or series of marks on something; characteristic arrangement of natural colouring (*the markings on a bird's egg*).

marking ink *n* an indelible ink used for marking line, etc.

marksman *n* (*pl* **marksmen**) one who shoots well.

markup *n* the act of selling at an increased price; the amount added to the price of something when selling it on.

marl *n* a mixture of clay and carbonate of lime, used as a fertilizer.

marlin[1] *n* any of various long-nosed marine fish hunted as game and used for food.

marlin[2], **marline** *n* (*naut*) a small line composed of two strands loosely twisted, used for winding round ropes to prevent their being chafed.

marlinspike, marlinespike *n* a pointed metal spike with an eye or hole on one end, used to separate the strands of a rope in splicing.

marmalade *n* a name applied to preserves made from various fruits, especially bitter and acid fruits, such as the orange, lemon, etc.

marmoreal, marmorean *adj* pertaining to marble; made of marble.

marmoset *n* an American monkey with a long tail, long fur and tufted ears.

marmot *n* a rodent quadruped, an inhabitant of northern latitudes, living in colonies in extensive burrows and hibernating in winter.

maroon[1] *vt* to put ashore and leave on a desolate island by way of punishment, as was done by buccaneers, etc; to abandon; to leave helpless and alone.

maroon[2] *adj* brownish-crimson; of a colour resembling claret.—*n* a brownish-crimson or claret colour.

maroon[3] *n* a rocket with the case bound round with tarred twine so that it explodes with a great noise, used as a warning device.

marplot *n* one who, by his or her officious interference, mars or defeats a design or plot.

marque *n* a brand of a product, especially a motorcar.

marquee *n* a large tent erected for a temporary purpose, such as a social reception.

marquess *n* same as **marquis**.

marquetry *n* inlaid work, often consisting of thin pieces of fine woods of different colours arranged on a ground so as to form various patterns.

marquis, marquess *n* a title of dignity in Britain next in rank to that of duke and hence the second of the five orders of English nobility.

marquisate *n* the dignity of a marquis.

marquisette *n* a sheer cloth of silk, cotton, rayon, etc, used to make clothes, curtains, etc.

marriage *n* the act of marrying; the legal union of a man and woman for life; the ceremony by which they are so united; a wedding.

marriageable *adj* of an age suitable for marriage.

marriage licence *n* a licence to marry without proclamation of banns in a church.

marrow *n* the fatty tissue in the cavities of bones; bone marrow; (*fig*) the essence; the best part; a kind of gourd yielding an oblong fruit used as a vegetable, a vegetable marrow.

marrowbone *n* a bone containing marrow.

marrowfat *n* a kind of rich pea.

marry[1] *vt* (**married, marrying**) to unite in wedlock or matrimony; to declare man and wife (*the clergyman married a couple*); to give in wedlock (as a father his daughter); to take for husband or wife; to wed; (*fig*) to unite by some close bond of connection.— *vi* to enter into a conjugal state; to take a husband or a wife.

marry[2] *interj* (*arch*) indeed, forsooth (used to express indignation or surprise or in emphasis).

Mars *n* the Roman god of war; the planet which comes next to the earth in the order of distance from the sun.

Marsala *n* a wine resembling sherry, from Marsala in Sicily.

Marseillaise *n* the national song of the French Republic, dating from the first revolution, being written in 1792 and first sung in Paris by revolutionaries from Marseilles.

marsh *n* a tract of low and very wet land; a fen, swamp, morass.—*adj* pertaining to marshes or swampy places; applied to various plants (*marsh mallow, marsh marigold*).

marshal *n* one who regulates rank and order at a ceremony, parade or any other assembly, directs the order of procession, etc; in some armies, a general officer of the highest rank.—*vt* (**marshalled, marshalling**) to dispose in due order (an army, troops); to arrange in a suitable or most effective order (arguments, evidence, etc).

marsh gas same as **firedamp**.

marsh harrier *n* a British bird of prey fre-

marmot

marquee

quenting marshes and living on water birds, mice, frogs, fish, etc.

marsh mallow *n* a plant of the hollyhock genus, growing naturally in marshes and possessing demulcent properties.

marshmallow *n* a soft, spongy sweet made of sugar, gelatine, etc; formerly, a sweet paste made from the root of the marsh mallow.

marsh marigold *n* a marsh plant with a bright yellow flower.

marshy *adj* of the nature of a marsh or swamp; swampy; fen-like; produced in marshes.

marsupial *adj* having an external abdominal pouch; belonging to the order of marsupials.—*n* one of an extensive group of mammals characterized by the absence of a placenta and the consequent premature production of the foetus, which immediately on its birth is placed by the mother in an external abdominal pouch in which are the teats and there nurtured until fully developed.

marsh marigold

marsupium *n* (*pl* **marsupia**) the pouch of the marsupials.

mart *n* a market; an emporium.

Martello tower *n* formerly, a small circular fort with very thick walls, chiefly built to defend the seaboard.

marten *n* a carnivorous quadruped of the weasel family, very destructive to game, poultry and eggs.

martial *adj* pertaining to war; suited to war; military; given to war; warlike.

martial art *n* any fighting technique which has been developed to the level of an art as a self-defence sport, such as karate or judo.

martial law *n* an arbitrary kind of law, proceeding directly from a military authority and proclaimed in times of war, insurrection, rebellion or other great emergency.

martin *n* a general name applied to various species of swallows.

martinet *n* one who lays stress on a rigid adherence to the details of discipline, dress, etc.

martingale *n* a strap from a horse's head to the girth, under its belly and passing between the forelegs, to prevent it from rearing.

mask

martini *n* a cocktail made of gin and dry vermouth.

Martinmas *n* the feast of St Martin, 11th November, a Scottish term day.

martyr *n* one who by his or her death bears witness to the truth; one who suffers death rather than renounce his or her religious opinions; one who suffers death or persecution in defence of any cause.—*vt* to persecute as a martyr; to torment or torture.

martyrdom *n* the state of being a martyr; the death of a martyr.

martyrology *n* a history or account of martyrs with their sufferings; a register of martyrs.

marvel *n* a wonder; an object of great astonishment.—*vi* (**marvelled, marvelling**) to be struck with surprise or astonishment; to wonder.

marvellous *adj* exciting wonder; wonderful; strange; astonishing; surpassing credit; partaking of the miraculous or supernatural.

Marxism *n* the theory developed by Karl Marx and Friedrich Engels that advocates public ownership of the means of production and the dictatorship of the proletariat until the establishment of a classless society; an analysis of society from the point of view of the struggle between the classes.

marzipan, marchpane *n* a kind of thick paste of ground almonds and sugar.

mascara *n* a coloured cosmetic applied to the eyelashes to make them appear darker or thicker.

mascot *n* a thing or person supposed to bring good luck.

masculine *adj* of the male sex; not female; strong; robust; powerful; manly; not soft or effeminate; coarse, bold, forward or unwomanly (said of a woman, as *her manners are rough and masculine*); (*gram*) denoting or pertaining to the gender of words which are especially applied to male beings or things regarded grammatically as male.—*n* (*gram*) the masculine gender; a word of this gender.

masculinity *n* the quality or state of being masculine.

mash *n* a mixture of ingredients beaten or blended together in an indiscriminate manner; especially, a mixture for feeding horses; in brewing, a mixture of ground malt and warm water yielding wort; (*colloq*) mashed potatoes.—*vt* to beat into a confused mass; to crush by beating or pressure; to mix (malt) and steep in warm water for brewing.

masher *n* a kitchen utensil with a slotted head for mashing vegetables.

mashie *n* formerly, a golf club with a lofted iron head mostly used for approach shots.

mask¹ *n* a cover for the face, often intended to conceal identity; a disguise, pretence or subterfuge; (*surg*) a protective gauze worn over the nose and mouth to prevent the spread of germs; (*photog*) a screen used to cover part of a sensitized surface to prevent exposure by light.—*vt* to cover with a mask; to disguise for concealment.

mask² *n* a masque.

masking tape *n* removable adhesive tape used to cover surfaces not to be painted.

masochism *n* a pathological condition in which pleasure, especially sexual, is derived from cruel treatment by another person.

mason *n* a builder in stone or brick; one who constructs the walls of buildings, etc.

Mason *n* a member of the fraternity of Freemasons.

Masonic *adj* pertaining to the craft or mysteries of Freemasons.

masonry *n* the art or occupation of a mason; the work produced by a mason; stonework or brickwork.

Masonry *n* the principles and practices of Freemasons.

masque *n* a masquerade; a piece of mummery; a sort of play or histrionic spectacle during the sixteenth and seventeenth centuries.

masquerade *n* an assembly of persons wearing masks and amusing themselves with various diversions, as dancing, walking in procession, etc; a disguise; a pretence; a false show.—*vi* (**masqueraded, masquerading**) to wear a mask; to take part in a masquerade; to go in disguise; to pretend to be what one is not.

mass *n* a body of matter collected into a lump; a lump; a collective body of fluid matter; a great quantity collected; an assemblage (*a mass of foliage*); bulk; magnitude; the main body of things collectively; the generality; the bulk (*the mass of the people*); (*physics*) the quantity of matter in any body, or the sum of all the material particles of a body, always proportional to the weight, whatever the bulk or figure.— **the masses** the great body of the people, more especially of the working class and lower orders; the populace.—*vt* to form into a mass; to collect into masses; to assemble in crowds.—*vi* to come together in a mass.

Mass *n* the service of the Eucharist in the Roman Catholic and Greek Churches; the Roman Catholic communion service; the elaborate musical setting of certain portions of the service of the Mass.

massacre *n* the indiscriminate killing of human beings, especially without authority or necessity; a great slaughter of people or animals; (*colloq*) a severe defeat.—*vt* (**massacred, massacring**) to kill with indiscriminate violence; to butcher; to slaughter; (*colloq*) to defeat thoroughly.

massage *n* the process of kneading, rubbing, pressing, slapping, etc, parts of a person's body to improve circulation, relieve stiffness, to induce relaxation, etc.—*vt* (**massaged, massaging**) to give a massage to.

masseur *n* a man who practises massage.

masseuse *n* a woman who practises massage.

massif *n* a central mountain mass; a large plateau with distinct edges.

massive *adj* forming or consisting of a large mass; having great size and weight; ponderous; (of a mineral) having a crystalline structure but not a regular form as a whole.

mass media *npl* means of communication, such as radio, television and newspapers with large circulations, able to reach a large number of people quickly over a wide area.

mass production *n* production of goods in large quantities, especially by machinery and division of labour.

massy *adj* possessing great mass or bulk; massive.

mast[1] *n* a long, round piece of timber or a hollow pillar of iron or steel standing upright in a vessel and supporting the yards, sails and rigging in general.—*vt* to fix a mast or masts in; to erect the masts of.

mast[2] *n* (no *pl*) the fruit of the oak and beech or other forest trees; nuts; acorns.

mastectomy *n* the surgical removal of a breast.

master *n* one who rules, governs or directs; one who has others under his immediate control; an employer; the counterpart of *slave*, *servant*, etc (often in compounds, as, *master printer*, *master builder*, etc); one who has possession and the power of controlling or using at pleasure; the owner; proprietor; a chief, principal, head, leader; the person entrusted with the care and navigation of a merchant ship, otherwise the captain; in the navy, formerly an officer who navigated the ship under the direction of the captain; the male head of, or a male teacher in, a school; a man eminently skilled in any pursuit, accomplishment, art or science; a proficient or adept (*a master of the violin*; *a master of sarcasm*); a civil or respectful title of address used before a person's name and written Mr (Mr John Smith), when applied to a boy or young gentleman, however, written in full; a title of dignity; a degree in colleges and universities (*Master of Arts*); the title of the head of some societies or corporations; the title of certain high legal or other functionaries (*Master of the Rolls*; *a master in chancery*).—*vt* to become the master of; to overpower; to subdue; to make oneself master of; to master or overcome the difficulties of; to become proficient or expert in.—*adj* belonging to a master; chief; principal (often used as the first element in a compound word, as, *masterpiece*, *mastermind*, etc).

masterful *adj* inclined to exercise mastery; imperious; domineering.

master key *n* a key that opens many locks; (*fig*) a general clue to lead out of many difficulties.

masterly *adj* formed or executed with superior skill; suitable to a master; most able or

mast

skilful (*a masterly design* or *performance*).

mastermind *n* a very clever person, especially one who plans or directs a project.— *vt* to be the mastermind of.

master mariner *n* the captain of a merchant vessel.

master of ceremonies *n* a person who presides at a public occasion and introduces guests, etc.

Master of the Rolls *n* one of the judges of chancery in England, keeper of the rolls of patents and grants that pass the great seal.

masterpiece *n* something superior to any other performance of the same person; anything done or made with superior skill.

mastery *n* the act of mastering; dominion or command over something; superiority in competition; pre-eminence; victory in war; eminent skill.

masthead *n* the top of a mast; the title, etc, of a newspaper or magazine, printed at the top of the front page.

mastic *n* a resin exuding from a tree of Southern Europe, etc, yielding a varnish; the tree itself; a kind of mortar or cement for plastering walls.

masticate *vt* (**masticated, masticating**) to grind with the teeth and prepare for swallowing and digestion; to chew.

mastication *n* the act of masticating.

mastiff *n* a variety of dog of old English breed, large and very stoutly built and with deep and pendulous lips.

mastitis *n* a bacterial inflammation of the mammary gland.

mastodon *n* any of a genus of extinct fossil quadrupeds resembling the elephant but larger.

mastoid *adj* resembling a nipple.—*n* the bony prominence behind the ear.

mat¹ *n* an article of interwoven rushes, straw, twine, etc, on the floor for cleaning the boots and shoes of those who enter a house or to keep the feet from the bare floor; some kind of coarse fabric used for packing or for covering floors, etc; an article of various materials, flat and of little thickness, put below dishes on a table, etc; a thick pad used in wrestling, gymnastics, etc; anything growing thickly or closely interwoven so as to resemble a mat in form or texture (*a mat of hair*).

mat², **matt**, **matte** *adj* without lustre; dull in surface; lustreless.

matador *n* the bullfighter who makes the final passes with the cape then kills the bull.

match¹ *n* a person equal to another; one who is able to mate or cope with another; an equal; a mate; the coming together of two parties suited to one another, as for a trial of strength or skill, etc; a contest or game; union by marriage; one to be married or gained in marriage.—*vt* to be a match or

match

mate for; to be able to compete with; to equal; to show an equal to; to place in competition or comparison with; to oppose as equal; to suit; to make to correspond; to marry; to give in marriage; to join in any way, combine, couple.—*vi* to be united in marriage; to be of equal size or quality; to tally, suit, correspond.

match² *n* a small slip of wood, cardboard or wax with a composition on one end that ignites on friction.

matchless *adj* having no match or equal; unequalled; unrivalled.

matchlock *n* originally, the lock of a musket containing a match for firing; hence, a musket fired by means of a match.

matchmaker *n* one who contrives or effects a union by marriage.

match play *n* in golf, scoring by the number of holes won as opposed to strokes played.

match point *n* in tennis, badminton, etc, the situation where the winner of the next point wins the match.

mate *n* one who customarily associates with another; a companion; an equal; a match; an officer in a ship whose duty is to assist the master or commander; a husband or wife; one of a pair of animals which associate for propagation and the care of their young; one of a matched pair, as of gloves, etc.—*vt* (**mated, mating**) to match; to marry; to match oneself against; to cope with; to equal.

maté *n* an evergreen South American shrub the dried leaves of which are used to make a mildly stimulating tea.

material *adj* pertaining to matter; consisting of matter; not spiritual; not mental; pertaining to the physical nature of human beings or to the bodily needs, interests and comforts; important; weighty; momentous; more or less necessary; (in logic) pertaining to the matter of a thing and not to the form.—*n* what is composed of matter; the substance or matter of which anything is made; fabric; cloth; (*pl*) the tools, equipment required to make or do something; a person regarded as fit for a particular task, position, etc.

materialism *n* the doctrine which denies the existence of spirit or anything but matter; concern with money and possessions rather than spiritual values.

materialist *n* one who holds the doctrine of materialism.

materialistic *adj* relating to or of materialism; believing in materialism; concerned with money and possessions.

materialization *n* the act of materializing; in spiritualism, the alleged assumption by a spirit of a material or bodily form.

materialize *vi* (**materialized, materializing**) to become fact; to be realized; to make an unexpected appearance.

materially *adv* in a material manner; in the state of matter; substantially; in an important manner or degree; essentially.

materia medica *n* the science of substances used in medicine, including pharmacology, pharmacy, etc; a substance employed as a medicine or in making drugs.

materiel, matériel *n* the baggage, munitions and provision of an army or of any other organization.

maternal *adj* pertaining to a mother; becoming a mother; motherly.

maternity *n* the state, character or relation of a mother.

mathematical, mathematic *adj* pertaining to mathematics; according to the principles of mathematics.

mathematician *n* one skilled in mathematics.

mathematics *n* the science dealing with the properties and relations of quantities, comprising pure mathematics, which considers quantity abstractly, as arithmetic, geometry, algebra, trigonometry; and applied mathematics, which treats of magnitude as subsisting in material bodies and is consequently interwoven with physical considerations (astronomy, optics, etc).

matins *n sing pl* morning worship or service; morning prayers or songs; time of morning service; (*RC Church*) the first canonical hour.

matinée *n* an afternoon performance at a theatre, cinema, etc.

matriarchy *n* the rule or predominance of the mother in a family; the principle of determining descent and inheritance on the mother's side and not on the father's.

matricide *n* the killing or murder of one's mother; the killer or murderer of his or her mother.

matriculate *vt* (**matriculated. matriculating**) to enter in a register; to enrol; especially, to admit to membership in a college or university by enrolling the name in a register.—*vi* to be entered as a member of a society.—*adj* matriculated; enrolled.—*n* one who is matriculated.

matriculation *n* the act of matriculating.

matrimonial *adj* pertaining to matrimony or marriage; connubial.

matrimony *n* marriage; the nuptial state.

matrix *n* (*pl* **matrices**) the womb; that which encloses anything or gives origin to anything; the form or mould in which something is shaped; the connective cellular substance in bone, cartilage or other tissue; formative cells that produce the teeth and nails; the rock or main substance in which a crystal, mineral or fossil is embedded; (*math*) a rectangular, usually square, array of symbols, regarded as having an individuality akin to that of a single quantity so that algebraic operations can be applied to matrices; a network of intersecting inputs and outputs in a computer.

matron *n* a married woman, especially a mature married woman; the mother of a family; a woman in charge of nursing and domestic arrangements in some institutions, such as private schools; the senior nursing officer in charge of nursing staff in a hospital.

matronly *adj* becoming a wife or matron; resembling a matron or what belongs to her; sedate.

matron of honour *n* a married woman acting as chief attendant to a bride.

matt, matte *adj* same as **mat**[2].

matter *n* that which occupies space and which becomes known by the senses; that of which the whole sensible universe is composed; body; substance; not mind; the substance of any speech or writing; the ideas or facts as distinct from the words; the meaning; in logic, that which forms the subject of any mental operation, as distinguished from the form; good sense; substance, as opposed to empty verbosity or frivolous jesting; thing treated; that about which we think, write or speak; affair or business (*thus the matter ended*); cause or occasion of trouble, disturbance, etc (*what is the matter?*); import; consequence; moment (as in *no matter which*); indefinite amount or quantity (*a matter of 7 miles*); substance excreted from living animal bodies; that which is discharged in a tumour, boil or abscess; pus.—*vi* to be of importance; to signify (*it does not matter; what does it matter?*).

matter-of-fact *adj* treating of facts or realities; not fanciful, imaginative or ideal; adhering to facts; not given to wander beyond realities; prosaic.

mattery *adj* purulent; generating pus.

mattock *n* a pickaxe with one or both of its ends broad instead of pointed.

mattock

mattress *n* a casing of strong cloth filled with cotton, foam, rubber, coiled springs, etc, used on a bed.

mature *adj* ripe; perfected by time or natural growth; brought by natural process to a complete state of development; ripe or ready to be put in action; (of fruit, cheese, etc) ripe; become payable; having reached the time fixed for payment; due.—*vt* (**matured, maturing**) to make mature; to ripen; to make ripe or ready for any special use.—*vi* to advance towards ripeness; to become mature or ripe; (*com*) to reach the time fixed for payment.

mattress

matureness *n* the state of being mature; maturity.

maturity *n* the state or quality of being mature; ripeness; a state of perfection or completeness; (*com*) the time when a note or bill of exchange becomes due.

matutinal *adj* pertaining to the morning; early in the day.

maudlin *adj* tearful; over-emotional; sickly sentimental; tearfully drunk.

maul *n* a kind of large hammer or mallet.—*vt* to beat with a maul or as with a maul; to maltreat severely; to paw.

maulstick, mahlstick *n* a stick used by painters to steady and support the hand in working.

maunder *vi* to mutter; to talk in a rambling way; to wander about aimlessly.

Maundy Thursday *n* the Thursday before Good Friday, when the British sovereign distributes alms.

Maundy money *n* small silver coins (including twopenny and penny pieces) struck for distribution on Maundy Thursday.

Mauser *n* (*trademark*) a kind of rifle or automatic pistol.

mausoleum *n* (*pl* **mausoleums, mausolea**) a magnificent tomb or stately sepulchral monument.

mauve *n* a pale purple colour.

mavis *n* the song thrush.

maw *n* the stomach, crop or throat of animals; the throat and stomach of a person who eats large quantities of food indiscriminately; the crop of fowls.

mawkish *adj* maudlin; insipid.

maxillar, maxillary *adj* pertaining to the jaw or the maxilla (*the maxillary bones* or *glands*).

maxim *n* an established principle; a principle or formula embodying a rule of conduct.

maximum *n* (*pl* **maximums, maxima**) the greatest quantity or degree attainable or attained in any given case, as opposed to *minimum*, the smallest.

may *vb aux* (*pret* **might**, used similarly to *can*, *could*, formerly often used in sense of *can*) implying personal power or ability; now to imply possibility with contingency (*it may be so*, *the king may be killed*); opportunity; moral power; permission granted (*you may now go*); desire, as in prayer, aspiration, imprecation, benediction, etc (*may he perish miserably!*); frequently used to form the compound tenses of the potential mood (*you might have gone had you pleased*).

May *n* the fifth month of the year; (*fig*) the early part of life; hawthorn blossom (so called as the hawthorn blooms then).

maybe *adv* perhaps; possibly; probably.—*n* a possibility; a probability.

mayday *n* the international radio-telephone signal indicating a ship or aircraft in distress.

May Day *n* the first day of May, on which various festivities were, and in some places still are, observed.

mayfly *n* a short-lived insect that appears first in May.

mayhap *adv* (*arch*) peradventure; it may happen; perhaps.

mayhem *n* (*law*) the act of maiming a person; violent destruction; utter confusion.

mayonnaise *n* a dish composed of yolks of eggs and salad oil beaten together, used as a sauce for salads, lobster, salmon, etc.

mayor *n* the chief magistrate of an English or other city or borough; the chief officer of a municipal corporation.

mayoralty *n* the office of a mayor and the time of service.

mayoress *n* the wife of a mayor.

mayorship *n* the office or dignity of a mayor.

maypole *n* a pole wreathed with flowers and set up to be danced round on May Day.

May queen *n* a young woman honoured as queen at games held on May Day.

mazarine *n* a deep blue colour.

maze *n* a confusing network of paths or passages; a winding and turning; an intricacy; a labyrinth; confusion of thought; perplexity.—*vt* (**mazed, mazing**) to confound; to stupefy; to bewilder.

mazy *adj* having the character of a maze; intricate; perplexed.

mazurka, mazourka *n* a lively Polish round dance in 3–8 or 3–4 time; the music written for this dance.

me *pron, pers* the objective or accusative, as also the dative, of I, the pronoun of the first person, it stands as a dative in *methinks*; *woe is me*; *give me a drink*, etc.

mead[1] *n* a fermented liquor made from honey and water flavoured with spices.

mead[2] *n* (*poet*) a meadow.

meadow *n* a low, level tract of land under grass and generally mown annually or oftener for hay; a piece of grassland in general.—*adj* belonging to or growing in a meadow.

meadow grass *n* a name of several British species of grass.

meadowsweet *n* a common British herbaceous plant with corymbs of white and fragrant flowers.

meagre *adj* having little flesh; thin; lean; lacking richness, fertility, strength, etc; small; scanty; (of a mineral) dry and harsh to the touch, as chalk.

meal[1] *n* a portion of food taken at one of the regular times for eating; occasion of taking food; a repast.

meal[2] *n* the edible part of wheat, oats, rye, barley, etc, ground into flour or a powdery state.

mealy-mouthed *adj* unwilling or hesitating to tell the truth in plain language; inclined to speak of anything in softer terms than the truth will warrant.

mausoleum

maze

mean[1] *vt* (*pret, pp* **meant**, *ppr* **meaning**) to have in the mind, view or contemplation; to intend; to purpose; to design; to signify or be intended to signify (*what does the word mean?*); to import; to denote.—*vi* to be minded or disposed; to have such and such intentions (*he means well*).

mean[2] *adj* occupying a middle position; middle; midway between extremes; intermediate; (*math*) having an intermediate value between two extremes (*mean distance, mean motion*).—*n* what is midway or intermediate between two extremes; the middle or average rate or degree; medium; (*math*) a quantity having an intermediate value between several others, the simple average formed by adding the quantities together and dividing by their number being called an *arithmetical mean*, while a *geometrical mean* is the square root of the product of the quantities; (*pl*) the medium or what is used to effect an object; measure or measures adopted; agency; instrumentality (though plural in form generally used as sing, as *by this means, a means to an end*); income, revenue, resources, estate (*his means were large*).

mean[3] *adj* selfish; ungenerous; spiritless; of little value; contemptible; despicable; bad-tempered; (*sl*) difficult; (*sl*) expert.

meander *n* the winding of a river; a winding course; a maze; a labyrinth.—*vt* to wind or flow over.—*vi* to wind or turn; to have an intricate or winding course.

meaning *adj* significant; intended to convey some idea (*a meaning look*).—*n* that which a person means; aim or purpose; intent; what is to be understood, whether by act or language; the sense of words; signification; import; force.

meanly *adv* in a mean manner; in a low condition; poorly; sordidly.

meanness *n* the state or quality of being mean; lack of dignity or rank; lack of spirit or honour; mean or base conduct or action.

meantime *adv* during the interval; in the interval between one specified period and another.—*n* the interval between one specified period and another.

mean time *n* the time according to an ordinary clock, which makes every day of exactly the same length, though if days are measured by the sun they are not so.

meanwhile *adv, n* meantime.

mease *n* the quantity of 500 (*a mease of herrings*).

measles *n* a contagious viral disease of the human body, usually characterized by a crimson rash on the skin.

measurable *adj* that may be measured; not beyond measure; moderate.

measurably *adv* in a measurable manner or degree; moderately.

measure *n* the extent of a thing in length, breadth and thickness, in circumference, capacity or in any other respect; a standard of measurement; a fixed unit of capacity or extent; the instrument by which extent or capacity is ascertained; a measuring rod or line; a certain definite quantity (*a measure of wine*); that which is allotted or dealt out to one; moderation; just degree, in such phrases as *beyond measure, within measure*; indefinite quantity or degree (*in some measure erroneous*); action or proceeding directed to an end; something done with a view to the accomplishment of purpose; (*mus*) that division by which the time of dwelling on each note is regulated; musical time; (*poet*) the metrical arrangement of the syllables in each line with respect to quantity or accent; a grave solemn dance with slow and measured steps, like the minuet; (*geol*) beds; strata (used in the term *coal measures*).—*vt* (**measured, measuring**) to ascertain the extent, dimensions or capacity of; to judge of the greatness of; to appreciate; to value; to pass through or over; to proportion; to allot or distribute by measure (often with *out*).—*vi* to take a measurement or measurements; to result or turn out on being measured; to be in extent.

measured *adj* deliberate and uniform; slow and steady; stately; formal; restricted; within bounds; moderate.

measureless *adj* immeasurable; without measure.

measurement *n* the act of measuring; the amount ascertained by measuring.

meat *n* food in general; anything eaten as nourishment; the flesh of animals used as food; the edible portion of something (*the meat of an egg*); the essence of something.

meatus *n* any passage in the body, e.g. *meatus auditorius* the ear canal.

meaty *n* abounding in meat; resembling meat; full of substance.

mechanic *n* a person skilled in repairing cars, etc.

mechanical *adj* pertaining to or in accordance with the laws of mechanics; resembling a machine; hence, acting without thought or independence of judgment; done as if by a machine, that is, by the mere force of habit (*a mechanical motion of the hand*); acting by or resulting from weight or momentum (*mechanical pressure*); physical; opposed to *chemical* (*a mechanical mixture*, that is, one in which the ingredients do not lose their identity).

mechanical engineering *n* that branch of engineering which refers strictly to machinery.

mechanically *adv* in a mechanical manner; without thought or intelligence; by the mere force of habit.

mechanics *n* the science which treats of

meander

motion and force, often divided into *statics* (embracing the principles which apply to bodies at rest), and *dynamics* (the principles of equilibrium and action of bodies in a state of motion); the technical aspects of something.

mechanism *n* the parts collectively or the arrangement and relation of the parts of a machine, contrivance or instrument; mechanical construction; machinery.

mechanist *n* a maker of machines or one skilled in machinery.

mechanize *vt* (**mechanized, mechanizing**) to subject to contrivance; to form mechanically.

medal *n* a coin or a piece of metal in the form of a coin, stamped with some figure or device, often issued to commemorate a noteworthy event or as a reward of merit.

medallion *n* a large antique medal, usually of gold or silver; anything resembling such a piece of metal, as a circular or oval tablet, bearing on it objects represented in relief.

medallist *n* an engraver, stamper or moulder of medals; a person skilled in medals; one who has gained a medal as the reward of merit.

meddle *vi* (**meddled, meddling**) to interfere; to take part in another person's affairs in an officious, impertinent or offensive manner (often followed by *with* or *in*).

meddlesome *adj* given to meddling; officiously intrusive.

meddling *adj* given to meddle; officious; officiously interposing or interfering in the affairs of others.

mediaeval *adj* same as **medieval**.

medial *adj* mean; pertaining to a mean or average.

median *adj* situated in the middle; passing through or along the middle; a line from an angular point of a triangle to the mid point of the opposite side.

median line *n* (*anat*) a vertical line, supposed to divide the body longitudinally into two equal parts.

mediant *n* (*mus*) an appellation given to the third above the keynote.

mediate *adj* being between two extremes; middle; acting as a means or medium; not direct or immediately; effected by the intervention of a medium.—*vi* (**mediated, mediating**) to interpose between parties as the equal friend of each; to negotiate between persons at variance with a view to reconciliation.—*vt* to effect by mediation or interposition between parties (*to mediate a peace*).

mediation *n* the act of mediating; entreaty for another; intercession; interposition; intervention.

mediative *adj* of or belonging to a mediator.

mediator *n* one who mediates or interposes

mechanism

medal

between parties at variance for the purpose of reconciling them.

medic[1] *n* (*colloq*) a medical student; (*colloq*) a physician, surgeon or medical orderly.

medic[2] *n* same as **medick**.

medical *adj* pertaining to or connected with medicine or the art of healing diseases; medicinal; tending to cure; intended or instituted to teach medical science.—*n* a medical examination.

medical jurisprudence *n* the application of the principles of medical science in aid of the administration of justice; forensic medicine.

medicament *n* anything used for healing diseases or wounds; a healing application.

medicate *vt* (**medicated, medicating**) to treat with healing substances.

medication *n* the act or process of medicating; a drug, medicine or remedy.

medicative *adj* tending to cure or heal.

medicinal *adj* having the property of healing or of lessening the effects of disease; containing healing ingredients (*medicinal springs*); pertaining to medicine.

medicine *n* any substance used as a remedy for or treatment of disease; a drug; physic; the science and art of preventing, curing or alleviating the diseases of the human body; the healing art.

medicine man *n* among the North American Indians, any man supposed to possess mysterious or supernatural powers.

medick, medic *n* one of certain pod-bearing plants yielding fodder and allied to clover; lucerne.

medieval, mediaeval *adj* relating to the Middle Ages or the period between the eighth and the middle of the fifteenth century AD.

mediocre *adj* of moderate degree or quality; of middle rate; average; middling; ordinary; not very good.

mediocrity *n* the quality or state of being mediocre; a middle state or degree; a person of mediocre talents or abilities of any kind.

meditate *vi* (**meditated, meditating**) to dwell on anything in thought; to cogitate; to turn or revolve any subject in the mind; to reflect; to engage in deep contemplation, especially as a religious or spiritual exercise.—*vt* to plan by revolving in the mind; to intend; to think on.

meditation *n* the act of meditating; close or continued thought; the revolving of a subject in the mind; religious or spiritual contemplation.

meditative *adj* addicted to meditation; pertaining to meditation.

Mediterranean *adj* pertaining to, situated on or near the Mediterranean Sea.

medium *n* (*pl* **media, mediums**) something

placed or ranked between other things; a mean between two extremes; a state of moderation; something serving as a means of transmission or communication; necessary means of motion or action; agency of transmission; that by or through which anything is accomplished, conveyed or carried on; agency; instrumentality; a person through whom spiritual manifestations are claimed to be made by believers in spiritualism, or who is said to be capable of holding intercourse with the spirits of the deceased; the liquid vehicle with which dry colours are ground and prepared for painting.—*adj* middle; middling.

medlar *n* a tree found wild in central Europe and cultivated in gardens for its fruit, which resembles a pear.

medley *n* a mingled and confused mass of ingredients; a jumble; a hotchpotch; a musical piece made up of scraps of different tunes or songs.

medulla *n* (*pl* **medullas, medullae**) (*anat*) the fat substance or marrow which fills the cavity of the bones; (*bot*) pith.

medusa *n* (*pl* **medusae, medusans**) the jellyfish or sea nettle, the latter name derived from the property which some of them have of stinging; in zoophytes, a free-swimming sexual stage (jellyfish).

Medusa *n* (*myth*) one of the Gorgons, who had her hair changed into serpents.

meed *n* that which is bestowed in consideration of merit; reward; recompense; a gift.

meek *adj* mild of temper; gentle; submissive; not easily provoked or irritated; marked by meekness.

meekly *adv* in a meek manner; gently; submissively.

meekness *n* the quality of being meek; mildness; gentleness; forbearance under injuries and provocation.

meerschaum *n* a silicate of magnesium occurring as a fine white clay and largely made into tobacco pipes; a tobacco pipe made of meerschaum.

meet *adj* fit; suitable; proper; appropriate.

meet *vt* (*pret, pp* **met**, *ppr* **meeting**) to come face to face with; to come in contact with; to come to be in company with; to come in hostile contact with; to encounter; to join battle with; to find; to light on; to get, gain or receive; to satisfy, gratify, answer (*to meet a demand, one's views* or *wishes*).—*vi* to come together by mutual approach; to come together in hostility; to encounter; to assemble; to come together by being extended; to join.—*n* a meeting as of huntsmen.

meeting *n* a coming together; an interview; an assembly; a congregation; a collection of people; a hostile encounter; a duel.

meeting house *n* a place of worship, especially one used by Quakers.

mega- *prefix* great; large; a million of; (*colloq*) greatest.

megalith *n* a huge stone, such as those in cromlechs, dolmens, the Cyclopean architecture of the Greeks, etc.

megalithic *adj* pertaining to megaliths.

megalomania *n* a form of mental abnormality, the victims of which have grandiose ideas about themselves; lust for power.

megaphone *n* a large speaking-trumpet, used to amplify and direct the voice.

megapode *n* any of a family of Australian birds that build mounds of sand, etc, for the incubation of eggs.

megatherium *n* a fossil genus of very large mammals, allied to the sloths but having feet adapted for walking on the ground.

megilp, magilp *n* a mixture of linseed oil and mastic varnish used by artists as a vehicle for colours.

meiosis *n* (*pl* **meioses**) a rhetorical figure by which a thing is represented as less than it is.

melancholia *n* abnormal melancholy; a mental disorder characterized by depression and misery.

melancholic *adj* disordered by melancholy; pertaining to melancholy; gloomy; mournful.

melancholy *n* dejection; gloominess; sadness.—*adj* gloomy; depressed in spirits; dejected; sombre.

mélange *n* a mixture; a medley.

melanic *adj* of or pertaining to melanism.

melanin *n* a dark brown pigment in the skin, hair and eyes of humans and animals.

melanism *n* an undue development of colouring material in the skin and its appendages; the opposite of *albinism*.

melanoma *n* a malignant skin tumour composed of darkly pigmented cells.

mêlée, melee *n* a fight in which the combatants are mingled in confused mass; an affray.

melic *adj* relating to song; lyric.

melilot *n* a pod-bearing annual or biennial plant allied to the clovers and cultivated for fodder; hart's-clover.

melinite *n* an explosive, the basis or chief ingredient of which is picric acid.

meliorate *vt* (**meliorated, meliorating**) to make better; to improve; to ameliorate.—*vi* to grow better.

melioration *n* improvement; amelioration.

melliferous *adj* producing honey.

mellifluence *n* the quality of being mellifluous; a flow of sweetness or a sweet smooth flow.

mellifluous, mellifluent *adj* flowing as with honey; sweetly flowing.

mellivorous *adj* honey-eating; fond of honey.

mellow *adj* soft with ripeness; soft to the senses; rich or delicate to the eye, ear, pal-

megaphone

ate, etc, as colour, sound, flavour, etc; toned down by the lapse of time; softened or matured by length of years; rendered good-humoured by liquor; half-tipsy.—*vt* to render mellow; to soften by a ripeness or age; to give richness, flavour or delicacy; to tone or smooth down; to soften in character; to mature.—*vi* to become mellow; to soften in character; to become toned down.

mellowness *n* the state or quality of being mellow.

melodeon *n* a wind instrument furnished with metallic free reeds and a keyboard; a type of harmonium; an improved accordion.

melodrama *n* a genre of play, generally of a serious character, in which effect is sought by startling incidents, striking situations and exaggerated sentiment, aided by splendid decoration and music.

melodramatic *adj* pertaining to, suitable for or having the character of a melodrama; sensational.

melodic *adj* of the nature of melody; relating to melody.

melodics *n* that branch of music which investigates the laws of melody.

melon

melodious *adj* containing or characterized by melody; musical; agreeable to the ear by a sweet succession of sounds.

melodize *vt* (**melodized, melodizing**) to make melodious.—*vi* to compose or sing melodies.

melody *n* an agreeable succession of sounds; sweetness of sound; sound highly pleasing to the ear; (*mus*) a succession of tones produced by a single voice or instrument and so arranged as to please the ear or to express some kind of sentiment; the particular air or tune of a musical piece.

melon *n* a climbing or trailing annual plant and its fruit, which is large, fleshy and highly flavoured.

melt *vt* to reduce from a solid to a liquid or flowing state by heat; to liquefy; to dissolve; to fuse; (*fig*) to soften, as by a warming and kindly influence; to render gentle or susceptible to mild influences, as to love, pity or tenderness.—*vi* to become liquid; to dissolve; to pass by imperceptible degrees; to blend; to shade; to become tender, mild or gentle; to be subdued as by fear.

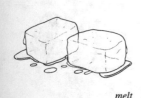

melt

melting *p, adj* fusing; dissolving; affecting; moving (*a melting speech*); feeling or showing tenderness (*melting charity*).

melting point *n* (*physics*) the temperature at which a substance changes from the solid to the liquid state at a standard pressure.

melting pot *n* a crucible.

member *n* a part of an animal body capable of performing a distinct office; an organ; a limb; part of an aggregate or a whole; one

of the persons composing a society, community, etc; a representative in a legislative body.

Member of Parliament *n* a representative elected by a constituency to that branch of the British legislature called the House of Commons (abbreviated **MP**).

membership *n* the state of being a member; the members of a body regarded collectively.

membrane *n* a thin tissue of the animal body which covers organs, lines the interior of cavities, takes part in the formation of the walls of canals, etc; a similar texture in vegetables; a thin pliable sheet or film.

membranous *adj* belonging to a membrane; consisting of membranes; resembling a membrane.

memento *n* (*pl* **mementos, mementoes**) a suggestion, notice or memorial to awaken memory; something that reminds.

memo *n* (*pl* **memos**) short for **memorandum**.

memoir *n* a notice of something remembered or deemed noteworthy; an account of transactions or events written familiarly; a biographical notice; recollections of one's life (in this sense usually in the plural); a biography or autobiography.

memorabilia *npl* things remarkable and worthy of remembrance or record.

memorable *adj* worthy to be remembered; illustrious; remarkable; distinguished.

memorably *adv* in a manner worthy to be remembered.

memorandum *n* (*pl* **memoranda, memorandums**) a note made of something to be remembered; a record or written statement of a business or other transaction.

memorial *adj* preservative of memory; serving as a memorial; contained in the memory.—*n* that which serves to perpetuate the memory of something; a monument; a written representation of facts made to a legislative or other body or to some person; an informal state paper much used in diplomatic negotiations.

memorize *vt* (**memorized, memorizing**) to cause to be remembered; to record; to hand down to memory by writing.

memory *n* the power, capacity or faculty of the mind by which it retains the knowledge of past events or ideas; that faculty which enables us to treasure up and preserve for future use the knowledge which we acquire; remembrance; the state of being remembered; that which is remembered about a person or event; the time within which a person may remember what is past; the part of a computer that stores information.

menace *vt* (**menaced, menacing**) to threaten; to show a disposition to inflict punishment or other evil on (followed by with before the evil threatened (*menaced him with death*); to hold out threats of.—*n* a threat or threatening; the indication of a probable evil or catastrophe to come.

menage *n* a household; housekeeping; household management.

menage à trois *n* a situation in which a couple and the lover of one of them live together.

menagerie *n* a collection of wild animals, especially of wild or foreign animals kept for exhibition.

menarche *n* the onset of menstruation in puberty.

mend *vt* to repair, as something broken, rent, decayed, etc; to restore to a sound state; to patch up; to alter for the better; to improve (*to mend one's manners*); to better; to improve on (to mend one's pace).—*vi* to advance to a better state; to improve; to act or behave better; to recover from ill-health or injury.

mendacious *adj* lying; false; given to telling untruths.

mendacity *n* the quality of being mendacious; lying; falsehood; a lie.

mendelevium *n* an artificially produced radioactive metallic element.

Mendelian *adj* of or pertaining to Mendelism.

Mendelism *n* a system of numerical laws of inheritance devised by the Austrian monk and geneticist Gregor Mendel with later modifications, determined by crossing related plants or animals differing in some easily recognized character and by observing the distribution of the character among the offspring of several generations.

mendicancy *n* beggary; a state of begging.

mendicant *adj* practising beggary; poor to a state of beggary; begging as part of religious discipline (*a mendicant friar*).—*n* a beggar; a member of a begging order or fraternity; a begging friar.

mendicity *n* the state or practice of begging; the life of a beggar.

menhaden *n* a saltwater fish of the herring family.

menhir *n* a tall monolithic stone, sometimes crudely sculptured, standing singly or in groups and dating from the Bronze Age in the UK or the Neolithic Age in Europe.

menial *adj* pertaining to household or domestic servants; consisting of work of little skill.—*n* a domestic servant.

meningitis *n* inflammation of the membranes of the brain or spinal cord.

meninx *n* (*pl* **meninges**) any of the three membranes covering and protecting the brain and the spinal cord.

menopause *n* the cessation of menstruation in a woman; the time of life during which a woman's menstrual cycle ceases permanently.

menorrhagia *n* an excessive flow of menstrual blood.

menses *npl* the monthly discharge of blood from a woman's uterus; the days during which this occurs.

menstrual *adj* pertaining to menstruation.

menstrual cycle *n* menstruation.

menstruate *vi* (**menstruated, menstruating**) to undergo menstruation; to have the menses; to have a period.

menstruation *n* the monthly discharge of blood from a woman's uterus; the act of menstruating; the period of menstruating.

menstruum *n* (*pl* **menstruums, menstrua**) a fluid which dissolves a solid; a solvent.

mensurable *adj* capable of being measured; measurable.

mensuration *n* the act or art of measuring or taking the dimensions of anything; the process of finding any dimension of a figure or its area or solid content, by means of the most simple measurements possible.

mental *adj* pertaining to the mind or intellect; wholly depending on the mind; intellectual; relating to a psychiatric disorder.

mental hospital *n* a hospital for the mentally ill.

mentality *n* the state of being mental; mental cast or habit.

mentally *adv* by or in the mind or intellect; intellectually; in thought.

mental reservation *n* an intentional reserving or holding back of some word or clause, the speaker thus intending to set his or her conscience at rest while being guilty of deceit or to keep his or her real sentiments secret.

menthol *n* a white crystalline substance obtained from oil of peppermint, used externally in cases of nervous headache.

mention *n* a brief notice or remark in regard to something; a cursory speaking of anything (often in the phrase *to make mention of*, to name or say something in regard to). —*vt* to make mention of.

mentor *n* a wise and trusted adviser.

menu *n* a list of the dishes, etc, to be served at a dinner, supper, etc; a bill of fare.

Mephistophelean *adj* resembling the character of Mephistopheles, the diabolic spirit of Goethe's *Faust* and the Faust legend generally; diabolical; sardonic.

mephitic, mephitical *adj* pertaining to mephitis; offensive to the sense of smell; noxious; pestilential.

mephitis *n* noxious gases from decomposing substances, filth or other source.

mercantile *adj* pertaining to merchants or their traffic; pertaining to trade or commerce; commercial.

Mercator's projection *n* a projection or map of the earth's surface with the meridians and parallels of latitude all straight lines.

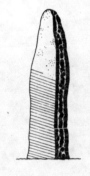

menhir

mercenary *adj* hired; obtained by hire (services, troops); that may be hired; moved by the love of money; greedy of gain; venal; entered into from motives of gain (*a mercenary marriage*).—*n* one who is hired; a soldier who is hired into foreign service.

mercer *n* one who has a shop for silks, woollens, linens, cottons, etc.

mercerize *vt* (**mercerized, mercerizing**) to subject to treatment with certain chemical agents, as caustic soda, sulphuric acid, zinc chloride, etc, in order to produce desired results on textile fabrics, especially cotton goods.

merchant *n* one who carries on trade on a large scale; especially, a person who exports and imports goods and sells them by wholesale; a trader or retailer.—*adj* relating to trade or commerce; commercial.

merchantman *n* (*pl* **merchantmen**) a merchant ship engaged in commerce; a trading vessel.

merchant seaman *n* a seaman employed in a merchant ship.

merchandise *n* the objects of commerce; wares; goods; commodities.

merciful *adj* full of mercy; unwilling to punish for injuries; compassionate; tender; not cruel.

merciless *adj* lacking mercy; pitiless; hardhearted.

mercurial *adj* like the god Mercury or what belongs to him; light-hearted; sprightly; flighty; fickle; pertaining to quicksilver; containing or consisting of quicksilver or mercury.

mercury *n* a heavy silvery liquid metallic element used in thermometers, etc; quicksilver.

Mercury *n* in Roman myth, the god of thieves, traders etc, and messenger of the gods; (*astron*) the planet that revolves round the sun within the orbit of the planet Venus and next to it.

mercy *n* that benevolence, mildness or tenderness of heart which disposes a person to overlook injuries; the disposition that tempers justice and leads to the infliction of a lighter punishment than law or justice will warrant; clemency; an act or exercise of mercy or favour; a blessing; compassion; pity; unrestrained exercise of will or authority (often in the phrase *at one's mercy*, that is, completely in one's power).

mere[1] *adj* this or that and nothing else; simple; absolute, entire, utter (*mere folly*).

mere[2] *n* a pool or small lake.

merely *adv* solely; simply; only; for this and no other purpose.

meretricious *adj* pertaining to prostitutes; alluring by false show; having a gaudy but deceitful appearance; showy but in bad taste; tawdry.

mermaid

merganser *n* an Arctic waterfowl, a not uncommon visitor to Britain; a goosander.

merge *vt* (**merged, merging**) to cause to be swallowed up, absorbed or incorporated; to sink; to cause to combine or unite; to bury (chiefly figurative, as *the smaller grief was merged in the greater*).—*vi* to be sunk, swallowed, incorporated or absorbed; to combine or unite.

merger *n* (*law*) absorption of one estate, contract, action, etc, in another; a combining together, especially of two or more commercial organizations.

meridian *adj* pertaining to midday or noon, when the sun is on the meridian.—*n* midday; noon; (*fig*) the culmination; the point of greatest splendour; one of the innumerable imaginary circles or lines on the surface of the earth passing through both poles and through any other given place and used in denoting the longitudes of places; a similar imaginary line in the heavens passing through the poles of the heavens and the zenith of any place (often called a *celestial meridian*), noon therefore occurring at all places directly under this line when the sun is on it.

meridional *adj* pertaining to the meridian; southern; having a southern aspect.—*n* an inhabitant of a meridional region.

merino *adj* belonging to a variety of sheep from Spain with long and fine wool; made of the wool of the merino sheep.—*n* a merino sheep; a fabric, twilled on both sides, manufactured from merino wool.

meristem *n* (*bot*) embryonic tissue.

merit *n* desert of good or evil; excellence entitling to honour or reward; worth; reward deserved or merited; (*pl*) the rights of a case or question; the essential points or circumstances.—*vt* to deserve, in a good sense; to have a right to claim, as a reward, regard, honour; to deserve, in a bad sense; to incur.

meritorious *adj* possessing merit; deserving reward or praise; praiseworthy.

merle *n* the blackbird.

merlin *n* a species of hawk about the size of a blackbird.

mermaid *n* a fabled marine creature, having the upper part of a woman and the lower of a fish.

merman *n* (*pl* **mermen**) the male corresponding to *mermaid*; a man of the sea, with the tail of a fish instead of legs.

meroblast *n* (*biol*) an ovum consisting both of a protoplasmic or germinal portion and an albuminous or nutritive one, as distinct from holoblast, an ovum entirely germinal.

merriment *n* gaiety with laughter or noise; mirth; hilarity.

merriness *n* the state or quality of being merry.

536

merry *adj* pleasant; causing cheerfulness; happy and noisy; in overflowing good spirits; hilarious; mirthful; sportive.—**to make merry** to be jovial; to indulge in hilarity; to feast with mirth.

merry-andrew *n* a buffoon.

merry-go-round *n* a circular frame, made to revolve and on which children are treated to a ride.

merrymaking *n* a convivial entertainment; a festival.

merrythought *n* the wishbone.

mescal *n* a round, spineless Central American cactus with tubercles that, when dried, are chewed as a drug.

mescaline *n* a hallucinogenic drug derived from mescal.

mesh *n* the opening or space between the threads of a net; engagement (of geared wheels).—*vt* to catch in a net; to ensnare.—*vi* to become entangled or interlocked.

mesial *adj* middle; median.

mesmeric *adj* pertaining to mesmerism.

mesmerism *n* hypnotism.

mesmerize *vt* (**mesmerized, mesmerizing**) to hypnotize; to bring into a hypnotic state.

mesne *adj* (*law*) middle, intervening, as, a *mesne lord*, i.e. one who holds land of a superior but grants a part of it to another person.

mesoblast *n* (*physiol*) the middle germinal layer of an ovum, the basis of muscles, bones, blood, etc.

mesocarp *n* (*bot*) the middle part or layer of the seed vessel of a fruit.

mesogastric *adj* (*anat*) applied to the membrane which sustains the stomach and by which it is attached to the abdomen.

Mesolithic *adj* of or pertaining to the period between the Palaeolithic and Neolithic ages, marked by the appearance of flint cutting tools and the development of fishing.—*n* the Mesolithic period.

meson *n* an unstable elementary particle having a mass between that of a proton and an electron.

Mesozoic *adj* (*geol*) pertaining to the secondary age, between the Palaeozoic and Cainozoic, marked by the predominance of reptilian life.—*n* the Mesozoic age.

mesquite *n* a pod-bearing tree or shrub of America, with edible pods.

mess[1] *n* a disorderly mixture; a state of dirt and disorder; (*fig*) a situation of confusion or embarrassment; a muddle.—*vt* to make a mess of; to bungle.

mess[2] *n* a dish or quantity of food set on a table at one time; food for a person at one meal; a number of persons who eat together at the same table, especially in the army or navy.—*vi* to take meals in common with others, as one of a mess; to associate at the same table.

message *n* any communication, written or verbal, sent from one person to another; an official communication delivered by a messenger; the chief idea that a writer, artist, etc, seeks to communicate in his or her work.

messenger *n* one who bears a message; one who conveys despatches from one prince or court to another; one who or that which foreshows; a harbinger.

Messiah *n* Christ, the Anointed; the Saviour of the world.

messianic *adj* relating to the Messiah.

messieurs *n* sirs; gentlemen; the plural of Mr, employed in addressing firms or companies of several persons and generally contracted into *Messrs*.

messuage *n* (*law*) a dwelling house with the adjacent buildings, etc, appropriated to the use of the household; a manor house.

metabolic *adj* pertaining to metabolism.

metabolism *n* the total processes in living organisms by which tissue is formed, energy produced and waste products eliminated.

metabolize *vt* (**metabolized, metabolizing**) to subject to metabolism; to process by metabolism; to assimilate.

metacarpal *adj* pertaining to the metacarpus.

metacarpus *n* (*pl* **metacarpi**) (*anat*) the part of the hand between the wrist and the fingers.

metacentre *n* (*physics*) that point in a floating body on the position of which its stability depends and which must be above the centre of gravity in order that the body does not turn over.

metagenesis *n* (*zool*) the changes of form which the representative of a species undergoes in passing, by a series of successively generated individuals, from the ovum or egg to the perfect state; alternation of generations.

metal *n* a name given to certain elementary substances of which gold, silver, iron, lead are examples, having a peculiar lustre and generally fusible by heat; any alloy of such elements as brass, bronze, etc; anything consisting of metal.—*vt* (**metalled, metalling**) to put metal on; to cover, as roads, with broken stones or metal.

metallic *adj* pertaining to metals; consisting of metal; like a metal.

metallist *adj* a worker in metals or one skilled in metals.

metallize *vt* (**metallized, metallizing**) to form into metal; to coat or treat with metal.

metallography *n* a branch of metallurgy dealing with the microscopic structure and physical properties of metals and alloys.

metalloid *n* a metallic base of a fixed alkali or alkaline earth; any non-metallic el-

mesh

ementary substance.—*adj* like metal; having the form or appearance of a metal.

metallurgic, metallurgical *adj* pertaining to metallurgy.

metallurgist *n* one engaged in metallurgy.

metallurgy *n* the art of working metals; the process of separating them from other matters in the ore, smelting, refining, etc.

metamerism *n* (*chem*) the character in certain compound bodies, differing in chemical properties, of having the same elements combined in the same proportion and with the same molecular weight.

metamorphic *adj* pertaining to or producing metamorphosis.

metamorphism *n* the process of metamorphosing; the change undergone by stratified rocks under the influence of heat and chemical or mechanical agents.

metamorphose *vt* (**metamorphosed, metamorphosing**) to change into a different form; to change the shape or character of; to transform; to change completely.

metamorphosis *n* (*pl* **metamorphoses**) change of form, shape or structure; transformation; complete change; (*zool*) the alterations which an animal undergoes after its exclusion from the egg and which alter extensively the general form and life of the individual; such changes as those from the caterpillar to the perfect butterfly.

metaphor *n* a figure of speech founded on resemblance, by which a word is transferred from an object to which it properly belongs to another in such a manner that a comparison is implied, though not formally expressed, thus, 'that man is a fox', is a metaphor; but 'that man is like a fox', is a simile or comparison.

metaphoric, metaphorical *adj* pertaining to metaphor; comprising a metaphor; not literal; figurative.

metaphorically *adv* in a metaphorical manner; not literally.

metaphrase *n* a verbal translation of one language into another, word for word, opposed to *paraphrase*.

metaphrast *n* a literal translator.

metaphrastic *adj* close or literal in translation.

metaphysic *n* metaphysics.

metaphysical, metaphysic *adj* pertaining to metaphysics; according to rules or principles of metaphysics.

metaphysician *n* one who is versed in metaphysics.

metaphysics *n* the branch of philosophy which seeks to trace the branches of human knowledge to their first principles or to find what is the nature of the human mind and its relations to the external world; a general philosophy that seeks to know the ultimate grounds of being or what it is that really exists.

metastasis *n* (*pl* **metastases**) a change or shift in the location of a disease, often used of the spreading of cancer cells; a transformation; a change.

metatarsal *adj* belonging to the metatarsus. —*n* a bone of the metatarsus.

metatarsus *n* (*pl* **metatarsi**) the middle of the foot or part between the ankle and the toes.

metathesis *n* (*pl* **metatheses**) (*gram*) transposition of the letters, sounds or syllables of a word.

mete *vt* (**meted, meting**) to measure; to ascertain the quantity, dimensions or capacity of by any rule or standard.

metempsychosis *n* (**metempsychoses**) transmigration of the soul of a person after death into some other animal body.

meteor *n* a transient luminous body seen in the atmosphere; an aerolite, a shooting star; (*fig*) something that transiently dazzles or strikes with wonder.

meteoric *adj* pertaining to a meteor or meteors; (*fig*) transiently or irregularly brilliant.

meteoric shower *n* shower of shooting stars occurring periodically.

meteorite *n* a meteor which falls on the surface of the earth without being vaporized and usually consisting of metallic iron and silicates.

meteorological, meteorologic *adj* pertaining to meteorology or to the atmosphere and its phenomena.

meteorologist *n* a person skilled in meteorology.

meteorology *n* the science which deals with atmospheric phenomena, especially as connected with or in relation to weather and climate.

meter *n* one who or that which measures; an instrument that measures and records automatically, as a gas meter, water meter, etc.

methane *n* a colourless, odourless, flammable gas formed by the decomposition of vegetable matter.

methinks *vb impers* (*pret* **methought**) (*arch*) it seems to me; I think.

method *n* a way or mode by which we proceed to the attainment of some aim; mode or manner of procedure; logical or scientific arrangement or mode of acting; systematic or orderly procedure; system; (*nat hist*) principle of classification (*the Linnaean method*).

methodical, methodic *adj* characterized by method; systematic; orderly.

Methodism *n* the doctrines and worship of the Methodists.

Methodist *n* one of a sect of Christians, founded by John Wesley, so called from the regularity of their lives and their strict observance of religious duties.

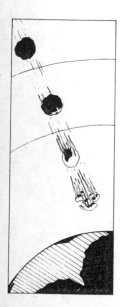

meteor

methodize *vt* (**methodized, methodizing**) to reduce to method; to dispose in due order.

methodology *n* the methods and procedures used by a science or discipline; the philosophical analysis of method and procedure.

methyl *n* a compound obtained from methane, composed of organic material and metals.

methylamine *n* a colourless gas with a strong odour of ammonia and resembling it in many of its reactions.

methylated *adj* impregnated or mixed with methyl.

methylated spirit *n* a form of alcohol containing 10 per cent wood naphtha, which renders it unfit for drinking, used as a solvent.

meticulous *adj* very precise, especially about small details; timidly scrupulous; too careful or fastidious.

métier *n* profession; speciality; role.

Metonic cycle *n* the cycle or period of nineteen years, in which the phases of the moon return to the same days of the month.

metonymy *n* (*rhet*) a figure by which one word is put for another on account of some actual relation between the things signified, as when we say, 'We read Virgil', that is, his poems or writings.

metre[1] *n* a metric measure of length, equal to 39.37 English inches.

metre[2] *n* rhythmical arrangement of syllables into verses, stanzas, strophes, etc; rhythm; measure; verse.

metric[1] *adj* pertaining to a system of weights, measures and moneys, first adopted in France; the decimal system.

metric[2], **metrical** *adj* pertaining to rhythm or metre; consisting of verse.

metrical *adj* pertaining to or employed in measuring.

metrist *n* a composer of verses.

metrology *n* an account of weights and measures; the art and science of mensuration.

metronome *n* an instrument, consisting of a pendulum set in motion by clockwork, that determines the quickness or slowness of musical compositions.

metropolis *n* the chief city or capital of a kingdom, state or country; the see or seat of a metropolitan bishop.

metropolitan *adj* belonging to a metropolis; (*eccles*) having the authority of a metropolitan; proceeding from a metropolitan.—*n* (*eccles*) a bishop having authority over the other bishops of a province; an archbishop; (*Greek Church*) a dignitary intermediate between patriarchs and archbishops.

mettle *n* moral or physical constitution;

stuff or material (*to try what mettle he is made of*); temper; spirit; constitutional ardour; courage; fire.—*to put a person on* or *to his or her mettle* to stimulate a person to do his or her uttermost; to put a person where he or she must do his or her utmost.

mettled *adj* full of mettle; high-spirited; ardent; full of fire.

mettlesome *adj* full of mettle or spirit; brisk; fiery.

mew[1] *n* the moulting of a hawk; a cage for hawks or other birds while moulting; a coop for fowls; a place of confinement in general.—*vt* to shed or cast; to moult; to shut up, enclose, confine, as in a cage or other enclosure.—*vi* to cast the feathers; to moult.

mew[2] *vi* to cry as a cat.—*n* the cry of a cat.

mew[3] *n* a sea mew; a gull.

mews *npl* a place where carriage horses were kept in large towns; a lane or alley in which stables or mews were situated, later often converted into living accommodation.

mezereon *n* a common garden shrub.

mezzo *adj* (*mus*) middle; mean.—*n* (*pl* **mezzos**) a mezzo soprano.

mezzo-soprano *n* (*pl* **mezzo-sopranos**) a treble voice of medium range, lower than soprano and higher than contralto; a singer with such a voice.

mezzotint *n* a manner of engraving on copper or steel in imitation of drawing in Indian ink, the lights being scraped and burnished out of a prepared dark ground.

mi *n* the third note in the musical scale, between re and fa.

miasma *n* (*pl* **miasmas, miasmata**) the unpleasant smell of particles of decaying matter rising and floating in the atmosphere; an unwholesome, foreboding atmosphere.

mica *n* a mineral of a foliated structure, consisting of thin flexible laminae or scales, having a shining and almost metallic lustre.

micaceous *adj* pertaining to or containing mica; resembling mica or partaking of its properties.

mica schist, mica slate *n* a metamorphic rock composed of mica and quartz, highly fissile and passing by insensible gradations into clay slate.

Michaelmas *n* the feast of St Michael, the archangel, which falls on 29th September and is one of the regular terms in England.

microbe *n* a microscopic organism such as a bacillus or bacterium.

microchip *n* a small wafer of silicon, etc, containing electronic circuits.

micrococcus *n* (*pl* **micrococci**) (*zool*) a microscopic organism of a round form.

microcosm *n* a little world or cosmos, applied to man, as supposed to be an epitome

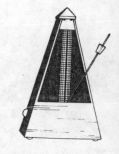

metronome

of the universe or great world (the *macrocosm*); a miniature universe or world.

microfiche *n* a sheet of microfilm containing pages of printed matter.

microfilm *n* a film on which documents, etc, are recorded on reduced scale.

micrometer *n* an instrument or appliance fitted to a telescope or microscope, for measuring very small distances or the apparent diameters of objects which subtend very small angles.

micrometre, micron *n* a unit of length of one thousandth of a millimetre.

micrometric, micrometrical *adj* belonging to the micrometer.

micrometry *n* the art of measuring with a micrometer.

micron *n* same as **micrometre**.

microorganism *n* a microscopic organism, as a bacterium or bacillus.

microphone *n* an instrument for transforming sound waves into electric signals, especially for transmission or recording.

microphone

microphotography *n* a photographic representation of microscopic size; the photography of microscopic objects.

microscope *n* an optical instrument consisting of a lens or combination of lenses for rendering minute objects distinctly visible.

microscopic, microscopical *adj* pertaining to the microscope; made by the aid of a microscope (*microscopic observations*); resembling a microscope; capable of seeing small objects; visible only by the aid of a microscope; very small.

microscopy *n* the use of the microscope; investigation with the microscope.

microtome *n* an instrument for making very fine sections or slices of objects for the microscope.

microwave *n* an electromagnetic wave between 1 and 100 centimetres in length; a microwave oven.—*vt* (**microwaved, microwaving**) to cook (food) in a microwave oven.

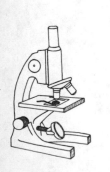

microscope

microwave oven *n* an oven in which food is cooked or heated up by microwaves.

micturate *vi* (**micturated, micturating**) to pass urine.

micturition *n* the frequent desire to pass urine; the act of urinating.

mid *adj* (*no compar*; *superl* **midmost**) middle; at equal distance from extremes; intervening.

midair *n* the middle of the air; a lofty position in the air.

midday *n* the middle of the day; noon.—*adj* pertaining to noon; meridional.

midden *n* a dunghill.

middle *adj* (no *compar*; *superl* **middlemost**) equally distant from the extremes; forming a mean; intermediate; intervening.—*n* the point or part equally distant from the extremities; an intervening

point or part in space, time or order; something intermediate; a mean.

middle-aged *adj* being about the middle of the ordinary age of a person.

Middle Ages *n* the period extending from the decline of the Roman Empire till the revival of letters in Europe or from the eighth to the middle of the fifteenth century of the Christian era.

middle-class *n* the class of people holding a social position between the working classes and the aristocracy.—*adj* of or relating to the middle classes.

middle ear *n* the central cavity of the ear behind the ear drum.

Middle East *n* the area extending from the eastern Mediterranean to the Gulf of Arabia; formerly, southern Asia from the Tigris and Euphrates rivers to Burma.

middleman *n* (*pl* **middlemen**) an agent or intermediary between two parties; one who hires land in large tracts and lets it again in smaller portions.

middlemost *adj* being in the middle or nearest the middle, of a number of things that are near the middle.

middle-of-the road *adj* avoiding extremes.

middling *adj* of middle state, size or quality; moderate; mediocre.

midge *n* the common name of numerous minute species of gnats or flies.

midget *n* a very small creature; something very small of its kind.

midland *adj* being in the interior country; distant from the coast or seashore; inland.—*n* the interior of a country.

midmost *adj* in the very middle; middlemost.

midnight *n* the middle of the night; twelve o'clock at night.—*adj* being or occurring in the middle of the night; dark as midnight; very dark.

midrib *n* (*bot*) a continuation of the petiole extending from the base to the apex of the lamina of a leaf.

midriff *n* the diaphragm; the muscular wall dividing the cavity of the thorax from that of the abdomen.

midship *adj* being or belonging to the middle of a ship.

midshipman *n* (*pl* **midshipmen**) in the navy, a rank intermediate between naval cadet and sublieutenant.

midst *n* the middle.

midstream *n* the middle of the stream.

midsummer *n* the middle of summer; the summer solstice, about 21st June.

midway *n* a middle way or the middle of the way.—*adj* being in the middle of the way or distance.—*adv* in the middle of the way or distance; halfway.

midwife *n* (*pl* **midwives**) a woman that assists other women in childbirth; a female practitioner of the obstetric art.

midwifery *n* the art or practice of a midwife; obstetrics.

midwinter *n* the middle of winter or the winter solstice, 21st December.

mien *n* external air or manner of a person; look; bearing; appearance; carriage.

miff *vt* (*colloq*) to offend.

might *n* strength; force; power; often bodily strength or physical power; but also mental power; power of will; political power.—**with might and main** with the utmost strength or bodily exertion.

mighty *adj* having great power or dominion; strong; powerful (often an epithet of honour (*most mighty prince*); very great; vast; eminent in intellect or acquirements; displaying great power; performed with great power (*mighty works*).

mignonette *n* an annual plant with spikes of small, sweet-smelling green-white flowers.

migraine *n* a neuralgic pain in the side of the head.

migrate *vi* (**migrated, migrating**) to remove from one place of residence to another at a distance, especially from one country to another.

migration *n* the act of migrating; (*zool*) transit of a species of animals from one locality or latitude to another.

migratory *adj* given to migration; migrating at certain seasons (as birds); roving or wandering in one's mode of life; unsettled.

mikado *n* (*pl* **mikados**) formerly, the emperor of Japan.

milch *adj* giving milk (applied only to beasts, as *a milch cow*).

mild *adj* tender and gentle in temper or disposition; not severe or cruel; not fierce, rough or angry; placid; not stern; not frowning; gently and pleasantly affecting the senses; not violent; soft; bland; gentle (*a mild temperature*); not acrid, pungent, corrosive or drastic; moderately sweet or pleasant to the taste (*mild fruit*).

mildew *n* decay produced in living and dead vegetable matter and in some manufactured products of vegetable matter, by very minute parasitic fungi; a sort of blight; the minute fungi causing this condition.—*vt* to affect with mildew.—*vi* to become affected with mildew.

mildness *n* the state or quality of being mild; gentleness; softness; clemency; blandness.

mile *n* a measure of length or distance, equal to about 1.61 kilometres.

mileage *n* total miles travelled; an allowance per mile for travelling expenses; the average number of miles that can be travelled, as per litre, gallon, etc, of petrol.

milestone *n* a stone or post set up on the side of a road or highway to mark the miles; an important event.

milfoil *n* a common plant in Britain with finely divided leaves and small, white or sometimes rose-coloured flowers; yarrow.

miliaria *n* a skin disease resulting from blocked sweat glands and characterized by an acute itchiness; heat rash; prickly heat.

miliary *adj* resembling tiny seeds; accompanied by an eruption resembling tiny seeds (*a miliary fever*).

militancy *n* warfare; militarism; the act of being militant.

militant *adj* fighting; serving as a soldier; ready to fight or be active, especially on behalf of a cause.

militarism *n* the system that leads a nation to pay excessive attention to military affairs; the keeping up of great armies.

militarist *n* one who favours a warlike policy.

military *adj* pertaining to soldiers or the profession of a soldier; becoming the profession of a soldier; pertaining to war; warlike; martial.—*n* a collective name of soldiers generally; soldiery; the army.

Military Cross *n* an army decoration awarded to captains, lieutenants and warrant officers.

military law *n* the body of regulations which governs soldiers both in peace and in war.

militate *vi* (**militated, militating**) to stand opposed; to have weight or influence on the opposite side (said of arguments, considerations, etc, and followed by *against*, as *another fact militated against that theory*).

militia *n* a body of people enrolled and trained as military for the defence of a country but not permanently organized in time of peace or, in general, liable to serve out of the country in time of war.

militiaman *n* (*pl* **militiamen**) one who belongs to the militia.

milk *n* a whitish fluid secreted by the mammary glands of females of the mammals, including the human species and drawn from the breasts for the nourishment of their young; the white juice of certain plants; an emulsion of which juice expressed from seeds is one of the constituents (*the milk of almonds*).—*vt* to draw milk from the breasts or udder of by the hand (*to milk a cow*); to extract (money, etc) from; to exploit.

milk-and-water *adj* tasteless; insipid; characterless; wishy-washy.

milk fever *n* a fever which sometimes accompanies the first secretion of milk in females after childbirth.

milkmaid *n* a woman that milks or is employed in the dairy.

milkman *n* (*pl* **milkmen**) a person that sells milk or carries milk to market.

milksop *n* a piece of bread sopped in milk; a

Military Cross

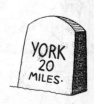

milestone

soft, effeminate, feeble-minded man; one devoid of manliness.

milky *adj* pertaining to, resembling or containing milk; yielding milk; soft; timorous.

Milky Way *n* the Galaxy.

mill *n* a machine for grinding and reducing to fine particles grain, fruit or other substances; applied also to many machines for grinding or polishing by circular motion or to complicated machinery for working up raw material, etc; the building where grinding or some process of manufacturing is carried on.—*vt* to grind in a mill; to pass through a mill; to stamp in a coining press; especially, to stamp so as to make a transversely grooved edge round; to throw, as silk; to full, as cloth.

millboard *adj* a stout kind of pasteboard.

milldam *n* a dam crossing a watercourse and raising the water to a height sufficient to turn a millwheel.

milled *adj* having the edge transversely grooved, as a coin.

millenary *n* the space of a thousand years; a thousandth anniversary.

millennial *adj* pertaining to the millennium or to a thousand years.

millwheel

millennium *n* (*pl* **millenniums, millennia**) an aggregate of a thousand years; the thousand years mentioned in Revelations 20, 1–5, during which some believe Christ will reign on earth with his saints.

millepede *n* same as **millipede**.

millepore *n* one of the reef-building corals, so named from their numerous minute cells or pores.

miller *n* one who keeps or attends a mill, especially a flour mill.

miller's thumb *n* a small fish found in streams; the bullhead.

millet *n* a common name for various species of small grain cultivated largely in many parts of Europe, Asia and Africa as food for humans; a British woodland grass.

milliard *n* a thousand millions.

millibar *n* (*meteor*) a unit of pressure of 1000 dynes per square centimetre.

milligram, milligramme *n* the thousandth part of a gram.

millilitre *n* a measure of capacity containing the thousandth part of a litre; equal to .06103 cubic inch.

minaret

millimetre *n* a lineal measure containing the thousandth part of a metre; equal to .03937 of an inch.

milliner *n* a person who makes and sells headdresses, hats or bonnets, etc, for females.

millinery *n* the business or occupation of a milliner; the articles made or sold by milliners.

milling *n* the process of passing through a mill; the grooves on the edge of a coin.

million *n* the number of ten hundred thou-

sand or a thousand thousand; a very large amount; (with the definite article) the great body of the people; the multitude; the public; the masses.

millionaire *n* a person worth a million of money; a person of great wealth.

millionth *adj* ten hundred thousandth; constituting one of a million.—*n* one of a million parts; a ten hundred thousandth part.

millipede, millepede *n* a worm-like articulated animal with many legs and a segmented body; a myriapod.

millrace, millrun *n* the stream of water that drives a millwheel or the channel in which it runs.

millstone *n* one of the stones for grinding the grain in a mill; stone or rock from which such stones are made; a very heavy burden.

millwheel *n* a wheel used to drive a mill; a waterwheel.

milt *n* the spleen of an animal; the soft roe of fishes or the spermatic organ of the males.

milter *n* a male fish or one having a milt.

mime *n* a kind of ancient entertainment in which gestures and mimicry predominate and no words are said; an actor in such performances.—*vi* (**mimed, miming**) to act or express by using gestures alone; to mouth the words of a song without singing.

mimetic *adj* apt to imitate; given to aping or mimicry; (*nat hist*) characterized by mimicry.

mimic *n* one who imitates or mimics; one who attempts to excite laughter or derision by acting or speaking in the manner of another.—*vt* (**mimicked, mimicking**) to imitate or ape, especially for sport; to ridicule by imitation; to act or speak like intentionally.—*adj* imitative; inclined to imitate or ape; imitating; consisting of or made in imitation (*mimic gestures*).

mimicry *n* imitation, often ludicrous imitation for sport or ridicule; (*nat hist*) the close resemblance presented by certain plants and animals to certain other plants or animals, or to the natural objects among which they live, this resemblance serving for protection.

mimosa *n* a genus of pod-bearing plants, usually with clustered yellow flowers, whose leaves fold when touched.

mimulus *n* one of a genus of plants with showy flowers.

mina *n* an Indian bird of the starling family that can be taught to speak.

minaret *n* a slender lofty turret rising by different stages or storeys, surrounded by one or more projecting balconies, common in mosques in Muslim countries and used for summoning people to prayers.

minatory *adj* threatening; menacing.

mince *vt* (**minced, mincing**) to cut or chop into very small pieces (*to mince meat*); to diminish in speaking; to extenuate; to palliate (*to mince the matter, to mince matters*); to pronounce with affected elegance; not to utter the full sound of.—*vi* to walk with short steps; to affect delicacy in manner; to speak with affected elegance.—*n* finely chopped meat, usually beef.

mincemeat *n* a mixture of chopped dried fruit, apples, etc, used as a pie filling, etc.

mince pie *n* a pie made with minced meat and other ingredients, baked in paste.

mincer *n* one who or that which minces, especially a utensil for mincing meat.

mincing *adj* speaking or walking affectedly; affectedly elegant.

mind *n* the intellectual power in humans; the understanding (*not in one's right mind*); cast of thought and feeling; opinion (*of the same mind*); intention; purpose; memory; remembrance (*to call to mind, to keep in mind*).—**to be in two minds about a thing** to be in doubt.—*vt* to attend to; to fix the thoughts on; to heed; to notice; to pay attention to; to attend with submission; to obey.

mindful *adj* attentive; bearing in mind; heedful.

mindless *adj* lacking mind; stupid; unthinking; inattentive; heedless; careless (with of.

mine[1] pronominal *adj* **my**; belonging to me.

mine[2] *n* a pit or excavation in the earth, from which coal, metallic ores or other mineral substances are taken by digging; a device floating on or near the surface of the sea to destroy ships by explosion; (*milit*) an underground gallery or passage dug under a fortification, in which a quantity of powder or other explosive may be lodged for blowing up the works; (*fig*) a rich source or store of wealth or anything highly valued.—*vi* (**mined, mining**) to dig a mine; to burrow.—*vt* to dig away the foundation from; to undermine; to sap.

minefield *n* an area sown with explosive mines; a situation containing hidden problems.

minelayer *n* a ship or aircraft involved in minelaying.

minelaying *n* the laying or dropping into the sea of mines intended to act against an enemy's vessels, such mines having a weight attached by way of anchor.

miner *n* one who mines; one who digs or works in a mine.

mineral *n* any ingredient in the earth's crust; an inorganic body with a definite chemical composition and which naturally exists within the earth or at its surface.—*adj* pertaining to minerals; consisting of minerals; impregnated with minerals or mineral matter (*mineral waters*).

mineralogist *n* one versed in the science of minerals.

mineralogy *n* the science which treats of the properties of mineral substances and teaches us to characterize, distinguish and classify them according to their properties.

mineral water *n* a water containing mineral salts or gases.

Minerva *n* one of the chief divinities of the Romans, a daughter of Jupiter; in later times identified with the Greek goddess Athene, the goddess of wisdom, of war and of the liberal arts.

minesweeper *n* a ship for clearing away explosive mines.

mingle *vt* (**mingled, mingling**) to mix up together so as to form one whole; to blend; to join in mutual intercourse or in society; to debase by mixture.—*vi* to become mixed; to become united in the same whole; to join (*to mingle with* or *in a crowd*).

miniature *n* a painting of very small dimensions, usually executed in watercolours, on ivory, vellum, etc; anything represented on a greatly reduced scale; a small scale (*shown in miniature*).—*adj* on a small scale; minute.

minibus *n* a small van-like bus for carrying up to 12 passengers.

minim *n* a note in music, equal in time to half a semibreve or two crotchets; the smallest liquid measure.

minimize *vt* (**minimized, minimizing**) to reduce to a minimum or the smallest possible proportion or part; to estimate at the lowest possible; to treat as being as insignificant as possible.

minimum *n* (*pl* **minimums, minima**) the smallest amount or degree; least quantity assignable in a given case, opposed to *maximum*.

mining *adj* of burrowing habits; insidious.

minion *n* a darling; an unworthy favourite; a servile dependant; one who is the creature of another.

minister *n* one who acts under the authority of another; a servant; an attendant; one to whom a sovereign entrusts the direction of affairs of state; one engaged in the administration of government; an official heading a government department; an ambassador; a diplomat; the pastor of a church.—*vt* to give; to supply.—*vi* to act as a minister or attendant; to perform service; to afford supplies; to give things needful; to supply the means of relief; to furnish (*to minister to one's necessities*).

ministerial *adj* pertaining to ministry or the performance of service; pertaining to a ministry or to ministers of state; pertaining to ministers of the gospel.

ministerialist *n* in politics, a supporter of the ministry in office.

mine

ministration *n* the act of ministering or performing service; service or attendance given; ecclesiastical function.

ministry *n* the act of ministering; service; aid; instrumentality; the office or functions of a minister of the gospel; the body of ministers of state or the chief officials of the executive government; duration of the office of a minister, civil or ecclesiastical.

minium *n* red oxide of lead; red lead.

miniver *n* the fur of the Siberian squirrel; a fine white fur.

mink *n* an American and European quadruped, allied to the polecat and weasel, yielding a fur of some value.

minnesinger *n* one of a class of German lyric poets of the twelfth and thirteenth centuries, so called from love being their chief theme.

minnow *n* a very small British fish inhabiting freshwater streams.

minnow

minor *adj* lesser; smaller (used relatively and opposed to *major*); absolutely small; petty; (*mus*) less by a lesser semitone, as applied to an interval; having a tone and semitone between the keynote and its third (applied to a scale.—*n* a person of either sex under full legal age (not yet eighteen years); one under the authority of his or her parents or guardians; in logic, the minor term or premise; (*mus*) the minor key.

Minorite, Minorist *n* a Franciscan friar.

minority *n* the state of being a minor or not come of age; the period or interval before one is of full legal age, generally the period from birth until eighteen years of age; the smaller number out of a whole divided into two, opposed to *majority*.

Minotaur *n* in Greek myth, a man-eating monster with the head of a bull and the body of a man.

minster *n* a cathedral church.

minstrel *n* a singer or musical performer; in the Middle Ages, one of a class of men who subsisted by the arts of poetry and music and sang to the harp or other instrument verses composed by themselves or others.

minstrelsy *n* the art or occupation of minstrels; music; song, especially song accompanied by instruments; a body of songs or ballads.

minstrel

mint[1] *n* an aromatic plant whose leaves are used for flavouring.

mint[2] *n* the place where money is coined by public authority; a great supply or store that may be drawn on (*a mint of reasons*). —*vt* to coin; to make and stamp into money; to invent; to fabricate.

mint sauce *n* mint chopped up with vinegar and sugar, used as a sauce for lamb.

minuet *n* a slow graceful dance and the tune or air for it.

minus *adj* less; (*alg*) applied to the negative or subtractive sign (-), which, when placed between two quantities, signifies that the latter is to be taken from the former; minus.—*n* a sign (-) indicating subtraction or negative quantity; a disadvantage.

minute[1] *n* a small portion of time, strictly the sixtieth part of an hour; sixty seconds; (*geom*) the sixtieth part of a degree of a circle; (*archit*) the sixtieth part of the diameter of a column at the base; a short summary of any agreement or other subject, taken in writing; (*pl*) an official record of a meeting.—*vt* (**minuted, minuting**) to set down in a short summary or note; to record or summarize the proceedings of.

minute[2] *adj* very small; characterized by attention to small things or details; precise; attentive to the smallest particulars.

minute gun *n* a gun discharged at intervals of a minute as a signal from a vessel in distress.

minutely *adv* with minuteness; exactly; nicely.

minuteness *n* extreme smallness; critical exactness.

minutiae *npl* (*sing* **minutia**) small, minor or unimportant particulars or details.

minx *n* a pert, wanton girl; a hussy.

Miocene *adj* (*geol*) of or pertaining to a middle subdivision of the Tertiary strata, being applied to those strata which overlie the Eocene and Oligocene and are below the Pliocene.—*n* (*geol*) the Miocene strata.

miracle *n* a wonder or wonderful thing; something that excites astonishment; a sensible deviation from the known laws of nature, held to be wrought by a supernatural being; a supernatural event.

miracle play *n* in the Middle Ages, a dramatic representation of the lives of saints or other sacred subjects.

miraculous *adj* of the nature of a miracle; effected by the direct agency of almighty power; exceedingly surprising or wonderful.

mirage *n* the name given to a natural optical illusion, consisting in an apparent elevation or approximation of coasts, mountains, ships, etc, accompanied by inverted images; in deserts often causing a plain to assume the appearance of a lake.

mire *n* wet, clayey soil; mud.—*vt* (**mired, miring**) to fix or sink in mire (as a carriage); to soil or daub with mud.—*vi* to sink in mud, so as to be unable to advance.

mirror *n* a looking glass; any polished substance that forms images by the reflection of rays of light; a pattern; an exemplar.—*vt* to furnish with mirrors; to reflect as in a mirror.

mirth *n* the feeling of being merry; merriment; noisy gaiety; glee; hilarity.

mirthful *adj* merry; jovial; causing or provoking mirth.

misadventure *n* a mischance; ill luck; an unlucky accident.

misalliance *n* any improper alliance or association; specifically, an improper connection by marriage.

misanthrope, misanthropist *n* a hater of humankind.

misanthropic *adj* pertaining to a misanthrope; hating humankind.

misanthropy *n* hatred or dislike of humankind.

misapplication *n* the act of misapplying.

misapply *vt* (**misapplied, misapplying**) to apply to a wrong purpose.

misapprehend *vt* to misunderstand; to take in a wrong sense.

misapprehension *n* a mistaking; wrong apprehension of one's meaning or of a fact.

misappropriate *vt* (**misappropriated, misappropriating**) to appropriate wrongly; to put to a wrong purpose.

misappropriation *n* wrong appropriation.

misbegotten *adj* unlawfully or irregularly begotten; illegitimate.

misbehave *vi* (**misbehaved, misbehaving**) to behave ill; to conduct oneself improperly (often used with reflexive pronouns).

misbehaviour *n* improper, rude or uncivil behaviour.

miscalculate *vt* (**miscalculated, miscalculating**) to calculate erroneously; to make a wrong guess or estimate of.

miscalculation *n* erroneous calculation or estimate.

miscall *vt* to call by a wrong name; to name improperly; to give a bad name or character to.

miscarriage *n* unfortunate issue or result of an undertaking; failure; non-success; the spontaneous expulsion of a foetus prematurely.

miscarry *vi* (**miscarried, miscarrying**) to fail to reach its destination, as a letter; to fail of the intended effect; not to succeed (*the project, scheme, design*, etc, *miscarried*); to expel a non-viable foetus from the uterus.

miscellaneous *adj* consisting of several kinds or things mingled; diversified; promiscuous; producing written compositions of various sorts (*a miscellaneous writer*).

miscellany *n* a mixture of various kinds; a collection of written compositions on various subjects; a collection of various kinds of compositions, treatises or extracts.

mischance *n* ill luck; misfortune; mishap; misadventure.

mischief *n* harm; hurt; injury; damage; evil, whether intended or not; source of vexation, trouble or annoyance; troublesome or annoying conduct; conduct causing injury; wrongdoing.

mischief-maker *n* one who makes mischief; one who excites or instigates quarrels or enmity.

mischievous *adj* harmful; injurious; fond of mischief; annoying or troublesome in conduct.

misconception *n* erroneous conception; false opinion; wrong notion or understanding of a thing.

misconduct *n* wrong or bad conduct; misbehaviour.—*vt* to conduct amiss; (*refl*) to misbehave.

misconstrue *vt* (**misconstrued, misconstruing**) to construe or interpret erroneously; to take in a wrong sense; to misjudge; to misunderstand.

miscount *vt* to count erroneously; to misjudge.—*vi* to make a wrong reckoning.—*n* an erroneous counting or numbering.

miscreant *n* a scoundrel; a detestable villain.

misdeed *n* an evil deed; a wicked action.

misdemeanour *n* a fault or transgression; (*law*) an offence of a less atrocious nature than a crime.

misdoing *n* a wrong done; a fault or crime; an offence.

miser *n* a niggardly person; one who hoards money for its own sake and hates to spend it.

miserable *adj* very unhappy; suffering misery; wretched; filled with misery; abounding in misery; causing misery; very poor or mean; worthless; despicable.

miserly *adj* like a miser in habits; pertaining to a miser; penurious; sordid; niggardly.

misery *n* great unhappiness; extreme distress; wretchedness; calamity; misfortune; cause of misery.

misfeasance *n* (*law*) a trespass; a wrong done.

misfire *vi* (**misfired, misfiring**) to fail to go off or explode from dampness or other cause (said of a gun).

misfit *n* a wrong or bad fit; a bad match; a maladjusted person; a person who does not fit in with his or her environment, job, etc.

misfortune *n* ill fortune; ill luck; calamity; some accident that prejudicially affects one's condition in life.

misgive *vt* (*pret* **misgave**, *pp* **misgiven**, *ppr* **misgiving**) to fill with doubt; to deprive of confidence; to fail (usually with 'heart' or 'mind', etc, as subject and a pronoun as object).

misgiving *n* a failing of confidence; doubt; distrust.

misgovern *vt* to govern ill; to administer unfaithfully.

misgovernment *n* the act of misgoverning; bad administration or management of public or private affairs; irregularity in conduct.

misguide *vt* (**misguided, misguiding**) to

lead or guide into error; to misdirect; to direct to a wrong purpose or end.

misguided *adj* misdirected; mistaken; foolish; ill-judged.

mishap *n* mischance; evil accident; ill luck; misfortune.

Mishna *n* the collection of precepts that constitute the basis of the Talmud.

misinform *vt* to give erroneous information to; to communicate an incorrect statement of facts to.

misinterpret *vt* to interpret erroneously; to understand or explain in a wrong sense.

misinterpretation *n* the act of interpreting erroneously.

misjudge *vt* (**misjudged, misjudging**) to mistake in judging of; to judge erroneously.—*vi* to err in judgment; to form false opinions or notions.

misjudgment *n* a wrong or unjust determination.

mislay *vt* (**mislaid, mislaying**) to lay in a wrong place; to lay wrongly; to lay in a place not recollected.

mislead *vt* to lead astray; to guide into error; to deceive.

misleading *p, adj* leading astray; leading into error; causing mistake.

mislike *vt* (**misliked, misliking**) to dislike; to disapprove; to have aversion to.

misnomer *n* a mistaken or inapplicable name or designation; a misapplied term.

misogynist *n* a woman-hater.

misogyny *n* hatred of the female sex.

misprint *vt* to mistake in printing; to print wrong.—*n* a mistake in printing; a deviation from the copy.

misprision *n* mistake; misconception; (*law*) any high offence under the degree of capital but nearly bordering thereon.

mispronounce *vti* (**mispronounced, mispronouncing**) to pronounce erroneously.

mispronunciation *n* a wrong or improper pronunciation.

misquotation *n* an erroneous quotation; the act of quoting wrong.

misquote *vti* (**misquoted, misquoting**) to quote erroneously; to cite incorrectly.

misread *vt* to read amiss; to mistake the sense of.

misrepresent *vt* to represent falsely or incorrectly; to give a false or erroneous representation of.

misrepresentation *n* the act of misrepresenting; a false or incorrect representation.

misrule *n* bad rule; disorder; confusion.

miss[1] *vt* to fail in hitting, reaching, obtaining, finding, seeing, etc; to discover the absence of; to feel or perceive the lack of; to mourn the loss of; to omit; to let slip; to pass over.—*vi* to fail to hit or strike what is aimed at.—*n* a failure to hit, reach, obtain, etc; loss; lack.

miss[2] *n* an unmarried female; a young unmarried lady; a girl; a title or address prefixed to the name of an unmarried woman.

missing *adj* absent from the place where it was expected to be found; not to be found; lacking; lost.

missal *n* the Roman Catholic mass book or book containing the office of the mass.

missel, missel thrush *n* a common British thrush rather larger than the common thrush.

misshapen *adj* ill formed; deformed; malformed; distorted.

missile *adj* capable of being thrown or projected from the hand or from any instrument or engine.—*n* a weapon or projectile thrown or to be thrown with a hostile intention, as a lance, an arrow, a bullet.

mission *n* a sending or delegating; duty on which one is sent; a commission; an errand; persons sent by authority to perform any service; particularly, persons sent on some political business or to propagate religion; a station of missionaries; the persons connected with such a station.

missionary *n* one who is sent on a religious mission; one who is sent to propagate religion.—*adj* pertaining to missions.

missive *n* that which is sent; a message; a letter sent.

misspell *vt* to spell wrong.

misspelling *n* a wrong spelling; false orthography.

misspend *vt* (**misspent, misspending**) to spend amiss, to no purpose or to a bad one; to waste.

misspent *adj* ill-spent; wasted.

misstate *vt* (**misstated, misstating**) to state wrongly; to make an erroneous statement of.

misstatement *n* the act of misstating; a wrong statement.

mist *n* visible watery vapour suspended in the atmosphere at or near the surface of the earth; aqueous vapour falling in numerous but separately almost imperceptible drops; cloudy matter; something which dims or darkens and obscures or intercepts vision.

mistake *vt* (*pret* **mistook**, *pp* **mistaken**, *ppr* **mistaking**) to take in error; to select wrongly; to conceive or understand erroneously; to regard otherwise than as the facts warrant; to misjudge; to take for a certain other person or thing; to regard as one when really another.—*vi* to be under a misapprehension or misconception; to be in error.—**to be mistaken** to be misunderstood or misapprehended; to make or have made a mistake; to be in error.—*n* an error in opinion or judgment; misapprehension; misunderstanding; a slip; a fault; a wrong act done unintentionally.

mistaken *adj* erroneous; incorrect; having made, or labouring under, a mistake; wrong.

missel thrush

mister *n* (*colloq*) sir.

Mister *n* (usually abbreviated to **Mr**) the title used before a man's surname.

mistletoe *n* a European evergreen plant growing parasitically on various trees, with oblong, entire leaves, small yellowish-green flowers and in winter small white berries.

mistral *n* a violent cold northwest wind experienced in southern France, especially in winter.

mistranslate *vt* (**mistranslated, mistranslating**) to translate erroneously.

mistranslation *n* an erroneous translation or version.

mistress *n* the female appellation corresponding to *master*; a woman who is chief or head in a certain sphere; a woman who has authority, command, ownership, etc; the female head of some establishment, as a family, school, etc; a woman who is well skilled in anything or has mastered it; a woman with whom a man is having a prolonged love affair outside marriage; a concubine; a title of address or term of courtesy pretty nearly equivalent to *madam* (now applied only to married or matronly women and written in the abbreviated form **Mrs**, used before personal names.

mistrust *n* lack of confidence or trust; suspicion.—*vt* to suspect; to doubt; to regard with jealousy or suspicion.

mistrustful *adj* suspicious; doubting; lacking confidence.

misty *adj* accompanied or characterized by mist; overspread with mist; dim; obscure; not perspicuous.

misunderstand *vt* to misconceive; to mistake; to take in a wrong sense.

misunderstanding *n* misconception; mistake of meaning; error; disagreement; dissension.

misuse *vt* (**misused, misusing**) to treat or use improperly; to use to a bad purpose; to abuse; to maltreat.—*n* improper use; employment in a wrong way or to a bad purpose; abuse; ill-treatment.

mite[1] *n* a name common to numerous small, in some cases microscopic, parasitic insects (cheese mite, sugar mite, itch mite, etc).

mite[2] *n* a small coin formerly current, equal to about one-third of a farthing; anything proverbially very small; a very little particle or quantity.

mitigant *adj* mitigating; softening; lenitive; soothing; alleviating.

mitigate *vt* (**mitigated, mitigating**) to alleviate or render less painful, rigorous, intense or severe; to assuage, lessen, abate, moderate; to become less severe, etc.

mitigation *n* the act of mitigating; alleviation; abatement; diminution.

mitre *n* a headdress worn in ancient times by the inhabitants of Asia Minor; a sort of cap, pointed and cleft at the top, worn on the head by bishops and archbishops (including the pope), cardinals and in some instances by abbots, on solemn occasions, as also by a Jewish high priest.—*vt* (**mitred, mitring**) to adorn with a mitre; to raise to a rank which entitles to a mitre; to unite or join by a mitre joint.

mitred *adj* wearing a mitre; entitled to wear a mitre; (in carpentry and masonry) cut or jointed at an angle of 45°.

mitred abbot *n* an abbot having episcopal authority within his own precincts.

mitre joint *n* in carpentry and masonry, a joint connecting two pieces of wood, stone, etc, at right angles, the line of the joint making an acute angle or an angle of 45° with both pieces.

mitten *n* a covering for the hand, differing from a glove in not having a separate cover for each finger, the thumb only being separate; also, a covering for the hand and wrist only and not for the fingers.

mix *vt* to unite or blend, as various ingredients, into one mass or compound; to mingle; to blend; to join; to associate; to unite with in company; to produce by blending different ingredients.—*vi* to become united or blended promiscuously in a mass or compound; to be joined or associated; to mingle.

mixed blessing *n* something that has both advantages and disadvantages.

mixer *n* a person or thing that mixes; an electric kitchen appliance for mixing; a sociable person; a person considered in terms of his or her ability to get on with people; a soft drink added to an alcoholic beverage.

mixture *n* the act of mixing or state of being mixed; a mass or compound, consisting of different ingredients blended without order; a liquid medicine formed by mixing several ingredients together.

mizzen, mizen *n* (*naut*) a fore-and-aft sail on the mast of a ship or barque next the stern (called also *spanker*).—*adj* (*naut*) belonging to the mizzen (applied to the mast supporting the mizzen and the rigging and shrouds connected with it.

mizzle *vi* (**mizzled, mizzling**) to rain in very fine drops; to drizzle.—*n* small rain.

mnemonics *n* the art of memory; the precepts and rules intended to teach some method of assisting the memory.

moa *n* the New Zealand name for the dinornis, an extinct wingless bird.

moan *vi* to utter a low dull sound under the influence of grief or pain; to make lamentations; to utter a prolonged groan; to give out a low dull noise.—*n* a low dull sound due to grief or pain; a sound resembling that made by a person moaning.

mistletoe

mitre

moat *n* a ditch or deep trench round the rampart of a castle or other fortified place to serve as a defence, often filled with water. —*vt* to surround with a ditch for defence

mob *n* a crowd; a disorderly or riotous crowd; the masses; the rabble; (*sl*) a gang of criminals; a riotous assembly.—*vt* (**mobbed, mobbing**) to crowd round and annoy.

mobile *adj* capable of being easily moved; readily liable to change (*mobile features*); changeable; fickle.

mobility *n* the state of being mobile; susceptibility of motion; readiness to move or change; fickleness; inconstancy.

mobilization *n* the act of mobilizing, calling or putting to use.

mobilize *vt* (**mobilized, mobilizing**) to put in a state of readiness for active military service; to organize for a particular reason; to put to use.

moccasin *n* a kind of shoe made of deerskin or other soft leather, without a stiff sole, worn by the North American Indians; a venomous serpent frequenting swamps in the warmer parts of America.

mock *vt* to imitate or mimic, especially in contempt or derision; to deride or flout; to ridicule; to fool, tantalize, disappoint, deceive; to set at naught; to defy.—*vi* to use ridicule; to gibe or jeer.—*n* ridicule; derision; gibe; flout; sneer.—*adj* false; counterfeit; assumed (often in compounds).

mockery *n* the act of mocking; derision; ridicule; sportive insult; sport; subject of laughter; imitation; counterfeit; appearance; false show; vain effort.

mock-heroic *adj* burlesquing the heroic in poetry, action, character, etc.

mockingbird *n* an American bird of the thrush family, much sought for on account of its wonderful faculty of imitating sounds.

modal *adj* relating to a mode or mood; pertaining to the mode, manner or form, not to the essence; (*gram*) expressing mood; (*philos*) asserting with qualification; (*mus*) of or composed in a mode.

mode *n* manner; method; custom; the mode, the prevailing fashion or style; (*gram, logic*) mood; (*mus*) any of the scales used in composition; in statistics, the predominant item in a series of items.

model *n* a pattern of something to be made; a form in miniature of something to be made on a larger scale; a copy, in miniature, of something already made or existing; an image, copy, facsimile; standard; that by which a thing is to be measured; anything serving or worthy of serving as a pattern; a person who sits for an artist or photographer; a person who displays clothes for sale by wearing them.—*vt*

moat

moccasin

(**modelled, modelling**) to plan or form after some model; to form in order to serve as a model; to mould; to shape.—*vi* to make a model; (*sculp*) to form a work of some plastic material, as clay.

modeller *n* one who models; especially, a moulder in clay, wax or plaster.

modem *n* a device which converts data from one computer into a form which can be transmitted along telephone lines to another computer.

moderate *vt* (**moderated, moderating**) to restrain from excess of any kind; to reduce in intensity (rage, passion, desire, joy, etc); to qualify; to temper; to lessen; to allay.—*vi* to become less violent or intense; to preside as a moderator.—*adj* (of persons) not going to extremes; temperate in opinions or views; (of things) not extreme or excessive; not very great; mediocre.—*n* a person who holds moderate views.

moderation *n* the act of moderating, tempering or repressing; the state or quality of being moderate; the keeping of a due mean between extremes; freedom from excess; due restraint; the act of presiding as a moderator.

moderator *n* one who or that which moderates or restrains; the person who presides at a meeting or discussion (now chiefly applied to the chairman of meetings or courts in Presbyterian churches).

modern *adj* pertaining to the present time or time not long past; recent; not ancient.—*n* a person of modern times, opposed to ancient.

modernism *n* the state of being modern; a deviation from ancient manner, practice or mode of expression, especially in art, architecture, literature, etc; a movement or tendency in Christian churches towards rationalistic interpretation of doctrine.

modernize *vt* (**modernized, modernizing**) to give a modern character to; to adapt to modern times; to cause to conform to modern ideas or style.

modest *adj* restrained by a sense of propriety; not forward or bold; unpretending; bashful; diffident; free from anything suggestive of sexual impurity; pure; moderate; not excessive, extreme or extravagant.

modesty *n* the state or quality of being modest; absence of tendency to forwardness, pretence or presumption; bashful reserve; absence of anything suggestive of sexual impurity; chastity; moderation; freedom from excess.

modicum *n* a little; a small quantity; a scanty allowance or allotment.

modification *n* the act of modifying; the state of being modified; some alteration in form, appearance or character; a particular form or manner of being; a mode.

modify *vt* (**modified, modifying**) to change

the external qualities of; to give a new form or external character to; to vary; to alter in some respect.

modish *adj* according to the mode or fashion; affectedly fashionable.

modiste *n* a milliner or dressmaker.

modulate *vt* (**modulated, modulating**) to proportion; to adjust; to vary or inflect the sound of in such a manner as to give expressiveness to what is uttered; to vary (the voice) in tone; (*mus*) to change the key or mode of in the course of composition; to transfer from one key to another.—*vi* (*mus*) to pass from one key into another.

modulation *n* the act of modulating; adjustment; the act of inflecting the voice or any instrument musically; melodious sound; music, the change from one scale or mode to another in the course of a composition.

modulator *n* one who or that which modulates; in the tonic sol-fa system of music, a sort of map of musical sounds representing the relative intervals of the notes of a scale, its chromatics and its more closely related scales.

module *n* a unit of measurement, especially used for building materials; a component made of standardized size so that it can be combined with others indifferent ways, used in building, furniture, electronics, etc.; a unit or section of an educational course treating a specific topic.

modus *n* (*pl* **modi**) mode, manner or method; (*law*) a fixed payment by way of tithe.—**modus operandi** method of working.—**modus vivendi** (*lit*) way of living; a temporary arrangement between parties pending the final settlement of matters in dispute.

mogul n a small mound or bump on a ski slope; (colloq) an important person, a magnate.

Mogul, Moghul *n* a ruler of the former Mogul Empire in India.

mohair *n* the hair of the Angora goat; cloth made of this hair; a wool-and-cotton cloth made in imitation of real mohair.

Mohammedan *adj* pertaining to Mohammed or the religion founded by him; Muslim.—*n* a follower of Mohammed; a Muslim.

Mohammedanism *n* the religion of Mohammed, contained in the Koran.

moiety *n* the half; one of two equal parts; a portion or share in general.

moire, moiré *n* a clouded or watered appearance on metals or textile fabrics; watered silk.

moist *adj* moderately wet; damp; not dry; humid.

moisten *vt* to make moist or damp; to wet in a small degree.—*vi* to become moist.

moistness *n* state of being moist; a small degree of wetness.

moisture *n* diffused and sensible wetness; damp.

mol *n* gram molecule.

molar *n* a basic tooth used for grinding food; a tooth having a flattened, triturating surface; a double tooth.

molasses *n* the uncrystallized syrup produced from sugar in the process of making.

mole[1] *n* an insectivorous animal which forms burrows or roads just under the surface of the ground, throwing up the excavated soil into little hills; a kind of plough for making drains.

mole[2] *n* a spot, mark or small discoloured protuberance on the human body.

mole[3] *n* a mound or breakwater formed so as partially to enclose a harbour or anchorage and protect it from the waves.

mole[4] *n* the basic SI unit of substance.

molecular *adj* pertaining to or consisting of molecules.

molecule *n* the simplest unit of a substance, retaining the chemical properties of that substance; a small particle.

molehill *n* a heap of earth thrown up by a mole; something insignificant as contrasted with something important.

moleskin *n* a strong twilled fustian or cotton cloth, so called from its being soft like the skin of a mole.

molest *vt* to annoy; to disturb; to vex; to attack or assault, especially sexually.

molestation *n* the act of molesting; disturbance; annoyance.

mollah *n* same as **mullah**.

mollification *n* the act of mollifying; mitigation; pacification.

mollify *vt* (**mollified, mollifying**) to soften; to assuage, as pain or irritation; to pacify or make less angry; to reduce in harshness; to tone down.

mollusc, mollusk *n* any of a group of soft invertebrates animals, such as oysters, snails, etc, usually with a shell of one or more pieces covering the body.

mollycoddle *n* an effeminate person.—*vt* (**mollycoddled, mollycoddling**) to pamper, coddle.

moloch *n* a spiny Australian lizard with a horned head, found in desert areas.

Moloch *n* the chief god of the Phoenicians and of the Ammonites, whose worship consisted chiefly of human sacrifices, ordeals by fire, mutilation, etc; anything that is said to demand great sacrifice

molten *adj* melted; made of melted metal.

molto *adv* (*mus*) very, as **molto allegro** very bright and lively.

molybdenum *n* a brittle and rare metal of a white colour.

moment *n* a minute portion of time; an instant; a particular point of time; importance; consequence.

molar

mole

momentary *adj* lasting but a moment or a very short time; fleeting.

momentous *adj* of moment or importance; weighty; of great consequence.

momentum *n* (*pl* **momenta, momentums**) the force possessed by a body in motion; the product of the mass and velocity of a body; impetus.

monachal *adj* pertaining to monks or a monastic life; monastic.

monachism *n* the monastic life or system.

monad *n* a unit, number one; (*philos*) the ultimate unit of being or evolution in the theory of Leibniz; (*zool*) a microscopic organism of an extremely simple character developed in organic infusions; (*chem*) a element, such as hydrogen, chlorine, etc, with a valence of one.

monadelphous *adj* (*bot*) (of a plant) having the stamens united in one body by the filaments.

monarch *n* a sole ruler; the supreme governor of a state; a sovereign, as an emperor, king, queen, prince, etc; one who is superior to others of the same kind (an oak is called *the monarch of the forest*).

monarchal *adj* pertaining to a monarch; suiting a monarch; sovereign.

monarchic, monarchical *adj* vested in a monarch or single ruler; pertaining to a monarchy.

monarchism *n* the principles of monarchy; love or preference of monarchy.

monarchist *n* an advocate of monarchy.

monarchy *n* a state or country in which the supreme power is either actually or nominally lodged in the hands of a single person; the system of government according to which the supreme power is vested in a single person; the territory ruled over by a monarch; a kingdom; an empire.

monastery *n* a house of religious retirement or of seclusion from ordinary temporal concerns, whether an abbey, a priory, a nunnery or convent (usually applied to the houses for monks.

monastic, monastical *adj* pertaining to monasteries; pertaining to religious or other seclusion.—*n* a member of a monastery; a monk.

monasticism *n* monastic life; the monastic system or condition.

Monday *n* the second day of the week.

monetary *adj* pertaining to money or consisting in money.

monetary unit *n* the standard of currency.

monetize *vt* (**monetized, monetizing**) to form into coin or money.

money *n* (*pl* **moneys, monies**) coin; gold, silver or other metal, stamped by public authority and used as the medium of exchange; in a wider sense, any equivalent for commodities and for which individuals readily exchange their goods or services; a circulating medium; wealth; affluence (*a man of money*), the plural is used in the sense of sums of money or denominations of money.—**a money of account** a denomination used merely for convenience in keeping accounts and not represented by any coin.

moneyed *adj* rich; wealthy; affluent.

moneylender *n* one who lends money on interest.

moneymaking *n* the process of accumulating money.—*adj* lucrative; profitable.

money market *n* the market or field for the investment or employment of money.

money order *n* an order granted on payment of the sum and a small commission, by one post office and payable at another.

money's worth *n* something as good as or that will bring money; full value.

monger *n* a trader; a dealer (now only or chiefly in composition).

mongolism *n* an old name for **Down's syndrome**.

mongoose *n* (*pl* **mongooses**) a small predatory animal about the size of a rat.

mongrel *adj* of a mixed breed; of mingled origins; hybrid.—*n* a cross between two plants or animal varieties (breeds, races), usually fertile, e.g. crosses between varieties of apple or breeds of sheep.

moniliform *adj* (*biol*) shaped like a necklace or like a series or string of beads.

monism *n* the doctrine which holds that in the universe there is only a single element or principle from which everything is developed, this single principle being either mind (*idealistic monism*) or matter (*materialistic monism*).

monition *n* admonition; warning; advice by way of caution; indication; intimation.

monitor *n* a pupil in a school appointed to perform certain duties; a prefect; any device for regulating the performance of a machine or process; a screen for viewing the image being produced by a television camera; a display screen connected to a computer; a genus of large lizards, popularly believed to give warning of the presence of crocodiles.—*vt* to watch or check on; to observe or listen to (a television or radio programme) for political or technical reasons; to regulate (a machine, etc).—*vi* to act as a monitor.

monitory *adj* admonitory; conveying admonition.

monitress *n* a female monitor.

monk *n* one of a community of males inhabiting a monastery and bound by vows to celibacy and religious exercises.

monkey *n* any of the primates except man and the lemurs, especially the smaller long-tailed primates; a mischievous child; a pile-driving apparatus; a sort of power hammer; (*sl*) a sum of £500.

monk

monkey

monkey business *n* mischief; underhand dealings.

monkey jacket *n* a close-fitting jacket, generally of some stout material.

monkey puzzle *n* a name for the araucaria.

monkey wrench *n* a screw key with a movable jaw, which can be adjusted by a screw.

monkfish *n* the angelfish

monkhood *n* character or condition of a monk.

monkish *adj* like a monk or pertaining to monks; monastic.

monkshood *n* aconite.

monobasic *adj* (*chem*) having only one hydrogen atom, replaceable by a basic atom or radical; having one hydrogen atom replaced, of several originally replaceable.

monocarp *n* (*bot*) a plant that perishes after having once borne fruit; an annual plant.

monocarpic, monocarpous *adj* (*bot*) bearing fruit only once.

monochord *n* (*mus*) a single string stretched across a sound board and having under it a movable bridge, used to show the lengths of string required to produce the notes of the scale, etc.

monochromatic *adj* consisting of one colour or presenting rays of light of one colour only.

monochrome *n* a painting in one colour but relieved by light and shade.

monocle *n* a single eyeglass.

monoclinal *adj* (*geol*) applied to strata that dip for an indefinite length in one direction.

monoclinic *adj* (of a mineral) having three unequal axes, two intersecting at an oblique angle and cut by the third at right angles.

monocotyledon *n* a plant with one cotyledon only; a monocotyledonous plant.

monocotyledonous *adj* (*bot*) having only one seed lobe or cotyledon, as endogenous plants have.

monodrama *n* a dramatic performance by a single person.

monody *n* a mournful kind of song, in which a single mourner is supposed to give vent to his or her grief.

monogamist *n* one who practises or upholds monogamy, as opposed to a bigamist or polygamist.

monogamous *adj* upholding or practising monogamy; (*zool*) having only one mate.

monogamy *n* the practice or principle of marrying only once; the marrying of only one at a time; (*zool*) the having only one mate.

monogenesis *n* (*biol*) direct development of an embryo from a parent similar to itself.

monogram *n* a character or cipher composed of one, two or more letters interwoven, being an abbreviation of a name, used for instance on seals, letter paper and envelopes, etc.

monograph *n* an account or description of a single thing or class of things; a learned paper written on one particular subject.

monolith *n* a pillar, column, etc, formed of a single stone, generally applied to such only as are noted for their magnitude; any massive unyielding structure.

monologue *n* that which is spoken by one person alone; a dramatic soliloquy; a long speech or dissertation, uttered by one person in company.

monomania *n* that form of mania in which the mind of the patient is absorbed by one idea or is irrational on one subject only.

monomaniac *n* a person affected by monomania.—*adj* affected with, pertaining to or resulting from monomania.

monometallism *n* the fact of having only one metal as a standard in the coinage of a country; the theory of a single metallic standard.

monomorphic, monomorphous *adj* (*biol*) retaining the same form throughout the various stages of development.

monopetalous *adj* (*bot*) having the petals united together into one piece by their edges.

monophyllous *adj* (*bot*) having one leaf only or formed of one leaf.

monoplane *n* a flying machine with its wings or carrying surfaces arranged in nearly the same plane.

monopolist, monopolizer *n* one that monopolizes or possesses a monopoly.

monopolize *vt* (**monopolized, monopolizing**) to obtain a monopoly of; to have full command of for trade purposes; to obtain or engross the whole of; to assume exclusive possession of.

monopoly *n* an exclusive trading privilege; the sole right or power of selling something or full command over the sale of it; that which is the subject of a monopoly; the possession or assumption of anything to the exclusion of others.

monorail *n* a single-track railway, often with suspended carriages.

monosepalous *adj* (*bot*) composed of sepals which are united by their edges.

monospermous, monospermal *adj* (*bot*) having one seed only.

monostich *n* a poem consisting of one verse only.

monosyllabic *adj* consisting of one syllable; consisting of words of one syllable.

monosyllable *n* a word of one syllable.

monotheism *n* the doctrine or belief of the existence of one God only.

monotheist *n* one who believes in one God only.

monotheistic *adj* pertaining to monotheism.

monotone *n* a sameness of sound or the ut-

monkey wrench

monorail

terance of successive syllables on one unvaried key, without inflection or cadence; a tiresome sameness of style in writing or speaking.

monotonous *adj* characterized by monotony or monotone; with dull uniformity; dull; wearisome.

monotony *n* uniformity of tone or sound; lack of inflections of voice in speaking or reading; lack of cadence or modulation; tiresome sameness; lack of variety; dull uniformity.

monotrematous *adj* belonging to or characteristic of the monotremes.

monotreme *n* one of a primitive order of Australian egg-laying mammals with a single vent for digestive, urinary and genital organs.

Monotype *n* (*trademark*) in printing, a mechanical method of setting and casting types in single letters.

monsieur *n* (*pl* **messieurs**) the common title of courtesy and respect in France, answering to the English Sir and Mr; abbreviated M.

Monsignor *n* (*RC Church*) a title given, usually by the Pope, to some prelates.

monsoon *n* a seasonal wind of Southern Asia; the rainy season.

monster *n* a plant or animal of abnormal structure or greatly different from the usual type; an animal exhibiting malformation in important parts; a person looked on with horror on account of extraordinary crimes, deformity or power to do harm; an imaginary creature, such as the sphinx, mermaid, etc.—*adj* of inordinate size or numbers (*a monster meeting*).

monstrance *n* (*RC Church*) the transparent or glass-faced shrine in which the consecrated host is presented for the adoration of the people.

monstrosity *n* the state of being monstrous; that which is monstrous; an unnatural production.

monstrous *adj* unnatural in form; out of the common course of nature; enormous; huge; extraordinary; shocking; frightful; horrible.—*adv* exceedingly; very much (now vulgar or colloquial.)

month *n* one of the twelve parts of the calendar year, consisting unequally of 30 or 31 days, except February, which has 28, and in leap year 29 days, called distinctively a calendar month; the period between change and change of the moon, reckoned as twenty-eight days.

monthly *adj* continued a month or performed in a month; happening once a month or every month.—*adv* once a month; in every month.—*n* a magazine or other literary periodical published once a month.

monument *n* anything by which the memory of a person, period or event is perpetuated; a memorial; especially something built or erected in memory of events, actions or persons; any enduring evidence or example; a singular or notable instance.

monumental *adj* pertaining to a monument; serving as a monument; memorial; preserving memory; colossal.

moo *vi* to low, as a cow (imitated from the sound).—*n* the low of a cow.

mood[1] *n* temper of mind; state of the mind in regard to passion or feeling; temporary disposition; humour; a gloomy feeling; a fit of temper or sullenness; a predominant feeling or spirit.

mood[2] *n* (*gram*) a special form of verbs expressive of certainty, contingency, possibility, etc; (*logic*) the determination of propositions according to their quantity and quality, that is, whether universal, affirmative, etc.

moody *adj* subject to or indulging in moods or humours; fretful; out of humour; gloomy; sullen; melancholy.

moon *n* the heavenly orb which revolves round the earth; a secondary planet or satellite of the earth; a satellite of any planet (*the moons of Jupiter*); the period of a revolution of the moon; a month; something in the shape of a moon or crescent.— *vi* to wander or gaze idly or moodily, as if moonstruck.

moonbeam *n* a ray of light from the moon.

mooncalf *n* (*pl* **mooncalves**) a monster; a deformed creature; a dolt; a stupid fellow.

Moonie *n* (*colloq*) an adherent of the Unification Church, a religious sect.

moonlight *n* the light afforded by the moon.—*adj* Illuminated by the moon; occurring during or by moonlight.

moonlit *adj* lit or illuminated by the moon.

moonraker, moonsail *n* a sail rigged above a sky sail.

moonshine *n* the light of the moon; show without substance or reality; pretence; empty show; nonsense; illegally distilled spirits.

moonstruck *adj* besotted with love or sentiment; demented.

moony *adj* pertaining to the moon; like a moon; moon-shaped; bewildered or silly, as if moonstruck.

moor[1] *n* a tract of waste land, especially when partly covered with heath; a tract of hilly ground on which game is strictly preserved for sport.

moor[2] *vt* to confine or secure (a ship) in a particular station, as by cables and anchors or by chains; to fix firmly.

Moor *n* a native of the northern coast of Africa.

moorcock, moorfowl *n* the red grouse.

moorhen *n* an aquatic bird of a dark colour with a red bill; the female of the red grouse.

mooring *n* (*naut*) the act of one who moors; that by which a ship is moored; (*pl*) the place where a ship is moored.

Moorish *adj* pertaining to the Moors or Saracens.

moorland *n* a waste, barren district; a moor.

moose *n* the North American variety of the elk.

moot *vt* to debate; to bring forward and discuss; to argue for and against.—*n* dispute; discussion; a debate on a hypothetical legal case by way of practice.—*adj* debatable; subject to discussion; discussed or debated (*a moot subject*).

moot point *n* a point debated or liable to be debated.

mop *n* a piece of cloth, sponge, etc, fastened to a long handle and used for cleaning floors, etc; a thick or tangled head of hair.—*vt* (**mopped, mopping**) to rub or wipe with a mop.

mope *vi* (**moped, moping**) to show a dull, downcast or listless air; to be spiritless or gloomy.—*n* one who mopes; a low-spirited person.

moraine *n* an accumulation of stones or other debris on the surface of glaciers or in the valleys at their foot, a regular feature in glacier phenomena.

moral *adj* relating to right and wrong as determined by duty; relating to morality or morals; ethical; capable of distinguishing between right and wrong; governed by the laws of right and wrong; real or effective if not apparent (*moral victory*); psychological (*moral support*); having a strong probability (*moral certainty*).—*n* the practical lesson inculcated by any story; (*pl*) general conduct or behaviour as right or wrong; principles and mode of life; also moral philosophy or ethics.

morale *n* degree of confidence, courage, optimism, etc.

moralist *n* one who teaches morals; a writer or lecturer on ethics; one who inculcates or practises moral duties.

morality *n* the doctrine of moral duties; morals; ethics; the practice of the moral duties; virtue; moral character or quality; the quality of an action, as estimated by a standard of right and wrong; a morality play.

morality play *n* a kind of medieval allegorical play in which the characters were representations of virtues, vices etc.

moralize *vt* (**moralized, moralizing**) to apply to a moral purpose; to draw a moral from.—*vi* to make moral pronouncements; to make moral reflections; to draw practical lessons from the facts of life.

morally *adv* in a moral manner; from a moral point of view; virtuously; uprightly; virtually; to all intents and purposes.

moral philosophy *n* the science which treats of the nature and grounds of moral obligation; ethics.

morass *n* a tract of low, soft, wet ground; a marsh; a swamp; a fen.

moratorium *n* (*pl* **moratoria, moratoriums**) a special period of delay granted by law to debtors.

morbid *adj* diseased; sickly; not sound and healthful; relating to disease.

morbidity *n* the state of being morbid; diseased state.

mordacious *adj* biting; sarcastic.

mordant *n* a substance employed in the process of dyeing which serves to fix the colours; sticky matter by which gold leaf is made to adhere—*adj* biting; caustic; severe.

more *adj* (serving as the *compar* of **much** and **many**, the *superl* being **most**) (with singular nouns, as *compar* of **much**) greater in amount, extent, degree, etc (*more land*, *more light*); (with plural nouns, as *compar* of **many**) greater in number; in greater numbers (*more men*); added to some former number; additional (*one day more* or *one more day*).—*adv* in a greater degree, extent or quantity; in addition; besides; again (*once more*, *no more*). —**to be no more** to be destroyed or dead; to have perished.—*n* what is more or greater; something farther or in addition.

morel *n* an edible European mushroom.

morello *n* a kind of cherry with a dark-red skin.

moreover *adv* beyond what has been said; further; besides.

morganatic *adj* denoting a marriage between a monarch or one of the highest nobility and a lady of inferior rank, the offspring of which do not inherit the father's rank or possessions but are considered legitimate in most other respects.

morgue *n* a mortuary.

moribund *adj* in a dying state.

Mormon *n* a member of a sect founded in the USA in 1830 by Joseph Smith, who practise polygamy and have a complete hierarchical organization.

morn *n* the first part of the day; the morning (used chiefly in poetry).

morning *n* the first part of the day, beginning at twelve o'clock at night and extending to twelve at noon; in a more limited sense, the time beginning at break of day and extending to the hour of breakfast and of beginning the labours of the day or considerably later; (*fig*) the first or early part (as of life).—*adj* of or in the morning.

morning star *n* the planet Venus when it rises before the sun.

morocco *n* a fine kind of leather made from the skins of goats, extensively used in the binding of books, upholstering furniture, making shoes, etc.

mop

moose

moron *n* a mentally retarded person; a foolish or stupid person.

morose *adj* of a sour temper; severe; sullen and austere.

moroseness *n* the quality of being morose; sourness of temper; sullenness.

Morpheus *n* in Greek myth, the god of sleep and dreams.

morphia *n* a former name for **morphine**.

morphine *n* an alkaloid derived from opium, used as an anaesthetic and sedative and causing addition after repeated use.

morphology *n* that department of science which treats of the form and arrangement of the structures of plants and animals; the science of form in the organic world.

morris, morris dance *n* a type of traditional English dance performed by men in costumes to the accompaniment of bells, tambourines, etc.

morrow *n* the day next after the present or after any day specified; (*arch*, *poet*) morning (*good morrow*).

morse *n* a jewelled clasp on a cope.

Morse alphabet *n* a system of symbols, consisting of dashes and dots, used in telegraphic messages; any system on the same principle, as carried out by long and short blasts of a steam whistle, etc.

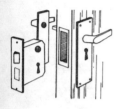

mortise lock

morsel *n* a bite; a mouthful; a small piece of food; a fragment; a little piece in general.

mortal *adj* subject to death; destined to die; deadly; destructive to life; causing death; fatal; incurring the penalty of death or divine condemnation; not venial (*mortal sin*); human; belonging to humans who is mortal.—*n* a being subject to death; a person; a human being.

mortality *n* the state of being mortal; death; frequency of death; death of numbers in proportion to a population; humanity; human nature; the human race.

mortally *adv* in the manner of a mortal; in a deadly manner or manner that must cause death.

mortar *n* a vessel, usually in form of an inverted bell, in which substances are pulverized or pounded with a pestle; a short piece of ordnance, thick and wide, used for throwing shells, etc; a mixture of lime and sand with water, used as a cement for stones and bricks in walls.

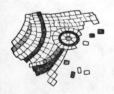

mosiac

mortgage *n* an assignment or conveyance of land or house property to a person as security for the payment of a debt due to him and on the condition that if the money shall be paid according to contract the grant shall be void; the deed by which this conveyance is effected.—*vt* (**mortgaged, mortgaging**) to grant or assign on mortgage; to pledge; to make liable to the payment of any debt.

mortgagee *n* the person to whom a property is mortgaged.

mortgagor, mortgager *n* the person who grants a mortgage.

mortice *n* same as **mortise**.

mortification *n* the act of mortifying or the condition of being mortified; (*med*) the death of a part of the body while the rest is alive; gangrene; the subduing of the passions and appetites by penance, abstinence, etc; humiliation; vexation or chagrin caused by damage to one's pride.

mortify *vt* (**mortified, mortifying**) to affect with gangrene or mortification; to subdue or bring into subjection by abstinence or penance; to humiliate; to chagrin; to affect with vexation.—*vi* to become gangrenous.

mortise, mortice *n* a deep rectangular cavity or slot in a surface into which a matching tapered end (a tenon) is fitted in order to fix the two together.—*vt* (**mortised, mortising**) to cut a mortise in; to join by tenon and mortise.

mortise lock *n* a lock fitted into a mortise in the frame of a door.

mortmain *n* (*law*) possession of lands by hands that cannot alienate, as those of a corporation; the holding of property, more particularly by religious houses, which has been restricted by various statutes.

mortuary *n* a place for the temporary reception of the dead; a dead-house.—*adj* pertaining to the burial of the dead.

mosaic *adj* a term applied to inlaid work formed by little pieces of enamel, glass, marble, precious stones, etc, of various colours.—*n* mosaic or inlaid work.

Mosaic *adj* relating to Moses, the Hebrew lawgiver or his writings and institutions.

Moslem *n*, *adj* same as **Muslim**.

mosque *n* a Muslim temple or place of religious worship.

mosquito *n* (*pl* **mosquitoes, mosquitos**) a name applied to several species of gnatlike flies, common in many regions and some species of which are the means of infecting human beings with certain diseases, such as malaria and yellow fever.

moss *n* a name common to many non-flowering plants of small size with simple branching stems and numerous, generally narrow, leaves; also a name of various lichens; a bog; a place where peat is found.

mossy *adj* overgrown with moss; abounding with moss; like moss.

most *adj* (*superl* of **more**) greatest in any way (with singular nouns, as *most wisdom*, *need*, etc); greatest in number; amounting to a considerable majority (with plurals, as *most men*; *most sorts of learning*).—*adv* in the greatest or highest or in a very great or high degree, quantity or extent; mostly; chiefly (often used before adjectives and adverbs to form the superlative degree, as *more* is to form the comparative).—*n* the greatest or greater number; the majority (in this case plural); greatest amount or advantage; utmost extent, degree, effect, etc (often with *the* and in this sense singular). —**at most** *or* **at the most** at furthest; at the utmost extent.

mostly *adv* for the most part; chiefly; mainly.

mot *n* a pithy or witty saying; a bon mot.

mote *n* a small particle; a mere atom; anything proverbially small.

motel *n* a kind of hotel which specializes in providing accommodation for motorists, often chalets with adjacent parking.

motet *n* (*mus*) a sacred cantata; a choral composition, usually of a sacred character.

moth *n* a lepidopteran related to the butterflies but seldom seen on the wing except in the evening or at night; the clothes moth, the caterpillar of which is destructive to clothes, etc.

mothball *n* a small ball of camphor, etc, used to protect stored clothes from moths.—**in mothballs** in storage; postponed.

moth-eaten *adj* eaten into by moths or rather their larvae; dilapidated.

mother¹ *n* a female parent, especially one of the human race; a woman who has borne a child; that which has produced anything; source of anything; a familiar term of address to elderly females; an abbess or other female holding an important position in religious or semi-religious institutions.— *adj* native; natural (*mother wit*); giving birth or origin; originating (*mother country*).

mother² *n* a thick slimy substance that gathers in liquors, particularly vinegar.

mother country *n* a country which has sent out colonies; in relation to its colonies; a country as the mother or producer of anything.

motherhood *n* the state of being a mother.

mother-in-law *n* the mother of one's husband or wife.

motherly *adj* pertaining to a mother; becoming a mother; tender and affectionate.

mother-of-pearl *n* the hard silvery brilliant internal layer of several kinds of shells extensively used in the arts (called also **nacre**).

mother wit *n* native wit; common sense.

motif *n* a recurrent theme in a musical composition; a repeated theme, subject or figure, e.g. in a design.

motile *adj* (*bot*) able to move without outside aid; exhibiting movement.—*n* (*psychol*) a person whose perception of the material world comprises, to a very strong degree, the imagery of movement, especially his or her own.

motion *n* the act or process of changing place; the passing of a body from one place to another, opposed to *rest*; the power of moving; a single act of motion; a movement; movement of the mind or soul; internal impulse; proposal made; a proposition made in a deliberative assembly; the proposing of any matter for the consideration of an assembly or meeting; a bowel movement; faeces.—*vti* to make a significant motion or gesture for guidance, as with the hand or head.

motionless *adj* lacking motion; being at rest.

motive *n* that which incites to action; that which determines the choice or moves the will; cause; object; inducement; prevailing design; a motif.—*adj* of, causing or relating to motion; moving to action.

mot juste *n* (*pl* **mots justes**) exactly the right word.

motley *adj* consisting of different colours; parti-coloured (*a motley coat*); exhibiting a combination of discordant elements; heterogeneous (*a motley style*).—*n* a dress of various colours; the usual dress of a court fool or jester.

motor *n* that which imparts motion; a machine for converting electrical energy into mechanical energy; a motorcar.—*adj* imparting motion.

moth

motorbike *n* a motorcycle.

motorbus *n* a bus driven by a motor engine.

motorcade *n* a procession of motor vehicles.

motorcar *n* a vehicle (usually with four wheels) powered by an internal-combustion engine.

motorcycle *n* a two-wheeled motor vehicle.—vi (**motorcycled, motorcycling**) to drive or ride on a motor cycle.

motor scooter *n* a small-wheeled motorcycle with an enclosed engine.

motorway *n* a divided highway with several lanes, no crossroads and limited entry and exit points, designed to speed up the flow of traffic.

mottle *n* a blotched or spotted sort of surface, as seen in woods employed in cabinet work when polished.—*vt* (**mottled, mottling**) to mark with spots or blotches as if mottled.

mottled *adj* spotted; marked with blotches of colour.

motto *n* (*pl* **mottoes, mottos**) a short pithy sentence or phrase, or even a single word, adopted as expressive of one's guiding idea or principle, appended to a coat of arms or otherwise put prominently forward.

mould

mould¹ *n* the matrix in which anything is cast and receives its form; a hollow tool for producing a form by percussion or compression; cast; form; shape; character—*vt* to form into a particular shape; to shape; to model; to fashion.

mould² *n* fine soft earth or earth easily pulverized, such as constitutes soil; mustiness or mildew; a minute fungoid or other vegetable growth of a low type, especially such as appears on bodies which lie long in warm and damp air, animal and vegetable tissues, etc; dust from incipient decay.—*vt* to cause to contract mould; to cover with mould or soil.—*vi* to become mouldy.

moulder *vi* to turn to dust by natural decay; to waste away by a gradual separation of the component particles; to crumble; to perish.—*vt* to turn to dust; to crumble; to waste.

moulding *n* something cast in a mould; (*archit*) a general term applied to the varieties of outline or contour given to cornices, bases, door or window jambs, lintels, etc.

mouldy *adj* overgrown with mould; mildewed; musty; fusty; decaying.

moult *vi* to shed or cast the feathers, hair, skin, horns, etc, as birds and other animals do (most commonly used of birds but also of crabs, serpents, etc).—*vt* to shed or cast, as feathers, hair, skin, etc.—*n* the act of moulting; the shedding or changing of feathers.

mound *n* an elevation of earth, generally artificial; a rampart; a hillock or knoll.

mount *n* a hill; a mountain, now chiefly poetical or used in proper names, as Mount Vesuvius, Mount Sinai; a bulwark for offence or defence; the cardboard or other material on which a picture or drawing is mounted or fixed; the setting of a gem or something similar; a horse, etc, for riding; the opportunity or means of riding on horseback.—*vi* to rise on high; to go up; to ascend; to be built to a great altitude; to get on or upon anything, specifically, to get on horseback; to amount; to reach in value.—*vt* to raise aloft; to ascend; to climb up to or upon; to place oneself on (a throne, etc); to furnish with a horse or horses; to put on or cover with something necessary, useful or ornamental (*to mount a map on cloth*); to prepare for use; to carry or be furnished with (*a fort mounts a hundred cannon*).

mountain *n* a huge mass of earth and rock rising above the common level of the earth or adjacent land; an elevated mass higher than a hill; something very large or great.—*adj* pertaining to a mountain; found on mountains; growing or dwelling on a mountain.

mountain ash *n* the rowan tree.

mountaineer *n* an inhabitant of a mountainous district; a climber of mountains.

mountainous *adj* full of mountains; diversified by many mountains; large as a mountain; huge.

mountebank *n* a quack doctor; any boastful and false pretender; a charlatan.

mouse

mouth organ

mounting *n* the act of ascending; that with which an article is mounted or set off or finished for use, as the setting of a gem, the furnishings of a sword, the cardboard on which a picture is pasted, etc.

mourn *vi* to express grief or sorrow; to grieve; to be sorrowful; to lament; to wear the dress or appearance of grief.—*vt* to grieve for; to lament; to deplore; to bewail.

mourner *n* one that mourns; one that follows a funeral in the habit of mourning.

mournful *adj* expressing sorrow; exhibiting the appearance of grief; doleful; causing sorrow; sad; calamitous; sorrowful; feeling grief.

mourning *n* the act of expressing grief; lamentation; the dress or customary habit worn by mourners.

mouse *n* (*pl* **mice**) a well-known small rodent quadruped that infests dwelling houses, granaries, fields, etc; a name of various allied animals; a term of endearment; a hand-held device used to position the cursor and control software on a computer screen.—*vi* (**moused, mousing**) to hunt for or catch mice.

mouser *n* one that catches mice; a cat good at catching mice.

mousse *n* a light fluffy desert made with cream, eggs, gelatine and flavouring; a foamy substance sold in a spray for cosmetic purposes, such as hair styling.

moustache *n* the hair on the upper lip of men; the unshaven hair of the upper lip (often plural).

Mousterian, Moustierian *adj* of an intermediate stage of Palaeolithic culture.

mousy, mousey *adj* mouse-like; grey-brown in colour; dull; timid; quiet.

mouth *n* (*pl* **mouths**) the aperture in the head of an animal through which food is received and voice uttered; the aperture between the lips or the portion of the face formed by the lips; the cavity within the lips; the opening of anything hollow, as of a pitcher or other vessel; the entrance to a cave, pit or den, the opening of a well, etc; the part of a river, creek, etc, by which it joins with the ocean or any large body of water.—*vt* to utter with a voice affectedly big or swelling; to seize or shake with the mouth.—*vi* to speak with a full, round or loud, affected voice; to vociferate; to rant; to make wry faces; to grimace.

mouthful *n* as much as the mouth contains at once; a small quantity.

mouth organ *n* a small popular wind instrument, flat in shape, with openings for the various notes, which are produced by inhalation and exhalation.

mouthpiece *n* the part of a musical instrument, tobacco pipe, etc, that is applied to the mouth; one who speaks on behalf of others.

mouth-to-mouth resuscitation a method of artificial respiration in which a person blows into the patient's mouth in order to force air into his/her lungs.

movable, moveable *adj* capable of being moved; changing from one time to another (*a movable feast*, that is, a feast or festival like Easter, the time for holding which varies within certain limits).—*n* any part of a person's goods capable of being moved; (*pl*) goods, wares, commodities, furniture.

move *vt* (**moved, moving**) to carry, convey or draw from one place to another; to cause to change place or posture; to set in motion; to stir; to excite into action; to influence; to prevail on; to rouse or excite the feelings of; to make an impression on; to affect, usually with tender feelings; to touch; to stir up; to awaken (laughter, terror); to offer formally, as a motion for consideration by a deliberative assembly; in chess, draughts, etc, to change the position of (a piece) in the regular course of play.—*vi* to change place or posture; to stir; to pass or go; to walk; to carry or bear oneself; to change residence; to take action; to begin to act; in chess, draughts, etc, to change the position of one of the pieces in the course of play.—*n* proceeding; action taken; the moving of a piece in playing chess, etc.

moveable *adj, n* same as **movable**.

movement *n* act of moving; course or process of change; motion; an individual act of motion; a gesture; an agitation set on foot by one or more persons for the purpose of bringing about some result desired; (*mus*) motion or progression in time, also a detached and independent portion of a composition; the train of wheel work in a watch or clock.

mover *n* one who or that which gives motion; one who or that which is in motion; one that offers a motion in an assembly; a driving force; an active person.

movie *n* a cinema film; a motion picture.

moving *adj* causing to move or act; impelling; exciting the feelings; touching; pathetic; affecting.

mow *vt* (*pret* **mowed**, *pp* **mowed** *or* **mown**, *ppr* **mowing**) to cut down with a scythe or mowing machine (*to mow grass*); to cut the grass from (*to mow a meadow*); to cut down (people, etc) indiscriminately or in great numbers or quantity.—*vi* to cut grass; to use the scythe or mowing machine.

mower *n* one who mows; a mowing machine.

MP abbreviation of **Member of Parliament**.

Mr abbreviation of **Mister**.

MS, MSS abbreviation of **manuscript**, **manuscripts**.

much *adj* (**more** and **most** serve as its *compar* and *superl*) great in quantity or amount; abundant; used with singular nouns (*much food, seed, water, money*, etc).—*adv* in a great degree; to a great amount or extent; greatly (used especially with comparatives and past participles, as *much better, larger, sooner, surprised*, etc); nearly (*much as it was*).—*n* a great quantity; a great deal; equivalent to an adjective with a noun omitted and often qualified by *too, as* and *so*.

mucilage *n* a gummy vegetable matter contained in gum tragacanth, many seeds, roots, etc; a solution in water of gummy matter of any kind.

mucilaginous *adj* pertaining to or secreting mucilage; slimy; ropy; soft and slightly viscid.

muck *n* dung in a moist state or a mass of dung and rotten vegetable matter; something mean, vile or filthy.

mucus *n* a viscid fluid secreted by the mucous membrane of animals, which it serves to moisten and defend; (*bot*) gummy matter soluble in water.

mucous, mucose *adj* pertaining to or resembling mucus; slimy; ropy; secreting a slimy substance.

mucous membrane *n* a membrane that lines all the cavities of the body which open externally (such as the mouth, nose, intestines) and secretes mucus.

mud *n* wet and soft earth or earthy matter as in a puddle; sediment from turbid waters; mire.

muddle *vt* (**muddled, muddling**) to intoxicate partially; to cloud or stupefy, particularly with liquor; to bring into a state of confusion; to make a mess of.—*vi* to become muddy; to be in a confused state.—*n* a mess; dirty confusion; intellectual confusion; bewilderment.

muddy *adj* abounding in mud; foul with mud; turbid; miry; cloudy in mind; confused; stupid; obscure; lacking in perspicuity.—*vt* (**muddied, muddying**) to soil with mud; to dirty; to make turbid; to cloud or make dull.

mudguard *n* a guard over the wheel of a vehicle serving as a protection against mud.

mudguard

muesli *n* a breakfast food consisting of whole-grain cereals, nuts and dried fruit.

muezzin *n* a Muslim crier attached to a mosque, whose duty it is to proclaim from the balcony of a minaret the summons to prayers five times a day.

muff *n* a cylindrical cover, usually made of fur, into which both hands may be thrust in order to keep them warm; a soft, useless fellow; a mean, poor-spirited person.

muffin *n* a light round spongy cake.

muffle *vt* (**muffled, muffling**) to wrap up so

as to conceal from view or protect from the weather; to wrap up or cover close, particularly the neck and face; to deaden the sound of (*to muffle an oar* or *a drum*); to restrain from speaking by wrapping up the head; to put to silence; (*fig*) to wrap up or envelop; to involve.—*n* an arched vessel, resisting the strongest fire and made to be placed over cupels in the operation of assaying, to preserve them from coming in contact with fuel, smoke or ashes; a pulley block containing several sheaves.

muffler *n* a wrapper for muffling or enveloping the neck and often also the face.

mufti *n* civilian dress.

Mufti *n* the chief of the ecclesiastical order among Muslims; a doctor of Islamic law.

mug[1] *n* an earthenware, porcelain or metal cylindrical vessel for drinking from.

mug[2] *n* (*sl*) the face or mouth; a fool; a dupe.

mug[3] *vt* (**mugged, mugging**) to attack violently, usually with intent to rob.

mugger *n* a person who mugs someone.

muggy *adj* damp and close (said of the atmosphere or weather); warm and humid; moist; mouldy.

mugwump *n* a person who takes an independent position in politics or any question; a highly superior person in his or her own eyes.

mulatto *n* (*pl* **mulattos, mulattoes**) a person with one Black and one White parent.

mulberry *n* the berry or fruit of a well-known tree and also the tree itself, long cultivated for silkworm rearing.

mulch *n* a moist mixture of straw and organic material spread around the roots of newly planted shrubs or trees, etc, to protect and fertilize them.—*vt* to cover with mulch.

mulct *n* a fine or penalty imposed on a person guilty of some offence or misdemeanour, usually a fine.—*vt* to punish by fine or forfeiture; to punish by depriving; to deprive (*to mulct a person of* or *in £300*).

mule *n* the offspring of a male donkey and a female horse as distinct from a hinny; also any animal produced by a mixture of different species; a hybrid; a hybrid plant; a machine for spinning cotton; an obstinate person.

muleteer *n* a mule driver

mulish *adj* like a mule; sullen; stubborn.

muliebrity *n* womanhood; the qualities of womanhood.

mull[1] *vti* to ponder (over); to reflect or consider.

mull[2] *vt* to heat, sweeten and flavour with spices (*to mull wine*).

mull[3] *n* (*Scots*) a cape or promontory.

mull[4] *n* dust or rubbish; a muddle; a mess.

mullah, mollah *n* a Muslim title of respect; a Muslim religious teacher or theologian.

mug

mullet

mullein *n* the common name of a genus of wild plants used in domestic medicine.

mullet *n* either of two spiny-rayed fishes of two somewhat widely separate families, the grey mullet and the red mullet.

mulligatawny *n* an Indian curry soup.

mullion *n* (*archit*) a vertical division between the lights of windows, screens, etc, in Gothic architecture; also a division between the panels in wainscoting.

mullioned *adj* having mullions.

multifarious *adj* having great multiplicity; having great diversity or variety; made up of many differing parts.

multifoil *adj* (*archit*) having more than five foils or divisions (*a multifoil arch*).

multiform *adj* having many forms, shapes or appearances; (*math*) having more than one value, opposite of *uniform*.

multiformity *n* the state of being multiform.

multilateral *adj* having many sides; polygonal; with several nations or participants (*multilateral talks*).

multilingual *adj* in many languages; speaking many languages.

multimillionaire *n* a person with two or more millions of money.

multinational *adj* (of a company) operating in several countries.—*n* a multinational company.

multiparous *adj* producing many at a birth.

multipartite *adj* divided into several or many parts.

multiple *adj* manifold; having many parts or divisions.—*n* a number which contains another an exact number of times without a remainder; a common multiple of two or more numbers containing each of them a certain number of times exactly (thus *24 is a common multiple of 3 and 4*); the least common multiple being the smallest number that will do this (thus *12 is the least common multiple of 3 and 4*).

multiple sclerosis *n* a disease causing progressive deterioration of the nervous system.

multiplex *n adj* manifold; complex; (*bot*) having petals lying over each other in folds.

multipliable *adj* capable of being multiplied.

multiplicand *n* (*arith*) the number to be multiplied by another, which is called the *multiplier*.

multiplication *n* the act or process of multiplying; the state of being multiplied; (*arith, alg*) the operation by which any given number or quantity may be added to itself any number of times proposed.

multiplication table *n* a table containing the product of all the simple digits multiplied into each other and onwards, to some assumed limit, as to 12 times 12.

multiplicative *adj* tending to multiply; having the power to multiply.

multiplicator *n* a multiplier.

multiplicity *n* the state of being multiplex, numerous or various; an extensive aggregate of individuals of the same kind; a great number.

multiplier *n* one who or that which multiplies; the number in arithmetic by which another is multiplied; (*physics*) an instrument for increasing an effect, strength, etc.

multiply *vt* (**multiplied, multiplying**) to increase in number; to make more by natural reproduction or by addition; to make more numerous; (*arith*) to add to itself any given number of times.—*vi* to grow or increase in number or to become more numerous by reproduction; to extend; to spread.

multipurpose *adj* having several purposes or uses.

multiracial *adj* of or involving different racial groups.

multistorey *adj* having several storeys.

multitude *n* the state of being many; a great number, collectively; a great many, indefinitely; a crowd or throng; a gathering of people.—**the multitude** the populace or the mass of people without reference to an assemblage.

multitudinous *adj* pertaining or belonging to a multitude; consisting of a multitude.

mum[1] *n* (*colloq*) mother.

mum[2] *adj* silent; not speaking.—*n* silence (*mum's the word*).

mum[3] *vi* to mask; to sport or make diversion in a mask or disguise.

mumble *vi* (**mumbled, mumbling**) to mutter; to speak so as to render the sounds inarticulate and imperfect; to chew or bite softly; to eat with the lips close.—*vt* to utter with a low inarticulate voice; to chew gently or to eat with a muttering sound.

mumbler *n* one who mumbles.

mumbo jumbo *n* meaningless ritual, talk, etc.

mummer *n* a masker; a masked buffoon.

mummery *n* a masking or masquerade; buffoonery; farcical show; hypocritical disguise and parade.

mummification *n* the act of mummifying; the process of becoming a mummy.

mummify *vt* (**mummified, mummifying**) to make into a mummy; to embalm and dry, as a mummy.

mummy[1] *n* (*colloq*) mother.

mummy[2] *n* a dead human body embalmed and dried after the manner of those taken from Egyptian tombs; a human body dried up and preserved, either artificially or by accident.

mumps *npl* a disease consisting in an inflammation of the salivary glands, with swelling along the neck; parotitis.

munch *vti* to chew audibly or steadily; to nibble.

mundane *adj* belonging to this world; worldly; terrestrial; earthly; ordinary; banal.

municipal *adj* pertaining to local self-government; pertaining to the corporation of a town or city or to the citizens of a state.

municipality *n* a town or city possessed of local self-government; a community under municipal jurisdiction.

municipal law *n* the law which pertains to the citizens of a state in their private capacity.

munificence *n* the quality of being munificent; a giving with great liberality; bounty; liberality.

munificent *adj* liberal in giving or bestowing; bounteous; generous.

muniment *n* a fortification; a stronghold; support; defence; a writing by which claims and rights are defended or maintained; a title deed, charter, record, etc.

munition *n* materials used in war; military stores; ammunition; material for any enterprise (usually plural).

mural *adj* pertaining to a wall; resembling a wall; perpendicular or steep.—*n* a picture or design painted directly onto a wall.

murder *n* the act of unlawfully killing a human being with premeditated malice, the person committing the act being of sound mind.—*vt* to kill (a human being) with premeditated malice; to slay feloniously; (*fig*) to abuse or violate grossly (*to murder the King's English*).

murderer *n* a person who commits murder.

murderess *n* a female who commits murder.

murderous *adj* pertaining to murder; guilty of murder; accompanied or marked by murder; bloody.

murex *n* (*pl* **murices**) a mollusc resembling the whelk, valued from the earliest ages on account of the purple dye that some of them yielded; the dye itself.

muriatic *adj* pertaining to or obtained from brine or sea salt.

murk *n* darkness or gloom.

murkiness *n* state of being murky; darkness; gloom.

murky *adj* dark; obscure; gloomy.

murmur *n* a low sound continued or continually repeated, as that of a stream; a low indistinct sound; a hum; a complaint uttered in a low muttering voice; a grumble or mutter.—*vi* to utter or give out a murmur or hum; to grumble; to utter complaints; to mutter.—*vt* to utter indistinctly; to mutter.

murmuring *n* a continued murmur; a low confused noise.

murrain *n* a disease among cattle; a cattle plague or epizootic disease of any kind; foot and mouth disease.

murrey *n* a dark-red or mulberry colour.

mummy

muscat *n* a kind of sweet white grape used in making wine.

muscatel *n* a kind of sweet wine made from the muscat grape.

muscle *n* fibrous tissue in the body that contracts and relaxes, serving to cause motion and the exertion of power; strength; power.—*vi* (**muscled, muscling**) to force one's way (in).

muscle-bound *adj* having some of the muscles abnormally enlarged and lacking elasticity, caused by excessive exercise; inflexible; rigid.

Muscovite *n* a native of Moscow; (*arch*) a native of Russia.

muscular *adj* pertaining to or consisting of muscles (*muscular fibre* or *tissue*, that which forms the substance of muscles); performed by or dependent on muscles (*muscular exertion*); having well-developed muscles; strong; brawny.

muscular dystrophy *n* a genetic disease characterized by progressive degeneration of the muscles.

muse[1] *vi* (**mused, musing**) to ponder; to think or meditate in silence; to be absent in mind.—*vt* to think or meditate on.—*n* a fit of abstraction.

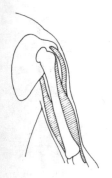

muscle

muse[2] *n* a power or spirit presiding over an art or science; poetic inspiration.

Muse *n* in Greek myth, one of the daughters of Zeus and Mnemosyne, who presided over the different kinds of poetry and the sciences and arts, nine in number: Clio (history), Thalia (comedy), Melpomene (tragedy), Calliope (epic poetry), Euterpe, Terpsichore, Erato, Polymnia and Urania.

musing *adj* meditative; absent-minded.—*n* meditation; absent-mindedness.

museum *n* a building for displaying interesting objects connected with history, literature, art or science; a cabinet of curiosities; a collection of objects in natural history.

mush *n* the meal of maize boiled in water.

mushroom *n* the common name of numerous fungi, especially such as are edible.—*adj* pertaining to mushrooms; resembling mushrooms in rapidity of growth.—*vi* to gather mushrooms; to spread quickly.

mushroom spawn *n* the reproductive matter or mycelium of mushrooms.

mushroom

music *n* a succession of sounds so modulated as to please the ear; melody or harmony; the science of harmonic sounds; the art of producing melody or harmony; the written or printed score of a composition; an agreeable sound.

musical *adj* belonging to music; producing music or agreeable sounds; melodious; harmonious; fond of or skilled in music.—*n* a play or film incorporating dialogue, singing and dancing.

musical box *n* a small instrument, having a toothed barrel operating on vibrating tongues, which plays one or more tunes on being wound up.

musician *n* a person skilled in music; one that sings or performs on instruments of music.

music master *n* one who teaches music.

music stand *n* a light frame for placing pieces of music on while being played.

music stool *n* a stool for one who performs on a piano or similar instrument.

musk *n* a substance obtained from a cyst or bag near the navel of the musk deer, with a strong odour, used in making perfume; a synthetic form of this; a musky smell; a plant with a similar smell.

musk beaver *n* the muskrat.

musk deer *n* a deer of Central Asia, the male of which has long tusks and yields musk.

musk duck *n* a duck with a musky smell.

musket *n* a general term formerly used for any handgun employed for military purposes.

musketeer *n* a soldier armed with a musket.

musketry *n* the art or science of firing small arms.

muskiness *n* the quality of being musky; the scent of musk.

musk ox *n* a kind of small hardy ox which inhabits the extreme north of North America and smells strongly of musk.

muskrat *n* an American rodent allied to the beaver, which smells of musk in summer, called also musquash; the name is also given to two insectivorous animals smelling of musk.

musk rose *n* a species of rose, so called from its fragrance.

musky *adj* having the odour of musk.

Muslim, Moslem *n* an adherent of Islam.—*adj* of Islam, its adherents and culture.

muslin *n* a fine thin cotton fabric, of which there are many different kinds.—*adj* made of muslin (*a muslin gown*).

musquash *n* a muskrat; the fur of the muskrat.

mussel *n* the common name of a genus of bivalve shellfish, one species of which is largely used for food.

Mussulman *n* (*pl* **Mussulmen, Mussulmans**) (*arch*) a Muslim.

must[1] *vi* (without inflection and used as a present or a past tense) a defective or auxiliary verb expressing obligation or necessity, physical or moral; or often merely expressing the conviction of the speaker (*you must be wrong*).

must[2] *n* wine or juice pressed from the grape but not fermented.

mustang *n* the wild horse of America, a descendant of horses imported.

mustard *n* an annual plant extensively cultivated for its pungent seeds, which, when ground, form the condiment of the same name; a paste made from the powdered seeds and used as a condiment.

mustard gas *n* a poisonous oily liquid used in warfare which evaporates very slowly as a gas and produces serious effects on the skin, eyes and lungs.

musteline *adj* pertaining to the weasel and related animals.

muster *vt* to collect, as troops for service, review, parade or exercise; to assemble or bring together generally; to summon (as courage); to collect for use or exhibition.—*vi* to assemble or meet in one place, as soldiers.—*n* an assembling of troops for review or for service; the act of assembling; an assemblage.—**to pass muster** to pass without censure, as one among a number on inspection; to be allowed to pass.

muster roll *n* a roll or register of the people in each company, troop or regiment; a roll or register of a ship's crew.

musty *adj* mouldy; turned sour; fusty; stale; spoiled by age; having an ill flavour; vapid.

mutable *adj* capable of being altered; subject to change; changeable; inconstant in mind or feelings; unsettled; unstable; variable.

mutability *n* the state of being mutable; changeability; inconstancy; instability; fickleness.

mutant *n* a mutation; an organism whose structure has undergone mutation.—*adj* mutating.

mutate *vi* (**mutated, mutating**) to experience alteration or change; to undergo mutation.—*vt* to cause to experience alteration or change.

mutation *n* the act or process of changing; change; alteration; modification; (*philol*) umlaut; (*biol*) a sudden change in some inheritable characteristic of a species.

mute[1] *adj* silent; not speaking; incapable of utterance; not having the power of speech; dumb; (*gram, philol*) silent, not pronounced or having its sound suddenly and completely checked by a contact of the vocal organs (applied to certain consonants, as *t, p*).—*n* a dumb person; one unable to use articulate speech; an actor in a dumb show; a hired attendant at a funeral; (*gram, philol*) a mute letter; (*mus*) a utensil applied to a musical instrument to deaden or soften the sounds.—*vt* (**muted, muting**) to deaden the sound of (a musical instrument).

mute[2] *vi* (of birds) to eject the contents of the bowels.

mutilate *vt* (**mutilated, mutilating**) to cut off a limb or essential part of; to maim; to remove any material part from so as to render the thing imperfect.

mutilation *n* the act of mutilating or state of being mutilated.

mutineer *n* one guilty of mutiny.

mutinous *adj* engaged in or disposed to mutiny.

mutiny *n* a resistance to or revolt against constituted authority; specifically, an insurrection of soldiers or naval crew against the authority of their commanders; open resistance to officers or opposition to their authority.—*vi* (**mutinied, mutinying**) to engage in mutiny; to rise against military or naval officers; to be guilty of mutinous conduct.

mutter *vi* to utter words with a low voice and compressed lips; to grumble; to murmur; to sound with a low rumbling noise.—*vt* to utter with a low murmuring voice.

mutton *n* the flesh of sheep, raw or dressed for food.

mutual *adj* reciprocally given and received; pertaining alike or reciprocally to both sides; interchanged; equally relating to, affecting, proceeding from two or more together; common to two or more combined; shared alike.

mutually *adv* in a mutual manner; reciprocally; conjointly; in common.

muzziness *n* the state of being muzzy.

muzzle *n* the projecting mouth and nose of an animal, as of a horse, dog, etc; the open end of a gun or pistol, etc; a fastening for the mouth which hinders an animal from biting.—*vt* (**muzzled, muzzling**) to put a muzzle on; to bind the mouth of, to prevent biting or eating; to put to silence.

muzzle-loader *n* a gun loaded by the muzzle, opposed to *breech-loader*.

muzzy *adj* confused; bewildered; tipsy; blurred; hazy.

my *pronominal adj* belonging to me (*this is my book*), always used before a noun or attributively, *mine* being used predicatively (*this book is mine*).

mycelium *n* (*pl* **mycelia**) a cellular spawn of fungi, consisting of whitish filaments spreading like a network.

mycology *n* that department of botany which investigates fungi.

myelitis *n* (*med*) inflammation of the substance of the brain or spinal marrow.

myography *n* a description of the muscles of the body; myology

myology *n* the scientific knowledge or description of the muscles of the human body.

myopia *n* short-sightedness.

myopic *adj* pertaining to or affected with myopia.

myosin *n* a constituent of muscle.

myosotis *n* the plant forget-me-not.

myriad *n* the number of ten thousand collectively; an immense number indefi-

muzzle

nitely.—*adj* innumerable; multitudinous; manifold.

myriapod *n* an individual belonging to the class of animals that includes the centipedes and millipedes, having bodies of a lengthened form and in numerous segments, each segment being provided with one pair of feet.

myrmecophilous *adj* (of an organism) protected by ants, to which it affords food and shelter.

myrobalan *n* an Asian tree with edible yellow or red fruit; its fruit, which when dried was formerly used in medicine, dyeing and tanning; the dye from such fruit.

myrrh *n* the gummy resin exuded by a spiny shrub of Arabia, India and eastern Africa, used in perfume, incense, etc; a European plant with fern-like foliage and large umbels of white flowers; sweet cicely.

myrtle *n* an evergreen shrub of the south of Europe having buds and berries that yield a volatile oil, while the distilled flowers yield a perfume.

myself *pron* (*pl* **ourselves**) as a nominative it is used, generally after *I*, to express emphasis and mark distinction; I and not another (in the objective often used reflexively and without any emphasis).

myriapod

mystagogue *n* one who instructs in or interprets mysteries.

mystagogy *n* the practice or doctrines of a mystagogue; the interpretation of mysteries.

mysterious *adj* partaking of or containing mystery; not revealed or explained; unintelligible; beyond human comprehension; occult; enigmatic.

mystery *n* something hidden from human knowledge and fitted to inspire a sense of awe; something incomprehensible through being above human intelligence; something intentionally kept hidden; a secret; an enigma; a species of dramatic performance in the Middle Ages, the characters and events of which were drawn from sacred history.

mystic *n* one who is addicted to mysticism.

mystical *adj* hidden from or obscure to human knowledge or comprehension; involving some secret meaning or import; mysterious; occult; pertaining to the ancient mysteries; pertaining to mystics or mysticism.

mysticism *n* views or tendencies in religion which aspire towards a communication between human beings and his or her Maker through the inward perception of the mind, more direct than that which is afforded us through revelation; a seeking to solve the mysteries of existence by internal illumination or special revelation; a dreamy contemplation on ideas that have no foundation in human experience.

mystification *n* the act of mystifying or state of being mystified.

mystify *vt* (**mystified, mystifying**) to perplex purposely; to play on the credulity of; to bewilder; to befog.

myth *n* a fable or legend of natural evolution, embodying the convictions of a people as to their gods or other divine personages, their own origin and early history and the heroes connected with it, the origin of the world, etc; in a looser sense, an invented story; something purely fabulous or having no existence in fact; a fictitious event.

mythic, mythical *adj* relating to myths; described in a myth; fabulous; fabled; fictitious.

mythological, mythologic *adj* relating to mythology; proceeding from mythology; of the nature of a myth; fabulous.

mythologist *n* one versed in mythology; a student of myths.

mythology *n* the science or doctrine of myths; the myths of a people or nation collectively.

mythopoeic *adj* myth-making; producing or tending to produce myths; suggesting or giving rise to myths.

myxoedema *n* a disease due to deficient secretion of the thyroid gland.

N

N the fourteenth letter and the eleventh consonant of the English alphabet.

nab *vt* (**nabbed, nabbing**) (*colloq*) to catch or seize suddenly or unexpectedly.

nabob *n* a governor of a province or commander of an army in India under the Mogul empire; a very wealthy person.

nacelle *n* the crew, cargo or engine housing area of an aircraft.

nacre *n* mother-of-pearl.

nacreous *adj* consisting of or resembling nacre or mother-of-pearl.

nadir *n* that point of the heavens or lower hemisphere directly opposite the zenith; the point directly underneath; (*fig*) the lowest point; the point or time of extreme depression.

naevus *n* (*pl* **naevi**) a natural mark, spot or blemish on the skin of a person; a birthmark.

nag[1] *vti* (**nagged, nagging**) to scold constantly; to find fault constantly.

nag[2] *n* a small horse; (*colloq*) any worn-out horse.

nagana *n* a disease transmitted by the tsetse fly.

naiad *n* (*pl* **naiads, naiades**) in Greek myth, a water nymph; a female divinity that presides over rivers and springs.

nail *n* the horny scale growing at the end of the human fingers and toes; a similar appendage in the lower animals; a claw; a small pointed piece of metal with some sort of a head used for driving through or into timber or other material for the purpose of holding separate pieces together or left projecting so that things may be hung on it; a stud or boss.—**to hit the nail on the head** to hit or touch the exact point (in a figurative sense).—*vt* to fasten with nails; to drive nails into; to stud with nails; to fix firmly; (*colloq*) to arrest.

naïve *adj* ingenuous; artless; showing candour or simplicity; unsophisticated.

naïveté *n* unaffected ingenuousness; artlessness; lack of sophistication.

naked *adj* not having clothes on; bare; nude; not having a covering, especially a customary covering (*a naked sword*); (*bot*) not having a calyx; not enclosed in a pod, etc; (*zool*) not having a calcareous shell; (*fig*) open to view; not concealed; manifest; unarmed; defenceless; (of the eye) without optical aid (*naked eye*).

nakedness *n* the state of being naked; nudity; bareness; plainness.

namby-pamby *adj* affectedly pretty; weakly sentimental; insipid; vapid (*namby-pamby sentiment, rhymes*).—*n* a namby-pamby person; an affected person.

name *n* that by which a person or thing is called or designated, in distinction from other persons or things; appellation; reputation; character (*one's good* or *bad name*); renown; fame; eminence; the mere word by which anything is called; sound only; not reality; authority; behalf; persons having a certain name.—*vt* (**named, naming**) to give a name or distinctive appellation to; to denominate; to mention by name; to nominate; to designate for any purpose by name; to pronounce to be; to speak of or mention as; to specify, as a date for an appointment.

name-drop *vi* to indulge in name-dropping.

name-dropper *n* one who name-drops.

name-dropping *n* the practice or habit of mentioning the names of well-known or influential people as if they were personal friends in order to try to impress others.

nameless *adj* without a name or appellation; not known to fame; obscure; that cannot or ought not to be named; inexpressible.

namely *adv* to mention by name; to particularize; that is to say.

namesake *n* one who or that which has the same name as another; one named after another for that other's sake.

nankeen *n* a sort of cotton cloth, usually of a yellowish colour, originally manufactured and imported from Nankin in China.

nanny *n* a child's nurse; a person employed to look after a young child.

nanny goat *n* a female domestic goat.

nap[1] *vi* (**napped, napping**) to have a short sleep; to drowse; to be in a careless, secure state.—*n* a short sleep or slumber.

nap[2] *n* the woolly substance on the surface

nail

of cloth, etc; the pile, as of a hat; what resembles this, as the downy substance on some plants.

nap³ *n* a game at cards.

napalm *n* a jelly-like incendiary substance mixed with petrol and used in bombs, flame-throwers, etc.

nape *n* the back part of the neck; the prominent part of the neck behind.

napery *n* a collective term for linen cloths used for domestic purposes, especially for the table.

naphtha *n* a variety of bitumen, fluid, inflammable, emitting a strong odour and generally of a yellow colour, used as a source of light, as a solvent, etc.

naphthalene *n* a white crystalline solid formed during the distillation of coal for gas or obtained by redistilling coal tar, used in making dyes, explosives, etc.

napkin *n* a cloth used for wiping the hands or mouth at table.

napoleon *n* formerly, a French gold coin worth 20 francs.

nappy *n* a piece of towelling or absorbent paper pad arranged between a baby's legs and fastened at the waist, used to absorb urine and faeces.

narcissism *n* an excessive interest in one's own appearance or interests.

narcissistic *adj* pertaining to or affected by narcissism; excessively interested in one's own appearance and interests.

narcissus *n* (*pl* **narcissuses, narcissi**) any of an extensive genus of bulbous plants with bright and fragrant flowers, including the daffodil, jonquil, etc.

narcolepsy *n* a disease characterized by uncontrollable fits of deep sleep.

narcoleptic *adj* pertaining to narcolepsy; suffering from narcolepsy.

narcosis *n* a state of unconsciousness or drowsiness induced by narcotics.

narcotic *adj* having the properties of a narcotic.—*n* a substance, often addictive, which relieves pain, produces sleep and in large doses brings on stupor, coma and even death, as opium, hemlock, alcohol, etc; (loosely) any illegal drug.

nard *n* a plant, same as spikenard; an unguent prepared from the plant.

narghile *n* a kind of Oriental tobacco pipe or smoking apparatus in which the smoke is passed through water.

nark *n* (*sl*) an informer, especially a police informer.—*vi* to nag.—*vt* to nag; to irritate.

narrate *vt* (**narrated, narrating**) to tell or recite, as a story; to relate the particulars of in speech or writing; to provide a spoken commentary for (a television programme, film, etc).

narration *n* the act of narrating; that which is related; a narrative.

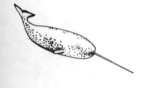

narwhal

nasturtium

narrative *adj* pertaining to narration.—*n* that which is narrated or related; a relation or narration; a relation in words or writing of the particulars of any transaction or event.

narrator *n* one who narrates or produces a narrative.

narrow *adj* of little breadth; having little distance from side to side; of little extent; limited or contracted; limited as to means; straitened; contracted in mind; of confined views; bigoted; not liberal or bountiful; niggardly; near; within but a little; hence, barely sufficient to avoid evil, etc (*a narrow escape*, *majority*); close; scrutinizing.—*n* a narrow channel of water between one sea or lake and another; a strait or sound (usually in the plural).—*vt* to make narrow or contracted, literally or figuratively.—*vi* to become narrow or narrower.

narrowly *adv* in a narrow manner; contractedly; sparingly; closely; rigorously; nearly; within a little.

narrow-minded *adj* of confined views or sentiments; illiberal; prejudiced; intolerant.

narrowness *n* the quality or condition of being narrow; illiberality; lack of tolerant views.

narwhal *n* an Arctic whale with no teeth except two canines in the upper jaw of which one is frequently developed into a long projecting tusk.

nasal *adj* pertaining to the nose; uttered through the nose or through both the nose and mouth simultaneously.—*n* a sound uttered through or partly through the nose.

nasally *adv* in a nasal manner; by or through the nose.

nascent *adj* beginning to exist or to grow; coming into being; arising.

nastiness *n* the quality of being nasty or what is nasty; filthiness; filthy matter; obscenity.

nasturtium *n* any of a group of garden plants with yellow, red or orange flowers, a pungent odour and edible leaves.

nasty *adj* filthy; dirty; indecent; obscene; disgusting to taste or smell; disagreeable; troublesome.

natal *adj* pertaining to one's birth; dating from one's birth.

natant *adj* floating on the surface of water; swimming, as the leaf of an aquatic plant.

natation *n* the art or act of swimming.

natatorial *adj* swimming or adapted to swimming.

natatory *adj* enabling to swim; adapted for swimming; natatorial.

nation *n* a people inhabiting a certain extent of territory and united by common political institutions; an aggregation of persons speaking the same or a cognate language.

national *adj* pertaining to a nation; common to a whole people or race; public; general.—*n* a citizen or subject of a specific country.

national anthem *n* a patriotic song or hymn adopted officially by a nation and sung on certain public and ceremonial occasions.

nationalism *n* nationality; a national idiom or trait; patriotic sentiments, principles, etc; strong attachment to one's own nation or countrymen; a policy of national independence or self-government; chauvinism.

nationalist *n* a supporter of nationalism.

nationality *n* the qualities that distinguish a nation; national character; the people constituting a nation; a nation; a race of people; separate existence as a nation; national unity and integrity.

nationalize *vt* (**nationalized, nationalizing**) to make national; to make the common property of the nation as a whole; to give the character of a distinct nation.

national park *n* a very large tract of land preserved in its natural state as an area of wildlife conservation.

nation-state *n* a sovereign state containing a relatively homogeneous population.

native *adj* pertaining to the place or circumstances of one's birth; being the scene of one's origin (*our native land*); conferred by birth; belonging to one's nature or constitution; not artificial or acquired; occurring in nature pure or unmixed with other substances (said of mineral bodies, as iron or silver when found almost pure).—*n* one born in a place or country and not a foreigner or immigrant; an indigenous plant or animal.

nativity *n* a coming into life or the world; birth; the circumstances attending birth

Nativity *n* the birth of Christ; a picture representing the birth of Christ.

natron *n* native carbonate of soda, or mineral alkali, found in the ashes of several marine plants, in some lakes and mineral springs.

natter *vi* (*colloq*) to chatter; to gossip.—*n* a chat; a gossip.

natterjack *n* a species of English toad.

natty *adj* neat; tidy; spruce.

natural *adj* pertaining to nature; produced by nature; not artificial, acquired or assumed (*natural colour, strength, heat*); in conformity with the laws of nature; regulated by the laws which govern events, actions, sentiments, etc (*a natural enemy, supposition*); happening in the ordinary course of things (*the natural consequence*); connected with the existing physical system of things or creation at large (*natural philosophy, laws*, etc); according to life and reality; without affectation or artificiality (*he was always natural*); born out of wedlock; bastard; in a state of nature; unregenerate; (*mus*) a term applied to the diatonic or normal scale of C.—*n* one born without the usual powers of reason or understanding; an idiot; a fool; (*mus*) a sign indicating that a sharpened note is to be made a semitone lower and a flattened one a semitone higher; such a note.

natural childbirth *n* childbirth using natural techniques, such as relaxation, controlled breathing, etc, rather than the use of pain-killing drugs.

natural gas *n* a mixture of hydrocarbon gases, usually containing methane, found under the earth or sea bed near oil fields and used as fuel and in making organic compounds.

natural history *n* the study of nature, especially the animal, vegetable and mineral world.

naturalist *n* a person who studies or is expert in natural science or natural history.

naturalization *n* the act of naturalizing; the act of investing an alien with the rights and privileges of a natural subject.

naturalize *vt* (**naturalized, naturalizing**) to confer the rights and privileges of a native subject or citizen on; to accustom to a climate; to acclimatize; to adopt as native or vernacular (*to naturalize foreign words*).

naturally *adv* in a natural manner; according to nature; not by art or habit; without affectation; according to the usual course of things; spontaneously; without cultivation.

naturalness *n* the state of being natural; conformity to nature; absence of affectation.

natural philosophy *n* the study of nature and the physical universe, especially studies that led to the science of physics; an old term for the physical sciences, especially physics.

natural selection *n* that process in nature by which plants and animals best fitted for the conditions in which they are placed survive, propagate and spread, while the less fitted die out and disappear; survival of the fittest.

nature *n* the universe; the system of things of which human beings are a part; the world of matter or of matter and mind; the creation, especially that part of it by which human beings are more immediately surrounded; often also the agent, author or producer of things or the powers that carry on the processes of the creation; the total of all agencies and forces in the creation; the inherent qualities of anything; the essential qualities which constitute it what it is; disposition of mind; personal character; individual constitution; quality; sort; natural affection; life or reality as distin-

natterjack

guished from that which is artificial; natural scenery.

naught *n* nought; nothing.—*adj* worthless; of no value or account; bad; vile.

naughtiness *n* the state of being naughty; misbehaviour, as of children.

naughty *adj* bad; mischievous; ill-behaved; very wrong (*a naughty child*).

nausea *n* a desire to vomit; sickness.

nauseate *vi* (**nauseated, nauseating**) to feel nausea; to be inclined to vomit.—*vt* to loathe; to cause to feel sick; to cause to vomit; to affect with disgust.

nauseous *adj* causing nausea; arousing a desire to vomit; loathsome; disgusting.

nauseousness *n* the quality of being nauseous; loathsomeness.

nautical *adj* pertaining to seamanship or navigation.

nautical mile *n* the sixtieth part of a degree of latitude or approximately 6080 feet (1.85 kilometres).

nautilus *n* (*pl* **nautiluses, nautili**) any of a group of aquatic molluscs related to the cuttlefish, having a spiral, chambered shell with pearly walls; a form of diving bell which requires no suspension, sinking and rising by means of condensed air.

naval *adj* consisting of ships or of forces fighting in ships; pertaining to a navy or to ships of war; maritime.

nave[1] *n* the middle part lengthways of a church; the part between the aisles and extending from the entrance.

nave[2] *n* the thick piece in the centre of a wheel in which the spokes are inserted; the hub.

navel *n* a depression in the centre of the abdomen, the point where the umbilical cord passes out of the foetus.

navigable *adj* capable of being navigated; affording passage to ships.

navigate *vi* (**navigated, navigating**) to pass on water in ships; to manage a ship; to sail; to find one's way and keep a course; to chart the route for a motor vehicle.—*vt* to pass over in ships; to sail on; to steer or manage in sailing; to direct the course of.

navigation *n* the act of navigating; the science or art of managing ships.

navigator *n* one who navigates; one who directs the course of a ship, aircraft, motor vehicle, etc.

navvy *n* a labourer engaged in such works as the making of canals, railways or roads.

navy *n* a collective term for all the ships, or all of a certain class, belonging to a country (*the mercantile navy of Britain*); especially, the whole of the ships of war belonging to a nation; the naval force of any country, including ships, personnel, stores, etc.

nay *adv* (*arch*) no; a word that expresses negation or refusal; also used to intimate that something is to be added to an expression; not only so; not this alone.—*n* a refusal or denial.

Nazi *n* a member of the German National Socialist party (1930s).

Neanderthal *adj* denoting or characteristic of Neanderthal man; primitive; extremely old-fashioned and reactionary.

Neanderthal man *n* a type of primitive human who inhabited Europe in Palaeolithic times and who is represented by a skull found in a cave at Neanderthal in Germany in 1857.

neap *adj* low or not rising high (applied to the lowest tides, being those that happen in the middle of the second and fourth quarters of the moon, taking place about four or five days before the new and full moons).—*n* a neap tide.

neap tide *n* one of the lowest tides or the time of one, opposite to *spring tide*.

near *adj* nigh; not far distant in place, time or degree; closely connected by blood (*near relations*); intimate; familiar (*a near friend*); closely affecting one's interest or feelings; close or literal; so as barely to avoid injury or danger; narrow (*a near escape*); on the left of a horse, vehicle, etc, opposed to *off*, in riding or driving (*the near side*); short or not circuitous (*a near way home*); (*arch*) close, narrow, niggardly.—*prep* at no great distance from; close to; nigh.—*adv* almost; within a little; closely; (*naut*) close to the wind, opposed to *off*.—*vti* to approach; to come near.

nearby *adj, adv* close by in position; not far away.

Near East *n* an old term for the Middle East, which included Turkey, the Balkans and the area of the Ottoman Empire.

nearly *adv* almost; within a little; not remotely; closely; intimately; (*arch*) in a parsimonious or niggardly manner.

near miss *n* a situation in which two aircraft narrowly avoid a mid-air collision.

nearness *n* the state or attribute of being near in any sense; closeness in time or place; proximity; (*arch*) parsimony.

nearside *n* the left-hand side of a vehicle where traffic drives on the left.

near-sighted *adj* short-sighted; seeing at a small distance only.

neat[1] *adj* having everything in perfect order; tidy; trim; expressed in few and well-chosen words; pure or unmixed with water (*a glass of brandy neat*); (*arch*) with all deductions made; net.

neat[2] *n* (*arch*) cattle of the bovine genus, as oxen or cows (used either collectively or of one individual).

neatness *n* the state or quality of being neat; tidiness; simple elegance.

neb *n* (*Scots*) the nose; the beak of a fowl; the bill.

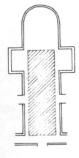

nave

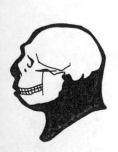

Neanderthal man

nebula *n* (*pl* **nebulae**) a cloudy, luminous or dark patch consisting of gas and dust in the night sky.

nebular *adj* pertaining to a nebula or nebulae.

nebular hypothesis *n* a hypothesis that the bodies composing the solar system once existed in the form of a nebula, from which, when condensed by refrigeration, the planets were constituted, the main body forming the sun.

nebulous *adj* cloudy; indistinct; formless; (*astron*) pertaining to or having the appearance of a nebula; nebular.

necessarily *adv* in a necessary manner; by necessity; indispensably.

necessary *adj* such as must be; inevitable; unavoidable; indispensable; essential; that cannot be absent; acting from necessity, opposed to *free* (as regards the will).—*n* anything necessary or indispensable.

necessitarianism, necessarianism *n* the doctrine of philosophical necessity.

necessitate *vt* (**necessitated, necessitating**) to make necessary or indispensable; to render necessary; to compel; to force.

necessitous *adj* exhibiting indigence; pressed with poverty; indigent; destitute.

necessity *n* the state of being necessary; condition demanding that something must be; unavoidability; indispensability; need; irresistible compulsion; compulsion of circumstances; the absolute determination of the will by motives; that which is requisite; a necessary; extreme indigence; pinching poverty.

neck *n* the part of the body between the head and the trunk and connecting them; part of a thing corresponding to the neck; the part of a garment nearest the neck; a narrow tract of land connecting two larger tracts; an isthmus; the slender part of a vessel, as a bottle; a strait; that part of a violin or similar instrument which connects the scroll or head and body.—*vti* (*sl*) to kiss and caress.

neckband *n* the band of a shirt round the neck to which the collar is attached.

neckcloth *n* a piece of linen or cotton cloth formerly worn round the neck as part of a man's dress.

neckerchief *n* a kerchief for the neck.

necklace *n* a string of beads, precious stones or other ornamental objects worn round the neck.

necklet *n* a small chain worn round the neck for suspending a locket.

necktie *n* a small band of cloth worn round the neck.

necromancer *n* one who practises necromancy; a sorcerer; a wizard.

necromancy *n* divination by means of a pretended communication with the dead; the black art; the art of magic or sorcery.

necrophilia *n* an erotic interest in corpses; sexual intercourse with corpses.

necrophiliac *adj* pertaining to necrophilia; affected by necrophilia.

necropolis *n* (*pl* **necropolises, necropoleis**) a cemetery, especially one that is extensive and ornamentally laid out.

necrosis *n* (*pathol*) death of living tissue due to disease, injury or interruption of the blood supply; (*bot*) a disease of plants chiefly found in the leaves and soft parts.

necrotic *adj* pertaining to necrosis; affected by necrosis.

nectar *n* in Greek myth, the drink of the gods, ambrosia being their solid food; hence, any delicious drink; (*bot*) the honey of a flower.

nectarine *adj* sweet as nectar.—*n* a variety of the common peach with a smoother rind and firmer pulp.

nectary *n* the part of a flower that contains or secretes the nectar.

nee, née *adj* born, a term placed before a married woman's maiden name to indicate her parentage.

need *n* a state that requires supply or relief; pressing occasion for something; urgent want; necessity; lack of the means of subsistence; poverty; indigence.—*vt* to have necessity or need for; to want, lack, require; often used as a sort of auxiliary, especially in negative and interrogative sentences without the personal termination of the 3rd person singular and without the infinitive sign *to* before the following verb (*he* or *they need not go*; *need he do it?*).—*vi* to be wanted; to be necessary (not used with a personal nominative, as *there needs nothing more*).

needful *adj* needy; necessitous; necessary; requisite.—**the needful** anything necessary; specifically, ready money.

neediness *n* want; poverty; indigence.

needle *n* a small instrument of steel pointed at one end and with an eye or hole at the other through which is passed a thread, used for sewing; an instrument of metal, plastic, wood, etc, used for interweaving or interlacing a thread or twine in knitting, netting, embroidery, etc; a name of sundry long and sharp-pointed surgical instruments; a magnetized bar of steel in a mariner's or other compass, etc; the sharp, slender metal tube at the end of a hypodermic syringe; a sharp pinnacle of rock; a needle-shaped crystal.—*vt* (**needled, needling**) to goad, prod or tease; to annoy or irritate.

needlepoint *n* a type of embroidery worked on canvas.

needless *adj* not wanted; unnecessary; not requisite.

needlewoman *n* (*pl* **needlewomen**) a woman who does needlework; a seamstress.

neck

needle

needlework *n* work executed with a needle; sewn work; embroidery; the business of a seamstress.

needly *adj* relating to or resembling a needle.

needs *adv* of necessity; necessarily; indispensably (generally with *must*).

needy *adj* necessitous; indigent; very poor; distressed by lack of the means of living.

ne'er (*poet*) a contraction of **never**.

nefarious *adj* wicked in the extreme; atrociously sinful or villainous; detestably vile.

negate *vt* (**negated, negating**) to nullify; to make ineffective or futile; to deny.

negation *n* denial; a declaration that something is not, has not been or will not be, opposed to *affirmation*; contradiction or contradictory condition.

negative *adj* implying or containing denial or negation, opposed to *affirmative*; tending in the direction of denial without directly denying or controverting, opposed to *positive* (*a negative result*); (of criticism, etc) not constructive or helpful; lacking positive attributes; (*photog*) having the lights and shades the opposite of those in nature; (*elect*) of the charge carried by electrons, opposed to *positive*; carrying such a charge.—*n* a proposition by which something is denied; an opposite or contradictory term or conception; a negative proposition; a word that denies (not, no); that side of a question which denies or refuses; a decision or answer expressive of negation; (*photog*) a photographic picture in which the lights and shades are the opposite of those in nature, used to print positive impressions.—*vt* (**negatived, negativing**) to disprove; to prove the contrary; to say no to; to reject; to refuse to enact or sanction, to veto (*the lords negatived the bill*).

neglect *vt* to treat with no regard or attention or with too little; to slight; to set at naught; to omit to do; to leave undone; to forbear (often with an infinitive as object, as *to neglect to pay a visit*).—*n* omission; forbearance to do anything that should be done; carelessness; omission of due attention or civilities; negligence; habitual lack of regard; state of being disregarded.

neglectful *adj* apt to neglect; treating with neglect; negligent; careless; inattentive.

negligée, negligee *n* a woman's loose decorative dressing gown of flimsy material.

negligence *n* the quality of being negligent; neglect; remissness; an act of negligence.

negligent *adj* characterized by neglect; apt to neglect; careless; heedless; neglectful.

negligible *adj* that may be neglected; that need not be regarded; unimportant; trifling.

negotiable *adj* capable of being negotiated; transferable by assignment from one person to another, as a bill or promissory note.

negotiate *vi* (**negotiated, negotiating**) to treat with another respecting purchase and sale; to hold discussions in bargaining or trade; to hold diplomatic discussions with another, as respecting a treaty, league, etc; to treat; to conduct communications in general.—*vt* to procure or bring about by negotiation (a treaty, a loan); to pass in the way of business; to put into circulation (*to negotiate a bill of exchange*); to negotiate a corner (said of a motorcar or other vehicle), taking an obstacle carefully in order to overcome it.

negotiation *n* the act of negotiating; the treating with another respecting sale or purchase; the intercourse of governments by their agents, in making treaties, etc.

Negro *n* (*pl* **Negroes**) a member of the dark-skinned indigenous peoples of Africa; a member of the Negroid group; a person with some Negro ancestors.—*adj* relating to Negroes; black.

Negroid *adj* of or relating to one of the major groups of humankind, including most of the peoples of Africa south of the Sahara.

negus *n* a beverage made of wine, hot water, sugar, nutmeg and lemon juice, or only of wine, water and sugar.

neigh *vi* to utter the cry of a horse; to whinny.—*n* the cry of a horse; a whinnying.

neighbour *n* one who lives near another; one in close proximity; one who lives on friendly terms with another.—*adj* being in the vicinity; adjoining; next.—*vt* to adjoin; to border on or be near to.

neighbourhood *n* vicinity; a particular community, area or district; a locality; the people in an area.—**in the neighbourhood of** approximately; somewhere about.

neighbouring *adj* living as neighbours; being situated near.

neighbourly *adj* becoming a neighbour; acting as a good neighbour; friendly; social; sociable.

neither *pron, pronominal adj* not one of two; not either; not the one or the other (used either alone or with a noun following).—*conj* not either (generally prefixed to the first of two or more coordinate negative propositions or clauses, the others being introduced by *nor*; sometimes used instead of *nor* in the second of two clauses, the former containing *not*).

nekton *n* the actively swimming fishes and other organisms living near the surface of the ocean.

nelson *n* in wrestling, a hold in which the arms are placed under an opponent's arms from behind so that pressure can be exerted by the palms on the back of the opponent's neck.

nelumbo *n* (*pl* **nelumbos**) the Hindu and Chinese lotus, a water plant with rose-coloured flowers.

nematode *n* any of a large group of worms with an unsegmented threadlike body, many of which are parasitic.

Nemesis *n* a female Greek divinity regarded as a personification of retributive justice.

Neolithic *adj* (*archaeol*) of or pertaining to the more recent of the two periods into which the Stone Age has been subdivided, marked by the use of polished stone implements, the domestication of animals, the growing of cereals and fruit trees, the making of pottery, weaving of linen and use of boats.

neologism *n* a new word or phrase or new use of a word; the use of new words or of old words in a new sense; new doctrines.

neologist, neologian *n* one who introduces new words or phrases; an innovator in doctrines or beliefs.

neology *n* the introduction of a new word or of new words into a language; novel doctrines; rationalistic views in theology.

neon *n* an inert gaseous element, present in small amounts in the air, which gives off a bright orange glow in an electrical discharge and is used in lighting and advertisements.

neophyte *n* a new convert or proselyte; a novice; one newly admitted to the order of priests; a tyro; a beginner in learning.

neoplasm *n* a diseased new growth of tissue; a tumour.

neoprene *n* a durable synthetic rubber used in waterproof products.

neoteric *adj* new; recent in origin; modern.

neoterism *n* the introduction of new words or phrases.

Neozoic *adj* (*geol*) of or formed in strata from the beginning of the Trias up to the most recent deposits, including the Mesozoic and Cainozoic divisions.—*n* the Neozoic period.

nepenthe *n* a drug supposed by the ancient Greeks to make persons forget their sorrows and misfortunes; any draught or drug capable of removing pain or care.

nephew *n* the son of a brother or sister; also, the son of a brother- or sister-in-law.

nephrite *n* a variety of jade.

nephritic *adj* pertaining to the kidneys; pertaining to kidney disease; suffering from kidney disease.

nephritis *n* inflammation of the kidneys.

ne plus ultra *n* the farthest attainable point; the acme.

nepotism *n* undue favouritism shown to relatives, especially in job allocation.

nepotistic *adj* pertaining to nepotism; practising or exhibiting nepotism.

Neptune *n* in Roman myth, the chief marine god; a planet beyond the orbit of Uranus, the remotest from the sun yet known in the solar system, with the exception of Pluto.

Neptunian *adj* pertaining to Neptune or the ocean or sea; formed by water or aqueous solution (as rocks).

neptunium *n* a radioactive metallic element.

Nereid *n* (*pl* **Nereides**) in Greek myth, a sea nymph.

nereis *n* (*pl* **nereides**) a marine annelid; a sea centipede.

nerve *n* a sinew or tendon; strength; muscular power; self-command or steadiness, especially under trying circumstances; firmness of mind; courage; (*colloq*) audacity, boldness; one of the whitish fibres which proceed from the brain and spinal cord or from the central ganglia and ramify through all parts of the body and whose function is to convey sensation and originate motion; courage; coolness in danger; a sensitive point or subject; the sensitive tissue in the pulp of a tooth; (*colloq*) audacity, boldness; (*pl*) nervousness, anxiety; (*pl*) the general tone of one's system; (*bot*) one of the ribs or principal veins in a leaf.—*vt* (**nerved, nerving**) to give nerve, strength or vigour to; to arm with force.

nerve cell, neuron, neurone *n* a cell transmitting impulses in nerve tissue; a type of cell that sends messages from one part of the body to another.

nerve centre *n* a group of closely connected nerve cells that performs a particular function; a place where a number of nerves join together; a centre of control from which instructions are sent out, as in military operations.

nerveless *adj* without nerve; lacking strength; weak; calm; cool.

nervous *adj* pertaining to the nerves; affecting the nerves; having the nerves affected; easily agitated; highly strung; anxious; apprehensive.

nervous breakdown *n* a loose term for a period of mental illness resulting from severe strain, mental fatigue, anxiety, etc.

nervous system *n* the brain, spinal cord and nerves collectively.

nervure *n* the veins of leaves; the horny ribs supporting the membranous wings of an insect.

nescience *n* the state of not knowing; lack of knowledge; ignorance.

ness *n* a promontory; a cape; a headland.

-ness *n suffix* (added to adjectives) indicating the state or quality of being (*nervous, nervousness*).

nest *n* the place or bed formed or used by a bird for incubation and rearing the young; a place where the eggs of insects, turtles, etc, are produced; a place in which the

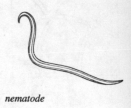

nematode

nest

young of various small animals (as mice) are reared; a number of persons frequenting the same haunt (*a nest of thieves*); a set of articles of diminishing sizes, each enveloping the one next smaller (*a nest of tables*).—*vi* to build a nest; to nestle; to raid nests in search of eggs; to fit together, as in a stack.—*vt* to place, as if in a nest; (*comput*) to enclose (one instruction) inside another.

nest egg *n* an egg left in the nest to prevent the hen from forsaking it; something laid up as a beginning or nucleus; money put aside as a reserve.

nestle *vi* (**nestled, nestling**) to make or occupy a nest; to take shelter; to lie close and snug.

nestling *n* a young bird in the nest or just taken from the nest.

net[1] *n* a fabric formed of thread, twine or other fibrous materials, woven into meshes and used for catching fish, birds, etc, and also for securing or containing articles of various kinds; a material of fine open texture; a snare.—*vt* (**netted, netting**) to make into a net or network; to take in a net; hence, to capture by wile or stratagem; to ensnare; to enclose in a net or network; to hit (a ball) into a net or goal.—*vi* to form network.

net

net[2], **nett** *adj* free from all deductions (*net profits, net produce, net rent, net weight*).—*vt* (**netted, netting**) to gain as clear profit.

nether *adj* lower; lying or being beneath or in the lower part, opposed to *upper*.

nethermost *adj* lowest.

netherwards *adv* in a direction downwards.

nett *adj* same as **net**[2].

netting *n* the process of making nets; a piece of network; netted fabric.

nettle *n* a sort of wild plant with stinging hairs.—*vt* (**nettled, nettling**) to irritate or vex; to cause to feel displeasure or vexation not amounting to anger.

nettle rash *n* an eruption on the skin resembling the effects of the sting of a nettle; urticaria.

network *n* work formed in the same manner as a net; any net-like fabric; an arrangement of intersecting lines; a chain of interconnected operations; a group of broadcasting stations connected to transmit the same programme simultaneously; a group of people with a common interest, often able to help each other.—*vt* to broadcast on a network; (*comput*) to connect systems so that data, software and peripheral devices can be shared.

nettle

networking *n* the making of contacts and trading information as for career advancement; the interconnection of computer systems.

network marketing *n* the selling of a product directly to customers gathered at a party.

neural *adj* pertaining to the nerve or nervous system.

neuralgia *n* pain in a nerve; an ailment, the chief symptom of which is acute pain, apparently seated in a nerve or nerves.

neurasthenia *n* (*med*) nervous debility or exhaustion.

neuritis *n* (*med*) inflammation of a nerve.

neurology *n* the study of the nervous systems and their diseases.

neuron, neurone *n* same as **nerve cell**.

neuropteran *n* any of an order of insects having four membranous, transparent, naked wings, reticulated with veins or nervures, as the dragonflies.

neurosis *n* a mental disorder with symptoms such as anxiety, obsession and phobias; psychoneurosis.

neurosurgery *n* the branch of surgery performed on the brain, spinal cord and other parts of the nervous system.

neurotic *adj* relating to or acting on the nerves; affected by neurosis; suffering from neurosis; highly strung.—*n* a neurotic person.

neurotransmitter *n* a chemical by which nerves cells communicate with each other or with muscles.

neuter *adj* neutral; (*gram*) of neither gender; neither masculine nor feminine (in English grammar applied to all names of things without life); neither active nor passive; intransitive (*a neuter verb*); (*bot*) having neither stamens nor pistils; (*zool*) having no fully developed sex (*neuter bees*).—*n* an animal of neither sex or incapable of propagation; one of the imperfectly developed females of certain social insects, as ants and bees; (*bot*) a plant which has neither stamens nor pistils; (*gram*) a noun of the neuter gender.—*vt* to castrate or spay.

neutral *adj* not taking an active part with one of certain contending parties; not interested one way or another; non-aligned; indifferent; of no definite colour; of no definite characteristics; (*chem*) neither acid nor alkaline; (*physics*) having zero charge.—*n* a person or nation that takes no part in a contest between others; a neutral colour; a position of a gear mechanism in which power is not transmitted.

neutrality *n* the state of being neutral; the state of taking no part on either side.

neutralization *n* the act of neutralizing.

neutralize *vt* (**neutralized, neutralizing**) to render neutral; to render ineffective; to counterbalance; to declare neutral; (*chem*) to make neutral.

neutron *n* an elementary particle with the same mass as a proton but no electric charge.

never *adv* not ever; at no time, whether past, present or future; in no degree (*never fear*); not at all; none (*never the better*); not, emphatically (*he answered never a word*).

nevermore *adv* never again; at no future time.

nevertheless *conj* not the less; notwithstanding; in spite of or without regarding that.

new *adj* lately made, invented, produced or come into being; recent in origin; novel, opposed to *old*; not before known; recently discovered; recently produced by change; different from a former (*to lead a new life*); not habituated; not familiar; unaccustomed; fresh after any event; never used before or recently brought into use; not second-hand (*a new copy of a book*); recently commenced; starting afresh (*the new year, a new week*).—*adv* again; newly; recently.

newcomer *n* one who has lately come or arrived.

newel *n* (*archit*) the upright cylinder or pillar round which in a winding staircase the steps turn and are supported from the bottom to the top.

newfangled *adj* new-fashioned; fond of change; formed with the affectation of novelty; easily captivated by what is new.

Newfoundland *n* a large variety of dog, originally from Newfoundland.

newly *adv* lately; freshly; recently; with a new form, different from the former; anew; afresh; as before; in a new and different manner.

news *n* recent intelligence regarding any event; fresh information of something that has lately taken place or of something before unknown; tidings; current events; recent happenings; a newspaper; a programme of news on television or radio.

news agency *n* an organization that gathers news for newspapers and other news media.

newsagent *n* a retailer of newspapers, magazines, etc.

newsletter *n* a bulletin regularly distributed among the members of a firm, organization, society, etc, containing information, news of activities, etc.

newspaper *n* a sheet of paper printed and distributed for conveying news; a printed periodical published daily or weekly that circulates news, advertisements, political intelligence, information regarding proceedings of parliament, public meetings, etc; newsprint.

newspeak *n* a style of misleading and confusing language often used by officials, such as politicians.

newsprint *n* an inexpensive paper on which newspapers are printed.

newsroom *n* the department of a broadcasting system, newspaper, etc, that prepares news for broadcasting or publication; a room, etc, where newspapers, magazines, etc, may be read.

newsworthy *adj* timely and important or interesting.

newt *n* one of a genus of small-tailed batrachians of lizard-like appearance, living in ponds, ditches and moist places; an eft.

New Testament *n* the second part of the Bible, including the story of the life and teachings of Christ.

newton *n* the SI unit of force which when acting for one second on a mass of one kilogram imparts an acceleration of one metre per second per second.

New World *n* a name frequently given to North and South America; the western hemisphere.

New Year's Day *n* the first day of the year; 1st January, a public holiday in many countries.

New Year's Eve *n* the evening of the last day of the year; 31st December.

next *adj* nearest in place, time, rank or degree.—*adv* at the time or turn nearest or immediately succeeding (*who follows next?*).

next of kin *n* the person most closely related to someone.

nib *n* the bill or beak of a fowl; the point of anything, particularly of a pen; a small pen adapted to be fitted into a holder.

nibble *vt* (**nibbled, nibbling**) to bite by little at a time; to eat in small bits; to bite, as a fish does the bait; just to catch by biting. —*vi* to bite gently; (*fig*) to carp; to show cautious interest (in).—*n* a little bite or the act of seizing with the mouth as if to bite.

niblick *n* a golf club with a round and heavy head.

nice *adj* over-scrupulous; fastidious; punctilious; distinguishing minutely; made with scrupulous exactness; precise; pleasant to the senses; delicious; dainty; pleasing or agreeable in general.

nicely *adv* in a nice manner; fastidiously; critically; with delicate perception; accurately; exactly; becomingly; pleasantly.

Nicene creed *n* a summary of Christian faith composed by the Council of Nice against Arianism, AD 325, altered and confirmed by the Council of Constantinople, AD 381.

niceness *n* state or quality of being nice; fastidiousness; minute exactness; agreeableness; pleasantness.

nicety *n* refinement; accuracy; a subtle point of distinction.

niche *n* a recess in a wall for holding a statue, vase or other ornament; a place, situation, post, use, etc, for which a person

newt

nib

571

is exceptionally suited; a profitable corner of the business market.

nick¹ *n* a notch; a small chip, cut, etc, made on a surface; (*colloq*) a prison; (*colloq*) a police station.—*vt* to make a nick or notch in; to cut in nicks or notches.

nick² *n* the exact point of time required by necessity or convenience (*in the nick of time*); the critical time.

Nick *n* originally, a goblin or spirit of the waters but now applied only to the devil, generally with the addition of *Old*.

nickel *n* a metallic element of a white colour, of great hardness, always magnetic and when perfectly pure malleable and ductile; the popular name in the USA and Canada given to a small coin worth five cents.

nickel silver *n* an alloy composed of copper, zinc and nickel.

nickname *n* a substitute name given to a person in fun; a familiar form of a proper name.—*vt* (**nicknamed, nicknaming**) to give a nickname to; to call by a contemptuous name.

nicotian *adj* pertaining to or derived from tobacco.

nicotine *n* a volatile alkaloid from tobacco, highly poisonous.

nicotinic acid *n* a vitamin of the B complex derived from milk, liver and yeast.

nictitate, nictate *vi* (**nictitated, nictitating** or **nictated, nictating**) to wink with the eyes.

nictitating membrane *n* a thin movable membrane, most largely developed in birds, which covers and protects the eyes from dust or too much light.

nidus *n* (*pl* **nidi**) the developing place of spores, seeds, germs, etc.

niece *n* the daughter of a brother or sister; also, the daughter of a brother- or sister-in-law.

niello *n* (*pl* **nielli, niellos**) a method of ornamenting metal plates by cutting lines in the metal and filling them up with a black or coloured composition.

nifty *adj* neat; smart; stylish; quick; agile.

niggard *adj* miserly; niggardly; meanly covetous; parsimonious.—*n* a miser; a meanly covetous person; a parsimonious person.

niggardliness *n* the quality of being niggardly; parsimony.

niggardly *adj* giving grudgingly, ungenerous.—*adv* like a niggard.

nigh *adj* (*compar* **nigher**, *superl* **next**) near; not distant or remote in place or time; closely at hand; ready to aid.—*adv* near; close; almost; nearly.—*prep* near to; at no great distance from.

night *n* that part of the natural day when the sun is beneath the horizon or the time from sunset to sunrise; (*fig*) a state or time of darkness, depression, misfortune, etc; a state of ignorance or intellectual darkness; obscurity; the darkness of death or the grave; a time of sadness or sorrow.

night blindness *n* a disease in which the eyes can see by daylight but not by night or poor light; nyctalopia.

nightcap *n* a cap worn in bed; a drink taken before going to bed.

nightclothes *npl* garments that are worn in bed, such as pyjamas.

nightclub *n* a place of entertainment for drinking, dancing, etc, in the evening.

nightdress *n* a loose garment worn by women and girls in bed.

nightfall *n* the fall of night; the close of the day; evening.

nightglasses *npl* binoculars adapted to enable objects to be seen at night.

nightgown *n* a loose gown worn in bed; a nightdress.

nightingale *n* a well-known migratory bird that sings at night.

nightjar *n* a name of the common or British goatsucker.

nightlife *n* public social entertainment in the evening, such as discos, nightclubs, etc.

night-light *n* a candle or taper for burning at night, often placed in a dish of water; a dim electric light kept burning at night.

nightly *adj* done by night; happening in the night; done every night.—*adv* by night; every night.

nightmare *adj* a state of oppression or feeling of suffocation felt during sleep and accompanied by a feeling of intense anxiety, fear or horror; a frightening dream; any horrible or frightening experience.

nightpiece *n* a picture representing a night scene; a written piece descriptive of a scene by night.

night porter *n* a worker who attends during the night in hotels, hospitals, etc.

nightshade *n* a flowering plant related to the potato and tomato which possess narcotic or poisonous properties, especially deadly nightshade (belladonna).

nightshirt *n* a long shirt for sleeping in.

night-watchman *n* a person employed to guard a building at night.

nigrescent *adj* growing black; approaching to blackness.

nigrification *n* the act of making black.

nigritude *n* blackness.

nihilism *n* nothingness; the belief that nothing has real existence; total scepticism; a total rejection of customary beliefs in morality, religion, etc.

nihilist *n* one who holds the doctrine or principles of nihilism.

nil *n* nothing (*his liabilities were over £5000 and his assets nil*)

nimble *adj* light and quick in motion; mov-

nightingale

ing with ease and celerity; agile; prompt; swift.

nimbleness *n* agility; quickness; celerity.

nimbus *n* (*pl* **nimbi, nimbuses**) a cloud; a rain cloud; a kind of halo or disc surrounding the head in representations of divine or sacred personages.

nincompoop *n* a fool; a blockhead; a simpleton.

nine *adj* one more than eight or one less than ten.—*n* the number composed of eight and one; a symbol representing this number, as 9, IX.

nine days' wonder *n* a sensational event that will be forgotten about it in a few days.

nine men's morris *n* an old game played with nine stones, placed in holes cut in the turf and moved alternately as at draughts.

ninepins *npl* a game with nine pins of wood set on end, at which a bowl is rolled.

nineteen *adj* nine and ten.—*n* the number composed of nine and ten; a symbol representing this number, as 19, XIX.

nineteenth *adj* the ordinal of nineteen.—*n* a nineteenth part.

ninetieth *adj* the ordinal of ninety.—*n* a ninetieth part.

ninety *adj, n* nine times ten.—*n* the number composed of nine times ten; a symbol representing this number, as 90, XC.

ninny *n* a fool; a simpleton.

ninth *adj* the ordinal of nine; the next preceding ten.—*n* a ninth part; (*mus*) an interval containing an octave and a tone.

ninthly *adv* in the ninth place.

niobium *n* a rare metallic element used in alloys.

nip[1] *vt* (**nipped, nipping**) to catch and compress sharply between two surfaces or points, as of the fingers; to pinch; to cut, bite or pinch off the end of; to blast, as by frost; to benumb; to chill.—**to nip in the bud** to destroy in the first stage of growth.—*n* a pinch, as with the points of the fingers, nails, etc; a blast by frost.

nip[2] *n* a sip or small draught, especially of some strong alcoholic drink.

nipper[1] *n* one who or that which nips; the pincer of a crab or a lobster.

nipper[2] *n* (*colloq*) a young child.

nippers *npl* small pincers.

nipple *n* the spongy protuberance by which milk is drawn from the breasts of females; a pap; a teat; something like a nipple, as that part of a grease gun through which grease is forced.

nirvana *n* the Buddhist doctrine of the extinction of all desire for existence and worldly good and the absorption of the soul into the Deity.

nisi *adj* (of a decree, order, etc) valid unless cause is shown to the contrary by a fixed date, at which it is made absolute.

nit *n* the egg of a louse or other small insect.

nitrate *n* a salt of nitric acid; a fertilizer made from this.

nitre *n* potassium nitrate, used for making gunpowder, in dyeing, metallurgy, medicine, etc.

nitric *adj* containing nitrogen.

nitric acid *n* an acid prepared from sulphuric acid and nitre, used in etching, metallurgy and assaying, and also in explosives and fertilizers.

nitriferous *adj* producing or containing nitre (*nitriferous strata*).

nitrite *n* a salt of nitrous acid.

nitrogen *n* the gaseous element which is the principal ingredient of atmospheric air, of which it constitutes about four-fifths, the rest being principally oxygen, possessing neither taste nor smell.

nitrogenous *adj* pertaining to or containing nitrogen.

nitroglycerine *n* a compound produced by the action of a mixture of strong nitric and sulphuric acids on glycerine at low temperatures, a most powerful explosive.

nitrous *adj* (*chem*) resembling, obtained from or impregnated with nitrogen.

nitrous oxide *n* a combination of nitrogen and oxygen which, when inhaled, causes insensibility, and hence is used as an anaesthetic during short surgical operations: diluted with air it produces an exhilarating or intoxicating effect; hence the old name of *laughing gas*.

nitty-gritty *n* the basic facts, details etc; the basic elements.

nitwit *n* a person of little intelligence.

nival *adj* abounding with snow; snowy; growing among snow or flowering during winter.

niveous *adj* snowy; resembling snow.

no[1] *adv* a word of denial or refusal, expressing a negative and opposed to *yes*: when repeated or when used with another negative it is specially emphatic; it may be used as the correlative of *whether* (*whether or no*), though now less common than *not*.—*n* (*pl* **noes**) a negative vote or a person who votes in the negative (*the noes have it*).

no[2] *adj* not any; not one; none.—**no end** an indefinitely great number or quantity (*no end of things*).—*adv* not in any degree; not at all; not (with comparatives, as *no sooner*).

nob[1] *n* (*colloq*) a member of the aristocracy.

nob[2] *n* (*colloq*) the head.

nobby *adj* (*colloq*) showy; stylish; smart.

nobility *n* the quality of being noble; nobleness; the state of being of noble birth or rank; the persons collectively who are of rank above commoners; the peerage.

noble *adj* high in excellence or worth; lofty in character; magnanimous (*a noble mind*); proceeding from or characteristic

nipper

of greatness of mind (*noble sentiments*); of the best kind; choice; pertaining to the nobility or peerage; magnificent; stately (*a noble edifice*).—*n* a nobleman; a peer; a gold coin, which was struck in the reign of Edward III.

noble gas *n* same as **inert gas**.

nobleman *n* (*pl* **noblemen**) one of the nobility; a noble; a peer.

noble metal *n* a metal which is not oxidized when heated in air, e.g. gold, silver, platinum, rhodium, iridium, osmium and mercury.

nobleness *n* the state or quality of being noble; nobility; noble rank; stateliness; magnificence.

noblesse oblige *n* the benevolent and honourable behaviour expected of persons of high birth or rank.

noblewoman *n* (*pl* **noblewomen**) a female of noble rank.

nobly *adv* in a noble manner; heroically; with magnanimity; splendidly; magnificently.

nobody *n* no person; no one; an insignificant or contemptible person; a person of no standing or position

nocturn *n* a religious service formerly used in the Roman Catholic Church at midnight, now a part of matins.

nocturnal *adj* pertaining or belonging to the night; done or occurring at night; (*zool*) active by night; (*bot*) closing during the day and expanding during the night (said of flowers).

nocturne *n* a painting exhibiting some of the characteristic effects of night light; a nightpiece; a piece of music of a pensive character.

nod *vi* (**nodded, nodding**) to incline the head with a quick motion, either forward or sideways; to let the head sink from sleep; to make an inclination of the head, as in assent or in beckoning; to bend or incline the top with a quick motion (*nodding plumes*); to be drowsy; to fall asleep (with *off*).—*vt* to incline, as the head or top; to signify by a nod; to beckon by a nod.—*n* a quick downward motion of the head as a sign of assent, salutation, from drowsiness, etc.

nodal *adj* pertaining to nodes.

noddle *n* (*colloq*) the head.

noddy *n* a simpleton; a fool; a tropical tern with dark brown body plumage and a white head.

node *n* a knot; a knob; a protuberance; (*med*) a swelling; (*bot*) a sort of knot on a stem where leaves grow; (*mus*) a nodal point; (*astron*) one of the two points in which two great circles of the celestial sphere (as the ecliptic and equator) intersect each other; one of the points in which the orbit of a satellite intersects the plane

of the orbit of its primary; in oscillatory or wave motion, a point where the disturbance considered vanishes.

nodical *adj* (*astron*) pertaining to nodes.

nodular *adj* pertaining to or like a nodule.

nodule *n* a little knot or lump; (*bot*) a small woody body found in bark; (*geol*) a rounded irregularly shaped mineral mass.

noetic *adj* relating to the mind or intellect.

no-fault *adj* (of insurance) providing damages without blame being fixed; (of a divorce) concluded without blame being charged.

nog *n* a wooden pin; a tree nail or pin used in shipbuilding; a brick-shaped piece of wood inserted in a wall; a timber brick; a square piece of wood used to prop up the roof of a mine.

noggin *n* a small mug or wooden cup; a measure equivalent to a gill.

noise *n* a sound of any kind or proceeding from any cause; more especially a din, a confused mixture of sounds; outcry; clamour; frequent talk; much public conversation or discussion; unwanted fluctuations in a transmitted signal; (pl) conventional sounds, words, etc, made in reaction, such as sympathy.—*vi* (**noised, noising**) to sound loud.—*vt* to spread by rumour or report; to report.

noiseless *adj* making no noise; silent.

noisome *adj* noxious to health; morally noxious or injurious; offensive to the smell or other senses; fetid.

noisy *adj* making a loud noise; clamorous; full of noise.

nomad *n* one of a people or tribe who move in search of food and water for their flocks, shifting their residence according to the state of the pasture; a wanderer.—*adj* nomadic.

nomadic *adj* pertaining to nomads; subsisting by the tending of cattle and wandering for the sake of pasturage; pastoral; wandering.

no-man's-land *n* the ground between hostile trenches, as belonging to neither side; an ambiguous area, subject, etc.

nom de plume *n* (*pl* **noms de plume**) a name other than his or her own name used by a writer.

nomenclature *n* a system of names; the systematic naming of things; the vocabulary of names or technical terms which are appropriated to any branch of science.

nominal *adj* pertaining to a name, term or noun; existing in name only; not real; merely so called.

nominalism *n* the principles of the nominalists.

nominalist *n* one of a sect of scholastic philosophers who maintained that general notions (such as the notion of a tree) have no realities corresponding to them and have no existence but as names or words, opposed to *realist*.

nominally *adv* in a nominal manner; in name only, not really (*nominally king*).

nominate *vt* (**nominated, nominating**) to name; to mention by name; to designate by name for an office or place; to propose by name or offer the name of as a candidate for an office or place.

nomination *n* the act of nominating; the act of proposing by name for an office; the state of being nominated; the power of nominating or appointing to office.

nominative *adj* (*gram*) a term applied to that form of a noun or pronoun which is used when the noun or pronoun is the subject of a sentence.—*n* the nominative case; a nominative word.

nominator *n* one who nominates.

nominee *n* a person nominated; one proposed to fill a place or office.

nonage *n* the time of life before a person becomes legally of age; minority; period of immaturity in general.

nonagenarian *n* a person ninety or between ninety and a hundred years old.

nonce *n* present occasion or purpose (used only in the phrase *for the nonce*).

nonchalance *n* lack of earnestness or feeling of interest; indifference; coolness.

nonchalant *adj* indifferent; careless; cool.

noncombatant *n* anyone connected with a military or naval force whose duty it is not to fight; civilians in a place occupied by troops.

noncommissioned *adj* not having a commission.

noncommissioned officer *n* a subordinate officer in the army below the rank of warrant officer, as sergeant and corporal.

noncommittal *adj* not revealing one's opinions.

noncompliance *n* neglect or failure of compliance.

nonconductor *n* a substance which does not conduct heat or electricity or which transmits it with difficulty.

nonconforming *adj* dissenting from the established religion of a country.

nonconformist *n* one who does not conform; especially, one who refuses to conform to an established church.

nonconformity *n* neglect or failure of conformity; the neglect or refusal to unite with an established church in its rites and mode of worship.

nondescript *adj* not hitherto described or classed; not easily described; abnormal or amorphous; odd; indescribable.—*n* anything that has not been described; a person or thing not easily classed.

none *n, pron* not one (used of persons or things); not any; not a part; not the least portion.—*adv* not at all.

nonentity *n* a thing not existing; a person utterly without consequence or importance.

nones *npl* in the Roman calendar, the fifth day of the months of January, February, April, June, August, September, November and December, and the seventh day of March, May, July and October: so called as falling on the ninth day before the ides, both days included; the office for the ninth hour, one of the breviary offices of the Roman Catholic Church.

nonesuch *n* (*arch*) a person or thing such as to have no parallel; a plant like clover used for fodder.

nonetheless *conj* nevertheless.

nonfiction *n* literature that is not fiction.

nonintervention *n* abstention from intervening; a policy of not interfering in foreign politics except where a country's own interests are distinctly involved.

noninterventionist *adj* pertaining to nonintervention; advocating nonintervention.

no-nonsense *adj* sensible, straightforward; not tolerating excess; strict.

nonpareil *n* a person or thing of peerless excellence; a paragon; a variety of apple. —*adj* unequalled; matchless.

nonplus *vt* (**nonplussed, nonplussing**) to puzzle; to confound.

non-profitmaking *adj* (of an organization) not conducted for the purpose of making money.

nonproliferation *n* restrictions on the acquisition or production of, especially nuclear weapons.

nonsense *n* words, actions, etc, that have no meaning or are absurd; absurdity; things of no importance.

nonsensical *adj* having no sense or meaning; absurd.

non sequitur *n* an inference or conclusion which does not follow from the premises; a statement that has no relevance to what preceded it.

nonsmoker *n* a person who does not smoke.

nonstick *adj* (of a saucepan, etc) coated with a surface that prevents food from sticking.

nonstop *adj* (of a train, plane, etc) not making any intermediate stops; not ceasing.— *adv* without stopping or pausing (*he talked nonstop*).

nonviolence *n* the absence of physical force in achieving civil rights or making a protest.

noodle[1] *n* (usually *pl*) a strip of pasta.

noodle[2] *n* (*colloq*) a simpleton; (*sl*) the head.

nook *n* a corner; a recess; a secluded retreat.

noon *n* the middle of the day; the time when the sun is in the meridian; twelve o'clock; the time of greatest brilliancy or power; the prime.

noonday *n* midday; twelve o'clock in the day.—*adj* pertaining to midday; meridional.

no one, no-one *pron* nobody.

noontide *n* the time of noon; midday.

noose *n* a running knot which binds the closer the more it is drawn, used in hanging, snaring, etc.—*vt* (**noosed, noosing**) to catch in a noose; to entrap; to ensnare.

nor *conj* a word used to render negative the second or a subsequent member of a clause or sentence: correlative to *neither* or other negative; also equivalent to *and not* and in this case not always corresponding to a foregoing negative.

Nordic *adj* of or belonging to those peoples of northern Europe who are long-headed, tall, blue-eyed and fair-haired; (of skiing) including cross-country runs and jumping.—*n* a person of the Nordic type.

Norfolk jacket *n* a loose sporting jacket with a waist belt fastened to the back.

noria *n* a hydraulic machine used in Spain and various Arab countries for raising water.

norm *n* a model or standard; the average behaviour, performance, etc, of a group of people.

normal *adj* according to a rule, principle or norm; conforming with a certain type or standard; not abnormal; regular; usual; (*geom*) perpendicular.

normalize *vti* (**normalized, normalizing**) to make or become normal.

Norman *n* a native or inhabitant of Normandy.—*adj* pertaining to Normandy or the Normans.

Norman architecture *n* the round-arched style of architecture, a variety of the Romanesque.

Norse *n* the language of Norway.—*adj* belonging to ancient Scandinavia or its language.

Norseman *n* (*pl* **Norsemen**) a native of ancient Scandinavia.

north *n* one of the cardinal points, being that point of the horizon which is directly opposite to the sun in the meridian, the opposite of *south*; a region, tract or country lying opposite to the south.—*adj* northern; being in the north.—*adv* in or towards the north.

northeast *n* the point midway between the north and east.—*adj* pertaining to, proceeding from or directed towards that point; northeastern.

northeastern *adj* pertaining to or being in the northeast or in a direction to the northeast.

northerly *adj* pertaining to or being in or towards the north; northern; proceeding from the north.

northern *adj* pertaining to or being in the north; in a direction towards the north;

noose

nostril

proceeding from the north (*the northern wind*).

northern lights *npl* the popular name of the **aurora borealis**.

northing *n* the distance of a planet from the equator northward; north declination; (*navig, surv*) the difference of latitude northward from the last point of reckoning, opposed to *southing*.

North Pole *n* the northern extremity of the earth's axis; that point of the heavens towards the north which is 90° distant from the equinoctial.

North Star *n* the Pole Star.

northward *adv, adj* toward the north.—*n* the northern part.

northwards *adv* towards the north; northward.

northwest *n* the point midway between the north and west.—*adj* pertaining to or being between the north and west; northwesterly; proceeding from the northwest (*a northwest wind*).

northwestern *adj* pertaining to or being in the northwest; from the northwest.

north wind *n* the wind that blows from the north.

Norwegian *adj* belonging to Norway.—*n* a native of Norway.

nose *n* the part of the face above the mouth having two nostrils and used for smelling and breathing; the power of smelling; scent; something supposed to resemble a nose; a nozzle.—*vt* (**nosed, nosing**) to smell; to detect, as if by the nose; to touch with the nose; to nuzzle; to push (away, etc) with the front forward.—*vi* to smell; to pry officiously; to inch forwards.

nosegay *n* a bunch of flowers to carry for smelling; a bouquet; a posy.

nose ring *n* a ring worn in the nose as an ornament; a ring for the nose of an animal, as a bull, a pig, etc.

nosology *n* a systematic arrangement or classification of diseases; that branch of medical science which deals with the classification of diseases.

nostalgia *n* a yearning for past times; a vehement desire to revisit places from one's past.

nostalgic *adj* feeling or expressing nostalgia; longing for one's youth.

nostril *n* one of the two apertures of the nose which give passage to air.

nostrum *n* a medicine, the ingredients of which are kept secret; a quack medicine; a patent medicine.

nosy *adj* (*colloq*) inquisitive, snooping.

nosy parker *n* (*colloq*) an inquisitive person; a busybody.

not *adv* a word that expresses negation, denial, refusal or prohibition.

notability *n* the quality of being notable; a notable person or thing; a person of note.

576

notable *adj* worthy of notice; remarkable; memorable; noted or distinguished; conspicuous; manifest; observable.—*n* a person or thing of note or distinction; in French history, one of the nobles or notable men selected by the king to form a parliament, before the Revolution.

notably *adv* in a notable manner; remarkably; eminently; especially.

notary, notary public *n* an officer authorized to attest written documents, contracts, etc.

notation *n* the act or practice of noting; the art of recording by marks or characters; a system of signs or characters used for expressing briefly facts connected with an art or science, as in arithmetic, algebra, music, etc.

notch *n* a hollow cut in anything; a nick; what resembles such a cutting; a gap in a mountain or hill.—*vt* to cut a notch or notches in; to nick; to indent; to fit to a string by the notch, as an arrow.

note *n* a mark in the margin of a book; a mark, character or symbol; a statement subsidiary to the text of a book elucidating or adding something; an explanatory or critical comment; an annotation; a memorandum or short writing intended to assist the memory or for later use or reference; a list of items; a reckoning, bill, account; a written or printed paper acknowledging a debt and promising payment (*a promissory note*; *a banknote*); a diplomatic or official communication in writing; a short letter; a short report; a billet; notice; heed; observation; reputation; consequence; distinction; (*mus*) a character which represents a sound; a musical sound; voice; harmonious or melodious sound.—*vt* (**noted, noting**) to observe carefully; to heed; to attend to; to set down in writing; to make a memorandum of.

notebook *n* a book in which notes or memoranda are written.

noted *adj* being of note; much known by reputation or report; celebrated.

notepaper *n* paper of a small size for writing notes or letters on.

noteworthy *adj* worthy of note; worthy of observation or notice.

nothing *n* not anything, opposed to *anything* and *something*; nothingness; a trifle; a thing of no consideration or importance; (*arith*) a cipher.—*adv* in no degree; not at all.

nothingness *n* the state of being nothing; insignificance; unconsciousness.

notice *n* the act of noting, observing or remarking; heed; regard; cognizance; note; information; intelligence; direction; order; premonition; warning; intimation beforehand; a paper that communicates information; attention; respectful treatment; civil-ity; a short statement; a brief review about a book, play, film, etc.—*vt* (**noticed, noticing**) to take cognizance or notice of; to perceive; to become aware of; to observe; to mention or make observations on; to treat with attention and civilities.—*vi* to be aware of.

noticeable *adj* worthy of being noticed or observed; observable; likely to attract attention.

notifiable disease *n* an infectious disease which must be reported to the health authorities.

notification *adj* the act of notifying or giving notice; notice given in words or writing or by signs; intimation; the writing which communicates information; an advertisement, citation, etc.

notify *vt* (**notified, notifying**) to make known; to declare; to publish; to give notice to; to inform by words or writing.

notion *n* a mental conception; mental apprehension of whatever may be known or imagined; idea; an opinion; a belief or view entertained; a whim.

notional *adj* hypothetical, abstract; imaginary.

notions *npl* small useful articles, such as thread, needles, etc; haberdashery.

notoriety *n* the state or attribute of being notorious; the state of being publicly known to disadvantage; discreditable publicity.

notorious *adj* publicly or generally known and spoken of; manifest to the world; known to disadvantage; publicly known from something discreditable.

notwithstanding *prep, conj* in spite of; without hindrance or obstruction from; despite; nevertheless; however.

nought *n* not anything; nothing; a cipher.

noumenon *n* (*pl* **noumena**) an object conceived by the understanding or thought of by the reason, as opposed to *phenomenon*.

noun *n* (*gram*) a word that names anything or anyone, whether animate or inanimate, material or immaterial.

nourish *vt* to feed and cause to grow; to supply with nutriment; (*fig*) to supply the means of support and increase to; to encourage; to foster; to cherish; to comfort.

nourishing *adj* promoting growth; nutritious.

nourishment *n* the act of nourishing; nutrition; food; sustenance; nutriment; (*fig*) that which promotes any kind of growth or development.

nous *n* common sense; gumption; mother wit.

nouveau riche *n* (*pl* **nouveaux riches**) the new rich, a parvenu.

nova *n* (*pl* **novas, novae**) a new star that explodes in bright luminosity before subsiding.

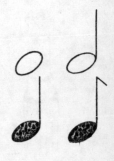

note

novel *n* a fictitious prose narrative involving a plot of greater or less intricacy and professing to give a picture of real life.—*adj* of recent origin or introduction; new and striking; of a kind not known before; unusual; strange.

novelette *n* a short novel.

novelist *n* a writer of a novel or of novels.

novelty *n* the quality of being novel; a noticeable newness; recentness of origin; freshness; something new or strange; (*pl*) small, mass-produced toys or trinkets.

November *n* the eleventh month of the year, containing 30 days.

novice *n* one who is new to the circumstances in which he or she is placed; one newly converted to the Christian faith; one who has entered a religious house but has not taken the vow; a probationer; one who is new in any business; a beginner; an inexperienced person.

noviciate, novitiate *n* the state or time of being a novice; apprenticeship; a year or other time of probation for the trial of a novice before he or she finally takes the vows of a religious order.

now *adv* at the present time; at a particular past time (*he was now king*); at that time; after this had happened, often implying a connection between a subsequent and a preceding proposition or introducing an inference or an explanation of what precedes ('now Barabbas was a robber').

nowadays *adv* at the present time; in these days.

no way *adv* in no way, manner or degree.—*interj* expressing emphatic denial or refusal.

noway, noways, nowise *adv* in no way, manner or degree.

nowhere *adv* not in or to any place.

no-win *adj* (of a policy, situation, etc) having no chance of success.

noxious *adj* hurtful; harmful; pernicious; unwholesome; injurious in a moral sense.

noyade *n* a putting to death by drowning.

nozzle *n* the projecting spout of something; a terminal pipe or terminal part of a pipe (*the nozzle of a bellows*).

nth *adj* (*math*) of or having an unspecified number; (*colloq*) utmost, extreme.

nuance *n* a gradation by which a colour passes from its lightest to its darkest shade; shade of colour; delicate degree in transition; a subtle difference in meaning.

nub *n* a lump or small piece; (*colloq*) the central point or gist of a matter.

nubile *adj* of an age suitable for marriage; marriageable.

nuclear *adj* pertaining to or having the character of a nucleus; constituted by a nucleus; using nuclear energy; having nuclear weapons.

nuclear fission *n* the splitting of a nucleus

nozzle

of an atom either spontaneously or by bombarding it with particles.

nuclear fusion *n* the combining of two nuclei into a heavier nucleus, releasing energy in the process.

nuclear power *n* electrical or motive power produced by a nuclear reactor; a country possessing nuclear weapons.

nuclear reactor *n* a device in which nuclear fission is maintained and harnessed to produce energy.

nuclear waste *n* radioactive waste.

nucleolus, nucleole *n* (*pl* **nucleoli, nucleoles**) the minute solid particle in the interior of the nucleus of some cells.

nucleus *n* (*pl* **nuclei**) a kernel or something similar; a central mass about which matter is collected; the part of an animal or plant cell containing genetic material; (*astron*) the body of a comet, called also its head; (*physics*) the centrally positively charged portion of an atom.

nude *adj* naked; not covered with clothes or drapery.—*n* a nude or naked figure or statue; generally *the nude*, that is, the undraped human figure.

nudge *n* a jog with the elbow or a poke in the ribs.—*vt* (**nudged, nudging**) to give a hint or signal by a slight touch with the hand, elbow or foot.

nudity *n* the state of being naked; nakedness.

nugatory *adj* trifling; futile; worthless; of no force; inoperative.

nugget *n* a lump; especially, one of the larger lumps of gold found in diggings.

nuisance *n* something that annoys or gives trouble; that which is offensive or irritating; an annoyance; a pest; a bore.

null *adj* of no legal or binding force or validity; void; invalid.

nullification *n* the act of nullifying; a rendering void and of no effect.

nullify *vt* (**nullified, nullifying**) to annul; to render invalid; to deprive of legal force or efficacy.

nullity *n* the state or quality of being null; lack of validity; that which is of no force or efficacy.

numb *adj* torpid, benumbed or deadened; having lost the power of sensation and motion.—*vt* to make numb or torpid.

number *n* that which may be counted; an aggregate of units or a single unit considered as part of a series; an aggregate of several individuals; not a few; many; one of a numbered series of things, as a division of a book published in parts; a part of a periodical; a single issue of a magazine, etc; metrical arrangement of syllables; poetical rhythm or measure; a song or piece of music, especially as an item in a performance; a telephone number; (*gram*) the form which a word assumes according to whether speaking of or expressing one or more than one (the form that denotes one individual being *the singular number*, that set apart for two *the dual number*, that which refers to two or more *the plural number*); (*pl*) arithmetic; (*pl*) numerical superiority.—*vt* to count; to reckon; to enumerate; to reckon, rank or consider; to put a number or numbers on; to amount to; to reach the number of.

numberless *adj* that cannot be counted; innumerable.

number one *n* the first in a list, series, etc; (*colloq*) oneself or one's own interests; (*colloq*) the most important person or thing; (*colloq*) a best-selling pop record.—*adj* most important, urgent, etc (*our number-one priority*).

number plate *n* a plate on the front or rear of a motor vehicle that displays its registration number.

Numbers *n* the fourth book of the Pentateuch.

numbles *npl* the entrails of a deer.

numbness *n* the state of being numb; torpidity; torpor.

numbskull *n* same as **numskull**.

numerable *adj* capable of being numbered or counted.

numeral *adj* pertaining to number; consisting of number; expressing number; representing number.—*n* a figure or character used to express a number; (*gram*) a word expressing a number (*one, two, three*, etc).

numerate *vti* (**numerated, numerating**) to count.—*adj* having a basic understanding of arithmetic.

numeration *n* the act or art of numbering; (*arith*) the art of expressing in figures any number proposed in words or of expressing in words any number proposed in figures.

numerator *n* one that numbers; (*arith*) the number in vulgar fractions which shows how many parts of a unit are taken—the number above the line.

numerical *adj* belonging to number; denoting number; consisting of numbers.

numerically *adv* in numbers; with respect to numerical quantity (*numerically greater*).

numerous *adj* consisting of many individuals; great in number; many.

numismatic *adj* pertaining to coins or medals.

numismatics *n* the science of coins and medals.

numismatist *n* one skilled in numismatics.

numskull, numbskull *n* a dunce; a stupid person.

nun *n* a woman devoted to a religious life who lives in a convent or nunnery under a vow of perpetual chastity; a kind of pigeon having on its head a tuft of feathers.

nuncio *n* (*pl* **nuncios**) an ambassador of the first rank (not a cardinal) representing the pope at the court of a sovereign.

nuncupative *adj* (*law*) oral; not written.

nuncupative will *n* one made by the verbal declaration of the testator.

nunnery *n* a convent in which nuns reside.

nuptial *adj* pertaining to marriage; used or done at a wedding.

nuptials *npl* a wedding or marriage.

nurse *n* one who tends or takes care of the young, sick or infirm; a female who has the care of a child or children; an attendant in a hospital; one who or that which nurtures, cherishes or protects.—*vt* (**nursed, nursing**) to feed and tend generally in infancy; to suckle; to rear; to nurture; to tend in sickness or infirmity; to promote growth or vigour in; to foment; to foster; to manage with care and economy with a view to increasing.

nursemaid *n* a maidservant employed in nursing children.

nursery *n* a place or apartment in a house set apart for children; a place where young children may be left in temporary care; a nursery school; a place where trees, shrubs, flowering plants, etc, are raised from seed or otherwise in order to be transplanted or where they are propagated in order to be sold; a place where anything is fostered and the growth promoted.

nurseryman *n* (*pl* **nurserymen**) one who has a nursery of plants or is employed in one.

nursery school *n* a school for children who are too young for primary school.

nursing *n* the profession of a nurse.

nursing home *n* an establishment providing care for convalescent, chronically ill or disabled people.

nursling *n* one who or that which is nursed; a child.

nurture *n* the act of nursing or nourishing; education; that which nourishes; food; diet.—*vt* (**nurtured, nurturing**) to nourish; to educate; to bring or train up.

nut *n* the fruit of certain trees and shrubs which have the seed enclosed in a bony, woody or leathery covering, not opening when ripe; (*bot*) a bony pericarp containing a single seed to which it is not closely attached; a small block of metal or wood with an internal or female screw put on the end of a bolt to keep it firmly in its place; (*colloq*) a mad or foolish person; (*colloq*) a devotee or fan.—*vt* (**nutted, nutting**) to gather nuts.

nutation *n* a nodding; (*astron*) a slight gyratory movement of the earth's axis tending to make the pole describe a minute ellipse, due to the attraction of the sun and moon; (*bot*) the turning of flowers towards the sun.

nut

nutcracker *n* an instrument for cracking hard-shelled nuts; a kind of bird, so called from feeding on nuts.

nuthatch *n* a European bird which eats the kernel of the hazelnut.

nutmeg *n* a tropical Asian evergreen tree; its hard, aromatic kernel, grated and used as a spice.

nutria *n* the commercial name for the skins or fur of the coypu.

nutrient *adj* nourishing; nutritious.—*n* any substance which nourishes.

nutriment *n* that which nourishes; nourishment; food; aliment.

nutrition *n* the act or process by which organisms, whether vegetable or animal, absorb into their system their proper food; the process of assimilating food; that which nourishes; nutriment.

nutritious *adj* containing or serving as nutriment; promoting the growth or repairing the waste of organic bodies; nourishing.

nuts *adj* (*colloq*) mad; very foolish.

nuts and bolts *npl* (*colloq*) the basic facts; the essential, practical details.

nutshell *n* the hard covering of a nut; a tiny receptacle; a compact way of expression (*in a nutshell*).

nutty *adj* abounding in nuts; having the flavour of nuts; (*sl*) crazy.

nutcracker

nux vomica *n* the fruit of an Asian tree which contains the virulent poison strychnine; a drug containing strychnine.

nuzzle *vt* (**nuzzled, nuzzling**) to put a ring into the nose of; to root up with the nose.—*vi* to work with the nose, as a pig; to hide the head, as a child in its mother's bosom; to nestle; to snuggle.

nyctalopia *n* night blindness; a defect of vision which causes a person who can see normally by day to be almost blind at night, the opposite of *hemeralopia*).

nylgau, nylghau *n* a large species of antelope, inhabiting northern India, Iran, etc.

nylon *n* any of numerous synthetic strong, elastic materials used in textiles and plastics; (*pl*) stockings made of nylon.

nymph *n* in mythology, a spirit of nature envisaged as a maiden; (*poet*) a young and attractive woman; a maiden; a damsel; the chrysalis of an insect.

nympho *n* (*colloq*) a nymphomaniac.

nymphomania *n* abnormal and uncontrollable sexual desire in females.

nymphomaniac *adj* of or pertaining to nymphomania.—*n* a woman affected by nymphomania.

nystagmus *n* a condition of the eye characterized by spasmodic movement of the eyeballs.

O

O[1] the fifteenth letter and the fourth vowel in the English alphabet.

O[2] *interj* an exclamation used in earnest or solemn address, appeal or invocation and prefixed to the noun of address; an exclamation indicating wonder, admiration, surprise, pain, etc.

oaf *n* a dolt; a lout.

oafish *adj* doltish; loutish.

oak *n* a large tree which produces acorns and a hard wood formerly used in ship-building and for furniture, the bark being used for tanning.

oak apple *n* a spongy excrescence growing on the leaves or young branches of the oak, caused by the gallfly.

oakum *n* a fibre of old ropes untwisted and pulled loose, used for caulking the seams of ships, stopping leaks, etc.

oar *n* a long piece of timber, flat at one end and round at the other, used to propel a boat, barge or galley through the water.

oarsman *n* (*pl* **oarsmen**) one who rows with an oar; a boatman.

oasis *n* (*pl* **oases**) a fertile tract where there is water, in the midst of a desert or waste; a green spot in the midst of barrenness; a peaceful spot or situation in the midst of turmoil or trouble.

oast *n* a kiln to dry hops or malt.

oat *n* a cereal plant valuable for the grain it produces; (*pl*) a quantity of the plant in cultivation or of the grain (*field of oats*).

oatcake *n* a cake made of the meal of oats.

oatmeal *n* meal made from oats.

oath *n* (*pl* **oaths**) a solemn affirmation or declaration, made with an appeal to God for the truth of what is affirmed; a solemn swearing; a blasphemous use of the name of God or Christ; an imprecation.

obbligato *n* (*pl* **obbligatos, obbligati**) in music, an instrumental part or accompaniment of such importance that it cannot be dispensed with.

obduracy *n* the state or quality of being obdurate.

obdurate *adj* hardened in heart; persisting obstinately in sin; stubborn; inflexible; inexorable; harsh or rough.

obeah *n* same as **obi**.

obedience *n* the act or habit of obeying; compliance with a command, prohibition or known law and rule prescribed; submission to authority.

obedient *adj* submission to authority; complying with all commands; yielding compliance; dutiful.

obeisance *n* a bow or courtesy; an act of reverence, deference or respect.

obelisk *n* a column or monumental structure of rectangular form, diminishing towards the top and generally finishing with a low pyramid; a mark (thus †) referring the reader to a note in the margin or at the foot of the page (called also **dagger**).

obese *adj* excessively corpulent; fat; fleshy.

obesity *n* the state or quality of being obese; excessive corpulence.

obey *vt* to give ear to; to comply with the commands of; to be under the government of; to be ruled by; to submit to the direction or control of.—*vi* to submit to commands or authority; to do as one is bid.

obfuscate *vt* (**obfuscated, obfuscating**) to darken; to obscure; to bewilder; to confuse; to muddle.

obfuscation *n* the act of obfuscating; confusion or bewilderment of mind.

obi, obeah *n* a system of sorcery or witchcraft among Africans.

obit *n* (*colloq*) a short form of **obituary**.

obituary *n* an announcement of a person's death; a short article about the life and achievement of a person who has just died.—*adj* relating to the decease of a person; written about a person at his or her death (*an obituary notice*).

obiter dictum *n* (*pl* **obiter dicta**) a remark by the way; an offhand aphorism or statement.

object *n* that towards which the mind is directed in any of its states or activities; what is thought about, believed or seen; some visible and tangible thing; a concrete reality (*objects of interest in a museum*); that to which efforts are directed; aim; end; ultimate purpose; (*gram*) the word, clause or member of a sentence expressing

oak

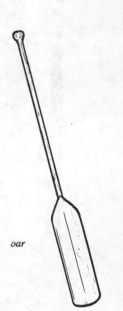

oar

that on which the action expressed by a transitive verb is exercised or the word or member governed by a preposition.—*vt* to place before or in the way; to bring forward as a matter of reproach or as an adverse ground or reason; to state or urge in opposition; to state as an objection (*I have nothing to object against him*).—*vi* to make opposition in words or arguments; to offer adverse reasons.

object glass *n* the lens of an optical instrument.

objection *n* the act of objecting; that which is or may be objected; adverse reason, argument or charge; fault found.

objectionable *adj* such as might reasonably be objected to; justly liable to objection; calling for disapproval; reprehensible (as actions, language, etc).

objective *adj* belonging to what is external to the mind; hence, when used of literature or art, containing no trace of the writer's or artist's own feelings or individuality, opposed to *subjective*; not influenced by one's feelings or thoughts; impartial; (*gram*) belonging to the object of a transitive verb or a preposition (*the objective case, an objective clause*).—*n* the objective case; an object glass; the thing or place aimed at; an aim; a goal.

objectivity *n* the quality or state of being objective.

object lesson *n* a lesson to the young by means of articles themselves or pictures of them; a warning or instructive experience.

objector *n* one that objects.

objet d'art *n* (*pl* **objets d'art**) an object valued for its artistic worth.

objurgate *vti* (**objurgated, objurgating**) to chide, reprove or reprehend.

objurgation *n* the act of objurgating; a reproof.

oblate *adj* (*geom*) flattened or depressed at the poles.

oblation *n* anything offered or presented in worship or sacred service.

obligate *vt* (**obligated, obligating**) to bring or place under some obligation; to hold to some duty.

obligation *n* that which binds or obliges to do something; binding or constraining power or effect; an external act or duty imposed by the relations of society; a claim upon one; the position in which one is bound or indebted to another for a favour received; a favour bestowed and binding to gratitude.

obligatory *adj* imposing obligation or duty; binding in law or conscience; requiring performance or forbearance of some act (*obligatory on a person*).

oblige *vt* (**obliged, obliging**) to constrain by any force, physical, moral or legal; to compel; to bind by any restraint; to bind

oblong

oboe

by some favour done; to lay under obligation of gratitude.

obligement *n* a favour conferred; obligation.

obliging *adj* having the disposition to do favours; conferring favours or kindnesses; kind; helpful.

oblique *adj* having a direction neither perpendicular nor parallel to some line or surface which is made the standard of reference; not direct; aslant; slanting; (*fig*) indirect or by allusion; not direct in descent; collateral.

oblique case *n* (*gram*) any case except the nominative.

obliquity *n* the state of being oblique; deviation from parallelism or a perpendicular; deviation from moral rectitude; a mental or moral twist.

obliterate *vt* (**obliterated, obliterating**) to efface; to erase or blot out; to make indecipherable; to cause to be forgotten.

obliteration *n* the act of obliterating or effacing.

oblivion *n* the state of being blotted out from the memory; a being forgotten; forgetfulness; the act of forgetting; a forgetting of offences or remission of punishment.

oblivious *adj* causing forgetfulness; forgetful; mentally absent.

oblong *adj* rectangular and having the length greater than the breadth; longer than broad.—*n* an oblong figure.

obloquy *n* censorious speech; reproachful language; language that causes reproach and odium to rest on men or their actions; odium.

obnoxious *adj* odious; hateful; offensive.

oboe *n* a wind instrument of wood, sounded through a double reed; a hautboy.

oboist *n* a player on the oboe.

obscene *adj* impure in language or action; indecent; lewd; offensive.

obsceneness, obscenity *n* the state or quality of being obscene; impurity; ribaldry; lewdness.

obscurant, obscurantist *n* one who obscures; one who opposes the progress of knowledge, enlightenment, inquiry or reform.

obscurantism *n* the system or principles of an obscurant.

obscure *adj* imperfectly illuminated; gloomy; not clear or distinct to view; dim; not easily understood; not obviously intelligible; abstruse; indistinct; not much known or observed; unknown to fame; unnoticed.—*vt* (**obscured, obscuring**) to darken; to make dark or dim; to make less intelligible, legible or visible; to hide; to prevent from being seen or known.

obscurity *n* the quality or state of being obscure; darkness; dimness; darkness of meaning; a state of being unknown to fame.

obsequies *npl* funeral rites, ceremonies or solemnities.

obsequious *adj* obedient or submissive to the will of another; compliant; servilely condescending; compliant to excess; cringing; fawning.

observance *n* the act of observing; performance; a rite or ceremony; an act of respect, worship, etc; obedient regard or attention; respectful or servile attention; homage.

observant *adj* characterized by observation; taking notice; attentively noticing; attentive to duties or commands; obedient; adhering to in practice (*observant of duties*).

observation *n* the act, power or habit of observing; a taking notice or paying attention; monitoring; the careful noting of someone or something, such as a patient's condition or a criminal suspect's movements; the observing of some phenomenon, often by the assistance of an instrument; information gained by such an act; a remark based or professing to be based on what has been observed; notice.

observatory *n* a place used for making observations of natural phenomena; a building constructed for astronomical observations; a place of outlook.

observe *vt* (**observed, observing**) to look on with attention; to regard attentively; to watch; to monitor; to notice; to perceive; to detect; to discover; to remark in words; to mention; to keep with due ceremonies; to celebrate; to keep or adhere to in practice; to comply with; to obey.—*vi* to be attentive; to remark; to comment.

obsess *vt* to occupy or dominate the thoughts or feelings of continually.

obsession *n* act of obsessing; that which obsesses; a persistent idea or preoccupation.

obsessive *adj* pertaining to obsession; resulting from an obsession; suffering from an obsession or obsessions.

obsidian *n* vitreous lava or volcanic glass, a glassy mineral of several varieties.

obsolescent *adj* becoming obsolete; going out of use; passing into desuetude.

obsolete *adj* gone into disuse; disused; neglected; out of fashion.

obstacle *n* anything that stands in the way and hinders progress; a hindrance; an obstruction or impediment, either physical or moral.

obstetric, obstetrical *adj* pertaining to obstetrics.

obstetrician *n* a doctor specializing in obstetrics.

obstetrics *n* the branch of medicine which deals with the care and treatment of women during pregnancy and childbirth.

obstinate *adj* pertinaciously adhering to an opinion or purpose; fixed firmly in resolution; not yielding to reason, arguments or other means; stubborn (said of persons); not yielding or not easily subdued or removed (*an obstinate fever*; *an obstinate cough*).

obstinacy *n* the state or quality of being obstinate.

obstreperous *adj* vociferous; noisy; loud.

obstruct *vt* to block up, stop up or close, as a passage; to fill with obstacles or impediments that prevent passing; to hinder from passing; to impede; to stand in the way of; to retard, interrupt, render slow.

obstruction *n* the act of obstructing; anything that stops or closes a way, passage or channel; obstacle; impediment; that which impedes progress; hindrance.

obstructionist *n* one who practises obstruction; an obstructive.

obstructive *adj* obstructing or tending to obstruct.

obtain *vt* to gain possession of; to gain, procure, receive, get, acquire.—*vi* to be received in customary or common use; to be established in practice; to hold good; to subsist (*the custom still obtains*).

obtrude *vt* (**obtruded, obtruding**) to thrust prominently forward; to push (an opinion, etc) on another, uninvited or unwanted; to intrude; to push oneself forward.—*vi* to intrude; to enter when not invited.

obtrusion *n* the act of obtruding.

obtrusive *adj* disposed to obtrude; forward; intrusive.

obtuse *adj* not pointed or acute; blunt; not having acute sensibility; stupid; dull.

obtuse angle *n* an angle larger than a right angle.

obverse *adj* (*numis*) bearing the face or head.—*n* that side of a coin or medal which has the face or head or principal device on it, the other being the reverse.

obviate *vt* (**obviated, obviating**) to meet, as difficulties or objections; to overcome; to clear out of the way; to make unnecessary.

obvious *adj* easily discovered, seen or understood; perfectly plain, manifest or evident.

ocarina *n* a small egg-shaped musical instrument played like a flute.

occasion *n* time of an occurrence, incident or event; a special occurrence or event; an opportunity; favourable time, season or circumstances; reason or grounds; incidental cause; a motive or reason; incidental need; requirement (*to have occasion* or *no occasion for a thing*).—*vt* to cause incidentally; to produce; to induce.

occasional *adj* incidental; occurring at times but not regular or systematic; intermittent; made or happening as opportunity requires or admits; produced for an occasion.

occasionally *adv* in an occasional manner; at times; sometimes but not often.

Occident *n* the western quarter of the hemisphere; the west, the opposite of *Orient*.

Occidental *adj* pertaining to the occident or west; western, opposed to *oriental*.

occipital *adj* of or pertaining to the occiput.

occiput *n* (*pl* **occiputs, occiputa**) the hinder part of the head.

occlude *vt* (**occluded, occluding**) to shut up or close; to shut out or in; to obstruct; (*chem*) to absorb or take up without chemical combination.

occlusion *n* the state of being occluded; the position of the teeth when the jaws are closed.

occult *adj* hidden from the eye or understanding; invisible and mysterious; unknown; secret; esoteric; supernatural; magical.—**the occult** *n* the supernatural; magic; black magic; necromancy; that which is mysterious or secret.

occultation *n* (*astron*) the hiding of a star or planet from our sight by passing behind some other of the heavenly bodies; the time of a planet or star being so hidden; hence, (*fig*) disappearance from view; withdrawal from public notice.

occultism *n* a system of occult or mysterious doctrines; the beliefs of the theosophists.

occult sciences *npl* certain so-called sciences of the Middle Ages, as alchemy, necromancy or magic, astrology.

occupancy *n* the act of occupying; the time of occupying; the fact of being an occupant.

occupant *n* an occupier.

occupation *n* the act of occupying or taking possession; possession; tenure; the time of occupation; state of being employed or occupied in any way; that which engages one's time and attention; the principal business of one's life; a vocation; calling; trade.

occupational therapy *n* a type of therapy involving work with arts and crafts to exercise the muscles, etc, and aid recovery after injury or illness.

occupier *n* one that occupies; an occupant.

occupy *vt* (**occupied, occupying**) to take possession of; to possess; to hold and use; to take up, as room or space; to cover or fill; to employ or use (one's time); to engage; to busy (often reflexive).—*vi* to be an occupant; to hold possession.

occur *vi* (**occurred, occurring**) to meet or come to the mind, imagination or memory; to happen; to take place; to exist so as to be capable of being found or seen; to be found; to be met with.

occurrence *n* the act of occurring or taking place; any incident or accidental event; an observed instance.

ocelot

octagon

ocean *n* the vast body of water which covers more than three-fifths of the surface of the globe; the sea; also, one of the great basins or areas into which it has been divided; any immense expanse (*the boundless ocean of eternity*).—*adj* pertaining to the main or great sea (*the ocean wave*).

oceanic *adj* pertaining to the ocean; occurring in or produced by the ocean, as distinguished from smaller seas.

oceanography *n* the department of knowledge that deals with oceanic phenomena.

ocellate, ocellated *adj* resembling an eye; studded with the figures of little eyes.

ocellus *n* (*pl* **ocelli**) one of the minute simple eyes of insects, many spiders, crustaceans, molluscs etc.

ocelot *n* a carnivorous animal of the cat kind, an inhabitant of Mexico.

ochlocracy *n* the rule or ascendancy of the multitude or common people.

ochre *n* a name generally applied to clays coloured with the oxides of iron in various proportions and varying in colour from pale yellow to brownish red, much used in painting.

octagon *n* (*geom*) a figure of eight sides and eight angles.

octagonal *adj* having eight sides and eight angles.

octahedron *n* (*geom*) a solid contained by eight faces, which take the form of equal and equilateral triangles.

octahedral *adj* having eight equal surfaces.

octangular *adj* having eight angles.

octave *n* the first eight lines of a sonnet; a stanza of eight lines; (*mus*) an eighth or an interval of seven degrees or twelve semitones; one sound corresponding to a frequency of vibration double that of another.—*adj* consisting of eight.

octavo *n* (*pl* **octavos**) the size of one leaf of a sheet of paper folded so as to make eight leaves, usually written 8vo; a book having eight leaves to each sheet.—often used as an adjective.

octet *n* (*mus*) a musical composition for eight parts.

October *n* the tenth month of the year.

octogenarian *n* a person eighty years of age; anyone whose age is between eighty and ninety.—*adj* of eighty years of age; between eighty and ninety years of age.

octopus *n* (*pl* **octopuses**) a genus of two-gilled cuttlefishes, having eight tentacles provided with suckers.

octosyllabic *adj* consisting of eight syllables.—*n* a word of eight syllables.

octuple *adj* eightfold.

ocular *adj* pertaining to the eye; depending on the eye; received by actual sight.

oculist *n* one skilled in diseases of the eyes.

odalisque, odalisk *n* a female slave or concubine in an oriental seraglio or a harem.

odd *adj* not even; not exactly divisible by 2; left over after the pairs have been reckoned; additional to a whole mentioned in round numbers; not included with others; hence, unheeded; of little value or account (*odd times*, *odd trifles*); incidental; casual; forming one of a pair of which the other is lacking; belonging to a broken set; singular; strange; peculiar; eccentric; queer.

oddity *n* the state or quality of being odd; singularity; something strange; an eccentric or strange person.

oddly *adv* in an odd manner; not evenly; strangely; whimsically; singularly.

oddment *n* an odd article or one left over.

oddness *n* the state of being odd; state of not being even; strangeness; eccentricity.

odds *n sing or pl* excess of one amount or quantity compared with another; difference in favour of one and against another; amount by which the bet of one party exceeds that of the other.—**at odds** at variance; in controversy or quarrel.

odds and ends *npl* small miscellaneous articles.

ode *n* a short poem or song; a poem to be set to music or sung; a lyric poem of a lofty kind.

Odin *n* same as **Woden** .

odious *adj* hateful; causing disgust or repugnance; offensive.

odium *n* hatred; dislike; the quality that provokes hatred.

odometer *n* an instrument for measuring the distance travelled by any vehicle.

odontoid *adj* tooth-like.

odontoid process *n* the part of the first vertebra of the neck, forming a pivot for the head.

odontology *n* that branch of anatomical science which treats of the teeth.

odoriferous *adj* giving odour or scent; diffusing fragrance; fragrant.

odorous *adj* having or emitting an odour; sweet of scent; fragrant.

odour *n* any scent or smell, whether pleasant or offensive; when used alone most commonly a sweet smell; fragrance.

odyssey *n* a long adventurous journey.

oedema *n* (*med*) a puffiness or swelling of parts arising from water collecting; an excess of fluid in the tissues.

Oedipus complex *n* an excessive attachment of a boy to his mother.

oenological *adj* pertaining to the study of wine.

oenologist *n* a wine expert.

oenology *n* the study of wine.

o'er (*poet*) a contraction of **over**.

oesophagus *n* (*pl* **oesophagi**) the gullet; the canal through which food and drink pass to the stomach

oestrogen *n* a hormone that develops and maintains female characteristics of the body, is secreted by the ovaries and controls part of the oestrus cycle.

oestrus *n* the period of ovulation of animals; heat; violent desire.

oeuvre *n* a work of art, literature, music, etc.; the life's work of an artist, writer or composer.

of *prep* a word used in regard to source, cause, origin, motive, etc; possession or ownership; attribute, quality or condition; the material of anything; an aggregate or whole with a partitive reference (*all*, *some of us*); the relation of object to a verbal notion (*a desire of fame*); to express concerning, relating to, about; distance or time (*within a mile of*); identity, equivalence or apposition—the appositive use of *of* (*the city of London*); on or in (with indefinite expressions of time, as *I often go there of an evening*; *so of late*, that is, in recent times; *of old*, in olden times).

off *adv* away; distant (*a mile off*); from or away by removal or separation (*to cut off*); not on; from, in the way of departure, abatement, remission (*the fever goes off*); away, not toward.—*adj* distant; as applied to horses, right hand (opposed to *near*); in cricket, applied to that part of the field which is on the left of the bowler; cancelled; having gone bad.—*prep* not on; away from; from or out of (*a lane leading off a street*); (*naut*) to seaward from (hence *offing*).—*interj* a command to depart; away! begone!

offal *n* the intestines (kidneys, heart, tongue, liver and other parts of an animal carcass) eaten as food; carrion; refuse.

offbeat *adj* unconventional; eccentric.

off chance *n* a remote possibility.

off-colour *n* a defective colour in gems, etc; indecent; obscene; slightly unwell.

off-day *n* a day on which any usual occupation is discontinued; a day on which a person is not performing as well as usual.

offence *n* hurt; injury; an affront, insult or wrong; the state of being offended; displeasure; any transgression of law; a crime or sin; a misdemeanour.

offend *vt* to displease; to make angry; to affront; to mortify; to shock, annoy or pain (the taste or smell); to sin against; to disobey.—*vi* to break the law; to sin; to cause dislike or anger; to take offence.

offender *n* one who offends; a criminal; a transgressor.

offensive *adj* causing offence; giving provocation; irritating; disgusting; disagreeable (as to the senses); pertaining to offence; used in attack, opposed to *defensive*; consisting in attack; proceeding by attack.—*n* (with the definite article) the act of attacking (*to act on the offensive*).

offensiveness *n* the quality of being offensive; unpleasantness.

offer *vt* to present for acceptance or rejection; to tender; to present to notice; to proffer; to present, as an act of worship; to sacrifice (often with *up*); to attempt or do with evil intent (*to offer violence, an insult*); to bid, as a price or wages.—*vi* to present itself (*an opportunity offers*); to declare a willingness; to make an attempt.—*n* the act of offering; a proposal to be accepted or rejected; the act of bidding a price or the sum bid.

offering *n* the act of an offerer; that which is offered; a gift offered or consecrated to a deity; a sacrifice; an oblation.

offertory *n* the sentences in the communion service of the Church of England read while the collection is being made; the money collected.

offhand *adv* impromptu; without thinking.—*adj* done without study or hesitation; curt; brusque.

office *n* employment or business; duty or duties falling on or entrusted to a person; that which is performed or assigned to be done by a particular thing; function; position; act of good or ill voluntarily tendered; service; (*eccles*) a book of devotion or a service appointed for a particular occasion; a room or building in which people transact business; a place where official acts are done; a body of persons entrusted with certain duties; people who transact business in an office; a department or branch of an organization or firm; (*pl*) kitchens, outhouses, etc, of a mansion, dwelling house or farm.

office-bearer *n* a person who holds an office or official position; one of the officials of a society, organization, etc.

officer *n* a person who holds an office; a person commissioned or authorized to fill a public situation or to perform any public duty; one who holds a commission in the army, navy or air force.

official *adj* pertaining to an office or public duty; relating to or authorized by a recognized authority; formal or ceremonious.—*n* one invested with an office of a public nature; (*eccles*) a deputy appointed by a bishop, chapter, archdeacon, etc.

officialism *n* a system of official government; a system of excessive official routine; bureaucracy.

officially *adv* in an official manner; by virtue of the proper authority.

officiate *vi* (**officiated, officiating**) to perform official duties; to act in an official capacity.

officiator *n* one who officiates.

officious *adj* excessively forward in offering unwelcome or unwanted advice or services; interfering; meddling.

offing *n* the position of a vessel, or of a portion of the sea, within sight of land, relatively to the coast; the near or foreseeable future.

offish *adj* (*colloq*) distant, stiff.

off-key *adj* sung or played in the wrong key; out of tune; jarring; discordant.

off-licence *n* a licence to sell alcohol for consumption away from the premises; a shop, etc, with such a licence.

off limits *adj* out of bounds.

off-line *adj* in computing, not connected to the central processor; not having a direct connection to a computer.

off-peak *adj* not at the maximum degree of activity, etc.

offprint *n* a copy of a magazine article, academic paper, etc, given to the author.

off-putting *adj* discouraging; daunting.

offscouring *n* refuse; dregs.

offset *n* a sum or amount set off against another as an equivalent; something that compensates; (*surv*) a perpendicular distance measured from a main line in order to get the area of an irregular portion; (*hortic*) a young bulb or a scion used to propagate a plant; an offshoot; a method of printing in which the image is transferred from the plate on to paper by a rubber-coated cylinder.—*vt* (**offset, offsetting**) to compensate for; to counterbalance.

offshoot *n* a branch from a main stem, stream, mountain range, etc; a by-product; something derivative.

offshore *adj* away from the shore; at a distance from the shore.

offside *adj* in football, hockey and some other games, said of a player who gets into such a position that for the moment he or she is debarred by the rules from taking part in the game; pertaining to the right-hand side of a vehicle where traffic drives on the left.

offspring *n sing pl* what is sprung from a stock or parent; a child or children; what arises or is produced from something.

offstage *adj, adv* out of sight of the audience; behind the scenes.

off-the-cuff *adj* (of a remark, speech, etc) spontaneous; unrehearsed; extempore.

off the record *adj* not intended to be made public; unofficial.

off the wall *adj* unusual; innovative.

off-white *adj* white tinged with yellow or grey.

oft *adv* (*poet*) often; frequently.

often *adv* frequently; many times; not seldom.—*adj* frequent.

oftentimes, ofttimes *adv* (*arch*) frequently, often.

ogee *n* (*archit*) a moulding consisting of two members, the one concave, the other convex.

ogham, ogam *n* an ancient Irish alphabet; any of the characters of this alphabet.

ogive *n* (*archit*) the Gothic or pointed arch.

ogle *vt* (**ogled, ogling**) to view with side glances, as in fondness or with a design to attract notice; to look at with lust.—*vi* to cast side glances; top look lustfully.—*n* a side glance or look.

ogre *n* a monster of popular legends who lived on human flesh; a person who is frightening, cruel or unpleasant.

ogress *n* a female ogre.

ogreish *adj* resembling or suggestive of an ogre.

oh *interj* expressing surprise, admiration, delight, pain, etc.

ohm *n* the SI unit of electrical resistance.

oil *n* a substance of animal and vegetable origin, liquid at ordinary temperatures, insoluble in water and burning with a more or less luminous flame; a substance of somewhat similar character of mineral origin (as petroleum)—oils are divided into fixed and volatile or essential oils, the latter being diffusible in vapour by heat; an oil colour; an oil painting.—*vt* to smear or rub over with oil.

oilcake *n* a cake or mass of compressed linseed, rape or other seed from which oil has been extracted, linseed cake being much used as food for cattle.

oilcloth *n* a waterproof fabric impregnated with oil or synthetic resin, used as a floor-covering, table-covering, etc.

oil colour, oil paint *n* a pigment made by grinding a colouring substance in oil.

oiliness *n* the quality of being oily; the quality of being over-smooth or too suave; unctuousness.

oil painting *n* the art of painting with oil colours; a picture painted in oil colours.

oilskin *n* a fabric made waterproof by treatment with oil; a waterproof garment of oilskin or plastic-coated fabric.

oilstone *n* a fine-grained stone on which tools receive a fine edge by the aid of oil.

oil well *n* a well sunk into an oil-bearing mineral bed.

oily *adj* consisting of or containing oil; resembling oil; fat; greasy; too smooth or suave; unctuous; sanctimonious; hypocritically pious.

ointment *n* any soft substance, such as a paste, cream or lotion, usually medicated, used for smearing, the body; an unguent.

okapi *n* an African animal akin to the giraffe but smaller and striped.

okra *n* a tall West African plant, the pods of which are used as a vegetable, also called **lady's fingers**.

old *adj* advanced far in years or life (*an old man* or *tree*); not new or fresh; long made or produced (*old clothes, wine*); not modern; ancient; of any duration whatever (*a year old*); former (*old habits*); long practised; experienced (*old offender*); having the feelings of an old person; crafty or cunning; a familiar term of affection or cordiality.

old age pensioner *n* a senior citizen.

old boy, old girl *n* a former pupil of a school.

old boy network *n* an official system by which people who attended the same school or a similar school (usually private) give preference to each other in employment, etc.

olden *adj* old; ancient.

old-fashioned *adj* formed according to obsolete fashion or custom; characterized by antiquated fashions or customs; aping old people.

oldish *adj* somewhat old.

old master *n* a painting by one of the leading early European painters, usually from the fifteenth century to the eighteenth century; one of these painters.

oldness *n* the state of being old; old age; antiquity.

Old Norse *n* the ancient language of Scandinavia, represented by the classical Icelandic and still with wonderful purity by modern Icelandic.

old wives' tale *n* a traditional superstitious belief.

old-world *adj* belonging to a far bygone age; antiquated.

Old World *n* a name frequently given to Europe, Asia and Africa; the eastern hemisphere.

oleaginous *adj* having the qualities of oil; unctuous; (*fig*) (applied to persons, manners, etc) smoothly sanctimonious; fawning.

oleander *n* a poisonous evergreen shrub with fragrant flowers.

oleaster *n* the wild olive, a yellow-flowered shrub resembling the olive.

olefin *n* any of a class of unsaturated hydrocarbons.

oleic acid *n* an oily acid obtained from butter, the oil of linseed, etc.

olein *n* one of the chief constituents of animal fat.

oleograph *n* a picture produced in oils by a process analogous to that of lithographic printing.

olfactory *adj* pertaining to smelling; connected with the sense of smelling.—*n* an organ of smelling.

olibanum *n* a kind of incense; frankincense.

oligarch *n* a member of an oligarchy.

oligarchic, oligarchical *adj* pertaining to oligarchy.

oligarchy *n* a form of government in which the supreme power is placed in the hands of a small exclusive class; those who form such a class or body.

Oligocene *adj* (*geol*) more recent than Eocene and older than Miocene.

olio *n* (*pl* **olios**) a dish of stewed meat; a

oil

oilskin

mixture; a medley; a miscellany or collection of various compositions.

olive *n* an evergreen tree much cultivated in Southern Europe, etc, for its edible hard-stoned fruit and the oil derived from this; its fruit; a yellowish-green colour; a brownish-green colour.—*adj* relating to the olive; of a yellowish-green colour; of a brownish-green colour.

olive branch *n* a branch of the olive tree, the emblem of peace.

olive green *n* a yellowish-green colour; a brownish-green colour.

olive oil *n* an oil obtained from the fruit of the olive and much used in cookery and for medicinal and manufacturing purposes.

olivine *n* an olive-green variety of chrysolite.

olla *n* a jar or urn.

Olympiad *n* a period of four years reckoned from one celebration of the Olympic games to another, by which the ancient Greeks computed time, from 776 BC.

Olympian, Olympic *adj* pertaining to Olympus, home of the Greek gods.

Olympic games *n sing pl* a national festival of the ancient Greeks, celebrated at intervals of four years on the plain of Olympia; an international athletics event held every four years in a different country.

omasum *n* (*pl* **omasa**) the third stomach of ruminating animals.

ombre *n* an old game at cards, usually played by three persons.

omega *n* the name of the last letter of the Greek alphabet, hence in Scripture omega denotes the last, the ending; the end of anything.

omelette *n* a kind of dish made with eggs, beaten up and flavoured with chopped herbs, etc, or jam, etc.

omen *n* an event or occurrence thought to portend good or evil; a prognostic; an augury.—*vi* to prognosticate as an omen; to augur; to betoken.—*vt* to divine; to predict.

ominous *adj* containing an ill omen; foreboding or betokening evil; threatening evil; inauspicious.

omission *n* the act of omitting; a neglect or failure to do something that should have been done; the act of leaving out; something omitted or left out.

omit *vt* (**omitted, omitting**) to pass over or neglect; to let slip; to fail to do or to use; to leave out; not to insert.

omnibus *n* a long-bodied covered vehicle for carrying passengers; a bus; a large book containing a variety of items.

omnifarious *adj* of all varieties, forms or kinds.

omnipotence *n* unlimited or infinite power; almighty power.

omnipotent *adj* almighty; all-powerful.

omnipresence *n* the faculty or power of being present in every place at the same time.

omnipresent *adj* present in all places at the same time; ubiquitous.

omniscience *n* the faculty of knowing everything.

omniscient *adj* having knowledge of all things.

omnium-gatherum *n* a miscellaneous collection of things or persons.

omnivorous *adj* all-devouring; eating food of every kind indiscriminately (*omnivorous animals*).

on *prep* above and so as to touch; not off; performing by means of (*to play on a harp, on a violin*); in addition to (*loss on loss*); at or near (*on the coast*); expressing reliance, dependence, basis, etc (*a statement founded on error*); at or in the time of (we say *on the day, at the hour, in the week, month, year*); at the time of or during (*on public occasions*); immediately after and as a result (*he retired on the ratification of the treaty*); in reference or relation to (*on our part*); toward or so as to affect (*mercy on him*); denoting a pledge, engagement or affirmation (*on my word, on his honour*); in betting, in support of the chances of; among the staff of or contributors to (with names of periodicals); pointing to a state, condition, occupation, etc (*on fire, on duty*).—*adv* forward, in progression (*move on*); forward, in succession (*and so on*); without interruption or ceasing (*sleep on, say on*); attached to the body (*his clothes are not on*).—also used elliptically as an imperative = *go on*, advance.—*adj* operating; working; taking place.

onager *n* the wild ass of Central Asia.

once *adv* one time; on one occasion only; at one former time; formerly; immediately after; as soon as.—used as a noun preceded by *this* or *that* (*this once, that once*).—**at once** at the same time; all together; suddenly; precipitately; not gradually; immediately; forthwith; without delay.

once-over *n* (*colloq*) a quick look; a superficial inspection.

oncologist *n* a person who specializes in oncology.

oncology *n* the branch of medicine dealing with tumours and cancer.

oncoming *adj* approaching; nearing.—*n* a coming or drawing near; approach.

one *adj* being but a single thing or a unit; not two or more; indicating a contrast or opposition to some other thing; closely united; forming a whole; undivided; single in kind.—*one* occurs in many compound words of obvious meaning, as *one-armed, one-handed, one-masted*, etc.—*n* the first

olive

of the simple units; the symbol representing this (= 1); a particular individual, whether thing or person (in this sense with a plural).—**at one** in union; in concord or agreement.—*pron* any single person; any man, any person (*one may speak one's mind*).—**one another** one or each the other.

one-horse *adj* drawn by a single horse; small or unimportant.

oneiromancy *n* divination by dreams.

oneness *n* the state of being one; singleness; unity.

one-night stand *n* a performance given for one night only in one place; a sexual encounter that last for one night only; the partner in such an encounter.

one-off *adj* produced or performed only once.

onerous *adj* burdensome; troublesome; oppressive.

oneself *pron* one's self; himself or herself.

one-sided *adj* related to or having but one side; partial; unjust; unfair.

one-upmanship *n* the art or practice of always securing and maintaining an advantage or superiority over opponents, often by cunning means.

ongoing *adj* progressing; continuing.

onion *n* a biennial cultivated plant of the lily family, and particularly its bulbous root, much used as an article of food.

on-line *adj* (of equipment) connected to and controlled by the central processor of a computer; having a direct connection to a computer.

onlooker *n* a looker-on; a spectator.

only *adj* single; alone in its class; solitary.—*adv* for one purpose alone; simply; merely; barely; solely; singly.—*conj* but; excepting that.

onomatopoeia *n* the formation of words by imitation of sounds; the expressing by sound of the thing signified, thus *buzz, hum, peewit, whip-poor-will*, etc, are produced by onomatopoeia.

onomastics *n* the study of proper names.

onrush *n* a rush or dash onwards; a rapid or violent onset.

onset *n* a violent attack; an assault; an assault by an army or body of troops.

onslaught *n* an attack or onset; an assault.

ontogeny, ontogenesis *n* (*biol*) the history of the individual development of an organized being.

ontology *n* the doctrine of being; that part of metaphysics which investigates and explains the nature of all things or existences, dealing with whatever does or can exist (sometimes equivalent to *metaphysics*).

onus *n* (*pl* **onuses**) a burden; the burden of proving what has been alleged.

onward *adv* toward the point before or in front; forward; on; in advance.—*adj* advanced or advancing (*an onward course*); carried so far towards an end; forward; advanced.

onwards *adv* same as **onward**.

onyx *n* a semi-pellucid gem with variously coloured zones or veins; an agate with layers of chalcedony, one of which is flesh-coloured, used for cameos.

oodles *npl* a great many; a huge quantity.

oolite *n* (*geol*) a type of limestone composed of globules clustered together, commonly without any visible cement or base.

oology *n* the scientific study of birds' eggs.

oologist *n* one skilled in oology.

ooze *vi* (**oozed, oozing**) to percolate, as a liquid, through the pores of a substance or through small openings; to flow in small quantities from the pores of a body (often used figuratively, as *the secret oozed out*).—*vt* to emit in the shape of moisture.—*n* soft mud or slime, as at the bottom of any sheet of water; in tanning, a solution of tannin; the liquor of a tan vat.

opah *n* a large and brightly coloured sea fish of tropical and temperate seas.

opal *n* a precious stone of various colours and varieties, the finest characterized by its iridescent reflection of light and formerly believed to possess magical virtues.

opalescence *n* a play of colours like that of the opal; the reflection of a milky and iridescent light.

opalescent *adj* resembling opal; having the iridescent tints of opal.

opaline *adj* pertaining to or like opal.

opaque *adj* impervious to the rays of light; not transparent.

opacity *n* state or quality of being opaque; lack of transparency.

open *adj* not shut; not closed; not covered; not stopped (as a bottle); unsealed (as a letter); free to be used or enjoyed; not restricted; affording free ingress; accessible; public; spread; expanded; not drawn together or contracted (*an open hand*; *open arms*); hence, free, liberal, bounteous; free from dissimulation; candid; not secret or concealed; clear; unobstructed (*an open view*; *an open country*); exposed to view; laid bare; exposed or liable to be assailed; fully prepared; attentive; not yet decided (*an open question*); available; ready for business; not settled, balanced or closed (*an open account*); enunciated without closing the mouth or with the full utterance (*an open vowel*); (*mus*) produced without stopping by the finger or without using a slide, key, piston, etc.—*n* an open or clear space.—*vt* to make open; to unclose; to remove any fastening or obstruction from, so as to afford an entrance, passage or view of the inner parts; to spread; to expand (the fingers, the arms);

onion

to enter upon; to commence (*to open a negotiation* or *correspondence*); to declare open; to set in operation with some ceremony; to reveal; to disclose (*to open one's mind*).—*vi* to unclose itself; to be unclosed; to be parted; to begin to be seen from a distance; to commence; to begin; to begin to fire (as a battery).

open day *n* a day on which visitors, such as potential pupils, etc, are invited to look around an institution, such as a school, etc.

open-handed *adj* generous; liberal; munificent.

open-hearted *adj* candid; frank; sincere; not sly.

opening *adj* first in order; commencing (*an opening speech*).—*n* the act of one who or that which opens; an open place; a break or breach in something; a hole or perforation; an aperture; beginning; commencement; a vacancy; an opportunity of commencing a business or profession; a thinly wooded space without undergrowth, as in a forest.

opera glass

openly *adv* in an open manner; publicly; candidly; frankly.

open-mouthed *adj* having the mouth open; gaping, as with astonishment.

openness *n* the state or quality of being open.

open verdict *n* a verdict of an inquest finding that a crime has been committed but without specifying the criminal or which finds that a sudden or violent death has occurred but does not decide on the cause.

openwork *n* ornamental work, so made as to show openings through its substance.

opera *n* a musical drama; a dramatic composition set to music and sung and acted on the stage, accompanied with musical instruments; the score or words of a musical drama.

opera bouffe *n* an exaggerated or farcical form of comic opera.

opera glass *n* a small binocular telescope of low magnifying power, used in theatres, etc; a lorgnette.

operate *vi* (**operated, operating**) to exert power or strength, physical or mechanical; to function; to act; to have agency; to produce an effect; to have a designed result; (*surg*) to cut open a human body in order to remove or repair a part of it.—*vt* to effect; to accomplish; to put into operation; to work; to drive (a machine).

opossum

operatic *adj* pertaining to the opera; exaggerated.

operating system *n* the software in a computer which controls basic operations.

operation *n* the act or process of operating; a functioning, working or proceeding; process; manipulation; the carrying out of planned measures by regular movements (*military* or *naval operations*); a surgical proceeding in which the human body is cut open in order to remove or repair a part of it.

operative *adj* operating; working; functioning; exerting force; active in the production of effects; efficacious; producing the effect; having to do with manual or other operations.—*n* a person who operates a machine, etc; a skilled worker.

operator *n* one who operates.

operculum *n* (*pl* **opercula, operculums**) (*biol*) a little lid or cover; the cover or lid of the spore cases of mosses; the lid of a pitcher form leaf; a plate closing the aperture of the shell of many molluscs when the animal is retracted within it; the bony apparatus which protects the gills of fishes.

operetta *n* a short musical drama of a light character.

ophicleide *n* (*mus*) an old large and powerful brass wind instrument with a compass of three octaves.

ophidian *adj* pertaining to snakes; having the characters of the snakes; serpentine.— *n* one of an order of reptiles which comprises all the snakes or serpents.

ophiology *n* that branch of zoology which deals with snakes; the natural history of snakes.

ophthalmia *n* inflammation of the eye.

ophthalmic *adj* pertaining to the eye; situated near the eye.

ophthalmology the branch of medicine dealing with disorders of the eye.

opiate *n* any medicine that contains opium and has the quality of inducing sleep or repose; a narcotic; anything that dulls sensation, mental or physical.—*adj* inducing sleep; soporific; narcotic.

opine *vti* (**opined, opining**) to think; to suppose; to be of opinion.

opinion *n* a judgment or belief formed without certain evidence; belief stronger than impression, less strong than positive knowledge; judgment or sentiments on persons or things as regards their character or qualities; settled judgment or persuasion; belief (*religious opinions*).

opinionated *adj* obstinate in opinion; opinionative; conceited.

opinionative *adj* unduly attached to one's own opinions; dogmatic; obstinate in beliefs.

opinion poll *n* a testing of public opinion by questioning a representative sample of the population on an issue, such as the relative popularity of political parties; the results of such a poll.

opium *n* a narcotic drug obtained from the juice of certain poppies; the juice of poppies.

opossum *n* the name of several marsupial mammals of America.

oppidan *n* an inhabitant of a town.

opponent *adj* opposing; antagonistic; opposite.—*n* one that opposes; an adversary; an antagonist; one that supports the opposite side in controversy, disputation or argument; a person who competes against someone.

opportune *adj* seasonable; timely; well timed; convenient.

opportunism *n* the practice of seizing or turning opportunities to advantage; a political attitude dispensing with a fixed and moral programme but merely waiting for something to turn up to be utilized for immediate service.

opportunity *n* fit or convenient time or occasion; a time favourable for the purpose; a suitable time, combined with other favourable circumstances.

oppose *vt* (**opposed, opposing**) to set opposite; to place as an obstacle; to put with a view to hinder, defeat, destroy or prevent effect; to act against; to resist, either by physical or other means; to act as an opponent to; to confront; to check; to withstand; to resist effectually.—*vi* to make objections; to act obstructively.

opposite *adj* standing or situated in front; facing; adverse; opposed; hostile; different in nature or quality; mutually antagonistic; contrary; inconsistent; repugnant; (*bot*) growing in pairs; each pair crosswise to that above or below it.—*n* one who or that which opposes; one who or that which is opposite or adverse.

opposite number *n* a person in a corresponding position on the other side; a counterpart.

opposition *n* situation so as to front something; a standing over against; the state of being opposed or contrasted; the state of being adverse; the act of opposing; attempt to check, restrain or defeat resistance; that which opposes; the collective body of opposers; the party in either house of parliament (or similar assembly) opposed to the administration for the time being; (*astron*) the situation of two heavenly bodies when diametrically opposite to each other or when their longitudes differ by 180°.

oppress *vt* to load or burden with cruel, unjust or unreasonable impositions; to treat with unjust severity, rigour or hardship; to overburden; to overwhelm; to subdue; to sit or lie heavy on (as food in the stomach).

oppression *n* the act of oppressing; excessively rigorous government; severity; hardship; calamity; depression; a sense of heaviness or weight in the mind or body.

oppressive *adj* unreasonably burdensome; unjustly severe; given to oppression; tyrannical; overpowering; overwhelming.

oppressor *n* one that oppresses or harasses.

opprobrious *adj* containing or expressive of opprobrium; scurrilous; abusive; infamous.

opprobrium *n* scurrilous or abusive language; contemptuous reproaches; scurrility; disgrace; infamy.

oppugn *vt* to attack by arguments, etc, not by weapons; to oppose; to resist; to exercise hostile reasoning against.

optative *adj* expressing desire or wish; (*gram*) applied to that mood of the verb in which wish or desire is expressed.—*n* (*gram*) the optative mood of a verb.

optic *adj* relating or pertaining to vision or sight; pertaining to the organ of vision; relating to the science of optics.—*n* an organ of sight; an eye.

optical *adj* relating to or connected with the science of optics; pertaining to vision; optic.

optician *n* a person skilled in the science of optics; one who makes or sells spectacles and instruments.

optics *n* that branch of physical science which treats of the nature and properties of light and vision, optical instruments, etc.

optimism *n* the doctrine that everything in nature is ordered for the best; the tendency always to take the most hopeful view of matters social or political; belief in the world's improvement.

optimist *n* one who believes in optimism

optimistic *adj* relating to or characterized by optimism.

optimize *vt* (**optimized, optimizing**) to make the best possible of.

option *n* the power or liberty of choosing; right of choice; the power of deciding on any course of action; choice; election; preference; in stock exchange, a right to effect a certain transaction or not at a certain date, at the desire of the person bargaining, who pays for the right.

optional *adj* left to one's option or choice; depending on choice or preference.

optometrist *n* a person who is qualified to test eyesight and to prescribe spectacles or contact lenses.

opulence *n* wealth; riches; affluence.

opulent *adj* wealthy; rich; affluent; having large means.

opus *n* (*pl* **opuses, opera**) a literary or artistic work; a musical composition, especially any of the numbered works of a composer.

or[1] *conj* a particle that marks, or seems to mark, an alternative, frequently corresponding to a preceding *either* and also to *whether*, with which words it is sometimes interchangeable in poetry; it often connects a series of words or propositions, presenting a choice between any two of them (*he may study law or medicine or divinity or he may enter into trade*); it also sometimes begins a sentence, in which case it expresses an alternative with the foregoing sentence or a transition to some fresh argument or illustration.

or² *n* (*heral*) gold, expressed in engraving by numerous small points or dots.

oracle *n* the answer of a god, or the inspired priest or priestess of a god, to an inquiry made respecting some affair; the deity who gave or was supposed to give answers to inquiries; the place where the answers were given; the sanctuary; a divine communication, revelation or message; any person reputed uncommonly wise and whose opinions have great weight.

oracular *adj* pertaining to an oracle or oracles; uttering oracles; resembling the utterance of an oracle; authoritative; sententious; ambiguous, like the ancient oracles.

oral *adj* of the mouth; uttered by the mouth or in words; spoken, not written; verbal; (of medicine) taken by the mouth.

orally *adv* in an oral manner; by word of mouth; verbally.

orange *n* a tree cultivated abundantly in the south of Europe, the Azores, America, etc; its round, reddish-yellow citrus fruit; a reddish-yellow colour.—*adj* belonging to an orange; coloured as an orange; reddish-yellow in colour.

orang-outang

orange blossom, orange flower *n* the blossom of the orange tree, a wreath of which is commonly worn by a bride at her marriage.

orange lily *n* a garden plant with large orange-coloured flowers.

orangery *n* a place where oranges are cultivated; a house for orange trees.

orang-outang, orang-utan *n* one of the largest of the anthropoid apes, a native of Sumatra and Borneo.

oration *n* a speech or discourse composed according to the rules of oratory and spoken in public; a set speech; a formal discourse pronounced on a special occasion.

orate *vi* (**orated, orating**) to deliver an oration, with undercurrent idea of pomposity.

orator *n* a public speaker; one who delivers an oration; one who is skilled as a speaker; an eloquent man.

oratorical *adj* pertaining to an orator or to oratory; rhetorical.

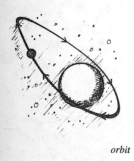

orbit

oratorio *n* (*pl* **oratorios**) a sacred musical composition, consisting of airs, recitatives, duets, trios, choruses, etc, the subject of which is generally taken from Scripture.

oratory *n* the art of public speaking; the art of an orator; exercise of eloquence; eloquence; a place for prayer; a small apartment for private devotions.

orb *n* a spherical body; a sphere or globe; also a circular body or disc; an ornamental sphere surmounted by a cross as part of a sovereign's regalia; a hollow globe or sphere believed by medieval astronomers to form part of the solar or sidereal system.

orbit *n* the path of a planet or comet through space; the curve line which a planet describes in its periodical revolution round its central body (*the orbit of Jupiter or Mercury*); a similar curved path of one body around another, such as that of an electron around the nucleus of an atom; the eye socket.—*vt* to put (a satellite, etc) into orbit; to circle around.

Orcadian *n* relating to the Orkney Islands.—*n* a native or inhabitant of Orkney.

orchard *n* an enclosure used for the culture of fruit trees.

orchestra *n* the part of a theatre assigned to the musicians; in the Grecian theatres, a part of the stage allotted to the chorus; the whole instrumental band performing together in public places.

orchestral *adj* pertaining to an orchestra.

orchestrate *vt* (**orchestrated, orchestrating**) to arrange (music) for performance by an orchestra; to arrange; to arrange or organize to best effect.

orchestration *n* the act of orchestrating; the arrangement of music for an orchestra; instrumentation.

orchid *n* any of an order of perennial plants with tuberous fleshy roots and unusually shaped flowers in brilliant colours comprising three petals of uneven size.

orchil, archil *n* a violet, mauve or purple dye obtained from lichens.

orchis *n* any of a genus of wild orchid.

ordain *vt* to set in order or arrange; to decree, appoint, establish, institute; to set apart for an office; to invest with ministerial or sacerdotal functions.

ordeal *n* an ancient form of trial to determine guilt or innocence, escape from injury being considered a proof of innocence; hence, any severe trial or strict test; an exacting or painful experience.

order *n* regular disposition or methodical arrangement; established succession; a method; a system; a proper state or condition; the established usage or settled method; regularity; public tranquillity; absence of confusion or disturbance; tidiness; a state or condition; a mandate, precept or authoritative direction; a rule or regulation, oral or written; a direction, demand or commission to supply goods; a written direction to pay money; something requested or demanded; a rank or class of people; a religious fraternity; a body of people having had a common honorary distinction conferred on them; the distinction, rank or dignity itself (*the order of the Garter*); a large division in the classification of natural objects, as plants or animals; a group above a family but below a class; (*archit*) one of the different ways in which a column and its entablature is moulded and related to the other columns, there being five architectural orders—Doric, Ionic, Tuscan, Corinthian and Composite.—*vt* to put in order; to dispose or arrange; to manage or conduct; to command; to give an order to; to give an order or commission for; to place a request for.—*vi* to give command or direction.

order book *n* a book for orders; a book in which a member of parliament must enter any motion he intends to propose.

orderliness *n* the state or quality of being orderly; regularity.

orderly *adj* in accordance with good order; well-ordered; methodical; regular; well-behaved; obedient.—*n* a private soldier or noncommissioned officer who attends on a superior officer to carry orders or messages; a hospital attendant.

ordinal *adj* applied to a number which expresses order or succession (*the ordinal numbers*, first, second, third, etc); (*nat hist*) pertaining to an order.—*n* a number denoting order (as *first*); a book containing the ordination service.

ordinance *n* a rule established by authority; a law, edict, decree, etc; an established rite or ceremony.

ordinarily *adv* in an ordinary manner; usually; generally; in most cases.

ordinary *adj* established; regular; customary; common; usual; normal; frequent; habitual; unexceptional; mediocre; somewhat inferior; of little merit.—*n* an archbishop in a province, a bishop in a diocese; a prescribed form of service; an ecclesiastical judge; a prison chaplain; (*heral*) that part of the escutcheon contained between straight and other lines.

ordinary seaman *n* a seaman of the lowest rank, below able-bodied seaman.

ordinate *adj* regular; methodical.—*n* (*geom*) one of those lines which determine the position of a point in coordinate geometry (the abscissa and ordinate, when spoken of together, are called *coordinates*).

ordination *n* the act of ordaining; the act of settling or establishing; appointment; settled order of thing; especially the act of conferring holy orders, as by a bishop of the English Church; the act of settling a Presbyterian clergyman in a charge.

ordnance *n* cannon or great guns, mortars and howitzers collectively; artillery.

Ordnance Survey *n* the survey of Britain carried out by a government department.

Ordovician *n* a series of strata succeeding the Cambrian.

ordure *n* dung; excrement; faeces.

ore *n* a mineral consisting of a metal and some other substance, as oxygen, sulphur or carbon, in combination, being the source from which metals are usually obtained by smelting (metals found free from such combination being called *native metals*); metal, sometimes gold.

oread *n* a mountain nymph.

oregano *n* an aromatic herb used in cooking.

organ *n* an instrument or means; that which performs some office, duty or function; more commonly, a part of an animal or vegetable by which some function is carried on (as the heart, the eye); a means of communication between one person or body of persons and another; a medium of conveying certain opinions; specifically, a newspaper; the largest and most harmonious of wind instruments of music, consisting of a great number of pipes and with keys similar to those of the piano.

organic *adj* pertaining to an organ or to organs of animals and plants; pertaining to objects that have organs, hence to the animal and vegetable worlds; exhibiting animal or vegetable life and functions (*organic bodies, tissues,* etc); forming a whole with a systematic arrangement of parts; organized; systematized.

organism *n* organic structure; a body exhibiting organization and organic life; a member of the animal or vegetable kingdoms; any living thing.

organist *n* one who plays on the organ.

organization *n* the act or process of organizing; the act of systematizing or arranging; a whole or aggregate that is organized; organic structure; arrangement of parts or organs for the performance of vital functions.

organize *vt* (**organized, organizing**) to give an organic structure to; to arrange the several parts of for action or work; to establish and systematize.

organizer *n* one who organizes, establishes or systematizes.

organography *n* a description of the organs of plants or animals.

organology *n* the physiology of the different organs of animals or plants.

organon, organum *n* (*pl* **organa**) a body of rules and canons for regulating scientific or philosophic investigation.

orgasm *n* the climax of sexual excitement.

orgy *n* secret rites or ceremonies connected with the worship of some of the pagan deities, particularly revels of the Greeks in honour of Dionysus (properly plural); a wild or frantic revel; drunken revelry.

oriel *n* a large window projecting from a wall and forming a bay or recess inside; a bay window.

orient *adj* rising, as the sun or moon; eastern; oriental; bright; shining.—*vt* to orientate.

Orient *n* the east; Oriental countries.

oriel

oriental *adj* eastern; situated in the east; proceeding from the east; applied to gems as a mark of excellence; precious, opposed to *occidental*.

Oriental *n* a native of some eastern part of the world; an Asiatic.—*adj* of or pertaining to the Orient.

Orientalist *n* a person skilled in eastern languages and literature.

orientate *vt* (**orientated, orientating**) to arrange in a direction, especially in relation to the points of the compass; to place or face in a particular position or direction; to adjust (oneself) to a particular situation.

orientation *n* the act of orientating; a position relative to a compass direction; arrangement; alignment; one's way of thinking; one's direction of interest.

orienteering *n* the sport of cross-country running over a set course on difficult terrain using a map and compass.

orifice *n* the mouth or aperture of a tube, pipe or other similar object; a perforation; an opening; a vent.

origin *n* the first existence or beginning of anything; the commencement; fountain; source; that from which anything primarily proceeds; of a muscle, the end attached to a relatively fixed part.

original *adj* pertaining or belonging to the origin or early state of something; primitive; pristine; having the power to originate new thoughts or combinations of thought; produced by an author; not copied.—*n* origin; source; first copy; archetype; that from which anything is copied; a work not copied from another but the work of an artist himself; the language in which any work is composed as distinguished from a translation; a person of marked individuality of character; a primary stock or type from which varieties have been developed.

originality *n* the quality or state of being original; the power of originating new thoughts or uncommon combinations of thought.

originally *adv* in an original manner; at the very beginning; from the first.

original sin *n* (*theol*) the first sin of Adam, namely the eating of the forbidden fruit; the inherent tendency of mankind to sin.

orpine

originate *vt* (**originated, originating**) to give origin or beginning to; to cause to be; to produce.—*vi* to take first existence; to have origin.

originator *n* a person who originates.

oriole *n* the name of certain birds of the crow family with plumage of a golden colour.

Orion *n* a constellation on the celestial equator represented by the figure of a man with a sword by his side, three stars on a line forming his belt.

orison *n* a prayer or supplication.

orle *n* (*heral*) a figure on an escutcheon resembling a smaller escutcheon with the interior cut out; (*archit*) a fillet under the ovolo of a capital.

orlop *n* (*naut*) the lowest deck in a ship of war or merchant vessel that has three decks; sometimes a temporary deck.

ormolu *n* an alloy of copper, zinc and tin, made to imitate gold and used to decorate clocks, furniture, etc.

ornament *n* that which embellishes or adorns; something which, added to another thing, renders it more beautiful to the eye; decoration; fair outward show; that which adds beauty to the mind or character.—*vt* to adorn; to embellish.

ornamental *adj* serving to ornament; pertaining to ornament.

ornamentation *n* the act of ornamenting; the ornaments or decorations produced.

ornate *adj* adorned; decorated; ornamental; richly and artistically finished; much embellished.

ornithological *adj* pertaining to ornithology.

ornithologist *n* a person skilled in ornithology.

ornithology *n* that branch of zoology which treats of the form, structure, classification and habits of birds.

ornithorhynchus *n* the duckbill.

orographic, orographical *adj* relating to orography.

orography *n* the science which describes or deals with the mountains and mountain systems of the globe; orology.

orological *adj* pertaining to orology.

orologist *n* a describer of mountains; one skilled in orology.

orology *n* a description of mountains; orography.

orotund *adj* (*rhet*) characterized by fullness, richness and clearness; rich and musical (applied to the voice or manner of utterance).

orphan *n* a child bereaved of both parents.—*adj* being an orphan; bereaved of parents.—*vt* to reduce to the state of an orphan; to bereave of parents.

orphanage *n* the state of an orphan; a home for orphans.

Orphean *adj* pertaining to Orpheus, the legendary poet and musician of ancient Greece; hence, melodious.

orpiment *n* a mineral substance, a compound of sulphur and arsenic, of a brilliant yellow colour, forming the basis of a yellow pigment.

orpine *n* a succulent plant with fleshy leaves and purple flowers.

orrery *n* a moving model of the solar system.

orris[1] *n* a sort of gold or silver lace; a pattern in which gold and silver lace is worked.

orris[2] *n* a plant from which orris root is obtained.

orris root *n* the root of three species of iris which, in its dried state, is used perfumery and medicine.

orthochromatic *adj* (*photog*) (of film) giving natural tone values of light and shade, excessive sensitiveness to violet and blue light being subdued by an absorbent dye or other special means.

orthoclase *n* a kind of feldspar with a straight flat fracture.

orthodontics *n* the branch of dentistry dealing with the correction of abnormally aligned or positioned teeth.

orthodox *adj* sound in opinion or doctrine; particularly, sound in religious opinions or doctrines, opposed to *heterodox*; in accordance with sound doctrine; sound; correct (*an orthodox faith* or *proceeding*); conventional; conforming with established behaviour or opinions.

orthodoxy *n* the state or quality of being orthodox; soundness of faith; correctness of opinion or doctrine, especially in religious matters; orthodox practice or belief.

orthoepic, orthoepical *adj* pertaining to orthoepy.

orthoepy *n* the science of correct pronunciation of words.

orthognathous, orthognathic *adj* having jaws that do not protrude; having a skull in which the forehead does not recede and the jaws project.

orthographer, orthographist *n* one skilled in orthography.

orthographic, orthographical *adj* pertaining to orthography.

orthography *n* the art of writing words with the proper letters; the way in which words are properly written; spelling; the part of grammar that deals with spelling.

orthopaedic *adj* relating to orthopaedics.

orthopaedics *n* the branch of surgery concerned with the treatment of bones; the art or process of curing deformities or diseases of the bones.

orthopaedist *n* one who practises or specializes in orthopaedics.

orthopteran *n* (*pl* **orthopterans, orthoptera**) one of an order of insects which have four wings, the anterior pair being leathery, the posterior pair folding longitudinally like a fan; such as the cockroaches, grasshoppers and locusts.

orthopterous *adj* pertaining to the orthopterans.

orthorhombic *adj* of that system of crystals in which the three axes are unequal and mutually at right angles.

ortolan *n* a European bird of the bunting family, eaten as a delicacy.

oryx *n* any of a species of antelope, a native of the countries on both sides of the Red Sea; also the gemsbok of South Africa.

Oscar *n* any of several gold statuettes awarded annually by the United States Academy of Motion Picture Arts and Sciences for outstanding performances or achievements.

oscillate *vi* (**oscillated, oscillating**) to swing; to move backward and forward; to vibrate; to vary or fluctuate between fixed limits; to vacillate between two forms of opinion.

oscillating *adj* moving backward and forward; vibrating.

oscillation *n* the act or state of oscillating or swinging backward and forward; vibration.

oscillator *n* one who or that which oscillates.

oscillatory *adj* moving backward and forward like a pendulum.

oscilloscope *n* a device for viewing oscillations on a display screen of a cathode-ray tube.

oscitancy, oscitance *n* the act of gaping or yawning; sleepiness; drowsiness.

oscitant *adj* yawning; gaping; drowsy; sluggish.

osculant *adj* kissing; osculating; having features bordering on those of two groups of plants or animals.

osculate *vt* (**osculated, osculating**) to salute with a kiss; to kiss; (*geom*) of curves and surfaces, to touch very closely.—*vi* to kiss one another; to kiss; (*geom*) to touch very closely, as two curves or surfaces.

osculation *n* the act of osculating; a kissing; specifically, (*geom*) specially close contact between two curves at a common point.

osier *n* the name of various species of willow, chiefly employed in basket-making. —*adj* made of osier or twigs; like osier.

Osiris *n* an Egyptian deity, the husband of Isis and the personification of all physical and moral good.

osmium *n* a bluish-white metallic element, very hard and more infusible than any other metal.

osmosis *n* the percolation and intermixture of fluids separated by a porous membrane; a gradual absorption or assimilation.

osmotic *adj* pertaining to or characterized by osmosis.

osmotic pressure *n* the pressure, analogous to gaseous pressure, which gives rise in liquids to diffusion and osmosis.

osmunda, osmund *n* a European flowering fern.

osprey *n* a bird which feeds almost entirely on fish captured by suddenly darting on them when near the surface.

osseous *adj* bony; resembling bone.

ortolan

Osiris

595

ossicle *n* a small bone; some of the small bones of the human skeleton, as those of the internal ear; a small hard structure in starfishes, etc.

ossification *n* the act of ossifying; the change or process of changing into a bony substance.

ossify *vt* (**ossified, ossifying**) to form into bone; to change from a soft animal substance into bone or a substance of the hardness of bones.—*vi* to become bone or bony.

ossuary *n* a charnel house; a place where the bones of the dead are deposited.

ostensible *adj* put forth as having a certain character, whether worthy of it or not; hence, frequently, apparent and not real; having something of sham or pretence; pretended; professed.

ostensive *adj* showing; exhibiting.

ostentation *n* ambitious display; pretentious parade; display dictated by vanity or to invite praise or flattery.

ostentatious *adj* characterized by ostentation; showy; intended for vain display.

osteoarthritis *n* a condition causing painful inflammation of the joints, in the hip, knee, etc.

ostrich

osteology *n* that branch of anatomy which deals with bones and bone tissue.

osteomyelitis *n* a bacterial disease of the bones causing inflammation of the bone marrow, pain and fever.

osteopath *n* a practitioner of osteopathy.

osteopathy *n* a system of medical treatment involving the manipulation of bones.

osteoporosis *n* a condition in which a porous structure develops in the bones causing them to become brittle, caused by a lack of calcium.

ostiary *n* (*arch*) the doorkeeper of a church.

ostler, hostler *n* formerly, the person who had the care of horses at an inn, the innkeeper; a stable boy.

ostracod *n* a minute freshwater crustacean.

ostracism *n* banishment from society; banishment from a group; expulsion; exclusion from friendship.

ostracize *vt* (**ostracized, ostracizing**) to exile by ostracism; to banish from society; to exclude from public or private favour; to exclude from friendship.

ostrich *n* a large running bird inhabiting the sandy plains of Africa and Arabia, the largest of all existing birds.

Ostrogoth *n* one of the eastern Goths, as distinguished from the Visigoths or western Goths.

otalgia *n* a pain in the ear; earache.

otter

other *adj, pron* not the same; different; second of two; additional (*get other knowledge as well*); not this; opposite (*the other side of the street*); often used reciprocally with each and applicable to any number of individuals (*help each other*).—it is also used substantively and may take the plural number and the sign of the possessive case and frequently is opposed to *some, one, I*, etc (*some were right, others were wrong*; *the one and the other*).—**the other day** on some day not long past; quite recently.—**every other** every second (*every other day, every other week*).

otherwise *adv* in a different manner; differently; not so; by other causes; in other respects.—**rather . . . than otherwise** rather than not (*rather pleased than otherwise*).—*conj* else; but for this; such not being the case.

otic *adj* belonging or relating to the ear.

otiose *adj* idle; unemployed; useless; futile; needless.

otitis *n* inflammation of the tympanum of the ear, accompanied by intense pain.

otology *n* that branch of anatomy which concerns itself with the ear.

ottava rima *n* an Italian form of versification consisting of eight lines, of which the first six rhyme alternately and the last two form a couplet.

otter *n* any of various aquatic carnivorous mammals having dense dark-brown fur and webbed feet.

otto of roses *n* same as **attar of roses**.

ottoman *n* (*pl* **ottomans**) a kind of couch or sofa.

Ottoman *adj* pertaining to or derived from the Turks.—*n* (*pl* **Ottomans**) a Turk.

oubliette *n* a dungeon with an opening only at the top for the admission of air.

ought *vb aux* to be held or bound in duty or moral obligation.

ought *n* aught; anything.

ounce[1] *n* a weight, the twelfth part of a pound troy and the sixteenth of a pound avoirdupois, about 28.349 grams; a very small amount.

ounce[2] snow leopard; (*poet*) the lynx or a similar animal.

our *adj* pertaining or belonging to us (*our country*; *our rights*).—**ours** is a later possessive form and is used in place of *our* and a noun (*the book is ours*).

ourself *pron* myself, used like *we* and *us* in the regal or formal style.

ourselves *pron* (*pl* of **ourself**) we or us, not others—often when used as a nominative added to *we* by way of emphasis or opposition; when in the objective often without emphasis and simply serving as the reflexive pronoun corresponding to *us*.

ousel *n* same as **ouzel**.

oust *vi* to eject; to turn out; to dispossess.

out *adv* on or towards the outside; not in or within; without; opposed to *in, into* or *within*; not indoors; abroad; beyond usual limits (*he was out when I called*); hence, engaged in a duel (*he has been out several* *times*); *to call a person out* = to challenge him; no longer concealed or kept secret; not in a state of obscurity; public (*the secret is out*); finished; exhausted; used up; deficient; having expended (*out of money*); extinguished; no longer burning (*the candle* or *fire is out*); not in employment; not in office; to an end or settlement (*hear me out*); loudly; in an open and free manner (*to laugh out*); not in the hands of the owner (*out on loan*); in an error; at a loss; in a puzzle; having taken her place as a woman in society (said of a girl).—*adj* external; outward; asleep; unconscious.— *n* one who is out; especially one out of office, politically (chiefly in the plural); a nook or corner; a projecting angle (*ins and outs*); hence, *the ins and outs of a question*, all its details.

out-and-out *adv* completely; thoroughly; without reservation. —*adj* thorough; thorough-paced; absolute; complete (*an out-and-out swindle*).

outbid *vt* to bid more than; to go beyond in the offer of a price.

outboard *adj* (*naut*) applied to anything that is on the outside of the ship (*the outboard works*, etc).

outbreak *n* a breaking out; a bursting forth; a sudden and violent manifestation (as of fever, anger, disease).—*vi* to break or burst forth.

outburst *n* a breaking or bursting out; an outbreak (*an outburst of wrath*).

outcast *n* one who is cast out or expelled; an exile; one driven from home or country.— *adj* cast out; thrown away; rejected as useless.

outcome *n* that which comes out of or results from something; the issue; the result; the consequence.

outcrop *vi* (**outcropped, outcropping**) (*geol*) to crop out or appear above the surface of the ground (said of strata).—*n* (*geol*) the exposure of an inclined stratum at the surface of the ground; the part so exposed.

outcry *n* a vehement or loud cry; cry of distress; clamour; noisy opposition; sale at public auction.

outdistance *vt* (**outdistanced, outdistancing**) to excel or leave far behind in any competition or career.

outdo *vt* (*pret* **outdid**, *pp* **outdone**, *ppr* **outdoing**) to excel; to surpass; to perform beyond another.

outdoor *adj* being without the house; exterior; in the open air; specifically used of paupers who are not required to reside in a union or poorhouse.

outdoors *adv* abroad; out of the house; in the open air.

outer *adj* being on the outside; external, opposed to *inner*; farthest or farther removed from a person or fixed point.

outermost *adj* being on the extreme external part; remotest from the midst; most distant of a series.

outer space *n* any region of space beyond the earth's atmosphere.

outfall *n* the mouth of a river; the lower end of a watercourse; the point of discharge for or the embouchure of a drain, culvert or sewer.

outfit *n* the equipment needed for a particular task; the set of clothes worn by a particular person (*wedding outfit*); an ensemble; a group or organization.—*vt* (**outfitted, outfitting**) to supply with an outfit or equipment.

outfitter *n* one who supplies or makes outfits.

outflank *vt* to go or extend beyond the flank or wing of; hence, to outmanoeuvre; to get the better of.

outgoing *adj* going out; departing; retiring; sociable; forthcoming.—*n* the act of going out; outlay; expenditure.

outgrow *vt* (*pret* **outgrow**, *pp* **outgrown**, *ppr* **outgrowing**) to surpass in growth; to grow too great or too old for.

outhouse *n* a small house or building near the main one.

outhouse

outing *n* the act of going out; an excursion; an airing.

outlandish *adj* belonging to or characteristic of a foreign country; foreign; strange; odd; bizarre.

outlaw *n* a person excluded from the benefit of the law or deprived of its protection.— *vt* to deprive of the benefit and protection of law; to proscribe.

outlay *n* a laying out or expending; that which is laid out or expended; expenditure.

outlet *n* the place or opening by which anything is let out, escapes or is discharged; a means of egress; a place of exit; a vent.— *vt* to let forth; to emit.

outline *n* the line by which a figure is defined; the exterior line; contour; a drawing in which an object or scene is represented merely by lines of contour without shading; first general sketch of any scheme or design; a summary.—*vt* (**outlined, outlining**) to draw in outline; to delineate.

outlive *vt* (**outlived, outliving**) to live beyond; to survive.

outlook *n* a vigilant watch (*to be on the outlook for something*); the place of watch; what lies before the eye; prospect; view; point of view; attitude; future.

outlying *adj* lying away from the main body or design; remote; being on the exterior or frontier.

outnumber *vt* to exceed in number.

outpatient *n* a patient not residing in a hospital but who receives medical treatment, etc, from the institution, at a clinic, etc.

outpost *n* a post or station without the limits of a camp or at a distance from the main body of an army; the troops placed at such a station; a distant or remote settlement.

output *n* the quantity of material put out or produced within a specified time, as coal from a pit or iron from a furnace, etc; information delivered by a computer, especially to a printer; (*elect*) the useful voltage, current or power delivered.—*vt* (**output, outputting**) (of a printer attached to a computer) to produce an output.

outrage *n* rude or injurious violence offered to persons or things; excessive abuse; an act of wanton mischief; an audacious transgression of law or decency.—*vt* (**outraged, outraging**) to treat with violence and wrong; to do violence to; to abuse; to maltreat; to commit a rape or indecent assault on.

outrageous *adj* characterized by outrage; violent; furious; turbulent; excessive; exceeding reason or decency; enormous; atrocious.

outré *adj* being out of the common course or limits; extravagant; exaggerated; bizarre.

outrigger *n* a structure of spars, etc, rigged out from the side of a sailing boat to steady it; an iron bracket on the outside of a boat, with the rowlock at the extremity; a light boat provided with such apparatus.

outright *adv* completely; wholly; altogether (*to kill him outright*).

outrun *vt* (*pret* **outrun**, *pp* **outrun**, *ppr* **outrunning**) to excel in running; to leave behind; to exceed or go beyond.

outset *n* a setting out; beginning; start.

outshine *vt* (*pret, pp* **outshone**, *ppr* **outshining**) to outdo in ability, success, etc; to be more splendid than.

outside *n* the external outer or exposed parts or surface; superficial appearance; external aspect or features; space immediately without or beyond an enclosure; the farthest limit; the utmost; extreme estimate (with *the*).—*adj* being on the outside; external; superficial.

outsider *n* one not belonging to a party, association or set; unconnected or not admitted.

outsize *adj* unusually large; very large.

outskirts *npl* the outer districts; the outlying districts of a town, etc.

outsmart *vt* to outwit.

outspoken *adj* free or bold of speech; candid; frank.

outspread *vt* (**outspread, outspreading**) to spread out; to extend.

outstanding *adj* not collected; unpaid (*outstanding debts*).

outvote *vt* (**outvoted, outvoting**) to exceed in the number of votes given; to defeat by plurality of votes.

outward *adj* forming the superficial part; exterior; external; visible; appearing; tending to the exterior; derived from without; not properly belonging; adventitious.—*adv* outwards; from a port or country.

outward-bound *adj* proceeding from a port or country.

outwardly *adv* externally; on the outside; in appearance only.

outwards *adv* towards the outer parts.

outweigh *vt* to exceed in weight or in value, influence or importance.

outwit *vt* (**outwitted, outwitting**) to defeat or frustrate by superior ingenuity; to prove too clever for; to overreach.

outwork *n* part of a fortification distant from the main fortress or citadel.

ouzel, ousel *n* a kind of small bird.

ova *npl* the plural form of **ovum**.

oval *adj* of the shape of the outline of an egg; resembling the longitudinal section of an egg; elliptical.—*n* a figure in the shape of the outline of an egg; an elliptical figure.

ovary *n* the female organ in which ova, reproductive germs or eggs, are formed and developed; (*bot*) a case enclosing ovules or young seeds and ultimately becoming the fruit.

ovate, ovated *adj* egg-shaped; oval.

ovation *n* enthusiastic applause.

oven *n* a closely built recess for baking, heating or drying any substance; a chamber in a stove or kitchen range.

over *prep* above in place or position; rising to or reaching a height above; across (implying motion); on the surface of; through the whole extent of; above in eminence or superiority; above in authority; with oversight or watchfulness in respect to (*to keep guard over*); denoting motive or occasion (*to rejoice over*); denoting superiority as the result of a struggle or contest; upwards of; more than.—*adj* upper; excessive; surplus; finished; remaining.—*n* (in cricket) the number of balls (six or eight) which the bowler delivers in succession from one end of the pitch, before a change is made to the other end.—*adv* from side to side; in width; across; from one side to the other or to another (*to roll over*); on all the surface; above the top, brim or edge; more than the quantity assigned; in excess; throughout; completely; having come to an end; past (*till this heat be over*); excessively; in a great degree.—*adj* upper; superior; covering; outer (*overshoes*).

overact *vt* to act or perform to excess.—*vi* to act more than is necessary.

overalls *npl* loose trousers worn over others to protect them from being soiled; (*sing*) a loose outer garment for the same purpose.

overbalance *vt* (**overbalanced, overbal-**

oven

overalls

ancing) to more than balance; to exceed in weight, value, etc; to surpass; to destroy the balance or equilibrium of (used reflexively).—*n* excess; something more than an equivalent.

overbear *vt* (*pret* **overbore**, *pp* **overborne**, *ppr* **overbearing**) to bear down; to overpower; to overcome by argument, effrontery, etc.

overbearing *adj* haughty and dogmatic; given to effrontery.

overblown *adj* too fully open; pretentious; excessive.

overboard *adv* over the side of a ship; out of a ship or from on board.—**thrown overboard** (*fig*) discarded; deserted; betrayed.

overburden *vt* to load with too great weight; to overload.

overcast *vt* (**overcast**, **overcasting**) to cloud; to obscure with clouds; to cover with gloom; to sew by running the thread over a rough edge.—*adj* clouded.

overcharge *vt* (**overcharged**, **overcharging**) to charge or burden to excess; to fill too numerously; to make an excessive charge against; to charge at too high a sum or price; to exaggerate.—*n* an excessive charge; a charge of more than is just in an account.

overcoat *n* a coat worn over all the other dress; a top-coat or greatcoat.

overcome *vt* (*pret* **overcame**, *pp* **overcome**, *ppr* **overcoming**) to conquer; to vanquish; to surmount; to get the better of.—*vi* to gain the superiority; to be victorious.

overcrowd *vt* to fill or crowd to excess, especially with human beings.

overdo *vt* (*pret* **overdid**, *pp* **overdone**, *ppr* **overdoing**) to do to excess; to overact; to surpass or exceed in performance; to boil, roast or otherwise cook too much.

overdose *n* an excessive dose, as of a drug, etc.—*vt* (**overdosed**, **overdosing**) to give an excessive dose to.—*vi* to commit suicide, or attempt to do so, by taking an excessive dose of a drug.

overdraw *vt* (*pret* **overdrew**, *pp* **overdrawn**, *ppr* **overdrawing**) to draw on for a larger sum than is standing at one's credit in the books of a bank, etc; to exaggerate in writing, speech or a picture.

overdue *adj* not arrived at the proper date or assigned limit (*an overdue ship*); past the time of payment (*an overdue bill*).

overeat *vt* (*pret* **overate**, *pp* **overeaten**, *ppr* **overeating**) to surfeit with eating (used reflexively, as *to overeat oneself*).

overestimate *vt* (**overestimated**, **overestimating**) to estimate too great an amount; to place too high a value on; to have too favourable an opinion of the ability, etc, of.

overflow *vt* (*pret* **overflowed**, *pp* **overflowed**, sometimes **overflown**, *ppr* **over-**

flowing) to flow or spread over; to inundate; to fill and run over the brim of; to deluge; to overwhelm.—*vi* to swell and run over the brim or banks; to be so full that the contents run over; to abound.—*n* an inundation; a flowing over; superabundance.

overflowing *adj* abundant; exuberant.

overflowingly *adv* exuberantly; in great abundance.

overgrow *vt* (*pret* **overgrew**, *pp* **overgrown**, *ppr* **overgrowing**) to cover with growth or herbage (*a ruin overgrown with ivy*).—*vi* to grow beyond the fit or natural size.

overhand *adj*, *adv* with the hand over the object; with the knuckle upward.

overhang *vt* (**overhung**, **overhanging**) to impend or hang over; to jut or project over; to jut or project over.

overhaul *vt* to turn over for examination; to examine thoroughly with a view to repairs; to re-examine (as accounts); to gain on or overtake.—**to overhaul a ship** to gain on her in following; to search for contraband goods.

overhaul, overhauling *n* examination; inspection; repair.

overhead *adv* aloft; in the zenith; in the ceiling or storey above.—*adj* applied to what is above or aloft.

overheads *npl* the general, continuing costs of running a business, such as rent, heating and lighting costs, etc.

overhear *vt* (**overheard**, **overhearing**) to hear though not intended or expected to hear (as low or whispered conversation); to hear by accident or stratagem.

overhung *adj* hung or covered over; adorned with hangings.

overjoyed *adj* highly delighted; thrilled.

overkill *n* the capacity of weapons to kill infinitely more people than is necessary to achieve victory; the capability to employ more weapons than are necessary to destroy the enemy; excess capacity for a task; unwarranted excess.

overland *adj* passing by land; made on or across the land (*an overland journey*).

overlap *vt* (**overlapped**, **overlapping**) to lap or fold over; to extend so as to lie or rest on.—*n* the lapping of one thing over another; (*geol*) the extension of a superior stratum over an inferior so as to cover and conceal it.

overlay *vt* (**overlaid**, **overlaying**) to cover or spread over the surface of; to coat or cover; to obscure by covering.—*n* a coating; a transparent sheet of written or graphic matter to be laid over an illustration, etc.

overload *vt* to load with too heavy a burden or cargo; to overburden.

overlook *vt* to view from a higher place; to

overcoat

rise or be elevated above; to see from behind or over the shoulder of another; to inspect or superintend; to pass over indulgently; to omit to censure or punish (a fault); to slight.

overlord *n* one who is lord over another; a feudal superior.

overmuch *adj* too much; exceeding what is necessary or proper.—*adv* in too great a degree.—*n* more than sufficient.

overnight *adv* through or during the night; in the course of the night or evening; in the evening before.

overpower *vt* to vanquish by power or force; to subdue; to be too intense or violent for (*his emotions overpowered him*).

overpowering *adj* bearing down by superior power; irresistible.

overrate *vt* to rate at too much; to regard as having greater talents, abilities or more valuable qualities than is really the case.

overreach *vt* to reach beyond; to rise above; to deceive by cunning, artifice or sagacity; to cheat; to outwit.

override *vt* (*pret* **overrode**, *pp* **overridden**, *ppr* **overriding**) to ride over; hence, to trample down; to supersede; to annul.

overripe *adj* ripe or matured to excess.

overrule *vt* (**overruled, overruling**) to influence or control by predominant power; to set aside (objections) as not sufficiently weighty or convincing; (*law*) to rule against or reject.—*vi* to govern; to exercise control.

overruling *adj* exerting superior and controlling power; having effective sway.

overrun *vt* (*pret* **overrun**, *pp* **overrun**, *ppr* **overrunning**) to run or spread over; to grow over; to cover all over (as with weeds); to harass by hostile incursions; to overcome and take possession of by an invasion; to outrun; to run faster and leave behind; to exceed (a time limit, etc).

overseas *adj* foreign; from beyond sea.—*adv* beyond or across the sea; abroad.

oversee *vt* (*pret* **oversaw**, *pp* **overseen**, *ppr* **overseeing**) to superintend; to overlook; to take charge of.

overseer *n* one who supervises; a superintendent.

overset *vti* (**overset, oversetting**) to upset, to disturb; to overthrow.

overshadow *vt* to throw a shadow over; to appear more prominent or more important than.

overshoe *n* a shoe worn over another; an outer waterproof shoe.

overshoot *vt* (**overshot, overshooting**) to shoot over; to shoot beyond (a mark); to pass swiftly over.—**to overshoot oneself** to venture too far.

oversight *n* superintendence; watchful care; a mistake of inadvertence; an overlooking; omission.

oviduct

overspend *vt* (**overspent, overspending**) to spend more than necessary; to wear out; to tire.—*vi* to spend more than one can afford.

overstate *vt* (**overstated, overstating**) to exaggerate in statement; to state in too strong terms.

overstatement *n* an exaggerated statement.

overstep *vt* (**overstepped, overstepping**) to step over or beyond; to exceed.

overstock *vt* to stock to too great an extent; to fill too full; to supply with more than is wanted (the market with goods; a farm with cattle).

overt *adj* open to view; public; apparent; (*law*) not covert or secret; manifest.

overtake *vt* (*pret* **overtook**, *pp* **overtaken**, *ppr* **overtaking**) to come up with in following; to follow and reach or catch; to catch up with and pass; to come upon; to take by surprise.

overthrow *vt* (*pret* **overthrow**, *pp* **overthrown**, *ppr* **overthrowing**) to turn upside down; to throw down; to demolish; to defeat, conquer, vanquish; to subvert or destroy.—*n* the act of overthrowing; ruin; subversion; defeat.

overtime *n* time during which one works beyond the regular hours.

overtone *n* (often *pl*) an additional subtle meaning; an implicit quality.

overture *n* a proposal; something offered for consideration; a musical introduction to precede important compositions, as oratorios, operas, etc, written for a full orchestra.

overturn *vt* to overset or overthrow; to turn or throw from a foundation; to subvert; to ruin.—*n* state of being overturned; overthrow.

overvalue *vt* (**overvalued, overvaluing**) to set too great value on; to rate at too high a price.

overweening *adj* haughty; arrogant; proud; conceited.

overwhelm *vt* to overcome entirely; to swallow up; (*fig*) to bear down; to crush.

overwork *vt* to work beyond strength; to cause to labour too much (often reflexive, as *to overwork oneself*).—*n* excessive work or labour; work done beyond the amount required by stipulation.

overwrought *adj* laboured to excess; worked all over; affected or excited to excess; tasked beyond strength.

oviduct *n* the tube that conducts the ovum from the ovary.

oviform *adj* having the form or figure of an egg.

ovine *adj* pertaining to sheep; consisting of sheep.

oviparous *adj* producing eggs, especially eggs that are hatched after exclusion from the body.

oviposit *vi* to deposit eggs (said of insects).

ovipositor *n* an organ at the extremity of the abdomen of many insects for depositing their eggs.

ovisac *n* the cavity in the ovary which immediately contains the ovum.

ovoid, ovoidal *adj* having a shape resembling that of an egg.

ovolo *n* (*pl* **ovoli**) (*archit*) a round moulding forming the quarter of a circle.

ovoviviparous *adj* producing eggs which are hatched within the body (as is the case with vipers).

ovulate *vi* (**ovulated, ovulating**) to discharge or produce eggs from an ovary.

ovulation *n* the formation and discharge of ova or an ovum from the ovary.

ovule *n* a small vesicle; (*bot*) a rudimentary seed; an immature ovum; a small pellucid body borne by the placenta of a plant and changing into a seed.

ovum *n* (*pl* **ova**) an unfertilized female egg cell.

owe *vt* (**owed, owing**) to possess or own; to be indebted in; to be bound to pay; to be obliged to ascribe; to be obliged for (*he owes his safety to me*); to be due or owing.

owing *adj* required by obligation to be paid; remaining as a debt; ascribable, as to a cause; due; imputable, as to an agent.

owl *n* one of the nocturnal birds of prey, well known for their somewhat cat-like heads and their harsh and screeching note.

owlet *n* an owl; a young owl.

own *adj* belonging to me, him, us, you, etc, distinctly and emphatically, always following a possessive pronoun or a noun in the possessive, as *my own, his own, John's own*, sometimes used to impart tenderness to an expression (*thine own true knight*).— **to hold one's own** to maintain one's own cause; not to lose ground.—*vt* to have the right of property in; to hold or possess by right; to acknowledge or avow (*owned him as his son*); to concede; to admit to be true.

owner *n* one who owns; the rightful proprietor.

ownership *n* the state of being an owner.

ox *n* (*pl* **oxen**) any animal of the cow or bovine kind; a full-grown castrated bull.

oxlip *n* a species of the primrose growing wild in Britain.

oxalate *n* (*chem*) a combination of oxalic acid with a base.

oxalic *adj* pertaining to sorrel.

oxalic acid *n* an acid obtained from sorrel, rhubarb, etc; a violent poison (erroneously called *salt of lemons*).

oxide *n* (*chem*) a compound of oxygen with another element.

oxidize *vt* (**oxidized, oxidizing**) to cause to combine with oxygen; to convert into an oxide.

Oxonian *n* a native or inhabitant of Oxford; a member or a graduate of the University of Oxford.

oxygen *n* a gaseous element which, along with nitrogen, forms atmospheric air and with hydrogen forms water and which is essential to respiration (and therefore to animal life) and to combustion.

oxygenate *vt* (**oxygenated, oxygenating**) to unite or cause to combine with oxygen.

oxygenize *vt* (**oxygenized, oxygenizing**) to oxygenate.

oxyhydrogen *adj* formed by a mixture or combination of oxygen and hydrogen (*oxyhydrogen gas*); adapted to the combustion of oxygen and hydrogen in combination (*oxyhydrogen blowpipe, lamp*).

oxymoron *n* (*rhet*) a figure in which an epithet of a quite contrary meaning is added to a word, as, *cruel kindness*.

oyez, oyes *interj* the introduction to a proclamation made by a public crier in order to secure silence and attention and repeated three times.

oyster *n* an edible mollusc with a shell composed of two irregular valves, living in the sea and adhering to other objects.

oyster bed *n* a breeding place of oysters; a place where they are artificially or naturally reared.

oystercatcher *n* a wading shore bird which feeds on small molluscs.

ozone *n* a modification of oxygen existing in the atmosphere to a minute extent and produced when an electric machine is worked and in other ways; (*colloq*) bracing sea air.

ozone layer *n* a layer of ozone in the stratosphere that absorbs ultraviolet rays from the sun.

ox

oyster

601

P

P the sixteenth letter of the English alphabet.—**to mind one's P's and Q's** to be very careful in behaviour.

pa *n* a shortened form of **papa**.

pabulum *n* food; aliment; (*fig*) food for the mind or intellect.

paca *n* a large rodent animal of South and Central America.

pace *n* a step or the space between the feet in walking; the distance from the place where either foot is taken up to that where the same foot is set down (*Roman pace*); manner of walking; walk; gait (*heavy, quick* or *slow pace*); degree of speed; rate of progress (*events followed at a great pace*); a way of stepping by a horse.—*vi* (**paced, pacing**) to step; to walk; to step slowly or with measured tread; to stride.—*vt* to measure by steps; to walk over with measured paces.

pachyderm *n* one of a group of large, non-ruminant, hoofed, thick-skinned mammals, including the elephant, hippopotamus, etc.

pachydermatous *adj* belonging to the pachyderms; thick-skinned; (*fig*) not sensitive to ridicule, sarcasm, etc.

pacific *adj* suited to make or restore peace; conciliatory; appeasing; pacifying; calm, peaceful, tranquil; not warlike (*pacific disposition*).

Pacific *adj* of or pertaining to the Pacific Ocean.—*n* the Pacific Ocean.

pacification *n* the act of pacifying; appeasement; reconciliation.

pacifism *n* opposition to the use of force under any circumstances, particularly the refusal to participate in war.

pacifist *n* one who advocates pacifism.

pacify *vt* (**pacified, pacifying**) to appease; to cause to give up anger or excited feeling; to allay the agitation or excitement of; to calm; to restore peace to; to tranquillize.

pack *n* a bundle made up to be carried; a bale; a haversack, a backpack; a complete set of playing cards; a group of animals living together, such as wolves; a number of hounds or dogs hunting or kept together; a number of persons united in a

package

bad design or practice (*a pack of rascals*); a large amount (*a pack of lies*); a compact mass (as of snow or ice).—*vt* to put together for transportation or storage; to make up into a package, bundle or bale; to stow; to fill methodically with contents (*to pack a suitcase*); to assemble or bring together with a view to favour a particular side (*to pack a meeting*); to dismiss without ceremony (with *off*); to make airtight by stuffing; to stuff; to preserve in close vessels (*to pack meat* or *fish*); (*sl*) to carry (a gun); (*sl*) to deliver (a punch) with force.—*vi* to make up bundles or packs; to put up things for transportation; to depart in haste (with *off* or *away*); to gather together into flocks or bands (*the grouse begin to pack*); (of snow or ice) to form into a hard mass.

package *n* a bundle or bale; a packet; a parcel.

package deal *n* a deal which includes a number of matters and has to be accepted as a unit, any unfavourable items along with the favourable.

package holiday *n* a holiday in which all the fares, accommodation, etc, are arranged beforehand for an all-inclusive price.

pack drill *n* punishment of military offences by compelling the offender to parade in full marching kit and order.

packet *n* a small pack or package; a little bundle or parcel; a parcel of letters; a vessel employed in carrying mails, goods and passengers on regular days of starting (*packet boat*); (*sl*) a great deal of money.

packhorse *n* a horse employed in carrying packs or goods and baggage on its back.

pack ice *n* sea ice formed into a mass by the crushing together of floes.

packing *n* any material used for filling up empty spaces or for making close or tight; stuffing.

packing case *n* a wooden box for moving and protecting goods.

packman *n* (*pl* **packmen**) one who carries a pack; a pedlar.

pact *n* a contract; an agreement or covenant.

pad¹ *n* a cushion, soft saddle, bolster, part of

a garment, etc, stuffed with some soft material; a protection for the leg in cricket, hockey, etc; a sheet of mount blotting paper, a blotter or a quantity of paper for writing on (*a blotting* or *writing pad*); the soft under part of an animal's sole; a piece of fold absorbent material used as a surgical dressing; a flat concrete surface; (*sl*) one's own home or room.—*vt* (**padded, padding**) to stuff so as to make a pad; to furnish with a pad; to embellished with unnecessary or misleading detail (often with *out*).

pad² *n* the dull sound of a footstep; (*arch*) an easy-paced horse.—*vi* (**padded, padding**) to walk, especially softly.

padding *n* the act of stuffing; the materials used for stuffing furniture, parts of a garment, a saddle, bolster, etc; literary matter inserted in a narrative, book, periodical, etc, merely to increase the bulk.

paddle *vi* (**paddled, paddling**) to play in the water with the hands or feet in swimming or sport; to use a paddle; to row with a paddle.—*vt* to propel by an oar or paddle.—*n* the act of paddling; a short broad oar used in propelling and steering canoes and boats by a vertical motion; something shaped like this, as the limb of a seal, the tail of a beaver, or an implement used to hit, beat or stir; one of the float-boards placed on the circumference of the wheel of a steamer.

paddle wheel *n* a wheel with boards or floats on its circumference, driven by steam and propelling a steamship.

paddock *n* a small field or enclosure, especially a small enclosure under pasture immediately adjoining a house; on a racecourse, a turf enclosure where the horses are assembled before the race.

paddy *n* rice in the husk whether in the field or gathered; a rice field.

padlock *n* a movable lock with a bow or semicircular link to be fastened through a staple.—*vt* to fasten or provide with a padlock or padlocks.

padre *n* a minister of religion; a chaplain.

paean *n* a song of triumph; a loud and joyous song.

paediatrician *n* a doctor who specializes in paediatrics.

paediatrics *npl* the branch of medicine that deals with the treatment of diseases and disorders in children.

paedophilia *n* an abnormal sexual attraction towards children.

paedophiliac *adj* pertaining to paedophilia.—*n* a person who is abnormally sexually attracted to children.

paeon *n* a four-syllable metrical foot comprising in any order three short and one long syllable.

pagan *n* one who worships false gods; one who is neither a Christian, a Jew, nor a Muslim; a heathen; an idolater.—*adj* pertaining to pagans or heathens; heathenish; idolatrous.

paganism *n* the worship of false gods; the religious opinions and worship of pagans; heathenism.

page¹ *n* one side of the leaf of a book, letter, etc; a writing or record (*the page of history*); printing, types set up for one side of a leaf.—*vt* (**paged, paging**) to mark or number the pages of; to paginate.

page² *n* a young male attendant on kings, nobles or other persons of distinction; a young uniformed man in the service of people of rank or wealth, hotels, etc, whose duty it is to run errands, attend to the door, etc.—*vt* (**paged, paging**) to attend as a page; to summon by messenger, loudspeaker, bleep, etc.

pageant *n* a spectacle or entertainment; a great display or show, as at some public rejoicing; a theatrical exhibition; anything showy, without stability or duration.

pageantry *n* pageants collectively; a showy exhibition or spectacle; splendid or ostentatious show.

pager *n* a device carried on a person so that he or she can be summoned; a bleep.

paginate *vt* (**paginated, paginating**) to number the pages of.

pagination *n* the act of paginating; the arrangement and number of pages of a book, etc; the marks or figures which indicate the number of pages.

pagoda *n* a Hindu or Buddhist temple in India or the Far East.

pah *interj* an exclamation expressing contempt or disgust.

pail *n* a bucket of plastic, metal or wood in which water is carried.

paillasse *n* same as **palliasse**.

pain *n* a sensation of hurting in animal bodies; bodily distress; suffering; the throes of travail or childbirth (generally in plural); mental distress; penalty; suffering associated with the commission of a crime (*under pain of death*); careful labour; close application in working; trouble (chiefly in plural).—*vt* to give pain to; to cause to endure physical or mental suffering; to afflict; to distress.

painful *adj* full of pain; giving or accompanied by pain; distressing; requiring labour or toil; difficult; executed with pains; attended with close and careful application or attention.

painstaking *adj* taking or given to taking pains; giving close application; laborious and careful.—*n* the taking of pains; careful labour.

paint *vt* to lay colour or colours on with a brush or otherwise; to colour; to produce (a representation) in colours; to form a

padlock

page

likeness or representation of in colours; to represent or exhibit to the mind; to describe vividly; to delineate; to depict; to adorn or beautify by laying artificial colours on (the face).—*vi* to practise painting; to lay artificial colour on the face with the view of beautifying it.—*n* a substance used in painting; a pigment; colour laid on the face; make-up.

painter[1] *n* one whose occupation is to paint; an artist who uses the mediums of colours or pigments, usually laid on paper, canvas, board, etc.

painter[2] *n* a rope used to fasten a boat to a ship or other object.

painting *n* the act, art or employment of laying on colours; the art of representing objects by means of figures and colours on a plane surface so as to produce the appearance of relief; a painted picture.

pair *n* two things similar in form and suited to each other or used together (*a pair of gloves* or *stockings*); a single thing composed of two pieces suiting each other (*a pair of scissors* or *of trousers*); two of a sort; a couple; a brace; distinctively, a man and his wife; in Parliament and similar bodies, two Members who would vote on opposite sides and agree not to vote for a specified time.—*vi* to join in pairs; to couple; to mate (as birds).—*vt* to unite in pairs or couples; to assort in twos.

paisley *n* an intricate pattern of curved shapes; a soft woollen fabric with this design; a shawl made of this material.—*adj* of this pattern or material.

pal *n* mate; partner; accomplice; chum.

palace *n* the building in which an emperor, king or other distinguished person resides; a splendid place of residence; a stately mansion.

paladin *n* a knight attached to a sovereign's court; a knight errant; a heroic champion; an eminent hero.

Palaeocene *n* the earliest division of the Tertiary epoch, preceding the Eocene, characterized by the appearance of mammals with placentas.

palaeographer *n* one skilled in palaeography.

palaeographic, palaeographical *adj* pertaining to palaeography.

palette knife

palaeography *n* an ancient manner of writing; ancient writings collectively; the art of deciphering ancient documents or inscriptions.

palaeolith *n* an unpolished stone, implement or other object belonging to the earlier Stone Age.

Palaeolithic *adj* belonging to the earlier Stone Age.

palaeontologist *n* one who studies or is versed in palaeontology.

palaeontology *n* the science of the ancient life of the earth; that branch of biological science which treats of fossil organic remains.

Palaeozoic *adj* (*geol*) applied to the lowest division of stratified groups, as distinguished from the Mesozoic and Cenozoic.

palanquin, palankeen *n* a covered conveyance used in India, China, etc, borne by poles on the shoulder and carrying a single person.

palatable *adj* agreeable to the taste or palate; acceptable.

palatal *adj* pertaining to the palate; uttered by the aid of the palate, as certain sounds. —*n* a sound pronounced by the aid of the palate (as that of *ch* in church and of *j*).

palate *n* the roof or upper part of the mouth; taste; relish; sometimes intellectual taste.

palatial *adj* pertaining to a palace; suitable for a palace; magnificent.

palatinate *n* the province or seignory of a palatine.

palatine *adj* pertaining to a palace; holding office in the king's palace; possessing royal privileges.—*n* a prince or noble who rules a palatinate.

palaver *n* a talk or conference; a conversation; superfluous or idle talk.—*vi* to talk idly; to indulge in a palaver or palavers.

pale[1] *adj* white or whitish; wan; not ruddy or fresh of colour; not bright; of a faint lustre; dim.—*vt* (**paled, paling**) to make pale; to diminish the brightness of.—*vi* to turn pale; to lose colour; to become or appear comparatively dull or feeble (*to pale into insignificance*).

pale[2] *n* a pointed stake used in fencing or enclosing, fixed upright in the ground or joined above and below to a rail; a picket; what surrounds and encloses; the space enclosed; an enclosure.—**beyond the pale** beyond the limits of convention; unacceptable.—*vt* (**paled, paling**) to enclose with pales or stakes; to encompass.

palea *n* (*pl* **paleae**) (*bot*) one of the bracts on the receptacle of composite plants between the florets; one of the interior bracts of the flowers of grasses.

palette *n* a thin oval board or tablet, with a thumbhole at one end, on which a painter lays the pigments with which he or she paints; the range of colours used by an artist.

palette knife *n* a flat flexible knife used in painting for mixing colours and in cooking for scraping, etc.

palfrey *n* an ordinary riding horse or a horse used by noblemen and others for state, distinguished from a war horse; a small horse fit for ladies.

palimpsest *n* a parchment or other piece of writing material from which one writing has been erased to make room for another, often leaving the first faintly visible, a process to which many ancient manuscripts were subjected.

palindrome *n* a word, verse or sentence that is the same when read backwards or forwards, as 'Madam, I'm Adam'.

paling *n* pales in general or a fence formed with pales.

palingenesis *n* (*pl* **palingeneses**) recapitulation of ancestral stages in a life history; a transformation from one state to another; a metamorphosis as of insects.

palinode *n* originally a poetical recantation; a piece in which a poet retracts the invectives contained in a former piece; hence, a recantation in general.

palisade *n* a fence or fortification consisting of a row of strong stakes or posts set firmly in the ground; also applied to one of the stakes.—*vt* (**palisaded, palisading**) to surround or fortify with palisades.

pall[1] *n* a large black cloth thrown over a coffin at a funeral or over a tomb; a mantle; a covering as of smoke; an atmosphere of gloom or grief; an outer mantle of dignity.—*vt* to cover with a pall; to cover or invest; to shroud.

pall[2] *vi* to become insipid; to become devoid of agreeableness or attraction (*pleasures begin to pall*).—*vt* to make vapid or insipid; to cloy; to dispirit or depress.

Palladian architecture *n* a type of Italian architecture founded by the Italian architect Andrea Palladio (1518–80) on the Roman classical style.

palladium[1] *n* a metallic element of a silvery colour, ductile and malleable, considerably harder and lighter than platinum.

palladium[2] *n* a sacred object thought to be the effectual defence of a city; a safeguard.

pallbearer *n* one of those who attend the coffin at a funeral.

pallet[1] *n* a wooden instrument used for forming and shaping clay; a palette; an instrument for applying gold leaf; a piece which receives the impulse from a pendulum or balance wheel; a portable platform for lifting and stacking goods.

pallet[2] *n* a small crude bed.

palliasse, paillasse *n* an underbed of straw; a straw mattress.

palliate *vt* (**palliated, palliating**) to extenuate; to soften or tone down by favourable representations; to mitigate, lessen or abate (*to palliate a disease*).

palliation *n* the act of palliating; what palliates or serves to excuse; extenuation; mitigating; alleviation.

palliative *adj* serving to palliate or extenuate; extenuating; mitigating.—*n* that which palliates.

pallid *adj* pale; wan; deficient in colour; not high coloured.

pallor *n* paleness.

palm *n* the inner part of the hand; a tropical tree with fan-shaped leaves; a branch or leaf of the palm borne in ancient times as a symbol of victory or triumph; hence, superiority, victory, triumph (*to carry off the palm*).—*vt* (**palmed, palming**) to conceal in the palm of the hand, as jugglers or cheats; to impose by fraud (*to palm off trash on the public*); to foist.

palmar *adj* pertaining to the palm of the hand; of the breadth of the hand.

palmate, palmated *adj* having the shape of the hand (*palmate leaves*); having the toes webbed (*the palmate feet of aquatic birds*).

palm civet *n* an animal of Southeastern Asia of the civet family, living in palm trees and able to curl its tail into a tight spiral.

palmer *n* in medieval times, a pilgrim who returned from the Holy Land with a branch of palm.

palmiped *adj* web-footed.—*n* a bird that has webbed feet.

palmist *n* one who deals in palmistry.

palmistry *n* the art of telling fortunes by the lines and marks in the palm of the hand; manual dexterity (humorous).

palm oil *n* an oil resembling butter obtained from palms, used in the manufacture of soap, candles, etc, and as food.

Palm Sunday *n* the Sunday before Easter, commemorating Christ's triumphal entry into Jerusalem, when the crowd strewed palm branches.

palmy *adj* abounding in palms; worthy of the palm; flourishing; prosperous (*the palmy days of Rome*).

palp, palpus *n* (*pl* **palps, palpi**) a jointed sensitive organ on the head of an insect or crustacean; a feeler.

palpable *adj* perceptible by the touch; capable of being felt; easily perceived and detected; plain; obvious; easily perceptible.

palpitate *vi* (**palpitated, palpitating**) to flutter or move with slight throbs; to throb; to pulsate violently (applied particularly to an abnormal movement of the heart, as from fright or disease); hence, to tremble; to quiver.

palpitation *n* a violent and unnatural beating or pulsation of the heart, as from violent action, fright or disease.

palsy *n* paralysis; a condition marked by an uncontrollable tremor of a part of the body.—*vt* (**palsied, palsying**) to affect with palsy or as with palsy; to paralyse.

palter *vi* to act insincerely; to equivocate; to dodge; to play tricks.

paltriness *n* the state of being paltry, vile or worthless.

paltry *adj* trifling; insignificant; worthless.

paludal *adj* pertaining to marshes; generated by marshes; malarial.

pampas *npl* the grassy treeless plains of South America.

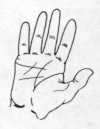

palm

pampas grass *n* a variety of tall-stemmed grass growing on the pampas, now widely cultivated for its feathery heads.

pamper *vt* to gratify to the full; to spoil; to indulge to excess; to indulge with rich food.

pampero *n* (*pl* **pamperos**) a cold wind blowing from the Andes north- or north-eastwards to the Atlantic.

pamphlet *n* a small book consisting of a sheet of paper or of a few sheets stitched together but not bound; a short treatise or essay published by itself.

pamphleteer *n* a writer of pamphlets; a scribbler.

pan[1] *n* a vessel of tin, iron or other metal, often rather shallow, used to separate gold from other matter by washing; a tray (of scales); a vessel of various kinds used for domestic purposes; an open vessel for boiling or evaporating or other operations (*a milk pan*, etc); the bowl of a lavatory; a pond for evaporating salt water to make salt (*a salt pan*); the part of a flintlock which holds the powder; the skull or cranium (*the brain pan*).—*vt* (**panned, panning**) to wash (gold-bearing gravel) in a pan; (*colloq*) to disparage or find fault with; to criticize severely.—**to pan out** (*colloq*) to turn out, especially to turn out well; to succeed.

pan

pan[2] *vti* (**panned, panning**) (of a film camera) to move horizontally to follow an object or provide a panoramic view.—*n* the act or an instance of panning; a horizontal shot.

Pan *n* in Greek myth, the chief god of pastures, forests and flocks.

panacea *n* a remedy for all diseases; a universal medicine or remedy.

Panama hat *n* a hat made of a fine straw-like material from the leaves of a palm-like plant, originally from Panama.

pancake *n* a thin cake of batter fried in a pan.

pancreas *n* a large glandular organ found in vertebrates, situated behind the stomach, which secretes insulin and digestive juices; in cattle, the sweetbread.

pancreatic *adj* pertaining to the pancreas.

panda *n* either of two mammals of the racoon family: the *giant panda*, a large black and white bear-like animal; the *lesser panda*, a smaller, reddish-brown animal with a ringed tail.

panda

Pandean *adj* pertaining to Pan.

pandect *n* a treatise which contains the whole of any science.

pandemic *adj* over a large area; universal; epidemic.

pandemonium *n* the place or abode of demons or evil spirits; hence, any lawless, disorderly place or assemblage; uproar; chaos.

pander *n* a pimp; a procurer; a go-between in sexual liaisons.—*vi* to act as agent for the lusts of others; to gratify a person's desires or weaknesses.

pandiculation *n* the stretching of oneself, as when newly woken from sleep; an abnormal restlessness and stretching.

Pandora's box *n* in Greek myth, a box given to Pandora which, forbidden to do so, she opened, letting all the evils escape to plague the world, leaving behind only hope; a source of many troubles.

pandore *n* same as **bandore**.

pane *n* a plate of glass inserted in a window, door, etc; a panel or division of a work; a distinct part of a flat surface; a sunken portion surrounded by a border.

panegyric *n* a laudatory oration; a formal eulogy; an elaborate encomium; praise bestowed.

panegyrical *adj* containing praise or eulogy.

panegyrist *n* one who bestows praise; a eulogist.

panegyrize *vt* (**panegyrized, panegyrizing**) to write or pronounce a panegyric or eulogy on.—*vi* to indulge in panegyric; to bestow praises.

panel *n* a surface or compartment of a surface more or less distinct from others; an area on a wall sunk from the general surface; a similar portion fixed in the framing of a door, shutter, etc; a piece of wood on which a picture is painted; a board for instruments or controls; a lengthways strip in a skirt, etc; a group of selected persons for judging, discussing, etc; (*law*) a document containing the names of persons summoned to serve on a jury; the jury; (*Scots law*) the accused person in a criminal action.—*vt* (**panelled, panelling**) to form with panels.

panelling *n* panelled work.

panellist *n* a member of a panel.

pang *n* a sudden brief spasm of hunger, pain, grief, etc.

pangolin *n* an insect-eating mammal, also known as the *scaly anteater*, found in Africa and Asia.

Panhellenic *adj* pertaining to all Greece.

Panhellenism *n* the proposed union of all the Greeks into one political body.

panic *n* a sudden overpowering fright or anxiety, particularly without real cause; an outbreak of this among many people at once.—*adj* of or resulting from overpowering fright (*panic measures*).—*vt* (**panicked, panicking**) to affect with panic.—*vi* to be affected with panic.

panicky *adj* showing or inspired by panic.

panicle *n* a branching form of inflorescence, as in the lilac or the oat.

panic-stricken, panic-struck *adj* struck with a panic or sudden fear.

pannier *n* a wicker basket, one of two baskets slung across a beast of burden, in which things are carried; a connected pair of bags slung over the back of a bicycle or motorcycle; formerly, a part of a woman's dress attached to the back of the skirt; (*archit*) a corbel.

pannikin *n* a small pan or cup.

panoply *n* complete armour of defence; a full suit of armour; a complete array.

panorama *n* a complete view in all directions; a comprehensive presentation of a subject; a constantly changing scene.

panoramic *adj* pertaining to or like a panorama or complete view.

Panpipes, panpipes *npl* a musical wind instrument composed of reeds of different lengths tied together; a syrinx.

pansy *n* a garden variety of violet; heartsease; (*colloq*) an effeminate man.

pant *vi* to breathe quickly, as after exertion or from excited eagerness; to gasp; to throb or heave with unusual violence, as the heart or the breast after hard labour; to desire ardently.—*vt* to breathe forth; to gasp out.—*n* a quick, short respiration; a gasp; a throb or palpitation.

pantalets, pantalettes *npl* loose drawers with ruffles worn by women and children in early Victorian days.

Pantaloon *n* a character in Italian comedy, so called from his dress; in pantomimes, a character usually represented as a very fatuous old man, the butt of the clown.

pantaloons *npl* formerly, a man's tight breeches fastened at the calf or foot; (*colloq*) baggy trousers.

pantechnicon *n* a place where all kinds of manufactured articles are collected and exposed for sale; a large furniture van.

pantheism *n* the doctrine that the universe, taken or conceived of as a whole, is God or that all things are simply modes or manifestations of God.

pantheist *n* one who believes in pantheism.

pantheon *n* a temple dedicated to all the gods; all the gods collectively worshipped by a people; a building in which the famous dead of a nation are buried or remembered.

panther *n* a leopard, a large feline animal of Asia and Africa, usually used to mean the black leopard.

pantile *n* a tile with a cross-section resembling the letter S, overlapping the tile by its side as well as the one beneath.

pantisocracy *n* a utopian community in which all the members are equal in rank and social position; the principle of such a scheme or community.

pantograph *n* an instrument by means of which drawings, maps, plans, etc, can be copied mechanically on the original scale or on one reduced or enlarged.

pantomime *n* a drama without words, using only actions and gestures; mime; a popular stage entertainment usually produced about the Christmas season, with jokes and music.

pantry *n* an apartment or closet in which provisions, kitchen utensils, etc, are kept or where silver and knives, etc, are cleaned.

pants *npl* underpants, knickers, briefs; trousers.

pap[1] *n* a kind of soft food for infants; the pulp of fruit; oversimplified or insipid writing, ideas, etc; drivel.

pap[2] *n* a nipple of the breast; a teat; a round hill resembling a pap.

papa *n* an informal word for **father**.

papacy *n* the office and dignity of the pope; papal authority and jurisdiction.

papal *adj* of or belonging to the pope or the papacy; proceeding from the pope.

paparazzo *n* (*pl* **paparazzi**) a freelancer photographer who pursues celebrities for candid or sensational shots for publication.

papaya, papaw *n* a tree indigenous to South America but now widely cultivated in tropical countries; its elongated melon-like fruit with edible yellow flesh and small black seeds.

pansy

paper *n* a substance used for writing and printing on and for various other purposes, manufactured principally of vegetable fibre reduced to a pulp; a piece, leaf or sheet of paper; a newspaper; a journal; an essay or article on some subject; any written or printed document; a set of written examination questions; collectively, such documents as promissory notes, bills of exchange, etc; (*pl*) personal documents.—**on paper** in theory but not in practice.—*adj* made of paper; appearing merely in certain documents without really existing (*a paper army*); thin; slight.—*vt* to cover with paper; to furnish with paper hangings; to fold or enclose in paper; (*colloq*) to fill (the empty seats of a theatre) by giving away free tickets (*to paper the house*).—**to paper over** to disguise; to conceal.

paperback *n* a book bound in a flexible paper cover.—*adj* pertaining to such a book or the publication of such books.

paperclip *n* a clip for holding paper.

paper-cutter *n* a paperknife; a machine for cutting paper in piles or for trimming the edges of books, etc.

paperhanger *n* one whose employment is to line walls with wallpaper; a device to help in hanging wallpaper.

paperknife *n* (*pl* **paperknives**) an instrument of bone, ivory, etc, with an edge like a blunt knife, used in cutting open envelopes, the leaves of books, etc, or for folding paper.

paperclip

607

paper money *n* paper currency authorized as representing value; banknotes.

paper tiger *n* a someone or something that has the outward appearance of being powerful and threatening but is in fact ineffective.

paperweight *n* a small weight laid on loose papers to keep them in place.

papery *adj* like paper; having the thinness and consistency of paper.

papier-mâché *n* a material prepared by pulping or layering paper mixed with glue or size, which is moulded into various articles, dried and japanned.

papilionaceous *adj* resembling the butterfly; (*bot*) having the corolla shaped like a butterfly, such as the flower of the pea.

papilla *n* (*pl* **papillae**) a small pap or nipple; a little eminence on the surface of the skin, as on the tongue.

papillary *adj* pertaining to or resembling the nipple.

papillon *n* a small breed of dog with a fine white coat with coloured patches.

papillote *n* a piece of curled paper used to decorate a cooked chop.

papist *n* (*derog*) a Roman Catholic.

papoose *n* among the American Indians, a baby or young child.

pappus *n* (*pl* **pappi**) (*bot*) the feathery appendage that crowns many single-seeded seed vessels; a form of calyx in composite plants of a downy or hairy character.

paprika *n* a mild red condiment ground from the fruit of certain peppers.

papula *n* (*pl* **papulae**) a pimple.

papular, papulose, papulous *adj* covered with pimples.

papyrus *n* (*pl* **papyri, papyruses**) a plant abundant in southern Europe and the valley of the Nile, the stems of which provided the earliest material for writing, used by the ancient Egyptians, Greeks and Romans; an ancient written scroll of papyrus.

par *n* state of equality; equality in circumstances or in value; the state of the shares of a public undertaking when they may be purchased at their face value or at par; (in golf) the average number of strokes that a first-class player should take for each hole or a number of holes.—**above par** above the nominal price; at a premium.—**below par** below the nominal price; at a discount; hence, not up to the usual standard; slightly unwell.—**par of exchange** the established value of the standard value of one country expressed in the standard value of another.

parabasis *n* (*pl* **parabases**) the part of an ancient Greek comedy in which the chorus addressed the audience in the name of the poet.

parable *n* originally, a comparison or similitude; now a fable or allegorical representation of something real in life or nature, from which a moral is drawn for instruction; (*scrip*) a proverbial or notable saying, a thing darkly or figuratively expressed.—*vt* (**parabled, parabling**) to represent by a parable.

parabola *n* a geometrical figure, one of the conic sections, shown when a cone is cut by a plane parallel to one of its sides; the curve which a projectile theoretically describes.

parabole *n* (*rhet*) similitude; comparison.

parabolic *adj* having the form of a parabola; pertaining to a parabola; pertaining to a parable.

paracetamol *n* a drug used to relieve headache, neuralgia, fever, etc.

parachute *n* an umbrella-shaped apparatus, consisting of a canopy of nylon (formerly silk) attached to a harness, for the purpose of enabling people or supplies to drop to the ground gradually without sustaining injury or damage, shape affording great resistance to air; also sometimes used to slow down a landing aircraft or missile.—*vt* (**parachuted, parachuting**) to drop by parachute.—*vi* to descend by parachute.

paraclete *n* one called to aid or support; hence, a term applied to the Holy Spirit.

parade *n* show; ostentation; display; a showy or pompous procession; a military display; the collection of troops for inspection, etc; the place where such display is held; a public walk or promenade.—*vt* (**paraded, parading**) to exhibit in a showy manner; to make a show of; to assemble and march in military order.—*vi* to assemble in military order; to go about in military procession; to walk about for show.

paradigm *n* an example; a model; (*gram*) an example of a word, as a noun, adjective or verb, in its various inflections.

paradise *n* according to various religions, a region of supreme felicity; the abode of sanctified souls after death; the Garden of Eden, in which Adam and Eve were at first placed; hence, any place of beauty and bliss.

parados *n* (*fort*) an elevation of earth behind a trench, etc, to protect it from attack from the rear.

paradox *n* a tenet or proposition contrary to received opinion; a statement which seems to be at variance with common sense or to contradict some previously ascertained truth, though when properly investigated it may be perfectly well founded; something with seemingly contradictory qualities, etc.

paradoxical *adj* having the nature of a paradox; inclined to paradox.

paraffin *n* a liquid distilled from petroleum

parachute

which in its highly refined form is used as a fuel in jet engines (when it is usually known as *kerosene*) and is otherwise principally used as a solvent and as a domestic and industrial fuel oil, formerly much used as a fuel for oil lamps, portable spirit stoves and in certain types of internal-combustion engine; (*chem*) also **alkane**) any of the methane series of hydrocarbons, called saturated hydrocarbons and including methane and propane, which remain gaseous at lower temperatures.

paraffin wax *n* a white wax-like substance, odourless and insoluble and having a very low melting point, derived principally from alkane hydrocarbons and used in the manufacture of candles, waxed paper and as a sealing agent.

paragon *n* a model or pattern of superior excellence or perfection.—*vt* (*arch*) to compare; to rival; to form a rival or equal to.

paragraph *n* a division in a written composition; the character ¶ used to mark such a division; a distinct part of a discourse or writing, consisting of one or several sentences; a portion or section which relates to a particular point and is generally distinguished by a break in the lines; a brief notice, as in a newspaper.

Paraguay tea *n* maté.

parakeet, parrakeet, paroquet *n* any of various parrots of the eastern hemisphere, generally of small size and having very long tail feathers.

parallax *n* the apparent change of position of an object relative to other objects when viewed from different places; (*astron*) the difference in direction of any celestial object as viewed from the surface of the earth and from the centre of either the earth or the sun; optics, the non-coincidence of the cross fibres of a telescope with the focus of the eyeglass.

parallel *adj* extended in the same direction and in all parts equally distant; being exactly at an equal distance throughout their length or breadth (said of lines or surfaces); hence, having the same direction or tendency; running in accordance with something; equal in all essential parts, points or features; exactly similar (*a parallel passage* or *incident*).—*n* a line which throughout its whole extent is equidistant from another line; one of the circles on a sphere parallel to its equator; a line on a map marking latitude; resemblance or conformity in essential points; likeness; comparison (*to draw a parallel between two historians*); one who corresponds essentially to another; a counterpart; (*print*) a mark of reference (thus ‖) used to direct attention to notes; (*elect*) an arrangement of part of an electric circuit, such that the conductors in that part form distinct branches, each of which carries a fraction of the total current.—*vt* (**paralleled, paralleling**) to make parallel; to form or serve as a parallel to; to match; to correspond to; to show or furnish an equal to; to compare.—*vi* to be parallel.

parallel bars *npl* a set of horizontal bars raised above the floor on posts used by gymnasts.

parallelepiped, parallelopiped *n* a solid body bounded by three pairs of parallel faces; a solid in the shape of a brick.

parallelism *n* state of being parallel; resemblance in a number of important particulars; correspondence; a comparison.

parallelogram *n* a four-sided figure composed of straight lines and having its opposite sides parallel and equal; popularly, a quadrilateral figure of greater length than breadth.

paralogism *n* a fallacious argument; an instance of false reasoning.

paralysis *n* a loss or diminution of muscular power in some part of the body, arising from some disorder of the nervous system; a loss of sensation in any part of the body; palsy; a condition of helpless inactivity.

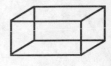

parallelepiped

paralyse *vt* (**paralysed, paralysing**) to affect with paralysis; to destroy physical or mental energy in; to bring to a complete stop.

paralytic *adj* pertaining to paralysis; affected with paralysis; inclined to paralysis; (*colloq*) very drunk.—*n* a person affected with paralysis.

paramedic *n* a person trained to provide emergency medical treatment and to support professional medical staff.

paramedical *adj* supplementing and assisting the work of professional medical staff.

parameter *n* (*math*) a variable quantity which is treated as constant while other variables are investigated, hence characterizing and limiting the other variables; a limit, boundary or condition.

paramilitary *adj* of a military structure or organization which is supplementary to the regular armed offices.

paramount *adj* eminent; of the highest order; superior to all others.—*n* chief; highest in rank or order; superior in power or jurisdiction (*lord paramount*, the supreme lord of a fee or of lands, etc).

parallelogram

paramour *n* a lover; a wooer; one who takes the place of a husband or wife without possessing the rights.

paranoia *n* a form of mental illness characterized by delusions of grandeur and persecution and feelings of distrust; (*colloq*) unfounded fear and suspicion.

paranoid *adj* of or like paranoia; (*colloq*) highly suspicious or fearful.—*n* a paranoid person.

609

paranormal *adj* beyond the scope of normal experience or scientific explanation.

parapet *n* (*archit*) a wall placed at the edges of roofs, platforms, sides of bridges, etc, to prevent people from falling over; (*milit*) a wall or rampart to cover the soldiers from the attacks of the enemy in front; a breastwork.

paraphernalia *npl* personal belongings; accessories; appendages; ornaments; trappings.

paraphrase *n* a restatement of a text, passage or work, giving the sense of the original in other words; the setting forth in clearer and ampler terms of the signification of a passage or work; a sacred song or hymn based on a selected portion of Scripture.—*vt* (**paraphrased, paraphrasing**) to make a paraphrase of; to explain or translate with latitude.—*vi* to interpret or explain amply.

paraphrast *n* one who paraphrases.

paraphrastic *adj* having the character of a paraphrase; explaining in words more clear and ample than those of the author.

paraplegia *n* a paralysis which affects the lower half of the body.

paraplegic *adj* of, relating to or suffering from paraplegia.—*n* a paraplegic person.

paraselene *n* (*pl* **paraselenae**) a bright spot sometimes seen on a lunar halo, bearing a resemblance to the moon; a mock moon.

parasite *n* an animal that lives on or in, and at the expense of, other animals; a plant which grows on another plant and feeds on its juices; a hanger-on; a person who lives on others and gives nothing in return.

parasitic, parasitical *adj* of the nature of a parasite; meanly dependent on others for support; (*bot, zool*) growing or living as a parasite.

parasitism *n* the behaviour or manners of a parasite; the state of being a parasite.

parasol *n* an umbrella, often of considerable size, used as protection from the sun; a sunshade.

parasol

parasynthesis *n* (*gram*) derivation from a compound plus affix (*light + heart + ed = light-hearted*).

parataxis *n* (*gram*) use of successive clauses without connecting words.

parathyroid *adj* of small gland-like masses near or embedded in, the thyroid gland.

paratyphoid fever *n* a disease closely resembling typhoid but caused by different bacteria.

paratroops *npl* infantry trained and equipped to be dropped by parachute into enemy-held areas.

paravane *n* a torpedo-shaped machine fitted with an apparatus for severing the moorings of sea mines.

parboil *vt* to boil in part; to boil in a moderate degree.

parbuckle *n* a sling formed by a single rope round a heavy object for hoisting or lowering.—*vt* (**parbuckled, parbuckling**) to hoist or lower by means of a parbuckle.

parcel *n* a bundle; a package; a portion of anything taken separately; a collection; a lot; a quantity or number of things put up together.—*vt* (**parcelled, parcelling**) to divide or put up into parts or portions; to make up into a mass.

parcener *n* a coheir.

parch *vt* to burn the surface of; to scorch; to dry to extremity; to make thirsty.—*vi* to become scorched or superficially burned; to become very dry; to become thirsty.

parchment *n* the skin of a young calf, sheep or goat dressed or prepared and rendered fit for writing on; paper like parchment.

pard *n* (*arch*) the leopard or panther.

pardon *vt* to release from liability to suffer punishment for a crime or a fault; to forgive (an offender); to remit the penalty or punishment of; to forgive (the offence).— **pardon me** forgive me; excuse me (a phrase often used when a person means civilly to deny or contradict what another affirms).—*n* forgiveness of an offender or of his offence; a passing over without, or not visiting with, punishment; remission of penalty; forgiveness; an official warrant of penalty remitted.

pardonable *adj* capable of being pardoned or forgiven; excusable; venial.

pardoner *n* one who pardons; (*hist*) one licensed to sell the pope's indulgences.

pare *vt* (**pared, paring**) to cut off, as the superficial substance or extremities of a thing; to shave off with a sharp instrument; to trim by shaving the surface; to diminish by little and little.

paregoric *adj* (*med*) mitigating or assuaging pain.—*n* a medicine that mitigates pain; an anodyne.

parenchyma *n* (*anat*) the tissue outside the blood vessels and derived from the blood; the cellular and fibrous substance of the glands and other solid organs; (*bot*) the pith or pulp of plants; the spongy and cellular tissue.

parent *n* a father or mother; he or she that produces young (used of animals and plants as well as of humans); one who or that which produces; cause; source.

parentage *n* extraction; birth; origin; condition with respect to the rank or character of parents.

parental *adj* pertaining to parents; suited to or characteristic of parents.

parenthesis *n* (*pl* **parentheses**) an explanatory or qualifying sentence, or part of a sentence, inserted into the midst of another sentence, without being grammatically connected with it, generally marked off by upright curves () (brackets, parentheses) but frequently by dashes (– —) and even by commas; (*print*) the parenthetical sign (), including the words inserted; an intervening period or event; an interlude.

parenthetic, parenthetical *adj* pertaining to a parenthesis; of the nature of a parenthesis; exhibiting parentheses

parenthood *n* the state of being a parent; the condition of a parent.

parergon *n* (*pl* **parerga**) something done incidentally; a by-product; something subsidiary; a superfluity; a superfluous detail.

parget *n* plaster laid on roofs or walls.—*vt* (**pargetted, pargetting**) to cover with plaster or parget.—*vi* to plaster.

parhelion *n* (*pl* **parhelia**) a bright spot sometimes seen on a solar halo, having the appearance of the sun itself; a mock sun.

pariah *n* one of the lowest class of people in India; hence, one despised and condemned by society; an outcast.

parietal *adj* (*anat*) pertaining to the walls of a cavity of the body or to the bones which form the sides and upper part of the skull; (*bot*) growing from the side of another organ.

paring *n* what is pared off; a piece clipped off; the rind.

parish *n* a district of a diocese under the charge of a parson, minister, etc; the inhabitants of such a district; in UK, an administrative subdivision of a rural county.—*adj* belonging to a parish; parochial.

parish clerk *n* a person appointed to assist in various church duties.

parishioner *n* one who belongs to a parish.

parish priest *n* a parson; a minister who holds a parish as a benefice.

parish register *n* a book in which the births, deaths and marriages that occur in a parish are registered.

parity *n* the condition of being equal or equivalent; like state or degree; equality; close correspondence; analogy.

park *n* formerly, a large piece of ground enclosed and set apart for hunting; an extensive area of pasture and woodland surrounding or adjoining a mansion house; a piece of public ground in or near a large town, laid out and kept for the sole purpose of pleasure and recreation; a national park; in Scotland, any field, as on a farm.—*vt* to draw up and leave (a vehicle) for a time in an enclosed space or at the side of a road; (*sl*) to put, to sit.

parka *n* a warm, hooded kind of anorak, often of fur or fur-lined, for wear in very cold conditions.

Parkinson's disease *n* a progressive disease of the nervous system characterized by uncontrollable shaking of the limbs, muscular rigidity, partial paralysis and weakness.

Parkinson's Law *n* a law, humorously expounded by C. N. Parkinson in 1958, that work expands to fill the time available for its completion.

parlance *n* a way of speaking, especially of a specialized nature (*political parlance, sales parlance*).

parley *vi* (**parleyed, parleying**) to confer or speak with a person on some point of mutual concern; especially, to confer with an enemy, as on an exchange of prisoners, a cessation of arms, etc—*n* mutual discourse or conversation; a conference with an enemy in war.

parliament *n* a meeting or assembly of persons for conference or deliberation; a legislative assembly made up of representatives of a nation.

Parliament *n* the supreme governing and legislative body of various countries, such as Britain.

Parliamentarian *n* one of those who adhered to Parliament in the time of the English Civil War (1542–52); a Roundhead.—*adj* serving Parliament in opposition to King Charles I.

parliamentary *adj* pertaining to Parliament or a parliament; enacted or done by a parliament; according to the rules and usages of a parliament or similar legislative body.

parlour *n* a room in a house for receiving guests; a sitting room; a shop or place of business (*funeral parlour*).

parlous *adj* dangerous; risky.

Parmesan cheese *n* a hard, dry cheese made round Parma in Italy.

Parnassian *adj* pertaining to Parnassus, the mountain in Greece sacred to Apollo and the Muses; hence, relating to poetry.

parochial *adj* belonging to a parish; provincial; narrow in outlook.

parochialism *n* the state of being parochial; narrowness.

parody *n* a literary, musical, etc, composition in which the form and expression of serious works are closely imitated but adapted to a ridiculous subject or a humorous method of treatment; a burlesque imitation of a serious work; a weak imitation.—*vt* (**parodied, parodying**) to turn into a parody; to write a parody on.

parodist *n* one who writes a parody.

parole *n* word of promise; word of honour; the release of a prisoner before the end of his or her sentence on condition of future good behaviour.

paronomasia *n* (*rhet*) a play on words; a pun.

paroquet *n* same as **parakeet**.

parotid gland *n* (*anat*) a salivary gland on either side of the face, in front of the ear and communicating with the mouth by a duct.

parotitis *n* inflammation of the parotid gland; mumps.

parrot

paroxysm *n* a fit or period of great intensity of a disease; convulsion; a sudden and violent outburst (as of rage or laughter).

parquet *n* flooring made of parquetry.—*vt* (**parqueted, parqueting**) to form in parquetry; to ornament with parquetry.

parquetry *n* a kind of inlaid woodwork in geometric or other patterns and generally of different colours, principally used for floors.

parr *n* a young salmon, trout, etc, up to two to three years of age.

parrakeet *n* same as **parakeet**.

parricidal *adj* pertaining to parricide; committing parricide.

parricide *n* the murder of a parent; a person who murders his or her father or mother.

parrot *n* any of an order of birds, including parakeets, macaws, lories, cockatoos, etc, or restricted to certain members of the family, all of which have hooked and rounded bills and fleshy tongues, some of them having the faculty of imitating the human voice.—*vt* to repeat as a parrot; to repeat by rote.

parry *vt* (**parried, parrying**) to ward off (a blow, a thrust); to stop or to put or turn aside; to prevent taking effect.—*vi* to put aside thrusts or strokes; to fence.—*n* a defensive movement in fencing; an evasive action.

parse *vt* (**parsed, parsing**) (*gram*) to analyse or describe grammatically; to show the several parts of speech composing (a sentence) and their relation to each other by government or agreement.

parsec *n* (*astron*) a unit of length for measuring stellar distances equal to 3.26 light years.

Parsee, Parsi *n* one of the adherents of the Zoroastrian or ancient Persian religion in India, originally from Persia.

Parseeism *n* the religion and customs of the Parsees.

parsimonious *adj* exhibiting or characterized by parsimony; niggardly; closefisted.

parsimony *adj* closeness or sparingness in the use or expenditure of money; niggardliness; miserliness.

parsley *n* a garden herb, used for flavouring in cooking.

parsley

parsnip *n* a biennial umbelliferous plant cultivated for its white, fleshy, cone-shaped root which is used as a vegetable; the root itself.

parson *n* the priest or incumbent of a parish; a clergyman; a man who is in orders or has been licensed to preach.

parsonage *n* the official dwelling house of a parson.

parson bird *n* the tui.

part *n* any portion of a thing; something less than the whole; a piece or fragment separated from a whole thing; a portion or quantity not separated in fact but considered as by itself; one of a number of equal portions or quantities that make up a whole; a constituent portion of a whole; a member of a whole; that which falls to each in division; share, portion, lot; concern or interest; side or party (*to take one's part*); allotted duty; particular office or business (*to perform one's part*); character assigned to an actor in a play or other like performance; (*mus*) one of the different melodies of a concerted composition, which, heard in union, compose its harmony (*the treble, tenor* or *bass part*); (*pl*) qualities, powers, faculties; (*pl*) often excellent or superior endowments (*a man of parts*); (*pl*) regions, districts; (*pl*) locality (*well-known in these parts*).—*vt* to divide; to separate or break into two or more pieces; to distribute; to share; to cause to sunder or go apart; to intervene betwixt; to interpose between; to separate, as combatants; (*naut*) to break; to suffer the breaking of (the ship parted her cables).—*vi* to become separate or detached; to divide; to move apart; to go away from another or others; to quit each other; to take leave (*to part with* or *from a person*); to break; to be torn asunder (*the rope parted*).—*adv* partly; in some measure.

partake *vi* (*pret* **partook**, *pp* **partaken**, *ppr* **partaking**) to take a part, portion or share in common with others; to have a share or part; to participate (*to partake of a repast, in festivities*); to have something of the character or nature of; to have features in common with (followed by *of*).—*vt* to have a part in; to share.

parterre *n* (*hortic*) a system of flower beds, connected together with intervening spaces of gravel or turf for walking on; the pit of a theatre.

parthenogenesis *n* (*zool*) the production of new individuals from an unfertilized ovum; the propagation by a plant or animal by any other method than impregnation.

partial *adj* affecting a part only; not general or universal; not total; inclined to favour one party in a cause or one side of a question more than the other; biased; not indifferent; inclined to favour without principle or reason (*a fond and partial parent*); having a predilection; inclined or favourable (with *to*).

partiality *n* the state or quality of being partial; unfair or undue bias; undue favour shown; a special liking or fondness.

participant *adj* sharing; having a share or part.—*n* one participating; a partaker.

participate *vt* (**participated, participating**) to partake; to take a part; to have a share in common with others (generally followed by *of* or *in*).—*vt* to partake, share, receive a part of.

participation *n* the state of participating or sharing in common with others.

participle *n* (*gram*) a part of speech, so called because although a verb it partakes of the character both of verb and adjective, and is also used in the formation of some compound tenses: the *past participle* in regular verbs is generally formed by adding '-ed' and the *present participle* by adding '-ing'.

particle *n* a minute part or portion of matter, the aggregation of which parts constitutes a whole mass; any very small portion or part; an atom; a jot; (*gram*) a word that is not varied or inflected, as the preposition, conjunction, etc.

parti-coloured *adj* coloured differently in different parts; of various colours.

particular *adj* pertaining to one and not to more; special; not general; individual; considered separately; peculiar; personal; private (*our own particular wrongs*); not ordinary; notable (*of no particular importance*); minute; circumstantial (*a full and particular account*); singularly nice in taste; precise; fastidious.—*n* a single instance; a single point; a distinct, separate or minute part; a detail.—**in particular** specially; particularly; to particularize.

particularize *vt* (**particularized, particularizing**) to specify or mention distinctly; to give the particulars of; to enumerate or specify in detail.—*vi* to mention or be attentive to single things or to small matters; to give full details.

particularly *adv* in a particular or especial manner.

parting *adj* serving to part; dividing; separating; given at separation (*a parting kiss*).—*n* the act of dividing or separating; a division; a separation; leave-taking; a line on the scalp where the hair falls or is combed in different directions; (*geol*) a fissure in strata.

partisan[1] *n* an adherent of a party or faction; one who is violently and passionately devoted to a party or interest.—*adj* pertaining to a party or faction; biased in favour of a party or interest.

partisan[2] *n* formerly, a kind of double-headed halberd or pike.

partite *adj* (*bot*) parted.

partition *n* the act of parting, dividing or separating into portions and distributing; division; separation; that by which different parts are separated; a wall separating apartments in a building; a division between the chambers or cells of a thing.—*vt* to divide by walls or partitions; to divide into shares.

partitive *adj* (*gram*) denoting a part or partition.—n (*gram*) a partitive word.

partly *adv* in part; in some measure or degree; not wholly, used in stating particulars that make up a whole.

partner *n* one who partakes or shares with another; an associate; one who has a share with another or others in some commercial, manufacturing or other undertaking; a member of a partnership; one who dances with another, either male or female; one who plays a sport with another; a husband or wife; either member of a married or non-married couple.

partnership *n* the state or condition of being a partner; an association of two or more persons for the purpose of undertaking and pursuing jointly any business, occupation or calling.

part of speech *n* each of the categories (e.g. verb, noun, adjective, etc) into which words are divided according to their grammatical and semantic functions.

partridge *n* any of several genera of game birds belonging to the same family as pheasants and quails.

parturition *n* the act of bringing forth or being delivered of young.

party *n* a selected company invited to an entertainment (*a tea party*, *an evening party*); a social gathering; a group of people with a common aim or interest (*a search party*, *a coach party*); a number of persons united in opinion or design in opposition to others in the community; persons in a state united by certain political views (*a political party*); a faction; a detached portion of a larger body or company; a detachment; one of two litigants; one concerned or interested in an affair (*a party to a plot*); a single person distinct from or opposed to another; a person under special consideration; hence, a person in general; an individual.

party-line *n* a telephone line shared by more than one household, each having a separate receiver; the official ideas or policies of a political party.

party politics *npl* politics involving the rivalry between different parties.

party wall *n* a wall between buildings to separate them from each other.

parvenu, parvenue *n* an upstart or one newly risen into notice or to high social or economic status.

parvis, parvise *n* a name formerly given to the porch of a church, now applied to the area round a church; also, a room above the church porch.

pas *n* in ballet, a step or series of steps; a dance sequence; right of going foremost; precedence.

paschal *adj* pertaining to Passover or to Easter.

paschal lamb *n* the lamb eaten on the first day of Passover.

partridge

Paschal Lamb *n* Jesus Christ.

pas de deux *n* (*pl* **pas de deux**) a ballet dance or part of a dance for two people.

pasha *n* in North Africa and the Middle East, a title conferred on high officials or military commanders; formerly, a provincial governor in the Ottoman Empire.

pasquinade *n* a lampoon or short satirical publication.

pass *vi* (**passed, passing**) to go; to proceed (*to pass away, from, into, over, under*, etc); to go past a certain person or place (*we saw him pass*); to alter or change condition or circumstances; to undergo transition; to vanish, disappear, be lost; hence, to depart from life; to die; to elapse; to be spent; to receive the sanction of a legislative house or body by a majority of votes (*the bill has passed*); to be current; to gain reception or be generally received (*banknotes pass as a substitute for coin*); to be regarded, held or considered; to occur; to take place (*what passes within our own mind*); to make a push in fencing or fighting; to go unheeded or neglected; to be transferred from an owner; to go successfully through an inspection or examination.—**to pass off** to take place; to disappear gradually; to impose fraudulently.—**to pass out** to distribute; to become unconscious; to complete military, etc, training.—*vt* to move near and go beyond; to move from side to side of; to live through; to spend (*to pass the summer*); to let go by without care or notice; to take no notice of; to transcend, exceed, excel, surpass; to transfer; to make to change hands; to hand over; to send; to circulate; to undergo successfully, as an examination, ordeal, etc; to obtain the legislative or official sanction of; to be enacted by (*the bill has passed the house*); to give legal or official sanction to; to enact or ratify; to allow as valid or just; to give forth officially; to pronounce (*to pass a sentence of death*); to void, as faeces or other matter.—**to pass up** to refuse or reject, as an opportunity.—*n* a passage; a way; a difficult or narrow way; a narrow road or defile between two mountains; permission to pass or to go or come; a ticket of free transit or admission; a thrust or push in fencing; a movement of the hand over or along anything; a manipulation of a mesmerist; state or condition of things; an embarrassing situation; the successful or satisfactory standing or going through an examination.

passable *adj* capable of being passed, travelled, traversed, penetrated, etc; capable of being passed from person to person; current; receivable; adequate; moderately good; tolerable; allowable; admissible.

passably *adv* tolerably; moderately.

passage *n* the act of passing; transit from one place to another; a going by, through, over, etc; transit by means of a conveyance; a journey by a conveyance, especially a ship; liberty of passing; access; entry or exit; way by which a person or thing may pass; avenue; way of entrance or exit; a gallery or corridor leading to the various divisions of a building; a part or portion quoted or referred to in a book, piece of music, etc; the act of carrying through all the steps necessary to render valid (*the passage of a bill* or *of a law*); an encounter (*a passage at arms, a passage of love*).

passant *adj* (*heral*) a term applied to an animal which appears to be walking.

passbook *n* a book held by the customer in which a record is kept by a bank or building society of credits and debits in certain types of account, such as a savings account; a bank book.

passenger *n* a person who travels in a public or private vehicle other than the driver or the operator; (*colloq*) one of a group who does not participate fully in the work of that group, allowing others to carry him or her along.

passer-by *n* (*pl* **passers-by**) one who goes by or near.

passerine *adj* perching (pertaining to the order of perching birds).—*n* a passerine bird.

passim *adv* here and there, an indication that something appears or recurs in a work (usually a book); in many different places or passages.

passion *n* an intense emotion; a strong feeling by which the mind is swayed, as joy, grief, love, hatred, ambition, avarice, revenge, fear, hope, etc; suffering (as of an early Christian martyr); violent agitation or excitement of mind; violent anger; zeal, ardour, vehement desire (*a passion for fame*); love; ardent affection; sexual desire; a passionate display; an exhibition of deep feeling (*a passion of tears*); a pursuit to which one is devoted; the object of any strong desire.

Passion *n* the last suffering of Christ; a description or depiction of this in the Bible, music, art, etc.

passionate *adj* characterized by passion; exhibiting or expressing passion; readily moved to anger; fiery; showing strong emotion; vehement; warm (*passionate affection*).

passionflower *n* any of a genus of plants with showy flowers, chiefly natives of tropical South America.

passionfruit *n* the edible fruit of certain varieties of passionflower.

Passion play *n* a mystery or miracle play representing the different scenes in the Passion of Christ.

Passion Sunday *n* the fifth Sunday in Lent.

Passion Week *n* the week between Passion Sunday and Palm Sunday; the week before Easter.

passive *adj* not active; inert; not acting, receiving or capable of receiving impressions from external objects; unresisting; not opposing; receiving or suffering without resistance; (*gram*) expressive of suffering or being affected by some action; expressing that the nominative is the object of some action or feeling (*the passive voice*, *a passive verb* or *inflection*).

passive smoking *n* involuntary inhalation of tobacco smoke from the cigarettes of other people.

passkey *n* a key for opening several locks; a latch key.

Passover *n* a feast of the Jews, instituted to commemorate the providential escape of the Hebrews in Egypt, when God, smiting the first-born of the Egyptians, passed over the houses of the Israelites, which were marked with the blood of the paschal lamb; the sacrifice offered at the feast of the Passover; the paschal lamb.

passport *n* an official document identifying an individual, giving authority for him or her to travel in a foreign country with the state's protection; something that enables one to pass with safety or certainty or to attain any object or reach any end (*ability is a passport to success*); something that secures admission or acceptance.

password *n* a secret word, sign or countersign by which members of a group, society, etc, might identify themselves to other members; a word by which a friend may be distinguished from a stranger and allowed to pass; a sequence of characters required to access a computer system.

past *adj* gone by; belonging to a time previous to this; not present nor future; spent; ended; over; existing no more.—*n* a past or former time or state; a bygone time; a state of matters no longer present.—*prep* beyond in time; after; having lost; no longer possessing (*past sense of feeling*); beyond; out of reach of; out of the scope or influence of (*past help*); beyond in position; further than.—*adv* by.

pasta *n* the flour paste or dough from which spaghetti, macaroni, etc, is made; a dish made of cooked pasta.

paste *n* a mixture or substance in which there is just sufficient moisture to soften without liquefying the mass, such as toothpaste; an adhesive mixture used to glue paper, etc; a mixture of flour with milk, water, etc, used in making pastry or dough; a kind of cement variously compounded; a composition of pounded rock crystal melted with alkaline salts and coloured with metallic oxides, used for making imitation gems; the mineral substance in which other minerals are embedded.—*vt* (**pasted, pasting**) to unite or cement with paste; to fasten with paste; (*sl*) to beat, to trounce.

pasteboard *n* a kind of thick paper formed of several single sheets pasted one upon another or by macerating paper and casting it in moulds, etc; cardboard.—*adj* made of pasteboard; insubstantial, unconvincing.

pastel *n* a coloured crayon; also the plant woad and the blue dye obtained from it.

pastern *n* the part of a horse's foot between the fetlock and the hoof.

pasteurization *n* the act of pasteurizing.

pasteurize *vt* (**pasteurized, pasteurizing**) to sterilize (milk, etc) by heat or radiation to destroy harmful organisms.

pastiche *n* a literary, musical or artistic work in imitation of another's style; such a work containing elements borrowed from other sources; a medley of styles or materials.

pastille, pastil *n* an aromatic or medicated lozenge; a small scented cone for disinfecting the air.

pastime *n* that which amuses and serves to make time pass agreeably; sport; amusement.

past master *n* one who has experience in his particular craft or business; one who is very good at something; one who has occupied the office or dignity of master, especially in such bodies as Freemasons, etc.

pastor *n* a minister or priest having the charge of a church and congregation.

pastoral *adj* pertaining to rustic life; rural; descriptive of the life of shepherds or of a country life (*a pastoral poem*); relating to pasture or grazing; relating to the cure of souls or to the pastor of a church.—*n* a poem describing the life and manners of shepherds; a bucolic poem; a pastoral letter or address.

pastorale *n* a musical composition with a pastoral subject.

pastry *n* a kind of dough made of flour, water and fat, baked and used for making pies, tarts, etc; the crust or cover of a pie, tart, etc; a baked food made with pastry.

pastrycook *n* one whose occupation is to make and sell pastry.

pasturage *n* the business of feeding or grazing cattle; grazing ground; growing grass on which cattle feed.

pasture *n* grass or herbage for feeding cattle or other animals; ground covered with grass for the food of animals; a grazing ground.—*vt* (**pastured, pasturing**) to feed on growing grass or to supply pasture for.—*vi* to graze.

pasty *adj* like paste; of the consistency of paste; pallid and unhealthy in appearance.—*n* a meat pie covered with pastry.

passport

pastry

615

pat¹ *vt* (**patted, patting**) to strike gently with the fingers or hand; to tap; to shape by patting; to apply by patting.—*n* a light quick blow with the fingers or hand; a light sound; a small lump of butter patted into shape.—*adj* apt; fit; convenient; exact; glib.

pat² *adj* apt; exact; glib.—*adv* conveniently; exactly; glibly.—**off pat** known completely; memorized.

patch *n* a piece of cloth sewed on a garment to repair it; any similar piece; a shield for an injured eye; a piece of protective dressing; a small piece of black silk formerly stuck on the face as adornment; an area or spot; an irregular spot or surface; a small piece of ground (*a carrot patch*); a plot of land; the name of the clown in patchwork or motley; the medieval fool; any sorry or poor creature.—*vt* to mend with patches or pieces; to repair clumsily; to adorn (the face) with a patch or with patches; to make up of pieces and shreds; (*fig*) to make hastily or without regard to forms (usually with *up*, as *to patch up a quarrel*).

patchouli *n* a plant of India and China, the leaves of which furnish an odorous oil; the perfume itself.

patchwork *n* work composed of various fabrics or colours sewn together; anything formed of ill-assorted parts.

pate *n* the head of a person; the top of the head; the mind.

pâté *n* a rich paste or spread made of meat, fish or vegetables.

paten, patin *n* a metallic plate or flat dish; the round metallic plate on which the bread is placed in the Eucharist.

patent *adj* open; spreading; expanded; open to the perusal of all (*letters patent*); secured by law or royal grant as an exclusive privilege; manifest to all; evident.—*n* a privilege from the crown, granted by letters patent, conveying to the individual or individuals specified therein the sole right to make, use or dispose of some new invention or discovery for a certain limited period.—*vt* to make the subject of a patent; to secure by patent right.

patentee *n* one who holds a patent; one by whom a patent is secured.

patent leather *n* a kind of leather or artificial leather to which a permanent polish is given by a process of japanning.

patent medicine *n* a medicine made and sold under patent and available without a prescription.

paterfamilias *n* (*pl* **paterfamilias**) the father or male head of a family.

paternal *adj* pertaining to a father; fatherly; derived from the father; hereditary.

paternalism *n* a system that provides for human needs but allows no individual responsibility.

paternity *n* fatherhood; the relation of a father to his offspring; derivation from a father (*the child's paternity*); hence, origin; authorship.

paternoster *n* a lift consisting of a continuously revolving belt of linked compartments; a type of fishing line with hooks at intervals.

Paternoster *n* the Lord's prayer; every tenth large bead in the rosary; the rosary itself.

path *n* (*pl* **paths**) a way beaten or trodden by the feet of man or beast or made hard by wheels; a narrow or unimportant road; a foot way; a way or route in general; the way or course which an animal or any object follows in the air, in water or in space; (*fig*) course of life; course of conduct or procedure.

pathetic *adj* full of pathos; moving the feelings; exciting pity, sorrow or other emotion; affecting; (*sl*) inadequate.

pathetic fallacy *n* the attribution of human emotions to inanimate objects.

pathogen *n* any organism that can cause disease.

pathological *adj* pertaining to pathology; caused by disease; involving disease; habitual, compulsive.

pathologist *n* one skilled in the nature of diseases.

pathology *n* that branch of medicine which explains the nature of diseases, their causes and symptoms.

pathos *n* that quality, attribute or element which awakens such emotions as pity, compassion or sympathy; the quality that touches the heart; expression of strong or deep feeling; touching or affecting influence.

pathway *n* a path; a narrow way to be passed on foot; a way; a course of life.

patience *n* the quality of being patient; the power or capacity of physical endurance; the character or habit of mind that enables one to suffer afflictions, provocation or other evil with a calm unruffled temper; calmness; composure; quietness or calmness in waiting for something to happen; forbearance; long-suffering; constancy in labour or exertion; perseverance; a card game played by one person alone.

patient *adj* physically able to support or endure; bearing pain or trial without murmur; sustaining afflictions with fortitude, calmness or submission; waiting with calmness; tolerant; not hasty; long-suffering; persevering; calmly diligent.—*n* one who or that which is passively affected; a sufferer from an ailment; a person who is under medical treatment.

patin *n* same as **paten**.

patina *n* the fine green rust or verdigris with which ancient bronzes and copper coins

patchwork

and medals become covered by exposure to air or certain acids; a superficial covering or exterior; a sheen; a bowl of metal or earthenware.

patio *n* (*pl* **patios**) a paved area adjoining a house; an inner, usually roofless, courtyard.

patisserie *n* a shop specializing in the sale of pastries and cakes; pastries generally.

patness *n* the quality of being pat; fitness.

patois *n* (*pl* **patois**) a regional dialect, especially of French; a provincial form of speech; jargon.

patriarch *n* the father and ruler of a family or tribe; an aged venerable man; in the Old Testament, one of the fathers of the human race or one of the ancestors of the Hebrew people; in various churches, the head or a high dignitary.

patriarchal *adj* belonging to patriarchs; subject to a patriarch.

patriarchate *n* the office or jurisdiction of a patriarch.

patrician *adj* pertaining to the senatorial order in ancient Rome; of noble birth, not plebeian.—*n* a person of patrician or noble birth; a nobleman.

patricide *n* the act of murdering one's father; a person who kills his or her father.

patrimony *n* a right or estate inherited from one's father or ancestors; heritage; a church estate or revenue

patriot *n* a person who loves his or her country and zealously supports and defends it and its interests.—*adj* patriotic.

patriotic *adj* having the feelings of a patriot; inspired by the love of one's country; directed by zeal for the public safety and welfare.

patriotism *n* love of one's country; the passion which leads a person to serve his or her country with zeal.

patristics *n* that branch of historical theology which is devoted to the doctrines of the Christian Fathers.

patrol *n* (*milit*) the marching round of a guard in the night to secure the peace and safety of a camp or other place; the persons who go the rounds; a unit of persons or vehicles employed for security, reconnaissance; a subdivision of a Scout or Guide group; a police constable who goes round a regular beat.—*vi* (**patrolled, patrolling**) to go the rounds as a guard in a camp or garrison; to walk around (a building, etc) in order to guard and inspect it; to go the rounds in a city, as is done by a body of police.—*vt* to pass through or walk round in the capacity of a patrol.

patron *n* a person of distinction who protects and supports another; one who or that which supports or protects either a person or a work; a person of rank or standing who assists another in an inferior position;

a sponsor, as of the arts; a regular client or customer; a patron saint; one who has the gift and disposition of an ecclesiastical benefice.

patronage *n* the act of patronizing; protection; encouragement; the power to grant political favours; such favours; guardianship, as of a saint; the right of presentation to a church or ecclesiastical benefice; the support given or custom brought by a patron, client or customer; business; trade; clientèle.

patroness *n* a female patron.

patronize *vt* (**patronized, patronizing**) to act as patron towards; to give support to; to favour; to assist; to sponsor; to be a regular customer or client of; to treat with condescension in an offensively superior manner.

patron saint *n* any saint under whose special protection a church, a society or a person is regarded as placed.

patronymic *n* a personal name derived from that of parent or ancestor; a surname.

patten *n* a wooden shoe or sole; a clog.

patter[1] *vi* to strike, as falling drops of water or hail, with a quick succession of small sounds; to move with quick steps, making a series of small sounds.—*n* a quick succession of small sounds.

patter[2] *vt* to repeat in a muttering way; to mutter; to talk quickly and rapidly.—*vi* to mutter; to chatter.—*n* a low dialect or patois; rapid speech, as of a salesman; glib talk; jargon; an arrangement, usually regular, of repeated or complementary motifs, etc.

pattern *n* an original or model proposed for imitation; that which is to be copied or imitated; a piece or part exhibited as a specimen of the whole; a design or figure corresponding in outline to an object that is to be fabricated and serving as a guide for determining its shape and dimensions; an ornamental design on fabrics, wallpaper, tiles, etc; the counterpart in wood of something that is to be cast in metal; a predictable route, set of events, etc.

patty *n* a little pie; a pasty.

paucity *n* smallness of number; fewness; smallness or scantiness of quantity.

paunch *n* the belly and its contents when protruding; the abdomen; the first and largest stomach in ruminating quadrupeds, into which the food is received before rumination.

pauper *n* a very poor person; one in a state of indigence; formerly, one who, on account of poverty, becomes chargeable to a parish.

pauperism *n* the state of being a pauper; a state of indigence in a community.

pauperize *vt* (**pauperized, pauperizing**) to reduce to pauperism.

pattern

pause *n* a temporary cessation; an intermission of action, of speaking, singing, etc; a short stop; cessation proceeding from doubt; suspense; a mark of suspension of the voice; a character marking a lengthened note in music.—*vi* (**paused, pausing**) to make a pause or short stop; to intermit speaking or action; to wait; to forbear for a time; to hesitate; to hold back; to be intermitted (*the music pauses*).

pave *vt* (**paved, paving**) to cover with a hard level surface by laying with stones, bricks, etc; to floor with brick, stone or other material.—**to pave the way** to make possible or easier.

pavement *n* a raised, paved way for pedestrians alongside a road; a paved path or road; a floor or surface that is trodden on, consisting of stones, bricks, etc; the stones or other material with which anything is paved.

pavilion *n* a tent; particularly, a large tent raised on posts and open on one side; a canopy; (*archit*) a small building or a part of a building having a tent-formed roof; a building attached to a sports ground.

pavonine *adj* belonging to a peacock; resembling a peacock.

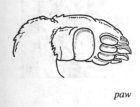

paw

paw *n* the foot of quadrupeds having claws. —*vi* to draw the forefoot along the ground; to scrape with the forefoot (as a horse).— *vt* to scrape or strike with the forefoot; to handle roughly; to handle indecently.

pawky *adj* humorous; dry and satiric in tone.

pawl *n* a device pivoted at one end, so as to catch in a notch of a revolving body, such as a ratchet wheel, and stop its motion.

pawn[1] *n* some article or chattel given or deposited as security for money borrowed; a pledge.—**in pawn, at pawn** in the state of being pawned or pledged.—*vt* to give or deposit in pledge; to pledge with a pawnbroker; to pledge for the fulfilment of a promise.

pawn[2] *n* a piece of the lowest rank at chess; hence, one of limited power made use of by another or others to further their own ends.

pawnbroker *n* a person licensed to lend money at a legally fixed rate of interest on goods deposited with him as surety.

pawnbroking *n* the business of a pawnbroker.

pawn

pawn ticket *n* a ticket given by a pawnbroker to the pledger as an evidence of the transaction; a dated receipt for the article pledged.

pax *n* (*RC Church*) a small tablet engraved with sacred figures or emblems, which, having been kissed by the priest, is then kissed by others ('the kiss of peace').— *interj* (*sl*) a call for a truce, especially in a children's game.

pay *vt* (**paid, paying**) to recompense for goods received or for service rendered; to discharge one's obligation to; to compensate, remunerate, reward, requite; to discharge (as a debt) by giving or doing that which is due; to give; to render or offer, without any sense of obligation (*to pay attention, respect, court, a visit*); (*naut*) to cover or coat, as the bottom of a vessel, a mast, etc, with tar or pitch, etc—*vi* to make payment or requital; to be worth the pains or efforts spent; to be remunerative.—*n* an equivalent given for money due, goods purchased or services performed; wages, salary.

payable *adj* capable of being paid; suitable to be paid; justly due.

payday *n* the day when payment is regularly made; the day for paying wages.

payee *n* the person to whom money is to be paid.

payer *n* one that pays; the person named in a bill or note who has to pay the holder.

paymaster *n* one from whom wages or reward is received; an officer in the army or navy who regularly pays the officers and soldiers.

payment *n* the act of paying; the discharge of a debt; the thing given in discharge of a debt; recompense; requital; reward.

paynim *n* (*arch*) a pagan; a heathen.

pea *n* an annual, climbing pod-bearing plant with small white flowers and green pods containing green seeds that are eaten as a vegetable, cultivated in widely in temperate regions; one of the edible seeds of the plant.

peace *n* a state of quiet or tranquillity; calm, quietness, repose; especially, freedom from war; a cessation of hostilities; absence of strife; tranquillity of mind; quiet of conscience; harmony; concord; public tranquillity.

peaceable *adj* tranquil; peaceful; disposed to peace; not quarrelsome.

peaceful *adj* possessing or enjoying peace; tranquil; quiet; removed from noise or tumult; pacific.

peacemaker *n* one who reconciles parties at variance.

peach[1] *n* a fruit tree of many varieties, related to the plum, cherry, apricot, etc, and bearing usually pink flowers, supposed to have been introduced into Europe from Persia; the fruit of the tree with reddish-yellow skin and yellowish flesh and of some size, containing a stone; the yellowish pink colour of peach; (*colloq*) an especially pleasing or attractive person or thing.

peach[2] *vi* to betray one's accomplice; to turn informer.

peachy *adj* of or resembling a peach; (*colloq*) great, excellent.

peacock *n* a male peafowl, distinguished by its large, brilliantly coloured, fan-like tale; a vain person.

peafowl *n* a large bird related to the pheasant.

peahen *n* a female peafowl.

pea jacket, pea coat *n* a thick loose woollen jacket worn by seamen, fishermen, etc.

peak[1] *n* the top of a hill or mountain, ending in a point; a projecting point; a projecting portion on a head covering (*the peak of a cap*); (*naut*) the upper corner of a sail which is extended by a gaff or yard; the extremity of the yard or gaff; the highest point; maximum value; the eye shade of a cap or visor.—*vi* to reach the height of power, popularity, etc; (of prices) to reach (and stay) at the highest level.

peak[2] *vi* (*arch*) to look sickly or thin; to look pale; to be or become emaciated.

peaky *adj* drawn or emaciated; sickly.

peal *n* a succession of loud sounds, as of bells, thunder, cannon, shouts of a multitude, etc; a set of bells tuned to each other; the changes rung on such bells.—*vi* to utter or give out a peal.—*vt* to cause to ring or sound; to utter loudly and sonorously.

peanut *n* a flowering plant with underground pods containing edible seeds; the pod or any of its seeds; (*pl*) (*sl*) a trifling thing or amount.

pear *n* a fruit tree relating to the apple, bearing white blossom and yielding an edible fruit of tapering oval shape; the fruit of the tree.

pearl *n* a silvery or bluish-white, hard, smooth, lustrous substance, usually round, valued as a gem and produced by certain molluscs, notably the oyster, by coating a foreign body, such as a piece of grit, with a calcareous substance; the calcareous substance itself, chiefly calcium carbonate, which the mollusc secretes and deposits around the foreign body; (*poet*) something round and clear, as a drop of dew; anything very valuable; what is choicest or best; a pale bluish-grey colour.—*adj* relating to, made of pearl.—*vt* to set or adorn with pearls.

pearly *adj* containing pearls; resembling pearls; lustrous.

peasant *n* a rustic or countryman; one occupied in rural labour.—*adj* rustic; rural.

peasantry *n* peasants collectively; the body of country people.

pease meal *n* meal or flour from peas.

pease pudding *n* a dish made chiefly of peas.

peashooter *n* a small tube used by children for shooting a small pellet which makes a 'pop' when it is expelled.

peat *n* a kind of turf used as fuel; the natural accumulation of vegetable matter, more or less decomposed, in hollows on land not in a state of cultivation; a small block of peat cut and dried for fuel.

peat bog *n* a bog or marsh containing peat.

peat moss *n* a moss that decays to produce peat.

peaty *adj* resembling peat; abounding in peat; composed of peat.

pebble *n* a small round stone; a stone worn and rounded by the action of water; a kind of clear rock crystal used in making lenses.

pebbled *adj* abounding with pebbles.

pebble-dash *n* mortar embedded with pebbles used for covering walls.

pebbly *adj* full of pebbles.

pecan, pecan nut *n* a species of hickory and its fruit.

peccadillo *n* (*pl* **peccadilloes**) a minor sin; a minor misdeed.

peccant *adj* sinning; guilty; abnormal; corrupt (*peccant humours*).

peccary *n* a wild ungulate mammal of tropical America, resembling a small pig with tusks.

peck[1] *vt* to strike with the beak; to pick up with the beak; to make by striking with the beak or a pointed instrument (*to peck a hole*); to kiss lightly; to pick at one's food.—*vi* to make strokes with a beak or a pointed instrument.

peck[2] *n* a little used unit of dry measure, the fourth part of a bushel.

peckish *adj* (*colloq*) somewhat hungry.

pecten *n* any of a genus of marine bivalves having a shell marked with diverging ribs and furrows; a comb-like structure of blood vessels in the eye of birds and reptiles.

pectic *adj* having the property of forming a jelly.

pectin *n* a kind of acid found in fruit and vegetables that readily forms a gel in sugar solutions and is therefore used in making jams and jellies to ensure that they set.

pectinal *adj* pertaining to a comb; resembling a comb.

pectinate, pectinated *adj* having resemblance to the teeth of a comb; toothed like a comb; serrated.

pectoral *adj* pertaining to the breast.—*n* a covering or protection for the breast; a breastplate; the breastplate of the Jewish high priest; in fishes, either of a pair of fins situated just behind the head.

peculate *vi* (**peculated, peculating**) to appropriate public money or goods, entrusted to one's care; to embezzle.

peculation *n* the act of peculating; embezzlement.

peculiar *adj* one's own; of private, personal or characteristic possession and use; specially belonging (*peculiar to that part of the country*); singular; striking; unusual; eccentric; odd.

peacock

peculiarity *n* the quality of being peculiar; that which is peculiar to a person or thing; a special characteristic or feature.

peculiarly *adv* in a peculiar manner; especially; in a manner not common to others.

pecuniary *adj* relating to or connected with money; consisting of money.

pedagogue *n* a teacher of children; a schoolmaster; a pedant.

pedagogy, pedagogics *n* the science or art of teaching.

pedal *adj* pertaining to a foot (*pedal digits*); (*mus*) relating to a pedal.—*n* a lever to be pressed down by the foot to operate machinery, vehicles, etc (*a bicycle pedal, an accelerator pedal*); a sort of treadle; a part of a musical instrument acted on by the feet, as in the piano for strengthening or softening the sound, on the organ for opening additional sets of pipes, on the harmonium for working the bellows, etc.—*vt* (**pedalled, pedalling**) to propel or operate by pressing pedals with the foot.

pedant *n* a person who attaches too much importance to academic learning; a person who insists on a strict interpretation of rules, etc; one who attaches too much importance to details.

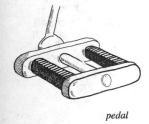

pedal

pedantic *adj* pertaining to a pedant or to pedantry.

pedantry *n* the manners or character of a pedant; ostentatious or boastful display of learning; obstinate adherence to rules or established forms; over-attachment to details; a tendency to correct others.

peddle *vi* (**peddle, peddling**) to travel about the country and sell small wares; to go about as a pedlar.—*vt* to sell in small quantities while travelling about; to sell (especially drugs) illegally.

peddler *n* one who peddles goods, especially drugs; a pedlar.

pedestal *n* a base or support for a column, a statue, a vase, etc.

pedestrian *adj* going on foot; performed on foot; walking; prosaic; unimaginative; commonplace.—*n* one who walks or journeys on foot.

pedestrianism *n* the art of a professional walker; the practice of walking; the quality of being prosaic or commonplace.

pedicel *n* (*bot*) the stalk that supports a single flower, leaf, etc; a subordinate stalk.

pedigree *n* a line of ancestors; lineage; a genealogy; a genealogical or family tree.

pediment *n* (*archit*) the low triangular mass resembling a gable at the end of buildings in the classical style, surrounded with a cornice and often ornamented with sculptures; a small gable or triangular decoration like a gable over a window, door, etc.

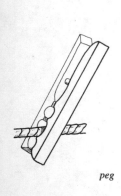

peg

pedipalp *n* in spiders, one of the second pair of head limbs.

pedlar *n* one who peddles; a dealer in small goods who carries his or her wares; a hawker.

pedometer *n* a small instrument by which paces are numbered as a person walks and the distance covered thus measured.

peduncle *n* (*bot*) the main stalk of a plant bearing several flowers; (*zool*) the stalk by which certain organisms anchor themselves to the substrate; (*anat*) a stalk-like band of fibres, especially nerve fibres in the brain.

peel[1] *vt* to strip the skin, bark or rind from; to strip by drawing or tearing off the skin; to strip (bark) from the surface.—*vi* to lose the skin or rind; to fall off (as bark or skin).—*n* the skin or rind of anything.

peel[2], **peel tower** *n* a name of certain strong square towers or strongholds common on the Scottish borders.

peeler *n* (*hist sl*) a policeman (from Sir Robert Peel, founder of the police force).

peep *vi* to cry, as chickens; to cheep; to chirp; to begin to appear; to look through a crevice; to look narrowly, closely or slyly.—*n* the cry of a chicken; a sly look or a look through a crevice.

peepshow *n* a show of small pictures viewed through a hole sometimes fitted with a magnifying lens.

peer[1] *vi* to look attentively; to look narrowly; to pry; to peep.

peer[2] *n* one of the same rank, qualities, etc; an equal; a match; a companion; an associate; a member of one of the five degrees of nobility (duke, marquis, earl, viscount, baron); a nobleman.

peerage *n* the rank or dignity of a peer; the body of peers.

peeress *n* the consort of a peer; a woman ennobled by descent, by creation or by marriage.

peerless *adj* unequalled; having no peer or equal; unrivalled.

peevish *adj* apt to mutter and complain; easily vexed or fretted; fretful; querulous; self-willed; forward.

peevishness *n* the state or quality of being peevish; fretfulness.

peewit *n* the lapwing.

peg *n* a pin used in fastening things, as a mark, etc; one of the pins on a musical instrument for stretching the strings; a pin on which or with which to hang anything; a predetermined level at which (a price) is fixed; a small alcoholic drink.—*vt* (**pegged, pegging**) to put pegs into for fastening, etc; to fasten on the sole of (a shoe) with pegs; to mark off by pegs.—*vi* to work diligently (generally followed by *away* or *on*).

Pegasus *n* the winged horse of Greek mythology.

peg top *n* a child's toy, a variety of top made to spin by a string.

peg-top *adj* (of trousers and skirts) wide at the hips and narrow at the bottom.

pejorative *adj* conveying a derogatory meaning.—*n* a word conveying such a meaning.

pekan *n* a species of North American marten.

pekoe *n* a fine black tea.

pelage *n* (*zool*) the hairy covering of an animal.

pelagic *adj* belonging to the ocean; inhabiting the open ocean.

pelargonium *n* a flowering plant of the geranium family, cultivated for its colourful flowers and ornamental foliage, commonly called geranium.

pelf *n* money or riches, especially when fraudulently obtained.

pelican *n* a big web-footed bird of tropical and subtropical waters with a large bill and a deep pouch beneath the jaw for holding fish.

pelisse *n* formerly, a long cloak lined or trimmed with fur worn by women.

pellagra *n* a disease caused by a deficiency in nicotinic acid, characterized by skin inflammation, diarrhoea and nervous disorders.

pellet *n* a small ball of paper, bread, etc; a pill; a small ball of hair, bones, etc, regurgitated by a bird of prey; a piece of shot.

pellicle *n* a thin skin or film on a surface; (*bot*) the thin outer covering of plants.

pellitory *n* any of several European flowering plants that grow on walls.

pell-mell *adv* with confused violence; in a disorderly body; in utter confusion.

pellucid *adj* transparent; admitting the passage of light; translucent; not opaque.

pelota *n* a Spanish (originally Basque) and Spanish-American ball game, resembling tennis and played with a wicker racket fastened to the wrist.

pelt[1] *vt* to strike or assail with something thrown; to bombard.—*vi* to throw missiles; (of rain) to pour down or fall heavily (usually with *down*); to rush, to hurry.—*n* a rush (*at full pelt*).

pelt[2] *n* the skin of a beast with the hair, wool or fur on it; a raw hide.

pelvic *adj* pertaining to the pelvis.

pelvis *n* (*anat*) the bony cavity of the body constituting a framework for the lower part of the abdomen.

pemmican *n* a North American Indian preparation consisting of dried meat with fat and other ingredients pounded into a paste and pressed into cakes so that it will keep.

pemphigus *n* a rare disease of the skin, characterized by watery blisters.

pen[1] *n* formerly, a quill or large feather; an instrument used for writing by means of a fluid ink, formerly made from the quill of a large bird but now commonly of metal, plastic, etc; style or quality of writing; the internal bone of some cuttlefishes.—*vt* (**penned, penning**) to write; to compose and commit to paper.

pen[2] *vt* (**penned** *or* **pent, penning**) to shut in a small enclosure; to coop up.—*n* a small enclosure, as for cows, sheep, fowls, etc; a fold; a coop.

penal *adj* pertaining to punishment; enacting punishment; inflicting punishment; incurring or entailing punishment.

penalize *vt* (**penalized, penalizing**) to subject to a penalty; to put under a disadvantage.

penal servitude *n* formerly, a punishment in Britain, consisting of imprisonment with hard labour, (abolished 1948).

penalty *n* the official punishment attached to the commission of a crime, offence or trespass; the suffering or loss to which a person subjects himself or herself by agreement, in case of non-fulfilment of stipulations; the sum forfeited for breaking an agreement; a disadvantage imposed for breaking a rule, as in sports; a disagreeable consequence of some act or error.

penance *n* an ecclesiastical punishment imposed for sin; the suffering to which a person subjects himself or herself as an expression of repentance; a sacrament of for remission of sin.

penchant *n* strong inclination; decided taste; liking; bias.

pencil *n* formerly, a small delicate brush used by painters for laying on pigment; a pointed, cylindrical instrument of wood, plastic or metal, containing a rod of graphite, crayon, etc, for marking, drawing or writing; in optics, an aggregate of rays of light which converge to or diverge from the same point.—*vt* (**pencilled, pencilling**) to write or mark with a pencil.—**to pencil in** to commit tentatively.

pendant *n* anything hanging down by way of ornament but particularly from the neck; (*naut*) a short line hanging from a masthead with an eye for attaching tackle, etc; a light fitting or chandelier hanging from a ceiling; one of a pair of companion pictures, statues, etc; an appendix or addition; (*archit*) a hanging ornament used in the vaults and timber roofs of Gothic architecture.

pendency *n* state of being pendent or suspended; the state of being continued as not yet decided.

pendent *adj* hanging; suspended; depending; overhanging; projecting.—*n* something pendent or hanging.

pendentive *n* (*archit*) the part of a groined ceiling springing from one pillar or impost.

pending *adj* remaining undecided; unfin-

pelican

pelvis

ished; imminent.—*prep* for the time of the continuance of; during.

pendragon *n* a chief leader, a title among the ancient British and Welsh.

pendulous *adj* hanging so as to swing freely; swinging.

pendulum *n* a body so suspended from a fixed point as to swing to and fro under the action of gravity; the swinging piece in a clock serving as the regulating power, the wheel work being attached to register the number of vibrations and the weight or spring serving to counteract the effects of friction and air resistance.

peneplain, peneplane *n* a tract of land which is almost a plain.

penetrable *adj* capable of being penetrated, entered or pierced by another body; susceptible of moral or intellectual impression.

penetralia *npl* the inner parts of a building, as of a temple or palace; a sanctuary; hidden things; mysteries.

penetrate *vt* (**penetrated, penetrating**) to enter or pierce; to make way into the interior of; to pass into or affect the mind of; to touch; to pierce into by the intellect; to arrive at the inner meaning of; to understand.—*vi* to enter into or pierce anything; to pass or make way in.

penetration *n* the act of penetrating; a seeing into something obscure or difficult; discernment; mental acuteness.

penetrative *adj* sharp; subtle; acute; discerning; achieving penetration.

penguin *n* any of several species of marine birds, native to the Antarctic and cold south, having rudimentary wings useless for flight but effective in swimming.

penicillin *n* an antibiotic obtained from a fungus and active against a broad spectrum of bacteria.

penile *adj* of, like or affecting the penis.

peninsula *n* a portion of land almost surrounded by water and connected with the mainland by an isthmus.

peninsular *adj* in the form of a peninsula; pertaining to a peninsula.

penis *n* the male sexual and urinary organ.

penitence *n* sorrow for the committing of sin or offences; repentance; contrition.

penitent *adj* suffering sorrow of heart on account of sins or offences; contrite; sorry for wrong-doing and resolved on amendment.—*n* one who is penitent; one under church censure but admitted to penance.

penitentiary *adj* relating to penance.—*n* a penitent; an official or office of the Roman Catholic Church connected with the granting of dispensations, etc; in North America, a house of correction in which offenders are confined for punishment and reformation and made to work.

penknife *n* (*pl* **penknives**) a small pocket

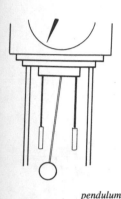

pendulum

penguin

knife, so called from its former use in making and mending quill pens.

penman *n* (*pl* **penmen**) a calligrapher; an author; a writer.

penmanship *n* the use of the pen; the art of writing; manner of writing.

pen name *n* a name assumed by an author in order to protect his or her anonymity.

pennant *n* a small flag; a pennon; one of two long tapering flags borne at the masthead of certain ships, one long, the other broad.

pennate, pennated *adj* (*biol*) having feathers, wings, etc; (*bot*) pinnate.

penniless *adj* moneyless; lacking money; poor.

pennon *n* formerly, a small pointed swallow-tailed flag carried by a knight attached to a spear or lance and generally bearing a badge or device; a pennant.

penny *n* (*pl* **pennies** denoting number, **pence** denoting value) in Britain, a coin worth one hundredth of a pound; an insignificant coin or value; money.

Penny Black *n* in Britain, the first adhesive stamp issued, bearing the head of Queen Victoria on a black background and costing one penny.

penny-farthing *n* an early type of bicycle with a large front wheel and a small rear wheel.

penny-pinching *adj* frugal; miserly.—*n* the condition of being penny-pinching.

pennyroyal *n* a European plant of the mint genus from which an aromatic oil is obtained.

pennyweight *n* a troy weight containing 24 grains or one twentieth of an ounce.

pennyworth *n* as much as is bought for a penny; a very small amount.

penology *n* the study of the punishment and rehabilitation of prisoners and prison management.

pensile *adj* hanging; suspended; pendulous.

pension[1] *n* a regular payment to a person, most often after that person has retired from employment, paid by the government, his or her former employers or out of a pension scheme to which he or she has contributed; an allowance to a person in consideration of past services; a regular payment to a person beyond retirement age, widowed, disabled, etc.—*vt* to grant a pension to; to dismiss or retire from service with a pension (with *off*).

pension[2] *n* a small hotel in Europe, especially in France

pensioner *n* one in receipt of a pension.

pensive *adj* thoughtful; employed in serious thought or reflection; thoughtful and somewhat melancholy; expressing thoughtfulness with sadness.

pent *pt, pp* of **pen**.—*adj* (*poet*) pent-up.

pentacle, pentagram *n* a figure consisting

of five straight lines so joined and intersecting as to form a five-pointed star; a pentacle, a pentangle; a mystic sign used in astrology, necromancy, devil worship, etc.

pentagon *n* (*geom*) a figure of five sides and five angles if the sides and angles are equal being a regular pentagon, otherwise irregular; (*fort*) a fort with five bastions.

Pentagon *n* the headquarters of the United States defence establishment (a five sided building); the American military leadership collectively.

pentagonal *adj* having five corners or angles.

pentagram *n* same as **pentacle**.

pentahedron *n* a solid with five faces.

pentameter *n* (*pros*) a ten-syllable line of verse forming five iambic feet; a verse of five feet, belonging more especially to Greek and Latin poetry, the elegiac couplet consisting of a hexameter and a pentameter.

pentangle *n* a pentacle.

Pentateuch *n* a collective term for the first five books of the Old Testament.

Pentecost *n* a solemn festival of the Jews, so called because celebrated on the fiftieth day after Passover; Whitsuntide, which is fifty days after Easter.

Pentecostal *adj* pertaining to Pentecost or Whitsuntide; denoting one of certain fundamentalist or revivalist Christian groups emphasizing the immediate presence of God in the Holy Spirit.

Pentecostalist *adj* pertaining to a Pentecostal church.—*n* a member of a Pentecostal church.

pentene *n* amylene.

penthouse *n* an apartment on the roof or in the top floor of a building; a roof sloping up against a wall.

pent roof *n* a roof formed like an inclined plane, the slope being all on one side.

pent-up *adj* (of emotions) confined, repressed.

penult, penultima *n* the last syllable but one of a word.

penultimate *adj* the last but one; pertaining to a penult.—*n* a penult.

penumbra *n* the partial shadow outside the total shadow caused by an opaque body intercepting the light from a luminous body, as in an eclipse; in painting, the boundary of shade and light where one blends with the other.

penurious *adj* pertaining to penury; destitute; parsimonious; poor; scanty.

penury *n* lack of financial means; indigence; extreme poverty.

peon *n* a South American labourer; formerly, a labourer compelled to work to pay off debts.

peony *n* any of a genus of herbaceous plants

cultivated in gardens for their large showy, red, pink, yellow or white flowers.

people *n sing pl* a race of human beings; the body of persons who compose a community, race or nation; persons considered indefinitely (*people may say what they please*); a person's family or relatives.— **the people** the commonalty, as distinct from people of rank; the public; the populace.—*vt* (**peopled, peopling**) to stock with people or inhabitants; to populate.

pepper *n* a plant cultivated in the tropics and its fruit, which latter has an aromatic, extremely hot, pungent taste and is used in seasoning, etc; any of various plants of the capsicum family whose fruit can be red, green, yellow, sweet or hot and is eaten as a vegetable.—*vt* to sprinkle with pepper; to pelt with shot or missiles; to drub thoroughly.

pepper-and-salt *adj* of a light ground colour (as white, drab, grey, etc) dotted with black, brown or like dark colour (said of greying hair).

peppercorn *n* the berry or fruit of the pepper plant; hence, an insignificant quantity; something of inconsiderable value.

peppercorn rent *n* a nominal rent.

peppermint *n* a plant of the mint genus the leaves of which yield an oil with a strong pungent taste, glowing like pepper and followed by a sense of coolness; a sweet flavoured with peppermint; a liqueur prepared from the peppermint plant.

peppery *adj* having the qualities of pepper; hot-tempered; fiery; irritable.

pepsin, pepsine *n* a digestive enzyme which acts on proteins contained in gastric juice.

peptic *adj* relating to digestion; digestive; promoting digestion.—*n* a medicine which promotes digestion.

per *prep* for or in each; through, by means of; according to.

peradventure *adv* (*arch*) perchance; perhaps; it may be.

perambulate *vt* (**perambulated, perambulating**) to walk through or over; to survey the boundaries of (*to perambulate a parish*).

perambulation *n* the act of perambulating; a travelling survey or inspection; a walking through or over ground for the purpose of settling boundaries.

perambulator *n* one who perambulates; a carriage for a child, pushed from behind, usually shortened to **pram**.

per annum *adv* by the year; in each year; annually.

per capita *adj, adv* per head; of or for each person.

perceive *vt* (**perceived, perceiving**) to have or obtain knowledge of by the senses; to apprehend or take cognizance of by the or-

pentagon

pepper

gans of sense; to apprehend by the mind; to discern, know, understand.

per cent, percent *adv* by, for or in every hundred.—*n* a percentage.

percentage *n* a rate per hundred parts; a proportion.

perceptibility *n* the state or quality of being perceptible; perception; power of perceiving.

perceptible *adj* capable of being perceived or noticed; plain; apparent.

perceptibly *adv* in a perceptible manner; so as to be perceived.

perception *n* the act of perceiving; that act or process of the mind which makes known an external object; discernment; insight; a way of perceiving; a view.

perceptive *adj* able to perceive or discern; observant; having insight; understanding; perspicacious.

perch[1] *n* a roost for birds; anything on which they alight; an elevated seat or position; a measure of length; a pole or rod.—*vi* to sit or roost; to light or settle, as a bird.—*vt* to place on a perch.

perch[2] *n* a kind of spiny-finned, freshwater, edible fish, one species of which is found in rivers and lakes throughout temperate Europe; the sea perch.

perch

perchance *adv* perhaps; peradventure.

percipience *n* act or power of perceiving; perception.

percipient *adj* perceiving; having the faculty of perception; perceptive.—*n* one who perceives.

percolate *vt* (**percolated, percolating**) to strain or filter; to brew (coffee).—*vi* to pass through small interstices or pores; to filter; to ooze through; to spread gradually.

percolation *n* the act of percolating; filtration.

percolator *n* one who or that which filters; a pot for the preparation of coffee, sometimes electrically operated, in which very hot water is passed through coffee grounds.

percussion *n* the act of striking one body against another with some violence; musical instruments that sound when struck with sticks or hammers, e.g. drums, cymbals, etc; such instruments as a section of an orchestra; forcible collision; the shock produced by the collision of bodies; the impression or effect of sound on the ear; (*med*) the method of eliciting sounds by striking the surface of the body, for the purpose of determining the condition of certain organs (as the lungs or heart).

percussion cap *n* a detonator consisting of a thin metal plate which explodes when struck.

percussionist *n* a person who plays a percussion instrument.

perdition *n* loss of final happiness in a fu-

ture state; future misery or eternal death; hell; entire ruin; utter destruction.

peregrinate *vi* (**peregrinated, peregrinating**) to travel from place to place; to wander.

peregrination *n* a travelling, roaming or wandering about; a journey.

peregrine *adj* (*arch*) foreign, not native; migratory.—*n* a peregrine falcon.

peregrine falcon *n* any of a species of falcon with a dark back and lighter coloured under parts, found in most parts of the world.

peremptory *adj* precluding debate or expostulation; decisive; authoritative; fully resolved; determined; positive in opinion or judgment; dogmatic; (*law*) final; determinate.

perennial *adj* lasting or continuing without cessation through the year; continuing without stop or intermission; unceasing; never-failing; (*bot*) continuing more than two years (*a perennial stem* or *root*)—*n* a plant whose root remains alive more years than two but whose stems flower and perish annually.

perfect *adj* brought to a consummation or completion; having received and possessing all its parts; finished; completed; of the best, highest or completest type; without blemish or defect; faultless; completely skilled (*perfect in discipline*); absolute.—*n* (*gram*) the perfect tense.—*vt* to finish or complete so as to leave nothing lacking; to make perfect; to instruct fully; to make fully skilful.

perfectible *adj* capable of being made perfect.

perfectibility *n* the quality of being perfectible; the capacity of becoming or being made perfect.

perfection *n* the state of being perfect or complete; supreme degree of moral or other excellence; a quality of the highest worth.

perfectly *adv* in a perfect manner; so as to reach perfection; completely; totally; thoroughly.

perfect tense *n* (*gram*) a tense which expresses an act completed, as in 'They have won'.

perfervid *adj* very fervid; very intense or ardent.

perfidious *adj* guilty of or involving perfidy or treachery; treacherous; consisting in breach of faith; traitorous.

perfidy *n* the act of violating faith or allegiance; breach of faith; treachery; faithlessness.

perforate *vt* (**perforated, perforating**) to bore through; to pierce with a pointed instrument; to make a hole or holes through by boring.

perforation *n* the act of perforating, boring

or piercing; a hole bored; a hole passing through anything; a row of holes in paper to facilitate tearing.

perforce *adv* by force or compulsion; of necessity.

perform *vt* to do; to execute; to accomplish; to fulfil, act up to, discharge (a duty); to act or represent as on the stage.—*vi* to act a part; to play on a musical instrument, represent a character on the stage, etc.

performable *adj* capable of being performed.

performance *n* the act of performing or condition of being performed; an action, deed or thing done; the acting or exhibition of character on the stage; an exhibition of skill and capacity; an entertainment provided at any place of amusement.

performer *n* one who performs; an actor, musician, etc, who exhibits his skill.

perfume *n* a substance that emits a pleasing scent; a mixture containing fragrant essential oils and a fixative; the scent or odour emitted from sweet-smelling substances. —*vt* (**perfumed, perfuming**) to fill or impregnate with a pleasant odour; to scent.

perfunctory *adj* done in a half-hearted or careless manner and merely for the sake of getting rid of the duty; careless, slight or not thorough; negligent.

pergola *n* a kind of arbour or bower on which plants may grow; the supported trellis on which the plants are trained.

perhaps *adv* it may be; possibly; peradventure; perchance.

peri *n* in Persian myth, a sort of spiritual being or fairy, represented as a descendant of fallen angels, excluded from paradise till the accomplishment of a task imposed as a penance.

perianth *n* (*bot*) the outer whorls of a flower collectively, especially when the calyx and corolla cannot be satisfactorily distinguished from each other.

pericarditis *n* inflammation of the pericardium.

pericardium *n* (*pl* **pericardia**) the membranous sac that encloses the heart.

pericarp *n* the seed vessel of a plant or the shell of the seed vessel; the part enclosing the seed.

periclinal *adj* dipping on all sides from a central point or apex (applied to strata).

pericranium *n* (*pl* **pericrania**) the membrane that envelops the skull.

peridot *n* a semiprecious stone of a yellowish-green colour, a form of chrysolite.

perigee *n* that point of the orbit of the moon or an artificial satellite which is nearest to the earth; formerly also this point in the orbit of any heavenly body.

perihelion *n* that part of the orbit of a planet or comet in which it is at its least distance from the sun, opposed to *aphelion*.

peril *n* danger; risk; hazard; jeopardy; exposure of person or property to injury, loss or destruction.—*vt* (**perilled, perilling**) to hazard; to risk; to expose to danger.

perilous *adj* full of peril; dangerous; hazardous.

perimeter *n* a boundary around an area; (*geom*) the boundary of a body or figure or the sum of all the sides.

perineum *n* (*pl* **perinea**) (*anat*) the area between the anus and the genitals.

period *n* originally a circuit; hence, the time taken up by the revolution of a heavenly body or the time till it returns to the point of its orbit where it began; any round of time or series of years, days, etc, in which a revolution is completed and the same course is to be begun; an indefinite portion of any continued state, existence or series of events (*the early period of life*); the time in which anything is performed; an age or era in history; a portion of time; an interval of time, as in a school day; termination or point of completion of any cycle or series of events; end; conclusion; limit; a complete sentence from one full stop to another; the point that marks the end of a complete sentence or indicates an abbreviation, etc; a full stop, thus (.).

periodic, periodical *adj* pertaining to a period or to periods; performed in a period or regular revolution; happening or returning regularly in a certain period of time; recurring; published at regular intervals, as a newspaper, magazine, etc (in this sense periodical is the only form).

periodical *n* a publication which appears in successive numbers at regular intervals, as a newspaper or magazine.

periodic function *n* (*math*) a function (e.g. sine or cosine) whose possible values all recur at regular intervals.

periodic table *n* a list of the chemical elements arranged by their atomic number.

periodontal *adj* of or pertaining to the gums or to periodontics.

periodontics *n* the branch of dentistry dealing with disorders of the gums and tissues around the teeth.

periosteum *n* (*pl* **periostea**) (*anat*) a membrane covering the bones and carrying nerves and blood vessels and essential to the bones' nutrition.

peripatetic *adj* walking about; itinerant; travelling.—*n* a peripatetic person.

periphery *n* the outside or surface of a body; the outermost boundary; (*geom*) the boundary line of a closed figure; the perimeter; in a circle, the circumference.

periphrase *n* a periphrasis.—*vt* (**periphrased, periphrasing**) to express by periphrasis or circumlocution.—*vi* to use circumlocution.

periphrasis *n* (*pl* **periphrases**) a roundabout phrase or expression; circumlocution; the use of more words than are necessary to express the idea.

periphrastic *adj* having the character of or characterized by periphrasis.

periscope *n* a tubular optical instrument capable of being raised or lowered and in which a series of mirrors or prisms enables the user to see objects not in the direct line of sight, as in a submerged submarine; a similar, small device that enables a view above (people in a crowd).

perish *vi* to lose life or vitality in any manner; to die; to be destroyed; to pass away, come to nothing, be ruined or lost; to deteriorate.

perishable *adj* liable to perish; subject to decay and destruction; liable to deteriorate.

peristaltic *adj* contracting all round or in successive circles (applied to the peculiar worm-like motion of the intestines, by which their contents are gradually forced downwards).

peristyle *n* (*archit*) a range of surrounding columns.

peritoneum *n* (*pl* peritonea, peritoneums) a membrane that lines the walls of the abdomen.

peritonitis *n* inflammation of the peritoneum.

periwig *n* a short wig; a peruke.

periwinkle[1] *n* an edible gastropod with a spiral shell found on rocks in great profusion in Europe and elsewhere, often called the **winkle**.

periwinkle[2] *n* one of various trailing plants with evergreen leaves and white, blue or purple flowers; a purply blue colour.—*adj* of the colour of periwinkle.

perjure *vt* (**perjured, perjuring**) to cause to be false to oaths or vows; to swear falsely to an oath in judicial proceedings; to forswear (generally used reflexively, as *the witness perjured himself*).

perjurer *n* one who wilfully takes a false oath.

perjury *n* the act of wilfully making a false oath; knowingly making a false oath in a judicial proceeding in a matter material to the issue or cause in question; the act of violating an oath or solemn promise.

perk[1] *vti* (*colloq*) to percolate.—**to perk up** to recover self-confidence; to become lively or cheerful; to smarten up; to prick up, as a dog's ears.

perk[2] *n* (*colloq*) a perquisite.

perky *adj* lively; jaunty.

perm *n* (short for **permanent wave**) a method of giving hair curls or waves that last several weeks, using heat and certain chemicals.— *vt* to curl or wave hair by means of a perm.

permafrost *n* frozen ground that is perma-

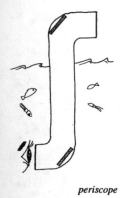

periscope

nently frozen except for surface melting in summer.

permanence, permanency *n* the state or quality of being permanent; continuance; fixedness.

permanent *adj* continuing in the same state or without any change that destroys the form or nature of the thing; remaining unaltered or unremoved; durable; lasting; abiding; fixed.

permanent wave *n* see **perm**.

permanent way *n* in railways, the finished road bed and track, including bridges, viaducts, crossings and switches.

permanganate *n* a salt of permanganic acid, a dark, purple, crystalline substance used in solution as an oxidizing agent.

permanganic acid *n* an unstable inorganic solution of potassium, manganese and oxygen.

permeability *n* the quality or state of being permeable.

permeable *adj* capable of being permeated; admitting the passage of a fluid.

permeate *vt* (**permeated, permeating**) to pass through the pores or interstices of; to penetrate and pass through by osmosis; to pervade.

permeation *n* the act of permeating.

Permian *adj* (*geol*) denoting a system of rocks lying beneath the Triassic rocks and immediately above the Carboniferous system and forming the uppermost of the Palaeozoic strata.—*n* the Permian period.

permissible *adj* being permitted or allowed; allowable; not forbidden.

permission *n* the act of permitting or allowing; authorization; allowance; licence or liberty granted; leave.

permissive *adj* permitting; granting liberty; allowing; lenient; allowing much freedom in sexual matters.

permit *vt* (**permitted, permitting**) to grant leave or liberty to by express consent; to allow expressly; to give leave to do or be done; to allow by silent consent or by not prohibiting; to suffer without giving express authority.—*vi* to grant leave or permission; to allow (*if circumstances permit*).—*n* a licence.

permutable *adj* capable of being permuted; exchangeable.

permutation *n* interchange; change among various things at once; (*math*) change or combination in different order of any number of quantities; any of the different ways in which a set of quantities can be arranged.

permute *vt* (**permuted, permuting**) to interchange; to change as regards order or arrangement.

pernicious *adj* having the effect of destroying or injuring; malicious or mischievous; destructive; noxious; deadly.

perorate *vi* (**perorated, perorating**) to make a peroration; also, to speechify; to spout.

peroration *n* the concluding part of an oration, in which the speaker recapitulates the principal points of his or her discourse or argument and urges them with greater earnestness; a rhetorical passage at the conclusion of a speech.

peroxide *n* hydrogen peroxide, an oxide of hydrogen, a colourless liquid used as an antiseptic and bleach.

perpendicular *adj* perfectly upright or vertical; extending in a straight line from any point towards the centre of the earth or at right angles (90°) with the plane of the horizon; (*geom*) falling directly on a line or surface at right angles; at right angles to a given line or surface or forming a right angle with a tangent plane at a point on a curved surface.—*n* a line at right angles to the plane of the horizon; a vertical line; (*geom*) a line falling at right angles on another line or on a plane.

Perpendicular style *n* (*archit*) the florid or Tudor style of Gothic, characterized by window tracery with vertical lines.

perpetrate *vt* (**perpetrated, perpetrating**) to do, execute or perform (generally in a bad sense); to be guilty of; to commit.

perpetration *n* the act of perpetrating; commission.

perpetrator *n* one who perpetrates.

perpetual *adj* continuing or lasting for ever in future time; destined to be eternal; continuing or continued without intermission; uninterrupted.

perpetuate *vt* (**perpetuated, perpetuating**) to make perpetual; to cause to endure or to be continued indefinitely; to preserve from extinction or oblivion.

perpetuity *n* the state or quality of being perpetual; something of which there will be no end; duration to all futurity; exemption from intermission or ceasing.

perplex *vt* to puzzle; to bewilder; to tease with suspense, anxiety or ambiguity; to involve, entangle, make complicated or intricate.

perplexity *n* the state of being perplexed, puzzled or at a loss; the state of being intricate or involved.

perquisite *n* something obtained from employment over and above the settled wages or emoluments; something in addition to regular wages or salary; a gratuity, a tip.

perry *n* a fermented liquor made from the juice of pears and resembling cider.

per se *adv* by or in itself; by its very nature, intrinsically; as such.

persecute *vt* (**persecuted, persecuting**) to harass or afflict with repeated acts of cruelty or annoyance; to afflict persistently; specifically, to afflict or punish on account of particular opinions held or of adherence to a particular creed or mode of worship.

persecution *n* the act or practice of persecuting; the state of being persecuted.

perseverance *n* the act or habit of persevering; persistence in anything undertaken.

persevere *vi* (**persevered, persevering**) to continue resolutely in any business or enterprise undertaken; to pursue steadily any design or course commenced; not to give over or abandon what is undertaken in spite of any obstacles.

persevering *adj* steadfast in purpose; persisting in any business or course begun.

Persian *adj* pertaining to Persia, now Iran, its people or their language.—*n* a native of Persia; the language spoken in Persia; a thin silk formerly used for lining.

persiflage *n* idle bantering talk; frivolous talk regarding any subject, serious or otherwise.

persimmon *n* a tropical tree of the ebony family and also its fruit, which is about the size of an apple and has a sweet flesh when ripe.

persist *vi* to continue steadily and firmly in the pursuit of any business or course commenced; to continue in the face of some amount of opposition; to persevere; (of things) to continue in a certain state.

persistence, persistency *n* the state of persisting or of being persistent; steady continuance in a course; perseverance, often in evil.

persistent *adj* inclined to persist; persevering; tenacious of purpose; obstinate.

person *n* an individual human being; a man, woman or child; bodily form; human frame, with its characteristic appearance (*to appear in person; cleanly in person*); a human being, indefinitely; one; a human being (*a person would think so*); (*gram*) one of three relations in which nouns and pronouns are regarded as standing to the act of speaking, a pronoun of the *first person* denoting the speaker, the *second person* one who is spoken to, and the *third person* one who or that which is spoken of (thus including all nouns); one of the three corresponding inflections of a verb singular and plural.—**in person** physically present, not represented.

personable *adj* having a well-formed body or person; of pleasant appearance and personality.

personage *n* a person; a man or woman of distinction (*an illustrious personage*); a being regarded as having an individuality like that of a human being (*a divine* or *a mythological personage*).

personal *adj* pertaining to a person as distinct from a thing; relating to or affecting some individual person; peculiar or proper to him or her, or to private actions or character; applying to the person, character or conduct of an individual, generally in a disparaging manner (*personal remarks*); belonging to face and figure (*personal charms*); done in person, not by representative (*a personal interview*); (*gram*) denoting or pointing to the person (a *personal pronoun*, as I, we, you, he, she, it, they); having the modifications of the three persons.

personal computer *n* a small, low-cost computer used, e.g. for word-processing or computer games.

personal identification number *n* see **PIN**.

personality *n* the state of being personal; what constitutes an individual a distinct person; the state of existing as a thinking intelligent being; application or applicability to a person; one's individual characteristics; distinctive or well-marked character; a celebrity; an application of remarks to the conduct, character or appearance of some person; a remark reflecting in some way on an individual (*to indulge in personalities*); (*law*) personal estate; personality.

personally *adv* in a personal manner; in person; with respect to an individual; as regards one's personal existence or individuality.

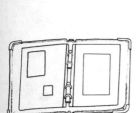
personal organizer

personal organizer *n* a kind of portable loose-leaf file containing an appointments diary, address book, notebook, etc.

personal pronoun *n* a pronoun such as *I, we, you, them*, used to denote a definite person or thing.

personal property *n* personal estate, movables; things belonging to a person, as money, jewels, furniture, etc, as distinct from real estate in land and houses.

personal stereo *n* a very small portable audio cassette player with lightweight headphones.

personalty *n* (*law*) personal property, in distinction from realty or real property.

persona non grata *n* (*pl* **personae non gratae**) a person who is not acceptable or welcome to someone.

personate *vt* (**personated, personating**) to assume the character or appearance of, whether in real life or on the stage; to represent by an assumed appearance; to act the part of; to assume or put on.

personation *n* the act of counterfeiting the person or character of another.

personator *n* one who personates; one who assumes the character of another.

personification *n* the act of personifying; an embodiment; an impersonation; (*rhet*) a kind of metaphor which represents inanimate objects or abstract notions as possessing the attributes of living beings.

personify *vt* (**personified, personifying**) to treat or regard as a person; to treat for liter-

personal stereo

ary purposes as if endowed with the characters of a rational being or person; to typify; to embody.

perspective *n* the art or science which teaches how to draw or paint objects or scenes so that they appear to have their natural dimensions, positions and relationships; a representation of objects on a plane surface, projected as they appear to the eye; quality of a picture as regards perspective; view; vista; a way of regarding things; a point of view; relative value (*to see matters in their true perspective*).— *adj* pertaining to the art of perspective; of or in perspective.

perspicacious *adj* quickly seeing through or understanding anything; of acute discernment; perceptive; shrewd.

perspicacity *n* the state or quality of being perspicacious; acuteness of discernment; penetration; sagacity; shrewdness.

perspicuity *n* the quality of being perspicuous; easily understood; freedom from obscurity or ambiguity.

perspicuous *adj* clear to the understanding; not obscure or ambiguous; lucid.

perspiration *n* the act of perspiring; sweat, the salty fluid secreted by sweat glands in the skin.

perspire *vi* (**perspired, perspiring**) to give out or exude watery matter through the pores of the skin; to sweat.—*vt* to emit through the pores of the skin.

persuade *vt* (**persuaded, persuading**) to influence by argument, advice or expostulation; to argue or reason into a certain course of action; to advise; to try to influence; to convince by argument or reasons offered.

persuasion *n* the act of persuading; the state of being persuaded or convinced; settled opinion or conviction; a creed or belief; a sect or party adhering to a creed or system of opinions.

persuasive *adj* having the power of persuading; influencing to a course of action.—*n* that which persuades; an incitement; an exhortation.

pert *adj* lively; brisk; dapper; smart; forward; saucy; indecorously free.

pertain *vi* to belong; to be the property, right, duty of; to appertain; to have relation or bearing (with *to*).

pertinacious *adj* holding or adhering to any opinion, purpose or design with obstinacy; obstinate; perversely persistent; resolute; constant.

pertinacity *n* firm or unyielding adherence to opinion or purpose; obstinacy; resolution; constancy.

pertinence, pertinency *n* the quality of being pertinent; justness of relation to the subject or matter in hand; fitness; appositeness.

pertinent *adj* related to the subject or matter in hand; just to the purpose; apposite; relevant to the question.

pertness *n* the state or quality of being pert; smartness; sauciness; forward boldness.

perturb *vt* to disturb; to agitate; to disorder; to confuse.

perturbable *adj* capable of being perturbed or agitated.

perturbation *n* the act of perturbing or state of being perturbed; disorder; especially, disquiet of mind; commotion of the passions; agitation; cause of disquiet.

peruke *n* an artificial cap of hair; a periwig.

perusal *n* the act of perusing or reading.

peruse *vt* (**perused, perusing**) to read through; to read with attention; to observe; to examine with careful survey.

Peruvian bark *n* the bark of the South American cinchona, yielding quinine.

pervade *vt* (**pervaded, pervading**) to pass or flow through; to extend through; to spread or be diffused through the whole extent of.

pervasion *n* the act of pervading.

pervasive *adj* tending or having power to pervade.

perverse *adj* turned aside from the right; persisting in wrongdoing; wayward; contrary; intractable.

perverseness *n* the quality of being perverse.

perversion *n* deviation from the normal, especially in sexual matters; diversion from the true intent or object; a change to something worse; the act of perverting

perversity *n* state or quality of being perverse; perverseness.

pervert *vt* to turn from truth, propriety or from its proper purpose; to distort from its true use or end; to misinterpret wilfully; to turn from the right; to corrupt.—*n* a person given to abnormal sexual behaviour; one who has been perverted.

pervious *adj* capable of being penetrated by another body or substance; penetrable.

pessary *n* a surgical plug worn in the vagina to support the womb; a suppository inserted into the vagina.

pessimism *n* the tendency to take a gloomy view of things and to expect the worst; the opinion or doctrine that takes the most unfavourable view of everything in nature and holds that the present state of things only tends to evil, opposed to *optimism*.

pessimist *n* one who is inclined to take a despondent view of things; one who believes in pessimism.

pessimistic *adj* pertaining to pessimism.

pest *n* an insect or organism that damages or destroys cultivated plants, crops, livestock, etc; someone or something that annoys persistently; a nuisance; (*arch*) a plague, a deadly epidemic disease.

pester *vt* to trouble; to disturb; to annoy with little vexations; to encumber.

pestiferous *adj* irritating; malignant; pestilential; noxious to health; infectious; noxious in any manner.

pestilence *n* any contagious and malignant disease that is epidemic and fatal; that which is pestilential or pestiferous; something morally evil or destructive.

pestilent *adj* pestilential; mischievous; noxious to morals or society; troublesome; corrupt.

pestilential *adj* having the nature of a pestilence, plague or other infectious and deadly disease; producing or tending to produce infectious disease; destructive; annoying.

pestle *n* a blunt-headed instrument for pounding and breaking substances in a mortar.

pesto *n* a kind of sauce served with pasta, made from basil, olive oil, etc.

pet[1] *n* a domesticated animal kept as a companion; a darling; a favourite child.—*vt* (**petted, petting**) to treat as a pet; to fondle; to indulge.—*adj* petted; favourite (*a pet lamb, a pet theory*).

pet[2] *n* a slight fit of peevishness or fretful discontent.

pestle

petal *n* (*bot*) one of the parts of a flower known collectively as the corolla, often the largest part of a flower and often brightly coloured, sometimes scented.

petaloid *adj* having the form of a petal; resembling petals.

petalous *adj* (*bot*) having petals; petalled.

petard *n* formerly, an explosive device used to break down a gate, barricade, etc.— **hoist with one's own petard** (*fig*) caught in one's own trap or scheme meant for others.

petasus *n* a broad-brimmed hat; the winged cap of Mercury.

peter *vi* to lessen and eventually dwindle to nothing (with *out* or *away*).

petersham *n* a thick corded ribbon used in dressmaking as a stiffening; a thick woollen fabric used for overcoats, etc.

Peter's pence *npl* an annual levy formerly offered to the popes (as the successors of St Peter); a similar contribution still voluntarily given by some Roman Catholics.

petiole *n* (*bot*) a leaf stalk; the stalk connecting the blade of the leaf with the branch or stem.

petal

petit *adj* (*law*) of lesser importance, minor.

petite *adj* little; small and trim in figure.

petition *n* an entreaty, supplication or prayer, as one to God or a superior in rank or power; a particular request or article among several in a prayer; a formal written request; a written supplication from an inferior to a superior soliciting some favour, grant, right or mercy; a written application in certain legal proceedings.—*vt* to make a petition, request or prayer to; to solicit; to address a written or printed petition or supplication to (*to petition government*).

petitionary *adj* offering a petition; supplicatory; containing a petition or request.

petitioner *n* one who presents a petition, either verbal or written.

petit larceny *n* the theft of property below a legal minimum value.

petit mal *n* a mild form of epilepsy.

petit point *n* a fine stitch used in needlepoint.

petrel *n* one of several species of web-footed oceanic birds related to the albatross and shearwater and found at great distances from land.

petrifaction *n* the process of changing into stone; an organic body rendered hard by deposition of a stony substance in its cavities; a fossil; a state of being paralysed as with astonishment.

petrify *vt* (**petrified, petrifying**) to convert to stone or stony substance; to turn into a fossil; to terrify; to paralyse or stupefy with fear or amazement.—*vi* to become stone or of a stony hardness.

petrochemical *n* a chemical substance obtained from petroleum or natural gas and used in the manufacture of many products, including plastics, synthetic fibres, detergents, drugs fertilizers, etc.

petrography *n* the study of rocks; a scientific description of rocks; petrology.

petrol *n* petroleum spirit; one of the products of refined petroleum used as the source of power for the internal-combustion engines of motorcars, etc.

petroleum *n* a thick, dark, flammable oil found in sedimentary rocks and refined to yield numerous products, such as petrol, paraffin, lubricating oil, petroleum jelly, asphalt and petrochemicals.

petroleum jelly *n* a greasy, jelly-like substance obtained from petroleum and used for ointments, etc.

petrologist *n* one skilled in petrology.

petrology *n* the study of rocks; that branch of geology which determines the constitution of rocks by investigating the chemical composition of the separate mineral ingredients of which they consist.

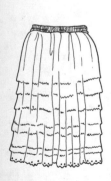
petticoat

petrous *adj* like stone; hard; stony.

petticoat *n* a loose undergarment in the form of a skirt with or without an upper part, worn by women.

petticoat government *n* female government, either political or domestic.

pettifog *vi* (**pettifogged, pettifogging**) to behave or act like a pettifogger.

pettifogger *n* an inferior or crooked lawyer; a person who quibbles over small details.

pettiness *n* small-mindedness; triviality.

pettish *adj* peevish; sulky.

pettitoes *npl* pig's trotters as a dish.

petty *adj* small-minded; trivial; trifling; having little power or few possessions; inferior, minor (*a petty prince*); (*law*) petit.

petty officer *n* an officer in the British navy whose rank corresponds with that of a non-commissioned officer in the army.

petulance *n* peevishness; pettishness; sulky impatience.

petulant *adj* manifesting pique, perversity or fretfulness; peevish; petty; impatient in a sulky way.

petunia *n* any of a genus of tropical American herbaceous plants of the tobacco plant family, widely cultivated for their variously coloured soft-petalled, funnel-shaped flowers.

pew *n* a fixed seat in a church, sometimes enclosed and separated from those adjoining by partitions; an enclosure containing more than one seat; (*colloq*) a seat.

pewit *n* the peewit or lapwing.

pewter *n* an alloy of tin and lead, sometimes with small amounts of antimony and copper, etc, dark silvery-grey in colour; a vessel, or vessels collectively, made of pewter; a silver-grey colour.—*adj* made of pewter.

pH, pH value *n* a measure of the acidity or alkalinity of solutions, soil, etc.

phaeton *n* an open four-wheeled carriage usually drawn by two horses.

phagocyte *n* any of various cells able to absorb and digest bacteria and dead or harmful matter, such phagocytic cells including white blood cells (leucocytes) which thus play a vital part in fighting disease.

phalange *n* (*anat*) same as **phalanx**; (*bot*) a collection of several stamens joined more or less by their filaments.

phalanger *n* an Australasian marsupial animal of several species, nocturnal in habits and living in trees, often called **possum**.

phalanx *n* (*pl* **phalanges, phalanxes**) in Greek antiquity, a battle formation of heavy-armed infantry of an army; any body of people in close array; hence, a group united by a common purpose; (*pl* **phalanges**) (*anat*) one of the small bones of the fingers or the toes.

phalarope *n* one of several species of small wading birds.

phallic *adj* pertaining to the phallus; resembling a phallus.

phallus *n* (*pl* **phalli, phalluses**) the male reproductive organ, the penis.

phanerogam *n* (*bot*) a flowering plant or a plant bearing flowers with stamens, pistils and seeds, opposed to a *cryptogam*.

phantasm *n* a creation of the fancy; an imaginary existence which seems to be real; an apparition; a phantom; an idea; a notion; a fancy.

phantasmagoria *n* formerly, an exhibition of images by means of shadows, as by a magic lantern; any mixed gathering of figures or illusive images, constantly changing.

phantasmal *adj* pertaining to or resembling a phantasm; spectral; illusive.

phantom *n* an apparition or spectre; a ghost; a fancied vision; a phantasm; something unreal.

Pharaoh *n* the Hebrew form of the name (meaning 'great house') of the ancient monarchs of Egypt.

pharisaic, pharisaical *adj* addicted to external forms and ceremonies; making a show of religion without the spirit of it; hypocritical.

Pharisaic *adj* pertaining to the Pharisees; resembling the Pharisees.

pharisee *n* a strict observer of the outward forms or ceremonies in religion without the spirit of it; a hypocrite.

Pharisee *n* one of a Jewish sect distinguished by their strict observance of rites and ceremonies.

pharmaceutical, pharmaceutic *adj* pertaining to the knowledge or art of pharmacy or preparing and dispensing drugs.

pharmaceutics *n* the science of pharmacy.

pharmacist *n* one skilled in pharmacy; one licensed to practise pharmacy.

pharmacologist *n* one who is skilled in pharmacology.

pharmacology *n* the science dealing with the effects of drugs on living organisms.

pharmacopoeia *n* an authoritative book listing medicinal drugs, their uses, formulas, preparation, dosage, etc.

pharmacy *n* the preparation of drugs and medicines and dispensing them according to the prescriptions of medical practitioners; a dispensary.

pharos *n* a lighthouse; a beacon.

pharyngeal *adj* belonging to or affecting the pharynx.

pharyngitis *n* inflammation of the pharynx.

pharynx *n* (*pl* **pharynges**) the back of the throat; the muscular cavity between the mouth and the oesophagus, its contraction aiding in swallowing.

phase *n* a stage in growth and development; an aspect or appearance of that which presents various aspects; one of the recurring appearances or states of the moon or a planet in respect to quantity of illumination or figure of enlightened disc; the particular state at a given instant of a continuously varying and periodic phenomenon (*the phases of a tide*, etc).—*vt* to do by stages or gradually.—**to phase in** to introduce or start gradually, one step at a time.—**to phase out** to eliminate or stop gradually.

pheasant *n* any of a genus of long-tailed game bird, the male having richly coloured plumage in contrast to the female's drabber appearance, reared and preserved for sport and food.

phenacetin *n* a drug related to paracetamol which is now widely used in its stead.

phenol *n* carbolic acid.

phenomenal *adj* connected with, relating to or constituted by phenomena; so surprising or extraordinary as to arrest the attention; extremely remarkable or extraordinary; astounding.

phenomenon *n* (*pl* **phenomena**) a visible manifestation or appearance; a fact or occurrence presented to our observation either in the external world or in the human mind; an appearance produced by the action of the different forces on matter; what strikes us as strange and uncommon; something extraordinary; an exceedingly remarkable thing or personage.

phenyl *n* the hydrocarbon radical of phenol.

pheon *n* (*heral*) a charge representing the barbed head of a dart or other weapon; the broad arrow.

pheromone *n* a molecule that functions as a chemical communication signal between individuals of the same species.

phial *n* a small glass vessel or bottle; a vial.

philander *vi* to flirt or have casual affairs with women; to womanize.

philanderer *n* a man who philanders; a womanizer.

philanthropic, philanthropical *adj* pertaining to philanthropy; possessing general benevolence and concern; entertaining goodwill towards all.

philanthropist *n* one who evinces philanthropy; a person of general benevolence; one who exerts himself or herself in doing good to his or her fellows; a humanitarian.

philanthropy *n* love towards humankind; benevolence towards the whole of humankind; charitable actions.

philatelist *n* one who collects and is knowledgeable about postage stamps.

philately *n* the practice of collecting and studying postage stamps and all that pertains to postal matters.

philhellene, philhellenist *n* one who loves Greece and Greek culture; one who supports the cause and interests of the Greeks (Hellenes).

philippic *n* a bitter denunciation; any discourse full of invective.

philistine *n* a person with no feeling for, or appreciation of, culture; an uncultured, conventional person.

Philistine *n* a member of a warlike race hostile to ancient Israel.

philological *adj* pertaining to philology.

philologist, philologer, philologian *n* one skilled in philology or the study of language in a scientific manner.

philology *n* the science of language; linguistic science; linguistics, often expressed by the qualified title of comparative philology.

philomath *n* a lover of learning.

philomel *n* (*poet*) the nightingale.

philosopher *n* a person versed in or devoted to philosophy; one who devotes himself or herself to the study of moral or intellectual science; one who conforms his or her life to the principles of philosophy; one who lives according to reason or the rules of practical wisdom; a person who acts calmly and rationally.

philosophers' stone *n* a stone or preparation formerly sought by alchemists as the means of converting baser metals into pure gold.

philosophical, philosophic *adj* pertaining, suitable or according to philosophy; characterized or constituted by philosophy; proceeding from philosophy; characteristic of a practical philosopher; based on the rules of practical wisdom; stoical; calm; temperate.

philosophize *vi* (**philosophized, philosophizing**) to reason like a philosopher; to form or attempt to form a philosophical system or theory; to moralize.

philosophy *n* the science which aims at an explanation of all the phenomena of the universe by ultimate causes; the knowledge of phenomena as explained by, and resolved into, causes and reasons, powers and laws; a particular philosophical system or theory; the calm and unexcitable state of mind of the wise man; practical wisdom.—**moral philosophy** ethics; personal outlook.

philtre *n* a potion supposed to have the power of exciting love.

phiz, phizog *n* (*sl*) the face or visage (from *physiognomy*).

phlebitis *n* inflammation of a vein.

phlebotomy *n* surgical incision into a vein for letting blood.

phlegm *n* thick viscid matter secreted in the respiratory passages and discharged by coughing or vomiting; bronchial mucus; (*fig*) coldness; sluggishness; indifference.

phlegmatic *adj* cold or sluggish in temperament; not easily excited into action or passion; not mercurial or lively; abounding in phlegm; generating phlegm.

phloem *n* (*bot*) the tissue which carries food around a plant.

phlox *n* a North American genus of plants, with red, purple or white flowers, cultivated in gardens.

phobia *n* (*psychol*) an abnormal and persistent fear of something, dominating the mind.

phocine *adj* pertaining to or resembling seals.

phoenix

phoenix *n* a bird of ancient legend said to be the only one of its kind and to live 500 or 600 years, at the end of which it built for itself a funeral pile, lighted it with the fanning of its wings and rose again from its ashes; hence, an emblem of immortality; a paragon; a person of singular distinction or beauty.

phone *n* a telephone.—*vt* (**phoned, phoning**) to telephone; to call.

phonetic *adj* relating to phonetics; relating to or representing speech sounds; according to pronunciation (*phonetic spelling*).

phonetic alphabet *n* a set of symbols used to transcribe words phonetically; a code identifying letters of the alphabet in voice communication.

phonetics *n* the study of speech processes; the science which treats of the sounds of the human voice and the art of representing them by writing.

phoney *adj* (*colloq*) not genuine or sincere.—*n* (*colloq*) a fake; an insincere person.

phonic *adj* pertaining to sound.

phonics *n* a phonetics-based method of teaching reading.

phonograph *n* formerly, an instrument capable of registering sound and reproducing it on wax cylinders; a gramophone.

phonography *n* the description of sounds; the representation of sounds by characters, each of which represents one sound and always the same sound; phonetic shorthand.

phonology *n* the study of speech sounds and their development; the speech sounds of a particular language.

phosgene *n* a poisonous gas, carbonyl chloride, with a sweetish, suffocating odour, used in the manufacture of dyes and other substances, and in chemical warfare.

phosphate *n* a salt of phosphoric acid; a chemical fertilizer supplying phosphorus.

phosphatic *adj* partaking of the nature of a phosphate; containing a phosphate.

phosphide *n* a compound of phosphorus and another element.

phosphite *n* a salt of phosphorous acid.

phosphor *n* any of a number of substances that give out light when activated by a beam of electrons or ultraviolet light.

phosphoresce *vi* (**phosphoresced, phosphorescing**) to give off light without noticeable heat for a short time after having absorbed energy, as phosphorus; to give out a phosphorescent light.

phosphorescence *n* the state or quality of being phosphorescent; the property which certain bodies possess of emitting a faint light without undergoing combustion for a short time after having absorbed energy, once the source of energy has gone.

phosphorescent *adj* shining with a faint light or luminosity and continuing to do so for a short time after its source of energy has gone.

phosphoric *adj* pertaining to, obtained from or containing phosphorus.

phosphorite *n* a mineral deposit that consists mainly of calcium phosphate.

phosphorous *adj* pertaining to or containing phosphorus.

phosphorus *n* a solid non-metallic combustible element occurring in several forms in organic and inorganic compounds, commonly *white phosphorus* which is a highly poisonous soft solid that ignites spontaneously, and *red phosphorus* which is more stable and non-poisonous, an important constituent in living animal and vegetable structures and minerals and much used in industry.

photo *n* (*pl* **photos**) a photograph; a snapshot.

photocell *n* a photoelectric cell.

photochemical *adj* of or relating to the effect of radiant energy, especially light.

photochemistry *n* that branch of chemistry which deals with the chemical action of light and other forms of electromagnetic radiation.

photoconductive *adj* conducting by exposure to light.

photocopy *n* a photographic reproduction of written or printed documents, etc.—*vt* (**photocopied, photocopying**) to copy in this way.

photoelectric *adj* related to light and electricity, especially to the production of either by means of the other.

photoelectric cell, photocell *n* a cell whose electrical properties are affected by light; any device in which light controls an electric circuit that operates a mechanical device, as for opening doors.

photoengraving *n* a process in which the action of light is used for obtaining a picture on a plate or block for subsequent printing.

photo finish *n* the finish of a race where the winner has to be decided on the basis of a photograph because the contestants are so close together; a race or contest where the winning margin is very small.

photogenic *adj* appearing attractive in photographs.

photograph *n* a picture obtained by means of photography.—*vt* to produce a likeness or representation of by photographic means.

photographer *n* one who takes pictures by means of photography.

photographic, photographical *adj* relating to photography; of or like a photograph; minutely accurate like a photograph.

photographic memory *n* a memory capable of retaining facts, etc, after reading for only a brief time.

photographic printing *n* the process of obtaining positives on sensitized paper from transparent negatives by exposure to light.

photography *n* the art of obtaining accurate representations of scenes and objects by means of the action of light on substances treated with certain chemicals.

photogravure *n* a printing process by which an engraving is produced on a metal plate by light acting on a sensitive surface; printed matter so produced.

photojournalism *n* a form of news reporting in which a story is presented mainly through photographs.

photolithograph *n* a picture produced by photolithography.

photolithography *n* a mode of lithographing using a photographically prepared plate.

photometer *n* an instrument for measuring the comparative intensity of different lights.

photometry *n* the measurement of the relative amounts of light emitted by different sources.

photomicrography *n* the photographing of minute objects magnified by a microscope.

photon *n* a quantum of electromagnetic radiation.

photosphere *n* an envelope of light; the luminous envelope surrounding the sun.

photosynthesis *n* in green plants, the utilization by protoplasm of the energy of light, aided by the green pigment chlorophyll, for building up organic matter from water and carbon dioxide.

phrasal *adj* of or consisting of a phrase or phrases.

phrasal verb *n* (*gram*) a usually simple verb that combines with a preposition or adverb, or both, to convey a meaning more than the sum of its parts, e.g. *to phase out.*

phrase *n* a brief expression; two or more words, usually not containing a finite verb, forming a complete expression by themselves or being a portion of a sentence; a particular or characteristic expression; a pointed saying; a high-flown expression; (*mus*) a short part of a composition usually occupying a distinct rhythmical period of from two to four bars.—*vt* (**phrased, phrasing**) to express orally; to put into words; to divide into melodic phrases.

phrasebook *n* a book in which phrases or idioms of a foreign language are collected and translated.

phraseology *n* manner of expression; particular words or phrases used in a sentence; diction; a collection of phrases in a language.

phrasing *n* the wording of a speech or a piece of writing; (*mus*) the division of a melodic line, etc, into musical phrases.

phrenetic adj an old spelling of **frenetic**.

phrenic adj (anat) belonging to the diaphragm; (arch) pertaining to the mind.

phrenitis n (med) encephalitis, an inflammation of the brain; delirium; frenzy.

phrenologist n one who practised phrenology.

phrenology n formerly, the theory that intelligence, ability and character may be judged from the shape of a person's skull; the study of the shape of the skull based on this belief.

phthisical adj relating to or affected by phthisis.

phthisis n a wasting disease, particularly tuberculosis.

pH value n same as **pH**.

phycology n that branch of botany which studies algae or seaweeds.

phylactery n a strip of parchment inscribed with certain texts from the Old Testament, enclosed within a small leather case and fastened on the forehead or on the left arm near the region of the heart of Jewish men; an amulet worn as a preservative from danger or disease.

phyle n in ancient Greece, a tribe or clan of people.

phylloxera n an insect which attacks the leaves and roots of the oak, vine, etc, one species of which has caused immense damage in some wine-producing countries.

phylogeny, phylogenesis n (biol) the origin and history of races or types of animal forms.

phylum n (pl **phyla**) one of the major divisions of the animal or vegetable kingdom.

physic n (arch) the science or knowledge of medicine; the art of healing; a medicine, popularly a medicine that purges; a purge; a cathartic.—vt (**physicked, physicking**) (arch) to treat with physic; to purge with a cathartic; to remedy.

physical adj pertaining to nature; relating to what is material and perceived by the senses; pertaining to the material part or structure of the body, as opposed to what is mental or moral (physical force); material (the physical world); pertaining to physics or natural philosophy; (of sports) involving much bodily contact.

physical education n the teaching and practice of sports and gymnastics.

physical geography n the science concerned with the study of the earth's physical features and the causes by which they have been modified, as well as of the climates, life, etc, of the globe; geomorphology; physiography.

physically adv in a physical manner; as regards the material world; as regards the bodily constitution.

physical science n any of the sciences dealing with inanimate matter or energy, e.g. physics, chemistry, geology, astronomy, etc.

physician n a doctor of medicine; a doctor who specializes in disease and disorder treated with medicines rather than by surgery.

physicist n a specialist in or one who studies physics.

physics n that branch of science which treats of the laws and properties of matter and energy; the department of science that deals with mechanics, dynamics, light, heat, sound, electricity, magnetism, nuclear studies, radiation, etc; natural philosophy.

physiognomy n the face or countenance as an index of the mind; particular cast or expression of countenance; the art of discerning the character of the mind from the features of the face; the physical features of an inanimate entity.

physiography n physical geography.

physiological adj pertaining to physiology.

physiologist n one who specializes in physiology.

physiology n the science of the functioning and processes of living organisms.

physique n a person's physical or bodily structure or constitution.

phytochemistry n the study of the chemistry of plants.

phytogenesis n the study of plant evolution.

phytography n the branch of botany concerned with describing and naming plants.

phytology n the science of plants; botany.

phyton n the smallest unit of a plant capable of growing into a new plant.

pia mater n (anat) the innermost of three vascular membranes (the meninges) covering the whole surface of the brain.

pianissimo adj, adv (mus) very soft, a direction to execute a passage in the softest manner.

pianist n a performer on the piano.

piano adj, adv (mus) soft, a direction to execute a passage softly or with diminished volume of tone.—n (pl **pianos**) a pianoforte.

pianoforte n a musical metal-stringed instrument with a keyboard by means of which the strings are struck by hammers to produce sound.

piastre n a unit of currency in Egypt, Lebanon, Sudan and Syria.

piazza n a public open space surrounded by buildings or colonnades.

pibroch n a kind of music performed on the bagpipe.

pica n a (print) a standard measurement equal to 12 points.

picador n one of the horsemen armed with a lance who excites and irritates the bull in a bullfight.

picaresque *adj* pertaining to rogues or picaroons; pertaining to episodic fiction describing the fortunes of rogues or adventurers (such as Henry Fielding's *Tom Jones*).

picaroon *n* (*arch*) a rogue or cheat; one who lives by his wits; an adventurer.

piccalilli *n* a pickle of various vegetables with mustard and other pungent spices.

piccolo *n* (*pl* **piccolos**) a small flute, the tones of which range an octave higher than those of the ordinary orchestral flute.

pice *n sing, pl* a former Indian coin of very small value.

pick *vt* to select; to choose (*to pick the best men*); to pluck; to gather, as fruit or things growing; to gather up here and there; to collect (often with *up*); to snatch thievishly (a purse); to steal the contents of (*to pick a pocket*); to strike at with anything pointed; to peck at, as a bird with its bill; to pierce; to clean, by removing with the teeth, fingers, claws or a small instrument, something that adheres (*to pick a bone*, *the teeth*); to separate from other things.—*vi* to eat slowly or by morsels; to nibble; to pilfer.—**to pick on** to criticize constantly; to bully.—**to pick out** to select; to distinguish; to identify.—**to pick up** to lift up; to give a lift in a car to; to collect by car, etc; to acquire in a casual way (*to pick up foreign languages*); to receive, as a radio transmission; to arrest; to improve gradually; to gather (*to pick up speed*); to make the acquaintance of in a casual way, often a sexual partner.—*n* right of selection; choice; the best (of); a heavy, sometimes double-pointed, iron tool with a wooden handle used for loosening hard earth, stones, etc, in digging, ditching, etc; a sharp hammer used in dressing stones.

pickaback *adj, adv* same as **piggyback**.

pickaxe *n* a pick with a sharp point at one end and a broad blade at the other; also, simply a pick.

picker *n* one who picks, culls, collects or gathers (*a rag-picker*, *a hop-picker*); a name of tools or apparatus of many various shapes.

pickerel *n* any of several small freshwater fishes of the pike family found in North America.

picket *n* a stake, post or narrow board sharpened or pointed, used in making fences, fortification and encampments; a pale; (*milit*) a detachment of troops in a camp kept fully equipped to protect the camp from surprise; a small detachment of men sent out on reconnaissance; a person or set of people posted by strikers outside a workplace to persuade others not to enter.—*vt* to fortify with pickets or pointed stakes; to fence with narrow pointed boards or pales; to fasten to a picket or stake; to place or post as a guard of observation; to place pickets at a workplace; to serve as a picket at a workplace.

pickings *npl* perquisites not over-honestly obtained; that which is left to be picked or gleaned; scraps, gleanings; profits, spoils or a share of spoils.

pickle *n* a solution of salt and water, brine or vinegar in which flesh, fish, vegetables, etc, are preserved; a thing preserved in this way; a state or condition of difficulty or disorder; (*colloq*) a plight (*we're in a fine pickle*); (*colloq*) a troublesome child.—*vt* (**pickled, pickling**) to preserve in brine or pickle; to treat with pickle.

pickled *adj* preserved in pickle; (*sl*) drunk.

picklock *n* an instrument for picking or opening locks without the key.

pickpocket *n* one who steals, or makes a practice of stealing, from people's pockets, handbags, etc.

picnic *n* a usually informal meal taken on an excursion and eaten outdoors; food so eaten; an excursion with such food; (*colloq*) an easy task (usually negatively, as *the war was no picnic*).—*vi* (**picnicked, picnicking**) to attend or take part in a picnic.

picotee *n* a variety of carnation.

picric *adj* a yellow crystalline toxic acid used as a dye, an antiseptic and in the manufacture of explosives.

Pict *n* one of an ancient race of people who inhabited the northeast of Scotland.

pictorial *adj* pertaining to pictures; illustrated by pictures; constituting a picture.

pictorially *adv* in a pictorial manner; with pictures or engravings.

picture *n* a painting, drawing, engraving or photograph exhibiting the resemblance of anything; any resemblance or representation, either to the eye or to the mind; a mental image; a likeness; an image; a representation or description in words; a film.—**to get the picture** to grasp the situation.—*vt* (**pictured, picturing**) to draw or paint a resemblance of; to form an ideal likeness of; to describe in a vivid manner; to see in the mind's eye; to imagine.

picture book *n* an illustrated book for children.

picture house *n* a former name for a cinema.

picturesque *adj* forming or fitted to form a pleasing picture; expressing that kind of beauty which is agreeable in a picture; abounding with vivid and striking imagery; graphic in style of writing.

picture window *n* a large window of plate glass usually overlooking a good view.

piddling *adj* (*colloq*) trifling; insignificant.

pidgin *n* a jargon using words and grammar from two or more languages.

pie[1] *n* an article of food consisting of pastry

pickaxe

baked with something sweet or savoury in it or under it.

pie² *n* the magpie.

piebald *adj* having spots or patches of white and black or other colour; having patches of various colours; pied; diversified.

piece *n* a fragment or part of anything separated from the whole, in any manner (*to tear in pieces*); a part of anything, though not separated or separated only in idea; a portion; a definite quantity or portion of certain things (*a piece of muslin, a piece of work*); an artistic or literary composition (*a piece of poetry* or *sculpture*); a coin (*a ten-pence piece*); a gun or single firearm (*a fowling piece*).—**of a piece** of the same sort, as if taken from the same whole; alike.—**a piece of one's mind** (*colloq*) a blunt and uncomplimentary statement.—*vt* (**pieced, piecing**) to mend by the addition of a piece; to patch; to unite; to join; to cement.

pièce de résistance *n* (*pl* **pièces de résistance**) the most important part or dish.

piecemeal *adv* in pieces; by pieces; by little and little in succession.

piecework *n* work done and paid for by the measure of quantity.

pie chart *n* a kind of circular graph divided into wedge-shaped segments in proportion to the relevant quantities.

pie chart

pied *adj* parti-coloured; variegated with spots of different colours; spotted with larger spots than if speckled.

pied-à-terre *n* (*pl* **pieds-à-terre**) a dwelling for occasional use; a second home.

pier *n* a mole or jetty carried out into the sea, serving to protect vessels from the open sea, to form a harbour, etc; a projecting quay, wharf or landing place; one of the supports of the arches of a bridge; (*archit*) the solid parts between openings in a wall, as between doors or windows; the square or other mass or post to which a gate is hung; the solid support from which an arch springs; a large pillar or shaft.

pierce *vt* (**pierced, piercing**) to stab or transfix with a pointed instrument; to penetrate; to force a way into; to affect keenly; to move deeply; to penetrate into, as into a secret or purpose.—*vi* to enter, as a pointed instrument; to penetrate.

pierced *adj* penetrated with a hole (*pierced ears*); perforated.

piercing *adj* penetrating; keen; (cold or pain) acute.

pier glass *n* a mirror or looking glass hanging between windows.

Pierrot *n* a male entertainer who wears a loose white suit and has a whitened face; a clown in such a costume.

pier table *n* a table placed between windows.

pietà *n* a picture or sculpture of the Virgin mourning over the dead Christ.

piety *n* veneration or reverence of God and love of his character; the exercise of these affections in obedience to his will and devotion to his service; filial reverence; reverence towards parents or friends, with affection and devotion to them.

piffle *n* nonsense.—*vi* (**piffled, piffling**) to talk nonsense.

pig *n* a hoofed, omnivorous mammal, descended from the European wild boar, widely domesticated and raised mainly for its meat; a swine; a greedy, filthy nasty person; an oblong mass of unforged iron, lead or other metal; the mould in which such metal is cast.—*vti* (**pigged, pigging**) to bring forth pigs; to act as pigs; to live or huddle as pigs.

pigeon *n* a common bird of many varieties; a dove, as the stock dove, the ring dove; a simpleton; a dupe; a person swindled by gamblers.

pigeonhole *n* one of the holes in a dovecote where pigeons go in and out; a small compartment or division in a case or cabinet for papers; a system of categorizing, usually one that is too rigid; a usually rigid category.—*vt* (**pigeonholed, pigeonholing**) to put into a pigeonhole; to classify methodically or too rigidly; to lay aside and delay action on.

piggery *n* a place with sties where pigs are reared.

piggin *n* a small wooden vessel with an erect handle.

piggish *adj* relating to or like pigs; swinish; greedy.

piggyback, pickaback *adj, adv* on the back or shoulders like a pack.

pig-headed *adj* stupidly obstinate; having a head like a pig.

pig iron *n* crude iron in pigs or moulds.

pig lead *n* lead in pigs or moulds, as when first extracted from the ore.

pigment *n* paint; a naturally occurring substance used by painters, dyers, etc, to impart colours.

pigmentation *n* the matter found in animals and plants that gives them their characteristic colour; the depositing of pigments by cells.

pigmy *n, adj* same as **pygmy**.

pignut *n* a plant of the carrot family with edible tuberous roots, common in woods and fields in Europe; in North America, the nut of several types of hickory.

pigskin *n* the skin of a pig, especially when prepared for use as leather.

pigsty *n* a sty or pen for pigs.

pigtail *n* the tail of a pig; the hair of the head tied behind in a tail or two tails, one on either side, usually braided; tobacco twisted into a long rope.

pike¹ *n* a freshwater fish, so named from its long predatory shape or from the form of its snout.

pike² *n* a medieval weapon, consisting of a long wooden shaft or staff with a flat pointed steel head; a pointed peak, hill or mountain summit (*Langdale Pikes*).

pike³ *n* a shortened form of **turnpike**.

pikeman *n* (*pl* **pikemen**) formerly, a soldier armed with a pike.

pikestaff *n* the staff or shaft of a pike; a long staff with a sharp pike in the lower end.

pilaster *n* a rectangular pillar projecting slightly from a wall.

pilau *n* a highly spiced oriental dish consisting of rice with meat, fish or fowl.

pilchard *n* a small European fish of the herring family caught for food.

pile¹ *n* a heap; a mass or collection of things in an elevated form; a (funeral) pyre; (*colloq*) a great deal of money; (*colloq*) a lot of (*a pile of things to do*); a large building or mass of buildings; an edifice; a voltaic battery (an early form of battery); a nuclear reactor; a long beam or column driven into the ground for the support of some superstructure or to form part of a wall, as of a quay; an heraldic figure resembling a wedge.—*vt* (**piled, piling**) to lay or throw into a heap; to heap up, to accumulate (with *up* or *on*); to drive piles into; to furnish or support with piles.—*vi* to become heaped up (with *up*, *out* or *on*); to move confusedly in a mass.—**to pile it on** (*colloq*) to exaggerate.—**to pile up** to accumulate; (*colloq*) (of vehicles) to collide.

pile² *n* the nap or fine hairy or woolly raised surface of cloth, as on a carpet; soft hair, down, fur, wool, etc; also the shag or hair on the skins of animals.

pile-driver *n* a machine that hammers piles into the ground.

piles *npl* abnormal dilatation of the veins of the lower part of the rectum near the anus, the veins often forming bleeding enlargements and growths; haemorrhoids.

pilfer *vi* to steal in small quantities; to practise petty theft.—*vt* to steal or gain by petty theft; to filch.

pilgrim *n* one who travels from his or her own country to visit a shrine or holy place, or to pay his or her devotion to the remains of dead saints; a wanderer; a traveller.

pilgrimage *n* a journey undertaken by a pilgrim; a journey to some place deemed sacred for a devotional purpose; the journey of human life.

pill *n* a small flattened round mass or little ball of medicinal substance to be swallowed whole; something unpleasant that has to be metaphorically swallowed or accepted.—*vt* to dose with pills; to form into pills.

pillage *n* the act of plundering; plunder; spoil; that which is taken by open force, particularly from enemies in war.—*vt* (**pillaged, pillaging**) to strip of money or goods by open violence and usually by a number of persons; to plunder; to despoil.

pillar *n* a column; a columnar mass or upright body; (*fig*) a supporter; one who or that which sustains or upholds; a person who is morally upright (*a pillar of the community*); a strong supporter of a cause.

pillar box *n* a public receptacle for letters that are to be sent by post.

pillbox *n* a box for holding pills; (*milit*) a small concrete blockhouse used as a machine-gun emplacement; a small round hat without a brim.

pillion *n* a seat behind the driver for a passenger to ride on a motorcycle, horse, etc; a low saddle; the pad of a saddle that rests on the horse's back.

pillory *n* a former instrument of punishment consisting of a frame of wood erected on a post with holes through which were put the head and hands of an offender, who had to stand there as the butt of public ridicule and abuse.—*vt* (**pilloried, pillorying**) to punish with the pillory; (*fig*) to expose to ridicule, contempt, abuse, etc.

pillow *n* a rectangular cushion to support the head of a person when reposing, filled with feathers, foam rubber, polyester fibre or other soft material; a supporting piece for an axle or shaft; a bearing.—*vt* to rest on for support.

pillowcase, pillow slip *n* the removable cover or case which is drawn over a pillow.

pilot *n* the person qualified to operate the controls of an aircraft, hovercraft or spacecraft; a person qualified to conduct ships into and out of particular harbours or along certain coasts, channels, etc; a guide or director of the course of another person; a television show produced as a sample of a proposed series.—*vt* to act as pilot of; to guide through dangers or difficulties; to lead.—*adj* serving as a test (*a pilot scheme*); guiding.

pilotage *n* the remuneration of a pilot; the act of piloting.

pilot boat *n* a boat used by pilots for reaching ships near shore.

pilot cloth *n* a coarse stout blue cloth for overcoats, such as are worn by sailors.

pilotfish *n* a fish marked with vertical stripes which is in the habit of accompanying and hiding below larger fish like sharks or below boats and ships.

pimiento, pimento *n* (*pl* **pimientos, pimentos**) a kind of sweet pepper, usually red or green but sometimes yellow or deep maroon; capsicum.

pimp *n* a man who solicits for a prostitute,

pillow

usually for money; a procurer; a pander.—
vi to solicit for prostitutes; to procure prostitutes for the gratification of others; to pander.

pimpernel *n* a wild flower of the primrose family found in cornfields, famously having red flowers but also pink, lilac, blue or yellow.

pimple *n* a small elevation of the skin, with an inflamed base.

pin *n* a piece of metal, wood, etc, usually pointed at the end with a rounded or flattened head at the other, used for fastening separate articles or pieces together or as a support from which a thing may be hung; a peg; a bolt; a brooch or badge; the part of a key stem entering a lock; the safety clasp on a hand grenade; in golf, the pole and flag marking a hole; a hold in wrestling; in bowling, one of the clubs at which the ball is rolled; the centre of a target; a small metal rod inserted in surgery; a tuning peg in stringed musical instruments; a central part; (*pl*) (*sl*) legs.—*vt* (**pinned, pinning**) to fasten with a pin or pins of any kind; to clutch; to hold fast; to transfix; (*colloq*) to attach (blame, etc) to someone (with *on*).—**to pin down** (*colloq*) to get (someone) to commit himself or herself as to plans, etc; to establish (a fact, etc).

PIN *n* (abbreviation for **personal identification number**) a secret number assigned by a bank, etc, which is used with a plastic card to receive money from a cash machine.

pinafore *n* a sort of apron worn especially by children or those who work in food retailing, etc, to protect the front part of their clothes; a kind of dress worn over a shirt or sweater.

pincers *npl* an instrument consisting of a pair of hinged arms ending in jaws by which anything is gripped in order to be drawn out, as a nail, or kept fast for some operation; the claws of certain animals, as lobsters or beetles.

pinch *vt* to press hard or squeeze between the ends of the fingers, the teeth, claws or with an instrument, etc; to nip; to distress; to afflict; to nip with frost; (*colloq*) to steal; (*colloq*) to arrest.—*vi* to act with pressing force; to press painfully, as shoes; to be sparing or niggardly.—*n* a close compression, as with the ends of the fingers; a nip; a gripe; a pang; distress inflicted or suffered; straits (*to feel the pinch*); difficulty; a strong iron lever; a crowbar; as much as is taken by the finger and thumb; a small quantity, generally of salt.

pinched *adj* appearing to be squeezed; drawn by cold, stress or pain.

pinchbeck *n* an alloy of copper and zinc, somewhat like gold in colour formerly

pineapple

much used for cheap jewellery.—*adj* made of pinchbeck; sham; not genuine.

pincushion *n* a small cushion or pad in which pins are stuck ready for use.

Pindaric *adj* in the style of an ode of Pindar, the Grecian lyric poet; in a complex metrical mode.—*n* a Pindaric ode.

pine[1] *n* any of a family of evergreen coniferous trees, of which about two hundred species are known in ten genera, having needle-like leaves, bearing cones and providing timber, turpentine, pitch and resin; (*colloq*) the pineapple.

pine[2] *vi* (**pined, pining**) to yearn; to languish; to lose flesh or grow weak under distress or anxiety; to languish with desire (*to pine for a thing*).

pineal *adj* resembling a pine cone in shape; relating to the pineal gland.

pineal body, pineal gland *n* a tiny organ found behind the third ventricle of the brain.

pineapple *n* an edible tropical fruit so called from its resemblance to the cone of the pine tree; the plant itself.

ping *n* a sudden, high-pitched ringing sound, as of a bullet or raindrop hitting a sheet of metal.—*vti* to strike with a ping; to emit a ping.

pingpong *n* table tennis.

Ping-Pong *n* a trademark for table tennis equipment.

pinhole *n* a small hole as made by a pin; a very small aperture.

pinion *n* the joint of a fowl's wing remotest from the body; a wing; a small wheel which gears with the teeth of a larger.—*vt* to restrain (a person's limbs) by holding or binding; to confine by binding the wings; to disable by cutting off the first joint of the wing; to bind the arms of; to shackle; to fetter.

pink[1] *n* a name of various garden flowers, as the clove pink or carnation and garden pink; a range of light red colours resembling those of the common garden pinks; anything supremely excellent (*the pink of perfection*); a fish, the minnow, so called from the colour of its abdomen in summer.—**in the pink** in good health.—*adj* of a light red colour, rose; (*colloq*) left-wing.

pink[2] *vt* to ornament with holes, etc; to make a scalloped or notched border like the serrated edges of the petals of a pink or carnation; to cut with pinking shears; to stab lightly; to prick with a sword or rapier.

pinkeye *n* a contagious form of ophthalmia in humans; acute conjunctivitis; a contagious fever affecting horses and cattle.

pin money *n* an allowance made by a husband to his wife for her separate use; money for small incidental expenses.

pinnace *n* a small vessel propelled by oars

and sails and having generally two masts rigged like those of a schooner; a boat usually rowed with eight oars.

pinnacle *n* a rocky peak; a sharp or pointed summit; (*archit*) any lesser structure, whatever its form, that rises above the roof of a building or that caps and terminates the higher parts of other buildings; the highest point (of a profession, of fame, etc); the climax.

pinnate *adj* (*bot*) shaped or branching like a feather; formed like a feather.

pinniform *adj* having the form of a fin or feather.

pinniped *n* any of an order of aquatic mammals with a streamlined body and limbs like fins or paddles, as the seal.—*adj* relating to or belonging to this order.

pint *n* a liquid measure of capacity equal to the eighth part of a gallon; a dry measure of capacity equal to one half of a quart; (*colloq*) a pint of beer.

pintail *n* a variety of duck with a sharp pointed tail.

pintle *n* a pin or bolt, often used as a pivot; (*naut*) an iron bolt by which the rudder is hung to the sternpost; a pin passing through an axle to hold on a wheel.

pinpoint *vt* to locate or identify accurately.—*n* the point of a pin.

pins and needles *npl* a tingling feeling in the fingers, toes, etc, caused by impeded blood circulation returning to normal.—**on pins and needles** in an expectant or anxious state.

pinwheel *n* a wheel of which the cogs are pins projecting outward.

pioneer *n* an early settler or explorer; one who originates or develops something new; (*milit*) one whose business is to march with or before an army to repair the road or clear it of obstructions, work at entrenchments, etc; anyone that goes before to prepare the way for another (*pioneers of civilization*).—*vt* to go before and prepare a way for; to initiate.—*vi* to act as pioneer; to clear the way.

pious *adj* having due respect and affection for parents or other relatives; more commonly, duly reverencing God; godly; devout; dictated by reverence to God; proceeding from piety; smug and sanctimonious; practised under the pretence of religion (*pious frauds*).

pip[1] *n* the seed of some fruits, as an apple or orange; a spot or device on cards, dice, etc; (*colloq*) an emblem on the shoulder of an officer of the British Army or Royal Marine; a short high-pitched sound, as on radio; a signal on a radar screen.

pip[2] *vt* (**pipped, pipping**) (*colloq*) to hit with a bullet; to beat or defeat at the last moment (*he was pipped at the post*).

pip[3] *n* a disease of fowls, characterized by secretion of thick mucus in the mouth which stops the nostrils; (*colloq*) a minor human ailment, bad temper and discontentedness; (*colloq*) annoyance or irritation (*he gives me the pip*).

pip[4] *vi* (**pipped, pipping**) to cry or chirp, as a chicken.

pipa *n* the Surinam toad, a South American toad the female of which carries her fertilized eggs on her back.

pipe *n* a wind instrument of music, consisting of a tube of wood or metal; a long tube or hollow body made of various materials and used for conveying water, gas, steam, etc; a tube of clay or other material with a bowl at one end, used in smoking tobacco, etc; the windpipe; the sound of the voice; a whistle or call of a bird; a wine measure, usually containing about 105 imperial or 126 wine gallons; (*naut*) the boatswain's whistle used to call the men to their duties; (*pl*) bagpipes.—*vi* (**piped, piping**) to sound or play on a pipe; to have a shrill sound; to whistle.—*vt* to convey (water, etc) by pipe; to play on a pipe or other wind instrument; to lead with the sound of a pipe; to utter in a sharp or high tone; (*naut*) to call by means of the boatswain's pipe or whistle; to trim with piping; to decorate food with icing, etc, pushed through a nozzle.

pipeclay *n* the purest kind of potter's clay, manufactured into tobacco pipes and used by soldiers for cleaning belts, etc.—*vt* to whiten with pipeclay.

pipe dream *n* a wish or idea that can never be realized.

pipefish *n* a long slender fish with a tube-like snout and bony plates covering its body.

pipeline *n* a pipe or line of pipes (often underground) for conveying liquids, e.g. petroleum, over long distances; a direct channel for information; the processes through which supplies pass from source to user.—**in the pipeline** due to be completed or delivered.

piper *n* one who plays on a pipe; a bagpiper.—**to pay the piper** to bear the expense (of an undertaking, etc) and therefore have control.

pipette *n* a small tube terminating in a perforated point, used by chemists for transferring liquids.

piping *adj* playing on a pipe; having or giving out a shrill whistling sound; boiling; hissing with heat (*piping hot*).—*n* pipes, as for gas, water, etc, collectively; the art of playing a pipe or bagpipes; a high-pitched sound; a thin strip of material, cord, etc, for edging hems or seams or decorating garments; a strip of icing, cream, etc, for decorating food; (*hortic*) a jointed stem used for propagating plants.

pintail

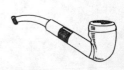

pipe

pipistrel, pipistrelle *n* one of several species of small bats found in most parts of the world.

pipit *n* one of several species of small birds of the same family as wagtails, some of which resemble the lark.

pipkin *n* a small earthen boiler.

pippin *n* one of several kinds of eating apple.

piquancy *n* the state or quality of being piquant; sharpness; pungency.

piquant *adj* sharp; racy; lively; sparkling; interesting; sharp or cutting to the feelings; pungent; strong-tasting; strong-smelling.

pique *n* an offence taken; slight anger at someone; a feeling arising from wounded pride, vanity or self-love, as resentment.—*vt* (**piqued, piquing**) to nettle; to irritate; to sting (less strong than *exasperate*); to stimulate; to touch with envy, jealousy or other passion; (*refl*) to pride or value oneself.—*vi* to cause irritation.

piquet *n* a game at cards played between two persons with thirty-two cards, the ace of spades being highest card.

piracy *n* the act, practice or crime of robbing on the high seas; the profession of pirate; literary theft; any infringement on the law of copyright.

piragua *n* same as **pirogue**.

pirate *n* a robber on the high seas; one who by open violence takes the property of another on the high seas; an armed ship or vessel engaged in piracy; a publisher or compiler who appropriates the literary labours of an author without compensation or permission.—*vi* (**pirated, pirating**) to play the pirate; to rob on the high seas.—*vt* to publish without right or permission.

piratical, piratic *adj* having the air or character of a pirate, often glamorized; robbing or plundering by open violence on the high seas; pertaining to or consisting of piracy.

pirogue, piragua *n* a kind of canoe made from a single trunk of a tree hollowed out.

pirouette *n* a rapid whirling on the point of one foot; the short turn of a horse so as to bring its head suddenly in the opposite direction to where it was before.—*vi* (**pirouetted, pirouetting**) to perform a pirouette, as in dancing.

piscatorial, piscatory *adj* relating to fish, fishermen or fishing; pertaining to angling.

Pisces *npl* (*astron*) the Fishes, the twelfth sign or constellation in the zodiac, next to Aries; the vertebrate animals of the class fishes.

pisciculture *n* the breeding, rearing, preservation and feeding of fish.

pisciform *adj* having the shape of a fish.

piscina *n* (*pl* **piscinae, piscinas**) a niche on the south side of the altar in churches, with a small basin and water drain connected, into which the priest empties any water used.

pisé *n* stiff earth or clay used to construct walls or floors by being rammed.

pish *exclam* a word expressing contempt.—*vi* to express contempt by *pish!*

pismire *n* (*arch*) the ant.

pissed *adj* (*sl*) drunk; (*sl*) angry or depressed (usually with *off*).

pistachio *n* (*pl* **pistachios**) a small tree cultivated over southern Europe and western Asia; its fruit, a small, hard-shelled, edible nut of the pistachio tree.

pistil *n* (*bot*) the seed-bearing organ of a flower, consisting of the ovary, the stigma and often also of a style.

pistol *n* a small firearm, the smallest used, designed to be fired with one hand only.—*vt* (**pistolled, pistolling**) to shoot with a pistol.

piston *n* (*mach*) a movable cylindrical piece which exactly fits a hollow cylinder, such as the barrel of a pump or the cylinder of a steam engine, and capable of being driven alternately in two directions.

piston rod *n* a connecting rod.

pit *n* a hollow or cavity, usually deep, either natural or made by digging in the earth; the shaft of a mine; a (coal) mine; a scooped-out place for burning something; a concealed hole in the ground for snaring wild beasts; any hollow, cavity or depression in the flesh (*the armpits*); a small indentation on any surface, including the skin, as the scar left by smallpox; the stone of a fruit; a place or area where cocks or dogs were formerly brought to fight or where dogs are trained to kill rats; part of a theatre on the floor of the house and below the level of the stage for the orchestra; a hole in the floor of a garage workshop or an area by the side of a motor-racing track for the repair and servicing of cars and other vehicles; (*sl*) bed.—**the pit** (*Scrip*) the place of the dead or the abode of evil spirits.—**the pits** (*colloq*) the worst possible.—**the bottomless pit** hell.—*vt* (**pitted, pitting**) to lay in a pit or hole; to mark with little hollows, as by smallpox; to set in competition; to set against one another, as in combat, as (*lit*) *like cocks in a pit*.

pitapat *adv* in a flutter; with palpitation or quick succession of beats.—*n* a light quick step.

pit bull terrier *n* a breed of dog developed from the bull terrier for dog-fighting.

pitch¹ *vt* to fling or throw; to cast forward; to hurl; to toss; to fix or plant, as stakes or pointed instruments; to fix by means of such; hence, to set in array; to marshal or arrange in order (*to pitch a tent, to pitch a camp*); to regulate or set the keynote of; to pave or face with stones, as an embank-

pistol

ment; to choose (with *on*).—*vi* to light; to settle; to come to rest from flight; to plunge or fall headlong; to fix choice (with *on* or *upon*); to fix a tent or temporary habitation; to encamp; to move vigorously and irregularly back and forth, to rise and fall irregularly, as the head and stern of a ship passing over waves.—*n* a point or degree of elevation or depression; height or depth; degree; rate; highest rise; the degree of slope or inclination (*the pitch of a hill* or *roof*); the rise of an arch; a throw; a toss; that part of a cricket field where the wickets are put up; a piece of ground reserved for playing a team game (*a football pitch*); a place where a street vendor works; sales talk; a cast or jerk of something from the hand; in music and acoustics, the relative height of a sound, the quality of a sound which depends on the number of vibrations per second; in a toothed wheel, the distance from centre to centre of two adjacent teeth, measured along either a circular arc (*pitch circle*) or the straight chord; in certain technical senses, a distance between two points (as *the pitch of a screw*, that is, the distance between its threads).

pitch² *n* a thick, tenacious oily substance, commonly obtained from tar and extensively used for closing up the seams of ships, for preserving wood from the effects of water, for coating ironwork, etc.—*vt* to smear or cover over with pitch.

pitch-and-toss *n* a game in which the players determine the order of tossing by pitching coins at a mark.

pitchblende *n* a mineral which constitutes one of the principal sources of radium and uranium.

pitch-dark *adj* dark as pitch; very dark.

pitched battle *n* a battle in which the armies are previously drawn up in form, with a regular disposition of the forces.

pitcher *n* a vessel with a spout for holding liquors; an earthen or metallic vessel for holding water for domestic purposes; a water pot, jug or jar with ears.

pitchfork *n* a long-handled fork with curved tines used in lifting or throwing hay or sheaves of grain.—*vt* to lift or throw with a pitchfork; hence, to put suddenly or accidentally into any position.

pitch pipe *n* a small flute or free-reed pipe used in regulating the pitch or elevation of the key or leading note of a tune.

piteous *adj* fitted to excite pity; moving to pity or compassion; mournful; affecting; lamentable.

pitfall *n* a pit slightly covered over, forming a kind of trap; a concealed danger; an unexpected difficulty.

pith *n* a soft cellular substance occupying the centre of the root, stem and branches of exogenous plants; the spinal cord or marrow of an animal; strength, vigour or force; closeness and vigour of thought and style; cogency; condensed substance or matter; quintessence.

pithead *n* the top of a pit shaft or the ground immediately around it.

pithecoid *adj* pertaining to apes; resembling an ape; ape-like.

pithy *adj* consisting of pith; containing pith; abounding with pith; terse and striking; forcible; energetic; uttering energetic words or expressions.

pitiable *adj* deserving or exciting pity.

pitiful *adj* miserable; moving compassion; paltry; insignificant; contemptible; (*arch*) full of pity and compassion.

pitiless *adj* lacking pity; hard-hearted; relentless; exciting no pity.

pitta bread *n* a small, flat, oval slightly leavened loaf of bread, usually split open for a filling.

pittance *n* formerly, an allowance of food or a gift bestowed in charity; a very small quantity of money allowed or assigned.

pituitary *adj* (*anat*) of or relating to the pituitary gland.

pituitary gland *n* (*anat*) a complex and extremely important two-lobed endocrine or ductless gland attached to the base of the brain, which secretes hormones affecting growth, sex glands and other endocrine glands, the birth process, regulation of the kidneys, etc.

pity *n* the sorrow of one person excited by the distress of another; commiseration; compassion; mercy; the ground or subject of pity; cause of grief; thing to be regretted (in this sense it has a plural, as *it is a thousand pities he should fail*).—*vt* (**pitied, pitying**) to feel pity or compassion towards; to feel pain or grief for; to have sympathy for; to commiserate.—*vi* to be compassionate; to exercise pity.

pivot *n* a pin on which anything turns; a short shaft or point on which a wheel or other body revolves; (*milit*) the person or position on whom or which the different wheelings are made in the various evolutions of drill, etc; that on which important results depend; a turning point; a key person on whom progress depends.—*vt* to place on a pivot; to furnish with a pivot.—*vi* to turn as if on a pivot.

pivotal *adj* relating to or acting as a pivot; upon whom or which everything depends; of vital importance.

pix *n* same as **pyx**.

pixie, pixy *n* a sort of fairy or elf.

pizza *n* a baked dough crust covered with tomatoes, cheese, olives, spiced sausage, etc, of Italian origin.

pizzazz *n* flamboyance; theatricality; glamour; energy.

pizza

pizzeria *n* a place where pizzas are made and sold.

pizzicato *adj* (*mus*) (of stringed instruments) to be plucked with the finger rather than played with the bow.—*n* (*pl* **pizzicati, pizzicatos**) a pizzicato passage in music.

placable *adj* easy to placate.

placard *n* a written or printed paper posted in a public place; a bill posted up to draw public attention; a poster.—*vt* to post placards on; to make known by placard.

placate *vt* (**placated, placating**) to appease, pacify or conciliate.

place *n* a broad way or open space in a city; an area of any size; a particular portion of space marked off by its use or character; a locality, spot or site; position; a town or village; a fortified post; a passage in a book; point or degree in order of proceeding (*in the first place*); a finishing position in a race (*he took third place*); rank; order of priority, dignity or importance; office; employment; official station; ground or occasion; room; station in life; house or home (*let's go to my place*); seat; calling; occupation; condition; room or stead, with the sense of substitution (*to act in place of another*); the position in the heavens of a heavenly body.—*vt* (**placed, placing**) to put or set in a particular place or spot; to set or put in a certain relative position; to find a place or seat for; to locate; to identify (*I can't place his face*); to appoint, set, induct or establish in an office; to put or set in any particular rank, state or condition; to set; to fix (*to place confidence in a friend*); to invest; to lend; to request material from a supplier (*to place an order*).— **to fall into place** to become understood when seen in relationship to other things.—**to go places** to be successful.— **to know one's place** to accept the lowliness of one's position and act accordingly.—**to put oneself in (someone's) place** to imagine what it would be like to be in (someone else's) circumstances.—**to put (someone) in his** *or* **her place** to remind (someone) of the lowliness of his or her position, lack of experience, etc.—**to take place** to happen.

placebo *n* (*pl* **placebos, placeboes**) a harmless substance given to a patient who thinks it is a medicine, used either in drug trials or for psychological effect.

placement *n* the act of placing or of putting in a certain spot or position; the act of assigning to a job; a job so assigned.

placenta *n* the afterbirth; a temporary organ developed in mammals during pregnancy and forming a connection between the mother and the foetus, providing oxygen to and removing waste products from the foetus; (*bot*) that part of a seed vessel on which the ovules or seeds are placed.

placer *n* a gravelly place where particles gold occur; a spot where gold dust is found in the soil.

placid *adj* gentle; quiet; undisturbed; equable; mild; serene; unruffled.

placket *n* an opening or slit in a skirt, etc, to make it easy to put on or take off or to reach a pocket.

plafond *n* (*archit*) the ceiling of a room; the underside of a beam, arch, etc.

plagal *adj* (*mus*) applied to a cadence in which the chord of the subdominant is followed by that of the tonic.

plagiarism *n* the act of plagiarizing; the crime of literary theft; that which is plagiarized.

plagiarist *n* one who plagiarizes; one who steals or purloins the words or ideas of another and passes them off as his or her own; a literary thief.

plagiarize *vti* (**plagiarized, plagiarizing**) to steal or purloin the words of another in literary composition.

plague *n* a highly dangerous pestilential disease that has in the past reached epidemic proportions; a disease of rodents transmitted by rat fleas, eminently contagious and attended by excessive debility with buboes (*bubonic plague*) or carbuncles with a form of pneumonia (*pneumonic plague*); an affliction; severe trouble; a nuisance.— *vt* (**plagued, plaguing**) to vex; to tease; to annoy; to harass; to trouble; to embarrass; to scourge with disease, calamity or natural evil of any kind.

plaice *n* a European species of flatfish, more flat and square than the halibut, valued as a food fish; any of several North American flatfishes.

plaid *n* a large rectangular outer garment or wrap, frequently of tartan, worn by the Highlanders and others in Scotland; cloth with a tartan or checked pattern.

plain *adj* without elevations and depressions; level; flat; even; smooth; void of ornament; without embellishment; simple; unadorned; without beauty; homely; sometimes used as a euphemism for ugly; artless; simple; unlearned; without disguise, cunning or affectation; without refinement; unsophisticated; honestly undisguised; open; unreserved; mere; absolute; unmistakable; without difficulties or intricacies; evident to the understanding; clear; manifest; not obscure; not highly seasoned; not rich or luxurious (*a plain diet*).—*adv* in a plain manner; plainly; frankly; bluntly.—*n* a piece of level land; a piece of ground with an even surface or a surface little varied by inequalities; (*geog*) the general term for all those parts of the dry land which cannot properly be called hilly or mountainous.

plain clothes *npl* the ordinary dress of society; non-official dress, opposed to *uniform*.

plainness *n* the state or quality of being plain; evenness of surface; openness; candour; intelligibility.

plain sailing *n* easy progress over an unobstructed course.

plainsong *n* (*mus*) a simple, unadorned, unaccompanied chant used in medieval church services, still heard in the Roman Catholic Church in the form of the Gregorian chant; the simple notes of an air without ornament or variation; hence, a plain unexaggerated statement.

plaint *n* (*arch*) lamentation; complaint; (*law*) representation made of injury or wrong done.

plaintiff *n* (*law*) the person who brings a lawsuit against another, opposed to *defendant*.

plaintive *adj* expressive of sorrow or melancholy; mournful; sad.

plait *n* a braid of three or more intertwined strands of hair, straw, etc.—*vt* to braid; to interweave the locks or strands of (*to plait the hair*).

plan *n* the representation of anything drawn on a plane and forming a map or chart (*the plan of a town*); the representation of a horizontal section of a building, showing the extent, division and distribution of its area into apartments, passages, etc; a scheme devised, often in considerable detail; a project; disposition of parts according to a certain design; a method or process; a way.—*vt* (**planned, planning**) to invent or contrive for construction; to scheme; to devise; to form in design; to intend (*I plan to finish this soon*).

plane[1] *n* same as **plane tree**.

plane[2] *n* a joiner's tool, consisting of a piece of edged steel or a chisel set obliquely in a smooth-soled stock, used in paring or smoothing boards or wood of any kind.—*vt* (**planed, planing**) to make smooth, especially by the use of a plane.

plane[3] *adj* without elevations or depressions; even; level; flat.—*n* a smooth or perfectly level surface; a smooth, level facet of something; the supporting surface of an aircraft, hydroplane, etc; an aeroplane or hydroplane; (*math*) a surface such that if any two points whatever in it be joined by a straight line, the whole of the straight line will be on the surface; an imaginary surface, supposed to cut and pass through solid bodies or in various directions, frequently used in astronomy (*the plane of the ecliptic, the plane of a planet's orbit*); level of thought, development or existence (*he lives on a different plane from the rest of us*).—*vi* (**planed, planing**) to glide or soar; to skim across the surface of water; to travel by aeroplane.

plane geometry *n* the geometry of plane figures, in contradistinction to solid geometry or the geometry of solids.

planet *n* a celestial body (such as the earth) which revolves about the sun or other star, from which it receives light.

planetarium *n* (*pl* **planetariums, planetaria**) an astronomical machine which, by the movement of its parts, represents the motions and orbits of the planets; a building for housing this machine; a model of the solar system.

planetary *adj* pertaining to the planets; having the nature of a planet.—**planetary years** the periods of time in which the several planets make their revolutions round the sun.

planetoid *n* one of a numerous group of very small planets revolving round the sun between the orbits of Mars and Jupiter; an asteroid.

plane tree, plane *n* a tree with a straight smooth branching stem and palmate leaves, used in towns as a shade tree for lining avenues, roads, etc; in Scotland, a name once commonly given to the sycamore.

plangent *adj* having a loud, deep, plaintive sound.

planimeter *n* an instrument for measuring the area of any plane figure.

planish *vt* to make smooth or plain, as wood; to condense, smooth and toughen, as a metallic plate, by light blows of a hammer; to polish.

planisphere *n* a sphere projected on a plane; a map exhibiting the circles of the sphere.

plank *n* a broad length of sawn timber, differing from a board only in being thicker; in political parlance, one of the principles in the system adopted by a party.—*vt* to cover or lay with planks.

plankton *n* the mass of minute organisms, plant or animal, floating or drifting in the ocean.

plant *n* an organism possessing cellulose cell walls, synthesizing its food from carbon dioxide, water and light and having the power of propagating itself by seeds or similar reproductive bodies; a soft-stemmed organism of this kind, as distinguished from a tree or shrub; a collective term for the fixtures, machinery, tools, apparatus, etc, necessary to carry on any industry or business, especially large machines used in construction; (*colloq*) something concealed in someone's possession in order to implicate that person in a crime, etc; (*colloq*) a swindle.—*vt* to put in earth and cover, as seed for growth; to set in the ground, pots, etc, for growth; to furnish with plants; to lay out and prepare with plants; to set upright; to set firmly; to

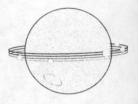

planet

fix; to put; to set and direct or point (*to plant cannon against a fort*); to furnish the first inhabitants of; to settle (*to plant a colony*); to introduce and establish (*to plant Christianity*); (*colloq*) to conceal (something) in someone's possession in order to implicate him or her in a crime, etc; (*sl*) to deliver a punch.

plantain[1] *n* any of a family of perennial or annual herbs, found in all temperate regions and represented in Britain by five species, of which the most common is ribwort plantain or rib grass.

plantain[2] *n* a large tropical flowering plant with a soft succulent stem, the banana-like fruit of which is an important food.

plantar *adj* (*anat*) relating or belonging to the sole of the foot.

plantation *n* the act of planting or setting in the earth for growth; the place planted; a large cultivated planting of trees; a grove; an estate, usually in the tropics, where crops such as tea, sugar cane, cotton, rubber, etc, are cultivated; a first planting; introduction; establishment.

planter *n* one who plants, sets, introduces or establishes; one who runs a plantation; a machine for planting; a decorative container for plants.

plantigrade *adj* walking on the sole of the foot and not on the toes (*digitigrade*), applied to a section of carnivorous animals, including humans and bears.

planting *n* the act or art of inserting plants in the soil; the art of forming plantations of trees; a plantation.

plaque *n* an inscribed or purely informative plate; a brooch; the plate of a clasp; a flat plate of metal on which enamels are painted; a sticky film which forms on teeth and which can cause gum disease, dental plaque.

plash[1] *n* a puddle; a splash.—*vi* to dabble in water; to fall with a dabbling sound; to splash.

plash[2] *vt* to bend and intertwine branches, etc, to make or mend a hedge.

plashy *adj* watery; abounding with puddles.

plasma *n* the pale amber fluid in which the red and white blood cells float; the viscous living matter of a cell, the protoplasm; (*physics*) an ionized gas produced at very high temperatures, containing positive and negative charges in equal amounts, conducting electricity and affected by magnetic fields; a green, near-translucent kind of quartz allied to chalcedony.

plaster *n* a composition of lime, water and sand, with or without hair or other fibres for binding, used for coating walls and partitions of houses; calcined gypsum, used, when mixed with water, for finishing walls, for casts, cement, etc; plaster of Paris; a plaster cast; an adhesive dressing

for cuts and minor wounds.—*vt* to overlay or cover with plaster; to lay coarsely on; to bedaub.

plaster cast *n* a rigid dressing of gauze impregnated with plaster of Paris, commonly used to hold in place a fractured limb; a sculptor's model in plaster of Paris.

plasterer *n* one who overlays with plaster.

plastering *n* the act or operation of overlaying with plaster; plasterwork; a covering of plaster.

plaster of Paris *n* a composition of several kinds of gypsum, originally obtained from Montmartre near Paris, used for various purposes.

plastic *n* any of various non-metallic compounds synthetically produced, usually from petroleum, that can be moulded, cast, squeezed or laminated into objects, films or filaments and that can be divided simply into those that become pliable when reheated (*thermoplastic*) and those that set (*thermosetting plastic*) and are much used. —*adj* having the power to give form or fashion to a mass of matter; capable of being moulded into various forms; capable of change or modification; capable of receiving a new bent or direction (as the mind); applied to sculpture and the kindred arts, as distinguished from painting and the graphic arts.

plasticity *n* the state or quality of being plastic.

plastic surgery *n* the branch of surgery which deals with the remodelling, repairing or restoring of external parts of the body, used either for remedial or cosmetic purposes.

plat *n* a small piece of ground marked out and devoted to some special purpose; a plot of ground.

plate *n* a flattened piece of metal, glass, etc, with a uniform thickness; armour composed of broad pieces or plates, domestic vessels or utensils made of gold or silver; a small shallow vessel of metal, porcelain or earthenware, from which food is eaten at table; a piece of timber laid horizontally in a wall to receive the ends of other timbers; a piece of metal on which anything is engraved for the purpose of being printed off on paper; a page of stereotype for printing. —*vt* (**plated, plating**) to cover with a plate or plates; to overlay with a thin coating of silver or other metal, used particularly of silver (*plated vessels*).

plate armour *n* defensive armour consisting of plates of metal.

plateau *n* (*pl* **plateaux, plateaus**) a broad, flat area of land in an elevated position; a tableland; a state or period of little variation.

plate glass *n* rolled, ground and polished sheet glass used for large windows, etc.

plate armour

644

platelayer *n* a worker on railways whose occupation is to lay down rails and fix them to the sleepers.

platelet *n* any of the many minute, irregularly shaped bodies in blood, necessary for clotting blood.

platen *n* the roller on a typewriter; (*print*) a plate which presses the paper against the type.

plater *n* one who coats articles with gold or silver; a race horse not of the highest class competing for a cup or piece of gold or silver plate in race.

platform *n* any flat or horizontal structure, especially if raised above some particular level; the flat roof of a building on the outside; the place where guns are mounted on a fortress or battery; the raised walk at a railway station for landing passengers and goods; a place raised above the floor of a hall set apart for the speakers at public meetings; the aggregate of principles adopted or avowed by any body of men, such as a political party; a declared system of policy (*a political platform*).

plating *n* the art of covering articles with a thin coating of metal, especially of overlaying articles made of the baser metals with a thin coating of gold or silver; a thin coating of one metal laid on another metal.

platinum *n* a metallic element of a white colour very much like silver but of inferior lustre, the heaviest of the ordinary metals, exceedingly ductile, malleable, tenacious and difficult to fuse, used in scientific and medical equipment, in the chemical industry and in jewellery.

platitude *n* a trite, dull or stupid remark; a truism; flatness; dullness; insipidity.

Platonic *adj* pertaining to Plato the philosopher or to his philosophy, his school or his opinions.

platonic love *n* a non-sexual affection subsisting between the sexes.

platoon *n* (*milit*) formerly, a small square body of soldiers; now, a body consisting of about three sections and some thirty soldiers commanded by a subaltern with a sergeant as second in command.

platter *n* a plate; a large shallow dish for holding eatables.

platypus *n* the duckbill.

plaudit *n* (usually *pl*) applause, praise bestowed.

plausible *adj* apparently truthful or reasonable; specious; using specious arguments or discourse; fair-spoken.

plausibility *n* the state or quality of being plausible; speciousness; superficial appearance of right.

play *vi* to do something not as a task or for profit but for amusement; to act wantonly or thoughtlessly; to dally, trifle, toy; to move irregularly; to flutter; to contend in a game; to gamble; to perform on an instrument of music; to act with free motion; to work freely (*the lungs play*); to act; to behave; to act a part on the stage; to impersonate a character; (of light) to flicker or shimmer; (of water) to discharge or direct on.—*vt* to perform in sport or for sport or for a prize; to make use of in a game (*to play a trump card*); to enter into a game with; to perform music on; to perform on a musical instrument (a tune); to act on the stage; to act or represent in general; to act like; to behave in the manner of (*to play the fool*); to perform; to execute (*to play a trick*); to direct (*to play a hose*); to give line to (a fish).—**to play along** to deceive.—**to play along with** to cooperate.—**to play back** to reproduce (previously recorded sound or pictures).—**to play down** to minimize or make little of.—**to play down to** to condescend.—**to play out** to finish.—**to play up** to cause trouble to or annoy.—**to play up to** to flatter for one's own advantage.—*n* any exercise intended for pleasure, amusement or diversion, as cricket, quoits, etc; a game; amusement; sport; frolic; jest; not earnest; gaming; practice in any contest (*sword play*); action; use; employment; practice; manner of acting or dealing (*fair play*); a dramatic composition; a comedy or tragedy; a dramatic performance; motion; movement, regular or irregular (*the play of a wheel*); hence, power or space for motion; liberty of action; scope; swing.

playact *vi* to make believe, pretend; to be affected or insincere; to act in a play.

playback *n* the act of reproducing recorded sound or pictures, especially soon after they are made; a mechanism in an audio or video record for doing this.

playbill *n* a poster advertising a play.

playboy, playgirl *n* a person who lives for pleasure.

played out *adj* exhausted; no longer of interest, influence or usefulness.

player *n* one who plays; an actor; a musician.

playful *adj* sportive; frolicsome; frisky; indulging in gambols; full of sprightly humour; pleasantly jocular or amusing.

playgoer *n* one who regularly goes to the theatre.

playground *n* a piece of ground set apart for open-air recreation, such as are connected with a school, etc, for the pupils.

playgroup *n* a supervised assembly of pre-school children where they can play.

playhouse *n* a theatre.

playing card *n* one of a set of cards used for playing games, each card having an identical pattern on one side and its own symbol on the reverse.

playing field *n* a place for playing sport.

platter

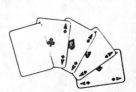

playing card

645

playmate *n* a playfellow; a companion in diversions.

playpen *n* a portable collapsible enclosure in which a young child may be left to play safely.

playschool *n* a nursery for children where there are educational activities based on play.

plaything *n* a toy; anything that serves to amuse.

playwright *n* a maker of plays.

plea *n* an earnest appeal or entreaty; an excuse; (*law*) that which is alleged by a party to an action in support of his or her demand; the answer of a defendant to the plaintiff's declaration; (*Scots law*) a suit or action; a cause in court; that which is alleged in support, justification or defence.

pleach *vt* to interweave; to plash.

plead *vi* (*pret, pp* **pleaded**, sometimes **pled**, *ppr* **pleading**) to appeal or implore; to argue in support of a claim or in defence against the claim of another; to urge reasons for or against; to attempt to persuade one by argument or supplication; (*law*) to present a plea; to present an answer to the declaration of a plaintiff; to deny the plaintiff's declaration and demand.—*vt* to discuss, defend and attempt to maintain by arguments or reasons (*to plead one's cause*); to allege or adduce in proof, support or vindication; to offer in excuse (*to plead poverty*); to allege and offer in a legal plea or defence, or for repelling a demand in law.

pleader *n* one who pleads; a lawyer who argues in a court of justice; one who forms pleas or pleadings (*a special pleader*).

pleading *n* the act of advocating any cause; the act or practice of advocating clients' causes in courts of law; one of the written statements containing the subject matter of a litigant's demand or claim, or of his defence or answer.

pleasant *adj* pleasing; agreeable to the mind or to the senses.

pleasantry *n* gaiety; merriment; a sprightly or humorous remark; a jest; good-humoured or lively talk (*we exchanged pleasantries*); a frolic.

please *vt* (**pleased, pleasing**) to excite agreeable sensations or emotions in; to delight; to gratify; to satisfy; to content; to seem good to (used impersonally).—*vi* to give pleasure; to gain approbation; to like; to choose; to prefer; to condescend; to be pleased; to be kind enough (used in polite commands, requests or appeals, as *please do it, do it, if you please*).

pleasing *adj* giving pleasure or satisfaction; agreeable; gratifying; delightful.

pleasurable *adj* pleasing; giving pleasure.

pleasure *n* the gratification of the senses or of the mind; agreeable sensations or emotions; the feeling produced by enjoyment or the expectation of good; delight, opposed to *pain*; sensual or sexual gratification; what the will dictates or prefers; choice; wish; desire; a favour; arbitrary will or choice (*to go* or *stay at pleasure*).—*vt* (**pleasured, pleasuring**) to give or afford pleasure to; to please; to gratify.

pleat *n* any of various kinds of permanent fold made in fabric, etc, by flattening a gather or doubling back the material, etc.—*vt* to arrange in pleats; to fold.

plebeian *adj* pertaining to the common people; vulgar; common; belonging to the lower ranks.—*n* one of the common people; an unrefined, uncultured person.

plebiscite *n* a direct vote of a whole people or community; a decree of a country obtained by an appeal to the entire electorate.

plectrum *n* (*pl* **plectra**) a small instrument of plastic, wood, horn or metal used for striking the strings of a lyre, guitar or other stringed instrument.

pledge *n* (*law*) the transfer of a chattel by a debtor to a creditor in security of a debt; the thing pawned as security for the repayment of money borrowed or for the performance of some agreement or obligation; a pawn; anything given or considered as a security for the performance of an act; a guarantee; a solemn promise; a surety; a hostage; the drinking of another's health; toast.—**to take the pledge** to swear to abstain from alcoholic drink.—*vt* (**pledged, pledging**) to give as a pledge or pawn; to deposit in possession of a person as a security; to give as a guarantee or security; to gage (*to pledge one's word* or *honour*); to engage solemnly (*to pledge oneself*); to drink a health to.

Pleiad *n* (*pl* **Pleiads, Pleiades**) one of a cluster of seven stars in the neck of the constellation Taurus.

Pleiocene *adj* same as **Pliocene**.

Pleistocene *adj* (*geol*) of or denoting the first epoch of the Quaternary era, during which Homo sapiens appeared and the fossil remains of which belong almost wholly to existing species.—*n* the Pleistocene epoch.

plenary *adj* full; entire; complete.

plenipotence *n* fullness or completeness of power.

plenipotentiary *n* a person invested with full power to transact any business; particularly, an ambassador or envoy to a foreign court with full power to negotiate a treaty or to transact other business.—*adj* invested with or containing full power.

plenitude *n* the state of being full or complete; plenty; abundance; repletion.

plenteous *adj* abundant; copious; sufficient for every purpose; yielding abundance; having an abundance.

plectrum

plentiful *adj* existing in great quantity; copious; abundant; ample; fruitful.

plenty *n* abundance; copiousness; a full or adequate supply; sufficiency; abundance of things necessary for human beings (*a time of plenty*).—*adj* plentiful; being in abundance; very many.

pleonasm *n* redundancy of words in speaking or writing; the use of more words to express ideas than are necessary; a superfluous or tautological word or phrase.

plesiosaur, plesiosaurus *n* an extinct marine reptile of the Jurassic and Cretaceous periods, chiefly remarkable for its length of neck, nearly allied to the ichthyosaurs.

plethora *n* overfullness; a superabundance; (*med*) formerly, an excess of red corpuscles in the blood.

pleura *n* (*pl* **pleurae**) (*anat*) a thin membrane which covers the inside of the thorax and also envelops the lungs.

pleural *adj* pertaining to the pleura.

pleurisy, pleuritis *n* an inflammation of the pleura.

pleuritic *adj* pertaining to pleurisy; diseased with pleurisy.

plexus *n* (*pl* **plexuses, plexus**) (*anat*) a network of vessels, nerves or fibres.

pliability *n* the quality of being pliable; flexibility; a yielding to force or to moral influence.

pliable *adj* easily bent; flexible; pliant; flexible in disposition; easily persuaded.

pliancy *n* the state or quality of being pliant; easiness to be bent; readiness to be influenced.

pliant *adj* capable of being easily bent; readily yielding to force or pressure without breaking; flexible; lithe; limber; plastic; easily yielding to moral influence; easy to persuade.

plicate, plicated *adj* (*bot*) pleated; folded like a fan.

plication *n* a folding or fold; (*geol*) a bending back of strata on themselves.

plicature *n* a plication; a folding.

pliers *npl* a small pair of pincers adapted to handle small articles and also for bending and shaping wire.

plight *vt* to pledge, as one's word, hand, faith, honour; to give as a security for the performance of some act (never applied to property or goods and therefore differing from pledge, which is applied to property as well as to word, honour, etc).—*n* a pledge or security; condition; state; predicament; generally, a risky or dangerous state; a distressed condition (*to be in a wretched plight*).

plimsoll, plimsole *n* a light rubber-soled canvas shoe.

Plimsoll line *n* the line on the hull of a ship, regulating the load carried.

plinth *n* (*archit*) a flat slab, which serves as the foundation of a column; the flat table under the moulding of the base and pedestal, at the bottom of the order.

Pliocene, Pleiocine *adj, n* a geological term applied to the last division of the Tertiary epoch, the others being the Palaeocene, the Eocene, Oligocene and Miocene, the Palaeocene being the earliest.

plod *vi* (**plodded, plodding**) to walk or make one's way slowly or with steady laborious diligence; to study or work dully but with steady diligence; to toil; to trudge; to moil.—*vt* to go or walk over in a heavy labouring manner; to accomplish by toilsome exertion.

plodder *n* a dull, heavy, laborious person.

plodding *adj* given to plod or work with slow and patient diligence; patiently laborious.

plot *n* a scheme, stratagem or plan, usually a secret and underhand; an intrigue; a conspiracy; the story of a play, poem, novel or romance, comprising a complication of incidents; an intrigue; a small extent of ground of a well-defined shape; (*surv*) a plan or draught of a field, farm, estate, etc, on paper.—*vt* (**plotted, plotting**) to make a plan of; to plan; to devise; to contrive.—*vi* to form a scheme of mischief against another or against a government or those who administer it; to conspire; to contrive a plan.

plotter *n* one who plots; a conspirator.

plough *n* an agricultural implement usually drawn by mechanical power but also by animals which breaks up the surface of the ground to render it fit for receiving seed or for other agricultural operations; also, a name of various implements or tools, as a snowplough, a joiner's instrument for grooving, an instrument for cutting and smoothing the edges of books.—*vt* to till and turn up with a plough; to make furrows, grooves or ridges in; to force a way through; to work at laboriously (with *on*); to run into (with *into*); to reinvest (with *back*); (*sl*) to fail at examinations.—*vi* to turn up the soil with a plough.

ploughman *n* (*pl* **ploughmen**) one who ploughs or holds a plough; a farm labourer.

ploughshare *n* the share or part of a plough which cuts the ground at the bottom of the furrow.

plover *n* the common name of several species of wading birds generally seen in meadows, on the banks of rivers or on the seashore, including the golden plover, the dotterel and the ringed plover.

pluck[1] *vt* to gather; to pick; to cull, as berries or flowers; to pull with sudden force or effort; to twitch; to pull or draw, literally or figuratively; to strip by plucking; to strip feathers from (*to pluck a fowl*).

plough

pluck² *n* courage or spirit.

plucky *adj* spirited; courageous.

plug *n* anything used to stop a hole or leak, as a *bath plug*; a device which is attached to the cable of an electrical appliance and by which, when it is inserted into a wall or other socket, mains, etc, electrical power is fed to the appliance; a sparking plug for an internal-combustion engine; (*geol*) a volcanic plug, molten rock sealing the throat of a volcano that is no longer active; a heavy, often jointed, lure used in spinning for fish; (*colloq*) an adulatory and repeated mention (of a book, film, product) in the mass media; free (often self-) advertising; a quid of tobacco.—*vt* (**plugged, plugging**) to stop with a plug; to make tight by stopping a hole; to insert into a hole, electric socket, etc; (*colloq*) to make repeated favourable mentions in the mass media; (colloq) to shoot with a gun; (*colloq*) to work, especially long and steadily (with *at* or *away*).

plum *n* a common fleshy fruit containing a stone or kernel and when dried being called a *prune*; also, the tree producing it; a reddish-purple colour; a choice thing; a handsome sum or fortune.

plumage *n* the feathers that cover a bird.

plumb *n* a weight on the end of a line, used to test depth or check verticality; a plummet.—*adj* standing according to a plumb line; perpendicular.—*adv* in a perpendicular direction; (*colloq*) entirely.—*vt* to adjust by a plumb line; to set in a perpendicular direction; to sound with a plumb line; hence, to ascertain the capacity of; to test; to text the extremes of despair, grief, depression, etc (*to plumb the depths of misery*); to fit, connect, adapt, repair, etc, plumbing; to connect (an appliance) to plumbing (with *in*).

plumbago *n* one of a genus of flowering plants, some species of which are grown in gardens or kept as house plants; another name for **graphite**.

plumber *n* one who fits and repairs, pipes, fittings, appliances, etc, for water, drainage, sewage, gas, etc; one who plumbs; (rare) one who works in lead.

plumbing *n* the business of work of a plumber; the pipes, fittings, appliances, etc, used for water supply, drainage, sewage, gas, etc; (rare) the business or skills of working in lead.

plumbism *n* poisoning by lead taken into the system.

plumb line *n* a line with a metal weight attached to one end, used to determine a perpendicular; a line perpendicular to the plane of the horizon.

plumb rule *n* a narrow board with a plumb line attached, used by masons, bricklayers, etc, for determining a perpendicular.

plum cake *n* cake containing raisins, currants or other fruits.

plume *n* the feather of a bird, particularly a large or conspicuous feather; a feather or collection of feathers worn as an ornament; anything resembling a feather (*a plume of spray*); token of honour; prize of contest.—*vt* (**plumed, pluming**) to pick and adjust the feathers of; to strip of feathers; to adorn with feathers or plumes; to pride (with *on* or *upon*); to boast (in this sense used reflexively).

plummet *n* a piece of lead or other metal attached to a line, used in sounding the depth of water; a plumb or plumb line.—*vi* to fall vertically; to plunge.

plump¹ *adj* swelled with fat or flesh to the full size; rounded; well filled; chubby; fat or stout in person.—*vt* to make plump; to fatten.—*vi* to become plump.

plump² *vt* to cause to fall suddenly and heavily.—*vi* to plunge or fall like a heavy mass or lump of dead matter; to fall suddenly or at once; to opt for.—*n* a sudden drop or plunge; the sound of this.—*adv* at once or with a sudden heavy fall; suddenly; heavily.

plum pudding *n* pudding containing raisins or currants.

plumule *n* (*bot*) the growing point of the embryo, situated at the apex of the radical and at the base of the cotyledons, by which it is protected when young; the rudiment of the future stem of a plant.

plunder *vt* to take goods or valuables forcibly from; to pillage; to spoil; to rob in a hostile way; to take by pillage or open force; (*colloq*) to take, often hastily or greedily.—*n* the act of plundering; robbery; that which is taken from an enemy by force; pillage; spoil; that which is taken by theft, robbery or fraud; loot.

plunge *vt* (**plunged, plunging**) to thrust into water or other fluid substance or into any substance easily penetrable; to immerse; to thrust; to thrust or drive into any state or condition (*to plunge a nation into war*); to baptize by immersion.—*vi* to thrust or drive oneself into water or other fluid; to dive or to rush in; to fall or rush into distress or any state or circumstances in which the person or thing is enveloped, enclosed or overwhelmed (*to plunge into war*); to throw the body forward and the hind legs up, as an unruly horse.—*n* a dive, rush or leap into something; the act of pitching or throwing the body forward and the hind legs up, as an unruly horse.

plunger *n* a solid cylinder that operates with a plunging motion, as a piston; a large rubber suction cup used to unblock drains; (*colloq*) an electrical device, operated by a plunger, for detonating explosive charges; (*colloq*) a rash or heedless gambler.

pluperfect *adj*, *n* (*gram*) (applied to) that tense of a verb which denotes that an action was finished at a certain period to which the speaker refers (*he had done it*).

plural *adj* containing more than one; consisting of two or more or designating two or more; (*gram*) the plural number is that number or form of a word which designates more than one.—*n* a form of a word expressing more than one; the plural number.

pluralism *n* the simultaneous holding of more than one office or benefice; a theory that reality is composed of a plurality of entities; a theory that there are at least two levels of ultimate reality; the coexistence in society of people of distinct ethnic, cultural or religious groups, each preserving their own traditions; a doctrine or policy advocating this condition.

pluralist *n* a clergyman who holds more ecclesiastical benefices than one; a person who adheres to or propounds a theory of society as a number of self-governing but interdependent groups of equal power.

plurality *n* the state of being plural; an aggregate of two or more of the same kind; (*math*) a number greater than one; the greater number; the majority; (*eccles*) the holding of two or more benefices together; one of two or more benefices held by the same clergyman.

plus *n* (*alg*, *arith*) the name of a character (+) which being placed between two numbers or quantities, signifies that they are to be added together; frequently used prepositionally, with the meaning of *in addition to* (*ability plus impudence*); an advantage; a benefit; an extra.

plus-fours *n* wide knickerbockers, with four inches overlap below the knee.

plush *n* a textile fabric with a sort of velvet nap or shag on one side resembling short hairs.—*adj* made of plush; (*colloq*) richly appointed; extravagantly comfortable.

Pluto *n* in Roman myth, the god of the dead and ruler of the underworld; (*astron*) the most remote of the planets, discovered in 1930.

plutocracy *n* the power or rule of wealth; a class or group that wields power because of its wealth; a nation governed by the rule of the wealthy.

plutocrat *n* a person possessing power or influence solely or mainly owing to his riches; a member of a plutocracy.

Plutonian *adj* of or relating to Pluto or to the regions of fire; subterranean; dark.

plutonic *adj* (*geol*) formed from magma cooling beneath the earth's surface.

plutonium *n* a man-made radioactive metallic element, discovered while the atomic bomb was being perfected and later used in nuclear power and nuclear weapons.

pluvial *adj* rainy; humid; relating to rain; (*geol*) applied to results and operations which depend on or arise from the action of rain.

pluviometer *n* a rain gauge.

pluvious *adj* rainy; pluvial.

ply *vt* (**plied, plying**) to employ with diligence (*to ply a needle* or *an oar*); to keep busy; to practise or perform with diligence; to busy oneself in; to press hard with blows or missiles; to assail briskly; to beset; to urge; to solicit, as for a favour.—*vi* to be steadily employed; to work steadily; to offer service; to run regularly between any two ports or places, as a vessel or vehicle; (*naut*) to endeavour to make way against the wind.—**to ply with** to present or offer to urgently and repeatedly; to press upon, especially with some ulterior object (*to ply one with flattery*).—*n* a fold; a plait; a twist, a layer (often used in composition to designate the number of twists, etc, as *a three-ply carpet*); bent; turn; direction; bias.

Plymouth Brethren *npl* a sect of Christians founded in Plymouth about 1827 and noted for its puritanical outlook.

plywood *n* compound wood made of three or more layers glued together in sheets under pressure and so arranged that the grains of adjacent layers run in different directions.

pneumatic *adj* consisting of or resembling air; having the properties of a gas; pertaining to air or to gases or their properties; moved or played by means of air; filled with or fitted to contain air; applied to numerous instruments, machines, apparatus, etc, for experimenting on gases or for working by means of the compression or exhaustion of air (*a pneumatic tyre*; *a pneumatic drill*).

pneumatics *n* the science dealing with the mechanical properties of air.

pneumonia *n* (*med*) an acute and serious inflammation of the lungs.

pneumonic *adj* pertaining to the lungs.

pneumonic plague *n* see **plague**.

pneumoskeleton *n* a hard structure connected with the breathing organs of certain animals, as the shell of a mollusc.

poach[1] *vt* to cook (eggs, fish, etc) by simmering in boiling water, stock, milk, wine, etc.

poach[2] *vi* to intrude or encroach on the property of another to steal or plunder; to steal game or carry it away clandestinely; to kill or destroy game contrary to law; to encroach on another's rights, etc; to take someone away (from employment, a team, etc) by the use of blandishment.

poacher[1] *n* a pan with shallow cups for poaching eggs; a dish for poaching fish, etc.

plus-fours

poacher² *n* one who poaches or steals game; one who kills game unlawfully.

pochard *n* any of a genus of migratory diving ducks, common in Europe.

pock *n* a pustule raised on the surface of the body in an eruptive disease, as smallpox.

pocket *n* a small bag inserted in a garment for carrying small articles; a small bag or net to receive the balls in billiards, etc; a small cavity in a rock or on its surface, containing gold; a mass of rich ore; an isolated or enclosed area.—**to be in pocket** to have gain or profit from some transaction.—**to be out of pocket** to expend or lose money.—*adj* small enough to fit the pocket (*a pocketknife*); hence, smaller than the norm (*pocket battleship, pocket Venus*).—*vt* to put or conceal in the pocket; to take clandestinely.

pocketbook *n* a small book or case, used for carrying papers in the pocket; a wallet; a small paperback book.

pocket borough *n* formerly, an English borough, the power of electing a member of parliament for which was in the hands of one or a few persons (abolished by the Reform Act of 1832).

pocketful *n* enough to fill a pocket; as much as a pocket will hold.

pocket handkerchief *n* a handkerchief carried in the pocket for use.

pocketknife *n* (*pl* **pocketknives**) a knife suited for carrying in the pocket with one or more blades which fold into the handle.

pocket money *n* a child's allowance; money for the pocket or for occasional expenses; a small or mean amount.

pockmark *n* a small skin depression or scar caused by acne, smallpox, etc; something resembling a pockmark.—*vt* to scar with pockmarks.

poco *adv* (*mus*) a little, a word frequently prefixed to another to lessen the strength of its meaning (*poco largo*, a little slow).

pococurante *n* one who cares little; an apathetic, careless, indifferent person.

pococurantism *n* the character, disposition or habits of a pococurante; extreme indifference, apathy or carelessness.

pod *n* a dry fruit or seed vessel, as of peas, beans, etc; a protective container or housing; a detachable compartment on a spacecraft.—*vi* (**podded, podding**) to swell and assume the appearance of a pod; to produce pods.—*vt* to remove the pod from.

podagra *n* gout in the foot.

podgy *adj* pudgy; fat and short.

podophthalmic *adj* having the eyes borne at the end of long foot stalks, as in certain crustaceans.

poe bird *n* the tui; the parson bird.

poem *n* a work of poetry; a metrical composition; a composition in which the verses consist of certain measures, whether in blank verse or in rhyme; a composition in which the language is that of excited imagination; (*colloq*) a performance, etc, the execution of which demonstrates a rare skill, beauty, etc; (*colloq*) someone or something of exceptional grace, fineness, beauty, etc.

poesy *n* the art of or skill in composing poems; poetry; metrical composition.

poet *n* the author of a poem; the composer of a metrical composition; one skilled in making poetry or who has a particular genius for metrical composition; one distinguished for poetic talents or whose principal work is the writing of poetry.

poetaster *n* a petty poet; a pitiful rhymer or writer of verses.

poetic, poetical *adj* pertaining to poetry; suitable to poetry; expressed in poetry; having a metrical form; possessing the peculiar beauties of poetry.

poetic justice *n* formerly, a distribution of rewards and punishments such as is common in poetry and works of fiction but hardly in accordance with the realities of life; now chiefly retribution.

poetic licence *n* a liberty or licence taken by a poet with regard to matters of fact or language in order to produce a desired effect, e.g. rhyming *poet* with *note*.

poetics *n* the theory, study or criticism of the nature and laws of poetry.

poet laureate *n* in the UK, an officer belonging to the Royal Household, who was formerly required to compose an ode annually for the sovereign's birthday, for a great national victory, etc, a requirement discontinued since the reign of George III, the post being now a sinecure; hence, a poet regarded as being at the head of his or her profession or excelling in some branch of his or her art.

poetry *n* that branch of the fine arts which exhibits its special character and powers by means of language; the art which has for its object the creation of intellectual pleasure by means of imaginative and passionate language, generally in verse; the language of the imagination or emotions rhythmically expressed, or such language expressed in an elevated style of prose; in a wide sense whatever appeals to the finer emotions or the sense of ideal beauty; metrical composition; verse; poems; (*colloq*) any act or thing that displays a special skill, grace or beauty.

pogo stick *n* a stilt with a powerful spring used to hop along the ground.

pogrom *n* an organized massacre or attack on a minority group of racial or religious origins different from those of the attackers; genocidal murder of large numbers of people.

poignant *adj* stimulating the organs of

pocket handkerchief

taste; piquant; pointed; keen; bitter; irritating; satirical; severe; piercing; very painful or acute; deeply moving.

poind *vt* (*Scots law*) to enclose in a pound or pen; to distrain; to seize and sell a debtor's goods under proper warrant.

point *n* the mark made by the end of a sharp piercing instrument, such as a pin, a needle, etc; hence, an indefinitely small space; (*geom*) that which has neither length, breadth, nor thickness—that by the motion of which a line is considered to be produced; a mark of punctuation, a full point or full stop; a dot placed before a decimal fraction to show that it is a decimal; a division of the card of the mariner's compass; north, south, east and west or any intermediate direction; any place marked in the heavens of importance in astronomical calculations; that which pricks, pierces or punctures; particularly the sharp end of a thorn, pin, needle, knife, sword, etc; a tool or instrument which pricks or pierces; a small cape or promontory; formerly, a lace, string, etc, with a tag used for fastening articles of dress; lace worked by the needle (*petit point*); a lively turn of thought or expression which strikes with force or agreeable surprise; the sting of an epigram; hence, force or expression generally (*his action gave point to his words*); a salient trait of character; a peculiarity; a characteristic (*the good* or *bad points of a man*); a certain external characteristic of an animal (*the points of a horse, dog,* etc); single thing or subject; matter (*right in every point*); particular thing desired or required; aim; purpose (*the point of the exercise*); a single part of a complicated question or of a whole; the purpose or salient principle of a discussion or argument (*to get the point, to come to the point*); an indivisible part of time or space; the eve or verge (*at the point of death*); an electrical socket; (*pl*) the switches or movable guiding rails at junctions or stations on railways; a fielder in the game of cricket who stands a little to the off side of the batter's wicket or the spot where he or she stands; (*pl*) the tips of a pair of ballet shoes; a mark to denote the degree of success or progress attained in certain trials of skill and games, as in rifle-shooting, rugby football, cards, etc, a single point counting one; a unit used to measure the performance of commodities and securities; (*print*) a unit for measuring the body of type equal to one seventy-second of an inch.—*vt* to give a point to; to cut, forge, grind or file to a point; to add to the force or expression of; to direct towards an object or place; to aim; to direct the eye or notice of; to indicate the purpose or point of; (*mus*) to mark the text of (a psalm) to indicate where the chant alters when it is sung; to punctuate; in masonry, to fill the joints of with mortar and smooth them with the point of a trowel.—*vi* to direct the finger or other object, such as a pencil, stick, etc, for designating an object and drawing attention to it (with *at*); to indicate the presence of game by standing and turning the nose in its direction, as pointer dogs do; to show distinctly by any means.

point-blank *adj* (of a firearm, especially an artillery piece) fired horizontally without allowance for the fall of shot; at so close a range that the shot has not travelled far enough to begin to fall (*point-blank range*); (*fig*) direct; plain; explicit; express.—*adv* closely, at close range; horizontally; (*fig*) directly; bluntly (*he told me point-blank*).

pointed *adj* having a sharp point; aimed at or expressly referring to some particular person (*a pointed remark*); epigrammatic; conspicuous.

pointer *n* one who or that which points; a breed of sporting dog noted for its habit of pointing game.

pointing *n* punctuation; marks or points made; the raking out of the mortar from between the joints of a stone or brick wall and replacing the same with new mortar.

point-lace *n* a fine kind of lace worked with a needle.

pointless *adj* having no point; blunt; purposeless; meaningless.

pointsman *n* (*pl* **pointsmen**) a man who has charge of the points or switches on a railway.

poise *vt* (**poised, poising**) to balance in weight; to make of equal weight; to hold or place in equilibrium; to load with weight for balancing.—*vi* to be balanced or suspended on the point of action; to hover; to be ready; (*fig*) to hang in suspense.—*n* a dignified, calm or imperturbable bearing; physical balance or confidence in a person or animal; equipoise; self-assurance; weight; gravity; a thing suspended or attached as a counterweight; a counterpoise; hence, regulating power; that which balances; the weight used in weighing with steelyards, to balance the substance weighed; balance; equilibrium.

poison *n* any agent capable of producing an abnormal, noxious, dangerous or deadly effect, when introduced either by absorption through the skin, respiration or ingestion; that which taints or destroys moral purity or health; malice.—*vt* to infect with poison; to put poison in or on; to add poison to; to attack, injure or kill by poison; to destroy; to taint; to mar, impair, vitiate, corrupt.

poisoner *n* one who or that which poisons or corrupts.

poison

poison fang *n* one of the long, sharp upper teeth of poisonous snakes, through which venom is conveyed into the wound when they bite.

poison gas *n* any noxious gas, such as chlorine or phosgene, especially when used against troops in warfare.

poisonous *adj* having the qualities of poison; containing poison; venomous; corrupting; malicious; pernicious; spiteful.

poison-pen letter *n* an abusive, often threatening, anonymous letter.

poke[1] *vt* (**poked, poking**) to thrust something long or pointed against, as the hand or a stick; hence, to feel or search, as in the dark or in a hole; (*sl*) to hit.—*vi* to grope; to search; to feel or push one's way, as in the dark; to busy oneself without a definite object (followed by *about*).—*n* a thrust; a jab; a sudden push.

poke[2] *n* a pocket; a pouch; a bag; a sack.

poker[1] *n* one who pokes; an iron or steel bar or rod used in poking or stirring a coal fire.

poker[2] *n* a game of cards in which players bet on the value of their hands to win a pool.

poker face *n* an expressionless face, like that of a poker player concealing his or her intentions or the worth of his or her hand of cards.

pokerwork *n* ornamental work produced by singeing the surface of white wood with a heated poker.

poky, pokey *adj* narrow or confined as to space; small and uncomfortable; slow or dull.

polar *adj* pertaining to a pole or the poles of a sphere; pertaining to one of the poles of the earth or of the heavens; proceeding from the poles of the earth; pertaining to a magnetic pole or poles; pertaining to the points of a body at which its attractive or repulsive energy is concentrated; having positive and negative electricity diametrically opposite.

polar bear *n* a large creamy-white bear that inhabits Arctic regions.

polarimeter *n* an instrument for measuring the polarization of light.

Polaris *n* the Pole Star; an American-built medium-range ballistic missile mainly designed to be fired from a submerged submarine.

pole vault

polariscope *n* an instrument for detecting polarized light.

polarity *n* the condition of being polar; (*elect*) the state, positive or negative, of a body; the magnet's property of turning north; attraction towards a particular object or in a specific direction; diametrical opposition; an instance of such opposition.

polarization *n* the act of polarizing or giving polarity to a body; the state of being polarized or of having polarity; the pro-

duction or acquirement of polarity; the process of causing light waves to vibrate in a uniform, circular or linear pattern; the separation of positive and negative electric charges; the grouping into opposing factions; concentration.

polarize *vt* (**polarized, polarizing**) to cause (light waves) to vibrate in a definite pattern; to give physical polarity to; to break up into opposite factions; to concentrate.

polder *n* in the Netherlands, a tract of land below the level of the sea or nearest river, which, being originally a morass or lake, has been drained and brought under cultivation.

pole[1] *n* a long slender piece of wood; a tall piece of timber (frequently used in composition, as *a fishing pole, a maypole*); a perch or rod, a measure of length equal to $5 \frac{1}{2}$ yards.—*vt* (**poled, poling**) to furnish with poles for support; to bear or convey on poles; to impel (a small vessel) by poles; to push forward by the use of poles.

pole[2] *n* one of the two points in which the axis of the earth meets its surface; one of the extremities of the earth's axis, the North or South Pole; the Pole Star; one of the points of a body at which its attractive or repulsive energy is concentrated or in which a polar force is exerted; in magnetism, one of the two points at which the magnetic strength of a magnet is principally concentrated; either of two opposed forces, parts, etc, as the terminals on a battery; either of two opposed principles.— **poles apart** completely different.

Pole *n* a native of Poland.

poleaxe *n* a kind of axe or hatchet; a butcher's axe, used for stunning animals.—*vt* (**poleaxed, poleaxing**) to hit with such an axe; to hit very hard.—*vi* to be stunned with surprise, grief, delight, etc.

polecat *n* a small, dark-brown animal of the weasel family, very destructive to poultry, rabbits, game, etc, and noted for its powerful musky smell; also, a name for the ferret or skunk.

polemic, polemical *adj* pertaining to polemics; given to controversy; engaged in supporting an opinion or system by controversy.

polemics *n* the art or practice of disputation; controversy; controversial writings.

polenta *n* in Italy, a kind of thick pudding made from semolina or maize meal.

pole star *n* that which serves as guide or director; a lode star.

Pole Star *n* the star nearest the North Pole, round which it describes a small circle.

pole vault *n* a field event in which competitors jump over a high bar using a long flexible pole.

police *n* the means instituted by a government or community to maintain public order, liberty, property and individual security; the organized civil body by which the municipal laws and regulations are enforced and public order maintained.—*vt* (**policed, policing**) to supply with police; to control, protect, etc, with police; to guard.

policeman, policewoman *n* (*pl* **policemen, policewomen**) one of the police.

police officer *n* a policeman or policewoman.

police state *n* a totalitarian state controlled by a repressive political police.

police station *n* the headquarters of the police or of a section of them, the place to which offenders are taken in the first instance.

policy[1] *n* the art or manner of governing a nation; the line of conduct which the rulers of a nation adopt on particular questions, especially with regard to foreign countries; the principles on which any measure or course of action is based; prudence or wisdom of governments or individuals in the management of their affairs public or private; dexterity of management; the grounds of a country house, especially those which have been improved by plantings, etc.

policy[2] *n* a written contract by which a corporation or other persons engage to pay a certain sum on certain contingencies, as in the case of fire or shipwreck, in the event of death, etc, on the condition of receiving a fixed sum or percentage on the amount of the risk or certain periodical payments or premiums.

poliomyelitis *n* an acute infectious viral disease marked by inflammation of the nerve cells in the spinal cord and sometimes causing paralysis; infantile paralysis.

polish *vt* to make smooth and glossy, usually by friction; to burnish; to deprive of rudeness, rusticity or coarseness; to make elegant and polite (*to polish life* or *manners*).—*vi* to become smooth; to take a smooth and glossy surface; to become refined.—*n* a substance used to impart a gloss; a smooth glossy surface produced by friction; artificial gloss; refinement; elegance of manners.

Polish *adj* pertaining to Poland or to its inhabitants.—*n* the language of the Poles.

polite *adj* polished or elegant in manners; refined in behaviour; well-bred; courteous.

politic *adj* consisting of citizens; constituting the state (*the body politic*); prudent and sagacious in devising and pursuing measures adapted to promote the public welfare; well devised and adapted to the public prosperity; ingenious in devising and pursuing any scheme of personal or national aggrandizement; cunning; artful;

shrewdly tactful; sagacious in adapting means to an end; well devised; adapted to its end, right or wrong.

political *adj* having a fixed or regular system or administration; concerned in state affairs or national measures; pertaining to a nation or state, or to nations or states, as distinguished from civil or municipal; treating of politics or government; full of intrigue.

political asylum protection given by one country to a refugee from another who has left because he or she was in danger from the authorities because of political views.

political correctness *n* (often abbreviated to **PC**) a movement aiming to remove discrimination against all minorities and to promote equal opportunities for them.

political economy *n* an old name for **economics**.

politician *n* one versed in the science of government and the art of governing; one skilled in politics; one who occupies himself or herself with politics.

politics *n* the science of government; that part of ethics which relates to the regulation and government of a nation or state for the preservation of its safety, peace and prosperity; political affairs or the conduct and contests of political parties; manoeuvring and intriguing.

polity *n* the form or constitution of civil government of a nation or state; the constitution or fundamental principles of government of any body of citizens; the recognized principles on which any institution is based.

polka *n* a dance of Bohemian origin, the music to which is in 2/4 time with the third quaver accented; a tune for the dance.

polka dot *n* any of a pattern of small round dots forming a pattern on cloth.

poll[1] *n* the head of a person or the back part of the head; a catalogue or register of heads, that is, of persons; the voting or registering of votes for candidates in elections (*the close of the poll*); a sampling of general opinion; an opinion poll.—*vt* to remove (the top or head of); to lop, clip, shear; to cut closely; to mow; to register or give (a vote); to bring to the poll; to receive or elicit, as a number of votes or voters; to canvass (people) for their opinions about specific subjects or questions, as in an opinion poll.—*vi* to vote at a poll; to record a vote, as an elector.

poll[2] *n* a familiar name often applied to a parrot.

pollack *n* a species of marine fish belonging to the cod family.

pollan, powan *n* a species of small freshwater fish found in the inland loughs and lochs of Ireland and Scotland.

pollard *n* a tree with the branches cut off at

some height from the ground to induce it to throw out new growth all round the section where amputation has taken place; a stag that has cast his horns; also, a cow, sheep, etc, that has cast its horns or had them removed; (*arch*) a coarse product of wheat but finer than bran.—*vt* to make a pollard of; to convert into a pollard by cutting off the branches; to de-horn or poll.

pollen *n* the male element in flowering plants; the fine dust or powder which by contact with the stigma effects the fertilization of the seeds.

polling booth *n* a temporary erection in a polling station in which to record votes at an election.

polling station *n* a place officially designed for the recording of votes in an election.

pollster *n* a person who conducts a public opinion poll or compiles data obtained from it.

poll tax *n* a tax of a fixed amount per person levied on a population; a capitation tax.

pollute *vt* (**polluted, polluting**) to make foul or unclean; to contaminate with toxic matter or effluent; to render impure; to defile; to soil; to taint; to corrupt or defile in a moral sense; to impair; to profane.

polo

polluter *n* one who pollutes or profanes.

pollution *n* the act of polluting; the state of being polluted; defilement; uncleanness; impurity.

polo *n* a ball game resembling hockey but played on horseback using long mallets; water polo; a polo neck.

polonaise *n* a stately or formal Polish dance in 3/4 time; a melody written for or in imitation of such a dance; a woman's dress modelled on Polish costume.

polo neck *n* a long tubular collar turned back on itself; a sweater with such a collar.

polonium *n* a naturally occurring radioactive chemical element.

polony *n* a kind of smoked sausage made of pork and other meats.

polo shirt *n* a sports shirt made of a knitted fabric with an open neck fastened by buttons.

poltergeist *n* a noisy type of spirit, which is supposed to manifest its presence by slamming doors, breaking crockery, etc.

poltroon *n* an arrant coward; a dastard; a wretch without spirit or courage.—*adj* base; vile; contemptible.

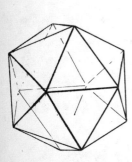

polygon

poltroonery *n* cowardice; lack of spirit.

polyandry *n* the practice of women having more husbands than one at the same time; plurality of husbands.

polyanthus *n* (*pl* **polyanthuses**) one of the many varieties of hybrid garden primrose with clusters of small coloured flowers.

polyatomic *adj* (*chem*) having more than one atom in the molecule; having more than one replaceable atom or radical.

polybasic *adj* (*chem*) of substances in which the molecule contains two or more hydrogen atoms capable of replacement by basic atoms or radicals.

polycotyledon *n* (*bot*) a plant that has many or more than two cotyledons or lobes to the seed.

polyester *n* any of a class of complex organic compounds used in making synthetic resins, plastics and mixed with other fibres in many crease-resistant fabrics.

polyethylene *n* same as **polythene**.

polygam *n* a polygamian plant.

polygamian *adj* (*bot*) pertaining to a class of plants producing hermaphrodite flowers, with male or female flowers or both.

polygamist *n* a person who practises polygamy or who maintains its lawfulness.

polygamous *adj* relating to or characterized by polygamy (*polygamous marriages*); having a plurality of wives; (*bot*) polygamian; (*zool*) having more than one mate in any breeding season.

polygamy *n* a plurality of wives at the same time or the having of such plurality; (*bot*) the condition of being polygamian; (*zool*) the practice of having more than one mate in a breeding season.

polygenesis *n* the doctrine that the human races descend from different original ancestors; (*biol*) the evolution of organisms descended from two or more ancestral groups.

polygenous *adj* consisting of many kinds.

polyglot —*adj* having command of many languages; composed of numerous languages; containing matter in several languages; composed of elements from different languages.—*n* a person who speaks many languages; a book containing many languages, particularly a Bible that presents the Scriptures in several languages; a mixture of languages.

polygon *n* (*geom*) a plane figure of many angles and straight sides or at least of more than three sides.

polygonal *adj* having the form of a polygon; having many angles.

polygyn *n* (*bot*) a plant having flowers with many pistils, more than twelve.

polygynist *n* one who practices polygyny.

polygyny *n* polygamy in male humans and animals; (*bot*) a state in certain flowers in which they show different styles, by virtue of their having many pistils.

polyhedral *adj* forming a polyhedron; having many sides.

polyhedron *n* (*geom*) a solid bounded by many polygonal faces or planes and when all the faces are regular polygons the solid becomes a regular body.

polymath *n* a person of deep and wide-ranging learning.

polymer *n* (*chem*) a compound, natural or

synthetic, that has large molecules composed of many simpler molecules.

polymorphic, polymorphous *adj* having many forms; assuming or going through many forms.

polymorphism *n* (*biol*) the property in a single species of existing in different forms; (*chem*) the property of crystallizing in two or more fundamental forms.

Polynesian *adj* of or pertaining to Polynesia, the region of many islands in the Pacific.—*n* a native or inhabitant of Polynesia.

polyp *n* (*zool*) a name loosely applied to what were once known as radiate animals, having the mouth surrounded by more or less numerous arms or tentacles, now commonly applied to the hydra, the sea anemone and their related coelenterates; a zoophyte; (*med*) a growth on mucous membrane.

polypean *adj* pertaining to a polyp.

polyphonic *adj* having or consisting of many voices or sounds; contrapuntal.

polyphony *n* multiplicity of sounds or voices; (*mus*) a composition consisting of two or more parts progressing simultaneously according to the rules of counterpoint.

polypiferous *adj* producing polyps.

polypite *n* the fundamental portion of a hydrozoan.

polypod *n* an animal having many feet, such as the millipede or the woodlouse.

polypody *n* a name of various ferns, one of them common to Britain and North America.

polypoid *adj* like a polyp.

polyprismatic *adj* (of a mineral) having crystals presenting numerous prisms in a single form.

polystyrene *n* a plastic material used in rigid form or in the form of a light white expanded foam for packing, insulating etc.

polysyllabic *adj* consisting of many syllables or of more than two.

polysyllable *n* a word of many syllables, that is, consisting of two or more syllables.

polytechnic *n* an educational institution that provides part- or full-time courses in many applied sciences and technical subjects.

polytheism *n* the doctrine of a plurality of gods; belief in or worship of more than one god.

polytheist *n* a person who believes in a plurality of gods.

polytheistic *adj* pertaining to polytheism; holding a plurality of gods.

polythene, polyethylene *n* a light, plastic, multipurpose synthetic material which is resistant to moisture and chemicals.

polytonality *n* (*mus*) the use of two or more keys at the same time.

polyunsaturated *adj* (of a fat or oil) lacking hydrogen bonds at several points in its carbon chain and thus reacting with other compounds.

polyvinyl chloride *n* (often abbreviated to **PVC**) a synthetic thermoplastic originating as a colourless solid, having a good resistance to water, alkalis, acids and alcohol, and used in making many industrial and domestic fabrics as well as hoses, insulation, shoes etc.

polyzoan, bryozoan *n* any of a class of invertebrate animals, chiefly marine polyps, forming compound groups or colonies, being the lowest members of the molluscs.

pomace *n* the substance of apples or of similar fruit crushed by grinding and then pressed.

pomaceous *adj* like pomace; pertaining to the apple family of trees.

pomade *n* perfumed ointment, especially ointment for the hair; pomatum.

pomander *n* a mixture of perfumes and spices contained in a sachet or a ball (originally a hollowed-out orange), formerly carried as a protection against infection or for its pleasant smell; a container for such a mixture.

pomatum *n* a perfumed unguent used in dressing the hair; pomade.

pomegranate *n* a fruit as large as an orange, with a hard rind filled with a soft red pulp and numerous grains or seeds; the shrub that bears such fruit, originally from Asia.

Pomeranian *n* a breed of small dog (black, white or chocolate) with a long coat, bushy tail, sharp muzzle and pointed ears, originally from Pomerania in Prussia.

pommel *n* a knob or ball; the knob on the hilt of a sword; the protuberant part of a saddle bow; a round knob on the frame of a chair.—*vt* (**pommelled, pommelling**) to pummel; to beat with repeated blows; to bruise.

pomology *n* the branch of knowledge that deals with the study of fruits and the cultivation of fruit trees.

pomp *n* stately and ceremonial magnificence; splendour; display; vanity or ostentation, especially in those standing upon their dignity or self-importance.

pom-pom *n* quick-firing automatic cannon, especially a light anti-aircraft weapon.

pompon *n* a ball of feathers, wool, artificial flowers, etc, worn as an ornament for a bonnet or hat, on a clown's costume, etc.

pomposity *n* pompousness; pompous display; show; ostentation; self-importance; vain and over-exaggerated sense of worth in a person's speech, manner, style, etc.

pompous *adj* showing self-importance; exhibiting an exaggerated sense of dignity; ostentatious; (*arch*) displaying pomp; splendid.

poncho *n* (*pl* **ponchos**) in Spanish America,

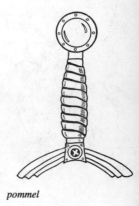

pommel

a garment like a narrow blanket with a slit in the middle for the head to pass through.

pond *n* a body of still water of less extent than a lake, either artificial or natural.

ponder *vt* to weigh carefully in the mind; to think about; to reflect on; to examine carefully.—*vi* to think; to muse; to deliberate (with *on* or *over*).

ponderable *adj* capable of being evaluated or estimated; substantial; capable of being weighed; having weight.

ponderous *adj* very heavy; of great weight; massive; weighty; forcible; without grace; awkward; heavy-footed; long-winded or circumlocutory.

pond lily *n* the waterlily.

pondweed *n* a name of several British water weeds.

poniard *n* a small dagger; a pointed weapon for stabbing.—*vt* (*arch*) to pierce with a poniard; to stab.

pontifex *n* (*pl* **pontifices**) the name by which the Romans designated the highest members of their great colleges of priests, the chief being termed Pontifex Maximus.

pontiff *n* a high priest; a designation of the pope; (*arch*) a bishop.

pontifical *adj* relating to pontiffs or priests; relating to a pope; belonging to the pope; in a lofty manner, expressive of infallibility of speaker; pompous.—*n* a book containing ecclesiastical rites and ceremonies (*pl*) the dress and ornaments of a pope, priest or bishop.

pontificate *n* the state or dignity of a high priest; the office or dignity of the pope; the papacy; the reign of a pope.—*vi* (**pontificated, pontificating**) to speak pompously or dogmatically, as if an expert on the subject; to officiate at a pontifical Mass.

pontoon *n* a flat-bottomed boat or any light framework or floating body used in the construction of a temporary military bridge over a river; a lighter; a low flat vessel resembling a barge; a watertight structure placed beneath a submerged vessel and then filled with air, to assist in refloating the vessel; a card game, also called **vingt-et-un** or **twenty-one**.

pony *n* any of a number of varieties of small horse; (*sl*) £25.

poodle *n* any of several varieties of dog, usually small and covered with long curling hair, often clipped.

pooh *interj* an expression of dislike, scorn or contempt.

pooh-pooh *vt* to express scorn or contempt for; to sneer at; to disparage or dismiss.

pool[1] *n* a small collection of water or other liquid in a hollow place; a small piece of stagnant water; a hole in the course of a stream deeper than the ordinary bed; a puddle of liquid; a subterranean deposit or reservoir of oil or gas; a swimming pool.

pool[2] *n* the receptacle for the stakes at certain games of cards, billiards, etc; the stakes themselves; a game played on a billiard table with six pockets; a combination of resources, funds, supplies, etc; the parties forming this combination.—*vti* to contribute to a common fund; to share.

poon *n* one of a genus of Southeast Asia trees valued for their wood; the wood of these trees.

poop[1] *n* the highest and aftermost part of a ship's deck, raised above the main deck of the vessel.—*vt* (*naut*) to break heavily over the stern or quarter of; to drive in the stern of.

poop[2] *vt* (*colloq*) to exhaust, to tire; to become exhausted.

poor *adj* lacking riches; not having property sufficient for a comfortable subsistence; needy; lacking good or desirable qualities; having little value or importance; trifling; insignificant; paltry; mean; lacking fertility; barren; lacking intellectual or artistic merit (*a poor discourse*); lacking in spirit or vigour; weak; impotent; worthy of pity; ill-fated; a word of tenderness or endearment (*poor thing*); a word of slight contempt; wretched.

poor box *n* a box to receive money for the poor.

poorhouse *n* (*hist*) a residence for persons receiving public charity.

poor law *n* (*hist*) a law or the laws collectively established for the management of the funds for the maintenance of the poor.

poorly *adv* in a poor manner or condition; in indigence; with little or no success; in an inferior manner; insufficiently; defectively.—*adj* somewhat ill; indisposed; not in health.

pop[1] *n* a small sharp sound or report; (*colloq*) any carbonated, non-alcoholic beverage.—*vi* (**popped, popping**) to make a small sharp sound; to burst open with this sound; to appear suddenly (*with up*); to enter or issue forth with a quick, sudden motion; to dart; to start from a place suddenly; (of the eyes) to bulge.—*vt* to thrust forward or offer suddenly; to thrust or push suddenly with a quick motion; to go or come quickly; to put suddenly; to roast (corn, maize) until it pops; (*sl*) to pawn; (*sl*) to take (especially pills) frequently.

pop[2] *adj* in a popular modern style.—*n* pop music; pop art

pop[3] *n* (*colloq*) father.

pop art *n* a form of modern art using techniques and subjects from commercial art, advertising literature, comic strips, etc.

popcorn *n* a kind of corn or maize, which, when heated, puffs up or pops.

pope[1] *n* the Bishop of Rome, the head of the Roman Catholic Church; in the Greek Orthodox Church, a priest or chaplain, or oc-

poodle

pony

casionally the patriarch of Alexandria; any figure of great authority.

pope² *n* the ruffe.

popery *n* (*derog*) the religion of the Church of Rome, comprehending doctrines and practice.

pop group a small group of musicians who, together with a singer or singers, play pop music.

popgun *n* a child's spring-operated gun, generally firing a cork that is attached to the muzzle by a long string and making a characteristic 'pop' when fired; (*joc*) a light or small-calibre firearm.

popinjay *n* a parrot; a trifling young man; a fop or coxcomb; (*hist*) a target for tilting or archery practice, shaped like a parrot.

popish *adj* (*derog*) pertaining to the pope or the Roman Catholic Church.

poplar *n* any of certain slender, quick-growing trees of the willow family, chiefly found in northern and temperate regions.

poplin *n* a fine-weave, corded fabric of silk, cotton, rayon, etc.

pop music *n* popular music, especially when characterized by a strong rhythmic element and the use of electrical amplification.

poppet *n* a term of endearment; a support for a ship in launching, dry dock, etc; one of the heads of a lathe.

poppet valve *n* a reciprocating, generally spring-loaded valve used in the cylinder heads of internal-combustion engines.

popply *adj* (of water) choppy, somewhat rough, tumbling.

poppy *n* a flowering plant of many species, from one of which, the white poppy, opium is collected.

poppycock *n*, *interj* (*colloq*) nonsense.

populace *n* the multitude, comprehending all persons not distinguished by rank, education, office or profession (usually with the definite article).

popular *adj* pertaining to the common people; constituted by or depending on the people; suitable to common people; easy to be comprehended; plain; familiar; beloved by the people; pleasing to people in general' generally liked and admired.

popularity *n* the state or quality of being popular or esteemed by the people at large; goodwill or favour proceeding from the people.

popularize *vt* (**popularized, popularizing**) to make popular; to treat in a popular manner or so as to be generally intelligible; to spread among the people; to make fashionable or sought-after.

popularly *adv* in a popular manner; so as to please the populace; among the people at large; currently; commonly.

populate *vt* (**populated, populating**) to furnish with inhabitants; to people.

population *n* the act or process of populating or peopling; the whole number of people in a country, town, etc; the populace; populousness.

populous *adj* full of inhabitants; thickly peopled.

porbeagle *n* any of a genus of shark found in northern waters, sometimes known as *mackerel shark*.

porcelain *n* the finest pottery ware, originally manufactured in China and Japan, formed from clays mixed with siliceous earths, which communicate a certain degree of translucency by means of their vitrification.—*adj* having the properties or attributes of porcelain; hence, delicate, light, white (*porcelain skin*).

porch *n* (*archit*) an exterior appendage to a building forming a covered approach or vestibule to a doorway; a covered walk or portico.

porcine *adj* pertaining to pigs; like a pig; hog-like.

porcupine *n* a large rodent of several species, found in Africa, America, Asia and southern Europe, which is covered with long spines mixed with bristly hairs, which the animal can erect at will and which serve for its defence.

pore¹ *n* a small opening in a solid body, especially one of the minute openings in the skin of animals or the leaves, stems, etc, of plants through which fluids and minute substances are excreted or exhaled or by which they are absorbed; a small opening in solid matter, such as rock, etc, or in membranes or coverings such as paint.

pore² *vi* (**pored, poring**) to look with steady continued attention or application; to read or examine anything with steady perseverance (generally followed by *on*, *upon* or *over*).

porgy *n* the name given to a number of species of marine fishes, especially the North American sea bream.

poriferan *n* any of an order of invertebrates that includes the marine and freshwater sponges.

pork *n* the flesh of the pig, fresh or salted, used for food.

pork chop *n* a slice from the rib of a pig.

porker *n* a hog; a pig; especially one fed for pork; hence, a glutton.

pork pie *n* a pie made of pastry and minced pork.

pork sausage *n* a sausage made of minced pork with various flavouring ingredients.

pornographic *adj* pertaining to pornography; obscene.

pornography *n* books, magazines, films, etc, intended to arouse sexual desire, often with explicitly sexual, titillating pictures and usually considered obscene; obscene writing.

porcupine

porosity *n* the state or quality of being porous or of having pores.

porous *n* having many pores or minute openings or interstices; capable of absorbing fluids or of allowing fluids to pass through.

porphyry *n* a reddish igneous rock containing crystals of feldspar.

porpoise *n* a cetacean mammal frequenting northern seas and frequently seen off shores pursuing shoals of herring, mackerel, etc; also, a name given to several dolphins.

porridge *n* a kind of food made with oatmeal and water or milk.

porringer *n* a porridge dish; a small vessel out of which children eat their food.

port[1] *n* a natural or artificial harbour; a haven; any bay, cove or inlet of the sea, of a lake, or the mouth of a river, which vessels can enter and where they can lie safe from injury by storms; any place of shelter.

port[2] *n* a gate; an entrance; a passageway in the side of a ship or a defensive wall; an opening in the side of a ship of war, fortification, etc, through which cannon were discharged; an aperture for the passage of gases or fluids (*exhaust port*); a circuit in a computer for inputting or outputting data.

port[3] *n* (*naut*) the larboard or left side of a ship.—*vti* (*naut*) to turn or put to the left or larboard side of a ship (said of the helm).

port[4] *n* a kind of sweet fortified wine originating in Portugal.

port[5] *n* (*milit*) a position in which the rifle is carried with the weapon's barrel slanting across the left shoulder and the stock on the right side at belt level.—*vt* to carry a weapon at the port; to carry something, as a suitcase.

portability *n* the state of being portable.

portable *adj* capable of being carried by the hand or about the person; capable of being carried or transported from place to place; easily carried; not bulky or heavy.

portage *n* the act of carrying; the price of carriage; a break in a waterway over which goods, boats, etc, have to be carried, as from one lake, river or canal to another or along the banks of rivers round waterfalls, rapids, etc.

portal *n* (*poet*) a door or gate; (*archit*) the lesser gate when there are two of different dimensions at the entrance of a building; a kind of arch over a door or gate or the framework of the gate.

portcullis *n* (*fort*) a strong grating of timber or iron, made to slide in vertical grooves in the jambs of the entrance gate of a fortified place and capable of being lowered to protect the gate in case of assault.

portend *vt* to foreshow ominously; to foretoken; to indicate something future by previous signs.

portrait

portent *n* that which portends or foretokens; especially, an omen of ill.

portentous *adj* of the nature of a portent; ominous; foreshowing ill; monstrous; prodigious; wonderful.

porter[1] *n* one who has charge of a door or gate; a doorkeeper; a person in charge of a building's security, minor maintenance, etc.

porter[2] *n* a person who carries or conveys luggage at railway stations, hotels, airports, etc; a person employed in a market, hospital, etc, to carry things; a dark-coloured ale made wholly or partially with high-dried malt, so called from its having been originally the favourite beverage of porters.

porterage *n* money charged or paid for the carriage of burdens or parcels by a porter.

portfolio *n* a portable case in the form of a large book, for holding loose drawings, prints, papers, etc; a collection of work; the office and functions of a minister of state; a list of stocks and shares.

porthole *n* the port of a ship.

portico *n* (*pl* **porticoes**) (*archit*) a kind of porch before the entrance of a building fronted with columns; a covered walkway of the same style.

portion *n* a part of anything separated from it; that which is divided off, as a part from a whole; a part, though not actually divided but considered by itself; a part assigned; an allotment; someone's fate, destiny or lot.—*vt* to divide or distribute into portions or shares; to parcel out; to apportion; to allot in shares; to endow with a portion or an inheritance.

Portland cement *n* a cement made from common limestone which has the property of hardening under water.

portly *adj* inclined to stoutness; (*arch*) grand or dignified in mien, stately.

portmanteau *n* (*pl* **portmanteaus, portmanteaux**) a large case or trunk for carrying apparel, etc, on journeys.

portmanteau word *n* a term coined by Lewis Carroll and applied to a word coined from two words and suggesting something of the sense of each, as *brunch*, a combination of *breakfast* and *lunch*.

portrait *n* a painted picture or representation of a person and especially of a face drawn from the life, also used generally for engravings, photographs, crayon drawings, etc, of this kind; a vivid description or delineation in words.

portraiture *n* a portrait; the art or practice of drawing portraits.

portray *vt* to paint or draw the likeness of; to depict; to describe in words.

portrayal *n* the act of portraying; delineation; representation.

Portuguese *adj* of or pertaining to Portugal.—*n* the language of Portugal; the people of Portugal.

pose *n* attitude or position taken naturally or assumed for effect; an artistic posture or attitude; an attitude deliberately adopted for effect.—*vi* (**posed, posing**) to sit for a painting, photograph, etc; to set oneself up as; to attitudinize; to assume characteristic airs.—*vt* to cause to assume a certain posture; to place so as to have a striking effect; to put forward (as a question, problem).

poser *n* a person who poses, as for a portrait; one who adopts attitudes or affects mannerisms in an effort to impress; a poseur; something that puzzles, as a difficult question.

poseur *n* a person who affects a certain style or adopts certain physical or intellectual poses as a means of impressing.

posh *adj* upper-class; high-class; stylish; exclusive.

posit *vt* to lay down as a position or principle; to present to the consciousness as an absolute fact.

position *n* state of being placed; place, location; situation (generally with reference to other objects or to different parts of the same object); relation with regard to other persons or to some subject; manner of standing or being placed; attitude; point of view; that on which one takes one's stand; hence, principle laid down; predication; affirmation; place or standing in society; social rank; state; condition of affairs; in any employment, the title or description of the job held; (*milit*) ground held by troops for strategic or tactical purposes; (in sport) a player's place on a field, or in an area, of play.—*vt* to place or locate.

positive *adj* definitely laid down or expressed; direct; explicit, opposed to *implied*; not admitting any condition or discretion; express; absolute; real; existing in fact; not negative; direct (*positive proof*); confident; fully assured; dogmatic; overconfident in opinion or assertion; demonstrable; distinctly ascertained or ascertainable; (*photog*) having the lights and shades rendered as they are in nature, opposed to *negative*; (*math*) greater than zero; (*med*) (of blood test result, etc) indicating the presence of an actual or potential disorder; (*med*) (of a course of treatment) beneficial; (*elect*) (of a terminal, etc) of the opposite polarity to negative; (*physics*) having the polarity of a proton as opposed to an electron; (*colloq*) great (*a positive disgrace*).—*n* (*photog*) a picture in which the lights and shades are rendered as they are in nature, opposed to *negative*.

positively *adv* in a positive manner; absolutely; really; not negatively; expressly; with full conviction.

positron *n* a particle of the same size as an electron but with a positive charge.

posse *n* in the USA, men of a district formally empowered by the sheriff to assist with upholding the law; a body of such men, especially when engaged in pursuing a criminal.

posse comitatus *n* (*lit*) the power of a county; (*law*) the body of men which the sheriff is empowered to raise in case of riot, etc, the formal legal form of *posse*.

possess *vt* to occupy in person; to have and hold; to have as a piece of property or as a personal belonging; to be owner of; to own; to affect strongly (*fear possessed them*); to pervade; to fill or take up entirely; to have full power or mastery over, as, an evil spirit, evil influence, violent passion, etc (*possessed with a fury*); to put in possession; to make master or owner (with *of* before the thing and now generally in the passive or with reflexive pronouns, as *to be possessed of a large fortune; to possess oneself of another's property*); to furnish or fill; to imbue or instil into (with *with* before the thing).

possession *n* the having or holding of property; the state of owning or having in one's hands or power; the thing possessed; land, estate or goods owned; the state of being mastered by some evil spirit or influence.

possessive *adj* pertaining to possession; expressing possession; having an excessive desire to possess or dominate.—*n* (*gram*) a pronoun or other word denoting possession; the possessive case.

possessive case *n* (*gram*) the genitive case, or case of nouns and pronouns which expresses possession.

posset *n* a drink composed of hot spiced milk curdled by some infusion, as wine or other liquor, used as a cure for a cold.

possibility *n* the state or condition of being possible; a chance of happening; a thing possible; that which may take place or come into being.

possible *adj* that may be or exist; that may be now or may happen or come to pass; that may be done; not contrary to the nature of things; capable of coming to pass but improbable.

possibly *adv* in a possible manner; perhaps; perchance; under any circumstances (*I couldn't possibly do it*).

post¹ *n* a piece of timber, metal or other solid substance set upright and often intended to support something else.

post² *n* the place at which some person or thing is stationed or fixed; a station or position occupied, especially a military station; the place where a single soldier or a body of troops is stationed; a bugle call giving notice to soldiers to retire to their quarters for the night; an office or employment; an appointment; an established system for the public conveyance of letters and parcels; letters and parcels so sent; the mail; a post office; (*hist*) a staging post, especially one established for the purposes of delivering mail; a courier who rode between staging posts, a post rider.—*vt* to fix up in a public place, as a notice or advertisement; to expose to public reproach; to expose to opprobrium by some public action; to place; to station (*to post troops on a hill*); in bookkeeping, to carry (accounts or items) from the journal to the ledger; to make the requisite entries in, for showing a true state of affairs; to place in the post office; to transmit by post (*to post letters*); to keep informed.

postage *n* the charge levied on letters or other articles conveyed by post.

postage stamp *n* an adhesive stamp of various values issued by the post office department for affixing to letters, packets, etc, as payment of cost of transmission.

postal *adj* relating to a post office or the carrying of mails.

postbox *n* a public box for depositing post.

postcard *n* a card, usually illustrated, for sending messages by post.

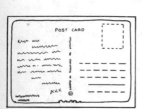
postcard

postchaise *n* formerly, a light, closed, horse-drawn carriage for conveying travellers and mail from one staging post to another and let for hire.

postcode *n* in Britain, a set of letters and digits which denote a postal address, to assist delivery.

postdate *vt* (**postdated, postdating**) to write a future date on a letter or cheque.

poster *n* a large printed bill or placard, usually illustrated, posted for advertising purposes.

poste restante *n* a department in a post office where letters so addressed are kept till the owners call for them.

posterior *adj* later or subsequent in time, opposed to *prior*; later in order; coming after; situated behind; hinder (*the posterior portion of the skull*), opposed to *anterior*.—*n* (*joc*) the buttocks.

posterity *n* descendants; the race that proceeds from a progenitor; succeeding generations.

postern *n* primarily, a back door or gate; a private entrance; hence, any small door or gate.

post-haste *adv* with speed or expedition.—*n* (*arch*) haste or speed in travelling, like that of a post or courier.

posthumous *n* born after the death of the father; published after the death of the author (*posthumous works*); being or continuing after one's decease (*posthumous fame*); awarded after death (*a posthumous VC*).

postilion, postillion *n* the rider on the near

leader of a travelling or other carriage; one who rides the near horse when one pair only is used.

postman, postwoman *n* (*pl* **postmen, postwomen**) a person employed to deliver mail.

postmark *n* the mark or stamp of a post office on a letter.

postmaster *n* the officer who has the superintendence and direction of a post office.

postmaster general *n* the officer in charge of a national postal service.

postmeridian *adj* (usually abbreviated to **p.m.**) coming after the sun has passed the meridian; being or belonging to the afternoon.—*n* the afternoon.

post-mortem *adj* after death.—*n* a postmortem examination; hence, an investigation into some recent incident or enterprise.

post-mortem examination *n* an examination of a corpse to determine the cause of death; an autopsy.

postnatal *adj* of or happening in the period immediately after the birth of a baby.

post office *n* a public building in which stamps are sold and other postal matters dealt with and to which letters, etc, are taken for onward transmission and from which mail for that area is delivered; a public department having responsibility for the postal service and also, in some countries, for telecommunications.

postpone *vt* (**postponed, postponing**) to put off; to defer to a future or later time.

postponement *n* the act of postponing or deferring to a future time.

post-prandial *adj* happening after a meal, especially dinner.

postscript *n* a note added to a letter after it has been written; any addition made to a book or composition after it has ostensibly been finished; something appended; an afterthought.

post-traumatic stress disorder *n* a medical condition characterized by anxiety, depression, etc, following or resulting from an injury or a traumatic experience.

postulant *n* a person who asks or applies, especially a candidate for admission to a religious order.

postulate *n* a position or supposition of which the truth is demanded or assumed for the purpose of future reasoning; a necessary assumption; a prerequisite; a basic principle; something assumed or taken for granted; the enunciation of a self-evident problem; an axiom.—*vt* (**postulated, postulating**) to assume without proof, to take for granted; to regard as self-evident or as too obvious to require further proof; to demand or claim; to nominate someone for a position.

posture *n* the disposition of the several

parts of the body with respect to each other or with respect to a particular purpose; carriage or bearing; attitude; an affected manner or bearing, a pose; situation; condition; particular state with regard to something else (*the posture of affairs*).—*vt* (**postured, posturing**) to place in a particular posture.—*vi* to dispose the body in particular postures; to contort the body into artificial attitudes; to adopt an affected physical or intellectual stance, to pose.

post-war *adj* belonging to the period after a war.

posy *n* a small bunch of flowers.

pot[1] *n* a hollow vessel used for various domestic and other purposes (*a cooking pot, a flower pot*); a mug; a jug containing a specified quantity of liquor; the quantity contained in a pot; the metal or earthenware top of a chimney; in gambling, money placed in a pool; a fish trap or creel, especially for crustaceans (*a lobster pot*); in billiards, etc, a shot by which a ball is to be, or is, pocketed; (*joc*) a cup, tankard, etc, given as a prize in a sporting competition; (*pl*) a lot of (especially of money).—**to go to pot** to be destroyed or ruined; to have deteriorated drastically.—*vt* (**potted, potting**) to put into pots; to preserve seasoned fish, meat, etc, in pots (*potted shrimps*); to plant in earth-filled pots; (*colloq*) to shoot some animal or person; to shoot for food rather than sport; to shoot in a rather aimless manner; (in billiards, etc) to pocket a ball.

pot[2] *n* a pothole; a deep hole in a riverbed; any deep hole.

pot[3] *n* (*colloq*) cannabis when taken as a drug.

potable *adj* suitable for drinking; capable of being drunk.

potash *n* alkali in an impure state, originally the evaporated lye of the ashes of plants; potassium carbonate, used in the manufacture of glass, soft soap and cleaning solutions; potassium hydroxide, used for liquid and solid soaps and detergents; lye.

potassium *n* a soft silvery-white alkali metallic element, the basis of potash, which reacts violently and rapidly oxidizes when exposed to the air and the compounds of which are used in many applications, notably as fertilizers.

potation *n* the act of drinking; a draught; a drink.

potato *n* (*pl* **potatoes**) the common plant, originally from South America, whose oval tubers are eaten as a vegetable; a tuber of this plant.

pot-bellied *adj* having a prominent belly.

pot belly *n* a protuberant belly.

potboy *n* a boy or man who carries pots of ale or beer for sale; a male menial in a public house.

poteen, potheen *n* in Ireland, spirit illicitly distilled and sold so as to avoid excise duty, often made from potatoes.

potency *n* the state or quality of being potent.

potent *adj* powerful; efficacious; having great authority, influence, strength, etc; producing powerful or violent effects (*a potent drug*); (of arguments, etc) forceful or persuasive; (of males) physically able to have sexual intercourse, not impotent;

potentate *n* a person who possesses great power or sway; a prince; a sovereign; an emperor, king or monarch.

potential *adj* possible but not yet actual; latent; that may be manifested.—*n* anything that may be possible; a possibility; the possible but as yet unrealized ability to do or become something.

potentiality *n* state of being potential; possibility but not actuality; inherent power or quality not actually exhibited.

potentiary *n* one having or assuming power, authority or influence.

potentilla *n* any of an extensive genus of flowering perennials of the rose family, which includes cinquefoil, silverweed and tormentil, and one species of which is used in Lapland and the Orkney Islands to tan and dye leather.

potheen *n* same as **poteen**.

pother *n* bustle; confusion; tumult; flutter.

potherb *n* any herb, plant or vegetable used in cooking.

pothole *n* a subterranean cavity caused by the action of water on limestone; a circular cavity in the rocky beds of rivers formed by stones being whirled round by the action of the current; a deep hole in the surface of a track or road.

pothook *n* a hook on which pots and kettles are hung over the fire; a letter or character like a pothook, written by children in learning to write.

pothouse *n* an alehouse; a tavern.

pothunter *n* a sportsman who has more regard for winning prizes than for sport; originally, someone who hunted for food alone, regardless of sporting rules or laws.

potion *n* a draught; a liquid medicine; a dose to be drunk.

potluck *n* what may chance to be in the pot or provided for a meal.—**to take potluck** (of an unexpected visitor) to partake of the family meal, whatever it may chance to be; hence, to take a chance on something, there being little alternative.

potpourri *n* a mixture of scented, dried flowers; a dish of different kinds of meat and vegetables cooked together; a miscellaneous collection; a medley.

potsherd *n* a piece or fragment of an earthenware pot; a shard.

pottage *n* a dish made of meat boiled to

potato

softness in water, usually with some vegetables; also, oatmeal or other porridge.

potter[1] *n* one who makes pottery.

potter[2] *vi* to busy or perplex oneself about trifles; to work with little energy or effect; to trifle; to waste time.

pottery *n* the ware or vessels made by potters; earthenware glazed and baked; the place where earthen vessels are manufactured; the business of a potter.

potty[1] *adj* (*colloq*) slightly mad; eccentric.

potty[2] *n* (*colloq*) a small chamber pot for young children.

pouch *n* a small bag; a pocket; a bag or sac belonging to or forming an appendage of certain animals, as that of a marsupial.—*vt* to put into a pouch or pocket.

poult *n* a young chicken, pheasant or other gallinaceous bird.

poulterer *n* a poultry dealer; one whose business is the rearing of domestic fowl for their meat or eggs.

poultice *n* a hot, soft, moist dressing for applying to a sore part of the body.

poultry *n* domestic fowl which are reared for their flesh as an article of food, for their eggs, feathers, etc, such as chickens, turkeys, ducks and geese.

pounce *n* a sudden leap or dive, as in securing prey; the claw or talon of a bird of prey.—*vi* (**pounced, pouncing**) to fall on and seize with the claws or talons; to make a sudden assault or attack on; to dart or dash on (with *on* or *upon*).

pound[1] *n* a standard of weight or mass; the legal standard of weight in Britain, or pound avoirdupois, equal to 7000 grains or 456.3 grams, and divided into 16 ounces; the pound troy, equal to 5760 grains, and divided into 12 ounces; a pound sterling.

pound[2] *n* a place of confinement; a municipal enclosure for stray animals; a depot for enclosing impounded personal property, such as cars, until claimed.—*vt* to shut up as in a pound; to confine in a public pound; to impound.

pound[3] *vt* to beat; to strike repeatedly with some heavy instrument; to pulverize by beating; to bruise or break into fine parts by a heavy instrument; to do heavily and repeatedly; to teach something by constant repetition (with *into*); to produce in a heavy manner (with *out*).—*vi* to deliver heavy blows repeatedly (at or on); to move with heavy steps; to throb; to work hard and continuously (*to pound away*).

poundage *n* a charge or payment of an amount per pound in weight; a charge or payment of an amount per pound sterling; weight when quoted in pounds.

poundal *n* the British absolute unit of force, equal to the force which in 1 second produces in 1 pound a velocity of 1 foot per second.

pouch

powder puff

pound sterling *n* the standard monetary unit of the UK (and of some other countries) consisting of 100 pence.

pour *vt* to cause to flow, as a liquid, either out of a vessel or into it; to send forth in a stream or continued succession; to emit; to give vent to, as under the influence of strong feeling; to throw in profusion.—*vi* to flow; to issue forth in a stream; to gush; to rush in continued procession.

pout *vi* to thrust out the lips, as in sullenness, contempt or displeasure; hence, to look sullen; to swell out, as the lips; to be prominent.—*vt* to speak while pouting.—*n* a thrusting out of the lips; a sulky state; (*pl*) a fit of pique.

poverty *n* the state of being poor or indigent; indigence; a deficiency of necessary or desirable elements; absence or dearth (*poverty of honour*); barrenness (*poverty of soil*); poorness; lack of ideas or information; lack or defect of words (*poverty of language*).

powan *n* same as **pollan**.

powder *n* any dry substance composed of minute particles; a substance comminuted or triturated to fine particles; gunpowder; face powder; hair powder; fresh loose snow.—*vt* to reduce to fine particles; to pulverize; to sprinkle with powder or as with powder.—*vi* to become like powder; to wear powder.

powdered *adj* reduced to powder; sprinkled with powder.

powder horn *n* formerly, a horn in which gunpowder was carried before the introduction of cartridges.

powder puff *n* a soft pad, usually of down, for applying powder to the skin.

power *n* ability or capacity to act; the faculty of doing or performing something; capability of producing an effect; strength, force or energy manifested in action; capacity; susceptibility (*great power of resistance*); natural strength; animal strength; influence; predominance (as of the mind, imagination); faculty of the mind as manifested by a particular mode of operation (*the power of thinking*); ability; capability; the employment of strength or influence among people; command; the right of governing or actual government; dominion; rule; authority; one who or that which exercises authority or control (*the powers that be*); a sovereign or the sovereign authority of a state; a state (*the great powers of Europe*); a spirit or superhuman agent having a certain sway (*celestial powers*); legal authority; warrant; military strength or force; a significant amount (*a power of good*); (*mech*) that which produces motion or force or that which may be applied to produce it; a mechanical agent; the moving force applied to produce the required effect; mechanical advantage or effect; force or effect considered as resulting from the action of a machine; rate of doing work; a shortened form of *horsepower*; domestic or industrial electricity; a particular form of energy (*water power*); (*math*) the product arising from the multiplication of a number or quantity into itself or the index denoting this; in optics, the degree to which an optical instrument magnifies the apparent dimensions of an object.

powerful *adj* having great power; able to produce great effects; strong; potent; energetic; efficacious.

power of attorney *n* a formal instrument by which one person authorizes another to act for him or her.

powwow *n* (*colloq*) a conference or get-together.

pox *n* eruptive pustules on the body; a disease characterized by pustules, the term being restricted to specific diseases, as smallpox, chickenpox, etc; (*arch*) syphilis.—*interj* (*arch*) meaning may the plague get you (*a pox on you!*).

practicable *adj* capable of being effected or performed by human means or by powers that can be applied; feasible; capable of being passed or travelled over; passable; assailable.

practicability *n* the quality of being practicable; feasibility.

practical *adj* relating to practice, use or employment, opposed to *speculative*, *ideal* or *theoretical*; that may be turned to use; reducible to use in the conduct of life; given to or concerned with action or practice; capable of reducing knowledge or theories to actual use; educated by practice or experience; skilled in actual work (*a practical gardener*); derived from practice or experience.

practically *adv* in a practical manner; not merely theoretically; so far as actual results or effects are concerned; in effect.

practice *n* a way of behaviour; a proceeding; a customary action; custom or habit; use or usage; state of being used; customary use; method or art of doing anything; actual performance (as opposed to theory); exercise of any profession (*the practice of law*); (*law*) the established method of conducting court proceedings; application of remedies; medical treatment of diseases; drill; repeated or systematic exercise for instruction or discipline; skilful or artful management; stratagem; artifice (usually in a bad sense); (*math*) a rule in arithmetic for expeditiously multiplying quantities expressed in different denominations.

practise *vt* (**practised, practising**) to do or perform frequently, customarily or habitually; to do (something) regularly in order to acquire skill at it; to use for instruction or discipline or as a profession or art (*to practise law* or *medicine*); to put into practice; to perform; to do; to teach by practice; to accustom; to train.—*vi* to perform certain acts frequently or customarily, for instruction, profit or amusement; to do something regularly in order to acquire skill at it; to exercise some profession, as that of medicine or of law.

practitioner *n* one who is engaged in the exercise of any art or profession, particularly in law or medicine.

pragmatic, pragmatical *adj* practical; concerned with what is practicable and expedient rather than with theories and ideals; matter-of-fact; realistic; (*philos*) concerning or relating to pragmatism.

pragmatism *n* philosophical views laying stress on practical consequences as a test of the importance or truth, of any theory.

prairie *n* an extensive tract of land mostly level or nearly so, generally lacking trees and covered with coarse grass and flowering plants.

prairie wolf *n* the coyote.

praise *n* commendation bestowed on a person; approbation; eulogy; laud; a joyful tribute of gratitude or homage paid to God, often expressed in song; the ground or reason for praise; what makes a person worthy of praise.—*vt* (**praised, praising**) to commend; to applaud; to express approbation of; to extol in words or song; to laud or magnify, especially applied to God.

praiseworthy *adj* commendable.

pram[1] *n* (*colloq*) a small wheeled carriage for a baby pushed by a handle, a perambulator.

pram[2] *n* a small dinghy with a flat bow.

prance *vi* (**pranced, prancing**) to spring or bound, as a horse in high mettle; to ride ostentatiously; to strut about in a showy manner or with warlike parade.

prandial *adj* relating to a dinner or meal in general.

prank *n* a playful or sportive action; a merry trick; a practical joke.

prate *vi* (**prated, prating**) to talk much and without weight; to chatter; to babble.—*vt* to utter foolishly.—*n* continued talk to little purpose; unmeaning loquacity.

prattle *vi* (**prattled, prattling**) to talk much and idly; to be loquacious on trifling subjects; to talk like a child.—*n* puerile or trifling talk.

prau *n* same as **proa**.

prawn *n* a small marine crustacean related to the shrimp, lobster and other decapods and prized as food.

pray *vi* to ask something with earnestness or zeal; to supplicate; to beg (*to pray for mercy*); to make petition to God; to address God with confession of sins and

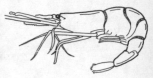

prawn

pray

supplication for benefits.—*pray* used elliptically for *I pray you tell me*, is a way of introducing a question.—*vt* to make earnest request to; to entreat; to address with a prayer for something such as God may grant; to ask earnestly for; to beseech; to petition.

prayer *n* the act of asking for a favour with earnestness; a petition, supplication, entreaty; a solemn petition for benefits addressed to God or to a figure connected with the deity, as a saint; the words of a supplication; a formula of church service or of worship, public or private; that part of a petition to a public body, especially to a court of law, which specifies the thing desired to be done or granted.

prayerbook *n* a book containing prayers.

Prayerbook *n* the Book of Common Prayer used by the Anglican Church.

prayer wheel *n* in Buddhism, an apparatus consisting of a wheel to which a written prayer is attached, each revolution of the wheel counting as an utterance of the prayer.

praying mantis *n* the mantis, so called from the position of the anterior legs resembling that of a person's hands at prayer.

preach *vi* to pronounce a public discourse on a religious subject or from a text of Scripture; to deliver a sermon; to give earnest advice (often unwanted or uncalled for); to discourse in the manner of a preacher.—*vt* to proclaim; to publish in religious discourses; to inculcate in public discourse; to deliver (a sermon).

preamble *n* an introduction, as to a discourse, piece of music, novel, etc; the introductory part of a statute or act of parliament which states the reasons and intent of the law.

prebend *n* the stipend granted to a canon of a cathedral or collegiate church out of its estate; the rents or other monies providing the stipend; (rare) a prebendary.

prebendary *n* an ecclesiastic who enjoys a prebend; a canon.

precarious *adj* dependent on chance; insecure; dangerous; likely to fail; (*arch*) dependent on the will of someone else.

precatory *adj* suppliant; beseeching.

precaution *n* a measure taken beforehand to prevent or circumvent an unpleasant or hazardous event; care beforehand; careful foresight; a preventive measure.

precautionary *adj* containing previous caution; proceeding from precaution.

precede *vt* (**preceded, preceding**) to go before in time; to be previous to; to go before in place, rank or importance; to introduce.

precedence *n* the act or state of preceding or going before; priority in time; the state of being before in rank or dignity; the right to a more honourable place; order or adjustment of place according to rank; formal order by rank in a ceremony, etc; superior importance or influence; priority.

precedent *adj* going before in time; anterior; antecedent.—*n* something done or said that may serve or be adduced as an example or rule to be followed in a subsequent act of the like kind; (*law*) a judicial decision, which serves as a rule for future decisions in similar or analogous cases.—*adj* going before; preceding.

precentor *n* the leader of the choir in a cathedral, usually a minor canon; in some churches, a person whose duty it is to lead the psalmody during services.

precept *n* a commandment intended as an authoritative rule of action; a command respecting moral conduct; a principle; an injunction; (*law*) a mandate in writing sent by a justice of the peace, etc, for bringing a person, record, etc, before him or her.

preceptive *adj* giving or containing precepts for the regulation of conduct; admonitory; instructive.

preceptor *n* a teacher, especially a doctor or surgeon; an instructor.

precession *n* the act of going before or forward.

precinct *n* the boundary line encompassing a place; a limit; a part near a border; a district within certain boundaries; a minor territorial division; a police district; (*pl*) surrounding district.

precious *adj* of great price; costly; of great value or worth; very valuable; much esteemed; highly cherished; much boasted about (*his precious children*); affected (*precious writing*); fastidious.

precipice *n* any steep sheer face, of a cliff, gorge, mountain, etc, or the cliff, etc, itself; hence, a difficult, dangerous or precarious situation.

precipitance, precipitancy *n* the quality of being precipitate; rash haste; haste in resolving, forming an opinion or executing a purpose.

precipitant *adj* falling or rushing headlong; precipitate.—*n* (*chem*) a substance which, when added to a solution, cause the formation of a precipitate.

precipitate *vt* (**precipitated, precipitating**) to throw headlong; to cast down from a precipice or height; to urge or press with eagerness or violence; to hasten (*to precipitate one's flight*); to hurry blindly or rashly; to cause moisture to condense and so fall as rain, etc.—*vi* to condense and fall as rain, etc.—*adj* falling, flowing or rushing steeply downwards; headlong; overhasty; rashly hasty; adopted with haste or without due deliberation; rash; hurried; violent; swift and sudden.—*n* (*chem*) any matter which, having been dissolved in a fluid, separates from the solution as a suspense of fine particles; the resulting matter in suspension or after settling.

precipitation *n* the act of precipitating or state of being precipitated; a falling or rushing down with violence and rapidity; rash, tumultuous haste; the result of the condensation of atmospheric moisture, as rain, snow, hail, etc; (*chem*) the process by which any substance in solution is made to separate, resulting in a suspension of fine particles.

precipitous *adj* very steep; like or forming a precipice; precipitate; over-hasty.

précis *n* a concise or abridged statement; a summary of the main points of a text; an abstract.—*vt* to make a précis of.

precise *adj* sharply or exactly limited or defined as to meaning; exact; definite, not loose, vague or equivocal; exact in conduct; using or performing with absolute accuracy; strict; formal; nice; punctilious.

precision *n* the state of being precise as to meaning; preciseness; exactness; absolute accuracy.

preclude *vt* (**precluded, precluding**) to exclude or prevent; to stop; to impede; to hinder; to hinder or make impossible by anticipatory action.

preclusion *n* the act of precluding.

preclusive *adj* tending to preclude; hindering by previous obstacles.

precocious *adj* ripe before the proper or natural time; ripe in understanding at an early period; developed or matured early in life.

precocity *n* the state or quality of being precocious; early development of the mental powers.

precognition *n* previous knowledge or cognition; (*psychol*) the supposed ability to foretell events in the future; (*Scots law*) a preliminary examination of a witness or witnesses to a criminal act, in order to know whether there is ground of trial.

preconceive *vt* (**preconceived, preconceiving**) to form a conception or opinion of beforehand; to form a previous notion or idea of.

preconception *n* the act of preconceiving; conception or opinion previously formed.

precursor *n* a predecessor; a harbinger; one who or that which precedes an event and indicates its approach.

precursory, precursive *adj* heralding; forerunning; introductory.

predacious, predaceous *adj* living by prey; given to preying on others.

predatory *adj* plundering; pillaging; (*zool*) predacious.

predecessor *n* one who precedes or goes before another in some position; one who has preceded another in any state, position, office, etc; a forerunner or ancestor.

predella *n* the basal part of an altar; a shelf or ledge at the back of an altar; a small painting or strip of paintings forming the lower edge of a large altarpiece.

predestinate *vt* (**predestinated, predestinating**) to predetermine or foreordain; to appoint or ordain beforehand by an unchangeable purpose.—*adj* foreordained.

predestination *n* the act of decreeing or foreordaining events; (*theol*) the doctrine that God has from eternity unchangeably appointed or determined what comes to pass, particularly the preordination of individuals to everlasting happiness or misery.

predestine *vt* (**predestined, predestining**) to decree beforehand; to foreordain.

predetermination *n* previous determination; purpose formed beforehand.

predetermine *vt* (**predetermined, predetermining**) to determine beforehand; to form or influence an opinion beforehand; to doom by previous decree.—*vi* to make a determination beforehand.

predicament *n* a dangerous or trying condition or state; a difficult or embarrassing state; a quandary or dilemma.

predicate *vt* (**predicated, predicating**) to affirm as an attribute of something (*to predicate whiteness of snow*); to declare one thing of another; to imply.—*vi* to make an affirmation.—*n* in logic, that which, in a proposition, is affirmed or denied of the subject; (*gram*) the word or words in a proposition which express what is affirmed or denied of the subject.

predication *n* the act of predicating; affirmation; assertion.

predicative *adj* expressing affirmation or predication; (*gram*) forming all or part of a predicate.

predict *vt* to foretell; to prophesy; to declare to be going to happen in the future; to make a reasoned statement about or assessment of in advance.

prediction *n* the act of predicting; a foretelling; a prophecy.

predictive *adj* foretelling; prophetic.

predictor *n* someone or something that predicts; a device used in anti-aircraft units to predict the course, weight, speech and range of an enemy aircraft.

predilection *n* a previous liking; a prepossession of mind in favour of something; preference; bias.

predispose *vt* (**predisposed, predisposing**) to incline beforehand; to give a previous disposition or tendency to; to fit or adapt previously; (*law*) to bequeath; (*med*) to make susceptible to (a disease, etc).

predisposition *n* the state of being previously disposed towards something; previous inclination or tendency; previous fitness or adaptation to any change, impression or purpose; (*med*) liability to affliction by a particular disease.

predominance *n* prevalence over others; superiority in power, influence or authority; ascendancy.

predominant *adj* prevalent over others; superior in strength, influence or authority; ruling; controlling.

predominate *vi* (**predominated, predominating**) to have surpassing power, influence or authority; to have controlling influence.—*vt* to rule over; to master.

pre-eminence *n* the state or quality of being notably eminent among others; superior or surpassing eminence; undoubted superiority, especially superiority in excellence.

pre-eminent *adj* eminent above others; surpassing or highly distinguished in excellence, sometimes also in evil; outstanding.

pre-empt *vt* to take action beforehand to prevent possible action by another; to seize (something) before anyone else can.

pre-emption *n* the act of pre-empting; the act or right of purchasing before others.

pre-emptive *adj* intended to pre-empt or actually pre-empting; (*milit*) attacking a hostile target (especially with missiles) in order to deny the enemy the chance of attacking first or to reduce forces before they can be deployed (*a pre-emptive strike*); (in bridge) denoting a high bid to exclude bids from the opposition.

preen *vt* (of birds) to trim with the beak, to clean and dress (their feathers); (of people) to take exaggerated care of one's appearance; to primp, especially in a vain or conceited manner.

preface *n* something spoken as introductory to a discourse or written as introductory to a book or other composition.—*vt* (**prefaced, prefacing**) to introduce by preliminary remarks or text.

prefatory *adj* pertaining to or having the character of a preface; introductory.

prefect *n* a monitor in a school; in some countries, an administrative official, a chief police officer, etc.

prefecture *n* the office or jurisdiction of a prefect; prefectship; the official residence of a prefect.

prefer *vt* (**preferred, preferring**) to find someone or something preferable; to like better or esteem more highly; to advance, as to an office or dignity; to raise; to exalt; to choose rather (*to prefer one to another*); (*law*) to bring charges before a court for deliberation and judgment.

preferable *adj* worthy of preference; more eligible; more desirable.

preference *n* the preferring of one thing before another; choice of one thing rather than another; higher place in esteem; the object of choice; choice.

preferential *adj* resulting from or displaying preference; in a position to which some preference is attached.

pregnant

preferment *n* advancement to a higher office, dignity or station; promotion; a superior or valuable place or office, especially in the church.

prefix *vt* to put or fix before or at the beginning of another thing (*to prefix a syllable to a word, an advertisement to a book*); to settle, fix or appoint beforehand.—*n* a letter, syllable or word put at the beginning of a word, usually to vary its meaning.

pregnancy *n* the state of being pregnant; the term of being with child, from conception to birth; the quality of being full of significance.

pregnant *adj* being with young; great with child; gravid; full of important matter; abounding with results; full of consequence or significance (*a silence pregnant with threat*).

prehensible *adj* capable of being seized.

prehensile *adj* capable of or adapted to seize or grasp (*a monkey's prehensile tail*).

prehension *n* a taking hold of; a seizing; grasp, understanding (of the mind or senses).

prehistoric *adj* relating to the history of events and conditions before the development of writing; (*colloq*) old-fashioned.

prehistory *n* the prehistoric ages; the study of the prehistoric period; the history of the earlier background of an incident, etc.

prejudge *vt* (**prejudged, prejudging**) to judge before hearing or before the arguments and facts are fully known; to decide by anticipation; to condemn beforehand or unheard.

prejudgment, prejudgement *n* the act of prejudging; judgment without a hearing or full examination.

prejudice *n* a bias or leaning, favourable or unfavourable, without reason or for some reason other than justice; a prepossession (when used absolutely generally with the unfavourable meaning of wrong or ignorant bias or view); hatred or intolerance of members of a particular religion or race (*racial prejudice*); mischief; damage; injury (*without prejudice to one's interests*).—*vt* to implant a prejudice in the mind of; to bias by hasty and incorrect notions; to injure by prejudices; to hurt, damage, impair; to injure in general (*to prejudice one's cause*).

prejudicial *adj* hurtful; mischievous; injurious; detrimental.

prelacy *n* the function or standing of a prelate; the system of church government by prelates; prelates collectively.

prelate *n* an ecclesiastic of the higher order having authority over the lower clergy, as an archbishop, bishop or patriarch; a dignitary of the church.

prelatic *adj* pertaining to prelates or prelacy.

preliminary *adj* introductory; preceding the main discourse or business; prefatory. —*n* something introductory or preparatory; something to be examined and determined before an affair can be treated of on its own merits; a preparatory act.

prelude *n* something preparatory or leading up to what follows; an introductory performance; (*mus*) a short introductory strain preceding the principal movement. —*vt* (**preluded, preluding**) to introduce with a prelude; to serve as prelude to. —*vi* to serve as a prelude.

premarital *adj* taking place before marriage.

premature *adj* happening, arriving, existing, performed or adopted before the proper time; done, said or believed too soon; too early; untimely.

premeditate *vt* (**premeditated, premeditating**) to think on and resolve in the mind beforehand; to contrive and design previously; to plan (a crime, etc) in advance. —*vi* to meditate beforehand.

premeditation *n* the act of premeditating; previous deliberation; forethought; previous contrivance or design; (*law*) the plotting of a crime beforehand, demonstrating intent to commit it.

premenstrual tension *n* (often abbreviated to **PMT**) nervous tension characterized by irritability, aggression or depression that may be experienced in the days before menstruation begins.

premier *adj* first; chief; principal; holding the most ancient title in any rank of the peerage (*the premier earl*). —*n* the first or chief minister of state; the prime or premier minister.

premiere, première *n* the first public performance of a play, film, etc. —*vt* (**premiered, premiering**) to give a premiere of. —*vi* to have a first performance; to appear for the first time as a star performer.

premiership *n* the office of premier.

premise *vt* (**premised, premising**) to state (an argument, theory, etc) as a premise; to postulate; to set forth or make known beforehand, as introductory to the main subject; to postulate. —*vi* to state as an introduction. —*n* a premiss; (*pl*) a piece of land and its buildings; (*pl*) the buildings and land where a business, etc, is situated.

premiss *n* (in logic) a proposition laid down as a base of argument on the assumption or in the belief that it is true; something assumed or taken for granted; one or other of the two propositions of a syllogism.

premium *n* a reward or prize offered for some specific thing; a bonus; an extra sum paid as an incentive; a bounty; something given free or at a reduced price with a purchase; a sum paid or to be paid periodically for an insurance policy; a high value. —**at a premium** much in demand and therefore difficult to obtain. —*adj* (of goods) of high quality.

premonition *n* a foreboding; a feeling of something about to happen.

premonitory *adj* conveying a warning or premonition.

preoccupation *n* the condition of being preoccupied; absorption; a chief interest; an obsession; an occupation or taking possession before another.

preoccupied *adj* having the attention taken up previously; engrossed; absorbed; lost in thought; obsessed with; already occupied.

preoccupy *vt* (**preoccupied, preoccupying**) to engage or occupy the attention or thoughts of; to engross; to absorb; to obsess; to occupy or take possession of before another.

preparation *n* the act of preparing; that which is prepared for a particular purpose; a substance compounded or made up for a certain use, especially medication; the state of being prepared or in readiness.

preparative *adj* tending or serving to prepare or make ready; preparatory. —*n* that which is preparative or preparatory; that which is done to prepare.

preparatory *adj* serving to prepare the way for some proceeding to follow; introductory; preparative.

prepare *vt* (**prepared, preparing**) to fit, adapt or qualify for a particular purpose; to put into such a state as to be fit for use or application; to make ready; to make ready for something that is to happen; to give notice to (*to prepare a person for ill news* or *calamity*); to provide; to mix, build, make, et from ingredients or components (to prepare a prescription); to fit out or equip; to procure as suitable (*to prepare arms, ammunition*, etc, *for troops*). —*vi* to make ready; to put things in suitable order; to take the necessary previous measures; to make oneself ready.

prepay *vt* (**prepaid, prepaying**) to pay before obtaining possession of; to pay in advance; to pay before the payment falls due.

prepayment *n* act of paying beforehand; payment in advance.

preponderance *n* the state or quality of preponderating or being preponderant.

preponderant *adj* outweighing; superior in number, amount, power, influence, etc.

preponderate *vt* (**preponderated, preponderating**) to outweigh; to be greater in number, amount, weight, importance, influence, etc. —*vi* to exceed in number, amount, weight, influence or power; to have the greater weight or influence; to have sway or power superior to others.

preposition *n* (*gram*) a part of speech which is used to show the relation of one noun or pronoun to another in a sentence and is usually placed before the word which expresses the object of the relation.

prepositional *adj* (*gram*) pertaining to or having the nature or function of a preposition.

prepossess *vt* to impress favourable; to prejudice.

prepossessing *adj* creating an favourable impression; engaging (said especially of the external characteristics of a person); attractive.

prepossession *n* the state of being prepossessed; a preconceived opinion or judgment.

preposterous *adj* contrary to nature, reason or common sense; utterly and glaringly foolish; totally opposed to the fitness of things; manifestly absurd.

prepuce *n* the foreskin.

prerequisite *adj* previously required; necessary to something subsequent.—*n* a prior necessity; something that is previously necessary.

prerogative *n* an exclusive or peculiar privilege or right; a privilege belonging to one by virtue of character or position; an official and hereditary right which may be asserted without question; a special right or privilege of a sovereign or an executive of a government.

presage *n* something which portends or foreshows a future event; a prognostication; an omen; a foreboding or presentiment; a feeling that something is to happen; a prophecy; foreknowledge.—*vt* (**presaged, presaging**) to forebode; to foreshow; to foretell, predict, prophesy.—*vi* to form or utter a prediction.

presbyopia *n* an imperfection of vision in which the eye's ability to focus progressively diminishes so that near objects are seen less distinctly than those at a distance.

presbyter *n* a priest; a minister; in the Presbyterian Church, an elder.

presbyterian *adj* pertaining to a presbyter; pertaining to ecclesiastical government by presbyteries or to those who uphold such government.

Presbyterian *adj* pertaining to a Presbyterian Church.—*n* a member of a Presbyterian Church.

Presbyterian Church *n* any of various churches in which government is vested in presbyteries or associations of ministers and elders and in which there are no bishops.

Presbyterianism *n* adherence to the Presbyterian faith; the doctrines, principles and discipline or government of any of the Presbyterian Churches.

presbytery *n* Presbyterianism; a church court consisting of Presbyterian ministers of all the churches of any particular denomination within a given district, along with one ruling elder from each church session; the churches and congregations within such a court's jurisdiction; the sanctuary of a church or cathedral where the high altar is situated; (*RC Church*) a parish priest's residence.

prescience *n* foreknowledge; knowledge of events before they take place; foresight.

prescribe *vt* (**prescribed, prescribing**) to lay down authoritatively for direction; to give as a rule of conduct; (*med*) to direct to be used as a remedy.—*vi* to lay down rules or directions; to dictate; to write or give medical directions, especially those concerning medication; to direct what remedies are to be used; (*law*) to become extinguished or of no validity through lapse of time, as a right, debt, obligation, etc.

prescript *adj* directed; set down as a rule; prescribed.—*n* direction; precept; something prescribed.

prescription *n* the act of prescribing; what is prescribed; a direction; prescript; (*med*) a written statement of the medicines or remedies to be used by a patient; (*law*) a claim, right or title based on long use or custom; (*law*) the loss of a right by lapse of time and neglect.

prescriptive *adj* composing or issuing rules, directions, etc; (*law*) consisting in or acquired by prescription.

presence *n* the state of being present; the existence of a person or thing in a certain place, opposed to *absence*; the being in company with; personal attendance; the state of being within sight or call; the state of being in view of a superior; the person of a superior, as a sovereign; mien; air; personal appearance; demeanour, especially an imposing or dignified bearing; an invisible supernatural being felt to be present.

presence of mind *n* coolness and readiness of invention or resource in occasions of difficulty; quickness in devising expedients on pressing occasions.

present *adj* being in a specific place or thing, opposed to *absent*; being in the presence of or near; being in company; near at hand, available; being now in view or under consideration; now existing or occurring or being done at this time; not past or future; (*arch*) quick in emergency (*a present help in trouble*); (*arch*) instant, immediate (*present death*).—*vt* to place or introduce into the presence or before the face of, especially of a superior; to bring before and introduce to the public; to suggest or submit for consideration (*to present an argument, to present the accounts*); (*law*) to bring a charge, or to lay a charge formally in court; to exhibit or offer to view or notice; to bestow; to make a gift or donation of, generally to give formally and ceremoniously; to bestow a gift on; to favour with a donation (*to present a person with a thing*); (*eccles*) to nominate to a benefice; to lay before a public body for consideration, as before a committee of enquiry, etc.—**to present arms** (*milit*) to carry out a drill movement in which the weapon is held vertically in front of the body, as in saluting a superior officer or in token of respect.—*n* that which is presented or given; a gift; (*pl*) (*law*) a term used in a legal deed to signify the document itself.

presentable *adj* capable of being presented; in such a condition as to be able to present oneself without embarrassment; well turned out; suitable to be exhibited or offered.

presentation *n* the act of presenting or state of being presented; (*eccles*) the act or right of presenting a clergyman or nominating a minister to a vacant parish.

presentiment *n* previous apprehension of something future; anticipation of impending evil; foreboding.

presently *adv* in a little time; soon; (*arch*) forthwith, immediately.

preservation *n* the act of preserving; the state of being preserved; escape from danger; safety.

preservative *n* that which preserves or has the power of preserving, especially an additive introduced into foodstuffs to slow down decomposition; something that is preventive of injury or decay.

preserve *vt* (**preserved, preserving**) to keep or save from injury or destruction; to defend from evil; to save; to keep in the same state; to uphold, sustain, guard; to maintain a hold on (*she preserved her dignity*); to inhibit or prevent decomposition (in foodstuffs) by treating with salt, sugar, etc, or by smoking, drying, freezing, etc; to limit the taking of (game, fish, etc) for sport to certain seasons; to protect (game, fish, etc) in areas where hunting or fishing for sport is limited or proscribed.—*vi* to treat foodstuffs, etc, so as to inhibit decomposition; to maintain a protected environment for game, fish, etc, in preserves.—*n* that which is preserved or which preserves; (usually *pl*) fruit, etc, that has been preserved by cooking with sugar; jam; an area where game, etc, is protected (and often reared) for purposes of sport; a specialized field or area of knowledge, study, experience, skill, etc (*bomb disposal is the preserve of experts*).

preside *vi* (**presided, presiding**) to be set over others; to have the place of authority over others, as a chairman or director (usually denoting temporary superintendence and government, as at a public meeting);

to exercise superintendence; to watch over as inspector.

presidency *n* the office of president, especially the president of a republic; the term during which a president holds his or her office.

president *n* the highest officer of state in a republic; an officer elected or appointed to preside over and control the proceedings of a number of persons; the chief officer of a corporation, company, society, etc; the chief officer of some colleges or universities; one who presides.

presidential *adj* pertaining to a president.

presidentship *n* the office of president or term of a president's tenure.

press[1] *vt* to act on with force or weight; to exert or maintain pressure on; to squeeze; to crush; to extract the juice of by squeezing; to apply pressure to, usually accompanied by heat, for the purpose of making smooth (*to press cloth* or *paper*); to make by pressing in a mould; to embrace closely; to constrain or compel; to put a case, claim, please, etc, vigorously or importunately; to urge by authority or necessity; to impose importunately (*to press a gift on one*); to cause to be in want of (*to be pressed for cash, time*, etc); to urge or solicit with earnestness; to importune; to harass; to inculcate with earnestness; (*arch*) to enforce, to oppress; to bear hard on.—*vi* to exert pressure; to act with compulsive force; to bear heavily; to strain or strive eagerly; to go forward with impulsive eagerness or energetic efforts; to hurry (often with *on*); to crowd; to throng; to force one's way; to urge.—*n* the act of pressing or state of being pressed; an instrument or machine by which anything is squeezed, crushed or forced into a more compact form; a machine for printing; a printing press; the printing process (*the book has gone to press*); a crowd; a throng; a multitude of individuals crowded together; an upright cupboard; urgent demands of affairs; attention in newspapers or the media generally (*a good* or *bad press*) a device for holding components firmly together while they are glued, etc; a framework for prevent warps (*a racket press*); a lift in weightlifting.—**the press** the gathering and distribution of news and those who perform these functions; newspapers in general; the news media.

press[2] *vt* to force into service, especially originally into naval service; to impress; to conscript forcibly; to bring someone or something into service or action, usually in a crisis and in tasks other than those for which they are trained, designed or fitted.

press agent *n* a person employed to generate favourable publicity in the press.

press conference *n* a group interview given

press

to members of the press by a politician, celebrity, etc.

press gang *n* a detachment of seamen formerly empowered to impress men into the naval service.

pressing *adj* urgent; importunate; distressing.—*n* a number of records made at one time form a master.

pressman *n* (*pl* **pressmen**) one who operates or supervises a printing press; a journalist or reporter; someone from the news media generally.

press release *n* a statement or announcement given to the press for publication.

pressure *n* the act of pressing; the state of being squeezed or crushed; the force of one body acting on another by weight or the continued application of power; a constraining force or impulse, especially a moral force acting on the mind; force, compulsion; severity of grievousness, as of personal circumstances; distress, strait or difficulty; urgency; demand on one's time or energies (*the pressure of business*); strain; (*physics*) force exerted on a surface; intensity of pressure.—*vt* (**pressured, pressuring**) to pressurize.

pressure cooker *n* a strong, sealed pan in which food can be cooked quickly by steam under pressure; (*colloq*) a situation beset with emotional or social pressure.

pressure group *n* a group of people which tries to influence legislators, public opinion, etc, in order to promote a particular area of interest.

pressure system *n* a body of moving air above or below normal atmospheric pressure.

pressurize *vt* (**pressurized, pressurizing**) to maintain nearly normal atmospheric pressure inside an aeroplane, etc, as at high altitudes; to exert pressure on; to attempt to compel, press.

prestidigitation *n* skill at conjuring; sleight of hand; the performance of conjuring tricks; originally, juggling.

prestige *n* status, power or influence, especially status derived from previous achievements; reputation or renown.

prestigious *adj* imparting prestige or renown.

presto *adv* (*mus*) a direction for a quick lively movement or performance.—*n* (*pl* **prestos**) (*mus*) a lively passage.—*interj* quickly, immediately, in haste.

presume *vt* (**presumed, presuming**) to take for granted, to suppose on reasonable grounds; (*law*) to consider proved until evidence to the contrary is adduced.—*vi* to suppose or believe without examination; to infer; to venture without permission or beyond what is justifiable; to take the liberty; to make bold; to act on overconfident conclusions; to make unwarranted advances (*to presume upon one's good nature*); to act in a forward way; to go beyond the boundaries laid down by reverence, respect or politeness.

presumption *n* a supposition; a ground for presuming; a strong probability; that which is supposed to be true without direct proof; blind or headstrong confidence; unreasonable adventurousness; presumptuousness; arrogance; assurance; (*law*) a deduction of the truth from other facts but without direct evidence.

presumptive *adj* based on presumption or probability; proving circumstantially, not directly (*presumptive evidence*).

presumptuous *adj* imbued with or characterized by presumption; taking undue liberties; given to presuming or acting in a forward manner; arrogant; overconfident.

presuppose *vt* (**presupposed, presupposing**) to assume or take for granted; to cause to be taken for granted; to imply as antecedent; to require as a prior condition.

presupposition *n* the act of presupposing; that which is presupposed.

pretence *n* the act of pretending; the presenting to others, either in words or actions, of a false or hypocritical appearance; false show intended to mislead, affectation; a pretext; a claim, true or (especially) false.

pretend *vt* to hold out falsely; to allege falsely; to use as a pretext; to make false appearance or representation of; to feign or affect (*to pretend zeal*); to claim or put in a claim for.—*vi* to feign, make believe or sham; to put in a claim, truly or falsely (usually with *to*).

pretender *n* one who pretends; one who lays claim to anything.

pretension *n* a false claim, specially of merit or importance; a holding out the appearance of possessing a certain character; an alleged or assumed right; assumption of superiority; affectation; pretentiousness.

pretentious *adj* full of pretension; attempting to pass for more than one is worth; pretending to an unmerited superiority.

preterit, preterite *adj* (*gram*) expressing past time; applied to the tense expressing action or existence perfectly past or finished; past (*he struck*); also used as equivalent to perfect.—*n* (*gram*) the preterit tense.

pretermit *vt* (**pretermitted, pretermitting**) (*arch*) to pass by deliberately; to omit or neglect to do.

preternatural *adj* beyond what is natural or different from what is natural, as distinguished from *supernatural*, above nature; unnatural, contrary to nature.

pretext *n* an ostensible reason or motive assigned or assumed as a cover for the real reason or motive; a pretence.

prettiness *n* state or quality of being pretty; charm or appeal, but not conforming to formal ideas of beauty.

pretty *adj* of a pleasing and attractive form without the strong lines of beauty or without gracefulness and dignity; pleasing; neatly arranged; (ironically) nice, fine, meaning the opposite (*a pretty muddle*); (*colloq*) effeminate, unmasculine; (*colloq*) facile, fussy, without depth (*his music is too pretty*).—*adv* in some degree; moderately expressing a degree less than very (*pretty well, large, sure,* etc); (*colloq*) rather or very (*a pretty enormous crowd*).

prevail *vi* to overcome; to gain the victory or superiority (often with *over* or *against*); to be in force; to have extensive power or influence (*a disease, a custom prevails in a place*); to have predominant influence; to succeed; to overcome or gain over by persuasion (with *on* or *upon*, as *they prevailed on him to go*).

prevalence *n* the state or quality of being prevalent; superiority; general reception or practice; general existence or extension (*the prevalence of vice* or *of a fashion*).

prevalent *adj* prevailing; predominant; most generally received or current; widespread.

prevaricate *vi* (**prevaricated, prevaricating**) to act or speak evasively or falsely; to evade or swerve from the truth; to play for time by being evasive; to quibble in giving answers.

prevarication *n* the act of prevaricating; a shuffling or quibbling to evade the truth or the disclosure of truth; the wilful concealment or misrepresentation of truth by giving evasive evidence.

prevaricator *n* one who prevaricates; a quibbler.

prevent *vt* to stop or intercept; to impede; to thwart, especially by acting beforehand.

preventable *adj* capable of being prevented or hindered.

prevention *n* the act of preventing; the act of hindering by something done before.

preventive *adj* tending to prevent or hinder; protective; prophylactic.—*n* that which prevents; that which intercepts the access or approach of something; something used to prevent disease; a prophylactic.

preview *n* an advance, restricted showing, as of a film, art exhibition, etc.—*vt* to view or show in advance of public presentation; to give a preliminary survey.

previous *adj* going before in time; being or happening before something else; antecedent; prior.

previously *adv* in time preceding; beforehand; antecedently.

pre-war *adj* belonging to the period before a war.

prey *n* a creature hunted or caught by another for food; spoil; booty; goods taken from an enemy in war; anything taken by violence and injustice; a victim.—*vi* to feed by the hunting or seizing of other creatures (with *on* or *upon*); to take prey or booty; to weigh heavily, as on the mind; to waste gradually (*grief preyed on him*).

priapism *n* (*med*) abnormally prolonged erection of the penis.

price *n* the sum of money or the value which a seller sets on goods; the current value of a commodity; the equivalent for which something is bought or sold; cost; value; worth (*a pearl of good price*); estimation.—*vt* (**priced, pricing**) to set a price on; to value; to ask the price of.

priceless *adj* invaluable; inestimable; too valuable to admit of a price being fixed.

prick *n* something sharply pointed, small, or relatively small, and slender; a thorn; a skewer; a puncture or wound by a prick or prickle; a sting; the act of prickling or the feeling or state of being pricked; (*fig*) a stinging or tormenting thought or emotion; remorse; (*arch*) a dot or small mark; (*vulg sl*) a penis; (*sl*) an objectionable or despised person.—*vt* to pierce with something sharp pointed; to puncture; to erect (said of the ears, hence, *to prick up the ears*, to listen with eager attention); (*fig*) to cause an acute emotional pain in (a person); to fix by a sharp point; to designate or set apart by a puncture or mark (*pricked off for duty*); to transplant seedlings (with *out*); to spur; to goad; to incite (often with *on*); to sting; to trace or transfer (a design) by puncturing.—*vi* to suffer or feel penetration by a point or sharp pain; to be punctured; (*arch*) to spur on, to ride rapidly.

prick

pricking *n* the act of piercing with a sharp point; (*fig*) a feeling as of something sharp penetrating the flesh.

prickle *n* a little prick; a small sharp point; (*bot*) a small pointed shoot or sharp process growing from the bark and thus distinguished from the thorn, which grows from the wood of a plant; a sharp-pointed process or projection, as from the skin of an animal; a feeling as of being pricked.—*vt* (**prickled, prickling**) to prick slightly; to pierce with fine sharp points.—*vi* to suffer a pricking sensation.

prickly *adj* full of sharp points or prickles; equipped with prickles; stinging in feeling; easily offended or irritated; ill humoured.

prickly heat *n* (*med*) miliaria.

prickly pear *n* any of several tropical species of cactus covered with clusters of spines, some species producing an edible fruit; the fruit itself.

pride *n* the quality or state of being proud; inordinate self-esteem; an unreasonable conceit about one's own superiority over others; self-respect; consciousness of worth; proud behaviour; insolence; that which is or may be a cause of pride; that of which people are proud; one who or that which gives rise to pride or glorification; highest pitch; splendid show; ostentation; the best, greatest or most glorious part (*the pride of the fleet*); a herd (of lions).—*vt* (**prided, priding**) to indulge in pride; to value oneself (used reflexively and with *on* or *upon*).

prie-dieu *n* (*pl* **prie-dieus, prie-dieux**) a desk with a low rest for kneeling on while saying prayers.

priest *n* someone ordained to mediate between a supplicant or a congregation and God and to carry out the sacred offices of his or her faith or church; a minister of public worship; a person who is set apart or consecrated to the ministry of the Gospels.

priestess *n* a priest who is a woman; a woman regarded as a leader (as of a movement).

priestcraft *n* the art of being a priest; priestly policy or system of management based on temporal or material interest; (*derog*) policy of clergy to advance the political influence and power of their own order.

priesthood *n* the office or character of a priest; the order composed of priests; priests collectively.

priestly *adj* pertaining to or characteristic of a priest or priests; sacerdotal; becoming to a priest.

prig *n* a smug, self-righteous person.

priggish *adj* smug; self-righteous and narrow-minded.

prim *adj* neat; formal; precise; demure; over-proper.

prima ballerina *n* the principal female dancer in a ballet company.

primacy *n* (*eccles*) the office or dignity of a primate, archbishop or pope; the state of being ranked first or highest.

prima donna *n* (*pl* **prima donnas**) the first or chief female singer in an opera; someone who is temperamental, melodramatic or difficult.

prima facie *adv* at first view or appearance. —*adj* true, valid or sufficient at first impression; self-evident; legally sufficient to establish a fact unless disproved (*prima facie evidence*).

primal *adj* primary; first in time, order or importance; original.

primary *adj* first in order of time; original; first; first in dignity or importance; chief; principal; elementary; preparatory or lowest in order (*primary schools*); first in intention.—*n* that which stands highest in rank or importance, as opposed to *second-*ary; any of the large feathers (quills) on the outermost joint of a bird's wing; in the USA, a preliminary election at which candidates are chosen for the final election; a primary school.

primary colour *n* any colour having no trace of another colour, that is red, green and blue (or violet); (loosely) any of the colours into which white light is divided by a prism—red, orange, yellow, green, blue, indigo and violet.

primary school *n* a school for children between the ages of five and eleven.

primate¹ *n* any of the highest order of mammals, including man, the apes, monkeys, lemurs, etc.

primate² *n* the chief ecclesiastic in certain churches, as the Anglican; an archbishop (the Archbishop of York is entitled *Primate of England*; the Archbishop of Canterbury, *Primate of all England*).

prime *adj* first in order of time; fundamental; original (*prime cost*); first in rank, degree or dignity (*prime minister*); first in excellence, value or importance; first-rate; early; in the first stage; (*math*) (of a number) divisible only by itself or 1.—*n* the earliest stage or beginning of anything; the dawn; the morning; the spring of the year; the spring of life; youth; full health, strength or beauty; the highest or most perfect or most flourishing condition; the best part; that which is best in quality; (*math*) a prime number; (*eccles*) one of the canonical hours of the Divine Office, fixed for the first hour, generally 6 a.m.; hence, the time of day at which prime takes place; (in fencing) the first guard position; (*mus*) the keynote or tonic of a scale; also, a unison.—*vt* (**primed, priming**) to cover with a coat of primer so as to prepare a surface for painting, filling, etc; to make something ready; to charge (a hydraulic device) with fluid prior to operating it; to charge (the carburettor of an internal-combustion engine) with fuel prior to starting; to equip (an explosive charge, e.g. a gun, mine, etc) with a primer for detonating the main charge; (chiefly *hist*) to equip (a muzzle-loading firearm) with priming powder for igniting the main charge; to provide (a person) with information beforehand; to brief; to instruct or prepare (a person) beforehand as to what to say or do.

prime minister *n* the first minister of state or of a sovereign; the head of a parliamentary government; the premier.

primeness *n* the quality of being prime; supreme excellence.

prime number *n* (*arith*) a number not divisible without remainder by any other number than itself or 1.

primer¹ *n* a small elementary book for religious instruction or for teaching children to read; a book of elementary principles.

primer² *n* a detonator or igniter for an explosive charge; a priming charge of gunpowder; an undercoat or size used to prepare a surface for painting, etc; priming.

primeval *adj* original; primitive; belonging to the first ages.

priming *n* (of a gun and blasting) the powder used to ignite the charge; in painting, the first layer of paint or size laid on a surface which is to be painted.

primipara *n* (*pl* **primiparas, primiparae**) (*obstet*) a woman due to give birth to her first child or who has given birth to only one child.

primiparous *adj* bearing young for the first time.

primitive *adj* pertaining to the beginning or origin; original; first; old-fashioned; characterized by the lack of sophistication, etc, of the dawn of civilization; crude, simple, rough, unpolished; crudely constructed; lacking civilized amenities (*a primitive cottage*); (of art) belonging to the pre-Renaissance period in art; characteristic of often deliberately unsophisticated modern works of art or of artists working in that genre; (*gram*) applied to a word in its simplest etymological form; not derived; radical; primary; (*bot*) original, in opposition to forms resulting from hybridization; (*biol*) of or pertaining to the earliest stages of evolution; (*biol*) (of a species, etc) little changed from the earliest ancestral type.— *n* a primitive person; hence, someone crude, unsophisticated, rough, etc; a work of art of the primitive period or primitive in style; the author of such works; (*gram*) a word from which another word is derived, a root form, opposed to *derivative*.

primogeniture *n* the state of being born first of the same parents; seniority by birth among children; the right or principle under which the eldest son of a family succeeds to the father's real estate, in preference to, and often in absolute exclusion of the younger sons and daughters.

primordial *adj* first in order; original; primeval; existing from the beginning.— *n* a first principle or element.

primrose *n* the common name for certain herbaceous perennial plants of the genus Primula, some species of which grow wild in Britain, and especially the European species with pale yellow flowers; a pale yellow colour.— *adj* resembling a primrose in colour; pale yellow; abounding with primroses; pleasant, bright

primrose path *n* the path of self-indulgence and (sensual) pleasure.

primus *n* the leading bishop of the Scottish Episcopal Church.

Primus *n* the trademark of a small portable paraffin cooking stove.

prince *n* a man holding the first or highest rank; a sovereign; a sovereign who has the government of a particular territory but owes certain services to a superior; the son of a sovereign; a male member of a royal family; the chief of any body of men; a man at the head of any class, profession, etc (*a merchant prince*).

princedom *n* the jurisdiction, rank or state of a prince.

princely *adj* pertaining to a prince; resembling a prince; noble; grand; august; magnificent.

princess *n* a female of the same rank as a prince; a female sovereign; the consort of a prince.

principal *adj* chief; highest in rank, character, authority or importance; first; main; essential; most considerable.— *n* a chief or head; one who takes a leading part; one primarily engaged; one chief in authority; the head of a school, college or university; (*law*) the perpetrator of a crime or an abettor; a capital sum lent on interest, due as a debt or used as a fund, so called in distinction to *interest*; in carpentry, a main timber in an assemblage of pieces.

principality *n* sovereignty; supreme power; a prince or one invested with sovereignty; the territory of a prince or the country which gives title to a prince.

principally *adv* in the chief place; chiefly; above all.

principle *n* a source of origin; the primary source from which anything proceeds; element; primordial substance; a general truth; a law comprehending many subordinate truths; a law on which others are founded or from which others are derived; an axiom; a maxim; a tenet; a governing law of conduct; a settled rule of action; a rule of moral conduct; uprightness (*a man of principle*); (*chem*) a component part; an element; a substance on the presence of which certain qualities common to a number of bodies depend.

print *vt* to impress; to imprint; to mark by pressing one thing on another; to take an impression of; to produce (on paper, cloth, etc) the impression of inked type, illustrations, designs, etc; to produce (a book, etc); to write (something) in capital or unjoined letters resembling printed ones; (*photog, cinematog*) to produce (a positive print) from a negative.— *vi* to use or practise the art of printing; to write in capital letters; to imprint upon the memory.— *n* a mark made by impression; a stamp; printed letters; the impression of types in general; printed matter; a picture or design produced by printing, especially an engraving, etching, lithograph, woodcut, etc; a photographic copy, especially from a negative; printed cloth; a fingerprint, foot-

primrose

print, etc.—**in print** (of a book) having been published; still available to buy.—**out of print** no longer available to buy.

printer *n* one who prints books, pamphlets, newspapers, etc; one who prints cloth or one who takes impressions from engraved plates, etc; a machine for printing from; a device that produces printout.

printing *n* the art or practice of impressing letters, type, illustrations, designs, etc, on paper, cloth or other material; the impression of letters, designs, etc, made from inked type, plates or blocks; the business of a printer; (*photog*) the act or art of obtaining a positive print from a negative.

prior *adj* preceding, especially in the order of time; earlier; antecedent; anterior.—*adv* previously; antecedently (*he had never been there prior to that time*).—*n* the superior of a priory or a monastery, ranking lower than an abbot; a monk next in dignity to an abbot.

prioress *n* the female head of a convent of nuns, next in rank to an abbess.

priority *n* the state of being prior or antecedent in time or of preceding something else; precedence in place or rank; a matter to which specified and often urgent attention is given.

priory *n* a religious house of which a prior or prioress is the superior, in dignity below an abbey.

prise, prize *vt* (**prised, prising**) to force open or up; to raise as by means of a lever; to obtain or extract with difficulty.

prism *n* a polyhedron whose bases or ends are any similar, equal and parallel plane figures and whose sides are parallelograms; a transparent polygonal solid, often of glass, with a triangular section, used to reflect or alter the direction of light or to disperse it into a spectrum.

prismatic, prismatical *adj* resembling or pertaining to a prism; formed or exhibited by a prism; operating by means of a prism.

prison *n* a place of confinement or involuntary restraint; especially, a public building for the confinement or safe custody of criminals and others committed by process of law; a jail.—*vt* to shut up in a prison; to confine; to imprison.

prisoner *n* one who is confined in a prison; a person under arrest, whether in prison or not; a captive; one taken by an enemy in war; one whose liberty is restrained; hence, a person who is a captive of his or her own ideas, emotions, etc.

pristine *adj* belonging to a primitive or early state or period; original; primitive; pure; unusual; not corrupted.

prithee *interj* (*arch*) a corruption of *pray thee, I pray thee.*

privacy *n* a state of being private or reclusive; seclusion; secrecy; solitude.

prism

private *adj* peculiar or special to oneself; belonging to or concerning an individual only; personal, opposed to *public* or *national*; not known, open or accessible to people in general; secret; not invested with public office or employment; not having a public or official rank or office; unconnected with others; solitary; withdrawn; reclusive.—*n* a soldier of the lowest rank in the army.

private detective *n* a person engaged privately to investigate crime or make enquiries.

privateer *n* (chiefly *hist*) a privately owned and outfitted armed vessel commissioned by a government for war service; one who serves on a privateer; (in sport) someone, such as a racing driver, who is not a member of an official team or who has not sponsorship and so funds his or her own efforts.

privation *n* the state of being deprived; deprivation of what is necessary for comfort; destitution; want; hardship.

privet *n* a bushy evergreen shrub, frequently planted to form ornamental hedges in gardens.

privilege *n* a right or advantage enjoyed by a person or body of persons beyond the common advantages of other individuals; a private or personal favour enjoyed; a special advantage, right or immunity; any of a citizen's constitutional rights; an honour (*it was a privilege to have known them*); (*law*) the right of a lawyer to refuse to divulge information given to him or her in confidence; a similar right granted to or claimed by certain officials or members of some professions, as journalists; the rights and immunities of members of most constitutional legislative bodies (*parliamentary privilege*).—*vt* (**privileged, privileging**) to grant some privilege, right or exemption to; to invest with a special right or immunity.

privy *adj* private; assigned to private uses; not public; secret; not seen openly; privately knowing; admitted to the participation of knowledge with another of a secret transaction (*privy to a thing*); (*arch*) pertaining to one person alone.—*n* a latrine or toilet.

Privy Council *n* the principal private council of the British sovereign, nominally including all present and former Cabinet ministers as well as other eminent people from public life, its role being now primarily advisory.

Privy Councillor *n* a member of the Privy Council.

prize[1] *n* that which is taken from an enemy in war, particularly a ship, with the property taken in it; that which is deemed a valuable acquisition; any gain or advantage; that which is obtained or offered as the reward of exertion or contest; that which is won in a lottery or in any similar way.

prize² *vt* (**prized, prizing**) to value highly; to consider of great worth; to esteem.

prize³ *vt* (**prized, prizing**) same as **prise**.

prizefight *n* a boxing match for a prize.

prizefighter *n* a boxer.

proa, prau *n* any of several types of canoe from the South China Sea and the South Pacific, usually having an outrigger and a sail.

proactive *adj* active in initiating; (*psychol*) affecting a subsequent process.

probability *n* the state or quality of being probable; likelihood; appearance of truth; anything that has the appearance of reality or truth (in this sense with a plural); (*math*) a measure of the likely chance of something occurring or the likely frequency of its occurrence.

probable *adj* likely to be true or likely to occur but with some room for doubt; likely; most likely, especially when evidence is absent (*the probable reason for his disappearance*); rendering something probable (*probable evidence*).

probably *adv* in a probable manner; in all likelihood; as is probable; likely.

probate *n* a proceeding before proper authorities by which a person's will or testament is established as such and registered; official proof of a will.

probation *n* the act of proving; proof; any proceeding designed to ascertain character, qualifications, etc; a preliminary or preparatory trial or examination; the period of trial; release from prison or conditional freedom from a prison sentence, allowing liberty under supervision on condition of good behaviour; the state or period of being on probation.

probationer *n* one who is on probation or trial, especially in UK a young offender; a person, as a trainee nurse or teacher, whose fitness is being tested under a trial period.

probation officer *n* an official who supervises offenders on probation.

probe *n* a surgeon's instrument for examining the depth or other circumstances of a wound, ulcer or cavity; a device, such as an unmanned spacecraft, used to obtain information about an environment; an instrument used to measure or test (*a heat probe*); an investigation.—*vt* (**probed, probing**) to apply a probe to; to examine by a probe; (*fig*) to search to the end; to examine thoroughly into.

probity *n* tried virtue or integrity; strict honesty; rectitude; uprightness; high principle.

problem *n* a question proposed for solution,

decision or determination; a point requiring to be cleared up; (*geom*) a proposition requiring some operation to be performed.—*adj* difficult to deal with or resolve (*a problem family*).

problematic, problematical *adj* questionable; uncertain; disputable; doubtful.

proboscis *n* (*pl* **proboscises, proboscides**) the snout or trunk projecting from the head of an elephant and certain other animals; the horny tube formed by the modified jaws of insects, used for sucking blood from animals or juice from plants; (*joc*) the nose.

procedure *n* manner of proceeding or acting; a course or mode of action; conduct; a step taken; a proceeding.

proceed *vi* to move, pass or go onward; to continue or renew motion or progress; to advance; to go on; to pass from one point, stage or topic to another; to issue or come, as from an origin, source or fountain; to set to work and go on in a certain way; to act according to some method; to begin and carry on a legal action.

proceeding *n* the act of one who proceeds; a measure or step taken; a transaction; a mode of conduct; (*pl*) the course of steps in the prosecution of actions at law; the record or account of the transactions of a society.

proceeds *npl* the amount accruing from some transaction; the value of goods sold or converted into money; profit; return on investment.

process *n* a proceeding or moving forward; progressive course; way in which something goes on or is done; gradual progress; course; series of actions or experiments (*a chemical process*); series of motions or changes going on, as in growth, decay, etc, in physical bodies; drift; lapse; a passing or elapsing (*the process of time*); (*law*) the whole course of proceedings in a legal action; (*law*) a summons compelling attendance at court; a projecting portion of something; (*anat*) any protuberance or projecting part of a bone or other body.—*vt* to handle following set procedures; to prepare or treat (food, etc) by a special process; to develop (film).

procession *n* the act of proceeding or issuing forth; a train of persons walking or riding on horseback or in vehicles in a formal march or moving with ceremonious solemnity.

processional *adj* pertaining to a procession; consisting in a procession.—*n* a processional hymn or hymn book.

proclaim *vt* to make known by public announcement; to promulgate; to announce; to publish; to praise or exalt.

proclamation *n* the act of proclaiming; an official public announcement or declaration; a public ordinance; a declaration or announcement of something by a person, often with some formality.

proclivity *n* inclination; propensity; proneness; tendency; readiness.

procrastinate *vt* (**procrastinated, procrastinating**) to put off from day to day; to delay; to defer to a future time.—*vi* to delay; to be dilatory.

procrastination *n* the act or habit of putting off to a future time; dilatoriness.

procreate *vt* (**procreated, procreating**) to beget; to generate, produce; to engender.

procreation *n* the act of procreating or begetting.

procreative *adj* having the power or function of procreating.

procreator *n* one that begets; a father or sire.

Procrustean *adj* compelling uniformity by violent means.

proctor *n* a person employed to manage another's cause in a court of civil or ecclesiastical law; (hist) a collector of tithes; in the Anglican Church, one of the clergy elected as a representative to the General Synod; an official in a university whose function is to see that good order is kept.

proctorial *adj* pertaining to a proctor.

procumbent *adj* lying down; prone; (*bot*) trailing; prostrate; lying on the ground but without putting forth roots (*a procumbent stem*).

procurable *adj* capable of being procured; obtainable.

procuration *n* the act or process of procuring; (*law*) management of another's affairs; the document by which a person is empowered to transact the affairs of another.

procurator *n* the manager of another's affairs; one who undertakes the care of legal proceedings for another; a governor of a province under the Roman emperors.

procurator fiscal *n* the title of officials in Scotland perform the duties of prosecutor and coroner.

procure *vt* (**procured, procuring**) to obtain, as by request, loan, effort, labour or purchase; to get, gain, come into possession of; to bring on; to cause, bring about, effect, contrive; to get and make available for sexual intercourse.—*vi* to pimp; to obtain or employ women for the purposes of prostitution.

procurement *n* the act of procuring or obtaining.

procurer *n* one that procures; a pimp.

procuress *n* a female pimp; a bawd.

prod *n* a pointed instrument, as a goad or an awl; a stab; a push or jab with the finger, elbow, etc.—*vt* (**prodded, prodding**) to prick with a pointed instrument; to goad; to push, jab or nudge; hence, to encourage or exhort (especially someone slow or reluctant).

Prod, Proddie *n* (*sl*) a Protestant.

prodigal *adj* given to extravagant expenditure; expending wastefully; profuse; lavish; wasteful; lavishly bountiful.—*n* one who expends money extravagantly; one who is profuse or lavish; a waster; a spendthrift.

prodigality *n* extravagance in expenditure; profusion; waste; excessive or profuse liberality.

prodigious *adj* of the nature of a prodigy; extraordinary; very great; huge; enormous; excessive; intense.

prodigy *n* someone, especially someone young, of remarkable talents; (*arch*) something extraordinary from which omens are drawn; a portent; anything very extraordinary; a wonder or miracle (*he is a prodigy of learning*); something out of the ordinary course of nature.

produce *vt* (**produced, producing**) to bring forward; to bring or offer to view or notice; to exhibit; to bring forth; to give birth to; to bear, furnish, yield; to cause, effect, bring about; to make; to bring into being or form; to cause to accrue (*money produces interest*); (*geom*) to draw out in length; to extend (*to produce a line for a certain distance*).—*vi* to bring forth or yield appropriate offspring, products or consequences.—*n* a product; a total produced, brought forth or yielded; the outcome yielded by labour and natural growth; yield or production (*the produce of a farm* or *of a country*).

producer *n* someone who produces, especially a farmer or manufacturer; a person who finances or supervises the putting on of a play or making of a film; an apparatus or plant for making gas.

product *n* a thing which is produced by nature, as fruits or grain crops; what is yielded by the soil; that which is produced by labour or mental application; a production; anything made or produced and offered for sale (*the client's product*); something resulting as a consequence; result; (*math*) the result of, or quantity produced by, the multiplication of two or more numbers or quantities together.

production *n* the act or process of producing; (*econ*) the producing of articles having an exchangeable value; that which is produced or made (*the productions of the earth, of art* or *manufacture*); the amount of something produced or the rate of production; mass production; a literary or artistic work; the presentation of a film, stage or television show, opera, etc; a particular version of a play, opera, etc, in performance (*this production of 'Pygmalion'*).

productive *adj* having the power of producing; fertile; producing good crops; bringing into being; causing to exist (*an age productive of great men*); (*econ*) producing commodities of value; adding to the wealth of the world.

productivity *n* the state of being productive; the ratio of the output of a manufacturing business to the input of materials, labour, etc.

proem *n* preface; introduction; preliminary observations to a book or writing.

profanation *n* the act of profaning; the violating of sacred things or the treating of them with contempt or irreverence; desecration; the act of treating with too little delicacy.

profane *adj* not sacred or devoted to sacred purposes; not possessing any sanctity; secular; irreverent towards God or holy things; speaking or spoken, acting or acted in contempt of sacred things or implying it; blasphemous; polluted.—*vt* (**profaned, profaning**) to treat as if not sacred or deserving reverence; to treat with irreverence, impiety or sacrilege; to desecrate (*to profane the name of God* or *the Sabbath*); to put to a wrong use; to employ basely or unworthily.

profanity *n* the quality of being profane; that which is profane; profane language or conduct.

profess *vt* to make open declaration of; to avow, acknowledge, own; to acknowledge or own publicly to be; to lay claim openly to the character of (used reflexively, as *to profess oneself a Christian*); to make a show of; to make protestations or a pretence of; to pretend (*to profess great friendship for a person*); to declare oneself skilled in, often falsely (*he professes surgery*).—*vi* to declare openly; to make any declaration or assertion.

profession *n* the act of professing; a public avowal or acknowledgement of one's sentiments or belief; a declaration; a representation or protestation (*professions of friendship* or *sincerity*); a calling superior to a mere trade or handicraft, as that of medicine, law, architecture, etc; a vocation; the collective body of persons engaged in such calling (*the medical profession*).

professional *adj* pertaining to a profession; engaged in a profession; efficient and competent in a job or activity (*a pianist of professional standard*); undertaken for pay or gain (*a professional killer*).—*n* a member of any profession; someone extremely competent in his or her job or chosen activity; one who makes a living from an activity in which amateurs also engage; one employed to instruct others in a sport or game (*a golf professional*).

professor *n* a senior teacher in a university or college, whose business is to deliver lectures or instruct students; one who professes his or her faith or beliefs.

professorial *adj* pertaining to a professor in a college, etc; professor-like.

professoriate *n* a body of professors; the teaching staff of professors.

professorship *n* the office of a professor.

proffer *vt* to offer or tender for acceptance, usually something intangible.—*n* the act of proffering.

proficiency *n* the quality of being proficient; competence; skill.

proficient *n* (*arch*) an adept, an expert.—*adj* skilled in any business or branch of learning; well qualified; competent.

profile *n* an outline or contour; especially, an outline of the human face seen sideways; the side face or half face; a drawing, photograph, etc, of someone or something in profile; a biographical sketch; a table or graph demonstrating the tested characteristics of a person or group of people, a machine, an area of interest, natural matter or features, etc.—*vt* (**profiled, profiling**) to represent in profile; to produce a profile of.

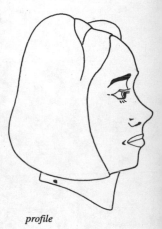

profile

profit *n* any advantage or gain, especially the advantage or gain resulting to the owner of capital from its employment in any undertaking; an excess of income over expenditure over a given period, usually expressed as profit for the year and applied in particular to the financial performance of businesses; the difference between the total cost and the selling price of anything; financial gain; emolument.—*vt* to benefit; to advantage; to be of service to; to advance.—*vi* to derive profit; to improve; to make progress intellectually or morally; to gain financially; to become richer; to be of use or advantage; to bring good.

profitable *adj* yielding or bringing profit or gain; gainful; lucrative; useful; advantageous.

profiteer *n* a trader who takes advantage of abnormal conditions, such as those which hold during war, to make excessive profit, especially by raising the prices of essential or vital commodities.—*vi* to make excess profits.

profligacy *n* shamelessly debauched or immoral behaviour; extravagance; wastefulness.

profligate *adj* abandoned to vice; lost to virtue or decency; debauched; wasteful; extravagant.—*n* an abandoned person; one who has lost all regard to good principles, virtue or decency; a wasteful or prodigal person.

profound *adj* deep; far below the surface; having great depth; intellectually deep; deep in knowledge or skill (*a profound* *scholar*); characterized by intensity; far-reaching; deeply felt (*profound grief*); exhibiting or expressing humility (*a profound bow*, *profound reverence*).—*n* (*arch*) the deep, the sea, the ocean (with *the*); an abyss; a deep immeasurable space.

profundity *n* the quality or condition of being profound; depth of place, of knowledge, etc.

profuse *adj* plentiful, copious; extravagant; lavish; liberal to excess; prodigal; generously or freely given.

profusion *n* profuse or lavish expenditure; rich abundance; lavish supply; exuberant plenty.

progenitor *n* an ancestor in the direct line; a forefather; a parent; a forerunner or precursor.

progeny *n* offspring collectively; children; human or animal descendants or offspring.

prognostic *adj* foreshowing; indicating something future by signs or symptoms.—*n* a sign by which a future event may be known or foretold; an omen; a token; a symptom; a foretelling; prediction.

prognosticate *vt* (**prognosticated, prognosticating**) to foretell by means of present signs; to predict; to foreshow or foretoken; to prophesy.—*vi* to judge or pronounce from prognostics.

prognostication *n* the act of prognosticating; that which foreshows; a prophecy; a foretoken; previous sign.

program *n* a sequence of instructions fed into a computer or the software containing such instructions.—*vt* (**programmed, programming**) to feed (a program) into a computer; to write a program for (a computer).

programme *n* a plan of proceedings sketched out beforehand; a list, schedule or order of things to be done; an outline or detailed sketch or advertisement, usually printed, of the order of proceedings or subjects in any entertainment, performance or public ceremony; a scheduled radio or television broadcast; a syllabus for a course of study.—*vti* (**programmed, programming**) to plan, to schedule.

progress *n* a moving or going forward; a proceeding onward; a moving forward in growth; increase; advance in matters of any kind; course; intellectual or moral improvement; a passage from place to place; a journey.—*vi* to move forward or onward; to advance; to proceed in any course; to advance towards something better; to make improvement.—*vt* to bring (a project, etc) closer to completion.

progression *n* the act of progressing, advancing or moving forward; progress; advance; course; movement forward in a defined, usually logical, sequence; (*math*) a numerical sequence following a simple law; thus 2, 4, 6, 8, 10 are numbers in *ar-*

ithmetical progression; 2, 4, 8, 16, etc, in *geometrical progression*; (*mus*) motion, usually in a logical sequence, from one note to another or one chord to another.

progressive *adj* pertaining to progress; moving forward; proceeding onward; advancing; supporting or encouraging political or social reform as a matter of the first importance (often advocating revolution as the means); pertaining to an educational system that seeks to match academic development to social development; (of taxes) graded so that the rate increases as the taxable sum does; (of a disease) advancing, worsening.—*n* one who advocates progress, especially in political or social reform.

prohibit *vt* to forbid authoritatively; to interdict by authority (*to prohibit a person from doing a thing; to prohibit the thing being done*); to prevent; to preclude.

prohibition *n* the act of prohibiting; a declaration to hinder some action; interdict; the forbidding by law of the manufacture, importation or sale of alcoholic liquors for ordinary use.

Prohibition *n* the period (1920–33) when the manufacture, importation, transport and sale of alcoholic liquors in the USA was banned by law.

prohibitionist *n* one who favours prohibition.

prohibitive, prohibitory *adj* serving to prohibit; forbidding; implying prohibition; (of a price, etc) tending to discourage purchase or sale.

project *vt* to throw out or forth; to cast or shoot forward; to cause (an image) to appear on a surface; to delineate; to make (one's voice) heard at a distance; to attribute (feelings, etc) to another; to imagine; to estimate or plan for the future.—*vi* to shoot forward; to extend beyond something else; to jut; to be prominent.—*n* that which is projected or devised; a plan; a scheme; a design; a substantial educational task in which a student is required to make his or her own research and to present the results.

projectile *adj* impelling forward (*a projectile force*); caused by impulse (*projectile motion*).—*n* an object projected or impelled through the air, as something thrown, a bullet fired from a gun, etc; a missile.

projection *n* the act of projecting, throwing or shooting forward; the state of projecting or jutting out; a part projecting or jutting out; a prominence; the representation of something by means of lines, etc, drawn on a surface; especially the representation of any object on a perspective plane; the delineation of the earth's surface or a portion of it by a map; the process by which images on film, slides, etc, are projected on to a screen or other surface; a forecast based on known facts; the unconscious process by which a person imputes his or her own secret feelings, motives, desires, etc, to another.

projectionist *n* a person who operates a projector; a map-maker.

projector *n* one who projects; one who forms a scheme or design; a device for hurling missiles or from which missiles are fired; a machine for projecting films, slides, etc.

prolapse *vi* (**prolapsed, prolapsing**) (*med*) (of an organ, etc) to fall or slip out of place.—*n* a prolapsed condition.

prolate *adj* extended beyond the line of an exact sphere.

prolegomenon *n* (*pl* **prolegomena**) a preliminary observation (chiefly used in plural); a critical introduction to a text.

prolepsis *n* (*pl* **prolepses**) something of the nature of an anticipation; (*rhet*) a figure by which a thing is represented as already done, though in reality it is to follow as a consequence of the action which is described.

proletarian *adj* pertaining to the working or wage-earning classes; belonging to the lowest or poorest class of the community; hence, mean; vulgar.—*n* a member of the working class or the poorest classes; (*derog*) one of the rabble.

proletariat *n* the working classes collectively; the lower classes; all wage-earners collectively, as distinct from those who earn salaries.

prolific *adj* producing young or fruit, especially in abundance; fruitful; productive; having the quality of generating abundantly (*a topic prolific of controversy*).

prolix *adj* long and wordy; extending to a great length; diffuse; indulging in lengthy discourse; discussing at great length; tedious.

prolixity *n* the state or quality of being prolix.

prologue *n* a preface or introduction; the discourse or poem spoken before a dramatic performance or play begins; the speaker of a prologue.—*vt* (**prologued, prologuing**) to introduce with a formal prologue; to preface.

prolong *vt* to lengthen in time; to extend the duration of; to put off to a distant time; to extend in space or length (*to prolong a line*).—*vi* to put off to a distant time.

prolongation *n* the act of prolonging; something that is or has been prolonged; an extension.

prom *n* (*colloq*) a promenade concert; in USA, a promenade.

promenade *n* a walk for pleasure and display or exercise; a place for walking in public; in USA, a formal dance in a school or college.—*vi* (**promenaded, promenading**) to walk for amusement, show or exercise.

promenade concert *n* a concert in which part of the audience is located in an area without seats.

promenade deck *n* an upper deck on a ship where passengers may promenade.

promenader *n* one who promenades; one who attends a promenade concert.

prominence, prominency *n* a standing out from the surface of something; that which juts out; protuberance; state of being distinguished among people; conspicuousness; distinction; relative eminence or importance.

prominent *adj* standing out beyond the line or surface of something; jutting; protuberant; distinguished above others (*a prominent character*); likely to attract special attention from size, position, etc; striking; conspicuous.

promiscuity *n* the state of being promiscuous, especially sexually.

promiscuous *adj* given to casual and indiscriminate sexual behaviour; consisting of individuals united in a body or mass without order; mingled indiscriminately; forming part of a confused crowd or mass; random; indiscriminate; not restricted to an individual; casual; careless or thoughtless.

promise *n* a declaration, written or verbal, made by one person to another, which binds the person who makes it to do or keep from doing a certain act specified; a declaration that something will be done or given for the benefit of another; ground or basis of expectation; an undertaking or pledge; an indication of future distinction or excellence (*a youth of great promise*). —*vt* (**promised, promising**) to make a promise of; to engage to do, give, grant or procure for someone; to afford reason to expect (*the year promises a good harvest*). —*vi* to make a promise; to assure by a promise; to afford hopes or expectations.

promising *adj* giving promise; affording reasonable ground of hope for the future; looking as if likely to turn out well.

promontory *n* a high point of land or rock projecting into the sea beyond the line of coast; a headland.

promote *vt* (**promoted, promoting**) to contribute to the growth, enlargement, increase or power of; to forward; to advance; to help onward; to excite; to stir up (as strife); to exalt or raise to a higher post or position; to elevate; to encourage sales by advertising or by publicity.

promotion *n* the act of promoting; advancement; encouragement; exaltation in rank or honour; preferment; the furtherance of sales by advertising or publicity.

prompt *adj* ready and quick to act as occasion demands; acting with cheerful alacrity; ready and willing; performed without delay; quick; ready; not delayed.—*vt* to move or excite to action or exertion; to incite; to instigate; to assist (a speaker) when at a loss by pronouncing the words forgotten or next in order (*to prompt an actor*); to dictate; to suggest to the mind.—*n* the act of prompting; a prompter; a reminder; (*com*) time limit allowed for payment; the contract specifying such a period; something that serves as a reminder; (*comput*) a message, generally a symbol or sentence, which appears on a screen to remind the operator to do something or to go through a procedure.

promptbook *n* the book used by a prompter of a theatre.

prompter *n* one who or that which prompts; specifically, a person placed behind the scenes in a theatre, whose business is to assist the actors when at a loss by uttering the first words of the forgotten lines.

promptitude *n* readiness; quickness of decision and action when occasion demands; readiness of will; cheerful ala ritv.

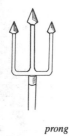

prong

promulgate *vt* (**promulgated, promulgating**) to make known by open declaration, as laws, decrees, tidings, etc; to publish abroad; to announce; to proclaim.

promulgation *n* the act of promulgating; publication; open declaration.

prone *adj* lying with the face downward; rushing or falling headlong or downward; sloping downward; inclined by disposition or natural tendency; disposed, usually in a bad sense (*men prone to evil, to strife*).

proneness *n* the state of being prone; inclination; propensity; readiness.

prong *n* a sharp-pointed instrument; the spike of a fork or of a similar instrument; a pointed projection (*the prongs of a deer's antlers*).

pronominal *adj* pertaining to pronouns; acting as a pronoun.

pronoun *n* (*gram*) one of a certain class of words or generalized terms often used instead of a noun or name, to prevent the repetition of it.

pronounce *vt* (**pronounced, pronouncing**) to form or articulate (words) by the organs of speech; to utter; to speak; to utter formally, officially or solemnly (*the court pronounced sentence of death*); to declare or affirm (*he pronounced it a forgery*).—*vi* to speak with confidence or authority; to utter an opinion; to use a certain pronunciation.

pronounced *adj* strongly marked or defined; decided (*a man of pronounced views*).

pronouncement *n* the act of pronouncing; a formal announcement.

pronunciamiento *n* (*pl* **pronunciamientos**) a manifesto or proclamation; a formal announcement or declaration.

pronunciation *n* the act of pronouncing or uttering with articulation; the manner of uttering words or letters; utterance.

proof *n* any effort, process or operation that ascertains truth, validity, quality or fact; a test; a trial; what serves as evidence, especially the full evidence upon which a verdict is based; what proves or establishes; that which convinces the mind and produces belief; a test applied to certain manufactured or other articles; a test of firearms for resistance to bursting; a test of the strength of gunpowder; the act of testing the strength of alcoholic liquors; hence, also the degree of strength in such liquors; (*math*) a sequence of calculations that establishes the truth of a proposition; (*print*) a rough impression of a piece of matter, taken for correction; an impression taken from an engraving to prove the state of it during the progress of executing; an early impression or one of a limited number taken before the letters to be inserted are engraved on the plate (called a *proof impression* and considered the best because taken before the plate is worn).—*adj* impenetrable; able to resist, physically or morally (*proof against shot, against temptation*); (*print*) used in making corrections.—*vt* to make proof against (water); to test or prove; (*print*) to take an impression of (an engraving, etc) or to print (text) as a proof or proofs.

proof-read *vt* (*pret, pp* **proof-read**, *ppr* **proof-reading**) to read and correct (printed proofs).—*vi* to correct proofs.

proof spirit *n* spirit of a certain alcoholic strength (49.28 per cent of alcohol by weight).

prop[1] *n* that which sustains an incumbent weight; a support; a stay; one who gives moral or spiritual support to another; in rugby football, one of two forwards at each end of the front row of the scrum.—*vt* (**propped, propping**) to support by placing something under or against; to support by standing under or against; to support or sustain, in a general sense.

prop[2] see **property**.

prop[3] a shortened form of **propeller**.

propaganda *n* the organized spread of ideas, doctrines, etc, to advance a cause, etc, or to destroy or damage another or rival causes; the ideas, cause, etc, so spread.

propagandist *n* one who devotes himself or herself to the spread of ideas, doctrine, etc.

propagandize *vt* (**propagandized, propagandizing**) to subject to propaganda; to spread (information or disinformation) by the use of propaganda.—*vi* to disseminate propaganda.

propagate *vt* (**propagated, propagating**) to continue or multiply by generation or successive reproduction; to cause to reproduce itself (applied to animals and plants); to spread from person to person or from place to place; to disseminate (ideas, news, etc); to diffuse; to generate, beget, produce, originate.—*vi* to have young or issue; to be reproduced or multiplied by generation or by new shoots or plants.

propagation *n* the act of propagating; the multiplication of a species by generation or reproduction; the spreading or extension of anything; dissemination; diffusion.

propane *n* a colourless inflammable gas obtained from petroleum and used as a fuel.

propel *vt* (**propelled, propelling**) to drive forward; to urge or press onwards, often by force.

propellant *n* a propelling agent, such as an explosive charge or rocket fuel; the gas that activates an aerosol spray.

propellent *adj* driving forward; propelling.

propeller *n* one who or that which propels; specifically, a device for propelling a steam or motor vessel or a piston-engined or turbo-prop aircraft, consisting of a hub bearing large angled blades which is rotated to produce thrust.

propensity *n* bent of mind, natural or acquired; inclination; natural tendency or disposition, particularly to evil.

proper *adj* correct in behaviour, manner or conduct; decent; respectable; over-correct in manner, prim; genuine; real, actual, strictly so called, according to correct usage (*this is a proper hotel, not a pub* or *the garden proper*); thorough, complete, utter (*a proper little madam*); fit, suitable, appropriate, suited or designed for its purpose (*the proper moment to tell him*); accurate (*the proper meaning of the expression*); belonging exclusively or particularly (with *to*, as *the conduct proper to a solder*); (*arch*) agreeable, pleasant, good; (*heral*) depicted in its natural colours (*a lion proper*); (*eccles*) appointed for a certain day or a particular occasion.

properly *adv* in a proper manner; fitly; suitably; rightly; in a strict sense; strictly.

proper noun *n* (*gram*) a noun that is the name of a particular person, thing, place, etc, and which is distinguished by the use of an initial capital letter (*James, Ireland, Rolls-Royce*).

property *n* anything of value, whether tangible, as possession, or intangible, as copyrights; a building, piece of land or estate; possessions collectively; hence, ownership in general, especially of things of value (*the watch is his property, this is private property*); (*law*) the exclusive right to own, enjoy and dispose of anything; a distinctive quality, attribute or feature, especially one that is characteristic (*one of the chief properties of aluminium is its lightness*); that which is inherent in a thing or naturally essential to it; in theatres or film sets, etc, any portable article necessary for a scene (usually abbreviated to **prop**).

property man, property woman *n* a person in charge of the properties or stage requisites of a theatre.

prophecy *n* a foretelling; a declaration of something to come; especially, a foretelling inspired by God; a book of prophecies; (*arch*) interpretation of Scripture; exhortation or instruction.

prophesy *vt* (**prophesied, prophesying**) to foretell; to predict.—*vi* to utter predictions; to make declaration of events to come; (*arch*) to interpret or explain Scripture or religious subjects.

prophet *n* one who foretells future events; a predictor; a foreteller; a person inspired or instructed by God to announce future events; (*arch*) an interpreter.

Prophet *n* Muhammad, the founder of the Islamic faith; a name given to the founder of the Mormon Church, Joseph Smith.

prophetess *n* a female prophet.

prophetic, prophetical *adj* pertaining or relating to a prophet or prophecy; having the character of prophecy; containing prophecy.

Prophets *npl* a major part of the Old Testament including accounts of the ancient Hebrew religious reformers and patriots and books written by prophets.

prophylactic *adj* (*med*) preventive; defending from or warding off disease; hence, protective or preventive in general.—*n* a medicine which preserves or defends against disease; a preventive; a condom.

prophylaxis *n* (*med*) preventive or preservative treatment.

propinquity *n* nearness in place; neighbourhood; nearness in time; nearness of blood; kindred.

propitiable *adj* capable of being propitiated.

propitiate *vt* (**propitiated, propitiating**) to appease and render favourable; to make propitious; to conciliate.

propitiation *n* the act of propitiating; (*theol*) the atonement or atoning sacrifice offered to God to assuage his wrath and render him propitious to sinners.

propitiatory *adj* having the power to make propitious; serving to propitiate.

propitious *adj* favourably disposed towards a person; disposed to be gracious or merciful; ready to forgive sins and bestow blessings; affording favourable conditions or circumstances (*a propitious season*).

proponent *n* one who makes a proposal or lays down a proposition; an advocate or supporter of something.

propeller

proportion *n* the comparative relation of one thing to another in respect of size, quantity or degree; suitable or corresponding degree; the relation of one part to another or to the whole, with respect to magnitude; ratio; relative size and arrangement of parts; symmetrical arrangement; the proper relation of parts in a whole; symmetry; just or equal share; lot; (*math*) the equality or similarity of ratios between two pairs of numbers, as 10:15, 29:30.—*vt* to adjust in a suitable proportion; to adjust harmoniously to something else as regards dimensions or extent; to form with symmetry.

proportional *adj* having a due proportion; being in suitable proportion or degree; (*math*) having the same or a constant ratio (*proportional quantities*).—*n* a quantity in proportion; (*math*) one of the terms of a proportion.

proportional representation *n* a system of voting in elections to representative bodies, designed to secure representation proportional to the number of votes a candidate or party polls.

proportionate *adj* having due proportion or relation; proportional.—*vt* (**proportionated, proportionating**) to make proportional; to adjust in due relation.

proposal *n* that which is proposed or offered for consideration; a scheme or design; an offer of marriage; terms or conditions proposed (*proposals of peace*).

propose *vt* (**proposed, proposing**) to offer for consideration or acceptance; to put forward as something to be done, attained or striven after (often governing an infinitive).—*vi* to form or declare an intention or design; to offer oneself in marriage (*to propose to a lady*).

proposition *n* that which is proposed or offered for consideration, acceptance or adoption; a proposal; term or offer advanced; a workable idea or scheme, especially one made informally (*I've a proposition for you*); someone or something that is to be dealt with (*a tricky proposition*); an indecent proposal; (*gram, logic*) a form of speech in which something is affirmed or denied of a subject; (*math*) a statement of either a truth to be demonstrated or an operation to be performed.—*vt* to propose (something); to offer to engage in sexual intercourse.

propound *vt* to offer for consideration; to propose; to put or set, as a question.

proprietary *n* a body of proprietors collectively; a drug protected by patent.—*adj* belonging to a proprietor or owner; belonging to private ownership; (of a drug or other agent) legally made only by a person or persons holding a patent and usually marketed under a trade name

proprietor *n* an owner; the person who has the legal right or exclusive title to anything.

proprietress, proprietrix *n* a female proprietor.

propriety *n* suitableness to an acknowledged or correct standard; consonance with established principles, rules or customs; fitness; justness.

propulsion *n* the act of driving forward or the state of being driven; the propelling force.

propulsive *adj* tending or having power to propel; driving or urging on.

pro rata *adj, adv* in proportion.

prorogue *vt* (**prorogued, proroguing**) to protract or prolong; to defer, put off, delay; to continue from one session to another; to adjourn to an indefinite period by royal authority, as the British parliament.

prosaic *adj* dull; uninteresting; commonplace; unimaginative; characteristic of prose.

proscenium *n* (*pl* **proscenia, prosceniums**) (*archit*) in a theatre, the arch and the space in front of it which separate the stage from the auditorium; in the ancient theatre, the whole stage.

prosciutto *n* a type of cured ham from northern Italy, sliced very finely and usually served as an hors d'oeuvre.

proscribe *vt* (**proscribed, proscribing**) in ancient Rome, to publish the name of, as doomed to destruction and seizure of property; hence, to put out of the protection of the law; to outlaw; to exile, to reject utterly; to interdict, exclude, condemn prohibit.

proscription *n* the act of proscribing or state of being proscribed; outlawry; exclusion; denunciation; prohibition; exile.

prose *n* the ordinary written or spoken language of human beings; language without poetical measure, as opposed to verse or metrical composition; hence, dull and commonplace language or discourse.—*adj* relating to or consisting of prose; prosaic.—*vi* (**prosed, prosing**) to write in prose; to write or speak tediously.

prosecute *vt* (**prosecuted, prosecuting**) to bring criminal proceedings against; to pursue; to apply to with continued purpose; to carry on or follow a course of action (*he prosecuted a policy of social reform*); to continue; (*law*) to seek to obtain by legal process; to pursue for redress or punishment before a legal tribunal.—*vi* to carry on a legal prosecution; to act as a prosecutor.

prosecution *n* the act or process of prosecuting or of being prosecuted; the proceeding with or following up of any matter in hand (*the prosecution of a design, an inquiry*, etc); the carrying on of a suit in a court of law; the process of exhibiting formal charges against an offender before a legal tribunal; the party by whom criminal proceedings are instituted, especially the lawyers acting for them in court.

prosecutor *n* one who prosecutes; the person who institutes and carries on proceedings in a court of justice.

proselyte *n* a new convert to some religion or religious sect (especially a convert to Judaism) or to some particular opinion, system or party.

proselytize *vt* (**proselytized, proselytizing**) to make a proselyte or convert of.—*vi* to engage in making proselytes.

prosody *n* the study of the art of versification and of poetical metres; the structure of speech sounds; a system of versification.

prospect *n* view, vista or scene, especially a wide or distant one (*a fine prospect*); a looking forward to the future or the likely course of the future (*the prospect before us is bleak*); moderate expectation or ground for expectation (*there is a prospect that he will come to Britain*); anticipation; reasonable potential for success or good in a person, project, plant etc (*as a client he is a sound prospect*); (*pl*) expectations, especially financial or social (*there are good prospects with this job*); in mining, an actual or potential ore deposit or its location; a test sample of ore or the mineral yield from such a sample.—*vi* to explore in search of oil, gold, minerals, etc.—*vt* to explore (an area or region) for minerals, etc; (*colloq*) to search for (*prospecting for a pub*, etc).

prospective *adj* looking forward; being in prospect or expectation; looked forward to (*prospective advantages*); future.

prospector *n* one who searches for minerals, oil, metals, etc, as preliminary to settled or continuous operations.

prospectus *n* (*pl* **prospectuses**) a brief sketch issued for the purpose of making known the chief features of some proposed commercial enterprise, as the plan of a literary work, the proposals of a new company or joint-stock association; a brochure showing the features of a school, college, etc.

prosper *vi* to be successful; to succeed; (of persons) to advance in wealth or any good; to be in a successful state; (of affairs) to turn out successfully; (of plants and animals) to be in a healthy growing state; to thrive.—*vt* (*arch*) to make prosperous or successful.

prosperity *n* the state of being prosperous or financially successful; good progress in any business or enterprise; success; attainment of the object desired; good fortune.

prosperous *adj* thriving; successful, especially financially; favourable; favouring success.

prostate, prostate gland *n* a gland surrounding the neck of the bladder in male mammals, which secretes a constituent of semen.

prostatic *adj* pertaining to the prostate.

prosthesis *n* (*pl* **prostheses**) the replacement of a lost limb, etc, with an artificial one; the replacement limb, etc.

prosthetic *adj* of or pertaining to prosthesis.—*n* a prosthetic device.

prostitute *vt* (**prostituted, prostituting**) to hire or to offer to hire out (oneself or another) for sexual intercourse or other immoral purpose; to give or offer to give (oneself or another or one's skills, experience, knowledge, etc, or another's) to base or unworthy purposes, often in return for money, fame, etc (*he prostituted his talents as a painter*).—*n* a woman or homosexual man or a bisexual of either sex who accepts money in exchange for sexual intercourse; a strumpet; a harlot.

prostitution *n* the act or practice of engaging in indiscriminate intercourse for hire; devotion to unworthy or shameful pursuits.

prostrate *adj* lying with the body extended on the ground; lying at mercy, as a suppliant; lying in the posture of humility or adoration; (*bot*) lying flat and spreading on the ground without taking root.—*vt* (**prostrated, prostrating**) to lay flat or prostrate; to render defenceless or helpless; to make exhausted; (*refl*) to throw oneself down as in humility or adoration; (*fig*) to exhaust; to overthrow; to ruin; to reduce to nothing.

prostration *n* the act of prostrating or laying flat; the act of falling down or of bowing in humility or adoration; great depression or reduction (as of strength or spirits).

prosy *adj* dull; tedious; having the quality or character of prose.

protagonist *n* the leading character or actor in a Greek play; hence, a leading character generally; a champion or advocate.

protasis *n* (*gram*) the first clause of a conditional sentence, being the condition on which the apodosis depends, as, 'if we run' (*protasis*) 'we shall be in time' (*apodosis*).

protean *adj* readily assuming different shapes; exceedingly variable.

protect *vt* to cover or shield from danger or injury; to serve as a cover or shelter to; to defend; to guard; to serve as protection against insects, weather, staining, etc.

protection *n* the act of protecting or state of being protected; defence; shelter from evil; that which protects or preserves from injury, damage or wear; a passport or other writing which secures from molestation;

exemption, as from arrest in civil suits; an artificial advantage conferred by a legislature on articles of home production, usually by taxes imposed on the same articles introduced from abroad; the advocacy or theory of this (also called **protectionism**); (*colloq*) an act of extortion in which criminals demand money from businesses, etc, in return for freedom from being molested; the money thus extorted (also called **protection money**).

protectionist *n* one who favours the protectionism, the protection of some branch of industry by legal enactments; one opposed to free trade.

protective *adj* affording protection; sheltering; defensive.—*n* that which protects; a condom.

protector *n* one who or that which protects; a defender; a guardian.

protectorate *n* government by a protector; the protection, and effectively the control, of a weaker country by a stronger, the former, however, not being annexed to the latter.

protégé, protégée *n* one under the care and protection of another; a person guided or helped in training for his or her career by someone.

protester

protein *n* one of a class of complex chemical compounds which contain carbon, hydrogen, nitrogen, oxygen and sulphur, are essential constituents of living matter and on decomposition yield various amino acids.

Proterozoic *adj* of or pertaining to the era preceding the Cambrian.—*n* the Proterozoic era.

protest *vi* to affirm with solemnity (*to protest one's innocence*); to asseverate; to make a solemn or formal declaration (often in writing) expressive of opposition to something; to object (often with *at* or *against*); to complain.—*vt* to make a solemn declaration or affirmation of; to assert; to make a forceful objection to (especially to an alleged injustice or failure of official protection. etc).—*n* a solemn declaration of opinion, commonly against some act; a formal statement (usually in writing), by which a person declares that he or she dissents from an act to which he or she might otherwise be deemed to have yielded assent; an objection, especially a forceful or violent objection; a public demonstration of dissent, often organized; a complaint; (*law*) a formal declaration that acceptance or payment of a bill or promissory note has been refused.

protractor

Protestant *n* originally, an adherent of Luther at the Reformation in 1529 and a protester against a decree of the Emperor Charles V and the Diet of Spires; now, a member of any of the Christian denominations that differ from the Roman Catholic Church and that sprang from the Reformation.—*adj* belonging to the religion of the Protestants.

Protestantism *n* the principles or religion of Protestants.

protestation *n* a solemn declaration; an asseveration (*a protestation of loyalty*); a solemn declaration of dissent; a protest; an objection; a complaint.

protester, protestor *n* one who protests; one who takes part in a protest.

Proteus *n* a sea god of the ancient Greeks who had the faculty of assuming different shapes; hence, one who easily changes his form or principles.

prothesis *n* (*pl* **protheses**) (*ling*) the addition of a letter or syllable at the beginning of a word.

protocol *n* the minutes or rough draft of some diplomatic document or instrument; a document serving as a preliminary to, or for the opening of, any diplomatic transaction; a record or registry; the ceremonial etiquette accepted as correct in official dealings, as between heads of states or diplomatic officials; hence, accepted rules governing etiquette, behaviour, precedence, etc, in general; the plan of a scientific experiment or treatment.

proton *n* the elementary positive charge of electricity, corresponding, and equal except for sign, to the negative *electron*; the nucleus of the hydrogen atom.

protophyte *n* a name given to the lowest organisms in the vegetable kingdom.

protoplasm *n* a transparent substance, a complex and unstable mixture of proteins and other compounds and constituting the basis of living matter in animal and plant cell structures.

prototype *n* an original or model after which anything is formed; a pattern; archetype.

protozoan, protozoon *n* any of a number of microscopic invertebrates consisting of a single cell or a group of single cells.

protract *vt* to draw out or lengthen in time; to prolong; to lengthen out in space; to delay, defer, put off; (*surv*) to draw to a scale.

protracted *adj* prolonged; extending over a long time.

protractile *adj* (*zool*) able to be extended.

protraction *n* the act of protracting; (*surv*) the act of laying down on paper the dimensions of a field, etc.

protractor *n* an instrument for laying down and measuring angles on paper.

protrude *vt* (**protruded, protruding**) to thrust forward; to shoot forth or project or cause to project.—*vi* to shoot forward; to stand out prominently.

protrusion *n* the act of protruding; anything that protrudes.

protuberance *n* a swelling or tumour; a prominence; anything swelled or pushed beyond the surrounding or adjacent surface.

protuberant *adj* swelling; prominent beyond the surrounding surface.

protuberate *vi* (**protuberated, protuberating**) to swell or be prominent beyond the adjacent surface; to bulge out.

proud *adj* possessing a high and often unreasonable opinion of one's own excellence; pleased or honoured by an achievement or distinction; possessing a praiseworthy self-esteem that avoids anything mean or base; possessing a high opinion of (*proud of his children*); haughty; arrogant; ready to boast; elated; taking satisfaction in or basking in reflected glory (*proud of one's country*); arising from pride; presumptuous; of fearless or untameable character; suggesting or exciting pride; ostentatious; grand; magnificent; distinguished.

prove *vt* (*pret* **proved**, *pp* **proved** *or* **proven**, *ppr* **proving**) to try or ascertain by an experiment; to test; to make trial of (*to prove gunpowder*); to establish the truth or reality of by reasoning, induction or evidence; to demonstrate; to establish the authenticity or validity of; to obtain probate of (*to prove a will*); to gain personal experience of; (*arith*) to show or ascertain the correctness of by a further calculation.—*vi* to be found or ascertained by experience or trial; to turn out to be (*the report proved to be false*); to attain certainty.

proven *pp* of **prove**.—**not proven** (*Scots law*) a verdict given by a jury in a criminal case when, although there is insufficient evidence to convict the prisoner (who is free to go after such a verdict), there is sufficient to warrant grave suspicion of his or her guilt.

provenance *n* source or place of origin; the date, origin and subsequent history of a work of art.

Provençal *n* a native of Provence, southern France; the Romance language of Provence.—*adj* of or pertaining to Provence.

Provençale *adj* (of food) cooked or prepared with garlic, tomatoes and olive oil.

provender *n* dry food for beasts, as hay, straw and corn; provisions; food in general.

proverb *n* a short pithy sentence expressing a truth ascertained by experience or observation; a sentence which briefly and forcibly expresses some practical truth; a wise saw; an adage; a maxim; a short dramatic composition in which some proverb or popular saying is taken as the foundation of the plot; a byword; (*Scrip*) a saying of the wise that requires interpretation.

proverbial *adj* comprised in a proverb; used or current as a proverb; resembling a proverb; generally known, especially as an example of something.

proverbially *adv* in a proverbial manner or style; by way of proverb.

Proverbs *n* one of the books of the Old Testament containing the wise sayings of Solomon and others.

provide *vt* (**provided, providing**) to procure beforehand; to prepare (*to provide warm clothing*); to furnish; to supply (*well provided with corn*); to lay down as a previous arrangement; to make a previous condition or understanding.—*vi* to make provision; to take measures beforehand (*we must provide for our wants, against mishaps*).

provided *conj* on condition; on these terms; this being conceded.

providence *n* foresight; timely care or preparation; prudence; something due to an act of providential intervention; a providential circumstance.

Providence *n* divine superintendence; God, regarded as exercising forecast, care and direction for and over His creatures; the divine being or power.

provident *adj* foreseeing wants and making provision to supply them; prudent in preparing for future exigencies; frugal; economical.

providential *adj* effected by the providence of God; resulting or arising from divine providence; very opportune or lucky.

province *n* a large territorial or political division of a state; in England, a division for ecclesiastical purposes under the jurisdiction of an archbishop, there being two provinces, that of Canterbury and that of York; (*fig*) the proper duty, office or business of a person (*insurance is his province*); sphere of action; a division in any department of knowledge or speculation; a department; (*pl*) the parts of a country at a distance from the major cities.

provincial *adj* pertaining to a province; forming a province; exhibiting the manners or characteristics of a province; characteristic of the inhabitants of a province; rustic; not polished; unsophisticated; narrow-minded; pertaining to an ecclesiastical province or to the jurisdiction of an archbishop.—*n* a person belonging to a province as distinct from a metropolis; a rustic, unsophisticated or narrow-minded person; in some religious orders, a monastic superior in a given district.

provincialism *n* a provincial attitude or point of view; lack of sophistication; narrow-mindedness; a special word or manner of speaking in a district of a country.

provision *n* the act of providing or making previous preparation; a measure taken beforehand; provident care; accumulation of stores or materials beforehand; a store or stock; a stock of food provided; hence, victuals, food (usually in the plural); a stipulation or measure proposed in an enactment, etc; a proviso.—*vt* to provide with things necessary, especially victuals or food.

provisional *adj* provided for present need or for the occasion; temporarily established; temporary.

provisionally *adv* in a provisional manner; for the present exigency; temporarily.

proviso *n* (*pl* **provisos**) an article or clause in any statute, agreement, contract, grant or other writing, by which a condition is introduced; a conditional stipulation; a condition.

provisory *adj* temporary; provisional; conditional.

provocation *n* the act of provoking; anything that excites anger; cause of resentment; incitement; stimulus.

provocative *adj* serving to provoke; exciting; apt to incense or enrage; intended to arouse or arousing, sexual desire.

provoke *vt* (**provoked, provoking**) to challenge; (*arch*) to summon; to stimulate to action; to induce by motive; to excite or arouse (as hunger); to call forth; to instigate; to excite to anger or passion; to irritate; to enrage.

provost *n* the chief or head of certain bodies, as of certain university colleges; the chief dignitary of a cathedral or collegiate church; the chief magistrate of a Scottish burgh, corresponding to the English mayor.

provost marshal *n* (*milit*) an officer whose duty it is to attend to offences committed against military discipline; in the navy, an officer who has the custody of prisoners at a court martial.

prow *n* the forepart of a vessel; the bow; the beak.

prowess *n* great skill or ability; valour; military bravery combined with skill; intrepidity and dexterity in war.

prowl *vi* to rove or wander stealthily, as a beast in search of prey (usually with *around* or *about*).—*vt* to wander stealthily over.—*n* the act of prowling.—**on the prowl** prowling around, especially in enthusiastic pursuit of members of the opposite sex.

prox a contraction of **proximo**.

proximity *n* the state of being proximate or next; immediate nearness, either in place, blood or alliance; propinquity.

proximo *adv* (often contracted to **prox**) in or of the next month.

proxy *n* the agency of a person who acts as a substitute for a principal; authority to act for another; the person authorized to act

prow

for another; a deputy; a document by which one person authorizes another to vote in his or her place.

prude *n* a person affecting great reserve, modesty, coyness and excessive virtue or delicacy of feeling, especially in regard to sex or who pretends to great propriety of conduct; a prim and proper person, easily shocked.

prudence *n* the state or quality of being prudent.

prudent *adj* cautious or circumspect in determining on any action or line of conduct; careful of the consequences of enterprises, measures or actions; dictated or directed by prudence (*prudent behaviour*); frugal; economical; correct and decorous in manner.

prudery *n* the conduct of a prude; affected delicacy of feeling; coyness; primness.

prudish *adj* pertaining to a prude; affecting excessive modesty or virtue; coy or reserved; prim.

prune[1] *vt* (**pruned, pruning**) to lop superfluous twigs or branches from; to trim with a knife; to clear from anything superfluous; to trim, cut back or economize on (*he pruned his budget*); to cut down in length (as a book, article, etc).

prune[2] *n* a dried plum.

prurience, pruriency *n* the state of being prurient; lascivious suggestiveness.

prurient *adj* unusually inclined or inclining to lascivious thoughts; having a lecherous imagination; encouraging lustful thoughts; erotic.

Prussian blue *n* a pigment for paints, dyes and printing inks; the deep blue colour of the pigment.

prussic acid *adj* the common name for hydrocyanic acid.

pry[1] *vi* (**pried, prying**) to peep narrowly; to look closely; to attempt to discover something with impertinent curiosity; to snoop into other people's affairs (often with *into*).—*n* close inspection; impertinent peeping.

pry[2] *vt* (**pried, prying**) to raise with a lever, to prise.

psalm *n* a sacred song or hymn; especially one of the hymns composed by King David and other Hebrew writers; also applied to versifications of the scriptural psalms composed for the use of churches; a musical setting for a psalm.

psalmist *n* a writer or composer of psalms.

psalmody *n* the singing or writing of psalms or psalm music; psalms collectively.

Psalms *n* the Book of Psalms in the Old Testament, a collection of 150 psalms.

Psalter *n* the Book of Psalms; a book containing the Psalms separately printed; the version of the Psalms in the Book of Common Prayer.

psaltery *n* a musical instrument used by the

Hebrews, the form of which is not known; a medieval stringed instrument of the zither type, similar in shape to a dulcimer, which became the forerunner of the harpsichord.

pseud *n* (*colloq*) a pretentious person, especially one claiming or seeking to demonstrate an intellectual capability which he or she does not possess.

pseudo *adj* false; pretended.

pseudo- *prefix* signifying false, counterfeit or spurious, used in many compound words (*pseudo-socialist*, *pseudo-sympathetic*, etc); closely resembling.

pseudonym *n* a false or feigned name; a pen name assumed by a writer; an alias.

pseudopod *n* an organism with pseudopodia.

pseudopodia *npl* (*sing* **pseudopodium**) (*zool*) the organs of locomotion characteristic of protozoans, consisting of threads or processes temporarily projected from any part of the body.

pshaw *exclam* an expression of contempt, disdain, impatience, disbelief, etc.

psittaceous *adj* of or relating to the parrots.

psittacosis *n* an infectious disease of parrots and other birds, which can be transmitted to humans when it affects the respiratory system.

psoriasis *n* a chronic skin disease characterized by red scaly spots or patches.

psyche *n* the soul.

Psyche *n* in Greek myth, a beautiful maiden beloved by Eros, later taken as the personification of the human soul.

psychedelic *adj* of greatly increased consciousness, sensitivity or perception, the result of taking hallucinogenic drugs; relating to any drug or other agent that brings about this state; having vivid or luminous colours.

psychiatry *n* the branch of medicine dealing with mental disorders and their treatment.

psychic *adj* sensitive to phenomena not known to natural laws; supposedly having contact with or sensitivity to forces that cannot be explained by natural laws; of the mind as opposed to the body; originating from the mind.—*n* someone sensitive to psychic forces; a spiritualist; a medium.

psychical *adj* psychic.

psychism *n* the doctrine which maintains the existence and power of psychic forces.

psychist *n* a believer in psychic force; a spiritualist.

psychoanalysis *n* the analysis of a patient's mental condition, as a preliminary to the treatment of mental or emotional disorders; a method of treating neuroses, phobias and other mental disorders by analysing conflicts, repressions, etc.

psychogenesis *n* the origin or generation of the mind as manifested by consciousness.

psychological *adj* pertaining to psychology.

psychologist *n* a person trained in psychology.

psychology *n* the scientific study of human and animal behaviour, particularly the science that studies the human mind and behaviour.

psychoneurosis *n* (*pl* **psychoneuroses**) neurosis.

psychopath *n* a person who suffers from a personality disorder that results in aggressively antisocial behaviour, lack of guilt, fluctuating moods, etc.

psychopathy *n* any mental disease or disorder.

psychosis *n* (*pl* **psychoses**) a term for all mental disorders other than neuroses, including schizophrenia; a mental illness in which the personality is very seriously disturbed and contact with reality is impaired.

psychosomatic *adj* (of a physical illness) caused or affected by the patient's mental or emotional condition rather than physical factors.

psychotherapist *n* one who practices psychotherapy.

psychotherapy *n* the treatment of mental disorders by psychological as distinct from physical methods.

psychotic *adj* of or like a psychosis; having a psychosis.—*n* a person suffering from a psychosis.

psychrometer *n* an instrument for measuring atmospheric humidity, a form of hygrometer.

ptarmigan *n* a European game bird of the grouse family, turning white in winter and partly so in autumn and inhabiting mountain tops, tundra and areas well above the treeline.

pterodactyl *n* an extinct species of flying dinosaur belonging to the Mesozoic period and exhibiting affinities to mammals, reptiles and birds.

ptisan *n* same as **tisane**.

Ptolemaic system *n* the system maintained by the second-century Greek astronomer geographer Ptolemy of Alexandria, who supposed the earth to be fixed in the centre of the universe and that the sun and known stars and planets revolved around it.

ptomaine *n* one of a class of alkaloids or organic bases which are generated in animal substances during putrefaction, or occasionally during life, some of them highly poisonous.

ptyalin *n* a ferment in saliva that converts starch into sugar.

ptyalism *n* salivation; an abnormal and copious excretion of saliva.

puberty *n* the period in both male and female adolescence marked by the functional development of the generative sys-

ptarmigan

pterodactyl

tem; the age at which persons are capable of begetting or bearing children.

pubes *npl* (*sing* **pubis**) (*anat*) the middle part of the hypogastric region, so called because covered with hair at puberty; (*bot*) the down or downy substance on plants; the pubic bones; pubic hair.

pubescence *n* the state of one who has reached puberty; puberty; (*bot*) the downy substance on plants.

pubescent *adj* arriving at puberty; (*bot*) covered with pubescence; (*zool*) covered with very fine short hairs.

pubic *adj* pertaining to the pubes.

pubis *n* (*pl* **pubes**) (*anat*) the foremost of the three sections of the hip bone that forms part of the pelvis.

public *adj* not private; pertaining to the whole people; relating to, regarding or affecting a state, nation or community (*the public service*); proceeding from many or the many; belonging to people in general (*a public subscription*); open to the knowledge of all; general; common; notorious (*public report*); regarding not private interest but the good of the community (*public spirit*); open to common use (*a public road*, *a public house*).—*n* the general body of mankind or of a nation, state or community; the people, indefinitely (with *the*); a part or those parts of the community linked by common interests or activities (*the race-going public*, *an author's public*, etc); (*colloq*) a public house.

publican *n* in ancient Rome, a contractor, especially one having the right to collect and keep public revenues; any collector of public dues or revenues; the keeper of a public house.

publication *n* the act of publishing or offering to public notice; notification to people at large; promulgation; the act of offering a book, map, print, etc, to the public by sale or gratuitous distribution; a printed and published work.

public house *n* a place for the retail of liquors, as beer, spirits, wines, etc, usually to be consumed on the premises.

publicist *n* a person who organizes publicity; a press agent; a journalist; a writer on current international and political topics.

publicity *n* the art, business or process of bringing products, people, etc, to public notice, especially through the mass media; public interest as a result of that process; the material or work used to attract the public's attention and interest; any information or action that brings a person or cause to public notice.

publicize *vt* (**publicized, publicizing**) to give publicity to.

public prosecutor *n* one who originates and conducts prosecutions in the interests of the public.

puck

pudding

public relations *n* the practice or techniques of establishing a favourable image or relationship for a company, government, etc, with the community.

public school *n* a private, independent, often boarding, secondary school financed by fees and endowments .

publish *vt* to make public; to make known to people in general; to promulgate; to cause to be printed and offered for sale; to issue from the press to the public; to communicate some information (especially defamatory) to a third party; to make known by putting up posters or by reading in a church (*to publish banns of matrimony*).

publishable *adj* capable of being published; fit for publication.

publisher *n* one who publishes; especially, one who, as the first source of supply, issues books and other literary works or other kinds of printed matter for sale.

puce *adj* dark-brown; reddish-brown.

puck *n* the flat disc, usually made of vulcanized rubber, used in ice hockey.

Puck *n* in English folklore, a mischievous goblin.

pucker *vt* to gather into small folds or wrinkles; to contract into ridges and furrows; to wrinkle.—*vi* to become wrinkled; to gather into folds.—*n* a fold or wrinkle or a collection of folds.

puckish *adj* resembling Puck; elfish; impish.

pudding *n* a dessert, generally cooked, concocted of flour, milk, eggs, etc, with fruit or other ingredients; a steamed or baked dessert; a dessert course; a savoury dish, usually combining cooked meat and vegetables with suet; cooked seasoned minced meat mixed with oatmeal, vegetables, etc, and forced into a skin, as a haggis; a type of large cooked sausage (*black pudding*, etc).

pudding stone *n* (*geol*) conglomerate.

puddle *n* a small collection of dirty water; a small muddy pool; spilled water or other liquid; clay or earth tempered with water and thoroughly worked so as to be impervious to water.—*vt* (**puddled, puddling**) to make turbid or muddy; to stir up the mud or sediment in; to make or line with puddle; to stir (molten iron) to free it from carbon.—*vi* to splash as if in a puddle; to dabble.

pudenda *npl* (*sing* **pudendum**) the external reproductive organs, especially of a woman.

pudgy *adj* fat and short; thick; fleshy.

puerile *adj* boyish; childish; trifling.

puerility *n* the state of being puerile; boyishness; that which is puerile; a childish or silly act, thought or expression.

puerperal *adj* pertaining to the period immediately following childbirth.

puerperal fever *n* infection of the genital tract following childbirth.

puff *n* a sudden and single emission of breath from the mouth; a sudden and short blast of wind; a puffball; a powder puff; an exaggerated or empty statement of commendation, as of a book, of a shopkeeper's goods, etc; a light pastry confection filled with cream, etc; a single draw on a cigarette, cigar, etc; the noise made by a puff or an imitation of it.—*vi* to blow with single and quick blasts; to blow, as an expression of scorn or contempt; to make a puffing noise; to move with a puffing noise; to draw on a cigarette, cigar, etc; to breathe with vehemence, as after violent exertion; to be dilated or inflated (often with *up* or *out*); to assume importance.—*vt* to drive with a blast of wind or air; to inflate or dilate with air; to swell or inflate, as with pride or vanity (often with *up*); to praise with exaggeration.

puff adder *n* a large African viper, one of the most deadly snakes in the world, capable of inflating the upper part of its body.

puffball *n* a fungus in the form of a ball which bursts when ripe and discharges its spores in the form of fine powder.

puffin *n* the common name for a northern genus of marine diving birds of the auk family, characterized by a bill resembling that of a parrot.

puff pastry *n* a rich dough for making the light, crisp flaky pastry covers of pies, tarts, etc.

puffy *adj* swelled with air or any soft matter; tumid; turgid; bombastic, vain, pompous (*a puffy style*).

pug *n* a pugdog.

pugdog *n* a breed of small dog with a very short, almost flattened nose and a curled tail.

pugging *n* the process of mixing and working clay for bricks, etc; a composition to prevent the transmission of sound through a floor or partition.

puggree, puggaree *n* a piece of muslin cloth wound round a hat or helmet to ward off the rays of the sun; an Indian word for a turban.

pugilism *n* the practice of boxing or fighting with the fists.

pugilist *n* a boxer.

pugilistic *adj* pertaining to boxing.

pugnacious *adj* disposed or inclined to fighting; quarrelsome.

pugnacity *n* inclination to fight; quarrelsomeness.

pug nose *n* a snub nose.

puisne *adj* (*law*) younger or inferior in rank (applied to certain English judges).

puissance *n* power; strength; might.

puissant *adj* powerful; strong; mighty; forcible.

puke *vi* (**puked, puking**) to vomit; to retch; to be disgusted.—*vt* to vomit or eject (something) from the stomach.

pukka *adj* solid; substantial; permanent; genuine (an Anglo-Indian term).

pule *vi* (**puled, puling**) to cry, as a complaining child; to whimper.

puling *adj* whining; infantile; childish.—*n* a plaintive cry; a whining.

pulkha *n* a Laplander's travelling sledge.

pull *vt* to draw; to draw towards one or make an effort to draw; to tug; to haul, opposed to *push*; to pluck; to extract (a tooth); to gather by the hand (*to pull fruit*); to tear, rend, draw apart (in this sense followed by some qualifying word or phrase, as *to pull to pieces, to pull asunder* or *apart*); (*print*) to take (an impression) from type; (*sl*) to draw out (a weapon); to hit (a ball) wrongly in cricket, golf, etc; (*colloq*) to draw or attract (*the event pulled a huge crowd*); to bring about or succeed in (usually with *off*); to put on or adopt (*to pull faces*); to move (something) away, ahead, etc; to cause (a horse) to stop or slow down, usually to prevent it winning; to take (something) out or away; to move by drawing or pulling (*to pull a bell, to pull a boat*).—*vi* to give a pull; to tug; to exert strength in drawing; to inhale or drink deeply; to move or draw away; to row a boat.—**to pull out** to extract; to withdraw troops; (of a vehicle) to move off from the side of the road; to overtake; to abandon; to level off from a dive.—**to pull over** to steer a vehicle to the side of the road; to move aside to let another pass.—**to pull through** to recover from an illness or from a period of distress.—**to pull up** to remove by the roots; to come to a halt; to stop; to criticize or rebuke.—*n* the act of pulling; an effort to move by drawing towards one; a pluck; a shake; a twitch; a single stroke with an oar or the act of making such a stroke; the force or effort required in pulling; (*print*) a single proof sheet; something used in pulling (*a bell-pull*); the act of slowing a ridden horse; the act of drinking or inhaling deeply; (*colloq*) the ability or facility to attract support; (*colloq*) power, influence or special advantage; the resistance offered by a bowstring or gun's trigger.

pullet *n* a young hen or chicken.

pulley *n* (*pl* **pulleys**) one of the simple machines or mechanical powers, used for raising weights and consisting of a small wheel movable about an axle and having a groove cut in its circumference over which a cord, rope, chain, etc, passes, used either singly or several in combination; a wheel placed on a shaft and transmitting power to or from the different parts of machinery or changing the direction of motion by

puffin

means of a belt or band which runs over it.

pullover *n* a knitted jersey, without buttons, pulled over the head when put on.

pulmonary *adj* pertaining to the lungs; affecting the lungs.

pulp *n* the soft fleshy tissue found in plants; the soft succulent part of fruit; material for making paper reduced to a soft uniform mass of moist fibres; a book or magazine printed on cheap paper and containing lurid and hackneyed material; the soft vascular substance in the interior of a tooth; any soft moist matter of a pulpy consistency.—*vt* to make into pulp; to deprive of the pulp.—*vi* to be reduced to pulp.

pulpiness *n* the state of being pulpy.

pulpit *n* an elevated place or enclosed stage in a church, in which the preacher stands; frequently used adjectivally and signifying belonging, pertaining or suitable to the pulpit (*pulpit eloquence*, *pulpit oratory*); any pulpit-like structure; a means of or platform for expressing views.

pulpy *adj* like pulp; soft; fleshy.

pulque *n* a vinous beverage obtained by fermenting the juice of various species of the agave.

pulsar *n* any of several very small stars that emit radio pulses at regular intervals.

pulsate *vi* (**pulsated, pulsating**) to beat or throb.

pulsation *n* the beating or throbbing of the heart or of an artery; a beat of the pulse; a throb; a beat or stroke by which some medium is affected, as in the transmission of sound.

pulse[1] *n* the beating or throbbing of the heart or blood vessels, especially of the arteries; the pulsation of the radial artery at the wrist; pulsation; vibration; the atmosphere of a place, environment, etc; an underlying opinion or sentiment or an indication of it; a short radio signal; (*elect*) an occasional sudden change in current, voltage or some other usually constant quantity.—**to feel one's pulse** (*fig*) to sound one's opinion; to try or to know one's mind.—*vi* (**pulsed, pulsing**) to beat or vibrate, as the arteries or heart.

pulse[2] *n* leguminous plants or their seeds; the plants whose pericarp is a legume, as beans, peas, etc.

pulveraceous *adj* (*bot*) having a powdery surface.

pulverization *n* the act of pulverizing.

pulverize *vt* (**pulverized, pulverizing**) to reduce to fine powder, as by beating, grinding, etc; to smash; (*colloq*) to beat or bludgeon severely; (*colloq*) to defeat.—*vi* to become reduced to fine powder; to fall to dust; (*colloq*) to lose a game, etc, heavily.

pulverous *adj* consisting of dust or powder.

puma *n* the cougar or American lion.

pump

pumpkin

pumice *n* a porous volcanic rock, lighter than water, used for polishing ivory, wood, marble, metals, glass, etc.

pummel *vt* (**pummelled, pummelling**) to strike repeatedly with the fists, to thump.

pump[1] *n* an instrument or machine for raising water or other liquid to a higher level or for exhausting or compressing air or other gases.—*vi* to work a pump; to raise water with a pump.—*vt* to raise with a pump; to free from water or other fluid by a pump (*to pump a ship*); to put artful questions to for the purpose of extracting information.

pump[2] *n* a low shoe or slipper with a low heel, used chiefly in dancing.

pumpernickel *n* a kind of coarse bread made from unbolted rye, originally from Germany.

pumpkin *n* any of several climbing plants, originally from India; the large round edible fruit of this plant with a thick, orange rind and pulpy flesh.

pump room *n* a room connected with a mineral spring, in which the waters are drunk; a room housing machinery for pumping.

pun *n* a play on words that agree or resemble in sound but differ in meaning; an expression in which two different applications of a word present an odd or ludicrous idea.—*vi* (**punned, punning**) to play on words so as to make puns.

punch[1] *n* a tool employed for making apertures, as in plates of metal, in impressing dies, driving out bolts, rivets, etc, usually made of steel and operated by hammering; a blow, as with the fist, elbow or knee.—*vt* to perforate, drive, stamp, mark or impress with a punch; to give a blow or stunning knock to, usually with the fist, as in boxing.

punch[2] *n* a beverage made from spirits or wine and water, sweetened and flavoured with sugar and fruit juice, often served hot.

punch[3] *n* a breed of large horse, an English draught breed (*a Suffolk punch*); (*arch*) a short fat fellow.

punchbowl *n* a bowl in which punch is made or from which it is served to be drunk; a large bowl-shaped depression or hollow in the ground.

puncheon *n* a measure of liquids; a large cask.

punch line *n* the final line or sentence of a joke on which the whole joke depends.

punctilio *n* (*pl* **punctilios**) a fine point in conduct, ceremony or proceeding; particularity or exactness in forms; petty formality.

punctilious *adj* attentive to forms of behaviour; scrupulously or over-scrupulously correct in etiquette; attentive to detail (*punctilious in his presentation of the facts*).

punctual *n* occurring or arriving at the agreed or appointed time; prompt; (of a person) exact to the time agreed on; made at the exact time (*punctual payment*); (*arch*) exact, precise, apt.

punctuality *n* the state or quality of being punctual; adherence to the exact time of attendance or appointment.

punctuate *vt* (**punctuated, punctuating**) to introduce (punctuation marks) into written or printed compositions; to use punctuation to separate (a text) into sentences, clauses or other divisions; to interrupt or insert frequently; to emphasize.

punctuation *n* the use of punctuation marks within a written text or discourse to enhance its meaning or fluency or to indicate aspects of pronunciation; the act or art of punctuating.

punctuation mark *n* one of the standard symbols used in punctuation, as the full stop, colon, semicolon, comma, etc.

puncture *n* the act of perforating with a pointed instrument or a small hole thus made; the deflation of a pneumatic tyre caused by a small hole; a small wound, as by a needle, prickle or sting.—*vt* (**punctured, puncturing**) to make a puncture in; to prick.

pundit *n* a learned person; an expert, especially a self-styled one; a critic.

pungency *n* the state or quality of being pungent; tartness; causticity.

pungent *adj* having a sharp, bitter or acrid taste or smell; (of humour) caustic, biting, savage.

puniness *n* the state or quality of being puny.

punish *vt* to inflict a penalty on; to visit judicially with a penalty; to castigate; to chastise; to inflict pain or suffering on; to treat or use roughly, heavy-handedly or harshly.

punishment *n* the act of punishing; pain or penalty inflicted on a person for a crime or offence; a penalty imposed in the enforcement of law; (*colloq*) rough treatment.

punitive *adj* pertaining to or involving punishment; awarding or inflicting punishment; having the intention of punishing or of taking reprisals.

punka, punkah *n* a large fan slung from the ceilings of rooms in India and elsewhere to produce an artificial current of air.

punnet *n* a small basket used for holding strawberries and other fruit when for sale.

punster *n* one skilled in or given to punning.

punt[1] *n* a small flat-bottomed boat used in fishing and wildfowl shooting, etc; a long flat-bottomed, square-ended river boat propelled with a pole.—*vt* to propel (a punt) by pushing with a pole against the bed of the river, etc; to convey in a punt.

punt[2] *vti* (in rugby football and certain other sports) to kick the ball after dropping it from the hands, before it has touched the ground.—*n* a kick in this manner.

punt[3] *vi* (in some gambling games) to bet against the bank; to bet; to gamble.—*n* a bet or gamble.

punter[1] *n* one who punts a boat; one who uses a punt.

punter[2] *n* one who punts or bets; one who plays in games of chance against the banker or dealer; (*sl*) a consumer, a customer.

puny *adj* small and weak; petty; insignificant.

pup *n* a young dog, a puppy; one of the young of certain other mammals, especially a young seal.—*vi* (**pupped, pupping**) to give birth to pups.

pupa *n* (*pl* **pupae**) the chrysalis form of a moth or butterfly and of a number of other insects; the stage in an emerging insect between larva and imago.

pupil *n* the round aperture in the centre of the iris of the eye through which light passes to reach the retina; a young person under the care of a teacher or tutor; a disciple; a ward; a young person under the care of a guardian.

pupillage *n* the state of being a pupil; the state or period of being a ward under the care of a guardian; the period which a newly qualified barrister spends in the chambers of a member of the bar.

puppet *n* a doll moved by strings attached to its limbs or by a hand inserted in its body; a marionette; a person controlled by the will of another; a person who is a mere tool.

puppet

puppet show *n* a drama performed by puppets.

puppy *n* a pup, a whelp; a young dog not grown up; an insolent, loud or impudent young man.

purblind *adj* partially or almost wholly blind; near-sighted or dim-sighted; seeing obscurely; hence, lacking understanding or insight; obtuse.

purchase *vt* (**purchased, purchasing**) to obtain (goods or services) by payment of money or its equivalent; to buy; to obtain by labour, danger, sacrifice or other means (*his efforts purchased her love*).—*n* acquisition in general; the acquisition of anything by rendering an equivalent in money; buying; that which is purchased; any mechanical advantage (as is gained by a lever) used in the raising or removing of heavy bodies; any firm hold or foothold, as in pushing (*his feet found purchase on the rock*).

purdah *n* the system of seclusion for

puppy

women practised by some Muslims and Hindus; a type of veil worn by high-caste Hindu women.

pure *adj* free from all heterogeneous or extraneous matter, especially from anything that impairs or pollutes; free from that which defiles or contaminates, especially morally; innocent; spotless; chaste; stainless; genuine; ceremonially clean; unpolluted; mere; sheer; absolute (*pure shame, hatred*); (of a subject under study) abstract and theoretical rather than practical (*pure physics*); (*mus*) not discordant, perfectly in tune; (*philos*) lacking empirical elements; (of humans) of unmixed ancestry or racial descent; (of animals) of unmixed ancestry; (*biol*) breeding true in at least one characteristic.

pureness *n* the state or quality of being pure; purity.

purgation *n* the act of purging; the act of carrying away impurities; purification; the act of cleansing of guilt.

purgative *adj* having the power of cleansing; having the power of evacuating the intestines; cathartic.—*n* a medicine that evacuates the intestines; a cathartic.

purgatory *adj* tending to cleanse; cleansing; expiatory.—*n* (*RC Church*) a place in which souls after death are purified from venial sins and suffer punishment for mortal sins not atoned for; (*colloq*) any place or state of irritating temporary suffering.

purge *vt* (**purged, purging**) to cleanse or purify by carrying off whatever is impure, foreign or superfluous; to clear from moral defilement; to clear from accusation or the charge of a crime; to evacuate the bowels; to operate on by means of a cathartic.—*vi* to produce evacuations by a cathartic.—*n* the act of purging; anything that purges; a cathartic medicine.

purification *n* the act of purifying or making pure; the act of cleansing ceremonially by removing any pollution or defilement; a cleansing of guilt or the pollution of sin.

purify *vt* (**purified, purifying**) to make pure; to free from extraneous polluting, debasing or contaminating matter; to free from pollution ceremonially; to cleanse from whatever renders unclean and unfit for sacred services; to free from guilt or the defilement of sin.—*vi* to grow or become pure or clear.

purist *n* one who scrupulously aims at purity of style and correctness of form, particularly in language; one who is a rigorous critic of purity in literary style; one who insists on traditional correctness in his or her chosen pastime, as fly-fishing.

puritan *n* a person who is extremely strict in religion or morals, especially one who denounces sensuousness, luxury, etc; hence, a person who wishes to limit or destroy another's pleasure or enjoyment.—*adj* of or like a puritan.

Puritan *n* one of the more extreme Protestant dissenters from the Church of England in the reign of Elizabeth I and the first two Stewarts, noted for strict religious observance, moral behaviour, etc, and for wishing to purge the church of ceremonial and trappings deemed to be Catholic.—*adj* pertaining to the Puritans.

puritanical, puritanic *adj* pertaining to puritans or their doctrines and practice; precise in religious matters; rigorously strict in religious or moral matters; rigidly condemnatory, especially of perceived moral failures or sensual pleasures.

Puritanism *n* the doctrines or practices of Puritans.

purity *n* the condition of being pure; freedom from foreign matter; cleanness; innocence; chastity; freedom from anything sinister or underhand; freedom from improper words or phrases.

purl[1] *n* an inversion of the stitches in knitting, giving a distinctive appearance.—*vt* to knit a row or rows in purl or to edge a piece of knitting with purl.

purl[2] *vi* to murmur, as a shallow stream flowing among stones; to flow with a gentle murmur; to ripple.—*n* a ripple; a murmuring sound, as of a shallow stream among stones.

purlieu *n* (*hist*) a piece of land set apart from an ancient royal forest; a part lying adjacent, a neighbouring area; the outer portion of any area; the environs.

purloin *vt* to steal; to filch; to take by plagiarism.—*vi* to practise theft.

purple *adj* of a colour composed of red and blue blended; imperial; regal; noble; (of writing) over-elaborate, over-worked with imagery; (*arch*) bloody or dyed with blood.—*n* a colour compounded by the blending of blue and red; a purple robe or dress; imperial or regal power; high rank, nobility.—**the purple** imperial dignity; the dignity of a cardinal; bishops collectively.

purport *n* meaning; tenor; import.—*vt* to convey, as a certain meaning; to import; to signify.—*vi* to have a certain purport or tenor.

purpose *n* that which a person sets before himself as an object to be reached or accomplished; end or aim; that which a person intends to do; design; plan; intention.—*vt* (**purposed, purposing**) to intend; to resolve; to mean; to wish.—*vi* to have intention or design; to intend.

purr *vi* to utter a soft, vibrant murmuring sound, as a cat when pleased.—*vt* to signify by purring.—*n* the low vibrant sound uttered by a cat when pleased; any purring sound.

purse *n* a small bag or pouch in which money is contained or carried in the pocket; a sum of money for a present or a prize; (*fig*) a treasury; finances; resources; riches.—*vt* (**pursed, pursing**) to contract into folds or wrinkles; to pucker.

purser *n* an officer on a passenger or merchant ship in charge of cabins, stewards, etc; an airline official responsible for the comfort and welfare of passengers.

purslane *n* a common annual flowering plant with fleshy leaves used in salads.

pursuance *n* a pursuing or carrying out (of a design); prosecution.—**in pursuance of** in fulfilment or execution of.

pursue *vt* (**pursued, pursuing**) to follow with a view to overtaking; to chase; to attend on (*misfortune pursues him*); to seek; to use measures to obtain; to prosecute, continue or proceed in; to carry on; to follow up; to proceed along, with a view to some end or object; to follow (*to pursue a course, hobby*, etc).—*vi* to go in pursuit; to proceed; (*law*) to act as a prosecutor.

pursuer *n* one who pursues; (*Scots law*) the party who institutes an ordinary action; the plaintiff.

pursuit *n* the act of pursuing or following with a view to overtaking; a following with a view to reaching or obtaining; endeavour to attain; a course of business or an occupation, pastime, hobby, etc; employment (*mercantile pursuits*).

pursuivant *n* (*hist*) a state messenger; an attendant on heralds; one of the third and lowest order of heraldic officers.

purtenance *n* appurtenance; that which pertains or belongs to anything; (*arch*) the internal organs.

purulence *n* the state of being purulent; pus.

purulent *adj* consisting of pus or matter; full of or resembling pus.

purvey *vt* to procure and supply (provisions); to provide, especially to provide provisions or other necessaries for a number of persons; to state, broadcast, sell or publish (*he purveyed his lies in the newspapers*).—*vi* to purchase provisions, especially for a number.

purveyance *n* act of purveying; the procuring of provisions; the provisions provided.

purveyor *n* one who purveys; one who supplies eatables for a number of persons; a caterer; one who makes available, publishes, sells or spreads information, gossip, etc.

purview *n* (*law*) the body of a statute as distinguished from the preamble; the limit or scope of a statute; limit of sphere of authority; scope; the extent or range of outlook.

pus *n* the white or yellowish matter produced as a result of infection of a wound, etc; matter produced in a festering sore.

push *vt* to press against with force; to impel by pressure; to drive by steady pressure, without striking, opposed to *draw*; to press or urge forward; to advance by exertions (*to push one's fortune*); to enforce, as in argument; to press or ply hard (as an opponent in argument); to urge; to importune; to prosecute energetically (*to push a trade*); (in cricket, tennis, etc) to make a pushing stroke; (*colloq*) to approach (an age); (*colloq*) to take to its limits (*to push one's luck*); (*sl*) to sell drugs illegally.—*vi* to make a thrust; to make an effort; to press oneself onward; to force one's way; to go or depart (with *off*); to support, advocate or promote (with *for*); (often *geol*) to extend (with *out* or *into*, as *the promontory pushes out from the northern shore*).—*n* the act of pushing; a short pressure or force applied; a thrust; a vigorous effort; an emergency; an extremity (*to come to the push*); persevering energy; enterprise; an attack on a large scale; an offensive; (in cricket, tennis, etc) a short stiff stroke with the bat, racket, etc.

pushchair *n* a wheeled conveyance designed to carry a small child in a sitting position, made of metal and cloth and usually collapsible.

pusher *n* a person or thing that pushes; a person who sells drugs illegally; a type of aircraft in which the propeller is situated behind the engine; a child's eating utensil for pushing food onto a spoon; (*sl*) an aggressively ambitious person.

pushing *adj* pressing forward in business; enterprising; energetic; assertive; presumptuous.

pushy *adj* (*colloq*) unnecessarily or offensively assertive; forceful; aggressively ambitious.

pusillanimity *n* weakness of spirit; cowardliness; timidity.

pusillanimous *adj* lacking strength and firmness of mind; being of weak courage; faint-hearted; cowardly.

puss[1] *n* a name for the cat; (*sl*) a girl; (*arch*) a name for the hare.

puss[2] *n* (*sl*) the mouth or face.

pussy *n* diminutive of **puss**[1]; (*vulg sl*) the female genitals.

pustular, pustulous *adj* having the character of or proceeding from a pustule or pustules.

pustule *n* (*med*) an inflamed elevation of the skin containing pus; (*bot*) a pimple or little blister.

put *vt* (*pret, pp* **put**, *ppr* **putting**) to place, set or lay in any position or situation; to place or cause to be in any state or condition (*to put to shame, to death, to put a house in order, to stay put*); to apply (*to put one's hand, one's mind to something*);

purse

to commit to an action, task, course, etc, often by coercion (*to put to work*); to set before or propose, especially in expectation or anticipation of an answer or reaction (*to put a question, I put it to you that the problem will not go away*); to state, aver, declare (*to put it mildly, he put his points with force*); to translate, adapt, portray, depict, set to (*to put into words, to put to music, I'll put it this way*); to guess, assess or estimate (with *at*, as *she put his age at thirty*); to employ, to deploy (with *to*, as *her experience was put to good use*); to bring together (a male and female domestic animal) for the purposes of mating and breeding (with *to*, as *the stockman put the stallion to the mare*); to set or make a limit (*to put an end to*); to expound or explain (with *over* or *across*, as *she put her points across well, he was unable to put over his sense of injustice*); to invest; to give, inspire, imbue or impart; to don or attach; to throw or hurl (*to put the shot*).—*vi* to proceed.—**to put about** to change the course of (a ship); to worry.—**to put aside** to reserve; to save for later use.—**to put away** to remove; to lay by; (*sl*) to consume.—**to put back** to replace; to postpone; to return to land.—**to put by** to thrust aside; to store up.—**to put down** to suppress; to silence; to kill or have killed; to write or enter; to reckon or assign; (*sl*) to belittle or humiliate.—**to put forth** to exert; to bud or shoot; to set out.—**to put forward** to propose (a person, plan, idea, etc) for some specific purpose.—**to put in** to interpose; to spend (time); to apply (for); to call (at).—**to put off** to doff, discard; to postpone; to evade; to get rid of; to discourage, repel; to foist (upon); to leave shore.—**to put on** to don; to assume, pretend; to increase; to add; to advance; to stage (a play, etc); (*sl*) to hoax.—**to put out** to eject; to extend; to exert; to dislocate; to quench; to publish; to place (money) at interest; to disconcert; to anger; to leave shore.—**to put over** to succeed in; to carry through.—**to put through** to carry out; to cause to do or undergo.—**to put up** to rouse; to offer (prayer); to propose as a candidate; to pack; to sheathe; to lodge; to build; to provide (money); to arrange (hair) on top; (*colloq*) to incite some action.—**to put up with** to endure, to tolerate.—**to put upon** to impose upon.—**to put wise** to disabuse, to enlighten.

putative *adj* supposed; reputed (*the putative father of a child*).

putrefaction *n* the act or process of putrefying; the decomposition of animal and vegetable substances, attended by the evolution of fetid gases; that which is or has putrefied.

putrefactive *adj* pertaining to putrefaction;

putter

tending to cause or causing putrefaction.

putrefy *vt* (**putrefied, putrefying**) to render putrid; to cause to rot with an offensive smell; to make carious or gangrenous.—*vi* to become putrid; to rot.

putrescence *n* the state of being putrescent; a putrid state.

putrescent *adj* becoming putrid; growing rotten; pertaining to the process of putrefaction.

putrid *adj* in a state of decay or putrefaction; corrupt; rotten; foul; proceeding from putrefaction or pertaining to it; (*colloq*) bad; (*colloq*) without merit, quality or worth; (*colloq*) morally rotten, corrupt.

putt *vt* to drive or attempt to drive (the ball) into the hole on the green of a golf course.

puttee *n* a long roll of cloth wound round a soldier's leg from ankle to knee as support and protection.

putter[1] *n* a short iron-headed golf club for putting the ball into the hole at golf; a player who putts.

putter[2] *n* someone who puts, as a proposal, argument, etc; an athlete who puts the shot.

putter[3] *vi* to busy oneself idly; to spend time; to potter.

putting green *n* the smooth grassy area round a hole in golf.

puttock *n* (*arch*) a bird of prey, usually the kite but sometimes the buzzard.

putty *n* a powder of calcined tin, used in polishing glass and steel; a kind of paste or cement compounded of whiting and linseed oil, used by glaziers for fixing panes of glass in window frames, etc; a fine cement made of lime and stone dust; the mixture of ground materials in which earthenware is dipped for glazing; any material of a putty-like consistency or with the same function.—*vt* (**puttied, puttying**) to cement with putty; to fill up with putty.

puzzle *vt* (**puzzled, puzzling**) to perplex; to nonplus; to make intricate; to entangle; to discover or resolve by long cogitation (with *out*).—*vi* to be bewildered; to be perplexed; to ponder (with *about* or *on*); to ponder; to try to solve (with *over*).—*n* a difficult problem; that which puzzles; the state or condition of being puzzled (*all in a puzzle*); a kind of riddle; a question, toy or contrivance which tests the ingenuity or skill.

puzzle-headed *adj* full of confused notions.

puzzlement *n* the state of being puzzled; bewilderment.

puzzler *n* one who or that which puzzles.

puzzling *adj* such as to puzzle; perplexing; embarrassing; bewildering.

PVC an abbreviation for **polyvinyl chloride**.

pyaemia *n* blood poisoning resulting from the introduction of pus, etc, into the system.

pyaemic *adj* pertaining to pyaemia; characterized by or of the nature of pyaemia.

pygarg *n* a species of antelope mentioned in the Bible and by Herodotus and Pliny, probably the addax; also, the sea eagle or osprey.

pygmean *adj* pertaining to a pygmy; abnormally undersized.

pygmy, pigmy *n* an abnormally small person; an insignificant person; anything little of its type.—*adj* pygmean; little; undersized; insignificant.

Pygmy, Pigmy *n* one of a people of equatorial Africa and Asia with a hereditary stature of less than five feet; one of a fabulous race of dwarfs, first mentioned by Homer.

pyjamas *npl* a loose garment consisting of trousers and jacket, worn at night in bed; a sleeping suit.

pylon *n* a tower-like structure of latticed steel used to carry electric cables across country; a structure on an aircraft to which are attached engines, weapons, fuel tanks, etc; a guide marker for pilots, or a marker in an aircraft race.

pylorus *n* (*pl* **pylori**) the outlet of the stomach, through which the food passes to the intestines.

pyorrhoea *n* a discharge of septic matter, especially from the gums.

pyramid *n* a solid structure with a rectilinear base and triangular sides that meet at a point; any object resembling a pyramid in form; one of the ancient masonry structure of this form erected in different parts of the world, especially in Egypt (to which the word was originally applied); (*geom*) a solid contained by a polygonal base and by other triangular planes meeting in a common point; (*com*) a group of holding companies structured in such a way that the controlling company manages the whole group with a comparatively small proportion of the total capital invested; (*pl*) a game similar to snooker played with fifteen red balls, arranged at the start into a triangular or pyramid pattern, and one white ball.—*vt* (*com*) to form companies into a pyramid; (in logic) to develop a proposition, theory, argument, etc, in a systematic fashion from a fundamental general premiss.

pyramidal, pyramidic, pyramidical *adj* pertaining to a pyramid; having the form of a pyramid.

Pyramids *npl* the three vast stone pyramids constructed as tombs for kings at Gizeh in Egypt about 2600 BC.

pyramid selling *n* the process of selling goods to agents who then sell batches to other distributors at a higher price, etc.

pyrargyrite *n* an ore of silver with hexagonal crystallization.

pyre *n* a heap of combustible materials, especially one on which a dead body is laid to be burned; a funeral pile; something used as a funeral pyre, such as a longship.

pyretic *adj* pertaining to or causing fever.

Pyrex *n* a trademark for heat-resistant glassware.

pyrexia *n* fever.

pyrexial, pyrexic *adj* pertaining to fever; feverish.

pyrheliometer *n* an instrument for measuring the intensity of the heat of the sun.

pyrite, pyrites *n* a hard yellow mineral in cubic crystalline form used in the manufacture of paper, sulphuric acid, etc; a mineral in which sulphur exists in combination with copper, cobalt, nickel, etc.

pyrolatry *n* the worship of fire

pyrology *n* the science of heat.

pyromancy *n* divination by fire.

pyromania *n* an uncontrollable urge to set things on fire.

pyromaniac *adj* of or pertaining to pyromania.—*n* a person who suffers from pyromania.

pyrometer *n* an instrument which is used to measure gradations of temperature above those that can be indicated by the mercurial thermometer.

pyrope *n* a dark-red variety of garnet.

pyrosis *n* heartburn.

pyrotechnic, pyrotechnical *adj* pertaining to fireworks or the art of making them.

pyrotechnics *n sing* the art of making fireworks; the use of artificial fireworks; the management and application of fire or fireworks in various operations, as for military purposes; (*pl*) a fireworks display; a brilliant display of virtuosity.

pyroxylin, pyroxyline *n* an inflammable substance derived from cellulose, used in making plastics.

pyrrhic *n* a metrical foot consisting of two short syllables.

Pyrrhic victory *n* a victory, as of that gained by King Pyrrhus of Epirus over the Romans at Asculum (279 BC), costing more to the victor than to the vanquished.

pyrrhonism *n* scepticism; universal doubt.

Pythagorean *adj* pertaining to Pythagoras or his system of philosophy, which taught the doctrine of the transmigration of souls and resolved all philosophy into the relations of numbers; (*mus*) pertaining to the diatonic eight-note scale, a succession of fifths, first developed by Pythagoras.—*n* a student or follower of Pythagoras.

python *n* any of a family of large, non-venomous constricting snakes native to Africa, southern Asia and Australia.

pyuria *n* the discharge of pus into the urine.

pyx, pix *n* a vessel used in church services for holding the consecrated Host; at the Royal Mint, a chest in which specimen gold and silver coins are placed for assay.

pyramids

Q

Q the seventeenth letter of the English alphabet, a consonant having the same sound as *k* or hard *c*.

quack *vi* to cry like the common domestic duck; to make vain and loud pretensions; to talk noisily and ostentatiously.—*n* the cry of a duck; one who pretends to skill or knowledge which he does not possess; an empty pretender; a charlatan; especially, a pretender to medical skill; (*sl*) a doctor.—*adj* pertaining to or characterized by quackery (*quack medicines, a quack doctor*).

quackery *n* the boastful pretensions or bad practice of a quack, particularly in medicine; humbug; imposture.

quad[1] *n* (*colloq*) the quadrangle or court, as of a college or jail; a small four-wheel drive cross-country vehicle with motorcycle controls.

quad[2] *n* a short form of **quadruplet**.

Quadragesima *n* Lent, so called because it consists of forty days.

Quadragesima Sunday *n* the first Sunday in Lent.

quadrangle *n* a quadrilateral figure; a figure having four sides and consequently four angles; a square or quadrangular court surrounded by buildings.

quadrangular *adj* of a square shape; having four sides and four angles.

quadrant *n* the quarter of a circle; the arc of a circle containing 90°; the space included between this arc and two radii drawn from the centre to each extremity; an instrument for measuring angular altitudes, in principle and application the same as the sextant, by which it is superseded.

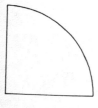

quadrant

quadraphonic *adj* of or relating to sound reproduction through four distinct sound sources.

quadrate *adj* square in form; square, by being the product of a number multiplied into itself.—*n* a square surface or figure.

quadratic *adj* pertaining to, denoting or containing a square; (*alg*) involving the square or second power of an unknown quantity (*a quadratic equation*).—*n* a quadratic equation; (*pl*) that branch of algebra which treats of quadratic equations.

quadrennial *adj* comprising four years; occurring once in four years.—*n* something occurring every four years.

quadrennially *adv* once in four years.

quadriga *n* (*pl* **quadrigae**) an ancient two-wheeled chariot drawn by four horses, harnessed all abreast.

quadrilateral *adj* having four sides and consequently four angles.—*n* a figure having four sides and four angles; the space enclosed between and defended by four fortresses or the four fortresses collectively.

quadrille *n* a game played by four persons with forty cards; a dance consisting generally of five figures or movements executed by four couples each forming the side of a square; the music for such a dance.

quadrillion *n* the fourth power of a million or the number represented by a unit with twenty-four ciphers annexed.

quadrinomial *adj* (*alg*) consisting of four denominations or terms.—*n* (*alg*) a quantity consisting of four terms.

quadriplegia *n* paralysis of all four limbs.

quadriplegic *adj* having the arms and the legs paralysed.—*n* a person suffering from quadriplegia.

quadrireme *n* a galley with four benches of oars, in use among the ancient Greeks and Romans.

quadrisyllabic *adj* consisting of four syllables.

quadrisyllable *n* a word consisting of four syllables.

quadrivalent *adj* (*chem*) applied to an element one atom of which is equivalent in combination to four atoms of hydrogen.

quadrivial *adj* having four roads meeting in a point.

quadrivium *n* (*pl* **quadrivia**) a collective term in the Middle Ages for the four lesser arts—arithmetic, music, geometry and astronomy.

quadroon *n* the offspring of a mulatto and a white person; a person who is one-fourth Negro-blooded.

quadrumanous *adj* (of apes, monkeys, baboons, lemurs, etc) usually characterized by all the four limbs terminating in prehensile hands.

quadruped *n* an animal having four legs, usually restricted to four-footed mammals, though many reptiles also have four legs.

quadrupedal *adj* belonging to a quadruped; having or walking on four feet.

quadruple *adj* four-fold; four times told.—*n* four times the sum or number.—*vt* (**quadrupled, quadrupling**) to make four times as much or as many; to multiply by four.—*vi* to become four times as much or as many.

quadruplet *n.* any of four offspring born at a single birth.

quadruplicate *vt* (**quadruplicated, quadruplicating**) to make fourfold; to double twice.—*adj* fourfold; four times repeated (*a quadruplicate ratio* or *proportion*).

quadruplication *n* the act of making fourfold or four times as great.

quadruply *adv* in a quadruple or fourfold degree; to a fourfold quantity.

quaestor *n* same as **questor**.

quaff *vt* to drink; to swallow in large draughts; to drink copiously.—*vi* to drink largely.

quagga *n* a wild horse of southern Africa, closely allied to the zebra, which became extinct in 1883 because of hunting.

quaggy *adj* trembling under the foot, as soft wet earth; boggy; spongy.

quagmire *n* a piece of soft boggy land that trembles under the foot; a bog; a fen; (colloq) a difficult or embarrassing situation, i.e. one where a person must go very carefully.

quahog *n* an edible North American clam with a rounded shell, found on the Atlantic coast.

quail[1] *n* the smallest European game bird allied to the partridge.

quail[2] *vi* to have the spirits sink or give way, as before danger or difficulty; to shrink; to lose heart; to cower.

quaint *adj* old-fashioned in an attractive way; curiously strange; attractive in an odd way.

quaintly *adv* in a quaint manner.

quaintness *n* the quality of being quaint.

quake *vi* (**quaked, quaking**) to shake; to tremble; to shudder (*to quake with fear*); to be shaken with more or less violent convulsions (*the earth quakes*); to shake or tremble, as the earth under the feet, through lack of solidity or firmness.—*n* a shake; a trembling; a tremulous agitation; (*colloq*) an earthquake.

Quaker *n* one of the Society of Friends, a religious sect advocating peace and simplicity and rejecting formal beliefs in favour of personal experience of divine revelation.

qualification *n* the act of qualifying or the state of being qualified; that which qualifies or fits a person or thing for any use or purpose, as for a place, an office, an employment; a quality, accomplishment, etc, which makes a person suitable for a job, etc; legal power; ability; a qualifying or extenuating circumstance; modification; restriction; limitation; an abatement; a diminution.

qualificative *adj* serving or having the power to qualify or modify.—*n* that which serves to qualify; a qualifying term, clause or statement.

qualify *vt* (**qualified, qualifying**) to make such as is required; to fit for any place, office or occupation; to furnish with knowledge, skill, etc, necessary for a purpose; to furnish with legal power or capacity (*to qualify persons for the franchise*); to limit or modify; to restrict; to limit by exceptions (*to qualify a statement*); to moderate, abate, soften; to modify the quality or strength of; to dilute or otherwise fit for taste (*to qualify spirits with water*).—*vi* to take the necessary steps for rendering oneself capable of holding any office or enjoying any privilege; to have the qualities, training, etc, necessary for something; to win a place in the later stages of a competition (usually sporting) by being sufficiently well placed in earlier heats (*to qualify for the final*); to establish a right to exercise any function (followed by *for*).

qualitative *adj* pertaining to quality; estimable according to quality.

quality *n* that which makes or helps to make anything such as it is; a distinguishing property, characteristic or attribute; a property; a trait; moral characteristic, good or bad; comparative rank; condition in relation to others; superior or high rank (*ladies of quality*).—*adj* of high quality.

quality time *n* a period time of time during which a person concentrates his or her full attention on a person or thing, used particularly of time spent by parents with their children.

qualm *n* a throb of pain; a sudden feeling of sickness at the stomach; a sensation of nausea; a sudden misgiving or apprehensive feeling; a scruple or twinge of conscience; compunction.

quandary *n* a state of difficulty, perplexity, uncertainty or hesitation; a dilemma; a pickle; a predicament.

quango *n* (*pl* **quangos**) a body of people appointed by a government to be responsible for a particular area of public interest.

quantitative *adj* estimable according to quantity; relating or having regard to quantity.

quantity *n* that property by which anything may be measured; greatness; extent; meas-

quadruped

quail

697

ure; size; any amount, bulk or aggregate (*a quantity of earth, a quantity of water*); often a large or considerable amount (*wheat shipped in quantities*); (*math*) anything which can be multiplied, divided or measured; anything to which mathematical processes are applicable; (*gram*) the measure of a syllable or the time in which it is pronounced; the metrical value of syllables as regards length or weight in pronunciation; (in logic), the extent in which the subject of a proposition is taken.

quantity surveyor *n* a person who estimates the quantities and costs of materials required for the construction of a building.

quantum *n* (*pl* **quanta**) a quantity; an amount; a sufficient amount; a share or portion; a fixed elemental unit of energy.

quantum leap *n* a sudden change in an atom, electron, etc. from one energy level or state to another; any sudden major change, especially one that is untypical or which takes an entirely new direction; any sudden major advance in one's understanding.

quarantine *n* a period of isolation imposed to prevent the spread of disease; the time or place of this.—*vt* (**quarantined, quarantining**) to put or keep in quarantine.

quark *n* in physics, a hypothetical elementary particle.

quarrel[1] *n* a brawl; an angry dispute; a wrangle; an altercation; a breach of friendship or concord; open variance between parties; the basis or ground of being at variance with another; ill-will or reason to complain; ground of objection.—*vi* (**quarrelled, quarrelling**) to dispute violently or with loud and angry words; to wrangle; to squabble; to fall out; to pick a quarrel; to get into hostilities; to find fault; to cavil.

quarrel[2] *n* a crossbow bolt, especially one with a somewhat square-shaped head; a lozenge-shaped pane of glass in a window; a small paving stone or tile of the square or lozenge form; a glazier's diamond; a kind of engraving tool.

quarrelsome *adj* apt to quarrel; easily irritated or provoked to contest; irascible; choleric.

quarry[1] *n* a place where stone, slate, etc, is dug from the earth or separated, as by blasting, from a large mass of rocks; an excavation for the extraction of stone, slate, etc; a source of information.—*vi* (**quarried, quarrying**) to dig or take from a quarry (*to quarry marble*).

quarry[2] *n* any animal pursued for prey; the game which a hawk or hound pursues; object of chase or pursuit in general; a part of the entrails of a beast of chase given to the dogs; a heap of game killed.

quart *n* the fourth part of an imperial gallon; two pints; equal to 69.3185 cubic inches; a vessel containing the fourth of a gallon.

quartan *adj* (of a fever, especially malaria) recurring every fourth day.

quarter *n* one of four parts into which anything is divided; a fourth part or portion; the fourth part of a hundredweight, that is, 28 pounds; the fourth of a ton in weight or 8 bushels of grain; the fourth part of the moon's period or monthly revolution; one of the four cardinal points; more widely, any region or point of the compass; a particular region of a town, city or country; a district; a locality; the fourth part of the year; in schools, the fourth part of the teaching period of the year; the fourth part of the carcass of a quadruped, including a limb; (*heral*) one of the divisions of a shield when it is divided into four portions by horizontal and perpendicular lines meeting in the fesse point; the part of a vessel's side which lies towards the stern; proper position; specific place; assigned or allotted position; the sparing of the life of a vanquished enemy; mercy shown by a conqueror (*to give* or *show quarter to a person*—perhaps originally to assign a lodging to or to give a share of one's own quarters); (*pl* in each of the following senses), temporary residence; shelter (*to find quarters somewhere*); a station or encampment occupied by troops (*winter quarters*); place of lodgement for officers and men; (*naut*) the post allotted to the officers and men at the commencement of an engagement (*to go to quarters*).—*vt* to divide into four equal parts; to separate into parts; to cut to pieces; to furnish with lodgings or shelter; to find lodgings and food for (*to quarter soldiers on the inhabitants*); (*heral*) to add to other arms on the shield by dividing it into four or more compartments.—*vi* to be stationed; to lodge; to have a temporary residence.

quarterdeck *n* (*naut*) that part of the upper deck of a vessel which is abaft the mainmast; the part of a naval vessel used for official or ceremonial business.

quarterfinal *n* one of four matches played before the semifinals in a competition or contest.

quartering *n* (*heral*) the conjoining of coats of arms in one shield to denote the alliances of one family with the heiresses of others; one of the compartments on such a shield.

quarterly *adj* recurring at the end of each quarter of the year (*quarterly payments of rent*).—*adv* once in a quarter of a year.—*n* a literary periodical issued once every three months.

quartermaster *n* (*milit*) an officer who has charge of the quarters, barracks, tents, etc, of a regiment and keeps the regimental

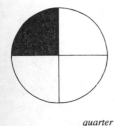

quarter

stores; (*naut*) a petty officer who has charge of the stowage of ballast and provisions and attends to the steering of the ship, etc.

quarterstaff *n* (*pl* **quarterstaves**) an old English weapon formed of a stout pole grasped by one hand in the middle and by the other between the middle and the end.

quartet, quartette *n* a set or group of four; a piece of music arranged for four voices or four instruments; the persons who execute a quartet; a stanza of four lines.

quarto *n* (*pl* **quartos**) a book of the size of the fourth of a sheet; a size made by twice folding a sheet, which then makes four leaves: abbreviated thus, *4to*.—*adj* denoting the size of a book in which a sheet makes four leaves.

quartz *n* a mineral formed of silicon dioxide occurring both crystallized and massive, and an important constituent of granite and the older rocks, varieties of it being known as rock crystal, flint, agate, amethyst, etc.

quartz clock, quartz watch *n* an extremely precise timepiece deriving its accuracy from the constant frequency of the vibrations of a quartz crystal.

quasar *n* a distant star-like celestial body that emits much light and radio waves.

quash *vt* to subdue, put down or quell; to extinguish; to put an end to (*to quash a rebellion*); (*law*) to make void from insufficiency or for other cause.

quasi *adv* as if; seemingly; having a resemblance only.

quasi- *prefix* almost; apparently.

quassia *n* any of several American tropical trees yielding a bitter bark and wood; the bark and wood used for making furniture; a bitter tonic obtained from the tree formerly used medicinally and now as an insecticide.

quatercentenary *n* a four-hundredth anniversary.

quarterlight *n* a usually triangular section within the side window of a car.

quaternary *adj* consisting of, arranged in or by fours; of the number 4; (*chem*) an atom bound to four other atoms or groups or containing such an atom; (*math*) with four variables.

Quaternary *adj* denoting strata more recent than the Upper Tertiary, i.e. the most recent geological period, of less than 1 million years ago.—*n* the Quaternary rock system, consisting of Pleistocene and Holocene epochs.

quatrain *n* a stanza of four lines, usually rhyming alternately.

quatrefoil *n* (*archit*) an aperture or ornament somewhat resembling four leaves about a common centre; an opening showing four radiating cusps.

quattrocento *n* the fifteenth century, especially in connection with Italian art and literature.

quaver *vi* to have a tremulous motion; to vibrate; to shake in vocal utterance; to sing with tremulous modulations of voice; to produce a shake on a musical instrument.—*vt* to utter with a tremulous sound.—*n* a shake or rapid vibration of the voice; (*mus*) a note equal to half a crotchet or the eighth of a semibreve.

quay *n* a built landing place along a line of coast or a river bank or forming the side of a harbour, at which vessels are loaded and unloaded; a wharf.

queasy *adj* sick at the stomach; affected with nausea; qualmish; apt to cause nausea.

QED an abbreviation of **quod erat demonstrandum**.

queen *n* the consort of a king; a woman who is the sovereign of a kingdom; a female sovereign; a female pre-eminent among others; the sovereign of a swarm of bees or the female of the hive; a playing card on which a queen is depicted; the most powerful of all the pieces in a set of chessmen; (*sl*) a homosexual male, especially one given to an overt and over-exaggerated homosexual manner.—*vi* to play the queen (with *it*); to act in an imperious or dominating manner, being especially resentful of criticism.—*vt* to promote (a pawn) to a queen in chess.

queen bee *n* the only fully developed and prolific female insect in a hive of bees; (*colloq*) a person who is the undoubted leader of a group, whether or not appointed to such a position.

queen consort *n* the wife of a king.

queen dowager *n* the widow of a deceased king.

queenly *adj* like a queen; becoming a queen.

queen mother *n* a queen dowager who is also mother of the reigning sovereign.

queen regent, queen regnant *n* a queen who holds the crown in her own right.

Queen's Counsel *n* (abbreviated to **QC**) during the reign of a queen, a barrister appointed counsel to the crown on the nomination of the Lord Chancellor and taking precedence over ordinary barristers.

queen's evidence *n* during the reign of a queen, evidence given by an accomplice, when the ordinary evidence is defective on the understanding that he or she shall go free for his or her share of the crime.

queer *adj* behaving or appearing otherwise than is usual; odd; singular; quaint; eccentric.—*n* (*sl*) a homosexual male.—*vt* to spoil the success of.

queerness *n* the state or quality of being queer; singularity.

quassia

queen bee

quell *vt* to subdue; to cause to cease by using force; to crush (an insurrection, etc); to quiet; to allay.

quench *vt* to extinguish; to put out (fire); to allay; to slake (thirst); to suppress, stifle, check, repress.—*vi* to be extinguished; to go out; to lose zeal.

quencher *n* one who or that which quenches.

quenelle *n* a ball of savoury cooked meat or fish, formed in various shapes and either fried or boiled in stock.

quercitron *n* the black or dyer's oak, a large forest tree of North America; the bark of this tree yielding a yellow dye; the dyestuff itself.

querist *n* one who puts a query; one who asks questions.

quern *n* a stone handmill for grinding grain, once commonly used by the Highlanders of Scotland.

querulous *adj* complaining or habitually complaining; apt to murmur; peevish; expressing complaint.

query *n* a question; an inquiry to be answered or resolved; the mark or sign of interrogation (?), a question mark.—*vi* (**queried, querying**) to ask a question or questions.—*vt* to seek by questioning; to examine by questions; to doubt of; to mark with a query.

quest *n* the act of seeking; search; pursuit; a journey in search of someone or something; searchers collectively; inquiry; examination.—*vti* to search (about) for, to seek.

question *n* an interrogation; something asked; an inquiry; a query; disquisition; discussion; the subject or matter of investigation or discussion; the theme of inquiry (*foreign to the question*); subject of debate; a point of doubt or difficulty; doubt; controversy (*true beyond question*).—*vi* to ask a question or questions; to debate; to doubt.—*vt* to inquire of by asking questions; to examine by interrogation; to doubt; to have no confidence in; to call in question; to challenge.

questionable *adj* capable of being questioned or inquired of; liable to question; suspicious; doubtful; dubious; uncertain; disputable.

questionnaire *n* a set of questions, usually printed on a form, designed to obtain a person's opinion or gather information for a survey, statistics, etc.

questor, quaestor *n* in ancient Rome, a magistrate whose chief office was the management of public finances; a receiver of taxes, tribute, etc.

quetzal *n* a brilliantly coloured, crested bird of Central and South America with long tail feathers, one of the trogons; the principal monetary unit of Guatemala.

queue

quiche

queue *n* the tail of a wig; a tail formed with a person's hair behind; a pigtail; a file of people, vehicles, etc, waiting in the order of arrival for admission to somewhere, to be served. for transport, etc.—*vi* (**queued, queuing**) to wait in turn.

quibble *n* a turn of language to evade the point in question; an evasion; a prevarication; a pun; a low conceit.—*vi* (**quibbled, quibbling**) to evade the point in question by artifice, play upon words or any conceit; to prevaricate; to pun.

quiche *n* a savoury tart made of beaten eggs, bacon, cheese or other ingredients baked in a pastry case.

quick *adj* characterized by liveliness or sprightliness; nimble; brisk; speedy; rapid; swift; perceptive in a high degree (*quick sight*); sensitive; hasty; precipitate; irritable (*quick of temper*); (*arch*) alive, living; (*arch*) pregnant.—*adv* in a quick manner; quickly.—*n* the living flesh; the sensitive flesh below a fingernail or toenail; (*fig*) the inmost sensibilities (*stung to the quick*); (*arch*) living people collectively (*the quick and the dead*); quickset.—*exclam* hurry!

quicken *vt* to make alive; to revive or resuscitate; to cheer or refresh; to make quicker; to accelerate; to sharpen; to give keener perception to; to stimulate.—*vi* to become alive; to become quicker; (of a mother) to be in that state of pregnancy in which the child gives indications of life; (of a foetus) to begin to give signs of life in the womb.

quickie *n* (*colloq*) anything done rapidly or in haste, especially an alcoholic drink taken quickly or a brief sexual union.

quicklime *n* lime (calcium oxide) burned and not yet slaked with water.

quickly *adv* speedily; rapidly; nimbly; soon; without delay.

quickness *n* speed; celerity; activity; briskness; acuteness of perception; keenness; sharpness; (*arch*) state of being quick or alive.

quicksand *n* a deep, constantly moving area of loose wet sand, usually on the shore of the sea, a lake or a river, which sucks down inextricably anything that becomes mired in it; (*fig*) something deceptive or treacherous.

quickset *n* a living plant set to grow, particularly for a hedge; hawthorn planted for a hedge.—*adj* made of quickset.

quicksilver *n* an old name for **mercury**.

quickstep *n* a ballroom dance in quick time; the music for this.

quid[1] *n* (*colloq*) one pound sterling.—**quids in** (*colloq*) in a fortunate position.

quid[2] *n* a piece of tobacco chewed and rolled about in the mouth.

quiddity *n* an old philosophical term

equivalent to essence and comprehending both the substance and qualities; a trifling nicety; a quirk or quibble.

quidnunc *n* one curious to know everything that passes; one who pretends to know all that goes on; a collector and retailer of gossip.

quid pro quo *n* (*pl* **quid pro quos**) something in return for something; a fair exchange; some advantage or thing that must be given before a bargain is struck or a service performed.

quiescence *n* the state or quality of being quiescent; rest; repose.

quiescent *adj* being in a state of repose; still; not moving; quiet; not excited; tranquil; (*gram*) silent; not sounded (*a quiescent letter*).

quiet *adj* noiseless; hushed; not in action or motion; still; in a state of rest; free from alarm or disturbance; left at rest; tranquil; peaceable; not turbulent; free from emotion; calm; patient; retired; secluded; free from fuss or bustle; not glaring or showy (*quiet colours*).—*n* absence or near-absence of noise; rest; stillness; tranquillity; repose; freedom from emotion of the mind; calmness.—*exclam* silence! make less noise!—*vt* to make or cause to be quiet; to calm; to pacify; to allay; to tranquillize; to bring to a state of rest.—*vi* to become quiet or still; to abate.

quieten *vti* to quiet; to pacify; to become quiet.

quietism *n* a mental tranquillity and passive attitude towards life; the absorption of the feelings or faculties in religious contemplation; the practice of a class of mystics who resigned themselves to mental inactivity in order to bring the soul into direct union with the Godhead.

quietist *n* one who believes in or practises quietism; especially applied to one of a sect of mystics founded by Molinos, a Spanish priest, in the latter part of the seventeenth century.

quietly *adv* in a quiet state or manner; peaceably; calmly; patiently; in a manner to attract little or no attention.

quietness *n* the state of being quiet; tranquillity; calmness.

quietude *n* rest; quiet; tranquillity.

quietus *n* (*pl* **quietuses**) a final discharge of an account; a final settlement; a quittance; death; anything that results in death or annihilation.

quill *n* the hollow steam of a feather; any of the large, wing or tail feathers of a bird; anything made of this, as a pen; any of the spines of a porcupine; a piece of small reed on which weavers wind the thread of the woof; a piece of quill attached to a slip of wood, by means of which certain stringed musical instruments like the harp-

sichord were played; the fold of a plaited ruff or ruffle, about the size and shape of a goose quill.—*vt* to plait with small ridges like quills.

quilt *n* a warm bedcover or coverlet made by stitching one piece of cloth over another, with some soft substance between; any thick or warm coverlet; a bedspread.—*vt* to stitch together, as two pieces of cloth, with some soft substance between; to stuff in the manner of a quilt.

quilting *n* the act or operation of forming a quilt; the material used for making quilts; quilted work.

quin *n* a short form of **quintuplet**.

quince *n* a small Asian tree, now widely cultivated; the pear-shaped golden-yellow fruit of the tree, used in making preserves.

quincentenary *n* the five-hundredth anniversary.

quincunx *n* an arrangement of five objects in a square, one at each corner and one in the middle; an arrangement, as of trees, in such squares continuously.

quinine *n* an important vegetable alkali, obtained from the bark of the cinchona tree and used in medicine, one of its salts being used as an anti-malarial drug.

quinquagesima *n* fiftieth.

Quinquagesima Sunday *n* the Sunday before Lent, being about the fiftieth day before Easter; Shrove Sunday.

quinquennial *adj* occurring once in five years or lasting five years.—*n* something that occurs every five years.

quinquennium *n* (*pl* **quinquennia**) the space of five years.

quinquereme *n* an ancient galley having five ranks of rowers.

quinsy *n* (*med*) an inflammation of the tonsils; any inflammation of the throat or parts adjacent.

quintain *n* a figure or other object used as a target for tilting practice, often an upright post on the top of which was a horizontal bar turning on a pivot with a sandbag attached to one end and a broad board on the other, it being a trial of skill to tilt at the broad end with a lance and pass on before the bag of sand could whirl round and strike the tilter.

quintal *n* a measure of weight of 100 kilograms (220 pounds).

quintessence *n* according to old notions, the fifth or highest essence or most ethereal element of natural bodies; hence, an extract from anything, containing its virtues or most essential part in a small but concentrated quantity; the best and purest part of a thing; a pure or perfect example of something.

quintessential *adj* consisting of the quintessence.

quintet, quintette *n* a set or group of five; a

quill

quince

piece of music arranged for five voices or five instruments; the people who execute a quintet.

quintuple *adj* fivefold; arranged in five or in fives; (*mus*) containing five notes of equal value in a bar.

quintuplet *n* one of five offspring born at a birth.

quip *n* a smart sarcastic turn; a sharp or cutting jest; a jibe; a witty remark.—*vt* (**quipped, quipping**) to utter quips on; to sneer at.—*vi* to use quips; to joke.

quire[1] *n* a collection of paper consisting of twenty-four or twenty-five sheets of equal size, one-twentieth of a ream.

quire[2] *n* an old form of **choir**.

quirk *n* a peculiarity of manner or action; a sudden, unexpected twist or turn.

quit *vt* (**quitted, quitting**) to discharge, as an obligation or duty; to meet and satisfy; to repay; to set free, absolve, acquit; to relieve; to rid; to discharge from; to meet expectations entertained of; to acquit (used reflexively, as *to quit oneself like a man*); to depart from; to leave; to resign; to give up; to abandon.—*vi* to leave; to resign; to give up.

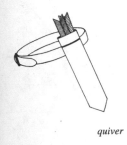

quiver

quite *adv* completely; wholly; entirely; totally; altogether; to a great extent or degree; very (*quite warm*); actually, truly; to a certain extent, somewhat (*it's quite nice*).—*interj* expressing firm agreement or concurrence (also **quite so**).

quits *adj* being on even terms.—**to be quits with one** to have got even with him or her.—*exclam* we are even!

quiver[1] *vi* to shake or tremble; to quake; to shiver; to show a slight tremulous motion; to be agitated.—*n* the act or state of quivering; a tremulous motion; a shiver.

quiver[2] *n* a case or sheath for arrows.

qui vive *n* the challenge of French sentries; equivalent to the English 'Who goes there?'.—**to be on the qui vive** to be on the alert.

quixotic, quixotical *adj* romantic to the point of extravagance; aiming at visionary ends; ideal; high-flown; unrealistically idealistic.

quixotism *n* romantic and absurd notions.

quoit

quiz *n* something designed to puzzle; a hoax; a jest; one who quizzes; an odd person; a form of entertainment where players are asked questions; a short written or oral test.—*vt* (**quizzed, quizzing**) to puzzle; to make sport of by means of obscure questions; to look at through an eyeglass; to look at inquisitively; to interrogate.

quizmaster *n* the person who puts the question to the contestants in a quiz or a quiz show.

quiz show *n* an entertainment programme o television or radio in which contestants answer questions to win prizes.

quizzical *adj* suggesting puzzlement; teasing or mocking; questioning.

quod erat demonstrandum (usually abbreviated to **QED**) (*geom*) 'that which was to be proved', used at the end of workings that have proved a theorem; hence, used in conversation to signify the speaker's believe that something is or has been proved.

quoin *n* an external solid angle; the external angle of a building or corner of a wall; a wedge-like piece of stone, wood, metal or other material; a cornerstone.

quoit *n* a flattish ring of iron, to be thrown at a fixed mark on the ground at play; (*pl*) the game played with such rings.

quondam *adj* having been formerly; former (*one's quondam friend*).

quorum *n* the minimum number that must be present at a meeting or assembly to make its proceedings valid.

quota *n* a proportional part or share; share or proportion assigned to each or which each of a number has to contribute; a prescribed amount, especially a figure to which quantities are restricted (*the milk quota*).

quotability *n* fitness for being quoted.

quotation *n* the act of quoting; the passage quoted or cited; (*com*) the current price of commodities or stocks published in prices current, etc; an estimated price.

quotation mark *n* a punctuation mark used to indicate the beginning (' or ") and end (' or ") of a quotation.

quote *vt* (**quoted, quoting**) to refer to some author or speaker; to refer to by way of authority or illustration; to cite or cite the words of (*to quote a passage, an author*); (*com*) to name, as the price of an article; to state the price of.—*n* (*colloq*) something quoted; (*colloq*) a quotation mark.

quoth *vt* (*arch*) said; spoke (used generally in the first and third persons preterit tense and followed instead of preceded by its nominative, as '*No,*' *quoth he*).

quotidian *adj* daily; occurring or returning daily.

quotient *n* (*arith*) the number resulting from the division of one number by another and showing how often a less number is contained in a greater.

R

R the eighteenth letter of the English alphabet.

rabbet *vt* to cut the edge of (as of a board) in a sloping manner, so that it may join by lapping with another piece cut in a similar manner; also, to cut a rectangular groove along the edge of to receive a corresponding projection.—*n* the cut or groove so made.

rabbi *n* (*pl* **rabbis**) a title of respect given to Jewish doctors or expounders of the law, especially the ordained spiritual leader of a synagogue.

rabbit *n* a common rodent mammal with long ears, long back legs and a short tail which feeds on grass or other herbage and burrows in the earth; the flesh of rabbits as food; the fur of rabbits.

rabbit warren *n* an area where rabbits live and breed.

rabble *n* a tumultuous crowd of vulgar, noisy people.—**the rabble** a mob; the common people.

Rabelaisian *adj* in the broad, indelicate style of the French author François Rabelais (*c.*1494–1553).

rabid *adj* infected with rabies; extreme in opinion, intolerant (*a rabid Tory*, *a rabid teetotaller*).

rabies *n* an acute infectious viral disease of dogs, etc, that may be transmitted to people if bitten by an infected animal, causing convulsions, delirium, frothing of the mouth and a terror of water.

raccoon, racoon *n* a small nocturnal flesh-eating American mammal with a bushy tail ringed in black and white.

race[1] *n* a rapid course; a contest of speed, especially in running but also in riding, driving, sailing, rowing, etc, in competition; (*pl*) horse races (*to go to the races*, *Doncaster races*); a strong or rapid current of water; a powerful current or heavy sea sometimes produced by the meeting of two tides; a canal or watercourse to and from a mill or waterwheel; a strong tidal rush of water (*the Race of Alderney*).—*vi* (**raced, racing**) to run swiftly; to hurry; to run or contend in running.—*vt* to cause to

run; to cause to contend in running; to drive quickly in a trial of speed.

race[2] *n* any of the divisions of humankind distinguished especially by colour of skin; any geographical, national or tribal ethnic grouping; a breed or stock; a perpetuated variety of animals or plants; a special or characteristic flavour, nature, etc.

racecourse *n* the ground or path on which races, especially horse races, are run.

racehorse *n* a horse bred or kept for racing; a horse that runs in competition.

raceme *n* (*bot*) a type of inflorescence, in which a number of flowers with short and equal stalks stand on a common slender axis, as in the currant.

rachis *n* (*pl* **rachises, rachides**) the vertebral column of mammals and birds; something similar to this, as the shaft of a feather, the stalk of the frond in ferns, the common stalk bearing the alternate spikelets in some grasses.

rachitic *adj* pertaining to rachitis; rickety.

rachitis *n* inflammation of the spine; rickets; a disease of plants which produces abortion of the fruit.

racial *adj* pertaining to race or lineage; pertaining to the races of humankind.

racism, racialism *n* a belief in the superiority of some races over others; prejudice against or hatred towards people of other races; discrimination on the grounds of race.

racist, racialist *adj* pertaining to racism; exhibiting racism.—*n* a person who believes in or practices racism.

rack[1] *vt* to stretch unduly; to strain vehemently (as in *to rack one's brains*, to strain or exercise one's thoughts to the utmost); to twist; to wrest; to distort; to put a false meaning on; to punish on the rack; to torment; to torture; to affect with extreme pain or anguish; to harass by exacting excessive rents; to heighten; to exaggerate; to place on or in a rack or frame (*to rack bottles*).—*n* an appliance for straining or stretching; formerly, an instrument for the judicial torture of criminals and suspected persons, consisting of a framework on

rabbit

which the victim's limbs were strained by cords and levers; hence, torture; extreme pain; anguish; an open wooden framework above a manger containing hay, grass, straw, etc, as fodder for horses and cattle; a framework on or in which articles are arranged and deposited (*a bottle rack, a hayrack, a letter rack*, etc); (*mach*) a straight or very slightly curved bar, with teeth on one of its edges, adapted to work into the teeth of a wheel or pinion.

rack[2] *n* thin flying broken clouds or any portion of floating vapour in the sky.—*vi* to fly, as vapour or broken clouds.

rack[3] *vt* to draw off from the lees; to draw off, as pure liquor from its sediments (*to rack cider* or *wine*).

rack[4] *n* wreck; ruin; destruction (*to go to rack and ruin*).

racket[1] *n* a confused, clattering noise; noisy talk; clamour; din; a scheme or activity to make money illegally or by exploitation.—*vi* to make a racket; to frolic; to move about in scenes of tumultuous pleasure.

racket[2], racquet *n* a long-handled bat strung with interlaced nylon or catgut for hitting the ball in tennis and squash.—*vt* to strike as with a racket; to toss.

racketeer *n* a person who extorts money by threats; a person who engages in an illegal profit-making enterprise.

rackety *adj* making a racket or tumultuous noise.

rack-rent *n* a rent raised to the uttermost or greater than any tenant can be reasonably expected to pay.—*vt* to subject to the payment of rack-rent.

raconteur *n* a teller of a good story; a conversationalist.

racoon *n* same as **raccoon**.

racquet *n* same as **racket[2]**.

racy *adj* strong and flavourful (*racy wine*); having a strong distinctive character of thought or language; spirited; pungent; piquant (*a racy style, a racy anecdote*).

radar *n* a system or device for detecting objects such as aircraft by using the reflection of radio waves.

raddle *n* same as **ruddle**.

raddled *adj* worn-out.

radial *adj* having the character of a radius; grouped or appearing like radii or rays; shooting out as from a centre; pertaining to the radius, one of the bones of the human forearm (*the radial artery* or *nerve*); (of a tyre) having the fabric cords of the outer casing lying radial to the hub for greater flexibility.

radian *n* the SI unit of plane angle equal to the angle at the centre of a circle formed by radii of an arc equal in length to the radius.

radiance, radiancy *n* the condition of being

racket

radar

radiant; brightness shooting in rays or beams; hence in general, brilliant or sparkling lustre; vivid brightness; brilliance; splendour; dazzling beauty; obvious happiness.

radiant *adj* radiating; giving out rays; darting, shooting or emitting rays of light or heat; transmitted by radiation; shining; beaming with brightness; emitting a vivid light or splendour; beautiful; beaming with happiness.—*n* in optics, the luminous point or object from which light radiates; (*astron*) the point in the heavens from which a star shower seems to proceed.

radiant energy *n* energy in the form of light or radiant heat.

radiant heat *n* heat conveyed by electromagnetic radiation rather than conduction or convection.

radiate *vi* (**radiated, radiating**) to issue and proceed in rays or straight lines from a point or surface, as heat or light; to beam forth; to emit rays; to be radiant; to proceed as from a centre.—*vt* to emit or send out in direct lines from a point or surface (*a body radiates heat*); to give forth.—*adj* having rays; having lines proceeding as from a centre like radii; (*zool*) with parts arranged radially; (*bot*) having a ray distinct from the disc.

radiation *n* the act of radiating or state of being radiated; the divergence or shooting forth of anything from a point or surface, like the diverging rays of light (*the radiation of heat, of sound*, etc); that which is radiated; any ray, energy or particle which is radiated; radiant particles emitted as energy; rays emitted in nuclear decay; medical treatment using a radioactive substance.

radiation sickness *n* an illness caused by excessive exposure to radiation from radioactive materials.

radiator *n* that which radiates; an appliance for heating a room by means of hot water, steam, gas or electricity; a nest of tubes for cooling circulating water, as in a motorcar engine.

radical *adj* pertaining to the root or origin; original; reaching to the principles; fundamental; thorough-going; extreme (*a radical error, a radical cure* or *reform*); implanted by nature; innate; native; (*philol*) belonging to or proceeding directly from a root; primitive; original; not derived (*the radical meaning of a word*); (*bot*) proceeding immediately from the root or from a stem and close to the root (*a radical root* or *peduncle*).—*n* (*philol*) a primitive word; a root or simple underived uncompounded word; a letter that belongs to the root; in politics, one who favours basic social or political change; (*chem*) a compound of two or more elements which has itself an elemental nature and performs elemental functions in other compounds; (*math*) a quantity involving square, cube or other roots; a surd.

radicalism *n* the doctrine or principles of a radical.

radically *adv* in a radical manner; in root or origin; fundamentally.

radical sign *n* the symbol √ placed before a number to show that the square root (or a higher root denoted by an index number over the sign) is to be extracted. ·

radicle *n* (*bot*) that part of the embryo or seed of a plant which, on vegetating, becomes the root; the fibrous parts of a root.

radii the plural of **radius**.

radio *n* (*pl* **radios**) the use of electromagnetic waves to send sounds or signals through space without wires to a receiving set; a radio receiving set; broadcasting by radio as an industry, form of entertainment, etc.—*vt* (**radioed, radioing**) to send a message to by radio. ·

radioactive *adj* giving off radiant energy in the form of particles or rays caused by the disintegration of atomic nuclei.

radioactivity *n* the property of some atomic nuclei to break down into simple nuclei and release alpha particles, beta particles, neutrons or gamma rays; the quality of being radioactive.

radio astronomy *n* astronomy dealing with radio waves in space in order to obtain information about the universe.

radio-control *n* remote control using radio signals.

radio-controlled *adj* remotely controlled by radio signals, as radio-controlled models.

radio frequency *n* a frequency intermediate between audio frequencies and infrared frequencies, used especially in radio and television transmission.

radiogram *n* an instrument consisting of a radio and a record player; a telegram; an X-ray photograph.

radiograph *n* a picture produced by X-rays.

radiography *n* the production of X-ray photographs for use in medicine, industry, etc.

radioisotope *n* a radioactive isotope.

radiology *n* the science of X-rays and of the rays emitted by radioactive bodies, with special reference to their use in medicine.

radio telescope *n* an instrument used in radio astronomy for picking up and focusing radio signals from objects in space.

radiotherapy *n* the use of X-rays and the rays from radium, etc, in medicine, especially in the treatment of cancer.

radio wave *n* an electromagnetic wave with radio frequency.

radish *n* a plant with a small red-skinned root used as a salad vegetable.

radium *n* an intensely radioactive chemical element extracted from pitchblende and used in medicine, especially in radiotherapy.

radius *n* (*pl* **radii, radiuses**) (*geom*) a straight line extending from the centre of a circle to the circumference or from the centre of a sphere to its surface, and hence the semi-diameter of the circle or sphere; (*anat*) the smaller of the two bones of the forelimb of vertebrate animals; (*bot*) a ray; the outer part or circumference of a compound flower, having a character distinct from the central disc.

radix *n* (*pl* **radices, radixes**) a root (of a plant, of a word); (*math*) any number which is arbitrarily made the fundamental number or base of any system, as 10 in decimals.

radon *n* a gaseous radioactive element.

raffia, raphia *n* a fibrous substance obtained from a palm and used in making baskets, hats, etc.

raffish *adj* disreputable.

raffle *n* a form of lottery in which the winners receive objects as prizes, usually held to make money for charity, etc.—*vi* (**raffled, raffling**) to try the chance of a raffle; to engage in a raffle.—*vt* to dispose of by means of a raffle.

raft *n* a float of logs, planks or other pieces of timber fastened together for transporting them by water; a floating structure used in shipwrecks, often formed of barrels, planks, spars, etc; a floating platform used to move goods or people over water or moored for use by divers, etc; a floating mass of trees, branches, etc.—*vt* to transport on a raft.

rafter *n* one of the sloping timbers of a roof, which support the outer covering.—*vt* to furnish with rafters.

rag[1] *n* any piece of cloth torn from the rest; a tattered cloth, torn or worn; a fragment of dress; a shred; a tatter; (*pl*) tattered garments or poor clothes; (*geol*) rock deposits consisting of hard irregular masses (*coral rag, Kentish rag*, etc); ragstone; ragtime.

rag[2] *vt* (**ragged, ragging**) to torment, tease or subject to annoyance, often petty or ludicrous.

ragamuffin *n* an unkempt, dirty person, especially a child.

rage *n* violent anger accompanied by furious words, gestures or agitation; anger excited to fury; vehemence or violent exacerbation (*the rage of a fever, of hunger* or *thirst*); fury; extreme violence (*the rage of a tempest*); violent desire; (*colloq*) a craze; (*colloq*) a party, an enjoyable time.—**the rage** the object of popular and eager desire; the fashion.—*vi* (**raged, raging**) to be furious with anger; to be exasperated to fury; to be in a passion; to act or move fu-

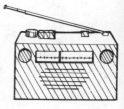

radio

radish

riously or with mischievous impetuosity (*the sea rages*); to ravage; to prevail with fatal effect (*the plague rages*).

ragged *adj* rent or worn into rags or tatters; tattered; having broken or rough edges; jagged; rough with sharp or irregular points; wearing tattered clothes; shabby.

ragged school *n* (*hist*) a school which provided free education, and in many cases food, lodging and clothing, for destitute children.

raglan *n* a type of loose sleeve cut or formed in one piece with the shoulder of a garment.

ragman *n* (*pl* **ragmen**) a man who collects or deals in rags.

ragout *n* a dish of stewed and highly seasoned meat.

ragstone *n* siliceous stone, so named from its rough fracture.

ragtime *n* music used with much inverted rhythm of note or tone, beginning on unaccented and sustaining into accented beat.

rag trade *n* (*colloq*) the clothes-manufacturing or fashion trade.

ragwort *n* one of several British weeds of the same genus as the groundsel.

raid *n* a hostile or predatory incursion; especially, an inroad or incursion of soldiers, police, etc; a foray; an attack by violence.

raider *n* one who makes a raid.

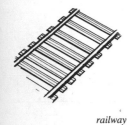

railway

rail[1] *n* a bar of wood or metal extending from one upright post to another, as in fences; a horizontal timber in any piece of framing or panelling; the upper pieces into which the balusters of a stair are mortised; a series of posts or balusters connected by crossbeams, bars or rods, for enclosure; a railing; one of the parallel iron or steel bars forming a smooth track for the wheels of a locomotive and its associated carriages, wagons, etc, or for a tramway car; a railway (*to travel* or *send goods by rail*).— *vt* to enclose with rails; to send by rail, as goods, etc.

rail[2] *n* one of several wading birds inhabiting damp places, moist herbage, etc, and comprising the land rail or corncrake and the water rail.

rail[3] *vi* to utter reproaches; to use insolent and reproachful language; to scold.

railhead *n* the most advanced point of a railway under construction; the point at which goods are transferred from a railway to some other means of transport.

rain guage

railing[1] *n* a fence or barrier of wood or iron, constructed of posts and rails; rails in general or the materials for rails.

railing[2] *adj* expressing reproach; insulting.

raillery *n* good-humoured pleasantry or slight satire; satirical merriment; jesting language; banter.

railroad *n* a railway.

railway *n* a road or way consisting of one or more series of pairs of iron or steel rails laid parallel to each other and several feet apart, on which the wheels of carriages are made to run in order to lessen friction; in an extended sense, all the land, works, buildings and machinery required for the support and use of the road or way, with its rails.

railway carriage *n* a passenger carriage on a railway.

railway crossing *n* the place where a road crosses a railway.

raiment *n* clothing in general; vestments; garments.

rain *n* the descent of water in drops from the clouds; the water thus falling; the moisture of the atmosphere condensed and deposited in drops; a shower or pouring down of anything.— *vi* to fall in drops from the clouds, as water (used mostly with *it* for a nominative, as *it rains, it will rain*); to fall or drop like rain (*tears rained from their eyes*).— *vt* to pour or shower down, like rain from the clouds; to pour or send down abundantly.

rainbow *n* a bow or arc of a circle consisting of all the prismatic colours and formed by the refraction and reflection of rays of light from drops of rain appearing in the part of the heavens opposite to the sun.

rain check *n* (*colloq*) the postponement of acceptance of an invitation.

rain cloud *n* a ragged and hanging cloud which resolves itself into rain.

rainfall *n* a fall of rain; the amount of water that falls as rain.

rain forest *n* a dense evergreen forest found in equatorial areas which has heavy rainfall and no dry season.

rain gauge *n* an instrument for measuring or gauging the quantity of rain which falls at a given place.

rainwater *n* water that has fallen from the clouds in rain.

rainy *adj* abounding with rain; wet; showery.— **a rainy day** (*fig*) less fortunate times.

raise *vt* (**raised, raising**) to cause to rise; to put, place or remove higher; to lift upward; to elevate; to heave; to elevate in social position, rank, dignity, etc; to increase the value or estimation of; to exalt, enhance, promote, advance; to increase the energy, strength, power or vigour of; to excite; to heighten (*to raise the courage, to raise the temperature of a room*); to cause to appear from the world of spirits; to recall from death (*to raise the dead*); to cause to assume an erect position or posture; to set upright; to awaken; to rouse to action; to incite; to stir up (*to raise the country, to raise a mutiny*); to cause to arise or come into being; to build up; to erect; to construct; to bring or get together;

to gather, collect; to levy (*to raise money, to raise an army*); to cause to be produced; to breed; to rear; to grow (*to raise wheat, to raise cattle, sheep*, etc); to give rise to; to originate (*to raise a false report*); to give vent or utterance to (*to raise a cry*); to strike up (*to raise the song of victory*); to cause to appear; to call up (*to raise a smile* or *a blush*); to heighten or elevate in pitch (*a sharp raises a note half a tone*); to increase the loudness of (*to raise the voice*); (*law*) to institute or originate (*to raise an action*); to cause to swell, as dough.—*n* a rise in wages.

raisin *n* a dried grape; a dried fruit of various species of vines.

raison d'être *n* (*pl* **raisons d'être**) the chief reason or justification for the existence of something.

raisonné *adj* supported by proofs, arguments or illustrations; arranged and digested systematically.

raita *n* a dish served cold with Indian food consisting of yoghurt mixed with a chopped vegetable, such as cucumber.

raj *n* the period of British rule in India.

rajah *n* formerly, an Indian ruler; an Indian or Malayan chief or prince.

rake[1] *n* an implement with wooden or metal teeth used for collecting hay or straw after mowing or reaping and in gardening for smoothing the soil, covering the seed, etc; a small implement like a hoe used for collecting the stakes on a gaming table.—*vt* (**raked, raking**) to apply a rake to or something that serves the same purpose; to gather with a rake; to smooth with a rake; to gather with labour or difficulty (*to rake together wealth*); to ransack; to pass swiftly over; to scour; (*milit*) to enfilade.—*vi* to use a rake; to seek by raking; to search with minute inspection into every part.

rake[2] *vi* (**raked, raking**) to incline; to slope; (*naut*) to incline from a perpendicular direction (*a mast rakes aft*).—*n* (*naut*) a slope or inclination; the projection of the stem or stern beyond the extremities of the keel; the inclination of a mast, funnel, etc, from a perpendicular direction.

rake[3] *n* a loose, disorderly, vicious person; a dissolute person; one addicted to lewdness; a libertine; a roué.

rakish *adj* dissolute; dashing; jaunty.

rallentando *adv, adj* (*mus*) a term indicating that the time of the passage over which it is written is to be gradually decreased.—*n* (*pl* **rallentandos**) a passage played in this way.

rally[1] *vt* (**rallied, rallying**) to collect and bring about order in, as troops dispersed or thrown into confusion; to bring together as for a fresh effort; to reunite.—*vi* to come back quickly to order; to re-form into an orderly body for a fresh effort; to resume or recover vigour or strength (*the patient begins to rally*); to improve.—*n* the act of one who rallies; a stand made by retreating troops; return of disordered troops to their ranks; the act of recovering strength.

rally[2] *vt* (**rallied, rallying**) to attack with raillery; to treat with good humour and pleasantry or with slight contempt or satire; to tease.—*vi* to use pleasantry or satirical merriment.

ram *n* the male of the sheep or ovine genus; a battering ram; formerly, a steam ironclad ship-of-war, armed at the prow below the waterline with a heavy iron or steel beak intended to destroy an enemy's ships by the force with which it was driven against them; the loose hammer of a pile-driving machine; the piston of a hydraulic press.—*vt* (**rammed, ramming**) to strike with a ram; to drive a ram or similar object against; to batter; to force in; to drive down; to fill or compact by pounding or driving; to stuff; to cram.—*vi* to use a battering ram or similar object.

Ram *n* Aries, one of the signs of the zodiac.

Ramadan *n* the ninth month of the Muslim year; the great annual Muslim fast, kept throughout the entire month from sunrise to sunset.

ramble *vi* (**rambled, rambling**) to rove; to wander; to go from place to place without any determinate object in view; to think or talk in an incoherent manner; to grow without constraint.—*n* a roving; an excursion or trip in which a person wanders from place to place; an irregular excursion.

rambler *n* one who rambles; a rover; a wanderer; a climbing rose.

rambling *adj* roving; wandering; straggling; without method; confused in ideas or language.

Ramboesque *adj* tough, aggressive and violent.

ramee *n* same as **ramie**.

ramekin *n* a baked dish of cheese, eggs, breadcrumbs, etc; the small pot in which it is cooked.

ramie, ramee *n* an Asian fibre, the produce of a species of nettle, used in textiles.

ramification *n* the act of ramifying; the process of branching out; a small branch or offshoot from a main stock or channel; a subordinate branch; a division or subdivision in a classification, etc; consequence; effect.

ramify *vt* (**ramified, ramifying**) to divide into branches or parts.—*vi* to shoot into branches, as the stem of a plant; to branch out; to be divided or subdivided; to branch out, as a main subject or scheme.

rammer *n* one who or that which rams or drives; a ramrod.

rake

ram

ramose, ramous *adj* (*bot*) belonging to a branch; growing on or shooting from a branch.

ramp *n* a sloping platform serving as a way between different levels; a wheeled staircase for boarding a plane; a sloping runway for launching boats.—*vi* to climb, as a plant; to rear on the hind legs; to assume a rampant attitude; to spring or move with violence; to rage; to bound; to romp.

rampage *vi* (**rampaged, rampaging**) to rush about with unrestrained spirits; to rush about in fury; to rage and storm.—*n* a state of passion or excitement; violent conduct (*on the rampage*).

rampageous *adj* boisterous; unruly.

rampancy *n* the state or quality of being rampant.

rampant *adj* springing or climbing unchecked; rank in growth; exuberant (*rampant weeds*); overleaping restraint or usual limits; excessively and obtrusively prevalent; predominant (*rampant vice*); (*heral*) (of a beast of prey, as the lion) standing upright on its hind legs (properly on one foot) as if attacking.

rampart *n* a bulwark; a defence; anything used for protection or defence; (*fort*) formerly, an elevation or mound of earth round a place, capable of resisting cannon shot and on which the parapet was raised, also sometimes including the parapet.

rampion *n* a perennial plant of the bellflower family, the root and leaves of which are used in salads.

ram raid *n* a shop, factory, etc, robbery carried out by driving a vehicle through the windows or security gates.

ramrod *n* a rod formerly used to ram down the charge of a muzzle-loading gun or other firearm.—*adj* (of a person) stiff and inflexible.

ramshackle *adj* liable to collapse; dilapidated.

ramson, ramsons *n* a species of garlic.

ranch *n* in America, a large kind of farm for rearing cattle and horses.

rancid *adj* having a rank smell; strong-scented, from turning bad with keeping (said of oils and fats, butter, etc); musty.

rancorous *adj* full of rancour; deeply malignant; intensely virulent; spiteful.

rancour *n* the deepest malignity, enmity or spite; deep-seated and implacable malice; inveterate enmity; malignity.

rand *n* a unit of money in South Africa.

random *adj* done at hazard or without settled aim or purpose; haphazard; left to chance; fortuitous.—**at random** in a haphazard or fortuitous manner.

random-access *adj* denoting direct access to data in any desired order.

randy *adj* (*colloq*) sexually aroused; (*colloq*) promiscuous.

ranee *n* same as **rani**.

range *vt* (**ranged, ranging**) to set in a row or in rows; to place in regular lines or ranks; to rank; to arrange systematically; to classify; to class; to rove through or over; to pass over.—*vi* to be placed in order; to be ranked; to rank; to rove at large; to wander without restraint; to pass from one point to another; to fluctuate (*the price ranges between £1 and £2*); (in guns) to have range or horizontal direction.—*n* a series of things in a line; a row; a rank (*a range of mountains*); space or room for excursion; the extent of country over which a plant or animal is naturally spread; compass or extent; discursive power; scope (*a wide range of thought*); the series of sounds belonging to a voice or a musical instrument; a kitchen grate and cooking apparatus; (in guns) the horizontal distance to which a shot or other projectile is carried; a place where gun or rifle practice is carried on.

ranger *n* one who ranges; a government official connected with a royal forest or park; the keeper of or an official superintending a public park.

rangy *adj* tall and thin; long-legged.

rani, ranee *n* the wife of a rajah; an Indian princess or queen.

rank[1] *n* a row; a line; a tier; a range; (*milit*) a line of soldiers; (*pl*) the order of common soldiers (*to reduce a sergeant to the ranks*); an aggregate of individuals together; a social class; an order; a division; degree of dignity, eminence or excellence; comparative station; relative place (*a writer of the first rank*); high social position; distinction; eminence (*a man of rank*).—*vt* to place abreast in a rank or line; to place in a particular class, order or division; to class or classify; to range.—*vi* to be ranged, classed or included, as in a particular class, order or division; to have a certain rank; to occupy a certain position as compared with others.

rank[2] *adj* luxuriant in growth; causing vigorous growth; fertile; strong-scented; rancid; strong to the taste; excessive; utter (*rank nonsense*); gross; coarse; disgusting.

rank and file *n* ordinary soldiers; the ordinary members of an organization, etc, as distinct from the leaders or office-bearers.

rankle *vi* (**rankled, rankling**) to fester, as a sore or wound; to produce a painful sensation; (*fig*) to produce bitterness or rancour in the mind; to continue to irritate.

rankness *n* the state or quality of being rank; vigorous growth; luxuriance; strength and coarseness in smell or taste.

ransack *vt* to search thoroughly; to enter and search every place and part of; to rummage; to plunder; to strip by plundering.

ransom *n* release from captivity or bondage

in exchange for payment; the price paid for such release.—*vt* to pay a ransom for; to redeem from captivity, bondage, forfeit or punishment.

rant *vi* to rave in violent or extravagant language; to be noisy and boisterous in words or declamation.—*n* boisterous, empty declamation; bombast.

ranunculus *n* (*pl* **ranunculuses, ranunculi**) any of a common genus of usually yellow-flowering plants including the buttercup.

rap *n* a quick smart blow; a knock; a sharp criticism; (*colloq*) a rebuke; (*colloq*) a chat; (*colloq*) a rapid, rhythmical chanting, often improvised and often rhyming, to an instrumental backing.—*vi* (**rapped, rapping**) to strike with a quick sharp blow; to knock.—*vt* to strike with a quick blow; to give a knock (*to rap one's knuckles*); to criticize sharply; to reprove; (*colloq*) to chat; (*colloq*) to talk or sing in the style of rap.

rapacious *adj* given to plunder; accustomed to seize or take possession of property by violence; subsisting on prey or animals seized by violence; avaricious; grasping.

rapacity *n* the quality of being rapacious; ravenousness; the act or practice of extorting or exacting by oppressive injustice.

rape[1] *n* the act of snatching by force; a seizing and carrying away by force or violence (*the rape of Proserpine*); (*law*) the forcing of a person to have sexual intercourse against his or her will.—*vt* (**raped, raping**) to perform the act of rape on.

rape[2] *n* a plant of the cabbage family, cultivated for its seeds from which oil is extracted by grinding and pressure.

rape[3] *n* refuse stalks and skins of raisins.

raphe *n* (*bot, zool*) a line between parts that makes them look as if they had been sewn or joined together; a suture or line of junction.

raphia *n* same as **raffia**.

rapid *adj* very swift or quick; moving with celerity; advancing with speed; speed in progression (*rapid growth*); quick or swift in performance.—*n* a swift current in a river where the channel is descending.

rapidity *n* the state or quality of being rapid; swiftness; celerity; velocity; haste in utterance; quickness.

rapier *n* a straight, two-edged sword with a narrow pointed blade used in thrusting.

rapine *n* the act of plundering; the seizing and carrying away of things by force.

rappel *n* the roll or beat of the drum to call soldiers to arms.

rapport *n* a resemblance; a correspondence; harmony; affinity.

rapscallion *n* a rascal.

rapt *adj* snatched away; transported; enraptured; in an ecstasy; entirely absorbed.

raptor *n* a bird of prey.

raptorial *adj* pertaining to raptors, the birds of prey; living by rapine or prey; adapted to the seizing of prey.

rapture *n* a transport of delight; ecstasy; extreme joy or pleasure; enthusiasm.

rapturous *adj* ecstatic; transporting; ravishing.

rare[1] *adj* uncommon; not frequent; possessing qualities seldom to be met with; excellent or valuable to a degree seldom found; (of gas, etc) thinly scattered; sparse; thin; porous; not dense or compact.

rare[2] *adj* not completely cooked, partly raw; underdone.

rare earth *n* (*chem*) one of a series of oxides of metallic elements occurring in certain rare minerals of the lanthanide series.

rarefy *vt* (**rarefied, rarefying**) to make rare, thin, porous or less dense; to expand by separation of constituent atoms or particles, opposed to *condense*.—*vi* to become rare, that is, not dense or less dense.

rarely *adv* in a rare degree or manner; seldom.

rareness *n* the state of being rare; uncommonness; thinness; tenuity; value arising from scarcity.

rarity *n* the state or quality of being rare; a thing valued for its scarcity or excellence.

rascal *n* a rogue or scoundrel; a mischievous person or child.

rascality *n* such qualities as make a rascal.

rascally *adj* like a rascal.

rase *vt* (**rased, rasing**) same as **raze**.

rash[1] *adj* hasty in counsel or action; precipitate; impetuous; resolving or entering on a project without due deliberation and caution; uttered, formed or undertaken with too little reflection.

rash[2] *n* an eruption on the skin, usually in the form of red spots or patches.

rasher *n* a slice of bacon for frying or grilling.

rashness *n* the quality of being rash; impetuosity; precipitation; inconsiderate readiness to decide or act; a rash act.

rasorial *adj* (of poultry) scratching the ground for food.

rasp *vt* to rub against with some rough implement; to file with a rasp; to grate; (*fig*) to grate harshly on.—*vi* to rub or grate.—*n* a coarse file with numerous separate projections or teeth; a raspberry.

raspberry *n* a small, juicy, edible red berry; (*colloq*) a harsh noise made with the tongue and lips to express contempt, etc.

Rastafarian *n* a member of a largely Jamaican religious and political movement that worships Ras Tafari, the former Emperor of Ethiopia.

rat *n* a long-tailed rodent mammal; one who deserts his or her political party from some interested motive (*rats desert a sinking*

raspberry

rat

ship); a worker who takes employment where the regular workers have gone on strike; a scab; a contemptible person, especially an informer.—*vi* (**ratted, ratting**) to catch or kill rats; to forsake one's associates; to desert a party from selfish or dishonourable motives; to work as a scab; to inform on.

ratable, rateable *adj* capable of being rated; reckoned according to a certain rate; liable by law to taxation.

ratafia *n* a liquor flavoured with the kernels of cherries, apricots, peaches, etc; a kind of liqueur

ratany *n* a shrubby South American plant with an excessively astringent root.

ratchet *n* a piece, one extremity of which abuts against the teeth of a ratchet wheel.

ratchet wheel *n* a wheel with pointed and angular teeth against which a ratchet abuts, used either for converting a reciprocating into a rotary motion or for allowing motion in one direction only.

rate¹ *n* the proportion or standard by which quantity or value is adjusted; price or amount fixed on anything with relation to a standard; a settled proportion; comparative value or estimate; degree as regards speed; a tax or sum assessed on property for public use according to its income or value; a local tax; (in navy) the order or class of a ship according to its magnitude or force; the daily gain or loss of a chronometer or other timepiece.—*vt* (**rated, rating**) to settle or fix the value, rank or degree of; to value or estimate; to fix the relative scale, rank or position of (*to rate a ship*); (*colloq*) to think highly of.—*vi* to be set or considered in a class.

rate² *vt* (**rated, rating**) to chide with vehemence; to reprove; to scold; to censure violently.

rateable *adj* same as **ratable**.

ratel *n* a carnivorous quadruped of the badger family, a native of India and South Africa.

ratepayer *n* one who is assessed and pays a rate or tax.

rath, rathe *adj* (*arch*) early; coming before others or before the usual time.

rather *adv* more readily or willingly; with preference or choice; with better reason; more properly; more correctly speaking; to the contrary of what has been just stated (*no better but rather worse*); somewhat (*rather pretty*).

ratification *n* the act of ratifying or confirming; confirmation; authorization.

ratify *vt* (**ratified, ratifying**) to confirm; to settle authoritatively; to approve and sanction; to make valid, as something done by a representative, agent or servant.

rating *n* the act of estimating; a fixing in rank or place; rank, as the rating of sailors

ratchet wheel

and ships in the navy; an evaluation; an assessment; in radio and television, the relative popularity of a programme according to sample polls.

ratio *n* (*pl* **ratios**) relation or proportion which one thing has to another in respect of magnitude or quantity.

ratiocinate *vi* (**ratiocinated, ratiocinating**) to reason; to argue.

ratiocination *n* the act or process of reasoning, especially of reasoning deductively.

ration *n* a fixed amount or quantity dealt out; an allowance; (*pl*) food supply.—*vt* to supply with rations; to restrict the supply of.

rational *adj* having reason or the faculty of reasoning; endowed with reason, opposed to *irrational*; agreeable to reason; not absurd, foolish, preposterous, etc; acting in conformity to reason; judicious.

rationale *n* a statement of reasons; an account or exposition of the principles of some process, phenomenon, etc.

rationalism *n* (*theol*) a system of opinions deduced from reason, as distinct from *inspiration* or *revelation* or opposed to it; the belief that reason can supply knowledge independently of personal experience.

rationalist *n* an adherent of rationalism; one who rejects the supernatural element in dealing with the Old and New Testaments and disbelieves in revelation.

rationality *n* the quality of being rational; power of reasoning; possession of reason; reasonableness.

rationalize *vti* (**rationalized, rationalizing**) to interpret as a rationalist; to bring to the test of pure reason; to perceive or understand the reason of; to justify one's reason for an action; to substitute a natural for a supernatural explanation of; to cut down on personnel or equipment.

rational number *n* a number which can be expressed as an ordinary vulgar fraction.

ratline, ratlin *n* (*naut*) one of a series of small ropes or lines which traverse the shrouds horizontally, forming ladders for going aloft.

rat race *n* the unscrupulous, competitive struggle for success in one's career, etc; a continual, hectic activity.

rattan *n* a climbing plant with a jointed stem; cane made from this used in wickerwork.

ratter *n* one who rats; one whose business it is to catch rats; a terrier which kills rats.

rattle *vi* (**rattled, rattling**) to make a quick sharp noise rapidly repeated, as by the collision of not very sonorous bodies; to clatter; to speak eagerly and noisily; to chatter fluently.—*vt* to cause to make a rapid succession of sharp sounds; (*colloq*) to disconcert, to fluster.—*n* a rapid succession of sharp clattering sounds; loud rapid talk;

an instrument with which a clattering sound is made, formerly used by watchmen; also a child's toy constructed to produce a rattling sound; one who talks rapidly and without constraint; the horny organ at the extremity of the tail of the rattlesnake; the peculiar sound heard in the throat which immediately precedes and prognosticates death; the death rattle.

rattlesnake *n* a venomous American snake with a tail terminating in a series of articulated horny pieces which it moves in such a manner as to make a rattling sound.

rattletrap *n* a shaky rickety object.

rattlewort *n* a plant the seeds of which rattle in the pods when shaken.

rattling *adj* making a quick succession of sharp sounds; lively; vigorous; first-rate (*a rattling good yarn*).

raucous *adj* hoarse; harsh, as the voice.

ravage *n* desolation; devastation; ruin.—*vt* (**ravaged, ravaging**) to lay waste by force; to devastate; to pillage.

rave *vi* (**raved, raving**) to wander in mind or intellect; to be delirious, wild, furious or raging, as a mad person; to speak enthusiastically.—*n* (*colloq*) a wild party; a very large organized party or disco, often held in a warehouse, etc, where the participants take part in long-lasting, very fast dances. —*adj* very enthusiastic (*a rave review*).

ravel *vt* (**ravelled, ravelling**) to untwist; to unweave; to disentangle; to entangle; to make intricate; to involve.—*vi* to become entangled; to fall into perplexity and confusion

ravelin *n* (*fort*) a detached triangular work with two embankments which form a projecting angle.

raven[1] *n* a large black bird of the crow family.—*adj* resembling a raven, especially in colour; black (*raven locks*).

raven[2], **ravin** *n* prey; plunder.—*vi* to prey with rapacity; to show rapacity.—*vt* to devour; to eat with voracity.

ravenous *adj* furiously voracious; starving; very hungry; eager for gratification (*a ravenous appetite*).

ravin *n*, *vti* same as **raven**[2].

ravine *n* a long deep hollow worn by a stream or torrent of water; any deep narrow gorge in a mountain, etc; a gully

raving *adj* furious with delirium; mad.—*n* furious exclamation; irrational incoherent talk.

ravioli *npl* an Italian dish consisting of envelopes of pasta filled with chopped meat, etc, and usually served with a tomato sauce.

ravish *vt* to seize and carry away by violence; to rape; to transport with joy or delight; to enrapture; to enchant.

ravishing *adj* such as to ravish; delightful; enchanting; charming; beautiful.

raw *adj* not altered from its natural state by cooking; not roasted, boiled, etc; not subjected to some industrial or manufacturing process; not manufactured (*raw silk, raw hides*); not mixed or diluted (*raw spirits*); not covered with the natural covering; having the flesh exposed; sore; skinned; sensitive; immature; inexperienced; cold and damp (*a raw day*).

raw material *n* unmanufactured material; material in its natural state.

rawness *n* the state or quality of being raw; lack of cooking; state of being inexperienced; chilliness with dampness.

ray[1] *n* a line of light, one of the lines that make up a beam; a beam of radiant energy or radioactive particles; a beam of intellectual light; a gleam; a small amount (*a ray of hope*); one of a number of diverging radii; (*bot*) the radiating part of a flower; the outer part or circumference of a compound radiate flower; one of the radiating bony spines in the fins of fishes.—*vt* to radiate; to shoot forth or emit; to cause to shine out.—*vi* to shine forth or out, as in rays.

ray[2] *n* one of a genus of cartilaginous fishes, of which the skate is a well-known example, having a flattened body, with extremely broad and fleshy pectoral fins.

rayon *n* a textile fibre made from cellulose; a fabric of such fibres.

raze, rase *vt* (**razed, razing**) to graze; to erase; to level with the ground; to overthrow; to demolish; to erase; to destroy.

razor *n* a kind of keen-edged knife used for shaving.

razorback *n* one of the largest species of whale; the rorqual.

razorbill *n* an aquatic bird, the common auk.

razzmatazz *n* any exciting, noisy and colourful activity or atmosphere.

re[1] *prep* (shortened form of Latin legal expression *in re*, adopted in business correspondence) with reference to, in the matter of, a former communication or subject.

re[2] *n* (*mus*) the name given to the second of the syllables used in solmization.

reach *vt* to extend or stretch out; to hold or put forth; to spread out (often followed by *out* and *forth*); to touch by extending the arm or something in the hand; to extend to; to stretch out as far or as high as; to give with the hand (*reach me a chair*); to arrive at; to come to; to get as far as (*the ship reached port*); to attain to by effort, labour or study; to gain or obtain; to extend in action or influence to.—*vi* to extend in space (*to reach to heaven*); to extend in scope or power; to stretch out the hand in order to touch; to make efforts at attainment.—*n* the act or power of reaching; distance to which one can reach; the sphere to which an agency or a power is limited; often the

raven

razor

711

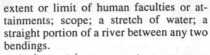

extent or limit of human faculties or attainments; scope; a stretch of water; a straight portion of a river between any two bendings.

react *vi* to act in response to a person or stimulus; to resist the action of another body by an opposite force; to act in opposition; to act mutually or reciprocally on each other, as two or more chemical agents.

reaction *n* the reciprocal action which two bodies or two minds exert on each other; action or tendency to revert from a present to a previous condition; (in politics) a tendency to revert from a more to a less advanced policy; (*physics*) the resistance made by a body to anything tending to change its state; (*chem*) the mutual or reciprocal action of chemical agents on each other.

reactionary *adj* pertaining to, proceeding from or favouring reaction, opposed to *progressive.*—*n* one who favours reaction; one who attempts to check or reverse political progress or change.

reactor *n* a person or thing that undergoes a reaction; a vessel in which a chemical reaction occurs; a nuclear reactor.

reader

read *vt* (*pret*, *pp* **read**, *ppr* **reading**) to peruse; to go over and gather the meaning of (*to read a book*, *a` author*); to utter aloud, following something written or printed; to reproduce in sound; to see through; to understand from superficial indications (*to read one's face*); to discover by marks; to study by reading (*to read law*); to explain; to interpret (*to read a riddle*).—*vi* to perform the act of perusing; to read many books; to study for a specific object; to stand written or printed (*the passage reads thus*); to have a certain effect when read; to be coherent; to make sense (said of a sentence).—*n* a reading over; perusal.

readable *adj* capable of being read; legible; worth reading.

reader *n* one who reads or peruses; one who studies; one whose office it is to read prayers, lessons, lectures, etc, to others; a reading book; one who corrects the errors in proof sheets; in some universities, a member of the teaching staff ranking below a professor but above a lecturer.

readily *adv* in a ready manner; quickly; promptly; cheerfully.

readiness *n* the state or quality of being ready; due preparation; aptitude; quickness; cheerfulness; alacrity.

reading *n* the act of one who reads; perusal; study of books (*a man of extensive reading*); a public recital or delivery of something written; a particular version of a passage; a view or interpretation of an author's meaning or intention; reproduction in accordance with such interpretation;

rendering; (in legislation) the formal recital of a bill by the proper officer before the house which is to consider it (*the bill passed the second reading*).

reading room *n* a room provided with books, newspapers, etc, to which people resort for reading.

read-only memory *n* (abbreviated to **ROM**) in computing a permanent memory which is built into the central processing unit and can be accessed but not altered.

ready *adj* prepared at the moment; fit for immediate use; causing no delay from lack of preparation; not slow, backward, dull or hesitating (*a ready apprehension*); prompt; dextrous; not backward or reluctant; willing; inclined; offering itself at once; at hand; opportune, near, easy, convenient; on the point, eve or brink (with *to*).—*n* the position of a firearm when ready to be raised to the shoulder and fired (*at the ready*).

ready-made *adj* made or prepared beforehand; kept in stock ready for use or sale (*ready-made clothes*).

ready-reckoner *n* a book of tabulated calculations or tables to facilitate calculations.

reaffirm *vt* to affirm again.

reagent *n* generally, anything that produces reaction; (*chem*) a substance employed to detect the presence of other bodies in a compound.

real *adj* actually being or existing; not fictitious or imaginary (*real life*); genuine; not artificial, counterfeit or fictitious; not affected; not assumed (*his real character*); (*law*) pertaining to things fixed, permanent or immovable (*real estate*), opposed to *personal* or *movable*.

real estate *n* property; land.

realgar *n* a mineral consisting of sulphur and arsenic; red sulphide of arsenic.

realism *n* a tendency to be practical or sensible or to see things as they really are; the portrayal of accurate or realistic detail, e.g. in a painting, book, film, etc; (*philol*) the doctrine that the physical world has an objective existence; the doctrine that general ideas have an objective existence.

realist *n* one who believes in or practises realism; a realistic person.

realistic *adj* relating to realism; matter-of-fact; not visionary; lifelike; relating to reality.

reality *n* the state or quality of being real; actual being or existence; actuality; truth; fact; that which is real as opposed to that which is imagination or pretence.

realization *n* the act of realizing.

realize *vt* (**realized, realizing**) to make real; to bring into being or act (*to realize a scheme* or *project*); to feel as vividly or strongly as if real; to bring home to one's own case or experience; to acquire as the result of labour or pains; to gain (*to realize profit from trade*); to sell for or convert into money (*to realize one's stock in a company*).—*vi* to turn any kind of property into money.

really *adv* in a real manner; in truth; actually; indeed; to tell the truth (often used familiarly as a slight corroboration of an opinion or declaration (*well, really, I cannot say*).

realm *n* a kingdom; a monarch's dominions; region, sphere, domain.

ream *n* a bundle or package of paper, consisting generally of 20 quires of 24 sheets each; (*pl*) (*colloq*) a great amount.

reanimate *vt* (**reanimated, reanimating**) to revive; to resuscitate; to restore to life or animation; to infuse new life or courage into.

reap *vt* to cut with a sickle, scythe, etc, as a grain crop; to cut down and gather; to gather when ripe or ready; to cut down the crop on; to clear of a grain crop (*to reap a field*); to receive as a reward or as the fruit of labour or of works.—*vi* to perform the act or operation of reaping; to receive the fruit of labour or works.

reaper *n* one who reaps; a machine for cutting grain.

reappear *vi* to appear again or anew.

rear[1] *n* the part behind or at the back; the hind part; the background; the part of an army or a fleet which is behind the rest.—*adj* pertaining to or in the rear; hindmost; last.

rear[2] *vt* to lift or set up; to erect; to raise; to bring up, as young; to foster; to educate; to breed, as cattle; to build up; to construct (*to rear an edifice*).—*vi* to rise on the hind legs, as a horse; to assume an erect posture.

rear admiral *n* an admiral next in rank to a vice admiral.

rearguard *n* the part of an army that marches in the rear of the main body to protect it and bring up stragglers.

rearmost *adj* farthest in the rear; last of all.

reason *n* a motive, ground or cause acting on the mind; the basis for any opinion, conclusion or determination; a ground or a principle; what accounts for or explains a fact or phenomenon; final cause; explanation; a faculty of the mind by which it distinguishes truth from falsehood and which enables the possessor to deduce inferences from facts or from propositions and to combine means for the attainment of particular ends; the act of deducing consequences from premises; justice; equity; fairness; that which is dictated or supported by reason; moderate demands; claims which reason and justice admit or prescribe (*to bring one to reason*).—*vi* to

exercise the faculty of reason; to deduce inferences justly from premises; to argue; to ratiocinate; to discuss, in order to make something understood.—*vt* to examine or discuss by arguments; to debate or discuss (*to reason the point*); to persuade by reasoning or argument.

reasonable *adj* having the faculty of reason; rational; governed by reason; not given to extravagant notions or expectations; conformable or agreeable to reason; not extravagant, excessive or immoderate; fair; equitable (*any reasonable demands*); moderate; tolerable.

reasoning *n* the act or process of exercising the faculty of reason; ratiocination; the arguments employed; the proofs or reasons when arranged and developed.

reassemble *vt* (**reassembled, reassembling**) to collect or assemble again.—*vi* to assemble or meet together again.

reassure *vt* (**reassured, reassuring**) to assure anew; to restore courage or confidence to; to free from fear or terror.

reassurance *n* the act or instance of reassuring.

Réaumur *n* a thermometric scale on which the fixed points are 0° (freezing point) and 80° (boiling point), denoted by **R**.

reave *vt* (*pret*, *pp* **reaved** *or* **reft**, *ppr* **reaving**) (*arch*) to take away by stealth or violence; to bereave; to deprive (with *of*).

reaver *n* (*arch*) one who reaves; a robber.

rebate *n* a refund of part of an amount paid; a discount; rebatement.

rebatement *n* diminution; (*com*) abatement in price; deduction.

rebec, rebeck *n* a stringed instrument introduced by the Moors into Spain, similar to the violin and played with a bow.

rebel *n* one who revolts from the government to which he or she owes allegiance; one who defies and seeks to overthrow the authority to which he or she is rightfully subject; a person who refuses to conform with convention.—*adj* rebellious; acting in revolt.—*vi* (**rebelled, rebelling**) to revolt; to take up arms against the government of constituted authorities; to refuse to obey a superior; to shake off subjection; to conceive a loathing (*his stomach rebelled at such food*).

rebellion *n* the act of rebelling; an armed rising against a government; the taking of arms traitorously to resist the authority of lawful government; open resistance to, or refusal to obey, lawful authority; defiance of authority.

rebellious *adj* engaged in or characterized by rebellion; mutinous.

rebound *vi* to spring or bound back; to fly back by elastic force after impact on another body.—*n* the act of flying back on collision with another body; resilience.

reap

rebuff *n* a beating, forcing or driving back; sudden check; a repulse; refusal; rejection of solicitation.—*vt* to beat back; to offer sudden resistance to; to repel the advances of.

rebuild *vt* to build again; to build after having been demolished.

rebuke *vt* (**rebuked, rebuking**) to check with reproof; to reprehend sharply and summarily; to reprimand; to reprove.—*n* a direct and severe reprimand; reproof; reprehension; a chiding.

rebus *n* (*pl* **rebuses**) a set of words written by figures or pictures of objects whose names resemble in sound those words or the syllables of which they are composed.

rebut *vt* (**rebutted, rebutting**) to repel, as by counter evidence; to refute; (*law*) to oppose by argument, plea or countervailing proof.

rebuttal *n* the act of rebutting; refutation; confutation.

recalcitrant *adj* exhibiting repugnance or opposition; not submissive; refractory.

reciever

recall *vt* to call or bring back; to take back; to revoke; to annul by a subsequent act; to revive in memory; to order to come back from a place or mission (*to recall a minister*).—*n* a calling back; revocation; the power of calling back or revoking.

recant *vti* to retract; to unsay; to make formal contradiction of something which one had previously asserted.

recantation *n* the act of recanting; retraction; a declaration that contradicts a former one.

recapitulate *vt* (**recapitulated, recapitulating**) to repeat or summarize, as the principal things mentioned in a preceding discourse; to give a summary of the principal facts, points or arguments of.—*vi* to repeat in brief what has been said before.

recapitulation *n* the act of recapitulating; a concise statement of the principal points in a preceding discourse, argument or essay.

recapture *n* (**recaptured, recapturing**) the act of retaking; the retaking of goods from a captor; a prize retaken.—*vt* to capture back; to retake.

recede *vi* (**receded, receding**) to move back; to retreat; to withdraw; to withdraw from a claim or pretension; to relinquish what had been proposed or asserted (*to recede from a demand, from propositions*).

receipt *n* the act of receiving (*the receipt of a letter*); that which is received; (*pl*) money drawn or received; drawings (*his receipts were £20 a day*); a recipe; a prescription of ingredients for any composition, as of medicines, etc; a written acknowledgment of something received, as money, goods, etc.—*vt* to give a receipt for; to discharge, as an account.

receive *vt* (**received, receiving**) to get or obtain; to take, as a thing given, sent, paid, communicated, etc; to accept; to take into the mind; to embrace; to allow or hold, as a belief, custom, tradition, etc; to give acceptance to (*a received belief*); to allow to enter in an official capacity; to welcome as a guest; to entertain; to take in or on; to hold, admit, contain, have capacity for (*a box to receive contributions*); to be the object of; to suffer (*to receive an injury*); to take from a thief, knowing the thing to be stolen.

Received Pronunciation *n* (often abbreviated to **RP**) the unlocalized accent of British English, regarded as a standard.

receiver *n* one who receives; a person appointed by a court to receive the rents and profits of land or other property which is in dispute; a person appointed in some business for the purpose of winding up the concern; one who takes stolen goods from a thief, knowing them to be stolen; equipment that receives electronic signals, especially in a telephone.

receivership *n* (*law*) the status of a business in the hands of a receiver.

recent *adj* of late origin, occurrence or existence; new; not of remote date, antiquated style, etc; modern; only made known or spoken of lately; fresh (*recent intelligence*); (*geol*) belonging exclusively to species still existing; occurring or formed since the glacial period.

receptacle *n* a place or vessel in which anything is received and contained; a repository.

reception *n* a receiving or manner of receiving; receipt; treatment at first coming; welcome; entertainment; a formal occasion or ceremony of receiving guests, official personages, etc; admission or credence, as of an opinion or doctrine; acceptance or allowance.

receptionist *n* a person employed to receive visitors or clients in a hotel, office, etc.

receptive *adj* such as to receive readily (*receptive of teaching*); taking in; able to take in, hold or contain.

receptivity *n* the state or quality of being receptive.

recess *n* a temporary halting of work; a holiday; the time or period during which school is suspended; a period of time when Parliament stops work; a cavity, niche or sunken space formed in a wall; an alcove or similar portion of a room.—*vt* to make a recess in; to put in a recess.

recession *n* the act of receding; withdrawal; position relatively withdrawn; a cession or granting back; a downturn in economic activity.

recessional *adj* of or belonging to the recess or non-session of Parliament.—*n* a hymn or other verses sung after service, when the choir and clergy withdraw from their places.

recessive *adj* receding; going back; (of a gene) remaining masked by a dominant gene and undetected in characteristics until pairing with an identical gene.—*n* a recessive gene.

rechauffé *n* (*lit*) a warmed-up dish; hence, a concoction of old materials; old literary matter worked up into a new form.

recherché *adj* much sought after; choice; rare; exquisite.

recidivism *n* an inevitable relapse into crime.

recipe *n* a list of ingredients and instructions on preparing food; a prescription of ingredients in a medicine; a set of circumstances leading to an end (*a recipe for disaster*).

recipient *n* a person or thing that receives; one to whom anything is communicated.—*adj* receiving.

reciprocal *adj* acting with a backward and forward motion; moving backwards and forwards; reciprocating; done by each to the other; mutual; mutually interchangeable; (*gram*) reflexive.—*n* that which is reciprocal to another thing.

reciprocate *vi* (**reciprocated, reciprocating**) to move backwards and forwards; to have an alternate movement; to alternate.—*vt* to interchange; to give and return mutually; to give in requital (*to reciprocate favours*).

reciprocity *n* the state or character of being reciprocal; reciprocal obligation or right; equal rights or benefits to be mutually yielded or enjoyed; especially equal commercial rights or privileges enjoyed mutually by two countries trading together.

recital *n* the act of reciting; the repetition of the words of another; narration; a telling of the particulars of an adventure or event; that which is recited; a story; a narrative; a musical entertainment given by a single performer (*an organ recital*).

recitation *n* the act of reciting; the delivery aloud, with appropriate gestures, before an audience of a composition committed to memory as an exhibition of elocution; the rehearsal of a lesson by pupils before their instructor.

recitative *n* (*mus*) a vocal composition which differs from an air in having no definite rhythmical arrangement and no strictly constructed melody; musical recitation or declamation.

recite *vt* (**recited, reciting**) to repeat, as something prepared, written down or committed to memory beforehand; to rehearse, with appropriate gestures, before an audience; to tell over; to relate or narrate; to go over in particulars; to recapitulate.—*vi* to rehearse before an audience compositions

committed to memory; to rehearse a lesson.

reckless *adj* careless; heedless of consequences; mindless (with *of* before an object).

reckon *vt* to count; to number; to tell one by one; to calculate; to estimate by rank or quality; to esteem, account, repute, hold.—*vi* to make computation; to compute; to calculate; to make up or render an account; to think, suppose, imagine.

reckoning *n* the act of computing; calculation; a statement and comparison of accounts for adjustment; the charges made in an hotel, etc (*to pay the reckoning*); (*naut*) the calculation of the position of a ship from the rate found by the log and the course as determined by the compass.

reclaim *vt* to claim back; to call back; (*arch*) to bring a hawk to the wrist by a certain call; (*arch*) to bring (a hawk, etc) from a wild to a tame or domestic state; to bring under cultivation; to bring back from error; to reform.—*n* the act of reclaiming; reformation.

reclamation *n* the act of reclaiming; the act of bringing into cultivation; the bringing back of a person from evil courses; a demand; claim made; a remonstrance or representation.

recline *vt* (**reclined, reclining**) to lean to one side or sideways; to lay down to rest (*to recline the head*).—*vi* to rest or repose; to take a recumbent position.

recluse *adj* living shut up or apart from the world; retired; sequestered; solitary.—*n* a person who lives in retirement or seclusion; a hermit; a religious devotee who lives in an isolated cell.

recognition *n* the act of recognizing or state of being recognized; a perceiving as being known; avowal; notice taken; acknowledgment.

recognizable *adj* capable of being recognized.

recognizance *n* act of recognizing; recognition; mark or badge of recognition; token.

recognize *vt* (**recognized, recognizing**) to perceive the identity of, with a person or thing formerly known; to know again; to avow or admit a knowledge of; to acknowledge formally; to indicate one's notice by a bow or nod; to indicate appreciation of (*to recognize services by a reward*).—*vi* (*law*) to enter into recognizances.

recoil *vi* to rebound; to fall back; to take a sudden backward motion after an advance; to be forced to retreat; to return after a certain strain or impetus (*the gun recoils*); to start or draw back, as from anything repulsive, alarming, etc; to shrink.—*n* a starting or falling back; rebound; the rebound or resilience of a firearm when discharged.

recipe

recollect *vt* to recover or recall the knowledge of; to bring back to the mind or memory; to remember; (*refl*) to recover resolution or composure of mind; to collect oneself.

re-collect *vt* to collect or gather again; to collect what has been scattered.

recollection *n* the act of recollecting or recalling to the memory; a bringing back to mind; remembrance; the power of recalling ideas to the mind or the period over which such power extends; that which is recollected; something recalled to mind.

recommend *vt* to commend to another's notice; to put in a favourable light before another; to commend or give favourable representations of; to make acceptable; to attract favour to; hence, to recommend itself, to make itself approved; to advise, as to an action, practice, measure, remedy, etc; to set forward as advisable.

recommendation *n* the act of recommending; a favourable representation; that which procures favour or a favourable reception.

recorder

recompense *vt* (**recompensed, recompensing**) to give or render an equivalent to, as for services, loss, etc; to reward; to requite; to compensate; to return an equivalent for; to make amends for by anything equivalent; to make compensation for.—*n* an equivalent returned for anything given, done or suffered; compensation; reward; amends.

reconcilable *adj* capable of being again brought to friendly feelings; capable of being made to agree or be consistent; capable of being harmonized.

reconcile *vt* (**reconciled, reconciling**) to conciliate anew; to restore to union and friendship after estrangement; to adjust or settle (differences, quarrels); to bring to acquiescence or quiet submission (*to reconcile oneself to afflictions*); to make consistent or congruous (followed by *with* or *to*); to remove apparent discrepancies from; to harmonize; to check (a financial account) with another account for accuracy.—*vi* to become reconciled.

reconcilement *n* reconciliation; renewal of friendship.

reconciliation *n* the act of reconciling parties at variance; renewal of friendship after disagreement or enmity; the act of harmonizing or making consistent; agreement of things seemingly opposite or inconsistent.

recondite *adj* hidden from the mental perception; abstruse; profound; dealing with things abstruse.

reconnaissance *n* the act or operation of reconnoitring; preliminary examination or survey of a territory or of an enemy's position for the purpose of directing military operations.

record player

reconnoitre *vt* (**reconnoitred, reconnoi-tring**) to make a preliminary survey of; to examine or survey, as a track or region, for military purposes.—*n* a preliminary survey; a reconnaissance.

reconsider *vt* to consider again; to turn over in the mind again; to take into consideration a second time, generally with the view of rescinding.

reconstruct *vt* to construct again; to rebuild; to build up, as from remains, an image of the original; to supply missing parts by conjecture.

reconstruction *n* act of constructing again; the recreation of an event by repeating the steps leading up to it.

record *vt* to register; to note; to chart; to write down or enter for the purpose of preserving evidence of; to imprint deeply on the mind or memory; to register on a disc, tape, etc, for later reproduction; to make a recording of.—*n* something set down in writing for the purpose of preserving the knowledge of it; a register; an authentic or official account of facts or proceedings, entered in a book for preservation; the book or document containing such; a public document; memory; remembrance; testimony; witness (*to bear record*); the known facts in a person's life, especially in that of a public person; one's personal history; an outstanding performance or achievement that surpasses others previously recorded; a grooved vinyl disc for playing on a record player; (*comput*) data in machine-readable form.

recorder *n* one who records; a person whose official duty is to register writings or transactions; a machine or device that records; a tape recorder; a wind instrument of the flute family.

record player a machine that reproduces sounds on a disc through a loudspeaker.

recount *vt* to relate in detail; to tell or narrate the particulars of; to rehearse; to count again.

recoup *vt* to recover; to regain; to receive compensation for.

recourse *n* resort for help or protection when in danger; that to which one turns when seeking help.

recover *vt* to regain; to get or obtain after being lost; to get back; to restore from sickness, faintness, etc; to revive; to cure; to heal; to retrieve; to make up for; to rescue.—*vi* to regain health after sickness; to grow well again; to regain a former state or condition, as after misfortune or disturbance of mind.

recovery *n* the act or power of regaining or getting again; restoration from sickness or faintness; restoration from low condition or misfortune.

recreant *adj* cowardly; mean-spirited; false; disloyal.—*n* one who basely yields;

716

one who begs for mercy; a cowardly person; a disloyal person.

recreate *vt* (**recreated, recreating**) to revive or refresh after toil or exertion; to reanimate, as languid spirits or exhausted strength; to amuse; to divert; to gratify.—*vi* to take recreation.

re-create *vt* (**re-created, re-creating**) to create or form anew.

recreation *n* the act of recreating or the state of being recreated; relaxation of the body or mind; amusement; entertainment; a sport or pastime.

recriminate *vi* (**recriminated, recriminating**) to return one accusation with another; to charge an accuser with the like.—*vt* to accuse in return.

recrimination *n* the act of recriminating; the return of one accusation with another; (*law*) an accusation brought by the accused against the accuser on the same fact; a counter-accusation.

recruit *vt* to enlist (military personnel); to enlist (new members) for an organization, etc (*to recruit helpers*).—*n* a soldier newly enlisted; a newly enlisted member.

rectangle *n* a right-angled parallelogram; a quadrilateral figure having all its angles right angles.

rectangular *adj* right-angled; having an angle or angles of ninety degrees.

rectification *n* the act or operation of rectifying; the act of setting right that which is wrong; the process of refining or purifying by repeated distillation.

rectifier *n* one who or that which rectifies; one who refines by repeated distillations; a device for obtaining direct electric current from alternating current.

rectify *vt* (**rectified, rectifying**) to make or put right; to correct when wrong, erroneous or false; to amend; (*elect*) to convert to direct current.

rectilinear *adj* bounded by straight lines; consisting of a straight line or of straight lines; straight.

rectitude *n* rightness of principle or practice; uprightness; integrity; honesty; probity; correctness.

recto *n* (*pl* **rectos**) the right-hand page of an open book; the right-hand side of a sheet of paper, as opposed to *verso*.

rector *n* a clergyman in the Anglican Church who has the charge of a parish; the chief elective officer of some universities, as in France and Scotland; in Scotland, the title of the head teacher of an academy or other senior school.

rectorial *adj* pertaining to a rector or to a rectory.

rectory *n* the house of a minister or priest.

rectum *n* (*pl* **recta, rectums**) (*anat*) the third and last part of the large intestine opening at the anus.

recumbence, recumbency *n* the state of being recumbent; the posture of reclining or lying; rest; repose; idle state.

recumbent *adj* leaning; reclining; lying down; reposing; inactive; (*zool, bot*) applied to a part that leans or reposes on anything.

recuperate *vt* (**recuperated, recuperating**) to recover; to regain.—*vi* to recover; to regain health.

recuperation *n* recovery.

recuperative, recuperatory *adj* tending to recovery; pertaining to recovery.

recur *vi* (**recurred, recurring**) to return; to return to the thought or mind; to occur again or be repeated at a stated interval or according to some regular rule.

recurrence *n* the act of recurring or state of being recurrent; return; resort; recourse.

recurrent *adj* returning from time to time.

recusancy *n* the state of being recusant; the tenets of a recusant; nonconformity.

recusant *adj* obstinate in refusal; refusing to acknowledge the supremacy of a sovereign or to conform to the established rites of a church.—*n* one obstinate in refusing; one who will not conform to general opinion or practice; specifically, (in English history) a nonconformist.

recycle *vt* (**recycled, recycling**) to pass (a substance) through a process again; to process (used matter) to regain re-usable material; to save from loss and restore to usefulness.

red *adj* of a bright warm colour resembling blood (applied to many different shades or hues, as crimson, scarlet, vermilion, etc).—*n* a red colour; a colour resembling that of arterial blood; one of the simple or primary colours; a red pigment.

redact *vt* to give a presentable literary form to; to act as editor of.

red admiral *n* a common European and American butterfly with black and red markings.

redan *n* (*fort*) the simplest kind of work, consisting of two parapets of earth raised so as to form a salient angle with the apex towards the enemy.

redbreast *n* a singing bird so called from the colour of its breast; the robin.

red card *n* in soccer, a red card held up by a referee indicating that a player is to be sent off the pitch for some misdemeanour.

red carpet *n* a strip of red carpet for royalty or dignitaries to walk on at official events; a grand or impressive welcome.

redcoat *n* (*hist*) a British soldier (from the red coats worn by most regiments).

Red Cross *n* the emblem adopted at the Geneva Convention of 1864 for the International Societies organized for the treatment of the sick and wounded in war.

red deer *n* the common stag, a native of the

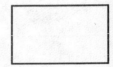

rectangle

redcoat

forests of Europe and Asia; still plentiful in the Highlands of Scotland.

redden *vt* to make red.—*vi* to grow or become red.

redeem *vt* to buy back; to release from captivity or bondage or from any obligation or liability to suffer or be forfeited by paying an equivalent; to pay ransom or equivalent for; to ransom; to rescue; to perform, as a promise; to make good by performance; to make amends for; to atone for; to improve or employ to the best advantage (*redeeming the time*).

redeemer *n* one who redeems or ransoms.

Redeemer *n* the Saviour of the world, Jesus Christ.

redemption *n* the act of redeeming; the state of being redeemed; ransom; (*theol*) the deliverance of sinners from the penalty of God's violated law by the sufferings and death of Christ.

red-handed *adj* caught in the act of committing a crime, indiscretion, etc.

red herring *n* the common herring highly salted, dried and smoked; (*fig*) something cast in the path as a means of diverting the attention of persons or the scent of hounds, from the real object; something intended to sidetrack an issue.

red-hot *adj* red with heat; heated to redness.

red lead *n* a poisonous oxide of lead much used as a pigment.

red-letter day *n* a memorable occasion; a day of significance.

red mullet *n* a European food fish with red colouring.

redness *n* the quality of being red; red colour.

redolence *n* the quality of being redolent; fragrance.

redolent *adj* having or diffusing a sweet scent; giving out an odour; odorous; fragrant (often with *of*).

redouble *vt* (**redoubled, redoubling**) to multiply; to repeat often; to increase by repeated or continued additions.—*vi* to become twice as much; to become greatly or repeatedly increased.

redoubt *n* (*fort*) a detached outpost wholly enclosed and defended by re-entering or flanking angles; a small enclosed temporary fieldwork.

redoubtable *adj* formidable; to be dreaded.

redound *vi* to roll or flow back, as a wave; to conduce; to contribute; to result (*this will redound to your benefit*).—*n* the coming back, as a consequence or effect; result.

red pepper *n* a variety of pepper grown for its large red fruit, used in cooking and salads, the capsicum; this fruit; cayenne pepper.

redpoll *n* a name given to several species of linnets.

redshank

redress *vt* to remedy or put right, as a wrong; to repair, as an injury; to relieve of anything unjust or oppressive; to compensate; to make amends to.—*n* deliverance from wrong, injury or oppression; undoing of wrong; reparation; indemnification.

redshank *n* a wading bird allied to the snipes, so called from its red legs.

redstart *n* a singing bird related to the redbreast, widely diffused over Europe, Asia and North Africa.

red tape *n* excessive regard to formality and routine without corresponding attention to essential duties.

reduce *vt* (**reduced, reducing**) to bring to any state or condition, good or bad; to bring (to power, to poverty, to order, etc); to diminish in size, quantity or value; to make thin; to make less or lower; to bring to an inferior condition; to subdue; to bring into subjection; to bring under rules or within certain limits of description; to bring from a form less fit to one more fit for operation; (*arith*) to change from one denomination into another without altering the value; (*alg*) to bring to the simplest form with the unknown quantity by itself on one side and all the known quantities on the other side; (in metallurgy) to separate, as a pure metal from a metallic ore; (*surg*) to restore to its proper place or state, as a dislocated or fractured bone.—**to reduce to the ranks** to degrade for misconduct to the position of a private soldier.

reducible *adj* capable of being reduced; convertible.

reductio ad absurdum *n* a reduction to an absurdity, a type of argument which proves not the thing asserted but the absurdity of everything which contradicts it.

reduction *n* the act of reducing; conversion into another state or form; diminution; conquest; subjugation; (*arith*) the bringing of numbers of one denomination into another; the arithmetical rule by which this is done; the act of making a copy of a map, design, etc, on a smaller scale, preserving the proper proportions; (*surg*) the operation of restoring a dislocated or fractured bone to its former place; the operation of obtaining pure metals from metallic ores.

reductive *adj* having the power of reducing; tending to reduce.

redundancy, redundance *n* the quality of being redundant; loss of one's job because of being no longer necessary.

redundant *adj* superfluous; exceeding what is natural or necessary; deprived of one's job as being no longer necessary; using more words than are necessary.

reduplicate *vt* (**reduplicated, reduplicating**) to double again; to multiply; to repeat; (*philol*) to repeat, as the initial syllable or the root of a word, for the purpose of marking past time.—*vi* (*philol*) to be doubled or repeated; to undergo reduplication.

reduplication *n* the act of doubling or reduplicating; (*philol*) the repetition of a root or of the initial syllable (more or less modified).

red-water *n* a disease of cattle, and occasionally of sheep, in which the urine becomes reddened with blood.

redwing *n* a species of thrush well known in Britain as a winter bird of passage.

redwood *n* an important tree of California that can reach a great height; any of various trees yielding a red dye or reddish wood.

re-echo *vti* to echo back; to reverberate again.—*n* the echo of an echo; a second or repeated echo.

reed *n* a tall broad-leaved grass that grows in marshy places; its hollow stem; a musical instrument made from a reed; a rustic or pastoral pipe; a vibrating tongue of cane, wood, etc, in the mouthpiece of certain wind instruments, e.g. the bassoon, oboe, clarinet and saxophone; one of the thin plates of metal whose vibrations produce the notes of an accordion, harmonium, etc; (in weaving) a frame of parallel flat strips of wood or metal for separating the threads of the warp and for beating the weft up to the web.

reed bunting, reed sparrow *n* one of the British buntings, a bird that frequents reeds, fens, etc.

reed pipe *n* a musical pipe made of reed; a pipe in an organ sounding by means of a reed.

reedy *adj* abounding with reeds; resembling a reed; (of a voice or musical instrument) having a thin, harsh tone.

reef[1] *n* a mass of rocks in the ocean lying at or near the surface of the water; in mining, a gold-bearing quartz vein.

reef[2] *n* (*naut*) that part of a sail which can be drawn together by small cords so as to contract the canvas in proportion to the increase of the wind.—*vt* (*naut*) to take in a reef or reefs in; to reduce the extent of a sail by folding a certain portion of it and making it fast to the yard.

reefer *n* one who reefs; a reefing jacket; (*colloq*) a cigarette containing marijuana.

reek *n* vapour; steam; exhalation; fume; smoke.—*vi* to smoke; to steam; to exhale; to emit vapour.

reel[1] *n* a roller or bobbin of wood, etc, for thread used in sewing; a winding device; a machine on which yarn is wound to form it into hanks, skeins, etc; a revolving appliance attached to the butt of a fishing rod and around which the line is wound; a length of photographic film.—*vt* to wind on a reel.

reel[2] *vi* to stagger or sway in walking; to whirl; to have a whirling or giddy sensation (*my brain reeled*).—*n* a staggering motion, as that of a drunk person.

reel[3] *n* a lively dance originating in Scotland.

re-elect *vt* to elect again.

re-election *n* election a second time or repeated election.

re-enact *vt* to enact again.

re-enter *vti* to enter again or anew.

re-entry *n* the act of entering or possession again; the return of a spacecraft to the earth's atmosphere.

reeve[1] *vti* (**reeved, reeving**) (*naut*) to pass the end of a rope through any hole in a block, thimble, etc; to run or pass through such a hole.

reeve[2] *n* a bird, the female of the ruff.

reeve[3] *n* (*hist*) a bailiff; a steward; a peace officer.

refectory *n* an eating room; an apartment in convents, schools, etc, where meals are taken.

refer *vt* (**referred, referring**) to impute; to assign; to attribute to, as the cause, motive or ground; to hand over, as to another person or tribunal for treatment, decision, etc (*to refer a matter to a third party*); to appeal; to assign, as to an order, genus or class (in all senses followed by *to*).—*vi* to respect; to have relation; to appeal; to have recourse; to apply; to consult (*to refer to one's notes*); to allude; to make allusion; to direct the attention.

referee *n* one to whom a matter in dispute has been referred for settlement or decision; an arbitrator; in football and other sports, an official who sees that the rules are observed and decides all points which may be matters of dispute; a person who provides a reference, particularly a character reference.

reference *n* the act of referring; the act of alluding; direct allusion; relation, respect or regard (generally in the phrase *in* or *with reference to*); one of whom inquiries may be made in regard to a person's character, abilities, etc; a written statement testifying to the abilities, character, etc, of someone; a testimonial; a passage or note in a work by which a person is referred to another passage.

referendum *n* (*pl* **referendums, referenda**) a public vote as a means of consulting public opinion when a public body is unable to make or take the responsibility on itself of a measure; a plebiscite.

refine *vt* (**refined, refining**) to reduce to a pure state; to free from impurities; to purify; to reduce from the ore; to separate from other metals or from dross or alloy; to purify from what is coarse, inelegant, rude, etc; to make elegant; to raise or educate, as the taste; to give culture to; to

redwing

reed

polish (*to refine the manners*, etc).—*vi* to become pure or purer; to affect nicety or subtlety in thought or language.

refined *adj* polished or elegant in character; free from anything coarse or vulgar; free from impurities.

refinement *n* the act of refining or purifying or state of being refined; the state of being free from what is coarse, rude, inelegant, etc; elegance of manners, language, etc; culture; a result of excessive elaboration, polish or nicety; over-nicety; an affected subtlety.

refinery *n* a place and apparatus for refining sugar, oil, metals, etc.

refit *vt* (**refitted, refitting**) to restore after damage or decay; to repair; to fit out anew. —*vi* to repair damages, especially to ships. —*n* a repairing; the repair of a ship.

refitment *n* the act of refitting.

reflect *vt* to bend back; to turn, cast or direct back; to throw off after striking or falling on any surface and in accordance with certain physical laws (*to reflect light*, *heat* or *sound*); to give back an image or likeness of; to mirror.—*vi* to throw back light, heat or sound, etc; to return rays or beams; to throw or turn back the thoughts on anything; to think or consider seriously; to revolve matters in the mind; to bring reproach; to cast censure or blame (*do not reflect on his errors*).

reflected *adj* cast or thrown back (*reflected light*); curved or turned back.

reflecting *adj* throwing back light, heat, etc, as a mirror or other polished surface does; given to reflection; thoughtful; meditative (*a reflecting mind*).

reflecting telescope *n* a telescope operated by a series of mirrors.

reflection *n* the act of reflecting or the state of being reflected; (*physics*) the change of direction which light, heat or sound experiences when it strikes on a surface and is thrown back into the same medium from which it approached; that which is produced by being reflected; an image given back from a reflecting surface; attentive or continued consideration; meditation, contemplation, deliberation; a censorious remark or one attaching blame; reproach.

reflector *n* one who reflects; that which reflects; a polished surface of metal or other material for reflecting light, heat or sound; a reflecting telescope.

reflex *adj* turned backwards; having a backward direction; reflective; introspective.—*n* reflection; image produced by reflection; a reflex action.

reflex action *n* an action of the nervous system which is performed involuntarily, and often unconsciously, as the contraction of the pupil of the eye when exposed to strong light.

reflexed *adj* turned or bent back.

reflexive *adj* reflective; bending or turning backward; having respect to something past; (*gram*) having for its direct object a pronoun which stands for the agent or subject (said of certain verbs, as *I bethought myself*, *the witness forswore himself*, also applied to pronouns of this class).

reflexology *n* a form of therapy used in alternative medicine involving massaging and applying pressure to the soles of the feet.

reflux *n* a flowing back (*the flux and reflux of the tides*).—*adj* returning or flowing back.

reform *vt* to change from worse to better; to introduce improvement in; to amend; to bring from a bad to a good state; to remove or abolish for something better.—*vi* to abandon evil and return to good; to amend one's behaviour.—*n* a rearrangement which either brings back a better order of things or reconstructs the present order in an entirely new form; reformation; amendment of what is defective, vicious, corrupt or depraved; specifically, a change in the regulations of parliamentary representation (often used adjectivally, as *a reform bill* or *act*).

re-form *vt* to form again or anew; to give the same or another disposition or arrangement to (*to re-form troops that have been scattered*).

reformation *n* the act of reforming or state of being reformed; correction or amendment of life, manners or of anything objectionable or bad; the redress of grievances or abuses.

Reformation *n* the religious revolution of the sixteenth century which divided the Western Church into the two sections known as Protestant and Roman Catholic.

reformatory *adj* tending to produce reformation.—*n* formerly, an institution for the reception and reformation of juveniles convicted of crime.

reformatory school *n* a reformatory.

reformer *n* one who effects a reformation or amendment; one who promotes or urges political reform.

Reformer *n* one of those who commenced or assisted in the reformation of religion in the sixteenth century.

refract *vt* to bend back sharply or abruptly; (in optics) to deflect (a ray of light) at a certain angle on passing from one medium into another of a different density.

refracting *adj* serving or tending to refract; turning from a direct course.

refracting telescope *n* a telescope in which the rays are refracted by an object glass, at the focus of which they are viewed by an eyepiece.

refraction *n* the act of refracting or state of

being refracted; a deflection or change of direction impressed on rays of light or heat passing from one transparent medium into another of different density, as from air into water or vice versa, or on rays traversing a medium the density of which is not uniform, as the atmosphere.

refractory *adj* sullen or perverse in opposition or disobedience; obstinate in non-compliance; stubborn and unmanageable (*a refractory child*); resisting ordinary treatment, as metals that are difficult to fuse.

refragable *adj* capable of being opposed or resisted; refutable.

refrain[1] *vt* to hold back; to restrain; to curb; to keep from action (often reflexive).—*vi* to forbear; to abstain; to keep oneself from action or interference (followed by *from*).

refrain[2] *n* the burden of a song; part of a poetic composition repeated at the end of every stanza; a kind of musical repetition.

refrangible *adj* capable of being refracted; subject to refraction, as rays of light.

refresh *vt* to make fresh or vigorous again; to restore vigour or energy to; to give new strength to; to reinvigorate; to recreate or revive after fatigue, want, pain, etc; to re-animate; to freshen.

refresher *n* one who or that which refreshes; a training course to improve or modernize one's skill or knowledge (*a refresher course*).

refreshing *adj* acting or operating so as to refresh; invigorating; reviving; reanimating.

refreshment *n* the act of refreshing; that which refreshes; that which gives fresh strength or vigour, as food, drink or rest (in the plural almost exclusively applied to food and drink).

refrigerate *vt* (**refrigerated, refrigerating**) to cool; to preserve by keeping cool.

refrigeration *n* the act of refrigerating; abatement of heat; the operating of cooling without exposure to evaporation.

refrigerator *n* that which refrigerates, cools or keeps cool; an apparatus for cooling; a chest or chamber for keeping food, etc, cool; an apparatus for cooling.

refuel *vi* (of an aircraft, etc) to take on more fuel.—*vt* (**refuelled, refuelling**) to supply with more fuel.

refuge *n* shelter or protection from danger or distress; that which shelters or protects from danger, distress or calamity; any place where one is out of the way of any evil or danger; an institution where the destitute, homeless, etc, find temporary shelter; a house of refuge; a retreat or sanctuary; an expedient to secure protection or defence.—*vt* (**refuged, refuging**) to shelter; to protect.—*vi* to take shelter.

refugee *n* one who flees for refuge; one who

in times of persecution or political commotion flees to a foreign country for safety.

refulgence, refulgency *n* the state or quality of being refulgent; splendour; brilliancy.

refulgent *adj* casting a bright light; shining; splendid.

refund *vt* to return in payment or compensation for what has been taken; to pay back; to restore; to reimburse.

refurbish *vt* to furbish a second time or anew; to renovate; to re-equip.

refurnish *vt* to furnish anew; to supply anew with furniture.

refusal *n* the act of refusing; denial of anything demanded, solicited or offered for acceptance; option of taking or buying (*first refusal*); pre-emption.

refuse[1] *vt* (**refused, refusing**) to deny, as a request, demand, invitation or command; to decline to do or grant (often with an infinitive as object, as *he refused to give me the book*); to decline to accept; to reject (*to refuse an office*); to deny the request of; to say no to (*I could not refuse him*).—*vi* to decline a request; not to comply.

refuse[2] *adj* rejected; worthless; left as of no value.—*n* that which is rejected as useless; waste matter; rubbish; garbage.

refutable *adj* capable of being refuted.

refutation *n* the act of refuting or proving to be false or erroneous; overthrow by argument or countervailing proof.

refute *vt* (**refuted, refuting**) to disprove and overthrow by argument, evidence or countervailing proof; to prove to be false or erroneous; to confute; to prove to be in error.

regain *vt* to gain anew; to recover what has been lost; to reach again (*they regained the shore*).

regal *adj* pertaining to a king or queen; royal.

regale *vt* (**regaled, regaling**) to entertain sumptuously or with something that gives great pleasure; to gratify, as the senses; to delight; to feast.—*vi* to feast; to fare sumptuously.—*n* a splendid repast; a treat.

regalia *npl* the symbols of royalty; the apparatus of a coronation, as the crown, sceptre, etc; the insignia or decorations of some society, as the Freemasons.

regality *n* royalty; sovereignty; kingship; in Scotland, a territorial jurisdiction formerly conferred by the monarch.

regally *adv* in a regal or royal manner; royally.

regard *vt* to look on; to observe; to notice with some care; to pay attention to; to observe a certain respect towards; to respect, reverence, honour, esteem; to mind; to care for; to have or to show certain feelings towards; to view in the light of; to put on the same footing as.—*n* look or gaze;

refrigerator

attention or care; heed; consideration; that feeling which springs from estimable qualities in the object; respect, esteem, reverence; relation; respect; reference; view (*in regard to, with regard to*); (*pl*) respects; good wishes; compliments (*give my regards to the family*).

regardful *adj* having or paying regard.

regarding *prep* respecting; concerning; in reference to (*to be at a loss regarding something*).

regardless *adj* not having regard or heed; heedless; careless.

regatta *n* a gathering of boats at which races and contests are held.

regency *n* rule; government; the office or jurisdiction of a regent; a body of people entrusted with the power of a regent.

regenerate *vt* (**regenerated, regenerating**) to generate or produce anew; to reproduce; to be reborn spiritually.

regent *n* one who governs a kingdom in the minority, absence or disability of the sovereign; a member of a governing board, as of a university.

reggae *n* a strongly accented West Indian musical form with four beats to the bar.

regicide *n* one who murders a king; the killing or murder of a king.

regime *n* mode or system of management; government, especially as connected with certain social features; administration; rule.

regimen *n* orderly government; the regulation of diet, exercise, etc.

regiment *n* a body of troops with a permanent organization and forming the command of a colonel (nominally), consisting of a varying number of battalions.—*vt* to organize in a strict manner; to subject to order or conformity.

regimental *adj* belonging to a regiment.

regimentals *npl* articles of military dress; the uniform worn by the troops of a regiment.

regimentation *n* the act of regimenting; excessive orderliness.

Regina *n* a reigning queen.

region *n* a large division of any space or surface considered as apart from others; a tract of land, sea, etc, of considerable but indefinite extent; a country; a district; an administrative area of a country; a part or division of the body (*the region of the heart*); area.

regional *adj* pertaining to a particular region; sectional.

regionalism *n* identification with or loyalty to a particular region; regional policy; a characteristic feature of a particular area, especially a word or custom; something that evokes the characteristics of an area.

register *n* an official written account or entry in a book regularly kept for preserva-

tion or for reference; a record; a list; the book in which records are kept; a document issued by customs authorities as evidence of a ship's nationality; a variety of language appropriate to a subject or occasion; (*comput*) a device in which data can be stored and operated on; (*print*) exact alignment; (*mus*) the compass of a voice or instrument or a portion of the compass; a tone of voice; a stop or set of pipes in an organ.—*vt* to record; to enter in a register; to send a letter, package, etc, by a special service which confers extra safety precautions; to express (some emotion) facially.—*vi* to make an impression.

registrar *n* one whose business it is to write or keep a register; a keeper of records; an officer who superintends a system of registration; an official who records births, deaths and marriages and is empowered to perform marriages.

registration *n* the act of inserting in a register.

registry *n* the act of entering in a register; the place where a register is kept; facts recorded; an entry.

registry office *n* an office where records of births, deaths and marriages are kept and where marriages are performed; a record office.

regius professor *n* a person appointed to a university chair founded by the crown.

regnant *adj* reigning as sovereign; predominant; prevalent; exercising sovereign power by hereditary right.

regret *n* grief or trouble caused by the lack or loss of something formerly possessed; sorrowful longing; pain or mind at something done or left undone; remorse.—*vt* (**regretted, regretting**) to lament the loss of or separation from; to look back at with sorrowful longing; to grieve at; to be sorry for.

regrettable *adj* admitting of or calling for regret.

regular *adj* conformed to a rule; agreeable to a prescribed mode or customary form; normal; acting or going on by rule or rules; steady or uniform; orderly; methodical; unvarying; (*geom*) applied to a figure or body whose sides and angles are equal, as a square, a cube, an equilateral triangle, an equilateral pentagon, etc; (*gram*) adhering to the common form in respect to inflectional terminations; (*eccles*) belonging to a monastic order and bound to certain rules; (*bot*) symmetrical as regards figure, size and proportion of parts; (*colloq*) thorough, out-and-out, complete.—*n* a monk who has taken the vows of a monastic order; a soldier belonging to a permanent army; (*colloq*) someone who attends regularly.

regularity *n* the state or quality of being regular; agreeableness to rule or established order; conformity to the customary type; steadiness or uniformity in a course.

regularly *adv* in a regular manner; in uniform order; at fixed intervals or periods; methodically; in due order.

regular verb *n* in English, one that forms the preterit and past participle with *d* or *ed*.

regulate *vt* (**regulated, regulating**) to adjust by rule or established mode; to govern by or subject to certain rules or restrictions; to direct; to put or keep in good order; to control and cause to act properly.

regulation *n* the act of regulating; a rule prescribed by a superior as to the actions of those under his or her control; a governing direction; a precept.

regulator *n* one who or that which regulates; a device or contrivance of which the object is to produce uniformity of motion or action; the governor of a steam engine.

regurgitate *vt* (**regurgitated, regurgitating**) to pour or cause to rush or surge back; to pour or throw back in great quantity.—*vi* to be poured back; to rush or surge back.

regurgitation *n* the act of regurgitating; (*med*) the rising of some of the contents of the stomach into the mouth.

rehabilitate *vt* (**rehabilitated, rehabilitating**) to restore to a former capacity or position; to reinstate; to put back in good condition; to re-establish in the esteem of others; to help to adapt to society after a stay in a hospital or institution.

rehash *vt* to work up old material in a new form.—*n* something made up of materials formerly used.

rehear *vt* to hear again; (*law*) to try a second time.

rehearsal *n* the act of rehearsing; narration; a telling or recounting; a trial performance (as of a play) made before exhibiting to the public.

rehearse *vt* (**rehearsed, rehearsing**) to repeat, as what has already been said or written; to recite; to narrate, recount, relate; to recite or repeat in private for experiment and improvement before giving a public representation (*to rehearse a tragedy*).—*vi* to go through some performance in private preparatory to public representation.

reign *vi* to possess or exercise sovereign power or authority; to hold the supreme power; to rule; to be predominant; to prevail; to have superior or uncontrolled dominion.—*n* royal authority; sovereignty; the time during which a king, queen or emperor reigns; empire; kingdom; power; sway.

reimburse *vt* (**reimbursed, reimbursing**) to replace in a treasury; to pay back; to refund; to pay back to; to render an equivalent to for money or other expenditure.

reimbursement *n* the act of reimbursing; repayment.

rein *n* the strap of a bridle, by which the rider or driver restrains and governs a horse, etc; any thong or cord for the same purpose; (*fig*) a means of curbing, restraining or governing; restraint.—*vt* to govern, guide or restrain by a bridle; to restrain; to control.

reindeer *n* a deer of northern Europe and Asia with broad branched antlers.

reindeer moss *n* a lichen which constitutes almost the sole winter food for reindeer.

reinforce *vt* (**reinforced, reinforcing**) to strengthen; to add to the strength of; to strengthen with more troops, ships, etc.

reinforced concrete *n* concrete in which steel bars are embedded, so as to increase the resistance of the structure to tension.

reinforcement *n* the act of reinforcing; additional support; (*pl*) additional troops or forces to augment an army or fleet.

reinstall *vt* (**reinstalled, reinstalling**) to install again.

reinstate *vt* (**reinstated, reinstating**) to place again in possession or in a former state.

reinstatement *n* the act of reinstating; re-establishment.

reintroduce *vt* (**reintroduced, reintroducing**) to introduce again.

reintroduction *n* a second introduction.

reinvigorate *vt* (**reinvigorated, reinvigorating**) to revive vigour in; to re-animate.

reissue *vi* (**reissued, reissuing**) to issue or go forth again.—*vt* to issue, send out or put forth a second time (*to reissue banknotes*).—*n* a second or renewed issue.

reiterate *vt* (**reiterated, reiterating**) to repeat again and again; to do or say (especially to say) repeatedly.—*adj* reiterated.

reiteration *n* the act of reiterating; repetition.

reiver *n* (*hist*) a robber.

reject *vt* to throw away as useless or vile; to cast off; to discard; to refuse to receive; to decline haughtily or harshly; to refuse to grant.—*n* something or someone rejected.

rejection *n* the act of rejecting; refusal to accept or grant.

rejoice *vi* (**rejoiced, rejoicing**) to experience joy and gladness in a high degree; to be joyful; to exult (often with *at, in, on account of*, etc, or a subordinate clause).—*vt* to make joyful; to gladden.

rejoicing *n* the act of expressing joy; procedure expressive of joy; festivity.

rejoin *vt* to join again; to unite after separation; to join the company of again; to answer; to say in answer; to reply (with a clause as object).—*vi* to answer to a reply.

rejoinder *n* an answer to a reply; (*law*) the fourth stage in the pleadings in an action, being the defendant's answer to the plaintiff's replication.

rein

reindeer

rejuvenate *vt* (**rejuvenated, rejuvenating**) to restore to youth; to make young again.

rejuvenation *n* the act of rejuvenating.

relapse *vi* (**relapsed, relapsing**) to slip or slide back; to return to a former bad state or practice; to backslide; to fall back or return from recovery or a convalescent state.—*n* a falling back into a former bad state, either of health or of morals.

relate *vt* (**related, relating**) to tell; to recite; to recount; to narrate the particulars of; to ally by connection or kindred.—*vi* to have reference or respect; to regard; to stand in some relation (with *to* following).

relation *n* the act of relating; that which is related or told; narrative; reference, respect or regard (*in relation to*); connection perceived or imagined between things; a certain position of one thing with regard to another; the condition of being such or such in respect to something else; due conformity or harmony of parts; kinship; a kinsman or kinswoman; (*math*) ratio; proportion.

relative *adj* having relation to or bearing on something; close in connection; pertinent; relevant; not absolute or existing by itself; depending on or incident to something else; (*gram*) applied to a word which relates to another word, sentence or part of a sentence called the antecedent, applied especially to certain pronouns, as *who*, *which* and *that*.—*n* something considered in its relation to something else; a person connected by blood or affinity, especially one allied by blood; a kinsman or kinswoman; a person related by marriage; (*gram*) a word which relates to or represents another word, called its antecedent, or refers back to a statement; a relative pronoun.

relay race

relative atomic mass *n* the mass of atoms of an element given in atomic mass units.

relatively *adv* in a relative manner; in relation to something else; not absolutely; comparatively (often followed by *to*, as *an expenditure large relatively to his income*).

relativity *n* the state of being relative; (*physics*) a theory based on the hypothesis that the distance between two points and the interval of time between two events are not absolute quantities but have different values for different observers.

relax *vt* to slacken; to make less tense or rigid; to make less severe or rigorous; to remit in strictness; to remit or abate in respect to attention, effort or labour; to relieve from constipation.—*vi* to become loose, feeble or languid; to abate in severity; to become more mild or less rigorous; to remit in close attention; to unbend.

relaxation *n* the act of relaxing or state of being relaxed; a diminution of tension or firmness; a diminution of the natural and healthy tone of parts of the human body; remission of attention or application; recreation; an occupation intended to give mental or bodily relief after effort.

relay *n* a team of fresh people, horses, etc, to replace others; a relay race; (*elect*) a device for enabling a weak current to control others; a relayed broadcast.—*vt* to spread in stages; to re-transmit by radio items received from a distance.

relay race *n* a race of several teams in which the second and succeeding members of every team take up the race as the preceding members finish, each member passing on to his or her successor a baton or other object.

release *vt* (**released, releasing**) to let loose again; to set free from restraint or confinement; to liberate; to free from pain, grief or any other evil; to free from obligation or penalty; (*law*) to give up or let go, as a claim.—*n* liberation from restraint of any kind, as from confinement or bondage; liberation from care, pain or burden; discharge from obligation or responsibility.

relegate *vt* (**relegated, relegating**) to send away or out of the way; to consign to some obscure or remote destination; to banish.

relent *vt* to become less harsh, cruel or obdurate; to soften in temper; to become more mild; to yield; to comply.

relentless *adj* incapable of relenting; insensible to the distresses of others; merciless; implacable; pitiless; unremitting.

relevance, relevancy *n* the quality of being relevant; pertinence.

relevant *adj* lending aid or support; to the purpose; pertinent; applicable; bearing on the matter in hand (*arguments not relevant to the case*).

reliability *n* the quality of being reliable.

reliable *adj* such as may be relied on; worthy of being relied on; to be depended on for support.

reliance *n* the act of relying; dependence; confidence; trust; ground of trust.

reliant *adj* having reliance; confident; self-reliant.

relic *n* that which is left after the loss or decay of the rest; a remaining fragment; the body of a deceased person (usually in plural); something preserved in remembrance; a memento, souvenir or keepsake; a bone or other part of saints or martyrs, or some part of their garments, etc, preserved and regarded as of extraordinary sanctity and often as possessing miraculous powers.

relict *n* a widow; a woman whose husband is dead.

relief *n* the removal of anything painful or burdensome by which some ease is obtained; ease from cessation of pain; alleviation; succour; what mitigates or removes pain, grief or other evil; assistance given under the poor laws to a pauper; release from duty by a substitute or substitutes; (*sculp*, *archit*) the projection or prominence of a figure above or beyond the ground or plane on which it is formed; (in painting) the appearance of projection and solidity in represented objects; hence, prominence or distinctness given to anything by something presenting a contrast to it; (*feudal law*) a payment by the heir of a tenant made to his lord for the privilege of taking up the estate.

relieve *vt* (**relieved, relieving**) to remove or lessen, as anything that pains or distresses; to mitigate, alleviate (pain, misery, needs); to free, wholly or partially, from pain, grief, anxiety or anything considered to be an evil; to help, aid or succour (the poor, the sick, etc); to release from a post or duty by substituting another person or party (*to relieve a sentry*); to obviate the monotony of by the introduction of some variety; to make conspicuous; to set off by contrast; to give the appearance of projection to.

religion *n* the feeling of reverence which people entertain towards a god; the recognition of God as an object of worship, love and obedience; piety; any system of faith and worship (*the religion of the Christians, Jews, Hindus, Muslims*, etc).

religious *adj* pertaining or relating to religion; concerned with religion; set apart for purposes connected with religion; imbued with religion; pious; devout; devoted by vows to the practice of religion or to a monastic life (*a religious order*); bound by some solemn obligation; scrupulously faithful.

relinquish *vt* to give up the possession or occupancy of; to withdraw from; to leave; to abandon; to give up the pursuit or practice of; to desist from; to renounce a claim to.

reliquary *n* a depository for relics; a casket in which relics are kept; a shrine.

relish *vt* to like the taste or flavour of; to be pleased with or gratified by; to have a liking for; to enjoy; to give an agreeable taste or flavour to; to savour or smack of.—*vi* to have a pleasing taste; to have a flavour.—*n* the sensation produced by anything on the palate; savour; taste, usually a pleasing taste; inclination; liking (*a relish for something*); delight given by anything; characteristic quality; savour or flavour; smack; a small quantity just perceptible; tincture; something taken with food to increase the pleasure of eating.

relocate *vi* (**relocated, relocating**) to move to a new location; to set up in a new place.—*vt* to establish in a new place; to move (employees, etc) to a new location.

reluctance, reluctancy *n* the state or quality of being reluctant; aversion; unwillingness; (*physics*) the resistance offered by a medium to the passage through it of lines of magnetic force, the reciprocal of permeability.

reluctant *adj* striving against doing something; unwilling to do what one feels called on to do; acting with repugnance; averse; loath; granted with unwillingness (*reluctant obedience*).

rely *vt* (**relied, relying**) to rest with confidence, as when satisfied of the veracity, integrity or ability of persons or of the certainty of facts or of evidence; to have confidence; to trust (with *on* or *upon*).

remain *vi* to continue in a place; to abide; to continue in an unchanged form or condition; to endure; to last; to stay behind after others have gone; to be left; to be left as not included or comprised; to be still to deal with.—*n* that which is left; remainder; relic (chiefly plural); (*pl*) that which is left of a human being after life is gone, the dead body; (*pl*) the productions, especially the literary works, of one who is dead.

remainder *n* that which remains; anything left after the removal of the rest; (*arith*) the sum or quantity that is left after subtraction or deduction; (*law*) an estate limited so as to be enjoyed after the death of the present possessor or otherwise; the copies of a book which are left unsold when the demand or sale has fallen off and which are then issued or sold at a reduced price.

remake *vt* (*pret, pp* **remade**, *ppr* **remaking**) to make or construct again.—*n* something which is made again; a new version of an old film.

remand *vt* to send, call or order back; (*law*) to hold (an accused party) in jail to await trial or in order to give time to collect more evidence.—*n* the state of being remanded; the act of remanding.

remark *n* the act of observing or taking notice; notice or observation; a brief statement taking notice of something; an observation; a comment.—*vt* to observe; to note in the mind; to express, as a thought that has occurred to the speaker; to utter by way of comment or observation.

remarkable *adj* observable; worthy of notice; extraordinary; unusual; striking; noteworthy; conspicuous; distinguished.

remarriage *n* any marriage after the first; a repeated marriage.

remarry *vt* (**remarried, remarrying**) to marry again or a second time.—*vi* to be married again or a second time.

remaster *vt* to make a new master recording from an original recording to provide improved sound quality.

remediable *adj* capable of being remedied.

remedial *adj* affording a remedy; intended

to remedy or cure something or for the removal of something bad (*remedial measures*); relating to the teaching of people with learning disabilities.

remedy *n* that which cures a disease; any medicine or application which puts an end to disease and restores health (*a remedy for gout*); that which corrects or counteracts an evil of any kind; relief; redress; legal means for recovery of a right.—*vt* (**remedied, remedying**) to cure; to heal; to repair or remove, as some evil; to redress; to counteract.

remember *vt* to have in the mind and capable of being brought back from the past; to bear or keep in mind; to be capable of recalling; not to forget; to put in mind; to remind; to think of; to keep in mind with gratitude, favour, affection or other emotion.—*vi* to have something in remembrance; to recollect.

remembrance *n* the keeping of a thing in mind; power or faculty of remembering; limit of time over which the memory extends; what is remembered; a memorial; a keepsake; state of being mindful; regard.

Remembrance Sunday *n* the Sunday nearest 11th November, on which the dead of the two World Wars are commemorated.

remind *vt* to put in mind; to cause to recollect or remember (*to remind a person of his promise*).

reminder *n* one who or that which reminds; a hint that serves to awaken remembrance.

reminisce *vi* (**reminisced, reminiscing**) to think, talk or write about past events.

reminiscence *n* recollection; that which is recollected or recalled to mind; a relation of what is recollected; a narration of past incidents within one's personal knowledge.

reminiscent *adj* having remembrance; calling to mind.—*n* one who calls to mind.

remiss *adj* not energetic or diligent in performance; careless in performing duty or business; negligent; dilatory; slack; lacking earnestness or activity.

remission *n* the act of remitting; diminution or cessation of intensity; abatement; moderation; a giving up; the act of forgiving; forgiveness; pardon; a temporary subsidence of the force or violence of a disease or of pain.

remit *vt* (**remitted, remitting**) to relax in intensity; to make less intense or violent; to abate; to refrain from exacting; to give up in whole or in part (*to remit punishment*); to pardon; to forgive; to refrain from exacting punishment for (sins); to surrender; to resign; to send back; to put again into custody; (*Scots law*) to transfer from one tribunal or judge to another; (*com*) to transmit or send, as money or other things, in payment for goods re-

ceived.—*vi* to slacken; to become less intense or rigorous; (*med*) to abate in violence for a time (*a fever remits at a certain hour every day*); (*com*) to transmit money, etc.—*n* (*Scots law*) the transferring of a case from one tribunal or judge to another.

remittance *n* the act of transmitting money, bills, etc, to a distant place, in return or payment for goods purchased; the sum remitted.

remittance man *n* someone dependent on remittances from home, often someone paid to stay away.

remittent *adj* temporarily ceasing; having remissions from time to time.

remix *vt* to adjust the balance and separation of a recording.

remnant *n* what remains after the removal of the rest of a thing; the remaining piece of a web of cloth after the rest is sold; that which remains after a part is done or past; a scrap, fragment, little bit.

remodel *vt* (**remodelled, remodelling**) to model or fashion anew.

remodification *n* the act of modifying again; a repeated modification or change.

remodify *vt* (**remodified, remodifying**) to modify again; to shape anew.

remonetize *vt* (**remonetized, remonetizing**) to restore to circulation in the shape of money.

remonstrance *n* the act of remonstrating or expostulating; an expostulation; a strong statement of reasons against something; a paper containing such a statement.

remonstrate *vi* (**remonstrated, remonstrating**) to exhibit or present strong reasons against an act, measure or any course of proceedings; to expostulate.

remora *n* a fish with a flattened, adhesive disc on the top of the head by which it attaches itself firmly to other fishes or to the bottoms of vessels, thought by the ancients to have miraculous powers of delaying ships.

remorse *n* the keen pain or anguish excited by a sense of guilt; compunction of conscience for a crime committed; painful memory of wrongdoing.

remote *adj* distant in place; far off; not near; out of the way; secluded; distant in time, past or future; not directly producing an effect; not proximate (*the remote causes of a disease*); distant in relationship or affinity (*a remote kinsman*); slight; inconsiderable (*a remote resemblance*); aloof.

remote control *n* the control of a device or activity from a distance, usually by means of an electric circuit or the making or breaking of radio waves.

remotely *adv* in a remote manner; at a distance; slightly; not closely.

remoteness *n* state of being remote; distance; farness.

remote control

remount *vti* to mount again.—*n* a fresh horse to mount.

removal *n* a moving from one place to another; change of place or site; the act of displacing from an office or post; the act of putting an end to (*the removal of a grievance*).

remove *vt* (**removed, removing**) to shift from the position occupied; to put from its place in any manner; to displace from an office, post or position; to take away by causing to cease; to cause to leave a person or thing; to put an end to; to banish (*to remove a disease* or *grievance*); to make away with; to cut off (*to remove a person by poison*).—*vi* to change place in any manner; to move from one place to another; to change the place of residence.—*n* the act of removing; a removal; change of place; the distance or space through which anything is removed; an interval; stage; a step in any scale of gradation; a dish removed from table to make room for something else.

remunerate *vt* (**remunerated, remunerating**) to reward; to recompense; to requite; to pay an equivalent to for any service, loss or sacrifice.

remuneration *n* the act of remunerating; what is given to remunerate.

remunerative *adj* affording remuneration; yielding a sufficient return.

renaissance, renascence *n* the revival of anything which has long been in decay or extinct.

Renaissance *n* the transitional movement in Europe from the Middle Ages to the modern world, especially applied to the time of the revival of art and literature under the influence of classical study during the fourteenth to sixteenth centuries.

Renaissance man, Renaissance woman *n* a person with wide knowledge, interests and accomplishments.

renal *adj* pertaining to the kidneys.

renascence *n* same as **renaissance**.

renascent *n* springing or rising into being again.

rend *vt* (*pret, pp* **rent**, *ppr* **rending**) to separate into parts with force or sudden violence; to tear asunder; to split; to take away with violence; to tear away.

render *vt* to give in return; to give or pay back; to give, often officially, or in compliance with a request or duty; to furnish; to report (*to render an account*); to afford; to give for use or benefit (*to render services*); to make or cause to be so or so (*he was rendered dumb*); to invest with qualities (*to render a fortress more secure*); to translate from one language into another; to interpret or bring into full expression to others; to reproduce (*to render a piece of music*); to boil down and clarify (*to render

butter*).—*vi* (*naut*) to yield or give way to force applied; (of a rope) to pass freely through a block.—*n* a return; a payment, especially a payment of rent.

rendering *n* the act of one who renders; a version; a translation; (in fine arts and drama) interpretation; representation; exhibition.

rendezvous *n* (*pl* **rendezvous**) a place of meeting; a place at which persons commonly meet; an arranged meeting.—*vi* (**rendezvoused, rendezvousing**) to meet by appointment.

rendition *n* a rendering or giving the meaning of a word or passage; translation; the act of reproducing or exhibiting artistically; the act of rendering up or yielding possession; surrender.

renegade *n* an apostate from a religious faith; one who deserts to an enemy or who deserts one party and joins another; a deserter.

renew *vt* to make new again; to restore to former freshness, completeness or perfection; to restore to a former state or to a good state, after decay or impairment; to make again (*to renew a treaty*); to begin again; to recommence (*renew a fight*); to grant or furnish again, as a new loan or a new note for the amount of a former one (*to renew a bill*).—*vi* to become new; to grow afresh; to begin again; not to desist.

renewal *n* the act of renewing or of forming anew.

rennet *n* the prepared inner membrane of a calf's stomach which has the property of coagulating milk.

renounce *vt* (**renounced, renouncing**) to disown, disclaim, abjure, forswear; to refuse to own or acknowledge as belonging; to cast off or reject.—*vi* (in card-playing) not to follow suit when one has a card of the same sort; to revoke.

renouncement *n* the act of disclaiming or rejecting; renunciation.

renovate *vt* (**renovated, renovating**) to renew; to repair and render as good as new; to restore to freshness or to a good condition.

renovation *n* the act of renovating; renewal; repair; restoration.

renovator *n* one who or that which renovates.

renown *n* fame; celebrity.

renowned *adj* famous; celebrated; eminent.

rent¹ *n* a sum of money payable for the occupancy of a house, etc; a sum of money payable for the hire of a piece of machinery, etc.—*vt* to grant the possession and enjoyment of for a certain rent; to let on lease; to take and hold on the payment of rent.—*vi* to be leased or let for rent.

rent² *n* an opening made by rending or tearing; a break or breach; a hole torn; schism.

727

rental *n* an amount paid or received as rent; a house, car, etc, for rent; an act of renting; a business that rents something.

rente *n* a public fund or stock bearing interest; French government stock.

rentier *n* one who has a fixed income, as from lands, stocks, etc; a fund-holder.

renunciation *n* the act of renouncing; a disowning or disclaiming; rejecting.

reopen *vt* to open again.—*vi* to be opened again; to open anew.

reorganization *adj* the act of organizing anew.

reorganize *vt* (**reorganized, reorganizing**) to organize anew; to reduce again to an organized condition.

rep[1] a shortened form of **repertory**.

rep[2] a shortened form of **representative**.

rep[3], **repp** *n* a dress fabric with a ribbed or corded appearance, the ribs being transverse.

repair[1] *vt* to carry out restoration or renovation on; to restore to a sound or good state after decay, injury, dilapidation or partial destruction; to make amends for, as for an injury, by an equivalent; to give indemnity for.—*n* restoration to a sound or good state; supply of loss; reparation; state as regards repairing (*a building in good* or *bad repair*).

repair[2] *vi* to go to some place; to betake oneself; to resort.—*n* the act of betaking oneself to any place; a resorting; haunt; resort.

reparation *n* the act of repairing; repair; what is done to repair a wrong; indemnification for loss or damage; satisfaction for injury; amends.

reparative *adj* capable of effecting repair; tending to amend defect or make good.—*n* that which restores to a good state; that which makes amends.

repartee *n* a smart, ready and witty reply.

repast *n* the act of taking food; a meal.

repatriate *vt* (**repatriated, repatriating**) to restore to one's own country.

repatriation *n* return or restoration to one's own country.

repay *vt* (**repaid, repaying**) to pay back; to refund; to make return or requital for.—*vi* to requite either good or evil.

repayment *n* the act of repaying or paying back; the money repaid.

repeal *vt* to recall, as a law or statute; to revoke; to abrogate by an authoritative act or by the same power that made or enacted.—*n* the act of repealing; revocation; abrogation.

repeat *vt* to do or perform again (*to repeat an attempt*); to go over, say, make, etc, again; to iterate; to recite; to rehearse; to say over (*to repeat a lesson*).—*n* the act of repeating; repetition; (*mus*) a sign that a movement or part of a movement is to be twice performed.—*vi* to strike the hours (*a repeating watch*).

repeatedly *adv* with repetition; more than once; again and again.

repeater *n* one that repeats; one that recites or rehearses; a watch that strikes the hours, etc, on the compression of a spring; (*arith*) a decimal in which the same figure continually recurs.

repel *vt* (**repelled, repelling**) to drive back; to force to return; to check the advance of; to repulse (*to repel an enemy*); to encounter with effectual resistance; to resist or oppose successfully (*to repel an encroachment, an argument*).—*vi* to cause repugnance; to shock; to act with force in opposition (*electricity sometimes repels*).

repellent *adj* having the effect of repelling; able or tending to repel; repulsive; deterring.—*n* a substance that repels, especially a spray for protection against insects.

repent *vi* to feel pain, sorrow or regret for something done or left undone by oneself; to experience such sorrow for sin as produces amendment of life; to be penitent.—*vt* to remember with compunction or self-reproach; to feel self-accusing pain or grief on account of (*to repent rash words*), frequently used in such phrases as *I repent me, it repented him* (impersonally).

repentance *n* the act of repenting; the state of being penitent; contrition for sin; such sorrow for past conduct as produces a new life.

repentant *adj* experiencing repentance; sorrowful for sin; expressing or showing sorrow for sin (*repentant tears*).

repercussion *n* the act of driving back; reverberation; a far-reaching, often indirect reaction to an event.

repertoire *n* a list of plays, operas, etc, which can be performed by a dramatic or operatic company; those parts, songs, etc, that are usually performed by an actor, vocalist, etc.

repertory *n* a repertoire; the system of alternating several plays through a season with a permanent acting group.

repetition *n* the act of doing or uttering a second time; the act of repeating or saying over; a reciting or rehearsing; what is repeated; something said or done a second time.

repine *vi* (**repined, repining**) to fret oneself; to feel inward discontent which preys on the spirits; to indulge in complaint; to murmur (with *at* or *against*).

replace *vt* (**replaced, replacing**) to put again in the former place; to repay; to refund; to fill the place of; to be a substitute for; to fulfil the end or office of.

replacement *n* the act of replacing.

replenish *vt* to fill again after having been emptied or diminished; hence, to fill completely; to stock with numbers or abundance.

replenishment *n* the act of replenishing.

replete *adj* completely filled; full; abounding; thoroughly imbued.—*vt* (**repleted, repleting**) to fill to repletion or satiety.

repletion *n* the state of being replete or completely filled; superabundant fullness; surfeit.

replica *n* a copy of a picture or piece of sculpture made by the hand that executed the original; a reproduction; an exact copy.

replicate *vt* (**replicated, replicating**) to fold over; to bend back; to reproduce, copy, duplicate or repeat.—*adj* (*bot*) folded over or bent back.

replication *n* the act of replicating; a fold; duplication; response: (*law*) a plaintiff's response to a defendant's answer or plea; (*biol*) the duplication of genetic material, generally before cell division.

replier *n* one who replies or answers; a respondent.

reply *vi* (**replied, replying**) to make answer in words or writing, as to something said or written by another; to answer; to respond; to do or give something in return for something else; to answer by deeds; to meet an attack by fitting action.—*vt* to return for an answer (often with a clause as object).—*n* that which is said or written in answer to what is said or written by another; an answer; that which is done in consequence of something else; an answer by deeds; a counterattack.

report *vt* to bear or bring back, as an answer; to relate, as what has been discovered by a person sent to examine or investigate; to give an account of; to relate; to tell; to circulate publicly, as a story (as in the phrase, *it is reported*, that is, it is said in public); to give an official or formal account or statement of; to give an account of for public reading; to write out or take down from the lips of the speaker (*the debate was fully reported*); to lay a charge or make a disclosure against (*I will report you*); to inform against; to complain about.—*vi* to make a statement of facts; to take down in writing speeches from a speaker's lips; to discharge the office of a reporter.—*n* an account brought back; a statement of facts given in reply to inquiry; a story circulated; hence, rumour; fame; repute; public character (*a man of good report*); an account of a judicial decision or of a case argued and determined in a court of law, etc; an official statement of facts; an account of the proceedings, debates, etc, of a legislative assembly or other meeting, intended for publication; an epitome or fully written account of a speech; sound of an explosion; loud noise (*the report of a gun*).

reportage *n* the art of reporting on current events; an accurate, observant and well-written account of an event.

reportedly *adv* as reported, not directly.

reporter *n* one who reports; a member of a newspaper, broadcasting or television staff who gathers and reports news.

repose *vt* (**reposed, reposing**) to lay at rest; to lay for the purpose of taking rest; to refresh by rest (frequently used reflexively); to lay, place or rest in full reliance (*to repose trust* or *confidence in a person*).—*vi* to lie at rest; to sleep; to rest in confidence; to reply (followed by *on*).—*n* the act or state of reposing; a lying at rest; sleep; rest; quiet; rest of mind; tranquillity; settled composure; absence of all show of feeling; (in painting) an avoidance of obtrusive tints or of striking action in figures.

repository *n* a place where things are or may be deposited for safety or preservation; a depository; a storehouse; a magazine; a warehouse; a shop.

repossess *vt* to take back possession of, especially because of non-payment of loan repayments, etc.

repoussé *adj* (of ornamentation in metal) effected by strokes of the hammer from behind until a rough image of the desired figure is produced, which is finished by chasing.

repp *n* same as **rep³**.

reprehend *vt* to charge with a fault; to chide sharply; to reprove; to take exception to; to speak of as a fault; to censure.

reprehensible *adj* deserving to be reprehended or censured; blameworthy; censurable; deserving reproof.

reprehension *n* the act of reprehending; reproof; censure; blame.

represent *vt* to exhibit the image or counterpart of; to typify; to portray by pictorial or plastic art; to act the part of; to exhibit to the mind in language; to bring before the mind; to give an account of; to describe; to supply the place of; to speak and act with authority on behalf of; to be a substitute or agent for; to serve as a sign or symbol of (*words represent ideas or things*).

re-present *vt* to present again.

representation *n* the act of representing, describing, exhibiting, portraying, etc; that which represents; an image or likeness; a picture or statue; exhibition of a play on the stage or of a character in a play; a dramatic performance; a statement of arguments or facts, etc; sometimes a written expostulation; a remonstrance; the representing of a constituency in a legislative assembly; delegates or representatives collectively.

representative *adj* fitted to represent, portray or typify; acting as a substitute for another or others; performing the functions of others (*a representative body*); conducted by the agency of delegates chosen by the people (*a representative government*).—*n* one who or that which represents; that by which anything is represented; something standing for something else; an agent, deputy or substitute who supplies the place of another or others, being invested with his, her or their authority; a salesman or saleswoman who travels around selling a firm's range of goods to shops, etc (often shortened to **rep**); (*law*) one that stands in the place of another as heir.

repress *vt* to press back or down effectually; to crush, quell, put down, subdue (sedition, a rising); to check; to restrain; to suppress; to exclude involuntarily from the conscious mind.

repressible *adj* capable of being repressed.

repression *n* the act of repressing, restraining or subduing; check; restraint; (*psychol*) involuntary suppression of unpleasant memories or impulses from the conscious mind.

repressive *adj* having power to repress; tending to subdue or restrain.

reprieve *n* the suspension of the execution of a criminal's sentence; respite; interval of ease or relief.—*vt* (**reprieved, reprieving**) to grant a reprieve or respite to; to suspend or delay the execution of for a time.

reprimand *n* a severe reproof for a fault; a sharp rebuke; reprehension.—*vt* to reprove severely; to reprehend; to reprove publicly and officially in execution of a sentence.

reprint *vt* to print again; to print a second or any new edition of; to renew the impression of.—*n* a second or new impression of any printed work.

reprisal *n* the seizure or taking of anything from an enemy by way of retaliation or indemnification; that which is so taken; any taking by way of retaliation; an act of severity done in retaliation.

reprise *n* (*mus*) the repetition of an earlier theme or passage.—*vt* (**reprised, reprising**) to make a reprise of; to repeat.

reproach *vt* to charge with a fault in severe language; to censure with severity, opprobrium or contempt or as having suffered wrong personally; to upbraid.—*n* a severe or cutting expression of censure or blame; blame for something considered outrageous or vile; source of blame; shame, infamy or disgrace; object of contempt, scorn or derision.

reprobate *adj* abandoned in sin; morally abandoned; depraved; profligate; lost to virtue or grace.—*n* one who is very profligate or abandoned; a hardened criminal or sinner; a scoundrel.

reproduce *vt* (**reproduced, reproducing**) to produce again or anew; to renew the production of; to make a copy, duplicate or likeness of; to portray or represent; to produce offspring.

reproduction *n* the act or process of reproducing; a copy or likeness; a representation; the process by which animals and plants breed; that which is produced or presented anew.

reproductive *adj* pertaining to reproduction.

reproof *n* the expression of blame or censure addressed to a person; blame expressed to the face; censure for a fault; reprehension; rebuke; reprimand.

reprove *vt* (**reproved, reproving**) to charge with a fault to the face; to chide; to reprehend; to express disapproval of (*to reprove sins*); to serve to admonish.

reptile *n* an animal that moves on its belly or by means of small, short legs; a crawling creature; (*zool*) a vertebrate animal of a class intermediate between fishes and birds, comprising the snakes, lizards, crocodiles, tortoises, etc, breathing by lungs and having cold blood and horny scales; a grovelling, abject or mean person.—*adj* pertaining to the reptiles; grovelling; low; mean; vile; (*arch*) creeping.

reptilian *adj* belonging or pertaining to the reptiles.—*n* a reptile.

republic *n* a commonwealth; a political community in which the supreme power in the state is vested either in certain privileged members of the community or in the whole community and thus varying from the most exclusive oligarchy to a pure democracy.

republican *adj* pertaining to or having the character of a republic; consonant to the principles of a republic.—*n* one who favours or prefers a republican form of government.

repudiate *vt* (**repudiated, repudiating**) to cast away; to reject; to discard; to disavow; to divorce; to refuse to acknowledge or to pay, as debt.

repudiation *n* the act of repudiating; rejection; disavowal; divorce; refusal on the part of a government to pay debts contracted by a former government.

repugnance, repugnancy *n* the state of being opposed in mind; feeling of dislike to some action; reluctance; unwillingness; opposition in nature or qualities; contrariety.

repugnant *adj* standing or being in opposition; contrary; at variance (usually followed by *to*, as *a statement repugnant to common sense*); highly distasteful.

repulse *n* the condition of being repelled or driven back by force; the act of driving back; a check or defeat; refusal; denial.—

vt (**repulsed, repulsing**) to repel; to drive back; to refuse; to reject.

repulsion *n* the act of repelling; a feeling of disgust; aversion; (*physics*) the action which two bodies exert on one another when they tend to increase their mutual distance.

repulsive *adj* acting so as to repel; exercising repulsion; tending to deter or forbid approach or familiarity; repellent; forbidding.

reputable *adj* being in good repute; held in esteem; not mean or disgraceful.

reputation *n* character by report; opinion of character generally entertained; character attributed; repute (in a good or bad sense); often favourable or honourable regard; good name.

repute *vt* (**reputed, reputing**) to hold in thought; to reckon, account or consider as such or such; to deem.—*n* reputation; character attributed by public report, especially good character; honourable name.

reputed *adj* generally considered; commonly believed, regarded or accounted.

reputedly *adv* in common opinion or estimation.

request *n* the expression of desire to some person for something to be granted or done; an asking; a petition, prayer, entreaty; the thing asked for or requested; a state of being esteemed and sought after or asked for (*an article in much request*).—*vt* to make a request for; to solicit or express desire for; to express a request to; to ask.

Requiem *n* a mass for the dead; music for this.

require *vt* (**required, requiring**) to demand; to ask as of right and by authority; to insist on having; to ask as a favour; to call on to act; to request; to have need or necessity for; to need or lack (*the matter requires great care, we require food*); to find it necessary; to have to (with infinitives, as *you will require to go*).

requirement *n* the act of requiring; demand; that which requires the doing of something; an essential condition; something required or necessary.

requisite *adj* required by the nature of things or by circumstances; necessary.—*n* that which is necessary; something indispensable.

requisition *n* an application made as of a right; a demand; a demand for or a levying of necessaries by hostile troops from the people in whose country they are; a written call or invitation (*a requisition for a public meeting*); state of being required or much sought after; request.—*vt* to make a requisition or demand on.

requital *n* return for any office, good or bad; recompense; reward.

requite *vt* (**requited, requiting**) to repay either good or evil, in a good sense, to recompense or reward, in a bad sense, to retaliate on.

reredos *n* the decorated portion of the wall behind and rising above the altar in a church; the back of a fireplace.

rerun *vt* to run (a race, etc) again; to show (a television programme, film, etc) again.

reschedule *vt* (**rescheduled, rescheduling**) to postpone (a debt) or extend repayment terms.

rescind *vt* to cut short; to abrogate; to revoke or annul by competent authority (*to rescind a law, a judgment*).

rescission *n* the act of rescinding; the act of abrogating or annulling.

rescue *vt* (**rescued, rescuing**) to free from confinement, danger or evil; to withdraw from a state of exposure to evil; (*law*) to take by forcible or illegal means from lawful custody.—*n* the act of rescuing; deliverance from restraint or danger; (*law*) a forcible taking out of the custody of the law.

research *n* diligent inquiry or examination in seeking facts or principles; laborious or continued search after truth; a systematic and careful investigation of a particular subject; a scientific search.—*vt* to search again; to examine anew.—*vi* to carry out an investigation; to study.

researcher *n* one engaged in research.

resemblance *n* the state or quality of resembling; likeness; similarity either of external form or of qualities; something similar; a similitude.

resemble *vt* (**resembled, resembling**) to be like to; to have similarity to in form, figure or qualities; to liken; to compare.

resent *vt* to consider as an injury or affront; to be in some degree angry or provoked at; to take ill; to show such feeling by words or acts.—*vi* to be indignant; to feel resentment.

resentment *n* the act of resenting; the feeling with which one who resents is impressed; a deep sense of injury; anger arising from a sense of wrong; strong displeasure.

reservation *n* the act of reserving or keeping back; concealment or withholding from disclosure; something not expressed, disclosed or brought forward; a limitation or proviso; an arrangement in advance to keep or hold (something, such as theatre tickets, accommodation, flight tickets, etc) until paid for or claimed; a booking; a tract of public land reserved for some special use; (*pl*) doubts, misgivings.

reserve *vt* (**reserved, reserving**) to keep in store for future or other use; to withhold from present use for another purpose; to keep back for a time; to have set aside; to have kept (as theatre tickets, accommodation, etc) until claimed or paid for; to book; to withdraw.—*n* the act of reserving or keeping back; that which is reserved or retained from present use or disposal; a store of something still kept or remaining; something in the mind withheld from disclosure; a reservation; the habit of keeping back or restraining the feelings; a certain closeness or coldness towards others; aloofness; caution in personal behaviour; banking capital retained in order to meet average liabilities; troops reserved to sustain other troops in battle as occasion may require; a body of troops kept for an exigency.—**in reserve** in store; in keeping for other or future use.

reserved *adj* kept for another or future use; showing reserve in behaviour; restrained; not open or frank; distant; cold.

reservist *n* a soldier or sailor belonging to a reserve.

reservoir *n* a place where anything is kept in store; a place where water is collected and kept for use; an artificial lake or pond from which pipes convey water to a town; a supply or store; an extra supply or store.

reset[1] *vt* (**resetted, resetting**) to set again (*to reset a diamond*); (*print*) to set over again, as a page of matter.—*n* the act of resetting; (*print*) matter set over again.

reset[2] *n* (*Scots law*) the receiving and harbouring of an outlaw, criminal or stolen goods.

reside *vi* (**resided, residing**) to dwell permanently or for a length of time; to have one's dwelling or home; to abide continuously; to abide or be inherent, as a quality; to inhere.

residence *n* the act of residing or abiding; period of abode; the place where a person resides; a dwelling; a habitation; a mansion or dwelling house.

residency *n* residence; the official residence of a British resident at the court of a native prince in India.

resident *adj* dwelling or having an abode in a place for a continuance of time; residing.—*n* one who resides or dwells in a place for some time; one residing.

residential *adj* relating or pertaining to residence or to residents; used for private houses.

residual *adj* having the character of a residue or residuum; remaining after a part is taken or dealt with.

residuary *adj* pertaining to a residue or part remaining; forming a residue or portion not dealt with.

residue *n* that which remains after a part is taken, separated or dealt with in some way; that which is still over; remainder; the rest; (*law*) the remainder of a testator's estate after payment of debts and legacies.

residuum *n* (*pl* **residua**) that which is left after any process of separation or purification; a residue; the dregs or refuse; (*law*) the part of an estate remaining after the payment of debts and legacies.

resign *vti* to assign or give back; to give up, as an office or post; to surrender or relinquish; to give over; to withdraw, as a claim; to submit, particularly to Providence; to reconcile oneself.

resignation *n* the act of resigning or giving up, as a claim, etc; the state of being resigned or submissive; patience; quiet submission to the will of Providence; submission without discontent or complaint.

resigned *adj* surrendered; given up; feeling resignation; submissive; patient.

resilience *n* the act of rebounding; rebound from being elastic; the quantity of work given out by a body, such as a spring, that is compressed and then allowed to resume its former shape.

resilient *adj* rebounding.

resin *n* an inflammable substance of sundry varieties found in most plants and often obtained by spontaneous emission, in some cases solid and brittle at ordinary temperatures, in others viscous or semifluid (in which case they are called *balsams*), valuable as ingredients in varnishes and several of them used in medicine.

resinous *adj* pertaining to or obtained from resin; partaking of the qualities of resin; like resin.

resist *vt* to withstand so as not to be impressed by; to form an impediment to; to oppose, passively (*certain bodies resist acids* or *a cutting tool*); to act in opposition to; to strive or struggle against, actively.—*vi* to make opposition.—*n* a sort of paste applied to calico goods to prevent colour or mordant from fixing on those parts not intended to be coloured.

resistance *n* the act of resisting, whether actively or passively; a being or acting in opposition; the quality or property in matter of not yielding to force or external impression; a force acting in opposition to another force so as to destroy it or diminish its effect; (*elect*) the property of a body that limits the strength of an electric current in it by causing part of the electrical energy to be dissipated in the form of heat, etc.

resolute *adj* having a fixed purpose; determined; steadfast; bold; firm.

resolution *n* the character of being resolute; a resolve taken; a fixed purpose or determination of mind; the character of acting with fixed purpose; firmness; determination; a formal decision of a legislative or other body; the operation of resolving or separating the component parts of a body; the act of unravelling a perplexing question or problem; solution; (*mus*) the succession of a concord immediately after a discord; (*med*) a removal or disappearance, as the disappearance of a tumour; (*math*) solution.

resolve *vt* (**resolved, resolving**) to separate the component parts of; to reduce to constituent elements; to reduce to simple parts; to analyse; to disentangle of perplexities; to clear of difficulties (*to resolve doubts*); to explain; to fix in determination or purpose; to determine (usually in *pp*); to melt; to dissolve; to form or constitute by resolution (*the house resolved itself into a committee*); to determine on; to express by resolution and vote; (*med*) to disperse or remove, as an inflammation or a tumour; (*math*) to solve.—*vi* to form an opinion or purpose; to determine; to determine by vote; to melt; to become fluid; to become separated into its component parts or into distinct principles.—*n* that which has been resolved on; fixed purpose of mind; a settled determination; a resolution.

resolved *adj* having the mind made up; determined.

resonance *n* the state or quality of being resonant; the act of resounding; (*physics*) in a system capable of oscillation of any kind, e.g. acoustic or electromagnetic, energetic response to disturbances of certain definite frequencies.

resonant *adj* capable of returning sound; resounding; full of sounds; echoing back.

resonate *vi* (**resonated, resonating**) to have or show resonance; to resound.

resonator *n* a device that produces or increases sound by resonance.

resort *vi* to have recourse; to betake oneself (*to resort to force*); to go (*to resort to a place*); to repair frequently.—*n* a betaking oneself; recourse; a source of help; the act of visiting or frequenting; a place frequented; a haunt; a popular holiday location.

resound *vt* to sound again; to echo; to extol.—*vi* to be filled with sound; to echo; to reverberate; to sound loudly; to be echoed; to be much mentioned.

resource *n* any source of aid or support; an expedient; means yet untried; resort; (*pl*) financial means, funds; (*pl*) available means or capabilities of any kind; (*pl*) raw materials.

respect *vt* to regard, heed or consider; to have reference or regard to; to relate to; to view with some degree of reverence.—*n* a respecting or noticing with attention; regard; attention; a holding in high estimation or honour; the deportment which proceeds from esteem, regard or reverence; partial or undue regard; bias (*respect of persons*); (*pl*) an expression of regard, esteem or deference (*give him my respects*);

a point or particular (*wrong in many respects*); relation; reference, especially in the phrase *in* or *with respect to.*

respectability *n* state or quality of being respectable.

respectable *adj* worthy of respect; having an honest or good reputation; belonging to a fairly good position in society; mediocre; not despicable (*a respectable number of citizens*).

respectful *adj* marked by respect; showing respect or outward regard; ceremonious.

respecting *prep* regarding; in regard to; concerning.

respective *adj* relating or pertaining severally each to each; severally connected or belonging; several (*our respective places of abode*); relative; not absolute.

respectively *adv* in their respective relations; as each belongs to each.

respirable *n* capable of or fit for being respired or breathed.

respiration *n* the act of respiring or breathing.

respirator *n* a device to maintain breathing by artificial means; a device or mask to prevent the inhaling of dangerous substances.

respire *vi* (**respired, respiring**) to breathe.—*vt* to breathe in and out, as air; to inhale and exhale; to breathe out.

respite *n* a temporary intermission of labour or suffering; prolongation of time for the payment of a debt; (*law*) a reprieve; temporary suspension of the execution of an offender.—*vt* (**respited, respiting**) to give or grant a respite to; to reprieve.

resplendent *adj* very bright; shining with brilliant lustre.

respond *vi* to make answer; to give a reply in words; to answer or reply in any way; to answer by action; to react to; to correspond; to suit.—*n* (in religious services) a short anthem or versicle chanted at intervals; a response.

respondent *adj* answering; conformable; corresponding.—*n* one who responds; one who answers in a lawsuit; one who maintains a thesis in reply.

response *n* the act of responding or replying; reply; answer; the answer of the congregation to the priest in the litany and other parts of divine service; a reply to an objection in formal disputation; a reaction to stimulation.

responsibility *n* the state of being responsible; that for which one is responsible; a trust, etc, resting on a person; ability to answer in payment.

responsible *adj* accountable; answerable; able to respond to any claim; involving responsibility.

responsive *adj* answering; responding; correspondent; suited to something else.

rest[1] *n* a state of quiet or repose; cessation of motion, labour or action of any kind; freedom from everything that disquiets; peace; tranquillity; sleep; (*fig*) the last sleep, death; a place of quiet; that on which anything leans for support; an article or appliance for support; (*mus*) an interval of silence between one sound and another or the mark or character denoting the interval.—*vi* to cease from action, motion or work of any kind; to stop; to be free from whatever harasses or disturbs; to be quiet or still; to lie for repose; to sleep; to sleep the final sleep; to die; to stand for support; to be supported; to be fixed in any state or opinion (*to rest content*); to rely (*to rest on a man's promise*); to be in a certain state or position, as an affair.—*vt* to lay at rest; to give rest or repose to; to quiet; to lay or place, as on a support.

rest[2] *n* that which is left after the separation of a part, either in fact or in contemplation (used with *the*); the remainder; the others; those not before included (in this sense plural); a surplus fund held in reserve by a bank or other such company, to fall back on in any great emergency.—*vi* to be left; to remain; to continue to be.

restaurant *n* an eating house; a place where food is cooked, bought and eaten.

restful *adj* full of rest; giving rest; quiet; being at rest.

restharrow *n* a pod-bearing plant with a woody, tough and strong root that catches in the prongs of a harrow.

resting place *n* a place for rest; used poetically for the grave.

restitution *n* the restoring of what is lost or taken away, especially taken away unjustly; amends; indemnification.

restive *adj* unwilling to go forward; refusing to rest or stand still; constantly fidgeting or moving about (said of horses); hence, impatient under restraint or opposition (applied to persons).

restless *adj* not resting; unquiet; continually moving; being without rest; unable to sleep; passed in unquietness; not satisfied to be at rest; unsettled; turbulent.

restoration *n* the act of restoring; replacement; renewal; re-establishment; the repairing of injuries suffered by works of art, buildings, etc; recovery of health.

Restoration *n* the return of King Charles II in 1660 and the re-establishment of the British monarchy.

restorative *adj* capable of restoring strength, vigour, etc.—*n* a medicine efficacious in restoring strength and vigour.

restore *vt* (**restored, restoring**) to bring back to a former and better state; to repair; to rebuild; to heal; to cure; to revive; to re-establish after interruption (*to restore peace*); to give back; to return after having

been taken away; to bring or put back to a former position; to recover or renew, as passages of an author defective or corrupted; (in fine arts) to bring back from a state of injury or decay (*to restore a painting*); to complete by adding the defective parts.

restrain *vt* to hold back; to hold in; to check; to hold from action; to repress; to restrict.

restraint *n* the act of restraining; a holding back or hindering from motion in any manner; hindrance of the will; a check to any tendency; abridgement of liberty; confinement; detention; that which restrains or hinders; a limitation.

restrict *vt* to limit; to confine; to restrain within bounds.

restriction *n* the act of restricting or state of being restricted; that which restricts; a restraint; reservation.

result *vi* to proceed, spring or rise, as a consequence, from facts, arguments, premises, combination of circumstances, etc; to ensue; to accrue; to have an issue; to terminate (followed by *in*, as *this measure will result in good* or *evil*).—*n* consequence; conclusion; outcome; issue; effect; product; that which proceeds naturally or logically from facts, premises or the state of things; a desired effect; in sport, the final score.

resultant *adj* following as a result or consequence; resulting from the combination of two or more agents.

resume *vt* (**resumed, resuming**) to take again; to take back; to take up again after interruption; to begin again.

résumé *n* a summing up; a recapitulation; a condensed statement; a summary; a curriculum vitae, CV.

resumption *n* the act of resuming, taking back or taking again.

resurrection *n* a rising again; a springing again into life; a rising from the dead; the revival of the dead of the human race at the general judgment.

resurrection *n* a rising again; a springing again into life; a rising from the dead.

Resurrection *n* the rising of Christ from the dead; the revival of the dead of the human race at the general judgment.

resurrectionist *n* one who steals bodies from the grave for dissection.

resuscitate *vt* (**resuscitated, resuscitating**) to stir up anew; to revivify; to revive; particularly, to recover from apparent death.—*vi* to revive; to come to life again.

resuscitation *n* the act of resuscitating; revivification; the restoring to animation of persons apparently dead.

resuscitator *n* one who resuscitates; an apparatus for forcing oxygen into the lungs.

ret *vt* (**retted, retting**) to steep or macerate

flax in water, in order to separate the fibre by incipient rotting.

retable *n* (*archit*) a shelf or ledge behind an altar for holding candles or vases.

retail *vt* to sell in small quantities directly to the consumer, opposed to selling by *wholesale*; to deal out in small quantities; to tell to many (*to retail slander* or *idle reports*).—*n* the sale of commodities in small quantities directly to the consumer; a dealing out in small portions.—*adj* applied to the sale of anything in small quantities (*a retail trade*).

retailer *n* one who retails.

retain *vt* to hold or keep in possession; to keep from departure or escape; to detain; to keep; not to lose or part with; to engage by the payment of a preliminary fee (*to retain counsel*).

retainer *n* one who or that which retains; one who is kept in service; a dependant; formerly, a servant; (*law*) a fee to retain the services of.

retaliate *vt* (**retaliated, retaliating**) to return the like for (*to retaliate injuries* or *wrongs*); to pay or requite by an act of the same kind as has been received, in a bad sense, that is, to return evil for evil.—*vi* to return like for like; to do injuries in return for injuries.

retaliation *n* the act of retaliating; the return of like for like; requital of evil by evil; reprisal; revenge.

retard *vt* to obstruct in swiftness of course; to keep delaying; to impede; to clog; to hinder.

retarded *adj* slow in physical or mental development; mentally underdeveloped.

retch *vi* to make an effort to vomit; to strain, as in vomiting.

retention *n* the act of retaining or power of retaining; the faculty of remembering; power of memory; (*med*) an abnormal accumulation of matter in the body that should be evacuated.

retentive *adj* characterized by retention; having strong power of recollecting.

reticence *n* the quality of observing studied and continued silence; a refraining from talking; the keeping of one's counsel.

reticent *adj* having a disposition to be silent; reserved; not apt to speak about or reveal any matters.

reticular *adj* having the form of a net or of network; formed with interstices.

reticulate, reticulated. *adj* netted; resembling network; having distinct lines or veins crossing like network.

reticulation *n* that which is reticulated; network; organization of substances resembling a net.

reticule *n* a kind of bag, usually of network, formerly used by ladies for carrying in the hand.

retina *n* a membrane lining the interior of the eye behind, being a reticular expansion of the optic nerve, which receives the impressions from external objects.

retinue *n* the attendants of a prince or other distinguished personage, chiefly on a journey or an excursion; a train of persons; a suite; a cortège.

retiral *n* the act of retiring or withdrawing.

retire *vi* (**retired, retiring**) to withdraw; to go back; to draw back; to go from company or from a public place into privacy; to retreat from action or danger (*to retire from battle*); to withdraw from business or work, usually when pensionable age is reached; to go to bed; to recede.—*vt* to arrange for the retirement of; to withdraw from use.

retired *adj* secluded from much society or from public notice; apart from public view (*a retired life, a retired locality*); private; secret; withdrawn from business or active life; having given up business (*a retired merchant*); given to seclusion; inclining to retirement.

retirement *n* the act of retiring; state of living a retired life; the state of having given up work, usually at pensionable age; seclusion; privacy; retired or private abode.

retort *vt* to return, as an argument, accusation, censure or incivility (*to retort the charge of vanity*); to bend or curve back (*a retorted line*).—*vi* to return an argument or charge; to make a severe reply; to curl or curve back, as a line.—*n* a censure or incivility returned; a severe reply; a repartee; a flask-shaped vessel, to which a long neck is attached, employed for the purpose of distilling or effecting decomposition by the aid of heat.

retrace *vt* (**retraced, retracing**) to trace or track back; to go over again in the reverse direction.

retract *vt* to draw back; to draw in (*to retract the claws*); to rescind; to withdraw, as a declaration, words or saying; to disavow; to recant.—*vi* to take back statements; to unsay one's words.

retractable, retractile *adj* capable of being drawn back.

retraction *n* the act of retracting or drawing back; the act of recalling what has been said; recantation.

retreat *n* the act of retiring; a withdrawing from any place; state of privacy or seclusion; place of retirement or privacy; a refuge; a place of safety or security; a military operation, either forced or strategic, by which troops retire before an enemy; a period of retirement with a view to self-examination, meditation and special prayer.—*vi* to make a retreat; to retire from any position or place; to withdraw; to take shelter; to retire before an enemy.

retrench *vt* to cut off, abridge; to limit or restrict; to curtail or cut down (expenses).—*vi* to live at less expense; to practise economy.

retrenchment *n* the removing of what is superfluous; the act of curtailing or lessening.

retrial *n* a second trial.

retribution *n* the act of requiting actions, whether good or bad; a reward, recompense or requital; especially, a requital or punishment for wrong or evil done; evil justly befalling the perpetrator of evil; the distribution of rewards and punishments in a future life.

retributive, retributory *adj* making retribution; rewarding for good deeds and punishing for offences.

retrievable *adj* capable of being retrieved or recovered.

retrieval *n* act of retrieving.

retrieve *vt* (**retrieved, retrieving**) to get again; to regain; to recover; to restore from loss or injury (*to retrieve the credit of a nation*); to make amends for; to repair.

retriever *n* one who retrieves; a dog that picks up the game which a sportsman has shot.

retro *adj* associated with a fashion revived from the past.

retrocede *vi* (**retroceded, retroceding**) to go back; to give place; to retire.—*vt* to yield or cede back.

retrocedent *adj* going back (applied to certain diseases which move from one part of the body to another).

retrocession *n* the act of retroceding.

retrograde *adj* going or moving backward; specifically, (*astron*) appearing to move from east to west in the sky, opposed to *direct*; declining from a better to a worse state.—*vi* (**retrograded, retrograding**) to go or move backwards.

retrogression *n* the act of going backwards; a backward movement.

retrogressive *adj* moving backward; declining from a more to a less perfect state.

retrorocket *n* a small rocket on an aircraft or spacecraft that produces thrust in the opposite direction to the line of flight to slow it down.

retrospect *n* a looking back on things past; a review of past events.

retrospection *n* the act or faculty of looking back on things past.

retrospective *adj* looking back on past events; having reference to what is past; affecting things past.—*n* an exhibition of an artist's lifetime's work.

retrude *vt* (**retruded, retruding**) to thrust back.

retsina *n* a Greek wine flavoured with resin.

return *vi* to come back; to come or go back to the same place or state; to pass back; to come again; to reappear; to recur; to answer; to retort.—*vt* to bring, carry or send back; to give back; to repay; to give in recompense or requital (*to return good for evil*); to give back in reply (*to return an answer*); to cast, throw or hurl back; to render, as an account to a superior; to report officially; to transmit; to elect as a member of parliament.—*n* the act of returning; the act of coming or going back (*the return of a traveller, of the seasons*); the act of giving or sending back; repayment; recompense; requital; restitution; that which is returned; the profit on labour, on an investment, undertaking, adventure, etc; an account or official or formal report; (*pl*) tabulated statistics for general information; also, a name for a light-coloured mild-flavoured kind of tobacco.

returnable *adj* capable of being returned; (*law*) legally required to be returned or delivered.

returning officer *n* presiding officer at an election who returns the persons duly elected.

return match *n* a second match or trial played by the same two players, sets of players or clubs.

return ticket *n* a ticket issued by railway, bus, shipping companies, etc, for the journey out and back, generally at a reduced charge.

reunion *n* a second union; union after separation or discord; an assembly or festive gathering, as of friends, associates, etc.

reunite *vt* (**reunited, reuniting**) to unite again; to join after separation; to reconcile after variance.—*vi* to be united again; to join and cohere again.

revaluation *n* a second valuation.

revalue *vt* (**revalued, revaluing**) to value again.

reveal *vt* to make known, as something secret or concealed; to disclose; to divulge; to lay open; to betray; to make known by divine means; to communicate by supernatural revelation.

reveille *n* (*milit*) the beat of drum, bugle sound or other signal given about break of day to awaken soldiers.

revel *n* a feast with loose and noisy jollity; a festivity; a merrymaking.—*vi* (**revelled, revelling**) to feast with boisterous merriment; to carouse; to take one's fill of pleasure.

revelation *n* the act of revealing; that which is revealed or made known.

Revelation *n* the Apocalypse; the last book of the New Testament, containing the prophecies of St John.

reveller *n* one who revels.

revelry *n* the act of engaging in a revel; noisy festivity; clamorous jollity.

revenge *vt* (**revenged, revenging**) to take

736

vengeance for or on account of; to exact satisfaction for, under a sense of wrong or injury; to exact retribution for or for the sake of; to avenge; to inflict injury for or on account of, in a spiteful, wrong or malignant spirit, and in order to gratify one's bitter feelings.—*vi* to take vengeance.—*n* the act of revenging; the executing of vengeance; retaliation; the deliberate infliction of pain or injury in return for an injury received; the desire of inflicting pain on one who has done an injury.

revenue *n* the annual rents or profits of any type of property; income; the annual income of a state.

reverberate *vt* (**reverberated, reverberating**) to return, as sound; to send back; to echo; to resound; to reflect, as heat or light.—*vi* to rebound; to be reflected, as rays of light; to echo; to resound.

reverberation *n* the act of reverberating; particularly, the act of reflecting or returning sound; a sound reverberated or echoed.

reverberatory *adj* producing reverberation; acting by reverberation; reverberating.

revere *vt* (**revered, revering**) to regard with awe mingled with respect and affection; to venerate; to reverence.

reverence *n* a feeling of deep respect and esteem mingled with affection; awe combined with respect; veneration; an obeisance; reverend character; a reverend personage; a common title of the clergy (used with the pronouns *his, your,* etc).—*vt* (**reverenced, reverencing**) to regard with reverence.

reverend *adj* worthy of reverence; a title of respect given to clergymen or ecclesiastics and sometimes to Jewish rabbis.

reverent *adj* expressing reverence or veneration; humble; impressed with reverence.

reverential *adj* proceeding from reverence or expressing it.

reverie *n* a waking dream; a brown study; a loose or irregular train of thoughts occurring in musing or meditation.

reversal *n* the act of reversing.

reverse *vt* (**reversed, reversing**) to turn or put in an opposite or contrary direction or position; to turn upside down; to alter to the opposite; to make quite the contrary or have contrary bearings or relations; to make void; to annul, repeal, revoke (*to reverse a judgment* or *decree*); (*mach*) to cause to revolve in a contrary direction; to change the motion of.—*n* the side presented when anything is turned in a direction opposite to its natural position; a complete change or turn of affairs (generally in a bad sense); a change for the worse; a misfortune; a cessation of success; a check; a defeat; that which is directly opposite or contrary; the contrary; the oppo-

site (with *the*); the back or under surface, as of a leaf or of a coin, not the obverse.—*adj* opposite; turned backward; having a contrary or opposite direction.

reversible *n* capable of being reversed; capable of being turned outside in; wearable with either side on the outside; with both sides usable.

reversion *n* a reverting or returning; succession to a post or office after the present holder's term; (*biol*) a return towards some ancestral type or character; atavism; (*law*) the returning of an estate to the grantor or his heirs; a remainder.

revert *vt* to turn or direct back; to reverse; to repel.—*vi* to return or come back to a former position; to turn back; to turn to something spoken of before; to go back to a former condition; (*law*) to return to the possession of the donor or of the former proprietor.

review *vt* to view or behold again; to revise; to notice critically; to write a critical notice of, after an examination in order to discover excellences or defects (*to review a newly published book*); to inspect; to make a formal or official examination of the state of, as of troops (*to review a regiment*); to look back on.—*n* a second or repeated view; a re-examination; a critical examination of a new publication, with remarks; a criticism; a critique; the name given to certain periodical publications, consisting of essays, with critical examinations of new publications; an official inspection of military or naval forces, which may be accompanied by manoeuvres and evolutions.—*vi* to make reviews; to be a reviewer (*he reviews for the Times*).

reviewer *n* one that reviews; a writer in a review; one who critically examines a new publication.

revile *vt* (**reviled, reviling**) to assail with opprobrious and contemptuous language; to vilify; to speak evil of.

revise *vt* (**revised, revising**) to examine or re-examine and make corrections on; to look over with care for correction; to review and amend; to read or study again, especially in preparation for an examination.—*n* a revision; a re-examination and correction; (*print*) a second or further proof sheet corrected.

revision *n* the act of revising; a re-examination for correction; that which is revised.

revisit *vt* to visit again; to come to see again.

revitalize *vt* (**revitalized, revitalizing**) to put new life in; to renew the strength or vigour of.

revival *n* the act of reviving or the state of being revived; recovery from apparent death; return to activity from a state of languor or depression; recovery from a state of neglect; a renewed and more active attention to religion; an awakening among large numbers of people to their spiritual concerns.

revivalism *n* the spirit of religious revivals; excited feeling with respect to religion.

revivalist *n* one who promotes revivals of religion.

revive *vi* (**revived, reviving**) to return to life; to recover life; to recover new life or vigour; to be reanimated after depression; to recover from a state of neglect, oblivion, obscurity or depression.—*vt* to bring again to life; to reanimate; to raise from depression or discouragement; to quicken; to refresh; to bring again into notice or vogue (*to revive a scheme*); to renew in the mind or memory.

revoke *vt* (**revoked, revoking**) to call back; to annul by recalling or taking back; to make void; to cancel; to repeal; to reverse.—*vi* in card playing, to neglect to follow suit when the player can follow.—*n* in card playing, the act of renouncing or failing to follow suit.

revolt *vi* to desert or go over to the opposite side; to renounce allegiance and subjection; to rise against a government in rebellion; to rebel; to be grossly offended or disgusted (with *at*).—*vt* to repel; to shock.—*n* the act of revolting; change of sides; a renunciation of allegiance and subjection to one's prince or government; rebellion.

revolting *adj* causing abhorrence or extreme disgust.

revolution *n* the act of revolving or rotating; rotation; the circular motion of a body on its axis; the course or motion of a body round a centre; one complete circuit made by a heavenly body round a centre; a cycle of time; a radical change of circumstances or of system; a sudden and violent change of government or in the political constitution of a country, mainly brought about by internal causes.

revolutionary *adj* pertaining to a revolution in government; tending to produce a revolution.—*n* a person disposed towards a revolution.

revolutionist *n* the favourer of a revolution.

revolutionize *vt* (**revolutionized, revolutionizing**) to bring about a revolution in; to effect a complete change in.

revolve *vi* (**revolved, revolving**) to turn or roll round an axis; to rotate; to move round a centre; to circle; to move in an orbit; to pass away in cycles or periods (*the years revolve*).—*vt* to cause to turn round; to turn over and over in the mind; to meditate on.

revolver *n* one who or that which revolves; a pistol having a revolving set of cartridge chambers, so constructed as to discharge

revolver

rhea

several shots in quick succession without being reloaded.

revue *n* a loosely constructed and spectacular theatrical exhibition, depending on music and scenic and staging effects.

revulsion *n* a violent separation; a sudden and violent change of feeling.

reward *vt* to give something to in return, either good or evil; to requite (commonly in a good sense); to bestow a recompense, remuneration or token of favour on (when evil is returned for injury *reward* signifies to punish).—*n* that which is given in return for good or evil done or received, especially that which is in return for good; recompense; in a bad sense, punishment or requital of evil; the fruit of men's labour or works; a sum of money offered for taking or detecting a criminal or for the recovery of anything lost.

rewind *vt* to wind again; to wind back; to wind (an audiotape, videotape, etc) back to the beginning.

rewire *vt* (**rewired, rewiring**) to put new electrical wiring in.

reword *vt* to change the wording of.

rewrite *vt* (*pret* **rewrote**, *pp* **rewritten**, *ppr* **rewriting**) to write a second time; to write over again.—*n* something rewritten; revision.

Rex *n* a reigning king.

Rhadamanthine *adj* severely or rigorously just.

rhapsodic, rhapsodical *adj* pertaining to or consisting of rhapsody.

rhapsodize *vi* (**rhapsodized, rhapsodizing**) to speak or write about with great enthusiasm or feeling.

rhapsody *n* originally, a short epic poem or portion of a longer epic; an irregular emotional piece of music; an ecstatic utterance; an expression of great enthusiasm or delight.

rhea *n* the three-toed ostrich of South America.

rhenium *n* a hard, heat-resistant chemical element allied to manganese, discovered in 1926.

rheostat *n* an instrument for regulating the strength of an electric current by means of adjustable resistances.

rhesus *n* a small monkey held sacred in India.

rhesus factor *n* (abbreviated to **Rh factor**) a substance usually present in the red blood cells of humans and the higher animals.

rhesus negative *adj* (abbreviated to **Rh negative**) lacking the rhesus factor in the blood.

rhesus positive *adj* (abbreviated to **Rh positive**) containing the rhesus factor in the blood.

rhetoric *n* the art or branch of knowledge

which treats of the rules or principles underlying all effective composition whether in prose or verse; the art which teaches oratory; the rules that govern the art of speaking with propriety, elegance and force; rhetoric exhibited in language; eloquence, especially artificial eloquence; flashy oratory; declamation.

rhetorical *adj* pertaining to, exhibiting or involving rhetoric.

rhetorician *n* one who teaches the art of rhetoric; one well versed in the rules and principles of rhetoric.

rheum *n* a thin serous fluid secreted by the mucous glands, etc, as in catarrh; humid matter which collects in the eyes, nose or mouth.

rheumatic *adj* pertaining to rheumatism or partaking of its nature; affected with rheumatism.

rheumatic fever *n* a disease causing fever, joint pains and inflammation and often affecting the lining of the heart, caused by a bacterial infection.

rheumatism *n* a painful inflammation affecting muscles and joints of the human body, attended by swelling and stiffness.

rheumatoid *adj* pertaining to rheumatism; affected by rheumatism.

rheumatoid arthritis *n* a chronic disease characterized by inflamed painful swelling of the joints.

rheumatology *n* the branch of medicine dealing with rheumatic disease.

rheumy *adj* full of rheum or watery matter; causing rheum.

Rh factor an abbreviation of **rhesus factor**.

rhinal *adj* pertaining to the nose.

rhinoceros *n* a large ungainly hoofed animal nearly allied to the hippopotamus, the tapir, etc, having a very thick skin which is usually thrown into deep folds and deriving its name from the nasal bones usually supporting one or two horns, composed of matter similar to that of hair.

rhinologist *n* one with a special knowledge of diseases of the nose.

rhinoplasty *n* plastic surgery of the nose.

rhinoscope *n* a small mirror for inspecting the passages of the nose.

rhizanth *n* a plant of a class lacking true leaves but with short amorphous stems, parasitic on roots.

rhizocarpous *adj* (*bot*) having roots that endure many years, though the stems perish annually.

rhizoid *n* in mosses, etc, one of the hair-like structures acting as roots.

rhizome *n* (*bot*) a stem running along the surface of the ground or partially subterranean, sending forth shoots at its upper end and decaying at the other, as in the ferns, iris, etc.

rhizopod *n* any of a class of protozoans containing minute animals lacking a mouth and capable of protruding root-like or finger-shaped masses from any part of their substance.

Rh negative an abbreviation of **rhesus negative**.

rhodium *n* a rare metal found associated with palladium in the ore of platinum, which it resembles in its general and chemical properties.

rhododendron *n* a genus of evergreen shrubs, with beautiful flowers disposed in corymbs, occurring both in the New and Old Worlds, especially in the Himalayas.

rhomb *n* a rhombus.

rhombic *adj* having the figure of a rhombus; in crystallography, the system of crystals having three unequal axes mutually at right angles.

rhombohedron *n* a solid bounded by six rhombic planes.

rhomboid *n* a quadrilateral figure whose opposite sides and angles are equal but which is neither equilateral nor equiangular; a solid having a rhomboidal form.—*a* In the form of a rhomboid; rhomboidal; diamond-shaped.

rhombus *n* (*pl* **rhombi, rhombuses**) a quadrilateral figure whose sides are equal and the opposite sides parallel but the angles not right angles; a figure of a diamond or lozenge form; a solid bounded by six equal and similar rhombic planes; a rhombohedron.

Rh positive an abbreviation of **rhesus positive**.

rhubarb *n* the common name of a large herbaceous plant which yields leaf stalks cooked and used for making tarts, etc.

rhumb *n* (*navig*) an imaginary line crossing all meridians at the same angle.

rhyme *n* a correspondence of sound in the final portions of two or more syllables, more especially the correspondence in sound of the terminating word or syllable of one line of poetry with the terminating word or syllable of another; poetry; metre; a composition in verse; a poem, especially a short one; a verse, word or termination rhyming with another.—*vi* (**rhymed, rhyming**) to accord in the terminational sounds; to form a rhyme; to make verses.—*vt* to put into rhyme.

rhymer *n* one who makes rhymes; a poor poet.

rhymster *n* a rhymer; a poor poet.

rhythm *n* the measure of time or movement by regularly recurring impulses, sounds, etc, as in poetry, prose composition and music, and by analogy, dancing; periodical emphasis; numerical proportion or harmony; rhyme; metre; verse; number.

rhythmic, rhythmical *adj* pertaining to rhythm; having rhythm.

rhinoceros

rhubarb

rial, ryal *n* a gold coin of varying value, formerly current in Britain.

rib[1] *n* one of the curved bones springing from the vertebral column and enclosing a certain number of the important organs and viscera in humans and other vertebrate animals; something resembling a rib in form, use, position, etc, as one of the bent timber or metallic bars which spring from the keel and form or strengthen the side of a ship; a piece of timber or iron supporting an arched roof, as in domes, vaults, etc; one of the principal veins or nerves in leaves of plants; one of the rods on which the cover of an umbrella is stretched; a prominent line or rising on cloth, as in corduroy.—*vt* (**ribbed, ribbing**) to furnish with ribs; to plough so as to leave rib-like ridges somewhat apart.

rib[2] *vt* (**ribbed, ribbing**) (*colloq*) to tease.

ribald *adj* humorously vulgar; coarsely humorous; irreverent.

ribaldry *n* ribald speech or behaviour; ribald humour.

ribbing[1] *n* an assemblage or arrangement of ribs, as of a vaulted ceiling, on cloth, etc; a kind of imperfect ploughing, every alternate strip only being moved.

ribbing[2] *n* (*colloq*) teasing.

ribbon *n* a fillet of silk, satin, etc; a narrow web of silk, satin, nylon, etc, generally used for an ornament or for fastening; that which resembles a ribbon in some respects; a narrow, thin strip of anything; a shred (*sails torn to ribbons*).

ribbonfish *n* a fish with a lengthened body much flattened on the sides.

ribonucleic acid *n* (abbreviated to **RNA**) any of a group of nucleic acids found in all living cells where they are essential to protein development.

ribwort plantain, ribgrass *n* a common member of the plantain family the pollen of which is a cause of hay fever.

rice *n* a cereal plant with white seeds, often grown in water in warm countries; its seeds used as food.

rice paper *n* a very thin edible paper made from rice; a paper made from the pith of a Chinese shrub.

rice pudding *n* a pudding made of milk and rice, with eggs and sugar.

rich *adj* having abundant material possessions; wealthy, opposed to *poor*; hence, generally, well supplied; abounding; producing ample supplies; productive; fertile; composed of valuable or costly materials or ingredients; sumptuous; highly valued; costly; abounding in nutritive or agreeable qualities; especially, as applied to articles of food and drink, sweet, luscious or highly flavoured; largely gratifying the sense of sight; vivid; bright; agreeable to the sense of hearing; sweet; mellow; abounding in humour; highly provocative of amusement (*a rich joke*).—**the rich** rich people.

riches *n* abundant possessions; wealth; affluence.

richly *adv* in a rich manner; with riches; opulently; abundantly; splendidly; magnificently; highly.

richness *n* the state or quality of being rich; opulence; productiveness; fertility; magnificence; costliness; lusciousness; brilliancy; sweetness.

rick *n* a stack or pile of corn or hay, the lower part generally of a cylindrical form and the top part rounded or conical, and often thatched so as to protect the pile from rain.—*vt* to pile up in ricks.

rickets *n* a disease of children in which there is usually some distortion of the bones, caused by a lack of vitamin D in the diet.

rickety *adj* affected with rickets; feeble or imperfect in general; threatening to fall; shaky; tottering.

rickshaw *n* a small two-wheeled carriage with an adjustable hood or cover, drawn by one or more men and extensively used in Japan, India, etc.

ricochet *n* a rebounding from a flat surface, as of a stone from water or of a shell from the ground.—*vi* (of a stone, bullet, etc) to skip or rebound one or more times from the first hit; to skim, as a stone, along the surface of water.

rid *vt* (*pret, pp* **rid** *or* **ridded**, *ppr* **ridding**) to free; to deliver; to clear; to disencumber (*to rid a person of pain, of a burden*); to make away with; to remove by violence.—*adj* free; clear (*to be rid of trouble*).—**to get rid of** to free oneself from.

riddance *n* the act of ridding; a clearing away; a getting rid of something.

riddle *n* a kind of large sieve with coarse meshes, employed for separating coarser materials from finer.—*vt* (**riddled, riddling**) to pass through or separate with a riddle; to perforate so as to make like a riddle (*a house riddled with shot*); to spread through; to permeate.

riddle *n* a proposition put in obscure or ambiguous terms to puzzle or exercise the ingenuity in discovering its meaning; something to be solved by conjecture; a puzzling question; an enigma; anything ambiguous or puzzling.

ride *vi* (*pret* **rode**, *pp* **ridden**, *ppr* **riding**) to travel or be carried on the back of an animal, as on a horse; to travel or be carried in a vehicle, as in a carriage or wagon; to be borne on or in a fluid (*a ship rides at anchor*); to have ability as an equestrian.—*vt* to sit or be supported on, so as to be carried (*to ride a horse*); to go over in riding (*he rode three miles*); to tyrannize or

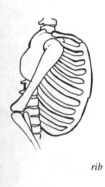

rib

ribbon

domineer over.—*n* an excursion on horseback or in a vehicle; a road cut in a wood or through pleasure ground, for the amusement of riding; a certain district established for excise purposes.

rider *n* one who rides; one who breaks or manages a horse; any addition to a manuscript, roll, record or other document, inserted after its first completion; an additional clause, as to a bill in parliament; a subsidiary problem in mathematics.

ridge *n* a long and narrow elevation on the earth's surface from which the ground slopes on either side; a long crest or summit (*the ridge of a mountain, the ridge of a wave*); a strip of ground thrown up by a plough or left between furrows; a strip of tilled land with a furrow on either side; the highest part of the roof of a building at the meeting of the upper end of the rafters.—*vt* (**ridged, ridging**) to form or make into a ridge; to furnish with a ridge or ridges.

ridged, ridgy *adj* having a ridge or ridges; rising in a ridge.

ridicule *n* expression or action intended to convey contempt and excite laughter; contemptuous mockery or jesting; wit of that kind which provokes contemptuous laughter; that kind of writing which excites contempt with laughter.—*vt* (**ridiculed, ridiculing**) to treat with ridicule; to mock; to make sport or game of; to deride.

ridiculous *adj* worthy of or fitted to excite ridicule; laughable and contemptible.

riding *n* one of the three districts (North, East and West Ridings) into which the county of York, in England, was formerly divided.

riding school *n* a place where the art of riding is taught.

rife *adj* prevailing; prevalent; abundant; common; supplied or filled with in large numbers or great quantity; abounding in; replete.

riff-raff *n* sweepings; refuse of anything; the rabble; disreputable people.

rifle[1] *n* a gun the inside of whose barrel is grooved or formed with spiral channels; (*pl*) a body of troops armed with rifles.—*vt* (**rifled, rifling**) to groove; to channel.

rifle[2] *vt* (**rifled, rifling**) to steal; to search through; to snatch away; to plunder.

rifleman *n* (*pl* **riflemen**) a soldier armed with a rifle; a private in a rifle regiment.

rift *n* a cleft; a fissure; an opening made by riving or splitting.—*vt* to cleave; to rive; to split.—*vi* to burst open; to split.

rift valley a narrow valley caused by land subsiding between two parallel faults.

rig *vt* (**rigged, rigging**) to dress; (*colloq*) to clothe (generally with *out*); to furnish with apparatus or tackling; to set up in working order; (*naut*) to equip with sails and tackle; to manipulate fraudulently.—*n*

dress, usually fanciful; (*naut*) the particular style of the masts, sails and rigging of any vessel.

rigger *n* one who rigs; one whose occupation is to fit the rigging of a ship.

rigging *n* the ropes which support the masts, extend and contract the sails, etc, of a ship.

right *adj* in conformity with the rules which ought to regulate human action; in accordance with duty, truth and justice or morality; not wrong; just; equitable; fit; suitable; proper (*the right man in the right place*); real; true; not spurious (*the right heir*); not erroneous; according to fact or reality; not mistaken or wrong; not in error; not left but its opposite; originally, no doubt, most useful or dextrous (*the right hand*); hence, being on the same side as the right hand (*the right ear* or *eye*); most favourable or convenient; opportune; properly done, made, placed, disposed or adjusted; correct; to be placed or worn outward (*the right side of cloth*); straight; not crooked (*a right line*); hence, (*math*) rising perpendicularly; having a perpendicular axis (*a right cone*); formed by one line or direction perpendicular to another (*a right angle*); politically conservative; rightwing.—*adv* in a right manner; justly; properly; correctly; in a great degree; very (*right well*), used especially in titles, as *right honourable, right reverend, right noble*; in a straight line; directly.—*n* what is right; the opposite of wrong; rectitude; a just claim (*a right to fair play*); legal or other claim or title; a prerogative; privilege belonging to one as member of a state, society or community (*natural, political, public rights*); that which justly belongs to one; power of action; authority; legal power (*a right to arrest malefactors*); the side opposite to the left (*on the right*); the conservative section of a political party, etc.—**in one's own right** by absolute right (*peeresses in their own right*, that is, as opposed to peeresses by marriage).—*vt* to put right; to restore to the natural or proper condition; to make correct from being wrong; to do justice to; to relieve from wrong.—*vi* to resume a vertical position, as a ship in the water after having been listed over.

right-about *adv* in an opposite direction (used substantively in the phrase *to send to the right-about*, to pack off); to dismiss; to cause to retreat.

right angle *n* an angle of 90°.

right-angled *adj* containing a right angle or right angles.

right ascension *n* (of the sun or of a star) the arc of the equator intercepted between the first point of Aries and that point of the equator which comes to the meridian at the same instant with the star.

rider

rifle

righteous *adj* upright; virtuous; acting in accordance with the dictates of religion or morality; free from guilt or sin; agreeing with right; just; equitable.

righteousness *n* the quality of being righteous; (*theol*) the state of being right with God; justification.

rightful *adj* having a right or just claim according to established laws (*the rightful heir*); being by right or by just claim (*one's rightful property*); just; consonant to justice (*a rightful cause*).

right-hand *adj* situated on the right hand or in a direction from the right side; applied to one who is essential to another (*our right-hand man*).

right-handed *adj* using the right hand more easily and readily than the left.

rightly *adv* according to right or justice; properly; fitly; suitably; according to truth or fact; not erroneously; correctly.

right-minded *adj* having a right or honest mind; well-disposed.

rightness *n* the state or quality of being right; correctness; rectitude.

right of way *n* (*pl* **rights of way**) the right of passing over land not one's own; the right of the public to a road or path over a certain piece of ground.

ring

right whale *n* the common or Greenland whale, from whose mouth whalebone is obtained.

right-wing *adj* of or relating to the conservative section of a political party, etc.

rigid *adj* stiff; stiffened; not pliant; not easily bent; (*physics*) theoretically such as to resist change of form when acted on by any force; strict in opinion, practice or discipline; severe in temper, opposed to *lax* or *indulgent*; inflexible; unmitigated; severely just (*a rigid law* or *rule*).

rigidity *n* the quality of being rigid.

rigmarole *n* a succession of confused or disjointed statements; an incoherent harangue; balderdash.

rigor *n* (*med*) a sudden coldness, attended by a shivering more or less perfect, a symptom which ushers in many diseases.

rigor mortis *n* the stiffening of the body after death.

rigorous *adj* characterized by rigour; severe; stringent; scrupulously accurate; very cold (*rigorous weather*).

rigour *n* rigidity; severity of life; austerity; strictness; exactness without allowance, latitude or indulgence (*to enforce moral duties with rigour*); sternness; harshness; intensity of atmospheric cold (*the rigour of winter*); (*med*) rigor.

rile *vt* (**riled, riling**) to stir to anger; to irritate.

rill *n* a small brook; a rivulet; a little stream.

rim *n* the border, edge or margin of a thing; a brim.

rime *n* white or hoar frost; congealed dew or vapour.

rimy *adj* abounding with rime; frosty.

rind *n* the outward coat or covering of trees, fruits, animals, etc; bark; peel; husk; skin.

rinderpest *n* a virulent and highly contagious disease or plague, affecting ruminant animals, especially cattle.

rinforzando *adj, adv* (*mus*) strengthening the power and emphasis.

ring¹ *n* anything in the form of a circular line or hoop; a circle of gold or other material worn on the fingers; a hoop of metal or other material used for a great variety of purposes; an area in which games or sports are performed; the arena of a hippodrome or circus; the enclosure in which pugilists fight; a space in which horses are exhibited or exercised; a circular group of persons; a combination of persons for a selfish end, as for controlling the market in stocks.—**the ring** the prize ring, a term given to pugilism or those connected with pugilism.—*vt* to encircle; to surround with a ring or as with a ring; to make a cutting circularly round (a tree or branch).

ring² *vt* (*pret* **rang** or **rung**, *pp* **rung**, *ppr* **ringing**) to cause to sound, as a sonorous metallic body (*to ring a bell*); to repeat often, loudly or earnestly; to sound (*to ring one's praises*); to attend on or celebrate by ringing.—**ring up** to get into communication with by telephone.—*vi* to sound, as a bell or other sonorous body; to resound; to have the sensation of sound continued; to tingle; to be filled with report or talk (*the whole town rings with his fame*).—*n* the sound of a bell or other sonorous body; any loud sound continued, repeated or reverberated; characteristic sound; a chime.

ringbolt *n* a bolt with an eye in the head through which a ring is fitted.

ring course *n* the outer course of stone or brick in an arch.

ringdove *n* a species of pigeon so called from a circular marking on the neck.

ringer *n* one who rings; one who rings chimes on bells; a person or thing that closely resembles another; a horse entered in a race under a false name, weight, etc.

ring finger *n* the third finger of the left hand, on which the ring is placed in marriage.

ringleader *n* one who leads a ring, as of dancers; the leader of any association of persons engaged in violation of law or an illegal enterprise.

ringlet *n* a curl; particularly, a curl of hair.

ringmaster *n* one who has charge of the performances in a circus ring.

ring-ouzel *n* a British thrush resembling the blackbird but with a white ring or bar on the breast.

ring-pull *n* a metal ring on the top of a tin

which is pulled back to break the metal seal attached to it and open the tin.

ring road *n* a road encircling a town or city or its inner part, allowing motorists to avoid the town or city centre.

ringtail *n* the female of the hen-harrier; a sort of studding sail set outside a spanker or a sloop's mainsail.

ringworm *n* a contagious skin disease appearing in the form of rings or patches on different parts of the body but most frequently on the scalp.

rink *n* that portion of a sheet of ice on which the game of curling is played; the players that make up a side at the games of curling and bowling; a smooth flooring, generally under cover, on which people skate with ordinary or roller skates.

rinse *vt* (**rinsed, rinsing**) to wash lightly; to wash in water to remove soap, etc; to cleanse the inner surface of by the introduction of water or other liquid.

riot *n* an uproar; a tumult; excessive and expensive feasting; wild and loose festivity; revelry; (*law*) a tumultuous disturbance of the peace.—*vi* to revel; to act in an unrestrained or wanton manner; to raise a riot, uproar or sedition.

rioter *n* one who riots or engages in a riot.

riotous *adj* indulging in riot or revelry; tumultuous; guilty of riot.

rip[1] *vt* (**ripped, ripping**) to separate or divide the parts of by cutting or tearing; to tear or cut open; to take out by cutting or tearing.—**to rip off** (*colloq*) to cheat (someone); to swindle (someone); to exploit (someone) financially; to plagiarize.—*n* a rent, a tear.

rip[2] *n* a stretch of broken water caused by currents and tides.

riparian *adj* pertaining to the bank of a river.

ripe *adj* ready for reaping; brought to perfection in growth or to the best state; mature; advanced to the state of being fit for use; fully developed; maturated; complete; finished; consummate (*a ripe scholar*); ready for action or effect (*ripe for a war*).

ripen *vi* to grow ripe; to be matured, as grain or fruit; to approach or come to perfection.—*vt* to mature; to make ripe.

rip-off *n* (*colloq*) a swindle; exploitation; the act of, or instance of, taking financial advantage of; plagiarization.

riposte *n* (in fencing) the thrust or blow with which one follows up a successful parry; hence, a smart reply or repartee.

ripple *vi* (**rippled, rippling**) to assume or wear a ruffled surface, as water when agitated or running over a rough bottom; to make a sound as of water running over a rough bottom.—*vt* to fret or dimple as the surface of water.—*n* the fretting or ruffling of the surface of water; little curling waves; a sound like that of water flowing in ripples (*a ripple of laughter*).

ripsaw *n* a saw used for cutting wood in the direction of the fibre.

rise *vi* (*pret* **rose**, *pp* **risen**, *ppr* **rising**) to move or pass from a lower position to a higher; to move upwards; to ascend; to mount up; to change from a sitting, lying or kneeling posture to a standing one; to become erect; to bring a sitting or a session to an end (*the house rose at 11 p.m.*); to get out of bed; to arise; to attain a height; to stand in height (*a tree rises to 60 feet*); to reach a higher level by increase of bulk or quantity (*the tide rises*); to swell or puff up in the process of fermentation, as dough, etc; to slope upwards; to have an upward direction; to seem to mount up; to appear above the horizon, as the sun, moon, stars, etc; to become apparent; to come forth; to appear (*an eruption rises on the skin*); to become audible (*there rose a shout*); to come into existence; to be produced; to spring; to increase in force, value, intensity, degree, etc (*the wind rises, a price rises*); to take up arms; to go to war; to rebel or revolt; to attain a higher social position or rank; to increase in power or interest (said of style, thought or discourse).—*n* the act of rising; ascent; the distance through which anything rises; elevation or degree of ascent (*a gradual rise in the land*); spring; source; origin; beginning; appearance above the horizon (*the rise of the sun*); increase; advance (*a rise in the price of wheat*); advance in rank, honour, property or fame.

riser *n* one who or that which rises; the vertical face of a step of a stair; a vertical pipe for carrying, air, etc, inside a building.

risible *adj* having the faculty or power of laughing; capable of exciting laughter; laughable; belonging to the phenomenon of laughter.

rising *adj* increasing in wealth, power or distinction (*a rising man*); advancing to adult years (*the rising generation*).—*n* the act of one who or that which rises; the appearance of the sun or a star above the horizon; the act of reviving from the dead; resurrection; an insurrection; a mutiny; an eminence or prominence.

risk *n* hazard; danger; peril; exposure to harm; (*com*) the hazard of loss, either of ship, goods or other property.—*vt* to hazard; to expose to injury or loss; to venture; to dare to undertake.

risky *adj* dangerous; hazardous; full of risk.

risqué *adj* verging on indecency.

rissole *n* a ball or cake of minced meat or fish mixed with yolk of egg, potato, etc, rolled in bread crumbs and fried.

ritardando *adv* (*mus*) retarding; a direction to sing or play slower and slower.

rite *n* a formal act of religion or other solemn duty; a religious ceremony or usage; ceremonial.

ritual *adj* pertaining to rites; consisting of rites; prescribing rites (*the ritual law*).—*n* a book containing the rites or ordinances of a church or of any special service; the manner of performing divine service; ceremonial.

ritualism *n* the system of rituals or prescribed forms of religious worship; observance of prescribed forms in religion; an excessive use of external forms in religion.

ritualistic *adj* of, pertaining to or favouring ritual or ritualism.

rival *n* one who is in pursuit of the same object as another; one striving to reach or obtain something which another is attempting to obtain and which one only can possess; a competitor; one who emulates or strives to equal or exceed another in excellence.—*adj* having the same pretensions or claims; standing in competition for superiority.—*vt* (**rivalled, rivalling**) to stand in competition with; to strive to equal or excel; to emulate.

rivalry *n* the act of rivalling; competition; a strife or effort to obtain an object which another is pursuing; emulation.

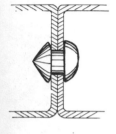

rivet

rive *vt* (*pret* **rived**, *pp* **rived** *or* **riven**, *ppr* **riving**) to split; to cleave; to rend asunder by force.—*vi* to be split or rent asunder.

river *n* a large stream of water flowing through a certain portion of the earth's surface and discharging itself into the sea, a lake, a marsh or into another such stream.

river basin *n* the region drained by all the rills, rivulets, streams or rivers which ultimately gather to form one river.

riverbed *n* the bed or bottom of a river.

rivet *n* a short metallic pin or bolt passing through a hole and keeping two pieces of metal (or sometimes other substances) together; especially, a short bolt or pin of wrought iron formed with a head and inserted into a hole at the junction of two pieces of metal, the point after insertion being hammered broad so as to keep the pieces closely bound together.—*vt* to fasten with a rivet or with rivets; to clinch; (*fig*) to fasten firmly; to make firm, strong or immovable; to engross the attention of; to fix one's eyes immovably on.

riveter *n* one who rivets.

rivulet *n* a small stream or brook; a rill.

RNA an abbreviation of **ribonucleic acid**.

roach[1] *n* a fish of the carp family, inhabiting lakes, ponds and slow-running rivers.

roach[2] *n* the curve in the foot of a sail.

road *n* an open way or public passage; a piece of ground appropriated for travel, forming a line of communication between one city, town or place and another for foot

roast

passengers, cattle, vehicles, etc; generally applied to highways, and as a generic term it includes highway, street, lane, etc; a means or way of approach or access; a path; a place where ships may ride at anchor at some distance from the shore, a roadstead (usually in the plural).

road hog *n* a reckless and selfish motorist.

road metal *n* broken stones used for macadamizing roads.

roadstead *n* a place where ships may ride at anchor off the shore.

roadway *n* a highway; the part of a road used by horses, carriages, etc.

roam *vi* to wander; to ramble; to rove; to walk or move about from place to place without any certain purpose or direction.—*vt* to range; to wander over.

roan *adj* applied formerly to a horse of a bay, sorrel or dark colour, with numerous spots of grey or white; now generally applied to a colour having a decided shade of red.—*n* a leather used largely in bookbinding to imitate morocco, prepared from sheepskin; a horse of a roan colour; a roan colour.

roar *vi* to cry with a full, loud, continued sound; to bellow, as a beast; to cry aloud, as in distress or anger; to make a loud, continued, confused sound, as winds, waves, a multitude of people shouting together, etc; to laugh out loudly and continuously.—*vt* to cry out aloud; to shout.—*n* a full loud sound of some continuance; the strong loud cry of a beast; the loud cry of a person in distress, pain, anger; a loud, continued, confused sound; outcry of joy or mirth.

roarer *n* one who or that which roars; a broken-winded horse.

roaring *n* a loud cry, as of a beast; a continuous roar; loud continued sound, as of the billows of the sea; a disease of the bronchial tubes in horses.—*adj* characterized by roars or noise; disorderly; riotous; brisk; flourishing.

roast *vt* to cook or prepare for the table by exposure to the direct action of heat, on a spit, in an oven, etc; to heat to excess; to dry and parch by exposure to heat; (in metallurgy) to burn in a heap, as broken ore, in order to free it from foreign matters; (*colloq*) to banter severely.—*vi* to become roasted or fit for eating by exposure to fire.—*n* that which is roasted, as a piece of beef; part of a slaughtered animal selected for roasting.—*adj* roasted (*roast beef*).

rob *vt* (**robbed, robbing**) to plunder or strip by force or violence; to deprive of something by stealing; to deprive unlawfully; to deprive (*to rob a person of his peace of mind*).

robber *n* one who robs; one who commits a robbery.

robbery *n* the act or practice of robbing; a taking away by violence or wrong; the forcible and felonious taking of something from the person of another.

robbin *n* (*naut*) a short flat plaited piece of rope, with an eye in one end, used in pairs to tie square sails to their yards.

robe *n* a kind of gown or long loose garment worn over other dress; a gown or dress of a rich, flowing or elegant style or make; a dressed buffalo (or bison) skin with the hair on.—*vt* (**robed, robing**) to clothe in a robe; to attire; to invest.

robing room *n* a room where robes of ceremony are put on and off.

robin *n* the well-known European bird called also redbreast and robin-redbreast; in America, a species of thrush with a red breast.

robot *n* any mechanical contrivance designed to perform work normally requiring the exercise of human intelligence; a machine in the shape of a person; a mechanism guided by automatic controls; a person who acts mechanically, an automaton.

robust *adj* possessed of or indicating great strength; strong; lusty; sinewy; muscular; vigorous.

robustness *n* the quality of being robust; strength; vigour.

roc *n* a monstrous bird of Arabian mythology.

rochet *n* a sort of short surplice, with tight sleeves and open at the sides, worn by bishops.

rock[1] *n* a large mass of stony matter; a large fixed stone or crag; the stony matter constituting the earth's crust, as distinguished from soil, mud, sand, gravel, clay, peat; (*geol*) any natural deposit or portion of the earth's crust, whatever be its hardness or softness; (*fig*) defence, means of safety; asylum; a cause or source of peril or disaster; a name for a kind of solid sweetmeat.

rock[2] *vt* to move backwards and forwards, as a body resting on a support beneath; to cause to reel or totter; to make to sway; to move backwards and forwards in a cradle, chair, etc; to lull; to quiet, as if by rocking in a cradle.—*vi* to be moved backwards and forwards; to reel.—*n* a rocking motion; rock-and-roll; a form of popular music which has developed from rock-and-roll.

rock[3] *n* a distaff used in spinning.

rock-and-roll *n* a form of popular music originating during the 1950s, characterized by a strong beat and repetitious melody and rhythm, which incorporates country and blues elements.

rock cork *n* mountain cork, a white or grey-coloured variety of asbestos.

rock crystal *n* crystallized quartz, found both colourless and of various gradations of colour, as yellowish white, amber, purple, etc.

rocker *n* one who rocks anything, as a cradle; the curving piece of wood on which a cradle or rocking chair rocks; a rocking horse; a cradle or trough for washing ore by agitation.

rockery *n* an artificial mound formed of fragments of rock, earth, etc, for plants, as ferns.

rocket *n* a structure shaped like a cylinder which moves by expelling burning gases, such as a firework, a distress signal or the propulsion mechanism of a spacecraft; (*colloq*) a severe reprimand.—*vi* to move like a rocket.

rocking chair *n* an armchair mounted on rockers.

rocking horse *n* a wooden horse mounted on rockers; a hobby-horse.

rocking stone *n* a large block of stone poised (usually by natural causes) so finely on the point of a rock that a moderate force applied to it causes it to rock or oscillate.

rock-'n-roll *n* same as **rock-and-roll**.

rock oil *n* petroleum.

rock pigeon *n* a species of pigeon that builds its nest in rocks.

rockrose *n* a plant or shrub with rose-like white, yellow or reddish flowers.

rock salt *n* mineral salt; common salt found in masses or beds in the new red sandstone.

rocky *adj* full of rocks; hard; stony; shaky; unstable.

rococo *n* an architectural style of the time of Louis XIV and XV, characterized by elaborate ornamentation.—*adj* in the style of rococo.

rod *n* a shoot or slender stem of any woody plant; a wand; a straight slender stick; hence, an instrument of punishment or correction; a means of chastisement; a kind of sceptre or badge of office; a fishing rod; an instrument for measuring; an enchanter's wand; a measure of length, often termed a *pole* or *perch*.

rodent *adj* gnawing; belonging or pertaining to the order of gnawing animals.—*n* an animal of an order of mammals, including the squirrel, rat, mouse, hare, rabbit, beaver, etc, characterized by a single pair of chisel-like cutting teeth in each jaw, between which and the grinding teeth there is a wide gap.

rodeo *n* a public exhibition of horse-breaking, lariat-throwing, etc.

rodomontade *n* vain boasting; empty bluster or vaunting; rant.—*adj* boasting; blustering.

roe[1] *n* a roebuck; the female of the hart.

roe[2] *n* the sperm or spawn of fishes; the roe of the male being called soft roe or milt,

rocket

rodent

that of the female hard roe or spawn.

roebuck, roedeer *n* a species of European deer with erect cylindrical branched horns.

roentgen, röntgen *n* the unit of measuring X-rays or gamma rays.

Roentgen ray, Röntgen ray *n* an old name for **X-ray**.

rogation *n* a supplication; a litany.

rogue *n* a dishonest person; a rascal; a mischievous person; a solitary and savage elephant.

roguery *n* knavish tricks; dishonest practices; rascality; arch tricks; mischievousness.

roguish *adj* knavish; fraudulent; dishonest; waggish; wanton; slightly mischievous.

roil *vt* to render turbid by stirring up the dregs or sediment.

roister *vi* to bluster; to swagger; to be noisy, vaunting or turbulent.

roisterer *n* one who roisters; a blustering or turbulent fellow.

role *n* a play or character represented by a stage-player; any conspicuous part or function performed by any one, as a leading public character; a person's job or function.

role-playing *n* the playing of imaginary parts, especially for educational or therapeutic purposes.; the practice of always behaving like a stereotype, for example men only having jobs and hobbies traditionally associated with the male sex.

role-playing game a game in which players assume the roles of imaginary characters who take part in adventures.

roll *vt* to cause to revolve by turning over and over; to drive onward by turning on itself; to move in a circular direction; to whirl or wheel (*to roll the eyes*); to turn about, as in one's mind; to revolve; to wrap round on itself by turning; to bind or involve in a bandage, etc; to enwrap; to press or level with a roller.—*vi* to move along a surface by revolving; to turn over and over; to rotate; to run on wheels; to move circularly; to be tossed about; to move, as waves or billows, with alternate swells and depressions; to tumble or fall over and over; to wallow; to sound with a deep prolonged sound.—**to roll up** to form into a roll or bundle; (*colloq*) to arrive or gather round.—*n* the act of rolling; something made or formed by rolling; that which is rolled up; a scroll; an official document; a list of the names of persons, as of students or soldiers; a register; a catalogue; a quantity of cloth or paper wound up in a cylindrical form; a small piece of dough rolled up into a cake before baking; a bread roll; the beating of a drum with strokes so rapid as to produce a continued sound; a prolonged deep sound.

roll call *n* the act of calling over a list of

roller skate

rolling pin

names, as of men who compose a military body.

roller *n* one who or that which rolls; a cylinder which turns on its axis, used for various purposes, as smoothing, crushing, spreading out, etc, in agriculture, gardening, roadmaking, etc; that on which something may be rolled up; that on which a body can be rolled or moved along; a bandage; a long broad bandage used in surgery; a long, heavy, swelling wave, such as is seen setting in on a coast after the subsiding of a storm; a bird of the crow family; a variety of canary.

roller coaster *n* an elevated open-car railway with sharp turns and steep slopes ridden for amusement in fairgrounds.

roller skate *n* a skate mounted on small wheels or rollers and used for skating on asphalt or other smooth flooring.

rollick *vi* to move in a careless, swaggering manner; to be jovial in behaviour.

rolling *adj* revolving; making a continuous noise; undulating; rising and falling in gentle slopes (*the rolling land of the prairies*).

rolling pin *n* a round piece of wood with which dough or paste is reduced to a proper thickness.

rolling stock *n* the carriages, vans, locomotive engines, etc, of a railway.

roll-on roll-off *adj* pertaining to a cargo ship or passenger ferry designed so that vehicles can be driven straight on and off.

rolltop desk *n* a desk with a cover made of connected slats, which runs into a recess at the top when the desk is opened.

roly-poly *n* a sheet of paste spread with jam and rolled into a pudding; (*colloq*) a small plump person.

ROM an abbreviation of **read-only memory**.

Roman *adj* pertaining to or resembling Rome or the Roman people; pertaining to or professing the Roman Catholic religion; applied to the common upright letter in printing, as distinguished from italic, and to numerals expressed by letters and not in the Arabic characters.—*n* a native or citizen of Rome; one enjoying the privileges of a Roman citizen.

Roman candle *n* a kind of firework, consisting of a tube which discharges upwards a stream of white or coloured stars.

Roman Catholic *adj* of or pertaining to that branch of the Christian Church of which the pope is the head.—*n* a member of the Roman Catholic Church.

Roman Catholic Church *n* the branch of the Christian Church of which the pope or bishop of Rome is the head.

Roman Catholicism *n* the principles, doctrines, rules, etc, of the Roman Catholic Church.

romance *n* originally, a tale in verse, written in one of the Romance dialects; hence, any popular epic or any fictitious and wonderful tale in prose or verse; a kind of novel dealing with extraordinary and often extravagant adventures or picturing an almost purely imaginary state or society; a love story; tendency of mind towards the wonderful and mysterious; romantic notions; something belonging rather to fiction than to everyday life; a fiction; a love affair.—*vi* (**romanced, romancing**) to devise and tell fictitious stories; to deal in extravagant stories.

Romance *adj* a term applied to the languages which arose in the south and west of Europe, based on the Latin as spoken in the provinces and including Italian, French, Provençal, Spanish, Portuguese and Romanian.—*n* the Romance languages.

roman cement *n* a dark-coloured hydraulic cement, which hardens very quickly and is very durable.

Romanesque *n* the style of architecture and ornament that prevailed in the later Roman Empire.—*adj* belonging to this style.

Roman law *n* the civil law; the system of jurisprudence finally elaborated in the ancient Roman Empire.

Romansch *n* a dialect based on Latin, spoken in Switzerland.

romantic *adj* pertaining to romance or romances; partaking of romance or the marvellous; fanciful, imaginative or ideal; extravagant; chimerical; not belonging to real life; wildly picturesque; having striking natural features; full of wild or fantastic scenery.

romanticism *n* the state or quality of being romantic; a reaction in literature or art from classical to medieval or modern forms; romantic feeling.

romanticist *n* one imbued with romanticism.

Romany *n* a gypsy; the language spoken by the gypsies.

romp *vi* to play boisterously; to leap and frisk about in play.—**to romp home** to win easily.—*n* a noisy game; a frolic.

rondeau *n* (*pl* **rondeaux**) a poem, commonly consisting of thirteen lines, of which eight have one rhyme and five another, and divided into three strophes, at the end of the second and third the beginning of the rondeau being repeated.

rondo *n* (*pl* **rondos**) a musical form of three strains with a leading theme to which return is made.

röntgen *n* same as **roentgen**.

Röntgen ray *n* same as **Roentgen ray**.

rood *n* a square measure, the fourth part of a statute acre, equal to 1210 square yards; a measure of $5\frac{1}{2}$ yards in length; a rod, pole or perch; also, a square pole or $272\frac{1}{4}$ square feet, used in estimating mason work; a cross or crucifix; a large crucifix placed at the entrance to the chancel, often supported on the rood beam or rood screen.

rood loft *n* a gallery over the rood screen in a church where the rood was placed.

rood screen *n* a screen or ornamental partition separating the choir of a church from the nave.

roof *n* the cover of any house or building irrespective of the materials of which it is composed; that which corresponds with or resembles the covering of a house, as the arch or top of a vault, a furnace, the top of a carriage, etc; a canopy; the palate; a house.—*vt* to cover with a roof; to enclose in a house; to shelter.

roofing *n* the act of covering with a roof; the materials of which a roof is composed; the roof itself.

roofless *adj* having no roof; having no house or home; unsheltered.

rooftree *n* a main beam in a roof.

rook[1] *n* a bird resembling the crow but differing from it in not feeding on carrion but on insects and grain, also in having the root of the bill bare of feathers; a cheat; a rapacious person.—*vti* to cheat; to defraud.

rook[2] *n* (in chess) one of the four pieces placed on the corner squares of the board; also called a **castle**.

rookery *n* a wood used for nesting places by rooks; the rooks belonging to a rookery; a breeding place of seabirds; a close assemblage of poor mean dwellings inhabited by the lowest class; a resort of thieves, etc.

room *n* space; compass; extent of place, great or small; space or place unoccupied or unobstructed; adequate space; fit occasion; opportunity; place or station once occupied by another; stead; an apartment in a house; any division separated from the rest by a partition; particular place or station; (*pl*) lodgings.—*vi* to lodge.

roomful *n* as much or as many as a room will hold.

roominess *n* state of being roomy; spaciousness.

roomy *adj* having ample room; spacious.

roost[1] *n* the pole or other support on which fowls rest at night; a collection of fowls roosting together.—*vi* to occupy a roost; to lodge; to settle.

roost[2] *n* the tidal race in the Orkney and Shetland Islands.

rooster *n* the male of the domestic fowl; a cock.

root[1] *n* that part of a plant which fixes itself in the earth and by means of its radicles imbibe nutriment; a bulb, tuber or similar part of a plant; that which resembles a root

roof

rook

in position or function; the part of anything that resembles the root of a plant (*the root of a tooth*); foundation or base; the origin or cause of anything; that part of a word which conveys its essential meaning, as distinguished from the formative parts by which this meaning is modified; an ultimate form or element from which words are derived or regarded as having arisen; (*math*) the root of any quantity is such a quantity as, when multiplied into itself a certain number of times, will exactly produce that quantity.—*vi* to fix the root; to be firmly fixed; to be established.—*vt* to fix by the root; to plant and fix deep in the earth; to plant deeply; to impress deeply and durably (*principles rooted in the mind*).

root² *vt* to dig or burrow in with the snout; to turn up with the snout, as a swine; to tear up or out as if by rooting; to remove or destroy utterly; to exterminate (generally with *up*, *out*, *away*, etc).—*vi* to turn up the earth with the snout, as swine.

root crop *n* a crop of plants with esculent roots, as turnips, beets, etc.

rooted *adj* having roots; firmly fixed; fixed in the heart (*a rooted antipathy*).

rope *n* a general name applied to cordage over 1 inch in circumference; a row or string consisting of a number of things united (*a rope of onions*).—*vi* (**roped, roping**) to be formed into filaments from any glutinous or adhesive quality.—*vt* to fasten or tie with a rope or ropes; to pull by a rope.

rope

rope dancer *n* one who dances or performs acrobatic feats on a rope extended at a greater or less height above the ground.

rope ladder *n* a ladder made of ropes.

rope walk *n* a long covered walk or a long building where ropes are manufactured.

rope yarn *n* yarn for ropes, consisting of a single thread which is twisted into strands.

ropy *adj* having such consistence that it may be drawn into viscous filaments; stringy; glutinous; (*colloq*) not good; (*colloq*) not well.

roric *adj* pertaining to or resembling dew; dewy.

roriferous *adj* generating or producing dew.

rorqual *n* a large whale of several species with dorsal fins and deep furrows on the skin of the throat and chest.

rosary *n* a chaplet; a garland; formerly often adopted as a title of books, consisting of pieces culled from various authors; a string of beads used by Roman Catholics, on which they count their prayers, there being so many small beads each for an Ave Maria and so many large ones each for a Paternoster.

rose *n* a common and universally cultivated plant and flower of many species and vari-

rose

eties, found in almost every country of the northern hemisphere, both in the Old and the New World; a knot of ribbon in the form of a rose, used as an ornament; a perforated nozzle of a pipe, spout, etc, to distribute water in fine shower-like jets; a popular name of the disease erysipelas (from its colour); a circular card or disc or diagram with radiating lines, as the compass card.—**under the rose** in secret; privately; in a manner that forbids disclosure.

rosé *n* a pink wine made from skinless red grapes or by mixing white and red wine.

roseate *adj* full of roses; of a rose colour; blooming.

rosebud *n* the bud of a rose; the flower of the rose just appearing.

rose carnation *n* a carnation the ground colour of whose petals is striped with rose colour.

rose-coloured *adj* rosy; overly optimistic.

rose diamond *n* a diamond nearly hemispherical, cut with twenty-four triangular faces round a hexagonal centre.

rosehip *n* the small round fruit of the rose plant.

rosemary *n* an evergreen shrub having a fragrant smell and a warm, pungent, bitterish taste and yielding by distillation a light, pale, essential oil of great fragrance.

roseola *n* (*med*) a kind of rose-coloured rash occurring in connection with different complaints, including measles.

rose quartz *n* a variety of quartz which is rose-red.

rosery *n* a place where roses grow; a nursery of rose bushes.

rosette *n* an imitation of a rose, as by ribbon, used as an ornament or badge; (*archit*) a flower ornament of frequent use in decorations and in all styles.

rose water *n* water tinctured with roses by distillation.

rose window *n* (*archit*) a circular window divided into compartments by mullions or tracery radiating or branching from a centre.

rosewood *n* the wood of South American trees, so named because when freshly cut it has a faint agreeable smell of roses, in the highest esteem for cabinet-work.

Rosicrucian *n* one of a secret sect or society said to have originated in the fourteenth century, whose members made great pretensions to a knowledge of the secrets of nature and especially as to the transmutation of metals, the prolongation of life, etc—*adj* pertaining to the Rosicrucians or their arts.

Rosicrucianism *n* the arts, practices or doctrines of the Rosicrucians.

rosin *n* the name given to resin when it is employed in a solid state for ordinary purposes.—*vt* to rub or cover over with rosin.

rosiness *n* the quality of being rosy or of resembling the colour of the rose.

roster *n* a list showing the rotation of those who relieve or succeed each other; a military list showing the rotation in which individuals, companies, regiments, etc, are called on to serve.

rostrate *adj* having a beak; beak-shaped; having a process resembling the beak of a bird.

rostrum *n* (*pl* **rostra, rostrums**) the beak or bill of a bird or other animal; the beak of a ship, especially of an ancient war galley; an elevated place in the forum at Rome where orations, funeral harangues, etc, were delivered (so called because adorned with the rostra of captured ships); hence, a platform from which any speaker addresses an audience.

rosy *n* resembling a rose in colour; blushing; blooming; (*fig*) very alluring or hopeful (*rosy prospects*).

rot *vi* (**rotted, rotting**) to decompose; to become putrid; to go to decay.—*vt* to make putrid; to cause to decompose; to expose to a process of partial rotting, as flax; to ret; used in the imperative as a sort of imprecation (*rot it*).—*n* putrefaction; a fatal distemper in sheep, caused by the liver fluke; a disease of the potato; (*colloq*) nonsense; (*colloq*) rubbish; (in cricket) sudden collapse of the batting side.

rota *n* an ecclesiastical court of Rome, composed of twelve prelates; a turn in succession; a list or roster of duties.

Rotarian *n* a member of a Rotary Club.

rotary *adj* turning, as a wheel on its axis; pertaining to rotation; rotatory.

Rotary Club *n* a club belonging to an international organization of business people for promoting community service.

rotate *vi* (**rotated, rotating**) to revolve or move round a centre; to turn round as a wheel; to act in turn or rotation.—*vt* to cause to turn round like a wheel.

rotation *n* the act of rotating or turning; the motion of a solid body, as a wheel or sphere, about an axis; a return or succession in a series; established succession; the course in which persons leave their places or duties at certain times and are succeeded by others; a recurring series of different crops grown on the same ground; the order of recurrence in cropping.

rotatory *adj* pertaining to or consisting in rotation; exhibiting rotation; rotary.

rote *n* repetition of words or sounds without attending to the meaning; mere effort of memory.—**by rote** by memory merely, without intelligence.

rotifer *n* any of a class of animalcules, which, through the microscope, appear like revolving wheels, whence they have been called wheel animalcules.

rotisserie *n* a rotating spit on which poultry is roasted; a place where such food is prepared.

rotor *n* the revolving part of an electric generator or motor.

rotten *adj* putrid; decaying; decomposed by the natural process of decay; unsound; defective in principle; corrupt; fetid; ill-smelling; (*colloq*) nasty; (*colloq*) not well.

rotten borough *n* a name given to certain boroughs in England before the reform of 1832, which had fallen into decay and had a mere handful of voters but which still retained the privilege of sending Members to Parliament.

rottenness *n* state of being rotten; putrefaction; unsoundness.

rotten stone *n* a soft stone much used for polishing household articles of brass or other metal, derived from the decomposition of siliceous limestone.

rotter *n* a worthless person; a waster.

Rottweiler *n* a breed of tall, strongly built, black and tan dog with a short coat, originating in Germany.

rotund *adj* round; spherical; globular; (*bot*) circumscribed by one unbroken curve or without angles.

rotunda *n* a round building; any building that is round both on the outside and inside.

rotundity *n* sphericity; circularity.

rouble *n* the unit of the Russian money system divided into 100 kopecks.

roué *n* a person devoted to a life of pleasure and sensuality; a rake.

rouge *n* a red or pink cosmetic for colouring the cheeks; a powder of a scarlet colour used for polishing gold, silver, etc.—*vi* (**rouged, rouging**) to paint the face or rather the cheeks, with rouge.—*vt* to paint or tinge with rouge.

rouge-et-noir *n* a game at cards played between a 'banker' and an unlimited number of persons, at a table marked with four spots of a diamond shape, two coloured black and two red.

rough *adj* having prominences or inequalities; not smooth; having many irregularities of surface; harsh to the feel; unfinished; unpolished; shaggy; ragged; coarse; swelling into billows or breakers; stormy, as the sea or weather; not mild or gentle in character; boisterous; untamed; not mild or courteous; rude and brusque; harsh; severe; cruel; not refined or delicate; astringent; sour; harsh to the ear; grating; inharmonious; vague; crude (*a rough guess*); (*colloq*) difficult, unpleasant.—*vt* to give a rough appearance to; to make rough; to break in, as a horse; to shape out roughly, as a stone; to rough-hew.—**to rough it** to submit to hardships; to put up for a time with rough accommodation.—*n* the state of being coarse or in the original material (*with the materials* or *work in the rough*); a rowdy; a rude coarse fellow; a bully.

roughage *n* any rough or coarse material; the coarser parts of fodder or food which are of little nutritional value but aid digestion; dietary fibre.

roughcast *vt* (**roughcast, roughcasting**) to form in its first rudiments; to mould without nicety or elegance; to cover with a coarse plaster of lime and gravel (*to roughcast a building*).—*n* the form of a thing in its first rudiments; a coarse kind of plastering for an external wall.

rough diamond *n* a diamond uncut; hence, (*fig*) a person of genuine worth but rude and unpolished manners.

roughen *vt* to make rough.—*vi* to grow or become rough.

roughly *adv* in a rough manner; with uneven surface; harshly; severely; uncivilly; rudely; violently; not gently; boisterously; tempestuously.

roughness *n* the state or quality of being rough; harshness to the taste or ear; unevenness of surface; ruggedness; asperity of temper; coarseness of behaviour or address; tempestuousness; violence.

rough-rider *n* one who breaks horses.

roughshod *adj* shod with shoes armed with points.—**to ride roughshod** (*fig*) to pursue a violent or selfish course, regardless of the pain it may cause others.

roulade *n* a cake, soufflé, etc, mixture served rolled up, usually with a filling.

rouleau *n* (*pl* **rouleaus, rouleaux**) a little roll; a roll of coin made up in paper.

roulette *n* a game of chance played with a ball at a table, in the centre of which is a cavity surmounted by a revolving disc having its circumference divided into compartments coloured black and red alternately, into any one of which the ball may drop; a tool furnished with a little toothed wheel, used by engravers for producing dotted work.

roulette

round *adj* having every part of the surface at an equal distance from the centre; spherical; globular; circular; cylindrical; having a curved form; swelling; plump; not given as extremely accurate (*in round numbers*); large; considerable (*a good round sum*); full in utterance; candid; free or plain in speech; without delicacy or reserve; without circumlocution; positive (*a round assertion*); smart or rapid (*a round trot*).—*n* that which is round, as a circle, a sphere, a globe; a series coming back to where it began (*a round of toasts*); a series of events or duties which come back to the point of commencement; the step of a ladder; a walk or circuit performed by a guard or an officer among sentries; a short musical composition in which three or more

voices, starting at the beginning of stated successive phrases, sing the same music (in unison or octave), the combination of all the parts producing correct harmony; a dance in a ring; a general discharge of firearms by a body of troops, in which each soldier fires once; ammunition for firing once.—*adv* on all sides; circularly; not in a direct line; through a circle, as of friends or houses.—*prep* on every side of; around; about, in a circular course.—*vt* to make round; to make full or complete; to make full, smooth and flowing.—*vi* to grow or become round; to become complete or full; to develop into the full type.—**to round to** (*naut*) to turn the head of the ship toward the wind.

roundabout *adj* indirect; going round; not straightforward.—*n* a large horizontal wheel on which children ride; a merry-go-round.

round-arm *adj* applied to a style of bowling in cricket in which the arm is brought round horizontally.

roundel *n* anything having a round form; a round figure; a circle; a roundelay.

roundelay *n* a sort of ancient poem, consisting of thirteen verses, of which eight are in one kind of rhyme and five in another; a song or tune in which the first strain is repeated; a dance in a circle.

rounders *npl* a game played with a short bat and a ball by two parties or sides, on a piece of ground marked off.

Roundhead *n* a name given by the Cavaliers or adherents of Charles I to members of the Puritan or parliamentary party, from the latter having their hair closely cut, while the Cavaliers wore theirs long.

roundhouse *n* a lock-up; a cabin on the afterpart of the quarterdeck of a ship, having the poop for its roof.

roundly *adv* in a round form; openly; plainly; without reserve; briskly; with speed; to the purpose; vigorously.

roundness *n* the quality of being round; circularity; sphericity; cylindrical form; fullness; smoothness of flow; plainness of speech; positiveness.

round robin *n* a written petition, memorial or remonstrance signed by names in a ring or circle so that it is impossible to ascertain who headed the list.

round shot *n* a spherical solid shot of cast iron or steel.

round tower *n* a kind of tall, slender tower tapering from the base upwards, generally with a conical top, often met with in Ireland.

roup[1] *n* a disease of poultry.

roup[2] *n* in Scotland, a sale of goods by auction or outcry.

rouse *vt* (**roused, rousing**) to wake from sleep; to excite to thought or action from a state of idleness, languor or inattention; to put into commotion; to agitate; to startle; to surprise; to drive from a lurking place or cover (a hunting term).—*vi* to awake from sleep or repose; to be excited to thought or action.—*n* a carousal; a drinking frolic or festival.

rousing *adj* having power to awaken or excite; stirring.

rout[1] *n* a company of persons; a rabble or multitude; a fashionable assembly or large evening party; an uproar; a brawl; the breaking or defeat of troops; the disorder and confusion of troops thus defeated.—*vt* to break the ranks of and put to flight in disorder; to defeat and throw into confusion; to drive or chase away; to dispel.

rout[2] *vt* to turn up with the snout (as pigs); to root.

route *n* the course or way which is travelled or passed or to be passed; a passing; a course; a march.—*vt* (**routed, routing**) to plan the route of; to send by a specified route.

route march *n* a march performed for exercise and training by a body of troops in full equipment.

routine *n* a round of business, amusements or pleasure, daily or frequently pursued; a course of business or duties regularly returning; habit or practice adhered to by force of habit.

roux *n* (*pl* **roux**) a mixture of flour and butter heated to form a binding element in sauces and soups.

rove[1] *vi* (**roved, roving**) to wander; to ramble; to range; to go, move or pass without certain direction in any manner.—*vt* to wander over.

rove[2] *vt* (**roved, roving**) to draw through an eye or aperture; to bring (wool or cotton) into that form which it receives before being spun into thread; to card into flakes, as wool, etc.—*n* a roll of wool, cotton, etc, drawn out and slightly twisted.

rover *n* one who roves or rambles about; a fickle or inconstant person; a pirate.

roving *n* the act of rambling or wandering.

row[1] *n* a series of persons or things arranged in a continued line; a line; a rank; a file.

row[2] *vt* to impel along the surface of water by oars; to transport by rowing.—*vi* to labour with the oar; to be moved by means of oars.—*n* an excursion taken in a boat with oars.

row[3] *n* a riotous noise; a turbulent, noisy disturbance; a riot; a noisy quarrel or dispute; a scolding.—*vt* to scold; to quarrel noisily.

rowan *n* mountain ash.

rowdy *n* a riotous, turbulent fellow; a rough.—*adj* disreputable; blackguard.

rowdyism *n* the conduct of a rowdy; turbulent blackguardism.

rowel *n* the little wheel of a spur with sharp points for pricking the horse.

rower *n* one that rows or manages an oar in rowing.

rowlock *n* a contrivance on a boat's gunwale on which the oar rests in rowing, formed with two upright pegs or of a single peg or otherwise.

royal *adj* pertaining or belonging to a king or queen; pertaining to the crown; regal; becoming a king or queen; kingly; queenly; princely; noble; generous; founded or originated by, in the service of, under the patronage of or receiving support from royalty (*royal navy*); a large size of paper.—*n* (*naut*) a square sail spread immediately above the top-gallant-sail; a gold coin formerly current in England.

royal assent the approbation given by the British sovereign in parliament to a bill which has passed both houses, after which it becomes law.

royalism *n* attachment to a royal government.

royalist *n* an adherent of a king or queen or one attached to a royal government.

Royalist *n* (in English history) an adherent of Charles I and Charles II, opposed to Roundhead.

royally *adv* in a royal manner; like a king or queen; as becomes a king or queen.

Royal Marines *npl* soldiers who serve in British warships, and also at dockyards and elsewhere on shore in certain circumstances.

royalty *n* the state or quality of being royal; condition or status of a person of royal rank; the person of a king or queen; majesty (*to stand in the presence of royalty*); a right or prerogative of a king or queen; a tax paid to the crown or to a superior on the produce of a mine, to an inventor for the use of his or her patent or to an author on the sales of his or her book.

rub *vt* (**rubbed, rubbing**) to move along the surface of, or backwards and forwards on, with friction; to apply friction to; to wipe; to clean; to scour; to smear all over; to gall or chafe; to gibe.—*vi* to move along the surface of a body with pressure; to grate; to fret; to chafe; to get on or along with difficulty (usually with *on*, *along* or *through*, as *to rub through the world*).—*n* an act of rubbing; something that renders motion or progress difficult; a difficulty or obstruction; a sarcasm; a gibe; something grating to the feelings; (in bowling) inequality of ground that hinders the motion of a bowl.

rubber[1] *n* an elastic substance made synthetically or from the sap of various tropical plants; one who or that which rubs; an instrument for rubbing; an eraser; (*American colloq*) a condom.

rower

751

rubber² *n* in whist, bridge, etc, two games out of three or a contest consisting of three games.

rubbish *n* refuse fragments of building materials; debris; waste or rejected matter; trash.

rubbishy *adj* characterized by rubbish; trashy; worthless.

rubble, rubblestone *n* the upper fragmentary and decomposed portion of a mass of stone; stones of irregular shapes and dimensions, broken bricks, etc, used in coarse masonry or to fill up between the facing courses of walls.

rubblework *n* walls or masonry built of rubblestone.

rubella *n* German measles.

Rubenesque *adj* of, like or pertaining to the art of the Florentine painter Rubens (1577–1640); opulent, colourful; (of a woman's figure) full-breasted and shapely.

Rubicon *n* the river forming the southern boundary of Caesar's province of Cisalpine Gaul, crossing which meant declaration of war.—**to cross the Rubicon** to take decisive steps which cannot be retraced.

rubicund *adj* inclining to redness; ruddy; blood-red (said especially of the face).

rubidium *n* a soft radioactive metallic element found in mineral waters.

rubigo *n* a kind of rust on plants, consisting of a parasitic fungus; mildew.

rubric *n* some part of a manuscript or printed matter that is, or in former times usually was, coloured red, to distinguish it from other portions; in law books, the title of a statute, formerly written in red letters; in prayerbooks, the directions and rules for the conduct of service, often printed in red; hence an ecclesiastical or episcopal rule or injunction; any formulated, fixed or authoritative injunction of duty.

ruby *n* a gem next to the diamond in hardness and value, of various shades of red, the most highly prized varieties being the crimson and carmine red; redness; red colour; (*print*) a type smaller than nonpareil and larger than pearl.—*adj* of the colour of the ruby; red.

ruche *n* goffered net, lace, silk, etc, used as trimming for dresses.—*vt* (**ruched, ruching**) to pleat, gather or flute fabric for use as a trimming.

ruck¹ *vt* to wrinkle; to crease.—*n* a wrinkle; a crease.

ruck² *n* an undistinguished crowd.

rucksack *n* a bag made to strap on the shoulders and used by walkers, climbers, etc.

ruction *n* disturbance; uproar; trouble.

rudd *n* a European freshwater fish.

rudder *n* the instrument by which a ship is steered; that part of the helm which con-

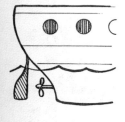

rudder

ruff

sists of a piece of timber, broad at the bottom and attached to the sternpost by hinges on which it turns; (*fig*) that which guides or governs a course; (in aviation) the subsidiary aerofoil (in an aeroplane more or less perpendicular to the main supporting surfaces) by means of which an aircraft is turned to left or right.

ruddiness *n* the state of being ruddy; that degree of redness which characterizes high health.

ruddle, raddle *n* a kind of red earth coloured by iron, used as a pigment and for marking sheep.

ruddy *adj* of a red colour or or of a colour approaching redness; of a lively flesh colour or the colour of the human skin in high health; of a reddish shining colour (*ruddy gold*).—*vt* (**ruddied, ruddying**) to make red or ruddy.

rude *adj* unformed by art, taste or skill; rough; rugged; coarse; primitive; ignorant; ill-mannered; uncivil; uncourteous; violent; boisterous.

rudely *adv* in a rude manner; roughly; unskilfully; coarsely; uncivilly; violently; boisterously.

rudiment *n* that which is in an undeveloped state; an unformed or unfinished beginning; an element or first principle of any art or science; especially in plural, the introduction to any branch of knowledge; the elements or elementary notions.

rudimentary, rudimental *adj* pertaining to rudiments; elementary; initial; in an undeveloped state; imperfectly developed; in the first stage of existence; embryonic.

rue¹ *vt* (**rued, ruing**) to regret; to grieve for; to repent; to repent of and withdraw or try to withdraw, from (*to rue a bargain*).—*vi* to have compassion; to become sorrowful, grieved or repentant.

rue² *n* a plant with evergreen leaves and greenish-yellow flowers, used as a sudorific and a vermifuge.

rueful *adj* causing to rue or lament; mournful; sorrowful; expressing sorrow; suggesting sorrow or melancholy; pitiful.

ruff¹ *n* a large muslin or linen collar plaited, crimped or fluted, formerly an important ornament of dress among both sexes; a species of pigeon with feathers round its neck in the form of a ruff; a male bird of the sandpiper family, having the feathers of the neck standing out like a ruff, the female being called *reeve*.

ruff² *n* an old game at cards, the predecessor or whist; the act of trumping when you have no cards of the suit led.—*vt* (in card playing) to trump instead of following suit.

ruff³, ruffe *n* a small European freshwater fish of the perch family, also known as *pope*.

ruffian *n* a boisterous brutal fellow; a fellow ready for any desperate crime.—*adj* like or belonging to a ruffian; brutal.

ruffianly *adj* like a ruffian; bold in crimes; violent.

ruffle *vt* (**ruffled, ruffling**) to disorder; to rumple; to derange; to disarrange; to disturb the surface of; to cause to ripple or rise in waves; to agitate; to disturb (*to ruffle the mind*); to furnish or adorn with ruffles; to contract into plaits or folds.—*vi* to grow rough or turbulent; to put on airs; to swagger (often with an indefinite *it*).—*n* a strip of plaited cambric or other fine cloth attached to some border of a garment, as to the wristband or bosom; a frill; a state of being disturbed or agitated; a low vibrating beat of the drum.

rug *n* a heavy woollen fabric used for various purposes, as to cover a bed, for protecting the carpet before a fireplace, for protecting the legs against the cold on a journey by rail, etc.

rugby *n* one of the two principal varieties of football, played by fifteen players a side, with an oval ball, handling being permitted.

rugged *adj* full of rough projections on the surface; broken into irregular points or prominences (*a rugged mountain, a rugged road*); rough; shaggy; rough in temper; hard; crabbed; austere; rough to the ear; harsh; grating (*rugged prose*).

ruin *n* that change of anything which destroys it or entirely unfits it for use; destruction; overthrow; downfall; what promotes injury, decay or destruction; a loss of fortune; a building or anything in a state of decay or dilapidation; (*pl*) the remains of a decayed or demolished city, house, fortress, etc; the state of being destroyed or rendered worthless (*to go to ruin*).—*vt* to bring to ruin or destruction; to damage essentially; to destroy, defeat, demolish.—*vi* to fall into ruin; to run to ruin.

ruination *n* the act of ruining; subversion; overthrow; demolition.

ruinous *adj* fallen to ruin; dilapidated; composed of ruins; bringing or tending to bring ruin.

rukh *n* the roc.

rule *n* government; sway; control; supreme command or authority; an established principle, standard or guide for action; something settled by authority or custom for guidance and direction; a maxim, canon or precept to be observed; the body of laws or regulations observed by a religious society and its members (*the rule of St Benedict*); a point of law settled by authority; an instrument by which straight lines are drawn; an instrument for measuring short lengths and performing various operations in mensuration; (*arith*) a deter-minate mode prescribed for performing any operation and producing a certain result; (*gram*) an established form of construction in a particular class of words or the expression of that form in words.—*vt* (**ruled, ruling**) to govern; to exercise authority or dominion over; to control, conduct, guide; to mark with lines by a ruler; (*law*) to establish by rule; to determine; to decide.—*vi* to have power or command; to exercise supreme authority (often followed by *over*); (*com*) to stand or maintain a level (*prices rule lower than formerly*).

rule of thumb *n* a rule suggested by a practical rather than a scientific knowledge; a rough common-sense approach as opposed to a precise or theoretical one.

ruler *n* one that rules or governs; one that assists in carrying on a government; an instrument made of wood, brass, ivory, etc, with straight edges or sides, by which straight lines may be drawn on paper or other substance, by guiding a pen or pencil along the edge.

ruling *adj* governing; reigning; chief; prevalent; predominant.—*n* a rule or point settled by a judge or court of law.

rug

rum[1] *n* spirit distilled from cane juice or from treacle or molasses.

rum[2] *adj* old fashioned; odd; queer.

rumble *vi* (**rumbled, rumbling**) to make a low, heavy, hoarse, continued sound.—*vt* (*sl*) to find out, to detect (*rumble his intentions*).—*n* a low, heavy, continuous sound; a rumbling; a seat for servants behind a carriage.

rumbling *adj* making a low, heavy, continued sound (*a rumbling noise*).—*n* a low, heavy, continued sound; a rumble.

ruminant *adj* chewing the cud; characterized by chewing again what has been swallowed (*ruminant animals*).—*n* a member of an order of herbivorous hoofed mammals that chew the cud, as the camel, deer, goat, ox, etc.

ruminate *vi* (**ruminated, ruminating**) to chew the cud; to chew again what has been slightly chewed and swallowed; to muse; to meditate; to think again and again; to ponder.—*vt* to chew over again; to muse or meditate on.

rumination *n* the act of ruminating; the act of meditating; a musing or continued thinking.

rummage *vt* (**rummaged, rummaging**) to search narrowly every place or part of, by looking into every corner and turning over goods or other things; to explore; to ransack.

rummer *n* a glass or drinking cup.

rummy *n* a simple card game for two or more players.

rumour *n* flying or popular report; the common voice; a current story passing from

ruler

one person to another, without any known authority for the truth of it; a mere report.

rump *n* the end of the backbone of an animal, with the parts adjacent; the buttocks.

Rump *n* (in English history) the remainder of the Long Parliament, after the expulsion of the majority of its members by Cromwell in 1648.

rumple *vt* (**rumpled, rumpling**) to wrinkle; to make uneven; to ruffle; to dishevel.—*n* a fold or plait.

rumpus *n* a riot; a great noise; disturbance.

run *vi* (*pret* **ran** *or* **run**, *pp* **run**, *ppr* **running**) to pass over the ground by using the legs more quickly than in walking; to contend in a race; hence, to enter into a contest; to flee for escape; to retreat hurriedly; to steal away; to extend quickly; to spread (*the fire runs over a field*); to rush or be carried along with violence (*a ship runs against a rock*); to move on wheels or runners, as a locomotive or sledge; to sail, as a ship; to pass or go back and forth from place to place; to ply (ships, railway trains, stagecoaches, etc, between different places); to move or pass, as a fluid, the sand in an hourglass, etc; to be wet with a flowing liquid; to become fluid; to fuse; to melt; to spread on a surface; to spread and blend (*colours run in washing*; *ink runs on damp paper*); to discharge pus or other matter (*an ulcer runs*); to unravel, come undone; to revolve on an axis or pivot; to turn, as a wheel; to continue going or in operation (*an engine runs, the mills are running*); to pass or proceed in thought or speech (*to run from one topic to another*); to pass from one state or condition to another (*to run into error* or *into debt*); to proceed or pass, as time; to have a certain course, track or direction; to extend, stretch, lie (*the street runs east and west*); to have a certain written form; to read so or so to the ear (*the lines run smoothly*); to have a continued tenor or purport (*the conversation ran as follows*); to be popularly spread or received; to continue or be repeated for a certain time (*the play ran for a hundred nights*); to be carried to a pitch; to rise (*debates run high*); to grow exuberantly; to proceed or tend in growing; to continue in time before it becomes due and payable (*a bill has ninety days to run*).—*vt* to cause to run or go quickly; to cause to be carried in a certain course (*to run a ship aground*); to cause to ply; to maintain in running (*to run a stagecoach*); to accomplish by running; to pursue, as a course; to incur; to encounter (*to run the risk of being killed*); to break through or evade (*to run a blockade*); hence, to smuggle; to import or export without paying duties; to push; to thrust; to pierce; to stab (*to run a person through with a rapier*); to carry on or con-

rune

rung

duct, as an hotel or other enterprise; to sew by passing the needle through and through in a continuous line.—**to run in** to operate carefully (a new vehicle) to bring to full working condition; (*colloq*) to arrest.—**to run into** to have a collision with; to meet unexpectedly; of costs, etc, to amount to. —**to run across** to meet or find unexpectedly.—**to run down** to knock down with a moving vehicle; to criticize persistently; to disparage; to reduce in quantity or scale; of a mechanism, etc, to slow down and stop.—**to run through** to pierce; to rehearse.—*n* the act of running; a course run (*a long run, a quick run*); a trip; a pleasure trip or excursion; particular or distinctive course, progress, tenor, etc; continued course (*a run of ill luck*); a trend; a series; a general or uncommon pressure or demand, as on a bank or treasury for payment of its notes; the distance sailed by a ship; a voyage; a passage from one place to another; a pair of millstones; (in cricket) one complete act of running from one wicket to the other by the batsman; a place where animals run or may run; a large extent of grazing ground, called variously a *cattle run*, a *sheep run*, etc, according to the animals pastured; (*mus*) a succession of notes, either ascending or descending, played or sung rapidly; a ladder in stockings or tights.—*adj* liquefied; melted; clarified (*run butter*); run or conveyed ashore secretly; contraband (*run brandy*).

runagate *n* (*arch*) a fugitive; a vagabond; an apostate; a renegade.

runaway *n* one that flies from danger or restraint; one that deserts lawful service; a fugitive.—*adj* acting the part of a runaway; escaping or breaking from restraint; accomplished or effected by running away or eloping (*a runaway match*).

rundale *n* same as **runrig**.

run-down *n* a brief review or summary.— *adj* in a poor or dilapidated condition; not in very good health.

rune *n* one of a particular set of alphabetic characters peculiar to the ancient northern nations of Europe, all the runes being formed almost entirely of straight lines, either single or in composition.

rung *n* a heavy staff; the round or step of a ladder.

runic *adj* pertaining to runes.

runlet *n* a small barrel of no certain dimensions.

runnel *n* a rivulet or small brook.

runner *n* one who runs; an athlete; a racer; a messenger; an old name for a criminal detective; a slender prostrate stem sending out leaves and roots, as in the strawberry; any running bird; that on which a thing runs or slides (*the runner* or *keel of a sleigh* or *skate*).

runner-up *n* the player who is next to the winner in a competition.

running *adj* kept for racing (*a running horse*); in succession; without any intervening day, year, etc (*to visit two days running*, *to sow land two years running*); discharging pus, matter, etc.—*n* the act of one who runs; a quantity run (*the first running of a still*).

runny *adj* tending to flow; liquid; discharging a liquid.

run-of-the mill *adj* ordinary; commonplace; mediocre.

runrig, rundale *n* a system of holding land in which successive strips or ridges belong to different owners.

runt *n* any animal below the usual size of the breed; a variety of pigeon; a root of kale or cabbage; a cudgel.

run-up *n* a preliminary period; the time leading up to an event.

rupee *n* a unit of money in India, Pakistan, Sri Lanka, etc.

rupture *n* the act of breaking or bursting; the state of being broken or violently parted; (*med*) same as hernia, especially hernia of the abdomen; a breach of concord either between individuals or nations; open hostility or war; a quarrel.—*vt* (**ruptured, rupturing**) to make a rupture in; to burst; to part by violence; to affect with or cause to suffer from rupture.—*vi* to suffer a breach or disruption.

rural *adj* pertaining to the country, as distinguished from a city or town; suiting the country or resembling it; pertaining to agriculture or farming.

rural dean *n* an ecclesiastic who has the care and inspection of the clergy and laity of a district.

ruse *n* an artifice, trick or stratagem; a wile.

rush[1] *vi* to move or drive forward with impetuosity, violence and tumultuous rapidity; to enter with undue eagerness or without due deliberation (*to rush into a scheme*).—*vt* to carry with violence, with a rush (*to rush a platform*).—*n* a driving forward with eagerness and haste; a violent motion or course; an eager demand; a run; an unedited film print.

rush[2] *n* a herbaceous plant, usually growing in damp meadows and swamps, with a round erect stem which is sometimes used for plaiting into mats, chair bottoms, etc, and which contains a large pith; the merest trifle; a straw.

rush candle *n* a small taper made by the pith of a rush in tallow.

rush hour a time of exceptionally heavy traffic, usually at the beginning and end of the working day.

rusk *n* a kind of light hard cake browned in a moderately cool oven and used as food for infants.

russet *adj* of a reddish-brown colour; coarse; homespun; rustic (from the general colour of homespun cloth).—*n* a kind of apple of a russet colour and rough skin; a pigment of a rich transparent brown colour obtained from madder.

Russian *adj* pertaining to Russia.—*n* a native of Russia; the language of Russia.

Russian roulette *n* a dangerous game of chance in which a revolver loaded with a bullet in only one of its chambers is spun and the muzzle held at one's head and fired; a dangerous act of bravado.

rust *n* the red or orange-yellow coating (an oxide of iron) which is formed on the surface of iron when exposed to air and moisture; a parasitic fungus which attacks the leaves, glumes, stalks, etc, of cereals and grasses; any foul extraneous matter; corrosive or injurious accretion or influence.—*vi* to contract or gather rust; to be oxidized; to assume an appearance as if coated with rust; to degenerate in idleness or inaction.—*vt* to cause to contract rust; to impair by time and inactivity.

rustic *adj* pertaining to the country; living in or found in the country; rural; plain; simple; not elegant, refined or costly.—*n* an inhabitant of the country; a swain.

rusticate *vi* (**rusticated, rusticating**) to dwell or reside in the country.—*vt* to suspend from studies at a university and send away for a time by way of punishment.

rusticity *n* the state or quality of being rustic.

rustle *vi* (**rustled, rustling**) to make a quick succession of small sounds like the rubbing of silk cloth or dry leaves; to give out a slightly sibilant sound when shaken.—*vt* to cause to rustle.—*n* the noise made by one who or that which rustles; a slight crackling sound as of dry leaves or silk clothes.

rusty *adj* covered or affected with rust; having the colour of rust; appearing as if covered with rust; impaired by inaction or neglect of use; out of practice.

rut[1] *n* the track of a wheel.

rut[2] *n* the seasonal period of sexual excitement in male ruminants, such as deer.—*vi* (**rutted, rutting**) (of deer, etc) to be in the seasonal period of sexual excitement.

ruth *n* mercy; pity; tenderness; sorrow for the misery of another; sorrowful or tender regret.

ruthenium *n* a hard rare metal of a grey colour occurring in platinum ore.

ruthless *adj* having no ruth or pity; cruel; pitiless; barbarous.

ryal *n* same as **rial**.

rye *n* a cereal plant the grain of which is used to make flour and whisky and as a food for cattle; whisky distilled from rye.

ryot *n* in India, a small farmer, a peasant.

rye

S

S the nineteenth letter of the English alphabet, a consonant representing a hissing sound.

Sabbath *n* the day which God appointed to be observed as a day of rest; originally the seventh day of the week but in the Christian church the first day of the week is held sacred, in commemoration of the resurrection of Christ on that day; the Lord's day; Sunday. *Sabbath* is not strictly synonymous with *Sunday*, *Sunday* being the mere name of the day and *Sabbath* the name of the institution. *Sunday* is the *Sabbath* of Christians, *Saturday* is the *Sabbath* of Jews.

Sabbatic, Sabbatical *adj* pertaining to the Sabbath.

sabbatical *n* a year's leave from a teaching post, often paid, for research or travel.

sabin *n* a unit of acoustic absorption.

sable *n* a carnivorous animal related to the marten, found chiefly in the northern regions of Asia and hunted for its black lustrous fur; the fur of the sable; a black or mourning suit or garment; (*heral*) black.—*adj* of the colour of the sable; black; dark.

sabot *n* a shoe made from a single piece of wood; a shoe with a wooden sole and cloth upper.

sabotage *n* malicious destruction of property or machinery by dissatisfied employees, enemy agents, etc.—*vt* (**sabotaged, sabotaging**) to practise sabotage on; to spoil, disrupt.

saboteur *n* a person who engages in sabotage.

sabre *n* a sword with a broad and heavy blade, thick at the back and a little curved towards the point, specially adapted for cutting; a cavalry sword.—*vt* (**sabred, sabring**) to strike, cut or kill with a sabre.

sabre-rattling *n* a conspicuous display of military power or aggression.

sac *n* a bag or cyst in an animal or plant; a pouch; a receptacle for a liquid (*the lacrymal sac*).

saccharin *n* an extremely sweet substance obtained from coal tar and used as a non-fattening substitute for sugar.

sack

saccharine *adj* pertaining to sugar; having the qualities of sugar; sugary; excessively sweet.

sacerdotal *adj* pertaining to priests or the priesthood; priestly.

sacerdotalism *n* sacerdotal system or spirit; a tendency to attribute a lofty and sacred character to the priesthood; priestcraft.

sachem *n* in North America, a chief among some of the American Indian tribes.

sachet *n* a sealed envelope or packet; a small bag containing perfumed substances.

sack[1] *n* a large bag of coarse cloth, paper, etc, used for holding and conveying corn, wool, cotton, hops, etc; the contents of this; a kind of loose dress.—**the sack** (*colloq*) dismissal.—*vt* to put in a sack or in bags; (*colloq*) to dismiss.

sack[2] *vt* to pillage; to plunder or loot; to devastate (usually said of a town).—*n* the act of one who sacks; the storm and plunder of a town or city; booty; spoil.

sack[3] *n* formerly, a general name for different sorts of dry wines, especially Spanish.

sackbut *n* a musical wind instrument similar to the trumpet.

sackcloth *n* cloth of which sacks are made; coarse cloth worn in mourning, distress or penance.

sackful *adj* as much as a sack will hold.

sacking *n* a coarse fabric of which sacks are made; (*colloq*) dismissal.

sacque *n* a kind of loose gown or upper robe worn by women in the seventeenth and eighteenth centuries.

sacrament *n* (*theol*) a religious ceremony forming an outward and visible sign of inward and spiritual grace, such as baptism and the Eucharist; the consecrated elements in the Eucharist, especially the bread; a sacred symbol or pledge.

sacramental *adj* constituting a sacrament or pertaining to it; having the character of a sacrament.

sacred *adj* set apart by solemn religious ceremony; dedicated to religious use; holy; not profane or common; relating to religion or the services of religion; not secular; consecrated; dedicated; devoted (with *to*, as *sacred to one's memory*); entitled to the highest respect or reverence; venerable; not to be profaned or violated; inviolable; inviolate (*a secret kept sacred*).

sacred cow *n* a person or thing that is regarded as being above criticism because of high reputation, popular esteem.

sacrifice *n* the offering of anything to God or to a god; a consecratory rite; anything consecrated and offered to God or to a divinity; an immolated victim on an altar; surrender or loss made for gaining something else; a giving up of some desirable object for a higher or more worthy object; the thing so devoted or given up; the selling of goods under cost price.—*vt* (**sacrificed, sacrificing**) to make an offering or sacrifice of; to consecrate or present to some divinity; to immolate on the altar of God either as an atonement for sin or to express gratitude; to destroy, surrender or suffer to be lost for the sake of obtaining something else; to devote or give up with loss or suffering; to destroy; to kill.—*vi* to offer up a sacrifice; to make offerings to God or to a deity by the slaughter and burning of victims, or some part of them, on an altar.

sacrificial *adj* pertaining to sacrifice; performing sacrifices; consisting of sacrifice.

sacrilege *n* the violation or profaning of sacred things; the appropriating to common purposes what has been reserved for religious uses.

sacrilegious *adj* guilty of or involving sacrilege; violating sacred things; profane; impious.

sacrist *n* a sacristan; a person employed in a cathedral to copy out music for the choir and to take care of books.

sacristan *n* an officer of the church who has the charge of the sacristy and its contents.

sacristy *n* an apartment in a church where the sacred utensils and the clerical vestments are deposited; the vestry.

sacrosanct *adj* sacred and inviolable; holy and venerable.

sacrum *n* (*pl* **sacra**) (*anat*) the bone which forms the basis or inferior extremity of the vertebral column.

sad *adj* serious; sedate or grave; sorrowful; melancholy; mournful; affected with grief; downcast; gloomy; having the external appearance of sorrow; afflictive; calamitous; causing sorrow; bad; naughty; wicked.

sadden *vt* to make sad or sorrowful; to render melancholy or gloomy.—*vi* to become sad or sorrowful.

saddle *n* a seat to be placed on an animal's back for the rider to sit on; a padded piece of harness on an animal's back supporting the shafts of a vehicle; something like a saddle in shape or use, as a rise and fall on the ridge of a hill.—*vt* (**saddled, saddling**) to put a saddle on; to load; to burden (*to saddle a person with expense*).

saddlebag *n* one of a pair of bags joined by straps for hanging over a horse's back, one bag on each side.

saddlebow *n* the upper front part of a saddle, formed of two curved pieces joined in an arch; a pommel.

saddler *n* one whose occupation is to make saddles or harness generally.

Sadducee *n* one of a sect or party among the ancient Jews who denied the existence of any spiritual beings except God, believed that the soul died with the body and therefore that there was no resurrection and adhered to the written law alone.

sadism *n* (*psychol*) a form of sexual perversion in which pleasure is taken in the cruel treatment of another; extreme cruelty.

sadness *n* the state or quality of being sad; sorrowfulness; dejection.

sadomasochism *n* a liking both for sadism and masochism; the gaining of sexual pleasure from both inflicting pain and submitting to pain; sexual pleasure so obtained.

safari *n* (*pl* **safaris**) a hunting or shooting expedition, especially in Africa.

safari park *n* an enclosed park where wild animals, mostly non-native, are kept uncaged on view to the public.

safe *adj* free from or not liable to danger of any kind; free from or having escaped hurt, injury or damage; not exposing to danger; securing from harm; no longer dangerous; placed beyond the power of doing harm; sound; whole (*a safe conscience*).—*n* a box or chamber of great strength for preserving money, jewels, account books and other valuable articles from thieves or against the action of fire; a ventilated or refrigerated receptacle in which meat is kept.

safe-conduct *n* a convoy or guard for a person travelling in a foreign or hostile country; a writing serving as a pass or warrant of security to a traveller.

safeguard *n* one who or that which defends or protects; a defence; protection; a convoy or guard to protect a traveller; a passport; a warrant of protection to a traveller.—*vt* to guard; to protect.

safe house *n* a refuge; a refuge for victims of domestic violence, sexual abuse, etc, run by social welfare organizations or charity organizations; a secret place used by intelligence services, escaped prisoners of war, terrorists, etc, as a refuge.

safekeeping *n* the act or process of keeping safely; protection.

safely *adv* in a safe manner; without incurring danger; without hurt or injury; in safety; securely; carefully.

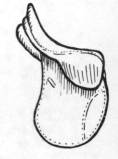

saddle

safe sex *n* sexual intercourse in which precautions, such as condoms, are used to lessen the risk of catching Aids or other sexually transmitted diseases.

safety *n* the state or quality of being safe; exemption from injury or loss; the state of not being liable to danger or injury; freedom from danger; preservation; the state or quality of not causing danger; close custody.

safety fuse *n* a fuse used in blasting operations, carefully made so as to burn at a certain known rate per minute.

safety lamp *n* a miner's lamp in which the flame is enclosed by a protective gauze to prevent it igniting combustible gases.

safety match *n* a match which will light only on being rubbed on a specially prepared friction substance.

safety pin *n* an oblong pin with a point fitting into a sheath so that it may not be withdrawn or prick the wearer.

safety razor *n* a type of razor in which the blade is covered by a comb-like guard.

safety valve *n* an automatic valve for relieving excess pressure of steam, etc; any outlet which is a relief for excitement or violent emotion.

saftey pin

safflower *n* a thistle-like plant with large orange or red flowers; a red dye and oil derived from it.

saffron *n* a kind of crocus whose bright yellow stigmas are used as a food colouring and flavouring; an orange-yellow colour.—*adj* having the colour of saffron flowers; orange-yellow.—*vt* to tinge with saffron; to make yellow; to gild.

sag *vi* (**sagged, sagging**) to incline or hang away owing to insufficiently supported weight; to sink in the middle; to hang off the perpendicular; to yield under the pressure of care, difficulties, etc; to waver; (*naut*) to incline to the leeward; to make leeway.—*vt* to cause to bend or give way.—*n* the state or act of sagging.

saga *n* an ancient Scandinavian legend or tradition of considerable length relating either mythical or historical events; a long tale, especially of heroic deeds.

sagacious *adj* intellectually keen or quick; acute in discernment; discerning and judicious; shrewd; full of wisdom; sage; showing intelligence resembling that of human beings (said of the lower animals).

sagacity *n* the quality of being sagacious; quickness of discernment; readiness of apprehension with soundness of judgment; shrewdness and common sense; intelligence resembling that of mankind (*the sagacity of a dog*).

sage[1] *adj* wise through reflection and experience; sagacious; serious.—*n* a wise person; a person of sound judgment and prudence.

sailor

sage[2] *n* a herb with leaves used in cooking as a flavouring agent.

Sagittarius *n* one of the zodiacal constellations which the sun enters 22nd November, represented by the figure of a centaur in the act of shooting an arrow from his bow.

sago *n* a starch produced from the stem of several Asian palms, forming light, wholesome, nutritious food.

sahib *n* a term of address formerly used by Indians to European men.

sai *n* a species of South American monkey.

saiga *n* a species of antelope found on the steppes of Russia.

sail *n* a piece of cloth spread to the wind to cause a vessel to move through the water, made of canvas, etc; that portion of the arm of a windmill which catches the wind; a ship or other vessel (used as a plural with the singular form, as *a fleet of twenty sail*); an excursion on water; a passage in a vessel.—*vi* to be impelled by the action of wind on sails, as a ship, or by steam, oars, etc; to be conveyed in a vessel on water; to pass by water; to set sail; to begin a voyage; to glide through the air; to pass smoothly along; to glide; to float (*the clouds sail*).—*vt* to pass over by means of sails; to move on or pass over, as in a ship (*to sail the seas*); to fly or glide through; to navigate; to direct or manage the motion of.

sailboard *n* a type of large surfboard with a sail used in windsurfing.

sailcloth *n* fabric used in making sails for yachts, etc; a strong, durable fabric for clothing.

sailer *n* a ship or other vessel with reference to her manner of sailing (*a fast sailer*).

sailing *n* the act of one who or that which sails; the art of navigation; a departure from a port.

sailor *n* a person who sails; one of a ship's crew; a mariner.

sainfoin *n* a leguminous plant cultivated for fodder.

saint *n* a person sanctified; one eminent for piety and virtue, particularly applied to the apostles and other holy persons of early Christian times; one of the blessed in heaven; an angel; a person canonized by the Roman Catholic Church (often contracted to **St** when coming before a personal name).

sainted *adj* canonized; holy; pious; entered into bliss; gone to heaven, often used as a euphemism for dead.

saintly *adj* resembling a saint; becoming a saint.

sajou *n* same as **sapajou**.

sake *n* purpose; account; behalf; interest; regard to any person or thing (always with *for*, as *for his sake*).

saké *n* a Japanese drink made from fermented rice.

saki *n* an American monkey with a non-prehensile bushy tail.

sal[1] *n* salt (a word used in pharmacy).

sal[2] *n* a valuable timber tree of India.

salaam *n* a ceremonious salutation or obeisance.—*vti* to perform the salaam; to salute with a salaam.

salacious *adj* lustful; lecherous.

salacity *n* the quality of being salacious; lecherousness.

salad *n* a general name for certain vegetables prepared and served so as to be eaten raw, such as tomatoes, spring onions, etc.

salad cream *n* a kind of bought, bottled mayonnaise used for dressing salads.

salad days *npl* days of youthful inexperience.

salad dressing *n* a mixture of oil, such as olive oil, vinegar and herbs, used to flavour a salad.

salamander *n* an amphibian reptile closely related to the newt, formerly believed to be capable of living in fire; a kind of fire spirit or being supposed to live in fire; a large iron poker.

salami *n* a highly seasoned sausage, usually sliced very thinly.

sal ammoniac *n* ammonium chloride.

salary *n* the recompense or consideration stipulated to be paid to a person periodically for services, usually a fixed sum to be paid by the month; stipend; wages.

sale *n* the act of selling; the exchange or transfer of a commodity for an agreed price in money; opportunity of selling; demand; market; public transfer to the highest bidder; exposure of goods in a market or shop; auction.

saleable *adj* capable of being sold; finding a ready market; in demand.

saleroom *n* a room in which goods are sold; an auction room.

salesman, saleswoman, salesperson *n* (*pl* **salesmen, saleswomen, salespersons**) one whose occupation is to sell goods or merchandise.

salicylic acid *n* an acid used as an antiseptic and for other purposes.

salience *n* the quality of being salient; projection; protrusion.

salient *adj* springing; shooting up or out; projecting outwardly (*a salient angle*); forcing itself on the notice or attention; conspicuous; prominent; a projecting angle or corner in a line of defence, forming a jumping-off place.

salimeter *n* an instrument for measuring the amount of salt present in any given solution.

salina *n* a salt marsh; a salt pond enclosed from the sea; a place where salt is made from salt water.

salination *n* the act of washing with or soaking in salt liquor.

saline *adj* consisting of salt; partaking of the qualities of salt; salt.—*n* a salt spring or a place where salt water is collected in the earth.

salinity *n* the state of being salt; salineness.

salinometer *n* a device for indicating the density of brine in the boilers of marine steam engines and thus showing when they should be cleansed.

saliva *n* the fluid which is secreted by certain glands of the mouth and which serves to moisten the mouth and tongue and to make the food more fitted for digestion.

salivary *adj* pertaining to the saliva; secreting or conveying saliva (*the salivary glands* or *ducts*).

salivate *vi* to secrete saliva, especially excessively.

sallow[1] *adj* of a pale, sickly colour, tinged with a dark yellow (said especially of the skin or complexion).—*vt* to tinge with a sallow colour.

sallow[2] *n* a broad-leaved shrub of the willow kind.

sally *n* a leaping forth; a rush of troops from a besieged place to attack the besiegers; a sudden attack; a spring or flight of intellect, fancy or imagination (*a sally of wit*); a lively remark; an act of levity or extravagance; a piece of wild gaiety; a frolic.—*vi* (**sallied, sallying**) to make a sally; to leap or rush out; to issue suddenly from a fortified place to attack besiegers.

salmagundi *n* a dish of chopped meat, eggs, anchovies, red pickled cabbage, etc; a mixture of various ingredients; a miscellany.

salmi, salmis *n* a spiced ragout of game birds cooked in wine.

salmon *n sing, pl* a large silvery fish with edible flesh that lives in salt water in northern Europe, America and Asia and spawns in freshwater rivers in autumn; the pinkish-orange colour of the flesh of the salmon.

salmon trout, sea trout *n* a fish resembling the salmon in form and colour and, like it, ascending rivers to deposit its spawn.

salon *n* an apartment for the reception of company; a saloon; a social gathering in the private house of a person of distinction; the shop of a hairdresser, beautician, etc.

saloon *n* any spacious apartment for the reception of company or for works of art; a large public room; an apartment for specific public use (*the saloon of a steamer*).

saloon bar an area in a public house that is comfortably furnished.

salopettes *npl* thick quilted trousers with shoulder straps, worn for skiing.

salsa *n* a spicy sauce made with tomatoes,

salami

onions. chillies and oil, used in Mexican cooking; a type of Puerto Rican dance; the music for this.

salsify *n* a purple-flowered plant with an edible root.

salt *n* a white crystalline substance used for seasoning and preserving food and obtained in the form of rock salt or from evaporation of sea water; (*chem*) a compound produced by the combination of a base (commonly a metallic oxide) with an acid; taste; smack; savour; wit; piquancy; pungency; sarcasm (*Attic salt*); a salt cellar; an old sailor.—*adj* impregnated with salt; abounding in or containing salt; prepared with or tasting of salt; sharp; pungent.—*vt* to sprinkle, impregnate or season with salt.

saltant *adj* leaping; jumping; dancing.

saltatory *adj* leaping or dancing; adapted for leaping.

saltbush *n* the name for Australian plants of the orache genus, which flourish in dry regions and are browsed by sheep.

saltcellar *n* a small vessel used for holding salt on the table.

saltcellar

salter *n* one who salts; one who sells salt; a drysalter.

saltire, saltier *n* (*heral*) an ordinary in the form of a St Andrew's cross, formed by two bends crossing each other.

salt lick *n* a salt spring.

salt marsh *n* land under pasture grasses subject to be overflowed by sea water.

salt mine *n* a mine where rock salt is obtained.

saltpan *n* a large shallow pan or a shallow pond in which salt water or brine is evaporated to obtain salt.

saltpetre *n* a white powder used in making gunpowder, etc.

salty *adj* of, containing or tasting of salt; witty; earthy; coarse.

salubrious *adj* favourable to health; healthful; healthy.

salubrity *n* the state or quality of being salubrious; healthfulness.

saluki *n* a breed of tall slender hound with a long silky coat, originally from Persia.

salutary *adj* wholesome; healthful; promoting health; contributing to some beneficial purpose; advantageous; profitable.

salutation *n* the act of saluting; that which is done or uttered in saluting; a greeting or salute.

salute *vt* (**saluted, saluting**) to address with expressions of kind wishes or in order to show homage or courtesy; to greet; to hail; to greet by some act, as by uncovering the head, a bow, etc; in the army or navy, to honour by a salute.—*vi* to perform a salutation; to greet each other.—*n* a salutation; a greeting; a kiss; a bow, etc; in the army or navy, a compliment paid to a royal or other distinguished personage when squadrons or other bodies meet and on various ceremonial occasions, by firing ordnance or small arms, dipping colours or topsails, presenting arms, manning the yards, etc.

salvage *n* the act of saving a ship or goods from danger, as from the sea, fire, an enemy, etc; a reward to someone by whose voluntary efforts ships or goods have been saved; property thus saved; waste material intended for future use.—*vt* (**salvaged, salvaging**) to save from loss or danger.

salvation *n* the act of saving; preservation from destruction, danger or great calamity; the redemption of a human being from the bondage of sin and liability to eternal death and the conferring on him or her of everlasting happiness; that which saves; the cause of saving.

Salvation Army *n* an international Christian and charitable society founded by William Booth in 1865, organized on military lines and conducted by generals, majors, captains, etc, of either sex.

salve[1] *n* a soothing substance applied to wounds or sores; a healing ointment; help; remedy.

salve[2] *vt* (**salved, salving**) to save a ship or goods from destruction, as by shipwreck or fire; to salvage.

salver *n* a small tray for table service or on which anything is presented to a person.

salvo *n* (*pl* **salvos, salvoes**) a general discharge of guns intended for a salute or for some special purpose; a sudden burst, as of applause or cheers; a spirited verbal attack.

salvo *n* (*pl* **salvos**) an exception or reservation; an excuse.

sal volatile *n* ammonia carbonate flavoured with aromatics and used as a remedy for faintness.

salvor *n* one who saves a ship or goods from wreck or destruction.

samara *n* (*bot*) a fruit with wing-like expansions, as in the fruit or key of the ash tree, elm, maple.

Samaritan *n* a native or inhabitant of Samaria, the principal city of the ten tribes of Israel; the language of Samaria; a charitable or benevolent person, in allusion to the 'good Samaritan' in the NT parable.

samarium *n* a silvery metallic element used in lasers and alloys.

samba *n* a lively Brazilian dance of African origin; the music for such a dance.

Sam Browne *n* formerly, a belt with a shoulder strap, worn by British officers and first-class warrant officers.

sambur *n* a large deer of northern India.

same *adj* identical; not different or other (*the same man*); of the identical kind, species or degree; exactly similar, though not the specific thing (*the same error*); just mentioned or denoted (always preceded by *the* or *this*, *that*, etc).—**all the same** nevertheless; notwithstanding.

sameness *n* the state of being the same; identity; similarity; lack of variety.

samite *n* formerly, a rich silk fabric interwoven with gold or embroidered.

samizdat *n* in the former Soviet Union, the illegal printing and distribution of banned literature.

samovar *n* a tea urn used in Russia in which the water is heated by a tube passing through it containing live coals.

sampan *n* a small flat-bottomed Chinese river boat.

samphire *n* any of a genus of plants whose leaves are used in pickles and salads.

sample *n* a pattern; an example; a small part or quantity of anything intended to be shown as evidence of the quality of the whole.—*vt* (**sampled, sampling**) to take a sample of; to take a quantity from to serve as a sample (*to sample sugar*, etc); to taste.

sampler *n* a piece of fancy sewn or embroidered work done for practice.

samurai *n* a member of an ancient Japanese warrior class.

sanatorium *n* (*pl* **sanatoriums, sanatoria**) a place to which people go for the sake of health.

sanctification *n* the act of sanctifying or state of being sanctified; the act of God's grace by which the affections of people are purified from sin; conformity to the will of God; consecration.

sanctify *vt* (**sanctified, sanctifying**) to make holy or sacred; to set apart to a holy or religious use; to hallow; to purify from sin or sinful affections; to make the means of holiness; to celebrate or confess as holy.

sanctimonious *adj* making a show of sanctity; affecting the appearance of sanctity.

sanctimony *n* piety; sanctity; the external appearance of devoutness; affected or hypocritical devoutness.

sanction *n* an official act of a superior by which he or she ratifies and gives validity to the act of some other person or body; ratification or confirmation; authority; penalty incurred by the infringement of a command.—*vt* to give sanction to; to ratify; to give countenance to.

sanctity *n* the state or quality of being sacred or holy; holiness; saintliness; sacredness; inviolability.

sanctuary *n* a sacred or consecrated place; the temple at Jerusalem, particularly the innermost part of it, called the holy of holies; a house consecrated to the worship of God; a church; (*RC Church*) that part of a church where the altar is placed; a place of protection; a sacred asylum; right of affording such protection, a privilege at-

tached to certain places by which criminals are protected from the law; refuge; shelter.

sanctum *n* (*pl* **sanctums, sancta**) a sacred place; a private retreat or room (*an editor's sanctum*).

sanctum sanctorum *n* the holy of holies; the innermost or holiest place of the Jewish temple.

Sanctus *n* an anthem beginning with the Latin word *Sanctus*, holy; a musical setting of this.

sand *n* fine particles of stone, particularly of siliceous stone in a loose state but not reduced to powder or dust, generally arising from disintegrated rock; (*pl*) a tract of land consisting of sandy soil, like the deserts of Arabia; tracts of sand exposed by the ebb of the tide.—*vt* to sprinkle with sand; to drive on a sandbank.

sandal *n* a kind of shoe, consisting of a sole fastened to the foot by means of straps crossed over and worn round the ankle; an open shoe.

sandalwood *n* the wood of several Asian trees with a strong scent which repels insects and used for making cabinets, boxes, etc.

sandarach *n* a resin which exudes from the bark of a North African timber tree, used as incense and for making varnish.

sandbag *n* a bag filled with sand or earth and used in a fortification, for ballast or to protect against flood water.

sandbank *n* a bank of sand; a bank of sand in the sea formed by tides or currents.

sand bath *n* a bath of hot sand for the body; hot sand used as an equable heater for retorts, etc, in chemical processes.

sandblast *vt* to clean by blasting with sand at high velocity.

sand castle *n* a model of a castle modelled from damp sand at the seaside.

sand eel, sand launce *n* a European fish that buries itself in the sand.

sanderling *n* a small wading bird which frequents the shores and feeds on small marine insects.

sandglass *n* a glass that measures time by the running of sand from one division of it to the other.

sandix, sandyx *n* red lead prepared by calcining carbonate of lead.

S & M an abbreviation for **sadomasochism**.

sand martin *n* the smallest of the British swallows, named from digging a hole for its nest in sandy banks, gravel pits, etc.

sandpaper *n* paper covered on one side with a fine gritty substance for smoothing woodwork.

sandpiper *n* one of several wading birds related to the snipe, plover, etc.

sandstone *n* stone composed of agglutinated grains of sand, which may be calcar-

samurai

sandal

eous, siliceous or of any other mineral nature, also called *freestone*.

sandstorm *n* a violent commotion of sand caused by wind.

sand wasp *n* an insect resembling a wasp, the female of which burrows in sandy banks.

sandwich *n* two thin slices of bread with meat, cheese, egg, salad, etc, between.—*vt* to place between two things or two layers; to make such a place for.

sandwich board *n* two usually hinged advertising boards hanging from the shoulders, one in front and one behind.

sandy *adj* consisting of or abounding with sand; resembling sand; of the colour of sand; of a yellowish-red colour.

sandyx *n* same as **sandix**.

sane *adj* mentally sound; not deranged; reasonable; sensible.

sangfroid *n* freedom from agitation or excitement of mind; coolness; calmness in trying circumstances.

sangreal *n* the Grail or holy vessel of medieval legends.

sangria *n* a Spanish drink made from red wine, fruit juice, fresh fruit, etc.

sandwich

sanguinary *adj* consisting of blood; bloody; attended with much bloodshed; murderous; bloodthirsty.

sanguine *adj* having the colour of blood; red; characterized by fullness of habit, vigour, activity of circulation, etc; cheerful in temper; anticipating the best; not desponding; confident.

sanicle *n* an umbelliferous plant of several species.

sanies *n* a watery mixture of blood and pus discharged from a sore or wound.

sanitarium *n* a health retreat; a sanatorium.

sanitary *adj* pertaining to or designed to secure health; relating to the preservation of health; hygienic.

sanitary engineering *n* the design, construction and installation of water and sewage systems.

sanitary towel *n* an absorbent pad worn externally during menstruation.

sanitation *n* the adoption of sanitary measures for the health of a community; hygiene.

sanitize *vt* (**sanitized, sanitizing**) to make sanitary; to make clean or hygienic; to sterilize; to clean up (language); to make (language) more acceptable by removing offensive elements.

sanity, saneness *n* the state of being sane or of sound mind.

sans *prep* without; deprived of.

Sanskrit *n* the ancient language of the Hindus, being that in which most of their vast literature is written, one of the Aryan or Indo-European family of tongues.—*adj* of or written in Sanskrit.

Santa Claus *n* a legendary fat, white-bearded old man who brings present to children at Christmas; Father Christmas.

saouari, souariwood *n* a timber obtained from tropical American trees which also yield edible nuts.

sap[1] *n* the juice or fluid which circulates in all plants, being as indispensable to vegetable life as the blood to animal life; vital juice; blood; (*colloq*) a fool.—*vt* (**sapped, sapping**) to drain the sap of; to exhaust the energy of.

sap[2] *vt* (**sapped, sapping**) to cause to fall or to render unstable by digging or wearing away the foundation; to undermine; to subvert; to destroy, as if by some secret, hidden or invisible process.—*vi* to proceed by secretly undermining.—*n* (*milit*) a ditch or trench by which approach is made to a fortress or besieged place within range of fire.

sapajou, sajou *n* any of certain small South American prehensile-tailed monkeys.

sapid *adj* possessing savour or relish; savoury.

sapidity, sapidness *n* the quality of being sapid; savour; relish.

sapience *n* the quality of being sapient; wisdom; sageness.

sapient *adj* wise; sage; knowing; discerning; proceeding from a wiseacre (now generally ironical or used of affected wisdom).

sapless *adj* lacking sap; dry; withered; lacking healthy vital juice.

sapling *n* a young tree full of sap.

sapodilla *n* a large tree of the West Indies, yielding a fine fruit.

saponaceous *adj* soapy; resembling soap; having the qualities of soap.

saponification *n* conversion into soap; the process in which fatty substances form soap through combination with an alkali.

saponify *vt* (**saponified, saponifying**) to convert into soap by combination with an alkali.

saponin *n* a vegetable principle found in the root of soapwort and other plants that causes water to froth like soap on being agitated.

saponite *n* a silicate of magnesia and alumina, occurring in soft, soapy, amorphous masses.

sapor *n* taste; savour.

saporific *adj* producing taste or relish.

sappanwood *n* a wood produced by a tree of southern Asia which yields a red colour used in dyeing.

sapper *n* a soldier of an engineer corps or who is trained in fortification or siege works; a member (any rank) of the Royal Engineers.

Sapphic *adj* pertaining to Sappho, a Grecian poetess; (*pros*) applied to a kind of verse said to have been invented by Sappho.—*n* a Sapphic verse.

sapphire *n* a precious stone, next in hardness to the diamond, belonging to the corundum class and of various shades of blue colour; hence, a rich blue colour; blue.—*adj* resembling sapphire; blue.

sappy *adj* abounding with sap; juicy; succulent; (*colloq*) foolish.

saprophagous *adj* feeding on substances in a state of decomposition.

saprophyte *n* a plant that grows on decaying vegetable matter.

saprophytic *adj* pertaining to saprophytes.

sapwood *n* the outer wood of branches and tree trunks, which contains living cells and conducts water and stores food as well as providing support.

saraband *n* a dance used in Spain, derived from the Saracens; a piece of music adapted to the dance.

Saracen *n* a member of a nomadic people of the Syrian desert; a Muslim at the time ot the Crusades.

sarcasm *n* a bitter cutting expression; a satirical remark; a bitter gibe; a taunt.

sarcastic *adj* characterized by sarcasm; bitterly cutting.

sarcenet, sarsenet *n* a species of fine thin woven silk used for linings, etc.

sarcode *n* structureless gelatinous matter forming the bodies of protozoans.

sarcoid *adj* resembling flesh.

sarcology *n* that part of anatomy which deals with the soft parts of the body.

sarcoma *n* (*pl* **sarcomata, sarcomas**) a fleshy growth; a malignant tumour of connective tissues; (*bot*) a fleshy disc.

sarcophagous *adj* feeding on flesh; flesh-eating.

sarcophagus *n* (*pl* **sarcophagi, sarcophaguses**) a coffin or tomb of stone; a kind of stone chest, generally more or less ornamented, for receiving a dead body.

sarcosis *n* the formation of flesh in a wound; a fleshy tumour; sarcoma.

sarcous *adj* belonging to flesh or muscle.

sard, sardius *n* a variety of carnelian of a translucent deep blood-red colour.

sardine *n* a small fish of the herring family, large quantities of which are caught, preserved, salted and hermetically sealed in tin boxes with oil.

sardius *n* same as **sard**.

sardonic *adj* bitterly ironical; sarcastic; derisive; mocking.

sardonyx *n* a precious stone, a beautiful variety of onyx, consisting of alternate layers of sard and white chalcedony.

sargasso, sargassum *n* gulf weed, floating on the surface of the sea, giving to part of the Atlantic the name Sargasso Sea.

sari *n* a woman's garment consisting of a long piece of cloth wrapped round the waist and across the shoulder, worn particularly by Hindu women.

sark *n* a shirt.

sarong *n* a garment consisting of a cloth wrapped round the lower part of the body, worn especially in the Malay archipelago and the Pacific islands.

sarsaparilla *n* any of various tropical American trailing plants; the dried roots used as a flavouring and formerly in medicine; a soft drink flavoured with the roots.

sarsen, sarsenstone *n* one of the large flat blocks of sandstone found on the chalk flats or downs of Wiltshire, etc.

sarsenet *n* same as **sarcenet**.

sartorial *adj* pertaining to a tailor; of or relating to the making of men's clothing.

sash[1] *n* a band or scarf worn over the shoulder or round the waist for ornament, usually of silk, variously made and ornamented.—*vt* to adorn with a sash.

sash[2] *n* the framed part of a window in which the glass is fixed; a similar part of a greenhouse, etc; the frame in which a saw is fixed to prevent its bending when worked.—*vt* to furnish with sash windows.

sash bar *n* one of the vertical and transverse pieces in a window frame.

sash cord *n* the rope by which a window sash is suspended in its frame.

sasin *n* a swift antelope abundant in the plains of India.

sassaby *n* a South African antelope.

sassafras *n* a North American laurel; the aromatic dried root of this used as a flavouring.

sassenach *n* a name applied by the Celts of the British Isles to persons of Saxon race; an English person.

Satan *n* the devil or prince of darkness; the chief of the fallen angels; the arch-fiend.

satanic, satanical *adj* pertaining to Satan; resembling Satan; extremely malicious or wicked; devilish; infernal.

Satanism *n* the evil and malicious disposition of Satan; the worship of Satan.

satchel *n* a little sack or bag; a bag in which school pupils carry their books to and from school.

sate *vt* (**sated, sating**) to satisfy the appetite or desire of; to feed beyond natural desire; to glut; to satiate.

sateen *n* a glossy fabric resembling satin but with a woollen or cotton instead of a silk face.

satellite *n* a subservient follower; a nation economically dependent on a more powerful one; a secondary planet or moon; a small planet revolving round a larger one; a man-made object orbiting the earth, moon, etc, to gather scientific information or for communications.

satiate *vt* (**satiated, satiating**) to satisfy the

sari

satchel

appetite or desire of; to feed or nourish to the full; to sate; to surfeit; to fill to repletion.—*adj* filled to satiety; glutted.

satiety *n* the state of being satiated; an excess of gratification which excites wearisomeness or loathing; a being surfeited.

satin *n* a glossy silk cloth of a thick, close texture with an overshot woof.—*adj* belonging to or made of satin.

satinbird *n* an Australian bird, so called from the glossy dark-purple plumage of the male.

satinet *n* a thin satin; a particular kind of twilled cloth, made of woollen weft and cotton warp, pressed and dressed to produce a glossy surface in imitation of satin.

satinwood *n* the wood of an Indian tree of a deep yellow colour, heavy and durable.

satiny *adj* resembling satin; having a surface or texture like satin.

satire *n* a literary composition in which people and their manners or actions are attacked with irony, sarcasm or similar weapons; sarcastic ridicule; trenchant invective.

satirical, satiric *adj* belonging to satire; conveying or containing satire; given to satire; severe in language.

satirist *n* one who satirizes; one who writes satire.

saucepan

satirize *vt* (**satirized, satirizing**) to attack with satire; to make the object of satire.

satisfaction *n* the act of satisfying or state of being satisfied; gratification of appetite or desire; contentment in possession and enjoyment; settlement of a claim due; payment; that which satisfies; compensation; atonement; the opportunity of satisfying one's honour by a duel.

satisfactory *adj* giving or producing satisfaction; yielding content; relieving the mind from doubt or uncertainty; making amends or recompense; atoning.

satisfy *vt* (**satisfied, satisfying**) to grant fully the needs, wishes or desires of; to supply to the full extent with what is wished for; to make content; to comply with the rightful demands of; to give what is due to; to pay, liquidate, requite; to fulfil the conditions of; to answer; to free from doubt, suspense or uncertainty; to set at rest the mind of.—*vi* to give satisfaction or content.

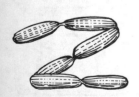

sausage

satrap *n* a governor of a province under the ancient Persian monarchy; a prince; a petty despot.

satsuma *n* a small, loose-skinned kind of orange.

saturate *vt* (**saturated, saturating**) to cause to become completely penetrated, impregnated or soaked; to fill fully; to imbue thoroughly; to impregnate or unite with till no more can be received (*air saturated with moisture*).

saturated *adj* being full; pure in colour; (*chem*) absorbing the maximum amount possible of a substance.

saturation *n* the act of saturation or state of being saturated; the combination of one body with another in such proportions that they neutralize each other; solution continued till the solvent can contain no more.

saturation point *n* the point at which a substance can absorb no more of another substance.

Saturday *n* the seventh or last day of the week.

Saturn *n* in Roman myth, the god of agriculture, gardening, etc; (*astron*) one of the planets, smaller than Jupiter and more remote from the sun.

Saturnalia *npl* in ancient Rome, the festival of Saturn, celebrated as a period of unrestrained licence and merriment; hence, any period of noisy licence and revelry; unconstrained, licentious revelling.

saturnine *adj* supposed to be under the influence of the planet Saturn, which tended to make people morose; morose; of a gloomy temper; heavy; grave; phlegmatic.

satyr *n* in classical myth, a sylvan deity or demigod, half man and half goat, an attendant on Bacchus and distinguished for lasciviousness.

sauce *n* a condiment or composition (usually liquid) to be eaten with food for improving its relish, for whetting the appetite or aiding digestion; pertness; insolence; saucy language.—*vt* (**sauced, saucing**) to add a sauce to; to season; to treat with pert language; to be saucy to.

sauceboat *n* a dish for holding sauce.

saucepan *n* a deep cooking pan, usually with a handle and a lid.

saucer *n* a piece of china or other ware in which a teacup or coffee cup is set; something resembling a saucer; a flying saucer.

saucy *adj* showing impertinent boldness or impudent flippancy; treating superiors with impertinence; rude; impudent; pert; forward; expressive of impudence (*a saucy eye*).

sauerkraut *n* a German dish consisting of cabbage cut fine, pressed into a cask with alternate layers of salt and allowed to ferment.

sauna *n* exposure of the body to hot steam; the room where this is done.

saunter *vi* to wander idly; to walk leisurely along; to loiter; to linger; to dawdle.—*n* a sauntering or place for sauntering.

saurian *adj* pertaining to the lizards; having lizard-like characteristics.—*n* formerly, a lizard.

sausage *n* an article of food consisting of chopped or minced meat, seasoned and stuffed into properly cleaned entrails of ox, sheep or pig or other casing.

sausage roll *n* meat minced and seasoned as for sausages, enveloped in pastry.

Sauterne *n* a white Bordeaux wine made near Sauternes in the Gironde department of France.

savage *adj* pertaining to the forest or wilderness; wild; uncultivated; untamed; violent; brutal; uncivilized; untaught; rude; cruel; barbarous; inhuman.—*n* a human being in his or her primitive state; one who is untaught or uncivilized; a person of brutal cruelty; a barbarian.

savageness *n* the quality of being savage; barbarism; cruelty; barbarousness.

savagery *n* the state of being savage; a wild, uncultivated condition; an act of cruelty or barbarity; an uncivilized state.

savanna, savannah *n* an extensive open grassy plain or meadow in a tropical region.

savant *n* a person of learning; a person of science; a person eminent for his or her acquirements.

save[1] *vt* (**saved, saving**) to preserve from destruction or evil of any kind; to snatch, keep or rescue from impending danger; to rescue from sin and eternal death; to deliver; to keep clear; to rescue from the power or influence of; to spare; to keep from doing or suffering (with a double object, as *to save a person trouble*); to hinder from being spent or lost (*to save time*); to hinder from being used; to reserve or lay by; to lay up or hoard; (*theol*) to deliver from sin.—*vi* to be economical; to avoid expense, waste, etc; to economize; to store up money or goods; (in sport) to keep an opponent from scoring or winning.—*n* the act of preventing one's opponent from scoring in football, etc.

save[2] *prep* except; not including.

saveloy *n* a highly seasoned dried sausage.

saving[1] *adj* preserving from evil or destruction; frugal; not lavish; avoiding unnecessary expense; incurring no loss though not gainful (*a saving voyage*); reserving, as some title or right (*a saving clause*).—*n* that which is saved; (*pl*) money saved for future use.

saving[2] *prep* with exception; excepting.

savings bank *n* a bank specially established for receiving and securely investing deposits and for their accumulation at interest.

saviour *n* one who saves, preserves or delivers from destruction or danger.

Saviour *n* Jesus Christ, the Redeemer.

savory *n* a herb used as a flavouring agent in food.

savour *n* flavour; taste; power or quality that affects the palate; characteristic property; distinctive quality.—*vi* to have a particular taste or flavour; to partake of the quality, nature or appearance of something else; to smack (followed by *of*, as *his conduct savours of pride*).—*vt* to like; to relish; to have the flavour or quality of.

savoury *adj* having savour or relish; spicy; not sweet; pleasing to the taste; palatable; agreeable in general.—*n* a savoury dish served either at the beginning or end of dinner; (*pl*) snacks served with drinks.

savoy *n* a variety of cabbage cultivated for winter use.

saw[1] *n* a cutting instrument consisting of a blade, band or disc of thin iron or steel with a toothed edge.—*vt* (*pret* **sawed**, *pp* **sawed** or **sawn**, *ppr* **sawing**) to cut with a saw; to form by cutting with a saw; to move through, as in the act of sawing (*to saw the air*).—*vi* to use a saw; to cut with a saw.

saw[2] *n* a saying; proverb; maxim.

sawdust *n* the small fragments of wood or other material produced by the cutting of a saw.

sawfish *n* a fish related to the sharks and rays (so called from the spines growing like teeth on both edges of its long bony snout).

sawfly *n* a insect, the female of which has an ovipositor with serrated or toothed edges.

sawmill *n* a mill for sawing timber.

sawn-off *adj* (of a shotgun) having the barrel shortened to aid concealment and increase the spread of shot.

sawyer *n* one whose occupation is to saw timber into planks or boards or to saw wood for fuel.

saxhorn *n* a brass wind instrument with a wide mouthpiece and three, four or five cylinders, much used in military bands.

saxifrage *n* any of various plants with small flowers and tufted leaves which mostly inhabit the colder and temperate parts of the northern zone and are mostly rock plants.

Saxon *n* one of the people who formerly dwelt in the northern part of Germany and who invaded and conquered England in the fifth and sixth centuries; a Saxon of England as opposed to an Angle or Anglian; an Anglo-Saxon; one of the English race; the language of the Saxons; Anglo-Saxon; a native or inhabitant of modern Saxony.—*adj* pertaining to the Saxons, their country or their language; Anglo-Saxon; pertaining to modern Saxony.

saxophone *n* a brass wind instrument with a conical bore, a single reed, finger keys and a clarinet mouthpiece.

say *vt* (*pret*, *pp* **said**, *ppr* **saying**) to utter or express in words; to speak; to argue; to allege by way of argument; to give as an opinion; to repeat, rehearse, recite; to recite without singing; to answer; to utter by way of reply; to tell; to suppose; to as-

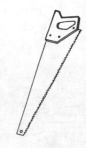

saw

saxophone

765

sume.—*vi* to tell; to express in words.—*adv* for example (*say 3000 men*).—*n* what one has to say (*he said his say*); something said; a statement.—*interj* expressing admiration, surprise, etc.

saying *n* that which is said; a sentence uttered; a proverbial expression; a maxim; an adage.

scab *n* a dry crust formed over a sore in healing; mange in horses; a disease of sheep; (*sl*) a worker who refuses to join a strike or who takes the job of a striker.—*vi* (**scabbed, scabbing**) to form a scab; to be covered with scabs; to work as a scab.

scabbard *n* the sheath of a sword or other similar weapon.—*vt* to put in a scabbard or sheath.

scabby *adj* abounding with scabs; diseased with scabs; mean; vile; worthless.

scabies *n* a contagious, itching skin disease.

scabious[1] *adj* consisting of scabs; rough; itchy.

scabious[2] *n* any of a genus of Mediterranean plants with tightly clustered blue, red or white flowers, formerly deemed efficacious against scabby eruptions of the skin.

scabrous *adj* (of a surface) rough or scaly; indecent, offensive; intractable.

scaffold *n* a temporary stage or platform; an elevated platform for the execution of a criminal; a temporary structure of timber, etc, for workers engaged in building or repairing houses, etc.—*vt* to provide with a scaffold.

scaffolding *n* a temporary framework of timber and metal for supporting workers engaged on some building; materials for a scaffold.

scald *vt* to burn and injure with or as with hot liquor; to expose to a strong heat over a fire or in water or other liquor (*to scald milk*).—*n* a burn or injury from scalding.

scalding *adj* so hot as to scald the skin; cutting.

scale[1] *n* one of the overlapping plates on the exterior of certain animals; one of the thin, small plates which protect the skin of many fishes; one of the somewhat similar laminae of reptiles; anything resembling the scale of a fish or other animal; a thin flake or lamina (*a scale of bone, iron*, etc); (*bot*) a rudimentary leaf on the exterior of a leaf bud.—*vt* (**scaled, scaling**) to strip or clear of scales; to take off in thin laminae or scales.—*vi* to come off in scales or thin layers.

scale[2] *n* the dish of a balance; the balance itself or whole instrument (in this sense generally in the plural).

scale[3] *n* anything graduated, especially when applied as a measure or rule; a mathematical instrument consisting of a slip of wood, ivory, etc, with spaces graduated and numbered on its surface, for measur-

scales

scalpel

ing or laying off distances; any succession of ascending or descending steps or degrees; series of ranks; relative dimensions without difference in proportion of parts; a basis for a numerical system (*the decimal scale*); (*mus*) a succession of notes arranged in the order of pitch and comprising the sounds that may occur in a piece of music written in a given key; the diatonic scale, having its eight notes ascending by five tones and two semitones; also the series of notes able to be produced by voices or instruments (*the scale of a violin*).—*vt* (**scaled, scaling**) to climb, as by a ladder (*to scale a wall*); to ascend by steps; to clamber up; to make or draw to scale; to increase or decrease in size.

scale armour *n* armour consisting of small plates of steel partly overlapping each other like the scales of a fish.

scale beam *n* the beam or lever of a balance.

scalene *adj* (*geom*) having three sides unequal.—*n* a scalene triangle.

scallion *n* a spring onion.

scallop, scollop *n* a marine bivalve of the oyster family; a kind of dish for baking oysters in; a curving on the edge of anything, like the segment of a circle.—*vt* to cut the edge or border of into scallops or segments of circles.

scallywag, scallawag *n* a rogue; a rascal; a scamp.

scalp *n* the outer covering of the skull, usually covered with hair; the skin of the head with the hair on it formerly torn off by certain American Indian tribes as a mark of victory; any victory trophy.—*vt* to deprive of the scalp; to criticize sharply.

scalpel *n* a short, thin, very sharp knife used in anatomical dissections and surgical operations.

scaly *adj* covered or abounding with scales; having the form of scales or thin laminae.

scaly anteater *n* a pangolin.

scam *n* (*colloq*) a swindle.

scamp *n* a rascal; a mischievous child.

scamper *vi* to run with speed; to hasten away.—*n* a hasty flight; a hurried run.

scan *vt* (**scanned, scanning**) to examine (poetry) by counting the metrical feet or syllables; to read so as to indicate the metrical structure; to examine minutely; to scrutinize; to make a pictorial record of (a body or part of a body) by various techniques, such as ultrasonics; to examine with a radiological device; to pass an electronic beam over; to check for recorded data by means of a mechanical or electronic device.—*vi* (of a poem) to conform to a rhythmical pattern.—*n* the action of scanning; an instance of being scanned; a pictorial record of a body or part of a body; the image produced by scanning.

scandal *n* offence given by the faults or

misdeeds of another; public reproach or reprobation; talk arising from immoral behaviour; a feeling of moral outrage; disgrace; opprobrium; shame; something uttered which is false and injurious to reputation; defamatory talk; slander.—*vt* to throw scandal on; to slander.

scandalize *vt* (**scandalized, scandalizing**) to offend by some action considered very wrong or outrageous; to shock; to give offence to; to disgrace; to slander.

scandalmonger *n* one who spreads scandal.

scandalous *adj* causing scandal or offence; shameful; disgraceful to reputation; libellous; slanderous.

scanner *n* a person or thing that scans; an electronic device that monitors or scans; a device for receiving or transmitting radar signals; an instrument which makes an image of an internal organ for medical purposes.

scansion *n* the act of scanning; the metrical structure of verse.

scansorial *adj* of, pertaining to or belonging to the climbing birds, such as the cuckoos, woodpeckers, parrots, etc, having feet with two toes turned backwards and two forwards.

scant *adj* scarcely sufficient; rather less than is needed for the purpose; not enough; having a limited supply; scarce; short (with *of*).—*vt* to limit; to stint; to keep on short allowance; to afford or give out sparingly; to be niggard of; to grudge.—*adv* scarcely; hardly; not quite.

scantling *n* a quantity cut for a particular purpose; a sample; a pattern; a small quantity; the dimensions of, timber, stones, etc, in length, breadth and thickness; timber less than five inches square; a kind of trestle for supporting a cask.

scanty *adj* lacking amplitude or extent; narrow; small; scant; not ample; hardly sufficient (*a scanty supply*).

scape[1] *n* (*bot*) a leafless stalk of a flower; (*archit*) the shaft of a column.

scape[2] *vti* (*arch*) escape.

scapegoat *n* in the Old Testament, a goat which was sent into the wilderness bearing the iniquities of the people which had been laid on him by the hands of the high priest; hence, one made to bear the blame of others.

scapegrace *n* a graceless hare-brained person; an incorrigible rascal.

scapula *n* (*pl* **scapulas, scapulae**) the shoulder blade.

scapular *adj* pertaining to the scapula or the shoulder.—*n* an ecclesiastical garment consisting of a wide piece of cloth worn over the shoulders and hanging down at the front and back; any of the feathers along the base of a bird's wing.

scapulary *n* a scapular.

scar[1] *n* the mark of a wound or an ulcer remaining after healing; a cicatrix; a hurt; a wound; (*bot*) a mark left after the fall of a leaf or on a seed after the separation of its stem.—*vt* (**scarred, scarring**) to mark with a scar or scars; to wound; to hurt.—*vi* to be covered with a scar; to form a scar.

scar[2] *n* a cliff; a naked detached rock; a bare and broken place on the side of a hill or mountain.

scarab *n* a dung beetle held to be sacred in ancient Egypt; a gem or seal in the shape of this.

Scaramouch *n* a boastful cowardly character in Italian comedy.

scarce *adj* not plentiful or abundant; being in small quantity in proportion to demand; deficient; seldom met with; rare; uncommon; unfrequent; scantily supplied; not having much (with *of*).—**to make oneself scarce** to disappear voluntarily; to get out of the way.—*adv* scarcely.

scarcely *adv* hardly; barely; scantly; but just; with difficulty.

scarcity *n* the state or condition of being scarce; dearth; lack; famine.

scare *vt* (**scared, scaring**) to frighten; to terrify suddenly; to strike with sudden terror.—*n* a sudden fright or panic; a sudden terror inspired by a trivial cause; a causeless alarm.

scarecrow *n* anything set up to frighten crows or other birds from crops; anything terrifying without danger; a person so poorly clad as to resemble a scarecrow.

scarf[1] *n* a rectangular or square piece of cloth worn round the neck, the head or loosely round the shoulders for warmth or decoration.

scarf[2] *n* in carpentry, the joint by which the ends of two pieces of timber are joined so as to overlap and form a continuous piece.—*vt* to cut a scarf on; to join by means of a scarf.

scarfskin *n* the cuticle or epidermis; the outer thin layer of skin.

scarify *vt* (**scarified, scarifying**) (*surg*) to make a small cut or incision in the skin; to scratch; to criticize savagely; to loosen the surface of (soil); to hasten germination by softening the wall (of a hard seed).

scarlatina *n* scarlet fever.

scarlet *n* a bright red colour, brighter than crimson; cloth of a scarlet colour; scarlet robe or dress.—*adj* of the colour scarlet; of a bright red colour; immoral; sinful.

scarp *n* a low steep slope; (*fort*) the interior slope of a ditch at the foot of a rampart.

scathing *adj* bitterly critical; cutting; damaging; harming; withering.

scatter *vt* to throw loosely about; to sprinkle; to strew; to disperse; to dissipate; to separate or remove to a distance from each other; to disunite; to frustrate, disappoint

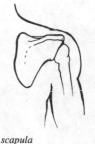

scapula

scarab

and overthrow (*to scatter hopes*, etc).—*vi* to disperse; to separate from each other; to straggle apart.

scatterbrain *n* a thoughtless person; one incapable of concentration.

scattered *adj* sprinkled or thinly spread; loose and irregular in distribution.

scaup *n* a species of diving duck which feeds on molluscs, etc.

scavenge *vi* (**scavenged, scavenging**) to gather things discarded by others; (of an animal) to eat decaying matter.

scavenger *n* one who or that which scavenges.

scenario *n* (*pl* **scenarios**) an abstract of the chief incidents in any dramatic work arranged according to act and scene, giving a skeleton of the piece; the plot or script of a film, etc; an outline of events; any imagined or projected sequence of events.

scene *n* a stage; that part of a theatre in which the acting is done; the imaginary place in which the action of a play is supposed to occur; the surroundings amid which anything is transacted; a whole series of actions and events connected and exhibited; an assemblage of objects displayed at one view; a place and objects seen together; a landscape; a view; one of the painted slides, hangings or other devices used to give an appearance of reality to the action of a play; a part of a play, being a division of an act; an exhibition of strong feeling between two or more persons; a theatrical display of emotion; an artificial or affected action or course of action; (*colloq*) an area of interest or activity (*the music scene*).

scenery *n* the paintings representing the scenes of a play; the general appearance or natural features of a place.

scene-shifter *n* a person who arranges the movable scenes in a theatre.

scenic *adj* pertaining to the stage; dramatic; theatrical; relating to natural scenery; picturesque.

scent *n* that which, issuing from a body, affects the olfactory nerves of animals; odour; smell; perfume; the power of smelling; odour left on the ground enabling an animal's track to be followed; course of pursuit or discovery; track.—*vt* to perceive by the olfactory organs; to smell; to perfume; to get wind of, detect.

sceptic *n* one who doubts the truth of any principle or system of principles or doctrines; one who disbelieves or hesitates to believe; a disbeliever; a person who doubts the existence of God or the truth of revelation; one who disbelieves in the divine origin of Christianity.

sceptical *adj* belonging to or characteristic of a sceptic or scepticism; holding the opinions of a sceptic.

sceptre

scepticism *n* the doctrines or opinions of a sceptic; disbelief or inability to believe; doubt; incredulity; a doubting of the truth of revelation or of the Christian religion.

sceptre *n* a staff or baton borne by a monarch or other ruler as a symbol of authority.—**the sceptre** royal power or authority.

sceptred *adj* bearing a sceptre; invested with royal power; regal.

schedule *n* a sheet of paper or parchment containing a written or printed list; a list annexed to a larger document, as to a will, lease, etc; a timed plan for a project.—*vt* (**scheduled, scheduling**) to place in a schedule or catalogue; to plan.

scheme *n* a combination of things connected and adjusted by design; a system; a plan of something to be done; a project; the representation of any design or geometrical figure; a diagram.—*vt* (**schemed, scheming**) to plan, contrive, plot, project, design.—*vi* to form a plan; to contrive.

schemer *n* one who schemes; a contriver; a plotter.

scheming *adj* given to forming schemes; artful; intriguing.

scherzando *adv* (*mus*) in a playful or sportive manner.—*n* (*pl* **scherzandos, scherzandi**) a piece of music played in this manner.

scherzo *n* (*pl* **scherzos, scherzi**) (*mus*) a lively passage of some length, as in a symphony.

schism *n* a split or division in a community; commonly, a division or separation in a church or denomination of Christians, occasioned by differing opinions; breach of unity among people of the same religious faith; discord; disharmony.

schismatic *adj* pertaining to schism; partaking of the nature of schism; tending to schism.—*n* one who takes part in a schism.

schist *n* (*geol*) rocks which have a foliated structure and split in thin irregular plates; properly confined to metamorphic rocks (as gneiss) consisting of layers of different minerals.

schizoid *adj* (*colloq*) mildly schizophrenic.—*n* a schizoid person.

schizophrenia *n* a mental disorder characterized by withdrawal from reality, delusions, deterioration of the personality, etc; the presence of mutually contradictory qualities or aspects.

schizophrenic *adj* suffering from schizophrenia; pertaining to schizophrenia.—*n* a person suffering from schizophrenia.

schmaltz *n* sickly sentimentality; overly sentimental music, literature, art or films.

schmaltzy *adj* overly sentimental.

schnapps *n* a Dutch alcoholic beverage distilled from potatoes; in Germany, any strong spirit.

schnauzer *n* a breed of terrier with a short wiry coat, originally from Germany.

scholar *n* one who attends a school; one who learns from a teacher; a pupil; a disciple; a person of letters; a learned person; a person of high attainments in learning; one who learns anything; a person who holds a scholarship.

scholarly *adj* like a scholar; becoming a scholar or person of learning.

scholarship *n* the character of a scholar; attainments in science or literature; erudition; learning; a regularly settled allowance of money for a scholar at some educational institution; a foundation for the support of a student.

scholastic *adj* pertaining to or suiting a scholar, school or schools; characteristic of a scholar; pertaining to scholars of the Middle Ages who adopted the system of Aristotle and spent much time on points of speculation; hence, pedantic; formal.—*n* one who adheres to the scholastic method.

scholiast *n* one who makes scholiums; a grammarian of ancient times who annotated the classics.

scholiastic *adj* pertaining to a scholiast.

scholium *n* (*pl* **scholiums, scholia**) a marginal note, annotation or remark; an explanatory comment, such as those annexed to the Latin and Greek authors by the early grammarians.

school[1] *n* a place in which persons are instructed in any kind of learning; an educational establishment; a place in which instruction is imparted to the young; one of the seminaries of the scholastic philosophy of the Middle Ages; a body of pupils; the disciples or followers of a teacher; those who hold a common doctrine or accept the same teachings or principles (*the Socratic school, painters of the Italian school*); a system or state of matters prevalent at a certain time (*the old school, the new school*); any place of discipline or training.—*adj* relating to a school or to education; scholastic.—*vt* to instruct; to educate; to discipline; to chide and admonish; to reprove.

school[2] *n* a shoal of porpoises, whales or other aquatic animals of one kind swimming together.

schoolbook *n* a book used in schools.

schoolboy *n* a boy attending school.

schoolfellow, schoolmate *n* an associate in school.

schoolgirl *n* a girl belonging to a school.

schoolhouse *n* a house appropriated for use as a school; a schoolteacher's dwelling house.

schooling *n* instruction in school; tuition; reproof; reprimand.

schoolmaster *n* a man who teaches in a school.

schoolmistress *n* a woman who teaches in a school.

schoolroom *n* a room for teaching.

schoolteacher *n* a person who gives regular instruction in a school; a teacher, instructor or preceptor of a school; one who or that which disciplines and instructs.

schooner *n* a vessel originally with two masts, now often with three or four, and her chief sails fore and aft sails, her mainsail and foresail being both extended by a gaff and a boom; a measure of beer about two-thirds of a pint; a large drinking glass for sherry, etc.

schorl *n* a mineral of a pitchy lustre and colour, brittle texture and capable of being rendered electric by heat or friction, usually occurring in granitic rocks and often embedded in feldspar and quartz; tourmaline.

schottische *n* a dance resembling a polka; the music suited for such a dance in 2-4 time.

sciagraphy *n* the act or art of correctly delineating shadows; the art of sketching objects with correct shading.

sciatica *n* pain along the sciatic nerve, especially in the back of the thigh; pain in the lower back or adjacent parts.

sciatic *adj* pertaining to the hip (*the sciatic artery* or *nerve*).

sciatic nerve *n* the major nerve in the leg, passing down the back of the thigh from the base of the spine.

science *n* knowledge; comprehension or understanding; knowledge coordinated, arranged and systematized; hence, the knowledge regarding any one department of mind or matter coordinated, arranged and systematized (*the science of botany, of astronomy*, etc); art derived from precepts or built on principles; skill resulting from training; special skill.

science fiction *n* a form of fiction dealing with a plot concerning supposed scientific and technological advances, set in the future and often including planets other than earth.

scientific *adj* pertaining to science; evincing or endowed with a knowledge of science; treating of science; skilled in science; according to the rules or principles of science.

scientist *n* a person skilled in or devoted to science; a scientific person; a specialist in a branch of science.

sci-fi *n* (*colloq*) an abbreviation of **science fiction**.

scilicet *adv* to wit; videlicet; namely.

scimitar *n* an oriental sword, the blade of which is single-edged, short, curved and broadest at the point end.

scintilla *n* a spark; a glimmer; the least particle; a trace.

schoolteacher

scientist

scintillate *vi* (**scintillated, scintillating**) to emit sparks; to sparkle or twinkle, as the stars; to sparkle.

scintillation *n* the act of scintillating or sparkling; the twinkling of the stars.

scintillation counter *n* an instrument for recording the intensity of a radioactive source.

sciolism *n* superficial knowledge.

sciolist *n* one who knows things superficially.

scion *n* a shoot or twig cut for the purpose of being grafted on some other tree or for planting; (*fig*) a descendant; an heir.

scirrhous *adj* proceeding from or of the nature of scirrhus; indurated; knotty.

scirrhus, scirrhosis *n* (*med*) a cancerous tumour consisting of fibrous tissue.

scission *n* the act of cutting or dividing by an edged instrument; the state of being cut; division.

scissorbill *n* the skimmer.

scissors *npl* a cutting instrument consisting of two blades movable on a pin in the centre which cut from opposite sides against an object placed between them.

sclerosis *n* hardening resulting from disease, especially of the nervous system and of arteries.

sclerotic *adj* (applied to the outer membrane of the eyeball) hard, firm; pertaining to sclerosis; affected with sclerosis.

scoff *n* an expression of derision, mockery, scorn or contempt; a gibe; a flout; an object of derision.—*vi* to show insolent ridicule or mockery; to utter contemptuous language; to mock (with *at* before the object).—*vt* to mock at; to ridicule.

scoffer *n* one who scoffs; a mocker or scorner.

scold *vi* to find fault in rude language; to utter harsh or rude rebuke; to make use of abuse or vituperation.—*vt* to chide with rudeness and ill-temper; to vituperate.—*n* one who scolds.

scolding *n* the act of one who scolds; a vituperative harangue; a rating.

scollop *n, vt* same as **scallop**.

sconce[1] *n* a cover or screen; a cover or protection for a light; a case for a candle; the tube in a candlestick in which the candle is inserted; a fixed candlestick on a wall.

sconce[2] *n* (*fort*) a work for defence; a bulwark; a fort, as at a pass or river; a covering for the head; a helmet; a headpiece; the head itself; the skull.—*vt* (**sconced, sconcing**) to shelter; to ensconce.

sconce[3] *n* a covering for the head; a helmet; a headpiece; the head itself; the skull.

scone *n* a small, round cake of flour and fat, baked and spread with butter, etc.

scoop *n* a thin metallic shovel with capacious sides for lifting grain; a similar but smaller utensil for lifting sugar, flour, etc;

a large ladle with a long handle for dipping in fluids; a spoon-shaped surgical instrument; a sort of pan for holding coals.—*vt* to take out with a scoop or as with a scoop; to ladle out; to empty as with a scoop; to hollow out; to excavate.

scooper *n* one who or that which scoops; a wading bird, the avocet, so named from its bill being curved upwards at the tip.

scoot *vi* to run quickly; to bolt or run away.

scooter *n* a child's two-wheeled vehicle with a footboard on which one foot rests while the other is used to propel it and with a handle for steering; a motor scooter.

scopalamine, hyoscine *n* an alkaloid extracted from certain plants and used as a sedative and for travel sickness.

scope *n* a mark shot at; an aim or end kept in view; ultimate design or purpose; intention; free or wide outlook or aim; amplitude of intellectual range; space; liberty; sweep; extent; range; the opportunity to use one's abilities; (*colloq*) an instrument for viewing, as a microscope, etc.

scorbutic *adj* pertaining to or affected with scurvy.

scorch *vt* to burn superficially; to subject to a degree of heat that injures the surface; to parch.—*vi* to be burnt on the surface; to be parched.

scorcher *n* (*colloq*) a very hot day.

score *n* a notch; a cut made on a tally for the purpose of keeping account of something; the number twenty, as being marked off by a special or larger score; in archery, twenty yards; an account or reckoning kept by notches, marks or otherwise; an account of dues; hence, what is due; a debt; the number of points made by players in certain games; account, reason, ground; a line drawn; a long superficial scratch; (*mus*) a written copy of a musical composition with the parts for all the different voices or instruments; the music composed for a film; a grievance for settling; a reason or motive; (*colloq*) the real facts; (*pl*) an indefinite, large number.—*vt* (**scored, scoring**) to make scores or scratches on; to furrow; to set down, as in an account; to record; to mark; to note; to enter or register; to make a score of; to get for oneself, as points, hits, runs, etc, in certain games; (*mus*) to write out, as the different parts of a composition, in proper order and arrangement.—*vi* to make or keep a score; to make a point or hit or a clever retort; to gain an advantage; (*sl*) to be successful in seduction.—**to score off** to get the better of someone.

scoreboard *n* a board on which the score of a game is displayed, as in cricket.

scorer *n* one who scores; one who keeps the score or tally at games, matches, etc.

scoria *n* (*pl* **scoriae**) the slag rejected after

scissors

scooter

the reduction of metallic ores; dross; (pl) the cinders of volcanic eruptions.

scorn n extreme and passionate contempt; disdain springing from a person's opinion of the meanness and unworthiness of an object; the expression of this feeling; a scoff; a subject of extreme contempt or disdain.—vt to hold in scorn; to despise; to disdain; to treat with scorn; to make a mock of.—vi to feel scorn or disdain; to show scorn.

scorner n one who scorns; a despiser; a scoffer; a derider; one who scoffs at religion.

scornful adj full of scorn; contemptuous; disdainful.

Scorpio n a constellation of the zodiac; the Scorpion.

scorpion n a small tropical insect-like animal with a pair of large nipping claws and a long jointed tail terminating in a poisonous sting; a kind of painful scourge or whip.

scot n formerly, a payment of money, a tax.—**to pay scot and lot** to settle all debts.

Scot n a native or inhabitant of Scotland; a member of a Celtic people from Ireland who settled in northern Britain in the fifth and sixth centuries.

scotch vt to put an end to; to quash (to scotch a rumour); (arch) to cut with shallow incisions, to notch; (arch) to maim.—n a slight cut or shallow incision; a line drawn on the ground, as in hopscotch.

Scotch n whisky made in Scotland.

Scotch mist n (colloq) a wetting mist like fine rain; a fine rain.

Scotch terrier n same as **Scottish terrier**.

scoter n a kind of sea duck abundant on some of the British coasts in winter.

scot-free adj free from payment or scot; untaxed; unhurt; safe.

Scots adj of or pertaining to Scotland, its law, money, people or language.—n the dialect of English developed in Lowland Scotland.

Scotsman, Scotswoman n (pl **Scotsmen, Scotswomen**) a native or inhabitant of Scotland; a Scot.

Scots pine n a European pine with needle-like leaves; its wood.

Scotticism n a Scots word or idiom.

Scottie n (colloq) a Scottish person; a Scottish terrier.

Scottish adj of or pertaining to Scotland or its people.

Scottish terrier, Scotch terrier n a small breed of terrier with a wiry hard coat, black or brindled in colour.

scoundrel n a base, mean, worthless person; a rascal; a person without honour or virtue.—adj belonging to a scoundrel; base; unprincipled.

scour[1] vt to rub hard with something for the purpose of cleaning; to make clean or bright on the surface; to take grease or dirt out of the fabric of, by washing or chemical appliances; to cleanse away; to flush out with a current of water; to purge.—vi to clean by rubbing; to take dirt or grease out of cloth.—n the act or process of scouring; a place scoured by running water; scouring action (as of a glacier); damage done by scouring action; a cleansing agent for cloth, etc; a kind of diarrhoea or dysentery among cattle.

scour[2] vt to pass swiftly over; to brush along; to pass swiftly over in search of something or to drive away something.—vi to rove or range; to run with celerity; to scamper.

scourge n an instrument like a whip for inflicting pain or punishment; a lash; a whip; hence, a punishment; a vindictive affliction; one who greatly afflicts, harasses or destroys; a whip for a top.—vt (**scourged, scourging**) to whip with a scourge; to whip severely; to lash; to chastise for correction; to afflict greatly; to harass.

scout[1] n one sent out to gain and bring in information, especially to observe the motions and obtain intelligence regarding an enemy; a person who seeks out new recruits for a football team, theatre, films, etc; in cricket, a fielder.

scout[2] vt to treat with disdain and contempt; to reject with scorn.

Scout n a member of the Scouting Association.

Scouting Association n an organization to encourage self-reliance and initiative, moral and physical courage and a courteous spirit in young people.

scoutmaster n the leader of a band of Scouts.

scow n a kind of large flat-bottomed boat used chiefly as a lighter or a ferryboat.

scowl vi to wrinkle the brows, as in frowning or displeasure; to let the brows droop; to look sullen or angry; to look gloomy, dark or tempestuous.—n a deep angry frown made by depressing the brows; dark or tempestuous aspect, as of the heavens; gloom.

scrabble vi (**scrabbled, scrabbling**) to make irregular, crooked marks; to scrawl; to scribble.—vt to mark with irregular lines or letters.—n a scribble; a scrawl.

Scrabble n the trademark of a game in which words are formed from individual lettered tiles on a grid.

scrag n something thin or lean, with roughness.

scraggy adj having an irregular broken surface; lean; bony.

scram vi (**scrammed, scramming**) (sl) to go away (usually in the imperative).

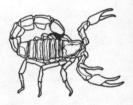

scorpion

Scotch

771

scramble *yi* (**scrambled, scrambling**) to move or climb by the aid of the hands; to move on all fours; to snatch eagerly at anything; to struggle to get somewhere before others.—*vt* to mix haphazardly; to cook eggs in a pan after mixing them with milk; to make (transmitted signals) unintelligible in transmission.—*n* the act of scrambling; a hard climb or advance; an eager contest for something in which one endeavours to get the thing before another; a rapid emergency take-off of fighter planes; a motorcycle rally over rough ground.

scrap[1] *n* a small piece; a detached, incomplete portion; a fragment; a fragment of something written or printed; a short or unconnected extract; (*pl*) bits of food.—*adj* in the form of pieces, leftovers, etc; used and discarded (*scrap metal*).—*vt* (**scrapped, scrapping**) to throw on the scrap heap (outworn or antiquated machinery, etc); to supersede; to discard; to cease to use; to abandon.

scrap[2] *n* (*colloq*) a fight or quarrel.—*vt* (**scrapped, scrapping**) to have a scrap.

scrapbook *n* a blank book for pasting in newspaper cuttings, etc.

scrape *vt* (**scraped, scraping**) to rub the surface of with a sharp or rough instrument or with something hard; to deprive of the surface coating by a sharp instrument; to grate harshly over; to clean with something sharp; to erase; to collect by laborious effort; to acquire, save or gather with difficulty (usually with *together*).—*vi* to roughen or remove a surface by rubbing; to make a harsh noise by rubbing; to play awkwardly on a violin, etc; to rub the feet on the ground; to make an awkward bow, with a drawing back of the foot.—**to scrape through** to manage or succeed with difficulty or by a slim margin—*n* a rubbing with something hard on a surface; an awkward bow accompanied by a scraping of the foot; a disagreeable predicament; a difficulty; perplexity; distress.

scraper *n* one who or that which scrapes; an instrument with which anything is scraped; a metal instrument placed at or near the door of a house on which to scrape or clean the shoes.

scrapie *n* a viral disease of sheep characterized by degeneration of the nervous system.

scrap metal *n* fragments of metal which are only of use for remelting.

scrappy *adj* consisting of scraps; disconnected; fragmentary.

scratch *vt* to rub, tear or mark the surface of with something sharp; to wound slightly by a point or points; to scrape with the nails so as not to wound; to write or draw awkwardly; to dig or excavate with the claws; to erase or blot out; to expunge; (in horse racing) to erase from the list of horses that are to compete in a race.—*vi* to use the nails, claws, etc, in tearing a surface or in digging; to withdraw from a competition.—*n* a break in a surface made by scratching; a slight furrow; a score; a slight wound; a superficial laceration; the starting point in a handicap of competitors who receive no odds.—*adj* taken at random or haphazard; heterogeneous; hastily collected (*a scratch company of actors* or *of cricketers*).

scratchy *adj* making a scratching noise; causing itching; uneven, ragged.

scrawl *vt* to draw or mark awkwardly and irregularly; to write awkwardly or imperfectly; to scribble; to make irregular lines or bad writing on.—*vi* to write unskilfully and inelegantly.—*n* a piece of unskilful, hasty or bad writing.

scrawny *adj* skinny; bony.

scream *vi* to cry out with a shrill voice; to utter a sudden, sharp outcry, as in a fright or in extreme pain; to shriek; to give out a shrill sound.—*n* a shriek or sharp, shrill cry; a sharp, harsh sound; (*colloq*) a very funny person or thing.

screamer *n* one who or that which screams; a South American wading bird with a harsh discordant voice; (*sl*) an exclamation mark.

scree *n* debris of rocks; shingle; loose stones.

screech *vi* to cry out with a sharp, shrill voice; to shriek.—*n* a sharp, shrill cry; a harsh scream; a sharp, shrill noise.

screech owl *n* an owl that screeches, in opposition to one that hoots.

screed *n* a harangue or tirade; a long tedious letter or speech.

screen *n* an appliance or article that shelters from the sun, rain, cold, etc, or from sight; an upright movable framework used in a room for excluding draughts or intercepting the heat of a fire; that which shelters, protects or conceals; a riddle or sieve; a wire sieve for sifting sand, lime, etc; (*archit*) an ornamental partition of wood, stone or metal in a church; a coarse wire mesh over a window or door to keep out insects; an electronic display (as in a television set, computer terminal, etc); a surface on which films or slides are projected.—*vt* to conceal or shelter; to grade by passing through a screen; to sort out by tests of ability, trustworthiness, etc; to test for illness, etc; to show (a film) on a screen; to make a film of.

screening *n* the refuse matter left after sifting coal, etc; a metal or plastic mesh, as for window screens; a showing of a film.

screenplay *n* a story written in a form suitable for a film.

screw *n* a cylinder of wood or metal with a spiral ridge (the *thread*) winding round it in a uniform manner so that the successive turns are all exactly the same distance from each other and a corresponding spiral groove is produced, forming one of the six mechanical powers; a propeller with revolving blades on a shaft; one who makes a sharp bargain; a skinflint; a small quantity of tobacco twisted up in a piece of paper.—*vt* to apply a screw to; to press, fasten or make firm by a screw; to force as by a screw; to wrench; to twist; to rack; to oppress by exactions; to distort; (*vulg sl*) to have sexual intercourse with.—*vi* to go together or come apart by being turned like a screw; to twist or turn with a writing movement; (*vulg sl*) to have sexual intercourse.—**to screw up** to gather (courage, etc); to bungle.

screwdriver *n* an instrument for turning and driving in screws; a cocktail based on vodka and orange juice.

screwtop *n* a bottle with a stopper that screws on, such as a beer bottle.

scribble *vt* (**scribbled**, **scribbling**) to write with haste or without care; to fill with careless or worthless writing.—*vi* to scrawl; to write without care or beauty.—*n* hasty or careless writing; a scrawl.

scribbler *n* one who scribbles or writes carelessly or badly; a petty author; a writer of no reputation.

scribe *n* one who writes; one skilled in penmanship; a secretary; an amanuensis; a notary; a copyist; a writer and doctor of the law among the ancient Hebrews; one who read and explained the law to the people.—*vt* (**scribed**, **scribing**) in carpentry, to mark by a rule or compasses; to mark for fitting accurately.

scriber *n* a tool used by joiners for marking lines on wood.

scrimmage, scrummage *n* a skirmish; a confused contest; a tussle.

scrimp *vt* to be sparing or frugal with; to make too small or short; to skimp; to limit.—*vi* to be sparing or frugal.

scrimshank *vi* to shirk duty of any kind, especially military duty.

scrip[1] *n* a small writing; a certificate or schedule; (*com*) a certificate of stock subscribed to a bank or other company; a interim writing entitling a party to a share or shares in any company, exchanged after registration for a formal certificate.

scrip[2] *n* a small bag; a wallet; a satchel.

scripholder *n* one who holds shares or stock by a written certificate or scrip.

script *n* handwriting; a style of writing; (*print*) type resembling or in imitation of handwriting; (*law*) the original or principal document; the text of a stage play, screenplay or broadcast.

scriptorium *n* (*pl* **scriptoriums, scriptoria**) a room set apart for the writing or copying of manuscripts; a writing room.

scriptural *adj* contained in or according to the Scriptures; biblical.

Scripture *n* (usually *pl*) the books of the Old and New Testaments; the Bible; what is contained in the Scriptures; a passage or quotation from the Scriptures; a Bible text.—*adj* relating to the Bible or the Scriptures; scriptural (*Scripture history*).

scrivener *n* formerly, a notary; a money-broker; a financial agent.

scrofula *n* tuberculosis of the lymph glands in the neck.

scroll *n* a roll of paper or parchment; a writing formed into a roll; a list or schedule; an ornament of a spiral form; the volute of the Ionic and Corinthian capitals; the curved head of instruments of the violin family; a kind of volute at a ship's bow; a flourish added to a person's name in signing.

scrotum *n* (*pl* **scrota, scrotums**) the pouch of skin which contains the testicles.

scrounge *vt* (**scrounged, scrounging**) to cadge; to seek or obtain (something) for nothing.—*vi* to try to get something for nothing.

scrub[1] *vt* (**scrubbed, scrubbing**) to rub hard, as with a brush or with something rough, for the purpose of cleaning, scouring or making bright; to scour by rubbing; (*colloq*) to remove, to cancel.—*vi* to clean or brighten by rubbing.—*n* the act of scrubbing.

scrub[2] *n* an arid area of low or stunted trees or brushwood; such vegetation; anything small or mean.—*adj* small, stunted, inferior, etc.

scrubber *n* one who or that which scrubs; a hard broom or brush; (*colloq*) an unattractive woman of loose morals.

scrubby *adj* small and mean; insignificant; stunted in growth.

scruff *n* the back of the neck, the nape (*to take by the scruff of the neck*).

scrum *n* in rugby, a closing-in of rival forwards round the ball on the ground or in readiness for its being inserted between the two packs; a large number of people jostling for position in a small space.

scrumptious *adj* (*colloq*) delicious.

scruple *n* hesitation as to action from perplexity; doubt, hesitation or perplexity arising from motives of conscience; a point causing hesitation; dubiety; a moral principle or belief causing doubt or hesitation; a weight of 20 grains.—*vi* (**scrupled, scrupling**) to have scruples; to hesitate; to doubt (often followed by an infinitive).

scrupulous *adj* full of scruples; hesitating to determine or to act; cautious in decision; careful; exact in regarding facts; precise; punctilious.

screwdriver

scroll

scrutineer *n* one who scrutinizes; one who acts as an examiner of votes, as at an election, etc.

scrutinize *vt* (**scrutinized, scrutinizing**) to subject to scrutiny; to investigate closely; to examine or inquire into critically.—*vi* to make a scrutiny.

scrutiny *n* close investigation or examination; a minute inquiry; a critical examination; an examination by a competent authority of the votes given at an election for the purpose of correcting the poll.

scuba *n* an apparatus used by skin-divers, consisting of a breathing tube attached to a cylinder or cylinders of compressed air.

scuba diver *n* a diver using a scuba.

scuba diving *n* diving using a scuba.

scud *vi* (**scudded, scudding**) to run quickly or with precipitation; to fly with haste; (*naut*) to run before a gale with little or no sail spread.—*n* the act of scudding; loose vapoury clouds driven swiftly by the wind; a type of missile.

scuffle *vi* (**scuffled, scuffling**) to struggle or contend with by grappling; to fight tumultuously or confusedly; to move by shuffling.—*n* a struggle in which the combatants grapple closely; any confused quarrel or contest; a tumultuous fight.

scull *n* an oar worked side to side over the stern of a boat; a light rowing boat for racing.—*vt* to propel by sculls or by moving and turning an oar over the stern.

scullery *n* a place where culinary utensils are cleaned and kept or where food, equipment, etc, is stored.

scullion *n* formerly, a servant who did menial services in a kitchen or scullery; a low, mean, worthless person.

sculpt *vt* to represent in sculpture; to carve.

sculptor *n* one who sculpts; one who carves or hews figures.

sculpture *n* the art of carving, cutting or hewing stone or other materials into images of people, beasts, etc; the art of imitating natural objects in solid substances; statuary; carved work; a figure cut in stone or other solid substance, representing some real or imaginary object.—*vt* (**sculptured, sculpturing**) to sculpt.

scum *n* the extraneous matter which rises to the surface of liquors in boiling or fermentation; the scoria of molten metals; refuse; the dregs of society; a despicable person.—*vt* (**scummed, scumming**) to take the scum from; to clear off the impure matter from the surface.

scumble *vt* (**scumbled, scumbling**) (in painting) to cover thinly with semi-opaque colours to modify the effect.—*n* the upper layer of colour applied for this purpose.

scumbling *n* the toning down of a picture by semi-transparent colours.

scupper *n* a channel cut through the side of

scuba diver

sculpture

a ship for carrying off the water from the deck.—*vt* to sink (a ship) deliberately; to ruin, as someone's chances.

scurf *n* matter composed of minute portions of the dry external scales of skin which are continually being detached from the surface of the body; a layer of matter adhering to a surface.

scurrility *n* the quality of being scurrilous; that which is scurrilous; low, vulgar, abusive language; grossness of abuse or invective; obscene jests, etc.

scurrilous *adj* using low and indecent language; containing low abuse; foul; vile; obscenely jocular; opprobrious; abusive.

scurry *vi* (**scurried, scurrying**) to run rapidly; to hurry.—*n* hurry; haste.

scurvily *adv* basely; meanly; with coarse and vulgar incivility.

scurvy *n* a disease characterized by livid spots and general bodily exhaustion and caused by a deficiency of vitamin C, obtainable from vegetables and fruit.—*adj* vile; mean; low; mischievous; malicious.

scut *n* a short tail such as that of a hare or deer.

scutage *n* (*hist*) a tax on feudal tenants holding lands by knight's service.

scutate *adj* (*bot*) formed like an ancient round buckler; (*zool*) protected or covered by large scales.

scutch *vt* to dress by beating; to separate the woody parts of the stalks of flax by beating.

scutcheon *n* a shield for armorial bearings; an escutcheon; the ornamental cover or frame to a keyhole.

scuttle[1] *n* a broad shallow basket; a wide-mouthed metal pan or pail for holding coal.

scuttle[2] *vi* (**scuttled, scuttling**) to run quickly; to hurry.—*n* a quick pace; a short run.

scuttle[3] *n* (*naut*) a small hatchway with a lid for covering it; the lid itself; a hole in the side of a ship.—*vt* (**scuttled, scuttling**) (*naut*) to sink by making holes through the bottom.

scythe *n* an instrument used in mowing or reaping, consisting of a long curving blade fixed to a handle which is swung by both arms.—*vt* (**scythed, scything**) to mow; to cut with a scythe.

sea *n* the continuous mass of salt water which covers great parts of the earth; the ocean; some special portion of this (*the Polar Sea, the Black Sea*); a name of certain lakes, especially when large (*the Caspian Sea, the Sea of Galilee*); a large wave; a surge (*the vessel shipped a sea*); the swell of the ocean; set of the waves; any large quantity (*a sea of difficulties*); a flood.

sea acorn *n* a barnacle.

sea anemone *n* any of various solitary brightly coloured polyps with a ring of petal-like tentacles surrounding the mouth.

seaboard *n* the sea coast; the country bordering on the sea.—*adj* bordering the sea.

sea cabbage, sea kale *n* a kind of cabbage found on sandy shores of the sea.

sea calf *n* the common seal.

sea cat *n* the wolf fish.

sea cow *n* a name given to the dugong and the manatee.

sea change *n* a complete transformation; a radical change.

sea cucumber *n* a name given to several of the holothurians; the trepang or bêche-de-mer.

seadog *n* the dogfish; the common seal; an old or experienced sailor.

sea eagle *n* the white-tailed eagle of Europe; the bald eagle of America, found generally on the sea coast, as it is a fish-loving bird.

sea elephant *n* the elephant seal.

seafarer *n* a traveller by sea; a mariner.

seafaring *adj* travelling by sea; following the business of a sailor.

seafood *n* edible fish or shellfish.

sea fox *n* the thresher shark.

seagoing *adj* (of a ship) made for use on the open sea, as opposed to working along coasts or on rivers.

sea-green *adj* having the green colour of sea water; being of a faint green colour.

seagull *n* a gull.

sea holly *n* the plant eryngo.

sea horse *n* in classical myth, an animal with foreparts like those of a horse and with hinder parts like those of a fish; a hippocampus.

sea-island cotton *n* a fine long-stapled variety of cotton grown on the islands off the coasts of South Carolina and Georgia.

seal[1] *n* a marine carnivorous mammal of numerous species with four webbed flippers, largely hunted for their fur and blubber; the fur of some seals.—*vi* to hunt seals.

seal[2] *n* a piece of stone, metal or other hard substance on which is engraved a figure or inscription, used for making an impression on a soft substance, as on the wax that formerly secured a letter, or is affixed to documents in token of authenticity; the wax or other substance so impressed; the wax, wafer or similar fastening of a letter or other paper; that which authenticates, confirms or ratifies; assurance; pledge; that which effectually shuts or secures; that which makes fast.—*vt* to affix a seal to, as a mark of authenticity; hence, to confirm or ratify; to establish; to settle; to fasten and mark with a seal; to fasten securely, as with a wafer or with wax; to close hermetically; to shut or keep close (*to seal one's lips*); to enclose; to confine securely.

sea lane *n* a route for ships.

sea legs *npl* the ability to walk steadily on a ship's deck when pitching or rolling and to be free from seasickness.

sea lemon *n* a mollusc of a lemon colour.

sea level *n* the level of the surface of the sea, usually taken as the point from which to measure heights or depressions of the land.

sealing wax *n* a composition of resinous materials used for fastening folded papers and envelopes and capable of receiving impressions of seals.

sea lion *n* a large seal of the Pacific Ocean which has a loud roar and the male of which has a mane.

sealskin *n* the skin of a seal; a coat of this.

sealyham *n* a variety of small wire-haired terrier with short legs and a longish, usually white coat.

seam *n* a joining line formed by the sewing of two different pieces of cloth, etc, together; a suture; a scar or cicatrix; the line or space between planks joined together; (*geol*) the line of separation between two strata; a thin layer or stratum, as of ore, coal, etc, between two thicker strata.—*vt* to form a seam on; to join with a seam; to mark with a cicatrix; to scar.

seaman *n* (*pl* **seamen**) a man whose occupation is to assist in the navigation of ships; a mariner; a sailor.

seamanship *n* the skill of a good seaman.

seamark *n* any elevated object on land which serves for a direction to mariners; a beacon; a mark indicating an upper tidal limit.

sea mew *n* a gull; a seagull.

sea mile *n* a nautical mile, the sixtieth part of a degree of latitude.

seamless *adj* having no seam.

seamy *adj* having a seam; containing seams or showing them, as the underside of a garment; unpleasant or sordid (*the seamy side of life*).

seance, séance *n* a meeting of spiritualists with the view of evoking spiritual manifestations or communicating with spirits.

sea nettle *n* a kind of stinging medusa or jellyfish.

sea otter *n* a marine mammal of North Pacific coasts related to the otter and feeding on shellfish.

sea parrot *n* the puffin, so called from its bill.

sea perch *n* a widely distributed sea fish with a spiny dorsal fin and an elongated body.

sea pink *n* a common European plant with pink flowers, growing on or near the seashore; thrift.

seaplane *n* an aeroplane fitted with floats to enable it to take off from and alight on water.

seal

sea lion

seaport *n* a port, or a town with a port, on or near the sea.

sear[1] *vt* to wither; to dry; to burn the surface of to dryness and hardness; to cauterize; to burn; to scorch; to make callous or insensible (*a seared conscience*); to brand with a heated iron.—*adj* dry; withered; no longer green and fresh (*a sear leaf*).

sear[2] *n* the pivoted piece in a gun lock which enters the notches of the tumbler and holds the hammer at full or half cock.

search *vt* to look over or through for the purpose of finding something; to examine; to explore; to probe (*to search a wound*); to put to the test.—*vi* to make a search; to make an inquiry; to inquire.—*n* the act of seeking or looking for something; inquiry; quest.

searchlight *n* a powerful movable ray of light used in warfare for detecting enemy aircraft, etc.

search warrant *n* a warrant granted by a judge or magistrate to authorize police to enter premises in search of stolen goods or articles kept contrary to law.

sea room *n* sufficient room at sea for a vessel to make any required movement.

seascape *n* a picture representing a scene at sea.

sea serpent *n* a legendary sea-dwelling monster resembling a snake or dragon.

seashell *n* the discarded or empty shell of a mollusc inhabiting the sea.

seashell

seashore *n* the shore of the sea; (*law*) the ground between the ordinary high-water mark and low-water mark.

seasick *adj* affected with sickness or nausea from the pitching or rolling of a vessel.

seasickness *n* nausea and vomiting, produced by the rolling or pitching of a vessel at sea.

seaside *n* the land or country bordering on the sea.

sea slug *n* a marine mollusc lacking a shell; the trepang.

season *n* one of the periods into which the year is naturally divided, as marked by its temperature, moisture, etc (as spring, summer, autumn and winter, or the wet and the dry *season* of tropical countries); a convenient or suitable time; a proper conjuncture; the right time; a period of time not very long; a while; a time; that time of the year when a particular locality is most frequented by visitors (*the London season*); that part of the year when a particular trade, profession or business is in its greatest activity (*the theatrical season*); that which gives a relish to food; seasoning.—*vt* to render suitable; to fit; to fit for any use by time or habit; to accustom; to inure; to acclimatize; to bring to the best state for use by any process (*to season timber by drying* or *hardening*); to render palatable;

seaweed

to flavour; to add salt and pepper to; to add herbs or spices to; to give a relish or zest to; to temper; to qualify by admixture.—*vi* to become suitable by time; to grow fit for use.

seasonable *adj* suitable as to time or season; opportune; happening or being done in due season.

seasonal *adj* pertaining to the seasons.

seasoning *n* that which is added to food to give it more flavour, as salt and pepper, herbs or spices; something added to enhance enjoyment.

season ticket *n* a ticket which entitles its holder to certain privileges during a specified period of time, as a pass for travelling by railway, etc, issued at a cheap rate.

seat *n* the place or thing on which one sits; something made to be sat in or on, as a chair, throne, bench, stool, etc; a regular place of sitting; hence, a right to sit; a sitting (*a seat in a church*); place of abode; residence; a mansion in the country; the place where anything is situated, fixed, settled or established; station; abode (*a seat of learning, the seat of war*).—*vt* to place on a seat; to cause to sit down; to place in a post of authority or a place of distinction; to settle; to fix in a particular place or country; to situate; to locate; to fix; to set firm; to assign seats to; to accommodate with room to sit; to fit up with seats.

seat-belt *n* an adjustable belt for holding someone firmly in his or her place in a car, aircraft, etc, in the case of accident.

sea trout *n* salmon trout.

sea unicorn *n* the narwhal.

sea urchin *n* a small marine animal with a round body enclosed in a shell covered with sharp spines.

seaward *adj* directed towards the sea.—*adv* towards the sea.

seaway *n* (*naut*) progress made by a vessel through the waves.

seaweed *n* a mass of plants growing in or under water; a sea plant, especially a marine alga.

seaworthy *adj* (of a ship) in good condition and fit for a voyage.

sebaceous *adj* pertaining to tallow or fat; made of, containing or secreting fatty matter; fatty; (*bot*) having the appearance of grease or wax.

sebaceous gland *n* one of the small skin glands that secrete sebum on to the skin surface.

seborrhoea *n* the excessive secretion of sebum.

sebum *n* a fatty substance secreted by the sebaceous glands to lubricate the skin and hair.

secant *adj* cutting; dividing into two parts. —*n* (*geom*) a line that cuts another or divides it into parts; a straight line cutting a curve in two or more points; a straight line from the centre of a circle cutting the circumference and proceeding till it meets a tangent to the same circle; (*trigon*) in a right-angled triangle, the secant of an acute angle = hypotenuse ÷ adjacent side.

secateurs *npl* a pair of small shears with curved blades used for gardening work, such as pruning.

secede *vi* (**seceded, seceding**) to withdraw from fellowship or association; to separate oneself; especially, to withdraw from a political or religious organization.

seceder *n* one who secedes.

secession *n* the act of seceding; the act of withdrawing from a political or religious organization.

seclude *vt* (**secluded, secluding**) to shut up apart from company or society and usually to keep apart for some time; (*refl*) to withdraw into solitude.

seclusion *n* the act of secluding; the state of being secluded; retirement; privacy; solitude.

second[1] *adj* immediately following the first; next the first in order of place or time; repeated again; other; next to the first in value, power, excellence or rank; inferior; secondary.—*n* one next to the first; one who assists and supports another; one who attends another (the principal) in a duel and sees that there is fair play; an aid or assistant to a boxer; the gear after low gear; the sixtieth part of a minute of time or of that of a degree, that is, the second division next to the hour or degree; (*mus*) the difference between any sound and the next nearest sound above or below it, also a lower part added to a melody when arranged for two voices or instruments; an article of merchandise not of first quality; (*pl*) a coarse kind of flour; (*pl*) (*colloq*) another helping of food.—*vt* to follow in the next place to; to follow up and support; to lend aid to; to assist; to promote; to encourage; to back; to support by one's voice or vote, as a motion or proposal brought forward in an assembly; to unite with in proposing some measure or motion.

second[2] *vt* to place on temporary service elsewhere.

secondary *adj* of second place, origin, rank or importance; not primary; subordinate.

second-best *adj* next to the best; inferior.—*adv* in second place.—*n* next to best; an inferior alternative.

Second Coming *n* the return to earth of Christ at the Last Judgment as prophesied.

second cousin *n* the child of a parent's first cousin.

seconder *n* one who seconds; one who supports what another attempts or what he or she affirms, moves or proposes.

second-hand *adj* not original or primary; received from another; not new; having been used or worn; dealing in second-hand goods (*a second-hand bookseller*).

second nature *n* a long-established habit, etc, deeply fixed in a person's nature.

second sight *n* the power of seeing things future or distant; prophetic vision.

second thoughts *npl* a change in decision, opinion, attitude, etc, after consideration.

secrecy *n* a state of being secret or hidden; concealment from the observation of others; secret mode of proceeding; retirement; privacy; the quality of being secret; fidelity to a secret; the act or habit of keeping secrets.

secret *adj* apart from the knowledge of others; private; known only to one or to a few; kept from general knowledge; not made public; affording privacy; retired; secluded (*a secret spot*); secretive; not inclined to betray confidence; occult; mysterious; not apparent; privy; not proper to be seen.—*n* something studiously concealed; a thing kept from general knowledge; what is not or should not be revealed; a thing not discovered or explained; a mystery.—**in secret** in privacy or secrecy; privately.

secret agent *n* a spy.

secretarial *adj* pertaining to a secretary.

secretariate *n* the office of a secretary; the place where a secretary transacts business.

secretary *n* a person employed to write letters, draw up reports, records, etc; one who carries on another's business correspondence or other matters requiring writing; a piece of furniture with conveniences for writing and for the arrangement of papers; an escritoire; an officer whose business is to superintend and manage the affairs of a particular department of government; a secretary of state.

secretary bird *n* an African bird of prey which kills and eats snakes and other reptiles, so called from the long plumes behind its ears, suggesting quills.

secretaryship *n* the office or post of a secretary.

secrete *vt* (**secreted, secreting**) to hide; to deposit in some secret place; (*physiol*) to separate from the circulating fluid, as from the blood, sap, etc, and elaborate into a new product.

secretion *n* the act or process of secreting; the physiological process by which there are separated from the blood substances differing from the blood itself or from any of its constituents, as bile, saliva, mucus, urine, etc; the process by which substances are separated from the sap of vegetables; the matter so secreted.

secretory *adj* performing the office of secretion.

secret police *n* a police force which oper-

secateurs

secretary

ates in secret, usually to suppress political opposition to the state rather than criminal activity.

sect *n* a body or number of persons who follow some teacher or leader or are joined in some settled tenets, chiefly in philosophy or religion; a group of people united by a common interest or belief.

sectarian *adj* pertaining to a sect or sects; strongly or bigotedly attached to a sect or religious denomination.—*n* one of a sect; a strict member or adherent of a special denomination or party.

sectarianism *n* the principles of sectarians; a narrow-minded devotion to the interests of a party.

sectary *n* one that belongs to a sect; a schismatic; a sectarian.

sectile *adj* capable of being cut, as with a knife.

section *n* the act of cutting; separation by cutting; a part cut or separated from the rest; a division; a portion; a distinct part or portion of a book or writing; the subdivision of a chapter; a paragraph; hence, the character §, often used to denote such a division; a distinct part of a country or people, community, class, etc; a representation of a building or other object as it would appear if cut through by any intersecting plane, showing the internal structure; a small division of some military body, more especially the fourth part of a platoon, consisting of about ten soldiers, commanded by a noncommissioned officer and forming the normal fire unit.—*vti* to cut or separate into sections; to represent in sections; to become separated or cut into parts.

sectional *adj* pertaining to a section; composed of or made up in several independent sections.

sector *n* (*geom*) a nearly triangular figure formed by two radii and the arc of a circle; a mathematical instrument useful in making diagrams, laying down plans, etc; (*milit*) an area of varying extent in war, over which operations are conducted.

secular *adj* pertaining to this present world or to things not spiritual or sacred; disassociated with religious teaching or principles; not devoted to sacred or religious use; temporal; profane; worldly (*secular education, secular music*); not bound by monastic vows or rules (*a secular priest* as opposed to a regular); coming or observed at long intervals; extending over, taking place in or accomplished during a very long period of time (*the secular refrigeration of the earth*).—*n* an ecclesiastic not bound by monastic rules; a secular priest.

secularist *n* one who theoretically rejects every form of religious faith and every kind of religious worship.

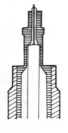

section

secularize *vt* (**secularized, secularizing**) to make secular; to convert from religious or ecclesiastical to secular or common use.

secure *adj* free from fear or apprehension; confident of safety; careless; unsuspecting; free from or not exposed to danger; in a state of safety; safe (often followed by *against* or *from*); such as to be depended on; capable of resisting assault or attack; stable; certain, sure or confident (with *of*); in safe custody.—*vt* (**secured, securing**) to make secure; to guard effectually from danger; to protect; to make certain; to put beyond hazard; to assure; to enclose or confine effectually; to guard effectually from escape; to seize and confine (*to secure a prisoner*); to make certain of payment; to warrant against loss; to make fast or firm (*to secure a door*); to get possession of; to make oneself owner of (*to secure an estate*).

security *n* the state of being secure; freedom from apprehension; confidence of safety; sometimes, overconfidence; freedom from danger or risk; safety; that which secures or makes safe; something that secures against financial loss; surety; a person who engages himself or herself for the performance of another's obligations; an evidence of property, as a bond, a certificate of stock, etc (*government securities*).

sedan *n* a car with two or four doors and a front and rear seat.

sedan chair *n* a covered chair for carrying one person, borne on poles by two people.

sedate *adj* calm or tranquil in feelings and manner; serene; unruffled by passion; staid; unmoved.

sedation *n* the act of calming; the condition of being calmed, especially by sedatives; the administration of sedatives to calm a patient.

sedative *adj* tending to calm or tranquillize; having a soothing, calming effect.—*n* a drug with a soothing, calming effect.

sedentary *adj* accustomed to sit much; requiring much sitting (*a sedentary occupation*); passed for the most part in sitting.

sedge *n* any of an extensive genus of grasslike plants growing mostly in marshes and swamps and on the banks of rivers, distinguished from the grasses by having the stem lacking joints.

sedge-warbler *n* a species of warbler, a summer visitor to Britain, frequenting the sedgy banks of streams.

sediment *n* the matter which subsides to the bottom of water or any other liquid; settlings; lees; dregs.

sedimentary *adj* consisting of sediment; formed by sediment or matter that has subsided.

sedition *n* incitement to rebel against a government, not amounting to an insurrection; offences against a state as have the same aim as, but do not amount to, treason.

seditious *adj* pertaining to sedition; exciting or aiding in sedition; guilty of sedition.

seduce *vt* (**seduced, seducing**) to draw aside or entice from the path of rectitude and duty; to lead astray; to corrupt; to entice into sexual intercourse.

seduction *n* the act of seducing; the act or crime of enticing someone into sexual intercourse.

seductive *adj* tending to seduce; designed to seduce; alluring; enticing.

sedulity *n* the state or quality of being sedulous; assiduity.

sedulous *adj* assiduous; diligent in application; steady and persevering in endeavours to effect an object; steadily industrious.

see[1] *vt* (*pret* **saw**, *pp* **seen**, *ppr* **seeing**) to perceive by the eye; to behold; to perceive mentally; to form a conception or idea of; to understand; to comprehend; to give attention to; to examine; to attend to escort (*to see a woman home*); to have communication with; to meet or associate with; to visit (*to go to see a friend*); to experience; to know by personal experience (*to see death*).—*vi* to have the power or sense of sight; to perceive mentally; to discern; to understand (often with *through* or *into*); to examine or inquire; to consider; to be attentive; to take heed; to take care.—**to see about** to deal with; to consider in detail.—**to see off** to be present when someone leaves on a journey, etc; to be rid of, as by defeating or outlasting.—**to see through** to persist or endure to the end; to assist (a friend) during a crisis, difficulty, etc; to recognize the true character of.—*interj* lo! look! observe! behold!

see[2] *n* the seat of episcopal power; the diocese or jurisdiction of a bishop or archbishop.

seed *n* the impregnated and matured ovule of a plant, containing an embryo which may be developed and converted into an individual similar to that from which it derives its origin; one of the grains or fruits of wheat and many other plants, though sometimes the seed is contained in the fruit; semen; that from which anything springs; first principle; progeny; offspring; children; descendants; a seeded tournament player or team.—*vi* to produce seed; to shed seed.—*vt* to sow; to supply with seed; to ornament with seed-like decorations; to remove seeds from; to sprinkle (clouds) with dry ice, etc, to induce rain; to arrange (a tournament, series of matches, etc) so that the best players or teams cannot meet until later rounds.

seedbed *n* a nursery bed for a plant; a place or source of growth or development.

seed cake *n* a sweet cake containing aromatic seeds.

seedling *n* a plant reared from seed and not from a layer, bud, etc.

seed money *n* money used to start a new project or enterprise.

seed pearl *n* a small pearl resembling a grain or seed in size or form.

seedy *adj* abounding with seeds; running to seed; worn-out; shabby; poor and miserable-looking; feeling or appearing wretched; indisposed, slightly unwell.

seeing *n* vision; sight.—*adj* having sight; observant.—*conj* because; inasmuch as; since; considering; taking into account that.

seek *vt* (*pret, pp* **sought**, *ppr* **seeking**) to go in search or quest of; to look for; to search for; to take pains to find (often followed by *out*); to ask for; to solicit; to try to gain; to go to; to resort to; to have recourse to; to aim at; to attempt; to strive after (*to seek a person's ruin*); to search.—*vi* to make search or inquiry; to endeavour; to make an effort or attempt; to try; to use solicitation.

seem *vi* to appear; to present the appearance of being; to be only in appearance and not really; to show oneself or itself; hence, to assume an air; to pretend; to appear to one's opinion or judgment; to be thought; to appear to oneself; to imagine; to feel as if (*I still seem to hear his voice*).

seeming *adj* appearing; having the appearance or semblance, whether real or not; specious or plausible in appearance.—*n* appearance; show; semblance, especially a false appearance.

seemingly *adv* as it would seem; apparently; ostensibly; in appearance.

seemly *adj* becoming; fitting; suitable; decent; proper.

seep *vi* to percolate; to ooze.

seer *n* one who sees; one who foresees future events; a prophet.

seesaw *n* a long piece of timber balanced on a support so that it is tilted alternately up and down by a person sitting on each end; a motion or action resembling that of a seesaw; vacillation.—*adj* moving up and down or to and fro.—*vti* to move as on a seesaw or upward and downward; to fluctuate.—*adj, adv* alternately rising and falling.

seethe *vi* (**seethed, seething**) to boil; to be very angry, often without showing it; to swarm (with people).

segment *n* a part cut off or marked as separate from others; one of the parts into which a body naturally divides itself; a section; (*geom*) a part cut off from any figure by a line or plane; the segment of a circle, being the part contained by an arc and its chord.—*vi* to divide or become divided up into segments.

seed

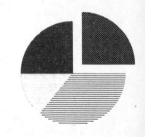

segment

segmentation *n* a division into segments; in animals, the division of the adult body into successive segments, e.g. in crustaceans.

segregate *vt* (**segregated, segregating**) to separate from others; to set apart; to separate racial or other minority groups.—*vi* to separate or go apart.—*adj* separate; select.

segregation *n* the act of segregating; separation from others.

seigneur, seignior *n* (*feudal law*) the lord of a fee or manor.

seigneurial, seigniorial *adj* pertaining to the lord of a manor; manorial.

seignory, seigniory *n* a lordship; power or authority as sovereign lord.

seine *n* a large net for catching fish.

seismic, seismal *adj* of, caused by or pertaining to earthquakes.

seismograph *n* an electromagnetic instrument for registering the shocks and concussions of earthquakes.

seismography *n* a description or account of earthquakes.

seismology *n* the science of earthquakes; that department of science which treats of volcanoes and earthquakes.

seismometer, seismoscope *n* an instrument for measuring the direction and force of earthquakes and similar shocks.

seize *vt* (**seized, seizing**) to lay hold of suddenly; to gripe or grasp suddenly; to take possession by force or by virtue of legal authority; to have a sudden and powerful effect on; to attack (*a fever seizes a patient*); to lay hold of by the mind; to comprehend; (*naut*) to fasten two ropes, or different parts of one rope, together with a cord; (*law*) to make possessed; to put in possession of (with *of* before the thing possessed).—*vi* to fall on and grasp (with *on* or *upon*); to take hold of; to take possession of; (of machinery) to become jammed.

seizin *n* (*law*) possession; the act of taking possession; the thing possessed.

seizing *n* (*naut*) the cord or cords used for fastening ropes together.

seizure *n* the act of seizing or taking sudden hold; a taking into possession; the thing seized or taken possession of; a sudden attack of illness, an apoplectic stroke.

seldom *adv* rarely; not often; not frequently.

select *vt* to choose and take from a number; to take by preference from among others; to pick out; to cull.—*adj* taken from a number by preference; picked out by reason of excellence; choice; picked; limited (*select membership*); exclusive.

selection *n* the act of selecting; a taking by preference from a number; a thing or things selected from others; the process by which certain animals or plants survive while others are eliminated; natural selection.

selective *adj* selecting; tending to select; highly specific in activity or effect.

selectivity *n* (*electron*) the property of a receiver of other circuit which allows it to be adjusted so as to respond to waves of any selected frequency.

selenium *n* a nonmetallic chemical element related to sulphur and tellurium, often occurring in pyrites and varying in electrical conductivity according to the intensity of the light.

self (*pl* **selves**) a word affixed to certain personal pronouns to express emphasis or distinction and when the pronoun is used reflexively (*I myself will write, I will examine for myself, he loves himself, we value ourselves*).—*n* the individual as an object to his or her own reflective consciousness (*my wretched self*); one's individual person; personal interest; one's own private interest (*he is always for self*).—*adj* same; very same (*self-same*); (of colour) matching, uniform.

self-abasement *n* degradation of oneself by one's own act.

self-abuse *n* misuse of one's abilities; abuse of one's health by drinking, taking drugs, etc; masturbation.

self-acting *adj* acting of itself; automatic.

self-addressed *adj* addressed to return to the sender; intended for oneself.

self-adjusting *adj* adjusting itself by special mechanism.

self-assertion *n* the act of asserting oneself or one's own rights or claims; a putting oneself forward in an assuming manner.

self-assertive *adj* forward in asserting oneself or one's rights and claims.

self-catering *adj* (of holiday accommodation) involving doing one's own cooking, cleaning, etc.

self-coloured *adj* all of one colour, as a piece of cloth.

self-complacent *adj* pleased with oneself or one's own doings; self-satisfied.

self-conceit *n* a high opinion of oneself; vanity.

self-confident *adj* confident of one's own strength or powers; relying on the correctness of one's own judgment or the competence of one's own powers, without other aid.

self-conscious *adj* conscious of one's states or acts as belonging to oneself; conscious of oneself as an object of observation to others; apt to think of how oneself appears.

self-contained *adj* reserved; not communicative; (of accommodation) complete in itself.

self-control *n* control exercised over oneself; self-restraint; self-command.

self-deception *n* deception concerning oneself, proceeding from one's own mistake.

self-defence *n* defence of one's own person, property or reputation.

self-denying *adj* denying oneself; forbearing to indulge one's appetites or desires.

self-determination *n* free will; the choice of action without compulsion; the right of a nation to choose its own national policy, free from interference by external governments.

self-drive *adj* (of a hired vehicle) driven by the person who hires.

self-educated *adj* educated by one's own efforts or without the aid of teachers.

self-effacement *n* the act of keeping oneself in the background out of sight or notice.

self-employed *adj* earning one's living in one's own business; not employed by another; freelance.

self-esteem *n* the esteem or good opinion of oneself.

self-evident *adj* evident without proof or reasoning; producing certainty or clear conviction on a bare presentation to the mind.

self-explanatory *adj* capable of explaining itself; bearing its meaning on its own face; obvious.

self-expression *n* the expression of one's own personality, especially through the creative arts, as in art, dance, etc.

self-fertilization *n* (*bot*) the fertilization of a flower by pollen from the same flower.

self-government *n* the government of oneself; self-control; a system of government by which the mass of a nation or people appoint the rulers; autonomy.

self-help *n* assistance of or by oneself; the use of one's own powers to attain an end.

self-image *n* one's sense of oneself or one's importance.

self-importance *n* high opinion of oneself; pride.

self-important *adj* important in one's own esteem; pompous.

self-imposed *adj* imposed or voluntarily taken on oneself (*a self-imposed task*).

self-induced *adj* brought on by oneself or itself.

self-indulgent *adj* indulging oneself; gratifying one's own passions, desires, etc.

self-inflicted *adj* brought on by oneself or itself.

self-interest *n* interest or concern for oneself; one's own advantage.

selfish *adj* caring only or chiefly for oneself; regarding one's own interest chiefly or solely; proceeding from love of self; influenced solely by private advantage.

selfishness *n* the quality of being selfish; devotion to one's own interests with carelessness of others.

self-knowledge *n* the knowledge of one's own real character, abilities, worth or demerit.

selfless *adj* with not thought of oneself; unselfish.

self-loading *adj* (of a firearm) semi-automatic.

self-love *n* the love of one's own person or happiness; the natural feeling which impels every rational creature to preserve his or her life and promote his or her own happiness.

self-made *adj* made by oneself; having risen in the world by one's own exertions (*a self-made man*).

self-opinionated *adj* valuing one's own opinion highly.

self-pity *n* pity for oneself.

self-possession *n* the possession of one's powers; presence of mind; calmness; self-command.

self-preservation *n* the preservation of oneself from destruction or injury.

self-propelled *adj* (of a vehicle) moving under its own power.

self-raising *adj* (of flour) containing a raising agent.

self-reliance *n* reliance on one's own powers.

self-reliant *adj* relying on oneself; trusting to one's own powers.

self-respect *n* respect for oneself or one's own character.

self-restraint *n* restraint or control imposed on oneself; self-control.

self-righteous *adj* righteous in one's own esteem; deeming oneself righteous above others; priggish.

self-righteousness *n* reliance on one's own supposed righteousness; false righteousness; priggishness.

self-sacrifice *n* sacrifice of oneself or of self-interest, feelings, etc.

self-same *adj* the very same; identical.

self-satisfied *adj* satisfied with oneself.

self-seeking *adj* seeking one's own interest or happiness; selfish.

self-service *adj* serving oneself in a shop, restaurant, petrol station, etc.

self-standing *adj* standing alone without being attached to something else; functioning alone without support.

self-starter *n* an electric device for starting an engine; a motivated employee who requires little supervision.

self-styled *adj* called by oneself; pretended.

self-sufficient *adj* independent of the aid of others; having undue confidence in one's own strength, ability or endowments; conceited; overbearing.

self-taught *adj* taught by oneself; educated without a teacher (a self-taught genius).

self-will *n* determination to have one's own way; wilfulness; obstinacy.

sell *vt* (*pret, pp* **sold**, *ppr* **selling**) to transfer to another for an equivalent; to give up for a consideration; to dispose of for some-

self-defence

thing else, especially for money, the counterpart of *buy*; to make a matter of bargain and sale of; to take a bribe for; to betray.—*vi* to practise selling; to be sold; to fetch a price.

seller *n* one who sells; a vendor.

Sellotape *n* the trademark of a kind of transparent adhesive tape used for sealing parcels, etc.

selvage, selvedge *n* a woven border or border of close work, on a fabric, made of the threads of the fabric; a list.

semaphore *n* a system of conveying information by signals visible at a distance made by the operators arms, by flags, etc.—*vt* (**semaphored, semaphoring**) to send (a signal) by semaphore.—*vi* to signal as by semaphore.

semblance *n* similarity; resemblance; external figure or appearance; form; a form or figure representing something; likeness; image.

semeiotics *n* same as **semiotics**.

semen *n* the sperm-carrying fluid in male animals; sperm.

semester *n* a period or term of six months.

semi *n* (*colloq*) a semidetached house; a semifinal.

semi- *prefix* signifying half; half of; in part; partially.

semiautomatic *adj* partly automatic; (of a firearm) self-loading but discharging in single shots only as the trigger is pulled.

semibreve *n* (*mus*) a note of half the duration or time of the breve, equivalent to two minims, four crotchets or eight quavers.

semicircle *n* the half of a circle; the part of a circle comprehended between its diameter and half of its circumference; any body in the form of a half circle.

semicircular *adj* having the form of a half circle.

semicolon *n* the punctuation mark or point (;), marking a pause of less duration than the colon and more than the comma and used to distinguish the conjunct parts of a sentence.

semiconductor *n* a substance in a transmitter, as silicon, used to control the flow of current.

semiconscious *adj* imperfectly conscious.

semidetached *adj* partly separated (applied to one of two houses which are detached from other buildings but joined together).

semifinal *adj* (of a match or round) before the final in a tournament.—*n* a semifinal match or round.

semifluid *adj* having qualities between those of a fluid and solid; viscous.

seminal *adj* of or pertaining to seed or semen or to the elements of reproduction; contained in seed; germinal; rudimentary; promising or contributing to further development; original, influential.

semi circle

seminary *n* a place of education, especially a training college for priests, ministers, etc; any school, college or university in which persons are instructed; a seed plot; a nursery.

semiology, semeiology *n* the study of signs and symbols.

semiotics, semeiotics *n* the science of signs and symbols, especially their use in language and relationship to the world of things and ideas; the study of the symptoms of disease in the human body.

semiprecious *adj* denoting gems of lower value than precious stones.

semiprofessional *adj* taking part in sport for pay but not on a full-time basis.

semiquaver *n* (*mus*) a note of half the duration of the quaver; the sixteenth of the semibreve.

semi-skimmed *adj* (of milk) having the cream partially removed.

Semite *n* a member of the group of peoples including Arabs and Jews.

Semitic *adj* of or relating to Semites; Jewish.

Semitic language *n* any of an important group or family of languages, comprising the Hebrew, Phoenician, Arabic, Abyssinian, Chaldean, Assyrian, Babylonian.

Semitism *n* a Semitic characteristic, idiom or word; any political or economic policy relating to Jews.

semitone *n* (*mus*) half a tone; an interval of sound, as between *mi* and *fa* in the diatonic scale, which is only half the distance of the interval between *ut* (*do*) and *re* or *sol* and *la*.

semivowel *n* a consonant that sounds like a vowel (e.g. *y* or *j*).

semolina *n* the large hard grains left after the sifting of wheat, sometimes used for puddings.

sempre *adv* (*mus*) always.

sempstress *n* a woman who lives by needlework.

senary *adj* of six; belonging to six; containing six.

senate *n* originally, in ancient Rome, a body of elderly citizens elected from among the nobles and having supreme legislative power; hence, the upper branch of a legislature in various countries, as in France, the USA, etc; in general, a legislative body; the legislative department of a government; the governing body of a university.

senate house *n* a house in which a senate meets or a place of public council.

senator *n* a member of a senate.

senatorial *adj* pertaining to a senator or senators; belonging to senators; in the USA, entitled to elect a senator.

send *vt* (*pret, pp* **sent**, *ppr* **sending**) to cause to go or pass from one place to another; to despatch; to cause to be conveyed or transmitted; to impel; to propel; to throw; to cast; to commission, authorize or direct to go and act; to cause to befall; to inflict (*to send destruction*); (before certain verbs of motion) to cause to do the act indicated by the respective verb (*to send the enemy flying in all directions*); (*sl*) to move (a person) to ecstasy.—*vi* to despatch a message or a messenger for some purpose.—**to send down** to expel from college; to imprison.—**to send for** to order to be brought; to summon.—**to send packing** to dismiss firmly and frankly.—**to send up** (*colloq*) to make fun of; to satirize.

send-off *n* a social gathering to express good wishes when someone is departing or setting out on a journey.

senescence *n* the state of growing old.

senescent *adj* beginning to grow old.

senile *adj* pertaining to old age; proceeding from age; characterized by the weakness of old age.

senility *n* the state of being senile; old age; dotage.

senior *adj* more advanced in age; older; elder; being the elder of two persons of the same name (*John Smith, senior*); higher or more advanced in rank, office, etc.—*n* a person who is older than another (*my senior by ten years*); one that is older in office than another; one prior or superior in rank or office; an aged person.

senior citizen *n* an elderly person, especially a retired one.

seniority *n* state of being senior; superior age; priority of birth; priority or superiority in rank or office.

senna *n* the leaves of various species of cassia used as a laxative.

señor *n* a Spanish title or form of address, corresponding to the English Mr or sir; a gentleman.

señora *n* the feminine of *señor*; madame or Mrs; a woman.

sensation *n* an impression made on the mind through the medium of one of the organs of sense; feeling produced by external objects or by some change in the internal state of the body; a feeling; the power of feeling or receiving impressions; feeling occasioned by causes that do not act on the senses; a purely spiritual or psychical affection (*a sensation of awe, novelty,* etc); a state of some excitement (*to create a sensation*); what produces excited interest or feeling.

sensational *adj* relating to or implying sensation or perception by the senses; causing or designed to cause a strong emotional reaction, especially excitement or horror; melodramatic; (*colloq*) excellent, marvellous.

sensationalism *n* the quality of being sensa-

tional; the use of sensational writing, language, etc, to excite emotion or shock; the use of melodramatic or lurid details to achieve a sensational effect.

sense *n* one of the faculties by which human beings and the higher animals perceive external objects by means of impressions made on certain organs of the body, the senses being usually spoken of as five, namely, sight, hearing, taste, smell and touch; perception by the senses; sensation; feeling; apprehension through the intellect; discernment; appreciation (*no sense of beauty*); moral perception; consciousness (*a sense of shame*); faculty of thinking and feeling; sound perception and reasoning; good judgment; understanding (*a man of sense*); rationality; view or opinion held in common (*to speak the sense of a public meeting*); meaning; import; (*pl*) conscious awareness.—*vt* (**sensed, sensing**) to perceive; to become aware of; to understand; to detect.

senseless *adj* lacking sense; having no power of sensation or perception; insensible; lacking feeling or sympathy; without sensibility; contrary to reason or sound judgment; unwise; foolish; nonsensical; lacking understanding; acting without judgment; stupid; unconscious.

sense organ *n* a bodily structure that reacts to stimuli and transmits them to the brain as nerve impulses.

sensibility *n* the state or quality of being sensible; capability of sensation; capacity to experience emotion or feeling; the capacity of being impressed with such sentiments as those of sublimity, awe, wonder, etc; delicacy or keenness of feeling; quick emotion or sympathy; that quality of an instrument which makes it indicate very slight changes of condition; sensitiveness (*the sensibility of a thermometer*).

sensible *adj* capable of being perceived by the senses; capable of exciting sensation; perceptible; felt; capable of sensation or impression (*the eye is sensible to light*); capable of emotional influences; liable to impression or emotion; easily affected; perceiving or having perception either by the senses or the intellect; cognizant; persuaded; capable of indicating slight changes of condition; sensitive (*a sensible thermometer*); possessing or containing sense, judgment or reason (*a sensible remark*); having good or sound sense; intelligent; reasonable; judicious.

sensitive *adj* having the capacity of receiving impressions from external objects; having feelings easily excited; readily and acutely affected; easily upset or hurt; allergic to; (of skin) easily irritated; (*physics*) easily affected, moved or exhibiting change from some influence (*a sensitive* *balance*); highly responsive to slight changes; (*photog*) reacting to light; (*chem*) readily affected by the action of appropriate agents.

sensitive plant *n* one of several plants which display movements of their leaves under the influence of light and darkness, and also under mechanical and other stimuli.

sensitivity *n* the state of being sensitive; responsiveness to stimuli, especially when excessive.

sensitize *vt* (**sensitized, sensitizing**) to make or become sensitive; to render sensitive to light.

sensual *adj* pertaining to the body, as distinct from the spirit; carnal; fleshly; pertaining to the gratification of the appetites; grossly luxurious; indulging in lust; voluptuous.

sensuality *n* the quality of being sensual; devotion to the gratification of the bodily appetites; indulgence in lust; carnality; fleshliness.

sensuous *adj* pertaining to the senses; appealing to the senses; readily affected through the senses; alive to the pleasure to be received through the senses.

sentence *n* a judgment; a decision; a judgment pronounced by a court or judge on a criminal; (*gram*) a number of words containing complete sense or a complete thought and followed by a full point.—*vt* (**sentenced, sentencing**) to pronounce sentence or judgment on; to condemn; to doom to punishment.

sententious *adj* abounding in axioms or maxims; showing a pompous, moralizing tone; rich in judicious observations; having brevity and weight of meaning; pithy; terse.

sentient *adj* capable of perceiving or feeling; having the faculty of perception; (*physiol*) more susceptible of feeling than others.

sentiment *n* a thought prompted by feeling; a feeling respecting some person or thing; a particular disposition of mind in view of some subject; tendency to be swayed by feeling; emotion; sensibility; a thought or opinion; the thought or opinion contained in words but considered as distinct from them; a thought expressed in striking words.

sentimental *adj* having sentiment; apt to be swayed by sentiment; manifesting an excess of sentiment; artificially or mawkishly tender; appealing to sentiment rather than to reason; foolishly emotional.

sentimentalist *n* one who affects sentiment; the character of being sentimental or swayed by sentiment.

sentimentality *n* proneness to sentiment; mawkish emotion.

sentry

sentinel *n* one who watches or keeps guard to prevent surprise; especially, a soldier set to guard any place from surprise; a sentry.

sentry *n* a soldier placed on guard; a sentinel; guard; watch; the duty of a sentinel.

sentry box *n* a small shed to cover and shelter a sentry at his or her post.

sepal *n* (*bot*) one of the separate divisions of a calyx when that organ is made up of various leaves.

separable *adj* capable of being separated or disjoined; divisible.

separate *vt* (**separated, separating**) to disunite; to divide; to part in almost any manner either things naturally or casually joined; to set apart from a number; to make a space between; to sever, as by an intervening space; to lie between.—*vi* to go apart; to withdraw from each other; to cease to live together as man and wife or as partners; to cleave or split; to come apart.—*adj* divided from the rest; parted from another or others; disjoined; unconnected; not joined; distinct; withdrawn; alone; without company.—*n* (*pl*) articles of clothing, such as skirts and blouses, forming separate coordinating parts of an outfit, designed to be interchangeable with others to form various outfits.

separately *adv* in a separate or unconnected state; apart; distinctly; singly.

separation *n* the act of separating; the state of being separate; disjunction; disunion; disconnection; a formal arrangement of husband and wife to live apart.

separatist *n* one who advocates or practices separation from an organization, church or government; one who withdraws or separates himself or herself from an established church; a dissenter.

separator *n* one who separates; a machine that separates liquid from solids or liquids of different specific gravities.

sepia *n* a brown pigment used in drawing, originally prepared from a black juice secreted by certain glands of the cuttlefish.

sepoy *n* formerly, an Indian soldier in the British army.

sepsis *n* putrefaction; blood poisoning; septicaemia.

sept *n* a clan; a branch of a race or family.

September *n* the ninth month of the year with 30 days, so called from being originally the seventh month from March, formerly the first month of the year.

septenary *adj* consisting of or relating to seven; lasting seven years; occurring once in seven years.

septennial *adj* lasting or continuing seven years; happening once in every seven years.

septentrion *n* (*arch*) the north or northern regions.

septic *adj* having power to promote putrefaction; causing putrefaction; infected by microorganisms.—*n* a substance causing putrefaction.

septicaemia *n* blood poisoning by absorption into the circulation of poisonous or putrid matter.

septuagenarian *n* a person seventy years of age or between seventy and eighty.

Septuagesima *n* the third Sunday before Lent, so called because it is about seventy days before Easter.

septum *n* (*pl* **septa**) a membrane separating cavities in animals or plants, as the cartilage between the nostrils; one of the partitions of an ovary or fruit.

sepulchral *adj* pertaining to burial, to the grave or to tombs; suggestive of a sepulchre; hence, deep, hollow in tone (*a sepulchral tone of voice*).

sepulchre *n* a tomb; a building, cave, etc, for interment; a burial vault.—*vt* (**sepulchred, sepulchring**) to bury; to inter; to entomb.

sepulture *n* burial; interment.

sequel *n* that which follows and forms a continuation; a succeeding part; consequence; result; event; the continuation of a story begun in an earlier literary work, film, etc.

sequence *n* a following or coming after; succession; a particular order or arrangement of succession; invariable order of succession; an observed instance of uniformity in following; a single, uninterrupted episode, as in a film; a series of things following in a certain order; a set of playing cards immediately following each other, as king, queen, knave, etc; (*mus*) the recurrence of a melodic figure in a different key to that in which it was first given.

sequential *adj* following; succeeding; following by logical consequence.

sequester *vt* to set apart or separate from other things; (*refl*) to retire or withdraw into obscurity; to seclude oneself; (*law*) to separate from the owner for a time; to set apart, as the property of a debtor, until the claims of creditors are satisfied.

sequestered *adj* secluded; private; retired; separated from others; (*law*) seized and detained for a time to satisfy a demand.

sequestrate *vt* (**sequestrated, sequestrating**) (*law*) to sequester; to take possession of on behalf of creditors, as of the estate of a bankrupt, with the view of realizing it and distributing it equitably.

sequestration *n* retirement; seclusion from society; (*law*) the separation of a thing in controversy from the possession of those who contend for it; the act of taking property from the owner for a time till the profits from it satisfy a demand.

sequin *n* a spangle of bright metal or foil, used to ornament dresses.

sequoia *n* a lofty coniferous tree found especially in California.

seraglio *n* (*pl* **seraglios**) a harem; a place for keeping wives or concubines.

serape *n* a blanket or shawl worn as an outer garment by Mexicans, etc.

seraph *n* (*pl* **seraphs, seraphim**) an angel of the highest order.

seraphic *adj* pertaining to a seraph; angelic; inflamed with holy love or zeal.

sere *adj* (*poet*) dry and withered.

serenade *n* an entertainment of music given at night under a person's window, especially by a lover, or performed as a mark of esteem and goodwill; a piece of music so played.—*vt* (**serenaded, serenading**) to entertain with a serenade.—*vi* to perform serenades or nocturnal music.

serene *adj* clear or fair and calm; placid; quiet; unruffled; undisturbed.

serenity *n* the quality or condition of being serene; clearness; calmness; quietness; stillness; peace.

serf *n* (*pl* **serfs**) a person in feudal service in the Middle Ages who was bound to the land and transferred with it and liable to the lowest services; a drudge.

serfdom *n* the state or condition of a serf.

serge *n* a kind of twilled worsted cloth.

sergeant *n* a noncommissioned officer in the army of the grade next above corporal; a police officer of superior rank.

sergeant major *n* the senior warrant officer (first class) in a battalion.

serial *adj* pertaining to a series; consisting of or constituted by a series; published, shown or broadcast by instalments at regular intervals.—*n* a story presented in a periodical or on radio or television in regular instalments with a connected plot.

serialize *vt* (**serialized, serializing**) to arrange in a series; to arrange, publish, broadcast or televise in serial form.

serial killer *n* a person who murders several people over a period, often killing the victims in the same way or choosing victims of the same type.

seriatim *adv* in regular order; one after the other.

sericeous *adj* (*bot*) pertaining to silk; consisting of silk; silky.

sericulture *n* the breeding and treatment of silkworms.

series *n sing, pl* a continued succession of similar things or of things bearing a similar relation to each other; an extended rank, line or course; a sequence; a succession; (*geol*) a set of strata possessing some common mineral or fossil characteristic; (*chem*) a group of compounds, each containing the same radical; (*arith, alg*) a number of terms or quantities in succession, each of which is related to the one before it according to a certain law; (*elect*)

sergeant

sequence

an end-to-end arrangement of conductors in an electric circuit, such that the current passes through each of them in turn; a radio or television serial whose episodes have self-contained plots; a set of books issued by one publisher.

seriocomic *adj* having a mixture of seriousness and comicality.

serious *adj* grave in manner or disposition; solemn; not light or volatile; really intending what is said; being in earnest; not jesting; important; weighty; not trifling; critical; significant; attended with danger.

sermon *n* a discourse delivered in public, especially by a clergyman or preacher, for the purpose of religious instruction or the inculcation of morality and grounded on some text or passage of Scripture; a similar discourse written or printed, whether delivered or not; a homily; a long, serious, usually tedious reproof.

serology *n* the scientific study of serums, their constituents and their properties.

sermonize *vi* (**sermonized, sermonizing**) to preach; to discourse; to direct a long speech of reproof at.

serous *adj* pertaining to serum; producing serum.

serpent *n* a reptile of an extremely eiongated form, without feet and moving by muscular contractions of the body; a snake; a powerful bass musical instrument, consisting of a conical tube of wood bent in a serpentine form; (*fig*) a subtle or malicious person.

serpent charmer *n* a snake charmer.

serpentine *adj* pertaining to or resembling a snake or serpent; having the qualities of a serpent; subtle; winding or turning one way and the other like a moving snake; spiral; crooked; treacherous.—*n* a rock, usually dark-coloured green, red, brown or grey with shades and spots resembling a snake's skin.

serpigo *n* a spreading skin complaint, such as ringworm.

serrate, serrated *adj* notched on the edge like a saw; toothed.

serration *n* formation in the shape of a saw.

serried *adj* crowded; compacted; in close order (*serried ranks of soldiers*).

serum *n* (*pl* **serums, sera**) the thin transparent part of the blood, a liquid of a pale straw-coloured or greenish-yellow colour; the lymph-like fluid secreted by certain membranes in the human body, such as the pericardium, pleura, peritoneum, etc, thence denominated serous membranes; any clear fluid resembling blood serum and containing cultures of bacteria or antibodies, used in the treatment of diseases.

serum hepatitis *n* a viral disease characterized by acute inflammation of the liver, usually transmitted by transfusion of in-

serration

fected blood or use of contaminated instruments, specially hypodermic needles, consequently often occurring in drug addicts.

serval *n* an African carnivorous animal, a kind of small leopard with a bushy tail.

servant *n* one who serves or does services; a person who is employed by another for menial offices or other labour; a subordinate assistant or helper.

serve *vt* (**served, serving**) to perform regular or continuous duties on behalf of; to be in the employment of, as a servant, hired assistant, etc; to work for; to render spiritual obedience and worship to; to minister to; to wait on at table or at meals; to set or arrange on a table for a meal (generally with *up*); to wait upon, to attend to the wants of (a customer); to conduce to; to be sufficient for; to promote; to be of use to (*to serve one's ends*); to help by good offices; to administer to the needs of; to be in the place or instead of anything to; to be in lieu of (*a sofa served him for a bed*); to regulate one's conduct in accordance with the fashion, spirit or demands of (*to serve the time* or *the hour*); to treat; to requite (*he served me ill*); to satisfy; to content (*nothing would serve them but war*); to handle, manage or work (*the guns were well served*); (of a male animal) to copulate with; (*naut*) to protect from friction by winding something round; (*law*) to deliver or transmit to; to present in due form; (in tennis) to put (the ball) into play.—*vi* to be or act as a servant; to perform domestic offices; to discharge the requirements of an office; to act as a soldier, seaman, etc; to answer a purpose; to be sufficient; to be of use; to suit (*when occasion serves*); to be convenient; (in tennis) to put the ball into play.

server *n* one who serves; a salver or small tray.

service *n* the act of serving; the performance of labour or offices for another; menial duties; employment as a servant; menial employ or capacity (*to be taken into a person's service*); assistance or kindness rendered to another; kind office (*he has done me many services*); duty performed; official function; especially military or naval duty; performance of the duties of a soldier or sailor (*to see much service abroad*); usefulness; benefit caused; public religious worship or ceremony; religious rites appropriate to any event or ceremony (*a marriage service*); a set of dishes or vessels for the table (*a tea service*); the duty which a tenant owes to a lord for his or her fee; a system of providing a utility, as gas, water, etc; professional aid; an overhaul of a vehicle; (in tennis) the act or manner of serving; (*pl*) friendly help or professional aid; (*pl*) a service area.—*adj* of or pertaining to military forces; providing services rather than producing goods (*service industries*).—*vt* (**serviced, servicing**) to provide with assistance; to overhaul.

serviceable *adj* capable of rendering useful service; fit for using; useful; doing service.

service area *n* a place offering a range of services such as restaurants, toilet facilities and petrol, especially beside a motorway.

service dress *n* military uniform worn when on active service or on ordinary occasions.

service flat *n* a set of rooms in which meals and service are supplied from a kitchen common to several such flats.

service station a place where petrol, oil, etc, and often some form of refreshment, may be purchased.

service tree *n* a European tree of the pear family, yielding a hard-grained timber and a small fruit, which is only pleasant in an overripe condition.

serviette *n* a table napkin.

servile *adj* pertaining to or befitting a servant or slave; slavish (*servile fear*); held in subjection; dependent; cringing; fawning; meanly submissive.

servility *n* the state or quality of being servile; mean submission; slavishness; slavish deference.

serving *n* a portion of food or drink.

servitor *n* a male servant; an attendant; a retainer.

servitude *n* the condition of a menial, underling or slave; involuntary subjection to a master; bondage; compulsory labour, such as a criminal has to undergo as a punishment (*penal servitude*); a state of slavish dependence.

servo a contracted form of **servomechanism.**

servomechanism *n* an automatic device which uses small amounts of power to control a system of much greater power.

sesame *n* an annual Asian herbaceous plant, the seeds of which yield an oil used in cooking; the seeds used as a flavouring agent in food.—**open sesame** the charm by which the door of the robbers' dungeon in the tale of Ali Baba and the Forty Thieves flew open; hence, a specific for gaining entrance from any place or means of exit from it.

sesquipedalian *adj* containing or measuring a foot and a half (humorously applied to long words).—*n* a very long word.

sessile *adj* (*zool, bot*) attached without any projecting support, a *sessile leaf* being one without a petiole or foot stalk, a *sessile flower* one having no peduncle, a *sessile gland* one not elevated on a stalk.

session *n* a sitting; the sitting of a court, academic body, council, legislature, etc, for the transaction of business; the time or term during which such a body transacts business regularly without breaking up; in Scotland, a kirk session; (*law*) (generally in *pl*) a sitting of justices in court upon commission; a period of study, classes, etc; a university year; a period of time passed in an activity.

session clerk *n* in Scotland, one who officially keeps the books and documents of a kirk session.

sesterce *n* an ancient Roman coin.

sestet *n* the two concluding stanzas of a sonnet, consisting of three verses each; the last six lines of a sonnet.

set *vt* (*pret, pp* **set**, *ppr* **setting**) to make or cause to sit; to place in a sitting, standing or any natural posture; to place upright (*to set a box on its end* or *a table on its feet*); to put, place or fix; to put in a certain place, position or station; to make or cause to be, do or act; to put from one state into another (*to set a person right, to set things in order*); to fix as regards amount or value (*to set a price on a house*); to fix or settle authoritatively or by arrangement; to appoint; to assign (*to set an hour for a journey*); to estimate or rate (*to set advice at naught*); to regulate or adjust (*to set a timepiece*); to fit to music; to plant, as distinguished from sowing; to fix for ornament, as in metal (*a diamond set in a ring*); to adorn, as with precious stones; to intersperse; to stud; to put in a normal position from a dislocated or fractured state (*to set a joint*); to fix mentally; to fix with settled purpose (*to set the heart* or *affections*); to embarrass; to perplex; to pose (*to be hard set*); to put in trim for use (*to set a razor* or *a saw*); to apply or use in action; to employ (with *to*, as *to set spurs to one's horse*); to incite; to instigate; to spur (often with *on*); to let to a tenant; (*print*) to place in proper order, as type; to compose; to arrange for printing; to put into type (*to set a manuscript*, often with *up*); to make stiff or solid; to convert into curd (*to set milk for cheese*); to fix (hair) in a particular style; to arrange (a table) for a meal.—*vi* to pass below the horizon; to sink; to decline; to congeal or concrete; to solidify; to have a certain direction in motion; to flow; to tend (*the current sets westward*); to point out game, as a sportsman's dog; to undertake earnestly; to apply oneself; to face one's partner in dancing.set.—**to set about** to begin; to attack physically or verbally.—**to set against** to compare or balance; to cause to be opposed to.—**to set aside** to discard; to reserve for a particular reason.—**to set down** to place (something) on a surface; to record, to put in writing; to

serviette

regard; to attribute (to); to allow to alight from (a vehicle).—**to set off** to set in motion; to cause to explode; to show up by contrast; to show to advantage; to counterbalance; to begin a journey.—**to set out** to display; to explain in detail; to begin a journey; to begin with an intention.—**to set up** to erect; to establish; to found.—*adj* placed, put, fixed, etc; regular; in due form; well arranged or put together (*a set speech* or *phrase*); fixed in opinion; determined; firm; obstinate; established; settled; appointed (*set forms of prayer*); predetermined; fixed beforehand (*a set purpose*); fixed; immovable.—*n* a collection of things of the same kind or to be used together, of which each is a complement of all the rest; a complete suit or assortment (*a set of chairs*); a number of persons customarily or officially associated; a clique; a number of things classed together; a number of particular things joined in the formation of a whole (*a set of features*); the five figures of a quadrille; the music for a quadrille; also, the number of couples required to execute the dance; the descent of the sun below the horizon; an attitude, position or posture; a permanent change of figure caused by pressure or being retained long in one position; a turn or bent; a direction or course (*the set of a current*); the scenery for a play, film, etc; assembled equipment for radio or television reception, etc; in tennis, a series of games forming a unit of a match; a badger's burrow, a sett.—**to make a dead set** to make a determined onset or an importunate application.

seta *n* (*pl* **setae**) a bristle or sharp hair; especially, a bristle or stiff hair-like appendage of plants and animals; the stalk that supports the capsule of mosses.

set-down *n* a rebuff; an unexpected and overwhelming answer.

set-off *n* that which is used to set off the appearance of anything; an ornament; a counter claim or demand; a cross debt; an equivalent; (*print*) the transferred impression from a printed page, the ink on which is not dry, to an opposite page.

setscrew *n* a screw screwed through one part tightly on another to bring pieces into close contact.

sett *n* a small block of granite or other stone for paving streets; a badge's burrow, a set.

settee *n* a long seat with a back to it; a large sofa-shaped seat for several persons to sit in at one time.

setter *n* one who or that which sets; a breed of large dog, named from its habit of setting or crouching when it perceives the scent of game and which is also trained to mark game by standing.

setting *n* the act of one who or that which sets; a sinking below the horizon; that in which something, as a jewel, is set (*a diamond in a gold setting*); a background scene, surroundings, environment; the music for a song, etc; the cutlery, dishes, etc, for a single place at table.

settle *n* a bench to sit on; a stool.—*vt* (**settled, settling**) to place in a fixed or permanent position; to establish or fix in any line of life, in an office, business, situation, etc; to change from a disturbed or troubled condition to one of tranquillity; to quiet, still, calm, compose (*to settle the mind when agitated*); to clear of dregs or sediment by causing them to sink; to cause to sink to the bottom; to determine, as something which is exposed to doubt or question; to free from uncertainty or wavering; to confirm; to adjust, as something in controversy; to bring to a conclusion; to finish (*to settle a dispute*); to make secure formally or legally (*to settle an annuity on a person*); to liquidate; to pay; to square or adjust (*to settle an account, claim*); to plant with inhabitants; to people; to colonize.—*vi* to become fixed or permanent; to assume a lasting form or condition; to establish a residence; to take up a permanent abode; to quit an irregular and desultory for a methodical life; to enter the married state; to change from a disturbed or turbid state to the opposite; to become free from dregs by their sinking to the bottom; to sink or fall gradually; to subside, as dregs from a liquid; to subside or to become lowered, as a building, by the sinking of its foundation; to become calm; to cease from agitation; to adjust differences; to come to an agreement.—**to settle for** to be content with.—**to settle up** to pay what one owes.—*n* a long wooden bench with a tall back.

settled *adj* established; stable; deep-rooted; unchanging (*settled gloom, a settled conviction*); orderly; methodical (*a settled life*).

settlement *n* the act of settling or state of being settled; arrangement; establishment in life; the act of colonizing or peopling; colonization; a tract of country colonized; a colony in its earlier condition; a small village; the liquidation of a claim or account; adjustment; arrangement; a legal deed by which property is settled; subsidence (of buildings); a financial arrangement.

settler *n* one who settles; one who fixes his or her residence in a new colony; a colonist; (*colloq*) that which settles or decides anything definitely.

set-to *n* a sharp contest; a fight at fisticuffs; a boxing match; any similar contest, as with foils.

seven *adj* one more than six or less than eight.—*n* this number; a group of things

settee

amounting to this number; the symbol representing this number, as 7 or VII.

sevenfold *adj* repeated or multiplied seven times.—*adv* seven times as much; in the proportion of seven to one.

seventeen *adj, n* seven and ten added.

seventeenth *adj* next in order after the sixteenth.—*n* the next in order after the sixteenth; one of the seventeen equal parts of a whole.

seventh *adj* next after the sixth; being one of seven equal parts of a whole.—**in seventh heaven** extremely happy.—*n* one next in order after the sixth; one of seven equal parts of a whole; (*mus*) the interval of five tones and a semitone, embracing seven degrees of the diatonic scale, as from C to B; the seventh note of the diatonic scale reckoning upwards; the B of the natural scale.

seventieth *adj* next in order after the sixty-ninth.—*n* one next after the sixty-ninth; one of seventy equal parts.

seventy *adj, n* seven times ten.—*n* the number made up of seven times ten; the symbol for this, 70, LXX.

sever *vt* to part or divide by violence; to separate by cutting or rending; to part from the rest by violence; to disjoin, referring to things that are distinct but joined by some tie (*friends severed by death*); to disunite.—*vi* to suffer disjunction; to be parted or rent asunder.

several *adj* separate; distinct; single; individual (*each several thing*); more than two but not very many; divers (used with plural nouns).—*n* a few separately or individually; a small number singly taken (with a plural verb).

severally *adv* separately; distinctly; each by himself or herself.

severance *n* the act of severing or state of being severed; separation; partition.

severe *adj* serious or earnest in feeling or manner; sedate; grave; austere; very strict in discipline or government; not indulgent; judging or criticizing harshly; strictly regulated by rule; rigidly methodical; not allowing unnecessary or florid ornament, etc (*the severest style of Greek architecture*); afflictive; distressing; violent; extreme; intense (*severe pain* or *cold*); difficult to be undergone; rigorous (*a severe test* or *examination*).

severity *n* the quality or state of being severe; extreme strictness; rigour; harshness; intensity; extremity; keenness; extreme coldness or inclemency; cruel treatment; sharpness of punishment; strictness.

Sèvres *n* a kind of fine porcelain manufactured at Sèvres in France.

sew *vt* (*pret* **sewed**, *pp* **sewn**, *ppr* **sewing**) to unite or fasten together with a needle and thread; to make or work by needle and thread.—*vi* to practise sewing; to join things with stitches.

sewage *n* waste matter which passes through drains, conduits or sewers, leading away from human habitations.

sewer *n* a subterranean channel or canal to carry off liquid waste matter; a main drain.

sewerage *n* the system of sewers that removes sewage.

sewing *n* the thread sewn in by the needle.

sewing machine *n* a machine for sewing.

sex *n* the distinction between male and female or that property or character by which an animal is male or female; the structure of plants which corresponds to sex in animals; one or other of the divisions of males and females; males or females collectively; the attraction between the sexes; (*colloq*) sexual intercourse.

sexagenarian *n* a person aged sixty or between sixty and seventy.—*adj* sixty years old; sexagenary.

sexagenary *adj* pertaining to the number sixty; composed of or proceeding by sixties.—*n* a sexagenarian.

Sexagesima *n* the second Sunday before Lent, so called as being about the sixtieth day before Easter.

sexagesimal *adj* sixtieth; pertaining to the number sixty.

sex chromosome *n* a chromosome that determines the sex of an animal.

sexed *adj* having a certain amount of sex or sexuality.

sex hormone *n* a hormone affecting the development of sexual organs and characteristics.

sexism *n* discrimination on the grounds of sex, often against women.

sex object *n* a person regarded solely in terms of their sexual attractiveness.

sextain *n* a stanza of six lines.

sextant *n* the sixth part of a circle contained by two radii and an arc; an improved form of quadrant, capable of measuring angles of 120° and having an arc embracing 60° of a circle, chiefly employed as a nautical instrument for measuring the altitudes of celestial objects and their angular distances.

sextet *n* a group of any six persons or things; a musical piece for six voices or instruments; the second part of the sonnet formation, opposed to the *octave*.

sextile *n* the aspect of two planets when distant from each other sixty degrees.

sexton *n* an officer of the church who takes care of the vessels, vestments, etc, and of the church generally.

sextuple *adj* sixfold; six times as much.

sexual *adj* pertaining to sex or the sexes; having sex.

sexual harassment *n* frequent unwelcome attention from a member of the opposite

sewing machine

sex in the form of sexually suggestive remarks, fondling, etc.

sexuality *n* the condition of being characterized by sex; a particular sexual nature.

sexually transmitted disease *n* any of various diseases, including Aids and syphilis, transmitted by sexual contact.

sexy *adj* exciting sexual desire; intended to excite sexual desire; exciting; attractive.

sforzando, sforzato *adj, adv* (*mus*) (generally contracted **sf**) signifying stronger emphasis than would otherwise be.—*n* a notation signifying this.

shabbiness *n* the quality of being shabby.

shabby *adj* threadbare or much worn; worn till no longer respectable; wearing much worn clothes; mean; despicable.

shack *n* a shanty; a hut.—**to shack up** (*sl*) to cohabit (with).

shackle *n* a fetter, handcuff, etc, that confines the limbs so as to restrain the use of them; (*fig*) that which obstructs or embarrasses free action (generally in plural).—*vt* (**shackled, shackling**) to fetter; to tie or confine the limbs of, so as to prevent free motion; (*fig*) to bind or confine so as to embarrass action.

shad *n sing, pl* a fish of the herring family which inhabits the sea near the mouths of rivers and ascends them to spawn.

shaddock *n* a tree and its fruit, which is a large species of orange, native to China.

shade *n* a comparative obscurity, dimness or gloom, caused by the interception of the rays of light; something that intercepts light, heat, dust, etc; a cover for the flame of a lamp; a cover that confines the light of a lamp within a given area; a cover for the eyes; the dark or darker part of a picture; degree or gradation of light or brightness of colour; a small or scarcely perceptible degree or amount (*a price a shade higher*); (*pl*) (*colloq*) sunglasses; a shadow; the soul after its separation from the body; a spirit; a ghost.—**the shades** the abode of spirits; Hades—*vt* (**shaded, shading**) to shelter or screen from light by intercepting its rays; to shelter from the light and heat of the sun; to cover with a shade or screen that intercepts light, heat, dust, etc; to overspread with darkness or obscurity; to obscure; to shelter; to protect; (in drawing and painting) to put in darker colours to show where the light is less intense; to mark with gradations of colour.

shading *n* the effect of light and shade represented in a picture.

shadow *n* the figure of a body projected on the ground or other surface by the interception of the light; a portion of space from which light is intercepted by an opaque body (*to be in shadow*); darkness or obscurity from intercepted light; (*fig*) the shelter, protection or security afforded

shadow

shaitsu

by someone; a dark part of a picture; anything unsubstantial or unreal, though having the appearance of reality; a spirit; a ghost; a shade; an imperfect and faint representation; adumbration; a dim bodying forth; an inseparable companion or one that follows like a shadow; a person (as a detective, etc) who shadows; a type or mystical representation; slight or faint appearance; a slight trace; a remnant; gloom.—*vt* to overspread with obscurity or shade; to intercept light or heat from; to shade; to cloud; to darken; to throw a gloom over; to protect; to screen from danger; to mark with slight gradations of colour or light; to paint in obscure colours; to represent faintly or imperfectly; to represent typically (often followed by *forth*); to follow closely; to attend on like a shadow; to maintain a position close to; to follow and watch, especially in secret.—*adj* having an indistinct pattern or darker section; (in an opposition party) matching a function or position of the party in power (*shadow cabinet*).

shadowy *adj* full of shade or shadow; causing shade; gloomy; faintly representative; unsubstantial; unreal; dimly seen; obscure; dim; indulging in fancies or dreamy imaginations.

shady *adj* abounding with shade or shades; casting or causing shade; sheltered from the glare of light or sultry heat; dark; tricky; ignoble.

shaft[1] *n* a narrow deep pit made into the earth as the entrance to a coal or other mine or for its ventilation; a vertical opening through a building, as for a lift or for ventilation or heating.

shaft[2] *n* an arrow; a spear or dart; the columnar part of anything; the body of a column between the base and the capital; the spire of a steeple; the handle of certain tools or instruments (*the shaft of a hammer, axe, whip,* etc); a kind of large axle, as of a flywheel or the screw or paddles of a steamer; one of the bars between a pair of which a horse is harnessed to a vehicle; the pole of a carriage; a critical remark or attack; (*sl*) harsh or unfair treatment.

shag *n* coarse hair or nap; rough woolly hair; a kind of cloth with a long coarse nap; a kind of tobacco cut into fine shreds; the crested or green cormorant.

shaggy *adj* rough with long hair or wool; rough; rugged.

shagreen *n* a granulated leather prepared without tanning from horse, ass or camel skin by means of embedding small seeds in the skin when soft; the rough skin of certain sharks, rays, etc.

shah *n* the title of the former ruler of Iran.

shaitsu *n* acupressure.

shake *vt* (*pret* **shook,** *pp* **shaken,** *ppr* **shak-**

ing) to cause to move with quick vibrations; to brandish; to clasp (another's hand) in greeting; to make to tremble, quiver or shiver; to agitate; to unnerve; to remove by agitating or by a jolting, jerking motion (generally with *away, off, out*, etc); to move from firmness; to threaten to overthrow; to cause to waver or doubt; to impair the resolution of; to depress the courage of; to give a tremulous sound to; to trill (a note in music).—*vi* to be agitated with a waving or vibratory motion; to tremble; to shiver; to totter; to shake hands.—**to shake off** to get rid off.—**to shake up** to shake together; to mix; to upset; to reorganize.—*n* a wavering rapid motion one way and the other; a shock or concussion; tremor; (*mus*) a rapid reiteration of two notes; a trill, marked by the sign *tr* placed over the note; a crack or fissure in timber; (*pl*) (*colloq*) convulsive trembling.

shaker *n* a container for holding condiments; a container in which cocktail ingredients are mixed.

Shaker *n* a member of a religious sect practising communal living and celibacy, founded in 1747 and so called from their ecstatic dance with shaking movements during ceremonies.

Shakespearean, Shakespearian *adj* relating to or like William Shakespeare (1564–1616) or his works.

shako *n* (*pl* **shakos, shakoes**) a kind of military cap somewhat resembling a truncated cone, with a peak in front.

shaky *adj* loosely put together; ready to come to pieces; insubstantial; tottering; cracked or split, as timber; unsteady; infirm.

shale *n* (*geol*) a species of schist or schistous clay; a clayey rock with a slaty fracture, often found in strata in coal mines, one variety being impregnated with bitumen and yielding paraffin, while another yields alum.

shall *vb aux* (*pres* **I shall, he shall**, *pl 1, 2 and 3* **shall**; *imperf* **should**) in the first persons singular and plural it forms part of the future tense and future perfect and simply foretells or declares what is to take place = am to, are to (*I shall go, we shall go*); in the second and third persons it implies control or authority on the part of the speaker and is used to express a promise, command or determination (*you shall go, he shall go*). Interrogatively, *shall I go? shall we go? shall he go? shall they go?* ask for direction or refer the matter to the determination of the person asked; *shall you go?* asks for information merely as to the future.—after *if*, etc, **shall**, in all persons, expresses simple futurity.—*should*, though in form the past of **shall**, is not used to express simple past futurity unless in the indirect speech (*I said I should go*); it is very commonly used to express present as well as past duty or obligation (*you should go, have gone*).—It is also used to express a merely hypothetical case or a contingent future event, standing in the same relation to *would* that **shall** does to *will* (*I should be glad if you would come*).—also often used in a modest way to soften a statement (*I should think so*).—nowadays **shall** and *will* are often used interchangeably.

shallop *n* a large boat with two masts, rigged like a schooner; a small light vessel with a small mainmast and foremast, with lugsails.

shallot *n* a species of onion cultivated for its edible bulb; a spring onion.

shallow *adj* not deep; having the bottom at no great distance from the surface (*shallow water*); having sides not raised much above the bottom (*a shallow trough*); not intellectually deep; not profound; superficial; silly.—*n* a place where the water is not deep; a shoal.—*vt* to make shallow.—*vi* to become shallow.

sham *n* one who or that which deceives expectation; a trick or fraud; something counterfeit; an imposture.—*adj* false; counterfeit; pretended.—*vt* (**shammed, shamming**) to make a pretence of in order to deceive; to feign (*to sham illness*).—*vi* to pretend; to make false pretences.

shaman *n* a priest of shamanism.

shamanism *n* a religion of northern Asia and elsewhere consisting mainly in a belief in sorcery and in demons who require to be propitiated by sacrifices and rites.

shamble *vi* (**shambled, shambling**) to walk awkwardly and unsteadily, as if the knees were weak.—*n* an awkward, unsteady style of walking.

shambles *npl* originally tables or benches where butchers laid meat for sale; hence, a slaughterhouse (often treated as a singular); a place of indiscriminate slaughter or butchery.

shame *n* a painful sensation caused by the exposure of that which nature or modesty prompts concealment of or by a consciousness of guilt or of having done something which injures reputation; the cause or reason of shame; a piece of unfairness; reproach; disgrace; contempt.—*vt* (**shamed, shaming**) to make ashamed; to cause to feel shame; to cover with reproach or ignominy.—*vi* to be ashamed.

shamefaced *adj* easily confused or put out of countenance; bashful; modest.

shameful *adj* bringing shame or disgrace; scandalous; disgraceful; raising shame in others; indecent.

shameless *adj* lacking shame; lacking mod-

shallot

esty; brazen-faced; insensible to disgrace; done without shame; indicating lack of shame.

shammy *n* the chamois; a kind of soft leather originally prepared from the skin of this animal but now commonly made of the skin of the goat and sheep.

shampoo *n* a liquid cleaning agent for washing the hair; a similar cleaning agent for cleaning carpets, upholstery, etc; the process of washing the hair or cleaning carpets, etc, with shampoo.—*vt* to rub the head vigorously with shampoo; to wash with shampoo.

shamrock *n* a three-leaved clover-like plant regarded as the national emblem of Ireland.

shandy *n* beer diluted with a non-alcoholic drink such as lemonade.

shanghai *vt* to force (a sailor, etc) to join a ship's crew by kidnapping or drugging; to trick or force (a person) into doing something.

Shangri-la *n* an imaginary earthly paradise.

shank *n* the leg from the knee to the ankle; the tibia or shinbone; the part of the foreleg of a horse between the knee and the fetlock; that part of a tool or other thing which connects the acting part with a handle; the stem of an anchor connecting the arms and the stock.

shamrock

shanks's pony, shanks's mare *n* one's legs, instead of another form of travel.

shanty[1] *n* a hut or mean dwelling; a slight temporary building.

shanty[2] *n* a rhythmic working song sung by sailors.

shape *vt* (**shaped, shaping**) to form or create; to make; to mould or make into a particular form; to give form or figure to; to adapt to a purpose; to suit; to conceive or conjure up.—*vi* to square; to suit; to be adjusted.—**to shape up** to develop to a definite or satisfactory form.—*n* external appearance of a body as determined by outlines or contours; (*colloq*) condition; make; figure; form; that which has form or figure; an appearance; a being; a pattern to be followed; a model; a mould; external manifestation of thought in words or action; condition; (in cookery) a dish made of blancmange, rice, cornflour, etc, which receives a particular form.

shark

shapeless *adj* lacking regular form; lacking symmetry of dimensions.

shapely *adj* well formed; having a regular and pleasing shape; symmetrical.

shard *n* a broken piece of an earthen vessel; a potsherd; a fragment in general; the wing case of a beetle; the leaves of the artichoke and some other vegetables whitened or blanched.

share *n* a certain allotted quantity; a part bestowed; a portion; a part or portion of a thing owned by a number in common (*shares in a bank*); one of the parts into which a company's capital stock is divided, entitling the holder to a share of profits; the iron blade of a plough which cuts the bottom of the furrow slice; a ploughshare.—*vt* (**shared, sharing**) to divide in portions; to part among two or more; to partake or enjoy with others; to seize and possess jointly or in common.—*vi* to have part; to get one's portion; to be a sharer.

shareholder *n* one who or that which holds or owns a share or shares in a joint-stock company or in some property.

shark[1] *n* a voracious carnivorous marine fish of which there are many species.

shark[2] *n* a greedy, artful person; a sharper; a cheat; an extortioner.—*vti* (*arch*) to swindle.

sharp *adj* having a very thin edge or fine point; not blunt; having a keen cutting edge; pointed; peaked; bent at or forming an acute angle; acute of mind; quick to discern or distinguish; ingenious; shrewd; subtle; keen as regards the organs of sense; quick of sight; vigilant; attentive; affecting the organs of taste like fine points; sour; acid; acrid; piercing to the ear; penetrating; shrill; acrimonious; severe; sarcastic; cutting (*a sharp rebuke*); severely rigid; intense; eager for food; feeling the calls of hunger; fierce; fiery; violent (*a sharp contest*); afflicting, distressing or painful; biting; piercing (*sharp frost*); gritty (*sharp sand*); emaciated (*a sharp visage*); keenly alive to one's own interest; barely honest; (*colloq*) smartly dressed; (in phonetics) applied to a sound pronounced or uttered with breath and not with voice; surd; not sonant (*the sharp mutes in p, t, k*); (*mus*) raised a semitone; too high; so high as to be out of tune or above true pitch.—*n* (*mus*) a note artificially raised a semitone, marked by the sign #; the sign itself.—*vt* to make sharp; to sharpen.—*adv* sharply; exactly; to the moment; not a minute behind.

sharpen *vt* to make sharp or sharper; to whet; to make more eager, active, intense, ingenious, etc; to make more eager for any gratification; (*mus*) to raise a semitone or a little above the true pitch.—*vi* to grow or become sharp.

sharpener *n* something that sharpens (*a pencil sharpener*).

sharper *n* a tricky person; a cheat; one who lives by cheating.

sharply *adv* in a sharp or keen manner; severely; rigorously; acrimoniously; keenly; violently; vehemently; with keen perception; wittily; abruptly; steeply.

sharpness *n* the state or quality of being sharp; keenness of edge or point; pungency; acidity; keenness of appetite; severity of pain or affliction; severity of language; acuteness of intellect; quickness of sense or perception; keenness; severity (*the sharpness of the air*); keenness in transacting business; equivocal honesty.

sharpshooter *n* formerly, a rifleman when skirmishing or sniping; a marksman.

shatter *vt* to break at once into many pieces; to dash into splinters; to break up violently; to overthrow (a government, a person's intellect).—*vi* to be broken into fragments.

shave *vt* (*pret* **shaved**, *pp* **shaved** *or* **shaven**, *ppr* **shaving**) to pare off from the surface of a body by a razor or other edged instrument; to pare close; to remove the hair from by a razor or other sharp instrument; to skim along or near the surface of; to sweep along; to oppress by extortion; to fleece.—*vi* to use a razor.—*n* a cutting off of the beard; a thin slice or shaving; the act of passing so closely as almost to graze; an exceedingly narrow miss or escape

shaver *n* one who shaves; an instrument for shaving, especially an electrical one; (*colloq*) a boy or lad; (*arch*) one who is close in bargains.

Shavian *adj* of, relating to or resembling the works of the writer George Bernard Shaw (1856–1950).

shaving *n* the act of one who shaves; a thin slice pared off with a plane or other cutting instrument.

shawl *n* an article of dress of various textures, usually of a square or oblong shape, worn as a shoulder covering, etc.—*vt* to cover with a shawl.

she *pron* (*possessive and dative* **her**, *objective* **her**; *pl* **they, their, them**) the nominative feminine of the pronoun of the third person; occasionally used as a noun; used also as a prefix denoting of the female sex (*she-bear, she-cat*).

shea *n* a tree of tropical Asia and Africa the trunk of which when pierced yields a copious milky juice, while a kind of vegetable butter is found in the nut.

sheading *n* one of the six local divisions of the Isle of Man.

sheaf *n* (*pl* **sheaves**) a quantity of the stalks of wheat, rye, oats or other plant, bound together; any similar bundle, as of arrows.—*vt* to collect and bind; to make sheaves of.

shealing *n* same as **shieling**.

shear *vt* (*pret* **sheared** *or* **shore**, *pp* **sheared** *or* **shorn**, *ppr* **shearing**) to cut or clip the wool from; to cut the nap from (*to shear cloth*); to separate by shears; to cut or clip from a surface; (*fig*) to strip of property; to fleece.—*vi* to cut; to penetrate by cutting; (of a piece of metal) to break off because of a heavy force or twist.—*n* a strain or

change of shape of a body in which parallel planes slide over each other.

shearing *n* a clipping by shears or by a machine; the result of the operation of clipping.

shearing stress *n* that form of stress which tends to make one part of a body slide over the adjacent part.

shearling *n* a sheep after its first shearing; its fleece.

shears *npl* an instrument consisting of two movable blades with bevel edges, used for cutting cloth and other substances by interception between the two blades; a tool for shearing sheep, cutting hedges, etc; something in the form of the blades of shears, as an apparatus for raising heavy weights.

shearwater *n* any of several marine birds belonging to the petrel family, which skim over the waves.

sheath *n* a case for holding a sword or other long and slender instrument; a scabbard; any similar covering; a petiole or leaf that embraces the branch from which it springs; the wing case of an insect; a condom; a closefitting dress.

sheathe *vi* (**sheathed, sheathing**) to put into a sheath or scabbard; to cover with a sheath or case; to protect by a casing or covering, as of copper (*to sheathe a ship*).

shebeen *n* an unlicensed or illegal drinking place; illicit whiskey.

shed[1] *vt* (*pret, pp* **shed**, *ppr* **shedding**) to let flow out; to let fall in drops (*to shed tears, to shed blood*); to cast or throw off, as a natural covering (*to shed leaves*); to emit or give out (*flowers shed fragrance*); to cause to flow off without penetrating (*a sloping roof sheds the rain*); to divide; to part (*to shed the hair*).—*vi* to let fall seed, a covering or envelope, etc.—*n* a parting of the streams of a district; a watershed; (in weaving) the interstice between the different parts of the warp of a loom through which the shuttle passes.

shed[2] *n* a hut or covering of boards, etc, for shelter; a poor house or hovel; a large open structure for the temporary storage of goods, etc; a warehouse.

sheen *n* brightness; splendour.—*adj* bright; shining; glittering; showy.

sheep *n sing, pl* a ruminant animal related to the goat and useful both for its wool and its flesh, called mutton; a person who always follows another's example; a silly person; a bashful person.

sheepcote *n* a small enclosure for sheep.

sheep-dip *n* a liquid disinfectant or insecticide into which sheep are plunged to destroy parasites.

sheepdog *n* a dog trained to tend, drive or guard sheep.

sheepfold *n* a fold or pen for sheep.

shed

sheepish *adj* like a sheep; foolishly bashful; over-modest; diffident.

sheep pen *n* an enclosure for sheep; a sheepfold.

sheep's eyes *npl* amorous glances.

sheepshank *n* (*naut*) a kind of knot made on a rope to shorten it temporarily.

sheepskin *n* the skin of a sheep, especially with the fleece; a rug, parchment or leather prepared from it; a garment made of or lined with sheepskin.

sheer[1] *adj* simple; mere; downright (*sheer ignorance*); straight up and down; perpendicular; precipitous, very steep; (of cloth) delicately fine, transparent.—*adv* outright; perpendicularly, steeply.

sheer[2] *vi* to deviate from the line of the proper course; to slip or move aside; to swerve.—*n* the act of sheering; the upward curve of a deck toward bow or stern of a ship; a change in course.

sheet[1] *n* a broad, large, thin piece of anything, as paper, linen, metal, glass, etc; a large piece of linen, cotton or other cloth forming part of a set of bedclothes; a broad piece of paper, either unfolded or folded into pages; a piece of writing paper folded in two leaves; (*colloq*) a newspaper; anything expanded; a broad expanse or surface (*a sheet of water* or *of ice*).—*vt* to furnish with sheets; to fold in a sheet; to cover as with a sheet.—*vi* to fall in sheets, as rain.

sheet *n* (*naut*) a rope fastened to the lower corner of a sail to extend and retain it in a particular situation.—*vt* to extend a sheet.

sheet anchor *n* the largest anchor of a ship, which is shot out in extreme danger; (*fig*) the chief support; the last refuge for safety.

sheet glass *n* a kind of glass made in large sheets or blown at first in the form of a cylinder which is afterwards opened out to form a sheet.

sheeting *n* cloth for sheets.

sheet iron *n* iron in sheets or broad thin plates.

sheet lightning *n* lightning appearing in wide expanded flashes.

sheik *n* an Arab chief.

shekel *n* the unit of money in Israel; (*pl*) (*sl*) money.

sheldrake *n* one of two species of Old World ducks with bright plumage.

shelduck *n* the female of the sheldrake.

shelf *n* (*pl* **shelves**) a board or platform of boards fixed horizontally to a wall for holding vessels, books, etc; a ledge; a projecting ledge of rocks; a ledge of rocks in the sea; a shoal.—*vt* to place on a shelf; to shelve.

shelf ice *n* a mass of ice extending from a glacier into coastal waters.

shelf life *n* the length of time a product can be stored without deterioration occurring.

shelf

shell *n* a hard outside covering, particularly that serving as a natural protection in certain plants and animals; the hard outside part of a nut; the hard covering or external skeleton of many invertebrate animals, as the crab, the oyster, etc; the hard covering of some vertebrates, as the armadillo, tortoise, etc; a carapace; the outside and calcareous layer of an egg; any outside framework; reserve, shyness (*to come out of one's shell*); any slight hollow structure; the outside plates of a boiler; a hollow projectile containing a bursting charge which is exploded by a time or percussion fuse; a light racing boat.—*vt* to strip or break off the shell of; to take out of the shell; to bombard (*to shell a fort*, *a town*, etc).—*vi* to fall off, as a shell, crust or exterior coat; to cast the shell.—**to shell out** (*colloq*) to pay out (money).

shellac *n* a resin usually produced in thin, flaky layers or shells; a thin varnish containing this and alcohol.

shellfish *n sing, pl* a mollusc or a crustacean the external covering of which consists of a shell, as oysters, crabs, etc.

shellproof *adj* proof against shells; impenetrable by shells; bombproof.

shell shock *n* a nervous disorder caused by the shock of being under fire on a battlefield.

shelter *n* that which covers or defends from injury or annoyance; a protection; a refuge; a position affording cover or protection; a safe place; security.—*vt* to provide shelter for; to cover from violence, injury, annoyance or attack; to protect; to place under cover; (*refl*) to betake oneself to cover or a safe place.—*vi* to take shelter.

sheltie *n* a Shetland pony.

shelve *vt* (**shelved, shelving**) to place on a shelf; hence, to put aside out of active employment or out of use; to delay consideration; to postpone; to dismiss; to furnish with shelves.—*vi* to slope, like a shelf or sandbank; to incline; to be sloping.

shelving *adj* inclining; sloping; having declivity.—*n* the shelves of a room, shop, etc, collectively; material for making shelves.

shepherd *n* a person employed in tending sheep in the pasture; one who exercises spiritual care over a community; a pastor.—*vt* to look after, as a shepherd; to manoeuvre or marshal in a particular direction.

shepherdess *n* a woman who tends sheep.

sherbet *n* a cooling drink made of fruit juices diluted with water and sweetened.

sheriff *n* in England, the chief officer of the crown in every county, to whom alone by letters patent is committed the custody of the county and whose duties are mainly honorary; in Scotland, a judge in the sheriff court or the chief judge of the sheriff court of a town or region; in the USA, the chief law officer in a county.

sheriff clerk *n* in Scotland, the clerk of the sheriff's court, who has charge of the records of the court.

sheriff court *n* in Scotland, a court dealing with civil and most criminal cases.

sheriff officer *n* in Scotland, an officer connected with the sheriff court who is charged with arrests, the serving of process, etc.

Sherpa *n* one of an eastern Tibetan people living on the southern side of the Himalayas, noted for their expertise as mountaineers and guides.

sherry *n* a type of fortified wine, so called from Xeres, in Spain where it was originally made.

Shetland pony *n* a small strong horse from Shetland with a shaggy mane.

shew *vt, vi* (*arch*) to show.

shibboleth *n* in the Old Testament, a word made the test to distinguish the Ephraimites from the Gileadites; hence, the watchword of any party; a pet phrase of a party; a party cry.

shield *n* a broad piece of defensive armour carried on the arm; a buckler, used in war for the protection of the body; anything that protects or defends; defence; protection; the person that defends or protects; a trophy in the shape of a shield; (*heral*) the escutcheon or field on which are placed the bearings in coats of arms.—*vt* to cover, as with a shield; to cover or protect from danger or anything hurtful or disagreeable; to defend; to protect.

shift *vt* to transfer from one place or position to another; to remove; to change; to substitute other clothes for; to dress in fresh clothes; to change the arrangement of (gears); (*colloq*) to remove (a dirty mark, etc).—*vi* to change; to pass into a different form, state, etc; to change place, position or direction; to resort to expedients; to adopt some course in a case of difficulty; to contrive.—*n* a change, a substitution of one thing for another; an expedient tried in difficulty; a contrivance; a resource; one thing tried when another fails; a base refuge or resort; an artifice; a woman's undergarment; a chemise; a straight dress; a squad of people to take a spell or turn of work at stated intervals; the working time of a squad or relay of people; the spell of work; a change in the arrangement of gears; (*mus*) a complete change of four notes by changing the position of the left hand in violin playing.—**to make (a) shift** to contrive; to find ways and means.

shiftless *adj* lacking expedients; not resorting to successful expedients; incapable; feckless.

shifty *adj* artful; evasive; dishonest.

Shiite *n* a member of one of the two great sects into which Muslims are divided (the other being the Sunni) who consider Ali as the only rightful successor of Mohammed.

shillelagh *n* an Irish name for an oaken sapling or other stick used as a cudgel.

shilling *n* formerly, a British coin and money of account, equal in value to twelve pennies or to one-twentieth of a pound sterling.

shillyshally *vi* (**shillyshallied, shillyshallying**) to act in an irresolute or undecided manner; to hesitate.—*n* foolish trifling; irresolution.

shimmer *vi* to emit a tremulous light; to gleam; to glisten.—*n* a tremulous gleam or glistening.

shin *n* the forepart of the leg between the ankle and the knee, particularly of the human leg.—*vti* (**shinned, shinning**) to climb (a tree, etc) by means of the hands and legs alone (with *up*).

shindig *n* (*colloq*) a a lively, noisy celebration; an uproar.

shine *vi* (*pret, pp* **shone**, *ppr* **shining**) to emit rays of light; to give light; to beam with steady radiance; to exhibit brightness or splendour; to glitter or be brilliant; to be splendid or beautiful; to be conspicuous or distinguished (*to shine in sport*); to be noticeably visible.—*vt* to cause or make to shine.—*n* fair weather (*shine and storm*); sunshine; brilliancy; brightness; splendour; lustre; gloss; (*sl*) a liking.

shingle[1] *n* a thin piece of wood, usually with parallel sides and thicker at one end than the other so as to lap with others, used as a roof covering instead of slates or tiles.—*vt* (**shingled, shingling**) to cover with shingles; to perform the process of shingling on (*to shingle iron*); to cut the hair short behind and wave it so as to form curving lines like those of a shingled roof.

shingle[2] *n* round, water-worn and loose gravel and pebbles as on a beach; an area covered with these.

shingles *npl* a painful eruptive viral skin disease which spreads around the body somewhat like a girdle; herpes.

shingly *adj* abounding with shingle or gravel.

Shinto, Shintoism *n* the ancient religion of Japan, a form of nature worship, though its essence is now ancestral worship and sacrifice to departed heroes.

shinty *n* a game similar to hockey, played mainly in Scotland.

shiny *adj* characterized by sunshine; bright; luminous; having a glittering appearance; glossy; brilliant.

ship *n* a vessel of some size navigating deep water; its officers and crew; a spacecraft.—*vt* (**shipped, shipping**) to put on

Shetland pony

shield

board a ship or vessel of any kind; to transport by any carrier; to take for service on board ship; to fix in its proper place (*to ship the tiller*); to take in (water) over the side.—*vi* to go on board a vessel to make a voyage with it; to embark; to engage for service on board a ship.

shipbuilder *n* one whose occupation is to construct ships; a shipwright.

shipbuilding *n* the art of constructing vessels for navigation.

ship canal *n* a canal through which vessels of large size can pass; a canal for seagoing vessels.

ship chandler *n* one who deals in cordage, canvas and other provisions for ships.

shipful *n* as much or as many as a ship will hold; enough to fill a ship.

shipmate *n* one who serves in the same ship with another; a fellow sailor.

shipment *n* the act of putting anything on board a ship; goods shipped; a consignment.

shipper *n* one who ships goods for transportation by any means.

shipping *n* ships in general; the collective body of ships belonging to a country, port, etc; the business of transporting goods generally.—*adj* relating to ships.

ship's biscuit *n* hard coarse biscuit prepared for long keeping and for use on board a ship.

shipshape *adj* having a seamanlike trim; hence, neat and trim; well arranged; in good order.

ship-to-shore *adj* (of communications) linking a ship with the shore.

shipworm *n* a mollusc that burrows in submerged wood.

shipwreck *n* the wreck of a ship; the destruction or loss at sea of a ship; destruction; ruin.—*vt* to destroy by shipwreck; to wreck; to cast away.

shipwright *n* a worker skilled in building ships.

shipyard *n* a yard or shed near water in which ships are constructed.

shire *n* in the UK, a county; a breed of large powerful working horse.

shirk *vti* to avoid or get off unfairly or meanly; to seek to avoid the performance of duty; to refuse to face (a duty, etc).—*n* one who seeks to avoid duty; the act of shirking.

shirker *n* one who shirks duty or danger.

shirr *vt* to gather (fabric) with parallel threads run through it; to bake (eggs) in buttered dishes.

shirring *n* a gathering made in cloth by drawing the material up on parallel rows of short stitches.

shirt

shirt *n* a sleeved garment of linen, cotton or other material, worn on the upper body, usually with a collar and cuffs and front buttons; (*colloq*) one's money or resources.

shiver[1] *vi* to tremble, as from cold; to shake, as with ague, fear, horror or excitement; to shudder; to quiver.—*n* a shaking fit; a tremulous motion.

shiver[2] *vt* to break into many small pieces or splinters; to shatter.—*vi* to fall at once into many small pieces or parts.—*n* a small fragment into which a thing breaks by sudden violence.

shivery *adj* pertaining to shivering; characterized by shivering.

shoal[1] *n* a place where the water of a river, lake or sea is shallow or of little depth; a sandbank or bar; a shallow.—*vi* to become more shallow (*the water shoals*).—*adj* shallow; of little depth (*shoal water*).

shoal[2] *n* a large number of fish swimming together; a large crowd; a throng.—*vi* to form shoals.

shock[1] *n* a violent collision of bodies; a concussion; a violent striking or dashing against; violent onset; hostile encounter; a strong and sudden agitation; any violent or sudden impression or sensation; a blow to the feelings; (*elect*) the effect on the body of a discharge of electricity; (*med*) a disorder of the blood circulation produced by displacement of body fluids, caused by injury; (*colloq*) a paralytic stroke.—*vt* to shake by sudden collision; to strike against suddenly; to strike, as with horror, fear or disgust; to offend extremely; to disgust; to scandalize.—*vi* to come together with a shock; to meet in sudden encounter; to experience extreme horror, outrage, etc.

shock[2] *n* a pile of sheaves of wheat, rye, etc; a stook.

shock[3] *n* a mass of close matted hair.—*adj* shaggy; having shaggy hair.

shock absorber *n* a device, as on the springs of a vehicle, that absorbs the force of bumps and jars.

shocker *n* (*colloq*) anything that shocks; (*colloq*) a horrible person; (*colloq*) a sensational novel.

shock-headed *adj* having a thick and bushy head of hair.

shocking *adj* causing a shock of horror, disgust or pain; causing to recoil with horror or disgust; extremely offensive or disgusting; very obnoxious or repugnant; very bad.

shock treatment *n* the treatment of certain kinds of mental illness by inducing convulsions, often by passing electric currents through the brain.

shock troops *npl* a highly disciplined force trained to lead an attack.

shoddy *n* the fibre from old woollen or worsted fabrics shredded and mixed with fresh but inferior wool to be respun and made into cheap cloth, etc; the coarse or inferior cloth made from this.—*adj* made of shoddy; (*fig*) of a trashy or inferior character (*shoddy literature*).

shoe *n* (*pl* **shoes**) a covering for the foot, not enclosing the ankle, composed of a thick kind for the sole and a thinner kind for the upper; a partial casing; a horseshoe; anything resembling a shoe in form or use; a drag for a wheel; a device to guid movement, provide contact or protect against wear or slipping; a dealing box that holds several decks of cards.—*vt* (*pret* **shod** *or* **shoed**, *pp* **shod, shoed** *or* **shodden**, *ppr* **shoeing**) to provide with shoes; to put shoes on; to cover at the lower end for strength or protection.

shoeblack *n* a person who cleans shoes.

shoehorn *n* a curved piece of plastic, polished horn or metal used for easing the heel into a shoe.

shoot *vt* (*pret, pp* **shot**, *ppr* **shooting**) to let fly with force; to propel, as from a bow or firearm (*to shoot an arrow, a ball*); to discharge; to let off; to fire (*to shoot a gun*); to hit, wound or kill with a missile discharged from a weapon; to discharge or propel with force; to empty out with rapidity or violence (*to shoot rubbish into a hole*); to push or thrust forward; to dart forth; to protrude; to put forth by way of vegetable growth; to pass rapidly through, under or over (*to shoot a rapid* or *a bridge*); to photograph (a film scene); to kick or drive (a ball) at goal; (*sl*) to inject (oneself) with a drug.—*vi* to perform the act of discharging a missile from an engine or instrument; to fire (*to shoot at a target* or *mark*); to be emitted; to dart forth; to rush or move along rapidly; to dart along (*shooting stars*); to be felt as if darting through one (*shooting pains*); to sprout; to put forth buds or shoots; to increase in growth; to grow taller or larger; to push or be pushed out; to project; to jut; (*sl*) to say what one has to say.—**to shoot down** to kill by shooting; to bring down (a plane) by shooting; to disprove strongly (an argument, etc); to rout.—**to shoot up** to grow very quickly; (*sl*) to inject (a drug).—*n* a young branch which shoots out from the main stock; an annual growth; a kind of sloping trough for conveying coal, grain, etc, into a particular receptacle; a place for shooting rubbish.

shooting *adj* pertaining to one who or that which shoots; connected with the killing of game by firearms (*a shooting licence, the shooting season*); sudden, quick (*a shooting pain*).—*n* the act of one who shoots; especially, the act or sport of killing game with firearms (*to be fond of shooting and fishing*); a tract of ground over which game is shot.

shooting box *n* a private house for the ac-

commodation of a person during the shooting season.

shooting gallery *n* an indoor range with targets for rifle practice.

shooting script *n* the final version of a script for a film or television programme with scenes arranged together for convenience of shooting.

shooting star *n* a meteor in a state of incandescence seen suddenly darting along some part of the sky.

shooting stick *n* a spiked stick with a handle that folds out into a small seat.

shop *n* a building or apartment in which goods are sold by retail, generally with a frontage to a street or road; a building in which workers carry on their occupation (*a joiner's shop, an engine shop*); the details and technicalities of one's work; talk about these.—**to talk shop** to speak of one's calling or profession only.—*vi* (**shopped, shopping**) to visit shops to buy goods.—*vt* (*sl*) to inform on (someone) to the police.—**to shop around** to hunt for articles that are the best value for money.

shop floor *n* the part of a factory where goods are manufactured; the work force employed there.

shopkeeper *n* a trader who sells goods in a shop or by retail, as distinct from a merchant or one who sells by wholesale; a tradesman.

shoplift *vi* to practice shoplifting.

shoplifter *n* one who is guilty of shoplifting.

shoplifting *n* stealing from a shop during shopping hours, usually under pretence of buying.

shop steward *n* a representative appointed from among themselves, subject to the approval of their union, by the workers in engineering and similar shops, to take charge of certain matters affecting their collective interests and to be the medium of complaints to the management.

shopwalker *n* an attendant in a large shop who directs customers to the proper department, sees that they are served, etc.

shore[1] *n* the land immediately adjacent to a great body of water, as an ocean or sea, or to a large lake or river; the land along the edge of the water.

shore[2] *n* a prop; a piece of timber or iron for the temporary support of something, often resting obliquely against it.—*vt* (**shored, shoring**) to support by a shore or shores; to prop (usually with *up*, as *to shore up a building*).

short *adj* not long; not having great length or linear extension; not extending in time; not of long duration; not reaching a certain point; limited in quantity; insufficient; inadequate; scanty; deficient (*a short supply, short weight*); scantily supplied or fur-

shoe

shooting

nished; not possessed of a reasonable or usual quantity or amount (*to be short of money* or *means*); not tenacious or retentive (*a short memory*); not containing many words; curt; brief; abrupt; sharp; severe; uncivil (*a short answer*); (of pastry) breaking or crumbling readily in the mouth; crisp; brittle; friable; not prolonged in sound (*a short vowel* or *syllable*); less than, below, inferior to (followed by *of*, as *his escape was nothing short of a miracle*); (of a drink) containing spirits without being diluted.—*adv* in a short manner; abruptly; suddenly.—*n* a summary account (*the short of the matter*); a short film; (*pl*) trousers not covering the knee; underpants; a short circuit.—**in short** in few words; briefly; to sum up in few words.—**the long and the short** a brief summing up in decisive, precise or explicit terms.

shortage *n* amount short or deficient; an amount by which a sum of money is deficient.

shortbread *n* a sweet and very brittle cake, in which butter or lard has been mixed with the flour.

short circuit *n* (*elect*) the deviation of an electric current by a path of small resistance; an interrupted electric current.—**short-circuit** *vt* to establish a short ciruit in; to cut off electric current to; to provide with a short cut; to bypass, impede, hinder or frustrate.

shortcoming *n* a failing of the usual quantity or amount, as of a crop; a failure of full performance, as of duty; a defect; any inadequacy.

shortcut *n* a shorter route; a quick way of doing something that saves time, effort, etc.

shorten *vt* to make short or shorter; to abridge; to curtail; to lessen; to diminish in extent or amount.—*vi* to become short or shorter; to contract.

shortfall *n* a deficit; the amount or extent of this.

shorthand *n* a method of rapid writing using signs or contractions; stenography.

shorthanded *adj* not having the necessary or regular number of hands or assistants.

short list *n* a selected list of candidates for a job from whom the successful candidate will be chosen.

shortly *adv* in a short or brief time or manner; soon; in few words.

short shrift *n* curt, dismissive treatment.

shortsighted *n* nearsightedness; myopia; vision accurate only when the object is near.—*adj* not able to see far; myopic; nearsighted; not able to look far into the future; not having foresight; characterized by a lack of foresight (*a shortsighted policy*).

shot-putter

shoulder

short-wave *adj* (of a radio wave) having a wavelength of less than 100 metres.

shot[1] *n* (*pl* **shot, shots**) the act of shooting; a discharge of a firearm or other missile weapon; one who shoots; a marksman; a missile, particularly a ball or bullet for firing from ordnance; small globular masses of lead for use with fowling pieces, etc (in collective sense, often called distinctively *small shot*); the flight of a missile or the range or distance through which it passes; range; reach; the whole sweep of a fishing net thrown out at one time; the number of fish caught in one haul of the net; (in weaving) a single thread of weft carried through the warp at one run of the shuttle; (in blasting) a charge of powder or other explosive in a blast hole, usually fired by a slow match; a photograph or a continuous film sequence; a hypodermic injection, as of vaccine; a turn; a spell; (*colloq*) a drink of alcohol.—*adj* having a changeable colour, like that produced in weaving by all the warp threads being of one colour and all the weft of another; chatoyant (*shot silk*); hence, interwoven; interspersed.

shot[2] *n* a reckoning or a person's share of a reckoning; share of expenses, as of a bill for drinks.

shotgun *n* a light, smooth-bored gun for firing shot at short range; a fowling piece.

shotgun wedding *n* an enforced wedding, usually because the bride is pregnant.

shot-put *n* a field event in which a heavy metal ball is propelled with an overhand thrust from the shoulder.

shot-putter *n* one who takes part in shot-put.

shoulder *n* the joint by which the arm of a human being or the foreleg of a quadruped is connected with the body; the bones and muscles of this part together; the upper joint of the foreleg of an animal cut for the market; that which resembles a human shoulder; a prominent or projecting part (*the shoulder of a hill*); a projection on various implements and articles.—*vt* to push or thrust with the shoulder; to push with violence; to take on the shoulder or shoulders; to assume responsibility for; (*milit*) to carry vertically at the side of the body and resting against the hollow of the shoulder (*to shoulder arms*).—*vi* to push forward; to force one's way, as through a crowd.

shoulder blade *n* the large flat triangular bone on either side of the back part of the human shoulder.

shout *vi* to utter a sudden and loud cry, as in joy or exultation or to call a person's attention.—*n* a loud cry; a vehement and sudden outcry, particularly of a multitude of people, expressing joy, triumph, exultation, etc.—*vt* to utter with a shout.

shove *vt* (**shoved, shoving**) to force or push along, usually without a sudden impulse; to cause to slide by pushing; to press against; to jostle.—*vi* to push or drive forward; to urge a course.—**to shove off** to push (a boat) off from the shore; (*colloq*) to depart.—*n* an act of shoving; a push.

shovel *n* an implement consisting of a broad and slightly hollow blade or a shallow scoop with a longish handle, used for removing coals, sand, earth or other loose matter.—*vt* (**shovelled, shovelling**) to take up and throw with a shovel; to move in large quantities.

shovel hat *n* a hat with a broad brim turned up at the sides and projecting in front.

shoveller *n* one who shovels; one of a species of duck with a broad bill.

show *vt* (*pret* **showed**, *pp* **shown** *or* **showed**, *ppr* **showing**) to exhibit or present to the view; to place in sight; to display; to let be seen; to communicate; to reveal; to make known; to make apparent or clear by evidence, reasoning, etc; to teach; to direct; to guide or usher; to conduct; to bestow, confer, afford (mercy, etc); to explain or expound; to indicate; to point out.—*vi* to appear; to become visible; to look; to be in appearance.—**to show off** to display ostentatiously; to behave boastfully or ostentatiously.—**to show up** (*colloq*) to show (faults, etc) by contrast; (*colloq*) to embarrass, to put to shame; to put in an appearance; to arrive.—*n* the act of showing; exposure to view or notice; appearance, whether true or false; semblance; outward aspect assumed; pretext; ostentatious display; parade; pomp; an object attracting notice; a sight or spectacle; an exhibition; a collection of curiosities exhibited for money (*a flower show*); an entertainment; a theatrical performance; a radio or television programme.

showcase *n* a case with glass on the top or front within which articles are placed for sale or exhibition; a setting or situation designed to exhibit something to best advantage.

shower *n* a fall of rain of short or not very great duration; also of snow or hail; a fall of things in thick and fast succession (*a shower of stones*); a method of washing in which the body is sprayed with water from above; a wash using this method; a party for the presentation of gifts, especially to a bride.—*vt* to pour down copiously and rapidly; to bestow liberally.—*vi* to rain in showers; to fall as a shower; to cleanse in a shower.

showery *adj* raining in showers; abounding with falls of rain.

showing *n* exhibition; performance.

showjumping *n* the competitive riding of horses to demonstrate their skill in jumping.

showman *n* (*pl* **showmen**) one who exhibits a show; the proprietor of a travelling exhibition.

showroom *n* a room in which a show is exhibited; a shop or other place where goods are displayed to the best advantage to attract purchasers.

showy *adj* making a great show or appearance; gaudy; gorgeous; ostentatious.

shrapnel *n* a shell filled with bullets and a small bursting charge just sufficient to split the shell open and release the bullets at any given point.

shred *vt* (*pret*, *pp* **shredded** *or* **shred**, *ppr* **shredding**) to tear or cut into small pieces, particularly narrow and long pieces, as cloth or leather.—*n* a piece torn or cut off; any torn fragment; a tatter; a fragment.

shrew *n* an ill-tempered woman; a virago; a scold; a shrewmouse.

shrewd *adj* astute; sagacious; discerning.

shrewdness *n* the quality of being shrewd; sagacity; acuteness of mind.

shrewish *adj* having the qualities of a shrew; vixenish.

shrewmouse *n* a small, brown nocturnal animal with a prolonged muzzle, resembling a mouse but belonging to the insectivores while the mouse is a rodent.

shrewmouse

shriek *vi* to utter a sharp shrill cry; to scream, as in a sudden fright, horror or anguish.—*n* a sharp shrill cry or scream; a shrill noise.—*vt* to utter with a shriek.

shrift *n* confession made to a priest; absolution.

shrike *n* any of certain birds which feed on mice, insects, small birds, etc, and often impale their prey on thorns.

shrill *adj* sharp or acute in tone; having a piercing sound; uttering an acute sound.—*vi* to utter an acute piercing sound.—*vt* to utter in a shrill tone.

shrillness *n* the quality of being shrill; acuteness of sound.

shrilly *adv* in a shrill manner; with a sharp sound or voice.—*adj* somewhat shrill.

shrimp *n* a small crustacean allied to the lobster and crayfish, which burrows in sand and is eaten as food; (*colloq*) a small or unimportant person.

shrimp

shrine *n* a box for holding the bones or other remains of departed saints; a reliquary; a tomb of shrine-like form; the mausoleum of a saint in a church; an altar; a place hallowed from its history or associations (*a shrine of art*).—*vt* (**shrined, shrining**) to place in a shrine; to enshrine.

shrink *vi* (*pret* **shrank** *or* **shrunk**, *pp* **shrunk**, **shrunken**, *ppr* **shrinking**) to contract spontaneously, as woollen cloth in water; to draw or be drawn into less compass by an inherent quality; to shrivel;

to become wrinkled; to draw back, as from danger; to decline action from fear; to recoil; to draw the body together as in fear or horror.—*vt* to cause to contract by immersing in water.—*n* the act of shrinking.

shrinkage *n* the contraction of a material into less compass, as by soaking or drying.

shrive *vt* (*pret* **shrove** *or* **shrived**, *pp* **shriven** *or* **shrived**, *ppr* **shriving**) to hear or receive the confession of; to administer confession to, as a priest does; to confess and absolve.

shrivel *vi* (**shrivelled, shrivelling**) to contract or shrink; to draw or be drawn into wrinkles; to dry up; to curl up with heat, etc.—*vt* to contract into wrinkles.

shroud *n* that which clothes, covers or conceals; a garment; a covering; the dress of the dead; a winding sheet; (*naut*) one of those large ropes that extend from the head of a mast to the right and left sides of the ship to support the mast.—*vt* to envelop with some covering; to cover; to hide; to veil; to put a shroud or winding sheet on.

Shrovetide *n* the time when the people were shriven preparatory to the Lenten season; the three days before Ash Wednesday.

Shrove Tuesday *n* confession Tuesday; the Tuesday preceding the first day of Lent or Ash Wednesday.

shrub *n* a low dwarf tree; a woody plant of a size less than a tree; a plant with several permanent woody stems dividing from the bottom.

shrubbery *n* an ornamental plantation of shrubs; growing shrubs.

shrug *vti* (**shrugged, shrugging**) to raise or draw up the shoulders, as in expressing dissatisfaction, aversion, etc.—*n* a drawing up of the shoulders, a motion usually expressing dislike.

shrunken *adj* having shrunk; shrivelled up; contracted.

shuck *n* a shell or husk.—*vt* to remove the shucks from.

shudder *vi* to tremble with fear, horror, aversion or cold; to shake or shiver; to quake.—*n* a tremor; a shaking with fear or horror.

shuffle *vt* (**shuffled, shuffling**) to mix together by pushing or shoving; to put into a fresh order at random, as playing cards; to mix up.—*vi* to change the position; to shift ground; to prevaricate; to practise shifts; to shift; to move with an irregular dragging gait; to shove the feet noisily to and fro on the floor or ground; to scrape the floor in dancing.—*n* the action of one who shuffles; an evasion; a trick; an artifice; (in dancing) a rapid scraping movement with the feet.

shuffleboard *n* a game played by pushing coins, etc, along a board towards certain marks; a game played on board ships by

shoving with a cue wooden discs so that they rest in one of nine squares drawn on the deck.

shuffler *n* one who shuffles; one who prevaricates or plays evasive mean tricks.

shun *vt* (**shunned, shunning**) to keep clear of; to get out of the way of; to avoid; to eschew.

shunt *vi* (in railways) to turn from one line of rails into another.—*vt* to cause to turn from one line of rails to another; to turn into a siding; hence, to shove off; to free oneself of.

shush *interj* used to demand silence; peace, silence.—*vt* to demand silence, as if by saying 'shush'.

shut *vt* (*pret, pp* **shut**, *ppr* **shutting**) to close so as to prevent entrance or exist; to close up by bringing the parts together (a book, etc); to forbid entrance into (*to shut a port*); to bar; to preclude; to exclude.—*vi* to close itself; to become closed.—**to shut down** to (cause to) stop working or operating.—**to shut in** to confine; to enclose; to block the view from.—**to shut off** to check the flow of; to debar.—**to shut out** to exclude.—**to shut up** to confine; to close, especially completely or finally; (*colloq*) to cease speaking; (*colloq*) to reduce to silence.—*adj* not resonant or sonorous; having the sound suddenly stopped by a succeeding consonant (as *o* in *got*).— *n* the act of closing; close; a shutter.

shutdown *n* a stoppage of work or activity.

shutter *n* one who or that which shuts; a movable covering for a window; a flap device for regulating the explosure of light to a camera lens.

shuttle *n* an instrument used by weavers for passing the thread of the weft from one side of the web to the other between the threads of the warp; (in sewing machines) the sliding thread holder which carries the lower thread between the needle and the upper thread to make a lock stitch; a bus, aircraft, etc, regularly making back-and-forth trips over a short route.—*vti* (**shuttled, shuttling**) to move back and forth rapidly.

shuttlecock *n* a cork stuck with feathers or a plastic imitation hit by a racket in badminton.—*vt* to throw or bandy backwards and forwards like a shuttlecock.

shy¹ *adj* keeping at a distance through caution or timidity; readily frightened; timid; sensitively timid; not inclined to be familiar; retiring; coy; reserved; cautious; wary; careful to avoid committing oneself (followed by *of*).—*vi* (**shied, shying**) to start away from an object that causes fear (said of a horse).—*n* a sudden start aside made by a horse.

shy² *vt* to throw (*to shy a stone*).—*n* a throw; (*colloq*) an attempt.

shuttlecock

shyness *n* the quality of state of being shy; reserve; coyness.

si *n* (*mus*) a name given in some systems to the seventh note of the natural or normal scale.

SI abbreviation of *Système international*, the International System of measurement, see **SI unit**.

Siamese cat *n* a domestic short-haired, fawn-coloured cat with blue eyes and a small head.

Siamese twins *npl* a set of twins born with their bodies joined at some point.

sib *adj* related to; akin to; consanguineous.—*n* a sibling.

sibilance, sibilancy *n* the quality of being sibilant; a hissing sound as of *s*.

sibilant *adj* hissing; making a hissing sound.—*n* a letter that is uttered with a hissing of the voice, as *s* and *z*.

sibilate *vt* (**sibilated, sibilating**) to pronounce with a hissing sound.

sibilation *n* the act of sibilating or hissing; a hissing sound; a hiss.

sibling *n* a brother or sister.

sibyl *n* in ancient Greece and Rome, a female prophet or oracle.

sibylline *adj* pertaining to a sibyl; like the productions of a sibyl; prophetic.

sic *adv* thus, as written (used in and placed within brackets to indicate that an error or doubtful usage is reproduced from the original).

sice *n* the number six at dice.

sick *adj* affected with nausea; inclined to vomit; disgusted; feeling tedium; wearied (*to be sick of flattery*); affected with disease of any kind; not in health; ill; languishing; used by or set apart for sick persons (*a sickbed*); (of humour) sadistic, gruesome.—**the sick** persons affected with disease.

sickbay *n* (*naut*) a portion of the main deck partitioned off for invalids; a room used for the treatment of the sick.

sickbed *n* a bed on which one is confined by sickness.

sicken *vt* to make sick; to disease; to make squeamish; to disgust.—*vi* to become sick; to fall ill; to feel sick; to become distempered; to languish.

sickening *adj* making sick; disgusting.

sickle *n* a reaping hook with a curved blade or hook of steel with a long handle for cutting grain, grass, etc; anything shaped like this.

sickle cell anaemia *n* a hereditary form of anaemia marked by the presence of sickle-shaped red blood cells.

sickly *adj* somewhat sick or ill; not healthy; attended with sickness; producing or tending to produce disease; faint; languid; appearing as if sick.—*adv* in a sick manner or condition.

sickness *n* the state of being sick; disease; ill-health; a disease; a malady; a particular state of the stomach which occurs under the forms of nausea, retching and vomiting; any disordered state.

side *n* the broad or long surface of a solid body, as distinguished from the end, which is of less extent; the exterior line of anything considered in length; the margin, edge, border; the part of an animal between the hip and shoulder (*the right* or *left side*); the part of persons on the right hand or the left; the part between the top and bottom; the slope of a hill or mountain (*the side of Mount Etna*); one of two principal surfaces opposed to each other; part whichever way directed; quarter in any direction; any party or interest opposed to another (*on the same side in politics*); line of descent traced through one parent (*by the father's side*); (*geom*) any line which forms one of the boundaries of a straight-lined figure; also, any of the bounding surfaces of a solid; swagger, pomposity.—*adj* lateral; being on the side; being from the side or toward the side; oblique; indirect (*a side view*).—*vi* (**sided, siding**) to embrace the opinions of one party when opposed to another party; to engage in a faction (often followed by *with*).

side arms *npl* arms carried by the side or in a belt, as sword, dagger, etc.

sideboard *n* a piece of dining-room furniture, consisting of a kind of table with drawers or compartments used to hold dining utensils, etc.

side dish *n* a food accompanying a main course at a meal.

side effect *n* an effect, often undesirable or harmful, which occurs in addition to the desired effect, as produced in certain people by some drugs.

sidekick *n* a deputy; an assistant; a partner.

sidelight *n* light admitted into a building, etc, laterally; a light on the side of a car, etc; information thrown indirectly on a subject; incidental information.

sidelong *adv* laterally; obliquely; in the direction of the side.—*adj* lateral; oblique; not directly in front.

sidereal *adj* pertaining to the stars; starry; measured or marked by the apparent motions of the stars (*sidereal time*).

sidereal day *n* the time in which the earth makes a complete revolution on its axis relative to the fixed stars, being 23 hours, 56 minutes, 4.092 seconds.

siderite *n* magnetic iron ore or loadstone; also native spathic iron ore and a blue variety of quartz.

side-saddle *n* a saddle that enables a rider to sit with both feet on the same side of a horse.—*adv* with the feet on one side, not astraddle.

sickle

sidesman *n* (*pl* **sidesmen**) in the Anglican Church, an assistant to a churchwarden.

sidetrack *vt* to prevent action by diversionary tactics; to shunt aside; to divert or be diverted from a main subject or course.—*n* a railway siding; an instance of sidetracking; a digression.

sideways, sidewise *adv* toward one side; laterally; on one side.

side wind *n* a wind blowing laterally, (*fig*) an indirect influence or means.

siding *n* a short additional line of rails laid at the side of a main railway line for the purpose of shunting.

sidle *vi* (**sidled, sidling**) to go or move side foremost; to move sideways in a furtive manner.

siege *n* the investment of a fortified place by an army and attack of it by passages and advance works that protect the besiegers; any continued endeavour to gain possession.

sienna *n* a ferruginous earth of a fine yellow colour, from Siena in Italy, used as a pigment; a reddish-brown colour; a yellowish-grown colour.

sierra *n* a chain of hills or mountains with jagged or saw-like ridges.

sieve

siesta *n* a sleep or rest in the hottest part of the day.

sieve *n* an instrument for separating the smaller particles of substances from the larger, usually in the form of a shallow circular vessel having its bottom made of basket work, interwoven wires, hair, canvas, network, etc, according to circumstances.—*vt* (**sieved, sieving**) to put through a sieve, to sift.

sift *vt* to operate on by a sieve; to separate by a sieve, as the fine part of a substance from the coarse; to part, as by a sieve; to examine minutely or critically; to scrutinize.

sigh *vi* to make a deep single respiration, as the involuntary expression of sorrow or melancholy; to grieve; to give out a similar sound (*the wind sighs*).—*vt* to emit in sighs; to mourn; to express by sighs.—*n* a single deep involuntary respiration; a simple respiration giving involuntary expression of some depressing emotion, as sorrow, melancholy, anxiety, etc.

sight *n* the act or power of seeing; perception of objects by the eye (*to gain sight of land*); the faculty of vision; range of unobstructed vision; open view (*in sight of land*); visibility; judgment or opinion from seeing; estimation (*to find favour in one's sight*); that which is beheld; a spectacle; particularly, something novel and remarkable; something worth seeing (*the sights of a town*); a great many individuals; something conspicuous or odd; an appliance for guiding the eye in an optical instrument; a

small elevated piece near the muzzle, or another near the breech, of a firearm, to aid the eye in taking aim.—*vt* to get or catch sight of; to come in sight of; to see (*to sight the land*); to give the proper elevation and direction to by means of a sight (*to sight a rifle* or *cannon*).

sightless *adj* lacking the power of seeing; blind.

sightly *adj* pleasing to the eye; striking to the view.

sightseeing *n* the act of seeing sights or visiting scenes of interest.

sightseer *n* one who goes to see sights or curiosities.

sign *n* that by which anything is made known or represented; anything visible that indicates the existence or approach of something else; a token; a mark; an indication; a motion or gesture by which a thought is expressed or intelligence communicated; a prodigy; an omen; a miracle; a wonder; any symbol or emblem; that which, being external, represents or signifies something internal or spiritual; something conspicuously placed on or near a house, indicating the occupation of the tenant or giving notice of what is sold or made within; a signboard; a board or placard with publicly displayed information; (*astron*) one of the twelve divisions of the ecliptic or zodiac, each containing 30 degrees and named in succession Aries, Taurus, Gemini, Cancer, Leo, Virgo, Libra, Scorpio, Sagittarius, Capricorn, Aquarius, Pisces; (*arith, math*) a character indicating the relation of quantities or an operation performed on them, as + (plus), - (minus), etc; (*mus*) any character, as a flat, sharp, dot, etc.—*vt* to express by a sign; to make known by gesture; to signify; to mark with a sign or symbol; to affix a signature to; to subscribe in one's own handwriting.—*vi* to make a sign or signal.

signal *n* a sign that is intended to communicate information, orders, etc, to persons at a distance, as by a motion of the hand, the raising of a flag, the showing of lights of various colours, etc.—*adj* distinguished from what is ordinary; remarkable; notable; conspicuous (said of things).—*vt* (**signalled, signalling**) to communicate or make known by a signal or signals; to make signals to (*the vessel signalled the forts*).—*vi* to give a signal or signals.

signal box *n* a small house in which railway signals are worked.

signalize *vt* (**signalized, signalizing**) to make remarkable; to render distinguished; to distinguish by some fact or exploit (often used reflexively).

signally *adv* in a signal manner; eminently; remarkably; memorably.

signalman *n* (*pl* **signalmen**) one who signals; specifically, an official on a railway who works the signals.

signatory *adj* relating to the signing of documents; setting a signature to a document; signing a public document, as a treaty.—*n* one who signs; the representative of a state who signs a public document.

signature *n* a stamp or mark impressed; the name of any person written with his or her own hand on a document; a sign manual; (*print*) a letter or figure at the bottom of the first page of each sheet or half sheet of a book to indicate their order; (*mus*) the sign placed at the beginning of a piece of music to indicate the time and key.

signboard *n* a board on which one sets a notice of his or her occupation or of articles for sale.

signet *n* a seal; particularly, a seal for the authentication of royal grants or warrants.

signet ring *n* a ring containing a signet or private seal.

significance, significancy *n* meaning; import; that which is intended to be expressed; expressiveness; impressiveness; force; importance; moment.

significant *adj* bearing a meaning; expressive in an eminent degree; expressive or suggestive of something more than what appears (*a significant look*); standing as a sign of something; important; momentous.

signification *n* the act of signifying; that which is signified or expressed by signs or words; meaning; import; sense; notion conveyed.

signify *vt* (**signified, signifying**) to make known by signs or words; to express or communicate to another by words, gestures, etc; to give notice; to announce, declare, proclaim; to convey as its meaning; to mean; to import; to indicate; to matter or be of consequence.

sign language *n* a system of manual signs and gestures for conveying meaning, used especially by deaf people.

sign manual *n* (*pl* **signs manual**) a signature; the subscription of one's own name to a document; a royal signature.

signora *n* an Italian title of address or respect, equivalent to madam, Mrs.

signore *n* an Italian title of respect equivalent to the English sir or Mr.

signorina *n* an Italian title equivalent to Miss.

sign-painter *n* a painter of signs for tradesmen, etc.

signpost *n* a post on which a sign hangs or is inscribed.—*vt* to provide with a signpost; to point out clearly or conspicuously.

Sikh *n* one of an Indian community, half religious, half military, which founded a state in the Punjab, annexed to British India in 1849.

silence *n* the condition prevailing when there is no noise; absence of sound; stillness; forbearance of speech; a holding of one's peace; taciturnity; a refraining from making known something; secrecy; absence of mention; oblivion.—*vt* (**silenced, silencing**) to put to silence; to oblige to hold the peace; to cause to cease speaking; to restrain in reference to liberty of speech; to cause to cease sounding; to stop the noise of; to still, quiet or appease (*to silence scruples*); to make to cease firing, especially by a vigorous cannonade (*to silence guns* or *a battery*).—*interj* used elliptically for *let there be silence* or *keep silence*.

silencer *n* a device on any form of engine or machine, for reducing the noise of escaping gases, in a motorcar usually consisting of a series of baffles in the exhaust pipe.

silent *adj* not speaking; mute; dumb; speechless; habitually taciturn; speaking little; not loquacious; not mentioning or proclaiming; making no noise; free from sound or noise; having or making no noise; having no sound in pronunciation (*e is silent in fable*).

silent majority *n* the section of society comprising the bulk who rarely express their views publicly but are generally assumed to hold moderate views.

silhouette *n* a profile or shadow outline portrait filled in with a black colour; the outline of a shape against a light or lighter background.—*vt* (**silhouetted, silhouetting**) to show up in outline; to depict in silhouette.

silica *n* a hard mineral, a compound of oxygen and silicone, found in quartz and flint.

silicate *n* a compound of silica with certain bases, as aluminium, lime, magnesia, potash, soda, etc.

silicle, silicula *n* (*bot*) a kind of seed vessel differing from a siliqua in being as broad as it is long or broader.

silicon *n* a common non-metallic element, used in glass, transistors, alloys, etc.

silicon chip in electronics, a microchip or chip.

silicone *n* any of a number of extremely stable organic derivatives of silicon, used in lubricants, polishes, rubbers, etc.

silicosis *n* a disease of the lungs caused by the prolonged inhalation of silica dust.

siliqua, silique *n* (*bot*) the long pod or seed vessel of crucifers (as wallflower), dehiscing by two valves which separate from a central portion.

siliquous, siliquose *adj* (*bot*) bearing siliquas.

silk *n* the fine, soft thread forming the cocoon of the larvae of various species of moths, the most important of which is the common silkworm moth, a native of the

sign language

silhouette

northern provinces of China; cloth made of silk; a garment made of this cloth.—*adj* made of silk; silken.—**silk gown** *n* the official robe of a queen's or king's counsel in England.—**to take silk** to attain the rank of queen's or king's counsel.

silken *adj* made of silk; like silk; silky.

silkworm *n* a worm which produces silk; the larva of various moths which spins a silken cocoon or case about the size of a pigeon's egg for the enclosure of the chrysalis.

silky *adj* made of silk; like silk; soft and smooth to the touch; delicate; tender.

sill *n* a stone or a piece of timber on which a structure rests; the horizontal piece of timber or stone at the bottom of a door, window or similar opening; (in mining) the floor of a gallery or passage in a mine.

sillabub *n* same as **syllabub**.

silly *adj* showing folly; unwise; stupid.

silo *n* (*pl* **silos**) the pit in which green fodder is preserved in the method of ensilage.

silt *n* a deposit of mud or fine soil from running or standing water; fine earthy sediment.—*vt* to choke or fill with silt or mud (often with *up*).—*vi* to percolate through crevices; to ooze.

silty *adj* consisting of or resembling silt; full of silt.

Silurian *adj* belonging to the Silures, an ancient people of South Wales.

Silurian rocks, Silurian strata, Silurian system *n* (*geol*) the name given to a great succession of Palaeozoic strata intervening between the Cambrian formation and the base of the old red sandstone; so called from the district where the strata were first investigated.

silvan *adj* same as **sylvan**.

silver *n* a precious metal which in its compact state is of a fine white colour and lively brilliancy, used for the purpose of coinage and also for the construction of ornaments and jewellery; money; coin made of silver; plate made of silver.—*adj* made of silver; resembling silver; silvery.—*vt* to cover superficially with a coat of silver; to cover with tinfoil amalgamated with quicksilver (*to silver glass*); to give a silvery sheen or silver-like lustre to; to make hoary; to tinge with grey.

silver fox *n* a fox of the northern parts of Asia, Europe and America, with a valuable fur of a shining black colour, intermingled with white.

silvering *n* the art of covering the surface of anything with silver or with an amalgam of tin and mercury; the silver or amalgam laid on.

silver lining *n* a favourable aspect of an otherwise unpleasant situation.

silver-plated *adj* covered with a thin coating of silver.

silversmith *n* one whose occupation is to work in silver.

silver stick *n* the name given to a field officer of the British Life Guards when on palace duty.

silver wedding *n* the twenty-fifth anniversary of a wedding.

silvery *adj* like silver; containing silver; having the appearance of silver; of silver-like lustre; clear and soft, as the sound of a silver bell.

simian *adj* pertaining to apes or monkeys; ape-like.

similar *adj* like; resembling; having a like form or appearance; like in quality; (*geom*) having like parts and relations but not of the same magnitude.—*n* that which is similar; something that resembles something else.

similarity *n* the state of being similar; close likeness; perfect or partial resemblance.

simile *n* (*rhet*) the likening together of two things which, however different in other respects, have some strong point or points of resemblance; a poetic or imaginative comparison.

similitude *n* likeness; resemblance, in nature, qualities or appearance; a comparison; a simile; a representation; a facsimile.

simmer *vi* to boil or bubble gently or with a gentle hissing.—**to simmer down** to calm down.

simony *n* the buying or selling of ecclesiastical preferment; the presentation of anyone to an ecclesiastical benefice for money or reward.

simoom, simoon *n* an intensely hot suffocating wind, laden with dust and sand, that blows occasionally in Africa and Arabia.

simper *vi* to smile in a silly, affected manner.—*n* a smile with an air of silliness; an affected smile or smirk.

simple *adj* not complex or compound; consisting of one thing or substance only; not complex or complicated; easily intelligible; clear; not given to deceit or duplicity; artless in manner; unaffected; not artificial; unadorned; plain; mere; being no more and no less (*a simple knight*); common; humble; weak in intellect; not wise or sagacious; silly; (*bot*) consisting of one; not exhibiting divisions; (*chem*) that has not been decomposed or separated into two or more elements; elementary.—*n* something not mixed or compounded; a medicinal herb or a medicine obtained from a herb (so called because each vegetable was supposed to have one particular virtue).

simple-minded *adj* artless; undesigning; unsuspecting.

simpleton *n* one who is very simple; a silly or foolish person; a person of weak intellect.

simplicity *n* the state or quality of being simple; unmixed, not compounded or not complex; artlessness of mind; freedom from slyness or cunning; sincerity; freedom from artificial ornament; plainness; weakness of intellect; silliness.

simplify *vt* (**simplified, simplifying**) to make simple; to bring to greater simplicity; to show an easier or shorter process for doing or making; to make plain or easy.

simply *adv* in a simple manner; without art or subtlety; plainly; merely; solely; weakly; foolishly.

simulate *vt* (**simulated, simulating**) to assume the mere appearance or character of, without the reality; to counterfeit; to feign.

simulation *n* the act of simulating or of feigning to be that which one is not.

simultaneous *adj* taking place or happening at the same time; done at the same time; coincident in time.

simultaneously *adv* at the same time; together; in conjunction.

sin *n* an offence against a religious or moral principle; transgression of the law of God; wickedness; iniquity; a wicked act; an offence in general; a transgression.—*vi* (**sinned, sinning**) to commit a sin; to violate any known rule of duty; to offend in general; to transgress; to trespass (with *against*, as *to sin against good taste*).

since *adv* from that time; after that time; from then till now; in the interval; before this or now; ago.—*prep* ever from the time of; subsequently to; after.—*conj* from the time when (*since I saw you last*); because that; seeing that; inasmuch as.

sincere *adj* being in reality what it appears to be; not feigned or simulated; not assumed; real; genuine; not dissembling; guileless; frank; true.

sincerity *n* the quality of being sincere; freedom from hypocrisy; truthfulness; genuineness; earnestness.

sine *n* (*trigon*) in a right-angled triangle, the *sine* of either acute angle is the ratio of the side opposite the angle to the hypotenuse.

sinecure *n* an ecclesiastical benefice without cure of souls; any office which has revenue without employment.

sine qua non *n* something absolutely necessary or indispensable.

sinew *n* the tough fibrous tissue which unites a muscle to a bone; a tendon; (*fig*) that which gives strength or vigour; that in which strength consists.—**sinews of war** money as a means of carrying it on.

sinful *adj* tainted with or full of sin; wicked; containing sin or consisting in sin.

sing *vi* (*pret* **sang** *or* **sung**, *pp* **sung**, *ppr* **singing**) to utter words or sounds with musical inflections or melodious modulations of voice; to utter sweet sounds, as birds; to give out a small shrill or humming sound (*the kettle sings*); to tell or relate something in poetry or verse.—*vt* to utter with musical modulations of voice; to celebrate in song; to give praises to in verse; to relate or rehearse in poetry; to act or produce an effect on by singing (*to sing one to sleep*).

singe *vt* (**singed, singeing**) to burn slightly or superficially; to burn the surface, ends or outside of; to scorch; to remove the nap from, as cloth, by passing it over a red-hot roller, through a gas flame, etc.—*n* a burning of the surface; a slight burn.

singer[1] *n* one who sings or whose occupation is to sing; a skilled or professional vocalist.

singer[2] *n* one who or that which singes.

single *adj* consisting of one alone; not double or more (*a single star, a single act*); (often emphatic) even one (*I shall not give you a single farthing*); individual; considered as apart; alone; having no companion or assistant; unmarried (*a single man, a single life*); performed by one person or by one person only opposed to another (*single combat*); (of a ticket for travel) for the outward journey only.—*vt* (**singled, singling**) to select individually from among a number; to choose out separately from others (with *out* or similar words).—*n* a single ticket; (*pl*) a game (of tennis, etc) between two people; a gramophone record with one tune or song on each side; a person without a permanent partner.

singer

single-handed *adj* unassisted; by oneself; alone.

singles bar a bar meant for unmarried people or people without permanent partners.

singlestick *n* a stick or cudgel for fencing with; fencing with such sticks.

singlet *n* a sleeveless vest or shirt.

singly *adv* individually; separately; each alone; without partners, companions or associates; honestly; sincerely.

singsong *n* a drawling or monotonous tone or wearying succession of tones; repetition of similar words or tones; an improvised concert.—*adj* drawling; monotonous.

singular *adj* belonging to one; (*gram*) denoting one person or thing (*a singular noun*); marked as apart from others; out of the usual course; remarkable; rare; peculiar; odd (*singular in his behaviour*).—*n* a particular instance; (*gram*) the singular number; a word in this number.

singularity *n* the state or quality of being singular; peculiarity; eccentricity; strangeness; oddity.

singularly *adv* in a singular manner; peculiarly; remarkably; oddly; strangely.

sinister *adj* on the left hand or left side; left; (*heral*) the term which denotes the left side of the escutcheon, that is, the right side of a drawing of it; evil; bad; ill-

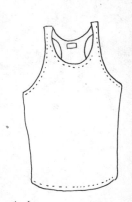

singlet

intentioned; baneful; malign; unlucky; inauspicious.

sink *vi* (*pret* **sunk** *or* **sank**, *pp* **sunk.— sunken** being used as a participial adjective.—*ppr* **sinking**) to fall by the force of gravity; to descend through a medium of little resisting power, as water; to go to the bottom; to fall as from lack of bodily strength; to take a lower position to the eye; to decline below the horizon; to be overwhelmed or depressed; to enter the mind and be impressed; to decline in worth, strength, estimation, etc; to fall off in value; to decay; to decrease and become less deep; to subside.—*vt* to cause to descend below the surface; to immerse in a fluid; to cause to fall or drop; to make by digging or delving (*to sink a pit* or *a well*); to depress; to degrade; to bring low; to ruin; to crush; to put or leave out of consideration; to lose sight of (oneself or one's own interest); to invest (money) more or less permanently in any undertaking or scheme.—*n* a receptacle for receiving liquid waste; a sewer; a receptacle for receiving waste water, as in kitchens, etc; any place where iniquity is gathered.

sinker *n* one who or that which sinks; a weight on something, as a fish line, net, etc, to sink it.

sinking fund *n* a fund or stock set apart, generally at certain intervals, for the reduction of a debt of a government or corporation.

sinless *adj* free from sin; innocent.

sinner *n* one who sins; one who fails in any duty or transgresses any law; an offender.

Sinology *n* the knowledge of the Chinese language, etc.

sinuate, sinuated *adj* winding; sinuous; (*bot*) having large curved breaks in the margin, as in the oak leaf.

sinuous *adj* bending or curving in and out; of an undulating form; winding; crooked.

sinus *n* a curved opening; a bending inward; a bay; a recess or opening into the land; (*anat*) an air cavity in the skull that opens into the nasal cavities; (*surg*) a cavity containing pus; a fistula; (*bot*) a curved hollow on a margin.

Sioux *n sing*, *pl* a race of Indians in North America.

sip *vt* (**sipped, sipping**) to imbibe or take into the mouth in small quantities by the lips; to drink in or absorb in small quantities; to draw into the mouth; to suck up.— *vi* to drink a small quantity; to take a fluid in small quantities with the lips.—*n* a small draught taken with the lips.

siphon, syphon *n* a bent tube whose legs are of unequal length, used for drawing liquid out of a vessel, the shorter leg being inserted in the liquid and the longer hanging down outside, when the air is sucked from the tube the pressure of the atmosphere causing the liquid to rise in it and flow over; a bottle with an internal tube and a tap at the top for aerated water; (*zool*) a tube in certain molluscs conveying water to or from the gills.—*vti* to draw off or be drawn off with a siphon.

sir *n* a common mode of address now used without consideration of rank or status; a general title by which a speaker addresses the person he or she is speaking to; the title distinctive of knights and baronets, always prefixed to the Christian name; a title formerly given to clergymen.

sirdar *n* a chieftain, captain or head man in India; the head of the Egyptian army.

sire *n* a respectful title used in addressing a king or other sovereign prince; a father; (*poet*) a progenitor; the male parent of a beast (particularly used of horses).—*vt* (**sired, siring**) to beget; to procreate (used especially of stallions).

siren *n* (in Greek myth) a name of several sea nymphs, who by their singing fascinated those that sailed by their island and then destroyed them; a charming, alluring or enticing woman; a woman dangerous from her enticing arts; a genus of amphibians peculiar to the southern parts of the USA, called also mud eels; an instrument for measuring the number of sound waves or vibrations; an instrument producing a loud piercing sound and used as a warning signal.—*adj* enticing; bewitching; fascinating (*a siren song*).

sirenian *n, adj* (of or pertaining to) any of an order of marine herbivorous mammals allied to the whales and comprising the manatee and the dugong.

Sirius *n* a large and bright star called also the Dogstar.

sirloin *n* the loin, or upper part of the loin, of beef or the part covering either kidney.

sirocco *n* an oppressive relaxing wind coming from Northern Africa to Italy, Sicily, etc; a variety of the simoom.

sirrah *n* formerly, a word of address, generally equivalent to *fellow* or to *sir*, with an angry or contemptuous force added.

sisal grass, sisal hemp *n* the prepared fibre of the American aloe, used for cordage, from Sisal, in Yucatan.

siskin *n* a European songbird of the finch family of a greenish colour.

sister *n* a female born of the same parents as another person, correlative to *brother*; a female fellow Christian; a female belonging to the same community (as the nuns in a convent).

sisterhood *n* the state of being a sister; a society of females united in one faith or one community.

sister-in-law *n* a husband's or wife's sister; also a brother's wife.

sisterly *adj* like a sister; becoming a sister.

sistrum *n* (*pl* **sistra**) a metal rattle used as a percussion instrument by the ancient Egyptians in their religious ceremonies.

Sisyphean *adj* entailing incessantly recurring toil; recurring unceasingly (*a Sisyphean task*).

sit *vi* (*pret, pp* **sat**, *ppr* **sitting**) to rest on the haunches; to repose on a seat; to remain, rest, abide; to lie, bear or weigh (*grief sits heavy on his heart*); to have a seat or position; to be placed; to incubate; to cover and warm eggs for hatching; to be suited to one's person; to fit or suit when put on; to assume a position in order to have one's portrait taken or a bust modelled; to have a seat in Parliament (*he sat for York*); to be convened, as an assembly; to hold a session; to be officially engaged in public business.—*vt* to keep the seat on (*he sits a horse well*); to place on a seat (used with *oneself, me, thee,* etc).—**to sit for** to act as an artist's model for (someone); to pose for (a portrait).—**to sit in** to attend a conference, discussion, etc, often as a visitor or observer; to take part in a sit-in.—**to sit up** to straighten one's back while sitting; not to go to bed; to keep watch during the night; to become startled; to become alert; (*colloq*) to be astonished.

sitcom *n* (short for **situation comedy**) a comedy in the form of a television or radio series in which the same characters appear in each episode.

site *n* situation, especially as regards relation to surroundings; local position; a plot of ground set apart for building; the place or scene of something.—*vt* (**sited, siting**) to locate; to place.

sit-in *n* the occupation of a building, especially as an organized protest against some kind of alleged injustice; a kind of strike in which workers refuse to leave the work premises.

sitter *n* one who sits; one who sits for his or her portrait; an artist's model; a person who looks after a child, dog, house, etc, while the parents, owners, etc, are out or away.

sitting *adj* holding the position of one who sits; incubating; occupying a place in an official capacity; holding a court.—*n* the act of one who sits; the occasion on which one sits for a portrait or a bust; a session; a business meeting; the time during which one sits, as for a meal, etc; the space occupied by one person in a church pew.

sitting room *n* sufficient space for sitting in; a room for sitting in; a parlour; a lounge; a drawing room.

situate *vt* (**situated, situating**) to place with respect to any other object; to fix permanently; to site.

situated *adj* having a site; placed or perma-nently fixed with respect to any other object; being in any state or condition with regard to people or things.

situation *n* position or location in respect to physical surroundings; state, condition or position with respect to society or circumstances; temporary state or position; a job or post.

situation comedy *n* see **sitcom.**

sitz bath *n* a form of bath in which one can bathe sitting; a bath taken in a sitting posture.

SI unit *n* the abbreviation of **Système international d'unités,** the universally used modern scientific system of units used in the measurement of all physical quantities, the principal units being the metre, kilogram, second, ampere, kelvin, candela and mole.

six *adj* twice three; one more than five.—*n* the number of six or twice three; a symbol representing this number, as 6.—**at sixes and sevens** in disorder and confusion.

sixpence *n* an English silver coin of the value of six pennies.

sixshooter *n* a six-chambered revolver.

sixteen *adj, n* six and ten; consisting of six and ten.

sixteenth *adj* next in order after the fifteenth.—*n* one of sixteen equal parts into which a thing is divided.

sixth *adj* the first after the fifth.—*n* a sixth part; (*mus*) an interval of two kinds, the minor sixth, composed of three tones and two semitones, and the major sixth, composed of four tones and a semitone.

sixtieth *adj* next in order after the fifty-ninth.—*n* one of sixty equal parts of a thing.

sixty *adj, n* ten times six; the sum of six times ten.

sizable, sizeable *adj* of considerable size.

size[1] *n* extent of volume or surface; dimensions great or small; comparative magnitude; bulk; a conventional relative measure of dimension, as of shoes, gloves, etc.—*vt* (**sized, sizing**) to adjust or arrange according to size; to fix the standard of.—**size up** to estimate, to value, to take correct estimate of a person or thing; to make a judgment of; to weigh up.

size[2] *n* a kind of weak glue used by painters (to mix with colours), paper manufacturers, etc; a tenacious varnish used by gilders; matter resembling size.—*vt* (**sized, sizing**) to cover with size; to prepare with size.

sizeable *adj* same as **sizable.**

sizzle *vi* (**sizzled, sizzling**) to make a spluttering sound, as things do when being fried; to be very hot.

sjambok *n* a long whip of rhinoceros hide.

skate[1] *n* a contrivance consisting of a steel runner or ridge fixed to a wooden sole or

sit

to a light iron framework, fastened under the foot and used to enable a person to glide rapidly over ice; a roller skate.—*vi* (**skated, skating**) to slide or move on skates.

skate² *n* one of several species of the ray family of fishes, having the body flat and more or less approaching to a rhomboidal form.

skateboard *n* a narrow oblong board made of wood, fibreglass, etc with two wheels at each side on which the user balances and rides, usually in a sitting position.

skateboarder *n* one who uses a skateboard.

skateboarding *n* the act or practice of using a skateboard.

skateboarder

skean-dhu *n* the knife which, when the Highland costume is worn, is stuck in the stocking.

skedaddle *vi* (*colloq*) (**skedaddled, skedaddling**) to run off hurriedly.

skein *n* a small hank of thread; a certain quantity of yarn put up together.

skeleton *n* the hard firm pieces constituting the framework which sustains the softer parts of any animal, in vertebrates consisting of bony pieces; the bones of an animal body separated from the flesh and retained in their natural position; the supporting framework of anything; a framework; an outline or rough draft; an abstract; a very thin or lean person; something shameful kept secret.

skerry *n* a rocky isle.

sketch *n* an outline or general delineation of anything; a first rough or incomplete draught; a picture rapidly executed and intended to give the general features or characteristic aspect; the first embodiment of an artist's idea in clay, on canvas or on paper; a short written description; a short humorous item for a revue, etc; a brief outline.—*vt* to draw a sketch of; to make a rough draft of; to give the principal points or ideas of; to delineate.—*vi* to practise sketching.

sketchy *adj* possessing the character of a sketch; not executed with finish or carefulness of detail; unfinished; incomplete; inadequate.

skew *adj* having an oblique position; turned or twisted to one side.—*adv* awry; obliquely.

skier

skewer *n* a pin of wood or iron for fastening meat to a spit or for keeping it in form while roasting.—*vt* to fasten with skewers; to pierce or transfix.

ski *n* a long, narrow runner of wood, metal or plastic that is fastened to a boot for moving across snow; a water-ski.—*vi* (**skied, skiing**) to travel on skis.

skid *n* the act of skidding; an instance of skidding; a fender for a ship's side; a log or something else forming an inclined plane in loading or unloading heavy articles from trucks, etc; a drag for the wheels of a wagon or carriage.—*vi* (**skidded, skidding**) to slip on a slippery surface without taking hold; to slip sideways.

skid row *n* a run-down, squalid district of a town or city where vagrants, alcoholics and drug addicts live.

skier *n* one who skis.

skiff *n* a popular name for any small boat.

skiffle *n* a type of popular music originating in the 1950s characterized by a strongly accented jazz-type beat and played by guitars, drums and often unconventional instruments, such as washboards.

skilful *adj* having skill; skilled; well versed in any art; dextrous; expert; displaying or done with skill; clever.

skill *n* proficiency; expertness; dexterity; a developed aptitude or ability; a type of work or craft requiring specialist training; power to discern and execute.

skilled *adj* having skill or familiar knowledge, together with readiness and dexterity; expert; skilful.

skillet *n* a small metal vessel with a long handle, used for cooking; a frying pan.

skim *vt* (**skimmed, skimming**) to lift the scum from; to clear from any substance floating on the top; to take off from a surface; to pass near the surface of; to pass over lightly; to glance over in a superficial manner (*to skim a newspaper article*).—*vi* to pass lightly; to glide along.

skimmer *n* one who or that which skims; a flat dish or ladle for skimming liquors; an aquatic swimming bird, with a long bill.

skim milk, skimmed milk *n* milk from which the cream has been taken.

skimp *adj* skimp measure, stinted.—*vt* to stint supplies.

skin *n* the external coating, layer or tissue of most animals; a hide; a pelt; the skin of an animal separated from the body; the skin of an animal used as a vessel (*wineskin*); any external covering resembling skin in appearance or use; the bark or husk of a plant; the exterior coat of fruits and plants.—*vt* (**skinned, skinning**) to strip the skin or hide from; to flay; to peel.—*vi* to become covered with skin (*a wound skins over*).

skin-deep *adj* not penetrating beyond the skin; superficial; slight.

skinflint *n* a very niggardly person.

skinhead a young person with closely cropped hair, usually applied to a member of a gang wearing simple, severe clothes and heavy boots and displaying aggressive behaviour.

skink *n* a small lizard of Egypt, etc.

skinny *adj* consisting of skin or of little more than skin; lacking flesh; very thin.

skinny-dip *vi* (**skinny-dipped, skinny-dip-**

ping) (*colloq*) to swim naked.—*n* a swim in the nude.

skip¹ *vi* (**skipped, skipping**) to take quick leaps or bounds; to spring; to jump lightly; to keep jumping over a rope as it is swung over; to pass without notice in reading; to make omissions in writing (often followed by *over*).—*vt* to pass with a bound; to pass over intentionally in reading; to leave (town, etc) hurriedly; to miss (an event, etc) deliberately.—*n* a leap; a bound; a spring.

skip² *n* a box or basket for raising material from mines; a large basket on wheels; a large metal receptacle for holding building debris, etc.

skip³ *n* in the games of bowls and curling, an experienced player chosen by each of the rival sides as their director or captain.

skipper *n* the master of a small trading or merchant vessel; a sea captain.

skipping *adj* given to skips; moving with leaps.

skipping rope *n* a small rope which people swing under their feet and over their heads in play or to exercise.

skirmish *n* a slight fight in war, especially between small parties; a short, desultory kind of engagement; a short contest of any kind; a contention.—*vi* to fight slightly or in small parties.

skirt *n* the lower and loose part of a coat or other garment; a woman's garment, either loose or fitted, for the lower part of the body; the edge of any part of dress; border; margin; extreme part; the diaphragm or midriff in animals.—*vt* to border; to form the border or edge of; to run along the edge of.—*vi* to be on the border.

skirting *n* material for making skirts; a skirting board.

skirting board *n* the board placed round the bottom of the wall of a room.

skit *n* a short humorous sketch performed in the theatre.

skittish *adj* easily frightened; playful; lively.

skittles *npl* a game played with nine pins set upright at one end of a skittle alley, the object of the player being to knock them over with as few throws as possible of a ball.

skua *n* a powerful predatory bird of the gull family with strong hooked beak and claws.

skulk *vi* to lurk; to keep to a place of concealment; to get out of the way in a sneaking manner; to shun doing one's duty.—*n* a skulker.

skulker *n* a person who skulks or avoids performing duties.

skull *n* the cranium or bony case that forms the framework of the head and encloses the brain; the brain as the seat of intelligence.

skull cap *n* a cap fitting closely to the head or skull.

skunk *n* an American carnivorous quadruped of the weasel family, provided with glands from which the animal can emit an extremely foul-smelling fluid when frightened; an obnoxious person.

sky *n* the apparent arch or vault over the earth; the firmament; heaven; the upper atmosphere; the region of clouds (the plural *skies* is often used in the same sense); weather; climate.

skylark *n* a lark that mounts and sings as it flies, the common lark of Britain.

skylarking *n* frolicking or tricks of various kinds.

skylight *n* a window placed in the roof of a house and having the same slope; a glazed aperture in a ship's deck.

skyline *n* the visible horizon; the outline, as of mountains, buildings, etc, as seen against the sky.

skyrocket *n* a rocket that ascends high and burns as it flies; a type of firework.

skyscraper *n* a high building of many storeys.

slab *n* a thin flat regularly shaped piece of anything, as of marble or other stone; an outside piece taken from round timber in sawing it into boards, planks, etc.

slack *adj* not tense or tightly drawn; loose; relaxed; backward; not using due diligence; not earnest or eager; inattentive; careless; not busy; slow as regards trade.—*adv* in a slack manner.—*n* the part of a rope that hangs loose; small coal screened from household coal of good quality.—*vi* to be lazy; to neglect (work, duty, etc).—*vt* to slacken (with *off*).

slacken *vi* to become less tense or tight; to become remiss or backward; to become less violent; to abate; to languish; to flag.—*vt* to lessen the tension of; to loosen; to relax; to remit for lack of eagerness; to abate; to retard; to repress; to check.

slacker *n* one who performs his or her work or duties remissly.

slackness *n* the state of being slack; looseness; remissness; inattention; slowness.

slacks *npl* trousers, especially trousers worn with military uniform instead of breeches and puttees.

slag *n* the scoria from a smelting furnace or from a volcano; vitrified mineral matter removed in the reduction of metals; the fused dross of metal in a smelting furnace; (*colloq*) a slut; (*colloq*) a slovenly or dissolute woman.

slake *vt* (**slaked, slaking**) to quench (thirst, fire, rage); to extinguish; to abate; to reduce (quicklime) to the state of powder by mixing with water.

slam *vt* (**slammed, slamming**) to close (a door, a lid) with force and noise; to shut with violence; to bang.—*vi* to shut or be

skipping rope

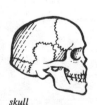

skull

closed violently or noisily, as a door.—*n* a violent shutting of a door; at bridge, thirteen tricks is called a *grand slam*, and twelve, a *little slam*.

slander *n* a false tale or report maliciously uttered and tending to injure the reputation of another; the uttering of such reports; aspersion; defamation; detraction.—*vt* to defame by slander; to injure by maliciously uttering a false report respecting; to calumniate.

slanderous *adj* given to slander; uttering slander; containing slander or defamation; calumnious.

slang *n* words or expressions used in speech or writing of a very familiar, informal nature but not regarded as standard English; jargon of a particular social class, age group, occupation, etc.—*adj* relating to slang; used as slang.—*vi* to use slang; to engage in vulgar, abusive language.—*vt* to address with slang or ribaldry; to abuse with vulgar language.

slangy *adj* of the nature of slang; addicted to the use of slang.

slant *adj* sloping; oblique; inclined from a direct line, whether horizontal or perpendicular.—*vt* to give a slant or sloping direction to; to tell (something) in such a way as to have a bias.—*vi* to slope; to lie obliquely.—*n* an oblique direction or plane; a slope; a bias or point of view.

slap *n* a blow given with the open hand or with something broad.—*vt* (**slapped, slapping**) to strike with the open hand or with something broad.—*adv* with a sudden and violent blow; plump.

slapdash *adv* all at once; in a careless manner; at random.

slapstick *n* a wooden stick with flapping ends, used for giving resounding but innocuous blows on the stage; a boisterous humour of a knockabout kind.—*adj* applied to comedies of a low farcical type.

slash *vt* to cut by striking at random; to cut with long incisions; to slit (*to slash a garment*); to reduce (prices) sharply.—*vi* to strike at random with an edged instrument.—*n* a long cut; a cut made at random; a large slit in the thighs and arms of old dresses, to show a rich coloured lining through the openings.

slashing *adj* cutting up, sarcastic or severe (*slashing criticism*).

slat *n* a long narrow slip of wood, as in a venetian blind.

slate *n* a name common to such rocks as are capable of being split readily into thin laminae in accordance with the planes of cleavage; a slab or thin piece of smooth argillaceous stone, used for covering buildings; a tablet for writing on, formed of slate or of an imitation of slate.—*vt* (**slated, slating**) to cover with slates.

slate[2] *vt* (**slated, slating**) to criticize severely; to reproach severely.

slate pencil *n* a pencil of soft slate, used for writing on slate tablets in schools, etc.

slater *n* one whose occupation is to slate buildings; a woodlouse.

slating[1] *n* the operation of covering roofs with slates; the slates thus put on.

slating[2] *n* severe criticism or reproach.

slattern *n* a untidily dressed woman; one who is not tidy; a slut.

slaty *adj* resembling slate; having the nature or properties of slate.

slaughter *n* the act of slaying or killing; great destruction of life by violent means; carnage; butchery; a killing of beasts for market.—*vt* to slay; to massacre; to butcher; to kill for the market.

slaughterhouse *n* a house where beasts are killed for the market; an abattoir.

Slav *n* one of a race of Eastern Europe, comprising the Russians, Bulgarians, Bohemians, Serbians, Poles, etc.

slave *n* a bondservant; a person who is wholly subject to the will of another; a human being who is the property of another; one wholly under the dominion of any power (*a slave to passion, to fear*); an abject wretch; a drudge.—*vi* (**slaved, slaving**) to drudge; to toil; to labour as a slave.

slave-driver *n* an overseer of slaves at their work; hence, a severe or cruel master.

slaver[1] *vi* to suffer the spittle to issue from the mouth; to be besmeared with saliva.—*n* saliva drivelling from the mouth; drivel.

slaver[2] *n* a person engaged in the slave trade; a slave trader; a vessel engaged in the slave trade.

slavery *n* the state or condition of a slave; bondage; complete subjection; the system of keeping or holding slaves; exhausting and mean labour; drudgery.

slavish *adj* pertaining to slaves; such as becomes a slave; servile; consisting in drudgery.

slay *vt* (*pret* **slew**, *pp* **slain**, *ppr* **slaying**) to put to death in any violent or sudden manner; to kill; to destroy; to ruin.

slayer *n* one that slays; a killer; a murderer.

sled *n* a sledge.—*vt* (**sledded, sledding**) to convey or transport on a sled.

sledge *n* a vehicle mounted on runners for the conveyance of loads over snow or ice or the bare ground; a sled; a travelling carriage mounted on runners; a sleigh; a toboggan; the hurdle on which traitors were formerly drawn to execution.—*vti* (**sledged, sledging**) to convey or travel in a sledge or sledges; to toboggan.

sledgehammer *n* a large heavy hammer used chiefly by smiths.

sleek *adj* having an even, smooth surface; having the hair smooth; glossy (*sleek hair*).—*vt* to make sleek; to render

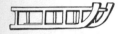

sledge

sledgehammer

smooth, soft and glossy; (*fig*) to soothe; to calm.

sleep *vi* (*pret, pp* **slept**, *ppr* **sleeping**) to be in that state in which there is a suspension of the voluntary exercise of the powers of the body and mind and which is periodically necessary to bodily health; to be dead; to lie in the grave; to be at rest; to be dormant or inactive (*the question sleeps for the present*).—*vt* to pass in sleeping (with *away*, as *to sleep away the time*); to get rid of, overcome or recover from by sleeping (usually with *off*, as *to sleep off a fit of sickness*).—**to sleep with** to have sexual intercourse with.—*n* that state of an animal in which the senses are more or less unaffected by external objects and the fancy or imagination only is active, and which is necessary to revive both body and mind; slumber; death; rest in the grave.

sleeper *n* a person or an animal that sleeps; an animal that lies dormant; a piece of timber on which are laid the ground joists of a floor; a beam on or near the ground for the support of some superstructure; (in railways) a beam of wood, etc, embedded in the ground to sustain the rails, which are usually fixed to the sleepers by means of cast-iron supports called chairs.

sleeping *adj* reposing in sleep; pertaining to sleep.

sleeping bag *n* a kind of long padded or quilted bag for sleeping in, especially out of doors.

sleeping policeman *n* a low transverse hump built into the surface of a road, intended to slow down traffic.

sleeping sickness *n* a tropical African disease due to microscopic animals introduced into the blood by the bites of tsetse flies and characterized by fever and lethargy.

sleepless *adj* without sleep; wakeful; having no rest; never resting.

sleepwalker *n* a person who walks in his or her sleep; a somnambulist.

sleepy *adj* drowsy; inclined to or overcome by sleep; tending to induce sleep; heavy; inactive; sluggish.

sleet *n* rain mingled with hail or snow.—*vi* to snow or hail with a mixture of rain.

sleeve *n* the part of a garment that is fitted to cover the arm.—**to laugh up one's sleeve** to laugh privately or unperceived.

sleigh *n* a vehicle mounted on runners for transporting persons on the snow or ice; a sledge; a toboggan.

sleight *n* an artful trick; a trick or feat so dextrously performed that the manner of performance escapes observation; dextrous practice; dexterity.

sleight of hand *n* manual dexterity, such as in conjuring or juggling; legerdemain; prestidigitation.

slender *adj* small in diameter or thickness compared with the length; not thick; slim; thin; weak; slight (*slender hope*); inconsiderable; insufficient; inadequate; meagre (*slender means*).

sleuth *n* (*colloq*) a detective.

sleuthhound *n* a bloodhound; a detective.

slew[1] *pret of* **slay**.

slew[2], **slue** *vt* to turn or swing round (as the yard of a ship).

slice *vt* (**sliced, slicing**) to cut into thin pieces or to cut off a thin broad piece from; to cut into parts; to cut off in a broad piece.—*n* a thin broad piece cut off; that which is thin and broad like a slice; a broad thin knife for serving fish at table; a share.

slide *vi* (*pret, pp* **slid**, *ppr* **sliding**) to move along a surface by slipping; to slip; to glide; to amuse oneself with gliding over a surface of ice; to pass along smoothly; to pass silently and gradually from one state to another, generally from a better to a worse.—*vt* to thrust smoothly along; to thrust or push forward by slipping; to pass or put imperceptibly; to slip.—*n* a smooth and easy passage; a prepared smooth surface of ice for sliding on; an inclined plane for facilitating the descent of heavy bodies; that part of an instrument or apparatus which slides or is slipped into or out of place.

slider *n* one who or that which slides; the part of an instrument that slides; ice cream sandwiched between two wafers.

slide rule *n* a kind of ruler with a graduated sliding part for making calculations.

sliding scale *n* a slide rule; a scale or rate of payment which varies under certain varying conditions; a scale to settle wages by the rise and fall of the market price of the product of labour; a flexible scale.

slight *adj* not decidedly marked; small; trifling; insignificant (*a slight difference*); not strong or forcible (*a slight impulse* or *effort*); not severe or serious (*a slight pain*); not thorough or exhaustive (*a slight examination*); not firm or of strong construction; slim; slender; paltry; contemptible.—*n* a moderate show of disrespect; contempt shown by neglect or inattention; intentional disregard.—*vt* to treat as unworthy of notice; to disregard intentionally; to treat with intentional neglect or superciliousness.

slightness *n* the quality of being slight; smallness; weakness; lack of strength; triviality.

slim *adj* slender; of small diameter or thickness in proportion to height; slight; insubstantial; not executed with due thoroughness; cunning.—*vti* (**slimmed, slimming**) to make or become slim; to reduce one's weight by diet, etc; to go on a diet.

sleeping bag

slime *n* a soft, ropy or glutinous substance; soft moist earth having an adhesive quality; viscous mud; asphalt or bitumen; a mucous or viscous substance exuded from the bodies of certain animals; (*fig*) anything of a clinging and offensive nature.—*vt* (**slimed, sliming**) to cover with slime; to make slimy.

slime pit *n* an asphalt or bitumen pit.

slimy *adj* abounding with slime; consisting of slime; overspread with slime.

sling *n* an instrument for throwing stones or bullets, consisting of a strap or piece of leather to hold the missile and two strings attached to it; a sweep or swing; a sweeping stroke; a hanging bandage in which a wounded limb is sustained; a rope or chain specially arranged for raising or lowering heavy articles, as casks, bales, etc; the strap to carry a rifle.—*vt* (*pret, pp* **slung**, *ppr* **slinging**) to throw with a sling; to fling or hurl; to hang so as to swing; to place in slings in order to hoist or lower.

sling *n* an American drink composed of equal parts of spirits and water sweetened.

slink *vi* (*pret, pp* **slunk**, *ppr* **slinking**) to sneak; to creep away meanly; to steal away.—*vt* to cast prematurely (said of the female of a beast).—*adj* born or cast prematurely, as a calf.—*n* a sneaking person; a calf brought away prematurely.

sling

slip *vi* (**slipped, slipping**) to move smoothly along a surface; to slide; to glide; to have the feet slide; to fall by a false step; to depart or withdraw secretly; to sneak or slink (with *away*); to fall into error or fault; to err; to pass unexpectedly or imperceptibly; to glide; to enter by oversight (with *in* or *into*, as *some errors have slipped in*); to escape insensibly, especially from the memory.—**to slip up** (*colloq*) to make a mistake.—*vt* to put secretly or unobserved (*slipped it into his pocket*); to let loose (*to slip the hounds*); to disengage oneself from; to cast or suffer abortion of; to make a slip or slips for planting.—*n* the act of slipping; an unintentional error or fault; a mistake inadvertently made (*a slip of the pen*); a departure from rectitude; a venial transgression; an indiscretion; a backsliding; a twig separated from the stock for planting or grafting; a scion; a leash or string by which a dog is held; a long narrow piece; a strip (*a slip of paper*); a portion of printed matter not yet formed into pages or columns; a proof from a galley of type; a child's pinafore; a loose covering or case (*pillow slip*); an inclined plane on which a vessel is supported while building or on which she is hauled up for repair; also, a contrivance for hauling vessels out of the water for repairs, etc; (in cricket) one of the fielders who stands behind the wicket on the off side.

slipper

slipknot *n* a knot which will not bear a strain but slips.

slipper *n* a loose light shoe for household wear.

slippery *adj* allowing or causing anything to slip or slide readily; so smooth as to cause slipping; not affording sure footing; not to be trusted to; ready to use evasions, etc; unstable; changeable; uncertain.

slip road a road that gives access to a motorway.

slipshod *adj* slovenly; careless.

slip-up *n* (*colloq*) a mistake; a lapse.

slipway *n* a sloping surface for launching or repairing ships; a sloped landing stage.

slit *vt* (*pret, pp* **slit**, *ppr* **slitting**) to cut lengthways; to cut into long pieces or strips; to cut a long fissure in (*to slit the ear* or *tongue*); to cut in general.—*n* a long cut; a long narrow opening; a slash.

slither *vi* to slide, as on a loose or wet surface; to slip or slide like a snake.

sliver *vt* to cut into long thin pieces; to cut or rend lengthways.—*n* a long piece cut or rent off; a splinter; a small branch; (in spinning) a continuous strand of wool, cotton or other fibre, in a loose untwisted condition.

slobber *vi* to drivel; to slaver.—*n* slaver; liquor spilled.

sloe *n* a British shrub of the plum genus, called also blackthorn; also its fruit, which is black and very astringent.

slog *vt* (**slogged, slogging**) to drive the ball violently at cricket; to work laboriously; to trudge doggedly.—*n* a hard hit; a hard, boring spell of work; a strenuous walk or hike.

slogan *n* the war cry or gathering word or phrase of a Highland clan; hence, the watchword used by soldiers in the field; a catchy phrase used in advertising or as a motto by a political party, etc.

sloop *n* a vessel with one mast, and often with nothing but fore-and-aft sails, the mainsail being extended by a gaff and a boom and attached to the mast on its foremost edge.

slop *vt* (**slopped, slopping**) to spill liquid on; to soil by letting a liquid fall on.—*vi* to be spilled; to spill over.—*n* a quantity of water carelessly thrown about, as on a floor; (*pl*) waste liquor or waste liquid food; the waste dirty water of a house.

slop basin, slop bowl *n* a dish for receiving the dregs from teacups at table.

slope *n* an oblique direction; a direction inclining obliquely downward; a declivity or acclivity; any ground whose surface forms an angle with the plane of the horizon; the angle of inclination of a surface to the horizontal plane.—*vt* (**sloped, sloping**) to form with a slope; to cause to slope; to direct obliquely; to incline.—*vi* to take an oblique direction; to descend in a slanting direction.

sloping *adj* oblique; inclining or inclined from a horizontal or other right line.

sloppy *adj* wet, so as to spatter easily; plashy; carelessly done or put together; foolishly sentimental.

sloshed *adj* (*sl*) drunk.

slot[1] *n* a bolt or bar; an oblong hole in a piece of metal, etc, as for the reception of a bolt; an aperture in an automatic machine for the insertion of the coin to start the apparatus inside; a trapdoor in the stage of a theatre; a particular position; a, usually regular, position in a radio or television programme, etc; a niche in an organization; a vacant position.—*vt* (**slotted, slotting**) to fit into a slot; to provide with a slot; (*colloq*) to place in a series.

slot[2] *n* the track of a deer, as shown by the marks of its feet.

sloth *n* slowness; disinclination to action; sluggishness; indolence; laziness; idleness; the name of two South American mammals, adapted for living in trees but moving with great slowness on the ground.

slothful *adj* sluggish; lazy; indolent.

slot machine *n* a machine operated by the insertion of a coin, used as a vending machine, fruit machine, etc.

slouch *n* a stoop in walking; a depression or hanging down, as of the brim of a hat; an awkward, ungainly person; (*colloq*) an inefficient or lazy person.—*vi* to have a downcast clownish gait or manner.

slouch hat *n* a hat with a hanging brim.

slough[1] *n* a place of deep mud or mire; a hole full of mire.—**the Slough of Despond** extreme despondency; great depression.

slough[2] *n* the cast skin of a snake or other animal; dead skin.—*vti* to come off, as kin; to shed or cast off.

sloven *n* a person careless of his or her dress or habitually negligent of neatness and order; a lazy person.

slovenly *adj* having the habits of a sloven; negligent of personal neatness; lacking neatness or tidiness; loose and careless (*slovenly dress*).

slow *adj* moving a small distance in a long time; not swift; not quick in motion; extending over a long time; gradual; not ready; not prompt; inactive; tardy; dilatory; not hasty; acting with deliberation; behind the correct time (*the clock is slow*); dull; heavy; not lively; stupid.—*vt* to delay; to retard; to slacken in speed.—*vi* to slacken in speed.

slow-motion *adj* moving slowly; slower than normal motion; pertaining to a filmed or taped scene with the original action slowed down.

slowworm *n* a name given to the blindworm.

sludge *n* mud; mire; soft mud.

slue *vt* (**slued, sluing**) same as **slew**[2].

slug[1] *n* a slow, heavy, lazy fellow; a sluggard; the popular name of a family of shell-less snails damaging to many plants.

slug[2] *n* a cylindrical, cubical or irregularly shaped piece of metal used for the charge of a gun; (*sl*) a hard blow; (*sl*) a drink of spirits.

sluggard *n* a person habitually lazy and inactive.

sluggish *adj* habitually indolent; slothful; inactive; having little motion (*a sluggish stream*); inert.

sluice *n* a contrivance for excluding or admitting the inflow of a body of water; a waterway provided with a gate by which the flow of water is controlled; a floodgate; any vent for water; that through which anything flows.—*vt* (**sluiced, sluicing**) to let in a copious flow of water on; to wet or lave abundantly; to scour out or cleanse by means of sluices.

slum *n* a low, dirty, back street or lane of a city; a low neighbourhood; a squalid rundown house.—*vi* (**slummed, slumming**) to visit slums, especially for amusement.—**to slum it** deliberately to adopt a lower standard of cultural or social activity than one would adopt normally.

slumber *vi* to sleep lightly; to doze; to sleep; to be inert or in a state of supineness or inactivity.—*n* light sleep; sleep not deep or sound; sleep; repose.

slump[1] *vi* to sink in walking, as in snow; to walk with sinking feet; to fall or drop heavily; (of prices) to fall steeply and suddenly.—*n* a sudden fall in prices or values.

slump[2] *n* the whole number taken in one lot; the gross amount (*to take things in the slump*).—*vt* to throw together into a single lot or mass.

slur *vt* (**slurred, slurring**) to soil or sully; to disparage by insinuation or innuendo; to speak slightingly of; to traduce; to pass lightly over; to say little of; to pronounce in an indistinct or sliding manner; (*mus*) to sing or perform in a smooth, gliding style; to run (notes) into each other.—*n* a slight reproach or disgrace; a stigma; (*mus*) the blending of two or more notes; a curved mark indicating this.

slush *n* sludge or watery mire; soft mud; wet, half-melted snow; a mixture of grease and other materials for lubrication; refuse fat or grease in ships; a mixture of white lead and lime with which the bright parts of machinery are covered to prevent them rusting.—*vt* to cover or grease with slush.

slushy *adj* consisting of soft mud or of snow and water; resembling slush.

slut *n* a woman who is negligent of cleanli-

slug

ness and tidiness in her person, clothes, furniture, etc; a name of contempt for a woman; an immoral woman.

sluttish *adj* like a slut or what is characteristic of a slut; devoid of tidiness or neatness; immoral.

sly *adj* meanly artful; crafty; cunning; proceeding by underhand ways; wily; cautious; shrewd; arch; knowing (*a sly remark*).

slyness *n* the quality of being sly; cunning; craftiness; archness.

smack *vi* to have a taste or flavour; to taste (*it smacks of onions*); to have a certain quality infused; to partake in character; to savour (*it smacks of vanity*).—*n* a slight taste or flavour; savour; tincture; a slight or superficial knowledge; a smattering.

smack[1] *vi* to make a sharp noise with the lips; to kiss so as to make a sound with the lips.—*vt* to kiss with a sharp noise; to make a sharp noise by opening the mouth; to make a sharp noise by striking; to crack; to give a sharp stroke to, as with the palm.—*n* a loud kiss; a quick sharp noise, as of a whip; a quick smart blow, as with the flat of the hand; a slap.—*adv* in a sudden and direct manner, as if with a smack or slap.

smack[2] *n* a large sloop with a gaff-topsail and a running bowsprit; a small sloop used in the fishing trade.

small *adj* little in size; not great or large; of minute dimensions; little in degree, quantity, amount, duration or number; of little moment; trivial; petty; trifling; of little genius or ability; insignificant; of little strength or force; weak; gentle; soft; not loud; characterized by narrowness of mind or character; narrow-minded; not generous; mean.

small arms *npl* a general name for rifles, carbines, pistols, etc, as distinguished from cannon.

small beer *n* a species of weak beer; something insignificant.

small fry *npl* people or things of little significance; young people.

small intestines *npl* the long thin tube connecting the stomach and the caecum, divided into three parts, the duodenum, the jejunum and the ileum.

smallpox *n* a dangerous, contagious viral disease characterized by fever and a skin eruption, which leaves the skin scarred and pitted.

smalls *npl* (*colloq*) underwear.

small talk *n* light conversation; gossip.

smalt *n* glass tinged a fine deep blue by cobalt, reduced to an impalpable powder and used as a pigment and colouring matter.

smarmy *adj* (*colloq*) unpleasantly flattering; obsequious.

smart *n* a sharp quick pain; a pricking local pain; severe pungent pain of mind.—*vi* to feel a lively pungent pain; to be acutely painful; to feel sharp pain of mind; to suffer acute mental pain.—*adj* causing a keen local pain; keen; intense; poignant; producing any effect with force and vigour; vigorous (*a smart blow*); sharp; severe (*a smart skirmish*); brisk; fresh (*a smart breeze*); acute and pertinent; witty; vivacious; lively; shrewd; fine in dress; spruce.

smart card *n* (*colloq*) a plastic card containing an integrated circuit that records transactions made with the card.

smarten *vt* to make smart; to render brisk, bright or lively.

smart money *n* money paid by a person to buy himself or herself off from some unpleasant engagement or painful situation; money formerly paid by a recruit to be free of his engagement; money invested or bet by experienced financiers or gamblers.

smash *vt* to break in pieces by violence; to dash to pieces; to crush by a sudden blow.—*vi* to go to pieces; to collide with force; to go to utter wreck.—*n* a breaking to pieces; a violent collision, as of cars; (*colloq*) a popular success; ruin; bankruptcy.

smatter *vi* to have a slight superficial knowledge; to talk superficially.—*n* slight superficial knowledge.

smattering *n* a slight superficial knowledge; an insignificant degree of acquirement (*a smattering of law*).

smear *vt* to overspread with anything unctuous, viscous or adhesive; to daub; to soil; to slander.—*n* a spot made as if by some unctuous substance; a smudge; a stain; a blot or blotch; a slanderous attack; a deposit of blood secretion, etc, on a glass slide for examination under a microscope.

smear test *n* a microscopic analysis of a smear of bodily cells, especially from the cervix, to test for traces of cancer.

smegma *n* the sebaceous secretion which accumulates as solid matter in the folds of the skin, especially under the foreskin.

smell *vt* (*pret, pp* **smelled** *or* **smelt**, *ppr* **smelling**) to perceive by the nose; to perceive the scent of; to perceive as if by the smell; to detect by sagacity.—*vi* to exercise the sense of smell; to give out odour or perfume; to affect the sense of smell; to have an odour or scent; to have an unpleasant smell; to have a smack of any quality.—*n* the sense or faculty of which the nose is the special organ; the faculty of perceiving by the nose; that which affects the olfactory organs; odour; scent.

smelling *n* the sense of smell.

smelling salts *npl* volatile salts used for exciting the organs of smell.

smelly *adj* having an unpleasant smell; malodorous.

smelt¹ *pret, pp of* **smell**.

smelt² *vt* to melt or fuse, as ore, for the purpose of separating the metal from extraneous substances.

smelt³ *n* a small edible European fish allied to the salmon, inhabiting the salt water about the mouths of rivers.

smelting *n* the process of obtaining metals from their ores by the action of heat, air and fluxes.

smew *n* a swimming bird of the merganser family.

smilax *n* a climbing plant grown in greenhouses for its beautiful foliage.

smile *vi* (**smiled, smiling**) to express pleasure or slight amusement by a special change of the features, especially the mouth, the contrary of *to frown*; to express slight contempt, sarcasm or pity by a look; to sneer; to look happy and joyous (*the desert smiled*); to appear propitious or favourable.—*vt* to express by a smile (*to smile content*); to put an end to or dispel by smiling (with *away*).—*n* a peculiar contraction of the features expressing pleasure, approbation or kindness, opposed to *frown*; joyous appearance; favour; countenance.

smirch *vt* to stain; to smear; to smudge.

smirk *vi* to smile affectedly or wantonly; to look affectedly soft or kind.—*n* an affected smile; a soft look.

smite *vt* (*pret* **smote**, *pp* **smitten** *or* **smote**, *ppr* **smiting**) to strike; to give a blow with the hand, something in the hand or something thrown; to slay; to kill; to assail or visit with something evil; to blast; to afflict, chasten, punish; to strike or affect with love or other feeling.—*vi* to strike; to knock.

smith *n* one who forges with the hammer; one who works in metals, often distinctively applied to a blacksmith.—*vt* to hammer into shape; to forge.

smithereens *npl* fragments; small bits and pieces.

smithy *n* the workshop of a smith.

smitten *adj* affected with some passion; excited by beauty or something impressive.

smock *n* a loose-fitting, shirt-like garment, often used to protect other clothes.

smog *n* a mixture of smoke and fog; polluted air.

smoke *n* the exhalation or vaporous matter that escapes from a burning substance; especially the volatile particles expelled from burning vegetable matter; what resembles smoke; vapour; (*fig*) idle talk; vanity; nothingness (*it all ended in smoke*); a continuous drawing in and puffing out of the fumes of burning tobacco.—*vi* (**smoked, smoking**) to emit smoke or vaporous matter; to give out visible vapour when heated; to inhale and exhale the fumes of burning tobacco; (*fig*) to burn or rage.—*vt* to apply smoke to; to foul by smoke; to hang in smoke; to fumigate; to drive out by smoke; to draw smoke from into the mouth and puff it out; to inhale the smoke of; to discover or find out; to make fun of (a person).

smokehouse *n* a building employed for the purpose of curing flesh or fish by smoking.

smoker *n* one who smokes, especially tobacco; a place, or part of a place, where smoking is allowed.

smoke screen *n* a dense cloud of smoke made to conceal military operations from enemy operations; something used to conceal or disguise the truth.

smokestack *n* in steam vessels, a name common to the funnel and the several escape pipes for steam beside it.

smoking *adj* emitting smoke; used for smoking or having its smoke inhaled; set apart for the purpose of smoking in.—*n* the act of one who or that which smokes; the act or practice of inhaling tobacco smoke from a pipe, cigar or cigarette.

smoking room *n* a room in a house, hotel, etc, in which smoking is permitted.

smoky *adj* emitting smoke, especially much smoke; resembling smoke; filled with smoke; tarnished with smoke.

smolt *n* a salmon when a year or two old and when it has acquired its silvery scales.

smooch *vi* (*colloq*) to, kiss and cuddle.

smooth *adj* having a very even surface; free from asperities; not rough; evenly spread; glossy; gently flowing; not ruffled or undulating; falling pleasantly on the ear; not harsh or rugged; using language not harsh or rugged; bland; soothing; insinuating; without jolt or shock; equable as to motion.—*vt* to make smooth; to make even on the surface by any means; to free from obstruction; to make easy; to palliate; to soften; to calm; to mollify; to allay.

smooth-bore *n* a firearm with a smooth-bored barrel and not rifled.

smoothing iron *n* an iron instrument with a flat polished face, used when heated for smoothing clothes, linen, etc.

smorgasbord *n* a type of buffet meal, mostly consisting of cold meat and fish dishes and salads.

smother *n* stifling smoke; a suffocating dust.—*vt* to suffocate or stifle; to suffocate by closely covering and by the exclusion of air; to cover close up, as with ashes, earth, etc; (*fig*) to suppress; to hide from public view.—*vi* to be suffocated; to smoulder.

smoulder *vi* to burn in a stifled manner; to burn and smoke without flame; (*fig*) to burn inwardly, as a thought, passion, etc; to exist in a suppressed state.

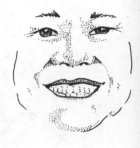

smile

815

smudge *vt* (**smudged, smudging**) to smear or stain with dirt or filth; to blacken with smoke.—*n* a foul spot; a stain; a smear; a fire of weeds, etc, kept smouldering to drive insects away.

smug *adj* neat; trim; spruce; fine; affectedly nice in dress; self-satisfied.

smuggle *vt* (**smuggled, smuggling**) to import or export secretly and contrary to law; to manage, convey or introduce clandestinely.—*vi* to practise smuggling.

smuggler *n* one who smuggles; a vessel employed in smuggling goods.

smuggling *n* the offence of importing or exporting prohibited goods or other goods without paying the legal duties.

smut *n* a spot made with soot or coal; or the foul matter itself; obscene and filthy language; indecent talk, writing, pictures, etc; pornography; a disease of cereals, the seed being converted into a black soot-like powder.—*vt* (**smutted, smutting**) to stain or mark with smut or other dirty substance; to affect with the disease called smut.

smutch *vt* (*arch*) to blacken with smoke, soot or coal; to smudge.—*n* (*arch*) a foul spot; a smudge; a black stain.

snake

smutty *adj* soiled with smut; affected with smut; obscene; pornographic; not modest or pure.

snack *n* a portion of food that can be eaten hastily; a slight, hasty meal; a light meal eaten between regular meals.

snaffle *n* a bridle, consisting of a slender bit with a single rein and without a curb; a snaffle-bit.—*vt* (**snaffled, snaffling**) (*colloq*) to snatch or steal.

snaffle-bit *n* a plain, slender snaffle with a joint in the middle.

snag *n* a small projecting stump of a branch; a branch broken from a tree; the trunk of a large tree stuck by chance in a river with one end projecting so that steamboats, etc, are liable to strike on it; any hidden obstacle or difficulty; an unexpected problem.—*vti* (**snagged, snagging**) to tear on a snag; to clear of snags.

snail *n* a slimy, slow-creeping, air-breathing mollusc differing from the slugs chiefly in having a spiral shell but the latter are also sometimes popularly called snails; a slow-moving person; a sluggard; a drone; a piece of spiral machinery; a piece of metal forming part of the striking work of a clock.

snap dragon

snake *n* a limbless, scaly reptile with a long, tapering body and with salivary glands often modified to produce venom; a sly, treacherous person.

snake charmer *n* one who charms or professes to charm snakes; one who makes snakes obey his or her will.

snaky *adj* pertaining to a snake or to snakes; resembling a snake; serpentine; winding; cunning; insinuating.

snap *vt* (**snapped, snapping**) to bite suddenly; to seize suddenly with the teeth; to snatch suddenly or unexpectedly; to crack; to make a sharp sound with (*to snap the fingers*); to shut with a sharp sound; to break with a sharp sound; to break short.—*vi* to make a sudden effort to bite; to aim to seize with the teeth (*to snap at a person's hand*); to accept promptly (*to snap at a proposal*); to break short; to part asunder suddenly; to give a sharp cracking sound, such as that of the hammer of a firearm when it descends without exploding the charge; to utter sharp, angry words.—*n* a sudden, eager bite; a sudden breaking or rupture of any substance; a sharp cracking sound; the spring catch of a purse, bracelet, etc; a crisp kind of gingerbread nut or small cake; a snapshot; a sudden spell of cold weather.

snapdragon *n* any of various plants with showy white, red or yellow flowers shaped like small jaws.

snappish *adj* apt to snap or bite; apt to use sharp words; sharp in reply; tart; crabbed.

snapshot *n* a photograph taken informally with a simple camera.

snare *n* a noose or set of nooses by which a bird or other living animal may be entangled; a gin; (*fig*) something that serves to entangle or entrap a person.—*vt* (**snared, snaring**) to catch with a snare; to catch or take by guile.

snarl[1] *vi* to growl, as an angry or surly dog; to talk in rude, murmuring terms.—*n* the act of snarling; the sound of this.

snarl[2] *vt* to entangle; to involve in knots.—*n* a knot; a complication; embarrassing difficulty.

snatch *vt* to seize hastily or abruptly; to seize without permission or ceremony; to seize and transport away; to kidnap.—*vi* to attempt to seize suddenly; to snap or catch (*to snatch at a thing*).—*n* a hasty catch or seizing; a catching at or attempt to seize suddenly; a small piece or fragment (*a snatch of a song*).

snazzy *adj* very smart; very well-dressed.

sneak *vi* to creep or steal privately; to go furtively, as if afraid or ashamed to be seen; to slink; to behave with meanness; to truckle.—*n* a mean fellow; a cowardly, mean, underhand fellow.

sneaker *n* one who sneaks; a kind of punchbowl; (*pl*) informal shoes with a cloth upper and soft robber soles.

sneer *vi* to show contempt by turning up the nose or by a particular cast of countenance; to insinuate contempt in words; to speak derisively.—*vt* to treat with sneers; to utter with a sneer.—*n* a look of contempt or disdain; an expression of contemptuous scorn; indirect expression of contempt.

sneeze *vi* (**sneezed, sneezing**) to emit air through the nose audibly and violently by involuntary convulsive force caused by irritation of the inner membrane of the nose. —*n* the act of one who sneezes.

sneezewort *n* a composite plant, so called because the dried flowers and roots when powdered cause sneezing.

sneezing *n* the act of ejecting air violently and audibly through the nose by a sudden and involuntary effort; sternutation.

snick *n* a small cut or mark.—*vt* to cut; to clip.

snickersnee *n* (*arch*) a large sword-shaped knife.

snicker *vi* to giggle; to snigger.

snide *adj* slyly nasty; sneering; malicious.

sniff *vi* to draw air audibly up the nose, sometimes as an expression of scorn; to snuff.—*vt* to draw in with the breath through the nose; to snuff; to smell.—*n* the act of sniffing; the sound so produced; that which is taken by sniffing (*a sniff of fresh air*).

snigger *vi* to snicker; to giggle.—*n* a suppressed laugh; a giggle.

snip *vt* (**snipped, snipping**) to cut off at once with shears or scissors; to clip; to shred.—*n* a cut with shears or scissors; a bit cut off; a small shred; (*colloq*) a bargain.

snipe *n* a wading bird frequenting marshy grounds, with a long straight bill, allied to the woodcock; a fool; a blockhead; a simpleton.—*vti* (**sniped, sniping**) to shoot at people with a rifle from a hidden position; to make critical or nasty remarks at.

sniper *n* a person with a rifle who shoots from ambush at people.

snippet *n* a small part or share.

snippety *adj* insignificant.

snivel *vi* (**snivelled, snivelling**) to run at the nose; to cry or fret, as children, with snuffing or snivelling; to whimper.

sniveller *n* one who snivels or whines; one who weeps for slight causes

snob *n* one who is always pretending to be something better than he or she is; a person who likes to associate with those of a higher social status and looks down of people whom he or she regards as being of inferior status.

snobbish, snobby *adj* belonging to or resembling a snob.

snog *vi* (**snogged, snogging**) (*colloq*) to kiss and cuddle.

snood *adj* a fillet or ribbon for the hair.

snooker *n* a game similar to billiards, using 22 balls of different colours, which are hit into pockets in various orders.

snooze *n* a nap or short sleep.—*vi* (**snoozed, snoozing**) to slumber; to take a short nap.

snore *vi* (**snored, snoring**) to breathe with a rough hoarse noise in sleep.—*n* a breathing with a harsh noise through the nose and mouth in sleep.

snorkel *n* a breathing- tube held in the mouth and projecting upwards so that a swimmer may breathe when just below the surface of the water.

snort *vi* to force the air with violence through the nose, so as to make an abrupt noise.—*n* a loud short sound produced by forcing the air through the nostrils.

snot *n* mucus discharged from or secreted in the nose.

snotty *adj* covered with snot; (*colloq*) irritatingly unpleasant; (*colloq*) snobbish.

snout *n* the long projecting nose of a beast, as that of swine; the nozzle or end of a pipe.

snow *n* watery particles congealed into white crystals in the air and falling to the earth in flakes.—*vi* to fall in snow (used chiefly impersonally, as *it snows, it snowed*).—*vt* to scatter or cause to fall like snow.

snowball *n* a ball of snow; a round mass of snow pressed or rolled together.—*vt* to pelt with snowballs.—*vi* to throw snowballs.

snow-blindness *n* an affection of the eyes caused by the reflection of light from the snow.

snowblink, snowlight *n* the peculiar reflection that arises from fields of ice or snow.

snowdrift *n* a driving snow; a bank of snow driven together by the wind.

snowdrop *n* a common garden plant, bearing solitary, drooping and bell-like white flowers, which appear very early in the year.

snow leopard *n* a large cat of the central Asian mountains with a tawny coat that becomes white in winter.

snow line *n* the line above which mountains are covered with perpetual snow, varying according to latitude and local circumstances, being highest near the equator and lowest near the poles.

snowplough *n* an implement for clearing away the snow from roads, railways, etc.

snowshoe *n* a kind of flat framework worn on the feet, made of wood alone or consisting of a light frame crossed and recrossed by thongs, the broad surface thus presented keeping the wearer from sinking in the snow.

snowstorm *n* a storm with a heavy, drifting fall of snow.

snowy *adj* white like snow; abounding with snow; covered with snow; white; pure; spotless; unblemished.

snub *vt* (**snubbed, snubbing**) to nip or check in growth; to check, stop or rebuke with a tart sarcastic reply or remark; to slight on purpose; to treat with contempt or neglect, as a forward or pretentious person.—*n* a check; a rebuke.

snub nose *n* a short or flat nose.

snuff *vt* to draw in with the breath; to inhale; to scent; to smell; to crop the snuff of, as of a candle.—*vi* to inhale air with noise, as dogs and horses; to snort or sniff; to sniff contemptuously.—**to snuff it** (*sl*) to die.—*n* an inhalation by the nose; a sniff; resentment; huff, expressed by a snuffing of the nose; a powdered preparation of tobacco inhaled through the nose; that part of a candle wick which has been charred by the flame.

snuffbox *n* a box for carrying snuff about the person.

snuffer *n* one that snuffs; (*pl*) an instrument for removing the snuff of a candle.

snuffle *vi* (**snuffled, snuffling**) to speak through the nose or with a nasal twang; to breathe hard through the nose.—*n* a sound made by the passage of air through the nostrils; a speaking through the nose; an affected nasal twang.

snuffles *npl* obstruction of the nose by mucus.

snug *adj* lying close and comfortable; cosy; warm and comfortable.—*vi* (**snugged, snugging**) to lie close; to snuggle.—*vt* to put in a snug position; to place snugly.

snuggery *n* (*colloq*) a snug, warm habitation or comfortable place.

snuggle *vi* (**snuggled, snuggling**) to lie close for convenience or warmth; to nestle; to cuddle.

so *adv* in this or that manner; so that degree (*so long*); thus (*he does it so*); in like manner or degree, after *as* (*as thou art so were they*); in such a manner; to such a degree, with *as* or *that* following (*so fortunate as to escape*); (*colloq*) extremely, very (*it is so beautiful*); as has been said or stated (*it is so, do so*); the case being such; accordingly; well (*so you are here again, are you?*); somewhere about this or that; thereby (*a year or so*); in wishes and asseverations (*so help me Heaven!* that is, may Heaven so help me as I speak truth).—*conj* provided that; on condition that; in case that.—*interj* enough! that will do!

soak *vt* to let lie in a fluid in order to imbibe what it can contain; to macerate in water or other fluid; to steep; to drench; to wet thoroughly; to draw in by pores; to penetrate or permeate by pores.—*vi* to lie steeped in water or other fluid; to steep; to enter into pores or interstices; to drink intemperately; to tipple constantly.

soaking *adj* steeping; macerating; wetting thoroughly.—*n* a wetting; a drenching.

so-and-so *n* (*pl* **so-and-sos**) (*colloq*) a certain person not mentioned by name; an in-

soap

definite person or thing; a mean or nasty person.

soap *n* a chemical compound of potash and soda with fat, soluble in water and used for detergent or cleansing purposes; (*sl*) flattery; a soap opera.—*vt* to rub or wash over with soap; (*sl*) to flatter.

soapbox *n* a place or means, originally an improvised platform, used to make a speech, express one's opinions, etc; such an improvised platform.

soap bubble *n* a thin film of soapsuds inflated by blowing through a pipe and forming a hollow globe with beautiful iridescent colours.

soap opera *n* a radio or television serial, usually long-running, concerned with the day-to-day lives of the members of a family or small community.

soapstone *n* a species of steatite.

soapwort *n* a perennial plant common in gardens, the stems of which, on being put in water, form a lather like soap.

soapy *adj* resembling soap; having the qualities of soap; smeared with soap; (*fig*) flattering; unctuous; (*colloq*) oily (said of persons, language, etc).

soar *vi* to fly aloft, as a bird; to mount upward on wings or as on wings; to mount intellectually; to rise above what is prosaic or commonplace, etc; to be transported with a lofty imagination, desires, etc.—*n* a towering flight; ascent.

sob *vi* (**sobbed, sobbing**) to weep with convulsive catching of the breath.—*n* a convulsive catching of the breath excited by mental emotion of a painful nature; a short convulsive sigh.

sober *adj* temperate in the use of intoxicating liquors; abstemious; not intoxicated; not drunk; not wild, visionary or heated with passion; having the regular exercise of cool, dispassionate reason; dispassionate; calm; serious; grave; not bright or brilliant in appearance; dull-looking.—*vt* to make sober; to cure of intoxication; to make temperate, calm or solemn.—*vi* to become sober, staid or sedate (often with *down*).

sober-minded *adj* having a calm and temperate disposition.

sobriety *n* temperance in the use of intoxicating liquors; abstemiousness; moderation; freedom from the influence of strong drink; calmness; coolness; seriousness; gravity.

sobriquet *n* a nickname.

sob story *n* a story intended to arouse sympathy or pity, especially when used as a n excuse.

socage *n* (*hist*) a tenure of lands in England by the performance of certain and determinate service.

soccer *n* a type of football which is played

with a spherical ball by two teams of 11 players and in which only the goalkeeper is allowed to handle the ball.

sociable *adj* inclined to associate or join in friendly intercourse; fond of companions; companionable; social.

social *adj* pertaining to society; relating to people living in society or to the public as an aggregate body; ready to mix with people; sociable; consisting in union or mutual activity; (*bot*) growing naturally in large groups or masses; (*zool*) living in communities, as wolves, deer, wild cattle, etc; or as ants, bees, etc, which form cooperative communities.

social class *n* a group of people in a society, classified by their sharing of similar occupations, incomes, background, etc, and forming part of a hierarchy.

socialism *n* the name applied to theories of social organization having for their aim the abolition of that individual action on which modern societies depend and the substitution of a regulated system of cooperative action; especially, a system which makes community of property a necessary condition of political improvement.

socialist *n* one who advocates socialism.

socialize *vi* (**socialized, socializing**) to take part in social activities; to meet other people socially.—*vt* to make an individual ready for life in a community, for example by acquiring accepted behaviour patterns; to establish or organize according to socialism (*to socialize medicine*).

social sciences *npl* the study of human social organization and relationships, using scientific methods; the study of subjects, such as economics, sociology, politics, etc, which relate to Man in society.

social security *n* the financial care provided by a government for the elderly, the sick and the unemployed.

social service *n* a welfare service provided by the state; the organized work of people trained to improve social conditions for people.

society *n* the relationship of people to one another when associated; companionship; fellowship; company; a body of persons united for the promotion of some object, either literary, scientific, political, religious, benevolent, convivial, etc; an association for mutual profit, pleasure or usefulness; the persons collectively who live in any region or at any period, viewed in regard to their manners and customs, civilization, moral or material condition; those who recognize each other as associates, friends and acquaintances; the more cultivated portion of any community in its social relations and influences; those who give and receive formal entertainments mutually (used without the article).

Society of Friends *n* the name assumed by the society of dissenters commonly called Quakers.

sociology *n* the science which investigates the laws that regulate human society in all its grades; the science which treats of the general structure of society, the laws of its development and the progress of civilization.

sock[1] *n* the shoe worn by the ancient actors of comedy; hence, *the sock*, comedy in distinction from tragedy, which is symbolized by the buskin; a knitted or woven covering for the foot, shorter than a stocking.

sock[2] *vt* (*sl*) to hit hard; to punch.—*n* (*sl*) a hard blow; a punch.

socket *n* an opening or cavity into which anything is fitted endwise; a hollow which receives and holds something else (*the sockets of the teeth* or *of the eyes*).

Socratic, Socratical *adj* pertaining to Socrates, the Greek philosopher, or to his language or manner of teaching and enquiring; reaching conclusions by means of question and answer.

sod *n* the surface layer of the ground with the grass growing on it; a piece lifted from that surface; turf; sward.

soda *n* a name for various compounds of sodium, as the oxide and hydroxide; popularly, sodium carbonate (*soda crystals* or *washing soda*), used in washing and in the manufacture of soap and glass and extensively made from salt; soda water.

soda water *n* a refreshing and effervescent drink generally consisting of ordinary water into which carbonic acid has been forced under pressure.

sodden *adj* boiled; seethed; soaked and softened, as in water; thoroughly saturated; not well baked; doughy.

sodium *n* a soft light silvery metallic element, of which soda is the oxide; never found in the uncombined state in nature but existing in many minerals and in almost all vegetable and animal organisms.

sodomite *n* one guilty of sodomy.

Sodomite *n* an inhabitant of Sodom, the wicked city of the Bible destroyed by God.

sodomy *n* the sin attributed to the inhabitants of Sodom; buggery; sexual intercourse involving the anal opening, especially between males.

sofa *n* a long seat with a stuffed bottom and raised stuffed back and ends.

soft *adj* easily yielding to pressure; yielding, the contrary of *hard*; not rough, rude or violent; affecting the senses in a pleasant manner; delicate or pleasing to the touch; gentle or melodious to the ear; not glaring; not repelling or striking to the sight; easily yielding to persuasion or motives; facile, weak; not harsh, severe or un-

sock

feeling; gentle; easily moved by pity; susceptible of tender affections; effeminate; not manly or courageous; foolish; simple; silly; quiet and refreshing (*soft slumbers*); readily forming a lather and washing well with soap (*soft water*); pronounced with more or less of a sibilant sound, as *c* in *cinder*, as opposed to *c* in *candle* and *g* in *gin*, as opposed to *g* in *gift*.—*adv* softly; gently; quietly.—*interj* be soft; hold; stop; not so fast.

softa *n* a Muslim student of theology and law.

soft-core *adj* (of pornography) not sexually explicit.

soft drink *n* a non-alcoholic drink.

soft drug *n* any drug which is considered to be non-addictive.

soften *vt* to make soft or more soft; to make less hard; to mollify; to make less implacable or angry; to make less severe, harsh or strong in language; to alleviate; to tone down.—*vi* to become soft or less hard; to become less harsh or cruel; to become milder.

softening *n* the act of making soft or softer.

softening of the brain *n* an affection of the brain, in which it becomes pulpy or pasty, often causing death; foolishness; stupidity.

soft-hearted *adj* having tenderness of heart.

softly *adv* in a soft manner; not with force or violence; gently; not loudly; mildly; tenderly.

softness *n* the quality of being soft; the opposite of hardness; penetrability; susceptibility of tender feeling; weakness of mind or will; mildness; gentleness.

soft soap *n* a coarse kind of soap in a viscid form; (*colloq*) flattery, blarney.—**soft-soap** *vt* (*colloq*) to flatter.

soft-spoken *adj* speaking softly; having a mild or gentle voice; mild; affable.

soft spot *n* a sentimental fondness for; a special liking for.

software *n* the programs used in computers.

soi-disant *adj* calling himself or herself; self-styled; pretended; would-be.

soil¹ *n* the upper stratum of the earth's crust; the mould or that compound substance which furnishes nutriment to plants; earth; ground; land; country.

soil² *vt* to make dirty on the surface; to dirty; to defile; to tarnish; to sully; to dung; to manure.—*vi* to take on dirt; to take a soil or stain; to tarnish.—*n* foul matter on another surface; stain; tarnish; defilement or taint.

soil pipe *n* a pipe for conveying from a house the foul or waste water, night soil, etc.

soirée *n* an evening party.

sojourn *vi* to dwell for a time; to dwell as a temporary resident or as a stranger, not considering the place a permanent habitation.—*n* a temporary residence, as that of a traveller in a foreign land.

sol¹ *n* in singing, a syllable used to denote the fifth tone of the diatonic scale.

sol² *n* a colloidal solution, composed of a liquid solvent and a liquid or very finely divided solid therein.

solace *vt* (**solaced, solacing**) to cheer in grief or under calamity; to relieve in affliction; to console; to comfort; to allay or assuage.—*n* comfort in grief; alleviation of grief or anxiety; what relieves in distress; recreation.

solan goose *n* the gannet.

solar *adj* pertaining to the sun; proceeding from or produced by the sun; measured by the progress of the sun or by its apparent revolution.

solar cycle *n* a period of twenty-eight year.

solar plexus *n* the network of nerves behind the stomach; (*colloq*) the pit of the stomach.

solar spot *n* a dark spot that appears on the sun's disc, sometimes so large as to be seen by the naked eye, very changeable in number, figure and dimensions.

solar system *n* the system of which the sun is the centre and to which belong the planets, satellites, comets and meteorites, all directly or indirectly revolving round the central sun.—**solar year** *n* the time which the earth takes to go round the sun, 365 days, 5 hours, 48 minutes, 46 seconds.

solatium *n* (*pl* **solatia**) anything that alleviates or compensates for suffering or loss; a compensation in money.

solder *vt* to join by a metallic substance in a state of fusion, which hardens in cooling and renders the joint solid; (*fig*) to unite or combine; to patch up.—*n* a metal or metallic composition used in joining other metals by being fused between them.

soldering iron *n* a tool consisting of a wedge-shaped piece of copper with a handle, the copper being heated and used to melt the solder in soldering.

soldier *n* a person who serves in an army; a common soldier or private; a person of military experience and skill or a person of distinguished valour.

soldierly *adj* like or becoming a soldier; brave; martial; honourable.

sole¹ *adj* single; being or acting without another; alone in its kind; individual; (*law*) single.

sole² *n* the underside of the foot; the bottom surface of a shoe or boot or the piece of leather which constitutes the bottom; the part of anything that forms the bottom and on which it stands; a marine fish belonging to the family of flat fishes, of an oblong form, probably so called from its shape.—*vt* (**soled, soling**) to furnish with a sole (*to sole a shoe*).

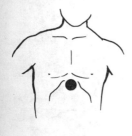

solar plexus

sole

solecism *n* an impropriety in the use of language, arising from ignorance; a gross deviation from the idiom of a language or a gross deviation from the rules of syntax; a violation of the rules of society; a social gaffe.

solely *adv* singly; alone; only; without another.

solemn *adj* marked by religious rites or ceremonious observances; fitted to excite reverent or serious reflections; awe-inspiring; grave; impressive (*a solemn silence*); accompanied by seriousness or impressiveness in language or demeanour; earnest (*a solemn promise*); affectedly grave.

solemnity *n* the state or quality of being solemn; gravity; impressiveness; mock gravity; a solemn or reverent rite or ceremony; a proceeding adapted to impress awe or reverence.

solemnize *vt* (**solemnized, solemnizing**) to dignify or honour by ceremonies; to celebrate; to perform with ritual ceremonies or according to legal forms (used especially of marriage; to make grave, serious and reverential.

solenoid *n* a coil of wire that produces a magnetic field when an electric current is passed through it.

sol-fa *n* same as **tonic sol-fa**.

solfeggio *n* (*mus*) a system of arranging the scale by the names *do* (or *ut*), *re*, *mi*, *fa*, *sol*, *la*, *si*; an exercise in scale singing; solmization.

solicit *vt* to ask from with some degree of earnestness; to make petition to; to ask for with some degree of earnestness; to seek by petition; to awake or excite to action; to invite; to disturb or disquiet; to make anxious; (*law*) to incite to commit a felony; to endeavour to influence by a bribe.—*vi* to make solicitation for someone or for a thing; to approach and offer sexual services to.

solicitation *n* the act of soliciting; an earnest request; endeavour to influence to grant something by bribery; the offence of inciting a person to commit a felony.

solicitor *n* one who solicits; an attorney; a law agent; one who represents another in court.

solicitor-general *n* an officer of the British crown, next in rank to the attorney general, with whom he or she is associated in the management of the legal business of the crown.

solicitous *adj* anxious; concerned; apprehensive; disturbed; restless.

solicitude *n* the state of being solicitous; uneasiness of mind occasioned by the fear of evil or the desire of good; concern; anxiety.

solid *adj* possessing the property of excluding all other bodies from the space occupied by itself; impenetrable; firm; compact, opposed to *liquid* and *gaseous*; not hollow; full of matter; having all the geometrical dimensions.—length, breadth and thickness; cubic (*a solid foot*); strong; sound; substantial, as opposed to frivolous, fallacious, etc; real; valid; financially sound or safe; reliable.—*n* a firm compact body with the particles firmly cohering and thus distinguished from a liquid or a gas, whose particles yield to the slightest impression; (*geom*) a body or magnitude which has three dimensions.—length, breadth and thickness.—**regular solid** *n* one which is bounded by equal and regular plane polygons.

solidarity *n* unity or communion of interests and responsibilities among nations or humankind in general.

solidify *vt* (**solidified, solidifying**) to make solid or compact; to cause to change from a liquid or a gas to a solid.—*vi* to become solid or compact.

solidity *n* the state or quality of being solid; firmness; density; compactness, opposed to *fluidity*; strength or stability; massiveness; soundness; strength or validity, as opposed to *weakness* or *fallaciousness*; the quantity of space occupied by a solid body; cubic content.

solidus *n* (*pl* **solidi**) an oblique stroke (/) used to separate items of text as in dates, alternative words, lists or the terms of fractions.

soliloquize *vi* (**soliloquized, soliloquizing**) to utter a soliloquy; to talk to oneself.

soliloquy *n* a talking to oneself; a monologue; a discourse not addressed to any person; a speech in a play that takes this form.

solitaire *n* an article of jewellery in which a single gem is set; a game for a single person played on a board indented with thirty-three or thirty-seven hemispherical hollows and an equal number of balls; a card game for one person; patience; a bird of the dodo family, long since extinct.

solitary *adj* being or living alone; being by oneself; not much visited or frequented; retired; lonely (*a solitary residence*); passed without company; shared by no companions (*a solitary life*); single; individual (*a solitary example*).—*n* one that lives alone or in solitude; a hermit; a recluse.

solitude *n* a state of being alone; loneliness; remoteness from society; destitution of inhabitants; a lonely place; a desert.

solmization *n* (*mus*) the act or art of giving to each of the seven notes of the scale its proper sound or relative pitch; solfeggio.

solo *n* (*pl* **soli, solos**) a tune, air or strain to be played by a single instrument or sung by a single voice without or with an accompaniment; a card game similar to whist, the chief distinction being that a single player often opposes the other three. —*adj* performed alone; performing alone. —*adv* alone; by oneself.

soloist *n* a musician who plays a solo.

solstice *n* the time of the year at which, owing to the annual revolution of the earth, the sun is at its greatest distance north or south of the equator and begins to turn back, which happens at midsummer and midwinter, or 21st June and 22nd December.

solubility *n* the quality of being soluble; susceptibility of being dissolved in a fluid; capability of being solved or cleared up.

soluble *adj* susceptible of being dissolved in a fluid; capable of solution; (*fig*) capable of being solved or resolved, as a mathematical problem; capable of being cleared up or settled by explanation, as a doubt, question, etc.

solution *n* the act of dissolving or state of being dissolved; the conversion of solid matter into liquid by means of a liquid (called the *solvent*); the combination of a liquid with a liquid or a gas to form a homogeneous liquid; the liquid thus produced; the preparation made by dissolving a solid in a liquid; the act of solving, clearing up or explaining; explanation; (*math*) the method of resolving a problem; (*med*) the termination or the crisis of a disease.

solve *vt* (**solved, solving**) to explain or clear up the difficulties in; to make clear; to remove perplexity regarding; to operate on by calculation or mathematical processes so as to bring out the required result (*to solve a problem*).

solvency *n* the state of being solvent; ability to pay all debts or just claims.

solvent *adj* having the power of dissolving; able to pay all just debts.—*n* any fluid or substance that dissolves or renders liquid other bodies; a menstruum.

solvent abuse *n* the use of various forms of solvent, including glue, as an inhalant to become intoxicated.

soma *n* (*pl* **somata, somas**) the body of a plant or animal exclusive of the germ cells.

somatic *adj* corporeal; pertaining to the body as opposed to the mind.

somatology *n* the branch of biology dealing with the anatomy and functions of the body; that branch of anthropology which deals with human physical characteristics.

sombre *adj* dark in hue or aspect; dusky; gloomy; dismal; melancholy.—*vt* to make sombre, dark or gloomy; to shade.

sombreness *n* state or quality of being sombre; gloominess.

sombrero *n* a broad-brimmed hat.

some *adj* expressing a certain indeterminate quantity or number, sometimes expressive

sombero

somersault

of a considerable quantity (*situated at some distance*); indicating a person or thing not definitely known or not specific (often followed by *or other*, as *some person or other*); used before a word or number, with the sense of about or near (*a village of some eighty houses*); applied to those of one party; certain, in distinction from others (*some men believe one thing, others another*). It is often used without a noun and often followed by *of* (*some of us, some of our provisions*).

somebody *n* a person unknown or uncertain; a person indeterminate; (*colloq*) a person of importance.

somehow *adv* one way or other; in some way not yet known.

something *n* an indeterminate or unknown event or thing; an indefinite quantity or degree; a little; a person or thing of importance.—*adv* in some degree or measure; somewhat; rather.

sometime *adv* once; formerly; at one time or other; at some time in the future, not specified or not yet known.—*adj* having been formerly; former; late.

sometimes *adv* at times; at intervals; not always; now and then; once.

somewhat *n* something, though uncertain what; more or less; a certain quantity or degree, indeterminate.—*adv* in some degree or measure; rather; a little.

somewhere *adv* in or to some place or other unknown or not specified; in one place or another.

somersault *n* a leap by which a person turns with the heels thrown over his or her head, completing a circuit and again alights on his or her feet; a complete reversal.—*vi* to make somersaults.

somnambulate *vi* (**somnambulated, somnambulating**) to walk in one's sleep.

somnambulism *n* the act or practice of walking in sleep, resulting from a peculiar perversion of the mental functions during sleep.

somnambulist *n* a sleepwalker.

somnolence *n* sleepiness; drowsiness; inclination to sleep; (*pathol*) a state intermediate between sleeping and waking.

somnolent *adj* sleepy; drowsy; inclined to sleep.

son *n* a male child; the male issue of a parent, father or mother (also used of animals); a male descendant; a term of affectionate address by an old man to a young one, a confessor to his penitent, a teacher to his disciple, etc; a native of a country; a person strongly imbued by some quality (*sons of light*).

Son *n* Christ, called also *Son of God* and *Son of Man*.

sonant *adj* pertaining to sound; sounding; uttered with voice and not breath merely;

voiced, as the letters *b*, *d* compared with *p*, *t*.—*n* a sonant letter.

sonata *n* a musical composition for one or two instruments, consisting of several movements, frequently allegro, adagio, minuetto or scherzo and rondo.

son et lumière *n* an evening entertainment staged at historical sites, using lighting displays, music and recorded speech to relate the history of the place.

song *n* that which is sung, whether by the human voice or a bird; a little poem to be sung; a vocal melody; an air for a single voice or several; a lay; a strain; poesy; verse.

songbird n a bird with a musical call.

songster *n* one who sings; especially, a bird that sings.

song thrush *n* a European songbird with a spotted breast and brown plumage.

sonic *adj* of, producing or involving sound waves.

sonic barrier *n* same as **sound barrier**.

sonic boom *n* a loud, explosive sound caused by an aircraft or missile moving faster than the speed of sound.

son-in-law *n* (*pl* **sons-in-law**) a man married to one's daughter.

sonnet *n* a short poem of fourteen lines, the rhymes being adjusted by a particular rule; a short poem; a song.

sonneteer *n* a composer of sonnets; a small poet (usually in contempt).

sonorous *adj* giving sound, as when struck; resonant; sounding; giving a clear, loud or full-volumed sound; high-sounding.

soon *adv* in a short time; shortly after any time specified or supposed; early; before any time supposed; quickly; speedily; readily; willingly; gladly (*I would as soon do it*).

soot *n* a black substance formed from fuel in combustion, rising in fine particles and adhering to the sides of the chimney or pipe conveying the smoke.—*vt* to cover or foul with soot.

sooth *n* truth; reality (used frequently with *in*, as *in sooth I know not*).

soothe *vt* (**soothed, soothing**) to please with blandishments or soft words; to cajole; to make less angry or violent; to pacify; to assuage; to mitigate, ease or allay.

soothsayer *n* one who foretells or predicts; a prophet.

soothsaying *n* a foretelling; a prediction.

sooty *adj* pertaining to, producing, covered with or resembling soot; dusky; dark.

sop *n* something dipped in broth or liquid food and intended to be eaten; something given to pacify or appease.—*vt* (**sopped, sopping**) to steep or dip in liquor.

sophism *n* a specious proposition; a specious but fallacious argument; a fallacy designed to deceive.

sophist *n* one of a class of leading public teachers in ancient Greece during the fifth and fourth centuries BC, many of whom were people who spent their time in verbal quibbles and philosophical enigmas, thus causing the term to take on a bad sense; one who reasons captiously or fallaciously; one who quibbles.

sophistic, sophistical *adj* fallaciously subtle; containing sophistry; quibbling.

sophisticate *vt* (**sophisticated, sophisticating**) to pervert; to wrest from the truth; to adulterate; to render spurious by admixture.

sophisticated *adj* complex; worldly; worldly-wise; refined, cultured.

sophistication *n* the act of adulterating; adulteration; the act or art of quibbling; a quibble; worldliness; refinement, culture.

sophistry *n* fallacious reasoning; reasoning sound in appearance only and intended to mislead.

sophomore *n* in American colleges, a student belonging to the second of the four classes; one next above a freshman.

soporific *adj* causing sleep; tending to cause sleep.—*n* a drug or other thing that has the quality of inducing sleep.

sopping *adj* soaking; wet through.

soppy *adj* sickly sentimental.

soprano *n* (*pl* **soprani, sopranos**) the highest kind of female voice, whose ordinary easy range is from C below the treble staff to G or A above it; equivalent to *treble*.

sorb *n* the service tree or its fruit.

sorb apple *n* the fruit of the service tree.

sorcerer, *n* a conjurer; an enchanter; a magician.

sorceress *n* a female sorcerer.

sorcery *n* divination by the assistance or supposed assistance of evil spirits; magic; enchantment; witchcraft.

sordid *adj* filthy; base; mean; meanly avaricious; covetous; niggardly.

sordidness *n* the state or quality of being sordid; niggardliness.

sore *adj* painful; being the seat of pain; violent with pain; severe; distressing; tender, as the mind; easily annoyed or vexed; feeling aggrieved; galled.—*n* a place in a body where the skin and flesh are ruptured or bruised, so as to be painful; a boil, ulcer, wound, etc.—*adv* with painful violence; severely; sorely.

sorghum *n* the cereal plant that yields Indian millet, one species also yielding sugar.

sorrel[1] *n* the popular name of certain perennial plants, a common species being a succulent acid herb used as a salad and potherb.

sorrel[2] *adj* of a reddish or yellowish brown colour.—*n* a reddish or yellow-brown colour.

sorriness *n* pitifulness; meanness; despicableness.

sorrow *n* pain of mind from loss of or disappointment in the expectation of good; grief; regret; sadness; mourning.—*vi* to be affected with sorrow; to feel sorry; to grieve; to be sad.

sorrowful *adj* full of sorrow; exhibiting or producing sorrow; sad; mournful; dejected.

sorry *adj* grieved for the loss of some good; pained at some evil experienced or committed; feeling regret (*I am sorry you cannot come*); mean; vile; worthless; pitiful (*a sorry excuse*).

sort *n* a kind, species, class or order (*a sort of men*); manner; form of being or acting; degree (*in some sort*); a set; a suit.—**out of sorts** out of order; not in one's usual state of health; unwell.—*vt* to separate and arrange in distinct classes or divisions; to assort; to arrange; to reduce to order.—*vi* to consort; to associate; to suit; to agree.

sorter *n* one who sorts (*a letter-sorter*; *a wool-sorter*).

sortie *n* the issuing of troops from a besieged place to attack the besiegers; a sally.

S.O.S

••• ——— •••

SOS

SOS the letters of the international signal of distress (three dots, three dashes, three dots) prescribed in 1912 for use at sea and subsequently used by airships, troops in action, etc.

so-so *adj* not very good; mediocre; middling; not very well.

sot *n* a stupid person; a dolt; a person stupefied by excessive drinking; an habitual drunkard.

sottish *adj* pertaining to a sot; having the character of a sot.

Sothic *adj* pertaining to the Dogstar.

sotto (*mus*) a term signifying below or inferior.

sotto voce *adv* in an undertone.

sou *n* an old low-value French copper coin; a very small sum of money.

soubrette *n* a waiting maid; the part of a pert or coquettish servant girl in a comedy, operetta, etc.

souchong *n* a kind of black tea.

soufflé *n* a light dish made with beaten white of eggs, variously flavoured and baked.

sough *vi* to emit a rushing, moaning or whistling sound, like that of the wind; to sound like the roar of the sea.—*n* a sound of this kind; a rushing sound like that of the wind; a deep sigh.

soul *n* the spiritual and immortal part in human beings; the immaterial spirit which inhabits the body; the moral and emotional part of man's nature; the seat of the sentiments or feelings; the animating or essential part; the vital principle; the essence (*he is the very soul of honour*); an inspirer or leader (*the soul of an enterprise*); courage or spirit; a spiritual being; a disembodied spirit; a human being; a person (*not a soul present*); a familiar term for a person (*poor soul, he was a good soul*); a type of Black music combining elements of gospel, jazz and rhythm and blues.

soul food *n* the kind of food, for example chitterlings, yams and ham hocks, traditionally eaten by American Black people.

soulful *adj* expressing profound sentiment.

soulless *adj* without a soul; lifeless; spiritless; base.

soul mate *n* a person with whom one has a strong affinity; a perfect companion or mate.

sound[1] *n* that which is heard; the effect which is produced by the vibrations of a body affecting the ear; a noise; noise without meaning; empty noise.—*vi* to make a noise; to give out a sound; to seem or appear when uttered; to appear on narration (*this story sounds like a fiction*); to be conveyed in sound; to be spread or published.—*vt* to cause to give out a sound; to play on; to utter audibly; to give a signal for by a certain sound (*to sound a retreat*); to publish or proclaim (*to sound the praises of a great man*).

sound[2] *adj* healthy; not diseased; not being in a morbid state (*a sound mind, a sound body*); uninjured; unhurt (*a sound limb*); free from imperfection or defect (*sound timber, sound fruit*); founded in truth; valid; that cannot be refuted (*sound reasoning*); correct; free from error; orthodox; founded in right and law; just (*a sound claim*); profound, unbroken, undisturbed (*a sound sleep*); heavy; laid on with force (*a sound beating*).

sound[3] *n* a narrow passage or channel of water, as between the mainland and an isle or connecting two seas; a strait.

sound[4] *vt* to measure the depth of; to fathom by sinking a plummet or lead attached to a line; (*surg*) to examine by means of a probe; (*fig*) to try or search out the intention, opinion, will or desires of.—*vi* to use the line and lead in searching the depth of water.—*n* (*surg*) any elongated instrument by which cavities of the body are sounded or explored.

sound[5] *n* the air bladder of a fish.

sound barrier, sonic barrier *n* the rapid increase in air resistance as an aeroplane reaches the speed of sound, the sonic barrier.

sound bite *n* a short, punchy phrase or sentence extracted from a speech or interview, often used by the media.

sound effects *npl* artificial sounds used for dramatic purposes in plays, television programmes, films, etc.

sounding[1] *n* a measurement of the depth of water in a river, harbour, at sea, etc; a test, sampling, e.g. of public opinion.

sounding[2] *adj* causing sound; sonorous; having a lofty sound.

sounding board *n* a canopy over a pulpit, etc, to direct the sound of a speaker's voice towards the audience; a thin board over which the strings of a pianoforte, violin, guitar, etc, are stretched; a person or thing used to test reaction to an idea or plan.

sounding post, soundpost *n* a small post in a violin, set under the bridge for a support and for propagating the sound.

soundless *adj* having no sound; noiseless; silent; dumb.

soundtrack *n* the sound accompanying a film; the area on a cinema film that carries the sound recording.

sound wave *n* a wave by which sound is transmitted.

soup *n* a kind of broth; a liquid food made from vegetables and water and sometimes meat.

soupçon *n* a very small quantity; a taste.

sour *adj* sharp to the taste; tart; acid; harsh of temper; crabbed; austere; morose; expressing discontent, displeasure or peevishness (*a sour word* or *look*); to become tart or acid by keeping, as milk.—*vt* to make acid or sour; to make cross, crabbed or discontented (*to sour the temper*); to embitter.—*vi* to become acid; to acquire tartness; to become peevish, crabbed or harsh in temper.

source *n* the spring or fountain head from which a stream of water proceeds; one who or that which originates or gives rise to anything; first cause; origin.

sour grapes *npl* pretending not to like something because it cannot be obtained or achieved by oneself.

sourly *adv* in a sour manner; acidly; morosely; peevishly; discontentedly.

sourness *n* the state or quality of being sour; acidity; sharpness to the taste; asperity; harshness of temper.

souse *n* pickle made with salt; sauce; pickled meat; the ears, feet, etc, of swine pickled.—*vt* (**soused, sousing**) to steep in pickle; to plunge into water.

south *n* one of the four cardinal points of the compass, directly opposite to the north; the region or locality lying opposite to the north; the wind that blows from the south.—*adj* situated in the south or in a southern direction; pertaining to the south; proceeding from the south.—*adv* toward the south; from the south.—*vi* to move or turn towards the south; (*astron*) to arrive at or pass the meridian of a place.

southeast *n* the point of the compass equally distant from the south and east.—*adj* pertaining to the southeast.

southeaster *n* a wind from the southeast.

southerly *adj* lying in the south; coming from the south.

southern *adj* belonging to the south; lying on the south side of the equator; coming from the south.

Southern Cross *n* a bright constellation in the southern hemisphere, the principal stars of which form a cross.

southerner *n* an inhabitant or native of the south.

southing *n* motion to the south; the time at which the moon or other heavenly body passes the meridian of a place; (*navig, surv*) the difference of latitude southward from the last point reckoning.

southmost *adj* farthest toward the south.

southward *adv* toward the south.—*adj* lying or situated toward the south; directed towards the south.

southwest the point of the compass equally distant from the south and west.—*adj* lying in the direction of the southwest; coming from the southwest.

southwester *n* a strong southwest wind; a waterproof hat with a flap hanging over the neck, worn in bad weather (frequently contracted into **sou'wester**).

souvenir *n* that which reminds or revives the memory of anything; a keepsake.

sovereign *adj* supreme in power; possessing supreme dominion; royal; princely; paramount efficacious in the highest degree (*a sovereign medicine*).—*n* a supreme ruler; the person having the highest power or authority in a state, as a king, queen, emperor, etc; a monarch; formerly, a gold coin of the value of 20 shillings.

sovereignty *n* the state of being a sovereign; the supreme power in a state; monarchical sway; supremacy; supreme excellence.

soviet *n* the local governing council in the former Soviet Union.

sow[1] *vt* (*pret* **sowed**, *pp* **sowed** or **sown**, *ppr* **sowing**) to scatter, as seed on the earth, for the purpose of growth; to plant by strewing; to stock with seed; to spread abroad; to disseminate; to propagate (*to sow discord*).—*vi* to scatter seed for growth and the production of a crop.

sow[2] *n* the female of the swine; (in founding) the main channel into which metal is run from a smelting furnace.

sower *n* one who sows; a disseminator.

soybean, soya bean *n* a nutritious seed of an Asian plant, used as a food and a source of oil.

soy sauce, soya sauce *n* a salty, brown sauce made by pickling fermented soya beans, used for flavouring in oriental cooking.

sozzled *adj* (*sl*) very drunk.

spa *n* a mineral spring; a place to which people resort for its mineral waters.

soup

space *n* extension, considered independently of anything which it may contain; extension in all directions; any portion of extension; the interval between any two or more points or objects; the part of the universe beyond the earth's atmosphere; quantity of time; the interval between two points of time (*print*) the interval between words in printed matter; also a kind of blank type for separating words; (*mus*) one of the four intervals between the five lines of a staff.—*vt* (**spaced, spacing**) to arrange at proper intervals; to arrange the spaces in.

spacecraft *n* a vehicle designed to travel outside the earth's atmosphere.

space-time continuum *n* (*physics*) the four-dimensional coordinate system comprising the three spatial and one temporal coordinates which together define a continuum in which any particle or event may be located.

spacial *adj* same as **spatial**.

spacious *adj* enclosing an extended space; large in extent; wide extended; not contracted or narrow; roomy.

spade *n* an instrument for digging, having abroad lade of iron and a stout handle, adapted to be used with both hands and one foot; (*pl*) one of the four suits of playing cards.—**to call a spade a spade** to call things by their proper names; to speak plainly and without mincing matters.—*vt* (**spaded, spading**) to dig with a spade; to pare the sward from with a spade.

spadework *n* hard, preliminary, detailed work before the adoption of final measures.

spadix *n* (*pl* **spadixes, spadices**) a spike of flowers clustered around a fleshy stem and enclosed in a spathe.

spaghetti *n* a pasta made into long thin, thin solid strings.

spake (*arch*) *pt* of **speak**.

span *n* the space from the point of the thumb to that of the little finger when extended; the distance between two edges or extremes of something, such as the tips of a pair of wings or two supports of a bridge; the full reach or extent of anything; a short space of time; a pair of horses; a yoke of animals; a team.—*vt* (**spanned, spanning**) to measure by the hand with the fingers extended or with the fingers encompassing the object; to measure or reach from one side of to the other.

spandrel *n* (*archit*) the irregular triangular space between the outer curve of an arch and a straight-sided figure surrounding it.

spangle *n* a small circular ornament of metal stitched on an article of dress; any little thing sparkling and brilliant; a small sparkling object.—*vt* (**spangled, spangling**) to sprinkle or adorn with spangles.

spaniel

spanner

Spaniard *n* a native of Spain.

spaniel *n* any of various breeds of dogs with large drooping ears and a long silky coat.

Spanish *adj* pertaining to Spain.—*n* the language of Spain.

spank *vi* to move with a quick, lively step; to move or run along quickly.—*vt* to slap or smack, as with the open hand.

spanking *adj* moving with a quick, lively pace; dashing; brisk.

spanner *n* a tool with jaws or sockets at the end or ends of a lever (used for tightening nuts).

span roof *n* a common roof formed by two meeting inclined planes.

spar[1] *n* a long piece of timber of no great thickness; a piece of sawed timber; a pole; (*naut*) a long beam; a general term for masts, yards, booms and gaffs.

spar[2] *n* any of various crystallized, earthy and some metallic substances which easily break into rhomboidal, cubical or laminated fragments with polished surfaces, as calcareous spar, fluorspar, etc.

spar[3] *vi* (**sparred, sparring**) to rise and strike with the feet or spurs (said of cocks); to move the arms in a way suitable for immediate attack or defence; to fight with boxing gloves; to argue or dispute.—*n* a preliminary flourish of the fists; a boxing match; a contest with boxing gloves.

spare *vt* (**spared, sparing**) to use frugally; not to be profuse of; to part with; to do without; to dispense with; to omit; to forbear (in this sense often with an infinitive as object); to treat with pity, mercy or forbearance; to forbear to afflict or punish; to forbear to inflict on; to withhold from; to save, withhold or gain, as from some engrossing occupation.—*vi* to be parsimonious or frugal; not to be liberal or profuse; to use mercy or forbearance.—*adj* scanty; not plentiful or abundant; such as may be spared; over and above what is necessary; superfluous; held in reserve; not required for present use (*a spare anchor, a spare bed*); lean; lacking flesh; meagre; thin.

spare rib *n* the piece of a hog taken from the side, consisting of the ribs with little flesh on them.

spark[1] *n* a small particle of fire emitted from bodies in combustion; a small shining body or transient light; the light accompanying electric discharge; a particle (*a spark of life, of courage*).—*vi* to emit particles of fire; to sparkle.

spark[2] *n* a brisk, showy gay, person; a lover; a gallant; a beau.

sparking plug *n* in internal-combustion engines, a plug screwed into the cylinder head, carrying the insulated secondary or high tension wire from the magneto to one end of the spark gap within the cylinder.

sparkle *vi* (**sparkled, sparkling**) to emit

sparks; to shine as if giving out sparks; to glitter; to flash; to twinkle.—*vt* to emit with coruscations; to shine with.—*n* a spark; a luminous particle; a scintillation; luminosity; lustre.

sparkler *n* one who or that which sparkles; a taper-like firework that gives off small sparks and is held in the hand; (*colloq*) a diamond.

sparkling *adj* emitting sparks; glittering; brilliant; lively.

sparrow *n* a well-known bird of the finch family, constantly seen near houses and even in the midst of large cities.

sparrowhawk *n* a small hawk, very destructive to pigeons and small birds.

sparse *adj* thinly scattered; set or planted here and there; not dense; (*bot*) not in any apparent regular order.

Spartan *adj* pertaining to ancient Sparta; hence, hardy; undaunted; rigorously austere.

spasm *n* (*med*) an abnormal, sudden and more or less violent contraction of one or more muscles or muscular fibres, sometimes attended with pain; a sudden outburst (of emotion or activity).

spasmodic *adj* relating to spasm; consisting in spasm; convulsive; marked by strong effort but of brief duration; violent and short-lived.

spastic *adj* affected by muscle spasm; suffering from continuous or uncontrollable muscle spasms, as in cerebral palsy.

spat[1] *n* the spawn of shellfish; the developing spawn of the oyster.

spat[2] *n* a gaiter covering the ankle and the instep and fastening under the shoe.

spat[3] *n* (*colloq*) a petty argument; a slight quarrel.

spatchcock *n* a fowl killed and immediately cooked, for some sudden occasion.

spate *n* a sudden heavy flood, especially in mountain streams, caused by heavy rainfall.

spathe *n* (*bot*) a large bract situated at the base of a spadix, which it encloses as a sheath.

spatial, spacial *adj* pertaining to space.

spatter *vt* to scatter a liquid substance on; to sprinkle with anything liquid or semi-liquid that befouls; to be spatter; to throw out in drops.

spatterdash *n* a covering of cloth or leather for the leg; a gaiter; a legging.

spatula *n* a sort of knife with a thin flexible blade, used by painters, cooks, etc,; (*surg*) a flat instrument for depressing the tongue in operations about the throat or for examining the throat.

spatulate *adj* shaped like a spatula; resembling a spatula in shape.

spavin *n* a disease of horses affecting the hock joint or joint of the hind leg between the knee and the fetlock, by which lameness is produced.

spawn *n* the eggs or ova of fishes, frogs, etc, when shed; the white fibrous matter from which fungi are produced; the mycelium of fungi; (contemptuously) any offspring or product.—*vt* to deposit in the form of spawn; contemptuously, to bring forth or generate.—*vi* to deposit eggs, as fish, frogs, etc.

spawner *n* a female fish

spay *vt* to remove or destroy the ovaries of.

speak *vi* (*pret* **spoke**, *pp* **spoken**, *ppr* **speaking**) to utter words; to express thoughts by words; to utter a speech, discourse or harangue; to talk; to discourse; to make mention; to tell by writing; to communicate ideas in any manner; to be expressive.—*vt* to utter with the mouth; to utter articulately; to say; to declare (*to speak the truth*); to proclaim; to talk or converse in (*to speak French*); to address; to accost; to express in any way (*her eyes spoke love*).

speaker *n* one who speaks; one that utters a speech in public or one that practises public speaking; a person who is the mouthpiece or spokesperson of another; a person who presides over a deliberative assembly (*the speaker in the House of Commons*).

speaking *adj* used for the purpose of conveying speech (*a speaking trumpet*); forcibly expressive (*a speaking likeness*); extending to mere phrases of civility (*a speaking acquaintance*).

spear *n* a long pointed weapon used in war and hunting, by thrusting or throwing; a lance; a pointed instrument with barbs, for stabbing fish, etc.—*vt* to pierce with, or as with, a spear; to kill with a spear.

spearhead *n* the metal point of a spear; a person or thing that leads an attack or other action.—*vt* to lead (an attack or other action); to serve as the leader of.

spearman *n* (*pl* **spearmen**) one who is armed with a spear.

spearmint *n* an aromatic plant having spear-shaped leaves.

special *adj* pertaining to something distinct or having a distinctive character; distinctive; particular; peculiar; differing from others; designed for a particular purpose or occasion; having a distinct field or scope.—*n* any person or thing appointed for a special purpose or occasion, as a constable, a railway train, etc.

specialism *n* a particular branch or department of knowledge; devotion to some one subject.

specialist *n* a person who devotes himself or herself to a particular branch of a profession, art or science; one who has a special knowledge of some particular subject.

speciality *n* that property by which a person

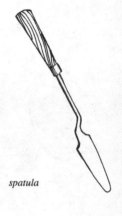

spatula

spearhead

or thing is specially characterized; that in which one is specially skilled; that in which one has studied to a high degree; a quality or attribute peculiar to a species.

specialization *n* the act of specializing or devoting to a particular use or function; special determination.

specialize *vt* (**specialized, specializing**) to assign a specific use or purpose to; to devote or apply to a specific use or function.—*vi* to engage in special study or occupation (used especially of students, medical practitioners, etc).

specially *adv* in a special manner; particularly; especially; for a particular purpose.

specialty *n* a particular point; that in which one is specially skilled in or good at; a speciality; (*law*) a special contract; an obligation or bond.

specie *n* gold or silver coined and used as a circulating medium; coin, as opposed to paper money.

species *n sing, pl* a kind, sort or variety; a class, collection or assemblage of things or beings classified according to attributes which are determined by scientific observation; a group of animals or plants which bear a close resemblance to each other in the more essential features of their organization and produce similar progeny, several species uniting to form a genus; (in logic) a group of individuals agreeing in common attributes and designated by a common name.

specific *adj* pertaining to, characterizing or constituting a species; marking something as a distinct species; tending to specify or particularize; particular; definite; precise; (*med*) possessed of peculiar efficacy in the cure of a particular disease.—*n* a remedy which exerts a special action in the prevention or cure of a disease; an infallible or supposed infallible remedy; something certain to effect the purpose for which it is used; an unfailing agent.

specifically *adv* in a specific manner; so far as concerns the species; definitely; particularly.

specification *n* the act of specifying; designation of particulars; particular mention; a statement describing the dimensions, details, etc, of any work about to be undertaken, as in building, engineering, etc; an article, item or particular specified.

specific gravity *n* the ratio of the weight of any given bulk of a substance to that of the same bulk of some standard substance, usually water for solids and liquids, air or hydrogen for gases.

specific heat *n* the ratio of the quantity of heat required to raise the temperature of a given mass of any substance through one degree to the quantity required to raise the same mass of a standard substance (water

speckled

spectacles

for solids and liquids, water or air for gases) through one degree.

specify *vt* (**specified, specifying**) to mention or name distinctively; to designate in words, so as clearly to distinguish or limit.

specimen *n* one of a number of similar things intended to show the character of the whole or of others not exhibited; a portion exhibited; a sample.

specious *adj* pleasing to the eye; superficially fair, just or correct; plausible; appearing well at first view (*a specious argument, a specious objection*).

speck *n* a spot; a small discoloured place in anything; a stain; a blemish; a small particle or patch.—*vt* to mark with small specks or spots.

speckle *n* a little spot in anything, of a different colour from that of the thing itself; a speck.—*vt* (**speckled, speckling**) to mark with small specks or spots.

speckled *adj* marked with specks or speckles; variegated with spots of a different colour from the ground or surface of the object.

spectacle *n* a show; something exhibited as worthy of being seen; a gorgeous or splendid show; anything seen; a sight; (*pl*) an optical instrument used to assist or correct some defect in the organs of vision, consisting of two lenses mounted in a light frame.

spectacular *adj* pertaining to or of the nature of a show or spectacle; impressive.

spectate *vi* (**spectated, spectating**) to be a spectator.

spectator *n* one who looks on; a beholder; one who is present at a play or spectacle.

spectral *adj* pertaining to a spectre; ghostlike; pertaining to spectra; pertaining to the solar or other spectrum.

spectre *n* an apparition; the disembodied spirit of a person who is dead; a ghost; a phantom.

spectroheliograph *n* an instrument for photographing the sun by monochromatic light.

spectrometer *n* (*physics*) a more elaborate form of spectroscope.

spectroscope *n* (*physics*) an instrument for producing and examining spectra, with the help of a collimator and a telescope.

spectroscopy *n* that branch of science which is concerned with the use of the spectroscope and with spectrum analysis.

spectrum *n* (*pl* **spectra**) an image of something seen, continuing after the eyes are closed, covered or turned away; the oblong figure or stripe, exhibiting the prismatic or rainbow colours or some of them, formed by a beam of light, as of the sun, received through a small slit and split up into its components of various wavelengths by means of a prism or a diffraction grating; any similar distribution of wave frequencies; a broad range of ideas, beliefs, emotions, etc.

speculate *vi* (**speculated, speculating**) to meditate; to consider a subject in its different aspects and relations; to theorize; to form hypotheses or opinions on the basis of little or no evidence; to undertake risky business or investments in the hope of making a large profit; to purchase goods, stock or other things with the expectation of an advance in price and of selling the articles with a profit by means of such advance; to engage in speculation.

speculation *n* mental view of anything in its various aspects and relations; contemplation; a theory or theoretical view; the laying out of money or incurring of extensive risks with a view to more than the usual success in trade; a hazardous commercial or other business transaction entered into in the hope of large profits.

speculative *adj* given to speculation; contemplative; pertaining to, involving or formed by speculation; theoretical; not verified by fact, experiment or practice; pertaining to, or given to, speculation in trade or finance.

speculator *n* one who speculates or forms theories; a theorizer; one who speculates in trade; one who incurs great risks in the hope of great gain.

speculum *n* (*pl* **specula, speculums**) a mirror or looking glass; (in optics) a reflecting surface, such as is used in reflecting telescopes, made of an alloy of copper and tin or of glass; (*surg*) an instrument with a reflecting mirror attached for examining certain openings of the body.

speech *n* the faculty of expressing thoughts by words or articulate sounds; the power of speaking; language; a particular language; the act of speaking with another; conversation; anything spoken; a discourse, oration or harangue.

speech day *n* annual school distribution of prizes, etc.

speechify *vi* (**speechified, speechifying**) to make a speech; to harangue.

speechless *adj* lacking or deprived of the faculty of speech; dumb; mute; not speaking for a time; silent.

speed *vi* (*pret, pp* **sped** *or* **speeded**, *ppr* **speeding**) to make haste; to move with celerity; to exceed the speed limit; to have success; to prosper; to succeed; to have any fortune, good or ill; to fare.—*vt* to despatch or send away in haste; to hasten; to accelerate; to expedite; to help forward; to make prosperous; to cause to succeed; to dismiss with good wishes or friendly services; to kill or destroy.—*n* a rapidity in moving, travelling, etc; excessive rapidity; (*sl*) any of various strong amphetamines.

speediness *n* the quality of being speedy; quickness; despatch.

speed limit *n* a legal maximum or minimum at which a vehicle may travel on specified roads.

speedometer *n* an instrument for indicating speed.

speedwell *n* any of various plants with small blue or white flowers.

speedy *adj* quick; nimble; rapid in motion; not dilatory or slow.

speleological *adj* pertaining to speleology.

speleology *n* the study and exploration of caves.

spell[1] *n* a charm consisting of some words of occult power; an incantation; any charm.—*vt* (*pret, pp* **spelled** *or* **spelt**, *ppr* **spelling**) to repeat, point out, write or print the proper letters of in their regular order; to form by letters; to read; to read with labour or difficulty (often with *out*); to act as a spell on; to fascinate; to charm.—*vi* to form words with the proper letters, either in reading or writing; to read.

spell[2] *n* a piece of work done by one person in relief of another,; a turn of work; a single period of labour; a period; a while or season.

spellbound *adj* bound as by a spell or charm.

spelling *n* the act of one who spells; orthography.

spelling bee *n* an assembly of people met for the purpose of exercising themselves or comparing their acquirements, in spelling.

spend *vt* (*pret, pp* **spent**, *ppr* **spending**) to lay out (money); to part with in purchasing; to exhaust (*to spend one's energies*); to waste; to pass, as time; to suffer to pass away; to exhaust of force or strength; to waste (*to spend efforts*).—*vi* to make expense; to spend money.

spender *n* one who spends; a prodigal; one who lavishes.

spendthrift *n* one who spends his or her means lavishly or improvidently; a prodigal (often used as an adjective, as *spendthrift ways*).

spent *pret, pp* of **spend**.—*adj* worn-out; wearied; exhausted; having deposited the spawn (said of a herring).

sperm *n* the seminal fluid of animals; semen; spawn of fishes or frogs; a microscopic male cell, usually motile.

spermaceti *n* a fatty material obtained from the sperm whale in the Pacific.

spermatic *adj* seminal; pertaining to the semen or conveying it.

spermatium *n* (*pl* **spermatia**) in fungi, a free non-motile male cell.

spermatoid *adj* sperm-like; resembling sperm or semen.

spermatophyte *n* any plant of the highest

phylum of plants, the seed plants or flowering plants.

spermatozoon *n* (*pl* **spermatozoa**) one of the microscopic animalcule-like bodies developed in the semen of animals and essential to impregnation; a male reproductive cell.

sperm cell *n* a cell in which spermatia are developed.

sperm oil *n* the oil of the sperm whale.

sperm whale *n* a large whale with a blunt head which was hunted for its oil and spermaceti.

spew *vt* to vomit; to eject from the stomach; to eject or to cast forth.—*vi* to vomit.

sphagnum *n* an important genus of mosses; peat moss, used for packing plants and formerly for dressing wounds.

sphenoid, sphenoidal *adj* resembling a wedge.—*n* a wedge-shaped body; the sphenoid bone.

sphenoid bone *n* a bone in the base of the skull, so named because it is wedged in amongst the other bones.

spheral *adj* pertaining to the spheres or heavenly bodies; rounded like a sphere.

sphere *n* a globular body; an orb or globe; a planet, star or sun; a solid body the surface of which in every part is equally distant from a point within it called its centre; the concave expanse of the heavens; circuit or range of action, knowledge or influence; a field of activity; compass; province; rank or order of society.—*vt* (**sphered, sphering**) to place in a sphere or among the spheres; to form into a sphere.

spherical, spheric *adj* having the form of a sphere; globular; pertaining or belonging to a sphere; relating to the orbs of the planets; planetary.

sphericity *n* the state or quality of being spherical; roundness.

spheroid *n* a body not perfectly spherical (*geom*) a solid generated by the revolution of an ellipse about one of its axes, being either oblate or prolate.

spheroidal, spheroidical *adj* having the form of a spheroid; (of a crystal) bounded by several convex faces.

spheroidicity *n* the quality of being spheroidal.

spherometer *n* an instrument for measuring the thickness of small bodies when great accuracy is required, as the curvature of optical glasses, etc.

spherule *n* a little sphere or spherical body.

spherulite *n* a variety of obsidian found in rounded grains.

sphinx *n* (*pl* **sphinxes**) (in Egyptian antiquity) a statue having the body of a lion and a human (male or female) or animal head; hence, a person who puts puzzling questions; a mysterious or enigmatic person; a name of the hawkmoths.

sperm whale

sphere

Sphinx *n* (*pl* **Sphinxes**) (in Greek myth) a she-monster often represented with the winged body of a lion and the breasts and head of a woman, said to have proposed a riddle to the Thebans and to have killed all who were not able to guess it, till Oedipus did so, whereupon the Sphinx slew herself; a massive sphinx at El Giza in Egypt.

sphragistics *n* the study of seals or signet rings, their history, peculiarities and distinctions.

sphygmic *adj* of or pertaining to the pulse.

sphygmograph *n* an instrument which, when applied over an artery, indicates the character of the pulse.

spicate *adj* (*bot*) having a spike or ear; eared like corn.

spice *n* a vegetable production, fragrant or aromatic to the smell and pungent to the taste, such as pepper, nutmeg, ginger, cinnamon and cloves, used in sauces and in cookery; (*fig*) a small admixture; a flavouring.—*vt* (**spiced, spicing**) to season with spice; to season, literally or figuratively.

spicery *n* spices collectively; a repository of spices.

spick-and-span *adj* very neat and clean.

spicula *n* (*pl* **spiculae**) (*bot*) a small spike or spikelet; a pointed, fleshy, superficial appendage.

spicy *adj* producing spice; abounding with spices; having the quality of spice; flavoured with spice; aromatic; (*fig*) pungent; piquant; keen.

spider *n* the common name of well-known arachnids, many of them remarkable for spinning webs for taking their prey.

spider monkey *n* a name given to many species of New World monkeys.

spiel *n* any glib or plausible talk, such as a salesman's prepared speech.

spigot *n* a pin or peg used to stop a faucet or a small hole in a cask of liquor.

spike *n* a large nail or pin; a piece of pointed iron like a long nail, as on the top of walls, gates, etc; a nail or instrument with which the vents of cannon were formerly filled up; a sharp metal projection on the sole of a running shoe; an ear of corn or other grain; (*bot*) a type of inflorescence in which the flowers are sessile along a common axis.—*vt* (**spiked, spiking**) to fasten with spikes or long nails; to set with spikes; to fix on a spike; (*colloq*) to add alcohol to; (*colloq*) to add drugs to.

spikelet *n* (*bot*) a small spike.

spikenard *n* an aromatic herbaceous plant of the East Indies, the root of which is highly prized for its aromatic properties; a name given to several other plants and to various fragrant essential oils.

spike oil *n* a volatile oil distilled from a species of lavender often called spikenard.

spiky *adj* in the shape of a spike; set with spikes.

spill[1] *vt* (*pret, pp* spilled *or* spilt, *ppr* spilling) to suffer to fall or run out of a vessel (applied to fluids and to substances whose particles are small and loose); to suffer or cause to flow out; to shed (*a man spills another's blood*); to throw from a horse or carriage; (*colloq*) to tell, to disclose.—*vi* to be shed; to be suffered to fall, to be lost or wasted.

spill[2] *n* a spigot; a small slip of wood or strip of paper rolled up, used to light a lamp, etc.

spin *vt* (*pret* spun *or* span, *pp* spun, *ppr* spinning) to draw out and twist into threads, either by the hand or machinery (*to spin wool, cotton or flax*); to draw out tediously (*to spin out a tale*); to extend to a great length; to whirl rapidly; to cause to turn with great speed (*to spin a top*); to form by the extrusion of a viscid fluid from their bodies, as spiders, silkworms, etc.—to spin a yarn to tell a long story.—*vi* to perform the act of making threads; to work at drawing and twisting threads; to move round rapidly; to whirl, as a top or a spindle; to run or drive with great rapidity; to go quickly.—*n* the act of spinning; a rapid run; a race; the rotation of an elongated projectile (a bullet or shell) about its long axis imparted to it by the rifling of the gun; a brief ride in a vehicle; an emphasis or slant imparted to information, proposals or policies.

spina bifida *n* a disabling congenital condition in which the spinal meninges protrude through their bony coverings.

spinach *n* a common annual plant, the young deep-green leaves of which are eaten in salads or cooked in various ways.

spinal *adj* pertaining to the spine or backbone of an animal.

spinal column *n* the backbone.

spinal cord, spinal marrow *n* the elongated mass of nervous matter contained in the osseous canal of the spine.

spindle *n* a slender rod by which the thread is twisted and wound in spinning; any slender pointed rod or pin which turns round or on which anything turns; an axis or arbour.

spindle legs, spindle shanks *n* long slender legs or a person having such.

spindle tree *n* a small tree found wild in Britain.

spin doctor *n* a person who imparts an emphasis or slant to information, proposals or policies.

spindrift *n* (*naut*) the blinding drift of salt water blown from the surface of the sea in hurricanes.

spine *n* the backbone of a vertebrate animal, so called from the thorn-like processes of the vertebrae; a thorn; a sharp process from the woody part of a plant; a stout, rigid and pointed process of the integument of an animal; a ridge of mountains, especially a central ridge; the part of the cover of a book which holds the pages together.

spine-chilling *adj* making one very frightened.

spinel *n* a species of corundum, which occurs in regular crystals and sometimes in rounded grains.

spineless *adj* lacking moral courage or resolution; weak-willed; lacking a spine.

spinet *n* a stringed musical instrument, which differed from the virginal only in being of a triangular form.

spinifex *n* an excessively spiny grass, growing in tussocks and covering large areas in Australia.

spinnaker *n* a triangular racing sail carried by yachts when running before the wind, on the opposite side to the mainsail.

spinner *n* one who or that which spins; a spider; a spinneret.

spinneret *n* one of the nipple-like organs with which spiders form their webs.

spinney *n* a small wood with undergrowth; a clump of trees; a small grove.

spinning jenny *n* the first spinning machine by which a number of threads could be spun at once (invented about 1767 by James Hargreaves).

spinning wheel *n* a machine for spinning wool, cotton or flax into threads by the hand.

spin-off *n* a product or benefit derived incidentally from existing research and development.

spinster *n* an unmarried woman.

spiny *adj* full of spines; thorny; like a spine; slender; perplexed; troublesome.

spiracle *n* a breathing hole; an aperture for exhalation or inhalation; one of the breathing pores or apertures of the breathing tubes of insects.

spiraea *n* any of a genus of plants with clusters of small pink or white flowers.

spiral *adj* winding round a fixed point or centre, like a watch spring; winding round a cylinder and at the same time rising or advancing forward, like a corkscrew; pointed or shaped like a spire.—*n* a curve which continually recedes from a centre or fixed point while continuing to revolve about it; a helix or curve which winds round a cylinder like a screw.

spire[1] *n* a body that shoots up to a point; the tapering portion of a steeple rising above the tower; a steeple; a stalk or blade of grass or other plant.

spire[2] *n* a winding line like the threads of a screw; a spiral; anything wreathed or contorted; a wreath; the convolutions of the

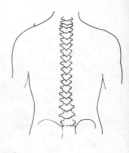

spine

spiral shell of a mollusc above the lowest or body whorl.

spirit *n* the intelligent, immaterial and immortal part of a human being; the soul, as distinguished from the body which it occupies; a person considered with respect to his or her mental or moral characteristics; the human soul after it has quitted the body; an apparition; a spectre; a ghost; a supernatural being; an angel, fairy, elf, sprite, demon, etc; vivacity, animation, ardour, enthusiasm, courage, etc; emotional state; mood; humour (often in the plural, as *to be in high* or *low spirits*); the vital or essential part of anything; inspiring or actuating principle; essence; real meaning; intent, as opposed to the letter or formal statement; a liquid obtained by distillation, especially alcohol; (*pl*) brandy, gin, rum, whisky or other distilled liquor containing much alcohol (*a glass of spirits*).—**animal spirits** liveliness of disposition; constitutional briskness and gaiety.—**the Spirit** the Holy Ghost.—*vt* to animate with vigour; to encourage; to convey away secretly, as if by the agency of a spirit; to kidnap.

spirited *adj* animated; full of life; lively; full of spirit or fire (*a spirited address*); having a spirit of a certain character (used in composition, as *high-spirited, low-spirited*).

spirit lamp *n* a lamp in which alcohol is used instead of oil.

spiritless *adj* lacking spirits; lacking courage or fire; depressed; pusillanimous.

spirit level *n* a glass tube nearly filled with spirit, for determining a line or plane parallel to the horizon, by the central position of an air bubble on its upper side.

spiritual *adj* pertaining to or consisting of spirit; not material; incorporeal; pertaining to the mind or intellect; mental; intellectual; pertaining to the soul or its affections as influenced by God; proceeding from or controlled and inspired by the Holy Spirit; holy; sacred; divine; relating to sacred things; not lay or temporal; ecclesiastical.—*n* a kind of religious song originated among the American Negroes in the southern USA.

spiritualism *n* the state of being spiritual; spiritual character; the doctrine of the existence of spirit as distinct from matter; that system of philosophy according to which all that is real is spirit, soul or mind, matter or the external world being either a succession of notions impressed on the mind by God or else a mere product of the mind itself; the belief that communication can be held with departed spirits by means of phenomena manifested through a person of special susceptibility, called a medium.

spirit level

spiritualist *n* one whose state is spiritual; an adherent of spiritualism; one who believes that intercourse may be held with departed spirits through the agency of a medium; one who pretends to hold such intercourse.

spirituality *n* the state or quality of being spiritual; spiritual character; what belongs to the church or to religion, as distinct from temporalities (generally in plural).

spirituous *adj* containing spirit as the characteristic ingredient; alcoholic.

spirt *vt* same as **spurt**.

spit[1] *vt* (*pret, pp* **spat** *or* **spit**, *ppr* **spitting**) to eject from the mouth; to eject or throw out with violence.—*vi* to throw out saliva from the mouth; (*colloq*) to rain slightly.—*n* what is ejected from the mouth; saliva.

spit[2] *n* a long pointed spike or prong of metal on which meat is roasted; a small point of land running into the sea; a long narrow shoal extending from the shore.—*vt* (**spitted, spitting**) to put on a spit; to thrust through; to pierce.

spitchcock *vt* to split an eel lengthways and grill or fry it.—*n* an eel split and grilled or fried.

spite *n* a disposition to thwart and disappoint the wishes of another; a feeling of ill-will or malevolence; a manifestation of malevolence or malignity; chagrin; vexation.—**in spite of** in defiance or contempt of; in opposition to all efforts of; notwithstanding.—*vt* (**spited, spiting**) to mortify; to thwart spitefully· to fill with spite or vexation.

spiteful *adj* filled with spite; having a malicious disposition; malignant; malicious.

spitfire *n* a violent or passionate person; one who is irascible or fiery.

spitting image *n* a person who is extremely like someone else.

spittle *n* the moist matter which is secreted by the salivary glands; saliva ejected from the mouth.

spittoon *n* a vessel to spit into.

splanchnic *adj* of or pertaining to the viscera.

splash *vt* to spatter with water or water and mud; to dash a liquid on or over; to spatter; to cast or dash in drops; to display prominently.—*vi* to strike and dash about water or something liquid.—*n* a small quantity of water, or water and dirt, thrown on anything; a stroke or fall of something in water; a noise from water dashed about; a spot of dirt or other matter; a blot; a daub; a prominent display; a sensation.

splatter *vi* to make a noise, as in water.

splay *vt* to dislocate or break a horse's shoulder bone; (*archit*) to slope or form with an angle, as the jambs or sides of a window.—*n* (*archit*) a sloped surface, as when the opening through a wall for a door, window, etc, widens inwards.—*adj* spreading out; turned outwards (*a splay foot*).

splay foot *n* a foot turning outward and with a flat under-surface; a flat foot.

spleen *n* a spongy glandular organ situated in the upper part of the abdomen, forming one of the ductless glands concerned in the elaboration of the blood, formerly supposed to be the seat of melancholy, anger or vexation; hence, anger; latent spite; ill humour; malice (*to vent one's spleen*); melancholy; low spirits; vapours.

splendid *adj* magnificent; gorgeous; dazzling; sumptuous; illustrious; grand; heroic; brilliant; noble; glorious.

splendour *n* great brightness, brilliant lustre; magnificence; pomp; parade; brilliance; glory; grandeur; eminence.

splenetic, splenetical *adj* affected with spleen; peevish.—*n* a person affected with spleen.

splice *vt* (**spliced, splicing**) to unite, as two end of rope, by interweaving the strands of the ends; to unite by overlapping, as two pieces of timber; (*colloq*) to unite in marriage.—*n* the joining of two ends of rope by interweaving the untwisted strands; the junction of two pieces of wood or metal by overlapping and fastening the ends.

splint *n* a splinter; (*surg*) a thin piece of wood or other substance, used to confine a broken bone when set or to maintain any part of the body in a fixed position; the splint bone of a horse; a disease affecting the splint bone.

splint bone *n* one of the two small bones extending from the knee to the fetlock of a horse, behind the shank bone.

splinter *n* a fragment of anything split or shivered off; a thin piece of wood or other solid substance rent from the main body; a splint.—*vt* to split or rend into splinters or long thin pieces; to shiver; to support by a splint.—*vi* to be split or rent into long pieces; to shiver.

splinter bar *n* a crossbar in front of a vehicle to which the traces of the horses are attached; also, the crossbar which supports the springs.

splinter group *n* a small group that has separated from the main body of an organization after a disagreement, etc.

split *vt* (*pret, pp* **split**, *ppr* **splitting**) to divide longitudinally or lengthways; to separate or part in two from end to end by force; to rive; to cleave; to tear asunder by violence; to burst; to rend; to divide or break into parts as by discord; to separate into parts or parties.—*vi* to part asunder, especially lengthways; to suffer disruption; to separate; to be divorced; to burst; to burst with laughter; to be dashed to pieces; to differ in opinion; to break up into parties; (*sl*) to inform on one's accom-

plices or divulge a secret; (*sl*) to run away, to leave.—*n* a crack, rent or straight fissure; a division or breach, as in a party; a flat strip of steel, cane etc; a cleft twig of willow, etc, used in basket-weaving.—*adj* divided; cleft; rent in two.

split infinitive *n* an infinitive with a word or words between 'to' and the verb.

split pea *n* a husked pea, split for cooking.

splotch *n* a spot or stain; a daub; a smear.

splotchy *adj* marked with splotches.

splurge *n* a showing off; great display or ostentation; an extravagant display of wealth; an occasion when a great deal of money is spent.—*vi* (**splurged, splurging**) to spend lavishly (on); to show off.

splutter *n* a bustle; a stir.—*vi* to speak hastily and confusedly; to sputter.

Spode *n* a fine variety of porcelain of which vases and ornaments are made.

spoil *vt* to plunder; to strip by violence; to rob; to seize by violence; to corrupt or vitiate; to mar; to render useless; to render less useful or valuable in some way; to injure fatally; to ruin; to destroy.—*vi* to practise plunder; to lose the valuable qualities; to be corrupted; (*colloq*) to be eager for (*to be spoiling for a fight*).—*n* that which is taken from others by violence; plunder; booty; the slough or cast skin of a snake or other animal.

spoiled, spoilt *adj* deprived of its valuable qualities; rendered useless; vitiated; destroyed; ruined.

spoke *n* the radius of a wheel; one of the bars which are inserted in the hub or nave and which serve to support the rim; the round of a ladder; one of the supporting rods of an umbrella.—**to put a spoke in one's wheel** to put an impediment in one's way; to thwart one's purpose or design.

spokesman, spokeswoman *n* (*pl* **spokesmen, spokeswomen**) a spokesperson.

spokesperson *n* one who speaks for another or others.

spoliate *vt* (**spoliated, spoliating**) to plunder; to pillage; to despoil.—*vi* to practise plunder; to commit robbery.

spoliation *n* the act of plundering; robbery; plunder.

spondaic *adj* pertaining to a spondee; composed of spondees.

spondee *n* a poetic foot of two long syllables, used in Greek and Latin poetry.

sponge *n* a name given to a class of animal growths or organisms belonging to the protozoans, also to the framework or skeleton of these bodies, which is composed of horny elastic fibres, soft, light and porous, easily compressible, readily imbibing fluids and as readily giving them out again on compression (in common domestic use); one who meanly lives on others; a sycophantic or cringing dependant; a parasite;

splint

sponge

(in baking) dough before it is kneaded and formed, when full of globules of carbonic acid, generated by the yeast; a light, fluffy cake; (in metallurgy) iron in a soft or pasty condition, as delivered from the puddling furnace.—**to throw in the sponge** to acknowledge that one is conquered or beaten; to submit (a phrase borrowed from the prize ring).—*vt* (**sponged, sponging**) to cleanse or wipe with a sponge; to efface; to destroy all traces of; to gain by sycophantic or mean arts.—*vi* to imbibe, as a sponge; to live as a parasite.

sponge cake *n* a light sweet cake.

spongy *adj* resembling a sponge; soft and full of cavities; of an open, loose, easily compressible texture.

sponsion *n* the act of becoming surety for another; an engagement made on behalf of a state by an agent not specially authorized.

sponsor *n* a surety; one who binds himself or herself to answer for another and is responsible for his or her default; a person who proposes or supports something; a person, business, etc, that finances or helps to finance a sport, cultural event, broadcast, etc, usually in return for advertising facilities; one who is surety for an infant at baptism; a godfather or godmother.

spontaneity *n* the quality of being spontaneous.

spontaneous *adj* proceeding from natural inclination and without constraint or external force; voluntary; acting by its own impulse, energy or natural law; self-originated.

spoof *n* a hoax; a joke; a light satire; a parody.

spook *n* (*colloq*) a ghost; a spy.—*vt* to frighten.

spooky, spookish *adj* (*colloq*) pertaining to spooks; ghostly; haunted; unearthly.

spool *n* a piece of cane or reed or a hollow cylinder of wood, etc, used to wind thread or yarn on; also, a cylinder for winding photographic and cinema film on.

spoon *n* a small domestic utensil, with a bowl or concave part and a handle, used at table for taking up and conveying to the mouth liquids and soft food; a kind of wooden-headed golf club.—*vt* to take up or out with a spoon or ladle; (in cricket) to hit a ball softly with the bat, affording an easy catch.—*vi* (*colloq*) to act in an amorous way, to cuddle and exchange kisses.

spoon

spoonbill *n* a wading bird of the heron family, so called from the shape of the bill, which is somewhat like a spoon at the end.

spoonful *n* as much as a spoon contains.

spoondrift *n* fine spray from the tops of waves; spindrift.

spoonerism *n* an inadvertent and usually

spoonbill

amusing transposition of sounds, e.g. *half-warmed fish* for *half-formed wish*.

spoor *n* the track or trail of a wild animal or animals.

sporadic *adj* separate; single; scattered; occurring here and there in a scattered manner.

sporangium *n* (*pl* **sporangia**) (*bot*) the case in which the spores of cryptogams are formed.

spore *n* (*bot*) the reproductive germ of a cryptogamic plant, as distinguished from a true seed; (*zool*) a minute germ of certain animal organisms.

sporogen *n* a plant producing spores instead of seed.

sporogonium *n* (*pl* **sporogonia**) in mosses, the spore-producing 'fruit'.

sporophyte *n* (*bot*) the asexual stage in the life history of a plant.

sporran *n* the fur or leather pouch worn by Highlanders in full dress in front of the kilt.

sport *n* a pastime or amusement in which a person engages; a game; a diversion; any activity for exercise or enjoyment, especially one involving physical skill and often organized with a set form, rules, etc, as football, cricket, tennis, etc; such activities collectively; amusement, fun or enjoyment experienced; jest, as opposed to *earnest*; mockery; derision; object of mockery; any plant or animal deviating from the normal or natural condition or type; a monstrosity; a person with a strong sense of fair play.—*vt* to divert; to make merry (used reflexively); to exhibit or wear in public.—*vi* to play; to frolic; to make merry; to trifle; to take part in a sport.

sporting *adj* belonging to or practising sport or sports; fair or honourable in competition.

sporting chance *n* a reasonable chance, given luck.

sportive *adj* engaging in sport; gay; frolicsome; playful; amorous; wanton.

sports *n* athletic games.

sportsman, sportswoman *n* (pl **sportsmen, sportswomen**) one who pursues the sports of the field; one skilled in hunting, shooting, fishing, etc; one with a strong sense of fair play.

spot *n* a mark on a substance made by foreign matter; a speck; a place discoloured; a stain on character or reputation; disgrace; reproach; blemish; a locality; any particular place; a small part of definite shape and different colour from the ground on which it is.—*vt* (**spotted, spotting**) to make a spot, speck or fleck on; to stain; to tarnish; to mark with spots of colour different from the ground; to note something as peculiar to, in order to identify; to catch with the eye; (*colloq*) to recognize.

spot-check *n* a sudden, random and unexpected examination of something.

spotless *adj* free from spots; free from stain or impurity; pure; unspotted; immaculate.

spotlight *n* a light with a strong, narrow beam, as used in the theatre; intense public attention.—*vt* (**spotlighted** *or* **spotlit**, **spotlighting**) to illuminate with a spotlight; to focus attention on.

spotted *adj* marked with spots.

spotted fever *n* cerebrospinal meningitis.

spouse *n* one joined in wedlock; a married person, husband or wife.

spout *n* a nozzle or projecting mouth of a vessel, used in directing the stream of a liquid poured out; a pipe or conduit; a pipe for conducting water as from a roof; a waterspout.—*vt* to pour out in a jet and with some force; to throw out through a spout or pipe; to utter at length and boringly; to mouth.—*vi* to issue in a strong jet; to run as from a spout; to spurt; to make a speech, especially in a pompous manner.

sprain *vt* to overstrain, as the muscles or ligaments of a joint so as to injure them but without dislocation.—*n* a violent straining or twisting of the soft parts surrounding a joint, without dislocation.

sprat *n* a small fish of the herring family found in great abundance on the British coasts.

sprawl *vi* to spread and stretch the body carelessly in a horizontal position; to lie or crawl with the limbs stretched out or struggling; to grow or spread irregularly or ungracefully.

spray[1] *n* water flying in small drops or particles, as by the force of wind or the dashing of waves or from a waterfall; the vapour from an atomizer.

spray[2] *n* a small shoot or branch (*a spray of pearls*, *diamonds*); the extremity of a branch; a twig; the small branches of a tree collectively.

spread *vt* (*pret*, *pp* **spread**, *ppr* **spreading**) to stretch or expand to a broader surface (a sheet, a carpet); to open out (the wings); to unfurl (a sail); to stretch; to cover by extending something; to overspread; to extend; to shoot to a greater distance in every direction (*a tree spreads its branches*); to put forth; to publish, as news or fame; to cause to be more extensively known; to propagate (a disease); to cause to affect greater numbers; to emit; to diffuse (perfume); to disperse; to scatter over a larger surface; to set and furnish with provisions.—*vi* to extend itself; to be extended or stretched; to be made known more extensively; to be propagated from one to another; to be diffused.—*n* the act of spreading or state of being spread; extent; compass; a table, as spread or furnished with a meal; (*colloq*) a feast.

spread-eagle *n* (*heral*) an eagle having the wings and legs extended on each side of the body; also 'an eagle with two heads displayed'.—*adj* (*also* **spread-eagled**) with the arms and the legs stretched out.

spree *n* a merry frolic; a drinking frolic; a carousal.

sprig *n* a small shoot or twig of a tree or other plant; a spray; an offshoot; a slip; a youth; a lad (used as a term of slight disparagement, as *a sprig of nobility*); an ornament resembling a sprig; a small square brad or nail without a head.

sprightly *adj* lively; spirited; brisk; airy; gay.

spring *vi* (*pret* **sprung** *or* **sprang**, *pp* **sprung**, *ppr* **springing**) to rise or come forth, as out of the ground; to shoot up, out or forth; to begin to appear; to come to light; to issue into sight or knowledge; to take rise or origin; to issue or originate, as from ancestors or from a country; to result, as from a cause, motive, principle, etc; to leap; to jump; to fly back by elastic force; to start; to start or rise suddenly from a covert; to shoot; to issue with speed and violence; to warp or become warped; to become cracked (as a mast).—*vt* to start or rouse, as game; to cause to rise from a covert; to produce quickly or unexpectedly; to propose on a sudden; to crack; to weaken by a crack in the timber (*to spring a mast*); to pass by leaping; to jump over (*to spring the fence*).—*n* a leap; a bound; a flying back of a body by its elasticity; elastic power or force; an elastic body, made of various materials, as a strip or wire of steel coiled spirally, a steel rod or plate, etc, which, when bent or forced from its natural state, has the power of recovering it again in virtue of its elasticity; (*fig*) that by which action is induced; mainspring; a natural fountain of water, owing its origin to the water which falls on the earth; an issue of water from the earth or the basin of water at the place of its issue; any source of supply; that from which supplies are drawn; one of the four seasons of the year (so called because plants *spring* or grow then); the vernal season; (*fig*) the first and freshest part of any state or time; a crack in a mast or yard running obliquely or transversely.

springbok

spring balance *n* a contrivance for weighing articles by observing the amount of deflection or compression which their weight produces on a steel spring properly adjusted.

springboard *n* an elastic board, used in vaulting, etc.

springbok *n* a species of antelope, related to the gazelle, common in South Africa.

spring-clean *vi* to clean or tidy thoroughly; to clean the whole house thoroughly in the spring.—*n* a thorough clean, especially of the whole house in the spring.

springe *n* a noose attached to a spring or elastic body so as to catch a bird or other animal; a gin; a snare.—*vt* to catch in a springe; to ensnare.

spring onion *n* an onion with a small bulb and long green shoots, usually eaten raw as part of a salad.

springer *n* one who springs; a breed of spaniel; (*archit*) the lowest voussoir or bottom stone of an arch; the bottom stone of the coping of a gable; the rib of a groined roof or vault.

springtail *n* an insect that can leap by means of an elastic caudal appendage.

springtide *n* the tide which happens at or soon after the new and full moon and which rises higher than common tides; the time or season of spring; springtime.

springtime *n* the spring; the vernal season.

springy *adj* having elasticity like that of a spring; elastic; light (*a springy step*); abounding with springs or fountains.

sprinkle *vt* (**sprinkled, sprinkling**) to scatter in drops or particles; to cast or let fall in fine separate particles; to strew; to besprinkle; to bestrew.—*n* a small quantity scattered; a sprinkling.

sprinkler *n* one who sprinkles; a device for sprinkling.

sprinkling *n* a small quantity falling in drops or particles; a small number or quantity scattered as if sprinkled.

sprint *n* a short race or run at high speed.—*vi* to run a race at full speed, especially over a short distance; to run at full speed.

sprit *n* a sprout; a small boom or spar which crosses the sail of a boat diagonally and thus extends and elevates it; also, the bowsprit of a vessel.

spritsail *n* a sail extended by a sprit; a sail, now disused, on a yard under a bowsprit.

sprite *n* a spirit; a kind of fairy, elf or goblin.

sprout *vi* to shoot, as the seed of a plant; to germinate; to push out new shoots.—*n* the shoot or bud of a plant; a fresh outgrowth from a plant or tree; (*pl*) Brussels sprouts.

spruce[1] *adj* neat or smart in dress; trim; smug; dandified.—*vt* (**spruced, sprucing**) to trim or dress in a spruce manner.—**to spruce up** to dress oneself sprucely or neatly.

spruce[2] *n* one of several species of trees of the pine family, yielding valuable timber, as the Norway spruce fir of Europe and the white spruce, the black spruce and the hemlock spruce of North America.

spry *adj* nimble; active; vigorous; lively.

spud *n* a straight narrow spade with a long handle for digging up weeds, etc; also, a small spade with a short handle; (*sl*) potato.

spur

spume *n* froth; foam; scum; frothy matter on liquors.—*vi* (**spumed, spuming**) to froth; to foam.

spumescence *n* frothiness.

spunk *n* touchwood; tinder; tinder made from a species of fungus; a quick, ardent temper; (*colloq*) mettle, pluck.

spur *n* an instrument having a rowel or little wheel with sharp points, worn on a rider's heels to prick the horses for hastening their pace; (*fig*) an incitement or stimulus; the hard pointed projection on a cock's leg which serves as an instrument of offence and defence; (*geog*) a mountain, or mountain mass, that shoots from another mountain mass and extends for some distance.—*vt* (**spurred, spurring**) to prick with spurs; to urge or encourage to action; to incite; to instigate; to impel; to stimulate; to put spurs on; to provide with spurs.—*vi* to spur one's horse to make it go fast; to ride fast; to press forward.

spurge *n* the common name of certain British plants, with an acrid milky juice powerfully purgative.

spurious *adj* not legitimate; not proceeding from the true source or from the source pretended; not genuine; counterfeit; adulterate.

spurn *vt* to drive back or away, as with the foot; to kick; to reject with disdain; to treat with contempt.—*vi* to kick or toss up the heels; to dash the foot against something; to manifest disdain or contempt in rejecting anything.—*n* disdainful rejection; contemptuous treatment.

spurred *adj* wearing spurs; having prolongations or shoots like spurs.

spurrey *n* a British plant growing in cornfields, etc, one species of which is cultivated as food for cattle.

spurt, spirt *vt* to throw out in a stream or jet, as water; to spout; to squirt.—*vi* to gush out.—*n* a forcible gush of liquid; a jet; a sudden extraordinary effort for an emergency; a short sudden act.

sputnik *n* any of the early man-made satellites used for space research.

sputter *vi* to emit saliva from the mouth in rapid speaking; to speak so rapidly as to emit saliva; to give out moisture (as green wood burning); to burn with some crackling or noise (as a candle).—*vt* to utter rapidly and with indistinctness; to jabber.

sputum *n* saliva and mucus; spittle; phlegm.

spy *vt* (**spied, spying**) to gain sight of; to discover at a distance or in concealment; to espy; to gain a knowledge of by artifice; to explore; to view and examine secretly.—*vi* to search narrowly; to scrutinize; to pry.—*n* a person who keeps a constant watch on the actions, motions, conduct, etc, of others; a secret emissary sent into the enemy's camp or territory to bring back intelligence.

spyglass *n* a telescope, especially a small telescope.

squab *adj* fat; short and stout; bulky; unfledged; not feathered.—*n* a young unfledged pigeon; a short fat person; a soft cushion.

squabble *vi* (**squabbled, squabbling**) to engage in a noisy quarrel; to quarrel and fight noisily; to brawl; to wrangle; to debate peevishly to dispute.—*n* a scuffle; a wrangle; a petty quarrel.

squad *n* any small party of people; (*milit*) a small number of soldiers assembled for drill or instruction.

squad car *n* a police patrol car.

squadron *n* a body of troops drawn up in a square; a body of cavalry consisting of four troops, each of three or four sections; a division of a fleet; a detachment of ships of war under the command of a commodore or junior flag officer.

squadron leader *n* an officer in the Royal Air Force, ranking with a major in the army.

squalid *adj* foul; filthy; extremely dirty.

squalor *n* foulness; filthiness; coarseness.

squall *vi* to cry out; to scream or cry violently.—*n* a loud scream; a harsh cry; a sudden and strong gust of wind; a sudden and vehement succession of gusts.

squally *adj* abounding with sudden and violent gusts of wind; gusty.

squama *n* (*pl* **squamae**) a scale or scaly part of plants; a horny scale on animals.

squamous, squamose *adj* covered with or consisting of scales; resembling scales; scaly.

squander *vt* to spend lavishly or profusely; to waste without economy or judgment.

square *adj* having four equal sides and four right angles; forming a right angle; having rectilinear and angular rather than curved outlines; fair, just or honest; adjusted so as to leave no balance (*to make accounts square*).—*n* a four-sided plane rectilinear figure, having all its sides equal and all its angles right angles; what nearly approaches this shape; a square surface; an area of four sides with houses on each side or on at least three; an instrument used by artificers, draughtsmen and others, for testing or describing right angles; (*arith, alg*) the number or quantity produced by multiplying a number or quantity by itself; (*milit*) a body of infantry formed into a rectangular figure with several ranks or rows of soldiers facing each side; (*sl*) a person considered to be conventional and old-fashioned.—*vt* (**squared, squaring**) to make square; to reduce or bring accurately to right angles and straight lines; to reduce to any given standard; to compare

with a standard; to adjust, regulate, accommodate, fit; to make even so as to leave no difference or balance; to settle (*to square accounts*); (*math*) to multiply by itself; (*naut*) to place at right angles with the mast or keel (*to square the yards*).—*vi* to suit; to fit; to accord or agree (*the facts do not square with the theory*).

squarely *adv* in a square form; fairly; honestly.

square number *n* the product of a number multiplied into itself.

square-rigged *adj* (*naut*) a term applied to a vessel most of whose sails are of a square shape and extended by yards suspended by the middle.

square root *n* (*arith, alg*) that root which being multiplied into itself produces the given number or quantity: thus, 8 is the square root of 64.

squash[1] *vt* to crush; to beat or press into pulp or a flat mass.—*n* something soft and easily crushed; something unripe and soft; a drink made with fruit juice or cordial as a base; an unripe pea pod; a crowd or crowded gathering; a sudden fall or shock of a heavy soft body; a variety of rackets, played with a soft ball.

squash[2] *n* a plant, a kind of gourd, cultivated in America as an article of food.

squat *vi* (**squatted, squatting**) to sit down on the buttocks or heels; to sit close to the ground; to cower, as an animal; to settle on land, especially public lands, without any title or right; to enter an unoccupied house unofficially and live there without paying rent.—*vt* to put on the buttocks or heels (used reflexively).—*adj* sitting close to the ground; cowering; short and thick, like the figure of an animal squatting.—*n* the posture of one who squats; a house that is occupied by squatters.

squatter *n* one that squats; one that settles on unoccupied land, particularly public land, without a title; one who occupies an unoccupied house unofficially and lives there without paying rent.

squaw *n* among American Indians, a female or wife.

squawk *vi* to cry with a loud, harsh voice.

squeak *vi* to utter a sharp, shrill cry; to cry with an acute tone, as a pig, a mouse, etc; or to make a sharp noise, as a wheel, a door, etc; to break secrecy.—*n* a sharp, shrill cry or noise.

squeal *vi* to cry with a sharp, shrill voice, as certain animals do.—*n* a shrill, sharp cry; a squeak.

squeamish *adj* having a stomach that is easily turned; easily nauseated; excessively nice as to taste; fastidious; easily disgusted; scrupulous.

squeegee *n* a long-handled implement with a rubber blade used for cleaning floors,

square

spyglass

washing windows, etc; a small roller used for drying photographs.

squeeze *vt* (**squeezed, squeezing**) to press between two bodies; to press closely; to crush; to clasp closely; to hug; to press lovingly; to oppress so as to make to give money; to harass by extortion; to force by pressure.—*vi* to press; to press among a number of persons; to pass by pressing.—*n* an application of pressure; a compression; a hug or embrace.

squelch *n* a flat heavy fall; sound of suction made in walking through mud, clay, etc.—*vi* to make a splashing, sucking sound.

squib *n* a small firework which sparkles and then explodes.

squid *n* an edible mollusc related to the cuttlefish, with a long body and ten arms.

squiggle *n* a short wavy line.

squill *n* a plant allied to the hyacinths, onions, etc, with a bulbous root used in medicine as a diuretic and expectorant; a crustacean; a kind of shrimp.

squint *adj* looking obliquely or askance; not having the optic axes coincident (said of the eyes); having distorted sight.—*vi* to look obliquely with the eyes; to have the axes of the eyes not coincident; to be affected with strabismus, to have an indirect reference.—*vt* to turn (the eye) to an oblique position; to cause to be squint.—*n* an oblique look; an affection of the eyes in which the optic axes do not coincide.

squire *n* the title of a gentleman next in rank to a knight; an attendant on a knight; the knight's shield or armour bearer; (*colloq*) a devoted male attendant on a woman; a beau; a gallant; a country gentleman.

squirm *vti* to move like a worm or eel, with writhing or contortions.—*n* a wriggling motion.

squirrel *n* any of various species of rodent mammals, mostly living in trees and distinguished by their powers of leaping and their usually long and bushy tails.

squirt *vt* to eject from a narrow pipe or orifice in a stream.—*vi* to be ejected in a rapid stream; to spurt.—*n* an instrument with which a liquid is ejected in a stream; a syringe; a small jet.

stab *vt* (**stabbed, stabbing**) to pierce or wound with a pointed weapon; to kill by a pointed weapon; to drive in; to pierce in a figurative sense; to inflict keen or severe pain on.—*vi* to aim a blow with a pointed weapon; to be extremely cutting.—*n* the thrust of a pointed weapon; a wound with a sharp-pointed weapon; keen, poignant pain; (*colloq*) an attempt (*a stab at the right answer*).

stability, stableness *n* the state or quality of being stable or firm; strength to stand without being moved or overthrown; steadiness or firmness of character; a con-

squirrel

dition of equilibrium in which a body tends to return to its position of rest when disturbed.

stabilize *vt* (**stabilized, stabilizing**) to give a stable character or value to (e.g. prices or the relation of the franc to the dollar).

stabilizer *n* a device for stabilizing (an aircraft, ship, bicycle, etc); something which stabilizes, such as a substance to limit or control chemical changes, etc, in other substances.

stable[1] *adj* firmly established; not to be easily moved, shaken or overthrown; firmly fixed or settled; steady in purpose; firm in resolution; not fickle or wavering; abiding; durable.

stable[2] *n* a building constructed for horses (rarely beasts generally) to lodge and feed in and furnished with stalls and necessary equipment.—*vt* (**stabled, stabling**) to put or keep in a stable.—*vi* to dwell or lodge in a stable; to dwell, as beasts; to kennel.

staccato *adj* (*mus*) a direction to perform the notes of a passage in a crisp, detached, distinct or pointed manner.

stack *n* corn in the sheaf, hay, straw, etc, piled up in a for keeping; a pile, as of wood, formerly of a specified measure; a pile of indefinite quantity; a number of funnels or chimneys standing together; a single tall chimney; the funnel of a locomotive or steam vessel; a high rock detached; a columnar rock rising out of the sea.—*vt* to pile or build into the form of a stack; to make into a large pile.

stadium *n* (*pl* **stadia, stadiums**) a sports ground, usually surrounded by raised banks of seats for spectators.

staff *n* (*pl* **staves, staffs**) a stick carried in the hand for support; a walking stick; (*fig*) that which props or upholds; a support; a stick used as a weapon; a straight stick used as symbol of office; a baton; a rod with a curved head belonging to a bishop; the long handle of an instrument or weapon; (*surv*) a graduated stick used in levelling; (*naut*) a light pole on which to hoist and display the colours; (*mus*) the five parallel lines, and the four spaces between them, on which notes and other musical characters are placed; (*milit*) a body of officers whose duties refer to an army or regiment as a whole and who are not attached to particular subdivisions; a number of persons, considered as one body, assisting in carrying on any undertaking (*the editorial staff of a newspaper, a hospital staff*, etc).

stag *n* the male red deer or a generic name of the red deer; the male of the hind; a hart (sometimes applied particularly to a hart in its fifth year; commercial slang, an outside irregular dealer in stocks, not a member of the exchange.

stag beetle *n* one of the largest of the British insects, distinguished by the enormous size of the horny and toothed mandibles in the males.

stage *n* a floor or platform elevated above the ground or a common surface, as for an exhibition of something to public view; a scaffold; a staging; the raised platform or floor on which theatrical performances are exhibited; hence, *the stage*, the theatre, the dramatic profession, the drama; the scene of any noted action or affair; a place of rest on a journey, as where a relay of horses is taken; a station; the distance between two places of rest on a road (*a stage of 15 miles*); a single step of a gradual process; degree of advance or progression, an increase or decrease, in rising or falling; a coach or other carriage running regularly from one place to another; a stagecoach; a wooden landing place at a quay or pier; a landing stage.—*vt* (**staged, staging**) to put on the theatrical stage.

stagecoach *n* formerly, a coach that ran by stages; a coach that ran regularly between two places for the conveying passengers.

stage door *n* the door giving access to the stage and the parts behind it in a theatre.

stage manager *n* one who superintends the production and performance of a play and who regulates all matters behind the scenes.

stage-struck *adj* smitten with a love for the stage; seized by a passionate desire to become an actor.

stage whisper *n* a loud whisper; what is spoken on the stage in a subdued voice meant to indicate a whisper but loud enough to be heard by the audience; an aside.

stagey *adj* pertaining to the stage; theatrical, in a depreciatory sense.

stageyness *n* the character or quality of being stage; theatricality.

stagger *vi* to sway helplessly to one side and the other in standing or walking; to reel; to cease to stand firm; to hesitate; to become less confident or determined.—*vt* to cause to doubt and waver; to make to hesitate; to make less confident; to strike as incredible; to amaze; to arrange working hours so that employees enter and leave their place of work at intervals in batches, instead of simultaneously.—*n* a sudden swing or reel of the body, as if the person were about to fall; divergence from straightness, as when spokes or rivets are arranged on the two sides of a median line or, in an aeroplane, when the leading edge of one plane falls behind that of the other; (*pl*) a disease of horses and cattle attended with reeling or giddiness.

staging *n* a temporary structure for support, as in building; scaffolding.

stagnant *adj* not flowing; not running in a current or stream; standing; hence, impure from lack of motion; inactive; dull; not brisk (*trade is stagnant*).

stagnate *vi* (**stagnated, stagnating**) to cease to run or flow; to have no current, as water; to become impure from lack of current; to cease to be brisk or active; to become dull, quiet or inactive (as trade).

stagnation *n* the condition of being stagnant; the state of being without flow or circulation; the stage of being very dull or inactive (as trade).

stag party *n* a party for men only, usually one given for a man who is going to be married.

staid *adj* sober; grave; steady; sedate; not volatile, flighty or fanciful.

stain *vt* to discolour by the application of foreign matter; to make foul; to spot; to colour, as wood, glass, etc, by a chemical or other process; to tinge with colours; to impress with figures or patterns in colours different from the ground (*to stain paper for hangings*); to soil or sully with guilt or infamy; to tarnish; to bring reproach on.—*vi* to take stains; to become stained or soiled; to grow dim.—*n* a spot; discoloration from foreign matter; taint of guilt or evil; blot; blemish; disgrace; reproach; shame.

stainless *adj* free from stains or spots; free from the reproach of guilt; unblemished; immaculate.

stainless steel *n* steel alloyed with some element, frequently chromium, so as to prevent corrosion.

stair *n* a succession of steps rising one above the other arranged as a way between two points at different heights in a building, etc (used often in plural in same sense while the singular is also employed to mean a single step).

staircase *n* the part of a building which contains the stairs.

stair

stake¹ *n* a piece of wood sharpened at one end and set in the ground or prepared for setting, as a support to something, as part of a fence, etc; the post to which one condemned to die by fire was fastened (*to suffer at the stake*).—*vt* (**staked, staking**) to set and plant like a stake; to fasten, support or defend with stakes.—**to stake out** to mark the limits of by stakes (*to stake out land*); to put under surveillance.

stake² *n* that which is pledged or wagered; that which is laid down to await the issue of a contest, to be gained by victory or lost by defeat; something hazarded; the state of being pledged or put at hazard (preceded by *at*, as *his honour is at stake*).—*vt* (**staked, staking**) to pledge; to lay down as a stake; to hazard on the issue of a competition or on a future contingency.

stake

stakeholder *n* one who holds stakes or with whom the stakes are deposited when a wager is laid.

stalactite *n* a mass of calcareous matter, usually in a conical or cylindrical form, pendent from the roofs of caverns and produced by the filtration of water containing particles of carbonate of lime through fissures and pores of rocks.

stalagmite *n* a deposit of calcareous matter on the floor of a cavern, sometimes rising into columns, which meet and blend with the stalactites above.

stale *adj* vapid or tasteless from age; having lost its life, spirit and flavour from being long kept; not new; not freshly made (*stale bread*); no longer interesting, from use or long familiarity; trite; common; musty.—*vt* (**staled, staling**) to make vapid, useless, cheap or worthless; to wear out.

stalemate *n* in chess-playing, the position of the king when so situated that, though not in check, he cannot move without being placed in check, there being no other available move (in this case the game is drawn); deadlock.—*vt* (**stalemated, stalemating**) to subject to a stalemate in chess; to bring into a position where nothing further can be done by either side; to bring into a situation of deadlock.

stalk[1] *n* the stem or main axis of a plant; the pedicel of a flower or the peduncle that supports the fructification of a plant; anything resembling a stalk.

stalk[2] *vi* to walk softly or in a stealthy manner; to walk behind a stalking horse; to pursue game by approaching softly and warily behind a cover; to walk in a lofty or dignified manner; to pace slowly.—*vt* in sport, to pursue stealthily; to watch and follow warily for the purpose of killing.—*n* a high, proud, stately step or walk.

stalked *adj* (*zool*) applied to crustaceans such as the lobster, shrimp and crab, which have the eyes set at the end of foot stalks.

stalking *n* in sport, the act of approaching game softly and warily, taking advantage of the inequalities of the ground, etc.

stalking horse *n* a means of concealing one's true intentions; a horse or dummy-horse behind which a hunter stands.

stall *n* the place where a horse or an ox is kept and fed; the division or compartment of a stable or cow house for one horse or ox; a bench or kind of table in the open air on which anything is exposed to sale; a small booth in which merchandise is exposed for sale or an occupation carried on (*a butcher's stall*); a fixed seat in the choir or chancel of a cathedral, church, etc, and mostly appropriated to some dignitary; a seat in the front part of the ground floor in the auditorium of a theatre; in mining, an opening made between pillars in the direc-

stamp

tion that the work is progressing or transversely.—*vt* to put into a stall or stable; to keep in a stall; to bring to a standstill unintentionally, e.g. a horse, carriage, motor or aeroplane.—*vi* to live as in a stall; to dwell.

stall-feed *vt* to fatten in a stall or stable (*to stall-feed an ox*).

stallion *n* a horse not castrated; an entire horse.

stalwart *adj* brave; bold; daring; tall and strong; large and strong in frame.

stamen *n* (*pl* **stamens, stamina**) (*bot*) the male organ of fructification in plants, situated immediately within the petals and composed in most cases of three parts, the filament, the anther and the pollen, of which the two latter are essential, the other not.

stamina *n* whatever constitutes the principal strength or support of anything; power of endurance; staying power; long-lasting strength or vigour.

stammer *vi* to make involuntary breaks or pauses in speaking; to hesitate or falter in speaking; to speak with stops and difficulty; to stutter.—*vt* to utter with hesitation or imperfectly (frequently with *out*).—*n* defective utterance; a stutter.

stammering *n* the act of one who stammers; defective articulation.—*adj* characterized by a stammer; stuttering.

stamp *vt* to strike or press forcibly by thrusting the foot downward; to impress with some mark or figure; to mark with an impression; to imprint; to fix deeply; to coin or mint; to affix a stamp (as a postage or receipt stamp) to; to cut out with a stamp; to crush by the downward action of a kind of pestle, as ore in a stamping mill.—**to stamp out** to extinguish, as fire, by stamping on with the foot; hence, to extirpate; to eradicate; to suppress at once by strong measures.—*vi* to strike the foot forcibly downward.—*n* the act of stamping; an instrument for making impressions on other bodies; a mark imprinted; an official mark set on things chargeable with some duty or tax, showing that the duty is paid (often used as a means of raising revenue); a small piece of stamped paper used by government; a postage stamp; an instrument for cutting materials (as paper, leather, etc) into various forms by a downward pressure; general character fixed on anything (*bears the stamp of genius*); sort or character (*a man of the same stamp*); (in metallurgy) a kind of hammer for crushing or beating ores to powder.

stamp collector *n* a collector or receiver of stamp duties; one who collects rare or foreign stamps.

stamp duty *n* a tax imposed by governments on many types of legal instrument.

stampede *n* a sudden fright seizing large bodies of cattle or horses on the prairies and causing them to run for long distances. —*vi* (**stampeded, stampeding**) to take sudden flight, as if under the influence of panic terror.—*vt* to cause to break off in a stampede.

stance *n* a standing place; position (for a stall at market, etc); in golf, etc, the position of the player when making a stroke.

stanch *vt, adj* same as **staunch**.

stanchness *n* same as **staunchness**.

stanchion *n* a prop or support; a post or beam used for a support; an upright post or beam of different forms in ships.

stand *vi* (*pret, pp* **stood**, *ppr* **standing**) to be stationary or at rest in an upright position; to be set upright; to be on end; to be as regards position or situation; to have its site or locality; to cease from progress; to come to a state of rest; to stop; to pause; to halt; to continue or remain without injury; to last; to endure; to maintain one's ground or position; to maintain a fixed or steady attitude; to persevere; to persist; to insist; to be placed as regards rank or order (*a stands first*); to be in a particular state or condition; to be (*how stands the matter?*); to be in the stead or place; to be equivalent (*v stands for 5*); to become a candidate; to hold a certain course, as a ship; to be directed towards any local point, to measure from feet to head or from bottom to top; to stagnate; to be valid; to have efficacy.— **stand to** (*milit*) to stand to arms; to assemble fully armed in preparation for an attack (in trench warfare this was done daily at dawn and dusk).—*vt* to place on end; to endure; to sustain; to bear; to await; to undergo.—*n* a cessation of progress, motion or activity; a stop; a halt; a point or condition beyond which no further progress is made; a state of hesitation or perplexity; a place or post where one stands; a station; a halt made for the purpose of resisting an attack; a small table or frame, on or in which articles may be put for support (*an umbrella stand*) or on which goods may be exposed for sale (*a fruit stand*); a place in a town where carriages, taxis, etc, stand ready for hire; an erection or raised platform for spectators at open-air gatherings.—**stand of arms** a rifle with its usual appendages, as a bayonet, etc.

standard *n* a flag or ensign set up and round which soldiers rally or under which they unite for a common purpose; a flag or carved symbolical figure, etc, erected on a long pole or staff; a banner (the heraldic standard is a long, narrow pennant with a gold or parti-coloured fringe); that which is established by competent authority as a rule or measure of quantity; a measure or weight by which others are to be regulated and adjusted; that which is established as a rule or model by public opinion, custom or general consent; that which serves as a test or measure (*a standard of morality* or *of taste*); (*hortic*) a tree or shrub which stands singly and not attached to any wall or support; (*bot*) the upper petal or banner of a papilionaceous corolla; (in carpentry) any upright in a framing.—*adj* serving as a standard; capable of satisfying certain conditions fixed by competent authority; fixed; settled; (*hortic*) not trained on a wall, etc.

standard-bearer *n* one who bears a standard.

standardize *vt* (**standardized, standardizing**) to accept as a standard; to make in certain fixed or standard sizes, qualities, etc.

standby *n* a person or thing held in readiness for use in an emergency, etc; a passenger with a stand-by ticket.—*adj* kept in readiness or reserve; of an airline ticket, issued immediately before a journey; of a passenger, travelling with a stand-by ticket.

standing *adj* permanent; not temporary; lasting; not transitory; stagnant; not flowing; fixed; not movable; remaining erect; not cut down.—*n* the act of one who stands; duration of existence (*a custom of long standing*); station; place to stand in; power to stand; condition in society; relative position; rank; reputation.

stand-off *n* deadlock; stalemate.

standpoint *n* a fixed point or station; a basis or fundamental principle; a position or point of view from which a matter is considered.

St Andrew's Cross *n* the Scottish flag, a silver cross on a blue ground.

standstill *n* a standing at rest; a stop.

stannary *adj* relating to tin works.—*n* a tin mine; tin works.

Stannary Court *n* a court in Devonshire and Cornwall for the administration of justice among those involved in tin mining.

stannic *adj* pertaining to tin; containing tin.

stanza *n* a number of lines of poetry connected with each other and properly ending in a full point or pause; a part of a poem containing every variation of measure in that poem and successively repeated.

staple[1] *n* the principal commodity grown or manufactured in a country, district or town; the principal element of or ingredient in anything; the chief constituent; the material or substance of anything; raw or unmanufactured material; the thread or pile of wool, cotton or flax (*wool of a long* or *coarse staple*).—*adj* pertaining to or being a mart or staple for commodities; mainly occupying commercial enterprise;

standard

established in commerce (*a staple trade*); chief; principal; regularly produced or made for market.—*vt* (**stapled, stapling**) to sort or adjust the different staples of, as wool.

staple[2] *n* a loop of iron formed with two points to be driven into wood, etc, to hold a hook, pin, bolt, etc.—*vt* (**stapled, stapling**) to join with staples.

stapler *n* a dealer in staple commodities; one employed in assorting wool according to its staple; a machine that staples.

star *n* any celestial body except the sun and moon; more strictly, one of those self-shining bodies constituted like the sun, situated at immense distances from earth and, like the sun, the centres of similar systems, distinctively called *fixed stars* (as different from planets); one of the planets in astrology, supposed to have influence over a person's life; that which resembles a star; a figure with points radiating like the spokes of a wheel; an ornamental figure rayed like a star worn on the breast to indicate rank or honour; a radiated mark in writing or printing; an asterisk, thus *, used as a reference to a note in the margin or to fill a blank in writing or printing where letters or words are omitted; a person of brilliant qualities; a brilliant film, theatrical or operatic performer.—*vt* (**starred, starring**) to set or adorn with stars; to bespangle; to have or present in the leading role.—*vi* to shine as a star; to be in the leading role.

starboard *n* (*naut*) the right-hand side of a ship looking towards the stem or prow (opposed to *port* or old *larboard*).—*adj* pertaining to the right-hand side of a ship; being or lying on the right side.

starch *n* a substance universally diffused in the vegetable world and forming the greater part of all farinaceous substances; this substance as prepared for commerce, chiefly extracted from wheat flour or potatoes and employed for stiffening linen or other cloth; (*fig*) stiffness of a person's behaviour or manner.—*vt* to stiffen with starch.

Star Chamber *n* in English history, a court of civil and criminal jurisdiction which inflicted often arbitrary and cruel punishments.

starched *adj* stiffened with starch; stiff; precise; formal.

starchy *adj* consisting of starch; resembling starch; stiff; formal in manner.

stare *vi* (**stared, staring**) to look with fixed eyes wide open; to gaze, as in admiration, surprise, horror, impudence, etc.—*vt* to affect or abash by gazing at; to look earnestly or fixedly at.—*n* the act of one who stares.

starfish *n* a marine animal which has the

staple

starfish

form of a star, with five or more rays radiating from a central disc.

stargazer *n* one who gazes at the stars; an astrologer.

staring *adj* gazing fixedly; fixed.—*adv* staringly; so as to stare wildly (*stark, staring mad*).

stark *adj* stiff; rigid, as in death; strong; rugged; powerful; mere; pure; downright (*stark nonsense*).—*adv* wholly; entirely (*stark mad, stark naked*).

starless *adj* having no stars visible or no starlight.

starlight *n* the light proceeding from the stars.—*adj* lighted by the stars.

starlike *adj* resembling a star; bright; lustrous.

starling *n* an insessorial bird of a family allied to the crows, found in almost all parts of Europe, capable of being taught to whistle tunes and even to speak.

starlit *adj* lighted by stars.

starred *adj* studded or adorned with stars; influenced by the stars (*ill-starred*); marked with a star to indicate importance.

starry *adj* abounding with stars; adorned with stars; consisting of or proceeding from stars; stellar; resembling stars; stellate.

star shell *n* a shell containing a number of stars that ignite and make a display when the shell bursts, serving to reveal the position of the enemy.

star-spangled *adj* spotted with stars.

start *vi* to move suddenly and spasmodically; to make a sudden and involuntary motion of the body, caused by surprise, pain or any sudden feeling; to shrink; to wince; to make a sudden or unexpected change of place; to spring up; to change condition at once; to set out; to commence a course, as a race, a journey, etc; to shift or spring from a fixed position; to be dislocated.—*vt* to rouse suddenly from concealment; to cause to flee or fly (*to start a hare*); to begin; to set going; to originate (*to start an enterprise, a newspaper*); to cause to jump from its place; to make to lose its hold (*to start a nail*); to dislocate.—*n* a sudden involuntary twitch, spring or motion, caused by surprise, fear, pain, etc; a sudden change of place; a quick movement; a bursting forth; a sally; a spasmodic effort; a beginning of action or motion; the setting of something going; first motion from a place; first motion in a race; the outset; a career opening.

startle *vi* (**startled, startling**) to move with a start or spasmodically; to start.—*vt* to excite by sudden alarm, surprise or apprehension; to alarm.—*n* a start of alarm.

startling *adj* such as to startle with fear or surprise; alarming; shocking.

starvation *n* the state of starving or being

starved; a suffering extremely from cold or lack of food.

starve *vi* (**starved, starving**) to perish with or suffer extremely from hunger; to suffer from want; to perish or suffer extremely from cold; to be hard put to it through lack of anything.—*vt* to kill or distress with hunger; to subdue by famine; to destroy by want; to kill, afflict or destroy with cold; to deprive of force or vigour.

starveling *adj* hungry; lean; pining with want.—*n* an animal or plant that is thin and weak through lack of nutriment.

stasis *n* a stoppage in the flow of bodily fluids, such as blood; a state of balance or inactivity.

state *n* condition as determined by whatever circumstances; the condition or circumstances of a being or thing at any given time; situation; position; rank, condition or quality; royal or gorgeous pomp; appearance of greatness; dignity; grandeur; a certain division of the community partaking in the government of their country; an estate (of the realm); a whole people united into one body politic; a commonwealth; the power wielded by the government of a country; the civil power (*the union of church and state*); one of the commonwealths or bodies politic which together make up a federal republic.—*adj* public; belonging to the community or body politic (*state affairs, state policy*).— *vt* (**stated, stating**) to express the particulars of; to set down in detail; to explain particularly; to narrate; to recite.

statecraft *n* the art of conducting state affairs; statesmanship.

stated *adj* settled; established; fixed (*stated hours* or *times*).

stateliness *n* the condition or quality of being stately; loftiness of mien; dignity.

stately *adj* august; lofty; majestic; magnificent.

statement *n* the act of stating; that which is stated; a narrative; a recital; the expression of a fact or of an opinion.

state-of-the-art *adj* using the most advanced technology possible.

state prisoner *n* one confined for a political offence.

stateroom *n* a magnificent room in a palace or great house; a private cabin, generally for two persons, in a steamer.

statesman *n* (*pl* **statesmen**) a person versed in the arts of government; a politician.

statesmanship *n* the qualifications of a statesman; political skill.

state trial *n* a trial of a person or persons for political offences.

statics *n* that branch of dynamics which treats of the properties and relations of forces in equilibrium, the body on which they act being in a state of rest.

station *n* the spot or place where anything stands, particularly where a person habitually stands or is appointed to remain for a time; post assigned; situation; position or locality; condition of life; social position; the place where the police force of any district is assembled when not on duty; a building or buildings on a railway for the reception of passengers and goods intended to be conveyed and where trains stop.—*vt* to assign a station or position to; to post; (*refl*) to take up a post or position.

stationariness *n* the quality of being stationary; fixity.

stationary *adj* remaining in the same station or place; not moving; fixed; remaining in the same condition.

stationer *n* one who sells paper, pens, pencils, ink and various other materials connected with writing.

stationery *n* the articles usually sold by stationers, as the various materials employed in connection with writing.

station master *n* the official in charge of a railway station.

statistics *n* a collection of facts which admit of numerical statement and of arrangement in tables, especially facts illustrating the physical, social, moral, intellectual, political, industrial and economic condition of communities or classes of people; that department of political science which deals with such facts; (*colloq*) a woman's bust, waist and hip measurements (*vital statistics*).

statistician *n* one skilled in statistics.

statuary *n* the art of carving or making statues, a branch of sculpture; statues regarded collectively; one that professes or practises the art of making statues.

statue *n* a lifelike representation of a human figure or animal in some solid substance, as marble, bronze, iron, wood; a sculptured cast or moulded figure of some size and in the round.

statuesque *adj* partaking of or having the character of a statue.

statuette *n* a small statue; a statue smaller than nature.

stature *n* the natural height of an animal body; bodily tallness (generally used of the human body); level of achievement.

status *n* (*pl* **statuses**) standing or position as regards rank or condition; position of affairs.

status quo *n* the condition in which the thing or things were at first.

status symbol *n* a possession, such as an expensive, car, etc, which is considered to indicate the owner's wealth, social position, etc.

statute *n* a law proceeding from the government of a state; an enactment of the legislature of a state; especially one passed by a

statuette

body of representatives; a written law; a permanent rule or law of a corporation.

statute book *n* a register of statutes; the statute book, the whole statutes of a country.

statute law *n* a statute; also, collectively, the enactments of a legislative assembly, as opposed to *common law*.

statutory *adj* enacted by statute; depending on statute for its authority.

staunch, stanch *vt* to prevent the flow of, as of blood; to stop the flow of blood from; to dry up.—*vi* to stop, as blood; to cease to flow.—*adj* strong and tight; sound; firm in principle; steady; hearty; loyal (*a staunch republican, a staunch friend*).

staunchness, stanchness *n* the state or quality of being staunch; strongness and soundness; firmness in principle.

steam

stave *n* a pole or piece of wood of some length; one of the thin narrow pieces of timber of which casks, tubs, buckets, etc, are made; a stanza; a verse; (*mus*) the staff.—*vt* (*pret, pp* **staved** *or* **stove**, *ppr* **staving**) to break in a stave or staves of or to break a hole in (in this sense *pret* and *pp* may be **stove**); to furnish with staves.—**to stave off** (*lit*) to push off with a staff; to keep away; to put off; to delay.

staves *n* the plural of **staff** as well as of **stave**.

stay[1] *vi* (*pret, pp* **stayed** *or* **staid**, *ppr* **staying**) to remain, continue or be in a place; to abide; to dwell; to delay; to tarry; to be steady or firm; to continue in a state; to remain; to wait; to forbear to act; to stop; to come to a stand.—*vt* to prop or support; to make to stop; to stop; to cause to cease (*to stay operations*); to delay; to keep back; to abide; to wait for; to await.—*n* a continuance in a place; abode for a time; continuance in a state or condition; stand; stop; obstacle; obstruction; a prop; a support; a piece in some structure performing the office of a brace or tie; (*pl*) a tightly fitting garment, stiffened with whalebone or other material, worn by women on the upper portion of the body; a bodice; a corset (so called from the support it gives to the figure).

steam engine

stay[2] *n* (*naut*) a strong rope used to support a mast and leading from the head of one mast down to some other or to some part of the vessel.

stead *adj* place or room which another had or might have (preceded by *in*, as, *David died and Solomon reigned in his stead*), hence, instead.

steadfast *adj* fast fixed; firm; constant or firm in resolution; resolute; not fickle or wavering.

steadfastness *n* the state of being steadfast; firmness of mind or purpose; constancy; resolution.

steading *n* a farm building; a holding.

steady *adj* firm in standing or position; firmly fixed; constant in mind or pursuit; not fickle; regular; constant; uniform.—*vt* (**steadied, steadying**) to make steady; to hold or keep from shaking, reeling or falling; to support firmly.—*vi* to become steady; to regain or maintain an upright position.

steak *n* a slice of meat or fish, etc, grilled or cut for grilling.

steal *vt* (*pret* **stole**, *pp* **stolen** *or* **stole**, *ppr* **stealing**) to take and carry away feloniously; to take clandestinely without right or leave; to gain or win by address or gradual and imperceptible means; to perform secretly; to try to accomplish clandestinely (*to steal a look*).—*vi* to practise or be guilty of theft; to withdraw or pass secretly; to slip unperceived; to go or come furtively.

stealing *n* the act of one who steals; theft.

stealth *n* the act of stealing; a secret or clandestine method of procedure; a proceeding by secrecy.

stealthy *adj* done by stealth; accompanied by efforts at concealment; done furtively; furtive; sly.

steam *n* the vaporous or gaseous substance into which water is converted under certain circumstances of heat and pressure; the elastic aeriform fluid generated by heating water to the boiling point; popularly, the visible moist vapour which rises from water and from all moist and liquid bodies when subjected to the action of heat.—*vi* to give out steam or vapour; to rise in a vaporous form; to pass off in visible vapour; to sail by the agency of steam.—*vt* to expose to steam; to apply steam to.

steamboat *n* a ship moved by the elastic power of steam acting on machinery.

steam boiler *n* a strong metallic vessel of iron or steel plates riveted together, in which water is converted into steam for supplying steam engines, etc.

steam engine *n* an engine in which the elastic or expansive force of steam is made available as a source of motive power in the arts and manufactures and in locomotion.

steamer *n* a steamship; a road-steamer; a fire engine the pumps of which are worked by steam; a vessel in which articles are subjected to the action of steam.

steam gauge *n* a gauge attached to a boiler to indicate the pressure of steam; a pressure gauge.

steam packet *n* a packet or vessel propelled by steam and running between certain ports.

steam power *n* the power of steam mechanically applied.

steamship, steam vessel *n* a ship propelled by steam.

steamy *adj* consisting of or abounding in steam; vaporous; misty; (*colloq*) sexy; (*colloq*) erotic.

stearic *adj* pertaining to stearine.

stearic acid *n* an acid abundant in fats.

stearine, stearin *n* the chief ingredient of suet and tallow or the harder ingredient of animal fats, olein being the softer one.

steatite *n* a mineral consisting of magnesia and alumina, used in the manufacture of porcelain, in polishing marble, in the composition of crayons, etc; soapstone.

steed *n* a horse; a horse for state or war (a word used chiefly in poetry and poetical or picturesque prose).

steel *n* iron combined with a small portion of carbon, capable of showing great hardness and elasticity and used in forming various kinds of instruments, edge-tools, springs, etc; (*fig*) a weapon, as a sword, spear, etc; a kind of steel file for sharpening knives; a piece of steel for striking sparks from flint to ignite tinder or match; used to typify extreme hardness; sternness; rigour (*a heart of steel*).—*adj* made of steel; resembling steel; unfeeling; rigorous.—*vt* to overlay, point or edge with steel; to make hard or stubborn; to render insensible or obdurate (*to steel one's heart against mercy*).

steeliness *n* the state of being steely; great hardness.

steeling *n* the welding of a piece of steel on that part of a cutting instrument which is to receive the edge; the covering of a metal plate (as an engraved copper plate) with steel electrolytically to render it more durable.

steel plate *n* a plate or broad piece of steel; a plate of polished steel on which a design is engraved; the print taken from such plate.

steely *adj* made of or resembling steel; hard; stubborn.

steelyard *n* an instrument for weighing bodies, consisting essentially of a lever of unequal arms, the body to be weighed being applied at the shorter arm, while a weight is made to balance the body by being moved along the longer arm at a proper distance from the fulcrum.

steenbok *n* a species of antelope of South Africa.

steep[1] *adj* ascending or descending with great inclination (as a roof, a slope); precipitous (hill, rock, etc).—*n* a precipitous place; a bold projecting rock; a precipice.

steep[2] *vt* to soak in a liquid; to macerate; to extract the essence of by soaking (often used figuratively, as *steeped to the lips in misery*).—*n* something that is steeped or used in steeping; that in which things are steeped.

steeple *n* a lofty erection attached to a church, town house or other edifice and generally intended to contain its bells; a tower surmounted by a spire.

steeplechase *n* a horse race across country in which obstacles have to be jumped as they come in the way (so called because originally a church steeple or other conspicuous object served as a goal).

steepled *adj* furnished with a steeple; having steeples.

steeplejack *n* a person employed to repair steeples, tall chimneys, etc.

steepness *n* the state of being steep; precipitousness.

steer[1] *vt* to direct and govern the course of by the movements of the helm; to control or govern; to direct; to guide.—*vi* to direct a vessel by the helm; to direct one's course at sea; to take a course at the direction of the helm; (*fig*) to take or pursue a course in life.

steer[2] *n* a young male of the common ox or ox kind.

steerage *n* the steering of a ship; the hinder or stern part of a ship; that part of a ship allotted to passengers paying a lower fare.

steering committee *n* a committee that organizes the content and order of business for a legislative assembly.

steersman *n* (pl **steersmen**) one that steers; the helmsman of a ship.

stele, stela *n* (pl **steles, stelae**) an upright slab of stone with inscriptions dating from prehistoric times; a small column without base or capital, serving as a monument, a milestone, etc; a sepulchral slab or column; the vascular tissue in the stems and roots of plants.

stellar *adj* pertaining to stars; starry; full of stars; set with stars.

stellate, stellated *adj* resembling a star; radiated; (*bot*) arranged in the form of a star.

stem[1] *n* the principal body of a tree, shrub or plant of any kind; the firm part which supports the branches; the ascending axis, as opposed to the root or descending axis; the stalk; also, a peduncle, pedicel or petiole or leaf stem; the stock of a family; a race or generation of progenitors; anything resembling the stem of a plant; (*mus*) the vertical line added to the head of a note.

stem[2] *n* a curved piece of timber or combination of pieces to which the two sides of a ship are joined at the fore end; the prow; the forward part of a vessel.—*vt* (**stemmed, stemming**) to make way against by sailing or swimming; to press forward through; to dash against with the stem.

stem[3] *vt* (**stemmed, stemming**) to dam up; to stop; to check, as a stream or moving force.

stench *n* an unpleasant smell; a stink.

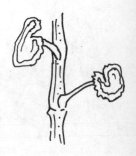

stem

stencil *n* a thin plate of metal, leather or other material, which has a pattern cut through it and which is laid flat on a surface and brushed over with colour so as to mark the surface below.—*vt* (**stencilled, stencilling**) to form by means of a stencil; to paint or colour with stencils.

stenographer *n* one who is skilled in the art of shorthand writing.

stenography *n* a generic term which embraces every system of shorthand.

stenosis *n* (*pl* **stenoses**) an abnormal narrowing of a bodily passage or orifice.

stentorian *adj* extremely loud or powerful (*a stentorian voice*); able to utter a very loud sound.

step *vi* (**stepped, stepping**) to move the leg and foot in walking; to advance or recede by a movement of the foot or feet; to go; to walk; especially, to go a little distance and with a limited purpose (*to step aside*); to advance or come as it were by chance or suddenly (*to step into an inheritance*).—*vt* (*naut*) to fix the foot of, as of a mast; to erect in readiness for setting sail.—*n* a pace; an advance made by one removal of the foot in walking; one remove in ascending or descending a stair; the distance between the feet in walking or running; a small space or distance; a grade in progress or rank; a forward move; a higher grade of rank; print or impression of the foot; footprint; gait; manner of walking; sound of the feet; footfall; a proceeding; one of a series of proceedings; measure (*to take steps in a matter*); a foot piece for ascending or descending from a carriage; the round of a ladder; (*pl*) a self-supporting ladder with flat steps; a stepladder, much used indoors; (*naut*) a block or a solid piece supporting the heel of a mast.

stepbrother *n* a brother by being a stepfather's or stepmother's son by a former wife or husband.

stepchild *n* the child of a husband or wife by a former wife or husband.

stepdaughter *n* the daughter of a husband or wife by a former wife or husband.

stepfather *n* a mother's second or subsequent husband.

stepladder *n* a portable ladder usually having flat steps and its own means of support attached.

stepmother *n* a father's second or subsequent wife.

step-parent *n* a stepfather or stepmother.

steppe *n* a name applied to those extensive plains which stretch across the southeast of European Russia, round the shores of the Caspian and Aral Seas and occupy the low lands of Siberia.

stepping stone *n* a raised stone in a stream or in a swampy place to keep the feet dry in crossing; an aid by which an end may be accomplished or an object gained; an assistance to progress.

stepsister *n* a stepfather's or stepmother's daughter by a former wife or husband.

stepson *n* the son of a husband or wife by a former wife or husband.

stereo *n* a hi-fi or record player with two loud-speakers; stereophonic sound.

stereophonic *adj* of or relating to sound reproduction through two distinct sound sources.

stereoscope *n* an optical instrument which blends two images viewed from a slightly different aspect into a single three-dimensional picture.

stereoscopic *adj* pertaining to a stereoscope; adapted to a stereoscope.

stereotype *n* a metal plate, presenting on its upper surface a facsimile of a page of arranged types, being cast in a papier mâché, stucco or other mould obtained from these types and being used to print from in the same way, thus saving the types and allowing them to be used afresh at once; a person or thing considered to represent a set or conventional type.—*adj* relating to the art of stereotyping or printing from stereotypes.—*vt* (**stereotyped, stereotyping**) to make a stereotype of; to prepare for printing by means of stereotype plates; (*fig*) to fix firmly or unchangeably; to consider a person as a stereotype.

stereotyped *adj* made or printed from stereotype plates; formed in a fixed, unchangeable manner (*stereotyped opinions*); conventional, conforming to a stock image.

sterile *adj* unfruitful; not fertile; barren; producing no young; not capable of producing young; not germinating; barren of ideas; lacking sentiment; (*bot*) bearing only stamens.

sterility *n* the state of being sterile; unfruitfulness; barrenness.

sterilize *vt* (**sterilized, sterilizing**) to make sterile or barren; to destroy the germs or microbes in.

sterlet *n* a small species of sturgeon.

sterling *adj* an epithet by which English money is distinguished, signifying that it is of the standard value (*a pound sterling*); hence, genuine; undoubted; of excellent quality (*a work of sterling merit*).

stern[1] *adj* severe, as regards facial expression; austere of aspect; gloomy; severe of manner; pitiless; harsh; rigidly steadfast; immovable.

stern[2] *n* the hind part of a ship or boat.

sternly *adv* in a stern manner; with an austere or stern countenance.

sternmost *adj* farthest in the rear; farthest astern.

sternness *n* the state or quality of being stern; severity of look; severity or harshness of manner; rigour.

stepladder

sternpost *n* a principal piece of timber in a vessel's stern.

sternutation *n* the act of sneezing.

stertorous *adj* characterized by a deep snoring, such as frequently accompanies apoplexy (*a stertorous breathing*).

stet *n* (*print*) a word written on proofs to signify that something which has been deleted or altered is after all to remain.

stethoscope *n* an instrument of a tubular form used by medical people for listening to sounds within the thorax and other cavities of the body.

stevedore *n* one whose occupation is to stow goods, packages, etc, in a ship's hold; one who loads or unloads vessels.

stew *vt* to boil slowly in a moderate manner or with a simmering heat.—*vi* to be boiled in a slow gentle manner or in heat and moisture; (*colloq*) to fret or worry.—*n* a dish cooked by stewing; (*colloq*) a state of agitation or excitement.

steward *n* a person employed on a large estate or establishment to manage the domestic concerns, superintend the other servants, keep the accounts, etc; one who has affairs to superintend for another; an officer of state (*the lord high steward of England*, one of the ancient great officers of state); a man who waits on passengers in a ship, aircraft, etc; a man who organizes or manages the details of a race, meeting, etc.

stewardess *n* a female steward; a female who waits on women in passenger vessels, etc.

stewardship *n* the office or functions of a steward.

St George's Cross *n* the English flag, a red cross on a white ground.

stich *n* a verse, of whatever measure or number of feet; a line of writing.

stick *n* a piece of wood of indefinite size and shape; a branch of a tree or shrub cut or broken off; a rod or wand; a staff; a walking stick; anything shaped like a stick (*a stick of sealing wax*); (*print*) a composing stick; (*colloq*) punishment; a joystick; (*pl*) (*colloq*) the outlying area of a town or city.

stick *vt* (*pret, pp* **stuck**, *ppr* **sticking**) to thrust so as to wound or penetrate; to fasten by piercing (*to stick a pin*); to thrust in; to attach by causing to adhere to the surface; to fix; to set; to fix in; to set with something inserted; to fix on a pointed instrument.—*vi* to cleave to the surface, as by tenacity or attraction; to adhere; to be fixed by being thrust in; to remain where placed; to cling; to be hindered from making progress; to be brought to a stop by some impediment; to scruple; to hesitate (often with *at*).

sticker *n* one who sticks (*a billsticker*).

stickiness *n* the quality of being sticky; viscousness; glutinousness.

sticking plaster *n* an adhesive plaster for dressing minor wounds.

stickleback *n* the popular name for certain very small British fishes found in ponds and streams and having spines on their backs, remarkable for building nests.

stickler *n* a person who is obstinate or scrupulous about something, often of little consequence.

sticky *adj* having the quality of adhering to a surface; gluey; viscous.

stiff *adj* not easily bent; not flexible; rigid; not liquid or fluid; thick and tenacious; drawn very tight; tense; not supple; not working smoothly or easily (*stiff joints*); not natural and easy; cramped; constrained (*a stiff style of writing*); haughty and unbending; formal in manner; blowing strongly; violent; not easily subdued; obstinate; stubborn; containing a good deal of spirits (*a stiff glass of grog*); (*naut*) bearing a press of canvas without careening much.

stiffen *vt* to make stiff; to make less pliant or flexible.—*vi* to become stiff or stiffer; to become more rigid or less flexible; to become less susceptible of impression; to grow more obstinate.

stiffener *n* one who or that which stiffens; a piece of stiff material inside a neckcloth.

stiffening *n* the act of making stiff; something that is used to make a substance stiff.

stiff neck *n* a condition of the neck in which movement causes extreme pain, due to rheumatism of the muscles on the side of the neck.

stiff-necked *adj* stubborn; inflexibly obstinate.

stiffness *n* the state or quality of being stiff; lack of pliability, suppleness or flexibility; rigidity; tension; stubbornness; formality or constraint of manner, expression or writing.

stifle[1] *vt* (**stifled, stifling**) to kill by impeding respiration; to suffocate or greatly oppress by foul or close air; to smother; to deaden (flame, sound); to suppress or conceal; to repress; to keep from being known.—*vi* to suffocate; to perish by suffocation.

stifle[2] *n* the joint of a horse next to the buttock and corresponding to the knee in human beings.

stigma *n* (*pl* **stigmas, stigmata**) a brand impressed with a red-hot iron on slaves and others; any mark of infamy; a brand of disgrace which attaches to a person; a natural mark on the skin; (*bot*) the upper extremity of the style and the part which in impregnation receives the pollen; (*entomol*) one of the apertures in the bodies of insects communicating with the air vessels; (*pl*

stick

St George's Cross

stigmata) marks said to have been supernaturally impressed on the bodies of certain persons in imitation of the wounds on the crucified body of Christ (*the stigmata of St Francis*).

stigmatize *vt* (**stigmatized, stigmatizing**) to mark with a stigma or brand; to set a mark of disgrace on; to call or characterize by some opprobrious epithet.

stilbite *n* a mineral of a shining pearly lustre; a kind of zeolite.

stile[1] *n* a step or series of steps, or a frame of bars and steps, for ascending and descending in getting over a fence.

stile[2] *n* the gnomon on the face of a dial to form the shadow.

stiletto *n* (*pl* **stilettos**) a small slender dagger; a pointed tool for piercing holes in leather, etc; a high heel tapering to a point on a woman's shoe.

still[1] *adj* silent; noiseless; not loud; soft; low (*a still small voice*); quiet or calm; without agitation; motionless; not sparkling or effervescing.—*vt* to bring to silence; to make quiet; to check or restrain; to appease or allay.—*adv* to this time; now no less than before; in future no less than formerly; always; time after time; continually; nevertheless; in spite of what has occurred; yet; in an increasing degree; even yet (very common with comparatives, as *still more*).

stiletto

still[2] *n* an apparatus for distilling or separating, by means of heat, volatile matters from substances containing them and recondensing them into the liquid form; a distillery.—*vt* to distil.

stillborn *adj* dead at the birth; abortive; produced unsuccessfully.

still house *n* a building containing a still.

still life *n* (*pl* **still lifes**) inanimate objects, such as flowers, furniture, fruit, etc, represented by the painter's art.

stillness *n* the state or quality of being still; freedom from noise or motion; calmness; quiet; silence.

still room *n* an apartment for distilling; a domestic laboratory; an apartment where liquors, preserves, etc, are kept.

stilly *adj* still; quiet.—*adv* silently; without noise; calmly; quietly.

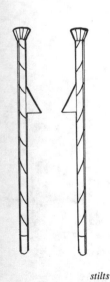

stilts

stilt *n* a long piece of wood with a rest for the foot, used in pairs for walking with the feet raised above the ground; a wading bird of no great size having remarkably long slender legs, whence its name.

stilted *adj* elevated as if on stilts; hence, pompous; inflated; stiff and bombastic (said of language); unnaturally formal.

Stilton *adj* applied to a well-known and highly esteemed solid, rich, white cheese, originally made at Stilton, Huntingdonshire but now chiefly made in Leicestershire.—*n* Stilton cheese.

stimulant *adj* serving to stimulate.—*n* that which stimulates; a stimulus; an agent which produces a quickly diffused and transient increase of energy in an organism or some part of it (often applied distinctively alcoholic or drugs).

stimulate *vt* (**stimulated, stimulating**) to excite or animate to action by some pungent motive or by persuasion; to spur on; to incite, instigate, rouse; to excite greater vitality or keenness in; to produce a quickly diffused and transient increase of vital energy and strength of action in.—*vi* to act as a stimulus.

stimulation *n* the act of stimulating; the effect produced.

stimulative *adj* having the quality of stimulating.—*n* that which stimulates.

stimulus *n* (*pl* **stimuli**) something that acts as an incentive; an agent that arouses or provokes a response in a living organism.

sting *vt* (*pret, pp* **stung**, *ppr* **stinging**) to pierce with the sharp-pointed organ with which certain animals and plants are furnished; to poison or goad with a sting; to give acute mental pain (*stung with remorse* or *taunts*); (*sl*) to cheat, such as by overcharging.—*vi* to use a sting, as a bee.—*n* a sharp-pointed weapon which certain insects possess and which they can thrust out from the hinder part of the body; a somewhat similar appendage of other animals, as scorpions; the thrust of a sting into the flesh; anything that gives acute pain; the biting, sarcastic or cutting effect of words; the point, as in an epigram; that which gives acute mental pain; an impulse; a stimulus; (*bot*) a hair which secretes a poisonous fluid, which, when introduced under the skin of animals, produces pain; (*sl*) a swindle.

stinginess *n* the quality of being stingy; mean covetousness; niggardliness.

stingray *n* a fish allied to the rays having a sharp bony spine on its tail.

stingy[1] *adj* extremely close-fisted and covetous; meanly avaricious; niggardly; scanty.

stingy[2] *adj* having power to sting; stinging.

stink *vi* (*pret, pp* **stank** or **stunk**, *ppr* **stinking**) to emit a strong offensive smell; (*fig*) to be in bad odour; to have a bad reputation.—*n* a strong offensive smell; a stench.

stinkpot *n* an earthen pot filled with a stinking combustible mixture, formerly used in attacking an enemy's vessel at sea.

stint *vt* to restrict to a scanty allowance; to limit or make scanty.—*vi* to cease; to stop; to desist.—*n* limit or restraint set or observed; restriction as to quantity (*to give money without stint*).

stipend *n* any periodical payment for services, especially the income of an ecclesiastical living.

stipendiary *adj* receiving wages or salary; performing services for a stated compensation.—*n* one who performs services for a settled salary or stipend (*a stipendiary magistrate*).

stipple *vt* (**stippled, stippling**) to engrave by means of dots, in distinction from engraving in lines.—*n* engraving by means of dots.

stipulate *vi* (**stipulated, stipulating**) to make an agreement or covenant to do or forbear anything; to contract; to settle terms; to bargain; to set as a condition.

stipulation *n* the act of stipulating; a contracting or bargaining; a point or matter settled by agreement; a particular article or item in a contract; a condition.

stipule *n* (*bot*) a small leaf-like appendage to a leaf commonly situated at the base of the petiole in pairs, either adhering to it or standing separate.

stir *vt* (**stirred, stirring**) to move or make to change place in any manner; to agitate the particles of; to bring into debate; to moot; to incite to action; to instigate; to excite; to awaken; to rouse, as from sleep; to agitate.—*vi* to move oneself; to change place; to be in motion; not to be still; to be on foot; to be already out of bed.—*n* agitation; tumult; bustle; public disturbance or commotion; excitement.

stir-fry *vt* (**stir-fried, stir-frying**) to cook (chopped vegetables, meat, poultry, etc) by stirring rapidly in hot oil in a wok or frying-pan.—*n* a dish cooked in this way.

stirk *n* a bullock or heifer between one and two years old.

stirrer *n* one who stirs or is in motion; one who or that which puts in motion; one who incites or excites; an instigator.

stirring *adj* active in business; bustling; animating; rousing; exciting.

stirrup *n* a strap hanging from a saddle and having at its lower end a suitable appliance for receiving the foot of the rider, used to assist persons in mounting a horse; hence, anything resembling in shape and functions the stirrup of a saddle.

stirrup cup *n* a cup of liquor presented to a rider on having mounted his or her horse at parting.

stitch *vt* to sew; to sew by passing the needle through and through in a continuous line; to unite together by sewing.—*vi* to practise stitching; to practise needlework.—*n* a single pass of a needle in sewing; a single turn of the thread round a needle in knitting; (*agric*) a furrow or ridge; a sharp pain in the side.

stithy *n* (*arch*) an anvil.

stoa *n* (*pl* **stoas, stoae**) (*Greek archit*) a porch or portico.

stoat *n* a small European mammal related to the weasel, the ermine.

stock *n* the stem or trunk of a tree or other plant; the stem in which a graft is inserted or that furnishes grafts; a block; hence, what is lifeless and senseless (*stocks and stones*); a principal supporting or holding part in certain implements or tools; the wooden support to which the barrel, etc, of a rifle or like firearm is attached; the bar or crosspiece at the upper end of the shank of an anchor; the original race or line of a family; the progenitors and their direct descendants; lineage; family; the property which a merchant, tradesman or company has invested in any business; capital invested in some commercial business or enterprise and contributed by individuals jointly; money funded in government securities at a fixed rate of interest (*3 per cent stock*); a fund lent to a government and forming part of the national debt; supply provided; store, provision, hoard; (*agric*) the collective animals used or reared on a farm or such animals collectively (*prices of stock are low*); a kind of stiff band or cravat worn round the neck; liquor in which meat, bones, vegetables, etc, have been boiled, used to form a foundation for soups and gravies; a garden plant of various species, with a very sweet smell; (*pl*) an instrument of punishment formerly used for petty offenders, consisting of a wooden frame in which their ankles or wrists were confined; (*pl*) the frame of timbers on which a ship is supported while building.—*vt* to lay up in store; to put aside or accumulate for future use; to provide or furnish with stock; to supply with stock (*to stock a farm*, *a warehouse*).—*adj* kept in stock; constantly ready for service; standing; permanent (*a stock play*, *a stock jest*).—*vi* to branch out into shoots or sprouts (applied to grasses or other plants).

stockade *n* (*fort*) a fence or barrier constructed by planting upright in the ground trunks of trees or rough piles of timber; an enclosure made with posts.

stockbreeder *n* a person who breeds live stock or domestic animals.

stockbroker *n* a broker who purchases and sells stocks or shares for his or her customers.

stock dove *n* a wild pigeon of Europe, probably so called because it lives in stocks of trees.

stock exchange *n* the building, place or mart where stocks or shares are bought and sold; an organized association of brokers or dealers in stocks.

stockfish *n* fish, as cod, etc, split open and dried in the sun without salting.

stockholder *n* one who is a proprietor of stock in the public funds or in any joint-stock company.

stoat

stocking *n* a close-fitting covering for the foot and leg, usually knitted from woollen, cotton, silk, nylon, etc, thread.

stockjobber *n* one who speculates or gambles in stocks or whose occupation is to buy and sell stocks or shares.

stockpot *n* (in cookery) a pot in which stock for soups or gravies is boiled.

stockstill *adj* still as a fixed post; perfectly still.

stocktaking *n* a periodical examination and valuation of the stock or goods in a shop, warehouse or other business premises.

stocky *adj* short and sturdy.

stodge *n* (*colloq*) heavy, starchy food.

stodgy *adj* indigestible; heavy and solid; dull; boring.

stoep *n* a veranda in front of a house in South Africa.

stoic *n* an apathetic person or one who is indifferent to pleasure or pain; a person who shows fortitude or self-control in situations involving pain, distress, adversity, etc.

Stoic *n* a disciple of the philosopher Zeno, who founded a sect about 308 BC, teaching that people should strive to be free from passion, unmoved by joy or grief and submit without complaint to the unavoidable necessity by which all things are governed, regarding virtue as the highest good.—*adj* pertaining to the Stoics or their teaching.

stoical *adj* pertaining to a stoic; able completely to repress feeling; manifesting or maintaining indifference to pleasure or pain; showing stoicism; having or show fortitude in adversity, etc.

stoicism *n* the opinions and maxims of stoics; the qualities of a stoic; the state of being stoic.

stoke *vt* (**stoked, stoking**) to supply a fire with fuel and attend to its combustion.—*vi* to act as a stoker.

stoker *n* one who feeds and trims a furnace or large fire.

stole *n* a long narrow band or scarf with fringed ends, worn by some ecclesiastics; a similar band or scarf worn round the shoulders by women.

stolid *adj* slow in intellect; dull; heavy; stupid.

stolidity *n* the state or quality of being stolid; dullness; stupidity.

stomach *n* a membranous receptacle in animal bodies, which is the principal organ of digestion and in which food is prepared for yielding its nourishment to the body; a specialized cavity for the digestion of food in some of the simpler forms of animals; the desire of food caused by hunger; appetite; inclination; liking.—*vt* to bear without open resentment or without opposition; to brook (*to stomach an affront*).

stomacher *n* formerly, an ornamental covering for the breast, forming part of a woman's dress.

stomachic, stomachal *adj* pertaining to the stomach; strengthening the stomach; exciting the action of the stomach.—*n* a medicine that strengthens the stomach and excites its action.

stomach pump *n* a small pump used in medical practice for emptying the stomach, as when a patient has taken an overdose of drugs.

stone *n* a hard concretion of some species of earth or mineral matter, as lime, clay, etc, being usually a mass of no great size and generally movable, as opposed to a rock which is a solid and immovable portion of the earth's crust; the material obtained from stones or rocks; the kind of substance they produce (*a house built of stone*); (*fig*) a type of hardness or insensibility (*a heart of stone*); a concretion in the kidneys or bladder; the disease arising from such; a testicle; the nut of a drupe or stone fruit; a common measure of weight, the English standard stone being 14 pounds avoirdupois, though other values are in regular use; (*print*) the imposing stone.—*adj* made of stone; like stone; pertaining to stone.—*vt* (**stoned, stoning**) to pelt with stones; to free from stones (*to stone raisins*).

Stone Age *n* the long period in the development of Man when weapons and tools were first made from stone before the use of metals was discovered.

stone-blind *adj* blind as a stone; perfectly blind.

stonechat *n* a bird of the family of warblers, common in Europe and often seen about heaps of stone in waste places.

stonecrop *n* any of a genus of plants that grow on rocks.

stonecutter *n* one whose occupation is to hew or cut stones for building, ornamental or other purposes.

stone-dead *adj* as lifeless as a stone.

stone-deaf *adj* deaf as a stone; totally deaf.

stone fruit *n* fruit whose seeds are covered with a hard shell enveloped in the pulp, as peaches, cherries, plums, etc; a drupe.

stone hammer *n* a hammer for breaking or rough-dressing stones; a hammer made of stone.

stonemason *n* one who dresses stones for building or builds with them.

stone plover, stone curlew *n* any of a species of European plover, a summer visitor to Britain.

stonewall *vi* (in cricket) to bet defensively, aiming to stay in rather than to score; to adopt a policy of obstruction.—*vt* to obstruct or hinder, as the passage of a parliamentary bill.

stoneware *n* a common species of glazed potter's ware made from a composition of clay and flint.

stony *adj* pertaining to, abounding in or resembling stone; pitiless; obdurate; with rigid features.

stony-broke *adj* financially ruined.

stook *n* a sheaf of corn.

stool *n* a seat without a back and with three or four legs, intended as a seat for one person; the seat used in evacuating the bowels; hence, an evacuation; a discharge from the bowels.

stoop¹ *vt* to bend down the head and upper half of the body; to have the back bowed or bent and the head forward; to yield or submit; to condescend; to lower oneself; to dart down on prey, as a hawk; to pounce; to sink when on the wing.—*vt* to bend or bow downward and forward; to bow down; to bend forward (*to stoop a cask of liquid*).—*n* the act of stooping; an habitual bend of the back or shoulders; a condescension; fall of a bird on its prey; swoop.

stoop² *n* the steps at the entrance of a house; a porch with seats.

stop *vt* (**stopped, stopping**) to close up by filling, stuffing or otherwise; to fill up a cavity or cavities in (*to stop a vent, the ears*); to staunch or prevent from bleeding; to obstruct or render impassable (*to stop a road* or *passage*); to check, stay, arrest, impede, keep back, in a variety of usages; to regulate the sounds of with the fingers or otherwise (*to stop a string*); to retain or refuse to pay for some reason (*to stop one's wages, an allowance of liquor*).—*vi* to cease to go forward; to come to a standstill; to cease from any motion, habit, practice or course of action; to check oneself; to stay; to reside temporarily.—*n* a cessation of progressive motion; a hindrance of progress or action; interruption; pause; that which hinders or obstructs; obstacle, impediment, hindrance; one of the vent holes of a wind instrument; a collection or series of pipes in an organ giving sounds of a distinctive tone and quality; a point or mark in writing, intended to distinguish the sentences, part of a sentence or clauses.

stopcock *n* a cock or faucet used to turn off or regulate the supply of water, gas, etc.

stopgap *n* that which fills up a gap; a temporary expedient.

stoppage *n* the act of stopping; arrest of progress or motion; a halt; an obstruction; a deduction made from pay or allowances; a concerted cessation of work by employees, as during a strike.

stopper *n* one who or that which stops; that which closes a vent or hole; the lid of a bottle.

stopping *n* the act of one who stops; that which stops or fills up.

stopwatch *n* a watch used in horse racing, etc, in which one of the hands can be stopped at once so as to mark with accuracy the time occupied.

stopple *n* that which stops or closes the mouth of a vessel; a stopper.

storage *n* the act of storing; the act of depositing in a store or warehouse; a price for keeping goods in a store; the storing of data in a computer memory or on a disk, tape, etc.

store *n* a quantity collected, hoarded or massed together; a supply, stock, hoard; specifically, (*pl*) supplies, as of provisions, ammunition, arms, clothing, etc, for an army, a ship, etc; a great quantity or a large number; abundance; a storehouse or warehouse; a place where goods are kept for sale either by wholesale or retail; a shop; a large shop.—*adj* kept in store; containing stores; obtained at a store.—*vt* (**stored, storing**) to collect or lay up in stock; to stock; to furnish or supply; to replenish (*to store the mind with knowledge*); to deposit in a store or warehouse; (*comput*) to put (data) into a computer memory or on to a disk, tape, etc.

storey *n* a stage or floor of a building; a set of rooms on the same floor or level.

storied *adj* adorned with historical paintings or designs; referred to or celebrated in story or history; having stories, tales or legends associated with it.

stork *n* a genus of tall wading birds resembling the herons, found in the vicinity of marshes and rivers, where they feed on frogs, lizards, fishes, etc.

storm *n* a violent commotion of the atmosphere, producing or accompanied by wind, rain, snow, hail or thunder and lightning; a tempest; a heavy fall of rain or snow; a violent disturbance in human society; a civil, political or domestic commotion; a tumult; (*milit*) a violent assault on a fortified place or strong position.—*vt* (*milit*) to take by storm; to assault (*to storm a fortified town*).—*vi* to be a storm (used impersonally, as *it storms*); to be in a violent agitation or passion; to fume.

stormy *adj* characterized by storm or tempest; tempestuous; boisterous; characterized by violence of feeling; passionate; angry.

story *n* a narrative; an account of past events or transactions; history; an account of an incident or event; a short narrative about a matter or a person; a fictitious narrative less elaborate than a novel; a tale; a short romance; a lie; a falsehood.

storybook *n* a book containing one or more stories; a book of short tales.

storyteller *n* one who tells stories, true or

stopwatch

stork

851

fictitious; a writer of stories; a euphemism for a liar.

stoup *n* a basin for holy water placed in a niche at the entrance of Roman Catholic churches; a deep narrow vessel for holding liquids; a flagon.

stout *adj* strong; vigorous; robust; bold; intrepid; firmly or strongly built; having strength; rather corpulent; bulky or thick-set in body.—*n* a kind of dark beer flavoured with roasted malt.

stove *n* an apparatus to contain a fire for warming a room or house or for cooking or other purposes; a cooker.

stow *vt* to put away in a suitable place; to lay up; to pack; to compactly arrange anything in; to fill by packing closely.

stowage *n* the act of stowing; room for things to be stowed; money paid for stowing goods.

stowaway *n* one who attempts to obtain a free passage by concealing himself or herself aboard a ship.

strabismus *n* squinting.

straddle *vi* (**straddled, straddling**) to part the legs wide; to stand or walk with the legs far apart; to sit astride.—*vt* to stride over; to stand or sit astride of.—*n* a standing or sitting with the legs far apart.

Stradivarius *n* (*pl* **Stradivarii**) a violin from Cremona in Italy, made by the celebrated maker there in the eighteenth century.

strafe *vt* (**strafed, strafing**) to punish; to bombard severely; to scold with severity.

straggle *vi* (**straggled, straggling**) to wander from the direct course or way; to scatter in marching; to rove; to shoot too far in growth; to grow with long irregular branches; to occur at intervals or apart from one another; to occur here and there.

straggler *n* one who straggles; one who wanders from or is left behind by his or her fellows; something that stands apart from others.

straight *adj* passing from one point to another by the nearest course; not curved, bent or crooked; direct (*a straight line*); according with justice and rectitude; not deviating from truth or fairness; upright; honest.—*adv* immediately; directly; in the shortest time; in a straight line.—*n* straight part; straight direction.

straight-edge *n* a slip of wood or metal made perfectly straight on the edge and used to test surfaces or for drawing straight lines.

straighten *vt* to make straight; to reduce from a crooked to a straight form.

straightforward *adj* proceeding in a straight course; not deviating; upright; honest; open.

straightly *adv* in a straight line; not crookedly; directly.

strand

straightway *adv* immediately; forthwith; without delay.

strain¹ *vt* to stretch or draw tightly; to make tighter; to squeeze or clasp in an embrace; to injure or weaken by stretching or overtasking; to subject to too great stress or exertion; to harm by a twist or wrench; hence, to sprain; to exert to the utmost; to push to the utmost strength or exertion; (*fig*) to push beyond the due limit; to carry too far; to do violence to (*to strain the meaning of a text*); to squeeze out; to purify by filtration; to filter; to sieve.—*vi* to exert oneself; to make violent efforts; to filter or be filtered; to percolate.—*n* a violent effort; an excessive exertion of the limbs or muscles or of the mind; an injurious stretching of the muscles or tendons; tension; stress; a continued course of action; general bearing; a poem; a song; a lay; a tune; a melody or part of a melody; especially, a section of a melody ending with a cadence; the subject or theme of a poem, discourse, etc; tenor of discourse; (*mech*) a definite alteration of form or dimensions experienced by a solid under the action of a stress; sometimes, in older usage, stress or force.

strain² *n* race; stock in a genealogical sense; family blood; quality or line in regard to breeding; natural disposition; turn; tendency.

strainer *n* an instrument for filtration; a sieve.

strait *adj* strict or rigorous; narrow; not wide.—*n* a narrow pass or passage; a narrow passage of water between two seas or oceans (the plural is often used of one, as the *Strait* or *Straits of Gibraltar*); distress; difficulty; distressing necessity.

straiten *vt* to make strait; to contract, confine, hem in, narrow; to make tense or tight; to distress; to press with poverty or other necessity; to put in pecuniary difficulties (used especially in *pp*).

straitjacket *n* a garment made of some strong material, with long sleeves, which are tied behind the body, used to restrain violent people; something that restricts or limits.

strait-laced *adj* having the stays or bodice tightly laced; constrained; strict in manners or morals; often excessively and puritanically strict.

strake *n* a continuous line of planking or plates on a ship's side, reaching from stem to stern.

strand¹ *n* a shore or beach of the sea or lake.—*vi* to drift or be driven on shore; to run aground; to have progress interrupted; to come to a standstill.—*vt* to drive or run aground on the seashore.

strand² *n* one of the twists or parts of which a rope is composed.

strange *adj* foreign; belonging to another country; not one's own; belonging to others; not before known, heard or seen; new; wonderful; causing surprise; extraordinary; odd; unusual; not according to the common way; estranged; not familiar; unacquainted; not knowing.

stranger *n* a foreigner; one of another place; one unknown or at least not familiar; one not knowing; one ignorant or unacquainted (*a stranger to the affair*); a guest; a visitor; one not admitted to fellowship.

strangle *vt* (**strangled, strangling**) to destroy the life of by compressing the windpipe; to choke; (*fig*) to suppress or stifle.

strangles *npl* a disorder which attacks horses, consisting of an abscess between the branches of the lower jaw.

strangulation *n* the act of strangling; the state of being strangled; (*med*) the state of a part too closely constricted, as the intestine in hernia.

strangury, stranguria *n* a disease in which there is pain in passing urine, which is given out by drops.

strap *n* a long narrow slip of leather or other substance of various forms and for various uses and often provided with a buckle; a plate, band or strip of metal to connect or hold other parts together; a piece of leather for sharpening razors, etc (in this sense often written **strop**); a piece of leather formerly used to punish children in schools.—*vt* (**strapped, strapping**) to chastise with a strap; to fasten or bind with a strap.

straphanger *n* a passenger in a bus, train, etc, who cannot get a seat and has to stand and hold on to a strap.

strapping *adj* tall and well built.

stratagem *n* an artifice in war; a plan or scheme for deceiving an enemy; a clever piece of generalship; any artifice; a trick to gain some advantage.

strategic, strategical *adj* pertaining to strategy; effected by strategy.

strategy *n* the science of forming and carrying out projects of military operations; generalship; the use of artifice or finesse in carrying out any project; a political, economic, etc, policy.

strath *n* in Scotland, a valley of considerable size, often having a river running through it.

strathspey *n* in Scotland, a type of dance in duple time, resembling a reel but slower.

stratification *n* the process by which are formed strata; an arrangement in strata or layers.

stratosphere *n* an upper part of the atmosphere, in which temperature does not vary with height.

stratum *n* (*pl* **strata**) a layer or bed of matter spread out; (*geol*) a layer of any substance, as sand, clay, limestone, etc, which is deposited over a certain surface by the action of water, especially such a layer when forming one of a number superposed.

stratus *n* (*pl* **strati**) a low, dense, horizontal cloud.

straw *n* the stalk or stem of certain species of grain, pulse, etc; such stalks collectively when cut and after being thrashed (no plural in this sense); used proverbially as typical of worthlessness (*I don't care a straw*).

strawberry *n* a well-known fruit and plant, the fruit being succulent and bearing the seeds on its surface.

straw colour *n* the colour of dry straw; a beautiful yellowish colour.

straw hat *n* a hat made of the plaited straw of cereals.

straw poll *n* an unofficial poll to test public opinion.

stray *vi* to wander, as from a direct course; to go astray; (*fig*) to wander from the path of duty or rectitude; to err; to roam or ramble; to run in a serpentine course; to wind.—*adj* having gone astray; straggling.—*n* any domestic animal that wanders at large or is lost; (*pl*) random electromagnetic waves, which interfere with the reception of normal wireless signalling.

streak *n* a line or long mark of a different colour from the ground; a layer in a mine; a stripe; (*naut*) a strake; the colour and appearance of a mineral when scratched.—*vt* to form streaks on; to variegate with lines of colour.

streaked, streaky *adj* having streaks; striped.

stream *n* any river, brook or course of running water; a flow or gush of any fluid substance; a flow of air or gas or of light; a steady current in the sea or in a river (*the Gulf Stream*); anything issuing as if in a flow (*a stream of words*); many individuals moving uniformly forward without interval.—*vi* to flow in a stream; to issue with continuance, not by fits; to issue or shoot in streaks or beams; to stretch in a long line; to float at full length in the air.—*vt* to send forth in a current or stream; to pour.

streamer *n* a long narrow flag; a pennon; a stream of light shooting upward from the horizon, as in some forms of the aurora borealis; a long narrow strip of coloured paper, used for decoration at Christmas, etc.

streamline *n* the path of an individual particle of fluid in fluid motion.

streamlined *adj* having a shape designed to offer resistance to air or water; made more modern, efficient, etc.

strangle

strawberry

853

street *n* a way or road in a city having houses on one or both sides, chiefly a main way, in distinction from a lane or alley; the houses as well as the open way.

streetwise *adj* (*colloq*) experienced in surviving or avoiding the potential dangers of urban life.

strength *n* the muscular force or energy which an animal is capable of exerting; animal force; the quality of bodies by which they sustain the application of force without breaking or yielding; solidity or toughness (*the strength of a bone*); power or vigour of any kind; capacity for exertion (*strength of mind, memory, evidence, argument, affection*); power of resisting attacks; that on which confidence or reliance is placed; support; force or power in expressing meaning by words; vividness; intensity; intensity of some distinguishing or essential constituent; potency (*strength of wine, poison, acid*); legal or moral force or efficacy; force as measured or stated in figures; amount or numbers of an army, fleet, etc; force proceeding from motion and proportioned to it; vehemence; impetuosity.

strength

strengthen *vt* to make strong or stronger; to add strength to; to confirm; to establish; to encourage; to fix in resolution; to make greater; to add intensity to.—*vi* to grow strong or stronger.

strenuous *adj* eager and constant in action; zealous; ardent; earnest.

strenuousness *n* earnestness; active zeal.

streptococcus *n* (*pl* **streptococci**) any of a genus of spherical bacteria which occur in chains of different lengths and may cause disease, such as throat infections.

stress *n* constraining, urging or impelling force; pressure; urgency; violence (*stress of weather*); an effort or exertion; a strain; tension; weight; any force tending to change the form or dimensions of a solid, that is, to produce a strain; also the reaction of the solid against the straining forces; importance or influence, imputed or ascribed (*to lay stress on some point in argument*); accent or emphasis; (*mech*) force exerted in any direction or manner on bodies (*tensile stress*, etc).

stressful *adj* causing stress or strain.

stretch *vt* to draw out; to extend in length; to draw tight; to make tense; to extend, spread, expand in any direction; to reach out; to hold forth; to extend or distend forcibly; to strain; to exaggerate; to extend too far (*to stretch a prerogative*).—*vi* to extend; to reach; to be continuous over a distance; to bear extension without breaking; to attain greater length.—*n* a stretching or the state of being stretched; an effort; a strain; utmost extent or reach; an extended portion; an expanse.

stretcher *n* one who or that which stretches; an instrument for widening gloves or for distending boots; a flat board on which corpses are laid out; a litter for carrying sick, wounded or dead persons; (in carpentry) a tie timber in a frame; (*naut*) a narrow piece of plank placed across a boat for the rowers to set their feet against.

strew *vt* (*pret* **strewed**, *pp* **strewed** *or* **strewn**, *ppr* **strewing**) to scatter or sprinkle (always applied to dry substances separable into parts or particles); to cover by scattering or being scattered over; to throw loosely apart; to spread abroad; to disseminate.

striated *adj* marked with small channels running parallel to each other.

strict *adj* carefully adhering to or governed by some rule; carefully observed; rigorously nice (*strict watch*); rigorous as to rules or conduct (*strict in religious observances*); definite as to terms; stringent; rigidly interpreted; not loose or vague (*the strict sense of a word*).

stricture *n* a touch of sharp criticism; a censorious remark; censure; a narrowing in a duct or vessel in the body, causing obstruction; something that restrains or limits.

stride *vi* (*pret* **strode**, *pp* **stridden**, *ppr* **striding**) to walk with long steps; to stand with the feet far apart; to straddle.—*vt* to pass over at a step; to bestride.—*n* a long step; a measured or pompous step; a lofty gait; the space measured by the legs far apart.

strident *adj* creaking; harsh; grating; shrill; raucous.

strife *n* exertion or contention for superiority; contest of emulation; emulation; contention in anger or enmity; discord; quarrel or war.

strike *vi* (*pret* **struck**, *pp* **struck, stricken**, *ppr* **striking**) to pass or dart with rapidity (*to strike into another path*; *the bullet struck through the door*); to penetrate (*the roots strike deep*); to make a quick blow or thrust; to use one's weapons; to knock; to sound an hour (as a clock); to reach (*light strikes on the wall*); to run or dash on the shore, a rock or bank; to be stranded; to lower a sail or a flag in token of respect or to signify surrender (*the ship struck*); to assume (an attitude); to yield; to quit work in order to compel an increase or prevent a reduction of wages or for other reasons.—*vt* to touch or hit with some force; to smite; to give a blow to; to give, deal or inflict (with *blow* or similar word as object); to dash; to knock (with the instrument as object); to produce by a blow or blows (*to strike fire*); to stamp with a stroke; hence, to mint; to coin; to thrust in; to cause to enter or penetrate (*a tree strikes its root*

854

deep); to cause to sound; to notify by sound; to impress (the mind) strongly; to affect sensibly with strong emotion (*the scene struck him*); to produce suddenly; to effect at once (*to strike terror*); to bring suddenly into some state or condition (*to strike one dumb*); to make and ratify (*to strike a bargain*); to lower, as the yards, flag, sails of a vessel.—**to strike down** to afflict or cause to die suddenly.—**to strike off** to delete or erase from (a list, etc); to prevent from continuing in a profession, especially due to malpractice.—**to strike out** to erase or delete; to begin on a journey.—**to strike up** to cause to begin, to bring about; (of a band, etc) to begin to play.—*n* an instrument for levelling a measure of grain, salt, etc; the act of a body of workers discontinuing work with the object of compelling their employer to concede certain demands made by them; a military attack; (*geol*) the horizontal direction of the outcropping edges of tilted strata, running at right angles to the dip.

striker *n* one who or that which strikes.

striking *adj* such as to strike with surprise or other feeling; remarkable; forcible; impressive.

string *n* a small rope, line or cord used for fastening or tying things; a twine; a thread; a thread on which things are filed; and hence, a set of things on a line (*a string of beads*); the chord of a musical instrument which gives a sound by its vibrations; hence, (*pl*) the stringed instruments of an orchestra; a line or chain of things following each other; (*pl*) a nerve or tendon of an animal body (*the heart strings*); a series of things connected or following in succession (*a string of arguments*).—*vt* (*pret, pp* **strung**, *ppr* **stringing**) to furnish with strings; to put in tune the strings of; to put on a string (*to string beads*).

string band *n* a band of musicians who play on stringed instruments.

string course *n* a narrow moulding continued horizontally along the face of a building.

stringed *adj* having strings; produced by strings.

stringent *adj* making strict claims or requirements; strict; rigid; making severe restrictions.

string-halt *n* a twitching of the hind leg of a horse, constituting a defect, being a convulsive motion of the muscles.

stringiness *n* the state of being stringy; fibrousness.

stringy *adj* consisting of strings or small threads; fibrous; ropy; sinewy; wiry.

strip *vt* (**stripped, stripping**) to pull or tear off (a covering); to deprive of a covering; to remove the clothes from; to skin; to peel (*to strip a tree of the bark*); to deprive; to bereave; to despoil; to tear off the thread of a screw or bolt; to milk dry; to unrig (*to strip a ship*).—*vi* to take off the covering or clothes; to remove all one's clothes.—*n* a narrow piece comparatively long; a stripe.

stripe *n* a long narrow division of anything of a different colour from the rest; a streak; a strip or long narrow piece; a stroke made with a lash, rod or scourge; a wale or weal; the distinctive mark of a noncommissioned officer in the army, one stripe denoting a lance corporal, two a corporal and three a sergeant.—*vt* (**striped, striping**) to make stripes on; to form with lines of different colours.

striped *adj* having stripes of different colours.

stripling *n* a youth in the state of adolescence or just passing from boyhood to manhood; a lad.

strive *vi* (*pret* **strove**, *pp* **striven**, *ppr* **striving**) to make efforts; to endeavour with earnestness; to try; to contend; to struggle in opposition; to fight; to quarrel or contend with each other; to be in dispute or altercation; to vie.

strobilus, strobile *n* (*pl* **strobili, strobiles**) (*bot*) a pine cone.

stroke[1] *n* a blow; a knock; the striking of one body against another; a fatal assault or attack; a sudden attack of disease or affliction; a calamity; the striking of a clock; a dash in writing or printing; a line; the touch of a pen or pencil (*a hair stroke*); a touch; a masterly effort (*a stroke of genius*); a successful attempt; the sweep of an oar; the stroke oar; (in steam engines) the entire movement of the piston from one end to the other of the cylinder; a sudden loss of consciousness and paralysis caused by a blocking in a blood vessel that supplies blood to parts of the brain.

stroke[2] *vt* to rub gently with the hand in kindness or tenderness; to rub gently in one direction; to make smooth by gentle rubbing.—*n* a caress; a gentle rubbing with the hand, expressive of kindness.

stroke oar *n* the aftermost oar of a boat; also, the person that uses it.

stroll *vi* to wander on foot slowly; to ramble idly or leisurely.—*n* a walking idly and leisurely; a ramble.

strong *adj* having physical power; having the power of exerting great bodily force; robust; muscular; able or powerful mentally or morally; of great power or capacity (*a strong mind, memory, imagination*); naturally sound or healthy; hale; not easily broken; firm; solid; compact; well fortified; not easily subdued or taken (*a strong fortress* or *position*); having great military or naval power or force; having great wealth or resources; having force from

striped

moving with rapidity; violent; impetuous; adapted to make a deep impression on the mind or imagination; effectual; cogent; ardent or zealous (*a strong supporter*); having a particular quality or qualities in a great degree (*a strong decoction, strong tea*); containing much alcohol; intoxicating; affecting the senses forcibly (*a strong light, scent, flavour*); substantial; solid but not of easy digestion; well-established; firm; not easily overthrown or altered; vehement; earnest (*a strong affection*); having great resources; powerful; mighty; having great force or expressiveness; forcibly expressed; (preceded by numerals) amounting to; powerful to the extent of (*an army 10,000 strong*); (*com*) tending upwards in price; rising (*a strong market*); (*gram*) applied to inflected words when inflection is effected by internal vowel change and not by adding syllables (*swim, swam, swum is a strong verb*).

stronghold *n* a fastness; a fortified place; a place of security.

strongroom *n* a fireproof and burglar-proof apartment in which valuables are kept.

strontium *n* a metal of a whitish yellow colour, ductile and malleable and somewhat harder than lead.

studs

strop *n* a strip of leather or a strip of wood covered with leather or other suitable material, used for sharpening razors; a razor strop.—*vt* (**stropped, stropping**) to sharpen with a strop.

strophe *n* the part of a Greek choral ode sung in turning from the right to the left of the orchestra, *antistrophe* being the reverse.

structure *n* a building of any kind but chiefly a building of some size or magnificence; an edifice; manner of building; make; construction; the arrangement of the parts in a whole.

struggle *vi* (**struggled, struggling**) to make efforts with contortions of the body; to use great efforts; to labour hard; to strive.—*n* a violent effort with contortions of the body; a contortion of distress; a forcible effort to attain an object; an effort to get on in the world; contest; strife.

strum *vi* (**strummed, strumming**) to play unskilfully and coarsely on a stringed instrument; to thrum.—*vt* to play on unskilfully or noisily.

student

struma *n* (*pl* **strumae**) a scrofulous swelling or tumour; scrofula.

strumpet *n* a prostitute; a harlot.

strut *vi* (**strutted, strutting**) to walk with a lofty, proud gait and erect head; to walk with affected dignity or pompousness.—*n* a lofty, proud step or walk with the head erect; affectation of dignity in walking; (in carpentry) a strengthening piece diagonally placed; a brace; a stretching piece.

strychnine *n* a vegetable alkaloid obtained from certain East Indian trees and especially from the seeds of nux vomica, a very strong poison but used in small quantities medically to stimulate the nervous system.

stub *n* the stump of a tree or that part which remains in the earth when the tree is cut down; a stub nail; the butt of a cigar, etc; the counterfoil of a cheque book.—*vt* (**stubbed, stubbing**) to grub up by the roots; to clear of roots.

stubble *n* the stumps of corn left in the ground; the part of the stalk left in the ground by the scythe or sickle.

stubborn *adj* unreasonably or perversely obstinate; not to be moved or persuaded by reason; inflexible; refractory; not easily worked (as soil, metal); stiff; not flexible.

stubby *adj* abounding with stubs; short and thick.

stucco *n* (*pl* **stuccos, stuccoes**) a kind of fine plaster, used for cornices, mouldings, etc, of rooms.—a composition of fine sand, pulverized marble and gypsum mixed with water; also, a popular name for plaster of Paris or gypsum.—*vt* (**stuccoed, stuccoing**) to overlay with stucco.

stud[1] *n* a nail with a large head, inserted chiefly for ornament; an ornamental knob; an ornamental button for a shirt front, transferable from one shirt to another; a supporting beam; a post or prop.—*vt* (**studded, studding**) to adorn with studs or knobs; to set thickly, as with studs.

stud[2] *n* a collection of breeding horses and mares; a person's horses collectively; (*colloq*) an attractive, virile man.

studbook *n* a book containing a genealogy or register of horses or cattle of particular breeds.

student *n* a person engaged in learning something from books or attending some educational institution, especially of the higher class; one studying anything; a scholar; a person devoted to books.

studied *adj* made the subject of study; well considered; qualified by study; premeditated; deliberate (*a studied insult*).

studio *n* (*pl* **studios**) the working room of a painter, sculptor, photographer, etc; a small flat containing one room and a kitchen and bathroom; a room or building with equipment for broadcasting, making films, etc.

studious *adj* given to study; devoted to the acquisition of knowledge from books; eager to discover something or to effect some object; earnest; eager (*studious to please*); attentive; careful (with *of*); deliberate; studied.

study *n* application of mind to books, to arts or science or to any subject for the purpose of learning what is not before known; earnest endeavour; diligence; a branch of learning studied; an object of study; a building or room devoted to study or reading and writing; a fit of thought; a reverie; (in fine arts) a work undertaken for improvement or a preparatory sketch to be used in the composition of more finished works.—*vi* (**studied, studying**) to apply the mind to books or learning; to dwell in thought; to ponder; to be zealous.—*vt* to apply the mind to for the purpose of learning; to consider attentively; to examine closely; to con over or to commit to memory; to have careful regard to (one's interest, comfort, etc); to be solicitous for the good of.

stuff *n* substance or matter indefinitely; the matter of which anything is formed; material; furniture; goods; refuse or worthless matter; hence, foolish or irrational language; trash; (*com*) a general name for fabrics of silk, wool, hair, cotton, etc; particularly woollen cloth of slight texture, for linings, etc.—*vt* to fill by packing or crowding material into; to cram; to crowd in together; to fill or pack with material necessary to make complete (*to stuff a cushion*); to fill the skin of, as of a dead animal, for presenting and preserving its form; to fill mentally full; to crowd with facts or idle tales or fancies; (in cookery) to fill with seasoning (*to stuff a leg of veal*).—*vi* to feed like a glutton.

stuffing *n* that which is used for filling anything, as a cushion, etc; a seasoned mixture used to stuff poultry, etc, before cooking.

stuffy *adj* difficult to breathe in; close; stifling (said of a room); prim or easily shocked (said of a person); blocked (said of a nose).

stultify *vt* (**stultified, stultifying**) to make useless; to make futile.

stumble *vi* (**stumbled, stumbling**) to trip in walking; to make a false step; to stagger; to walk unsteadily; to fall into crime or error; to err; to make a mistake; to strike on without design; to light by chance (with *on* or *upon*).—*n* the act of stumbling; a trip in walking or running; a blunder.

stumbling block *n* any cause of stumbling; that which forms a difficulty in one's way or which causes offence (used in figurative sense).

stump *n* the root part of a tree remaining in the earth after the tree is cut down; the part of a limb or other body remaining after the rest is cut off or destroyed (*the stump of a tooth, of a lead pencil*); one of the three upright sticks constituting the wicket in a game of cricket.—*vt* to lop; to make a tour through delivering speeches for political or personal purposes (*to stump the country*); (in cricket) to put out of play by knocking down a stump or stumps whilst

the batsman is out of the crease.—*vi* to walk stiffly, heavily or noisily; to campaign for political election.—**to stump up** (*colloq*) to pay or hand over money.

stump orator *n* a person who harangues the populace from an improvised platform; a bombastic speaker.

stumpy *adj* full of stumps; (*colloq*) short or stubby.

stun *vt* (**stunned, stunning**) to overpower the sense of hearing of; to confound by loud noise; to render insensible or dizzy by force or violence; to render senseless by a blow; to surprise completely; to overpower.

stunner *n* (*colloq*) something first-rate; (*colloq*) a person or thing of very showy appearance, especially a very beautiful person.

stunning *adj* first-rate; excellent; very beautiful.

stunt[1] *vt* to hinder from free growth; to check in growth; to dwarf.—*n* a check in growth.

stunt[2] *n* a remarkable feat of skill; a daring or spectacular feat; any enterprise, task or undertaking; an action meant to attract attention (*an advertising stunt*).

stunted *adj* checked in growth; of dwarfish growth.

stuntman, stuntwoman *n* (*pl* **stuntmen, stuntwomen**) a person employed to replace an actor or actress during dangerous scenes and stunts.

stupe *n* flannel, flax or similar substance wrung out of hot water, plain or medicated, applied to a wound or sore.

stupefaction *n* the state of being stupefied or stunned; a senseless state; insensibility; torpor.

stupefy *vt* (**stupefied, stupefying**) to deprive of sensibility; to make dull or dead to external influences; to make torpid.

stupendous *adj* striking dumb by magnitude; great and wonderful; of astonishing magnitude or elevation; grand.

stupid *adj* bereft of consciousness, sense or feeling; in a state of stupor; insensible; stupefied; devoid of understanding; possessed of dull gross folly; extremely dull of perception or understanding; nonsensical.

stupidity *n* the state or quality of being stupid; astonishment; extreme dullness of understanding; dull foolishness.

stupor *n* great diminution or total suspension of sensibility; a state in which the faculties are deadened or dazed; torpor.

sturdy *adj* forcible; vigorous; robust in body; strong; stout; vigorous and hardy.

sturgeon *n* a genus of large fishes having a skin protected with rows of bony plates; flesh used as food; roes converted into caviar and an air bladder into isinglass.

stump

sturgeon

stutter *vi* to stammer; to hesitate in uttering words.—*n* a stammer; a hesitation in speaking.

sty[1] *n* a pen or enclosure for swine; any filthy hovel or place; a place of bestial debauchery.

sty[2] *n* a small inflammatory tumour on the edge of the eyelid.

style *n* a pointed instrument used by the ancients for writing by scratching on wax tablets; anything of a similar kind; a pointed tool used in graving; a pointed surgical instrument; the pin or gnomon of a sundial; (*bot*) the prolongation of the summit of the ovary which supports the stigma; manner of writing with regard to language; a distinctive manner of writing belonging to an author or body of authors; a characteristic mode of presentation in any of the fine arts; particular type of architecture pervading a building (*the Gothic style*); external manner, mode or fashion; manner deemed elegant and appropriate; fashion (*a person dressed in the style*); a person's manner of dressing; a way of dressing the hair; a formal or official designation; title (*a person's style and title*).—*vt* (**styled, styling**) to term; to name or call; to designate or denominate; to dress or cut (hair).

stylish *adj* being in fashionable form or in high style; fashionable; elegant.

stylist *n* a writer or speaker who is careful of his or her style; a master of style; a person who creates hairstyles.

stylite *n* a pillar saint, one of those ascetics who, by way of penance, passed the greater part of their lives on the top of high columns or pillars.

stylize *vt* (**stylized, stylizing**) to give a conventional style to; to represent or treat in accordance with a principle of design or style, rather than as it is in nature.

stymie *n* the position in golf when the opponent's ball lies between the player's ball and the hole.

styptic *adj* astringent; having the quality of stopping the bleeding of a wound.—*n* a substance that checks a flow of blood by application to the bleeding surface.

suave *adj* gracious or agreeable in manner; blandly polite; pleasant; urbane.

suavity *n* the state or quality of being suave; graciousness and politeness of address; pleasantness.

sub *n* (*colloq*) a submarine; a substitute; a subeditor; a subscription.—*vt* (**subbed, subbing**) (*colloq*) to subedit.

sub- *prefix* under, below; subordinate, next in rank to.

subaltern *adj* holding a subordinate position; in the army, below the rank of a captain.—*n* a commissioned military officer below the rank of a captain.

subaquatic, subaqueous *adj* being under or partially under water; (*geol*) formed under water; deposited under water.

subarctic *adj* applied to a region or climate next to the Arctic; approximately Arctic.

subcommittee *n* an under committee; a part or division of a committee.

subconscious *adj* happening without one's awareness; outside the immediate field of consciousness but able to be recalled to conscious awareness under hypnosis, etc; not clearly perceived by the thinking subject.—*n* the part of the mind that is active without one's conscious awareness.

subconsciousness *n* the state of being subconscious.

subcontinent *n* a land mass of great size but smaller than a recognized continent.

subcontract *n* a secondary contract under which work or supply of materials is let out to a firm other than the main part of the contract.—*vti* to make a subcontract.

subcontractor *n* one who subcontracts.

subculture *n* a distinct group with its own customs, language, dress, etc, within an existing culture.

subcutaneous *adj* situated immediately under the skin.

subdivide *vt* (**subdivided, subdividing**) to divide the parts of into more parts; to part into subdivisions.—*vi* to be subdivided.

subdivision *n* the act of subdividing; one of the parts of a larger part.

subdominant *n* (*mus*) the fourth note of the diatonic scale lying a tone under the dominant or fifth of the scale.

subdue *vt* (**subdued, subduing**) to conquer and bring into permanent subjection; to reduce under dominion; to overpower by superior force; to vanquish; to overcome by discipline; to tame; to prevail over by some mild or softening influence; to gain complete sway over; to melt or soften (the heart, opposition); to tone down or make less glaring.

subdued *adj* vanquished; made mild or tractable; submissive; toned down or softened.

subedit *vt* to edit and prepare (newspaper material) for publication.

subeditor *n* a journalist who edits and prepares newspaper material for publication.

subjacent *adj* lying under or below; (*geol*) applied to rocks, beds or strata which lie under or are covered by others.

subject *adj* placed under; being under the power and dominion of another; ruled by another state; liable, from extraneous or inherent causes; open to (*subject to appeal*); dependent on (*subject to the council's approval*).—*n* one who owes allegiance to a sovereign; one who lives under and owes allegiance to a government; a person as the recipient of certain treatment; that which is treated or operated on; a dead body for the purposes of dissection; that which is spoken of, thought of, treated of or handled; matter dealt with; theme of discourse; any area of knowledge which may be studied; in logic, that term of a proposition of which the other is affirmed or denied; (*gram*) that which is spoken of; the nominative of a verb; (*philos*) the mind, soul or personality of the thinker.— the Ego; the thinking agent or principle, the object, which is its correlative, being anything or everything external to the mind; (*mus*) the principal theme of a movement; in fine arts, the incident chosen by an artist; the design of a composition or picture.—*vt* to bring under; to subdue; to expose; to make liable; to cause to undergo; to expose, as in chemical or other operations (usually with *to* following in all senses, as *to subject a person to ridicule*).

subjection *n* the act of subjecting or subduing; the state of being under the control and government of another; subjugation; enthralment.

subjective *adj* relating to the subject, as opposed to the object; belonging to one's own mind and not to what is external; belonging to ourselves, the conscious subject; influenced by one's own personal interests, opinions, emotions or prejudices; (in literature and art) characterized by prominence of the personality of the author or artist (*the writings of Shelley and Byron are subjective*).

subjectivism *n* (*metaph*) the doctrine that all human knowledge is merely relative.

subjectivity *n* the state of being subjective or in the mind alone; the character of exhibiting the individuality of an author or artist.

subject matter *n* the theme or matter discussed or spoken of.

subjoin *vt* to add at the end; to add after something else has been said or written.

subjugate *vt* (**subjugated, subjugating**) to subdue and bring under dominion; to conquer and compel to submit.

subjugation *n* the act of subjugating; subjection.

subjunctive *adj* (*gram*) designating a mood or form of verbs expressing condition, hypothesis or contingency, generally subjoined or subordinate to another verb and preceded by a conjunction.—*n* (*gram*) the subjunctive mood.

sublease *n* (*law*) a lease granted to a subtenant.—*vt* to lease to another property that one is leasing from someone else.

sublet *vt* (*pret*, *pp* **sublet**, *ppr* **subletting**) to let to another property that one is renting from someone else.—*n* an act of subletting; a property that is sublet.

sublieutenant *n* a junior naval officer, holding rank next below that of lieutenant.

sublimate *vt* (**sublimated, sublimating**) to bring by heat from a solid state into a state of vapour; (*fig*) to refine and exalt; to elevate; to redirect unconsciously (a primitive or unacceptable impulse such as sexual or aggressive impulse) into a higher or more socially acceptable impulse or activity.—*n* what is produced by sublimation.—*adj* exalted.

sublimation *n* the process of sublimating; a process by which solids are by heat converted into vapour that again becomes solid; the unconscious diversion of primitive or unacceptable impulses, such as aggressive and sexual impulses, towards more socially acceptable impulses or activities.

sublime *adj* high in place; elevated; high in excellence; elevated far above people in general by lofty or noble traits (said of persons); striking the mind with a sense of grandeur or power; calculated to awaken or expressive of, awe, veneration or lofty feeling; grand; noble (said of objects, of scenery, of an action or exploit, etc).

subliminal *adj* below consciousness; in the mind without awareness; perceived below the threshold of consciousness.

sublimity *n* the state or quality of being sublime; grandeur; loftiness of nature or character; moral grandeur; loftiness of conception, sentiment or style; elevation, whether exhibited in the works of nature or of art; the emotion produced by what is sublime.

sublunary *adj* (*lit*) situated under the moon; hence, pertaining to this world; mundane; earthly; worldly.

sub-machine gun *n* a light automatic or semiautomatic gun designed to be fired from the hip or shoulder.

submarine *adj* situated, existing, acting or growing at some depth in the waters of the sea; remaining at the bottom or under the surface of the sea (*submarine plants*).—*n* a vessel that can be submerged at will and sail under the water.

submediant *n* (*mus*) the sixth note of the diatonic scale or middle note between the octave and subdominant.—*adj* of or relating to the submediant.

submerge *vt* (**submerged, submerging**) to put under water; to plunge; to cover or overflow with water; to drown.—*vi* to plunge under water; to sink out of sight.

submergence *n* act of submerging.

submersible *n* a submarine, especially one with projecting ballast tanks.

submersion *n* the act of putting or state of being put under water or other fluid; a dipping or plunging; a state of being overflowed.

submission *n* the act of submitting, yielding

submarine

or surrendering; the state of being submissive; humble or suppliant behaviour; meekness; resignation; compliance with the commands of a superior; obedience.

submissive *adj* disposed or ready to submit; compliant; obedient; humble; meek.

submissiveness *n* the character of being submissive; ready compliance; meekness.

submit *vt* (**submitted, submitting**) to yield to the power or will of another (used reflexively); to place under the control of another; to surrender; to leave to the discretion or judgment of another; to refer.— *vi* to yield one's person to the power of another; to surrender; to yield one's opinion; to acquiesce; to be submissive; to yield without murmuring.

subnormal *adj* less than normal; having lower intelligence than usual.

subordinate *adj* placed in a low order, class or rank; occupying a lower position in a scale; inferior in nature, power, importance, etc.—*vt* (**subordinated, subordinating**) to place below something else; to make or consider as of less value or importance; to make subject.—*n* one inferior in power, rank, dignity, office, etc; one below and under the orders of another.

subordination *n* the act of subordinating; gradation of ranks one below another; the state of being under control or government; subjection.

suborn *vt* to bribe to commit perjury; to induce to give false testimony or do some other wickedness.

subornation *n* the crime of suborning.

subplot *n* an incidental or secondary plot in a novel, play, film, etc.

subpoena *n* (*law*) a writ or process commanding the attendance in a court of justice of the person on whom it is served under a penalty.—*vt* (**subpoenaed, subpoenaing**) to serve with a writ of subpoena.

subscribe *vt* (**subscribed, subscribing**) to write one's signature beneath; to sign with one's own hand; to consent or bind oneself to by writing one's name beneath; to attest by writing one's name; to promise to give by writing one's name (*to subscribe money*); to contribute (a sum of money).— *vi* to promise along with others a certain sum by setting one's name to a paper; to give consent; to assent; to express agreement with or approval of; to enter one's name for a newspaper, a book, etc.

subscriber *n* one who subscribes; one who admits, confirms or binds himself or herself to a promise or obligation by signing his or her name; one who contributes to an undertaking by paying or promising; one who enters his or her name for a newspaper, periodical, book, etc.

subscript *n* a character written or printed below another character.

subscription *n* the act of subscribing or signing; the signature attached to a paper; a sum subscribed or promised by signature; a sum contributed along with other subscribers; the amount subscribed.

subsequent *adj* following in time; coming or being after something else at any time, indefinitely; following in the order of place or succession; succeeding.

subsequently *adv* in a subsequent manner, time or position; afterwards; later on.

subservience, subserviency *n* the state of being subservient.

subservient *adj* useful as an instrument to promote a purpose; serving to promote some end; acting as a subordinate instrument; servile; tame; submissive.

subside *vi* (**subsided, subsiding**) to sink or fall to the bottom; to settle, as lees; to sink or settle to a lower level, as a building; to fall into a state of quiet; to become tranquil; to abate.

subsidence *n* the act or progress of subsiding; a gradually settling lower; a sinking into the ground (*the subsidence of ground*).

subsidiary *adj* lending some aid or assistance; furnishing help; aiding or assisting; subordinate; contributory; pertaining to a subsidy.—*n* one who or that which is subsidiary; an auxiliary; an assistant.

subsidize *vt* (**subsidized, subsidizing**) to furnish with a subsidy; to purchase the assistance of by a subsidy.

subsidy *n* a sum of money granted for a purpose; a sum paid by one government to another to meet the expenses of carrying on a war; financial assistance; government funds used to keep down the cost of food, etc; government financial aid given to a private person or company for a particular enterprise, such as setting up a business in an area of low employment.

subsist *vi* to exist; to have continued existence; to continue to retain the present state; to be maintained with food and clothing; to be supported; to live; to inhere in something else.—*vt* to support with provisions.

subsistence *n* actual existence; that which furnishes support to animal life; means of support; support; livelihood; inherence in something else.

subsoil *n* the undersoil; the bed or stratum of earth or earthy matter which lies immediately under the surface soil.

substance *n* that of which a thing consists or is made up; matter; material; a distinct portion of matter; a body; that which is real; that which constitutes a thing really a thing; the characteristic constituents collectively; the essential or material part; the purport; solidity; firmness; substantiality; material means and resources; goods; estate; (*philos*) that which underlies all phenomena; that which exists independently and unchangeably, in contradistinction to accident or quality; (*theol*) that in which the divine attributes inhere.

substantial *adj* actually existing; real; not seeming or imaginary; corporeal; material; firm in substance or material; strong; solid; possessed of considerable substance, goods or estate; moderately wealthy; of a considerable size, importance, value, etc.

substantiate *vt* (**substantiated, substantiating**) to make real or actual; to establish by proof or competent evidence; to verify; to make good; to prove.

substantiation *n* the act of substantiating or proving; evidence; proof.

substantival *adj* (*gram*) relating to or like a substantive.

substantive *adj* betokening or expressing existence; depending on itself; having an independent existence; independent; essential or basic.—*n* (*gram*) a noun or a group of words acting as a noun.

substitute *vt* (**substituted, substituting**) to put in the place of another; to put in exchange.—*n* a person acting for or put in place of another; one thing put in the place of another or serving the purpose of another.

substitution *n* the act of substituting or putting in place of another; a person or thing substituted for another.

substrate *n* (*biol*) the surface upon which an organism lives and from which it may derive its food; a substance in a reaction that is catalysed by an enzyme.

substratum *n* (*pl* **substrata**) that which is laid or spread under something; a stratum lying under another; subsoil; (*metaph*) matter or substance in which qualities inhere.

subtend *vt* to extend under or be opposite to (a geometrical term said of the side of a triangle opposite an angle).

subterfuge *n* an underhand method used to escape or avoid an awkward situation, etc; a trick used to conceal something; such underhand methods or trickery.

subterranean *adj* being or lying at some depth in the earth; situated within the earth; underground.

subtext *n* an underlying meaning or construction, especially in a work of literature or art.

subtitle *n* an explanatory title to a book; a printed translation of a foreign language film at the bottom of the screen; a caption inserted between shots in a silent film; text printed at the bottom of the screen in television programme for the benefit of deaf people.—*vt* (**subtitled, subtitling**) to add subtitles to.

subtle *adj* slight; fine; delicate; acute or penetrating in intellect; capable of drawing nice distinctions; sly in design; cunning; artful; insinuating; cunningly devised.

subtlety *n* the quality of being subtle; delicacy; fineness; cunning; craftiness; wiliness; acuteness of intellect; nicety of distinction or discrimination.

subtract *vt* to withdraw or take from a number or quantity; to deduct.

subtraction *n* the act or operation of subtracting; the taking of a lesser number from a greater.

subtropical *adj* of or characteristic of the regions bordering on the tropics.

suburb *n* an outlying part of a city or town, usually residential with its own shops and services; (*pl*) the residential areas near or outside the edge of a town or city.

suburban *adj* pertaining to the suburbs of a city.

subvene *vi* (**subvened, subvening**) to arrive or happen so as to obviate something or afford relief.

subvention *n* the act of coming to relieve or aid; a government grant or aid; financial aid granted.

subversion *n* the act of subverting or overthrowing; overthrow; utter ruin; destruction.

subversive *adj* tending to subvert, overthrow or ruin.

subvert *vt* to overthrow from the foundation; to ruin utterly; to destroy; to corrupt or pervert, as the mind.

subway *n* a passage under a road for use by pedestrians; an underground railway.

succeed *vt* to take the place of in some post or position; to be heir or successor to; to come after; to be subsequent or consequent to.—*vi* to follow; to come next; to become heir; to ascend a throne after the removal or death of the occupant; to come down by order of succession; to devolve; to be fortunate or prosperous in any endeavour; to obtain the object desired; to achieve the desired or intended result; to turn out as wished; to have the desired result.

success *n* a favourable or prosperous termination of anything attempted; the achievement of what is attempted, intended or desire; a person or thing that succeeds.

successful *adj* having or resulting in success; prosperous; fortunate.

succession *n* a following of things in order, either in time or place; a series following one after the other; a series or line of descendants; successors collectively; a succession or coming to an inheritance; the act or right of entering on an office, rank, etc, held by a predecessor.

successive *adj* following in an uninterrupted course or series, as persons or things, and either in time or place; coming one after another; consecutive.

successor *n* one that succeeds or follows; one that takes the place which another has left and sustains the like part or character, correlative to *predecessor*.

succinct *adj* compressed into few words; characterized by verbal brevity; brief; concise.

succour *vt* to help when in difficulty or distress; to assist and deliver from suffering; to aid or relieve.—*n* aid; help; assistance; particularly, assistance in difficulty or distress; the person or thing that brings relief.

succulence *n* the quality of being succulent; juiciness.

succulent *n* full of juice; juicy.

succumb *vi* to sink or give way without resistance; to yield; to submit.

such *adj* of that or the like kind or degree; similar; like; the same as mentioned; so great (*such baseness*).—**such like** of the like kind; similar persons or things; et cetera (used at the close of enumeration).

suck *vt* to draw into the mouth by the action of the lips and tongue; to draw something from with the mouth; specifically, to draw milk from; to hold and moisten in the mouth, as sweets; to draw in or imbibe; to inhale; to absorb; to draw in as a whirlpool; to swallow up; to engulf.—*vi* to draw fluid into the mouth; to draw milk from the breast.—*n* the act of drawing with the mouth; milk drawn from the breast by the mouth.

sucker *n* one who or that which sucks; an organ in animals for sucking; the piston of a suction pump; a shoot or branch which proceeds from the roots or lower part of a stem; the sucking fish; the lumpfish or lumpsucker; a person who is easily deceived.

sucking fish *n* the remora.

suckle *vt* (**suckled, suckling**) to give suck to; to nurse at the breast.

suckling *n* a young child at the breast.

suction *n* the act of sucking; the sucking up of any fluid by the pressure of the external air when a vacuum is made; the process of removing, or attempting to remove, gas from an enclosed space.

suctorial *adj* (*biol*) adapted for sucking; living by sucking; capable of adhering by sucking.

sudden *adj* happening without or with scarcely a moment's notice; coming unexpectedly; hastily put in use, employed or prepared; quick; rapid; hasty; violent; passionate.—**all of a sudden** all at once; hastily; unexpectedly.

sudden infant death syndrome *n* cot death.

suddenly *adv* in a sudden manner; unexpectedly; all at once.

sudorific *adj* causing sweat.—*n* a medicine that produces sweat.

suds *npl* a lye of soap and water or water impregnated with soap and forming a frothy mass; soapy water.

sue *vt* (**sued, suing**) to seek in marriage; to seek justice or right from by legal process; to institute a process in law against.—*vi* to woo or be a wooer; to prosecute; to make legal claim; to seek by request; to petition; to plead.

suède, suede *n* a soft, undressed leather made of kidskin and used for gloves, shoes, clothes, etc.

suet *n* the fatty tissue situated about the loins and kidneys of the ox, sheep, deer, etc, and which is harder than the fat from other parts, used to make dumplings and puddings.

suffer *vt* to feel or bear with painful, disagreeable or distressing effects; to undergo (*to suffer pain*); to be affected by (*to suffer change, a loss*); not to forbid or hinder; to allow.—*vi* to feel or undergo pain of body or mind; to undergo punishment; to be executed; to be injured; to sustain loss or damage.

sufferable *adj* capable of being permitted or endured.

sufferance *n* the state of suffering; endurance; patient endurance; passive consent by not forbidding or hindering; toleration; permission.—**on sufferance** by passive permission or consent; without being positively forbidden; tolerated.

sufferer *n* one who suffers; one who undergoes pain; one who sustains inconvenience or loss; one that permits or allows.

suffering *n* the bearing of pain, inconvenience or loss; pain endured; distress.

suffice *vi* (**sufficed, sufficing**) to be enough or sufficient; to be equal to the end proposed.—*vt* to satisfy; to be equal to the wants or demands of.

sufficiency *n* the state of being sufficient or adequate; adequacy; capacity; adequate substance or means; a competence; a comfortable fortune; a supply equal to needs; self-conceit; self-confidence.

sufficient *adj* equal to the end proposed; adequate to needs; enough; of competent power or ability; qualified; capable.

suffix *n* a letter or syllable added or annexed to the end of a word to form another word; an affix.—*vt* to add or annex (a letter or syllable) to a word.

suffocate *vt* (**suffocated, suffocating**) to choke or kill by stopping respiration; to stifle, as by depriving of air; to smother.—*vi* to become choked, stifled or smothered.

suffocation *n* the act of suffocating; the condition of being suffocated, choked or stifled.

suffragan *adj* assisting in ecclesiastical duties (said of bishops).—*n* a bishop consecrated to assist another bishop in a portion of his diocese; any bishop in relation to his archbishop.

suffrage *n* a vote given in deciding a question or in choice of a person; an opinion expressed; one's voice given; right to vote; the parliamentary franchise.

suffragette *n* a female advocate of female suffrage; a campaigner for women's rights to vote.

suffragist *n* a supporter of some form of suffrage; a suffragette.

suffuse *vt* (**suffused, suffusing**) to overspread, as with a fluid or tincture; to fill or cover, as with something fluid (*eyes suffused with tears, suffused with blushes*).

suffusion *n* the act of suffusing or state of being suffused; a spreading over.

Sufism *n* the doctrine of the Sufis, or Muslim mystics, of a pantheistic nature.

sugar *n* a common sweet granular substance, prepared chiefly from the expressed juice of the sugar cane but obtained also from many other plants, as maple, beet, birch, parsnip, etc; something resembling sugar in any of its properties; (*fig*) honeyed or soothing words.—*adj* made of sugar.—*vt* to impregnate, season, sprinkle or mix with sugar; (*fig*) to sweeten, honey or render acceptable.

sugar cane *n* a tall tropical plant from whose juice sugar is obtained.

sugar loaf *n* a conical mass of refined sugar; anything shaped like a sugar loaf.

sugar maple *n* a maple of North America, the juice of which, obtained in early spring by tapping, is converted into sugar.

sugar plum *n* a comfit or small sweet meat made of boiled sugar, with flavouring and colouring ingredients.

sugar tongs *npl* a small instrument of silver or plated metal for lifting lumps of sugar at table.

sugary *adj* resembling, containing or composed of sugar; sweet; (*fig*) honeyed; oversweet.

suggest *vt* to introduce indirectly to the mind or thoughts; to call up to the mind; to cause to be thought of; to recall; to propose with diffidence or modesty; to hint.—*vi* to make suggestions of evil.

suggestion *n* the act of suggesting or that which is suggested; a hint; a prompting, especially a prompting to do evil; temptation.

suggestive *adj* calculated to suggest thoughts or ideas; suggesting what does not appear on the surface; suggesting something indecent.

suicidal *adj* pertaining to or of the nature of suicide.

suicide *n* self-murder; the act of destroying one's own life; one guilty of self-murder; a person who intentionally kills himself or herself; the ruin of one's own interests.

suit *n* a following; pursuit; the act of suing; a seeking for something by petition or entreaty; a request; a prayer; an attempt to win a person in marriage; courtship; a set or number of things used together; a set of clothes designed to be worn together, such as trousers or a skirt and matching jacket, usually of the same colour and material; an outfit for a particular purpose (*a bathing suit*); a set of things of the same kind or stamp; any of the four classes into which playing cards are divided; a retinue or train of attendants or followers (in this sense usually written *suite*); (*law*) an action or process for the recovery of a right or claim.—*vt* to adapt; to be suitable; to become or be adapted to; to be suitable to; to fit; to be agreeable to; to fall in with the wishes or convenience of.—*vi* to agree; to correspond.

suitable *adj* suiting or being in accordance; correct or adequate for a particular purpose, situation, etc; fitting; proper; becoming.

suitcase *n* a flat case made of leather, fibre, etc, used for carrying clothes, etc, when travelling.

suite *n* a company or number of attendants or followers; a retinue; a train; a connected series forming one whole; a group of connected or related things forming a set or series.

suitor *n* a petitioner; an applicant; one who sues or entreats; one who solicits a person in marriage; a wooer; a lover; (*law*) a party to a lawsuit.

sulk *vi* to indulge in a sullen fit or mood; to be silent in a gloomy or resentful manner. —*n* (*often pl*) the state of being in a sulky fit or mood.

sulkiness *n* the state of being sulky.

sulky[1] *adj* sullen; morose; resentfully silent or angry.

sulky[2] *n* a light two-wheeled carriage for a single person.

sullen *adj* gloomily angry and silent; morose; sour; sulky; dismal; of a threatening aspect; sombre.

sullenness *n* the state or quality of being sullen; ill nature with silence; silent moroseness.

sully *vt* (**sullied, sullying**) to soil; to spot; to tarnish; to dim; (*fig*) to stain, tarnish or pollute (*character sullied by infamous vices*).—*vi* to be soiled or tarnished.

sulphate *n* a salt of sulphuric acid or a compound of sulphuric acid and a base.

sulphide *n* a combination of sulphur with a metal or other element.

sulphite *n* a salt composed of sulphurous acid with a base.

sulphur *n* a nonmetallic chemical element

suit

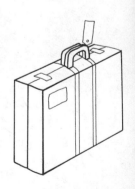

suitcase

of a greenish-yellow colour, occurring abundantly in minerals, sparingly in vegetable and animal matter, nearly tasteless, readily melted, burning with a blue flame and then emitting suffocating fumes.

sulphurate *vt* (**sulphurated, sulphurating**) to impregnate or combine with sulphur; to subject to the action of sulphur.

sulphureous *adj* consisting of or having the qualities of sulphur; sulphurous.

sulphuric *adj* pertaining to sulphur.

sulphuric acid *n* oil of vitriol as it is called, from being first prepared from green vitriol (sulphate of iron), a compound of sulphur, oxygen and hydrogen, colourless, oily and strongly corrosive, used in the arts for innumerable purposes.

sulphurous *adj* impregnated with sulphur; like sulphur; containing sulphur.

sultan *n* the ordinary title of Muslim rulers, especially the former ruler of Turkey.

sultana *n* the consort of a sultan; a kind of large raisin.

sultry *adj* very hot, burning and oppressive; very hot and moist or hot, close and heavy (*a sultry atmosphere*).

sum *n* the aggregate of two or more numbers, magnitudes, quantities or particulars; the amount or total of any number of things added together; the whole or totality; a quantity of money; any amount indefinitely; the principal points viewed or aggregated together; the essence; the substance; an arithmetical problem to be solved.—*vt* (**summed, summing**) to add into one whole; to cast up; to bring or collect into a small compass; to comprise in a few words (*to sum up arguments*).

sumach, sumac *n* a genus of shrubs the leaves of which are much used for tanning; the leaves, shoots, etc.

summarily *adv* in a summary manner; briefly; concisely; in a short way or method; without delay.

summarize *vt* (**summarized, summarizing**) to make a summary or abstract of; to represent briefly.

summary *adj* reduced into a narrow compass or into few words; succinct; concise; compendious; quickly executed; effected by a short way or method; (*law*) (said of proceedings) carried on by methods intended to facilitate the despatch of business.—*n* an abridged or condensed statement or account; an abridgement or compendium containing the important points or details of a fuller statement.

summer[1] *n* that season of the year when the sun shines most directly on any region; the warmest season of the year, which, north of the equator, may be roughly said to include the months of June, July and August.

summer[2] *n* building, a lintel; a girder; a supporting beam.

summit

sun

summerhouse *n* a small house or pavilion in a garden to be used in summer.

summertime *n* the summer season

summer time *n* a system of reckoning time in which clocks are kept one hour in advance of Greenwich mean time during the summer months to increase the number of daylight hours in the working day.

summit *n* the top; the highest point; utmost elevation, as of rank, prosperity, etc; a meeting between leaders of countries, especially the more powerful countries.

summon *vt* to call or cite by authority to appear at a place specified; especially, to command to appear in a court of justice; to send for; to ask the attendance of; to call on; to send for; to call on to surrender; to call up; to excite into action or exertion (with *up*, as *summon up your courage*).

summoner *n* one who summons; also, a former name for an apparitor.

summons *n* a call by authority to appear at a place named or to attend to some public duty; an invitation or asking to go to or appear at, some place; law, a call by authority to appear in a court; also, the written or printed document by which such call is given; (*milit*) a call to surrender.

sump *n* a pond of water for use in salt works; a pit for receiving metal on its first fusion; a reservoir at the lowest point of a machine, pump circulation system, etc, into which fluid drains before recalculating or in which wastes gather before dispersal.

sumpter *n* a horse that carries necessaries for a journey; a baggage horse; a pack-horse.—*adj* applied to a horse or mule that carries necessaries.

sumptuary *adj* relating to expense; regulating expense or expenditure.

sumptuary law *n* a law made to restrain excess in apparel, food or any luxuries.

sumptuous *adj* costly; expensive; hence, splendid; magnificent.

sun *n* the self-luminous orb which, being in or near the centre of our system of worlds, gives light and heat to the earth and other planets; the sunshine or sunlight (*to lie in the sun*); anything eminently splendid or luminous; that which is the chief source of light, honour, glory or prosperity; the luminary which constitutes the centre of any system of worlds; a revolution of the earth round the sun; a year.—*vt* (**sunned, sunning**) to expose to the sun's rays; to dry in the sun.

sunbathe *vi* (**sunbathed, sunbathing**) to expose the body to the sun's rays, especially in order to acquire a suntan.

sunbeam *n* a ray of the sun.

sunbonnet *n* a bonnet having a shade as a protection from the sun.

sunburn *vt* (*pret, pp* **sunburned, sunburnt,**

ppr **sunburning**) to discolour or scorch by the sun; to inflame (the skin or oneself) by overexposure to the sun's rays.—*n* inflammation and blistering of the skin from to much exposure to the sun's rays.

sunburnt *adj* discoloured by the heat or rays of the sun; suffering from an inflamed, blistered skin caused by overexposure to the sun's rays.

sundae *n* an ice cream served with crushed fruits, syrups, nuts, etc.

Sunday *n* the first day of the week; the Christian Sabbath; the Lord's day.—*adj* belonging to the Lord's day or Christian Sabbath.

Sunday school *n* a school for religious instruction held on the Lord's day.

sunder *vt* to part; to divide; to disunite in almost any manner, as by rending, cutting or breaking.—*vi* to part; to be separated.—*n* a separation or division into parts (used chiefly, if not exclusively, in the phrase *in sunder*, in two.

sundial *n* an instrument to show the time of day by means of a shadow cast by the sun.

sundown *n* sunset.

sundries *npl* various small things too minute or numerous to be individually specified.

sundry *adj* several; more than one or two.

sunfish *n* a genus of large fishes, so called on account of the almost circular form and shining surface of the typical species.

sunflower *n* a genus of plants, so named from the form and colour of the flower or from its habit of turning to the sun.

sunk *pret, pp of* **sink**.

sunken *adj* lying on the bottom of the sea or other water; low.

sunk fence *n* a ditch with a retaining wall on one side.

sunlight *n* the light of the sun; sunshine.

sunlit *adj* lit or lighted by the sun.

sunn, sunn hemp *n* an Asian material similar to hemp, used for cordage, canvas, etc.

Sunni *n* the branch of Islam that accepts the Sunna or traditional law as of equal importance with the Koran.

Sunnite *adj* of or pertaining to the Sunni.—*n* a member of the Sunni.

sunny *adj* like the sun; shining or dazzling with light or splendour; full of sunlight; bright; exposed to the rays of the sun; lighted up or warmed by the direct rays of the sun; cheerful.

sunrise *n* the rising or appearance of the sun above the horizon; dawn; morning; the region where the sun rises; the east.—*adj* of or pertaining to sunrise; developing (*sunrise industry*).

sunset *n* the descent of the sun below the horizon; the time when the sun sets; evening; (*fig*) close or decline; the region where the sun sets; the west.

sunshine *n* the light of the sun; sunlight; (*fig*) an influence acting like the rays of the sun; warmth; pleasantness; brightness; cheerfulness.—*adj* sunshiny.

sunshiny *adj* bright with the rays of the sun; bright like the sun.

sunspot *n* a dark, irregular, variable spot, sometimes visible on the surface of the sun.

sunstroke *n* a serious affection of the nervous system frequent in tropical climates and in temperate regions during very warm weather, generally caused by exposure of the head and neck to the direct rays of the sun.

suntan *n* browning of the skin by the sun.

sup *vt* (**supped, supping**) to take into the mouth with the lips, as a liquid; to imbibe; to sip; to have as one's lot; to be afflicted with (*to sup sorrow*).—*vi* to eat the evening meal.—*n* a little taken with the lips; a sip.

super- *prefix* indicating a position above or outside (*superstructure*); indicating superiority in size or quality (*superman*); indicating something greater to an unusual degree (*supercharge*).

superable *adj* capable of being overcome or conquered.

superabound *vi* to be very, or excessively, abundant.

superabundance *n* more than enough; excessive abundance.

superabundant *adj* abounding to excess; being more than is sufficient.

superadd *vt* to add over and above; to add or join in addition.

superannuate *vt* (**superannuated, superannuating**) to allow to retire from service on a pension, on account of old age or infirmity; to give a retiring pension to.—*vi* to retire on a pension.—*vt* to pension off on account of age or illness.

superannuation *n* the state of being too old for office or business; retirement or removal from office with a pension, on account of long service or infirmity; a regular contribution from an employee's salary or wages towards a pension scheme.

superb *adj* grand; august; stately; splendid; rich; sumptuous; showy; very fine; first-rate.

supercharge *vt* (**supercharged, supercharging**) to increase the power of an engine by using a device that supplies air or fuel in increased quantities by raising the intake pressure; to charge (the atmosphere, a conversation, etc) with excess tension or emotion.

supercilious *adj* having a haughty air or manner; acting as if others were our inferiors; haughty; overbearing; arrogant.

superconductivity *n* (*physics*) the complete loss of electrical resistance exhibited by

sunflower

certain materials at very low temperatures.

superconductor *n* a material capable of superconductivity.

supererogation *n* performance of more than duty requires.

superficial *adj* lying on or pertaining to the surface; not penetrating the substance of a thing; not sinking deep; not deep or profound as regards knowledge; not learned or thorough; not going to the heart of things.

superfine *adj* very fine; surpassing others in fineness; excessively or faultily subtle.

superfluity *n* a quantity that is over and above what is necessary; a greater quantity than is wanted; redundancy; something for show or luxury rather than use.

superfluous *adj* being more than is wanted or sufficient; unnecessary from being in excess; redundant.

superheat *vt* to heat to an extreme degree; specifically, to heat steam, apart from contact with water, until it resembles a perfect gas.

superhuman *adj* above or beyond what is human; hence, sometimes, divine.

superimpose *vt* (**superimposed, superimposing**) to lay or impose on something else.

superincumbent *adj* lying or resting on something else.

superintend *vt* to have the charge and oversight of; to oversee with the power of direction; to take care of with authority.

superintendence *n* the act of superintending; care and oversight for the purpose of direction and with authority to direct.

superintendent *n* one who superintends or has the oversight and charge of something; a police officer next above the rank of inspector.—*adj* overlooking others with authority.

superior *adj* more elevated in place; higher; higher in rank, office or dignity; higher or greater in excellence; being beyond some power or influence; too great or firm to be affected by (*superior to revenge*); (*bot*) growing above or on anything (as the ovary when growing above the origin of the calyx); next the axis.—*n* one who is superior to or above another; one who is higher or greater than another in social station, rank, power, excellence or qualities of any kind; the chief of a monastery, convent or abbey.

superiority *n* the state or quality of being superior; pre-eminence; higher rank or excellency.

superior planet *n* any of those planets that are more distant from the sun than the earth, namely Mars, Jupiter, Saturn, Uranus, Neptune and Pluto.

superlative *adj* of the highest degree or quality; most eminent; surpassing all other

(*superlative wisdom* or *beauty*); (*gram*) applied to that form of an adjective or adverb which expresses the highest or utmost degree of the quality or manner.—*n* that which is superlative; (*gram*) the superlative degree of adjectives or adverbs; a word in the superlative degree.

superman, superwoman *n* (*pl* **supermen, superwomen**) a person of considerably more than human powers or qualities.

supernatural *adj* being beyond or exceeding the powers or laws of nature; a term stronger than preternatural and often equivalent to miraculous.

supernumerary *adj* exceeding a number stated or prescribed; exceeding a necessary or usual number.—*n* a person or thing beyond a certain number or beyond what is necessary or usual; especially, a person not formally a member of an ordinary or regular body or staff of officials or employees; (*milit*) in drill, the warrant officers, non-commissioned officers, etc, who do not fall in with the rank and file.

superscribe *vt* (**superscribed, superscribing**) to write on the top, outside or surface; to put an inscription on; to write the name or address of one on the outside or cover of.

superscript *n* a character written or printed above another character.

superscription *n* the act of superscribing; what is written or engraved on the outside or above something else; especially, an address on a letter.

supersede *vt* (**superseded, superseding**) to make void, ineffectual or useless by superior power or by coming in the place of; to come or be placed in the place of; to displace; to replace (*one person supersedes another*).

supersensitive *adj* abnormally sensitive.

superstition *n* belief in and reverence of things which are not proper objects of worship; a practice or observance founded on such a belief; credulity regarding the supernatural; belief in the direct agency of superior powers in certain affairs, as a belief in witchcraft or magic or in supernatural phenomena, as apparitions, omens, etc.

superstitious *adj* pertaining or addicted to superstition; credulous in regard to the supernatural; proceeding from superstition.

superstructure *n* any structure built on something else; anything erected on a foundation or basis.

supertax *n* an extra tax, usually graded, on incomes above some fixed amount.

supervene *vi* (**supervened, supervening**) to come on as something extraneous; to be added or joined; to take place; to happen.

supervise *vt* (**supervised, supervising**) to oversee for direction; to superintend; to inspect.

supervision *n* the act of supervising; super-intendence; direction.

supervisor *n* one who supervises; an over-seer; an inspector; a superintendent.

supine *adj* lying on the back or with the face upward, opposed to *prone*; inclined or sloping; negligent; listless; indolent; inat-tentive.—*n* a part of the Latin verb, really a verbal noun with two cases, an accusa-tive in -*um* and an ablative in -*u*.

supper *n* the main evening meal; a snack taken in the evening.—*vi* to take supper; to sup.—*vt* to give supper to.

suppertime *n* the time when supper is taken; evening.

supplant *vt* to displace and take the place of.

supple *adj* pliant; flexible; easily bent; yielding; not obstinate; capable of mould-ing oneself to suit a purpose; flattering; fawning.

supplejack *n* a popular name given to vari-ous strong twining and climbing tropical American shrubs, the branches of which are made into walking sticks.

supplement *n* an addition to anything, by which it is made more full and complete, especially an addition to a book, to a peri-odical publication, etc.—*vt* to increase or complete by a supplement.

supplemental, supplementary *adj* of the nature of a supplement; serving to supple-ment; additional.

suppleness *n* the quality of being supple or easily bent; pliancy; readiness of compli-ance; facility.

suppliant *adj* entreating or begging ear-nestly; asking earnestly and submissively; supplicating; expressive of supplica-tion.—*n* a humble petitioner; one who en-treats submissively.

supplicant *n* one who supplicates or hum-bly entreats; a humble petitioner; a suppli-ant.—*adj* earnestly entreating; suppliant.

supplicate *vt* (**supplicated, supplicating**) to entreat or beg humbly for; to seek by earnest prayer (*to supplicate blessings*); to address in prayer; to petition humbly (*to supplicate God*).—*vi* to petition with ear-nestness and submission; to implore; to beseech.

supplication *n* the act of supplicating; hum-ble and earnest prayer in worship; a peti-tion; an earnest request.

supply *vt* to furnish with what is wanted (*to supply a person with a thing*); to afford or furnish a sufficiency for (*to supply needs*); to provide or furnish (*to supply provi-sions*); to serve instead of; to take the place of.—*n* the act of supplying; a quantity sup-plied; a stock; a store; (*pl*) the stores or ar-ticles necessary for an army or other great body of people; a grant of money provided by a national assembly to meet the ex-penses of government; the extent to which goods are produced to meet the demand.

support *vt* to bear, uphold, prop up; to keep from falling or sinking; to endure without being overcome; to bear; to undergo; to uphold by aid or encouragement; to fur-ther, second, aid, assist; to keep from sink-ing, failing or declining (*to support the courage*); to represent in acting on the stage; to act (*to support a part*); to be able to supply funds for or the means of con-tinuing; to be able to carry on or continue; to maintain with the means of living; to provide for; to keep up by nutriment; to sustain (*to support life*, *to support combus-tion*); to make good or substantiate (a statement, an accusation); to second, as a proposal or motion at a public meeting.—*n* the act of supporting; that which upholds or keeps from falling; a base, prop, foun-dation of any kind; sustenance or what maintains life; maintenance; livelihood; one who furnishes another's livelihood; the act of assisting, maintaining, vindicat-ing, etc; aid; help; succour; assistance.

supporter *n* one who supports or maintains; a defender, advocate, adherent; one who accompanies and aids another; that which supports or keeps up; a prop, a pillar, etc; (*heral*) a figure on each side of a shield appearing to support it; a band or truss for the support of any part.

supportive *adj* providing support or help; tending to provide psychological or emo-tional support.

suppose *vt* (**supposed, supposing**) to lay down or regard as matter of fact for the sake of argument or illustration; to assume hypothetically; to take for granted; to im-agine; to think to be the case; to require to exist or be true; to imply (*creation sup-poses a creator*).—*vi* to make or form a supposition; to think; to imagine.

supposition *n* the act of supposing; hypoth-esis; what is assumed hypothetically; an assumption; a conjecture.

suppress *vt* to overpower and crush; to put down; to quell; to destroy (a revolt, mutiny or riot); to restrain from utterance or vent; to check or keep in (*to suppress the breath*); to conceal; not to tell or reveal; to retain without making public.

suppression *n* the act of suppressing, crush-ing or putting down; the act of retaining from utterance, vent or disclosure; con-cealment; the retaining of anything from public notice.

suppurate *vi* (**suppurated, suppurating**) to generate pus or matter; to have a gather-ing of pus; to fester.

suppuration *n* the process of forming pus, as in a wound or abscess.

supremacy *n* the state or character of being supreme; highest authority or power.

supple

867

supreme *adj* highest in authority; holding the highest place in government or power; highest as to degree; greatest possible; utmost.

supremely *adv* with the highest authority; in the highest degree; to the utmost extent.

supremo *n* (*pl* **supremos**) (*colloq*) a person with supreme power.

sura *n* a chapter of the Koran.

surcharge *vt* (**surcharged, surcharging**) to overload; to overburden; to overcharge; to put an extra charge on.—*n* an excessive or extra charge or burden; an overcharge.

surcingle *n* a belt or girth fastening a saddle or anything else on a horse's back; the girdle round a clergyman's cassock.

surcoat *n* an outer garment formerly worn in a variety of forms; a loose sleeveless wrapper embroidered with the arms of a knight and girded round the waist with a sword belt, formerly worn by him over a coat of mail to protect it from wet.

surd *n* in phonetics, a non-sonant consonant; (*math*) an irrational quantity; a quantity that cannot be expressed in finite terms, as the square root of 2.

sure *adj* perfectly confident; certainly knowing and believing; certain; fully persuaded; certain to find or retain (*sure of success*); to be depended on; unfailing; firm; stable; secure; infallible (*a sure remedy*).—*adv* certainly; without doubt.

sure-footed *adj* not liable to stumble, slip or fall.

surely *adv* certainly; undoubtedly; firmly; securely; verily.

surety *n* certainty; security; ground of security; security against loss or damage or for payment; law, one bound with and for another who is primarily liable and who is called the principal; one who binds himself or herself to stand good for another; a bail.

surf *n* the swell of the sea which breaks on the shore or on sand banks or rocks.—*vi* to ride on the surf by means of a surfboard.

surface *n* the exterior part of anything that has length and breadth; the outside or outer boundary of something; the top level; (*fig*) outward or external appearance; what appears on a slight or casual view.—a *plane surface* is that in which any two points being taken the straight line between them lies wholly in that surface.—*adj* pertaining to the surface; external; superficial.—*vt* (**surfaced, surfacing**) to give a particular surface to; to work over the surface of.—*vi* to rise to the surface of.

surface tension *n* (of a liquid) the condition of the surface layer, which behaves like a stretched film.

surfboard *n* a long, narrow board used in the sport of surfing.

surfing

surfeit *n* an overloading of the stomach by excess in eating and drinking; too much of anything; disgust caused by excess; satiety.—*vt* to derange the stomach by excess in eating; to overload the stomach of; to give too much of anything to; to fill to satiety and disgust; to cloy.—*vi* to suffer from a surfeit.

surfing *n* the sport of riding in towards shore on the top of a wave, especially on a surfboard.

surge *n* a large wave or billow; a great rolling swell of water; a heaving or swelling up; an undulation.—*vi* (**surged, surging**) to swell; to rise high and roll, as waves; to rush or swell strongly.

surgeon *n* a medical person whose profession is to cure diseases or injuries of the body by manual operation or by medical appliances employed externally or internally, as distinguished from a physician.

surgery *n* that branch of medical science and practice which involves the performance of operations on the human body; a room where patients consult a general practitioner or dentist; a place where constituents may consult their MP.

surgical *adj* pertaining to surgery; done by means of surgery.

suricate *n* a carnivorous mongoose of southern Africa with a long tail.

Surinam toad *n* the pipa.

surly *adj* gloomily morose; sternly sour; cross and rude; churlish; rough or tempestuous.

surmise *n* a thought or supposition with little or no ground to go on; a guess or conjecture.—*vt* (**surmised, surmising**) to guess; to conjecture.

surmount *vt* to mount or rise above; to conquer; to overcome; to surpass.

surmullet *n* a name for a variety of fishes allied to the perch family.

surname *n* a name or appellation added to the Christian name or first name and which becomes a family name.

surpass *vt* to exceed; to excel; to go beyond in anything good or bad.

surplice *n* a white garment worn by priests, deacons and choristers in the Anglican and Roman Catholic Churches over their other dress at religious services.

surplus *n* that which remains when use or need is satisfied; more than suffices.—*adj* constituting an excess (*surplus population*).

surprise *n* the act of coming on unawares or of taking suddenly and without preparation; an emotion excited by something happening suddenly and unexpectedly; wonder; astonishment.—*vt* (**surprised, surprising**) to fall on suddenly and unexpectedly; to attack or take unawares; to confuse or perplex; to strike with wonder or astonishment; to astonish; to lead, bring or betray unawares.

surprising *adj* exciting surprise; wonderful; extraordinary.

surreal *adj* dreamlike; surrealistic; distorted.

surrealism *n* a movement in art characterized by the expression of the activities of the unconscious mind and dream elements.

surrealistic *adj* pertaining to surrealism.

surrender *vt* to yield to the power of another; to give or deliver up on compulsion or demand; to resign in favour of another; to cease to claim or use; to relinquish; (*refl*) to yield to any influence, passion or power (*to surrender oneself to grief*).—*vi* to yield; to give up oneself into the power of another.—*n* the act of surrendering; a yielding or giving up; the abandonment of an assurance policy by the party assured on receiving a portion of the premiums paid.

surreptitious *adj* done by stealth or without proper authority; secret; stealthy.

surrogate *n* a person or thing acting as a substitute for another person or thing.

surrogate mother *n* a woman who bears a child on behalf of another woman, usually a woman who is unable to bear children.

surround *vt* to encompass, environ or enclose on all sides; to invest, as a city; to lie or be on all sides of; to form an enclosure round.

surroundings *npl* those things that surround or environ; an environment; everything around or about a person, thing or place; an environment.

surtax *n* a tax increased for a particular purpose; an extra tax.

surtout *n* originally, a man's coat to be worn over his other garments; in later usage, an upper coat with long wide skirts; a frockcoat.

surveillance *n* watch kept over some person or thing; oversight; superintendence.

survey *vt* to inspect or take a view of; to view as from a high place; to view with a scrutinizing eye; to examine; to examine with reference to condition, situation or value; to inspect for a purpose; to determine the boundaries, extent, position, natural features, etc, of, as of any portion of the earth's surface by means of measurements and the application of geometry and trigonometry.—*n* a general view; a look at or over; a close examination or inspection to ascertain condition, quantity, quality, etc; the determination of dimensions and other topographical particulars of any part of the earth's surface; the plan or account drawn up of such particulars.

surveying *n* the act of one who surveys; the operation or art of making a survey of a portion of the earth's surface by means of measurements and calculations.

surveyor *n* one who surveys; an overseer; one that views and examines for the purpose of ascertaining the condition or state of anything; one who practises the art of surveying.

survival *n* the act of surviving; a living beyond the life of another person or beyond any event; any habit, usage or belief remaining from ancient times and existing merely from custom.

survive *vt* (**survived, surviving**) to outlive; to live beyond the life of; to live longer than; to live beyond (*to survive one's usefulness*).—*vi* to remain alive; to live after the death of another or after anything else.

survivor *n* one who lives after the death of another or after some event or time; (*law*) the longer liver of two persons who have a joint interest in anything.

susceptibility *n* the state or quality of being susceptible; sensitiveness; capacity for feeling or emotional excitement; sensibility.

susceptible *adj* capable of being acted on or affected in any way; admitting any change (*susceptible of pain* or *alteration*); capable of emotional impression; readily impressed; sensitive.

suspect *vt* to have a vague belief or fear of the existence of; to imagine as probably existing (*to suspect danger*); to mistrust; to imagine to be guilty but on slight evidence or without proof; to hold to be uncertain; to doubt.—*n* a suspected person; one suspected of a crime offence, etc.

suspend *vt* to cause to hang; to hang up; to cause to cease for a time; to interrupt temporarily; to stay; to hold in a state undetermined (*to suspend one's choice*); to debar for a time from any privilege; to remove temporarily from an office; to cause to cease for a time from operation or effect.—*vi* to cease from operation; to stop payment or be unable to meet one's engagements.

suspender *n* one that suspends; a strip of elastic with a fastener for holding up socks or stockings.

suspense *n* the state of having the mind or thoughts uncertain; uncertainty, with more or less apprehension or anxiety; indecision; (*law*) a temporary cessation.

suspension *n* the act of suspending or hanging up; the act of delaying, interrupting or stopping for a time; a cessation of operation; a stoppage; temporary abeyance; the state of being in the form of particles floating undissolved in a fluid.

suspension bridge *n* a bridge carrying a roadway suspended by cables anchored to towers at either end.

suspicion *n* the act of suspecting; the feel-

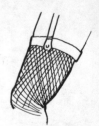

suspender

ing of one who suspects; the thought that there is probably something wrong; a notion that something is so or so.

suspicious *adj* inclined to suspect; ready to entertain or entertaining suspicion; distrustful (*suspicious of a person* or *his motives*); indicating or exhibiting suspicion; adapted to raise suspicion (*suspicious circumstances*).

sustain *vt* to rest under and bear up; to support; to hold suspended; to keep from sinking in despondence; to keep alive; to furnish sustenance for; to nourish; to aid effectually; to keep from ruin; to endure without failing or yielding; to bear up against; to suffer; to undergo; to allow (an action) to proceed before a court; to hold valid in law; to establish by evidence; to confirm or corroborate.

sustenance *n* the act of sustaining; maintenance; subsistence; that which supports life; food; provisions.

sutler *n* formerly, a person who followed an army and sold provisions, liquors, etc, to the troops.

sutra *n* a collection or string of aphorisms in the Sanskrit literature.

suttee *n* a Hindu widow who throws herself on the funeral pile of her husband to die; the voluntary self-destruction by fire of a Hindu widow.

suture *n* the act of sewing; a seam; the line along which two things or parts are joined; (*surg*) the uniting of the lips or edges of a wound by stitching; (*anat*) one of the seams uniting the bones of the skull; (*bot*) the seam of a dehiscent pericarp where the valves unite.

suzerain *n* a feudal lord or baron; a lord paramount.

suzerainty *n* the office or dignity of a suzerain; paramount authority or command.

swab *n* a mop for cleaning floors, ships' decks, etc; in medicine, a small piece of fabric used to wipe away fluids, apply medication or take samples of bodily secretions for analysis; the sample taken.— *vt* (**swabbed, swabbing**) to clean with a swab or mop: to take a medicinal specimen with a swab from.

swaddle *vt* (**swaddled, swaddling**) to bind as with a bandage; to swathe (used generally of infants).—*n* a cloth band round the body of an infant.

swaddling band, swaddling cloth *n* a band or cloth wrapped round an infant.

swag *n* plunder, booty.

swagger *vi* to boast noisily; to bluster; to hector; to strut with a defiant or insolent air.—*vt* to influence by blustering or threats.—*n* a piece of bluster; bravado or insolence in manner; an insolent strut.

swaggerer *n* one who swaggers or blusters; a bully.

swallow

swan

swagger stick *n* stick or cane carried by soldier in uniform when not on parade.

swain *n* a young man dwelling in the country; a peasant or rustic; a country gallant; a lover.

swallow¹ *vt* to receive through the gullet into the stomach; to draw into an abyss or gulf; to engulf; to absorb; to take into the mind readily; to receive or embrace, as opinions; to drink in; to occupy or take up (*to swallow time*); to exhaust or consume; to put up with; to bear or take patiently (*to swallow an affront*); (*colloq*) to believe.— *n* capacity for swallowing; voracity.

swallow² *n* one of certain birds remarkable for their extreme length of wing and velocity of flight, living on insects which they catch in the air and in temperate climates coming in spring and departing when summer is over.

swallowtail *n* a plant, a species of willow; a swallow-tailed coat.

swallow-tailed *adj* of the form of a swallow's tail; having tapering or pointed skirts (*a swallow-tailed coat*).

swamp *n* a piece of spongy land or low ground saturated with water; a bog, fen, marsh or morass.—*vt* to plunge or sink in a swamp or as in a swamp; to plunge into inextricable difficulties; (*naut*) to overset, sink or cause to become filled, as a boat in water; to overwhelm.

swampy *adj* consisting of swamp; low, wet and spongy.

swan *n* a long-necked web-footed bird of several species, frequenting rivers and ponds of fresh water, of great size, very graceful in the water and generally having plumage of snowy whiteness, though a black species exists in Australia.

swank *n* conceit.—*vi* to behave ostentatiously; to swagger.

swannery *n* a place where swans are bred and reared.

swan song *n* the last work or creation of a writer, artist, composer, etc; a last performance before retirement, departure or death.

swap, swop *vt* (**swapped, swapping**) to strike with a sweeping stroke; to knock down; to barter; to exchange.—*n* a blow; an exchange or barter.

sward *n* the grassy surface of land; turf; green-sward.—*vt* to cover with sward.

swarm¹ *n* a large number or body of insects; the cluster of bees which emigrate from a hive at once and seek new lodgings; any great number or multitude; a multitude of people in motion.—*vi* to depart from a hive in a swarm; to give out a swarm of bees; to throng in multitudes; to crowd; to be crowded or thronged with a multitude; to abound.

swarm² *vi* to climb a tree, pole, etc, by embracing it with the arms and legs and scrambling; to shin.

swarthy *adj* being of a dark hue or dusky complexion; tawny or black.

swashbuckler *n* a swaggering fellow; a bravo; a bully.

swastika *n* an ancient Aryan symbol adopted by Nazi Germany, consisting of a cross with arms of equal length, each arm having a prolongation at right angles and intended to represent the sun.

swat *vt* (**swatted, swatting**) to crush flat or squash (used of flies, wasps, etc).

swath *n* a band or bandage; a line of grass or corn cut and lying; the reach or sweep of a scythe.

swathe *vt* (**swathed, swathing**) to bind with a band or bandage; to tie up in bundles or sheaves; to bind or wind about; to wrap.— *n* a bandage.

sway *vi* to swing backwards and forwards; to be drawn to one side by weight; to incline or hang; to move or advance to one side; to have the judgment or feelings inclining one way; to have weight or influence; to bear rule; to govern.—*vt* to move backwards and forwards; to wield with the hand (a sceptre); to bias; to cause to incline to one side; to prejudice; to rule; to influence, govern or direct.—*n* a swing or sweep; power exerted in governing; rule; influence; weight or authority that inclines to one side.

swear *vi* (*pret* **swore**, *pp* **sworn**, *ppr* **swearing**) to utter a solemn declaration, with an appeal to God for the truth of what is affirmed; to declare or affirm in a solemn manner; to promise on oath; to give evidence on oath; to use profane language; to utter profane oaths.—*vt* to affirm with an appeal to God; to utter on oath; to promise solemnly; to vow; to put to an oath; to bind by an oath; to utter in a profane manner.

sweat *n* the moisture which comes out on the skin of an animal; perspiration; the state of one who sweats; moisture exuded from any substance.—*vi* to have sweat exuding from the skin; to perspire; to toil; to drudge; to emit moisture, as green plants in a heap.—*vt* to cause to give out sweat; to emit from the pores; to exude.

sweater *n* one who sweats; a grinding employer; thick jersey.

sweat gland *n* any of the glands in the skin of mammals that are responsible for the secretion of sweat and whose distribution varies according to the species.

sweatshop *n* a small factory or workshop where employees work long hours in poor conditions for low wages.

sweaty *adj* moist with sweat; having the character of sweat; consisting of sweat.

swede *n* a round root vegetable with yellow flesh; a turnip.

Swede *n* a native of Sweden.

Swedish *adj* pertaining to Sweden or its inhabitants.—*n* the language of the Swedes.

sweep[1] *vt* (*pret*, *pp* **swept**, *ppr* **sweeping**) to rub over with a broom or brush, for removing loose dirt; to clean by brushing; to remove or strike by a brushing stroke; to carry along or off (*the wind sweeps the snow, a river sweeps away a dam*); to destroy or carry off at a blow; to rub or trail over (*to sweep the ground*); to pass over so as to clear (*to sweep the seas of ships*); to move swiftly over or along; to carry the eye over; to draw or drag something over.—*vi* to pass or flow with swiftness and violence; to pass or brush along with celerity; to pass with pomp; to take in a view with progressive rapidity; to range.—*n* the act of sweeping; the reach or range of a continued motion or stroke; the compass or reach of anything flowing or brushing along; the direction or turn of a curve, as of a road; compass or extent of excursion; range; a rapid survey with the eye; (*naut*) a large oar used in small vessels to aid their progress; one who sweeps chimneys; the depth of strata of air disturbed by an aeroplane in motion.

sweep[2] *n* a short form of **sweepstake**.

sweeping *adj* including many individuals or particulars in a single act or assertion; wide and comprehensive (*a sweeping charge*); of very wide range.—*npl* things collected by sweeping; rubbish.

sweepstake *n* a gaming transaction in which a number of persons join in contributing a certain stake which becomes the property of one or of several of the contributors under certain conditions; a prize made up of several stakes.

sweet *adj* having a pleasant taste or flavour like that of sugar or honey, opposed to *bitter*; pleasing to the smell; fragrant; pleasing to the ear; soft; melodious; pleasing to the eye; beautiful; pleasing to the mind; mild; gentle; kind; obliging; bland; not salt or salted; not stale; not sour.—*npl* sweet things; sweetmeats; things that please (*the sweets of domestic life*).

sweetbread *n* the pancreas of an animal used as food.

sweetbrier, sweetbriar *n* a species of wild rose remarkable for the sweet smell of its leaves.

sweeten *vt* to make sweet to the taste; to make pleasing or grateful to the mind; to make mild or kind; to increase the agreeable qualities of; to make pure and wholesome; to make mellow and fertile; to restore to purity.—*vi* to become sweet.

sweetening *n* the act of one who sweetens; that which sweetens.

sweetheart *n* a lover, male or female; a boyfriend or girlfriend.

sweetmeat *n* an article of confectionery made wholly or principally of sugar; fruit preserved with sugar.

sweet pea *n* an annual much cultivated in gardens for its showy sweet-scented flowers.

sweet potato *n* a tropical climbing plant with an edible tuberous root, the yam; the root itself used as food.

sweet william *n* a species of pink of many varieties, cultivated in gardens.

swell *vi* (*pret* **swelled**, *pp* **swelled** *or* **swollen**, *ppr* **swelling**) to grow bulkier; to dilate; to increase in size or extent; to rise or be driven into billows; to be protuberant; to bulge out; to rise in altitude; to be puffed up with some feeling; hence, to strut; to look big; to grow and increase in the mind; to become larger in amount; to increase in intensity or volume, as sound.—*vt* to increase the size of; to cause to dilate or increase; to aggravate; to heighten; to inflate; to puff up.—*n* the act of swelling; gradual increase; an elevation of land; an undulation; a succession of long unbroken waves setting in one direction, as after a storm; a billow; a surge; a gradual increase and decrease in the volume of musical sound; an arrangement in an organ whereby the player can increase or diminish the intensity of the sound; a familiar word for a person of rank or high standing or for a showy, fashionable person; a dandy, a fop, etc.

swelling *n* a swollen part; a protuberance; an increase in size.

swelter *vi* to be overcome and faint with heat.—*vt* to oppress with heat.

swerve *vi* (**swerved, swerving**) to wander from any line prescribed or from a rule of duty; to deviate; to run aside suddenly or sharply from a course; to turn to one side.

swift *adj* moving with great speed or rapidity; fleet; rapid; ready; prompt; coming suddenly or without delay; of short continuance; rapidly passing.—*adv* in a swift or rapid manner; swiftly.—*n* the name of birds which have an outward resemblance to the swallows, the common swift having the greatest powers of flight of any bird that visits Britain.

swig *vt* (**swigged, swigging**) to drink by large draughts; to drink off rapidly and greedily.—*vi* to take deep draughts.—*n* a large draught.

swill *vt* to drink grossly or greedily; to inebriate; to rinse.—*vi* to drink greedily or to excess.—*n* drink taken in excessive quantities; the wash or mixture of liquid substances given to swine; a rinse.

swim *vi* (*pret* **swam** *or* **swum**, *pp* **swum**, *ppr* **swimming**) to be supported on water or other fluid; to float; to move through water by the motion of the hands and feet or of fins; to glide with a smooth motion; to be flooded; to be drenched; to overflow; to be dizzy or giddy (*the head swims*).—*vt* to pass or cross by swimming; to cause to swim or float.—*n* the act of swimming; period or extent of swimming; a smooth, gliding motion; the air bladder or sound of fishes.

swim bladder *n* an air-filled sac in fish that regulates buoyancy.

swimmer *n* one who swims; a bird that swims, as the duck and goose.

swimming *n* the act or art of sustaining and propelling the body in water; a dizziness or giddiness.

swimming baths *npl* a public swimming pool, sometimes with public baths and showers.

swimmingly *adv* in an easy gliding manner, as if swimming; smoothly; successfully.

swimming pool *n* an artificial outdoor or covered pool in which swimming is learned or practised.

swindle *vt* (**swindled, swindling**) to cheat and defraud grossly or with deliberate artifice.—*n* a fraudulent scheme intended to dupe people out of money; an imposition.

swindler *n* one who swindles; a cheat.

swine *n sing, pl* a hoofed mammal, the female of which is the sow and whose flesh is much eaten under the name of pork; a pig or hog; a brutish person; a nasty, vicious person.

swineherd *n* a herd or keeper of swine.

swinish *adj* befitting swine; like the swine in filthiness; hoggish; brutish; nasty.

swing *vi* (*pret, pp* **swung**, *ppr* **swinging**) to move to and fro, as a body suspended in the air; to oscillate; to sway; to be carried to and fro while hanging on something; (*colloq*) to bring about, to achieve; to have a lively rhythm; (*colloq*) (of a party, etc) to be very lively; (*colloq*) to hang, as a criminal.—*vt* to make to sway or oscillate loosely; to whirl in the air; to wave; to brandish.—*n* the act of swinging; an oscillation; the sweep of a moving body; an apparatus suspended for persons to swing in; free course of conduct; unrestrained liberty or licence; a type of popular jazz with a lively, steady rhythm; liveliness.

swing bridge *n* a bridge that may be moved by swinging, so as to afford passage for ships on a river, canal, at the mouth of docks, etc.

swingeing *adj* great; large; huge; severe.

swing-tree, swingle-tree *n* a crossbar by which a horse is yoked to a carriage, plough, etc, and to which the traces are fastened.

swipe *vti* (**swiped, swiping**) to strike with a sweeping blow; to strike or drive with great force; (*colloq*) to steal.

swirl *vi* to form eddies; to whirl in eddies.—

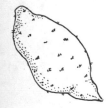

sweet potato

swimmer

n a whirling motion; an eddy, as of water; a twist or curl in the grain of wood.

Swiss *n sing, pl* a native or inhabitant (natives or inhabitants) of Switzerland.—*adj* belonging to the Swiss or to Switzerland.

swiss roll *n* a kind of light spongy cake, spread with jam or other sweet filling while still hot and then rolled up.

switch *n* a small flexible twig or rod; a movable piece of rail for turning a railway train from one line to another; a device for making or breaking an electric circuit or changing direction of current.—*vt* to strike with a switch; to lash; to transfer from one line of rails to another; to shunt; (*elect*) to turn on or off or into a new circuit.

switchboard *n* an installation in a building where phone calls are connected.

switchback *n* a zigzag road in a mountain region.

switchback railway *n* a short railway with cars that get an impetus from starting on a slope and again rise nearly as high as the start.

swivel *n* a fastening that allows the thing fastened to turn freely round on its axis; a link in a chain partly consisting of a pivot turning in a hole formed in the next link.—*vi* (**swivelled, swivelling**) to turn as if on a pivot.

swoon *vi* to faint; to sink into a fainting fit.—*n* the state of one who swoons; a fainting fit.

swoop *vt* to dash on while on the wing; to take with a sweep.—*vi* to descend on prey suddenly from a height, as a hawk; to stoop.—*n* the sudden pouncing of a rapacious bird on its prey; a falling on and seizing, as of a bird on its prey.

swop *vt* (**swopped, swopping**) same as **swap**.

sword *n* a weapon having a long metal blade (usually steel), either straight and with a sharp point for thrusting, as the rapier; with a sharp point and one or two cutting edges for thrusting and striking, as the broadsword; or curved and with a sharp convex edge for striking, as the scimitar.

sword dance *n* a dance by one performer over crossed swords among the Scottish Highlanders.

swordfish *n* a fish allied to the mackerel tribe, remarkable for its elongated upper jaw, which forms a sword-like weapon.

swordsman *n* (*pl* **swordsmen**) a man who carries a sword; one skilled in the use of the sword.

swordstick *n* a walking stick in which is concealed a sword.

sybarite *n* a person devoted to luxury and pleasure; an effeminate person.

sybaritic, sybaritical *adj* luxurious; devoted to luxury or pleasure.

sycamore *n* a fruit tree of the fig family, common in Palestine, Arabia, etc; a kind of maple, a well-known timber tree, long naturalized in England and usually called plane tree in Scotland; a name frequently given in America to the plane tree, buttonwood or cottonwood.

sycophant *n* a parasite; a servile flatterer.

sycophantic, sycophantical *adj* belonging to or resembling a sycophant; obsequiously flattering.

sycosis *n* a disease which consists of an eruption of tubercles on the bearded portion of the face and on the scalp.

syenite *n* a granitic rock of a greyish colour, composed of quartz, hornblende and feldspar (so called because abundant near Syene in Upper Egypt).

syllabic *adj* pertaining to a syllable or syllables; consisting of a syllable or syllables.

syllable *n* the smallest unit of speech, consisting of a vowel sound with or without one or more consonant sounds.

syllabub, sillabub *n* a dish of wine or cider with cream or milk forming a soft curd.

syllabus *n* (*pl* **syllabi, syllabuses**) a brief statement of the subject of a discourse, of a course of lectures, etc; an abstract; the set programme of a course of study.

syllepsis *n* (*pl* **syllepses**) a figure of speech by which one word is referred to another in the sentence to which it does not grammatically belong; zeugma.

syllogism *n* (in logic) a form of reasoning or argument, consisting of three propositions, of which the two first are called the premises (major and minor) and the last the conclusion, the conclusion necessarily following from the premises.

sylph *n* an elemental spirit of the air; a woman of graceful and slender proportions.

sylva *n* the forest trees of any region or country collectively.

sylvan, silvan *adj* pertaining to a wood or forest; abounding with trees; rural.

symbiosis *n* a sort of parasitism in which two kinds of animals or plants, or a plant and animal, live in close relationship, the one being of service to the other for protection or food.

symbol *n* an object animate or inanimate standing for or calling up something moral or intellectual; an emblem; a type (*the olive branch is the symbol of peace*); a letter or character which is significant; a sign (as in chemistry, astronomy, etc); a distinctive mark or attribute of office or duty; (*theol*) a creed or confession of faith.—*vt* to symbolize.

symbolic, symbolical *adj* pertaining to a symbol or symbols; of the nature of a symbol; representative.

symbolism *n* the investing of objects or animals with a symbolic meaning; meaning

sword

swordfish

expressed by symbols; symbols collectively.

symbolize *vt* (**symbolized, symbolizing**) to represent by a symbol or by symbols; to serve as the symbol of; to regard or treat as symbolic.—*vi* to express or represent in symbols.

symmetric *adj* symmetrical (used chiefly in mathematics).

symmetrical *adj* possessing symmetry; well proportioned in all parts; handsome; finely made; (*bot*) having the number of parts of one series corresponding with that of the other series (as, having five sepals, five petals and five or ten or fifteen stamens); (*math*) having corresponding parts or relations.

symmetry *n* a due proportion in size and form of the parts of a body or structure to each other; such harmony of parts as produces a pleasing whole; the character of being well proportioned.

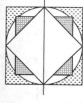

symetry

sympathetic *adj* expressive of, produced by or exhibiting sympathy; having sympathy or common feeling with another; feeling-hearted; (*physiol*) produced by sympathy.

sympathize *vi* (**sympathized, sympathizing**) to have a common feeling, as of bodily pleasure or pain; to feel in consequence of what another feels; to have fellow-feeling; to be sorry for another's suffering, etc.

sympathy *n* feeling corresponding to that which another feels; a feeling that enables a person to enter into and in part share another's feelings; fellow-feeling; compassion; commiseration; (*physiol, pathol*) that relation of the organs and parts of a living body to each other whereby a disordered condition of one part induces more or less disorder in another part.

symphonic *adj* pertaining to a symphony.

symphonious *adj* agreeing in sound; harmonious.

symphonist *n* a composer of symphonies.

symphony *n* a consonance or harmony of sounds agreeable to the ear; harmony; (*mus*) an elaborate composition for a full orchestra, consisting usually, like the sonata, of three or four contrasted but intimately related movements.

symphysis *n* (*pl* **symphyses**) (*anat*) a growing together; the union of bones by cartilage; the point of union between two parts.

symposium *n* (*pl* **symposia**) a meeting to discuss a particular topic; a collection of writings by different authors on the same subject.

symptom *n* what serves as evidence of something not seen; (*med*) a bodily sensation which accompanies a disease and from which the existence and nature of a disease may be inferred; a sign of the existence of something.

symptomatic *adj* being or serving as a symptom; indicating the existence of something else.

synaeresis *n* (*pl* **synaereses**) (*gram*) the contraction of two syllables or vowels into one.

synagogue *n* a congregation of Jews met for the purpose of worship; a Jewish place of worship.

syncarpous *adj* (*bot*) having the carpels completely united, as in the apple and pear.

synchronism *n* concurrence of two or more events or facts in time; simultaneousness; arrangement of contemporaneous events in tabular form.

synchronize *vi* (**synchronized, synchronizing**) to occur at the same time; to move or take place at the same rate or exactly together.—*vt* to make to agree in time; to cause to indicate the same time, as one timepiece with another.

synchronous *adj* happening at the same time; contemporaneous; simultaneous.

syncope *n* a contraction of a word by elision in the middle, as in *ne'er* for *never*; a suspension or sudden pause; (*med*) a fainting or swooning; (*mus*) syncopation.

syncopate *vt* (**syncopated, syncopating**) to contract by syncope; (*mus*) to treat with syncopation.

syncopation *n* the contraction of a word by elision; (*mus*) the alteration of rhythm by driving the accent to that part of a bar not usually accented, the accented part of a bar being usually the first note.

syncretism *n* the attempted blending of irreconcilable principles or parties, as in philosophy or religion, opposed to eclecticism.

syndactylous *adj* (*ornithol*) having the external toe nearly as long as the middle and partly joined to it, as in the bee-eater, kingfisher, etc; or with some of the digits closely bound together.

syndicate *n* an association of persons formed with the view of promoting some particular enterprise, financial scheme, etc; an organization selling articles to many newspapers or magazines.—*vt* (**syndicated, syndicating**) to manage as a syndicate; to form into a syndicate; to sell (a news article) through a syndicate.

syndrome *n* a characteristic pattern of signs and symptoms of a disease; a distinctive pattern of behaviour.

synod *n* a council or meeting of ecclesiastics, especially bishops and clergy, to consult on matters of religion; among Presbyterians, a church court consisting of the members of several adjoining presbyteries; also, a meeting, convention or council in general.

synodic *adj* pertaining to a synod; transacted in a synod.

synonym *n* a word having the same, or nearly the same, meaning as another in the same language; one of two or more words in the same language which have the same meaning.

synonymous *adj* having the character of a synonym; expressing the same thing; having the same meaning.

synopsis *n* (*pl* **synopses**) a summary or brief statement giving a general view of some subject, as by means of short paragraphs; a conspectus.

synoptic, synoptical *adj* affording a synopsis or general view.

synovia *n* a thick, viscid, yellowish-white fluid, somewhat resembling white of egg in appearance, secreted at the joints for the purpose of lubricating their surfaces.

synovial *adj* pertaining to or consisting of synovia.

synovitis *n* inflammation of the synovial membrane.

syntactic, syntactical *adj* pertaining or according to the rules of syntax.

syntax *n* (*gram*) the construction of sentences; the due arrangement of words or members of sentences in their mutual relations according to established usage.

synthesis *n* (*pl* **syntheses**) the putting of two or more things together to form a whole, opposed to analysis; (in logic) the combination of separate elements of thought into a whole; (*surg*) the operation by which divided parts are joined; (*chem*) the uniting of elements into a compound; composition or combination.

synthesize *vt* (**synthesized, synthesizing**) to make up by combining parts or elements; to combine into a whole.

synthesizer *n* an electronic device producing sounds and music by using a computer to combine individual sounds previously recorded.

synthetic, synthetical *adj* pertaining to synthesis; consisting in synthesis; made by mixing certain ingredients; produced by chemical synthesis; artificial.

syphilis *n* a contagious and hereditary venereal disease.

syphilitic *adj* pertaining to or infected with syphilis.

syphon *n*, *vti* same as **siphon**.

syringa *n* any of a genus of plants of which the lilac is the type; also a name of the mock orange.

syringe *n* a hollow tube with a piston which can be fitted on to a hypodermic needle and used to inject fluids into, or to withdraw them from, the body, etc.—*vt* (**syringed, syringing**) to wash and cleanse or water by means of a syringe; to apply a spray of liquid thus; to inject by means of a syringe.

syrinx *n* (*pl* **syringes**) the Pan pipes.

syrup *n* a saturated or nearly saturated solution of sugar in water; any sweet and somewhat viscous fluid; the uncrystallizable fluid finally separated from crystallized sugar in the refining process.

syrupy *adj* like syrup.

systaltic *adj* (*med*) having alternate contraction and dilatation, as the heart.

system *n* any assemblage of things forming a regular and connected whole; things connected according to a scheme; a number of heavenly bodies acting on each other according to certain laws (*the solar system*); an assemblage or connected series of parts or organs in an animal body (*the nervous system*); also, the body itself as a functional unity or whole (*to take poison into the system*); a plan or scheme according to which things are connected into a whole (*a system of philosophy*); regular method or order (*to have no system in working*).

systematic, systematical *adj* pertaining to or consisting in system; methodical; proceeding according to system.

systematize *vt* (**systematized, systematizing**) to reduce to system or regular method.

systemic *adj* pertaining to a system as a whole; (of an insecticide, etc) designed to be taken up into the plant tissues.

systole *n* the contraction of the heart and arteries for forcing the blood through the system and carrying on the circulation, opposite to diastole; (*gram*) the shortening of a long syllable.

systolic *adj* of or pertaining to the systole.

syzygy *n* (*astron*) the conjunction or opposition of a planet with the sum or of any two of the heavenly bodies.

T

T the twentieth letter of the English alphabet, closely allied to *d*, both being dentals.—**to a T** exactly; with the utmost exactness (*to suit to a T*), the allusion being to a T-square.

tab[1] *n* a tabulator; a tablet.—*vt* (**tabbed, tabbing**) to tabulate.

tab[2] *n* a strip, flap or loop on a garment; (*colloq*) a bill, as in a restaurant, etc.

tabard *n* a garment open at the sides, with wide sleeves or flaps reaching to the elbows.

tabby *n* a cat of a mixed or brindled colour, especially a female cat.

tabernacle *n* the movable building, so contrived as to be taken to pieces with ease, carried by the ancient Hebrews during their wanderings in the wilderness; a temple; a place of worship; a small cell or repository for holy things; an ornamental chest on Roman Catholic altars for the consecrated vessels; (*Gothic archit*) a canopied stall or niche; an arched canopy over a tomb; a tomb.

tabes *n* a disease consisting in a gradual wasting away of the whole body, accompanied with languor and depressed spirits.

tablature *n* an old name for musical notation, especially for the manner of writing music by letters, etc, for certain instruments.

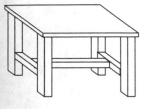

table

table *n* an article of furniture consisting of a horizontal frame with a flat upper surface supported by legs; any detached flat surface, especially when horizontal; the food served on a table; the persons sitting at table; a thin piece of something for writing on; a tablet; a series of many items or particulars presented in one connected group, especially when the items are in lists or columns; a syllabus or index; a series of numbers which proceed according to some given law (*tables of logarithms*); in jewellery, the upper and flat surface of a diamond or other precious stone; (*pl*) an old name for the game of backgammon or a similar game.—*vt* (**tabled, tabling**) to form into a table or catalogue; to tabulate; to lay or place on a table; to lay on the table in business meetings, whether public or private; to enter in the record.—*adj* appertaining to or provided for a table.

tableau *n* (*pl* **tableaux**) a picture; a striking representation; performers grouped in a dramatic scene or any persons regarded as forming a dramatic group.

tableau vivant *n* (*pl* **tableaux vivants**) (*lit*) a living picture, a group of persons dressed and placed so as to represent an historical or fictitious scene.

tablecloth *n* a cloth, usually of linen, for covering a table before the dishes are set for meals.

table d'hôte *n* a meal at a fixed price in a restaurant, offering either no choice of dishes or a limited choice.

tableland *n* a stretch of elevated flat land; a plateau.

table linen *n* the linen used for and at the table; napery.

table mat *n* a mat of cloth, wood, cork, etc, used to prevent hot dishes from spoiling the polish of a table.

table napkin *n* a linen cloth used as a protection for clothes at meals; a serviette.

table of contents *n* a summary of index of all the matters treated in a book.

tablespoon *n* a large oval spoon used to serve food or measure ingredients in cooking.

tablet *n* a small flat piece of wood, metal, ivory, etc, for writing or drawing on; a slab of wood or stone or a metal plate, bearing some device or inscription; (*pl*) a pocket memorandum book; a small flattish cake, as of soap; a medicinal pill.

table tennis, ping-pong *n* a game like tennis played on a table with small bats and a light plastic ball.

table-turning *n* one of the alleged phenomena of spiritualism, consisting of certain movements of tables attributed to spirits or spiritual forces.

tabloid *n* a small-format newspaper which has an emphasis on condensed news items, popular features and photographs.

taboo, tabu *n* the setting of something apart and away from human contact, either as consecrated or accursed, practised among certain indigenous peoples; the state of being so set apart; prohibition of contact or intercourse.—*adj* forbidden from contact, use, mention, etc; being banned by social custom (*a taboo subject of conversation*). —*vt* to put under taboo; to prohibit approach to, contact or intercourse with.

tabor, tabour *n* a small drum beaten with one stick, used as an accompaniment to a pipe or fife.

tabu *n* same as **taboo**.

tabular *adj* in the form of a table; having a flat surface; having the form of laminae or plates; set down in or forming a table or statement of items in columns; computed by the use of tables.

tabulate *vt* (**tabulated, tabulating**) to reduce to tables or synopses; to set down in a table of items.—*adj* table-shaped; tabular.

tabulation *n* the compilation of data into a tabular form.

tacheometer *n* an instrument used in rapid surveying.

tachometer *n* an instrument for measuring velocity, as of running water; an instrument used to measure the rate at which something, such as an engine, is running.

tacit *adj* implied but not expressed in words; silent (*tacit consent, a tacit agreement*).

taciturn *adj* habitually silent; not apt to talk or speak.

taciturnity *n* the state or quality of being taciturn; habitual silence or reserve in speaking.

tack[1] *n* a small, short nail, usually with a broad head; a slight fastening or connection, as by a few stitches; a long, loose stitch used to fasten seams in preparation for more thorough sewing; (*naut*) a rope for pulling the foremost lower corners of certain sails; (*naut*) the part of the sail to which the tack is fastened; (*naut*) a course of a ship as regards having the wind impelling her on the starboard or port side; a course of action; adhesiveness.—*vt* to fasten; to attach; to join in a slight or hasty manner; to sew with long, loose stitches; to add on as a supplement or addition; to append.—*vi* to change the course of a ship so as to have the wind act from the starboard instead of the port side or vice versa.

tack[2] *n* all the equipment, such as saddle, bridle, etc, used for horse riding.

tackle *n* apparatus, appliances or equipment for various kinds of work or sport, as angling; gear; one or more pulleys with a single rope, used for raising and lowering weights; the ropes and rigging, etc, of a ship; the act of tackling, for example in football.—*vt* (**tackled, tackling**) to supply with tackle; to apply tackle to; to set vigorously to work on; to attack for the purpose

of controlling or mastering; (in football) to intercept (a player) in an effort to get possession of the ball.—*vi* to go vigorously to work (followed by *to*).

tackling *n* tackle; gear, rigging, etc; instruments of action; harness, etc.

tacky *adj* sticky; slightly adhesive to the touch; (*colloq*) shabby; (*colloq*) seedy; (*colloq*) ostentatious and vulgar.

tact *n* skill or adroitness in doing or saying exactly what is required by circumstances; skill or adroitness in dealing with the feelings of a person; the stroke in beating time in music.

tactic *n* a manoeuvre; a ploy.—*adj* tactical.

tactical *adj* of or pertaining to tactics; choosing by pragmatism rather than preference (*tactical voting*).

tactician *n* one versed in tactics.

tactics *n* the science and art of disposing military or naval forces in order for battle or manoeuvring them in the presence of the enemy or within the range of fire; stratagem; ploy.

tactile *adj* capable of being touched or felt; tangible; pertaining to the sense of touch.

tad *n* (*colloq*) a small amount.

tadpole *n* the young of the frog or allied animal in its first state from the spawn.

ta'en (*poet*) contraction of **taken**.

taffeta *n* a thin glossy fabric with a silky lustre.

taffrail *n* (*naut*) the rail over the heads of the stern timbers; originally the upper flat part of a ship's stern.

Taffy *n* (*colloq*) a Welshman.

tag[1] *n* a metallic point at the end of a string; anything hanging loosely attached or affixed to another; a strip of paper, metal, etc, attached to something, as a label; an electronic device attached to a person or animal in order to record the whereabouts of the person or animal; a word applied as characteristic of a person; the end or catchword of an actor's speech.—*vt* (**tagged, tagging**) to fit with a tag or point; to fit one thing to another; to tack or join; to follow closely, to trail along behind (*tag along after*).

tag[2] *n* a children's game in which one person chases the other players until he or she touches someone who then becomes the chaser, often called 'it'.

tagliatelle *n* a form of pasta made in narrow strips.

tag-rag *n* the lowest class of people; the rabble.

tahini *n* a thick paste made from pulverized sesame seeds.

tai chi *n* a Chinese form of physical exercise involving slow, controlled, coordinated movements.

tail *n* that part of an animal which consists of the projecting termination of the spinal

tadpole

tail

column and terminates its body behind; the hinder or inferior part of a thing, as opposed to the *head*; the buttocks; any long terminal appendage or anything resembling or suggesting the tail of an animal; the other side of a coin from that which bears the head; the reverse; (*colloq*) a person who follows another in order to observe his or her movements.—*vi* to follow, droop or hang like a tail.

tailback *n* a long line of heavy stationary or slow-moving vehicles caused by an obstruction in the road or by heavy traffic.

tailboard *n* the movable board at the rear end of a cart or wagon.

tail end *n* the latter end; the back; the rear.

tailgate *n* the hinged board at the rear of a truck which can be let down or removed.

tail-light *n* a red warning light at the back of a vehicle.

tailor *n* one whose occupation is to cut out and make chiefly men's outer clothing, as coats, waistcoats, trousers, etc.—*vi* to practise making men's clothes.

tailorbird *n* an Asian bird of the warbler family, so called because it constructs its nest by sewing leaves together, using the bill as a needle and a fibre as thread.

tailor-made *adj* made by a tailor; specially designed for a particular need, occasion or person.

tailpiece *n* a piece forming a tail; an end piece; an appendage; a small picture or ornamental design at the end of a chapter or section in a book; the piece at the lower end of musical instruments, as the violin, etc, to which the strings are fastened.

tailrace *n* the water which runs from a water mill after it has produced the motion of the wheel.

tail wind *n* a wind blowing in the same direction as a ship or aircraft is travelling.

taint *vt* to imbue or impregnate with something noxious or poisonous; to infect; to corrupt, as by incipient putrefaction; to sully or pollute.—*vi* to become infected or corrupted; to be affected with incipient putrefaction.—*n* something that infects or contaminates; infection; corruption; a stain; a blemish on reputation.

take *vt* (*pret* **took**, *pp* **taken**, *ppr* **taking**) to receive or accept, correlative to *give*, and opposed to *refuse* or *reject*; to lay hold of; to seize; to grasp (*took him by the throat*); to lay hold of and remove; to carry off; to abstract (*to take one's goods*); to catch suddenly; to entrap; to circumvent; to surprise; to make prisoner of; to capture; to obtain possession of by arms (*to take a town*); to captivate, attract, allure; to understand or comprehend; to receive with good or ill will; to feel concerning (*take an act amiss*); to look on as; to suppose, regard, consider (*I take this to be right*); to

avail oneself of; to employ; to use (precaution, advice, etc); to require or render necessary (*the journey takes a week*); not to let slip; to choose and make one's own; to select; to have recourse to; to betake oneself to (*to take a course, shelter*); to form or adopt (a resolution, a plan); to put on; to assume (*to take shape*); to receive and swallow (food, medicine); to copy; to draw (a portrait, a sketch); to put into writing; to note down; to fasten on, attack or assail, as by a blast, a disease, etc; to be infected or seized with (*to take a cold*); to experience, indulge, feel (comfort, pride); to bear or submit to; to put up with; to enter into possession of by renting or leasing; to conduct, guide, convey, carry (*to take one home*); to leap over; to clear; to place oneself in; to occupy (*to take a seat*).—*vi* to direct one's course; to betake oneself; to turn in some direction; to suit the public taste; to please; to have the intended effect; to catch hold; to admit of being made a portrait of.—**to take after** to resemble in appearance, character, etc.—**to take off** (of an aircraft) to leave the ground; (*colloq*) to mimic, to imitate.—**to take over** to assume or acquire control of, as a business.—*n* the quantity of anything taken; the quantity of fish taken at one haul or on one cruise; a scene filmed without stopping the camera.

takeaway *n* cooked food, usually quick-cooking food, that is sold for consumption outside the premises where it is sold; a shop or restaurant that provides such food.

take-off *n* a caricature; a burlesque imitation; a skit; the place at which the feet leave the ground in jumping; the process of an aircraft becoming airborne.

taking *adj* alluring; engaging.—*n* a seizing; agitation or distress of mind.

talbot *n* (*heral*) a hound with a broad mouth, deep chops, large pendulous ears and usually pure white.

talc *n* a magnesia-laminated mineral, oily to the touch, of a shining lustre, translucent and usually white, apple-green or yellow, differing from mica in being flexible but not elastic.

talc schist *n* a schistose foliated rock consisting of quartz and talc.

talc slate *n* a slaty rock consisting of talc and quartz in laminae.

talcum powder *n* a purified, whitened and perfumed form of talc used on the skin.

tale *n* a narrative of events that have really happened or are imagined to have happened; a short story, true or fictitious; a lie.

tale-bearer *n* a person who tells tales likely to breed mischief; one who carries stories and makes mischief by his or her officiousness.

tale-bearing *n* the act of spreading stories

tailgate

officiously; communication of secrets maliciously.

talent *n* an ancient weight and denomination of money; a gift, endowment or faculty (*a talent for mimicry*); mental endowments or capacities of a superior kind; general mental power.

talented *adj* furnished with talents or great mental powers.

tale-teller *n* one who tells tales or stories; a tale-bearer.

talion *n* the law of retaliation, according to which the punishment inflicted is the same in kind and degree as the injury, as an eye for an eye, a tooth for a tooth, etc.

talipot *n* a tropical Asian palm with large leaves used for roofing, umbrellas, etc.

talisman *n* (*pl* **talismans**) a charm consisting of a magical figure cut or engraved on stone or metal and supposed to preserve the bearer from injury, disease or sudden death; hence, something that produces extraordinary effects; an amulet; a charm.

talismanic *adj* having the properties of a talisman; preserving against evil; magical.

talk *vi* to utter words; to speak; to converse familiarly; to hold converse; to prate; to confer; to reason.—*vt* to use as a means of conversation or communication (*to talk French* or *German*); to speak; to utter (*to talk nonsense*); to have a certain effect on by talking.—**to talk back** to answer in an impertinent or impudent way.—**to talk down to** to speak condescendingly to.—*n* familiar conversation; discourse; report; rumour; subject of discourse; a discussion; a short lecture.

talkative *adj* apt to engage in conversation; freely communicative; chatty.

talker *n* one who talks; a loquacious person.

talking picture, talkie *n* old terms for a film with a soundtrack.

talk show *n* a television or radio programme with informal interviews and conversation.

tall *adj* high in stature; long and comparatively slender (said of upright things); having height, great or small (*how tall is he?*); having a height as specified; (of a story) exaggerated.

tallboy *n* a tall chest of drawers mounted on short legs.

tallow *n* the harder and less fusible fat of animals melted and separated from the fibrous or membranous matter; also a fat obtained from some plants.—*vt* to grease or smear with tallow.

tally *n* a piece of wood on which notches or scores were cut, as marks of number, often split into two parts, so that each part contained one half of every notch (formerly used so as to answer the double purpose of receipts and records); a score; an account; anything made to suit or correspond to another; a label of wood or metal used in gardens, etc, bearing the name of the plant with which it is connected.—*vt* (**tallied, tallying**) to reckon; to count; to make to correspond.—*vi* to correspond; to agree exactly (*your information tallies with mine*).

tally system, tally trade *n* an old name for a system of dealing by which shopkeepers furnished articles on credit, the stipulated price being paid by weekly or monthly instalments.

tally-ho *interj*, *n* a hunting cry to urge on hounds.

Talmud *n* the body of the Hebrew civil and canonical laws, traditions and explanations or the book that contains them.

talon *n* the claw of a bird of prey.

tamable, tameable *adj* capable of being tamed or subdued; capable of being reclaimed from a wild or savage state.

tamarind *n* a tropical pod-bearing tree; its edible fruit, consisting of a long pod with acid-tasting flesh.

tamarisk *n* a genus of shrubs or small trees belonging to Southern Europe and Asia, some of them yielding 'manna'.

tambour *n* a drum; (*archit*) the naked part of Corinthian and Composite capitals, bearing some resemblance to a drum; the circular vertical part both below and above a cupola; a cylindrical stone as in the shaft of a column; a circular frame on which silk or other stuff is stretched to be embroidered.

tambourine *n* a musical instrument formed of a hoop, over which parchment is stretched like one end of a drum and having small pieces of metal called jingles inserted in the hoop.

tame *adj* having lost its native wildness and shyness; accustomed to people; domesticated (*a tame deer*); lacking in spirit; submissive; spiritless; not animated; without liveliness or interest; insipid; dull; flat (*a tame poem*, *tame scenery*); listless; cold.—*vt* (**tamed, taming**) to make tame; to reduce from a wild to a domestic state; to subdue; to crush; to depress.

tameable *adj* same as **tamable**.

tameness *n* the quality of being tame; domestication; lack of spirit or liveliness; dullness; flatness.

tamer *n* one who tames.

Tamil *n* a member of a people inhabiting southeastern India and Sri Lanka; the language they speak.

Tammany *n* Tammany Hall, the head centre of the Democratic party in New York.

tam o'shanter *n* a loosely woven round woollen cap.

tamp *vt* to ram tight with tough clay or other substance, as a hole bored for blasting, after the charge is lodged.

talon

tam o' shanter

tamper *vi* to meddle or interfere; to try little experiments; to meddle so as to alter by corruption or adulteration; to influence towards a certain course by secret and unfair means (generally followed by *with*, as *to tamper with a document, a witness*, etc).

tampion, tompion *n* the stopper of a cannon or other piece of ordnance; a plug.

tampon *n* a firm plug of absorbent material inserted in the vagina during menstruation to absorb blood.

tam-tam *n* a kind of Asian drum.

tan *vt* (**tanned, tanning**) to convert into leather, as animal skins, by steeping them in an infusion of oak or some other bark, by which they are rendered firm, durable and in some degree impervious to water; to make brown by exposure to the rays of the sun; to make sunburnt; to beat, flog or thrash.—*vi* to become tanned (*leather tans easily*); to become tan-coloured or sunburnt.—*n* the bark of the oak, willow or other trees, as broken by a mill and used for tanning; a yellowish-brown colour like that of tan; a brown colour produced on the skin by the sun.—*adj* of the colour of tan; resembling tan; tawny.

tangent

tanager *n* a genus of tropical American birds of the finch family, remarkable for their bright colours.

tanagra *n* a type of small terracotta statuette found at Tanagra in Boeotia and elsewhere.

tandem *n* a vehicle drawn by two horses harnessed one before the other; a cycle for two persons, one before the other.

tang¹ *n* a twang or sharp sound; a taste or flavour; characteristic flavour, quality or property; a smack or taste.

tang² *n* a projecting part of an object which is inserted into and so secured to another; the part of a table knife or tool which fits into the handle; the tongue of a buckle.

tangent *n* (*geom*) a straight line which touches a circle or curve and which being produced does not cut it; (*trigon*) in a right-angled triangle, the tangent of an acute angle = opposite side ± adjacent side.

tangerine *n* a type of small orange with a loose skin; a reddish-orange colour.

tangible *adj* capable of being touched or grasped; perceptible by the touch; capable of being possessed or realized; real; actual; evident (*tangible proofs*).

tank

tangle *vt* (**tangled, tangling**) to knit together confusedly; to interweave or interlace so as to be difficult to unravel; to entangle or entrap; to involve; to complicate.—*n* a knot of threads or other things confusedly interwoven; a perplexity or embarrassment; a name given to some species of seaweed.

tango *n* (*pl* **tangos**) a dance in two-four

time, with a great variety of steps.—*vt* to dance the tango.

tangy *adj* sharp in taste.

tank *n* a cistern or vessel of large size to contain liquids; a reservoir; a pond for storing water in India; (*milit*) an armoured car with caterpillar wheels, protected by guns fired from inside, used for clearing trenches, destruction of barbed wire, etc.

tankard *n* a large drinking vessel, with a cover, usually made of metal; a pitcher.

tanner *n* one whose occupation is to tan hides.

tannery *n* a place where the operations of tanning are carried on; the art or process of tanning.

tannic *adj* of, resembling or derived from tannin.

tannic acid *n* tannin.

tannin *n* a yellow or brown chemical found in plants or tea, used in tanning.

tanning *n* the operation and art of converting raw hides and skins of animals into leather; the process of acquiring a tan on the skin.

tansy *n* the popular name of a strongly scented perennial herb with much divided leaves and yellow flowers.

tantalize *vt* (**tantalized, tantalizing**) to tease or torment by presenting something desirable to the view, but continually frustrating the expectations by keeping it out of reach; to excite by expectations or fears which will not be realized.

tantalum *n* a rare metallic element, formerly used for electric lamp filaments but now superseded by tungsten.

tantalus *n* a stand for spirit bottles which is provided with a lock and so constructed that, whilst the bottles are plainly visible, their contents cannot be got at without unlocking the stand.

tantamount *adj* equivalent, as in value, force, effect or meaning.

tantrum *n* a burst of ill humour; a sudden, violent display of temper.

Taoism *n* a Chinese religion, non-theistic, teaching a pure morality, but associated with belief in magic, etc.

tap¹ *vt* (**tapped, tapping**) to strike with something small or to strike with a very gentle blow; to pat gently.—*vi* to strike a gentle blow.—*n* a gentle blow; a slight blow with a small thing; tap-dancing.

tap² *n* a pipe or hole through which liquor is drawn from a cask; a plug to stop a hole in a cask; a spigot; (*engin*) a small tool for forming threads in drilled holes.—*vt* (**tapped, tapping**) to pierce so as to let out a fluid (*to tap a cask*); to treat in any analogous way for the purpose of drawing something from (*to tap telephone wires*); to draw on (resources, etc); (*colloq*) to ask for money from.

tap dance *n* a dance in which rhythms are tapped by the heels and toes in rapid, intricate steps by a dancer wearing shoes with special taps.—**tap-dance** *vi* (**tap-danced, tap-dancing**) to perform a tap dance.

tape *n* a narrow fillet or band; a narrow woven band of cotton or linen, used for strings, etc; a plastic ribbon coated with a magnetic substance and used to record sounds; a magnetic tape.—*vt* (**taped, taping**) to tie up or bind with tape; to record on tape; to record on videotape.

tape deck *n* a tape recorder in a hi-fi system.

tape measure *n* a tape painted to give it firmness and marked with inches, centimetres, etc, used in measuring.

taper *n* a small candle; a long wick coated with wax or other suitable material; a small light; tapering form; gradual diminution of thickness in an elongated object.—*adj* long and regularly becoming more slender towards the point; becoming small towards one end (*taper fingers*).—*vi* to become gradually more slender or less in diameter; to diminish; to grow gradually less.—*vt* to cause to taper.

tape recorder *n* a machine using magnetic tape wound from one spool to another to record and reproduce sound.

tape recording *n* a recording made on magnetic tape; a magnetic tape on which sound has been recorded.

tapering *adj* becoming regularly smaller in diameter toward one end; gradually diminishing toward a point.

tapestry *n* a kind of woven hangings of wool and silk, often enriched with gold and silver, ornamented with figures of people, animals, landscapes, etc, and formerly much used for covering the walls and furniture of apartments, churches, etc.

tapeworm *n* the name of certain internal parasites composed of a number of flattened joints or segments, found in the intestines of warm-blooded vertebrates.

taphouse *n* formerly, a tavern.

tapioca *n* a farinaceous substance prepared from cassava meal.

tapir *n* a South American hoofed animal allied both to the hog and to the rhinoceros, with a nose resembling a small proboscis.

tappet *n* a small lever connected with the valve of the cylinder of a steam engine; a small cam.

tapping *n* the surgical operation of letting out a fluid by perforation, as in dropsy.

taproom *n* a bar.

taproot *n* the main root of a plant, long and tapering and penetrating the earth downwards.

tar *n* a thick, dark-coloured viscid product obtained by the destructive distillation of organic substances and bituminous minerals, as pine or fir, coal, shale, etc, used for coating and preserving timber and iron, for impregnating ships' ropes and cordage, etc; a sailor, contraction of tarpaulin.—*vt* (**tarred, tarring**) to smear with tar.

taradiddle *n* same as **tarradiddle**.

tarantass *n* a covered Russian carriage without springs.

tarantella *n* a swift, whirling Italian dance in six-eight measure; the music for the dance.

tarantula *n* a kind of large, hairy spider the bite of which is poisonous and painful but not deadly.

taraxacum *n* dandelion or its roots as used medicinally.

tarboosh, tarbush *n* a red woollen skullcap worn by Muslim men; a fez.

tardiness *n* the state or quality of being tardy; slowness; dilatoriness; unwillingness; reluctance.

tardy *adj* moving with a slow pace or motion; slow; late; dilatory; not up to time; reluctant.

tare[1] *n* a name of different species of leguminous plants; vetch.

tare[2] *n* (*com*) a deduction from the gross weight of goods as equivalent to the weight of the package containing them.

target *n* a shield or buckler of a small kind, circular in form; the mark set up to be aimed at in archery, musketry or artillery practice, etc; an objective or ambition.—*vt* to make a target of; to aim or direct (*to target aid*); to make the object of one's aim (*to target the wealthy buyer*).

Targum *n* (*pl* **Targum, Targumim**) a translation or paraphrase of the Hebrew Scriptures in the Aramaic or Chaldee language, made after Hebrew began to die out as the popular language.

tariff *n* a list of goods with the duties or customs to be paid for the same, either on importation or exportation; a table or scale of charges generally (*an hotel tariff*).

tarn *n* a small mountain lake or pool, especially one which has no visible feeders.

tarnish *vt* to diminish or destroy the lustre of; to soil or sully; to cast a stain or disgrace on.—*vi* to lose lustre; to become dull.—*n* a spot; a blot; soiled state.

taro *n* a plant of the arum family, cultivated in the Pacific Islands for its edible root.

tarot card *n* a kind of playing card used in predicting future events.

tarpaulin *n* tarred canvas or other waterproof material used as a protective covering.

tarpon *n* a fine large sea fish of the Southern USA and West Indies, belonging to the herring family and giving excellent sport to the angler.

tarradiddle, taradiddle *n* a slight lie, fib, equivocation.

tape recorder

target

tarragon *n* a herb with narrow green leaves used as a flavouring agent in cooking, vinegar and salads.

tarry[1] *vi* to stay; to abide; to remain behind; to wait; to put off going or coming; to delay; to linger.

tarry[2] *adj* consisting of tar or like tar; partaking of the character of tar; smeared with tar.

tarsier *n* a nocturnal animal of the lemur family inhabiting the Eastern Archipelago.

tarsus *n* (*pl* **tarsi**) (*anat*) that part of the lower limb which in human beings is known as the ankle.

tart[1] *n* a piece of pastry, consisting of fruit, vegetables, etc, baked and enclosed in pastry; (*colloq*) a prostitute; (*colloq*) a loose woman.—**to tart up** to decorate, especially cheaply and gaudily.

tart[2] *adj* sharp to the taste; acidulous; snappish in words; severe.

tartan *n* a kind of cloth, chequered or cross-barred in various colours, associated with different Scottish clans.—*adj* consisting of or resembling tartan.

tartan

tartar[1] *n* a hard pink or red crust deposited from wines not completely fermented, a compound of tartaric acid and potassium (also called **argal**); a hard, yellow, crusty deposit which forms on the teeth.

tartar[2] *n* a savage, cruel person; a shrew; a vixen.—**to catch a tartar** to assail a person who proves too strong for the assailant.

tartaric *adj* pertaining to or obtained from tartar.

Tartarus *n* in Greek myth, a name for the lower world or infernal regions; hell.

tartlet *n* a small tart.

tartly *adv* in a tart manner; snappishly.

tartness *n* acidity; sharpness; asperity.

task *n* a labour or work imposed by another; a piece of work to be done; what duty or necessity imposes; a lesson to be learned; a portion of study imposed by a teacher; an undertaking; burdensome employment; toil.—**to take to task** to reprove; to reprimand.—*vt* to impose a task on; to oppress with severe labour.

taskmaster *n* one who imposes a task; one who assigns tasks to others.

Tasmanian *adj* pertaining to Tasmania.—*n* a native or inhabitant of Tasmania.

Tasmanian devil *n* a burrowing flesh-eating marsupial of Tasmania with a black coat and long tail.

tart

Tasmanian wolf *n* a carnivorous marsupial of Tasmania, of nocturnal habits and very destructive to sheep.

tassel *n* a pendent ornament, consisting generally of a roundish mould covered with twisted threads of silk, wool, etc, and having threads hanging down in a fringe; anything resembling a tassel.—*vi* (**tasselled**, **tasselling**) to put forth a tassel or flower, as maize.—*vt* to adorn with tassels.

taste *vt* (**tasted**, **tasting**) to try by the touch of the tongue; to perceive the relish or flavour of; to try by eating; to eat; to become acquainted with by trial; to experience (*to taste death*); to partake of (*to taste happiness*).—*vi* to eat or drink a little by way of trial; to have a smack or flavour; to have a particular relish or savour; to smack or savour (*it tastes of garlic*); to have experience or enjoyment.—*n* the act of tasting; a particular sensation excited by certain bodies when applied to the tongue, palate, etc, and moistened with saliva; the sense by which we perceive this by means of special organs in the mouth; intellectual relish or discernment; appreciation and liking; fine perception; the faculty of discerning beauty, proportion, symmetry, congruity or whatever constitutes excellence, particularly in the fine arts and literature; discernment of what is fit or becoming; manner or style as tested by this faculty; manner, with respect to what is pleasing (*a work in good taste*, *a remark in bad taste*); a small portion tasted; a small bit.

tasteful *adj* having much flavour; savoury; possessing good taste; showing or produced in good taste.

tasteless *adj* having no taste; insipid; having no power of giving pleasure; stale; flat; void of good taste; showing or executed with bad taste.

taster *n* one who tastes; one who tests food, provisions or liquors by tasting samples; an instrument by which something is tasted in order to judge of its quality.

tasty *adj* palatable; good to the taste; tasteful; showing good taste.

ta-ta *n*, *interj* (*colloq*) a salutation at parting; goodbye.

tatter *n* a rag or a part torn and hanging to the thing.

tatterdemalion *n* a ragged fellow.

tatting *n* a kind of lace woven or knitted from sewing thread, with a somewhat shuttle-shaped implement; the act of making such lace.

tattle *vi* (**tattled**, **tattling**) to prate; to talk idly; to use many words with little meaning; to tell tales; to reveal secrets.—*vt* to utter in a prating way.—*n* idle talk or chat; trifling talk; tale-telling.

tattoo[1] *n* a beat of drum and bugle call at night, giving notice to soldiers to repair to their quarters; a public military display, usually outdoors.

tattoo[2] *vti* to prick the skin and stain the punctured spots with a colouring substance, forming a permanent design of lines and figures on the body.

taunt *vt* to reproach with severe or insulting

words; to twit scornfully or insultingly; to upbraid.—*n* a bitter or sarcastic reproach; insulting invective.

Taurus *n* the Bull, one of the twelve signs of the zodiac, which the sun enters about 20th April.

taut *adj* tight; not slack (applied to a rope or sail).

tautological *adj* involving tautology; repeating the same thing.

tautology *n* a repetition of the same idea or meaning in different words; needless repetition.

tavern *n* a public house; an inn.

taverner *n* one who keeps a tavern.

taw[1] *vt* to dress with alum and other matters and make into white leather (as distinguished from tanning), the leather being used for gloves, etc.

taw[2] *n* a marble to be played with; a game at marbles.

tawdry *adj* tastelessly but showily ornamental; cheap and gaudy.

tawny *adj* of a yellowish brown colour.

tawse *n* a leather strap with which corporal punishment was formerly inflicted on schoolchildren in Scotland.

tax *n* a contribution levied by authority from people to defray the expenses of government or other public services; an impost or duty on income or property; a disagreeable or burdensome duty or charge; an exaction; an oppressive demand.—*vt* to impose a tax on; to levy money or other contributions from; to load with a burden or burdens; ,o put to a certain strain (*to tax one's strength*); to accuse or charge (*to tax a person with perfidy*); (*law*) to examine and allow or disallow items of charge in.

taxable *adj* capable of being or liable to be taxed.

taxation *n* the act of laying a tax or of imposing taxes by the proper authority; the raising of revenue required for public service by means of taxes; the aggregate of taxes.

tax gatherer *n* a collector of taxes.

taxi *n* (short for **taxicab**) a car which may be hired with its driver, usually fitted with a taximeter which calculates the distance and indicates the fare due.—*vi* (**taxied**, **taxiing**) (of an aeroplane) to advance along the ground with the engine running, but not fast enough to give flying speed.

taxicab *n* a taxi.

taxidermist *n* a person skilled in taxidermy; one who stuffs dead animals.

taxidermy *n* the art of treating the skins of dead animals so that they retain their natural appearance, and also of stuffing and mounting them.

taximeter *n* an instrument attached to a taxi to show distance run and fare due.

taxonomic *adj* pertaining to taxonomy.

taxonomy *n* a process or system of classification; the classification of living things into groups based on similarities of biological origin, function, etc.

tea *n* the dried leaves of a shrub extensively cultivated in China, Assam, etc; the plant itself; a decoction or infusion of tea leaves in boiling water, used as a beverage; any similar infusion (*camomile tea, fennel tea,* etc); the evening meal at which tea is usually served.

tea caddy *n* a small box for holding the tea used in a household.

teacake *n* a kind of currant bun, often sliced, toasted and buttered, eaten at tea time.

teach *vt* (*pret, pp* **taught,** *ppr* **teaching**) to impart instruction to; to guide the studies of; to instruct; to impart the knowledge of; to instruct, train or give skill in the use, management or handling of; to let be known; to tell; to show how; to show.—*vi* to practise giving instruction; to perform the business of a preceptor.

teacher *n* one who teaches or instructs; a preceptor; a tutor; a preacher; a minister of the gospel.

tea chest *n* a large wooden box used to transport tea.

teaching *n* the act or business of instructing; instruction.

teacup *n* a small cup for drinking tea from.

teak *n* a tree growing in different parts of the East Indies and yielding a strong, durable, valuable timber; the timber used in making furniture, etc.

teal *n* a small British duck which frequents freshwater lakes and ponds; also the name of two American species.

team *n* two or more horses, oxen or other beasts harnessed together for drawing; the persons forming one of the parties or sides in a game, match, etc.

teapot *n* a vessel with a spout in which tea is infused and from which it is poured into teacups.

tear[1] *n* a drop of the limpid fluid secreted by a special gland and appearing in the eyes or flowing from them, especially through excessive grief or joy; any transparent drop of fluid matter; also a solid, transparent drop, as of some resins.

tear[2] *vt* (*pret* **tore** (formerly **tare**), *pp* **torn,** *ppr* **tearing**) to separate the parts of by pulling; to pull apart by force; to form fissures or furrows in by violence; to lacerate; to wound; to divide by violent measures; to disturb, excite or disorganize violently (*torn by factions*); to drag; to move or remove by pulling or violently; to cause or make by rending (*to tear a hole*).—*vi* to be rent or torn; to rage; to act with turbulent violence.—*n* a rent; a fissure.

teardrop *n* a tear.—*adj* shaped like a tear.

teacup

teapot

tearful *adj* abounding with tears; shedding tears.

tear gas *n* a gas that irritates the eyes and nasal passages, used in riot control.

tearing *adj* (*colloq*) violent or headlong (*a tearing rush*).

tearoom, teashop *n* a restaurant or cafe where tea and light refreshments are served.

tease *vt* (**teased, teasing**) to pull apart the adhering fibres of; to comb or card, as wool or flax; to taunt playfully; to torment; to annoy or irritate; to fluff up (hair) by combing it towards the roots, to backcomb.

teasel, teazel *n* the fuller's thistle, cultivated for its heads or burrs, which have numerous hooked bracts and were formerly used to raise the nap of woollen cloths; any device similarly used in the dressing of woollen cloth.—*vt* (**teaselled, teaselling**) to subject to the action of teasels.

tea service, tea set *n* a set of cups, saucers, etc, used for serving tea.

teashop *n* same as **tearoom**.

teasing *adj* vexing; irritating; annoying.

teaspoon *n* a small spoon used for stirring tea, coffee, etc, and for measuring small quantities.

teat *n* the projecting organ through which milk is drawn from the breast or udder of females; a nipple; a dug of a beast; a pap.

teazel *n, vt* same as **teasel**.

technetium *n* an artificially produced metallic element whose radioisotope is used in radiotherapy.

technical *adj* relating to or belonging to technology or to a particular science, trade, etc; peculiar to a particular field of activity.

technicality *n* the character of being technical; a technical feature or peculiarity; a technical point; a petty distinction, especially one based only on theory; a technical expression.

Technicolor *n* the trademark of a process of making colour films by superimposing primary colours to produce a final colour print.

technique *n* method of manipulation in any art; artistic execution; the particular method or procedure for doing something; a knack.

technology *n* that branch of knowledge which deals with the various industrial arts; the science or systematic knowledge of the industrial arts; the application of mechanical and applied sciences to industrial use.

tectonic *adj* pertaining to building or construction; (*geol*) resulting from deformation of the earth's crust.

tectonics *n sing pl* the art or science of constructing buildings, etc; the study of the forces which shape the earth's geological structure.

ted *vt* (**tedded, tedding**) (*agric*) to spread to the air after being mown; to turn and scatter newly mown grass or hay.

tedder *n* one who teds; an implement that spreads newly mown grass.

teddy bear *n* a stuffed toy bear.

Te Deum *n* the title of a celebrated hymn of praise, usually ascribed to St Ambrose, familiar from its translation in the Book of Common Prayer.

tedium *n* irksomeness; wearisomeness; boredom.

tedious *adj* involving or causing tedium; tiresome from continuance or slowness; wearisome; monotonous; boring.

tee *n* a point of aim or starting point in certain games, as quoits, curling and golf; more particularly, the little heap of sand on which golfers set the ball for the first stroke towards each hole; a small cone of wood or other material used for the same purpose.—*vt* (**teed, teeing**) to set the ball in this position.

teem *vi* to bring forth young; to be pregnant; to be stocked to overflowing; to be prolific or abundantly fertile.—*vt* to produce; to bring forth.

teen *n* grief; sorrow.

teens *npl* the years of one's age having the termination *-teen*, beginning with thirteen and ending with nineteen, during which period a person is said to be in his or her teens.

teeny *adj* (*colloq*) tiny; very small.

teepee *n* same as **tepee**.

tee-shirt *n* same as **T-shirt**.

teeter *vi* to move or stand unsteadily; to totter; to wobble.

teeth *pl* of **tooth**.

teethe *vi* (**teethed, teething**) to have the teeth grow.

teething *n* the growth of the teeth in the young; dentition.

teething troubles, teething problems *npl* difficulties encountered in the early stages of a project, etc.

teetotal *adj* pertaining to total abstinence from alcoholic drinks; totally abstaining from alcoholic drinks.

teetotaller *n* one who abstains totally from alcoholic drinks.

Teflon *n* the trademark of a kind of tough, waxy plastic substance, polytetrafluoroethylene, used in bearings and as a coating for pots and pans to prevent food sticking to them.

teg *n* a young sheep.

tegular *adj* resembling a tile; consisting of tiles.

tegulated *adj* composed of plates or scales overlapping like tiles.

teddy bear

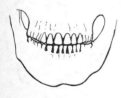

teeth

tegument *n* a cover or covering; a natural covering, as of an animal; an integument.

telecast *n* a television broadcast.—*vt* to broadcast by television.

telecommunication *n* communication of information, such as sounds, signals or pictures, over long distances by telephone and radio; (*pl*) the technology of telephone, telegraph, radio and television communication.

teledu *n* an Asian carnivorous animal related to the skunk and, like it, able to give out a strong smell.

telegram *n* a communication sent by telegraph; a telegraphic message or despatch.

telegraph *n* a system for transmitting messages over long distances, using electricity, wires and a code; a telegraphic communication; a telegram.—*vt* to convey or announce by telegraph.

telegraphy *n* the art or practice of communicating by telegraph.

telemessage *n* a message sent by telex or telephone, superseding the telegram.

teleology *n* the science or doctrine of final causes; the science treating of the end or design for which things were created.

telepathy *n* the communication of feelings or impressions between persons at a distance from each other.

telephone *n* an apparatus for sending or receiving voice messages, usually along electrical wires; the method or system for doing this.—*vi* (**telephoned, telephoning**) to call (someone) by telephone.

telephone directory *n* a book listing the names, addresses and telephone numbers of subscribers in a given area.

telephonic *adj* relating to the telephone; communicated by the telephone.

telephonist *n* a person who operates a telephone switchboard.

telephony *n* the use of the telephone.

telephotography *n* the photographing of distant objects by means of a specially constructed lens.

teleprinter *n* a telegraph apparatus that sends or receives messages.

telerpeton *n* a lizard-like reptilian fossil found in certain sandstones of the Triassic period.

telescope *n* an optical instrument essentially consisting of a set of lenses fixed in a tube or a number of sliding tubes, by which distant objects are brought within the range of distinct or more distinct vision.—*vt* (**telescoped. telescoping**) to drive the parts of into each other, like the movable joints of a pocket telescope (*the train was telescoped by the collision*); to condense or shorten.

telescopic *adj* pertaining to a telescope; performed by a telescope; seen only by a telescope; seeing at a great distance; having

the power of extension by joints sliding one within another.

teletext *n* a system of broadcasting information, such as news, weather forecasts, etc, by printed text which can be received on a modified television set.

televise *vt* (**televised, televising**) to make, send or receive pictures by television.

television *n* the transmission of visual images and accompanying sound through electrical and sound waves; television broadcasting; a television receiving set.

telex *n* a communication system whereby subscribers hire teleprinters for transmitting messages; a teleprinter; a message received by a teleprinter.

tell *vt* (*pret, pp* **told**, *ppr* **telling**) to express in words; to say; to relate, narrate, rehearse (*to tell a story*); to make known by words; to disclose; to confess; to acknowledge (*to tell a secret*); to discern so as to be able to say (*to tell one from another*); to distinguish; to decide on; to enumerate; to count; to inform; to give an order or request to.—*vi* to give an account; to make report; to play the informer; to blab; to take effect; to produce a marked effect (*every shot tells*).—**to tell off** to count off, select for a special duty; to rebuke.

teller *n* one that tells; one who numbers; one appointed to count votes on a division in the House of Commons; an employee in a bank, etc, whose job it is to receive and pay money over the counter.

telling *adj* operating with great effect; highly effective; impressive (*a telling speech*).—*n* the act of one that tells.

telltale *adj* telling tales; revealing what is meant to be hidden; blabbing.—*n* what is meant to be hidden; a person who informs on others.

tellurian *adj* pertaining to the earth or to an inhabitant of the earth.—*n* an inhabitant of the earth.

telluric *adj* pertaining to the earth or to tellurium.

tellurium *n* a non-metallic element of a tin-white crystalline appearance and closely resembling selenium and sulphur in its chemical relations.

tellurous *adj* pertaining to or obtained from tellurium.

telly *n* (*colloq*) television; a television set.

telson *n* the last joint in the abdomen of crustaceans.

temerity *n* heedlessness of consequences; extreme recklessness; rashness.

temp *n* (*colloq*) a temporary employee.

temper *vt* to proportion duly as regards constituent parts; to mix or combine in due proportion; to mix and work up; to qualify by intermixture (*to temper justice with mercy*); to reduce the excess, violence or severity of; to moderate; to calm; to form

telephone

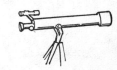

telescope

to a proper degree of hardness (*to temper steel*).—*n* due mixture of different qualities; disposition or constitution of the mind, particularly with regard to the passions and affections; a frame of mind; a fit of anger; irritation; the state of a metal as to its hardness; middle character; mean or medium.

temperament *n* the emotional nature of a person; disposition; (*mus*) a certain adjustment of the tones or intervals of the scale of fixed-toned instruments, as the organ, piano, etc.

temperance *n* the observance of moderation; temperateness; moderation in regard to the indulgence of the natural appetites and passions; restrained or moderate indulgence; sobriety; total abstinence from alcoholic drinks.

temperate *adj* moderate; showing moderation; moderate as regards the indulgence of the appetites or desires; abstemious; sober; not violent or excessive as regards the use of language; reasonable; calm; measured; not going beyond due bounds; moderate as regards amount of heat; not liable to excessive heats (*a temperate climate*).

Temperate Zone *n* one of the spaces on the earth between the tropics and the polar circles where the heat is less than in the tropics and the cold less than in the polar circles.

temperature *n* constitution or temperament; the state of a body or of a region of the earth with regard to heat; the degree or intensity of the heat effects of a body.

tempest *n* an extensive current of wind rushing with great velocity and violence; a storm of extreme violence; a hurricane; a violent tumult or commotion.

tempestuous *adj* belonging to a tempest; very stormy; blowing with violence; subject to fits of stormy passion.

Templar *n* one of a religious military order first established at Jerusalem for the protection of pilgrims travelling to the Holy Land and so named from their residence at Jerusalem being connected with the church and convent of the temple.

template, templet *n* a pattern gauge or mould used as a guide; a flat thin board or piece of sheet iron whose edge is shaped in some particular way, so that it may serve as a guide or test in making an article with a corresponding contour; a short piece of timber or a stone placed in a wall to support a girder, beam, etc.

temple[1] *n* an edifice dedicated to the service of some deity or deities; originally, an edifice erected for some Roman deity; one of the three successive edifices at Jerusalem dedicated to the worship of Jehovah; an edifice erected among Christians as a place of public worship; a church.

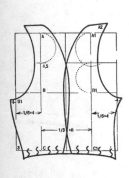
template

temple[2] *n* the flat portion of either side of the head between the forehead and ear.

templet *n* same as **template**.

tempo *n* (*pl* **tempos, tempi**) (*mus*) a word used to express the degree of quickness with which a piece of music is to be executed; musical time; speed; pace.

temporal *adj* pertaining to this life or this world; secular, opposed to *spiritual* and *ecclesiastical*; measured or limited by time or by this life or state of things; of or relating to time; having limited existence, opposed to *eternal*; (*gram*) relating to a tense; pertaining to the temple or temples of the head.—*n* anything temporal or secular; a temporality.

temporarily *adv* in a temporary manner; for a time; provisionally.

temporary *adj* lasting for a time only; existing or continuing for a limited time; transient; provisional.

temporize *vi* (**temporized, temporizing**) to delay in order to gain time; to act to fit the occasion.

tempt *vt* to incite or solicit to an evil act; to entice to something wrong by some specious argument or inducement; to seduce; to invite; to try to induce; to try the patience of; to put to a test.

temptation *n* the act of tempting or state of being tempted; enticement to evil; that which is presented as an inducement to evil; an enticement; an allurement to anything indifferent or even good.

temptress *n* a female who tempts or entices.

ten *adj* twice five; nine and one.—*n* the number of twice five; a figure or symbol denoting ten units, as 10 or X; a playing card with ten spots.

tenable *adj* capable of being held, maintained or defended against an assailant or against attempts to take it; able to be believed.

tenacious *adj* holding fast or inclined to hold fast; inclined to retain (with *of* before the thing held); retentive; apt to retain long what is committed to it (*a tenacious memory*); apt to adhere to another substance; adhesive; tough; having great cohesive force among the constituent particles.

tenacity *n* the quality of being tenacious; adhesiveness; that property of material bodies by which their parts resist an effort to force or pull them asunder or the measure of the resistance of bodies to tearing or crushing.

tenancy *n* a holding or possession as tenant; period of occupancy as tenant; tenure.

tenant *n* a person who holds or possesses lands or tenements by any kind of title, either in fee, for life, for years or at will; one who occupies land or houses for which he or she pays rent; one who has possession of any place; a dweller; an occupant.—*vt* to hold or possess as a tenant.—*vi* to live as a tenant; to dwell.

tench *n* a fish of the carp family inhabiting most of the lakes of Europe.

tend[1] *vi* to move in a certain direction; to be directed; to have influence towards producing a certain effect; to conduce or contribute.

tend[2] *vt* to accompany as an assistant or protector; to watch; to guard; to look after; to take care of; to attend to.—*vi* to attend; to wait, as attendants or servants; to attend as something inseparable; to be attentive.

tendency *n* an inclining or contributing influence; aptness to take a certain course; inclination; effect of giving a certain bent or direction.

tender[1] *adj* easily injured; delicate; very sensible to pain; very susceptible of any sensation; not hardy; weak; easily affected by the distresses of another (*a tender heart*); sympathetic; affectionate; fond; pathetic; careful not to hurt or injure; gentle; unwilling to pain; apt to give pain or to annoy when spoken of (*a tender subject*).

tender[2] *vt* to present for acceptance; to offer in payment or satisfaction of a demand.—*n* an offer of money or any other thing in satisfaction of a debt or liability; any offer for acceptance; an offer in writing to execute some specified work or to supply certain specified articles, at a certain rate; the thing offered.

tender[3] *n* one that tends; (*naut*) a small vessel attending a larger one with stores and passengers or to convey intelligence; (*rail*) a carriage attached to the locomotive, for carrying fuel, water, etc.

tenderfoot *n* a newcomer, one who is unaccustomed to the ways of a place; an inexperienced beginner.

tender-hearted *adj* very susceptible of the softer passions of love, pity or kindness.

tenderness *n* the state or character of being tender; delicacy; readiness to be hurt; susceptibility; affection; pathos.

tendon *n* (*anat*) a hard, insensible cord or bundle of fibres by which a muscle is attached to a bone or other part which it serves to move.

tendril *n* (*bot*) a slender spiral shoot of a plant that winds round another body for the purpose of support.

tenement *n* an abode; a habitation; a dwelling; an apartment or apartments in a building used by one family; (*law*) any kind of permanent property that may be held.

tenement house *n* a house or block of building divided into dwellings for separate families.

tenet *n* any opinion, principle, dogma or doctrine which a person believes or maintains as true.

tennis *n* a ball game for two or four people played on a court divided by a central net over which the ball is hit with a racket.

tenon *n* a projecting piece on the end of a piece of wood fitted for insertion into a corresponding cavity or mortise in order to form a joint.—*vt* to fit with a tenon.

tenon saw *n* a small saw with a brass or steel back, used for cutting tenons.

tenor *n* prevailing course or direction; general course or drift of thought; general spirit or meaning; purport; substance (the tenor of a discourse); (*mus*) the highest of the adult male chest voices (so called because in former times the leading melody was given to this voice; the part above the bass in harmonized music; one who sings a tenor part.—*adj* (*mus*) adapted for singing or playing the tenor.

ten-pin bowling *n* a bowling game involving the rolling of a large ball along a long lane or alleyway in an attempt to knock over as many as possible of the bottle-shaped objects (called **tenpins**) at the other end.

tenrec *n* an animal resembling the hedgehog, inhabiting Madagascar.

tense[1] *adj* stretched until tight; strained to stiffness; rigid; not lax; under strain; strained; stressed; nervous; apprehensive.

tense[2] *n* (*gram*) one of the forms which a verb takes in order to express the time of action or of that which is affirmed.

tensile *adj* pertaining to tension; capable of tension.

tension *n* the act of stretching or straining; the state of being stretched or strained to stiffness; tightness; mental strain; stress; (*mech*) the force by which a bar, rod or string is pulled when forming part of any system; (*physics*) elastic force.

tent *n* a portable shelter consisting of some flexible covering, such as skins, matting, canvas, plastic or other waterproof fabric stretched and sustained by poles and fixed to the ground by ropes and pegs.—*vi* to camp in a tent.

tentacle *n* (*zool*) an elongated appendage on the head or cephalic extremity of many of the lower forms of animals, used as an instrument for grasping or as a feeler.

tentative *adj* based on or consisting in trial or experiment; experimental; provisional; not definite; hesitant.—*n* an essay; a trial.

tenter *n* a frame used in cloth manufacture to stretch the pieces of cloth and make them set or dry even and square.

tenterhook *n* a hook for stretching cloth on a tenter; (*fig*) anything that painfully strains, racks or tortures.—**on tenterhooks** in a state of anxious suspense.

tenth *adj* first after the ninth.—*n* the tenth part; one of ten equal parts into which a whole is divided.

tennis

tent

tenuity *n* the state of being thin or fine; slenderness; rarity; thinness (as of a fluid).

tenuous *adj* thin; slender; rare; subtle; not dense; not substantial; flimsy; weak.

tenure *n* the act, manner or right of holding property, especially real estate; manner of holding or possessing in general; the terms or conditions on which anything is held or possessed (*life is held on a precarious tenure*).

teocalli *n* a temple among the Mexicans and other original inhabitants of America.

tepee, teepee *n* a cone-shaped North American Indian tent formed of animal hides or bark.

tepid *adj* moderately warm; lukewarm.

tepidity *n* moderate warmth; lukewarmness.

tequila *n* a Mexican alcoholic drink made from a cactus-like plant.

terbium *n* a rare element found along with erbium and yttrium at Ytterby in Sweden.

tercel, tiercel *n* a male hawk or falcon.

tercentenary *adj* comprising three hundred years.—*n* a festival in commemoration of some event that happened three hundred years before; the three-hundredth anniversary of any event.

tepee

terebinth *n* a European tree that yields turpentine.

teredo *n* (*pl* **teredos**) a worm-like mollusc that burrows in submerged wood in order to form a habitation; the shipworm.

tergiversate *vi* (**tergiversated, tergiversating**) to practise evasion; to make use of shifts or subterfuges.

tergiversation *n* the act of tergiversating; subterfuge; evasion; the act of changing one's opinions; a turning against a cause formerly advocated.

term *n* a limit; a bound or boundary; the time for which anything lasts; a time or period fixed in some way; a period during which instruction is regularly given to students in schools, universities and colleges; a day on which rent or interest is regularly payable, such as Lady Day or Michaelmas Day; a word by which something fixed and definite is expressed; particularly, a word having a technical meaning; (*pl*) in a general way, words or language (to speak in vague terms); (*pl*) conditions or propositions stated and offered for acceptance (state your terms); (*pl*) relative position or footing (on good terms with a person); (in logic) the expression in language of the notion obtained in an act of apprehension; the subject or the predicate of a proposition; (*alg*) a member of a compound quantity connected with another or others by the signs of addition and subtraction.—*vt* to name; to denominate.

termagant *n* a brawling, turbulent woman; a virago.—*adj* furious; scolding.

terminable *adj* capable of being terminated; coming to an end after a certain term.

terminal *adj* relating to or forming the end or extremity; placed at the end of something; (of a disease) incurable, fatal.—*n* that which terminates; an extremity; the clamping screw at each end of a voltaic battery for connecting it with the wires which complete the circuit; a bus, coach or railway station at the end of the line; a building at a bus terminus, airport, etc; the point at which an electrical current enters or leaves a device; a device with a keyboard and monitor for inputting or viewing data from a computer.

terminate *vt* (**terminated, terminating**) to bound; to limit; to form the extreme point or side of; to put an end to; to complete; to put the finishing touch to.—*vi* to be limited in space; to stop short; to end; to come to a limit in time.—*adj* capable of coming to an end (*a terminate decimal*).

termination *n* the act of terminating; an ending or concluding; the end of a thing or point where it ends; limit in space; end in time; (*gram*) a part annexed to the root or stem of an inflected word; the syllable or letter that ends a word; conclusion; issue; result.

terminology *n* the science of technical terms; theory regarding the proper use of terms; collectively, the special terms used in any art, science or specialized subject; nomenclature.

terminus *n* (*pl* **termini, terminuses**) a boundary; a limit; a landmark; the extreme station at either end of a railway line, bus or air route, etc.

termite *n* a wood-eating, white, ant-like insect.

tern *n* a long-winged bird of the gull family, which, from its manner of flight, forked tail and size, has received the name of sea swallow.

Terpsichore *n* (in Greek myth) one of the Muses, the inventor and patron of the art of dancing and lyrical poetry.

terpsichorean *adj* pertaining to Terpsichore; pertaining to dancing.

terra *n* earth; the earth.

terrace *n* a raised level space or platform of earth, supported on one or more sides by masonry, a bank of turf, etc; a level space on a sloping surface; an unroofed paved area adjoining a house; a balcony; a patio; a row or street of houses.

terraced house *n* a house in a terrace or row of houses, usually attached to each other.

terracotta *n* a mixture of fine clay and fine-grained white sand with crushed pottery, first slowly air-dried, then baked in a kiln into the hardness of stone, much used for statues, figures, vases, etc.

terra firma *n* firm or solid earth; dry land, in opposition to water.

terrain *n* land from a military point of view.

terra incognita *n* an unknown or unexplored region.

terrapin *n* a name of several species of freshwater tortoises.

terrestrial *adj* pertaining to the earth; existing on this earth; earthly, as opposed to *celestial*; pertaining to the world; mundane; pertaining to land as opposed to water; confined to or living on land, opposed to *aquatic*.

terrible *adj* adapted to excite fear, awe or dread; dreadful; formidable; excessive; extreme; (*colloq*) very bad; (*colloq*) very unpleasant.

terrier *n* one of various breeds of small dog, originally bred to pursue game into a hole or burrow.

terrific *adj* dreadful; terrifying; causing terror; (*colloq*) very great, very good.

terrify *vt* (**terrified, terrifying**) to frighten extremely; to alarm or shock with fear.

territorial *adj* pertaining to a territory; limited to a certain district.—*n* a member of the Territorial Army.

Territorial Army *n* a volunteer army reserve force.

territory *n* any separate tract of land as belonging to a state, city or other body; a dominion; a region; a country; an area assigned to a sales representative; an area which an animal claims as its own; an area of knowledge.

terror *n* fear that agitates the body and mind; dread; fright; the cause of extreme fear; a person or thing that causes fear or dread; (*colloq*) a nuisance.

terrorism *n* the use of violence and threats to generate fear, especially for political purposes.

terrorist *n* a person who uses, or favours the use of, terrorism.

terrorize *vt* (**terrorized, terrorizing**) to impress with terror; to repress or domineer over by means of terror; to intimidate by threats, etc.

terse *adj* free from superfluity; neat and concise; pithy (said of style or language).

tertian *adj* (*med*) having its paroxysm every other day (*a tertian fever*).

tertiary *adj* of the third order, rank or formation; third.

Tertiary *n* (*geol*) the era and group, now called Cainozoic, comprising the Eocene, Oligocene, Miocene and Pliocene periods and systems.

tertiary colour *n* a colour produced by the mixture of two secondary colours.

Tertiary formation *n* (*geol*) the third or Cainozoic group of stratified rocks, lying immediately above the secondary or Mesozoic and resting on the chalk.

terza rima *n* (*pl* **terze rime**) the rhyming arrangement in triple lines adopted in Dante's *Divina Commedia*.

tessellated *adj* formed by inlaying differently coloured materials in little squares, triangles or other geometrical figures, or by mosaic work.

tessera *n* (*pl* **tesserae**) a small cube of marble, precious stone, ivory, glass, wood, etc, used to form tessellated pavements and in mosaics; a small square of bone, wood, etc, used as a token or ticket in ancient Rome.

test *n* a critical trial and examination; means of trial; a touchstone; a standard; means of discrimination; anything used to distinguish or detect substances; a chemical reaction to test a substance or to test for a disease, etc; a series of questions to test knowledge.—*vt* to bring to trial and examination; to examine critically; to prove by experiment or by some fixed standard; to try; (*chem*) to examine by the application of some reagent.

testacy *n* the state of being testate.

testament *n* (*law*) a duly executed document in writing, by which a person declares his or her will as to the disposal of his or her estate and effects after his or her death; a will; the name of each general division of the canonical books of the sacred Scriptures (*the Old Testament, the New Testament*): when used alone the word is often limited to the New Testament.

testamentary *adj* pertaining to a will or to wills; bequeathed or arranged by will.

testate *adj* having made and left a will.

testator *n* a man who makes and leaves a will at death.

testatrix *n* a woman who makes and leaves a will at death.

test case *n* a legal action that establishes a precedent.

tester[1] *n* one who or that which tests; a sample, as of perfume, for trying before purchase.

tester[2] *n* the square canopy over a four-post bedstead; a flat canopy, as over a pulpit, tomb, etc.

testes *npl* (*anat*) the testicles.

test furnace *n* a kind of refining furnace.

testicle *n* one of the glands which secrete the seminal fluid in males.

testify *vi* (**testified, testifying**) to make a solemn declaration, verbal or written, to establish some fact; (*law*) to give evidence under oath; to declare a charge.—*vt* to affirm or declare solemnly; (*law*) to affirm under oath before a tribunal, for the purpose of proving some fact.

testimonial *n* a certificate in favour of someone's character; a certificate of qualifications; a gift or token of appreciation raised by subscription in acknowledgment

terrier

of an individual's services or to show respect for his or her worth.

testimony *n* a solemn declaration or affirmation made for the purpose of establishing or proving some fact; evidence; declaration; attestation; witness; anything equivalent to a declaration or protest; divine revelation.

test match *n* a cricket match played between representative teams of two countries.

testosterone *n* the hormone made in the testes of animals which produces male characteristics.

test paper *n* a paper impregnated with some chemical reagent and serving to detect the presence of certain substances by change of colour when they touch it; a set of questions to test knowledge of a subject.

test tube *n* a glass tube to contain substances to be chemically tested.

test-tube baby *n* a baby whose conception or part of its development is produced scientifically outside the mother's body.

testudo *n* (*pl* **testudines**) among the ancient Romans, a protection from missiles formed by soldiers holding their shields over their heads and standing close to each other.

testy *adj* fretful; peevish; easily irritated.

tetanus *n* spasm with rigidity; a bacterial disease characterized by a more or less violent and rigid spasm of many or all of the muscles of voluntary motion, one form being lockjaw.

tetchy *adj* peevish; fretful; irritable; testy.

tête-à-tête *adv* face to face; in private; in close confabulation.—*n* (*pl* **tête-à-têtes, tête-à-tête**) a private interview with no one present but the parties concerned.

tether *n* a rope or chain by which a grazing animal is confined within certain limits; the limit of one's endurance.—*vt* to confine with a tether; to limit.

tetrad *n* the number four; a collection of four things.

tetragon *n* (*geom*) a figure having four angles; a quadrangle, as a square, a rhombus, etc.

tetragonal *adj* having four angles or sides; of a system of crystals having all three axes equal and two of them at right angles to each other.

tetrahedron *n* a triangular pyramid having four equal and equilateral faces; a solid bounded by four equal triangles.

tetralogy *n* a collection of four dramatic compositions, three tragedies and one satire, which were exhibited together on the Athenian stage; any series of four related works, such as novels or plays.

tetrarch *n* a Roman governor of the fourth part of a province; a petty king or sovereign.

test tube

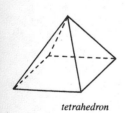

tetrahedron

tetrasyllable *n* a word consisting of four syllables.

Teutonic *adj* belonging to the Teutons or the peoples of Germanic origin in general; Germanic; pertaining to the languages spoken by these peoples, which include Anglo-Saxon and English, Dutch, German, Icelandic, Norse, Danish and Swedish.—*n* the language or languages collectively of the Teutons.

text *n* a discourse or composition on which notes or a commentary is written; the actual words of something written or printed; an author's own work as distinct from notes or annotations on it; a passage of Scripture, especially one selected as the theme of a sermon or discourse; any subject chosen to comment on; a topic.

textbook *n* a book used by students as a manual for a particular branch of study; a manual of instruction.

textile *adj* woven or capable of being woven; formed by weaving.—*n* a fabric made by weaving.

textual *adj* pertaining to or contained in the text.

texture *n* a fabric formed by weaving; the way in which threads in a material are interwoven; the composition or structure of a substance, especially as conveyed to the touch; the characteristic appearance, arrangement or feel of a thing.

thalamus *n* (*pl* **thalami**) (*bot*) the receptacle of a flower or part on which the carpels are placed; (*anat*) either of the two masses of tissue which sit close together at the base of the brain.

Thalia *n* in Greek myth, the Muse of comedy and the patron of pastoral and comic poetry.

thalidomide *n* a drug used as a sedative but withdrawn from use when it was found to cause malformation in foetuses.

thallium *n* a soft, heavy, greyish metallic element resembling lead in appearance, discovered in 1861.

thallus *n* (*pl* **thallia, thalluses**) (*bot*) a solid mass of cells or cellular tissue without woody fibre.

than *conj* a particle used after certain adjectives and adverbs which expresses comparison or diversity, such as *more, better, other, otherwise, rather, else*, etc, for the purpose of introducing the second member of the comparison (sometimes used to govern an objective like a preposition).

thane *n* a title of honour among the Anglo-Saxons; an Anglo-Saxon baron; a landed proprietor.

thank *vt* to express gratitude to for a favour; to make acknowledgments to for kindness bestowed.—**thank you** a colloquial or informal contraction of the phrase *I thank you*.

thankful *adj* impressed with a sense of kindness received and ready to acknowledge it; grateful; expressive of thanks.

thankless *adj* unthankful; ungrateful; not deserving or not likely to gain thanks (*a thankless task*).

thanks *npl* expression of gratitude; an acknowledgment made to express a sense of favour or kindness received or offered.—**thanks!** a common contraction for *I give* (*offer*, *render*, etc) *thanks*.

thanksgiving *n* the act of rendering thanks; a public celebration of divine goodness; a day set apart for such a celebration; a form of words expressive of thanks to God.

that *adj*, *pron* (*pl* **those**) a word used as pointing to a person or thing before mentioned or supposed to be understood (*that man, that city*); frequently used in opposition to *this* (*I will take this book, you can take that one*): often used without a noun as a demonstrative pronoun and also as a relative pronoun, in many cases equivalent to *who* or *which*; *who* being generally used for persons, *which* for things and *that* for either—when governed by a preposition the latter is put at the end of the clause (*the book that I read from*).—*conj* introducing a reason; because (*not that I care*); introducing an end or purpose (*speak that I may hear*); introducing a result or consequence (*so weak that he cannot stand*); introducing a clause as the subject or object of the principal verb (*we know that he is dead*); used to introduce a wish (*would that he were dead!*).

thatch *n* straw, rushes, reeds, heath, etc, used to cover the roofs of buildings or stacks of hay or grain.—*vt* to cover with straw, reeds or some similar substance.

thaumaturgy *n* the act of performing something wonderful; wonder-working; legerdemain; magic.

thaw *vi* to melt, as ice or snow; to become so warm as to melt ice and snow (said of the weather and used impersonally); (*fig*) to become less cold, formal or reserved; to become genial.—*vt* to melt ice or snow; to make less cold or reserved.—*n* the melting of ice or snow; warmth of weather, such as liquefies ice.

the *definite art* or *definitive adj* used before nouns with a specifying or limiting effect (*the laws of our country*); used before a noun in the singular to denote a species by way of distinction or a single thing representing the whole (*the elephant is sagacious*); prefixed to adjectives to give them the force of abstract nouns (*a passion for the sublime and beautiful*); used before adjectives and adverbs in the comparative degree it means *by that*; *by how much*; *by so much* (*the longer we continue in sin the more difficult it is to reform*).

theatre *n* a building appropriated to the representation of dramatic spectacles; a playhouse; a room with seats rising stepwise for public lectures, anatomical demonstrations, etc; the locality where events take place (*the theatre of war*).

theatrical *adj* pertaining to a theatre or to scenic representations; calculated for display; meretricious; artificial; false; affected; melodramatic.

theatricals *npl* a dramatic performance, especially in a private house.

thee *pron* the objective and dative case of **thou**.

theft *n* the wrongful removal of the goods of another with intent to deprive him or her of them; the act of stealing.

theine *n* caffeine.

their *adj* pertaining or belonging to them.

theirs a possessive or genitive, properly a double genitive of *they*, used without a noun following, either as a nominative, objective or simple predicate.

theism *n* the belief or acknowledgment of the existence of a God, as opposed to *atheism*.

theist *n* one who believes in the existence of God.

them *pron* the dative and objective case of **they**; those persons or things; those.

theme *n* a subject or topic on which a person writes or speaks; a subject of discourse or discussion; a short dissertation composed by a student on a given subject; (*philol*) the part of a noun or a verb unchanged in declension or conjugation; (*mus*) a series of notes selected as the text or subject of a new composition; the leading subject in a composition or movement.

theme park *n* a leisure area in which the buildings and settings all follow a particular theme, such as a particular period of history.

theme song *n* a recurring song or tune heard often throughout a film or play, that becomes associated with the film or play or with a particular character.

Themis *n* in Greek myth, the goddess of law and justice.

themselves *pron pl* of **himself, herself, itself**.

then *adv* at that time, referring to a time specified, either past or future; soon afterward or immediately; at another time (*now and then*).—*conj* in that case; in consequence; therefore; for this reason.

thence *adv* from that place; from that time; for that reason; from this; out of this; not there; elsewhere; absent.—**from thence** though pleonastic, is supported by custom and good usage.

thenceforth *adv* from that time forward.

thenceforward *adv* from that time or place onward.

thatch

theobromine *n* a crystalline compound found in the seeds of cacao.

theocracy *n* government of a state by the immediate direction of God; the state thus governed.

theocrat *n* one who lives under a theocracy.

theodolite *n* a surveying instrument for measuring horizontal and vertical angles by means of a telescope the movement of which can be accurately marked on two graduated circles.

theogony *n* a poem dealing with the generation and descent of gods; doctrine as to the genealogy or origin of gods.

theologian *n* a person well versed in theology; a divine.

theological *adj* pertaining to theology.

theology *n* the science of divine things or of the Christian religion; the science which treats of God and human beings in all their known relations to each other; the study of religious doctrine and matters of divinity.

theorbo *n* (*pl* **theorbos**) a seventeenth-century musical instrument like a large lute with two necks, to one of which the bass strings were attached.

theorem *n* a position laid down as an acknowledged truth or established principle; (*math*) a proposition to be proved by a chain of reasoning; (*alg, analysis*) a statement of relations expressed by symbols or formulae (*the binomial theorem*).

theoretical, theoretic *adj* pertaining to theory; depending on theory or speculation; speculative; hypothetical; conjectural; not practical.

theoretics *npl* the speculative parts of a science; speculation.

theorist *n* one who forms theories.

theorize *vi* (**theorized, theorizing**) to form a theory; to form opinions solely by theory; to speculate.

theory *n* a supposition explaining something; a doctrine or scheme of things resting merely on speculation; hypothesis; plan or system suggested; an exposition of the general or abstract principles of any science (*the theory of music* or *of medicine*); the science or rules of an art, as distinguished from the practice; a philosophical explanation of phenomena; a connected arrangement of facts according to their bearing on some real or hypothetical law or laws.

theosophy *n* knowledge of divine things; a knowledge of God obtained by spiritual ecstasy, direct intuition or special individual relations.

theosophist *n* one who pretends to divine illumination or to derive his or her knowledge from divine revelation.

therapeutic *adj* curative; pertaining to the healing art; pertaining to the treatment of disease.

therapeutics *n* that part of medicine which relates to the composition, application and operation of remedies; the curative branch of medicine.

therapist *n* one versed in therapy.

therapy *n* the treatment of disease or disorders; the power or quality of curing; the remedial treatment of physical or mental illness.

there *adv* in that place; at that place, often opposed to *here*, *there* generally denoting the place most distant; in that object or matter; at that point; after going to such a length; into that place; to that place; thither; often used to begin sentences before a verb when there is an inversion of the subject (*there came many strangers to the town*).

thereabouts, thereabout *adv* near that place; near that number, degree or quantity.

thereafter *adv* according to that; accordingly; after that; afterward.

thereat *adv* at that place; at that place or event; on that account.

thereby *adv* by that; by that means; annexed or attached to that; by or near that place; near that number or quantity.

therefor *adv* for that or this or it.

therefore *conj, adv* for that or this reason, referring to something previously stated; consequently; in return or recompense for this or that.

therefrom *adv* from this or that.

therein *adv* in that or this place, time or thing; in that or this particular point or respect.

thereof *adv* of that or this.

thereon *adv* on that or this; thereupon.

thereto, thereunto *adv* to that or this.

thereunder *adv* under that or this.

thereupon *adv* upon that or this; in consequence of that; at once; without delay.

therewith, therewithal *adv* with that or this.

therm *n* a measurement of energy or heat, used as a unit in calculating the amount of gas used to be paid for.

thermal *adj* pertaining to heat; warm; relating to temperature; (of underwear) made of a knitted material with air spaces for insulation.—*n* a rising current of warm air.

thermic *adj* thermal.

thermion *n* an electron emitted by a material at high temperature.

thermionic *adj* having reference to the ions or electrons given off by hot bodies; pertaining to, or worked by, thermions.

thermionic valve *n* a radio valve which contains a heated cathode.

thermodynamics *n* the branch of physics which deals with the conversion of heat into mechanical force or energy and vice versa.

thermometer *n* an instrument used to measure temperature.

thermoplastic see **plastic.**

thermosetting see **plastic.**

Thermos flask, Thermos *n* the trademark of a brand of vacuum flask, a double-walled container with a vacuum between, usually of silvered glass or stainless steel, used to keep substances at a constant temperature.

thermostat *n* a self-acting apparatus for regulating temperature.

thermostatics *n* a branch of the science of heat dealing with the equilibrium of heat.

thermotherapy *n* the treatment of disease by heat.

thesaurus *n* (*pl* **thesauri, thesauruses**) a book of words and phrases grouped according to theme or meaning; a book of synonyms; a lexicon or treasury of words.

thesis *n* (*pl* **theses**) a position or proposition which a person advances and maintains; a subject propounded for a school, college or university exercise; the exercise itself; an essay or dissertation; (*pros*) the part of a foot on which the depression of the voice falls, opposed to *arsis.*

thespian *adj* of or pertaining to drama.—*n* an actor or actress.

thews *npl* muscles, sinews, strength.

they *pron* (*possessive case* **their**, *objective case* **them**) the plural form for **he, she** or **it,** thus denoting more than one person or thing.

thick *adj* having more or less extent measured through and through or otherwise than in length or breadth (said of solid bodies); relatively of great dimensions when thus measured, opposed to *thin, slender, slim*; dense; having great consistence (*thick fog* or *smoke*); foggy or misty; close set or planted; closely crowded together; close; following each other closely (*blows thick as hail*); without due flexibility or articulation (*thick utterance*); (*colloq*) stupid; (*colloq*) very friendly or familiar.—*n* the thickest part, or the time when anything is thickest.—**thick and thin** whatever is in the way; all obstacles or hindrances.—*adv* in close succession one upon another; fast or close together.

thicken *vt* to make thick or thicker.—*vi* to become thick or thicker.

thicket *n* a wood or collection of trees or shrubs closely set.

thick-head *n* a stupid fellow; a blockhead; a numskull.

thick-headed *adj* dull; stupid.

thick-knee *n* the stone plover or stone curlew.

thickly *adv* in a thick manner or condition; to considerable depth on a surface; closely.

thickness *n* the state of being thick in any sense of the word; measure through from surface to surface; density; consistence; closeness or crowded state; clumsy indistinctness of speech; (*colloq*) stupidity.

thickset *adj* close set or planted; having a short thick body; thick; stout; stumpy.—*n* a close or thick hedge; dense undergrowth.

thick-skinned *adj* having a thick skin or rind; not easily moved or irritated, as by taunts, ridicule, etc.

thief *n* (*pl* **thieves**) a person who steals or is guilty of theft; one who deprives another of property secretly or without open force, as opposed to a robber, who openly uses violence.

thieve *vi* (**thieved, thieving**) to steal; to practise theft.—*vt* to take by theft; to steal.

thievery *n* the practice of stealing; theft.

thievish *adj* given to stealing; of the nature of theft.

thigh *n* the thick fleshy portion of the leg between the knee and the trunk.

thighbone *n* the bone of the thigh; the femur.

thill *n* the shaft of a cart, gig or other carriage.

thimble *n* a metal, etc, cap or cover for the finger, used in sewing for driving the needle through; (*naut*) an iron ring with a rope spliced round it.

thimbleful *n* as much as a thimble would hold; hence, a very small quantity.

thin *adj* not thick; having little extent from one surface to the opposite (*a thin plate, a thin board*); slight; flimsy (*a thin veil*); rare; not dense (said of gaseous fluids); deficient in body or substance (said of liquids or semi-liquids); not close or crowded; sparse; not abundant (*thin grass*); not numerously filled; slim; slender; lean; faint; feeble; lacking fullness or volume, as sound; often used adverbially in composition as the first element in compounds (*thin-clad*).—*vt* (**thinned, thinning**) to make thin in all its senses.—*vi* to diminish in thickness; to grow or become thin (with *out, away*, etc).

thine *pronominal adj* thy; belonging to thee—**thine**, like *thou*, is now used only in poetry or the solemn style, *your* and *yours* otherwise taking its place.

thing *n* whatever exists or is conceived to exist, as a separate entity; whatever may be spoken or thought of; an inanimate object; a creature; applied to human beings and animals in pity, contempt, tenderness or admiration; a transaction, matter, circumstance, event; (*pl*) clothes, personal belongings, luggage; (*pl*) the general state of affairs (*How are things?*); an unaccountable attitude or feeling; an aversion.—**the thing** (*colloq*) as it ought to be (applied to an ideal or typical condition).

think *vi* (*pret, pp* **thought**, *ppr* **thinking**) to have the mind occupied on some subject;

thimble

to revolve ideas in the mind; to perform any mental operation; to cogitate; to muse; to meditate; to consider; to deliberate; to judge, conclude, be of opinion (*I think it will rain*); to purpose, design, intend; to imagine, suppose, fancy.—*vt* to form in the mind; to imagine; to hold in opinion; to regard, consider, esteem; to form a conception of.

thinker *n* one who thinks; one who reasons or meditates (*a deep thinker*); one who writes on speculative subjects.

think tank *n* a group of people, usually having specialized knowledge and experience, appointed to analyse a particular problem or area of policy and advise the government, etc, on how to handle this.

thinness *n* the state of being thin.

thin-skinned *adj* having a thin skin; unduly sensitive; easily offended; irritable.

third *adj* next after the second; being one of three equal parts into which anything is divided.—*n* the third part of anything; the sixtieth part of a second of time; (*mus*) an interval consisting of three conjunct degrees of the scale; the upper of the two notes including this interval.

third degree *n* ruthless examination or treatment of a suspect by the police in order to extract a confession.

thirst *n* the desire, uneasiness or suffering occasioned by lack of drink; vehement desire for drink; a lack and eager desire after anything (*a thirst for knowledge*).—*vi* to experience thirst; to have desire to drink; to have a vehement desire for anything.

thirsty *adj* feeling a painful sensation for lack of drink; having thirst; very dry; parched; having a vehement desire for anything.

thirteen *adj* ten and three.—*n* the number which consists of ten and three; a symbol for this, as 13, XIII.

thirteenth *adj* the third after the tenth; being one of thirteen equal parts of a thing.—*n* one of thirteen equal parts of anything.

thirtieth *adj* the next in order after the twenty-ninth; being one of thirty equal parts of a thing.—*n* one of thirty equal parts of anything.

thirty *adj* thrice ten; ten three times repeated.—*n* the number which consists of three times ten.

this *adj*, *pron* (*pl* **these**) a demonstrative used with or without a noun to denote something that is present or near in place or time or something just mentioned, often opposed to *that* (the latter referring to something more remote); applied to time, this may refer to the present time; now; to time next to come or to time immediately ended; frequently used to signify present state, condition, etc.

thistle

thistle *n* the common name of a prickly plant of numerous species, most of them inhabitants of Europe; regarded as the national emblem of Scotland.

thistledown *n* the feathery cluster of seeds produced by the thistle.

thither *adv* to that place, opposed to hither; to that end or result.—**hither and thither** to this place and that; one way and another.

tho' a contraction of **though**.

thole¹, tholepin *n* a pin inserted into the gunwale of a boat to serve as a fulcrum for the oar in rowing, often in pairs with the oar resting between.

thole² *vt* (**tholed, tholing**) to bear; to endure; to undergo.

thong *n* a strap of leather used for fastening anything; a long narrow strip of leather or similar material.

Thor *n* the second principal god of the ancient Scandinavians, the god of thunder and son of Odin, after whom Thursday is named.

thorax *n* (*pl* **thoraxes, thoraces**) the cavity of the body formed by the spine, ribs and breastbone and containing the lungs, heart, etc; the chest; the corresponding portion of animals; the portion of an insect between the head and abdomen.

thorium *n* a comparatively rare radioactive metal, the oxide of which is used in the construction of incandescent gas mantles.

thorn *n* a common name of trees and shrubs armed with spines or prickles, as the blackthorn, buckthorn and especially the common hawthorn; any sharp-pointed spiny or prickly process growing on a plant; (*fig*) anything that annoys or torments sharply; a care or trouble.

thorn apple *n* an annual plant of the potato family with narcotic properties, used medicinally.

thorn hedge *n* a hedge of hawthorn.

thorny *adj* full of thorns, spines or prickles; prickly; vexatious; harassing.

thorough *adj* going completely to the end; extending to all particulars; complete; perfect.

thorough-bred *adj* of pure or unmixed breed, bred from a sire and dam of purest blood.—*n* an animal, especially a horse, of pure blood.

thoroughfare *n* a way through; a public highway; right of passing through.

thorough-going *adj* very thoroughly; out-and-out.

thoroughly *adv* in a thorough manner; completely; fully.

thoroughness *n* the state of being thorough; a painstaking or exhaustive approach.

thorp, thorpe *n* (*arch*) a group of houses standing together in the country; a hamlet; a village.

those *adj, pron* historically the plural of *this*, being another form of *these*, but used as plural of **that**.

Thoth *n* in Egyptian myth, the god of learning and wisdom associated with the ibis.

thou *pron* (*objective and dative* **thee**, *pl* **ye** *or* **you**) the second personal pronoun in the singular number (used to indicate the person spoken to but in ordinary language the plural form *you* is now universally substituted, *thou* being used in the poetical or solemn style).

though *conj* granting or allowing it to be the fact that; notwithstanding that.—*adv* however; for all that.

thought *n* the act of power of thinking; cogitation; meditation; that which is thought; an idea; a conception; a judgment; a fancy; a conceit; deliberation; reflection; solicitude.—**second thoughts** more mature reflection; after-consideration.

thoughtful *adj* full of thought; contemplative; meditative; attentive; careful; mindful; full of anxiety; solicitous.

thoughtfulness *n* serious attention; solicitude.

thoughtless *adj* free from thought or care; heedless; negligent; light-minded.

thoughtlessly *adv* without thought; carelessly.

thoughtlessness *n* the quality of being thoughtless; heedlessness; inattention.

thought-reading *n* a so-called psychical power by which it is claimed some persons are able to read the thoughts of others or at least tell the object of their thoughts.

thousand *n* the number of ten hundred; proverbially, a great number.—*adj* denoting the number of ten hundred, or proverbially, a great number indefinitely.

thousandth *adj* completing the number of a thousand; being one of a thousand equal parts of anything.—*n* the thousandth part of anything.

thraldom *n* slavery; bondage.

thrall *n* a slave; a bondsman.

thrash, thresh *vt* to beat out or separate the grain or seeds from by a flail or thrashing machine or by treading with oxen; to beat soundly with a stick or whip; to drub.—*vi* to drive out grain from straw.

thrasher, thresher *n* one who thrashes grain; a species of shark which uses its tail as a weapon.

thrashing, threshing *n* the operation by which grain is thrashed; a beating or drubbing.

thrashing floor *n* a floor or area on which grain is beaten out.

thrashing machine, thrashing mill *n* a machine for separating grain from the straw in which the moving power is that of horses, oxen, wind, water or steam.

thread *n* a fine cord, especially such as is used for sewing; the filaments of fibrous substances, such as cotton, flax, silk or wool, spun out into a slender line; anything resembling this; any slender filament; continued course or tenor (*the thread of a discourse*); the prominent spiral part of a screw.—*vt* to pass a thread through the eye or aperture of; to pass or go through, as through a narrow way or any intricate course.

threadbare *adj* having the nap worn off so as to show the separate threads; hence, trite; hackneyed; used till it has lost novelty or interest.

threadworm *n* a thread-like worm found as a parasite in the human intestine.

threat *n* a menace; a declaration of an intention to inflict punishment, loss or pain on another.

threaten *vt* to use threats towards; to declare an intention of injuring; to menace; to menace by action; to act as if intending to injure; to exhibit the appearance of bringing something evil or unpleasant on (*the clouds threaten us with rain*); to show to be impending (*the sky threatens a storm*).—*vi* to use threats or menaces.

threatening *adj* indicating a threat or menace; indicating something impending.

three *adj* two and one.—*n* the number which consists of two and one; a symbol representing this, as 3, III.—**rule of three** the arithmetical rule otherwise called *proportion*.

three-cornered *adj* having three corners or angles; triangular.

three-D, 3-D *adj* three-dimensional.

three-dimensional *adj* having three dimensions; appearing to have three dimensions.

three-ply *adj* threefold; consisting of three strands, as cord, yarn etc.

three-quarter *n* one of the four backs, in rugby football, who play between the halfbacks and the full-back.—*adj* being three-quarters of the normal size or length.

three-score *adj* thrice twenty; sixty.

threnody *n* a song of lamentation; a dirge.

thresh *vti* same as **thrash**.

thresher shark *n* a shark with a tail whose upper lobe is very long (so called because of lashing other animals with its tail).

threshold *n* a door sill; the stone or piece of timber which lies under a door; hence, entrance; beginning; outset (*the threshold of an argument*).

threshold of consciousness *n* (*psychol*) the point at which a stimulus to the sensory organism is just sufficiently intense to be felt.

thrice *adv* three times; also often used for emphasis or intensity (*thrice blessed*, etc).

thrift *n* a thriving state or condition; economical management in regard to prop-

thread

erty; economy; frugality; a plant which grows on the coasts of Britain and is often planted in gardens as a border plant; sea pink.

thrifty *adj* having thrift; careful in husbanding resources; frugal; economical.

thrill *vt* to pierce in a figurative sense; to affect with a pricking or tingling sensation through the whole body.—*vi* to pass through the system so as to cause a slight shiver or quiver; to feel a shivering sensation running through the body; to shiver; to quiver or move with a tremulous movement.—*n* a warbling; a trill; a thrilling sensation.

thriller *n* a novel, film or play dealing with exciting or mysterious events.

thrips *n* any of a genus of minute insects that feed on and damage plants.

thrive *vi* (*pret* **throve**, *pp* **thriven**, *ppr* **thriving**) to prosper or succeed; to be fortunate; to increase in goods and estate; to keep increasing one's acquisitions; to be marked by prosperity (*a thriving business*); to go on or turn out well; to have a good issue; to grow vigorously or luxuriantly; to flourish.

thriving *adj* being prosperous; advancing in wealth; flourishing.

thro' contraction of **through**.

throat *n* the anterior part of the neck of an animal in which are the gullet and windpipe; the fauces; the pharynx; an opening or entrance resembling the throat (*the throat of a valley*).

throaty *adj* guttural; uttered back in the throat.

throb *vi* (**throbbed, throbbing**) to beat, as the heart or pulse, with more than usual force or rapidity; to palpitate; to quiver or vibrate.—*n* a beat or strong pulsation; palpitation.

throes *npl* violent pangs or pain.

thrombosis *n* (*pl* **thromboses**) the formation of a stationary clot which develops inside a blood vessel and blocks the flow of blood.

thrombus *n* (*pl* **thrombi**) the blood clot that blocks a vessel in thrombosis.

throne *n* an elevated and ornamental chair of state used by a king, emperor, pope, bishop, etc; the official chair of a presiding official of certain societies; sovereign power and dignity; also, the wielder of that power (usually with *the*).—*vt* (**throned, throning**) to place on a royal seat; to enthrone; to exalt.

throng *n* a multitude of persons pressed into a close body; a crowd; a great number; a number of things crowded or close together (*a throng of words*).—*vi* to crowd together; to come in multitudes.—*vt* to crowd or press; to annoy with a crowd of living beings; to fill with a crowd.

throstle *n* (*poet*) the thrush or song thrush; a machine for spinning wool, cotton, etc.

throttle *n* the windpipe or trachea; the throat.—*vt* (**throttled, throttling**) to choke; to stop the breath of by compressing the throat; to strangle.

through *prep* from end to end or from side to side of; between the sides or walls of (*to pass through a gate*); by the agency of; by means of; on account of; over the whole surface or extent of; throughout; among or in the midst of, in the way of passage; among, in the way of experiencing; from beginning to end of.—*adv* from one end or side to the other; from beginning to end; to the end; to completion.—*adj* going with little or no interruption from one important place or centre to another (*a through passenger, a through journey*).

throughly *adv* (*arch*) completely, thoroughly.

throughout *prep* quite through in every part of; from one extremity to the other of.—*adv* everywhere; in every part.

throw *vt* (*pret* **threw**, *pp* **thrown**, *ppr* **throwing**) to fling or cast in any manner; to hurl; to dash (often reflexive, as *he threw himself on the enemy*); to prostrate, as in wrestling; to overturn; to divest oneself of; to shed; to give violent utterance or expression to; to send (*to throw defiance*); to put on or over with haste or negligence; to wind or twist two or more filaments of, as of silk, so as to form one thread; (in pottery) to form or shape roughly on a wheel or throwing engine; to hold (a party, etc); (*colloq*) to confuse or disconcert.—*vi* to perform the act of casting or flinging; to cast dice.—**to throw up** (*colloq*) to vomit; to abandon, as throw up one's job.—*n* the act of one who throws; a cast; a cast of dice; hence, risk; venture; decision of fortune; (in geology and in mining) a dislocation of strata up or down.

throwback *n* reversion to an ancestral or earlier type; atavism,.

thrum *vi* (**thrummed, thrumming**) to play coarsely or unskilfully on a stringed instrument; to make a drumming noise.—*vt* to play roughly on with the fingers; to drum; to tap.

thrush[1] *n* a songbird with a brown back and spotted breast.

thrush[2] *n* a fungal disease of mucous membranes, as the mouth or the vagina; an inflammatory and suppurating disease in the feet of the horse.

thrust *vt* (*pret, pp* **thrust**, *ppr* **thrusting**) to push or drive with force; to impel (usually followed by *away, from, in, off*, etc).—*vi* to make a push; to make a lunge with a weapon.—*n* a violent push or drive, as with the hand or foot or with a pointed weapon; a lunge; a stab; (*mech*) the force exerted by any body against another body, such as the force exerted by rafters or beams against the walls supporting them; the main point; the basic meaning.

thud *n* the sound produced by a blow on a comparatively soft substance; a blow causing a dull sound.—*vi* (**thudded, thudding**) to make such a sound.

thug *n* a violent and rough person, especially a criminal.

thumb *n* the short, thick finger of the human hand or the corresponding member of other animals.—*vt* to soil or wear with the thumb or fingers or by frequent handling.

thumbed *adj* having thumbs; soiled or worn with the thumb or the fingers.

thumbscrew *n* an instrument of torture for compressing the thumbs by means of screws; a screw to be turned by the finger and thumb.

thump *n* the sound made by the sudden fall of a heavy body; hence, a heavy blow given with anything that is thick.—*vt* to strike or beat with something thick or heavy.—*vi* to strike or fall with a heavy blow.

thumper *n* one who thumps; (*colloq*) a person or thing which is huge or great.

thumping *adj* (*colloq*) large; heavy.

thunder *n* the sound which follows a flash of lightning; a report due to the sudden disturbance of the air produced by a violent discharge of atmospheric electricity or lightning; any loud noise (*thunders of applause*); an awful or startling denunciation or threat (*the thunders of the Vatican*).—*vi* to make thunder (often impersonal, as *it thundered yesterday*); to make a loud noise, particularly a heavy sound of some continuance.—*vt* to emit as with the noise of thunder; to utter or issue by way of threat or denunciation.

thunderbolt *n* a destructive flash of lightning, formerly supposed to be accompanied by the fall of a solid body; a dreadful threat, denunciation or censure; any sudden or unforeseen event.

thunderclap *n* a clap or burst of thunder.

thunder cloud *n* a cloud that produces lightning and thunder, of dark and dense appearance.

thundering *adj* producing or characterized by a loud rumbling or rattling noise, as that of thunder or artillery; (*colloq*) large or extraordinary.

thunderstorm *n* a storm accompanied with thunder.

thunderstruck *adj* astonished; amazed; struck dumb by something surprising or terrible suddenly presented.

thurible *n* a kind of censer in the shape of a covered vase, perforated to allow the fumes of incense to escape.

Thursday *n* the fifth day of the week.

thus *adv* in this way, manner or state; accordingly; things being so; to this degree or extent; so (*thus wise*).—**thus far, thus much** to this point; to this degree.

thwack *vt* to strike, bang, beat or thrash.—*n* a heavy blow with something flat or heavy; a bang.

thwart *adj* transverse; being across something else.—*vt* to frustrate or defeat (a design, a person).—*n* the seat of a boat placed athwart it.

thy *pron* belonging or pertaining to thee: possessive pronoun of the second person singular.

thylacine *n* the Tasmanian wolf.

thyme *n* an aromatic shrub; its leaves used as a cooking herb.

thymol *n* a crystalline substance obtained from oil of thyme and used as an antiseptic and disinfectant.

thymus *n* (*anat*) (*pl* **thymi, thymuses**) a glandular body situated behind the sternum or breastbone in children, often entirely disappearing at puberty.

thyroid *adj* resembling a shield (applied to one of the cartilages of the larynx, to a gland situated near that cartilage and to the arteries and veins of the gland).—*n* a thyroid gland.

thyroid gland *n* a ductless gland attached to the front of the larynx, producing an internal secretion that helps to regulate the nutrition of the body and affects growth and metabolism.

thyself *pron* a pronoun used after *thou*, to express distinction with emphasis; or used without thou, its usage being similar to that of *myself*, etc.

ti *n* a flowering plant of the Pacific islands, etc, with a highly nutritious root.

tiara *n* a semi-circular crown decorated with jewels.

tibia *n* (*pl* **tibiae, tibias**) a kind of pipe, the commonest musical instrument of the Greeks and Romans; (*anat*) the large bone of the lower leg; the shinbone; (*entom*) the fourth joint of the leg.

tic *n* a convulsive twitching of certain muscles of the face; tic-douloureux.

tic douloureux *n* trigeminal neuralgia.

tick[1] *vi* to make a small noise by beating or otherwise, as a watch; to give out a succession of small sharp noises; (*colloq*) to work or function.—*n* a small distinct noise, as that of a watch or clock; a small dot.—*vt* to mark with a tick or dot; to check by writing down a small mark (generally with *off*).

tick[2] *n* the name common to certain small parasitic arachnids or mites which infest sheep, oxen, dogs, goats, etc.

tick[3] *n* the cover or case which contains the feathers, wool or other materials of a bed; ticking.

thumb

tiara

tick⁴ *n* (*colloq*) credit; trust.—**to buy on tick** to buy on a ticket or note or on credit.

ticket *n* a label stuck on the outside of anything to give notice of something concerning it; a small piece of paper, cardboard, etc, with something written or printed on it and serving as a notice, acknowledgement, etc; a certificate or token of a share in a lottery, etc; a card or slip of paper given as a certificate of right of entry to a place of public amusement, or to travel by public transport; (*colloq*) a fine or a summons for a parking offence.—**the ticket** the right or correct thing.—*vt* to distinguish by a ticket; to put a ticket on.

ticket of leave *n* formerly, a licence given to a convict before the expiry of his or her sentence to be, under certain restrictions, at large and labour for himself or herself.

ticking *n* a strong striped linen or cotton fabric used for the ticks of beds, mattresses, etc.

tickle *vt* (**tickled, tickling**) to touch lightly and cause a peculiar thrilling sensation, which commonly causes laughter; to titillate; to please by slight gratification; to stir up to pleasure; to flatter; to cajole; to puzzle.

ticket

ticklish *adj* easily tickled; in an unsteady or critical state; difficult; critical; nice.

tidal *adj* pertaining to tides; showing tides.

tidal harbour *n* a harbour in which the tide ebbs and flows, not having a dock with floodgates.

tidal wave *n* a large wave as a result of high winds with spring tides; a huge destructive wave caused by earthquakes; something overwhelming.

tide *n* time; season; the alternate rising and falling of the waters of the ocean and of bays, rivers, etc, connected therewith, depending on the relative position of the moon and in a less degree of the sun; the whole interval between high and low water; (*Shak*) a state of being at the height or acme; stream; flow; current (*a tide of blood*); course or tendency of influences or circumstances; current.—*vti* (**tided, tiding**) to drive with the tide or stream.— **to tide over** to surmount by favourable incidents, by prudence and management, or by aid from another.

tie

tide-gate *n* a gate through which water passes when the tide flows and which is shut to retain it.

tide table *n* a table showing the time of high water at any place, or at different places, throughout the year.

tidings *npl* news; information; intelligence; account of what has taken place and was not before known.

tidy *adj* arranged in good order or with neatness; dressed or kept with neatness; neat; trim; practising neatness; (*colloq*)

moderately large or great.—*vt* (**tidied, tidying**) to make neat or tidy; to put in good order.

tie *vt* (**tied, tying**) to fasten with a band or cord and knot; to bind; to fasten; to knit; to unite so as not to be easily parted; to limit or bind by authority or moral influence; to restrain; to confine; to oblige.—*n* something used to fasten or bind; a fastening; an ornamental knot; a necktie; a bond; an obligation, moral or legal (*the ties of blood* or *of friendship*); (in a building) a beam or rod which secures parts together and is subjected to a tensile strain; (*mus*) a curved line written over or under notes of the same pitch to indicate that the sound is to be unbrokenly continued to the time value of the combined notes; a state of equality among competing or opposed parties, as in certain games, competitions among marksmen, etc; a contest in which two or more competitors are equally successful; a draw.—**to play** *or* **shoot off a tie** to go through a second contest (the first being indecisive) to decide who is to be the winner.

tie beam *n* the beam which connects the bottom of a pair of principal rafters in a roof.

tiebreak, tiebreaker *n* any means of deciding a contest which has ended in a tie.

tier *n* a row; a rank, particularly when two or more rows are placed one above another.

tierce *n* formerly, a liquid measure equal to one-third of a pipe; a cask for salt provisions, etc; (*mus*) a major or minor third; (in fencing) a position in which the wrist and nails are turned downwards, the weapon of the opponent being on the right of the fencer.

tiercel *n* same as **tercel**.

tiff *n* a small draught of liquor; a pet or fit of peevishness; a slight altercation or quarrel.

tiffin *n* in India, a lunch or slight repast between breakfast and dinner.

tiger *n* a large and fierce carnivorous mammal of the cat family found in Southern Asia, about the size of the lion, but more cat-like and having a striped skin.

tiger beetle *n* a name given to certain beetles that feed on other insects.

tiger cat *n* a name for various animals of the cat family of medium size.

tiger lily *n* a plant common in English gardens, having scarlet flowers turned downward, with the perianth reflexed.

tigress *n* the female of the tiger.

tight *adj* having the parts or joints so close as to prevent the passage of fluids; impervious to air, gas, water, etc; compactly or firmly built or made; sound and strong; as applied to persons, well-knit, sinewy, strong; firmly packed or inserted; not loose; fitting too close to the body; tensely stretched or strained; taut; not slack (*a tight rope*); not easy to be obtained; not to be had on ordinary terms (said of money when capitalists are disinclined to speculate); (*colloq*) mean, stingy; (*colloq*) tipsy.

tighten *vt* to make tight; to draw tighter.

tightness *n* the state or quality of being tight; closeness of parts; imperviousness; compactness; tenseness.

tightrope *n* a tightly stretched rope on which an acrobat performs feats.

tights *npl* a close-fitting garment covering the lower part of the body and legs, as worn by ballet dancers, acrobats, etc; a similar garment worn by women instead of stockings.

tike *n* same as **tyke**.

til *n* Indian sesame.

tilbury *n* a gig or two-wheeled carriage without a top or cover.

tilde *n* the mark over the Spanish *n* when pronounced with a slightly added *y* sound, as in *señor, cañon*, etc.

tile *n* a slab of baked clay of similar substance used to cover the roofs, line furnaces and ovens, construct drains, etc; a tube- or tunnel-shaped piece of baked clay, plastic, etc, for drains; a slab of baked clay, etc, glazed on one side and used to cover walls, floors, etc; a piece of vinyl, carpet, etc, used to cover floors; a tall stiff hat.—*vt* (**tiled, tiling**) to cover with tiles.

tiler *n* a person who makes or who lays tiles.

till[1] *n* a money box in a shop, warehouse, etc; a cash drawer.

till[2] *n* a kind of hard clayey earth; boulder clay.

till[3] *prep* to the time of; until (*wait till next week*); often used before verbs and clauses (*I will wait till you arrive*); to, as far as, up to.

till[4] *vt* to plough and prepare for seed and to dress the crops of; to cultivate; to labour.

tillage *n* the operation or art of tilling land; cultivation; culture; husbandry.

tiller[1] *n* (*naut*) the bar or lever fitted to the head of a rudder and employed to turn the helm of a ship or boat in steering.

tiller[2] *n* one who tills; a cultivator.

tilt *n* a tent; the cloth covering of a cart or wagon; a canopy or awning over the after part of a boat.

tilt *vt* to raise one end of, as of a cask, for discharging liquor; to heave up at an angle; to hammer or forge with a tilt hammer.—**to tilt up** (*geol*) to throw up abruptly at a high angle of inclination (*the strata are tilted up*).—*vi* to run or ride and thrust with a lance; to joust, as in a tournament; to fight similarly; to rush as in combat; to rise into a sloping position; to heel.—*n* a thrust; a military exercise on

horseback, in which the combatants attacked each other with lances; a tilt hammer; inclination forward (*the tilt of a cask*); (*geol*) the throwing up of strata at a high angle of inclination.

tilth *n* the operation of tilling; tillage; husbandry; the state of being tilled; tilled ground.

timbal, tymbal *n* a kind of kettledrum.

timbale *n* a dish of fish, meat, vegetables, etc, cooked in a rich sauce in a fireproof mould lined with pastry or potato; the round, fireproof, straight-sided mould in which this dish is cooked.

timber *n* trees cut down and suitable for building purposes; trees felled and partly prepared for use; growing trees yielding wood suitable for constructive purposes; one of the main beams of a fabric; (*naut*) a curving piece of wood forming the rib of a ship (with a plural in this and preceding sense).

timbre *n* (*mus*) the quality which distinguishes any given tone or sound of one instrument or voice from the same tone or sound of another instrument or voice and which depends on the harmonics co-existing with the fundamental tone and their relative intensities.

timbrel *n* a kind of drum or tabor; a tambourine.

time *n* the measure of duration; a particular portion or part of duration, whether past, present or future, and either a space or a point, a period or a moment; occasion; season; moment; a proper occasion; opportunity (*to bide our time*); period at which any definite event occurred or person lived; an age (*the time of James I*); an allotted period of life; the present life; existence in this world; prevailing state of circumstances (generally in plural, as *good times, bad times*); leisure (*I have not time to speak with you*); hour of death or of travail (*his time was come*); a performance or repetition among others; (*mus*) the style of movement marked by the regular grouping of a certain and equal number of notes, or of more or less notes equal in time value to that certain number through all the bars of a movement; rhythm; the absolute velocity or rate of movement at which a piece is executed.—*vt* (**timed, timing**) to adapt to the time or occasion; to regulate as to time; to mark or ascertain the time or rate of.—*vi* to keep time; to harmonize.

time bomb *n* a bomb designed to explode at a predetermined time; something with a potentially delayed reaction.

time-honoured *adj* honoured for a long time; venerable and worthy of honour by reason of antiquity and long continuance.

timekeeper *adj* a clock, watch or chronom-

tiller

eter; a person who keeps or marks the time, as that during which a number of workers work.

timely *adj* seasonable; being in good time; sufficiently early.

timepiece *n* a clock, watch or other instrument to measure time, especially a small portable clock.

timer *n* a device for measuring, recording or controlling time; a device for controlling lights, heating, etc, by setting an electric clock to regulate their operations.

time-server *n* one who meanly and for selfish ends adapts his or her opinions and manners to the times; one who obsequiously complies with the ruling power.

time-serving *adj* obsequiously complying with the humours of people in power.—*n* the conduct of a time-server.

timesharing *n* a system which enables several users to have simultaneous access to the same computer from different terminals; joint ownership of a holiday property by which each owner is entitled to use the property for a specified amount of time at a specified time each year.

timetable *n* a table or register of times, as of the hours to be observed in a school, of the departure and arrival of railway trains, steamboats, etc.

timid *adj* fearful; lacking courage to meet danger; timorous; not bold.

timidity *n* the state or quality of being timid.

timorous *adj* fearful of danger; timid; lacking courage; indicating or marked by fear.

timpani, tympani *npl* a set of kettledrums.

timpanist, tympanist *n* a performer on kettledrums.

tin *n* a metal of a white colour tinged with grey, in hardness intermediate between gold and lead and very malleable; thin plates of iron covered with tin; tinplate; (*sl*) money.—*vt* (**tinned, tinning**) to cover with tin or overlay with tinfoil.

tinamou *n* a bird of South America, the species varying in size from a pheasant to a quail.

tincture *n* a tinge or shade of colour; slight taste added to any substance; slight quality added to anything; (*med*) an extract or solution of the active principles of some substance in a solvent, the latter being often proof spirit (so called from usually possessing colour); *tinctures* is the heraldic name for what are commonly called 'colours'.

tinder *n* an inflammable substance generally composed of partially burned linen, used for kindling fire from a spark struck with a steel and flint.

tine *n* the tooth or spike of a fork; a prong; the tooth of a harrow; a point or prong of a deer's horn.

tinfoil *n* pure tin, or the metal alloyed with a little lead, beaten and rolled into thin sheets.

ting *n* a sharp sound, as of a bell; a tinkling.—*vi* to sound or ring.

tinge *vt* (**tinged, tingeing** *or* **tinging**) to mix or imbue with some foreign substance so as to affect or modify the colour, taste or qualities of; to give a certain smack, flavour or quality to; to colour.—*n* a slight degree of colour, taste, flavour or quality infused or added to something; tincture; tint; smack.

tingle *vi* (**tingled, tingling**) to feel a kind of thrilling sensation, as in hearing a small sharp ringing sound; to feel a sharp prickling or stinging pain; to have a prickling, sharp or penetrating sensation.—*vt* to cause to give a sharp ringing sound; to ring.

tingling *n* a thrilling, jarring, tremulous sensation; a sharp, prickling feeling.

tinker *n* a mender of kettles, pans, etc; a repair; a cobbling or botching.—*vt* to mend like a tinker; to mend clumsily; to attempt to repair; to fiddle with.—*vi* to work at tinker's work; to cobble; to keep making petty repairs; to fiddle.

tinkle *vi* (**tinkled, tinkling**) to make small, quick, sharp sounds, as by striking on metal; to clink; to jingle; to resound with a small sharp sound; to tingle.—*vt* to cause to make sharp, quick, ringing sounds; to ring.—*n* a small, quick, sharp, ringing noise; (*colloq*) a telephone call.

tinkling *n* a small, quick, sharp sound.

tinny *adj* pertaining to, abounding with or resembling tin; having a high metallic sound.

tinsel *n* thin shining metallic plate or foil for ornamental purposes; cloth or tissue of silk and silver threads; cloth overlaid with foil; something superficially showy and more bright than valuable.—*adj* consisting of tinsel; showy to excess; specious; superficial.

tinsmith *n* one who makes articles of tin or tinplate.

tint *n* a slight colouring or tincture distinct from the ground or principal colour; a hue; a tinge; degree of intensity of a colour.—*vt* to tinge; to give a slight colouring to.

tiny *adj* very small; little; puny.

tip *n* a small pointed or tapering end or extremity; a gentle stroke; a tap; a small present of money, a gratuity to a waiter, etc; (*sl*) an item of private information, especially in regard to the chances of horses in a race, for betting purposes; a helpful hint; a piece of inside information.—*vt* (**tipped, tipping**) to form the tip of; to cover the tip of; to tilt to overturn; to dump rubbish; to give a small money gift or gratuity to.

tipcat *n* a game in which a small pointed piece of wood called a cat is made to jump from the ground by being struck on the tip with a stick, then being knocked to a distance by the same player.

tippet *n* a sort of cape covering the shoulders and sometimes descending as far as the waist.

tipple *vi* (**tippled, tippling**) to drink spirituous or intoxicating liquors habitually; to drink frequently, but without getting drunk.—*vt* to drink, sip or imbibe often.—*n* liquor taken in tippling; drink.

tipstaff *n* (*pl* **tipstaves, tipstaffs**) (*arch*) a staff tipped with metal; an officer who bears such a staff; a constable; a sheriff's officer.

tipster *n* one who for a fee sends tips for betting purposes.

tipsy *adj* (*colloq*) overpowered or muddled with strong drink; intoxicated, but not helplessly drunk; fuddled.

tipsy cake *n* a cake saturated with Madeira, stuck with almonds, etc, and served with custard.

tiptoe *n* the tip or end of the toe.—**on tiptoe** (*fig*) on the strain; interested or anxious.—*vi* (**tiptoed, tiptoeing**) to walk very quietly or carefully.

tiptop *adj* first-rate; excellent or perfect in the highest degree.

tirade *n* a long violent speech; a declamatory flight of censure or reproof; a series of invectives; a harangue.

tire *vt* to exhaust the strength of by toil or labour; to fatigue; to weary; to exhaust the attention or patience of, with dullness or tediousness.—**to tire out,** to weary or fatigue to excess; to exhaust.—*vi* to become weary; to have the patience exhausted.

tiredness *n* the state of being wearied; weariness.

tiresome *adj* fitted or tending to tire; fatiguing; wearisome; tedious.

tiro *n* same as **tyro.**

tisane, ptisan *n* a herbal drink with a slight medicinal effect.

tissue *n* a woven or textile fabric; cloth interwoven with gold or silver, or with coloured figures; (*fig*) a mass of connected particulars (*a tissue of falsehood*); one of the primary layers composing any of the parts of animal bodies; the minute elementary structures of which the organs of plants are composed.

tissue paper *n* a very thin, gauze-like paper, used for protecting engravings in books, wrapping delicate articles, etc.

tit *n* a small bit; a morsel; a small horse; the titmouse.—**tit for tat** an equivalent in the way of revenge or repartee.

titan *n* a person of great strength, size or ability.

Titan *n* in Greek myth, one of the twelve children of Uranus and Gaea, said to have been of gigantic size and enormous strength and to have been defeated by Zeus and the Olympian gods; (*astron*) the largest satellite of Saturn.

Titania *n* the queen of Fairyland and consort of Oberon.

titanic *adj* pertaining to a titan; enormous in size or strength; huge; vast.

Titanic *adj* pertaining to a Titan.

titanium *n* a metallic element belonging to the same group as silicon and tin and occurring widely in small quantities.

titbit *n* a small and delicious morsel; a particularly nice piece.

tithe *n* the tenth part of anything; the tenth part of the profits of land and stock and the personal industry of the inhabitants, allotted to the clergy for their support; hence, any small part or proportion.—*vt* to levy a tithe on; to tax to the amount of a tenth.—*vi* to pay tithes.

titian *adj* a reddish-brown colour.

titillate *vi* (**titillated, titillating**) to tickle; to arouse or excite pleasurably.

titillation *n* the act of titillating; any slight pleasure, especially sexual.

titivate, tittivate *vt* (**titivated, titivating**) to make look smart or spruce; to adorn.

titlark *n* a common European bird somewhat resembling a lark; a pipit.

title *n* an inscription or superscription on anything as a name by which it is known; a label; the inscription at the beginning of a book or other composition, containing the subject of the work or its particular designation; a particular section or division of a writing, especially a chapter or section of a law book; an appellation of dignity, distinction or pre-eminence given to persons; the appellation or honour distinctive of a sovereign, prince or nobleman; a name or appellation in general; a claim; a right; (*law*) right of ownership or the sources of such right; the instrument or document which is evidence of a right.—*vt* (**titled, titling**) to name; to call; to entitle.

titled *adj* having a title; especially, having a title of nobility.

title deed *n* a writing evidencing a person's right or title to property.

title page *n* the page of a book which contains the title.

titmouse *n* (*pl* **titmice**) a name of several common perching birds, small and active, feeding on seeds, insects, etc, with shrill, wild notes.

titter *vi* to laugh with a stifled sound or with restraint.—*n* a restrained laugh.

tittivate *vt* (**tittivated, tittivating**) same as **titivate.**

tittle *n* a small particle; a jot; an iota.

tittle-tattle *n* idle trifling talk; empty prattle.—*vi* to talk idly; to prate.

Titan

901

titular *adj* being such or such by title or name only; having the title to an office without the duties of it.—*n* one who has merely the title of an office; one who may lawfully enjoy an ecclesiastical benefice without performing its duties.

tizzy *n* (*colloq*) state of agitation; state of excitement; state of confusion.

TNT an abbreviation of **trinitrotoluene**.

to *prep* denoting motion towards a place or thing (*going to church*); towards (*point to the sky*), opposed to *from*; indicating a point or limit reached (*count to ten*); denoting destination, aim or design (*born to poverty*); denoting an end or consequence (*to our cost*); denoting addition, junction or union (*tied to a tree*); compared with; often used in expressing ratios or proportions (*three is to twelve as four is to sixteen*); denoting opposition or contrast (*face to face*); often used in betting phrases (*my hat to a halfpenny*); according to; in congruity or harmony with (*suited to his taste*); denoting correspondence or accompaniment (*dance to an air*); in the character or quality of (*took her to wife*); for; denoting the relation of the dative in other languages (*given to me*); marking an object (*a dislike to spirituous liquors*); the sign of the infinitive mood of a verb or governing the gerundial infinitive or gerund (*slow to believe; we have to pay it*).—*adv* forward; on; often denoting motion towards a junction, union or closing (*shut the door to*).—**to and fro** forward and backward; up and down.

toad *n* a reptile somewhat resembling the frog, with a heavy bulky body.

toadfish *n* a fish, the angler or fishing frog.

toadflax *n* a common perennial plant with yellow and orange flowers.

toad-in-the-hole *n* sausages cooked in batter.

toadstool *n* a popular name of fungi.

toadstool

toady *n* a sycophant; a flatterer.—*vt* (**toadied, toadying**) to fawn upon in a servile manner; to play the toady or sycophant to.

toadyism *n* mean sycophancy; servile adulation; nauseous flattery.

toast *vt* to dry and scorch (a piece of bread) by the heat of a fire, under a grill or in an electric toaster; to warm thoroughly (*to toast the feet*); to drink to the success of or in honour of.—*n* bread heated by fire, under a grill or in an electric toaster so that it becomes crisp and brown; a piece of such bread put in a beverage; a woman whose health is drunk in honour or respect; anyone or anything named in honour in drinking; a sentiment proposed for general acceptance in drinking.

toastmaster, toastmistress *n* a person who at a formal entertainment announces the toasts.

toggle

toast rack *n* a stand for a table for slices of dry toast.

tobacco *n* a narcotic plant, a native of the warmer parts of America and now extensively cultivated in various regions; also the prepared leaves, used for smoking and chewing or in the form of snuff.

tobacconist *n* a dealer in tobacco; a manufacturer of tobacco.

tobacco pipe *n* an implement used in smoking tobacco, consisting essentially of a bowl for the tobacco and a stem through which the tobacco smoke is drawn into the mouth, varying in form and material.

tobacco pouch *n* a small pouch for holding tobacco.

toboggan *n* a kind of sled used for sliding down snow-covered slopes; also, a sledge to be drawn by dogs over snow.—*vi* to use such a sled.

toby jug *n* a large drinking mug in the shape of a stout old man wearing a three-cornered hat.

tocsin *n* an alarm bell; a bell rung as a signal or for the purpose of giving an alarm.

today *n* the present day.—*adv* on this day.

toddle *vi* (**toddled, toddling**) to walk with short steps in a tottering way, as a child or an old person.—*n* a little toddling walk.

toddler *n* one who toddles; a young child.

toddy *n* the sweet juice of certain palms; palm wine; also, a mixture of spirit and hot water sweetened.

to-do *n* (*colloq*) ado; bustle; hurry; commotion.

tody *n* a tropical bird of gaudy plumage, allied to the kingfishers.

toe *n* one of the small members which form the extremity of the foot, corresponding to a finger on the hand; the fore part of the hoof of a horse or other hoofed animal; the member of an animal's foot corresponding to the toe in human beings.

toff *n* (*colloq*) a swell; a dandy; a member of the upper classes.

toffee *n* a kind of hard sweetmeat or candy, composed of boiled sugar with a proportion of butter.

tofu *n* a soft solid substance obtained from soya beans, used as a high-protein food.

toga *n* the principal outer garment worn by males among the ancient Romans; a sort of loose robe.

together *adv* in company; unitedly; in concert; in the same place; at the same time; so as to be contemporaneous; the one with the other; mutually; into junction or a state of union; without intermission; on end.

toggle *n* a peg attached to a rope to prevent it from passing through a loop or knot; a button of this form, as on a duffel coat, etc; (*comput*) a software instruction for starting or stopping a style, etc.

toil *vi* to exert strength continuously with

pain and fatigue of body or mind, particularly of the body; to labour; to work; to drudge.—*vt* to labour on; to exhaust or over-labour.—*n* labour with pain and fatigue; labour that oppresses the body or mind.

toiler *n* one who toils.

toilet *n* the act of washing and dressing oneself; an old word for a costume or outfit; a bowl-like receptacle for urination and defecation, filled with a device to flush it clean with water and connected by a pipe to the drains; a room containing such apparatus.—**to make one's toilet** to dress; to adjust one's dress with care.

token *n* something intended or supposed to represent or indicate another thing or an event; a sign; a mark; indication; symptom; a memorial of friendship; a souvenir; a love token; something that serves by way of pledge of authenticity, good faith, etc; a voucher exchangeable in shops for goods, such as books; a metal disc for a slot machine.—*adj* nominal; symbolic.

tokenism *n* the policy of making only token or nominal concessions to a demand, such as employing one woman in an all-male firm.

tolerable *adj* capable of being borne or endured; supportable, either physically or mentally; sufferable; moderately good or agreeable; not contemptible; passable; middling.

tolerance *n* the quality of being tolerant; the capacity or the act of enduring; a disposition to be patient and indulgent towards those whose opinions or practices differ from one's own; (*engin*) the permitted amount of deviation from exact dimensions as specified.

tolerant *adj* inclined or disposed to tolerate; favouring toleration; forbearing; able to endure or suffer.

tolerate *vt* (**tolerated, tolerating**) to suffer to be or to be done without prohibition or hindrance; to allow or permit; to treat in a spirit of patience and forbearance; not to judge of or condemn with bigotry.

toleration *n* the act of tolerating; allowance given to that which is not wholly approved; the recognition by the state of the right of private judgment in matters of faith and worship; a disposition to tolerate or not to judge or deal harshly in cases of difference of opinion or conduct; tolerance.

toll[1] *n* a tax or duty imposed for some liberty or privilege, as the sum charged for leave to offer goods in a market or fair; a fixed charge made for the use of a road, bridge, etc.—*vi* to pay toll; to exact or levy toll.

toll[2] *vi* to give out the slowly measured sounds of a bell when struck at uniform intervals, as at funerals.—*vt* to cause (a bell) to sound with strokes slowly and uniformly repeated; to indicate by tolling or striking; to draw attention to by slowly repeated sounds of a bell; to ring for or on account of.—*n* the sounding of a bell with slow, measured strokes.

tollbooth, tolbooth *n* a place where duties or tolls are collected.

tomahawk *n* an American Indian hatchet, used in hunting and war, not only in close fighting, but by being thrown to a considerable distance.

tomato *n* (*pl* **tomatoes**) a medium-sized, fleshy, red fruit with many pips, used in salads, etc.

tomb *n* a grave; a chamber or vault formed for the reception of the dead; a monument erected in memory of the dead; any sepulchral structure.—*vt* to bury; to entomb.

tombola *n* a kind of lottery, in which articles of various kinds are the prizes.

tomboy *n* a wild, romping girl; a hoyden.

tombstone *n* a stone erected over a grave; a sepulchral stone.

tomcat *n* a male cat, especially a full-grown male cat.

tome *n* a volume, forming part of a larger work; a book, usually a heavy one.

tomfool *n* a great fool; a trifler.

tomfoolery *n* foolish trifling; ridiculous behaviour.

tommy *n* (*sl*) a private soldier in the British Army.

tommy gun *n* a sub-machine gun.

tommyrot *n* complete nonsense.

tomorrow *n* the day after the present; the future; the morrow.—*adv* on the day after the present.—*adj* of the day after the present (*tomorrow night*).

tompion *n* same as **tampion**.

tomtit *n* the titmouse.

tom-tom *n* a long small-headed drum, usually beaten with the hands.

ton[1] *n* a weight equal to 20 hundredweight or 2240 pounds avoirdupois; a certain weight or space (tonnage), by which the burden of a ship is reckoned (*a ship of 300 tons*).

ton[2] *n* the prevailing fashion; high mode (*ladies of ton*).

tonality *n* (*mus*) the peculiarity characteristic of modern compositions due to their being written in definite keys, thereby conforming to certain defined arrangements of tones and semitones in the diatonic scale.

tone *n* any sound considered with relation to its pitch, its quality or timbre, or its strength or volume; a modulation of the voice, as expressing some feeling; accent; a singsong manner of speaking; a drawl; a musical sound; also one of the larger intervals between certain contiguous notes of

tomahawk

the diatonic scale (known as *major* or *minor*); the peculiar quality of sound of any voice or instrument; timbre; that state of a living body in which all the parts and organs have due tension or are well-strung; healthy activity of the organs; state or temper of mind; mood; the general or prevailing character, as of morals, manners or sentiments; in painting, a harmonious relation of the colours of a picture in light and shade; the characteristic expression of a picture as distinguished by its colour.—*vt* (**toned, toning**) to give a certain tone to; to utter in an affected tone.—**to tone down** to soften the colouring of; to give a lower tone to; to render less pronounced or decided (*to tone down a statement*); to soften.

tongs *npl* an instrument of metal, a kind of large nippers, used for handling things, particularly fire or heated metals.

tongue *n* the fleshy movable organ in the mouth, used for tasting, eating, swallowing, and in human beings for articulation or speech; the instrument of speech (*a bitter tongue*); speech; the whole sum of words used by a particular nation; a language; a nation as distinguished by their language; anything considered to resemble an animal's tongue; a point or strip of land running out into a sea or lake; a long low promontory; a tapering jet of flame; the pin of a buckle or brooch which pierces the strap, ribbon or object to be fastened.—*vt* (**tongued, tonguing**) to scold; (*mus*) to modify with the tongue in playing, as in the flute.

tongue-tied *adj* unable to articulate distinctly; having an impediment in the speech; unable to speak freely from whatever cause.

tongue-twister *n* a series of words that are difficult to pronounce quickly and clearly.

tonic *adj* producing or restoring tone or vigour; relating to tones or sounds; (*mus*) pertaining to or founded on the keynote.—*n* a medicine that improves physical well-being; something that imparts vigour; a carbonated mineral water with a bitter taste; (*mus*) the keynote or fundamental note of a scale.

tonic sol-fa *n* (*mus*) a term applied to a system of writing and teaching music, the leading features of which are the substitution of letters denoting sounds and of strokes, commas and colons, denoting time, for the notes, etc, of the ordinary notation.

tonight *n* the present night—*adv* in the present night, or in the night after the present day.

tonka bean *n* the fruit of a shrubby leguminous plant of Guyana containing a single seed with an agreeable odour.

tonsure

toothpaste

tonnage *n* the cubic content or burden of a ship; the number of tons a ship can carry with safety; the ships of a port or nation collectively estimated by their burden in tons.

tonsil *n* (*anat*) one of two oblong glands on each side of the throat or fauces which secretes mucus.

tonsillectomy *n* the surgical removal of the tonsils.

tonsillitis *n* inflammation of the tonsils.

tonsure *n* the act of clipping or shaving; the round bare place on the heads of the Roman Catholic priests and monks formed by shaving or cutting the hair.

tontine *n* an annuity shared by subscribers to a loan, the annuity being increased as the subscribers die until at last the whole goes to the last survivor or to the last two or three.

too *adv* over; more than enough; denoting excess (*too long, too short*); sometimes with merely an intensive force = very, exceedingly (*I should be only too glad*); likewise; also; in addition; besides; over and above (*a painter and a poet too*).

tool *n* any implement used by a craftsman or labourer at his or her work; an instrument employed in the manual arts for facilitating mechanical operations; a person used by another as an instrument to accomplish certain ends (a word of reproach).—*vt* to shape with a tool.

tooling *n* skilled work with a tool; carving; ornamental embossing or gilding by heated tools on the binding of books.

toot *vi* to make a noise like that of a pipe or horn.—*vt* to sound, as a horn.—*n* a sound blown on a horn; a similar noise.

tooth *n* (*pl* **teeth**) one of the projecting bony growths in the jaws of vertebrate animals, serving as the instrument of mastication; taste; palate; any projection resembling the tooth of an animal in shape, position or office; a small, narrow, projecting piece, usually one of a set (as of a comb, a saw, a rake, a wheel).—*vt* to furnish with teeth; to cut into teeth.

toothache *n* pain in a tooth or in the teeth arising from decay.

toothbrush *n* a small brush for cleaning the teeth.

toothed *adj* having teeth or cogs; having projecting points somewhat like teeth.

toothless *adj* having no teeth; deprived of teeth.

toothpaste *n* a paste for cleaning the teeth, used with a toothbrush; a dentifrice.

toothpick *n* a small instrument for picking substances from the teeth.

toothsome *adj* palatable; grateful to the taste.

top[1] *n* the highest part of anything; the most elevated or uppermost point; the summit;

upper surface; the highest place or rank; the most honourable position; the utmost degree; the height; the crown of the head (*from top to toe*); the head or upper part of a plant; a person or thing that has the highest place or position; a lid or covering; a garment for the upper part of the body; (*naut*) a sort of platform surrounding the head of the lower masts, serving to extend the shrouds and for the convenience of sailors aloft.—*adj* being on the top or summit; highest (*top speed*).—*vi* (**topped, topping**) to rise aloft; to be eminent.—*vt* to cover on the top; to cap; to rise above; to surpass; to take off the top or upper part of; to rise to the top of; (*sl*) to kill or execute.—**to top off** to complete by putting on the top; to finish; to complete.—**to top up** to raise up to the full capacity or amount.

top² *n* a child's toy shaped like a pear which spins on its point.

topaz *n* a gem harder than quartz, transparent or translucent and having the colour yellow, white, green or blue.

top boots *npl* boots having tops of light-coloured leather, used chiefly for riding.

topcoat *n* an upper or over coat.

top-draining *n* the act or practice of draining the surface of land.

top dressing *n* a dressing of manure laid on the surface of land.

tope¹ *vi* (**toped, toping**) to drink hard; to drink strong or spirituous liquors to excess.

tope² *n* a small grey European shark.

tope³ *n* a kind of Buddhist monument.

toper *n* one who drinks to excess; a drunkard; a sot.

topgallant *adj* (*naut*) being the third of the kind above the deck; above the topmast and below the royal mast (*the topgallant mast, yards*, etc).

top hat *n* a tall silk hat.

top-heavy *adj* having the top or upper part too heavy for the lower.

topiary *adj* shaped by clipping, pruning or training.

topiary work *n* the trimming of thickets, trees or hedges into fantastic shapes.

topic *n* the subject of a discourse; any subject that is discussed or spoken of for the time being; the matter treated of.

topical *adj* pertaining to a topic; pertaining to a place or locality; local; of current interest.

topknot *n* an ornamental knot or bow worn on the top of the head, as by women; the crest of a bird.

topmast *n* (*naut*) the second mast from the deck or that which is next above the lower mast, main, fore or mizzen.

topmost *adj* highest; uppermost.

topographic, topographical *adj* pertaining to topography; descriptive of a place or country.

topography *n* the description of a particular place, city, town, parish or tract of land; the detailed description of any country or region, distinguished from geography in dealing with the minuter features.

topper *n* one who tops or excels; anything superior; a top hat; a sturdy rectangular case with a wide lid for carrying things.

topping *adj* rising aloft; pre-eminent; surpassing; fine; noble; gallant.—*n* something added on top, such as a creamy mixture on a dessert.

topple *vi* (**toppled, toppling**) to fall forward, as something tall or high; to tumble down; to be on the point of falling.—*vt* to throw down.

topsail *n* (*naut*) the second sail above the deck on any mast (main, fore or mizzen).

topsoil *n* the upper part or surface of the soil.

topsy-turvy *adj*, *adv* in an inverted posture; with the top or head downward and the bottom upward.

toque *n* a kind of bonnet or headdress.

tor *n* a high pointed rock or hill.

Torah *n* in Mosaic law, the Pentateuch.

torch *n* a light carried in the hand, formed of some combustible substance, as of twisted flax, hemp, etc, soaked with tallow; a flambeau; a small electric lamp powered by batteries.

toreador *n* a general name for a bullfighter in Spain, especially one who fights on horseback.

torment *n* extreme pain; anguish of body or mind; torture; what causes such pain.—*vt* to put to extreme pain or anguish; to inflict excruciating pain on; to torture; to afflict; to tease, vex or harass; to annoy.

tormentor *n* one who or that which torments; a kind of harrow with wheels, used for breaking up stiff soils.

tormentil *n* a common weed with small yellow flowers and large woody roots sometimes used in tanning.

tornado *n* (*pl* **tornadoes**) a violent whirling wind; a whirlwind or tempest, usually accompanied with severe thunder, lightning and torrents of rain; a typhoon or hurricane.

torpedo *n* (*pl* **torpedoes**) a fish allied to the rays, noted for its power of discharging electric shocks when irritated; a destructive engine to be propelled under water against an enemy's ship and then exploded with deadly effect.—*vt* (**torpedoed, torpedoing**) to attack or destroy by a torpedo.

torpedo boat *n* a vessel specially intended to attack with torpedoes.

torpid *adj* having lost motion or the power of motion and feeling; numb; dull; sluggish; inactive.

top hat

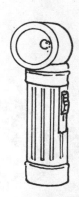

torch

torpidity *n* the state of being torpid; lethargy.

torpor *n* loss of motion or sensation; torpidity; numbness; sluggishness.

torque[1] *n* a force that causes rotation around a central point, such as an axle.

torque[2] *n* a personal ornament, consisting of a stiff collar, formed of a number of gold wires twisted together, or of a thin twisted metal plate, worn round the neck as a symbol of rank by certain ancient nations, as by the ancient Britons, Gauls, etc.

torrefaction *n* the operation of drying or parching by a fire.

torrefy *vt* (**torrefied, torrefying**) to dry, roast, scorch or parch by a fire; (in metallurgy) to roast, as metallic ores.

torrent *n* a violent stream, as of water, lava, etc; (*fig*) a violent or rapid flow; a flood (*a torrent of words* or *eloquence*).

torrential *adj* pertaining to a torrent.

torrid *adj* dried with heat; parched; violently hot; burning or parching.

Torrid Zone *n* (*geog*) the broad belt round the middle of the earth which is included between the tropics and divided into two parts by the equator and where the heat is always great.

torso

torsion *n* the act of twisting; the twisting, wrenching or straining of a body; (*mech*) the strain produced in a body, such as a thread, wire or slender rod, when equal and opposite twisting couples are applied to it in the planes of its two ends; (*surg*) the twisting of the cut end of a small artery for the purpose of checking haemorrhage.

torsk *n* a European fish of the cod family, caught in great quantities and salted and dried as food.

torso *n* (*pl* **torsos, torsi**) (*sculp*) the trunk of a statue deprived of head and limbs; the trunk of the human body.

tort *n* a legal term for any wrong or injury to person or property.

tortilla *n* a large thin cake of maize, usually eaten hot with a topping or a filling.

tortoise *n* a name common to a family of land reptiles covered with a flattened shell, a kind of bony box, from which the head and legs protrude.

tortoise

tortoiseshell *n* the shell, or more strictly the scales, of the tortoise and other allied reptiles, usually yellow and brown, used in the manufacture of combs, snuffboxes, etc, and in inlaying and other ornamental work; a long-haired domestic cat with a yellowish and black coat.

tortuous *adj* twisted; wreathed; winding; (*fig*) proceeding in a circuitous and underhand manner; taking an oblique and deceitful course; not open and straightforward.

torture *n* excruciating pain; extreme anguish of body or mind; agony; torment; severe pain inflicted judicially, either as a punishment for a crime or for the purpose of extorting a confession; the act of inflicting excruciating pain.—*vt* (**tortured, torturing**) to pain to extremity; to torment bodily or mentally; to punish with torture; to wrest greatly from the right meaning.

torturer *n* one who tortures; a tormentor.

torus *n* (*pl* **tori**) (*archit*) a large moulding used in the bases of columns, having a semicircular section; (*bot*) the receptacle of a flower; (*math*) a surface, or solid, generated by the revolution of a circle about an axis in its plane.

Tory *n* (*hist*) a member of the British political party which supported the monarchy and the established order of the Church and state; a member or supporter of the modern Conservative party.—*adj* pertaining to Tories.

Toryism *n* the principles or practices of the Tories.

toss *vt* to throw with the hand; to pitch; to fling; to cast; to throw up with a sudden or violent motion; to jerk (*to toss the head*); to dash about (*to be tossed on the waves*); to agitate; to make restless.—*vi* to roll and tumble; to be in violent commotion; to writhe; to be flung or dashed about.—*n* a throwing with a jerk; the act of tossing; a throw or jerk of the head; the tossing up of a coin to decide something.

toss-up *n* the throwing up of a coin to decide something; hence, an even chance or hazard.

tot[1] *n* anything small or insignificant (used as a term of endearment); a small child; a small quantity of liquor.

tot[2] *vt* (**totted, totting**) to sum (generally with *up*).

total *adj* pertaining to the whole; comprehending the whole; entire (*the total sum*); complete in degree; absolute (*a total wreck*); thorough.—*n* the whole; the whole sum or amount; an aggregate.—*vt* (**totalled, totalling**) to add up.

totalisator *n* the registration machine on the pari-mutuel system of betting, which registers the bets made on each race; familiarly called the **tote**.

totalitarian *adj* applied to states under a highly centralized government which suppresses all rival political parties.

totality *n* the whole or total sum; whole quantity or amount.

totally *adv* in a total manner; wholly; entirely; fully; completely.

tote[1] *n* (*colloq*) a contraction of **totalisator**.

tote[2] *vt* (**toted, toting**) (*colloq*) to carry.

totem *n* an object regarded as a symbol and treated with respect by a particular group of people.

totemic *adj* pertaining to a totem.

totem pole *n* a large pole covered with totemic symbols set up by North American Indian tribes as a tribal symbol.

totter *vi* to appear as if about to fall when standing or walking; to walk unsteadily; to be on the point of falling; to threaten to topple down.

tottery *adj* unsteady; shaking.

toucan *n* the name of a family of climbing birds of tropical America, distinguished by their enormous beak.

touch *vt* to perceive by the sense of feeling; to come in contact with in any manner, but particularly by means of the hand, finger, etc; to hit or strike against; to harm; to meddle or interfere with; hence, to taste or eat; to come to; to reach or arrive at; to relate to or concern (a person or thing); to mark or delineate slightly; to add a slight stroke or strokes to, as with a pen, pencil, brush, etc; to handle in a skilful or special manner (as a musical instrument); to discourse of; to write about; to make a mere reference to; to move or strike mentally; to excite with compassion or other tender emotion; to melt or soften the heart of; to make an impression on physically; to act on; (*geom*) to meet without cutting; to be in contact with; (*sl*) to ask for money from.—*vi* to be in contact; to take effect; to say a few words in discourse.—**to touch off** to cause to explode; to cause; to start.—**to touch up** to improve by making minor alterations or additions to; (*colloq*) to caress or fondle sexually.—*n* the act of touching or the state of being touched; contact; the sense of feeling which resides in the nervous papillae of the skin and forms one of the five senses; a state in which one or other of two parties has a knowledge of the other's position, opinions, etc; a certain degree of some feeling or emotion (*a touch of pity*); a trait; a characteristic; a small quantity or degree; a smack; a little; a successful effort or attempt; a stroke (*a touch of genius*); a stroke of a pen, pencil, etc; the act of the hand on a musical instrument; the peculiar handling usual to an artist and by which his or her works may be known; the resistance of the keys of a musical instrument to the fingers; in football, that part of the ground outside the side lines bounding the field of play.

touchable *adj* able to be touched.

touch-and-go *adj* precarious; risky.

touché *interj* used in fencing to acknowledge an opponent's hit; an acknowledgement of a valid or accomplished reply, remark, witty comment, etc.

touched *adj* emotionally affected; (*colloq*) mentally disturbed; (*colloq*) mentally retarded.

touchhole *n* the vent of a cannon or other kind of early firearm by which fire was communicated to the charge.

touching *adj* affecting; moving; pathetic.—*prep* concerning; relating to; with respect to.

touchstone *n* a hard black siliceous stone used in ascertaining the purity of gold and silver, the streak made by rubbing the article on it being compared with that made by the touch needle, the quality of which is known; (*fig*) any test or criterion by which the qualities of a thing are tried.

touchwood *n* the soft white substance into which wood is converted by the action of several fungi, serving the purpose of tinder.

touchy *adj* apt to take offence; irritable; irascible.

tough *adj* having the quality of flexibility without brittleness; yielding to force without breaking; having tenacity; tenacious; strong; able to endure hardship; viscous; durable; stubborn; unmanageable; difficult; rough and violent.

toughen *vi* to grow tough.—*vt* to make tough.

toughness *n* the quality of being tough; flexibility with firm adhesion of parts; viscosity; tenacity; strength of constitution or texture.

toupee *n* a small wig or hairpiece worn to cover a bald patch.

tour *n* a round or circuit; a journey in a circuit; a roving journey; a lengthy jaunt or excursion; turn or succession (*a tour of duty*) (a military use); a long trip, as for sightseeing.—*vi* to make a tour; to go on a sightseeing trip.—*vt* to go on a sightseeing trip of.

tour de force *n* (*pl* **tours de force**) a feat of skill or sustained effort; an outstanding achievement or performance.

tourist *n* one who makes a tour; one who travels for pleasure and for sightseeing.

touristy *adj* having many tourists; attracting many tourists.

tourmaline *n* a mineral of various colours, frequently black or colourless, crystallized in three-sided or six-sided prisms, often found in granitic rocks.

tournament *n* a martial sport or kind of combat performed in former times by knights on horseback for the purpose of exercising and exhibiting their courage, prowess and skill in arms; a tilting match among a number; hence, any contest of skill in which a number take part (*a chess tournament*).

tourney *n* a tournament.

tourniquet *n* a device used to prevent bleeding by compressing blood vessels.

tousle *vt* (**tousled, tousling**) to put into disorder; to dishevel; to rumple.

tout *vi* to solicit business in a brazen or pestering way; to try to gain something in a persistent manner; to sell information re-

toucan

garding race horses.—*n* a person who touts; a person who clandestinely watches the trials of race horses at their training quarters and for a fee gives information for betting purposes.

tow¹ *vt* to drag, as a boat or ship, through the water by means of a rope.—*n* the state of being towed (*to take a boat in tow*).

tow² *n* the coarse and broken part of flax or hemp separated from the finer part.

towage *n* the act of towing.

toward *adj* pliable; docile; ready to do or learn; apt.—*prep, adv* towards.

towards *prep* in the direction of; in regard or with respect to (*well-disposed towards us*); tending or contributing to; in aid of; for; nearly; about (*towards three o'clock*).—*adv* in a state of preparation; being carried on.

towboat *n* a boat employed in towing a vessel; a boat that is towed.

towel *n* a cloth, usually of linen, for wiping the hands and face, especially after washing; a similar cloth for wiping in domestic use.—**to throw in the towel** to admit defeat.—*vti* (**towelled, towelling**) to rub (oneself) with a towel.

tower *n* a lofty narrow building of a round, square or polygonal form, either insulated or forming part of a church, castle or other edifice; a tall, movable wooden structure used in ancient times for storming a fortified place; a citadel; a fortress.—*vi* to rise or fly high; to soar; to be lofty; to stand sublime.

tower block *n* a block of high-rise flats; a skyscraper.

towering *adj* very high or lofty; extreme; violent; outrageous (*a towering rage*).

tow-headed *adj* having pale yellow hair.

towing path *n* a path used by men and horses in towing boats along a canal or river.

towline, tow rope *n* a rope or hawser used to tow vessels.

town *n* a collection of houses larger than a village; a large assemblage of adjacent houses intersected by streets, often opposed to *country*; the metropolis or county town, or the particular city, etc, in or near which the speaker or writer is (*to go to town, to be in town*); the inhabitants of a town (*all the town talks of it*).—*adj* pertaining to or characteristic of a town; urban.

town council *n* the elected governing body in a town.

town councillor *n* a member of a town council.

town crier *n* a public crier in a town.

town hall *n* a large hall or building belonging to a town or borough housing the official administrative offices and often with a hall for public meetings.

tower block

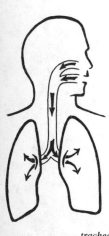

trachea

township *n* the district or territory of a town; a division of certain parishes; in the USA, a territorial district subordinate to a county, the inhabitants of which have certain powers for regulating their own affairs; in South Africa, an area outside a large town reserved for non-whites.

townsman *n* (*pl* **townsmen**) an inhabitant of a town; one of the same town with another.

toxaemia *n* blood poisoning.

toxic *adj* pertaining to poisons; poisonous.

toxicologist *n* one who treats of poisons.

toxicology *n* the doctrine of poisons; that branch of medicine which treats of poisons and their antidotes.

toxocariasis *n* a disease in humans caused by the larvae of a parasitic roundworm found in dogs and cats.

toxoplasmosis *n* a disease affecting the central nervous system caused by a parasitic worm.

toy *n* a plaything for children; a bauble; a thing for amusement and of no real value; a trifling object.—*vi* to dally amorously; to trifle; to play.

trace *n* a mark left by anything passing; a track; any mark, impression or appearance left when the thing itself no longer exists; visible evidence of something having been; token; vestige; a minute quantity or insignificant particle; one of the straps, chains or ropes by which a carriage, wagon, etc, is drawn.—*vt* (**traced, tracing**) to follow by traces left; to track out; to follow by vestiges or indications; to draw or delineate with marks; to draw in outline; to copy, as a drawing or engraving, by following the lines and marking them on a sheet superimposed, through which they appear.—*vi* to walk; to travel.

tracery *n* (*archit*) ornamental open-work in stone in the head of a Gothic window, showing curves and flowing lines intersecting in various ways and enriched with foliation; any similar ornamental work.

trachea *n* (*pl* **tracheae**) the windpipe, a cartilaginous and membranous pipe through which the air passes into and out of the lungs; (*bot*) one of the spiral vessels of plants; (*zool*) one of those vessels in insects, etc, which receive air and distribute it to every part of the interior of the body.

tracheotomy *n* (*surg*) the operation of cutting into the trachea, as for suffocation.

trachyte *n* a type of light-coloured volcanic rock.

tracing *n* the act of one who traces; a copy of an original design or drawing made by following its lines through a transparent medium.

tracing paper *n* transparent paper which is laid on a drawing, so that the outlines of the original may be drawn on it.

track *n* a mark left by something that has passed along; a mark left by the foot of a person or beast; a trace; a footprint; a road; a beaten path; course followed; path; the course of a railway; the permanent way; a path or course, frequently circular or oval, laid out for racing, etc.—*vt* to follow when guided by a track; to follow by tracks; (*naut*) to tow by a line from the shore.

track-and-field *adj* denoting various competitive athletic events (as running, jumping, weight-throwing, etc) performed on a track and adjacent field.

tracker *n* one who tracks; one who hunts by following a track.

track event *n* an athletic event that takes place on a running track.

track record *n* (*colloq*) a record of past achievements or failures.

track shoe *n* a spiked running shoe.

tracksuit *n* a loose suit worn by athletes to keep warm between sports events.

tract[1] *n* a region or quantity of land or water of indefinite extent; a part of a bodily system or organ; (*arch*) a length or extent of time.

tract[2] *n* a dissertation or treatise, particularly on religion.

tractable *adj* capable of being easily trained or managed; very amenable to discipline; docile; governable.

tractate *n* a treatise; a tract.

traction *n* the act of drawing, pulling or dragging; the using of weights to pull a muscle to correct an abnormal condition.

traction engine *n* a steam locomotive engine for dragging heavy loads on common roads.

tractor *n* that which draws; a vehicle driven by an internal-combustion engine, especially as used in agriculture.

trade *n* regular employment or way of life; the business which a person carries on for procuring subsistence or for profit; occupation; particularly a mechanical or mercantile employment or a handicraft, as distinguished from an art or profession; the business of exchanging commodities for other commodities or for money; commerce; traffic; collectively, those who are engaged in any trade; a trade wind.—*adj* pertaining to trade or a particular trade.—*vi* (**traded, trading**) to barter or to buy and sell; to traffic; to carry on commerce; to engage in affairs generally; to deal or have dealings.—*vt* to sell or exchange in commerce; to barter.

trademark *n* a distinctive mark or device adopted by a manufacturer or producer and impressed on his or her goods, labels, etc, to distinguish them from those of others, especially when legally protected.

trade price *n* the price charged to dealers for articles that are to be sold again.

trader *n* one engaged in trade or commerce; a vessel employed regularly in any particular trade.

tradesman *n* (*pl* **tradesmen**) a person involved in a trade; shopkeeper; a skilled worker.

trade union, trades union *n* a combination of workers of any particular trade, branch of manufacture or profession to enable them all to secure the conditions most favourable for labour and the redress of any of their grievances.

trade wind *n* one of those constant winds which occur in all open seas on both sides of the equator and to the distance of about 30° north and south of it, blowing always or for half the year in the same direction.

trading *adj* carrying on commerce; engaged in trade; venal.

tradition *n* the handing down of opinions, doctrines, practices, rites and customs from one generation to another, or from ancestors to posterity by oral communication; that which is handed down from age to age by oral communication; a doctrine or statement of facts so handed down.

traditional *adj* pertaining to or derived from tradition; communicated from ancestors to descendants by word only; transmitted from age to age without writing.

traduce *vt* (**traduced, traducing**) to misrepresent wilfully; to defame; to calumniate; to vilify.

traducer *n* one that traduces; a slanderer; a calumniator.

traffic *n* an interchange of goods or merchandise between countries, communities or individuals; trade; commerce; goods or persons passing along a road, railway, canal, steamboat route, etc, viewed collectively; vehicles passing along a road, street, etc; dealings; intercourse.—*vi* (**trafficked, trafficking**) to trade; to buy and sell wares; to carry on commerce; to have business or dealings; to deal, especially in illegal drugs.

traffic jam *n* a stoppage of traffic because of congested roads.

tragacanth *n* a leguminous plant yielding a gummy juice used in pharmacy and calico printing.

tragedian *n* a writer of tragedy; an actor of tragedy.

tragedy *n* a dramatic poem representing an important event or a series of events in the life of some person or persons, in which the diction is elevated and the catastrophe melancholy; that kind of drama in which some fatal or mournful event is the main theme; a fatal and mournful event; any event in which human lives are sacrificed; an event causing great suffering or distress.

tragic, tragical *adj* pertaining to tragedy; of

tractor

the nature or character of tragedy (in this sense *tragic* is now the more common form); connected with or characterized by bloodshed or loss of life; murderous; characterized by great suffering or distress; dreadful; calamitous.

tragicomedy *n* a kind of dramatic piece in which serious and comic scenes are blended and of which the event is not unhappy.

trail *vt* to draw behind or along the ground; to drag; to follow slowly behind.—*vi* to sweep over a surface by being pulled or dragged; to grow with long slender and creeping shoots or stems, as a plant.—*n* a track followed by a hunter; anything drawn to length (*a trail of smoke*); the end of the stock of a gun carriage which rests on the ground when a gun is in position for firing.

trailblazer *n* a person who is a pioneer or innovator in a particular field.

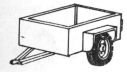
trailer

trailer *n* one who trails; a plant which cannot grow upward without support; a carriage dragged by a motor vehicle or cycle; a small vehicle drawn by another; a caravan; a short film containing scenes from a feature film coming to a cinema soon or of a television programme being shown soon.

train *vt* to educate; to rear and instruct (often followed by *up*); to form to any practice by exercise; to drill; to discipline; to break; to tame and reduce to docility; to teach to perform certain actions (*to train dogs*); to subject to proper regimen and exercise for the performance of some special exertion or feat (*to train horses for the Derby*); (in gardening) to form to a desired shape by growth and pruning, etc—*vi* to undergo some special drill or discipline; to subject oneself to a special course of exercise and regimen for an athletic or other feat.—*n* that which is drawn along behind; that part of a gown or robe which trails behind the wearer; the tail of a comet, meteor, etc; the tail of a bird; the after part of a gun carriage; a succession of connected things; a series; way or course of procedure; regular method; course; a number or body of followers or attendants; a retinue; a procession; a connected line of carriages on a railway, together with the engine; a line of combustible material to lead fire to a charge or mine; a set of wheels, or wheels and pinions, as in a watch.

trainband *n* (*hist*) a band or company of militia from the sixteenth to eighteenth centuries.

trainbearer *n* one who holds up a person's train or long state robe.

trained *adj* formed by training; exercised; educated; instructed; skilled by practice; qualified.

trainer *n* one who trains; one who prepares

trainers

people, horses, etc, for the performance of certain feats, as an oarsman for a boat race or a horse for racing.

trainers *npl* a kind of sports shoes worn for running, jogging, etc, or for leisure wear.

training *adj* teaching and forming by practice.—*n* the act of one who trains; the process of educating; education; drill; course of exercise and regimen.

training college an educational institution, especially for vocational subjects such as teaching.

training ship *n* a ship equipped with instructors, officers, etc, to train lads for the sea.

train oil *n* the oil procured from the blubber or fat of whales.

traipse *vi* (**traipsed, traipsing**) to walk casually or carelessly; to walk aimlessly.

trait *n* a stroke; a touch; a distinguishing or peculiar feature; a peculiarity.

traitor *n* one who violates his or her allegiance and betrays his or her country; one guilty of treason; one who, in breach of trust, plays into the hands of an enemy; one guilty of perfidy or treachery.

traitorous *adj* acting the traitor; treacherous; perfidious; consisting in or partaking of treason.

traitress *n* a female traitor; a woman who betrays her country or her trust.

trajectory *n* the path described by a body, such as a planet, comet, projectile, etc, under the action of given forces.

tram *n* a passenger vehicle running on rails in the street and usually powered by electricity from an overhead wire; one of the rails or tracks of a tramway; a four-wheeled wagon running on a tramway used in coal mines.

trammel *n* a kind of net for catching birds or fishes; a kind of shackles for regulating the motions of a horse and making it amble; whatever hinders activity, freedom or progress; an instrument for drawing ellipses, used by joiners and other artificers; a beam compass.—*vt* (**trammelled, trammelling**) to confine; to hamper; to shackle.

tramp *vt* to tread under foot; to trample; to travel over on foot (*to tramp a country*).—*vi* to travel on foot.—*n* the sound made by the feet coming in contact with the ground in walking or marching; an excursion on foot; a vagrant; a stroller; a cargo steamer which makes irregular and usually short voyages; (*colloq*) a promiscuous woman.

trample *vt* (**trampled, trampling**) to tread under foot; to tread down; to prostrate by treading; to crush with the feet; to treat with pride, contempt and insult.—*vi* to tread in contempt; to tread with force; to stamp.

tramway *n* a railway laid along a road or the street of a town, on which cars for passengers or for goods are drawn by horses or driven by some mechanical power.

trance *n* an ecstasy; a state in which the soul seems to have passed out of the body or to be rapt into visions; a state of insensibility to the things of this world; a state of perplexity or bewilderment; (*med*) catalepsy.

tranquil *adj* quiet; calm; undisturbed; peaceful; not agitated.

tranquillity *n* the state of being tranquil; quietness; calmness; freedom from agitation.

tranquillize *vt* (**tranquillized, tranquillizing**) to make tranquil, especially by administering a drug.

tranquillizer *n* a drug which has a calming effect without inducing sleep.

transact *vt* to carry through, perform or conduct (business affairs, etc); to do; to perform; to manage; to complete; to carry through.

transaction *n* the doing or performing of any business; some piece of business; a proceeding; an affair; (*pl*) reports containing papers or abstracts of papers, speeches, discussions, etc, read or delivered at the meetings of certain learned societies.

transatlantic *adj* lying or being beyond the Atlantic; crossing the Atlantic (*a transatlantic line of steamers*).

transcend *vt* to rise above or beyond; to be or go beyond the grasp or comprehension of; to surpass, outgo, excel, exceed.

transcendence, transcendency *n* the state of transcending; superior excellence.

transcendent *adj* superior or supreme in excellence; surpassing others; going beyond or transcending human experience.

transcendental *adj* transcendent; transcending the sphere of knowledge acquired by experience; beyond physical experience; beyond the reach of ordinary, everyday or common thought and experience; (*math*) applied to what cannot be represented by an algebraic expression of a finite number of terms.

transcendentalism *n* the quality of being transcendental; a system of philosophy which claims to have a true knowledge of all things material and immaterial, human and divine, so far as the mind is capable of knowing them; sometimes used for that which is vague and illusive in philosophy.

transcontinental *adj* extending or travelling across a continent.

transcribe *vt* (**transcribed, transcribing**) to write over again or in the same words; to copy.

transcriber *n* one who transcribes; a copier or copyist.

transcript *n* a writing made from and according to an original; a copy; an imitation.

transcription *n* the act of transcribing or copying; a copy; a transcript; (*mus*) the arrangement of a composition for some instrument or voice other than that for which it was originally composed.

transducer *n* a device that converts energy from one form into another.

transept *n* (*archit*) that portion of a church built in the form of a cross, which is between the nave and choir and projects externally on each side so as to form the short arms of the cross.

transfer *vt* to convey from one place or person to another; to transport or remove to another place or person; to make over the possession or control of; to convey, as a right, from one person to another; lithography, to produce a facsimile of on a prepared stone by means of prepared paper and ink.—*n* the act of transferring; that which is transferred; in lithography, a picture drawn or printed with a special ink on specially prepared paper and transferred to the surface of a stone to be printed from.

transference *n* the act of transferring; the act of conveying from one place, person or thing to another; the passage of anything from one place to another.

transfiguration *n* a change of form or figure.

Transfiguration *n* the supernatural change in the personal appearance of Christ on the mount; an ecclesiastical feast held on 6th August in commemoration of this.

transfigure *vt* (**transfigured, transfiguring**) to change the outward form or appearance of; to transform in appearance; to give an elevated or glorified appearance to; to elevate and glorify; to idealize.

transfix *vt* to pierce through as with a pointed weapon; to paralyse with shock or horror.

transform *vt* to change the form of; to give a new form to; to metamorphose; to change into another substance; to transmute; to change the character or disposition of.—*vt* to be changed in form; to be metamorphosed.

transformation *n* the act or operation of transforming; the state of being transformed; an entire change in form, appearance, nature, disposition, etc; a metamorphosis; (*math*) a type of operation of great theoretical and practical importance, applicable to equations, groups and geometrical figures which the operation changes into a more convenient form.

transformer *n* (*elect*) an instrument for converting an alternating current at one pressure into an alternating current at a different pressure.

transfuse *vt* (**transfused, transfusing**) to transfer by pouring; to cause to be instilled or imbibed; to instil; (*surg*) to transfer

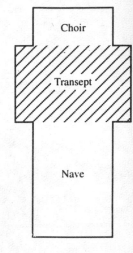

transept

(blood) from the veins or arteries of one animal to those of another.

transfusion *n* the act of transfusing; the transmission of blood from the veins of one person or animal to those of another, with the intention of restoring vigour.

transgress *vt* to overpass, as a law or rule prescribed; to break or violate; to infringe. —*vi* to offend by violating a law; to sin.

transgression *n* the act of transgressing; the breaking or violation of any law; a trespass; an offence.

transgressor *n* one who transgresses; an offender; an evildoer.

tranship *vt* (**transhipped, transhipping**) same as **transship**.

transhipment *n* the act of transhipping.

transient *adj* passing quickly away; of short duration; not permanent, lasting or durable; momentary; passing.

transistor *n* a device using a semiconductor to amplify sound, as in a radio or television; a small portable radio.

transit *n* the act of passing; a passing over or through; the process of conveying; passage; conveyance (*the transit of goods through a country*); (*astron*) the passage of a heavenly body across the meridian of any place; the passage of one heavenly body over the disc of a larger one, as of the planets Mercury and Venus over the sun's disc.

transition *n* passage from one place or state to another; change or process of change; (*mus*) a change in the course of a composition from one key to another, or the passage from one major scale to another more or less related.

transitional *adj* containing or involving transition.

transitive *adj* having the power of passing or making transition; (*gram*) taking an object after it; denoting action passing to an object that is expressed (*a transitive verb*).—*n* a transitive verb.

transitory *adj* passing away without continuance; unstable and fleeting; short and uncertain.

translate *vt* (**translated, translating**) to remove from one place to another; (NT) to take up to heaven without dying; to transfer from one office or charge to another; to remove a bishop from one see to another; (*Shak*) to transform; to render into another language; to interpret; to explain by using other words; to express in other terms.

translation *n* the act of translating; a removal or motion from one place to another; the removal of a person from one office to another; especially, the removal of a bishop from one see to another; also applied to the removal of the relics of a saint from one place to another; the removal of a person to heaven without sub-

jecting him or her to death; the act of turning into another language; that which is produced by turning into another language; a version.

translator *n* one who translates.

transliterate *vt* (**transliterated, transliterating**) to express or write in the alphabetic characters of another language; to spell in different characters intended to express the same sound.

transliteration *n* the act of transliterating; a rendering in equivalent alphabetic characters.

translucent *adj* transmitting rays of light, but not so as to render the form or colour of objects beyond distinctly visible.

transmigrate *vi* (**transmigrated, transmigrating**) to migrate; to pass from one country or region to another; to pass from one animal body into another.

transmigration *n* the act of transmigrating; the passing of a soul into another body after death; metempsychosis.

transmission *n* the act of transmitting or the state of being transmitted; transference; a passing through, as of light through glass or other transparent body; the sending of electromagnetic waves from a transmitter to a receiver; the transfer of motion from one part of a machine to another; any device for doing this, such as a gear system in a vehicle; a radio or television broadcast.

transmit *vt* (**transmitted, transmitting**) to cause to pass or be conveyed from one point to another; to communicate by sending; to send from one person or place to another; to hand down; to suffer to pass through or form a medium or passage; to let penetrate; to send out (radio or television signals).

transmitter *n* one who or that which transmits; an apparatus for broadcasting radio or television programmes.

transmogrify *vt* (**transmogrified, transmogrifying**) to transform into some other person or thing; to change entirely the appearance of.

transmutation *n* the act of transmuting or state of being transmuted; change into another substance, form or nature.

transmute *vt* (**transmuted, transmuting**) to change from one nature, form or substance into another; to change into another thing or body; to metamorphose; to transform.

transom *n* one of several transverse beams bolted to the sternpost of a ship and supporting the ends of the decks; a horizontal bar of stone or timber across a mullioned window; the crossbar separating a door from the fanlight above it; the piece of wood or iron joining the cheeks of gun carriages.

transparency *n* the quality or condition of being transparent; perviousness to light; something transparent; an image on transparent or semi-transparent materials to be viewed by light shining through it.

transparent *adj* having the property of transmitting rays of light so that bodies can be distinctly seen through; pervious to light; diaphanous; pellucid; (*fig*) such as to be easily seen through; not sufficient to hide underlying feelings.

transpire *vt* (**transpired, transpiring**) to emit through the pores of the skin; to send off in vapour.—*vi* to be emitted through the pores of the skin; to exhale; to pass off in insensible perspiration; to become public gradually; to come to light; to ooze out; (*colloq*) to happen, to take place.

transplant *vt* to remove and plant in another place; to remove from one place to another; to remove and settle or establish for residence in another place; (*surg*) to remove an organ from one person and transfer it to another.—*n* the process of transplanting; something which is transplanted.

transplantation *n* the act of transplanting; the shifting of a plant from one spot to another; (*surg*) the removal of a part of the human body to supply a part that has been lost.

transplanter *n* one who or that which transplants.

transponder *n* a device that automatically transmits a radio signal on receiving a predetermined signal.

transpontine *adj* situated beyond the bridge; across the bridge.

transport *vt* to carry or convey from one place to another; to carry into banishment, as a criminal; to hurry or carry away by violence of passion; to carry away or ravish with pleasure; to absorb.—*n* transportation; a system of transporting goods or passengers; a vehicle for this purpose; carriage; conveyance; a ship employed by government for carrying soldiers, warlike stores, etc; a vehement emotion; passion; rapture; ecstasy.

transportable *adj* capable of being transported; subjecting to transportation.

transportation *n* the act of transporting; a conveyance from one place to another; a vehicle used as a means of transport; carriage; the banishing of a person convicted of crime to a penal settlement.

transported *adj* carried to ecstasy or rapture; ravished with delight.

transport ship *n* a vessel employed in conveying soldiers, military stores, etc; a transport.

transpose *vt* (**transposed, transposing**) to change the place or order of by putting each in the place of the other; to cause to change places; (*alg*) to bring, as any term of an equation, over from one side to the other side; (*gram*) to change the natural order of words; (*mus*) to change the key of.

transposition *n* the act of transposing or state of being transposed; (*alg*) the bringing over of any term of an equation from one side to the other side; (*rhet*) a change of the natural order of words for effect; (*mus*) the change of a composition to a key either higher or lower than the original.

transship, tranship *vt* (**transshipped, transshipping**) to convey or transfer from one ship to another.

transubstantiate *vt* (**transubstantiated, transubstantiating**) to change to another substance.

transubstantiation *n* change of substance; (*theol*) the conversion of the substance of the bread and wine in the Eucharist into the substance of the body and blood of Christ, whilst the accidents remain unchanged, a belief held by Roman Catholics and others.

transverse *adj* lying or being across or in a cross direction; lying in a direction across other parts.

trap[1] *n* a contrivance that shuts suddenly and often with a spring, used for taking game and other animals; any device or contrivance to betray or catch unawares; a trick to catch someone out; an ambush; a game and also one of the instruments used in playing it, the others being a small bat and a ball; a drain trap; (*colloq*) a carriage, on springs, of any kind.—*vt* (**trapped, trapping**) to catch in a trap; to ensnare; to take by stratagem; to trick.—*vi* to set traps for game.

trap[2] *n* a kind of movable ladder or steps; a kind of ladder leading up to a loft; (*geol*) a name applied to the multifarious igneous rocks of the Palaeozoic and secondary epochs that cannot be classed as either granitic or volcanic, comprising basalt, clink stone, greenstone, etc.

trap[3] *vt* (**trapped, trapping**) to adorn; to dress with ornaments.

trapan *vt* (**trapanned, trapanning**) same as **trepan**[2].

trapdoor *n* a hinged or sliding door in a floor or roof.

trapeze *n* a trapezium; (in gymnastics) a sort of swing, consisting of one or more crossbars suspended by two cords at some distance from the ground, on which various feats are performed.

trapezium *n* (*pl* **trapeziums, trapezia**) (*geom*) a plane figure contained by four straight lines, two of them parallel; (*anat*) a bone of the wrist, so named from its shape.

trapezoid *n* (*geom*) a plane four-sided figure having none of its opposite sides parallel.

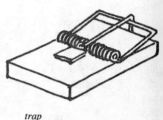

trap

trapezoid

trapper *n* one who sets traps to catch animals, usually for furs.

trappings *npl* ornamental accessories, as the ornaments put on horses; ornaments generally; dress; finery.

Trappist *n* a member of a religious order of the Roman Catholic Church, founded in 1664 and remarkable for the austere life led by the monks.

traps *npl* small or portable articles for dress, furniture, etc; goods; furniture; luggage.

trash *n* loppings of trees; sugar canes from which the juice has been expressed; waste or worthless matter; rubbish; refuse; dross; dregs; a worthless person.—*vt* to free from superfluous twigs or branches; to lop.

trashy *adj* composed of or resembling trash, rubbish or dross; waste; rejected; worthless; useless.

trass *n* a volcanic production consisting of ashes and scoriae and used as a cement.

trauma *n* an injury or wound, often produced by violence of some kind; an emotional shock; an upsetting experience.

traumatic *adj* of or causing trauma; (*colloq*) unpleasant.

travail *vi* to toil; to suffer the pangs of childbirth.—*n* severe toil; parturition; childbirth.

traveller

travel *vi* (**travelled, travelling**) to pass or make a journey from place to place on foot, on horseback or in any conveyance; to visit distant or foreign places; to journey; to go from place to place for the purpose of obtaining orders for goods, collecting accounts, etc, for a business; to proceed or advance in any way; to pass.—*vt* to journey over; to pass.—*n* the act of travelling or journeying; journeying to a distant country or countries; (*pl*) an account of occurrences and observations made during a journey.

travel agent *n* an agent who arranges travel bookings, such as flights, hotels, package tours, etc.

traveller *n* one who travels; a wayfarer; one who visits foreign countries; one who explores regions more or less unknown; a person who goes from place to place to solicit orders for goods, collect accounts, etc; a representative.

traveller's cheque *n* a cheque or draft issued by a bank, etc, and signed by the bearer at the time of purchase and again at the time of cashing, able to be cashed at banks, etc, in many foreign countries.

traverse *adj* transverse; being in a direction across something else.—**traverse sailing** where a ship makes several courses in succession, the track being zigzag and the directions of its several parts lying more or less athwart each other.—*n* a transverse piece; an untoward accident; (*fort*) a por-

trawler

tion of parapet thrown across the covered way at certain points; (*naut*) the zigzag track described by a ship when compelled to sail on different courses; a horizontal move in rock climbing, skiing, etc; (*archit*) a gallery or loft of communication in a church or other large building; (*law*) a denial of what the opposite party has advanced in any stage of the pleadings; (*surv*) a number of measured lengths and bearings forming a connected series.—*vt* (**traversed, traversing**) to cross; to lay in a cross direction; to thwart; to bring to nought; to wander over; to cross in travelling; (of a gun) to turn and point in any direction; (in carpentry) to plane in a direction across the grain of the wood; (*law*) to deny what the opposite party has alleged.—*vi* to turn, as on a pivot; to swivel.—*adv* athwart; crosswise.

travesty *n* a burlesque treatment or setting of a subject which had been originally handled in a serious or lofty manner; a parody; a poor imitation.

trawl *n* a long line from which short lines with baited hooks are suspended, used in sea fishing; a trawl net.—*vi* to fish with a trawl net.

trawler *n* one who trawls; a fishing vessel which uses a trawl net.

trawling *n* the act of fishing with a trawl net.

trawl net *n* a long purse-shaped net for dragging behind a boat, employed in deep-sea fishing, being useful for taking fish which lie near or on the bottom.

tray *n* a small shallow wooden vessel used for various domestic purposes, as kneading, mincing, etc; a sort of salver or waiter on which dishes, etc, are presented.

treacherous *adj* characterized by treason or violation of allegiance or faith pledge; faithless; traitorous; deceptive; illusory.

treachery *n* violation of allegiance or of faith and confidence; treason; perfidy.

treacle *n* the uncrystallizable matter separated from sugar in sugar refineries; molasses.

tread *vi* (*pret* **trod**, *pp* **trod** *or* **trodden**, *ppr* **treading**) to set the foot down or on the ground; to press with the foot; to step; to walk with a more or less measured or cautious step; to copulate, as fowls.—*vt* to step or walk on; to beat or press with the feet; to perform by motions of the feet; to dance; to crush under the foot; to trample in contempt or hatred; to copulate with, as a male bird.—*n* a step or stepping; way of walking; gait; the flat horizontal part of the step of a stair.

treadle *n* the part of a loom or other machine which is moved by the foot.—*vt* (**treadled, treadling**) to operate with a treadle.

treadmill *n* a machine formerly employed in prison discipline, the usual form of which was a wheel caused to revolve by the weight of the prisoners treading on steps on its periphery; a mechanism operated by a human or animal walking; a monotonous routine.

treason *n* a betraying, treachery or breach of faith, especially by a subject against the sovereign, liege lord or chief authority of the state.

treasure *n* wealth accumulated; particularly, a stock or store of money in reserve; a great quantity of anything collected for future use; something or someone very much valued.—*vt* (**treasured, treasuring**) to hoard up; to collect for future use; to accumulate; to store; to retain carefully in the mind; to regard as precious; to prize.

treasurer *n* one who has the care of a treasure or treasury; one who has the charge of collected funds, such as those belonging to incorporated companies or private societies.

treasure trove *n* (*law*) money, gold, silver plate or bullion of unknown ownership found hidden in the earth or in any private place; any valuable find.

treasury *n* a place or building in which wealth or valuables are deposited; a place where public moneys are deposited and kept and where money is disbursed for government expenses; any repository of valuable objects; (*fig*) a book containing much valuable information (*a treasury of botany*).

Treasury *n* a department of government which has control over the management of the public revenue.

treat *vt* to behave to or towards; to act well or ill towards; to use in any manner; to handle in a particular manner, in writing or speaking, or by any of the processes of art; to entertain (a guest) without expense to the guest; to give food or drink to; to manage in the application of remedies (*to treat a patient*); (*chem*) to subject to the action of some other substance.—*vi* to discourse; to handle in writing or speaking (followed usually by *of*); to negotiate; to propose terms of accommodation.—*n* an entertainment given as a compliment or expression of regard; anything which affords much pleasure; some unusual gratification.

treatise *n* a written composition on some subject, in which the principles of it are discussed or explained (usually of considerable length).

treatment *n* the act or the manner of treating; management; manipulation; manner of dealing with substances; usage; good or bad behaviour towards a person; manner of applying remedies to cure.

treaty *n* the act of treating or negotiating for the adjustment of differences or for forming an agreement; negotiation; an agreement, league or contract between two or more nations or sovereigns.

treble *adj* threefold; triple; (*mus*) pertaining to the highest or most acute sounds; playing or singing the highest part or most acute sounds.—*n* the highest vocal or instrumental part in a concerted piece of music; a soprano voice; a soprano singer.—*vt* to make thrice as much; to multiply by three; to triple.—*vi* (**trebled, trebling**) to become threefold.

treble clef *n* (*mus*) a clef that places **G** above middle **C** on the second line of the staff.

treble clef

tree *n* a perennial plant having a woody trunk of considerable size, from which spring branches, or, in the palms, fronds; something resembling a tree, consisting of a stem or stalk and branches (as *a genealogical tree*); a generic name for many wooden pieces in machines or structures (as, *axletree, saddletree*, etc).—*vt* to drive to a tree; to cause to take refuge in a tree (*a dog trees a squirrel*).

tree line *n* the height or latitude beyond which no trees grow on mountains or in cold regions.

trefoil *n* a three-leafed plant, as the white and red clover, etc, so well known as fodder plants; an ornament used in Gothic architecture representing the form of a three-lobed leaf.

trek *vi* (**trekked, trekking**) to travel by slowly or laboriously; (*colloq*) to go on foot; to migrate.—*n* a long and difficult journey; a migration.

trellis *n* a structure or frame of cross-barred work or latticework, used for supporting plants; a kind of espalier for climbing plants or for training fruit trees; a reticulated framing or latticework of wood or metal, for screens, doors or windows.

tremble *vi* (**trembled, trembling**) to shake involuntarily, as with fear, cold, weakness, etc; to shudder (said of persons); to be moved with a quivering motion; to shake; to totter (said of things); to quaver, as sound.—*n* the act or state of trembling; an involuntary shaking or shivering through cold or fear.

tremendous *adj* sufficient to excite fear or terror; terrible; awful; dreadful; such as may astonish by magnitude, force or violence; (*colloq*) wonderful, marvellous.

tree

tremolo *n* (*mus*) a rapid quavering effect in playing or singing; a vibration of the voice in singing, suitable for the production of certain effects.

tremor *n* an involuntary trembling; a shivering or shaking; a quivering or vibratory motion.

tremulous *adj* trembling; affected with fear or timidity; shaking; shivering.

trench *vt* to cut or dig, as a ditch; to furrow deeply with the spade or plough; to break up and prepare for crops by deep digging; to fortify by a ditch and rampart of earth; to entrench.—*vi* to encroach (with *on* or *upon*).—*n* a long narrow cut in the earth; a ditch; (*milit*) a deep ditch, with a parapet, cut for defence (as in a siege or a position taken up) or to interrupt the approach of an enemy.

trench coat *n* a kind of waterproof coat.

trenchant *adj* cutting; sharp; keen; unsparing; severe.

trencher *n* one who trenches or cuts; a wooden plate on which meat may be cut or carved, or on which it is eaten.

trencher cap *n* a cap with a flat square top like a square board set on it, such as that worn at universities.

trencherman *n* (*pl* **trenchermen**) a hearty eater; a table companion.

trench fever *n* an infectious disease with feverish symptoms, transmitted by vermin.

trench foot *n* a degenerative condition of the feet resembling frostbite, caused by prolonged exposure to wet and cold.

trend *n* tendency; a current style or fashion.

trepan[1] *n* (*surg*) an instrument in the form of a crown saw for removing portions of the bones of the skull and thus relieving the brain from pressure.—*vt* (**trepanned, trepanning**) to operate on by the trepan.

trepan[2], **trapan** *vt* (**trepanned, trepanning**) to ensnare or entrap; to inveigle in some deceitful manner.

trepang *n* the sea slug, sea cucumber or bêche-de-mer, found in the eastern seas and used in Chinese cookery.

trephine *n* an improved form of the trepan.

trepidation *n* a state of anxiety or apprehension; a state of terror; a trembling of the limbs, as in paralytic affections.

trespass *vi* to pass over a boundary line and enter unlawfully on the land of another; to intrude; to encroach; to commit any offence; to transgress; to violate any divine law or any known rule of duty.—*n* the act of one who trespasses; a violation of some law or rule laid down; any voluntary transgression of the moral law; sin; (*law*) any transgression of the law not amounting to felony; especially wrong done by entering on the grounds of another.

tress *n* a lock or curl of hair; a ringlet.

trestle *n* a sort of frame for supporting things; a frame with three or four legs attached to a horizontal piece.

trews *npl* tight-fitting tartan trousers of a Highlander or a soldier in Highland regiments.

triad *n* a set of three; a group of three; a trio; a trinity; (*mus*) the common chord formed of three radical sounds, a fundamental note, its third and its fifth.

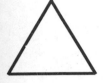

triangle

trencher cap

triage *n* the sorting and treatment of the wounded according to chance of survival.

trial *n* the act of trying or testing in any manner; an attempt; a test; experiment; a becoming acquainted by experience; that which tries or afflicts; that which tries the character or principle; a person causing annoyance; affliction; temptation; the state of being tried; a process for testing qualification; an examination; a preliminary race, game, etc, in a competition; (*law*) the examination of a cause in controversy between parties before a proper tribunal.— **trial and error** the solution of a problem by trying various solutions and rejecting the least successful.

trial balance *n* in bookkeeping, the compilation in two lists of the debit and credit items in a double-entry ledger to ensure that they are equal.

trial run *n* an opportunity to test something before purchase, as a vehicle; a rehearsal.

triangle *n* (*geom*) a figure bounded by three lines and containing three angles, the lines or sides being straight in a plane triangle and parts of circles in spherical triangles; a musical instrument of percussion, made of a rod of steel bent into this shape, open at one of the angles; a three-cornered straight edge, used by draughtsmen, etc.

triangular *adj* having three angles; having the form of a triangle; three-cornered.

triangulation *n* the reduction of the surface of an area to triangles for the purpose of a trigonometric survey.

Trias *n* the Triassic period.

Triassic *adj* (*geol*) of, pertaining to or belonging to the first period of the Mesozoic era, older than the Jurassic period.—*n* the Triassic period; Trias.

triatomic *adj* (*chem*) consisting of three atoms; having three atoms in the molecule.

tribal *adj* belonging to a tribe; characteristic of a tribe.

tribe *n* a division, class or distinct portion of a people or nation; a family or race descending from the same progenitor and kept distinct (*the twelve tribes of Israel*); a nation or family of people, forming a subdivision of a race; a number of persons of any character or profession (in contempt).

tribrach *n* (*pros*) a poetic foot of three short syllables; a word of three short syllables.

tribulation *n* that which occasions affliction or distress; severe affliction; distress; trouble; trial.

tribunal *n* the seat of a judge; a bench for judges; a court of justice; a committee that investigates and decides on a particular problem.

tribune *n* in ancient Rome, an officer or magistrate chosen by the common people to protect them from the oppression of the patricians; a sort of pulpit or rostrum where a speaker stands to address an assembly.

tributary *n* an individual, government or state that pays tribute; (*geog*) an affluent; a river which adds water to another river.

tribute *n* an annual or stated sum paid by one prince or nation to another, either as an acknowledgement of submission or by virtue of some treaty; the obligation of contributing; a personal contribution; anything done or given, as that which is due or observed (*a tribute of respect*).

trice[1] *n* a very short time; a moment.—**in a trice** in an instant or moment.

trice[2] *vt* (**triced, tricing**) (*naut*) to haul or tie up by means of a small rope; to hoist.

triceps *adj, n* three-headed (applied to certain muscles).

trichina *n* (*pl* **trichinae**) a minute roundworm, the larva of which is found in the tissue of the muscles of human beings and several other mammals, giving rise to the disease trichinosis.

trichinosis, trichiniasis *n* a painful disease caused by eating meat, either raw or insufficiently cooked, infested with trichinae.

trichotomy *n* division into three parts.

trichromatic *adj* pertaining to three colours, especially to red, green and violet, which, according to the *trichromatic theory*, are fundamental in colour sensation; or to red, yellow and blue, which are primary colours so far as regards mixtures of pigments.

trick[1] *n* an artifice; a stratagem; a fraudulent contrivance for an evil purpose; a cheat; a knack or art; a sleight-of-hand performance; the legerdemain of a juggler; a particular practice or habit; an action peculiar to a person (*a trick of frowning*); anything mischievously and roguishly done; a prank; a frolic; card playing, all the cards played in one round; (*naut*) a spell; a turn; the time allotted to a person to stand at the helm.—*vt* to deceive; to impose on; to defraud; to cheat.

trick[2] *vt* to dress; to decorate; to set off; to adorn fantastically (often followed by *out*).

trickery *n* the practice of tricks; imposture; cheating; artifice.

trickiness *n* the quality of being tricky.

trickish *adj* given to tricks; artful; knavish.

trickle *vt* (**trickled, trickling**) to flow in a small gentle stream; to run down in drops.

trickster *n* one who practises tricks; a deceiver; a cheat.

tricky *adj* trickish; mischievous; difficult; problematic.

triclinic *adj* (of a crystal) having three unequal axes intersecting obliquely.

tricolour *n* a flag having three colours; a flag having three colours arranged in equal stripes, as adopted in France, etc.

tricuspid, tricuspidal, tricuspidate *adj* having three cusps or points; (*bot*) three-pointed; ending in three points.

tricycle *n* a vehicle with three wheels, generally two driving wheels parallel to each other and a steering wheel either in front or in the rear.

tricyclist *n* one who rides on a tricycle.

trident *n* any instrument of the form of a fork with three prongs; the sceptre or spear with three barbed prongs with which Poseidon (Neptune), the sea god, is represented.

tridentate, tridentated *adj* having three teeth.

tridimensional *adj* having three dimensions; three-dimensional.

triennial *adj* continuing three years; happening every three years.

triennially *adv* once in three years.

trifle *n* a thing of very little value or importance; a paltry toy, bauble or luxury; a silly or unimportant action, remark, etc; a dessert made of sponge cake, custard, fruit, cream, etc.—*vi* (**trifled, trifling**) to act or talk without seriousness or with levity; to indulge in light amusements.—*vt* to waste to no good purpose; to spend (usually followed by *away*).

trifling *adj* acting with levity; frivolous; being of small value or importance; trivial.

trifoliate, trifoliated *adj* having three leaves.

triforium *n* (*pl* **triforia**) (*Gothic archit*) a gallery above the arches of the nave of a church, generally in the form of an arcade.

trig[1] *adj* trim; spruce; neat.

trig[2] *n* a shortened form of **trigonometry**.

trigeminal nerve *n* either of a pair of cranial nerves that supply various facial muscles.

trigeminal neuralgia *n* a sudden stabbing pain in the trigeminal nerve; tic douloureux.

trigger *n* the catch or lever which, on being pulled back, liberates the hammer of the lock of a gun or pistol; any similar device.

triggerfish *n* any of certain fishes which have a dorsal fin with a strong ray or spine in front that cannot be pressed down till the second ray is depressed.

triglyph *n* (*archit*) an ornamental block in Doric friezes, repeated at equal intervals, having on its face two small perpendicular channels and a half channel on either side.

trigon *n* (*arch*) a triangle; (*astrol*) the junction of three signs of the zodiac; (*mus*) an ancient triangular lyre.

trigonometry *n* the branch of mathematics concerned with calculating the angles of triangles or the lengths of their sides.

trigonometric, trigonometrical *adj* pertaining to trigonometry; performed by or according to the rules of trigonometry.

trilingual *adj* consisting of three languages.

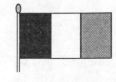

tricolour

trigger

917

trilithon, trilith *n* three large blocks of stone placed together like doorposts with a lintel and standing by themselves, as in ancient monuments like Stonehenge.

trill[1] *n* a warbling, quavering sound; a rapid, trembling series or succession of tones.— *vt* to sing with a quavering or tremulousness of voice; to sing.—*vi* to shake or quaver; to sound with tremulous vibrations; to sing with quavers; to pipe.

trill[2] *vi* to flow in a small stream; to trickle.

trillion *n* originally in UK one million million; (*colloq*) a very large number.

trilobate, trilobed *adj* (*bot*) having three lobes.

trilobite *n* one of an extinct and widely distributed family of Palaeozoic crustaceans abundant in the Silurian strata, having the body divided into three lobes which run parallel to its axis.

trilobitic *adj* pertaining to or resembling a trilobite.

trilogy *n* a series of three literary or operatic works, each in a certain sense complete in itself, yet together forming one connected whole.

trim *vt* (**trimmed, trimming**) to put in due order for any purpose; to adjust; to invest, embellish or decorate, as with ribbons, braid, lace, etc (*to trim a gown*); to bring to a neat or orderly condition by removing superfluous appendages or matter; to clip, pare, shave, prune, lop, etc (*to trim the hair, a hedge* or *a tree*); (in carpentry) to dress, as timber; to adjust the weights in a ship or aircraft so that it is balanced.—*vi* to hold a middle course or position between parties so as to appear to favour each.—*adj* being neat and in good order; properly adjusted; having everything appropriate and in its right place; tight; snug; neat; tidy; smart.—*n* dress; garb; state of preparation; order; condition; mood; disposition; the state of a ship or aircraft by which it is prepared for sailing or flying.

trimming *n* the act of one who trims; the act of one who fluctuates between parties; ornamental appendages to a garment, etc; (*pl*) (*colloq*) the accessories to any dish or article of food.

trimeter *n* a line or verse or poetry consisting of three measures (often of two iambic feet each).

trimorphic, trimorphous *adj* characterized by trimorphism; having three distinct forms.

trimorphism *n* the state or property of having three distinct forms; (*crystal*) the property of crystallizing in three fundamentally different forms.

Trimurti *n* the Hindu trinity: Brahma the creator, Vishnu the preserver and Siva the destroyer.

trinal *adj* threefold; triple.

trine *n* the aspect of planets distant from each other 120 degrees; a triad.

Trinitarian *adj* pertaining to the Trinity or to the doctrine of the Trinity.—*n* one who believes the doctrine of the Trinity.

trinitrotoluene *n* a high explosive, made by treating toluene with nitric acid; also called **TNT**.

trinity *n* a union of three in one; the state of being three.

Trinity *n* (*theol*) the union of three persons in one Godhead: the Father, the Son and the Holy Spirit; a symbolical representation of the mystery of the Trinity frequent in Christian art.

Trinity Sunday *n* the Sunday next after Whitsunday, observed in honour of the Trinity.

trinket *n* a small ornament, as a jewel, a ring, etc; a thing of no great value; a trifle.

trinomial *adj* (*alg*) consisting of three terms connected by the signs + or -.—*n* (*alg*) a quantity of three terms.

trio *n* (*pl* **trios**) a set of three; (*mus*) a composition for three voices or three instruments; the performers of a trio.

triolet *n* a stanza of eight lines in which the first line is repeated after the third, and the first and second lines after the sixth.

trip *vi* (**tripped, tripping**) to run or step lightly; to move the feet nimbly, as in running, walking, dancing; to stumble and come near to fall; to make a false step; to lose the footing; to offend against morality, propriety or rule; to err; to go wrong.—*vt* to cause to fall by striking the feet suddenly from under the person; to cause to stumble or make a false step (often followed by *up*); (*Shak*) to catch in a fault or mistake; (*naut*) to loose (an anchor) from the bottom by its cable.—*n* a light short step; a lively movement of the feet; a short journey or voyage; a tour; an excursion or jaunt; a causing to stumble or fall; a stumble; a false step; an error; a mistake.

tripartite *adj* divided into three parts; having three corresponding parts; made between three parties (*a tripartite treaty*); (*bot*) divided into three parts down to the base, but not wholly separate.

tripe *n* the stomach of ruminating animals when prepared for food.

triphthong *n* a combination of three vowels in a single syllable; three vowel characters representing a single sound (*eau* in *beau*).

triple *adj* consisting of three united; threefold; three times repeated; treble.—*vt* (**tripled, tripling**) to make threefold or thrice as much or as many; to treble.

triple crown *n* the crown worn by the popes, consisting of three crowns placed one above another, surrounding a high cap or tiara.

918

triplet *n* a collection or combination of three of a kind or three united; three verses or lines of poetry rhyming together; (*mus*) a group of three notes of equal time value, to be performed in the time of two, indicated by a slur and the figure 3; a combination of three lenses; one of three children born at a birth.

triple time *n* (*mus*) time or rhythm of three beats, or of three times three beats, in a bar.

triplicate *adj* made thrice as much; threefold.—*n* a third thing corresponding to two others.

triply *adv* in a triple or threefold manner; trebly.

tripod *n* a name for various ancient utensils or articles of furniture resting on three feet; a three-legged frame or stand for supporting a theodolite, compass, etc.

tripoli *n* a kind of siliceous stone used in polishing metals, marbles, glass etc.

tripper *n* one who trips or trips up; one who walks nimbly; one who takes a trip; a person who goes on a pleasure excursion; a tourist.

tripping *adj* stepping quickly or lightly; quick; nimble.

triptych *n* a series of altar paintings on three panels fixed or hinged side by side.

trireme *n* an ancient Greek galley or vessel with three benches or ranks of oars on a side.

trisect *vt* to cut or divide into three equal parts.

trisection *n* the division of a thing into three parts; particularly, in geometry, the division of an angle into three equal parts.

trisyllabic *adj* pertaining to a trisyllable; consisting of three syllables.

trisyllable *n* a word consisting of three syllables.

trite *adj* commonplace; hackneyed; banal.

triteness *n* the quality of being trite; commonness; banality.

tritheism *n* (*theol*) the opinion that the Father, Son and Holy Spirit are three beings or Gods.

tritheist *n* (*theol*) one who believes that there are three distinct Gods in the Godhead, that is, three distinct substances, essences or hypostases.

triton *n* one of a genus of molluscs with trumpet-like shells; one of a genus of reptiles including the newts.

Triton *n* one of certain subordinate sea deities among the Greeks and Romans, having their lower extremities fish-like.

triturate *vt* (**triturated, triturating**) to rub or grind to a very fine powder.

trituration *n* the act of triturating.

triumph *n* the state of being victorious; victory; conquest; joy or exultation for success; great gladness; rejoicing.—*vi* to enjoy a triumph; to celebrate victory with pomp; hence, to rejoice for victory; to obtain victory; to meet with success; to prevail; to exult upon an advantage gained; especially, to exult or boast insolently.

triumphal *adj* pertaining to triumph; commemorating or used in celebrating a triumph or victory.

triumphant *adj* rejoicing for victory or as for victory; triumphing; exulting; victorious; graced with conquest.

triumvir *n* one of three men united in office.

triumvirate *n* a coalition of three in office or authority; government by three people in coalition; a party of three people; three people in company or forming one company.

triune *n* three in one (applied to express the unity of the Godhead in a trinity of persons).

trivalent *adj* having a valence of three.

trivet *n* anything supported by three feet; a kind of iron frame or stand whereon to place vessels for boiling, etc, or to receive something placed before the fire (frequently used as a proverbial comparison indicating stability, as *right as a trivet*).

trivia *npl* (*sing* **trivium**) unimportant details.

trivial *adj* commonplace; trifling; insignificant; of little worth or importance; inconsiderable; occupying oneself with trifles; trifling.

triviality *n* the state or quality of being trivial; a trivial thing; a trifle.

trivially *adv* in a trivial or trifling manner; lightly; inconsiderably; insignificantly.

trocar *n* a perforating surgical instrument used for drawing off fluid.

trochaic *adj* pertaining to or consisting of trochees.—*n* a trochaic verse.

trochanter *n* (*anat*) a process of the upper part of the thighbone to which are attached the muscles which rotate the limb.

trochee *n* (*pros*) a foot of two syllables, the first long and the second short.

trochlea *n* (*pl* **trochleae**) (*anat*) a pulley-like cartilage connected with one of the superior muscles of the eye.

troglodyte *n* a cave-dweller.

trogon *n* any of certain tropical birds with long tail plumes and colourful plumage.

troika *n* a Russian vehicle drawn by a team of three horses running abreast; a triumvirate.

Trojan *adj* pertaining to ancient Troy.—*n* an inhabitant of ancient Troy; a person of great courage or determination.

troll¹ *n* in Scandinavian myth and literature, a supernatural being dwelling in the interior of hills and mounds.

troll² *vt* to fish for by trailing a baited line in water from a boat; to move in a circular

tripod

direction; to pass round or cause to circle, as a vessel of liquor at table; (*arch*) to sing the parts of in succession, especially in a full, jovial voice.—*vi* to fish by trolling; to go round; to move round.—*n* a lure for fishing; the act of going or moving round; (*arch*) a song the parts of which are sung in succession.

trolley *n* a kind of small truck; a small narrow cart; in electric railways and tramways, a grooved metal wheel at the end of a flexible pole, used to collect the electric energy from the overhead wire; a table on wheels for carrying or serving food; a cart for transporting luggage; a cart for carrying shopping in a supermarket.

trollop *n* a slattern; a slut; a slovenly woman; a loose woman; a prostitute.

trombone *n* a deep-toned instrument of the trumpet kind, consisting of three tubes of which the middle one is doubled and slides into the other two like the tube of a telescope.

troop *n* a collection of people; a number; a multitude; a body of soldiers; (*pl*) soldiers in general, whether more or less numerous; a body of cavalry forming the command of a captain; a band or company of performers; a troupe.—*vi* to collect in numbers; to gather in crowds; to march in a body or in company; to march in haste (often with *off*).

trooper *n* a private soldier in a body of cavalry; a horse soldier.

troopship *n* a ship for the conveyance of troops; a transport.

tropaeolum *n* (*pl* **tropaeolums, tropaeola**) a plant of a genus of South American trailing or climbing plants of the geranium family, some of them well known as nasturtium.

trope *n* (*rhet*) a figurative use of a word; a word or expression used in a different sense from that which it properly possesses; a figure of speech.

trophy *n* anything taken and preserved as a memorial of victory, as captured arms, standards, etc; anything serving as an evidence of victory; a cup, shield, etc.

tropic *n* one of the two corresponding parallels of latitude or circles going round the globe at the same distance north and south of the equator and including between them the Torrid Zone, having the equator for its central line; (*pl*) the regions lying between the tropics or near them on either side.—*adj* tropical; pertaining to the tropics.

tropical[1] *adj* pertaining to the tropics; being within the tropics; incident to the tropics (*tropical diseases*).

tropical[2] *adj* figurative; rhetorically changed from its original sense.

tropicbird *n* a tropical web-footed bird of the pelican family powerful in flight.

tropic of Cancer *n* the tropic lying about $23\frac{1}{2}°$ north of the equator.

tropic of Capricorn *n* the tropic lying about $23\frac{1}{2}°$ south of the equator.

trot *vi* (**trotted, trotting**) to move faster than in walking; to walk or move fast; to run.—*vt* to cause to trot; to ride at a trot.—*n* the pace of a horse or other quadruped more rapid than a walk; a contemptuous term for an old woman.

troth *n* truth; faith; fidelity; veracity.—**to plight one's troth** to pledge one's faith; to betroth oneself.

trotter *n* one who trots; a trotting horse; the foot of an animal, especially of a pig.

troubadour *n* a name given to any of a class of early poets who first appeared in Provence in France and flourished from the eleventh to the latter part of the thirteenth century, their poetry being lyrical and amatory.

trouble *vt* (**troubled, troubling**) to agitate; to disturb; to annoy, fret or molest; to afflict; to distress; to put to some slight labour or pains (used in courteous phraseology).—*n* distress of mind or what causes such; grief; great perplexity; affliction; anxiety; annoyance; pains; labour; exertion; disturbance; unrest.—**to take the trouble** to be at the pains; to give oneself inconvenience.

troublesome *adj* giving or causing trouble; harassing; annoying; vexatious; importunate.

trough *n* a vessel of wood, stone or metal, generally rather long and not very deep, for holding water, feeding stuffs for animals, etc; a channel or spout for conveying water; anything resembling a trough in shape, as a depression between two ridges or between two waves; a basin-shaped or oblong hollow.

trounce *vt* (**trounced, trouncing**) to punish or to beat severely; to castigate.

troupe *n* a troop; a company; particularly, a company of players, dancers, acrobats, etc.

trousers *npl* a garment extending from the waist to the ankles, covering the lower part of the trunk and each leg separately.

trousseau *n* (*pl* **trousseaux, trousseaus**) the clothes and general outfit of a bride.

trout *n* the common name of various species of the salmon family, as the bull trout, the salmon trout, the common trout, etc.

trow *vi* to believe; to trust; to think or suppose.

trowel *n* a tool somewhat resembling a small spade, used for spreading and dressing mortar and plaster, etc; a similar gardener's tool, used in taking up plants and for other purposes.

troy, troy weight *n* a weight chiefly used in weighing gold and silver, divided into 12

trolley

trophy

ounces, each of 20 pennyweights, each of 24 grains. the pound troy = 5760 grains; the pound avoirdupois 7000.

truant *n* one who shirks or neglects his or her duty; an idler; especially, a child who stays from school without leave.—*adj* shirking duty; wilfully absent from an appointed place; idle.

truce *n* (*milit*) a suspension of arms by agreement of the commanders of the opposing armies; an armistice; any temporary intermission or cessation.

truck[1] *n* a heavy motor vehicle for transporting goods; a wheeled structure for moving heavy goods, such as a railway wagon or a railway porter's handcart.—*vt* to put in a truck; to send or convey by truck.

truck[2] *vi* to exchange commodities; to barter—*vt* to exchange; to give in exchange; to barter.—*n* exchange of commodities; barter; payment of wages in goods; commodities appropriate for barter or for small trade; dealings.

truckle[1] *vi* (**truckled, truckling**) to yield or bend obsequiously to the will of another; to cringe (usually with *to*).

truckle[2] *n* a small wheel or castor; a truckle bed.—*vt* (**truckled, truckling**) to move on rollers; to trundle.

truckle bed *n* a bed that runs on wheels and may be pushed under another; a trundle bed.

truck system *n* formerly, the practice of paying the wages of workers in goods instead of money, which prevailed particularly in the mining and manufacturing districts of Britain though prohibited by law.

truculent *adj* aggressive; belligerent; sullen.

trudge *vi* to travel on foot with fatigue or more or less painful exertion; to travel or march with labour or effort.

true *adj* conformable to fact; not false or erroneous; free from falsehood; truthful; genuine; not counterfeit, false or pretended; firm or steady in adhering to promises to friends, etc; faithful; loyal; honest; exact; correct; right; conformable to law and justice; legitimate; rightful.—*vt* (**trued, truing**) to give a right form to; to make exactly straight, square, level, etc.

true-blue *adj* (of a person) of utter honesty and fidelity; staunch.—*n* a person of inflexible honesty or staunchness.

trueness *n* the quality of being true; sincerity; genuineness; accuracy.

truffle *n* an edible and much esteemed fungus growing a few inches beneath the surface of the ground, of a dark colour, of a roundish form and without visible root; a rich sweet made with chocolate, butter and sugar.

truism *n* an undoubted or self-evident truth.

truly *adv* in a true manner; exactly; faithfully; honestly; legitimately; in reality; in fact.

trump *n* a winning card; one of the suit of cards which takes any of the other suits; a good fellow; a person on whom one can depend.—*vt* to take with a trump card; to put a trump card on in order to win.—**to trump up** to devise; to forge (*to trump up a story*).

trumpery *n* worthless finery; things worn out and of no value; rubbish.—*adj* trifling; worthless.

trumpet *n* a wind instrument of music made of brass or silver, having a clear ringing tone; one who praises or propagates praise.—*vt* to publish by sound of trumpet; hence, to blaze or noise abroad; to proclaim.

trumpeter *n* one who sounds a trumpet; one who proclaims, publishes or denounces; a variety of the domestic pigeon; a wading bird of South America.

truncate *vt* (**truncated, truncating**) to shorten by cutting abruptly; to lop; to cut short.—*adj* truncated; (*bot*) appearing as if cut short at the tip (*a truncate leaf*).

truncated *adj* cut short abruptly; having a part abruptly cut off, especially at the apex or top, or having the appearance of being so cut.

truncheon *n* a short staff; a cudgel; a baton or staff of authority.

trundle bed *n* a truckle bed.

trundle *vi* (**trundled, trundling**) to roll, as on little wheels; to roll; to bowl along.—*vt* to wheel or move on wheels; to cause to roll (*to trundle a hoop*).—*n* a little wheel; a castor; a small carriage with low wheels; a truck.

trunk *n* the woody stem of trees; that part which supports the branches; the body without the limbs or considered as apart from the limbs; the main body of anything relatively to its branches or ramifications; a large box or chest with a hinged lid used for carrying or storing clothes, etc; the long snout or proboscis of an elephant; also, a similar organ of other animals, as the proboscis of an insect; a tube, usually wooden, to convey air, dust, broken matter, grain, etc; a trough to convey water from a race to a waterwheel, etc; a flume; a boxed passage for air to or from a blast apparatus or blowing engine; the boot of a car; (*pl*) a man's shorts, specially designed for swimming in.

trunk line *n* the main line of a railway, canal, etc.

trunk road *n* a highway or main road.

trunnion *n* each of any similar pair of opposite pins or pivots on which anything is supported, especially formerly on a cannon.

trvmpet

truss *n* a bundle, especially a small hand-packed bundle of dry goods; a quantity, as of hay or straw tied together; (*surg*) a bandage used in cases of rupture to keep up the parts or for other purposes; a tuft of flowers at the top of the main stalk of certain plants; an umbel; in a building, a combination of timbers, of iron or of timbers and ironwork, so arranged as to constitute an unyielding frame; (*archit*) a large corbel, etc, supporting some object projecting from the face of a wall.—*vt* to put in a bundle; to pack up (often with *up*); to seize and carry off (said of birds of prey); to draw tight and tie the laces of, as of garments; to make fast, as the wings of a fowl to the body in cooking it; to skewer; to pull up by a rope or ropes; to hang.

T-shirt

trust *n* a reliance or resting of the mind on the integrity, truth, justice, friendship, etc, of another person; a firm reliance on promises or on laws or principles; confidence; confident expectation; assured anticipation; belief; hope; reliance or belief without examination (*to take opinions on trust*); the transfer of goods, property, etc, in confidence of future payment; credit; a person confided in and relied on; that which is committed or entrusted to one; something committed to one's care for use of for safekeeping; the state of being confided to another's care and guard; safekeeping; care; management; (*law*) the conveying of property to one party (the *trustee*) in confidence that he or she will apply it for the benefit of a third party or to some specified purpose.—*vt* to place confidence in; to rely on; to depend upon; to believe; to receive as true; to rely on with regard to the care of; to entrust (*to trust him with money*); to commit, as to one's care; to leave to oneself or to itself without fear of consequences; to sell to on credit or in confidence of future payment; to be confident; to hope confidently (followed by a clause).—*vi* to have trust or reliance; to confide readily; to practise giving credit; to sell in reliance upon future payment.—*adj* held in trust (*trust property*).

trustee *n* a person appointed to hold property, to take care of and apply the same for the benefit of those entitled to it.

trustworthy *adj* worthy of trust or confidence.

trusty *adj* admitting of being safely trusted; deserving confidence; fit to be confided in; not liable to fail a person (*a trusty sword*).

truth *n* the state or quality of being true; conformity to fact or reality; veracity; purity from falsehood; fidelity; constancy; genuineness; that which is true; a true statement; fact; reality; verity; a verified fact.—**in truth** in reality; in sincerity.

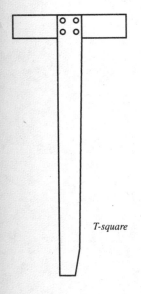

T-square

try *vt* (**tried, trying**) to test or prove by experiment; to subject to some severe test or experience; to cause suffering or trouble to; to examine or inquire into, especially, to examine judicially; to subject to the examination and decision or sentence of a tribunal; to attempt; to undertake; to make experiment with; to see what will result from using or employing.—**to try on** to put on, as a garment, to see if it fits.—*vi* to exert strength; to endeavour; to prove by a test; to attempt to deceive someone.—*n* the act of trying; a trial; experiment; in rugby football, the right of trying to kick a goal, obtained by carrying the ball behind the opponents' goal line and touching it down.

trying *adj* annoying; irritating.

trypanosome *n* a parasitic protozoan, infesting the blood of animals, including human beings, being usually introduced by the bite of an insect: it is the cause of various diseases, e.g. sleeping sickness.

tryst *n* an appointment to meet; a rendezvous.—*vi* to agree to meet at any particular time or place.

tsar, tzar, czar *n* formerly, a title of the emperor of Russia.

tsarina, tzarina, czarina *n* formerly, a title of the empress of Russia.

tsetse *n* a South African two-winged fly, whose bite is often fatal to horses, dogs and cattle and the cause of sleeping sickness in human beings.

T-shirt, tee-shirt *n* a light short-sleeved cotton top for casual wear.

T-square *n* an instrument used in drawing, consisting of two slips of hardwood of unequal length, the longer fixed into the shorter like a T and both having their edges dressed exactly straight and parallel.

tub *n* an open wooden vessel formed with staves, bottom and hoops; a half barrel open above; a small cask or barrel for liquor; any wooden structure resembling a tub; in mining, a bucket for raising coal or ore from the mine.—**a tale of a tub** an idle or silly fiction; a cock-and-bull story.—*vt* (**tubbed, tubbing**) to plant or set in a tub (*to tub plants*).—*vi* to wash; to make use of a bathing tub.

tuba *n* a large valved musical instrument of brass, low in pitch and resembling the bombardon.

tubby *adj* plump.

tube *n* a pipe; a hollow cylinder of wood, metal, glass, rubber, etc, used for the conveyance of fluids and for various other purposes; any similar object; a vessel of animal bodies or plants which conveys a fluid or other substance; (*elect*) a hollow vessel, usually of glass, fitted with electrodes and various adjuncts and containing air or other gas at a low or an adjustable pressure; the underground electric railway system in London.

tuber *n* an underground fleshy stem or modification of the root of plants (as in the potato), roundish in shape, of annual duration and with buds from which new plants are produced; (*surg*) a knot or swelling in any part.

tubercle *n* a small tuber; a little projecting knob; (*anat*) a natural small rounded body or mass; (*pathol*) one of certain small masses of abnormal matter which may be developed in different parts of the body, but are most frequently observed in the lungs (in tuberculosis).

tubercular *adj* of the character of a tubercle; caused by tubercles; affected with tubercles.

tuberculin *n* a sterile liquid prepared with weakened tubercle bacillus and used in the diagnosis of tuberculosis.

tuberculosis *n* a disease due to the formation of tubercles in various organs of the body; a consumptive state of the system.

tuberose *n* a bulbous Mexican plant with fragrant white flowers.

tubing *n* the act of making or providing with tubes; a series of tubes; material for tubes.

tubular *adj* having the form of a tube or pipe; consisting of a pipe.

tubular bells *npl* an orchestral percussion instrument consisting of a set of long metal tubes played with a mallet to simulate the sound of bells.

tuck *vt* to put into smaller compass by folding; to fold in or under; to gather up; to draw up; to gather the bedclothes close around (*to tuck a child into a bed*).—*vi* to contract; to draw together.—**tuck in** (*colloq*) to partake freely of food or dainties.—*n* a fold sewed in some part of a dress to shorten it, especially a horizontal fold made on a skirt; (*colloq*) food.

tucker *n* (*colloq*) food.

tuckshop *n* a shop in or near a school selling sweets, snacks, soft drinks, etc, to the pupils.

Tudor *adj* of the dynasty and the style of architecture during the reigns of Henry VII, Henry VIII, Edward VI, Mary, Elizabeth, deriving from Owen Tudor, grandfather of Henry VII.

Tudor rose *n* (*heral*) a double rose, having a white centre with red petals, or vice versa, and intended to conjoin the emblems of the Houses of York and of Lancaster.

Tuesday *n* the third day of the week.

tufa, tuff *n* (*geol*) a term originally applied to a light porous rock composed of cemented scoriae and ashes, but now to any porous vesicular compound.

tuft *n* a collection of small flexible or soft things in a knot or bunch (*a tuft of flowers*,

a tuft of feathers); a cluster; a clump (*a tuft of trees*).

tug *vt* (**tugged, tugging**) to pull with effort; to haul; to strain at; to drag by means of a steam tug.—*vi* to pull with great effort; to labour; to strive; to struggle.—*n* a pull with the utmost effort; a supreme effort; the severest strain or struggle (*the tug of war*); a tugboat.

tugboat *n* a strongly built steamboat used for towing sailing and other vessels.

tug of love *n* (*colloq*) a struggle involving the custody of a child.

tug of war *n* a trial of strength between two parties at opposite ends of a rope, each striving to pull the other over a certain mark.

tui *n* a New Zealand bird noted for its song and its ability to mimic human speech and the calls of other birds.

tuition *n* guardianship or superintendence; instruction; tutorship; teaching.

tulip *n* a highly coloured, cup-shaped flower grown from a bulb.

tulle *n* a delicate semi-transparent fabric of rayon, silk, etc, used for scarves, veils, etc.

tumble *vi* (**tumbled, tumbling**) to roll about by turning one way and the other; to toss the body about; to roll; to lose footing and fall; to be precipitated; to play acrobats' tricks.—*vt* to turn or throw about for examination or search; to toss over carelessly; to disorder; to rumple; to throw down; to precipitate.—*n* a fall; a rolling over.

tumbler *n* one who tumbles; one who plays the tricks of an acrobat turning somersaults, etc; a large drinking glass; a variety of the domestic pigeon, so called from its practice of turning over in flight; a sort of spring latch in a lock which detains the bolt until a key lifts it.

tumbrel, tumbril *n* a dung cart; a low vehicle with two wheels used by farmers; a covered cart or carriage with two wheels, which accompanied troops for conveying the tools of pioneers, ammunition, etc.

tumid *adj* being swelled, enlarged or distended; swollen; protuberant; swelling in sound or sense; pompous; bombastic.

tummy *n* (*colloq*) stomach.

tumour *n* (*surg*) an abnormal enlargement or swelling; more strictly, a permanent swelling occasioned by a new growth and not a mere enlargement of a natural part, which may be benign or malignant.

tumult *n* the commotion, disturbance or agitation of a multitude; an uproar; violent commotion or agitation, with confusion of sounds; irregular or confused motion.

tumultuous *adj* full of tumult, disorder or confusion; conducted with tumult; disorderly; agitated; disturbed, as by passion, etc; turbulent; violent.

tumbler

tumulus *n* (*pl* **tumuli**) a mound; a barrow or artificial burial mound of earth.

tun *n* originally any large cask or vessel for containing liquids; hence, a certain measure or quantity, as the old English tun of wine, which contained 4 hogsheads or 252 gallons.

tuna, tunny *n* a large food fish of the mackerel family.

tunable, tuneable *adj* capable of being put in tune or made harmonious; musical; tuneful.

tundra *n* a term applied to the immense stretches of flat boggy country in the northern part of Siberia, where vegetation takes an Arctic character.

tune *n* a rhythmical, melodious series of musical tones produced by one voice or instrument, or by several voices or instruments in unison; an air; a melody; correct intonation in singing or playing; adjustment of a musical instrument so as to produce its tones in correct key relationship or in harmony with other instruments; frame of mind; mood; temper for the time being.—**to the tune of** (*colloq*) to the sum or amount of.—**in tune with** in agreement with; compatible with.—*vt* (**tuned, tuning**) to put into or cause to be in tune; to sing with melody or harmony; to attune; to put into the proper state; to adapt; to adjust (an engine) so that it yields its maximum power; to adjust the capacity or inductance of a radio receiving set so as to put it in resonance with radiation of a given wavelength.

tunic

tuneable *adj* same as **tunable**.

tuneful *adj* harmonious; melodious; musical.

tungsten, wolfram *n* a hard, greyish-white, brittle and heavy metal, used for the filaments of electric lamps and to form a hard alloy with steel.

tunic *n* a loose garment drawn in at the waist and reaching not far below it, often worn with a belt; the garment worn by a knight over his armour; the full-dress scarlet or green coat worn by soldiers; (*anat*) a membrane that covers or composes some part or organ (*the tunics* or *coats of the eye, the tunics of the stomach*, etc); a natural covering; an integument; (*bot*) any loose membranous skin not formed from epidermis; the skin of a seed.

tureen

tunicate *n* any of an order of molluscs, which are enveloped in a tough membrane; an ascidian or sea squirt.—*adj* having or enclosed in a membrane; (of bulbs) made up from concentric layers of tissue.

tuning fork *n* a steel instrument with two prongs, designed when set in vibration to give a musical sound of a certain fixed pitch.

tunnel *n* a subterranean passage cut through a hill, a rock or any eminence, or under a river, a town, etc, to carry a canal, a road or a railway in an advantageous course.—*vt* (**tunnelled, tunnelling**) to form or cut a tunnel through or under.

tunnel vision *n* a condition in which peripheral vision is impaired; a narrowness of viewpoint owing to a preoccupation with one idea, plan, etc.

tunny *n* same as **tuna**.

tup *n* a ram.

turban *n* a form of headdress consisting of cloth wound in folds around the head, worn by some Muslim men, etc; a woman's hat of this shape.

turbellarian *n* any of an order of worms, nearly all aquatic and nonparasitic, including the nematodes and others.

turbid *adj* muddy; not clear (said of liquids of any kind).

turbinate, turbinated *adj* shaped like a whipping top; (of a conch) spiral or wreathed conically from a larger base to the apex like a top; (*bot*) shaped like an inverted top or cone.

turbine *n* a machine in which power is produced when the forced passage of steam water, etc, causes the blades to rotate.

turbit *n* a variety of domestic pigeon with a short beak.

turbo- *prefix* coupled direct to a turbine; constructed like a turbine.

turbojet *n* a jet engine or aircraft with a turbo-driven compressor.

turboprop *n* a jet engine which produces thrust by a propeller connected to the turbine shaft; an aircraft driven by one or more such engines.

turbot *n* a large, common, flat edible species of flatfish plentiful off the British shores.

turbulence *n* the state of quality of being turbulent; riotous disposition; unruliness.

turbulent *adj* being in violent commotion; tumultuous; disposed to insubordination and disorder; riotous; disorderly.

turd *n* (*colloq*) a piece of excrement.

tureen *n* a large deep vessel for holding soup or other liquid food at the table.

turf *n* (*pl* **turfs, turves**) the surface layer of grass; a piece of earth with the grass growing on it; a sod; a kind of peaty substance cut from the surface of the ground and used as fuel.—**the turf** the racecourse; and hence, the occupation or profession of horse racing.—*vt* to cover with turf or sod.

turgescence *n* the act of swelling or state of being swelled; inflation; bombast.

turgescent *adj* growing turgid; in a swelling state.

turgid *adj* swelled; bloated; distended beyond its natural state; inflated; bombastic (*a turgid style*).

turgidity *n* the state or quality of being turgid; distension beyond its natural state; inflated manner of writing or speaking; bombast.

Turk *n* a native or inhabitant of Turkey.

turkey *n* a large bird farmed for its meat.

turkey buzzard *n* an American bird of the vulture family resembling a turkey.

turkey cock *n* a male turkey.

Turkey red *n* a brilliant and durable red colour produced by madder, etc, on cotton cloth.

Turkish *adj* pertaining to Turkey or to the Turks.

Turkish bath *n* a hot-air or steam bath inducing copious perspiration followed by massage, etc.

Turkish delight *n* a sweetmeat made of gelatine and coated with powdered sugar.

turmeric *n* a tropical Indian plant; its yellow powdered root used as a spice and a dye.

turmoil *n* harassing labour; molestation by tumult; commotion; disturbance.

turn *vt* to cause to move round on a centre or axis or as on a centre or axis; to put into circular motion; to rotate or revolve; to shape by means of a lathe; to direct or put into a different way, course, direction or channel (*to turn a person from a purpose, to turn the eyes towards*); to apply or devote (*to turn oneself to trade*); to put to some use or purpose; to shift or change with respect to the top, bottom, front, back, sides, etc; to reverse; to invert; to bring the inside of out; to change to another opinion or party; to convert; to translate; to alter into something else; to metamorphose; to transform, transmute, change; to revolve or ponder (*turn the matter over*); to consider and reconsider; to change from a fresh, sweet or natural condition; to cause to ferment, become sour, etc; to put, bring or place in a certain state or condition (*turned into ridicule*).— *vi* to have a circular or rotatory motion; to move round; to revolve or rotate; (*fig*) to depend, as on the chief point for decision or the like; to hinge (*the question turns on this*); to move the body, face or head in another direction; to change the position or posture of the body, as in bed; to retrace one's steps; to go or come back; to return; to offer opposition; to show fight; to take an opposite or a new course; to be directed (*the road turns to the right*); to have recourse (*knew not where to turn*); to be transformed or transmuted; to be converted; in a general sense, to become; to grow (*to turn pale*); to change from a fresh or sweet condition; to become sour or spoiled, as milk, wine, cider; to become dizzy or giddy, as the head or brain; to reel; to become nauseated or qualmish, as the stomach; to become inclined in an-

other direction; to change from ebb to flow or from flow to ebb, as the tide; to have a consequence; to result (*to turn to account*).—**to turn down** to lessen in volume, flow, etc; to reject; to refuse.—**to turn off** to switch off; (*sl*) to cause (someone) to lose interest in; (*sl*) to repel.—**to turn on** to switch on; to attack suddenly; to depend on; (*sl*) to excite sexually; (*sl*) to attract the interest of.—*n* the act of turning; a revolution or rotation; one round of a rope or cord; the point or place of deviation from a straight line; a winding; a bend; a flexure; an angle; a short walk, promenade or excursion; alteration of course; new direction or tendency; change or alteration generally; a turning point or crisis; vicissitude; opportunity enjoyed in alternation with another or others, or in rotation; due chance, time or opportunity; occasion; occasional act of kindness or malice (*a good* or *bad turn*); purpose; requirement; use; exigency (*to serve our turn*); form, shape or mould; manner; fashion; character or temper; (*colloq*) a short spell or a little job; (*colloq*) a nervous shock, such as is caused by alarm or sudden excitement; a performer's act; (*mus*) the sign ~ indicating a certain way of playing a group of notes.—**by turns** one after another; alternately; at intervals.—**in turn** in due order of succession.—**to a turn** to a nicety; exactly; perfectly.—**to take turns** to take each other's place alternately.

turncoat *n* one who forsakes his or her party or principles; a renegade.

turner *n* one who turns; one whose occupation is to form things with a lathe.

turning *n* a bend or flexure; the place where a road or street diverges from another road or street; the art or operation of shaping articles in a lathe.

turning point *n* the point where a thing or person turns back; the point at which a deciding change takes place, as from good to bad, increase to decrease or the opposite.

turnip *n* a biennial plant, allied to the cabbage, with a solid bulbous root, much cultivated as a vegetable and as food for sheep and cattle.

turnkey *n* a person who has charge of the keys of a prison for opening and fastening the doors.

turnout *n* a coming forth; a number of persons who have come out on some particular occasion (*a great turnout of spectators*); that which is brought prominently forward or exhibited; hence, an equipage; a horse or horses and carriage; the net quantity of produce yielded.

turnover *n* the act or result of turning over; the amount of money turned over or drawn in a business, as in a retail shop, in a given time; a fruit or meat pastry.

turn

turnip

turnpike *n* a turnstile; a gate set across a road in order to stop traffic or travellers, till toll is paid; a toll bar or toll gate; a turnpike road.

turnstile *n* a mechanical gate across a footpath or entrance which admits only one person at a time, used to control entry at sports grounds, etc.

turnstone *n* a bird of the plover family, so called from its practice of turning up small stones in search of worms, etc, on which it feeds.

turntable *n* a circular revolving platform used for shifting railway carriages from one line of rails to another and for reversing engines on the same line of rails; the part of a record player on which the record sits and revolves.

turpentine *n* an oily resin flowing naturally or by incision from coniferous trees, as the pine, larch, fir, etc; the oil or spirit of turpentine, used as a solvent, paint-thinner, etc.

turpitude *n* inherent baseness or vileness of principle, words or actions; shameful wickedness; moral depravity.

turquoise *n* a greenish-blue opaque precious stone, a favourite gem in rings and other articles of jewellery.

turret *n* a little tower on a building; an armoured shelter on a warship containing and revolving with, a gun.

turreted *adj* formed like a turret; furnished with turrets.

turtle *n* any of an order of aquatic reptiles living in the sea or fresh water, with legs modified for swimming and having a soft body encased in a hard shell.

turtle dove *n* a bird of the pigeon family, smaller than the ordinary domestic pigeon, celebrated for the constancy of its affection.

turtleneck *n* a high close-fitting tubular collar on a sweater.

Tuscan *adj* pertaining to Tuscany, in Italy.—*n* an inhabitant of Tuscany; (*archit*) the Tuscan order.

Tuscan order *n* one of the five orders of architecture, devoid of ornaments and having columns that are never fluted.

tusk *n* the long, pointed and often protruding tooth on each side of the jaw of certain animals, as the elephant; the canine tooth of the boar, walrus, hippopotamus, etc; the share of a plough, a harrow tooth, etc.

tusker *n* an animal with developed tusks, such as the elephant, boar, walrus, etc.

tussah silk *n* a strong, coarse, brown silk obtained from the cocoons of a wild Bengal silkworm.

tussle *n* a struggle; a conflict; a scuffle.—*vi* (**tussled, tussling**) to struggle; to scuffle.

tussock *n* a clump, tuft or small hillock of growing grass.

tusker

tussore *n* tussah silk.

tut *interj* an exclamation used to check or rebuke, or to express impatience or contempt.

tutelage *n* guardianship; protection bestowed; the state of being under a guardian; protection enjoyed.

tutelary, tutelar *adj* having the guardianship or charge of protecting a person or a thing; protecting.

tutor *n* one who has the care of the education of another; a private instructor; a teacher or instructor in anything; a university or college lecturer responsible for the teaching and supervision of a group of undergraduate students; (*law*) a guardian.—*vt* to instruct; to teach; to train or discipline.

tutorial *adj* belonging to a tutor or instructor.—*n* a period of tuition by a tutor to an individual or a small group.

tutorship *n* the office of a tutor, guardianship; tutelage.

tutti *adj, adv* (*mus*) all; a direction to every performer to take part in the execution of the passage or movement.—*n* a musical piece or passage so performed.

tutti-frutti *n* a type of ice cream containing pieces of chopped candied fruit.

tutu *n* a short, projecting, layered skirt worn by a ballerina.

tuxedo *n* (*pl* **tuxedos**) a dinner jacket.

tuyère *n* the nozzle of the pipe that introduces the blast of a blast furnace; the blast pipe itself, of which there are usually two.

TV abbreviation of **television**.

twaddle *vi* (**twaddled, twaddling**) to talk in a weak, silly or tedious manner; to prate. —*n* empty, silly talk; one who twaddles.

twain *adj* (*arch*) two.—*n* (*arch*) a pair or couple.

twang *n* a sharp, quick sound; an affected modulation of the voice; a kind of nasal sound; aftertaste; tang.—*vi* to sound with a quick, sharp noise; to make the sound of a string which is stretched and suddenly pulled; to utter with a sharp or nasal sound.—*vt* to make to sound, as by pulling and letting go suddenly; to utter with a short, sharp sound.—*interj* imitative of a sharp, quick sound, as that made by a bowstring.

tweak *vt* to twitch; to pinch and pull with a sudden jerk.—*n* a sharp pinch or jerk; a twitch.

twee *n* affectedly dainty; excessively or affectedly quaint.

tweed *n* a twilled woollen fabric.

tweeny *n* formerly, a young servant girl who helped two other maids with their work.

tweezers *npl* small pincers used to pluck out hairs, etc; small forceps.

twelfth *adj* the second after the tenth; the ordinal of twelve; being one of twelve equal parts of anything.—*n* one of twelve equal parts of anything.

Twelfth Night *n* the evening of the festival of the Epiphany.

twelve *adj* the sum of two and ten; twice six; a dozen.—*n* the number which consists of ten and two; a symbol representing twelve units, as 12 or XII.

twelvemonth *n* a year.

twentieth *adj* the ordinal of twenty; being one of twenty equal parts of anything.—*n* one of twenty equal parts.

twenty *adj* twice ten; proverbially, an indefinite number.—*n* the number of twice ten; a score; a symbol representing this, as 20 or XX.

twenty-one *n* the game of pontoon.

twice *adv* two times; doubly.

twiddle *vt* (**twiddled, twiddling**) to twirl, in a small way; to touch lightly or play with. —*vi* to play with a tremulous quivering motion; to fiddle with idly.

twig[1] *n* a small shoot or branch of a tree or other plant, of no definite length or size.

twig[2] *vt* (**twigged, twigging**) (*colloq*) to take notice of, to observe keenly.—*vi* (*colloq*) to see; to apprehend or understand.

twilight *n* the faint light which is reflected on the earth after sunset and before sunrise; crepuscular light; usually applied to evening twilight, morning twilight being called *dawn*; a faint light in general; hence, a dubious or uncertain medium through which anything is seen or examined (*the twilight of early history*).—*adj* imperfectly illuminated; seen, done or appearing by twilight.

twill *vt* to weave in such a manner as to produce a kind of diagonal ribbed appearance on the surface of the cloth.—*n* a variety of textile fabric so woven as to have the appearance of parallel diagonal lines or ribs over the surface; the raised lines made by twilling.

twin *n* one of two young produced at a birth by an animal that ordinarily bears but one; one very much resembling another.—*adj* applied to one or two born at a birth; very much resembling something else.—*vt* (**twinned, twinning**) to pair together.

twine *vt* (**twined, twining**) to twist; to form by twisting two or more threads or fibres; to entwine; to encircle.—*vi* to wind circularly or spirally; to make flexures; to ascend or grow up in convolutions about a support (*the plant twines*).—*n* a strong thread composed of two or three smaller threads or strands twisted together; a small cord or string.

twinge *vt* (**twinged, twinging**) to affect with a sharp, sudden pain; to torment with pinching or sharp pains; to pinch; to tweak.—*vi* to have a sudden, sharp, local pain.—a sudden, sharp pain; a darting, lo-

cal pain of short duration; a pinch; a tweak.

twinkle *vi* (**twinkled, twinkling**) to open and shut the eyes rapidly; to gleam; to sparkle (said of the eyes); to flash at intervals; to shine with a tremulous, intermittent light; to scintillate.—*n* a wink or quick motion of the eye; a gleam or sparkle of the eye or of a star; a twinkling.

twinkling *n* the act of that which twinkles; a quick movement of the eye; a wink; the time taken up in winking the eye; an instant.

Twins *npl* a constellation and sign of the zodiac; Gemini.

twinset *n* a jumper and cardigan designed to be worn together.

twirl *vt* to cause to turn round with rapidity; to cause to rotate rapidly, especially with the finger.—*vi* to revolve with velocity; to be whirled round.—*n* a rapid circular motion; a twist; a convolution.

twist *vt* to form by winding strands together; to twine; to form into a thread from many fine filaments; to contort; to crook spirally; to wreathe; to insinuate; to pervert; to turn from the true form or meaning.—*vi* to be joined by winding round each other; to be twisted; to writhe.—*n* the act of twisting; the result of the act; a convolution; a contortion; a flexure; what is formed by twisting, as a cord, thread, etc; a wrench; an unexpected event; manufactured tobacco in the form of a thick cord; the spiral in the bore of a rifled gun.

twig

twister *n* one that twists; a tornado; a dishonest person.

twit[1] *n* (*colloq*) a silly or foolish person.

twit[2] *vt* (**twitted, twitting**) to vex or annoy by bringing to remembrance a fault, imperfection, etc; to taunt; to upbraid, as for some previous act.

twitch *vt* to pull with a sudden jerk; to snatch.—*vi* to be suddenly contracted, as a muscle.—*n* a pull with a jerk; a short, quick pull; a short, spastic contraction of the muscles.

twitter *vi* to utter a succession of small, tremulous, intermitted notes, as certain birds do.—*n* a small intermittent noise or series of chirpings, as the sound made by a swallow.

two *adj* one and one together (often used indefinitely for a small number, as *a word or two*, *two or three hours*).—**in two** into two parts; asunder.—*n* the number which consists of one and one; the symbol representing it, as 2 or II.

two-edged *adj* having two cutting edges, one on each side; double-edged.

two-faced *adj* having two visages, like the Roman deity Janus; given to equivocation or double-dealing; insincere; hypocritical.

twofold *adj* double; multiplied by two; (*bot*)

two and two together growing from the same place (*twofold leaves*).—*adv* in a double degree; doubly.

two-handed *adj* having two hands; requiring the two hands to grasp (*a two-handed sword*); requiring two people.

twopence *n* the sum of two pence; a coin of this value; something of little value.

twopenny *adj* of the value of twopence; of little worth.

two-ply *adj* having two strands, as cord, or two thicknesses, as cloth, carpets, etc.

two-step *n* a dance in polka time.

two-stroke cycle *n* the cycle in one type of internal-combustion engine, completed in two strokes of the piston, or one revolution of the crankshaft.

two-time *vt* (**two-timed, two-timing**) (*colloq*) to deceive; to double-cross.

two-way *adj* allowing movement or operation in two opposite directions; involving two participants; involving mutual obligation; (of a radio, telephone, etc) capable of transmitting and receiving messages; (of a mirror) reflecting as a mirror on one side but able to be seen through from the other.

tyke, tike *n* a mongrel dog; (*colloq*) a cheeky child.

typewriter

tymbal *n* same as **timbal**.

tympani, tympanist *n* same as **timpani, timpanist**.

tympanitis *n* inflammation of the lining membrane of the middle ear or tympanum.

tympanum *n* (*pl* **tympana, tympanums**) (*anat*) the drum of the ear, a cavity of an irregular shape, constituting the middle ear; (*archit*) the triangular space in a pediment.

Tynewald *n* the legislative assembly of the Isle of Man.

type *n* a distinguishing mark or stamp; an emblem; an allegorical or symbolic representation of some object, which is called the antitype; a symbol; what prefigures something else; an example of any class considered as eminently possessing the properties or characters of the class; the ideal representative of a group; distinctive plan of structure; the model or pattern which becomes the subject of a copy; (*print*) a rectangular piece of metal, wood or other hard material having a raised letter, figure or other character on the upper end, which, when inked, gives impressions on paper; such types collectively.—**in type** set up, ready for printing; style of print.—*vt* (**typed, typing**) to serve as type of; to typify; to typewrite.

tyre

typescript *n* matter produced by a typewriter; a typed copy of a book, document, etc.

typesetter *n* one who sets up type.

typesetting *n* the act or process by which type is set up to be printed from.

typewriter *n* a machine with a keyboard for printing characters.

typhoid *adj* pertaining to or resembling typhus.—*n* typhoid fever.

typhoid fever *n* an infectious bacterial disease characterized by abdominal pains and diarrhoea and spread by contaminated food and water.

typhoon *n* a violent tropical cyclone originating in the western Pacific.

typhus *n* a disease characterized by fever, debility and rash, spread by body lice.

typical *adj* pertaining to a type; conforming to a particular type or character; representative of a particular type; characteristic.

typify *vt* (**typified, typifying**) to represent by an image or resemblance; to serve as the type of; to prefigure; to exemplify; to characterize.

typist *n* one who uses a typewriter.

typographer *n* a person who is employed or skilled in typography.

typographic, typographical *adj* pertaining to typography.

typography *n* the art of printing or typesetting; the way in which printed material is designed or set for printing; style in which anything is printed.

tyrannical *adj* pertaining to or acting as a tyrant; unjustly severe in government; oppressive to subordinates; despotic; cruel.

tyrannize *vi* (**tyrannized, tyrannizing**) to act the tyrant; to exercise arbitrary power; to rule with unjust and oppressive severity.

tyrannosaur, tyrannosaurus *n* a very large carnivorous dinosaur which walked erect on its hind limbs.

tyrannous *adj* tyrannical; unjustly severe; oppressive.

tyranny *n* the rule of a tyrant; despotic exercise of power; cruel government; severity; oppression.

tyrant *n* a monarch or other ruler or master who uses power to oppress those under him or her; a cruel sovereign or master; an oppressor.

tyre *n* a band of hollow, inflated rubber around the rim of a wheel to grip the road and cushion vibration.

tyro, tiro *n* (*pl* **tyro, tiros**) a novice or mere beginner; a beginner in learning.

tzar, tzarina *n* same as **tsar, tsarina**.

U

U the twenty-first letter and the fifth vowel in the English alphabet.

ubiquitous *adj* existing or being everywhere; omnipresent.

ubiquity *n* the state of being ubiquitous; existing everywhere at the same time; omnipresence.

U-boat *n* a German submarine (from German *Unterseeboot*).

udal *adj* a term in Orkney and Shetland equivalent to *allodial* or *freehold* .

udaller, udalman *n* a freeholder without feudal superior.

udder *n* the glandular organ of cows and other quadrupeds in which milk is secreted and retained for the nourishment of their young.

UFO an abbreviation of **unidentified flying object**.

ugh *interj* an expression of horror or recoil: usually accompanied by a shudder.

ugly *adj* possessing qualities opposite to beauty; offensive to the sight; deformed; morally repulsive; hateful.—*n* a kind of sunshade formerly worn by ladies in front of their bonnets.

ugly duckling *n* an apparently unattractive or untalented child who grows up to be, or who has the potential to grow up to be, very attractive or talented.

UHF an abbreviation of **ultra-high frequency**.

ukase *n* a Russian edict or order, which had the force of law, emanating from the former imperial government.

ukulele *n* a small four-stringed guitar.

ulcer *n* a sore on the surface of the skin or a mucous membrane, accompanied by secretion of pus or some kind of discharge.

ulcerate *vti* (**ulcerated, ulcerating**) to make or become ulcerous.

ulceration *n* the process of becoming ulcerous; the state of being ulcerated; an ulcer.

ulcerous *adj* affected with an ulcer or with ulcers; like an ulcer.

ullage *n* the quantity that a cask lacks of being full.

ulna *n* (*pl* **ulnae**) the larger of the two bones of the forearm, reaching from the elbow to the wrist, its upper extremity forming the point of the elbow.

ulotrichous *adj* pertaining to crisp or woolly hair.

ulster *n* a long loose overcoat originally made of heavy cloth in Ulster.

ult contracted form of **ultimo**.

ulterior *adj* being beyond or on the further side; not at present in view or consideration; more remote; distant (*ulterior views* or *objects*); hidden, not evident (*ulterior motives*).

ultimate *adj* furthest; most remote in place; last or final; arrived at as a final result; such that we cannot go beyond; incapable of further resolution or analysis.

ultimatum *n* (*pl* **ultimatums, ultimata**) any final proposal or statement of conditions, refusal of which causes negotiation to end and other action to be taken; in diplomatic negotiations, the final terms offered by a negotiator or party.

ultimo *adj* last, as distinguished from the current month and all others (usually contracted to **ult**).

ultra- *prefix* beyond; exceedingly; in a high degree (*ultraconservative, ultrahigh*).—*adj* signifying beyond due limit; extreme (*ultra measures*).

ultra-high frequency *n* (often abbreviated to **UHF**) a radio frequency in the range between 300 megahertz and 3000 megahertz, used for television and some kinds of radar.

ultramarine *adj* situated or being beyond the sea .—*n* a brilliant pure blue colour or pigment.

ultramontane *adj* being or lying beyond mountains.—*n* someone who lives beyond mountains, particularly south of the Alps.

ultrasonic *adj* of waves and vibrations, having a frequency beyond the range of human hearing.

ultrasound *n* in medicine, the use of ultrasonic waves to detect abnormalities in human tissue.

ultraviolet *adj* (of light waves) shorter than the wavelengths of visible light and longer than X-rays.

udder

ultra vires *adv* exceeding the legal powers of a court, etc.

ululate *vi* (**ululated, ululating**) to howl, as a dog or wolf.

umbel *n* (*bot*) a particular type of inflorescence which consists of a number of flower stalks or pedicels nearly equal in length and spreading from a common centre, each bearing a single flower, as in the ivy, carrot, etc.

umbelliferous *adj* producing umbels; bearing umbels.

umber *n* a soft earthy combination forming a pigment of an olive-brown colour in its raw state but much redder when burnt.

umbilical *adj* pertaining to the navel; formed in the middle like a navel; navel-shaped; central.

umbilical cord *n* (*anat*) a cord-like structure which passes from the navel of the foetus or embryo of the higher mammals to the placenta.

umbilicus *n* (*pl* **umbilici**) (*anat*) the navel.

umble pie *n* (*arch*) humble pie.

umbles *npl* (*arch*) the humbles or entrails of a deer.

umbo *n* (*pl* **umbones, umbos**) the boss or protuberant part in the centre of a shield; a similarly shaped part, as in the centre of the cap of a mushroom or in the centre of the tympanum.

umbra *n* (*astron*) the total shadow of the earth or moon in an eclipse or the dark cone projected from a planet or satellite on the side opposite to the sun, as contrasted with the *penumbra*; the dark central portion of a sun spot surrounded by a brighter annular portion.

umbrage *n* a shade; shadow; shade caused by foliage; hence, the feeling of being overshadowed; jealousy of another, as standing in one's light or way; suspicion of injury; offence; resentment.

umbrella *n* a portable shade, screen or canopy of silk, cotton, etc, extended on an expanding frame of bars of steel, cane, etc, inserted in or fastened to a rod or stick and carried in the hand for sheltering a person from the rays of the sun or from rain or snow; a general protection.

umiak *n* a flat-bottomed skin boat rowed by the Inuit.

umlaut *n* (*philol*) the change of a vowel in one syllable through the influence of one of the vowels, *a, i, u*, in the syllable immediately following and marked by ¨.

umpire *n* a person to whose sole decision a controversy or question between parties is referred; one agreed upon as a judge, arbiter or referee in case of conflict of opinions; an official who enforces the rules in certain sports.—*vt* (**umpired, umpiring**) to referee (a match); to adjudicate.—*vi* to act as an umpire.

umbrella

umpteen *adj* (*colloq*) an indefinite number.

un- *prefix* not; opposite of; contrary to; reversal of an action or state.

unabashed *adj* not abashed or daunted.

unabated *adj* not diminished in strength or violence.

unable *adj* not able; not having sufficient ability; not equal for some task.

unabridged *adj* not abridged; not shortened.

unacceptable *adj* not acceptable or pleasing; not welcome; not such as will be received with pleasure.

unaccommodating *adj* not ready to accommodate or oblige.

unaccompanied *adj* having no attendants, companions or followers; (*mus*) performed or written without an accompaniment.

unaccountable *adj* not to be accounted for; not explicable; such that no reason or explanation can be given.

unacknowledged *adj* not acknowledged or recognized; not owned, confessed or avowed.

unacquainted *adj* not having formed an acquaintance; not having knowledge: followed by with.

unadorned *adj* not adorned; not decorated; not embellished; plain.

unadulterated *adj* not adulterated; pure; unmixed.

unadvised *adj* unwise, imprudent; not advised.

unaffected *adj* not having the feelings moved; not influenced; not showing affectation; natural; not artificial; simple; sincere.

unalloyed *adj* not alloyed; having no admixture of alloy; without disturbing elements (*unalloyed happiness*).

unalterable *adj* not alterable; unchangeable; immutable.

unambiguous *adj* not of doubtful meaning; plain; clear; certain.

unambitious *adj* free from ambition; not affecting show; not showy or prominent.

unanimity *n* the state of being unanimous.

unanimous *adj* being of one mind; agreeing in opinion or determination; formed by unanimity (*a unanimous vote*).

unanswerable *adj* not to be satisfactorily answered; not capable of refutation.

unapproachable *adj* that cannot be approached; inaccessible; not to be equalled or rivalled; aloof; unfriendly.

unarmed *adj* not having on arms or armour; not equipped.

unasked *adj* not asked; not invited; unsolicited; not sought by entreaty or care.

unassailable *adj* incapable of being assailed; not to be moved or shaken from a purpose; not open to attack; not open to criticism or doubt.

unassimilated *adj* not assimilated; (*physiol*) not taken into the system by way of digestion.

unassuming *adj* not assuming; not bold or forward; not arrogant; modest.

unattached *adj* not attached; not married, not engaged, not having a permanent partner; not belonging to a particular, group, organization, etc.

unattended *adj* not accompanied; having no retinue or attendance.

unau *n* the two-toed sloth of Brazil.

unauthorized *adj* not warranted by proper authority; not duly commissioned; not having official permission.

unavailing *adj* not having the effect desired; of no avail; ineffectual; useless; vain.

unavenged *adj* not avenged; not having obtained revenge or satisfaction; not punished; not atoned for.

unavoidable *adj* not avoidable; inevitable; compulsory.

unaware *adj* not aware; not knowing; not cognizant.—*adv* unawares.

unawares *adv* unexpectedly; without previous preparation; inadvertently.

unbalanced *adj* not balanced; not in equipoise; mentally unstable; lacking soundness of judgment; not brought to an equality of debit and credit.

unbar *vt* (**unbarred, unbarring**) to remove a bar or bars from; to unfasten; to unlock.

unbearable *adj* not to be borne or endured; intolerable.

unbecoming *adj* not becoming; improper; indecorous; not attractive.

unbelief *n* disbelief; scepticism or lack of belief, especially in religious matters.

unbeliever *n* one who does not believe, especially in a religion.

unbelieving *adj* incredulous; lacking belief, especially in religious matters; sceptical.

unbend *vi* (*pret, pp* **unbent**, *ppr* **unbending**) to straighten from a bent shape; to become relaxed or not bent; to rid oneself of constraint; to act with freedom; to give up stiffness or austerity of manner.—*vt* to free from bend or flexure; to relax; to set at ease for a time (*to unbend the mind*); (*naut*) to unfasten from the yards and stays, as sails.

unbending *adj* unyielding; resolute; inflexible.

unbiased *adj* without bias; unprejudiced.

unbidden *adj* not commanded; spontaneous; uninvited; not requested to attend.

unblemished *adj* not blemished or tarnished; pure; spotless (*unblemished reputation*); free from fault.

unblushing *adj* not blushing; lacking shame; impudent.

unborn *adj* not yet born; future; to come; never born or brought into existence.

unbosom *vt* (*refl*) to disclose, as one's secret opinions or feelings .

unbounded *adj* having no bound or limit; unlimited in extent; very great; excessive.

unbridled *adj* unrestrained; violent.

unbroken *adj* not broken; whole; not subdued; not tamed and rendered tractable; not interrupted; continuous.

unburden *vt* to rid of a load or burden; (*refl*) to relieve the mind or heart of, as by disclosing troubles, secrets, etc, to another.

uncalled-for *adj* not required; not needed or demanded; unwarranted; not properly brought forward.

uncanny *adj* not canny; eerie; mysterious; not of this world; of evil and supernatural character.

unceasing *adj* not ceasing; not intermitting; continual.

unceasingly *adv* in an unceasing manner; without intermission; continually.

unceremonious *adj* not using ceremony or form; not ceremonious; familiar; abrupt; rude.

uncertain *adj* not certain; doubtful; not certainly known; ambiguous; not having certain knowledge; not sure; unreliable; not to be depended on; undecided; not having the mind made up; not steady; fitful; fickle; inconstant; capricious.

uncertainty *n* the quality or state of being uncertain; lack of certainty; doubtfulness; state of doubting; dubiety; hesitation; something not certainly and exactly known; a contingency.

unchallenged *adj* not challenged or called to account; not objected to; not called in question.

unchanging *adj* not changing; not subject to changes; unalterable.

uncharitable *adj* not charitable; ready to think evil or impute bad motives; harsh; censorious; severe in judging.

uncial *adj* a term applied to letters of a large size used in ancient Latin and Greek manuscripts.—*n* an uncial letter.

uncivil *adj* not courteous; ill-mannered; rude; coarse.

uncivilized *adj* not civilized; barbarous; savage; unsophisticated.

uncle *n* the brother of one's father or mother; also applied to the husband of one's aunt; (*colloq*) pawnbroker.

unclean *adj* not clean; foul; dirty; filthy; morally impure; foul with sin; wicked; evil; ceremonially impure according to Jewish law.

unclothe *vt* (**unclothed, unclothing**) to strip of clothes; to make naked; to divest of covering; to uncover.

unclothed *adj* stripped of clothing; not clothed; lacking clothes.

unclouded *adj* free from clouds; free from gloom; clear; bright.

uncoil *vti* to unwind or open, as the turns of a rope or a spiral spring; to open out its coils, as a snake.

uncoloured *adj* not coloured; not heightened or exaggerated in description.

uncomfortable *adj* affording no comfort; causing bodily discomfort; giving uneasiness; uneasy; ill at ease.

uncomfortably *adv* in an uncomfortable manner.

uncommon *adj* not common; infrequent; rare; remarkable; extraordinary.

uncommonly *adv* rarely; not usually; remarkably.

uncommunicative *adj* not apt to communicate to others; not willing to talk or express an opinion; reserved.

uncompanionable *adj* not companionable or sociable.

uncompromising *adj* not accepting of any compromise; not prepared to compromise; not agreeing to terms; inflexible.

unconcern *n* lack of concern; freedom from solicitude; cool and undisturbed state of mind.

unconcerned *adj* feeling no concern or solicitude; not involved; having or taking no interest; not affected.

unconditional *adj* not limited by any conditions; absolute; unreserved.

unconditionally *adv* without terms or conditions.

unconfined *adj* not confined; free from restraint or control; not having narrow limits.

unconfirmed *adj* not firmly established; not strengthened or established by additional testimony; not confirmed according to the church ritual.

unconscionable *adj* not conscionable; exceeding the limits of any reasonable claim or expectation; inordinate; unreasonable (*an unconscionable demand* or *claim*).

unconscious *adj* not conscious; devoid of consciousness; having no mental perception; not knowing; not perceiving.— *n* the deepest level of the mind containing feelings and emotions of which one is unaware and unable to control.

unconsciously *adv* in an unconscious manner; without perception.

unconsciousness *n* the state of being unconscious; lack of perception.

unconstitutional *adj* not .agreeable to the constitution of a country; contrary to the principles of the constitution.

unconstrained *adj* free from constraint; voluntary; having no feeling that checks one's words or actions.

uncontested *adj* not contested or disputed.

uncontrollable *adj* that cannot be controlled, ruled or restrained; ungovernable.

unconvinced *adj* not convinced; not persuaded.

uncoil

unconvincing *adj* not sufficient to convince.

uncork *vt* to draw the cork from.

uncouple *vt* (**uncoupled, uncoupling**) to loose or disconnect.

uncouth *adj* lacking in manners; rough.

uncover *vt* to remove a cover or covering from; to divest of a cover or covering; hence, to lay bare; to disclose.—*vi* to bare the head; to take off one's hat.

uncovered *adj* deprived of or not provided with a cover or covering; bare; naked.

uncritical *adj* not critical; lacking in critical powers; not according to the rules of criticism.

uncrossed *adj* not crossed; not traversed; not thwarted; (of a cheque) not crossed so as to indicate that it must be paid through an account at a bank.

unction *n* the act of anointing or rubbing with an unguent, ointment or oil; an unguent; a salve; (*fig*) something soothing; that quality in language, mode of address or manner which excites devotion or sympathy; religious fervour; sham devotional fervour; oiliness.

unctuous *adj* of an oily or greasy character; fat and clammy; soapy; greasy or soapy to the feel when rubbed or touched by the fingers, a characteristic of steatite and other minerals; oily; smarmy; too suave; insincerely charming.

uncultivated *adj* not cultivated or tilled; rough or rude in manners; not improved by labour, study, care, etc.

uncurl *vt* to straighten out, as something curled.—*vi* to fall from a curled state, as ringlets; to become straight.

uncut *adj* not cut; not cut open at the edges, as the leaves of a book.

undaunted *adj* not daunted; not depressed by fear; fearless; intrepid.

undeceive *vt* (**undeceived, undeceiving**) to free from deception, misapprehension or mistake, whether caused by others or by oneself.

undecided *adj* not decided or determined; not settled; not having the mind made up; hesitating; irresolute.

undefended *adj* not defended; being without works of defence; (*law*) not characterized by a defence being put forward.

undefinable *adj* not definable; indefinable.

undefined *adj* not defined; not having its limits distinctly marked or seen.

undemonstrative *adj* not demonstrative; not apt to let the feelings betray themselves; reserved; cold in manner.

undeniable *adj* incapable of being denied; indisputable; obviously true.

under *prep* in a lower place or position than; so as to be overtopped, overhung or covered by; beneath; denoting a state of being loaded, oppressed or distressed by;

subject to the government, direction, instruction or influence of; in a state of liability or limitation with respect to; inferior to in rank, social position, etc; inferior to or less than with respect to number, quantity, value, etc; falling short of; included in; in the same category division, class, etc, as; with the character, pretext or cover of; being the subject of (*under discussion*).—**under the breath** with a low voice; in a whisper; very softly.—**under the rose** in secret.—**under way** (*naut*) having just weighed anchor or left moorings and making progress through the water.—*adv* in a lower or subordinate condition or degree (*to keep a person under*).—*adj* lower in position, rank or degree; subject; subordinate (*under sheriff*).

undercharge *vt* (**undercharged, undercharging**) to charge less than a fair price for; to take too low a price from.—*n* too low a charge or price.

underclothes, underclothing *n* clothes worn under others or next the skin; underwear; undergarments.

undercurrent *n* a current below the surface of the water; (*fig*) an influence at work out of sight or not readily apparent.

undercut *n* the meat on the under side of the bone of a sirloin of beef; a blow delivered with an upward swing.—*vt* (*pret, pp* **undercut**, *ppr* **undercutting**) to reduce prices so as to sell cheaper than a competitor; (in golf) to hit a ball so that it rises sharply and falls almost dead.

underdog *n* a person in an inferior position; the loser in an encounter, competition or contest; the person most likely to lose in an encounter, contest, etc.

underdone *adj* (of meat, etc) cooked lightly or cooked insufficiently.

underestimate *vt* (**underestimated, underestimating**) to estimate at too low a rate.—*n* an estimate at too low a rate.

undergo *vt* (*pret* **underwent**, *pp* **undergone**, *ppr* **undergoing**) to pass through; to be subjected to; to experience (*to undergo changes*).

undergraduate *n* a student or member of a university or college who has not taken his or her first degree.

undergrowth *n* shrubs or small trees growing among large ones.

underground *adj* below the surface of the ground; secret; subversive; (of non-commercial newspapers, films, etc) that are radical, unconventional, anti-establishment, etc.—*n* a railway system running through underground tunnels; a movement or organization which is secret or outside the established or accepted society; a secret group working for the overthrow of the government or the expulsion of occupying forces.

underhand *adv* by secret means; in a clandestine manner and often with a bad design.—*adj* working by stealth; clandestine; sly and devious; (in cricket) bowling with the hand under the ball and lower than the shoulder.

underlie *vt* (*pret* **underlay**, *pp* **underlain**, *ppr* **underlying**) to lie beneath; to be situated under; to be at the basis of; to form the foundation of; to be subject or liable to.—*vi* to lie beneath.

underline *vt* (**underlined, underlining**) to mark underneath or below with a line; to underscore; to emphasize; to stress.

underling *n* an inferior person or agent; a subordinate.

underlying *adj* lying beneath or under; (*geol*) applied to rocks or strata lying below others; basic; fundamental.

undermine *vt* (**undermined, undermining**) to wear away or weaken; to injure or weaken, especially by subtle or insidious means.

undermost *adj* lowest in place, rank or condition.

underneath *adv* beneath; in a lower place.—*prep* under; beneath.

underpants *npl* an undergarment worn over the buttocks, hips and the lower part of the abdomen, particularly applied to such an undergarment worn by males.

underpin *vt* (**underpinned, underpinning**) to pin or support underneath; to place something under for support or foundation when a previous support is removed.

underprivileged *adj* lacking the basic rights or standard of living of other members of society.

underrate *vt* (**underrated, underrating**) to rate too low; to undervalue.

under-secretary *n* a secretary subordinate to the principal secretary, especially in a government department.

undershoot *vt* (*pret, pp* **undershot**, *ppr* **undershooting**) to shoot short of; to fail to reach in aiming at; (of an aeroplane) to land before the start of the runway.

undersized *adj* being of a size or stature less than common.

underskirt *n* a woman's undergarment worn beneath a skirt; a waist-length petticoat or slip.

understand *vt* (*pret, pp* **understood**, *ppr* **understanding**) to apprehend or comprehend fully; to know or apprehend the meaning of; to perceive or discern by the mind; to have just and adequate ideas of; to comprehend; to see through; to be informed; to learn; governing a clause; to suppose to mean; to interpret (*how do you understand it?*); to take as meant or implied; to infer; to assume; to supply or leave to be supplied mentally; to recognize as implied or meant although not ex-

underpin

933

pressed.—*vi* to have the use of the intellectual faculties; to have understanding; to be informed by another; to learn.

understanding *adj* knowing; skilful; intelligent.—*n* the act of one who understands or comprehends; comprehension; apprehension and appreciation; discernment; intelligence between two or more persons; anything mutually understood or agreed upon; that power by which we perceive, conceive and apprehend; that mental faculty which comprehends the just import, relations and value of all notions and ideas, however derived; the faculty of forming judgments on the communications made through the senses; in a more popular sense, clear insight and intelligence in practical matters; wisdom and discernment.

understate *vt* (**understated, understating**) to state (something) in restrained terms; to state less forcefully than is necessary or desirable; to declare to be less than is the actual case.

understudy *n* a performer who makes a study of a theatrical part so as to be able to take it in the absence of the regular performer.—*vti* (**understudied, understudying**) to learn a role or part so as to be able to replace (the actor playing it); to act as an understudy (to).

undertake *vt* (*pret* **undertook**, *pp* **undertaken**, *ppr* **undertaking**) to take on oneself; to lay oneself under obligations to perform or execute; to pledge oneself to do (often with infinitives); to engage in; to take in hand; to set about; to attempt; to warrant; to answer for; to guarantee (often governing a clause, as *undertook that he would go*).

undertaker *n* one who undertakes any business; one who manages and provides things necessary for funerals.

undertaking *n* that which a person undertakes; an enterprise; a task; a promise; an obligation.

undertone *n* a low or subdued tone; a tone lower than is usual, as in speaking.

undertow *n* a current of water below the surface in a different direction from that at the surface; the backward flow of a wave breaking on a beach.

undervalue *vt* (**undervalued, undervaluing**) to value or estimate below the real worth; to esteem lightly; to hold in too low an estimation.

underwear *n* clothes worn next to the skin under outer clothing; underclothes; undergarments.

underwhelm *vt* (*colloq*) to fail to impress; to disappoint.

underwood *n* small trees and bushes that grow among large trees; coppice; underbrush.

underworld *n* the place of departed souls; Hades; the criminal world of society.

underwrite *vt* (*pret* **underwrite**, *pp* **underwritten**, *ppr* **underwriting**) to write below or under; to agree to finance (an undertaking); to set one's name to a policy of insurance along with others, for the purpose of becoming answerable for loss or damage to a certain amount.

undeviating *adj* not departing from a rule, principle or purpose; steady; regular.

undine *n* a female water spirit resembling in character the sylphs or spirits of the air and corresponding somewhat to the naiads of classical mythology.

undiscerning *adj* not discerning; lacking judgment or discrimination.

undiscovered *adj* not discovered; not laid open to view; lying hid.

undisguised *adj* not disguised; not covered with a mask; hence, open; candid; artless.

undistinguished *adj* not having any distinguishing mark; not treated with any particular respect; not famous; not distinguished by any particular eminence.

undisturbed *adj* free from interruption; not molested or hindered; calm; tranquil; not agitated.

undivided *adj* not divided; unbroken; whole (*one's undivided attention*).

undo *vt* (*pret* **undid**, *pp* **undone**, *ppr* **undoing**) to reverse, as something which has been done; to annul; to untie or unfasten; to unravel; to open out; to bring ruin or distress upon; to ruin the morals, reputation or prospects of; to destroy; to impoverish.

undoing *n* the reversal of what has been done; ruin; destruction.

undone *adj* untied or unfastened; reversed; ruined.

undoubted *adj* not doubted; not called in question; indubitable; indisputable.

undreamed-of, undreamt-of *adj* not thought of or imagined.

undress *vi* to take off one's clothes.—*vt* to take off the clothes of.—*n* in the services, uniform worn normally.

undressed *adj* divested of dress; not clothed; not prepared; in a raw state.

undue *adj* improper; unworthy; excessive; inordinate (*an undue attachment to forms*).

undulate *vi* (**undulated, undulating**) to have a wavy motion; to rise and fall in waves; to move in curving or bending lines; to wave.—*vt* to cause to wave or move with a wavy motion.

undulation *n* the act of undulating; a waving motion; a wavy form.

undulatory *adj* having an undulating character; moving in the manner of waves; pertaining to such a motion.

unduly *adv* improperly; excessively; inordinately.

unearned *adj* not earned by labour or services; not deserved.

unearth *vt* to drive or bring forth from an earth or burrow; to bring to light; to discover or find out.

unearthly *adj* not earthly; not terrestrial; supernatural; weird.

uneasy *adj* troubled; anxious; awkward; causing constraint, discomfort or lack of ease; irksome.

uneconomical *adj* wasteful; not profitable.

uneducated *adj* not educated; illiterate.

unemployed *adj* not employed; having no work or occupation; not being in use.— **the unemployed** people who are out of work.

unending *adj* not ending; having no end; perpetual; continuous.

unenterprising *adj* not enterprising; not adventurous; not resourceful.

unenviable *adj* not enviable; not to be envied or viewed with envy (*an unenviable notoriety*).

unequal *adj* not equal; not of the same size, length, breadth, quantity, quality, strength, talents, age, station; inadequate; insufficient; not equable or uniform.

unequalled *adj* not to be equalled; unparalleled; unrivalled.

unequivocal *adj* not equivocal; not doubtful; clear; evident; not ambiguous.

unerring *adj* committing no mistake; incapable of error; incapable of missing the mark; certain.

uneven *adj* not level, smooth or plain; rough; not straight; crooked; not uniform or equable; changeable; not fair, just or true; (*arith*) odd; not divisible by 2 without a remainder.

unevenness *n* the state or quality of being uneven; inequality of surface; lack of uniformity; variability.

uneventful *adj* ordinary; routine; without exciting incidents.

unexceptionable *adj* not liable to any exception or objection; unobjectionable; irreproachable; faultless.

unexpected *adj* not expected; not looked for; unforeseen; sudden.

unexplored *adj* not explored; not examined by any traveller.

unfailing *adj* not liable to fail; ever fulfilling a hope, promise or want; sure; certain.

unfair *adj* not fair; not honest; not impartial; disingenuous; using trick or artifice; proceeding from trick or dishonesty.

unfaithful *adj* not observant of promises, vows, allegiance or duty; faithless; violating trust or confidence; violating the wedding vow; committing adultery.

unfamiliar *adj* not familiar; not well known by frequent use; having an element of strangeness.

unfasten *vt* to loose; to unbind; to untie.

unfavourable *adj* not favourable; not propitious; discouraging; giving an adverse judgment or opinion; somewhat prejudicial.

unfeeling *adj* devoid of feeling; insensible; without sensibility; devoid of sympathy with others; hard-hearted.

unfetter *vt* to loose from fetters; to unchain; to unshackle; to free from restraint; to set at liberty.

unfinished *adj* not finished; not complete; imperfect; lacking the last hand or touch.

unfit *adj* not fit; improper; unsuitable; unbecoming (said of things); lacking suitable qualifications, physical or moral; not suited or adapted; not competent (of persons).—*vt* (**unfitted, unfitting**) to render unfit; to make unsuitable; to deprive of the strength, skill or proper qualities for anything.

unfitting *adj* improper; unbecoming.

unflagging *adj* not flagging; not drooping; maintaining strength or spirit.

unflappable *adj* (*colloq*) not easily agitated; calm.

unflinching *adj* not flinching; not shrinking.

unfold *vt* to open the folds of; to expand; to spread out; to lay open to view or contemplation; to disclose; to reveal.—*vi* to become gradually expanded; to open out; to become disclosed or developed; to develop itself.

unforced *adj* not forced or compelled; not constrained; not feigned; not artificially assumed or heightened; not strained; easy; natural.

unforeseen *adj* not foreseen; not suspected.—**the unforeseen** that which is not foreseen or expected.

unforgettable *adj* never to be forgotten; not lost to memory; impressive; exceptional.

unforgivable *adj* incapable of being forgiven; unpardonable.

unforgiven *adj* not forgiven; not pardoned.

unforgiving *adj* not forgiving; not disposed to overlook or pardon offences; implacable.

unformed *adj* not having been formed; not fashioned; not moulded into regular shape.

unfortunate *adj* not successful; not prosperous; unlucky; unhappy.—*n* one who is unfortunate.

unfounded *adj* having no real foundation; groundless; idle; baseless.

unfriendliness *n* the quality of being unfriendly; lack of kindness.

unfriendly *adj* not friendly; not kind or benevolent; not favourable.—*adv* in an unkind manner; not as a friend.

unfrock *vi* to deprive or divest of a frock; hence, to deprive of the character and privileges of a priest or clergyman.

unfruitful *adj* not producing fruit or offspring; barren; unproductive; not fertile (*an unfruitful soil*); not productive of good (*an unfruitful life*); fruitless; ineffectual.

unfulfilled *adj* not fulfilled; not accomplished.

unfurl *vt* to loose from a furled state; to expand to the wind.

unfurnished *adj* not furnished; not supplied with furniture.

ungainliness *n* the state or character of being ungainly; clumsiness; awkwardness.

ungainly *adj* clumsy; awkward; uncouth; ill-shaped in person.

unglazed *adj* not furnished with glass (as windows); lacking glass windows; not covered with vitreous matter (*unglazed pottery*).

ungodly *adj* not godly; godless; wicked; impious; sinful; (*colloq*) outrageous.

ungovernable *adj* incapable of being governed, ruled or restrained; refractory; unruly, wild; unbridled.

ungoverned *adj* not governed; unbridled; licentious.

ungraceful *adj* not graceful; lacking in grace and elegance; inelegant; clumsy.

ungracious *adj* unmannerly; rude; not well received; not favoured.

ungrammatical *adj* not according to the rules of grammar.

ungrateful *adj* not grateful; not feeling thankful or showing gratitude; making ill returns for kindness; unpleasant; unacceptable; disagreeable; harsh.

ungrounded *adj* having no foundation or support; groundless; baseless; unfounded.

ungrudging *adj* not grudging; freely giving; liberal; hearty.

unguarded *adj* not guarded; having no guard or watch; not being on one's guard; not attentive to danger; not cautious; negligent; not done or spoken with caution.

unguent *n* any soft composition used as an ointment or for the lubrication of machinery.

unguided *adj* not guided, led or conducted; not regulated; ungoverned.

ungulate *n* a hoofed mammal, one of a large order including the horse, rhinoceros, tapir, hippopotamus, swine, camel, deer, giraffe, ox, sheep, goat, elephant and cony.

unhallowed *adj* not hallowed, consecrated or dedicated to sacred purposes; unholy; profane; impious.

unhampered *adj* not hampered, hindered or restricted.

unhand *vt* to take the hand or hands from; to release from a grasp; to let go.

unhappily *adv* in an unhappy manner; unfortunately; by ill fortune; as ill luck would have it.

unhappiness *n* the state of being unhappy; misfortune; ill luck.

unhappy *adj* not happy; not cheerful; in

unicorn

some degree miserable or wretched; marked by ill fortune or mishap; ill-omened; evil.

unhealthy *adj* lacking health; not sound and vigorous of body; habitually weak or indisposed; lacking vigour of growth; unfavourable to the preservation of health (*an unhealthy season* or *city*); adapted to generate disease; unwholesome; insalubrious (*an unhealthy climate*); not indicating health; resulting from bad health; morbid.

unheard *adj* not heard; not perceived by the ear; not admitted to audience.

unheard-of *adj* unprecedented; such as was never known before; not known to fame; not celebrated.

unheeded *adj* not heeded; disregarded; neglected; unnoticed.

unheeding *adj* not heeding; careless; negligent.

unheralded *adj* not announced in advance; not expected.

unhesitating *adj* not hesitating; not remaining in doubt; prompt; ready.

unhinge *vt* (**unhinged, unhinging**) to take from the hinges; to unsettle; to render unstable or wavering; to render mentally unstable; to discompose or disorder (the mind, opinions); to put quite out of sorts; to incapacitate by disturbing the nerves.

unhitch *vt* to disengage from a fastening.

unholy *adj* not holy; not sacred; not hallowed or consecrated; impious; wicked.

unhonoured *adj* not honoured; not regarded with veneration; not celebrated.

unhook *vt* to loose from a hook; to undo the hook or hooks of.

unhoped-for *adj* not hoped for.

unhurt *adj* not hurt; not harmed; free from wound or injury.

unicameral *adj* consisting of a single chamber (said of a legislative body).

unicellular *adj* consisting of a single cell; exhibiting only a single cell.

uniclinal *adj* inclined in one direction only; (*geol*) applied to a bend or inclination of a stratum either up or down, opposed to *anticlinal* and *synclinal*.

unicorn *n* a legendary animal with the head, neck and body of a horse, the legs of a deer, the tail of a lion and a long horn growing out of the forehead.

unidentified flying object *n* (often abbreviated to **UFO**) any object which is detected in the sky but cannot be identified, sometimes alleged to have come from another planet.

unification *n* the act of unifying.

uniform *adj* having always the same form; not changing in shape, appearance, character, etc; not varying in degree or rate; equable; invariable; of the same kind or matter all through; homogeneous; consistent at all times; conforming to one rule or mode.—*n* a dress of the same kind, fabrics, fashion or general appearance as others worn by the members of the same body, whether military, naval or any other, intended as a distinctive costume.

uniformity *n* the state or character of being uniform; a state of matters in which sameness is exhibited; freedom from variation or difference; conformity to one type.

unify *vt* (**unified, unifying**) to form into one; to reduce to unity; to view as one.

unilateral *adj* one-sided; pertaining to one side; of or by one side only; (*bot*) growing chiefly to one side.

unilluminated *adj* not illuminated; not enlightened; dark; ignorant.

unimaginable *adj* not capable of being imagined, conceived or thought of; inconceivable.

unimagined *adj* not imagined, conceived or formed in idea.

unimpaired *adj* not impaired; not diminished; not enfeebled by time or injury.

unimpassioned *adj* not impassioned; not moved or actuated by passion; calm; tranquil; not violent.

unimpeachable *adj* not impeachable; not to be called in question; blameless; irreproachable.

unimportant *adj* not important; not of great moment.

uninhabitable *adj* not inhabitable; unfit to be the residence of people.

uninhabited *adj* not inhabited; having no inhabitants.

uninhibited *adj* free from restraints or inhibitions; not repressed; spontaneous; relaxed.

uninjured *adj* not injured; not hurt; suffering no harm.

uninspired *adj* not having received any supernatural instruction or illumination; not produced under the direction or influence of inspiration; unimaginative; dull; dreary.

uninstructed *adj* not instructed or taught; not educated; not furnished with instructions.

unintelligent *adj* not having reason or understanding; not having the mental faculties acute; not showing intelligence; dull.

unintelligible *adj* not intelligible; not capable of being understood; meaningless.

unintentional *adj* not intentional; done or happening without design.

uninterested *adj* not interested; not personally concerned; not having the mind or feelings engaged.

uninteresting *adj* not capable of exciting an interest or of engaging the mind or passions.

uninterrupted *adj* not interrupted; incessant.

uninvited *adj* not having received an invitation; unbidden.

union *n* the act of joining two or more things into one and thus forming a compound body; the state of being united; junction; coalition; concord; agreement and conjunction of mind, will, affections or interest; that which is formed by a combination of individual things or persons; a combination; a confederation; a confederacy; a permanent combination among workers engaged in the same occupation or trade; a trade union; marriage; a joint, screw, etc, uniting parts of machinery, etc; a kind of coupling.

unionist *n* one who promotes or advocates union.

Union Jack *n* the national flag of the United Kingdom, formed by the union of the cross of St George, the diagonal crosses of St Andrew and St Patrick (used alone or in the upper inner corner of another flag).

unique *adj* without a like or equal; unmatched; unequalled; single in its kind of excellence.

unisex *adj* of or for both sexes; not distinguishing between the sexes.

unison *n* (*mus*) the state of sounding at the same pitch; the combination of two or more sounds equal in pitch or at one or more octaves apart; hence, accordance; harmony.

unit *n* a single thing or person regarded as having oneness for the main attribute; a single one of a number; an individual; (*arith*) one, the least whole number; (*math*, *physics*), any known determinate quantity by the constant repetition of which any other quantity of the same kind is measured (as a foot pound, a gram, a dyne); (in war) any self-contained portion of a military force, comprising soldiers, vehicles, etc, ready to act or to be employed together: there may be fighting, medical, transport, etc, units; a group of people who carry out a specific function; a piece of furniture fitting together with other pieces.

Unitarian *n* one who ascribes divinity to God the Father only; one of a religious sect distinguished by the denial of the doctrine of the Trinity; also, a monotheist.—*adj* pertaining to Unitarians or their doctrines.

Unitarianism *n* the doctrines of Unitarians.

unite *vt* (**united, uniting**) to combine or conjoin, so as to form one; to incorporate in one; to associate by some bond, legal or other; to join in interest, affection, etc; to ally; to couple; to cause to adhere; to attach.—*vi* to become one; to become incorporated; to coalesce; to commingle; to join in an act; to concur.

united *adj* joined or combined; made one.

unit trust *n* a company which spreads subscribers' funds over a wide range of shares

Union Jack

and distributes the proceeds to each subscriber in proportion to the number of units which he or she has bought.

unity *n* the property of being one; oneness; concord; agreement; oneness of sentiment, affection, etc; the principle by which a uniform tenor of story and propriety of representation are preserved in literary compositions; (*math*) any definite quantity taken as one or for which 1 is made to stand in calculation.—**the unities** (of time, place and action), formerly deemed essential to a classical drama, demanded that there should be no shifting of the scene from place to place, that the whole series of events should be such as might occur within the space of a single day and that nothing should be admitted irrelevant to the development of the single plot.

univalent *adj* (*chem*) having a valence of one, like a hydrogen atom.

univalve *adj* (*zool*) having one valve only, as a shell or pericarp.—*n* a shell having one valve only; a mollusc with a shell composed of a single piece, usually of a conical and spiral form.

universal *adj* relating to the universe or all of the world; relating to or applicable to all of mankind; extending to or comprehending the whole number, quantity or space; pervading all or the whole; all-embracing; all-reaching; total; whole; comprising all the particulars.—*n* a general notion or idea; a predicable; a universal proposition.

universe *n* the general system of things; all created things viewed as constituting one system or whole; the world; the totality of space, stars and planets and other forms of matter and energy.

university *n* an establishment or corporation for the purposes of instruction in all or some of the most important branches of science and literature and having the power of conferring degrees in several faculties, as arts, medicine, law and theology.

unjust *adj* not just; not acting according to law and justice; contrary to justice and right.

unjustifiable *adj* not justifiable; not to be vindicated or defended.

unkempt *adj* uncombed; hence, rough; unpolished.

unkind *adj* lacking in kindness, affection, etc; harsh; cruel.

unkindness *n* the quality of being unkind; lack of kindness or affection; unkind conduct; an unkind act.

unknowing *adj* not knowing; ignorant.

unknown *adj* not known; not discovered or found out; not ascertained; not famous.—**unknown to** without the knowledge of (*he did it unknown to me*).—*n* an unknown person or thing.

unlawful *adj* contrary to law; illegal; begotten out of wedlock; illegitimate.

unleavened *adj* not leavened; not raised by leaven or yeast.

unless *conj* if it be not that; if . . . not; supposing that . . . not; except; excepting; by omission of a verb *unless* may have the force of a preposition = except, but for.

unlicensed *adj* not having a licence or legal permission; done or undertaken without due licence.

unlike *adj* not like; having no resemblance.

unlikelihood, unlikeliness *n* the state of being unlikely; improbability.

unlikely *adj* such as cannot be reasonably expected; improbable; not holding out a prospect of success; likely to fail; unpromising.

unlimited *adj* not limited; boundless; indefinite; unconfined; not restrained.

unload *vt* to take the load from; to discharge or disburden; to remove from a vessel or vehicle; (*fig*) to relieve from anything onerous or troublesome; to withdraw the charge from (*to unload a gun*).

unlock *vt* to unfasten something which has been locked; to open, in general; to lay open.

unlooked-for *adj* not looked for; not expected; not foreseen.

unloose *vt* (**unloosed, unloosing**) to loose; to untie; to undo; to set free from hold or fastening; to set at liberty.

unlovely *adj* not lovely; tending rather to repel; not beautiful or attractive.

unlucky *adj* not lucky or fortunate; not successful in one's undertakings; resulting in failure, disaster or misfortune; ill-omened; inauspicious.

unman *vt* (**unmanned, unmanning**) to deprive of the character or qualities of a human being; to deprive of manly courage and fortitude; to dishearten; to overpower with womanish weakness; to unnerve.

unmanageable *adj* not manageable; not easily restrained or directed; not controllable; beyond control.

unmanly *adj* not manly or the reverse of manly; effeminate; womanish; childish; unbecoming in a man; cowardly.

unmanned *adj* not manned.

unmannerly *adj* not mannerly; not having good manners; rude; ill-bred.

unmask *vt* to strip of a mask or of any disguise; to lay open to view.—*vi* to put off a mask.

unmatched *adj* matchless; having no equal.

unmerciful *adj* not merciful; cruel; inhuman; merciless; unconscionable.

unmerited *adj* not merited or deserved; obtained without service or equivalent; not deserved through wrongdoing.

unmindful *adj* not mindful; not heedful; regardless.

unmistakable *adj* not capable of being mistaken or misunderstood; clear; evident.

unmitigated *adj* not mitigated; not softened or toned down; perfect in badness; having no redeeming feature (*an unmitigated scoundrel*).

unmixed *adj* not mixed; pure; unadulterated; unalloyed.

unmoved *adj* not moved; not changed in place; not changed in purpose or resolution; unshaken; firm; not touched by passion or emotion; calm; cool.

unmuzzle *vt* (**unmuzzled, unmuzzling**) to remove a muzzle from; to free from restraint.

unnamed *adj* not having received a name; not mentioned.

unnatural *adj* not natural; contrary to the laws of nature; contrary to natural feelings; acting without the affections of our common nature; not representing nature; forced; affected; artificial.

unnecessary *adj* not necessary; needless; not required by the circumstances of a case.

unneighbourly *adj* not neighbourly; not suitable to the duties of a neighbour; not kind and friendly.

unnerve *vt* (**unnerved, unnerving**) to deprive of nerve, force or strength; to enfeeble; to deprive of coolness or composure of mind.

unnoticed *adj* not observed; not regarded; not treated with the usual marks of respect.

unnumbered *adj* not numbered; innumerable; indefinitely numerous.

unobservant *adj* not observant; not attentive; heedless.

unobserved *adj* not observed, noticed or regarded; not heeded.

unobstructed *adj* not obstructed; not filled with impediments; not hindered.

unobtrusive *adj* not obtrusive; not forward; modest.

unoccupied *adj* not occupied; not possessed; not employed or taken up in business or otherwise.

unopposed *adj* not opposed; not resisted; not meeting with any obstruction or opposition.

unorthodox *adj* heterodox; heretical.

unostentatious *adj* not ostentatious; not making show and parade; modest; not glaring or showy.

unpack *vt* to take from a package; to remove a wrapper from; to unload; to remove the contents from (a suitcase).—*vi* to take clothes, etc, from a suitcase, etc.

unpaid *adj* not paid; not discharged, as a debt; not having received what is due; not receiving a salary or wages.

unpalatable *adj* not palatable; disgusting to the taste; not such as to be relished; disagreeable to the feelings.

unparalleled *adj* having no parallel or equal; unequalled; matchless; such that nothing similar was ever seen.

unparliamentary *adj* contrary to the usage or rules of proceeding in parliament; not such as can be used or uttered in parliament; unseemly, as language.

unpeople *vt* (**unpeopled, unpeopling**) to deprive of inhabitants; to depopulate.

unperturbed *adj* not perturbed; not disturbed.

unpin *vt* (**unpinned, unpinning**) to loose from pins; to unfasten or undo what is held together by a pin or pins.

unpitying *adj* having no pity; showing no compassion.

unpleasant *adj* not pleasant; not affording pleasure; disagreeable.

unpleasing *adj* unpleasant; offensive; disagreeable.

unplumbed *adj* not plumbed or measured by a plumb line; unfathomed.

unpoetic, unpoetical *adj* not poetical; not having poetical qualities; not proper to or becoming a poet.

unpolished *adj* not polished; not made smooth or bright by rubbing; not refined in manners; rude; plain.

unpopular *adj* not popular; not having the public favour.

unpopularity *n* the state of being unpopular.

unpractical *adj* not practical; impractical.

unpractised *adj* not having been taught by practice; raw; unskilful.

unprecedented *adj* having no precedent; not matched by any other instance; unexampled.

unprejudiced *adj* not prejudiced; free from undue bias or prepossession; unbiased; impartial.

unpremeditated *adj* not previously meditated or prepared in the mind; not previously purposed or intended; not done by design.

unprepared *adj* not prepared; not fitted or made suitable or ready; not brought into a right or suitable condition in view of a future event, contingency, danger, etc.

unprepossessing *adj* unattractive.

unprincipled *adj* not having settled principles; lacking virtue; profligate; immoral; iniquitous; wicked.

unprintable *adj* not considered fit to be printed; too bad, libellous, obscene, etc to be printed.

unproductive *adj* not productive; not producing large crops; not making profitable returns for labour; not producing profit or interest; not producing articles for consumption or distribution; not producing any effect.

unprofessional *adj* not pertaining to one's profession; contrary to the rules or usage of a profession; not belonging to a profession.

unprofitable *adj* not profitable; bringing no profit; serving no useful end; useless; profitless.

unpromising *adj* not affording a favourable prospect of success, of excellence, of profit, etc.

unpropitious *adj* not propitious or favourable; inauspicious.

unprotected *adj* not protected or defended; without protector or guardian.

unproved *adj* not tested or known by trial; not established as true by proof.

unprovoked *adj* not provoked; not proceeding from provocation or just cause.

unpunished *adj* receiving no punishment.

unqualified *adj* not having the requisite qualifications; without sufficient talents, abilities or accomplishments; not legally competent to act; not having passed the necessary examinations and received a diploma or licence; not modified by conditions or exceptions (*unqualified praise*).

unquenchable *adj* incapable of being quenched, extinguished, etc.

unquestionable *adj* not to be doubted or called in question; indubitable; certain.

unquiet *adj* not calm or tranquil; restless; agitated; disturbed.

unravel *vt* (**unravelled, unravelling**) to disentangle; to disengage or separate; to clear from complication or difficulty; to unfold or bring to a denouement, as the plot of a play.—*vi* to be unfolded; to be disentangled.

unread *adj* not perused; not instructed by books.

unreadable *adj* incapable of being read or deciphered; illegible; not worth reading; so dull or ill-written as to repel readers.

unreadiness *n* lack of promptness or of preparation.

unready *adj* not prepared; not fit; not prompt.

unreal *adj* not real; not substantial; having appearance only.

unreality *n* lack of real existence; that which has no reality.

unreason *n* lack of reason; folly; absurdity.

unreasonable *adj* not agreeable to reason; not guided by reason; exceeding the bounds of reason; exorbitant; immoderate; unconscionable.

unreasonableness *n* the state or quality of being unreasonable.

unreasonably *adv* in an unreasonable manner; excessively; immoderately.

unreconciled *adj* not reconciled; not made consistent; not restored to friendship or favour; still at enmity.

unrecorded *adj* not recorded or registered; not kept in remembrance by public monuments.

unredeemed *adj* not redeemed; unmitigated.

unrefined *adj* not purified; not polished in manners, taste, etc.

unrelated *adj* not connected by blood or affinity; having no connection of any kind.

unrelenting *adj* not becoming lenient, gentle or merciful; relentless; hard; pitiless.

unreliable *adj* not reliable; not to be relied or depended on.

unremitting *adj* not abating; not relaxing for a time; incessant; continued.

unrepentant *adj* not penitent; not contrite for sin.

unrequited *adj* not requited; not recompensed; not reciprocated.

unreserved *adj* not reserved or restricted; not withheld in part; full; entire; open; frank; concealing nothing.

unreservedly *adv* without limitation or reservation; frankly; without concealment.

unresisted *adj* not resisted or opposed.

unresisting *adj* not making resistance; submissive.

unrest *n* disquiet; lack of tranquillity; uneasiness; unhappiness.

unrestrained *adj* not restrained or controlled; not limited; uncontrolled; licentious; loose.

unrighteous *adj* not righteous; not just; wicked; not honest and upright (of persons or things).

unrighteousness *n* injustice; a violation of the principles of justice and equity; wickedness.

unripe *adj* not ripe; not mature; not fully prepared; not completed.

unrivalled *adj* having no rival or equal; peerless; incomparable.

unroll *vt* to open out, as something rolled; to lay open or display.—*vi* to unfold; to uncoil.

unromantic *adj* not romantic; not given to romantic fancies; having nothing of romance connected with it.

unruffled *adj* calm; tranquil; not agitated; not disturbed.

unruly *adj* disregarding restraint; disposed to violate laws; turbulent; ungovernable; disorderly.

unsafe *adj* not affording or accompanied by complete safety; not free from danger; perilous; hazardous.

unsaleable *adj* not saleable; not meeting a ready sale; that cannot find a purchaser.

unsatisfactory *adj* not satisfactory; not satisfying; not giving satisfaction.

unsatisfied *adj* not having enough; not gratified to the full; not content; not pleased; not convinced or fully persuaded; unpaid.

unsatisfying *adj* not affording full gratification; not convincing the mind.

unsavoury *adj* not savoury; tasteless; insipid; disagreeable to the taste or smell; offensive.

unsay *vt* (*pret, pp* **unsaid**, *ppr* **unsaying**) to recant or recall after having been said; to retract; to take back.

unscathed *adj* not scathed or injured; without scathe; uninjured.

unscrew *vt* to draw the screws from; to unfasten by screwing back; to loosen (a lid, etc) by turning.

unscrupulous *adj* having no scruples; regardless of principle.

unseal *vt* to open after having been sealed.

unseasonable *adj* not seasonable; not agreeable to the time of the year; ill-timed; untimely; not suited to the time or occasion.

unseasoned *adj* not seasoned; not kept and made fit for use; not inured; not flavoured with seasoning.

unseat *vt* to remove from a seat; to throw from one's seat on horseback; to depose from a seat in the House of Commons.

unseaworthy *adj* not fit for a voyage (said of ships not in a fit state to encounter the ordinary perils of a sea voyage).

unseemly *adj* not seemly; not becoming; indecorous; indecent.

unseen *adj* not seen; invisible.—**the unseen** *n* that which is unseen, especially, the world of spirits; the hereafter.

unselfish *adj* not selfish or unduly attached to one's own interest.

unsettle *vt* (**unsettled, unsettling**) to change from a settled state; to unhinge; to make uncertain or fluctuating; to disorder the mind of; to derange.

unsettled *adj* not fixed in resolution; unsteady or wavering; disturbed or troubled; not calm or composed; having no fixed place of abode; apt to change one's abode or occupation; displaced from a fixed or permanent position; not adjusted; unpaid; not occupied by permanent inhabitants.

unsex *vt* to deprive of the qualities of sex; to transform in respect to sex; usually, to deprive of the qualities of a woman.

unshackle *vt* (**unshackled, unshackling**) to unfetter; to set free from restraint.

unshaken *adj* not shaken; not agitated; not moved in resolution; firm; steady.

unsheathe *vt* (**unsheathed, unsheathing**) to draw from the sheath or scabbard.—**to unsheathe the sword** to make war.

unship *vt* (**unshipped, unshipping**) to take out of a ship or other water craft; (*naut*) to remove from the place where it is fixed or fitted.

unsightliness *n* repulsiveness; deformity; ugliness.

unsightly *adj* disagreeable to the eye; repulsive; ugly; deformed.

unskilful *adj* not skilful; having little or no skill; lacking knowledge and dexterity.

unskilfulness *n* the quality of being unskilful; lack of skill.

unskilled *adj* lacking skill or practical knowledge.

unskilled labour *n* labour not requiring special skill or training; simple manual labour.

unslaked *adj* not slaked or quenched; not mixed with water and so reduced to powder (*unslaked lime*).

unsociability *n* the state or quality of being unsociable.

unsociable *adj* not sociable; not suitable for society; not inclined to mix with others; not inclined for society; not free in conversation; not companionable.

unsocial *adj* not social; not adapted to society; not caring to mix with one's fellows.

unsolicited *adj* not solicited; not applied to or petitioned; not asked for; not eagerly requested.

unsophisticated *adj* not sophisticated; not adulterated; unmixed; pure; in the natural and simple state; natural; void of the conventionalities of polite society; naive; inexperienced.

unsought *adj* not searched for; unasked for; unsolicited.

unsound *adj* not sound or healthy; corrupt; decayed; not solid, firm, etc; not founded on truth or correct principles; not valid; erroneous; not orthodox.

unsparing *adj* not parsimonious; profuse; not merciful or forgiving; severe; rigorous in treatment.

unspeakable *adj* incapable of being spoken or uttered; unutterable; ineffable.

unspoken *adj* not spoken or uttered.

unstable *adj* not stable; inconstant; irresolute; wavering.

unsteady *adj* not steady; shaking; staggering; reeling; wavering; fluctuating; not constant in mind; fickle; unsettled; not regular, equable or uniform; varying.

unstinted *adj* not stinted; rather profuse or lavish; bestowed abundantly.

unstrung *adj* deprived of strings; having the nerves shaken.

unstudied *adj* not studied; not premeditated; not laboured; easy; natural; unaffected.

unsuccessful *adj* not successful; having met with no success; not fortunate in the result or issue.

unsuitable *adj* not suitable, fit or adapted; unfit; improper.

unsullied *adj* not sullied; not stained or tarnished; free from imputation of evil; pure; stainless.

unsupported *adj* not supported; not upheld; not sustained; not countenanced; not aided.

unsurpassable *adj* not capable of being surpassed, excelled or exceeded.

unscrew

unsurpassed *adj* not excelled, exceeded or outdone.

unsuspected *adj* not suspected; not an object of suspicion.

unsuspecting *adj* not imagining that any ill is designed; free from suspicion.

unswerving *adj* not deviating from any rule or standard; unwavering; firm.

unsystematic *adj* not systematic; lacking a proper system.

untainted *adj* not tainted; not impregnated with foul matter; not sullied; unblemished.

untamable, untameable *adj* not capable of being tamed.

untamed *adj* not reclaimed from wildness; not domesticated; not subdued or brought under control.

untaught *adj* not instructed or educated; unlettered; unskilled; unschooled; not made the subject of teaching.

untempered *adj* not tempered; not duly mixed; not regulated, moderated or controlled.

untenable *adj* not tenable; that cannot be held in possession; that cannot be maintained by argument; not defensible.

unthinkable *adj* inconceivable; out of the question.

unthinking *adj* not heedful; inconsiderate; not indicating thought or reflection.

unthrifty *adj* prodigal; profuse; lavish; wasteful.

untidy *adj* not tidy; not neat; disordered.

untie *vt* (**untied, untying**) to loosen, as a knot; to undo; to unfasten; to unbind; to set loose.

until *prep* till; to (used before nouns of time); (preceding a sentence or clause) till the time that; till the point or degree that.

untimely *adj* not timely; not done or happening in the right season; inopportune; premature.—*adv* before the natural time; unseasonably.

untiring *adj* not becoming tired or exhausted; unwearied.

unto *prep* to; **unto** is now antiquated, though still sometimes used in the solemn or elevated style.

untold *adj* not told; not related; not revealed; not numbered.

untouched *adj* not hit; not meddled with; uninjured; not mentioned; not affected; not affected emotionally.

untoward *adj* unseemly; unfavourable; adverse.—*adv* in an untoward manner; perversely.

untrained *adj* not trained; not disciplined; not instructed.

untrammelled *adj* not trammelled or fettered; quite free to act.

untried *adj* not tried; not attempted; not showing capabilities by trial or proof given; not having passed trial; not heard and determined in a court of law.

untrodden *adj* not having been trod; not marked by the feet; unfrequented.

untroubled *adj* free from trouble; not disturbed by care, sorrow or business; not agitated or ruffled; not raised into waves.

untrue *adj* not true; false; contrary to the fact; not faithful to another; not to be trusted; inconstant in love.

untrustworthy *adj* not worthy of being trusted; not deserving of confidence.

untruth *n* the quality of being untrue; contrariety to truth; lack of veracity; lack of fidelity; a false assertion; a lie.

untruthful *adj* lacking in truth or veracity.

unused *adj* not employed; disused; that has never been used; not accustomed.

unusual *adj* not usual; not common; rare.

unutterable *adj* incapable of being uttered or expressed; ineffable; inexpressible.

unvaried *adj* not varied; not altered; not diversified; always the same.

unvarnished *adj* not overlaid with varnish; (*fig*) not artfully embellished; plain.

unvarying *adj* not altering; uniform.

unveil *vt* to remove a veil from; to disclose to view; to reveal.—*vi* to remove one's veil.

unversed *adj* not versed or skilled; unacquainted.

unwaged *adj* not receiving a wage or salary; unemployed.

unwarrantable *adj* not defensible; not justifiable; improper.

unwarranted *adj* not authorized; not assured or certain; not guaranteed.

unwary *adj* not wary or vigilant against danger; not cautious; unguarded.

unwashed *adj* not washed; not cleansed by water; filthy.

unwavering *adj* not wavering; not unstable; fixed; steadfast.

unwearied *adj* not tired; not fatigued; indefatigable; assiduous.

unwelcome *adj* not welcome; not pleasing or grateful; not well received.

unwell *adj* indisposed; not in good health; ailing.

unwholesome *adj* not wholesome; unfavourable or prejudicial to health; unhealthy; insalubrious; causing sickness; not sound; diseased.

unwieldy *adj* movable with difficulty; too bulky and clumsy to move or be moved easily; unmanageable from weight; ponderous.

unwilling *adj* not willing; loath; disinclined; reluctant.

unwinking *adj* not winking; not shutting the eyes; not ceasing to wake or watch.

unwise *adj* not wise; defective in wisdom; foolish; injudicious.

unwitting *adj* not knowing; unconscious; unaware.

unwittingly *adv* without knowledge or consciousness; inadvertently.

unwomanly *adj* unbecoming a woman.

unwonted *adj* not wonted; not common; unusual; infrequent; unaccustomed.

unworldly *adj* not influenced by worldly or sordid motives; spiritual.

unworthy *adj* not deserving; not worthy (*unworthy of confidence*); worthless; vile; base; beneath the character (*work unworthy of the man*).

unwrap *vt* (**unwrapped, unwrapping**) to open or undo, as what is wrapped up; to take off a wrapper from.

unwritten *adj* not reduced to writing; oral; not written upon; blank.

unwritten law *n* a law based on custom, not formulated in any written document.

unyielding *adj* unbending; not pliant; stiff; firm; obstinate.

up *adv* the opposite of down; to a higher place or position; from a lower to a higher place; on high; aloft; raised; upright; erect; no longer in bed; in a state of action; in commotion, excitement, insurrection, etc; higher or advanced in price, rank, social standing, etc; to a more complete or mature condition; reaching a certain point; as far as (with *to*, as *up to the roof*); not below or inferior (with *to*, as *up to one's expectations*); denoting approach or arrival (*to bring up troops*); quite; thoroughly; often used to intensify a verb (*to eat up all the food*); in a place where it is kept when not used; in a state of being brought together or into close compass or being erected or raised (*up with the flag*).—*prep* from a lower to a higher place or point on; at or in a high or higher position on; towards the interior (generally the more elevated part) of a country; in a direction from the coast or towards the head or source of a stream.—*n* ascent; high point.—**ups and downs** rises and falls; alternate states of prosperity and the contrary; vicissitudes.—*adj* moving or directed upwards; at an end; (*colloq*) well-informed.—*vt* (**upped, upping**) to raise; to increase; to take up.

upas *n* a tree of Java and the neighbouring islands yielding a poisonous sap.

upbraid *vt* to cast some fault or offence in the teeth of; to charge reproachfully (followed by *with* or *for* before the thing imputed); to reprove with severity; to chide; to be a reproach to.

upbringing *n* the process of bringing up; training; education; breeding.

upheaval *n* the act of upheaving; a radical or violent change or disturbance(*geol*) a lifting up of a portion of the earth's crust by some expansion or elevating power from below.

upheave *vt* (**upheaved, upheaving**) to lift up (a heavy weight, etc).

upheld *pret, pp* of **uphold**.

uphill *adj* leading or going up a rising ground; attended with exertion; difficult; fatiguing.

uphold *vt* (*pret, pp* **upheld**, *ppr* **upholding**) to raise on high; to keep elevated; to keep erect; to support; to sustain; to keep from declining.

upholder *n* a supporter; a defender.

upholster *vt* to furnish with upholstery.

upholsterer *n* one who furnishes houses with curtains, carpets, cushions for chairs and sofas, etc.

upholstery *n* the business or goods of an upholsterer; materials used to make a soft covering for a seat, etc.

upkeep *n* maintenance in a state of efficiency; the cost of such maintenance.

upland *n* the higher ground of a district; ground elevated above meadows and valleys; slopes of hills, etc.—*adj* pertaining to uplands or higher grounds.

uplift *vt* to raise aloft; to elevate; to improve the standard or condition of.

up-line *n* a line of railway which leads to the metropolis or to a main terminus from the provinces.

upmost *adj* highest; topmost; uppermost.

upon *prep* on; especially, resting on; at or in contact with the upper or outer part of a thing; resting, lying or placed in contact with (all but synonymous with *on*, though sometimes rather more emphatic).

upper *adj* higher as contrasted with lower; higher in place; superior in rank or dignity (*the upper house of a legislature*).—*n* the part of a boot or shoe above the sole; (*sl*) a drug used as a stimulant.

upper case *n* (*print*) the top one of a pair of cases, used by compositors to hold capital letters, reference marks and other less used type.

upper class people occupying the highest social rank.—*adj* pertaining to such people.

upper crust (*colloq*) the upper class; the aristocracy.

upper hand *n* superiority; advantage.

Upper House *n* in England, the House of Lords, as distinguished from the Lower House, or House of Commons.

uppermost *adj* highest in place; highest in power or authority.

uppish *adj* (*colloq*) proud; arrogant; putting on airs.

uppishness *n* (*colloq*) the quality of being uppish.

upraise *vt* (**upraised, upraising**) to raise or lift up.

upright *adj* erect; perpendicular; erect on one's feet; pricked up; shooting directly from the body; adhering to rectitude; honest; honourable; having integrity.—*n* something standing erect; a vertical piece in some structure.

uprightness *n* the quality or condition of being upright; honesty; integrity; probity.

uprising *n* the act of rising up; rise; an ascent or declivity; a riot; a rebellion.

uproar *n* a violent disturbance and noise; bustle and clamour; a commotion; a noisy tumult; an outcry.

uproarious *adj* making an uproar or tumult; tumultuous; very funny; boisterous.

uproot *vt* to tear up by the roots or as if by the roots; to eradicate.

upset *vt* (*pret*, *pp* **upset**, *ppr* **upsetting**) to overturn; to overthrow; to overset; to put out of one's normal state; to discompose completely.—*n* the act of upsetting.—*adj* fixed; determined.

upset price *n* the price at which anything is exposed to sale by auction.

upshot *n* final issue; conclusion.

upside *n* the upper side.

upside-down *adj* the upper part undermost; hence, in complete disorder.

upstairs *adj* pertaining or relating to an upper storey or flat.—*adv* in or towards an upper storey.

upstanding *adj* standing upright; upright; honest.

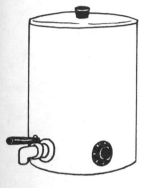

urn

upstart *vi* to start or spring up suddenly.—*n* one who suddenly rises from a humble position to wealth, power or consequence; a parvenu; a presumptuous, arrogant person.

uptight *adj* (*colloq*) very tense; very anxious.

up-to-date *adj* modern; fashionable.

upturn *n* an upward trend; an economic improvement; an improvement.—*vt* to turn upside down.

upward *adj* directed or turned to a higher place.—*adv* upwards.

upwards *adv* towards a higher place; in an upward direction; towards heaven and God; with respect to the higher part; towards the source or origin.—**upwards of, upward of** more than; above.

upwardly mobile *adj* aspiring to improve one's social and economic status.

Urania *n* in Greek myth, the Muse of astronomy.

uranium *n* a radioactive metallic element used as a source of nuclear energy.

Uranus *n* in Greek myth, a deity personified with heaven; (*astron*) one of the primary planets, the seventh from the sun.

urban *adj* belonging to or included in a town or city (*urban population*).

urbane *adj* courteous; polite; suave; elegant or refined; sophisticated.

urbanity *n* civility or courtesy of manners; refinement; sophistication.

urchin *n* a raggedly dressed, mischievous child; a sea urchin.

Urdu *n* a Hindustani language which is the official language of Pakistan and also spoken in India and Afghanistan.

urea *n* a crystalline compound which exists in urine, produced by protein metabolism.

ureter *n* the duct or tube that conveys the urine from the kidney to the bladder.

urethra *n* (*pl* **urethrae**, **urethras**) the canal by which the urine is conducted from the bladder and discharged.

urge *vt* (**urged, urging**) to press, impel or force onward; to press the mind or will of; to serve as a motive or impelling cause; to stimulate; to press or ply hard with arguments, entreaties, etc; to importune; to solicit earnestly; to press upon attention; to insist on (*to urge an argument*).—*vi* to press forward.

urgency *n* the state or character of being urgent; importunity; earnest solicitation; pressure of necessity.

urgent *adj* pressing; necessitating or calling for immediate action; eagerly soliciting; pressing with importunity.

urgently *adv* in an urgent manner; with pressing importunity; vehemently.

uric *adj* pertaining to or obtained from urine.

uric acid *n* a white odourless acid found in the urine of birds, reptiles and some mammals.

urinal *n* a bowl or trough in a public lavatory for males to urinate into; a room or building with such a fixture.

urinate *vi* (**urinated, urinating**) to pass urine.

urine *n* a fluid secreted by the kidneys from where it is conveyed into the bladder by the ureters and discharged through the urethra.

urn *n* a vase or large vessel; a large metal container with a stopcock for boiling water for tea or coffee; a vessel in which the ashes of the dead are kept.

urogenital, urinogenital *adj* of or relating to the urinary and genital organs and their functions.

urology *n* the branch of medicine that deals with urogenital diseases and disorders.

Ursa Major *n* a constellation, the Great Bear, one of the most conspicuous of the northern constellations, situated near the pole and popularly called the Plough.

Ursa Minor *n* a constellation, the Little Bear, the constellation which contains the Pole Star.

ursine *adj* of or relating to bears.

urticaceous *adj* (*bot*) pertaining to plants of the nettle family.

urticaria *n* an allergic reaction causing raised, whitish, itchy patches on the skin; nettlerash.

urus *n* (*pl* **uruses**) the aurochs.

us *pron* (the objective or accusative case of **we**; the dative of **we**) used after certain verbs, such as verbs of giving.

usable *adj* capable of being used.

usage *n* treatment; behaviour of one person

towards another; long-continued practice; customary way of acting; custom; practice; established mode of employing some particular word.

use *n* the act of employing anything or the state of being employed; employment; conversion to a purpose (*to make use of*); the quality that makes a thing proper for a purpose; utility; service; convenience; need for employing; exigency (*I have no use for it*); continued or repeated practice; wont; usage.—*vt* (**used, using**) to employ or make use of; to act with or by means of; to do work with; to consume or exhaust by employment (*to use flour for food*); to practice or employ (*to use treachery*); to make a practice of; to act or behave towards; to treat (*to use one ill*); to accustom; to render familiar by practice.—**to use up** to consume entirely by using; to exhaust or wear out the strength of—*vi* to be accustomed; to be in the habit.

useful *adj* valuable for use; suited or adapted to the purpose; beneficial; profitable.

useless *adj* having no use; unserviceable; producing no good end; not advancing the end proposed.

user *n* one who uses; (*colloq*) a drug addict.

user-friendly *adj* reasonably easy to understand or to operate.

usher *n* a person who shows people to their seats in a church, cinema, theatre, etc; an official in court who acts as doorkeeper and maintains order.—*vt* to act as an usher towards; to escort or conduct; to introduce, as forerunner (with *in, forth,* etc).

usual *adj* in common use; customary; ordinary; frequent.

usually *adv* customarily; ordinarily.

usufruct *n* (*law*) the use and enjoyment of property without the right to alienate such.

usurer *n* formerly, any person who lent money on interest; now, one who lends money at an exorbitant rate of interest.

usurious *adj* pertaining to or practising usury; taking exorbitant interest for the use of money.

usurp *vt* to seize and hold possession of by force or without right; to appropriate or assume illegally or wrongfully (a throne, power or rank).—*vi* to be or act as a usurper; to encroach.

usurper *n* one who usurps; one who seizes power or position without right.

usury *n* interest for money; an excessive or inordinate premium for the use of money borrowed; exorbitant interest; the practice of taking exorbitant or excessive interest.

ut *n* the first or key note in a musical scale of tonic sol-fa, now superseded by **do.**

utensil *n* an implement; an instrument; particularly one used in a kitchen.

uterus *n* (*pl* **uteri**) the female organ in which offspring grow between fertilization and birth.

utilitarian *adj* consisting in or pertaining to utilitarianism; designed to be of practical use.—*n* one who holds the doctrine of utilitarianism.

utilitarianism *n* the doctrine that the greatest happiness of the greatest number should be the aim of all social and political institutions; or the doctrine that utility is the standard of morality, that actions are right in proportion as they tend to promote happiness, wrong as they tend to produce the reverse of happiness.

utility *n* the state or quality of being useful; usefulness; a public service, such as telephone, electricity, gas, etc; a company providing such a service.

utility room *n* a room containing laundry appliances, heating equipment, etc.

utilization *n* the act of utilizing or turning to account.

utilize *vt* (**utilized, utilizing**) to turn to profitable account or use; to make useful; to adapt to some useful purpose.

utmost *adj* being at the farthest point or extremity; farthest out; most distant; extreme; being in the greatest or highest degree (often used substantively, signifying the most that can be); greatest power, degree or effort (*try your utmost*).

Utopia *n* a name invented by Sir Thomas More and applied by him to an imaginary island which he represents as enjoying the utmost perfection in laws, politics, etc, as contrasted with the defects of those which then existed; hence, a place or state of ideal perfection.

utopian *adj* pertaining to Utopia; founded upon or involving imaginary or ideal perfection.—*n* an inhabitant of Utopia; an ardent but impracticable reformer.

utter *adj* outer; situated at or beyond the limits of something; complete; total; entire; perfect.—*vt* to put into circulation, as money, notes, base coin, etc; to give expression to; to give vent to by the vocal organs; to pronounce; to speak.

utterance *n* the act of uttering; manner of speaking; expression; circulation, as of money.

utterly *adv* to the full extent; fully; perfectly; totally.

uttermost *adj* extreme; being in the furthest, greatest or highest degree; utmost (used also substantively, like *utmost*).

uvula *n* (*pl* **uvulae, uvulas**) the small conical fleshy substance which hangs from the soft palate over the roof of the tongue.

uxorious *adj* excessively or foolishly fond of one's wife; doting on one's wife.

V

V the twenty-second letter of the English alphabet.

vacancy *n* the quality or state of being vacant; empty space; vacuity; a space between objects; an unoccupied space; an unoccupied interval of time; an unoccupied post, position or office; a situation or office lacking a person to fill it; vacuity or inanity.

vacuum cleaner

vacant *adj* having no contents; empty; unfilled; void; not occupied or filled by an incumbent, possessor or official; unoccupied; unemployed; not required to be spent in work; leisure; free (*vacant hours*); free from thought; not given to thinking, study, reflection, etc; lacking intelligent facial expression; inane.

vacate *vt* (**vacated, vacating**) to make vacant; to quit the occupancy or possession of; to leave empty or unoccupied; to make void or of no validity.

vacation *n* the act of vacating; the act of leaving without an occupant; a stated interval in a round of duties; holidays.

vaccinate *vt* (**vaccinated, vaccinating**) to inoculate with vaccine for the purpose of procuring immunity from a disease.

vaccination *n* the act of vaccinating; the resulting scar.

vaccine *n* a modified, and thus harmless, virus or other microorganism used for inoculation to give immunity from certain diseases by stimulating antibody production; cowpox used in this way against smallpox.

vacillate *vi* (**vacillated, vacillating**) to waver; to move one way and the other; to fluctuate in mind or opinion; to be unsteady or inconstant.

vacillation *n* the act of vacillating; a wavering; vacillating conduct; fluctuation of mind; unsteadiness; change from one object to another; inconstancy.

vacuity *n* the state of being empty or unfilled; emptiness; a space unfilled or unoccupied or occupied with an invisible fluid only; a vacuum; freedom from mental exertion; absence of thought; absence of intelligence in look; vacant expression.

vacuous *adj* empty; unfilled; void; vacant.

vacuum *n* (pl **vacuums, vacua**) empty space or space devoid of all matter or body; an enclosed space from which air is more or less completely removed, as from the receiver of an air pump, a portion of a barometric tube, etc.—*vt* to clean with a vacuum cleaner.—*adj* of, having or creating a vacuum; working by suction or maintenance of a partial vacuum.

vacuum cleaner *n* an electrical appliance which sucks up dust and dirt from carpets, upholstery, etc.

vacuum flask *n* a double-walled flask with a vacuum between the walls which enables liquids to be kept either hot or cold for some time.

vacuum-packed *adj* sealed in an airtight container from which the air has been removed.

vade mecum *n* a book or other thing that a person constantly carries with him or her; a manual; a pocket companion.

vagabond *adj* wandering; going from place to place without settled habitation; pertaining to a vagrant or idle stroller.—*n* one who goes from place to place without fixed habitation or visible means of earning a living; a vagrant.

vagary *n* a wandering of the thoughts; a wild freak; a whim; a whimsical purpose.

vagina *n* (pl **vaginae, vaginas**) (*bot, anat*) any part having the character of a sheath; the canal in females connecting the external sex organs with the uterus.

vagrant *adj* wandering without any settled habitation; pertaining to one who wanders; unsettled; moving without any certain direction.—*n* a wanderer; one without a settled home or habitation; a vagabond; a tramp; a beggar.

vague *adj* wandering; unsettled as regards meaning, scope, etc; indefinite; hazy; uncertain; doubtful; proceeding from no known authority; of uncertain origin or foundation (*a vague report*); (of a person) absent-minded.

vain *adj* having no real value or importance; unsubstantial; empty; idle; worthless; unsatisfying; producing no good result; fruit-less; ineffectual; light-minded; foolish; silly; proud of petty things or of trifling attainments; having a foolish craving for the admiration or applause of others; puffed up; inflated; conceited.—**in vain** to no purpose; without effect; ineffectually.

vainglorious *adj* feeling or proceeding from vainglory; vain to excess of one's own achievements; boastful.

vainglory *n* glory, pride or boastfulness that is vain or empty; tendency unduly to exalt oneself or one's own performances; vain pomp or show.

vainly *adv* in a vain manner; without effect; to no purpose; in vain; in a conceited manner; foolishly.

vainness *n* the state of being vain; empty pride; vanity.

valance *n* drapery round the base of a bed; a canopy for a window frame to hide rods, etc; a pelmet.

vale[1] *n* a tract of low ground between hills; a valley.

vale[2] *n* (*arch*) farewell, adieu.

valediction *n* a farewell; a bidding farewell.

valedictory *adj* bidding farewell; pertaining to a leave-taking or farewell.—*n* a valedictory oration; a statement or speech made on leaving a position, etc.

valence, valency *n* (*chem*) the combining strength or capacity of atoms, referred to hydrogen as a standard; the number of atoms of hydrogen which one atom of an element can replace in compounds.

valentine *n* a sweetheart selected or obtained on St Valentine's Day, 14th February; a card or gift sent by one person to another on St Valentine's Day.

valerian *n* an ornamental flowering plant with a root formerly used as a sedative.

valet *n* a manservant who attends on a gentleman; a steward in a hotel or on board ship.—*vt* to attend (someone) as a valet.—*vi* to work as a valet.

valetudinarian *adj* sickly; in a poor state of health; infirm; seeking to recover health.—*n* a person of an infirm or sickly constitution; one who is seeking to recover health.

Valhalla, Walhalla *n* in Scandinavian myth, the palace of immortality, inhabited by the souls of heroes slain in battle.

valiant *adj* brave; courageous; intrepid in danger; performed with valour; heroic.

valid *adj* sufficiently supported by fact; well grounded; sound; just; good; not weak or defective; having sufficient legal strength or force; good or sufficient in point of law.

validate *vt* (**validated, validating**) to corroborate; to legalize.

validity *n* the state or quality of being valid; strength or cogency from being supported by fact; justness; soundness; legal strength or force; sufficiency in point of law.

valise *n* a small leather bag or case for holding a traveller's equipment; a portmanteau.

Valkyrie, Valkyr, Walkyrie *n* one of the sisters of Odin, who led to Valhalla the souls of those who fell in battle, where they ministered at their feasts.

valley *n* any hollow or surface depression of some width bounded by hills or mountains and usually traversed by a stream or river; a vale; the internal angle formed by the meeting of the two inclined sides of a roof.

vallum *n* a rampart; a palisaded rampart, such as that with which the Romans enclosed their camps.

valour *n* that quality which enables a person to encounter danger with firmness; personal bravery, especially as regards fighting; intrepidity; prowess.

valuable *adj* having value or worth; having a high value; having qualities which are useful and esteemed; precious.—*n* a thing, especially a small thing, of value; a choice article of personal property (usually in the plural).

valuate *vt* (**valuated, valuating**) to estimate the worth of; to value.

valuation *n* the act of valuing; the act of setting a price; appraisement; estimation; value set on a thing; estimated worth.

valuator *n* one who sets a value; an appraiser.

value *n* worth; that property or those properties of a thing which render it useful or estimable; the degree of such property or properties; utility; importance; what makes a person of some account, estimation or worth; estimate of worth; price equal to the worth; market price; the money for which a thing is sold or will sell; equivalence in the market; import; precise meaning (*the value of a word* or *phrase*); (*mus*) the relative length or duration of a tone or note.—*vt* (**valued, valuing**) to estimate the worth of; to rate at a certain price; to appraise; to consider with respect to importance; to rate, whether high or low; to have in high esteem; to prize; to regard; to hold in respect and estimation.

value-added tax *n* (often shortened to **VAT**) a tax on the rise in value of a product due to the manufacturing and marketing processes; a tax on the value added to an article at each stage of manufacture.

valve *n* one of the leaves of a folding door; a kind of movable lid or partition adapted to a tube or orifice and so formed as to open communication in one direction and to close it in the other, used to regulate the admission or escape of water, gas or steam; (*anat*) a partition within the cavity

valley

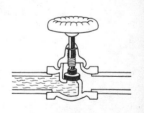

valve

of a vessel opening to allow the passage of a fluid in one direction and shutting to prevent its return (*the valves of the heart*); (*bot*) one of the divisions of any dehiscent body; one of the separable portions of the shell of a mollusc.

valvular *adj* containing valves; having the character of or acting as a valve.

vamp[1] *n* the upper leather of a boot or shoe; any piece or patch intended to give an old thing a new appearance; a piece added for sake of appearance; (*mus*) an improvised accompaniment.—*vt* to put a new vamp or upper leather on; to furbish up; to give a new appearance to; to patch.

vamp[2] *n* a seductive woman, especially one who exploits men.—*vt* to fascinate or exploit by seducing.—*vi* to act as a vamp.

vampire *n* in folklore, a spectral being or ghost still with a human body believed to leave the grave during the night and suck the blood of living men and women while they are asleep; a person who preys on others; an extortioner or bloodsucker; a vampire bat.—*adj* pertaining to or resembling a vampire in character.

vampire bat *n* a bloodsucking bat of South America of several species, with long sharp teeth.

van[1] *n* a caravan; a covered motor vehicle used by tradesmen and others for carrying goods; a closed railway carriage for carrying luggage or for other purposes.

van[2] *n* the vanguard.

vanadium *n* a silvery brittle metallic element used to toughen steel.

vandal *n* a person who wilfully destroys or defaces something.

Vandal *n* one of a Teutonic race who pillaged Rome in the fifth century AD and unsparingly destroyed art and writings.

vandalism *n* the act of a vandal; the deliberate destruction or defacement of something.

vandalize *vt* (**vandalized, vandalizing**) to carry out an act of vandalism.

vane *n* a weathercock, arrow or thin slip of metal, wood, etc, placed on a spindle at the top of a spire, tower, etc, for the purpose of showing by its turning and direction which way the wind blows; any similar device; the broad part of a feather on either side of the shaft; one of the plates or blades of a windmill, propeller, etc.

vanguard *n* the troops who march in the front part of an army; the advance guard; the forefront of any movement; those in this position.

vanilla *n* any of a genus of orchidaceous plants, natives of tropical America, the fleshy pod-like fruit of several species of which has a fragrant odour and is used as a flavouring.

vanish *vi* to disappear; to pass from a vis-

ible to an invisible state; to pass beyond the limit of vision; to be annihilated or lost; to be no more; (*math*) to become less and less till the value is nothing or is denoted by 0.

vanishing point *n* the point in a view or picture at which all parallel lines in the same plane tend to meet when correctly represented.

vanity *n* the quality or state of being vain; worthlessness; falsity; unrealness; lack of substance to satisfy desire; the desire of indiscriminate admiration; empty pride inspired by an overweening conceit of one's personal attainments or decorations; ambitious display; anything empty or unsubstantial.

vanquish *vt* to conquer, overcome or subdue in battle; to defeat in any contest; to get the better of; to confute; to overpower; to prostrate; to be too much for.

vantage *n* advantage; superiority of position or place; the place or condition which gives one an advantage over another; favourable position (*vantage ground*); in lawn tennis, the state of being able to win the game by winning the next point.

vapid *adj* having lost life and spirit; insipid; dead; flat; dull; unanimated; spiritless.

vaporize *vt* (**vaporized, vaporizing**) to convert into vapour by the application of heat or artificial means; to cause to evaporate; to sublimate.—*vi* to pass off in vapour.

vaporizer *n* a device for converting liquid into a fine spray.

vaporous *adj* being in the form of or having the character of vapour; full of vapours or exhalations; promoting exhalation; unsubstantial; vainly imaginative or soaring; whimsical.

vapour *n* an exhalation or fume; a gaseous substance; visible steam; the gaseous form which any solid or liquid substance assumes when heated; also specifically used of a gas below its critical temperature; any visible diffused substance floating in the atmosphere, as fog or mist; hazy matter; something unsubstantial, fleeting or transitory; a vain imagination; an unreal fancy; (*pl*) an old name for hysteria or low spirits.—*vi* to vaporize; to boast or vaunt with ostentatious display; to bully; to hector; to brag; to bounce.

variable *adj* capable of varying, changing or altering; liable to change; often changing; changeable (*variable winds*); fickle; unsteady; inconstant; capable of being varied or changed.—*n* that which is variable; a variable quantity; a shifting wind as opposed to a trade wind; (*pl*) the region between the northeast and the southeast trade winds where variable winds occur.

variable quantity *n* (*math*) a quantity

vanishing point

which may take a number of different values or even any value.

variable star *n* a star which undergoes a periodical increase and diminution of its lustre.

variance *n* difference that produces dispute or controversy; disagreement; dissension; discord; (*law*) a discrepancy between two statements or documents.—**at variance** in disagreement; in a state of dissension; in enmity.

variant *adj* different; diverse; variable; varying.—*n* something that is really the same though with a different form; a different reading or version.

variation *n* the act or process of varying; partial change in the form, position, state or qualities of the same thing; alteration; mutation; change; modification; the extent to which a thing varies; the amount or rate of change; the act of deviating; deviation; (*gram*) change of termination of words; inflection; (*astron*) any deviation from the mean orbit or mean motion of a heavenly body occasioned by another disturbing body; (*physics, navig*) declination; (*mus*) one of a series of ornamental changes or embellishments in the treatment of a tune, movement or theme during several successive repetitions.

varicose *adj* (of veins) abnormally enlarged and swollen.

varied *adj* altered; changed; characterized by variety; diversified; consisting of various kinds or sorts differing from each other; diverse; various.

variegate *vt* (**variegated, variegating**) to diversify by means of different tints or hues.

variegated *adj* diversified with tints or hues; (*bot*) irregularly marked with spots of a light colour (said of leaves).

variety *n* the state or quality of being varied or various; intermixture or succession of different things or of things different in form; diversity; multifariousness; manysidedness; a collection or number of different things; a varied assortment; something different from others of the same general kind; a sort; a kind; in scientific classifications, a subdivision of a species of animals or plants; a species in process of evolving.

variety show *n* a light, mixed theatrical show.

variola *n* smallpox.

variorum *n* an edition of some work in which the notes of different commentators are inserted.—*adj* denoting or pertaining to a variorum (*a variorum edition of Shakespeare*).

various *adj* differing from each other; different; diverse; manifold; several; exhibiting different characters; multiform.

varlet *n* (*arch*) a page or knight's attendant; a scoundrel; a rascal.

varnish *n* a solution of resinous matter forming a clear limpid fluid and used by painters, cabinet-makers, etc, for coating the surface of their work in order to give it a shining, transparent and hard surface capable of resisting the influences of air and moisture; what resembles varnish either naturally or artificially; a glossy or lustrous appearance; outside show; gloss.—*vt* to lay varnish on; to give an improved appearance to; to give a fair colouring to; to gloss over.

vary *vt* (**varied, varying**) to alter in form, appearance, substance or position; to make different by a partial change; to change; to diversify; (*mus*) to embellish, as a melody or theme with passing notes, arpeggios, etc.—*vi* to alter or be altered in any manner; to suffer change; to appear in different forms; to differ or be different; to be unlike or diverse; to change, as in purpose, opinion, etc; to deviate; to swerve; to alternate; to disagree; to be at variance; (*math*) to be subject to continual increase or decrease.

vascular *adj* (*biol*) of, consisting of or containing vessels as part of a structure of animal and vegetable organisms for conveying blood, sap, etc.

vascular bundle *n* a strand of conducting vascular tissue of xylem and phloem occurring in seed plants and ferns and extending from the root to the leaves.

vascular system *n* the network that circulates fluids through the body tissues, comprising the heart, veins, arteries and capillaries; (*bot*) vascular tissue.

vascular tissue *n* the tissue of xylem and phloem that transports nutrients and water through the body of seed plants and ferns.

vas deferens *n* (*pl* **vasa deferentia**) either of a pair of tubes in the testicle which carry semen to the penis.

vase *n* a vessel of some size of various materials, forms and purposes, used for displaying flowers or for ornament; (*archit*) a sculptured ornament representing the vessels of the ancients, as incense pots, flowerpots, etc; the body of a Corinthian or Composite capital.

vasectomy *n* the excision of all or part of the vas deferens, especially to cause sterility.

vassal *n* a feudal tenant holding lands under a lord and bound by his tenure to feudal services; a subject; a dependant; a retainer; a servant; a bondsman; a slave.

vast *adj* waste or desert; lonely; of great extent; boundless; huge in bulk and extent; immense; very great in numbers or amount; very great as to degree or intensity.

variegated

vastness *n* the quality of being vast; great extent; immensity; greatness in general.

vat *n* a large vessel for holding liquors; a large tub; a tank or cistern.

VAT an abbreviation of **value-added tax**.

Vatican *n* an extensive palace in Rome on the Vatican hill, the residence of the pope.—**the Vatican** papal power or government.

vaudeville *n* a stage show consisting of several acts, including singing, dancing and comedy; a dramatic piece whose dialogue is intermingled with light or comic songs set to popular airs; a variety entertainment.

vault[1] *n* an arched roof; a concave roof or roof-like covering (*the vault of heaven*); (*archit*) a continued arch; an arched apartment; a subterranean chamber used for a place of interment; a cellar.—*vt* to form with a vault or arched roof; to arch.

vault[2] *n* a leap or spring; a bound; a leap by means of a pole or assisted by resting the hand or hands on something.—*vi* to leap; to bound; to spring; to exhibit equestrian or other feats of tumbling or leaping.

vaunt *vi* to boast; to talk with ostentation; to brag; to glory; to exult.—*vt* to boast of; to magnify or glorify with vanity; to display or put forward boastfully.—*n* a boast; a brag.

vaunting *n* vain boasting; bragging.

VDU an abbreviation of **visual display unit**.

veal *n* the flesh of a calf killed for food.

vector *n* a quantity, such as a velocity or a force, which has direction as well as magnitude and is compounded by the parallelogram law.

Veda *n* the body of ancient Sanskrit hymns with accompanying comments believed by the Hindus to have been revealed by Brahma and on which the Brahmanical system is based.

vedette, vidette *n* a sentry on horseback stationed on an outpost or elevated point to watch an enemy and give notice of danger; a small patrol boat.

veer *vi* to shift or change direction, as the wind, especially to shift in a clockwise direction, the opposite of *back*; to go round; to change the direction of its course by turning (as a ship); to turn round, vary, be otherwise minded (said in regard to persons, feelings, intentions).—*vt* (*naut*) to direct into a different course; to wear or cause to change a course by turning the stern to windward, in opposition to *tacking*.

vegan *n* a vegetarian who does not eat eggs or any form of dairy produce.

vegetable *adj* belonging, pertaining or peculiar to plants; having the characteristics of a plant or plants.—*n* a plant; often distinctively, a plant used for food; a person who leads an inactive, uninteresting existence.

vegetarian *n* one who abstains from animal food, eating vegetables, fruit, eggs and dairy produce.—*adj* belonging to the diet or system of vegetarians.

vegetate *vi* (**vegetated, vegetating**) to grow in the manner of plants; hence, to live a monotonous, inactive life; to have a mere existence.

vegetation *n* the process of growing exhibited by plants; vegetable growth; vegetables or plants in general or collectively.

vehemence *n* the character or quality of being vehement; violent ardour; fervour; impetuosity; fire; impetuous force; boisterousness; violence.

vehement *adj* proceeding from or characterized by strength or impetuosity of feeling; very eager or urgent; fervent; passionate; acting with great force or energy (*vehement wind, fire*); energetic; violent; very forcible.

vehicle *n* any kind of conveyance, such as a motorcar, lorry, etc, moving on land; a conveyance; that which is used as the instrument of conveyance, transmission or communication (*language is the vehicle for conveying ideas*); a substance in which medicine is taken; a menstruum or medium in which paints, gums, varnishes, etc, are dissolved and prepared for use.

vehicular *adj* of or pertaining to a vehicle.

veil *n* something hung up or spread out to intercept the view; a screen; a curtain; a piece of thin fabric worn to conceal, shade or protect the face; (*fig*) anything that prevents observation; a covering, mask, disguise, etc.—**to take the veil** to assume the veil on becoming a nun; to retire to a nunnery.—*vt* to cover or conceal with a veil; to enshroud; to envelop; to keep from being seen; to conceal from view; to conceal; to mask; to disguise.

vein *n* one of a system of membranous canals or tubes distributed throughout the bodies of animals for the purpose of returning the impure blood from the extremities, surfaces and viscera to the heart and lungs; a tube or an assemblage of tubes through which the sap of plants is transmitted along the leaves; a crack or fissure in a rock filled up by substances different from the rock and which may either be metallic or nonmetallic; a streak or wave of different colour appearing in wood, marble, etc; disposition or cast of mind; particular mood, humour or disposition for the time being.—*vt* to fill or furnish with veins; to streak or variegate with veins.

veined *adj* full of veins; streaked; variegated; (*bot*) having vessels branching over the surface, as a leaf.

veined

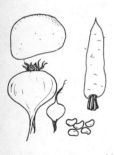

vegetable

Velcro *n* the trademark for a nylon material made of matching strips of tiny hooks and pile that are easily pressed together or pulled apart.

veld, veldt *n* a term in South Africa for open unenclosed country.

vellum *n* a fine kind of parchment made of calfskin and rendered clear, smooth and white for writing on.

velocipede *n* an early form of bicycle consisting of wheels and driven or impelled by the feet of the rider or pair of riders.

velocity *n* quickness or speed in motion or movement; swiftness; rapidity (rarely applied to the movements of animals); (*physics*) rate of motion, differing from speed in involving direction as well as magnitude.

velour, velours *n* a velvet-like fabric.

velure *n* a substance of felt or other velvety combinations used in hats, etc.

velvet *n* a rich fabric of silk, rayon, etc, covered on the outside with a close, short, fine, soft shag or nap; a delicate hairy integument covering a deer's antlers in the first stages of growth.—*adj* made of velvet; soft and delicate like velvet.

velveteen *n* a cloth made of cotton in imitation of velvet; cotton velvet.

velvety *adj* made of or resembling velvet; smooth, soft or delicate in surface.

vena cava *n* (*pl* **venae cavae**) one of the two major veins that empty blood into the right chamber of the heart in air-breathing vertebrates.

venal *adj* ready to sell oneself for money or other consideration and entirely from sordid motives; ready to accept a bribe; mercenary.

venality *n* prostitution of talents, offices or services for money or reward; mercenariness.

vend *vt* to sell.

vendace *n* a fish of the salmon family.

vendetta *n* a blood feud; the practice of the nearest of kin executing vengeance on the murderer of a relative; the taking of private vengeance.

vendible *adj* capable of being sold; saleable; marketable.

vending machine *n* a coin-operated machine dispensing small articles for sale, including soft drinks, chocolate, cigarettes, etc.

vendor *n* a seller.

veneer *n* a thin piece of wood (sometimes ivory or other substance) laid on another of a less valuable kind so that the whole article appears to be of the more valuable kind.—*vt* to overlay or face over with veneer; (*fig*) to put a fine superficial show on; to gild.

veneering *n* the act of one who veneers; the material laid on; (*fig*) superficial show.

venerable *adj* worthy of veneration; deserving of honour and respect; to be regarded with awe and reverence; hallowed by associations; a title given by Church of England to archdeacons and by the Roman Catholic Church to those who have passed the first stage of canonization.

venerate *vt* (**venerated, venerating**) to regard with respect and reverence; to reverence; to revere; to regard as hallowed.

veneration *n* the highest degree of respect and reverence; a feeling or sentiment excited by the dignity, wisdom and goodness of a person or by the sacredness of his or her character, and with regard to place by whatever makes us regard it as hallowed.

venereal *adj* pertaining to sexual relations or their indulgence; relating to or arising from sexual intercourse.

venereal disease *n* any disease transmitted by sexual intercourse.

venery[1] *n* (*arch*) sexual indulgence.

venery[2] *n* (*arch*) the act or exercise of hunting; the sports of the chase.

Venetian *adj* pertaining to Venice in Northern Italy.

Venetian blind *n* a window blind with overlapping slats which may be opened, closed or raised by pulling a cord.

Venetian red *n* a burnt ochre which owes its colour to the presence of an oxide of iron.

vengeance *n* punishment inflicted in return for an injury or an offence, generally implying indignation on the part of the punisher and more or less justice in the nature of the punishment, often used in curses or imprecations (*a vengeance on you!*).—**with a vengeance** very strongly, much, etc (*it's snowing with a vengeance*).

vengeful *adj* vindictive; retributive; revengeful.

venial *adj* that may be forgiven; pardonable; not deeply sinful; excusable; that may pass without censure.

venison *n* the flesh of deer used as food.

venom *n* the poisonous fluid secreted by certain animals and introduced into the bodies of other animals by biting in the case of snakes and stinging in the case of scorpions, bees, etc; hence, spite; malice; malignity; virulency.

venomous *adj* full of venom; noxious to animal life from venom; poisonous; malignant; spiteful; malicious.

venous *adj* pertaining to a vein or to veins; contained in veins (*venous blood*, distinguishable from *arterial blood* by its darker colour); consisting of veins; (*bot*) veined.

vent *n* a small aperture or opening; the priming and firing aperture of a gun; the touchhole; the anus; the opening at which the excrements of birds and fishes are discharged; the flue or funnel of a chimney; an outlet; means of outward manifestation or expression (*a vent for one's feelings*);

utterance; expression.—**to give vent to** to suffer to escape; to keep no longer pent up (anger, etc).—*vt* to let out; to give passage to; to emit; to keep no longer pent up in one's mind; to pour forth; to utter; to publish.

ventilate *vt* (**ventilated, ventilating**) to expose to the free passage of air or wind; to supply with fresh and remove exhausted air; to expose to common talk or consideration; to let be freely discussed.

ventilation *n* the act of ventilating; the replacement of exhausted air by pure fresh air; the art or operation of supplying buildings, mines and other confined places with a necessary quantity of fresh air; public examination or discussion of questions or topics.

ventilator *n* a device for keeping air fresh in any close space; a device for enabling a patient to breathe normally or more easily.

ventricle *n* a small cavity in an animal body serving some function; (*anat*) one of two cavities of the heart (distinguished as right and left) which propel the blood into the arteries.

ventriloquism *n* the act, art or practice of speaking or uttering sounds by employing the vocal organs in such a manner that the voice appears to come not from the person but from some distance, as from the opposite side of the room, from the cellar, etc.

ventriloquist *n* one who practises or is skilled in ventriloquism.

venture *n* an undertaking of chance or danger; the risking or staking something; a hazard; a scheme for making gain by way of trade; a commercial speculation; the thing put to hazard; a dangerous expedition; chance; luck; contingency.—**at a venture** at hazard; without seeing the end or mark or without foreseeing the issue.— *vi* (**ventured, venturing**) to dare; to have courage or presumption to do, undertake or say something; to run a hazard or risk; to risk oneself.—*vt* to expose to hazard; to risk; to expose oneself to.

venture capital *n* capital available for investment in risky but potentially very profitable enterprises and repayable at higher than normal interest rates.

venturesome *adj* inclined to venture; venturous.

venue *n* the place where an action or event takes place.

Venus *n* in Roman myth, the goddess of beauty and love; (*astron*) the planet second from the sun and having its orbit between Mercury and the earth, seen as a bright star sometimes in the morning and sometimes in the evening.

veracious *adj* observant of truth; habitually disposed to speak truth; characterized by truth; true.

veracity *n* the state or quality of being veracious or true; regard to or observance of truth; truthfulness; truth; agreement with actual fact.

veranda, verandah *n* a kind of open portico or a sort of light external gallery attached to the front of a building with a sloping roof supported on slender pillars; a roofed porch.

verb *n* (*gram*) that part of speech whose essential function is to predicate or assert something in regard to something else (the subject or thing spoken of), divided into active and neuter, transitive and intransitive, etc.

verbal *adj* spoken; expressed to the ear in words; oral; respecting words only and not things; literal; having word answering to word (*a verbal translation*); (*gram*) derived from a verb (*a verbal noun*).

verbally *adv* in a verbal manner; by words uttered; orally; word for word.

verbatim *adv* word for word; in the same words (*to repeat a story verbatim*).

verbena *n* one of a genus of plants, mostly American, with red, white or purple flowers.

verbiage *n* verbosity; use of many words without necessity; wordiness.

verbose *adj* abounding in words; using or containing more words than are necessary; wordy; prolix.

verbosity *n* the state or quality of being verbose; wordiness; prolixity.

verdant *adj* green with herbage or foliage; covered with growing plants or grass; (*colloq*) green in knowledge; (*colloq*) simple by reason of inexperience.

verderer *n* formerly, an official having charge of the trees, etc, in a royal forest.

verdict *n* the answer of a jury given to the court concerning any matter of fact in any cause committed to their trial and examination; hence, a decision, judgment or opinion pronounced in general.

verdigris *n* a substance obtained by exposing copper to the air in contact with acetic acid, used as a pigment, as a mordant and otherwise.

verdure *n* greenness or freshness of vegetation; green plants or foliage.

verge[1] *n* the extreme side or edge of anything; a grass border beside a road; the brink, border, margin, limit; compass; space; room; scope.

verge[2] *vi* (**verged, verging**) to tend downwards; to bend; to slope; to tend; to incline; to approach; to border.

verge[3] *n* a rod or staff of office; a mace.

verger *n* one who carries a verge; an officer who bears the verge or staff of office before a bishop, dean or other dignitary; the official who takes care of the interior of the fabric of a church.

verge

verification *n* the act of verifying; authentication; confirmation.

verify *vt* (**verified, verifying**) to prove to be true; to confirm; to establish the truth, correctness or authenticity of.

verily *adv* in truth; in very truth or deed; in fact; certainly; really; in sincere earnestness.

verisimilitude *n* the appearance of truth; probability; likelihood.

verismo *n* a term used to describe a type of opera concerned with representing contemporary life of ordinary people in an honest and realistic way.

veritable *adj* true; agreeable to truth or fact; real; actual.

verity *n* the quality of being true or real; true or real nature; reality; truth; fact; a true assertion or tenet; a truth.

verjuice *n* an acid liquor expressed from crab apples, unripe grapes, etc, used for culinary and other purposes; (*fig*) sourness or acidity of temper, manner or expression.

vermicelli *n* a pasta in the form of long, thin threads.

vermicide *n* a substance which destroys intestinal worms; a worm-killer.

vermicular *adj* pertaining to worms; resembling a worm; particularly resembling the motion of a worm.

vermiform *adj* having the form or shape of a worm or of its motions.

vermiform appendix *n* the worm-shaped structure attached to the caecum vestigially in humans and certain other mammals, the appendix.

vermifuge *n* a medicine or substance that destroys or expels intestinal worms; an anthelmintic.

vermilion *n* the red sulphide of mercury or cinnabar; a bright red pigment formed of this or artificially prepared from a preparation of sulphur and mercury; a colour such as that of the above pigment; a red colour.—*vt* to colour with vermilion; to cover with a delicate red.

vermin *n sing, pl* (used chiefly in plural) the smaller mammals or certain birds which damage crops or other belongings and to destructive insects, etc; human beings dangerous to society.

vermouth *n* a liquor compounded of white wine, absinthe, angelica and other aromatics, used to whet the appetite.

vernacular *adj* belonging to the country of or place of one's birth; belonging to speech naturally acquired or more particularly to the everyday idiom of a place.—*n* one's native tongue; the native idiom of a place.

vernal *adj* belonging to the spring; appearing in spring; belonging to youth; the spring of life.

vernier *n* a small sliding scale parallel with the fixed scale of a barometer, theodolite or other instrument, used for measuring fractional parts of the divisions on the fixed graduated scale; an additional apparatus used to tune or adjust an instrument.

veronica[1] *n* any of a genus of plants including the various species of speedwell.

veronica[2] *n* the image of Christ's face that in legend appeared on a handkerchief given to him by St Veronica on the way to the crucifixion; this handkerchief.

veronica[3] *n* in bullfighting, a manoeuvre by a matador in which he swings the cape slowly before the bull while standing still.

verruca *n* a wart on the hand or foot; (*biol*) a wart-like excrescence.

versatile *adj* capable of being moved or turned round; turning with ease from one thing to another; readily applying oneself to a new task or to various subjects; many-sided; (*bot*) turning like the needle of a compass; fixed but freely movable.

versatility *n* the state or quality of being versatile; the faculty of easily turning one's mind to new tasks or subjects; facility in taking up various intellectual pursuits.

verse *n* a line of poetry consisting of a certain number of metrical feet; poetry; metrical language; poetical composition; versification; a short division of the chapters in the Scriptures; a short division of a poetical composition; a stanza.

versed *adj* thoroughly acquainted; practised; skilled (with *in*).

versicle *n* a little verse; a short verse in a church service spoken or chanted by the priest or minister alternately with a response by the people.

versification *n* the act or practice of composing poetic verse; a turning into verse; the construction of poetry; metrical composition.

versify *vi* (**versified, versifying**) to make verses.—*vt* to relate in verse; to treat as the subject of verse; to turn into verse.

version *n* the act of translating from one language into another; a translation; that which is rendered from another language (*the revised version of the Scriptures*); a statement or account of incidents or proceedings from some particular point of view.

verso *n* (*pl* **versos**) the left-hand page of an open book; the left-hand side of a sheet of paper, as opposed to *recto*; the reverse of a coin.

verst *n* a Russian measure of length.

versus *prep* against; in contrast to.

vert *n* formerly, the legal right to collect whatever grows and bears a green leaf in a forest; (*heral*) a green colour.

vertebra *n* (*pl* **vertebrae**) one of the bones

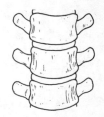

vertebrae

of which the spine or backbone consists; (*pl*) the spine.

vertebral *adj* pertaining to the vertebrae (*the vertebral column*); vertebrate.—*n* a vertebrate animal.

vertebral column *n* the backbone; the spine; the spinal column.

vertebrate *n* (*zool*) an animal possessing a vertebral column or spine, including fish, amphibians, birds, reptiles, quadrupeds and human beings.

vertex *n* (*pl* **vertexes, vertices**) the highest or principal point; apex; top; crown; summit; (*math*) the point in any figure opposite to and most distant from the base; the point of a conic section where the axis meets the curve.

vertical *adj* relating to the vertex; situated at the vertex; directly overhead; in a position perpendicular to the plane of the horizon; upright; plumb.—*n* a vertical line or plane.

vertigo *n* (*pl* **vertigoes, vertigines**) dizziness or swimming of the head; giddiness arising from some disorder of the system.

vertu *n* same as **virtu**.

verve *n* poetic or artistic rapture; great spirit; energy; rapture; enthusiasm.

very *adv* in a high degree; to a great extent; extremely; exceedingly.—*adj* veritable; real; true; actual; often placed before nouns to indicate that they must be understood in their full, unrestricted sense (*my very heartstrings*); to denote exact conformity with what is expressed by the word or to express identity (*the very words*); to give emphasis or force generally (*even your very eyes*).

very high frequency *n* (often shortened to **VHF**) a radio frequency between 300 and 30 megahertz, the frequency which is used in short-range radio and which is relatively free from interference.

Very light *n* a coloured flare fired to give temporary light or to serve as a signal.

very low frequency *n* the frequency used for maritime radio navigation, etc.

vesicant *n* a blistering application or agent with applications in chemical warfare.—*adj* raising blisters.

vesicle *n* any small bladder-like structure, cavity, cell, etc, in a body; a little sac or cyst; a small blister or pustule on the skin.

vesper *n* the evening star; hence, the evening; (*pl*) the time of evening service in some churches; (*pl*) evening worship or service.

vessel *n* a utensil for holding liquids and other things, as a barrel, kettle, cup, dish, etc; a ship; a craft of any kind but usually one larger than a mere boat; (*anat*) any tube or canal in which the blood or other fluids are contained, secreted or circulated; (*bot*) a canal or tube in which the sap

vest

vetch

is contained and conveyed; (*fig*) in scriptural phraseology, a person into whom anything is conceived as poured or infused (*a chosen vessel, vessels of wrath*).

vest *n* a short sleeveless garment worn under a garment, covering the upper part of the body; a waistcoat.—*vt* to clothe; to invest or clothe, as with authority; to endow; to confer on (*vested with power*); to confer possession or enjoyment of (*to vest dominion in a person*).—*vi* to devolve; to take effect, as a title or right (*the estate vests in the heir*).

vesta *n* a wax or wooden match which ignites by friction.

Vesta *n* in Roman myth, the virgin goddess of the hearth in honour of whom a sacred fire was kept constantly burning under the care of six virgins; (*astron*) one of the asteroids.

vestal *adj* pertaining to Vesta; pure; chaste.—*n* among the ancient Romans, a virgin consecrated to Vesta; hence, a virgin or woman of spotless chastity.

vested *adj* clothed; habited; (*law*) not in a state of contingency or suspension; fixed.

vested interest *n* (*law*) a permanent entitlement to the possession and use of property now and in the future; a strong reason for acting in a certain way, usually on account of personal gain.

vestibule *n* a passage, hall or antechamber next the outer door of a house; a lobby; a hall.

vestige *n* a footprint; a trace, mark or appearance of something which is no longer present or in existence; remains of something long passed away; (*biol*) a structure which has been reduced as a result of adaptation.

vestigial *adj* of or relating to a vestige; (*biol*) having lost use or importance in adaptation and reduced in size.

vestment *n* a covering or garment, especially that worn by a priest or official; some part of clothing or dress; especially, some part of outer clothing.

vestry *n* a place or room attached to a church where the ecclesiastical vestments are kept and where the clergy robe themselves.

vesture *n* (*arch*) a garment or garments generally; clothing; that which invests or covers; envelope; integument.—*vt* (**vestured, vesturing**) (*arch*) to clothe.

vet *n* (*colloq*) a veterinary surgeon.—*vt* (**vetted, vetting**) (*colloq*) to examine or treat an animal medically or surgically; (*colloq*) to examine and correct a literary work; (*colloq*) to check carefully.

vetch *n* a common plant allied to the bean with blue or purple flowers and a stem with tendrils found in temperate climates and cultivated for fodder.

veteran *adj* having long experience in anything; long practised or experienced in war and the duties of a soldier.—*n* one who has long experience in any service or art, originally particularly in war.

veterinary *adj* pertaining to the art or science of treating the diseases of animals.

veterinary surgeon *n* a person trained in treating sick or injured animals.

veto *n* (*pl* **vetoes**) the power which one branch of a legislature has to negative the resolutions of another branch; the act of exercising this power or right; any authoritative prohibition, interdict, refusal or negative.—*vt* (**vetoed, vetoing**) to put a veto on; to forbid; to interdict.

vex *vt* to cause slight anger or displeasure in; to trouble by petty or light annoyances; to irritate, fret, plague, annoy; to make sorrowful; to grieve or distress.

vexation *n* the act of vexing or state of being vexed; irritation; annoyance; cause of irritation; affliction.

vexatious *adj* causing vexation; annoying; mortifying.

via *prep* by way of (*to send a letter via Falmouth*).

viable *adj* capable of sustaining independent life (said of a newborn child); practicable; workable.

viaduct *n* a long bridge or series of arches carrying a railway or road over a valley or district of low level.

vial *n* a glass vessel or bottle; especially, a small glass bottle used for holding liquors and particularly liquid medicines.

viand *n* meat dressed; food; victuals (used chiefly in the plural).

vibes *npl* (short for **vibrations**) one's instinctive emotional reaction to a situation, atmosphere, etc.

vibraphone *n* a percussion instrument consisting of tuned metal bars which are struck with small mechanical hammers.

vibrate *vi* (**vibrated, vibrating**) to swing; to oscillate; to move one way and the other; to play to and fro; to produce a vibratory or resonant effect; to quiver.—*vt* to move or wave to and fro; to oscillate; to cause to quiver; to measure by vibrating or oscillating (*a pendulum which vibrates seconds*).

vibration *n* the act of vibrating; an oscillation or swing of a pendulum or similar body; one of a series of rapid tremulous motions produced in a body or substance; the tremulous motion of a sonorous body; (*pl*) feelings instinctively sensed; (*pl*) feelings experienced or communicated.

vicar *n* a substitute in office; a representative (*the vicar of Christ*); an Anglican clergyman in charge of a parish.

vicarage *n* the benefice of a vicar; the house or residence of a vicar.

vicarious *adj* belonging to a deputy or substitute; delegated; filling the place of another; performed or suffered for, or instead of, another.

vice[1] *n* a defect, fault or blemish; any immoral or evil habit or practice; a moral failing; a particular form of wickedness or depravity; the indulgence of impure or degrading appetites or passions; depravity or corruption of manners (*an age of vice*).

vice[2] *n* an instrument with a pair of iron jaws brought together by means of a screw so that they can take a fast hold of anything placed between them.

Vice *n* a character in the old morality plays dressed in the habit of a fool and carrying a dagger whose chief employment was to belabour the devil.

vice- *prefix* denoting position second in rank (sometimes used by itself as a noun, the context making the meaning clear).

vice-admiral *n* an officer next in rank and command to the admiral.

vice-chancellor *n* an officer next to a chancellor; a judge in the chancery division of the High Court of Justice in England; an officer of a university who discharges certain duties of the chancellor.

viceregal *adj* pertaining to a viceroy.

vice-regent *n* an officer who is deputed to exercise the powers of another; a substitute; one having a delegated power.

viceroy *n* one who rules in the name of the queen (or king) with regal authority.

vice versa *adv* contrariwise; the reverse; the terms or the case being reversed.

vicinity *n* the quality of being near; propinquity; proximity; nearness in place; neighbourhood; the adjoining district, space or country.

vicious *adj* characterized by vice; faulty; defective; imperfect; addicted to vice; depraved; wicked; contrary to morality; evil; bad (*vicious examples*); not genuine or pure; faulty; incorrect (*a vicious style in language*); addicted to bad tricks (*a vicious horse*).

vicissitude *n* a passing from one state or condition to another; change, especially in regard to the affairs of life or the world; mutation.

victim *n* a living being sacrificed to some deity or in the performance of a religious rite; a person or thing destroyed; a person sacrificed in the pursuit of an object; a person who suffers severe injury from another; one who is cheated or duped; a gull.

victimize *vt* (**victimized, victimizing**) to make a victim of; to cause to suffer; to make the victim of a swindling transaction.

victor *n* one who wins or gains the advantage in a contest; especially, one who conquers in war.—*adj* victorious.

viaduct

vice

victoria *n* a four-wheeled carriage for two persons and with an elevated driver's seat in front; a very large African water lily; a type of plum.

Victoria Cross *n* the highest British decoration granted for individual acts of bravery, founded by Queen Victoria in 1856.

Victorian *adj* of or living in the reign of Queen Victoria; old-fashioned, prudish.—*n* one who lived in the reign of Queen Victoria; one with characteristics of the reign of Queen Victoria.

victorious *adj* having conquered in battle or contest; being victor; conquering; associated with victory; indicating victory.

victory *n* the defeat of an enemy in battle or of an antagonist in a contest; the superiority gained in any contest (as over passions, temptations, etc).

victual *n* provision of food; provisions (now generally in plural and signifying food for human beings, prepared for eating).—*vt* (**victualled, victualling**) to supply or store with victuals; to provide with stores of food.

victualler *n* formerly, a supplier of provisions; an innkeeper.

vicuña, vicuna *n* a South American animal of the camel family, closely allied to the llama and yielding short, soft, silken fur used for making delicate fabrics.

videlicet *adv* (usually abbreviated to **viz**) to wit; that is; namely.

video *n* the visual part of a television broadcast; a video cassette recorder; a film recorded on a video cassette.—*vt* (**videoed, videoing**) to record (a television programme, etc) on a video cassette recorder.

video cassette *n* a cassette containing videotape.

video cassette recorder *n* a tape-recorder for visual and sound signals, used for recording and playing back television programmes.

videotape *n* magnetic tape used for recording visual images, as of a television programme.

vidette *n* same as **vedette**.

vie *vi* (**vied, vying**) in old games of cards, to wager on one's hand against an opponent; to strive for superiority; to contend (followed by *with* and said of persons or things).

video cassette

view *n* the act of looking, seeing or beholding; survey; look; sight; a mental survey; consideration; range of vision; power of seeing or perception, either physical or mental; that which is viewed, seen or beheld; a sight or spectacle presented; scene; prospect; a scene portrayed; a representation of a landscape, etc; manner or mode of looking at things; judgment; opinion; way of thinking; something looked towards or forming the subject of considera-

tion; intention; purpose (*to act with a view to happiness*).—*vt* to see; to look on; to examine with the eye; to inspect; to survey; to survey intellectually; to consider.—*vi* to look; to take a view.

viewer *n* a person who views, especially television; an optical device used in viewing.

viewfinder *n* a device in a camera showing the view to be photographed.

vigil *n* the act of keeping awake; forbearance from sleep; a period of sleeplessness; a watch or watching; a devotional watching; devotions performed during the customary hours of sleep; (*eccles*) the eve or evening or whole day preceding a festival, as Christmas, Easter or some principal saint's day.

vigilance *n* the state or quality of being vigilant; watchfulness; circumspection.

vigilant *adj* watchful; ever awake and on the alert; circumspect.

vignette *n* a woodcut, engraving or illustration not enclosed within a definite border; a picture, the edges of which shade off into the background; a short word portrait.—*vt* (**vignetted, vignetting**) to depict in vignette; to shade off into the background.

vigorous *adj* possessing vigour or physical strength; strong; lusty; exhibiting or resulting from vigour, energy or strength, either of body or mind; powerful; energetic.

vigour *n* active strength or force of body in animals; physical strength; strength of mind; intellectual force; energy; strength in animal or vegetable nature or action.

Viking *n* one of the Norse pirates who ravaged the European seas during the eighth, ninth and tenth centuries.

vile *adj* worthless; despicable; morally base; depraved; bad; wicked; villainous.

vilify *vt* (**vilified, vilifying**) to attempt to degrace by slander; to defame; to traduce.

villa *n* a country residence, usually of some size and pretension; a rural or suburban detached house.

village *n* an assemblage of houses smaller than a town or city and larger than a hamlet.

villain *n* a depraved person capable or guilty of great crimes; a vile, wicked person; the main evil chracter in a play, film or novel; a villein; (*arch*) a boor.

villainous *adj* pertaining to a villain; very wicked or depraved; vile; proceeding from depravity; sorry; mean.

villainy *n* the quality of being villainous; extreme depravity; great wickedness; a villainous act; a crime; an action of deep depravity.

villein *n* a feudal tenant of the lowest class.

vim *n* (*colloq*) vigour, energy.

vinaigrette *n* a small box of perforated gold, silver, etc, for holding an aromatic substance or smelling salts; a salad dressing made from oil, vinegar and seasoning.

vindicate *vt* (**vindicated, vindicating**) to assert a right or claim to; to prove (a claim) to be just or valid; to maintain the cause or rights of; to deliver from wrong, oppression, etc; to support or maintain against denial, censure or objections; to defend (*to vindicate a theory*); to justify.

vindication *n* the act of vindicating; justification against censure, objections or accusations; the proving of anything to be just; defence from wrong or oppression, by force or otherwise.

vindictive *adj* revengeful; given to revenge; (of damages) exemplary, punitive.

vindictiveness *n* revengeful spirit; revengefulness.

vine *n* a climbing plant with a woody stem producing grapes; a grapevine; the trailing or climbing stem of a plant; a sphere of activity.

vinegar *n* a sour liquid of diluted acetic acid obtained by fermenting wine, etc, and used for flavouring, pickling, etc; anything really or metaphorically sour; sourness of temper.

vinery *n* a place where vines are cultivated or wine is made.

vineyard *n* a plantation of vines producing grapes.

vintage *n* the gathering of a crop of grapes; the crop produced; the wine from the crop of grapes in one season; any especially good wine made in a good year; the product of a particular period.—*adj* (of wine) made or harvested during a particularly good year; especially good; characteristic of the best; (of a car) old, specifically of one built between 1918 and 1930.

vintner *n* one who deals in wine; a wine seller.

viol *n* a medieval stringed musical instrument of much the same form as the violin but softer.

viola[1] *n* a large kind of violin, to which the part between the second violin and the bass is generally assigned.

viola[2] *n* any of several plants of the genus that includes violets and pansies.

violate *vt* (**violated, violating**) to treat roughly and injuriously; to do injury to; to outrage; to break in on; to disturb; to desecrate; to treat with irreverence; to profane or profanely meddle with; to infringe; to sin against; to transgress; to ravish; to commit rape on.

violation *n* the act of violating; desecration; profanation; infringement; transgression; rape.

violator *n* one who violates; one who infringes or transgresses; one who profanes or desecrates; one who rapes.

violence *n* the quality of being violent; vehemence; intensity of action or motion;

highly excited feeling; impetuosity; injury done to anything which is entitled to respect or reverence; profanation; violation; unjust force; outrage; attack; assault.

violent *adj* characterized by the exertion of force accompanied by rapidity; impetuous; furious; effected by violence; not coming by natural means (*a violent death*); acting or produced by unlawful, unjust or improper force; unreasonably vehement; passionate; severe; extreme; sharp or acute (*violent pains*).

violet *n* a small plant with bluish-purple flowers; a bluish-purple colour.

violin *n* a musical instrument of wood with four strings stretched by means of a bridge over a hollow body and played with a bow; a fiddle.

violinist *n* a person skilled in playing on a violin.

violoncello *n* (*pl* **violoncellos**) a large four-stringed bass instrument of the violin family, held by the performer between the knees and filling a place between the violin and double bass.

VIP (an abbreviation of *very important person*) someone of great importance or seniority in an organization, etc.; a celebrity.

viper *n* a name of certain poisonous snakes, one of them the common viper or adder found in Europe; a mischievous or malignant person.

viperish *adj* inclining to the character of a viper.

virago *n* (*pl* **viragoes, viragos**) a bold, impudent, turbulent woman; a termagant.

viral *adj* of or caused by a virus.

virelai, virelay *n* a short poem with a refrain, based throughout on two rhymes.

Virgilian *adj* pertaining to Virgil, the Roman poet; resembling the style of Virgil.

virgin *n* a person who has not had sexual intercourse, especially a woman; a person who has preserved his or her chastity.—*adj* pertaining to a virgin; maidenly; modest; chaste; untouched; fresh; unsullied.

Virgin *n* Mary, the mother of Christ; a painting or statue of Mary; the sign or the constellation Virgo.

virginal[1] *adj* of or pertaining to a virgin or virginity; chaste, pure, innocent; fresh, unsullied, untouched.

virginal[2] *n* an ancient keyed musical instrument resembling the spinet.

virginity *n* the state of being a virgin; perfect chastity.

Virgo *n* one of the twelve signs of the zodiac, which the sun enters about 22nd August.

virile *adj* pertaining to a man as opposed to a woman; masculine; sexually potent.

virility *n* manhood; sexual potency; masculine conduct or action.

virtu, vertu *n* excellence in objects of art or

violin

viper

curiosity; objects of art, antiquity or curiosity taken collectively.

virtual *adj* being in essence or effect, not in fact; not actual but equivalent, so far as result is concerned (*a virtual denial of a statement*); (*comput*) denoting memory created by software and not actually present in hardware.

virtually *adv* in a virtual manner; in efficacy or effect if not in actuality.

virtue *n* moral goodness; uprightness; morality, the opposite of *vice*; a particular moral excellence (*the virtue of temperance*); specifically, female purity; chastity; any good quality, merit or accomplishment; an inherent power or property (*the medicinal virtues of plants*); efficacy; active, efficacious power.

virtuoso *n* (*pl* **virtuosi**) one skilled in or having a taste for artistic excellence; one skilled in antiquities, curiosities, etc; a person highly skilled in playing a musical instrument.—*adj* skilled or masterly in technique.

virtuous *adj* imbued with or proceeding from virtue; morally good; practising the moral duties and abstaining from vice; chaste; pure.

virulence *n* the quality of being virulent; intensity of destructive quality; acrimony of temper; rancour or malignity.

virulent *adj* extremely poisonous or venomous; very actively injurious to life; hostile; vicious; malignant.

virus *n* (*pl* **viruses**) a very simple microorganism capable of replicating within living cells, producing disease; the disease caused by a virus; (*fig*) extreme acrimony or bitterness; malignity; (*comput*) a hidden program that, when activated, corrupts other programs or data.

visa *n* an endorsement made in a passport denoting that it has been examined and found correct; an official permit from a foreign country allowing a person to visit it.

visage *n* the face, countenance or look of a person or of other animal (chiefly applied to human beings).

vis-à-vis *adv* in a position facing each other; standing or sitting face to face.—*n* one who is face to face with another.

viscera *npl* (*sing* **viscus**) the entrails; the bowels.

viscid *adj* sticking or adhering and having a ropy or glutinous consistency; semi-fluid and sticky.

viscose *n* a derivative of cellulose, obtained from wood pulp and other substances and extensively used in the manufacture of artificial silk.

viscosity *n* the quality of being viscous; stickiness; glutinousness.

viscount *n* a degree or title of nobility next

visor

in rank to an earl and above that of a baron.

viscountess *n* the wife of a viscount or a woman having equal rank.

viscous *adj* glutinous; sticky; adhesive; tenacious.

visibility *n* the state or quality of being visible; condition of the atmosphere with reference to the ease which objects can be seen through it (chiefly used in aviation and with such adjectives as *good*, *low*, *poor*, *moderate*).

visible *adj* perceivable by the eye; capable of being seen; in view; apparent.

visibly *adv* perceptibly to the eye; manifestly; obviously.

vision *n* the act or faculty of seeing; the power or faculty by which we perceive the forms and colours of objects; sight; that which is seen; an object of sight; something supposed to be seen otherwise than by the ordinary organs of sight; something seen in a dream, trance, etc; an apparition; a phantom; a mere creation of fancy; fanciful view.

visionary *adj* apt to behold visions of the imagination; given to indulging in daydreams, fanciful theories, etc; not real; having no solid foundation; imaginary.—*n* one who sees visions or unreal sights; one who forms impracticable schemes.

visit *vt* to go or come to see (a person or thing); to make a call on; to proceed to in order to view; to come or go to generally; to afflict; to overtake or come upon (said especially of diseases or calamities); to send a judgment on; to inflict punishment for.—*vi* to practise going to see others; to make calls.—*n* the act of visiting; a going to see a person, place or thing; a short stay of friendship, ceremony, business, curiosity, etc; a call.

visitant *n* a migratory bird; a visitor, especially a pilgrim; a ghost.—*adj* (*arch*) visiting.

visitation *n* a visit; a formal or judicial visit by a superior, superintending officer, etc; a special dispensation or judgment from heaven; communication of divine favour or goodness, more usually of divine indignation and retribution.

visiting card *n* a small card bearing one's name, etc, to be left in making calls or paying visits.

visitor *n* one who visits; a caller; guest.

visor, vizor *n* a mask used to conceal the face or disguise the wearer; the movable face guard of a helmet.

vista *n* a view or prospect through an avenue, as between rows of trees; a mental view or vision.

visual *adj* pertaining to sight; used in sight; serving as the instrument of seeing.

visual aid *n* a film, slide, overhead projector, etc, used in conveying information in a school lesson, lecture, etc.

visual display unit *n* (often shortened to **VDU**) in computers, a screen which displays information.

visualize *vt* (**visualized, visualizing**) to form a mental image or picture of anything.

vital *adj* pertaining to life, either animal or vegetable; contributing to life; necessary to life; being the seat of life; being that on which life depends (*a vital part*); hence, absolutely necessary; essential; indispensable.

vitality *n* the state of showing vital powers; the principle of life; animation; manifestation of life or of a capacity for lasting.

vitals *npl* internal parts or organs of animal bodies essential to life.

vital statistics *npl* data recording births, marriages, deaths, etc; (*colloq*) the measurements of a person's figure, usually of a woman's.

vitamin *n* one of several organic substances necessary for nutrition and occurring in minute quantities in natural foods, distinguished and designated by the letters of the alphabet.

vitiate *vt* (**vitiated, vitiating**) to render faulty or imperfect; to injure the quality or substance of; to impair; to spoil; to render invalid or of no effect; to invalidate.

viticulture *n* the science, culture or cultivation of grapes.

vitreous *adj* pertaining to or obtained from glass; consisting of glass; resembling glass.

vitreous humour *n* the transparent gelatinous fluid of the eyeball.

vitrify *vt* (**vitrified, vitrifying**) to convert into glass by fusion or the action of heat.—*vi* to become glass; to be converted into glass.

vitriol *n* sulphuric acid and of many of its compounds, which, in certain states, have a glassy appearance; savage criticism.—*vt* (**vitriolled, vitriolling**) to throw vitriol over; to poison with vitriol.

vitriolic *adj* pertaining to vitriol; having the qualities of vitriol; scathing; bitter.

vituperate *vt* (**vituperated, vituperating**) to blame with abusive language; to abuse; to berate; to objurgate.

vituperation *n* the act of vituperating; abuse; railing.

vituperative *adj* containing or expressing abusive censure; abusive.

viva[1] *interj* long live.

viva[2] *n* an oral examination; a viva voce.

vivacious *adj* lively; active; sprightly in temper or conduct; proceeding from or characterized by sprightliness.

vivacity *n* liveliness of manner or character; sprightliness of temper or behaviour; animation; briskness; cheerfulness; spirit.

vivarium *n* (*pl* **vivaria, vivaria**) a place artificially prepared for keeping animals alive in as nearly as possible their natural state.

viva voce *adj, adv* by word of mouth; orally. —*n* an oral examination, a viva.

vive *interj* long live; success to (*vive le roi*).

vivid *adj* exhibiting the appearance of life or freshness; bright; clear; lively; fresh (*vivid colours*); forming brilliant images or painting in lively colours; realistic.

vividly *adv* in a vivid or lively manner; with strength or intensity; in bright or glowing colours.

vivify *vt* (**vivified, vivifying**) to endue with life; to animate; to make to be living.—*vi* to impart life or animation.

viviparous *adj* (*zool*) producing young in a living state, as distinct from *oviparous*.

vivisect *vt* to subject to vivisection.

vivisection *n* the dissection of, or otherwise experimenting on, a living animal for the purpose of ascertaining or demonstrating some fact in physiology or pathology.

vixen *n* a female fox; a turbulent, quarrelsome woman; a scold; a termagant.

viz a contraction of **videlicet** namely.

vizier *n* a high political officer in the former Turkish empire and other Muslim states; a minister of state.

vizor *n* same as **visor**.

vlej, vlei *n* in South Africa, a swampy hollow or pool that dries up at certain seasons.

vocable *adj* able to be spoken.—*n* a word looked on as a pattern of characters or sounds with no regard to meaning; a sound; a vowel.

vocabulary *n* a list or collection of words arranged in alphabetical order and briefly explained; a word book; sum or stock of words employed; range of language (*a limited vocabulary*).

vocal *adj* pertaining to the voice or speech; uttered or modulated by the voice; endowed or as if endowed with a voice; (in phonetics) voiced or sonant (said of certain sounds); having a vowel character; outspoken; noisy.—*n* a vowel; (*pl*) music for the voice, not another instrument.

vocal chord *n* one of two elastic membranous folds so attached to the cartilages of the larynx and to muscles that they may be stretched or relaxed so as to modify the sounds produced by their vibration.

vocalist *n* a vocal musician; a singer.

vocalize *vt* (**vocalized, vocalizing**) to form into voice; to make vocal; to utter with voice and not merely breath; to make sonant.

vocally *adv* in a vocal manner; with voice; verbally.

vocation *n* a calling or designation to a particular state or profession; a summons; a

visual display unit

call; employment; calling; occupation; trade.

vocative *adj* relating to calling or addressing by name (applied to the grammatical case in which a person or thing is addressed).—*n* the vocative case.

vociferant *adj* clamorous, noisy.—*n* a clamorous, noisy person.

vociferate *vi* (**vociferated, vociferating**) to cry out with vehemence; to exclaim.—*vt* to utter with a loud voice or clamorously; to shout.

vociferous *adj* making a loud outcry; clamorous; noisy.

vodka *n* an intoxicating spirit distilled from rye, potatoes, etc.

voe *n* an inlet, bay or creek.

vogue *n* the prevalent mode or fashion; fashion at a specified time; popularity.

voice *n* the sound uttered by the mouths of living creatures, especially human utterance in speaking, singing or otherwise; the sound made when a person speaks or sings; the faculty of uttering audible sounds; the faculty of speaking; language; a sound produced by an inanimate object; sound emitted; the right of expressing an opinion; vote; suffrage (*you have no voice in the matter*); in phonetics, sound uttered with resonance of the vocal chords and not with breath merely; sonant utterance; (*gram*) a form of verb inflection (*active voice, middle voice, passive voice*); (*mus*) to regulate so as to give the correct tone.—*vi* (**voiced, voicing**) to utter, declare or proclaim.

voiced *adj* having a voice, especially of a specified kind, quality or tone; (in phonetics) sonant.

voice-over *n* the voice of an unseen narrator, especially in a film, television commercial, etc.

void *adj* empty or not containing matter; having no holder or possessor; vacant; unoccupied; devoid; destitute (*void of learning*); not producing any effect; ineffectual; in vain; having no legal or binding force; null (*a deed not duly signed and sealed is void*).—*n* an empty space; a vacuum.—*vt* to make or leave vacant; to quit or vacate; to emit, throw or send out; to evacuate from the bowels.

voile *n* a thin semi-transparent fabric used for dresses, scarves, etc.

volatile *adj* having the quality of passing off by spontaneous evaporation; diffusing more or less freely in the atmosphere; passing off insensibly in vapour; of a lively, brisk temperament; fickle; apt to change.

volatilize *vt* (**volatilized, volatilizing**) to cause to exhale or evaporate; to cause to pass off in vapour.

volcanic *adj* pertaining to volcanoes;

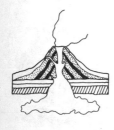

volcano

vole

changed or affected by the heat of a volcano; violent; intense.

volcano *n* (*pl* **volcanoes**) a hill or mountain more or less perfectly cone-shaped with a circular cup-like opening or basin (called a crater) at its summit from which are sent out clouds of vapour, gases, showers of ashes, hot fragments of rocks and streams of lava.

vole *n* a small rat-like rodent with a short tail.

volition *n* the act of willing; the exercise of the will; the power of willing; will.

volley *n* a flight of missiles, as of shot, arrows, etc; a simultaneous discharge of a number of missile weapons, as small arms; a barrage; a string, as of oaths; in tennis, a return of the ball before it touches the ground.—*vt* to discharge with a volley or as if with a volley.—*vi* to be discharged at once or with a volley; to sound like a volley of artillery.

volleyball *n* a team game played by hitting a large inflated ball over a net with the hands; the ball used.

volplane *n* in aviation, a descent by means of a steep glide with the engine shut off.—*vi* (**volplaned, volplaning**) to descend in this manner.

volt *n* the SI unit of electric potential.

voltage *n* electrical energy that moves a charge around a circuit, measured in volts.

voltaic *adj* pertaining to electricity generated by chemical action or galvanism.

volte-face *n* (*pl* **volte-faces, volte-face**) a wheel about; a sudden change in speaking, acting, etc.

volubility *n* the quality of being voluble in speech; excessive fluency or readiness of the tongue; unchecked flow of speech.

voluble *adj* having a great flow of words or glibness of utterance; speaking with excessive fluency; over-fluent; (*bot*) twining.

volume *n* a roll of manuscript such as formed a book in ancient times; a book; a tome; a part or portion of an extended work that is bound up together in one cover; the amount of space a body takes up; a quantity or amount, especially a large quantity; the bulk or solid content of a body measured in cubic feet or cubic centimetres; (*mus*) quantity, fullness, power or strength of tone or sound.

volumetric *adj* relating to measurement by volume.

voluminous *adj* of great volume; bulky; having written much; producing books that are bulky or writing many of them (*a voluminous writer*); (of clothes) loose.

voluntarism *n* the theory that the will is over the intellect; a belief in voluntary participation not compulsion in a course of action.

voluntary *adj* done of one's own accord or free choice; spontaneous; not prompted or suggested by another; of one's or its own accord or choice; occurring through conscious control; supported by voluntary effort or contribution.—*n* (*mus*) an organ solo performed at the beginning, during or at the end of a church service.

volunteer *n* a person who enters into any service of his or her own free will; a person who of his or her own free will offers the state his or her services in a military capacity; a person who carries out a task voluntarily.—*vt* to offer or bestow voluntarily.—*vi* to enter into any service of one's free will.

voluptuary *n* a person wholly given up to luxury or the gratification of the appetite and sensual pleasures; a sensualist.

voluptuous *adj* pertaining to sensual pleasure; gratifying the senses; exciting or tending to excite sensual desires; sensual; having an attractive, full figure.

volute *n* a spiral; a whorl; anything shaped to resemble a spiral or otherwise convoluted form; (*archit*) a spiral scroll used in the Ionic, Corinthian and Composite capitals, of which it is a principal ornament; a tropical shellfish with a spiral shell; any of the whorls found on the shells of snails; an auxiliary curved part of an engine that collects waste gases or liquids from that engine.—*adj* spiral-shaped; (of machinery) moving spirally; (*bot*) rolled up.

vomit *vt* to throw up or eject from the stomach; to belch forth; to emit.—*vi* to eject the contents of the stomach by the mouth; to spew.—*n* the matter ejected from the stomach.

voodoo *n* (*pl* **voodoos**) in the West Indian, a person who professes to be a sorcerer or to possess mysterious powers; such mysterious and malign powers collectively; an evil spirit; a religious cult based on a belief in sorcery, etc.—*vt* to affect by voodoo.

voracious *adj* greedy for eating; eating food in large quantities; rapacious; ready to devour or swallow up.

vortex *n* (*pl* **vortices or vortexes**) a whirling or gyratory motion in any fluid, whether liquid or aeriform; a whirlpool or a whirlwind; an eddy.

vorticist *n* a follower of an English movement in art of the 1920s and 1930s.

votaress *n* a woman devoted to any service, worship or state of life.

votarist *n* a votary.

votary *n* one devoted, consecrated or engaged by a vow or promise; a person devoted, given or addicted to some particular service, worship, study or state of life; an ardent follower or fan.—*adj* ardently devoted to a deity or saint.

vote *n* the expression of a desire, preference or choice in regard to any measure proposed in which the person voting has an interest in common with others; a suffrage; that by which will or preference is expressed in elections or in deciding proposals; a ballot, a ticket, etc; a thing conferred by vote; a grant.—*vi* (**voted, voting**) to give a vote; to express or signify the mind, will or preference in electing persons to office, etc.—*vt* to elect by some expression of will; to enact, establish or grant by vote.

voter *n* one who votes or has a legal right to vote; an elector.

voting paper *n* a paper by which a person gives his or her vote.

votive *adj* given, paid or consecrated in consequence of some vow.

votive offering *n* a tablet, picture, etc, dedicated in consequence of the vow of a worshipper.

vouch *vt* to declare, assert, affirm or attest; to maintain by affirmation; to warrant; to answer for.—*vi* to bear witness; to give testimony or attestation; to maintain; to assert; to aver.

voucher *n* one who vouches; a paper or document which serves to confirm and establish facts of any kind; the written evidence of the payment of a debt, as a discharged account, etc.

vouchsafe *vt* (**vouchsafed, vouchsafing**) to condescend to grant; to concede (*to vouchsafe an answer*); to give; to grant.—*vi* to condescend; to deign; to yield.

voussoir *n* one of a series of stones, etc, shaped like truncated wedges, with which an arch is constructed, the uppermost or middle one of which is called the keystone.

vow *n* a solemn promise; an engagement solemnly entered into; an oath made to God or to some deity, to perform some act on the fulfilment of certain conditions; a promise to follow out some line of conduct or to devote oneself to some act or service.—*vt* to promise solemnly; to give, consecrate or dedicate by a solemn promise, as to a divine power; to threaten solemnly or on oath (*to vow vengeance*).—*vi* to make vows or solemn promises.

vowel *n* a sound uttered by opening the mouth and giving vent to voice; a sound uttered when the vocal organs are in an open position, as of *a* or *o*; the letter or character which represents such a sound.

voyage *n* formerly, a journey by sea or by land; now, a journey by sea from one place, port or country to another, especially a journey by water to a distant place or country; a journey by spacecraft.—*vi* (**voyaged, voyaging**) to take a journey or voyage; to sail or pass by water.—*vt* to travel; to pass over.

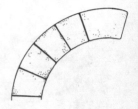

voussoir

voyager *n* one who makes a voyage.

voyeur *n* a person who gets sexual pleasure from watching people undress, perform sexual acts, etc.

Vulcan *n* in Roman myth, the god of fire and the working of metals; (*arch*) a planet once though to orbit Mercury.

vulcanite *n* a kind of vulcanized rubber differing from ordinary vulcanized rubber in containing a larger proportion of sulphur and in being made at a higher temperature, used for combs, brooches, bracelets, etc; ebonite; a name for pyroxene, from its being found in ejected blocks and lavas.

vulcanization *n* the process of vulcanizing; the condition of being vulcanized.

vulcanize *vt* (**vulcanized, vulcanizing**) to treat (rubber) with sulphur, white lead and other substances at high temperatures under pressure to improve its strength and elasticity or render it hard and non-elastic; to change the properties (of any material) in a similar way.

vulgar *adj* pertaining to the common people or the multitude; plebeian; common; ordinary; in general use; hence, national; vernacular (*the vulgar tongue*); pertaining to the less refined class of people; coarse; rude; unrefined; offensive; indecent.

vulture

vulgarian *n* a vulgar person.

vulgarism *n* vulgarity; a vulgar phrase or expression.

vulgarity *n* the quality of being vulgar; coarseness of manners or language; a vulgar act; a vulgar expression.

vulgarize *vt* (**vulgarized, vulgarizing**) to make vulgar or common.

vulgarly *adv* in a vulgar manner.

Vulgate *n* a Latin translation of the Scriptures made towards the end of the fourth century; a revised form of this recognized as authoritative by the Roman Catholic Church.—*adj* pertaining to or contained in the Vulgate.

vulnerable *adj* capable of being wounded; liable to injury; subject to be affected injuriously; (in contract bridge) having already won one game of the rubber and liable to doubled penalties.

vulpine *adj* pertaining to the fox; resembling the fox; cunning.

vulture *n* a large bird of prey which has no feathers on the neck or head and which lives chiefly on carrion; a rapacious person.

vulva *n* (*pl* **vulvae, vulvas**) (*anat*) the opening of the genitals in the female.

W

W the twenty-third letter of the English alphabet, taking its form and name from the union of two V's or U's.

wacky *adj* (*colloq*) crazy; eccentric.

wad *n* a soft mass of fibrous material, as cotton wool, etc, used for stuffing, stopping an aperture, etc; a little mass of some soft or flexible material, used for stopping the charge of powder in a gun and pressing it close to the shot.—*vt* (**wadded, wadding**) to furnish with a wad; to stuff or line with wadding, as a garment.

wadding *n* a fabric of cotton fibre, etc, used for stuffing various parts of articles of dress; material for ramming down above the charge of firearms.

waddle *vi* (**waddled, waddling**) to sway or rock from side to side in walking; to walk in a tottering or vacillating manner; to toddle.

wade *vi* (**waded, wading**) to walk through any substance that impedes or hinders the free motion of the limbs (as water, mud, long grass or snow); to proceed with difficulty or labour.—*vt* to pass or cross by wading; to ford.

wader *n* one who wades; a bird that wades, as the heron, snipe, rail, etc; (*pl*) high waterproof boots worn by anglers.

wadi *n* the channel of a watercourse which is dry, except in the rainy season; a watercourse.

wafer *n* a small thin sweet cake; a thin, flat sheet or slice; (*RC Church*) a thin circular portion of unleavened bread, used in the celebration and administration of the Eucharist.

waffle *n* a kind of thick crisp pancake made in a special mould.

waft *vt* to convey through water or air; to make to sail or float; to buoy up; to keep from sinking.—*vi* to sail or float.—*n* the act of one who or that which wafts; a sweep; a breath or current, as of wind.

wag *vt* (**wagged, wagging**) to cause to move backwards and forwards or from side to side alternately; to cause to oscillate or vibrate slightly; to wave.—*vi* to move backwards and forwards; to hang loosely and shake; to oscillate; to sway; to be in motion or action; to move off or away; to be gone.—*n* a person who is fond of making jokes; one who is full of frolicsome tricks; a humorist; a wit; a joker.

wage *vt* (**waged, waging**) to engage in (a contest); to carry on (war); to undertake.—*n* a gage or pledge; hire; wages.

wager *n* an occasion on which two parties bet; a bet; the stake laid; the subject of a bet.—*vt* to hazard on the issue of some question that is to be decided; to bet; to stake.—*vi* to make a bet; to bet.

wages *npl* the payment given for services performed; the price paid for labour; hire; recompense.

waggle *vi* (**waggled, waggling**) to move with a wagging motion; to sway or move from side to side.—*vt* to cause to wag frequently and with short motions.

wagon, waggon *n* a four-wheeled vehicle for the transport of heavy loads; an open four-wheeled vehicle for the conveyance of goods on railways.

wagon

wagoner *n* one who drives a wagon.

wagtail *n* a small bird of several species, distinguished by its brisk and lively motions, as well as by the length of its tail, which it jerks up and down incessantly.

waif *n* a neglected, homeless wretch, especially a child.

wail *vt* to lament; to bewail.—*vi* to express sorrow audibly; to lament.—*n* loud weeping; violent lamentation.

wain *n* a four-wheeled vehicle for the transport of goods; a wagon.

wainscot *n* a wooden lining or boarding of the walls of apartments, usually made in panels.—*vt* to line with wainscot.

waistcoat

waist *n* that part of the human body which is immediately below the ribs or thorax or between the thorax and hips; the middle part of a ship or that part between the fore- and main-masts.

waistcoat *n* a garment without sleeves, under the coat, covering the chest and waist.

wait *vi* to stay or rest in expectation or patience; to perform the duties of a servant or attendant; to serve at table.—**wait up** not to go to bed at night in order to wait for someone or something.—*vt* to stay or wait for; to await.—*n* the act of waiting; a waiting in concealment; ambush; a musician who with others promenades the streets in the night about Christmas time, performing music appropriate to the season.—**to lie in wait** to lie in ambush; hence, (*fig*) to lay snares or make insidious attempts.

waiter *n* one who waits; a male attendant on the guests in a restaurant, hotel, etc.

waiting *n* the act of staying in expectation; attendance.—**in waiting** in attendance (*lords in waiting*, certain officers of the royal household).

waitress *n* a female attendant in a restaurant, hotel, etc.

waive *vt* (**waived, waiving**) to relinquish or give up; not to insist on or claim; to forego.

waiver *n* (*law*) a waiving of a right, claim, etc.

wake[1] *vi* (*pret, pp* **woke** *or* **waked**, *ppr* **waking**) to be awake; to continue awake; not to sleep; to cease to sleep; to be aroused; to be excited from a torpid or inactive state; to be put in motion; to revel or carouse late at night.—*vt* to rouse from sleep; to excite or stir; to put in motion or action (often with *up*); to hold a wake for.—*n* vigils; the feast of the dedication of a parish church, formerly kept by watching all night; the watching of a dead body prior to burial by the friends and neighbours of the deceased.

wake[2] *n* the track which is left by a ship in the water and which may be seen to a considerable distance behind.

wakeful *adj* keeping awake after going to bed; watchful; vigilant.

waken *vi* to wake; to cease to sleep.—*vt* to excite or rouse from sleep; to awaken; to excite to action; to rouse; to stir; to produce; to call forth (*to waken love* or *fear*).

waking *adj* being awake; rousing from sleep; exciting.

wale *n* a streak or stripe produced by the stroke of a rod or whip on animal flesh; a weal; a plank from one end of a ship to another a little above the waterline.

Walhalla *n* same as **Valhalla**.

walk *vi* to step along; to advance by alternate steps, lifting one foot past the other without running; to go or travel on foot; to go or come, as used in the ceremonious language of invitation (*walk in*); to haunt or show itself in some place, as a spectre; to conduct oneself; to pursue a particular course of life.—*vt* to pass over or through on foot; to cause to walk or step slowly.—*n* the act of one who walks; the pace of one who walks; a short excursion on foot, for pleasure or exercise; manner of walking; gait; a place in which one is accustomed to

walk; an avenue, promenade, etc; sphere of action; a department, as of art, science or literature; way of living; a tract or piece of ground in which animals graze; a district habitually served by an itinerant vendor of any commodity.

walkabout *n* a period of wandering through the bush by an Australian Aboriginal; an informal stroll through a crowd by a member of the royal family, a politician, etc.

walker *n* one who walks; a pedestrian.

walkie-talkie *n* a light radio device which combines a transmitter and receiver and which can be carried and operated while the operator is moving.

Walkman *n* the trademark of a kind of personal stereo.

walkover *n* (*colloq*) an unopposed or easy victory.

wall *n* a structure of stone, brick or other materials, of some height and breadth, serving to enclose a space, form a division, support weights, etc; the side of a building or room; a solid and permanent enclosing fence; a rampart; a fortified barrier (in this sense often plural); means of securing or protection; in mining, the rock enclosing a vein.—*vt* to enclose with a wall; to defend by walls; to fill up with a wall.

wallaby *n* a small Australian kangaroo-like animal.

wallah *n* a person employed about or concerned with something.

wallet *n* a small folding holder for paper money, driving licence, credit cards, etc.

walleye *n* an eye with an abnormal amount of white in the iris, often associated with blindness.

wallflower *n* the name of a plant that exudes a perfume and is cultivated in gardens; so called because in its wild state it grows on old walls and in stony places.

Walloon *n* a member of a French-speaking people of southern Belgium; the language of the Walloons.

wallop *vt* (*colloq*) to thrash, beat soundly.

wallow *vi* to roll one's body on the earth, in mire or in other substance; to tumble and roll in anything soft; to indulge oneself fully in.

wallpaper *n* paper for covering room walls; paper-hangings.

walnut *n* a large handsome tree and its fruit, a native of Persia, yielding timber of great value as a cabinet and furniture wood.

walrus *n* a large marine carnivorous mammal of the Arctic regions allied to the seal and hunted for its oil and for the ivory of its tusks.

waltz *n* a dance performed to music in triple time by couples who swing round and round, moving on as they do so; the music composed for the dance.—*vi* to dance a waltz.

waiter

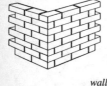

wall

wampum *n* small beads made of shells, used by the American Indians as money or wrought into belts, etc, as an ornament.

wan *adj* having a pale or sickly hue; languid of look; pale; gloomy.

wand *n* a long slender stick; a rod; a rod or similar article with a special use or character; a rod used by conjurers or diviners.

wander *vi* to ramble here and there without any certain course or object in view; to roam; to stroll; to leave home; to go through the world; to deviate; to err; to be delirious; not to be under the guidance of reason.—*vt* to travel over without a certain course; to traverse.

wandering *adj* given to wander; roaming; unsettled.—*n* a travelling without a settled course; peregrination; aberration; deviation; mental aberration.

wanderlust *n* a strong urge to travel.

wane *vi* (**waned, waning**) to diminish; to decrease or grow less, particularly applied to the illuminated part of the moon, as opposed to *wax*; to decline; to approach its end (*the autumn wanes*).—*n* decrease of the illuminated part of the moon to the eye of the spectator; decline (*his fortunes were on the wane*).

wangle *vti* (**wangled, wangling**) to gain one's ends by devious or unscrupulous methods.

want *n* the state of not having; absence or scarcity of what is needed or desired; lack; need; necessity (*to supply one's wants*); poverty; indigence; lack of the necessaries of life (*to suffer from want*).—*vt* to be without; not to have; to lack; to have occasion for; to require; to need; to feel a desire for; to long for.—*vi* to be deficient; to be lacking; to be absent or not present where required or expected; to be in want.

wanton *adj* indulging the natural impulses or appetites without restraint; licentious, lustful; unrestrained in various ways, as in gaiety or sport; playful; frolicsome; sportive; playing freely or without constraint (*wanton ringlets*); unrestrained in growth; growing too luxuriantly; arising from recklessness or disregard of right or consequences; unprovoked (*wanton mischief*).—*n* a lascivious man or woman; a pampered, petted creature.—*vi* to revel; to frolic unrestrainedly; to sport or dally in lewdness.

wapiti *n* the North American stag, closely resembling the European red deer, although larger and popularly called **elk**.

war *n* a contest between nations or states (*international war*) or between parties in the same state (*civil war*), carried on by force of arms; the profession of arms; art of war; a state of violent opposition or contest; hostility; enmity (*feelings at war with each other*).—*vi* (**warred, warring**) to make or carry on war; to carry on hostilities; to contend; to strive; to be in a state of opposition.

warble *vt* (**warbled, warbling**) to sing in a trilling, quavering or vibrating manner; to modulate with turns or variations; to sing or carol generally; to utter musically.—*vi* to have a trilling, quavering or vibrating sound; to carol or sing with smoothly gliding tones; to trill.—*n* a soft, sweet flow of melodious sounds; a trilling, flexible melody; a carol; a song.

warbler *n* one who warbles; any of a family of small Old World songbird which includes the nightingale and robin.

war cry *n* a cry or phrase used in common by a body of troops, etc, in charging an enemy.

ward *vt* to fend off; to keep from hitting; to turn aside, as anything mischievous that approaches (often followed by *off*).—*n* the act of guarding; guard (*to keep watch and ward*); a defensive motion or position in fencing, etc; the state of being under a guard; confinement; custody; guardianship; one who is guarded; specifically, a minor who is under guardianship; a certain division or section of a town or city, such as is constituted for the convenient transaction of local public business; one of the apartments into which a hospital is divided.

war dance *n* a dance engaged in by savage tribes before a warlike excursion; a dance simulating a battle.

warden *n* a guard or watchman; an officer of rank in charge of something; a keeper; a person having control or superintendence over; the title given to the head of some colleges.

warder *n* one who guards or keeps; a keeper; a guard; a prison guard.

wardrobe *n* a place in which clothes are kept, often a piece of furniture resembling a cupboard; wearing apparel in general.

wardroom *n* a room for use by officers in a warship.

ware *n* articles of merchandise; goods; commodities; manufactures of a particular kind: properly a collective noun, as in the compounds *chinaware, hardware, tinware*, etc, but generally used in the plural form when articles for sale of different kinds are meant.

warehouse *n* a house in which wares or goods are kept; a building for storing imported goods on which customs dues have not been paid; a store for the sale of goods wholesale; also a large retail establishment.

warfare *n* military service; military life; hostilities; war.

warlike *adj* fit for war; disposed or inclined for war; military; pertaining to war; hav-

wardrobe

ing a martial appearance; having the qualities of a soldier.

warlock *n* a male witch; a wizard or sorcerer.

warm *adj* having heat in a moderate degree; not cold; having the sensation of heat; feeling hot; flushed; subject to heat; having prevalence of heat (*a warm climate*); full of zeal, ardour or affection; zealous; ardent (*a warm friend*); somewhat ardent or excitable; irritable (*a warm temper*); somewhat excited; nettled; brisk; keen (*a warm contest*); (*colloq*) wealthy; moderately rich; well-off.—*vt* to make warm; to communicate a moderate degree of heat to; to interest; to excite ardour or zeal in; to animate; to inspirit; to give life to; to flush; to cause to glow.—*vi* to become moderately heated; to become ardent or animated.

warm-blooded *adj* (*zool*) having warm blood (said of mammals and birds as opposed to fishes, amphibians and reptiles or cold-blooded animals).

warming pan *n* a covered pan with a long handle formerly used for warming a bed with ignited coals.

warming pan

warmonger *n* a person eager to provoke war.

warmth *n* the quality or state of being warm; the sensation of heat; gentle heat; hearty kindness or good feeling; ardour; zeal; fervour; earnestness; slight anger or irritation.

warn *vt* to give notice of approaching or probable danger or evil, that it may be avoided; to caution against anything that may prove injurious; to advise; to expostulate with; to inform previously; to give notice to.

warning *n* caution against danger or against faults or evil practices which incur danger; previous notice; a notice given to terminate the relation of master and servant or landlord and tenant.

warp *vt* to turn or twist out of shape or out of a straight direction, by contraction (*the heat of the sun warps boards*); to turn aside from the true direction; to pervert (the mind or judgment); (*naut*) to tow or move, as a ship into a required position, by means of a rope attached to something.—*vi* to twist or be twisted from straightness; to turn from a straight, true or proper course; to deviate; to swerve; to wind yarn off bobbins to form the warp of a web; (*naut*) to work forward by means of a rope.—*n* in weaving, the threads which are extended lengthways in the loom and crossed by the woof; (*naut*) a rope used in moving a ship by attachment to an anchor, post, etc; a towing line; the twist of wood in drying.

wart hog

war paint *n* paint put on the face and other parts of the body by savages before going to war.

warpath *n* the route or path taken on going to war; a warlike expedition or excursion (used chiefly in regard to the American Indians).**on the warpath** (*colloq*) very angry.

warped *adj* twisted by shrinking; perverted; unnatural.

warrant *vt* to give an assurance or surety to; to guarantee; to give authority or power to do or forbear anything; to justify, sanction, support, allow; to give one's word for or concerning; to assert as undoubted; to furnish sufficient grounds or evidence to; to give a pledge or assurance to or in regard to (*to warrant goods to be as said*).—*n* an authority granted by one person to another to do something which he or she has not otherwise a right to do; a document or anything that authorizes an act; security; guarantee; pledge; a voucher; an attestation; a document or negotiable writing authorizing a person to receive money or other thing; an instrument giving power to arrest or execute an offender; in the army and navy, a writ or authority inferior to a commission.

warrant officer *n* an officer in the army or navy next below a commissioned officer, acting under a warrant from a department of state and not under a commission.

warren *n* a piece of ground appropriated to the breeding and preservation of game or rabbits; a preserve for keeping fish in a river.

warrior *n* a soldier; a person engaged in military life; a brave soldier.

wart *n* a small dry hard growth in the skin, most common on the hands; a spongy excrescence on the hinder pasterns of a horse; a roundish protuberance on the surface of plants.

wart hog *n* a species of pig found in Africa, notable for its large tusks and warty growths on the cheeks.

wary *adj* carefully watching against deception, artifices and dangers; ever on one's guard; cautious; circumspect; prudent; careful, as to doing or not doing something.

was the past tense of the verb to **be**.

wash *vt* to apply water or other liquid to, for the purpose of cleansing; to scour, scrub, etc, with water or other liquid; to cover with water or other liquid; to overflow or flow along; to wet copiously; to remove by ablution, literally or figuratively (with *away*, *off*, *out*, etc); to sweep away by a rush of water (*a man washed overboard*); to cover with a watery or thin coat of colour; to tint lightly or thinly; to overlay with a thin coat of metal; to separate from earthy and lighter matters by the action of water (*to wash gold*, *to wash ores*).—*vi* to perform the act of ablution on one's own person; to perform the business of cleansing clothes in water; to stand the operation of washing without being injured, spoiled or destroyed; hence, to stand being put to the proof; (*colloq*) to stand the test.—**to wash up** to wash dishes, cutlery, etc, after a meal; to wash one's face and hands; (of waves) to sweep (something) up onto a shore.—*n* the act of washing; the clothes washed on one occasion; the flow or sweep of water; a piece of ground sometimes overflowed; a shallow; waste liquor containing the refuse of food, such as is often given to pigs; swill; the fermented malt from which spirit is extracted; a liquid used for washing; a lotion; a thin coat of colour spread over surfaces; a thin coat of metal.

washboard *n* a board or frame with a ridged surface on which clothes are rubbed while being washed; such a device scratched or scraped as an accompaniment in some forms of popular music.

washed-out *adj* pale; faded; exhausted.

washed-up *adj* (*sl*) ruined; (*colloq*) finished.

washer *n* one who or that which washes; an annular disc or flat ring of metal, leather or other material, used to reduce friction, form an airtight or watertight packing, etc.

washerwoman *n* (*pl* **washerwoman**) a woman who washes clothes for hire.

washing *n* a cleansing with water; ablution; clothes washed at one time; a wash.

wash leather *n* a kind of soft leather, usually from split sheepskins, used for domestic purposes, as cleaning glass or plate, polishing, etc.

washout *n* the washing out or away of earth by rain or a flood; a shot which misses the target; (*colloq*) a complete failure (used of persons and things).

wasp *n* any of various hymenopterous insects which live in societies and consist of males, females and neuters, the two latter classes being armed with powerful and in some cases highly venomous stings.

wassail *n* formerly, a toast made at festivities; a festive occasion with much drinking and celebration; the liquor used on such occasions, especially about Christmas or the New Year.

wastage *n* loss by use, decay, leakage, etc.

waste *vt* (**wasted, wasting**) to bring to desolation; to devastate; to desolate; to ravage; to wear away gradually; to spend uselessly, vainly or foolishly; to squander; (*law*) to damage, injure or impair, as an estate, voluntarily or by allowing the buildings, fences, etc, to go to decay.—*vi* to decrease gradually; to be consumed; to dwindle.—*adj* resembling a desert or wil-

derness; desolate; not cultivated; producing no crops nor timber; rendered unfit for its intended use; spoiled in making or handling; refuse.—*n* the act of wasting or process of being wasted; lavish expenditure; gradual decrease in quantity, strength, value, etc; discarded material; refuse; excrement; effluent; a desert region; a wilderness; a tract of land not in cultivation and producing little or no herbage or wood.

wasteful *adj* causing waste; grossly thriftless; ruinous; lavish; prodigal.

waste pipe *n* a pipe for waste water, etc; an overflow pipe.

waster *n* one who wastes or squanders; a useless person; a good-for-nothing.

wasting *adj* desolating; laying waste; sapping the bodily strength (*a wasting disease*).

wastrel *n* an idle, worthless person; a waster.

watch *n* a keeping awake for the purpose of attending, guarding, preserving, etc; a vigil; vigilant attention; vigilance; a guard or number of guards; a watchman or body of watchmen; the time during which a person or body of persons are on guard; a division of the night, when the precautionary setting of a watch is most generally necessary; (*naut*) the period of time occupied by each part of a ship's crew alternately while on duty; a certain part of the officers and crew of a vessel who together attend to working her for an allotted time; a small timepiece to be carried in the pocket or strapped to the wrist.—*vi* to be or continue without sleep; to keep vigil; to be attentive, circumspect or vigilant; to be closely observant; to give heed; to act as a watchman, guard, sentinel, etc; to look forward with expectation; to be expectant; to wait.—*vt* to look with close attention at or on; to keep a sharp lookout on or for; to regard with vigilance and care; to have in keeping; to tend; to guard; to look for; to wait for.

watchdog *n* a dog kept to watch or guard premises and property; a person or group that monitors safety, quality, etc.

watchful *adj* careful to observe; observant; giving wary attention; vigilant.

watchman *n* (*pl* **watchmen**) a person set to pay heedful attention over something; one who holds a post of observation; a guard; the caretaker of a building at night.

watchword *n* the word given to sentries and such as have occasion to visit guards, as a token by which a friend is known from an enemy; a countersign; a password, motto or maxim.

water *n* a compound substance, consisting of hydrogen and oxygen in the proportion of 2 volumes of the former gas to 1 volume

washer

wasp

of the latter; a fluid covering about three-fifths of the entire surface of the earth and forming an essential constituent of vegetable and animal organisms; this fluid as opposed to land (*to travel by water*); any natural collection of it; sometimes used of other fluids, humours, etc; urine; the colour or lustre of a diamond or other precious stone (*a diamond of the first water*, that is, perfectly pure and transparent).— *vt* to irrigate; to overflow or wet with water; to supply with water or streams of water (*a country well watered*); to supply with water for drink (*to water horses*); to subject to a calendering process, as silk, etc, in order to make it exhibit a variety of undulated reflections and plays of light.— *vi* to shed water or liquid matter (*his eyes water*); to take in water (*the ship put into port to water*); to gather saliva as a symptom of appetite; to have a longing desire (*his mouth watered*).

water bed *n* a bed with a water-filled mattress.

water boatman *n* any of various aquatic bugs adapted for swimming.

water bottle *n* a bottle for holding drinking water.

water butt *n* a large open-headed cask as a reservoir for rain water.

water cart *n* a cart carrying water for sale or for watering streets, gardens, etc.

water closet *n* (usually abbreviated to **WC**) a lavatory; a toilet.

watercolour *n* a pigment or colour carefully ground up with water and isinglass or other liquid instead of oil; a picture painted with watercolours.

watercourse *n* a stream of water; a channel for the conveyance of water.

watercress *n* an aquatic plant much used as a salad.

watered *adj* having a wavy appearance on the surface (*watered silk* or *paper*).

waterfall *n* a fall or perpendicular descent of the water of a river or stream; a cascade; a cataract.

water gas *n* a gas used as a fuel and produced by the decomposition of steam forced against glowing carbon.

water glass *n* a soluble alkaline silicate made by boiling silica in an alkali and used to give a protective covering.

water hen *n* the gallinule or moorhen.

watering can, watering pot *n* a hand vessel for sprinkling water on plants.

watering can

watering place *n* a place where water may be obtained, as for a ship, for cattle, etc; a place to which people resort at certain seasons in order to drink mineral waters or for bathing, etc, as at the seaside.

watering trough *n* a trough in which cattle and horses drink.

water jacket *n* an outer casing containing

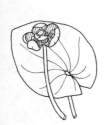
water lily

cooling water, e.g. in an internal-combustion engine.

waterless *adj* lacking water.

water level *n* a levelling instrument in which water is employed, consisting of a bent glass tube open at both ends and having the ends turned up.

water lily *n* any of several aquatic plants with showy flowers and large floating leaves.

waterline *n* the line of floatation in a ship.

waterlogged *adj* excessively filled or saturated with water.

water main *n* a main pipe or conduit for carrying water.

waterman *n* (*pl* **watermen**) a boatman; a ferryman; one who plies for hire on rivers, etc.

watermark *n* the mark indicating the rise and fall of water; any distinguishing device or devices indelibly stamped in the substance of a sheet of paper during the process of manufacture.

watermelon *n* a large fruit with a hard green rind and edible red watery flesh.

water mill *n* a mill whose machinery is moved by water.

water ouzel *n* the dipper, a European bird of the thrush family that can walk about under the surface of water.

water pipe *n* a pipe for the conveyance of water.

water polo *n* a ball game played by swimmers, who try to throw the ball into their opponents' goal.

water power *n* the power of water employed or capable of being employed as a prime mover in machinery.

waterproof *adj* impervious to water; so firm and compact as not to admit water.— *n* cloth rendered waterproof; an overcoat or other article of dress made of such cloth.—*vt* to render impervious to water, as cloth, leather, etc.

water rail *n* a bird, a species of rail, the only one found in Europe.

water rat *n* a rodent animal of the vole genus which lives in the banks of streams or lakes.

water rate *n* a rate or tax for the supply of water.

watershed *n* an imaginary line which runs along the ridge of separation between adjacent seas, lakes or river basins and represents the limit from which water naturally flows in opposite directions; a turning point; a dividing point.

waterside *n* the bank or margin of a stream or lake; the seashore.

water-ski *vi* (**water-skied, water-skiing**) to take part in water-skiing.—*n* a ski designed for water-skiing.

water-skier *n* a person who takes part in water-skiing.

water-skiing the sport of skimming over water on skis when towed by a motor boat.

water spaniel *n* the name of two varieties of the spaniel, excellent swimmers.

waterspout *n* a meteorological phenomenon frequently observed at sea and consisting of a pillar of dark cloud caused to revolve by a whirlwind and forming a vast funnel, which descends to the surface of the sea and draws up a certain quantity of spray or water; a down pipe.

watertight *adj* so tight as to retain or not admit water; staunch.

waterway *n* that part of a river, arm of the sea, etc, through which vessels enter or depart; the fairway; also, a name given to the thick planks along the scuppers of a ship.

waterworks *npl* the aggregate of constructions and appliances for the collection, storage and distribution of water for the use of communities; (*colloq*) tears.

watery *adj* pertaining to water; resembling water; thin or transparent, as a liquid; consisting of water; abounding in, filled with or containing water; wet; moist; tasteless; insipid; vapid; spiritless.

watt *n* the SI unit of power.

wattle *n* a hurdle made of interwoven rods or wands; the fleshy lobe that grows under the throat of the domestic fowl or any appendage of the like kind; a wattle tree.—*vt* (**wattled, wattling**) to twist, interweave or interlace (twigs or branches); to plat (*to wattle a hedge*); to form by platting twigs.

wattlebird *n* any of certain Australian birds of the honey-eater family, having wattles hanging below the ear.

wattle tree *n* a name in Australia for various species of acacia, some of them with beautiful flowers.

wave *vi* (**waved, waving**) to move loosely backwards and forwards; to float or flutter; to undulate; to be moved as a signal; to beckon.—*vt* to move one way and the other; to brandish; to signal to by waving the hand, etc; to beckon.—*n* a swell or ridge on the surface of water or other liquid resulting from the oscillatory motion of its component particles, when disturbed from their position of rest by any force; especially, a swell or surge on the surface of the sea or other large body of water by the action of the wind; a billow; (*physics*) a vibration propagated from one set of particles of an elastic medium to the adjoining set, and so on; anything resembling a wave; one of a series of undulating inequalities on a surface; an undulation; a swelling outline; that which advances and recedes, rises and falls, comes and goes, etc, like a wave; the undulating line or streak of lustre on cloth watered and calendered; a signal made by waving the hand, a flag, etc.

waveband *n* a range of radio frequencies allocated for particular purposes or to broadcasting or other telecommunication stations.

wavelength *n* the distance between the crests of or hollows between two adjacent waves; the distance a wave travels in a time equal to the period of vibration.—**on the same wavelength** having the same attitude, point of view, background knowledge and so getting on very well.

waver *vi* to play or move to and fro; to flutter; to be unsettled in opinion; to be undetermined; to fluctuate; to vacillate; to hesitate; to be in danger of falling or failing; to totter; to reel.—*n* the act of wavering.

waverer *n* one who wavers; one who is unsettled in faith or opinion.

wavy *adj* rising or swelling in waves; full of waves.

wax[1] *n* a thick, viscid, tenacious substance, excreted by bees from their bodies and employed in the construction of their cells; any substance resembling this in appearance or properties; a vegetable product which may be regarded as a concrete fixed oil; vegetable wax; a tenacious substance excreted in the ear; earwax; a substance used in sealing letters; sealing wax; a thick resinous substance used by shoemakers for rubbing their thread.—*vt* to smear or rub with wax.

wax[2] *vi* to increase in size; to grow; to become larger or show a larger disc (as the moon); to become (*to wax strong*).

waxwing *n* a bird with small, oval, horny appendages on the secondary feathers of the wings of the colour of red sealing wax.

waxwork *n* work in wax; figures formed of wax in imitation of real beings; (*pl*) a place where a collection of such figures is exhibited.

waxy *adj* resembling wax; made of wax; abounding in wax.

way *n* a track or path along or over which one passes or journeys; a path, route or road of any kind; distance (*a good way off*); path or course in life; direction of motion; means by which anything is accomplished; scheme; device; plan; method or manner of proceeding; mode; style; usual or habitual mode of acting or behaving; plan or mode of action selected; course approved of as one's own; sphere of observation (*to come in one's way*); (*naut*) progress or motion through the water; (*pl*) the timbers on which a ship is launched.

waybill *n* a list of passengers or goods carried by rail or other public conveyance.

wayfarer *n* one who journeys or travels; a traveller; a passenger.

wayfaring *adj* being on a journey; travelling.

waylay *vt* (*pret, pp* **waylaid**, *ppr* **waylay-**

water-skiing

wavelength

ing) to watch insidiously in the way, with a view to seize, rob or slay; to beset in ambush.

wayleave *n* permission, or right, to cross land.

way-out *adj* (*colloq*) unconventional; eccentric; unusual; amazing.

wayside *n* the side, border or edge of a road or highway.—*adj* growing, situated, etc, by or near the side of the way (*wayside flowers*).

wayward *adj* full of peevish caprices or whims; wilful; perverse.

WC an abbreviation of **water closet**.

we *pron* (*pl* of **I**) I and another or others; I and he or she, or I and they; **we** is frequently used by individuals, as editors, authors, etc, when alluding to themselves in order to avoid the appearance of egotism; the plural style is also used by monarchs and other potentates.

weak *adj* not strong; lacking physical strength; feeble; infirm; not able to sustain a great weight or strain; easily broken; brittle; frail; lacking in ability to perform functions or office (*a weak stomach*, *weak eyes*); deficient in force of utterance (*a weak voice*); unfit for effective attack or defence (*a weak fortress* or *body of troops*); deficient in essential or characteristic ingredients (*weak tea*, etc); deficient in intellectual power or judgment; silly; not decided or confirmed (*weak faith*); vacillating; lacking resolution; easily moved or worked on; facile; lacking moral courage; not supported by the force of reason or truth (*weak arguments*); ineffective; not founded in right or justice; deficient in force of expression; not affecting the mind or the senses strongly; slight; (*gram*) a term applied when inflection is effected by adding a letter or syllable (*dawn*, *dawned* as compared with *rise*, *rose*), distinguished from *strong*.

weaken *vt* to make weak or weaker; to enervate; to enfeeble.—*vi* to become weak or weaker.

weak-kneed *adj* easily frightened; cowardly; easily intimidated.

weakling *n* a feeble creature.

weakly *adv* in a weak manner; with little physical strength; faintly; not forcibly; with feebleness of mind or intellect; injudiciously.—*adj* not strong of constitution; infirm.

weakness *n* the state or quality of being weak; lack of physical, mental or moral strength; feebleness; lack of strength of will or resolution; lack of cogency; a defect; a failing.

weal[1] *n* a sound, healthy, prosperous state; welfare; prosperity; happiness.

weal[2] *n* the mark of a stripe.

weald *n* (*arch*) a piece of open forest land.

wealth *n* well-being or welfare; a collective term for riches; material possessions in all their variety; affluence; opulence; profusion; abundance; (*econ*) all objects and resources having economic value and therefore able to be exchanged.

wealthy *adj* having wealth; having large possessions in lands; affluent; rich; opulent; large in point of value; ample.

wean *vt* to accustom to do without the mother's milk as food; to reconcile to the lack or loss of something; to disengage from any habit.

weapon *n* any instrument of offence or defence; an instrument for contest or for combating enemies; an instrument that may be classed among arms.

wear[1] *vt* (*pret* **wore**, *pp* **worn**, *ppr* **wearing**) to carry covering or attachments to the body, as clothes, weapons, ornaments, etc; to have on; to deteriorate or destroy (clothes, etc) by frequent or habitual use; to waste or impair by rubbing or attrition; to destroy by degrees; to produce by constant rubbing or attrition (*to wear a channel*); to have or exhibit an appearance of; to exhibit; to show (*to wear a glad face*).—*vi* to be undergoing gradual impairment or diminution; to waste gradually; to pass away, as time; to make gradual progress (*winter wore over*).—*n* the act of wearing; the state of being worn; diminution by friction, use, time, etc; style of dress; fashion or vogue in costume.

wear[2] *vt* (*pret* **wore**, *pp* **worn**, *ppr* **wearing**) (*naut*) to bring on the other tack by turning the vessel round, stern towards the wind.

wearable *adj* capable of being worn.

weariness *n* the state of being weary or tired; lassitude or exhaustion of strength induced by labour; fatigue; tedium; ennui; languor.

wearisome *adj* causing weariness; tiresome; irksome; monotonous.

weary *adj* having the strength much exhausted by toil or violent exertion; tired; fatigued; impatient of the continuance of something painful, irksome, etc; sick; disgusted (*weary of life*); tiresome; irksome.—*vt* (**wearied**, **wearying**) to make weary; to tire; to fatigue; to exhaust the patience of; to harass by anything irksome.—*vi* to become weary; to tire.

weasand *n* (*arch*) the windpipe.

weasel *n* a small carnivorous ferret-like animal distinguished by the length and slenderness of its body, feeding on mice, rats, moles and small birds; a cunning, sneaky person.

weather *n* the atmospheric conditions at any particular time; the state of the atmosphere with respect to its temperature, pressure, humidity, motions or any other meteorological phenomena.—*vt* to bear up against and come through, though with difficulty (*to weather a gale*); hence, to bear up against and overcome, as danger or difficulty; (*naut*) to sail to the windward of.—*vi* (*geol*) to suffer change, disintegration or waste by exposure to the weather, as a rock or cliff.—*adj* (*naut*) towards the wind; windward, opposite of *lee*.

weather-beaten *adj* seasoned by exposure to every kind of weather.

weathercock *n* a vane or figure on the top of a spire, which turns with the wind and shows its direction (so called from the figure of a cock being a favourite form of vane); a fickle, inconstant person.

weather eye *n* the eye that looks at the sky to forecast the weather.—**to keep a weather eye open** to be on one's guard; to be alert.

weatherglass *n* an instrument to indicate the state of the atmosphere; a barometer.

weathervane *n* a weathercock.

weave *vt* (*pret* **wove**, *pp* **woven**, *ppr* **weaving**) to form by interlacing anything flexible, such as thread, yarn, filaments or strips of different materials; to form by a loom; to form a tissue with; to entwine into a fabric; to unite by intermixture or close connection; to work up into one whole (*to weave incidents into a story*); to contrive or construct with design (*to weave a plot*).—*vi* to work with a loom; to become woven.

weaver *n* one who weaves or whose occupation is to weave; a weaverbird.

weaverbird *n* a tropical songbird, so called from its nest being woven of grass, twigs, etc.

weaving *n* the act of one who weaves; the act or art of producing cloth or other textile fabrics.

web *n* that which is woven; the whole piece of cloth woven in a loom; something resembling this; a large roll of paper such as is used for newspapers, etc; the blade of a saw; a flat portion of various things; the membrane which unites the toes of many waterfowl; the threads or filaments which a spider spins; a cobweb; (*fig*) anything carefully contrived and put together, as a plot or scheme.

webbing *n* a strong narrow fabric of hemp, cotton, etc, for supporting the seats of stuffed chairs, sofas, etc.

weber *n* the derived SI unit of magnetic flux.

web-footed *adj* having a foot whose toes are united by a web or membrane.

wed *vt* (**wedded, wedding**) to marry; to take for husband or for wife; to join in marriage; to unite closely by passion or prejudice; to unite inseparably.—*vi* to marry; to contract matrimony.

wedded *adj* pertaining to matrimony (*wed-*

ded life); intimately connected or joined together.

wedding *n* marriage; nuptial ceremony; nuptial festivities.

wedding ring *n* a plain gold ring placed by the bridegroom on the third finger of the bride's left hand at the marriage ceremony.

wedge *n* a piece of wood or metal, thick at one end and sloping to a thin edge at the other, used in splitting wood, rocks, etc; a golf club with a wedge-shaped based used to lift the ball out of sand, etc; anything in the form of a wedge (*a wedge of pie*).— **the thin end of the wedge** a first step of small apparent importance but calculated to produce ultimately an important effect.—*vt* (**wedged, wedging**) to split with a wedge or with wedges; to rive; to drive as a wedge is driven; to crowd or compress closely; to fasten with a wedge or with wedges; to fix in the manner of a wedge.

wedlock *n* marriage; matrimony.

Wednesday *n* the fourth day of the week; the next day after Tuesday.

wee *adj* (*colloq*) small, little

weed[1] *n* the general name of any plant that is useless or troublesome; a plant such as grows where it is not wanted and is either of no use to people or injurious to crops; (*colloq*) a thin, weak, unhealthy-looking person; (*sl*) a cigar or cigarette.—*vt* to free from weeds or noxious plants; to extirpate; to free from anything hurtful or offensive.

weed[2] *n* a garment; (*pl*) mourning, especially the mourning dress of a widow.

weedy *adj* consisting of weeds; abounding with weeds; (*colloq*) thin, weak and unhealthy-looking.

week *n* the space of seven days; the space from one Sunday to another.

weekday *n* any day of the week except Sunday, sometimes except Saturday and Sunday.

weekly *adj* pertaining to a week or weekdays; lasting for a week; happening or done once a week.—*adv* once a week.—*n* a periodical, as a newspaper, appearing once a week.

ween *vi* (*arch*) to be of opinion; to have the notion; to think; to imagine.

weep *vi* (*pret*, *pp* **wept**, *ppr* **weeping**) to manifest grief or other strong passion by shedding tears; to drop or flow like tears; to let fall drops; to rain; to give out moisture; to have the branches drooping or hanging downwards; to droop.—*vi* to lament, bewail or bemoan; to shed tears for; to shed or let fall drop by drop; to pour forth in drops, as if tears; to get rid of by weeping (followed by *away*, *out*, etc).

weevil *n* the name applied to various insects of the beetle family, distinguished by the prolongation of the head, so as to form a sort of snout or proboscis; dangerous en-

weathercock

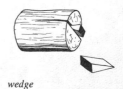

wedge

emies to the agriculturist, from destroying grain, fruit, etc.

weft *n* the woof of cloth; the threads that are carried in the shuttle and cross the warp.

weigh *vt* to raise or bear up; to lift so that it hangs in the air (*to weigh anchor*); to examine by the balance so as to ascertain how heavy a thing is; to pay, allot or take by weight; to consider for the purpose of forming an opinion or coming to a conclusion; to estimate; to balance; to compare.—*vi* to have weight; to be equal in weight to (*to weigh a pound*); to be considered as important; to have weight in the intellectual balance; to bear heavily; to press hard.

weighbridge *n* a machine for weighing trucks, wagons, etc, with their load.

weigh-in *n* the checking of the weight of a sports contestant, especially of a jockey after a race or of a boxer before a bout.

weight *n* that property of bodies by which they tend toward the centre of the earth; the measure of the force of gravity as determined for any particular body; the amount which anything weighs; a certain mass of brass, iron or other substance to be used for determining the weight of other bodies (*a pound weight*); a heavy mass; something heavy; an object used in weightlifting; in some clocks, one of the two masses of metal that by their weight actuate the machinery; pressure; burden (*the weight of grief*); importance; influence; efficacy; consequence; moment; impressiveness; (*med*) a sensation of oppression or heaviness.—*vt* to add or attach a weight or weights to; to add to the heaviness of.

weightlessness *n* the state of having no or little reaction to gravity, especially in space travel.

weightlifting *n* the sport of lifting barbells, dumbbells, etc, to improve one's physique.

weight training *n* physical exercise involving weight-lifting.

weighty *adj* having great weight; heavy; ponderous; important; momentous; grave; adapted to turn the balance in the mind or to convince; cogent; grave or serious.

weir *n* a dam across a stream to stop and raise the water, for the purpose of conveying water to a mill for irrigation, etc; a fence of twigs or stakes set in a stream for catching fish.

weird *n* destiny; a person's allotted fate.—*adj* pertaining to the supernatural; unearthly; suggestive of unearthliness; mysterious; bizarre.

welch *vi* same as **welsh**.

welcher *n* same as **welsher**.

welcome *adj* received with gladness; admitted willingly to one's house and company;

weightlifting

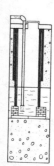

well

producing gladness on its reception; grateful; pleasing; free to have or enjoy (in phrases of courtesy).—*n* greeting of a newcomer; kind reception of a guest or newcomer.—*vt* (**welcomed, welcoming**) to salute a newcomer with kindness; to receive hospitably and cheerfully; to accept or meet with gladness (*to welcome death*).

weld *vt* to unite or join together into firm union, as two pieces of metal, by hammering or compression when raised to a white heat; hence, (*fig*) to unite very closely (*welded by affection*).—*n* a junction of two pieces of iron by hammering when heated to a white heat.

welfare *n* well-being; prosperity; assistance or financial aid granted to the poor, the unemployed, etc.

welkin *n* (*poet*) the sky; the vault of heaven.

well[1] *adj* not ill; in accordance with wish or desire (*the business turned out well*); satisfactory (often in impersonal usage, as *it is well*); being in health; not ailing or sick; having recovered; comfortable; being in favour; favoured (*to be well with the king*); just; right; proper (*was it well to do this?*).—*adv* in a proper manner; justly; rightly; not ill or wickedly; in a satisfactory manner; skilfully; with due art (*the work is well done*); sufficiently; to a degree that gives pleasure; with praise; commendably (*to speak well of one*); conveniently; suitably (*I cannot well go*); easily; fully; adequately; thoroughly; considerably; not a little (*well advanced in life*); often used as an expletive or used to avoid abruptness (*well, the work is done*; *well, let us go*; *well, well, be it so*).

well[2] *n* a spring; a fountain; an artificial structure from which water is obtained, often a round pit sunk perpendicularly into the earth to reach a supply of water; a compartment at the bottom of certain things; a compartment in a fishing vessel having holes to let in water so that fish may be kept alive; (*archit*) the space in a building in which winding stairs are placed; (*fig*) a spring, source or origin.—*vi* to spring or issue forth, as water from the earth; to flow; to bubble up.

welladay, wellaway *interj* (*arch*) alas! lackaday!

well-appointed *adj* fully furnished and equipped.

well-being *n* welfare; happiness; prosperity.

well-born *adj* born of a noble or respectable family; not of mean birth.

well-bred *adj* of good breeding; polite; cultivated; refined; of good breed, stock or race.

well-educated *adj* having a good education; well-instructed.

well-founded *adj* founded on good and valid reasons.

well-heeled *adj* (*colloq*) well-off; in comfortable financial circumstances; wealthy.

well-informed *adj* well furnished with information; intelligent.

wellington, wellington boot *n* a kind of high waterproof boot.

wellingtonia *n* a popular name for the sequoia.

well-knit *adj* firmly compacted; having a strong bodily frame.

well-known *adj* fully known; generally known or acknowledge.

well-meaning *adj* having a good intention.

well-meant *adj* rightly intended; sincere; not feigned.

well met *interj* (*arch*) a term of salutation denoting joy at meeting.

well-off *adj* in comfortable circumstances; having a good store of wealth; fortunate.

well-read *adj* having read a great deal; conversant with books.

well-regulated *adj* having good regulations; well-ordered.

wellspring *n* a fountain; a source of continual supply.

well-timed *adj* done at a proper time; opportune.

well-to-do *adj* being in easy circumstances; well-off; prosperous.

well-wisher *n* one who wishes the good of another.

welsh, welch *vi* to avoid paying a gambling debt; to run off without paying.

Welsh *adj* pertaining to Wales or to its people.—*n* the language of Wales, a member of the Celtic family, forming with the Breton and now extinct Cornish the Cymric group; the inhabitants of Wales.

welsher, welcher *n* a person who welshes.

Welshman, Welshwoman *n* (*pl* **Welshmen, Welshwomen**) a native of the principality of Wales.

Welsh rarebit, Welsh rabbit *n* a dish consisting of seasoned melted cheese on toast.

welt *n* a border; a kind of hem or edging; a strip of leather sewn round the edge of the upper of a boot or shoe and the inner sole, and to which the outer sole is afterwards fashioned.—*vt* to furnish with a welt.

welter *vi* to wallow; to tumble about.

wen *n* a tumour without inflammation or change of colour of the skin.

wench *n* a girl or young woman; (*arch*) a prostitute.—*vi* to frequent the company of loose women.

wend *vi* (*pret, pp* **wended—went**, the *pret* of this verb, is now detached from it and used as *pret* of *go*, *ppr* **wending**) to go; to pass to or from a place; to travel.—*vi* to go; to direct (*to wend one's way*); also used reflexively (*wend thee homewards*).

werewolf *n* (*pl* **werewolves**) in legend, a man transformed for a time or periodically into a wolf; a lycanthrope.

wergild, wergeld *n* (*hist*) a fine of varying amounts for manslaughter and other crimes against the person, by paying which the offender got rid of every further obligation or punishment.

Wesleyan *adj* pertaining to John Wesley or the religious sect (the Methodists) established by him about 1739.—*n* one who adopts the principles and doctrines of the Methodists.

west *n* that point of the horizon where the sun sets at the equinox and midway between the north and south points; the region of the heavens near this point; the region or tract lying opposite the east or nearer the west point than another point of reckoning.—*adj* being in the west or lying towards the west; western; coming or moving from the west or western region.—*adv* to the western region; at the westward; more westward.—*vi* to pass to the west; to assume a westerly direction.

West *n* the western region of a country; Europe and the Western Hemisphere.

westerly *adj* being toward the west; situated in the western region; coming from the westward.—*adv* tending, going or moving toward the west.—*n* a wind blowing from the west.

western *adj* being in the west or in the direction of west; moving or directed to the west; proceeding from the west (*a western breeze*).—*n* a film, novel, etc, about the American West.

westing *n* space or distance westward; space reckoned from one point to another westward from it.

westward, westwards *adv* toward the west.

westwardly *adv* in a direction toward the west.

wet *adj* containing water; soaked with water; having water or other liquid on the surface; rainy; drizzly; very damp (*wet weather*); allowing the consumption of alcohol (*a wet American state*); (*colloq*) ineffective; (in politics) moderately conservative.—*n* water or wetness; moisture or humidity in considerable degree; rainy weather; rain.—*vt* (*pret, pp* **wet** or **wetted**—the latter regularly in the passive to avoid confusion with the adjective *wet*—*ppr* **wetting**) to make wet; to moisten, drench or soak with water or other liquid; to dip or soak in liquor.

wet blanket *n* a person who dampens the enthusiasm of others.

wether *n* a ram, especially a castrated ram.

wetness *n* the state of being wet; a watery or moist state of the atmosphere; moisture.

wet nurse *n* a woman who suckles and nurses a child not her own, opposed to *dry nurse*.

wet suit *n* a close-fitting suit worn by divers, etc, to retain body heat.

whack *vt* to thwack; to give a hearty or resounding blow to.—*vi* to strike or continue striking anything with smart blows.

whacking *adj* (*colloq*) very big.

whale *n* a very large sea mammal that breathes through a blowhole and resembles a fish in shape; something very large; something very good or enjoyable (*a whale of a time*).—*vi* (**whaled, whaling**) to hunt whales.

whalebone *n* an elastic horny substance which adheres in thin parallel plates to the upper jaw of certain species of whales; baleen.

whaler *n* a person or ship employed in whale fishery.

wham *n* the sound of a heavy blow; a solid blow or impact.—*vti* (**whammed, whamming**) to hit or strike with a loud noise.

wharf *n* (*pl* **wharves, wharfs**) a quay of wood or stone on a harbour or river, alongside which ships are brought to load or unload.—*vt* to place or lodge on a wharf.

wharfinger *n* a person who owns or who has the charge of a wharf.

what *pron* an interrogative pronoun used in asking questions as to things and corresponding in many respects to *who* but used adjectively as well as substantively (*what's the matter?*; *I do not know what the matter is*; *what stuff is this?*).—used alone in introducing a question it has an emphatic force or is almost an interjection, equivalent to is it possible that? really? (*what, do you believe that?*); hence, such expressions as *what if* = what would be the consequence if?, what will it matter if?; *what of* = what follows from? why need you speak of?; *what though* = what does it matter though?, granting or admitting that.—*interj* used to introduce an intensive or emphatic phrase or exclamation and when employed adjectively it is equivalent to how great . . .! how remarkable . . .! how extraordinary . . .! (*what a season it has been!*).

whatever *pron* anything that; be it what it may that; all that (used substantively); of any kind; be what may the (used adjectivally).

whatnot *n* a stand or piece of household furniture having shelves for papers, books, etc.

whatsoever *pron* no matter what thing or things (more emphatic than *whatever*).

wheat *n* a plant belonging to the grass family, of several varieties; the seeds collectively of the plant, a well-known grain which furnishes a white nutritious flour.

wheatear *n* a bird akin to the stonechat, a common summer visitor to Britain, having a conspicuous white patch at the base of the tail.

wheaten *adj* made of wheat.

wheelbarrow

whelk

wheedle *vt* (**wheedled, wheedling**) to entice by soft words; to gain over by coaxing and flattery; to cajole; to procure by coaxing.—*vi* to flatter; to coax.

wheel *n* a circular frame or solid disc turning on an axis; as applied to carriages, a wheel usually consists of a nave, into which are inserted radiating spokes connecting it with the periphery or circular ring; any apparatus or machine the essential feature of which is a wheel (*a spinning wheel, a potter's wheel*); a circular frame with projecting handles and an axle on which are wound the ropes or chains connecting it with the rudder for steering a ship; an instrument of torture formerly used, the victim being fastened on it and his or her limbs being broken by successive blows; a whirling round; a revolution or rotation.—*vt* to cause to turn round or revolve; to give a circular motion to; to rotate; to whirl; to convey in a wheeled vehicle; to give a circular direction or form to.—*vi* to turn on an axis or as on an axis; to revolve; to rotate; to turn round; to make a circular flight; to roll forward or along; to march, as a body of troops, round a point that serves as a pivot.

wheelbarrow *n* a frame or box with a wheel in front and two handles behind, rolled by a single individual.

wheelchair *n* a chair with wheels, operated by hand or mechanically, used by people who are unable to walk easily.

wheel clamp *n* a clamp locked on a car illegally parked to immobilize it until the required fine is paid.

wheeler-dealer *n* a shrewd or cunning operator in business, politics, etc.

wheelwright *n* a person whose occupation is to make wheels.

wheeze *vi* (**wheezed, wheezing**) to breathe hard and with an audible sound, as persons affected with asthma.—*n* the act of wheezing; the sound of wheezing; (*colloq*) a joke; (*colloq*) a hoax; (*colloq*) a cunning plan.

wheezy *adj* making a wheezing sound; asthmatic.

whelk *n* an edible mollusc with a spiral shell, used for food in England.

whelp *n* the young of the canine species and of several other beasts of prey; a puppy; a cub; a son; a young man.—*vi* to bring forth whelps.—*vt* to bring forth, as a bitch does; hence to give birth to or originate.

when *adv* at what or which time (used interrogatively, as *when did he come?*); at the time that; at or just after the moment that (used relatively, as *he came when I went*); at which time; at the same time that; while; whereas (*you were absent when you should have been present*); which time; then (preceded by *since* or *till*).

whence *adv* from what place; from what or

which source, origin, premises, antecedents, principles, facts, etc; how; used interrogatively (*whence and what art thou?*); from which (referring to place, source, origin, facts, arguments, etc, and used relatively, as *the place whence he came*).—**from whence** although pleonastic, is used by good writers.

whenever *adv* at whatever time.

whensoever *adv* at whatever time.

where *adv* at or in what place; in what position, situation or circumstances (used interrogatively); at or in the place in which; in which case, position, circumstances, etc (used relatively); to which place; whither (used both interrogatively and relatively).

whereabouts *adv* near what or which place; the place near which; concerning or about which.—*n* an approximate location (*a notice of your whereabouts*).

whereas *conj* the fact or case really being that; when in fact; the thing being so that; considering that things are such that.

whereat *adv* at which (used relatively); at what (used interrogatively).

whereby *adv* by which (used relatively); by what (used interrogatively).

wherefore *adv*, *conj* for which reason (used relatively); why; for what reason (used interrogatively).

wherein *adv* in which; in which thing, time, respect, etc (used relatively); in what thing, time, etc (used interrogatively).

whereof *adv* of which (used relatively; of what (used interrogatively).

whereon *adv* on which (used relatively); on what (used interrogatively).

wheresoever *adv* in what place; in whatever place.

whereupon *adv* upon which; upon what; immediately after and in consequence of which.

wherever *adv* at whatever place.

wherewith, wherewithal *adv* with which (used relatively); with what (used interrogatively).—**the wherewithal** a sufficiency of resources or money.

wherry *n* a light shallow boat, seated for passengers and plying on rivers.

whet *vt* (**whetted, whetting**) to sharpen by rubbing on or with a stone; to sharpen in general; to make keen or eager; to excite; to stimulate (*to whet the appetite*); to provoke.—*n* the act of sharpening; something that provokes or stimulates the appetite.

whether *pron* which of two; which one of the two (used interrogatively and relatively).—*conj* which of two or more alternatives (used to introduce the first of a series of alternative clauses, the succeeding clause or clauses being connected by *or* or by *or whether*).—**whether or no** in either alternative; in any case.

whetstone *n* a stone for sharpening cutlery or tools by friction.

whew *interj* a sound expressing astonishment, aversion or contempt.

whey *n* the watery part of milk separated from the curds, particularly in the process of making cheese.

which *pron* an interrogative pronoun, by which one or more among a number of persons or things (frequently one of two) is inquired for (used adjectivally or substantively, as *which man is it? which are the articles you mean?*); a relative pronoun, serving as the neuter of *who* (often used adjectivally, the relative coming before the noun by a kind of inversion, as *within which city he resides*); used as an indefinite pronoun, standing for any one which (*take which you will*).

whichever *pron* no matter which; anyone (used both as an adjective and as a noun).

whiff *n* a sudden expulsion of air, smoke, etc, from the mouth; a puff; a faint smell.—*vt* to puff; to throw out in whiffs; to smoke.—*vi* to emit puffs, as of smoke; to puff; to smoke.

Whig *n* a name once given to the members of a political party in Britain, opposed to Tory; later applied to the more conservative section of the Liberal party and opposed to *Radical*.—*adj* belonging to or composed of Whigs.

while *n* a time; a space of time; especially, a short space of time during which something happens or is to happen or be done.—*conj* during the time that; as long as; at the same time that.—*vt* (**whiled, whiling**) to cause to pass pleasantly and bother, languor or weariness (usually with *away*, as *to while away time*).

whilst *conj* the same as *while* but less commonly used.

whim *n* a sudden turn of the mind; a freak; a capricious notion; an irrational thought.

whimbrel *n* a British bird closely allied to the curlew but considerably smaller.

whimper *vi* to cry with a low, whining, broken voice.—*vt* to utter in a low, whining or crying tone.—*n* a low, broken, unhappy cry.

whimsical *adj* full of whims; freakish; capricious; odd in appearance; fantastic.

whimsy, whimsey *n* a whim; a freak; a capricious notion.

whin *n* gorse; furze.

whinchat *n* a passerine bird visiting Britain in summer and commonly found among broom and furze.

whine *vi* (**whined, whining**) to express distress or complaint by a plaintive drawling cry; to complain in a mean or unmanly way; to make a similar noise, as dogs or other animals.—*n* a drawling plaintive tone; a mean or affected complaint.

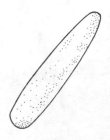

whetstone

whinny *vi* (**whinnied, whinnying**) to neigh. —*n* the neigh of a horse; a low neigh.

whinstone *n* a name for greenstone and also applied to any dark-coloured and hard unstratified rock.

whip *vt* (**whipped, whipping**) to take or seize with a sudden motion; to carry or convey suddenly and rapidly (with *away*, *out*, *up*, etc); to sew slightly; to form into gathers; to overlay, as a rope or cord, with a cord, twine or thread going round and round; to strike with a lash or with anything tough and flexible; to lash; to flog; to drive with lashes; to make to spin round with lashes (*to whip a top*); to lash in a figurative sense; to treat with cutting severity; to fish in with rod and line; to beat into a froth, as eggs, cream, etc.—*vi* to start suddenly and run; to turn and run (with *away*, *round*, etc).—*n* an instrument for driving horses, cattle, etc, or for correction, consisting commonly of a handle, to which is attached a thong of plaited leather; a lash; a coachman or driver of a carriage (*a good whip*); a member of parliament or other legislative body who secures the attendance of as many members as possible at important divisions; a call made on members to be in their places at a certain time.

whip

whipcord *n* a hard-twisted cord of which lashes for whips are made; a strong tough worsted material, used for riding breeches, uniforms, etc.

whip hand *n* the hand that holds the whip in riding or driving; the dominant position; the dominant person.—**to have the whip hand of** to have an advantage over.

whiplash *n* the lash of a whip; a sudden jerking movement, as of the head thrown either backwards or forwards in a car collision.

whipper-in *n* one who keeps hounds from wandering and whips them in, if necessary.

whippersnapper *n* an insignificant, impertinent person.

whippet *n* a breed of dog resembling the greyhound but smaller, used chiefly for coursing and racing.

whip-poor-will *n* the popular name of an American bird, allied to the European goatsucker or nightjar, so called from its cry.

whistle

whir *vi* (**whirred, whirring**) to whiz; to fly, dart, revolve or otherwise move quickly with a whizzing or buzzing sound.—*n* the buzzing or whirring sound made by a quickly revolving wheel, a partridge's wings, etc.

whirl *vt* to turn round or cause to revolve rapidly; to turn with velocity; to carry away by means of something that turns round.—*vi* to turn round rapidly; to re- volve or rotate swiftly; to move along swiftly as in a wheeled vehicle.—*n* a turning with velocity; rapid rotation; something that moves with a whirling motion; a hook used in twisting, as in a rope machine; (*colloq*) an attempt or try.

whirlpool *n* a circular eddy or current in a river or the sea produced by the configuration of the channel, by meeting currents, by winds meeting tides, etc.

whirlwind *n* a whirling wind; a violent wind moving in a circle or rather in a spiral form, as if moving round an axis, this axis having at the same time a progressive motion.

whisk *vt* to sweep, brush or agitate with a light, rapid motion; to move with a quick, sweeping motion; to beat (eggs or cream).—*vi* to move nimbly and with velocity.—*n* a rapid, sweeping motion, as of something light; a sudden puff or gale; a wisp or small bunch; in cookery, an instrument for rapidly agitating certain articles, as cream, eggs, etc.

whisker *n* the hair growing on the cheeks of a man; the bristly hairs growing on the upper lip of a cat or other animal at each side.

whiskey *n* a spirit distilled from barley in Ireland and from corn or rye in the USA.

whisky *n* a spirit distilled from barley in Scotland and from corn or rye in Canada.

whisper *vi* to speak with a low, hissing or sibilant voice; to speak softly or without sonant breath; to make a low, sibilant sound, as the wind.—*vt* to say in a whisper or under the breath.—*n* a low, soft, sibilant voice; the utterance of words with the breath merely; what is uttered by whispering; a low, sibilant sound, as of the wind.

whispering *adj* speaking in a whisper; making secret insinuations of evil; backbiting; making a low, sibilant sound.

whist *interj* silence! hush! be still!—*adj* silent; still.—*n* a well-known game at cards, played by four persons and with the full pack, said to be so called because the parties playing it have to be *whist* or silent.

whistle *vi* (**whistled, whistling**) to utter a kind of musical sound by pressing the breath through a small orifice formed by contracting the lips; to utter a sharp or piercing tone or series of tones, as birds; to pipe; to produce a shrill sound; to sound with a loud shrill wind instrument; to sound shrill or like a pipe.—*vt* to utter or modulate by whistling; to call, direct or signal by a whistle.—*n* the sound produced by one who whistles; any similar sound; the shrill note of a bird; a sound of this kind from an instrument; an instrument or apparatus for producing such a sound; the instrument sounded by escaping steam used on railway engines, steamships, etc.

whit *n* the smallest part or particle imaginable; an iota; a tittle; used generally with a negative (*not a whit better*).

white *adj* being of the colour of pure snow; not tinged or tinted with any of the proper colours of their compounds; snowy; the opposite of *black* or *dark*; pale; pallid; bloodless, as from fear or cowardice; pure and unsullied; grey, greyish-white or hoary, as from age, grief, fear, etc (*white hair*); lucky; favourable (*a white day*).—*n* the colour of snow; the lightest colouring matter or pigment or the hue produced by such; a part of something having the colour of snow; the central part of the butt in archery; the albumen of an egg; that part of the ball of the eye surrounding the iris or coloured part; a member of the white race of mankind.—*vt* (**whited, whiting**) to make white; to whiten.

white ant *n* a termite.

whitebait *n* the fry of several kinds of small fish abounding in the Thames and much prized as a delicacy.

white-collar worker *n* a person employed in professional or office work.

white feather *n* the symbol of cowardice, a term introduced from cockfighting, a game cock having no white feathers.

white flag *n* a flag of plain white material indicating surrender or willingness to take part in a truce.

white friar *n* a friar of the Carmelite order, from their white cloaks.

white heat *n* that degree of heat at which iron becomes glowing white.

white knight *n* a person who comes to someone else's rescue; a company or person that rescues a company facing a take-over bid from an unwelcome source.

white lead *n* a carbonate of lead much used in painting.

white lie *n* a lie for which some kind of excuse can be offered; a harmless or non-malicious falsehood.

white metal *n* a general name for any alloy in which zinc, tin, nickel or lead is used in such quantity as to give it a white colour, as Britannia metal, German silver, queen's metal, etc.

whiten *vt* to make white; to bleach; to blanch.—*vi* to grow white; to turn or become white.

whiteness *n* the state of being white; lack of blood in the face; paleness; purity; cleanness.

whitethorn *n* the common hawthorn.

whitethroat *n* a small British bird of the warbler family.

whitewash *n* a wash or liquid for whitening something; a composition of lime and water, or of whiting, size and water, for whitening walls, ceilings, etc; concealment of the truth.—*vt* to cover with whitewash;

hence, (*fig*) to try to clear from imputations; to try to conceal the truth of.

white wine *n* any wine of a clear transparent colour, varying from the palest straw colour to a deep golden tint.

white witch *n* a witch who does not user her supposed magical powers for evil purposes.

whither *adv* to what place (used interrogatively); to which place (used relatively).—*where* has now to a considerable extent taken the place of *whither*.

whiting *n* a small fish of the cod tribe which abounds on all the British coasts and forms a delicate article of food; chalk pulverized and freed from impurities, used in white-washing, for cleaning plate, etc.

whitlow *n* a painful inflammation at the tip of a finger, generally terminating in an abscess.

Whit Monday *n* the Monday following Whitsunday; in England generally observed as a holiday.

Whitsun *adj* pertaining to Whitsuntide.

Whitsunday *n* the seventh Sunday after Easter; a festival of the Church in commemoration of the descent of the Holy Spirit on the day of Pentecost; in Scotland, a term day (15th May, or 26th May, Old Style).

Whitsuntide *n* the season of Pentecost.

whittle *vt* (**whittled, whittling**) to cut or shape with a knife; to reduce.

whiz, whizz *vi* (**whizzed, whizzing**) to make a humming or hissing sound, like an arrow or ball flying through the air; to move with such a sound.—*n* a sound between hissing and humming.—*n* (*colloq*) an expert.

whiz kid, whizz kid *n* a person of exceptional achievements at a relatively young age, especially in business.

who *relative pron* (possessive **whose** objective **whom**) a relative and interrogative pronoun always used substantively (that is, not joined with a noun) and with relation to a person or persons; used interrogatively *who* = what or which person or persons? of what personality (*who is he?, I do not know who he is*); used relatively = that; which person; sometimes used elliptically for *he* or *she*, *they* or *those, who* or *whom*.

whoa *exclam* stop! stand still!

whodunit, whodunnit *n* (*colloq*) a detective novel play, etc.

whoever *pron* any person whatever; no matter who.

whole *adj* in a healthy state; sound; well; restored to a sound state; healed; unimpaired; uninjured; not broken or fractured; not defective or imperfect; entire; complete; comprising all parts, units, etc, that make up an aggregate; all the; total (*the* *whole city*).—*n* an entire thing; a thing complete in itself, the entire or total assemblage of parts; a complete system; a regular combination of parts.

wholefood *n* any food which has had a minimum of processing or refinement, such as brown bread which still contains the bran, etc.

wholemeal, wholewheat *adj* (of bread, flour, etc) made with complete wheat grains.

whole number *n* (*math*) an integer, as opposed to a *fraction*.

wholesale *n* sale of goods by the entire piece or large quantity, as distinguished from *retail*.—*adj* pertaining to the trade by wholesale; dealing by wholesale; (*fig*) in great quantities; extensive and indiscriminate.

wholesome *adj* tending to promote health; good for the bodily system; nourishing; healthful; favourable to morals, religion or prosperity; salutary.

wholewheat *n* same as **wholemeal**.

wholly *adv* entirely; completely; perfectly; totally; exclusively.

whom *pron* objective case of **who**.

whoop *vi* to shout with a loud, clear voice; to call out loudly, as in excitement; to halloo; to hoot, as an owl.—*n* a shout; a loud clear call.

whooping cough *n* an infectious disease, most common in children, characterized by violent coughing spasms followed by a whooping noise.

whop *vt* (**whopped, whopping**) to strike; to beat; to defeat completely.—*n* a heavy thud or blow.

whopper *n* (*colloq*) anything uncommonly large; a manifest lie.

whore *n* a harlot; a prostitute; a lewd woman.—*vi* (**whored, whoring**) to have to do with prostitutes.

whorl *n* a ring of leaves or other organs of a plant all on the same plane; a turn of the spire of a univalve cell; the fly of a spindle, generally made of wood, sometimes of hard stone.

whortleberry *n* the bilberry and its fruit.

whose *pron* possessive case of **who**.

whosoever *pron* whoever; whatever person.

why *adv* for what cause, reason or purpose; wherefore (interrogatively—direct or indirect); for what reason or cause; for what; wherefore (used relatively).—sometimes used as a noun (*the how and the why*).— *interj* used emphatically or to enliven the speech or to draw attention.

wick *n* a sort of loose spongy string or band which draws up the oil in lamps or the melted tallow or wax in candles to be burned.

wicked *adj* evil in principle or practice; doing evil; sinful; bad; wrong; iniquitous;

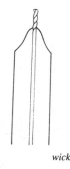

wick

wickerwork

mischievous; prone or disposed to mischief, often good-natured mischief; roguish.

wicker *adj* made of plaited twigs or osiers; covered with such plaited work.—*n* a small pliant twig; a withe; a basket.

wickerwork *n* a texture of woven wicker; an object made of this.

wicket *n* a small gate or doorway, especially a small door forming part of a larger one; a hole in a door; (in cricket) the object at which the bowler aims, consisting of three upright rods (stumps) with two small pieces (bails) lying in grooves along their tops; the ground on which the wickets are set.

widdershins *adv* same as **withershins**.

wide *adj* having a great or considerable distance or extent between the sides; broad, opposed to *narrow*; having a great extent every way; vast; extensive; (*fig*) not narrow or limited; enlarged; liberal; broad to a certain degree (*three feet wide*); failing to hit a mark; hence, remote or distant from anything, as truth, propriety, etc.—*n* (in cricket) a ball bowled so as to pass the wicket out of the batsman's reach.—*adv* to a distance; to a considerable extent or space; far; far from the mark or from the purpose; astray.

widely *adv* in a wide manner or degree; with great extent each way; very much; greatly; far.

widen *vt* to make wide or wider; to extend the breadth of.—*vi* to grow wide or wider; to extend itself.

widespread *adj* extending over a wide area; extensive; general.

widgeon *n* a migratory bird of the duck family, which breeds in high northern latitudes.

widow *n* a woman who has lost her husband by death and who remains still unmarried.—*vt* to reduce to the condition of a widow; to bereave of a husband or mate; to strip of anything good.

widower *n* a man who has lost his wife by death.

width *n* breadth; wideness.

wield *vt* to use in the hand or hands with full command or power; to hold aloft or swing freely with the arm; to use or employ with the hand; to manage, employ or have full control over.

wife *n* (*pl* **wives**) originally, any woman of mature age (still so used in compounds, as *ale wife, fishwife*); a woman or female of any age who is united to a man in wedlock, the counterpart of *husband*.

wifely *adj* like a wife; becoming a wife.

wig *n* an artificial covering of real or synthetic hair for the head.

wigging *n* a berating; a scolding.

wight[1] *adj* (*arch*) having warlike prowess; strong and active; agile.

wight² *n* (*arch*) a being; a human being; a person either male or female.

wigwam *n* a kind of tent used by North American Indians, made of bark or animal hides stretched over a frame of poles.

wild *adj* living in a state of nature; roving at will; not tame; not domestic; savage; uncivilized; ferocious; sanguinary; growing or produced without culture; not cultivated; desert; uncultivated; as left by nature (*a wild scene*); turbulent; tempestuous; stormy; furious (in both a physical and moral sense); violent; unregulated; passionate (*a wild outbreak of rage*); disorderly in conduct; frolicsome; wayward; reckless; rash; not based on reason or prudence; lacking order or regularity; extravagant; fantastic; indicating strong emotion or excitement; excited; bewildered; distracted (*a wild look*); excessively eager; ardent to pursue, perform or obtain.—*n* a desert; an uninhabited and uncultivated tract or region.

wild boar *n* an animal of the hog kind, the ancestor of the domesticated swine.

wildcat *n* a ferocious animal closely akin to the domestic cat but with a shorter, bushier tail, formerly abundant in Britain.

wildcat strike *n* an unofficial industrial strike.

wild duck *n* a web-footed bird, the stock of the common domestic duck; the mallard.

wilderness *n* a desert; a tract of land or region uncultivated and uninhabited by human beings, whether a forest or a wide barren plain; a portion of a garden set apart for things to grow in unchecked.

wildfire *n* a composition of inflammable materials readily catching fire and hard to be extinguished; a kind of lightning unaccompanied by thunder.

wild goose *n* the stock of the domestic goose, formerly abundant in England but now only a winter visitor.

wild-goose chase *n* a foolish or hopeless pursuit or enterprise.

wildness *n* the state of being wild; desert or uncultivated state; savageness; fierceness; distraction; great perturbation of look.

wile *n* a trick or stratagem practised for ensnaring or deception; a sly, insidious artifice.—*vt* (**wiled, wiling**) to draw or turn away, as by diverting the mind; to cajole or to wheedle.

wilful *adj* governed by one's own will without yielding to reason; not to be moved from one's notions or inclinations; obstinate; refractory; wayward; done by design; intentional (*wilful murder*).

wilfulness *n* obstinacy; stubbornness; perverseness; intention; character of being done by design.

wiliness *n* the character of being wily; cunning; guile.

will *n* that faculty or power of the mind by which we determine either to do or not to do something; the power of control which the mind possesses over its own operations; volition; power of resisting impulse; determination; the determination or choice of one possessing authority; wish or pleasure of a superior; strong wish or inclination (*it is against my will*); (*law*) the legal declaration of a person's intentions as to what he or she wishes to be performed after his or her death in relation to his or her property; a testament; the written paper containing such a disposition of property.—*vb aux* (*pres* **I will, he** *or* **she will**; *past* **would**, no past participle) a word denoting either simple futurity or futurity combined with volition according to the subject of the verb—in the first person it expresses willingness, consent, intention or promise; and when emphasized, determination or fixed purpose (*I will go*); simple futurity with the first person being expressed by *shall*; in the second and third persons *will* expresses only a simple future or certainty, the idea of volition, purpose or wish being then lost (in modern usage, the distinction between *will* and *shall* is fading).—*vt* (*pres ind* **I will, he** *or* **she wills**, etc, *pret*, *pp* **willed**, *ppr* **willing**) to determine by an act of choice (*a man may move if he wills it*); to ordain; to decree; to desire or wish; to intend; to dispose of by testament; to give as a legacy; to bequeath.—*vi* to form a volition; to exercise an act of the will; to desire; to wish; to determine; to decree.

willies *npl* (*colloq*) a feeling of dislike; a feeling of nervousness.

willing *adj* ready to do or grant; having the mind inclined; not averse; desirous; ready; borne or accepted voluntarily; voluntary.

will-o'-the-wisp *n* an ignis fatuus.

willow *n* a name for numerous well-known species of plants of a tree-like or shrubby habit, loving moist grounds and valuable for a variety of purposes, including basket-making.

willowy *adj* abounding with willows; resembling a willow; slender and graceful.

willy-nilly *adv* whether it is desired or not; in a haphazard or disorganized way.

wilt *vi* to fade; to droop.

wily *adj* capable of using wiles; full of wiles; subtle; cunning; crafty.

wimble *n* a hand tool such as a gimlet, auger or brace, used for boring holes.

wimp *n* a weak or ineffectual person.

wimple *n* formerly, a headdress laid in plaits over the head and round the chin, sides of the face and neck, still worn by some nuns.

win *vt* (*pret*, *pp* **won**, *ppr* **winning**) to gain by proving oneself superior in a contest; to be victorious in; to gain as victor; to gain

wildcat

possession of by fighting; to get into one's possession by conquest (*to win a fortress*); to gain, procure or obtain in a general sense but especially implying labour, effort or struggle; to allure to kindness or compliance; to gain or obtain, as by solicitation or courtship; to gain to one's side or party, as by solicitation or other influence.—*vi* to be superior in a contest or competition; to be victorious; to gain the victory.

wince *vi* (**winced, wincing**) to twist or turn, as in pain or uneasiness; to flinch; to shrink; to start back.—*n* the act of one who winces; a start, as from pain.

winceyette *n* a soft, cotton fabric used for nightclothes.

winch *n* the crank for turning an axle; a hoisting machine in which an axis is turned by a crank handle and a rope or chain wound round it so as to raise a weight.

winch

wind[1] *n* air naturally in motion with any degree of velocity; a current of air; a current in the atmosphere, as coming from a particular point; air artificially put in motion (*the wind of a projectile*); breath modulated by the respiratory organs or by an instrument; power of respiration; lung power; breath; empty or unmeaning words; idle or vain threats; gas generated in the stomach and bowels; flatulence.—*vt* (*pret, pp* generally **winded**, sometimes **wound**, *ppr* **winding**) to blow; to sound by blowing.—*vt* to perceive or follow by the scent; to nose (*hounds wind an animal*); to expose to the wind; to render scant of wind by riding or driving (a horse); to let rest and recover wind.

wind[2] *vt* (*pret, pp* **wound**—occasionally **winded**—*ppr* **winding**) to coil round something; to form into a ball or coil by turning; to turn by shifts and expedients; (*refl*) to insinuate; to bend or turn to one's pleasure; to enfold or encircle.—*vi* to turn around something; to have a spiral direction; to have a course marked by bendings; to meander; to make one's way by bendings.

windbag *n* a bag filled with wind; a person of mere words; a noisy pretender.

winder *n* one who or that which winds yarn, etc; an instrument or machine for winding.

windfall *n* fruit blown from a tree; timber blown down; an unexpected legacy; any unexpected piece of good fortune.

windflower *n* the anemone.

windgall *n* a soft tumour on the fetlock joints of a horse; a streak of light on the edge of a cloud, reckoned a sign of approaching stormy weather.

wind gauge *n* an instrument for ascertaining the velocity and force of wind; an anemometer.

windmill

windhover *n* a name of the kestrel.

winding *adj* bending; having curves or bends; spirals.—*n* a turn or turning; a bend.

winding sheet *n* a sheet in which a corpse is wrapped; a piece of tallow or wax hanging down from a burning candle, regarded as an omen of death.

wind instrument *n* an instrument of music, played by breath or wind, as the flute, horn, organ, harmonium, etc.

windjammer *n* a sailing ship.

windlass *n* a modification of the wheel and axle, consisting of a horizontal barrel turned by a winch or by levers, for raising a weight that hangs at the end of a rope or chain wound on to the barrel.

windmill *n* a mill driven by the force of the wind and used for grinding corn, pumping water, etc.

window *n* an opening in the wall of a building for the admission of light or of light and air when necessary; an opening resembling or suggestive of a window; the sash or other thing that covers the aperture; the transparent part of an envelope through which the address can be read; (*comput*) a rectangular area of a screen that can be manipulated separately from the rest of the screen; a period of free time in an appointments diary or schedule.

window box *n* a container for growing plants, placed on a windowsill.

window dressing *n* the art of arranging goods in a shop window to attract customers; the presenting of something in its most attractive or appealing form, usually to disguise its less appealing features.

window glass *n* glass for windows, of an inferior quality to plate glass.

window-shop *vi* (**window-shopped, window-shopping**) to occupy oneself in window-shopping.

window-shopper *n* a person who occupies himself or herself in window-shopping.

window-shopping *n* the occupation of looking at goods in shop windows without buying anything.

windowsill *n* an interior or exterior ledge built along the bottom of a window.

windpipe *n* the passage for the breath to and from the lungs; the trachea.

windscreen *n* a protective shield of glass in the front of a vehicle.

wind-up *n* the conclusion or final settlement of any matter; the closing act; the close.

windward *n* the point from which the wind blows.—*adj* on the side toward which the wind blows.—*adv* toward the wind.

windy *adj* consisting of wind; formed by gales; tempestuous; boisterous; exposed to the wind; resembling the wind; as empty as the wind; flatulent.

wine *n* an alcoholic liquor obtained by the fermentation of the juice of the grape or fruit of the vine; also, the juice of certain fruits prepared in imitation of this (*elderberry wine, gooseberry wine*).—*adj* dark purplish red; wine-coloured.

wine cellar *n* an apartment or cellar for stowing wine.

wine cooler *n* a vessel for cooling wine before it is drunk.

wine glass *n* a small glass in which wine is drunk.

wine press *n* an apparatus in which the juice is pressed out of grapes.

wine vault *n* a vault or cellar for wine, a name frequently used by a public house.

wing *n* one of the anterior limbs in birds, specially modified and provided with feathers, in most cases serving as organs of flight; an organ used for flying by some other animals, as insects and bats; act of flying; flight (*to take wing*); that which moves or acts like a wing, as the sail of a windmill, of a ship, etc; a projection of a building on one side of the central or main portion; a lateral extension of anything; a leaf of a gate or double door; one of the sides of the stage of a theatre; also, one of the long narrow scenes which fill up the picture on the side of the stage; the half of a regiment or larger body, termed 'right' and 'left' when in line, 'leading' and 'rear' when in column; in a football side, position to right or left of the centre line, looking towards the opponent's goal.—*vt* to furnish with wings; to enable to fly; to transport by flight (*to wing me home*); to move in flight through; to traverse by flying (*to wing the air*); to wound in the wing; to disable a wing or limb of.

wing case *n* the hard case which covers the wings of beetles, etc; the elytron.

wing chair *n* an armchair with high sides for excluding draughts.

wing collar *n* a stiff upturned shirt collar with the points turned down.

wing commander *n* an officer in Royal Air Force corresponding in rank to a commander in the navy or a lieutenant colonel in the army.

wing nut *n* a nut that is tightened manually using flat wings that project on each side.

wingspan *n* the width of a bird or aeroplane between the tips of the wings.

wink *vi* to close and open the eyelids quickly and involuntarily; to blink; to nictitate; to give a significant hint by motion of the eyelids; to twinkle; to connive; to seem not to see; to shut the eyes wilfully (with *at*, as *to wink at faults*).—*n* the act of closing the eyelids quickly; no more time than is necessary to shut the eyes; a hint given by shutting the eye with a significant cast.

winkle *n* a common abbreviation of **periwinkle**.

winkle-pickers *npl* (*colloq*) shoes or boots with sharp pointed toes.

winning *adj* attracting; adapted to gain favour; charming (*a winning manner*).—*n* (*usually pl*) the sum won or gained by success in competition or contest.

winnow *vt* to drive the chaff from by means of wind; to fan; (*fig*) to examine, sift or try, as for the purpose of separating falsehood from truth.—*vi* to separate chaff from corn.

winsome *adj* attractive; agreeable; engaging.

winter *n* the cold season of the year, which in northern latitudes may be roughly said to comprise December, January and February; a year—the part being used for the whole; also often used as an emblem of any cheerless situation.—*adj* belonging to winter.—*vi* to pass the winter; to hibernate.—*vt* to keep, feed or manage during the winter (*to winter cattle*).

wintergreen *n* the common name of certain perennial plants allied to the heaths, some of which are medicinal, while an American species yields an oil, used in confectionery and to disguise the taste of disagreeable medicines.

winter quarters *npl* the quarters of an army during the winter; a winter residence or station.

wintry *adj* suitable to winter; cold; bleak and cheerless.

winy *adj* having the taste or qualities of wine.

wipe *vt* (**wiped, wiping**) to rub with something soft for cleaning; to clean by gentle rubbing; to strike or brush gently (often with *off, up, away*, etc).—*n* the act of one who wipes; a rub for the purpose of cleaning.

wiper *n* one who wipes; a thing which wipes; a wiper on a car windscreen.

wire *n* a thread of metal; a fine or slender metal rod of uniform diameter; such metallic threads collectively; a telegraph wire; hence, a telegram; (*colloq*) a hidden electronic recording or listening device.—*vt* (**wired, wiring**) to bind with wire; to apply wire to; to snare by means of a wire; to send by telegraph.—*vt* to send a telegram; to fit (a building) with a series of wires to provide electricity.

wired *adj* (*colloq*) wearing a hidden electronic recording or listening device; (*sl*) nervous, edgy, especially as a result of taking stimulating drugs.

wire fence *n* a fence made of parallel wires attached to upright posts.

wire gauze *n* a kind of stiff close fabric made of fine wire.

wireless *n* radio; a radio.

wine glass

wing

wire netting *n* a texture of wire used for light fencing, etc.

wire-puller *n* one who pulls the wires of puppets; hence, one who instigates the actions of others without his or her influence appearing; an intriguer.

wiretap *vi* (**wiretapped, wiretapping**) to connect to a telephone wire in order to listen in to a private conversation.

wireworm *n* a name for several kinds of larvae or grubs very destructive to crops, the name being given from the cylindrical form and hardness of the grubs.

wiry *adj* made of wire; like wire; tough; lean and sinewy.

wisdom *n* the quality of being wise; the power or faculty of forming the fittest and best judgment in any matter presented for consideration; sound judgment and sagacity; prudence; discretion; sound common sense, often opposed to *folly*.

wisdom tooth *n* a large back double tooth, so named because not appearing till a person is grown up.

wise[1] *adj* having the power of discerning and judging correctly; possessed of discernment, judgment and discretion; prudent; sensible; sage; judicious; experienced; skilled; (*Scrip*) godly; pious.—**wise man** *n* a man skilled in hidden arts; a sorcerer.—**wise woman** *n* a witch; a fortune-teller.

wise[2] *n* manner; mode; now used only in such phrases as *in any wise*, *in no wise*, etc, or in composition, as in *likewise*, *lengthwise*, etc, having then much the same force as *-ways* in *lengthways*, etc.

wiseacre *n* one who makes pretensions to great wisdom; a would-be wise person.

wish *vi* to have a desire; to long (with *for* before the object).—*vt* to desire; to long for (often governing an infinitive or a clause); to frame or express desires concerning; to desire to be (with words completing the sense: *to wish one well, to wish himself rich*); to imprecate; to invoke (*to wish one evil*).—*n* a desire; a longing; an expression of desire; a request; a petition; the thing desired.

wishbone *n* the forked bone at the front of the breastbone of a bird, consisting of the fused clavicles.

wishful *adj* having a desire; desirous (with *of* before an object); showing desire; longing.

wishy-washy *adj* very thin and weak; diluted; hence, feeble; lacking in substantial qualities.

wisp *n* a thin strand of straw or other like substance; a bunch of fibrous matter; a small frail person.

wistful *adj* anxiously observant; pensive from the absence or lack of something; earnest from a feeling of desire; longing

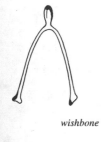

wishbone

wit[1] *n* intellect, understanding or mental powers collectively; a faculty or power of the mind (*he has all his wits about him*); wisdom; sagacity; the faculty of associating ideas in a new and ingenious, and at the same time natural and pleasing way exhibited in apt language; a quality or faculty akin to humour but depending more on point or brilliancy of language; facetiousness; a person possessing this faculty; one distinguished for bright or amusing sayings; a humorist.

wit[2] *vti* (*arch*) to know; to be or become aware; to learn.—**to wit** namely, that is to say.

witan *n* same as **witenagemot**.

witch *n* originally, a person of either sex given to the black art; later, a woman supposed to have formed a compact with the devil or with evil spirits and by their means to operate supernaturally; one who practises sorcery or enchantment; a bewitching or charming young woman.

witchcraft *n* the practices of witches; sorcery; power more than natural; enchantment; fascination.

witch doctor *n* a man in certain tribes who appears to be able to cure sickness or cause harm to people.

witch hazel, wych hazel *n* a winter-flowering garden shrub; an astringent liquid prepared from this shrub, used to reduce swelling, bruising, etc.

witch hunt *n* formerly, the search for and persecution of those accused of witchcraft; a campaign of harassment of those with dissenting opinions.

witenagemot, witan *n* among the Anglo-Saxons, a national council or parliament.

with *prep* against, competing against (*to fight, contend* or *vie with*); not apart from; in the company of; on the side of or in favour of; in the estimation, consideration or judgment of (*with you art is useless*); having as a concomitant, consequence or appendage (*with a blush*); so as to contrast or correspond; immediately after (*with that he left*); correspondence; through or by, as means, cause or consequence (*pale with fear*).

withal *adv* with the rest; together with that; likewise.—*prep* with (used after relatives or equivalent words and transposed to the end of a sentence or clause).

withdraw *vt* (*pret* **withdrew**, *pp* **withdrawn**, *ppr* **withdrawing**) to draw back or in a contrary direction; to lead, bring or take back; to recall; to retract.—*vi* to retire from or quit a company or place; to go away; to retreat.

withe, withy *n* a willow or osier; a willow or osier twig; a flexible twig used to bind something; a fastening of plaited or twisted twigs.

wither *vi* to dry and shrivel up, as a plant; to lose freshness and bloom; to fade; to become dry and wrinkled, as from the loss of moisture; to lose pristine freshness, bloom or vigour; to decline; to pass away.—*vt* to cause to fade; to make sapless and shrunken; to cause to lose bloom; to shrivel; to blight, injure or destroy, as by some malign or baleful influence.

withers *npl* the junction of the shoulder bones of a horse, forming an elevation at the springing of the neck.

withershins, widdershins *adv* in a direction contrary to the apparent course of the sun, anticlockwise, a direction considered to be of evil omen.

withhold *vt* (*pret, pp* **withheld**, *ppr* **withholding**) to hold back; to restrain; to keep from action; to retain; to keep back; not to grant.

within *prep* in the inner or interior part or parts of; inside of, opposed to *without*; in the limits, range, reach or compass of; not beyond; inside or comprehended by the scope, limits, reach or influence of; not exceeding, not overstepping, etc.—*adv* in the interior or centre; inwardly; internally; in the mind, heart or soul; in the house or dwelling; indoors; at home.

without *prep* on or at the outside or exterior of; out of, opposed to *within*; out of the limits, compass, range or reach of; beyond; not having or not being with; in absence or lack of; deprived of; not having. —*adv* on the outside; outwardly; externally; out of doors.

withstand *vt* (*pret, pp* **withstood**, *ppr* **withstanding**) to resist, either with physical or moral force; to oppose.—*vi* to resist; to make a stand.

withy *n* same as **withe**.

witless *adj* lacking sense or understanding; silly; senseless; foolish.

witness *n* attestation of a fact or event; testimony; that which furnishes evidence or proof; a person who knows or sees anything; a person who is present at and hears or sees something; (*law*) one who sees the execution of an instrument and subscribes it for confirmation of its authenticity; a person who gives testimony or evidence in a judicial proceeding.—*vt* to attest; to testify; to see or know by personal presence; to be a witness of; to give or serve as evidence or token of; to subscribe as witness.—*vi* to bear testimony; to give evidence.

witticism *n* a witty sentence, phrase or remark; an observation characterized by wit.

wittingly *adv* knowingly; not inadvertently or ignorantly.

witty *adj* possessed of wit; smartly or cleverly facetious; bright and amusing.

wivern *n* same as **wyvern**.

wizard *n* originally, a wise man; a sage; later, an adept in the black art; a sorcerer; an enchanter; a magician; a conjurer.

wizened *adj* hard, dry and shrivelled; withered.

woad *n* a European plant of the mustard family, the pulped and fermented leaves of which yield an blue dye.

wobble *vi* (**wobbled, wobbling**) to move unsteadily in rotating or spinning; to rock; to vacillate.

Woden, Odin *n* the chief god of Northern mythology, after whom is named Wednesday.

woe *n* grief; sorrow; misery; heavy calamity.—**woe** is frequently used in denunciations either with a verb or alone; it is also used in exclamations of sorrow, a pronoun following being then in the dative (*woe is me*).

woebegone *adj* overwhelmed with woe; immersed in grief and sorrow.

woeful *adj* full of woe; afflicted; sorrowful; expressing woe; doleful; distressful; piteous; wretched.

wok *n* a kind of frying pan with a curved base like a bowl, used in stir-frying, etc.

wold *n* open country; a low hill; a down; (*pl*) a hilly district or a range of hills.

wolf *n* (*pl* **wolves**) a carnivorous quadruped belonging to the dog family and closely related to the dog; a flirtatious man who is always chasing women.

Wolf Cub *n* a junior Scout, between the ages of 8 and 11.

wolfish *adj* like a wolf; savage.

wolfram *n* a native tungsten of iron and manganese, the ore from which tungsten is usually obtained; a name of the metal tungsten.

wolfsbane *n* an aconite.

wolverine *n* a voracious carnivorous mammal of northern forests of Europe, North America and Asia with thick black fur, the glutton.

woman *n* (*pl* **women**) the female of the human race; an adult or grown-up female, as distinguished from a girl; a female attendant on a person of rank.

womanhood *n* the state, character or collective qualities of a woman.

womanish *adj* suitable to a woman; feminine; (of men) effeminate.

womankind *n* women in general; the female sex.

womanly *adj* becoming or suiting a woman; feminine.

womb *n* the uterus of a female; something likened to this; any large or deep cavity that receives or contains anything.

wombat *n* a marsupial mammal of Australia and Tasmania, about the size of a badger.

wonder *n* that emotion which is excited by something new, strange and extraordinary

woad

wok

or that arrests the attention by its novelty, grandeur or inexplicability; a feeling less than astonishment and much less than amazement; a cause of such feeling; a strange or extraordinary thing; a prodigy.—*vi* to be struck with wonder; to marvel; to be amazed; to look with or feel admiration; to entertain some doubt and curiosity; to be in a state of expectation, mingled with doubt and slight anxiety (followed by a clause).

wonderful *adj* adapted to excite wonder; strange; astonishing; marvellous.

wonderfully *adv* in a wonderful manner; surprisingly; strangely; (*colloq*) often equivalent to *very*.

wondrous *adj* such as to excite wonder; wonderful; marvellous; strange.—*adv* in a wonderful degree; remarkably; exceedingly (*wondrous wise*).

wont *adj* accustomed; having a certain habit or custom; using or doing customarily.—*n* custom; habit; use.—*vi* (*pret* **wont**, *pp* **wont** *or* **wonted**, *ppr* **wonting**) to be accustomed or habituated; to use; to be used.

won't a contraction for **will not**.

wonted *adj* customary or familiar from use or habit; usual; accustomed; made or having become familiar by using, frequenting, etc.

woo *vt* to court; to solicit in love; to invite; to seek to gain or bring about; to court (*to woo destruction*).—*vi* to make love.

wood *n* a large collection of growing trees; a forest; the substance of trees or their trunks; timber; (*pl*) wind instruments in an orchestra, such as the flute, clarinet, oboe, etc.—*vi* to take in or get supplies of wood.—*vt* to supply with wood or get supplies of wood for.

woodbine *n* the wild honeysuckle.

woodchuck *n* a species of marmot common in the USA and Canada; the groundhog.

woodcock *n* a bird allied to the snipe but with a stronger bill and shorter legs, a winter visitor to Britain, where it sometimes breeds; esteemed for the table.

woodcraft *n* skill in anything which pertains to woods or forests.

woodcut *n* an engraving on wood or a print from such engraving.

wooden *adj* made of wood; consisting of wood; ungainly; awkward; without spirit or expression.

wood engraving *n* the art of engraving on wood or of producing by special cutting tools a design or picture in relief on the surface of a block of wood (generally box), from which impressions can be taken by means of an ink or pigment.

woodenly *adv* in a wooden manner; stiffly; clumsily; awkwardly.

woodiness *n* state or quality of being woody.

woodlouse

woodpecker

woodland *n* land covered with wood.—*adj* relating to woods; sylvan.

woodlark *n* a small species of lark which usually sings perched on the branch of a tree.

woodlouse *n* (*pl* **woodlice**) a small slate-coloured ground-dwelling wingless crustacean with a segmented body that it can roll into a ball.

woodpecker *n* the name for certain climbing birds which feed on insects and their larvae that they find on trees.

wood pigeon *n* the ring dove or cushat.

woodruff *n* a common plant of woods and shady places and cultivated in gardens for its whorled leaves and simple white blossoms but chiefly for the fragrance of its leaves.

wood sage *n* a species of germander, extremely bitter and sometimes used as a substitute for hops.

wood sorrel *n* a small species of sorrel, supposed by some to be the Irish shamrock.

wood spirit *n* a crude spirit obtained by distilling wood in closed vessels.

wood warbler *n* a small bird visiting England in summer.

woodwork *n* work formed of wood; the part of any structure that is made of wood; carpentry.

woody *adj* abounding with wood; consisting of wood; ligneous; pertaining to woods.

wooer *n* one who woos; one who courts or solicits in love; a suitor.

woof[1] *n* the threads that cross the warp in weaving; the weft; texture.

woof[2] *n* a dog's bark.—*vi* (of a dog) to bark.

woofer *n* a kind of loudspeaker.

wooing *n* courtship; time of courtship

wool *n* that soft species of hair which grows on sheep and some other animals; the fleecy coat of the sheep; also applied to other kinds of hair, especially short, crisped and curled hair like that of a Negro; any fibrous or fleecy substance resembling wool.

woolgathering *n* the act of gathering wool; idle daydreaming.

woollen *adj* made of wool; consisting of wool; pertaining to wool.—*n* cloth made of wool, such as serges, flannels, tweeds, broadcloth, etc.

woolly *adj* consisting of wool; resembling wool; clothed or covered with wool; (*bot*) covered with a pubescence resembling wool; confused; indistinct.—*n* (*colloq*) a woollen garment.

woolpack *n* a large bag for wool; a bundle or bale of wool.

woolsack *n* a sack or bag of wool; the seat of the Lord Chancellor in the House of Lords, a large square bag of wool without back or arms and covered with red cloth.

woozy *adj* dazed; dizzy; slightly drunk.

word *n* a single articulate sound or a combination of articulate sounds or syllables, uttered by the human voice and by custom expressing an idea or ideas; a vocable; a term; speech exchanged; conversation; talk (in this sense plural); information; tidings (in this sense without an article and only as a singular, as *to send word of one's safe arrival*); a watchword; a password; a motto; a term or phrase of command; an injunction; an order; an assertion or promise; an affirmation on honour; a declaration (with possessives, as *to take him at his word*); terms or phrases interchanged in contention, anger or reproach (in plural and often qualified by *high, hot, harsh, sharp,* etc).—*vt* to express in words; to phrase.

wording *n* expression in words; form of expression.

word-perfect *adj* able to repeat something without mistake.

word processing *n* a system for the input, editing, storage and retrieval of written material electronically.

word processor *n* a microprocessor with monitor, keyboard and printer used in word processing.

wordy *adj* using many more words than are necessary; verbose; consisting of words; verbal.

work *n* exertion of energy, physical or mental; effort directed to some purpose or end; toil; labour; employment; the matter on which one is employed, engaged or labouring; that which engages one's time or attention; an undertaking; an enterprise; a task; that which is done; performance; deed; feat; achievement; goings-on; that which is made or produced; a product of nature or art; a literary or artistic performance; a composition; some extensive structure, as a dock, bridge, fortification, etc; any establishment where labour is carried on extensively (the plural being often applied to such an establishment, as *ironworks*); (*mech*) the overcoming of resistance; the act of producing a change of configuration in a system in opposition to a force which resists that change; when the point of application of force moves, the force is said to do *work*, the measure of which is found by multiplying the force by the component displacement of the point in the direction of the force.—*vi* (*pret, pp* **worked** *or* **wrought**, *ppr* **working**) to make exertion for some end or purpose; to be engaged or employed on some task, labour, duty, etc; to labour; to toil; to be engaged in an employment or occupation; to perform the duties of a labourer, workman, person of business, etc; to be in motion, operation or activity (*the machine works well*); to act; to operate; to have or take effect; to exercise influence; to tend or conduce (*things work to some end*); to be tossed or agitated, as the sea; to be in agitation; to boil (*passion works in him*); to make way laboriously and slowly; to act as a purgative or cathartic; to ferment, as liquors.—*vt* to bestow manual labour on; to carry on the operations of (*to work a mine or quarry*); to bring about; to effect, perform, do (*to work mischief*); to keep at work; to keep busy or employed (*he works his horses*); to bring by action to any state (*to work oneself out*); to make or get by labour or exertion (*to work one's way*); to make into shape; to fashion; to mould; to embroider; to operate on, as a purgative; to purge; to cause to ferment, as liquor.

workable *adj* that can be worked or that is worth working; practicable.

workaday *adj* everyday; ordinary.

workaholic *n* a person with a compulsive need to work.

workbag *n* a small bag for containing needlework, etc; a reticule.

workbox *n* a small box for holding tools for work; a small box for holding needles, thread, etc.

worker *n* one who works; a labourer; a toiler; a performer; a working bee.

work force *n* the number of workers who are engaged in a particular industry; the total number of workers who are potentially available.

workhouse *n* formerly, a house in which able-bodied paupers were compelled to work.

working *adj* engaged in or devoted to bodily toil (*the working classes*); laborious; industrious; taking an active part in a business (*a working partner*).—*n* the act of labouring; fermentation; movement; operation.

working capital *n* liquid capital available for the daily operation of a business.

working class *n* a collective name for those who earn money by manual labour.

working day *n* any day on which work is ordinarily performed as distinguished from Sundays and holidays; such part of the day as is devoted or allotted to work.

working party *n* a committee established to investigate a particular problem.

workman *n* (*pl* **workmen**) any man employed in work, especially manual labour; a labourer; a toiler; a worker; a tradesman.

workmanlike *adj* skilful; well performed.

workmanship *n* the art or skill of a workman; the style or character of work performed on anything; operative skill; the result or objects produced by a workman, artificer or operator.

work-out *n* a session of strenuous physical exercises.

workbox

workshop *n* a shop or building where any work or handicraft is carried on.

work-to-rule *n* a form of industrial action in which employees adhere strictly to rules and regulations in the workplace with the aim of slowing down production.

world *n* the earth and all created things thereon; the globe; the universe; any celestial orb or planetary body; a large portion or division of our globe (*the Old World*, or eastern hemisphere; *the New World*, or western hemisphere; *the Roman world*); the earth as the scene of human existence and action; any state or sphere of existence (*a future world*); a domain, region or realm (*the world of dreams, of art*); the human race; the aggregate of humanity; the public; the people among whom one lives; the life of humanity at large; the people united by a common faith, aim, pursuit, etc (*the religious world, the heathen world*); the people exclusively interested in secular affairs; the unregenerate or ungodly part of humanity.

World Cup *n* an international soccer championship competition held every four years, alternately in Europe and North or South America.

worldliness *n* the condition of being worldly.

worldling *n* one who is devoted exclusively to the affairs and interests of this life.

worldly *adj* belonging to the world or present state of human existence; temporal; secular; seeking temporal benefit or enjoyment merely; earthly as opposed to heavenly or spiritual; carnal; sordid; sophisticated.

worldwide *adj* universal.

worm *n* a term loosely applied to many small creeping animals, entirely lacking feet or having only very short ones; any somewhat similar creature; an intestinal parasite of lengthened form; (*pl*) the disease due to the presence of such parasites; a maggot; a canker; an epithet of scorn, disgust or contempt; anything vermicular or spiral; the thread of a screw; the spiral pipe of a still placed in a vessel of cold water and through which the vapour of the substance distilled is conducted to cool and condense it.—*vi* to advance by wriggling; (*refl*) to insinuate oneself; to work gradually and secretly.—*vt* to effect by slow and stealthy means; to extract or get at slyly or cunningly (*to worm a secret out of a person*).

wormcast *n* a small mass of fine earth voided by the earthworm after all the nutritive matter has been extracted from it.

worm-eaten *adj* gnawed by worms; having a number of internal cavities made by worms.

wormwood *n* a well-known plant, cel-

worm

ebrated for its intensely bitter, tonic and stimulating qualities; bitter feeling, mortification (*gall and wormwood*).

worry *vt* (**worried, worrying**) to seize by the throat with the teeth; to tear with the teeth, as dogs when fighting; to harass with importunity or with care and anxiety; to plague, tease, bother, vex, persecute.—*vi* to be unduly careful and anxious; to be in solicitude or trouble; to fret.—*n* the act of worrying or mangling with the teeth; perplexity; trouble; anxiety; harassing turmoil.

worse *adj* bad or ill in a greater degree; less good or perfect; of less value; inferior; more unwell; more sick; in poorer health; in a less favourable situation; more ill off. —*n* loss; defeat; disadvantage; something less good or desirable (*worse remains behind*).—*adv* in a manner more evil or bad; in a smaller or lower degree; less (*it pleases him worse*); in a greater manner or degree; with a notion of evil (*he hates him worse*).

worship *n* excellence of character; worth; honour; a title used in addressing certain magistrates and others of rank or station; the performance of devotional acts in honour of a deity; the act of paying divine honours to God; religious exercises; reverence; submissive respect; loving or admiring devotion.—*vt* (**worshipped, worshipping**) to pay divine honours to; to reverence with supreme respect and veneration; to perform religious service to; to adore; to idolize.—*vi* to perform acts of adoration; to perform religious service.

worshipful *adj* worthy of honour; honourable; a term of respect specially applied to magistrates and corporate bodies.

worshipper *n* one who worships; one who pays divine honours to any being; one who adores.

worst *adj* bad in the highest degree, whether in a moral or physical sense.—*n* the most evil, aggravated or calamitous state or condition (usually with *the*).—*adv* most ill or extreme; most intensely (*he hates us worst*).—*vt* to get the advantage over in conquest; to defeat; to overthrow.

worsted *n* a variety of woollen yarn or thread, spun from long-staple wool, used in knitting stockings, etc.

wort *n* new beer unfermented or in the act of fermentation; the sweet infusion of malt.

worth *n* that quality of a thing which renders it valuable; value; money value; price; rate; value in respect of mental or moral qualities; desert; merit; excellence.—*adj* equal in value or price to; deserving of (*a castle worth defending*); having estate to the value of; possessing (*a man worth £10,000*).

worthless *adj* having no value; having no dignity or excellence; mean; contemptible; unworthy; not deserving.

worthy *adj* having worth; excellent; deserving praise; valuable; estimable; applied to persons and things; such as merits; deserving (*worthy of love* or *hatred*); suitable; proper; fitting.—*n* a person of worth or distinguished for estimable qualities; a local celebrity; a character (*a village worthy*).

would *vb aux* (past tense of **will**) stands in the same relation to *will* that *should* does to *shall*, being seldom or never a preterit indicative pure and simple but mainly employed in subjunctive, conditional or optative senses, in the latter case having often the force of an independent verb.

would-be *adj* wishing to be; vainly pretending to be (*a would-be philosopher*).

wound[1] *n* a cut, breach or rupture in the skin and flesh of an animal caused by violence; an injury in a soft part of the body from external violence; a similar injury to a plant; any injury, hurt or pain, as to the feelings.—*vt* to inflict a wound on; to cut, slash or lacerate; to hurt the feelings of; to pain.—*vi* to inflict hurt or injury.

wound *pret*, *pp* of **wind**[2].

wrack[1] *n* destruction.—**wrack and ruin** the remains of something destroyed.

wrack[2] *n* seaweed, especially when thrown ashore by the waves.

wraith *n* an apparition in the exact likeness of a person, supposed to be seen before or soon after the person's death.

wrangle *vi* (**wrangled, wrangling**) to dispute angrily; to brawl; to altercate; to engage in discussion and disputation; to argue; to debate.—*n* an angry dispute; a noisy quarrel.

wrangler *n* one who wrangles.

wrangling *n* angry disputation or altercation.

wrap *vt* (**wrapped, wrapping**) to fold together; to arrange so as to cover something; to envelop or muffle; to cover up or involve generally.—**to be wrapped up in** to be bound up with or in; to be involved in; to be engrossed in or entirely devoted to (*wrapped up in his studies*).—*n* an outer article of dress for warmth; a wrapper.

wrapper *n* one who wraps; that in which anything is wrapped; an outer covering; a loose upper garment; a woman's dressing gown, etc.

wrasse *n* any of a genus of prickly-spined fish with an oblong scaly body and a single dorsal fin, inhabiting the rocky parts of the British coast.

wrath *n* violent anger; vehement exasperation; indignation; rage.

wrathful *adj* full of wrath; wroth; greatly incensed; raging; furious; impetuous.

wreak *vt* to revenge or avenge; to inflict or cause to take effect (*to wreak vengeance, rage*, etc).

wreath *n* something twisted or curled; a twist or curl; a garland; a chaplet; an ornamental twisted bandage to be worn on the head; a circular band of flowers, leaves, etc, put on a grave or used as a Christmas decoration, etc.

wreathe *vt* (**wreathed, wreathing**) to form into a wreath; to make or fashion by twining or twisting the parts together; to entwine; to intertwine; to surround with a wreath; to twine round; to encircle.—*vi* to twine circularly; to be interwoven or entwined.

wreck *n* the destruction of a vessel by being driven ashore, dashed against rocks, etc; shipwreck; the ruins of a ship stranded or floating about; goods which, after a shipwreck, have been thrown ashore by the sea; destruction or ruin generally; a person whose constitution is quite ruined; the remains of anything destroyed, ruined or fatally injured; something completely ruined.—*vt* to cause to become a wreck; to cast away, as a vessel, by violence, collision or otherwise; to cause to suffer shipwreck; to ruin or destroy generally, physically or morally.

wreckage *n* the act of wrecking; the remains of a ship or cargo that has been wrecked; material cast up by the sea from a wrecked vessel.

wrecker *n* one who plunders the wrecks of ships; one who, by delusive lights or other signals, causes ships to be cast ashore, that he or she may obtain plunder from the wreck; one whose occupation is to recover cargo or goods from wrecked vessels.

wren *n* any of various small birds, especially a small brownish songbird with a short erect tail.

wrench *n* a violent twist or a pull with twisting; a sprain; an injury by twisting, as in a joint; an instrument consisting essentially of a bar of metal having jaws adapted to catch on the head of a bolt or a nut to turn it; a screw key; the combination of a single force and a couple in a plane at right angles to its line of action.—any system of forces whatever can be reduced to a wrench.—*vt* to pull with a twist; to wrest, twist or force by violence; to sprain; to distort; (*fig*) to pervert; to wrest.

Wren *n* formerly, a member of the Women's Royal Naval Service.

wrest *vt* to twist; to wrench; to apply a violent twisting force to; to extort or bring out, as by a twisting, painful force; to force, as by torture; to turn from truth or twist from the natural meaning by violence; to pervert.

wrestle *vi* (**wrestled, wrestling**) to contend

wrack

wrench

by grappling and trying to throw down; to struggle, strive or contend.—*vt* to contend with in wrestling.

wrestler *n* one who wrestles or is skilful in wrestling.

wretch *n* a miserable person; one sunk in the deepest distress; one who is supremely unhappy; a worthless person.

wretched *adj* miserable or unhappy; sunk into deep affliction or distress; calamitous; very afflicting; worthless; paltry; poor or mean; despicable.

wriggle *vi* (**wriggled, wriggling**) to move the body to and fro with short motions like a worm or an eel; to move with writhing or twisting of the body; hence, to proceed in a mean, grovelling manner; to work by shifts or schemes (*to wriggle into one's confidence*).—*n* the motion of one who wriggles; a quick twisting motion like that of a worm or an eel.

wright *n* a builder (*shipwright, wheelwright*); a maker (*playwright*).

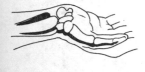

wrist

wring *vt* (*pret, pp* **wrung**, *ppr* **wringing**) to twist and squeeze or compress; to pain, as by twisting, squeezing or racking; to torture; to distress (*to wring one's heart*); to squeeze or press out; hence, to extort or force (*to wring a confession* or *money from a person*).—*vi* to writhe; to twist, as with anguish.

wringer *n* one who wrings; an apparatus for forcing water from clothes after they have been washed by compression between rollers.

wrinkle[1] *n* a small ridge or a furrow, formed by the shrinking or contraction of any smooth substance; a crease; a fold.—*vt* (**wrinkled, wrinkling**) to contract into wrinkles or furrows; to furrow; to crease. —*vi* to become contracted into wrinkles.

wrinkle[2] *n* a valuable hint; a new or good idea; a notion; a device.

wrinkly *adj* somewhat wrinkled; puckered; creased.

wrist *n* the joint by which the hand is united to the arm and by means of which the hand moves on the forearm; the carpus.

writ *n* that which is written, particularly applied to the Scriptures (*holy writ, sacred writ*); a formal document or instrument in writing; (*law*) a written court order.

write *vt* (*pret* **wrote**, *pp* **written**, *ppr* **writing**) to form or trace by a pen, pencil, graver or other instrument; to produce by tracing legible characters expressive of ideas; to set down in letters or words; to inscribe; to cover with characters or letters; to make known or express by means of characters formed by the pen, etc; to compose and produce as author; to style in writing; to entitle; (*fig*) to impress deeply or durably.—*vi* to trace or form characters

writing

with a pen, pencil, etc, on paper or other material; to be engaged in literary work; to be an author; to conduct correspondence; to convey information by letter, etc.

writer *n* one who writes; a member of the literary profession; a person who makes his or her living by writing books.

Writer to the Signet *n* (*Scots law*) one of a class of legal practitioners in Edinburgh who act as agents or attorneys in conducting causes before the Court of Session.

writhe *vt* (**writhed, writhing**) to twist with violence (*to writhe the body*); to distort; to wrest.—*vi* to twist the body about, as in pain.

writing *n* the act or art of setting down words or characters on paper or other material for the purpose of recording ideas; anything written; a literary or other composition; a manuscript; a book; an inscription.

writing paper *n* paper treated to accept ink and used especially for letters.

written *adj* in writing, as opposed to *oral* or *spoken*.

wrong *adj* not right; not fit or suitable; not according to rule, wish, design, etc; not what ought to be; not according to the divine or moral law; deviating from rectitude; not according to facts or truth; inaccurate; erroneous; holding erroneous notions; being in error; mistaken.—*n* what is not right, especially morally, a wrong, unfair or unjust act; a breach of law to the injury of another; an injustice; any injury, hurt, pain or damage.—**in the wrong** holding a wrong or unjustifiable position as regards another person; blameworthy; guilty of error.—*adv* in a wrong manner; erroneously; incorrectly.—*vt* to treat with injustice; to deal harshly or unfairly with; to do wrong to; to do injustice to; to think ill of unfairly.

wrongdoer *n* one who does wrong or evil.

wrongful *adj* injurious; unjust; illegal.

wrongly *adv* unjustly; amiss.

wrought *pret, pp* of **work**.

wrought iron *n* iron that is forged or rolled, not cast.

wry *adj* abnormally bent or turned to one side; twisted; distorted; crooked; ironic.

wryneck *n* a twisted or distorted neck; a small European bird allied to the woodpeckers, so called from the manner in which it twists its neck.

wych elm *n* a variety of elm with large leaves and sometimes hanging branches, forming a 'weeping' tree.

wych hazel *n* same as **witch hazel**.

wynd *n* (*Scots*) a lane or alley.

wyvern, wivern *n* an heraldic monster, a sort of dragon, with two wings, two legs and a tapering body.

X

X the twenty-fourth letter of the English alphabet, representing a double consonant sound and = *cs* or *ks*.

xanthophyll *n* (*bot*) an orange or yellow pigment in autumn leaves.

xanthous *adj* yellow; yellowish.

x-axis *n* the reference axis of graph along which the x coordinate is measured.

X-chromosome *n* one of a pair of chromosomes associated with sex determination, the other being the **Y-chromosome**.

xebec *n* a small three-masted vessel having both square and lateen sails, used in the Mediterranean.

xenolith *n* (*geol*) a rock occurring in a system of rocks to which it does not belong.

xenon *n* an inert gaseous element present in the atmosphere in tiny quantities.

xenophobe *n* a person who has a fear of strangers or foreigners.

xenophobia *n* fear or dislike of strangers or foreigners.

xenophobic *adj* afraid of strangers or foreigners.

xerography *n* photocopying by using light to form an electrostatic image on a photoconductive plate to which powder adheres, the particles then being fused by heat and the image transferred onto paper.

xerophyte *n* a plant adapted to live in surroundings where water is scarce (deserts) or difficult to absorb (moors).

Xerox *n* a trademark for a photocopying process using xerography; the copy produced by this.—*vt* to produce a copy in this way.

Xmas *n* a contracted form of **Christmas**.

X-ray *n* (formerly **Röntgen ray**) radiation of very short wavelengths capable of penetrating solid bodies and printing on a photographic plate a shadow picture of objects not permeable by light rays; a photograph of the interior part of a solid substance, especially a part of the body, by a machine using X-rays which can show up fractures, tumours, etc.—*vt* to photograph by X-rays.

xylem *n* (*bot*) the woody plant tissue that transports water and nutrients and also functions in support.

xylophone *n* a musical instrument consisting of a series of wooden bars and played by means of a hammer.

xylophonist *n* a performer on a xylophone.

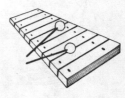

xylophone

Y

Y the twenty-fifth letter of the alphabet, sometimes a vowel, sometimes a consonant.

yacht *n* a light vessel used either for pleasure trips or racing or as a vessel of state.—*vi* to race, sail or cruise in a yacht.

yacht club *n* a club or union of yacht owners for racing purposes, etc.

yachting *adj* belonging to a yacht or yachts. —*n* the act or practice of sailing in a yacht.

yachtsman, yachtswoman *n* (*pl* **yachtsmen, yachtswomen**) one who keeps or sails a yacht.

yacht

yahoo *n* (*pl* **yahoos**) a name given by Jonathan Swift in *Gulliver's Travels* to a race of brutes with the form of man and all his degrading passions; hence, a rude, boorish, uncultivated person.

Yahweh, Yahveh *n* Jehovah.

yak[1] *n* a kind of ox with long silky hair, a bushy mane and horse-like tail, inhabiting Tibet and the Himalayas.

yak[2] *vi* (**yakked, yakking**) (*colloq*) to chatter constantly.—*n* (*colloq*) constant chatter; a person who yaks.

Yale lock *n* the trademark for a kind of lock with a cylinder mechanism into which a specially grooved key is placed to release the barrel and open the lock.

yam *n* a large tuber or root produced by a genus of tropical plants, forming a wholesome, nutritious food, the sweet potato.

yang *n* one of the two complementary forces in Chinese philosophy, representing the creative, active and positive aspects of the universe, the complement of **yin**.

yank *vt* to pull suddenly or sharply; to jerk. —*n*. a sudden, sharp pull; a jerk.

yak

yankee *n* (*colloq*) a citizen of New England or a northern state in the USA; in Britain often applied more widely to a native of any state of the USA.

yap *vi* (**yapped, yapping**) to yelp; to bark; to talk noisily or foolishly.—*n* the cry of a dog; a bark; a yelp.

yarborough *n* a hand at bridge or whist containing no card higher than a nine.

yard[1] *n* a small piece of enclosed ground adjoining a building; an enclosure within which any work or industry is carried on (*a brickyard*, *a dockyard*, etc).—*vt* to enclose or shut up in a yard, as cattle.

yard[2] *n* a unit of length equivalent to 0.914 metre; a long cylindrical piece of timber in a ship, slung crosswise to a mast and supporting and extending a sail.

yardage[1] *n* the use of a yard; the charge for this.

yardage[2] *n* a length measured in yards.

yardarm *n* the end of a ship's yard.

yardstick *n* a stick measuring a yard, used as a measure of cloth, etc; any standard used in judging.

yarn *n* any kind of thread prepared for weaving into cloth; one of the threads of which a rope is composed; (*fig*) a long story or tale.

yarrow *n* a strongly scented astringent plant with clusters of small flowers.

yataghan *n* a dagger-like sabre without a cross guard, worn in Muslim countries.

yaw *vi* to steer wild; to deviate from the line of her course in steering (said of a ship); to turn from side to side about the vertical axis (said of an aircraft).—*vt* to cause to yaw.—*n* a yawing movement or course.

yawl *n* a small ship's boat, usually rowed by four or six oars; a jollyboat; the smallest boat used by fishermen; a two-masted vessel, similar to a cutter but with a mizzenmast stepped well aft.

yawn *vi* to have the mouth open involuntarily through drowsiness or dullness; to gape; to open wide; to stand open, as a chasm or gulf, etc.—*n* an involuntary opening of the mouth from drowsiness; a gaping or opening wide; (*colloq*) something or someone very boring.

yaws *n* a contagious disease characterized by cutaneous tumours growing to the size of a raspberry.

y-axis *n* the reference axis of a graph along which the y coordinate is measured.

Y-chromosome *n* one of a pair of chromosomes associated with sex determination, the other being the **X-chromosome**.

yclept *adj* (*arch*) named.

ye[1] *pron* properly the nominative plural of

the second personal pronoun but in later times also used as an objective, now used only in the sacred and solemn style, in common discourse and writing *you* being exclusively used.

ye² the old method of printing **the**.

yea *adv* (*arch*) yes, the opposite of *nay*; not this alone, not only so but also.

year *n* the period of time during which the earth makes one complete revolution in its orbit, comprising the twelve calendar months or 365 days from 1st January to 31st December; (*pl*) age or old age.

yearbook *n* a book published every year, each issue supplying fresh information on matters in regard to which changes are continually taking place.

yearling *n* an animal one year old or in the second year of its age.—*adj* being a year old.

yearlong *adj* lasting a year.

yearly *adj* annual; happening every year.—*adv* annually; once a year.

yearn *vi* to be filled with eager longing; to have a wistful feeling.

yearning *adj* longing; having longing desire.—*n* the feeling of one who yearns; a strong feeling of longing desire.

yeast *n* a fungus that causes alcoholic fermentation, used in brewing and baking; a preparation consisting of living yeast cells, compressed or powdered, used as a raising agent in baking.

yeasty *adj* resembling or containing yeast; frothy; foamy.

yell *vi* to cry out with a sharp, disagreeable noise, to shriek hideously; to cry or scream as with agony or horror; to shout.—*n* a sharp, loud, harsh outcry; a scream or cry of horror, distress or agony; a shout.

yellow *adj* being of a pure bright golden colour or of a similar hue; (*colloq*) cowardly.—*n* a bright golden colour, the type of which may be found in the field buttercup.—*vt* to render yellow.—*vi* to grow yellow.

yellow fever *n* an infectious tropical fever caused by a virus transmitted by certain mosquitoes, characterized by aching limbs and yellowing of the skin.

yellowhammer, yellow bunting *n* a small songbird of Europe with a yellow head, neck and breast.

yellow pages *npl* a telephone directory, or part of one, which lists business subscribers according to trade.

yellow press *n* sensational or jingoistic press.

yellow spot *n* (*anat*) the point of acutest vision in the retina.

yelp *vi* to utter a sharp or shrill bark; to give a sharp, quick cry, as a dog, either in eagerness or in pain or fear.—*n* a sharp bark or cry caused by fear or pain.

yen¹ *n* the Japanese basic money unit.

yen² *n* (*colloq*) a desire; a longing.

yeoman *n* (*pl* **yeomen**) (*hist*) a man of small estate in land, not ranking as one of the gentry; formerly, a gentleman farmer or one who farms his own land; a petty officer on a warship with clerical duties.

yeoman of the guard *n* a bodyguard of the British sovereign, dressed in the costume of Henry VIII's time.—also called **beefeater**.

yeomanry *n* yeomen collectively; a British volunteer cavalry force raised from country districts as a home guard (1761–1907).

yerba, yerba maté *n* an infusion of dried leaves of the maté which makes a mildly stimulating tea.

yes *adv* a word which expresses affirmation or consent, opposed to *no*.

yester *adj* belonging to the day preceding the present; next before the present (mostly in composition, as *yesteryear*).

yesterday *n* the day next before the present; often used for time not long gone by (used without the preposition *on* or *during*).

yet *adv* in addition; over and above; further; still (used especially with comparatives, as *yet more surprising*); at this or at that time, as formerly; now or then, as at a previous period (*while yet young*); at or before some future time; before all is done (*he'll suffer yet*); thus far; hitherto (*a letter not yet sent off*), often accompanied by *as* in this sense (*I have not met him as yet*); though the case be such; nevertheless.—*conj* nevertheless; however; notwithstanding.

yeti *n* a large hairy creature alleged to live high in the Himalayas, also called **abominable snowman**.

yew *n* an evergreen tree allied to the conifers and indigenous in Europe and Asia, with thin, sharp, poisonous leaves and red berries and yielding a hard and durable timber used for cabinet work and formerly for making bows.

Yiddish *n* a mixed dialect with German, Hebrew and Slavonic elements, used by European and American Jews.—*adj* spoken, written, etc, in Yiddish.

yield *vt* to pay; to requite; to give in return or by way of recompense; to produce as return for labour or capital; to produce generally; to bring forth, give out or provide (*trees yield fruit*); to afford; to grant or give (*to yield consent*); to give up, as to superior power; to relinquish; to surrender (in this sense often followed by *up*).—*vi* to give way, as to superior force; to submit; to surrender; to give way, as to entreaty, argument, etc; to comply; to consent; to give place, as inferior in rank or excellence.—*n* amount yielded; product; return; particularly product resulting from growth or cultivation.

yew

yielding *adj* ready to submit, comply or yield; compliant; unresisting.

yin *n* one of the two complementary forces in Chinese philosophy, representing the receptive, passive and negative aspects of the universe, the complement of **yang**.

yip *n* a cry; an exclamation.—*vi* (**yipped, yipping**) to utter a yip.

yippee *interj* used to express exuberant delight.

yodel *vti* (**yodelled, yodelling**) to sing by suddenly changing from the natural voice to the falsetto and vice versa.

yoga *n* any of the forms of mental, physical or moral discipline practised in the Hindu religion to achieve spiritual union with the absolute, usually stressing the importance of physical exercises, positions and breathing control in promoting physical and mental well-being; a system of such exercises.

yoghurt, yogurt *n* a semi-liquid food made from milk curdled by bacteria, often flavoured with fruit, etc.

yogi *n* a devotee or practitioner of yoga.

yoke

yoke *n* a part of the gear or tackle of draught animals, particularly oxen, passing across their necks so that two are connected for drawing; a pair of draught animals, especially oxen, yoked together; something resembling a yoke in form or use; a frame to fit the shoulders and neck of a person for carrying pails or the like; (*fig*) servitude, slavery or burden imposed; something which couples or binds together; a bond of connection; a tie; a shaped part of a garment, usually below the neck, from which the rest of the garment hangs.—*vt* (**yoked, yoking**) to put a yoke on; to join in a yoke; to couple; to join with another.—*vi* to be joined together.

yokel *n* a rustic or country person who is considered to be unsophisticated and simple-minded.

yolk *n* the nutritive yellow part of an egg; a greasy secretion from the skin of sheep which renders the pile soft and pliable.

Yom Kippur *n* an annual Jewish holiday marked by fasting and prayer.

yomp *vi* to march laboriously carrying heavy equipment, especially over rough terrain.

yo-yo

yon *adj* that; those (referring to an object at a distance); (*poet*) yonder.

yonder *adj* being at a distance within view; that or those (referring to persons or things far off).—*adv* at or in that place there.

yore *adv* in time long past; long since; in old time.—**of yore** of old time; long ago (*in days of yore*).

yorker *n* in cricket, a ball which pitches immediately in front of a batsman's block.

Yorkshire terrier *n* a breed of very small long-haired terrier.

you *pron* the second person singuar or plural; the person or persons spoken to.

young *adj* being in the first or early stage of life or growth; not yet arrived at maturity; not old; being in the early part of existence; not yet far advanced; having the appearance of early life; fresh or vigorous; having little experience; raw; green; pertaining to one's early life.—*n* the offspring of an animal collectively; young people.—**with young** pregnant; gravid.

younger *n* one who is not so old as another; a junior.—*adj compar* more young; less old.

youngling *n* (*arch*) an animal in the first part of life.

youngster *n* a young person.

your *adj* pertaining or belonging to you.

yours *pron* of or belonging to you; that or those which belong to you; your property; your friends or relations.

yourself *pron* (*pl* **yourselves**) you, not another or others; you, in your own person or individually (used distinctively or reflexively).

youth *n* the state or quality of being young; youthfulness; the part of life between childhood and adulthood; a young man; young persons collectively.

youthful *adj* being in the early stage of life; young; pertaining to the early part of life; suitable to the first part of life; fresh or vigorous, as in youth.

youth hostel *n* a supervised hostel for young travellers.

yowl *vi* to give a long distressful or mournful cry, as a dog.—*n* a long distressful or mournful cry, as that of a dog.

yoyo *n* (*pl* **yoyos**) a round toy containing string around its grooved centre so that it spins up and down as the string winds and unwinds.

ytterbium *n* a soft metallic element.

yttria *n* a metallic oxide of yttrium with the appearance of a white powder.

yttrium *n* a metallic element found in Sweden of a scaly texture, a greyish black colour and a perfectly metallic lustre.

yucca *n* a large American plant of the lily family with white flowers in large panicles and long rigid, pointed leaves, cultivated in British gardens.

yucky *adj* (*colloq*) disgusting; nasty.

yule *n* Christmas.

yule log *n* a large log of wood traditionally burnt at Christmas; a cake shaped like this.

yuletide *n* the time or season of yule or Christmas.

yummy *adj* (*colloq*) delicious; tasty.

yuppie *n* a young, ambitious and successful person (an acronym of young upwardly mobile professional or young urban professional).

Z

Z the last letter of the English alphabet, equivalent to the *s* in *wise*, *ease*, etc.

zamindar, zemindar *n* in India, a landholder or landed proprietor subject to the payment of the land tax or government land revenue.

zander *n* a European freshwater fish.

zany *adj* clownish; comical; eccentric.

zap *vt* (**zapped, zapping**) (*colloq*) to hit; to shoot; to kill suddenly, as with heavy firepower or electric current; (*comput*) to get rid of (data); to change (television channels) rapidly.—*vi* to change television channels rapidly by means of a hand-held remote control device.

zax *n* an instrument used by slaters for cutting and dressing slates.

z-axis *n* the reference axis of a three-dimensional coordinate system along which the z coordinate is measured.

zeal *n* passionate ardour in the pursuit of anything; eagerness in any cause or behalf, good or bad; earnestness; fervency; enthusiasm.

zealot *n* one who is zealous or full of zeal; one carried away by excess of zeal; a fanatical partisan.

zealous *adj* inspired with zeal; warmly engaged or ardent in the pursuit of an object; fervent; eager; earnest.

zebra *n* a quadruped of southern Africa allied to the horse and ass, nearly as large as a horse, white, striped with numerous brownish-black bands.

zebra crossing *n* a street crossing for pedestrians marked by broad white and black stripes.

zebu *n* a species of ox found in Asia and Africa with a prominent hump on its shoulders.

zedoary *n* an Asiatic root used for similar purposes as ginger.

Zeitgeist *n* the spirit of the time; the beliefs, attitudes, tastes, etc, of a particular period.

zemindar *n* same as **zamindar**.

Zen *n* a form of Buddhism that emphasizes the importance of self-awareness and self-mastery as a means to enlightenment.

zenana *n* the portion of a house exclusively for the women in a family of good caste in India.

Zend *n* an ancient Iranian language belonging to the Aryan family and closely allied to Sanskrit, in which are composed the sacred writings of the Zoroastrians.

Zenda-Vesta *n* the collective name for the sacred writings of the Parsees, ascribed to Zoroaster.

zenith *n* the vertical point of the heavens at any place or point right above a spectator's head; the upper pole of the celestial horizon; (*fig*) the highest point of a person's fortune; culminating point.

zephyr *n* the west wind; (*poet*) any soft, mild, gentle breeze.

zeppelin *n* a rigid, cigar-shaped airship.

zero *n* no number or quantity; number or quantity diminished to nothing; a cipher; nothing; (*physics*) the point of a graduated instrument at which its scale commences; the starting point on a graduated scale, generally represented by the mark 0; the symbol 0; freezing point; 0° Celsius.

zero gravity *n* weightlessness.

zero hour *n* the time set for any planned move or activity to begin.

zest *n* the outer part of the skin of an orange or lemon used to give flavour; that which serves to enhance enjoyment; a relish; keen enjoyment; gusto.

zuegma *n* syllepsis.

Zeus *n* in Greek myth, the supreme god.

zibet *n* an animal closely akin to the civet.

zigzag *n* something that consists of straight lines or pieces with short sharp turns or angles; a zigzag moulding; a chevron.—*adj* having sharp and quick turns or bends.—*vi* (**zigzagged, zigzagging**) to move or advance in a zigzag fashion; to form zigzags.

zilch (*colloq*) *n* nothing.

zinc *n* a metallic element with a strong lustre and a bluish-white colour, used in brass and other alloys and as a protective coating.—*vt* to coat or cover with zinc.

zincography *n* an art similar to lithography, the stone printing surface being replaced by that of a plate of polished zinc.

zebra

zeppelin

zing *vi* (*colloq*) to move with a high-pitched buzzing noise.— *n* a high-pitched buzzing noise; vitality; exuberance; enthusiasm.

zinnia *n* a tropical American plant with showy flowers.

Zionism *n* a Jewish national movement formerly concerned with the re-establishment of the Jews in Palestine, now concerned with the development of Israel.

zip *n* a light whizzing sound of a bullet, etc; (*sl*) brisk energy; a kind of fastener, pulled open or shut by a tag and joining two edges together, used on clothing, purses, etc.—*vi* (**zipped, zipping**) to move at high speed, to dart.—*vt* to fasten with a zip.

zip fastener, zipper *n* a zip.

zircon *n* a variously coloured, hard, translucent mineral, some varieties of which are cut as gemstones.

zither, zithern *n* a flat, stringed musical instrument consisting of a sounding box with thirty-one strings played with the right hand, the strings being stopped with the left.

zodiac *n* an imaginary belt or zone in the heavens, extending about 8° on each side of the ecliptic, within which the motions of the sun, moon and principal planets are confined, divided crosswise into twelve equal areas, called signs of the zodiac, each named after a constellation.

zodiacal *adj* pertaining to the zodiac.

zodiacal light *n* a luminous tract lying nearly in the ecliptic, its base being on the horizon, seen at certain seasons either in the west after sunset or in the east before sunrise.

zombie *n* a dead body supposed to be brought to life by witchcraft; a person who is lifeless and apathetic

zone *n* a girdle or belt; any well-marked band or stripe running round an object; (*geog*) one of the five great divisions of the earth, bounded by circles parallel to the equator, named according to the temperature prevailing in each: the Torrid Zone, two Temperate Zones and two Frigid Zones; (*nat hist*) any well-defined belt within which certain forms of plant or animal life are confined; a region; an area; any area with a specified use or specified restrictions.—*vt* (**zoned, zoning**) to divide or mark off into zones; to designate as a zone; to encircle with a zone.

zoo *n* (*pl* **zoos**) a place in which a collection of living animals is kept for public viewing; a zoological garden

zoography *n* a description of animals, their forms and habits.

zooid *adj* resembling or pertaining to an animal.—*n* an organic body, as a cell or a spermatozoon, in some respects resembling a distinct animal; one of the more or less completely independent organisms produced by gemmation or fission, as in polyzoa, tapeworms, etc.

zoological *adj* pertaining to zoology.

zoological garden *n* a zoo.

zoologist *n* one who studies or specializes in zoology.

zoology *n* that science which treats of the natural history of animals or their structure, physiology, classification, habits and distribution.

zoomorphic *adj* pertaining to animal forms; exhibiting animal forms.

zoomorphism *n* the state of being zoomorphic.

zoom *vi* (*colloq*) to move quickly; to rise rapidly and sharply, as an aircraft; to focus in on an object using a zoom lens.—*n* the act of zooming; a zoom lens.

zoom lens *n* a camera lens of variable focal length, used, for example, to make distant objects appear closer without moving the camera.

-zoon *n* an animal having a distinct and independent existence (*spermatozoon*).

zoophyte *n* a name loosely applied to many plant-like animals, as sponges, corals, sea anemones, etc.

zoophytic *adj* relating to zoophytes.

zoosperm *n* spermatozoon.

zoospore *n* a spore of algae, fungi, etc, which can move spontaneously to some extent by its cilia.

Zoroastrian *adj* pertaining to Zoroaster, whose system of religion was the national faith of ancient Persia and is embodied in the Zend-Avesta.—*n* a believer in this religion.

Zoroastrianism *n* the religion founded by Zoroaster, one feature of which was a belief in a good and an evil power or deity perpetually striving against each other.

zounds *exclam* (*arch*) contracted from 'God's wounds', expressing anger and astonishment.

zucchini *n* a courgette.

zygospore *n* (*bot*) a spore formed by union of two gametes.

zygote *n* the cell formed by the union of an ovum and a sperm; the developing organism from such a cell.

zymic *adj* pertaining to a ferment or to fermentation; causing fermentation.

zymology *n* the science of ferments and fermentation.

zymosis *n* an infectious disease caused by a virus or organism that acts like a ferment.

zymotic *adj* caused by or relating to an infection or an infectious disease; pertaining to or produced by fermentation.

zymurgy *n* the chemistry of fermentation in brewing, etc.

zip

Abbreviations, Acronyms and Contractions

A Adult; alcohol; alto; America; American; ampere; angstrom; anode; answer; April; (*math*) area; (*chem*) argon; Associate; atomic weight; IVR Austria.

Å Angstrom unit.

a acre; are (measure).

a. adjective; alto; ampere; *anno* (*Latin* year); anode; answer; *ante* (*Latin* before); *aqua* (*Latin* water); area.

A1 first class.

AA Alcoholics Anonymous; anti-aircraft; Automobile Association.

AAA Amateur Athletic Association; American Automobile Association.

AAC Amateur Athletic Club; *anno ante Christum* (*Latin* in the year before Christ).

AAM air-to-air missile.

A & A additions and amendments.

A & M Hymns Ancient and Modern.

A & N Army and Navy.

A & R Artist and Repertoire.

AAPO African Peoples' Organization.

aar against all risks; average annual rainfall.

AAU Amateur Athletic Union.

AB able-bodied seaman; *Artium Baccalaureus* (*Latin* Bachelor of Arts).

Ab (*chem*) alabamine.

ABA Amateur Boxing Association.

Abb. Abbess; Abbey; Abbot.

abbr., abbrev. abbreviated; abbreviation.

ABC Advance Booking Charter; American Broadcasting Company; Associated British Cinemas; Audit Bureau of Circulations; automatic binary computer.

abd abdicated abridged.

ab init. *ab initio* (*Latin* from the beginning).

abl. ablative.

ABM anti-ballistic missile.

ABMEWS anti-ballistic missile early warning system.

ABP arterial blood pressure.

Abp Archbishop.

abr. abridged; abridgement.

abs. absence; absent; absolute; abstract.

absol. absolute.

abstr. abstract.

abt about.

ABTA Association of British Travel Agents.

abv. above.

AC Air Command; Air Corps; Aircraftman; Alternating Current; analog computer; Annual Conference; *ante Christum* (*Latin* before Christ); Appeal Case; Appeal Court; Army Corps; Arts Council; Assistant Commissioner; Athletic Club.

A/C account; account current.

Ac (*chem*) actinium.

ac. acre.

a.c. *ante cibum* (*Latin* before meals).

acad. academic; academy.

ACAS Advisory, Conciliation and Arbitration Service.

ACC Army Catering Corps.

acc. acceleration; accent; accepted; accompanied; according; account; accusative.

accel. (*mus*) *accelerando* (*Italian* more quickly).

Accred Accredited.

acct account.

accy accountancy.

ACF Army Cadet Force.

ACG automatic control gear.

ACGB Arts Council of Great Britain.

ack. acknowledge(d).

ackt acknowledgment.

ACLS Automatic Carrier Landing System.

ACM Air Chief Marshal.

ACN *ante Christum natum* (*Latin* before the birth of Christ).

ACOP Association of Chief Officers of Police.

ACORN (*comput*) automatic checkout and recording network.

ACP American College of Physicians.

acpt. acceptance.

ACSIR Advisory Council for Scientific and Industrial Research.

Act. Acting.

act. active.

actg acting.

ACTH adrenocorticotrophic hormone, an anti-rheumatic drug.

ACV actual cash value; air cushion vehicle (hovercraft).

ACW Aircraftwoman; alternating continuous waves.

AD (*milit*) active duty; air defence; *anno Domini* (*Latin* in the year of our Lord).

ad. adverb; advertisement.

ADC Aide-de-Camp; (*comput*) analog to digital converter; automatic digital calculator.

add. addendum; addition; additional; address.

ADF automatic direction finder.

ad fin. *ad finem* (*Latin* near the end).

ad inf. *ad infinitum* (*Latin* to infinity).

ad imt. *ad initium* (*Latin* at the beginning).

ad int. *ad interim* (*Latin* in the meantime).

adj, adj. adjacent; adjective; adjoining; adjourned; adjudged; adjunct; adjustment; adjutant.

Adjt Adjutant.

Adjt-Gen. Adjutant-General.

ad lib. *ad libitum* (*Latin* at will).

ad loc. *ad locum* (*Latin* at the place).

adm. administration; administrative; admitted.

admin. administration.

ADN IVR People's Democratic Republic of Yemen.

ADP automatic data processing.

adv. advance; advent; adverb; adverbial; *adversus* (*Latin* against); advertisement; advisory; advocate.

ad val. *ad valorem* (*Latin* according to the value).

advt advertisement.

ADW Air Defence Warning.

AE Atomic Energy.

AEA Atomic Energy Authority.

AE & P Ambassador Extraordinary and Plenipotentiary.

AEF Amalgamated Union of Engineering and Foundry Workers.

AEI Associated Electrical Industries.

AELTC All England Lawn Tennis Club.

aer. aeronautics; aeroplane.

AERE Atomic Energy Research Establishment.

aeron. aeronautical; aeronautics.

AEU Amalgamated Engineering Union (now AUEW).

AEW airborne early warning.

AF Admiral of the Fleet; Air Force; Anglo-French; audio-frequency.

A/F as found.

AFA Amateur Football Association.

AFC Association Football Club; automatic frequency control.

affil. affiliated.

afft affidavit.
AFG IVR Afghanistan.
AFI American Film Institute.
AFM Air Force Medal.
AFN American Forces Network; Armed Forces Network.
Afr. Africa; African.
Afrik. Afrikaans.
AFS Auxiliary Fire Service.
afsd aforesaid.
AFV armoured fighting vehicle.
AG Adjutant General; Attorney General.
Ag (*chem*) silver.
AGC automatic gain control.
AGCA automatic ground controlled approach.
AGCL automatic ground controlled landing.
agcy agency.
AGM air-to-ground missile; Annual General Meeting.
AGR advanced gas-cooled reactor.
agr., agric. agricultural; agriculture.
agst against.
agt agent; agreement.
a.g.w. actual gross weight.
AH *anno Hegirae* (*Latin* in the year of the Hegira).
AI Amnesty International; artificial insemination.
a.i. *ad interim* (*Latin* in the meantime).
AID acute infectious disease; Army Intelligence Department; artificial insemination by donor.
AIH artificial insemination by husband.
AL IVR Albania; Anglo-Latin.
Al (*chem*) aluminium.
al. alcohol; alcoholic.
ALBM air-launched ballistic missile.
Ald. Alderman.
Alg. Algeria; Algerian.
alg, alg. algebra.
ALGOL (*comput*) algorithmic language.
alk. alkali.
alt. alteration; alternate; alternative; altitude; alto.
alter. alteration.
alum. aluminium.
AM Air Marshal; Air Ministry; Albert Medal; amplitude modulation; *anno mundi* (*Latin* in the year of the world); *ante meridiem* (*Latin* before noon); arithmetic mean; *Artium Magister* (*Latin* Master of Arts); Associate Member.
Am (*chem*) americium.
Am. America; American.
a.m. ante meridiem.
amal. amalgamated.
AMDG *ad majorem Dei gloriam* (*Latin* to the greater glory of God).
Amer. America; American.
AMM anti-missile missile.
amn. amunition.
amp. amperage; ampere; amplifier; amplitude.
AMS Ancient Monuments Society.
amt amount.
AMU atomic mass unit.

AN Anglo-Norman.
An (*chem*) actinon.
an. *anno* (*Latin* in the year); anonymous; *ante* (*Latin* before).
anag. anagram.
anal. analogous; analogy; analysis; analytic.
anat. anatomical; anatomist; anatomy.
ANC African National Congress.
anc. ancient; anciently.
AND IVR Andorra.
and. (*mus*) *andante* (*Italian* moderately slow).
Angl. Anglican; Anglicized.
anim. (*mus*) *animato* (*Italian* animated).
ann. annual; annuity.
anniv. anniversary.
annot. annotated; annotation; annotator.
anon. anonymous.
ANS Army Nursing Service.
ans. answer.
ant. antenna; antiquarian; antique; antonym.
anthol. anthology.
anthrop. anthropological; anthropology.
antiq. antiquarian; antiquity.
ANZAC Australian and New Zealand Army Corps.
a/o account of.
AOB any other business.
AOCB any other competent business.
AOC-in-C Air Officer Commander-in-Chief.
AP *ante prandium* (*Latin* before meals); Associated Press; atmospheric pressure.
Ap. Apostle; April.
ap. apothecary.
APC automatic phase control; automatic pitch control.
APEX Advance Purchase Excursion.
aph. aphorism.
apo. apogee.
Apoc. Apocalypse; Apocrypha.
app. apparatus; apparent; appendix; applied; appointed; apprentice; approved; approximate.
appro. approbation; approval.
approx. approximate; approximately.
apptd appointed.
Apr, Apr. April.
APT advanced passenger train.
apt. apartment.
APWU Amalgamated Postal Workers' Union.
aq. *aqua* (*Latin* water).
AR Autonomous Republic.
Ar (*chem*) argon.
Ar. Arabic; Aramaic.
ar. arrival; arrives.
a.r. *anno regni* (*Latin* in the year of the reign).
ARA Associate of the Royal Academy.
Arab Arabian; Arabic.
arb. arbiter; arbitration.
ARC Aeronautical Research Council; American Red Cross; automatic relay calculator.
Arch. Archbishop; Archdcacon; Archduke; Archipelago; Architecture.

arch. archaic; archaism; archery; archipelago; architect; architecture; archive.
archaeol. archaeology.
Archd. Archdeacon; Archduke.
archit. architecture.
ARCS Australian Red Cross Society.
ARD acute respiratory disease.
Arg. Argentina; Argyll (former county).
arg. *argentum* (*Latin* silver).
arith. arithmetic(al).
Ariz. Arizona.
Ark. Arkansas.
ARM anti-radar missile.
ARP air raid precautions.
ARR *anno regni regis* or *regine* (*Latin* in the year of the king's or queen's reign).
arr. arranged; arrangement; arrival.
art. article; artificial; artillery.
ARTC Air Route Traffic Control.
AS Anglo-Saxon; *anno salutis* (*Latin* in the year of salvation); anti-submarine; Assistant Secretary.
As (*chem*) arsenic.
ASA Advertising Standards Authority.
a.s.a.p. as soon as possible.
ASAT Anti-Satellite.
ASCII (*comput*) American Standard Code for Information Interchange.
ASDIC Allied Submarine Detection Investigation Committee.
ASE American Stock Exchange.
a.s.e. air standard efficiency.
ASH Action on Smoking and Health.
ASI air speed indicator.
ASLEF Associated Society of Locomotive Engineers and Firemen.
ASLIB Association of Special Libraries and Information Bureaux.
ASM air-to-surface missile.
ASN Army Service Number.
ASPCA American Society for the Prevention of Cruelty to Animals.
Ass. Assembly.
ass. assistant; association; assorted.
Asscn., Assn. Association.
Assoc. Associate; Association.
asst assistant.
AST Atlantic Standard Time.
ASTMS Association of Scientific, Technical, and Managerial Staffs.
astr. astronomer; astronomical; astronomy.
astrol. astrologer; astrological; astrology.
astron. astronomer; astronomical; astronomy.
ASW anti-submarine warfare.
AT alternativetechnology; anti-tank.
At (*chem*) astatine.
at. airtight; atmosphere; atomic.
ATA Atlantic Treaty Association.
ATC Air Traffic Control; Air Training Corps.
Atl. Atlantic.
atm. atmosphere; atmospheric.
at. no. atomic number.
ATS (*comput*) Administrative Terminal System; anti-tetanus serum; Auxiliary Territorial Service (now WRAC).

a.t.s. (*law*) at the suit of.
att. attached; attention; attorney.
attn. attention.
attrib. attribute; attributive.
at. vol. atomic volume.
at. wt. atomic weight.
AU Angstrom unit; astronomical unit.
Au (*chem*) gold.
AUBTW Amalgamated Union of Building Trade Workers.
AUEW Amalgamated Union of Engineering Workers.
Aug. August.
AUM air-to-underwater missile.
AUS IVR Australia.
Aust. Australia; Australian.
Austl. Australasia.
AUT Association of University Teachers.
aut. automatic.
auth. author; authority; authorized.
Auth. Ver. Authorized Version.
auto. automatic; automobile; automotive.
aux. auxiliary.
AV audio-visual; Authorized Version.
Av. Avenue.
av. average; avoirdupois.
a.v. *ad valorem* (*Latin* according to the value).
avdp. avoirdupois.
Ave Avenue.
avg. average.
AVM Air Vice-Marshal.
AVR Army Volunteer Reserve.
a.w. atomic weight.
AWOL absent without official leave.
ax. axiom; axis.
az. azimuth.
B Bachelor; bacillus; Baron; base; (*mus*) bass; IVR Belgium; Bible; Blessed; book; born; (*chem*) boron; bowled (in cricket); breadth; British; Brother.
BA *Baccalaureus Artium* (*Latin* Bachelor of Arts); British Academy; British Airways; Buenos Aires.
Ba (*chem*) barium.
BAA British Airports Authority.
BAAB British Amateur Athletic Board.
Bach. Bachelor.
bact. bacteria; bacteriology; bacterium.
bacteriol. bacteriological; bacteriology.
BAFO British Army Forces Overseas.
BAL (*comput*) basic assembly language.
bal. balance.
ball. ballast; ballistics.
BALPA British Air Line Pilots' Association.
B & B bed and breakfast.
b & s brandy and soda.
b & w black and white.
BAOR British Army of the Rhine.
Bap. Baptist.
bap. baptized.
bar. barometer; barometric; barrel; barrister.
barit. baritone.
barr. barrister.
Bart. Baronet.
BASIC (*comput*) Beginners' All-purpose Symbolic Instruction Code.

bat., batt. battalion; battery.
BB Boys' Brigade; double black (pencils).
bb. books.
BBB triple black (pencils).
BBBG British Boxing Board of Control.
BBC British Broadcasting Corporation.
BBFC British Board of Film Censors.
bbl. barrel.
BC before Christ; British Council.
BCC British Council of Churches.
BCD (*comput*) binary coded decimal notation.
BCG Bacillus Calmette-Guerin, antituberculosis vaccine.
BCh *Baccalaureus Chirurgiae* (*Latin* Bachelor of Surgery).
BD Bachelor of Divinity.
B/D bank draft.
bd. board; bond; bound; bundle.
BDA British Dental Association.
bdl. bundle.
BDS Bachelor of Dental Surgery; IVR Barbados.
BDU Bomb Disposal Unit.
BE Bachelor of Education; Bank of England; Bill of Exchange; British Embassy.
Be (*chem*) beryllium.
BEAB British Electrical Approvals Board.
bec. because.
BEd Bachelor of Education.
Beds. Bedfordshire.
BEF British Expeditionary Force.
bef. before.
beg. begin; beginning.
Belg. Belgian; Belgium.
BEM British Empire Medal.
BEng Bachelor of Engineering.
Beng. Bengal, Bengali.
beq. bequeath; bequeathed.
beqt bequest.
Berks. Berkshire.
bet. between.
BeV billion electron-volts.
B/F brought forward.
b.f. bloody fool; (*print*) bold face; *bona fide* (*Latin* genuine, genuinely).
BFBS British Forces Broadcasting Service.
BFI British Film Institute.
BFN British Forces Network.
BG BrigadierGeneral; IVR Bulgaria.
bg bag.
BH IVR British Honduras.
B'ham Birmingham.
BHC British High Commissioner.
b.h.p. brake horsepower.
Bi (*chem*) bismuth.
Bib. Bible; Biblical.
Bibl. Biblical.
bibliog. bibliographer; bibliography.
bicarb. bicarbonate of soda.
b.i.d. *bis in die* (*Latin* twice daily).
BIM British Institute of Management.
biog. biographical; biographer; biography.
biol. biological; biologist; biology.
BIT (*comput*) binary digit.

Bk (*chem*) berkelium.
bk. bank; bark; block; book; break.
bkcy. bankruptcy.
bkg. banking.
bkpt. bankrupt.
bkt. basket; bracket.
BL Bachelor of Laws; Bachelor of Letters; British Legion (now RBL); British Library.
B/L Bill of Lading.
bldlg. building.
BLit Bachelor of Literature.
BLitt *Baccalaureus Litterarum* (*Latin* Bachelor of Letters).
blk black; block; bulk.
B.LL. Bachelor of Laws.
blvd boulevard.
BM Bachelor of Medicine; *Beatae Memoriae* (*Latin* of blessed memory); bench mark; bowel movement; British Museum.
BMA British Medical Association.
BMC British Medical Council.
BMJ British Medical Journal.
BML British Museum Library.
BMR basal metabolic rate.
BMus Bachelor of Music.
BN banknote.
Bn Baron; Battalion.
BO body odour; Box Office; Broker's Order; Buyer's Option.
b/o brought over.
BOA British Olympic Association.
BOD biochemical oxygen demand.
Boh. Bohemia, Bohemian.
Bol. Bolivia, Bolivian.
bor. borough.
BOT Board of Trade.
bot. botanical; botanist; botany; bottle; bought.
boul. boulevard.
BP British Petroleum; British Pharmacopoeia.
b/p bills payable; blueprint.
bp. baptized; birthplace; bishop.
b.p. below proof; bill of parcels; boiling point.
BPh, BPhil Bachelor of Philosolphy.
bpl. birthplace.
BR IVR Brazil; British Rail.
B/R bills receivable.
Br (*chem*) bromine.
Br. Breton; Britain; British; Brother.
br. branch; brand; brig; bronze; brother; brown.
Braz. Brazil, Brazilian.
BRCS British Red Cross Society.
BRDC British Research and Development Corporation.
Brig. Brigade; Brigadier.
Brig. Gen. Brigadier General.
Brit. Britain; Britannia; British; Briton.
BRN IVR Bahrain.
bro. brother.
BRU IVR Brunei.
BS Bachelor of Science; Bachelor of Surgery; IVR Bahamas; Balance Sheet; Bill of Sale; Blessed Sacrament; British Standards.
b.s. balance sheet; bill of sale.

BSc *Baccalaureus Scientiae* (*Latin* Bachelor of Science).
BSG British Standard Gauge.
BSI British Standards Institution; Building Societies' Institute.
bskt basket.
BSS British Standards Specification.
BST British Standard Time; British Summer Time.
Bt. Baronet.
BTA British Travel Association.
BTh Bachelor of Theology.
BThU British thermal unit.
btl. bottle.
BTU Board of Trade Unit.
Btu British thermal unit.
bu. bureau; bushel.
Bucks. Buckinghamshire.
BUP British United Press.
BUPA British United Provident Association.
BUR IVR Burma.
Bur. Burma; Burmese.
bus. business.
BV *beata virgo* (*Latin* Blessed Virgin); *bene vale* (*Latin* farewell).
b/w black and white.
bx. box; boxes.
Bz (*chem*) benzene.
C Canon; (*physics*) capacitance; Cape; Captain; (*chem*) carbon; Catechism; Catholic; Celsius; Celtic; Centigrade; Central; Century; Chancellor; Chancery; Chapter; Chief; Church; Circuit; Collected; Commander; Confessor; Confidential; Congregational; Congress; Conservative; Constable; Consul; Contralto; Contrast; Corps; coulomb; Count; County; Court; IVR Cuba; Cubic; (*physics*) heat capacity; 100 (Roman numeral).
c. candle; canon; carat; case; cathode; cent; centavo; centigram; centimetre; central; centre; century; chapter; charge; *circa* (*Latin* about); city; class; college; (*math*) constant; contralto; copyright; cubic; cup; currency; current; cycle; (*physics*) specific heat capacity.
CA Central America; Chartered Accountant; Civil Aviation; Consumers' Association; Court of Appeal; Crown Agent.
C/A Credit Account; Current Account.
Ca (*chem*) calcium.
ca. *circa* (*Latin* about).
CAA Civil Aviation Authority.
CAB Citizens' Advice Bureau.
CAD (*comput*) computer-aided design.
cad. (*mus*) *cadenza* (*Italian* final flourish).
Caern. Caernarvonshire (former county).
Caith. Caithness (former county).
cal. calendar; calibre; calorie.
Cambs. Cambridgeshire.
Can. Canon; Canto.
can. canal; cancel; cannon; canton.
Canad. Canadian.
canc. cancellation; cancelled.
cand. candidate.

C & W (*mus*) country and western.
Cantab. *Cantabrigiensis* (*Latin* of Cambridge).
CAP Code of Advertising Practice; Common Agricultural Policy (of EC).
cap. capacity; capital; capitalize; captain; *caput* (*Latin* chapter).
caps. capital letters; capsule.
Capt. Captain.
car. carat.
Card. Cardiganshire (former county); Cardinal.
Carms. Carmarthenshire (former county).
carp. carpenter; carpentry.
carr. carriage.
cartog. cartography.
cas. casual; casualty.
CAT College of Advanced Technology.
cat. catalogue; catechism.
Cath. Cathedral; Catholic.
cath. cathode.
caus. causation; causative.
cav. cavalier; cavalry.
CB Cape Breton; Citizens' Band; Companion of the Order of the Bath; (*milit*) confinement to barracks.
Cb (*chem*) columbium.
CBC Canadian Broadcasting Corporation.
c.b.d. cash before delivery.
CBE Commander of the Order of the British Empire.
CBI Central Bureau of Investigation (USA); Confederation of British Industry.
CBS Columbia Broadcasting System.
CBW chemical and biological warfare.
CC carbon copy; Chamber of Commerce; Chief Clerk; closed circuit; County Council; Cricket Club.
cc cubic centimetre; cubic centimetres.
cc. centuries; chapters; copies.
CCC County Cricket Club.
CCF Combined Cadet Force.
CCP Chinese Communist Party.
CCTV closed circuit television.
c.c.w. counter-clockwise.
CD Civil Defence; contagious disease; Corps Diplomatique; compact disc.
Cd (*chem*) cadmium.
cd candela.
cd. cord; could.
c.d. cash discount.
c/d carried down.
CDC Commonwealth Development Corporation.
CDN IVR Canada.
Cdr Commander; Conductor.
Cdre Commodore.
CDSO Companion of the Distinguished Service Order.
CE Chancellor of the Exchequer; Church of England; Civil Engineer; Council of Europe.
Ce (*chem*) cerium.
Cel. Celsius.
Celt. Celtic.
Cem. Cemetery.
cen. central; centre; century.
cent. centavo; centigrade; centime; cen-

timetre; central; *centum* (*Latin* a hundred; century.
cer. ceramics.
cert. certain; certificate; certification; certified; certify.
CET Central European Time.
CF Chaplain to the Forces.
Cf (*chem*) californium.
cf. *confer* (*Latin* compare).
c/f carried forward.
cfm cubic feet per minute.
cfs cubic feet per second.
cft cubic foot or feet.
CG Coast Guard; Commanding General; Consul General.
cg centigram.
c.g. centre of gravity.
CGI City and Guilds Institute.
CGM Conspicuous Gallantry Medal.
cgm centigram.
cgs centimetre-gram-second.
CH Companion of Honour; IVR Switzerland.
Ch. Chairman; China; Chinese.
ch. chain; champion; chaplain; chapter; check; chemical; chemistry; chief; child; choir; church.
c.h. central heating.
Chal. Chaldaic; Chaldee.
Chanc. Chancellor; Chancery.
Chap. Chapel; Chaplain.
chap. chapter.
char. character.
ChB *Chirurgiae Baccalaureus* (*Latin* Bachelor of Surgery).
chem, chem. chemical; chemist; chemistry.
Ches. Cheshire.
chg. change; charge.
Chin. China; Chinese.
Chm Chairman.
chq. cheque.
Chr. Christ; Christian; Chronicles.
chron. chronicle; chronological.
chs chapters.
CI Channel Islands; Commonwealth Institute; IVR Ivory Coast.
Ci. cirrus; curie.
CIA Central Intelligence Agency (USA).
Cicestr. *Cicestrensis* (*Latin* of Chichester).
CID Criminal Investigation Department.
cif cost, insurance and freight.
C-in-C Commander-in-Chief.
CIS Commonwealth of Independent States.
cit. cited.
ckw clockwise.
CL IVR Sri Lanka.
Cl (*chem*) chlorine.
cl centilitre.
cl. class; classical; classification; clause.
cld. called; cancelled; cleared; coloured; could.
clin. clinical.
Cllr Councillor.
Cm (*chem*) curium.
cm centimetre.
Cmdr Commander.
Cmdre Commodore.

Cmdt Commandant.

CMG Companion of the Order of St Michael and St George.

CMO Chief Medical Officer.

CND Campaign for Nuclear Disarmament.

CNS central nervous system; Chief of Naval Staff.

CO Cash Order; IVR Colombia; Commanding Officer; conscientious objector; Criminal Office; Crown Office.

Co (*chem*) cobalt.

Co. Company; County.

c/o care of; carried over.

COBOL (*comput*) common business oriented language.

COD cash on delivery.

cod. codicil.

coef. coefficient.

C of E Church of England; Council of Europe.

C of I Church of Ireland.

C of S Chief of Staff; Church of Scotland.

c.o.h. cash on hand.

COHSE Confederation of Health Service Employees.

COI Central Office of Information.

COL computer-oriented language.

Col. Colonel; Colorado; (*Scrip*) Colossians; Columbia; Columbian.

col. column.

coll. collateral; colleague; collection; collector; college; collegiate; colloquial.

colloq, colloq. colloquial; colloquialism; colloquially.

comp. companion; comparative; compare; comparison; compensation; competitor; compiled; compilation; complete; composer; composition; compositor; compound; comprehensive; comprising.

compar. comparative; comparison.

compd compound.

compl. complement; complete; compliment; complimentary.

COMSAT Communications Satellite (USA).

con. concentration; concerning; concerto; conclusion; *conjunx* (*Latin* wife); connection; consolidated; *contra* (*Latin* against); convenience.

conc. concentrate; concentrated; concentration; concerning.

conf. *confer* (*Latin* compare); conference.

conj, conj. conjugation; conjunction.

conn. connected; connection; connotation.

Cons. Conservative; Constable.

const. constant.

Cont. Continental.

cont. containing; contents; continent; continental; continued; *contra* (*Latin* against); contract.

contd contained; continued.

contr. contract; contraction; contralto; contrary; contrast; control; controller.

contrib. contribution; contributor.

co-op co-operative.

corr. correct; correction; correspondence; corresponding; corrugated; corruption.

cos (*math*) cosine.

cosec (*math*) cosecant.

cosh (*math*) hyperbolic cosine.

cot, cotan (*math*) cotangent.

Cox. Coxswain.

CP Carriage Paid; Common Prayer; Communist Party.

cp. compare.

CPI consumer price index.

cpi characters per inch.

Cpl. Corporal.

cpm cycles per minute.

CPR Canadian Pacific Railway.

cps characters per second; cycles per second.

CPU (*comput*) central processing unit.

CR IVR Costa Rica.

Cr (*chem*) chromium.

CRE Commission for Racial Equality.

Cres. Crescent.

cres. (*mus*) *crescendo* (*Italian* increasing).

crit. criticism; criticize.

CRO cathode-ray oscillograph; Criminal Records Office.

CRT cathode-ray tube.

cryst. crystalline; crystallized; crystallography.

CS IVR Czechoslovakia.

Cs (*chem*) caesium; (*meteor*) cirrostratus.

csch (*math*) hyperbolic cosecant.

CSE Certificate of Secondary Education.

CSEU Confederation of Shipbuilding and Engineering Unions.

CSM Company Sergeant-Major.

CSU Civil Service Union.

ct. carat; cent; *centum* (*Latin* hundred); certificate; county; court.

Cu (*chem*) copper.

cu. cubic.

Cumb. Cumberland (former county).

CUP Cambridge University Press.

CV Curriculum Vitae.

Cwlth Commonwealth.

c.w.o. cash with order.

cwt. hundredweight.

CY IVR Cyprus.

D Democratic; Department; *Deus* (*Latin* God); (*chem*) deuterium; dimension; Director; *Dominus* (*Latin* Lord); Duchess; Duke; Dutch; IVR Germany; 500 (Roman numeral).

d. date; day; dead; deceased; decree; degree; delete; *denarius* (*Latin* penny); density; departs; deputy; diameter; died.

DA Deposit Account; District Attorney.

Dak. Dakota.

Dan. (*Scrip*) Daniel; Danish.

D & C dilation and curettage.

dat. dative.

dB decibel.

d.b.a. doing business as.

DBE Dame Commander of the Order of the British Empire.

D. Bib. Douay Bible.

dbl. double.

DBST Double British Summer Time.

DC Death Certificate; Depth Charge; Diplomatic Corps; direct current; District of Columbia.

d.c. (*mus*) *da capo* (*Italian* repeat from beginning); direct current.

DCB Dame Commander of the Order of the Bath.

DCM Distinguished Conduct Medal.

DCMG Dame Commander of the Order of St Michael and St George.

dct document.

DCVO Dame Commander of the Royal Victorian Order.

DD direct debit; *Divinitatis Doctor* (*Latin* Doctor of Divinity).

DDC Dewey Decimal Classification.

DDR Deutsche Demokratische Republik (German Democratic Republic).

DDT dichlorodiphenyltrichlorethane, an insecticide.

deb. debenture; debit.

Dec. December.

dec. deceased; decimal; decimetre; declaration; declension; declination; decrease; (*mus*) *decrescendo* (*Italian* becoming softer).

decd deceased.

decl. declaration; declension.

def. defective; defence; defendant; deferred; deficit; definite; definition.

deg. degree.

Del. Delaware.

del. delegate; delegation; delete.

Dem. Democratic.

Den. Denmark.

Denb. Denbighshire (former county).

dep. department; departs; departure; deponent; deposed; deposit; depot; deputy.

dept department.

der., deriv. derivation; derivative; derived.

Derbys. Derbyshire.

DERV diesel engined road vehicle.

DES Department of Education and Science.

Det. Detective.

det. detachment; detail.

Det. Con. Detective Constable.

Det. Insp. Detective Inspector.

Det. Sgt. Detective Sergeant.

Deut. (*Scrip*) Deuteronomy.

dev. development; deviation.

DF *Defensor Fidei* (*Latin* Defender of the Faith).

DFC Distinguished Flying Cross.

DFM Diploma in Forensic Medicine.

DG *Dei gratia* (*Latin* by the grace of God); *Deo gratias* (*Latin* thanks to God).

dia. diagram; dialect; diameter.

diag. diagonal; diagram.

dial. dialect; dialogue.

diam. diameter.

dict. dictionary.

diff. difference; different; differential.

dig. digest; digit; digital.

dim. dimension; diminished; (*mus*) *diminuendo* (*Italian* becoming softer).

dimin. (*mus*) *diminuendo* (*Italian* becoming softer); diminutive.

Dioc. Diocesan; Diocese.

Dip. Diploma.

Dir. Director.

dis. discontinued; discount; distance; distant; distribute.

disc. discount; discovered.

disp. dispensary; dispensation.

dist distant; district.

distr. distribute; distributed; distribution; distributor.

div. dividend; division; divorce.

DIY do-it-yourself.

DJ dinner jacket; disc jockey.

DK IVR Denmark.

dlvy delivery.

dly daily.

DM Deutsche Mark.

dm decimetre.

DMZ demilitarized zone.

DNA (*chem*) deoxyribonucleic acid.

do. *ditto* (*Italian* the same).

DOA dead on arrival.

d.o.b. date of birth.

doc. document.

DOE Department of the Environment.

dol. (*mus*) *dolce* (*Italian* sweet); dollar.

DOM *Deo optimo maximo* (*Latin* to God, the best and greatest); IVR Dominican Republic.

doz. dozen.

DP data processing; displaced person.

DPh, DPhil Doctor of Philosophy.

DPP Director of Public Prosecutions.

dpt department; deponent; deposit; depot.

Dr Doctor.

Dr. Drive.

dram. pers. *dramatis personae* (*Latin* characters present in the drama).

DS (*mus*) *dal segno* (*Italian* from the sign); disseminated sclerosis.

DSC Distinguished Service Cross.

DSM Distinguished Service Medal.

DSO Distinguished Service Order.

d.s.p. *decessit sine prole* (*Latin* died without issue).

DST Daylight Saving Time.

DT data transmission; delirium tremens.

DTI Department of Trade and Industry.

Du. Duchy; Duke; Dutch.

Dumb. Dumbarton.

Dumf. Dumfriesshire (former county).

Dunb. Dunbartonshire (former county).

dup. duplicate.

DV defective vision; *Deo volente* (*Latin* God willing); Douay Version (of the Bible).

DY IVR Dahomey.

Dy (*chem*) dysprosium.

DZ IVR Algeria.

dz. dozen.

E East; Easter; Eastern; England; English; IVR Spain.

e. elder; electric.

ea. each.

EAK IVR Kenya.

E & OE errors and omissions excepted.

EAT IVR Tanzania.

EAU IVR Uganda.

EAZ IVR Tanzania.

EC East Central; IVR Ecuador; European Community.

eccles ecclesiastical.

Eccles. (*Scrip*) Ecclesiastes.

ECG electrocardiogram; electrocardiograph.

ecol. ecological; ecology.

econ. economical; ecomics; economy.

ECT electroconvulsive therapy.

ed. edited; edition; editor; education.

EDC (*med*) expected date of confinement.

EDD (*med*) expected date of delivery.

edit. edited; edition; editor.

EDP electronic data processing.

educ. educated; education; educational.

EEC European Economic Community.

EEG electroencephalogram; electroencephalograph.

EEOC Equal Employment Opportunities Commission.

EFL English as a foreign language.

EFT electronic funds transfer.

EFTA European Free Trade Association.

e.g. *exempli gratia* (*Latin* for example).

EHF extremely high frequency.

elect. electric; electrical; electricity.

elem. element; elementary.

elev. elevation.

Eliz. Elizabethan.

ELT English Language Teaching.

EM electromagnetic; electromotive.

EMF, emf electromotive force.

EMI Electrical and Musical Industries.

Emp. Emperor; Empire; Empress.

EMR electronic magnetic resonance.

EMS European Monetary System.

EMU, emu electromagnetic unit; European monetary unit.

enc., encl enclosed; enclosure.

ENE east-northeast.

Eng. England; English.

eng. engine; engineer; engineering; engraved; engraver.

enl. enlarged; enlisted.

Ens. Ensign.

ENSA Entertainments National Services Association.

ENT ear, nose and throat.

entom. entomology.

env. envelope.

EO Executive Officer.

EoC Equal Opportunities Commission.

EP electroplate; extended play (record).

Ep. Epistle.

EPNS electroplated nickel silver.

eq. equal.

ER *Elizabeth Regina* (*Latin* Queen Elizabeth).

Er (*chem*) erbium.

ERNIE Electronic Random Number Indicator Equipment.

Es (*chem*) einsteinium.

ESE east-southeast.

ESL English as a second language.

ESN educationally subnormal.

ESP extrasensory perception.

esp, esp. especially.

Esq. Esquire.

ESRO European Space Research Organization.

Est. Established; Estate.

est. estimated; estuary.

ET IVR Egypt; extra-terrestrial.

ETA estimated time of arrival.

et al. *et alii* (*Latin* and others).

etc, etc. *et cetera* (*Latin* and so on).

ETD estimated time of departure.

ethnol. ethnology.

ETU Electrical Trades Union.

etym. etymological; etymology.

Eu (*chem*) europium.

Eu., Eur. Europe; European.

EV, e.v. electron volt.

ex. examination; excellent; except; exchange; excluding; excursion; executed; executive; exempt; express; export; extra.

exam. examination.

Exe. Excellency.

exch. exchange; exchequer.

excl. exclamation; excluding.

exclam, exclam. exclamation.

exec. executive; executor.

ex lib. *ex libris* (*Latin* from the library of).

ex off. *ex officio* (*Latin* by virtue of office).

ext. extension; exterior; external; extinct; extra; extract; extreme.

F Fahrenheit; farad; Father; fathom; February; Fellow; Finance; (*chem*) fluorine; folio; (*mus*) *forte* (*Italian* loud); IVR France; French; frequency; Friday; function.

f. farad; farthing; fathom; feet; female; feminine; filly; fine; fluid; folio; following; foot; (*mus*) *forte* (*Italian* loud); foul; franc; frequency; from; furlong.

FA Fanny Adams; Football Association.

f.a. free alongside.

Fac. Faculty.

fam. family.

FAO Food and Agriculture Organization.

f.a.s. free alongside ship.

fath. fathom.

FBI Federal Bureau of Investigation (USA).

FC Football Club.

FCI Foreign and Commonwealth Office.

FD *Fidei Defensor* (*Latin* Defender of the Faith).

fd. forward; found; founded.

Fe (*chem*) iron.

Feb, Feb. February.

fec. *fecit* (*Latin* he or she made).

fed. federal; federated; federation.

fem. female; feminine.

ff (*mus*) *fortissimo* (*Italian* very loud).

ff. folios; the following.

fict. fiction; fictitious.

Fid. Def. *Fidei Defensor* (*Latin* Defender of the Faith).

fig. figuratively; figure.

Fin. Finland; Finnish.

fin. final; finance; financial; finish.

Finn. Finnish.

FJI IVR Fiji.

FL Flight Lieutenant; IVR Liechtenstein.

Fl. Flanders; Flemish.

fl. floor; florin; *floruit* (*Latin* flourished); fluid.

Flem. Flemish.

Flor. Florida.

flor. *floruit* (*Latin* flourished).

fl. oz. fluid ounce.

FMD foot and mouth disease.

fn. footnote.

FO Flying Officer; Foreign Office.

fo. folio.

f.o.b. free on board.

FOC (*print*) Father of the Chapel (union official); free of charge.

fol. folio; followed; following.

foll. following.

for. foreign; forestry.

fort, fort. fortification; fortified.

FORTRAN (*comput*) Formula Translation.

FP former pupil; freezing point.

fp (*mus*) *forte piano* (*Italian* loud and then immediately soft).

f.p. freezing point.

FPA Family Planning Association.

f.p.s. feet per second; foot-pound-second; (*photog*) frames per second.

Fr (*chem*) francium.

Fr. Father; France; *frater* (*Latin* brother); French; Friar; Friday.

fr. fragment; franc; frequent; from.

f.r. *folio recto* (*Latin* right-hand page).

FRCP Fellow of the Royal College of Physicians.

FRCS Fellow of the Royal College of Surgeons.

freq. frequent; frequentative; frequently.

Fri. Friday.

front. frontispiece.

FRS Fellow of the Royal Society.

FSH follicle-stimulating hormone.

ft, ft. feet; foot; fort; fortification.

fur. furlong.

fut. future.

f.v. *folio verso* (*Latin* left-hand page).

fwd forward.

f.w.d. four-wheel drive; front-wheel drive.

FYI for your information.

fz (*mus*) *forzando* (*Italian* to be strongly accentuated).

G (*physics*) conductance; gauge; German; giga; grain; gram; grand; (*physics*) gravitational constant; guilder; guinea; gulp; gravity.

g gram, gramme; (*physics*) gravitational acceleration.

g. genitive; guinea.

Ga (*chem*) gallium.

Ga. Georgia.

Gael. Gaelic.

gal., gall. gallon.

galv. galvanic; galvanism.

GATT General Agreement on Tariffs and Trade.

gaz. gazette; gazetteer.

GB IVR Great Britain and Northern Ireland.

GBA IVR Alderney.

GBE Grand Cross of the Order of the British Empire.

GBG IVR Guernsey.

g.b.h. grievous bodily harm.

GBJ IVR Jersey.

GBM IVR Isle of Man.

GBZ IVR Gibraltar.

GC George Cross; Golf Club.

GCA IVR Guatemala.

GCE General Certificate of Education.

GCF greatest common factor.

GCMG Knight *or* Dame Grand Cross of the Order of St Michael and St George.

GCVO Grand Cross of the Royal Victorian Order.

Gd (*chem*) gadolinium.

gd good; guard.

Gdns Gardens.

GDR German Democratic Republic.

gds goods.

Ge (*chem*) germanium.

GEC General Electric Company.

Gen. General; (*Scrip*) Genesis.

gen. gender; general; generally; generator; generic; genetics; genitive; genuine; genus.

gent gentleman.

Geo. Georgia.

geog. geographer; geographic; geographical; geography.

geol. geologic; geological; geologist; geology.

geom. geometric; geometrical; geometrician; geometry.

Ger. German; Germany.

ger. gerund; gerundive.

GeV giga-electronvolts.

GG Girl Guides; Governor General.

GH IVR Ghana.

GHQ General Headquarters.

GI gastrointestinal; general issue; Government Issue.

Gib. Gibraltar.

Gk. Greek.

gl. glass.

g/l grams per litre.

Glam. Glamorganshire (former county).

Glas. Glasgow.

GLC Greater London Council.

Glos. Gloucestershire.

gloss. glossary.

GM Geiger-Müller counter; General Manager; George Medal; Grand Master; Guided Missile.

gm gram.

gm² grames per square metre.

GMB Grand Master of the Order of the Bath.

GMBE Grand Master of the Order of the British Empire.

GMC General Medical Council.

Gmc Germanic.

GMT Greenwich Mean Time.

GMWU National Union of General and Municipal Workers.

GNP Gross National Product.

gns. guineas.

GOC General Officer Commanding.

Goth. Gothic.

Gov. Governor.

Govt Government.

GP Gallup Poll; (*med*) general paresis; (*mus*) general pause; General Practitioner; general purpose; *Gloria Patri* (*Latin* Glory to the Father); Grand Prix.

gp group.

Gp Capt. Group Captain.

GPO General Post Office.

GR *Geogius Rex* (*Latin* King George).

Gr. Grecian; Greece; Greek.

gr. grade; grain; grammar; gravity; great; gross; group.

grad. gradient; graduate.

gram. grammar; grammarian; grammatical.

Gr. Br. Great Britain.

gr. wt. gross weight.

GS General Secretary; General Staff; ground speed.

gs. guineas.

gsm grams per square metre.

GT Grand Tourer.

gtd guaranteed.

GTS Greenwich Time Signal.

GU gastriculcer; genitourinary.

guar. guaranteed.

GUY IVR Guyana.

GW gigawatt.

gym. gymnasium; gymnastics.

gyn. gynaecological; gynaecology.

H hard (pencils); hecto-; (*physics*) henry; heroin; hospital; IVR Hungary; hydrant; (*chem*) hydrogen.

h hour.

h. harbour; hard; height; high; hit; horizontal; (*mus*) horn; hour; hundred; husband.

ha hectare.

hab. habitat.

Haw. Hawaii; Hawaiian.

HB hard black (pencils).

HC House of Commons.

HCF highest common factor.

HCJ High Court Judge.

HD heavy duty.

hd hand; head.

hdbk handbook.

hdqrs headquarters.

HE high explosive; His Eminence; His *or* Her Excellency.

He (*chem*) helium.

Heb. Hebrew.

her., heral. heraldic; heraldry.

Herts. Hertfordshire.

hex. hexagon; hexagonal.

HF high frequency.

Hf (*chem*) hafnium.

hf half.

HG High German; Horse Guards.

Hg (*chem*) mercury.

hgt. height.

HGV heavy goods vehicle.

HH double hard (pencils); His *or* Her Highness; His Holiness; His *or* Her Honour.

Hind. Hindi; Hindu.

hist. histology; historian; historical; history.

HIV human immunodeficiency virus.

HJ *hic jacet* (*Latin* here lies).

HJS *hic jacet sepultus* (*Latin* here lies buried).

HK IVR Hong Kong; House of Keys (Manx Parliament).

HKJ IVR Jordan.

HL Honours List; House of Lords.

hl hectolitre.

HM His *or* Her Majesty.

HMG Higher Middle German; His *or* Her Majesty's Government.

HMI His *or* Her Majesty's Inspector.

HMS His *or* Her Majesty's Service; His *or* Her Majesty's Ship.

HMSO His *or* Her Majesty's Stationery Office.

HMV His Master's Voice.

HNC Higher National Certificate.

HND Higher National Diploma.

HO Home Office.

Ho (*chem*) holmium.

ho. house.

Hon. Honorary; Honourable.

Hons Honours.

Hon. Sec. Honorary Secretary.

hort. horticultural; horticulture.

hosp. hospital.

HP hire purchase; horse power; Houses of Parliament.

HQ Headquarters.

hr hour.

HRH His *or* Her Royal Highness.

HS *hic sepultus* (*Latin* here is buried); High School; Home Secretary.

HT high tension.

ht. heat; height.

Hung. Hungarian; Hungary.

Hunts. Huntingdonshire (former county).

HV high velocity; high voltage.

hwy highway.

hyd. hydraudics; hydrostatics.

Hz hertz.

I (*physics*) current; incisor; Independence; (*physics*) inertia; Institute; Institution; Interest; International; intransitive; (*chem*) iodine; Island; Isle; (*physics*) isospin; IVR Italy; 1 (Roman numeral).

IABA International Amateur Boxing Association.

IAM Institute of Advanced Motorists.

ib. *ibidem* (*Latin* in the same place).

IBA Independent Broadcasting Authority.

ibid. *ibidem* (*Latin* in the same place).

IC integrated circuit.

i/c in charge; internal combustion.

ICA Institute of Contemporary Art.

ICBM intercontinental ballistic missile.

ICI Imperial Chemical Industries.

icon. iconographic; iconography.

ICU intensive care unit.

ID identification.

id. *idem* (*Latin* the same).

IDP integrated data processing.

i.e. *id est* (*Latin* that is).

IL IVR Israel.

ILEA Inner London Education Authority.

Ill. Illinois.

ill., illus. illustrated; illustration.

ILO International Labour Organization.

ILP Independent Labour Party.

ILTF International Lawn Tennis Federation.

IM Isle of Man.

IMF International Monetary Fund.

imit. imitation; imitative.

imp. imperative; imperfect; imperial; impersonal; implemerlt; import; important; importer; *imprimatur* (*Latin* let it be printed); imprint; improper; improved; improvement.

imper. imperative.

imperf. imperfect.

impers. impersonal.

impf. imperfect.

imp. gall. imperial gallon.

In (*chem*) indium.

in. inch.

Inc. Incorporated.

inc. included; including; inclusive; income; incomplete; increase.

incl. including; inclusive.

incog. incognito.

incor. incorporated.

incr. increase; increased; increasing.

IND IVR India.

Ind. Independent; India; Indian; Indies.

ind. independence; independent; index; indicative; indirect; industrial; industry.

indef. indefinite.

indic. indicating; indicative; indicator.

individ. individual.

Inf. Infantry.

inf. inferior; infinitive; influence; information; *infra* (*Latin* below).

infin. infinitive.

init. initial; *initio* (*Latin* in the beginning).

in loc. cit. *in loco citato* (*Latin* in the place cited).

ins. inches; inspector; insulated; insulation; insurance.

Insp. inspected; inspector.

Inst. Institute.

inst. instant; instantaneous; instrumental.

instr. instructor; instrument; instrumental.

int. interest; interim; interior; interjection; internal; international; interpreter; intransitive.

intens. intensified; intensive.

inter. intermediate.

interj. interjection.

INTERPOL International Criminal Police Commission.

interrog. interrogation; interrogative.

intr., intrans. intransitive.

intro. introduction; introductory.

inv. invented; invention; inventor; invoice.

I/O (*comput*) input/output.

Io (*chem*) ionium.

Io. Iowa.

IOC International Olympic Committee.

IOM Isle of Man.

IOU I owe you.

IOW Isle of Wight.

IPA International Phonetic Alphabet or Association.

IPBM interplanetary ballistic missile.

IQ intelligence quotient.

IR infrared; Inland Revenue; IVR Iran.

Ir (*chem*) iridium.

Ir. Ireland; Irish.

IRA Irish Republican Army.

IRBM intermediate range ballistic missile.

IRC International Red Cross.

IRL IVR Republic of Ireland.

IRQ IVR Iraq.

IS IVR Iceland.

Is. (*Scrip*) Isaiah; Island; Isle.

ISBN International Standard Book Number.

isl. island; isle.

isth. isthmus.

It. Italian; Italic; Italy.

ITA Independent Television Authority; Initial Teaching Alphabet.

Ital. Italian; Italic.

ITN Independent Television News.

ITV Independent Television.

IUD intra-uterine device.

i.v. intravenous.

IVR International Vehicle Registration.

IVS International Voluntary Service.

IW Isle of Wight.

J IVR Japan; (*physics*) joule; Journal; Judge; Justice.

JA IVR Jamaica.

Ja. January.

Jan. January.

Jap. Japan; Japanese.

Jas James.

JATO jet-assisted take-off.

JC Jesus Christ; Jockey Club.

JCB (trademark) Joseph Cyril Bamford (manufacturer of an earth-moving vehicle).

jct. junction.

Jl. July.

Jnr Junior.

JP Justice of the Peace.

Jr Junior.

jt joint.

Ju. June.

Jul. July.

Jun. June; Junior.

junc. junction.

Junr Junior.

Jus. Justice.

juv. juvenile.

Jy July.

K (*elect*) capacity; carat; (*math*) constant; (*physics*) kaon; (*physics*) kelvin; IVR Khmer Republic; kilo; King; knight; knit; kopeck; (*chem*) potassium.

K. (*mus*) Köchel (number) (Mozart catalogue).

KB King's Bench; Knight of the Order of the Bath.

KBE Knight of the Order of the British Empire.

KC Kennel Club; King's Counsel; Knight Commander.

kc kilocycle.

KCB Knight Commander of the Order of the Bath.

KCMG Knight Commander of the Order of St Michael and St Gearge.

KCVC Knight Commander of the Royal Victorian Order.

keV kilo-electronvolt.

KG Knight of the Order of the Garter.

kg kilogram.

KGB Komitet Gosudarstvennoi Bezopasnosti (*Russian* Committee of State Security, former USSR).

KGCB Knight of the Grand Cross of the Order of the Bath.

kHz kilohertz.

KIA killed in action.

kilo kilogram.

kJ kilojoule.

KJV King James Version (of the Bible).

KKK Ku Klux Klan.

kl kilolitre.

km kilometre.

km/h kilometres per hour.

kn (*naut*) knot.

KO knock-out.

Kr (*chem*) krypton.

Kt Knight.

kV kilovolt.

kW kilowatt.

kWh kilowatt-hour.

KWT IVR Kuwait.

L (*elect*) inductance; Lake; Latin; learner driver; Liberal; longitude; IVR Luxembourg; 50 (Roman numeral).

l litre.

l. lake; land; latitude; left; length; *liber* (*Latin* book); *libra* (*Latin* pound); line; lire; low.

LA Los Angeles.

La (*chem*) lanthanum.

Lab. Labour; Labrador.

lab. labial; laboratory.

Lancs. Lancashire.

lang. language.

LAO IVR Laos.

LAR IVR Libya.

Lat. Latin.

lat. latitude.

LB IVR Liberia.

lb. pound.

l.b.w. leg before wicket (in cricket).

LC Lance Corporal.

L/C Letter of Credit.

lc, l.c. *loco citato* (*Latin* in the place cited); (*print*) lower case.

LCC London County Council.

LCD lowest common denominator.

LCM lowest common multiple.

L/Cpl Lance Corporal.

Ld. Lord.

Ldg. Leading.

LEA Local Education Authority.

leg. legal; (*mus*) *legato* (*Italian* smooth).

Leics. Leicestershire.

LEM lunar excursion module.

LEV lunar excursion vehicle.

LF low frequency.

LG Low German.

lg. large.

lgth length.

LH luteinizing hormone.

l.h. left hand.

l.h.d. left hand drive.

Li (*chem*) lithium.

Lib. Liberal.

Lieut, Lieut. Lieutenant.

Lincs. Lincolnshire.

ling. linguistics.

lit. literal; literary; literature; litre.

LL Lord Lieutenant.

ll. lines.

LL.B. *Legum Baccalaureus* (*Latin* Bachelor of Laws).

LL.D. *Legum Doctor* (*Latin* Doctor of Laws).

lm (*physics*) lumen.

LMT local mean time.

LNG liquefied natural gas.

LOA leave of absence.

loc. cit. *loco citato* (*Latin* in the place cited).

log. logarithm.

long. longitude.

loq. *loquitur* (*Latin* he or she speaks).

LP long-playing (record); London Philharmonia.

LPG liquefied petroleum gas.

LPO London Philharmonic Orchestra.

L'pool Liverpool.

Lr (*chem*) lawrencium.

LRBM long range ballistic missile.

LRS Lloyd's Register of Shipping.

LS IVR Lesotho.

LSD *librae, solidi, denarii* (*Latin* pounds, shillings, pence); lysergic acid diethylamide.

LSE London School of Economics.

LSO London Symphony Orchestra.

Lt. Lieutenant.

l.t. local time.

LTA Lawn Tennis Association.

Lt. Col. Lieutenant Colonel.

Lt. Comdr Lieutenant Commander.

Ltd Limited.

Lu (*chem*) lutetium.

LV luncheon voucher.

LW long wave.

Lw (*chem*) lawrencium.

LWM low water mark.

lx (*physics*) lux.

M mach (number); Majesty; IVR Malta; Manitoba; Marquis; Master; (*physics*) maxwell; Medieval; Member; (*mus*) *mezzo* (*Italian* half); Middle; Monday; Monsieur; motorway; Mountain; 1000 (Roman numeral).

m (*physics*) mass; metre.

m. male; married; masculine; medium; meridian; mile; million; minim; minute; modulus; month; moon; morning.

MA *Magister Artium* (*Latin* Master of Arts); IVR Morocco.

mach. machine; machinery; machinist.

mag. magazine; magnetic; magnetism; magnesium; magneto; magnitude.

Maj. Major.

MAL IVR Malaysia.

manuf. manufacture.

MAO (*chem*) monoamine oxidase.

Mar. March.

mar. marine; maritime.

March. Marchioness; margin, marginal.

marg. margin; marginal.

Marq. Marquess; Marquis.

masc. masculine.

Mass. Massachusetts.

math. mathematics.

Matt. Matthew.

max. maximum.

MB *Medicinae Baccalaureus* (*Latin* Bachelor of Medicine).

MC Master of Ceremonies; Medical Corps; Military Cross; IVR Monaco.

mc megacycle; millicurie.

MCC Marylebone Cricket Club.

MCP male chauvinist pig.

MCS missile control system.

MD Managing Director; *Medicinae Doctor* (*Latin* Doctor of Medicine); mentally deficient.

Md (*chem*) mendelivium.

Md. Maryland.

Mdm Madam.

ME myalgic encephalomyelitis.

Me (*chem*) methyl.

Me. Maine.

mech. mechanical; mechanics; mechanism.

Med. Mediterranean.

med. medical; medicine; medieval; medium.

Medit. Mediterranean.

mem. member; *memento* (*Latin* remember); memoir; memorandum; memorial.

MEP Member of the European Parliament.

met. metaphor; metaphysics; meteorological; meteorology; metropolitan.

metal. metallurgical; metallurgy.

metaph. metaphor; metaphysics.

meteor. meteorological; meteorology.

MeV mega-electron-volt; million electron-volts.

MEX IVR Mexico.

MF medium frequency.

mf (*mus*) *mezzo forte* (*Italian* moderately loud).

mfd manufactured.

mfr. manufacture; manufacturer.

Mg (*chem*) magnesium; megagram.

mg milligram.

Mgr Manager.

mgt management.

MHF medium high frequency.

MHG Middle High German.

MHz megahertz.

MI MilitaryIntelligence.

mi. mile.

MI5 Military Intelligence, section 5.

MIA missing in action.

MICR (*comput*) magnetic ink character recognition.

Middx Middlesex (former county).

mil millilitre.

mil., milit military.

Min. Ministry.
min. mineralogical; mineralogy; minim; minimum; mining; minister; ministry; minor; minute.
mineral. mineralogical; mineralogy.
MIRAS mortgage interest relief at source.
MIRV multiple independently targetted re-entry vehicle.
misc. miscellaneous; miscellany.
mk mark.
mks metre-kilogram-second.
mkt market.
ml mile; millilitre.
Mlle Mademoiselle.
MLR minimum lending rate.
MM Military Medal.
mm millimetre.
Mme Madame.
MMR measles, mumps and rubella (combined vaccine against these).
Mn (*chem*) manganese.
MO Medical Officer; *modus operandi* (*Latin* mode of operation); Money Order.
Mo (*chem*) molybdenum.
Mo. Monday.
mo. month.
MOD Ministry of Defence.
mod. moderate; modern; modulus.
mod. cons. modern conveniences.
MOH Medical Officer of Health.
mol (*chem*) mole.
mol. molecular; molecule.
mol. wt. molecular weight.
Mon. Monday; Monmouthshire (former county).
Mont. Montgomeryshire (former county).
MOR middle-of-the-road.
MORI Market and Opinion Research Institute.
morph. morphological; morphology.
MOT Ministry of Transport.
MP Member of Parliament; Metropolitan Police; Military Police; Mounted Police.
mp (*mus*) *mezzo piano* (*Italian* moderately soft).
m.p. melting point.
mph miles per hour.
Mr, Mr. Mister.
MRBM medium range ballistic missile.
MRC Medical Research Council.
MRCP Member of the Royal College of Physicians.
MRCS Member of the Royal College of Surgeons.
MRP Manufacturer's Recommended Price.
Ms a title used before a woman's name instead of Miss or Mrs.
MS manuscript; IVR Mauritius; multiple sclerosis.
ms millisecond.
m/s metres per second.
MSC Manpower Services Commission.
MSc Master of Science.
MSG (*chem*) monosodium glutamate.
Msgr. Monseigneur; Monsignor.
msl mean sea level.

MT mean time.
Mt Mount.
mtg. meeting; mortgage.
mth month.
mtn mountain.
Mt. Rev. Most Reverend.
mun. municipal.
mus. museum; music; musical; musician.
mV millivolt.
m.v. (*mus*) *mezzo voce* (*Italian* half the power of voice); motor vessel.
MW IVR Malawi; medium wave; megawatt.
mW milliwatt.
Mx Middlesex (former county).
MY motor yacht.
mycol. mycological; mycology.
myth. mythological; mythology.
N National; Nationalist; Navy; (*physics*) newton; (*chem*) nitrogen; Norse; North; IVR Norway; November.
n. name; *natus* (*Latin* born); navy; nephew; net; neuter; (*physics*) neutron; new; nominative; noon; note; noun; number.
NA IVR Netherlands Antilles; North America.
Na (*chem*) sodium.
n/a no account; not applicable; not available.
NAAFI Navy, Army and Air Force Institutes.
NALGO National and Local Government Officers' Association.
NASA National Aeronautics and Space Administration (USA).
nat. national; native; natural.
NATO North Atlantic Treaty Organization.
NATSOPA National Society of Operative Printers and Assistants.
naut. nautical.
nav. naval; navigable; navigation; navy.
navig. navigation; navigator.
NB *nota bene* (*Latin* note well).
Nb (*chem*) niobium.
NBC National Broadcasting Corporation (USA).
NCB National Coal Board.
NCCL National Council for Civil Liberties.
NCO Noncommissioned Officer.
ncv no commercial value.
Nd (*chem*) neodymium.
NE northeast.
Ne (*chem*) neon.
NEB New English Bible.
NEC National Executive Committee.
NEDC National Economic Development Council.
neg. negative; negatively.
nem. con. *nemine contradicente* (*Latin* no one opposing).
neurol. neurol. neurology.
neut. neuter; neutral.
NF no funds.
NFT National Film Theatre.
NFU National Farmers' Union.
NHS National Health Service.

NI National Insurance; Northern Ireland.
Ni (*chem*) nickel.
NIC IVR Nicaragua.
NIG IVR Niger.
NL IVR Netherlands.
n.l. new line.
NMR nuclear magnetic resonance.
NNE north-northeast.
NNW north-northwest.
No (*chem*) nobelium.
No. Number.
n.o. not out (in cricket).
nol. pros. *nolle prosequi* (*Latin* do not continue).
nom. nominal; nominative.
noncom. noncommissioned.
non seq. *non sequitur* (*Latin* it does not follow logically).
Nor. Norman; North; Norway; Norwegian.
norm. normal.
Northants. Northamptonshire.
Northumb. Northumberland.
nos. numbers.
Notts. Nottinghamshire.
Nov. November.
NP Notary Public.
Np (*chem*) neptunium.
n.p. new paragraph.
NPT normal pressure and temperature.
nr near.
NRC Nuclear Research Council.
ns nanosecond.
n.s. new style.
NSB National Savings Bank.
n.s.f. not sufficient funds.
NSPCC National Society for the Prevention of Cruelty to Children.
NSU (*med*) non-specific urethritis.
NT National Trust; New Testament.
NTS National Trust for Scotland.
NUGMW National Union of General and Municipal Workers.
NUJ National Union of Journalists.
NUM National Union of Mineworkers.
num. number; numeral.
numis. numismatics.
NUPE National Union of Public Employees.
NUR National Union of Railwaymen.
NUS National Union of Seamen; National Union of Students.
NUT National Union of Teachers.
NV New Version (of the Bible).
n.v.d. no value declared.
NVQ National Vocational Qualification.
NW northwest.
NY New York.
NYC New York City.
NZ IVR New Zealand.
O Ocean; octavo; October; Ohio; Old; Ontario; Oregon; (*chem*) oxygen.
O & M Organization and Methods.
OAP Old Age Pensioner; Old Age Pensioner.
OB outside broadcast.
ob. *obiit* (*Latin* he *or* she died).
obb. (*mus*) *obbligato* (*Italian* obligatory).
OBE Officer of the Order of the British Empire.

obj. object; objection; objective.

obl. obligation; oblique; oblong.

obs. obsolete.

obstet. obstetrics.

obv. obverse.

OC Officer Commanding.

OCR (*comput*) Optical Character Reader; Optical Character Recognition.

Oct. October.

oct. octave; octavo.

OD Officer of the Day; overdose; overdraft.

OE Old English.

OECD Organization for Economic Co-operation and Development.

OED Oxford English Dictionary.

OF Old French.

off. offer; office; office; official.

OFT Office of Fair Trading.

OGM Ordinary General Meeting.

OHG Old High German.

OHMS On His *or* Her Majesty's Service.

OM Order of Merit.

o.n.o. or nearest offer.

Ont. Ontario.

o.p. out of print.

op. cit. *opere citato* (*Latin* in the work cited).

OPEC Organization of Petroleum Exporting Countries.

opp. opposed; opposite.

OR Official Receiver; operational research; other ranks.

orch. orchestra; orchestral.

ord. ordained; order; ordinal; ordinance; ordinary; ordnance.

Ore. Oregon.

org. organic; organization.

orig. origin; original; originally.

ornith. ornithology.

orth. orthography; orthopaedic; orthodox.

OS Old Style; Ordinary Seaman; Ordnance Survey; Outsize.

Os (*chem*) osmium.

o.s. out of stock; outsize.

OT Old Testament.

OU Open University.

OXFAM Oxford Committee for Famine Relief.

Oxon. *Oxoniensis* (*Latin* of Oxford).

oz. ounce.

P (*chem*) phosphorus; IVR Portugal; President.

p. page; paragraph; part; participle; past; penny; per; pint; *post* (*Latin* after); power; *pro* (*Latin* in favour of); purl.

PA IVR Panama; Personal Assistant; Press Agent; Press Association; Public Address.

p.a. per annum.

PAK IVR Pakistan.

P & L Profit and Loss.

P & O Peninsular and Oriental (Steamship Company).

p & p postage and packing.

par. paragraph; parallel; parenthesis.

Parl. Parliament(ary).

part. participial; participle; partner.

partn. partnership.

pass. passage; passenger; *passim* (*Latin* here and there); passive.

pat. patent; patented.

path., pathol. pathological; pathology.

Pat. Off. Patent Office.

pat. pend. patent pending.

patt. pattern.

PAYE Pay As You Earn.

Pb (*chem*) lead.

PBS Public Broadcasting System (US).

PBT President of the Board of Trade.

PC personal computer; Police Constable; politically correct; political correctness; Privy Council.

p.c. per cent; postcard; *post cibum* (*Latin* after meals).

Pd (*chem*) palladium.

pd paid; passed.

pdq (*colloq*) pretty damn quickly.

PDSA People's Dispensary for Sick Animals.

PE IVR Peru; physical education.

PEI Prince Edward Island.

pen. peninsula; penitentiary.

per. period; person.

perf. perfect.

perm. permanent; permutation.

perp. perpendicular.

per pro. *per procurationem* (*Latin* on behalf of).

pers. person; personal.

PFA Professional Footballers' Association.

PG paying guest; Postgraduate.

pg. page.

PGA Professional Golfers' Association.

pharm. pharmacist; pharmacology; pharmacy.

PhD *Philosophiae Doctor* (*Latin* Doctor of Philosophy).

Phil. Philadelphia; Philharmonic.

phil. philology; philosopher; philosophical; philosophy.

philos. philosopher; philosophical; philosophy.

phon. phonetics; phonology.

phot. photograph; photography.

phr. phrase; phraseology.

phys. physical; physician; physics; physiological; physiology.

PI IVR Philippine Islands.

PIN personal identification number.

pizz. (*mus*) *pizzicato* (*Italian* plucking strings with fingers).

pk. pack; park; peak; peck.

pkg. package; packing.

pkt. packet; pocket.

PL Poet Laureate; IVR Poland.

P/L Profit and Loss.

Pl. Place.

pl. place; plate; platoon; plural.

PLA Port of London Authority.

PLC, plc public limited company.

PLO Palestine Liberation Organization.

PLP Parliamentary Labour Party.

PLR Public Lending Right.

plupf. pluperfect.

plur. plural.

PM *post meridiem* (*Latin* after noon); Post Mortem; Prime Minister.

Pm (*chem*) promethium.

p.m. *post meridiem* (*Latin* after noon).

PMT pre-menstrual tension.

PNdb perceived noise decibel.

PO Personnel Officer; Postal Order; Post Office.

Po (*chem*) polonium.

POD pay on delivery.

poet. poetic; poetical; poetry.

pol. political; politics.

pop. popular; popularly; population.

POS point of sale.

pos. position; positive.

poss. possessive; possible; possibly.

pot. potential.

POW prisoner of war.

PP Past President.

pp *per procurationem* (*Latin* on behalf of); (*mus*) *pianissimo* (*Italian* very soft).

pp. pages.

p.p. past participle; *post prandium* (*Latin* after meals).

PPE Philosophy, Politics and Economics.

PPS Parliamentary Private Secretary; *post postscriptum* (*Latin* additional postscript).

PR Proportional Representation; Public Relations.

Pr (*chem*) praseodymium.

pr. pair; paper; power; preferred; present; price; pronoun.

PRC People's Republic of China.

prec. preceding.

pred. predicate.

pref. preface; prefatory; preference; preferred; prefix.

prelim. preliminary.

prep. preparation; preparatory; preposition.

Pres. Presbyterian; President.

pres. present.

pres. part. present participle.

pret. preterit.

prev. previous; previously.

prim. primary; primitive.

prin. principal; principally; principle.

priv. private; privative.

PRO Public Records Office; Public Relations Officer.

pro. professional; prostitute.

proc. proceedings.

prod. product.

Prof. Professor.

prog. programme; progress; progressive.

prom. promenade.

pron. pronoun; pronounced.

prop. proper ; proprietor.

pros. prosody.

Prot. Protectorate; Protestant.

Prov. (*Scrip*) Proverbs; Province.

prov. proverb; proverbial; province; provincial; provisional.

prox. *proximo* (*Latin* next month).

prs. pairs.

PS Parliamentary Secretary; permanent secretary; postscript; Private Secretary.

Ps. (*Scrip*) Psalms.

PSBR public sector borrowing requirement.

pseud. pseudonym.

psi pounds per square inch.

PSV Public Service Vehicle.

psych. psychological; psychology.

PT Pacific Time; physical training.

Pt (*chem*) platinum.

pt. part; patient; payment; pint; point; port; preterit.

p.t. past tense.

PTA Parent-Teacher Association.

ptg printing.

PTO please turn over.

Pty Proprietary.

Pu (*chem*) plutonium.

pub. public; publication; published; publisher; publishing.

PVC polyvinyl chloride.

PVS post-viral symdrome.

Pvt., Pvte Private.

PW Policewoman; prisoner of war.

PY IVR Paraguay.

Q Quebec; Queen.

q. quart; quarter; quarto; quasi; question.

QB Queen 's Bench.

QC Queen's Counsel.

QED *quod erat demonstrandum* (*Latin* that was to be proved).

q.i.d. *quater in die* (*Latin* four times daily).

qlty quality.

QMG Quartermaster General.

qnty quantity.

qt quart.

q.t. quiet.

qto quarto.

qtr. quarter; quarterly.

qty quantity.

quad. quadrangle; quadrant; quadrilateral.

Quango quasi autonomous non-governmental organization.

quot. quotation.

q.v. *quod vide* (*Latin* which see).

R *Regina* (*Latin* Queen); *Rex* (*Latin* King); (*physics*) roentgen, röntgen; IVR Romania.

r. radius; right; river; road.

RA IVR Argentina; Royal Academician.

Ra (*chem*) radium.

RAC Royal Automobile Club.

RADA Royal Academy of Dramatic Art.

RAF Royal Air Force.

rall. (*mus*) *rallentando* (*Italian* gradually decreasing speed).

R & B (*mus*) rhythm and blues.

R & D research and development.

RB IVR Botswana.

Rb (*chem*) rubidium.

RC IVR China; Red Cross; Roman Catholic.

RCA IVR Central African Republic; Royal College of Art.

RCB IVR Congo.

rcd received.

RCH IVR Republic of Chile.

RCM Royal College of Music.

RCMP Royal Canadian Mounted Police.

rcpt receipt.

R/D Refer to Drawer.

Rd Road.

RDC Rural District Council.

RE (*chem*) rare earth elements; Royal Engineers.

Re (*chem*) rhenium.

rec. receipt; recipe; record; recorded; recorder; recording.

recd received.

recit. (*mus*) *recitativo* (*Italian* recitative).

rect. receipt; rectangle.

ref. refer; referee; reference.

refl. reflection; reflective; reflex.

Reg. Regent; Regiment; *Regina* (*Latin* Queen).

reg. regiment; region; register; registrar; registry; regular; regulation.

regd registered.

Regt Regent; Regiment.

rel. relating; relative; relatively.

relig. religion; religious.

REM rapid eye movement.

REME Royal Electrical and Mechanical Engineers.

Renf. Renfrewshire (former county).

Rep. Repertory; Representative; Republic; Republican.

rep. repeat; report; reported; reporter; representative; reprint.

repro. reproduction.

req. request; required; requisition.

res. research; reserve; residence.

resp. respective; respectively.

ret. retain; retired; return; returned.

Rev. (*Scrip*) Revelation; Reverend.

rev. revenue; reverse; revise; revision; revolution.

Revd Reverend.

RF radio frequency.

rgd registered.

Rgt Regiment.

RH IVR Republic of Haiti; Royal Highness.

Rh rhesus; (*chem*) rhodium.

r.h. right hand.

r.h.d. right hand drive.

rhet. rhetoric; rhetorical.

RHF Royal Highland Fusiliers.

RHG Royal Horse Guards.

RHS Royal Horticultural Society.

RI religious instruction; IVR Republic of Indonesia; Rhode Island.

RIBA Royal Institute of British Architects.

RIM IVR Republic of Mauritania.

RIP *requiescat in pace* (*Latin* may he or she rest in peace).

rit. (*mus*) *ritardando* (*Italian* decrease pace).

RL IVR Republic of Lebanon; Rugby League.

rly railway.

RM IVR Malagasy Republic; Royal Mail.

rm ream; room.

RMA Royal Military Academy.

RMM IVR Republic of Mali.

RN Registered Nurse; Royal Navy.

Rn (*chem*) radon.

RNA ribonucleic acid.

RNIB Royal National Institute for the Blind.

RNID Royal National Institute for the Deaf.

RNLI Royal National Lifeboat Institution.

RNR Royal Naval Reserve; IVR Zambia.

RNVR Royal Naval Volunteer Reserve.

ROC Royal Observer Corps.

ROK IVR Republic of Korea.

Rom. Roman; Romania; (*Scrip*) Romans.

rom. roman (type).

RoSPA Royal Society for the Prevention of Accidents.

RP Received Pronunciation.

RPI retail price index.

rpm revolutions per minute.

rps revolutions per second.

rpt. repeat; report.

RRP recommended retail price.

RS Royal Society.

r.s. right side.

RSA Royal Scottish Academy.

RSFSR Russian Soviet Federated Socialist Republic.

RSM Regimental Sergeant-Major; IVR San Marino.

RSPB Royal Society for the Protection of Birds.

RSPCA Royal Society for the Prevention of Cruelty to Animals.

RSPCC Royal Scottish Society for the Prevention of Cruelty to Children.

RSR IVR Rhodesia.

RSV Revised Standard Version (of the Bible).

RSVP *répondez s'il vous plait* (*French* please reply).

rt right.

Rt Hon. Right Honourable.

Rt Rev. Right Reverend.

RU IVR Burundi; Rugby Union.

Ru (*chem*) ruthenium.

RUC Royal Uster Constabulary.

Russ. Russia; Russian.

RV Revised Version (of the Bible).

RWA IVR Rwanda.

S Saint; Saturday; Saxon; School; Senate; September; Society; South; Southern; (*chem*) sulphur; Sunday; IVR Sweden.

S second.

S. section; series; shilling; signed; singular; soprano.

SA Salvation Army; South Africa; South America; South Australia.

Sab. Sabbath.

SAD seasonal affective disorder.

s.a.e. stamped addressed envelope.

SALT Strategic Arms Limitation Talks.

SAM surface-to-air missile.

Sans., Sansk. Sanskrit.

SARAH Search and Rescue and Homing.

Sat. Saturday; Saturn.

Sax. Saxon; Saxony.

sax. saxophone.

SAYE Save As You Earn.

SB Special Branch.

Sb (*chem*) antimony.

sb. substantive.

SBN Standard Book Number.

Sc (*chem*) scandium.

Sc. Scots; Scottish.

sc. scene; science; *sculpsit* (*Latin* he or she engraved it).

s.c. small capitals.

Scand. Scandinavia; Scandinavian.

SCE Scottish Certificate of Education.

SCF Save the Children Fund.

sci. science; scientific.

sci-fi science fiction.

Scot. Scotland; Scottish.

sculp. *sculpsit* (*Latin* he or she engraved it); sculptor; sculpture.

SD IVR Swazilarld.

sd sound.

s.d. *sine die* (*Latin* without date); standard deviation.

SDLP Social and Democratic Labour Party (Northern Ireland).

SDP Social Democratic Party.

SE southeast.

Se (*chem*) selenium.

SEATO Southeast Asia Treaty Organization.

sec. secant; second; secondary; secretary; section; security.

sect. section.

Secy Secretary.

Selk. Selkirkshire (former county).

SEN State Enrolled Nurse.

Sen. Senate; Senator; Senior.

Sep. September; Septuagint.

sep. separate.

Sept. September; Septuagint.

seq. sequel; *sequens* (*Latin* the following).

ser. serial; series; sermon.

Serg. Sergeant.

SF IVR Finland; San Francisco; Science Fiction; Sinn Fein.

sf. (*mus*) *sforzando* (*Italian* with a strong accent on a single note or chord).

SFA Scottish Football Association; (*colloq*) Sweet Fanny Adams, i.e. nothing.

sgd signed.

SGP IVR Singapore.

Sgt Sergeant.

Sgt Maj. Sergeant Major.

Shak. Shakespeare.

SHAPE Supreme Headquarters Allied Powers Europe.

SHO (*med*) senior house officer.

SI *Système Internationale* (*French* international system).

Si (*chem*) silicon.

SIDS sudden infant death syndrome.

sig. signal; signature.

sing. singular.

sinh (*math*) hyperbolic sine.

SLADE Society of Lithographic Artists, Designers, Engravers and Process Workers.

SLP Socialist Labour Party.

SM Sergeant Major.

Sm (*chem*) samarium.

SME IVR Surinam.

SN IVR Senegal.

Sn (*chem*) tin.

SNP Scottish National Party.

Snr Senior.

SOB (*sl*) son of a bitch.

Soc. Socialist; Society.

SOGAT Society of Graphical and Allied Trades.

Som. Somerset.

SONAR Sound Navigation and Ranging.

sop. soprano.

SOR sale or return.

SoS Save our Souls.

SP starting price.

Sp. Spain; Spaniard; Spanish.

sp. special; species; specific; specimen; spelling; spirit; sport.

s.p. *sine prole* (*Latin* without issue).

spec special; specification; speculation.

sp. gr. specific gravity.

SPQR *Senatus Populusque Romanus* (*Latin* the senate and people of Rome).

Sq. Squadron; Square.

sq. sequence; *sequens* (*Latin* the following); squadron; square.

sq. ft square foot.

sq. in. square inch.

SR self-raising.

Sr (*chem*) strontium.

Sr. Senior; Sister.

SRBM short range ballistic missile.

SRC Science Research Council; Student RepresentativeCouncil.

SRN State Registered Nurse.

SRO standing room only; Statutory Rules and Orders.

SS Secretary of State; Social Security; steamship; *supra scriptum* (*Latin* written above).

SSE south-southeast.

SSM surface-to-surface missile.

SSPCA Scottish Society for the Prevention of Cruelty to Animals.

SSR Soviet Socialist Republic.

SSW south-southwest.

St Saint; Strait; Street.

Sta. Station.

Staffs. Staffordshire.

Stir. Stirlingshire (former county).

STOL short take-off and landing.

str. strait.

STUC Scottish Trades Union Congress.

STV Scottish Television.

sub. subaltern; subeditor; subject; submarine; subscription; substitute; suburb; suburban; subway.

subj. subject; subjective; subjectively; subjunctive.

subst. substantive; substitute.

Suff. Suffolk.

suff. suffix.

SUM surface-to-underwater missile.

Sun. Sunday.

supp., suppl. supplement; supplementary.

Supt Superintendent.

surg. surgeon; sulgery; surgical.

surv. survey; surveying; surveyor.

SW shortwave; southwest.

Sw. Sweden; Swedish; Swiss.

SWA IVR South West Africa.

SWG standard wire gauge.

Swit., Switz. Switzerland.

SWAPO South West Africa People's Organization.

Sx Sussex.

SY IVR Seychelles.

syll. syllable; syllabus.

sym. symbol; symmetrical; symphony; symptom.

syn. synonym.

SYR IVR Syria.

T temperature; Testament; IVR Thailand; (*chem*) tritium; Tuesday.

t. tense; ton.

TA TerritorialArmy.

Ta (*chem*) tantalum.

tab. table; tablet.

tan (*math*) tangent.

TB tuberculosis.

Tb (*chem*) terbium.

tbs. tablespoon.

TC Tennis Club; Town Councillor.

Tc (*chem*) technetium.

Te (*chem*) tellurium.

tech. technical.

technol. technological; technology.

telecomm. telecommunications.

teleg. telegram; telegraph.

temp. temperate; temperature; temporary; *tempore* (*Latin* in the time of).

ten. (*mus*) *tenuto* (*Italian* sustained).

Terr. Terrace; Territory.

Test. Testament.

TF Task Force.

TG IVR Togo.

TGWU Transport and General Workers' Union.

Th (*chem*) thorium.

Th. Thursday.

theat. theatrical.

theol. theologian; theological; theology.

theor. theorem.

Thos Thomas.

Thurs. Thursday.

Ti (*chem*) titanium.

t.i.d. *tres in die* (*Latin* three times daily).

tkt ticket.

Tl (*chem*) thallium.

TM trademark; transcendental meditation.

Tm (*chem*) thulium.

TN IVR Tunisia.

tn town.

TNT (*chem*) trinitrotoluene, an explosive.

t.o. turn over.

tog. together.

topog. topographical; topography.

TR IVR Turkey.

tr. transitive; transpose.

trad. traditional.

trans. transaction; transferred; transitive; transpose.

transl. translated; translation; translator.

transp. transport.

TRH Their Royal Highnesses.

trig. trigonometrical; trigonometry.

tripl. triplicate.

TRM trademark.

trs. transfer; transpose.

tsp. teaspoon.

TT teetotal; teetotaller; IVR Trinidad and Tobago; tuberculin tested.

TU Trade Union.

Tu. Tuesday.

TUC Trades Union Congress.
Tues. Tuesday.
TV television.
U (*chem*) uranium; IVR Uruguay.
u. unit; upper.
UAE United Arab Emirates.
UAM underwater-to-air missile.
UAR United Arab Republic.
u.c. upper case.
UCCA Universities Central Council on Admissions.
UDC Urban District Council.
UDI Unilateral Declaration of Independence.
UDR Ulster Defence Regiment.
UEFA Union of European Football Associations.
UFO unidentified flying object.
UGC University Grants Committee.
UHF ultrahigh frequency.
UHT ultra-heat treated.
UK United Kingdom.
UKAEA United Kingdom Atomic Energy Authority.
ult. ultimate; *ultimo* (*Latin* last month).
UN United Nations.
UNA United Nations Association.
UNESCO United Nations Educational, Scientific and Cultural Organization.
UNICEF United Nations International Children's Emergency Fund.
univ. university.
UNO United Nations Organization.
US United States.
USA Union of South Africa; IVR United States of America.
USDAW Union of Shop, Distributive and Allied Workers.
USM underwater-to-surface missile.
USSR Union of Soviet Socialist Republics.
usu. usually.
USW ultrashort waves; ultrasonic waves.
UT Universal Time.
UV ultraviolet.
V 5 (Roman numeral); (*chem*) vanadium; IVR Vatican City; (*math*) vector; velocity; volt.
v. verb; verse; *verso* (*Latin* left-hand page); *versus* (*Latin* against); very; *vice* (*Latin* in the place of); *vide* (*Latin* see); voice; volt; voltage.
vac. vacancy; vacant.
val. valuation; value.
var. variant; variety; various.
VAT Value Added Tax.
Vat. Vatican.
vb verb.
VC Victoria Cross; Viet Cong.
VDU (*comput*) visual display unit.
VE Victory in Europe.

veg. vegetable.
vet. veteran.
VF video frequency; voice frequency.
v.g. very good.
VHF very high frequency.
VI Virgin Islands.
v.i. verb intransitive; *vide infra* (*Latin* see below).
Vic. Victoria.
VIP very important person.
Vis. Viscount.
viz. *videlicit* (*Latin* namely).
VJ Victory in Japan.
VLF very low frequency.
VM Victoria Medal.
VN IVR Vietnam.
vo. *verso* (**Latin** left-hand page).
voc. vocative.
vocab. vocabulary.
vol. volume.
vs. *versus* (*Latin* against).
VSO very superior old; Voluntary Service Overseas.
VSOP very superior old pale.
v.t. verb transitive.
VTOL vertical take-off and landing.
VTR videotape recorder.
vulg. vulgar.
Vulg. Vulgate.
v.v. *viva voce* (*Latin* spoken aloud).
W (*chem*) tungsten; Wales; Wednesday; Welsh; west; western; women's.
w. week; weight; width; with; won.
WA West Africa; Western Australia.
WAAA Women's Amateur Athletic Association.
WAAC Women's Auxiliary Army Corps.
WAAF Women's Auxiliary Air Force.
WAG IVR Gambia.
WAL IVR Sierra Leone.
WAN IVR Nigeria.
War. Warwickshire.
WASP White Anglo-Saxon Protestant.
Wb (*physics*) weber.
WBA World Boxing Association.
WBC World Boxing Council.
WC West Central.
w.c. watercloset.
WCC World Council of Churches.
W/Cdr Wing Commander.
WD IVR Dominica.
wd. ward; word; would.
WEA Workers' Educational Association.
Wed. Wednesday.
w.e.f. with effect from.
w.f. (*print*) wrong fount.
WG IVR Grenada.
w.g. wire gauge.
WHO World Health Organization.
WI Women's Institute.
Wilts. Wiltshire.

wk week; work.
WL IVR St Lucia; wavelength.
WNP Welsh Nationalist Party.
WNW west-northwest.
WO War Office; Warrant Officer.
w/o without.
Worcs. Worcestershire (former county).
WPC Woman Police Constable.
wpm words per minute.
WRAC Women's Royal Army Corps.
WRAF Women's Royal Air Force.
WRI Women's Rural Institute.
WRNS Women's Royal Naval Service.
WRVS Women's Royal Voluntary Service.
WS IVR Western Samoa; West Saxon; Writer to the Signet.
WSW west-southwest.
wt weight.
WV IVR St Vincent.
WVS Women's Voluntary Service.
WWI World War I (First World War).
WWII World War II (Second World War).
WX women's extra large size.
WYSIWYG (*comput*) what you see is what you get.
X 10 (Roman numeral).
Xe (*chem*) xenon.
XL extra large.
Xmas Christmas.
x.ref. cross reference.
xs. expenses.
Y (*chem*) yttrium.
y. year.
YB (*chem*) ytterbium.
yd. yard.
YHA Youth Hostels Association.
YMCA Young Men's Christian Association.
Yorks. Yorkshire.
yr. year; younger; your.
yrs. years; yours.
YTS Youth Training Scheme.
YU IVR Yugoslavia.
YV IVR Venezuela.
YWCA Young Women's Christian Association.
Z (*chem*) atomic number; IVR Zambia.
z. zero; zone.
ZA IVR South Africa.
ZANU Zimbabwe African National Union.
ZAIPU Zimbabwe African People's Union.
Zn (*chem*) zinc.
zool. zoological; zoology.
ZPG zero population growth.
ZR IVR Zaire.
Zr (*chem*) zirconium.